LAROUSSE

DICCIONARIO
Pocket

**ESPAÑOL
INGLÉS**

**INGLÉS
ESPAÑOL**

LAROUSSE

Para esta edición

For this edition

Antonio Fortin, José A. Gálvez, Sharon J. Hunter, Janice McNeillie,

Carol Styles Carvajal, David Tarradas Agea

Para las ediciones anteriores

For previous editions

Joaquín A. Blasco, Dileri Borunda Johnston, Isabel Ferrer Marrades,

José A. Gálvez, Sharon J. Hunter, Ana Cristina Llompart Lucas,

Janice McNeillie, Julie Muleba, Victoria Ordóñez Diví, José María Ruiz

Vaca, Carol Styles Carvajal, Eduardo Vallejo

ISBN 978-2-0354-2084-8

Distribución/Sales: Houghton Mifflin Company, Boston

LAROUSSE

Pocket
DICTIONARY

**SPANISH
ENGLISH**

**ENGLISH
SPANISH**

LAROUSSE

A NUESTROS LECTORES

El nuevo Diccionario POCKET Larousse es la herramienta de trabajo ideal para todas las situaciones lingüísticas, desde el aprendizaje de idiomas en la escuela y en casa hasta los viajes al extranjero.

Este diccionario está pensado para responder de manera práctica y rápida a los diferentes problemas que plantea la lectura del inglés actual. Con sus más de 55.000 palabras y expresiones y por encima de las 80.000 traducciones, este diccionario permitirá al lector comprender con claridad un amplio espectro de textos y realizar traducciones del inglés de uso corriente con rapidez y corrección.

Esta nueva obra recoge también numerosas siglas y abreviaturas actuales, además de nombres propios y términos comerciales e informáticos.

Gracias al análisis claro y detallado del vocabulario básico, así como de los indicadores de sentido que guían hacia la traducción más adecuada, se ayuda al usuario a escribir en inglés con precisión y seguridad.

Se ha puesto especial cuidado en la presentación de las entradas, tanto desde el punto de vista de su estructura como de la tipografía empleada. Para aquellos lectores que todavía están en un nivel básico o intermedio en su aprendizaje del inglés, el POCKET es el diccionario ideal.

Le invitamos a que se ponga en contacto con nosotros si tiene cualquier observación o crítica que hacer; entre todos podemos hacer del POCKET un diccionario aún mejor.

El Editor

TO OUR READERS

This new edition of the Larousse POCKET dictionary continues to be a reliable and user-friendly tool for all your language needs, from language learning at school and at home to travelling abroad. This handy dictionary is designed to provide fast and practical solutions to the various problems encountered when reading present-day Spanish. With over 55,000 references and 80,000 translations, it enables the user to read and enjoy a wide range of texts and to translate everyday Spanish quickly and accurately. This new dictionary also features up-to-date coverage of common abbreviations and acronyms; proper names, business terms and computing vocabulary.

Writing basic Spanish accurately and confidently is no longer a problem thanks to the POCKET's detailed coverage of essential vocabulary, and helpful sense-markers which guide the user to the most appropriate translation.

Careful thought has gone into the presentation of the entries, both in terms of layout and typography. The POCKET is the ideal reference work for all learners from beginners up to intermediate level.

Send us your comments or queries – you will be helping to make this dictionary an even better book.

The Publisher

Abbreviations

Abreviaturas

abbreviation	*abbr/abrev*	abreviatura
adjective	*adj*	adjetivo
administration	ADMIN	administración
adverb	*adv*	adverbio
aeronautics, aviation	AERON	aeronáutica
agriculture	AGR	agricultura
Latin American Spanish	*Amér*	español latinoamericano
anatomy	ANAT	anatomía
Andean Spanish	*Andes*	español de los Andes
before noun	*antes de s*	antes de sustantivo
archeology	ARCHEOL	arqueología
architecture	ARCHIT/ARQUIT	arquitectura
Argentinian Spanish	*Arg*	español de Argentina
article	*art*	artículo
astrology	ASTROL	astrología
astronomy	ASTRON	astronomía
automobile, cars	AUT(OM)	automóviles
auxiliary	*aux*	auxiliar
biology	BIOL	biología
Bolivian Spanish	*Bol*	español de Bolivia
botany	BOT	botánica
Central American Spanish	*CAm*	español de Centroamérica
Caribbean Spanish	*Carib*	español del Caribe
chemistry	CHEM	química
Chilean Spanish	*Chile*	español de Chile
cinema, film-making	CIN(EMA)	cine
Colombian Spanish	*Col*	español de Colombia
commerce, business	COM(M)	comercio
comparative	*compar*	comparativo
information technology	COMPUT	informática
conjunction	*conj*	conjunción
construction, building	CONSTR	construcción
continuous	*cont*	continuo
Costa Rican Spanish	*CRica*	español de Costa Rica
Cono Sur Spanish	*CSur*	español del Cono Sur
Cuban Spanish	*Cuba*	español de Cuba
culinary, cooking	CULIN	cocina
definite	*def*	determinado
demonstrative	*demos*	demostrativo
sport	DEP	deporte
juridical, legal	DER	derecho
pejorative	*despec*	despectivo
dated	*desus*	desusado
ecology	ECOLOG	ecología
economics	ECON	economía
school, education	EDUC	educación, escuela
electricity, electronics	ELEC(TR)	electricidad, electrónica
especially	*esp*	especialmente
exclamation	*excl*	interjección
feminine noun	*f*	sustantivo femenino
informal	*fam*	familiar
pharmacology, pharmaceuticals	FARM	farmacología, farmacia
figurative	*fig*	figurado
finance, financial	FIN	finanzas

Abbreviations

Abreviaturas

physics	FÍS	física
formal	*fml*	formal, culto
photography	FOTO	fotografía
soccer	FTBL	fútbol
inseparable	*fus*	inseparable
generally	*gen*	generalmente
geography	GEOGR	geografía
geology, geological	GEOL	geología
geometry	GEOM	geometría
grammar	GRAM(M)	gramática
Guatemalan Spanish	*Guat*	español de Guatemala
history	HIST	historia
humorous	*hum*	humorístico
industry	IND	industria
indefinite	*indef*	indeterminado
informal	*inf*	familiar
information technology	INFORM	informática
exclamation	*interj*	interjección
invariable	*inv*	invariable
ironic	*iro/irón*	irónico
juridical, legal	JUR	jurídico, derecho
linguistics	LING	lingüística
literal	*lit*	literal
literature	LITER	literatura
phrase(s)	*loc*	locución, locuciones
masculine noun	*m*	sustantivo masculino
mathematics	MAT(H)	matemáticas
mechanical engineering	MEC	mecánica
medicine	MED	medicina
metallurgy	METAL	metalurgia
weather, meteorology	METEOR	meteorología
Mexican Spanish	*Méx*	español de México
military	MIL	militar
mining	MIN	mineralogía
mythology	MYTH/MITOL	mitología
music	MUS/MÚS	música
noun	*n*	sustantivo
nautical, maritime	NAUT/NÁUT	náutica
Nicaraguan Spanish	*Nic*	español de Nicaragua
numeral	*num/núm*	número
oneself	*o.s*	
Panamanian Spanish	*Pan*	español de Panamá
pejorative	*pej*	despectivo
personal	*pers*	personal
Peruvian Spanish	*Perú*	español de Perú
pharmacology, pharmaceuticals	PHARM	farmacología, farmacia
photography	PHOT	fotografía
phrase(s)	*phr*	locución, locuciones
physics	PHYS	física
plural	*pl*	plural
politics	POL(ÍT)	política
possessive	*poss/poses*	posesivo
past participle	*pp*	participio pasado
press, journalism	PRENS	periodismo

Abbreviations

Abreviaturas

preposition	*prep*	preposición
Porto Rican Spanish	*PRico*	español de Puerto Rico
pronoun	*pron*	pronombre
psychology	PSYCH/PSICOL	psicología
past tense	*pt*	pasado, pretérito
chemistry	QUÍM	química
registered trademark	®	marca registrada
railways	RAIL	ferrocarril
relative	*relat*	relativo
religion	RELIG	religión
River Plate Spanish	*RP*	español del Río de la Plata
noun	*s*	sustantivo
someone, somebody	*sb*	
school, education	SCH	educación, escuela
Scottish English	*Scot*	inglés de Escocia
separable	*sep*	separable
singular	*sg*	singular
slang	*sl*	argot
sociology	SOCIOL	sociología
Stock Exchange	ST EX	bolsa
something	*sthg*	
subject	*subj/suj*	sujeto
superlative	*superl*	superlativo
bullfighting	TAUROM	tauromaquia
theatre	TEATR	teatro
technical, technology	TECH/TECN	técnico, tecnología
telecommunications	TELEC(OM)	telecomunicaciones
television	TV	televisión
printing, typography	TYPO	imprenta
uncountable noun	U	sustantivo 'incontable'
British English	UK	inglés británico
university	UNI	universidad
Uruguayan Spanish	*Urug*	español de Uruguay
American English	US	inglés americano
verb	*vb/v*	verbo
Venezuelan Spanish	*Ven*	español de Venezuela
veterinary science	VETER	veterinaria
intransitive verb	*vi*	verbo intransitivo
impersonal verb	*v impers*	verbo impersonal
pronominal verb	*vpr*	verbo pronominal
transitive verb	*vt*	verbo transitivo
vulgar	*vulg*	vulgar
zoology	ZOOL	zoología
cultural equivalent	≃	equivalente cultural

La ordenación alfabética en español

En este diccionario se ha seguido la ordenación alfabética internacional. Esto significa que las entradas con **ch** aparecerán después de **cg** y no al final de **c**; del mismo modo las entradas con **ll** vendrán después de **lk** y no al final de **l**. Adviértase, sin embargo, que la letra **ñ** sí se considera letra aparte y sigue a la **n**.

Spanish alphabetical order

The dictionary follows international alphabetical order. Thus entries with **ch** appear after **cg** and not at the end of **c**. Similarly, entries with **ll** appear after **lk** and not at the end of **l**. Note, however, that **ñ** is treated as a separate letter and follows **n**.

Los compuestos en inglés

En inglés se llama compuesto a una locución sustantiva de significado único pero formada por más de una palabra; p.ej. **point of view**, **kiss of life** o **virtual reality**. Uno de los rasgos distintivos de este diccionario es la inclusión de estos compuestos con entrada propia y en riguroso orden alfabético. De esta forma **blood test** vendrá después de **bloodshot**, el cual sigue a **blood pressure**.

English compounds

A compound is a word or expression which has a single meaning but is made up of more than one word, e.g. **point of view**, **kiss of life** and **virtual reality**. It is a feature of this dictionary that English compounds appear in the A-Z list in strict alphabetical order. The compound **blood test** will therefore come after **bloodshot** which itself follows **blood pressure**.

Marcas registradas

Los nombres de marca aparecen señalados en este diccionario con el símbolo ®. Sin embargo, ni este símbolo ni su ausencia son representativos de la situación legal de la marca.

Trademarks

Words considered to be trademarks have been designated in this dictionary by the symbol ®. However, neither the presence nor the absence of such designation should be regarded as affecting the legal status of any trademark.

Phonetics

English vowels

[ɪ]   pit, big, rid
[e]   pet, tend
[æ]   pat, bag, mad
[ʌ]   run, cut
[ɒ]   pot, log
[ʊ]   put, full
[ə]   mother, suppose

[iː]   bean, weed
[ɑː]   barn, car, laugh
[ɔː]   born, lawn
[uː]   loop, loose
[ɜː]   burn, learn, bird

English diphthongs

[eɪ]   bay, late, great
[aɪ]   buy, light, aisle
[ɔɪ]   boy, foil
[əʊ]   no, road, blow
[aʊ]   now, shout, town
[ɪə]   peer, fierce, idea
[eə]   pair, bear, share
[ʊə]   poor, sure, tour

English semi-vowels

[j]   you, spaniel
[w]   wet, why, twin

English consonants

[p]   pop, people
[b]   bottle, bib
[t]   train, tip
[d]   dog, did
[k]   come, kitchen
[g]   gag, great
[tʃ]   chain, wretched
[dʒ]   jet, fridge
[f]   fib, physical
[v]   vine, live
[θ]   think, fifth
[ð]   this, with
[s]   seal, peace
[z]   zip, his
[ʃ]   sheep, machine

Fonética

Vocales españolas

[i]   piso, imagen
[e]   tela, eso
[a]   pata, amigo
[o]   bola, otro
[u]   luz, luna

Diptongos españoles

[ei]   ley, peine
[ai]   aire, caiga
[oi]   soy, boina
[au]   causa, aula
[eu]   Europa, deuda

Semivocales españoles

[j]   hierba, miedo
[w]   agua, hueso

Consonantes españoles

[p]   papá, campo
[b]   vaca, bomba
[β]   curvo, caballo
[t]   toro, pato
[d]   donde, caldo
[k]   que, cosa
[g]   grande, guerra
[ɣ]   aguijón, iglesia
[tʃ]   ocho, chusma
[f]   fui, afán
[θ]   cera, paz
[ð]   cada, pardo
[s]   solo, paso
[z]   andinismo
[x]   gemir, jamón

[ʒ]	usual, measure	[m]	madre, cama
[h]	how, perhaps	[n]	no, pena
[m]	metal, comb	[ŋ]	banca, encanto
[n]	night, dinner	[ɲ]	caña
[ŋ]	sung, parking	[l]	ala, luz
[l]	little, help	[ɾ]	atar, paro
[r]	right, carry	[r]	perro, rosa
		[ʎ]	llave, collar

Los símbolos ['] y [,] indican que la sílaba siguiente lleva un acento primario o secundario respectivamente.

The symbol ['] indicates that the following syllable carries primary stress and the symbol [,] that the following syllable carries secondary stress.

El símbolo [ʳ] en fonética inglesa indica que la r al final de palabra se pronuncia sólo cuando precede a una palabra que comienza por vocal. Adviértase que casi siempre se pronuncia en inglés americano.

The symbol [ʳ] in English phonetics indicates that the final r is pronounced only when followed by a word beginning with a vowel. Note that it is nearly always pronounced in American English.

CONJUGACIONES ESPAÑOLAS

ENGLISH VERB TABLES

Conjugaciones españolas

Llave: A = presente indicativo, **B** = imperfecto indicativo, **C** = pretérito perfecto simple, **D** = futuro, **E** = condicional, **F** = presente subjuntivo, **G** = imperfecto subjuntivo, **H** = imperativo, **I** = gerundio, **J** = participio

acertar A acierto, acertamos, etc., **F** acierte, acertemos, etc., **H** acierta, acierte, acertemos, acertad, etc.

adquirir A adquiero, adquirimos, etc., **F** adquiera, adquiramos, etc.,**H** adquiere, adquiramos, adquirid, etc.

AMAR A amo, amas, ama, amamos, amáis, aman, **B** amaba, amabas, amaba, amábamos, amabais, amaban, **C** amé, amaste, amó, amamos, amasteis, amaron, **D** amaré, amarás, amará, amaremos, amaréis, amarán, **E** amaría, amarías, amaría, amaríamos, amaríais, amarían, **F** ame, ames, ame, amemos, améis, amen, **G** amara, amaras, amara, amáramos, amarais, amaran, **H** ama, ame, amemos, amad, amen, **I** amando, **J** amado, -da

andar C anduve, anduvimos, etc., **G** anduviera, anduviéramos, etc.

avergonzar A avergüenzo, avergonzamos, etc., **C** avergoncé, avergonzó, avergonzamos, etc., **F** avergüence, avergoncemos, etc., **H** avergüenza, avergüence, avergoncemos, avergonzad, etc.

caber A quepo, cabe, cabemos, etc., **C** cupe, cupimos, etc., **D** cabré, cabremos, etc., **E** cabría, cabríamos, etc., **F** quepa, quepamos, cabed, etc., **G** cupiera, cupiéramos, etc., **H** cabe, quepa, quepamos, etc.

caer A caigo, cae, caemos, etc., **C** cayó, caímos, cayeron, etc., **F** caiga, caigamos, etc., **G** cayera, cayéramos, etc., **H** cae, caiga, caigamos, caed, etc., **I** cayendo

conducir A conduzco, conduce, conducimos, etc., **C** conduje, condujimos, etc., **F** conduzca, conduzcamos, etc., **G** condujera, condujé-ramos, etc., **H** conduce, conduzca, conduzcamos, conducid, etc.

conocer A conozco, conoce, conocemos, etc., **F** conozca, conozcamos, etc. **H** conoce, conozca, conozcamos, etc.

dar A doy, da, damos, etc., **C** di, dio, dimos, etc., **F** dé, demos, etc., **G** diera, diéramos, etc., **H** da, dé, demos, dad, etc.

decir A digo, dice, decimos, etc., **C** dije, dijimos, etc., **D** diré, diremos, etc., **E** diría, diríamos, etc., **F** diga, digamos, etc., **G** dijera, dijéramos, etc., **H** di, diga, digamos, decid, etc., **I** diciendo, **J** dicho, -cha

dormir A duermo, dormimos, etc., **C** durmió, dormimos, durmieron, etc., **F** duerma, durmamos, etc., **G** durmiera, durmiéramos, etc., **H** duerme, duerma, durmamos, dormid, etc., **I** durmiendo

errar A yerro, erramos, etc., **F** yerre, erremos, etc., **H** yerra, yerre, erremos, errad, etc.

estar A estoy, está, estamos, etc., **C** estuve, estuvimos, etc., **F** esté, estemos, etc., **G** estuviera, estuviéramos, etc., **H** está, esté, estemos, estad, etc.

HABER A he, has, ha, hemos, habéis, han, **B** había, habías, había, habíamos, habíais, habían, **C** hube, hubiste, hubo, hubimos, hubisteis, hubieron, **D** habré, habrás, habrá, habremos, habréis, habrán, **E** habría, habrías, habría, habríamos, habríais, habrían, **F** haya, hayas, haya, hayamos, hayáis, hayan, **G** hubiera, hubieras, hubiera, hubiéramos, hubierais, hubieran, **H** he, haya, hayamos, habed, hayan, **I** habiendo, **J** habido, -da

hacer A hago, hace, hacemos, etc., **C** hice, hizo, hicimos, etc., **D** haré, haremos, etc., **E** haría, haríamos, etc., **F** haga, hagamos, etc., **G** hiciera, hiciéramos, etc., **H** haz, haga, hagamos, haced, etc., **J** hecho, -cha

huir A huyo, huimos, etc., **C** huyó, huimos, huyeron, **F** huya, huyamos, etc. **G** huyera, huyéramos, etc. **H** huye, huya, huyamos, huid, etc., **I** huyendo

ir A voy, va, vamos, etc., **C** fui, fue, fuimos, etc., **F** vaya, vayamos, etc., **G** fuera, fuéramos, etc., **H** ve, vaya, vayamos, id, etc., I yendo

leer C leyó, leímos, leyeron, etc., G leyera, leyéramos, etc., I leyendo

lucir A luzco, luce, lucimos, etc., F luzca, luzcamos, H luce, luzca, luzcamos, lucid, etc.

mover A muevo, movemos, etc., F mueva, movamos, etc., H mueve, mueva, movamos, moved, etc.

nacer A nazco, nace, nacemos, etc., F nazca, nazcamos, etc., H nace, nazca, nazcamos, naced, etc.

oír A oigo, oye, oímos, etc., C oyó, oímos, oyeron, etc., F oiga, oigamos, etc., G oyera, oyéramos, etc., H oye, oiga, oigamos, oíd, etc., I oyendo

oler A huelo, olemos, etc., F huela, olamos, etc., H huele, huela, olamos, oled, etc.

parecer A parezco, parece, parecemos, etc., F parezca, parezcamos, etc., H parece, parezca, parezcamos, pareced, etc.

PARTIR A parto, partes, parte, partimos, partís, parten, B partía, partías, partía, partíamos, partíais, partían, C partí, partiste, partió, partimos, partisteis, partieron, D partiré, partirás, partirá, partiremos, partiréis, partirán, E partiría, partirías, partiría, partiríamos, partiríais, partirían, F parta, partas, parta, partamos, partáis, partan, G partiera, partieras, partiera, partiéramos, partierais, partieran, H parte, parta, partamos, partid, partan, I partiendo, J partido, -da.

pedir A pido, pedimos, etc., C pidió, pedimos, pidieron, etc., F pida, pidamos, etc., G pidiera, pidiéramos, etc., H pide, pida, pidamos, pedid, etc., I pidiendo

poder A puedo, podemos, etc., C pude, pudimos, etc., D podré, podremos, etc., E podría, podríamos, etc., F pueda, podamos, etc., H puede, pueda, podamos, poded, etc., I pudiendo

poner A pongo, pone, ponemos, etc., C puse, pusimos, etc., D pondré, pondremos, etc., E pondría, pondríamos, etc., F ponga, pongamos, etc., G pusiera, pusiéramos, etc., H pon, ponga, pongamos, poned, etc., J puesto, -ta

querer A quiero, queremos, etc., C quise, quisimos, etc., D querré, querremos, etc., E querría, querríamos, etc., F quiera, queramos, etc., G quisiera, quisiéramos, etc., H quiere, quiera, queramos, quered, etc.

reír A río, reímos, etc., C rió, reímos, rieron, etc., F ría, riamos, etc., G riera, riéramos, etc., H ríe, ría, riamos, reíd, etc., I riendo

saber A sé, sabe, sabemos, etc., C supe, supimos, etc., D sabré, sabremos, etc., E sabría, sabríamos, etc., F sepa, sepamos, etc., G supiera, supiéramos, etc., H sabe, sepa, sepamos, sabed, etc.

salir A salgo, sale, salimos, etc., D saldré, saldremos, etc., E saldría, saldríamos, etc., F salga, salgamos, etc., H sal, salga, salgamos, salid, etc.

sentir A siento, sentimos, etc., C sintió, sentimos, sintieron, etc., F sienta, sintamos, etc., G sintiera, sintiéramos, etc., H siente, sienta, sintamos, sentid, etc., I sintiendo

SER A soy, eres, es, somos, sois, son, B era, eras, era, éramos, erais, eran, C fui, fuiste, fue, fuimos, fuisteis, fueron, D seré, serás, será, seremos, seréis, serán, E sería, serías, sería, seríamos, seríais, serían, F sea, seas, sea, seamos, seáis, sean, G fuera, fueras, fuera, fuéramos, fuerais, fueran, H sé, sea, seamos, sed, sean, I siendo, J sido, -da

sonar A sueno, sonamos, etc., F suene, sonemos, etc., H suena, suene, sonemos, sonad, etc.

TEMER A temo, temes, teme, tememos, teméis, temen, B temía, temías, temía, temíamos, temíais, temían, C temí, temiste, temió, temimos, temisteis, temieron, D temeré, temerás, temerá, temeremos, temeréis, temerán, E temería, temerías, temería, temeríamos, temeríais, temerían, F tema, temas, tema, temamos, temáis, teman, G temiera, temieras, temiera, temiéramos, temierais, temieran, H teme, tema, temamos, temed, teman, I temiendo, J temido, -da

tender A tiendo, tendemos, etc., F tienda, tendamos, etc., H tiende, tendamos, etc.

tener A tengo, tiene, tenemos, etc., C tuve, tuvimos, etc., D tendré, tendremos, etc., E tendría, tendríamos, etc., F tenga, tengamos, etc., G tuviera, tuviéramos, etc., H ten, tenga, tengamos, tened, etc.

traer A traigo, trae, traemos, etc., C traje, trajimos, etc., F traiga, traigamos, etc., G trajera, trajéramos, etc., H trae, traiga, traigamos, traed, etc., I trayendo

valer A valgo, vale, valemos, etc., D valdré, valdremos, etc., F valga, valga-mos, etc., H vale, valga, valgamos, valed, etc.

venir A vengo, viene, venimos, etc., C vine, vinimos, etc., D vendré, vendremos, etc., E vendría, vendríamos, etc., F venga, vengamos, etc., G viniera, viniéramos, etc., H ven, venga, vengamos, venid, etc., I viniendo

ver A veo, ve, vemos, etc., C vi, vio, vimos, etc., G viera, viéramos, etc., H ve, vea, veamos, ved, etc., I viendo, J visto, -ta.

English Irregular Verbs

Infinitive	Past Tense	Past Participle	Infinitive	Past Tense	Past Participle
arise	arose	arisen	forget	forgot	forgotten
awake	awoke	awoken	freeze	froze	frozen
be	was/were	been	get	got	got (US gotten)
bear	bore	born(e)			
beat	beat	beaten	give	gave	given
begin	began	begun	go	went	gone
bend	bent	bent	grind	ground	ground
bet	bet/ betted	bet/ betted	grow	grew	grown
			hang	hung/ hanged	hung/ hanged
bid	bid	bid	have	had	had
bind	bound	bound	hear	heard	heard
bite	bit	bitten	hide	hid	hidden
bleed	bled	bled	hit	hit	hit
blow	blew	blown	hold	held	held
break	broke	broken	hurt	hurt	hurt
breed	bred	bred	keep	kept	kept
bring	brought	brought	kneel	knelt/ kneeled	knelt/ kneeled
build	built	built			
burn	burnt/ burned	burnt/ burned	know	knew	known
burst	burst	burst	lay	laid	laid
buy	bought	bought	lead	led	led
can	could	-	lean	leant/ leaned	leant/ leaned
cast	cast	cast			
catch	caught	caught	leap	leapt/ leaped	leapt/ leaped
choose	chose	chosen			
come	came	come	learn	learnt/ learned	learnt/ learned
cost	cost	cost			
creep	crept	crept	leave	left	left
cut	cut	cut	lend	lent	lent
deal	dealt	dealt	let	let	let
dig	dug	dug	lie	lay	lain
do	did	done	light	lit/lighted	lit/lighted
draw	drew	drawn	lose	lost	lost
dream	dreamed/ dreamt	dreamed/ dreamt	make	made	made
			may	might	-
drink	drank	drunk	mean	meant	meant
drive	drove	driven	meet	met	met
eat	ate	eaten	mow	mowed	mown/ mowed
fall	fell	fallen			
feed	fed	fed	pay	paid	paid
feel	felt	felt	put	put	put
fight	fought	fought	quit	quit/ quitted	quit/ quitted
find	found	found			
fling	flung	flung	read	read	read
fly	flew	flown	rid	rid	rid

Infinitive	Past Tense	Past Participle	Infinitive	Past Tense	Past Participle
ride	rode	ridden	spin	spun	spun
ring	rang	rung	spit	spat	spat
rise	rose	risen	split	split	split
run	ran	run	spoil	spoiled/ spoilt	spoiled/ spoilt
saw	sawed	sawn			
say	said	said	spread	spread	spread
see	saw	seen	spring	sprang	sprung
seek	sought	sought	stand	stood	stood
sell	sold	sold	steal	stole	stolen
send	sent	sent	stick	stuck	stuck
set	set	set	sting	stung	stung
shake	shook	shaken	stink	stank	stunk
shall	should	-	strike	struck	struck/ stricken
shed	shed	shed			
shine	shone	shone	swear	swore	sworn
shoot	shot	shot	sweep	swept	swept
show	showed	shown	swell	swelled	swollen/ swelled
shrink	shrank	shrunk			
shut	shut	shut	swim	swam	swum
sing	sang	sung	swing	swung	swung
sink	sank	sunk	take	took	taken
sit	sat	sat	teach	taught	taught
sleep	slept	slept	tear	tore	torn
slide	slid	slid	tell	told	told
sling	slung	slung	think	thought	thought
smell	smelt/ smelled	smelt/ smelled	throw	threw	thrown
			tread	trod	trodden
sow	sowed	sown/ sowed	wake	woke/ waked	woken/ waked
speak	spoke	spoken	wear	wore	worn
speed	sped/ speeded	sped/ speeded	weave	wove/ weaved	woven/ weaved
spell	spelt/ spelled	spelt/ spelled	weep	wept	wept
			win	won	won
spend	spent	spent	wind	wound	wound
spill	spilt/ spilled	spilt/ spilled	wring	wrung	wrung
			write	wrote	written

ESPAÑOL-INGLÉS
SPANISH-ENGLISH

a¹ (*pl* aes), **A** (*pl* Aes) *sf* [letra] a, A.

a² *prep* (a + el = al) - **1.** [periodo de tiempo]: **a las pocas semanas** a few weeks later; **al día siguiente** the following day - **2.** [momento preciso] at; **a las siete** at seven o'clock; **a los 11 años** at the age of 11; **al caer la noche** at nightfall; **al oír la noticia, se desmayó** on hearing the news, she fainted - **3.** [frecuencia]: **40 horas a la semana** 40 hours per O a week; **tres veces al día** three times a day - **4.** [dirección] to; **voy a Sevilla** I'm going to Seville; **me voy al extranjero** I'm going abroad; **llegó a Barcelona/la fiesta** he arrived in Barcelona/at the party - **5.** [posición]: **a la puerta** at the door - **6.** [distancia]: **está a más de cien kilómetros de aquí** it's more than a hundred kilometres from here - **7.** [con complemento indirecto] to; **dáselo a Juan** give it to Juan; **dile a Juan que venga** tell Juan to come - **8.** [con complemento directo]: **quiere a sus hijos/su gato** she loves her children/her cat - **9.** [cantidad, medida, precio]: **a cientos/miles/docenas** by the hundred/thousand/dozen; **a 90 km por hora** (at) 90 km per hour; **¿a cuánto están las peras?** how much are the pears?; **tiene las peras a tres euros** she's selling pears for O at three euros; **ganaron tres a cero** they won three nil - **10.** [modo]: **lo hace a la antigua** he does it the old way; **a lo Mozart** in Mozart's style; **a cuadros** checked; **a escondidas** secretly; **poco a poco** little by little - **11.** [instrumento]: **escribir a máquina** to use a typewriter; **a lápiz** in pencil; **a mano** by hand - **12.** *(después de v y antes de infinitivo)* [finalidad] to; **entró a pagar** he came in to pay; **aprender a nadar** to learn to swim - **13.** *(después de s y antes de infinitivo)* [complemento de nombre]: **temas a tratar** matters to be discussed - **14.** [en oraciones imperativas]: **¡a la cama!** go to bed!; **¡a bailar!** let's dance!

AA (*abrev de* Alcohólicos Anónimos) *smpl* AA.

abad, esa *sm, f* abbot (*f* abbess).

abadía *sf* abbey.

abajo <> *adv* - **1.** [posición - gen] below; [- en edificio] downstairs; **vive (en el piso de) abajo** she lives downstairs; **más abajo** further down - **2.** [dirección] down; **ve abajo** [en edificio] go downstairs; **hacia/para abajo** down, downwards; **calle/escaleras abajo** down the street/stairs; **río abajo** downstream - **3.** [en un texto] below. <> *interj*: **¡abajo la dictadura!** down with the dictatorship! ➤ **de abajo** *loc adj* bottom.

abalanzarse *vprnl*: **abalanzarse sobre** to fall upon; **abalanzarse hacia** to rush towards.

abalear *vt Andes, Amér C & Ven* to shoot at.

abalorio *sm* (*gen pl*) [bisutería] trinket.

abanderado *sm lit & fig* standard-bearer.

abandonado, da *adj* - **1.** [desierto] deserted - **2.** [desamparado] abandoned - **3.** [descuidado - jardín, casa] neglected; **dejar abandonado** to abandon.

abandonar *vt* - **1.** [gen] to abandon; [lugar, profesión, cónyuge] to leave - **2.** [desatender - obligaciones, estudios] to neglect. ➤ **abandonarse** *vprnl* [a una emoción]: **abandonarse a** [desesperación, dolor] to succumb to; [bebida, drogas] to give o.s. over to.

abandono *sm* - **1.** [acción - gen] abandonment; [- de lugar, profesión, cónyuge] leaving; [- de obligaciones, estudios] neglect - **2.** [estado] state of abandon - **3.** DEP: **ganar por abandono** to win by default.

abanicar *vt* to fan.

abanico *sm* [para dar aire] fan.

abaratar *vt* to reduce the price of. ➤ **abaratarse** *vprnl* to become cheaper.

abarcar *vt* [incluir] to embrace, to cover.

abarrotado, da *adj*: abarrotado (de) [teatro, autobús] packed (with); [desván, baúl] crammed (with).

abarrotar *vt*: abarrotar algo (de O con) [teatro, autobús] to pack sthg (with); [desván, baúl] to cram sthg full (of).

abarrotería *sf* Amér C & Méx grocer's (shop) *UK*, grocery store *US*.

abarrotero, ra *sm, f* Amér C & Méx grocer.

abarrotes *smpl* Amér groceries.

abastecer *vt*: abastecer algo/a alguien (de) to supply sthg/sb (with).

abastecimiento *sm* [cantidad] supply; [acción] supplying.

abasto *sm*: no dar abasto para hacer algo to be unable to cope with doing sthg; no doy abasto con tanto trabajo I can't cope with all this work.

abatible *adj* reclining; de alas abatibles gate-legged.

abatido, da *adj* dejected.

abatir *vt* - 1. [derribar - muro] to knock down; [- avión] to shoot down - 2. [desanimar] to depress. ◆ **abatirse** *vprnl*: abatirse (sobre) to swoop (down on).

abdicación *sf* abdication.

abdicar *vi* to abdicate; abdicar de algo *fig* to renounce sthg.

abdomen *sm* abdomen.

abdominal *adj* abdominal.

abecé *sm lit & fig* ABC.

abecedario *sm* [alfabeto] alphabet.

abedul *sm* birch (tree).

abeja *sf* bee.

abejorro *sm* bumblebee.

aberración *sf* aberration; eso es una aberración that's absurd.

abertura *sf* opening.

abertzale [aβer'tʃale] *adj & smf* Basque nationalist.

abeto *sm* fir (tree).

abierto, ta ◇ *pp* ▷ **abrir**. ◇ *adj* [gen] open; dejar el grifo abierto to leave the tap on; bien O muy abierto wide open.

abigarrado, da *adj* multi-coloured; *fig* motley.

abismal *adj* vast, colossal.

abismo *sm* [profundidad] abyss.

abjurar *culto vi*: abjurar de algo to abjure sthg.

ablandar *vt* [material] to soften. ◆ **ablandarse** *vprnl* [material] to soften.

abnegación *sf* abnegation, self-denial.

abochornar *vt* to embarrass. ◆ **abochornarse** *vprnl* to get embarrassed.

abofetear *vt* to slap.

abogacía *sf* legal profession.

abogado, da *sm, f* lawyer, attorney *US*; abogado defensor counsel for the defence; abogado del estado public prosecutor.

abogar *vi fig* [defender]: abogar por algo to advocate sthg; abogar por alguien to stand up for sb.

abolengo *sm* lineage.

abolición *sf* abolition.

abolir *vt* to abolish.

abolladura *sf* dent.

abollar *vt* to dent.

abominable *adj* abominable.

abonado, da *sm, f* [de teléfono, revista] subscriber; [al fútbol, teatro, transporte] season-ticket holder.

abonar *vt* - 1. [pagar] to pay; abonar algo en la cuenta de alguien to credit sb's account with sthg - 2. [tierra] to fertilize. ◆ **abonarse** *vprnl*: abonarse (a) [revista] to subscribe (to); [fútbol, teatro, transporte] to buy a season ticket (for).

abonero, ra *sm, f* Méx hawker, street trader.

abono *sm* - 1. [pase] season ticket - 2. [fertilizante] fertilizer - 3. [pago] payment - 4. Méx [plazo] instalment.

abordar *vt* - 1. [embarcación] to board - 2. *fig* [tema, tarea] to tackle.

aborigen *adj* [indígena] indigenous; [de Australia] aboriginal.

aborrecer *vt* [actividad] to abhor; [persona] to loathe.

abortar *vi* [MED - espontáneamente] to have a miscarriage; [- intencionadamente] to have an abortion.

aborto *sm* [MED - espontáneo] miscarriage; [- intencionado] abortion.

abotonar *vt* to button up. ◆ **abotonarse** *vprnl* to do one's buttons up; [abrigo, camisa] to button up.

abovedado, da *adj* arched, vaulted.

abrasar *vt* - 1. [quemar - casa, bosque] to burn down; [- persona, mano, garganta] to burn; murieron abrasados they were burned to death - 2. [desecar - suj: sol, calor, lejía] to scorch; [- suj: sed] to parch.

abrazadera *sf* TECNOL brace, bracket; [en carpintería] clamp.

abrazar *vt* [con los brazos] to hug, to embrace; abrazar fuerte a alguien to hold sb tight. ◆ **abrazarse** *vprnl* to hug O embrace (each other).

abrazo *sm* embrace, hug.

abrebotellas *sm inv* bottle opener.

abrecartas *sm inv* paper knife.

abrelatas *sm inv* tin opener *UK*, can opener *US*.

abreviar *vt* [gen] to shorten, [texto] to abridge; [palabra] to abbreviate; [viaje, estancia] to cut short.

abreviatura *sf* abbreviation.

abridor *sm* - **1.** [abrebotellas] (bottle) opener - **2.** [abrelatas] (tin) opener *UK*, (can) opener *US*.

abrigar *vt* - **1.** [arropar - suj: persona] to wrap up; [- suj: ropa] to keep warm - **2.** *fig* [albergar - esperanza] to cherish; [- sospechas, malas intenciones] to harbour. ◆ **abrigarse** *vprnl* [arroparse] to wrap up.

abrigo *sm* - **1.** [prenda] coat, overcoat - **2.** [refugio] shelter.

abril *sm* April; *ver también* **septiembre**.

abrillantar *vt* to polish.

abrir ◇ *vt* - **1.** [gen] to open; [alas] to spread; [melón] to cut open - **2.** [puerta] to unlock, to open; [pestillo] to pull back; [grifo] to turn on; [cremallera] to undo - **3.** [túnel] to dig; [canal, camino] to build; [agujero, surco] to make. ◇ *vi* [establecimiento] to open. ◆ **abrirse** *vprnl* - **1.** [sincerarse]: **abrirse a alguien** to open up to sb, to confide in sb - **2.** [cielo] to clear.

abrochar *vt* [camisa, botón] to do up; [cinturón] to fasten. ◆ **abrocharse** *vprnl* to do up; [cinturón] to fasten.

abrumar *vt* [agobiar] to overwhelm.

abrupto, ta *adj* [escarpado] sheer; [accidentado] rugged.

absceso *sm* abscess.

absentismo *sm* [de terrateniente] absentee landownership.

ábside *sm* apse.

absolución *sf* - **1.** DER acquittal - **2.** RELIG absolution.

absoluto, ta *adj* [gen] absolute; [silencio, obediencia] total. ◆ **en absoluto** *loc adv* [en negativas] at all; [tras pregunta] not at all; **¿te gusta? – en absoluto** do you like it? – not at all; **nada en absoluto** nothing at all.

absolver *vt*: **absolver a alguien (de algo)** DER to acquit sb (of sthg); RELIG to absolve sb (of sthg).

absorbente *adj* - **1.** [que empapa] absorbent - **2.** [actividad] absorbing.

absorber *vt* - **1.** [gen] to absorb - **2.** [consumir, gastar] to soak up.

absorción *sf* absorption.

absorto, ta *adj*: **absorto (en)** absorbed O engrossed (in).

abstemio, mia *adj* teetotal.

abstención *sf* abstention.

abstenerse *vprnl*: **abstenerse (de algo/de hacer algo)** to abstain (from sthg/from doing sthg); **le han recomendado que se abstenga del alcohol** she has been advised to stay off the alcohol.

abstinencia *sf* abstinence.

abstracción *sf* [gen] abstraction.

abstracto, ta *adj* abstract.

abstraer *vt* to consider separately.

abstraído, da *adj* lost in thought.

absuelto, ta *pp* ▷ **absolver**.

absurdo, da *adj* absurd. ◆ **absurdo** *sm*: **decir/hacer un absurdo** to say/do something ridiculous.

abuchear *vt* to boo.

abuelo, la *sm, f* [familiar] grandfather (*f* grandmother). ◆ **abuelos** *smpl* grandparents.

abulia *sf* apathy, lethargy.

abúlico, ca *adj* apathetic, lethargic.

abultado, da *adj* [paquete] bulky; [labios] thick; [cantidad, cifra] inflated.

abultar ◇ *vt* - **1.** [hinchar] to swell - **2.** [exagerar] to blow up. ◇ *vi* [ser muy grande] to be bulky.

abundancia *sf* - **1.** [gran cantidad] abundance; **en abundancia** in abundance - **2.** [riqueza] plenty, prosperity.

abundante *adj* abundant.

abundar *vi* [ser abundante] to abound.

aburguesarse *vprnl* to adopt middle-class ways.

aburrido, da ◇ *adj* - **1.** [harto, fastidiado] bored; **estar aburrido de hacer algo** to be fed up with doing sthg - **2.** [que aburre] boring. ◇ *sm, f* bore.

aburrimiento *sm* boredom; **¡qué aburrimiento!** what a bore!

aburrir *vt* to bore; **me aburre** I'm bored of it. ◆ **aburrirse** *vprnl* to get bored; [estar aburrido] to be bored.

abusado, da *adj Méx* astute, shrewd.

abusar *vi* - **1.** [excederse] to go too far; **abusar de algo** to abuse sthg; **abusar del alcohol** to drink too much; **abusar de alguien** to take advantage of sb - **2.** [forzar sexualmente]: **abusar de alguien** to sexually abuse sb.

abusivo, va *adj* [trato] very bad, appalling; [precio] extortionate.

abuso *sm* [uso excesivo]: **abuso (de)** abuse (of); **abuso de confianza** breach of confidence; **abusos deshonestos** sexual abuse *(U)*.

abyecto, ta *adj culto* vile, wretched.

a. C. (*abrev de* antes de Cristo) BC.

acá *adv* - **1.** [lugar] here; **de acá para allá** back and forth - **2.** [tiempo]: **de una semana acá** during the last week.

acabado, da adj - 1. [completo] perfect, consummate - 2. [fracasado] finished. ◆ **acabado** sm [de producto] finish; [de piso] décor.

acabar ◇ vt - 1. [concluir] to finish - 2. [consumir - provisiones, dinero] to use up; [- comida] to finish. ◇ vi - 1. [gen] to finish, to end; **acabar de hacer algo** to finish doing sthg - 2. [haber hecho recientemente]: **acabar de hacer algo** to have just done sthg; **acabo de llegar** I've just arrived - 3. [terminar por - persona]: **acabar por hacer algo, acabar haciendo algo** to end up doing sthg - 4. [destruir]: **acabar con** [gen] to destroy; [salud] to ruin; [paciencia] to exhaust; [violencia, crimen] to put an end to. ◆ **acabarse** vprnl - 1. [agotarse] to be used up; **se nos ha acabado el petróleo** we're out of petrol; **se ha acabado la comida** there's no more food left, all the food has gone - 2. [concluir] to finish, to be over - 3. loc: **¡se acabó!** [¡basta ya!] that's enough!; [se terminó] that's it, then!

acabose sm fam: **¡es el acabose!** it really is the limit!

academia sf - 1. [para aprender] school - 2. [institución] academy. ◆ **Real Academia Española** sf institution that sets lexical and syntactical standards for Spanish.

académico, ca adj academic.

acaecer v impers culto to occur.

acallar vt to silence.

acalorado, da adj - 1. [por calor] hot - 2. [apasionado - debate] heated.

acalorar vt [enfadar]: **acalorar a alguien** to make sb hot under the collar. ◆ **acalorarse** vprnl [enfadarse] to get aroused O excited.

acampanado, da adj flared.

acampar vi to camp.

acanalado, da adj [columna] fluted; [tejido] ribbed; [hierro, uralita] corrugated.

acantilado sm cliff.

acaparar vt - 1. [monopolizar] to monopolize; [mercado] to corner - 2. [guardarse] to hoard.

acápite sm Amér paragraph.

acaramelado, da adj fig [pegajoso] sickly sweet.

acariciar vt - 1. [persona] to caress; [animal] to stroke - 2. fig [idea, proyecto] to cherish.

acarrear vt - 1. [transportar] to carry; [carbón] to haul - 2. fig [ocasionar] to bring, to give rise to.

acaso adv perhaps; **¿acaso no lo sabías?** are you trying to tell me you didn't know?; **por si acaso** (just) in case; **¿acaso es culpa mía?** is it my fault? ◆ **si acaso** ◇ loc adv [en todo caso] if anything. ◇ loc conj [en caso de que] if.

acatar vt to respect, to comply with.

acatarrarse vprnl to catch a cold.

acaudalado, da adj well-to-do.

acaudillar vt to lead.

acceder vi - 1. [consentir]: **acceder (a algo/hacer algo)** to agree (to sthg/to do sthg) - 2. [tener acceso]: **acceder a** to enter - 3. [alcanzar]: **acceder a** [trono] to accede to; [poder] to come to; [cargo] to obtain.

accesible adj [lugar] accessible.

accésit sm inv consolation prize.

acceso sm - 1. [entrada]: **acceso (a)** entrance (to) - 2. [paso]: **acceso (a)** access (to); **acceso a Internet** Internet access; **acceso remoto** remote access - 3. [carretera] access road, ramp US - 4. fig & MED [de tos] fit; [de fiebre, gripe] bout.

accesorio, ria adj incidental. ◆ **accesorio** (gen pl) sm accessory.

accidentado, da ◇ adj - 1. [vida, viaje] eventful - 2. [terreno, camino] rough, rugged. ◇ sm, f injured person, victim.

accidental adj [imprevisto] accidental; [encuentro] chance.

accidentarse vprnl to be involved in O have an accident.

accidente sm - 1. [desgracia] accident; **accidente laboral/mortal** industrial/fatal accident; **accidente de tráfico** road accident - 2. (gen pl) [del terreno] unevenness (U).

acción sf - 1. [gen] action - 2. [hecho] deed, act - 3. FIN share.

accionar vt to activate.

accionista smf shareholder.

acechar vt - 1. [vigilar] to keep under surveillance; [suj: cazador] to stalk - 2. [amenazar] to be lying in wait for.

acecho sm: **estar al acecho de** to lie in wait for; fig to be on the lookout for.

aceite sm oil.

aceitera sf oil can. ◆ **aceiteras** sfpl cruet sing.

aceitoso, sa adj oily.

aceituna sf olive.

aceleración sf acceleration.

acelerador, ra adj accelerating. ◆ **acelerador** sm accelerator.

acelerar ◇ vt [avivar] to speed up; TECNOL to accelerate. ◇ vi to accelerate. ◆ **acelerarse** vprnl to hurry up.

acelga sf chard.

acento sm - 1. [gen] accent - 2. [intensidad] stress, accent.

acentuación sf accentuation.

acentuar vt - 1. [palabra, letra - al escribir] to put an accent on; [- al hablar] to stress - 2. fig [realzar] to accentuate. ◆ **acentuarse** vprnl [intensificarse] to deepen, to increase.

acepción sf meaning, sense.

aceptable adj acceptable.

aceptación *sf* - **1.** [aprobación] acceptance - **2.** [éxito] success, popularity.

aceptar *vt* to accept.

acequia *sf* irrigation channel.

acera *sf* [para peatones] pavement *UK*, sidewalk *US*; **ser de la otra acera, ser de la acera de enfrente** *fam despec* to be one of them, to be queer.

acerbo, ba *adj culto* [mordaz] caustic.

acerca ➡ **acerca de** *loc adv* about.

acercar *vt* to bring nearer *O* closer; **¡acércame el pan!** could you pass me the bread? ➡ **acercarse** *vprnl* [arrimarse - viniendo] to come closer; [- yendo] to go over.

acero *sm* steel; **acero inoxidable** stainless steel.

acérrimo, ma *adj* [defensor] diehard *(antes de s)*; [enemigo] bitter.

acertado, da *adj* - **1.** [con acierto - respuesta] correct; [- comentario] appropriate - **2.** [oportuno] good, clever.

acertar ⬦ *vt* - **1.** [adivinar] to guess (correctly) - **2.** [el blanco] to hit - **3.** [elegir bien] to choose well. ⬦ *vi* - **1.** [atinar]: **acertar (al hacer algo)** to be right (to do sthg) - **2.** [conseguir]: **acertar a hacer algo** to manage to do sthg - **3.** [hallar]: **acertar con** to find.

acertijo *sm* riddle.

acervo *sm* [patrimonio] heritage.

achacar *vt*: **achacar algo a alguien/algo** to attribute sthg to sb/sthg.

achantar *vt fam* to put the wind up. ➡ **achantarse** *vprnl fam* to get the wind up.

achaparrado, da *adj* squat.

achaque *sm* ailment.

achatado, da *adj* flattened.

achicar *vt* - **1.** [tamaño] to make smaller - **2.** [agua - de barco] to bale out - **3.** *fig* [acobardar] to intimidate.

achicharrar *vt* [chamuscar] to burn. ➡ **achicharrarse** *vprnl* - **1.** *fig* [de calor] to fry - **2.** [chamuscarse] to burn.

achicoria *sf* chicory.

achuchado, da *adj fam* hard, tough.

achuchar *vt fam* [abrazar] to hug.

aciago, ga *adj culto* black, fateful.

acicalar *vt* [arreglar] to do up. ➡ **acicalarse** *vprnl* to do o.s. up.

acicate *sm fig* [estímulo] incentive.

acidez *sf* - **1.** [cualidad] acidity - **2.** MED: **acidez (de estómago)** heartburn.

ácido, da *adj* - **1.** QUÍM acidic - **2.** [bebida, sabor, carácter] acid, sour. ➡ **ácido** *sm* QUÍM acid; **ácido clorhídrico/desoxirribonucleico/ribonucleico/sulfúrico** hydrochloric/deoxyribonucleic/ribonucleic/sulphuric acid.

acierto *sm* - **1.** [a pregunta] correct answer - **2.** [habilidad, tino] good *O* sound judgment - **3.** [éxito] success.

aclamación *sf* [ovación] acclamation, acclaim; **por aclamación** unanimously; **entre aclamaciones** to great acclaim.

aclamar *vt* to acclaim.

aclaración *sf* explanation.

aclarar *vt* - **1.** [ropa] to rinse - **2.** [explicar] to clarify, to explain - **3.**: **aclarar la voz** [carraspeando] to clear one's throat. ➡ **aclararse** *vprnl* - **1.** [entender] to understand - **2.** [explicarse] to explain o.s.

aclaratorio, ria *adj* explanatory.

aclimatación *sf* acclimatization.

aclimatar *vt* - **1.** [al clima]: **aclimatar algo/a alguien (a)** to acclimatize sthg/sb (to) - **2.** [al ambiente]: **aclimatar algo/a alguien a algo** to get sthg/sb used to sthg. ➡ **aclimatarse** *vprnl* - **1.** [al clima]: **aclimatarse (a algo)** to acclimatize (to sthg) - **2.** [al ambiente] to settle in; **aclimatarse a algo** to get used to sthg.

acné *sm* acne.

acobardar *vt* to frighten, to scare. ➡ **acobardarse** *vprnl* to get frightened *O* scared; **acobardarse ante** to shrink back from.

acodarse *vprnl*: **acodarse (en)** to lean (on).

acogedor, ra *adj* [país, persona] welcoming; [casa, ambiente] cosy.

acoger *vt* - **1.** [recibir] to welcome - **2.** [dar refugio] to take in. ➡ **acogerse a** *vprnl* [inmunidad parlamentaria etc] to take refuge in; [ley] to have recourse to.

acogida *sf* reception; **acogida familiar** fostering.

acolchar *vt* to pad.

acometer ⬦ *vt* - **1.** [atacar] to attack - **2.** [emprender] to undertake. ⬦ *vi* [embestir]: **acometer contra** to hurtle into.

acometida *sf* - **1.** [ataque] attack, charge - **2.** [de luz, gas etc] (mains) connection.

acomodado, da *adj* [rico] well-off.

acomodador, ra *sm, f* usher (*f* usherette).

acomodar *vt* - **1.** [instalar - persona] to seat, to instal; [- cosa] to place - **2.** [adaptar] to fit. ➡ **acomodarse** *vprnl* [instalarse] to make o.s. comfortable; **acomodarse en** to settle down in.

acomodaticio, cia *adj* [complaciente] accommodating.

acompañamiento *sm* CULIN & MÚS accompaniment.

acompañante *smf* [compañero] companion; MÚS accompanist.

acompañar *vt* - **1.** [ir con]: **acompañar a alguien** [gen] to go with *O* accompany sb; [a la puerta] to show sb out; [a casa] to walk sb

home; **te acompaño** I'll come with you
- **2.** [estar con]: **acompañar a alguien** to keep sb
company - **3.** [adjuntar] to enclose - **4.** MÚS to
accompany.

acompasar *vt*: **acompasar algo (a)** to synchronize sthg (with).

acomplejar *vt* to give a complex. ▸ **acom-
plejarse** *vprnl* to develop a complex.

acondicionado, da *adj* equipped; **estar
bien/mal acondicionado** to be in a fit/no fit
state; **aire acondicionado** air conditioned.

acondicionador *sm* - **1.** [de aire] (air) conditioner - **2.** [de pelo] conditioner.

acondicionar *vt* - **1.** [reformar] to condition,
to convert, to upgrade - **2.** [preparar] to prepare, to get ready.

acongojar *vt* to distress.

aconsejar *vt* [dar consejos]: **aconsejar a alguien (que haga algo)** to advise sb (to do
sthg); **te aconsejo que vayas al médico** I'd advise you to see a doctor.

acontecer *v impers* to take place, to happen.

acontecimiento *sm* event.

acopio *sm* stock, store.

acoplar *vt* - **1.** [encajar] to attach, to fit together - **2.** FERROC to couple - **3.** *fig* [adaptar] to
adapt, to fit.

acorazado, da *adj* armour-plated. ▸ **acorazado** *sm* battleship.

acordar *vt*: **acordar algo/hacer algo** to agree
on sthg/to do sthg. ▸ **acordarse** *vprnl*:
acordarse (de algo/de hacer algo) to remember (sthg/to do sthg); **acordarse de haber hecho algo** to remember doing sthg.

acorde ◇ *adj* [en consonancia]: **acorde con** in
keeping with. ◇ *sm* MÚS chord.

acordeón *sm* accordion.

acordonar *vt* [lugar] to cordon off.

acorralar *vt lit & fig* to corner.

acortar *vt* - **1.** [falda, pantalón etc] to take up;
[cable] to shorten - **2.** [plazo, vacaciones] to cut
short - **3.** [extensión] to shorten. ▸ **acortarse** *vprnl* [días] to get shorter; [reunión] to end
early.

acosar *vt* - **1.** [hostigar] to harass - **2.** [perseguir]
to pursue relentlessly.

acoso *sm* [hostigamiento] harassment; **acoso
sexual** sexual harassment.

acostar *vt* [en la cama] to put to bed.
▸ **acostarse** *vprnl* - **1.** [irse a la cama] to go to
bed - **2.** [tumbarse] to lie down - **3.** *fam* [tener
relaciones sexuales]: **acostarse con alguien** to
sleep with sb.

acostumbrado, da *adj* - **1.** [habitual] usual
- **2.** [habituado]: **estar acostumbrado a** to be
used to.

acostumbrar ◇ *vt* [habituar]: **acostumbrar a
alguien a algo/a hacer algo** to get sb used to
sthg/to doing sthg. ◇ *vi* [soler]: **acostumbrar
a hacer algo** to be in the habit of doing sthg;
acostumbro a levantarme temprano I usually
get up early. ▸ **acostumbrarse** *vprnl* [habi-
tuarse]: **acostumbrarse a algo/a hacer algo** to
get used to sthg/to doing sthg.

acotación *sf* [nota] note in the margin.

acotar *vt* - **1.** [terreno, campo] to enclose; *fig*
[tema etc] to delimit - **2.** [texto] to write notes
in the margin of.

acrecentar *vt* to increase.

acreditado, da *adj* - **1.** [médico, abogado etc]
distinguished; [marca] reputable - **2.** [embaja-
dor, representante] accredited.

acreditar *vt* - **1.** [certificar] to certify; [autori-
zar] to authorize - **2.** [confirmar] to confirm
- **3.** [embajador] to accredit - **4.** FIN to credit.

acreedor, ra ◇ *adj*: **hacerse acreedor de algo** to earn sthg, to show o.s. to be worthy of
sthg. ◇ *sm, f* creditor.

acribillar *vt* [herir]: **acribillar (a)** to pepper *O*
riddle (with); **acribillar a balazos** to riddle
with bullets.

acrílico, ca *adj* acrylic.

acrimonia = acritud.

acritud, acrimonia *sf* - **1.** [de olor] acridity,
pungency; [de sabor] bitterness - **2.** *fig* [morda-
cidad] venom - **3.** [desavenencia] acrimony.

acrobacia *sf* [en circo] acrobatics *pl*.

acróbata *smf* acrobat.

acta *sf (el)* - **1.** [de junta, reunión] minutes *pl*;
levantar acta to take the minutes - **2.** [de defunción etc] certificate; **acta notarial** affidavit.
▸ **actas** *sfpl* minutes.

actitud *sf* [disposición de ánimo] attitude.

activar *vt* - **1.** [gen] to activate - **2.** [explosivo]
to detonate.

actividad *sf* [acción] activity; [trabajo] work.

activo, va *adj* - **1.** [gen & GRAM] active - **2.** [tra-
bajador] hard-working. ▸ **activo** *sm* FIN as-
sets *pl*; **activo fijo/líquido/financiero** fixed/li-
quid/financial assets; **activo y pasivo** assets
and liabilities.

acto *sm* - **1.** [acción] act; **hacer acto de presencia** to show one's face; **acto de solidaridad**
show of solidarity - **2.** [ceremonia] ceremony
- **3.** TEATRO act. ▸ **en el acto** *loc adv* on the
spot; **murió en el acto** she died instantly.

actor, triz *sm, f* actor (*f* actress).

actuación *sf* - **1.** [conducta, proceder] conduct,
behaviour - **2.** [interpretación] performance.

actual *adj* - **1.** [existente] present, current
- **2.** [de moda] modern, present-day - **3.** [de ac-
tualidad] topical.

actualidad *sf* - **1.** [momento presente] current
situation; **de actualidad** [moderno] in fashion;

[de interés actual] topical; **en la actualidad** at the present time, these days - **2.** [noticial news (U)] **ser actualidad** to be making the news.

actualizar vt [información] to update; [tecnología, industria] to modernize; INFORM to upgrade.

actualmente adv [hoy día] these days, nowadays; [en este momento] at the (present) moment.

actuar vi [gen] to act; **actuar de** to act as.

acuarela sf watercolour.

acuario sm aquarium. ◆ **acuario** ◇ sm [zodiaco] Aquarius. ◇ smf [persona] Aquarius.

acuartelar vt to confine to barracks.

acuático, ca adj aquatic.

acuchillar vt - **1.** [apuñalar] to stab - **2.** [mueble, parqué] to grind down.

acuciar vt culto [suj: persona] to goad; [suj: necesidad, deseo] to press.

acuclillarse vprnl to squat (down).

acudir vi - **1.** [ir] to go; [venir] to come - **2.** [recurrir]: **acudir a** to go O turn to - **3.** [presentarse]: **acudir (a)** [escuela, iglesia] to attend; [cita, examen] to turn up (for); fig [memoria, mente] to come (to).

acueducto sm aqueduct.

acuerdo sm agreement; **de acuerdo** all right, O.K.; **de acuerdo con** [conforme a] in accordance with; **estar de acuerdo (con alguien/en hacer algo)** to agree (with sb/to do sthg).

acumular vt to accumulate.

acunar vt to rock.

acuñar vt - **1.** [moneda] to mint - **2.** [palabra] to coin.

acuoso, sa adj watery.

acupuntura sf acupuncture.

acurrucarse vprnl [por frío] to huddle up; [en sitio agradable] to curl up.

acusación sf [inculpación] charge.

acusado, da ◇ adj [marcado] marked. ◇ sm, f [procesado] accused, defendant.

acusar vt - **1.** [culpar] to accuse; DER to charge; **acusar a alguien de algo** [gen] to accuse sb of sthg; DER to charge sb with sthg - **2.** [mostrar] to show.

acusativo sm accusative.

acuse ◆ **acuse de recibo** sm acknowledgement of receipt.

acústico, ca adj acoustic. ◆ **acústica** sf [de local] acoustics pl.

AD sf (abrev de **Acción Democrática**) Venezuelan political party.

adagio sm [sentencia breve] adage.

adaptación sf - **1.** [aclimatación]: **adaptación (a)** adjustment (to) - **2.** [modificación] adaptation.

adaptar vt - **1.** [acomodar, ajustar] to adjust - **2.** [modificar] to adapt. ◆ **adaptarse** vprnl: **adaptarse (a)** to adjust (to).

adecentar vt to tidy up.

adecuado, da adj appropriate, suitable.

adecuar vt to adapt. ◆ **adecuarse a** vprnl - **1.** [ser adecuado] to be appropriate for - **2.** [adaptarse] to adjust to.

adefesio sm fam [persona fea] fright.

a. de JC., a.JC. (abrev de antes de Jesucristo) BC.

adelantado, da adj advanced; **llevo el reloj adelantado** my watch is fast; **por adelantado** in advance.

adelantamiento sm AUTO overtaking.

adelantar ◇ vt - **1.** [dejar atrás] to overtake - **2.** [mover hacia adelante] to move forward; [pie, reloj] to put forward - **3.** [en el tiempo - trabajo, viaje] to bring forward; [- dinero] to pay in advance. ◇ vi - **1.** [progresar] to make progress - **2.** [reloj] to be fast. ◆ **adelantarse** vprnl - **1.** [en el tiempo] to be early; [frío, verano] to arrive early; [reloj] to gain; **adelantarse a alguien** to beat sb to it - **2.** [en el espacio] to go on ahead.

adelante ◇ adv forward, ahead; **(de ahora) en adelante** from now on, in future; **más adelante** [en el tiempo] later (on); [en el espacio] further on. ◇ interj: **¡adelante!** [¡siga!] go ahead!; [¡pase!] come in!

adelanto sm advance.

adelgazar ◇ vi to lose weight, to slim. ◇ vt to lose.

ademán sm [gesto - con manos etc] gesture; [- con cara] face, expression; **en ademán de** as if to.

además adv [con énfasis] moreover, besides; [también] also; **además de** as well as, in addition to.

adentrarse vprnl: **adentrarse en** [jungla etc] to enter the heart of; [tema etc] to study in depth.

adentro adv inside; **tierra adentro** inland; **mar adentro** out to sea.

adepto, ta sm, f: **adepto (a)** follower (of).

aderezar vt [sazonar - ensalada] to dress; [- comida] to season.

aderezo sm [aliño - de ensalada] dressing; [- de comida] seasoning.

adeudar vt - **1.** [deber] to owe - **2.** COM to debit. ◆ **adeudarse** vprnl to get into debt.

adherir vt to stick. ◆ **adherirse** vprnl - **1.** [pegarse] to stick - **2.** [mostrarse de acuerdo]: **adherirse a** to adhere to.

adhesión sf [apoyo] support.

adhesivo, va adj adhesive. ◆ **adhesivo** sm [pegatina] sticker.

adicción *sf*: adicción (a) addiction (to).

adición *sf* addition.

adicional *adj* additional.

adicto, ta ⟨⟩ *adj*: adicto (a) addicted (to). ⟨⟩ *sm, f*: adicto (a) addict (of).

adiestrar *vt* to train; **adiestrar a alguien en algo/para hacer algo** to train sb in sthg/to do sthg.

adinerado, da *adj* wealthy.

adiós ⟨⟩ *sm* goodbye. ⟨⟩ *interj*: ¡adiós! goodbye!; [al cruzarse con alguien] hello!

adiposo, sa *adj* adipose.

aditivo *sm* additive.

adivinanza *sf* riddle.

adivinar *vt* - **1.** [predecir] to foretell; [el futuro] to tell - **2.** [acertar] to guess (correctly).

adivino, na *sm, f* fortune-teller.

adjudicación *sf* awarding.

adjudicar *vt* [asignar] to award. ⬦ **adjudicarse** *vprnl* [apropiarse] to take for o.s.; **adjudicarse un premio** to win a prize.

adjuntar *vt* to enclose.

adjunto, ta ⟨⟩ *adj* [incluido] enclosed; 'adjunto le remito...' 'please find enclosed...' ⟨⟩ *sm, f* [auxiliar] assistant.

administración *sf* - **1.** [suministro] supply; [de medicamento, justicia] administering - **2.** [gestión] administration - **3.** [gerentes] management; [oficina] manager's office. ⬦ **Administración** *sf* [gobierno] administration; **Administración local** local government; **Administración pública** civil service.

administrador, ra *sm, f* - **1.** [de empresa] manager - **2.** [de bienes ajenos] administrator.

administrar *vt* - **1.** [gestionar - empresa, finca etc] to manage, to run; [- casa] to run - **2.** [país] to run the affairs of - **3.** [suministrar] to administer.

administrativo, va *adj* administrative.

admirable *adj* admirable.

admiración *sf* - **1.** [sentimiento] admiration; **causar admiración** to be admired; **sentir admiración por alguien** to admire sb - **2.** [signo ortográfico] exclamation mark.

admirar *vt* - **1.** [gen] to admire - **2.** [sorprender] to amaze. ⬦ **admirarse** *vprnl*: **admirarse (de)** to be amazed (by).

admisible *adj* acceptable.

admisión *sf* - **1.** [de persona] admission - **2.** [de solicitudes etc] acceptance; **prueba de admisión** entrance exam.

admitir *vt* - **1.** [acoger, reconocer] to admit; **admitir a alguien en** to admit sb to - **2.** [aceptar] to accept.

ADN (*abrev de* **ácido desoxirribonucleico**) *sm* DNA.

adobar *vt* to marinate.

adobe *sm* adobe.

adobo *sm* [salsa] marinade.

adoctrinar *vt* to instruct.

adolecer ⬦ **adolecer de** *vi* to suffer from.

adolescencia *sf* adolescence.

adolescente *adj* & *smf* adolescent.

adonde *adv* where; **la ciudad adonde vamos** the city we are going to, the city where we are going.

adónde *adv* where.

adopción *sf* [de hijo, propuesta] adoption; [de ley] passing.

adoptar *vt* [hijo, propuesta] to adopt; [ley] to pass.

adoptivo, va *adj* [hijo, país] adopted; [padre] adoptive.

adoquín (*pl* **adoquines**) *sm* cobblestone.

adorable *adj* [persona] adorable; [ambiente, película] wonderful.

adoración *sf* adoration; **sentir adoración por alguien** to worship sb.

adorar *vt* - **1.** [dios, ídolo] to worship - **2.** [persona, comida] to adore.

adormecer *vt* [producir sueño] to lull to sleep. ⬦ **adormecerse** *vprnl* to nod off.

adormilarse *vprnl* to doze.

adornar *vt* to decorate.

adorno *sm* decoration; **de adorno** [árbol, figura] decorative, ornamental; [person] serving no useful purpose.

adosado, da *adj* [casa] semi-detached.

adquirir *vt* - **1.** [comprar] to acquire, to purchase - **2.** [conseguir - conocimientos, hábito, cultura] to acquire; [- éxito, popularidad] to achieve; [- compromiso] to undertake.

adquisición *sf* - **1.** [compra, cosa comprada] purchase; **ser una buena/mala adquisición** to be a good/bad buy - **2.** [obtención] acquisition - **3.** [de costumbres] adoption.

adquisitivo, va *adj* purchasing (*antes de s*).

adrede *adv* on purpose, deliberately.

adrenalina *sf* adrenalin.

adscribir *vt* - **1.** [asignar] to assign - **2.** [destinar] to appoint O assign to. ⬦ **adscribirse** *vprnl*: **adscribirse (a)** [grupo, partido] to become a member (of); [ideología] to subscribe (to).

adscrito, ta ⟨⟩ *pp* ▷ **adscribir**. ⟨⟩ *adj* assigned.

aduana *sf* [administración] customs *pl*; **pasar por la aduana** to go through customs.

aducir *vt* to adduce.

adueñarse ⬦ **adueñarse de** *vprnl* - **1.** [apoderarse] to take over - **2.** [dominar] to take hold of.

adulación *sf* flattery.

adulador, ra *adj* flattering.

9

adular *vt* to flatter.

adulterar *vt* [alimento] to adulterate.

adulterio *sm* adultery.

adúltero, ra <> *adj* adulterous. <> *sm, f* adulterer (*f* adulteress).

adulto, ta *adj* & *sm, f* adult.

adusto, ta *adj* dour.

advenedizo, za *adj* & *sm, f* parvenu (*f* parvenue).

advenimiento *sm* [llegada] advent; [al trono] accession.

adverbio *sm* adverb; **adverbio de cantidad/lugar/modo/tiempo** adverb of degree/place/manner/time.

adversario, ria *sm, f* adversary.

adversidad *sf* adversity.

adverso, sa *adj* [gen] adverse; [destino] unkind; [suerte] bad; [viento] unfavourable.

advertencia *sf* warning; **servir de advertencia** to serve as a warning; **hacer una advertencia a alguien** to warn sb.

advertir *vt* - **1.** [notar] to notice - **2.** [prevenir, avisar] to warn; **te advierto que no deberías hacerlo** I'd advise against you doing it; **te advierto que no me sorprende** mind you, it doesn't surprise me.

adviento *sm* Advent.

adyacente *adj* adjacent.

aéreo, a *adj* - **1.** [del aire] aerial - **2.** AERON air (antes de s).

aeroclub (*pl* aeroclubes) *sm* flying club.

aerodeslizador *sm* hovercraft.

aerodinámico, ca *adj* - **1.** FÍS aerodynamic - **2.** [forma, línea] streamlined.

aeródromo *sm* airfield, aerodrome.

aeroespacial *adj* aerospace (antes de s).

aerógrafo *sm* airbrush.

aerolínea *sf* airline.

aeromozo, za *sm, f* Amér air steward (*f* air hostess).

aeronauta *smf* aeronaut.

aeronaval *adj* air and sea (antes de s).

aeronave *sf* [gen] aircraft; [dirigible] airship.

aeroplano *sm* aeroplane.

aeropuerto *sm* airport.

aerosol *sm* aerosol.

aerostático, ca *adj* aerostatic.

aeróstato *sm* hot-air balloon.

aerotaxi *sm* light aircraft (for hire).

afabilidad *sf* affability.

afable *adj* affable.

afamado, da *adj* famous.

afán *sm* - **1.** [esfuerzo] hard work (*U*) - **2.** [anhelo] urge; **tener afán de algo** to be eager for sthg; **afán de conocimiento** thirst for knowledge.

afanador, ra *sm, f* Méx cleaner.

afanar *vt fam* [robar] to pinch. ◆ **afanarse** *vprnl* [obstinarse]: **afanarse (por hacer algo)** to do everything one can (to do sthg).

afanoso, sa *adj* - **1.** [trabajoso] demanding - **2.** [que se afana] eager.

afear *vt* to make ugly.

afección *sf* MED complaint, disease.

afectación *sf* affectation.

afectado, da *adj* - **1.** [gen] affected - **2.** [afligido] upset, badly affected.

afectar *vt* - **1.** [gen] to affect - **2.** [afligir] to upset, to affect badly.

afectísimo, ma *adj* [en cartas]: **'suyo afectísimo'** 'yours faithfully'.

afectivo, va *adj* - **1.** [emocional] emotional - **2.** [cariñoso] affectionate.

afecto *sm* affection, fondness; **sentir afecto por alguien, tenerle afecto a alguien** to be fond of sb.

afectuoso, sa *adj* affectionate, loving.

afeitar *vt* [pelo, barba] to shave. ◆ **afeitarse** *vprnl* to shave.

afeminado, da *adj* effeminate.

aferrarse *vprnl*: **aferrarse a** lit & fig to cling to.

Afganistán *n pr* Afghanistan.

AFI *sm* (abrev de alfabeto fonético internacional) IPA.

afianzar *vt* [objeto] to secure. ◆ **afianzarse** *vprnl* to steady o.s.; **afianzarse en algo** [opinión etc] to become sure *O* convinced of sthg; [cargo, liderazgo] to consolidate sthg.

afiche *sm* Amér poster.

afición *sf* - **1.** [inclinación] fondness, liking; **tener afición a algo** to be keen on sthg - **2.** [en tiempo libre] hobby; **por afición** as a hobby - **3.** [aficionados] fans *pl*.

aficionado, da <> *adj* - **1.** [interesado] keen; **ser aficionado a algo** to be keen on sthg - **2.** [no profesional] amateur. <> *sm, f* - **1.** [interesado] fan; **aficionado al cine** film buff - **2.** [amateur] amateur.

aficionar *vt*: **aficionar a alguien a algo** to make sb keen on sthg. ◆ **aficionarse** *vprnl*: **aficionarse a algo** to become keen on sthg.

afilado, da *adj* [borde, filo] sharp; [dedos] pointed.

afilar *vt* to sharpen.

afiliado, da *sm, f*: **afiliado (a)** member (of).

afiliarse *vprnl*: **afiliarse a** to join, to become a member of.

afín *adj* [semejante] similar, like.

afinar *vt* - **1.** MÚS [instrumento] to tune; **afinar la voz** to sing in tune - **2.** [perfeccionar, mejorar] to fine-tune - **3.** [pulir] to refine.

afinidad *sf* [gen & QUÍM] affinity.

afirmación *sf* statement, assertion.

afirmar *vt* - 1. [confirmar] to confirm - 2. [decir] to say, to declare - 3. [consolidar] to reaffirm - 4. CONSTR to reinforce.

afirmativo, va *adj* affirmative.

aflicción *sf* suffering, sorrow.

afligir *vt* [afectar] to afflict; [causar pena] to distress.

aflojar ◇ *vt* [destensar] to loosen; [cuerda] to slacken. ◇ *vi* - 1. [disminuir] to abate, to die down - 2. fig [ceder] to ease off. ◆ **aflojarse** *vprnl* [gen] to come loose; [cuerda] to slacken.

aflorar *vi* fig [surgir] to (come to the) surface, to show.

afluencia *sf* stream, volume.

afluente *sm* tributary.

afluir ◆ **afluir a** *vi* - 1. [gente] to flock to - 2. [sangre, fluido] to flow to.

afonía *sf* loss of voice.

afónico, ca *adj*: quedarse afónico to lose one's voice.

aforo *sm* [cabida] seating capacity.

afortunadamente *adv* fortunately.

afortunado, da *adj* - 1. [agraciado] lucky, fortunate - 2. [oportuno] happy, felicitous.

afrenta *sf* [ofensa, agravio] affront.

África *n pr* Africa.

africano, na *adj* & *sm, f* African.

afrontar *vt* [hacer frente a] to face.

afuera *adv* outside; por (la parte de) afuera on the outside. ◆ **afueras** *sfpl*: las afueras the outskirts.

afuerita *adv* Amér fam right outside.

afusilar *vt* Amér fam to shoot.

agachar *vt* to lower; [la cabeza] to bow. ◆ **agacharse** *vprnl* [acuclillarse] to crouch down; [inclinar la cabeza] to stoop.

agalla *sf* ZOOL gill. ◆ **agallas** *sfpl* fig guts; tener agallas to have guts.

agarradero *sm* - 1. [asa] hold - 2. fam fig [pretexto] pretext, excuse.

agarrado, da *adj* - 1. [asido]: agarrado (de) gripped (by); agarrados del brazo arm in arm; agarrados de la mano hand in hand - 2. fam [tacaño] tight, stingy.

agarrar *vt* - 1. [asir] to grab - 2. [pillar - ladrón, resfriado] to catch; Amér [- tomar] to take. ◆ **agarrarse** *vprnl* [sujetarse] to hold on; agarrarse de O a algo to hold on to O clutch sthg.

agarrón *sm* [tirón] pull, tug.

agarrotar *vt* [parte del cuerpo] to cut off the circulation in; [mente] to numb. ◆ **agarrotarse** *vprnl* - 1. [parte del cuerpo] to go numb - 2. [mecanismo] to seize up.

agasajar *vt* to lavish attention on.

ágata *sf (el)* agate.

agazaparse *vprnl* - 1. [para esconderse] to crouch - 2. [agacharse] to bend down.

agencia *sf* - 1. [empresa] agency; agencia matrimonial marriage bureau; agencia de viajes travel agency - 2. [sucursal] branch.

agenda *sf* - 1. [de notas, fechas] diary; [de teléfonos, direcciones] book - 2. [de trabajo] agenda.

agente ◇ *sm, f* [persona] agent; agente de policía O de la autoridad policeman (f policewoman); agente de aduanas customs officer; agente de cambio (y bolsa) stockbroker; agente secreto secret agent. ◇ *sm* [causa activa] agent.

ágil *adj* [movimiento, persona] agile.

agilidad *sf* agility.

agilizar *vt* to speed up.

agitación *sf* - 1. [intranquilidad] restlessness - 2. [jaleo] racket, commotion - 3. [conflicto] unrest.

agitar *vt* - 1. [mover - botella] to shake; [- líquido] to stir; [- brazos] to wave - 2. [inquietar] to perturb, to worry - 3. [alterar, perturbar] to stir up. ◆ **agitarse** *vprnl* [inquietarse] to get worried.

aglomeración *sf* build-up; [de gente] crowd.

aglomerar *vt* to bring together. ◆ **aglomerarse** *vprnl* to amass.

agnóstico, ca *adj* & *sm, f* agnostic.

agobiado, da *adj*: agobiado (de) [trabajo] snowed under (with); [problemas] weighed down (with).

agobiar *vt* to overwhelm. ◆ **agobiarse** *vprnl* to feel overwhelmed, to let things get one down.

agobio *sm* - 1. [físico] choking, suffocation - 2. [psíquico] pressure.

agolparse *vprnl* [gente] to crowd round; [sangre] to rush.

agonía *sf* - 1. [pena] agony - 2. [del moribundo] death throes pl.

agonizante *adj* dying.

agonizar *vi* [expirar] to be dying.

agosto *sm* - 1. [mes] August - 2. loc: hacer su agosto to line one's pockets; ver también septiembre.

agotado, da *adj* - 1. [cansado]: agotado (de) exhausted (from) - 2. [producto] out of stock, sold out - 3. [pila, batería] flat.

agotador, ra *adj* exhausting.

agotamiento *sm* [cansancio] exhaustion.

agotar *vt* [gen] to exhaust; [producto] to sell out of; [agua] to drain. ◆ **agotarse** *vprnl* - 1. [cansarse] to tire o.s. out - 2. [acabarse] to run out; [libro, disco, entradas] to be sold out; [pila, batería] to go flat.

agraciado, da adj - 1. [atractivo] attractive, fetching - 2. [afortunado] **agraciado con algo** lucky enough to win sthg.

agraciar vt [embellecer] to make more attractive O fetching.

agradable adj pleasant.

agradar vt to please.

agradecer vt [suj: persona]: **agradecer algo a alguien** [dar las gracias] to thank sb for sthg; [estar agradecido] to be grateful to sb for sthg.

agradecido, da adj [ser] grateful; [estar] appreciative.

agradecimiento sm gratitude.

agrado sm [gusto] pleasure; **esto no es de mi agrado** this is not to my liking.

agrandar vt to make bigger.

agrario, ria adj [reforma] agrarian; [producto, política] agricultural.

agravante ◇ adj aggravating. ◇ sm o sf - 1. [problema] additional problem - 2. DER aggravating circumstance.

agravar vt [situación] to aggravate; [impuestos etc] to increase (the burden of). **agravarse** vprnl to get worse.

agraviar vt to offend.

agravio sm - 1. [ofensa] offence, insult - 2. [perjuicio] wrong.

agredir vt to attack.

agregado, da sm, f - 1. EDUC assistant teacher - 2. [de embajada] attaché; **agregado cultural** cultural attaché. **agregado** sm [añadido] addition.

agregar vt: **agregar (algo a algo)** to add (sthg to sthg).

agresión sf [ataque] act of aggression, attack.

agresividad sf aggression.

agresivo, va adj lit & fig aggressive.

agresor, ra sm, f attacker, assailant.

agreste adj [abrupto, rocoso] rugged.

agriar vt [vino, leche] to (turn) sour. **agriarse** vprnl lit & fig to turn sour.

agrícola adj agricultural; [pueblo] farming (antes de s).

agricultor, ra sm, f farmer.

agricultura sf agriculture.

agridulce adj bittersweet; CULIN sweet and sour.

agrietar vt - 1. [muro, tierra] to crack - 2. [labios, manos] to chap. **agrietarse** vprnl [la piel] to chap.

agrio, agria adj - 1. [ácido] sour - 2. fig [áspero] acerbic, bitter.

agronomía sf agronomy.

agropecuario, ria adj farming and livestock (antes de s).

agrupación sf [asociación] group.

agrupamiento sm [concentración] grouping.

agrupar vt to group (together). **agruparse** vprnl - 1. [congregarse] to gather (round) - 2. [unirse] to form a group.

agua sf (el) water; **agua bendita/dulce/destilada/potable/salada** holy/fresh/distilled/drinking/salt water; **venir como agua de mayo** to be a godsend. **aguas** sfpl - 1. [manantial] waters, spring sing - 2. [de río, mar] waters; **aguas territoriales** O **jurisdiccionales** territorial waters; **aguas internacionales** international waters - 3. [de diamantes, telas] water (U). **agua de colonia** sf eau de cologne. **agua oxigenada** sf hydrogen peroxide. **aguas residuales** sfpl sewage (U).

aguacate sm [fruto] avocado (pear).

aguacero sm shower.

aguachirle sf dishwater (U), revolting drink.

aguado, da adj [con demasiada agua] watery; [diluido a propósito] watered-down.

aguafiestas smf inv spoilsport.

aguafuerte sm etching.

aguamarina sf aquamarine.

aguamiel sf Amér [bebida] water mixed with honey or cane syrup; Caribe & Méx [jugo] maguey juice.

aguanieve sf sleet.

aguantar vt - 1. [sostener] to hold - 2. [resistir - peso] to bear - 3. [tolerar, soportar] to bear, to stand; **no sé cómo la aguantas** I don't know how you put up with her - 4. [contener - risa] to contain; [- respiración] to hold. **aguantarse** vprnl - 1. [contenerse] to restrain o.s. - 2. [resignarse]: **no quiere aguantarse** he refuses to put up with it.

aguante sm - 1. [paciencia] self-restraint - 2. [resistencia] strength; [de persona] stamina.

aguar vt - 1. [mezclar con agua] to water down - 2. fig [estropear] to spoil.

aguardar vt to wait for, to await.

aguardiente sm spirit, liquor.

aguarrás sm turpentine.

agudeza sf [gen] sharpness.

agudizar vt fig [acentuar] to exacerbate. **agudizarse** vprnl [crisis] to get worse.

agudo, da adj - 1. [gen] sharp; [crisis, problema, enfermedad] serious, acute - 2. fig [perspicaz] keen, sharp - 3. fig [ingenioso] witty - 4. MÚS [nota, voz] high, high-pitched.

agüero sm: **de buen/mal agüero** that bodes well/ill.

aguijón sm - 1. [de insecto] sting - 2. fig [estímulo] spur, stimulus.

aguijonear vt - 1. [espolear]: **aguijonear a alguien para que haga algo** to goad sb into doing sthg - 2. fig [estimular] to drive on.

águila *sf (el)* - **1.** [ave] eagle - **2.** *fig* [vivo, listo] sharp O perceptive person.

aguileño, ña *adj* aquiline.

aguilucho *sm* eaglet.

aguinaldo *sm* Christmas box.

aguja *sf* - **1.** [de coser, jeringuilla] needle; [de hacer punto] knitting needle - **2.** [de reloj] hand; [de brújula] pointer; [de iglesia] spire - **3.** FERROC point - **4.** [de tocadiscos] stylus, needle.
  ➡ **agujas** *sfpl* [de res] ribs.

agujerear *vt* to make a hole O holes in.

agujero *sm* hole; **agujero negro** ASTRON black hole.

agujetas *sfpl*: **tener agujetas** to feel stiff.

aguzar *vt* - **1.** [afilar] to sharpen - **2.** *fig* [apetito] to whet; [ingenio] to sharpen.

ah *interj*: **¡ah!** [admiración] ooh!; [sorpresa] oh!; [pena] ah!

ahí *adv* there; **vino por ahí** he came that way; **la solución está ahí** that's where the solution lies; **¡ahí tienes!** here you are!, there you go!; **de ahí que** [por eso] and consequently, so; **está por ahí** [en lugar indefinido] he/she is around (somewhere); [en la calle] he/she is out; **por ahí, por ahí** *fig* something like that; **por ahí va la cosa** you're not too far wrong.

ahijado, da *sm, f* [de padrinos] godson (*f* goddaughter).

ahínco *sm* enthusiasm, devotion.

ahíto, ta *adj culto* [saciado]: **estar ahíto** to be full.

ahogar *vt* - **1.** [en el agua] to drown; [asfixiar] to smother, to suffocate - **2.** [estrangular] to strangle - **3.** [extinguir] to extinguish, to put out - **4.** *fig* [controlar - levantamiento] to quell; [- pena] to hold back - **5.** [motor] to flood.
  ➡ **ahogarse** *vprnl* - **1.** [en el agua] to drown - **2.** [asfixiarse] to suffocate.

ahogo *sm* - **1.** [asfixia] breathlessness - **2.** *fig* [económico] financial difficulty.

ahondar *vi* [profundizar] to go into detail; **ahondar en** [penetrar] to penetrate deep into; [profundizar] to study in depth.

ahora ◇ *adv* - **1.** [en el presente] now; **ahora mismo** right now; **por ahora** for the time being; **de ahora en adelante** from now on - **2.** [pronto] in a second O moment; **¡hasta ahora!** see you in a minute! ◇ *conj* [pero] but, however; **ahora que** but, though; **ahora bien** but, however.

ahorcar *vt* to hang. ➡ **ahorcarse** *vprnl* to hang o.s.

ahorita, ahoritita *adv Amér C & Méx fam* right now.

ahorrador, ra ◇ *adj* thrifty, careful with money. ◇ *sm, f* thrifty person.

ahorrar *vt* to save. ➡ **ahorrarse** *vprnl*: **ahorrarse algo** to save O spare o.s. sthg.

ahorro *sm* - **1.** [gen] saving - **2.** *(gen pl)* [cantidad ahorrada] savings *pl*.

ahuecar *vt* [poner hueco - manos] to cup.

ahuevado, da *adj Andes & Amér C fam* [tonto] daft.

ahumado, da *adj* smoked.

ahumar *vt* - **1.** [jamón, pescado] to smoke - **2.** [habitación etc] to fill with smoke.

ahuyentar *vt* - **1.** [espantar, asustar] to scare away - **2.** *fig* [apartar] to drive away.

airado, da *adj* angry.

airar *vt* to anger, to make angry. ➡ **airarse** *vprnl* to get angry.

aire *sm* - **1.** [fluido] air; **al aire** exposed; **al aire libre** in the open air; **estar en el aire** to be in the air; **saltar** O **volar por los aires** to be blown sky high, to explode; **tomar el aire** to go for a breath of fresh air - **2.** [viento] wind; [corriente] draught; **hoy hace (mucho) aire** it's (very) windy today - **3.** *fig* [aspecto] air, appearance.
  ➡ **aires** *smpl* [vanidad] airs (and graces).
  ➡ **aire (acondicionado)** *sm* air-conditioning.

airear *vt fig* [contar] to air (publicly). ➡ **airearse** *vprnl* to get a breath of fresh air.

airoso, sa *adj* - **1.** [garboso] graceful - **2.** [triunfante]: **salir airoso de algo** to come out of sthg with flying colours.

aislado, da *adj* - **1.** [gen] isolated - **2.** TECNOL insulated.

aislar *vt* - **1.** [gen] to isolate - **2.** TECNOL to insulate.

ajá *interj*: **¡ajá!** [sorpresa] aha!; *fam* [aprobación] great!

ajar *vt* [flores] to wither, to cause to fade; [piel] to wrinkle; [colores] to make faded; [ropa] to wear out. ➡ **ajarse** *vprnl* [flores] to fade, to wither; [piel] to wrinkle, to become wrinkled.

ajardinado, da *adj* landscaped.

ajedrez *sm inv* chess.

ajeno, na *adj* - **1.** [de otro] of others; **jugar en campo ajeno** to play away from home - **2.** [extraño]: **ajeno a** having nothing to do with; **ajeno a nuestra voluntad** beyond our control.

ajetreo *sm* - **1.** [tarea] running around, hard work - **2.** [animación] (hustle and) bustle.

ají *sm Andes & R Dom* chilli (pepper).

ajiaco *sm Andes & Caribe* chilli-based stew.

ajillo ➡ **al ajillo** *loc adj* CULIN *in a sauce made with oil, garlic and chilli.*

ajo *sm* garlic; **andar** O **estar en el ajo** *fig* to be in on it.

ajustado, da *adj* [ceñido - ropa] tight-fitting; [- tuerca, pieza] tight; [- resultado, final] close.

ajustar *vt* - **1.** [arreglar] to adjust - **2.** [apretar] to tighten - **3.** [encajar - piezas de motor] to fit;

[- puerta, ventana] to push to - **4.** [pactar - matrimonial to arrange; [- pleito] to settle; [- paz] to negotiate; [- precio] to fix, to agree.

ajuste *sm* [de pieza] fitting; [de mecanismo] adjustment; [de salario] agreement.

al *prep* ⊳ **a²**.

ala *sf (el)* - **1.** ZOOL & POLÍT wing - **2.** [parte lateral - de tejado] eaves *pl*; [- de sombrero] brim - **3.** DEP winger, wing. ⬩ **ala delta** *sf* [aparato] hang glider.

alabanza *sf* praise.

alabar *vt* to praise.

alabastro *sm* alabaster.

alacena *sf* kitchen cupboard.

alacrán *sm* [animal] scorpion.

alado, da *adj* [con alas] winged.

alambique *sm* still.

alambre *sm* wire; **alambre de espino** *O* **púas** barbed wire.

alameda *sf* - **1.** [sitio con álamos] poplar grove - **2.** [paseo] tree-lined avenue.

álamo *sm* poplar.

alano *sm* [perro] mastiff.

alarde *sm*: **alarde (de)** show *O* display (of); **hacer alarde de algo** to show sthg off, to flaunt sthg.

alardear *vi*: **alardear de** to show off about.

alargar *vt* - **1.** [ropa] to lengthen - **2.** [viaje, visita, plazo] to extend; [conversación] to spin out. ⬩ **alargarse** *vprnl* [hacerse más largo - días] to get longer; [- reunión] to be prolonged.

alarido *sm* shriek, howl.

alarma *sf* [gen] alarm; **dar la alarma** to raise the alarm; **alarma de coche** car alarm.

alarmante *adj* alarming.

alarmar *vt* - **1.** [avisar] to alert - **2.** *fig* [asustar] to alarm. ⬩ **alarmarse** *vprnl* [inquietarse] to be alarmed.

alazán, ana *adj* chestnut.

alba *sf (el)* [amanecer] dawn.

albacea *smf* executor (*f* executrix).

albahaca *sf* basil.

albanés, esa *adj* & *sm, f* Albanian. ⬩ **albanés** *sm* [lengua] Albanian.

Albania *n pr* Albania.

albañil *sm* bricklayer.

albañilería *sf* [obra] brickwork.

albarán *sm* delivery note.

albaricoque *sm* apricot.

albedrío *sm* [antojo, elección] fancy, whim; **a su albedrío** as takes his/her fancy; **libre albedrío** free will; **a su libre albedrío** of his/her own free will.

alberca *sf* - **1.** [depósito] water tank - **2.** *Méx* [piscina] swimming pool.

albergar *vt* - **1.** [personas] to accommodate, to put up - **2.** [odio] to harbour, [esperanzas] to cherish. ⬩ **albergarse** *vprnl* to stay.

albergue *sm* accommodation (*U*), lodgings *pl*; [de montaña] shelter, refuge; **albergue de juventud** *O* **juvenil** youth hostel.

albino, na *adj* & *sm, f* albino.

albis ⬩ **in albis** *loc adv*: **estar in albis** to be in the dark; **quedarse in albis** not to have a clue *O* the faintest idea.

albóndiga *sf* meatball.

alborada *sf* [amanecer] dawn.

alborear *v impers*: **empezaba a alborear** dawn was breaking.

albornoz *sm* bathrobe.

alborotar ◇ *vi* to be noisy *O* rowdy. ◇ *vt* [amotinar] to stir up, to rouse. ⬩ **alborotarse** *vprnl* [perturbarse] to get worked up.

alboroto *sm* - **1.** [ruido] din - **2.** [jaleo] fuss, to-do; **armar un alboroto** to cause a commotion.

alborozar *vt* to delight.

alborozo *sm* delight, joy.

albufera *sf* lagoon.

álbum (*pl* **álbumes**) *sm* album.

ALCA *sf* (*abrev de* **Área de Libre Comercio de América**) LAFTA.

alcachofa *sf* BOT artichoke.

alcahuete, ta *sm, f* [mediador] go-between.

alcalde, esa *sm, f* mayor (*f* mayoress).

alcaldía *sf* [cargo] mayoralty.

alcance *sm* - **1.** [de arma, misil, emisora] range; **de corto/largo alcance** short-/long-range - **2.** [de persona]: **a mi/a tu** *etc* **alcance** within my/your *etc* reach; **al alcance de la vista** within sight; **fuera del alcance de** beyond the reach of - **3.** [de reformas etc] scope, extent.

alcanfor *sm* camphor.

alcantarilla *sf* sewer; [boca] drain.

alcantarillado *sm* sewers *pl*.

alcanzar ◇ *vt* - **1.** [llegar a] to reach - **2.** [igualarse con] to catch up with - **3.** [entregar] to pass - **4.** [suj: bala etc] to hit - **5.** [autobús, tren] to manage to catch. ◇ *vi* - **1.** [ser suficiente]: **alcanzar para algo/hacer algo** to be enough for sthg/to do sthg - **2.** [poder]: **alcanzar a hacer algo** to be able to do sthg.

alcaparra *sf* caper.

alcayata *sf* hook.

alcázar *sm* fortress.

alce *sm* elk, moose.

alcoba *sf* bedroom.

alcohol *sm* alcohol.

alcohólico, ca *adj* & *sm, f* alcoholic.

alcoholímetro *sm* [para la sangre] Breathalyzer® *UK*, drunkometer *US*.

alcoholismo *sm* alcoholism.

alcohotest (*pl* alcohotests) *sm* Breathalyzer® *UK*, drunkometer *US*.

alcornoque *sm* - 1. [árbol] cork oak - 2. *fig* [persona] idiot, fool.

aldaba *sf* [llamador] doorknocker.

aldea *sf* small village.

aldeano, **na** *sm*, *f* villager.

aleación *sf* [producto] alloy; **aleación ligera** light alloy.

aleatorio, **ria** *adj* [número] random; [suceso] chance *(antes de s)*.

aleccionar *vt* to instruct, to teach.

alegación *sf* allegation.

alegar *vt* [motivos, pruebas] to put forward; **alegar que** to claim (that).

alegato *sm* - 1. *fig* & DER plea - 2. [ataque] diatribe.

alegoría *sf* allegory.

alegórico, **ca** *adj* allegorical.

alegrar *vt* [persona] to cheer up, to make happy; **me alegra que me lo preguntes** I'm glad you asked me that; [fiesta] to liven up. ◆ **alegrarse** *vprnl* [sentir alegría]: **alegrarse (de algo/por alguien)** to be pleased (about sthg/for sb).

alegre *adj* - 1. [contento] happy - 2. [que da alegría] cheerful, bright - 3. *fam* [borracho] tipsy.

alegría *sf* - 1. [gozo] happiness, joy - 2. [motivo de gozo] joy.

alejamiento *sm* - 1. [distancia] distance - 2. [separación - de objetos etc] separation; [- entre personas] estrangement.

alejar *vt* - 1. [poner más lejos] to move away - 2. *fig* [ahuyentar] to drive out. ◆ **alejarse** *vprnl*: **alejarse (de)** [ponerse más lejos] to go O move away (from); [retirarse] to leave.

aleluya *interj*: ¡aleluya! Hallelujah!

alemán, **ana** *adj* & *sm*, *f* German. ◆ **alemán** *sm* [lengua] German.

Alemania *n pr* Germany.

alentador, **ra** *adj* encouraging.

alentar *vt* to encourage.

alergia *sf lit* & *fig* allergy; **tener alergia a algo** to be allergic to sthg; **alergia primaveral** hay fever.

alérgico, **ca** *adj lit* & *fig*: **alérgico (a)** allergic (to).

alero *sm* - 1. [del tejado] eaves *pl* - 2. DEP winger, wing.

alerta ◇ *adj inv* & *adv* alert. ◇ *sf* alert.

alertar *vt* to alert.

aleta *sf* - 1. [de pez] fin; **aleta dorsal** dorsal fin - 2. [de buzo, foca] flipper - 3. [de coche] wing.

aletargar *vt* to make drowsy. ◆ **aletargarse** *vprnl* to become drowsy O sleepy.

aletear *vi* to flap O flutter its wings.

alevín *sm* - 1. [cría de pez] fry, young fish - 2. *fig* [persona] novice, beginner.

alevosía *sf* [traición] treachery.

alfabetizar *vt* - 1. [personas] to teach to read and write - 2. [ordenar] to put into alphabetical order.

alfabeto *sm* alphabet.

alfalfa *sf* alfalfa, lucerne.

alfarería *sf* [técnica] pottery.

alféizar *sm* window-sill.

alférez *sm* ≃ second lieutenant.

alfil *sm* bishop.

alfiler *sm* - 1. [aguja] pin - 2. [joya] brooch, pin.

alfombra *sf* [grande] carpet; [pequeña] rug.

alfombrar *vt* to carpet.

alfombrilla *sf* - 1. [alfombra pequeña] rug - 2. [felpudo] doormat - 3. [del baño] bathmat - 4. INFORM: **alfombrilla (del ratón)** mouse mat.

alforja *sf* (gen *pl*) [de caballo] saddlebag.

alga *sf* (el) [de mar] seaweed *(U)*; [de río] algae *pl*.

algarroba *sf* [fruto] carob O locust bean.

álgebra *sf* (el) algebra.

álgido, **da** *adj* [culminante] critical.

algo ◇ *pron* - 1. [alguna cosa] something; [en interrogativas] anything; **¿te pasa algo?** is anything the matter?; **algo es algo** something is better than nothing; **por algo lo habrá dicho** he must have said it for a reason; **o algo así** or something like that - 2. [cantidad pequeña] a bit, a little; **algo de** some, a little - 3. *fig* [cosa importante] something; **se cree que es algo** he thinks he's something (special). ◇ *adv* [un poco] rather, somewhat. ◇ *sm*: **tiene un algo** there's something attractive about him.

algodón *sm* cotton; **criado entre algodones** *fig* pampered, mollycoddled.

algoritmo *sm* INFORM algorithm.

alguacil *sm* [del juzgado] bailiff.

alguien *pron* - 1. [alguna persona] someone, somebody; [en interrogativas] anyone, anybody; **¿hay alguien ahí?** is anyone there? - 2. *fig* [persona de importancia] somebody; **se cree alguien** she thinks she's somebody (special).

alguno, **na** ◇ *adj* (antes de *sm*: **algún**) - 1. [indeterminado] some; [en interrogativas] any; **¿tienes algún libro?** do you have any books?; **algún día** some O one day; **ha surgido algún (que otro) problema** the odd problem has come up - 2. *(después de s)* [ninguno] any; **no tengo interés alguno** I have no interest, I haven't any interest. ◇ *pron* - 1. [persona] someone, somebody; *(pl)* some people; [en interrogativas] anyone, anybody; **¿conocisteis a algunos?** did you get to know any?; **algunos de, algunos (de) entre** some O a few of - 2. [cosa] the odd one, some *pl*, a few *pl*; [en interrogativas] any; **me salió mal alguno** I got the odd one wrong.

alhaja *sf* [joya] jewel.

alhelí (*pl* alhelíes) *sm* wallflower.

aliado, da *adj* allied.

alianza *sf* - **1.** [pacto, parentesco] alliance - **2.** [anillo] wedding ring.

aliar *vt* [naciones] to ally. ◆ **aliarse** *vprnl* to form an alliance.

alias ◇ *adv* alias. ◇ *sm inv* alias; [entre amigos] nickname.

alicaído, da *adj* [triste] depressed.

alicates *smpl* pliers.

aliciente *sm* - **1.** [incentivo] incentive - **2.** [atractivo] attraction.

alienación *sf* - **1.** [gen] alienation - **2.** [trastorno psíquico] derangement.

aliento *sm* [respiración] breath; **tener mal aliento** to have bad breath; **cobrar aliento** to catch one's breath; **sin aliento** breathless.

aligerar *vt* - **1.** [peso] to lighten - **2.** [ritmo] to speed up; [el paso] to quicken - **3.** *fig* [aliviar] to relieve, to ease.

alijo *sm* contraband (U).

alimaña *sf* pest (fox, weasel etc).

alimentación *sf* - **1.** [acción] feeding - **2.** [comida] food - **3.** [régimen alimenticio] diet.

alimentar *vt* [gen] to feed; [motor, coche] to fuel. ◆ **alimentarse** *vprnl* [comer]: **alimentarse de** to live on.

alimenticio, cia *adj* nourishing; **productos alimenticios** foodstuffs; **valor alimenticio** food value.

alimento *sm* [gen] food; [valor nutritivo] nourishment; **alimentos transgénicos** GM foods.

alineación *sf* - **1.** [en el espacio] alignment - **2.** DEP line-up.

alinear *vt* - **1.** [en el espacio] to line up - **2.** DEP to select. ◆ **alinearse** *vprnl* POLIT to align.

aliñar *vt* [ensalada] to dress; [carne] to season.

aliño *sm* [para ensalada] dressing; [para carne] seasoning.

alioli *sm* garlic mayonnaise.

alisar *vt* to smooth (down).

alistarse *vprnl* to enlist; *Amér* [aprontarse] to get ready.

aliviar *vt* - **1.** [atenuar] to soothe - **2.** [aligerar - persona] to relieve; [- carga] to lighten.

alivio *sm* relief; **¡qué alivio!** what a relief!

aljibe *sm* [de agua] cistern.

allá *adv* - **1.** [espacio] over there; **allá abajo/arriba** down/up there; **más allá** further on; **más allá de** beyond; **¡allá voy!** I'm coming! - **2.** [tiempo]: **allá por los años cincuenta** back in

the 50s; **allá para el mes de agosto** around August some time. **- 3.** [en] **allá él/ella etc** that's his/her etc problem.

allanamiento *sm* forceful entry; **allanamiento de morada** breaking and entering.

allanar *vt* - **1.** [terreno] to flatten, to level - **2.** [irrumpir en] to break into.

allegado, da *sm, f* - **1.** [familiar] relative - **2.** [amigo] close friend.

allí *adv* there; **allí abajo/arriba** down/up there; **allí mismo** right there; **está por allí** it's around there somewhere; **hasta allí** up until then.

alma *sf* (el) - **1.** [gen] soul - **2.** [de bastón, ovillo] core.

almacén *sm* warehouse. ◆ **(grandes) almacenes** *smpl* department store *sing*.

almacenar *vt* - **1.** [gen & INFORM] to store - **2.** [reunir] to collect.

almendra *sf* almond.

almendro *sm* almond (tree).

almíbar *sm* syrup.

almidón *sm* starch.

almidonar *vt* to starch.

almirantazgo *sm* [dignidad] admiralty.

almirante *sm* admiral.

almirez *sm* mortar.

almizcle *sm* musk.

almohada *sf* pillow; **consultarlo con la almohada** *fig* to sleep on it.

almohadilla *sf* [gen, TECNOL & ZOOL] pad; [cojín] small cushion.

almorrana *sf* (gen pl) piles *pl*.

almorzar ◇ *vt* [al mediodía] to have for lunch. ◇ *vi* [al mediodía] to have lunch.

almuerzo *sm* [al mediodía] lunch.

aló *interj Andes & Caribe* [al teléfono] hello؟

alocado, da *sm, f* crazy person.

alojamiento *sm* accommodation; **buscar alojamiento** to look for accommodation.

alojar *vt* to put up. ◆ **alojarse** *vprnl* - **1.** [hospedarse] to stay - **2.** [introducirse] to lodge.

alondra *sf* lark.

alpargata *sf* (gen pl) espadrille.

Alpes *smpl*: **los Alpes** the Alps.

alpinismo *sm* mountaineering.

alpinista *smf* mountaineer.

alpiste *sm* [semilla] birdseed.

alquilar *vt* [casa, TV, oficina] to rent; [coche] to hire. ◆ **alquilarse** *vprnl* [casa, TV, oficina] to be for rent; [coche] to be for hire; **'se alquila'** 'to let'.

alquiler *sm* - **1.** [acción - de casa, TV, oficina] renting; [- de coche] hiring *UK*, rental *US*; **de alquiler** [- casa] rented; [- coche] hire (*antes de*

s) UK, rental *(antes de s)* US; **tenemos pisos de alquiler** we have flats to let UK, we have apartments to rent US - **2.** [precio - de casa, oficina] rent; [- de televisión] rental; [- de coche] hire UK, rental US.

alquimia *sf* alchemy.

alquitrán *sm* tar.

alrededor *adv* - **1.** [en torno] around; **mira a tu alrededor** look around you; **de alrededor** surrounding - **2.** [aproximadamente]: **alrededor de** around, about. ◆ **alrededores** *smpl* surrounding area *sing*; **en los alrededores de Londres** in the area around London. ◆ **alrededor de** *loc prep* around.

alta *sf* ➭ **alto**.

altanero, ra *adj* haughty.

altar *sm* altar; **conducir** O **llevar a alguien al altar** *fig* to lead sb down the aisle.

altavoz *sm* [gen] speaker; [para anuncios] loudspeaker.

alteración *sf* - **1.** [cambio] alteration - **2.** [excitación] agitation - **3.** [alboroto] disturbance; **alteración del orden público** breach of the peace.

alterar *vt* - **1.** [cambiar] to alter - **2.** [perturbar - persona] to agitate, to fluster; [- orden público] to disrupt. ◆ **alterarse** *vprnl* [perturbarse] to get agitated O flustered.

altercado *sm* argument, row.

alternar ◇ *vt* to alternate. ◇ *vi* - **1.** [relacionarse]: **alternar (con)** to mix (with), to socialize (with) - **2.** [sucederse]: **alternar con** to alternate with. ◆ **alternarse** *vprnl* - **1.** [en el tiempo] to take turns - **2.** [en el espacio] to alternate.

alternativa *sf* ➭ **alternativo**.

alternativamente *adv* [moverse] alternately.

alternativo, va *adj* - **1.** [movimiento] alternating - **2.** [posibilidad] alternative. ◆ **alternativa** *sf* [opción] alternative.

alterno, na *adj* alternate; ELECTR alternating.

alteza *sf fig* [de sentimientos] loftiness. ◆ **Alteza** *sf* [tratamiento] Highness; **Su Alteza Real** His Royal Highness (*f* Her Royal Highness).

altibajos *smpl fig* [de vida etc] ups and downs.

altiplano *sm* high plateau.

altisonante *adj* high-sounding.

altitud *sf* altitude.

altivez *sf* haughtiness.

altivo, va *adj* haughty.

alto, ta *adj* - **1.** [gen] high; [persona, árbol, edificio] tall; [piso] top, upper; **alta fidelidad** high fidelity; **altos hornos** blast furnace - **2.** [ruidoso] loud - **3.** [avanzado] late; **a altas horas de la noche** late at night, in the small hours. ◆ **al-**

to ◇ *sm* - **1.** [altura] height - **2.** [interrupción] stop - **3.** [lugar elevado] height; **en lo alto de** at the top of - **4.** MÚS alto - **5.** *loc*: **pasar por alto algo** to pass over sthg; **por todo lo alto** [lujoso] grand, luxurious; [a lo grande] in (great) style. ◇ *adv* - **1.** [arriba] high (up) - **2.** [hablar etc] loud. ◇ *interj* ¡alto! halt!, stop! ◆ **alta** *sf (el)* [del hospital] discharge.

altoparlante *sm Amér* loudspeaker.

altramuz *sm* lupin.

altruismo *sm* altruism.

altura *sf* - **1.** [gen] height; [en el mar] depth; **ganar altura** to climb - **2.** [nivel] level; **está a la altura del ayuntamiento** it's next to the town hall - **3.** [latitud] latitude. ◆ **alturas** *sfpl* [el cielo] Heaven *sing*; **a estas alturas** *fig* this far on, this late.

alubia *sf* bean.

alucinación *sf* hallucination.

alucinado, da *adj* - **1.** MED hallucinating - **2.** *fam* [sorprendido] gobsmacked.

alucinante *adj* - **1.** MED hallucinatory - **2.** *fam* [extraordinario] amazing.

alucinar ◇ *vi* MED to hallucinate. ◇ *vt fam fig* [seducir] to captivate.

alud *sm lit & fig* avalanche.

aludido, da *sm, f*: **el aludido** the aforesaid; **darse por aludido** [ofenderse] to take it personally; [reaccionar] to take the hint.

aludir *vi*: **aludir a** [sin mencionar] to allude to; [mencionando] to refer to.

alumbrado *sm* lighting.

alumbramiento *sm* [parto] delivery.

alumbrar *vt* - **1.** [iluminar] to light up - **2.** [instruir] to enlighten - **3.** [dar a luz] to give birth to.

aluminio *sm* aluminium.

alumnado *sm* [de escuela] pupils *pl*; [de universidad] students *pl*.

alumno, na *sm, f* [de escuela, profesor particular] pupil; [de universidad] student.

alunizar *vi* to land on the moon.

alusión *sf* [sin mencionar] allusion; [mencionando] reference.

alusivo, va *adj* allusive.

aluvión *sm* - **1.** [gen] flood - **2.** GEOL alluvium.

alza *sf (el)* rise; **jugar al alza** FIN to bull the market.

alzamiento *sm* uprising, revolt.

alzar *vt* - **1.** [levantar] to lift, to raise; [voz] to raise; [vela] to hoist; [cuello de abrigo] to turn up; [mangas] to pull up - **2.** [aumentar] to raise. ◆ **alzarse** *vprnl* - **1.** [levantarse] to rise - **2.** [sublevarse] to rise up, to revolt.

a.m. *(abrev de ante merídiem)* a.m.

ama ➭ **amo**.

amabilidad *sf* kindness; **¿tendría la amabilidad de...?** would you be so kind as to...?

amable *adj* kind; ¿sería tan amable de...? would you be so kind as to...?

amaestrado, da *adj* [que] trained: [en circo] performing.

amaestrar *vt* to train.

amagar ◇ *vt* - **1.** [dar indicios de] to show signs of - **2.** [mostrar intención] to threaten; **le amagó un golpe** he threatened to hit him. ◇ *vi* [tormenta] to be imminent, to threaten.

amago *sm* - **1.** [indicio] sign, hint - **2.** [amenaza] threat.

amainar *vi lit & fig* to abate.

amalgama *sf fig* & QUÍM amalgam.

amalgamar *vt fig* & QUÍM to amalgamate.

amamantar *vt* [animal] to suckle; [bebé] to breastfeed.

amanecer ◇ *sm* dawn; **al amanecer** at dawn. ◇ *v impers*: **amaneció a las siete** dawn broke at seven.

amanerado, da *adj* [afectado] mannered, affected.

amansar *vt* - **1.** [animal] to tame - **2.** *fig* [persona] to calm down.

amante *smf* - **1.** [querido] lover - **2.** *fig* [aficionado]: **ser amante de algo/hacer algo** to be keen on sthg/doing sthg; **los amantes del arte** art lovers.

amañar *vt* [falsear] to fix; [elecciones, resultado] to rig; [documento] to doctor.

amaño *sm* (gen pl) [treta] ruse, trick.

amapola *sf* poppy.

amar *vt* to love.

amarar *vi* [hidroavión] to land at sea; [vehículo espacial] to splash down.

amargado, da *adj* [resentido] bitter.

amargar *vt* to make bitter; *fig* to spoil.

amargo, ga *adj lit & fig* bitter.

amargoso, sa *adj Amér* bitter.

amargura *sf* [sentimiento] sorrow.

amarillento, ta *adj* yellowish.

amarillo, lla *adj* [color] yellow. ◆ **amarillo** *sm* [color] yellow.

amarilloso, sa *adj Amér* yellowish.

amarra *sf* mooring rope O line; **largar** O **soltar amarras** to cast off.

amarrar *vt* - **1.** NÁUT to moor - **2.** [atar] to tie (up); **amarrar algo/a alguien a algo** to tie sthg/sb to sthg. ◆ **amarrarse** *vprnl Amér salvo R Plata* - **1.** [pelo] to tie up - **2.** [zapatos] to tie.

amarre *sm* mooring.

amarrete *adj Andes & R Plata fam despec* mean, tight.

amasar *vt* - **1.** [masa] to knead; [yeso] to mix - **2.** *fam fig* [riquezas] to amass.

amasia *sf C Rica, Méx & Perú* mistress.

amasijo *sm fam fig* [mezcla] hotchpotch.

amateur [ama'ter] (*pl* amateurs) *adj inv* & *smf* amateur.

amatista *sf* amethyst.

amazona *sf fig* [jinete] horsewoman.

Amazonas *sm*: **el Amazonas** the Amazon.

ambages *smpl*: **sin ambages** without beating about the bush, in plain English.

ámbar *sm* amber.

ambición *sf* ambition.

ambicionar *vt* to have as one's ambition.

ambicioso, sa *adj* ambitious.

ambidextro, tra ◇ *adj* ambidextrous. ◇ *sm, f* ambidextrous person.

ambientación *sf* - **1.** CINE, LITER & TEATRO setting - **2.** RADIO & TV sound effects *pl*.

ambientador *sm* air freshener.

ambiental *adj* - **1.** [físico, atmosférico] ambient - **2.** [ecológico] environmental.

ambiente *sm* - **1.** [aire] air, atmosphere - **2.** [circunstancias] environment - **3.** [ámbito] world, circles *pl* - **4.** [animación] life, atmosphere - **5.** *Andes & R Dom* [habitación] room.

ambigüedad *sf* ambiguity.

ambiguo, gua *adj* [gen] ambiguous.

ámbito *sm* - **1.** [espacio, límites] confines *pl*; **una ley de ámbito provincial** an act which is provincial in its scope - **2.** [ambiente] world, circles *pl*.

ambivalente *adj* ambivalent.

ambos, bas ◇ *adj pl* both. ◇ *pron pl* both (of them).

ambulancia *sf* ambulance.

ambulante *adj* travelling; [biblioteca] mobile.

ambulatorio *sm* state-run surgery O clinic.

ameba *sf* amoeba.

amedrentar *vt* to scare, to frighten.

amén *adv* [en plegaria] amen; **decir amén a** *fig* to accept unquestioningly. ◆ **amén de** *loc prep* - **1.** [además de] in addition to - **2.** [excepto] except for, apart from.

amenaza *sf* threat; **amenaza de bomba** bomb scare; **amenaza de muerte** death threat.

amenazar *vt* to threaten; **amenazar a alguien con hacerle algo** to threaten to do sthg to sb; **amenazar a alguien con hacer algo** to threaten sb with doing sthg; **amenazar a alguien de muerte/con el despido** to threaten to kill/sack sb; **amenaza lluvia** it's threatening to rain.

amenidad *sf* [entretenimiento] entertaining qualities *pl*.

ameno, na *adj* [entretenido] entertaining.

América *n pr* America; **América del Sur** South America; **América Central** Central America.

americana *sf* ▷ **americano**.

americano, na adj & sm, f American. ◆ **americana** sf [chaqueta] jacket.

ameritar vt Amér to deserve.

amerizar vi [hidroavión] to land at sea; [vehículo espacial] to splash down.

ametralladora sf machine gun.

ametrallar vt [con ametralladora] to machinegun.

amianto sm asbestos.

amígdala sf tonsil.

amigdalitis sf inv tonsillitis.

amigo, ga ◇ adj [gen] friendly. ◇ sm, f - 1. [persona] friend; **hacerse amigo de** to make friends with; **hacerse amigos** to become friends; **amigo íntimo** close friend - 2. fam [compañero, novio] partner; [amante] lover.

amigote, amiguete sm fam pal.

amiguismo sm: **hay mucho amiguismo** there are always jobs for the boys.

aminoácido sm amino acid.

aminorar vt to reduce.

amistad sf friendship. ◆ **amistades** sfpl friends.

amistoso, sa adj friendly.

amnesia sf amnesia.

amnistía sf amnesty.

amo, ama sm, f - 1. [gen] owner - 2. [de criado, situación etc] master (f mistress). ◆ **ama de casa** sf housewife. ◆ **ama de llaves** sf housekeeper.

amodorrarse vprnl to get drowsy.

amoldar vt [adaptar]: **amoldar (a)** to adapt (to). ◆ **amoldarse** vprnl [adaptarse]: **amoldarse (a)** to adapt (to).

amonestación sf - 1. [reprimenda] reprimand - 2. DEP warning.

amonestar vt - 1. [reprender] to reprimand - 2. DEP to warn.

amoníaco, amoniaco sm [gas] ammonia.

amontonar vt - 1. [apilar] to pile up - 2. [reunir] to accumulate. ◆ **amontonarse** vprnl - 1. [personas] to form a crowd - 2. [problemas, trabajo] to pile up; [ideas, solicitudes] to come thick and fast.

amor sm love; **hacer el amor** to make love; **por amor al arte** for the love of it. ◆ **amor propio** sm pride.

amoral adj amoral.

amoratado, da adj [de frío] blue; [por golpes] black and blue.

amordazar vt [persona] to gag; [perro] to muzzle.

amorfo, fa adj [sin forma] amorphous.

amorío sm fam [romance] fling.

amoroso, sa adj - 1. [gen] loving; [carta, relación] love (antes de s) - 2. C Sur [encantador] charming.

amortajar vt [difunto] to shroud.

amortiguador, ra adj [de ruido] muffling; [de golpe] softening, cushioning. ◆ **amortiguador** sm AUTO shock absorber.

amortiguar vt [ruido] to muffle; [golpe] to soften, to cushion.

amortización sf ECON [de deuda, préstamo] paying-off; [de inversión, capital] recouping; [de bonos, acciones] redemption; [de bienes de equipo] depreciation.

amortizar vt - 1. [sacar provecho] to get one's money's worth out of - 2. [ECON - deuda, préstamo] to pay off; [- inversión, capital] to recoup; [- bonos, acciones] to redeem.

amotinar vt to incite to riot; [a marineros] to incite to mutiny. ◆ **amotinarse** vprnl to riot; [marineros] to mutiny.

amparar vt - 1. [proteger] to protect - 2. [dar cobijo a] to give shelter to. ◆ **ampararse** vprnl - 1. fig [apoyarse]: **ampararse en** [ley] to have recourse to; [excusas] to draw on - 2. [cobijarse]: **ampararse de** O **contra** to (take) shelter from.

amparo sm [protección] protection; **al amparo de** [persona, caridad] with the help of; [ley] under the protection of.

amperio sm amp, ampere.

ampliación sf - 1. [aumento] expansion; [de edificio, plazo] extension; **ampliación de capital** ECON increase in capital - 2. FOTO enlargement.

ampliar vt - 1. [gen] to expand; [local] to add an extension to; [plazo] to extend - 2. FOTO to enlarge, to blow up.

amplificación sf amplification.

amplificador sm ELECTRÓN amplifier.

amplificar vt to amplify.

amplio, plia adj - 1. [sala etc] roomy, spacious; [avenida, gama] wide - 2. [ropa] loose - 3. [explicación etc] comprehensive; **en el sentido más amplio de la palabra** in the broadest sense of the word.

amplitud sf - 1. [espaciosidad] roominess, spaciousness; [de avenida] wideness - 2. [de ropa] looseness - 3. fig [extensión] extent, comprehensiveness.

ampolla sf - 1. [en piel] blister - 2. [para inyecciones] ampoule - 3. [frasco] phial.

ampuloso, sa adj pompous.

amputar vt to amputate.

amueblar vt to furnish.

amurallar vt to build a wall around.

anacronismo sm anachronism.

anagrama sm anagram.

anal adj ANAT anal.

anales smpl lit & fig annals.

analfabetismo sm illiteracy.

analfabeto, ta adj & sm, f illiterate.

analgésico, ca *adj* analgesic. ➤ **analgésico** *sm* analgesic.

análisis *sm inv* analysis; **análisis de sangre** blood test.

analizar *vt* to analyse.

analogía *sf* similarity; **por analogía** by analogy.

analógico, ca *adj* INFORM & TECNOL analogue, analog.

análogo, ga *adj*: **análogo (a)** analogous *O* similar (to).

ananá, ananás *sm R Dom* pineapple.

anaquel *sm* shelf.

anarquía *sf* - **1.** [falta de gobierno] anarchy - **2.** [doctrina política] anarchism.

anárquico, ca *adj* anarchic.

anarquista *adj* & *smf* anarchist.

anatema *sm* [maldición] curse.

anatomía *sf* anatomy.

anca *sf* (el) haunch; **ancas de rana** frogs' legs.

ancestral *adj* ancestral; [costumbre] age-old.

ancho, cha *adj* [gen] wide; [prenda] loose-fitting; **te va** *O* **está ancho** it's too big for you; **a mis/tus** *etc* **anchas** *fig* at ease; **quedarse tan ancho** not to care less. ➤ **ancho** *sm* width; **a lo ancho** crosswise; **cinco metros de ancho** five metres wide; **a lo ancho de** across (the width of); **ancho de vía** gauge.

anchoa *sf* anchovy *(salted)*.

anchura *sf* - **1.** [medida] width - **2.** [de ropa] bagginess.

anciano, na ⬦ *adj* old. ⬦ *sm, f* old person, old man (*f* old woman). ➤ **anciano** *sm* [de tribu] elder.

ancla *sf* (el) anchor; **echar/levar anclas** to drop/weigh anchor.

anclar *vi* to anchor.

andadas *sfpl*: **volver a las andadas** *fam fig* to return to one's evil ways.

andadura *sf* walking.

ándale *interj* *Amér C & Méx fam* come on!

Andalucía *n pr* Andalusia.

andaluz, za *adj* & *sm, f* Andalusian.

andamio *sm* scaffold.

andanada *sf* *fig* & MIL broadside.

andando *interj*: **¡andando!** come on!, let's get a move on!

andante *adj* [que anda] walking.

andanza *sf* *(gen pl)* [aventura] adventure.

andar ⬦ *vi* - **1.** [caminar] to walk; [moverse] to move - **2.** [funcionar] to work, to go; **las cosas andan mal** things are going badly - **3.** [estar] to be; **andar preocupado** to be worried; **andar tras algo/alguien** *fig* to be after sthg/sb - **4.** *(antes de gerundio)*: **andar haciendo algo** to be doing sthg; **anda echando broncas a to-** dos he's going round telling everybody off; **anda buscando algo** he's looking for sthg - **5.** [ocuparse] **andar en** [asuntos, líos] to be involved in; [papeleos, negocios] to be busy with - **6.** [hurgar]: **andar en** to rummage around in - **7.** [alcanzar, rondar]: **anda por los 60** he's about sixty. ⬦ *vt* - **1.** [recorrer] to go, to travel - **2.** *Amér C* [llevar puesto] to wear. ⬦ *sm* gait, walk. ➤ **andares** *smpl* [de persona] gait *sing*. ➤ **anda** *interj* [sorpresa, desilusión] oh!; [¡vamos!] come on!; [¡por favor!] go on!; **¡anda ya!** [incredulidad] come off it!

andén *sm* FERROC platform.

Andes *smpl*: **los Andes** the Andes.

andinismo *sm* *Amér* mountaineering.

andinista *smf* *Amér* mountaineer.

Andorra *n pr* Andorra.

andorrano, na *adj* & *sm, f* Andorran.

andrajo *sm* [harapo] rag.

andrajoso, sa *adj* ragged.

andrógino, na *adj* androgynous.

androide *sm* [autómata] android.

anduviera *etc* ▭ **andar**.

anécdota *sf* anecdote.

anecdótico, ca *adj* - **1.** [con historietas] anecdotal - **2.** [no esencial] incidental.

anegar *vt* [inundar] to flood. ➤ **anegarse** *vprnl* - **1.** [inundarse] to flood; **sus ojos se anegaron de lágrimas** tears welled up in his eyes - **2.** [ahogarse] to drown.

anejo, ja *adj*: **anejo (a)** [edificio] connected (to); [documento] attached (to). ➤ **anejo** *sm* annexe.

anemia *sf* anaemia.

anémona *sf* anemone.

anestesia *sf* anaesthesia; **anestesia general/local** general/local anaesthesia.

anestésico, ca *adj* anaesthetic. ➤ **anestésico** *sm* anaesthetic.

anexar *vt* [documento] to attach.

anexión *sf* annexation.

anexionar *vt* to annex.

anexo, xa *adj* [edificio] connected; [documento] attached. ➤ **anexo** *sm* annexe.

anfetamina *sf* amphetamine.

anfibio, bia *adj* *lit* & *fig* amphibious.

anfiteatro *sm* - **1.** CINE & TEATRO circle - **2.** [edificio] amphitheatre.

anfitrión, ona *sm, f* host (*f* hostess).

ángel *sm* *lit* & *fig* angel; **ángel custodio** *O* **de la guarda** guardian angel; **tener ángel** to have something special.

angelical *adj* angelic.

angina *sf* *(gen pl)* [amigdalitis] sore throat; **tener anginas** to have a sore throat. ➤ **angina de pecho** *sf* angina (pectoris).

anglicano, na *adj* & *sm, f* Anglican.

anglosajón, ona *adj* & *sm, f* Anglo-Saxon.

Angola *n pr* Angola.

angora *sf* [de conejo] angora; [de cabra] mohair.

angosto, ta *adj culto* narrow.

angostura *sf* [bebida] angostura.

anguila *sf* eel.

angula *sf* elver.

angular *adj* angular. ◆ **gran angular** *sm* FOTO wide-angle lens.

ángulo *sm* - 1. [gen] angle; **ángulo de tiro** [para disparar] elevation - 2. [rincón] corner.

anguloso, sa *adj* angular.

angustia *sf* [aflicción] anxiety.

angustiar *vt* to distress. ◆ **angustiarse** *vprnl* [agobiarse]: **angustiarse (por)** to get worried (about).

angustioso, sa *adj* [espera, momentos] anxious; [situación, noticia] distressing.

anhelante *adj*: **anhelante (por algo/hacer algo)** longing (for sthg/to do sthg), desperate (for sthg/to do sthg).

anhelar *vt* to long O wish for; **anhelar hacer algo** to long to do sthg.

anhelo *sm* longing.

anhídrido *sm* anhydride; **anhídrido carbónico** carbon dioxide.

anidar *vi* [pájaro] to nest.

anilla *sf* ring.

anillo *sm* [gen & ASTRON] ring; **anillo de boda** wedding ring.

ánima *sf* (el) soul.

animación *sf* - 1. [alegría] liveliness - 2. [bullicio] hustle and bustle, activity - 3. CINE animation.

animado, da *adj* - 1. [con buen ánimo] cheerful - 2. [divertido] lively - 3. CINE animated.

animador, ra *sm, f* - 1. [en espectáculo] compere - 2. [en fiesta de niños] children's entertainer - 3. [en béisbol etc] cheerleader.

animadversión *sf* animosity.

animal ◇ *adj* - 1. [reino, funciones] animal *(antes de s)* - 2. *fam* [persona - basto] rough; [- ignorante] ignorant. ◇ *smf fam fig* [persona] animal, brute. ◇ *sm* animal; **animal doméstico** [de granja etc] domestic animal; [de compañía] pet; **animal de tiro** draught animal.

animar *vt* - 1. [estimular] to encourage; **animar a alguien a O para hacer algo** to encourage sb to do sthg - 2. [alegrar - persona] to cheer up - 3. [avivar - fuego, diálogo, fiesta] to liven up; [comercio] to stimulate. ◆ **animarse** *vprnl* - 1. [alegrarse - persona] to cheer up; [- fiesta etc] to liven up - 2. [decidir]: **animarse (a hacer algo)** to finally decide (to do sthg).

ánimo ◇ *sm* - 1. [valor] courage - 2. [aliento] encouragement; **dar ánimos a alguien** to encourage sb - 3. [humor] disposition. ◇ *interj* [para alentar]: **¡ánimo!** come on!

animoso, sa *adj* [valiente] courageous; [decidido] undaunted.

aniñado, da *adj* [comportamiento] childish; [voz, rostro] childlike.

aniquilar *vt* to annihilate, to wipe out.

anís *(pl anises) sm* - 1. [grano] aniseed - 2. [licor] anisette.

aniversario *sm* [gen] anniversary; [cumpleaños] birthday.

ano *sm* anus.

anoche *adv* last night, yesterday evening; **antes de anoche** the night before last.

anochecer ◇ *sm* dusk, nightfall; **al anochecer** at dusk. ◇ *v impers* to get dark.

anodino, na *adj* [sin gracia] dull, insipid.

anomalía *sf* anomaly.

anómalo, la *adj* anomalous.

anonimato *sm* anonymity; **permanecer en el anonimato** to remain nameless.

anónimo, ma *adj* anonymous. ◆ **anónimo** *sm* anonymous letter.

anorak *(pl anoraks) sm* anorak.

anorexia *sf* anorexia.

anormal *adj* [anómalo] abnormal.

anotación *sf* [gen] note; [en registro] entry; **anotación al margen** marginal note; **anotación contable** COM book entry.

anotar *vt* - 1. [apuntar] to note down - 2. [tantear] to notch up. ◆ **anotarse** *vprnl* [matricularse] to enrol.

anquilosamiento *sm* - 1. [estancamiento] stagnation - 2. MED paralysis.

anquilosarse *vprnl* - 1. [estancarse] to stagnate - 2. MED to become paralysed.

ansia *sf* (el) - 1. [afán]: **ansia de** longing O yearning for - 2. [ansiedad] anxiousness; [angustia] anguish; **comer con ansia** to eat ravenously.

ansiar *vt*: **ansiar hacer algo** to long O be desperate to do sthg.

ansiedad *sf* - 1. [inquietud] anxiety; **con ansiedad** anxiously - 2. PSICOL nervous tension.

ansioso, sa *adj* [impaciente] impatient; **estar ansioso por O de hacer algo** to be impatient to do sthg.

antagónico, ca *adj* antagonistic.

antagonista *smf* opponent.

antaño *adv* in days gone by.

antártico, ca *adj* Antarctic. ◆ **Antártico** *sm*: **el Antártico** the Antarctic; **el océano Glacial Antártico** the Antarctic Ocean.

Antártida *sf*: **la Antártida** the Antarctic.

ante [1] *sm* - 1. [piel] suede - 2. [animal] elk.

ante² *prep* - 1. [delante de, en presencia de] before - 2. [frente a - hecho, circunstancial] in the face of ▪ **ante todo** *loc adv* [sobre todo] above all - 2. [en primer lugar] first of all.

anteanoche *adv* the night before last.

anteayer *adv* the day before yesterday.

antebrazo *sm* forearm.

antecedente ◇ *adj* preceding, previous. ◇ *sm* [precedente] precedent. ▪ **antecedentes** *smpl* [de persona] record *sing*; [de asunto] background *sing*; **poner a alguien en antecedentes de** [informar] to fill sb in on; **una persona sin antecedentes** a person with a clean record.

anteceder *vt* to precede.

antecesor, ra *sm, f* [predecesor] predecessor.

antedicho, cha *adj* aforementioned.

antelación *sf*: **con antelación** in advance, beforehand; **con dos horas de antelación** two hours in advance.

antemano ▪ **de antemano** *loc adv* beforehand, in advance.

antena *sf* - 1. RADIO & TV aerial *UK*, antenna *US*; **antena parabólica** satellite dish - 2. ZOOL antenna.

anteojos *smpl Amér* glasses.

antepasado, da *sm, f* ancestor.

antepenúltimo, ma *adj* & *sm, f* last but two.

anteponer *vt*: **anteponer algo a algo** to put sthg before sthg.

anterior *adj* - 1. [previo]: **anterior (a)** previous (to); **el día anterior** the day before - 2. [delantero] front *(antes de s)*.

anterioridad *sf*: **con anterioridad** beforehand; **con anterioridad a** before, prior to.

anteriormente *adv* previously.

antes *adv* - 1. [gen] before; **no importa si venís antes** it doesn't matter if you come earlier; **ya no nado como antes** I can't swim as I used to; **mucho/poco antes** long/shortly before; **lo antes posible** as soon as possible; **mi coche de antes** my old car - 2. [primero] first; **esta señora está antes** this lady is first - 3. [expresa preferencia]: **antes... que** rather... than; **prefiero la sierra antes que el mar** I like the mountains better than the sea; **iría a la cárcel antes que mentir** I'd rather go to prison than lie. ▪ **antes de** *loc prep* before; **antes de hacer algo** before doing sthg. ▪ **antes (de) que** *loc conj* before; **antes (de) que llegarais** before you arrived.

antesala *sf* anteroom; **hacer antesala** [esperar] to wait.

antiadherente *adj* non-stick.

antiaéreo, a *adj* anti-aircraft.

antibala, antibalas *adj inv* bullet-proof.

antibiótico, ca *adj* antibiotic. ▪ **antibiótico** *sm* antibiotic.

anticipación *sf* antidepression.

anticipación *sf* earliness; **con anticipación** in advance; **con un mes de anticipación** a month in advance; **con anticipación a** prior to.

anticipado, da *adj* [elecciones] early; [pago] advance; **por anticipado** in advance.

anticipar *vt* - 1. [prever] to anticipate - 2. [adelantar] to bring forward - 3. [dinero] to pay in advance. ▪ **anticiparse** *vprnl* - 1. [suceder antes] to arrive early; **se anticipó a su tiempo** he was ahead of his time - 2. [adelantarse]: **anticiparse a alguien** to beat sb to it.

anticipo *sm* [de dinero] advance.

anticonceptivo, va *adj* contraceptive. ▪ **anticonceptivo** *sm* contraceptive.

anticongelante *adj* & *sm* antifreeze.

anticonstitucional *adj* unconstitutional.

anticorrosivo, va *adj* anticorrosive.

anticuado, da *adj* old-fashioned.

anticuario, ria *sm, f* [comerciante] antique dealer; [experto] antiquarian.

anticuerpo *sm* antibody.

antidepresivo, va *adj* antidepressant. ▪ **antidepresivo** *sm* antidepressant (drug).

antidisturbios *smpl* [policía] riot police.

antidopaje *sm* doping tests *pl*.

antidoping [anti'ðopin] *adj* doping *(antes de s)*.

antídoto *sm* antidote.

antier *adv Amér fam* the day before yesterday.

antiestético, ca *adj* unsightly.

antifaz *sm* mask.

antigás *adj inv* gas *(antes de s)*.

antiglobalización *sf* antiglobalization.

antigualla *sf despec* [cosa] museum piece; [persona] old fogey, old fossil.

antiguamente *adv* [hace mucho] long ago; [previamente] formerly.

antigubernamental *adj* anti-government.

antigüedad *sf* - 1. [gen] antiquity - 2. [veteranía] seniority. ▪ **antigüedades** *sfpl* [objetos] antiques; **tienda de antigüedades** antique shop.

antiguo, gua *adj* - 1. [viejo] old; [inmemorial] ancient - 2. [anterior, previo] former.

antihéroe *sm* antihero.

antihigiénico, ca *adj* unhygienic.

antihistamínico *sm* antihistamine.

antiinflamatorio *sm* anti-inflammatory drug.

antílope *sm* antelope.

antinatural *adj* unnatural.

antiniebla ▷ **faro**.

antioxidante sm rustproofing agent.

antipatía sf dislike; **tener antipatía a alguien** to dislike sb.

antipático, ca adj unpleasant.

antípodas sfpl: **las antípodas** the Antipodes.

antirrobo sm [en coche] antitheft device; [en edificio] burglar alarm.

antisemita adj anti-Semitic.

antiséptico, ca adj antiseptic. ⬦ **antiséptico** sm antiseptic.

antiterrorista adj anti-terrorist.

antítesis sf inv antithesis.

antitetánico, ca adj anti-tetanus (antes de s).

antivirus sm inv INFORM antivirus system.

antojarse vprnl - 1. [capricho]: **se le antojaron esos zapatos** he fancied those shoes; **se le ha antojado ir al cine** he felt like going to the cinema; **cuando se me antoje** when I feel like it - 2. [posibilidad]: **se me antoja que...** I have a feeling that...

antojitos smpl Méx snacks, appetizers.

antojo sm - 1. [capricho] whim; [de embarazada] craving - 2. [en la piel] birthmark.

antología sf anthology.

antónimo sm antonym.

antonomasia sf: **por antonomasia** par excellence.

antorcha sf torch.

antracita sf anthracite.

antro sm despec dive, dump.

antropófago, ga sm, f cannibal.

antropología sf anthropology.

anual adj annual.

anualidad sf annuity, yearly payment.

anuario sm yearbook.

anudar vt to knot, to tie in a knot.

anulación sf [cancelación] cancellation; [de ley] repeal; [de matrimonio, contrato] annulment.

anular[1] sm ▷ **dedo**.

anular[2] vt - 1. [cancelar - gen] to cancel; [- ley] to repeal; [- matrimonio, contrato] to annul - 2. [DEP - gol] to disallow; [- resultado] to declare void.

anunciación sf announcement. ⬦ **Anunciación** sf RELIG Annunciation.

anunciante smf advertiser.

anunciar vt - 1. [notificar] to announce - 2. [hacer publicidad de] to advertise - 3. [presagiar] to herald. ⬦ **anunciarse** vprnl: **anunciarse en** to advertise in, to put an advert in.

anuncio sm - 1. [notificación] announcement; [cartel, aviso] notice; [póster] poster - 2.: **anuncio (publicitario)** advertisement, advert; **anuncios por palabras** classified adverts - 3. [presagio] sign, herald.

anverso sm [de moneda] head, obverse; [de hoja] front.

anzuelo sm [para pescar] (fish) hook.

añadido, da adj: **añadido (a)** added (to).

añadidura sf addition; **por añadidura** in addition, what is more.

añadir vt to add.

añejo, ja adj - 1. [vino, licor] mature; [tocino] cured - 2. [costumbre] age-old.

añicos smpl: **hacer** O **hacerse añicos** to shatter.

añil adj & sm [color] indigo.

año sm year; **en el año 1939** in 1939; **los años 30** the thirties; **año académico/escolar/fiscal** academic/school/tax year; **año bisiesto/solar** leap/solar year; **año nuevo** New Year; **¡Feliz Año Nuevo!** Happy New Year! ⬦ **años** smpl [edad] age sing; **¿cuántos años tienes? – tengo 17 años** how old are you? – I'm 17 (years old); **los de 25 años** the 25-year-olds; **cumplir años** to have one's birthday; **cumplo años el 25** it's my birthday on the 25th.

añoranza sf: **añoranza (de)** [gen] nostalgia (for); [hogar, patria] homesickness (for).

añorar vt to miss.

apabullar vt to overwhelm.

apacentar vt to graze.

apacible adj [gen] mild, gentle; [lugar, ambiente] pleasant.

apaciguar vt - 1. [tranquilizar] to calm down - 2. [aplacar - dolor etc] to soothe. ⬦ **apaciguarse** vprnl - 1. [tranquilizarse] to calm down - 2. [aplacarse - dolor etc] to abate.

apadrinar vt - 1. [niño] to act as a godparent to - 2. [artista] to sponsor.

apagado, da adj - 1. [luz, fuego] out; [aparato] off - 2. [color, persona] subdued - 3. [sonido] muffled; [voz] quiet.

apagar vt - 1. [extinguir - fuego] to put out; [- luz] to put off; [- vela] to extinguish - 2. [desconectar] to turn O switch off; **apaga y vámonos** fig we have nothing more to talk about - 3. [aplacar - sed] to quench - 4. [rebajar - sonido] to muffle. ⬦ **apagarse** vprnl [extinguirse - fuego, vela, luz] to go out; [- dolor, ilusión, rencor] to die down; [- sonido] to die away.

apagón sm power cut.

apaisado, da adj oblong.

apalabrar vt [concertar] to make a verbal agreement regarding; [contratar] to engage on the basis of a verbal agreement.

apalancar vt [para abrir] to lever open; [para mover] to lever.

apalear *vt* to beat up.

apañado, da *adj fam* [hábil, mañoso] clever, resourceful; **estar apañado** *fig* to have had it.

apañar *vt fam* - 1. [reparar] to mend - 2. [amañar] to fix, to arrange. ➤ **apañarse** *vprnl fam* to cope, to manage; **apañárselas (para hacer algo)** to manage (to do sthg).

apaño *sm fam* - 1. [reparación] patch - 2. [chanchullo] fix, shady deal - 3. [acuerdo] compromise.

apapachar *vt Méx* [mimar] to cuddle; [consentir] to spoil.

aparador *sm* [mueble] sideboard.

aparato *sm* - 1. [máquina] machine; [de laboratorio] apparatus (U); [electrodoméstico] appliance; **aparato de radio** radio; **aparato de televisión** television set - 2. [dispositivo] device - 3. [teléfono]: **¿quién está al aparato?** who's speaking? - 4. [MED - prótesis] aid; [- para dientes] brace - 5. ANAT system - 6. POLIT machinery - 7. [ostentación] pomp, ostentation.

aparatoso, sa *adj* - 1. [ostentoso] ostentatious - 2. [espectacular] spectacular.

aparcamiento *sm* - 1. [acción] parking - 2. [parking] car park UK, parking lot US; [hueco] parking place.

aparcar ◇ *vt* [estacionar] to park. ◇ *vi* [estacionar] to park.

aparcero, ra *sm, f* sharecropper.

aparear *vt* [animales] to mate. ➤ **aparearse** *vprnl* [animales] to mate.

aparecer *vi* - 1. [gen] to appear - 2. [acudir]: **aparecer por (un lugar)** to turn up at (a place) - 3. [ser encontrado] to turn up.

aparejador, ra *sm, f* quantity surveyor.

aparejo *sm* - 1. [de caballerías] harness - 2. MECÁN block and tackle - 3. NÁUT rigging. ➤ **aparejos** *smpl* equipment (U); [de pesca] tackle (U).

aparentar ◇ *vt* - 1. [fingir] to feign - 2. [edad] to look. ◇ *vi* [presumir] to show off.

aparente *adj* [falso, supuesto] apparent.

aparición *sf* - 1. [gen] appearance - 2. [de ser sobrenatural] apparition.

apariencia *sf* [aspecto] appearance; **guardar las apariencias** to keep up appearances; **las apariencias engañan** appearances can be deceptive.

apartado, da *adj* - 1. [separado]: **apartado de** away from - 2. [alejado] remote. ➤ **apartado** *sm* [párrafo] paragraph; [sección] section. ➤ **apartado de correos** *sm* PO Box.

apartamento *sm* apartment, flat UK.

apartar *vt* - 1. [alejar] to move away; [quitar] to remove - 2. [separar] to separate - 3. [escoger] to take, to select. ➤ **apartarse** *vprnl* - 1. [hacerse a un lado] to move to one side - 2. [separarse] to separate; **apartarse de** [gen] to move away from; [tema] to get away from; [mundo, sociedad] to cut o.s. off from.

aparte ◇ *adv* - 1. [en otro lugar, a un lado] aside, to one side; **bromas aparte** joking apart; **dejar algo aparte** to leave sthg aside; **poner algo aparte** to put sthg aside; **impuestos aparte** before tax - 2. [además] besides; **aparte de fea...** besides being ugly... - 3. [por separado] separately. ◇ *sm* - 1. [párrafo] new paragraph - 2. TEATRO aside. ➤ **aparte de** *loc prep* [excepto] apart from, except from.

apasionado, da ◇ *adj* passionate. ◇ *sm, f* lover, enthusiast.

apasionante *adj* fascinating.

apasionar *vt* to fascinate; **le apasiona la música** he's mad about music. ➤ **apasionarse** *vprnl* to get excited; **apasionarse por** O **con** to be mad about.

apatía *sf* apathy.

apático, ca *adj* apathetic.

apátrida *adj* stateless.

apdo. *abrev de* **apartado**.

apeadero *sm* [de tren] halt.

apear *vt* [bajar] to take down. ➤ **apearse** *vprnl* [bajarse]: **apearse (de)** [tren] to alight (from), to get off; [coche] to get out (of); [caballo] to dismount (from).

apechugar *vi*: **apechugar con** to put up with, to live with.

apedrear *vt* [persona] to stone; [cosa] to throw stones at.

apegarse *vprnl*: **apegarse a** to become fond of O attached to.

apego *sm* fondness, attachment; **tener/tomar apego a** to be/become fond of.

apelación *sf* appeal.

apelar *vi* - 1. DER to (lodge an) appeal; **apelar ante/contra** to appeal to/against - 2. [recurrir]: **apelar a** [persona] to go to; [sentido común, bondad] to appeal to; [violencia] to resort to.

apelativo *sm* name.

apellidarse *vprnl*: **se apellida Suárez** her surname is Suárez.

apellido *sm* surname.

apelmazar *vt* - 1. [jersey] to shrink - 2. [arroz, bizcocho] to make stodgy. ➤ **apelmazarse** *vprnl* - 1. [jersey] to shrink - 2. [arroz, bizcocho] to go stodgy.

apelotonar *vt* to bundle up. ➤ **apelotonarse** *vprnl* [gente] to crowd together.

apenado, da *adj Andes, Amér C, Caribe & Méx* [avergonzado] ashamed, embarrassed.

apenar *vt* to sadden.

apenas *adv* - 1. [casi no] scarcely, hardly; **apenas me puedo mover** I can hardly move - 2. [tan sólo] only; **apenas hace dos minutos**

only two minutes ago - **3.** [tan pronto como] as soon as; **apenas llegó, sonó el teléfono** no sooner had he arrived than the phone rang.

apéndice *sm* appendix.

apendicitis *sf inv* appendicitis.

apercibir *vt* [amonestar] to reprimand. ◆ **apercibirse de** *vprnl* to notice.

aperitivo *sm* [bebida] aperitif; [comida] appetizer.

apero *sm (gen pl)* tool; **aperos de labranza** farming implements.

apertura *sf* - **1.** [gen] opening; [de año académico, temporada] start - **2.** POLIT [liberalización] liberalization *(especially that introduced in Spain by the Franco regime after 1970)*.

aperturista *adj* & *smf* progressive.

apesadumbrar *vt* to weigh down. ◆ **apesadumbrarse** *vprnl* to be weighed down.

apestar *vi*: **apestar (a)** to stink (of).

apetecer *vi*: **¿te apetece un café?** do you fancy a coffee?; **me apetece salir** I feel like going out.

apetecible *adj* [comida] appetizing, tempting; [vacaciones etc] desirable.

apetito *sm* appetite; **abrir el apetito** to whet one's appetite; **perder el apetito** to lose one's appetite; **tener apetito** to be hungry.

apetitoso, sa *adj* [comida] appetizing.

apiadar *vt* to earn the pity of. ◆ **apiadarse** *vprnl* to show compassion; **apiadarse de** to take pity on.

ápice *sm* - **1.** [pizca] iota; **no ceder un ápice** not to budge an inch - **2.** [punto culminante] peak, height.

apicultura *sf* beekeeping.

apilar *vt* to pile up. ◆ **apilarse** *vprnl* to pile up.

apiñar *vt* to pack *O* cram together. ◆ **apiñarse** *vprnl* to crowd together; [para protegerse, por miedo] to huddle together.

apio *sm* celery.

apisonadora *sf* steamroller.

aplacar *vt* to placate; [hambre] to satisfy; [sed] to quench. ◆ **aplacarse** *vprnl* to calm down; [dolor] to abate.

aplanar *vt* to level.

aplastante *adj fig* [apabullante] overwhelming, devastating.

aplastar *vt* - **1.** [por el peso] to flatten - **2.** [derrotar] to crush.

aplatanar *vt fam* to make listless.

aplaudir *vt* & *vi* to applaud.

aplauso *sm* - **1.** [ovación] round of applause; **aplausos** applause *(U)* - **2.** *fig* [alabanza] applause.

aplazamiento *sm* postponement.

aplazar *vt* - **1.** [retrasar] to postpone - **2.** *R Plata* [suspender] to fail.

aplicación *sf* [gen & INFORM] application.

aplicado, da *adj* [estudioso] diligent.

aplicar *vt* [gen] to apply; [nombre, calificativo] to give. ◆ **aplicarse** *vprnl* [esmerarse]: **aplicarse (en algo)** to apply o.s. (to sthg).

aplique *sm* wall lamp.

aplomo *sm* composure; **perder el aplomo** to lose one's composure.

apocado, da *adj* timid.

apocalipsis *sm inv* calamity. ◆ **Apocalipsis** *sm* Apocalypse.

apocarse *vprnl* [intimidarse] to be frightened *O* scared; [humillarse] to humble o.s.

apodar *vt* to nickname.

apoderado, da *sm, f* - **1.** [representante] (official) representative - **2.** TAUROM agent, manager.

apoderar *vt* [gen] to authorize; DER to grant power of attorney to. ◆ **apoderarse de** *vprnl* - **1.** [adueñarse de] to seize - **2.** *fig* [dominar] to take hold of, to grip.

apodo *sm* nickname.

apogeo *sm fig* height, apogee; **estar en (pleno) apogeo** to be at its height.

apolillar *vt* to eat holes in. ◆ **apolillarse** *vprnl* to get moth-eaten.

apolítico, ca *adj* apolitical.

apología *sf* apology, eulogy.

apoltronarse *vprnl* - **1.** [apalancarse]: **apoltronarse (en)** to become lazy *O* idle (in) - **2.** [acomodarse]: **apoltronarse en** to lounge in.

apoplejía *sf* apoplexy.

apoquinar *vt* & *vi fam* to fork out.

aporrear *vt* to bang.

aportación *sf* [contribución] contribution.

aportar *vt* [contribuir con] to contribute.

aposentar *vt* to put up, to lodge. ◆ **aposentarse** *vprnl* to take up lodgings.

aposento *sm* - **1.** [habitación] room; **retirarse a sus aposentos** *desus* & *hum* to withdraw (to one's chamber) - **2.** [alojamiento] lodgings *pl*.

apósito *sm* dressing.

aposta *adv* on purpose.

apostar ◇ *vt* - **1.** [jugarse] to bet - **2.** [emplazar] to post. ◇ *vi*: **apostar (por)** to bet (on). ◆ **apostarse** *vprnl* [jugarse] to bet; **apostarse algo con alguien** to bet sb sthg.

apostilla *sf* note.

apóstol *sm lit* & *fig* apostle.

apóstrofo *sm* GRAM apostrophe.

apoteósico, ca *adj* tremendous.

apoyar *vt* - **1.** [inclinar] to lean, to rest - **2.** *fig* [basar, respaldar] to support. ◆ **apoyarse** *vprnl* - **1.** [sostenerse]: **apoyarse en** to lean on

- **2.** *fig* [basarse]: **apoyarse en** [suj: tesis, conclusiones] to be based on, to rest on; [suj: personal to base one's argument on] [respaldarse] to support one another.

apoyo *sm lit & fig* support.

APRA *sf* (*abrev de* **Alianza Popular Revolucionaria Americana**) *Peruvian political party.*

apreciable *adj* - **1.** [perceptible] appreciable - **2.** *fig* [estimable] worthy.

apreciación *sf* [consideración] appreciation; [estimación] evaluation.

apreciar *vt* - **1.** [valorar] to appreciate; [sopesar] to appraise, to evaluate - **2.** [sentir afecto por] to think highly of - **3.** [percibir] to tell, to make out.

aprecio *sm* esteem.

aprehender *vt* [coger - persona] to apprehend; [- alijo, mercancía] to seize.

aprehensión *sf* [de persona] arrest, capture; [de alijo, mercancía] seizure.

apremiante *adj* pressing, urgent.

apremiar ◇ *vt* [meter prisa]: **apremiar a alguien para que haga algo** to urge sb to do sthg. ◇ *vi* [ser urgente] to be pressing.

apremio *sm* [urgencia] urgency.

aprender ◇ *vt* - **1.** [estudiar] to learn - **2.** [memorizar] to memorize. ◇ *vi*: **aprender (a hacer algo)** to learn (to do sthg).

aprendiz, za *sm, f* - **1.** [ayudante] apprentice, trainee - **2.** [novato] beginner.

aprendizaje *sm* - **1.** [acción] learning - **2.** [tiempo, situación] apprenticeship.

aprensión *sf*: **aprensión (por)** [miedo] apprehension (about); [escrúpulo] squeamishness (about).

aprensivo, va *adj* - **1.** [miedoso] apprehensive - **2.** [hipocondríaco] hypochondriac.

apresar *vt* [suj: animal] to catch; [suj: persona] to capture.

aprestar *vt* - **1.** [preparar] to prepare, to get ready - **2.** [tela] to size. ◆ **aprestarse a** *vprnl*: **aprestarse a hacer algo** to get ready to do sthg.

apresto *sm* size.

apresurado, da *adj* hasty, hurried.

apresurar *vt* to hurry along, to speed up; **apresurar a alguien para que haga algo** to try to make sb do sthg more quickly. ◆ **apresurarse** *vprnl* to hurry.

apretado, da *adj* - **1.** [gen] tight; [triunfo] narrow; [esprint] close; [caligrafía] cramped - **2.** [apiñado] packed.

apretar ◇ *vt* - **1.** [oprimir - botón, tecla] to press; [- gatillo] to pull; [- nudo, tuerca, cinturón] to tighten; **el zapato me aprieta** my shoe is pinching - **2.** [estrechar] to squeeze; [abrazar] to

hug - **3.** [comprimir - ropa, objetos] to pack tight - **4.** [juntar - dientes] to grit; [- labios] to press together. ◇ *vi* [zapatos, ropa] to be too tight. ◆ **apretarse** *vprnl* [agolparse] to crowd together; [acercarse] to squeeze up.

apretón *sm* [estrechamiento] squeeze; **apretón de manos** handshake.

apretujar *vt* - **1.** [gen] to squash - **2.** [hacer una bola con] to screw up. ◆ **apretujarse** *vprnl* [en banco, autobús] to squeeze together; [por frío] to huddle up.

apretujón *sm fam* [abrazo] bearhug.

aprieto *sm fig* fix, difficult situation; **poner en un aprieto a alguien** to put sb in a difficult position; **verse** *O* **estar en un aprieto** to be in a fix.

aprisa *adv* quickly.

aprisionar *vt* - **1.** [encarcelar] to imprison - **2.** [inmovilizar - atando, con camisa de fuerza] to strap down; [- suj: viga etc] to trap.

aprobación *sf* approval.

aprobado, da *adj* [aceptado] approved. ◆ **aprobado** *sm* EDUC pass.

aprobar *vt* - **1.** [proyecto, moción, medida] to approve; [ley] to pass - **2.** [comportamiento etc] to approve of - **3.** [examen, asignatura] to pass.

apropiación *sf* [robo] theft.

apropiado, da *adj* suitable, appropriate.

apropiar *vt*: **apropiar (a)** to adapt (to). ◆ **apropiarse de** *vprnl lit & fig* to appropriate.

aprovechable *adj* usable.

aprovechado, da *adj* - **1.** [caradura]: **es muy aprovechado** he's always sponging off other people - **2.** [bien empleado - tiempo] well-spent; [- espacio] well-planned.

aprovechamiento *sm* [utilización] use.

aprovechar ◇ *vt* - **1.** [gen] to make the most of; [oferta, ocasión] to take advantage of; [conocimientos, experiencia] to use, to make use of - **2.** [lo inservible] to put to good use. ◇ *vi* [ser provechoso] to be beneficial; **¡que aproveche!** enjoy your meal! ◆ **aprovecharse** *vprnl*: **aprovecharse (de)** to take advantage (of).

aprovisionamiento *sm* supplying.

aprox. (*abrev de* **aproximadamente**) approx.

aproximación *sf* - **1.** [acercamiento] approach - **2.** [en cálculo] approximation.

aproximadamente *adv* approximately.

aproximado, da *adj* approximate.

aproximar *vt* to move closer. ◆ **aproximarse** *vprnl* to come closer.

aptitud *sf* ability, aptitude; **tener aptitud para algo** to have an aptitude for sthg.

apto, ta *adj* - **1.** [adecuado, conveniente]: **apto (para)** suitable (for) - **2.** [capacitado - intelectualmente] capable, able; [- físicamente] fit - **3.** CINE: apto/no apto para menores suitable/unsuitable for children.

apto. (*abrev de* apartamento) Apt.

apuesta *sf* bet.

apuesto, ta *adj* dashing.

apuntador, ra *sm, f* prompter.

apuntalar *vt lit & fig* to underpin.

apuntar *vt* - **1.** [anotar] to note down; **apuntar a alguien** [en lista] to put sb down - **2.** [dirigir - dedo] to point; [- arma] to aim; **apuntar a alguien** [- con el dedo] to point at sb; [- con un arma] to aim at sb - **3.** TEATRO to prompt - **4.** *fig* [indicar] to point out. ◆ **apuntarse** *vprnl* - **1.** [en lista] to put one's name down; [en curso] to enrol - **2.** [participar]: **apuntarse (a hacer algo)** to join in (doing sthg).

apunte *sm* [nota] note. ◆ **apuntes** *smpl* EDUC notes.

apuñalar *vt* to stab.

apurado, da *adj* - **1.** [necesitado] in need; **apurado de** short of - **2.** [avergonzado] embarrassed - **3.** [difícil] awkward - **4.** *Amér* [con prisa]: **estar apurado** to be in a hurry.

apurar *vt* - **1.** [agotar] to finish off; [existencias, la paciencia] to exhaust - **2.** [meter prisa] to hurry - **3.** [preocupar] to trouble - **4.** [avergonzar] to embarrass. ◆ **apurarse** *vprnl* - **1.** [preocuparse]: **apurarse (por)** to worry (about) - **2.** [darse prisa] to hurry.

apuro *sm* - **1.** [dificultad] fix; **estar en apuros** to be in a tight spot - **2.** [penuria] hardship (U) - **3.** [vergüenza] embarrassment; **me da apuro (decírselo)** I'm embarrassed (to tell her).

aquejado, da *adj*: **aquejado de** suffering from.

aquejar *vt* to afflict.

aquel, aquella (*mpl* aquellos, *fpl* aquellas) *adj demos* that (*pl* those).

aquél, aquélla (*mpl* aquéllos, *fpl* aquéllas) *pron demos* - **1.** [ése] that (one), those (ones) *pl*; **este cuadro me gusta pero aquél del fondo no** I like this picture, but I don't like that one at the back; **aquél fue mi último día en Londres** that was my last day in London - **2.** [nombrado antes] the former - **3.** [con oraciones relativas] whoever, anyone who; **aquél que quiera hablar que levante la mano** whoever wishes O anyone wishing to speak should raise their hand; **aquéllos que...** those who...

aquella ▷ **aquel**.

aquélla ▷ **aquél**.

aquello *pron demos (neutro)* that; **aquello de su mujer es una mentira** all that about his wife is a lie.

aquellos, aquellas ▷ **aquel**.

aquéllos, aquéllas ▷ **aquél**.

aquí *adv* - **1.** [gen] here; **aquí abajo/arriba** down/up here; **aquí dentro/fuera** in/out here; **aquí mismo** right here; **de aquí para allá** [de un lado a otro] to and fro; **por aquí** over here - **2.** [ahora] now; **de aquí a mañana** between now and tomorrow; **de aquí a poco** shortly, soon; **de aquí a un mes** a month from now, in a month.

ara *sf (el)* [altar] altar. ◆ **en aras de** *loc prep culto* for the sake of.

árabe ◇ *adj* Arab, Arabian. ◇ *smf* [persona] Arab. ◇ *sm* [lengua] Arabic.

Arabia Saudí, Arabia Saudita *n pr* Saudi Arabia.

arábigo, ga *adj* - **1.** [de Arabia] Arab, Arabian - **2.** [numeración] Arabic.

arado *sm* plough.

arancel *sm* tariff.

arándano *sm* bilberry, blueberry *US*.

arandela *sf* TECNOL washer.

araña *sf* - **1.** [animal] spider - **2.** [lámpara] chandelier.

arañar *vt* [gen] to scratch.

arañazo *sm* scratch.

arar *vt* to plough.

arbitraje *sm* - **1.** [DEP - en fútbol etc] refereeing; [- en tenis, cricket] umpiring - **2.** DER arbitration.

arbitrar ◇ *vt* - **1.** [DEP - en fútbol etc] to referee; [- en tenis, cricket] to umpire - **2.** DER to arbitrate. ◇ *vi* - **1.** [DEP - en fútbol etc] to referee; [- en tenis, cricket] to umpire - **2.** DER to arbitrate.

arbitrariedad *sf* [cualidad] arbitrariness.

arbitrario, ria *adj* arbitrary.

arbitrio *sm* [decisión] judgment.

árbitro *sm* - **1.** [DEP - en fútbol etc] referee; **árbitro asistente** asisstant referee; [- en tenis, cricket] umpire - **2.** DER arbitrator.

árbol *sm* - **1.** BOT tree - **2.** TECNOL shaft; **árbol de levas** camshaft - **3.** NÁUT mast. ◆ **árbol genealógico** *sm* family tree.

arboleda *sf* grove.

arbusto *sm* bush, shrub.

arca *sf (el)* [arcón] chest. ◆ **arcas** *sfpl* coffers; **arcas públicas** Treasury *sing*.

arcada *sf* - **1.** (*gen pl*) [de estómago] retching (U); **me dieron arcadas** I retched - **2.** [ARQUIT - arcos] arcade; [- de puente] arch.

arcaico, ca *adj* archaic.

arce *sm* maple.

arcén *sm* [de autopista] hard shoulder *UK*, shoulder *US*; [de carretera] verge.

archiconocido, da *adj fam* very well-known.

archiduque, esa *sm, f* archduke (*f* archduchess).

archipiélago *sm* archipelago.

archivador, ra sm, f archivist. ◆ **archivador** sm filing cabinet.

archivar vt [guardar, documento, fichero etc] to file.

archivo sm - 1. [lugar] archive; [documentos] archives pl - 2. [informe, ficha] file - 3. INFORM file.

arcilla sf clay.

arco sm - 1. GEOM arc - 2. ARQUIT arch; **arco de herradura** horseshoe arch; **arco triunfal** O **de triunfo** triumphal arch - 3. DEP, MIL & MÚS bow. ◆ **arco iris** sm rainbow.

arcón sm large chest.

arder vi to burn; [sin llama] to smoulder; **arder de** fig to burn with; **está que arde** [persona] he's fuming; [reunión] it's getting pretty heated.

ardid sm ruse, trick.

ardiente adj [gen] burning; [líquido] scalding; [admirador, defensor] ardent.

ardilla sf squirrel.

ardor sm - 1. [quemazón] burning (sensation); **ardor de estómago** heartburn - 2. fig [entusiasmo] fervour.

arduo, dua adj arduous.

área sf (el) - 1. [gen] area; **área de libre cambio** ECON free exchange area - 2. DEP: **área (de castigo** O **penalti)** (penalty) area.

arena sf - 1. [de playa etc] sand; **arenas movedizas** quicksand (U) - 2. [para luchar] arena - 3. TAUROM bullring.

ARENA sf (abrev de Alianza Republicana Nacionalista) Salvadorean political party.

arenal sm sandy ground (U).

arenga sf harangue.

arenilla sf [polvo] dust.

arenoso, sa adj sandy.

arenque sm herring.

aretes smpl Andes & Cuba earrings.

argamasa sf mortar.

Argelia n pr Algeria.

Argentina n pr Argentina.

argentino, na adj & sm, f Argentinian.

argolla sf - 1. [aro] (large) ring - 2. Andes & Cuba [alianza] wedding ring.

argot sm - 1. [popular] slang - 2. [técnico] jargon.

argucia sf sophism.

argüir ⬦ vt culto - 1. [argumentar] to argue - 2. [demostrar] to prove. ⬦ vi [argumentar] to argue.

argumentación sf line of argument.

argumentar vt - 1. [teoría, opinión] to argue - 2. [razones, excusas] to allege.

argumento sm - 1. [razonamiento] argument - 2. [trama] plot.

aria sf MÚS aria.

aridez sf [gen] dryness; [de zona, clima] aridity.

árido, da adj [gen] dry, [zona, clima] arid. ◆ **áridos** smpl dry goods.

Aries ⬦ sm [zodiaco] Aries. ⬦ smf [persona] Aries.

ariete sm HIST & MIL battering ram.

ario, ria adj & sm, f Aryan.

arisco, ca adj surly.

arista sf edge.

aristocracia sf aristocracy.

aristócrata smf aristocrat.

aritmético, ca adj arithmetic. ◆ **aritmética** sf arithmetic.

arma sf (el) - 1. [instrumento] arm, weapon; **arma biológica/nuclear/química** biological/nuclear/chemical weapon; **armas de destrucción masiva** weapons of mass destruction; **arma blanca** blade, weapon with a sharp blade; **arma de fuego** firearm; **arma homicida** murder weapon - 2. fig [medio] weapon.

armada sf ⊳ **armado**.

armadillo sm armadillo.

armado, da adj - 1. [con armas] armed - 2. [con armazón] reinforced. ◆ **armada** sf [marina] navy; [escuadra] fleet.

armador, ra sm, f shipowner.

armadura sf - 1. [de barco, tejado] framework; [de gafas] frame - 2. [de guerrero] armour.

armamentista, armamentístico, ca adj arms (antes de s).

armamento sm [armas] arms pl.

armar vt - 1. [montar - mueble etc] to assemble; [- tienda] to pitch - 2. [ejército, personas] to arm - 3. fam fig [provocar] to cause; **armarla** fam to cause trouble. ◆ **armarse** vprnl - 1. [con armas] to arm o.s. - 2. [prepararse]: **armarse de** [valor, paciencia] to summon up - 3. loc: **se armó la gorda** O **la de San Quintín** O **la de Dios es Cristo** fam all hell broke loose.

armario sm [para objetos] cupboard, closet US; [para ropa] wardrobe UK, closet US; **armario empotrado** fitted cupboard/wardrobe; **salir del armario** fam to come out of the closet.

armatoste sm [mueble, objeto] unwieldy object; [máquina] contraption.

armazón sf [gen] framework, frame; [de avión, coche] chassis; [de edificio] skeleton.

armería sf - 1. [museo] military O war museum - 2. [depósito] armoury - 3. [tienda] gunsmith's (shop).

armiño sm [piel] ermine; [animal] stoat.

armisticio sm armistice.

armonía sf harmony.

armónico, ca adj harmonic. ◆ **armónica** sf harmonica.

armonioso, sa adj harmonious.

armonizar ⬦ vt - **1.** [concordar] to match - **2.** MÚS to harmonize. ⬦ vi [concordar]: **armonizar con** to match.

arnés sm armour. ⬥ **arneses** smpl [de animales] harness (U).

aro sm - **1.** [círculo] hoop; TECNOL ring; **los aros olímpicos** the Olympic rings; **entrar O pasar por el aro** to knuckle under - **2.** Amér [pendiente] earring.

aroma sm [gen] aroma; [de vino] bouquet; CULIN flavouring.

aromático, ca adj aromatic.

arpa sf (el) harp.

arpía sf fig [mujer] old hag.

arpillera sf sackcloth, hessian.

arpón sm harpoon.

arquear vt [gen] to bend; [cejas, espalda, lomo] to arch. ⬥ **arquearse** vprnl to bend.

arqueología sf archeology.

arqueólogo, ga sm, f archeologist.

arquero sm - **1.** DEP & MIL archer - **2.** Amér [portero de fútbol] goalkeeper.

arquetipo sm archetype.

arquitecto, ta sm, f architect.

arquitectura sf lit & fig architecture.

arrabal sm [barrio pobre] slum (on city outskirts); [barrio periférico] outlying district.

arrabalero, ra adj - **1.** [periférico] outlying - **2.** [barriobajero] rough, coarse.

arracimarse vprnl to cluster together.

arraigado, da adj [costumbre, idea] deeply rooted; [persona] established.

arraigar vi lit & fig to take root. ⬥ **arraigarse** vprnl [establecerse] to settle down.

arraigo sm roots pl; **tener mucho arraigo** to be deeply rooted.

arrancar ⬦ vt - **1.** [desarraigar - árbol] to uproot; [- malas hierbas, flor] to pull up - **2.** [quitar, separar] to tear O rip off; [cable, página, pelo] to tear out; [cartel, cortinas] to tear down; [muela] to pull out; [ojos] to gouge out - **3.** [arrebatar]: **arrancar algo a alguien** to grab O snatch sthg from sb - **4.** AUTO & TECNOL to start; INFORM to start up - **5.** fig [obtener]: **arrancar algo a alguien** [confesión, promesa, secreto] to extract sthg from sb; [sonrisa, dinero, ovación] to get sthg out of sb; [suspiro, carcajada] to bring sthg from sb. ⬦ vi - **1.** [partir] to set off - **2.** [suj: máquina, coche] to start - **3.** [provenir]: **arrancar de** to stem from.

arranque sm - **1.** [comienzo] start - **2.** AUTO starter motor - **3.** fig [arrebato] fit.

arrasar vt to destroy, to devastate.

arrastrar ⬦ vt - **1.** [gen] to drag O pull along; [pies] to drag; [carro, vagón] to pull; [suj: corriente, aire] to carry away - **2.** fig [convencer] to win over; **arrastrar a alguien a algo/a hacer**

algo to lead sb into sthg/to do sthg; **dejarse arrastrar por algo/alguien** to allow o.s. to be swayed by sthg/sb - **3.** INFORM to drag; **arrastrar y soltar algo** to drag and drop sthg - **4.** fig [producir] to bring. ⬦ vi [rozar el suelo] to drag (along) the ground. ⬥ **arrastrarse** vprnl to crawl; fig to grovel.

arrastre sm - **1.** [acarreo] dragging - **2.** [pesca] trawling - **3.** Esp fam: **estar para el arrastre** to have had it - **4.** R Dom fam: **tener arrastre** to be popular with members of the opposite sex.

arre interj: **¡arre!** gee up!

arrear vt - **1.** [azuzar] to gee up - **2.** fam [propinar] to give.

arrebatado, da adj - **1.** [impetuoso] impulsive, impetuous - **2.** [ruborizado] flushed - **3.** [iracundo] enraged.

arrebatar vt - **1.** [arrancar]: **arrebatar algo a alguien** to snatch sthg from sb - **2.** fig [cautivar] to captivate. ⬥ **arrebatarse** vprnl [enfurecerse] to get furious.

arrebato sm - **1.** [arranque] fit, outburst; **un arrebato de amor** a crush - **2.** [furia] rage.

arrebujar vt [amontonar] to bundle (up). ⬥ **arrebujarse** vprnl [arroparse] to wrap o.s. up.

arreciar vi - **1.** [temporal etc] to get worse - **2.** fig [críticas etc] to intensify.

arrecife sm reef.

arreglado, da adj - **1.** [reparado] fixed; [ropa] mended - **2.** [ordenado] tidy - **3.** [bien vestido] smart - **4.** [solucionado] sorted out - **5.** fig [precio] reasonable.

arreglar vt - **1.** [reparar] to fix, to repair; [ropa] to mend - **2.** [ordenar] to tidy (up) - **3.** [solucionar] to sort out - **4.** MÚS to arrange - **5.** [acicalar] to smarten up; [cabello] to do. ⬥ **arreglarse** vprnl - **1.** [apañarse]: **arreglarse (con algo)** to make do (with sthg); **arreglárselas (para hacer algo)** to manage (to do sthg) - **2.** [acicalarse] to smarten up.

arreglo sm - **1.** [reparación] mending, repair; [de ropa] mending - **2.** [solución] settlement - **3.** MÚS (musical) arrangement - **4.** [acuerdo] agreement; **llegar a un arreglo** to reach agreement.

arrellanarse vprnl to settle back.

arremangar = **remangar**.

arremeter ⬥ **arremeter contra** vi to attack.

arremetida sf attack.

arremolinarse vprnl - **1.** fig [personas]: **arremolinarse alrededor de** to crowd around - **2.** [agua, hojas] to swirl (about).

arrendamiento, arriendo sm - **1.** [acción] renting, leasing - **2.** [precio] rent, lease.

arrendar vt - **1.** [dar en arriendo] to let, to lease - **2.** [tomar en arriendo] to rent, to lease.

arrendatario, ria *sm, f* leaseholder, tenant.

arreos *smpl* harness (U).

arrepentido, da ‹›   *adj*   repentant.
‹› *sm, f* POLÍT person who renounces terrorist
activities.

arrepentimiento *sm* regret, repentance.

arrepentirse *vprnl* to repent.

arrestar *vt* to arrest.

arresto *sm* [detención] arrest.

arriar *vt* to lower.

arriba ‹› *adv* - 1. [posición - gen] above; *Amér*
[- encima de] above; [- en edificio] upstairs; vive (en el piso de) arriba she lives upstairs; está aquí/allí arriba it's up here/there; arriba del
todo right at the top; más arriba further up
- 2. [dirección] up; ve arriba [en edificio] go upstairs; hacia/para arriba up, upwards; calle/
escaleras arriba up the street/stairs; río arriba upstream - 3. [en un texto] above; 'el arriba
mencionado...'   'the   above-mentioned...'
- 4. *loc:* de arriba abajo [cosa] from top to bottom; [persona] from head to toe O foot; mirar a
alguien de arriba abajo [con desdén] to look sb
up and down. ‹› *prep:* arriba (de) *Amér* [en-
cima de] on top of. ‹› *interj:* ¡arriba...! up
(with)...!; ¡arriba los mineros! up (with) the
miners!; ¡arriba las manos! hands up!
➡ **arriba de** *loc prep* more than. ➡ **de
arriba** *loc adj* top; el estante de arriba the top
shelf.

arribar *vi* to arrive; NÁUT to reach port.

arribeño, ña *sm, f* Amér fam highlander.

arribista *adj* & *smf* arriviste.

arriendo *sm* = **arrendamiento**.

arriesgado, da *adj* [peligroso] risky.

arriesgar *vt* to risk; [hipótesis] to venture, to
suggest. ➡ **arriesgarse** *vprnl* to take risks/a
risk.

arrimar *vt* [acercar] to move O bring closer;
arrimar algo a [pared, mesa] to move sthg up
against. ➡ **arrimarse** *vprnl* [acercarse] to
come closer O nearer; arrimarse a algo [acer-
cándose] to move closer to sthg; [apoyándose]
to lean on sthg.

arrinconar *vt* - 1. [apartar] to put in a corner
- 2. [abandonar] to discard, to put away - 3. *fig*
[persona - dar de lado] to cold-shoulder; [- aco-
rralar] to corner.

arrodillarse *vprnl* to kneel down; *fig* to go
down on one's knees, to grovel.

arrogancia *sf* arrogance.

arrogante *adj* arrogant.

arrojar *vt* - 1. [lanzar] to throw; [con violencia]
to hurl, to fling - 2. [despedir - humo] to send
out; [- olor] to give off; [- lava] to spew out
- 3. [echar]: arrojar a alguien de to throw sb out

of - 4. [resultado] to produce, to yield - 5. [vo-
mitar] to throw up. ➡ **arrojarse** *vprnl* to hurl
o.s.

arrojo *sm* courage, fearlessness.

arrollador, ra *adj* overwhelming; [belleza,
personalidad] dazzling.

arrollar *vt* - 1. [atropellar] to run over - 2. [tirar
- suj: agua, viento] to sweep away - 3. [vencer] to
crush.

arropar *vt* [con ropa] to wrap up; [en cama] to
tuck up. ➡ **arroparse** *vprnl* to wrap o.s. up.

arroyo *sm* [riachuelo] stream.

arroz *sm* rice; arroz blanco white rice; arroz
con leche rice pudding.

arruga *sf* - 1. [en ropa, papel] crease - 2. [en piel]
wrinkle, line.

arrugar *vt* - 1. [ropa, papel] to crease, to
crumple - 2. [piel] to wrinkle. ➡ **arrugarse**
vprnl - 1. [ropa] to get creased - 2. [piel] to get
wrinkled.

arruinar *vt* lit & fig to ruin. ➡ **arruinarse**
vprnl to go bankrupt, to be ruined.

arrullar *vt* to lull to sleep. ➡ **arrullarse**
vprnl [animales] to coo.

arrumar *vt* Andes & Ven to pile up.

arsenal *sm* - 1. [de barcos] shipyard - 2. [de ar-
mas] arsenal - 3. [de cosas] array.

arsénico *sm* arsenic.

art. (abrev de **artículo**). art.

arte *sm o sf* (en sing gen m; en pl f) - 1. [gen]
art; arte abstracto/figurativo abstract/figurat-
ive art; arte dramático drama - 2. [don] artistry
- 3. [astucia] artfulness, cunning; malas artes
trickery (U). ➡ **artes** *sfpl* arts; bellas artes
fine arts.

artefacto *sm* [aparato] device; [máquina] machine.

arteria *sf* lit & fig artery.

artesa *sf* trough.

artesanal *adj* [hecho a mano] handmade.

artesanía *sf* craftsmanship; de artesanía
[producto] handmade.

artesano, na *sm, f* craftsman (f craftswo-
man).

ártico, ca *adj* arctic. ➡ **Ártico** *sm:* el Ártico
the Arctic; el océano Glacial Ártico the Arctic
Ocean.

articulación *sf* - 1. ANAT & TECNOL joint - 2. LING
articulation.

articulado, da *adj* articulated.

articular *vt* [palabras, piezas] to articulate.

artículo *sm* [gen] article; artículo básico ECON
basic product; artículo de fondo editorial,
leader; artículo de primera necesidad basic
commodity.

artífice *smf* fig architect.

artificial *adj* artificial.

artificio *sm fig* [falsedad] artifice; [artimaña] trick.

artificioso, sa *adj fig* [engañoso] deceptive.

artillería *sf* artillery.

artillero *sm* artilleryman.

artilugio *sm* gadget, contrivance.

artimaña *sf (gen pl)* trick, ruse.

artista *smf* - 1. [gen] artist - 2. [de espectáculos] artiste; **artista de cine** movie actor (*f* actress).

artístico, ca *adj* artistic.

artritis *sf inv* arthritis.

arzobispo *sm* archbishop.

as *sm* - 1. [carta, dado] ace - 2. [campeón]: **un as del volante** an ace driver.

asa *sf (el)* handle.

asado, da *adj* roasted. ◆ **asado** *sm* - 1. [carne] roast - 2. *Col & C Sur* [barbacoa] barbecue.

asador *sm* - 1. [aparato] roaster - 2. [varilla] spit.

asaduras *sfpl* offal (*U*); [de pollo, pavo] giblets.

asalariado, da ◇ *adj* wage-earning. ◇ *sm, f* wage earner.

asalmonado, da *adj* salmon (pink).

asaltante *smf* [agresor] attacker; [atracador] robber.

asaltar *vt* - 1. [atacar] to attack; [castillo, ciudad etc] to storm - 2. [robar] to rob - 3. *fig* [suj: dudas etc] to assail.

asalto *sm* - 1. [ataque] attack; [de castillo, ciudad] storming - 2. [robo] robbery - 3. DEP round.

asamblea *sf* assembly; POLÍT mass meeting.

asar *vt* [alimentos - al horno] to bake; [- a la parrilla] to grill; [- en asador] to roast.

ascendencia *sf* - 1. [linaje] descent - 2. [extracción social] extraction - 3. *fig* [influencia] ascendancy.

ascender ◇ *vi* - 1. [subir] to go up, to climb - 2. [aumentar, elevarse] to rise, to go up - 3. [en empleo, deportes]: **ascender (a)** to be promoted (to) - 4. [totalizar - precio etc]: **ascender a** to come O amount to. ◇ *vt*: **ascender a alguien (a)** to promote sb (to).

ascendiente *smf* [antepasado] ancestor.

ascensión *sf* ascent. ◆ **Ascensión** *sf* RELIG Ascension.

ascenso *sm* - 1. [en empleo, deportes] promotion - 2. [escalada] ascent - 3. [de precios, temperaturas] rise.

ascensor *sm* lift *UK*, elevator *US*.

ascético, ca *adj* ascetic.

asco *sm* [sensación] revulsion; **siento asco** I feel sick; **¡qué asco de tiempo!** what foul weather!; **me da asco** I find it disgusting; **¡qué asco!** how disgusting O revolting!; **hacer ascos a** to turn one's nose up at.

ascua *sf (el)* ember; **en O sobre ascuas** on tenterhooks.

aseado, da *adj* [limpio] clean; [arreglado] smart.

asear *vt* to clean. ◆ **asearse** *vprnl* to get washed and dressed.

asediar *vt* to lay siege to; *fig* to pester.

asedio *sm* siege; *fig* pestering.

asegurado, da *sm, f* policy-holder.

asegurar *vt* - 1. [fijar] to secure - 2. [garantizar] to assure; **te lo aseguro** I assure you; **asegurar a alguien que...** to assure sb that... - 3. COM: **asegurar (contra)** to insure (against); **asegurar algo en** [cantidad] to insure sthg for. ◆ **asegurarse** *vprnl* [cerciorarse]: **asegurarse de que...** to make sure that...

asemejar ◆ **asemejar a** *vi* to be similar to, to be like. ◆ **asemejarse** *vprnl* to be similar O alike; **asemejarse a** to be similar to, to be like.

asentamiento *sm* [campamento] settlement.

asentar *vt* - 1. [instalar - empresa, campamento] to set up; [- comunidad, pueblo] to settle - 2. [asegurar] to secure; [cimientos] to lay. ◆ **asentarse** *vprnl* - 1. [instalarse] to settle down - 2. [sedimentarse] to settle.

asentir *vi* - 1. [estar conforme]: **asentir (a)** to agree (to) - 2. [afirmar con la cabeza] to nod.

aseo *sm* [limpieza - acción] cleaning; [- cualidad] cleanliness. ◆ **aseos** *smpl* toilets *UK*, restroom *sing US*.

aséptico, ca *adj* MED aseptic.

asequible *adj* - 1. [accesible, comprensible] accessible - 2. [precio, producto] affordable.

aserradero *sm* sawmill.

aserrar *vt* to saw.

asesinar *vt* to murder; [rey, jefe de estado] to assassinate.

asesinato *sm* murder; [de rey, jefe de estado] assassination.

asesino, na *sm, f* murderer (*f* murderess); [de rey, jefe de estado] assassin; **asesino en serie** serial killer.

asesor, ra *sm, f* adviser; FIN consultant; **asesor fiscal** tax consultant.

asesorar *vt* to advise; FIN to provide with consultancy services. ◆ **asesorarse** *vprnl* to seek advice; **asesorarse de** to consult.

asesoría *sf* [oficina] consultant's office.

asestar *vt* [golpe] to deal; [tiro] to fire.

aseveración *sf* assertion.

asfaltado *sm* [acción] asphalting, surfacing; [asfalto] asphalt, (road) surface.

asfalto *sm* asphalt.

asfixia *sf* asphyxiation, suffocation.

asfixiar *vt* [ahogar] to asphyxiate, to suffoc-ate. ➡ **asfixiarse** *vprnl* [ahogarse] to as-phyxiate, to suffocate.

así <> *adv* [de este modo] in this way, like this; [de ese modo] in that way, like that; **era así de largo** it was this/that long; **así es/era/fue como...** that is how...; **así así** [no muy bien] so so; **algo así como** [algo igual a] something like; **así es** [para asentir] that is correct, yes; **y así todos los días** and the same thing hap-pens day after day; **así como** [también] as well as, and also; [tal como] just as, exactly as; **así no más** *Amér fam* [de repente] just like that. <> *conj* - **1.** [de modo que]: **así (es) que** so - **2.** [aunque] although - **3.** [tan pronto como]: **así que** as soon as - **4.** *Amér* [aun si] even if. <> *adj inv* [como éste] like this; [como ése] like that. ➡ **así y todo, aun así** *loc adv* even so.

Asia *n pr* Asia.

asiático, ca *adj* & *sm, f* Asian, Asiatic.

asidero *sm* [agarradero] handle.

asiduidad *sf* frequency.

asiduo, dua *adj* & *sm, f* regular.

asiento *sm* [en casa, teatro] seat; **tomar asien-to** to sit down.

asignación *sf* - **1.** [atribución] allocation - **2.** [sueldo] salary.

asignar *vt* - **1.** [atribuir]: **asignar algo a alguien** to assign *O* allocate sthg to sb - **2.** [destinar]: **asignar a alguien a** to send sb to.

asignatura *sf* EDUC subject.

asilado, da *sm, f* person living in an old people's home, convalescent home etc.

asilo *sm* - **1.** [hospicio] home; **asilo de ancianos** old people's home - **2.** *fig* [amparo] asylum; **asilo político** political asylum - **3.** [hospedaje] accommodation.

asimilación *sf* [gen & LING] assimilation.

asimilar *vt* [gen] to assimilate.

asimismo *adv* [también] also, as well; (a prin-cipio de frase) likewise.

asir *vt* to grasp, to take hold of.

asistencia *sf* - **1.** [presencia - acción] attend-ance; [- hecho] presence - **2.** [ayuda] assist-ance; **asistencia letrada** *O* **jurídica** legal ad-vice; **asistencia médica** medical attention; **asistencia sanitaria** health care; **asistencia téc-nica** technical assistance - **3.** [afluencia] audi-ence - **4.** DEP assist.

asistenta *sf* cleaning lady.

asistente *smf* - **1.** [ayudante] assistant, help-er; **asistente personal** INFORM personal digital assistant; **asistente social** social worker - **2.** [presente] person present; **los asistentes** the audience sing.

asistido, da *adj* AUTO power (antes de s); IN-FORM computer-assisted.

asistir <> *vt* [ayudar] to attend to. <> *vi*: **asis-tir a** to attend, to go to.

asma *sf* (el) asthma.

asno *sm* lit & fig ass.

asociación *sf* association; **asociación de pa-dres de alumnos** parent-teacher association; **asociación de vecinos** residents' association.

asociado, da <> *adj* [miembro] associate. <> *sm, f* [miembro] associate, partner.

asociar *vt* [relacionar] to associate. ➡ **aso-ciarse** *vprnl* to form a partnership.

asolar *vt* to devastate.

asomar <> *vi* [gen] to peep up; [del interior de algo] to peep out. <> *vt* to stick; **asomar la ca-beza por la ventana** to stick one's head out of the window. ➡ **asomarse a** *vprnl* [ventana] to stick one's head out of; [balcón] to come/go out onto.

asombrar *vt* [causar admiración] to amaze; [causar sorpresa] to surprise. ➡ **asombrarse** *vprnl*: **asombrarse (de)** [sentir admiración] to be amazed (at); [sentir sorpresa] to be surprised (at).

asombro *sm* [admiración] amazement; [sor-presa] surprise.

asombroso, sa *adj* [sensacional] amazing; [sorprendente] surprising.

asomo *sm* [indicio] trace, hint; [de esperanza] glimmer.

aspa *sf* (el) X-shaped cross; [de molino] arms *pl*.

aspaviento *sm* (gen pl) furious gesticula-tions *pl*.

aspecto *sm* - **1.** [apariencia] appearance - **2.** [faceta] aspect; **en todos los aspectos** in every respect.

aspereza *sf* roughness; *fig* sourness.

áspero, ra *adj* - **1.** [rugoso] rough - **2.** *fig* [des-agradable] sharp, sour.

aspersión *sf* [de jardín] sprinkling; [de cultivos] spraying.

aspersor *sm* [para jardín] sprinkler; [para culti-vos] sprayer.

aspiración *sf* - **1.** [ambición & LING] aspiration - **2.** [de aire - por una persona] breathing in; [- por una máquina] suction.

aspirador *sm* = **aspiradora**.

aspiradora *sf* vacuum cleaner, hoover®; **pa-sar la aspiradora** to vacuum, to hoover.

aspirante *smf*: **aspirante (a)** candidate (for); [en deportes, concursos] contender (for).

aspirar <> *vt* [aire - suj: persona] to breathe in, to inhale. <> *vi*: **aspirar a algo** [ansiar] to aspire to sthg.

aspirina® *sf* aspirin.

asquear *vt* to disgust, to make sick.

asqueroso, sa *adj* disgusting, revolting.

asta *sf (el)* - **1.** [de bandera] flagpole, mast - **2.** [de lanza] shaft; [de brocha] handle - **3.** [de toro] horn.

asterisco *sm* asterisk.

astigmatismo *sm* astigmatism.

astilla *sf* splinter; **hacer astillas** *fig* to smash to smithereens.

astillero *sm* shipyard.

astringente *adj* astringent.

astro *sm* ASTRON heavenly body; *fig* star.

astrofísica *sf* astrophysics (U).

astrología *sf* astrology.

astrólogo, ga *sm, f* astrologer.

astronauta *smf* astronaut.

astronomía *sf* astronomy.

astrónomo, ma *sm, f* astronomer.

astucia *sf* - **1.** [picardía] cunning, astuteness - **2.** *(gen pl)* [treta] cunning trick.

astuto, ta *adj* [ladino, tramposo] cunning; [sagaz, listo] astute.

asueto *sm* break, rest; **unos días de asueto** a few days off.

asumir *vt* - **1.** [gen] to assume - **2.** [aceptar] to accept.

asunción *sf* assumption. **Asunción** *sf*: **la Asunción** RELIG the Assumption.

Asunción *n pr* GEOGR Asunción.

asunto *sm* - **1.** [tema - general] subject; [- específico] matter; [- de obra, libro] theme; **asuntos a tratar** agenda *sing* - **2.** [cuestión, problema] issue - **3.** [negocio] affair, business (U); **no es asunto tuyo** it's none of your business. **asuntos** *smpl* POLÍT affairs; **asuntos exteriores** foreign affairs.

asustado, da *adj* frightened, scared.

asustar *vt* to frighten, to scare. **asustarse** *vprnl*: **asustarse (de)** to be frightened O scared (of).

atacar *vt* [gen] to attack; **me ataca los nervios** *fig* it gets on my nerves.

atadura *sf lit & fig* tie.

atajar *vi* [acortar]: **atajar (por)** to take a short cut (through). *vt* [contener] to put a stop to; [hemorragia, inundación] to stem.

atajo *sm* - **1.** [camino corto, medio rápido] short cut; **coger** O **tomar un atajo** to take a short cut - **2.** *despec* [panda] bunch.

atalaya *sf* - **1.** [torre] watchtower - **2.** [altura] vantage point.

atañer *vi* - **1.** [concernir]: **atañer a** to concern - **2.** [corresponder]: **atañer a** to be the responsibility of.

ataque *sm* - **1.** [gen & DEP] attack - **2.** *fig* [acceso] fit, bout; **ataque cardíaco** O **al corazón** heart attack; **ataque de nervios** nervous breakdown.

atar *vt* - **1.** [unir] to tie (up) - **2.** *fig* [constreñir] to tie down.

atardecer *sm* dusk; **al atardecer** at dusk. *v impers* to get dark.

atareado, da *adj* busy.

atascar *vt* to block (up). **atascarse** *vprnl* - **1.** [obstruirse] to get blocked up - **2.** *fig* [detenerse] to get stuck; [al hablar] to dry up.

atasco *sm* - **1.** [obstrucción] blockage - **2.** AUTO traffic jam.

ataúd *sm* coffin.

ataviar *vt* [cosa] to deck out; [persona] to dress up. **ataviarse** *vprnl* to dress up.

atavío *sm* [indumentaria] attire (U).

atemorizar *vt* to frighten. **atemorizarse** *vprnl* to get frightened.

atenazar *vt* - **1.** [sujetar] to clench - **2.** *fig* [suj: dudas] to torment, to rack; [suj: miedo, nervios] to grip.

atención *sf* - **1.** [interés] attention; **poner** O **prestar atención** to pay attention; **atención al cliente** customer service department; **atención personalizada** personalized service; **atención psiquiátrica** psychiatric treatment - **2.** [cortesía] attentiveness (U). *interj*: **¡atención!** [en aeropuerto, conferencia] your attention please! **atenciones** *sfpl* attentions.

atender *vt* - **1.** [satisfacer - petición, ruego] to attend to; [- consejo, instrucciones] to heed; [- propuesta] to agree to - **2.** [cuidar de - necesitados, invitados] to look after; [- enfermo] to care for; [- cliente] to serve; **¿le atienden?** are you being served? *vi* [estar atento]: **atender (a)** to pay attention (to).

atenerse **atenerse a** *vprnl* - **1.** [promesa, orden] to stick to; [ley, normas] to abide by - **2.** [consecuencias] to bear in mind.

atentado *sm*: **atentado contra alguien** attempt on sb's life; **atentado contra algo** crime against sthg.

atentamente *adv* [en cartas] Yours sincerely O faithfully.

atentar *vi*: **atentar contra (la vida de) alguien** to make an attempt on sb's life; **atentar contra algo** [principio etc] to be a crime against sthg.

atento, ta *adj* - **1.** [pendiente] attentive; **estar atento a** [explicación, programa, lección] to pay attention to; [ruido, sonido] to listen out for; [acontecimientos, cambios, avances] to keep up with - **2.** [cortés] considerate, thoughtful.

atenuante *sm* DER extenuating circumstance.

atenuar *vt* [gen] to diminish; [dolor] to ease; [luz] to filter.

ateo, a *adj* atheistic. *sm, f* atheist.

aterrador, ra *adj* terrifying.

aterrar *vt* to terrify.

aterrizaje *sm* landing; **aterrizaje de emergencia** *o* **forzoso** emergency landing.

aterrizar *vi* [avión] to land.

aterrorizar *vt* to terrify; [suj: agresor] to terrorize.

atesorar *vt* [riquezas] to amass.

atestado *sm* official report.

atestar *vt* - **1.** [llenar] to pack, to cram - **2.** DER to testify to.

atestiguar *vt* to testify to.

atiborrar *vt* to stuff full. ◆ **atiborrarse** *vprnl*: **atiborrarse (de)** *fam* *fig* to stuff one's face (with).

ático *sm* [para vivir] penthouse; [desván] attic.

atinar *vi* [adivinar] to guess correctly; [dar en el blanco] to hit the target; **atinar a hacer algo** to succeed in doing sthg; **atinar con** to hit upon.

atingencia *sf* Amér [relación] connection.

atípico, ca *adj* atypical.

atisbar *vt* - **1.** [divisar, prever] to make out - **2.** [acechar] to observe, to spy on.

atisbo *sm* (gen pl) trace, hint; [de esperanza] glimmer.

atizar *vt* - **1.** [fuego] to poke, to stir - **2.** *fam* [puñetazo, patada] to land, to deal.

atlántico, ca *adj* Atlantic. ◆ **Atlántico** *sm*: **el (océano) Atlántico** the Atlantic (Ocean).

atlas *sm inv* atlas.

atleta *smf* athlete.

atlético, ca *adj* athletic.

atletismo *sm* athletics (U).

atmósfera *sf* lit & fig atmosphere.

atole *sm* Amér C & Méx drink made of corn meal.

atolladero *sm* [apuro] fix, jam.

atolondrado, da *adj* - **1.** [precipitado] hasty, disorganized - **2.** [aturdido] bewildered.

atómico, ca *adj* atomic; [central, armas] nuclear.

atomizador *sm* atomizer, spray.

átomo *sm* lit & fig atom; **ni un átomo de** without a trace of.

atónito, ta *adj* astonished, astounded.

atontado, da *adj* - **1.** [aturdido] dazed - **2.** [tonto] stupid.

atontar *vt* [aturdir] to daze.

atormentar *vt* to torture; *fig* to torment.

atornillar *vt* to screw.

atorón *sm* Méx traffic jam.

atorrante *adj* R Dom [holgazán] lazy.

atosigar *vt* *fig* to harass.

atracador, ra *sm, f* [de banco] armed robber; [en la calle] mugger.

atracar ◇ *vi* NÁUT: **atracar (en)** to dock (at). ◇ *vt* [banco] to rob; [persona] to mug. ◆ **atracarse** *vprnl*: **atracarse de** to eat one's fill of.

atracción *sf* - **1.** [gen] attraction - **2.** [espectáculo] act - **3.** *fig* [centro de atención] centre of attention - **4.** (gen pl) [atracción de feria] fairground attraction.

atraco *sm* robbery.

atracón *sm* *fam* feast; **darse un atracón** to stuff one's face.

atractivo, va *adj* attractive. ◆ **atractivo** *sm* [de persona] attractiveness, charm; [de cosa] attraction.

atraer *vt* [gen] to attract.

atragantarse *vprnl*: **atragantarse (con)** to choke (on).

atrancar *vt* - **1.** [cerrar] to bar - **2.** [obturar] to block. ◆ **atrancarse** *vprnl* - **1.** [atascarse] to get blocked - **2.** *fig* [al hablar, escribir] to dry up.

atrapar *vt* [agarrar, alcanzar] to catch.

atrás *adv* - **1.** [detrás - posición] behind, at the back; [- movimiento] backwards; **quedarse atrás** *fig* to fall behind - **2.** [antes] earlier, before.

atrasado, da *adj* - **1.** [en el tiempo] delayed; [reloj] slow; [pago] overdue, late; [número, copia] back (antes de s) - **2.** [en evolución, capacidad] backward.

atrasar ◇ *vt* to put back. ◇ *vi* to be slow. ◆ **atrasarse** *vprnl* - **1.** [demorarse] to be late - **2.** [quedarse atrás] to fall behind.

atraso *sm* [de evolución] backwardness. ◆ **atrasos** *smpl* *fam* arrears.

atravesar *vt* - **1.** [interponer] to put across - **2.** [cruzar] to cross - **3.** [perforar] to go through - **4.** *fig* [vivir] to go through. ◆ **atravesarse** *vprnl* [interponerse] to be in the way; **se me ha atravesado la vecina** *fig* I can't stand my neighbour.

atrayente *adj* attractive.

atreverse *vprnl*: **atreverse (a hacer algo)** to dare (to do sthg); **se atreve con todo** he can tackle anything.

atrevido, da *adj* [osado] daring; [caradura] cheeky.

atrevimiento *sm* - **1.** [osadía] daring - **2.** [insolencia] cheek.

atribución *sf* - **1.** [imputación] attribution - **2.** [competencia] responsibility.

atribuir *vt* [imputar]: **atribuir algo a** to attribute sthg to. ◆ **atribuirse** *vprnl* [méritos] to claim for o.s.; [poderes] to assume; **atribuirse la responsabilidad** to claim responsibility.

atributo *sm* attribute.

atril *sm* [para libros] bookrest; MÚS music stand.

atrocidad *sf* [crueldad] atrocity.

atropellado, da *adj* hasty.

atropellar *vt* - **1.** [suj: vehículo] to run over - **2.** *fig* [suj: persona] to trample on. ➡ **atropellarse** *vprnl* [al hablar] to trip over one's words.

atropello *sm* - **1.** [por vehículo] running over - **2.** *fig* [moral] abuse.

atroz *adj* atrocious; [dolor] awful.

ATS (*abrev de* **ayudante técnico sanitario**) *smf Esp* qualified nurse.

atte. *abrev de* **atentamente**.

atuendo *sm* attire.

atún *sm* tuna.

aturdido, da *adj* dazed.

aturdir *vt* [gen] to stun; [suj: alcohol] to fuddle; [suj: ruido, luz] to bewilder.

audacia *sf* [intrepidez] daring.

audaz *adj* [intrépido] daring.

audición *sf* - **1.** [gen] hearing - **2.** MÚS & TEATRO audition.

audiencia *sf* - **1.** [público, recepción] audience; **índice de audiencia** audience ratings - **2.** [DER - juicio] hearing; [- tribunal, edificio] court.

audífono *sm* hearing aid.

audiovisual *adj* audiovisual.

auditivo, va *adj* ear (*antes de s*).

auditor, ra *sm, f* FIN auditor.

auditorio *sm* - **1.** [público] audience - **2.** [lugar] auditorium.

auge *sm* [gen & ECON] boom.

augurar *vt* [suj: persona] to predict; [suj: suceso] to augur.

augurio *sm* omen, sign.

aula *sf* (el) [de escuela] classroom; [de universidad] lecture room.

aullar *vi* to howl.

aullido *sm* howl.

aumentar ◇ *vt* - **1.** [gen] to increase; [peso] to put on - **2.** [en óptica] to magnify - **3.** [sonido] to amplify. ◇ *vi* to increase; [precios] to rise.

aumento *sm* - **1.** [incremento] increase; [de sueldo, precios] rise; **ir en aumento** to be on the increase - **2.** [en óptica] magnification.

aun ◇ *adv* even. ◇ *conj*: **aun estando cansado, lo hizo** even though he was tired, he did it; **ni aun puesta de puntillas llega** she can't reach it, even on tiptoe; **aun cuando** even though; **aun así** even so.

aún *adv* [todavía] still; (*en negativas*) yet; **no ha llegado aún** he hasn't arrived yet, he still hasn't arrived.

aunar *vt* to join, to pool. ➡ **aunarse** *vprnl* [aliarse] to unite.

aunque *conj* - **1.** [a pesar de que] even though, although; [incluso si] even if - **2.** [pero] although.

aúpa *interj*: ¡**aúpa**! [¡levántate!] get up!; ¡**aúpa el Atleti!** up the Athletic!

aupar *vt* to help up; *fig* [animar] to cheer on. ➡ **auparse** *vprnl* to climb up.

aureola *sf* - **1.** ASTRON & RELIG halo - **2.** *fig* [fama] aura.

auricular *sm* [de teléfono] receiver. ➡ **auriculares** *smpl* [cascos] headphones.

aurora *sf* first light of dawn.

auscultar *vt* to sound (*with a stethoscope*).

ausencia *sf* absence; **brillar por su ausencia** to be conspicuous by one's/its absence.

ausentarse *vprnl* to go away.

ausente ◇ *adj* - **1.** [no presente] absent; **estará ausente todo el día** he'll be away all day - **2.** [distraído] absent-minded. ◇ *smf* - **1.** [no presente]: **criticó a los ausentes** he criticized the people who weren't there - **2.** DER missing person.

auspicio *sm* [protección] protection; **bajo los auspicios de** under the auspices of.

austeridad *sf* austerity.

austero, ra *adj* [gen] austere.

austral ◇ *adj* southern. ◇ *sm* [moneda] austral.

Australia *n pr* Australia.

australiano, na *adj* & *sm, f* Australian.

Austria *n pr* Austria.

austriaco, ca, **austríaco, ca** *adj* & *sm, f* Austrian.

autarquía *sf* - **1.** POLÍT autarchy - **2.** ECON autarky.

auténtico, ca *adj* [gen] genuine; [piel, joyas] genuine, real; **un auténtico imbécil** a real idiot; **es un tío auténtico** he's a genuine bloke.

auto *sm* - **1.** *fam* [coche] car; *C Sur* [vehículo] car - **2.** DER judicial decree.

autoadhesivo, va *adj* self-adhesive.

autobiografía *sf* autobiography.

autobús *sm* bus.

autocar *sm Esp* coach.

autocontrol *sm* self-control.

autóctono, na *adj* indigenous.

autodefensa *sf* self-defence.

autodeterminación *sf* self-determination.

autodidacta *adj* self-taught.

autoescuela *sf* driving school.

autoestop, autostop *sm* hitch-hiking; **hacer autoestop** to hitch-hike.

autoestopista, autostopista *smf* hitch-hiker.

autógrafo *sm* autograph.

autómata *sm lit & fig* automaton.

automático, ca *adj* automatic. ➡ **automático** *sm* [botón] press-stud.

automatización *sf* automation.

automóvil *sm* car *UK*, automobile *US*.

automovilismo *sm* motoring; DEP motor racing.

automovilista *smf* motorist, driver.

automovilístico, ca *adj* motor (antes de s); DEP motor-racing (antes de s).

autonomía *sf* [POLÍT - facultad] autonomy; [- territorio] autonomous region.

autonómico, ca *adj* autonomous.

autónomo, ma <> *adj* - 1. POLÍT autonomous - 2. [trabajador] self-employed; [traductor, periodista] freelance. <> *sm, f* self-employed person; [traductor, periodista] freelance.

autopista *sf* motorway *UK*, freeway *US*.

autopsia *sf* autopsy, post-mortem.

autor, ra *sm, f* - 1. LITER author - 2. [de crimen] perpetrator.

autoridad *sf* - 1. [gen] authority - 2. [ley]: **la autoridad** the authorities *pl*.

autoritario, ria *adj & sm, f* authoritarian.

autorización *sf* authorization.

autorizado, da *adj* - 1. [permitido] authorized - 2. [digno de crédito] authoritative.

autorizar *vt* - 1. [dar permiso] to allow; [en situaciones oficiales] to authorize - 2. [capacitar] to allow, to entitle.

autorretrato *sm* self-portrait.

autoservicio *sm* - 1. [tienda] self-service shop - 2. [restaurante] self-service restaurant.

autostop = autoestop.

autostopista = autoestopista.

autosuficiencia *sf* self-sufficiency.

autovía *sf* dual carriageway *UK*, state highway *US*.

auxiliar <> *adj* [gen & GRAM] auxiliary. <> *smf* assistant; **auxiliar administrativo** office clerk. <> *vt* to assist, to help.

auxilio *sm* assistance, help; **pedir/prestar auxilio** to call for/give help; **primeros auxilios** first aid (U); **¡socorro, auxilio!** help! help!

av., avda. (abrev de avenida) Ave.

aval *sm* - 1. [persona] guarantor - 2. [documento] guarantee, reference.

avalancha *sf lit & fig* avalanche.

avalar *vt* to endorse, to guarantee.

avance *sm* - 1. [gen] advance - 2. FIN [anticipo] advance payment - 3. RADIO & TV [- meteorológico etc] summary; [- de futura programación] preview; **avance informativo** news (U) in brief.

avanzar <> *vi* to advance. <> *vt* - 1. [adelantar] to move forward - 2. [anticipar] to tell in advance.

avaricia *sf* greed, avarice.

avaricioso, sa *adj* avaricious.

avaro, ra *adj* miserly, mean.

avasallar *vt* [arrollar] to overwhelm.

avatar *sm* (gen pl) vagary.

avda. (abrev de avenida) = **av.**

ave *sf* (el) [gen] bird; **ser un ave pasajera** O **de paso** *fig* to be a rolling stone.

AVE (abrev de **alta velocidad española**) *sm* Spanish high-speed train.

avecinarse *vprnl* to be on the way.

avellana *sf* hazelnut.

avemaría *sf* (el) [oración] Hail Mary.

avena *sf* [grano] oats *pl*.

avenencia *sf* [acuerdo] compromise.

avenida *sf* avenue.

avenido, da *adj*: **bien/mal avenidos** on good/bad terms.

avenirse *vprnl* [ponerse de acuerdo] to come to an agreement; **avenirse a algo/a hacer algo** to agree on sthg/to do sthg.

aventajado, da *adj* [adelantado] outstanding.

aventajar *vt* [rebasar] to overtake; [estar por delante de] to be ahead of; **aventajar a alguien en algo** to surpass sb in sthg.

aventón *sm Amér C, Méx & Perú*: **dar aventón a alguien** to give sb a lift.

aventura *sf* - 1. [gen] adventure - 2. [relación amorosa] affair.

aventurado, da *adj* risky.

aventurero, ra <> *adj* adventurous. <> *sm, f* adventurer (*f* adventuress).

avergonzar *vt* - 1. [deshonrar] to shame - 2. [abochornar] to embarrass. ◆ **avergonzarse** *vprnl*: **avergonzarse (de)** [por culpa] to be ashamed (of); [por timidez] to be embarrassed (about).

avería *sf* [de máquina] fault; AUTO breakdown.

averiado, da *adj* [máquina] out of order; [coche] broken down.

averiar *vt* to damage. ◆ **averiarse** *vprnl* [máquina] to be out of order; AUTO to break down.

averiguación *sf* investigation.

averiguar *vt* to find out.

aversión *sf* aversion.

avestruz *sm* ostrich.

aviación *sf* - 1. [navegación] aviation - 2. [ejército] airforce.

aviador, ra *sm, f* aviator.

aviar *vt* [comida] to prepare.

avicultura *sf* poultry farming.

avidez *sf* eagerness.

ávido, da *adj*: **ávido de** eager for.

avinagrado, da *adj lit & fig* sour.

avío *sm* [preparativo] preparation. ◆ **avíos** *smpl* - 1. *fam* [equipo] things, kit (U) - 2. [víveres] provisions *pl*.

avión *sm* plane, airplane *US*; **en avión** by plane; **avión a reacción** jet; **avión de papel** paper aeroplane.

avioneta *sf* light aircraft.

avisar *vt* - **1.** [informar]: **avisar a alguien** to let sb know, to tell sb - **2.** [advertir]: **avisar (de)** to warn (of) - **3.** [llamar] to call, to send for.

aviso *sm* - **1.** [advertencia, amenaza] warning - **2.** *Amér* [anuncio] advertisement, advert; **aviso clasificado** classified advertisement - **3.** [notificación] notice; [en teatros, aeropuertos] call; **hasta nuevo aviso** until further notice; **sin previo aviso** without notice.

avispa *sf* wasp.

avispado, da *adj fam* sharp, quick-witted.

avispero *sm* [nido] wasp's nest.

avituallar *vt* to provide with food.

avivar *vt* - **1.** [sentimiento] to rekindle - **2.** [color] to brighten - **3.** [fuego] to stoke up.

axila *sf* armpit.

axioma *sm* axiom.

ay (*pl* **ayes**) *interj*: **¡ay!** [dolor físico] ouch!; [sorpresa, pena] oh!; **¡ay de ti si te cojo!** Heaven help you if I catch you!

aya ⊳ **ayo**.

ayer ◇ *adv* yesterday; *fig* in the past; **ayer (por la) noche** last night; **ayer por la mañana** yesterday morning; **antes de ayer** the day before yesterday. ◇ *sm fig* yesteryear.

ayo, aya *sm, f* [tutor] tutor (*f* governess).

ayuda *sf* help, assistance; ECON & POLIT aid; **ayuda en carretera** breakdown service; **ayuda humanitaria** humanitarian aid.

ayudante *adj & smf* assistant.

ayudar *vt* to help; **ayudar a alguien a hacer algo** to help sb (to) do sthg; **¿en qué puedo ayudarle?** how can I help you? ◆ **ayudarse** *vprnl*: **ayudarse de** to make use of.

ayunar *vi* to fast.

ayunas *sfpl*: **en ayunas** [sin comer] without having eaten; *fig* [sin enterarse] in the dark.

ayuno *sm* fast; **hacer ayuno** to fast.

ayuntamiento *sm* - **1.** [corporación] ≃ town council - **2.** [edificio] town hall *UK*, city hall *US*.

azabache *sm* jet; **negro como el azabache** jet-black.

azada *sf* hoe.

azafata *sf*: **azafata (de vuelo)** air hostess *UK*, air stewardess.

azafate *sm Amér C, Caribe, Méx & Perú* [bandeja] tray.

azafrán *sm* saffron, crocus.

azahar *sm* [del naranjo] orange blossom; [del limonero] lemon blossom.

azalea *sf* azalea.

azar *sm* chance, fate; **al azar** at random; **por (puro) azar** by (pure) chance.

azorar *vt* to embarrass. ◆ **azorarse** *vprnl* to be embarrassed.

azotar *vt* [suj: persona] to beat; [en el trasero] to smack; [con látigo] to whip.

azote *sm* - **1.** [golpe] blow; [en el trasero] smack; [latigazo] lash - **2.** *fig* [calamidad] scourge.

azotea *sf* [de edificio] terraced roof; **estar mal de la azotea** *fam fig* to be funny in the head.

azteca *adj & smf* Aztec.

azúcar *sm o sf* sugar.

azucarado, da *adj* sweet, sugary.

azucarero, ra *adj* sugar *(antes de s)*. ◆ **azucarero** *sm* sugar bowl.

azucena *sf* white lily.

azufre *sm* sulphur.

azul *adj & sm* blue.

azulejo *sm* (glazed) tile.

azuzar *vt* [animal] to set on.

b, B *sf* [letra] b, B.

baba *sf* [saliva - de niño] dribble; [- de adulto] saliva; [- de perro] slobber; **echar babas** to drool.

babear *vi* [niño] to dribble; [adulto, animal] to slobber; *fig* to drool.

babero *sm* bib.

babi *sm* child's overall.

bable *sm* Asturian dialect.

babor *sm*: **a babor** to port.

babosada *sf Amér C & Méx fam* daft thing.

baboso, sa *adj Amér fam* [tonto] daft, stupid. ◆ **babosa** *sf* ZOOL slug.

babucha *sf* slipper.

baca *sf* roof O luggage rack.

bacalao *sm* [fresco] cod; [salado] dried salted cod; **partir** O **cortar el bacalao** *fam fig* to be the boss.

bacanal *sf* orgy.

bache *sm* - **1.** [en carretera] pothole - **2.** *fig* [dificultades] bad patch - **3.** [en un vuelo] air pocket.

bachillerato *sm Spanish two-year course of secondary studies for academically orientated 16-18-year-olds*.

bacinica *sf Amér* chamber pot.

bacon ['beikon] *sm inv* bacon.

bacteria *sf* germ; **bacterias** bacteria.

badén *sm* [de carretera] ditch.

bádminton ['baðminton] *sm inv* badminton.

bafle, baffle *sm* loudspeaker.

bagaje *sm fig* background; **bagaje cultural** cultural baggage.

bagatela *sf* trifle.

Bahamas *sfpl*: **las Bahamas** the Bahamas.

bahía *sf* bay.

bailaor, ra *sm, f* flamenco dancer.

bailar ◇ *vt* to dance. ◇ *vi* [danzar] to dance.

bailarín, ina *sm, f* dancer; [de ballet] ballet dancer; **prima bailarina** prima ballerina.

baile *sm* - 1. [gen] dance; **baile clásico** ballet; **baile de salón** ballroom dancing - 2. [fiesta] ball.

baja *sf* ⮌ **bajo**.

bajada *sf* - 1. [descenso] descent; **bajada de bandera** [de taxi] minimum fare - 2. [pendiente] (downward) slope - 3. [disminución] decrease, drop.

bajamar *sf* low tide.

bajar ◇ *vt* - 1. [poner abajo - libro, cuadro etc] to take/bring down; [- telón, ventanilla, mano] to lower - 2. [descender - montaña, escaleras] to go/come down - 3. [precios, inflación, hinchazón] to reduce; [música, volumen, radio] to turn down; [fiebre] to bring down - 4. [ojos, cabeza, voz] to lower. ◇ *vi* - 1. [descender] to go/come down; **bajar por algo** to go/come down to get sthg; **bajar corriendo** to run down - 2. [disminuir] to fall, to drop; [fiebre, hinchazón] to go/come down; [Bolsa] to suffer a fall. ⮌ **bajarse** *vprnl*: **bajarse (de)** [coche] to get out (of); [moto, tren, avión] to get off; [árbol, escalera, silla] to get/come down (from).

bajeza *sf* - 1. [cualidad] baseness - 2. [acción] nasty deed.

bajial *sm Méx & Perú* lowland.

bajo, ja *adj* - 1. [gen] low; [persona] short; [planta] ground *(antes de s)*; [sonido] soft, faint; **en voz baja** in a low voice - 2. [territorio, época] lower; **el bajo Amazonas** the lower Amazon - 3. [pobre] lower-class - 4. [vil] base. ⮌ **bajo** ◇ *sm* - 1. *(gen pl)* [dobladillo] hem - 2. [piso] ground floor flat - 3. [MÚS - instrumento, cantante] bass; [- instrumentista] bassist. ◇ *adv* - 1. [gen] low - 2. [hablar] quietly. ◇ *prep* - 1. [gen] under - 2. [con temperaturas] below. ⮌ **baja** *sf* - 1. [descenso] drop, fall - 2. [cese]: **dar de baja a alguien** [en una empresa]

to lay sb off; [en un club, sindicato] to expel sb; **darse de baja (de)** [dimitir] to resign (from); [salirse] to drop (of) - 3. [por enfermedad - permiso] sick leave *(U)*; [- documento] sick note, **estar/darse de baja** to be on/to take sick leave; **baja por maternidad/paternidad** maternity/paternity leave - 4. MIL loss, casualty.

bajón *sm* slump; **dar un bajón** to slump; [suj - mercado, producción] to slump; [- persona] to go downhill.

bala *sf* - 1. [proyectil] bullet - 2. [fardo] bale.

balacear *vt Amér* [tirotear] to shoot.

balada *sf* ballad.

balance *sm* - 1. [COM - operación] balance; [- documento] balance sheet - 2. [resultado] outcome; **hacer balance (de)** to take stock (of).

balancear *vt* [cuna] to rock; [columpio] to swing. ⮌ **balancearse** *vprnl* [en cuna, mecedora] to rock; [en columpio] to swing; [barco] to roll.

balanceo *sm* - 1. [gen] swinging; [de cuna, mecedora] rocking; [de barco] roll - 2. *Amér* AUTO wheel balance.

balancín *sm* - 1. [mecedora] rocking chair; [en jardín] swing hammock - 2. [columpio] seesaw.

balanza *sf* - 1. [báscula] scales *pl* - 2. COM: **balanza comercial/de pagos** balance of trade/payments.

balar *vi* to bleat.

balaustrada *sf* balustrade.

balazo *sm* [disparo] shot; [herida] bullet wound.

balbucear = **balbucir**.

balbuceo *sm* babbling.

balbucir, balbucear *vi & vt* to babble.

Balcanes *smpl*: **los Balcanes** the Balkans.

balcón *sm* [terraza] balcony.

balde *sm* pail, bucket. ⮌ **en balde** *loc adv* in vain; **no ha sido en balde** it wasn't in vain.

baldosa *sf* [en casa, edificio] floor tile; [en la acera] paving stone.

baldosín *sm* tile.

balear ◇ *vt Amér* to shoot. ◇ *adj* Balearic.

Baleares *sfpl*: **las (islas) Baleares** the Balearic Islands.

baleo *sm Amér* shootout.

balido *sm* bleat, bleating *(U)*.

balín *sm* pellet.

balístico, ca *adj* ballistic.

baliza *sf* NÁUT marker buoy; AERON beacon.

ballena *sf* [animal] whale.

ballesta *sf* - 1. HIST crossbow - 2. AUTO (suspension) spring.

ballet [ba'le] *(pl* ballets*)* *sm* ballet.

balneario *sm* - **1.** [con baños termales] spa - **2.** *Amér* [con piscinas, etc] ≃ lido.

balompié *sm* football.

balón *sm* [pelota] ball; **balón de reglamento** regulation ball.

baloncesto *sm* basketball.

balonmano *sm* handball.

balonvolea *sm* volleyball.

balsa *sf* - **1.** [embarcación] raft - **2.** [estanque] pond, pool.

bálsamo *sm* - **1.** [medicamento] balsam - **2.** [alivio] balm.

balsero, ra *sm, f Cuba* refugee fleeing Cuba on a raft.

Báltico *sm*: **el (mar) Báltico** the Baltic (Sea).

baluarte *sm* - **1.** [fortificación] bulwark - **2.** *fig* [bastión] bastion, stronghold.

bambolear *vi* to shake. ◆ **bambolearse** *vprnl* [gen] to sway; [mesa, silla] to wobble.

bambú (*pl* bambúes *O* bambús) *sm* bamboo.

banal *adj* banal.

banana *sf Amér* banana.

banca *sf* - **1.** [actividad] banking; **banca por Internet** Internet banking; **banca en línea** online banking; **banca telefónica** telephone banking - **2.** [institución]: **la banca** the banks *pl* - **3.** [en juegos] bank - **4.** *Andes & R Plata* [escaño] seat.

bancario, ria *adj* banking (*antes de s*).

bancarrota *sf* bankruptcy; **en bancarrota** bankrupt.

banco *sm* - **1.** [asiento] bench; [de iglesia] pew - **2.** *FIN* bank - **3.** [de peces] shoal - **4.** [de ojos, semen etc] bank - **5.** [de carpintero, artesano etc] workbench. ◆ **banco de arena** *sm* sandbank. ◆ **Banco Mundial** *sm*: **el Banco Mundial** the World Bank.

banda *sf* - **1.** [cuadrilla] gang; **banda terrorista** terrorist organization - **2.** *MÚS* band - **3.** [faja] sash - **4.** [cinta] ribbon - **5.** [franja] stripe - **6.** *RADIO* waveband - **7.** [margen] side; [en billar] cushion; [en fútbol] touchline; **fuera de banda** out of play; **sacar de banda** to throw the ball in. ◆ **banda ancha** *sf INFORM* broadband. ◆ **banda magnética** *sf* magnetic strip. ◆ **banda sonora** *sf* soundtrack.

bandada *sf* [de aves] flock; [de peces] shoal.

bandazo *sm* [del barco] lurch; **dar bandazos** [barco, borracho] to lurch; *fig* [ir sin rumbo] to chop and change.

bandeja *sf* tray; **servir** *O* **dar algo a alguien en bandeja** *fig* to hand sthg to sb on a plate; **bandeja de entrada** *INFORM* inbox; **bandeja de salida** *INFORM* outbox.

bandera *sf* flag; **jurar bandera** to swear allegiance (to the flag); **estar hasta la bandera** to be packed.

banderilla *sf TAUROM* banderilla (*barbed dart thrust into bull's back*).

banderín *sm* [bandera] pennant.

bandido, da *sm, f* - **1.** [delincuente] bandit - **2.** [granuja] rascal.

bando *sm* - **1.** [facción] side; **pasarse al otro bando** to change sides - **2.** [de alcalde] edict.

bandolero, ra *sm, f* bandit. ◆ **bandolera** *sf* [correa] bandoleer; **en bandolera** slung across one's chest.

bandurria *sf* small 12-stringed guitar.

banjo [ˈbanʤo] *sm* banjo.

banquero, ra *sm, f* banker.

banqueta *sf* - **1.** [asiento] stool - **2.** *Amér C & Méx* [acera] pavement *UK*, sidewalk *US*.

banquete *sm* [comida] banquet.

banquillo *sm* - **1.** [asiento] low stool - **2.** *DEP* bench.

bañadera *sf Arg* [bañera] bath.

bañador *sm* [for women] swimsuit; [for men] swimming trunks *pl*.

bañar *vt* - **1.** [asear] to bath; *MED* to bathe - **2.** [sumergir] to soak, to submerge - **3.** [revestir] to coat. ◆ **bañarse** *vprnl* - **1.** [en el baño] to have *O* take a bath, to bathe *US* - **2.** [en playa, piscina] to go swimming.

bañera *sf* bathtub, bath; **bañera de hidromasaje** whirlpool bath.

bañista *smf* bather.

baño *sm* - **1.** [acción - en bañera] bath; [en playa, piscina] swim; **darse un baño** [en bañera] to have *O* take a bath; [en playa, piscina] to go for a swim - **2.** [bañera] bathtub, bath - **3.** [cuarto de aseo] bathroom - **4.** [capa] coat.

bar *sm* bar.

barahúnda *sf* racket, din.

baraja *sf* pack (of cards).

barajar *vt* - **1.** [cartas] to shuffle - **2.** [considerar - nombres, posibilidades] to consider; [- datos, cifras] to marshal, to draw on.

baranda, barandilla *sf* [de escalera] handrail; [de balcón] rail.

baratero, ra *sm, f Amér* [comerciante] discount retailer.

baratija *sf* trinket, knick-knack.

baratillo *sm* [tienda] junkshop; [mercadillo] flea market.

barato, ta *adj* cheap. ◆ **barato** *adv* cheap, cheaply.

barba *sf* beard; **barba incipiente** stubble; **por barba** [cada uno] per head.

barbacoa *sf* barbecue.

barbaridad *sf* - **1.** [cualidad] cruelty; **¡qué barbaridad!** how terrible! - **2.** [disparate] nonsense (*U*) - **3.** [montón]: **una barbaridad (de)** tons (of); **se gastó una barbaridad** she spent a fortune.

barbarie *sf* [crueldad - cualidad] cruelty, savagery; [- acción] atrocity.

barbarismo *sm* - 1. [extranjerismo] foreign word - 2. [incorrección] substandard usage.

bárbaro, ra ⬦ *adj* - 1. HIST barbarian - 2. [cruel] barbaric, cruel - 3. [bruto] uncouth, coarse - 4. *fam* [extraordinario] brilliant, great. ⬦ *sm, f* HIST barbarian. ◆ **bárbaro** *adv fam* [magníficamente]: **pasarlo bárbaro** to have a wild time.

barbecho *sm* fallow (land); **estar en barbecho** to be left fallow.

barbería *sf* barber's (shop).

barbero, ra *sm, f* barber.

barbilampiño, ña *adj* beardless.

barbilla *sf* chin.

barbo *sm* barbel; **barbo de mar** red mullet.

barbotar *vi & vt* to mutter.

barbudo, da *adj* bearded.

barca *sf* dinghy, small boat.

barcaza *sf* barge.

barco *sm* [gen] boat; [de gran tamaño] ship; **en barco** by boat; **barco cisterna** tanker; **barco de guerra** warship; **barco mercante** cargo ship; **barco de vapor** steamer, steamboat; **barco de vela** sailing boat, sail boat US.

baremo *sm* [escala] scale.

bario *sm* barium.

barítono *sm* baritone.

barman ['barman] (*pl* barmans) *sm* barman, bartender US.

barniz *sm* [para madera] varnish; [para loza, cerámica] glaze.

barnizar *vt* [madera] to varnish; [loza, cerámica] to glaze.

barómetro *sm* barometer.

barón, onesa *sm, f* baron (*f* baroness).

barquero, ra *sm, f* boatman (*f* boatwoman).

barquillo *sm* CULIN cornet, cone.

barra *sf* - 1. [gen] bar; [de hielo] block; [para cortinas] rod; [en bicicleta] crossbar; **la barra** [de tribunal] the bar; **barra de labios** lipstick; **barra de pan** baguette, French stick - 2. [de bar, café] bar *(counter)*; **barra libre** *unlimited drink for a fixed price* - 3. [signo gráfico] slash, oblique stroke - 4. *Andes & R Plata* [de amigos] gang; **barra brava** *R Dom* group of violent soccer fans - 5. INFORM: **barra de estado** status bar; **barra de herramientas** tool bar; **barra de menús** menu bar.

barrabasada *sf fam* mischief (U).

barraca *sf* - 1. [chabola] shack - 2. [caseta de feria] stall - 3. [en Valencia y Murcia] thatched farmhouse.

barranco *sm* - 1. [precipicio] precipice - 2. [cauce] ravine.

barraquismo *sm* shanty towns *pl*.

barrena *sf* drill.

barrenar *vt* [taladrar] to drill.

barrendero, ra *sm, f* street sweeper.

barreno *sm* - 1. [instrumento] large drill - 2. [agujero - para explosiones] blast hole.

barreño *sm* washing-up bowl.

barrer *vt* - 1. [con escoba, reflectores] to sweep - 2. [suj: viento, olas] to sweep away.

barrera *sf* - 1. [gen] barrier; FERROC crossing gate; [de campo, casa] fence; **barreras arancelarias** tariff barriers - 2. DEP wall. ◆ **barrera de seguridad** *sf* [en carretera] safety barrier.

barriada *sf* - 1. neighbourhood, area - 2. *Amér* [pobre] shanty town.

barricada *sf* barricade.

barrido *sm* - 1. [con escoba] sweep, sweeping (U) - 2. TECNOL scan, scanning (U) - 3. CINE pan, panning (U).

barriga *sf* belly.

barrigón, ona *adj* paunchy.

barril *sm* barrel; **de barril** [bebida] draught.

barrio *sm* [vecindario] area, neighborhood US.

barriobajero, ra *despec adj* low-life *(antes de s)*.

barrizal *sm* mire.

barro *sm* - 1. [fango] mud - 2. [arcilla] clay - 3. [grano] blackhead.

barroco, ca *adj* ARTE baroque. ◆ **barroco** *sm* ARTE baroque.

barrote *sm* bar.

bartola ◆ **a la bartola** *loc adv fam*: **tumbarse a la bartola** to lounge around.

bártulos *smpl* things, bits and pieces.

barullo *sm fam* - 1. [ruido] din, racket; **armar barullo** to raise hell - 2. [desorden] mess.

basar *vt* [fundamentar] to base. ◆ **basarse en** *vprnl* [suj: teoría, obra etc] to be based on; [suj: persona] to base one's argument on.

basca *sf* [náusea] nausea.

báscula *sf* scales *pl*.

bascular *vi* to tilt.

base *sf* - 1. [gen, MAT & MIL] base; [de edificio] foundations *pl*; **base naval** naval base - 2. [fundamento, origen] basis; **sentar las bases para** to lay the foundations of - 3. [de partido, sindicato]: **las bases** the grass roots *pl*, the rank and file - 4. *loc*: **a base de** by (means of); **me alimento a base de verduras** I live on vegetables; **a base de bien** extremely well; **a base de trabajar mucho** by working hard. ◆ **base de datos** *sf* INFORM database.

básico, ca *adj* basic; **lo básico de** the basics of.

basílica *sf* basilica.

basta *interj*: ¡**basta**! that's enough!; ¡**basta de chistes/tonterías**! that's enough jokes/of this nonsense!

bastante ◇ *adv* - **1.** [suficientemente] enough; **es lo bastante lista para...** she's smart enough to... - **2.** [considerablemente - antes de adj o adv] quite, pretty; [- después de verbo] quite a lot; **me gustó bastante** I quite enjoyed it, I enjoyed it quite a lot. ◇ *adj* - **1.** [suficiente] enough; **no tengo dinero bastante** I haven't enough money - **2.** [mucho]: **éramos bastantes** there were quite a few of us; **tengo bastante frío** I'm quite O pretty cold.

bastar *vi* to be enough; **basta con que se lo digas** it's enough for you to tell her; **con ocho basta** eight is enough; **baste decir que...** suffice it to say that...; **con la intención basta** it's the thought that counts. ◆ **bastarse** *vprnl* to be self-sufficient.

bastardilla ▷ **letra**.

bastardo, da *adj* - **1.** [hijo etc] bastard *(antes de s)* - **2.** *despec* [innoble] mean, base.

bastidor *sm* [armazón] frame. ◆ **bastidores** *smpl* TEATRO wings.

basto, ta *adj* coarse. ◆ **bastos** *smpl* [naipes] ≃ clubs.

bastón *sm* - **1.** [para andar] walking stick - **2.** [de mando] baton; **empuñar el bastón** *fig* to take the helm - **3.** [para esquiar] ski stick.

basura *sf* *lit & fig* rubbish *UK*, garbage *US*, trash *US*; **tirar algo a la basura** to throw sthg away; **basura radiactiva** radioactive waste.

basurero *sm* - **1.** [persona] dustman *UK*, garbage man *US* - **2.** [vertedero] rubbish dump.

bata *sf* - **1.** [de casa] housecoat; [para baño, al levantarse] dressing gown, robe *US* - **2.** [de médico] white coat; [de laboratorio] lab coat.

batacazo *sm* bump, bang.

batalla *sf* battle.

batallar *vi* [con armas] to fight.

batallón *sm* MIL battalion.

batata *sf* sweet potato.

bate *sm* DEP bat.

batear ◇ *vt* to hit. ◇ *vi* to bat.

batería *sf* - **1.** ELECTR & MIL battery - **2.** MÚS drums *pl* - **3.** [conjunto] set; [de preguntas] barrage; **batería de cocina** pots *pl* and pans.

batido, da *adj* - **1.** [nata] whipped; [clara] whisked - **2.** [senda, camino] well-trodden. ◆ **batido** *sm* [bebida] milkshake. ◆ **batida** *sf* - **1.** [de caza] beat - **2.** [de policía] combing, search.

batidora *sf* [eléctrica] mixer.

batín *sm* short dressing gown.

batir *vt* - **1.** [gen] to beat; [nata] to whip; [récord] to break - **2.** [suj: olas, lluvia, viento] to beat

against - **3.** [derribar] to knock down - **4.** [explorar - suj: policía etc] to comb, to search. ◆ **batirse** *vprnl* [luchar] to fight.

batuta *sf* baton; **llevar la batuta** *fig* to call the tune.

baúl *sm* - **1.** [cofre] trunk - **2.** *Arg & Col* [maletero] boot *UK*, trunk *US*.

bautismo *sm* baptism.

bautizar *vt* - **1.** RELIG to baptize, to christen - **2.** *fam fig* [aguar] to dilute.

bautizo *sm* RELIG baptism, christening.

baya *sf* berry.

bayeta *sf* - **1.** [tejido] flannel - **2.** [para fregar] cloth; [de gamuza] chamois.

bayo, ya *adj* bay.

bayoneta *sf* bayonet.

baza *sf* - **1.** [en naipes] trick - **2.** *loc*: **meter baza en algo** to butt in on sthg; **no pude meter baza (en la conversación)** I couldn't get a word in edgeways; **no jugó bien su baza** he didn't play his cards right.

bazar *sm* bazaar.

bazo *sm* ANAT spleen.

bazofia *sf* - **1.** [comida] pigswill (U) - **2.** *fig* [libro, película etc] rubbish (U).

bazuca, bazooka *sm* bazooka.

BCE (*abrev de* **Banco Central Europeo**) *sm* ECB.

be *sf* *Amér*: **be larga** O **grande** b.

beatificar *vt* to beatify.

beato, ta *adj* - **1.** [beatificado] blessed - **2.** [piadoso] devout - **3.** *fig* [santurrón] sanctimonious.

bebe, ba *sm, f* *C Sur fam* baby.

bebé *sm* baby; **bebé probeta** test-tube baby.

bebedero *sm* [de jaula] water dish.

bebedor, ra *sm, f* heavy drinker.

beber ◇ *vt* [líquido] to drink. ◇ *vi* [tomar líquido] to drink.

bebida *sf* drink; **darse** O **entregarse a la bebida** to take to the bottle; **bebida alcohólica** alcoholic drink.

bebido, da *adj* drunk.

beca *sf* [del gobierno] grant; [de organización privada] scholarship.

becar *vt* [suj: gobierno] to award a grant to; [suj: organización privada] to award a scholarship to.

becario, ria *sm, f* - **1.** [del gobierno] grant holder; [de organización privada] scholarship holder - **2.** [en prácticas] *person on a work placement*, intern *US*.

becerro, rra *sm, f* calf.

béchamel [betʃa'mel] = **besamel**.

bedel *sm* janitor.

befa *sf* jeer; **hacer befa de** to jeer at.

begonia *sf* begonia.

beige [beis] *adj inv* & *sm inv* beige.

béisbol *sm* baseball.

belén *sm* [de Navidad] crib, Nativity scene.

belfo, **fa** *adj* thick-lipped.

belga *adj* & *smf* Belgian.

Bélgica *n pr* Belgium.

Belice *n pr* Belize.

bélico, **ca** *adj* [gen] war *(antes de s)*; [actitud] bellicose, warlike.

belicoso, **sa** *adj* bellicose; *fig* aggressive.

beligerante *adj* & *smf* belligerent.

bellaco, **ca** *sm*, *f* villain, scoundrel.

belleza *sf* beauty.

bello, **lla** *adj* beautiful.

bellota *sf* acorn.

bemol <> *adj* flat. <> *sm* MÚS flat; **tener (muchos) bemoles** [ser difícil] to be tricky; [tener valor] to have guts; [ser un abuso] to be a bit rich *O* much.

bencina *sf Chile* petrol *UK*, gas *US*.

bencinera *sf Chile* petrol station *UK*, gas station *US*.

bendecir *vt* to bless.

bendición *sf* blessing.

bendito, **ta** *adj* - **1.** [santo] holy; [alma] blessed - **2.** [dichoso] lucky - **3.** [para enfatizar] damned.

benefactor, **ra** *sm*, *f* benefactor (*f* benefactress).

beneficencia *sf* charity.

beneficiar *vt* to benefit. ◆ **beneficiarse** *vprnl* to benefit; **beneficiarse de algo** to do well out of sthg.

beneficiario, **ria** *sm*, *f* [de herencia, póliza] beneficiary; [de cheque] payee.

beneficio *sm* - **1.** [bien] benefit; **a beneficio de** [gala, concierto] in aid of; **en beneficio de** for the good of; **en beneficio de todos** in everyone's interest; **en beneficio propio** for one's own good - **2.** [ganancia] profit; **beneficio bruto/neto** gross/net profit.

beneficioso, **sa** *adj*: **beneficioso (para)** beneficial (to).

benéfico, **ca** *adj* - **1.** [favorable] beneficial - **2.** [rifa, función] charity *(antes de s)*; [organización] charitable.

beneplácito *sm* consent.

benevolencia *sf* benevolence.

benevolente, **benévolo**, **la** *adj* benevolent.

bengala *sf* - **1.** [para pedir ayuda, iluminar etc] flare - **2.** [fuego artificial] sparkler.

benigno, **na** *adj* - **1.** [gen] benign - **2.** [clima, temperatura] mild.

benjamín, **ina** *sm*, *f* youngest child.

berberecho *sm* cockle.

berenjena *sf* aubergine *UK*, eggplant *US*.

bermejo, **ja** *adj* reddish.

bermellón *adj inv* & *sm* vermilion.

bermudas *stpl* Bermuda shorts.

berrear *vi* - **1.** [animal] to bellow - **2.** [persona] to howl.

berrido *sm* - **1.** [del becerro] bellow, bellowing *(U)* - **2.** [de persona] howl, howling *(U)*.

berrinche *sm fam* tantrum; **coger** *O* **agarrarse un berrinche** to throw a tantrum.

berro *sm* watercress.

berza *sf* cabbage.

besamel, **bechamel** *sf* béchamel sauce.

besar *vt* to kiss. ◆ **besarse** *vprnl* to kiss.

beso *sm* kiss; **dar un beso a alguien** to kiss sb, to give sb a kiss.

bestia <> *adj* - **1.** [ignorante] thick, stupid - **2.** [torpe] clumsy - **3.** [maleducado] rude. <> *smf* [ignorante, torpe] brute. <> *sf* [animal] beast; **bestia de carga** beast of burden.

bestial *adj* - **1.** [brutal] animal, brutal; [apetito] tremendous - **2.** *fam* [formidable] terrific.

bestialidad *sf* - **1.** [brutalidad] brutality - **2.** *fam* [tontería] rubbish *(U)*, nonsense *(U)* - **3.** *fam* [montón]: **una bestialidad de** tons *pl* *O* stacks *pl* of.

best-seller [bes'seler] (*pl* **best-sellers**) *sm* best-seller.

besucón, **ona** *fam adj* kissy.

besugo *sm* - **1.** [pez] sea bream - **2.** *fam* [persona] idiot.

besuquear *fam vt* to smother with kisses. ◆ **besuquearse** *vprnl fam* to smooch.

bético, **ca** *adj* [andaluz] Andalusian.

betún *sm* - **1.** [para calzado] shoe polish - **2.** QUÍM bitumen.

bianual *adj* - **1.** [dos veces al año] twice-yearly - **2.** [cada dos años] biennial.

biberón *sm* (baby's) bottle; **dar el biberón a** to bottle-feed.

Biblia *sf* Bible.

bibliografía *sf* bibliography.

bibliorato *sm R Dom* lever arch file.

biblioteca *sf* - **1.** [gen] library - **2.** [mueble] bookcase.

bibliotecario, **ria** *sm*, *f* librarian.

bicarbonato *sm* [medicamento] bicarbonate of soda.

bicentenario *sm* bicentenary.

bíceps *sm inv* biceps.

bicho *sm* - **1.** [animal] beast, animal; [insecto] bug - **2.** [pillo] little terror.

bici *sf fam* bike.

bicicleta *sf* bicycle.

bicolor *adj* two-coloured.

bidé *sm* bidet.

bidimensional *adj* two-dimensional.

bidón *sm* drum *(for oil etc)*; [lata] can, canister; [de plástico] (large) bottle.

biela *sf* connecting rod.

bien ⟨⟩ *adv* - **1.** [como es debido, adecuado] well; **has hecho bien** you did the right thing; **habla inglés bien** she speaks English well; **cierra bien la puerta** shut the door properly; **hiciste bien en decírmelo** you were right to tell me - **2.** [expresa opinión favorable]: **estar bien** [de aspecto] to be nice; [de salud] to be O feel well; [de calidad] to be good; [de comodidad] to be comfortable; **está bien que te vayas, pero antes despídete** it's all right for you to go, but say goodbye first; **oler bien** to smell nice; **pasarlo bien** to have a good time; **sentar bien a alguien** [ropa] to suit sb; [comida] to agree with sb; [comentario] to please sb - **3.** [muy, bastante] very; **hoy me he levantado bien temprano** I got up nice and early today; **quiero un vaso de agua bien fría** I'd like a nice cold glass of water - **4.** [vale, de acuerdo] all right, OK; **¿nos vamos? – bien** shall we go? – all right O OK - **5.** [de buena gana, fácilmente] quite happily; **ella bien que lo haría, pero no la dejan** she'd be happy to do it, but they won't let her - **6.** *loc*: **¡está bien!** [bueno, vale] all right then!; [es suficiente] that's enough; **¡ya está bien!** that's enough!; **¡muy bien!** very good!, excellent! ⟨⟩ *adj inv* [adinerado] well-to-do. ⟨⟩ *conj*: **bien... bien** either... or; **dáselo bien a mi hermano, bien a mi padre** either give it to my brother or my father. ⟨⟩ *sm* good; **el bien y el mal** good and evil; **por el bien de** for the sake of; **lo hice por tu bien** I did it for your own good. ◆ **bienes** *smpl* - **1.** [patrimonio] property *(U)*; **bienes inmuebles** O **raíces** real estate *(U)*; **bienes gananciales** shared possessions; **bienes muebles** personal property *(U)* - **2.** [productos] goods; **bienes de consumo** consumer goods. ◆ **más bien** *loc adv* rather; **no estoy contento, más bien estupefacto** I'm not so much happy as stunned. ◆ **no bien** *loc adv* no sooner, as soon as; **no bien me había marchado cuando empezaron a...** no sooner had I gone than they started... ◆ **si bien** *loc conj* although, even though.

bienal *sf* biennial exhibition.

bienaventurado, da *sm, f* RELIG blessed person.

bienestar *sm* wellbeing.

bienhechor, ra *sm, f* benefactor *(f* benefactress).

bienio *sm* [periodo] two years *pl.*

bienvenido, da ⟨⟩ *adj* welcome. ⟨⟩ *interj*: **¡bienvenido!** welcome! ◆ **bienvenida** *sf* welcome; **dar la bienvenida a alguien** to welcome sb.

bies *sm inv* bias binding.

bife *sm Andes & R Plata* steak.

bífido, da *adj* forked.

biftec = **bistec**.

bifurcación *sf* [entre calles] fork; TECNOL bifurcation.

bifurcarse *vprnl* to fork.

bigamia *sf* bigamy.

bígamo, ma ⟨⟩ *adj* bigamous. ⟨⟩ *sm, f* bigamist.

bigote *sm* moustache.

bigotudo, da *adj* with a big moustache.

bikini = **biquini**.

bilateral *adj* bilateral.

biliar *adj* bile *(antes de s)*.

bilingüe *adj* bilingual.

bilis *sf inv* lit & fig bile.

billar *sm* - **1.** [juego] billiards *(U)* - **2.** [sala] billiard hall.

billete *sm* - **1.** [dinero] note *UK*, bill *US* - **2.** [de rifa, transporte, cine etc] ticket; **billete de ida** single (ticket); **billete de ida y vuelta** return (ticket) *UK*, round-trip (ticket) *US*; **billete sencillo** single (ticket) *UK*, one-way (ticket) *US* - **3.** [de lotería] lottery ticket.

billetera *sf* wallet.

billetero *sm* = **billetera**.

billón *num* billion *UK*, trillion *US*; *ver también* **seis**.

bingo *sm* - **1.** [juego] bingo - **2.** [sala] bingo hall - **3.** [premio] (full) house.

binóculo *sm* pince-nez.

biocombustible *sm* biofuel.

biodegradable *adj* biodegradable.

bioética *sf* bioethics.

biografía *sf* biography.

biográfico, ca *adj* biographical.

biógrafo, fa *sm, f* [persona] biographer.

biología *sf* biology.

biológico, ca *adj* biological.

biólogo, ga *sm, f* biologist.

biombo *sm* (folding) screen.

biopsia *sf* biopsy.

bioquímico, ca ⟨⟩ *adj* biochemical. ⟨⟩ *sm, f* [persona] biochemist. ◆ **bioquímica** *sf* [ciencia] biochemistry.

biorritmo *sm* biorhythm.

biotecnología *sf* biotechnology.

bipartidismo *sm* two-party system.

bipartito, ta *adj* bipartite.

biplaza *sm* two-seater.

biquini, bikini *sm* [bañador] bikini.

birlar *vt fam* to pinch, to nick.

Birmania *n pr* Burma.

birra *sf fam* beer.

birrete *sm* - **1.** [de clérigo] biretta - **2.** [de catedrático] mortarboard.

birria *sf fam* [fealdad - persona] sight, fright; [- cosa] monstrosity.

bis (*pl* bises) <> *adj inv*: viven en el 150 bis they live at 150a. <> *sm* encore.

bisabuelo, la *sm,* *f* great-grandfather (*f* great-grandmother); **bisabuelos** great-grandparents.

bisagra *sf* hinge.

bisección *sf* bisection.

bisectriz *sf* bisector.

biselar *vt* to bevel.

bisexual *adj* & *smf* bisexual.

bisiesto ▷ **año**.

bisnieto, ta *sm, f* great-grandchild, great-grandson (*f* great-granddaughter).

bisonte *sm* bison.

bisoño, ña *sm, f* novice.

bistec, biftec *sm* steak.

bisturí (*pl* bisturíes *o* bisturís) *sm* scalpel.

bisutería *sf* imitation jewellery.

bit [bit] (*pl* bits) *sm* INFORM bit.

bíter, bitter *sm* bitters (*U*).

bizco, ca *adj* cross-eyed.

bizcocho *sm* [de repostería] sponge.

bizquear *vi* to squint.

blanco, ca <> *adj* white. <> *sm, f* [persona] white (person). <> *sm* - **1.** [color] white - **2.** [diana] target; **dar en el blanco** DEP & MIL to hit the target; *fig* to hit the nail on the head - **3.** *fig* [objetivo] target; [de miradas] object - **4.** [espacio vacío] blank (space). ◆ **blanca** *sf* MÚS minim; **estar** *o* **quedarse sin blanca** *fig* to be flat broke. ◆ **blanco del ojo** *sm* white of the eye. ◆ **en blanco** *loc adv* - **1.** [gen] blank; **se quedó con la mente en blanco** his mind went blank - **2.** [sin dormir]: **una noche en blanco** a sleepless night.

blancura *sf* whiteness.

blandengue *adj lit* & *fig* weak.

blandir *vt* to brandish.

blando, da *adj* - **1.** [gen] soft; [carne] tender - **2.** *fig* [persona - débil] weak; [- indulgente] lenient, soft.

blandura *sf* - **1.** [gen] softness; [de carne] tenderness - **2.** *fig* [debilidad] weakness; [indulgencia] leniency.

blanquear *vt* - **1.** [ropa] to whiten; [con lejía] to bleach - **2.** [con cal] to whitewash - **3.** *fig* [dinero] to launder.

blanquecino, na *adj* off-white.

blanqueo *sm* - **1.** [de ropa] whitening; [con lejía] bleaching - **2.** [encalado] whitewashing - **3.** *fig* [de dinero] laundering.

blanquillo *sm Amér C* & *Méx* [huevo] egg.

blasfemar *vi* RELIG: **blasfemar (contra)** to blaspheme (against).

blasfemia *sf* RELIG blasphemy.

blasfemo, ma *adj* blasphemous.

bledo *sm*: **me importa un bledo (lo que diga)** *fam* I don't give a damn (about what he says).

blindado, da *adj* armour-plated; [coche] armoured.

bloc [blok] (*pl* blocs) *sm* pad; **bloc de dibujo** sketchpad; **bloc de notas** notepad.

bloque *sm* - **1.** [gen & INFORM] block - **2.** POLÍT bloc - **3.** MECÁN cylinder block.

bloquear *vt* - **1.** [gen & DEP] to block - **2.** [aislar - suj: ejército, barcos] to blockade; [- suj: nieve, inundación] to cut off - **3.** FIN to freeze.

bloqueo *sm* - **1.** [gen & DEP] blocking; **bloqueo mental** mental block - **2.** ECON & MIL blockade - **3.** FIN freeze, freezing (*U*).

blues [blus] *sm inv* MÚS blues.

blusa *sf* blouse.

blusón *sm* [camisa] long shirt; [de pintor] smock.

bluyín *sm* jeans *pl*.

bluyines *Amér, Andes* & *Ven smpl* = **bluyín**.

boa *sf* ZOOL boa.

bobada *sf fam*: **decir bobadas** to talk nonsense.

bobina *sf* - **1.** [gen] reel; [en máquina de coser] bobbin - **2.** ELECTR coil.

bobo, ba <> *adj* - **1.** [tonto] stupid, daft - **2.** [ingenuo] naïve. <> *sm, f* - **1.** [tonto] idiot - **2.** [ingenuo] simpleton.

boca *sf* - **1.** [gen] mouth; **boca arriba/abajo** face up/down; **se me hace la boca agua** it makes my mouth water - **2.** [entrada] opening; [de cañón] muzzle; **boca de metro** tube *o* underground entrance *UK*, subway entrance *US*. ◆ **boca a boca** *sm* mouth-to-mouth (resuscitation).

bocacalle *sf* [entrada] entrance (*to a street*); [calle] side street; **gire en la tercera bocacalle** take the third turning.

bocadillo *sm* CULIN sandwich.

bocado *sm* - **1.** [comida] mouthful; **no probar bocado** [por estar desganado] not to touch one's food; [no haber podido comer] not to have a bite (to eat) - **2.** [mordisco] bite.

bocajarro ◆ **a bocajarro** *loc adv* [disparar] point-blank; **se lo dije a bocajarro** I told him to his face.

bocanada *sf* [de líquido] mouthful; [de humo] puff; [de viento] gust.

bocata *sm fam* sarnie.

bocazas *smf inv fam despec* big mouth, blabbermouth.

boceto *sm* sketch, rough outline.

bocha *sf* [bolo] bowl. ↪ **bochas** *sfpl* [juego] bowls *(U)*.

bochorno *sm* - **1.** [calor] stifling *O* muggy heat - **2.** [vergüenza] embarrassment.

bochornoso, sa *adj* - **1.** [tiempo] muggy - **2.** [vergonzoso] embarrassing.

bocina *sf* - **1.** AUTO & MÚS horn - **2.** [megáfono] megaphone, loudhailer.

boda *sf* [ceremonia] wedding; [convite] reception; **bodas de diamante/oro/plata** diamond/golden/silver wedding *sing*.

bodega *sf* - **1.** [cava] wine cellar - **2.** [tienda] wine shop; [bar] bar - **3.** [en buque, avión] hold.

bodegón *sm* ARTE still life.

bodrio *sm fam despec* [gen] rubbish *(U)*; [comida] pigswill *(U)*; **¡qué bodrio!** what a load of rubbish!

body ['boði] *(pl* bodies) *sm* body.

BOE *(abrev de* Boletín Oficial del Estado) *sm official Spanish gazette.*

bofetada *sf* slap (in the face).

bofetón *sm* hard slap (in the face).

bofia *sf*: **la bofia** *fam* the cops *pl*.

boga *sf*: **estar en boga** to be in vogue.

bogavante *sm* lobster.

Bogotá *n pr* Bogotá.

bohemio, mia *adj* - **1.** [vida etc] bohemian - **2.** [de Bohemia] Bohemian.

boicot *(pl* boicots) *sm* boycott.

boicotear *vt* to boycott.

boina *sf* beret.

boj *(pl* bojes) *sm* [árbol] box.

bol *(pl* boles) *sm* bowl.

bola *sf* - **1.** [gen] ball; [canica] marble; **bola del mundo** globe; **bolas de naftalina** mothballs; **convertirse en una bola de nieve** *fig* to snowball - **2.** *fam* [mentira] fib.

bolada *sf R Dom fam* opportunity.

bolea *sf* DEP volley.

bolear *vt Méx* [embetunar] to shine, to polish.

bolera *sf* bowling alley.

bolero, ra *sm, f Méx* shoeshine, bootblack UK.

boleta *sf Amér* [recibo] receipt; *Amér C & C Sur* [multa] parking ticket; *Cuba & Méx* [para voto] ballot, voting slip.

boletería *sf Amér* [de cine, teatro] box office; [de estación] ticket office.

boletero, ra *sm, f Amér* box office attendant.

boletín *sm* journal, periodical; **boletín de noticias** *O* **informativo** news bulletin; **boletín meteorológico** weather forecast; **boletín de prensa** press release; **Boletín Oficial del Estado** *official Spanish gazette.*

boleto *sm* - **1.** [de lotería, rifa] ticket; [de quinielas] coupon - **2.** *Amér* [para medio de transporte] ticket.

boli *sm fam* Biro®.

boliche *sm* - **1.** [en la petanca] jack - **2.** [bolos] ten-pin bowling - **3.** [bolera] bowling alley - **4.** *Amér* [tienda] small grocery store - **5.** *C Sur fam* [bar] cheap bar or café.

bólido *sm* racing car; **ir como un bólido** *fig* to go like the clappers.

bolígrafo *sm* ballpoint pen, Biro®.

bolívar *sm* bolivar.

Bolivia *n pr* Bolivia.

boliviano, na *adj & sm, f* Bolivian.

bollo *sm* - **1.** [para comer - de pan] (bread) roll; [- dulce] bun - **2.** [abolladura] dent; [abultamiento] bump.

bolo *sm* - **1.** DEP [pieza] skittle - **2.** [actuación] show - **3.** *Amér C fam* [borracho] boozer. ↪ **bolos** *smpl* [deporte] skittles.

bolsa *sf* - **1.** [gen] bag; **bolsa de aire** air pocket; **bolsa de basura** bin liner; **bolsa de deportes** holdall, sports bag; **bolsa de plástico** [en tiendas] carrier *O* plastic bag; **bolsa de viaje** travel bag; **bolsa de patatas fritas** packet of crisps - **2.** FIN: **bolsa (de valores)** stock exchange, stock market; **la bolsa ha subido/bajado** share prices have gone up/down; **jugar a la bolsa** to speculate on the stock market - **3.** [acumulación de mineral] pocket - **4.** ANAT sac - **5.** *R Dom* [saco de dormir] sleeping bag.

bolsillo *sm* pocket; **de bolsillo** pocket *(antes de s)*; **lo pagué de mi bolsillo** I paid for it out of my own pocket.

bolso *sm* bag; [de mujer] handbag, purse US.

boludear *vi R Dom fam* [decir tonterías] to talk nonsense; [hacer tonterías, perder el tiempo] to mess about *O* around.

boludo, da *sm, f R Dom fam* [estúpido] prat UK, jerk US; [perezoso] lazy slob.

bomba ◇ *sf* - **1.** [explosivo] bomb; **bomba atómica** atom *O* nuclear bomb; **bomba de mano** (hand) grenade - **2.** [máquina] pump - **3.** *fig* [acontecimiento] bombshell - **4.** *Chile, Col, Ecuad & Ven* [surtidor de gasolina] petrol station UK, gas station US - **5.** *loc*: **pasarlo bomba** *fam* to have a great time. ◇ *adj inv fam* astounding.

bombachos *smpl* baggy trousers.

bombardear *vt lit & fig* to bombard.

bombardeo *sm* bombardment.

bombardero *sm* [avión] bomber.

bombazo *sm fig* [noticia] bombshell.

bombear *vt* [gen & DEP] to pump.

bombero, ra *sm, f* - **1.** [de incendios] fireman (f firewoman) - **2.** *Ven* [de gasolinera] petrol-pump UK *O* gas-pump US attendant.

bombilla *sf* - **1.** [de lámpara] light bulb - **2.** *R Plata* [para mate] *tube for drinking maté tea.*

bombillo *sm Amér C, Col & Méx* light bulb.

bombín *sm* bowler (hat).

bombo *sm* - **1.** MÚS bass drum; **estar con bombo** *fam fig* to be in the family way - **2.** *fam fig* [elogio] hype; **a bombo y platillo** with a lot of hype - **3.** MECÁN drum.

bombón *sm* [golosina] chocolate.

bombona *sf* cylinder; **bombona de butano** (butane) gas cylinder.

bonachón, ona *fam adj* kindly.

bonanza *sf* - **1.** [de tiempo] fair weather; [de mar] calm at sea - **2.** *fig* [prosperidad] prosperity.

bondad *sf* [cualidad] goodness; [inclinación] kindness; **tener la bondad de hacer algo** to be kind enough to do sthg.

bondadoso, sa *adj* kind, good-natured.

boniato *sm* sweet potato.

bonificar *vt* - **1.** [descontar] to give a discount of - **2.** [mejorar] to improve.

bonito, ta *adj* pretty; [bueno] nice. ◆ **bonito** *sm* bonito (tuna).

bono *sm* - **1.** [vale] voucher - **2.** COM bond; **bono del Estado/del tesoro** government/treasury bond.

bonobús *sm* ten-journey bus ticket.

bonoloto *sm Spanish state-run lottery.*

boñiga *sf* cowpat.

boquerón *sm* (fresh) anchovy.

boquete *sm* hole.

boquiabierto, ta *adj* open-mouthed; *fig* astounded, speechless.

boquilla *sf* - **1.** [para fumar] cigarette holder - **2.** [de pipa, instrumento musical] mouthpiece - **3.** [de tubo, aparato] nozzle.

borbotear, borbotar *vi* to bubble.

borbotón *sm*: **salir a borbotones** to gush out.

borda *sf* NÁUT gunwale; **tirar** *O* **echar algo por la borda** *fig* to throw sthg overboard. ◆ **fuera borda** *sm* [barco] outboard motorboat; [motor] outboard motor.

bordado, da *adj* embroidered. ◆ **bordado** *sm* embroidery.

bordar *vt* [al coser] to embroider.

borde ◇ *adj fam* [antipático] stroppy, miserable. ◇ *sm* [gen] edge; [de carretera] side; [del mar] shore, seaside; [de río] bank; [de vaso, botella] rim; **al borde de** *fig* on the verge *O* brink of.

bordear *vt* [estar alrededor de] to border; [moverse alrededor de] to skirt (round).

bordillo *sm* kerb.

bordo ◆ **a bordo** *loc adv* on board.

borla *sf* tassel; [pompón] pompom.

borrachera *sf* - **1.** [embriaguez] drunkenness (U); **agarrar** *O Esp* **coger una borrachera** to get drunk - **2.** *fig* [emoción] intoxication.

borracho, cha ◇ *adj* [ebrio] drunk. ◇ *sm, f* [persona] drunk. ◆ **borracho** *sm* [bizcocho] ≃ rum baba.

borrador *sm* - **1.** [de escrito] rough draft; [de dibujo] sketch - **2.** [goma de borrar] rubber *UK*, eraser *US*.

borrar *vt* - **1.** [hacer desaparecer - con goma] to rub out *UK*, to erase *US*; [- en ordenador] to delete; [- en casete] to erase - **2.** [tachar] to cross out; *fig* [de lista etc] to take off - **3.** *fig* [olvidar] to erase.

borrasca *sf* area of low pressure.

borrego, ga *sm, f* [animal] lamb.

borrón *sm* blot; *fig* blemish; **hacer borrón y cuenta nueva** to wipe the slate clean.

borroso, sa *adj* [foto, visión] blurred; [escritura, texto] smudgy.

Bosnia *n pr* Bosnia.

bosnio, nia *adj & sm, f* Bosnian.

bosque *sm* [pequeño] wood; [grande] forest.

bosquejar *vt* [esbozar] to sketch (out).

bosquejo *sm* [esbozo] sketch.

bostezar *vi* to yawn.

bostezo *sm* yawn.

bota *sf* - **1.** [calzado] boot; **botas camperas/de montar** cowboy/riding boots - **2.** [de vino] *small leather container in which wine is kept.*

botana *sf Méx* snack, appetizer.

botánico, ca ◇ *adj* botanical. ◇ *sm, f* [persona] botanist. ◆ **botánica** *sf* [ciencia] botany.

botar ◇ *vt* - **1.** NÁUT to launch - **2.** *fam* [despedir] to throw *O* kick out - **3.** [pelota] to bounce - **4.** *Andes, Amér C, Caribe & Méx* [tirar] to throw away. ◇ *vi* - **1.** [saltar] to jump - **2.** [pelota] to bounce.

bote *sm* - **1.** [tarro] jar - **2.** [lata] can - **3.** [botella de plástico] bottle - **4.** [barca] boat; **bote salvavidas** lifeboat - **5.** [salto] jump; **dar botes** [gen] to jump up and down; [en tren, coche] to bump up and down - **6.** [de pelota] bounce; **dar botes** to bounce.

botella *sf* bottle; **de botella** bottled; *Cuba*: **pedir botella** to hitchhike; **dar botella a alguien** to give sb a ride, to give sb a lift.

botellín *sm* small bottle.

boticario, ria *sm, f desus* pharmacist.

botijo *sm* earthenware jug.

botín *sm* - **1.** [de guerra, atraco] plunder, loot - **2.** [calzado] ankle boot.

botiquín *sm* [caja] first-aid kit; [mueble] first-aid cupboard; [enfermería] first-aid post.

botón *sm* button; **botón de marcado abrevia-do** TELECOM speed-dial button. ◆ **botones** *sm inv* [de hotel] bellboy, bellhop *US*; [de oficinas etc] errand boy.

boutique [bu'tik] *sf* boutique.

bóveda *sf* ARQUIT vault.

box *(pl* boxes) *sm* - 1. [de coches] pit; **entrar en boxes** to make a pit stop - 2. *Amér* boxing.

boxeador, ra *sm, f* boxer.

boxear *vi* to box.

boxeo *sm* boxing.

bóxer *(pl* boxers) *sm* boxer.

boya *sf* - 1. [en el mar] buoy - 2. [de una red] float.

boyante *adj* - 1. [feliz] happy - 2. [próspero - empresa, negocio] prosperous; [- economía, comercio] buoyant.

bozal *sm* [gen] muzzle.

bracear *vi* [nadar] to swim.

braga *(gen pl) sf* knickers *pl*.

bragueta *sf* flies *pl* UK, zipper *US*; **tienes la bragueta abierta** your flies are undone.

braille ['braile] *sm* Braille.

bramar *vi* - 1. [animal] to bellow - 2. [persona - de dolor] to groan; [- de ira] to roar.

bramido *sm* - 1. [de animal] bellow - 2. [de persona - de dolor] groan; [- de ira] roar.

brandy *sm* brandy.

branquia *(gen pl) sf* gill.

brasa *sf* ember; **a la brasa** CULIN barbecued.

brasero *sm* brazier.

brasier, brassier *sm Caribe, Col & Méx* bra.

Brasil *n pr* Brazil.

brasileño, ña, brasilero, ra *adj & sm, f Andes, C Sur & Ven* Brazilian.

brassier = **brasier.**

bravata *(gen pl) sf* - 1. [amenaza] threat - 2. [fanfarronería] bravado *(U).*

braveza *sf* bravery.

bravío, a *adj* [salvaje] wild; [feroz] fierce.

bravo, va *adj* - 1. [valiente] brave - 2. [animal] wild - 3. [mar] rough. ◆ **bravo** ◇ *sm* [aplauso] cheer. ◇ *interj:* **¡bravo!** bravo!

bravuconear *vi despec* to brag.

bravura *sf* - 1. [de persona] bravery - 2. [de animal] ferocity.

braza *sf* - 1. DEP breaststroke; **nadar a braza** to swim breaststroke - 2. [medida] fathom.

brazada *sf* stroke.

brazalete *sm* - 1. [en la muñeca] bracelet - 2. [en el brazo] armband.

brazo *sm* - 1. [gen & ANAT] arm; [de animal] foreleg; [cogidos del brazo] arm in arm; **en brazos** in one's arms; **luchar a brazo partido** [con empeño] to fight tooth and nail; **ser el brazo derecho de alguien** to be sb's right-hand man

(f woman) - 2. [de árbol, río, candelabro] branch; [de grúa] boom, jib. ◆ **brazo de gitano** *sm* ≃ swiss roll.

brea *sf* - 1. [sustancia] tar - 2. [para barco] pitch.

brebaje *sm* concoction, foul drink.

brecha *sf* - 1. [abertura] hole, opening - 2. MIL breach - 3. *fig* [impresión] impression.

bregar *vi* - 1. [luchar] to struggle - 2. [trabajar] to work hard - 3. [reñir] to quarrel.

breve ◇ *adj* brief; **en breve** [pronto] shortly; [en pocas palabras] in short. ◇ *sf* MÚS breve.

brevedad *sf* shortness; **a O con la mayor brevedad** as soon as possible.

brezo *sm* heather.

bribón, ona *sm, f* scoundrel, rogue.

bricolaje *sm* D.I.Y., do-it-yourself.

brida *sf* [de caballo] bridle.

bridge [britʃ] *sm* bridge.

brigada ◇ *sm* MIL ≃ warrant officer. ◇ *sf* - 1. MIL brigade - 2. [equipo] squad, team.

brillante ◇ *adj* - 1. [reluciente - luz, astro] shining; [- metal, zapatos, pelo] shiny; [- ojos, sonrisa, diamante] sparkling - 2. [magnífico] brilliant. ◇ *sm* diamond.

brillantina *sf* brilliantine, Brylcreem®.

brillar *vi lit & fig* to shine.

brillo *sm* - 1. [resplandor - de luz] brilliance; [- de estrellas] shining; [- de zapatos] shine - 2. [lucimiento] splendour.

brilloso, sa *adj Amér* shining.

brincar *vi* [saltar] to skip (about); **brincar de alegría** to jump for joy.

brinco *sm* jump; **en un brinco** *fig* in a second, quickly.

brindar ◇ *vi* to drink a toast; **brindar por algo/alguien** to drink to sthg/sb. ◇ *vt* to offer. ◆ **brindarse** *vprnl:* **brindarse a hacer algo** to offer to do sthg.

brindis *sm inv* toast.

brío *sm* [energía, decisión] spirit, verve.

brisa *sf* breeze.

británico, ca ◇ *adj* British. ◇ *sm, f* British person, Briton; **los británicos** the British.

brizna *sf* - 1. [filamento - de hierba] blade; [- de tabaco] strand - 2. *fig* [un poco] trace, bit.

broca *sf* (drill) bit.

brocha *sf* brush; **brocha de afeitar** shaving brush.

brochazo *sm* brushstroke.

broche *sm* - 1. [cierre] clasp, fastener - 2. [joya] brooch - 3. *R Plata* [para papeles] staple - 4. *Méx & Urug* [para el cabello] hair slide *UK*, barrette *US* - 5. *Arg* [para ropa] clothespin. ◆ **broche de oro** *sm fig* final flourish.

broma *sf* [ocurrencia, chiste] joke; [jugarreta] prank, practical joke; **en broma** as a joke; **gastar una broma a alguien** to play a joke Ω prank on sb.

bromear *vi* to joke.

bromista *smf* joker.

bronca *sf* ⊳ **bronco**.

bronce *sm* [aleación] bronze.

bronceado, da *adj* tanned. ◆ **bronceado** *sm* tan.

bronceador, ra *adj* tanning *(antes de s)*, suntan *(antes de s)*. ◆ **bronceador** *sm* [loción] suntan lotion; [leche] suntan cream.

broncear *vt* to tan. ◆ **broncearse** *vprnl* to get a tan.

bronco, ca *adj* **- 1.** [grave - voz] harsh; [- tos] throaty **- 2.** *fig* [brusco] gruff. ◆ **bronca** *sf* **- 1.** [jaleo] row **- 2.** [regañina] scolding; **echar una bronca a alguien** to give sb a row, to tell sb off **- 3.** *R Dom fam* [rabia]: **me da bronca** it hacks me off; **el jefe le tiene bronca** the boss has got it in for her.

bronquio *sm* bronchial tube.

bronquitis *sf inv* bronchitis.

brotar *vi* **- 1.** [planta] to sprout, to bud **- 2.** [agua, sangre etc]: **brotar de** to well up out of **- 3.** *fig* [esperanza, sospechas, pasiones] to stir **- 4.** [en la piel]: **le brotó un sarpullido** he broke out in a rash.

brote *sm* **- 1.** [de planta] bud, shoot **- 2.** *fig* [inicios] sign, hint.

broza *sf* [maleza] brush, scrub.

bruces ◆ **de bruces** *loc adv* face down; **se cayó de bruces** he fell headlong, he fell flat on his face.

bruja *sf* ⊳ **brujo**.

brujería *sf* witchcraft, sorcery.

brujo, ja *adj* [hechicero] enchanting. ◆ **brujo** *sm* wizard, sorcerer. ◆ **bruja** ◇ *sf* **- 1.** [hechicera] witch, sorceress **- 2.** [mujer fea] hag **- 3.** [mujer mala] (old) witch. ◇ *adj inv Méx:* **estar bruja** *fam* to be broke.

brújula *sf* compass.

bruma *sf* [niebla] mist; [en el mar] sea mist.

bruñido *sm* polishing.

brusco, ca *adj* **- 1.** [repentino, imprevisto] sudden **- 2.** [tosco, grosero] brusque.

brusquedad *sf* **- 1.** [imprevisión] suddenness **- 2.** [grosería] brusqueness.

brutal *adj* [violento] brutal.

brutalidad *sf* [cualidad] brutality.

bruto, ta ◇ *adj* **- 1.** [torpe] clumsy; [ignorante] thick, stupid; [maleducado] rude **- 2.** [sin tratar]: **en bruto** [diamante] uncut; [petróleo] crude **- 3.** [sueldo, peso etc] gross. ◇ *sm, f* brute.

bucear *vi* [en agua] to dive.

buceo *sm* (underwater) diving.

bucle *sm* [rizo] curl, ringlet.

budismo *sm* Buddhism.

buen ⊳ **bueno**.

buenas ⊳ **bueno**.

buenaventura *sf* [adivinación] fortune; **leer la buenaventura a alguien** to tell sb's fortune.

bueno, na *(mejor es el comparativo y el superlativo de bueno) adj (antes de s m sing:* **buen**) **- 1.** [gen] good **- 2.** [bondadoso] kind, good; **ser bueno con alguien** to be good to sb **- 3.** [curado, sano] well, all right **- 4.** [apacible - tiempo, clima] nice, fine **- 5.** [aprovechable] all right; [comida] fresh **- 6.** [uso enfático]: **ese buen hombre** that good man; **un buen día** one fine day **- 7.** *loc:* **de buen ver** good-looking, attractive; **de buenas a primeras** [de repente] all of a sudden; [a simple vista] at first sight, on the face of it; **estar bueno** *fam* [persona] to be a bit of all right, to be tasty; **estar de buenas** to be in a good mood; **lo bueno es que...** the best thing about it is that... ◇ *sm* CINE: **el bueno** the goody. ◇ *adv* **- 1.** [vale, de acuerdo] all right, O.K. **- 2.** [pues] well. ◇ *interj Méx* [al teléfono]: **¡bueno!** hello. ◆ **buenas** *interj:* **¡buenas!** hello!; *Col & Méx:* **¿buenas?** [al teléfono] hello.

Buenos Aires *n pr* Buenos Aires.

buey *(pl* **bueyes)** *sm* ox.

búfalo *sm* buffalo.

bufanda *sf* scarf.

bufar *vi* [toro, caballo] to snort.

bufé, buffet *(pl* **buffets)** *sm* [en restaurante] buffet.

bufete *sm* lawyer's practice.

buffet = **bufé**.

bufido *sm* [de toro, caballo] snort.

bufón *sm* buffoon, jester.

buhardilla *sf* [habitación] attic.

búho *sm* owl.

buitre *sm lit & fig* vulture.

bujía *sf* AUTO spark plug.

bulbo *sm* ANAT & BOT bulb.

buldozer *(pl* **buldozers), bulldozer** *(pl* **bulldozers)** [bul'doθer] *sm* bulldozer.

bulevar *(pl* **bulevares)** *sm* boulevard.

Bulgaria *n pr* Bulgaria.

búlgaro, ra *adj & sm, f* Bulgarian. ◆ **búlgaro** *sm* [lengua] Bulgarian.

bulín *sm R Dom* bachelor pad.

bulla *sf* racket, uproar; **armar bulla** to kick up a racket.

bullanguero, ra ◇ *adj* noisy, rowdy. ◇ *sm, f* noisy Ο boisterous person.

bulldozer = **buldozer**.

bullicio *sm* [de ciudad, mercado] hustle and bustle; [de reunión] hubbub.

bullicioso, sa *adj* **- 1.** [agitado - reunión, multitud] noisy; [- calle, mercado] busy, bustling **- 2.** [inquieto] rowdy.

bullir *vi* - **1**. [hervir] to boil; [burbujear] to bubble - **2**. *fig* [multitud] to bustle; [ratas, hormigas etc] to swarm; [mar] to boil; **bullir de** to seethe with.

bulto *sm* - **1**. [volumen] bulk, size; **escurrir el bulto** [trabajo] to shirk; [cuestión] to evade the issue - **2**. [abombamiento - en rodilla, superficie etc] bump; [- en maleta, bolsillo etc] bulge - **3**. [forma imprecisa] blurred shape - **4**. [paquete] package; [maleta] item of luggage; [fardo] bundle; **bulto de mano** piece *O* item of hand luggage.

bumerán (*pl* bumeranes), **bumerang** (*pl* bumerangs) *sm* boomerang.

bungalow [buŋga'lo] (*pl* bungalows) *sm* bungalow.

búnquer (*pl* bunquers), **bunker** (*pl* bunkers) *sm* [refugio] bunker.

buñuelo *sm* [CULIN - dulce] ≃ doughnut; [- de bacalao etc] ≃ dumpling.

BUP *sm academically oriented secondary-school course formerly taught in Spain for pupils aged 14-17, now known as the bachillerato.*

buque *sm* ship; **buque nodriza** supply ship; **buque de vapor** streamer, steamship.

burbuja *sf* bubble; **con burbujas** fizzy; **hacer burbujas** to bubble.

burbujear *vi* to bubble.

burdel *sm* brothel.

burdo, da *adj* [gen] crude; [tela] coarse.

burgués, esa *adj* middle-class, bourgeois.

burguesía *sf* middle class; HIST & POLIT bourgeoisie.

burla *sf* - **1**. [mofa] taunt; **hacer burla de** to mock - **2**. [broma] joke; **burlas aparte** joking aside - **3**. [engaño] trick. ➤ **burlas** *sfpl* ridicule (U), mockery (U).

burlar *vt* [esquivar] to evade; [ley] to flout; **burla burlando** *fig* without anyone noticing. ➤ **burlarse de** *vprnl* to make fun of.

burlesco, ca *adj* [tono] jocular; LITER burlesque.

burlón, ona *adj* [sarcástico] mocking.

burocracia *sf* bureaucracy.

burócrata *smf* bureaucrat.

burrada *sf* [acción, dicho]: **hacer burradas** to act stupidly; **decir burradas** to talk nonsense.

burro, rra *sm, f* - **1**. [animal] donkey; **apearse** *O* **bajarse del burro** *fam* to back down; **no ver tres en un burro** *fam* to be as blind as a bat - **2**. *fam* [necio] dimwit. ➤ **burro** *sm* - **1**. *Caribe & Méx* [escalera] stepladder - **2**. *Méx* [tabla de planchar] ironing board.

bursátil *adj* stock-market *(antes de s)*.

bus (*pl* buses) *sm* AUTO & INFORM bus.

busca ◇ *sf* search; **en busca de** in search of; **la busca de** the search for; **andar a la busca** *fig* to find a way of getting by. ◇ *sm* = **buscapersonas**.

buscapersonas, busca *sm inv* bleeper.

buscar ◇ *vt* - **1**. [gen] to look for; [provecho, beneficio propio] to seek; **voy a buscar el periódico** I'm going for the paper *O* to get the paper; **ir a buscar a alguien** to pick sb up; **'se busca camarero'** 'waiter wanted' - **2**. [en diccionario, índice, horario] to look up - **3**. INFORM to search for. ◇ *vi* to look. ➤ **buscarse** *vprnl*: **buscársela** to be asking for it.

buscón, ona *sm, f* [estafador] swindler.

búsqueda *sf* search.

busto *sm* - **1**. [pecho] chest; [de mujer] bust - **2**. [escultura] bust.

butaca *sf* - **1**. [mueble] armchair - **2**. [en cine] seat.

butano *sm* butane (gas).

butifarra *sf* type of Catalan pork sausage.

buzo *sm* - **1**. [persona] diver - **2**. *Arg & Col* [sudadera] sweatshirt - **3**. *Arg, Chile & Perú* [chándal] tracksuit - **4**. *Urug* [suéter] sweater, jumper UK.

buzón *sm* letter box; **echar algo al buzón** to post sthg; **buzón electrónico** electronic mailbox; **buzón de sugerencias** suggestion box; **buzón de voz** voice mail.

byte [bait] *sm* INFORM byte.

c, C *sf* [letra] c, C.

c. (*abrev de* **calle**) St.

c/ - **1**. (*abrev de* **calle**) St. - **2**. (*abrev de* **cuenta**) a/c.

cabal *adj* - **1**. [honrado] honest - **2**. [exacto] exact; [completo] complete. ➤ **cabales** *smpl*: **no estar en sus cabales** not to be in one's right mind.

cábala *sf* (gen pl) [conjeturas] guess.

cabalgar *vi* to ride.

cabalgata *sf* cavalcade, procession.

caballa *sf* mackerel.

caballería *sf* - **1.** [animal] mount, horse - **2.** [cuerpo militar] cavalry.

caballeriza *sf* stable.

caballero ⌣ *adj* [cortés] gentlemanly. ◇ *sm* - **1.** [gen] gentleman; [al dirigir la palabra] sir; **ser todo un caballero** to be a real gentleman - **2.** [miembro de una orden] knight.

caballete *sm* - **1.** [de lienzo] easel - **2.** [de mesa] trestle - **3.** [de nariz] bridge.

caballito *sm* small horse, pony. ◆ **caballitos** *smpl* [de feria] merry-go-round *sing*.

caballo *sm* - **1.** [animal] horse; **montar a caballo** to ride - **2.** [pieza de ajedrez] knight - **3.** [naipe] ≃ queen - **4.** MECÁN: **caballo (de fuerza** *O* **de vapor)** horsepower. ◆ **caballo de Troya** *sm* Trojan horse.

cabaña *sf* - **1.** [choza] hut, cabin - **2.** [ganado] livestock *(U)*.

cabaré *sm* cabaret.

cabecear *vi* - **1.** [persona - negando] to shake one's head; [- afirmando] to nod one's head - **2.** [caballo] to toss its head - **3.** [dormir] to nod (off).

cabecera *sf* - **1.** [gen] head; [de cama] headboard - **2.** [de texto] heading; [de periódico] headline - **3.** [de río] headwaters *pl*.

cabecilla *smf* ringleader.

cabellera *sf* long hair *(U)*.

cabello *sm* hair *(U)*.

caber *vi* - **1.** [gen] to fit; **no cabe nadie más** there's no room for anyone else; **no me cabe en el dedo** it won't fit my finger - **2.** MAT: **nueve entre tres caben a tres** three into nine goes three (times) - **3.** [ser posible] to be possible; **cabe destacar que...** it's worth pointing out that...

cabestrillo ◆ **en cabestrillo** *loc adj* in a sling.

cabestro *sm* [animal] leading ox.

cabeza *sf* - **1.** [gen] head; **por cabeza** per head; **obrar con cabeza** to use one's head; **tirarse de cabeza (a)** to dive (into); **venir a la cabeza** to come to mind; **cabeza (lectora)** [gen] head; [de tocadiscos] pickup - **2.** [pelo] hair - **3.** [posición] front, head - **4.** *loc*: **alzar** *O* **levantar cabeza** to get back on one's feet, to recover; **se le ha metido en la cabeza que...** he has got it into his head that...; **sentar la cabeza** to settle down. ◆ **cabeza de ajo** *sf* head of garlic. ◆ **cabeza rapada** *smf* skinhead. ◆ **cabeza de turco** *sf* scapegoat.

cabezada *sf* - **1.** [de sueño] nod, nodding *(U)*; **dar cabezadas** to nod off - **2.** [golpe] butt.

cabezal *sm* [de aparato] head.

cabezón, ona *adj* [terco] pigheaded, stubborn.

cabida *sf* capacity; **dar cabida a, tener cabida para** to hold, to have room for.

cabina *sf* - **1.** [locutorio] booth, cabin, **cabina de prensa** press box - **2.**: **cabina telefónica** phone box *UK*, **phone booth** - **3.** [de avión] cockpit; [de camión] cab; **cabina de mandos** flight deck - **4.** [vestuario - en playa] bathing hut; [- en piscina] changing cubicle.

cabizbajo, ja *adj* crestfallen.

cable *sm* cable; **echar un cable** *fam fig* to help out, to lend a hand; **televisión por cable** cable television.

cablegrafiar *vt* to cable.

cabo *sm* - **1.** GEOGR cape - **2.** NÁUT cable, rope - **3.** MIL corporal - **4.** [trozo] bit, piece; [trozo final] stub, stump; [de cuerda] end - **5.** *loc*: **llevar algo a cabo** to carry sthg out. ◆ **cabo suelto** *sm* loose end. ◆ **al cabo de** *loc prep* after.

cabra *sf* [animal] goat; **estar como una cabra** *fam* to be off one's head; **la cabra siempre tira al monte** *prov* you can't make a leopard change his spots.

cabré ▷ **caber**.

cabrear *vt mfam*: **cabrear a alguien** to get sb's goat, to annoy sb.

cabría ▷ **caber**.

cabriola *sf* prance; **hacer cabriolas** to prance about.

cabrito *sm* [animal] kid (goat).

cabro, bra *sm, f Chile fam* kid.

cabrón, ona *vulg* ◇ *adj*: ¡**qué cabrón eres!** you bastard! ◇ *sm, f* bastard (*f* bitch).

cabuya *sf Amér C, Col & Ven* rope.

caca *sf fam* - **1.** [excremento] pooh - **2.** [cosa sucia] nasty *O* dirty thing.

cacahuate *sm Amér C & Méx* peanut.

cacahuete *sm* [fruto] peanut.

cacao *sm* - **1.** [bebida] cocoa - **2.** [árbol] cacao.

cacarear *vi* [gallo] to cluck, to cackle.

cacatúa *sf* [ave] cockatoo.

cacería *sf* hunt.

cacerola *sf* pot, pan.

cachalote *sm* sperm whale.

cacharro *sm* - **1.** [recipiente] pot; **fregar los cacharros** to do the dishes - **2.** *fam* [trasto] junk *(U)*, rubbish *(U)* - **3.** [máquina] crock; [coche] banger.

cachear *vt* to frisk.

cachemir *sm* cashmere.

cachemira *sf* = **cachemir**.

cacheo *sm* frisk, frisking *(U)*.

cachet [ka'tʃe] *sm* - **1.** [distinción] cachet - **2.** [cotización de artista] fee.

cachetada *sf fam* smack.

cachete *sm* - **1.** [moflete] chubby cheek - **2.** [bofetada] slap.

cachirulo *sm* [chisme] thingamajig.

cachivache *sm fam* knick-knack.

cacho *sm* - 1. *fam* [pedazo] piece, bit - 2. *Andes & Ven* [asta] horn.

cachondearse *vprnl:* **cachondearse (de)** *fam* to take the mickey (out of).

cachondeo *sm fam* - 1. [diversión] lark - 2. *despec* [cosa poco seria] joke.

cachondo, da *fam adj* - 1. [divertido] funny - 2. [salido] randy.

cachorro, rra *sm, f* [de perro] puppy; [de león, lobo, oso] cub.

cacique *sm* - 1. [persona influyente] cacique, local political boss - 2. [jefe indio] chief.

caco *sm fam* thief.

cacto, cactus (*pl* cactus) *sm* cactus.

cada *adj inv* - 1. [gen] each; [con números, tiempo] every; **cada dos meses** every two months; **cada cosa a su tiempo** one thing at a time; **cada cual** each one, every one; **cada uno de** each of - 2. [valor progresivo]: **cada vez más** more and more; **cada vez más largo** longer and longer; **cada día más** more and more each day - 3. [valor enfático] such; **¡se pone cada sombrero!** she wears such hats!

cadalso *sm* scaffold.

cadáver *sm* corpse, (dead) body.

cadena *sf* - 1. [gen] chain - 2. TV channel - 3. [RADIO - emisora] station; [- red de emisoras] network - 4. [de proceso industrial] line; **cadena de montaje** assembly line - 5. [aparato de música] sound system - 6. GEOGR range. ◆ **cadena perpetua** *sf* life imprisonment.

cadencia *sf* [ritmo] rhythm, cadence.

cadera *sf* hip.

cadete *sm* - 1. cadet - 2. *R Dom* [recadero] errand boy, office junior.

caducar *vi* - 1. [carné, ley, pasaporte etc] to expire - 2. [medicamento] to pass its use-by date; [alimento] to pass its sell-by date.

caducidad *sf* expiry.

caduco, ca *adj* - 1. [viejo] decrepit; [idea] outmoded - 2. [desfasado] no longer valid.

caer *vi* - 1. [gen] to fall; [diente, pelo] to fall out; **dejar caer algo** to drop sthg; **caer bajo** to sink (very) low; **estar al caer** to be about to arrive - 2. [al perder equilibrio] to fall over *O* down; **caer de un tejado/caballo** to fall from a roof/horse - 3. *fig* [sentar]: **caer bien/mal (a alguien)** [comentario, noticia etc] to go down well/badly (with sb) - 4. *fig* [mostrarse]: **me cae bien/mal** I like/don't like him - 5. *fig* [estar situado]: **cae cerca de aquí** it's not far from here - 6. *fig* [recordar]: **caer (en algo)** to be able to remember (sthg). ◆ **caer en** *vi* - 1. [entender] to get, to understand; [solución] to hit upon - 2. [coincidir - fecha] to fall on; **cae en domingo** it falls on a Sunday - 3. [incurrir] to fall into. ◆ **caerse** *vprnl* - 1. [persona] to fall over *O* down; **caerse de ingenuo/listo** *fig* to be incredibly naive/

clever - 2. [objetos] to drop, to fall - 3. [desprenderse - diente, pelo etc] to fall out; [- botón] to fall off; [- cuadro] to fall down.

café *sm* - 1. [gen] coffee; **café solo/con leche** black/white coffee - 2. [establecimiento] cafe.

cafeína *sf* caffeine.

cafetera *sf* ▷ **cafetero**.

cafetería *sf* cafe.

cafetero, ra *sm, f* - 1. [cultivador] coffee grower - 2. [comerciante] coffee merchant. ◆ **cafetera** *sf* - 1. [gen] coffee pot - 2. [en bares] expresso machine; [eléctrica] percolator, coffee machine.

cafiche *sm Andes fam* pimp.

cagar *vi vulg* [defecar] to shit. ◆ **cagarse** *vprnl vulg lit & fig* to shit o.s.

caído, da *adj* [árbol, hoja] fallen. ◆ **caída** *sf* - 1. [gen] fall, falling (*U*); [de diente, pelo] loss - 2. [de paro, precios, terreno]: **caída (de)** drop (in) - 3. [de falda, vestido etc] drape. ◆ **caídos** *smpl*: **los caídos** the fallen.

caiga *etc* ▷ **caer**.

caimán *sm* - 1. [animal] alligator, cayman - 2. *fig* [persona] sly fox.

caja *sf* - 1. [gen] box; [para transporte, embalaje] crate; **caja de zapatos** shoebox; **una caja de cervezas** a crate of beer; **caja torácica** thorax - 2. [de reloj] case; [de engranajes etc] housing; **caja de cambios** gearbox - 3. [ataúd] coffin - 4. [de dinero] cash box; **caja fuerte** *O* **de caudales** safe, strongbox - 5. [en tienda, supermercado] till; [en banco] cashier's desk - 6. [banco]: **caja (de ahorros)** savings bank, ≈ savings and loan association *US* - 7. [hueco - de chimenea, ascensor] shaft - 8. IMPR case - 9. [de instrumento musical] body; **caja de resonancia** sound box; **caja de ritmos** drum machine. ◆ **caja negra** *sf* black box. ◆ **caja registradora** *sf* cash register.

cajero, ra *sm, f* [en tienda] cashier; [en banco] teller. ◆ **cajero** *sm:* **cajero (automático)** cash machine, cash dispenser, ATM *US*.

cajetilla *sf* - 1. [de cigarrillos] packet - 2. [de cerillas] box.

cajón *sm* - 1. [de mueble] drawer - 2. [recipiente] crate, case. ◆ **cajón de sastre** *sm* muddle, jumble.

cajuela *sf Méx* boot *UK*, trunk *US*.

cal *sf* lime.

cala *sf* - 1. [bahía pequeña] cove - 2. [del barco] hold.

calabacín *sm* courgette *UK*, zucchini *US*.

calabaza *sf* pumpkin, squash *US*, gourd.

calabozo *sm* cell.

calada *sf* ▷ **calado**.

calado, da *adj* soaked. ◆ **calado** *sm* NÁUT draught. ◆ **calada** *sf* [de cigarrillo] drag.

calamar *sm* squid.

calambre *sm* - 1. [descarga eléctrica] (electric) shock - 2. [contracción muscular] cramp (U).

calamidad *sf* calamity; **ser una calamidad** *fig* to be a dead loss.

calaña *sf*: de esa calaña *despec* of that ilk.

calar <> *vt* - 1. [empapar] to soak - 2. *fig* [persona] to see through - 3. [gorro, sombrero] to jam on - 4. [sandía, melón] to cut a sample of - 5. [perforar] to pierce. <> *vi* - 1. NÁUT to draw - 2. *fig* [penetrar]: **calar en** to have an impact on. <> **calarse** *vprnl* - 1. [empaparse] to get soaked - 2. [motor] to stall.

calavera *sf* [cráneo] skull. <> **calaveras** *sfpl* Méx [luces] tail lights.

calcar *vt* - 1. [dibujo] to trace - 2. [imitar] to copy.

calce *sm* - 1. [cuña] wedge - 2. *Guat, Méx & P Rico* DER footnote.

calceta *sf* stocking; **hacer calceta** to knit.

calcetín *sm* sock.

calcificarse *vprnl* to calcify.

calcinar *vt* [quemar] to char.

calcio *sm* calcium.

calco *sm* - 1. [reproducción] tracing - 2. *fig* [imitación] carbon copy.

calcomanía *sf* transfer.

calculador, ra *adj lit & fig* calculating. <> **calculadora** *sf* calculator.

calcular *vt* - 1. [cantidades] to calculate - 2. [suponer] to reckon.

cálculo *sm* - 1. [operación] calculation - 2. [ciencia] calculus - 3. [evaluación] estimate - 4. MED stone, calculus.

caldear *vt* - 1. [calentar] to heat (up) - 2. *fig* [excitar] to warm up, to liven up.

caldera *sf* - 1. [recipiente] cauldron - 2. [máquina] boiler.

calderilla *sf* small change.

caldero *sm* cauldron.

caldo *sm* - 1. [sopa] broth - 2. [caldillo] stock - 3. [vino] wine.

calefacción *sf* heating; **calefacción central** central heating.

calefactor *sm* heater.

calendario *sm* calendar; **calendario escolar/laboral** school/working year.

calentador *sm* - 1. [aparato] heater - 2. [prenda] legwarmer.

calentar <> *vt* [subir la temperatura de] to heat (up), to warm (up). <> *vi* [entrenarse] to warm up. <> **calentarse** *vprnl* [por calor - suj: persona] to warm o.s., to get warm; [- suj: cosa] to heat up.

calentura *sf* - 1. [fiebre] fever, temperature - 2. [herida] cold sore.

calibrar *vt* - 1. [medir] to calibrate, to gauge - 2. [dar calibre a - arma] to bore - 3. *fig* [juzgar] to gauge.

calibre *sm* - 1. [diámetro - de pistola] calibre; [- de alambre] gauge; [- de tubo] bore - 2. [instrumento] gauge - 3. *fig* [tamaño] size.

calidad *sf* - 1. [gen] quality; **de calidad** quality (antes de s); **calidad de vida** quality of life - 2. [clase] class - 3. [condición]: **en calidad de** in one's capacity as.

cálido, da *adj* warm.

caliente *adj* - 1. [gen] hot; [templado] warm; **en caliente** *fig* in the heat of the moment - 2. *fig* [acalorado] heated.

calificación *sf* - 1. [de película] rating - 2. EDUC mark.

calificar *vt* - 1. [denominar]: **calificar a alguien de algo** to call sb sthg, to describe sb as sthg - 2. EDUC to mark - 3. GRAM to qualify.

calificativo, va *adj* qualifying. <> **calificativo** *sm* epithet.

caligrafía *sf* - 1. [arte] calligraphy - 2. [tipo de letra] handwriting.

cáliz *sm* RELIG chalice.

calizo, za *adj* chalky. <> **caliza** *sf* limestone.

callado, da *adj* quiet, silent.

callar <> *vi* - 1. [no hablar] to keep quiet, to be silent - 2. [dejar de hablar] to be quiet, to stop talking. <> *vt* - 1. [ocultar] to keep quiet about; [secreto] to keep - 2. [acallar] to silence. <> **callarse** *vprnl* - 1. [no hablar] to keep quiet, to be silent - 2. [dejar de hablar] to be quiet, to stop talking; **¡cállate!** shut up! - 3. [ocultar] to keep quiet about; [secreto] to keep.

calle *sf* - 1. [vía de circulación] street, road; **calle arriba/abajo** up/down the street; **calle de dirección única** one-way street; **calle peatonal** pedestrian precinct; **calle sin salida** dead end, blind alley - 2. DEP lane - 3. *loc*: **dejar a alguien en la calle** to put sb out of a job; **traer O llevar a alguien por la calle de la amargura** to make sb's life a misery.

callejear *vi* to wander the streets.

callejero, ra *adj* [gen] street (antes de s); [perro] stray. <> **callejero** *sm* [guía] street map.

callejón *sm* alley; **callejón sin salida** cul-de-sac; *fig* blind alley, impasse.

callejuela *sf* backstreet, side street.

callista *smf* chiropodist.

callo *sm* [dureza] callus; [en el pie] corn; **dar el callo** *fam fig* to slog. <> **callos** *smpl* CULIN tripe (U).

calma *sf* - 1. [sin ruido o movimiento] calm; **en calma** calm - 2. [sosiego] tranquility; **tómatelo con calma** take it easy - 3. [apatía] sluggishness, indifference.

calmante ⬦ *adj* soothing. ⬦ *sm* sedative.

calmar *vt* - 1. [mitigar] to relieve - 2. [tranquilizar] to calm, to soothe. ➤ **calmarse** *vprnl* to calm down; [dolor, tempestad] to abate.

caló *sm* gypsy dialect.

calor *sm* [gen] heat; [sin quemar] warmth; **entrar en calor** [gen] to get warm; [público, deportista] to warm up; **hacer calor** to be warm *O* hot; **tener calor** to be warm *O* hot.

caloría *sf* calorie.

calumnia *sf* [oral] slander; [escrita] libel.

calumniar *vt* [oralmente] to slander; [por escrito] to libel.

calumnioso, sa *adj* [de palabra] slanderous; [por escrito] libellous.

caluroso, sa *adj* - 1. [gen] hot; [templado] warm - 2. *fig* [afectuoso] warm.

calva *sf* ➪ **calvo**.

calvario *sm fig* [sufrimiento] ordeal.

calvicie *sf* baldness.

calvo, va *adj* bald. ➤ **calva** *sf* [en la cabeza] bald patch.

calza *sf* [cuña] wedge, block.

calzado, da *adj* [con zapatos] shod. ➤ **calzado** *sm* footwear. ➤ **calzada** *sf* road.

calzar *vt* - 1. [poner calzado] to put on - 2. [llevar un calzado] to wear; **¿qué número calza?** what size do you take? - 3. [poner cuña a] to wedge. ➤ **calzarse** *vprnl* to put on.

calzo *sm* [cuña] wedge.

calzón *sm* - 1. *Esp* [deportivo] shorts - 2. *Andes, Méx & R Plata* [braga] knickers *UK*, panties *US*.

calzoncillo *sm (gen pl)* underpants *pl*, shorts *pl US*.

cama *sf* bed; **estar en** *O* **guardar cama** to be in bed; **hacer la cama** to make the bed; **hacerle** *O* **ponerle la cama a alguien** *fig* to plot against sb.

camada *sf* litter.

camafeo *sm* cameo.

camaleón *sm lit & fig* chameleon.

cámara ⬦ *sf* - 1. [gen & TECNOL] chamber; **cámara alta/baja** upper/lower house - 2. CINE, FOTO & TV camera; **cámara de seguridad** security camera; **cámara de vídeo** video camera - 3. [de balón, neumático] inner tube - 4. [habitáculo] cabin. ⬦ *smf* [persona] cameraman (*f* camerawoman).

camarada *smf* POLÍT comrade.

camarero, ra *sm, f* [de restaurante] waiter (*f* waitress); [de hotel] steward (*f* chambermaid).

camarilla *sf* clique; POLÍT lobby.

camarón *sm* shrimp.

camarote *sm* cabin.

cambiante *adj* changeable.

cambiar ⬦ *vt* - 1. [gen] to change; **cambiar libras por euros** to change pounds into euros

- 2. [canjear]: **cambiar algo (por)** to exchange sthg (for). ⬦ *vi* - 1. [gen] to change; **cambiar de** [gen] to change; **cambiar de casa** to move house; **cambiar de trabajo** to move jobs - 2. AUTO: **cambiar de marcha** to change gear. ➤ **cambiarse** *vprnl*: **cambiarse (de)** [ropa] to change; [casa] to move; **cambiarse de vestido** to change one's dress.

cambio *sm* - 1. [gen] change; **cambio climático** climate change; **cambio de domicilio** change of address; **cambio de guardia** changing of the guard - 2. [trueque] exchange; **a cambio (de)** in exchange *O* return (for) - 3. [FIN - de acciones] price; [- de divisas] exchange rate; **'cambio'** 'bureau de change' - 4. AUTO: **cambio de marchas** *O* **velocidades** gear change; **cambio de sentido** U-turn. ➤ **cambio de rasante** *sm* brow of a hill. ➤ **libre cambio** *sm* - 1. ECON [librecambismo] free trade - 2. FIN [de divisas] floating exchange rates *pl*. ➤ **en cambio** *loc adv* - 1. [por otra parte] on the other hand, however - 2. [en su lugar] instead.

camelar *vt fam* [seducir, engañar] to butter up, to win over.

camelia *sf* camellia.

camello, lla *sm, f* [animal] camel. ➤ **camello** *sm fam* [traficante] drug pusher *O* dealer.

camellón *sm Col & Méx* central reservation *UK*, median (strip) *US*.

camerino *sm* dressing room.

camilla ⬦ *sf* [gen] stretcher; [de psiquiatra, dentista] couch. ⬦ *adj* ➪ **mesa**.

caminante *smf* walker.

caminar ⬦ *vi* - 1. [a pie] to walk - 2. *fig* [ir]: **caminar (hacia)** to head (for). ⬦ *vt* [una distancia] to travel, to cover.

caminata *sf* long walk.

camino *sm* - 1. [sendero] path, track; [carretera] road; **camino de montaña** mountain path; **abrir camino a** to clear the way for; **abrirse camino** to get on *O* ahead - 2. [ruta] way; **a medio camino** halfway; **estar a medio camino** to be halfway there; **quedarse a medio camino** to stop halfway through; **camino de** on the way to; **en el** *O* **de camino** on the way; **ir camino de** to be heading for - 3. [viaje] journey; **ponerse en camino** to set off - 4. *fig* [medio] way.

camión *sm* - 1. [de mercancías] lorry *UK*, truck *US*; **camión articulado** articulated lorry *UK O* truck *US*; **camión cisterna** tanker; **camión de la mudanza** removal van - 2. *Amér C & Méx* [bus] bus.

camionero, ra ⬦ *adj Amér C & Méx* bus. ⬦ *sm, f* lorry driver *UK*, trucker *US*.

camioneta *sf* van.

camisa *sf* - 1. [prenda] shirt - 2. *loc*: **meterse en camisa de once varas** to complicate matters unnecessarily. ➤ **camisa de fuerza** *sf* straitjacket.

camisería sf [tienda] outfitter's.

camiseta sf - 1. [prenda interior] vest UK, undershirt US - 2. [de verano] T-shirt - 3. [DEP - de tirantes] vest; [- de mangas] shirt.

camisola sf - 1. [prenda interior] camisole - 2. Amér DEP sports shirt.

camisón sm nightdress.

camorra sf trouble; **buscar camorra** to look for trouble.

campamento sm camp.

campana sf bell; **campana de buzo** O **de salvamento** diving bell; **campana extractora de humos** extractor hood.

campanada sf - 1. [de campana] peal - 2. [de reloj] stroke - 3. fig [suceso] sensation.

campanario sm belfry, bell tower.

campanilla sf - 1. [de la puerta] (small) bell; [con mango] handbell - 2. [flor] campanula, bellflower.

campanilleo sm tinkling (U).

campaña sf - 1. [gen] campaign; **hacer campaña (de/contra)** to campaign (for/against); **de campaña** MIL field (antes de s) - 2. R Dom [campo] countryside.

campechano, na adj fam genial, good-natured.

campeón, ona sm, f champion.

campeonato sm championship; **de campeonato** fig terrific, great.

campero, ra adj country (antes de s); [al aire libre] open-air. ➤ **campera** sf - 1. [bota] ≃ cowboy boot - 2. R Dom [chaqueta] jacket.

campesino, na sm, f [gen] farmer; [muy pobre] peasant.

campestre adj country (antes de s).

camping ['kampin] (pl campings) sm - 1. [actividad] camping; **ir de camping** to go camping - 2. [lugar de acampada] campsite.

campo sm - 1. [gen & INFORM] field; **campo de aviación** airfield; **campo de batalla** battlefield; **campo de tiro** firing range - 2. [campiña] country, countryside; **a campo traviesa** cross country - 3. [DEP - de fútbol] pitch; [- de tenis] court; [- de golf] course - 4. C Sur [hacienda] cattle ranch - 5. Andes [lugar] room, space. ➤ **campo de concentración** sm concentration camp.

camuflaje sm camouflage.

cana sf ⊳ **cano**.

Canadá n pr: **(el) Canadá** Canada.

canadiense adj & smf Canadian.

canal sm - 1. [cauce artificial] canal; **canal de riego** irrigation channel - 2. GEOGR channel, strait - 3. RADIO & TV channel; **canal por cable** cable channel - 4. ANAT canal, duct - 5. [de agua, gas] conduit, pipe - 6. fig [medio, vía] channel.

canalizar vt - 1. [territorio] to canalize; [agua] to channel - 2. fig [orientar] to channel.

canalla smf fam swine, dog.

canalón sm [de tejado] gutter; [en la pared] drainpipe.

canapé sm - 1. CULIN canapé - 2. [sofá] sofa, couch.

Canarias sfpl: **las (islas) Canarias** the Canary Islands, the Canaries.

canario, ria ⊳ adj of the Canary Islands. ⊳ sm, f [persona] Canary Islander. ➤ **canario** sm [pájaro] canary.

canasta sf [gen & DEP] basket.

canastilla sf - 1. [cesto pequeño] basket - 2. [de bebé] layette.

canasto sm large basket.

cancán, cancanes sm o sf R Dom tights UK, pantyhose US.

cancela sf wrought-iron gate.

cancelación sf cancellation.

cancelar vt - 1. [anular] to cancel - 2. [deuda] to pay, to settle - 3. Chile & Perú [cuenta] to pay.

cáncer sm fig & MED cancer. ➤ **Cáncer** ⊳ sm [zodiaco] Cancer. ⊳ smf [persona] Cancer.

cancerígeno, na adj carcinogenic.

canceroso, sa adj [úlcera, tejido] cancerous; [enfermo] suffering from cancer.

canciller sm - 1. [de gobierno, embajada] chancellor - 2. [de asuntos exteriores] foreign minister.

canción sf song; **canción de cuna** lullaby; **la misma canción** fig the same old story.

cancionero sm songbook.

candado sm padlock.

candela sf - 1. [vela] candle - 2. Amér [fuego] fire.

candelabro sm candelabra.

candelero sm candlestick.

candente adj - 1. [incandescente] red-hot - 2. fig [actual] burning (antes de s).

candidato, ta sm, f candidate.

candidatura sf [para un cargo] candidacy.

candidez sf ingenuousness.

cándido, da adj ingenuous, simple.

candil sm - 1. [lámpara] oil lamp - 2. Méx [araña] chandelier.

candilejas sfpl footlights.

canelo, la adj fam fig [inocentón] gullible. ➤ **canela** sf cinnamon.

canelón sm CULIN cannelloni pl.

cangrejo sm crab.

canguro ⊳ sm [animal] kangaroo. ⊳ smf fam [persona] babysitter; **hacer de canguro** to babysit.

caníbal smf cannibal.

canica *sf* [pieza] marble. ➤ **canicas** *sfpl* [juego] marbles.

caniche *sm* poodle.

canijo, ja *adj* sickly.

canilla *sf* - **1.** [espinilla] shinbone - **2.** *R Dom* [grifo] tap *UK*, faucet *US* - **3.** *Amér* [pierna] leg.

canillita *sm R Dom fam* newspaper vendor.

canino, na *adj* canine. ➤ **canino** *sm* [diente] canine (tooth).

canjear *vt* to exchange.

cano, na *adj* grey. ➤ **cana** *sf* grey hair; **echar una cana al aire** *fig* to let one's hair down.

canoa *sf* canoe.

canódromo *sm* greyhound track.

canon *sm* - **1.** [norma] canon; **como mandan los cánones** according to the rules - **2.** [modelo] ideal - **3.** [impuesto] tax - **4.** MÚS canon.

canónigo *sm* canon.

canonizar *vt* to canonize.

canoso, sa *adj* [pelo] grey; [persona] grey-haired.

cansado, da *adj* - **1.** [agotado] tired; **cansado de algo/de hacer algo** tired of sthg/of doing sthg - **2.** [pesado, cargante] tiring.

cansador, ra *adj Andes & R Plata* [que cansa] tiring; [que aburre] tiresome, boring.

cansancio *sm* tiredness.

cansar ⬦ *vt* to tire (out). ⬦ *vi* to be tiring. ➤ **cansarse** *vprnl*: **cansarse (de)** *lit & fig* to get tired (of).

Cantábrico *sm*: **el (mar) Cantábrico** the Cantabrian Sea.

cantaleta *sf Amér* nagging.

cantante ⬦ *adj* singing. ⬦ *smf* singer.

cantaor, ra *sm, f* flamenco singer.

cantar ⬦ *vt* - **1.** [canción] to sing - **2.** [bingo, línea, el gordo] to call (out); **cantar victoria** to claim victory; **cantar a alguien las cuarenta** to give sb a piece of one's mind. ⬦ *vi* - **1.** [persona, ave] to sing; [gallo] to crow; [grillo] to chirp - **2.** *fam fig* [confesar] to talk.

cántaro *sm* large pitcher; **llover a cántaros** to rain cats and dogs.

cante *sm*: **cante (jondo O hondo)** flamenco singing.

cantera *sf* [de piedra] quarry.

cantero *sm C Sur & Cuba* [de flores] flowerbed.

cantidad *sf* - **1.** [medida] quantity - **2.** [abundancia] abundance, large number; **en cantidad** in abundance; **cantidad de** lots of; **en cantidades industriales** in industrial quantities - **3.** [número] number - **4.** [suma de dinero] sum (of money).

cantilena, cantinela *sf*: **la misma cantilena** *fig* the same old story.

cantimplora *sf* water bottle.

cantina *sf* [de soldados] mess; [en fábrica] canteen; [en estación de tren] buffet; [bar] snack bar.

cantinela = **cantilena**.

canto *sm* - **1.** [acción, arte] singing - **2.** [canción] song - **3.** [lado, borde] edge; **de canto** edgeways - **4.** [de cuchillo] blunt edge - **5.** [guijarro] pebble; **canto rodado** [pequeño] pebble; [grande] boulder.

cantor, ra *sm, f* singer.

canturrear *vt & vi fam* to sing softly.

canuto *sm* - **1.** [tubo] tube - **2.** *fam* [porro] joint.

caña *sf* - **1.** BOT cane; **caña de azúcar** sugarcane - **2.** *Esp* [de cerveza] half; **una caña** one beer - **3.** *Andes, Cuba & R Plata* [aguardiente] type of rum made using sugar cane spirit. ➤ **caña de pescar** *sf* fishing rod.

cañabrava *sf Cuba & R Dom* kind of cane.

cáñamo *sm* hemp.

cañería *sf* pipe.

cañero, ra *sm, f Amér* [trabajador] sugar plantation worker.

caño *sm* [de fuente] jet.

cañón *sm* - **1.** [arma] gun; HIST cannon; **cañón antiaéreo** anti-aircraft gun; **cañón de nieve** snow cannon - **2.** [de fusil] barrel; [de chimenea] flue; [de órgano] pipe - **3.** GEOGR canyon.

caoba *sf* mahogany.

caos *sm inv* chaos.

caótico, ca *adj* chaotic.

cap. (*abrev de* **capítulo**) ch.

capa *sf* - **1.** [manto] cloak, cape; **andar de capa caída** to be in a bad way; **de capa y espada** cloak and dagger - **2.** [baño - de barniz, pintura] coat; [- de chocolate etc] coating - **3.** [estrato] layer; GEOL stratum; **capa de ozono** ozone layer; **capa de hielo** sheet of ice - **4.** [grupo social] stratum, class - **5.** TAUROM cape.

capacidad *sf* - **1.** [gen] capacity; **con capacidad para 500 personas** with a capacity of 500 - **2.** [aptitud] ability; **no tener capacidad para algo/para hacer algo** to be no good at sthg/at doing sthg. ➤ **capacidad de decisión** *sf* decision-making ability. ➤ **capacidad de trabajo** *sf* capacity for hard work.

capacitación *sf* training.

capacitar *vt*: **capacitar a alguien para algo** [habilitar] to qualify sb for sthg; [formar] to train sb for sthg.

capar *vt* to castrate.

caparazón *sm lit & fig* shell.

capataz *sm, f* foreman (*f* forewoman).

capaz *adj* - **1.** [gen] capable; **capaz de algo/de hacer algo** capable of sthg/of doing sthg - **2.** [atrevido]: **ser capaz** to dare; **ser capaz de**

hacer algo to bring oneself to do sthg - **3.** [espacioso]: **muy/poco capaz** with a large/small capacity; **capaz para** with room for.

capazo sm large wicker basket.

capellán sm chaplain.

caperuza sf [gorro] hood.

capicúa adj inv reversible.

capilla sf chapel; **capilla ardiente** funeral chapel.

cápita ◆ **per cápita** loc adj per capita.

capital ◇ adj - **1.** [importante] supreme - **2.** [principal] main. ◇ sm ECON capital. ◇ sf [ciudad] capital; **soy de Barcelona capital** I'm from the city of Barcelona.

capitalismo sm capitalism.

capitalista adj & smf capitalist.

capitalizar vt - **1.** ECON to capitalize - **2.** fig [sacar provecho] to capitalize on.

capitán, ana sm, f captain.

capitanear vt DEP & MIL to captain.

capitel sm capital.

capitoste smf despec big boss.

capitulación sf capitulation, surrender.

capitular vi to capitulate, to surrender.

capítulo sm - **1.** [sección, división] chapter - **2.** fig [tema] subject.

capó, capot [ka'po] sm bonnet UK, hood US.

caporal sm MIL ≃ corporal.

capot = **capó.**

capota sf hood UK, top US.

capote sm - **1.** [capa] cape with sleeves; [militar] greatcoat - **2.** TAUROM cape.

capricho sm - **1.** [antojo] whim, caprice; **darse un capricho** to treat o.s. - **2.** MÚS & ARTE caprice.

caprichoso, sa adj capricious.

Capricornio ◇ sm [zodiaco] Capricorn. ◇ smf [persona] Capricorn.

cápsula sf - **1.** [gen & ANAT] capsule - **2.** [tapón] cap. ◆ **cápsula espacial** sf space capsule.

captar vt - **1.** [atraer - simpatía] to win; [- interés] to gain, to capture - **2.** [entender] to grasp - **3.** [sintonizar] to pick up, to receive - **4.** [aguas] to collect.

captura sf capture.

capturar vt to capture.

capucha sf hood.

capuchón sm cap, top.

capullo, lla vulg sm, f [persona] prat. ◆ **capullo** sm - **1.** [de flor] bud - **2.** [de gusano] cocoon.

caqui, kaki adj inv [color] khaki.

cara sf - **1.** [rostro, aspecto] face; **cara a cara** face to face - **2.** [lado] side; GEOM face - **3.** [de moneda] heads (U); **cara o cruz** heads or tails; **echar algo a cara o cruz** to toss (a coin) for sthg - **4.** fam [osadía] cheek - **5.** loc: **de cara a** with a

view to; **decir algo a alguien en O a la cara** to say sthg to sb's face; **echar en cara algo a alguien** to reproach sb for sthg; **por su linda cara, por su cara bonita** because his/her face fits; **verse las caras** [pelearse] to have it out; [enfrentarse] to fight it out.

carabina sf - **1.** [arma] carbine, rifle - **2.** fam fig [mujer] chaperone.

Caracas n pr Caracas.

caracol sm - **1.** [animal] snail - **2.** [concha] shell - **3.** [rizo] curl. ◆ **escalera de caracol** sf spiral staircase.

caracola sf conch.

carácter (pl **caracteres**) sm - **1.** [de persona] character; **tener buen/mal carácter** to be good-natured/bad-tempered - **2.** [índole] nature; **con carácter de urgencia** as a matter of urgency; **una reunión de carácter privado/oficial** a private/official meeting - **3.** INFORM character; **carácter alfanumérico** alphanumeric character; **caracteres de imprenta** typeface sing - **4.** BIOL trait.

característico, ca adj characteristic. ◆ **característica** sf characteristic.

caracterización sf - **1.** [gen] characterization - **2.** [maquillaje] make-up.

caracterizar vt - **1.** [definir] to characterize - **2.** [representar] to portray - **3.** [maquillar] to make up. ◆ **caracterizarse por** vprnl to be characterized by.

caradura fam adj cheeky.

carajillo sm coffee with a dash of liqueur.

carajo mfam interj: **¡carajo!** damn it!

caramba interj: **¡caramba!** [sorpresa] good heavens!; [enfado] for heaven's sake!

carambola sf - **1.** cannon (in billiards) - **2.** [fruta] starfruit. ◆ **carambolas** interj Amér: **¡carambolas!** good heavens!

caramelo sm - **1.** [golosina] sweet - **2.** [azúcar fundido] caramel; **de caramelo** fig great.

carátula sf - **1.** [de libro] front cover; [de disco] sleeve - **2.** [máscara] mask.

caravana sf - **1.** [gen] caravan UK, trailer US - **2.** [de coches] tailback. ◆ **caravanas** sfpl Amér [pendientes] earrings.

caray interj: **¡caray!** [sorpresa] good heavens!; [enfado] damn it!

carbón sm [para quemar] coal; **carbón mineral** O **de piedra** coal.

carboncillo sm charcoal; **al carboncillo** in charcoal.

carbonilla sf [ceniza] cinder.

carbonizar vt to char, to carbonize.

carbono sm carbon.

carburador sm carburettor.

carburante sm fuel.

carca fam despec adj old-fashioned.

carcajada sf guffaw; **reír a carcajadas** to roar with laughter.

carcamal smf fam despec old crock.

cárcel sf prison; **estar en la cárcel** to be in prison.

carcelero, ra sm, f warder, jailer.

carcoma sf - 1. [insecto] woodworm - 2. [polvo] wood dust.

carcomer vt lit & fig to eat away at.

cardar vt - 1. [lana] to card - 2. [pelo] to backcomb.

cardenal sm - 1. RELIG cardinal - 2. [hematoma] bruise.

cardiaco, ca, cardíaco, ca adj cardiac, heart (antes de s).

cárdigan, cardigán sm cardigan.

cardinal adj cardinal.

cardiólogo, ga sm, f cardiologist.

cardo sm [planta] thistle.

carecer vi: **carecer de algo** to lack sthg.

carencia sf [ausencia] lack; [defecto] deficiency.

carente adj: **carente de** lacking (in).

carestía sf [escasez] scarcity, shortage.

careta sf - 1. [máscara] mask; **careta antigás** gas mask - 2. fig [engaño] front.

carey sm [material] tortoiseshell.

carga sf - 1. [acción] loading; **de carga frontal** front-loading - 2. [cargamento - de avión, barco] cargo; [- de tren] freight; [- de camión] load - 3. [peso] load - 4. fig [sufrimiento] burden - 5. [ataque, explosivo] charge; **volver a la carga** fig to persist - 6. [de batería, condensador] charge - 7. [para mechero, bolígrafo] refill - 8. [impuesto] tax; **carga fiscal** tax burden.

cargado, da adj - 1. [abarrotado]: **cargado (de)** loaded (with); **un árbol cargado de fruta** a tree laden with fruit - 2. [arma] loaded - 3. [bebida] strong - 4. [bochornoso - habitación] stuffy; [- tiempo] sultry, close; [- cielo] overcast - 5.: **cargado de hombros** round-shouldered (s).

cargador sm [de arma] chamber.

cargamento sm cargo.

cargante adj fam fig annoying.

cargar ⟨> vt - 1. [gen] to load; [pluma, mechero] to refill - 2. [peso encima] to throw over one's shoulder - 3. ELECTR to charge; INFORM to load - 4. fig [responsabilidad, tarea] to give, to lay upon; **cargar a alguien de deudas** to encumber sb with debts - 5. [producir pesadez - suj: humo] to make stuffy; [- suj: comida] to bloat - 6. [gravar]: **cargar un impuesto a algo/alguien** to tax sthg/sb - 7. [importe, factura, deuda]: **cargar algo (a)** to charge sthg (to); **cárguelo a mi cuenta** charge it to my account. ⟨> vi [atacar]: **cargar (contra)** to charge. ⬛ **cargar con** vi - 1. [paquete etc] to carry away - 2. fig

[coste, responsabilidad] to bear; [consecuencias] to accept; [culpa] to get. ⬛ **cargarse** vprnl - 1. fam [romper] to break - 2. fam [matar - persona] to bump off; [- animal] to kill - 3. [de humo] to get stuffy - 4. ELECTR to become charged; INFORM to load.

cargo sm - 1. [gen, ECON & DER] charge; **sin cargo** free of charge; **correr a cargo de** to be borne by; **estar a cargo de algo, tener algo a cargo de uno** to be in charge of sthg; **las personas a mi cargo** the people in my care; **hacerse cargo de** [asumir el control de] to take charge of; [ocuparse de] to take care of; [comprender] to understand - 2. [empleo] post; **es un cargo público** he holds public office.

cargosear vt C Sur to annoy, to pester.

cargoso, sa adj C Sur annoying.

carguero sm cargo boat.

Caribe sm: **el (mar) Caribe** the Caribbean (Sea).

caribeño, ña adj Caribbean.

caricatura sf - 1. [de personaje, situación] caricature - 2. Méx [dibujos animados] cartoon.

caricia sf [a persona] caress; [a perro, gato etc] stroke.

caridad sf charity.

caries sf inv tooth decay; **tengo dos caries** I have two cavities.

cariño sm - 1. [afecto] affection; **tomar cariño a** to grow fond of; **con mucho cariño** with great affection - 2. [cuidado] loving care - 3. [apelativo] love.

cariñoso, sa adj affectionate.

carisma sm charisma.

carismático, ca adj charismatic.

Cáritas sf charitable organization run by the Catholic Church.

caritativo, va adj charitable.

cariz sm look, appearance; **tomar mal/buen cariz** to take a turn for the worse/better.

carmesí (pl carmesíes O carmesís) adj & sm crimson.

carmín ⟨> adj [color] carmine. ⟨> sm - 1. [color] carmine - 2. [lápiz de labios] lipstick.

carnada sf lit & fig bait.

carnal ⟨> adj - 1. [de la carne] carnal - 2. [primo] first (antes de s). ⟨> sm Méx fam [amigo] mate.

carnaval sm carnival.

carnaza sf lit & fig bait.

carne sf - 1. [de persona, fruta] flesh; **en carne viva** raw; **entrado** O **metido en carnes** plump; **ser de carne y hueso** fig to be human - 2. [alimento] meat; **carne de cerdo** pork; **carne de cordero** lamb; **carne picada** mince; **carne de ternera** veal; **carne de vaca** beef; **poner toda la carne en el asador** fig to go for broke; **ser car-**

ne de cañón to be cannon fodder; poner la carne de gallina a alguien [de frío] to give sb goose pimples; [de miedo] to give sb the creeps. ━ carne de membrillo sf quince jelly.

carné, carnet (pl carnets) sm [documento] card; carné de conducir driving licence; carné de identidad identity card; carné de estudiante student card; carné de prensa press pass.

carnicería sf - 1. [tienda] butcher's - 2. fig [masacre] carnage (U).

carnicero, ra sm, f lit & fig [persona] butcher.

carnitas sfpl Méx small pieces of braised pork.

carnívoro, ra adj carnivorous. ━ carnívoro sm carnivore.

carnoso, sa adj fleshy; [labios] full.

caro, ra adj [precio] expensive. ━ caro adv: costar caro to be expensive; fig to cost dear; vender caro algo to sell sthg at a high price; fig not to give sthg up easily; pagar caro algo fig to pay dearly for sthg; salir caro to be expensive; fig to cost dear.

carozo sm R Dom stone, pit US.

carpa sf - 1. [pez] carp - 2. [de circo] big top; [para fiestas etc] marquee - 3. Amér [tienda de campaña] tent.

carpeta sf file, folder.

carpintería sf - 1. [arte] carpentry; [de puertas y ventanas] joinery - 2. [taller] carpenter's/joiner's shop.

carpintero, ra sm, f carpenter; [de puertas y ventanas] joiner.

carraca sf [instrumento] rattle.

carraspear vi [toser] to clear one's throat.

carraspera sf hoarseness.

carrera sf - 1. [acción de correr] run, running (U) - 2. fig & DEP race; carrera ciclista cycle race; carrera de coches motor race; carrera de obstáculos steeplechase - 3. [trayecto] route - 4. [de taxi] ride - 5. [estudios] university course; hacer la carrera de derecho to study law (at university) - 6. [profesión] career - 7. [en medias] ladder UK, run US.

carreta sf cart.

carrete sm - 1. [de hilo] bobbin, reel; [de alambre] coil - 2. FOTO roll (of film) - 3. [para pescar] reel - 4. [de máquina de escribir] spool.

carretera sf road; viaje por carretera road journey; carretera de circunvalación ring road; carretera comarcal ≃ B road UK; carretera de cuota Méx toll road; carretera nacional ≃ A road UK, state highway US.

carretilla sf wheelbarrow.

carril sm - 1. [de carretera] lane; carril bici cycle lane; carril bus bus lane - 2. [de vía de tren] rail.

carrillo sm cheek; comer a dos carrillos fig to cram one's face with food.

carrito sm trolley UK, cart US.

carro sm - 1. [vehículo] cart; carro de combate MIL tank - 2. [de máquina de escribir] carriage - 3. Andes, Amér C, Caribe & Méx [automóvil] car - 4. Méx: carro comedor [en tren] dining car, restaurant car.

carrocería sf bodywork UK, body.

carromato sm [carro] wagon.

carroña sf carrion.

carroza sf [vehículo] carriage.

carruaje sm carriage.

carrusel sm [tiovivo] carousel.

carta sf - 1. letter; echar una carta to post a letter; carta certificada/urgente registered/express letter; carta de presentación letter of introduction; carta de recomendación reference (letter) - 2. [naipe] (playing) card; echar las cartas a alguien to tell sb's fortune (with cards) - 3. [en restaurante] menu - 4. [mapa] map; NÁUT chart - 5. [documento] charter; carta verde green card - 6. loc: jugarse todo a una carta to put all one's eggs in one basket; dar carta blanca a alguien to give sb carte blanche. ━ carta de ajuste sf test card. ━ Carta de Derechos sf Bill of Rights. ━ Carta Magna sf Constitution.

cartabón sm set square.

cartapacio sm [carpeta] folder.

cartearse vprnl to correspond.

cartel sm - 1. [póster] poster; 'prohibido fijar carteles' 'billposters will be prosecuted' - 2. [letrero] sign.

cártel sm cartel.

cartelera sf - 1. [tablón] hoarding, billboard - 2. PRENSA entertainments page; estar en cartelera to be showing; lleva un año en cartelera it's been running for a year.

cárter sm AUTO housing.

cartera sf - 1. [para dinero] wallet - 2. [para documentos] briefcase; [sin asa] portfolio; [de colegial] satchel - 3. COM, FIN & POLÍT portfolio - 4. [bolsillo] pocket flap - 5. Andes & C Sur [bolso] handbag UK, purse US.

carterista smf pickpocket.

cartero, ra sm, f postman (f postwoman).

cartílago sm cartilage.

cartilla sf - 1. [documento] book; cartilla (de ahorros) savings book - 2. [para aprender a leer] primer.

cartón sm - 1. [material] cardboard; cartón piedra papier mâché - 2. [de cigarrillos, leche] carton; [de huevos] box.

cartucho sm [de arma] cartridge; quemar el último cartucho to play one's last card.

cartujo, ja adj Carthusian.

cartulina sf card; cartulina amarilla/roja FÚT yellow/red card.

casa *sf* - 1. [edificio] house; **casa adosada** semi-detached house; **casa de campo** country house; **casa unifamiliar** *house (usually detached) on an estate*; **se le cae la casa encima** [se deprime] it's the end of the world for him; **en casa del herrero cuchillo de palo** *prov* the shoemaker's wife is always worst shod - 2. [hogar] home; **en casa** at home; **ir a casa** to go home; **pásate por mi casa** come round to my place; **jugar en casa/fuera de casa** to play at home/away - 3. [empresa] company; **vino de la casa** house wine - 4. [organismo]: **casa Consistorial** town hall; **casa de huéspedes** guesthouse; **casa de juego** gambling house; **casa de putas** brothel; **casa de socorro** first-aid post.

casaca *sf* frock coat.

casado, da *adj*: **casado (con)** married (to).

casamiento *sm* wedding, marriage.

casar ◇ *vt* - 1. [en matrimonio] to marry - 2. [unir] to fit together. ◇ *vi* to match. ◆ **casarse** *vprnl*: **casarse (con)** to get married (to).

cascabel *sm* (small) bell.

cascado, da *adj* - 1. *fam* [estropeado] bust; [persona, ropa] worn-out - 2. [ronco] rasping. ◆ **cascada** *sf* [de agua] waterfall.

cascanueces *sm inv* nutcracker.

cascar *vt* - 1. [romper] to crack - 2. *fam* [pegar] to thump. ◆ **cascarse** *vprnl* [romperse] to crack; **cascársela** *vulg* to jerk off.

cáscara *sf* - 1. [de almendra, huevo etc] shell - 2. [de limón, naranja] skin, peel - 3. [de plátano] skin.

cascarilla *sf* husk.

cascarón *sm* eggshell; **salir del cascarón** *fig* to leave the nest.

cascarrabias *smf inv* grouch.

casco *sm* - 1. [para la cabeza] helmet; [de motorista] crash helmet - 2. [de barco] hull - 3. [de ciudad]: **casco antiguo** old (part of) town; **casco urbano** city centre - 4. [de caballo] hoof - 5. [envase] empty bottle.

caserío *sm* [casa de campo] country house.

casero, ra ◇ *adj* - 1. [de casa - comida] home-made; [- trabajos] domestic; [- reunión, velada] at home; [de la familia] family *(antes de s)* - 2. [hogareño] home-loving. ◇ *sm, f* [propietario] landlord (*f* landlady).

caserón *sm* large, rambling house.

caseta *sf* - 1. [casa pequeña] hut - 2. [en la playa] bathing hut - 3. [de feria] stall, booth - 4. [para perro] kennel - 5. *Méx*: **caseta de cobro** tollbooth; **caseta telefónica** phone box, phone booth *US*.

casete, cassette [ka'sete] ◇ *sf* [cinta] cassette. ◇ *sm* [aparato] cassette recorder.

casi *adv* almost; **casi me muero** I almost O nearly died; **casi no dormí** I hardly slept at all; **casi, casi** almost, just about; **casi nunca** hardly ever; **casi nada** hardly anything.

casilla *sf* - 1. [de caja, armario] compartment; [para cartas] pigeonhole; **casilla de correos** *Andes* & *R Dom* PO Box; **casilla postal** *Amér C, Caribe* & *Méx* PO Box - 2. [en un impreso] box - 3. [de ajedrez etc] square - 4. *Méx* [de votación] polling booth.

casillero *sm* - 1. [mueble] set of pigeonholes - 2. [casilla] pigeonhole.

casino *sm* [para jugar] casino.

caso *sm* - 1. [gen, DER & GRAM] case; **el caso es que... que...** the fact is (that)...; **en el mejor/peor de los casos** at best/worst; **en todo caso** in any case; **caso clínico** clinical case - 2. [ocasión] occasion; **en caso de** in the event of; **en caso de que** if; **(en) caso de que venga** should she come; **en cualquier** O **todo caso** in any event O case - 3. *loc*: **hacer caso a** to pay attention to; **tú ni caso** take no notice.

caspa *sf* dandruff.

casquete *sm* [gorro] skullcap.

casquillo *sm* [de munición] case; **casquillo de bala** bullet shell.

cassette = casete.

casta *sf* ➞ **casto.**

castaña *sf* ➞ **castaño.**

castañetear *vi* [dientes] to chatter.

castaño, ña *adj* [color] chestnut. ◆ **castaño** *sm* - 1. [color] chestnut - 2. [árbol] chestnut (tree). ◆ **castaña** *sf* [fruto] chestnut.

castañuela *sf* castanet; **estar como unas castañuelas** to be very happy.

castellano, na *adj* & *sm, f* Castilian. ◆ **castellano** *sm* [lengua] (Castilian) Spanish.

castidad *sf* chastity.

castigador, ra *fam adj* seductive.

castigar *vt* - 1. [imponer castigo] to punish - 2. DEP to penalize - 3. [maltratar] to damage.

castigo *sm* - 1. [sanción] punishment - 2. [sufrimiento] suffering *(U)*; [daño] damage *(U)* - 3. DEP penalty.

castillo *sm* [edificio] castle; **castillos en el aire** O **de naipes** *fig* castles in the air; **castillo de naipes** house of cards.

castizo, za *adj* pure; [autor] purist.

casto, ta *adj* chaste. ◆ **casta** *sf* - 1. [linaje] lineage - 2. [especie, calidad] breed - 3. [en la India] caste.

castor *sm* beaver.

castrar *vt* [animal, persona] to castrate; [gato] to doctor.

castrense *adj* military.

casual *adj* chance, accidental.

casualidad *sf* coincidence; **fue pura casualidad** it was sheer coincidence; **dio la casualidad de que...** it so happened that..., **por casualidad** by chance; **¡qué casualidad!** what a coincidence!

casualmente *adv* by chance.

casulla *sf* chasuble.

cataclismo *sm* cataclysm.

catacumbas *sfpl* catacombs.

catador, ra *sm, f* taster.

catalán, ana *adj & sm, f* Catalan, Catalonian. **catalán** *sm* [lengua] Catalan.

catalejo *sm* telescope.

catalizador, ra *adj fig* [impulsor] catalysing *(antes de s).* **catalizador** *sm* - **1.** *fig & QUÍM* catalyst - **2.** AUTO catalytic converter.

catalogar *vt* - **1.** [en catálogo] to catalogue - **2.** [clasificar]: **catalogar a alguien (de)** to class sb (as).

catálogo *sm* catalogue.

Cataluña *n pr* Catalonia.

catamarán *sm* catamaran.

cataplasma *sf* MED poultice.

catapulta *sf* catapult.

catar *vt* to taste.

catarata *sf* - **1.** [de agua] waterfall - **2.** *(gen pl)* MED cataract.

catarro *sm* cold.

catastro *sm* land registry.

catástrofe *sf* catastrophe; [accidente] disaster; **catástrofe aérea** air disaster; **catástrofe natural** natural disaster.

catastrófico, ca *adj* catastrophic.

catch [katʃ] *sm* DEP all-in wrestling.

catchup ['katʃup], **ketchup** *sm inv* ketchup.

catear *vt fam* - **1.** *Esp*: **he cateado las matemáticas** I failed *O* flunked *US* maths - **2.** *Amér* [registrar] to search.

catecismo *sm* catechism.

Catedr. *(abrev de catedrático)* Prof.

cátedra *sf* - **1.** [cargo - en universidad] chair; [- en instituto] post of head of department - **2.** [departamento] department.

catedral *sf* cathedral.

catedrático, ca *sm, f* [de universidad] professor; [de instituto] head of department.

categoría *sf* - **1.** [gen] category; **categoría gramatical** part of speech - **2.** [posición social] standing; **de categoría** important - **3.** [calidad] quality; **de (primera) categoría** first-class.

categórico, ca *adj* categorical.

catequesis *sf inv* catechesis.

cateto *ta despec sm, f* country bumpkin.

catolicismo *sm* Catholicism.

católico, ca *adj* Catholic. *sm, f* Catholic.

catorce *num* fourteen; *ver también* **seis**.

catorceavo, va *num* fourteenth.

catre *sm* [cama] camp bed; **irse al catre** *fam* to hit the sack.

catrín, ina *sm, f Amér C & Méx fam* toff.

cauce *sm* - **1.** *fig & AGRIC* channel - **2.** [de río] river-bed; **volver a su cauce** to return to normal.

caucho *sm* [sustancia] rubber; **caucho vulcanizado** vulcanized rubber.

caudaloso, sa *adj* - **1.** [río] with a large flow - **2.** [persona] wealthy, rich.

caudillo *sm* [en la guerra] leader, head.

causa *sf* - **1.** [origen, ideal] cause; **por una buena causa** for a good cause - **2.** [razón] reason; **a causa de** because of - **3.** DER case.

causalidad *sf* causality.

causante *adj*: **la razón causante** the cause.

causar *vt* [gen] to cause; [impresión] to make; [placer] to give; **causar asombro a alguien** to amaze sb.

cáustico, ca *adj lit & fig* caustic.

cautela *sf* caution, cautiousness.

cauteloso, sa *adj* cautious, careful.

cautivador, ra *adj* captivating, enchanting. *sm, f* charmer.

cautivar *vt* - **1.** [apresar] to capture - **2.** [seducir] to captivate, to enchant.

cautiverio *sm* captivity.

cautividad *sf* = **cautiverio**.

cautivo, va *adj & sm, f* captive.

cauto, ta *adj* cautious, careful.

cava *sm* [bebida] cava. *sf* [bodega] wine cellar.

cavar *vt & vi* [gen] to dig; [con azada] to hoe.

caverna *sf* cave; [más grande] cavern.

cavernícola *smf* caveman (*f* cavewoman).

caviar *sm* caviar.

cavidad *sf* cavity; [formada con las manos] cup.

cavilar *vi* to think deeply, to ponder.

cayado *sm* [de pastor] crook.

cayera *etc* **caer**.

caza *sf* - **1.** [acción de cazar] hunting; **dar caza a** to hunt down; **caza de brujas** *fig* witch-hunt - **2.** [animales, carne] game. *sm* fighter (plane).

cazabombardero *sm* fighter-bomber.

cazador, ra *sm, f* [persona] hunter; **cazador furtivo** poacher. **cazadora** *sf* [prenda] bomber jacket.

cazalla *sf* [bebida] aniseed-flavoured spirit.

cazar *vt* - **1.** [animales etc] to hunt - **2.** *fig* [pillar, atrapar] to catch; [en matrimonio] to trap.

cazo *sm* saucepan.

cazoleta *sf* - **1.** [recipiente] pot - **2.** [de pipa] bowl.

cazuela *sf* - **1.** [recipiente] pot; [de barro] earthenware pot; [para el horno] casserole (dish) - **2.** [guiso] casserole, stew; **a la cazuela** casseroled.

cazurro, rra *adj* [bruto] stupid.

cc - **1.** (*abrev de* **centímetro cúbico**) cc *(cubic centimetre)* - **2.** (*abrev de* **copia de carbón**) cc *(carbon copy)*.

c/c (*abrev de* **cuenta corriente**) a/c.

CC (*abrev de* **corriente continua**) DC.

CC OO (*abrev de* **Comisiones Obreras**) *sfpl* Spanish Communist-inspired trade union.

CD *sm* - **1.** (*abrev de* **compact disc**) CD - **2.** (*abrev de* **club deportivo**) sports club; [en fútbol] FC.

CE *sf* - **1.** (*abrev de* **Comunidad Europea**) EC - **2.** (*abrev de* **Comisión Europea**) EC.

cebada *sf* barley.

cebar *vt* - **1.** [sobrealimentar] to fatten (up) - **2.** [máquina, arma] to prime - **3.** [anzuelo] to bait - **4.** *R Dom* [mate] to prepare, to brew. ➤ **cebarse en** *vprnl* to take it out on.

cebo *sm* - **1.** [para cazar] bait - **2.** *fig* [para atraer] incentive.

cebolla *sf* onion.

cebolleta *sf* - **1.** BOT spring onion - **2.** [en vinagre] pickled onion; [muy pequeña] silverskin onion.

cebollino *sm* - **1.** BOT chive; [cebolleta] spring onion - **2.** *fam* [necio] idiot.

cebra *sf* zebra.

cecear *vi* to lisp.

ceceo *sm* lisp.

cecina *sf* dried, salted meat.

cedazo *sm* sieve.

ceder ◇ *vt* - **1.** [traspasar, transferir] to hand over - **2.** [conceder] to give up; **'ceda el paso'** 'give way'; **ceder la palabra a alguien** to give the floor to sb. ◇ *vi* - **1.** [venirse abajo] to give way - **2.** [destensarse] to give, to become loose - **3.** [disminuir] to abate - **4.** [rendirse] to give up; **ceder a** to give in to - **5.** [ensancharse] to stretch.

cedro *sm* cedar.

cédula *sf* document; **cédula hipotecaria** mortgage bond.

cegar *vt* - **1.** [gen] to blind - **2.** [tapar - ventana] to block off; [- tubo] to block up. ➤ **cegarse** *vprnl lit & fig* to be blinded.

cegato, ta *fam adj* short-sighted.

ceguera *sf lit & fig* blindness.

ceja *sf* ANAT eyebrow; **quemarse las cejas** *fam* to burn the midnight oil; **tener a alguien entre ceja y ceja** *fam* not to be able to stand the sight of sb.

cejar *vi*: **cejar en** to give up on.

CELAM *sm* (*abrev de* **Consejo Episcopal Latinoamericano**) *Latin American Episcopal Council*.

celda *sf* cell; **celda de castigo** solitary confinement cell.

celebración *sf* - **1.** [festejo] celebration - **2.** [realización] holding.

celebrar *vt* - **1.** [festejar] to celebrate - **2.** [llevar a cabo] to hold; [oficio religioso] to celebrate - **3.** [alegrarse de] to be delighted with - **4.** [alabar] to praise. ➤ **celebrarse** *vprnl* - **1.** [festejarse] to be celebrated; **esa fiesta se celebra el 24 de julio** that festival falls on 24th July - **2.** [llevarse a cabo] to take place.

célebre *adj* famous, celebrated.

celebridad *sf* - **1.** [fama] fame - **2.** [persona famosa] celebrity.

celeridad *sf* speed.

celeste *adj* [del cielo] celestial, heavenly.

celestial *adj* celestial, heavenly.

celestina *sf* lovers' go-between.

celibato *sm* celibacy.

célibe *adj* & *smf* celibate.

celo *sm* - **1.** [esmero] zeal, keenness - **2.** [devoción] devotion - **3.** [de animal] heat; **en celo** on heat, in season - **4.** [cinta adhesiva] Sellotape® UK, Scotch tape® US. ➤ **celos** *smpl* jealousy (U); **dar celos a alguien** to make sb jealous; **tener celos de alguien** to be jealous of sb.

celofán *sm* cellophane.

celosía *sf* lattice window, jalousie.

celoso, sa *adj* - **1.** [con celos] jealous - **2.** [cumplidor] keen, eager.

celta ◇ *adj* Celtic. ◇ *smf* [persona] Celt. ◇ *sm* [lengua] Celtic.

céltico, ca *adj* Celtic.

célula *sf* cell. ➤ **célula fotoeléctrica** *sf* photoelectric cell, electric eye. ➤ **célula madre** *sf* stem cell.

celulitis *sf inv* cellulitis.

celulosa *sf* cellulose.

cementerio *sm* - **1.** [para personas] cemetery, graveyard - **2.** [de cosas inutilizables] dump; **cementerio nuclear** *O* **radioactivo** nuclear dumping ground.

cemento *sm* [gen] cement; [hormigón] concrete; **cemento armado** reinforced concrete.

cena *sf* dinner, evening meal; **cena de despedida** farewell dinner; **cena de negocios** business dinner.

cenagal *sm* bog, marsh.

cenagoso, sa *adj* muddy, boggy.

cenar ◇ *vt* to have for dinner. ◇ *vi* to have dinner.

cencerro *sm* cowbell; **estar como un cencerro** *fam fig* to be as mad as a hatter.

cenefa *sf* border.

cenicero *sm* ashtray.

cenit, zenit *sm lit & fig* zenith.

cenizo, za *adj* ashen, ash-grey. ➤ **cenizo** *sm* - **1.** [mala suerte] bad luck - **2.** [gafe] jinx. ➤ **ceniza** *sf* ash. ➤ **cenizas** *sfpl* [de cadáver] ashes.

censar *vt* to take a census of.

censo *sm* - **1.** [padrón] census; **censo de población** population census; **censo electoral** electoral roll - **2.** [tributo] tax.

censor, ra *sm, f* [funcionario] censor.

censura *sf* - **1.** [prohibición] censorship - **2.** [organismo] censors *pl* - **3.** [reprobación] censure, severe criticism.

censurar *vt* - **1.** [prohibir] to censor - **2.** [reprobar] to censure.

centavo, va *num* hundredth.

centella *sf* - **1.** [rayo] flash - **2.** [chispa] spark.

centellear *vi* [luz] to sparkle; [estrella] to twinkle.

centelleo *sm* [de luz] sparkle, sparkling *(U)*; [de estrella] twinkle, twinkling *(U)*.

centena *sf* hundred; **una centena de** a hundred.

centenar *sm* hundred; **a centenares** by the hundred.

centenario, ria *adj* [persona] in one's hundreds; [cifra] three-figure *(antes de s)*. ➤ **centenario** *sm* centenary.

centeno *sm* rye.

centésimo, ma *num* hundredth.

centígrado, da *adj* centigrade.

centigramo *sm* centigram.

centilitro *sm* centilitre.

centímetro *sm* centimetre.

céntimo *sm* [moneda] cent; **estar sin un céntimo** *fig* to be flat broke.

centinela *sm* sentry.

centollo *sm* spider crab.

centrado, da *adj* - **1.** [basado]: **centrado en** based on - **2.** [equilibrado] stable, steady - **3.** [rueda, cuadro etc] centred.

central ◇ *adj* central. ◇ *sf* - **1.** [oficina] headquarters, head office; [de correos, comunicaciones] main office - **2.** [de energía] power station; **central hidroeléctrica** *O* **hidráulica/nuclear/térmica** hydroelectric/nuclear/thermal power station; **central camionera** *Méx* bus station.

centralista *adj & smf* centralist.

centralita *sf* switchboard.

centralización *sf* centralization.

centralizar *vt* to centralize.

centrar *vt* - **1.** [gen & DEP] to centre - **2.** [arma] to aim - **3.** [persona] to steady - **4.** [atención, in-

terés] to be the centre of. ➤ **centrarse** *vprnl* - **1.** [concentrarse]: **centrarse en** to concentrate *O* focus on - **2.** [equilibrarse] to find one's feet.

céntrico, ca *adj* central.

centrifugadora *sf* [para secar ropa] spin-dryer.

centrifugar *vt* [ropa] to spin-dry.

centrista *adj* centre *(antes de s)*.

centro *sm* - **1.** [gen] centre; **centro nervioso/óptico** nerve/optic centre; **centro de desintoxicación** detoxification centre; **centro de planificación familiar** family planning clinic; **centro social** community centre - **2.** [de ciudad] town centre; **me voy al centro** I'm going to town; **centro urbano** town centre. ➤ **centro comercial** *sm* shopping centre. ➤ **centro de mesa** *sm* centrepiece. ➤ **centro de salud** *sm* health centre.

Centroamérica *sf* Central America.

centroamericano, na *adj* Central American.

centrocampista *smf* DEP midfielder.

ceñir *vt* - **1.** [apretar] to be tight on - **2.** [abrazar] to embrace. ➤ **ceñirse** *vprnl* - **1.** [apretarse] to tighten - **2.** [limitarse]: **ceñirse a** to keep *O* stick to.

ceño *sm* frown, scowl.

cepa *sf lit & fig* stock; **de pura cepa** [auténtico] real, genuine; [pura sangre] thoroughbred.

cepillar *vt* - **1.** [ropa, pelo, dientes] to brush - **2.** [madera] to plane.

cepillo *sm* - **1.** [para limpiar] brush; [para pelo] hairbrush; **cepillo de dientes** toothbrush - **2.** [de carpintero] plane.

cepo *sm* - **1.** [para cazar] trap - **2.** [para vehículos] wheel clamp - **3.** [para sujetar] clamp.

cera *sf* [gen] wax; [de abeja] beeswax; **hacerse la cera en las piernas** to wax one's legs; **cera depilatoria** hair-removing wax.

cerámica *sf* - **1.** [arte] ceramics *(U)*, pottery - **2.** [objeto] piece of pottery.

ceramista *smf* potter.

cebiche = ceviche

cerca ◇ *sf* [valla] fence. ◇ *adv* near, close; **por aquí cerca** nearby; **de cerca** [examinar, ver] closely; [afectar, vivir] deeply. ➤ **cerca de** *loc prep* - **1.** [en el espacio] near, close to - **2.** [aproximadamente] nearly, about.

cercado *sm* - **1.** [valla] fence - **2.** [lugar] enclosure.

cercanía *sf* [proximidad] nearness. ➤ **cercanías** *sfpl* [de ciudad] outskirts, suburbs.

cercano, na *adj* - **1.** [pueblo, lugar] nearby - **2.** [tiempo] near - **3.** [pariente, fuente de información]: **cercano (a)** close (to).

cercar *vt* - **1.** [vallar] to fence (off) - **2.** [rodear, acorralar] to surround.

cerciorar *vt* to assure.

cerco *sm* - **1.** [gen] circle, ring - **2.** [de puerta, ventana] frame - **3.** [asedio] siege; **poner cerco a** to lay siege to - **4.** *Amér* [valla] fence.

cerdo, da *sm, f* - **1.** [animal] pig (*f* sow) - **2.** *fam fig* [persona] pig, swine. ◆ **cerda** *sf* [pelo - de cerdo, jabalí] bristle; [- de caballo] horsehair.

cereal *sm* cereal; **cereales** (breakfast) cereal *(U)*.

cerebro *sm* - **1.** [gen] brain - **2.** *fig* [cabecilla] brains *sing* - **3.** *fig* [inteligencia] brains *pl*.

ceremonia *sf* ceremony.

ceremonial *adj* & *sm* ceremonial.

ceremonioso, sa *adj* ceremonious.

cereza *sf* cherry.

cerezo *sm* [árbol] cherry tree.

cerilla *sf* match.

cerillo *sm Amér C, Ecuad & Méx* match.

cerner, cernir *vt* [cribar] to sieve. ◆ **cernerse** *vprnl* - **1.** [ave, avión] to hover - **2.** *fig* [amenaza, peligro] to loom.

cernícalo *sm* - **1.** [ave] kestrel - **2.** *fam* [bruto] brute.

cernir = cerner.

cero ◇ *adj inv* zero. ◇ *sm* - **1.** [signo] nought, zero; [en fútbol] nil; [en tenis] love; **dos goles a cero** two goals to nil, two nil - **2.** [cantidad] nothing - **3.** FÍS & METEOR zero; **cero absoluto** absolute zero - **4.** *loc*: **ser un cero a la izquierda** *fam* [un inútil] to be useless; [un don nadie] to be a nobody; **partir de cero** to start from scratch; *ver también* **seis**.

cerquillo *sm Amér* fringe *UK*, bangs *US pl*.

cerrado, da *adj* - **1.** [al exterior] closed, shut; [con llave, pestillo etc] locked; **cerrado a** closed to - **2.** [tiempo, cielo] overcast; **era noche cerrada** it was completely dark - **3.** [rodeado] surrounded; [por montañas] walled in - **4.** [circuito] closed - **5.** [curva] sharp, tight - **6.** [vocal] close - **7.** [acento, deje] broad, thick.

cerradura *sf* lock.

cerrajero, ra *sm, f* locksmith.

cerrar ◇ *vt* - **1.** [gen] to close; [puerta, cajón, boca] to shut, to close; [puños] to clench; [con llave, pestillo etc] to lock - **2.** [tienda, negocio - definitivamente] to close down - **3.** [apagar] to turn off - **4.** [bloquear - suj: accidente, inundación etc] to block; [- suj: policía etc] to close off - **5.** [tapar - agujero, hueco] to fill, to block (up); [- bote] to put the lid *O* top on - **6.** [cercar] to fence (off) - **7.** [cicatrizar] to heal - **8.** [ir último en] to bring up the rear of - **9.:** **cerrar un trato** to seal a deal. ◇ *vi* to close, to shut; [con llave, pestillo etc] to lock up. ◆ **cerrarse** *vprnl* - **1.** [al exterior] to close, to shut - **2.** [incomuni-

carse] to clam up; **cerrarse a** to close one's mind to - **3.** [herida] to heal, to close up - **4.** [acto, debate, discusión etc] to close - **5.** [vocal] to close.

cerrazón *sf fig* stubbornness, obstinacy.

cerro *sm* hill; **irse por los cerros de Úbeda** to stray from the point.

cerrojo *sm* bolt.

certamen *sm* competition, contest.

certero, ra *adj* - **1.** [tiro] accurate - **2.** [opinión, respuesta etc] correct.

certeza *sf* certainty.

certidumbre *sf* certainty.

certificación *sf* - **1.** [hecho] certification - **2.** [documento] certificate.

certificado, da *adj* - **1.** [gen] certified; [carta, paquete] registered. ◆ **certificado** *sm* certificate; **certificado de depósito** BANCA certificate of deposit; **certificado de estudios** school-leaving certificate; **certificado de origen** COM certificate of origin.

certificar *vt* - **1.** [constatar] to certify - **2.** [en correos] to register.

cerumen *sm* earwax.

cervato *sm* fawn.

cervecería *sf* - **1.** [fábrica] brewery - **2.** [bar] bar.

cervecero, ra *sm, f* [que hace cerveza] brewer.

cerveza *sf* beer; **cerveza de barril** draught beer; **cerveza negra** stout; **cerveza rubia** lager.

cesante *adj* - **1.** [destituido] sacked; [ministro] removed from office - **2.** *C Sur & Méx* [en paro] unemployed.

cesantear *vt Chile & R Dom* to make redundant.

cesar ◇ *vt* [destituir] to sack; [ministro] to remove from office. ◇ *vi* [parar]: **cesar (de hacer algo)** to stop *O* cease (doing sthg); **no cesaba de llorar** he didn't stop crying; **no cesa de intentarlo** she keeps trying; **sin cesar** nonstop, incessantly.

cesárea *sf* caesarean (section).

cese *sm* - **1.** [detención, paro] stopping, ceasing - **2.** [destitución] sacking; [de ministro] removal from office.

cesión *sf* cession, transfer; **cesión de bienes** surrender of property.

césped *sm* [hierba] lawn, grass *(U)*. ◆ **césped artificial** *sm* artificial turf.

cesta *sf* basket. ◆ **cesta de la compra** *sf* - **1.** *fig* cost of living - **2.** [para compras en Internet] shopping basket. ◆ **cesta de Navidad** *sf* Christmas hamper.

cesto *sm* [cesta] (large) basket.

cetro *sm* - **1.** [vara] sceptre - **2.** *fig* [reinado] reign.

ceviche, cebiche *sm Méx* dish with raw fish or seafood, marinated in onion, lemon juice and pepper.

cf., cfr. *(abrev de* **confróntese)** cf.

cg *(abrev de centigramo)* cg.

chabacano, na *adj* vulgar. ◆ **chabacano** *sm Méx* [fruto] apricot.

chabola *sf* shack; **barrios de chabolas** shanty town *sing*.

chacal *sm* jackal.

chacarero, ra *sm, f Andes & R Plata* [agricultor] farmer.

chacha *sf* maid.

chachachá *sm* cha-cha.

cháchara *sf fam* chatter, nattering; **estar de cháchara** to have a natter.

chacra *sf Andes & R Plata* farm.

chafar *vt* - **1.** [aplastar] to flatten - **2.** *fig* [estropear] to spoil, to ruin. ◆ **chafarse** *vprnl* [estropearse] to be ruined.

chaflán *sm* [de edificio] corner.

chagra *Amér* ◇ *smf* peasant, person from the country. ◇ *sf* farm.

chal *sm* shawl.

chalado, da *fam adj* crazy, mad.

chalar *vt* to drive round the bend.

chalé, chalet *(pl* **chalets)** *sm* [gen] detached house (with garden); [en el campo] cottage; [de alta montaña] chalet;: **chalé pareado** semi-detached house.

chaleco *sm* waistcoat, vest *US*; [de punto] tank-top; **chaleco salvavidas** life jacket.

chalet = chalé.

chamaco, ca *sm, f Méx fam* kid.

chamarra *sf* sheepskin jacket.

chamba *sf Amér C, Méx, Perú & Ven fam* odd job.

chamiza *sf* [hierba] thatch.

chamizo *sm* - **1.** [leña] half-burnt wood *(U)* - **2.** [casa] thatched hut.

champán, champaña *sm* champagne.

champiñón *sm* mushroom.

champú *(pl* **champús** *O* **champúes)** *sm* shampoo.

chamuscar *vt* to scorch; [cabello, barba, tela] to singe. ◆ **chamuscarse** *vprnl* [cabello, barba, tela] to get singed.

chamusquina *sf* scorch, scorching *(U)*; **me huele a chamusquina** *fam fig* it smells a bit fishy to me.

chance ◇ *sf Amér* opportunity, chance. ◇ *adv Méx* maybe.

chanchada *sf Amér* [trastada] dirty trick.

chancho, cha *fam adj* [sucio] filthy. ◆ **chancho** *sm* - **1.** [animal] pig *(f* **sow)** - **2.** [persona] slob - **3.** [carne] pork.

chanchullo *sm fam* fiddle, racket.

chancla *sf* [chancleta] low sandal; [para la playa] flip-flop.

chancleta *sf* low sandal; [para la playa] flip-flop.

chándal *(pl* **chándales** *O* **chandals), chandal** *(pl* **chandals)** *sm* tracksuit.

changarro *sm Méx* small store.

chantaje *sm* blackmail; **hacer chantaje a** to blackmail; **chantaje emocional** emotional blackmail.

chantajear *vt* to blackmail.

chanza *sf* joke; **estar de chanza** to be joking.

chao *interj:* **¡chao!** *fam* bye!, see you!

chapa *sf* - **1.** [lámina - de metal] sheet; [- de madera] board; **de tres chapas** three-ply - **2.** [tapón] top, cap - **3.** [insignia] badge - **4.** [ficha de guardarropa] metal token *O* disc - **5.** *Col, Cuba & Méx* [cerradura] lock - **6.** *R Dom* [de matrícula] number plate *UK*, license plate *US*. ◆ **chapas** *sfpl* [juego] children's game played with bottle tops.

chapado, da *adj* [con metal] plated; [con madera] veneered; **chapado a la antigua** *fig* stuck in the past, old-fashioned.

chaparro, rra ◇ *adj* short and squat. ◇ *sm, f* [persona] short, squat person.

chaparrón *sm* downpour; *fam fig* [gran cantidad] torrent.

chapata *sf* ciabatta.

chapopote *sm Caribe & Méx* bitumen, pitch.

chapotear *vi* to splash about.

chapucear *vt* to botch (up).

chapucero, ra ◇ *adj* [trabajo] shoddy; [persona] bungling. ◇ *sm, f* bungler.

chapulín *sm Amér C & Méx* - **1.** [saltamontes] grasshopper - **2.** *fam* [niño] kid.

chapurrear, chapurrar *vt* to speak badly.

chapuza *sf* - **1.** [trabajo mal hecho] botch (job) - **2.** [trabajo ocasional] odd job.

chapuzón *sm* dip; **darse un chapuzón** to go for a dip.

chaqué *sm* morning coat.

chaqueta *sf* jacket; [de punto] cardigan.

chaquetón *sm* short coat.

charanga *sf* [banda] brass band.

charca *sf* pool, pond.

charco *sm* puddle; **cruzar el charco** *fig* to cross the pond *O* Atlantic.

charcutería *sf* - **1.** [tienda] shop selling cold cooked meats and cheeses, ≃ delicatessen - **2.** [productos] cold cuts *pl* and cheese.

charla *sf* - **1.** [conversación] chat - **2.** [conferencia] talk.

charlar *vi* to chat.

charlatán, ana <> adj talkative. <> sm, f
- **1.** [hablador] chatterbox - **2.** [mentiroso] trickster, charlatan.

charlotada sf [payasada] clowning around
(U).

charlotear vi to chat.

charnego, ga sm, f pejorative term referring
to immigrant to Catalonia from another part
of Spain.

charol sm - **1.** [piel] patent leather - **2.** Andes
[bandeja] tray.

charola sf Bol, Amér C & Méx tray.

chárter adj inv charter (antes de s).

chasca sf Andes [greña] mop of hair.

chascar <> vt - **1.** [lengua] to click - **2.** [dedos]
to snap. <> vi - **1.** [madera] to crack - **2.** [lengua]
to click.

chasco sm [decepción] disappointment; llevarse un chasco to be disappointed.

chasis sm inv AUTO chassis.

chasquear <> vt - **1.** [látigo] to crack - **2.** [la
lengua] to click. <> vi [madera] to crack.

chasquido sm [de látigo, madera, hueso] crack;
[de lengua, arma] click; [de dedos] snap.

chatarra sf - **1.** [metal] scrap (metal) - **2.** [obje-
tos, piezas] junk.

chateo sm - **1.** [en bar] pub crawl; ir de chateo
to go out drinking - **2.** INFORM chatting.

chato, ta <> adj - **1.** [nariz] snub; [persona]
snub-nosed - **2.** [aplanado] flat - **3.** R Dom [me-
diocre] commonplace. <> sm, f fam [apelativo]
love, dear. ◆ **chato** sm [de vino] small glass
of wine.

chau, chaucito interj Bol, C Sur & Perú fam
bye!, see you!

chauvinista = **chovinista**.

chaval, la sm, f fam kid, lad (f lass).

chavo, va fam sm, f Méx [joven] boy (f girl).
◆ **chavo** sm [dinero]: no tener un chavo to be
penniless.

che interj R Dom fam: ¿como andás, che? hey,
how's it going?; ¡che, vení para acá! hey, over
here, you!

Chechenia Chechnya.

checheno adj & sm, f Chechen.

checo, ca adj & sm, f Czech. ◆ **checo** sm
[lengua] Czech.

chef [tʃef] (pl chefs) sm chef.

chele, la Amér C <> adj [rubio] blond (f
blonde); [de piel blanca] fair-skinned. <> sm, f
[rubio] blond(e); [de piel blanca] fair-skinned
person.

chelín sm shilling.

chelo, la <> adj Amér blond (f blonde).
<> sm, f MÚS [instrumentista] cellist. ◆ **chelo**
sm MÚS [instrumento] cello.

cheque sm cheque UK, check US; **extender
un cheque** to make out a cheque; **cheque en
blanco/sin fondos** blank/bad cheque; **cheque
cruzado** O **barrado** crossed cheque; **cheque
(de) gasolina** petrol voucher; **cheque nomina-
tivo** cheque in favour of a specific person;
cheque al portador cheque payable to the
bearer; **cheque de viaje** O **de viajero** traveller's
cheque; **cheque regalo** gift voucher.

chequear vt - **1.** MED: **chequear a alguien** to
examine sb, to give sb a checkup - **2.** [compro-
bar] to check.

chequeo sm - **1.** MED checkup - **2.** [comproba-
ción] check, checking (U).

chequera sf chequebook UK, checkbook US.

chévere adj Andes, Amér C, Caribe & Méx
fam great, fantastic.

chic adj inv chic.

chica sf - **1.** [criada] maid - **2.** ver también **chico**.

chicano, na adj & sm, f Chicano, Mexican-
American. ◆ **chicano** sm [lengua] Chicano.

chicarrón, ona sm, f strapping lad (f strapping lass).

chícharo sm Amér C & Méx pea.

chicharra sf ZOOL cicada.

chicharro sm [pez] horse mackerel.

chicharrón sm [frito] pork crackling. ◆ **chi-
charrones** smpl [embutido] cold processed
meat made from pork.

chichón sm bump.

chicle sm chewing gum.

chiclé, chicler sm AUTO jet.

chico, ca <> adj [pequeño] small; [joven]
young; **cuando era chico** when I was little.
<> sm, f - **1.** [joven] boy (f girl) - **2.** [tratamien-
to - hombre] sonny, mate; [- mujer] darling.
◆ **chico** sm [recadero] messenger, office-
boy.

chicote sm Amér [látigo] whip.

chifla sf [silbido] whistle.

chiflado, da fam adj crazy, mad.

chiflar <> vt fam [encantar]: me chiflan las patatas fritas I'm mad about chips. <> vi [silbar]
to whistle.

chiflido sm Amér whistling.

chigüín, güina sm, f Amér C fam kid.

chile sm chilli; **chile con carne** CULIN chilli con
carne.

Chile n pr Chile.

chileno, na adj & sm, f Chilean.

chillar <> vi - **1.** [gritar - personas] to scream,
to yell; [- ave, mono] to screech; [- cerdo] to
squeal; [- ratón] to squeak - **2.** [chirriar] to
screech; [puerta, madera] to creak; [bisagras] to
squeak. <> vt fam [reñir] to yell at.

chillido sm [de persona] scream, yell; [de ave, mono] screech; [de cerdo] squeal; [de ratón] squeak.

chillón, ona adj - 1. [voz] piercing - 2. [persona] noisy - 3. [color] gaudy.

chimenea sf - 1. [hogar] fireplace - 2. [en tejado] chimney.

chimpancé sm chimpanzee.

china ➤ **chino**.

China n pr: **(la) China** China.

chinchar vt fam to pester, to bug. ◆ **chincharse** vprnl fam: **ahora te chinchas** now you can lump it.

chinche ◇ adj fam fig annoying. ◇ sf [insecto] bedbug.

chincheta sf drawing pin UK, thumbtack US.

chinchín sm [brindis] toast; ¡**chinchín!** cheers!

chinchón sm strong aniseed liquor.

chinga sf Méx mfam [paliza]: **me dieron una chinga** they kicked the shit out of me; [trabajo duro]: **es una chinga** it's a bitch of a job.

chingar Esp & Méx ◇ vt - 1. mfam [molestar]: **chingar a alguien** to get up sb's nose, to piss sb off - 2. mfam [estropear] to bust, to knacker UK - 3. vulg [acostarse con] to screw, to fuck. ◇ vi vulg [fornicar] to screw.

chino, na adj & sm, f - 1. Chinese - 2. Andes & R Plata [mestizo] person of mixed ancestry. ◆ **chino** sm - 1. [lengua] Chinese - 2. [piedra] pebble. ◆ **china** sf - 1. [piedra] pebble - 2. [porcelana] china.

chip (pl **chips**) sm INFORM chip.

chipirón sm baby squid.

Chipre n pr Cyprus.

chipriota adj & smf Cypriot.

chiquillo, lla sm, f kid.

chiquito, ta adj tiny; **no andarse con chiquitas** fig not to mess about. ◆ **chiquito** sm [de vino] small glass of wine.

chiribita sf [chispa] spark.

chirimbolo sm fam thingamajig.

chirimoya sf custard apple.

chiringuito sm fam [bar] refreshment stall.

chiripa sf fam fig fluke; **de O por chiripa** by luck.

chirivía sf BOT parsnip.

chirla sf small clam.

chirona sf fam clink, slammer; **en chirona** in the clink.

chirriar vi [gen] to screech; [puerta, madera] to creak; [bisagra, muelles] to squeak.

chirrido sm [gen] screech; [de puerta, madera] creak; [de bisagra, muelles] squeak.

chis, chist interj: ¡**chis!** ssh!

chisme sm - 1. [cotilleo] rumour, piece of gossip - 2. fam [cosa] thingamajig.

chismorrear vi to spread rumours, to gossip.

chismoso, sa ◇ adj gossipy. ◇ sm, f gossip, scandalmonger.

chispa sf - 1. [de fuego, electricidad] spark; **echar chispas** fam to be hopping mad - 2. [de lluvia] spot (of rain) - 3. fig [pizca] bit; **una chispa de sal** a pinch of salt - 4. fig [agudeza] sparkle.

chispear ◇ vi - 1. [chisporrotear] to spark - 2. [relucir] to sparkle. ◇ v impers [llover] to spit (with rain).

chisporrotear vi [fuego, leña] to crackle; [aceite] to splutter; [comida] to sizzle.

chist = **chis**.

chistar vi: **me fui sin chistar** I left without a word.

chiste sm joke; **contar chistes** to tell jokes; **chiste verde** dirty joke.

chistera sf [sombrero] top hat.

chistorra sf type of cured pork sausage typical of Aragon and Navarre.

chistoso, sa adj funny.

chita ◆ **a la chita callando** loc adv fam quietly, on the quiet.

chitón interj: ¡**chitón!** quiet!

chivar vt fam to tell secretly. ◆ **chivarse** vprnl fam: **chivarse (de/a)** [niños] to split (on/to); [delincuentes] to grass (on/to).

chivatazo sm fam tip-off; **dar el chivatazo** to grass.

chivato, ta sm, f fam [delator] grass, informer; [acústica] telltale.

chivo, va sm, f kid, young goat; **ser el chivo expiatorio** fig to be the scapegoat.

choc (pl **chocs**), **choque, shock** [tʃok] sm shock.

chocante adj startling.

chocar ◇ vi - 1. [colisionar]: **chocar (contra)** to crash (into), to collide (with) - 2. fig [enfrentarse] to clash. ◇ vt fig [sorprender] to startle.

chochear vi [viejo] to be senile.

chocho, cha adj - 1. [viejo] senile - 2. fam fig [encariñado] soft, doting.

choclo sm Andes & R Plata corncob, ear of maize O corn US.

chocolate sm [para comer, beber] chocolate; **chocolate (a la taza)** thick drinking chocolate; **chocolate blanco** white chocolate; **chocolate con leche** milk chocolate.

chocolatina sf chocolate bar.

chófer (pl **chóferes**) smf - 1. [como oficio - de automóvil] chauffeur; [- de autobús] driver - 2. Amér [conductor] driver.

chollo sm fam [producto, compra] bargain; [trabajo, situación] cushy number.

cholo, la *Amér* ◇ *adj* mestizo, mixed race. ◇ *sm, f* - **1.** [mestizo] *person of mixed race* - **2.** [indio] country bumpkin.

chomba, chompa *sf Andes* sweater.

chompipe *sm Amér C & Méx* turkey.

chongo *sm Méx* [moño] bun.

chopo *sm* poplar.

choque *sm* - **1.** [impacto] impact; [de coche, avión etc] crash; **choque frontal** head-on collision - **2.** *fig* [enfrentamiento] clash; **choque cultural** culture shock - **3.** = **choc.**

chorizar *vt fam* to nick, to pinch.

chorizo *sm* - **1.** [embutido] *highly seasoned pork sausage* - **2.** *fam* [ladrón] thief.

choro *sm Andes* mussel.

chorrada *sf mfam* rubbish (U); **eso es una chorrada** that's rubbish; **decir chorradas** to talk rubbish.

chorrear *vi* - **1.** [gotear - gota a gota] to drip; [- en un hilo] to trickle - **2.** [brotar] to spurt (out), to gush (out).

chorro *sm* - **1.** [de líquido - borbotón] jet, spurt; [- hilo] trickle; **salir a chorros** to spurt O gush out; **chorro de vapor** steam jet - **2.** *fig* [de luz, gente etc] stream; **tiene un chorro de dinero** she has loads of money; **a chorros** in abundance.

choteo *sm fam* joking, kidding; **tomar algo a choteo** to take sthg as a joke.

choto, ta *sm, f* - **1.** [cabrito] kid, young goat - **2.** [ternero] calf.

chovinista, chauvinista [tʃoβi'nista] ◇ *adj* chauvinistic. ◇ *smf* chauvinist.

choza *sf* hut.

christmas = **crismas.**

chubasco *sm* shower.

chubasquero *sm* raincoat, mac.

chúcaro, ra *adj Andes, Amér C & R Plata fam* [animal] wild; [persona] unsociable.

chuchería *sf* - **1.** [golosina] sweet - **2.** [objeto] trinket.

chucho *sm fam* mutt, dog.

chueco, ca *adj Amér* [torcido] twisted; *Méx fam* [proyecto, razonamiento] shady; *Amér* [patizambo] bowlegged.

chufa *sf* [tubérculo] tiger nut.

chulear *fam vi* [fanfarronear]: **chulear (de)** to be cocky (about).

chulería *sf* [descaro] cockiness.

chuleta *sf* - **1.** [de carne] chop; **chuleta de cordero** lamb chop - **2.** *fam* [en exámenes] crib note.

chulo, la ◇ *adj* - **1.** [descarado] cocky; **ponerse chulo** to get cocky - **2.** *fam* [bonito] lovely. ◇ *sm, f* [descarado] cocky person. ◆ **chulo** *sm* [proxeneta] pimp.

chumbera *sf* prickly pear.

chumbo ▷ **higo.**

chungo, ga *adj fam* [persona] horrible, nasty; [cosa] lousy. ◆ **chunga** *sf*: **tomarse algo a chunga** *fam* to take sthg as a joke.

chupa *sf fam*: **chupa de cuero** leather jacket.

chupachup® (*pl* chupachups) *sm* lollipop.

chupado, da *adj* - **1.** [delgado] skinny - **2.** *fam* [fácil]: **estar chupado** to be dead easy O a piece of cake. ◆ **chupada** *sf* [gen] suck; [fumando] puff, drag.

chupar *vt* - **1.** [succionar] to suck; [fumando] to puff at - **2.** [absorber] to soak up - **3.** [quitar]: **chuparle algo a alguien** to milk sb for sthg; **chuparle la sangre a alguien** *fig* to bleed sb dry.

chupe *sm Andes & Arg* stew.

chupete *sm* dummy *UK*, pacifier *US*.

chupi *adj fam* great, brill.

chupón, ona *sm, f fam* [gorrón] sponger, cadger. ◆ **chupón** *sm Méx* [chupete] dummy *UK*, pacifier *US*.

churrería *sf* shop selling "churros".

churro *sm* [para comer] *dough formed into sticks or rings and fried in oil*.

churrusco *sm* piece of burnt toast.

churumbel *sm fam* kid.

chusco, ca *adj* funny. ◆ **chusco** *sm fam* bread bun.

chusma *sf* rabble, mob.

chut (*pl* chuts) *sm* kick.

chutar *vi* [lanzar] to shoot. ◆ **chutarse** *vprnl mfam* to shoot up.

chute *sm* - **1.** FÚT shot - **2.** *mfam* [de droga] fix.

CIA (*abrev de* **Central Intelligence Agency**) *sf* CIA.

cía., Cía. (*abrev de* **compañía**) Co.

cianuro *sm* cyanide.

ciático, ca *adj* sciatic. ◆ **ciática** *sf* sciatica.

cibercafé *sm* cybercafe, Internet cafe.

ciberespacio *sm* cyberspace.

cicatero, ra *adj* stingy, mean.

cicatriz *sf lit & fig* scar.

cicatrizar ◇ *vi* to heal (up). ◇ *vt fig* to heal.

cicerone *smf* guide.

cíclico, ca *adj* cyclical.

ciclismo *sm* cycling.

ciclista *smf* cyclist.

ciclo *sm* - **1.** [gen] cycle; **ciclo vital** life cycle - **2.** [de conferencias, actos] series - **3.** [de enseñanza] stage.

ciclocrós *sm* cyclo-cross.

ciclomotor *sm* moped.

ciclón *sm* cyclone.

cicuta *sf* hemlock.

ciego, ga <> adj - **1.** [invidente] blind; **quedarse ciego** to go blind; **a ciegas** *lit & fig* blindly - **2.** *fig* [enloquecido]: **ciego (de)** blinded (by) - **3.** [pozo, tubería] blocked (up). <> *sm, f* [invidente] blind person; **los ciegos** the blind.

cielo *sm* - **1.** [gen] sky; [mina] opencast - **2.** RELIG heaven - **3.** [nombre cariñoso] my love, my dear - **4.** *loc:* **clama al cielo** it's outrageous; **ser un cielo** to be an angel. ➡ **cielos** *interj:* ¡cielos! good heavens!

ciempiés *sm inv* centipede.

cien ▷ **ciento**.

ciénaga *sf* marsh, bog.

ciencia *sf* [gen] science. ➡ **ciencias** *sfpl* EDUC science (U). ➡ **ciencia ficción** *sf* science fiction. ➡ **a ciencia cierta** *loc adv* for certain.

cieno *sm* mud, sludge.

científico, ca <> adj scientific. <> *sm, f* scientist.

cientista *smf C Sur:* **cientista social** social scientist.

ciento, cien *num* a O one hundred; **ciento cincuenta** a O one hundred and fifty; **cien mil** a O one hundred thousand; **cientos de** hundreds of; **por ciento** per cent; **ciento por ciento, cien por cien** a hundred per cent; **cientos de veces** hundreds of times; **a cientos** by the hundred; *ver también* **seis**.

cierne ➡ **en ciernes** *loc adv:* **estar en ciernes** to be in its infancy; **una campeona en ciernes** a budding champion.

cierre *sm* - **1.** [gen] closing, shutting; [con llave] locking; [de fábrica] shutdown; RADIO & TV closedown; **cierre patronal** lockout - **2.** [mecanismo] fastener; **cierre metálico** [de tienda etc] metal shutter; **cierre relámpago** *Andes, Arg & Méx* [cremallera] zip UK, zipper US.

cierto, ta *adj* - **1.** [verdadero] true; **estar en lo cierto** to be right; **lo cierto es que...** the fact is that... - **2.** [seguro] certain, definite - **3.** [algún] certain; **cierto hombre** a certain man; **en cierta ocasión** once, on one occasion; **durante cierto tiempo** for a while. ➡ **cierto** *adv* right, certainly. ➡ **por cierto** *loc adv* by the way.

ciervo, va *sm, f* deer, stag (f hind).

CIF (*abrev de* código de identificación fiscal) *sm* tax code.

cifra *sf* [gen] figure; **cifra de negocios** ECON turnover; **cifra de ventas** sales figures.

cifrar *vt* - **1.** [codificar] to code - **2.** *fig* [centrar] to concentrate, to centre. ➡ **cifrarse en** *vprnl* to amount to.

cigala *sf* Dublin Bay prawn.

cigarra *sf* cicada.

cigarrillo *sm* cigarette.

cigarro *sm* - **1.** [habano] cigar - **2.** [cigarrillo] cigarette.

cigüeña *sf* stork.

cigüeñal *sm* crankshaft.

cilindrada *sf* cylinder capacity.

cilíndrico, ca *adj* cylindrical.

cilindro *sm* [gen] cylinder; [de imprenta] roller.

cima *sf* - **1.** [punta - de montaña] peak, summit; [- de árbol] top - **2.** *fig* [apogeo] peak, high point.

cimbrear *vt* - **1.** [vara] to waggle - **2.** [caderas] to sway.

cimentar *vt* - **1.** [edificio] to lay the foundations of; [ciudad] to found, to build - **2.** *fig* [idea, paz, fama] to cement.

cimiento *sm (gen pl)* CONSTR foundation; **echar los cimientos** *lit & fig* to lay the foundations.

cinc, zinc *sm* zinc.

cincel *sm* chisel.

cincelar *vt* to chisel.

cincha *sf* girth.

cinco *num* five; ¡**choca esos cinco!** *fig* put it there!; **estar sin cinco** *fig* to be broke; *ver también* **seis**.

cincuenta *num* fifty; **los (años) cincuenta** the fifties; *ver también* **seis**.

cincuentón, ona *sm, f* fifty-year-old.

cine *sm* cinema; **hacer cine** to make films; **cine de estreno/de verano** first-run/open-air cinema; **cine de terror** horror films.

cineasta *smf* film maker O director.

cineclub *sm* - **1.** [asociación] film society - **2.** [sala] club cinema.

cinéfilo, la *sm, f* film buff.

cinematografía *sf* cinematography.

cinematográfico, ca *adj* film (*antes de s*).

cinematógrafo *sm* [local] cinema.

cínico, ca <> adj cynical. <> *sm, f* cynic.

cinismo *sm* cynicism.

cinta *sf* - **1.** [tira - de plástico, papel] strip, band; [- de tela] ribbon; **cinta métrica** tape measure - **2.** [de imagen, sonido, ordenadores] tape; **cinta digital/magnética** digital/magnetic tape; **cinta limpiadora** head-cleaning tape; **cinta magnetofónica** recording tape; **cinta de vídeo** videotape - **3.** [mecanismo] belt; **cinta transportadora** conveyor belt; **cinta de equipajes** baggage carousel - **4.** [película] film.

cintura *sf* waist.

cinturilla *sf* waistband.

cinturón *sm* - **1.** [cinto] belt - **2.** AUTO ring road - **3.** [cordón] cordon. ➡ **cinturón de castidad** *sm* chastity belt. ➡ **cinturón de seguridad** *sm* seat O safety belt. ➡ **cinturón de miseria** *sm Amér* slum or shanty town area round a large city.

ciprés *sm* cypress.

circo *sm* [gen] circus.

circuito sm - 1. DEP & ELECTRÓN.circuit - 2. [recorrido] tour.

circulación sf - 1. [gen] circulation; **circulación de la sangre** circulation of the blood; **circulación fiduciaria** O **monetaria** paper currency - 2. [tráfico] traffic.

circular ◇ adj & sf circular. ◇ vi - 1. [de mano en mano] to circulate; [moneda] to be in circulation - 2. [difundirse] to go round.

círculo sm lit & fig circle. ◈ **círculos** smpl [medios] circles. ◈ **círculo polar** sm polar circle; **el círculo polar ártico/antártico** the Arctic/Antarctic Circle. ◈ **círculo vicioso** sm vicious circle.

circuncisión sf circumcision.

circundante adj surrounding.

circundar vt to surround.

circunferencia sf circumference.

circunloquio sm circumlocution.

circunscribir vt - 1. [limitar] to restrict, to confine - 2. GEOM to circumscribe. ◈ **circunscribirse** a vprnl to confine o.s. to.

circunscripción sf [distrito] district; MIL division; POLÍT constituency.

circunscrito, ta ◇ pp ▷ **circunscribir**. ◇ adj restricted, limited.

circunstancia sf circumstance; **en estas circunstancias** under the circumstances.

circunstancial adj [accidental] chance (antes de s).

circunvalar vt to go round.

cirio sm (wax) candle; **montar un cirio** to make a row.

cirrosis sf inv cirrhosis.

ciruela sf plum; **ciruela pasa** prune.

cirugía sf surgery; **cirugía estética** O **plástica** cosmetic O plastic surgery.

cirujano, na sm, f surgeon.

cisco sm - 1. [carbón]·slack; **hecho cisco** fig shattered - 2. fam [alboroto] row, rumpus.

cisma sm - 1. [separación] schism - 2. [discordia] split.

cisne sm swan.

cisterna sf [de retrete] cistern.

cistitis sf inv cystitis.

cita sf - 1. [entrevista] appointment; [de novios] date; **concertar una cita** to make an appointment; **darse cita** to meet; **tener una cita** to have an appointment - 2. [referencia] quotation.

citación sf DER summons sing.

citar vt - 1. [convocar] to make an appointment with - 2. [aludir] to mention; [textualmente] to quote - 3. DER to summons. ◈ **citarse** vprnl: **citarse (con alguien)** to arrange to meet (sb).

citología sf - 1. [análisis] smear test - 2. BIOL cytology.

cítrico, ca adj citric. ◈ **cítricos** smpl citrus fruits.

CiU (abrev de **Convergència i Unió**) sf Catalan coalition party to the centre-right of the political spectrum.

ciudad sf [localidad] city; [pequeña] town. ◈ **Ciudad del Cabo** sf Cape Town. ◈ **Ciudad del Vaticano** sf Vatican City. ◈ **Ciudad de México** sf Mexico City.

ciudadanía sf - 1. [nacionalidad] citizenship - 2. [población] citizens pl.

ciudadano, na sm, f citizen.

cívico, ca adj civic; [conducta] public-spirited.

civil ◇ adj lit & fig civil. ◇ sm [no militar] civilian.

civilización sf civilization.

civilizado, da adj civilized.

civilizar vt to civilize.

civismo sm - 1. [urbanidad] community spirit - 2. [cortesía] civility, politeness.

cizaña sf BOT darnel.

cl (abrev de **centilitro**) cl.

clamar ◇ vt - 1. [expresar] to exclaim - 2. [exigir] to cry out for. ◇ vi - 1. [implorar] to appeal - 2. [protestar] to cry out.

clamor sm clamour.

clamoroso, sa adj - 1. [rotundo] resounding - 2. [vociferante] loud, clamorous.

clan sm - 1. [tribu, familia] clan - 2. [banda] faction.

clandestino, na adj clandestine; POLÍT underground.

claqué sm tap dancing.

claqueta sf clapperboard.

clara sf ▷ **claro**.

claraboya sf skylight.

clarear v impers - 1. [amanecer]: **empezaba a clarear** dawn was breaking - 2. [despejarse] to clear up. ◈ **clarearse** vprnl [transparentarse] to be see-through.

claridad sf - 1. [transparencia] clearness, clarity - 2. [luz] light - 3. [franqueza] candidness - 4. [lucidez] clarity; **explicar algo con claridad** to explain sthg clearly.

clarificar vt - 1. [gen] to clarify; [misterio] to clear up - 2. [purificar] to refine.

clarín sm [instrumento] bugle.

clarinete sm [instrumento] clarinet.

clarividencia sf farsightedness.

claro, ra adj - 1. [gen] clear; **claro está que...** of course...; **dejar algo claro** to make sthg clear; **a las claras** clearly; **pasar una noche en claro** to spend a sleepless night; **poner algo en claro** to get sthg clear, to clear sthg up; **sacar**

algo en claro (de) to make sthg out (from); **tener algo claro** to be sure of sthg - **2.** [luminoso] bright - **3.** [color] light - **4.** [diluido - té, café] weak. ◆ **claro** ◇ *sm* - **1.** [en bosque] clearing; [en multitud, texto] space, gap - **2.** METEOR bright spell. ◇ *adv* clearly. ◇ *interj* ¡claro! of course!; **¡claro que no!** of course not!; **¡claro que sí!** yes, of course. ◆ **clara** *sf* [de huevo] white.

clase *sf* - **1.** [gen] class; **clase alta/media** upper/middle class; **clase obrera** O **trabajadora** working class; **clase social** social class; **clase salón** *Amér* FERROC first class; **primera clase** first class - **2.** [tipo] sort, kind; **toda clase de** all sorts O kinds of - **3.** [EDUC - asignatura, alumnos] class; [- aula] classroom; **dar clases** [- en un colegio] to teach; [- en una universidad] to lecture; **clases particulares** private classes O lessons.

clásico, ca ◇ *adj* - **1.** [de la Antigüedad] classical - **2.** [ejemplar, prototípico] classic - **3.** [peinado, estilo, música etc] classical - **4.** [habitual] customary - **5.** [peculiar]: **clásico de** typical of. ◇ *sm, f* [persona] classic.

clasificación *sf* classification; DEP (league) table.

clasificar *vt* to classify. ◆ **clasificarse** *vprnl* [ganar acceso]: **clasificarse (para)** to qualify (for); DEP to get through (to).

clasista *adj* class-conscious; *despec* snobbish.

claudicar *vi* [ceder] to give in.

claustro *sm* - **1.** ARQUIT & RELIG cloister - **2.** [de universidad] senate.

claustrofobia *sf* claustrophobia.

cláusula *sf* clause.

clausura *sf* - **1.** [acto solemne] closing ceremony - **2.** [cierre] closing down - **3.** RELIG religious seclusion.

clausurar *vt* - **1.** [acto] to close, to conclude - **2.** [local] to close down.

clavadista *smf* *Amér C & Méx* diver.

clavado, da *adj* - **1.** [en punto - hora] on the dot - **2.** [parecido] almost identical; **ser clavado a alguien** to be the spitting image of sb.

clavar *vt* - **1.** [clavo, estaca etc] to drive; [cuchillo] to thrust; [chincheta, alfiler] to stick - **2.** [cartel, placa etc] to nail, to fix - **3.** *fig* [mirada, atención] to fix, to rivet.

clave ◇ *adj inv* key; **palabra clave** keyword. ◇ *sm* MÚS harpsichord. ◇ *sf* - **1.** [código] code; **en clave** in code - **2.** *fig* [solución] key; **la clave del problema** the key to the problem - **3.** MÚS clef; **clave de sol** treble clef - **4.** INFORM key.

clavel *sm* carnation.

clavicémbalo *sm* harpsichord.

clavicordio *sm* clavichord.

clavícula *sf* collar bone.

clavija *sf* - **1.** ELECTR & TECNOL pin; [de auriculares, teléfono] jack - **2.** MÚS peg.

clavo *sm* - **1.** [pieza metálica] nail, agarrarse a un clavo ardiendo to clutch at straws; **dar en el clavo** to hit the nail on the head; **¡por los clavos de Cristo!** for heaven's sake - **2.** BOT & CULIN clove - **3.** MED [para huesos] pin.

claxon® *(pl* **cláxones)** *sm* horn; **tocar el claxon** to sound the horn.

clemencia *sf* mercy, clemency.

clemente *adj* [persona] merciful.

cleptómano, na *sm, f* kleptomaniac.

clerical *adj* clerical.

clérigo *sm* [católico] priest; [anglicano] clergyman.

clero *sm* clergy.

clic *sm* INFORM click; **hacer clic en algo** to click on sthg.

cliché, clisé *sm* - **1.** FOTO negative - **2.** IMPR plate - **3.** *fig* [tópico] cliché.

cliente, ta *sm, f* [de tienda, garaje, bar] customer; [de banco, abogado etc] client; [de hotel] guest; **cliente habitual** regular customer.

clientela *sf* [de tienda, garaje] customers *pl*; [de banco, abogado etc] clients *pl*; [de hotel] guests *pl*; [de bar, restaurante] clientele.

clima *sm* *lit & fig* climate; **clima mediterráneo/tropical** Mediterranean/tropical climate.

climatizado, da *adj* air-conditioned.

climatizar *vt* to air-condition.

climatología *sf* - **1.** [tiempo] weather - **2.** [ciencia] climatology.

clímax *sm inv* climax.

clínico, ca *adj* clinical. ◆ **clínica** *sf* clinic.

clip *sm* [para papel] paper clip.

clisé = cliché.

clítoris *sm inv* clitoris. ·

cloaca *sf* sewer.

cloquear *vi* to cluck.

cloro *sm* - **1.** QUÍM chlorine - **2.** *Amér C & Chile* [lejía] bleach.

cloruro *sm* chloride; **cloruro de sodio** O **sódico** sodium chloride.

clóset, closets *sm* *Amér* fitted cupboard.

clown [klawn] *sm* clown.

club *(pl* **clubes** O **clubs)** *sm* club; **club de fans** fan club; **club de fútbol** football club; **club náutico** yacht club; **club nocturno** nightclub.

cm *(abrev de* **centímetro)** cm.

CNT *(abrev de* **Confederación Nacional del Trabajo)** *sf* Spanish anarchist trade union federation created in 1911.

Co. *(abrev de* **compañía)** Co.

coacción *sf* coercion.

coaccionar *vt* to coerce.

coagular *vt* [gen] to coagulate; [sangre] to clot; [leche] to curdle. ◆ **coagularse** *vprnl* [gen] to coagulate; [sangre] to clot; [leche] to curdle.

coágulo *sm* clot.

coalición *sf* coalition; **formar una coalición** to form a coalition.

coartada *sf* alibi.

coartar *vt* to limit, to restrict.

coba *sf fam* [halago] flattery; **dar coba a alguien** [hacer la pelota] to suck up O crawl to sb; [aplacar] to soft-soap sb.

cobalto *sm* cobalt.

cobarde ◇ *adj* cowardly. ◇ *smf* coward.

cobardía *sf* cowardice.

cobertizo *sm* - 1. [tejado adosado] lean-to - 2. [barracón] shed.

cobertura *sf* - 1. [gen] cover - 2. [de un edificio] covering - 3. PRENSA: **cobertura informativa** news coverage - 4. TELECOM: **no tengo cobertura** my network doesn't cover this area.

cobija *sf Amér* [manta] blanket.

cobijar *vt* - 1. [albergar] to house - 2. [proteger] to shelter. ◆ **cobijarse** *vprnl* to take shelter.

cobijo *sm* shelter; **dar cobijo a alguien** to give shelter to sb, to take sb in.

cobra *sf* cobra.

cobrador, ra *sm, f* [del autobús] conductor (*f* conductress); [de deudas, recibos] collector.

cobrar ◇ *vt* - 1. [COM - dinero] to charge; [- cheque] to cash; [- deuda] to collect; **cantidades por cobrar** amounts due; **¿me cobra, por favor?** how much do I owe you? - 2. [en el trabajo] to earn - 3. [adquirir - importancia] to get, to acquire; **cobrar fama** to become famous - 4. [sentir - cariño, afecto] to start to feel. ◇ *vi* [en el trabajo] to get paid.

cobre *sm* copper; **no tener un cobre** *Amér* to be flat broke.

cobrizo, za *adj* [color, piel] copper *(antes de s)*.

cobro *sm* [de talón] cashing; [de pago] collection; **llamada a cobro revertido** reverse charge call *UK*, collect call *US*; **llamar a cobro revertido** to reverse the charges *UK*, to call collect *US*.

coca *sf* - 1. [planta] coca - 2. *fam* [cocaína] coke.

cocaína *sf* cocaine.

cocción *sf* [gen] cooking; [en agua] boiling; [en horno] baking.

cóccix, coxis *sm inv* coccyx.

cocear *vi* to kick.

cocer *vt* - 1. [gen] to cook; [hervir] to boil; [en horno] to bake - 2. [cerámica, ladrillos] to fire. ◆ **cocerse** *vprnl fig* [plan] to be afoot.

coche *sm* - 1. [automóvil] car, automobile *US*; **ir en coche** [montado] to go by car; [conduciendo] to drive; **coche de alquiler** hire car; **coche blindado** armoured car; **coche de bomberos** fire engine; **coche de carreras** racing car; **coche celular** police van; **coche familiar** estate car *UK*, station wagon *US* - 2. [de tren] coach, carriage; **coche cama** sleeping car, sleeper; **coche restaurante** restaurant O dining car - 3. [de caballos] carriage. ◆ **coche bomba** *sm* car bomb.

cochera *sf* [para coches] garage; [de autobuses, tranvías] depot.

cochinilla *sf* - 1. [crustáceo] woodlouse - 2. [insecto] cochineal.

cochinillo *sm* sucking pig.

cochino, na ◇ *adj* - 1. [persona] filthy - 2. [tiempo, dinero] lousy. ◇ *sm, f* [animal - macho] pig; [- hembra] sow.

cocido *sm* stew; **cocido madrileño** CULIN *stew made with chickpeas, bacon, meat and root vegetables, typical of Madrid.*

cociente *sm* quotient; **cociente intelectual** intelligence quotient, I.Q.

cocina *sf* - 1. [habitación] kitchen - 2. [electrodoméstico] cooker, stove; **cocina eléctrica/de gas** electric/gas cooker - 3. [arte] cooking; **alta cocina** haute cuisine; **cocina casera** home cooking; **cocina española** Spanish cuisine O cooking; **libro/clase de cocina** cookery book/class.

cocinar *vt & vi* to cook.

cocinero, ra *sm, f* cook; **haber sido cocinero antes que fraile** to know what one is talking about.

cocker *sm* cocker spaniel.

coco *sm* [árbol] coconut palm; [fruto] coconut.

cocodrilo *sm* crocodile.

cocotero *sm* coconut palm.

cóctel, coctel *sm* - 1. [bebida, comida] cocktail; **cóctel de gambas** prawn cocktail - 2. [reunión] cocktail party. ◆ **cóctel molotov** *sm* Molotov cocktail.

coctelera *sf* cocktail shaker.

codazo *sm* nudge, jab *(with one's elbow)*; **abrirse paso a codazos** to elbow one's way through; **dar un codazo a alguien** [con disimulo] to give sb a nudge, to nudge sb; [con fuerza] to elbow sb.

codearse *vprnl*: **codearse (con)** to rub shoulders (with).

codera *sf* elbow patch.

codicia *sf* [avaricia] greed.

codiciar *vt* to covet.

codicioso, sa *adj* greedy.

codificar *vt* - 1. [ley] to codify - 2. [un mensaje] to encode - 3. INFORM to code.

código *sm* [gen & INFORM] code; **código postal** post *UK* O zip *US* code; **código territorial** area code; **código de barras/de señales** bar/signal code; **código de circulación** highway code; **código civil/penal** civil/penal code; **código máquina** machine code.

codillo *sm* [de jamón] shoulder.

codo *sm* [en brazo, tubería] elbow; **estaba de codos sobre la mesa** she was leaning (with her elbows) on the table; **dar con el codo** to nudge.

codorniz *sf* quail.

coeficiente *sm* - **1.** [gen] coefficient; **coeficiente intelectual** *O* **de inteligencia** intelligence quotient, I.Q. - **2.** [índice] rate.

coercer *vt* to restrict, to constrain.

coetáneo, a *adj* & *sm, f* contemporary.

coexistir *vi* to coexist.

cofia *sf* [de enfermera, camarera] cap; [de monja] coif.

cofradía *sf* - **1.** [religiosa] brotherhood (*f* sisterhood) - **2.** [no religiosa] guild.

cofre *sm* - **1.** [arca] chest, trunk - **2.** [para joyas] jewel box.

coger ⟷ *vt* - **1.** [asir, agarrar] to take; **coger a alguien de** *O* **por la mano** to take sb by the hand - **2.** [atrapar - ladrón, pez, pájaro] to catch - **3.** [alcanzar - persona, vehículo] to catch up with - **4.** [recoger - frutos, flores] to pick - **5.** [quedarse con - propina, empleo, piso] to take - **6.** [quitar]: **coger algo (a alguien)** to take sthg (from sb) - **7.** [tren, autobús] to take, to catch - **8.** [contraer - gripe, resfriado] to catch, to get - **9.** [sentir - manía, odio, afecto] to start to feel - **10.** [oír] to catch; [entender] to get - **11.** [sorprender, encontrar]: **coger a alguien haciendo algo** to catch sb doing sthg; **lo cogieron robando** they caught him stealing - **12.** [sintonizar - canal, emisora] to get, to receive - **13.** *Méx, R Plata & Ven vulg* [tener relaciones sexuales con] to screw, to fuck. ⟷ *vi* [dirigirse]: **coger a la derecha/la izquierda** to turn right/left. ⟜ **cogerse** *vprnl* - **1.** [agarrarse]: **cogerse de** *O* **a algo** to cling to *O* clutch sthg - **2.** [pillarse]: **cogerse los dedos/la falda en la puerta** to catch one's fingers/skirt in the door.

cogida *sf* [de torero]: **sufrir una cogida** to be gored.

cognac = coñac.

cogollo *sm* - **1.** [de lechuga] heart - **2.** [brote - de árbol, planta] shoot.

cogorza *sf fam*: **agarrarse una cogorza** to get smashed, to get blind drunk; **llevar una cogorza** to be smashed, to be blind drunk.

cogote *sm* nape, back of the neck.

cohabitar *vi* to cohabit, to live together.

cohecho *sm* bribery.

coherencia *sf* [de razonamiento] coherence.

coherente *adj* coherent.

cohesión *sf* cohesion.

cohete *sm* rocket.

cohibido, da *adj* inhibited.

cohibir *vt* to inhibit. ⟜ **cohibirse** *vprnl* to become inhibited.

COI (*abrev de* **Comité Olímpico Internacional**) *sm* IOC.

coima *sf Andes & R Dom fam* bribe, backhander *UK*.

coincidencia *sf* coincidence; **¡qué coincidencia!** what a coincidence!

coincidir *vi* - **1.** [superficies, versiones, gustos] to coincide - **2.** [personas - encontrarse] to meet; [- estar de acuerdo] to agree; **coincidimos en una fiesta** we saw each other at a party.

coito *sm* (sexual) intercourse.

coja ⟹ **coger.**

cojear *vi* - **1.** [persona] to limp - **2.** [mueble] to wobble.

cojera *sf* [acción] limp; [estado] lameness.

cojín *sm* cushion.

cojinete *sm* [en eje] bearing; [en un riel de ferrocarril] chair.

cojo, ja ⟷ *adj* - **1.** [persona] lame - **2.** [mueble] wobbly. ⟷ *sm, f* cripple. ⟷ *v* ⟹ **coger.**

cojón *sm* (gen pl) vulg ball. ⟜ **cojones** *interj vulg*: **¡cojones!** [enfado] for fuck's sake!

cojonudo, da *adj vulg* bloody brilliant.

cojudez *sf Andes mfam*: **¡que cojudez!** [acto] what a bloody *UK O* goddamn *US* stupid thing to do!; [dicho] what a bloody *UK O* goddamn *US* stupid thing to say!

cojudo, da *adj Andes mfam* bloody *UK O* goddamn *US* stupid.

col *sf* cabbage; **col de Bruselas** Brussels sprout; **entre col y col, lechuga** *fam* variety is the spice of life.

cola *sf* - **1.** [de animal, avión] tail - **2.** [fila] queue *UK*, line *US*; **¡a la cola!** get in the queue! *UK*, get in line! *US*; **hacer cola** to queue (up) *UK*, to stand in line *US*; **ponerse a la cola** to join the end of the queue *UK O* line *US* - **3.** [de clase, lista] bottom; [de desfile] end - **4.** [pegamento] glue - **5.** [peinado]: **cola (de caballo)** pony tail - **6.** *Amér fam* [nalgas] bum *UK*, fanny *US*.

colaboración *sf* - **1.** [gen] collaboration - **2.** [de prensa] contribution, article.

colaborador, ra *sm, f* - **1.** [gen] collaborator - **2.** [de prensa] contributor.

colaborar *vi* - **1.** [ayudar] to collaborate - **2.** [en prensa]: **colaborar en** *O* **con** to write for - **3.** [contribuir] to contribute.

colación *sf*: **sacar** *O* **traer algo a colación** [tema] to bring sthg up.

colado, da *adj* - **1.** [líquido] strained - **2.** [enamorado]: **estar colado por alguien** *fam* to have a crush on sb. ⟜ **colada** *sf* [ropa] laundry; **hacer la colada** to do the washing.

colador *sm* [para líquidos] strainer, sieve; [para verdura] colander.

colapsar ⟷ *vt* to bring to a halt, to stop. ⟷ *vi* to come O grind to a halt.

colapso *sm* - **1.** MED collapse, breakdown; **sufrir un colapso** to collapse; **colapso nervioso** nervous breakdown - **2.** [de actividad] stoppage; [de tráfico] traffic jam, hold-up.

colar ⟷ *vt* [verdura, té] to strain; [café] to filter. ⟷ *vi fam* [pasar por bueno]: **esto no colará** this won't wash. ⟷ **colarse** *vprnl* - **1.** [líquido]: **colarse por** to seep through - **2.** [persona] to slip, to sneak; [en una cola] to jump the queue UK O line US; **colarse en una fiesta** to gatecrash a party.

colateral *adj* [lateral] on either side.

colcha *sf* bedspread.

colchón *sm* [de cama] mattress; **colchón inflable** air bed.

colchoneta *sf* [para playa] beach mat; [en gimnasio] mat.

cole *sm fam* school.

colear *vi* [animal] to wag its tail.

colección *sf lit & fig* collection.

coleccionable ⟷ *adj* collectable. ⟷ *sm* special supplement in serialized form.

coleccionar *vt* to collect.

coleccionista *smf* collector.

colecta *sf* collection.

colectividad *sf* community.

colectivo, va *adj* collective. ⟷ **colectivo** *sm* - **1.** [grupo] group - **2.** *Andes* [taxi] collective taxi - **3.** *Andes & Bol* [autobús] bus.

colector, ra ⟷ **colector** *sm* - **1.** [sumidero] sewer; **colector de basuras** chute - **2.** MECÁN [de motor] manifold.

colega *smf* - **1.** [compañero profesional] colleague - **2.** [homólogo] counterpart, opposite number - **3.** *fam* [amigo] mate.

colegiado, da *adj* who belongs to a professional association. ⟷ **colegiado** *sm* DEP referee.

colegial, la *sm, f* schoolboy (f schoolgirl).

colegio *sm* - **1.** [escuela] school; **colegio concertado** private school with state subsidy; **colegio de curas** school run by priests; **colegio de monjas** convent school - **2.** [de profesionales]: **colegio (profesional)** professional association. ⟷ **colegio electoral** *sm* [lugar] polling station; [votantes] ward. ⟷ **colegio mayor** *sm* hall of residence.

cólera ⟷ *sm* MED cholera. ⟷ *sf* [ira] anger, rage; **montar en cólera** to get angry.

colérico, ca *adj* [carácter] bad-tempered.

colesterol *sm* cholesterol.

coleta *sf* pigtail.

coletilla *sf* postscript.

colgado, da *adj* - **1.** [cuadro, jamón etc]: **colgado (de)** hanging (from) - **2.** [teléfono] on the hook.

colgador *sm* hanger, coathanger.

colgante ⟷ *adj* hanging. ⟷ *sm* pendant.

colgar ⟷ *vt* - **1.** [suspender, ahorcar] to hang; **colgar el teléfono** to hang up - **2.** [imputar]: **colgar algo a alguien** to blame sthg on sb. ⟷ *vi* - **1.** [pender]: **colgar (de)** to hang (from) - **2.** [hablando por teléfono] to hang up.

colibrí *sm* hummingbird.

cólico *sm* stomachache; **cólico nefrítico** O **renal** renal colic.

coliflor *sf* cauliflower.

colilla *sf* (cigarette) butt O stub.

colimba *sf Arg fam* military service.

colina *sf* hill.

colindante *adj* neighbouring, adjacent.

colisión *sf* [de automóviles] collision, crash; [de ideas, intereses] clash.

colisionar *vi* [coche]: **colisionar (contra)** to collide (with), to crash (into).

collar *sm* - **1.** [de personas] necklace - **2.** [para animales] collar.

collarín *sm* surgical collar.

colmado, da *adj*: **colmado (de)** full to the brim (with). ⟷ **colmado** *sm* grocer's (shop).

colmar *vt* - **1.** [recipiente] to fill (to the brim) - **2.** *fig* [aspiración, deseo] to fulfil; **colmar a alguien de regalos/elogios** to shower gifts/ praise on sb.

colmena *sf* beehive.

colmillo *sm* - **1.** [de persona] eye-tooth - **2.** [de perro] fang; [de elefante] tusk.

colmo *sm* height; **para colmo de desgracias** to crown it all; **es el colmo de la locura** it's sheer madness; **¡eso es el colmo!** *fam* that's the last straw!

colocación *sf* - **1.** [acción] placing, positioning; [situación] place, position - **2.** [empleo] position, job.

colocado, da *adj* - **1.** [gen] placed; **estar muy bien colocado** to have a very good job - **2.** *fam* [borracho] legless; [drogado] high, stoned.

colocar *vt* - **1.** [en su sitio] to place, to put - **2.** [en un empleo] to find a job for - **3.** [invertir] to place, to invest. ⟷ **colocarse** *vprnl* - **1.** [en un trabajo] to get a job - **2.** *fam* [emborracharse] to get legless; [drogarse] to get high O stoned.

colofón *sm* [remate, fin] climax.

Colombia *n pr* Colombia.

colombiano, na *adj & sm, f* Colombian.

colon *sm* colon.

colonia *sf* - **1.** [gen] colony - **2.** [perfume] eau de cologne - **3.** *Méx* [barrio] district; **colonia proletaria** shanty town, slum area.

colonial *adj* colonial.

colonización *sf* colonization.

colonizador, ra *sm, f* colonist.

colonizar *vt* to colonize.

colono *sm* settler, colonist.

coloquial *adj* colloquial.

coloquio *sm* - **1.** [conversación] conversation - **2.** [debate] discussion, debate.

color *sm* [gen] colour; **color rojo** red; **color azul** blue; **¿de qué color?** what colour?; **una falda de color rosa** a pink skirt; **a todo color** in full colour; **de color** [persona] coloured.

colorado, da *adj* [color] red; **ponerse colorado** to blush, to go red.

colorante *sm* colouring.

colorear *vt* to colour (in).

colorete *sm* rouge, blusher.

colorido *sm* colours *pl.*

colosal *adj* - **1.** [estatura, tamaño] colossal - **2.** [extraordinario] great, enormous.

coloso *sm* - **1.** [estatua] colossus - **2.** *fig* [cosa, persona] giant.

columna *sf* - **1.** [gen] column - **2.** *fig* [pilar] pillar. ◆ **columna vertebral** *sf* spinal column.

columnista *smf* columnist.

columpiar *vt* to swing. ◆ **columpiarse** *vprnl* to swing.

columpio *sm* swing.

colza *sf* BOT rape.

coma ◇ *sm* MED coma; **en coma** in a coma. ◇ *sf* - **1.** GRAM comma - **2.** MAT ≃ decimal point.

comadreja *sf* weasel.

comadrona *sf* midwife.

comandancia *sf* - **1.** [rango] command - **2.** [edificio] command headquarters.

comandante *sm* [MIL - rango] major; [- de un puesto] commander, commandant.

comandar *vt* MIL to command.

comando *sm* MIL commando.

comarca *sf* region, area.

comba *sf* - **1.** [juego] skipping - **2.** [cuerda] skipping rope.

combar *vt* to bend. ◆ **combarse** *vprnl* [gen] to bend; [madera] to warp; [pared] to bulge.

combate *sm* [gen] fight; [batalla] battle; **dejar a alguien fuera de combate** [en boxeo] to knock sb out; *fig* to put sb out of the running.

combatiente *smf* combatant, fighter.

combatir ◇ *vt* to combat, to fight. ◇ *vi*: **combatir (contra)** to fight (against).

combativo, va *adj* combative.

combi *sm* [frigorífico] fridge-freezer.

combinación *sf* - **1.** [gen] combination - **2.** [de bebidas] cocktail - **3.** [prenda] slip - **4.** [de medios de transporte] connections *pl.*

combinado *sm* - **1.** [bebida] cocktail - **2.** DEP combined team - **3.** *Amér* [radiograma] radiogram.

combinar *vt* - **1.** [gen] to combine - **2.** [bebidas] to mix - **3.** [colores] to match.

combustible ◇ *adj* combustible. ◇ *sm* fuel.

combustión *sf* combustion.

comecocos *sm inv fam* [para convencer]: **este panfleto es un comecocos** this pamphlet is designed to brainwash you.

comedia *sf* - **1.** [obra, película, género] comedy - **2.** *fig* [engaño] farce; **hacer la comedia** to pretend, to make believe.

comediante, ta *sm, f* actor (*f* actress); *fig* [farsante] fraud.

comedido, da *adj* moderate.

comedirse *vprnl* to be restrained.

comedor *sm* [habitación - de casa] dining room; [- de fábrica] canteen.

comensal *smf* fellow diner.

comentar *vt* [opinar sobre] to comment on; [hablar de] to discuss.

comentario *sm* - **1.** [observación] comment, remark - **2.** [crítica] commentary. ◆ **comentarios** *smpl* [murmuraciones] gossip (*U*).

comentarista *smf* commentator.

comenzar ◇ *vt* to start, to begin; **comenzar a hacer algo** to start doing O to do sthg; **comenzar diciendo que...** to start O begin by saying that... ◇ *vi* to start, to begin.

comer ◇ *vi* [ingerir alimentos - gen] to eat; [- al mediodía] to have lunch. ◇ *vt* - **1.** [alimentos] to eat - **2.** [en juegos de tablero] to take, to capture - **3.** *fig* [consumir] to eat up. ◆ **comerse** *vprnl* - **1.** [alimentos] to eat - **2.** [desgastar - recursos] to eat up; [- metal] to corrode - **3.** [en los juegos de tablero] to take, to capture - **4.** *Amér vulg* [fornicar] to fuck.

comercial ◇ *adj* commercial. ◇ *sm Amér* [anuncio] advert.

comercializar *vt* to market.

comerciante *smf* tradesman (*f* tradeswoman); [tendero] shopkeeper.

comerciar *vi* to trade, to do business.

comercio *sm* - **1.** [de productos] trade; **comercio electrónico** e-business; **comercio exterior/interior** foreign/domestic trade; **comercio justo** fair trade; **libre comercio** free trade - **2.** [actividad] business, commerce - **3.** [tienda] shop.

comestible *adj* edible, eatable. ◆ **comestibles** *smpl* [gen] food (*U*); [en una tienda] groceries.

cometa <> *sm* ASTRON comet. <> *sf* kite.

cometer *vt* [crimen] to commit; [error] to make.

cometido *sm* - 1. [objetivo] mission, task - 2. [deber] duty.

comezón *sf* [picor] itch, itching *(U)*.

cómic (*pl* comics) *sm* (adult) comic.

comicios *smpl* elections.

cómico, ca <> *adj* - 1. [de la comedia] comedy *(antes de s)*, comic - 2. [gracioso] comic, comical. <> *sm, f* [actor de teatro] actor (*f* actress); [humorista] comedian (*f* comedienne), comic.

comida *sf* - 1. [alimento] food *(U)*; **comida basura** junk food; **comida chatarra** *Amér* junk food; **comida rápida** fast food - 2. [almuerzo, cena etc] meal - 3. [al mediodía] lunch; **comida de negocios** business lunch.

comidilla *sf*: **ser/convertirse en la comidilla del pueblo** *fam* to be/to become the talk of the town.

comienzo *sm* start, beginning; **a comienzos de los años 50** in the early 1950s; **dar comienzo** to start, to begin.

comillas *sfpl* inverted commas, quotation marks; **entre comillas** in inverted commas.

comilona *sf fam* [festín] blow-out.

comino *sm* [planta] cumin, cummin; **me importa un comino** *fam* I don't give a damn.

comisaría *sf* police station, precinct *US*.

comisario, ria *sm, f* - 1.: **comisario (de policía)** police superintendent - 2. [delegado] commissioner.

comisión *sf* - 1. [de un delito] perpetration - 2. COM commission; **(trabajar) a comisión** (to work) on a commission basis; **comisión fija** ECON flat fee - 3. [delegación] commission, committee; **Comisión Europea** European Comission; **comisión investigadora** committee of inquiry; **comisión permanente** standing commission; **Comisiones Obreras** Spanish Communist-inspired trade union.

comisura *sf* corner *(of mouth, eyes)*.

comité *sm* committee.

comitiva *sf* retinue.

como <> *adv* - 1. *(compar)*: **tan... como...** as... as...; **es (tan) negro como el carbón** it's as black as coal; **ser como algo** to be like sthg; **vive como un rey** he lives like a king; **lo que dijo fue como para ruborizarse** his words were enough to make you blush - 2. [de la manera que] as; **lo he hecho como es debido** I did it as O the way it should be done; **me encanta como bailas** I love the way you dance - 3. [según] as; **como te decía ayer...** as I was telling you yesterday... - 4. [en calidad de] as; **trabaja como bombero** he works as a fireman; **dieron el dinero como anticipo** they gave the money as

an advance - 5. [aproximadamente] about; **me quedan como cien euros** I've got about a hundred euros left; **tiene un sabor como a naranja** it tastes a bit like an orange. <> *conj* - 1. [ya que] as, since; **como no llegabas, nos fuimos** as O since you didn't arrive, we left - 2. [si] if; **como no me hagas caso, lo pasarás mal** if you don't listen to me, there will be trouble.

◆ **como que** *loc conj* - 1. [que] that; **le pareció como que lloraban** it seemed to him (that) they were crying - 2. [expresa causa]: **pareces cansado – como que he trabajado toda la noche** you seem tired – well, I've been up all night working. ◆ **como quiera** *loc adv* [de cualquier modo] anyway, anyhow. ◆ **como quiera que** *loc conj* - 1. [de cualquier modo que] whichever way, however; **como quiera que sea** whatever the case may be - 2. [dado que] since, given that. ◆ **como si** *loc conj* as if.

cómo *adv* - 1. [de qué modo, por qué motivo] how; **¿cómo lo has hecho?** how did you do it?; **¿cómo son?** what are they like?; **no sé cómo has podido decir eso** I don't know how you could say that; **¿cómo que no la has visto nunca?** what do you mean you've never seen her?; **¿a cómo están los tomates?** how much are the tomatoes?; **¿cómo es eso?** *fam* [¿por qué?] how come? - 2. [exclamativo] how; **¡cómo pasan los años!** how time flies!; **¡cómo no!** of course!; **está lloviendo, ¡y cómo!** it isn't half raining!

cómoda *sf* chest of drawers.

comodidad *sf* comfort, convenience *(U)*; **para su comodidad** for your convenience.

comodín *sm* [naipe] joker.

cómodo, da *adj* - 1. [confortable] comfortable; **ponte cómodo** make yourself comfortable, make yourself at home; **sentirse cómodo con alguien** to feel comfortable with sb - 2. [útil] convenient - 3. [oportuno, fácil] easy.

comoquiera *adv*: **comoquiera que** [de cualquier manera que] whichever way, however; [dado que] since, seeing as.

compa *smf fam* pal, mate *UK*, buddy *US*.

compactar *vt* to compress.

compact disk, compact disc *sm* compact disc.

compacto, ta *adj* compact.

compadecer *vt* to pity, to feel sorry for. ◆ **compadecerse de** *vprnl* to pity, to feel sorry for.

compadre *sm fam* [amigo] friend, mate *UK*, buddy *US*.

compadrear *vi R Dom fam* to brag, to boast.

compaginar *vt* [combinar] to reconcile. ◆ **compaginarse** *vprnl*: **compaginarse con** to square with, to go together with.

compañerismo *sm* comradeship.

compañero, ra *sm, f* - **1.** [acompañante] companion - **2.** [pareja] partner; **compañero sentimental** partner - **3.** [colega] colleague; **compañero de clase** classmate; **compañero de piso** flatmate.

compañía *sf* company; **le perdieron las malas compañías** he was led astray by the bad company he kept; **en compañía de** accompanied by, in the company of; **hacer compañía a alguien** to keep sb company; **compañía de seguros** insurance company; **compañía teatral** O **de teatro** theatre company.

comparación *sf* comparison; **en comparación con** in comparison with, compared to.

comparar *vt*: **comparar algo (con)** to compare sthg (to).

comparativo, va *adj* comparative.

comparecer *vi* to appear.

comparsa ◇ *sf* TEATRO extras *pl*. ◇ *smf* - **1.** TEATRO extra - **2.** *fig* [en carreras, competiciones] also-ran; [en organizaciones, empresas] nobody.

compartimento, compartimiento *sm* compartment; **compartimento de fumadores** smoking compartment.

compartir *vt* - **1.** [ganancias] to share (out) - **2.** [piso, ideas] to share.

compás *sm* - **1.** [instrumento] pair of compasses - **2.** [MÚS - periodo] bar; [- ritmo] rhythm, beat; **al compás (de la música)** in time (with the music); **llevar el compás** to keep time; **perder el compás** to lose the beat.

compasión *sf* compassion, pity; **¡por compasión!** for pity's sake!; **tener compasión de** to feel sorry for.

compasivo, va *adj* compassionate.

compatibilizar *vt* to make compatible.

compatible *adj* [gen & INFORM] compatible.

compatriota *smf* compatriot, fellow countryman (*f* fellow countrywoman).

compendiar *vt* [cualidades, características] to summarize; [libro, historia] to abridge.

compendio *sm* - **1.** [libro] compendium - **2.** *fig* [síntesis] epitome, essence.

compenetración *sf* mutual understanding.

compenetrarse *vprnl* to understand each other.

compensación *sf* [gen] compensation; **en compensación (por)** in return (for); **compensación económica** financial compensation.

compensar *vt* - **1.** [valer la pena] to make up for; **no me compensa (perder tanto tiempo)** it's not worth my while (wasting all that time) - **2.** [indemnizar]: **compensar a alguien (de** O **por)** to compensate sb (for).

competencia *sf* - **1.** [entre personas, empresas] competition; **hacer la competencia a** to compete with; **competencia desleal** ECON unfair competition, dumping - **2.** [incumbencia] field, province - **3.** [aptitud, atribuciones] competence.

competente *adj* competent; **competente en materia de** responsible for.

competer ◈ **competer a** *vi* [gen] to be up to, to be the responsibility of; [una autoridad] to come under the jurisdiction of.

competición *sf* competition.

competidor, ra *sm, f* competitor.

competir *vi*: **competir (con/por)** to compete (with/for).

competitividad *sf* competitiveness.

competitivo, va *adj* competitive.

compilar *vt* [gen & INFORM] to compile.

compinche *smf fam* crony.

complacencia *sf* pleasure, satisfaction.

complacer *vt* to please.

complaciente *adj* - **1.** [amable] obliging, helpful - **2.** [indulgente] indulgent.

complejo, ja *adj* complex. ◈ **complejo** *sm* complex; **complejo de Edipo/de inferioridad/de superioridad** Oedipus/inferiority/superiority complex; **complejo deportivo** sports complex; **complejo hotelero** hotel complex; **complejo industrial** industrial park; **complejo turístico** tourist development; **complejo vitamínico** vitamin complex.

complementar *vt* to complement. ◈ **complementarse** *vprnl* to complement each other.

complementario, ria *adj* complementary.

complemento *sm* - **1.** [añadido] complement - **2.** GRAM object, complement; **complemento directo/indirecto** direct/indirect object.

completamente *adv* completely, totally.

completar *vt* to complete.

completo, ta *adj* - **1.** [entero, perfecto] complete; **por completo** completely; **un deportista muy completo** an all-round sportsman - **2.** [lleno] full.

complexión *sf* build; **de complexión atlética** with an athletic build; **de complexión fuerte** well-built, with a strong constitution.

complicación *sf* - **1.** [gen] complication - **2.** [complejidad] complexity.

complicado, da *adj* - **1.** [difícil] complicated - **2.** [implicado]: **complicado (en)** involved (in).

complicar *vt* [dificultar] to complicate.

cómplice *smf* accomplice.

complicidad *sf* complicity.

complot, compló *sm* plot, conspiracy.

componente ◇ *sm* [gen & ELECTR] component. ◇ *smf* [persona] member.

componer *vt* - **1.** [constituir, ser parte de] to make up - **2.** [música, versos] to compose

- 3. [arreglar - algo roto] to repair. ◆ **componerse** *vprnl* [estar formado]: **componerse de** to be made up of, to consist of.

comportamiento *sm* behaviour.

comportar *vt* to involve, to entail. ◆ **comportarse** *vprnl* to behave.

composición *sf* composition.

compositor, ra *sm, f* composer.

compostura *sf* **- 1.** [reparación] repair **- 2.** [de persona, rostro] composure **- 3.** [en comportamiento] restraint.

compota *sf* CULIN stewed fruit *(U)*.

compra *sf* purchase; **ir de compras** to go shopping; **ir a** O **hacer la compra** to do the shopping; **compra al contado** cash purchase; **compra a plazos** hire purchase.

comprador, ra *sm, f* [gen] buyer; [en una tienda] shopper, customer.

comprar *vt* **- 1.** [adquirir] to buy, to purchase; **comprar algo a alguien** to buy sthg from sb **- 2.** [sobornar] to buy (off).

compraventa *sf* buying and selling, trading.

comprender *vt* **- 1.** [incluir] to include, to comprise **- 2.** [entender] to understand; **hacerse comprender** to make o.s. understood. ◆ **comprenderse** *vprnl* [personas] to understand each other.

comprensión *sf* understanding.

comprensivo, va *adj* understanding.

compresa *sf* [para menstruación] sanitary towel *UK*, sanitary napkin *US*.

comprimido, da *adj* compressed. ◆ **comprimido** *sm* pill, tablet.

comprimir *vt* to compress.

comprobante *sm* [documento] supporting document, proof; [recibo] receipt.

comprobar *vt* [averiguar] to check; [demostrar] to prove.

comprometer *vt* **- 1.** [poner en peligro - éxito etc] to jeopardize; [- persona] to compromise **- 2.** [avergonzar] to embarrass. ◆ **comprometerse** *vprnl* **- 1.** [hacerse responsable]: **comprometerse (a hacer algo)** to commit o.s. (to doing sthg) **- 2.** [ideológicamente, moralmente]: **comprometerse (en algo)** to become involved (in sthg).

comprometido, da *adj* **- 1.** [con una idea] committed **- 2.** [difícil] compromising, awkward.

compromiso *sm* **- 1.** [obligación] commitment; [acuerdo] agreement **- 2.** [cita] engagement; **sin compromiso** without obligation **- 3.** [de matrimonio] engagement; **compromiso matrimonial** engagement **- 4.** [dificultad, aprieto] compromising O difficult situation; **me pones en un compromiso** you're putting me in an awkward position.

compuerta *sf* sluice, floodgate.

compuesto, ta ◇ *pp* ▷ **componer**. ◇ *adj* [formado]: **compuesto de** composed of, made up of. ◆ **compuesto** *sm* GRAM & QUÍM compound.

compungido, da *adj* contrite.

computador *sm* = **computadora**.

computadora *sf* computer.

computar *vt* [calcular] to calculate.

cómputo *sm* calculation.

comulgar *vi* RELIG to take communion.

común *adj* **- 1.** [gen] common; **por lo común** generally; **poco común** unusual **- 2.** [compartido - amigo, interés] mutual; [- bienes, pastos] communal **- 3.** [ordinario - vino etc] ordinary, average; **común y corriente** perfectly ordinary.

comuna *sf* **- 1.** commune **- 2.** *Amér* [municipalidad] municipality.

comunicación *sf* **- 1.** [gen] communication; **ponerse en comunicación con alguien** to get in touch with sb **- 2.** [escrito oficial] communiqué; [informe] report. ◆ **comunicaciones** *sfpl* communications.

comunicado, da *adj*: **bien comunicado** [lugar] well-served, with good connections. ◆ **comunicado** *sm* announcement, statement; **comunicado oficial** communiqué; **comunicado a la prensa** press release.

comunicar ◇ *vt* **- 1.** [transmitir - sentimientos, ideas] to convey; [- movimiento, virus] to transmit **- 2.** [información]: **comunicar algo a alguien** to inform sb of sthg, to tell sb sthg. ◇ *vi* **- 1.** [hablar - gen] to communicate; [- al teléfono] to get through; [escribir] to get in touch **- 2.** [dos lugares]: **comunicar con algo** to connect with sthg, to join sthg **- 3.** [suj: el teléfono] to be engaged *UK*, to be busy *US*. ◆ **comunicarse** *vprnl* **- 1.** [hablarse] to communicate (with each other) **- 2.** [dos lugares] to be connected.

comunicativo, va *adj* communicative.

comunidad *sf* community; **comunidad autónoma** autonomous region; **Comunidad Económica Europea** HIST European Economic Community.

comunión *sf* lit & fig communion; **hacer la primera comunión** to take one's First Communion.

comunismo *sm* communism.

comunista *adj* & *smf* communist.

comunitario, ria *adj* **- 1.** [de la comunidad] community *(antes de s)* **- 2.** [de la UE] Community *(antes de s)*, of the European Community; **política comunitaria** EU O Community policy.

con *prep* **- 1.** [gen] with; **¿con quién vas?** who are you going with?; **lo ha conseguido con su**

esfuerzo he has achieved it through his own efforts; **una cartera con varios documentos** a briefcase containing several documents - **2.** [a pesar de] in spite of; **con todo** despite everything; **con lo estudioso que es, lo suspendieron** for all his hard work, they still failed him - **3.** [hacia]: **para con** towards; **es amable para con todos** she is friendly towards O with everyone - **4.** (+ infinitivo) [para introducir una condición] by (+ gerundio); **con hacerlo así** by doing it this way; **con salir a las diez es suficiente** if we leave at ten, we'll have plenty of time - **5.** [a condición de que]: **con (tal) que** (+ subjuntivo) as long as; **con que llegue a tiempo me conformo** I don't mind as long as he arrives on time.

conato sm attempt; **conato de robo** attempted robbery; **un conato de incendio** the beginnings of a fire.

concatenar, concadenar vt to link together.

concavidad sf [lugar] hollow.

cóncavo, va adj concave.

concebir ⟨⟩ vt [plan, hijo] to conceive; [imaginar] to imagine. ⟨⟩ vi to conceive.

conceder vt - **1.** [dar] to grant; [premio] to award - **2.** [asentir] to admit, to concede.

concejal, la sm, f (town) councillor.

concentración sf - **1.** [gen] concentration - **2.** [de gente] gathering; **concentración parcelaria** ECON land consolidation.

concentrado sm concentrate.

concentrar vt - **1.** [gen] to concentrate - **2.** [reunir - gente] to bring together; [- tropas] to assemble. ⇐ **concentrarse** vprnl to concentrate.

concéntrico, ca adj concentric.

concepción sf conception.

concepto sm - **1.** [idea] concept - **2.** [opinión] opinion; **te tiene en muy buen concepto** she thinks highly of you - **3.** [motivo]: **bajo ningún concepto** under no circumstances; **en concepto de** by way of, as.

concernir v impers to concern; **en lo que concierne a** as regards; **por lo que a mí me concierne** as far as I'm concerned.

concertado, da adj [centro de enseñanza] state-assisted, ≃ grant-maintained UK; **hospital concertado** private hospital that has been contracted to provide free treatment for social security patients.

concertar ⟨⟩ vt [precio] to agree on; [cita] to arrange; [pacto] to reach. ⟨⟩ vi [concordar]: **concertar (con)** to tally (with), to fit in (with).

concertina sf concertina.

concesión sf - **1.** [de préstamo etc] granting; [de premio] awarding - **2.** fig & COM concession.

concesionario, ria sm, f [persona con derecho exclusivo de venta] licensed dealer; [titular de una concesión] concessionaire, licensee.

concha sf - **1.** [de los animales] shell - **2.** [material] tortoiseshell - **3.** Ven [de frutas] peel, rind.

conchabarse vprnl: **conchabarse (contra)** fam to gang up (on).

conciencia, consciencia sf - **1.** [conocimiento] consciousness, awareness; **tener/tomar conciencia de** to be/become aware of; **conciencia de clase** class consciousness; **conciencia social** social conscience - **2.** [moral, integridad] conscience; **a conciencia** conscientiously; **me remuerde la conciencia** I have a guilty conscience; **tener la conciencia tranquila** to have a clear conscience.

concienciar vt to make aware. ⇐ **concienciarse** vprnl to become aware.

concientizar Amér vt: **concientizar a alguien de algo** to make sb aware of sthg. ⇐ **concientizarse** vprnl: **concientizarse (de)** to become aware (of).

concienzudo, da adj conscientious.

concierto sm - **1.** [actuación] concert - **2.** [composición] concerto.

conciliar vt to reconcile; **conciliar el sueño** to get to sleep.

concilio sm council.

concisión sf conciseness.

conciso, sa adj concise.

conciudadano, na sm, f fellow citizen.

cónclave, conclave sm conclave.

concluir ⟨⟩ vt to conclude; **concluir haciendo O por hacer algo** to end up doing sthg. ⟨⟩ vi to (come to an) end.

conclusión sf conclusion; **llegar a una conclusión** to come to O to reach a conclusion; **en conclusión** in conclusion.

concluyente adj conclusive.

concordancia sf [gen & GRAM] agreement.

concordar ⟨⟩ vt to reconcile. ⟨⟩ vi - **1.** [estar de acuerdo]: **concordar (con)** to agree O tally (with) - **2.** GRAM: **concordar (con)** to agree (with).

concordia sf harmony.

concretar vt [precisar] to specify, to state exactly. ⇐ **concretarse** vprnl [materializarse] to take shape.

concreto, ta adj specific, particular; **en concreto** [en resumen] in short; [específicamente] specifically; **nada en concreto** nothing definite. ⇐ **concreto armado** sm Amér reinforced concrete.

concurrencia sf - **1.** [asistencia] attendance; [espectadores] crowd, audience - **2.** [de sucesos] concurrence.

concurrido, da adj [bar, calle] crowded; [espectáculo] well-attended.

concurrir vi - 1. [reunirse]: **concurrir a algo** to go to sthg, to attend sthg - 2. [participar]: **concurrir a** [concurso] to take part in, to compete in; [examen] to sit UK, to take.

concursante smf [en concurso] competitor, contestant; [en oposiciones] candidate.

concursar vi [competir] to compete; [en oposiciones] to be a candidate.

concurso sm - 1. [prueba - literaria, deportiva] competition; [- de televisión] game show; **fuera de concurso** out of the running - 2. [para una obra] tender; **salir a concurso** to be put out to tender - 3. [ayuda] cooperation.

condado sm [territorio] county.

condal adj: **la Ciudad Condal** Barcelona.

conde, esa sm, f count (f countess).

condecoración sf [insignia] medal.

condecorar vt to decorate.

condena sf sentence.

condenado, da adj - 1. [a una pena] convicted, sentenced; [a un sufrimiento] condemned - 2. fam [maldito] damned.

condenar vt - 1. [declarar culpable] to convict - 2. [castigar]: **condenar a alguien a algo** to sentence sb to sthg - 3. [recriminar] to condemn.

condensar vt lit & fig to condense.

condescendencia sf [benevolencia] graciousness; [altivez] condescension.

condescender vi: **condescender a** [con amabilidad] to consent to, to accede to; [con desprecio] to deign to, to condescend to.

condescendiente adj obliging.

condición sf - 1. [gen] condition; **condiciones de un contrato** terms of a contract; **con una sola condición** on one condition - 2. [naturaleza] nature - 3. [clase social] social class. ➤ **condiciones** sfpl - 1. [aptitud] talent (U), ability (U) - 2. [circunstancias] conditions; **condiciones atmosféricas/de vida** weather/living conditions - 3. [estado] condition (U); **estar en condiciones de O para hacer algo** [físicamente] to be in a fit state to do sthg; [por la situación] to be in a position to do sthg; **estar en buenas condiciones** [casa, coche] to be in good condition; [carne, pescado] to be fresh; **estar en malas condiciones** [casa, coche] to be in bad condition; [carne, pescado] to be off.

condicional adj & sm conditional.

condicionar vt: **condicionar algo a algo** to make sthg dependent on sthg.

condimento sm seasoning (U).

condolencia sf condolence.

condolerse vprnl: **condolerse (de)** to feel pity (for).

condón sm condom.

cóndor sm condor.

conducción sf [de vehículo] driving.

conducir <> vt - 1. [vehículo] to drive - 2. [dirigir - empresa] to manage, to run; [- ejército] to lead; [- asunto] to handle - 3. [a una persona a un lugar] to lead. <> vi - 1. [en vehículo] to drive - 2. [a sitio, situación]: **conducir a** to lead to.

conducta sf behaviour, conduct.

conducto sm - 1. [de fluido] pipe - 2. fig [vía] channel - 3. ANAT duct.

conductor, ra sm, f - 1. [de vehículo] driver - 2. FÍS conductor.

conectar vt: **conectar algo (a O con)** to connect sthg (to O up to).

conejillo ➤ **conejillo de Indias** sm guinea pig.

conejo, ja sm, f rabbit (f doe); **conejo a la cazadora** CULIN rabbit cooked in olive oil with chopped onion, garlic and parsley.

conexión sf - 1. [gen] connection - 2. RADIO & TV link-up; **conexión a Internet** Internet connection; **conexión vía satélite** satellite link.

conexo, xa adj related, connected.

confabular ➤ **confabularse** vprnl: **confabularse (para)** to plot O conspire (to).

confección sf - 1. [de ropa] tailoring, dressmaking - 2. [de comida] preparation, making; [de lista] drawing up.

confeccionar vt - 1. [ropa] to make (up); [lista] to draw up - 2. [plato] to prepare; [bebida] to mix.

confederación sf confederation.

conferencia sf - 1. [charla] lecture; **dar una conferencia** to give a talk O lecture - 2. [reunión] conference - 3. [por teléfono] (long-distance) call; **poner una conferencia** to make a long-distance call; **conferencia a cobro revertido** reverse-charge call UK, collect call US.

conferir vt - 1.: **conferir algo a alguien** [honor, dignidad] to confer O bestow sthg upon sb; [responsabilidades] to give sthg to sb - 2. [cualidad] to give.

confesar vt [gen] to confess; [debilidad] to admit. ➤ **confesarse** vprnl RELIG: **confesarse (de algo)** to confess (sthg).

confesión sf - 1. [gen] confession - 2. [credo] religion, (religious) persuasion.

confesionario sm confessional.

confeti sm confetti (U).

confiado, da adj [seguro] confident; [crédulo] trusting.

confianza sf - 1. [seguridad]: **confianza (en)** confidence (in); **confianza en uno mismo** self-confidence - 2. [fe] trust; **de confianza** trustworthy; **ser digno de confianza** to be trustworthy - 3. [familiaridad] familiarity; **con toda confianza** in all confidence; **puedes hablar con toda confianza** you can talk quite freely; **en**

confianza in confidence; **en confianza, no creo que apruebe** don't tell anyone I said this, but I doubt she'll pass.

confiar *vt* - **1.** [secreto] to confide - **2.** [responsabilidad, persona, asunto]: **confiar algo a alguien** to entrust sthg to sb. ◆ **confiar en** *vi* - **1.** [tener fe] to trust in - **2.** [suponer]: **confiar en que** to be confident that. ◆ **confiarse** *vprnl* [despreocuparse] to be too sure (of o.s.)

confidencia *sf* confidence, secret; **hacer confidencias a alguien** to confide in sb.

confidencial *adj* confidential.

confidente *smf* - **1.** [amigo] confidant (*f* confidante) - **2.** [soplón] informer.

configurar *vt* [formar] to shape, to form.

confín *(gen pl) sm* - **1.** [límite] border, boundary - **2.** [extremo - del reino, universo] outer reaches *pl*; **en los confines de** on the very edge of.

confinar *vt* - **1.** [detener]: **confinar (en)** to confine (to) - **2.** [desterrar]: **confinar (en)** to banish (to).

confirmación *sf* [gen & RELIG] confirmation.

confirmar *vt* to confirm.

confiscar *vt* to confiscate.

confitado, da *adj* candied; **frutas confitadas** crystallized fruit.

confite *sm* sweet *UK*, candy *US*.

confitería *sf* - **1.** [tienda] sweetshop, confectioner's - **2.** *R Dom* [café] cafe.

confitura *sf* preserve, jam.

conflictivo, va *adj* [asunto] controversial; [situación] troubled; [trabajador] difficult.

conflicto *sm* [gen] conflict; [de intereses, opiniones] clash; **estar en conflicto** to be in conflict; **conflicto armado** armed conflict; **conflicto generacional** generation gap; **conflicto laboral** industrial dispute.

confluir *vi* - **1.** [corriente, cauce]: **confluir (en)** to converge *O* meet (at) - **2.** [personas]: **confluir (en)** to come together *O* to gather (in).

conformar *vt* [configurar] to shape. ◆ **conformarse con** *vprnl* [suerte, destino] to resign o.s. to; [apañárselas con] to make do with; [contentarse con] to settle for.

conforme ◇ *adj* - **1.** [acorde]: **conforme a** in accordance with - **2.** [de acuerdo]: **conforme (con)** in agreement (with) - **3.** [contento]: **conforme (con)** happy (with). ◇ *adv* [gen] as; **conforme envejecía** as he got older.

conformidad *sf* [aprobación]: **conformidad (con)** approval (of).

conformista *adj & smf* conformist.

confort *(pl conforts) sm* comfort; '**todo confort**' 'all mod cons'.

confortable *adj* comfortable.

confortar *vt* to console, to comfort.

confrontar *vt* - **1.** [enfrentar] to confront - **2.** [comparar] to compare.

confundir *vt* - **1.** [tractocar]: **confundir una cosa con otra** to mistake one thing for another; **confundir dos cosas** to get two things mixed up - **2.** [liar] to confuse - **3.** [mezclar] to mix up. ◆ **confundirse** *vprnl* - **1.** [equivocarse] to make a mistake; **confundirse de piso** to get the wrong flat - **2.** [liarse] to get confused - **3.** [mezclarse - colores, siluetas]: **confundirse (en)** to merge (into); [- personas]: **confundirse entre la gente** to lose o.s. in the crowd.

confusión *sf* - **1.** [gen] confusion - **2.** [error] mix-up.

confuso, sa *adj* - **1.** [incomprensible - estilo, explicación] obscure - **2.** [poco claro - rumor] muffled; [- clamor, griterío] confused; [- contorno, forma] blurred - **3.** [turbado] confused, bewildered.

congelación *sf* - **1.** [de alimentos] freezing - **2.** ECON [de precios, salarios] freeze.

congelador *sm* freezer.

congelados *smpl* frozen foods.

congelar *vt* [gen & ECON] to freeze. ◆ **congelarse** *vprnl* to freeze.

congeniar *vi*: **congeniar (con)** to get on (with).

congénito, ta *adj* [enfermedad] congenital; [talento] innate.

congestión *sf* congestion.

congestionar *vt* to block. ◆ **congestionarse** *vprnl* - **1.** AUTO & MED to become congested - **2.** [cara - de rabia etc] to flush, to turn purple.

congoja *sf* anguish.

congraciarse *vprnl*: **congraciarse con alguien** to win sb over.

congratular *vt*: **congratular a alguien (por)** to congratulate sb (on).

congregación *sf* congregation.

congregar *vt* to assemble.

congresista *smf* - **1.** [en un congreso] delegate - **2.** [político] congressman (*f* congresswoman).

congreso *sm* - **1.** [de una especialidad] congress - **2.** [asamblea nacional]: **congreso de diputados** [en España] *lower house of Spanish Parliament; UK* ≃ House of Commons; *US* ≃ House of Representatives; **el Congreso** [en Estados Unidos] Congress.

congrio *sm* conger eel.

congruente *adj* consistent, congruous.

conjetura *sf* conjecture; **hacer conjeturas, hacerse una conjetura** to conjecture.

conjugación *sf* GRAM conjugation.

conjugar *vt* - **1.** GRAM to conjugate - **2.** [opiniones] to bring together, to combine; [esfuerzos, ideas] to pool.

conjunción *sf* ASTRON & GRAM conjunction.

conjunto, ta *adj* [gen] joint; [hechos, acontecimientos] combined. ► **conjunto** *sm* - **1.** [gen] set, collection; **un conjunto de circunstancias** a number of reasons - **2.** [de ropa] outfit - **3.** [MÚS - de rock] group, band; [- de música clásica] ensemble - **4.** [totalidad] whole; **en conjunto** overall, as a whole - **5.** MAT set.

conjurar ◇ *vi* [conspirar] to conspire, to plot. ◇ *vt* - **1.** [exorcizar] to exorcise - **2.** [evitar - un peligro] to ward off, to avert.

conjuro *sm* spell, incantation.

conllevar *vt* [implicar] to entail.

conmemoración *sf* commemoration.

conmemorar *vt* to commemorate.

conmigo *pron pers* with me; **conmigo mismo/misma** with myself.

conmoción *sf* - **1.** [física o psíquica] shock; **conmoción cerebral** concussion - **2.** *fig* [trastorno, disturbio] upheaval.

conmocionar *vt* - **1.** [psíquicamente] to shock - **2.** [físicamente] to concuss.

conmovedor, ra *adj* moving, touching.

conmover *vt* - **1.** [emocionar] to move, to touch - **2.** [sacudir] to shake.

conmutador *sm* - **1.** ELECTR switch - **2.** *Amér* [centralita] switchboard.

connotación *sf* connotation; **una connotación irónica** a hint of irony.

cono *sm* cone.

conocedor, ra *sm, f*: **conocedor (de)** [gen] expert (on); [de vinos] connoisseur (of).

conocer *vt* - **1.** [gen] to know; **darse a conocer** to make o.s. known; **conocer bien un tema** to know a lot about a subject; **conocer alguien de vista** to know sb by sight; **conocer a alguien de oídas** to have heard of sb - **2.** [descubrir - lugar, país] to get to know - **3.** [a una persona - por primera vez] to meet - **4.** [reconocer]: **conocer a alguien (por algo)** to recognize sb (by sthg). ► **conocerse** *vprnl* - **1.** [a uno mismo] to know o.s. - **2.** [dos o más personas - por primera vez] to meet, to get to know each other; [- desde hace tiempo] to know each other.

conocido, da ◇ *adj* well-known. ◇ *sm, f* acquaintance.

conocimiento *sm* - **1.** [gen] knowledge - **2.** MED [sentido] consciousness; **perder/recobrar el conocimiento** to lose/regain consciousness. ► **conocimientos** *smpl* knowledge (U); **tener muchos conocimientos** to be very knowledgeable.

conozca *etc* ▷ **conocer**.

conque *conj* so; **¿conque te has cansado?** so you're tired, are you?

conquista *sf* [de tierras, persona] conquest.

conquistador, ra *sm, f* - **1.** [de tierras] conqueror - **2.** HIST conquistador.

conquistar *vt* [tierras] to conquer.

consabido, da *adj* [conocido] well-known; [habitual] usual.

consagrar *vt* - **1.** RELIG to consecrate - **2.** [dedicar]: **consagrar algo a algo/alguien** [tiempo, espacio] to devote sthg to sthg/sb; [monumento, lápida] to dedicate sthg to sthg/sb - **3.** [acreditar, confirmar] to confirm, to establish.

consciencia = **conciencia**.

consciente *adj* conscious; **ser consciente de** to be aware of; **estar consciente** [físicamente] to be conscious.

consecución *sf* [de un deseo] realization; [de un objetivo] attainment; [de un premio] winning.

consecuencia *sf* [resultado] consequence; **a O como consecuencia de** as a consequence O result of; **atenerse a las consecuencias** to accept the consequences; **traer como consecuencia** to result in.

consecuente *adj* [coherente] consistent.

consecutivo, va *adj* consecutive.

conseguir *vt* [gen] to obtain, to get; [un objetivo] to achieve; **conseguir hacer algo** to manage to do sthg; **conseguir que alguien haga algo** to get sb to do sthg.

consejero, ra *sm, f* - **1.** [en asuntos personales] counsellor; [en asuntos técnicos] adviser, consultant - **2.** [de un consejo de administración] member; POLIT [en España] minister *(in an autonomous government)*.

consejo *sm* - **1.** [advertencia] advice *(U)*; **dar un consejo** to give some advice - **2.** [organismo] council; **consejo de administración** board of directors - **3.** [reunión] meeting. ► **Consejo de Europa** *sm* Council of Europe. ► **consejo de guerra** *sm* court martial. ► **consejo de ministros** *sm* cabinet.

consenso *sm* [acuerdo] consensus; [consentimiento] consent.

consentimiento *sm* consent.

consentir ◇ *vt* - **1.** [tolerar] to allow, to permit - **2.** [mimar] to spoil. ◇ *vi*: **consentir en algo/en hacer algo** to agree to sthg/to do sthg.

conserje *smf* [portero] porter; [encargado] caretaker.

conserjería *sf* - **1.** [de un hotel] reception desk - **2.** [de un edificio público o privado] porter's lodge.

conserva *sf*: **conserva de carne** tinned meat; **en conserva** tinned, canned.

conservación *sf* [gen] conservation; [de alimentos] preservation.

conservacionista ◇ *adj* conservation *(antes de s.)*. ◇ *smf* conservationist.

conservante *smf* preservative.

conservar *vt* - **1.** [gen & CULIN] to preserve; [amistad] to keep up; [salud] to look after; [calor]

to retain - **2.** [guardar - libros, cartas, secreto] to keep. ◆ **conservarse** *vprnl* to keep; **se conserva bien** he's keeping well.

conservatorio *sm* conservatoire.

considerable *adj* [gen] considerable; [importante, eminente] notable.

consideración *sf* - **1.** [valoración] consideration - **2.** [respeto] respect; **tratar a alguien con consideración** to be nice to sb; **tratar a alguien sin consideración** to show no consideration to sb; **en consideración a algo** in recognition of sthg - **3.** [importancia]: **de consideración** serious.

considerado, da *adj* [atento] considerate, thoughtful; [respetado] respected.

considerar *vt* - **1.** [valorar] to consider - **2.** [juzgar, estimar] to think. ◆ **considerarse** *vprnl* to consider o.s.; **me considero feliz** I consider myself happy.

consigna *sf* - **1.** [órdenes] instructions *pl* - **2.** [para el equipaje] left-luggage office *UK*, checkroom *US*.

consignar *vt* - **1.** [poner por escrito] to record, to write down - **2.** [enviar - mercancía] to dispatch - **3.** [equipaje] to deposit in the left-luggage office.

consigo *pron pers* with him/her, *pl* with them; [con usted] with you; [con uno mismo] with o.s.; **consigo mismo/misma** with himself/herself; **hablar consigo mismo** to talk to o.s.

consiguiente *adj* consequent; **por consiguiente** consequently, therefore.

consistencia *sf lit & fig* consistency.

consistente *adj* - **1.** [sólido - material] solid - **2.** [coherente - argumento] sound - **3.** [compuesto]: **consistente en** consisting of.

consistir ◆ **consistir en** *vi* - **1.** [gen] to consist of - **2.** [deberse a] to lie in, to be based on.

consola *sf* - **1.** [mesa] console table - **2.** INFORM & TECNOL console; **consola de videojuegos** video console.

consolación *sf* consolation.

consolar *vt* to console.

consolidar *vt* to consolidate.

consomé *sm* consommé.

consonancia *sf* harmony; **en consonancia con** in keeping with.

consonante *sf* consonant.

consorcio *sm* consortium.

conspiración *sf* plot, conspiracy.

conspirador, ra *sm, f* conspirator.

conspirar *vi* to conspire, to plot.

constancia *sf* - **1.** [perseverancia - en una empresa] perseverance; [- en las ideas, opiniones]

steadfastness - **2.** [testimonio] record; **dejar constancia de algo** [registrar] to put sthg on record; [probar] to demonstrate sthg.

constante ◇ *adj* **1.** [persona - en una empresa] persistent - **2.** [acción] constant. ◇ *sf* constant.

constar *vi* - **1.** [una información]: **constar (en)** to appear (in), to figure (in); **constarle a alguien** to be clear to sb; **me consta que...** I am quite sure that...; **que conste que...** let it be clearly understood that..., let there be no doubt that...; **hacer constar** to put on record; **hacer constar por escrito** to confirm in writing - **2.** [estar constituido por]: **constar de** to consist of.

constatar *vt* [observar] to confirm; [comprobar] to check.

constelación *sf* constellation.

consternación *sf* consternation.

constipado, da *adj*: **estar constipado** to have a cold. ◆ **constipado** *sm* cold; **coger un constipado** to catch a cold.

constiparse *vprnl* to catch a cold.

constitución *sf* constitution.

constitucional *adj* constitutional.

constituir *vt* - **1.** [componer] to make up - **2.** [ser] to be - **3.** [crear] to set up.

constituyente *adj & sm* constituent.

constreñir *vt* [oprimir, limitar] to restrict.

construcción *sf* - **1.** [gen] construction; **en construcción** under construction - **2.** [edificio] building.

constructivo, va *adj* constructive.

constructor, ra *adj* building (*antes de s*), construction (*antes de s*). ◆ **constructor** *sm* [de edificios] builder.

construir *vt* [edificio, barco] to build; [aviones, coches] to manufacture; [frase, teoría] to construct.

consuelo *sm* consolation, solace.

cónsul, consulesa *sm, f* consul.

consulado *sm* [oficina] consulate; [cargo] consulship.

consulta *sf* - **1.** [pregunta] consultation; **hacer una consulta a alguien** to seek sb's advice; **consulta popular** referendum, plebiscite - **2.** [despacho de médico] consulting room; **horas de consulta** surgery hours.

consultar ◇ *vt* [dato, fecha] to look up; [libro, persona] to consult. ◇ *vi*: **consultar con** to consult, to seek advice from.

consultor, ra *sm, f* consultant.

consultorio *sm* - **1.** [de un médico] consulting room - **2.** [en periódico] problem page; [en radio] *programme answering listeners' questions* - **3.** [asesoría] advice bureau.

consumar *vt* [gen] to complete; [un crimen] to perpetrate; [el matrimonio] to consummate.

consumición *sf* - **1.** [acción] consumption; **está prohibida la consumición de bebidas alcohólicas** the consumption of alcohol is prohibited - **2.** [bebida] drink; [comida] food; **consumición mínima** cover charge.

consumidor, ra *sm, f* [gen] consumer; [en un bar, restaurante] patron.

consumir ◇ *vt* - **1.** [gen] to consume; **consumieron los refrescos en el bar** they had their drinks at the bar - **2.** [destruir - suj: fuego] to destroy. ◇ *vi* to consume. ➡ **consumirse** *vprnl* - **1.** [persona] to waste away - **2.** [fuego] to burn out.

consumismo *sm* consumerism.

consumo *sm* consumption; **no apto para el consumo** unfit for human consumption; **bienes/sociedad de consumo** consumer goods/ society.

contabilidad *sf* - **1.** [oficio] accountancy - **2.** [de persona, empresa] bookkeeping, accounting; **llevar la contabilidad** to do the accounts.

contable *smf* accountant.

contacto *sm* - **1.** [gen] contact; **perder el contacto** to lose touch - **2.** AUTO ignition.

contado, da *adj* [raro] rare, infrequent; **contadas veces** very rarely. ➡ **al contado** *loc adv*: **pagar al contado** to pay (in) cash.

contador, ra *sm, f Amér* [contable] accountant; **contador público** chartered accountant *UK*, certified public accountant *US*. ➡ **contador** *sm* [aparato] meter.

contaduría *sf Amér*: **contaduría general** audit office.

contagiar *vt* [persona] to infect; [enfermedad] to transmit. ➡ **contagiarse** *vprnl* [enfermedad, risa] to be contagious; [persona] to become infected.

contagio *sm* infection, contagion.

contagioso, sa *adj* [enfermedad] contagious, infectious; [risa etc] infectious.

container = **contenedor**.

contaminación *sf* [gen] contamination; [del medio ambiente] pollution.

contaminar *vt* [gen] to contaminate; [el medio ambiente] to pollute.

contar ◇ *vt* - **1.** [enumerar, incluir] to count - **2.** [narrar] to tell; **¡a mí me lo vas a contar!** you're telling me!, tell me about it! ◇ *vi* to count. ➡ **contar con** *vi* - **1.** [confiar en] to count on - **2.** [tener, poseer] to have - **3.** [tener en cuenta] to take into account; **con esto no contaba** I hadn't reckoned with that.

contemplación *sf* contemplation.

contemplar *vt* [mirar, considerar] to contemplate.

contemporáneo, a *adj* & *sm, f* contemporary.

contenedor, ra *adj* containing. ➡ **contenedor** *sm* [gen] container; [para escombros] skip; **contenedor de basura** large rubbish bin for collecting rubbish from blocks of flats etc; **contenedor de vidrio reciclable** bottle bank.

contener *vt* - **1.** [encerrar] to contain - **2.** [detener, reprimir] to restrain. ➡ **contenerse** *vprnl* to restrain o.s.

contenido *sm* [gen] contents *pl*; [de discurso, redacción] content.

contentar *vt* to please, to keep happy. ➡ **contentarse** *vprnl*: **contentarse con** to make do with.

contento, ta *adj* [alegre] happy; [satisfecho] pleased; **estar contento con alguien/algo** to be pleased with sb/sthg; **tener contento a alguien** to keep sb happy.

contestación *sf* answer.

contestador ➡ **contestador (automático)** *sm* answering machine.

contestar ◇ *vt* to answer; **contestó que vendría** she answered that she'd come. ◇ *vi* - **1.** [responder] to answer; **no contestan** there's no answer - **2.** [replicar] to answer back; **no contestes a tu madre** don't answer back to your mother.

contestatario, ria *adj* anti-establishment.

contexto *sm* context.

contienda *sf* [competición, combate] contest; [guerra] conflict, war.

contigo *pron pers* with you; **contigo mismo/ misma** with yourself.

contiguo, gua *adj* adjacent.

continencia *sf* self-restraint.

continental *adj* continental.

continente *sm* GEOGR continent.

contingente ◇ *adj* unforeseeable. ◇ *sm* - **1.** [grupo] contingent - **2.** COM quota.

continuación *sf* continuation; **a continuación** next, then.

continuar ◇ *vt* to continue, to carry on with. ◇ *vi* to continue, to go on; **continuar haciendo algo** to continue doing O to do sthg; **continúa lloviendo** it's still raining; **'continuará'** 'to be continued'.

continuidad *sf* [en una sucesión] continuity; [permanencia] continuation.

continuo, nua *adj* - **1.** [ininterrumpido] continuous - **2.** [constante, perseverante] continual.

contonearse *vprnl* [hombre] to swagger; [mujer] to swing one's hips.

contorno *sm* - **1.** GEOGR contour; [línea] outline - **2.** *(gen pl)* [vecindad] neighbourhood; [de una ciudad] outskirts *pl*.

contorsionarse *vprnl* [gen] to do contortions; [de dolor] to writhe.

contra ⟨⟩ *prep* against; un jarabe contra la tos a cough syrup; en contra against, estar en contra de algo to be opposed to sthg; en contra de [a diferencia de] contrary to. ⟨⟩ *sm*: los pros y los contras the pros and cons.

contraataque *sm* counterattack.

contrabajo *sm* - 1. [instrumento] double-bass - 2. [voz, cantante] low bass.

contrabandista *smf* smuggler.

contrabando *sm* [acto] smuggling; [mercancías] contraband; pasar algo de contrabando to smuggle sthg in; contrabando de armas gunrunning.

contracción *sf* contraction.

contrachapado, da *adj* made of plywood. ⟐ **contrachapado** *sm* plywood.

contradecir *vt* to contradict.

contradicción *sf* contradiction; estar en contradicción con to be in (direct) contradiction to.

contradicho, cha *pp* ▷ **contradecir**.

contradictorio, ria *adj* contradictory.

contraer *vt* - 1. [gen] to contract - 2. [costumbre, acento etc] to acquire - 3. [enfermedad] to catch. ⟐ **contraerse** *vprnl* to contract.

contrafuerte *sm* ARQUIT buttress.

contraindicación *sf*: 'contraindicaciones:...' 'not to be taken with...'

contralor *sm* Chile inspector of public spending.

contralto *sm* [voz] contralto.

contraluz *sm* back lighting; a contraluz against the light.

contramaestre *sm* - 1. NÁUT boatswain; MIL warrant officer - 2. [capataz] foreman.

contrapartida *sf* compensation; como contrapartida to make up for it.

contrapelo ⟐ **a contrapelo** *loc adv* - 1. [acariciar] the wrong way - 2. [vivir, actuar] against the grain.

contrapesar *vt* [físicamente] to counterbalance.

contrapeso *sm* - 1. [en ascensores, poleas] counterweight - 2. *fig* [fuerza que iguala] counterbalance.

contraponer *vt* [oponer]: contraponer (a) to set up (against). ⟐ **contraponerse** *vprnl* to oppose.

contraportada *sf* [de periódico, revista] back page; [de libro, disco] back cover.

contraproducente *adj* counterproductive.

contrariar *vt* - 1. [contradecir] to go against - 2. [disgustar] to upset.

contrariedad *sf* - 1. [dificultad] setback - 2. [disgusto] annoyance.

contrario, ria *adj* - 1. [opuesto - dirección, sentido] opposite; [- parte] opposing; [- opinión] contrary; ser contrario a algo to be opposed to sthg - 2. [perjudicial]: contrario a contrary to. ⟐ **contrario** *sm* - 1. [rival] opponent - 2. [opuesto] opposite; al contrario, por el contrario on the contrary; de lo contrario otherwise; todo lo contrario quite the contrary.

contrarreloj *adj inv*: etapa contrarreloj time trial.

contrarrestar *vt* [neutralizar] to counteract.

contrasentido *sm* nonsense (U); es un contrasentido hacer eso it doesn't make sense to do that.

contraseña *sf* password.

contrastar ⟨⟩ *vi* to contrast. ⟨⟩ *vt* - 1. [probar - hechos] to check, to verify - 2. [resistir] to resist.

contraste *sm* contrast; hacer contraste con algo to contrast with sthg; en contraste con in contrast to; por contraste in contrast.

contratar *vt* - 1. [obreros, personal, detective] to hire; [deportista] to sign - 2. [servicio, obra, mercancía]: contratar algo a alguien to contract for sthg with sb.

contratiempo *sm* [accidente] mishap; [dificultad] setback.

contratista *smf* contractor.

contrato *sm* contract; bajo contrato under contract; contrato matrimonial marriage contract.

contraventana *sf* shutter.

contribución *sf* - 1. [gen] contribution - 2. [impuesto] tax.

contribuir *vi* - 1. [gen]: contribuir (a) to contribute (to); contribuir con algo para to contribute sthg towards - 2. [pagar impuestos] to pay taxes.

contribuyente *smf* taxpayer.

contrincante *smf* rival, opponent.

control *sm* - 1. [gen] control; bajo control under control; fuera de control out of control; perder el control to lose one's temper; control del estrés stress management; control remoto remote control - 2. [verificación] examination, inspection; (bajo) control médico (under) medical supervision; control antidoping dope test - 3. [puesto policial] checkpoint; control de pasaportes passport control.

controlador, ra *sm, f* [gen & INFORM] controller; controlador aéreo air traffic controller. ⟐ **controlador de disco** *sm* disk controller.

controlar *vt* - 1. [gen] to control; [cuentas] to audit - 2. [comprobar] to check.

controversia *sf* controversy.

contundente *adj* - **1.** [arma, objeto] blunt; [golpe] thudding - **2.** *fig* [razonamiento, argumento] forceful.

contusión *sf* bruise.

convalecencia *sf* convalescence.

convaleciente *adj* convalescent.

convalidar *vt* [estudios] to recognize; [asignaturas] to validate.

convencer *vt* to convince; **convencer a alguien de algo** to convince sb of sthg. **◆ convencerse** *vprnl*: **convencerse de** to become convinced of.

convencimiento *sm* [certeza] conviction; [acción] convincing.

convención *sf* convention.

convencional *adj* conventional.

conveniencia *sf* - **1.** [utilidad] usefulness; [oportunidad] suitability - **2.** [interés] convenience; **sólo mira su conveniencia** he only looks after his own interests.

conveniente *adj* [útil] useful; [oportuno] suitable, appropriate; [lugar, hora] convenient; [aconsejable] advisable; **sería conveniente asistir** it would be a good idea to go.

convenio *sm* agreement.

convenir *vi* - **1.** [venir bien] to be suitable; **conviene analizar la situación** it would be a good idea to analyse the situation; **no te conviene hacerlo** you shouldn't do it - **2.** [acordar]: **convenir en** to agree on.

convento *sm* [de monjas] convent; [de monjes] monastery.

converger *vi* to converge.

conversación *sf* conversation; **cambiar de conversación** to change the subject; **trabar conversación con alguien** to strike up a conversation with sb. **◆ conversaciones** *sfpl* [negociaciones] talks.

conversada *sf* *Amér* chat.

conversar *vi* to talk, to converse.

conversión *sf* conversion.

converso, sa *adj* converted.

convertir *vt* - **1.** RELIG to convert - **2.** [transformar]: **convertir algo/a alguien en** to convert sthg/sb into, to turn sthg/sb into. **◆ convertirse** *vprnl* - **1.** RELIG: **convertirse (a)** to convert (to) - **2.** [transformarse]: **convertirse en** to become, to turn into.

convexo, xa *adj* convex.

convicción *sf* conviction; **tener la convicción de que** to be convinced that.

convicto, ta *adj* convicted.

convidar *vt* [invitar] to invite.

convincente *adj* convincing.

convite *sm* - **1.** [invitación] invitation - **2.** [fiesta] banquet.

convivencia *sf* living together.

convivir *vi* to live together; **convivir con** to live with.

convocar *vt* [reunión] to convene; [huelga, elecciones] to call.

convocatoria *sf* - **1.** [anuncio, escrito] notice - **2.** [de examen] diet.

convulsión *sf* - **1.** [de músculos] convulsion - **2.** [política, social] upheaval (U).

conyugal *adj* conjugal; **vida conyugal** married life.

cónyuge *smf* spouse; **los cónyuges** husband and wife.

coñac (*pl* coñacs), **cognac** (*pl* cognacs) *sm* brandy, cognac.

coñazo *sm* *fam* pain, drag.

coño *vulg* ◇ *sm* [genital] cunt. ◇ *interj* - **1.** [enfado]: **¡coño!** for fuck's sake! - **2.** [asombro]: **¡coño!** fucking hell!

cooperación *sf* cooperation.

cooperar *vi*: **cooperar (con alguien en algo)** to cooperate (with sb in sthg).

cooperativo, va *adj* cooperative. **◆ cooperativa** *sf* cooperative.

coordinador, ra ◇ *adj* coordinating. ◇ *sm, f* coordinator.

coordinar *vt* - **1.** [movimientos, gestos] to coordinate - **2.** [esfuerzos, medios] to combine, to pool.

copa *sf* - **1.** [vaso] glass; **ir de copas** to go out drinking; **¿quieres (tomar) una copa?** would you like (to have) a drink?; **lleva unas copas de más** she's had one too many - **2.** [de árbol] top; **es un profesional como la copa de un pino** *fam* he's a consummate professional; **es una mentira como la copa de un pino** *fam* it's a whopper of a lie - **3.** [en deporte] cup. **◆ copas** *sfpl* [naipes] *suit with pictures of goblets in Spanish playing cards.*

copete *sm* [de ave] crest.

copetín *sm* *Amér* [bebida] aperitif; [comida] appetizer.

copia *sf* [reproducción] copy; **sacar una copia** to make a copy; **copia al carbón** carbon copy; **copia de seguridad** INFORM backup; **hacer una copia de seguridad de algo** to back sthg up, to make a back-up of sthg.

copiar ◇ *vt* [gen] to copy; [al dictado] to take down. ◇ *vi* [en examen] to cheat, to copy.

copiloto *smf* copilot.

copión, ona *sm, f* [imitador] copycat; [en examen] cheat.

copioso, sa *adj* copious.

copla *sf* - **1.** [canción] folksong, popular song - **2.** [estrofa] verse, stanza.

copo *sm* [de nieve, cereales] flake; **copos de avena** rolled oats; **copos de maíz** cornflakes.

copropietario, ria *sm, f* co-owner.

copular *vi* to copulate.

copulativo, **va** *adj* copulative.

coquetear *vi* to flirt.

coqueto, **ta** *adj* [persona - que flirtea] flirtatious, coquettish; [- que se arregla mucho] concerned with one's appearance.

coraje *sm* - **1.** [valor] courage - **2.** [rabia] anger; **me da mucho coraje** it makes me furious.

coral <> *adj* choral. <> *sm* coral. <> *sf* - **1.** [coro] choir - **2.** [composición] chorale.

Corán *sm*: **el Corán** the Koran.

coraza *sf* - **1.** [de soldado] cuirasse, armour - **2.** [de tortuga] shell.

corazón *sm* - **1.** [órgano] heart - **2.** [centro - de ciudad, alcachofa] heart; [- de manzana] core - **3.** ⊏> **dedo.**

corazonada *sf* - **1.** [presentimiento] hunch - **2.** [impulso] sudden impulse.

corbata *sf* tie.

Córcega *n pr* Corsica.

corchea *sf* quaver.

corchete *sm* - **1.** [broche] hook and eye - **2.** [signo ortográfico] square bracket.

corcho *sm* cork.

cordel *sm* cord.

cordero, **ra** *sm*, *f* *lit & fig* lamb.

cordial *adj* cordial.

cordialidad *sf* cordiality.

cordillera *sf* mountain range; **la cordillera Cantábrica** the Cantabrian Mountains.

cordón *sm* - **1.** [gen & ANAT] cord; [de zapato] lace; [cordón umbilical] umbilical cord - **2.** [cable eléctrico] flex - **3.** *fig* [para protección, vigilancia] cordon; **cordón sanitario** cordon sanitaire - **4.** *C Sur* [de la vereda] kerb *UK*, curb *US*.

cordura *sf* [juicio] sanity; [sensatez] sense.

Corea *n pr*: **Corea del Norte/Sur** North/South Korea.

corear *vt* to chorus.

coreógrafo, **fa** *sm*, *f* choreographer.

corista *smf* [en coro] chorus singer.

cornada *sf* goring.

cornamenta *sf* [de toro] horns *pl*; [de ciervo] antlers *pl*.

córner *sm* corner (kick); **lanzar** *O* **sacar un córner** to take a corner.

corneta *sf* [instrumento] bugle.

cornisa *sf* ARQUIT cornice.

coro *sm* - **1.** [gen] choir; **contestar a coro** to answer all at once - **2.** [de obra musical] chorus.

corona *sf* - **1.** [gen] crown - **2.** [de flores] garland; **corona fúnebre/de laurel** funeral/laurel wreath - **3.** [de santos] halo.

coronación *sf* [de monarca] coronation.

coronar *vt* - **1.** [persona] to crown - **2.** *fig* [terminar] to complete; [culminar] to crown, to cap.

coronel *sm* colonel.

coronilla *sf* crown (of the head); **estar hasta la coronilla (de)** to be sick and tired (of).

corpiño *sm* - **1.** [bodice ar.] *Arg* [corsé] bra.

corporación *sf* corporation.

corporal *adj* corporal.

corporativo, **va** *adj* corporate.

corpulento, **ta** *adj* corpulent.

corral *sm* [gen] yard; [para cerdos, ovejas] pen.

correa *sf* - **1.** [de bolso, reloj] strap; [de pantalón] belt; [de perro] lead, leash - **2.** TECNOL belt; **correa del ventilador** fan belt.

corrección *sf* - **1.** [de errores] correction; **corrección de pruebas** proofreading - **2.** [de exámenes] marking - **3.** [de texto] revision - **4.** [de comportamiento] correctness.

correctivo, **va** *adj* corrective. ➡ **correctivo** *sm* punishment.

correcto, **ta** *adj* - **1.** [resultado, texto, respuesta] correct - **2.** [persona] polite; [conducta] proper.

corredor, **ra** <> *adj* running. <> *sm*, *f* - **1.** [deportista] runner - **2.** [intermediario]: **corredor de bolsa** stockbroker; **corredor de comercio** COM registered broker; **corredor de seguros** COM insurance broker. ➡ **corredor** *sm* [pasillo] corridor.

corregir *vt* [gen] to correct; [exámenes] to mark. ➡ **corregirse** *vprnl* to change for the better.

correlación *sf* correlation.

correo *sm* post *UK*, mail *US*; **echar al correo** to post; **a vuelta de correo** by return (of post); **correo aéreo** air mail; **correo basura** INFORM spam; **correo comercial** direct mail; **correo electrónico** e-mail; **correo urgente** special delivery; **correo de voz** voice mail. ➡ **Correos** *sm* [organismo] the post office.

correr <> *vi* - **1.** [andar de prisa] to run; **a todo correr** at full speed *O* pelt; **(ella) corre que se las pela** she runs like the wind - **2.** [conducir de prisa] to drive fast - **3.** [pasar por - río] to flow; [- camino, agua del grifo] to run; **deja correr el agua del grifo** leave the tap running - **4.** [el tiempo, las horas] to pass, to go by - **5.** [propagarse - noticia etc] to spread. <> *vt* - **1.** [recorrer - una distancia] to cover; **corrió los 100 metros** he ran the 100 metres - **2.** [deslizar - mesa, silla] to move *O* pull up - **3.** [cortinas] to draw; **correr el pestillo** to bolt the door - **4.** [experimentar - aventuras, vicisitudes] to have; [- riesgo] to run - **5.** *Amér fam* [despedir] to throw out. ➡ **correrse** *vprnl* - **1.** [desplazarse - persona] to move over; [- cosa] to slide - **2.** [pintura, colores] to run.

correspondencia *sf* - **1.** [gen] correspondence; **curso por correspondencia** correspondence course - **2.** [de metro, tren] connection.

corresponder *vi* - **1.** [compensar]: **corresponder (con algo) a alguien/algo** to repay sb/sthg (with sthg) - **2.** [pertenecer] to belong - **3.** [coincidir]: **corresponder (a/con)** to correspond (to/with) - **4.** [tocar]: **corresponderle a alguien hacer algo** to be sb's responsibility to do sthg - **5.** [a un sentimiento] to reciprocate. ◆ **corresponderse** *vprnl* - **1.** [escribirse] to correspond - **2.** [amarse] to love each other.

correspondiente *adj* - **1.** [gen]: **correspondiente (a)** corresponding (to) - **2.** [respectivo] respective.

corresponsal *smf* PRENSA correspondent.

corretear *vi* [correr] to run about.

corrido, da *adj* [avergonzado] embarrassed. ◆ **corrida** *sf* - **1.** TAUROM bull fight - **2.** [acción de correr] run; **dar una corrido** to make a dash; **en una corrido** inan instant O a flash. ◆ **de corrido** *loc prep* by heart.

corriente ◇ *adj* - **1.** [normal] ordinary, normal; **corriente y moliente** run-of-the-mill - **2.** [agua] running - **3.** [mes, año, cuenta] current. ◇ *sf* - **1.** [de río, electricidad] current - **2.** [de aire] draught - **3.** *fig* [tendencia] trend, current; [de opinión] tide - **4.** *loc*: **dejarse llevar de** O **por la corriente** to follow the crowd; **ir contra corriente** to go against the tide; **llevarle** O **seguirle la corriente a alguien** to humour sb. ◇ *sm*: **estar al corriente de** to be up to date with; **poner al corriente** to bring up to date; **ponerse al corriente** to bring o.s. up to date; **tener a alguien al corriente** to keep sb informed.

corro *sm* [círculo] circle, ring; **en corro** in a circle.

corroborar *vt* to corroborate.

corroer *vt* [gen] to corrode; GEOL to erode.

corromper *vt* - **1.** [pudrir - madera] to rot; [- alimentos] to turn bad, to spoil - **2.** [pervertir] to corrupt.

corrosivo, va *adj lit & fig* corrosive.

corrupción *sf* - **1.** [gen] corruption; **corrupción de menores** corruption of minors - **2.** [de una substancia] decay.

corrusco *sm* hard crust.

corsario, ria *adj* pirate *(antes de s)*. ◆ **corsario** *sm* corsair, pirate.

corsé *sm* corset.

cortacésped *(pl* cortacéspedes*)* *sm* lawn-mower.

cortado, da *adj* - **1.** [labios, manos] chapped - **2.** [leche] sour, off; [salsa] curdled - **3.** *fam fig* [tímido] inhibited. ◆ **cortado** *sm* [café] *small coffee with just a little milk.*

cortafuego *sm* firebreak.

cortafuegos *sm inv* INFORM firewall.

cortante *adj* - **1.** [afilado] sharp - **2.** *fig* [frase] cutting; [viento] biting; [frío] bitter.

cortapisa *sf* limitation, restriction; **poner cortapisas a algo** to hinder sb.

cortar ◇ *vt* - **1.** [seccionar - pelo, uñas] to cut; [- papel] to cut up; [- ramas] to cut off; [- árbol] to cut down - **2.** [amputar] to amputate, to cut off - **3.** [tela, figura de papel] to cut out - **4.** [interrumpir - retirada, luz, teléfono] to cut off; [- carretera] to block (off); [- hemorragia] to stop, to staunch; [- discurso, conversación] to interrupt - **5.** [labios, piel] to chap. ◇ *vi* - **1.** *R Dom* [comunicación] to hang up - **2.** [producir un corte] to cut - **3.** [cesar una relación] to break O split up; **he cortado con mi novio** I've split up with my boyfriend. ◆ **cortarse** *vprnl* - **1.** [herirse] to cut o.s.; **cortarse el pelo** to have a haircut - **2.** [alimento] to curdle - **3.** *fam* [turbarse] to become tongue-tied.

cortaúñas *sm inv* nail clippers *pl*.

corte ◇ *sm* - **1.** [raja] cut; [en pantalones, camisa etc] tear; **corte y confección** [para mujeres] dressmaking; [para hombres] tailoring - **2.** [interrupción]: **corte de digestión** stomach cramps - **3.** [sección] section - **4.** [concepción, estilo] style - **5.** *fam* [vergüenza] embarrassment. ◇ *sf* [palacio] court; **hacer la corte a alguien** *fig* to court sb. ◆ **Cortes** *sfpl* POLÍT *the Spanish parliament.*

cortejar *vt* to court.

cortejo *sm* retinue; **cortejo fúnebre** funeral cortège O procession.

cortés *adj* polite, courteous.

cortesía *sf* courtesy; **por cortesía de** courtesy of.

corteza *sf* - **1.** [del árbol] bark - **2.** [de pan] crust; [de queso, tocino, limón] rind; [de naranja etc] peel - **3.** [terrestre] crust.

cortina *sf* [de tela] curtain; *fig*: **cortina de agua** sheet of water.

cortisona *sf* cortisone.

corto, ta *adj* - **1.** [gen] short - **2.** [escaso - raciones] meagre; [- disparo] short of the target; **corto de** [dinero etc] short of - **3.** *fig* [bobo] dim, simple - **4.** *loc*: **ni corto ni perezoso** as bold as brass; **quedarse corto** [al calcular] to underestimate; **decir que es bueno es quedarse corto** it's an understatement to call it good.

cortocircuito *sm* short circuit.

cortometraje *sm* short (film).

cosa *sf* - **1.** [gen] thing; **¿queréis alguna cosa?** is there anything you want?; **no es gran cosa** it's not important, it's no big deal; **poca cosa** nothing much - **2.** [asunto] matter; **esto es otra cosa** that's another matter; **no es cosa de risa** it's no laughing matter - **3.** *loc*: **¡otra cosa, mariposa!** let's change the subject!; **decir cuatro cosas a alguien** to give sb a piece of one's mind; **eso es cosa mía** that's my affair O business; **hacer algo como quien no quiere la cosa** [disimuladamente] to do sthg as if one wasn't intending to; [sin querer] to do sthg almost without realizing it; **son cosas de mamá** that's just the way Mum is, that's just one of Mum's little idiosyncrasies; **son las cosas de la vida** that's life. ➭ **cosa de** *loc adv* about; **es cosa de tres semanas** it takes about three weeks.

coscorrón *sm* bump on the head.

cosecha *sf* - **1.** [gen] harvest; **ser de la (propia) cosecha de alguien** to be made up O invented by sb - **2.** [del vino] vintage.

cosechar ⬦ *vt* - **1.** [cultivar] to grow - **2.** [recolectar] to harvest. ⬦ *vi* to (bring in the) harvest.

coser ⬦ *vt* [con hilo] to sew. ⬦ *vi* to sew; **coser a cuchilladas** to stab repeatedly; **ser cosa de coser y cantar** to be child's play O a piece of cake.

cosido *sm* stitching.

cosmético, ca *adj* cosmetic *(antes de s)*. ➭ **cosmético** *sm* cosmetic. ➭ **cosmética** *sf* cosmetics (U).

cosmopolita *adj* & *smf* cosmopolitan.

cosmos *sm inv* cosmos.

cosquillas *sfpl*: **hacer cosquillas** to tickle; **buscarle las cosquillas a alguien** to wind sb up, to irritate sb.

costa *sf* GEOGR coast. ➭ **a costa de** *loc prep* at the expense of; **lo hizo a costa de grandes esfuerzos** he did it by dint of much effort; **vive a costa de sus padres** she lives off her parents. ➭ **a toda costa** *loc prep* at all costs.

costado *sm* side; **es francés por los cuatro costados** he's French through and through.

costal *sm* sack.

costanera *sf C Sur* promenade.

costar ⬦ *vt* - **1.** [dinero] to cost - **2.** [tiempo] to take. ⬦ *vi* [ser difícil]: **costar caro a alguien** to cost sb dear.

Costa Rica *n pr* Costa Rica.

costarricense, costarriqueño, ña *adj* & *sm, f* Costa Rican.

coste *sm* [de producción] cost; [de un objeto] price; **coste unitario** ECON unit cost.

costear *vt* [pagar] to pay for.

costilla *sf* - **1.** [de persona, barco] rib - **2.** [de animal] cutlet.

costo *sm* [de una mercancía] price; [de un producto, de la vida] cost.

costoso, sa *adj* [operación, maquinaria] expensive.

costra *sf* [de herida] scab.

costumbre *sf* habit, custom; **coger/perder la costumbre de hacer algo** to get into/out of the habit of doing sthg; **como de costumbre** as usual; **por costumbre** through force of habit, out of habit.

costura *sf* - **1.** [labor] sewing, needlework - **2.** [puntadas] seam - **3.** [oficio] dressmaking; **alta costura** haute couture.

costurero *sm* [caja] sewing box.

cota *sf* - **1.** [altura] altitude, height above sea level - **2.** *fig* [nivel] level, height.

cotarro *sm* riotous gathering; **alborotar el cotarro** to stir up trouble; **dirigir el cotarro** to rule the roost.

cotejar *vt* to compare.

cotejo *sm* comparison.

cotidiano, na *adj* daily.

cotilla *smf fam* gossip, busybody.

cotillear *vi fam* to gossip.

cotilleo *sm fam* gossip, tittle-tattle.

cotillón *sm* New Year's Eve party.

cotización *sf* - **1.** [valor] price - **2.** [en Bolsa] quotation, price.

cotizar ⬦ *vt* - **1.** [valorar] to quote, to price - **2.** [pagar] to pay. ⬦ *vi* to pay contributions. ➭ **cotizarse** *vprnl* - **1.** [estimarse - persona] to be valued O prized - **2.**: **cotizarse a** [producto] to sell for, to fetch; [bonos, valores] to be quoted at.

coto *sm* preserve; **coto de caza** game preserve; **poner coto a** to put a stop to.

cotorra *sf* [ave] parrot.

COU (*abrev de* **Curso de Orientación Universitaria**) *sm formerly, a one-year course which prepared pupils aged 17-18 for Spanish university entrance examinations.*

coxis = **cóccix.**

coyote *sm* - **1.** [animal] coyote - **2.** *Méx fam* [guía] guide - **3.** *Méx fam* [intermediario] fixer, middleman.

coyuntura *sf* - **1.** [situación] moment - **2.** ANAT joint.

coz *sf* kick.

crac (*pl* cracs), **crack** (*pl* cracks) *sm* FIN crash.

crack (*pl* cracks) *sm* - **1.** FIN = **crac** - **2.** [droga] crack.

cráneo *sm* cranium, skull.

crápula *smf* libertine.

cráter *sm* crater.

creación *sf* creation.

creador, ra ⬦ *adj* creative. ⬦ *sm, f* creator; **creador gráfico** creator *(of cartoon etc).*

crear *vt* - **1.** [gen] to create - **2.** [fundar - una academia] to found.

creatividad *sf* creativity.

creativo, va *adj* creative.

crecer *vi* - **1.** [persona, planta] to grow - **2.** [días, noches] to grow longer - **3.** [río, marea] to rise

- **4.** [aumentar - animosidad etc] to grow, to increase; [- rumores] to spread. ➤ **crecerse** *vprnl* to become more self-confident.

creces ➤ **con creces** *adv* with interest.

crecido, da *adj* [cantidad] large; [hijo] grown-up. ➤ **crecida** *sf* spate, flood.

creciente *adj* [gen] growing; [luna] crescent.

crecimiento *sm* [gen] growth; [de precios] rise; **crecimiento económico** ECON economic growth.

credibilidad *sf* credibility.

crédito *sm* - **1.** [préstamo] loan; **a crédito** on credit; **crédito personal** ECON personal loan - **2.** [plazo de préstamo] credit - **3.** [confianza] trust, belief; **digno de crédito** trustworthy; **dar crédito a algo** to believe sthg - **4.** [en universidad] credit.

credo *sm* [religioso] creed.

crédulo, la *adj* credulous.

creencia *sf* belief.

creer *vt* - **1.** [gen] to believe; **¡ya lo creo!** of course!, I should say so! - **2.** [suponer] to think; **creo que no** I don't think so; **creo que sí** I think so; **según creo** to the best of my knowledge - **3.** [estimar] to think; **lo creo muy capaz de hacerlo** I think he's quite capable of doing it. ➤ **creer en** *vi* to believe in. ➤ **creerse** *vprnl* [considerarse] to believe o.s. to be.

creíble *adj* credible, believable.

creído, da *sm, f* [presumido] conceited.

crema *sf* - **1.** [gen] cream; **crema batida** whipped cream; **la crema del mundo literario** the cream of the literary world - **2.** [cosmético, betún] cream; **crema de afeitar** shaving cream; **crema dental** toothpaste; **crema depilatoria** hair remover; **crema facial** face cream; **crema hidratante** moisturizer - **3.** [licor] crème - **4.** [dulce, postre] custard.

cremallera *sf* [para cerrar] zip (fastener), zipper *US*.

crematorio, ria *adj*: **horno crematorio** cremator. ➤ **crematorio** *sm* crematorium.

cremoso, sa *adj* creamy.

crepe [krep] *sf* crepe.

crepitar *vi* to crackle.

crepúsculo *sm* [al amanecer] first light; [al anochecer] twilight, dusk.

crespo, pa *adj* tightly curled, frizzy.

cresta *sf* - **1.** [gen] crest; **estar en la cresta (de la ola)** to be riding high - **2.** [del gallo] comb.

cretino, na *sm, f* cretin.

creyente *smf* believer.

cría ▷ **crío**.

criadero *sm* [de animales] farm *(breeding place)*; [de árboles, plantas] nursery.

criadillas *sfpl* bull's testicles.

criado, da *sm, f* servant (*f* maid).

criador, ra *sm, f* [de animales] breeder; [de vinos] grower.

crianza *sf* - **1.** [de animales] breeding - **2.** [del vino] vintage - **3.** [educación] breeding.

criar *vt* - **1.** [amamantar - suj: mujer] to breast-feed; [- suj: animal] to suckle - **2.** [animales] to breed, to rear; [flores, árboles] to grow - **3.** [vino] to mature, to make - **4.** [educar] to bring up. ➤ **criarse** *vprnl* [crecer] to grow up.

criatura *sf* - **1.** [niño] child; [bebé] baby - **2.** [ser vivo] creature.

criba *sf* - **1.** [tamiz] sieve - **2.** [selección] screening.

cricket ['kriket] *sm* cricket.

crimen *sm* crime.

criminal *adj & smf* criminal; **criminal de guerra** war criminal.

crin *sf* mane.

crío, cría *sm, f* [niño] kid. ➤ **cría** *sf* - **1.** [hijo del animal] young - **2.** [crianza - de animales] breeding; [- de plantas] growing.

criogenia *sf* cryogenics *(sing)*.

criollo, lla *adj* - **1.** [persona] native to Latin America - **2.** [comida, lengua] creole.

cripta *sf* crypt.

crisantemo *sm* chrysanthemum.

crisis *sf inv* [gen] crisis; **crisis cardíaca** cardiac arrest, heart failure; **crisis de los cuarenta** mid-life crisis; **crisis económica** recession.

crisma *sf fam* bonce, nut; **romperle la crisma a alguien** to bash sb's head in.

crismas, christmas *sm inv* Christmas card.

crispar *vt* [los nervios] to set on edge; [los músculos] to tense; [las manos] to clench.

cristal *sm* - **1.** [material] glass *(U)*; [vidrio fino] crystal; **cristal de roca** rock crystal - **2.** [en la ventana] (window) pane - **3.** [en mineralogía] crystal.

cristalera *sf* [puerta] French window; [techo] glass roof; [armario] glass-fronted cabinet.

cristalino, na *adj* crystalline. ➤ **cristalino** *sm* crystalline lens.

cristalizar *vt* - **1.** [una sustancia] to crystallize - **2.** *fig* [un asunto] to bring to a head. ➤ **cristalizarse** *vprnl* to crystallize. ➤ **cristalizarse en** *vprnl fig* to develop into.

cristiandad *sf* Christianity.

cristianismo *sm* Christianity.

cristiano, na *adj & sm, f* Christian.

cristo *sm* crucifix. ➤ **Cristo** *sm* Christ; **estar hecho un Cristo** *fam* to be a pitiful sight.

criterio *sm* - **1.** [norma] criterion; **criterios de convergencia** [en UE] convergence criteria - **2.** [juicio] taste - **3.** [opinión] opinion.

crítica ▷ **crítico**.

criticar *vt* - **1.** [enjuiciar - literatura, arte] to review - **2.** [censurar] to criticize.

crítico, ca ◇ *adj* critical. ◇ *sm, f* [persona] critic. ◆ **crítica** *sf* - **1.** [juicio - sobre arte, literatura] review - **2.** [conjunto de críticos]: **la crítica** the critics *pl* - **3.** [ataque] criticism.

criticón, ona ◇ *adj* nit-picking. ◇ *sm, f* nitpicker.

Croacia *n pr* Croatia.

croar *vi* to croak.

croata ◇ *adj* Croatian. ◇ *smf* Croat.

crol *sm* DEP crawl.

cromo *sm* - **1.** [metal] chrome - **2.** [estampa] picture card; **ir hecho un cromo** to be dressed up to the nines.

cromosoma *sm* chromosome.

crónico, ca *adj* chronic. ◆ **crónica** *sf* - **1.** [de la historia] chronicle - **2.** [de un periódico] column; [de la televisión] feature, programme.

cronista *smf* [historiador] chronicler; [periodista] columnist.

cronología *sf* chronology.

cronometrar *vt* to time.

cronómetro *sm* DEP stopwatch; TECNOL chronometer.

croqueta *sf* croquette.

croquis *sm inv* sketch.

cross *sm inv* [carrera] cross-country race; [deporte] cross-country (running).

cruasán, croissant [krwa'san] (*pl* croissants) *sm* croissant.

cruce *sm* - **1.** [de líneas] crossing, intersection; [de carreteras] crossroads - **2.** [paso] crossing; **cruce a nivel** level crossing *UK*, grade crossing *US*; **cruce de peatones** pedestrian crossing - **3.** [de animales] cross.

crucero *sm* - **1.** [viaje] cruise - **2.** [barco] cruiser - **3.** [de iglesias] transept.

crucial *adj* crucial.

crucificar *vt* [en una cruz] to crucify.

crucifijo *sm* crucifix.

crucifixión *sf* crucifixion.

crucigrama *sm* crossword (puzzle).

cruda *sf* ▷ **crudo**.

crudeza *sf* - **1.** [gen] harshness; **con crudeza** harshly - **2.** [de descripción, imágenes] brutality.

crudo, da *adj* - **1.** [natural] raw; [petróleo] crude - **2.** [sin cocer completamente] undercooked - **3.** [realidad, clima, tiempo] harsh; [novela] harshly realistic, hard-hitting - **4.** [cruel] cruel. ◆ **crudo** *sm* crude (oil). ◆ **cruda** *sf* Guat & Méx fam [resaca] hangover.

cruel *adj* [gen] cruel.

crueldad *sf* - **1.** [gen] cruelty - **2.** [acción cruel] act of cruelty.

crujido *sm* [de madera] creak, creaking *(U)*; [de hojas secas] crackle, crackling *(U)*.

crujiente *adj* [madera] creaky; [hojas secas] rustling; [patatas fritas] crunchy.

crujir *vi* [madera] to creak; [patatas fritas, nieve] to crunch; [hojas secas] to crackle; [dientes] to grind.

cruz *sf* - **1.** [gen] cross; **cruz gamada** swastika - **2.** [de una moneda] tails *(U)* - **3.** *fig* [aflicción] burden. ◆ **Cruz Roja** *sf* Red Cross.

cruza *sf* Amér cross, crossbreed.

cruzado, da *adj* - **1.** [cheque, piernas, brazos] crossed - **2.** [animal] crossbred - **3.** [abrigo, chaqueta] double-breasted. ◆ **cruzada** *sf* lit & fig crusade.

cruzar *vt* - **1.** [gen] to cross; **cruzar los dedos** to cross one's fingers - **2.** [unas palabras] to exchange. ◆ **cruzarse** *vprnl* - **1.** [gen] to cross; **cruzarse de brazos** to fold one's arms - **2.** [personas]: **cruzarse con alguien** to pass sb.

cta. *(abrev de* cuenta*)* a/c.

cte. *(abrev de* corriente*)* inst.

cuaderno *sm* [gen] notebook; [en el colegio] exercise book. ◆ **cuaderno de bitácora** *sm* logbook.

cuadra *sf* - **1.** [de caballos] stable - **2.** Amér [en calle] block.

cuadrado, da *adj* [gen & MAT] square; **elevar al cuadrado** to square. ◆ **cuadrado** *sm* square.

cuadragésimo, ma *num* fortieth.

cuadrar ◇ *vi* - **1.** [información, hechos]: **cuadrar (con)** to square *O* agree (with) - **2.** [números, cuentas] to tally, to add up. ◇ *vt* [gen] to square. ◆ **cuadrarse** *vprnl* MIL to stand to attention.

cuadrícula *sf* grid.

cuadrilátero *sm* - **1.** GEOM quadrilateral - **2.** DEP ring.

cuadrilla *sf* [de amigos, trabajadores] group; [de maleantes] gang.

cuadro *sm* - **1.** [pintura] painting, picture - **2.** [escena] scene, spectacle - **3.** [descripción] portrait - **4.** [cuadrado] square; **a cuadros** check *(antes de s)*; **quedarse a cuadros** *fam* to be gobsmacked, to be flabbergasted; **quedarse en cuadros** to be down to a skeleton staff - **5.** [equipo] team; **cuadros medios** middle management - **6.** [gráfico] chart, diagram - **7.** [de la bicicleta] frame - **8.** TEATRO scene.

cuádruple *sm* quadruple.

cuajar ◇ *vt* [solidificar - leche] to curdle; [- huevo] to set; [- sangre] to clot, to coagulate. ◇ *vi* - **1.** [lograrse - acuerdo] to be settled; [- negocio] to take off, to get going - **2.** [ser aceptado - persona] to fit in; [- moda] to catch on - **3.** [nieve] to settle. ◆ **cuajarse** *vprnl* [leche] to curdle; [sangre] to clot, to coagulate.

cuajo *sm* rennet. ◆ **de cuajo** *loc adv*: **arrancar de cuajo** [árbol] to uproot; [brazo etc] to tear right off.

cual *pron relat*: **el/la cual** *etc* [de persona] *(sujeto)* who, *(complemento)* whom; [de cosas] which; **lo cual** which; **conoció a una española, la cual vivía en Buenos Aires** he met a Spanish girl who lived in Buenos Aires; **está muy enfadada, lo cual es comprensible** she's very angry, which is understandable; **todo lo cual** all of which; **sea cual sea** *O* **fuere su decisión** whatever his decision (may be).

cuál *pron (interrogativo)* what; [en concreto, especificando] which one; **¿cuál es tu nombre?** what is your name?; **¿cuál es la diferencia?** what's the difference?; **no sé cuáles son mejores** I don't know which are best; **¿cuál prefieres?** which one do you prefer?

cualesquiera ▷ **cualquiera**.

cualidad *sf* quality.

cualificado, da *adj* skilled.

cualitativo, va *adj* qualitative.

cualquiera (*pl* **cualesquiera**) ◇ *adj (antes de s: **cualquier**)* any; **cualquier día vendré a visitarte** I'll drop by one of these days; **en cualquier momento** at any time; **en cualquier lugar** anywhere. ◇ *pron* anyone; **cualquiera te lo dirá** anyone will tell you; **cualquiera que** [persona] anyone who; [cosa] whatever; **cualquiera que sea la razón** whatever the reason (may be). ◇ *sm, f* [don nadie] nobody.

cuan *adv* [todo lo que]: **se desplomó cuan largo era** he fell flat on the ground.

cuán *adv* how.

cuando ◇ *adv* when; **de cuando en cuando** from time to time; **de vez en cuando** now and again. ◇ *conj* - **1.** [de tiempo] when; **cuando llegue el verano iremos de viaje** when summer comes we'll go travelling - **2.** [si] if; **cuando tú lo dices será verdad** it must be true if you say so - **3.** *(después de 'aun')* [aunque]: **no mentiría aun cuando le fuera en ello la vida** she wouldn't lie even if her life depended on it. ◆ **cuando más** *loc adv* at the most. ◆ **cuando menos** *loc adv* at least. ◆ **cuando quiera que** *loc conj* whenever.

cuándo *adv* when; **¿cuándo vas a venir?** when are you coming?; **quisiera saber cuándo sale el tren** I'd like to know when *O* at what time the train leaves.

cuantía *sf* [suma] quantity; [alcance] extent.

cuantificar *vt* to quantify.

cuantioso, sa *adj* large, substantial.

cuantitativo, va *adj* quantitative.

cuanto, ta ◇ *adj* - **1.** [todo]: **despilfarra cuanto dinero gana** he squanders all the money he earns; **soporté todas cuantas críticas me hizo** I put up with every single criticism he made of me - **2.** *(antes de adv)* [compara cantidades]: **cuantas más mentiras digas, menos te creerán** the more you lie, the less people will believe you. ◇ *pron relat (gen*

pl) [de personas] everyone who; [de cosas] everything (that); **cuantos fueron alabaron el espectáculo** everyone who went said the show was excellent; **dio las gracias a todos cuantos le ayudaron** he thanked everyone who helped him. ◆ **cuanto** ◇ *pron relat (neutro)* - **1.** [todo lo que] everything, as much as; **come cuanto quieras** eat as much as you like; **comprendo cuanto dice** I understand everything he says; **todo cuanto** everything - **2.** [compara cantidades]: **cuanto más se tiene, más se quiere** the more you have, the more you want. ◇ *adv* [compara cantidades]: **cuanto más come, más gordo está** the more he eats, the fatter he gets. ◆ **cuanto antes** *loc adv* as soon as possible. ◆ **en cuanto** ◇ *loc conj* [tan pronto como] as soon as; **en cuanto acabe** as soon as I've finished. ◇ *loc prep* [en calidad de] as; **en cuanto cabeza de familia** as head of the family. ◆ **en cuanto a** *loc prep* as regards.

cuánto, ta ◇ *adj* - **1.** *(interrogativo)* how much (*pl* how many); **¿cuántas manzanas tienes?** how many apples do you have?; **¿cuánto pan quieres?** how much bread do you want?; **no sé cuántos hombres había** I don't know how many men were there - **2.** *(exclamativo)* what a lot of; **¡cuánta gente (había)!** what a lot of people (were there)! ◇ *pron (gen pl)* - **1.** *(interrogativo)* how much (*pl* how many); **¿cuántos han venido?** how many came?; **dime cuántas quieres** tell me how many you want - **2.** *(exclamativo)*: **¡cuántos quisieran conocerte!** there are so many people who would like to meet you! ◆ **cuánto** *pron (neutro)* - **1.** *(interrogativo)* how much; **¿cuánto quieres?** how much do you want?; **me gustaría saber cuánto te costarán** I'd like to know how much they'll cost you - **2.** *(exclamativo)*: **¡cuánto han cambiado las cosas!** how things have changed!

cuarenta *num* forty; **los (años) cuarenta** the forties; *ver también* **seis**.

cuarentena *sf* [por epidemia] quarantine; **poner en cuarentena** [enfermos] to (put in) quarantine; [noticia] to put on hold.

cuaresma *sf* Lent.

cuartear *vt* to cut *O* chop up.

cuartel *sm* MIL barracks *pl*; **cuartel general** headquarters *pl*.

cuartelazo *sm Amér* military uprising.

cuarteto *sm* quartet.

cuarto, ta *num* fourth; **la cuarta parte** a quarter. ◆ **cuarto** *sm* - **1.** [parte] quarter; **un cuarto de hora** a quarter of an hour; **son las dos y cuarto** it's a quarter past *UK O* after *US* two; **son las dos menos cuarto** it's a quarter to *UK O* of *US* two - **2.** [habitación] room; **cuarto de baño** bathroom; **cuarto de estar** living room; **cuarto de huéspedes** guestroom; **cuarto oscuro** FOTO darkroom; **cuarto secreto** *R Dom* voting booth. ⟶ **cuarta** *sf* [palmo] span.

cuarzo *sm* quartz.

cuate, ta *sm, f Amér C, Ecuad & Méx fam* pal, mate *UK*, buddy *US*.

cuatro ⟷ *num* four; **más de cuatro** quite a few. ⟷ *adj fig* [poco] a few; **hace cuatro días** a few days ago; *ver también* **seis**.

cuatrocientos, tas *num* four hundred; *ver también* **seis**.

cuba *sf* barrel, cask; **beber como una cuba** to drink like a fish; **estar como una cuba** to be legless *O* blind drunk.

Cuba *n pr* Cuba.

cubalibre *sm* rum and coke.

cubano, na *adj & sm, f* Cuban.

cubertería *sf* set of cutlery, cutlery *(U)*.

cúbico, ca *adj* cubic.

cubierto, ta ⟷ *pp* ▷ **cubrir**. ⟷ *adj* - **1.** [gen]: **cubierto (de)** covered (with); **estar a cubierto** [protegido] to be under cover; [con saldo acreedor] to be in the black; **ponerse a cubierto** to take cover - **2.** [cielo] overcast. ⟶ **cubierto** *sm* - **1.** [pieza de cubertería] piece of cutlery - **2.** [para cada persona] place setting. ⟶ **cubierta** *sf* - **1.** [gen] cover - **2.** [de neumático] tyre - **3.** [de barco] deck.

cubilete *sm* [en juegos] cup.

cubito *sm* - **1.** [de hielo] ice cube - **2.** [de caldo] stock cube.

cubo *sm* - **1.** [recipiente] bucket; **cubo de la basura** rubbish bin *UK*, trashcan *US*, garbage can *US* - **2.** GEOM & MAT cube; **elevar al cubo** to cube.

cubrecama *sm* bedspread.

cubrir *vt* - **1.** [gen] to cover - **2.** [proteger] to protect - **3.** [disimular] to cover up, to hide - **4.** [puesto, vacante] to fill. ⟶ **cubrir de** *vt*: **cubrir de algo a alguien** to heap sthg on sb. ⟶ **cubrirse** *vprnl* - **1.** [taparse]: **cubrirse (de)** to become covered (with) - **2.** [protegerse]: **cubrirse (de)** to shelter (from) - **3.** [con sombrero] to put one's hat on - **4.** [con ropa]: **cubrirse (con)** to cover o.s. (with) - **5.** [cielo] to cloud over.

cucaracha *sf* cockroach *UK*, roach *US*.

cuchara *sf* [para comer] spoon; **cuchara de palo** wooden spoon; **cuchara de postre** dessert spoon; **meter la cuchara** *fam* to butt in.

cucharada *sf* spoonful.

cucharilla *sf* teaspoon.

cucharón *sm* ladle.

cuchichear *vi* to whisper.

cuchilla *sf* blade; **cuchilla de afeitar** razor blade.

cuchillo *sm* knife; **cuchillo de cocina** kitchen knife; **cuchillo de trinchar** carving knife.

cuchitril *sm* hovel.

cuclillas ⟶ **en cuclillas** *loc adv* squatting; **ponerse en cuclillas to squat (down)**.

cuclillo *sm* cuckoo.

cuco, ca *adj fam* - **1.** [bonito] pretty - **2.** [astuto] shrewd, canny. ⟶ **cuco** *sm* cuckoo.

cucurucho *sm* - **1.** [de papel] paper cone - **2.** [para helado] cornet, cone.

cuello *sm* - **1.** [gen] neck; **alargar el cuello** to stretch *O* crane one's neck; **cuello de botella** bottleneck; **cuello uterino** cervix - **2.** [de prendas] collar; **cuello de pico** V-neck; **cuello alto** *O* **de cisne** polo neck *UK*, turtleneck *US*; **hablar para el cuello de su camisa** *fam* to talk to o.s.

cuenca *sf* - **1.** [de río] basin - **2.** [del ojo] (eye) socket - **3.** [región minera] coalfield.

cuenco *sm* earthenware bowl.

cuenta *sf* - **1.** [acción de contar] count; **echar cuentas** to reckon up; **llevar/perder la cuenta de** to keep/lose count of; **cuenta atrás** countdown - **2.** [cálculo] sum - **3.** BANCA & COM account; **abonar algo en cuenta a alguien** to credit sthg to sb's account; **cuenta de gastos** expenditure account; **pagar mil euros a cuenta** to pay a thousand euros down; **cuenta de ahorros** savings account; **cuenta corriente** current account *UK*, checking account *US*; **cuenta de crédito** current account with an overdraft facility; **cuenta deudora** overdrawn account; **cuenta a plazo fijo** deposit account - **4.** [factura] bill *UK*, check *US*; **pasar la cuenta** to send the bill; **cuenta por cobrar/pagar** account receivable/payable - **5.** [bolita - de collar, rosario] bead - **6.** *loc*: **a fin de cuentas** in the end; **ajustarle a alguien las cuentas** to settle an account *O* a score with sb; **caer en la cuenta de algo** to realize sthg; **darse cuenta de algo** to realize sthg; **más de la cuenta** too much; **por mi/tu** *etc* **cuenta** on my/your *etc* own; **tener en cuenta algo** to bear sthg in mind.

cuentagotas *sm inv* dropper; **a** *O* **con cuentagotas** in dribs and drabs.

cuentakilómetros *sm inv* [de distancia recorrida] ≃ milometer; [de velocidad] speedometer.

cuentarrevoluciones *sm inv* tachometer, rev counter.

cuento *sm* - **1.** [fábula] tale; **cuento de hadas** fairy tale; **el cuento de la lechera** *fig* wishful thinking - **2.** [narración] short story - **3.** [mentira, exageración] story, lie; **¡puro cuento!** what nonsense!; **cuento chino** tall story - **4.** *loc*: **tener cuento** to put it on.

cuerda *sf* - **1.** [para atar - fina] string; [- más gruesa] rope; **cuerda floja** tightrope - **2.** [de instrumento] string - **3.** [de reloj] spring; **dar cuerda a** [reloj] to wind up - **4.** GEOM chord. ⟶ **cuerdas vocales** *sfpl* vocal cords.

cuerdo, da adj - **1.** [sano de juicio] sane - **2.** [sensato] sensible.

cueriza sf Andes fam beating, leathering.

cuerno sm [gen] horn; [de ciervo] antler; **saber a cuerno quemado** fam to be fishy; **¡vete al cuerno!** fam go to hell!

cuero sm - **1.** [piel de animal] skin; [piel curtida] hide; **cuero cabelludo** scalp; **en cueros, en cueros vivos** stark naked - **2.** [material] leather.

cuerpo sm - **1.** [gen] body; **cuerpo celeste** heavenly body; **a cuerpo** without a coat on; **luchar cuerpo a cuerpo** to fight hand-to-hand; **tomar cuerpo** to take shape; **en cuerpo y alma** body and soul - **2.** [tronco] trunk - **3.** [corporación consular, militar etc] corps; **cuerpo de bomberos** fire brigade; **cuerpo diplomático** diplomatic corps.

cuervo sm crow.

cuesta sf slope; **cuesta arriba** uphill; **cuesta abajo** downhill; **a cuestas** on one's back, over one's shoulders; **ir cuesta abajo** to decline, to go downhill.

cuestión sf - **1.** [pregunta] question - **2.** [problema] problem - **3.** [asunto] matter, issue; **en cuestión** in question, at issue; **ser cuestión de** to be a question of.

cuestionar vt to question.

cuestionario sm questionnaire.

cueva sf cave; **cueva de ladrones** den of thieves.

cuico sm Méx fam cop.

cuidado <> sm care; **con cuidado** [con esmero] carefully; [con cautela] cautiously; **tener cuidado con** to be careful with; **cuidados intensivos** intensive care (U); **eso me tiene** O **trae sin cuidado** I couldn't care less about that. <> interj: **¡cuidado!** careful!, look out!

cuidadoso, sa adj careful.

cuidar vt [gen] to look after; [estilo etc] to take care over; [detalles] to pay attention to. ⬥ **cuidar de** vi to look after; **cuida de que no lo haga** make sure she doesn't do it. ⬥ **cuidarse** vprnl to take care of O to look after o.s.; **cuidarse de** to worry about.

culata sf - **1.** [de arma] butt - **2.** [de motor] cylinder head.

culebra sf snake.

culebrón sm TV soap opera.

culinario, ria adj culinary.

culminación sf culmination.

culminar <> vt: **culminar (con)** to crown (with). <> vi to finish, to culminate.

culo sm fam - **1.** [de personas] backside, bum UK; **caerse de culo** fam to be flabbergasted, to be gobsmacked; **estar en el culo del mundo** fam to be in the back of beyond; **lamer el culo**

a alguien fam to lick sb's arse UK, to lick sb's ass US; **ser un culo de mal asiento** to be fidgety - **2.** [de objetos] bottom.

culpa sf [responsabilidad] fault; **tener la culpa de algo** to be to blame for sthg; **echar la culpa a alguien (de)** to blame sb (for); **por culpa de** because of.

culpabilidad sf guilt.

culpable <> adj: **culpable (de)** guilty (of); **declararse culpable** to plead guilty. <> smf DER guilty party; **tú eres el culpable** you're to blame.

culpar vt: **culpar a alguien (de)** [atribuir la culpa] to blame sb (for); [acusar] to accuse sb (of).

cultivar vt [tierra] to farm, to cultivate; [plantas] to grow. ⬥ **cultivarse** vprnl [persona] to improve o.s.

cultivo sm - **1.** [de tierra] farming; [de plantas] growing - **2.** [plantación] crop.

culto, ta adj [persona] cultured, educated; [estilo] refined; [palabra] literary. ⬥ **culto** sm - **1.** [devoción] worship; **libertad de culto** freedom of worship - **2.** [religión] cult.

cultura sf - **1.** [de sociedad] culture - **2.** [sabiduría] learning, knowledge; **cultura general** general knowledge.

cultural adj cultural.

culturismo sm body-building.

cumbre sf - **1.** [de montaña] summit - **2.** fig [punto culminante] peak - **3.** POLÍT summit (conference).

cumpleaños sm inv birthday.

cumplido, da adj - **1.** [completo, lleno] full, complete - **2.** [cortés] courteous. ⬥ **cumplido** sm compliment; **andarse con cumplidos** to stand on ceremony; **visita de cumplido** courtesy call.

cumplidor, ra adj reliable.

cumplimentar vt - **1.** [felicitar] to congratulate - **2.** [cumplir - orden] to carry out; [- contrato] to fulfil.

cumplimiento sm [de un deber] performance; [de contrato, promesa] fulfilment; [de la ley] observance; [de órdenes] carrying out; [de condena] completion; [de plazo] expiry.

cumplir <> vt - **1.** [orden] to carry out; [promesa] to keep; [ley] to observe; [contrato] to fulfil - **2.** [años] to reach; **mañana cumplo los 20** I'm 20 O it's my 20th birthday tomorrow - **3.** [condena] to serve; [servicio militar] to do. <> vi - **1.** [plazo, garantía] to expire - **2.** [realizar el deber] to do one's duty; **para** O **por cumplir** out of politeness; **cumplir con el deber** to do one's duty; **cumplir con la palabra** to keep one's word.

cúmulo sm - **1.** [de objetos] pile - **2.** fig [de asuntos, acontecimientos] series.

cuna sf [para dormir] cot, cradle.

cundir *vi* - **1.** [propagarse] to spread - **2.** [dar de sí - comida, reservas, tiempo] to go a long way.

cuneta *sf* [de una carretera] ditch; [de una calle] gutter.

cuña *sf* - **1.** [pieza] wedge - **2.** [de publicidad] commercial break - **3.** *Andes & R Plata fam*: **tener cuña** to have friends in high places.

cuñado, da *sm, f* brother-in-law (*f* sister-in-law).

cuño *sm* - **1.** [troquel] die - **2.** [sello, impresión] stamp.

cuota *sf* - **1.** [contribución - a entidad, club] membership fee, subscription - **2.** [cupo] quota - **3.** *Méx* [peaje] toll.

cupiera *etc* ⊳ **caber.**

cupo ⬦ *sm* - **1.** [cantidad máxima] quota - **2.** [cantidad proporcional] share; [de una cosa racionada] ration - **3.** *Amér* [cabida] capacity. ⬦ *v* ⊳ **caber.**

cupón *sm* [gen] coupon; [de lotería, rifa] ticket.

cúpula *sf* - **1.** ARQUIT dome, cupola - **2.** *fig* [mandos] leaders *pl*.

cura ⬦ *sm* priest. ⬦ *sf* - **1.** [curación] recovery; **tener cura** to be curable - **2.** [tratamiento] treatment, cure; **cura de emergencia** first aid; **cura de reposo** rest cure.

curación *sf* - **1.** [de un enfermo - recuperación] recovery; [- tratamiento] treatment; [de una herida] healing - **2.** [de jamón] curing.

curado, da *adj* [alimento] cured; [pieles] tanned; **curado de espanto** unshockable.

curandero, ra *sm, f* quack.

curar ⬦ *vt* - **1.** [gen] to cure - **2.** [herida] to dress - **3.** [pieles] to tan. ⬦ *vi* [enfermo] to recover; [herida] to heal up. ⬥ **curarse** *vprnl* - **1.** [sanar]: **curarse (de)** to recover (from) - **2.** [alimento] to cure.

curcuncho, cha ⬦ *adj Andes fam* [jorobado] hunchbacked. ⬦ *sm* [joroba] hump; [jorobado] hunchback.

curiosear ⬦ *vi* [fisgonear] to nose around; [por una tienda] to browse round. ⬦ *vt* [libros, revistas] to browse through.

curiosidad *sf* curiosity; **sentir** *O* **tener curiosidad por** to be curious about.

curioso, sa ⬦ *adj* - **1.** [por saber, averiguar] curious, inquisitive - **2.** [raro] odd, strange. ⬦ *sm, f* onlooker.

curita *sm Amér* sticking plaster, Band-Aid® US.

currante *adj fam* hard-working.

currar, currelar *vi fam* to work.

curre = curro.

currelar = currar.

currículum (vitae) [ku'rrikulum('bite)] (*pl* **currícula (vitae)** *O* **currículums**), **currículo** (*pl* **currículos**) *sm* curriculum vitae *UK*, résumé *US*.

curro, curre *sm fam* work.

cursar *vt* - **1.** [estudiar] to study - **2.** [enviar] to send - **3.** [dar - órdenes etc] to give, to issue - **4.** [tramitar] to submit.

cursi *adj fam* [vestido, canción etc] naff, tacky; [modales, persona] affected.

cursilería *sf* [cualidad] tackiness.

cursillo *sm* [curso] short course.

cursiva ⊳ **letra.**

curso *sm* - **1.** [año académico] year - **2.** [lecciones] course; **curso intensivo** crash course; **curso por correspondencia** correspondence course - **3.** [dirección - de río, acontecimientos] course; [- de la economía] trend; **seguir su curso** to go on, to continue; **el resfriado debe seguir su curso** you should allow the cold to run its course.

cursor *sm* INFORM cursor.

curtido, da *adj* - **1.** [piel, cuero] tanned - **2.** *fig* [experimentado] seasoned.

curtir *vt* - **1.** [piel] to tan - **2.** *fig* [persona] to harden.

curva ⊳ **curvo.**

curvatura *sf* curvature.

curvo, va *adj* [gen] curved; [doblado] bent. ⬥ **curva** *sf* [gen]. curve; [en carretera] bend; **curva cerrada** sharp bend; **curva de la felicidad** *fig* [barriga] paunch; **curva de nivel** contour line.

cúspide *sf* - **1.** [de montaña] summit, top - **2.** *fig* [apogeo] peak - **3.** GEOM apex.

custodia *sf* - **1.** [de cosas] safekeeping - **2.** [de personas] custody; **custodia preventiva** protective custody.

custodiar *vt* - **1.** [vigilar] to guard - **2.** [proteger] to look after.

custodio *sm* guard.

cutáneo, a *adj* skin (*antes de s*).

cutícula *sf* cuticle.

cutis *sm inv* skin, complexion.

cutre *adj fam* - **1.** [de bajo precio, calidad] cheap and nasty - **2.** [sórdido] shabby - **3.** [tacaño] tight, stingy.

cutter (*pl* **cutters**) *sm* (artist's) scalpel (*with retractable blade*).

cuyo, ya *adj* [posesión - por parte de personas] whose; [- por parte de cosas] of which, whose; **ésos son los amigos en cuya casa nos hospedamos** those are the friends in whose house we spent the night; **ese señor, cuyo hijo conociste ayer** that man, whose son you met yesterday; **un equipo cuya principal estrella...** a team, the star player of which *O* whose star player...; **en cuyo caso** in which case.

CV (*abrev de* **currículum vitae**) *sm* CV.

D

d, D *sf* [letra] d, D.

D. *abrev de* **don**.

dactilar ⟼ **huella**.

dádiva *sf* [regalo] gift; [donativo] donation.

dado, da *adj* given; **en un momento dado** at a certain point; **ser dado a** to be fond of.
➤ **dado** *sm* dice, die; **echar** *O* **tirar los dados** to throw the dice; **jugar a los dados** to play dice. ➤ **dado que** *loc conj* since, seeing as.

daga *sf* dagger.

dale *interj* ¡dale! - ¡otra vez con lo mismo!
there you go again!

dalia *sf* dahlia.

dálmata *adj* & *smf* [perro] Dalmatian.

daltónico, ca *adj* colour-blind.

daltonismo *sm* colour blindness.

dama *sf* - **1.** [mujer] lady; **primera dama** TEA-TRO leading lady; POLIT first lady US - **2.** [en damas] king; [en ajedrez, naipes] queen. ➤ **damas** *sfpl* [juego] draughts *(U)* UK, checkers *(U)* US.

damisela *sf desus* damsel.

damnificar *vt* [cosa] to damage; [persona] to harm, to injure.

danés, esa ⟨⟩ *adj* Danish. ⟨⟩ *sm, f* [persona] Dane. ➤ **danés** *sm* [lengua] Danish.

danza *sf* [gen] dancing; [baile] dance.

danzar *vi* - **1.** [bailar] to dance - **2.** *fig* [ir de un sitio a otro] to run about.

dañar *vt* [vista, cosecha] to harm, to damage; [persona] to hurt; [pieza, objeto] to damage.
➤ **dañarse** *vprnl* [persona] to hurt o.s.; [cosa] to become damaged.

dañino, na *adj* harmful.

daño *sm* - **1.** [dolor] pain, hurt; **hacer daño a alguien** to hurt sb; **hacerse daño** to hurt o.s. - **2.** [perjuicio a algo] damage; [- a persona] harm; **daños colaterales** collateral damage; **daños y perjuicios** damages.

dar ⟨⟩ *vt* - **1.** [gen] to give; [baile, fiesta] to hold, to give; [naipes] to deal; **dar algo a alguien** to give sthg to sb, to give sb sthg - **2.** [producir - gen] to give, to produce; [- frutos, flores] to bear; [- beneficios, intereses] to yield - **3.** [suj: reloj] to strike; **el reloj ha dado las doce** the clock struck twelve - **4.** [suministrar luz etc - por primera vez] to connect; [- tras un corte] to turn back on; [encender] to turn *O* switch on - **5.** CINE, TEATRO & TV to show; [concierto, interpretación] to give - **6.** [mostrar - señales etc] to show

- **7.** [untar con] to apply; **dar barniz a una silla** to varnish a chair - **8.** [provocar - gusto, escalofríos etc] to give; **me da vergüenza/pena** it makes me ashamed/sad; **me da risa** it makes me laugh; **me da miedo** it frightens me - **9.** [expresa acción]: **dar un grito** to give a cry; **darle un golpe/una puñalada a alguien** to hit/stab sb; **voy a dar un paseo** I'm going (to go) for a walk - **10.** [considerar]: **dar algo por** to consider sthg as; **eso lo doy por hecho** I take that for granted; **dar a alguien por muerto** to give sb up for dead. ⟨⟩ *vi* - **1.** [repartir - naipes] to deal - **2.** [horas] to strike; **han dado las tres en el reloj** three o'clock struck - **3.** [golpear]: **le dieron en la cabeza** they hit him on the head; **la piedra dio contra el cristal** the stone hit the window - **4.** [accionar]: **dar a** [llave de paso] to turn; [botón, timbre] to press - **5.** [estar orientado]: **dar a** [suj: ventana, balcón] to look out onto, to overlook; [suj: pasillo, puerta] to lead to; [suj: casa, fachada] to face - **6.** [encontrar]: **dar con algo/alguien** to find sthg/sb; **he dado con la solución** I've hit upon the solution - **7.** [proporcionar]: **dar de beber a alguien** to give sb sthg to drink; **le da de mamar a su hijo** she breast-feeds her son - **8.** *loc*: **dar de sí** [ropa, calzado] to give, to stretch. ➤ **darse** *vprnl* - **1.** [suceder] to occur, to happen; **se da pocas veces** it rarely happens - **2.** [entregarse]: **darse a** [droga etc] to take to - **3.** [golpearse]: **darse contra** to bump into - **4.** [tener aptitud]: **se me da bien/mal el latín** I'm good/bad at Latin - **5.** [considerarse]: **darse por** to consider o.s. (to be); **darse por vencido** to give in - **6.** *loc*: **dársela a alguien** [engañar] to take sb in; **se las da de listo** he makes out (that) he is clever.

dardo *sm* dart.

dársena *sf* dock.

datar *vt* to date. ➤ **datar de** *vi* to date from.

dátil *sm* BOT & CULIN date.

dato *sm* [gen] piece of information, fact; **datos** [gen] information; INFORM data; **datos personales** personal details; **datos bancarios** bank details.

dcha. (*abrev de* **derecha**) rt.

d. de JC., d.JC. (*abrev de* **después de Jesucristo**) AD.

de *prep* (*de + el = del*) - **1.** [posesión, pertenencia] of; **el coche de mi padre/mis padres** my father's/parents' car; **es de ella** it's hers; **la pata de la mesa** the table leg - **2.** [materia] (made) of; **un vaso de plástico** a plastic cup; **un reloj de oro** a gold watch - **3.** [en descripciones]: **un vaso de agua** a glass of water; **de fácil manejo** user-friendly; **la señora de verde** the lady in green; **el chico de la coleta** the boy with the ponytail; **he comprado las peras de dos euros**

el kilo I bought the pears that were O at two euros a kilo; **un sello de 50 céntimos** a 50 cent stamp - **4.** [asunto] about; **hablábamos de ti** we were talking about you; **libros de historia** history books - **5.** [uso]: **una bici de carreras** a racer; **ropa de deporte** sportswear - **6.** [en calidad de] as; **trabaja de bombero** he works as a fireman - **7.** [tiempo - desde] from; [- durante] in; **trabaja de nueve a cinco** she works from nine to five; **de madrugada** early in the morning; **a las cuatro de la tarde** at four in the afternoon; **trabaja de noche y duerme de día** he works at night and sleeps during the day - **8.** [procedencia, distancia] from; **salir de casa** to leave home; **soy de Bilbao** I'm from Bilbao - **9.** [causa, modo] with; **morirse de hambre** to die of hunger; **llorar de alegría** to cry with joy; **de una patada** with a kick; **de una sola vez** in one go - **10.** [con superlativos]: **el mejor de todos** the best of all; **el más importante del mundo** the most important in the world - **11.** [en comparaciones]: **más/menos de...** more/less than... - **12.** (antes de infinitivo) [condición] if; **de querer ayudarme, lo haría** if she wanted to help me, she'd do it; **de no ser por ti, me hubiese hundido** if it hadn't been for you, I wouldn't have made it - **13.** (después de adj y antes de s) [enfatiza cualidad]: **el idiota de tu hermano** your stupid brother - **14.** (adj): **es difícil de creer** it's hard to believe.

dé ▷ **dar**.

deambular vi to wander (about).

debajo adv underneath; **debajo de** underneath, under; **por debajo de lo normal** below normal.

debate sm debate.

debatir vt to debate. ◆ **debatirse** vprnl [luchar] to struggle; **se debate la vida y la muerte** she's fighting for her life.

debe sm debit (side).

deber ◇ vt [adeudar] to owe; **deber algo a alguien** to owe sb sthg, to owe sthg to sb. ◇ vi - **1.** (después de adj y antes de infinitivo) [expresa obligación]: **debo hacerlo** I have to do it, I must do it; **deberían abolir esa ley** they ought to O should abolish that law; **debes dominar tus impulsos** you must O should control your impulses - **2.** [expresa posibilidad]: **deber de: el tren debe de llegar alrededor de las diez** the train should arrive at about ten; **deben de ser las diez** it must be ten o'clock; **no debe de ser muy mayor** she can't be very old. ◇ sm duty. ◆ **deberse a** vprnl - **1.** [ser consecuencia de] to be due to - **2.** [dedicarse a] to have a responsibility towards. ◆ **deberes** smpl [trabajo escolar] homework (U).

debidamente adv properly.

debido, da adj [justo, conveniente] due, proper; **a su debido tiempo** in due course; **como es**

debido properly. ◆ **debido a** loc conj (a principio de frase) owing to; (en mitad de frase) due to.

débil adj - **1.** [persona - sin fuerzas] weak - **2.** [voz, sonido] faint; [luz] dim.

debilidad sf [gen] weakness; **tener debilidad por** to have a soft spot for.

debilitar vt to weaken. ◆ **debilitarse** vprnl to become O grow weak.

debutar vi to make one's debut.

década sf decade; **la década de los sesenta** the sixties.

decadencia sf [gen] decadence.

decadente adj decadent.

decaer vi [gen] to decline; [enfermo] to get weaker; [salud] to fail; [entusiasmo] to flag; [restaurante etc] to go downhill.

decaído, da adj [desalentado] gloomy, downhearted; [débil] frail.

decaimiento sm [desaliento] gloominess; [decadencia] decline; [falta de fuerzas] weakness.

decano, na sm, f [de corporación, facultad] dean.

decapitar vt to decapitate, to behead.

decena sf ten; **una decena de veces** about ten times.

decencia sf - **1.** [gen] decency; [en el vestir] modesty - **2.** [dignidad] dignity.

decenio sm decade.

decente adj - **1.** [gen] decent - **2.** [en el comportamiento] proper; [en el vestir] modest - **3.** [limpio] clean.

decepción sf disappointment; **llevarse una decepción** to be disappointed.

decepcionar vt to disappoint.

decibelio sm decibel.

decidido, da adj determined.

decidir ◇ vt - **1.** [gen] to decide; **decidir hacer algo** to decide to do sthg - **2.** [determinar] to determine. ◇ vi to decide. ◆ **decidirse** vprnl to decide, to make up one's mind; **decidirse a hacer algo** to decide to do sthg; **decidirse por** to decide on, to choose.

décima ▷ **décimo**.

decimal adj [sistema] decimal.

décimo, ma num tenth; **la décima parte** a tenth. ◆ **décimo** sm - **1.** [fracción] tenth - **2.** [en lotería] tenth part of a lottery ticket. ◆ **décima** sf [en medidas] tenth; **una décima de segundo** a tenth of a second.

decir vt - **1.** [gen] to say; **¿cómo se dice "estación" en inglés?** how do you say "estación" in English?; **¿diga?, ¿dígame?** [al teléfono] hello? - **2.** [contar, ordenar] to tell; **decir a alguien que haga algo** to tell sb to do sthg; **se dice que** they O people say (that); **decir la verdad** to tell the truth - **3.** fig [revelar] to tell, to show; **eso**

lo dice todo that says it all - **4.** *loc*: **como quien dice, como si dijéramos** so to speak; **decir para sí** to say to o.s.; **es decir** that is, that's to say; **(o) mejor dicho** or rather; **querer decir** to mean; **¿qué quieres decir con eso?** what do you mean by that?

decisión *sf* - **1.** [dictamen, resolución] decision; **tomar una decisión** to make O take a decision - **2.** [empeño, tesón] determination; [seguridad, resolución] decisiveness.

decisivo, va *adj* decisive.

declamar *vt* & *vi* to declaim, to recite.

declaración *sf* - **1.** [gen] statement; [de amor, guerra] declaration; **prestar declaración** to give evidence; **declaración de derechos** bill of rights - **2.** [de impuestos] tax return; **tengo que hacer la declaración** I have to do my tax return; **declaración conjunta** joint tax return; **declaración del impuesto sobre la renta** income tax return.

declarar ⟨⟩ *vt* [gen] to declare; [afirmar] to state, to say; **declarar culpable/inocente a alguien** to find sb guilty/not guilty. ⟨⟩ *vi* DER to testify, to give evidence. ➤ **declararse** *vprnl* - **1.** [incendio, epidemia] to break out - **2.** [confesar el amor] to declare one's feelings O love - **3.** [dar una opinión]: **declararse a favor de algo** to say that one supports sthg; **declararse en contra de algo** to say that one is opposed to sthg; **declararse culpable/inocente** to plead guilty/not guilty.

declinar ⟨⟩ *vt* [gen & GRAM] to decline; [responsabilidad] to disclaim. ⟨⟩ *vi* [día, tarde] to draw to a close; [fiebre] to subside; [economía] to decline.

declive *sm* - **1.** [decadencia] decline, fall; **en declive** in decline - **2.** [pendiente] slope.

decodificador = **descodificador**.

decoración *sf* - **1.** [acción] decoration; [efecto] décor - **2.** [adorno] decorations *pl*.

decorado *sm* CINE & TEATRO set.

decorar *vt* to decorate.

decorativo, va *adj* decorative.

decoro *sm* [pudor] decency.

decoroso, sa *adj* [decente] decent; [correcto] seemly, proper.

decrecer *vi* [gen] to decrease, to decline; [caudal del río] to go down.

decrépito, ta *adj despec* decrepit.

decretar *vt* to decree.

decreto *sm* decree; **decreto ley** decree, ≈ order in council UK.

dedal *sm* thimble.

dedicación *sf* dedication.

dedicar *vt* - **1.** [tiempo, dinero, energía] to devote - **2.** [libro, monumento] to dedicate. ➤ **dedicarse a** *vprnl* - **1.** [a una profesión]: **¿a qué se dedica usted?** what do you do for a

living?; **se dedica a la enseñanza** she works as a teacher - **2.** [a una actividad, persona] to spend time on; **los domingos me dedico al estudio** I spend Sundays studying.

dedicatoria *sf* dedication.

dedo *sm* - **1.** [de la mano] finger; **contar con los dedos** to count on one's fingers; **dos dedos de whisky** two fingers of whisky; **meterse el dedo en la nariz** to pick one's nose; **dedo anular/corazón** ring/middle finger; **dedo gordo** O **pulgar** thumb - **2.** [del pie] toe - **3.** *loc*: **estar a dos dedos de** to be within an inch of; **hacer dedo** *fam* to hitchhike; **nombrar a alguien a dedo** to handpick sb; **no mover un dedo** not to lift a finger; **pillarse** O **cogerse los dedos** *fig* to get one's fingers burnt; **poner el dedo en la llaga** to put one's finger on it.

deducción *sf* deduction.

deducir *vt* - **1.** [inferir] to guess, to deduce - **2.** [descontar] to deduct.

defecar *vi* to defecate.

defecto *sm* [físico] defect; [moral] fault; **defecto de pronunciación** speech defect. ➤ **por defecto** *loc adv* by default.

defectuoso, sa *adj* [mercancía] defective, faulty; [trabajo] inaccurate.

defender *vt* [gen] to defend; [amigo etc] to stand up for. ➤ **defenderse** *vprnl* [protegerse]: **defenderse (de)** to defend o.s. (against).

defensa ⟨⟩ *sf* defence; **defensa personal** self-defence. ⟨⟩ *smf* DEP defence; **defensa central** centre-back. ➤ **defensas** *sfpl* MED defences; **estoy baja de defensas** my body's defences are low.

defensivo, va *adj* defensive. ➤ **defensiva** *sf*: **ponerse/estar a la defensiva** to go/be on the defensive.

defensor, ra ⟨⟩ *adj* ▷ **abogado**. ⟨⟩ *sm, f* [gen] defender; [abogado] counsel for the defence; [adalid] champion; **defensor del pueblo** ≈ ombudsman.

deferencia *sf* deference.

deficiencia *sf* [defecto] deficiency, shortcoming; [insuficiencia] lack.

deficiente *adj* [defectuoso - gen] deficient; [audición, vista] defective. ➤ **deficiente (mental)** *smf* mentally handicapped person.

déficit *sm inv* ECON deficit.

deficitario, ria *adj* [empresa, operación] loss-making; [balance] negative.

definición *sf* - **1.** [gen] definition; **por definición** by definition - **2.** [en televisión] resolution.

definir *vt* [gen] to define. ➤ **definirse** *vprnl* to take a clear stance.

definitivamente *adv* - **1.** [sin duda] definitely - **2.** [para siempre] for good.

definitivo, va *adj* [texto etc] definitive; [respuesta] definite; **en definitiva** in short, anyway.

deforestación *sf* deforestation.

deformación *sf* [de huesos, objetos etc] deformation; [de la verdad etc] distortion; **deformación física** (physical) deformity; **tener deformación profesional** to be always acting as if one were still at work.

deformar *vt* - **1.** [huesos, objetos etc] to deform - **2.** *fig* [la verdad etc] to distort. ➤ **deformarse** *vprnl* to go out of shape.

deforme *adj* [cuerpo] deformed; [imagen] distorted; [objeto] misshapen.

defraudar *vt* - **1.** [decepcionar] to disappoint - **2.** [estafar] to defraud; **defraudar a Hacienda** to practise tax evasion.

defunción *sf* decease, death.

degeneración *sf* degeneration.

degenerado, da *adj* & *sm, f* degenerate.

degenerar *vi*: **degenerar (en)** to degenerate (into).

degollar *vt* [cortar la garganta] to cut *O* slit the throat of; [decapitar] to behead.

degradar *vt* - **1.** [moralmente] to degrade - **2.** [de un cargo] to demote. ➤ **degradarse** *vprnl* to degrade *O* lower o.s.

degustación *sf* tasting (of wines etc).

dehesa *sf* meadow.

dejadez *sf* neglect; [en aspecto] slovenliness.

dejado, da *adj* careless; [aspecto] slovenly.

dejar ◇ *vt* - **1.** [gen] to leave; **deja esa pera en el plato** put that pear on the plate; **deja el abrigo en la percha** leave your coat on the hanger; **dejar a alguien en algún sitio** [con el coche] to drop sb off somewhere; **deja algo de café para mí** leave some coffee for me; **dejar algo/a alguien a alguien** [encomendar] to leave sthg/sb with sb - **2.** [prestar]: **dejar algo a alguien** to lend sb sthg, to lend sthg to sb - **3.** [abandonar - casa, trabajo, país] to leave; [- tabaco, estudios] to give up; [- familia] to abandon; **dejar algo por imposible** to give sthg up as a lost cause; **dejar a alguien atrás** to leave sb behind - **4.** [permitir]: **dejar a alguien hacer algo** to let sb do sthg, to allow sb to do sthg; **sus gritos no me dejaron dormir** his cries prevented me from sleeping; **deja que tu hijo venga con nosotros** let your son come with us; **dejar correr algo** *fig* to let sthg be - **5.** [omitir] to leave out; **dejar algo por *O* sin hacer** to fail to do sthg; **dejó lo más importante por resolver** he left the most important question unsolved - **6.** [esperar]: **dejar que** to wait until; **dejó que acabara de llover para salir** he waited until it had stopped raining before going out. ◇ *vi* - **1.** [parar]: **dejar de hacer algo** to stop doing sthg; **no deja de venir ni un**

solo día he never fails to come - **2.** [expresando promesa]: **no dejar de** to be sure to; **¡no dejar de escribirmel** be sure to write to me! ➤ **dejarse** *vprnl* - **1.** [olvidar]: **dejarse algo en algún sitio** to leave sthg somewhere - **2.** [permitir]: **dejarse engañar** to allow o.s. to be taken in.

deje *sm* [acento] accent.

dejo *sm* [acento] accent.

del ⯈ **de**.

delantal *sm* apron.

delante *adv* - **1.** [en primer lugar, en la parte delantera] in front; **el de delante** the one in front; **el asiento de delante** the seat in front - **2.** [enfrente] opposite - **3.** [presente] present. ➤ **delante de** *loc prep* in front of.

delantero, ra ◇ *adj* front. ◇ *sm, f* DEP forward; **delantero centro** centre forward. ➤ **delantera** *sf* - **1.** DEP forwards *pl*, attack - **2.** *loc*: **coger *O* tomar la delantera** to take the lead; **coger *O* tomar la delantera a alguien** to beat sb to it; **llevar la delantera** to be in the lead.

delatar *vt* to denounce; *fig* [suj: sonrisa, ojos etc] to betray. ➤ **delatarse** *vprnl* to give o.s. away.

delator, ra *sm, f* informer.

delegación *sf* - **1.** [autorización, embajada] delegation; **delegación de poderes** devolution (of power) - **2.** [sucursal] branch - **3.** [oficina pública] local office - **4.** *Méx* [comisaria] police station, precinct *US*, station house *US*.

delegado, da *sm, f* - **1.** [gen] delegate; **delegado de curso** class representative - **2.** COM representative.

delegar *vt*: **delegar algo (en *O* a)** to delegate sthg (to).

deleite *sm* delight.

deletrear *vt* to spell (out).

deleznable *adj fig* [malo - clima, libro, actuación] appalling; [- conducta, razón] contemptible.

delfín *sm* [animal] dolphin.

delgado, da *adj* [gen] thin; [esbelto] slim.

deliberación *sf* deliberation.

deliberar *vi* to deliberate.

delicadeza *sf* - **1.** [miramiento - con cosas] care; [- con personas] kindness, attentiveness; **tener la delicadeza de** to be thoughtful enough to - **2.** [finura - de perfume, rostro] delicacy; [- de persona] sensitivity - **3.** [de un asunto, situación] delicacy. .

delicado, da *adj* - **1.** [gen] delicate; [perfume, gusto] subtle; [paladar] refined - **2.** [persona - sensible] sensitive; [- muy exigente] fussy; [- educado] polite; **estar delicado de salud** to be very weak.

delicia *sf* delight.

delicioso, sa *adj* [comida] delicious; [persona] lovely, delightful.

delimitar *vt* [finca etc] to set out the boundaries of; [funciones etc] to define.

delincuencia *sf* crime; **delincuencia juvenil** juvenile delinquency.

delincuente *smf* criminal; **delincuente habitual** habitual offender; **delincuente juvenil** juvenile delinquent.

delineante *sm, f* draughtsman (*f* draughtswoman).

delinquir *vi* to commit a crime.

delirante *adj* [gen] delirious.

delirar *vi* [un enfermo] to be delirious; [desbarrar] to talk nonsense.

delirio *sm* [por la fiebre] delirium; [de un enfermo mental] ravings *pl*; **delirios de grandeza** delusions of grandeur; **con delirio** madly.

delito *sm* crime, offence; **delito común** common law offence; **delito ecológico** ecological crime; **delito fiscal** tax offence; **delito informático** computer crime.

delta *sm* delta. *sf* delta.

demacrado, da *adj* gaunt.

demagogo, ga *sm, f* demagogue.

demanda *sf* - 1. [petición] request; [reivindicación] demand; **demanda salarial** wage claim; **en demanda de** asking for - 2. ECON demand - 3. DER lawsuit; [por daños o perjuicios] claim; **presentar una demanda contra** to take legal action against.

demandante *smf* plaintiff.

demandar *vt* - 1. DER: **demandar a alguien (por)** to sue sb (for) - 2. [pedir] to ask for.

demarcación *sf* - 1. [señalización] demarcation - 2. [territorio demarcado] area; [jurisdicción] district.

demás *adj* other; **los demás invitados** the other O remaining guests. *pron*: **lo demás** the rest; **todo lo demás** everything else; **los/las demás** the others, the rest; **por lo demás** apart from that, otherwise; **y demás** and so on.

demasiado, da *adj* too much (*pl* too many); **demasiada comida** too much food; **demasiados niños** too many children. *adv* [gen] too much; *(antes de adj o adv)* too; **habla demasiado** she talks too much; **iba demasiado rápido** he was going too fast.

demencia *sf* madness, insanity; **demencia senil** senile dementia.

demencial *adj* [disparatado] chaotic.

demente *adj* mad.

democracia *sf* democracy.

demócrata *adj* democratic. *smf* democrat.

democrático, ca *adj* democratic.

demografía *sf* demography.

demoler *vt* [edificio] to demolish, to pull down; *fig* to destroy.

demolición *sf* demolition.

demonio *sm* - 1. *lit & fig* devil; **un pesado de mil demonios** one hell of a bore - 2. [para enfatizar]: **¿qué/dónde demonios...?** what/where the hell...? **demonios** *interj*: **¡demonios!** damn (it)!

demora *sf* delay.

demorar *vt* - 1. to delay - 2. *Amér* [tardar]: **demoraron 3 días en hacerlo** it took them three days to do it; **demora una hora para vestirse** it takes her one hour to get dressed. *vi Amér* [tardar]: **¡no demores!** don't be late! **demorarse** *vprnl* - 1. [retrasarse] to be delayed - 2. [detenerse] to stop (somewhere).

demostración *sf* - 1. [gen] demonstration; **hacer una demostración** [de cómo funciona algo] to demonstrate; [de gimnasia etc] to put on a display; **demostración de afecto** show of affection - 2. [de un teorema] proof - 3. [exhibición] display; [señal] sign; [prueba] proof.

demostrar *vt* - 1. [hipótesis, teoría, verdad] to prove - 2. [alegría, impaciencia, dolor] to show - 3. [funcionamiento, procedimiento] to demonstrate, to show.

denegar *vt* to turn down, to reject.

denigrante *adj* [humillante] degrading; [insultante] insulting.

denigrar *vt* [humillar] to denigrate, to vilify; [insultar] to insult.

denominación *sf* naming; **'denominación de origen'** 'appellation d'origine'.

denominador *sm* denominator; **denominador común** *fig* & MAT common denominator.

denotar *vt* to indicate, to show.

densidad *sf* [gen & INFORM] density; **densidad de población** population density; **alta/doble densidad** INFORM high/double density.

denso, sa *adj* [gen] dense; [líquido] thick.

dentadura *sf* teeth *pl*; **dentadura postiza** false teeth *pl*, dentures *pl*.

dentera *sf*: **dar dentera a alguien** to set sb's teeth on edge.

dentífrico, ca *adj* tooth *(antes de s)*. **dentífrico** *sm* toothpaste.

dentista *smf* dentist.

dentro *adv* inside; **está ahí dentro** it's in there; **hacia/para dentro** inwards; **por dentro** (on the) inside; *fig* inside, deep down. **dentro de** *loc prep* in; **dentro del coche** in O inside the car; **dentro de poco/un año** in a while/a year; **dentro de un año terminaré los estudios** I'll have finished my studies within a year; **dentro de lo posible** as far as possible.

denuncia sf [acusación] accusation; [condena] denunciation; [a la policía] complaint; **presentar una denuncia contra** to file a complaint against.

denunciar vt to denounce; [delito] to report.

departamento sm - **1.** [gen] department - **2.** [división territorial] administrative district; [en Francia] department - **3.** [de maleta, cajón, tren] compartment - **4.** *Arg* [apartamento] flat *UK*, apartment *US*.

dependencia sf - **1.** [de una persona] dependence; [de país, drogas, alcohol] dependency - **2.** [departamento] section; [sucursal] branch. ➡ **dependencias** sfpl [habitaciones] rooms; [edificios] outbuildings.

depender vi to depend; **depende...** it depends... ➡ **depender de** vi: **depender de algo** to depend on sthg; **depender de alguien** to be dependent on sb; **depende de ti** it's up to you.

dependienta sf shop assistant, saleswoman.

dependiente ◇ adj dependent; **un organismo dependiente del gobierno central** a body which forms part of the central government. ◇ sm salesman, shop assistant *UK*, salesclerk *US*.

depilar vt [gen] to remove the hair from; [cejas] to pluck; [con cera] to wax.

depilatorio, ria adj hair-removing. ➡ **depilatorio** sm hair-remover.

deplorable adj [suceso, comportamiento] deplorable; [aspecto] sorry, pitiful.

deponer vt - **1.** [abandonar - actitud] to drop, to set aside; [las armas] to lay down - **2.** [destituir - ministro, secretario] to remove from office; [- líder, rey] to depose.

deportar vt to deport.

deporte sm sport; **hacer deporte** to do O practise sports; **hacer deporte es bueno para la salud** sport is good for your health; **practicar un deporte** to do a sport; **deportes de competición** competitive sports; **deportes extremos** extreme sports; **deportes náuticos** water sports.

deportista sm, f sportsman (f sportswoman).

deportivo, va adj - **1.** [revista, evento] sports (antes de s) - **2.** [conducta, espíritu] sportsmanlike. ➡ **deportivo** sm sports car.

depositar vt - **1.** [gen] to place; **depositar algo en alguien** [confianza, ilusiones] to place sthg in sb - **2.** [en el banco etc] to deposit. ➡ **depositarse** vprnl [asentarse] to settle.

depositario, ria sm, f - **1.** [de dinero] trustee - **2.** [de confianza etc] repository - **3.** [de mercancías etc] depositary.

depósito sm - **1.** [almacén - de mercancías] store, warehouse; [- de armas] dump; **depósito de cadáveres** morgue, mortuary; **depósito de equipaje** left luggage office *UK*, baggage room *US* - **2.** [recipiente] tank; **depósito de agua** [cisterna] water tank; [embalse] reservoir; **depósito de gasolina** petrol tank *UK*, gas tank *US* - **3.** [de dinero] deposit.

depravado, da adj depraved.

depreciar vt to (cause to) depreciate. ➡ **depreciarse** vprnl to depreciate.

depredador, ra ◇ adj predatory. ◇ sm, f predator.

depresión sf [gen] depression; **depresión nerviosa** nervous breakdown; **depresión posparto** postnatal depression.

depresivo, va ◇ adj PSICOL depressive; [deprimente] depressing. ◇ sm, f depressive.

deprimido, da adj depressed.

deprimir vt to depress. ➡ **deprimirse** vprnl to get depressed.

deprisa, de prisa adv fast, quickly; **¡deprisa!** quick!

depuración sf - **1.** [de agua, metal, gas] purification - **2.** fig [de organismo, sociedad] purge.

depurar vt - **1.** [agua, metal, gas] to purify - **2.** fig [organismo, sociedad] to purge.

derecha ➩ **derecho**.

derecho, cha ◇ adj - **1.** [diestro] right; **el margen derecho** the right-hand margin - **2.** [vertical] upright; **siempre anda muy derecha** she always walks with a very upright posture - **3.** [recto] straight. ◇ adv - **1.** [en posición vertical] upright - **2.** [en línea recta] straight; **todo derecho** straight ahead; **siga todo derecho y llegará al museo** continue straight ahead and you'll come to the museum - **3.** [directamente] straight; **se fue derecha a casa** she went straight home. ➡ **derecho** sm - **1.** [leyes, estudio] law; **un estudiante de derecho** a law student; **derecho canónico/fiscal** canon/tax law - **2.** [prerrogativa] right; **con derecho a** with a right to; **de pleno derecho** fully-fledged; **el derecho al voto** the right to vote; **hacer valer sus derechos** to exercise one's rights; **¡no hay derecho!** it's not fair!; **reservado el derecho de admisión** the management reserves the right of admission; **derecho de asilo** right of asylum; **derecho de réplica** right to reply; **derecho de retención** ECON right of retention - **3.** [de una tela, prenda] right side; **del derecho** right side out. ➡ **derecha** sf - **1.** [contrario de izquierda] right, right-hand side; **a la derecha** to the right; **girar a la derecha** to turn right - **2.** POLÍT right (wing); **ser de derechas** to be right-wing. ➡ **derechos** smpl [tasas] duties; [profesionales] fees; **derechos de aduana** customs duty (U); **derechos de**

inscripción membership fee *sing*; **derechos de autor** [potestad] copyright *(U)*; [dinero] royalties.

deriva *sf* drift; **a la deriva** adrift; **ir a la deriva** to drift.

derivado, da *adj* GRAM derived. ➡ **derivado** *sm* - **1.** [producto] by-product; **derivados lácteos** dairy products - **2.** QUIM derivative.

derivar ◇ *vt* - **1.** [desviar] to divert - **2.** MAT to derive. ◇ *vi* [desviarse] to change direction, to drift. ➡ **derivar de** *vi* - **1.** [proceder] to derive from - **2.** GRAM to be derived from. ➡ **derivar en** *vi* to result in, to lead to.

derogación *sf* repeal.

derramamiento *sm* spilling; **derramamiento de sangre** bloodshed.

derramar *vt* [por accidente] to spill; [verter] to pour.

derrame *sm* - **1.** MED discharge - **2.** [de líquido] spilling; [de sangre] shedding.

derrapar *vi* to skid.

derretir *vt* [gen] to melt; [nieve] to thaw. ➡ **derretirse** *vprnl* [metal, mantequilla] to melt; [hielo, nieve] to thaw.

derribar *vt* - **1.** [construcción] to knock down, to demolish - **2.** [hacer caer - árbol] to fell; [- avión] to bring down - **3.** [gobierno, gobernante] to overthrow.

derribo *sm* [material] rubble.

derrocar *vt* [gobierno] to bring down, to overthrow; [ministro] to oust.

derrochar *vt* [malgastar] to squander.

derroche *sm* [malgaste] waste, squandering.

derrota *sf* [fracaso] defeat.

derrotar *vt* to defeat.

derrotero *sm* [camino] direction; **tomar diferentes derroteros** to follow a different course.

derrotista *adj* & *smf* defeatist.

derruir *vt* to demolish.

derrumbamiento *sm* - **1.** [de puente, edificio - por accidente] collapse; [- intencionado] demolition - **2.** *fig* [de imperio] fall; [de empresa etc] collapse.

derrumbar *vt* [puente, edificio] to demolish. ➡ **derrumbarse** *vprnl* [puente, edificio] to collapse; [techo] to fall O cave in.

desabotonar *vt* to unbutton. ➡ **desabotonarse** *vprnl* [suj: persona] to undo one's buttons; [suj: ropa] to come undone.

desabrochar *vt* to undo. ➡ **desabrocharse** *vprnl* [suj: persona] to undo one's buttons; [suj: ropa] to come undone.

desacato *sm* - **1.** [gen]: **desacato (a)** lack of respect (for), disrespect (for) - **2.** DER contempt of court.

desacierto *sm* [error] error.

desaconsejar *vt*: **desaconsejar algo (a alguien)** to advise (sb) against sthg; **desaconsejar a alguien que haga algo** to advise sb not to do sthg.

desacreditar *vt* to discredit.

desactivar *vt* to defuse.

desacuerdo *sm* disagreement.

desafiante *adj* defiant.

desafiar *vt* - **1.** [persona] to challenge; **desafiar a alguien a algo/a que haga algo** to challenge sb to sthg/to do sthg - **2.** [peligro] to defy.

desafinar *vi* MÚS to be out of tune.

desafío *sm* challenge.

desaforado, da *adj* - **1.** [excesivo - apetito] uncontrolled - **2.** [furioso - grito] furious, wild.

desafortunadamente *adv* unfortunately.

desafortunado, da *adj* - **1.** [gen] unfortunate - **2.** [sin suerte] unlucky.

desagradable *adj* unpleasant.

desagradar *vi* to displease; **su actitud le desagradó** he was displeased at her attitude.

desagradecido, da *sm, f* ungrateful person.

desagrado *sm* displeasure; **con desagrado** reluctantly.

desagraviar *vt*: **desagraviar a alguien por algo** [por una ofensa] to make amends to sb for sthg; [por un perjuicio] to compensate sb for sthg.

desagüe *sm* [vaciado] drain; [cañería] drainpipe.

desaguisado *sm* [destrozo] damage *(U)*.

desahogado, da *adj* - **1.** [de espacio] spacious - **2.** [de dinero] well-off.

desahogar *vt* [ira] to vent; [pena] to relieve, to ease. ➡ **desahogarse** *vprnl* - **1.** [contar penas]: **desahogarse con alguien** to pour out one's woes O to tell one's troubles to sb - **2.** [desfogarse] to let off steam.

desahogo *sm* - **1.** [moral] relief - **2.** [de espacio] space, room - **3.** [económico] ease.

desahuciar *vt* - **1.** [inquilino] to evict - **2.** [enfermo]: **desahuciar a alguien** to give up all hope of saving sb.

desahucio *sm* eviction.

desaire *sm* snub, slight; **hacer un desaire a alguien** to snub sb; **sufrir un desaire** to receive a rebuff.

desajuste *sm* - **1.** [de piezas] misalignment; [de máquina] breakdown - **2.** [de declaraciones] inconsistency; [económico etc] imbalance.

desalentar *vt* to discourage.

desaliento *sm* dismay, dejection.

desaliñado, da *adj* scruffy.

desaliño *sm* scruffiness.

desalmado, da *adj* heartless.

desalojar vt - **1.** [por una emergencia - edificio, personas] to evacuate - **2.** [por la fuerza - suj: policía, ejército] to clear; [- inquilinos etc] to evict - **3.** [por propia voluntad] to abandon, to move out of.

desamor sm [falta de afecto] indifference, coldness; [odio] dislike.

desamparado, da adj [niño] helpless; [lugar] desolate, forsaken.

desamparar vt to abandon.

desamparo sm [abandono] abandonment; [aflicción] helplessness.

desangrar vt - **1.** [animal, persona] to bleed - **2.** fig [económicamente] to bleed dry. ➡ **desangrarse** vprnl to lose a lot of blood.

desanimado, da adj [persona] downhearted.

desanimar vt to discourage. ➡ **desanimarse** vprnl to get downhearted O discouraged.

desánimo sm [gen] dejection; [depresión] depression.

desapacible adj unpleasant.

desaparecer vi - **1.** [gen] to disappear - **2.** [en guerra, accidente] to go missing.

desaparecido, da sm, f missing person.

desaparición sf disappearance.

desapego sm indifference.

desapercibido, da adj: pasar desapercibido to go unnoticed.

desaprensivo, va sm, f unscrupulous person.

desaprobar vt [gen] to disapprove of; [un plan etc] to reject.

desaprovechar vt to waste.

desarmador sm Méx - **1.** [herramienta] screwdriver - **2.** [cóctel] vodka and orange.

desarmar vt - **1.** [gen] to disarm - **2.** [desmontar] to take apart, to dismantle.

desarme sm MIL disarmament.

desarraigar vt - **1.** [vicio, costumbre] to root out - **2.** [persona, pueblo] to banish, to drive (out).

desarraigo sm [de árbol] uprooting; [de vicio, costumbre] rooting out; [de persona, pueblo] banishment.

desarreglar vt [armario, pelo] to mess up; [planes, horario] to upset.

desarreglo sm [de cuarto, persona] untidiness; [de vida] disorder.

desarrollado, da adj developed.

desarrollar vt - **1.** [mejorar - crecimiento, país] to develop - **2.** [exponer - teoría, tema, fórmula] to expound - **3.** [realizar - actividad, trabajo] to carry out. ➡ **desarrollarse** vprnl - **1.** [crecer, mejorar] to develop - **2.** [suceder - reunión] to take place; [- película] to be set.

desarrollo sm - **1.** [mejora] development; **países en vías de desarrollo** developing countries - **2.** [crecimiento] growth, development - **3.** [de idea, argumento, acontecimiento] development.

desarticular vt - **1.** [huesos] to dislocate - **2.** fig [organización, banda] to break up; [plan] to foil.

desasosegar vt to make uneasy.

desasosiego sm - **1.** [mal presentimiento] unease - **2.** [nerviosismo] restlessness.

desastrado, da adj [desaseado] scruffy; [sucio] dirty.

desastre sm disaster; **su madre es un desastre** her mother is hopeless; **desastre natural** natural disaster.

desastroso, sa adj disastrous.

desatar vt - **1.** [nudo, lazo] to untie; [paquete] to undo; [animal] to unleash - **2.** fig [tormenta, iras, pasión] to unleash; [entusiasmo] to arouse; [lengua] to loosen. ➡ **desatarse** vprnl - **1.** [nudo, lazo] to come undone - **2.** fig [desencadenarse - tormenta] to break; [- ira, cólera] to erupt.

desatascar vt to unblock.

desatender vt - **1.** [obligación, persona] to neglect - **2.** [ruegos, consejos] to ignore.

desatino sm - **1.** [locura] foolishness - **2.** [desacierto] foolish act.

desautorizar vt - **1.** [desmentir - noticia] to deny - **2.** [prohibir - manifestación, huelga] to ban - **3.** [desacreditar] to discredit.

desavenencia sf [desacuerdo] friction, tension; [riña] quarrel.

desavenirse vprnl to fall out.

desayunar ◇ vi to have breakfast. ◇ vt to have for breakfast.

desayuno sm breakfast; **desayuno continental** continental breakfast; **desayuno de trabajo** working breakfast.

desazón sf unease, anxiety.

desbancar vt fig [ocupar el puesto de] to oust, to replace.

desbandada sf breaking up, scattering; **a la desbandada** in great disorder.

desbarajuste sm disorder, confusion.

desbaratar vt to ruin, to wreck.

desbloquear vt [cuenta] to unfreeze; [país] to lift the blockade on; [negociación] to end the deadlock in.

desbocado, da adj [caballo] runaway.

desbocarse vprnl [caballo] to bolt.

desbole sm R Dom fam mess, chaos.

desbordar vt - **1.** [cauce, ribera] to overflow, to burst - **2.** [límites, previsiones] to exceed; [paciencia] to push beyond the limit. ➡ **desbor-**

darse *vprnl* - 1. [líquido]: **desbordarse (de)** to overflow (from) - 2. [río] to overflow - 3. *fig* [sentimiento] to erupt.

descabalgar *vi* to dismount.

descabellado, da *adj* crazy.

descafeinado, da *adj* [sin cafeína] decaffeinated. ► **descafeinado** *sm* decaffeinated coffee.

descalabro *sm* setback, damage *(U)*.

descalificar *vt* - 1. [en una competición] to disqualify - 2. [desprestigiar] to discredit.

descalzar *vt*: **descalzar a alguien** to take sb's shoes off. ► **descalzarse** *vprnl* to take off one's shoes.

descalzo, za *adj* barefoot.

descaminado, da *adj fig* [equivocado]: **andar** O **ir descaminado** to be on the wrong track.

descampado *sm* open country.

descansar ◇ *vi* - 1. [reposar] to rest - 2. [dormir] to sleep; **¡que descanses!** sleep well! ◇ *vt* - 1. to rest; **descansar la vista** to rest one's eyes; **descansa la cabeza en mi hombro** rest your head on my shoulder - 2. [dormir] to sleep.

descansillo *sm* landing.

descanso *sm* - 1. [reposo] rest; **tomarse un descanso** to take a rest; **día de descanso** day off - 2. [pausa] break; CINE & TEATRO interval; DEP half-time - 3. *fig* [alivio] relief.

descapotable *adj* & *sm* convertible.

descarado, da *adj* - 1. [desvergonzado - persona] cheeky, impertinent - 2. [flagrante - intento etc] barefaced.

descarga *sf* - 1. [de mercancías] unloading - 2. [de electricidad] shock - 3. [disparo] firing, shots *pl* - 4. INFORM download.

descargar *vt* - 1. [vaciar - mercancías, pistola] to unload - 2. [disparar - munición, arma, ráfaga]: **descargar (sobre)** to fire (at) - 3. ELECTR to run down. ► **descargarse** *vprnl* - 1. [desahogarse]: **descargarse con alguien** to take it out on sb - 2. ELECTR to go flat.

descargo *sm* - 1. [excusa]: **descargo a** argument against - 2. DER defence - 3. [COM - de deuda] discharge; [- recibo] receipt.

descarnado, da *adj* - 1. [descripción] brutal - 2. [persona, animal] scrawny.

descaro *sm* cheek, impertinence.

descarriarse *vprnl* - 1. [ovejas, ganado] to stray - 2. *fig* [pervertirse] to go astray.

descarrilamiento *sm* derailment.

descarrilar *vi* to be derailed.

descartar *vt* [ayuda] to refuse, to reject; [posibilidad] to rule out.

descendencia *sf* - 1. [hijos] offspring - 2. [linaje] lineage, descent.

descender *vi* - 1. [en estimación] to go down; **descender a segunda** to be relegated to the second division - 2. [cantidad, valor, temperatura, nivel] to fall, to drop. ► **descender de** *vi* - 1. [avión] to get off - 2. [linaje] to be descended from.

descenso *sm* - 1. [en el espacio] descent - 2. [de cantidad, valor, temperatura, nivel] drop.

descentralizar *vt* to decentralize.

descentrar *vt* - 1. [sacar del centro] to knock off-centre - 2. *fig* [desconcentrar] to distract.

descifrar *vt* - 1. [clave, mensaje] to decipher - 2. [motivos, intenciones] to work out; [misterio] to solve; [problemas] to puzzle out.

descodificador, decodificador *sm* decoder.

descolgar *vt* - 1. [una cosa colgada] to take down - 2. [teléfono] to pick up. ► **descolgarse** *vprnl* [bajar]: **descolgarse (por algo)** to let oneself down O to slide down (sthg).

descolorido, da *adj* faded.

descompasado, da *adj* excessive, uncontrollable.

descomponer *vt* - 1. [pudrir - fruta] to rot; [- cadáver] to decompose - 2. [dividir] to break down; **descomponer algo en** to break sthg down into - 3. [desordenar] to mess up - 4. [estropear] to damage. ► **descomponerse** *vprnl* - 1. [pudrirse - fruta] to rot; [- cadáver] to decompose - 2. [averiarse] to break down.

descomposición *sf* - 1. [de elementos] decomposition - 2. [putrefacción - de fruta] rotting; [- de cadáver] decomposition - 3. [alteración] distortion - 4. [diarrea] diarrhoea.

descompostura *sf* - 1. [falta de mesura] lack of respect, rudeness - 2. *Méx & R Dom* [avería] breakdown - 3. *Amér* [malestar] sickness - 4. *Amér* [diarrea] diarrhoea - 5. *Méx & R Plata* [avería] breakdown.

descompuesto, ta ◇ *pp* ▷ **descomponer**. ◇ *adj* - 1. [putrefacto - fruta] rotten; [- cadáver] decomposed - 2. [alterado - rostro] distorted, twisted - 3. *Méx & R Plata* [mecanismo, máquina] broken, broken down.

descomunal *adj* enormous.

desconcentrar *vt* to distract.

desconcertante *adj* disconcerting.

desconcertar *vt* to disconcert, to throw. ► **desconcertarse** *vprnl* to be thrown O bewildered.

desconchado *sm* [de pintura] peeling paint; [de enyesado] peeling plaster.

desconcierto *sm* [desorden] disorder; [desorientación, confusión] confusion.

desconectar *vt* [aparato] to switch off; [línea] to disconnect; [desenchufar] to unplug.

desconfianza *sf* distrust.

desconfiar ◆ **desconfiar de** *vi* - **1.** [sospechar de] to distrust - **2.** [no confiar en] to have no faith in

descongelar *vt* **1.** [producto] to thaw; [nevera] to defrost - **2.** *fig* [precios] to free; [créditos, salarios] to unfreeze.

descongestionar *vt* - **1.** MED to clear - **2.** *fig* [calle, centro de ciudad] to make less congested; **descongestionar el tráfico** to reduce congestion.

desconocer *vt* [ignorar] not to know.

desconocido, da ◇ *adj* [no conocido] unknown. ◇ *sm, f* stranger.

desconocimiento *sm* ignorance.

desconsiderado, da *adj* thoughtless, inconsiderate.

desconsolar *vt* to distress.

desconsuelo *sm* distress, grief.

descontado, da *adj* discounted. ◆ **por descontado** *loc adv* obviously; **dar algo por descontado** to take sthg for granted.

descontar *vt* - **1.** [una cantidad] to deduct - **2.** COM to discount.

descontentar *vt* to upset.

descontento, ta *adj* unhappy, dissatisfied. ◆ **descontento** *sm* dissatisfaction.

desconvocar *vt* to cancel, to call off.

descorazonador, ra *adj* discouraging.

descorazonar *vt* to discourage.

descorchar *vt* to uncork.

descorrer *vt* - **1.** [cortinas] to draw back - **2.** [cerrojo, pestillo] to draw back.

descortés *adj* rude.

descoser *vt* to unstitch. ◆ **descoserse** *vprnl* to come unstitched.

descosido, da *adj* unstitched.

descoyuntar *vt* to dislocate.

descrédito *sm* discredit; **ir en descrédito de algo/alguien** to count against sthg/sb.

descreído, da *sm, f* non-believer.

descremado, da *adj* skimmed.

describir *vt* to describe.

descripción *sf* description.

descrito, ta *pp* ▷ **describir**.

descuartizar *vt* [persona] to quarter; [res] to carve up.

descubierto, ta ◇ *pp* ▷ **descubrir**. ◇ *adj* - **1.** [gen] uncovered; [coche] open - **2.** [cielo] clear - **3.** [sin sombrero] bareheaded. ◆ **descubierto** *sm* [FIN - de empresa] deficit; [- de cuenta bancaria] overdraft. ◆ **al descubierto** *loc adv* - **1.** [al raso] in the open - **2.** BANCA overdrawn; **quedar al descubierto** *fig* to be exposed *O* uncovered.

descubrimiento *sm* - **1.** [de continentes, invenciones] discovery - **2.** [de placa, busto] unveiling - **3.** [de complots] uncovering; [de asesinos] detection.

descubrir *vt* - **1.** [gen] to discover; [petróleo] to strike; [complot] to uncover - **2.** [destapar - estatua, placa] to unveil - **3.** [vislumbrar] to spot, to spy - **4.** [delatar] to give away. ◆ **descubrirse** *vprnl* [quitarse el sombrero] to take one's hat off; **descubrirse ante algo** *fig* to take one's hat off to sthg.

descuento *sm* discount; **hacer descuento** to give a discount; **con descuento** at a discount; **un descuento del 10%** a 10% discount.

descuidado, da *adj* - **1.** [desaseado - persona, aspecto] untidy; [- jardín] neglected - **2.** [negligente] careless - **3.** [distraído] off one's guard.

descuidar ◇ *vt* [desatender] to neglect. ◇ *vi* [no preocuparse] not to worry; **descuida, que yo me encargo** don't worry, I'll take care of it. ◆ **descuidarse** *vprnl* - **1.** [abandonarse] to neglect one's appearance - **2.** [despistarse] not to be careful.

descuido *sm* - **1.** [falta de aseo] carelessness - **2.** [olvido] oversight; [error] slip; **en un descuido** by mistake.

desde *prep* - **1.** [tiempo] since; **no lo veo desde el mes pasado/desde ayer** I haven't seen him since last month/yesterday; **desde ahora** from now on; **desde hace mucho/un mes** for ages/a month; **desde... hasta...** from... until...; **desde el lunes hasta el viernes** from Monday till Friday; **desde entonces** since then; **desde que** since; **desde que murió mi madre** since my mother died - **2.** [espacio] from; **desde... hasta...** from... to...; **desde aquí hasta el centro** from here to the centre. ◆ **desde luego** *loc adv* - **1.** [por supuesto] of course - **2.** [en tono de reproche] for goodness' sake!

desdecir ◆ **desdecir de** *vi* [desmerecer] to be unworthy of; [no cuadrar con] not to go with, to clash with. ◆ **desdecirse** *vprnl* to go back on one's word; **desdecirse de** to go back on.

desdén *sm* disdain, scorn.

desdeñar *vt* to scorn.

desdeñoso, sa *adj* disdainful.

desdibujarse *vprnl* to become blurred.

desdicha *sf* [desgracia - situación] misery; [- suceso] misfortune; **por desdicha** unfortunately.

desdichado, da *adj* [decisión, situación] unfortunate; [persona - sin suerte] unlucky; [- sin felicidad] unhappy.

desdicho, cha *pp* ▷ **desdecir**.

desdoblar *vt* [servilleta, carta] to unfold; [alambre] to straighten out.

desear vt - **1.** [querer] to want; [anhelar] to wish; **¿qué desea?** [en tienda] what can I do for you?; **desearía estar allí** I wish I was there; **dejar mucho/no dejar nada que desear** to leave much/nothing to be desired - **2.** [sexualmente] to desire.

desecar vt to dry out. ◆ **desecarse** vprnl to dry out.

desechable adj disposable.

desechar vt - **1.** [tirar - ropa, piezas] to throw out, to discard - **2.** [rechazar - ayuda, oferta] to refuse, to turn down - **3.** [desestimar - idea] to reject; [- plan, proyecto] to drop.

desecho sm [objeto usado] unwanted object; [ropa] castoff; **material de desecho** [gen] waste products pl; [metal] scrap. ◆ **desechos** smpl [basura] rubbish (U); [residuos] waste products; **desechos radiactivos** radioactive waste (U).

desembalar vt to unpack.

desembarazar vt to clear. ◆ **desembarazarse** vprnl: **desembarazarse de** to get rid of.

desembarcar ⟨⟩ vt [pasajeros] to disembark; [mercancías] to unload. ⟨⟩ vi - **1.** [de barco, avión] to disembark - **2.** Amér [de autobús, tren] to get off. ◆ **desembarcarse** vprnl Amér to get off.

desembarco sm - **1.** [de pasajeros] disembarkation - **2.** MIL landing.

desembarque sm [de mercancías] unloading.

desembocadura sf [de río] mouth; [de calle] opening.

desembocar ◆ **desembocar en** vi - **1.** [río] to flow into - **2.** [asunto] to result in.

desembolso sm payment; **desembolso inicial** down payment.

desempaquetar vt [paquete] to unwrap; [caja] to unpack.

desempatar vi to decide the contest; **jugar para desempatar** to have a play-off.

desempate sm final result; **partido de desempate** decider.

desempeñar vt - **1.** [función, misión] to carry out; [cargo, puesto] to hold - **2.** [papel] to play - **3.** [joyas] to redeem.

desempeño sm - **1.** [de función] carrying out - **2.** [de papel] performance - **3.** [de objeto] redemption.

desempleado, da adj unemployed.

desempleo sm - **1.** [falta de empleo] unemployment - **2.** [subsidio] unemployment benefit; **cobrar el desempleo** to receive unemployment benefit.

desempolvar vt - **1.** [mueble, jarrón] to dust - **2.** fig [recuerdos] to revive.

desencadenar vt - **1.** [preso, perro] to unchain - **2.** fig [suceso, polémica] to give rise to; [pasión, furia] to unleash. ◆ **desencadenarse** vprnl - **1.** [pasiones, odios, conflicto] to erupt; [guerra] to break out - **2.** [viento] to blow up; [tormenta] to burst; [terremoto] to strike.

desencajar vt - **1.** [mecanismo, piezas - sin querer] to knock out of place; [- intencionadamente] to take apart - **2.** [hueso] to dislocate. ◆ **desencajarse** vprnl - **1.** [piezas] to come apart - **2.** [rostro] to distort, to become distorted.

desencanto sm disappointment.

desenchufar vt to unplug.

desenfadado, da adj [persona, conducta] relaxed, easy-going; [comedia, programa de TV] light-hearted; [estilo] light; [en el vestir] casual.

desenfado sm [seguridad en sí mismo] self-assurance; [desenvoltura] ease; [desparpajo] uninhibited nature.

desenfocado, da adj [imagen] out of focus; [visión] blurred.

desenfrenado, da adj [ritmo, baile] frantic, frenzied; [comportamiento] uncontrolled; [apetito] insatiable.

desenfreno sm - **1.** [gen] lack of restraint - **2.** [vicio] debauchery.

desenfundar vt [pistola] to draw.

desenganchar vt - **1.** [vagón] to uncouple - **2.** [caballo] to unhitch - **3.** [pelo, jersey] to free.

desengañar vt - **1.** [a persona equivocada]: **desengañar a alguien** to reveal the truth to sb - **2.** [a persona esperanzada] to disillusion.

desengaño sm disappointment; **llevarse un desengaño con alguien** to be disappointed in sb.

desenlace sm denouement, ending.

desenmarañar vt - **1.** [ovillo, pelo] to untangle - **2.** fig [asunto] to sort out; [problema] to resolve.

desenmascarar vt [descubrir] to unmask.

desenredar vt - **1.** [hilos, pelo] to untangle - **2.** fig [asunto] to sort out; [problema] to resolve. ◆ **desenredarse** vprnl: **desenredarse (de algo)** to extricate oneself (from sthg).

desenrollar vt [hilo, cinta] to unwind; [persiana] to roll down; [pergamino, papel] to unroll.

desenroscar vt to unscrew.

desentenderse vprnl to pretend not to hear/know etc.

desenterrar vt - **1.** [cadáver] to disinter; [tesoro, escultura] to dig up - **2.** fig [recordar]: **desenterrar algo (de)** to recall O revive sthg (from).

desentonar vi - **1.** [MÚS - cantante] to sing out of tune; [- instrumento] to be out of tune - **2.** [color, cortinas, edificio]: **desentonar (con)** to clash (with).

desentumecer vt to stretch. ◆ **desentumecerse** vprnl to loosen up.

desenvoltura *sf* [al moverse, comportarse] ease; [al hablar] fluency.

desenvolver *vt* to unwrap. ➤ **desenvolverse** *vprnl* - **1.** [asunto, proceso] to progress; [trama] to unfold - **2.** [persona] to cope, to manage.

desenvuelto, ta ◇ *pp* ▷ **desenvolver**. ◇ *adj* [al moverse, comportarse] natural; [al hablar] fluent.

deseo *sm* - **1.** [anhelo] wish, desire; **su deseo se hizo realidad** her wish came true; **buenos deseos** good intentions; **pedir un deseo** to make a wish - **2.** [apetito sexual] desire.

deseoso, sa *adj*: **estar deseoso de algo/hacer algo** to long for sthg/to do sthg.

desequilibrado, da *adj* - **1.** [persona] unbalanced - **2.** [balanza, eje] off-centre.

desequilibrio *sm* [mecánico] lack of balance; [mental] mental instability.

desertar *vi* to desert.

desértico, ca *adj* [del desierto] desert *(antes de s)*; [despoblado] deserted.

desertización *sf* [del terreno] desertification; [de la población] depopulation.

desertor, ra *sm, f* deserter.

desesperación *sf* [falta de esperanza] despair, desperation; **con desesperación** in despair.

desesperado, da *adj* [persona, intento] desperate; [estado, situación] hopeless; [esfuerzo] furious.

desesperante *adj* infuriating.

desesperar ◇ *vt* to exasperate, to drive mad. ◇ *vi* to despair, to give up O lose hope. ➤ **desesperarse** *vprnl* - **1.** [perder la esperanza] to be driven to despair - **2.** [irritarse, enojarse] to get mad O exasperated.

desestabilizar *vt* to destabilize.

desestatización *sf Amér* privatization.

desestatizar *vt Amér* to privatize, to sell off.

desestimar *vt* - **1.** [rechazar] to turn down - **2.** [despreciar] to turn one's nose up at.

desfachatez *sf fam* cheek.

desfalco *sm* embezzlement.

desfallecer *vi* - **1.** [debilitarse] to be exhausted; **desfallecer de** to feel faint from - **2.** [desmayarse] to faint.

desfasado, da *adj* [persona] out of touch; [libro, moda] out of date.

desfase *sm* [diferencia] gap; **desfase horario** jet lag.

desfavorable *adj* unfavourable.

desfigurar *vt* - **1.** [rostro, cuerpo] to disfigure - **2.** *fig* [la verdad] to distort.

desfiladero *sm* narrow mountain pass.

desfilar *vi* MIL to parade.

desfile *sm* MIL parade; [de carrozas] procession.

desfogar *vt* to vent. ➤ **desfogarse** *vprnl* to let off steam.

desgajar *vt* [página] to tear out; [rama] to break off, [libro, periódico] to rip up; [naranja] to split into segments. ➤ **desgajarse** *vprnl* [rama] to break off; [hoja] to fall.

desgana *sf* - **1.** [falta de hambre] lack of appetite - **2.** [falta de ánimo] lack of enthusiasm; **con desgana** unwillingly, reluctantly.

desganado, da *adj* [sin apetito]: **estar desganado** to be off one's food.

desgarbado, da *adj* clumsy, ungainly.

desgarrador, ra *adj* harrowing.

desgarrar *vt* to rip; **desgarrar el corazón** to break one's heart.

desgarro *sm* tear.

desgastar *vt* to wear out. ➤ **desgastarse** *vprnl* to wear o.s. out.

desgaste *sm* - **1.** [de tela, muebles etc] wear and tear; [de roca] erosion; [de pilas] running down; [de cuerdas] fraying; [de metal] corrosion - **2.** [de persona] wear and tear; **desgaste político** erosion of voter confidence.

desglosar *vt* to break down.

desglose *sm* breakdown.

desgracia *sf* - **1.** [mala suerte] misfortune; **por desgracia** unfortunately; **tener la desgracia de** to be unfortunate enough to - **2.** [catástrofe] disaster; **desgracias personales** casualties; **es una desgracia que...** it's a terrible shame that... - **3.** *loc*: **caer en desgracia** to fall into disgrace; **las desgracias nunca vienen solas** it never rains but it pours.

desgraciado, da *adj* - **1.** [gen] unfortunate - **2.** [sin suerte] unlucky - **3.** [infeliz] unhappy.

desgravar *vt* to deduct from one's tax bill.

desgreñado, da *adj* dishevelled.

desguace *sm* [de coches] scrapping; [de buques] breaking.

deshabitado, da *adj* uninhabited.

deshabituar *vt*: **deshabituar a alguien (de)** to get sb out of the habit (of).

deshacer *vt* - **1.** [costura, nudo, paquete] to undo; [maleta] to unpack; [castillo de arena] to destroy - **2.** [disolver - helado, mantequilla] to melt; [- pastilla, terrón de azúcar] to dissolve - **3.** [poner fin a - contrato, negocio] to cancel; [- pacto, tratado] to break; [- plan, intriga] to foil; [- organización] to dissolve - **4.** [destruir - enemigo] to rout; [- matrimonio] to ruin - **5.** INFORM to undo. ➤ **deshacerse** *vprnl* - **1.** [desvanecerse] to disappear - **2.** *fig* [librarse]: **deshacerse de** to get rid of - **3.** *fig*: **deshacerse en algo (con** O **hacia alguien)** [cumplidos] to lavish sthg (on sb); [insultos] to heap sthg (on sb).

desharrapado, da *adj* ragged.

deshecho, cha ◇ *pp* ▷ **deshacer**. ◇ *adj* - **1.** [costura, nudo, paquete] undone; [cama] unmade; [maleta] unpacked - **2.** [enemigo] destroyed; [tarta, matrimonio] ruined - **3.** [derretido - pastilla, terrón de azúcar] dissolved; [- helado, mantequilla] melted - **4.** [afligido] devastated - **5.** [cansado] tired out.

desheredar *vt* to disinherit.

deshidratar *vt* to dehydrate.

deshielo *sm* thaw.

deshilachar *vt* to unravel. ➡ **deshilacharse** *vprnl* to fray.

deshinchar *vt* - **1.** [globo, rueda] to let down, to deflate - **2.** [hinchazón] to reduce the swelling in. ➡ **deshincharse** *vprnl* [globo, hinchazón] to go down; [neumático] to go flat.

deshojar *vt* [árbol] to strip the leaves off; [flor] to pull the petals off; [libro] to pull the pages out of. ➡ **deshojarse** *vprnl* [árbol] to shed its leaves; [flor] to drop its petals.

deshonesto, ta *adj* [sin honradez] dishonest; [sin pudor] indecent.

deshonor *sm* dishonour.

deshonra *sf* = **deshonor**.

deshonrar *vt* to dishonour.

deshora ➡ **a deshora, a deshoras** *loc adv* [en momento inoportuno] at a bad time; [en horas poco habituales] at an unearthly hour.

deshuesar *vt* [carne] to bone; [fruto] to stone.

desidia *sf* [en el trabajo] neglect; [en el aspecto] slovenliness.

desierto, ta *adj* - **1.** [gen] deserted - **2.** [vacante - premio] deferred. ➡ **desierto** *sm* desert.

designar *vt* - **1.** [nombrar] to appoint - **2.** [fijar, determinar] to name, to fix.

designio *sm* intention, plan.

desigual *adj* - **1.** [diferente] different; [terreno] uneven - **2.** [tiempo, persona, humor] changeable; [alumno, actuación] inconsistent; [lucha] unevenly matched, unequal; [tratamiento] unfair, unequal.

desilusión *sf* disappointment, disillusionment *(U)*; **llevarse una desilusión** to be disappointed.

desilusionar *vt* [desengañar] to reveal the truth to; [decepcionar] to disappoint, to disillusion. ➡ **desilusionarse** *vprnl* [decepcionarse] to be disappointed *O* disillusioned; [desengañarse] to realize the truth.

desinfección *sf* disinfection.

desinfectar *vt* to disinfect.

desinflar *vt* [quitar aire a] to deflate. ➡ **desinflarse** *vprnl* [perder aire - gen] to go down; [- neumático] to go flat.

desinstalar *vt* INFORM to uninstall.

desintegración *sf* - **1.** [de objetos] disintegration - **2.** [de grupos, organizaciones] breaking up.

desintegrar *vt* - **1.** [objetos] to disintegrate; [átomo] to split - **2.** [grupos, organizaciones] to break up.

desinterés *sm* - **1.** [indiferencia] disinterest - **2.** [generosidad] unselfishness.

desinteresado, da *adj* unselfish.

desinteresarse *vprnl*: **desinteresarse de** *O* **por algo** to lose interest in sthg.

desistir *vi*: **desistir (de hacer algo)** to give up *O* to stop (doing sthg).

desleal *adj* [competencia] unfair; **desleal (con)** disloyal (to).

deslealtad *sf* disloyalty.

desleír *vt* [sólido] to dissolve; [líquido] to dilute.

desligar *vt* - **1.** [desatar] to untie - **2.** *fig* [separar]: **desligar algo (de)** to separate sthg (from). ➡ **desligarse** *vprnl* - **1.** [desatarse] to untie oneself - **2.** *fig* [separarse]: **desligarse de** to become separated from; **desligarse de un grupo** to distance o.s. from a group.

deslindar *vt* - **1.** [limitar] to mark out (the boundaries of) - **2.** *fig* [separar] to define.

desliz *sm* slip, error; **tener** *O* **cometer un desliz** to slip up.

deslizar *vt* [mano, objeto]: **deslizar algo en** to slip sthg into; **deslizar algo por algo** to slide sthg along sthg. ➡ **deslizarse** *vprnl* [resbalar]: **deslizarse por** to slide along.

deslomar *vt* [a golpes] to thrash.

deslucido, da *adj* - **1.** [sin brillo] faded; [plata] tarnished - **2.** [sin gracia - acto, ceremonia] dull.

deslumbrar *vt lit & fig* to dazzle.

desmadrarse *vprnl fam* to go wild.

desmadre *sm fam* chaos.

desmán *sm* - **1.** [con la bebida, comida etc] excess - **2.** [abuso de poder] abuse (of power).

desmandarse *vprnl* - **1.** [desobedecer] to be disobedient - **2.** [insubordinarse] to get out of hand.

desmantelar *vt* [casa, fábrica] to clear out, to strip; [organización] to disband; [arsenal, andamio] to dismantle; [barco] to unrig.

desmaquillador *sm* make-up remover.

desmayar *vi* to lose heart. ➡ **desmayarse** *vprnl* to faint.

desmayo *sm* [físico] fainting fit; **sufrir desmayos** to have fainting fits.

desmedido, da *adj* excessive, disproportionate.

desmelenado, da *adj* - **1.** [persona] reckless, wild - **2.** [cabello] tousled.

desmembrar *vt* - **1.** [trocear - cuerpo] to dismember; [- miembro, extremidad] to cut off - **2.** [disgregar] to break up.

desmemoriado, da *adj* forgetful.

desmentir *vt* - **1.** [negar] to deny - **2.** [no corresponder] to belie.

desmenuzar *vt* - **1.** [trocear - pan, pastel, roca] to crumble; [- carne] to chop up; [- papel] to tear up into little pieces - **2.** *fig* [examinar, analizar] to scrutinize.

desmerecer ◇ *vt* to be unworthy of. ◇ *vi* to lose value; **desmerecer (en algo) de alguien** to be inferior to sb (in sthg).

desmesurado, da *adj* [excesivo] excessive, disproportionate; [enorme] enormous.

desmitificar *vt* to demythologize.

desmontar *vt* - **1.** [desarmar - máquina] to take apart O to pieces; [- motor] to strip down; [- piezas] to dismantle; [- rueda] to remove, to take off; [- tienda de campaña] to take down; [- arma] to uncock - **2.** [jinete - suj: caballo] to unseat; [- suj: persona] to help down.

desmoralizar *vt* to demoralize.

desmoronar *vt* [edificios, rocas] to cause to crumble. ➤ **desmoronarse** *vprnl* [edificio, roca, ideales] to crumble.

desnatado, da *adj* skimmed.

desnaturalizado, da *adj* [sustancia] adulterated; [alcohol] denatured.

desnivel *sm* [del terreno] irregularity, unevenness (U).

desnivelar *vt* to make uneven; [balanza] to tip.

desnucar *vt* to break the neck of.

desnudar *vt* to undress. ➤ **desnudarse** *vprnl* to get undressed.

desnudez *sf* [de persona] nakedness, nudity; [de cosa] bareness.

desnudo, da *adj* - **1.** [persona, cuerpo] naked - **2.** *fig* [salón, hombro, árbol] bare; [verdad] plain; [paisaje] barren. ➤ **desnudo** *sm* nude.

desnutrición *sf* malnutrition.

desobedecer *vt* to disobey.

desobediencia *sf* disobedience; **desobediencia civil** civil disobedience.

desobediente *adj* disobedient.

desocupado, da *adj* - **1.** [persona - ocioso] free, unoccupied; [- sin empleo] unemployed - **2.** [lugar] vacant.

desocupar *vt* [edificio] to vacate; [habitación, mesa] to leave.

desodorante *sm* deodorant.

desolación *sf* - **1.** [destrucción] desolation - **2.** [desconsuelo] distress, grief.

desolar *vt* - **1.** [destruir] to devastate, to lay waste - **2.** [afligir] to cause anguish to.

desorbitado, da *adj* - **1.** [gen] disproportionate; [precio] exorbitant - **2.** *loc*: **con los ojos desorbitados** pop-eyed.

desorden *sm* - **1.** [confusión] disorder, chaos; [falta de orden] mess; **en desorden** topsy-turvy, **poner en desorden** to upset, to disarrange - **2.** [disturbio] disturbance

desordenado, da *adj* [habitación, persona] untidy, messy; [documentos, fichas] jumbled (up).

desorganización *sf* disorganization.

desorganizar *vt* to disrupt, to disorganize.

desorientar *vt* - **1.** [en el espacio] to disorientate, to mislead - **2.** *fig* [aturdir] to confuse.
➤ **desorientarse** *vprnl* - **1.** [en el espacio] to lose one's way O bearings - **2.** *fig* [aturdirse] to get confused.

despabilado, da *adj* - **1.** [despierto] wide-awake - **2.** [listo] smart, quick.

despabilar *vt* - **1.** [despertar] to wake up - **2.** [hacer más avispado] to make streetwise. ➤ **despabilarse** *vprnl* - **1.** [despertarse] to wake up - **2.** [darse prisa] to hurry up.

despachar ◇ *vt* - **1.** [mercancía] to dispatch - **2.** [en tienda - cliente] to serve; [- entradas, bebidas etc] to sell - **3.** *fam fig* [terminar - trabajo, discurso] to finish off - **4.** [asunto, negocio] to settle - **5.** *Amér* [equipaje] to check in. ◇ *vi* [en una tienda] to serve.

despacho *sm* - **1.** [oficina] office; [en casa] study - **2.** [comunicación oficial] dispatch - **3.** [venta] sale; [lugar de venta]: **despacho de billetes/localidades** ticket/box office.

despacio *adv* - **1.** [lentamente] slowly - **2.** *esp Amér* [en voz baja] quietly.

desparpajo *sm fam* forwardness, self-assurance.

desparramar *vt* [líquido] to spill; [objetos] to spread, to scatter.

despecho *sm* [rencor, venganza] spite; [desengaño] bitterness; **(hacer algo) por despecho** (to do sthg) out of spite.

despectivo, va *adj* - **1.** [despreciativo] contemptuous - **2.** GRAM pejorative.

despedazar *vt* - **1.** [físicamente] to tear apart - **2.** *fig* [moralmente] to shatter.

despedida *sf* [adiós] farewell.

despedir *vt* - **1.** [decir adiós a] to say goodbye to; **fuimos a despedirle a la estación** we went to see him off at the station - **2.** [echar - de un empleo] to dismiss, to sack; [- de un club] to throw out - **3.** [lanzar, arrojar] to fling; **salir despedido de/por/hacia algo** to fly out of/through/towards sthg - **4.** *fig* [difundir, desprender] to give off. ➤ **despedirse** *vprnl*: **despedirse (de)** to say goodbye (to).

despegar ◇ *vt* to unstick. ◇ *vi* [avión] to take off. ➤ **despegarse** *vprnl* [etiqueta, pegatina, sello] to come unstuck.

despegue *sm* takeoff; **despegue vertical** vertical takeoff.

despeinar vt [pelo] to ruffle; **despeinar a alguien** to mess up sb's hair. **despeinarse** vprnl to mess up one's hair.

despejado, da adj - **1.** [tiempo, día] clear - **2.** fig [persona, mente] alert - **3.** [espacio - ancho] spacious; [- sin estorbos] clear, uncluttered.

despejar vt [gen] to clear. **despejarse** vprnl - **1.** [persona - espabilarse] to clear one's head; [- despertarse] to wake o.s. up - **2.** [tiempo] to clear up; [cielo] to clear.

despeje sm DEP clearance.

despellejar vt [animal] to skin.

despensa sf larder, pantry.

despeñadero sm precipice.

despeñar vt to throw over a cliff. **despeñarse** vprnl to fall over a cliff.

desperdiciar vt [tiempo, comida] to waste; [dinero] to squander; [ocasión] to throw away.

desperdicio sm - **1.** [acción] waste - **2.** [residuo]: **desperdicios** scraps.

desperdigar vt to scatter, to disperse.

desperezarse vprnl to stretch.

desperfecto sm [deterioro] damage (U); [defecto] flaw, imperfection.

despertador sm alarm clock.

despertar ⬦ vt - **1.** [persona, animal] to wake (up) - **2.** fig [reacción] to arouse - **3.** fig [recuerdo] to revive, to awaken. ⬦ vi to wake up. ⬦ sm awakening. **despertarse** vprnl to wake up.

despiadado, da adj pitiless, merciless.

despido sm dismissal, sacking; **despido colectivo** collective dismissal.

despierto, ta adj - **1.** [sin dormir] awake - **2.** fig [espabilado, listo] sharp.

despilfarrar vt [dinero] to squander; [electricidad, agua etc] to waste.

despilfarro sm [de dinero] squandering; [de energía, agua etc] waste.

despiole sm R Dom fam rumpus, shindy.

despistado, da adj absent-minded.

despistar vt - **1.** [dar esquinazo a] to throw off the scent - **2.** fig [confundir] to mislead. **despistarse** vprnl - **1.** [perderse] to lose one's way, to get lost - **2.** fig [distraerse] to get confused.

despiste sm [distracción] absent-mindedness; [error] mistake, slip.

desplante sm rude remark; **hacer un desplante a alguien** to snub sb.

desplazamiento sm - **1.** [viaje] journey; [traslado] move - **2.** NÁUT displacement.

desplazar vt - **1.** [trasladar] to move - **2.** fig [desbancar] to take the place of. **desplazarse** vprnl [viajar] to travel.

desplegar vt - **1.** [tela, periódico, mapa] to unfold; [alas] to spread, to open; [bandera] to unfurl - **2.** [cualidad] to display - **3.** MIL to deploy.

despliegue sm - **1.** [de cualidad] display - **2.** MIL deployment.

desplomarse vprnl [gen] to collapse; [techo] to fall in.

desplumar vt - **1.** [ave] to pluck - **2.** fig [estafar] to fleece.

despoblado, da adj unpopulated, deserted.

despojar vt: **despojar a alguien de algo** to strip sb of sthg. **despojarse** vprnl: **despojarse de algo** [bienes, alimentos] to give sthg up; [abrigo, chandal] to take sthg off.

despojo sm [acción] plundering. **despojos** smpl - **1.** [sobras, residuos] leftovers - **2.** [de animales] offal (U).

desposar vt to marry. **desposarse** vprnl to get married.

desposeer vt: **desposeer a alguien de** to dispossess sb of.

déspota smf despot.

despotricar vi: **despotricar (contra)** to rant on (at).

despreciar vt - **1.** [desdeñar] to scorn - **2.** [rechazar] to spurn.

desprecio sm scorn, contempt.

desprender vt - **1.** [lo que estaba fijo] to remove, to detach - **2.** [olor, luz] to give off. **desprenderse** vprnl - **1.** [caerse, soltarse] to come O fall off - **2.** fig [deducirse]: **de sus palabras se desprende que...** from his words it is clear O it can be seen that... - **3.** [librarse]: **desprenderse de** to get rid of.

desprendimiento sm [separación] detachment; **desprendimiento de tierras** landslide.

despreocupado, da adj [libre de preocupaciones] unworried, unconcerned; [en el vestir] casual.

despreocuparse **despreocuparse de** vprnl [asunto] to stop worrying about.

desprestigiar vt to discredit.

desprevenido, da adj unprepared; **coger O pillar desprevenido a alguien** to catch sb unawares, to take sb by surprise.

desprolijo, ja adj Amér [casa, cuaderno] untidy; [persona] unkempt, dishevelled.

desproporcionado, da adj disproportionate.

despropósito sm stupid remark.

desprovisto, ta adj: **desprovisto de** lacking in, devoid of.

después adv - **1.** [en el tiempo - más tarde] afterwards, later; [- entonces] then; [- justo lo siguiente] next; **poco después** soon after; **años después** years later; **ellos llegaron después**

they arrived later; **llamé primero y después entré** I knocked first and then I went in; **yo voy después** It's my turn next - **2.** [en el espacio] next, after; **¿qué viene después?** what comes next O after¿; **hay una farmacia y después está mi casa** there's a chemist's and then there's my house - **3.** [en una lista] further down. ➤ **después de** loc prep after; **llegó después de ti** she arrived after you; **después de él, nadie lo ha conseguido** since he did it, no one else has; **después de hacer algo** after doing sthg. ➤ **después de todo** loc ad · after all.

despuntar ◇ vt [romper] to break the point off; [desgastar] to blunt. ◇ vi - **1.** fig [persona] to excel - **2.** [alba] to break; [día] to dawn.

desquiciar vt fig [desequilibrar] to derange; [sacar de quicio] to drive mad.

desquite sm revenge.

destacamento sm detachment; **destacamento de tropas** task force.

destacar ◇ vt - **1.** [poner de relieve] to emphasize, to highlight; **cabe destacar que...** it is important to point out that... - **2.** MIL to detach, to detail. ◇ vi [sobresalir] to stand out. ➤ **destacarse** vprnl: **destacarse (de/por)** to stand out (from/because of).

destajo sm piecework; **trabajar a destajo** [por trabajo hecho] to do piecework; fig [afanosamente] to work flat out.

destapador sm Amér bottle opener.

destapar vt - **1.** [abrir - caja, botella] to open; [olla] to take the lid off; [descorchar] to uncork - **2.** [descubrir] to uncover - **3.** R Dom [desobstruir] to unblock. ➤ **destaparse** vprnl [desabrigarse] to lose the covers.

destartalado, da adj [viejo, deteriorado] dilapidated; [desordenado] untidy.

destello sm - **1.** [de luz, brillo] sparkle; [de estrella] twinkle - **2.** fig [manifestación momentánea] glimmer.

destemplado, da adj - **1.** [persona] out of sorts - **2.** [tiempo, clima] unpleasant - **3.** [carácter, actitud] irritable.

desteñir ◇ vt to fade, to bleach. ◇ vi to run, not to be colour fast.

desternillarse vprnl: **desternillarse de risa** to split one's sides laughing O with laughter.

desterrar vt [persona] to banish, to exile.

destetar vt to wean.

destiempo ➤ **a destiempo** loc adv at the wrong time.

destierro sm exile; **en el destierro** in exile.

destilar vt [agua, petróleo] to distil.

destilería sf distillery; **destilería de petróleo** oil refinery.

destinar vt - **1.**: **destinar algo a** O **para** [cantidad, edificio] to set sthg aside for; [empleo, cargo] to assign sthg to; [carta] to address sthg to; [medidas, programa, publicación] to aim sthg at - **2.**: **destinar a alguien a** [cargo, empleo] to appoint sb to, [plaza, lugar] to post sb to.

destinatario, ria sm,f addressee.

destino sm - **1.** [sino] destiny, fate - **2.** [rumbo] destination; **(ir) con destino a** (to be) bound for O going to; **un vuelo con destino a...** a flight to... - **3.** [empleo, plaza] position, post - **4.** [finalidad] function.

destitución sf dismissal.

destituir vt to dismiss.

destornillador sm screwdriver.

destornillar vt to unscrew.

destreza sf skill, dexterity.

destrozar vt - **1.** [físicamente - romper] to smash; [- estropear] to ruin - **2.** [moralmente - persona] to shatter, to devastate; [- vida] to ruin.

destrozo sm damage (U); **ocasionar grandes destrozos** to cause a lot of damage.

destrucción sf destruction.

destruir vt - **1.** [gen] to destroy; [casa, argumento] to demolish - **2.** [proyecto] to ruin, to wreck; [ilusión] to dash.

desuso sm disuse; **caer en desuso** to become obsolete, to fall into disuse.

desvaído, da adj [color] pale, washed-out; [forma, contorno] blurred; [mirada] vague.

desvalido, da adj needy, destitute.

desvalijar vt [casa] to burgle, to burglarize US; [persona] to rob.

desván sm attic, loft.

desvanecer vt - **1.** [humo, nubes] to dissipate - **2.** [sospechas, temores] to dispel. ➤ **desvanecerse** vprnl - **1.** [desmayarse] to faint - **2.** [disiparse - humo, nubes] to clear, to disappear; [- sonido, sospechas, temores] to fade away.

desvanecimiento sm [desmayo] fainting fit.

desvariar vi [delirar] to be delirious; [decir locuras] to talk nonsense, to rave.

desvarío sm - **1.** [dicho] raving; [hecho] act of madness - **2.** [delirio] delirium.

desvelar vt - **1.** [quitar el sueño a] to keep awake - **2.** [noticia, secreto etc] to reveal. ➤ **desvelarse** vprnl Amér C & Méx [quedarse despierto] to stay up O awake. ➤ **desvelarse por** vprnl: **desvelarse por hacer algo** to make every effort to do sthg.

desvelo sm [esfuerzo] effort.

desvencijado, da adj [silla, mesa] rickety; [camión, coche] battered.

desventaja sf disadvantage; **en desventaja** at a disadvantage.

desventura sf misfortune.

desvergonzado, da adj shameless.

desvergüenza *sf* [atrevimiento, frescura] shamelessness.

desvestir *vt* to undress. ◆ **desvestirse** *vprnl* to undress (o.s.)

desviación *sf* - 1. [de dirección, cauce, norma] deviation - 2. [en la carretera] diversion, detour.

desviar *vt* [río, carretera, tráfico] to divert; [dirección] to change; [golpe] to parry; [pelota, disparo] to deflect; [pregunta] to evade; [conversación] to change the direction of; [mirada, ojos] to avert. ◆ **desviarse** *vprnl* [cambiar de dirección - conductor] to take a detour; [- avión, barco] to go off course; **desviarse de** to turn off.

desvío *sm* diversion, detour.

desvirtuar *vt* [gen] to detract from; [estropear] to spoil; [verdadero sentido] to distort.

desvivirse *vprnl*: **desvivirse (por alguien/algo)** to do everything one can (for sb/sthg); **desvivirse por hacer algo** to bend over backwards to do sthg.

detallado, da *adj* detailed, thorough.

detallar *vt* [historia, hechos] to detail, to give a rundown of; [cuenta, gastos] to itemize.

detalle *sm* - 1. [gen] detail; **con detalle** in detail; **entrar en detalles** to go into detail - 2. [atención] kind gesture O thought; **¡qué detalle!** what a kind gesture!, how thoughtful!; **tener un detalle con alguien** to be thoughtful O considerate to sb. ◆ **al detalle** *loc adv* COM retail.

detallista *smf* COM retailer.

detectar *vt* to detect.

detective *smf* detective.

detener *vt* - 1. [arrestar] to arrest - 2. [parar] to stop; [retrasar] to hold up. ◆ **detenerse** *vprnl* - 1. [pararse] to stop - 2. [demorarse] to linger.

detenidamente *adv* carefully, thoroughly.

detenido, da ◇ *adj* - 1. [detallado] thorough - 2. [arrestado]: **(estar) detenido** (to be) under arrest. ◇ *sm, f* prisoner.

detenimiento ◆ **con detenimiento** *loc adv* carefully, thoroughly.

detergente *sm* detergent.

deteriorar *vt* to damage, to spoil. ◆ **deteriorarse** *vprnl* fig [empeorar] to deteriorate, to get worse.

deterioro *sm* [daño] damage; [empeoramiento] deterioration.

determinación *sf* - 1. [fijación - de precio etc] settling, fixing - 2. [resolución] determination, resolution - 3. [decisión]: **tomar una determinación** to take a decision.

determinado, da *adj* - 1. [concreto] specific; [en particular] particular - 2. [resuelto] determined - 3. GRAM definite.

determinar *vt* - 1. [fijar - fecha, precio] to settle, to fix - 2. [averiguar] to determine - 3. [motivar] to cause, to bring about - 4. [decidir] to decide; **determinar hacer algo** to decide to do sthg. ◆ **determinarse** *vprnl*: **determinarse a hacer algo** to make up one's mind to do sthg.

detestar *vt* to detest.

detonante *sm* [explosivo] explosive.

detractor, ra *sm, f* detractor.

detrás *adv* - 1. [en el espacio] behind; **tus amigos vienen detrás** your friends are coming on behind; **el interruptor está detrás** the switch is at the back - 2. [en el orden] then, afterwards; **Portugal y detrás Puerto Rico** Portugal and then Puerto Rico. ◆ **detrás de** *loc prep* [gen] behind. ◆ **por detrás** *loc adv* at the back; **hablar de alguien por detrás** to talk about sb behind his/her back.

detrimento *sm* damage; **en detrimento de** to the detriment of.

detrito *sm* BIOL detritus. ◆ **detritos** *smpl* [residuos] waste *(U)*.

deuda *sf* debt; **deuda pública** ECON national debt *UK*, public debt *US*.

deudor, ra ◇ *adj* [saldo] debit *(antes de s)*; [entidad] indebted. ◇ *sm, f* debtor.

devaluación *sf* devaluation.

devaluar *vt* to devalue.

devaneos *smpl* [amoríos] affairs; [coqueteos] flirting *(U)*.

devastar *vt* to devastate.

devoción *sf*: **devoción (por)** devotion (to).

devolución *sf* [gen] return; [de dinero] refund.

devolver ◇ *vt* - 1. [restituir]: **devolver algo (a)** [coche, dinero etc] to give sthg back (to); [producto defectuoso, carta] to return sthg (to) - 2. [restablecer, colocar en su sitio]: **devolver algo a** to return sthg to - 3. [favor, agravio] to pay back for; [visita] to return - 4. [vomitar] to bring O throw up. ◇ *vi* to throw up. ◆ **devolverse** *vprnl* Andes, Amér, Caribe & Méx to come back.

devorar *vt* lit & fig to devour.

devoto, ta ◇ *adj* [piadoso] devout; **ser devoto de** to have a devotion for. ◇ *sm, f* [admirador] devotee.

devuelto, ta *pp* ▷ **devolver**.

dg (*abrev de* **decigramo**) dg.

di *etc* ▷ **dar**. ▷ **decir**.

día *sm* - 1. [gen] day; **me voy el día ocho** I'm going on the eighth; **¿a qué día estamos?** what day is it today?; **¿qué tal día hace?** what's the weather like today?; **todos los días** every day; **día de la Madre** Mother's Day; **día de los enamorados** St Valentine's Day; **día de los inocentes** *28th December*, ≈ April Fools' Day; **día de pago** payday; **día festivo** (public) holiday; **de día en día** from day to day, day by day; **del día** fresh; **hoy (en) día** nowadays; **todo el santo día** all day long, **el día de mañana** in the future; **al día siguiente** on the following day; **un día sí y otro no** every other day; **menú del día** today's menu - 2. [luz] daytime, day; **es de día** it's daytime; **hacer algo de día** to do sthg in the daytime O during the day; **día y noche** day and night - 3. loc: **estar/ponerse al día (de)** to be/get up to date (with); **poner algo/a alguien al día** to update sthg/sb; **vivir al día** to live from hand to mouth. ➡ **buen día** interj Amér: **¡buen día!** good morning! ➡ **buenos días** interj: **¡buenos días!** [gen] hello!; [por la mañana] good morning!

diabético, ca adj & sm, f diabetic.

diablo sm lit & fig devil; **pobre diablo** poor devil.

diablura sf prank.

diabólico, ca adj - 1. [del diablo] diabolic - 2. fig [muy malo, difícil] diabolical.

diadema sf [para el pelo] hairband.

diáfano, na adj - 1. [transparente] transparent, diaphanous - 2. fig [claro] clear.

diafragma sm diaphragm.

diagnosticar vt to diagnose.

diagnóstico sm diagnosis; **diagnóstico precoz** early diagnosis.

diagonal adj & sf diagonal.

diagrama sm diagram; **diagrama de flujo** INFORM flow chart O diagram.

dial sm dial.

dialecto sm dialect.

dialogar vi: **dialogar (con)** [hablar] to have a conversation (with), to talk (to); [negociar] to hold a dialogue O talks (with).

diálogo sm [conversación] conversation; LITER & POLÍT dialogue.

diamante sm [piedra preciosa] diamond; **diamante en bruto** uncut diamond; **ser un diamante en bruto** fig to have a lot of potential.

diámetro sm diameter.

diana sf - 1. [en blanco de tiro] bull's-eye, bull - 2. [en cuartel] reveille.

diapasón sm tuning fork.

diapositiva sf slide, transparency.

diariero, ra sm, f Andes & R Plata newspaper seller.

diario, ria adj daily; **a diario** every day; **de diario** daily, everyday; **ropa de diario** everyday clothes. ➡ **diario** sm - 1. [periódico] newspaper, daily - 2. [relación día a día] diary; **diario de sesiones** parliamentary report; **diario de vuelo** log, logbook.

diarrea sf diarrhoea.

dibujante sm, f [gen] sketcher; [de dibujos animados] cartoonist; [de dibujo técnico] draughtsman (f draughtswoman)

dibujar vt & vi to draw, to sketch.

dibujo sm - 1. [gen] drawing; **no se le da bien el dibujo** he's no good at drawing; **dibujos animados** cartoons; **dibujo artístico** art; **dibujo lineal** technical drawing; **dibujo al natural** drawing from life - 2. [de tela, prenda etc] pattern.

diccionario sm dictionary.

dice ⊳ **decir**.

dicha sf [alegría] joy.

dicho, cha ⬦ pp ⊳ **decir**. ⬦ adj said, aforementioned; **dichos hombres** the said men, these men; **lo dicho** what I/we etc said; **o mejor dicho** or rather; **dicho y hecho** no sooner said than done. ➡ **dicho** sm saying; **del dicho al hecho hay un gran O mucho trecho** it's easier said than done.

dichoso, sa adj [feliz] happy; [afortunado] fortunate.

diciembre sm December; ver también **septiembre**.

dictado sm dictation; **escribir al dictado** to take dictation.

dictador, ra sm, f dictator.

dictadura sf dictatorship.

dictamen sm [opinión] opinion, judgment; [informe] report.

dictar vt - 1. [texto] to dictate - 2. [emitir - sentencia, fallo] to pronounce, to pass; [- ley] to enact; [- decreto] to issue.

didáctico, ca adj didactic.

diecinueve num nineteen; ver también **seis**.

dieciocho num eighteen; ver también **seis**.

dieciséis num sixteen; ver también **seis**.

diecisiete num seventeen; ver también **seis**.

diente sm tooth; **está echando O le están saliendo los dientes** she's teething; **diente de leche** milk tooth; **dientes postizos** false teeth; **armado hasta los dientes** armed to the teeth; **hablar entre dientes** to mumble, to mutter; **reírse entre dientes** to chuckle. ➡ **diente de ajo** sm clove of garlic.

diera ⊳ **dar**.

diéresis sf inv diaeresis.

dieron etc ⊳ **dar**.

diesel, diésel adj diesel.

diestro, tra adj [hábil]: **diestro (en)** skilful (at); **a diestro y siniestro** fig left, right and centre, all over the place.

dieta sf MED diet; **estar/ponerse a dieta** to be/go on a diet; **dieta blanda** soft-food diet; **dieta equilibrada** balanced diet; **dieta mediterránea** Mediterranean diet. ➡ **dietas** sfpl COM expenses.

dietético, ca *adj* dietetic, dietary. ◆ **dietética** *sf* dietetics (U).

dietista *smf Amér* dietician.

diez ◇ *num* ten. ◇ *sm* [en la escuela] A, top marks *pl; ver también* **seis.**

difamar *vt* [verbalmente] to slander; [por escrito] to libel.

diferencia *sf* difference; **con diferencia** by a long chalk, by far; **es, con diferencia, el más listo** he's the smartest by far; **partir la diferencia** to split the difference; **diferencia horaria** time difference.

diferenciar ◇ *vt:* **diferenciar (de)** to distinguish (from). ◇ *vi:* **diferenciar (entre)** to distinguish O differentiate (between). ◆ **diferenciarse** *vprnl* [diferir]: **diferenciarse (de/en)** to differ (from/in), to be different (from/in).

diferente ◇ *adj:* **diferente (de** O **a)** different (from O to). ◇ *adv* differently.

diferido ◆ **en diferido** *loc adv* TV recorded.

diferir *vi* [diferenciarse] to differ.

difícil *adj* difficult; **difícil de hacer** difficult to do; **es difícil que ganen** they are unlikely to win.

dificultad *sf* - 1. [calidad de difícil] difficulty - 2. [obstáculo] problem.

dificultar *vt* [estorbar] to hinder; [obstruir] to obstruct.

difuminar *vt* to blur.

difundir *vt* - 1. [noticia, doctrina, epidemia] to spread - 2. [luz, calor] to diffuse; [emisión radiofónica] to broadcast. ◆ **difundirse** *vprnl* - 1. [noticia, doctrina, epidemia] to spread - 2. [luz, calor] to be diffused.

difunto, ta *sm, f:* **el difunto** the deceased.

difusión *sf* - 1. [de cultura, noticia, doctrina] dissemination - 2. [de programa] broadcasting.

diga ⊳ **decir.**

digerir *vt* to digest; *fig* [hechos] to assimilate, to take in.

digestión *sf* digestion; **hacer la digestión** to digest one's food.

digestivo, va *adj* digestive.

digital *adj* INFORM & TECNOL digital.

dígito *sm* digit.

dignarse *vprnl:* **dignarse a** to deign to.

dignidad *sf* [cualidad] dignity.

digno, na *adj* - 1. [noble - actitud, respuesta] dignified; [- persona] honourable, noble - 2. [merecedor]: **digno de** worthy of; **digno de elogio** praiseworthy; **digno de mención/de ver** worth mentioning/seeing - 3. [adecuado]: **digno de** appropriate for, fitting for - 4. [decente - sueldo, actuación etc] decent.

digo ⊳ **decir.**

dijera *etc* ⊳ **decir.**

dilapidar *vt* to squander, to waste.

dilatar *vt* - 1. [extender] to expand; [retina, útero] to dilate - 2. [prolongar] to prolong - 3. [demorar] to delay.

dilema *sm* dilemma.

diligencia *sf* - 1. [esmero, cuidado] diligence - 2. [trámite, gestión] business (U); **hacer una diligencia** to run an errand - 3. [vehículo] stagecoach. ◆ **diligencias** *sfpl* DER proceedings; **instruir diligencias** to start proceedings.

diligente *adj* diligent.

diluir *vt* to dilute. ◆ **diluirse** *vprnl* to dissolve.

diluvio *sm lit & fig* flood; **el Diluvio Universal** the Flood.

dimensión *sf* dimension; **las dimensiones de la tragedia** the extent of the tragedy.

diminutivo *sm* diminutive.

diminuto, ta *adj* tiny, minute.

dimisión *sf* resignation; **presentar la dimisión** to hand in one's resignation.

dimitir *vi:* **dimitir (de)** to resign (from).

dimos ⊳ **dar.**

Dinamarca *n pr* Denmark.

dinámico, ca *adj* dynamic.

dinamismo *sm* dynamism.

dinamita *sf* dynamite.

dinamo, dínamo *sf* dynamo.

dinastía *sf* dynasty.

dineral *sm fam* fortune.

dinero *sm* money; **andar bien/mal de dinero** to be well off for/short of money; **hacer dinero** to make money; **tirar el dinero** to throw money away; **dinero en metálico** cash.

dinosaurio *sm* dinosaur.

dintel *sm* ARQUIT lintel.

dio ⊳ **dar.**

diócesis *sf* diocese.

dios, osa *sm, f* god (*f* goddess). ◆ **Dios** *sm* God; **a la buena de Dios** any old how; **Dios los cría y ellos se juntan** *prov* birds of a feather flock together *prov;* **¡Dios me libre!** God O heaven forbid!; **Dios mediante, si Dios quiere** God willing; **¡Dios mío!** good God!, (oh) my God!; **Dios sabe, sabe Dios** God (alone) knows; **¡que Dios se lo pague!** God bless you!; **¡por Dios!** for God's sake!; **¡vaya por Dios!** for Heaven's sake!, honestly!

diploma *sm* diploma.

diplomacia *sf* [gen] diplomacy.

diplomado, da *adj* qualified.

diplomático, ca ◇ *adj lit & fig* diplomatic. ◇ *sm, f* diplomat.

diptongo *sm* diphthong.

diputación *sf* [corporación] committee; **diputación provincial** *governing body of each province of an autonomous region in Spain*, ~ county council *UK*.

diputado, **da** *sm, f* ≃ Member of Parliament, MP *UK*, representative *US*.

dique *sm* - 1. [en río] dike - 2. [en puerto] dock; **estar en (el) dique seco** *fig* to be out of action.

dirá ▷ **decir**.

dirección *sf* - 1. [sentido, rumbo] direction; **calle de dirección única** one-way street; **'dirección prohibida'** 'no entry'; **en dirección a** towards, in the direction of - 2. [domicilio] address; **dirección comercial** business address; **dirección electrónica** O **de correo electrónico** e-mail address; **dirección particular** home address - 3. [mando - de empresa, hospital] management; [- de partido] leadership; [- de colegio] headship; [- de periódico] editorship; [- de película] direction; [- de obra de teatro] production; [- de orquesta] conducting - 4. [junta directiva] management - 5. [de vehículo] steering; **dirección asistida** power steering. ➤ **Dirección** *sf*: **Dirección General de Tráfico** *traffic department (part of the Ministry of the Interior)*.

directivo, va ◇ *adj* managerial. ◇ *sm, f* [jefe] manager. ➤ **directiva** *sf* [junta] board (of directors).

directo, ta *adj* - 1. [gen] direct - 2. [derecho] straight. ➤ **directo** *adv* straight; **directo a** straight to. ➤ **directa** *sf* AUTO top gear. ➤ **en directo** *loc adv* live.

director, ra *sm, f* - 1. [de empresa] director; [de hotel, hospital] manager (*f* manageress); [de periódico] editor; [de cárcel] governor - 2. [de obra artística]: **director de cine** film director; **director de orquesta** conductor - 3. [de colegio] headmaster (*f* headmistress) - 4. [de tesis, trabajo de investigación] supervisor.

directorio *sm* - 1. [gen & INFORM] directory - 2.: **directorio telefónico** *Andes, Amér C, Caribe & Méx* directory.

directriz *sf* GEOM directrix. ➤ **directrices** *sfpl* [normas] guidelines.

diría ▷ **decir**.

dirigente *smf* [de partido político] leader; [de empresa] manager.

dirigir *vt* - 1. [conducir - coche, barco] to steer; [- avión] to pilot; *fig* [- mirada] to direct - 2. [llevar - empresa, hotel, hospital] to manage; [- colegio, cárcel, periódico] to run; [- partido, revuelta] to lead; [- expedición] to head - 3. [película, obra de teatro] to direct; [orquesta] to conduct - 4. [carta, paquete] to address - 5. [guiar - persona] to guide - 6. [dedicar]: **dirigir algo a** to aim sthg at. ➤ **dirigirse** *vprnl* - 1. [encaminarse]:

dirigirse a O **hacia** to head for - 2. [hablar]: **dirigirse a** to address, to speak to - 3. [escribir]: **dirigirse a** to write to.

discar *vt Andes & R Dom* to dial.

discapacidad *sf* disability.

discernir *vt* to discern, to distinguish.

disciplina *sf* discipline.

discípulo, la *sm, f* disciple.

disco *sm* - 1. ANAT, ASTRON & GEOM disc - 2. [de música] record; **parecer un disco rayado** *fam* to go on like a cracked record; **disco compacto** compact disc; **disco de larga duración** LP, long-playing record - 3. [semáforo] (traffic) light - 4. DEP discus - 5. INFORM disk; **disco de arranque/del sistema** startup/system disk.

discografía *sf* records previously released *(by an artist or group)*.

disconforme *adj* in disagreement; **estar disconforme con** to disagree with.

discontinuo, nua *adj* [esfuerzo] intermittent; [línea] broken, dotted.

discordante *adj* [sonidos] discordant; [opiniones] clashing.

discordia *sf* discord.

discoteca *sf* [local] disco.

discreción *sf* discretion. ➤ **a discreción** *loc adv* as much as one wants, freely.

discrecional *adj* [gen] optional; [parada] request *(antes de s)*.

discrepancia *sf* [diferencia] difference, discrepancy; [desacuerdo] disagreement.

discrepar *vi*: **discrepar (de)** [diferenciarse] to differ (from); [disentir] to disagree (with).

discreto, ta *adj* - 1. [prudente] discreet - 2. [cantidad] moderate, modest - 3. [normal - actuación] fair, reasonable.

discriminación *sf* discrimination; **discriminación racial/sexual** racial/sexual discrimination.

discriminar *vt* - 1. [cosa]: **discriminar algo de** to discriminate O distinguish sthg from - 2. [persona, colectividad] to discriminate against.

disculpa *sf* [pretexto] excuse; [excusa, perdón] apology; **dar disculpas** to make excuses; **pedir disculpas a alguien (por)** to apologize to sb (for).

disculpar *vt* to excuse; **disculpar a alguien (de** O **por algo)** to forgive sb (for sthg). ➤ **disculparse** *vprnl*: **disculparse (de** O **por algo)** to apologize (for sthg).

discurrir *vi* - 1. [pasar - personas] to wander, to walk; [- tiempo, vida, sesión] to go by, to pass; [- río, tráfico] to flow - 2. [pensar] to think, to reflect.

discurso *sm* speech.

discusión sf - 1. [conversación] discussion - 2. [pelea] argument.

discutible adj debatable.

discutir ⬦ vi - 1. [hablar] to discuss - 2. [pelear]: **discutir (de)** to argue (about). ⬦ vt [hablar] to discuss; [contradecir] to dispute.

disecar vt [animal] to stuff; [planta] to dry.

diseminar vt [semillas] to scatter; [ideas] to disseminate.

disentir vi: **disentir (de/en)** to disagree (with/on).

diseñar vt to design.

diseño sm design; **ropa de diseño** designer clothes; **diseño asistido por ordenador** INFORM computer-aided design; **diseño gráfico** graphic design.

disertación sf [oral] lecture, discourse; [escrita] dissertation.

disfraz sm [gen] disguise; [para baile, fiesta etc] fancy dress (U).

disfrazar vt to disguise. ⬦ **disfrazarse** vprnl to disguise o.s.; **disfrazarse de** to dress up as.

disfrutar ⬦ vi - 1. [sentir placer] to enjoy o.s. - 2. [disponer de]: **disfrutar de algo** to enjoy sthg. ⬦ vt to enjoy.

disgregar vt - 1. [multitud, manifestación] to disperse - 2. [roca, imperio, estado] to break up; [átomo] to split. ⬦ **disgregarse** vprnl - 1. [multitud, manifestación] to disperse - 2. [roca, imperio, estado] to break up.

disgustar vt [suj: comentario, críticas, noticia] to upset. ⬦ **disgustarse** vprnl: **disgustarse (con alguien/por algo)** [sentir enfado] to get upset (with sb/about sthg); [enemistarse] to fall out (with sb/over sthg).

disgusto sm - 1. [enfado] annoyance; [pesadumbre] sorrow; **dar un disgusto a alguien** to upset sb; **llevarse un disgusto** to be upset - 2. [pelea]: **tener un disgusto con alguien** to have a quarrel with sb.

disidente smf [político] dissident; [religioso] dissenter.

disimular ⬦ vt to hide, to conceal. ⬦ vi to pretend.

disimulo sm pretence, concealment.

disipar vt - 1. [dudas, sospechas] to dispel; [ilusiones] to shatter - 2. [fortuna, herencia] to squander, to throw away. ⬦ **disiparse** vprnl - 1. [dudas, sospechas] to be dispelled; [ilusiones] to be shattered - 2. [niebla, humo, vapor] to vanish.

diskette = **disquete**.

dislexia sm dyslexia.

dislocar vt to dislocate. ⬦ **dislocarse** vprnl to dislocate.

disminución sf decrease, drop.

disminuido, da adj handicapped.

disminuir ⬦ vt to reduce, to decrease. ⬦ vi [gen] to decrease; [precios, temperatura] to drop, to fall; [vista, memoria] to fail; [días] to get shorter; [beneficios] to fall off.

disolución sf - 1. [en un líquido] dissolving - 2. [de matrimonio, sociedad, partido] dissolution - 3. [mezcla] solution.

disolvente adj & sm solvent.

disolver vt - 1. [gen] to dissolve - 2. [reunión, manifestación, familia] to break up. ⬦ **disolverse** vprnl - 1. [gen] to dissolve - 2. [reunión, manifestación, familia] to break up.

disparar ⬦ vt to shoot; [pedrada] to throw. ⬦ vi to shoot, to fire.

disparatado, da adj absurd, crazy.

disparate sm [acción] silly thing; [comentario] foolish remark; [idea] crazy idea; **hacer disparates** to do silly things; **decir disparates** to make foolish remarks, to talk nonsense.

disparo sm shot; **disparo de advertencia** warning shot; **disparo de salida** starting shot.

dispensar vt - 1. [disculpar] to excuse, to forgive - 2. [rendir]: **dispensar algo (a alguien)** [honores] to confer sthg (upon sb); [bienvenida, ayuda] to give sthg (to sb) - 3. [eximir]: **dispensar a alguien de** to excuse O exempt sb from.

dispensario sm dispensary.

dispersar vt - 1. [esparcir - objetos] to scatter - 2. [disolver - gentío] to disperse; [- manifestación] to break up. ⬦ **dispersarse** vprnl to scatter.

dispersión sf [de objetos] scattering.

disperso, sa adj scattered.

disponer ⬦ vt - 1. [gen] to arrange - 2. [cena, comida] to lay on - 3. [decidir - suj: persona] to decide; [suj: ley] to stipulate. ⬦ vi - 1. [poseer]: **disponer de** to have - 2. [usar]: **disponer de** to make use of. ⬦ **disponerse a** vprnl: **disponerse a hacer algo** to prepare O get ready to do sthg.

disponibilidad sf [gen] availability.

disponible adj [gen] available; [tiempo] free, spare.

disposición sf - 1. [colocación] arrangement, layout - 2. [orden] order; [de ley] provision - 3. [uso]: **a disposición de** at the disposal of; **pasar a disposición policial** to be brought before the judge.

dispositivo sm device; **dispositivo intrauterino** intrauterine device, IUD.

dispuesto, ta ⬦ pp ▷ **disponer**. ⬦ adj [preparado] ready; **estar dispuesto a hacer algo** to be prepared to do sthg; **estar poco dispuesto a hacer algo** to be reluctant to do sthg.

disputa sf dispute.

disputar *vt* - **1.** [cuestión, tema] to argue about - **2.** [trofeo, puesto] to compete for; [carrera, par-tido] to compete in.

disquete, diskette [dis'kete] *sm* INFORM diskette, floppy disk.

disquetera *sf* INFORM disk drive.

distancia *sf* - **1.** [gen] distance; **a distancia** from a distance; **mantener a distancia** to keep at a distance; **mantener las distancias** to keep one's distance; **recorrer una gran distancia** to cover a lot of ground - **2.** [en el tiempo] gap, space.

distanciar *vt* [gen] to drive apart; [rival] to forge ahead of. ◆ **distanciarse** *vprnl* [alejarse - afectivamente] to grow apart; [- físicamente] to distance o.s.

distante *adj* - **1.** [en el espacio]: **distante (de)** far away (from) - **2.** [en el trato] distant.

distar *vi* [hallarse a]: **ese sitio dista varios kilómetros de aquí** that place is several kilometres away from here.

diste *etc* ▷ **dar**.

distendido, da *adj* [informal] relaxed, informal.

distensión *sf* - **1.** [entre países] détente; [entre personas] easing of tension - **2.** MED strain.

distinción *sf* - **1.** [diferencia] distinction; **a distinción de** in contrast to, unlike; **sin distinción** alike - **2.** [privilegio] privilege - **3.** [elegancia] refinement.

distinguido, da *adj* - **1.** [notable] distinguished - **2.** [elegante] refined.

distinguir *vt* - **1.** [diferenciar] to distinguish; **distinguir algo de algo** to tell sthg from sthg - **2.** [separar] to pick out - **3.** [caracterizar] to characterize. ◆ **distinguirse** *vprnl* [destacarse] to stand out.

distintivo, va *adj* distinctive; [señal] distinguishing. ◆ **distintivo** *sm* badge.

distinto, ta *adj* [diferente] different. ◆ **distintos, tas** *adj pl* [varios] various.

distorsión *sf* [de tobillo, rodilla] sprain; [de imágenes, sonidos, palabras] distortion.

distracción *sf* - **1.** [entretenimiento] entertainment; [pasatiempo] hobby, pastime - **2.** [despiste] slip; [falta de atención] absent-mindedness.

distraer *vt* - **1.** [divertir] to amuse, to entertain - **2.** [despistar] to distract. ◆ **distraerse** *vprnl* - **1.** [divertirse] to enjoy o.s.; [pasar el tiempo] to pass the time - **2.** [despistarse] to let one's mind wander.

distraído, da *adj* - **1.** [entretenido] amusing, entertaining - **2.** [despistado] absent-minded.

distribución *sf* - **1.** [gen] distribution; **distribución de premios** prizegiving - **2.** [de correo, mercancías] delivery - **3.** [de casa, habitaciones] layout.

distribuidor, ra ▷ *adj* [entidad] wholesale; [red] supply *(antes de s)*. ▷ *sm, f* [persona] deliveryman (f deliverywoman). ◆ **distribuidor** *sm* [aparato] vending machine.

distribuir *vt* - **1.** [gen] to distribute; [carga, trabajo] to spread; [pastel, ganancias] to divide up - **2.** [correo, mercancías] to deliver - **3.** [casa, habitaciones] to arrange.

distrito *sm* district.

disturbio *sm* disturbance; [violento] riot; **disturbios raciales** race riots.

disuadir *vt*: **disuadir (de)** to dissuade (from).

disuasión *sf* deterrence.

disuasivo, va *adj* deterrent.

disuelto, ta *pp* ▷ **disolver**.

DIU *(abrev de dispositivo intrauterino)* *sm* IUD.

diurno, na *adj* [gen] daytime *(antes de s)*; [planta, animal] diurnal.

diva ▷ **divo**.

divagar *vi* to digress.

diván *sm* divan; [de psiquiatra] couch.

divergencia *sf* - **1.** [de líneas] divergence - **2.** [de opinión] difference of opinion.

divergir *vi* - **1.** [calles, líneas] to diverge - **2.** *fig* [opiniones]: **divergir (en)** to differ (on).

diversidad *sf* diversity.

diversificar *vt* to diversify.

diversión *sf* entertainment, amusement.

diverso, sa *adj* [diferente] different. ◆ **diversos, sas** *adj pl* [varios] several, various.

divertido, da *adj* [entretenido - película, libro] entertaining; [- fiesta] enjoyable; [que hace reír] funny.

divertir *vt* to entertain, to amuse. ◆ **divertirse** *vprnl* to enjoy o.s.

dividendo *sm* FIN & MAT dividend.

dividir *vt*: **dividir (en)** to divide (into); **dividir entre** [gen] to divide between; MAT to divide by.

divinidad *sf* divinity, god.

divino, na *adj* lit & fig divine.

divisa *sf* - **1.** *(gen pl)* [moneda] foreign currency - **2.** [distintivo] emblem.

divisar *vt* to spy, to make out.

división *sf* [gen] division; [partición] splitting up.

divo, va *sm, f* [MÚS - mujer] diva, prima donna; [- hombre] opera singer.

divorciado, da ▷ *adj* divorced. ▷ *sm, f* divorcé (f divorcée).

divorciar *vt* lit & fig to divorce. ◆ **divorciarse** *vprnl* to get divorced.

divorcio *sm* DER divorce.

divulgar *vt* [noticia, secreto] to reveal; [rumor] to spread; [cultura, ciencia, doctrina] to popularize.

DNI (*abrev de* documento nacional de identidad) *sm* ID card.

Dña *abrev de* doña.

do *sm* MÚS C; [en solfeo] doh; **dar el do de pecho** *fam fig* to give one's all.

dobladillo *sm* [de traje, vestido] hem; [de pantalón] turn-up UK, cuff US; **hacer un dobladillo** to turn up, to hem.

doblado, da *adj* - 1. [papel, camisa] folded - 2. [voz, película] dubbed.

doblar ◇ *vt* - 1. [duplicar] to double - 2. [plegar] to fold - 3. [torcer] to bend - 4. [esquina] to turn, to go round - 5. [voz, actor] to dub. ◇ *vi* - 1. [girar] to turn - 2. [campanas] to toll. ● **doblarse** *vprnl* [someterse]: **doblarse a** to give in to.

doble ◇ *adj* double; **tiene doble número de habitantes** it has double O twice the number of inhabitants; **es doble de ancho** it's twice as wide; **una frase de doble sentido** a phrase with a double meaning; **doble clic** INFORM double click. ◇ *smf* [gen & CINE] double. ◇ *sm* [duplo]: **el doble** twice as much; **gana el doble que yo** she earns twice as much as I do, she earns double what I do. ◇ *adv* double; **trabajar doble** to work twice as hard. ● **dobles** *smpl* DEP doubles.

doblegar *vt* [someter] to bend, to cause to give in. ● **doblegarse** *vprnl*: **doblegarse (ante)** to give in O yield (to).

doblez *sm* [pliegue] fold, crease.

doce *num* twelve; *ver también* **seis**.

doceavo, va *num* twelfth.

docena *sf* dozen; **a** O **por docenas** by the dozen.

docente *adj* teaching; **centro docente** educational institution.

dócil *adj* obedient.

doctor, ra *sm, f*: **doctor (en)** doctor (of).

doctrina *sf* doctrine.

documentación *sf* [identificación personal] papers *pl*.

documentado, da *adj* [informado - película, informe] researched; [- persona] informed.

documental *adj* & *sm* documentary.

documentar *vt* - 1. [evidenciar] to document - 2. [informar] to brief. ● **documentarse** *vprnl* to do research.

documento *sm* - 1. [escrito] document; **documento nacional de identidad** identity card - 2. [testimonio] record.

dogma *sm* dogma.

dogmático, ca *adj* dogmatic.

dólar *sm* dollar.

dolencia *sf* pain.

doler *vi* to hurt; **me duele la pierna** my leg hurts; **¿te duele?** does it hurt? ● **dolerse** *vprnl*: **dolerse de** O **por algo** [quejarse] to complain about sthg; [arrepentirse] to be sorry about sthg.

dolido, da *adj* hurt.

dolor *sm* - 1. [físico] pain; **siento un dolor en el brazo** I have a pain in my arm; **(tener) dolor de cabeza** (to have a) headache; **dolor de estómago** stomachache; **dolor de muelas** toothache - 2. [moral] grief, sorrow.

dolorido, da *adj* [físicamente] sore; [moralmente] grieving, sorrowing.

doloroso, sa *adj* [físicamente] painful; [moralmente] distressing.

domador, ra *sm, f* [de caballos] breaker; [de leones] tamer.

domar *vt* [gen] to tame; [caballo] to break in; *fig* [personas] to control.

domesticar *vt lit & fig* to tame.

doméstico, ca *adj* domestic.

domiciliación *sf*: **domiciliación (bancaria)** standing order, direct debit (U).

domiciliar *vt* [pago] to pay by direct debit O standing order.

domicilio *sm* - 1. [vivienda] residence, home; **domicilio particular** private residence - 2. [dirección] address; **sin domicilio fijo** of no fixed abode; **domicilio social** head office.

dominante *adj* - 1. [nación, religión, tendencia] dominant; [vientos] prevailing - 2. [persona] domineering.

dominar ◇ *vt* - 1. [controlar - país, territorio] to dominate, to rule (over); [- pasión, nervios, caballo] to control; [- situación] to be in control of; [- incendio] to bring under control; [- rebelión] to put down - 2. [divisar] to overlook - 3. [conocer - técnica, tema] to master; [- lengua] to be fluent in. ◇ *vi* [predominar] to predominate. ● **dominarse** *vprnl* to control o.s.

domingo *sm* Sunday; **domingo de Resurrección** O **de Pascua** Easter Sunday; *ver también* **sábado**.

dominguero, ra *sm, f* Sunday tripper/driver *etc*.

dominical *adj* Sunday (antes de s).

dominicano, na *adj* & *sm, f* Dominican.

dominico, ca *adj* & *sm, f* Dominican.

dominio *sm* - 1. [dominación, posesión]: **dominio (sobre)** control (over); **dominio de** O **sobre sí mismo** self-control - 2. [autoridad] authority, power - 3. *fig* [territorio] domain; [ámbito] realm - 4. [conocimiento - de arte, técnica] mastery; [- de idiomas] command - 5. INFORM domain.

dominó *sm* - **1.** [juego] dominoes *(U)* - **2.** [fichas] set of dominoes.

don *sm* - **1.** [tratamiento]. **don Luis García** [gen] Mr Luis García; [en cartas] Luis García Esquire; **don Luis** *not translated in modern English or translated as 'Mr' + surname, if known* - **2.** [habilidad] gift; **el don de la palabra** the gift of the gab.

donaire *sm* [al expresarse] wit; [al andar etc] grace.

donante *smf* donor; **donante de sangre** blood donor.

donar *vt* to donate.

donativo *sm* donation.

doncella *sf* maid.

donde ⬦ *adv* where; **el bolso está donde lo dejaste** the bag is where you left it; **puedes marcharte donde quieras** you can go wherever you want; **hasta donde** as far as, up to where; **por donde** wherever. ⬦ *pron* where; **la casa donde nací** the house where I was born; **la ciudad de donde viene** the town (where) she comes from, the town from which she comes. ➡ **de donde** *loc adv* [de lo cual] from which.

dónde *adv (interrogativo)* where; **¿dónde está el niño?** where's the child?; **no sé dónde se habrá metido** I don't know where she can be; **¿a dónde vas?** where are you going?; **¿de dónde eres?** where are you from?; **¿hacia dónde vas?** where are you heading?; **¿por dónde?** whereabouts?; **¿por dónde se va al teatro?** how do you get to the theatre from here?

dondequiera ➡ **dondequiera que** *adv* wherever.

doña *sf*: **doña Luisa García** Mrs Luisa García; **doña Luisa** *not translated in modern English or translated as 'Mrs' + surname, if known*.

dopado, **da** *adj* having taken performance-enhancing drugs.

dopar *vt* to dope.

doping ['dopin] *sm* doping.

doquier ➡ **por doquier** *loc adv* everywhere.

dorado, **da** *adj lit & fig* golden. ➡ **dorada** *sf* [pez] gilthead.

dorar *vt* - **1.** [cubrir con oro] to gild - **2.** [alimento] to brown.

dormilón, **ona** *fam sm, f* [persona] sleepyhead.

dormir ⬦ *vt* [niño, animal] to put to bed; **dormir la siesta** to have an afternoon nap. ⬦ *vi* to sleep. ➡ **dormirse** *vprnl* - **1.** [persona] to fall asleep - **2.** [brazo, mano] to go to sleep.

dormitar *vi* to doze.

dormitorio *sm* [de casa] bedroom; [de colegio] dormitory.

dorsal ⬦ *adj* dorsal. ⬦ *sm* number (on player's back).

dorso *sm* back; **al dorso, en el dorso** on the back; **'véase al dorso'** 'see overleaf'; **dorso de la mano** back of one's hand.

dos *num* two; **cada dos por tres** every five minutes, continually; *ver también* **seis**.

doscientos, **tas** *num* two hundred; *ver también* **seis**.

dosificar *vt fig* [fuerzas, palabras] to use sparingly.

dosis *sf inv lit & fig* dose; **en pequeñas dosis** in small doses.

dossier [do'sjer] *sm inv* dossier, file.

dotación *sf* - **1.** [de dinero, armas, medios] amount granted - **2.** [personal] personnel; [tripulantes] crew; [patrulla] squad.

dotado, **da** *adj* gifted; **dotado de** [persona] blessed with; [edificio, instalación, aparato] equipped with.

dotar *vt* - **1.** [proveer]: **dotar algo de** to provide sthg with - **2.** *fig* [suj: la naturaleza]: **dotar a algo/alguien de** to endow sthg/sb with.

dote *sf* [en boda] dowry. ➡ **dotes** *sfpl* [dones] qualities; **dotes de mando** leadership qualities.

doy ➡ **dar**.

Dr. *(abrev de doctor)* Dr.

Dra. *(abrev de doctora)* Dr.

dragar *vt* to dredge.

dragón *sm* dragon.

drama *sm* [gen] drama; [obra] play.

dramático, **ca** *adj* dramatic.

dramatizar *vt* to dramatize.

dramaturgo, **ga** *sm, f* playwright, dramatist.

drástico, **ca** *adj* drastic.

drenar *vt* to drain.

driblar *vt* DEP to dribble.

droga *sf* drug; **la droga** drugs *pl*; **droga blanda/dura** soft/hard drug; **droga de diseño** designer drug.

drogadicto, **ta** *sm, f* drug addict.

drogar *vt* to drug. ➡ **drogarse** *vprnl* to take drugs.

droguería *sf* - **1.** [tienda] *shop selling paint, cleaning materials etc* - **2.** *Col* [farmacia] pharmacy, drugstore *US*.

dromedario *sm* dromedary.

dto. *abrev de* **descuento**.

dual *adj* dual.

Dublín *n pr* Dublin.

ducha *sf* shower; **una ducha de agua fría** *fam fig* a bucket of cold water; **ducha de teléfono** hand-held shower.

duchar *vt* to shower. ◆ **ducharse** *vprnl* to have a shower.

duda *sf* doubt; **poner algo en duda** to call sthg into question; **salir de dudas** to set one's mind at rest; **sin duda** doubtless, undoubtedly; **sin la menor duda** without the slightest doubt; **sin sombra de duda** beyond the shadow of a doubt; **no cabe duda** there is no doubt about it.

dudar ◇ *vi* - **1.** [desconfiar]: **dudar de algo/alguien** to have one's doubts about sthg/sb - **2.** [no estar seguro]: **dudar sobre algo** to be unsure about sthg - **3.** [vacilar] to hesitate; **dudar entre hacer una cosa u otra** to be unsure whether to do one thing or another. ◇ *vt* to doubt; **dudo que venga** I doubt whether he'll come.

dudoso, sa *adj* - **1.** [improbable]: **ser dudoso (que)** to be doubtful (whether), to be unlikely (that) - **2.** [vacilante] hesitant, indecisive - **3.** [sospechoso] suspect.

duelo *sm* - **1.** [combate] duel; **batirse en duelo** to fight a duel - **2.** [sentimiento] grief, sorrow.

duende *sm* [personaje] imp, goblin.

dueño, ña *sm, f* [gen] owner; [de piso etc] landlord (*f* landlady); **cambiar de dueño** to change hands.

duerma *etc* ▷ **dormir**.

dulce ◇ *adj* - **1.** [gen] sweet - **2.** [agua] fresh - **3.** [mirada] tender. ◇ *sm* [caramelo, postre] sweet; [pastel] cake, pastry; **a nadie le amarga un dulce** *fig* anything's better than nothing.

dulcificar *vt* [endulzar] to sweeten.

dulzura *sf* [gen] sweetness.

duna *sf* dune.

dúo *sm* - **1.** MÚS duet - **2.** [pareja] duo; **a dúo** together.

duodécimo, ma *num* twelfth.

dúplex, duplex *sm inv* [piso] duplex.

duplicado, da *adj* in duplicate. ◆ **duplicado** *sm*: **(por) duplicado** (in) duplicate.

duplicar *vt* - **1.** [cantidad] to double - **2.** [documento] to duplicate. ◆ **duplicarse** *vprnl* to double.

duque, esa *sm, f* duke (*f* duchess).

duración *sf* length; **de larga duración** [pila, bombilla] long-life; [parado] long-term; [disco] long-playing.

duradero, ra *adj* [gen] lasting; [ropa, zapatos] hard-wearing.

durante *prep* during; **le escribí durante las vacaciones** I wrote to him during the holidays; **estuve escribiendo durante una hora** I was writing for an hour; **durante toda la semana** all week.

durar *vi* [gen] to last; [permanecer, subsistir] to remain, to stay; [ropa] to wear well; **aún dura la fiesta** the party's still going on.

durazno *sm Amér* peach.

dureza *sf* - **1.** [de objeto, metal etc] hardness - **2.** [de clima, persona] harshness.

durmiera *etc* ▷ **dormir**.

duro, ra *adj* - **1.** [gen] hard; [carne] tough - **2.** [resistente] tough - **3.** [palabras, clima] harsh. ◆ **duro** ◇ *sm* [moneda] five-peseta piece. ◇ *adv* hard.

e¹, E *sf* [letra] e, E. ◆ **E** *sm* (*abrev de este*) E.

e² *conj* (*en lugar de 'y' ante palabras que empiecen por 'i' o 'hi'*) and.

ebanista *smf* cabinet-maker.

ébano *sm* ebony.

ebrio, ebria *adj* [borracho] drunk.

Ebro *sm*: **el Ebro** the Ebro.

ebullición *sf* boiling; **punto de ebullición** boiling point.

eccema *sm* eczema.

echar ◇ *vt* - **1.** [tirar] to throw; [red] to cast - **2.** [añadir]: **echar algo (a** *O* **en algo)** [vino etc] to pour sthg (into sthg); [sal, azúcar etc] to add sthg (to sthg) - **3.** [carta, postal] to post - **4.** [humo, vapor, chispas] to give off, to emit - **5.** [hojas, flores] to shoot - **6.** [expulsar]: **echar a alguien (de)** to throw sb out (of) - **7.** [despedir]: **echar a alguien (de)** to sack sb (from) - **8.** [accionar]: **echar la llave/el cerrojo** to lock/bolt the door; **echar el freno** to brake, to put the brakes on - **9.** [acostar] to lie (down) - **10.** *fam* [en televisión, cine] to show; **¿qué echan esta noche en la tele?** what's on telly tonight? - **11.** *loc*: **echar abajo** [edificio] to pull down, to demolish; [gobierno] to bring down; [proyecto] to ruin; [vestido, alimentos, plan] to ruin; [ocasión] to waste; **echar de menos** to miss. ◇ *vi* [empezar]: **echar a hacer algo** to begin to do sthg, to start doing sthg; **echar a correr** to break into a run; **echar a llorar** to burst into tears; **echar a reír** to burst out laughing. ◆ **echarse** *vprnl* - **1.** [acostarse] to lie down

- **2.** [apartarse]: **echarse (a un lado)** to move (aside); **echarse atrás** *fig* to back out - **3.** *loc*: **echarse a perder** [comida] to go off, to spoil; [plan] to fall through.

echarpe *sm* shawl.

eclesiástico, ca *adj* ecclesiastical.

eclipsar *vt lit & fig* to eclipse.

eclipse *sm* eclipse; **eclipse lunar** O **de luna** lunar eclipse, eclipse of the moon; **eclipse solar** O **de sol** solar eclipse, eclipse of the sun; **eclipse total** total eclipse.

eco *sm* [gen] echo; **hacerse eco de** to report; **tener eco** to arouse interest.

ecología *sf* ecology.

ecológico, ca *adj* [gen] ecological; [alimentos] organic.

ecologista <> *adj* environmental, ecological. <> *smf* environmentalist.

economato *sm* company cooperative shop.

economía *sf* - **1.** [gen] economy; **economía sumergida** black economy O market - **2.** [estudio] economics (U); **economía familiar** home economics - **3.** [ahorro] saving.

económico, ca *adj* - **1.** [problema, doctrina etc] economic - **2.** [barato] cheap, low-cost - **3.** [que gasta poco - motor etc] economical; [- persona] thrifty.

economista *smf* economist.

economizar *vt lit & fig* to save.

ecosistema *sm* ecosystem.

ecotasa *sf* ecotax.

ecoturismo *sm* ecotourism.

ecuación *sf* equation.

ecuador *sm* equator; **pasar el ecuador** to pass the halfway mark.

Ecuador *n pr* Ecuador.

ecuánime *adj* - **1.** [en el ánimo] level-headed - **2.** [en el juicio] impartial.

ecuatoriano, na *adj & sm, f* Ecuadorian, Ecuadoran.

ecuestre *adj* equestrian.

edad *sf* age; **¿qué edad tienes?** how old are you?; **tiene 25 años de edad** she's 25 (years old); **una persona de edad** an elderly person; **edad adulta** adulthood; **edad avanzada** old age; **edad del juicio** O **de la razón** age of reason; **edad escolar** school age; **Edad Media** Middle Ages *pl*; **edad mental** mental age; **edad del pavo** awkward age.

edecán *sm Méx* assistant, aide.

edén *sm* RELIG Eden; *fig* paradise.

edición *sf* - **1.** [acción - IMPR] publication; IN-FORM, RADIO & TV editing - **2.** [ejemplares] edition.

edicto *sm* edict.

edificante *adj* [conducta] exemplary; [libro, discurso] edifying.

edificar *vt* [construir] to build.

edificio *sm* building.

edil *sm* (town) councillor.

Edimburgo *n pr* Edinburgh.

editar *vt* - **1.** [libro, periódico] to publish; [disco] to release - **2.** INFORM, RADIO & TV to edit.

editor, ra <> *adj* publishing *(antes de s)*. <> *sm, f* - **1.** [de libro, periódico] publisher - **2.** RADIO & TV editor.

editorial <> *adj* publishing *(antes de s)*. <> *sm* editorial, leader. <> *sf* publisher, publishing house.

edredón *sm* eiderdown, comforter US; **edredón nórdico** duvet.

educación *sf* - **1.** [enseñanza] education; **educación física/sexual** physical/sex education; **educación primaria/secundaria** primary/secondary education - **2.** [modales] good manners *pl*; **¡qué poca educación!** how rude!; **mala educación** bad manners *pl*.

educado, da *adj* polite, well-mannered; **mal educado** rude, ill-mannered.

educador, ra *sm, f* teacher.

educar *vt* - **1.** [enseñar] to educate - **2.** [criar] to bring up - **3.** [cuerpo, voz, oído] to train.

edulcorante *sm* sweetener.

edulcorar *vt* to sweeten.

EE UU *(abrev de* **Estados Unidos**) *smpl* USA.

efectivamente *adv* [en respuestas] precisely, exactly.

efectividad *sf* effectiveness.

efectivo, va *adj* - **1.** [útil] effective - **2.** [real] actual, true; **hacer efectivo** [gen] to carry out; [promesa] to keep; [dinero, crédito] to pay; [cheque] to cash. ◆ **efectivo** *sm* [dinero] cash; **en efectivo** in cash; **efectivo en caja** cash in hand. ◆ **efectivos** *smpl* [personal] forces.

efecto *sm* - **1.** [gen] effect; **de efecto retardado** delayed-action; **tener efecto** [vigencia] to come into O take effect; **efecto 2000** INFORM millennium bug; **efecto dominó** domino effect; **efecto invernadero** greenhouse effect; **efecto óptico** optical illusion; **efectos sonoros/visuales** sound/visual effects; **efectos especiales** special effects; **efectos secundarios** side effects - **2.** [finalidad] aim, purpose; **a tal efecto** to that end; **a efectos** O **para los efectos de algo** as far as sthg is concerned - **3.** [impresión] impression; **producir buen/mal efecto** to make a good/bad impression - **4.** [de balón, bola] spin; **dar efecto a** to put spin on - **5.** COM [documento] bill. ◆ **efectos personales** *smpl* personal possessions O effects. ◆ **en efecto** *loc adv* indeed.

efectuar *vt* [gen] to carry out; [compra, pago, viaje] to make. ◆ **efectuarse** *vprnl* to take place.

efeméride *sf* [suceso] major event; [conmemoración] anniversary.

efervescencia *sf* [de líquido] effervescence; [de bebida] fizziness.

efervescente *adj* [bebida] fizzy.

eficacia *sf* [eficiencia] efficiency; [efectividad] effectiveness.

eficaz *adj* - **1.** [eficiente] efficient - **2.** [efectivo] effective.

eficiencia *sf* efficiency.

eficiente *adj* efficient.

efímero, ra *adj* ephemeral.

efusión *sf* [cordialidad] effusiveness.

efusivo, va *adj* effusive.

EGB (*abrev de* **Educación General Básica**) *sf* former Spanish primary education system.

egipcio, cia *adj* & *sm,* f Egyptian.

Egipto *n pr* Egypt.

egocéntrico, ca *adj* egocentric.

egoísmo *sm* selfishness, egoism.

egoísta <> *adj* egoistic, selfish. <> *smf* egoist, selfish person.

ególatra <> *adj* egotistical. <> *smf* egotist.

egresado, da *sm,* f Amér graduate.

egresar *vi* Amér to graduate.

egreso *sm* Amér graduation.

eh *interj:* ¡eh! hey!

ej. *abrev de* **ejemplo.**

eje *sm* - **1.** [de rueda] axle; [de máquina] shaft - **2.** GEOM axis - **3.** *fig* [idea central] central idea, basis.

ejecución *sf* - **1.** [realización] carrying out - **2.** [de condenado] execution - **3.** [de concierto] performance, rendition.

ejecutar *vt* - **1.** [realizar] to carry out - **2.** [condenado] to execute - **3.** [concierto] to perform - **4.** INFORM [programa] to run.

ejecutivo, va <> *adj* executive. <> *sm,* f [persona] executive. ➤ **ejecutivo** *sm* POLÍT: el ejecutivo the government.

ejem *interj:* ¡ejem! [expresa duda] um!; [expresa ironía] ahem!

ejemplar <> *adj* exemplary. <> *sm* [de libro] copy; [de revista] issue; [de moneda] example; [de especie, raza] specimen; **ejemplar de muestra** specimen copy.

ejemplificar *vt* to exemplify.

ejemplo *sm* example; **por ejemplo** for example; **predicar con el ejemplo** to practise what one preaches.

ejercer <> *vt* - **1.** [profesión] to practise; [cargo] to hold - **2.** [poder, derecho] to exercise; [influencia, dominio] to exert; **ejercer presión sobre** to put pressure on. <> *vi* to practise (one's profession); **ejercer de** to practise O work as.

ejercicio *sm* - **1.** [gen] exercise; **hacer ejercicio** to (do) exercise; **ejercicio escrito** written exercise; **ejercicio físico** physical exercise; **ejercicios de calentamiento** warm-up exercises; **ejercicios de mantenimiento** keep-fit exercises - **2.** [de profesión] practising; [de cargo, funciones] carrying out - **3.** [de poder, derecho] exercising - **4.** MIL drill - **5.** ECON: **ejercicio económico/fiscal** financial/tax year.

ejercitar *vt* [derecho] to exercise. ➤ **ejercitarse** *vprnl:* ejercitarse (en) to train (in).

ejército *sm fig* & MIL army.

ejote *sm* Amér C & Méx green bean.

el, la (*mpl* los, *fpl* las) *art* (el antes de sf que empiece por 'a' o 'ha' tónica; a + el = al; de + el = del) - **1.** [gen] the; [en sentido genérico] no se traduce; **el coche** the car; **la casa** the house; **los niños** the children; **el agua/hacha/águila** the water/axe/eagle; **fui a recoger a los niños** I went to pick up the children; **los niños imitan a los adultos** children copy adults - **2.** [con sustantivo abstracto] no se traduce; **el amor** love; **la vida** life - **3.** [indica posesión, pertenencia]: **se partió la pierna** he broke his leg; **se quitó los zapatos** she took her shoes off; **tiene el pelo oscuro** he has dark hair - **4.** [con días de la semana]: **vuelven el sábado** they're coming back on Saturday - **5.** [con nombres propios geográficos] the; **el Sena** the (River) Seine; **el Everest** (Mount) Everest; **la España de la postguerra** post-war Spain - **6.** [con complemento de nombre, especificativo]: **el de** the one; **he perdido el tren, cogeré el de las nueve** I've missed the train, I'll get the nine o'clock one; **el azul** the one in blue - **7.** [con complemento de nombre, posesivo]: **mi hermano y el de Juan** my brother and Juan's - **8.** [antes de frase]: **el que** [cosa] the one, whichever; [persona] whoever; **coge el que quieras** take whichever you like; **el que más corra** whoever runs fastest - **9.** [antes de adjetivo]: **prefiero el rojo al azul** I prefer the red one to the blue one.

él, ella *pron pers* - **1.** [sujeto, predicado - persona] he (f she); [- animal, cosa] it; **mi hermana es ella** she's the one who is my sister - **2.** (después de prep) [complemento] him (f her); **voy a ir de vacaciones con ella** I'm going on holiday with her; **díselo a ella** tell her it - **3.** [posesivo]: **de él** his; **de ella** hers.

elaborar *vt* [producto] to make, to manufacture; [idea] to work out; [plan, informe] to draw up.

elasticidad *sf* [gen] elasticity.

elástico, ca *adj* [gen] elastic. ➤ **elástico** *sm* [cinta] elastic.

elección *sf* - **1.** [nombramiento] election - **2.** [opción] choice. ➤ **elecciones** *sfpl* POLÍT election *sing.*

electo, ta *adj* elect; **el presidente electo** the president elect.

elector, ra *sm,* f voter, elector.

electorado *sm* electorate.

electoral adj electoral.

electricidad sf electricity; **electricidad estática** static electricity.

electricista smf electrician.

eléctrico, **ca** adj electric.

electrificar vt to electrify.

electrizar vt fig [exaltar] to electrify.

electrocutar vt to electrocute.

electrodoméstico (gen pl) sm electrical household appliance.

electromagnético, **ca** adj electromagnetic.

electrón sm electron.

electrónico, **ca** adj [de la electrónica] electronic. ◆ **electrónica** sf electronics (U).

elefante, **ta** sm, f elephant.

elegancia sf elegance.

elegante adj - **1.** [persona, traje, estilo] elegant - **2.** [conducta, actitud, respuesta] dignified.

elegantoso, **sa** adj Amér elegant.

elegía sf elegy.

elegir vt - **1.** [escoger] to choose, to select - **2.** [por votación] to elect.

elemental adj - **1.** [básico] basic - **2.** [obvio] obvious.

elemento ◇ sm - **1.** [gen] element - **2.** [factor] factor - **3.** [persona - en equipo, colectivo] individual. ◇ smf fam: **una elementa de cuidado** a bad lot; **¡menudo elemento está hecho tu sobrino!** your nephew is a real tearaway!

elenco sm [reparto] cast.

elepé sm LP (record).

elevación sf - **1.** [de pesos, objetos etc] lifting; [de nivel, altura, precios] rise - **2.** [de terreno] elevation, rise.

elevado, **da** adj [alto] high; fig [sublime] lofty.

elevador sm - **1.** [montacargas] hoist - **2.** Méx [ascensor] lift UK, elevator US.

elevalunas sm inv window winder.

elevar vt - **1.** [gen & MAT] to raise; [peso, objeto] to lift - **2.** [ascender]: **elevar a alguien (a)** to elevate sb (to). ◆ **elevarse** vprnl [gen] to rise; [edificio, montaña] to rise up; **elevarse a** [altura] to reach; [gastos, daños] to amount O come to.

elidir vt to elide.

eliminar vt [gen] to eliminate; [contaminación, enfermedad] to get rid of.

eliminatorio, **ria** adj qualifying (antes de s). ◆ **eliminatoria** sf [gen] qualifying round; [en atletismo] heat.

elipse sf ellipse.

élite, **elite** sf elite.

elitista adj & smf elitist.

elixir, **elíxir** sm - **1.** [producto medicinal]: **elixir bucal** mouthwash - **2.** fig [remedio milagroso] elixir.

ella ⊳ **él**.

ellas ⊳ **ellos**.

ello pron pers (neutro) it; **no nos llevamos bien, pero ello no nos impide formar un buen equipo** we don't get on very well, but it O that doesn't stop us making a good team; **no quiero hablar de ello** I don't want to talk about it; **por ello** for that reason.

ellos, **ellas** pron pers - **1.** [sujeto, predicado] they; **los invitados son ellos** they are the guests, it is they who are the guests - **2.** (después de prep) [complemento] them; **me voy al bar con ellas** I'm going with them to the bar; **díselo a ellos** tell them it - **3.** [posesivo]: **de ellos/ellas** theirs.

elocuencia sf eloquence.

elocuente adj eloquent; **se hizo un silencio elocuente** the silence said it all.

elogiar vt to praise.

elogio sm praise.

elote sm Amér C & Méx corncob, ear of maize O corn US.

El Salvador n pr El Salvador.

elucidar vt to elucidate.

elucubración sf - **1.** [reflexión] reflection, meditation - **2.** despec [divagación] mental meandering.

elucubrar vt - **1.** [reflexionar] to reflect O meditate upon - **2.** despec [divagar] to theorize about.

eludir vt [gen] to avoid; [perseguidores] to escape.

emanar ◆ **emanar de** vi to emanate from.

emancipación sf [de mujeres, esclavos] emancipation; [de menores de edad] coming of age; [de países] obtaining of independence.

emancipar vt [gen] to emancipate; [países] to grant independence (to). ◆ **emanciparse** vprnl to free o.s., to become independent.

embadurnar vt: **embadurnar algo (de)** to smear sthg (with).

embajada sf [edificio] embassy.

embajador, **ra** sm, f ambassador.

embalaje sm [acción] packing.

embalar vt to wrap up, to pack. ◆ **embalarse** vprnl [acelerar - corredor] to race away; [- vehículo] to pick up speed.

embalsamar vt to embalm.

embalse sm reservoir.

embarazada ◇ adj f pregnant; **dejar embarazada a alguien** to get sb pregnant; **quedarse embarazada** to get pregnant. ◇ sf pregnant woman.

embarazar *vt* - **1.** [impedir] to restrict - **2.** [cohibir] to inhibit.

embarazo *sm* - **1.** [preñez] pregnancy; **interrumpir un embarazo** to terminate a pregnancy; **prueba del embarazo** pregnancy test; **embarazo ectópico** *O* **extrauterino** ectopic pregnancy - **2.** [timidez] embarrassment.

embarazoso, sa *adj* awkward, embarrassing.

embarcación *sf* [barco] craft, boat; **embarcación pesquera** fishing boat; **embarcación de recreo** pleasure boat.

embarcadero *sm* jetty.

embarcar <> *vt* [personas] to board; [mercancías] to ship. <> *vi* to board. <> **embarcarse** *vprnl* [para viajar] to board.

embargar *vt* - **1.** DER to seize - **2.** [suj: emoción etc] to overcome.

embargo *sm* - **1.** DER seizure - **2.** ECON embargo. <> **sin embargo** *loc adv* however, nevertheless.

embarque *sm* [de personas] boarding; [de mercancías] embarkation.

embarrancar *vi* to run aground.

embarullar *vt fam* to mess up. <> **embarullarse** *vprnl fam* to get into a muddle.

embaucar *vt* to swindle, to deceive.

embeber *vt* to soak up. <> **embeberse** *vprnl*: **embeberse (en algo)** [ensimismarse] to become absorbed (in sthg); *fig* [empaparse] to immerse o.s. (in sthg).

embellecer *vt* to adorn, to embellish.

embestida *sf* [gen] attack; [de toro] charge.

embestir *vt* [gen] to attack; [toro] to charge.

emblema *sm* - **1.** [divisa, distintivo] emblem, badge - **2.** [símbolo] symbol.

embobar *vt* to captivate.

embocadura *sf* [de instrumento] mouthpiece.

embolia *sf* embolism.

émbolo *sm* AUTO piston.

embolsarse *vprnl* [ganar] to earn.

embonar *vt Andes, Cuba & Méx fam* - **1.** [ajustar] to suit - **2.** [abonar] to manure - **3.** [ensamblar] to join.

emborrachar *vt* to make drunk. <> **emborracharse** *vprnl* to get drunk.

emborronar *vt* [garabatear] to scribble on; [manchar] to smudge.

emboscada *sf lit & fig* ambush.

embotellado, da *adj* bottled.

embotellamiento *sm* [de tráfico] traffic jam.

embotellar *vt* [líquido] to bottle.

embragar *vi* to engage the clutch.

embrague *sm* clutch; **embrague automático** automatic clutch.

embriagar *vt* - **1.** [extasiar] to intoxicate - **2.** [emborrachar] to make drunk. <> **embriagarse** *vprnl* [emborracharse]: **embriagarse (con)** to get drunk (on).

embriaguez *sf* - **1.** [borrachera] drunkenness - **2.** [éxtasis] intoxication.

embrión *sm* embryo.

embrollo *sm* - **1.** [de hilos] tangle - **2.** *fig* [lío] mess; [mentira] lie.

embromado, da *adj Andes, Caribe & R Plata fam* [complicado] tricky.

embrujar *vt lit & fig* to bewitch.

embrujo *sm* [maleficio] curse, spell; *fig* [de ciudad, ojos] charm, magic.

embrutecer *vt* to brutalize. <> **embrutecerse** *vprnl* to become brutalized.

embuchado, da *adj*: **carne embuchada** cured cold meat.

embudo *sm* funnel.

embuste *sm* lie.

embustero, ra <> *adj* lying. <> *sm, f* liar.

embute *sm Amér fam* bribe.

embutido *sm* [comida] cold cured meat.

embutir *vt lit & fig* to stuff.

emergencia *sf* - **1.** [urgencia] emergency; **en caso de emergencia** in case of emergency - **2.** [brote] emergence.

emerger *vi* [salir del agua] to emerge; [aparecer] to come into view, to appear.

emigración *sf* [de personas] emigration; [de aves] migration.

emigrante *adj & smf* emigrant.

emigrar *vi* [persona] to emigrate; [ave] to migrate.

eminencia *sf* [persona] leading light. <> **Eminencia** *sf*: **Su Eminencia** His Eminence.

eminente *adj* [distinguido] eminent.

emirato *sm* emirate.

Emiratos Árabes Unidos *smpl*: **los Emiratos Árabes Unidos** United Arab Emirates.

emisión *sf* - **1.** [de energía, rayos etc] emission - **2.** [de bonos, sellos, monedas] issue; **emisión de obligaciones** COM debentures issue - **3.** RADIO & TV [- transmisión] broadcasting; [- programa] programme, broadcast.

emisor, ra *adj* transmitting *(antes de s)*. <> **emisora** *sf* radio station; **emisora pirata** pirate radio station.

emitir <> *vt* - **1.** [rayos, calor, sonidos] to emit - **2.** [moneda, sellos, bonos] to issue - **3.** [expresar - juicio, opinión] to express; [- fallo] to pronounce - **4.** RADIO & TV to broadcast. <> *vi* to broadcast.

emoción *sf* - **1.** [conmoción, sentimiento] emotion - **2.** [expectación] excitement; **¡qué emoción!** how exciting!

emocionante *adj* - **1.** [conmovedor] moving, touching - **2.** [apasionante] exciting, thrilling.

emocionar *vt* - **1.** [conmover] to move - **2.** [excitar, apasionar] to thrill, to excite **emocionarse** *vprnl* - **1.** [conmoverse] to be moved - **2.** [excitarse, apasionarse] to get excited.

emotivo, va *adj* [persona] emotional; [escena, palabras] moving.

empacar *vi Amér* to pack.

empachar *vt* to give indigestion to. **empacharse** *vprnl* [hartarse] to stuff o.s.; [sufrir indigestión] to get indigestion.

empacho *sm* [indigestión] upset stomach, indigestion.

empadronar *vt* ≃ to register on the electoral roll. **empadronarse** *vprnl* ≃ to register on the electoral roll.

empalagoso, sa *adj* sickly, cloying.

empalizada *sf* [cerca] fence; MIL stockade.

empalmar ⟨⟩ *vt* [tubos, cables] to connect, to join. ⟨⟩ *vi* - **1.** [autocares, trenes] to connect - **2.** [carreteras] to link O join (up).

empalme *sm* - **1.** [entre cables, tubos] joint, connection - **2.** [de líneas férreas, carreteras] junction.

empanada *sf* pasty.

empanadilla *sf* small pasty.

empanar *vt* CULIN to coat in breadcrumbs.

empantanar *vt* to flood. **empantanarse** *vprnl* - **1.** [inundarse] to be flooded O waterlogged - **2.** *fig* [atascarse] to get bogged down.

empañar *vt* - **1.** [cristal] to mist O steam up - **2.** *fig* [reputación] to tarnish. **empañarse** *vprnl* to mist O steam up.

empapar *vt* - **1.** [mojar] to soak - **2.** [absorber] to soak up. **empaparse** *vprnl* - **1.** [mojarse] to get soaked - **2.** [enterarse bien]: **se empapó de sociología antes de dar la conferencia** she did a lot of reading up about sociology before giving her speech; **¡para que te empapes!** *fam* so there!

empapelar *vt* [pared] to paper.

empaque *sm Méx* [en paquetes, bolsas, cajas] packing; [en latas] canning; [en botellas] bottling.

empaquetar *vt* to pack, to package.

emparedado, da *adj* confined. **emparedado** *sm* sandwich.

emparedar *vt* to lock away.

emparejar *vt* [aparejar - personas] to pair off; [- zapatos etc] to match (up).

emparentar *vi*: **emparentar con** to marry into.

empastar *vt* to fill.

empaste *sm* filling.

empatar *vi* DEP to draw; [en elecciones etc] to tie; **empatar a cero** to draw nil-nil.

empate *sm* [resultado] draw; **un empate a cero/dos** a goalless/two-all draw.

empedernido, da *adj* [bebedor, fumador] heavy, [criminal, jugador] hardened.

empedrado *sm* paving.

empedrar *vt* to pave.

empeine *sm* [de pie, zapato] instep.

empellón *sm* push, shove; **abrirse paso a empellones** to shove O push one's way through.

empeñado, da *adj* - **1.** [en préstamo] in pawn - **2.** [obstinado] determined; **estar empeñado en hacer algo** to be determined to do sthg.

empeñar *vt* [joyas etc] to pawn. **empeñarse** *vprnl* - **1.** [obstinarse] to insist; **empeñarse en hacer algo** [obstinarse] to insist on doing sthg; [persistir] to persist in doing sthg - **2.** [endeudarse] to get into debt.

empeño *sm* - **1.** [de joyas etc] pawning; **casa de empeños** pawnshop - **2.** [obstinación] determination; **poner mucho empeño en algo** to put a lot of effort into sthg; **tener empeño en hacer algo** to be determined to do sthg.

empeorar *vi* to get worse, to deteriorate.

empequeñecer *vt* [quitar importancia a] to diminish; [en una comparación] to overshadow, to dwarf.

emperador, emperatriz *sm, f* emperor (*f* empress). **emperador** *sm* [pez] swordfish.

emperifollar *vt fam* to doll O tart up.

emperrarse *vprnl*: **emperrarse (en hacer algo)** to insist (on doing sthg).

empezar ⟨⟩ *vt* to begin, to start. ⟨⟩ *vi*: **empezar (a hacer algo)** to begin O start (to do sthg); **empezar (por hacer algo)** to begin O start (by doing sthg); **para empezar** to begin O start with; **por algo se empieza** you've got to start somewhere.

empinado, da *adj* steep.

empinar *vt* [levantar] to raise. **empinarse** *vprnl* - **1.** [animal] to stand up on its hind legs - **2.** [persona] to stand on tiptoe.

empírico, ca *adj* empirical.

emplasto *sm* poultice.

emplazamiento *sm* [ubicación] location.

emplazar *vt* - **1.** [situar] to locate; MIL to position - **2.** [citar] to summon, DER to summons.

empleado, da *sm, f* [gen] employee; [de banco, administración, oficina] clerk.

emplear *vt* - **1.** [usar - objetos, materiales etc] to use; [- tiempo] to spend; **emplear algo en hacer algo** to use sthg to do sthg - **2.** [contratar] to employ. **emplearse** *vprnl* - **1.** [colocarse] to find a job - **2.** [usarse] to be used.

empleo *sm* - 1. [uso] use; **'modo de empleo'** 'instructions for use' - 2. [trabajo] employment; [puesto] job; **estar sin empleo** to be out of work.

emplomadura *sf R Dom* [de diente] filling.

empobrecer *vt* to impoverish. ◆ **empobrecerse** *vprnl* to get poorer.

empollar ⬦ *vt* - 1. [huevo] to incubate - 2. *fam* [estudiar] to swot up on. ⬦ *vi fam* to swot.

empollón, ona *fam sm, f* swot.

empolvarse *vprnl* to powder one's face.

empotrado, da *adj* fitted, built-in.

empotrar *vt* to fit, to build in.

emprendedor, ra *adj* enterprising.

emprender *vt* - 1. [trabajo] to start; [viaje, marcha] to set off on; **emprender vuelo** to fly off - 2. *loc*: **emprenderla con alguien** to take it out on sb; **emprenderla a golpes con alguien** to start hitting sb.

empresa *sf* - 1. [sociedad] company; **pequeña y mediana empresa** small and medium-sized business; **empresa de trabajo temporal** temping agency - 2. [acción] enterprise, undertaking.

empresarial *adj* management *(antes de s)*. ◆ **empresariales** *sfpl* business studies.

empresario, ria *sm, f* [patrono] employer; [hombre, mujer de negocios] businessman (*f* businesswoman); [de teatro] impresario.

empréstito *sm* debenture loan.

empujar *vt* to push; **empujar a alguien a que haga algo** to push sb into doing sthg.

empuje *sm* - 1. [presión] pressure - 2. [energía] energy, drive.

empujón *sm* [empellón] shove, push; **abrirse paso a empujones** to shove O push one's way through.

empuñadura *sf* handle; [de espada] hilt.

empuñar *vt* to take hold of, to grasp.

emulsión *sf* emulsion.

en *prep* - 1. [lugar - en el interior de] in; [- sobre la superficie de] on; [- en un punto concreto de] at; **viven en la capital** they live in the capital; **tiene el dinero en el banco** he keeps his money in the bank; **en la mesa/el plato** on the table/plate; **en casa/el trabajo** at home/work - 2. [dirección] into; **el avión cayó en el mar** the plane fell into the sea; **entraron en la habitación** they came into the room - 3. [tiempo - mes, año etc] in; [- día] on; **nació en 1940/mayo** he was born in 1940/May; **en aquel día** on that day; **en Nochebuena** on Christmas Eve; **en Navidades** at Christmas; **en aquella época** at that time, in those days; **en un par de días** in a couple of days - 4. [medio de transporte] by; **ir en tren/coche/avión/barco** to go by train/car/plane/boat - 5. [modo] in; **en voz baja** in a low voice; **lo dijo en inglés** she said it in English; **pagar en libras** to pay in pounds; **la inflación aumentó en un 10%** inflation increased by 10%; **todo se lo gasta en ropa** he spends everything on clothes - 6. [precio] in; **las ganancias se calculan en millones** profits are calculated in millions; **te lo dejo en 5.000** I'll let you have it for 5,000 - 7. [tema]: **es un experto en la materia** he's an expert on the subject; **es doctor en medicina** he's a doctor of medicine - 8. [causa] from; **lo detecté en su forma de hablar** I could tell from the way he was speaking - 9. [materia] in, made of; **en seda** in silk - 10. [cualidad] in terms of; **le supera en inteligencia** she is more intelligent than he is.

enagua *sf (gen pl)* petticoat.

enajenación *sf* [locura] insanity; [éxtasis] rapture.

enajenamiento *sm* = **enajenación**.

enajenar *vt* - 1. [volver loco] to drive mad; [extasiar] to enrapture - 2. [propiedad] to alienate.

enaltecer *vt* to praise.

enamoradizo, za *adj* who falls in love easily.

enamorado, da ⬦ *adj*: **enamorado (de)** in love (with). ⬦ *sm, f* lover.

enamorar *vt* to win the heart of. ◆ **enamorarse** *vprnl*: **enamorarse (de)** to fall in love (with).

enano, na *adj & sm, f* dwarf; **disfrutar como un enano** *fam* to have a whale of a time.

enarbolar *vt* [bandera] to raise, to hoist; [pancarta] to hold up; [arma] to brandish.

enardecer *vt* [gen] to inflame; [persona, multitud] to fill with enthusiasm.

encabezamiento *sm* [de carta, escrito] heading; [de artículo periodístico] headline; [preámbulo] foreword.

encabezar *vt* - 1. [artículo de periódico] to headline; [libro] to write the foreword for - 2. [lista, carta] to head - 3. [marcha, expedición] to lead.

encabritarse *vprnl* - 1. [caballo, moto] to rear up - 2. *fam* [persona] to get shirty.

encadenar *vt* - 1. [atar] to chain (up) - 2. [enlazar] to link (together).

encajar ⬦ *vt* - 1. [meter ajustando]: **encajar (en)** to fit (into) - 2. [meter con fuerza]: **encajar (en)** to push (into) - 3. [hueso dislocado] to set - 4. [recibir - golpe, noticia, críticas] to take. ⬦ *vi* - 1. [piezas, objetos] to fit - 2. [hechos, declaraciones, datos]: **encajar (con)** to square (with), to match.

encaje *sm* [tejido] lace.

encalar *vt* to whitewash.

encallar *vi* [barco] to run aground.

encaminar *vt* - **1.** [persona, pasos] to direct - **2.** [medidas, leyes, actividades] to aim; **encaminado a** aimed at. ➤ **encaminarse** *vprnl*: encaminarse a/hacia to set off for/towards.

encamotarse *vprnl Andes & Amér C fam* to fall in love.

encandilar *vt* to dazzle.

encantado, da *adj* - **1.** [contento] delighted; estar encantado con algo/alguien to be delighted with sthg/sb; **encantado de conocerle** pleased to meet you - **2.** [hechizado - casa, lugar] haunted; [- persona] bewitched.

encantador, ra *adj* delightful, charming.

encantar *vt* - **1.** [gustar]: encantarle a alguien algo/hacer algo to love sthg/doing sthg; me encanta el chocolate I love chocolate; le encanta bailar she loves dancing - **2.** [embrujar] to cast a spell on.

encanto *sm* - **1.** [atractivo] charm; ser un encanto to be a treasure O a delight - **2.** [hechizo] spell.

encapotado, da *adj* overcast.

encapotarse *vprnl* to cloud over.

encapricharse *vprnl* [obstinarse]: encapricharse con algo/hacer algo to set one's mind on sthg/doing sthg.

encapuchado, da *adj* hooded.

encaramar *vt* to lift up. ➤ **encaramarse** *vprnl*: encaramarse (a O en) to climb up (onto).

encarar *vt* [hacer frente a] to confront, to face up to. ➤ **encararse** *vprnl* [enfrentarse]: encararse a O con to stand up to.

encarcelar *vt* to imprison.

encarecer *vt* [productos, precios] to make more expensive. ➤ **encarecerse** *vprnl* to become more expensive.

encarecidamente *adv* earnestly.

encarecimiento *sm* [de producto, coste] increase in price.

encargado, da <> *adj*: encargado (de) responsible (for), in charge (of). <> *sm, f* [gen] person in charge; COM manager (*f* manageress); encargado de negocios POLÍT chargé d'affaires.

encargar *vt* - **1.** [poner al cargo]: encargar a alguien de algo to put sb in charge of sthg; encargar a alguien que haga algo to tell sb to do sthg - **2.** [pedir] to order. ➤ **encargarse** *vprnl* [ocuparse]: encargarse de to be in charge of; yo me encargaré de eso I'll take care of O see to that.

encargo *sm* - **1.** [pedido] order; por encargo to order - **2.** [recado] errand - **3.** [tarea] task, assignment.

encariñarse *vprnl*: encariñarse con to become fond of.

encarnación *sf* [personificación - cosa] embodiment; [- persona] personification.

encarnado, da *adj* - **1.** [personificado] incarnate - **2.** [color] red.

encarnizado, da *adj* bloody, bitter.

encarnizarse *vprnl*: encarnizarse con [presa] to fall upon; [prisionero, enemigo] to treat savagely.

encarrilar *vt fig* [negocio, situación] to put on the right track.

encasillar *vt* [clasificar] to pigeonhole; TEATRO to typecast.

encasquetar *vt* - **1.** [imponer]: encasquetar algo a alguien [idea, teoría] to drum sthg into sb; [discurso, lección] to force sb to sit through sthg - **2.** [sombrero] to pull on.

encasquillarse *vprnl* to get jammed.

encauzar *vt* - **1.** [corriente] to channel - **2.** [orientar] to direct.

encendedor *sm* lighter.

encender *vt* - **1.** [vela, cigarro, chimenea] to light - **2.** [aparato] to switch on - **3.** *fig* [avivar - entusiasmo, ira] to arouse; [- pasión, discusión] to inflame. ➤ **encenderse** *vprnl* - **1.** [fuego, gas] to ignite; [luz, estufa] to come on - **2.** *fig* [ojos] to light up; [persona, rostro] to go red, to blush; [de ira] to flare up.

encendido, da *adj* [luz, colilla] burning; la luz está encendida the light is on. ➤ **encendido** *sm* AUTO ignition; encendido electrónico electronic ignition.

encerado, da *adj* waxed, polished. ➤ **encerado** *sm* [pizarra] blackboard.

encerar *vt* to wax, to polish.

encerrar *vt* - **1.** [recluir - gen] to shut (up O in); [- con llave] to lock (up O in); [- en la cárcel] to lock away O up - **2.** [contener] to contain. ➤ **encerrarse** *vprnl* [gen] to shut o.s. away; [con llave] to lock o.s. away.

encestar *vt* & *vi* to score *(in basketball)*.

enceste *sm* basket.

encharcar *vt* to waterlog. ➤ **encharcarse** *vprnl* - **1.** [terreno] to become waterlogged - **2.** [pulmones] to become flooded.

enchilada *sf Méx* filled tortilla.

enchilarse *vprnl Méx fam* [enfadarse] to get angry.

enchufado, da *adj fam*: estar enchufado to get where one is through connections.

enchufar *vt* - **1.** [aparato] to plug in - **2.** *fam* [a una persona] to pull strings for.

enchufe *sm* - **1.** [ELECTR - macho] plug; [- hembra] socket; enchufe múltiple adapter - **2.** *fam* [recomendación] connections *pl*; obtener algo por enchufe to get sthg by pulling strings O through one's connections.

encía *sf* gum.

encíclica *sf* encyclical.

enciclopedia *sf* encyclopedia.

encierro *sm* [protesta] sit-in.

encima *adv* - **1.** [arriba] on top; **yo vivo encima** I live upstairs; **por encima** [superficialmente] superficially - **2.** [además] on top of that - **3.** [sobre sí]: **lleva un abrigo encima** she has a coat on; **¿llevas dinero encima?** have you got any money on you? **encima de** *loc prep* - **1.** [en lugar superior que] above; **vivo encima de tu casa** I live upstairs from you - **2.** [sobre, en] on (top of); **el pan está encima de la mesa** the bread is on (top of) the table - **3.** [además] on top of. **por encima de** *loc prep* - **1.** [gen] over; **vive por encima de sus posibilidades** he lives beyond his means - **2.** *fig* [más que] more than; **por encima de todo** more than anything else.

encina *sf* holm oak.

encinta *adj f* pregnant.

enclave *sm* enclave.

enclenque *adj* sickly, frail.

encoger <> *vt* - **1.** [ropa] to shrink - **2.** [miembro, músculo] to contract. <> *vi* to shrink. **encogerse** *vprnl* - **1.** [ropa] to shrink; [músculos etc] to contract; **encogerse de hombros** to shrug one's shoulders - **2.** *fig* [apocarse] to cringe.

encolar *vt* [silla etc] to glue; [pared] to size, to paste.

encolerizar *vt* to infuriate, to enrage. **encolerizarse** *vprnl* to get angry.

encomendar *vt* to entrust. **encomendarse** *vprnl*: **encomendarse a** [persona] to entrust o.s. to; [Dios, santos] to put one's trust in.

encomienda *sf* - **1.** [encargo] assignment, mission - **2.** *Amér* [paquete] parcel.

encontrado, da *adj* conflicting.

encontrar *vt* - **1.** [gen] to find - **2.** [dificultades] to encounter - **3.** [persona] to meet, to come across. **encontrarse** *vprnl* - **1.** [hallarse] to be; **se encuentra en París** she's in Paris - **2.** [coincidir]: **encontrarse (con alguien)** to meet (sb); **me encontré con Juan** I ran into O met Juan - **3.** [de ánimo] to feel; **¿cómo te encuentras?** how do you feel?, how are you feeling?; **encontrarse bien/mal** to feel fine/ill - **4.** [chocar] to collide.

encorvar *vt* to bend. **encorvarse** *vprnl* to bend down O over.

encrespar *vt* - **1.** [pelo] to curl; [mar] to make choppy O rough - **2.** [irritar] to irritate. **encresparse** *vprnl* - **1.** [mar] to get rough - **2.** [persona] to get irritated.

encrucijada *sf lit & fig* crossroads *sing*.

encuadernación *sf* binding; **encuadernación en cuero** leather binding; **encuadernación en tela** cloth binding.

encuadernador, ra *sm, f* bookbinder.

encuadernar *vt* to bind.

encuadrar *vt* - **1.** [enmarcar - cuadro, tema] to frame - **2.** [encerrar] to contain - **3.** [encajar] to fit.

encubierto, ta <> *pp* ▷ **encubrir**. <> *adj* [intento] covert; [insulto, significado] hidden.

encubridor, ra *sm, f*: **encubridor (de)** accessory (to).

encubrir *vt* [delito] to conceal; [persona] to harbour.

encuentro *sm* - **1.** [acción] meeting, encounter; **salir al encuentro de alguien** [para recibir] to go to meet sb; [para atacar] to confront sb - **2.** DEP game, match - **3.** [hallazgo] find.

encuesta *sf* - **1.** [de opinión] survey, opinion poll - **2.** [investigación] investigation, inquiry.

encuestador, ra *sm, f* pollster.

encuestar *vt* to poll.

endeble *adj* [persona, argumento] weak, feeble; [objeto] fragile.

endémico, ca *adj* MED endemic.

endemoniado, da *adj* - **1.** *fam* [molesto - niño] wicked; [- trabajo] very tricky - **2.** [desagradable] terrible, foul - **3.** [poseído] possessed (of the devil).

endenantes *adv Amér fam* before.

enderezar *vt* - **1.** [poner derecho] to straighten - **2.** [poner vertical] to put upright - **3.** *fig* [corregir] to set right. **enderezarse** *vprnl* [sentado] to sit up straight; [de pie] to stand up straight.

endeudamiento *sm* debt.

endeudarse *vprnl* to get into debt.

endiablado, da *adj* [persona] wicked; [tiempo, genio] foul; [problema, crucigrama] fiendishly difficult.

endibia, endivia *sf* endive.

endiñar *vt fam*: **endiñar algo a alguien** [golpe] to land O deal sb sthg; [trabajo, tarea] to lumber sb with sthg.

endivia = endibia.

endomingado, da *adj fam* dolled-up.

endorfina *sf* MED endorphin.

endosar *vt* - **1.** [tarea, trabajo]: **endosar algo a alguien** to lumber sb with sthg - **2.** COM to endorse.

endulzar *vt* [con azúcar] to sweeten; *fig* [hacer agradable] to ease.

endurecer *vt* - **1.** [gen] to harden - **2.** [fortalecer] to strengthen.

enemigo, ga <> *adj* enemy *(antes de s)*; **ser enemigo de algo** to hate sthg. <> *sm, f* enemy; **pasarse al enemigo** to go over to the enemy.

enemistad *sf* enmity.

enemistar *vt* to make enemies of. ➡ **enemistarse** *vprnl*: enemistarse (con) to fall out (with).

energético, ca *adj* energy *(antes de s)*.

energía *sf* - 1. [gen] energy; **energía atómica** O **nuclear** nuclear power; **energía eléctrica/eólica/hidráulica** electric/wind/water power; **energía solar** solar energy O power - 2. [fuerza] strength; **hay que empujar con energía** you have to push hard.

enérgico, ca *adj* [gen] energetic; [carácter] forceful; [gesto, medida] vigorous; [decisión, postura] emphatic.

energúmeno, na *sm, f* madman (*f* madwoman); **gritaba como un energúmeno** he was screaming like one possessed.

enero *sm* January; *ver también* **septiembre**.

enervar *vt* - 1. [debilitar] to sap, to weaken - 2. [poner nervioso] to exasperate.

enésimo, ma *adj* - 1. MAT nth - 2. *fig* umpteenth; **por enésima vez** for the umpteenth time.

enfadado, da *adj* angry.

enfadar *vt* to anger. ➡ **enfadarse** *vprnl*: enfadarse (con) to get angry (with).

enfado *sm* anger.

énfasis *sm inv* emphasis; **poner énfasis en algo** to emphasize sthg.

enfático, ca *adj* emphatic.

enfatizar *vt* to emphasize, to stress.

enfermar ⬦ *vt* [causar enfermedad a] to make ill, ⬦ *vi* to fall ill; **enfermar del pecho** to develop a chest complaint.

enfermedad *sf* illness; **contraer una enfermedad** to catch an illness; **enfermedad contagiosa** contagious disease; **enfermedad de Creutzfeldt-Jakob** Creutzfeldt-Jakob disease, CJD; **enfermedad infecciosa/venérea** infectious/venereal disease; **enfermedad mental** mental illness; **enfermedad profesional** occupational disease; **enfermedad terminal** terminal illness.

enfermera ▷ **enfermero**.

enfermería *sf* sick bay.

enfermero, ra *sm, f* nurse.

enfermizo, za *adj lit & fig* unhealthy.

enfermo, ma ⬦ *adj* ill, sick; **caer enfermo** to fall ill. ⬦ *sm, f* [gen] invalid, sick person; [en el hospital] patient; **enfermo terminal** terminally ill patient.

enfilar *vt* - 1. [ir por - camino] to go O head straight along - 2. [apuntar - arma] to aim.

enflaquecer *vi* to grow thin.

enfocar *vt* - 1. [imagen, objetivo] to focus - 2. [suj: luz, foco] to shine on - 3. [tema, asunto] to approach, to look at.

enfoque *sm* - 1. [de imagen] focus - 2. [de asunto] approach, angle; **dar un enfoque nuevo a algo** to adopt a new approach to sthg.

enfrascar *vt* to bottle. ➡ **enfrascarse en** *vprnl* [riña] to get embroiled in; [lectura, conversación] to become engrossed in.

enfrentar *vt* - 1. [hacer frente a] to confront, to face - 2. [poner frente a frente] to bring face to face. ➡ **enfrentarse** *vprnl* - 1. [luchar, encontrarse] to meet, to clash - 2. [oponerse]: enfrentarse con alguien to confront sb.

enfrente *adv* - 1. [delante] opposite; **la tienda de enfrente** the shop across the road; **enfrente de** opposite - 2. [en contra]: **tiene a todos enfrente** everyone's against her.

enfriamiento *sm* - 1. [catarro] cold - 2. [acción] cooling.

enfriar *vt lit & fig* to cool. ➡ **enfriarse** *vprnl* - 1. [líquido, pasión, amistad] to cool down - 2. [quedarse demasiado frío] to go cold - 3. MED to catch a cold.

enfundar *vt* [espada] to sheathe; [pistola] to put away.

enfurecer *vt* to infuriate, to madden. ➡ **enfurecerse** *vprnl* [gen] to get furious.

enfurruñarse *vprnl fam* to sulk.

engalanar *vt* to decorate. ➡ **engalanarse** *vprnl* to dress up.

enganchar *vt* - 1. [agarrar - vagones] to couple; [- remolque, caballos] to hitch up; [- pez] to hook - 2. [colgar de un gancho] to hang up. ➡ **engancharse** *vprnl* - 1. [prenderse]: engancharse algo con algo to catch sthg on sthg - 2. [alistarse] to enlist, to join up - 3. [hacerse adicto]: engancharse (a) to get hooked (on).

enganche *sm* - 1. [de trenes] coupling - 2. [gancho] hook - 3. [reclutamiento] enlistment - 4. *Méx* [depósito] deposit.

engañar *vt* - 1. [gen] to deceive; **engaña a su marido** she cheats on her husband - 2. [estafar] to cheat, to swindle. ➡ **engañarse** *vprnl* - 1. [hacerse ilusiones] to delude o.s. - 2. [equivocarse] to be wrong.

engaño *sm* [gen] deceit; [estafa] swindle.

engañoso, sa *adj* [persona, palabras] deceitful; [aspecto, apariencia] deceptive; [consejo] misleading.

engarzar *vt* - 1. [encadenar - abalorios] to thread; [- perlas] to string - 2. [enlazar - palabras] to string together.

engatusar *vt fam* to get round; **engatusar a alguien para que haga algo** to coax O cajole sb into doing sthg.

engendrar *vt* - 1. [procrear] to give birth to - 2. [originar] to give rise to.

engendro *sm* - 1. [obra de mala calidad] monstrosity - 2. [ser deforme] freak; [niño] malformed child.

englobar *vt* to bring together.

engomar *vt* to stick, to glue.

engordar ⋄ *vt* - 1. [cebar] to fatten up - 2. *fig* [aumentar] to swell. ⋄ *vi* to put on weight.

engorroso, sa *adj* bothersome.

engranaje *sm* - 1. [piezas - de reloj, piñón] cogs *pl*; AUTO gears *pl* - 2. [aparato - político, burocrático] machinery.

engrandecer *vt* - 1. *fig* [enaltecer] to exalt - 2. [aumentar] to increase, to enlarge.

engrasar *vt* [gen] to lubricate; [bisagra, mecanismo] to oil; [eje, bandeja] to grease.

engreído, da *adj* conceited, full of one's own importance.

engrosar *vt fig* [aumentar] to swell.

engullir *vt* to gobble up.

enhebrar *vt* [gen] to thread; [perlas] to string.

enhorabuena ⋄ *sf* congratulations *pl*; **dar la enhorabuena a alguien** to congratulate sb. ⋄ *interj*: **¡enhorabuena (por...)!** congratulations (on...)!

enigma *sm* enigma.

enigmático, ca *adj* enigmatic.

enjabonar *vt* [con jabón] to soap.

enjambre *sm lit & fig* swarm.

enjaular *vt* [en jaula] to cage; *fam* [en prisión] to jail, to lock up.

enjuagar *vt* to rinse.

enjuague *sm* rinse.

enjugar *vt* - 1. [secar] to dry, to wipe away - 2. [pagar - deuda] to pay off; [- déficit] to cancel out.

enjuiciar *vt* - 1. DER to try - 2. [opinar] to judge.

enjuto, ta *adj* [delgado] lean.

enlace *sm* - 1. [acción] link - 2. [persona] go-between; **enlace sindical** shop steward - 3. [casamiento]: **enlace (matrimonial)** marriage - 4. [de trenes] connection; **estación de enlace** junction; **vía de enlace** crossover - 5. INFORM: **enlace de datos** data link; **enlace hipertextual** *O* **de hipertexto** hypertext link.

enlatar *vt* to can, to tin.

enlazar ⋄ *vt*: **enlazar algo a** [atar] to tie sthg up to; [trabar, relacionar] to link *O* connect sthg with. ⋄ *vi*: **enlazar en** [trenes] to connect at.

enloquecer ⋄ *vt* - 1. [volver loco] to drive mad - 2. *fig* [gustar mucho] to drive wild *O* crazy. ⋄ *vi* to go mad.

enlutado, da *adj* in mourning.

enmarañar *vt* - 1. [enredar] to tangle (up) - 2. [complicar] to complicate. ⬗ **enmara-**

ñarse *vprnl* - 1. [enredarse] to become tangled - 2. [complicarse] to become confused *O* complicated.

enmarcar *vt* to frame.

enmascarado, da *adj* masked.

enmascarar *vt* [rostro] to mask; *fig* [encubrir] to disguise.

enmendar *vt* [error] to correct; [ley, dictamen] to amend; [comportamiento] to mend; [daño, perjuicio] to redress. ⬗ **enmendarse** *vprnl* to mend one's ways.

enmienda *sf* - 1. [en un texto] corrections *pl* - 2. POLÍT amendment.

enmohecer *vt* [gen] to turn mouldy; [metal] to rust. ⬗ **enmohecerse** *vprnl* [gen] to grow mouldy; [metal, conocimientos] to go rusty.

enmoquetar *vt* to carpet.

enmudecer ⋄ *vt* to silence. ⋄ *vi* [callarse] to fall silent, to go quiet; [perder el habla] to be struck dumb.

ennegrecer *vt* [gen] to blacken; [suj: nubes] to darken. ⬗ **ennegrecerse** *vprnl* [gen] to become blackened; [nublarse] to darken, to grow dark.

ennoblecer *vt* - 1. *fig* [dignificar] to lend distinction to - 2. [dar un título a] to ennoble.

enojar *vt* [enfadar] to anger; [molestar] to annoy. ⬗ **enojarse** *vprnl*: **enojarse (con)** [enfadarse] to get angry (with); [molestarse] to get annoyed (with).

enojo *sm* [enfado] anger; [molestia] annoyance.

enojoso, sa *adj* [molesto] annoying; [delicado, espinoso] awkward.

enorgullecer *vt* to fill with pride. ⬗ **enorgullecerse de** *vprnl* to be proud of.

enorme *adj* [en tamaño] enormous, huge; [en gravedad] monstrous.

enormidad *sf* [de tamaño] enormity, hugeness.

enrarecer *vt* - 1. [contaminar] to pollute - 2. [rarificar] to rarefy. ⬗ **enrarecerse** *vprnl* - 1. [contaminarse] to become polluted - 2. [rarificarse] to become rarefied - 3. *fig* [situación, ambiente] to become tense.

enredadera *sf* creeper.

enredar *vt* - 1. [madeja, pelo] to tangle up; [situación, asunto] to complicate, to confuse - 2. [implicar]: **enredar a alguien (en)** to embroil sb (in), to involve sb (in). ⬗ **enredarse** *vprnl* [plantas] to climb; [madeja, pelo] to get tangled up; [situación, asunto] to become confused.

enredo *sm* - 1. [maraña] tangle, knot - 2. [lío] mess, complicated affair; [asunto ilícito] shady affair - 3. [amoroso] (love) affair.

enrejado *sm* - **1.** [barrotes - de balcón, verja] railings *pl*; [- de jaula, celda, ventana] bars *pl* - **2.** [de cañas] trellis.

enrevesado, da *adj* complex, complicated.

enriquecer *vt* - **1.** [hacer rico] to make rich - **2.** *fig* [engrandecer] to enrich. ➡ **enriquecerse** *vprnl* to get rich.

enrojecer ◇ *vt* [gen] to redden; [rostro, mejillas] to cause to blush. ◇ *vi* [por calor] to flush; [por turbación] to blush. ➡ **enrojecerse** *vprnl* [por calor] to flush; [por turbación] to blush.

enrolar *vt* to enlist. ➡ **enrolarse en** *vprnl* [la marina] to enlist in; [un buque] to sign up for.

enrollar *vt* - **1.** [arrollar] to roll up - **2.** *fam* [gustar]: **me enrolla mucho** I love it, I think it's great.

enroscar *vt* - **1.** [atornillar] to screw in - **2.** [enrollar] to roll up; [cuerpo, cola] to curl up.

ensaimada *sf* cake made of sweet coiled pastry.

ensalada *sf* [de lechuga etc] salad; **ensalada de frutas** fruit salad; **ensalada mixta** mixed salad; **ensalada rusa** Russian salad.

ensaladilla *sf*: **ensaladilla (rusa)** Russian salad.

ensalzar *vt* to praise.

ensambladura *sf* = **ensamblaje**.

ensamblaje *sm* [acción] assembly; [pieza] joint.

ensanchar *vt* [orificio, calle] to widen; [ropa] to let out; [ciudad] to expand.

ensanche *sm* - **1.** [de calle etc] widening - **2.** [en la ciudad] new suburb.

ensangrentar *vt* to cover with blood.

ensañarse *vprnl*: **ensañarse con** to torment, to treat cruelly.

ensartar *vt* - **1.** [perlas] to string; [aguja] to thread - **2.** [atravesar - torero] to gore; [puñal] to plunge, to bury.

ensayar *vt* - **1.** [gen] to test - **2.** TEATRO to rehearse.

ensayista *smf* essayist.

ensayo *sm* - **1.** TEATRO rehearsal; **ensayo general** dress rehearsal - **2.** [prueba] test; **ensayo nuclear** nuclear test - **3.** LITER essay - **4.** [en rugby] try.

enseguida *adv* [inmediatamente] immediately, at once; [pronto] very soon; **llegará enseguida** he'll be here any minute now.

ensenada *sf* cove, inlet.

enseñanza *sf* [gen] education; [instrucción] teaching; **enseñanza superior/universitaria** higher/university education.

enseñar *vt* - **1.** [instruir, aleccionar] to teach; **enseñar a alguien a hacer algo** to teach sb (how) to do sthg - **2.** [mostrar] to show.

enseres *smpl* - **1.** [efectos personales] belongings - **2.** [utensilios] equipment (U); **enseres domésticos** household goods.

ensillar *vt* to saddle up.

ensimismarse *vprnl* [enfrascarse] to become absorbed; [abstraerse] to be lost in thought.

ensombrecer *vt* *lit & fig* to cast a shadow over. ➡ **ensombrecerse** *vprnl* to darken.

ensoñación *sf* daydream.

ensopar *vt* *Andes, R Plata & Ven* to soak.

ensordecer ◇ *vt* [suj: sonido] to deafen. ◇ *vi* to go deaf.

ensuciar *vt* to (make) dirty; *fig* [desprestigiar] to sully, to tarnish. ➡ **ensuciarse** *vprnl* to get dirty.

ensueño *sm* *lit & fig* dream; **de ensueño** dream *(antes de s)*, ideal.

entablado *sm* [armazón] wooden platform; [suelo] floorboards *pl*.

entablar *vt* - **1.** [iniciar - conversación, amistad] to strike up - **2.** [entablillar] to put in a splint.

entallar *vt* - **1.** [prenda] to cut, to tailor - **2.** [madera] to carve, to sculpt.

entarimado *sm* [plataforma] wooden platform; [suelo] floorboards *pl*.

ente *sm* - **1.** [ser] being - **2.** [corporación] body, organization; **ente público** [gen] state-owned body O institution; [televisión] Spanish state broadcasting company.

entender ◇ *vt* - **1.** [gen] to understand; **¿tú qué entiendes por 'amistad'?** what do you understand by 'friendship'?; **dar algo a entender** to imply sthg - **2.** [darse cuenta] to realize - **3.** [oír] to hear - **4.** [juzgar] to think; **yo no lo entiendo así** I don't see it that way. ◇ *vi* - **1.** [comprender] to understand - **2.** [saber]: **entender de O en algo** to be an expert on sthg; **entender poco/algo de** to know very little/a little about. ◇ *sm*: **a mi entender...** the way I see it... ➡ **entenderse** *vprnl* - **1.** [comprenderse - uno mismo] to know what one means; [- dos personas] to understand each other - **2.** [llevarse bien] to get on - **3.** [ponerse de acuerdo] to reach an agreement - **4.** [comunicarse] to communicate (with each other).

entendido, da *sm, f*: **entendido (en)** expert (on). ➡ **entendido** *interj*: ¡**entendido!** all right!, okay!

entendimiento *sm* - **1.** [comprensión] understanding; [juicio] judgment; [inteligencia] mind, intellect - **2.** [acuerdo] understanding; **llegar a un entendimiento** to come to O reach an understanding.

enterado, da *adj*: **enterado (en)** well-informed (about); **estar enterado de algo** to be aware of sthg; **darse por enterado** to get the message; **no darse por enterado** to turn a deaf ear.

enterarse *vprnl* - **1.** [descubrir]: **enterarse (de)** to find out (about) - **2.** *fam* [comprender] to get it, to understand - **3.** [darse cuenta]: **enterarse (de algo)** to realize (sthg).

entereza *sf* [serenidad] composure; [honradez] integrity; [firmeza] firmness.

enternecer *vt* to move, to touch. ◆ **enternecerse** *vprnl* to be moved.

entero, ra *adj* - **1.** [completo] whole - **2.** [sereno] composed - **3.** [honrado] upright, honest.

enterrador, ra *sm, f* gravedigger.

enterrar *vt* [gen] to bury.

entibiar *vt* - **1.** [enfriar] to cool - **2.** [templar] to warm. ◆ **entibiarse** *vprnl* [sentimiento] to cool.

entidad *sf* - **1.** [corporación] body; [empresa] firm, company - **2.** FILOS entity - **3.** [importancia] importance.

entierro *sm* [acción] burial; [ceremonia] funeral.

entlo. *abrev de* **entresuelo.**

entoldado *sm* [toldo] awning; [para fiestas, bailes] marquee.

entonación *sf* intonation.

entonar ◇ *vt* - **1.** [cantar] to sing - **2.** [tonificar] to pick up. ◇ *vi* - **1.** [al cantar] to sing in tune - **2.** [armonizar]: **entonar (con algo)** to match (sthg).

entonces ◇ *adv* then; **desde entonces** since then; **en** O **por aquel entonces** at that time. ◇ *interj*: **¡entonces!** well, then!

entornar *vt* to half-close.

entorno *sm* - **1.** [ambiente] environment, surroundings *pl* - **2.** INFORM environment; **entorno gráfico** graphic environment; **entorno de programación** programming environment.

entorpecer *vt* - **1.** [debilitar - movimientos] to hinder; [- mente] to cloud - **2.** [dificultar] to obstruct, to hinder.

entrada *sf* - **1.** [acción] entry; [llegada] arrival; **'prohibida la entrada'** 'no entry' - **2.** [lugar] entrance; [puerta] doorway; **'entrada'** 'way in', 'entrance'; **entrada principal** main entrance; **entrada de servicio** tradesman's entrance - **3.** TECNOL inlet, intake; **entrada de aire** air intake - **4.** [en espectáculos - billete] ticket; [- recaudación] receipts *pl*, takings *pl*; **entrada gratuita** admission free; **entrada libre** admission free; **sacar una entrada** to buy a ticket - **5.** [público] audience; DEP attendance - **6.** [pago inicial] down payment - **7.** [en contabilidad] income - **8.** [plato] starter - **9.** [en la frente]: **tener entradas** to have a receding hairline - **10.** [en un diccionario] entry - **11.** [principio]: **de entrada** right from the beginning O the word go.

entrante ◇ *adj* [año, mes] coming; [presidente, gobierno] incoming. ◇ *sm* - **1.** [plato] starter - **2.** [hueco] recess.

entraña *(gen pl)* *sf* - **1.** [víscera] entrails *pl*, insides *pl* - **2.** *fig* [centro, esencia] heart.

entrañable *adj* intimate.

entrañar *vt* to involve.

entrar ◇ *vi* - **1.** [introducirse - viniendo] to enter, to come in; [- yendo] to enter, to go in; **entrar en algo** to enter sthg, to come/go into sthg; **entré por la ventana** I got in through the window - **2.** [penetrar - clavo etc] to go in; **entrar en algo** to go into sthg - **3.** [caber]: **entrar (en)** to fit (in); **este anillo no te entra** this ring won't fit you - **4.** [incorporarse]: **entrar (en algo)** [colegio, empresa] to start (at sthg); [club, partido político] to join (sthg); **entrar de** [botones etc] to start off as - **5.** [estado físico o de ánimo]: **le entraron ganas de hablar** he suddenly felt like talking; **me está entrando frío** I'm getting cold; **me entró mucha pena** I was filled with pity - **6.** [periodo de tiempo] to start; **entrar en** [edad, vejez] to reach; [año nuevo] to enter - **7.** [cantidad]: **¿cuántos entran en un kilo?** how many do you get to the kilo? - **8.** [concepto, asignatura etc]: **no le entra la geometría** he can't get the hang of geometry - **9.** AUTO to engage. ◇ *vt* [introducir] to bring in.

entre *prep* - **1.** [gen] between; **entre nosotros** [en confianza] between you and me, between ourselves; **entre una cosa y otra** what with one thing and another - **2.** [en medio de muchos] among, amongst; **estaba entre los asistentes** she was among those present; **entre sí** amongst themselves; **discutían entre sí** they were arguing with each other.

entreabierto, ta *pp* ▷ **entreabrir.**

entreabrir *vt* to half-open.

entreacto *sm* interval.

entrecejo *sm* space between the brows; **fruncir el entrecejo** to frown.

entrecortado, da *adj* [voz, habla] faltering; [respiración] laboured; [señal, sonido] intermittent.

entrecot, entrecote *sm* entrecôte.

entredicho *sm*: **estar en entredicho** to be in doubt; **poner en entredicho** to question, to call into question.

entrega *sf* - **1.** [gen] handing over; [de pedido, paquete] delivery; [de premios] presentation; **entrega a domicilio** home delivery - **2.** [dedicación]: **entrega (a)** devotion (to) - **3.** [fascículo] instalment; **publicar por entregas** to serialize.

entregar *vt* [gen] to hand over; [pedido, paquete] to deliver; [examen, informe] to hand in; [persona] to turn over. ◆ **entregarse** *vprnl* [rendirse - soldado, ejército] to surrender; [- criminal] to turn o.s. in. ◆ **entregarse a** *vprnl* - **1.** [persona, trabajo] to devote o.s. to - **2.** [vicio, pasión] to give o.s. over to.

entreguerras ◆ **de entreguerras** *loc adj* between the wars.

entrelazar *vt* to interlace, to interlink.

entremés *sm (gen pl)* CULIN hors d'œuvres.

entremeter *vt* to insert, to put in. ◆ **entremeterse** *vprnl* [inmiscuirse]: **entremeterse (en)** to meddle (in).

entremezclar *vt* to mix up. ◆ **entremezclarse** *vprnl* to mix.

entrenador, ra *sm, f* coach; [seleccionador] manager.

entrenamiento *sm* training.

entrenar *vt & vi* to train. ◆ **entrenarse** *vprnl* to train.

entrepierna *sf* crotch.

entresacar *vt* to pick out.

entresijos *smpl* ins and outs.

entresuelo *sm* mezzanine.

entretanto *adv* meanwhile.

entretención *sf* Chile entertainment.

entretener *vt* - **1.** [despistar] to distract - **2.** [retrasar] to hold up, to keep - **3.** [divertir] to entertain. ◆ **entretenerse** *vprnl* - **1.** [despistarse] to get distracted - **2.** [divertirse] to amuse o.s. - **3.** [retrasarse] to be held up.

entretenido, da *adj* entertaining, enjoyable.

entretenimiento *sm* - **1.** [acción] entertainment - **2.** [pasatiempo] pastime.

entrever *vt* [vislumbrar] to barely make out; [por un instante] to glimpse.

entreverar *C Sur vt* to mix. ◆ **entreverarse** *vprnl* to get tangled.

entrevero *sm C Sur* [lío] tangle, mess; [pelea] brawl.

entrevista *sf* - **1.** [periodística, de trabajo] interview; **hacer una entrevista a alguien** to interview sb - **2.** [reunión] meeting.

entrevistar *vt* to interview. ◆ **entrevistarse** *vprnl*: **entrevistarse (con)** to have a meeting (with).

entrevisto, ta *pp* ▷ **entrever**.

entristecer *vt* to make sad. ◆ **entristecerse** *vprnl* to become sad.

entrometerse *vprnl*: **entrometerse (en)** to interfere (in).

entrometido, da *sm, f* meddler.

entroncar *vi* - **1.** [trenes etc] to connect - **2.** *fig* [relacionarse]: **entroncar (con)** to be related (to).

entuerto *sm* wrong, injustice.

entumecer *vt* to numb. ◆ **entumecerse** *vprnl* to become numb.

entumecido, da *adj* numb.

enturbiar *vt lit & fig* to cloud. ◆ **enturbiarse** *vprnl lit & fig* to become cloudy.

entusiasmar *vt* - **1.** [animar] to fill with enthusiasm - **2.** [gustar]: **le entusiasma la música** he loves music ◆ **entusiasmarse** *vprnl*: **entusiasmarse (con)** to get excited (about).

entusiasmo *sm* enthusiasm; **con entusiasmo** enthusiastically.

entusiasta ◇ *adj* enthusiastic. ◇ *smf* enthusiast.

enumeración *sf* enumeration, listing.

enumerar *vt* to enumerate, to list.

enunciar *vt* to formulate, to enunciate.

envainar *vt* to sheathe.

envalentonar *vt* to urge on, to fill with courage. ◆ **envalentonarse** *vprnl* to become daring.

envanecer *vt* to make vain. ◆ **envanecerse** *vprnl* to become vain.

envasado *sm* [en botellas] bottling; [en latas] canning; [en paquetes] packing.

envasar *vt* [en botellas] to bottle; [en latas] to can; [en paquetes] to pack.

envase *sm* - **1.** [envasado - en botellas] bottling; [- en latas] canning; [- en paquetes] packing - **2.** [recipiente] container; [botella] bottle; **envase desechable** disposable container; **envase retornable** returnable bottle; **envase sin retorno** non-returnable bottle.

envejecer ◇ *vi* [hacerse viejo] to grow old; [parecer viejo] to age. ◇ *vt* to age.

envejecimiento *sm* ageing.

envenenamiento *sm* poisoning.

envenenar *vt* to poison.

envergadura *sf* - **1.** [importancia] size, extent; [complejidad] complexity; **una reforma de gran envergadura** a wide-ranging reform - **2.** [anchura] span.

envés *sm* reverse (side), back; [de tela] wrong side.

enviado, da *sm, f* POLÍT envoy; PRENSA correspondent.

enviar *vt* to send; **enviar a alguien a hacer algo** to send sb to do sthg.

enviciar *vt* to addict, to get hooked. ◆ **enviciarse** *vprnl* to become addicted.

envidia *sf* envy; **era la envidia de todos** it was the envy of everyone; **dar envidia a alguien** to make sb jealous O envious; **tener envidia de alguien/algo** to envy sb/sthg, to be jealous O envious of sb/sthg; **morirse de envidia** to be green with envy.

envidiar *vt* to envy.

envidioso, sa *adj* envious.

envilecer *vt* to debase.

envío *sm* - **1.** COM dispatch; [de correo] delivery; [de víveres, mercancías] consignment; **gastos de envío** postage and packing UK, postage and handling *US*; **envío a domicilio** home delivery; **envío contra reembolso** cash on delivery - **2.** [paquete] package.

enviudar *vi* to be widowed.

envoltorio *sm* wrapper, wrapping.

envoltura *sf* = **envoltorio**.

envolver *vt* - **1.** [embalar] to wrap (up) - **2.** [enrollar] to wind - **3.** [implicar]: **envolver a alguien en** to involve sb in.

envuelto, ta *pp* ⊳ **envolver**.

enyesar *vt* - **1.** MED to put in plaster - **2.** CONSTR to plaster.

enzarzar *vt* to entangle, to embroil. ➡ **enzarzarse** *vprnl*: **enzarzarse en** to get entangled O embroiled in.

enzima *sf* enzyme.

e.p.d. (*abrev de* **en paz descanse**) RIP.

épica ⊳ **épico**.

épico, ca *adj* epic. ➡ **épica** *sf* epic.

epidemia *sf* epidemic.

epígrafe *sm* heading.

epilepsia *sf* epilepsy.

epílogo *sm* epilogue.

episodio *sm* [gen] episode.

epístola *sf culto* [carta] epistle; RELIG Epistle.

epitafio *sm* epitaph.

epíteto *sm* epithet.

época *sf* period; [estación] season; **de época** period (*antes de s*); **en aquella época** at that time; **época dorada** golden age.

epopeya *sf* - **1.** [gen] epic - **2.** *fig* [hazaña] feat.

equidad *sf* fairness.

equidistante *adj* equidistant.

equilibrado, da *adj* - **1.** [gen] balanced - **2.** [sensato] sensible.

equilibrar *vt* to balance.

equilibrio *sm* balance; **hacer equilibrios** *fig* to perform a balancing act.

equilibrista *smf* [trapecista] trapeze artist; [funambulista] tightrope walker.

equino, na *adj* equine.

equinoccio *sm* equinox.

equipaje *sm* luggage *UK*, baggage *US*; **hacer el equipaje** to pack; **equipaje de mano** hand luggage.

equipar *vt*: **equipar (de)** [gen] to equip (with); [ropa] to fit out (with).

equiparar *vt* to compare. ➡ **equipararse** *vprnl* to be compared.

equipo *sm* - **1.** [equipamiento] equipment; **caerse con todo el equipo** *fam* to get it in the neck - **2.** [personas, jugadores] team; **equipo de rescate** rescue team - **3.** [de música] system.

equis *adj* X; **un número equis de personas** x number of people.

equitación *sf* [arte] equestrianism; [actividad] horse riding.

equitativo, va *adj* fair, even-handed.

equivalente *adj* & *sm* equivalent.

equivaler ➡ **equivaler a** *vi* to be equivalent to; *fig* [significar] to amount to.

equivocación *sf* mistake; **por equivocación** by mistake.

equivocado, da *adj* mistaken.

equivocar *vt* to choose wrongly; **equivocar algo con algo** to mistake sthg for sthg. ➡ **equivocarse** *vprnl* to be wrong; **equivocarse en** to make a mistake in; **se equivocó de nombre** he got the wrong name.

equívoco, ca *adj* - **1.** [ambiguo] ambiguous, equivocal - **2.** [sospechoso] suspicious. ➡ **equívoco** *sm* misunderstanding.

era *sf* [periodo] era; ⊳ **ser**.

erario *sm* funds *pl*.

erección *sf* erection.

erecto, ta *adj* erect.

eres ⊳ **ser**.

erguir *vt* to raise. ➡ **erguirse** *vprnl* to rise up.

erigir *vt* [construir] to erect, to build.

erizado, da *adj* [de punta] on end; [con púas o espinas] spiky.

erizar *vt* to cause to stand on end. ➡ **erizarse** *vprnl* [pelo] to stand on end; [persona] to stiffen.

erizo *sm* - **1.** [mamífero] hedgehog - **2.** [pez] globefish; **erizo de mar** sea urchin.

ermita *sf* hermitage.

erosionar *vt* to erode. ➡ **erosionarse** *vprnl* to erode.

erótico, ca *adj* erotic.

erotismo *sm* eroticism.

erradicación *sf* eradication.

erradicar *vt* to eradicate.

errante *adj* wandering.

errar ◇ *vt* [vocación, camino] to choose wrongly; [disparo, golpe] to miss. ◇ *vi* - **1.** [vagar] to wander - **2.** [equivocarse] to make a mistake - **3.** [al disparar] to miss.

errata *sf* misprint.

erróneo, a *adj* mistaken.

error *sm* mistake, error; **cometer un error** to make a mistake; **estar en un error** to be mistaken; **salvo error u omisión** errors and omissions excepted; **error de cálculo** miscalculation; **error humano** human error; **error de imprenta** misprint; **error judicial** miscarriage of justice; **error tipográfico** typo, typographical error.

ertzaintza [er'tʃaintʃa] *sf Basque regional police force*.

eructar *vi* to belch.

eructo *sm* belch.

erudito, ta *adj* erudite.

erupción *sf* - 1. GEOL eruption; **en erupción** erupting; **entrar en erupción** to erupt - 2. MED rash.

es ⊳ **ser**.

esa ⊳ **ese**.

ésa ⊳ **ése**.

esbelto, ta *adj* slender, slim.

esbozar *vt* to sketch, to outline; [sonrisa] to give a hint of.

esbozo *sm* sketch, outline.

escabechado, da *adj* CULIN marinated.

escabeche *sm* CULIN marinade.

escabroso, sa *adj* - 1. [abrupto] rough - 2. [obsceno] risqué - 3. [espinoso] awkward, thorny.

escabullirse *vprnl* [desaparecer]: **escabullirse (de)** to slip away (from).

escacharrar *vt fam* to knacker.

escafandra *sf* diving suit.

escala *sf* - 1. [gen] scale; [de colores] range; **a escala** [gráfica] to scale; **a escala mundial** *fig* on a worldwide scale; **a gran escala** on a large scale; **a pequeña escala** small-scale; **en pequeña escala** on a small scale; **escala salarial** salary scale - 2. [en un viaje] stopover; **hacer escala** to stop over; **escala técnica** refuelling stop *UK*, refueling stop *US*.

escalada *sf* - 1. [de montaña] climb; **escalada libre** free climbing - 2. [de violencia, precios] escalation, rise.

escalador, ra *sm, f* [alpinista] climber.

escalafón *sm* scale, ladder.

escalar *vt* to climb.

escaldar *vt* to scald.

escalera *sf* - 1. [gen] stairs *pl*, staircase; [escala] ladder; **escalera mecánica** *O* **automática** escalator; **escalera de caracol** spiral staircase - 2. [en naipes] run.

escalfar *vt* to poach.

escalinata *sf* staircase.

escalofriante *adj* spine-chilling.

escalofrío *(gen pl) sm* shiver; **dar escalofríos a alguien** to give sb the shivers; **tener escalofríos** to have the shivers.

escalón *sm* step; *fig* grade.

escalonar *vt* - 1. [gen] to spread out - 2. [terreno] to terrace.

escalope *sm* escalope.

escama *sf* - 1. [de peces, reptiles] scale - 2. [de jabón, en la piel] flake.

escamar *vt fam fig* [mosquear] to make suspicious.

escamotear *vt*: **escamotear algo a alguien** [estafar] to do *O* swindle sb out of sthg; [hurtar] to rob sb of sthg.

escampar *v impers* to stop raining.

escandalizar *vt* to scandalize, to shock. ⬥ **escandalizarse** *vprnl* to be shocked.

escándalo *sm* - 1. [inmoralidad] scandal; [indignación] outrage - 2. [alboroto] uproar; **armar un escándalo** to kick up a fuss.

escandaloso, sa *adj* - 1. [inmoral] outrageous - 2. [ruidoso] very noisy.

Escandinavia *n pr* Scandinavia.

escandinavo, va *adj & sm, f* Scandinavian.

escanear *vt* to scan.

escáner *(pl escaners) sm* - 1. [aparato] scanner - 2. [exploración] scan; **hacerse un escáner** to have a scan.

escaño *sm* - 1. [cargo] seat *(in parliament)* - 2. [asiento] bench *(in parliament)*.

escapada *sf* - 1. [huida] escape, flight; DEP breakaway - 2. [viaje] quick trip.

escapar *vi* [huir]: **escapar (de)** to get away *O* escape (from). ⬥ **escaparse** *vprnl* - 1. [huir]: **escaparse (de)** to get away *O* escape (from); **escaparse de casa** to run away from home - 2. [salir - gas, agua etc] to leak.

escaparate *sm* - 1. [de tienda] (shop) window - 2. *Cuba & Ven* [ropero] wardrobe.

escapatoria *sf* [fuga] escape; **no tener escapatoria** to have no way out.

escape *sm* [de gas etc] leak; [de coche] exhaust; **a escape** in a rush, at high speed.

escaquearse *vprnl fam* to duck out; **escaquearse de algo/de hacer algo** to worm one's way out of sthg/doing sthg.

escarabajo *sm* beetle.

escaramuza *sf fig & MIL* skirmish.

escarbar *vt* to scratch, to scrape.

escarcha *sf* frost.

escarlata *adj & sm* scarlet.

escarlatina *sf* scarlet fever.

escarmentar *vi* to learn (one's lesson); **¡no escarmienta!** he never learns!; **¡para que escarmientes!** that'll teach you!

escarmiento *sm* lesson; **servir de escarmiento** to serve as a lesson.

escarnio *sm* mockery, ridicule.

escarola *sf* endive.

escarpado, da *adj* [inclinado] steep; [abrupto] craggy.

escasear *vi* to be scarce.

escasez *sf* [insuficiencia] shortage; [pobreza] poverty.

escaso, sa *adj* - 1. [insuficiente - conocimientos, recursos] limited, scant; [- tiempo] short; [- cantidad, número] low; [- víveres, trabajo] scarce; [- visibilidad, luz] poor; **andar escaso de** to be short of - 2. [casi completo]: **un metro escaso** barely a metre.

escatimar *vt* [gastos, comida] to be sparing with, to skimp on; [esfuerzo, energías] to use as little as possible; **no escatimar gastos** to spare no expense.

escay, skai *sm* Leatherette®.

escayola *sf* CONSTR plaster of Paris; MED plaster.

escena *sf* - 1. [gen] scene; **hacer una escena** to make a scene - 2. [escenario] stage; **llevar a la escena** to dramatize; **poner en escena** to stage; **salir a escena** to go on stage.

escenario *sm* - 1. [tablas, escena] stage; CINE & TEATRO [lugar de la acción] setting - 2. *fig* [de suceso] scene.

escenificar *vt* [novela] to dramatize; [obra de teatro] to stage.

escenografía *sf* set design.

escepticismo *sm* scepticism.

escéptico, ca <> *adj* [incrédulo] sceptical. <> *sm, f* sceptic.

escindir *vt* to split. ➠ **escindirse** *vprnl*: **escindirse (en)** to split (into).

escisión *sf* [del átomo] splitting; [de partido político] split.

esclarecer *vt* to clear up, to shed light on.

esclava ▷ **esclavo**.

esclavitud *sf lit & fig* slavery.

esclavizar *vt lit & fig* to enslave.

esclavo, va *sm, f lit & fig* [persona] slave; **es un esclavo del trabajo** he's a slave to his work.

esclerosis *sf inv* MED sclerosis; **esclerosis múltiple** multiple sclerosis.

esclusa *sf* [de canal] lock; [compuerta] floodgate.

escoba *sf* broom; **pasar la escoba** to sweep (up).

escocedura *sf* [sensación] stinging.

escocer *vi lit & fig* to sting.

escocés, esa <> *adj* [gen] Scottish; [whisky] Scotch; [tejido] tartan, plaid. <> *sm, f* [persona] Scot, Scotsman (*f* Scotswoman); **los escoceses** the Scottish, the Scots. ➠ **escocés** *sm* [lengua] Scots (U).

Escocia *n pr* Scotland.

escoger *vt* to choose.

escogido, da *adj* [elegido] selected, chosen; [selecto] choice, select.

escolar <> *adj* school (*antes de s*). <> *sm, f* pupil, schoolboy (*f* schoolgirl).

escolarizar *vt* to provide with schooling.

escollo *sm* - 1. [en el mar] reef - 2. *fig* stumbling block.

escolta *sf* escort.

escoltar *vt* to escort.

escombros *smpl* rubble (U), debris (U).

esconder *vt* to hide, to conceal. ➠ **esconderse** *vprnl*: **esconderse (de)** to hide (from).

escondido, da *adj* [lugar] secluded. ➠ **a escondidas** *loc adv* in secret; **hacer algo a escondidas de alguien** to do sthg behind sb's back.

escondite *sm* - 1. [lugar] hiding place - 2. [juego] hide-and-seek.

escondrijo *sm* hiding place.

escopeta *sf* shotgun; **escopeta de aire comprimido** air gun.

escoria *sf fig* dregs *pl*, scum.

Escorpio, Escorpión <> *sm* [zodiaco] Scorpio; **ser Escorpio** to be (a) Scorpio. <> *smf* [persona] Scorpio.

escorpión *sm* scorpion. ➠ **Escorpión = Escorpio**.

escotado, da *adj* low-cut.

escote *sm* [de prendas] neckline; [de persona] neck; **pagar a escote** to go Dutch; **escote en pico** V-neck; **escote redondo** round neck.

escotilla *sf* hatch, hatchway.

escozor *sm* stinging.

escribanía *sf Andes, C Rica & R Plata* [notaría] ≃ notary public's office.

escribano, na *sm, f Andes, C Rica & R Plata* [notario] notary (public).

escribir *vt & vi* to write; **escribir a lápiz** to write in pencil; **escribir a mano** to write by hand, to write in longhand; **escribir a máquina** to type. ➠ **escribirse** *vprnl* - 1. [personas] to write to one another - 2. [palabras]: **se escribe con 'h'** it is spelt with an 'h'.

escrito, ta <> *pp* ▷ **escribir**. <> *adj* written; **por escrito** in writing. ➠ **escrito** *sm* [gen] text; [documento] document; [obra literaria] writing, work.

escritor, ra *sm, f* writer.

escritorio *sm* [mueble] desk, bureau.

escritura *sf* - 1. [arte] writing - 2. [sistema de signos] script - 3. DER deed.

escrúpulo *sm* - 1. [duda, recelo] scruple - 2. [minuciosidad] scrupulousness, great care - 3. [aprensión] qualm; **le da escrúpulo** he has qualms about it.

escrupuloso, sa *adj* - 1. [gen] scrupulous - 2. [aprensivo] particular, fussy.

escrutar *vt* [con la mirada] to scrutinize, to examine; [votos] to count.

escrutinio *sm* count (*of votes*).

escuadra *sf* - 1. GEOM square - 2. [de buques] squadron - 3. [de soldados] squad.

escuadrilla *sf* squadron.

escuadrón *sm* squadron; **escuadrón de la muerte** death squad.

escuálido, da *adj culto* emaciated.

escucha *sf* listening-in, monitoring; **estar** *O* **permanecer a la escucha** to listen in; **escuchas telefónicas** telephone tapping *(U)*.

escuchar ⟩ *vt* to listen to. ⟩ *vi* to listen.

escudería *sf* team *(in motor racing)*.

escudo *sm* - **1.** [arma] shield - **2.** [moneda] escudo - **3.** [emblema] coat of arms.

escudriñar *vt* [examinar] to scrutinize, to examine; [otear] to search.

escuela *sf* school; **escuela normal** teacher training college; **escuela nocturna** night school; **escuela parroquial** parish school; **escuela privada** private school, public school *UK*; **escuela pública** state school; **ser de la vieja escuela** to be of the old school.

escueto, ta *adj* [sucinto] concise; [sobrio] plain, unadorned.

escuincle, cla *sm, f Méx fam* [muchacho] nipper, kid.

esculpir *vt* to sculpt, to carve.

escultor, ra *sm, f* sculptor *(f* sculptress).

escultura *sf* sculpture.

escupir ⟩ *vi* to spit. ⟩ *vt* [suj: persona, animal] to spit out; [suj: volcán, chimenea etc] to belch out.

escupitajo *sm* gob, spit.

escurreplatos *sm inv* dish rack.

escurridizo, za *adj lit & fig* slippery.

escurridor *sm* colander.

escurrir ⟩ *vt* [gen] to drain; [ropa] to wring out; [en lavadora] to spin-dry. ⟩ *vi* [gotear] to drip. ➡ **escurrirse** *vprnl* [resbalarse] to slip.

ese ¹ *sf* [figura] zigzag; **hacer eses** [en carretera] to zigzag; [al andar] to stagger about.

ese ² *(pl* esos), **esa** *(pl* esas) *adj demos* - **1.** [gen] that *(pl* those) - **2.** *(después de s) fam despec* that *(pl* those); **el hombre ese no me inspira confianza** I don't trust that guy.

ése *(pl* ésos), **ésa** *(pl* ésas) *pron demos* - **1.** [gen] that one *(pl* those ones) - **2.** [mencionado antes] the former - **3.** *fam despec*: **ése fue el que me pegó** that's the guy who hit me - **4.** *loc*: **¡a ése!** stop that man!; **ni por ésas** not even then; **no me lo vendió ni por ésas** even then he wouldn't sell me it.

esencia *sf* essence; **quinta esencia** quintessence.

esencial *adj* essential.

esfera *sf* - **1.** [gen] sphere; **esfera terrestre** (terrestrial) globe - **2.** [de reloj] face - **3.** [círculo social] circle; **esfera de influencia** sphere of influence - **4.** INFORM: **esfera de arrastre** *O* **de desplazamiento** trackball.

esférico, ca *adj* spherical.

esfinge *sf* sphinx; **parecer una esfinge** to be inscrutable.

esforzar *vt* [voz] to strain. ➡ **esforzarse** *vprnl* to make an effort; **esforzarse en** *O* **por hacer algo** to try very hard to do sthg, to do one's best to do sthg.

esfuerzo *sm* effort; **hacer un esfuerzo** to make an effort, to try hard.

esfumarse *vprnl* [esperanzas, posibilidades] to fade away; [persona] to vanish.

esgrima *sf* fencing.

esgrimir *vt* - **1.** [arma] to brandish, to wield - **2.** [argumento, hecho, idea] to use, to employ.

esguince *sm* sprain.

eslabón *sm* link; **el eslabón perdido** the missing link.

eslogan *(pl* eslóganes), **slogan** *(pl* slogans) *sm* slogan.

eslora *sf* NÁUT length.

eslovaco, ca *adj & sm, f* Slovak, Slovakian. ➡ **eslovaco** *sm* [lengua] Slovak.

Eslovaquia *n pr* Slovakia.

esloveno *adj & sm, f* Slovene.

esmaltar *vt* to enamel.

esmalte *sm* [sustancia - en dientes, cerámica etc] enamel; [- de uñas] (nail) varnish *O* polish.

esmerado, da *adj* [persona] painstaking, careful; [trabajo] polished.

esmeralda *sf* emerald.

esmerarse *vprnl*: **esmerarse (en algo/hacer algo)** [esforzarse] to take great pains (over sthg/doing sthg).

esmerilar *vt* [pulir] to polish with emery.

esmero *sm* great care.

esmoquin *(pl* esmóquines), **smoking** *(pl* smokings) *sm* dinner jacket *UK*, tuxedo *US*.

esnifar *vt fam* to sniff *(drugs)*.

esnob *(pl* esnobs), **snob** *(pl* snobs) *sm, f* person who wants to be trendy.

eso *pron demos (neutro)* that; **eso es la Torre Eiffel** that's the Eiffel Tower; **eso es lo que yo pienso** that's just what I think; **eso que propones es irrealizable** what you're proposing is impossible; **eso de vivir solo no me gusta** I don't like the idea of living on my own; **¡eso, eso!** that's right!, yes!; **¡eso es!** that's it; **¿cómo es eso?, ¿y eso?** [¿por qué?] how come?; **para eso es mejor no ir** if that's all it is, you might as well not go; **por eso vine** that's why I came. ➡ **a eso de** *loc prep* (at) about *O* around. ➡ **en eso** *loc adv* at that very moment. ➡ **y eso que** *loc conj* even though.

esófago *sm* oesophagus.

esos, esas ▷ **ese ²**.

ésos, ésas ▷ **ése**.

esotérico, ca *adj* esoteric.

espabilar *vt* - **1.** [despertar] to wake up - **2.** [avispar]: **espabilar a alguien** to sharpen sb's wits. ➡ **espabilarse** *vprnl* - **1.** [despertarse] to wake up, to brighten up - **2.** [darse prisa] to get a move on - **3.** [avisparse] to sharpen one's wits.

espacial *adj* space *(antes de s)*.

espaciar *vt* to space out.

espacio *sm* - **1.** [gen] space; **no tengo mucho espacio** I don't have much room; **a doble espacio** double-spaced; **por espacio de** over a period of; **espacio aéreo** air space - **2.** RADIO & TV programme.

espacioso, sa *adj* spacious.

espada *sf* [arma] sword; **espada de dos filos** *fig* double-edged sword. ➡ **espadas** *sfpl* [naipes] ≃ spades.

espagueti, spaghetti *sm* spaghetti *(U)*.

espalda *sf* - **1.** [gen] back; **cargado de espaldas** round-shouldered; **por la espalda** from behind; *fig* behind one's back; **tumbarse de espaldas** to lie on one's back; **echarse algo sobre las espaldas** to take sthg on; **tirar** *O* **tumbar de espaldas** to be amazing *O* stunning - **2.** [en natación] backstroke.

espantadizo, za *adj* nervous, easily frightened.

espantajo *sm* [persona fea] fright, sight.

espantapájaros *sm inv* scarecrow.

espantar *vt* - **1.** [ahuyentar] to frighten *O* scare away - **2.** [asustar] to frighten, to scare. ➡ **espantarse** *vprnl* to get frightened *O* scared.

espanto *sm* fright.

espantoso, sa *adj* - **1.** [terrorífico] horrific - **2.** [enorme] terrible - **3.** [feísimo] frightful, horrible.

España *n pr* Spain.

español, la ◇ *adj* Spanish. ◇ *sm, f* [persona] Spaniard. ➡ **español** *sm* [lengua] Spanish.

esparadrapo *sm* (sticking) plaster, Band-Aid® *US.*

esparcido, da *adj* scattered.

esparcir *vt* [gen] to spread; [semillas, papeles, objetos] to scatter. ➡ **esparcirse** *vprnl* to spread (out).

espárrago *sm* asparagus *(U)*; **mandar a alguien a freír espárragos** *fam* to tell sb to get lost.

esparto *sm* esparto (grass).

espasmo *sm* spasm.

espasmódico, ca *adj* spasmodic.

espatarrarse *vprnl fam* to sprawl (with one's legs wide open).

espátula *sf* CULIN & MED spatula; ARTE palette knife; CONSTR bricklayer's trowel; [de empapelador] stripping knife.

especia *sf* spice.

especial *adj* - **1.** [gen] special; **especial para** specially for; **en especial** especially, particularly - **2.** [peculiar - carácter, gusto, persona] peculiar, strange.

especialidad *sf* speciality, specialty *US*; **especialidad de la casa** house speciality.

especialista *sm, f* - **1.** [experto]: **especialista (en)** specialist (in) - **2.** CINE stuntman (*f* stuntwoman).

especializado, da *adj*: **especializado en** specialized (in).

especializar *vt* to specialize.

especie *sf* - **1.** BIOL species *sing*; **especie protegida** protected species - **2.** [clase] kind, sort.

especificar *vt* to specify.

específico, ca *adj* specific.

espécimen (*pl* **especímenes**) *sm* specimen.

espectacular *adj* spectacular.

espectáculo *sm* - **1.** [diversión] entertainment - **2.** [función] show, performance; **espectáculo de variedades** variety show - **3.** [suceso, escena] sight.

espectador, ra *sm, f* TV viewer; CINE & TEATRO member of the audience; DEP spectator; [de suceso, discusión] onlooker.

espectro *sm* - **1.** [fantasma] spectre, ghost - **2.** FÍS & MED spectrum.

especulación *sf* speculation.

especular *vi*: **especular (sobre)** to speculate (about).

espejismo *sm* mirage; *fig* illusion.

espejo *sm lit & fig* mirror; **espejo retrovisor** rear-view mirror.

espeleología *sf* potholing.

espeluznante *adj* hair-raising, lurid.

espera *sf* [acción] wait.

esperanza *sf* [deseo, ganas] hope; [confianza, expectativas] expectation; **dar esperanzas** to encourage, to give hope to; **perder la esperanza** to lose hope; **tener esperanza de hacer algo** to hope to be able to do sthg.

esperanzar *vt* to give hope to, to encourage.

esperar ◇ *vt* - **1.** [aguardar] to wait for; **esperar a que alguien haga algo** to wait for sb to do sthg - **2.** [tener esperanza de]: **esperar que** to hope that; **espero que sí** I hope so; **esperar hacer algo** to hope to do sthg - **3.** [tener confianza en] to expect; **esperar que** to expect (that) - **4.** [ser inminente para] to await, to be in store for. ◇ *vi* [aguardar] to wait; **espera y verás** wait and see; **como era de esperar** as was to be expected. ➡ **esperarse** *vprnl* - **1.** [imaginarse, figurarse] to expect - **2.** [aguardar] to wait; **esperarse a que alguien haga algo** to wait for sb to do sthg.

esperma ◇ *sm o sf* BIOL sperm. ◇ *sf Amér* [vela] candle.

esperpento *sm* [persona] grotesque sight; [cosa] piece of nonsense.

espeso, sa *adj* [gen] thick; [bosque, niebla] dense; [nieve] deep.

espesor *sm* - 1. [grosor] thickness; **tiene 2 metros de espesor** it's 2 metres thick - 2. [densidad · de niebla, bosque] density; [- de nieve] depth.

espesura *sf* - 1. [vegetación] thicket - 2. [grosor] thickness; [densidad] density.

espía *smf* spy.

espiar *vt* to spy on.

espiga *sf* - 1. [de trigo etc] ear - 2. [en telas] herringbone - 3. [pieza - de madera] peg; [- de hierro] pin.

espigado, da *adj* [persona] tall and slim.

espigón *sm* breakwater.

espina *sf* [de pez] bone; [de planta] thorn; **me da mala espina** it makes me uneasy, there's something fishy about it; **tener una espina clavada** to bear a great burden; **sacarse la espina** to get even. ➤ **espina dorsal** *sf* spine. ➤ **espina bífida** *sf* spina bifida.

espinaca *sf (gen pl)* spinach *(U)*.

espinazo *sm* spine, backbone.

espinilla *sf* - 1. [hueso] shin, shinbone - 2. [grano] blackhead.

espinoso, sa *adj lit & fig* thorny.

espionaje *sm* espionage.

espiral *sf lit & fig* spiral.

espirar *vi & vt* to exhale, to breathe out.

espiritista *adj* spiritualist.

espíritu *sm* [gen] spirit; RELIG soul; **espíritu de equipo** team spirit. ➤ **Espíritu Santo** *sm* Holy Ghost.

espiritual *adj & sm* spiritual.

espléndido, da *adj* - 1. [magnífico] splendid, magnificent - 2. [generoso] generous, lavish.

esplendor *sm* - 1. [magnificencia] splendour - 2. [apogeo] greatness.

espliego *sm* lavender.

espoleta *sf* [de proyectil] fuse.

espolvorear *vt* to dust, to sprinkle.

esponja *sf* sponge; **esponja vegetal** loofah, vegetable sponge; **beber como una esponja** *fam* to drink like a fish; **tirar la esponja** to throw in the towel.

esponjoso, sa *adj* spongy.

espontaneidad *sf* spontaneity.

espontáneo, a *adj* spontaneous.

esporádico, ca *adj* sporadic.

esposa ▷ **esposo**.

esposar *vt* to handcuff.

esposo, sa *sm, f* [persona] husband (*f* wife). ➤ **esposas** *sfpl* [objeto] handcuffs.

espot (*pl* **espots**) = **spot**.

espray (*pl* **esprays**) *sm* spray.

esprint (*pl* **esprints**) *sm* sprint.

espuela *sf* [gen] spur.

espuma *sf* - 1. [gen] foam; [de cerveza] head; [de jabón] lather; [de olas] surf; [de caldo] scum; **hacer espuma** to foam; **crecer como la espuma** to mushroom; **espuma de afeitar** shaving foam; **espuma seca** carpet shampoo - 2. [para pelo] (styling) mousse.

espumadera *sf* skimmer.

espumoso, sa *adj* [gen] foamy, frothy; [vino] sparkling; [jabón] lathery.

esputo *sm* [gen] spittle; MED sputum.

esqueje *sm* cutting.

esquela *sf* obituary.

esqueleto *sm* [de persona] skeleton; **menear O mover el esqueleto** *fam* to boogie (on down).

esquema *sm* [gráfico] diagram; [resumen] outline; **su respuesta me rompe los esquemas** her answer has thrown all my plans up in the air.

esquemático, ca *adj* schematic.

esquí (*pl* **esquís**), **ski** (*pl* **skis**) *sm* - 1. [tabla] ski - 2. [deporte] skiing; **esquí de fondo** O **nórdico** cross-country skiing.

esquiador, ra *sm, f* skier.

esquiar *vi* to ski.

esquilar *vt* to shear.

esquimal *adj & smf* Eskimo.

esquina *sf* corner; **a la vuelta de la esquina** just round the corner; **doblar la esquina** to turn the corner.

esquinazo *sm* corner; **dar (el) esquinazo a alguien** to give sb the slip.

esquirol *sm fam* blackleg, scab.

esquivar *vt* [gen] to avoid; [golpe] to dodge.

esquivo, va *adj* shy.

esquizofrenia *sf* schizophrenia.

esta ▷ **este²**.

ésta ▷ **éste**.

estabilidad *sf* stability.

estabilizar *vt* to stabilize. ➤ **estabilizarse** *vprnl* to stabilize.

estable *adj* - 1. [firme] stable - 2. [permanente - huésped] permanent; [- cliente] regular.

establecer *vt* - 1. [gen] to establish; [récord] to set - 2. [negocio, campamento] to set up - 3. [inmigrantes etc] to settle. ➤ **establecerse** *vprnl* - 1. [instalarse] to settle - 2. [poner un negocio] to set up a business.

establecimiento *sm* - 1. [gen] establishment; [de récord] setting - 2. [de negocio, colonia] setting up.

establo *sm* cowshed.

estaca *sf* - 1. [para clavar, delimitar] stake; [de tienda de campaña] peg - 2. [garrote] cudgel.

estacada *sf* [valla] picket fence; MIL stockade, palisade; **dejar a alguien en la estacada** to leave sb in the lurch.

estación *sf* - **1.** [gen & INFORM] station; **estación de autocares/de tren** coach/railway station; **estación de esquí** ski resort; **estación de gasolina** petrol station; **estación de servicio** service station; **estación de trabajo** workstation; **estación meteorológica** weather station - **2.** [del año, temporada] season.

estacionamiento *sm* AUTO parking; **estacionamiento indebido** parking offence.

estacionar *vt* AUTO to park.

estacionario, ria *adj* [gen] stationary; ECON stagnant.

estadía *sf* C Sur stay, stop.

estadio *sm* - **1.** DEP stadium - **2.** [fase] stage.

estadista *smf* statesman (*f* stateswoman).

estadístico, ca *adj* statistical. ◆ **estadística** *sf* - **1.** [ciencia] statistics (U) - **2.** [datos] statistics *pl*.

estado *sm* state; **su estado es grave** his condition is serious; **estar en buen/mal estado** [coche, terreno etc] to be in good/bad condition; [alimento, bebida] to be fresh/off; **estado de ánimo** state of mind; **estado civil** marital status; **estado de bienestar** welfare state; **estado de excepción** O **emergencia** state of emergency; **estado de salud** (state of) health; **estar en estado (de esperanza** O **buena esperanza)** to be expecting. ◆ **Estado** *sm* [gobierno] State; **Estado Mayor** MIL general staff. ◆ **Estados Unidos (de América)** *n pr* United States (of America).

estadounidense ◇ *adj* United States (antes de s). ◇ *smf* United States citizen.

estafa *sf* [gen] swindle; COM fraud.

estafador, ra *sm, f* swindler.

estafar *vt* [gen] to swindle; COM to defraud.

estafeta *sf* sub-post office.

estallar *vi* - **1.** [reventar - bomba] to explode; [- neumático] to burst - **2.** [guerra, epidemia etc] to break out.

estallido *sm* - **1.** [de bomba] explosion; [de trueno] crash; [de látigo] crack - **2.** [de guerra etc] outbreak.

Estambul *n pr* Istanbul.

estamento *sm* stratum, class.

estampa *sf* - **1.** [imagen, tarjeta] print - **2.** [aspecto] appearance.

estampado, da *adj* printed. ◆ **estampado** *sm* [dibujo] (cotton) print.

estampar *vt* - **1.** [imprimir - gen] to print; [- metal] to stamp - **2.** [escribir]: **estampar la firma** to sign one's name.

estampida *sf* stampede.

estampido *sm* report, bang.

estampilla *sf* - **1.** [para marcar] rubber stamp - **2.** Amér [sello de correos] stamp.

estancado, da *adj* [agua] stagnant; [situación, proyecto] at a standstill.

estancarse *vprnl* [líquido] to stagnate; [situación] to come to a standstill.

estancia *sf* - **1.** [tiempo] stay - **2.** [habitación] room - **3.** C Sur [hacienda] cattle ranch.

estanciero *sm* C Sur ranch owner.

estanco, ca *adj* watertight. ◆ **estanco** *sm* tobacconist's.

estándar (*pl* **estándares**)**, standard** (*pl* **standards**) *adj inv* & *sm* standard.

estandarizar *vt* to standardize.

estandarte *sm* standard, banner.

estanque *sm* - **1.** [alberca] pond; [para riego] reservoir - **2.** Amér [depósito] tank (of petrol).

estanquero, ra *sm, f* tobacconist.

estante *sm* shelf.

estantería *sf* [gen] shelves *pl*, shelving (U); [para libros] bookcase.

estaño *sm* tin.

estar ◇ *vi* - **1.** [hallarse] to be; **¿dónde está la llave?** where is the key?; **¿está María?** is Maria in?; **no está** she's not in - **2.** [con fechas]: **¿a qué estamos hoy?** what's the date today?; **hoy estamos a martes/a 15 de julio** today is Tuesday/the 15th of July; **estábamos en octubre** it was October - **3.** [quedarse] to stay, to be; **estaré un par de horas y me iré** I'll stay a couple of hours and then I'll go - **4.** (antes de 'a') [expresa valores, grados]: **estamos a veinte grados** it's twenty degrees here; **están a dos euros el kilo** they're two euros a kilo - **5.** [hallarse listo] to be ready; **¿aún no está ese trabajo?** is that piece of work still not ready? - **6.** [servir]: **estar para** to be (there) for; **para eso están los amigos** that's what friends are for - **7.** (antes de gerundio) [expresa duración] to be; **están golpeando la puerta** they're banging on the door - **8.** (antes de sin + infinitivo) [expresa negación]: **estoy sin dormir desde ayer** I haven't slept since yesterday; **está sin acabar** it's not finished - **9.** [faltar]: **eso está aún por escribir** that has yet to be written - **10.** [hallarse a punto de]: **estar por hacer algo** to be on the verge of doing sthg - **11.** [expresa disposición]: **estar para algo** to be in the mood for sthg. ◇ *v cop* - **1.** (antes de adj) [expresa cualidad, estado] to be; **los pasteles están ricos** the cakes are delicious; **esta calle está sucia** this street is dirty - **2.** (antes de con o sin + adj) [expresa estado] to be; **estamos sin agua** we have no water, we're without water - **3.** [expresa situación, acción]: **estar de: estar de camarero** to work as a waiter, to be a waiter; **estar de vacaciones** to be on holiday; **estar de viaje** to be on a trip; **estar de mudanza** to be (in the process of) moving - **4.** [expresa permanencia]: **estar en**

uso to be in use; **estar en guardia** to be on guard - **5.** [expresa apoyo, predilección]: **estar por** to be in favour of - **6.** [empresa ocupación] **estar como** to be; **está como cajera** she's a checkout girl - **7.** [consistir]: **estar en** to be, to lie in; **el problema está en la fecha** the problem is the date - **8.** [sentar - ropa]: **este traje te está bien** this suit looks good on you - **9.** (antes de 'que' + v) [expresa actitud]: **está que muerde porque ha suspendido** he's furious because he failed.

◆ estarse vprnl [permanecer] to stay; **te puedes estar con nosotros unos días** you can stay O spend a few days with us.

estárter (pl **estárters**), **starter** (pl **starters**) sm starter.

estatal adj state (antes de s).

estático, ca adj [inmóvil] stock-still.

estatización sf Amér nationalization.

estatizar vt Amér to nationalize.

estatua sf statue.

estatura sf height; **de estatura media** O **mediana de** of average O medium height.

estatus, status sm inv status.

estatuto sm [gen] statute; [de empresa] article (of association); [de ciudad] by-law.

este¹ ⬦ adj [posición, parte] east, eastern; [dirección, viento] easterly. ⬦ sm east; **los países del Este** the Eastern bloc countries.

este² (pl **estos**), **esta** adj demos - **1.** [gen] this (pl these); **esta camisa** this shirt; **este año** this year - **2.** fam despec that (pl those); **no soporto a la niña esta** I can't stand that girl.

éste (pl **éstos**), **ésta** pron demos - **1.** [gen] this one (pl these ones); **dame otro boli; éste no funciona** give me another pen; this one doesn't work; **aquellos cuadros no están mal, aunque éstos me gustan más** those paintings aren't bad, but I like these (ones) better; **ésta ha sido la semana más feliz de mi vida** this has been the happiest week of my life - **2.** [recién mencionado] the latter; **entraron Juan y Pedro, éste con un abrigo verde** Juan and Pedro came in, the latter wearing a green coat - **3.** fam despec: **éste es el que me pegó** this is the guy who hit me. **◆ en éstas** loc adv fam just then, at that very moment.

estela sf - **1.** [de barco] wake; [de avión, estrella fugaz] trail - **2.** fig [rastro] trail.

estelar adj - **1.** ASTRON stellar - **2.** CINE & TEATRO star (antes de s).

estepa sf steppe.

estera sf [tejido] matting; [alfombrilla] mat.

estéreo, stereo adj inv & sm stereo.

estereofónico, ca adj stereo.

estereotipo sm stereotype.

estéril adj - **1.** [persona, terreno, imaginación] sterile - **2.** [inútil] futile.

esterilizar vt to sterilize.

esterlina ⬦ **libra**.

esternón sm breastbone, sternum.

esteroides smpl steroids.

estética ⬦ **estético**.

esteticista, esthéticienne [esteti'θjen] sf beautician.

estético, ca adj aesthetic. **◆ estética** sf FILOS aesthetics (U).

esthéticienne = **esteticista**.

estiércol sm [excrementos] dung; [abono] manure.

estigma sm fig [deshonor] stigma.

estilarse vprnl fam to be in (fashion).

estilo sm - **1.** [gen] style; **al estilo de** in the style of; **estilo de vida** lifestyle - **2.** [en natación] stroke - **3.** GRAM speech; **estilo directo/indirecto** direct/indirect speech - **4.** loc: **algo por el estilo** something of the sort.

estilográfica sf fountain pen.

estima sf esteem, respect.

estimación sf - **1.** [aprecio] esteem, respect - **2.** [valoración] valuation - **3.** [en impuestos] assessment.

estimado, da adj [querido] esteemed, respected; **Estimado señor** Dear Sir.

estimar vt - **1.** [valorar - gen] to value; [- valor] to estimate - **2.** [apreciar] to think highly of - **3.** [creer] to consider.

estimulante ⬦ adj [que excita] stimulating. ⬦ sm stimulant.

estimular vt - **1.** [animar] to encourage - **2.** [excitar] to stimulate.

estímulo sm - **1.** [aliciente] incentive; [ánimo] encouragement - **2.** [de un órgano] stimulus.

estío sm culto summer.

estipulación sf - **1.** [acuerdo] agreement - **2.** DER stipulation.

estipular vt to stipulate.

estirado, da adj [persona - altanero] haughty; [- adusto] uptight.

estirar ⬦ vt - **1.** [alargar - gen] to stretch; [- cuello] to crane - **2.** [desarrugar] to straighten - **3.** fig [dinero etc] to make last; [discurso, tema] to spin out. ⬦ vi: **estirar (de)** to pull. **◆ estirarse** vprnl - **1.** [desperezarse] to stretch - **2.** [tumbarse] to stretch out.

estirón sm [acción] tug, pull.

estirpe sf stock, lineage.

estival adj summer (antes de s).

esto pron demos (neutro) this thing; **esto es tu regalo de cumpleaños** this is your birthday present; **esto que acabas de decir no tiene sentido** what you just said doesn't make sense; **esto de trabajar de noche no me gusta** I don't like this business of working at night; **esto es**

that is (to say). **a todo esto** *loc adv* meanwhile, in the meantime. **en esto** *loc adv* just then, at that very moment.

estofa *sf*: de baja estofa [gente] low-class; [cosas] poor-quality.

estofado *sm* stew.

estofar *vt* CULIN to stew.

estoicismo *sm* stoicism.

estoico, ca *adj* stoic, stoical.

estomacal *adj* [dolencia] stomach *(antes de s)*; [bebida] digestive.

estómago *sm* stomach; **revolver el estómago a alguien** to turn sb's stomach; **tener buen estómago** to be tough, to be able to stand a lot.

Estonia *n pr* Estonia.

estop = stop.

estorbar ◇ *vt* [obstaculizar] to hinder; [molestar] to bother. ◇ *vi* [estar en medio] to be in the way.

estorbo *sm* [obstáculo] hindrance; [molestia] nuisance.

estornudar *vi* to sneeze.

estos, tas ⊳ **este²**.

éstos, tas ⊳ **éste**.

estoy ⊳ **estar**.

estrabismo *sm* squint.

estrado *sm* platform.

estrafalario, ria *adj* outlandish, eccentric.

estragón *sm* tarragon.

estragos *smpl*: causar *O* hacer estragos en [físicos] to wreak havoc with; [morales] to destroy, to ruin.

estrambótico, ca *adj* outlandish.

estrangulador, ra *sm, f* strangler.

estrangular *vt* [ahogar] to strangle; MED to strangulate.

estraperlo *sm* black market; **de estraperlo** black market *(antes de s)*.

estratagema *sf* MIL stratagem; *fig* [astucia] artifice, trick.

estrategia *sf* strategy.

estratégico, ca *adj* strategic.

estrato *sm* fig & GEOL stratum.

estrechar *vt* - 1. [hacer estrecho - gen] to narrow; [- ropa] to take in - 2. *fig* [relaciones] to make closer - 3. [apretar] to squeeze, to hug; **estrechar la mano a alguien** to shake sb's hand. **estrecharse** *vprnl* [hacerse estrecho] to narrow.

estrechez *sf* - 1. [falta de anchura] narrowness; [falta de espacio] lack of space; [de ropa] tightness; **estrechez de miras** narrow-mindedness - 2. *fig* [falta de dinero] hardship; **pasar estrecheces** to be hard up - 3. [intimidad] closeness.

estrecho, cha *adj* - 1. [no ancho - gen] narrow; [- ropa] tight; [- habitación] cramped; **estrecho de miras** narrow-minded - 2. *fig* [íntimo] close. **estrecho** *sm* GEOGR strait.

estrella *sf* [gen] star; *fig* [destino] fate; **estrella de cine** film star *UK*, movie star *US*; **estrella fugaz** shooting star. **estrella de mar** *sf* starfish.

estrellado, da *adj* - 1. [con estrellas] starry - 2. [por la forma] star-shaped.

estrellar *vt* [arrojar] to smash. **estrellarse** *vprnl* [chocar]: **estrellarse (contra)** [gen] to smash (against); [avión, coche] to crash (into).

estrellón *sm* Amér crash.

estremecer *vt* to shake. **estremecerse** *vprnl*: **estremecerse (de)** [horror, miedo] to tremble *O* shudder (with); [frío] to shiver (with).

estremecimiento *sm* [de miedo] shudder; [de frío] shiver.

estrenar *vt* - 1. [gen] to use for the first time; [ropa] to wear for the first time; [piso] to move into - 2. CINE to release; TEATRO to premiere. **estrenarse** *vprnl* [persona] to make one's debut, to start.

estreno *sm* [de espectáculo] premiere, first night; [de cosa] first use; [en un empleo] debut.

estreñido, da *adj* constipated.

estreñimiento *sm* constipation.

estrépito *sm* [ruido] racket, din; *fig* [ostentación] fanfare.

estrepitoso, sa *adj* - 1. [gen] noisy; [aplausos] deafening - 2. [derrota] resounding; [fracaso] spectacular.

estrés, stress *sm inv* stress.

estría *sf* [gen] groove; [en la piel] stretch mark.

estribar **estribar en** *vi* to be based on, to lie in.

estribillo *sm* MÚS chorus; LITER refrain.

estribo *sm* - 1. [de montura] stirrup - 2. [de coche, tren] step - 3. *loc*: estar con un pie en el estribo to be ready to leave; **perder los estribos** to fly off the handle.

estribor *sm* starboard.

estricto, ta *adj* strict.

estridente *adj* - 1. [ruido] strident, shrill - 2. [color] garish, loud.

estrofa *sf* stanza, verse.

estropajo *sm* scourer.

estropear *vt* - 1. [averiar] to break - 2. [dañar] to damage - 3. [echar a perder] to ruin, to spoil. **estropearse** *vprnl* - 1. [máquina] to break down - 2. [comida] to go off, to spoil; [piel] to get damaged - 3. [plan] to fall through.

estropicio *sm*: hacer *O* causar un estropicio to wreak havoc.

estructura sf structure; **estructura profunda/ superficial** deep/surface structure.

estruendo sm - **1.** [estrépito] din, roar, [de trueno] crash - **2.** [alboroto] uproar, tumult.

estrujar vt - **1.** [limón] to squeeze; [trapo, ropa] to wring (out); [papel] to screw up; [caja] to crush - **2.** [abrazar - persona, mano] to squeeze - **3.** fig [sacar partido de] to bleed dry.

estuario sm estuary.

estuche sm - **1.** [caja] case; [de joyas] jewellery box - **2.** [utensilios] set.

estuco sm stucco.

estudiante smf student.

estudiantil adj student (antes de s).

estudiar <> vt [gen] to study. <> vi to study; **estudiar para médico** to be studying to be a doctor.

estudio sm - **1.** [gen] study; **estar en estudio** to be under consideration; **estudio de mercado** [técnica] market research; [investigación] market survey - **2.** [oficina] study; [de fotógrafo, pintor] studio - **3.** [apartamento] studio apartment - **4.** (gen pl) CINE, RADIO & TV studio. ◆ **estudios** smpl [serie de cursos] studies; [educación] education (U); **dar estudios a alguien** to pay for sb's education; **tener estudios** to be well-educated; **estudios primarios/ secundarios** primary/secondary education.

estudioso, sa adj studious.

estufa sf - **1.** [calefacción] heater, fire; **estufa de gas** gas heater; **estufa eléctrica** electric heater - **2.** Col & Méx [cocina] cooker.

estupefaciente sm narcotic, drug.

estupefacto, ta adj astonished.

estupendamente adv wonderfully; **estoy estupendamente** I feel wonderful.

estupendo, da adj great, fantastic. ◆ **estupendo** interj: ¡estupendo! great!

estupidez sf stupidity; **decir/hacer una estupidez** to say/do sthg stupid.

estúpido, da adj stupid.

estupor sm astonishment.

esturión sm sturgeon.

estuviera etc ▷ **estar**.

esvástica sf swastika.

ETA (abrev de Euskadi ta Askatasuna) sf ETA.

etapa sf stage; **por etapas** in stages.

etarra smf member of ETA.

etc. (abrev de etcétera) etc.

etcétera adv etcetera.

etéreo, a adj fig ethereal.

eternidad sf eternity; **hace una eternidad que no la veo** fam it's ages since I last saw her.

eterno, na adj eternal; fam [larguísimo] never-ending, interminable.

ético, ca adj ethical. ◆ **ética** sf [moralidad] ethics pl.

etílico, ca adj QUÍM ethyl (antes de s); **intoxicación etílica** alcohol poisoning.

etimología sf etymology.

Etiopía n pr Ethiopia.

etiqueta sf - **1.** [gen & INFORM] label; **etiqueta autoadhesiva** sticky label; **etiqueta del precio** price tag - **2.** [ceremonial] etiquette; **de etiqueta** formal; **vestir de etiqueta** to wear formal dress.

etiquetar vt lit & fig to label; **etiquetar a alguien de algo** to label sb sthg.

etnia sf ethnic group.

étnico, ca adj ethnic.

EUA (abrev de Estados Unidos de América) smpl USA.

eucalipto sm eucalyptus.

eucaristía sf: **la Eucaristía** the Eucharist.

eufemismo sm euphemism.

euforia sf euphoria, elation.

eufórico, ca adj euphoric, elated.

eunuco sm eunuch.

euro sm [unidad monetaria] euro.

Eurocámara sf European Parliament.

eurocheque sm eurocheque UK, eurocheck US.

eurócrata adj & smf Eurocrat.

eurodiputado, da sm, f Euro-M.P., M.E.P.

Europa n pr Europe.

europeo, a adj & sm, f European.

Euskadi n pr the Basque Country.

euskara, euskera sm Basque.

eutanasia sf euthanasia.

evacuación sf evacuation.

evacuar vt [gen] to evacuate; [vientre] to empty, to void.

evadir vt to evade; [respuesta, peligro] to avoid. ◆ **evadirse** vprnl: **evadirse (de)** to escape (from).

evaluación sf - **1.** [gen] evaluation - **2.** [EDUC - examen] assessment.

evaluar vt to evaluate, to assess.

evangélico, ca adj & sm, f evangelical.

evangelio sm gospel.

evaporar vt to evaporate. ◆ **evaporarse** vprnl [líquido etc] to evaporate.

evasión sf - **1.** [huida] escape - **2.** [de dinero]: **evasión de capitales** O **divisas** capital flight; **evasión fiscal** tax evasion - **3.** [entretenimiento] amusement, recreation; [escapismo] escapism; **de evasión** escapist.

evasivo, va adj evasive. ◆ **evasiva** sf evasive answer.

evento *sm* event.

eventual *adj* - **1.** [no fijo - trabajador] temporary, casual; [- gastos] incidental - **2.** [posible] possible.

eventualidad *sf* - **1.** [temporalidad] temporariness - **2.** [hecho incierto] eventuality; [posibilidad] possibility.

evidencia *sf* - **1.** [prueba] evidence, proof; **negar la evidencia** to refuse to accept the obvious; **rendirse ante la evidencia** to bow to the evidence - **2.** [claridad] obviousness; **poner algo en evidencia** to demonstrate sthg; **poner a alguien en evidencia** to show sb up.

evidenciar *vt* to show, to demonstrate. ➡ **evidenciarse** *vprnl* to be obvious O evident.

evidente *adj* evident, obvious.

evitar *vt* [gen] to avoid; [desastre, accidente] to avert; **evitar hacer algo** to avoid doing sthg; **evitar que alguien haga algo** to prevent sb from doing sthg.

evocación *sf* recollection, evocation.

evocar *vt* [recordar] to evoke.

evolución *sf* - **1.** [gen] evolution; [de enfermedad] development, progress - **2.** MIL manoeuvre.

evolucionar *vi* - **1.** [gen] to evolve; [enfermedad] to develop, to progress; [cambiar] to change - **2.** MIL to carry out manoeuvres.

ex *prep* ex; **el ex presidente** the ex-president, the former president.

exacerbar *vt* - **1.** [agudizar] to exacerbate, to aggravate - **2.** [irritar] to irritate, to infuriate.

exactitud *sf* accuracy, precision.

exacto, ta *adj* - **1.** [justo - cálculo, medida] exact; **tres metros exactos** exactly three metres - **2.** [preciso] accurate, precise; [correcto] correct, right - **3.** [idéntico]: **exacto (a)** identical (to), exactly the same (as). ➡ **exacto** *interj*: **¡exacto!** exactly!, precisely!

exageración *sf* exaggeration; **este precio es una exageración** this price is over the top.

exagerado, da *adj* [gen] exaggerated; [persona] overly dramatic; [precio] exorbitant; [gesto] flamboyant.

exagerar *vt & vi* to exaggerate.

exaltado, da *adj* [jubiloso] elated; [acalorado - persona] worked up; [- discusión] heated; [excitable] hotheaded.

exaltar *vt* - **1.** [elevar] to promote, to raise - **2.** [glorificar] to exalt. ➡ **exaltarse** *vprnl* to get excited O worked up.

examen *sm* - **1.** [ejercicio] exam, examination; **presentarse a un examen** to sit an exam; **examen de conducir** driving test; **examen final/oral** final/oral (exam); **examen parcial** ≈ end-of-term exam - **2.** [indagación] consideration, examination; **someter algo a examen** to examine sthg, to subject sthg to examination.

examinar *vt* to examine. ➡ **examinarse** *vprnl* to sit O take an exam.

exánime *adj* - **1.** [muerto] dead - **2.** [desmayado] lifeless.

exasperar *vt* to exasperate. ➡ **exasperarse** *vprnl* to get exasperated.

excavación *sf* [lugar] dig, excavation.

excavar *vt* [gen] to dig; [en arqueología] to excavate.

excedencia *sf* leave (of absence); EDUC sabbatical; **excedencia por maternidad** maternity leave.

excedente <> *adj* [producción etc] surplus. <> *sm* COM surplus.

exceder *vt* to exceed, to surpass. ➡ **excederse** *vprnl* - **1.** [pasarse de la raya]: **excederse (en)** to go too far O overstep the mark (in) - **2.** [rebasar el límite]: **se excede en el peso** it's too heavy.

excelencia *sf* [cualidad] excellence; **por excelencia** par excellence. ➡ **Su Excelencia** *sm, f* His Excellency (f Her Excellency).

excelente *adj* excellent.

excelentísimo, ma *adj* most excellent.

excentricidad *sf* eccentricity.

excéntrico, ca *adj & sm, f* eccentric.

excepción *sf* exception; **la excepción confirma la regla** *prov* the exception proves the rule. ➡ **de excepción** *loc adj* exceptional.

excepcional *adj* exceptional.

excepto *adv* except (for).

exceptuar *vt*: **exceptuar (de)** [excluir] to exclude (from); [eximir] to exempt (from); **exceptuando a...** excluding...

excesivo, va *adj* excessive.

exceso *sm* [demasía] excess; **exceso de equipaje** excess baggage; **exceso de peso** [obesidad] excess weight.

excitación *sf* [nerviosismo] agitation; [por enfado, sexo] arousal.

excitado, da *adj* [nervioso] agitated; [por enfado, sexo] aroused.

excitante *sm* stimulant.

excitar *vt* - **1.** [inquietar] to upset, to agitate - **2.** [estimular - sentidos] to stimulate; [- apetito] to whet; [- pasión, curiosidad, persona] to arouse. ➡ **excitarse** *vprnl* [alterarse] to get worked up O excited.

exclamación *sf* [interjección] exclamation; [grito] cry.

exclamar *vt & vi* to exclaim, to shout out.

excluir *vt* to exclude; [hipótesis, opción] to rule out; [hacer imposible] to preclude; **excluir a alguien de algo** to exclude sb from sthg.

exclusión *sf* exclusion.

exclusivo, va *adj* exclusive. ◆ **exclusiva** *sf* - 1. PRENSA exclusive - 2. COM exclusive O sole right.

Excma. *abrev de* **excelentísimo**.

Excmo. *abrev de* **excelentísimo**.

excombatiente *smf* ex-serviceman (*f* ex-servicewoman) *UK*, war veteran *US*.

excomulgar *vt* to excommunicate.

excomunión *sf* excommunication.

excremento *(gen pl) sm* excrement *(U)*.

excursión *sf* [viaje] excursion, trip; **ir de excursión** to go on an outing O a trip.

excursionista *smf* [en la ciudad] sightseer, tripper; [en el campo] rambler; [en la montaña] hiker.

excusa *sf* - 1. [gen] excuse; **¡nada de excusas!** no excuses!; **buscar una excusa** to look for an excuse; **dar excusas** to make excuses - 2. [petición de perdón] apology; **presentar uno sus excusas** to apologize, to make one's excuses.

excusar *vt* [disculpar a] to excuse; [disculparse por] to apologize for. ◆ **excusarse** *vprnl* to apologize.

exento, ta *adj* exempt; **exento de** [sin] free from, without; [eximido de] exempt from; **exento de impuestos** tax free.

exequias *sfpl* funeral *sing*, funeral rites.

exhalación *sf* [emanación] exhalation, vapour; [suspiro] breath.

exhalar *vt* - 1. [aire] to exhale, to breathe out; [suspiros] to heave - 2. [olor] to give off - 3. [quejas] to utter.

exhaustivo, va *adj* exhaustive.

exhausto, ta *adj* exhausted.

exhibición *sf* - 1. [demostración] show, display - 2. [deportiva, artística etc] exhibition - 3. [de películas] showing.

exhibir *vt* - 1. [exponer - cuadros, fotografías] to exhibit; [- modelos] to show; [- productos] to display - 2. [lucir - joyas, cualidades etc] to show off - 3. [película] to show, to screen.

exhortación *sf* exhortation.

exhortar *vt*: **exhortar a alguien a** to exhort sb to.

exigencia *sf* - 1. [obligación] demand, requirement - 2. [capricho] fussiness *(U)*.

exigente *adj* demanding.

exigir *vt* - 1. [gen] to demand; **exigir algo de** O **a alguien** to demand sthg from sb - 2. [requerir, necesitar] to require.

exiguo, gua *adj* [escaso] meagre, paltry; [pequeño] minute.

exiliado, da ◇ *adj* exiled, in exile. ◇ *sm, f* exile.

exiliar *vt* to exile. ◆ **exiliarse** *vprnl* to go into exile.

exilio *sm* exile.

eximir *vt*: **eximir (de)** to exempt (from).

existencia *sf* existence. ◆ **existencias** *sfpl* COM stock *(U)*; **reponer las existencias** to restock.

existir *vi* to exist; **existe mucha pobreza** there is a lot of poverty.

éxito *sm* - 1. [gen] success; **con éxito** successfully; **tener éxito** to be successful - 2. [libro] bestseller; [canción] hit.

exitoso, sa *adj* successful.

éxodo *sm* exodus.

exorbitante *adj* exorbitant.

exorcizar *vt* to exorcize.

exótico, ca *adj* exotic.

expandir *vt* to spread; FÍS to expand. ◆ **expandirse** *vprnl* to spread; FÍS to expand.

expansión *sf* - 1. FÍS expansion - 2. ECON growth; **en expansión** expanding - 3. [recreo] relaxation, amusement.

expansionarse *vprnl* - 1. [desahogarse]: **expansionarse (con)** to open one's heart (to) - 2. [divertirse] to relax, to let off steam - 3. [desarrollarse] to expand.

expansivo, va *adj* - 1. [gen] expansive - 2. [persona] open, frank.

expatriar *vt* to expatriate; [exiliar] to exile. ◆ **expatriarse** *vprnl* to emigrate; [exiliarse] to go into exile.

expectación *sf* expectancy, anticipation.

expectativa *sf* [espera] expectation; [esperanza] hope; [perspectiva] prospect; **estar a la expectativa** to wait and see; **estar a la expectativa de** [atento] to be on the lookout for; [a la espera] to be hoping for; **expectativa de vida** life expectancy.

expedición *sf* [viaje, grupo] expedition; **expedición militar** military expedition; **expedición de salvamento** rescue mission.

expediente *sm* - 1. [documentación] documents *pl*; [ficha] file - 2. [historial] record; **expediente académico** academic record *UK*, transcript *US* - 3. [investigación] inquiry; **abrir expediente a alguien** [castigar] to take disciplinary action against sb; [investigar] to start proceedings against sb.

expedir *vt* [carta, pedido] to send, to dispatch; [pasaporte, decreto] to issue; [contrato, documento] to draw up.

expedito, ta *adj* clear, free.

expeler *vt* [humo - suj: persona] to blow out; [- suj: chimenea, tubo de escape] to emit; [- suj: extractor, volcán] to expel.

expendedor, ra *sm, f* dealer; [de lotería] seller, vendor.

expendeduría *sf* [de tabaco] tobacconist's *UK*, cigar store *US*.

expensas *sfpl* [gastos] expenses, costs. ➤ **a expensas de** *loc prep* at the expense of.

experiencia *sf* [gen] experience; **por (propia) experiencia** from (one's own) experience.

experimentado, da *adj* [persona] experienced; [método] tried and tested.

experimentar *vt* - **1.** [gen] to experience; [derrota, pérdidas] to suffer - **2.** [probar] to test; [hacer experimentos con] to experiment with O on.

experimento *sm* experiment.

experto, ta *adj* & *sm, f* expert; **ser experto en la materia** to be a specialist in the subject; **ser experto en hacer algo** to be an expert at doing sthg.

expiar *vt* to atone for, to expiate.

expirar *vi* to expire.

explanada *sf* [llanura] flat O level ground (U).

explayar *vt* to extend. ➤ **explayarse** *vprnl* - **1.** [divertirse] to amuse o.s., to enjoy o.s. - **2.** [hablar mucho] to talk at length - **3.** [desahogarse]: **explayarse (con)** to pour out one's heart (to).

explicación *sf* explanation; **dar/pedir explicaciones** to give/demand an explanation.

explicar *vt* [gen] to explain; [teoría] to expound. ➤ **explicarse** *vprnl* - **1.** [comprender] to understand; **no me lo explico** I can't understand it - **2.** [dar explicaciones] to explain o.s. - **3.** [expresarse] to make o.s. understood.

explícito, ta *adj* explicit.

exploración *sf* [gen & MED] exploration.

explorador, ra *sm, f* explorer; [scout] boy scout (*f* girl guide).

explorar *vt* - **1.** [gen] to explore; MIL to scout - **2.** MED to examine; [internamente] to explore, to probe.

explosión *sf* lit & fig explosion; **hacer explosión** to explode.

explosivo, va *adj* [gen] explosive. ➤ **explosivo** *sm* explosive.

explotación *sf* - **1.** [acción] exploitation; [de fábrica etc] running; [de yacimiento minero] mining; [agrícola] farming; [de petróleo] drilling - **2.** [instalaciones]: **explotación agrícola** farm.

explotar ◇ *vt* - **1.** [gen] to exploit - **2.** [fábrica] to run, to operate; [terreno] to farm; [mina] to work. ◇ *vi* to explode.

expoliar *vt* to pillage, to plunder.

exponer *vt* - **1.** [gen] to expose - **2.** [teoría] to expound; [ideas, propuesta] to set out, to explain - **3.** [cuadro, obra] to exhibit; [objetos en vitrinas] to display - **4.** [vida, prestigio] to risk.

exportación *sf* - **1.** [acción] export - **2.** [mercancías] exports *pl*.

exportar *vt* COM & INFORM to export.

exposición *sf* - **1.** [gen & FOTO] exposure - **2.** [de arte etc] exhibition; [de objetos en vitrina] display; **exposición universal** world fair - **3.** [de teoría] exposition; [de ideas, propuesta] setting out, explanation.

expositor, ra *sm, f* [de arte] exhibitor; [de teoría] exponent.

exprés ◇ *adj* - **1.** [tren] express - **2.** [café] espresso. ◇ *sm* = **expreso**.

expresamente *adv* [a propósito] expressly; [explícitamente] explicitly.

expresar *vt* to express; [suj: rostro] to show.

expresión *sf* expression.

expresivo, va *adj* expressive; [cariñoso] affectionate.

expreso, sa *adj* [explícito] specific; [deliberado] express; [claro] clear. ➤ **expreso** ◇ *sm* - **1.** [tren] express train - **2.** [café] expresso. ◇ *adv* on purpose, expressly.

exprimidor *sm* squeezer.

exprimir *vt* [fruta] to squeeze; [zumo] to squeeze out.

expropiar *vt* to expropriate.

expuesto, ta ◇ *pp* ➡ **exponer**. ◇ *adj* - **1.** [dicho] stated, expressed - **2.** [desprotegido]: **expuesto (a)** exposed (to) - **3.** [arriesgado] dangerous, risky - **4.** [exhibido] on display.

expulsar *vt* - **1.** [persona - de clase, local, asociación] to throw out; [- de colegio] to expel - **2.** DEP to send off - **3.** [humo] to emit, to give off.

expulsión *sf* [gen] expulsion; [de clase, local, asociación] throwing-out; DEP sending-off.

exquisitez *sf* [cualidad] exquisiteness.

exquisito, ta *adj* exquisite; [comida] delicious, sublime.

extasiarse *vprnl*: **extasiarse (ante** O **con)** to go into ecstasies (over).

éxtasis *sm inv* ecstasy.

extender *vt* - **1.** [desplegar - tela, plano, alas] to spread (out); [- brazos, piernas] to stretch out - **2.** [esparcir - mantequilla] to spread; [- pintura] to smear; [- objetos etc] to spread out - **3.** [ampliar - castigo, influencia etc] to extend - **4.** [documento] to draw up; [cheque] to make out; [pasaporte, certificado] to issue. ➤ **extenderse** *vprnl* - **1.** [ocupar]: **extenderse (por)** to stretch O extend across - **2.** [hablar mucho]: **extenderse (en)** to enlarge O expand (on) - **3.** [durar] to extend, to last - **4.** [difundirse]: **extenderse (por)** to spread (across) - **5.** [tenderse] to stretch out.

extensión *sf* - **1.** [superficie - de terreno etc] area, expanse - **2.** [amplitud - de país etc] size; [- de conocimientos] extent - **3.** [duración] duration, length - **4.** [sentido - de concepto, palabra] range of meaning; **en toda la extensión de la palabra** in every sense of the word - **5.** INFORM Í, INNIMINARIALIÓN

extensivo, **va** adj extensive.

extenso, **sa** adj extensive; [país] vast; [libro, película] long.

extenuar vt to exhaust completely.

exterior ◇ adj - **1.** [de fuera] outside; [capa] outer, exterior - **2.** [visible] outward - **3.** [extranjero] foreign. ◇ sm - **1.** [superficie] outside; **en el exterior** outside - **2.** [extranjero] foreign countries pl; **en el exterior** abroad - **3.** [aspecto] appearance. ⬥ **exteriores** smpl CINE outside shots; **rodar en exteriores** to film on location.

exteriorizar vt to show, to reveal.

exterminar vt [aniquilar] to exterminate.

exterminio sm extermination.

externalización sf outsourcing.

externalizar vt to outsource.

externo, **na** adj - **1.** [gen] external; [parte, capa] outer; [influencia] outside; [signo, aspecto] outward - **2.** [alumno] day (antes de s).

extinción sf [gen] extinction; [de esperanzas] loss.

extinguir vt [incendio] to put out, to extinguish; [raza] to wipe out; [afecto, entusiasmo] to put an end to. ⬥ **extinguirse** vprnl [fuego, luz] to go out; [animal, raza] to become extinct; [ruido] to die out; [afecto] to die.

extinto, **ta** adj extinguished; [animal, volcán] extinct.

extintor sm fire extinguisher.

extirpar vt [tumor] to remove; [muela] to extract; fig to eradicate.

extorsión sf - **1.** [molestia] trouble, bother - **2.** DER extortion.

extorsionista smf extortionist.

extra ◇ adj - **1.** [adicional] extra - **2.** [de gran calidad] top quality, superior. ◇ smf CINE extra. ◇ sm [gasto etc] extra. ◇ sf ▷ **paga**.

extracción sf - **1.** [gen] extraction - **2.** [en sorteos] draw - **3.** [de carbón] mining.

extracto sm - **1.** [resumen] summary, résumé; **extracto de cuentas** statement (of account) - **2.** [concentrado] extract.

extraditar vt to extradite.

extraer vt: **extraer (de)** [gen] to extract (from); [sangre] to draw (from); [carbón] to mine (from); [conclusiones] to come to O draw (from).

extralimitarse vprnl fig to go too far.

extranjero, **ra** ◇ adj foreign. ◇ sm, f [persona] foreigner. ⬥ **extranjero** sm [territorio] foreign countries pl; **estar en el/ir al extranjero** to be/go abroad.

extrañar vt - **1.** [sorprender] to surprise; **me extraña (que digas esto)** I'm surprised (that you should say that) - **2.** [echar de menos] to miss ⬥ **extrañarse de** vprnl [sorprenderse de] to be surprised at.

extrañeza sf [sorpresa] surprise.

extraño, **ña** ◇ adj - **1.** [raro] strange; **¡qué extraño!** how odd O strange! - **2.** [ajeno] detached, uninvolved - **3.** MED foreign. ◇ sm, f stranger.

extraoficial adj unofficial.

extraordinario, **ria** adj - **1.** [gen] extraordinary; **no tiene nada de extraordinario** there's nothing extraordinary about that - **2.** [gastos] additional; [edición, suplemento] special - **3.** ▷ **paga**. ⬥ **extraordinario** sm PRENSA special edition.

extraparlamentario, **ria** adj non-parliamentary.

extrapolar vt to generalize about.

extrarradio sm outskirts pl, suburbs pl.

extraterrestre adj & smf extraterrestrial.

extravagancia sf eccentricity.

extravagante adj eccentric, outlandish.

extravertido, **da**, **extrovertido**, **da** adj & sm, f extrovert.

extraviado, **da** adj [perdido] lost; [animal] stray.

extraviar vt - **1.** [objeto] to lose, to mislay - **2.** [excursionista] to mislead. ⬥ **extraviarse** vprnl - **1.** [persona] to get lost - **2.** [objeto] to go missing.

extravío sm [pérdida] loss, mislaying.

extremado, **da** adj extreme.

extremar vt to maximize. ⬥ **extremarse** vprnl to take great pains O care.

extremaunción sf extreme unction.

extremidad sf [extremo] end. ⬥ **extremidades** sfpl ANAT extremities.

extremista adj & smf extremist.

extremo, **ma** adj [gen] extreme; [en el espacio] far, furthest. ⬥ **extremo** sm - **1.** [punta] end - **2.** [límite] extreme; **en último extremo** as a last resort; **ir** O **pasar de un extremo al otro** to go from one extreme to the other; **ser el extremo opuesto** to be the complete opposite.

extrovertido, **da** = **extravertido**.

exuberancia sf exuberance.

exuberante adj exuberant.

exudar vt to exude, to ooze.

exultante adj exultant.

eyaculación sf ejaculation.

eyacular vi to ejaculate.

F

f, F *sf* [letra] f, F. ➤ **23 F** *sm 23rd February, day of the failed coup d'état in Spain in 1981.*

f. - 1. (*abrev de* factura) inv. - 2. (*abrev de folio*) f.

fa *sm* MÚS F; [en solfeo] fa.

fabada *sf Asturian stew made of beans, pork sausage and bacon.*

fábrica *sf* [establecimiento] factory; **fábrica de cerveza** brewery; **fábrica de conservas** canning plant, cannery; **fábrica de papel** paper mill.

fabricación *sf* manufacture; **de fabricación casera** home-made; **fabricación en serie** mass production.

fabricante *smf* manufacturer.

fabricar *vt* - 1. [producir] to manufacture, to make - 2. [construir] to build, to construct - 3. *fig* [inventar] to fabricate, to make up.

fábula *sf* LITER fable; [leyenda] legend.

fabuloso, sa *adj* - 1. [ficticio] mythical - 2. [muy bueno] fabulous, fantastic.

facción *sf* POLIT faction. ➤ **facciones** *sfpl* [rasgos] features.

faceta *sf* facet.

facha *sf* - 1. [aspecto] appearance, look - 2. [mamarracho] mess; **vas hecho una facha** you look a mess.

fachada *sf* ARQUIT façade.

facial *adj* facial.

fácil *adj* - 1. [gen] easy; **fácil de hacer** easy to do - 2. [probable] likely.

facilidad *sf* - 1. [simplicidad] ease, easiness; **con facilidad** easily; **con la mayor facilidad** with the greatest of ease - 2. [aptitud] aptitude; **tener facilidad para algo** to have a gift for sthg. ➤ **facilidades** *sfpl* [comodidades] facilities; **dar facilidades a alguien para algo** to make sthg easy for sb; **facilidades de pago** easy (payment) terms.

facilitar *vt* - 1. [simplificar] to facilitate, to make easy; [posibilitar] to make possible - 2. [proporcionar] to provide; **facilitar algo a alguien** to provide O supply sb with sthg.

facsímil, facsímile *sm* facsimile.

factible *adj* feasible.

fáctico ▷ **poder**[1].

factor *sm* [gen] factor; **factor humano** human factor; **factor de riesgo** risk factor.

factoría *sf* [fábrica] factory.

factura *sf* - 1. [por mercancías, trabajo realizado] invoice; **factura pro forma** O **proforma** COM proforma invoice - 2. [de gas, teléfono] bill; [en tienda, hotel] bill - 3. *Arg* [repostería] cakes and pastries.

facturación *sf* - 1. [ventas] turnover *UK*, net revenue *US* - 2. [de equipaje - en aeropuerto] checking-in; [- en estación] registration; **mostrador de facturación** check-in desk.

facturar *vt* - 1. [cobrar]: **facturarle a alguien algo** to invoice O bill sb for sthg - 2. [vender] to turn over - 3. [equipaje - en aeropuerto] to check in; [- en estación] to register.

facultad *sf* - 1. [capacidad & UNIV] faculty; **facultades mentales** mental faculties - 2. [poder] power, right.

facultativo, va ◇ *adj* - 1. [voluntario] optional - 2. [médico] medical. ◇ *sm, f* doctor.

faena *sf* [tarea] task, work (U); **estar en plena faena** to be hard at work.

faenar *vi* to fish.

fagot *sm* [instrumento] bassoon.

faisán *sm* pheasant.

faja *sf* - 1. [prenda de mujer, terapéutica] corset; [banda] sash, cummerbund - 2. [de terreno - pequeña] strip; [- grande] belt.

fajo *sm* [de billetes, papel] wad; [de leña, cañas] bundle.

falacia *sf* deceit, trick.

falda *sf* - 1. [prenda] skirt; **estar pegado** O **cosido a las faldas de su madre** to to be tied to one's mother's apron strings; **falda escocesa** kilt; **falda pantalón** culottes *pl*; **falda plisada** O **tableada** pleated skirt - 2. [de montaña] slope, mountainside.

faldón *sm* [de ropa] tail; [de cortina, mesa camilla] folds *pl*.

falla *sf* [gen & GEOL] fault. ➤ **fallas** *sfpl* [fiesta] *celebrations in Valencia during which cardboard figures are burnt.*

fallar ◇ *vt* - 1. [sentenciar] to pass sentence on; [premio] to award - 2. [equivocar - respuesta] to get wrong; [- tiro] to miss. ◇ *vi* - 1. [equivocarse] to get it wrong; [no acertar] to miss - 2. [fracasar, flaquear] to fail; [plan] to go wrong - 3. [decepcionar]: **fallarle a alguien** to let sb down - 4. [sentenciar]: **fallar a favor/en contra de** to find in favour of/against.

fallecer *vi* to pass away, to die.

fallecimiento *sm* decease, death.

fallo *sm* - 1. [error] mistake; DEP miss; **¡qué fallo!** what a stupid mistake!; **fallo humano** human error - 2. [sentencia - de juez, jurado] verdict.

falo *sm* phallus.

falsear *vt* [hechos, historia] to falsify, to distort; [moneda, firma] to forge.

falsedad *sf* - 1. [falta de verdad, autenticidad] falseness - 2. [mentira] falsehood.

falsete *sm* falsetto.

falsificar *vt* to forge.

falso, sa *adj* - 1. [rumor, excusa etc] false, untrue - 2. [dinero, firma, cuadro] forged; [joyas] fake; **jurar en falso** to commit perjury - 3. [hipócrita] deceitful.

falta *sf* - 1. [carencia] lack; **hacer falta** to be necessary; **me hace falta suerte** I need some luck; **por falta de** for want O lack of - 2. [escasez] shortage - 3. [ausencia] absence; **echar en falta algo/a alguien** [notar la ausencia de] to notice that sthg/sb is missing; [echar de menos] to miss sthg/sb - 4. [imperfección] fault; [error] mistake; **falta de educación** bad manners *pl*; **falta de ortografía** spelling mistake; **falta de respeto** disrespect, lack of respect - 5. DEP foul; [en tenis] fault; **doble falta** double fault - 6. DER offence. ⟐ **a falta de** *loc prep* in the absence of; **a falta de pan, buenas son tortas** *prov* half a loaf is better than none. ⟐ **sin falta** *loc adv* without fail.

faltante *sm Amér* deficit.

faltar *vi* - 1. [no haber] to be lacking, to be needed; **falta aire** there's not enough air; **falta sal** it needs a bit of salt - 2. [estar ausente] to be absent O missing; **falta Elena** Elena is missing - 3. [carecer]: **le faltan las fuerzas** he lacks O doesn't have the strength - 4. [hacer falta] to be necessary; **me falta tiempo** I need time - 5. [quedar]: **falta un mes para las vacaciones** there's a month to go till the holidays; **sólo te falta firmar** all you have to do is sign; **¿cuánto falta para Leeds?** how much further is it to Leeds?; **falta mucho por hacer** there is still a lot to be done; **falta poco para que llegue** it won't be long till he arrives - 6. *loc*: **¡no faltaba O faltaría más!** [asentimiento] of course!; [rechazo] that tops it all!, that's a bit much! ⟐ **faltar a** *vi* - 1. [palabra, promesa] to break, not to keep; [deber, obligación] to neglect - 2. [cita, trabajo] not to turn up at; **¡no faltes (a la cita)!** don't miss it!, be there! - 3. [no respetar] to be disrespectful towards; **faltar a alguien en algo** to offend sb in sthg.

falto, ta *adj*: **falto de** lacking in, short of.

fama *sf* - 1. [renombre] fame; **tener fama** to be famous - 2. [reputación] reputation; **cría fama y échate a dormir** *prov* build yourself a good reputation, then you can rest on your laurels.

famélico, ca *adj* starving, famished.

familia *sf* family; **en familia** in private; **ser de buena familia** to come from a good family; **ser como de la familia** to be like one of the family; **familia de acogida** host family; **familia monoparental** one-parent family; **familia política** in-laws *pl*; **familia real** royal family.

familiar ⟐ *adj* - 1. [de familia] family *(antes de s)* - 2. [en el trato - agradable] friendly; [- en demasía] overly familiar - 3. [lenguaje, estilo] informal - 4. [conocido] familiar. ⟐ *smf* relative, relation.

familiaridad *sf* familiarity.

familiarizar *vt*: **familiarizar (con)** to familiarize (with). ⟐ **familiarizarse** *vprnl*: **familiarizarse con** [estudiar] to familiarize o.s. with; [acostumbrarse a] to get used to.

famoso, sa *adj* famous.

fanático, ca ⟐ *adj* fanatical. ⟐ *sm, f* [gen] fanatic; DEP fan.

fanatismo *sm* fanaticism.

fanfarria *sf* - 1. *fam* [jactancia] bragging - 2. [pieza musical] fanfare; [banda] brass band.

fanfarrón, ona *adj* boastful.

fango *sm* mud.

fantasear *vi* to fantasize.

fantasía *sf* [imaginación] imagination; [cosa imaginada] fantasy; **de fantasía** [ropa] fancy; [bisutería] imitation.

fantasma ⟐ *sm* [espectro] ghost, phantom. ⟐ *smf fam* [fanfarrón] show-off.

fantástico, ca *adj* fantastic.

fantoche *sm* - 1. [títere] puppet - 2. [mamarracho] (ridiculous) sight.

fardo *sm* bundle.

farfullar *vt & vi* to gabble, to splutter.

faringitis *sf inv* sore throat.

farmacéutico, ca ⟐ *adj* pharmaceutical. ⟐ *sm, f* chemist, pharmacist.

farmacia *sf* [establecimiento] chemist's (shop) *UK*, pharmacy, drugstore *US*; **farmacia de turno** O **de guardia** duty chemist's.

fármaco *sm* medicine, drug.

faro *sm* - 1. [para barcos] lighthouse - 2. [de coche] headlight, headlamp; **faro antiniebla** foglamp.

farol *sm* [farola] street lamp O light; [linterna] lantern, lamp.

farola *sf* [farol] street lamp O light; [poste] lamppost.

farsa *sf lit & fig* farce.

farsante *adj* deceitful.

fascículo *sm* part, instalment *(of serialization)*.

fascinante *adj* fascinating.

fascinar *vt* to fascinate.

fascismo *sm* fascism.

fascista *adj & smf* fascist.

fase *sf* phase; **en fase terminal** in terminal phase.

fastidiado, da *adj* [de salud] ill; **ando fastidiado del estómago** I've got a bad stomach.

fastidiar vt - **1.** [estropear - fiesta etc] to spoil, to ruin; [- máquina, objeto etc] to break - **2.** [molestar] to annoy, to bother. ◆ **fastidiarse** vprnl - **1.** [estropearse - fiesta etc] to be ruined; [- máquina] to break down - **2.** [aguantarse] to put up with it.

fastidio sm - **1.** [molestia] nuisance, bother; ¡qué fastidio! what a nuisance! - **2.** [enfado] annoyance.

fastidioso, sa adj [molesto] annoying.

fastuoso, sa adj lavish, sumptuous.

fatal ◇ adj - **1.** [mortal] fatal - **2.** [muy malo] terrible, awful - **3.** [inevitable] inevitable. ◇ adv terribly; **pasarlo fatal** to have an awful time; **sentirse fatal** to feel terrible.

fatalidad sf - **1.** [destino] fate, destiny - **2.** [desgracia] misfortune.

fatalismo sm fatalism.

fatídico, ca adj fateful, ominous.

fatiga sf [cansancio] tiredness, fatigue. ◆ **fatigas** sfpl [penas] hardships.

fatigar vt to tire, to weary. ◆ **fatigarse** vprnl to get tired.

fatigoso, sa adj tiring, fatiguing.

fatuo, tua adj - **1.** [necio] fatuous, foolish - **2.** [engreído] conceited.

fauna sf fauna.

favor sm favour; **a favor de** in favour of; **hacerle un favor a alguien** [ayudar a] to do sb a favour; fam fig [acostarse con] to go to bed with sb; **pedir un favor a alguien** to ask sb a favour; **tener a O en su favor a alguien** to enjoy sb's support. ◆ **por favor** loc adv please.

favorable adj favourable; **ser favorable a algo** to be in favour of sthg.

favorecer vt - **1.** [gen] to favour; [ayudar] to help, to assist - **2.** [sentar bien] to suit.

favoritismo sm favouritism.

favorito, ta adj & sm, f favourite.

fax sm inv - **1.** [aparato] fax (machine); **mandar algo por fax** to fax sthg - **2.** [documento] fax.

fayuquero, ra sm, f Méx fam smuggler.

faz sf culto - **1.** [cara] countenance, face - **2.** [del mundo, de la tierra] face.

fe sf - **1.** [gen] faith; **hacer algo de buena fe** to do sthg in good faith; **tener fe en** to have faith in, to believe in - **2.** [documento] certificate; **fe de bautismo** certificate of baptism; **fe de erratas** errata pl - **3.** loc: **dar fe de que** to testify that.

fealdad sf [de rostro etc] ugliness.

febrero sm February; ver también **septiembre**.

febril adj feverish; fig [actividad] hectic.

fecha sf [gen] date; [momento actual] current date; **a partir de esta fecha** from today; **hasta la fecha** to date, so far; **fecha de caducidad** [de alimentos] sell-by date; [de carne, pasaporte] expiry date; [de medicamento] 'use before' date; **fecha de nacimiento** date of birth; **fecha tope** O **límite** deadline.

fechar vt to date.

fechoría sf bad deed, misdemeanour.

fécula sf starch (in food).

fecundación sf fertilization; **fecundación artificial** artificial insemination; **fecundación asistida** assisted fertilization; **fecundación in vitro** in vitro fertilization.

fecundar vt - **1.** [fertilizar] to fertilize - **2.** [hacer productivo] to make fertile.

fecundo, da adj [gen] fertile; [artista] prolific.

federación sf federation.

federal adj & smf federal.

federar vt to federate. ◆ **federarse** vprnl - **1.** [formar federación] to become O form a federation - **2.** [ingresar en federación] to join a federation.

felicidad sf happiness. ◆ **felicidades** interj: ¡felicidades! [gen] congratulations!; [en cumpleaños] happy birthday!

felicitación sf - **1.** [acción]: **felicitaciones** congratulations - **2.** [postal] greetings card; **felicitación de Navidad** Christmas card.

felicitar vt to congratulate; ¡te felicito! congratulations!; **felicitar a alguien por algo** to congratulate sb on sthg.

feligrés, esa sm, f parishioner.

felino, na adj feline.

feliz adj - **1.** [dichoso] happy; **hacer feliz a alguien** to make sb happy - **2.** [afortunado] lucky - **3.** [oportuno] timely.

felpa sf [de seda] plush; [de algodón] towelling.

felpudo sm doormat.

femenino, na adj [gen] feminine; BOT & ZOOL female. ◆ **femenino** sm GRAM feminine.

fémina sf woman, female.

feminismo sm feminism.

feminista adj & smf feminist.

fémur (pl fémures) sm femur, thighbone.

fénix sm inv [ave] phoenix.

fenomenal adj [magnífico] wonderful.

fenómeno ◇ sm [gen] phenomenon. ◇ adv fam brilliantly, fantastically; **pasarlo fenómeno** to have a great time. ◇ interj: ¡fenómeno! great!, terrific!

feo, a adj - **1.** [persona] ugly; **le tocó bailar con la más fea** he drew the short straw; **ser más feo que Picio** to be as ugly as sin - **2.** [aspecto, herida, conducta] nasty; **es feo escupir** it's rude to spit.

féretro sm coffin.

feria sf - **1.** [gen] fair; **feria (de muestras)** trade fair - **2.** [fiesta popular] festival.

feriado *sm Amér* (public) holiday.

fermentación *sf* fermentation.

fermentar *vt & vi* to ferment.

ferocidad *sf* ferocity, fierceness.

feroz *adj* - **1.** [animal, bestia] fierce, ferocious - **2.** *fig* [criminal, asesino] cruel, savage - **3.** *fig* [dolor, angustia] terrible.

férreo, a *adj lit & fig* iron *(antes de s)*.

ferretería *sf* ironmonger's (shop) *UK*, hardware store.

ferrocarril *sm* [sistema, medio] railway, railroad *US*; [tren] train; **por ferrocarril** by train.

ferroviario, ria *adj* railway *(antes de s) UK*, rail *(antes de s)*, railroad *(antes de s) US*.

ferry *sm* ferry.

fértil *adj lit & fig* fertile.

fertilidad *sf lit & fig* fertility.

fertilizante *sm* fertilizer.

fertilizar *vt* to fertilize.

ferviente *adj* fervent.

fervor *sm* fervour.

festejar *vt* [celebrar] to celebrate.

festejo *sm* [fiesta] party. ◆ **festejos** *smpl* [fiestas] public festivities.

festín *sm* banquet, feast.

festival *sm* festival.

festividad *sf* festivity.

festivo, va *adj* - **1.** [de fiesta] festive; **día festivo** (public) holiday - **2.** [alegre] cheerful, jolly; [chistoso] funny, witty.

fetiche *sm* fetish.

fétido, da *adj* fetid, foul-smelling.

feto *sm* foetus.

feudal *adj* feudal.

FF AA *(abrev de Fuerzas Armadas) sfpl* Spanish armed forces.

fiable *adj* [máquina] reliable; [persona] trustworthy.

fiador, ra *sm, f* guarantor, surety; **salir fiador por** to vouch for.

fiambre *sm* [comida] cold meat *UK*, cold cuts *US*.

fiambrera *sf* lunch *O* sandwich box.

fianza *sf* - **1.** [depósito] deposit - **2.** DER bail; **bajo fianza** on bail - **3.** [garantía] security, bond.

fiar ◇ *vt* COM to sell on credit. ◇ *vi* COM to sell on credit; **ser de fiar** to be trustworthy. ◆ **fiarse** *vprnl*: **¡no te fíes!** don't be too sure (about it)!; **fiarse de algo/alguien** to trust sthg/sb.

fibra *sf* [gen] fibre; [de madera] grain; **fibra de vidrio** fibreglass.

ficción *sf* [gen] fiction.

ficha *sf* - **1.** [tarjeta] (index) card; [con detalles personales] file, record card - **2.** [de guardarropa, aparcamiento] ticket - **3.** [de teléfono] token

- **4.** [de juego - gen] counter; [en ajedrez] piece; [en casino] chip; **mover ficha** to act - **5.** INFORM card.

fichaje *sm* DEP [contratación] signing (up); [importe] transfer fee.

fichar ◇ *vt* - **1.** [archivar] to note down on an index card, to file - **2.** [suj: policía] to put on police files *O* records - **3.** DEP to sign up. ◇ *vi* - **1.** [suj: trabajador - al entrar] to clock in; [- al salir] to clock out - **2.** DEP: **fichar (por)** to sign up (for).

fichero *sm* - **1.** [mueble] filing cabinet - **2.** INFORM file.

ficticio, cia *adj* [imaginario] fictitious.

ficus *sm inv* rubber plant.

fidedigno, na *adj* reliable.

fidelidad *sf* - **1.** [lealtad] loyalty; [de cónyuge, perro] faithfulness - **2.** [precisión] accuracy; **alta fidelidad** high fidelity.

fideo *sm* noodle; **estar** *O* **quedarse como un fideo** to be as thin as a rake.

fiebre *sf* fever; **tener fiebre** to have a temperature; **fiebre aftosa** foot-and-mouth disease; **fiebre amarilla/de Malta** yellow/Malta fever; **fiebre del heno** hay fever.

fiel *adj* - **1.** [leal - amigo, seguidor] loyal; [- cónyuge, perro] faithful - **2.** [preciso] accurate. ◆ **fieles** *smpl* RELIG: **los fieles** the faithful.

fieltro *sm* felt.

fiero, ra *adj* savage, ferocious. ◆ **fiera** *sf* [animal] wild animal.

fierro *sm Amér* - **1.** [hierro] iron - **2.** [navaja] penknife.

fiesta *sf* - **1.** [reunión] party; [de pueblo etc] (local) festivities *pl*; **fiesta benéfica** fête; **fiesta de disfraces** fancy-dress party; **fiesta mayor** *local celebrations for the festival of a town's patron saint*; **no estar para fiestas** to be in no mood for joking - **2.** [día] public holiday; **ser fiesta** to be a public holiday; **hacer fiesta** to be on holiday. ◆ **fiestas** *sfpl* [vacaciones] holidays.

figura *sf* - **1.** [gen] figure; [forma] shape; **tener buena figura** to have a good figure - **2.** [en naipes] picture card.

figuraciones *sfpl* imaginings.

figurado, da *adj* figurative.

figurar ◇ *vi* - **1.** [aparecer]: **figurar (en)** to appear (in), to figure (in) - **2.** [ser importante] to be prominent *O* important. ◇ *vt* - **1.** [representar] to represent - **2.** [simular] to feign, to simulate. ◆ **figurarse** *vprnl* [imaginarse] to imagine; **ya me lo figuraba yo** I thought as much.

fijación *sf* - **1.** [gen & FOTO] fixing - **2.** [obsesión] fixation.

fijador *sm* [líquido] fixative; **fijador de pelo** [crema] hair gel; [espray] hair spray.

fijar vt - **1.** [gen] to fix; [asegurar] to fasten; [cartel] to stick up; [sello] to stick on - **2.** [significado] to establish; **fijar el domicilio** to take up residence; **fijar la mirada/la atención en** to fix one's gaze/attention on. ● **fijarse** vprnl to pay attention; **fijarse en algo** [darse cuenta] to notice sthg; [prestar atención] to pay attention to sthg.

fijo, ja adj - **1.** [gen] fixed; [sujeto] secure - **2.** [cliente] regular - **3.** [fecha] definite - **4.** [empleado, trabajo] permanent.

fila sf [hilera - gen] line; [- de asientos] row; **en fila, en fila india** in line, in single file; **ponerse en fila** to line up. ● **filas** sfpl MIL ranks; **cerrar filas** fig to close ranks.

filántropo, pa sm, f philanthropist.

filarmónico, ca adj philharmonic.

filatelia sf philately.

filete sm [CULIN - grueso] (fillet) steak; [- delgado] fillet; [solomillo] sirloin.

filiación sf POLIT affiliation.

filial ◇ adj - **1.** [de hijo] filial - **2.** [de empresa] subsidiary. ◇ sf subsidiary.

filigrana sf [en orfebrería] filigree.

Filipinas sfpl: **(las) Filipinas** the Philippines sing.

filipino, na adj & sm, f Filipino. ● **filipino** sm [lengua] Filipino.

film = **filme**.

filmar vt to film, to shoot.

filme, film (pl films) sm film UK, movie US.

filmoteca sf [archivo] film library; [sala de cine] film institute.

filo sm (cutting) edge; **de doble filo, de dos filos** lit & fig double-edged. ● **al filo de** loc prep just before.

filología sf - **1.** [ciencia] philology - **2.** [carrera] language and literature.

filón sm - **1.** [de carbón etc] seam - **2.** fig [mina] gold mine.

filoso, sa, filudo, da adj Amér sharp.

filosofía sf [ciencia] philosophy.

filósofo, fa sm, f philosopher.

filtración sf - **1.** [de agua] filtration - **2.** fig [de noticia etc] leak.

filtrar vt - **1.** [tamizar] to filter - **2.** fig [datos, noticia] to leak. ● **filtrarse** vprnl - **1.** [penetrar]: **filtrarse (por)** to filter O seep (through) - **2.** fig [datos, noticia] to be leaked.

filtro sm [gen] filter; [de cigarrillo] filter, filter tip; **filtro del aceite** oil filter.

filudo, da = **filoso**.

fin sm - **1.** [final] end; **dar** O **poner fin a algo** to put an end to sthg; **tocar a su fin** to come to a close; **fin de semana** weekend; **a fines de** at the end of; **al** O **por fin** at last, finally; **a fin de cuentas** after all; **al fin y al cabo** after all

- **2.** [objetivo] aim, goal; **el fin justifica los medios** prov the end justifies the means. ● **a fin de** loc conj in order to. ● **a fin de que** loc conj so that. ● **en fin** loc adv anyway.

final ◇ adj final, end (antes de s). ◇ sm end; **final feliz** happy ending; **a finales de** at the end of. ◇ sf final.

finalidad sf aim, purpose.

finalista smf finalist.

finalizar ◇ vt to finish, to complete. ◇ vi: **finalizar (con)** to end O finish (in).

financiación sf financing.

financiar vt to finance.

financiero, ra ◇ adj financial. ◇ sm, f [persona] financier. ● **financiera** sf [firma] finance company.

financista smf Amér financier.

finanzas sfpl finance (U).

finca sf [gen] property; [casa de campo] country residence.

fingir ◇ vt to feign. ◇ vi to pretend.

finiquito sm settlement.

finito, ta adj finite.

finlandés, esa ◇ adj Finnish. ◇ sm, f [persona] Finn. ● **finlandés** sm [lengua] Finnish.

Finlandia n pr Finland.

fino, na adj - **1.** [gen] fine; [delgado] thin; [cintura] slim - **2.** [cortés] refined - **3.** [agudo - oído, olfato] sharp, keen; [- gusto, humor, ironía] refined. ● **fino** sm dry sherry.

finura sf [gen] fineness; [delgadez] thinness; [cortesía] refinement; [de oído, olfato] sharpness, keenness; [de gusto, humor, ironía] refinement.

firma sf - **1.** [rúbrica] signature; [acción] signing - **2.** [empresa] firm.

firmamento sm firmament.

firmar vt to sign; **firmar algo en blanco** fig to rubber-stamp sthg.

firme adj - **1.** [gen] firm; [mueble, andamio, edificio] stable - **2.** [argumento, base] solid - **3.** [carácter, actitud, paso] resolute.

firmeza sf - **1.** [gen] firmness; [de mueble, edificio] stability - **2.** [de argumento] solidity - **3.** [de carácter, actitud] resolution.

fiscal ◇ adj tax (antes de s), fiscal. ◇ smf public prosecutor UK, district attorney US.

fisco sm treasury, exchequer.

fisgar, fisgonear vi [gen] to pry; [escuchando] to eavesdrop.

fisgón, ona sm, f nosy parker.

fisgonear = **fisgar**.

físico, ca ◇ adj physical. ◇ sm, f [persona] physicist. ● **físico** sm [complexión] physique. ● **física** sf [ciencia] physics (U).

fisiológico, ca adj physiological.

fisionomía = fisonomía.

fisioterapeuta *smf* physiotherapist.

fisonomía, fisionomía *sf* features *pl*, appearance.

fisura *sf* [grieta] fissure.

flacidez, flaccidez *sf* flabbiness.

flácido, da, **fláccido, da** *adj* flaccid, flabby.

flaco, ca ◇ *adj* thin, skinny. ◇ *sm, f Amér* [como apelativo]: ¿cómo estás, flaca? hey, how are you doing?

flagelar *vt* to flagellate.

flagrante *adj* flagrant.

flamante *adj* [vistoso] resplendent; [nuevo] brand-new.

flambear *vt* to flambé.

flamenco, ca ◇ *adj* - **1.** MÚS flamenco *(antes de s)* - **2.** [de Flandes] Flemish - **3.** [achulado] cocky; **ponerse flamenco** to get cocky. ◇ *sm, f* [de Flandes] Fleming. ◆ **flamenco** *sm* - **1.** [ave] flamingo - **2.** [lengua] Flemish - **3.** MÚS flamenco.

flan *sm* crème caramel; **estar hecho** O **como un flan** to shake like a jelly, to be a bundle of nerves.

flanco *sm* flank.

flanquear *vt* to flank.

flaquear *vi* to weaken; *fig* to flag.

flaqueza *sf* weakness.

flash [flaʃ] *(pl* **flashes**) *sm* - **1.** FOTO flash - **2.** [informativo] newsflash.

flato *sm*: **tener flato** to have a stitch.

flatulento, ta *adj* flatulent.

flauta ◇ *sf* flute; **flauta dulce** recorder; **de la gran flauta** *Chile & R Dom fig* tremendous. ◇ *interj*: **¡(la gran) flauta!** *Chile & R Dom* good grief!, good heavens!

flecha *sf* [gen] arrow; ARQUIT spire; **salir como una flecha** to shoot out, to fly out.

flechazo *sm fam fig* [amoroso]: **fue un flechazo** it was love at first sight.

fleco *sm* [adorno] fringe.

flema *sf* phlegm.

flemático, ca *adj* [tranquilo] phlegmatic.

flemón *sm* gumboil.

flequillo *sm* fringe, bangs *pl* US.

flete *sm* - **1.** [precio] freightage - **2.** [carga] cargo, freight.

flexible *adj* flexible.

flexo *sm* adjustable table lamp O light.

flipar *fam vi* - **1.** [disfrutar] to have a wild time - **2.** [asombrarse] to be gobsmacked - **3.** [con una droga] to be stoned O high.

flirtear *vi* to flirt.

flojear *vi* - **1.** [decaer - piernas, fuerzas etc] to weaken; [- memoria] to be failing; [- película, libro] to flag; [- calor, trabajo] to ease off; [- ventas] to fall off - **2.** *Andes* [holgazanear] to laze about O around.

flojera *sf* lethargy, feeling of weakness.

flojo, ja *adj* - **1.** [suelto] loose - **2.** [débil - persona, bebida] weak; [- sonido] faint; [- tela] thin; [- salud] poor; [- viento] light - **3.** [inactivo - mercado, negocio] slack.

flor *sf* - **1.** BOT flower; **de flores** flowered; **echar flores a alguien** to pay sb compliments; **no tener ni flores (de)** *fam* not to have a clue (about); **ser flor de un día** *fig* to be a flash in the pan - **2.** [lo mejor]: **la flor (y nata)** the crème de la crème, the cream; **en la flor de la edad** O **de la vida** in the flower of life. ◆ **a flor de** *loc adv*: **a flor de agua/tierra** at water/ground level.

flora *sf* flora.

florecer *vi* to flower; *fig* to flourish.

floreciente *adj fig* flourishing.

florero *sm* vase.

florido, da *adj* [con flores] flowery; [estilo, lenguaje] florid.

florista *smf* florist.

floristería *sf* florist's (shop).

flota *sf* fleet.

flotación *sf* [gen & ECON] flotation.

flotador *sm* - **1.** [para nadar] rubber ring - **2.** [de caña de pescar] float.

flotar *vi* [gen & ECON] to float; [banderas] to flutter.

flote ◆ **a flote** *loc adv* afloat; **sacar algo a flote** *fig* to get sthg back on its feet; **salir a flote** *fig* to get back on one's feet.

flotilla *sf* flotilla.

fluctuar *vi* [variar] to fluctuate.

fluidez *sf* - **1.** [gen] fluidity; [del tráfico] free flow; [de relaciones] smoothness - **2.** *fig* [en el lenguaje] fluency.

fluido, da *adj* - **1.** [gen] fluid; [tráfico] free-flowing - **2.** [relaciones] smooth - **3.** *fig* [lenguaje] fluent. ◆ **fluido** *sm* fluid; **fluido eléctrico** electric current O power.

fluir *vi* to flow.

flujo *sm* flow; **flujo de caja** cash flow.

flúor *sm* fluorine.

fluorescente *sm* strip light.

fluvial *adj* river *(antes de s)*.

FM *(abrev de* **frecuencia modulada)** *sf* FM.

FMI *(abrev de* **Fondo Monetario Internacional)** *sm* IMF.

fobia *sf* phobia.

foca *sf* seal.

foco *sm* - **1.** *fig* [centro] centre, focal point - **2.** [lámpara - para un punto] spotlight; [- para una zona] floodlight - **3.** FÍS & GEOM focus - **4.** *Col, Ecuad, Méx & Perú* [bombilla] light bulb.

fofo, fa *adj* flabby.

fogata *sf* bonfire, fire.

fogón *sm* [para cocinar] stove.

fogoso, sa *adj* passionate.

fogueo *sm*: de fogueo blank.

foie-gras [fwa'γras] *sm* (pâté de) foie-gras.

folclore, folclor, folklor *sm* folklore.

folio *sm* [hoja] leaf, sheet; [tamaño] folio.

folklor = folclore.

follaje *sm* foliage.

folletín *sm* [dramón] melodrama.

folleto *sm* [turístico, publicitario] brochure; [explicativo, de instrucciones] leaflet.

follón *sm fam* - **1.** [discusión] row; se armó follón there was an almighty row - **2.** [lío] mess; ¡vaya follón! what a mess!

fomentar *vt* to encourage, to foster.

fomento *sm* encouragement, fostering.

fonda *sf* boarding house.

fondear ◇ *vi* to anchor. ◇ *vt* [sondear] to sound; [registrar - barco] to search.

fondo *sm* - **1.** [de recipiente, mar, piscina] bottom; tocar fondo [embarcación] to scrape along the sea/river bed; *fig* to hit rock bottom; doble fondo false bottom - **2.** [de habitación etc] back; al fondo de [calle, pasillo] at the end of; [sala] at the back of - **3.** [dimensión] depth - **4.** [de tela, cuadro, foto] background; al fondo in the background - **5.** *R Dom* [patio] back patio - **6.** [de asunto, tema] heart, bottom - **7.** ECON fund; a fondo perdido non-returnable; fondo común kitty - **8.** [de biblioteca, archivo] catalogue, collection - **9.** DEP stamina - **10.** *Méx* [combinación] petticoat. ◆ **fondos** *smpl* ECON [capital] funds; recaudar fondos to raise funds. ◆ **a fondo** ◇ *loc adv* thoroughly; emplearse a fondo *fig* to do one's utmost. ◇ *loc adj* thorough. ◆ **en el fondo** *loc adv* - **1.** [en lo más íntimo] deep down - **2.** [en lo esencial] basically.

fonético, ca *adj* phonetic. ◆ **fonética** *sf* [ciencia] phonetics *(U)*.

fono *sm Amér fam* phone.

fontanería *sf* plumbing.

fontanero, ra *sm, f* plumber.

football = fútbol.

footing ['futin] *sm* jogging; hacer footing to go jogging.

forajido, da *sm, f* outlaw.

foráneo, a *adj* foreign.

forastero, ra *sm, f* stranger.

forcejear *vi* to struggle.

fórceps *sm inv* forceps.

forense ◇ *adj* forensic. ◇ *smf* pathologist.

forestal *adj* forest *(antes de s)*.

forja *sf* [fragua] forge; [forjadura] forging.

forjar *vt* - **1.** [metal] to forge - **2.** *fig* [inventarse] to invent; [crear] to build up. ◆ **forjarse** *vprnl fig* [labrarse] to carve out for o.s.

forma *sf* - **1.** [gen] shape, form; dar forma a to shape, to form; en forma de in the shape of; tomar forma to take shape; guardar las formas to keep up appearances - **2.** [manera] way, manner; de cualquier forma, de todas formas anyway, in any case; de esta forma in this way; de forma que in such a way that, so that - **3.** ARTE & LITER form - **4.** [condición física] fitness; estar en forma to be fit; estar bajo de forma, estar en baja forma to be in poor shape. ◆ **formas** *sfpl* - **1.** [silueta] figure *sing* - **2.** [modales] social conventions.

formación *sf* - **1.** [gen & MIL] formation - **2.** [educación] training; formación profesional vocational training - **3.** [conjunto] grouping.

formal *adj* - **1.** [gen] formal - **2.** [que se porta bien] well-behaved, good - **3.** [de confianza] reliable - **4.** [serio] serious.

formalidad *sf* - **1.** [gen] formality - **2.** [educación] (good) manners *pl* - **3.** [fiabilidad] reliability - **4.** [seriedad] seriousness.

formalizar *vt* to formalize.

formar ◇ *vt* - **1.** [gen] to form - **2.** [educar] to train, to educate. ◇ *vi* MIL to fall in. ◆ **formarse** *vprnl* - **1.** [gen] to form - **2.** [educarse] to be trained *O* educated.

formatear *vt* INFORM to format.

formato *sm* [gen & INFORM] format.

formica® *sf* Formica®.

formidable *adj* [enorme] tremendous; [extraordinario] amazing, fantastic.

fórmula *sf* formula; fórmula uno formula one; por pura fórmula purely as a matter of form.

formular *vt* to formulate.

formulario *sm* form.

fornido, da *adj* well-built.

foro *sm* - **1.** [tribunal] court (of law) - **2.** TEATRO back of the stage; desaparecer por el foro to slip away unnoticed - **3.** [debate] forum; foro de discusión INFORM forum.

forofo, fa *sm, f fam* fan, supporter.

forraje *sm* fodder.

forrar *vt*: forrar (de) [libro] to cover (with); [ropa] to line (with); [asiento] to upholster (with).

forro sm - **1.** [de libro] cover; [de ropa] lining; [de asiento] upholstery - **2.** R Dom fam [preservativo] rubber, johnny UK.

fortalecer vt to strengthen.

fortaleza sf - **1.** [gen] strength - **2.** [recinto] fortress.

fortificación sf fortification.

fortuito, ta adj chance (antes de s).

fortuna sf - **1.** [suerte] (good) luck; **por fortuna** fortunately, luckily - **2.** [destino] fortune, fate - **3.** [riqueza] fortune.

forúnculo, furúnculo sm boil.

forzado, da adj forced.

forzar vt - **1.** [gen] to force; **forzar la vista** to strain one's eyes - **2.** [violar] to rape.

forzoso, sa adj [obligatorio] obligatory, compulsory; [inevitable] inevitable; [necesario] necessary.

forzudo, da adj strong.

fosa sf - **1.** [sepultura] grave - **2.** ANAT cavity; **fosas nasales** nostrils - **3.** [hoyo] pit; **fosa marina** ocean trough.

fosfato sm phosphate.

fosforescente adj phosphorescent.

fósforo sm - **1.** QUÍM phosphorus - **2.** [cerilla] match.

fósil sm GEOL fossil.

foso sm [hoyo] ditch; [de fortaleza] moat; [de garaje] pit; DEP & TEATRO pit.

foto sf photo, picture.

fotocomponer vt IMPR to typeset.

fotocopia sf [objeto] photocopy.

fotocopiadora sf photocopier.

fotocopiar vt to photocopy.

fotoeléctrico, ca adj photoelectric.

fotogénico, ca adj photogenic.

fotografía sf - **1.** [arte] photography - **2.** [imagen] photograph.

fotografiar vt to photograph.

fotógrafo, fa sm, f photographer.

fotomatón sm passport photo machine.

fotonovela sf photo story.

fotorrobot (pl fotorrobots) sf Identikit® picture.

fotosíntesis sf inv photosynthesis.

FP (abrev de **formación profesional**) sf vocational training.

frac (pl fracs) sm tails pl, dress coat.

fracasar vi: fracasar (en/como) to fail (at/as).

fracaso sm failure; **todo fue un fracaso** the whole thing was a disaster.

fracción sf - **1.** [gen] fraction; **en una fracción de segundo** in a split second - **2.** POLÍT faction.

fraccionario, ria adj fractional; **moneda fraccionaria** small change.

fractura sf fracture.

fragancia sf fragrance.

fraganti ➤ **in fraganti** loc adv: **coger a alguien in fraganti** to catch sb red-handed O in the act.

fragata sf frigate.

frágil adj [objeto] fragile; [persona] frail.

fragilidad sf [de objeto] fragility; [de persona] frailty.

fragmentar vt [romper] to fragment; [dividir] to divide.

fragmento sm fragment, piece; [de obra] excerpt.

fragor sm [de batalla] clamour; [de trueno] crash.

fragua sf forge.

fraguar ◇ vt - **1.** [forjar] to forge - **2.** fig [idear] to think up. ◇ vi to set, to harden. ➤ **fraguarse** vprnl to be in the offing.

fraile sm friar.

frambuesa sf raspberry.

francés, esa ◇ adj French. ◇ sm, f Frenchman (f Frenchwoman); **los franceses** the French; **marcharse** O **despedirse a la francesa** to leave without even saying goodbye. ➤ **francés** sm [lengua] French.

Francia n pr France.

franco, ca adj - **1.** [sincero] frank, open; [directo] frank - **2.** [sin obstáculos, gastos] free - **3.** C Sur [de permiso]: **me dieron el día franco** they gave me the day off. ➤ **franco** sm [moneda] franc.

francotirador, ra sm, f MIL sniper.

franela sf flannel.

franja sf strip; [en bandera, uniforme] stripe; **franja horaria** time zone.

franquear vt - **1.** [paso, camino] to clear - **2.** [río, montaña etc] to negotiate, to cross - **3.** [correo] to frank.

franqueo sm postage.

franqueza sf [sinceridad] frankness.

franquicia sf exemption.

franquismo sm: **el franquismo** [régimen] the Franco regime; [doctrina] Franco's doctrine.

frasco sm small bottle.

frase sf - **1.** [oración] sentence - **2.** [locución] expression; **frase hecha** [modismo] set phrase; [tópico] cliché.

fraternidad, fraternización sf brotherhood, fraternity.

fraterno, na adj brotherly, fraternal.

fraude sm fraud; **fraude electoral** election O electoral fraud; **fraude fiscal** tax evasion.

fraudulento, ta *adj* fraudulent.

frazada *sf Amér* blanket; **frazada eléctrica** electric blanket.

frecuencia *sf* frequency; **con frecuencia** often; **alta/baja frecuencia** high/low frequency; **frecuencia modulada, modulación de frecuencia** frequency modulation.

frecuentar *vt* [lugar] to frequent; [persona] to see, to visit.

frecuente *adj* [reiterado] frequent; [habitual] common.

fregadero *sm* (kitchen) sink.

fregado, da *adj Andes, Méx & Ven fam* [persona - ser] annoying; [- estar]: **perdí las llaves, ¡estoy fregada!** I've lost my keys, I've had it!; [roto] bust.

fregar *vt* - **1.** [limpiar] to wash; **fregar los platos** to do the washing-up - **2.** [frotar] scrub - **3.** *Amér fam* [molestar] to bother, to pester - **4.** *Andes, Méx & Ven* [estropear]: **vas a fregar la televisión** you're going to bust the television.

fregona *sf* - **1.** *despec* [criada] skivvy - **2.** [utensilio] mop; **pasar la fregona** to mop.

freidora *sf* [gen] deep fat fryer; [para patatas fritas] chip pan.

freír *vt* CULIN to fry.

fréjol *sm Andes, Amér C & Méx* bean.

frenar ◇ *vt* - **1.** AUTO to brake - **2.** [contener] to check. ◇ *vi* to stop; AUTO to brake.

frenazo *sm* - **1.** AUTO: **dar un frenazo** to brake hard - **2.** *fig* [parón] sudden stop.

frenesí (*pl* frenesíes *O* frenesís) *sm* frenzy.

frenético, ca *adj* - **1.** [colérico] furious, mad - **2.** [enloquecido] frenzied, frantic.

freno *sm* - **1.** AUTO brake; **freno de mano** handbrake - **2.** [de caballerías] bit - **3.** *fig* [contención] check; **poner freno a** to put a stop to.

frente ◇ *sf* forehead; **arrugar la frente** to knit one's brow, to frown; **frente a frente** face to face; **con la frente muy alta** with one's head held high. ◇ *sm* front; **estar al frente (de)** to be at the head (of); **hacer frente a** to face up to; **frente cálido/frío** warm/cold front. ◆ **de frente** *loc adv* - **1.** [hacia delante] forwards - **2.** [uno contra otro] head on. ◆ **en frente** *loc adv* opposite. ◆ **en frente de** *loc adv* opposite. ◆ **frente a** *loc prep* - **1.** [enfrente de] opposite - **2.** [con relación a] towards.

fresa *sf* [planta, fruto] strawberry.

fresco, ca ◇ *adj* - **1.** [gen] fresh; [temperatura] cool; [pintura, tinta] wet - **2.** [caradura] cheeky; **¡qué fresco!** what a nerve! ◇ *sm, f* [caradura] cheeky person. ◆ **fresco** *sm* - **1.** ARTE fresco; **al fresco** in fresco - **2.** [frescor] coolness; **hace fresco** it's chilly; **tomar el fresco** to get a breath of fresh air.

frescor *sm* coolness, freshness.

frescura *sf* - **1.** [gen] freshness - **2.** [descaro] cheek, nerve.

fresno *sm* ash (tree).

fresón *sm* large strawberry.

frialdad *sf lit & fig* coldness.

fricción *sf* [gen] friction; [friega] rub, massage.

friega *sf* rub, massage.

frigidez *sf* frigidity.

frigorífico, ca *adj* [camión] refrigerator *(antes de s)*; [cámara] cold. ◆ **frigorífico** *sm* refrigerator, fridge *UK*, icebox *US*.

frijol, fríjol *sm Andes, Amér C, Caribe & Méx* bean.

frío, a *adj* [gen] cold; [inmutable] cool; **dejar a alguien frío** to leave sb cold. ◆ **frío** *sm* cold; **coger frío** to catch a chill; **hace frío** it's cold; **hacer un frío que pela** to be freezing cold; **tener frío** to be cold; **no darle a alguien ni frío ni calor** *fig* to leave sb cold.

friolento, ta *Amér* ◇ *adj* sensitive to the cold. ◇ *sm, f*: **es un friolento** he really feels the cold.

friolero, ra *adj* sensitive to the cold.

frito, ta ◇ *pp* ▷ **freír**. ◇ *adj* - **1.** [alimento] fried - **2.** *fam fig* [persona - harta] fed up (to the back teeth); [- dormida] flaked out, asleep. ◆ **frito** *sm* (*gen pl*) fried food (*U*).

frívolo, la *adj* frivolous.

frondoso, sa *adj* leafy.

frontal *adj* frontal.

frontera *sf* border; *fig* [límite] bounds *pl*.

fronterizo, za *adj* border *(antes de s)*.

frontispicio *sm* - **1.** [de edificio - remate] pediment - **2.** [de libro] frontispiece.

frontón *sm* [deporte] pelota; [cancha] pelota court.

frotar *vt* to rub. ◆ **frotarse** *vprnl*: **frotarse las manos** to rub one's hands.

fructífero, ra *adj* fruitful.

frugal *adj* frugal.

fruncir *vt* - **1.** [labios] to purse; **fruncir el ceño** to frown - **2.** [tela] to gather.

fruslería *sf* triviality, trifle.

frustración *sf* frustration.

frustrar *vt* [persona] to frustrate. ◆ **frustrarse** *vprnl* - **1.** [persona] to get frustrated - **2.** [ilusiones] to be thwarted; [proyecto] to fail.

fruta *sf* fruit; **fruta confitada** candied fruit; **fruta de la pasión** passion fruit; **fruta del tiempo** seasonal fruit.

frutal *sm* fruit tree.

frutería *sf* fruit shop.

frutero, ra *sm, f* [persona] fruiterer. ◆ **frutero** *sm* [recipiente] fruit bowl.

frutilla *sf Bol, C Sur & Ecuad* strawberry.

fruto *sm* - **1.** [naranja, plátano etc] fruit; [nuez, avellana etc] nut; **frutos secos** dried fruit and nuts. **2.** [resultado] fruit; **dar fruto** to bear fruit; **sacar fruto a** O **de algo** to profit from sthg.

FSLN *sm (abrev de* **Frente Sandinista de Liberación Nacional)** SNLF.

fucsia *sf* [planta] fuchsia.

fue ▷ ir, ser.

fuego *sm* - **1.** [gen & MIL] fire; [de cocina, fogón] ring, burner; **pegar fuego a algo** to set sthg on fire, to set fire to sthg; **pedir/dar fuego** to ask for/give a light; **¿tiene fuego?** have you got a light?; **fuegos artificiales** fireworks - **2.** [apasionamiento] passion, ardour.

fuelle *sm* [gen] bellows *pl*.

fuente *sf* - **1.** [manantial] spring - **2.** [construcción] fountain - **3.** [bandeja] (serving) dish - **4.** [origen] source; **fuentes oficiales** official sources; **fuente de información/ingresos** source of information/income - **5.**: **fuente de soda** *Caribe, Chile, Col & Méx* cafe.

fuera ▷ *adv* - **1.** [en el exterior] outside; **le echó fuera** she threw him out; **hacia fuera** outwards; **por fuera** (on the) outside - **2.** [en otro lugar] away; [en el extranjero] abroad; **de fuera** [extranjero] from abroad - **3.** *fig* [alejado]: **fuera de** [alcance, peligro] out of; [cálculos, competencia] outside; **estar fuera de sí** to be beside o.s. (with rage) - **4.** DEP: **fuera de juego** offside. ▷ *interj*: **¡fuera!** [gen] (get) out!; [en el teatro] (get) off!; ▷ ir, ser. ▪ **fuera de** *loc prep* [excepto] except for, apart from. ▪ **fuera de serie** *adj* exceptional.

fueraborda *sm inv* outboard motor O engine.

fuero *sm* - **1.** *(gen pl)* [ley local] *ancient regional law* still existing in some parts of Spain - **2.** [jurisdicción] code of laws.

fuerte ▷ *adj* - **1.** [gen] strong - **2.** [carácter] strong - **3.** [frío, dolor, color] intense; [lluvia] heavy; [ruido] loud; [golpe, pelea] hard - **4.** [comida, salsa] rich - **5.** [nudo] tight. ▷ *adv* - **1.** [intensamente - gen] hard; [- abrazar, agarrar] tight - **2.** [abundantemente] a lot - **3.** [en voz alta] loudly. ▷ *sm* - **1.** [fortificación] fort - **2.** [punto fuerte] strong point, forte.

fuerza *sf* - **1.** [gen] strength; [violencia] force; [de sonido] loudness; [de dolor] intensity; **cobrar fuerza** to gather strength; **por fuerza** of necessity; **tener fuerza** to be strong; **tener fuerzas para** to have the strength to; **fuerza mayor** DER force majeure; [en seguros] act of God; **no llegué por un caso de fuerza mayor** I didn't make it due to circumstances beyond my control; **a fuerza de** by dint of; **a la fuerza** [contra la voluntad] by force; [por necesidad] of necessity; **por la fuerza** by force; **írsele a alguien la fuerza por la boca** to be all talk and no action, to be all mouth; **fuerza bruta** brute force; **fuerza de voluntad** willpower - **2.** FÍS & MIL force; **fuerza aérea** airforce; **fuerza disuasoria** deterrent; **fuerza de la gravedad** force of gravity; **fuerza motriz** [gen] motive power; *fig* driving force; **fuerzas armadas** armed forces; **fuerzas del orden público** police *pl*; **fuerzas de seguridad** security forces - **3.** ELECTR power; **fuerza hidráulica** water power. ▪ **fuerzas** *sfpl* [grupo] forces.

fuese ▷ ir, ser.

fuga *sf* - **1.** [huida] escape; **fuga de capitales** flight of capital - **2.** [escape] leak - **3.** MÚS fugue.

fugarse *vprnl* to escape; **fugarse de casa** to run away from home; **fugarse con alguien** to run off with sb.

fugaz *adj* fleeting.

fugitivo, va *sm, f* fugitive.

fui ▷ ir, ser.

fulano, na *sm, f* what's his/her name, so-and-so. ▪ **fulana** *sf* [prostituta] tart, whore.

fulgor *sm* shining; [de disparo] flash.

fulminante *adj fig* [despido, muerte] sudden; [enfermedad] devastating; [mirada] withering.

fulminar *vt* [suj: enfermedad] to strike down; **fulminar a alguien con la mirada** to look daggers at sb.

fumador, ra *sm, f* smoker; **fumador empedernido** chain-smoker; **fumador pasivo** passive smoker; **no fumador** nonsmoker.

fumar *vt & vi* to smoke.

fumigar *vt* to fumigate.

función *sf* - **1.** [gen] function; [trabajo] duty; **director en funciones** acting director; **entrar en funciones** to take up one's duties - **2.** CINE & TEATRO show. ▪ **en función de** *loc prep* depending on.

funcional *adj* functional.

funcionamiento *sm* operation, functioning.

funcionar *vi* to work; **funcionar con gasolina** to run on petrol; **'no funciona'** 'out of order'.

funcionario, ria *sm, f* civil servant.

funda *sf* [de sofá, máquina de escribir] cover; [de almohada] case; [de disco] sleeve; [de pistola] sheath.

fundación *sf* foundation.

fundador, ra *sm, f* founder.

fundamental *adj* fundamental.

fundamentar *vt* - **1.** *fig* [basar] to base - **2.** CONSTR to lay the foundations of. ▪ **fundamentarse en** *vprnl fig* [basarse] to be based O founded on.

fundamento *sm* - **1.** [base] foundation, basis - **2.** [razón] reason, grounds *pl*; **sin fundamento** unfounded, groundless.

fundar *vt* - **1.** [crear] to found - **2.** [basar]: **fundar (en)** to base (on). ⬥ **fundarse** *vprnl* [basarse]: **fundarse (en)** to be based (on).

fundición *sf* - **1.** [fusión - de vidrio] melting; [- de metal] smelting - **2.** [taller] foundry.

fundir *vt* - **1.** [metalurgia] [plomo] to melt; [hierro] to smelt - **2.** ELECTR to fuse; [bombilla, fusible] to blow - **3.** *fig* & COM to merge. ⬥ **fundirse** *vprnl* - **1.** ELECTR to blow - **2.** [derretirse] to melt - **3.** *fig* & COM to merge - **4.** *Amér* [arruinarse] to go bust.

fúnebre *adj* funeral *(antes de s)*.

funeral *(gen pl)* *sm* funeral.

funerario, ria *adj* funeral *(antes de s)*. ⬥ **funeraria** *sf* undertaker's *UK*, mortician's *US*.

funesto, ta *adj* fateful, disastrous.

fungir *vi Méx & Perú*: **fungir (de** O **como)** to act (as), to serve (as).

funicular *sm* - **1.** [por tierra] funicular - **2.** [por aire] cable car.

furgón *sm* AUTO van; FERROC wagon; **furgón celular** O **policial** police van; **furgón de cola** guard's van *UK*, caboose *US*.

furgoneta *sf* van.

furia *sf* fury; **estar hecho una furia** to be furious.

furioso, sa *adj* furious.

furor *sm* - **1.** [enfado] fury, rage - **2.** *loc*: **hacer furor** to be all the rage.

furtivo, va *adj* [mirada, sonrisa] furtive.

furúnculo = forúnculo.

fusible *sm* fuse.

fusil *sm* rifle.

fusilar *vt* [ejecutar] to execute by firing squad, to shoot.

fusión *sf* - **1.** [agrupación] merging - **2.** [de empresas, bancos] merger - **3.** [derretimiento] melting - **4.** FÍS fusion.

fusionar *vt* - **1.** [gen & ECON] to merge - **2.** FÍS to fuse. ⬥ **fusionarse** *vprnl* ECON to merge.

fusta *sf* riding crop.

fustán *sm Amér* petticoat.

fuste *sm* shaft.

fútbol, futbol *Amér C & Méx* ['fudbol] *sm* football, soccer *US*; **fútbol sala** indoor five-a-side.

futbolín *sm* table football.

futbolista *smf* footballer.

fútil *adj* trivial.

futilidad *sf* triviality.

futón *sm* futon.

futuro, ra ⬦ *adj* future. ⬦ *adv*: **a futuro** *C Sur & Méx* in the future. ⬥ **futuro** *sm* [gen & GRAM] future; **en un futuro próximo** in the near future. ⬥ **futuros** *smpl* ECON futures.

futurología *sf* futurology.

G

g¹, G *sf* [letra] g, G.

g² *(abrev de gramo)* g.

gabacho, cha *fam despec sm, f* Frog.

gabán *sm* overcoat.

gabardina *sf* [prenda] raincoat, mac.

gabinete *sm* - **1.** [gobierno] cabinet - **2.** [despacho] office; **gabinete de prensa** press office - **3.** [sala] study.

gacela *sf* gazelle.

gaceta *sf* gazette.

gachas *sfpl* CULIN (corn) porridge *(U)*.

gacho, cha *adj* drooping.

gafas *sfpl* glasses; **gafas bifocales** bifocals; **gafas graduadas** prescription glasses; **gafas de sol** sunglasses.

gafe ⬦ *adj* jinxed. ⬦ *smf* jinxed person.

gaita *sf* [instrumento] bagpipes *pl*.

gajes *smpl*: **gajes del oficio** occupational hazards.

gajo *sm* [trozo de fruta] segment.

gala *sf* - **1.** [fiesta] gala; **ropa/uniforme de gala** [ropa] full dress/uniform; **cena de gala** black tie dinner, formal dinner - **2.** [ropa]: **galas** finery *(U)*, best clothes - **3.** [actuación] show - **4.** *loc*: **hacer gala de algo** [preciarse] to be proud of sthg; [exhibir] to demonstrate sthg.

galán *sm* TEATRO leading man, lead.

galante *adj* gallant.

galantear *vt* to court, to woo.

galantería *sf* - **1.** [cualidad] politeness - **2.** [acción] gallantry, compliment.

galápago *sm* turtle.

galardón *sm* award, prize.

galaxia *sf* galaxy.

galera *sf* galley.

galería *sf* - **1.** [gen] gallery; [corredor descubierto] verandah - **2.** *fig* [vulgo] masses *pl*. ⬥ **galerías (comerciales)** *sfpl* shopping arcade *sing*.

Gales *n pr*: **(el país de) Gales** Wales.

galés, esa ⬦ *adj* Welsh. ⬦ *sm, f* Welshman, *m* (f Welshwoman); **los galeses** the Welsh. ⬥ **galés** *sm* [lengua] Welsh.

galgo *sm* greyhound; **¡échale un galgo!** you can forget it!

galimatías *sm inv* [lenguaje] gibberish *(U)*; [lío] jumble.

gallardía *sf* - **1.** [valentía] bravery - **2.** [elegancia] elegance.

gallego, ga adj & sm, f - **1.** Galician - **2.** C Sur fam [español] sometimes pejorative term used to refer to someone or something Spanish. ◆ **gallego** sm [lengua] Galician.

galleta sf CULIN biscuit UK, cookie US; **galleta salada** cracker.

gallina ◇ sf [ave] hen; **la gallina ciega** blind man's buff; **acostarse con las gallinas** to go to bed early; **estar como gallina en corral ajeno** to be like a fish out of water. ◇ smf fam [persona] chicken, coward.

gallinero sm - **1.** [corral] henhouse - **2.** fam TEATRO gods sing.

gallo sm - **1.** [ave] cock UK, rooster US, cockerel; **en menos que canta un gallo** fam in no time at all; **otro gallo cantaría** things would be very different - **2.** [al cantar] false note; [al hablar] squeak - **3.** [pez] John Dory.

galo, la ◇ adj HIST Gallic; [francés] French. ◇ sm, f [persona] Gaul.

galón sm - **1.** [adorno] braid; MIL stripe - **2.** [medida] gallon.

galopar vi to gallop.

galope sm gallop; **al galope** at a gallop; **a galope tendido** at full gallop.

galpón sm Andes, Caribe & R Plata shed.

gama sf [gen] range; MÚS scale.

gamba sf prawn.

gamberro, rra ◇ adj loutish. ◇ sm, f vandal; [en fútbol etc] hooligan; **hacer el gamberro** to behave loutishly.

gamo sm fallow deer.

gamonal sm Andes, Amér C & Ven [cacique] village chief; [caudillo] cacique, local political boss.

gamuza sf - **1.** [tejido] chamois (leather); [trapo] duster - **2.** [animal] chamois.

gana sf - **1.** [afán]: **gana (de)** desire O wish (to); **de buena gana** willingly; **de mala gana** unwillingly; **me da/no me da la gana hacerlo** I damn well feel like/don't damn well feel like doing it - **2.** [apetito] appetite. ◆ **ganas** sfpl [deseo]: **tener ganas de algo/hacer algo, sentir ganas de algo/hacer algo** to feel like sthg/doing sthg; **no tengo ganas de que me pongan una multa** I don't fancy getting a fine; **morirse de ganas de hacer algo** to be dying to do sthg; **quedarse con ganas de hacer algo** not to manage to do sthg; **tenerle ganas a alguien** to have it in for sb.

ganadería sf - **1.** [actividad] livestock farming - **2.** [ganado] livestock.

ganado sm livestock, stock; **ganado porcino** pigs pl; **ganado vacuno** cattle pl.

ganador, ra ◇ adj winning. ◇ sm, f winner.

ganancia sf [rendimiento] profit; [ingreso] earnings pl; **ganancias y pérdidas** profit and loss; **ganancia líquida** net profit.

ganancial ⊳ **bien**

ganar ◇ vt - **1.** [gen] to win; [sueldo, dinero] to earn; [peso, tiempo, terreno] to gain - **2.** [derrotar] to beat; **ganar a alguien a algo** to beat sb at sthg - **3.** [aventajar]: **ganar a alguien en algo** to be better than sb as regards sthg. ◇ vi - **1.** [vencer] to win - **2.** [lograr dinero] to earn money - **3.** [mejorar]: **ganar en algo** to gain in sthg. ◆ **ganarse** vprnl - **1.** [conquistar - simpatía, respeto] to earn; [- persona] to win over - **2.** [merecer] to deserve.

ganchillo sm [aguja] crochet hook; [labor] crochet; **hacer ganchillo** to crochet.

gancho sm - **1.** [gen] hook; [de percha] peg - **2.** Andes, Amér C, Méx & Ven [percha] hanger - **3.** [cómplice - de timador] decoy; [- de vendedor] person who attracts buyers - **4.** fam [atractivo] sex appeal.

gandul, la fam ◇ adj lazy. ◇ sm, f lazybones, layabout.

ganga sf fam snip, bargain.

gangrena sf gangrene.

gángster (pl gángsters) sm gangster.

ganso, sa sm, f - **1.** [ave - hembra] goose; [- macho] gander - **2.** fam [persona] idiot, fool.

garabatear vi & vt to scribble.

garabato sm scribble.

garaje sm garage.

garante smf guarantor; **salir garante** to act as guarantor.

garantía sf - **1.** [gen] guarantee; **de garantía** reliable, dependable; **ser garantía de algo** to guarantee sthg; **garantías constitucionales** constitutional rights - **2.** [fianza] surety.

garantizar vt - **1.** [gen] to guarantee; **garantizar algo a alguien** to assure sb of sthg - **2.** [avalar] to vouch for.

garbanzo sm chickpea; **ser el garbanzo negro de la familia** to be the black sheep of the family.

garbeo sm fam stroll; **dar un garbeo** to go for O take a stroll.

garbo sm [de persona] grace; [de escritura] stylishness, style.

garete sm: **ir** O **irse al garete** fam to come adrift.

garfio sm hook.

gargajo sm phlegm.

garganta sf - **1.** ANAT throat; **lo tengo atravesado en la garganta** fig he/it sticks in my gullet - **2.** [desfiladero] gorge.

gargantilla sf choker, necklace.

gárgara *sf (gen pl)* gargle, gargling *(U)*; **hacer gárgaras** to gargle; **mandar a alguien a hacer gárgaras** *fam* to send sb packing; **¡vete a hacer gárgaras!** *fam* get lost!

garita *sf* [gen] cabin; [de conserje] porter's lodge; MIL sentry box.

garito *sm despec* [casa de juego] gambling den; [establecimiento] dive.

garra *sf* [de animal] claw; [de ave de rapiña] talon; *despec* [de persona] paw, hand; **caer en las garras de alguien** to fall into sb's clutches; **tener garra** [persona] to have charisma; [novela, canción etc] to be gripping.

garrafa *sf* carafe.

garrafal *adj* monumental, enormous.

garrapata *sf* tick.

garrapiñar *vt* [fruta] to candy; [almendras etc] to coat with sugar.

garrote *sm* - **1.** [palo] club, stick - **2.** [instrumento] garrotte.

garúa *sf Andes, R Plata & Ven* drizzle.

garza *sf* heron; **garza real** grey heron.

gas *sm* gas; **con gas** [agua] sparkling, carbonated; [refresco] fizzy, carbonated; **gas ciudad/natural** town/natural gas; **gas butano** butane (gas); **gas licuado de petróleo** liquified petroleum gas; **gas lacrimógeno** tear gas. ➣ **gases** *smpl* [en el estómago] wind *(U)*. ➣ **a todo gas** *loc adv* flat out.

gasa *sf* gauze.

gaseoducto *sm* gas pipeline.

gaseoso, sa *adj* gaseous; [bebida] fizzy. ➣ **gaseosa** *sf* lemonade *UK*, soda *US*.

gasfitería *sf Chile, Ecuad & Perú* plumber's (shop).

gasfitero, ra *sm, f Chile, Ecuad & Perú* plumber.

gasóleo *sm* diesel oil.

gasolina *sf* petrol *UK*, gas *US*; **poner gasolina** to fill up (with petrol).

gasolinera *sf* petrol station *UK*, gas station *US*.

gastado, da *adj* [ropa, pieza etc] worn out; [frase, tema] hackneyed; [persona] broken, burnt out.

gastar ➣ *vt* - **1.** [consumir - dinero, tiempo] to spend; [- gasolina, electricidad] to use (up); [- ropa, zapatos] to wear out - **2.** *fig* [usar - gen] to use; [- ropa] to wear; [- número de zapatos] to take; **gastar una broma (a alguien)** to play a joke (on sb) - **3.** [malgastar] to waste. ➣ *vi* [despilfarrar] to spend (money). ➣ **gastarse** *vprnl* - **1.** [deteriorarse] to wear out - **2.** [terminarse] to run out.

gasto *sm* [acción de gastar] outlay, expenditure; [cosa que pagar] expense; [de energía, gasolina] consumption; [despilfarro] waste; **cubrir gastos** to cover costs, to break even; **gasto**

deducible ECON tax-deductible expense; **gasto público** public expenditure; **gastos de envío** postage and packing; **gastos fijos** COM fixed charges *O* costs; [en una casa] overheads; **gastos generales** overheads; **gastos de mantenimiento** maintenance costs; **gastos de representación** entertainment allowance *sing*.

gastritis *sf inv* gastritis.

gastronomía *sf* gastronomy.

gastrónomo, ma *sm, f* gourmet.

gatas ➣ **a gatas** *loc adv* on all fours.

gatear *vi* to crawl.

gatillo *sm* trigger; **apretar el gatillo** to press *O* pull the trigger.

gato, ta *sm, f* cat; **dar gato por liebre a alguien** to swindle *O* cheat sb; **buscar tres pies al gato** to overcomplicate matters; **jugar al gato y al ratón** to play cat and mouse; **llevarse el gato al agua** to pull it off; **aquí hay gato encerrado** there's something fishy going on here; **el gato escaldado del agua fría huye** *prov* once bitten twice shy. ➣ **gato** *sm* AUTO jack.

gauchada *sf C Sur* favour; **hacerle una gauchada a alguien** to do sb a favour.

gaucho, cha *adj R Dom* helpful, obliging. ➣ **gaucho** *sm* gaucho.

gavilán *sm* sparrowhawk.

gavilla *sf* sheaf.

gaviota *sf* seagull.

gay *adj inv & smf* gay *(homosexual)*.

gazmoño, ña *adj* sanctimonious.

gazpacho *sm* gazpacho *(Andalusian soup made from tomatoes, peppers, cucumbers and bread, served chilled)*.

géiser *(pl* géiseres*)*, **géyser** *(pl* géyseres*) sm* geyser.

gel *sm* gel.

gelatina *sf* [de carne] gelatine; [de fruta] jelly.

gema *sf* gem.

gemelo, la ➣ *adj* twin *(antes de s)*. ➣ *sm, f* [persona] twin. ➣ **gemelo** *sm* [músculo] calf. ➣ **gemelos** *smpl* - **1.** [de camisa] cufflinks - **2.** [prismáticos] binoculars; [para teatro] opera glasses.

gemido *sm* [de persona] moan, groan; [de animal] whine.

Géminis ➣ *sm* [zodiaco] Gemini. ➣ *smf* [persona] Gemini.

gemir *vi* - **1.** [persona] to moan, to groan; [animal] to whine - **2.** [viento] to howl.

genealogía *sf* genealogy.

generación *sf* generation.

generador, ra *adj* generating. ➣ **generador** *sm* generator.

general ➣ *adj* - **1.** [gen] general; **por lo general, en general** in general, generally

- 2. [usual] usual. <> *sm* MIL general; **general de brigada** brigadier *UK*, brigadier general *US*; **general de división** major general.

generalidad *sf* - **1.** [mayoría] majority - **2.** [vaguedad] generalization.

generalísimo *sm* supreme commander, generalissimo.

Generalitat [xenerali'tat] *sf* autonomous government of Catalonia or Valencia.

generalizar <> *vt* to spread, to make widespread. <> *vi* to generalize. ◆ **generalizarse** *vprnl* to become widespread.

generalmente *adv* generally.

generar *vt* [gen] to generate; [engendrar] to create.

genérico, ca *adj* [común] generic.

género *sm* - **1.** [clase] kind, type - **2.** GRAM gender - **3.** LITER genre - **4.** BIOL genus; **el género humano** the human race - **5.** [productos] merchandise, goods *pl* - **6.** [tejido] cloth, material; **géneros de punto** knitwear *(U)*.

generosidad *sf* generosity.

generoso, sa *adj* generous.

genético, ca *adj* genetic. ◆ **genética** *sf* genetics *(U)*.

genial *adj* - **1.** [autor, compositor etc] of genius - **2.** [estupendo] brilliant, great.

genio *sm* - **1.** [talento] genius - **2.** [carácter] nature, disposition - **3.** [mal carácter] bad temper; **estar de/tener mal genio** to be in a mood/bad-tempered - **4.** [ser sobrenatural] genie.

genital *adj* genital. ◆ **genitales** *smpl* genitals.

genocidio *sm* genocide.

genoma *sm* genome; **genoma humano** human genome.

gente *sf* - **1.** [gen] people *pl*; **gente bien** well-to-do people; **gente menuda** kids *pl* - **2.** *fam* [familia] folks *pl*.

gentileza *sf* courtesy, kindness.

gentío *sm* crowd.

gentuza *sf* riffraff.

genuflexión *sf* genuflection.

genuino, na *adj* genuine.

GEO (*abrev de* Grupo Especial de Operaciones) *sm* specially trained police force, ≃ SAS *UK*, ≃ SWAT *US*.

geografía *sf* geography; *fig*: **varios puntos de la geografía nacional** several parts of the country; **geografía física** physical geography; **geografía política** political geography.

geógrafo, fa *sm, f* geographer.

geología *sf* geology.

geólogo, ga *sm, f* geologist.

geometría *sf* geometry; **geometría del espacio** solid geometry.

geranio *sm* geranium.

gerencia *sf* [gen] management.

gerente *smf* manager, director.

geriatría *sf* geriatrics *(U)*.

germen *sm* lit & fig germ; **germen de trigo** wheatgerm.

germinar *vi* lit & fig to germinate.

gerundio *sm* gerund.

gestar *vi* to gestate. ◆ **gestarse** *vprnl*: **se estaba gestando un cambio sin precedentes** the seeds of an unprecedented change had been sown.

gesticulación *sf* gesticulation; [de cara] face-pulling.

gesticular *vi* to gesticulate; [con la cara] to pull faces.

gestión *sf* - **1.** [diligencia] step, thing that has to be done; **tengo que hacer unas gestiones** I have a few things to do - **2.** [administración] management; **gestión de cartera** ECON portfolio management; **gestión de datos** INFORM data management; **gestión de ficheros** INFORM file management.

gestionar *vt* - **1.** [tramitar] to negotiate - **2.** [administrar] to manage.

gesto *sm* - **1.** [gen] gesture; **hacer gestos** to gesture, to gesticulate - **2.** [mueca] face, grimace; **torcer el gesto** to pull a face.

gestor, ra <> *adj* managing (*antes de s*). <> *sm, f* person who carries out dealings with public bodies on behalf of private customers or companies, combining the role of solicitor and accountant.

géyser = **géiser**.

ghetto = **gueto**.

giba *sf* [de camello] hump.

Gibraltar *n pr* Gibraltar.

gibraltareño, ña *adj* & *sm, f* Gibraltarian.

gigabyte [xiɣa'βait] *sm* INFORM gigabyte.

gigahercio *sm* INFORM gigahertz.

gigante, ta *sm, f* giant. ◆ **gigante** *adj* gigantic.

gigantesco, ca *adj* gigantic.

gil, gila *C Sur fam* <> *adj* stupid. <> *sm* jerk, twit *UK*.

gilipollada, jilipollada *sf fam*: **hacer/decir una gilipollada** to do/say sthg bloody stupid.

gilipollas, jilipollas *fam* <> *adj inv* daft, dumb *US*. <> *smf inv* prat.

gimnasia *sf* [deporte] gymnastics *(U)*; [ejercicio] gymnastics *pl*.

gimnasio *sm* gymnasium.

gimnasta *smf* gymnast.

gimotear *vi* to whine, to whimper.

gin [ʤin] ◆ **gin tonic** *sm* gin and tonic.

ginebra *sf* gin.

ginecología *sf* gynaecology.

ginecólogo, ga sm, f gynaecologist.

gira sf tour.

girar <> vi - **1.** [dar vueltas, torcer] to turn; [rápidamente] to spin - **2.** fig [centrarse]: **girar en torno a** O **alrededor de** to be centred around, to centre on. <> vt - **1.** [hacer dar vueltas a] to turn; [rápidamente] to spin - **2.** COM to draw - **3.** [dinero - por correo, telégrafo] to transfer, to remit.

girasol sm sunflower.

giratorio, ria adj revolving; [silla] swivel (antes de s).

giro sm - **1.** [gen] turn; **giro de 180 grados** lit & fig U-turn - **2.** [postal, telegráfico] money order; **giro postal** postal order - **3.** [de letras, órdenes de pago] draft; **giro en descubierto** overdraft - **4.** [expresión] turn of phrase.

gis sm Méx chalk.

gitano, na sm, f gypsy.

glacial adj glacial; [viento, acogida] icy.

glaciar <> adj glacial. <> sm glacier.

gladiolo, gladíolo sm gladiolus.

glándula sf gland; **glándula endocrina** endocrine gland; **glándula sebácea** sebaceous gland.

glicerina sf glycerine.

global adj global, overall.

globalización sf globalization.

globo sm - **1.** [Tierra] globe, earth - **2.** [aeróstato, juguete] balloon - **3.** [esfera] sphere.

glóbulo sm MED corpuscle; **glóbulo blanco/ rojo** white/red corpuscle.

gloria sf - **1.** [gen] glory - **2.** [placer] delight.

glorieta sf - **1.** [de casa, jardín] arbour - **2.** [plaza - redonda] circus, roundabout UK, traffic circle US.

glorificar vt to glorify.

glorioso, sa adj [importante] glorious.

glosa sf marginal note.

glosar vt - **1.** [anotar] to annotate - **2.** [comentar] to comment on.

glosario sm glossary.

glotón, ona <> adj gluttonous, greedy. <> sm, f glutton.

glúcido sm carbohydrate.

glucosa sf glucose.

gluten sm gluten.

gnomo, nomo sm gnome.

gobernador, ra sm, f governor.

gobernanta sf cleaning and laundry staff manageress.

gobernante <> adj ruling (antes de s). <> smf ruler, leader.

gobernar vt - **1.** [gen] to govern, to rule; [casa, negocio] to run, to manage - **2.** [barco] to steer; [avión] to fly.

gobierno sm - **1.** [gen] government - **2.** [administración, gestión] running, management - **3.** [control] control.

goce sm pleasure.

godo, da <> adj Gothic. <> sm, f HIST Goth.

gol (pl **goles**) sm goal; **marcar** O **meter un gol** to score a goal; **gol del empate** equalizer; **gol de penalti** penalty goal; **gol en propia meta** own goal; **meter un gol a alguien** to put one over on sb.

goleador, ra sm, f goalscorer.

golear vt to score a lot of goals against, to thrash.

golf sm golf.

golfear vi fam [vaguear] to loaf around.

golfista smf golfer.

golfo, fa sm, f [gamberro] lout; [vago] layabout. ◆ **golfo** sm GEOGR gulf, bay. ◆ **Golfo Pérsico** sm: **el Golfo Pérsico** the Persian Gulf.

golondrina sf [ave] swallow.

golosina sf [dulce] sweet; [exquisitez] titbit, delicacy.

goloso, sa adj sweet-toothed.

golpe sm - **1.** [gen] blow; [bofetada] smack; [con puño] punch; [en puerta etc] knock; [en tenis, golf] shot; [entre coches] bump, collision; **a golpes** by force; fig in fits and starts; **un golpe bajo** fig & DEP a blow below the belt; **golpe de castigo** [en rugby] penalty (kick); **golpe franco** free kick; **golpe de tos** coughing fit; **golpe de viento** gust of wind - **2.** [disgusto] blow - **3.** [atraco] raid, job, heist US - **4.** POLÍT: **golpe (de Estado)** coup (d'état) - **5.** loc: **dar el golpe** fam to cause a sensation, to be a hit; **errar** O **fallar el golpe** to miss the mark; **no dar** O **pegar golpe** not to lift a finger, not to do a stroke of work. ◆ **de golpe** loc adv suddenly. ◆ **de un golpe** loc adv at one fell swoop, all at once. ◆ **golpe de gracia** sm coup de grâce. ◆ **golpe maestro** sm masterstroke. ◆ **golpe de suerte** sm stroke of luck. ◆ **golpe de vista** sm glance; **al primer golpe de vista** at a glance.

golpear vt & vi [gen] to hit; [puerta] to bang; [con puño] to punch.

golpista smf person involved in military coup.

golpiza sf Amér beating.

goma sf - **1.** [sustancia viscosa, pegajosa] gum; **goma arábiga** gum arabic; **goma de mascar** chewing gum; **goma de pegar** glue, gum - **2.** [tira elástica] rubber band, elastic band UK; **goma elástica** elastic - **3.** [caucho] rubber; **goma espuma** foam rubber; **goma de borrar** rubber UK, eraser US - **4.** Cuba & C Sur [neumático] tyre UK, tire US - **5.** Amér C [fam] [resaca] hangover. ◆ **Goma 2** sf plastic explosive.

gomina *sf* hair gel.

gong *sm inv* gong.

gordinflón, ona *sm, f* fatty.

gordo, da <> *adj* - **1.** [persona] fat; **me cae gordo** I can't stand him - **2.** [grueso] thick - **3.** [grande] big - **4.** [grave] big, serious. <> *sm, f* - **1.** [persona obesa] fat man (*f* fat woman); **armar la gorda** *fig* to kick up a row *O* stink - **2.** *Amér* [querido] sweetheart, darling - **3.** *Amér* [como apelativo]: **¿cómo estás, gordo?** hey, how's it going? <> **gordo** *sm* [en lotería] first prize, jackpot; **el gordo** *first prize in the Spanish national lottery.*

gordura *sf* fatness.

gorgorito *sm* warble.

gorila *sm* - **1.** ZOOL gorilla - **2.** [guardaespaldas] bodyguard - **3.** [en discoteca etc] bouncer.

gorjear *vi* to chirp, to twitter.

gorra *sf* (peaked) cap; **de gorra** for free; **vivir de gorra** to scrounge.

gorrear = **gorronear**.

gorrinada *sf* [guarrada - acción] disgusting behaviour (*U*); [- lugar] pigsty.

gorrión *sm* sparrow.

gorro *sm* [gen] cap; [de niño] bonnet; **gorro de baño** [para ducha] shower cap; [para piscina] swimming cap.

gorrón, ona *fam sm, f* sponger.

gorronear, gorrear *vt* & *vi fam* to sponge, to scrounge.

gota *sf* - **1.** [de agua, leche, sangre] drop; [de sudor] bead; **caer cuatro gotas** to spit (with rain); **la gota que colma el vaso** the last straw, the straw that breaks the camel's back; **sudar la gota gorda** to sweat blood, to work very hard - **2.** [cantidad pequeña]: **una gota de** a (tiny) drop of; **ni gota: no se veía ni gota** you couldn't see a thing; **no tienes ni gota de sentido común** you haven't got an ounce of common sense - **3.** [enfermedad] gout. <> **gotas** *sfpl* [medicamento] drops. <> **gota a gota** *sm* MED intravenous drip. <> **gota fría** *sf* METEOR *cold front that remains in one place for some time, causing continuous heavy rain.*

gotear <> *vi* [líquido] to drip; [techo, depósito etc] to leak; *fig* to trickle through. <> *v impers* [chispear] to spit, to drizzle.

gotera *sf* [filtración] leak.

gótico, ca *adj* Gothic.

gozada *sf fam*: **es una gozada** it's wonderful.

gozar *vi* to enjoy o.s.; **gozar de algo** to enjoy sthg; **gozar con** to take delight in.

gozne *sm* hinge.

gozo *sm* joy, pleasure.

grabación *sf* recording; **grabación digital** digital recording; **grabación en vídeo** video recording.

grabado *sm* - **1.** [gen] engraving; [en madera] carving - **2.** [en papel - acción] printing; [- lámina] print.

grabar *vt* - **1.** [gen] to engrave; [en madera] to carve; [en papel] to print - **2.** [sonido, cinta] to record. <> **grabarse** *en vprnl fig*: **grabársele a alguien en la memoria** to become engraved on sb's mind.

gracia *sf* - **1.** [humor, comicidad] humour; **hacer gracia a alguien** to amuse sb; **no me hizo gracia** I didn't find it funny; **¡maldita la gracia!** it's not a bit funny!; **¡qué gracia!** how funny!; **tener gracia** (ser divertido) to be funny; **tiene gracia** (es curioso) it's funny; **caer en gracia** to be liked - **2.** [arte, habilidad] skill, natural ability - **3.** [encanto] grace, elegance - **4.** [chiste] joke; **hacer una gracia a alguien** to play a prank on sb; **no le rías las gracias** don't laugh when he says something silly. <> **gracias** *sfpl* thank you, thanks; **gracia a Dios** thank God; **dar las gracias a alguien (por)** to thank sb (for); **muchas gracias** thank you, thanks very much.

gracioso, sa <> *adj* [divertido] funny, amusing; **¡qué gracioso!** how funny!; **es gracioso que...** it's funny how... <> *sm, f* comedian; **hacerse el gracioso** to try to be funny.

grada *sf* - **1.** [peldaño] step - **2.** TEATRO row. <> **gradas** *sfpl* DEP terraces.

gradación *sf* [escalonamiento] scale.

gradería *sf* = **graderío**.

graderío *sm* TEATRO rows *pl*; DEP terraces *pl*.

grado *sm* - **1.** [gen] degree - **2.** [fase] stage, level; [índice, nivel] extent, level; **en grado sumo** greatly - **3.** [rango - gen] grade; MIL rank - **4.** EDUC year, class, grade *US* - **5.** [voluntad]: **hacer algo de buen/mal grado** to do sthg willingly/unwillingly.

graduación *sf* - **1.** [acción] grading; [de la vista] eye-test - **2.** EDUC graduation - **3.** [de bebidas] strength, ≃ proof - **4.** MIL rank.

graduado, da *sm, f* [persona] graduate. <> **graduado** *sm* [título - gen] certificate.

gradual *adj* gradual.

graduar *vt* - **1.** [medir] to gauge, to measure; [regular] to regulate; [vista] to test - **2.** [escalonar] to stagger - **3.** EDUC to confer a degree on - **4.** MIL to commission. <> **graduarse** *vprnl*: **graduarse (en)** to graduate (in).

grafía *sf* written symbol.

gráfico, ca <> *adj* graphic. <> **gráfico** *sm* [gráfica] graph, chart; [dibujo] diagram; **gráfico de barras** bar chart. <> **gráfica** *sf* graph, chart.

gragea *sf* MED pill, tablet.

grajo *sm* rook.

gral. (*abrev de* **general**) gen.

gramática ▷ **gramático**.

gramatical *adj* grammatical.

gramático, ca *adj* grammatical. ▶ **gramática** *sf* [disciplina, libro] grammar.

gramo *sm* gram.

gramófono *sm* gramophone.

gramola *sf* gramophone.

gran ▷ **grande**.

granada *sf* - 1. [fruta] pomegranate - 2. [proyectil] grenade.

granate ◇ *sm* garnet. ◇ *adj inv* garnet-coloured.

Gran Bretaña *sf* Great Britain.

grande ◇ *adj (antes de m sing: gran)* - 1. [de tamaño] big, large; [de altura] tall; [de intensidad, importancia] great; **un hombre grande** a big man; **un gran hombre** a great man; **este traje me está grande** this suit is too big for me - 2. *loc:* **hacer algo a lo grande** to do sthg in style; **pasarlo en grande** *fam* to have a great time; **vivir a lo grande** to live in style. ◇ *sm* [noble] grandee. ▶ **grandes** *smpl* [adultos] grown-ups. ▶ **a lo grande** *loc adv* in style.

grandeza *sf* - 1. [de tamaño] (great) size - 2. [de sentimientos] generosity.

grandioso, sa *adj* grand, splendid.

grandullón, ona *sm, f* big boy (*f* big girl).

granel ▶ **a granel** *loc adv* [sin envase - gen] loose; [- en gran cantidad] in bulk.

granero *sm* granary.

granito *sm* granite.

granizada *sf* METEOR hailstorm.

granizado *sm* iced drink.

granizar *v impers* to hail.

granizo *sm* hail.

granja *sf* farm; **granja avícola** chicken *O* poultry farm.

granjearse *vprnl* to gain, to earn.

granjero, ra *sm, f* farmer.

grano *sm* - 1. [semilla - de cereales] grain; **grano de café** coffee bean; **grano de pimienta** peppercorn - 2. [partícula] grain - 3. [en la piel] spot, pimple - 4. *loc:* **apartar el grano de la paja** to separate the wheat from the chaff; **aportar** *O* **poner uno su grano de arena** to do one's bit; **ir al grano** to get to the point.

granuja *smf* [pillo] rogue, scoundrel; [canalla] trickster, swindler.

granulado, da *adj* granulated.

grapa *sf* - 1. [para papeles etc] staple; [para heridas] stitch, (wire) suture - 2. *C Sur* [bebida] grappa.

grapadora *sf* stapler.

grapar *vt* to staple.

grasa *sf* ▷ **graso**.

grasiento, ta *adj* greasy.

graso, sa *adj* [gen] greasy; [con alto contenido en grasas] fatty. ▶ **grasa** *sf* - 1. [en comestibles] fat; [de cerdo] lard; **grasa animal** animal fat; **grasa saturada** saturated fat - 2. [lubricante] grease, oil - 3. [suciedad] grease.

gratén *sm* gratin; **al gratén** au gratin.

gratificación *sf* - 1. [moral] reward - 2. [monetaria] bonus.

gratificante *adj* rewarding.

gratificar *vt* [complacer] to reward; [retribuir] to give a bonus to; [dar propina a] to tip.

gratinado, da *adj* au gratin.

gratis *adv* [sin dinero] free, for nothing; [sin esfuerzo] for nothing.

gratitud *sf* gratitude.

grato, ta *adj* pleasant; **nos es grato comunicarle que...** we are pleased to inform you that...

gratuito, ta *adj* - 1. [sin dinero] free - 2. [arbitrario] gratuitous; [infundado] unfair, uncalled for.

grava *sf* gravel.

gravamen *sm* - 1. [impuesto] tax - 2. [obligación moral] burden.

gravar *vt* [con impuestos] to tax.

grave *adj* - 1. [gen] serious; [estilo] formal; **estar grave** to be seriously ill - 2. [sonido, voz] low, deep.

gravedad *sf* - 1. [cualidad] seriousness - 2. FÍS gravity.

gravilla *sf* gravel.

gravitar *vi* to gravitate; *fig* [pender]: **gravitar sobre** to hang *O* loom over.

graznar *vi* [cuervo] to caw; [ganso] to honk; [pato] to quack; [persona] to squawk.

graznido *sm* [de cuervo] caw, cawing (*U*); [de ganso] honk, honking (*U*); [de pato] quack, quacking (*U*); [de personas] squawk, squawking (*U*).

Grecia *n pr* Greece.

gremio *sm* [sindicato] (trade) union; [profesión] profession, trade; HIST guild; **ser del gremio** to be in the trade.

greña (*gen pl*) *sf* tangle of hair; **andar a la greña (con alguien)** to be at daggers drawn (with sb).

gres *sm* stoneware.

gresca *sf* row.

griego, ga *adj & sm, f* Greek. ▶ **griego** *sm* [lengua] Greek.

grieta *sf* crack; [entre montañas] crevice; [que deja pasar luz] chink.

grifería *sf* taps *pl*, plumbing.

grifo *sm* [llave] tap *UK*, faucet *US*; **grifo monomando** mixer tap.

grillado, da *adj fam* crazy, loopy.

grillete *sm* shackle.

grillo sm cricket.

grima sf [dentera]: **dar grima** to set one's teeth on edge.

gringo, ga <> adj despec Esp [estadounidense] gringo, Yankee; Amér [extranjero] gringo, foreign. <> sm, f Esp [estadounidense] gringo, Yank; Amér [extranjero] gringo, foreigner.

gripa sf Col & Méx flu.

gripe sf flu.

gris <> adj [color] grey; [triste] gloomy, miserable. <> sm grey.

gritar <> vi [hablar alto] to shout; [chillar] to scream, to yell. <> vt: **gritar (algo) a alguien** to shout (sthg) at sb.

griterío sm screaming, shouting.

grito sm [gen] shout; [de dolor, miedo] cry, scream; [de sorpresa, de animal] cry; **dar** O **pegar un grito** to shout O scream (out); **a grito limpio** O **pelado** at the top of one's voice; **pedir algo a gritos** fig to be crying out for sthg; **poner el grito en el cielo** to hit the roof; **ser el último grito** to be the latest fashion O craze, to be the in thing.

Groenlandia n pr Greenland.

grogui adj lit & fig groggy.

grosella sf redcurrant; **grosella negra** blackcurrant; **grosella silvestre** gooseberry.

grosería sf [cualidad] rudeness; [acción] rude thing; [palabrota] swear word.

grosero, ra adj - **1.** [maleducado] rude, crude - **2.** [tosco] coarse, rough.

grosor sm thickness.

grotesco, ca adj grotesque.

grúa sf - **1.** CONSTR crane - **2.** AUTO breakdown truck - **3.** [de la policía] tow truck.

grueso, sa adj - **1.** [espeso] thick - **2.** [corpulento] thickset; [obeso] fat - **3.** [grande] large, big - **4.** [mar] stormy. ◆ **grueso** sm [grosor] thickness.

grulla sf crane.

grumete sm cabin boy.

grumo sm [gen] lump; [de sangre] clot.

gruñido sm - **1.** [gen] growl; [de cerdo] grunt; **dar gruñidos** to growl, to grunt - **2.** [de persona] grumble.

gruñir vi - **1.** [gen] to growl; [cerdo] to grunt - **2.** [persona] to grumble.

gruñón, ona fam adj grumpy.

grupa sf hindquarters.

grupo sm [gen] group; [de árboles] cluster; TECNOL unit, set; **en grupo** in a group; **grupo de discusión** INFORM forum; **grupo electrógeno** generator; **grupo de noticias** INFORM newsgroup. ◆ **grupo sanguíneo** sm blood group.

gruta sf grotto.

guacal sm Amér C & Méx [calabaza] gourd; Col, Méx & Caribe [jaula] cage.

guachada sf R Dom fam mean trick.

guachimán sm Amér night watchman.

guacho, cha sm, f Andes & R Dom fam bastard.

guaco sm Amér pottery object found in pre-Columbian Indian tomb.

guadaña sf scythe.

guagua sf Caribe [autobús] bus; Andes [niño] baby.

guajolote sm Amér C & Méx [pavo] turkey; fig [tonto] fool, idiot.

guampa sf Bol & C Sur horn.

guanajo sm Caribe turkey.

guantazo sm fam slap.

guante sm glove; **echar el guante a algo** fam to get hold of sthg, to get one's hands on sthg; **echar el guante a alguien** fam to nab sb.

guantera sf glove compartment.

guapo, pa adj - **1.** [gen] good-looking; [hombre] handsome; [mujer] pretty - **2.** fam [bonito] cool.

guarangada sf Bol & C Sur rude remark.

guarda <> smf [vigilante] guard, keeper; **guarda jurado** security guard. <> sf - **1.** [tutela] guardianship - **2.** [de libros] flyleaf.

guardabarros sm inv mudguard UK, fender US.

guardabosque smf forest ranger.

guardacoches smf inv parking attendant.

guardacostas sm inv [barco] coastguard boat.

guardaespaldas smf inv bodyguard.

guardameta smf goalkeeper.

guardapolvo sm overalls pl.

guardar vt - **1.** [gen] to keep; [en su sitio] to put away - **2.** [vigilar] to keep watch over; [proteger] to guard - **3.** [reservar, ahorrar]: **guardar algo (a** O **para alguien)** to save sthg (for sb) - **4.** [cumplir - ley] to observe; [- secreto, promesa] to keep. ◆ **guardarse de** vprnl: **guardarse de hacer algo** [evitar] to avoid doing sthg; [abstenerse de] to be careful not to do sthg.

guardarropa sm [gen] wardrobe; [de cine, discoteca etc] cloakroom.

guardarropía sf TEATRO wardrobe.

guardavallas smf inv Amér goalkeeper.

guardería sf nursery; [en el lugar de trabajo] crèche.

guardia <> sf - **1.** [gen] guard; [vigilancia] watch, guard; **montar (la) guardia** to mount guard; **guardia municipal** urban police - **2.** [turno] duty; **estar de guardia** to be on duty. <> sm, f [policía] policeman (f policewoman); **guardia de tráfico** traffic warden. ◆ **Guardia Civil** sf: **la Guardia Civil** the Civil Guard.

guardián, ana *sm, f* [de persona] guardian; [de cosa] watchman, keeper.

guarecer *vt*: **guarecer (de)** to protect *O* shelter (from). ◆ **guarecerse** *vprnl*: **guarecerse (de)** to shelter (from).

guarida *sf* lair; *fig* hideout.

guarnición *sf* - 1. CULIN garnish - 2. MIL garrison.

guarrería *sf* - 1. [suciedad] filth, muck - 2. [acción] filthy thing.

guarro, rra ◇ *adj* filthy. ◇ *sm, f* - 1. [animal] pig - 2. *fam* [persona] filthy *O* dirty pig.

guarura *sm Méx fam* bodyguard.

guasa *sf fam* [gracia] humour; [ironía] irony; **estar de guasa** to be joking.

guasearse *vprnl fam*: **guasearse (de)** to take the mickey (out of).

guasón, ona *sm, f* joker, tease.

Guatemala *n pr* - 1. [país] Guatemala - 2. [ciudad] Guatemala City.

guatemalteco, ca, guatemaltés, esa *adj* & *sm, f* Guatemalan.

guau *sm* woof.

guay *adj fam* cool, neat.

guayín *sm Méx* van.

gubernativo, va *adj* government *(antes de s)*.

guepardo *sm* cheetah.

güero, ra *adj Méx fam* blond (*f* blonde), fair-haired.

guerra *sf* war; [referido al tipo de conflicto] warfare; [pugna] struggle, conflict; [de intereses, ideas] conflict; **declarar la guerra** to declare war; **en guerra** at war; **hacer la guerra** to wage war; **guerra bacteriológica/química** germ/chemical warfare; **guerra espacial** *O* **de las galaxias** star wars; **guerra fría** cold war; **guerra de guerrillas** guerrilla warfare; **guerra a muerte** fight to the death; **guerra psicológica** psychological warfare; **dar guerra** to be a pain, to be annoying.

guerrear *vi* to (wage) war.

guerrero, ra ◇ *adj* warlike. ◇ *sm, f* [luchador] warrior.

guerrilla *sf* [grupo] guerrilla group.

guerrillero, ra *sm, f* guerrilla.

gueto, ghetto ['geto] *sm* ghetto.

güevón *sm Andes, Arg & Ven vulg* prat *UK*, pillock *UK*, jerk *US*.

guía ◇ *smf* [persona] guide; **guía turístico** tourist guide. ◇ *sf* - 1. [indicación] guidance - 2. [libro] guide (book); **guía de carreteras** road atlas; **guía de ferrocarriles** train timetable; **guía telefónica** telephone book *O* directory.

guiar *vt* - 1. [indicar dirección a] to guide, to lead; [aconsejar] to guide, to direct - 2. AUTO to drive; NÁUT to steer. ◆ **guiarse** *vprnl*: **guiarse por algo** to be guided by *O* to follow sthg.

guijarro *sm* pebble.

guillotina *sf* guillotine.

guinda *sf* morello cherry.

guindilla *sf* chilli (pepper).

guiñapo *sm* [persona] (physical) wreck.

guiño *sm* wink.

guiñol *sm* puppet theatre.

guión *sm* - 1. CINE & TV script - 2. GRAM [signo] hyphen.

guionista *smf* scriptwriter.

guiri *fam despec smf* foreigner.

guirigay *sm fam* [jaleo] racket.

guirlache *sm brittle sweet made of roasted almonds or hazelnuts and toffee.*

guirnalda *sf* garland.

guisa *sf* way; **a guisa de** by way of.

guisado *sm* stew.

guisante *sm* pea.

guisar *vt* & *vi* to cook. ◆ **guisarse** *vprnl fig* to be cooking, to be going on.

guiso *sm* dish.

güisqui, whisky *sm* whisky.

guitarra *sf* guitar; **guitarra acústica** acoustic guitar.

guitarrista *smf* guitarist.

gula *sf* gluttony.

gurí, risa *sm, f R Dom fam* [niño] kid, child; [chico] lad, boy; [chica] lass, girl.

guru, gurú *sm* guru.

gusanillo *sm fam*: **el gusanillo de la conciencia** conscience; **entrarle a uno el gusanillo de los videojuegos** to be bitten by the video-game bug; **matar el gusanillo** [bebiendo] to have a drink on an empty stomach; [comiendo] to have a snack between meals; **sentir un gusanillo en el estómago** to have butterflies (in one's stomach).

gusano *sm lit & fig* worm.

gustar ◇ *vi* [agradar] to be pleasing; **me gusta esa chica/ir al cine** I like that girl/going to the cinema; **me gustan las novelas** I like novels; **como guste** as you wish. ◇ *vt* to taste, to try.

gustazo *sm fam* great pleasure; **darse el gustazo de algo/hacer algo** to allow o.s. the pleasure of sthg/doing sthg.

gusto *sm* - 1. [gen] taste; [sabor] taste, flavour; **de buen/mal gusto** in good/bad taste - 2. [placer] pleasure; **con mucho gusto** gladly, with pleasure; **da gusto estar aquí** it's a real pleasure to be here; **dar gusto a alguien** to please sb; **mucho** *O* **tanto gusto** pleased to meet you; **tener el gusto de** to have the pleasure of; **tengo el gusto de invitarle** I have the pleasure of inviting you; **tomar gusto a algo** to take a liking to sthg - **3.** [capricho] whim.

➥ **a gusto** *loc adv*: **hacer algo a gusto** [de buena gana] to do sthg willingly *O* gladly; [cómodamente] to do sthg comfortably; **estar a gusto** to be comfortable *O* at ease.

gustoso, sa *adj* - **1.** [sabroso] tasty - **2.** [con placer]: **hacer algo gustoso** to do sthg gladly *O* willingly.

gutural *adj* guttural.

h¹, H *sf* [letra] h, H; **por h o por b** *fig* for one reason or another.

h², h. (*abrev de* **hora**) hr, h.

ha ◇ ▷ **haber**. ◇ (*abrev de* **hectárea**) ha.

haba *sf* broad bean.

habano, na *adj* Havanan. ➥ **habano** *sm* Havana cigar.

haber ◇ *v aux* - **1.** [en tiempos compuestos] to have; **lo he/había hecho** I have/had done it; **los niños ya han comido** the children have already eaten; **en el estreno ha habido mucha gente** there were a lot of people at the premiere - **2.** [expresa reproche]: **haber venido antes** you could have come a bit earlier; **¡haberlo dicho!** why didn't you say so? - **3.** [expresa obligación]: **haber de hacer algo** to have to do sthg; **has de estudiar más** you have to study more. ◇ *v impers* - **1.** [existir, estar]: **hay** there is/are; **hay mucha gente en la calle** there are a lot of people in the street; **había/hubo muchos problemas** there were many problems; **habrá dos mil** [expresa futuro] there will be two thousand; [expresa hipótesis] there must be two thousand - **2.** [expresa obligación]: **haber que hacer algo** to have to do sthg; **hay que hacer más ejercicio** one *O* you should do more exercise; **habrá que soportar su mal humor** we'll have to put up with his bad mood - **3.** *loc*: **algo habrá** there must be something

in it; **allá se las haya** that's his/her/your *etc* problem; **habérselas con alguien** to face *O* confront sb; **¡hay que ver!** well I never!; **no hay de que** don't mention it; **¿qué hay?** fam [saludo] how are you doing?. ◇ *sm* - **1.** [bienes] assets *pl* - **2.** [en cuentas, contabilidad] credit (side). ➥ **haberes** *smpl* [sueldo] remuneration *(U)*.

habichuela *sf* bean.

hábil *adj* - **1.** [diestro] skilful; [inteligente] clever - **2.** [utilizable - lugar] suitable, fit - **3.** DER: **días hábiles** working days.

habilidad *sf* [destreza] skill; [inteligencia] cleverness; **tener habilidad para algo** to be good at sthg.

habilitar *vt* - **1.** [acondicionar] to fit out, to equip - **2.** [autorizar] to authorize.

habiloso, sa *adj Chile fam* shrewd, astute.

habitación *sf* [gen] room; [dormitorio] bedroom; **habitación doble** [con cama de matrimonio] double room; [con dos camas] twin room; **habitación individual** *O* **simple** single room; **habitación para invitados** guest room.

habitante *sm* [de ciudad, país] inhabitant; [de barrio] resident.

habitar ◇ *vi* to live. ◇ *vt* to live in, to inhabit.

hábitat (*pl* **hábitats**) *sm* [gen] habitat.

hábito *sm* habit; **tener el hábito de hacer algo** to be in the habit of doing sthg.

habitual *adj* habitual; [cliente, lector] regular.

habituar *vt*: **habituar a alguien a** to accustom sb to. ➥ **habituarse** *vprnl*: **habituarse a** [gen] to get used *O* accustomed to; [drogas etc] to become addicted to.

habla *sf (el)* - **1.** [idioma] language; [dialecto] dialect; **de habla española** Spanish-speaking - **2.** [facultad] speech; **dejar a alguien sin habla** to leave sb speechless; **quedarse sin habla** to be left speechless - **3.** LING discourse - **4.** [al teléfono]: **estar al habla con alguien** to be on the line to sb.

hablador, ra *adj* talkative.

habladurías *sfpl* [rumores] rumours; [chismes] gossip *(U)*.

hablante ◇ *adj* speaking. ◇ *smf* speaker.

hablar ◇ *vi*: **hablar (con)** to talk (to), to speak (to); **hablar de** to talk about; **hablar bien/mal de** to speak well/badly of; **hablar en español/inglés** to speak Spanish/English; **¡mira quién habla!, ¡mira quién fue a hablar!** look who's talking!; **¡ni hablar!** no way! ◇ *vt* - **1.** [idioma] to speak - **2.** [asunto]: **hablar algo (con)** to discuss sthg (with). ➥ **hablarse** *vprnl* to speak (to each other); **no hablarse** not to be speaking, not to be on speaking terms; **'se habla inglés'** 'English spoken'.

habrá *etc* ▷ **haber**.

hacendado, **da** *sm*, *f* landowner.

hacer ◇ *vt* - 1. [elaborar, crear, cocinar] to make; **hacer un vestido/planes** to make a dress/plans; **hacer un poema/una sinfonía** to write a poem/symphony; **para hacer la carne...** to cook the meat... - 2. [construir] to build; **han hecho un edificio nuevo** they've put up a new building - 3. [generar] to produce; **el árbol hace sombra** the tree gives shade; **la carretera hace una curva** there's a bend in the road - 4. [movimientos, sonidos, gestos] to make; **le hice señas** I signalled to her; **el reloj hace tic-tac** the clock goes tick-tock; **hacer ruido** to make a noise - 5. [obtener - fotocopia] to make; [- retrato] to paint; [- fotografía] to take - 6. [realizar - trabajo, estudios] to do; [- viaje] to make; [- comunión] to take; **hoy hace guardia** she's on duty today; **estoy haciendo segundo** I'm in my second year - 7. [practicar - gen] to do; [- tenis, fútbol] to play; **debes hacer deporte** you should start doing some sport - 8. [arreglar - casa, colada] to do; [- cama] to make - 9. [transformar en]: **hacer a alguien feliz** to make sb happy; **la guerra no le hizo un hombre** the war didn't make him (into) a man; **hizo pedazos el papel** he tore the paper to pieces; **hacer de algo/alguien algo** to make sthg/sb into sthg; **hizo de ella una buena cantante** he made a good singer of her - 10. [comportarse como]: **hacer el tonto** to act the fool; **hacer el vándalo** to act like a hooligan - 11. [causar]: **hacer daño a alguien** to hurt sb; **me hizo gracia** I thought it was funny - 12. CINE & TEATRO to play; **hace el papel de la hija del rey** she plays (the part of) the king's daughter - 13. [ser causa de]: **hacer que alguien haga algo** to make sb do sthg; **me hizo reír** it made me laugh; **has hecho que se enfadara** you've made him angry - 14. [mandar]: **hacer que se haga algo** to have sthg done; **voy a hacer teñir este traje** I'm going to have the dress dyed. ◇ *vi* - 1. [actuar]: **hacer de** CINE & TEATRO to play; [trabajar] to act as - 2. [aparentar]: **hacer como si** to act as if; **haz como que no te importa** act as if you don't care - 3. [procurar, intentar]: **hacer por hacer algo** to try to do sthg; **haré por verle esta noche** I'll try to see him tonight - 4. *loc*: **¿hace?** all right? ◇ *v impers* - 1. [tiempo meteorológico]: **hace frío/sol/viento** it's cold/sunny/windy; **hace un día precioso** it's a beautiful day - 2. [tiempo transcurrido]: **hace diez años** ten years ago; **hace mucho/poco** a long time/not long ago; **hace un mes que llegué** it's a month since I arrived; **no la veo desde hace un año** I haven't seen her for a year. ◆ **hacerse** *vprnl* - 1. [formarse] to form - 2. [desarrollarse, crecer] to grow - 3. [guisarse, cocerse] to cook - 4. [convertirse] to become; **hacerse musulmán** to become a Moslem - 5. [crearse en la mente]: **hacer-**

se ilusiones to get one's hopes up; **hacerse una idea de algo** to imagine what sthg is like - 6. [mostrarse]: **se hace el gracioso/el simpático** he tries to act the comedian/the nice guy; **hacerse el distraído** to pretend to be miles away.

hacha *sf* (el) axe; **enterrar el hacha de guerra** to bury the hatchet.

hachís, **hash** [xaˈʃis] *sm* hashish.

hacia *prep* - 1. [dirección, tendencia, sentimiento] towards; **hacia aquí/allí** this/that way; **hacia abajo** downwards; **hacia arriba** upwards; **hacia atrás** backwards; **hacia adelante** forwards - 2. [tiempo] around, about; **hacia las diez** around O about ten o'clock.

hacienda *sf* - 1. [finca] country estate O property - 2. [bienes] property; **hacienda pública** public purse - 3. *R Plata* [ganadería] ranch. ◆ **Hacienda** *sf*: **Ministerio de Hacienda** the Treasury.

hada *sf* (el) fairy; **hada madrina** fairy godmother.

haga *etc* ▷ **hacer**.

Haití *n pr* Haiti.

hala *interj*: ¡**hala!** [para dar ánimo, prisa] come on!; [para expresar incredulidad] no!, you're joking!; [para expresar admiración, sorpresa] wow!

halagador, **ra** *adj* flattering.

halagar *vt* to flatter.

halago *sm* flattery.

halagüeño, **ña** *adj* [prometedor] promising, encouraging.

halcón *sm* - 1. ZOOL falcon, hawk - 2. *Amér fam* [matón] *government-paid killer.*

hálito *sm* [aliento] breath.

halitosis *sf inv* bad breath.

hall [xol] (*pl* halls) *sm* foyer.

hallar *vt* [gen] to find; [averiguar] to find out. ◆ **hallarse** *vprnl* - 1. [en un lugar - persona] to be, to find o.s.; [- casa etc] to be (situated) - 2. [en una situación] to be; **hallarse enfermo** to be ill.

hallazgo *sm* - 1. [descubrimiento] discovery - 2. [objeto] find.

halo *sm* [de astros, santos] halo; [de objetos, personas] aura.

halógeno, **na** *adj* QUÍM halogenous; [faro] halogen (*antes de s*).

halterofilia *sf* weightlifting.

hamaca *sf* - 1. [para colgar] hammock - 2. [tumbona - silla] deckchair; [- canapé] sunlounger - 3. *R Plata* [columpio] swing - 4. *R Plata* [mecedora] rocking chair.

hambre *sf* (el) - 1. [apetito] hunger; [inanición] starvation; **tener hambre** to be hungry; **matar de hambre a alguien** to starve sb to death; **matar el hambre** to satisfy one's hunger; **morirse de hambre** to be starving, to be dying of hunger; **pasar hambre** to starve - **2.** [epidemia] fam-ine - **3.** *fig* [deseo]: **hambre de** hunger O thirst for.

hambriento, ta *adj* starving.

hamburguesa *sf* hamburger.

hampa *sf (el)* underworld.

hámster ['xamster] *(pl* hámsters) *sm* ham-ster.

hándicap ['xandikap] *(pl* hándicaps) *sm* han-dicap.

hará *etc* ▷ **hacer**.

haraganear *vi* to laze about.

harapiento, ta *adj* ragged, tattered.

harapo *sm* rag, tatter.

hardware ['xar'wer] *sm* INFORM hardware.

harén *sm* harem.

harina *sf* flour; **estar metido en harina** to be right in the middle of sthg.

harinoso, sa *adj* floury; [manzana] mealy.

hartar *vt* - **1.** [atiborrar] to stuff (full) - **2.** [fasti-diar]: **hartar a alguien** to annoy sb, to get on sb's nerves. ◆ **hartarse** *vprnl* - **1.** [atiborrar-se] to stuff O gorge o.s. - **2.** [cansarse]: **hartarse (de)** to get fed up (with) - **3.** [no parar]: **hartarse de algo** to do sthg non-stop.

hartazgo, hartón *sm* fill; **darse un hartazgo (de)** to have one's fill (of).

harto, ta *adj* - **1.** [de comida] full - **2.** [cansado]: **harto (de)** tired (of), fed up (with) - **3.** *Andes, Amér C, Caribe & Méx* [mucho] a lot of, lots of; **tiene harto dinero** she has a lot of O lots of money; **de este aeropuerto salen hartos aviones** a lot of O lots of planes fly from this airport. ◆ **harto** *adv* - **1.** somewhat, rather - **2.** *Andes, Amér C, Caribe & Méx fam* [mucho] a lot, very much; [muy] very, really.

hartón = **hartazgo**.

hash = **hachís**.

hasta ◇ *prep* - **1.** [en el espacio] as far as, up to; **desde aquí hasta allí** from here to there; **¿hasta dónde va este tren?** where does this train go? - **2.** [en el tiempo] until, till; **hasta aho-ra** (up) until now, so far; **hasta el final** right up until the end; **hasta luego** O **pronto** O **la vis-ta** see you (later) - **3.** [con cantidades] up to. ◇ *adv* - **1.** [incluso] even - **2.** *Amér C, Col, Ecuad & Méx* [no antes de]: **pintaremos la casa hasta fin de mes** we won't start painting the house until the end of the month. ◆ **hasta que** *loc conj* until, till.

hastiar *vt* [aburrir] to bore; [asquear] to sicken, to disgust. ◆ **hastiarse de** *vprnl* to tire of.

hastío *sm* [tedio] boredom (U); [repugnancia] disgust.

hatillo *sm* bundle of clothes.

haya ◇ ▷ **haber**. ◇ *sf (el)* [árbol] beech (tree); [madera] beech (wood).

haz *sm* - **1.** [de leña] bundle; [de cereales] sheaf - **2.** [de luz] beam; ▷ **hacer**.

hazaña *sf* feat, exploit.

hazmerreír *sm* laughing stock.

he ▷ **haber**.

hebilla *sf* buckle.

hebra *sf* - **1.** [de hilo] thread; [de judías, puerros] string; [de tabaco] strand (of tobacco) - **2.** *loc*: **pegar la hebra** *fam* to strike up a conversa-tion; **perder la hebra** to lose the thread.

hebreo, a *adj & sm, f* Hebrew. ◆ **hebreo** *sm* [lengua] Hebrew.

hechicero, ra *sm, f* wizard (*f* witch), sorcer-er (*f* sorceress).

hechizar *vt* to cast a spell on; *fig* to bewitch, to captivate.

hechizo *sm* - **1.** [maleficio] spell - **2.** *fig* [encan-to] magic, charm.

hecho, cha ◇ *pp* ▷ **hacer**. ◇ *adj* - **1.** [acabado, realizado] done; **bien/mal hecho** well/badly done - **2.** [manufacturado] made; **hecho a mano** handmade; **hecho a máquina** machine-made - **3.** [convertido en]: **estás he-cho un artista** you've become quite an artist - **4.** [formado]: **una mujer hecha y derecha** a fully-grown woman - **5.** [carne] done. ◆ **he-cho** *sm* - **1.** [obra] action, deed - **2.** [suceso] event - **3.** [realidad, dato] fact. ◆ **de hecho** *loc adv* in fact, actually.

hechura *sf* - **1.** [de traje] cut - **2.** [forma] shape.

hectárea *sf* hectare.

heder *vi* [apestar] to stink, to reek.

hediondo, da *adj* [pestilente] stinking.

hedor *sm* stink, stench.

hegemonía *sf* [gen] dominance; POLÍT hege-mony.

helada ▷ **helado**.

heladería *sf* [tienda] ice-cream parlour; [pues-to] ice-cream stall.

helado, da *adj* - **1.** [hecho hielo - agua] frozen; [- lago] frozen over - **2.** [muy frío - manos, agua] freezing. ◆ **helado** *sm* ice-cream. ◆ **hela-da** *sf* frost.

helar ◇ *vt* [líquido] to freeze. ◇ *v impers*: **ayer heló** there was a frost last night. ◆ **he-larse** *vprnl* to freeze; [plantas] to be frostbit-ten.

helecho *sm* fern, bracken.

hélice *sf* - **1.** TECNOL propeller - **2.** [espiral] spir-al.

helicóptero *sm* helicopter.

helio *sm* helium.

hematoma *sm* bruise; MED haematoma.

hembra *sf* - **1.** BIOL female; [mujer] woman; [ni-ña] girl - **2.** [del enchufe] socket.

hemiciclo *sm* [en el parlamento] floor.

hemisferio *sm* hemisphere.

hemofilia *sf* haemophilia.

hemorragia *sf* haemorrhage; **hemorragia nasal** nosebleed.

hemorroides *sfpl* haemorrhoids, piles.

hender, hendir *vt* [carne, piel] to carve open, to cleave; [piedra, madera] to crack open; [aire, agua] to cut *O* slice through.

hendidura *sf* [en carne, piel] cut, split; [en piedra, madera] crack.

hendir = **hender**.

heno *sm* hay.

hepatitis *sf inv* hepatitis.

herbicida *sm* weedkiller.

herbolario, ria *sm, f* [persona] herbalist.

hercio ['erθjo], **hertz** *sm* hertz.

heredar *vt*: **heredar (de)** to inherit (from).

heredero, ra *sm, f* heir (*f* heiress); **heredero forzoso** heir apparent; **heredero universal** residuary legatee.

hereditario, ria *adj* hereditary.

hereje *smf* heretic.

herejía *sf* heresy.

herencia *sf* [de bienes] inheritance; [de características] legacy; BIOL heredity.

herido, da <> *adj* [gen] injured; [en lucha, atentado] wounded; [sentimentalmente] hurt, wounded. <> *sm, f* [gen] injured person; [en lucha, atentado] wounded person; **no hubo heridos** there were no casualties; **los heridos** the wounded. ◆ **herida** *sf* [lesión] injury; [en lucha, atentado] wound; **herida superficial** flesh wound; **heridas múltiples** multiple injuries.

herir *vt* - **1.** [físicamente] to injure; [en lucha, atentado] to wound; [vista] to hurt; [oído] to pierce - **2.** [sentimentalmente] to hurt.

hermanado, da *adj* [gen] united, joined; [ciudades] twinned.

hermanar *vt* [ciudades] to twin.

hermanastro, tra *sm, f* stepbrother (*f* stepsister).

hermandad *sf* [asociación] association; [RELIG - de hombres] brotherhood; [- de mujeres] sisterhood.

hermano, na *sm, f* brother (*f* sister); **hermano gemelo** twin brother; **hermano mayor** older brother, big brother; **hermano menor** younger brother, little brother; **hermano de sangre** blood brother.

hermético, ca *adj* - **1.** [al aire] airtight, hermetic; [al agua] watertight, hermetic - **2.** *fig* [persona] inscrutable.

hermoso, sa *adj* [gen] beautiful, lovely; [hombre] handsome; [excelente] wonderful.

hermosura *sf* [gen] beauty; [de hombre] handsomeness.

hernia *sf* hernia, rupture; **hernia discal** slipped disc.

herniarse *vprnl* MED to rupture o.s.

héroe *sm* hero.

heroico, ca *adj* heroic.

heroína *sf* - **1.** [mujer] heroine - **2.** [droga] heroin.

heroinómano, na *sm, f* heroin addict.

heroísmo *sm* heroism.

herpes *sm inv* herpes (*U*).

herradura *sf* horseshoe.

herramienta *sf* tool.

herrería *sf* [taller] smithy, forge.

herrero *sm* blacksmith, smith.

herrumbre *sf* [óxido] rust.

hertz = **hercio**.

hervidero *sm* - **1.** [de pasiones, intrigas] hotbed - **2.** [de gente - muchedumbre] swarm, throng; [- sitio] place throbbing *O* swarming with people.

hervir <> *vt* to boil. <> *vi* - **1.** [líquido] to boil - **2.** *fig* [lugar]: **hervir de** to swarm with.

hervor *sm* boiling; **dar un hervor a algo** to blanch sthg.

heterodoxo, xa *adj* unorthodox.

heterogéneo, a *adj* heterogeneous.

heterosexual *adj* & *smf* heterosexual.

hexágono *sm* hexagon.

hez *sf* lit & fig dregs *pl*. ◆ **heces** *sfpl* [excrementos] faeces.

hibernar *vi* to hibernate.

híbrido, da *adj* lit & fig hybrid. ◆ **híbrido** *sm* [animal, planta] hybrid.

hice *etc* ⊳ **hacer**.

hidalgo, ga *sm, f* nobleman (*f* noblewoman).

hidratante *sm* moisturizing cream.

hidratar *vt* [piel] to moisturize; QUÍM to hydrate.

hidrato *sm*: **hidrato de carbono** carbohydrate.

hidráulico, ca *adj* hydraulic.

hidroavión *sm* seaplane.

hidroeléctrico, ca *adj* hydroelectric.

hidrógeno *sm* hydrogen.

hidroplano *sm* [barco] hydrofoil.

hiedra *sf* ivy.

hiel *sf* - **1.** [bilis] bile; **echar la hiel** to sweat blood - **2.** [mala intención] spleen, bitterness.

hielo *sm* ice; **con hielo** [whisky] with ice, on the rocks; **romper el hielo** *fig* to break the ice; **ser más frío que el hielo** to be as cold as ice.

hiena *sf* hyena.

hierático, ca *adj* solemn.

hierba, yerba *sf* - **1.** [planta] herb; **mala hierba** weed - **2.** [césped] grass - **3.** *fam* [droga] grass.

hierbabuena *sf* mint.

hierro *sm* [metal] iron; **de hierro** [severo] iron (*antes de s*); **hierro forjado** wrought iron; hierro fundido cast iron; hierro laminado sheet metal.

hígado *sm* liver.

higiene *sf* hygiene; **higiene personal** personal hygiene.

higiénico, ca *adj* hygienic; **papel higiénico** toilet paper.

higienizar *vt* to sterilize.

higo *sm* fig; **higo chumbo** prickly pear; **de higos a brevas** once in a blue moon; **me importa un higo** *fam* I couldn't care less.

higuera *sf* fig tree; **estar en la higuera** *fig* to live in a world of one's own.

hijastro, tra *sm, f* stepson (*f* stepdaughter).

hijo, ja *sm, f* [descendiente] child, son (*f* daughter); **hijo adoptivo** adopted child; **hijo de la chingada** *Méx O* **de puta** *vulg* fucking bastard, motherfucker (*f* fucking bitch); **hijo de papá** *fam* daddy's boy; **hijo ilegítimo** *O* natural illegitimate child; **hijo no deseado** unwanted child; **hijo único** only child; **cualquier** *O* **todo hijo de vecino** *fam fig* any Tom, Dick or Harry. ◆ **hijos** *smpl* children.

hilacha *sf* loose thread.

hilada *sf* row.

hilar *vt* [hilo, tela] to spin; [ideas, planes] to think up.

hilaridad *sf* hilarity.

hilera *sf* row.

hilo *sm* - 1. [fibra, hebra] thread; **colgar** *O* **pender de un hilo** to be hanging by a thread; **mover los hilos** to pull some strings - 2. [tejido] linen - 3. [de metal, teléfono] wire; **sin hilos** wireless - 4. [de agua, sangre] trickle - 5. [de pensamiento] train; [de discurso, conversación] thread; **perder el hilo** to lose the thread; **seguir el hilo** to follow (the thread).

hilvanar *vt* - 1. [ropa] to tack *UK*, to baste *US* - 2. [coordinar - ideas] to piece together.

himno *sm* hymn; **himno nacional** national anthem.

hincapié *sm*: **hacer hincapié en** [insistir] to insist on; [subrayar] to emphasize, to stress.

hincar *vt*: **hincar algo en** to stick sthg into. ◆ **hincarse** *vprnl*: **hincarse de rodillas** to fall to one's knees.

hinchado, da *adj* - 1. [rueda, globo] inflated; [cara, tobillo] swollen - 2. *fig* [persona] bigheaded, conceited; [lenguaje, estilo] bombastic.

hinchar *vt lit & fig* to blow up. ◆ **hincharse** *vprnl* - 1. [pierna, mano] to swell (up) - 2. *fig*

[de comida]: **hincharse (a)** to stuff o.s. (with). ◆ **hincharse a** *vprnl* [no parar de]: **hincharse a hacer algo** to do sthg a lot.

hinchazón *sf* swelling.

hindú (*pl* **hindúes** *O* **hindús**) *adj & smf* - 1. [de la India] Indian - 2. RELIG Hindu.

hinduismo *sm* Hinduism.

hinojo *sm* fennel.

hipar *vi* to hiccup, to have hiccups.

híper *sm fam* hypermarket.

hiperactivo, va *adj* hyperactive.

hipérbola *sf* hyperbola.

hiperenlace *sm* INFORM hyperlink.

hipermercado *sm* hypermarket.

hipertensión *sf* high blood pressure.

hipertexto *sm* INFORM hypertext.

hípico, ca *adj* [de las carreras] horseracing (*antes de s*); [de la equitación] showjumping (*antes de s*). ◆ **hípica** *sf* [carreras de caballos] horseracing; [equitación] showjumping.

hipnosis *sf inv* hypnosis.

hipnótico, ca *adj* hypnotic.

hipnotismo *sm* hypnotism.

hipnotizador, ra *adj* hypnotic; *fig* spellbinding, mesmerizing.

hipnotizar *vt* to hypnotize; *fig* to mesmerize.

hipo *sm* hiccups *pl*; **tener hipo** to have (the) hiccups; **quitar el hipo a uno** *fig* to take one's breath away.

hipocondriaco, ca *adj & sm, f* hypochondriac.

hipocresía *sf* hypocrisy.

hipócrita ◇ *adj* hypocritical. ◇ *smf* hypocrite.

hipodérmico, ca *adj* hypodermic.

hipódromo *sm* racecourse, racetrack.

hipopótamo *sm* hippopotamus.

hipoteca *sf* mortgage.

hipotecar *vt* [bienes] to mortgage.

hipotecario, ria *adj* mortgage (*antes de s*).

hipotenusa *sf* hypotenuse.

hipótesis *sf inv* hypothesis.

hipotético, ca *adj* hypothetical.

hippy, hippie ['xipi] (*pl* **hippies**) *adj & smf* hippy.

hiriente *adj* [palabras] hurtful, cutting.

hirsuto, ta *adj* [cabello] wiry; [brazo, pecho] hairy.

hispánico, ca *adj & sm, f* Hispanic, Spanish-speaking.

hispanidad *sf* [cultura] Spanishness; [pueblos] Spanish-speaking world.

hispano, na <> adj [español] Spanish; [hispanoamericano] Spanish-American; [en Estados Unidos] Hispanic. <> sm, f [español] Spaniard; [estadounidense] Hispanic.

hispanoamericano, na <> adj Spanish-American. <> sm, f Spanish American.

hispanohablante <> adj Spanish-speaking. <> smf Spanish speaker.

histeria sf fig & MED hysteria.

histérico, ca adj fig & MED hysterical; **ponerse histérico** to get hysterical.

histerismo sm fig & MED hysteria.

historia sf - **1.** [gen] history; **historia antigua/universal** ancient/world history; **historia del arte** art history; **hacer historia** to make history; **pasar a la historia** to go down in history - **2.** [narración, chisme] story; **dejarse de historias** to stop beating about the bush.

historiador, ra sm, f historian.

historial sm [gen] record; [profesional] curriculum vitae, résumé US.

histórico, ca adj - **1.** [de la historia] historical - **2.** [verídico] factual - **3.** [importante] historic.

historieta sf - **1.** [chiste] funny story, anecdote - **2.** [tira cómica] comic strip.

hito sm lit & fig milestone.

hizo ⊳ **hacer**.

hobby ['xoβi] (pl hobbies) sm hobby.

Hno. (abrev de hermano) Br.

Hnos. (abrev de hermanos) Bros.

hocico sm [de perro] muzzle; [de gato] nose; [de cerdo] snout.

hockey ['xokei] sm hockey; **hockey sobre hielo/patines** ice/roller hockey; **hockey sobre hierba** (field) hockey.

hogar sm - **1.** [de chimenea] fireplace; [de horno, cocina] grate - **2.** [domicilio] home; **artículos para el hogar** household goods; **labores del hogar** housework; **hogar, dulce hogar** home, sweet home; **hogar de ancianos** old people's home.

hogareño, ña adj [gen] family (antes de s); [amante del hogar] home-loving.

hogaza sf large loaf.

hoguera sf bonfire; **morir en la hoguera** to be burned at the stake.

hoja sf - **1.** [de plantas] leaf; **de hoja caduca** deciduous; **de hoja perenne** evergreen; [de flor] petal; [de hierba] blade - **2.** [de papel] sheet (of paper); [de libro] page - **3.** [de cuchillo] blade; **hoja de afeitar** razor blade - **4.** [de puertas, ventanas] leaf. ➡ **hoja de cálculo** sf INFORM spreadsheet.

hojalata sf tinplate.

hojaldre sm puff pastry.

hojarasca sf - **1.** [hojas secas] (dead) leaves pl; [frondosidad] tangle of leaves - **2.** fig [paja] rubbish.

hojear vt to leaf through.

hola interj: ¡hola! hello!

Holanda n pr Holland.

holandés, esa <> adj Dutch. <> sm, f [persona] Dutchman (f Dutchwoman). ➡ **holandés** sm [lengua] Dutch. ➡ **holandesa** sf [papel] piece of paper measuring 22 x 28 cm.

holding ['xoldin] (pl holdings) sm holding company.

holgado, da adj - **1.** [ropa] baggy, loose-fitting; [habitación, espacio] roomy - **2.** [victoria, situación económica] comfortable.

holgar vi [sobrar] to be unnecessary; **huelga decir que...** needless to say...

holgazán, ana <> adj idle, good-for-nothing. <> sm, f good-for-nothing.

holgazanear vi to laze about.

holgura sf - **1.** [anchura - de espacio] room; [- de ropa] bagginess, looseness; [- entre piezas] play, give - **2.** [bienestar] comfort, affluence.

hollar vt to tread (on).

hollín sm soot.

holocausto sm holocaust.

hombre <> sm man; **el hombre de la calle** O **de a pie** the man in the street; **hombre de las cavernas** caveman; **hombre de negocios** businessman; **hombre de palabra** man of his word; **un pobre hombre** a nobody; **¡pobre hombre!** poor chap UK O guy!; **de hombre a hombre** man to man; **ser un hombre hecho y derecho** to be a grown man; **hombre precavido vale por dos** prov forewarned is forearmed prov. <> interj: **¡hombre! ¡qué alegría verte!** (hey,) how nice to see you! ➡ **hombre orquesta** (pl hombres orquesta) sm one-man band. ➡ **hombre rana** (pl hombres rana) sm frogman.

hombrera sf [de traje, vestido] shoulder pad; [de uniforme] epaulette.

hombría sf manliness.

hombro sm shoulder; **a hombros** over one's shoulders; **hombro con hombro** shoulder to shoulder; **encogerse de hombros** to shrug one's shoulders; **arrimar el hombro** fig to lend a hand; **mirar por encima del hombro a alguien** fig to look down one's nose at sb.

hombruno, na adj mannish.

homenaje sm [gen] tribute; [al soberano] homage; **partido (de) homenaje** testimonial (match); **en homenaje de** O **a** in honour of, as a tribute to; **rendir homenaje a** to pay tribute to.

homenajeado, da sm, f guest of honour.

homenajear vt to pay tribute to.

homeopatía sf homeopathy.

homicida <> *adj* [mirada etc] murderous; **arma homicida** murder weapon. <> *smf* murderer.

homicidio *sm* homicide, murder; **homicidio frustrado** attempted murder.

homilía *sf* homily, sermon.

homogeneizar *vt* to homogenize.

homogéneo, a *adj* homogenous.

homologar *vt* - **1.** [equiparar]: **homologar (con)** to bring into line (with), to make comparable (with) - **2.** [dar por válido - producto] to authorize officially; [- récord] to confirm officially.

homólogo, ga <> *adj* [semejante] equivalent. <> *sm, f* counterpart.

homosexual *adj* & *smf* homosexual.

hondo, da *adj* - **1.** *lit* & *fig* [gen] deep; **tiene tres metros de hondo** it's three metres deep; **lo hondo the depths** *pl*; **calar hondo en** to strike a chord with; **en lo más hondo de** in the depths of - **2.** ⊳ **cante.** ➡ **honda** *sf* sling.

hondonada *sf* hollow.

hondura *sf* depth.

Honduras *n pr* Honduras.

hondureño, ña *adj* & *sm, f* Honduran.

honestidad *sf* [honradez] honesty; [decencia] modesty, decency; [justicia] fairness.

honesto, ta *adj* [honrado] honest; [decente] modest, decent; [justo] fair.

hongo *sm* - **1.** [planta - comestible] mushroom; [- no comestible] toadstool - **2.** [enfermedad] fungus.

honor *sm* honour; **hacer honor a** to live up to; **en honor a la verdad** to be (quite) honest. ➡ **honores** *smpl* [ceremonial] honours.

honorable *adj* honourable.

honorario, ria *adj* honorary. ➡ **honorarios** *smpl* fees.

honorífico, ca *adj* honorific.

honra *sf* honour; **¡y a mucha honra!** and proud of it! ➡ **honras fúnebres** *sfpl* funeral *sing*.

honradez *sf* honesty.

honrado, da *adj* honest.

honrar *vt* to honour. ➡ **honrarse** *vprnl*: **honrarse (con algo/de hacer algo)** to be honoured (by sthg/to do sthg).

honroso, sa *adj* - **1.** [que da honra] honorary - **2.** [respetable] honourable, respectable.

hora *sf* - **1.** [del día] hour; **a primera hora** first thing in the morning; **a última hora** [al final del día] at the end of the day; [en el último momento] at the last moment; **dar la hora** to strike the hour; **de última hora** [noticia] latest; [preparativos] last-minute; **'última hora'** 'stop press'; **(pagar) por horas** (to pay) by the hour; **hora de dormir** bedtime; **horas**

de oficina/trabajo office/working hours; **hora local/oficial** local/official time; **hora punta** O pico Amér rush hour; **horas extraordinarias** overtime *(U)*; **horas libres** free time *(U)*; **horas de visita** visiting times; **horas de vuelo** flying time *sing*; **media hora** half an hour - **2.** [momento determinado] time; **¿a qué hora sale?** what time O when does it leave?; **es hora de irse** it's time to go; **es hora de cenar** it's time for supper; **a la hora** on time; **cada hora** hourly; **en su hora** when the time comes, at the appropriate time; **¿qué hora es?** what time is it?; **hora de cerrar** closing time - **3.** [cita] appointment; **pedir/dar hora** to ask for/give an appointment; **tener hora en/con** to have an appointment at/with - **4.** *loc*: **a altas horas de la noche** in the small hours; **en mala hora** unluckily; **la hora de la verdad** the moment of truth; **¡ya era hora!** and about time too!

horadar *vt* to pierce; [con máquina] to bore through.

horario, ria *adj* time *(antes de s)*. ➡ **horario** *sm* timetable; **horario comercial/laboral** opening/working hours *pl*; **horario intensivo** working day without a long break for lunch; **horario de visitas** visiting hours *pl*.

horca *sf* - **1.** [patíbulo] gallows *pl* - **2.** AGRIC pitchfork.

horcajadas ➡ **a horcajadas** *loc adv* astride.

horchata *sf* cold drink made from ground tiger nuts or almonds, milk and sugar.

horizontal *adj* horizontal.

horizonte *sm* horizon.

horma *sf* [gen] mould, pattern; [para arreglar zapatos] last; [para conservar zapatos] shoe tree; [de sombrero] hat block.

hormiga *sf* ant; **ser una hormiga** *fig* to be hard-working and thrifty.

hormigón *sm* concrete; **hormigón armado** reinforced concrete.

hormigueo *sm* pins and needles *pl*.

hormiguero *sm* ants' nest; ⊳ **oso.**

hormona *sf* hormone.

hornada *sf* *lit* & *fig* batch.

hornear *vt* to bake.

hornillo *sm* [para cocinar] camping O portable stove; [de laboratorio] small furnace.

horno *sm* CULIN oven; TECNOL furnace; [de cerámica, ladrillos] kiln; **alto horno** blast furnace; **altos hornos** [factoría] iron and steelworks; **horno eléctrico** electric oven; **horno de gas** gas oven; **horno microondas** microwave (oven).

horóscopo *sm* - **1.** [signo zodiacal] star sign - **2.** [predicción] horoscope.

horquilla *sf* [para el pelo] hairpin, bobby pin US.

horrendo, **da** *adj* [gen] horrendous; [muy malo] terrible, awful.

horrible *adj* [gen] horrible; [muy malo] terrible, awful.

horripilante *adj* [terrorífico] horrifying, spine-chilling.

horripilar *vt* to terrify.

horror *sm* - **1.** [miedo] terror, horror; **¡qué horror!** how awful! - **2.** *(gen pl)* [atrocidad] atrocity.

horrorizado, **da** *adj* terrified, horrified.

horrorizar *vt* to terrify, to horrify. ➨ **horrorizarse** *vprnl* to be terrified O horrified.

horroroso, **sa** *adj* - **1.** [gen] awful - **2.** [muy feo] horrible, hideous.

hortaliza *sf* (garden) vegetable.

hortelano, **na** *sm, f* market gardener.

hortensia *sf* hydrangea.

hortera *fam adj* tasteless, tacky.

horticultura *sf* horticulture.

hosco, **ca** *adj* [persona] sullen, gruff; [lugar] grim, gloomy.

hospedar *vt* - **1.** to put up - **2.** INFORM to host. ➨ **hospedarse** *vprnl* to stay.

hospicio *sm* [para niños] children's home; [para pobres] poorhouse.

hospital *sm* hospital.

hospitalario, **ria** *adj* [acogedor] hospitable.

hospitalidad *sf* hospitality.

hospitalizar *vt* to hospitalize, to take O send to hospital.

hostal *sm* guesthouse.

hostelería *sf* catering.

hostia *sf* - **1.** RELIG host - **2.** *vulg* [bofetada] bash, punch - **3.** *vulg* [accidente] smash-up; **darse** O **pegarse una hostia** to have a smash-up. ➨ **hostias** *interj vulg*: **¡hostias!** bloody hell!, damn it!

hostiar *vt vulg* to bash.

hostigar *vt* - **1.** [acosar] to pester, to bother - **2.** MIL to harass.

hostil *adj* hostile.

hostilidad *sf* [sentimiento] hostility. ➨ **hostilidades** *sfpl* MIL hostilities.

hotel *sm* hotel.

hotelero, **ra** *adj* hotel *(antes de s)*.

hoy *adv* - **1.** [en este día] today; **de hoy en adelante** from now on; **hoy mismo** this very day; **por hoy** for now, for the time being - **2.** [en la actualidad] nowadays, today; **hoy día, hoy en día, hoy por hoy** these days, nowadays.

hoyo *sm* [gen] hole, pit; [de golf] hole.

hoyuelo *sm* dimple.

hoz *sf* sickle; **la hoz y el martillo** the hammer and sickle.

HTML *(abrev de hypertext markup language)* *sm* INFORM HTML.

huacal *sm Méx* - **1.** [jaula] cage - **2.** [cajón] drawer.

hubiera *etc* ➩ **haber**.

hucha *sf* moneybox.

hueco, **ca** *adj* - **1.** [vacío] hollow - **2.** [sonido] resonant, hollow - **3.** [sin ideas] empty. ➨ **hueco** *sm* - **1.** [cavidad - gen] hole; [- en pared] recess - **2.** [tiempo libre] spare moment - **3.** [espacio libre] space, gap; [de escalera] well; [de ascensor] shaft; **hacer un hueco a alguien** to make space for sb.

huela *etc* ➩ **oler**.

huelga *sf* strike; **estar/declararse en huelga** to be/to go on strike; **huelga de brazos caídos** O **cruzados** sit-down (strike); **huelga de celo** work-to-rule; **huelga de hambre** hunger strike; **huelga general** general strike; **huelga salvaje** wildcat strike.

huelguista *smf* striker.

huella *sf* - **1.** [de persona] footprint; [de animal, rueda] track; **huella digital** O **dactilar** fingerprint - **2.** *fig* [vestigio] trace; **sin dejar huella** without (a) trace - **3.** *fig* [impresión profunda] mark; **dejar huella** to leave one's mark.

huérfano, **na** *adj* & *sm, f* orphan; **es huérfano de madre** his mother is dead, he's lost his mother.

huerta *sf* [huerto] market garden *UK*, truck farm *US*.

huerto *sm* [de hortalizas] vegetable garden; [de frutales] orchard.

hueso *sm* - **1.** [del cuerpo] bone; **estar calado hasta los huesos** to be soaked to the skin; **ser un hueso duro de roer** to be a hard nut to crack - **2.** [de fruto] stone *UK*, pit *US* - **3.** *Amér* & *Méx fam* [enchufe] contacts *pl*, influence - **4.** *Méx fam* [trabajo fácil] cushy job.

huésped, **da** *sm, f* guest.

huesudo, **da** *adj* bony.

hueva *sf* roe.

huevo *sm* - **1.** [de animales] egg; **huevo a la copa** O **tibio** *Andes* soft-boiled egg; **huevo escalfado/frito** poached/fried egg; **huevo pasado por agua/duro** soft-boiled/hard-boiled egg; **huevo de Pascua** Easter egg; **huevos revueltos** scrambled eggs; **parecerse como un huevo a una castaña** to be like chalk and cheese - **2.** *(gen pl) vulg* [testículos] balls *pl*.

huevón, **ona** *sm, f Andes, Arg* & *Ven vulg* prat *UK*, pillock *UK*, jerk *US*.

huida *sf* escape, flight.

huidizo, **za** *adj* shy, elusive.

huir *vi* - **1.** [escapar]: **huir (de)** [gen] to flee (from); [de cárcel etc] to escape (from); **huir del país** to flee the country - **2.** [evitar]: **huir de algo** to avoid sthg, to keep away from sthg.

hule *sm* oilskin.

humanidad *sf* humanity. **humanidades** *sfpl* [letras] humanities.

humanitario, ria *adj* humanitarian.

humanizar *vt* to humanize.

humano, na *adj* - **1.** [del hombre] human - **2.** [compasivo] humane. **humano** *sm* human being; **los humanos** mankind *(U)*.

humareda *sf* cloud of smoke.

humear *vi* [salir humo] to (give off) smoke; [salir vapor] to steam.

humedad *sf* - **1.** [gen] dampness; [en pared, techo] damp; [de algo chorreando] wetness; [de piel, ojos etc] moistness - **2.** [de atmósfera etc] humidity; **humedad absoluta/relativa** absolute/relative humidity.

humedecer *vt* to moisten. **humedecerse** *vprnl* to become moist; **humedecerse los labios** to moisten one's lips.

húmedo, da *adj* - **1.** [gen] damp; [chorreando] wet; [piel, ojos etc] moist - **2.** [aire, clima, atmósfera] humid.

humidificar *vt* to humidify.

humildad *sf* humility.

humilde *adj* humble.

humillación *sf* humiliation.

humillado, da *adj* humiliated.

humillante *adj* humiliating.

humillar *vt* to humiliate. **humillarse** *vprnl* to humble o.s..

humo *sm* [gen] smoke; [vapor] steam; [de coches etc] fumes *pl*; **echar humo** [gen] to smoke; *fig* to be fuming; **tragarse el humo** [al fumar] to inhale. **humos** *smpl fig* [aires] airs; **bajarle a alguien los humos** to take sb down a peg or two; **tener muchos humos** to put on airs.

humor *sm* - **1.** [estado de ánimo] mood; [carácter] temperament; **estar de buen/mal humor** to be in a good/bad mood - **2.** [gracia] humour; **un programa de humor** a comedy programme; **humor negro** black humour - **3.** [ganas] mood; **no estoy de humor** I'm not in the mood.

humorismo *sm* humour; TEATRO & TV comedy.

humorista *smf* humorist; TEATRO & TV comedian (*f* comedienne).

humorístico, ca *adj* humorous.

hundimiento *sm* - **1.** [naufragio] sinking - **2.** [ruina] collapse.

hundir *vt* - **1.** [gen] to sink; **hundir algo en el agua** to put sthg underwater - **2.** [afligir] to devastate, to destroy - **3.** [hacer fracasar] to ruin. **hundirse** *vprnl* - **1.** [sumergirse] to sink; [intencionadamente] to dive - **2.** [derrumbarse] to collapse; [techo] to cave in - **3.** [fracasar] to be ruined.

húngaro, ra *adj* & *sm,* *f* Hungarian. **húngaro** *sm* [lengua] Hungarian.

Hungría *n pr* Hungary.

huracán *sm* hurricane.

huraño, ña *adj* unsociable.

hurgar *vi*: **hurgar (en)** [gen] to rummage around (in); [con el dedo, un palo] to poke around (in). **hurgarse** *vprnl*: **hurgarse la nariz** to pick one's nose; **hurgarse los bolsillos** to rummage around in one's pockets.

hurón *sm* ZOOL ferret.

hurra *interj*: ¡**hurra!** hurray!

hurtadillas **a hurtadillas** *loc adv* on the sly, stealthily.

hurtar *vt* to steal.

hurto *sm* theft.

husmear *vt* [olfatear] to sniff out, to scent. *vi* [curiosear] to nose around.

huso *sm* spindle; [en máquina] bobbin.

huy *interj*: ¡**huy!** [dolor] ouch!; [sorpresa] gosh!

i (*pl* **íes**), **I** (*pl* **íes**) *sf* [letra] i, I.

IAE (*abrev de* **impuesto sobre actividades económicas**) *sm Spanish tax paid by professionals and shop owners.*

iba ir.

ibérico, ca *adj* Iberian.

íbero, ra, ibero, ra *adj* & *sm,* *f* Iberian. **íbero, ibero** *sm* [lengua] Iberian.

iberoamericano, na *adj* & *sm,* *f* Latin American.

iceberg (*pl* **icebergs**) *sm* iceberg.

icono *sm* icon.

iconoclasta *smf* iconoclast.

id ir.

ida *sf* outward journey; **(billete de) ida y vuelta** return (ticket).

idea *sf* - **1.** [gen] idea; [propósito] intention; **con la idea de** with the idea O intention of; **hacerse a la idea de que...** to get used to the idea that...; **hacerse una idea de algo** to get an idea of sthg; **idea fija** obsession; **idea preconcebida** preconception; **cuando se le mete una**

idea en la cabeza... when he gets an idea into his head...; **¡ni idea!** *fam* search me!, I haven't got a clue!; **no tener ni idea (de)** not to have a clue (about) - 2. [opinión] impression; **cambiar de idea** to change one's mind.

ideal *adj & sm* ideal; **lo ideal sería hacerlo mañana** ideally, we would do it tomorrow.

idealista ◇ *adj* idealistic. ◇ *smf* idealist.

idealizar *vt* to idealize.

idear *vt* - 1. [planear] to think up, to devise - 2. [inventar] to invent.

ideario *sm* ideology.

ídem *pron* ditto.

idéntico, ca *adj*: **idéntico (a)** identical (to).

identidad *sf* [gen] identity.

identificación *sf* identification.

identificar *vt* to identify. ➠ **identificarse** *vprnl*: **identificarse (con)** to identify (with).

ideología *sf* ideology.

idílico, ca *adj* idyllic.

idilio *sm* love affair.

idioma *sm* language.

idiosincrasia *sf* individual character.

idiota ◇ *adj despec* [tonto] stupid. ◇ *smf* idiot.

idiotez *sf* [tontería] stupid thing, stupidity *(U)*.

ido, ida *adj* - 1. [loco] mad, touched - 2. [distraído]: **estar ido** to be miles away.

idolatrar *vt* to worship; *fig* to idolize.

ídolo *sm* idol.

idóneo, a *adj*: **idóneo (para)** suitable (for).

iglesia *sf* church.

iglú *(pl* **iglúes** *O* **iglús**) *sm* igloo.

ignorancia *sf* ignorance.

ignorante ◇ *adj* ignorant. ◇ *smf* ignoramus.

ignorar *vt* - 1. [desconocer] not to know, to be ignorant of - 2. [no tener en cuenta] to ignore.

igual ◇ *adj* - 1. [idéntico]: **igual (que)** the same (as); **llevan jerseys iguales** they're wearing the same jumper; **son iguales** they're the same - 2. [parecido]: **igual (que)** similar (to) - 3. [equivalente]: **igual (a)** equal (to) - 4. [liso] even - 5. [constante - velocidad] constant; [- clima, temperatura] even - 6. MAT: **A más B es igual a C** A plus B equals C. ◇ *smf* equal; **sin igual** without equal, unrivalled. ◇ *adv* - 1. [de la misma manera] the same; **yo pienso igual** I think the same, I think so too; **al igual que** just like; **por igual** equally - 2. [posiblemente] perhaps; **igual llueve** it could well rain - 3. DEP: **van iguales** the scores are level - 4. *loc*: **dar O ser igual a alguien** to be all the same to sb; **es O da igual** it doesn't matter, it doesn't make any difference.

igualado, da *adj* level.

igualar *vt* - 1. [gen] to make equal; DEP to equalize; **igualar algo a O con** to equate sthg with - 2. [persona] to be equal to; **nadie le iguala en generosidad** nobody is as generous as he is - 3. [terreno] to level; [superficie] to smooth. ➠ **igualarse** *vprnl* - 1. [gen] to be equal; **igualarse a O con** to be equated with - 2. [a otra persona]: **igualarse a O con alguien** to treat sb as an equal.

igualdad *sf* - 1. [equivalencia] equality; **en igualdad de condiciones** on equal terms; **igualdad de oportunidades** equal opportunities *pl* - 2. [identidad] sameness.

igualitario, ria *adj* egalitarian.

igualmente *adv* - 1. [también] also, likewise - 2. [fórmula de cortesía] the same to you, likewise.

ikurriña *sf* Basque national flag.

ilegal *adj* illegal.

ilegible *adj* illegible.

ilegítimo, ma *adj* illegitimate.

ileso, sa *adj* unhurt, unharmed; **salir O resultar ileso** to escape unharmed.

ilícito, ta *adj* illicit.

ilimitado, da *adj* unlimited, limitless.

iluminación *sf* - 1. [gen] lighting; [acción] illumination - 2. RELIG enlightenment.

iluminar *vt* [gen] to illuminate, to light up. ➠ **iluminarse** *vprnl* to light up.

ilusión *sf* - 1. [esperanza - gen] hope; [- infundada] delusion, illusion; **hacerse O forjarse ilusiones** to build up one's hopes; **hacerse la ilusión de** to imagine that; **tener ilusión por** to look forward to - 2. [emoción] thrill, excitement *(U)*; **¡qué ilusión!** how exciting!; **me hace mucha ilusión** I'm really looking forward to it - 3. [espejismo] illusion; **ilusión óptica** optical illusion.

ilusionar *vt* - 1. [esperanzar]: **ilusionar a alguien (con algo)** to build up sb's hopes (about sthg) - 2. [emocionar] to excite, to thrill. ➠ **ilusionarse** *vprnl* [emocionarse]: **ilusionarse (con)** to get excited (about).

ilusionista *smf* conjurer.

iluso, sa *adj* gullible.

ilusorio, ria *adj* illusory; [promesa] empty.

ilustración *sf* - 1. [estampa] illustration - 2. [cultura] learning. ➠ **Ilustración** *sf* HIST: **la Ilustración** the Enlightenment.

ilustrado, da *adj* - 1. [publicación] illustrated - 2. [persona] learned - 3. HIST enlightened.

ilustrar *vt* - 1. [explicar] to illustrate, to explain - 2. [publicación] to illustrate.

ilustre *adj* [gen] illustrious, distinguished.

imagen *sf* [gen] image; TV picture; **ser la viva imagen de alguien** to be the spitting image of sb; **imagen borrosa** blur; **imagen congelada** freeze frame; **imagen corporativa** corporate identity.

imaginación *sf* - **1.** [facultad] imagination; **se deja llevar por la imaginación** he lets his imagination run away with him; **pasar por la imaginación de alguien** to occur to sb, to cross sb's mind - **2.** *(gen pl)* [idea falsa] delusion.

imaginar *vt* - **1.** [gen] to imagine - **2.** [idear] to think up, to invent. **imaginarse** *vprnl* to imagine; **¡imagínate!** just think *O* imagine!; **me imagino que sí** I suppose so.

imaginario, ria *adj* imaginary.

imaginativo, va *adj* imaginative.

imán *sm* [para atraer] magnet.

imbécil <> *adj* stupid. <> *smf* idiot.

imbecilidad *sf* stupidity; **decir/hacer una imbecilidad** to say/do sthg stupid.

imborrable *adj fig* indelible; [recuerdo] unforgettable.

imbuir *vt*: **imbuir (de)** to imbue (with).

imitación *sf* imitation; [de humorista] impersonation; **a imitación de** in imitation of; **piel de imitación** imitation leather.

imitador, ra *sm, f* imitator; [humorista] impersonator.

imitar *vt* [gen] to imitate, to copy; [a personajes famosos] to impersonate; [producto, material] to simulate.

impaciencia *sf* impatience.

impacientar *vt* to make impatient. **impacientarse** *vprnl* to grow impatient.

impaciente *adj* impatient; **impaciente por hacer algo** impatient *O* anxious to do sthg.

impactante *adj* [imagen] hard-hitting; [belleza] striking.

impactar <> *vt* [suj: noticia] to have an impact on. <> *vi* [bala] to hit.

impacto *sm* - **1.** [gen] impact; [de bala] hit - **2.** [señal] (impact) mark; **impacto de bala** bullethole.

impagado, da *adj* unpaid.

impar *adj* MAT odd.

imparable *adj* unstoppable.

imparcial *adj* impartial.

impartir *vt* to give.

impase, impasse [im'pas] *sm* impasse.

impasible *adj* impassive.

impávido, da *adj* [valeroso] fearless, courageous; [impasible] impassive.

impecable *adj* impeccable.

impedido, da *adj* disabled; **estar impedido de un brazo** to have the use of only one arm.

impedimento *sm* [gen] obstacle; [contra un matrimonio] impediment.

impedir *vt* - **1.** [imposibilitar] to prevent; **impedir a alguien hacer algo** to prevent sb from doing sthg - **2.** [dificultar] to hinder, to obstruct.

impenetrable *adj lit & fig* impenetrable.

impensable *adj* unthinkable.

imperante *adj* prevailing.

imperar *vi* to prevail.

imperativo, va *adj* - **1.** [gen & GRAM] imperative - **2.** [autoritario] imperious. **imperativo** *sm* [gen & GRAM] imperative.

imperceptible *adj* imperceptible.

imperdible *sm* safety pin.

imperdonable *adj* unforgivable.

imperfección *sf* - **1.** [cualidad] imperfection - **2.** [defecto] flaw, defect.

imperfecto, ta *adj* [gen] imperfect; [defectuoso] faulty, defective. **imperfecto** *sm* GRAM imperfect.

imperial *adj* imperial.

imperialismo *sm* imperialism.

impericia *sf* lack of skill; [inexperiencia] inexperience.

imperio *sm* - **1.** [territorio] empire - **2.** [dominio] rule.

imperioso, sa *adj* - **1.** [autoritario] imperious - **2.** [apremiante] urgent.

impermeable <> *adj* waterproof. <> *sm* raincoat, mac *UK*.

impersonal *adj* impersonal.

impertinencia *sf* - **1.** [gen] impertinence - **2.** [comentario] impertinent remark.

impertinente *adj* impertinent.

imperturbable *adj* imperturbable.

ímpetu *sm* - **1.** [brusquedad] force - **2.** [energía] energy - **3.** FÍS impetus.

impetuoso, sa *adj* - **1.** [olas, viento, ataque] violent - **2.** [persona] impulsive, impetuous.

impío, a *adj* godless, impious.

implacable *adj* implacable, relentless.

implantar *vt* - **1.** [establecer] to introduce - **2.** MED to insert. **implantarse** *vprnl* [establecerse] to be introduced.

implicación *sf* - **1.** [participación] involvement - **2.** *(gen pl)* [consecuencia] implication.

implicar *vt* - **1.** [involucrar]: **implicar (en)** to involve (in); DER to implicate (in) - **2.** [significar] to mean. **implicarse** *vprnl* DER to incriminate o.s.; **implicarse en** to become involved in.

implícito, ta *adj* implicit.

implorar *vt* to implore.

imponente *adj* - **1.** [impresionante] imposing, impressive - **2.** [estupendo] sensational, terrific.

imponer ⬦ *vt* - 1.: **imponer algo (a alguien)** [gen] to impose sthg (on sb); [respeto] to command sthg (from sb) - 2. [moda] to set; [costumbre] to introduce. ⬦ *vi* to be imposing. ⬦ **imponerse** *vprnl* - 1. [hacerse respetar] to command respect, to show authority - 2. [prevalecer] to prevail - 3. [ser necesario] to be necessary - 4. DEP to win, to prevail.

impopular *adj* unpopular.

importación *sf* [acción] importing; [artículo] import.

importador, ra *sm, f* importer.

importancia *sf* importance; **dar importancia a algo** to attach importance to sthg; **quitar importancia a algo** to play sthg down; **darse importancia** to give o.s. airs, to show off.

importante *adj* - 1. [gen] important; [lesión] serious - 2. [cantidad] considerable.

importar ⬦ *vt* - 1. [gen & INFORM] to import - 2. [suj: factura, coste] to amount to, to come to. ⬦ *vi* - 1. [preocupar] to matter; **no me importa** I don't care, it doesn't matter to me; **¿y a ti qué te importa?** what's it got to do with you?; **me importa un bledo** O **comino** O **pito** *fam* I don't give a damn, I couldn't care less - 2. [en preguntas] to mind; **¿le importa que me siente?** do you mind if I sit down?; **¿te importaría acompañarme?** would you mind coming with me? ⬦ *v impers* to matter; **no importa** it doesn't matter.

importe *sm* [gen] price, cost; [de factura] total.

importunar *vt* to bother, to pester.

importuno, na = **inoportuno**.

imposibilidad *sf* impossibility; **su imposibilidad para contestar la pregunta** his inability to answer the question.

imposibilitado, da *adj* disabled; **estar imposibilitado para hacer algo** to be unable to do sthg.

imposibilitar *vt*: **imposibilitar a alguien para hacer algo** to make it impossible for sb to do sthg, to prevent sb from doing sthg.

imposible *adj* - 1. [irrealizable] impossible - 2. [insoportable] unbearable, impossible.

imposición *sf* - 1. [obligación] imposition - 2. [impuesto] tax - 3. BANCA deposit; **hacer** O **efectuar una imposición** to make a deposit.

impostor, ra *sm, f* [suplantador] impostor.

impotencia *sf* impotence.

impotente *adj* impotent.

impracticable *adj* - 1. [irrealizable] impracticable - 2. [intransitable] impassable.

imprecisión *sf* imprecision, vagueness (U).

impreciso, sa *adj* imprecise, vague.

impredecible *adj* unforeseeable; [variable] unpredictable.

impregnar *vt*: **impregnar (de)** to impregnate (with). ⬦ **impregnarse** *vprnl*: **impregnarse (de)** to become impregnated (with).

imprenta *sf* - 1. [arte] printing - 2. [máquina] (printing) press - 3. [establecimiento] printing house.

imprescindible *adj* indispensable, essential.

impresentable *adj* unpresentable.

impresión *sf* - 1. [gen] impression; [sensación física] feeling; **causar (una) buena/mala impresión** to make a good/bad impression; **dar la impresión de** to give the impression of; **tener la impresión de que** to have the impression that - 2. [huella] imprint - 3. [IMPR - acción] printing; [- edición] edition.

impresionable *adj* impressionable.

impresionante *adj* impressive; [error] enormous.

impresionar ⬦ *vt* - 1. [maravillar] to impress - 2. [conmocionar] to move - 3. [horrorizar] to shock - 4. FOTO to expose. ⬦ *vi* [maravillar] to make an impression. ⬦ **impresionarse** *vprnl* - 1. [maravillarse] to be impressed - 2. [conmocionarse] to be moved - 3. [horrorizarse] to be shocked.

impreso, sa ⬦ *pp* ▷ **imprimir**. ⬦ *adj* printed. ⬦ **impreso** *sm* - 1. [texto] printed matter (U) - 2. [formulario] form.

impresor, ra *sm, f* [persona] printer. ⬦ **impresora** *sf* INFORM printer; **impresora láser/térmica** laser/thermal printer; **impresora de matriz** O **de agujas** dot-matrix printer; **impresora de chorro de tinta** ink-jet printer.

imprevisible *adj* unforeseeable; [variable] unpredictable.

imprevisto, ta *adj* unexpected. ⬦ **imprevisto** *sm* [hecho]: **salvo imprevistos** barring accidents.

imprimir *vt* - 1. [gen] to print; [huella, paso] to leave - 2. *fig* [transmitir]: **imprimir algo a** to impart O bring sthg to.

improbable *adj* improbable, unlikely.

improcedente *adj* - 1. [inoportuno] inappropriate - 2. DER inadmissible.

improperio *sm* insult.

impropio, pia *adj*: **impropio (de)** improper (for), unbecoming (to).

improvisado, da *adj* [gen] improvised; [discurso, truco] impromptu; [comentario] ad-lib; [cama etc] makeshift.

improvisar ⬦ *vt* [gen] to improvise; [comida] to rustle up; **improvisar una cama** to make (up) a makeshift bed. ⬦ *vi* [gen] to improvise; MÚS to extemporize.

improviso ⬦ **de improviso** *loc adv* unexpectedly, suddenly; **coger a alguien de improviso** to catch sb unawares.

imprudencia *sf* [en los actos] carelessness (U); [en los comentarios] indiscretion.

imprudente *adj* [en los actos] careless, rash; [en los comentarios] indiscreet.

impúdico, ca *adj* immodest, indecent.

impuesto, ta *pp* ▷ **imponer**. ◆ **impuesto** *sm* tax; **impuesto de circulación** road tax; **impuesto sobre el valor añadido** value-added tax; **impuesto sobre la renta** ≃ income tax.

impugnar *vt* to contest, to challenge.

impulsar *vt* - **1.** [empujar] to propel, to drive - **2.** [promocionar] to stimulate.

impulsivo, va *adj* impulsive..

impulso *sm* - **1.** [progreso] stimulus, boost - **2.** [fuerza] momentum - **3.** [motivación] impulse, urge.

impulsor, ra *sm, f* dynamic force.

impune *adj* unpunished.

impunidad *sf* impunity.

impureza *sf* (gen pl) impurity.

impuro, ra *adj* lit & fig impure.

imputación *sf* accusation.

imputar *vt* [atribuir]: **imputar algo a alguien** [delito] to accuse sb of sthg; [fracaso, error] to attribute sthg to sb.

inacabable *adj* interminable, endless.

inaccesible *adj* inaccessible.

inaceptable *adj* unacceptable.

inactividad *sf* inactivity.

inactivo, va *adj* inactive.

inadaptado, da *adj* maladjusted.

inadecuado, da *adj* [inapropiado] unsuitable, inappropriate.

inadmisible *adj* inadmissible.

inadvertido, da *adj* unnoticed; **pasar inadvertido** to go unnoticed.

inagotable *adj* inexhaustible.

inaguantable *adj* unbearable.

inalámbrico, ca *adj* cordless; INFORM wireless.

inalcanzable *adj* unattainable.

inalterable *adj* - **1.** [gen] unalterable; [salud] stable; [amistad] undying - **2.** [color] fast - **3.** [rostro, carácter] impassive - **4.** [resultado, marcador] unchanged.

inamovible *adj* immovable, fixed.

inanición *sf* starvation.

inanimado, da *adj* inanimate.

inánime *adj* lifeless.

inapreciable *adj* - **1.** [incalculable] invaluable - **2.** [insignificante] imperceptible.

inapropiado, da *adj* inappropriate.

inaudito, ta *adj* unheard-of.

inauguración *sf* inauguration, opening.

inaugurar *vt* to inaugurate, to open.

inca *adj* & *smf* Inca.

incalculable *adj* incalculable.

incalificable *adj* unspeakable.

incandescente *adj* incandescent.

incansable *adj* untiring, tireless.

incapacidad *sf* - **1.** [imposibilidad] inability - **2.** [inaptitud] incompetence - **3.** DER incapacity.

incapacitado, da *adj* [DER - gen] disqualified; [- para testar] incapacitated; [- para trabajar] unfit.

incapacitar *vt*: **incapacitar (para)** [gen] to disqualify (from); [para trabajar etc] to render unfit (for).

incapaz *adj* - **1.** [gen]: **incapaz de** incapable of - **2.** [sin talento]: **incapaz para** incompetent at, no good at - **3.** DER incompetent.

incautación *sf* seizure, confiscation.

incautarse ◆ **incautarse de** *vprnl* DER to seize, to confiscate.

incauto, ta *adj* gullible.

incendiar *vt* to set fire to. ◆ **incendiarse** *vprnl* to catch fire.

incendiario, ria ◇ *adj* - **1.** [bomba etc] incendiary - **2.** [artículo, libro etc] inflammatory. ◇ *sm, f* arsonist.

incendio *sm* fire; **incendio forestal** forest fire; **incendio provocado** arson.

incentivo *sm* incentive; **incentivo fiscal** tax incentive.

incertidumbre *sf* uncertainty.

incesto *sm* incest.

incidencia *sf* - **1.** [repercusión] impact, effect - **2.** [suceso] event.

incidente *sm* incident; **incidente diplomático** diplomatic incident.

incidir ◆ **incidir en** *vi* - **1.** [incurrir en] to fall into, to lapse into - **2.** [insistir en] to focus on - **3.** [influir en] to have an impact on, to affect.

incienso *sm* incense.

incierto, ta *adj* - **1.** [dudoso] uncertain - **2.** [falso] untrue.

incineración *sf* [de cadáver] cremation; [de basura] incineration.

incinerar *vt* [cadáver] to cremate; [basura] to incinerate.

incipiente *adj* incipient; [estado, etapa] early.

incisión *sf* incision.

incisivo, va *adj* - **1.** [instrumento] sharp, cutting - **2.** fig [mordaz] incisive.

inciso, sa *adj* cut. ◆ **inciso** *sm* passing remark.

incitar *vt*: **incitar a alguien a algo** [violencia, rebelión etc] to incite sb to sthg; **incitar a alguien a la fuga/venganza** to urge sb to flee/

avenge himself; **incitar a alguien a hacer algo** [rebelarse etc] to incite sb to do sthg; [fugarse, vengarse] to urge sb to do sthg.

inclemencia *sf* harshness, inclemency.

inclinación *sf* - **1.** [desviación] slant, inclination; [de terreno] slope - **2.** *fig* [afición]: **inclinación (a** *O* **por)** penchant *O* propensity (for) - **3.** [cariño]: **inclinación hacia alguien** fondness towards sb - **4.** [saludo] bow.

inclinar *vt* - **1.** [doblar] to bend; [ladear] to tilt - **2.** [cabeza] to bow. ➣ **inclinarse** *vprnl* - **1.** [doblarse] to lean - **2.** [para saludar]: **inclinarse (ante)** to bow (before). ➣ **inclinarse a** *vi* [tender a] to be *O* feel inclined to. ➣ **inclinarse por** *vi* [preferir] to favour, to lean towards.

incluir *vt* [gen] to include; [adjuntar - en cartas] to enclose.

inclusive *adv* inclusive.

incluso, sa *adj* enclosed. ➣ **incluso** *adv* & *prep* even.

incógnito, ta *adj* unknown. ➣ **incógnita** *sf* - **1.** MAT unknown quantity - **2.** [misterio] mystery. ➣ **de incógnito** *loc adv* incognito.

incoherencia *sf* - **1.** [cualidad] incoherence - **2.** [comentario] nonsensical remark.

incoherente *adj* - **1.** [inconexo] incoherent - **2.** [inconsecuente] inconsistent.

incoloro, ra *adj lit* & *fig* colourless.

incomodar *vt* - **1.** [causar molestia] to bother, to inconvenience - **2.** [enfadar] to annoy.

incomodidad *sf* - **1.** [de silla etc] uncomfortableness - **2.** [de situación, persona] awkwardness.

incómodo, da *adj* - **1.** [silla etc] uncomfortable - **2.** [situación, persona] awkward, uncomfortable; **sentirse incómodo** to feel awkward *O* uncomfortable.

incomparable *adj* incomparable.

incompatible *adj*: **incompatible (con)** incompatible (with).

incompetencia *sf* incompetence.

incompetente *adj* incompetent.

incompleto, ta *adj* - **1.** [gen] incomplete - **2.** [inacabado] unfinished.

incomprendido, da *adj* misunderstood.

incomprensible *adj* incomprehensible.

incomprensión *sf* lack of understanding.

incomunicado, da *adj* - **1.** [gen] isolated - **2.** [por la nieve etc] cut off - **3.** [preso] in solitary confinement.

inconcebible *adj* inconceivable.

inconcluso, sa *adj* unfinished.

incondicional ◇ *adj* unconditional; [ayuda] wholehearted; [seguidor] staunch. ◇ *smf* staunch supporter.

inconexo, xa *adj* [gen] unconnected; [pensamiento, texto] disjointed.

inconformista *adj* & *smf* nonconformist.

inconfundible *adj* unmistakable; [prueba] irrefutable.

incongruente *adj* incongruous.

inconsciencia *sf* - **1.** [gen] unconsciousness - **2.** *fig* [falta de juicio] thoughtlessness.

inconsciente *adj* - **1.** [gen] unconscious - **2.** *fig* [irreflexivo] thoughtless.

inconsecuente *adj* inconsistent.

inconsistente *adj* [tela, pared etc] flimsy; [salsa] runny; [argumento, discurso etc] lacking in substance.

inconstancia *sf* - **1.** [en el trabajo, la conducta] unreliability - **2.** [de opinión, ideas] changeability.

inconstante *adj* - **1.** [en el trabajo, la conducta] unreliable - **2.** [de opinión, ideas] changeable.

inconstitucional *adj* unconstitutional.

incontable *adj* [innumerable] countless.

incontestable *adj* indisputable.

incontinencia *sf* incontinence.

incontrolable *adj* uncontrollable.

inconveniencia *sf* - **1.** [inoportunidad] inappropriateness - **2.** [comentario] tactless remark; [acto] mistake.

inconveniente ◇ *adj* - **1.** [inoportuno] inappropriate - **2.** [descortés] rude. ◇ *sm* - **1.** [dificultad] obstacle, problem; **no tener inconveniente en hacer algo** to have no objection to doing sthg - **2.** [desventaja] drawback.

incordiar *vt fam* to bother, to pester.

incorporación *sf*: **incorporación (a)** [gen] incorporation (into); [a un puesto] induction (into).

incorporar *vt* - **1.** [añadir]: **incorporar (a)** [gen] to incorporate (into); CULIN to mix (into) - **2.** [levantar] to sit up. ➣ **incorporarse** *vprnl* [levantarse] to sit up.

incorrección *sf* - **1.** [inexactitud] incorrectness; [error gramatical] mistake - **2.** [descortesía] lack of courtesy, rudeness (*U*).

incorrecto, ta *adj* - **1.** [equivocado] incorrect, wrong - **2.** [descortés] rude, impolite.

incorregible *adj* incorrigible.

incredulidad *sf* incredulity.

incrédulo, la *adj* sceptical, incredulous; RELIG unbelieving.

increíble *adj* - **1.** [difícil de creer] unconvincing - **2.** *fig* [extraordinario] incredible - **3.** *fig* [inconcebible] unbelievable; **es increíble que pasen cosas así** it's hard to believe that such things can happen.

incrementar *vt* to increase. ➣ **incrementarse** *vprnl* to increase.

incremento *sm* increase; [de temperatura] rise; **incremento salarial** pay increase.

increpar *vt* - **1.** [reprender] to reprimand - **2.** [insultar] to abuse, insult.

incriminar *vt* to accuse.

incrustar *vt* - **1.** TECNOL to inlay; [en joyería] to set - **2.** *fam fig* [empotrar]: **incrustar algo en algo** to sink sthg into sthg. ➡ **incrustarse** *vprnl* [cal etc] to become encrusted.

incubar *vt* - **1.** [huevo] to incubate - **2.** [enfermedad] to be sickening for.

inculcar *vt*: **inculcar algo a alguien** to instil sthg into sb.

inculpar *vt*: **inculpar a alguien (de)** [gen] to accuse sb (of); DER to charge sb (with).

inculto, ta ◇ *adj* [persona] uneducated. ◇ *sm, f* ignoramus.

incumbencia *sf*: **no es asunto de tu incumbencia** it's none of your business.

incumbir ➡ **incumbir a** *vi*: **incumbir a alguien** to be a matter for sb; **esto no te incumbe** this is none of your business.

incumplimiento *sm* [de deber] failure to fulfil; [de orden, ley] non-compliance; [de promesa] failure to keep; **incumplimiento de contrato** breach of contract.

incumplir *vt* [deber] to fail to fulfil, to neglect; [orden, ley] to fail to comply with; [promesa] to break; [contrato] to breach.

incurable *adj* incurable.

incurrir ➡ **incurrir en** *vi* - **1.** [delito, falta] to commit; [error] to make - **2.** [desprecio etc] to incur.

incursión *sf* incursion.

indagación *sf* investigation, inquiry.

indagar ◇ *vt* to investigate, to inquire into. ◇ *vi* to investigate, to inquire.

indecencia *sf* - **1.** [cualidad] indecency - **2.** [acción] outrage, crime.

indecente *adj* - **1.** [impúdico] indecent - **2.** [indigno] miserable, wretched.

indecible *adj* [alegría] indescribable; [dolor] unspeakable.

indecisión *sf* indecisiveness.

indeciso, sa ◇ *adj* - **1.** [persona - inseguro] indecisive; [- que está dudoso] undecided - **2.** [pregunta, respuesta] hesitant; [resultado] undecided. ◇ *sm, f* undecided voter.

indefenso, sa *adj* defenceless.

indefinido, da *adj* - **1.** [ilimitado] indefinite; [contrato] open-ended - **2.** [impreciso] vague - **3.** GRAM indefinite.

indeleble *adj culto* indelible.

indemne *adj* unhurt, unharmed.

indemnización *sf* [gen] compensation; [por despido] severance pay; **indemnización por daños y perjuicios** DER damages *pl*.

indemnizar *vt*: **indemnizar a alguien (por)** to compensate sb (for).

independencia *sf* independence; **con independencia de** independently of.

independiente *adj* - **1.** [gen] independent - **2.** [aparte] separate.

independizar *vt* to grant independence to. ➡ **independizarse** *vprnl*: **independizarse (de)** to become independent (of).

indeseable *adj* undesirable.

indeterminación *sf* indecisiveness.

indeterminado, da *adj* - **1.** [sin determinar] indeterminate; **por tiempo indeterminado** indefinitely - **2.** [impreciso] vague.

indexar *vt* INFORM to index.

India *n pr*: **(la) India** India.

indiano, na *sm, f* - **1.** [indígena] (Latin American) Indian - **2.** [emigrante] *Spanish emigrant to Latin America who returned to Spain having made his fortune.*

indicación *sf* - **1.** [señal, gesto] sign, signal - **2.** *(gen pl)* [instrucción] instruction; [para llegar a un sitio] directions *pl* - **3.** [nota, corrección] note.

indicado, da *adj* suitable, appropriate.

indicador, ra *adj* indicating *(antes de s)*. ➡ **indicador** *sm* [gen] indicator; TECNOL gauge, meter; **indicador económico** economic indicator; **indicador de velocidad** speedometer.

indicar *vt* [señalar] to indicate; [suj: aguja etc] to read.

indicativo, va *adj* indicative. ➡ **indicativo** *sm* GRAM indicative.

índice *sm* - **1.** [gen] index; [proporción] level, rate; **índice alfabético** alphabetical index; **índice del coste de la vida** cost of living index; **índice de materias** O **temático** table of contents; **índice de natalidad** birth rate - **2.** [señal] sign, indicator; **índice económico** economic indicator - **3.** [catálogo] catalogue - **4.** [dedo] index finger.

indicio *sm* sign; [pista] clue; [cantidad pequeña] trace.

Índico *sm*: **el (océano) Índico** the Indian Ocean.

indiferencia *sf* indifference.

indiferente *adj* indifferent.

indígena ◇ *adj* indigenous, native. ◇ *smf* native.

indigencia *sf culto* destitution.

indigente *adj* destitute.

indigestarse *vprnl* to get indigestion; **se me ha indigestado esa chica** *fam fig* I can't stomach that girl.

indigestión *sf* indigestion.

indigesto, ta adj indigestible; fam fig [pesado] stodgy, heavy.

indignación sf indignation.

indignar vt to anger. ◆ **indignarse** vprnl: **indignarse (por)** to get angry O indignant (about).

indigno, na adj - 1. [gen]: **indigno (de)** unworthy (of) - 2. [impropio] not fitting, wrong - 3. [vergonzoso] contemptible.

indio, dia ◇ adj Indian. ◇ sm, f Indian; **indio americano** Native American; **hacer el indio** to play the fool.

indirecto, ta adj indirect. ◆ **indirecta** sf hint; **lanzar una indirecta a alguien** to drop a hint to sb.

indisciplina sf indiscipline.

indiscreción sf - 1. [cualidad] indiscretion - 2. [comentario] indiscreet remark; **si no es indiscreción** if you don't mind my asking.

indiscreto, ta adj indiscreet.

indiscriminado, da adj indiscriminate.

indiscutible adj [gen] indisputable; [poder] undisputed.

indispensable adj indispensable.

indisponer vt - 1. [enfermar] to make ill, to upset - 2. [enemistar] to set at odds.

indisposición sf [malestar] indisposition.

indispuesto, ta ◇ pp ▷ **indisponer**. ◇ adj indisposed, unwell.

indistinto, ta adj - 1. [indiferente]: **es indistinto** it doesn't matter, it makes no difference - 2. [cuenta, cartilla] joint - 3. [perfil, figura] indistinct, blurred.

individual adj - 1. [gen] individual; [habitación, cama] single; [despacho] personal - 2. [prueba, competición] singles (antes de s). ◆ **individuales** smpl DEP singles.

individualizar vi to single people out.

individuo, dua sm, f person; despec individual.

indocumentado, da adj - 1. [sin documentación] without identity papers - 2. [ignorante] ignorant.

índole sf [naturaleza] nature; [tipo] type, kind.

indolencia sf indolence, laziness.

indoloro, ra adj painless.

indómito, ta adj - 1. [animal] untameable - 2. [carácter] rebellious; [pueblo] unruly.

Indonesia n pr Indonesia.

inducir vt [incitar]: **inducir a alguien a algo/a hacer algo** to lead sb into sthg/into doing sthg; **inducir a error** to mislead.

inductor, ra adj instigating.

indudable adj undoubted.

indulgencia sf indulgence.

indultar vt to pardon.

indulto sm pardon.

indumentaria sf attire.

industria sf [gen] industry.

industrial ◇ adj industrial. ◇ smf industrialist.

industrializar vt to industrialize.

INE sm (abrev de Instituto Nacional de Estadísticas) National Institute of Statistics in Bolivia, Chile, Guatemala and Uruguay.

inédito, ta adj - 1. [no publicado] unpublished - 2. [sorprendente] unprecedented.

inefable adj ineffable, inexpressible.

ineficaz adj - 1. [de bajo rendimiento] inefficient - 2. [de baja efectividad] ineffective.

ineficiente adj - 1. [de bajo rendimiento] inefficient - 2. [de baja efectividad] ineffective.

ineludible adj unavoidable.

INEM (abrev de Instituto Nacional de Empleo) sm Spanish department of employment.

inenarrable adj spectacular.

ineptitud sf ineptitude.

inepto, ta adj inept.

inequívoco, ca adj [apoyo, resultado] unequivocal; [señal, voz] unmistakeable.

inercia sf lit & fig inertia.

inerme adj [sin armas] unarmed; [sin defensa] defenceless.

inerte adj - 1. [materia] inert - 2. [cuerpo, cadáver] lifeless.

inesperado, da adj unexpected.

inestable adj lit & fig unstable.

inevitable adj inevitable.

inexacto, ta adj - 1. [impreciso] inaccurate - 2. [erróneo] incorrect, wrong.

inexistente adj nonexistent.

inexperiencia sf inexperience.

inexperto, ta adj - 1. [falto de experiencia] inexperienced - 2. [falto de habilidad] unskilful.

inexpresivo, va adj expressionless.

infalible adj infallible.

infame adj vile, base.

infamia sf [deshonra] infamy, disgrace.

infancia sf [periodo] childhood.

infante, ta sm, f - 1. [niño] infant - 2. [hijo del rey] infante (f infanta), prince (f princess).

infantería sf infantry; **infantería ligera** light infantry.

infantil adj - 1. [para niños] children's; [de niños] child (antes de s) - 2. fig [inmaduro] infantile, childish.

infarto sm: **infarto cerebral** stroke; **de infarto** fam heart-stopping.

infatigable adj indefatigable, tireless.

infección sf infection.

infeccioso, sa adj infectious.

infectar vt to infect. ◆ **infectarse** vprnl to become infected.

infeliz *adj* - **1.** [desgraciado] unhappy - **2.** *fig* [ingenuo] gullible.

inferior ◇ *adj* **inferior (a)** [en espacio, cantidad] lower (than); [en calidad] inferior (to). ◇ *smf* inferior.

inferioridad *sf* inferiority; **estar en inferioridad de condiciones** to be at a disadvantage.

inferir *vt* [ocasionar - herida] to inflict; [- mal] to cause.

infernal *adj lit & fig* infernal.

infestar *vt* to infest; [suj: carteles, propaganda etc] to be plastered across.

infidelidad *sf* [conyugal] infidelity; [a la patria, un amigo] disloyalty.

infiel ◇ *adj* - **1.** [desleal - cónyuge] unfaithful; [- amigo] disloyal - **2.** [inexacto] inaccurate, unfaithful. ◇ *smf* RELIG infidel.

infiernillo *sm* portable stove.

infierno *sm lit & fig* hell; **en el quinto infierno** in the middle of nowhere; **¡vete al infierno!** go to hell!

infiltrado, da *sm, f* infiltrator.

infiltrar *vt* [inyectar] to inject. ◆ **infiltrarse en** *vprnl* to infiltrate.

ínfimo, ma *adj* [calidad, categoría] extremely low; [precio] giveaway; [importancia] minimal.

infinidad *sf*: **una infinidad de** an infinite number of; *fig* masses of.

infinitivo *sm* infinitive.

infinito, ta *adj lit & fig* infinite. ◆ **infinito** *sm* infinity.

inflación *sf* ECON inflation; **inflación subyacente** underlying inflation.

inflamable *adj* inflammable.

inflamación *sf* MED inflammation.

inflamar *vt fig & MED* to inflame. ◆ **inflamarse** *vprnl* [hincharse] to become inflamed.

inflamatorio, ria *adj* inflammatory.

inflar *vt* - **1.** [soplando] to blow up, to inflate; [con bomba] to pump up - **2.** *fig* [exagerar] to blow up, to exaggerate. ◆ **inflarse** *vprnl*: **inflarse (de)** [hartarse] to stuff o.s. (with).

inflexible *adj lit & fig* inflexible.

inflexión *sf* inflection.

infligir *vt* to inflict; [castigo] to impose.

influencia *sf* influence; **bajo la influencia del alcohol** under the influence of alcohol.

influenciable *adj* easily influenced.

influenciar *vt* to influence.

influir ◇ *vt* to influence. ◇ *vi* to have influence; **influir en** to influence.

influjo *sm* influence.

influyente *adj* influential.

infografía *sf* computer graphics.

información *sf* - **1.** [conocimiento] información - **2.** [PRENSA - noticias] news *(U)*; [- noticia]

report, piece of news; [- sección] section, news *(U)*; **información meteorológica** weather report O forecast - **3.** [oficina] information office; [mostrador] information desk - **4.** TELECOM directory enquiries *pl UK*, directory assistance *US*.

informal *adj* - **1.** [desenfadado] informal - **2.** [irresponsable] unreliable.

informante *smf* informant.

informar ◇ *vt*: **informar a alguien (de)** to inform O tell sb (about). ◇ *vi* to inform; PRENSA to report. ◆ **informarse** *vprnl* to find out (details); **informarse de** to find out about.

informático, ca ◇ *adj* computer *(antes de s)*. ◇ *sm, f* [persona] computer expert. ◆ **informática** *sf* [ciencia] information technology, computing.

informativo, va *adj* - **1.** [instructivo, esclarecedor] informative - **2.** [que da noticias] news *(antes de s)*; [que da información] information *(antes de s)*. ◆ **informativo** *sm* news (bulletin).

informatizar *vt* to computerize.

informe ◇ *adj* shapeless. ◇ *sm* - **1.** [gen] report - **2.** DER plea. ◆ **informes** *smpl* [gen] information *(U)*; [sobre comportamiento] report *sing*; [para un empleo] references.

infortunio *sm* misfortune, bad luck *(U)*.

infracción *sf* infringement; [de circulación] offence.

infraestructura *sf* [de organización] infrastructure.

in fraganti *loc adv* red-handed, in the act; **coger a alguien in fraganti** to catch sb red-handed O in the act.

infrahumano, na *adj* subhuman.

infranqueable *adj* impassable; *fig* insurmountable.

infrarrojo, ja *adj* infrared.

infravalorar *vt* to undervalue, to underestimate.

infringir *vt* [quebrantar] to infringe, to break.

infundado, da *adj* unfounded.

infundir *vt*: **infundir algo a alguien** to fill sb with sthg, to inspire sthg in sb; **infundir miedo** to inspire fear.

infusión *sf* infusion; **infusión de manzanilla** camomile tea.

ingeniar *vt* to invent, to devise. ◆ **ingeniarse** *vprnl*: **ingeniárselas** to manage, to engineer it; **ingeniárselas para hacer algo** to manage O contrive to do sthg.

ingeniería *sf* engineering.

ingeniero, ra *sm, f* engineer; **ingeniero de caminos, canales y puertos** civil engineer.

ingenio *sm* - **1.** [inteligencia] ingenuity - **2.** [agudeza] wit - **3.** [máquina] device; **ingenio nuclear** nuclear device.

ingenioso, sa *adj* [inteligente] ingenious, clever; [agudo] witty.

ingenuidad *sf* ingenuousness, naivety.

ingenuo, nua *adj* ingenuous, naive.

ingerir *vt* to consume, to ingest.

Inglaterra *n pr* England.

ingle *sf* groin.

inglés, esa ◇ *adj* English. ◇ *sm, f* [persona] Englishman (*f* Englishwoman); **los ingleses** the English. ◆ **inglés** *sm* [lengua] English.

ingratitud *sf* ingratitude.

ingrato, ta *adj* ungrateful; [trabajo] thankless.

ingrávido, da *adj* weightless.

ingrediente *sm* ingredient.

ingresar ◇ *vt* BANCA to deposit, to pay in. ◇ *vi*: **ingresar (en)** [asociación, ejército] to join; [hospital] to be admitted (to); [convento, universidad] to enter; **ingresar cadáver** to be dead on arrival.

ingreso *sm* - **1.** [gen] entry; [en asociación, ejército] joining; [en hospital, universidad] admission - **2.** BANCA deposit; **hacer un ingreso** to make a deposit. ◆ **ingresos** *smpl* - **1.** [sueldo etc] income (*U*); **ingresos brutos/netos** gross/net income - **2.** [recaudación] revenue (*U*).

inhabilitar *vt* to disqualify.

inhabitable *adj* uninhabitable.

inhabitado, da *adj* uninhabited.

inhalador *sm* inhaler.

inhalar *vt* to inhale.

inherente *adj*: **inherente (a)** inherent (in).

inhibir *vt* to inhibit. ◆ **inhibirse de** *vprnl* [gen] to keep out of, to stay away from; [responsabilidades] to shirk.

inhóspito, ta *adj* inhospitable.

inhumano, na *adj* [despiadado] inhuman; [desconsiderado] inhumane.

iniciación *sf* - **1.** [gen] initiation - **2.** [de suceso, curso] start, beginning.

inicial *adj* & *sf* initial.

inicializar *vt* INFORM to initialize.

iniciar *vt* [gen] to start, to initiate; [debate, discusión] to start off.

iniciativa *sf* initiative; **no tener iniciativa** to lack initiative; **por iniciativa propia** on one's own initiative; **iniciativa de paz** peace initiative.

inicio *sm* start, beginning.

inigualable *adj* unrivalled.

ininteligible *adj* unintelligible.

ininterrumpido, da *adj* uninterrupted.

injerencia *sf* interference, meddling.

injerir *vt* to introduce, to insert. ◆ **injerirse** *vprnl* [entrometerse]: **injerirse (en)** to interfere (in), to meddle (in).

injertar *vt* to graft.

injerto *sm* graft.

injuria *sf* [insulto] insult, abuse (*U*); [agravio] offence; DER slander.

injuriar *vt* [insultar] to insult, to abuse; [agraviar] to offend; DER to slander.

injurioso, sa *adj* insulting, abusive; DER slanderous.

injusticia *sf* injustice; **¡es una injusticia!** that's unfair!; **cometer una injusticia con alguien** to do sb an injustice.

injustificado, da *adj* unjustified.

injusto, ta *adj* unfair, unjust.

inmadurez *sf* immaturity.

inmaduro, ra *adj* [persona] immature.

inmediaciones *sfpl* [de localidad] surrounding area *sing*; [de lugar, casa] vicinity *sing*.

inmediatamente *adv* immediately.

inmediato, ta *adj* - **1.** [gen] immediate; **de inmediato** immediately, at once - **2.** [contiguo] next, adjoining.

inmejorable *adj* unbeatable.

inmensidad *sf* [grandeza] immensity.

inmenso, sa *adj* [gen] immense.

inmersión *sf* immersion; [de submarinista] dive; **inmersión lingüística** language immersion.

inmerso, sa *adj*: **inmerso (en)** immersed (in).

inmigración *sf* immigration.

inmigrante *smf* immigrant.

inmigrar *vi* to immigrate.

inminente *adj* imminent, impending.

inmiscuirse *vprnl*: **inmiscuirse (en)** to interfere O meddle (in).

inmobiliario, ria *adj* property (*antes de s*), real estate US (*antes de s*). ◆ **inmobiliaria** *sf* [agencia] estate agency UK, real estate agent US.

inmoral *adj* immoral.

inmortal *adj* immortal.

inmortalizar *vt* to immortalize.

inmóvil *adj* motionless, still; [coche, tren] stationary.

inmovilizar *vt* to immobilize.

inmueble ◇ *adj*: **bienes inmuebles** real estate (*U*). ◇ *sm* [edificio] building.

inmundicia *sf* [suciedad] filth, filthiness; [basura] rubbish.

inmundo, da *adj* filthy, dirty.

inmune *adj* MED immune.

inmunidad *sf* immunity; **inmunidad diplo-mática/parlamentaria** diplomatic/parliament-ary immunity.

inmunizar *vt* to immunize.

inmutar *vt* to upset, to perturb. ◆ **inmu-tarse** *vprnl* to get upset, to be perturbed; **ni se inmutó** he didn't bat an eyelid.

innato, ta *adj* innate.

innecesario, ria *adj* unnecessary.

innoble *adj* ignoble.

innovación *sf* innovation.

innovador, ra ◇ *adj* innovative. ◇ *sm, f* innovator.

innovar *vt* [método, técnica] to improve on.

innumerable *adj* countless, innumerable.

inocencia *sf* innocence.

inocentada *sf* practical joke, trick.

inocente *adj* - 1. [gen & DER] innocent; **decla-rar inocente a alguien** to find sb innocent *O* not guilty - 2. [ingenuo - persona] naive, inno-cent - 3. [sin maldad - persona] harmless.

inodoro, ra *adj* odourless. ◆ **inodoro** *sm* toilet *UK*, washroom *US*.

inofensivo, va *adj* inoffensive, harmless.

inolvidable *adj* unforgettable.

inoperante *adj* ineffective.

inoportuno, na, importuno, na *adj* - 1. [en mal momento] inopportune, untimely - 2. [molesto] inconvenient - 3. [inadecuado] in-appropriate.

inoxidable *adj* rustproof; [acero] stainless.

inquebrantable *adj* unshakeable; [lealtad] unswerving.

inquietar *vt* to worry, to trouble. ◆ **in-quietarse** *vprnl* to worry.

inquieto, ta *adj* - 1. [preocupado]: **inquieto (por)** worried *O* anxious (about) - 2. [agitado, emprendedor] restless.

inquietud *sf* [preocupación] worry, anxiety.

inquilino, na *sm, f* tenant.

inquirir *vt culto* to inquire into, to investig-ate.

inquisición *sf* [indagación] inquiry, investig-ation. ◆ **Inquisición** *sf* [tribunal] Inquisition.

inquisidor, ra *adj* inquisitive. ◆ **inquisi-dor** *sm* inquisitor.

insaciable *adj* insatiable.

insalubre *adj culto* insalubrious, unhealthy.

insatisfecho, cha *adj* - 1. [descontento] dis-satisfied - 2. [no saciado] not full, unsatisfied.

inscribir *vt* - 1. [grabar]: **inscribir algo (en)** to engrave *O* inscribe sthg (on) - 2. [apuntar]: **inscribir algo/a alguien (en)** to register sthg/sb (on). ◆ **inscribirse** *vprnl*: **inscribirse (en)** [gen] to enrol (on); [asociación] to enrol (with); [concurso] to enter.

inscripción *sf* - 1. EDUC registration, enrol-ment; [en censo, registro] registration; [en parti-do etc] enrolment; [en concurso etc] **entry** - 2. [escrito] inscription.

inscrito, ta *pp* ▷ **inscribir**.

insecticida *sm* insecticide.

insecto *sm* insect.

inseguridad *sf* - 1. [falta de confianza] insec-urity - 2. [duda] uncertainty - 3. [peligro] lack of safety.

inseguro, ra *adj* - 1. [sin confianza] insecure - 2. [dudoso] uncertain - 3. [peligroso] unsafe.

inseminación *sf* insemination; **insemina-ción artificial** artificial insemination.

insensatez *sf* foolishness; **hacer/decir una insensatez** to do/say sthg foolish.

insensato, ta ◇ *adj* foolish, senseless. ◇ *sm, f* fool.

insensibilidad *sf* [emocional] insensitivity; [física] numbness.

insensible *adj* - 1. [indiferente]: **insensible (a)** insensitive (to) - 2. [entumecido] numb - 3. [im-perceptible] imperceptible.

insertar *vt* [gen & INFORM]: **insertar (en)** to in-sert (into).

inservible *adj* useless, unserviceable.

insidioso, sa *adj* malicious.

insigne *adj* distinguished, illustrious.

insignia *sf* - 1. [distintivo] badge; MIL insignia - 2. [bandera] flag, banner.

insignificante *adj* insignificant.

insinuar *vt*: **insinuar algo (a)** to hint at *O* in-sinuate sthg (to). ◆ **insinuarse** *vprnl* - 1. [amorosamente]: **insinuarse (a)** to make ad-vances (to) - 2. [asomar]: **insinuarse detrás de algo** to peep out from behind sthg.

insípido, da *adj lit & fig* insipid.

insistencia *sf* insistence.

insistir *vi*: **insistir (en)** to insist (on).

insociable *adj* unsociable.

insolación *sf* MED sunstroke *(U)*; **coger una insolación** to get sunstroke.

insolencia *sf* insolence.

insolente *adj* [descarado] insolent; [orgulloso] haughty.

insolidario, ria *adj* lacking in solidarity.

insólito, ta *adj* very unusual.

insoluble *adj* insoluble.

insolvencia *sf* insolvency.

insolvente *adj* insolvent.

insomnio *sm* insomnia.

insondable *adj lit & fig* unfathomable.

insonorizar *vt* to soundproof.

insoportable *adj* unbearable, intolerable.

insostenible *adj* untenable.

inspección *sf* inspection; [policial] search; **inspección ocular** visual inspection.

inspeccionar *vt* to inspect; [suj: policía] to search.

inspector, ra *sm, f* inspector; **inspector de aduanas** customs official; **inspector de Hacienda** tax inspector.

inspiración *sf* - 1. [gen] inspiration - 2. [respiración] inhalation, breath.

inspirar *vt* - 1. [gen] to inspire - 2. [respirar] to inhale, to breathe in. **inspirarse** *vprnl:* **inspirarse (en)** to be inspired (by).

instalación *sf* - 1. [gen] installation; **instalación eléctrica** wiring - 2. [de gente] settling. **instalaciones** *sfpl* [deportivas etc] facilities.

instalar *vt* - 1. [montar - antena etc] to instal, to fit; [- local, puesto etc] to set up - 2. [situar - objeto] to place; [- gente] to settle. **instalarse** *vprnl* [establecerse]: **instalarse en** to settle (down) in; [nueva casa] to move into.

instancia *sf* - 1. [solicitud] application (form) - 2. [ruego] request; **a instancias de** at the request O bidding of; **en última instancia** as a last resort.

instantáneo, a *adj* - 1. [momentáneo] momentary - 2. [rápido] instantaneous. **instantánea** *sf* snapshot, snap.

instante *sm* moment; **a cada instante** all the time, constantly; **al instante** instantly, immediately; **en un instante** in a second.

instar *vt:* **instar a alguien a que haga algo** to urge O press sb to do sthg.

instaurar *vt* to establish, to set up.

instigar *vt:* **instigar a alguien (a que haga algo)** to instigate sb (to do sthg); **instigar a algo** to incite to sthg.

instintivo, va *adj* instinctive.

instinto *sm* instinct; **por instinto** instinctively; **instinto maternal** maternal instinct; **instinto de supervivencia** survival instinct.

institución *sf* - 1. [gen] institution; **ser una institución** *fig* to be an institution - 2. [de ley, sistema] introduction; [de organismo] establishment; [de premio] foundation.

instituir *vt* [fundar - gobierno] to establish; [- premio, sociedad] to found; [- sistema, reglas] to introduce.

instituto *sm* - 1. [corporación] institute - 2. EDUC: **instituto (de Enseñanza Secundaria)** state secondary school; **instituto de Formación Profesional** ≃ technical college. **instituto de belleza** *sm* beauty salon.

institutriz *sf* governess.

instrucción *sf* - 1. [conocimientos] education; [docencia] instruction - 2. [DER - investigación]

preliminary investigation; [- curso del proceso] proceedings *pl*. **instrucciones** *sfpl* [de uso] instructions.

instructivo, va *adj* [gen] instructive; [juguete, película] educational.

instructor, ra ◇ *adj* training. ◇ *sm, f* [gen] instructor, teacher; DEP coach.

instruido, da *adj* educated.

instruir *vt* [enseñar] to instruct.

instrumental *sm* instruments *pl*.

instrumentista *smf* - 1. MÚS instrumentalist - 2. MED surgeon's assistant.

instrumento *sm* - 1. *fig* & MÚS instrument - 2. [herramienta] tool, instrument.

insubordinado, da *adj* insubordinate.

insubordinar *vt* to incite to rebellion. **insubordinarse** *vprnl* to rebel.

insubstancial = **insustancial**.

insuficiencia *sf* - 1. [escasez] lack, shortage - 2. MED failure; **insuficiencia cardiaca/renal** heart/kidney failure.

insuficiente ◇ *adj* insufficient. ◇ *sm* [nota] fail.

insufrible *adj* intolerable, insufferable.

insular *adj* insular, island *(antes de s)*.

insulina *sf* insulin.

insulso, sa *adj lit & fig* bland, insipid.

insultar *vt* to insult.

insulto *sm* insult.

insumiso, sa ◇ *adj* rebellious. ◇ *sm, f* [gen] rebel; MIL *person who refuses to do military or community service*.

insuperable *adj* - 1. [inmejorable] unsurpassable - 2. [sin solución] insurmountable, insuperable.

insurrección *sf* insurrection, revolt.

insustancial, insubstancial *adj* insubstantial.

intachable *adj* irreproachable.

intacto, ta *adj* untouched; *fig* intact.

integral *adj* - 1. [total] total, complete - 2. [sin refinar - pan, harina, pasta] wholemeal; [- arroz] brown.

integrante ◇ *adj* integral, constituent; **estado integrante de la CE** member state of the EC. ◇ *smf* member.

integrar *vt* - 1. [gen & MAT] to integrate - 2. [componer] to make up. **integrarse** *vprnl* to integrate.

integridad *sf* [gen] integrity; [totalidad] wholeness.

íntegro, gra *adj* - 1. [completo] whole, entire; [versión etc] unabridged - 2. [honrado] honourable.

intelecto *sm* intellect.

intelectual *adj* & *smf* intellectual.

inteligencia sf intelligence; **inteligencia artificial** INFORM artificial intelligence; **inteligencia emocional** emotional intelligence.

inteligente adj [gen & INFORM] intelligent.

inteligible adj intelligible.

intemperie sf: **a la intemperie** in the open air.

intempestivo, va adj [clima, comentario] harsh; [hora] ungodly, unearthly; [proposición, visita] inopportune.

intención sf intention; **con intención** intentionally; **sin intención** without meaning to; **tener la intención de** to intend to; **tener malas intenciones** to be up to no good; **buena/mala intención** good/bad intentions pl; **segunda intención** underhandedness, duplicity; **intención de voto** voting intention; **de buenas intenciones está el infierno lleno** prov the road to hell is paved with good intentions.

intencionado, da adj intentional, deliberate; **bien intencionado** [acción] well-meant; [persona] well-meaning.

intensidad sf [gen] intensity; [de lluvia] heaviness; [de luz, color] brightness; [de amor] passion, strength.

intensificar vt to intensify. ➡ **intensificarse** vprnl to intensify.

intensivo, va adj intensive.

intenso, sa adj [gen] intense; [lluvia] heavy; [luz, color] bright; [amor] passionate, strong.

intentar vt: **intentar (hacer algo)** to try (to do sthg).

intento sm [tentativa] attempt; [intención] intention; **intento de golpe/robo** attempted coup/robbery; **intento de suicidio** suicide attempt.

interactivo, va adj INFORM interactive.

intercalar vt to insert, to put in.

intercambiable adj interchangeable.

intercambio sm exchange; **hacer un intercambio** to go on an exchange programme; **intercambio comercial** trade.

interceder vi: **interceder (por alguien)** to intercede (on sb's behalf).

interceptar vt - **1.** [detener] to intercept - **2.** [obstruir] to block.

interés sm - **1.** [gen & FIN] interest; **de interés** interesting; **esperar algo con interés** to await sthg with interest; **tener interés en** O **por** to be interested in; **tengo interés en que venga pronto** it's in my interest that he should come soon; **interés acumulado** accrued interest; **interés compuesto** compound interest; **interés simple** simple interest; **intereses creados** vested interests - **2.** [egoísmo] self-interest; **por interés** out of selfishness.

interesado, da ⬦ adj - **1.** [gen]: **interesado (en** O **por)** interested (in) - **2.** [egoísta] selfish, self-interested. ⬦ sm, f [deseoso] interested person; **los interesados** those interested.

interesante adj interesting; **hacerse el/la interesante** to try to draw attention to oneself.

interesar vi to interest; **le interesa el arte** she's interested in art. ➡ **interesarse** vprnl: **interesarse (en** O **por)** to take an interest (in), to be interested (in); **se interesó por tu salud** she asked after your health.

interfaz sf INFORM interface.

interferencia sf interference.

interferir ⬦ vt - **1.** TELECOM, RADIO & TV to jam - **2.** [interponerse] to interfere with. ⬦ vi: **interferir (en)** to interfere (in).

interfono sm intercom.

interino, na ⬦ adj [gen] temporary; [presidente, director etc] acting; [gobierno] interim. ⬦ sm, f [gen] stand-in; [médico, juez] locum; [profesor] supply teacher. ➡ **interina** sf [asistenta] cleaning lady.

interior ⬦ adj - **1.** [gen] inside, inner; [patio, jardín etc] interior, inside; [habitación, vida] inner - **2.** POLÍT domestic - **3.** GEOGR inland. ⬦ sm - **1.** [parte de dentro] inside, interior - **2.** GEOGR interior - **3.** [de una persona] inner self; **en mi interior** deep down. ➡ **interiores** sfpl CINE interiors.

interiorismo sm interior design.

interiorizar vt to internalize; [sentimientos] to bottle up.

interjección sf interjection.

interlocutor, ra sm, f interlocutor, speaker; **su interlocutor** the person she was speaking to.

intermediario, ria sm, f [gen] intermediary; COM middleman; [en disputas] mediator.

intermedio, dia adj - **1.** [etapa] intermediate, halfway; [calidad] average; [tamaño] medium - **2.** [tiempo] intervening; [espacio] in between. ➡ **intermedio** sm [gen & TEATRO] interval; CINE intermission.

interminable adj endless, interminable.

intermitente ⬦ adj intermittent. ⬦ sm indicator.

internacional adj international.

internado, da adj [en manicomio] confined; [en colegio] boarding; POLÍT interned. ➡ **internado** sm [colegio] boarding school.

internar vt: **internar (en)** [internado] to send to boarding school (at); [manicomio] to commit (to); [campo de concentración] to intern (in). ➡ **internarse** vprnl: **internarse (en)** [un lugar] to go O penetrate deep (into); [un tema] to become deeply involved (in).

internauta smf Internet user.

Internet *sf*: (la) Internet the Internet; **en Internet** on the Internet.

interno, **na** ◇ *adj* - **1.** [gen] internal; POLÍT domestic - **2.** [alumno] boarding. ◇ *sm, f* - **1.** [alumno] boarder - **2.** ▷ **médico** - **3.** [preso] prisoner, inmate.

interpelación *sf* formal question.

interpolar *vt* to interpolate, to put in.

interponer *vt* - **1.** [gen] to interpose, to put in - **2.** DER to lodge, to make. ◆ **interponerse** *vprnl* to intervene.

interpretación *sf* - **1.** [explicación] interpretation; **mala interpretación** misinterpretation - **2.** [artística] performance - **3.** [traducción] interpreting.

interpretar *vt* - **1.** [gen] to interpret - **2.** [artísticamente] to perform.

intérprete *smf* - **1.** [traductor & INFORM] interpreter - **2.** [artista] performer.

interpuesto, **ta** *pp* ▷ **interponer**.

interrogación *sf* - **1.** [acción] questioning - **2.** [signo] question mark.

interrogante *sm o sf* [incógnita] question mark.

interrogar *vt* [gen] to question; [con amenazas etc] to interrogate.

interrogatorio *sm* [gen] questioning; [con amenazas] interrogation.

interrumpir *vt* - **1.** [gen] to interrupt - **2.** [discurso, trabajo] to break off; [viaje, vacaciones] to cut short.

interrupción *sf* - **1.** [gen] interruption; **interrupción (voluntaria) del embarazo** termination of pregnancy - **2.** [de discurso, trabajo] breaking-off; [de viaje, vacaciones] cutting-short.

interruptor *sm* switch.

intersección *sf* intersection.

interurbano, **na** *adj* inter-city; TELECOM long-distance.

intervalo *sm* - **1.** [gen & MÚS] interval; [de espacio] space, gap; **a intervalos** at intervals - **2.** [duración]: **en el intervalo de un mes** in the space of a month.

intervención *sf* - **1.** [gen] intervention - **2.** [discurso] speech; [interpelación] contribution - **3.** COM auditing - **4.** MED operation - **5.** TELECOM tapping.

intervenir ◇ *vi* - **1.** [participar]: **intervenir (en)** [gen] to take part (in); [pelea] to get involved (in); [discusión etc] to make a contribution (to) - **2.** [dar un discurso] to make a speech - **3.** [interferir]: **intervenir (en)** to intervene (in) - **4.** MED to operate. ◇ *vt* - **1.** MED to operate on - **2.** TELECOM to tap - **3.** [incautar] to seize - **4.** COM to audit.

interventor, **ra** *sm, f* COM auditor.

interviú (*pl* interviús) *sf* interview.

intestino, **na** *adj* internecine. ◆ **intestino** *sm* intestine; **intestino delgado/grueso** small/large intestine.

intimar *vi*: **intimar (con)** to become intimate O very friendly (with).

intimidad *sf* - **1.** [vida privada] private life; [privacidad] privacy; **en la intimidad** in private - **2.** [amistad] intimacy.

íntimo, **ma** ◇ *adj* - **1.** [vida, fiesta] private; [ambiente, restaurante] intimate - **2.** [relación, amistad] close - **3.** [sentimiento etc] innermost; **en lo (más) íntimo de su corazón/alma** deep down in her heart/soul. ◇ *sm, f* close friend.

intolerable *adj* intolerable, unacceptable; [dolor, ruido] unbearable.

intolerancia *sf* [actitud] intolerance.

intoxicación *sf* poisoning (U); **intoxicación alimenticia** food poisoning; **intoxicación etílica** alcohol poisoning.

intoxicar *vt* to poison.

intranquilizar *vt* to worry. ◆ **intranquilizarse** *vprnl* to get worried.

intranquilo, **la** *adj* [preocupado] worried, uneasy; [nervioso] restless.

intransferible *adj* non-transferable.

intransigente *adj* intransigent.

intransitable *adj* impassable.

intrascendente *adj* insignificant, unimportant.

intrépido, **da** *adj* intrepid.

intriga *sf* - **1.** [curiosidad] curiosity; **de intriga** suspense (*antes de s*) - **2.** [maquinación] intrigue - **3.** [trama] plot.

intrigar *vt* & *vi* to intrigue.

intrincado, **da** *adj* [problema etc] intricate.

intríngulis *sm inv fam*: **tiene su intríngulis** it is quite tricky.

intrínseco, **ca** *adj* intrinsic.

introducción *sf*: **introducción (a)** introduction (to).

introducir *vt* - **1.** [meter - llave, carta etc] to put in, to insert - **2.** [mercancías etc] to bring in, to introduce - **3.** [dar a conocer]: **introducir a alguien en** to introduce sb to; **introducir algo en** to introduce O bring sthg to. ◆ **introducirse** *vprnl*: **introducirse en** to get into.

introductorio, **ria** *adj* introductory.

intromisión *sf* meddling, interfering.

introspectivo, **va** *adj* introspective.

introvertido, **da** *adj* & *sm, f* introvert.

intruso, **sa** *sm, f* intruder; **intruso informático** hacker.

intuición *sf* intuition.

intuir *vt* to know by intuition, to sense.

intuitivo, **va** *adj* intuitive.

inundación *sf* flood, flooding (U).

inundar vt to flood; fig to inundate.
➤ **inundarse** vprnl to flood; **inundarse de** fig to be inundated O swamped with.

inusitado, da adj uncommon, rare.

inútil adj - 1. [gen] useless; [intento, esfuerzo] unsuccessful, vain - 2. [inválido] disabled.

inutilidad sf [gen] uselessness; [falta de sentido] pointlessness.

inutilizar vt [gen] to make unusable; [máquinas, dispositivos] to disable.

invadir vt to invade; **la invade la tristeza** she's overcome by sadness.

invalidez sf - 1. MED disability; **invalidez permanente/temporal** permanent/temporary disability - 2. DER invalidity.

inválido, da ◇ adj - 1. MED disabled - 2. DER invalid. ◇ sm, f invalid, disabled person; **los inválidos** the disabled.

invariable adj invariable.

invasión sf invasion.

invasor, ra ◇ adj invading. ◇ sm, f invader.

invención sf invention.

inventar vt [gen] to invent; [narración, falsedades] to make up. ➤ **inventarse** vprnl to make up.

inventario sm inventory.

inventiva sf inventiveness.

invento sm invention.

inventor, ra sm, f inventor.

invernadero, invernáculo sm greenhouse.

invernar vi [pasar el invierno] to (spend the) winter; [hibernar] to hibernate.

inverosímil adj unlikely, improbable.

inversión sf - 1. [del orden] inversion - 2. [de dinero, tiempo] investment.

inverso, sa adj opposite, inverse; **a la inversa** the other way round; **en orden inverso** in reverse order.

inversor, ra sm, f COM & FIN investor.

invertebrado, da adj invertebrate. ➤ **invertebrado** sm invertebrate.

invertido, da adj - 1. [al revés] reversed, inverted; [sentido, dirección] opposite - 2. [homosexual] homosexual.

invertir vt - 1. [gen] to reverse; [poner boca abajo] to turn upside down - 2. [dinero, tiempo, esfuerzo] to invest - 3. [tardar - tiempo] to spend.

investidura sf investiture.

investigación sf - 1. [estudio] research; **investigación y desarrollo** research and development - 2. [indagación] investigation, inquiry; **investigación judicial** judicial inquiry.

investigador, ra sm, f - 1. [estudioso] researcher - 2. [detective] investigator.

investigar ◇ vt - 1. [estudiar] to research - 2. [indagar] to investigate. ◇ vi - 1. [estudiar] to do research - 2. [indagar] to investigate.

investir vt: **investir a alguien con algo** to invest sb with sthg.

inveterado, da adj deep-rooted.

inviable adj impractical, unviable.

invidente smf blind O sightless person; **los invidentes** the blind.

invierno sm winter; **invierno nuclear** nuclear winter.

invisible adj invisible.

invitación sf invitation.

invitado, da sm, f guest.

invitar ◇ vt - 1. [convidar]: **invitar a alguien (a algo/a hacer algo)** to invite sb (to sthg/to do sthg) - 2. [pagar]: **os invito** it's my treat, this one's on me; **te invito a cenar fuera** I'll take you out for dinner. ◇ vi to pay; **invita la casa** it's on the house. ➤ **invitar a** vi fig [incitar]: **invitar a algo** to encourage sthg; **la lluvia invita a quedarse en casa** the rain makes you want to stay at home.

in vitro loc adv - 1. [de probeta] in vitro - 2. ▷ **fecundación**.

invocar vt to invoke.

involucrar vt: **involucrar a alguien (en)** to involve sb (in). ➤ **involucrarse** vprnl: **involucrarse (en)** to get involved (in).

involuntario, ria adj [espontáneo] involuntary; [sin querer] unintentional.

inyección sf injection.

inyectar vt to inject. ➤ **inyectarse** vprnl [drogas] to take drugs intravenously; **inyectarse algo** to inject o.s. with sthg.

iodo = yodo.

ion sm ion.

IPC (abrev de índice de precios al consumo) sm Spanish cost of living index, ≃ RPI UK.

ir vi - 1. [gen] to go; **ir hacia el sur/al cine** to go south/to the cinema; **ir en autobús/coche** to go by bus/car; **ir en avión** to fly; **ir en bicicleta** to ride; **ir andando** to go on foot, to walk; **¡vamos!** let's go! - 2. [expresa duración gradual]: **ir haciendo algo** to be (gradually) doing sthg; **va anocheciendo** it's getting dark; **voy mejorando mi estilo** I'm working on improving my style - 3. [expresa intención, opinión]: **ir a hacer algo** to be going to do sthg; **voy a decírselo a tu padre** I'm going to tell your father - 4. [cambiar]: **ir a mejor/peor** etc to get better/worse etc - 5. [funcionar] to work; **la manivela va floja** the crank is loose; **la televisión no va** the television isn't working - 6. [desenvolverse] to go; **le va bien en su nuevo trabajo** things are going well for him in his new job; **su negocio va mal** his business is going badly; **¿cómo te va?** how are you doing? - **7.** [vestir]: **ir en/con** to wear; **iba en camisa y con corbata** he was wearing a shirt and tie; **ir de azul/de uniforme** to be dressed in blue/in uniform - **8.** [tener aspecto físico] to look like; **iba hecho un pordiosero** he looked like a beggar - **9.** [vacaciones, tratamiento]: **irle bien a alguien** to do sb good - **10.** [ropa]: **irle (bien) a alguien** to suit sb; **ir con algo** to go with sthg - **11.** [comentario, indirecta]: **ir con O por alguien** to be meant for sb, to be aimed at sb - **12.** *loc:* **fue y dijo que...** he went and said that...; **ni me va ni me viene** *fam* I don't care; **¡qué va!** you must be joking!; **ser el no va más** to be the ultimate. ➤ **ir de** *vi* - **1.** [película, novela] to be about - **2.** *fig* [persona] to think o.s.; **va de listo** he thinks he's clever. ➤ **ir por** *vi* - **1.** [buscar]: **ir por algo/alguien** to go and get sthg/sb, to go and fetch sthg/sb - **2.** [alcanzar]: **va por el cuarto vaso de vino** he's already on his fourth glass of wine; **vamos por la mitad de la asignatura** we covered about half the subject. ➤ **irse** *vprnl* - **1.** [marcharse] to go, to leave; **irse a** to go to; **¡vete!** go away! - **2.** [gastarse, desaparecer] to go - **3.** *loc:* **irse abajo** [edificio] to fall down; [negocio] to collapse; [planes] to fall through.

ira *sf* anger, rage.

iracundo, da *adj* angry, irate; [irascible] irascible.

Irán *n pr:* **(el) Irán** Iran.

iraní (*pl* **iraníes** O **iranís**) *adj* & *smf* Iranian.

Iraq *n pr:* **(el) Iraq** Iraq.

iraquí (*pl* **iraquíes** O **iraquís**) *adj* & *smf* Iraqi.

irascible *adj* irascible.

iris *sm inv* iris.

Irlanda *n pr* Ireland.

irlandés, esa ◇ *adj* Irish. ◇ *sm, f* [persona] Irishman (*f* Irishwoman); **los irlandeses** the Irish. ➤ **irlandés** *sm* [lengua] Irish.

ironía *sf* irony.

irónico, ca *adj* ironic, ironical.

ironizar ◇ *vt* to ridicule. ◇ *vi:* **ironizar (sobre)** to be ironical (about).

IRPF (*abrev de* **impuesto sobre la renta de las personas físicas**) *sm* Spanish personal income tax.

irracional *adj* irrational.

irradiar *vt lit* & *fig* to radiate.

irreal *adj* unreal.

irreconciliable *adj* irreconcilable.

irreconocible *adj* unrecognizable.

irrecuperable *adj* irretrievable.

irreflexión *sf* rashness.

irreflexivo, va *adj* rash.

irrefutable *adj* irrefutable.

irregular *adj* [gen] irregular; [terreno, superficie] uneven.

irrelevante *adj* irrelevant.

irremediable *adj* irremediable.

irreparable *adj* irreparable.

irresistible *adj* irresistible.

irresoluto, ta *adj culto* irresolute.

irrespetuoso, sa *adj* disrespectful.

irrespirable *adj* unbreathable.

irresponsable *adj* irresponsible.

irreverente *adj* irreverent.

irreversible *adj* irreversible.

irrevocable *adj* irrevocable.

irrigar *vt* to irrigate.

irrisorio, ria *adj* - **1.** [excusa etc] laughable, derisory - **2.** [precio etc] ridiculously low.

irritable *adj* irritable.

irritar *vt* to irritate. ➤ **irritarse** *vprnl* - **1.** [enfadarse] to get angry O annoyed - **2.** [suj: piel etc] to become irritated.

irrompible *adj* unbreakable.

irrupción *sf* bursting in.

isla *sf* island.

islam *sm* Islam.

islamismo *sm* Islam.

islandés, esa ◇ *adj* Icelandic. ◇ *sm, f* [persona] Icelander. ➤ **islandés** *sm* [lengua] Icelandic.

Islandia *n pr* Iceland.

isleño, ña ◇ *adj* island (*antes de s*). ◇ *sm, f* islander.

islote *sm* small, rocky island.

Israel *n pr* Israel.

israelí (*pl* **israelíes** O **israelís**) *adj* & *smf* Israeli.

istmo *sm* isthmus.

Italia *n pr* Italy.

italiano, na *adj* & *sm, f* Italian. ➤ **italiano** *sm* [lengua] Italian.

itálico, ca *adj* ⊳ **letra**.

itinerante *adj* itinerant; [embajador] roving.

itinerario *sm* route, itinerary.

ITV (*abrev de* **inspección técnica de vehículos**) *sf* annual technical inspection for motor vehicles of ten years or more, ≃ MOT *UK*.

IVA (*abrev de* **impuesto sobre el valor añadido**) *sm* VAT.

izar *vt* to raise, to hoist.

izda (*abrev de* **izquierda**) L, l.

izquierda *sf* ⊳ **izquierdo**.

izquierdo, da *adj* left. ➤ **izquierda** *sf* - **1.** [lado] left; **a la izquierda (de)** on O to the left (of); **girar a la izquierda** to turn left - **2.** [mano] left hand - **3.** POLÍT left (wing); **de izquierdas** left-wing.

J

j, J *sf* [letra] j, J.

ja *interj*: ¡ja! ha!

jabalí (*pl* jabalíes *O* jabalís) *sm* wild boar.

jabalina *sf* DEP javelin.

jabón *sm* soap.

jabonar *vt* to soap.

jabonera *sf* soap dish.

jaca *sf* [caballo pequeño] pony; [yegua] mare.

jacal *sm* Méx hut.

jacinto *sm* hyacinth.

jactarse *vprnl*: jactarse (de) to boast (about *O* of).

jadear *vi* to pant.

jadeo *sm* panting.

jaguar (*pl* jaguars) *sm* jaguar.

jaiba *sf* Andes, Amér C, Caribe & Méx crayfish.

jalea *sf* jelly; jalea real royal jelly.

jalear *vt* to cheer on.

jaleo *sm* - **1.** *fam* [alboroto] row, rumpus - **2.** *fam* [lío] mess, confusion.

jalonar *vt* to stake *O* mark out; *fig* to mark.

Jamaica *n pr* Jamaica.

jamás *adv* never; no lo he visto jamás I've never seen him; la mejor película que jamás se haya hecho the best film ever made; jamás de los jamases never ever.

jamón *sm* ham; jamón (de) York *O* (en) dulce boiled ham; jamón serrano cured ham, ≃ Parma ham.

Japón *n pr*: (el) Japón Japan.

japonés, esa *adj* & *sm, f* Japanese. ◆ **japonés** *sm* [lengua] Japanese.

jaque *sm*: jaque mate checkmate.

jaqueca *sf* migraine.

jarabe *sm* syrup; jarabe para la tos cough mixture *O* syrup.

jarana *sf* [juerga]: estar/irse de jarana to be/go out on the town.

jaranero, ra *adj* fond of partying.

jardín *sm* garden, yard *US*; jardín botánico botanical garden; jardín zoológico zoological garden, zoo. ◆ **jardín de infancia** *sm* kindergarten, nursery school.

jardinera ⊳ **jardinero**.

jardinería *sf* gardening.

jardinero, ra *sm, f* gardener. ◆ **jardinera** *sf* flowerpot stand.

jarra *sf* - **1.** [para servir] jug - **2.** [para beber] tankard. ◆ **en jarras** *loc adv* [postura] hands on hips.

jarro *sm* jug.

jarrón *sm* vase.

jaspeado, da *adj* mottled, speckled.

jauja *sf fam* paradise.

jaula *sf* cage.

jauría *sf* pack of dogs.

jazmín *sm* jasmine.

jazz [jas] *sm* jazz.

JC (*abrev de* Jesucristo) JC.

je *interj*: ¡je! ha!

jeep [jip] (*pl* jeeps) *sm* jeep.

jefa ⊳ **jefe**.

jefatura *sf* - **1.** [cargo] leadership - **2.** [organismo] headquarters, head office.

jefe, fa *sm, f* [gen] boss; COM manager (*f* manageress); [líder] leader; [de tribu, ejército] chief; [de departamento etc] head; en jefe MIL in-chief; jefe de cocina chef; jefe de estación stationmaster; jefe de Estado head of state; jefe de estudios deputy head; jefe de producción/ventas production/sales manager; jefe de redacción editor-in-chief.

jején *sm Amér* [insecto] ≃ midge.

jengibre *sm* ginger.

jeque *sm* sheikh.

jerarquía *sf* - **1.** [organización] hierarchy - **2.** [persona] high-ranking person, leader.

jerárquico, ca *adj* hierarchical.

jerez *sm* sherry.

jerga *sf* jargon; [argot] slang.

jeringuilla *sf* syringe.

jeroglífico, ca *adj* hieroglyphic. ◆ **jeroglífico** *sm* - **1.** [inscripción] hieroglyphic - **2.** [pasatiempo] rebus.

jerséi (*pl* jerséis), **jersey** (*pl* jerseys) *sm* jumper, pullover.

Jerusalén *n pr* Jerusalem.

jesuita *adj* & *sm* Jesuit.

jesús *interj*: ¡jesús! [sorpresa] good heavens!; [tras estornudo] bless you!

jet [jet] (*pl* jets) *sm* jet.

jeta *mfam* [cara] mug, face; tener (mucha) jeta to be a cheeky bugger.

jet-set ['jetset] *sf* jet set.

Jibuti *n pr* Djibouti.

jilguero *sm* goldfinch.

jilipollada = **gilipollada**.

jilipollas = **gilipollas**.

jinete *smf* rider; [yóquey] jockey.

jirafa *sf* ZOOL giraffe.

jirón *sm* [andrajo] shred, rag; hecho jirones in tatters.

jitomate *sm Amér C & Méx* tomato.

JJ OO (*abrev de* **juegos olímpicos**) *smpl* Olympic Games.

jockey ['jokei] = **yóquey**.

jocoso, sa *adj* jocular.

joder *vulg vi* - **1.** [copular] to fuck - **2.** [fastidiar] to be a pain in the arse; **¡no jodas!** [incredulidad] bollocks!, pull the other one!

jofaina *sf* wash basin.

jolgorio *sm* merrymaking.

jolín, jolines *interj fam*: **¡jolín!** hell!, Christ!

jondo ▷ **cante**.

jornada *sf* - **1.** [de trabajo] working day; **jornada intensiva** *working day from 8 to 3 with only a short lunch break*; **jornada laboral** working day; **media jornada** half day; **jornada partida** *typical Spanish working day from 9 to 1 and 4 to 7* - **2.** [de viaje] day's journey - **3.** DEP round of matches, programme. ◆ **jornadas** *sfpl* [conferencia] conference *sing.*

jornal *sm* day's wage.

jornalero, ra *sm, f* day labourer.

joroba *sf* hump.

jorobado, da ◇ *adj* [con joroba] hunchbacked. ◇ *sm, f* hunchback.

jorongo *sm Méx* - **1.** [manta] blanket - **2.** [poncho] poncho.

jota *sf* [baile] *Aragonese folk song and dance.*

joto *sm Méx fam despec* queer *UK*, faggot *US*.

joven ◇ *adj* young. ◇ *smf* young man (*f* young woman); **los jóvenes** young people.

jovial *adj* jovial, cheerful.

joya *sf* jewel; *fig* gem.

joyería *sf* - **1.** [tienda] jeweller's (shop) - **2.** [arte, comercio] jewellery.

joyero, ra *sm, f* [persona] jeweller. ◆ **joyero** *sm* [estuche] jewellery box.

juanete *sm* bunion.

jubilación *sf* [retiro] retirement; **jubilación anticipada** early retirement; **jubilación forzosa** compulsory retirement; **jubilación voluntaria** voluntary retirement.

jubilado, da ◇ *adj* retired. ◇ *sm, f* pensioner *UK*, senior citizen.

jubilar *vt*: **jubilar a alguien (de)** to pension sb off *O* retire sb (from). ◆ **jubilarse** *vprnl* to retire.

jubileo *sm* RELIG jubilee.

júbilo *sm* jubilation, joy.

judía *sf* bean.

judicial *adj* judicial.

judío, a ◇ *adj* Jewish. ◇ *sm, f* Jew (*f* Jewess).

judo = **yudo**.

juega ▷ **jugar**.

juego *sm* - **1.** [gen & DEP] game; [acción] play, playing; [con dinero] gambling; **abrir/cerrar el juego** to begin/finish the game; **juego de azar** game of chance; **juego de manos** conjuring trick; **juego de palabras** play on words, pun; **juego sucio/limpio** foul/clean play; **descubrirle el juego a alguien** to see through sb; **estar (en) fuera de juego** DEP to be offside; *fig* not to know what's going on - **2.** [conjunto de objetos] set; **juego de herramientas** tool kit; **juego de llaves/sábanas** set of keys/sheets; **hacer juego (con)** to match. ◆ **Juegos Olímpicos** *smpl* Olympic Games.

juerga *sf fam* rave-up.

juerguista *fam smf* reveller.

jueves *sm inv* Thursday; **Jueves Santo** Maundy Thursday; *ver también* **sábado**.

juez *smf* - **1.** DER judge; **juez de paz** Justice of the Peace - **2.** [DEP - gen] judge; [- en atletismo] official; **juez de línea** [- fútbol] linesman; [- rugby] touch judge; **juez de salida** starter; **juez de silla** umpire.

jugada *sf* - **1.** DEP period of play; [en tenis, ping-pong] rally; [en fútbol, rugby etc] move; [en ajedrez etc] move; [en billar] shot - **2.** [treta] dirty trick; **hacer una mala jugada a alguien** to play a dirty trick on sb.

jugador, ra *sm, f* [gen] player; [de juego de azar] gambler.

jugar ◇ *vi* - **1.** [gen] to play; **jugar al ajedrez** to play chess; **jugar en un equipo** to play for a team; **te toca jugar** it's your turn *O* go; **jugar limpio/sucio** to play clean/dirty; **jugar con algo** to play with sthg; **jugar contra alguien** to play (against) sb - **2.** [con dinero]: **jugar (a)** to gamble (on); **jugar (a la Bolsa)** to speculate (on the Stock Exchange). ◇ *vt* - **1.** [gen] to play; [ficha, pieza] to move - **2.** [dinero]: **jugar algo (a algo)** to gamble sthg (on sthg). ◆ **jugarse** *vprnl* - **1.** [apostarse] to bet - **2.** [arriesgar] to risk - **3.** *loc*: **jugársela a alguien** to play a dirty trick on sb.

jugarreta *sf fam* dirty trick.

juglar *sm* minstrel.

jugo *sm* - **1.** [gen & ANAT] juice; BOT sap; **jugos gástricos** gastric juices - **2.** [interés] meat, substance; **sacar jugo a algo/alguien** to get the most out of sthg/sb.

jugoso, sa *adj* - **1.** [con jugo] juicy - **2.** *fig* [picante] juicy; [sustancioso] meaty, substantial.

juguete *sm lit & fig* toy; **de juguete** toy (*antes de s*); **juguete educativo** educational toy.

juguetear *vi* to play (around); **juguetear con algo** to toy with sthg.

juguetería *sf* toy shop.

juguetón, ona *adj* playful.

juicio *sm* - **1.** DER trial; **juicio civil** civil action; **juicio criminal** criminal trial - **2.** [sensatez] (sound) judgement; [cordura] sanity, reason; **estar/no estar en su (sano) juicio** to be/not to be in one's right mind; **perder el juicio** to lose one's reason, to go mad - **3.** [opinión] opinion; **a mi juicio** in my opinion. ● **Juicio Final** *sm*: **el Juicio Final** the Last Judgement.

juicioso, sa *adj* sensible, wise.

julio *sm* - **1.** [mes] July - **2.** FÍS joule; *ver también* **septiembre**.

junco *sm* - **1.** [planta] rush, reed - **2.** [embarcación] junk.

jungla *sf* jungle.

junio *sm* June; *ver también* **septiembre**.

júnior (*pl* **juniors**) *adj inv* - **1.** DEP under-21 - **2.** [hijo] junior.

junta *sf* - **1.** [gen] committee; [de empresa, examinadores] board; **junta directiva** board of directors; **junta militar** military junta - **2.** [reunión] meeting - **3.** [juntura] joint; **junta de culata** gasket.

juntar *vt* [gen] to put together; [fondos] to raise; [personas] to bring together. ● **juntarse** *vprnl* - **1.** [reunirse - personas] to get together; [- ríos, caminos] to meet - **2.** [arrimarse] to draw *O* move closer - **3.** [convivir] to live together.

junto, ta ⟨⟩ *adj* - **1.** [gen] together - **2.** [próximo] close together. ⟨⟩ *adv*: **todo junto** [ocurrir etc] all at the same time; [escribirse] as one word. ● **junto a** *loc prep* - **1.** [al lado de] next to - **2.** [cerca de] right by, near. ● **junto con** *loc prep* together with.

juntura *sf* joint.

Júpiter *sm* Jupiter.

jurado, da *adj* - **1.** [declaración etc] sworn - **2.** ▷ **guarda**. ● **jurado** *sm* - **1.** [tribunal] jury - **2.** [miembro] member of the jury.

juramento *sm* - **1.** [promesa] oath - **2.** [blasfemia] oath, curse.

jurar ⟨⟩ *vt* to swear; [constitución etc] to pledge allegiance to; **te lo juro** I promise, I swear it; **jurar por... que** to swear by... that. ⟨⟩ *vi* [blasfemar] to swear; **tenérsela jurada a alguien** to have it in for sb.

jurel *sm* scad, horse mackerel.

jurídico, ca *adj* legal.

jurisdicción *sf* jurisdiction.

jurisdiccional *adj* jurisdictional; [aguas] territorial.

jurisprudencia *sf* [ciencia] jurisprudence; [casos previos] case law.

jurista *smf* jurist.

justa *sf* HIST joust.

justamente *adv* - **1.** [con justicia] justly - **2.** [exactamente] exactly.

justicia *sf* - **1.** [gen] justice; [equidad] fairness, justice; **hacer justicia** to do justice; **ser de justicia** to be only fair - **2.** [organización]: **la justicia** the law.

justiciero, ra *adj* righteous.

justificación *sf* [gen & IMPR] justification.

justificante *sm* documentary evidence (U).

justificar *vt* - **1.** [gen & IMPR] to justify - **2.** [excusar]: **justificar a alguien** to make excuses for sb. ● **justificarse** *vprnl* [suj: persona] to justify *O* excuse o.s.

justo, ta *adj* - **1.** [equitativo] fair - **2.** [merecido - recompensa, victoria] deserved; [- castigo] just - **3.** [exacto - medida, hora] exact - **4.** [idóneo] right - **5.** [apretado] tight; **estar** *O* **venir justo** to be a tight fit. ● **justo** *adv* just; **justo ahora iba a llamarte** I was just about to ring you; **justo en medio** right in the middle.

juvenil *adj* youthful; DEP youth (*antes de s*).

juventud *sf* - **1.** [edad] youth; **¡juventud, divino tesoro!** what it is to be young! - **2.** [conjunto] young people *pl*.

juzgado *sm* [tribunal] court; **juzgado de guardia** *court open during the night or at other times when ordinary courts are shut*.

juzgar *vt* - **1.** [enjuiciar] to judge; DER to try; **juzgar mal a alguien** to misjudge sb; **a juzgar por (como)** judging by (how) - **2.** [estimar] to consider, to judge.

k, K *sf* [letra] k, K.

kaki = caqui.

kárate, cárate *sm* karate.

kart (*pl* **karts**) *sm* go-kart.

Kazajstán *n pr* Kazakhstan.

Kenia *n pr* Kenya.

ketchup ['ketʃup] *sm* ketchup.

kg (*abrev de* **kilogramo**) kg.

kibutz [ki'βuθ] (*pl* **kibutzim**) *sm* kibbutz.

kilo, quilo *sm* [peso] kilo.

kilogramo, quilogramo *sm* kilogram.

kilometraje, quilometraje *sm* ≃ mileage, distance in kilometres.

kilométrico, ca,   **quilométrico, ca** *adj* [distancia] kilometric.

kilómetro, quilómetro *sm* kilometre; **kilómetro cuadrado** square kilometre; **kilómetros por hora** kilometres per hour.

kilovatio, quilovatio *sm* kilowatt.

kínder *sm Andes & Cuba* nursery school *UK*, kindergarten *US*.

kiosco = quiosco

kiwi *sm* [fruto] kiwi (fruit).

km (*abrev de* **kilómetro**) km.

km/h (*abrev de* **kilómetro por hora**) km/h.

KO (*abrev de* **knockout**) *sm* KO.

kurdo, da ◇ *adj* Kurdish. ◇ *sm, f* Kurd.

Kuwait [ku'βait] *n pr* Kuwait.

l¹, L *sf* [letra] l, L.

l² (*abrev de* **litro**) l.

la¹ *sm* MÚS A; [en solfeo] lah.

la² ◇ *art* ➭ **el**. ◇ *pron* ➭ **lo**.

laberinto *sm lit & fig* labyrinth.

labia *sf fam* smooth talk; **tener mucha labia** to have the gift of the gab.

labio *sm* - **1.** ANAT lip; **leer los labios** to lip-read - **2.** [borde] edge.

labor *sf* - **1.** [trabajo] work; [tarea] task; **labores domésticas** household chores; **ser de profesión sus labores** to be a housewife; **no estar por la labor** [distraerse] not to have one's mind on the job; [ser reacio] not to be keen on the idea - **2.** [de costura] needlework; **labores de punto** knitting.

laboral *adj* labour; [semana, condiciones] working (*antes de s*).

laboratorio *sm* laboratory; **laboratorio espacial** space laboratory; **laboratorio fotográfico** photographic laboratory; **laboratorio de idiomas** O **lenguas** language laboratory.

laborioso, sa *adj* [difícil] laborious.

laborista ◇ *adj* Labour. ◇ *smf* Labour Party supporter O member; **los laboristas** Labour.

labrador, ra *sm, f* [agricultor] farmer; [trabajador] farm worker.

labranza *sf* farming.

labrar *vt* - **1.** [campo - cultivar] to cultivate; [- arar] to plough - **2.** [piedra, metal etc] to work - **3.** *fig* [desgracia etc] to bring about; [porvenir, fortuna] to carve out. ➭ **labrarse** *vprnl* [porvenir etc] to carve out for o.s.

labriego, ga *sm, f* farmworker.

laburar *vi R Dom fam* [trabajar] to work.

laburo *sm R Dom fam* [trabajo] job.

laca *sf* - **1.** [gen] lacquer; [para cuadros] lake - **2.** [para el pelo] hairspray.

lacar *vt* to lacquer.

lacayo *sm* footman; *fig* lackey.

lacerar *vt* to lacerate; *fig* to wound.

lacio, cia *adj* - **1.** [cabello - liso] straight; [- sin fuerza] lank - **2.** [planta] wilted - **3.** *fig* [sin fuerza] limp.

lacón *sm* shoulder of pork.

lacónico, ca *adj* laconic.

lacra *sf* scourge.

lacrar *vt* to seal with sealing wax.

lacre *sm* sealing wax.

lacrimógeno, na *adj* - **1.** [novela etc] weepy, tear-jerking - **2.** ➭ **gas**.

lacrimoso, sa *adj* - **1.** [ojos etc] tearful - **2.** [historia etc] weepy, tear-jerking.

lactancia *sf* lactation; **lactancia artificial** bottlefeeding; **lactancia materna** breastfeeding.

lactante *smf* breast-fed baby.

lácteo, a *adj* [gen] milk (*antes de s*); [industria, productos] dairy.

ladear *vt* to tilt.

ladera *sf* slope, mountainside.

ladino, na ◇ *adj* crafty. ◇ *sm, f Amér C, Méx & Ven* [mestizo hispanohablante] *non-white Spanish-speaking person.* ➭ **ladino** *sm* [dialecto] Ladino.

lado *sm* - **1.** [gen] side; **en el lado de arriba/abajo** on the top/bottom; **a ambos lados** on both sides; **al otro lado de** on the other side of; **estoy de su lado** I'm on her side; **de lado** [torcido] crooked; **dormir de lado** to sleep on one's side; **de lado a lado** from side to side; **echar a un lado** to push aside; **echarse O hacerse a un lado** to move aside; **ponerse del lado de alguien** to side with sb; **por un lado** on the one hand; **por otro lado** on the other hand - **2.** [lugar] place; **debe estar en otro lado** it must be somewhere else; **de un lado para O a otro** to and fro; **por todos lados** on all sides, all round - **3.** *loc*: **dar de lado a alguien** to cold-shoulder sb. ➭ **al lado** *loc adv* [cerca] nearby. ➭ **al lado de** *loc prep* [junto a] beside. ➭ **de al lado** *loc adj* next door; **la casa de al lado** the house next door.

ladrar *vi lit & fig* to bark.

ladrido *sm lit & fig* bark, barking *(U)*.

ladrillo *sm* CONSTR brick.

ladrón, ona *sm, f* [persona] thief, robber.
➡ **ladrón** *sm* [para varios enchufes] adapter.

lagartija *sf* (small) lizard.

lagarto, ta *sm, f* ZOOL lizard.

lago *sm* lake.

lágrima *sf* tear; **deshacerse en lágrimas** to dissolve into tears; **llorar a lágrima viva** to cry buckets.

lagrimal *sm* corner of the eye.

laguna *sf* - 1. [lago] lagoon - 2. *fig* [en colección, memoria] gap; [en leyes, reglamento] loophole.

La Habana *n pr* Havana.

laico, ca *adj* lay, secular.

lama *sm* lama.

lamber *vt Amér fam* to lick.

La Meca *n pr* Mecca.

lamentable *adj* - 1. [triste] terribly sad - 2. [malo] lamentable, deplorable.

lamentar *vt* to regret, to be sorry about; **lo lamento** I'm very sorry.

lamento *sm* moan.

lamer *vt* to lick. ➡ **lamerse** *vprnl* to lick o.s.

lamido, da *adj* skinny. ➡ **lamido** *sm* lick.

lámina *sf* - 1. [plancha] sheet; [placa] plate - 2. [rodaja] slice - 3. [plancha grabada] engraving - 4. [dibujo] plate.

laminar *vt* to laminate, to roll.

lámpara *sf* - 1. [aparato] lamp; **lámpara de pie** standard lamp; **lámpara de soldar** blowtorch; **lámpara de techo** ceiling lamp - 2. [bombilla] bulb - 3. TECNOL valve.

lamparón *sm* grease stain.

lampiño, ña *adj* [sin barba] beardless; [sin vello] hairless.

lamprea *sf* lamprey.

lana *sf* - 1. wool; **de lana** woollen; **pura lana virgen** pure new wool; **ir a por lana y volver trasquilado** *prov* to be hoist by one's own petard; **unos cardan la lana y otros llevan la fama** *prov* some do all the work and others get all the credit - 2. *Andes & Cuba fam* [dinero] dough, cash.

lance *sm* - 1. [en juegos, deportes] incident; [acontecimiento] event - 2. [riña] dispute.

lanceta *sf Andes & Cuba* sting.

lancha *sf* [embarcación - grande] launch; [- pequeña] boat; **lancha motora** motorboat, motor launch; **lancha salvavidas** lifeboat.

lanero, ra *adj* wool *(antes de s)*.

langosta *sf* - 1. [crustáceo] lobster - 2. [insecto] locust.

langostino *sm* king prawn.

languidecer *vi* to languish; [conversación, entusiasmo] to flag.

languidez *sf* [debilidad] listlessness, [falta de ánimo] disinterest.

lánguido, da *adj* [débil] listless; [falto de ánimo] disinterested.

lanilla *sf* - 1. [pelillo] nap - 2. [tejido] flannel.

lanolina *sf* lanolin.

lanza *sf* [arma - arrojadiza] spear; [- en justas, torneos] lance; **estar lanza en ristre** to be ready for action; **romper una lanza por alguien** to fight for sb.

lanzado, da *adj* [atrevido] forward; [valeroso] fearless.

lanzagranadas *sm inv* grenade launcher.

lanzamiento *sm* - 1. [de objeto] throwing; [de cohete] launching - 2. [DEP - con la mano] throw; [- con el pie] kick; [- en béisbol] pitch; **lanzamiento de peso** shot put - 3. [de producto, artista] launch; [de disco] release.

lanzamisiles *sm inv* rocket launcher.

lanzar *vt* - 1. [gen] to throw; [con fuerza] to hurl, to fling; [de una patada] to kick; [bomba] to drop; [flecha, misil] to fire; [cohete] to launch - 2. [proferir] to let out; [acusación, insulto] to hurl; [suspiro] to heave - 3. [COM - producto, artista, periódico] to launch; [- disco] to release.
➡ **lanzarse** *vprnl* - 1. [tirarse] to throw o.s. - 2. [abalanzarse]: **lanzarse (sobre)** to throw o.s. (upon).

lapa *sf* ZOOL limpet.

La Paz *n pr* La Paz.

lapicera *sf C Sur* ballpoint (pen), Biro®.

lapicero *sm* - 1. pencil - 2. *Amér C & Perú* [bolígrafo] ballpoint pen, Biro®.

lápida *sf* memorial stone; **lápida mortuoria** tombstone.

lapidar *vt* to stone.

lapidario, ria *adj* solemn.

lápiz *(pl lápices) sm* pencil; **escribir algo a lápiz** to write sthg in pencil; **lápiz de cejas** eyebrow pencil; **lápiz de labios** lipstick; **lápiz de ojos** eyeliner; **lápiz óptico** INFORM light pen.

lapón, ona *adj & sm, f* Lapp. ➡ **lapón** *sm* [lengua] Lapp.

lapso *sm* space, interval; **lapso de tiempo** space O interval of time.

lapsus *sm inv* lapse, slip.

larga ▷ **largo**.

largar *vt* - 1. [aflojar] to pay out - 2. *fam* [dar, decir] to give; **le largué un bofetón** I gave him a smack. ➡ **largarse** *vprnl fam* to clear off.

largavistas *sm inv Bol & C Sur* binoculars *pl*.

largo, ga *adj* - 1. [en espacio, tiempo] long - 2. [alto] tall - 3. [sobrado]: **media hora larga** a good half hour. ➡ **largo** ◇ *sm* length; **a lo**

largo lengthways; **tiene dos metros de largo** it's two metres long; **pasar de largo** to pass by; **a lo largo de** [en el espacio] along; [en el tiempo] throughout; **¡largo de aquí!** go away!, get out of here! ◆ *adv* at length; **largo y tendido** at great length. ◆ **larga** *sf*: **a la larga** in the long run; **dar largas a algo** to put sthg off.

largometraje *sm* feature film.

larguero *sm* - **1.** CONSTR main beam - **2.** DEP crossbar.

largura *sf* length.

laringe *sf* larynx.

laringitis *sf inv* laryngitis.

larva *sf* larva.

las ◇ *art* ▷ **el**. ◇ *pron* ▷ **lo**.

lasaña *sf* lasagne, lasagna.

lascivo, va *adj* lascivious, lewd.

láser ◇ *adj inv* ▷ **rayo**. ◇ *sm inv* laser.

lástima *sf* - **1.** [compasión] pity - **2.** [pena] shame, pity; **da lástima ver gente así** it's sad to see people in that state; **es una lástima que** it's a shame *O* pity that; **¡qué lástima!** what a shame *O* pity!; **tener** *O* **sentir lástima de** to feel sorry for; **quedarse hecho una lástima** to be a sorry *O* pitiful sight.

lastimar *vt* to hurt. ◆ **lastimarse** *vprnl* to hurt o.s.

lastimoso, sa *adj* pitiful, woeful.

lastre *sm* - **1.** [peso] ballast - **2.** *fig* [estorbo] burden.

lata *sf* - **1.** [envase] can, tin; [de bebidas] can; **en lata** tinned, canned - **2.** *fam* [fastidio] pain; **¡qué lata!** what a pain!; **dar la lata a alguien** to pester sb.

latente *adj* latent.

lateral ◇ *adj* [del lado - gen] lateral; [- puerta, pared] side. ◇ *sm* [lado] side.

latido *sm* [del corazón] beat; [en dedo etc] throb, throbbing *(U)*.

latifundio *sm* large rural estate.

latigazo *sm* - **1.** [golpe] lash - **2.** [chasquido] crack (of the whip).

látigo *sm* whip.

latín *sm* Latin; **latín de cocina** *O* **macarrónico** dog Latin; **saber (mucho) latín** *fig* to be sharp, to be on the ball.

latinajo *sm fam despec* Latin word used in an attempt to sound academic.

latino, na *adj* & *sm, f* Latin.

latinoamericano, na *adj* & *sm, f* Latin American.

latir *vi* [suj: corazón] to beat.

latitud *sf* GEOGR latitude. ◆ **latitudes** *sfpl* [parajes] region *sing*, area *sing*.

latón *sm* brass.

latoso, sa *fam adj* tiresome.

laúd *sm* lute.

laureado, da *adj* prize-winning.

laurel *sm* BOT laurel; CULIN bay leaf. ◆ **laureles** *smpl* [honores] laurels; **dormirse en los laureles** *fig* to rest on one's laurels.

lava *sf* lava.

lavabo *sm* - **1.** [objeto] washbasin - **2.** [habitación] lavatory *UK*, washroom *US*; **ir al lavabo** to go to the toilet.

lavadero *sm* [en casa] laundry room; [público] washing place.

lavado *sm* wash, washing *(U)*; **lavado a mano** hand-wash; **lavado de cerebro** brainwashing; **lavado de dinero** money-laundering; **lavado en seco** dry cleaning.

lavadora *sf* washing machine; **lavadora secadora** washer-drier.

lavamanos *sm inv* washbasin.

lavanda *sf* lavender.

lavandería *sf* laundry; [automática] launderette.

lavaplatos *sm inv* - **1.** [aparato] dishwasher - **2.** *Chile, Col, Méx & Ven* [fregadero] kitchen sink.

lavar *vt* [limpiar] to wash; **lavar a mano** to wash by hand; **lavar en seco** to dry-clean; **lavar y marcar** shampoo and set. ◆ **lavarse** *vprnl* [gen] to wash o.s.; [cara, manos, pelo] to wash; [dientes] to clean.

lavarropas *sm inv R Plata* washing machine.

lavativa *sf* enema.

lavavajillas *sm inv* dishwasher.

laxante *sm* laxative.

laxar *vt* [vientre] to loosen.

lazada *sf* bow.

lazarillo *sm* - **1.** [persona] blind person's guide - **2.** ▷ **perro**.

lazo *sm* - **1.** [atadura] bow; **hacer un lazo** to tie a bow - **2.** [trampa] snare; [de vaquero] lasso - **3.** *(gen pl) fig* [vínculo] tie, bond.

Lda. *abrev de* **licenciado**.

Ldo. *abrev de* **licenciado**.

le *pron pers* - **1.** *(complemento indirecto)* [hombre] (to) him; [mujer] (to) her; [cosa] to it; [usted] to you; **le expliqué el motivo** I explained the reason to him/her; **le tengo miedo** I'm afraid of him/her; **ya le dije lo que pasaría** [a usted] I told you what would happen - **2.** *(complemento directo)* him; [usted] you.

leal *adj*: **leal (a)** loyal (to).

lealtad *sf*: **lealtad (a)** loyalty (to).

leasing ['lisin] *(pl leasings) sm* system of leasing whereby the lessee has the option of purchasing the property after a certain time.

lección *sf* lesson; **aprenderse la lección** to learn one's lesson.

lechal *sm* sucking lamb.

leche *sf* - **1**. [gen] milk; **leche esterilizada/homogeneizada** sterilized/homogenized milk; **leche merengada** drink made from milk, egg whites, sugar and cinnamon - **2**. *mfam* [bofetada]: **pegar una leche a alguien** to belt *O* clobber sb - **3**. *mfam* [mal humor] bloody awful mood; **estar de mala leche** to be in a bloody awful mood; **tener mala leche** to be a miserable git.

lechera ⊳ **lechero**.

lechería *sf* dairy.

lechero, ra ◇ *adj* milk *(antes de s)*, dairy. ◇ *sm, f* [persona] milkman *(f* milkwoman). ◆ **lechera** *sf* [para transportar] milk churn; [para beber] milk jug.

lecho *sm* [gen] bed; **lecho de muerte** deathbed.

lechón *sm* sucking pig.

lechuga *sf* lettuce; **lechuga iceberg/romana** iceberg/cos lettuce; **ser más fresco que una lechuga** to be a cheeky devil.

lechuza *sf* (barn) owl.

lectivo, va *adj* school *(antes de s)*.

lector, ra *sm, f* - **1**. [gen] reader - **2**. EDUC language assistant. ◆ **lector** *sm* [de microfilms etc] reader, scanner; **lector óptico** optical scanner.

lectura *sf* - **1**. [gen] reading; **dar lectura a algo** to read sthg out loud - **2**. [de tesis] viva voce - **3**. [escrito] reading (matter) *(U)* - **4**. [de datos] scanning; **lectura óptica** optical scanning.

leer ◇ *vt* [gen & INFORM] to read. ◇ *vi* to read; **leer de corrido** to read fluently.

legado *sm* - **1**. [herencia] legacy - **2**. [representante - persona] legate.

legajo *sm* file.

legal *adj* - **1**. [gen] legal; [hora] standard - **2**. *fam* [persona] honest, decent.

legalidad *sf* legality.

legalizar *vt* [gen] to legalize.

legañoso, sa *adj* full of sleep.

legar *vt* - **1**. [gen] to bequeath - **2**. [delegar] to delegate.

legendario, ria *adj* legendary.

legible *adj* legible.

legión *sf* lit & fig legion.

legionario, ria *adj* legionary. ◆ **legionario** *sm* HIST legionary; MIL legionnaire.

legislación *sf* [leyes] legislation.

legislar *vi* to legislate.

legislatura *sf* [periodo] period of office.

legitimar *vt* - **1**. [legalizar] to legitimize - **2**. [certificar] to authenticate.

legítimo, ma *adj* [gen] legitimate; [auténtico] real, genuine; [oro] pure.

lego, ga ◇ *adj* - **1**. [gen] lay - **2**. [ignorante] ignorant. ◇ *sm, f* [gen] layman *(f* laywoman).

legua *sf* league; **legua marina** marine league.

legumbre *(gen pl)* *sf* pulse, pod vegetable.

lehendakari = **lendakari**.

leído, da *adj* [persona] well-read. ◆ **leída** *sf* reading.

lejanía *sf* distance.

lejano, na *adj* distant; **no está lejos** it's not far (away).

lejía *sf* bleach.

lejos *adv* - **1**. [en el espacio] far (away); **¿está lejos?** is it far?; **a lo lejos** in the distance; **de** *O* **desde lejos** from a distance - **2**. [en el pasado] long ago; [en el futuro] far in the future; **eso queda ya lejos** that happened a long time ago - **3**. *loc*: **ir demasiado lejos** to go too far; **llegar lejos** to go far; **sin ir más lejos** indeed. ◆ **lejos de** ◇ *loc conj* far from; **lejos de mejorar...** far from getting better... ◇ *loc prep* far (away) from.

lelo, la ◇ *adj* stupid; **quedarse lelo** to be stunned. ◇ *sm, f* idiot.

lema *sm* - **1**. [norma] motto; [político, publicitario] slogan - **2**. LING & MAT lemma.

lencería *sf* - **1**. [ropa] linen - **2**. [tienda] draper's.

lendakari, lehendakari [lenda'kari] *sm* president of the autonomous Basque government.

lengua *sf* - **1**. [gen] tongue; **sacarle la lengua a alguien** to stick one's tongue out at sb; **con la lengua fuera** out of breath; **lengua de gato** CULIN ≈ chocolate finger (biscuit); **lengua de fuego/tierra** tongue of flame/land; **lengua de víbora** *O* **viperina** malicious tongue; **darle a la lengua** *fam* to chatter; **irse de la lengua** to let the cat out of the bag; **las malas lenguas dicen que...** according to the gossip...; **morderse la lengua** to bite one's tongue; **¿te ha comido la lengua el gato?** has the cat got your tongue?, have you lost your tongue?; **tirar a alguien de la lengua** to draw sb out - **2**. [idioma, lenguaje] language; **lengua materna** mother tongue; **lengua oficial** official language.

lenguado *sm* sole.

lenguaje *sm* [gen & INFORM] language; **lenguaje coloquial/comercial** colloquial/business language; **lenguaje cifrado** code; **lenguaje corporal** body language; **lenguaje gestual** gestures *pl*; **lenguaje máquina** machine language; **lenguaje de alto nivel/de bajo nivel** high-level/low-level language; **lenguaje de programación** programming language; **lenguaje de los sordomudos** sign language.

lengüeta *sf* [gen & MÚS] tongue.

lengüetada *sf* = **lengüetazo**.

lengüetazo sm lick.

lente sf lens; **lente de aumento** magnifying glass; **lentes de contacto** contact lenses. ➤ **lentes** smpl [gafas] glasses.

lenteja sf lentil; **ganarse las lentejas** to earn one's daily bread.

lentejuela sf sequin.

lentilla (gen pl) sf contact lens.

lentitud sf slowness; **con lentitud** slowly.

lento, ta adj slow; [veneno] slow-working; [agonía, enfermedad] lingering.

leña sf [madera] firewood; **echar leña al fuego** to add fuel to the flames O fire; **llevar leña al monte** to carry coals to Newcastle.

leñador, ra sm, f woodcutter.

leño sm [de madera] log; **dormir como un leño** to sleep like a log.

Leo ⬥ sm [zodiaco] Leo. ⬥ smf [persona] Leo.

león, ona sm, f lion (f lioness); fig fierce person; **no es tan fiero el león como lo pintan** prov he/it etc is not as bad as he/it etc is made out to be. ➤ **león marino** sm sea lion.

leonera sf fam fig [cuarto sucio] pigsty.

leonino, na adj [contrato, condiciones] one-sided.

leopardo sm leopard.

leotardo sm - 1. (gen pl) [medias] stockings pl, thick tights pl - 2. [de gimnasta etc] leotard.

lépero, ra adj Amér C & Méx fam [vulgar] coarse, vulgar; Cuba fam [astuto] smart, crafty.

leproso, sa sm, f leper.

lerdo, da adj [idiota] dim, slow-witted; [torpe] useless.

les pron pers pl - 1. (complemento indirecto) (to) them; [ustedes] (to) you; **les expliqué el motivo** I explained the reason to them; **les tengo miedo** I'm afraid of them; **ya les dije lo que pasaría** [a ustedes] I told you what would happen - 2. (complemento directo) them; [ustedes] you.

lesbiano, na adj lesbian. ➤ **lesbiana** sf lesbian.

leseras sfpl Chile fam nonsense, rubbish UK.

lesión sf - 1. [herida] injury; **lesión cerebral** brain damage - 2. DER: **lesión grave** grievous bodily harm.

lesionado, da ⬥ adj injured. ⬥ sm, f injured person.

lesionar vt to injure; fig to damage, to harm. ➤ **lesionarse** vprnl to injure o.s.

letal adj lethal.

letanía (gen pl) sf lit & fig litany.

letargo sm ZOOL hibernation.

Letonia n pr Latvia.

letra sf - 1. [signo] letter - 2. [caligrafía] handwriting - 3. [estilo] script; IMPR typeface; **letra bastardilla** O **cursiva** O **itálica** italic type, italics pl; **letra de imprenta** O **molde** IMPR print; [en formularios etc] block capitals pl; **letra mayúscula/minúscula** capital/small letter; **letra negrita** O **negrilla** bold (face); **letra versalita** small capital; **la letra con sangre entra** prov spare the rod and spoil the child; **leer la letra pequeña** to read the small print; **mandar cuatro letras a alguien** to drop sb a line - 4. [de canción] lyrics pl - 5. COM: **letra (de cambio)** bill of exchange. ➤ **letras** sfpl EDUC arts.

letrado, da ⬥ adj learned. ⬥ sm, f lawyer.

letrero sm sign; **letrero luminoso** neon sign.

letrina sf latrine.

leucemia sf leukaemia.

leva sf MIL levy.

levadura sf yeast; **levadura de cerveza** brewer's yeast; **levadura en polvo** baking powder.

levantamiento sm - 1. [sublevación] uprising - 2. [elevación] raising; **levantamiento de pesas** DEP weightlifting - 3. [supresión] lifting, removal.

levantar vt - 1. [gen] to raise; [peso, capó, trampilla] to lift; **levantar el ánimo** to cheer up; **levantar la vista** O **mirada** to look up - 2. [separar - pintura, venda, tapa] to remove - 3. [recoger - campamento] to strike; [- tienda de campaña, puesto] to take down; [- mesa] to clear - 4. [encender - protestas, polémica] to stir up; **levantar a alguien contra** to stir sb up against - 5. [suspender - embargo, prohibición] to lift; [- pena, castigo] to suspend; [- sesión] to adjourn - 6. [redactar - acta, atestado] to draw up. ➤ **levantarse** vprnl - 1. [ponerse de pie] to stand up - 2. [de la cama] to get up; **levantar tarde** to sleep in - 3. [elevarse - avión etc] to take off; [- niebla] to lift - 4. [sublevarse] to rise up - 5. [empezar - viento, oleaje] to get up; [- tormenta] to gather.

levante sm - 1. [este] east; [región] east coast - 2. [viento] east wind.

levar vt to weigh.

leve adj - 1. [gen] light; [olor, sabor, temblor] slight - 2. [pecado, falta, herida] minor - 3. [enfermedad] mild, slight.

levedad sf lightness; [de temblor etc] slightness; [de pecado, falto, herida] minor nature; [de enfermedad] mildness.

levita sf frock coat.

levitar vi to levitate.

léxico, ca adj lexical. ➤ **léxico** sm [vocabulario] vocabulary.

lexicografía sf lexicography.

lexicón sm lexicon.

ley *sf* - **1.** [gen] law; [parlamentaria] act; **aprobar una ley** to pass a law; **ley de incompatibilidades** *act regulating which other positions may be held by people holding public office*; **ley marcial** martial law; **con todas las de la ley** in due form, properly - **2.** [regla] rule; **ley del embudo** one law for o.s. and another for everyone else; **ley de la ventaja** DEP advantage (law); **ley de la oferta y de la demanda** law of supply and demand - **3.** [de un metal]: **de ley** [oro] pure; [plata] sterling. ➤ **leyes** *sfpl* [derecho] law *sing*.

leyenda *sf* [narración] legend.

liar *vt* - **1.** [atar] to tie up - **2.** [envolver - cigarrillo] to roll; **liar algo en** [- papel] to wrap sthg up in; [- toalla etc] to roll sthg up in - **3.** [involucrar]: **liar a alguien (en)** to get sb mixed up (in) - **4.** [complicar - asunto etc] to confuse; **¡ya me has liado!** now you've really got me confused! ➤ **liarse** *vprnl* - **1.** [enredarse] to get muddled up - **2.** [empezar] to begin, to start.

Líbano *sm*: **el Líbano** the Lebanon.

libélula *sf* dragonfly.

liberación *sf* [gen] liberation; [de preso] release.

liberado, da *adj* [gen] liberated; [preso] freed.

liberal *adj* & *smf* liberal.

liberar *vt* [gen] to liberate; [preso] to free; **liberar de algo a alguien** to free sb from sthg. ➤ **liberarse** *vprnl* to liberate o.s.; **liberarse de algo** to free O liberate o.s. from sthg.

Liberia *n pr* Liberia.

libertad *sf* freedom, liberty; **tener libertad para hacer algo** to be free to do sthg; **tomarse la libertad de hacer algo** to take the liberty of doing sthg; **libertad de circulación de capitales/trabajadores** ECON free movement of capital/workers; **libertad de conciencia** freedom of conscience; **libertad condicional** probation; **libertad de expresión** freedom of speech.

libertar *vt* [gen] to liberate; [preso] to set free.

libertino, na ◇ *adj* licentious. ◇ *sm, f* libertine.

Libia *n pr* Libya.

libido *sf* libido.

libra *sf* [peso, moneda] pound; **libra esterlina** pound sterling. ➤ **Libra** ◇ *sm* [zodiaco] Libra. ◇ *smf* [persona] Libran.

librador, ra *sm, f* drawer.

libramiento *sm* order of payment.

libranza *sf* = **libramiento**.

librar ◇ *vt* - **1.** [eximir]: **librar a alguien (de algo/de hacer algo)** [gen] to free sb (from sthg/from doing sthg); [pagos, impuestos] to exempt sb (from sthg/from doing sthg) - **2.** [entablar - pelea, lucha] to engage in; [- batalla, combate] to join, to wage - **3.** COM to draw. ◇ *vi* [no tra-

bajar] to be off work. ➤ **librarse** *vprnl* - **1.** [salvarse]: **librarse (de hacer algo)** to escape (from doing sthg); **de buena te libraste** you had a narrow escape - **2.** [deshacerse]: **librarse de algo/alguien** to get rid of sthg/sb.

libre *adj* - **1.** [gen] free; [rato, tiempo] spare; [camino, vía] clear; [espacio, piso, lavabo] empty, vacant; **200 metros libres** 200 metres freestyle; **libre de** [gen] free from; [exento] exempt from; **libre de franqueo** post-free; **libre de impuestos** tax-free; **ser libre de O para hacer algo** to be free to do sthg; **ir por libre** to go it alone - **2.** [alumno] external; **estudiar por libre** to be an external student.

librecambio *sm* free trade.

librería *sf* - **1.** [tienda] bookshop; **librería de ocasión** second-hand bookshop - **2.** [mueble] bookcase.

librero, ra ◇ *sm, f* [persona] bookseller. ◇ *sm* Amér C, Col & Méx [mueble] bookcase.

libreta *sf* - **1.** [para escribir] notebook; **libreta de direcciones** address book - **2.** [del banco]: **libreta (de ahorros)** savings book.

libretista *smf* Amér [guionista] screenwriter, scriptwriter.

libreto *sm* - **1.** MÚS libretto - **2.** Amér [guión] script.

libro *sm* [gen & COM] book; **llevar los libros** to keep the books; **libro de bolsillo** paperback; **libro de cuentas** O **contabilidad** accounts book; **libro de ejercicios** workbook; **libro de escolaridad** school report; **libro de familia** *document containing personal details of the members of a family*; **libro de reclamaciones** complaints book; **libro de registro (de entradas)** register; **libro de texto** textbook; **libro de visitas** visitor's book; **colgar los libros** to give up one's studies; **ser como un libro abierto** to be an open book.

Lic. *abrev de* **licenciado**.

licencia *sf* - **1.** [documento] licence, permit; [autorización] permission; **licencia de exportación/importación** export/import licence; **licencia de obras** planning permission; **licencia poética** poetic licence - **2.** MIL discharge - **3.** [confianza] licence, freedom.

licenciado, da *sm, f* - **1.** EDUC graduate; **licenciado en económicas** economics graduate - **2.** MIL discharged soldier.

licenciar *vt* MIL to discharge. ➤ **licenciarse** *vprnl* - **1.** EDUC: **licenciarse (en)** to graduate (in) - **2.** MIL to be discharged.

licenciatura *sf* degree.

licencioso, sa *adj* licentious.

liceo *sm* - **1.** EDUC lycée - **2.** C Sur & Ven [instituto] secondary school UK, high school US.

lícito, ta *adj* - **1.** [legal] lawful - **2.** [correcto] right - **3.** [justo] fair.

licor *sm* liquor.

licuado *sm Amér* [batido] milk shake.

licuadora *sf* liquidizer, blender.

licuar *vt* CULIN to liquidize.

líder <> *adj* leading. <> *smf* leader.

liderato, liderazgo *sm* - **1.** [primer puesto] lead; [en liga] first place - **2.** [dirección] leadership.

lidia *sf* - **1.** [arte] bullfighting - **2.** [corrida] bullfight.

lidiar <> *vi* [luchar]: **lidiar (con)** to struggle (with). <> *vt* TAUROM to fight.

liebre *sf* ZOOL hare.

lienzo *sm* - **1.** [para pintar] canvas - **2.** [cuadro] painting.

lifting ['liftin] (*pl* **liftings**) *sm* facelift.

liga *sf* - **1.** [gen] league - **2.** [de medias] suspender.

ligadura *sf* - **1.** MED & MÚS ligature - **2.** [atadura] bond, tie.

ligamento *sm* ANAT ligament.

ligar <> *vt* [gen & CULIN] to bind; [atar] to tie (up). <> *vi* - **1.** [coincidir]: **ligar (con)** to tally (with) - **2.** *fam* [conquistar]: **ligar (con)** to get off (with).

ligazón *sf* link, connection.

ligereza *sf* - **1.** [levedad] lightness - **2.** [agilidad] agility - **3.** [irreflexión - cualidad] rashness; [- acto] rash act; **con ligereza** in a superficial manner.

ligero, ra *adj* - **1.** [gen] light; [dolor, rumor, descenso] slight; [traje, tela] thin - **2.** [ágil] agile, nimble - **3.** [rápido] quick, swift - **4.** [irreflexivo] flippant; **hacer algo a la ligera** to do sthg without much thought; **juzgar a alguien a la ligera** to be quick to judge sb; **tomarse algo a la ligera** not to take sthg seriously.

light [lait] *adj inv* [comida] low-calorie; [refresco] diet (*antes de s*); [cigarrillos] light.

ligón, ona *fam adj:* **es muy ligón** he's always getting off with sb or other.

liguero, ra *adj* DEP league (*antes de s*). ➡ **liguero** *sm* suspender belt *UK*, garter belt *US*.

lija *sf* [papel] sandpaper.

lila <> *sf* [flor] lilac. <> *adj inv* & *sm* [color] lilac.

lima *sf* - **1.** [utensilio] file; **lima de uñas** nail file - **2.** BOT lime.

Lima *n pr* Lima.

limar *vt* - **1.** [pulir] to file down - **2.** [perfeccionar] to polish.

limitación *sf* - **1.** [restricción] limitation, limit - **2.** [distrito] boundaries *pl*.

limitado, da *adj* - **1.** [gen] limited - **2.** [poco inteligente] dim-witted.

limitar <> *vt* - **1.** [gen] to limit - **2.** [terreno] to mark out - **3.** [atribuciones, derechos etc] to set out, to define. <> *vi*: **limitar (con)** to border (on). ➡ **limitarse a** *vprnl* to limit o.s. to.

límite <> *adj inv* - **1.** [precio, velocidad, edad] maximum - **2.** [situación] extreme; [caso] borderline. <> *sm* - **1.** [tope] limit; **dentro de un límite** within limits; **su pasión no tiene límite** her passion knows no bounds; **límite de velocidad** speed limit - **2.** [confín] boundary.

limítrofe *adj* [país, territorio] bordering; [terreno, finca] neighbouring.

limón *sm* lemon.

limonada *sf* lemonade.

limonero, ra *adj* lemon (*antes de s*). ➡ **limonero** *sm* lemon tree.

limosna *sf* alms *pl*; **pedir limosna** to beg.

limpia *sf Amér* cleaning.

limpiabotas *smf inv* shoeshine, bootblack *UK*.

limpiacristales *sm inv* window-cleaning fluid.

limpiamente *adv* - **1.** [con destreza] cleanly - **2.** [honradamente] honestly.

limpiaparabrisas *sm inv* windscreen wiper *UK*, windshield wiper *US*.

limpiar *vt* - **1.** [gen] to clean; [con trapo] to wipe; [mancha] to wipe away; [zapatos] to polish - **2.** *fig* [desembarazar]: **limpiar algo de algo** to clear sthg of sthg.

limpieza *sf* - **1.** [cualidad] cleanliness - **2.** [acción] cleaning; **limpieza en seco** dry cleaning - **3.** [destreza] skill, cleanness - **4.** [honradez] honesty.

limpio, pia *adj* - **1.** [gen] clean; [pulcro] neat; [cielo, imagen] clear - **2.** [neto - sueldo etc] net - **3.** [honrado] honest; [intenciones] honourable; [juego] clean - **4.** [sin culpa]: **estar limpio** to be in the clear. ➡ **limpio** *adv* cleanly, fair; **pasar a** O **poner en limpio** to make a fair copy of; **sacar algo en limpio de** to make sthg out from.

linaje *sm* lineage.

linaza *sf* linseed.

lince *sm* lynx; **ser un lince para algo** to be very sharp at sthg.

linchar *vt* to lynch.

lindar ➡ **lindar con** *vi* - **1.** [terreno] to adjoin, to be next to - **2.** [conceptos, ideas] to border on.

linde *sm* o *sf* boundary.

lindero, ra *adj* [terreno] adjoining. ➡ **lindero** *sm* boundary.

lindo, da *adj* pretty, lovely; **de lo lindo** a great deal.

línea *sf* - **1.** [gen, DEP & TELECOM] line; **cortar la línea (telefónica)** to cut off the phone; **línea aérea** airline; **línea de conducta** course of action; **línea continua** AUTO solid white line; **línea de mira** O **tiro** line of fire; **línea de puntos** dotted line - 2. [de un coche etc] lines *pl*, shape - 3. [silueta] figure; **guardar la línea** to watch one's figure - 4. [estilo] style; **de línea clásica** classical - 5. [categoría] class, category; **de primera línea** first-rate - 6. INFORM: **en línea** online; **fuera de línea** off-line - 7. *loc*: **en líneas generales** in broad terms; **en toda la línea** [completamente] all along the line; **leer entre líneas** to read between the lines.

lineamientos *smpl Amér* [generalidades] outline; [directrices] guidelines.

lingote *sm* ingot.

lingüista *smf* linguist.

lingüístico, ca *adj* linguistic. ➤ **lingüística** *sf* linguistics.

linier [li'njer] (*pl* **liniers**) *sm* linesman.

linimento *sm* liniment.

lino *sm* - 1. [planta] flax - 2. [tejido] linen.

linterna *sf* - 1. [farol] lantern, lamp - 2. [de pilas] torch *UK*, flashlight *US*.

lío *sm* - 1. [paquete] bundle - 2. *fam* [enredo] mess; **hacerse un lío** to get muddled up; **meterse en líos** to get into trouble - 3. *fam* [jaleo] racket, row - 4. *fam* [amorío] affair.

liposucción *sf* liposuction.

liquen *sm* lichen.

liquidación *sf* - 1. [pago] settlement, payment - 2. [rebaja] clearance sale - 3. [fin] liquidation.

liquidar *vt* - 1. [pagar - deuda] to pay; [- cuenta] to settle - 2. [rebajar] to sell off - 3. [malgastar] to throw away - 4. [acabar - asunto] to settle; [- negocio, sociedad] to wind up.

líquido, da *adj* - 1. [gen] liquid - 2. ECON [neto] net. ➤ **líquido** *sm* - 1. [gen] liquid - 2. ECON liquid assets *pl* - 3. MED fluid.

lira *sf* - 1. MÚS lyre - 2. [moneda] lira.

lírico, ca *adj* LITER lyrical. ➤ **lírica** *sf* lyric poetry.

lirio *sm* iris.

lirón *sm* ZOOL dormouse; **dormir como un lirón** to sleep like a log.

lisiado, da ◇ *adj* crippled. ◇ *sm, f* cripple.

lisiar *vt* to maim, to cripple.

liso, sa ◇ *adj* - 1. [llano] flat; [sin asperezas] smooth; [pelo] straight; **los 400 metros lisos** the 400 metres; **lisa y llanamente** quite simply; **hablando lisa y llanamente** to put it plainly - 2. [no estampado] plain. ◇ *sm, f Andes, Amér C & Ven* [insolente] cheeky person.

lisonja *sf* flattering remark.

lisonjear *vt* to flatter.

lista *sf* - 1. [enumeración] list; **pasar lista** to call the register - 2. [de tela, madera] strip; [de papel] slip; [de color] stripe. ➤ **lista de correos** *sf* poste restante.

listado, da *adj* striped.

listado, da ➤ **listín (de teléfonos)** *sm* (telephone) directory.

listo, ta *adj* - 1. [inteligente, hábil] clever, smart; **dárselas de listo** to make o.s. out to be clever; **pasarse de listo** to be too clever by half; **ser más listo que el hambre** to be nobody's fool - 2. [preparado] ready; **¿estáis listos?** are you ready?

listón *sm* lath; DEP bar; **poner el listón muy alto** *fig* to set very high standards.

litera *sf* - 1. [cama] bunk (bed); [de barco] berth; [de tren] couchette - 2. [vehículo] litter.

literal *adj* literal.

literario, ria *adj* literary.

literato, ta *sm, f* writer.

literatura *sf* literature.

litigar *vi* to go to law.

litigio *sm* DER litigation *(U)*; *fig* dispute; **en litigio** in dispute.

litografía *sf* - 1. [arte] lithography - 2. [grabado] lithograph.

litoral ◇ *adj* coastal. ◇ *sm* coast.

litro *sm* litre.

Lituania *n pr* Lithuania.

liturgia *sf* liturgy.

liviano, na *adj* - 1. [ligero - blusa] thin; [- carga] light - 2. [sin importancia] slight.

lívido, da *adj* - 1. [pálido] very pale - 2. [amoratado] livid.

living ['liβin] *sm C Sur* living room.

ll, Ll *sf* [letra] ll, Ll.

llaga *sf lit & fig* wound.

llagar *vt* to wound.

llama *sf* - 1. [de fuego, pasión] flame; **en llamas** ablaze - 2. ZOOL llama.

llamada *sf* - 1. [gen] call; [a la puerta] knock; [con timbre] ring - 2. TELECOM telephone call; **devolver una llamada** to phone back; **hacer una llamada** to make a phone call.

llamado, da *adj* so-called. ➤ **llamado** *sm Amér* [de teléfono] call.

llamamiento *sm* [apelación] appeal, call.

llamar ◇ *vt* - 1. [gen] to call; [con gestos] to beckon - 2. [por teléfono] to phone, to call - 3. [convocar] to summon, to call; **llamar (a filas)** MIL to call up - 4. [atraer] to attract, to call. ◇ *vi* - 1. [a la puerta etc - con golpes] to knock; [- con timbre] to ring; **están llamando** there's somebody at the door - 2. [por teléfono] llamarada

to phone. ➟ **llamarse** *vprnl* [tener por nombre] to be called; **¿cómo te llamas?** what's your name?; **me llamo Pepe** my name's Pepe.

llamarada *sf* [de fuego, ira etc] blaze.

llamativo, va *adj* [color] bright, gaudy; [ropa] showy.

llamear *vi* to burn, to blaze.

llano, na *adj* - **1.** [campo, superficie] flat - **2.** [trato, persona] natural, straightforward - **3.** [pueblo, clase] ordinary - **4.** [lenguaje, expresión] simple, plain. ➟ **llano** *sm* [llanura] plain.

llanta *sf* - **1.** rim - **2.** *Amér* [cubierta] tyre *UK*, tire *US*.

llanto *sm* tears *pl*, crying.

llanura *sf* plain.

llave *sf* - **1.** [gen] key; **bajo llave** under lock and key; **cerrar con llave** to lock; **echar la llave** to lock up; **llave en mano** [vivienda] ready for immediate occupation; **llave de contacto** ignition key; **llave maestra** master key - **2.** [del agua, gas] tap *UK*, faucet *US*; [de la electricidad] switch; **cerrar la llave de paso** to turn the water/gas off at the mains - **3.** [herramienta] spanner; **llave inglesa** monkey wrench - **4.** [de judo etc] hold, lock - **5.** [signo ortográfico] curly bracket.

llavero *sm* keyring.

llavín *sm* latchkey.

llegada *sf* - **1.** [gen] arrival - **2.** DEP finish.

llegar *vi* - **1.** [a un sitio]: **llegar (de)** to arrive (from); **llegar a un hotel/una ciudad** to arrive at a hotel/in a city; **llegaré pronto** I'll be there early - **2.** [un tiempo, la noche etc] to come - **3.** [durar]: **llegar a** O **hasta** to last until - **4.** [alcanzar]: **llegar a** to reach; **no llego al techo** I can't reach the ceiling; **llegar hasta** to reach up to - **5.** [ser suficiente]: **llegar (para)** to be enough (for) - **6.** [lograr]: **llegar a (ser) algo** to get to be sthg, to become sthg; **si llego a saberlo** if I get to know of it. ➟ **llegarse a** *vprnl* to go round to.

llenar *vt* - **1.** [ocupar]: **llenar algo (de)** [vaso, hoyo, habitación] to fill sthg (with); [pared, suelo] to cover sthg (with) - **2.** [satisfacer] to satisfy - **3.** [rellenar - impreso] to fill in O out - **4.** [colmar]: **llenar a alguien de** to fill sb with. ➟ **llenarse** *vprnl* - **1.** [ocuparse] to fill up - **2.** [saciarse] to be full - **3.** [cubrirse]: **llenarse de** to become covered in.

lleno, na *adj* - **1.** [gen] full; [cubierto] covered; **lleno de** [gen] full of; [manchas, pósters] covered in; **lleno hasta los topes** full to bursting, packed out - **2.** *fam* [regordete] chubby. ➟ **de lleno** *loc adv* full in the face; **acertó de lleno** he was bang on target.

llevadero, ra *adj* bearable.

llevar ◇ *vt* - **1.** [gen] to carry - **2.** [acompañar, coger y depositar] to take; **llevar algo/a alguien a** to take sthg/sb to; **me llevó en coche** he drove me there - **3.** [prenda, objeto personal] to wear; **llevo gafas** I wear glasses; **no llevo dinero** I haven't got any money on me - **4.** [caballo, coche etc] to handle - **5.** [conducir]: **llevar a alguien a algo** to lead sb to sthg; **llevar a alguien a hacer algo** to lead O cause sb to do sthg - **6.** [ocuparse de, dirigir] to be in charge of; [casa, negocio] to run; **lleva la contabilidad** she keeps the books - **7.** [hacer - de alguna manera]: **lleva muy bien sus estudios** he's doing very well in his studies - **8.** [tener - de alguna manera] to have; **llevar el pelo largo** to have long hair; **llevas las manos sucias** your hands are dirty - **9.** [soportar] to deal O cope with - **10.** [mantener] to keep; **llevar el paso** to keep in step - **11.** [pasarse - tiempo]: **lleva tres semanas sin venir** she hasn't come for three weeks now, it's three weeks since she came last - **12.** [ocupar - tiempo] to take; **me llevó un día hacer este guiso** it took me a day to make this dish - **13.** [sobrepasar en]: **te llevo seis puntos** I'm six points ahead of you; **me lleva dos centímetros** he's two centimetres taller than me - **14.** *loc*: **llevar consigo** [implicar] to lead to, to bring about; **llevar las de perder** to be heading for defeat. ◇ *vi* - **1.** [conducir]: **llevar a** to lead to; **esta carretera lleva al norte** this road leads north - **2.** *(antes de pp)* [haber]: **llevo leída media novela** I'm halfway through the novel; **llevo dicho esto mismo docenas de veces** I've said the same thing time and again - **3.** *(antes de gerundio)* [estar]: **llevar mucho tiempo haciendo algo** to have been doing sthg for a long time. ➟ **llevarse** *vprnl* - **1.** [coger] to take, to steal - **2.** [conseguir] to get; **se ha llevado el premio** she has carried off the prize; **yo me llevo siempre las culpas** I always get the blame - **3.** [recibir - susto, sorpresa etc] to get, to receive; **me llevé un disgusto** I was upset - **4.** [entenderse]: **llevarse bien/mal (con alguien)** to get on well/badly (with sb) - **5.** [estar de moda] to be in (fashion); **este año se lleva el verde** green is in this year - **6.** MAT: **me llevo una** carry the (one) one.

llorar *vi* [con lágrimas] to cry.

lloriquear *vi* to whine, to snivel.

lloro *sm* crying (U), tears *pl*.

llorón, ona *sm, f* crybaby.

lloroso, sa *adj* tearful.

llover *v impers* to rain; **está lloviendo** it's raining.

llovizna *sf* drizzle.

lloviznar *v impers* to drizzle.

lluvia *sf* METEOR rain; **bajo la lluvia** in the rain; **lluvia ácida** acid rain; **lluvia radiactiva** (nuclear) fallout; **lluvia torrencial** torrential rain.

lluvioso, sa adj rainy.

lo, la (mpl los, fpl las) pron pers (complemento directo) [cosa] it (pl them); [persona] him (f her, pl them), [usted] you. ◆ **lo** ◇ pron pers (neutro, predicado) it; **su hermana es muy guapa pero él no lo es** his sister is very good-looking, but he isn't; **es muy bueno aunque no lo parezca** it's very good, even if it doesn't look it. ◇ art det (neutro): **lo antiguo me gusta más que lo moderno** I like old things better than modern things; **lo mejor/peor** the best/worst part; **no te imaginas lo grande que era** you can't imagine how big it was. ◆ **lo de** loc prep: **¿y lo de la fiesta?** what about the party, then?; **siento lo de ayer** I'm sorry about yesterday. ◆ **lo que** loc conj what; **acepté lo que me ofrecieron** I accepted what they offered me.

loa sf - 1. [gen] praise - 2. LITER eulogy.

loable adj praiseworthy.

loar vt to praise.

lobato, lobezno sm wolf cub.

lobby ['loβi] (pl lobbies) sm lobby, pressure group.

lobezno = lobato.

lobo, ba sm, f wolf. ◆ **lobo de mar** sm [marinero] sea dog.

lóbrego, ga adj gloomy, murky.

lóbulo sm lobe.

local ◇ adj local. ◇ sm - 1. [edificio] premises pl - 2. [sede] headquarters pl.

localidad sf - 1. [población] place, town - 2. [asiento] seat - 3. [entrada] ticket; **'no hay localidades'** 'sold out'.

localizar vt - 1. [encontrar] to locate - 2. [circunscribir] to localize.

loción sf lotion.

loco, ca ◇ adj - 1. [gen] mad; **volverse loco por** to be mad about; **loco de atar** O **remate** stark raving mad - 2. [extraordinario - interés, ilusión] tremendous; [- amor, alegría] wild. ◇ sm, f - 1. lit & fig madman (f madwoman), lunatic; **conduce como un loco** he drives like a madman - 2. Chile [molusco] false abalone.

locomoción sf transport; [de tren] locomotion.

locomotor, ra O **triz** adj locomotive. ◆ **locomotora** sf engine, locomotive.

locuaz adj loquacious, talkative.

locución sf phrase.

locura sf - 1. [demencia] madness - 2. [imprudencia] folly; **hacer locuras** to do crazy things; **ser una locura** to be madness.

locutor, ra sm, f [de radio] announcer; [de televisión] presenter.

locutorio sm - 1. TELECOM phone box O booth - 2. RADIO & TV studio.

lodo sm lit & fig mud.

logaritmo sm logarithm.

lógico, ca adj logical; **es lógico que se enfade** it stands to reason that he should get angry. ◆ **lógica** sf [ciencia] logic.

logístico, ca adj logistic. ◆ **logística** sf logistics pl.

logopeda smf speech therapist.

logotipo sm logo.

logrado, da adj [bien hecho] accomplished.

lograr vt [gen] to achieve; [puesto, beca, divorcio] to get, to obtain; [resultado] to obtain, to achieve; [perfección] to attain; [victoria, premio] to win; [deseo, aspiración] to fulfil; **lograr hacer algo** to manage to do sthg; **lograr que alguien haga algo** to manage to get sb to do sthg.

logro sm achievement.

LOGSE (abrev de **Ley de Ordenación General del Sistema Educativo**) sf Spanish Education Act.

loma sf hillock.

lombarda sf red cabbage.

lombriz sf earthworm, worm.

lomo sm - 1. [espalda] back - 2. [carne] loin - 3. [de libro] spine.

lona sf canvas.

loncha sf slice; [de beicon] rasher.

lonche sm Perú & Ven - 1. [merienda] snack eaten during break time - 2. Méx [torta] filled roll.

londinense ◇ adj London (antes de s). ◇ smf Londoner.

Londres n pr London.

longaniza sf type of spicy, cold pork sausage.

longitud sf - 1. [dimensión] length; **tiene medio metro de longitud** it's half a metre long; **longitud de onda** wavelength - 2. ASTRON & GEOGR longitude.

lonja sf - 1. [loncha] slice - 2. [edificio] exchange; **lonja de pescado** fish market.

loro sm - 1. [animal] parrot - 2. loc: **estar al loro** vulg to have one's finger on the pulse.

los ◇ art ⊳ **el**. ◇ pron ⊳ **lo**.

losa sf - 1. [gen] paving stone, flagstone; [de tumba] tombstone; **losa.: losa radiante** R Dom underfloor heating.

loseta sf floor tile.

lote sm - 1. [parte] share - 2. [conjunto] batch, lot - 3. Amér [de tierra] plot (of land).

lotería sf - 1. [gen] lottery; **jugar a la lotería** to play the lottery; **le tocó la lotería** she won the lottery; **lotería primitiva** twice-weekly state-run lottery - 2. [juego de mesa] lotto.

loza sf - 1. [material] earthenware; [porcelana] china - 2. [objetos] crockery.

lozanía sf [de persona] youthful vigour.

lozano, na adj - 1. [planta] lush - 2. [persona] youthfully vigorous.

lubina sf sea bass.

lubricante, lubrificante <> adj lubricating. <> sm lubricant.

lubricar, lubrificar vt to lubricate.

lucero sm bright star.

lucha sf fight; fig struggle; **abandonar la lucha** to give up the struggle; **lucha armada** armed struggle; **lucha libre** all-in wrestling.

luchar vi to fight; fig to struggle; **luchar contra/por** to fight against/for.

lucidez sf lucidity, clarity.

lúcido, da adj lucid.

luciérnaga sf glow-worm.

lucimiento sm [de ceremonia etc] sparkle; [de actriz etc] brilliant performance.

lucir <> vi - 1. [gen] to shine - 2. [llevar puesto] to wear - 3. Amér [parecer] to look. <> vt [gen] to show off; [ropa] to sport. <> **lucirse** vprnl - 1. [destacar]: **lucirse (en)** to shine (at) - 2. fam fig & irón [quedar mal] to mess things up.

lucrativo, va adj lucrative; **no lucrativo** non profit-making.

lucro sm profit, gain.

lucubrar vt to rack one's brains over.

lúdico, ca adj [del juego] game (antes de s); [ocioso] of enjoyment, of pleasure.

ludopatía sf pathological addiction to gambling.

luego <> adv - 1. [justo después] then, next; **primero aquí y luego allí** first here and then there - 2. [más tarde] later; **¡hasta luego!** see you!, bye!; **hazlo luego** do it later - 3. Chile, Méx & Ven [pronto] soon. <> conj - 1. [así que] so, therefore - 2.: **luego luego** Méx fam [inmediatamente] immediately, straight away; [de vez en cuando] from time to time.

lugar sm - 1. [gen] place; [localidad] place, town; [del crimen, accidente etc] scene; [para acampar, merendar etc] spot; **en primer lugar** in the first place, firstly; **en último lugar** lastly, last; **fuera de lugar** out of place; **no hay lugar a duda** there's no room for doubt; **ponte en mi lugar** put yourself in my place; **sin lugar a dudas** without a doubt, undoubtedly; **yo en tu lugar** if I were you; **dejar a alguien en buen/mal lugar** to make sb look good/bad; **poner las cosas en su lugar** to set things straight; **tener lugar** to take place; **lugar de nacimiento** birthplace; **lugar de trabajo** workplace - 2. [motivo] cause, reason; **dar lugar a** to bring about, to cause - 3. [puesto] position. <> **en lugar de** loc prep instead of. <> **lugar común** sm platitude.

lugareño, ña sm, f villager.

lúgubre adj gloomy, mournful.

lujo sm luxury; fig profusion; **permitirse el lujo de algo/de hacer algo** to be able to afford sthg/to do sthg.

lujoso, sa adj luxurious.

lujuria sf lust.

lumbago sm lumbago.

lumbre sf [fuego] fire; **dar lumbre a alguien** to give sb a light.

lumbrera sf fam leading light.

luminoso, sa adj [gen] bright; [fuente, energía] light (antes de s).

luna sf - 1. [astro] moon - 2. [cristal] window (pane) - 3. loc: **estar de mala luna** to be in a bad mood; **estar en la luna** to be miles away. <> **luna de miel** sf honeymoon.

lunar <> adj lunar. <> sm - 1. [en la piel] mole, beauty spot - 2. [en telas] spot; **a lunares** spotted.

lunático, ca sm, f lunatic.

lunes sm inv Monday; ver también **sábado**.

luneta sf [de coche] windscreen; **luneta térmica** demister.

lupa sf magnifying glass.

lustrabotas sm inv Andes & R Dom shoeshine, bootblack UK.

lustrador sm Andes & R Plata shoeshine, bootblack UK.

lustrar vt to polish.

lustre sm [brillo] shine.

lustro sm five-year period.

lustroso, sa adj shiny.

luto sm mourning; **de luto** in mourning.

luxación sf dislocation.

Luxemburgo n pr Luxembourg.

luxemburgués, esa <> adj Luxembourg (antes de s). <> sm, f Luxembourger.

luz sf [gen] light; [electricidad] electricity; [destello] flash (of light); **apagar la luz** to switch off the light; **a plena luz del día** in broad daylight; **cortar la luz** to cut off the electricity supply; **dar O encender la luz** to switch on the light; **pagar (el recibo de) la luz** to pay the electricity (bill); **se ha ido la luz** the lights have gone out; **luz eléctrica** electric light; **luz solar** sunlight; **a la luz de** [una vela, la luna etc] by the light of; [los acontecimientos etc] in the light of; **arrojar luz sobre** to shed light on; **dar a luz (un niño)** to give birth (to a child); **sacar algo a la luz** [secreto] to bring sthg to light; [obra] to bring sthg out, to publish sthg; **salir a la luz** [descubrirse] to come to light; [publicarse] to come out; **ver la luz** to see the light. <> **luces** sfpl AUTO lights; **poner las luces de carretera O largas** to put (one's headlights) on full beam; **luces de tráfico O de señalización** traffic lights.

lycra® sf Lycra®.

m¹, M *sf* [letra] m, M.

m² (*abrev de* **metro**) m.

m. (*abrev de* **muerto**) d.

macabro, bra *adj* macabre.

macana *sf* C Sur, Perú & Ven *fam* [disparate] stupid thing; [fastidio] pain, drag; [pena] shame.

macanear *vi* C Sur *fam* [decir tonterías] to talk nonsense; [hacer tonterías] to be stupid.

macarra *sm fam* [de prostitutas] pimp; [rufián] thug.

macarrón *sm* [tubo] sheath (*of cable*).
➡ **macarrones** *smpl* [pasta] macaroni (U).

macedonia *sf* salad; **macedonia de frutas** fruit salad.

macerar *vt* CULIN to soak, to macerate.

maceta *sf* [tiesto] flowerpot.

macetero *sm* flowerpot holder.

machaca *smf* [trabajador] dogsbody.

machacar ◇ *vt* - 1. [triturar] to crush - 2. *fig* [insistir] to keep going on about. ◇ *vi fig:* **machacar (sobre)** to go on (about).

machete *sm* machete.

machista *adj* & *smf* male chauvinist.

macho ◇ *adj* - 1. BIOL male - 2. *fig* [hombre] macho. ◇ *sm* - 1. BIOL male - 2. *fig* [hombre] he-man - 3. TECNOL male part; [de enchufe] pin. ◇ *interj fam:* **¡oye, macho!** oy, mate!

macizo, za *adj* solid; **estar macizo** *fam* [hombre] to be hunky; [mujer] to be gorgeous.
➡ **macizo** *sm* - 1. GEOGR massif - 2. BOT: **macizo de flores** flowerbed.

macro *sf* INFORM macro.

macrobiótico, ca *adj* macrobiotic.

mácula *sf* spot; *fig* blemish.

macuto *sm* backpack.

madeja *sf* hank, skein; **enredar la madeja** to complicate matters.

madera *sf* - 1. [gen] wood; CONSTR timber; [tabla] piece of wood; **de madera** wooden; **madera contrachapada** plywood; **tocar madera** to touch wood UK, to knock on wood US - 2. [disposición]: **tener madera de algo** to have the makings of sthg.

madero *sm* [tabla] log.

madrastra *sf* stepmother.

madre *sf* - 1. [gen] mother; **es madre de tres niños** she's a mother of three; **madre adoptiva/de alquiler** foster/surrogate mother; **madre biológica** biological mother; **madre de familia** mother; **madre política** mother-in-law; **madre soltera** single mother; **madre superiora** mother superior - 2. [poso] dregs *pl* ➡ **madre mía** *interj:* **¡madre mía!** Jesus!, Christ!

Madrid *n pr* Madrid.

madriguera *sf lit & fig* den; [de conejo] burrow.

madrileño, ña *sm, f* native/inhabitant of Madrid.

madrina *sf* [gen] patroness; [de boda] bridesmaid; [de bautizo] godmother.

madroño *sm* - 1. [árbol] strawberry tree - 2. [fruto] strawberry-tree berry.

madrugada *sf* - 1. [amanecer] dawn; **de madrugada** at daybreak - 2. [noche] early morning; **las tres de la madrugada** three in the morning.

madrugador, ra *adj* early-rising.

madrugar *vi* to get up early; *fig* to be quick off the mark; **no por mucho madrugar amanece más temprano** *prov* time must take its course.

madurar ◇ *vt* - 1. [gen] to mature; [fruta, mies] to ripen - 2. [idea, proyecto etc] to think through. ◇ *vi* [gen] to mature; [fruta] to ripen.

madurez *sf* - 1. [cualidad - gen] maturity; [- de fruta, mies] ripeness - 2. [edad adulta] adulthood.

maduro, ra *adj* [gen] mature; [fruta, mies] ripe; **de edad madura** middle-aged.

maestra ▷ **maestro**.

maestría *sf* - 1. [habilidad] mastery, skill - 2. *Amér* [título] master's degree.

maestro, tra ◇ *adj* - 1. [perfecto] masterly - 2. [principal] main; [llave] master (*antes de s*). ◇ *sm, f* - 1. [profesor] teacher - 2. [sabio] master - 3. MÚS maestro - 4. *Méx* [de universidad] lecturer UK, professor US - 5. [director]: **maestro de ceremonias** master of ceremonies; **maestro de cocina** chef; **maestro de obras** foreman; **maestro de orquesta** conductor.

mafia *sf* mafia.

mafioso, sa *sm, f* mafioso.

magdalena *sf* fairy cake.

magia *sf* magic; **magia blanca/negra** white/black magic.

mágico, ca *adj* - 1. [con magia] magic - 2. [atractivo] magical.

magisterio *sm* - 1. [enseñanza] teaching - 2. [profesión] teaching profession.

magistrado, da *sm, f* [juez] judge.

magistral *adj* - 1. [de maestro] magisterial - 2. [genial] masterly.

magistratura *sf* - 1. [jueces] magistrature - 2. [tribunal] tribunal; **magistratura de trabajo** industrial tribunal.

magnánimo, ma *adj* magnanimous.

magnate *sm* magnate; **magnate del petró-leo/de la prensa** oil/press baron.

magnesia *sf* magnesia.

magnesio *sm* magnesium.

magnético, ca *adj lit & fig* magnetic.

magnetizar *vt* to magnetize; *fig* to mesmer-ize.

magnetófono *sm* tape recorder.

magnicidio *sm* assassination *(of somebody important)*.

magnificencia *sf* magnificence.

magnífico, ca *adj* wonderful, magnificent.

magnitud *sf* magnitude.

magnolia *sf* magnolia.

mago, ga *sm, f* - **1.** [prestidigitador] magician - **2.** [en cuentos etc] wizard.

magro, gra *adj* - **1.** [sin grasa] lean - **2.** [pobre] poor. ➡ **magro** *sm* lean meat.

magulladura *sf* bruise.

magullar *vt* to bruise.

mahometano, na *adj & sm, f* Muslim.

mahonesa = mayonesa.

maicena® *sf* cornflour *UK*, cornstarch *US*.

maíz *sm* maize *UK*, corn *US*; **maíz dulce** sweetcorn.

majadero, ra *sm, f* idiot.

majareta *fam* ◇ *adj* nutty. ◇ *smf* nut-case.

majestad *sf* majesty. ➡ **Su Majestad** *sf* His/Her Majesty.

majestuoso, sa *adj* majestic.

majo, ja *adj* - **1.** [simpático] nice - **2.** [bonito] pretty.

mal ◇ *adj* ▷ **malo**. ◇ *sm* - **1.** [perver-sión]: **el mal** evil - **2.** [daño] harm, damage - **3.** [enfermedad] illness; **mal de montaña** altitude *O* mountain sickness; **mal de ojo** evil eye - **4.** [inconveniente] bad thing; **un mal necesa-rio** a necessary evil. ◇ *adv* - **1.** [incorrectamen-te] wrong; **esto está mal hecho** this has been done wrong; **has escrito mal esta palabra** you've spelt that word wrong - **2.** [inadecua-damente] badly; **la fiesta salió mal** the party went off badly; **oigo/veo mal** I can't hear/see very well; **encontrarse mal** [enfermo] to feel ill; [incómodo] to feel uncomfortable; **oler mal** [te-ner mal olor] to smell bad; *fam* [tener mal cariz] to smell fishy; **sentar mal a alguien** [ropa] not to suit sb; [comida] to disagree with sb; [co-mentario, actitud] to upset sb; **tomar algo a mal** to take sthg the wrong way - **3.** [difícilmente] hardly; **mal puede saberlo si no se lo cuentas** he's hardly going to know it if you don't tell him - **4.** *loc:* **estar a mal con alguien** to have fallen out with sb; **ir de mal en peor** to go from bad to worse; **no estaría mal que...** it

would be nice if... ➡ **mal que** *loc conj* al-though, even though. ➡ **mal que bien** *loc adv* somehow or other.

malabarismo *sm lit & fig* juggling *(U)*.

malabarista *smf* juggler.

malacostumbrado, da *adj* spoiled.

malaria *sf* malaria.

Malasia *n pr* Malaysia.

malcriado, da *adj* spoiled.

maldad *sf* - **1.** [cualidad] evil - **2.** [acción] evil thing.

maldecir ◇ *vt* to curse. ◇ *vi* to curse.

maldición *sf* curse.

maldito, ta *adj* - **1.** [embrujado] cursed - **2.** *fam* [para enfatizar] damned; **¡maldita sea!** damn it!

maleable *adj lit & fig* malleable.

maleante *smf* crook.

malecón *sm* [atracadero] jetty.

maleducado, da *adj* rude.

maleficio *sm* curse.

malentendido *sm* misunderstanding.

malestar *sm* - **1.** [dolor] upset, discomfort; **siento un malestar en el estómago** I've got an upset stomach; **sentir malestar general** to feel unwell - **2.** [inquietud] uneasiness, unrest.

maleta *sf* suitcase; **hacer** *O* **preparar la male-ta** to pack (one's bags).

maletero *sm* boot *UK*, trunk *US*.

maletín *sm* briefcase.

malévolo, la *adj* malevolent, wicked.

maleza *sf* [arbustos] undergrowth; [malas hier-bas] weeds *pl*.

malformación *sf* malformation; **malforma-ción congénita** congenital malformation.

malgastar *vt* [dinero, tiempo] to waste; [salud] to ruin.

malhablado, da *adj* foul-mouthed.

malhechor, ra *adj & sm, f* criminal.

malhumorado, da *adj* bad-tempered; [en-fadado] in a bad mood.

malicia *sf* [maldad] wickedness, evil; [mala in-tención] malice.

malicioso, sa *adj* [malo] wicked, evil; [malin-tencionado] malicious.

maligno, na *adj* malignant.

malla *sf* - **1.** [tejido] mesh; **malla de alambre** wire mesh - **2.** [red] net - **3.** *R Dom* [traje de ba-ño] swimsuit. ➡ **mallas** *sfpl* - **1.** [de gimnasia] leotard *sing*; [de ballet] tights - **2.** [de portería] net *sing*.

Mallorca *n pr* Majorca.

malo, la *(peor es el comparativo y el superla-tivo de* **malo**; *antes de sm sing:* **mal**) *adj* - **1.** [gen] bad; [calidad] poor, bad; **lo malo fue**

que... the problem was (that)...; **más vale malo conocido que bueno por conocer** prov better the devil you know (than the devil you don't) - **2.** [malicioso] wicked - **3.** [enfermo] ill, sick; **estar/ponerse malo** to be/fall ill - **4.** [travieso] naughty. ◆ **malo, la** sm, f [de película etc] villain, baddie. ◆ **malas** sfpl: **estar de malas** to be in a bad mood; **por las malas** by force.

malograr vt - **1.** to waste - **2.** Andes [estropear] to make a mess of, to ruin. ◆ **malograrse** vprnl - **1.** [fracasar] to fail - **2.** [morir] to die before one's time - **3.** Andes [estropearse - máquina] to break down; [- alimento] to go off, to spoil.

malparado, da adj: **salir malparado de algo** to come out of sthg badly.

malpensado, da adj   malicious, evilminded.

malsano, na adj unhealthy.

malsonante adj rude.

malta sm malt.

malteada sf Amér [batido] milkshake.

maltés, esa adj & sm, f Maltese.

maltratar vt - **1.** [pegar, insultar] to ill-treat - **2.** [estropear] to damage.

maltrecho, cha adj battered; **dejar maltrecho a alguien** to leave sb in a bad way.

malva ◇ sf BOT mallow; **criar malvas** fam fig to push up daisies. ◇ adj inv mauve. ◇ sm [color] mauve.

malvado, da adj evil, wicked.

malversación sf: **malversación (de fondos)** embezzlement (of funds).

malversar vt to embezzle.

Malvinas sfpl: **las (islas) Malvinas** the Falkland Islands, the Falklands.

malvivir vi to scrape together an existence.

mama sf - **1.** [órgano - de mujer] breast; ZOOL udder - **2.** fam [madre] mum.

mamá sf - **1.** fam mum, mummy - **2.**: **mamá grande** Col & Méx fam grandma.

mamadera sf C Sur & Perú [biberón] (baby's) bottle.

mamar ◇ vt - **1.** [suj: bebé] to suckle - **2.** [aprender]: **lo mamó desde pequeño** he was immersed in it as a child. ◇ vi to suckle.

mamarracho sm [fantoche] mess.

mambo sm mambo.

mamífero, ra adj mammal. ◆ **mamífero** sm mammal.

mamografía sf - **1.** MED [técnica] breast scanning, mammography - **2.** MED [resultado] breast scan, mammogram.

mamotreto sm - **1.** despec [libro] hefty tome - **2.** [objeto grande] monstrosity.

mampara sf screen.

manada sf [ZOOL - gen] herd; [- de lobos] pack; [- de ovejas] flock; [- de leones] pride.

manager (pl **managers**) sm manager.

Managua n pr Managua.

manantial sm spring; fig source.

manar vi lit & fig: **manar (de)** to flow (from).

manazas adj inv clumsy.

mancha sf - **1.** [gen] stain, spot; [de tinta] blot; [de color] spot, mark; **extenderse como una mancha de aceite** to spread like wildfire - **2.** ASTRON spot - **3.** [deshonra] blemish; **sin mancha** unblemished.

manchar vt - **1.** [ensuciar]: **manchar algo (de O con)** [gen] to make sthg dirty (with); [con manchas] to stain sthg (with); [emborronar] to smudge sthg (with) - **2.** [deshonrar] to tarnish.

manchego, ga adj of/relating to La Mancha. ◆ **manchego** ▷ **queso**.

manco, ca adj [sin una mano] one-handed; [sin manos] handless; [sin un brazo] one-armed; [sin brazos] armless; **no ser manco para O en** to be a dab hand at.

mancomunidad sf association.

mancorna, mancuerna sf Andes, Amér C, Méx & Ven cufflink.

mandado, da sm, f [subordinado] underling. ◆ **mandado** sm [recado] errand.

mandamás (pl **mandamases**) smf bigwig.

mandamiento sm - **1.** [orden - militar] order, command; [- judicial] writ - **2.** RELIG commandment; **los diez mandamientos** the Ten Commandments.

mandar ◇ vt - **1.** [dar órdenes a] to order; **mandar a alguien hacer algo** to order sb to do sthg; **mandar hacer algo** to have sthg done - **2.** [enviar] to send - **3.** [dirigir, gobernar] to lead, to be in charge of; [país] to rule. ◇ vi - **1.** [gen] to be in charge; [jefe de estado] to rule; **aquí mando yo** I'm in charge here; **mandar en algo** to be in charge of sthg - **2.** despec [dar órdenes] to order people around - **3.** loc: **¿mande?** fam eh?, you what?

mandarina sf mandarin.

mandatario, ria sm, f representative, agent; **primer mandatario** [jefe de estado] head of state.

mandato sm - **1.** [gen] order, command - **2.** [poderes de representación, disposición] mandate; **mandato judicial** warrant - **3.** POLÍT term of office; [reinado] period of rule.

mandíbula sf jaw.

mandil sm [delantal] apron.

mando sm - **1.** [poder] command, authority; **al mando de** in charge of; **entregar el mando** to hand over command - **2.** [periodo en poder] term of office - **3.** (gen pl) [autoridades] leadership (U); MIL command (U); **alto mando** MIL high command; **mandos intermedios** middle

management *sing* - **4.** [dispositivo] control; **mando automático/a distancia** automatic/remote control.

mandolina *sf* mandolin.

mandón, ona ◇ *adj* bossy. ◇ *sm, f* bossy-boots.

manecilla *sf* [del reloj] hand.

manejable *adj* [gen] manageable; [herramienta] easy to use.

manejar ◇ *vt* - **1.** [conocimientos, datos] to use, to marshal - **2.** [máquina, mandos] to operate; [caballo, bicicleta] to handle; [arma] to wield - **3.** [negocio etc] to manage, to run; [gente] to handle - **4.** *Amér* [vehículo] to drive. ◇ *vi Amér* [conducir] to drive. ➥ **manejarse** *vprnl* - **1.** [moverse] to move O get about - **2.** [desenvolverse] to manage.

manejo *sm* - **1.** [de máquina, mandos] operation; [de armas, herramientas] use; **de fácil manejo** user-friendly - **2.** [de conocimientos, datos] marshalling; [de idiomas] command - **3.** [de caballo, bicicleta] handling - **4.** [de negocio etc] management, running - **5.** *(gen pl) fig* [intriga] intrigue.

manera *sf* way, manner; **lo haremos a mi manera** we'll do it my way; **a mi manera de ver** the way I see it; **de cualquier manera** [sin cuidado] any old how; [de todos modos] anyway, in any case; **de esta manera** in this way; **de la misma manera** similarly, in the same way; **de ninguna manera, en manera alguna** [refuerza negación] by no means, under no circumstances; [respuesta exclamativa] no way!, certainly not!; **de todas maneras** anyway; **en cierta manera** in a way; **manera de ser** way of being, nature; **de manera que** [para] so (that); **no hay manera** there is no way, it's impossible; **¡qué manera de...!** what a way to...! ➥ **maneras** *sfpl* [modales] manners; **buenas/malas maneras** good/bad manners.

manga *sf* - **1.** [de prenda] sleeve; **en mangas de camisa** in shirtsleeves; **sin mangas** sleeveless; **manga raglán** O **ranglán** raglan sleeve; **andar manga por hombro** to be a mess; **ser de manga ancha, tener manga ancha** to be over-indulgent - **2.** [manguera] hosepipe - **3.** [de pastelería] forcing O piping bag - **4.** DEP stage, round.

mangante *fam smf* thief.

mango *sm* - **1.** [asa] handle - **2.** [árbol] mango tree; [fruta] mango.

mangonear *vi fam* - **1.** [entrometerse] to meddle - **2.** [mandar] to be bossy - **3.** [manipular] to fiddle about.

manguera *sf* hosepipe; [de bombero] fire hose.

maní, manises *sm Andes, Caribe & R Plata* peanut.

manía *sf* - **1.** [idea fija] obsession - **2.** [peculiaridad] idiosyncracy - **3.** [mala costumbre] bad habit - **4.** [afición exagerada] mania, craze - **5.** *fam* [ojeriza] dislike - **6.** PSICOL mania.

maniaco, ca, maníaco, ca ◇ *adj* manic. ◇ *sm, f* maniac.

maniatar *vt* to tie the hands of.

maniático, ca ◇ *adj* fussy. ◇ *sm, f* fussy person; **es un maniático del fútbol** he's football-crazy.

manicomio *sm* mental O psychiatric hospital *UK*, insane asylum *US*.

manicuro, ra *sm, f* [persona] manicurist. ➥ **manicura** *sf* [técnica] manicure.

manido, da *adj* [tema etc] hackneyed.

manifestación *sf* - **1.** [de alegría, dolor etc] show, display; [de opinión] declaration, expression; [indicio] sign - **2.** [por la calle] demonstration; **hacer una manifestación** to hold a demonstration.

manifestar *vt* - **1.** [alegría, dolor etc] to show - **2.** [opinión etc] to express. ➥ **manifestarse** *vprnl* - **1.** [por la calle] to demonstrate - **2.** [hacerse evidente] to become clear O apparent.

manifiesto, ta *adj* clear, evident; **poner de manifiesto algo** [revelar] to reveal sthg; [hacer patente] to make sthg clear. ➥ **manifiesto** *sm* manifesto.

manillar *sm* handlebars *pl*.

maniobra *sf* - **1.** [gen] manoeuvre; **estar de maniobras** MIL to be on manoeuvres - **2.** [treta] trick.

maniobrar *vi* to manoeuvre.

manipulación *sf* - **1.** [gen] handling - **2.** [engaño] manipulation.

manipular *vt* - **1.** [manejar] to handle - **2.** [mangonear - información, resultados] to manipulate; [- negocios, asuntos] to interfere in.

maniquí *(pl maniquíes O maniquís)* ◇ *sm* dummy. ◇ *sm, f* [modelo] model.

manirroto, ta ◇ *adj* extravagant. ◇ *sm, f* spendthrift.

manitas *smf inv* handy person.

manito *sm Méx fam* pal, mate *UK*, buddy *US*.

manivela *sf* crank.

manjar *sm* delicious food *(U)*.

mano ◇ *sf* - **1.** [gen] hand; **a mano armada** armed; **dar** O **estrechar la mano a alguien** to shake hands with sb; **darse** O **estrecharse la mano** to shake hands; **echar/tender una mano** to give/offer a hand; **¡manos arriba!, ¡arriba las manos!** hands up!; **mano de obra** [capacidad de trabajo] labour; [trabajadores] workforce - **2.** [ZOOL - gen] forefoot; [- de perro, gato] (front) paw; [- de cerdo] (front) trotter - **3.** [lado] to **mano derecha/izquierda** on the right/left - **4.:** **calle de una sola mano** *R Dom* one-way street - **5.** [de pintura etc] coat - **6.** [influencia] influence - **7.** [partida de naipes] game - **8.** [serie, tanda] series - **9.** *loc:* **bajo mano** secretly; **caer en manos de alguien** to fall into sb's hands; **con las manos cruzadas**, **mano sobre mano** sitting around doing nothing; **coger a alguien con las manos en la masa** to catch sb red-handed O in the act; **de primera mano** [coche etc] brand new; [noticias etc] first-hand; **de segunda mano** second-hand; **mano a mano** tête-à-tête; **¡manos a la obra!** let's get down to it!; **tener buena mano para algo** to have a knack for sthg. ⬦ *sm Andes, Amér C, Caribe & Méx* pal, mate *UK*, buddy *US*.

manojo *sm* bunch.

manoletina *sf* [zapato] *type of open, low-heeled shoe, often with a bow.*

manómetro *sm* pressure gauge.

manopla *sf* mitten.

manosear *vt* - **1.** [gen] to handle roughly; [papel, tela] to rumple - **2.** [persona] to fondle.

manotazo *sm* slap.

mansalva ⬥ **a mansalva** *loc adv* [en abundancia] in abundance.

mansedumbre *sf* [gen] calmness, gentleness; [de animal] tameness.

mansión *sf* mansion.

manso, sa *adj* - **1.** [apacible] calm, gentle - **2.** [domesticado] tame - **3.** *Chile* [extraordinario] tremendous.

manta *sf* [para abrigarse] blanket; **manta eléctrica** electric blanket; **manta de viaje** travelling rug; **liarse la manta a la cabeza** to take the plunge.

manteca *sf* fat; [mantequilla] butter; **manteca de cacao** cocoa butter; **manteca de cerdo** lard.

mantecado *sm* - **1.** [pastel] shortcake - **2.** [helado] *ice-cream made of milk, eggs and sugar.*

mantel *sm* tablecloth.

mantener *vt* - **1.** [sustentar, aguantar] to support - **2.** [conservar] to keep; [en buen estado] to maintain, to service - **3.** [tener - relaciones, conversación] to have - **4.** [defender - opinión] to stick to, to maintain; [- candidatura] to refuse to withdraw. ⬥ **mantenerse** *vprnl* - **1.** [sustentarse] to subsist, to support o.s. - **2.** [permanecer, continuar] to remain; [edificio] to remain standing; **mantenerse aparte** [en discusión] to stay out of it.

mantenimiento *sm* - **1.** [sustento] sustenance - **2.** [conservación] upkeep, maintenance.

mantequilla *sf* butter.

mantilla *sf* - **1.** [de mujer] mantilla - **2.** [de bebé] shawl.

manto *sm* [gen] cloak.

mantón *sm* shawl.

manual ⬦ *adj* [con las manos] manual. ⬦ *sm* manual.

manubrio *sm* - **1.** crank - **2.** *Amér* [manillar] handlebars *pl*.

manufacturar *vt* to manufacture.

manuscrito, ta *adj* handwritten. ⬥ **manuscrito** *sm* manuscript.

manutención *sf* - **1.** [sustento] support, maintenance - **2.** [alimento] food.

manzana *sf* - **1.** [fruta] apple - **2.** [grupo de casas] block (of houses).

manzanilla *sf* - **1.** [planta] camomile - **2.** [infusión] camomile tea.

manzano *sm* apple tree.

maña *sf* - **1.** [destreza] skill; **tener maña para** to have a knack for - **2.** [astucia] wits *pl*, guile *(U)*.

mañana ⬦ *sf* morning; **a la mañana siguiente** the next morning; **a las dos de la mañana** at two in the morning; **por la mañana** in the morning. ⬦ *sm*: **el mañana** tomorrow, the future. ⬦ *adv* tomorrow; **a partir de mañana** starting tomorrow, as of tomorrow; **¡hasta mañana!** see you tomorrow!; **mañana por la mañana** tomorrow morning; **pasado mañana** the day after tomorrow.

mañanitas *sfpl Méx* birthday song *sing*.

mañoso, sa *adj* skilful.

mapa *sm* map; **mapa de carreteras** road map.

mapamundi *sm* world map.

maqueta *sf* - **1.** [reproducción a escala] (scale) model - **2.** [de libro] dummy.

maquila *sf Amér* [de máquinas] assembly; [de ropas] making-up.

maquiladora *sf Amér* assembly plant.

maquillaje *sm* - **1.** [producto] make-up - **2.** [acción] making-up.

maquillar *vt* [pintar] to make up. ⬥ **maquillarse** *vprnl* to make o.s. up.

máquina *sf* - **1.** [gen] machine; **a toda máquina** at full pelt; **coser a máquina** to machine-sew; **escribir a máquina** to type; **hecho a máquina** machine-made; **máquina de afeitar** electric razor; **máquina de coser** sewing machine; **máquina de escribir** typewriter; **máquina fotográfica** camera; **máquina tragaperras** O **traganíqueles** *Amér* slot machine, fruit machine *UK* - **2.** [locomotora] engine; **máquina de vapor** steam engine - **3.** [mecanismo] mechanism - **4.** *Cuba* [vehículo] car - **5.** [de estado, partido etc] machinery *(U)*.

maquinación *sf* machination.

maquinal *adj* mechanical.

maquinar *vt* to machinate, to plot.

maquinaria *sf* - **1.** [gen] machinery - **2.** [de reloj etc] mechanism.

maquinilla *sf*: **maquinilla de afeitar** razor; **maquinilla eléctrica** electric razor.

maquinista smf [de tren] engine driver UK, engineer US; [de barco] engineer.

mar sm o sf lit & fig sea; **alta mar** high seas pl; **mar de fondo** lit & fig groundswell; **mar gruesa** heavy sea; **el mar del Norte** the North Sea; **llover a mares** to rain buckets.

marabunta sf [muchedumbre] crowd.

maraca sf maraca.

maracujá sf Amér passion fruit.

maraña sf - 1. [maleza] thicket - 2. fig [enredo] tangle.

maratón sm o sf lit & fig marathon.

maravilla sf - 1. [gen] marvel, wonder; **es una maravilla** it's wonderful; **hacer maravillas** to do O work wonders; **a las mil maravillas, de maravilla** wonderfully; **venir de maravilla** to be just the thing O ticket - 2. BOT marigold.

maravillar vt to amaze. ◆ **maravillarse** vprnl: **maravillarse (con)** to be amazed (by).

maravilloso, sa adj marvellous, wonderful.

marca sf - 1. [señal] mark; [de rueda, animal] track; [en ganado] brand; [en papel] watermark; **marca de nacimiento** birthmark - 2. [COM - de tabaco, café etc] brand; [- de coche, ordenador etc] make; **de marca** designer (antes de s); **marca de fábrica** trademark; **marca registrada** registered trademark - 3. [etiqueta] label - 4. [DEP - gen] performance; [- en carreras] time; [- plusmarca] record.

marcado, da adj [gen] marked. ◆ **marcado** sm - 1. [señalado] marking - 2. [peinado] set.

marcador, ra adj marking. ◆ **marcador** sm - 1. [tablero] scoreboard - 2. [DEP - defensor] marker; [- goleador] scorer - 3. Amér [rotulador] felt-tip pen; Méx [fluorescente] highlighter pen.

marcapasos sm inv pacemaker.

marcar ◇ vt - 1. [gen] to mark - 2. [poner precio a] to price - 3. [indicar] to indicate - 4. [resaltar] to emphasise - 5. [número de teléfono] to dial - 6. [suj: termómetro, contador etc] to read; [suj: reloj] to say - 7. [DEP - tanto] to score; [- a un jugador] to mark - 8. [cabello] to set. ◇ vi - 1. [dejar secuelas] to leave a mark - 2. DEP [anotar un tanto] to score.

marcha sf - 1. [partida] departure - 2. [ritmo] speed; **en marcha** [motor] running; [plan] underway; **poner en marcha** [gen] to start; [dispositivo, alarma] to activate; **ponerse en marcha** [persona] to start off; [máquina] to start; **hacer algo sobre la marcha** to do sthg as one goes along - 3. AUTO gear; **marcha atrás** reverse - 4. MIL & POLÍT march - 5. MÚS march - 6. [transcurso] course; [progreso] progress - 7. DEP walk - 8. fam [animación] liveliness, life; **hay mucha marcha** there's a great atmosphere.

marchar vi - 1. [andar] to walk - 2. [partir] to leave, to go - 3. [funcionar] to work - 4. [desarrollarse] to progress; **el negocio marcha** business is going well. ◆ **marcharse** vprnl to leave, to go.

marchitar vt lit & fig to wither. ◆ **marchitarse** vprnl - 1. [planta] to fade, to wither - 2. fig [persona] to languish.

marchito, ta adj [planta] faded.

marcial adj martial.

marco sm - 1. [cerco] frame - 2. fig [ambiente, paisaje] setting - 3. [ámbito] framework - 4. [moneda] mark - 5. [portería] goalmouth.

marea sf [del mar] tide; **marea alta/baja** high/low tide; **marea negra** oil slick.

marear vt - 1. [provocar náuseas a] to make sick; [en coche, avión etc] to make travelsick; [en barco] to make seasick - 2. [aturdir] to make dizzy - 3. fam [fastidiar] to annoy. ◆ **marearse** vprnl - 1. [tener náuseas] to feel sick; [en coche, avión etc] to feel travelsick; [en barco] to get seasick - 2. [estar aturdido] to get dizzy - 3. [emborracharse] to get drunk.

marejada sf [mar rizada] heavy sea.

maremoto sm tidal wave.

mareo sm - 1. [náuseas] sickness; [en coche, avión etc] travelsickness; [en barco] seasickness - 2. [aturdimiento] dizziness - 3. fam fig [fastidio] drag, pain.

marfil sm ivory.

margarina sf margarine.

margarita sf - 1. BOT daisy; **echar margaritas a los cerdos** to cast pearls before swine - 2. IMPR daisy wheel.

margen sm o sf - 1. (gen f) [de río] bank; (gen m) [de camino] side - 2. (gen m) [de página] margin - 3. (gen m) COM margin - 4. (gen m) [límites] leeway; **dejar al margen** to exclude; **estar al margen de** to have nothing to do with; **mantenerse al margen de** to keep out of; **margen de error** margin of error - 5. (gen m) [ocasión]: **dar margen a alguien para hacer algo** to give sb the chance to do sthg.

marginación sf exclusion.

marginado, da ◇ adj excluded. ◇ sm, f outcast.

marica sm mfam despec queer, poof.

Maricastaña ▷ **tiempo**.

maricón sm mfam despec queer, poof.

marido sm husband.

marihuana sf marijuana.

marimacho sm fam mannish woman; despec butch woman.

marina ▷ **marino**.

marinero, ra adj [gen] sea (antes de s); [buque] seaworthy; [pueblo] seafaring. ◆ **marinero** sm sailor.

marino, na adj sea (antes de s), marine. → **marino** sm sailor. → **marina** sf MIL: marino (de guerra) navy.

marioneta sf [muñeco] marionette, puppet. → **marionetas** sfpl [teatro] puppet show sing.

mariposa sf - 1. [insecto] butterfly - 2. [en natación] butterfly.

mariquita sf [insecto] ladybird UK, ladybug US.

marisco sm seafood (U), shellfish (U).

marisma sf salt marsh.

marisquería sf seafood restaurant.

marítimo, ma adj [del mar] maritime; [cercano al mar] seaside (antes de s).

marketing ['marketin] sm marketing; **marketing direct** direct marketing.

mármol sm marble.

marmota sf marmot.

mar Muerto sm: el mar Muerto the Dead Sea.

mar Negro sm: el mar Negro the Black Sea.

marqués, esa sm marquis (f marchioness).

marquesina sf glass canopy; [parada de autobús] bus-shelter.

marrano, na sm, f - 1. [animal] pig - 2. fam fig [sucio] (filthy) pig.

mar Rojo sm: el mar Rojo the Red Sea.

marrón adj & sm brown.

marroquí (pl **marroquíes** O **marroquís**) adj & sm, f Moroccan.

Marruecos n pr Morocco.

Marte sm Mars.

martes sm inv Tuesday; **martes de Carnaval** Shrove Tuesday; **martes y trece** ≃ Friday 13th; ver también **sábado**.

martillear, martillar vt to hammer.

martillo sm - 1. hammer - 2. Col [subasta] auction.

mártir smf lit & fig martyr.

martirio sm - 1. RELIG martyrdom - 2. fig [sufrimiento] trial, torment; **ser un martirio chino** to be torture.

martirizar vt - 1. [torturar] to martyr - 2. fig [hacer sufrir] to torment.

marxismo sm Marxism.

marxista adj & smf Marxist.

marzo sm March; ver también **septiembre**.

mas conj but.

más ◇ adv - 1. (compar) more; **Pepe es más alto/ambicioso** Pepe is taller/more ambitious; **tener más hambre** to be hungrier O more hungry; **más de/que** more than; **más... que...** more... than...; **Juan es más alto que tú** Juan is taller than you; **de más** [de sobra] left over; **hay diez euros de más** there are ten euros left over; **eso está de más** that's not necessary - 2. (superl): **el/la/lo más** the most; **el más listo/ambicioso** the cleverest/most ambitious - 3. (en frases negativas) any more; **no necesito más (trabajo)** I don't need any more (work) - 4. (con pronombres interrogativos e indefinidos) else; **¿qué/quién más?** what/who else?; **nadie más vino** nobody else came - 5. [indica suma] plus; **dos más dos igual a cuatro** two plus two is four - 6. [indica intensidad]: **no le aguanto, ¡es más tonto!** I can't stand him, he's so stupid!; **¡qué día más bonito!** what a lovely day! - 7. [indica preferencia]: **más vale que nos vayamos a casa** it would be better for us to go home - 8. loc: **el que más y el que menos** everyone; **es más** indeed, what is more; **más bien** rather; **más o menos** more or less; **¿qué más da?** what difference does it make?; **sin más (ni más)** just like that. ◇ sm inv MAT plus (sign); **tiene sus más y sus menos** it has its good points and its bad points.

→ **por más que** loc conj however much; **por más que lo intente no lo conseguirá** however much O hard she tries, she'll never manage it.

masa sf - 1. [gen] mass - 2. CULIN dough - 3. R Dom [pastelillo] cake. → **masas** sfpl: **las masas** the masses.

masacre sf massacre.

masaje sm massage.

masajista smf masseur (f masseuse).

mascar vt & vi to chew.

máscara sf [gen] mask; **máscara antigás** gas mask; **máscara de oxígeno** oxygen mask.

mascarilla sf - 1. MED mask - 2. [cosmética] face pack.

mascota sf mascot.

masculino, na adj - 1. BIOL male - 2. [varonil] manly - 3. GRAM masculine.

mascullar vt to mutter.

masificación sf overcrowding.

masilla sf putty.

masivo, va adj mass (antes de s).

masón, ona ◇ adj masonic. ◇ sm, f mason, freemason.

masoquista ◇ adj masochistic. ◇ smf masochist.

máster (pl **masters**) sm Master's (degree).

masticar vt [mascar] to chew.

mástil sm - 1. NÁUT mast - 2. [palo] pole - 3. MÚS neck.

mastín sm mastiff.

masturbación sf masturbation.

masturbar vt to masturbate. → **masturbarse** vprnl to masturbate.

mata sf [arbusto] bush, shrub; [matojo] tuft; **matas** scrub. → **mata de pelo** sf mop of hair.

matadero *sm* abattoir, slaughterhouse.

matador, **ra** *fam adj* [cansado] killing, exhausting. ➡ **matador** *sm* matador.

matambre *sm Andes & Ven* [carne] flank O UK skirt steak; [plato] *flank steak rolled with boiled egg, olives and red pepper, which is cooked and then sliced and served cold.*

matamoscas *sm inv* [pala] flyswat; [espray] flyspray.

matanza *sf* [masacre] slaughter.

matar *vt* - 1. [gen] to kill; **matarlas callando** to be up to sthg on the quiet - 2. [apagar - sed] to quench; [- hambre] to stay. ➡ **matarse** *vprnl* - 1. [morir] to die - 2. [suicidarse, esforzarse] to kill o.s.

matasellos *smf inv* postmark.

mate ◇ *adj* matt. ◇ *sm* - 1. [en ajedrez] mate, checkmate - 2. [en baloncesto] dunk; [en tenis] smash - 3. BOT [bebida] maté.

matemático, **ca** ◇ *adj* mathematical. ◇ *sm, f* [científico] mathematician. ➡ **matemáticas** *sfpl* [ciencia] mathematics (U).

materia *sf* - 1. [sustancia] matter - 2. [material] material; **materia prima, primera materia** raw material - 3. [tema, asignatura] subject; **en materia de** on the subject of, concerning.

material ◇ *adj* - 1. [gen] physical; [daños, consecuencias] material - 2. [real] real, actual. ◇ *sm* - 1. [gen] material - 2. [instrumentos] equipment; **material bélico** O **de guerra** war material; **material de oficina** office stationery.

materialismo *sm* materialism; **materialismo dialéctico/histórico** dialectical/historical materialism.

materialista ◇ *adj* materialistic. ◇ *smf* materialist.

materializar *vt* - 1. [idea, proyecto] to realize - 2. [hacer tangible] to produce. ➡ **materializarse** *vprnl* to materialize.

maternal *adj* motherly, maternal.

maternidad *sf* - 1. [cualidad] motherhood - 2. [hospital] maternity hospital.

materno, **na** *adj* maternal; [lengua] mother (antes de s).

matinal *adj* morning (antes de s).

matiz *sm* - 1. [variedad - de color, opinión] shade; [- de sentido] nuance, shade of meaning - 2. [atisbo] trace, hint.

matizar *vt* - 1. [teñir]: **matizar (de)** to tinge (with) - 2. *fig* [distinguir - rasgos, aspectos] to distinguish; [- tema] to explain in detail - 3. *fig* [dar tono especial] to tinge - 4. ARTE to blend.

matojo *sm* [mata] tuft; [arbusto] bush, shrub.

matón, **ona** *sm, f fam* bully.

matorral *sm* thicket.

matraca *sf* [instrumento] rattle.

matriarcado *sm* matriarchy.

matrícula *sf* - 1. [inscripción] registration - 2. [documento] registration document - 3. AUTO number plate. ➡ **matrícula de honor** *sf* top marks *pl*.

matricular *vt* to register. ➡ **matricularse** *vprnl* to register.

matrimonial *adj* marital; [vida] married.

matrimonio *sm* - 1. [gen] marriage; **fuera del matrimonio** out of wedlock; **matrimonio de conveniencia** marriage of convenience; **matrimonio religioso** church wedding - 2. [pareja] married couple.

matriz ◇ *sf* - 1. ANAT womb - 2. [de talonario] (cheque) stub - 3. [molde] mould - 4. MAT matrix. ◇ *adj* [empresa] parent (antes de s); [casa] head (antes de s); [iglesia] mother (antes de s).

matrona *sf* - 1. [madre] matron - 2. [comadrona] midwife.

matutino, **na** *adj* morning (antes de s).

maullar *vi* to miaow.

maxilar *sm* jaw.

máxima ▷ **máximo**.

máxime *adv* especially.

máximo, **ma** ◇ *superl de* **grande**. ◇ *adj* maximum; [galardón, puntuación] highest. ➡ **máximo** *sm* maximum; **al máximo** to the utmost; **llegar al máximo** to reach the limit; **como máximo** [a más tardar] at the latest; [como mucho] at the most. ➡ **máxima** *sf* - 1. [sentencia, principio] maxim - 2. [temperatura] high, highest temperature.

mayo *sm* May; *ver también* **septiembre**.

mayonesa, **mahonesa** *sf* mayonnaise.

mayor ◇ *adj* - 1. *(compar)*: **mayor (que)** [de tamaño] bigger (than); [de importancia etc] greater (than); [de edad] older (than); [de número] higher (than) - 2. *(superl)*: **el/la mayor...** [de tamaño] the biggest...; [de importancia etc] the greatest...; [de edad] the oldest...; [de número] the highest... - 3. [adulto] grown-up; **hacerse mayor** to grow up - 4. [anciano] elderly - 5. MÚS: **en do mayor** in C major - 6. *loc*: **al por mayor** COM wholesale. ◇ *smf*: **el/la mayor** [hijo, hermano] the eldest. ◇ *sm* MIL major. ➡ **mayores** *smpl* - 1. [adultos] grown-ups - 2. [antepasados] ancestors.

mayoral *sm* [capataz] foreman.

mayordomo *sm* butler.

mayoreo *sm Amér* wholesale; **al mayoreo** wholesale.

mayoría *sf* majority; **la mayoría de** most of; **la mayoría de los españoles** most Spaniards; **la mayoría de las veces** usually, most often; **en su mayoría** in the main; **mayoría simple** simple majority. ➡ **mayoría de edad** *sf*: **llegar a la mayoría de edad** to come of age.

mayorista *smf* wholesaler.

mayoritario, **ria** *adj* majority (antes de s).

mayúscula ⊳ **letra**.

mayúsculo, la adj tremendous, enormous.

maza sf mace; [del bombo] drumstick.

mazapán sm marzipan.

mazmorra sf dungeon.

mazo sm - 1. [martillo] mallet - 2. [de mortero] pestle - 3. [conjunto - de naipes] balance (of the deck).

MDSMA sm (abrev de **Ministerio de Desarrollo Sostenible y Medio Ambiente**) Bolivian Department of Sustainable Development and the Environment.

me pron pers - 1. (complemento directo) me; **le gustaría verme** she'd like to see me - 2. (complemento indirecto) (to) me; **me lo dio** he gave it to me; **me tiene miedo** he's afraid of me - 3. (reflexivo) myself.

mear vi vulg to piss.

MEC sm (abrev de **Ministerio de Educación y Cultura**), Uruguayan Department of Education and Culture.

mecachis interj fam eufem: **¡mecachis!** sugar! UK, shoot! US

mecánico, ca ⬦ adj mechanical. ⬦ sm, f [persona] mechanic. ➤ **mecánica** sf - 1. [ciencia] mechanics (U) - 2. [funcionamiento] mechanics pl.

mecanismo sm [estructura] mechanism.

mecanografía sf typing.

mecanógrafo, fa sm, f typist.

mecapal sm Amér C & Méx porter's leather harness.

mecedora sf rocking chair.

mecenas smf inv patron.

mecer vt to rock. ➤ **mecerse** vprnl to rock back and forth; [en columpio] to swing.

mecha sf - 1. [de vela] wick - 2. [de explosivos] fuse - 3. [de pelo] streak.

mechero sm (cigarette) lighter.

mechón sm [de pelo] lock; [de lana] tuft.

medalla sf medal; **ponerse medallas** fig to show off.

medallón sm - 1. [joya] medallion - 2. [rodaja] médaillon; **medallón de pescado** [empanado] fishcake.

media sf - 1. ⊳ **medio** - 2. Amér [calcetín] sock.

mediación sf mediation; **por mediación de** through.

mediado, da adj [medio lleno] half-full; **mediada la película** halfway through the film. ➤ **a mediados de** loc prep in the middle of, halfway through.

medialuna sf Amér croissant.

mediana ⊳ **mediano**.

mediano, na adj - 1. [intermedio - de tamaño] medium; [- de calidad] average; **de mediana edad** middle-aged; **de mediana estatura** of medium O average height - 2. [mediocre] average, ordinary. ➤ **mediana** sf - 1. GEOM median - 2. [de carretera] central reservation.

medianoche (pl **medianoches**) sf [hora] midnight; **a medianoche** at midnight.

mediante prep by means of.

mediar vi - 1. [llegar a la mitad] to be halfway through; **mediaba julio** it was mid-July - 2. [estar en medio - tiempo, distancia, espacio]: **mediar entre** to be between; **media un jardín/un kilómetro entre las dos casas** there is a garden/one kilometre between the two houses; **medió una semana** a week passed by - 3. [intervenir]: **mediar (en/entre)** to mediate (in/between) - 4. [interceder]: **mediar (en favor de** O **por)** to intercede (on behalf of O for).

mediatizar vt to determine.

medicación sf medication.

medicamento sm medicine.

medicar vt to give medicine to. ➤ **medicarse** vprnl to take medicine.

medicina sf medicine.

medicinal adj medicinal.

medición sf measurement.

médico, ca ⬦ adj medical. ⬦ sm, f doctor; **médico de cabecera** O **familia** family doctor, general practitioner; **médico de guardia** duty doctor; **médico interno** houseman UK, intern US.

medida sf - 1. [gen] measure; [medición] measurement - 2. [disposición] measure, step; **tomar medidas** to take measures O steps; **medida cautelar** precautionary measure; **medidas de seguridad** security measures - 3. [moderación] moderation - 4. [grado] extent, degree; **en cierta/gran medida** to some/a large extent; **en la medida de lo posible** as far as possible; **en mayor/menor medida** to a greater/lesser extent; **a medida que entraban** as they were coming in. ➤ **medidas** sfpl [del cuerpo] measurements.

medidor sm Amér meter.

medieval adj medieval.

medievo, medioevo sm Middle Ages pl.

medio, dia adj - 1. [gen] half; **a medio camino** [en viaje] halfway there; [en trabajo etc] halfway through; **media docena/hora** a dozen/an hour; **medio pueblo estaba allí** half the town was there; **a media luz** in the half-light; **hacer algo a medias** to half-do sthg; **pagar a medias** to go halves, to share the cost; **un kilo y medio** one and a half kilos; **son (las dos) y media** it's half past (two) - 2. [intermedio - estatura, tamaño] medium; [- posición, punto] middle - 3. [de promedio - temperatura, velocidad] average. ➤ **medio** ⬦ adv half; **medio borracho** half drunk; **a medio hacer** half done.

◇ sm - **1.** [mitad] half - **2.** [centro] middle, centre; **en medio (de)** in the middle (of); **estar por (en) medio** to be in the way; **meterse** O **ponerse de por medio** to get in the way; fig to interfere; **quitar de en medio a alguien** to get rid of sb, to get sb out of the way - **3.** [sistema, manera] means, method; **por medio de** by means of, through - **4.** [elemento físico] environment; **medio ambiente** environment - **5.** [ambiente social] circle; **en medios bien informados** in well-informed circles - **6.** DEP midfielder. ◆ **medios** smpl [recursos] means, resources. ◆ **media** sf - **1.** [promedio] average - **2.** [hora]: **al dar la media** on the half-hour - **3.** (gen pl) [prenda] tights pl, stockings pl - **4.** DEP midfielders pl.

medioambiental adj environmental.

mediocre adj mediocre, average.

mediodía (pl **mediodías**) sm [hora] midday, noon; **al mediodía** at noon O midday.

medioevo = medievo.

medir vt - **1.** [gen] to measure; **¿cuánto mides?** how tall are you?; **mido 1,80** ≃ I'm 6 foot (tall); **mide diez metros** it's ten metres long - **2.** [pros, contras etc] to weigh up - **3.** [palabras] to weigh carefully.

meditar ◇ vi: **meditar (sobre)** to meditate (on). ◇ vt - **1.** [gen] to meditate, to ponder - **2.** [planear] to plan, to think through.

mediterráneo, a adj Mediterranean. ◆ **Mediterráneo** sm: **el (mar) Mediterráneo** the Mediterranean (Sea).

médium smf inv medium.

médula sf - **1.** ANAT [bone] marrow; **médula espinal** spinal cord; **médula ósea** bone marrow - **2.** [esencia] core; **hasta la médula** to the core.

medusa sf jellyfish.

megafonía sf public-address system; **llamar por megafonía a alguien** to page sb.

megáfono sm megaphone.

mejicano, na = mexicano.

Méjico n pr **= México**.

mejilla sf cheek.

mejillón sm mussel.

mejor ◇ adj (compar) better; **mejor (que)** better (than). ◇ smf: **el/la mejor (de)** the best (in); **el mejor de todos** the best of all; **lo mejor fue que...** the best thing was that... ◇ adv - **1.** (compar): **mejor (que)** better (than); **ahora veo mejor** I can see better now; **es mejor que no vengas** it would be better if you didn't come - **2.** (superl): **mejor** best; **el que la conoce mejor** the one who knows her best. ◆ **a lo mejor** loc adv maybe, perhaps. ◆ **mejor dicho** loc adv (or) rather.

mejora sf [progreso] improvement.

mejorar ◇ vt [gen] to improve; [enfermo] to make better. ◇ vi to improve, to get better. ◆ **mejorarse** vprnl to improve, to get better; **¡que te mejores!** get well soon!

mejoría sf improvement.

mejunje sm lit & fig concoction.

melancolía sf melancholy.

melancólico, ca adj melancholic.

melaza sf molasses pl.

melena sf - **1.** [de persona] long hair (U); **soltarse la melena** to let one's hair down - **2.** [de león] mane.

melenudo, da despec adj with a mop of hair.

mellado, da adj - **1.** [con hendiduras] nicked - **2.** [sin dientes] gap-toothed.

mellizo, za adj & sm, f twin.

melocotón sm peach.

melodía sf - **1.** MÚS melody, tune - **2.** [de teléfono móvil] ring tone.

melódico, ca adj melodic.

melodioso, sa adj melodious.

melodrama sm melodrama.

melómano, na sm, f music lover.

melón sm [fruta] melon.

meloso, sa adj - **1.** [como la miel] honey; fig sweet - **2.** [empalagoso] sickly.

membrana sf membrane.

membresía sf Amér membership.

membrete sm letterhead.

membrillo sm - **1.** [fruto] quince - **2.** [dulce] quince jelly.

memorable adj memorable.

memorándum (pl **memorándum** O **memorandos**) sm - **1.** [cuaderno] notebook - **2.** [nota diplomática] memorandum.

memoria sf - **1.** [gen & INFORM] memory; **si la memoria no me falla** if my memory serves me right; **¡qué memoria la mía!** what a memory I have!; **de memoria** by heart; **falta de memoria** forgetfulness; **hacer memoria** to try to remember; **tener buena/mala memoria** to have a good/bad memory; **traer a la memoria** to call to mind; **venir a la memoria** to come to mind - **2.** [recuerdo] remembrance; **ser de feliz/ingrata memoria** to be a happy/an unhappy memory - **3.** [disertación] (academic) paper - **4.** [informe]: **memoria (anual)** (annual) report. ◆ **memorias** sfpl [biografía] memoirs.

memorizar vt to memorize.

menaje sm household goods and furnishings pl; **menaje de cocina** kitchenware.

mención sf mention; **mención honorífica** honourable mention.

mencionar vt to mention.

menda ◇ *pron fam* [el que habla] yours truly. ◇ *smf* [uno cualquiera]: **vino un menda y** this bloke came along and...

mendigar ⌐ *vt* to beg for ◇ *vi* to beg.

mendigo, ga *sm, f* beggar.

mendrugo *sm* crust (of bread).

menear *vt* [mover - gen] to move; [- cabeza] to shake; [- cola] to wag; [- caderas] to wiggle. ➡ **menearse** *vprnl* - **1.** [moverse] to move (about); [agitarse] to shake; [oscilar] to sway - **2.** [darse prisa, espabilarse] to get a move on.

menester *sm* necessity. ➡ **menesteres** *smpl* [asuntos] business *(U)*, matters *pl*.

menestra *sf* vegetable stew.

mengano, na *sm, f* so-and-so.

menguante *adj* [luna] waning.

menguar ◇ *vi* [disminuir] to decrease, to diminish; [luna] to wane. ◇ *vt* [disminuir] to lessen, to diminish.

menopausia *sf* menopause.

menor ◇ *adj* - **1.** *(compar)*: **menor (que)** [de tamaño] smaller (than); [de edad] younger (than); [de importancia etc] less *O* lesser (than); [de número] lower (than) - **2.** *(superl)*: **el/la menor...** [de tamaño] the smallest...; [de edad] the youngest...; [de importancia] the slightest...; [de número] the lowest... - **3.** [de poca importancia] minor; **un problema menor** a minor problem - **4.** [joven]: **ser menor de edad** [para votar, conducir etc] to be under age; DER to be a minor - **5.** MÚS: **en do menor** in C minor - **6.** *loc*: **al por menor** COM retail. ◇ *smf* - **1.** *(superl)*: **el/la menor** [hijo, hermano] the youngest - **2.** DER [niño] minor.

Menorca *n pr* Minorca.

menos ◇ *adj inv* - **1.** *(compar)* [cantidad] less; [número] fewer; **menos aire** less air; **menos manzanas** fewer apples; **menos... que...** less/fewer... than...; **tiene menos experiencia que tú** she has less experience than you; **hace menos calor que ayer** it's not as hot as it was yesterday - **2.** *(superl)* [cantidad] the least; [número] the fewest; **el que compró menos acciones** the one who bought the fewest shares; **lo que menos tiempo llevó** the thing that took the least time - **3.** *fam* [peor]: **éste es menos coche que el mío** that car isn't as good as mine. ◇ *adv* - **1.** *(compar)* less; **menos de/que** less than; **estás menos gordo** you're not as fat - **2.** *(superl)*: **el/la/lo menos** the least; **él es el menos indicado para criticar** he's the last person who should be criticizing; **ella es la menos adecuada para el cargo** she's the least suitable person for the job; **es lo menos que puedo hacer** it's the least I can do - **3.** [expresa resta] minus; **tres menos dos igual a uno** three minus two is one - **4.** [con las horas] to; **son (las dos) menos diez** it's ten to (two) - **5.** *loc*: **es lo de menos** that's the least of it, that's of no

importance; **hacer de menos a alguien** to snub sb; **¡menos mal!** just as well!, thank God!; **no es para menos** not without (good) reason; **venir a menos** to go down in the world. ◇ *sm inv* MAT minus (sign). ◇ *prep* [excepto] except (for); **todo menos eso** anything but that.
➡ **al menos, por lo menos** *loc adv* at least.
➡ **a menos que** *loc conj* unless; **no iré a menos que me acompañes** I won't go unless you come with me. ➡ **de menos** *loc adj* [que falta] missing; **hay dos euros de menos** there's two euros missing.

menoscabar *vt* [fama, honra etc] to damage; [derechos, intereses, salud] to harm; [belleza, perfección] to diminish.

menospreciar *vt* [despreciar] to scorn, to despise; [infravalorar] to undervalue.

mensaje *sm* [gen & INFORM] message; **mensaje de texto** [en teléfono móvil] text message.

mensajero, ra *sm, f* [gen] messenger; [de mensajería] courier.

menstruación *sf* menstruation.

menstruar *vi* to menstruate, to have a period.

mensual *adj* monthly; **1.000 euros mensuales** 1,000 euros a month.

mensualidad *sf* - **1.** [sueldo] monthly salary - **2.** [pago] monthly payment *O* instalment.

menta *sf* mint.

mental *adj* mental.

mentalidad *sf* mentality.

mentalizar *vt* to put into a frame of mind.
➡ **mentalizarse** *vprnl* to get into a frame of mind.

mentar *vt* to mention.

mente *sf* [gen] mind; **traer a la mente** to bring to mind.

mentecato, ta *sm, f* idiot.

mentir *vi* to lie.

mentira *sf* lie; [acción] lying; **aunque parezca mentira** strange as it may seem; **de mentira** pretend, false; **parece mentira (que...)** it hardly seems possible (that...); **mentira piadosa** white lie.

mentirijillas ➡ **de mentirijillas** *fam* ◇ *loc adv* [en broma] as a joke, in fun. ◇ *loc adj* [falso] pretend, make-believe.

mentiroso, sa ◇ *adj* lying; [engañoso] deceptive. ◇ *sm, f* liar.

mentón *sm* chin.

menú (*pl* menús) *sm* - **1.** [lista] menu; [comida] food; **menú del día** set meal - **2.** INFORM menu.

menudencia *sf* trifle, insignificant thing.

menudeo *sm* *Amér* COM retailing.

menudillos *smpl* giblets.

menudo, da adj - 1. [pequeño] small - 2. [insignificante] trifling, insignificant - 3. *(antes de s)* [para enfatizar] what!; **¡menudo lío/gol!** what a mess/goal! ◆ **a menudo** *loc adv* often.

meollo *sm* core, heart; **llegar al meollo de la cuestión** to come to the heart of the matter.

mercader *smf* trader.

mercadería *sf* merchandise, goods *pl*.

mercadillo *sm* flea market.

mercado *sm* market; **mercado común** Common Market; **mercado libre/negro** free/black market; **Mercado Único Europeo** European Single Market.

mercancía *sf* merchandise *(U)*, goods *pl*. ◆ **mercancías** *sm inv* FERROC goods train, freight train *US*.

mercante *adj* merchant.

mercantil *adj* mercantile, commercial.

mercenario, ria *adj* & *sm, f* mercenary.

mercería *sf* [tienda] haberdasher's (shop) *UK*, notions store *US*.

MERCOSUR *sm* *(abrev de Mercado Común del Sur)* MERCOSUR.

mercurio *sm* mercury.

Mercurio *sm* Mercury.

merecedor, ra *adj*: **merecedor de** worthy of.

merecer ◇ *vt* to deserve, to be worthy of; **la isla merece una visita** the island is worth a visit; **no merece la pena** it's not worth it. ◇ *vi* to be worthy.

merecido *sm*: **recibir su merecido** to get one's just deserts.

merendar ◇ *vi* to have tea *(as a light afternoon meal)*. ◇ *vt* to have for tea.

merendero *sm* open-air café or bar *(in the country or on the beach)*.

merengue *sm* - 1. CULIN meringue - 2. [baile] merengue.

meridiano, na *adj* - 1. [hora etc] midday - 2. *fig* [claro] crystal-clear. ◆ **meridiano** *sm* meridian.

merienda *sf* tea *(as a light afternoon meal)*; [en el campo] picnic.

mérito *sm* - 1. [cualidad] merit - 2. [valor] value, worth; **tiene mucho mérito** it's no mean achievement; **de mérito** worthy, deserving.

merluza *sf* [pez, pescado] hake.

merma *sf* decrease, reduction.

mermar ◇ *vi* to diminish, to lessen. ◇ *vt* to reduce, to diminish.

mermelada *sf* jam; **mermelada de naranja** marmalade.

mero, ra *adj (antes de s)* mere. ◆ **mero** *sm* grouper.

merodear *vi*: **merodear (por)** to snoop *O* prowl (about).

mes *sm* - 1. [del año] month - 2. [salario] monthly salary.

mesa *sf* - 1. [gen] table; [de oficina, despacho] desk; **bendecir la mesa** to say grace; **mesa camilla** *small round table under which a heater is placed*; **mesa de billar** billiard table; **mesa de mezclas** mixing desk; **mesa plegable** folding table - 2. [comité] board, committee; [en un debate etc] panel; **mesa directiva** executive board *O* committee. ◆ **mesa redonda** *sf* [coloquio] round table.

mesada *sf* - 1. *Amér* [mensualidad] monthly payment, monthly instalment - 2. *R Dom* [encimera] worktop.

mesero, ra *sm, f Amér C, Col & Méx* waiter (*f* waitress).

meseta *sf* plateau, tableland.

mesías *sm fig* Messiah.

mesilla *sf* small table; **mesilla de noche** bedside table.

mesón *sm* - 1. HIST inn - 2. [bar-restaurante] *old, country-style restaurant and bar*.

mestizo, za ◇ *adj* [persona] half-caste; [animal, planta] cross-bred. ◇ *sm, f* half-caste.

mesura *sf* - 1. [moderación] moderation, restraint - 2. [cortesía] courtesy.

meta *sf* - 1. [DEP - llegada] finishing line; [- portería] goal - 2. [objetivo] aim, goal.

metabolismo *sm* metabolism.

metáfora *sf* metaphor.

metal *sm* - 1. [material] metal - 2. MÚS brass.

metálico, ca ◇ *adj* [sonido, color] metallic; [objeto] metal. ◇ *sm*: **pagar en metálico** to pay (in) cash.

metalizado, da *adj* [pintura] metallic.

metalurgia *sf* metallurgy.

metamorfosis *sf inv lit & fig* metamorphosis.

metedura ◆ **metedura de pata** *sf* clanger.

meteorito *sm* meteorite.

meteoro *sm* meteor.

meteorología *sf* meteorology.

meteorológico, ca *adj* meteorological.

meteorólogo, ga *sm, f* meteorologist; RADIO & TV weatherman (*f* weatherwoman).

meter *vt* - 1. [gen] to put in; **meter algo/a alguien en algo** to put sthg/sb in sthg; **meter la llave en la cerradura** to get the key into the lock; **lo metieron en la cárcel** they put him in prison; **meter dinero en el banco** to put money in the bank - 2. [hacer participar]: **meter a alguien en algo** to get sb into sthg - 3. [obligar a]: **meter a alguien a hacer algo** to make sb start doing sthg - 4. [causar]: **meter prisa/mie-**

do a alguien to rush/scare sb; **meter ruido** to make a noise - **5.** *fam* [asestar] to give; **le metió un puñetazo** he gave him a punch - **6.** [estrechar - prenda] to take in; **meter el bajo de una falda** to take up a skirt. ➡ **meterse** *vprnl* - **1.** [entrar] to get in; **meterse en** to get into - **2.** *(en frase interrogativa)* [estar] to get to; **¿dónde se ha metido ese chico?** where has that boy got to? - **3.** [dedicarse]: **meterse a** to become; **meterse a torero** to become a bullfighter - **4.** [involucrarse]: **meterse (en)** to get involved (in) - **5.** [entrometerse] to meddle; **se mete en todo** he never minds his own business; **meterse por medio** to interfere - **6.** [empezar]: **meterse a hacer algo** to get started on doing sthg. ➡ **meterse con** *vprnl* - **1.** [incordiar] to hassle - **2.** [atacar] to go for.

meterete *smf C Sur fam* busybody, nosey-parker *UK*.

metete *smf Andes & Amér C fam* busybody, nosey-parker *UK*.

meticuloso, sa *adj* meticulous.

metido, da *adj* - **1.** [envuelto]: **andar O estar metido en** to be involved in - **2.** [abundante]: **metido en años** elderly; **metido en carnes** plump.

metódico, ca *adj* methodical.

método *sm* - **1.** [sistema] method - **2.** EDUC course.

metodología *sf* methodology.

metomentodo *fam smf* busybody.

metralla *sf* shrapnel.

metralleta *sf* submachine gun.

métrico, ca *adj* [del metro] metric.

metro *sm* - **1.** [gen] metre - **2.** [transporte] underground *UK*, tube *UK*, subway *US* - **3.** [cinta métrica] tape measure.

metrópoli *sf* [ciudad] metropolis.

metrópolis *sf inv* = **metrópoli**.

metropolitano, na *adj* metropolitan.

mexicano, na, mejicano, na *adj & sm, f* Mexican.

México, Méjico *n pr* Mexico.

mezcla *sf* - **1.** [gen] mixture; [tejido] blend; [de grabación] mix - **2.** [acción] mixing.

mezclar *vt* - **1.** [gen] to mix; [combinar, armonizar] to blend - **2.** [confundir, desordenar] to mix up - **3.** [implicar]: **mezclar a alguien en** to get sb mixed up in. ➡ **mezclarse** *vprnl* - **1.** [gen]: **mezclarse (con)** to mix (with) - **2.** [esfumarse]: **mezclarse entre** to disappear O blend into - **3.** [implicarse]: **mezclarse en** to get mixed up in.

mezquino, na *adj* mean, cheap *US*.

mezquita *sf* mosque.

mg *(abrev de miligramo)* mg.

MHz *(abrev de megahercio)* MHz.

mi¹ *sm* MÚS E; [en solfeo] mi.

mi² *(pl mis)* *adj poses* my; **mi casa** my house; **mis libros** my books.

mí *pron pers (después de prep)* - **1.** [gen] me; **este trabajo no es para mí** this job isn't for me; **no se fía de mí** he doesn't trust me - **2.** *(reflexivo)* myself - **3.** *loc*: **¡a mí qué!** so what?, why should I care?; **para mí** [yo creo] as far as I'm concerned, in my opinion; **por mí** as far as I'm concerned; **por mí, no hay inconveniente** it's fine by me.

mía ⟜ **mío**.

miaja *sf* crumb; *fig* tiny bit.

miau *sm* miaow.

michelines *smpl fam* spare tyre *sing*.

mico *sm fam* [persona] ugly devil; **se volvió mico para abrir la puerta** he had a hell of a job opening the door.

micro ⟜ *sm fam (abrev de micrófono)* mike. ⟜ *sm o sf Chile* [microbús] bus, coach *UK*.

microbio *sm* germ, microbe.

microbús *sm* - **1.** minibus - **2.** *Méx* [taxi] (collective) taxi.

microfilm *(pl microfilms)*, **microfilme** *sm* microfilm.

micrófono *sm* microphone.

microondas *sm inv* microwave (oven).

microordenador *sm* INFORM microcomputer.

microprocesador *sm* INFORM microprocessor.

microscópico, ca *adj* microscopic.

microscopio *sm* microscope; **microscopio electrónico** electron microscope.

MIDA *sm (abrev de Ministerio de Desarrollo Agropecuario) Panamanian Department of Agricultural Development*.

miedo *sm* fear; **coger miedo a algo** to develop a fear of sthg; **dar miedo** to be frightening; **me de miedo conducir** I'm afraid O frightened of driving; **por miedo de que...** for fear that...; **temblar de miedo** to tremble with fear; **tener miedo** to be frightened O scared ▸▸▸ **de miedo** *fam*: **esta película está de miedo** this film is brilliant; **lo pasamos de miedo** we had a whale of a time.

miedoso, sa *adj* fearful.

miel *sf* honey.

miembro *sm* - **1.** [gen] member - **2.** [extremidad] limb, member; **miembros superiores/inferiores** upper/lower limbs; **miembro (viril)** penis.

miércoles *sm* Wednesday; **miércoles de ceniza** Ash Wednesday; *ver también* **sábado**.

mierda *vulg sf* - **1.** [excremento] shit - **2.** [suciedad] filth, shit - **3.** [cosa sin valor]: **es una mierda** it's (a load of) crap - **4.** *loc*: **¡vete a la mierda!** go to hell!, piss off!

mies *sf* [cereal] ripe corn. ➤ **mieses** *sfpl* [campo] cornfields.

miga *sf* [de pan] crumb; **tener miga** *fam* [ser sustancioso] to have a lot to it; [ser complicado] to have more to it than meets the eye. ➤ **migas** *sfpl* CULIN fried breadcrumbs; **hacer migas a alguien** *fam* [desmoralizar] to shatter sb.

migra *sf* Méx fam despec: **la migra** US police border patrol.

migración *sf* migration.

migraña *sf* migraine.

migrar *vi* to migrate.

migratorio, ria *adj* migratory.

mijo *sm* millet.

mil *num* thousand; **dos mil** two thousand; **mil euros** a thousand euros; *ver también* **seis**.

milagro *sm* miracle; **de milagro** miraculously.

milagroso, sa *adj* miraculous; *fig* amazing.

milenario, ria *adj* ancient. ➤ **milenario** *sm* millennium.

milenio *sm* millennium.

milésimo, ma *num* thousandth.

mili *sf fam* military service; **hacer la mili** to do one's military service.

milicia *sf* - 1. [profesión] military (profession) - 2. [grupo armado] militia.

miliciano, na *sm, f* militiaman (*f* female soldier).

miligramo *sm* milligram.

milímetro *sm* millimetre.

militante *adj & smf* militant.

militar ◇ *adj* military. ◇ *smf* soldier; **los militares** the military. ◇ *vi*: **militar (en)** to be active (in).

milla *sf* mile; **milla (marina)** nautical mile.

millar *sm* thousand; **un millar de personas** a thousand people.

millón *num* million; **dos millones** two million; **un millón de personas** a million people; **un millón de cosas que hacer** a million things to do; **un millón de gracias** thanks a million. ➤ **millones** *smpl* [dineral] a fortune *sing*.

millonario, ria *sm, f* millionaire (*f* millionairess).

millonésimo, ma *num* millionth.

mimado, da *adj* spoilt.

mimar *vt* to spoil, to pamper.

mimbre *sm* wicker; **de mimbre** wickerwork.

mímica *sf* - 1. [mimo] mime - 2. [lenguaje] sign language.

mimo *sm* - 1. [zalamería] mollycoddling - 2. [cariño] show of affection - 3. TEATRO mime.

mimosa *sf* BOT mimosa.

min (*abrev de* **minuto**) min.

mina *sf* GEOL & MIL mine; **mina de carbón** coalmine.

minar *vt* - 1. MIL to mine - 2. *fig* [aminorar] to undermine.

mineral ◇ *adj* mineral. ◇ *sm* - 1. GEOL mineral - 2. [en mineralogía] ore.

minería *sf* - 1. [técnica] mining - 2. [sector] mining industry.

minero, ra ◇ *adj* mining (*antes de s*); [producción, riqueza] mineral. ◇ *sm, f* miner.

miniatura *sf* miniature.

minicadena *sf* midi system.

minifalda *sf* mini skirt.

minigolf (*pl* **minigolfs**) *sm* [juego] crazy golf.

mínimo, ma ◇ *superl de* **pequeño**. ◇ *adj* - 1. [lo más bajo posible o necesario] minimum - 2. [lo más bajo temporalmente] lowest - 3. [muy pequeño - efecto, importancia etc] minimal, very small; [- protesta, ruido etc] slightest; **no tengo la más mínima idea** I haven't the slightest idea; **como mínimo** at the very least; **en lo más mínimo** in the slightest. ➤ **mínimo** *sm* [límite] minimum. ➤ **mínima** *sf* METEOR low, lowest temperature.

ministerio *sm* - 1. POLÍT ministry UK, department US - 2. RELIG ministry. ➤ **Ministerio de Asuntos Exteriores** *sm* ≃ Foreign Office UK, ≃ State Department US. ➤ **Ministerio de Economía y Hacienda** *sm* ≃ Treasury UK, ≃ Treasury Department US. ➤ **Ministerio del Interior** *sm* ≃ Home Office UK, ≃ Department of the Interior US.

ministro, tra *sm, f* POLÍT minister UK, secretary US; **primer ministro** prime minister.

minoría *sf* minority; **estar en minoría** to be in a O the minority; **minorías étnicas** ethnic minorities.

minorista ◇ *adj* retail. ◇ *smf* retailer.

minoritario, ria *adj* minority (*antes de s*).

minucia *sf* trifle, insignificant thing.

minucioso, sa *adj* - 1. [meticuloso] meticulous - 2. [detallado] highly detailed.

minúsculo, la *adj* - 1. [tamaño] tiny, minute - 2. [letra] small; IMPR lower-case. ➤ **minúscula** *sf* small letter; IMPR lower-case letter.

minusvalía *sf* [física] handicap, disability.

minusválido, da ◇ *adj* disabled, handicapped. ◇ *sm, f* disabled O handicapped person.

minuta *sf* - 1. [factura] fee - 2. [menú] menu - 3. R Dom [comida] quick meal.

minutero *sm* minute hand.

minuto *sm* minute; **guardar un minuto de silencio** to observe a minute's silence.

mío, mía ◇ *adj poses* mine; **este libro es mío** this book is mine; **un amigo mío** a friend of mine; **no es asunto mío** it's none of my business. <> pron **póses: el mío** mine; **el mío es rojo** mine is red; **esta es la mía** fam this is the chance I've been waiting for; **lo mío es el teatro** [lo que me va] theatre is what I should be doing; **los míos** fam [mi familia] my folks; [mi bando] my lot, my side.

miope adj shortsighted, myopic.

miopía sf shortsightedness, myopia.

mira <> sf sight; fig intention; **con miras a** with a view to, with the intention of. <> interj: **¡mira!** look!

mirado, da adj [prudente] careful; **bien mirado** [bien pensado] if you look at it closely. ➤ **mirada** sf [gen] look; [rápida] glance; [de cariño, placer, admiración] gaze; **apartar la mirada** to look away; **dirigir** O **lanzar la mirada a** to glance at; **echar una mirada (a algo)** to glance O to have a quick look (at sthg); **fulminar con la mirada a alguien** to look daggers at sb; **hay miradas que matan** if looks could kill; **levantar la mirada** to look up; **mirada fija** stare.

mirador sm - **1.** [balcón] enclosed balcony - **2.** [para ver un paisaje] viewpoint.

miramiento sm circumspection; **andarse con miramientos** to stand on ceremony; **sin miramientos** just like that, without the least consideration.

mirar <> vt - **1.** [gen] to look at; [observar] to watch; [fijamente] to stare at; **mirar algo de cerca/lejos** to look at sthg closely/from a distance; **mirar algo por encima** to glance over sthg, to have a quick look at sthg - **2.** [fijarse en] to keep an eye on - **3.** [examinar, averiguar] to check, to look through; **le miraron todas las maletas** they searched all her luggage; **mira si ha llegado la carta** go and see if the letter has arrived - **4.** [considerar] to consider, to take a look at. <> vi - **1.** [gen] to look; [observar] to watch; [fijamente] to stare; **mira, yo creo que...** look, I think that... - **2.** [buscar] to check, to look; **he mirado en todas partes** I've looked everywhere - **3.** [orientarse]: **mirar a** to face - **4.** [cuidar]: **mirar por alguien/algo** to look after sb/sthg. ➤ **mirarse** vprnl [uno mismo] to look at o.s.

mirilla sf spyhole.

mirlo sm blackbird.

mirón, ona fam sm, f - **1.** [espectador] onlooker - **2.** [curioso] nosy parker - **3.** [voyeur] peeping Tom.

misa sf mass; **cantar/decir/oír misa** to sing/say/hear mass.

misal sm missal.

misántropo, pa sm, f misanthropist.

miscelánea sf - **1.** miscellany - **2.** Méx [tienda] small general store.

miserable <> adj - **1.** [pobre] poor; [vivienda] wretched, squalid - **2.** [penoso] insuficiente] miserable - **3.** [vil] contemptible, base - **4.** [tacaño] mean. <> smf [ruin] wretch, vile person.

miseria sf - **1.** [pobreza] poverty; **vivir en la miseria** to live in poverty - **2.** [cantidad muy pequeña] pittance - **3.** [desgracia] misfortune - **4.** [tacañería] meanness.

misericordia sf compassion; **pedir misericordia** to beg for mercy.

mísero, ra adj [pobre] wretched; **ni un mísero...** not even a measly O miserable...

misil (pl misiles) sm missile; **misil de crucero** cruise missile.

misión sf - **1.** [gen] mission; [cometido] task - **2.** [expedición científica] expedition.

misionero, ra adj & sm, f missionary.

misiva sf culto missive.

mismo, ma <> adj - **1.** [igual] same; **el mismo piso** the same flat; **del mismo color que** the same colour as - **2.** [para enfatizar]: **yo mismo** I myself; **en este mismo cuarto** in this very room; **en su misma calle** right in the street where he lives; **por mí/ti mismo** by myself/yourself; **¡tú mismo!** it's up to you. <> pron: **el mismo** the same; **el mismo que vi ayer** the same one I saw yesterday; **lo mismo** the same (thing); **lo mismo que** the same as; **da** O **es lo mismo** it doesn't matter, it doesn't make any difference; **me da lo mismo** I don't care. ➤ **mismo** (después de s) adv - **1.** [para enfatizar]: **lo vi desde mi casa mismo** I saw it from my own house; **ahora/aquí mismo** right now/here; **ayer mismo** only yesterday; **por eso mismo** precisely for that reason - **2.** [por ejemplo]: **escoge uno – cualquiera este mismo** choose any – this one, for instance.

misógino, na adj misogynistic.

misterio sm mystery.

misterioso, sa adj mysterious.

mística ⊳ **místico.**

místico, ca adj mystical. ➤ **mística** sf [práctica] mysticism.

mitad sf - **1.** [gen] half; **a mitad de precio** at half price; **a mitad de camino** halfway there; **a mitad de película** halfway through the film; **la mitad de** half (of); **la mitad del tiempo no está** half the time she's not in; **mitad y mitad** half and half - **2.** [centro] middle; **en mitad de** in the middle of; **(cortar algo) por la mitad** (to cut sthg) in half.

mítico, ca adj mythical.

mitigar vt - **1.** [gen] to alleviate, to reduce; [ánimos] to calm; [sed] to slake; [hambre] to take the edge off; [choque, golpe] to soften; [dudas, sospechas] to allay - **2.** [justificar] to mitigate.

mitin (pl mítines) sm rally, meeting.

mito sm [gen] myth.

mitología *sf* mythology.

mitote *sm Méx fam* [bulla] racket.

mixto, ta *adj* mixed; [comisión] joint.

ml (*abrev de* mililitro) ml.

mm (*abrev de* milímetro) mm.

mobiliario *sm* furniture; **mobiliario urbano** street furniture.

mocasín *sm* moccasin.

mochila *sf* backpack.

mochuelo *sm* little owl.

moción *sf* motion.

moco *sm fam* snot (U); MED mucus (U); **limpiarse los mocos** to wipe one's nose; **sorberse los mocos** to sniffle, to snuffle.

mocoso, sa *sm, f fam despec* brat.

moda *sf* [gen] fashion; [furor pasajero] craze; **estar de moda** to be fashionable O in fashion; **estar pasado de moda** to be unfashionable O out of fashion; **ponerse de moda** to come into fashion; **moda pasajera** fad.

modal *adj* modal. ➡ **modales** *smpl* manners.

modalidad *sf* form, type; DEP discipline.

modelar *vt* to model; *fig* to shape.

modelo ◇ *adj* model. ◇ *smf* model. ◇ *sm* - **1.** [gen] model; **modelo económico** ECON economic model - **2.** [prenda de vestir] number.

módem ['moðem] (*pl* modems) *sm* INFORM modem; **módem fax** fax modem.

moderación *sf* moderation.

moderado, da *adj & sm, f* moderate.

moderador, ra *sm, f* chair, chairperson.

moderar *vt* - **1.** [gen] to moderate; [velocidad] to reduce - **2.** [debate] to chair. ➡ **moderarse** *vprnl* to restrain o.s.

modernizar *vt* to modernize.

moderno, na *adj* modern.

modestia *sf* modesty.

modesto, ta *adj* modest.

módico, ca *adj* modest.

modificar *vt* - **1.** [variar] to alter - **2.** GRAM to modify.

modista *smf* - **1.** [diseñador] fashion designer - **2.** [que cose] tailor (*f* dressmaker).

modisto *sm* - **1.** [diseñador] fashion designer - **2.** [sastre] tailor.

modo *sm* [manera, forma] way; **a modo de** as, by way of; **a mi modo** (in) my own way; **de ese modo** in that way; **de ningún modo** in no way; **de todos modos** in any case, anyway; **de un modo u otro** one way or another; **en cierto modo** in some ways; **modo de empleo** instructions *pl* for use; **modo de pensar/ser** way of thinking/being; **modo de vida** way of life; **de modo que** [de manera que] in such a way

that; [así que] so. ➡ **modos** *smpl* [modales] manners; **buenos/malos modos** good/bad manners.

modorra *sf fam* drowsiness.

modoso, sa *adj* [recatado] modest; [formal] well-behaved.

modular *vt* to modulate.

módulo *sm* - **1.** [gen] module; **módulo lunar** lunar module - **2.** [de muebles] unit.

mofa *sf* mockery.

mofarse *vprnl* to scoff; **mofarse de** to mock.

moflete *sm* chubby cheek.

mogollón *sm mfam* - **1.** [muchos]: **mogollón de** tons *pl* of, loads *pl* of - **2.** [lío] row, commotion; **entraron/salieron a mogollón** everyone rushed in/out at once.

moho *sm* - **1.** [hongo] mould; **criar moho** to go mouldy - **2.** [herrumbre] rust.

mohoso, sa *adj* - **1.** [con hongo] mouldy - **2.** [oxidado] rusty.

moisés *sm inv* Moses basket.

mojado, da *adj* wet; [húmedo] damp.

mojar *vt* [sin querer] to get wet; [a propósito] to wet; [humedecer] to dampen; [comida] to dunk; **moja el pan en la salsa** dip your bread in the sauce. ➡ **mojarse** *vprnl* [con agua] to get wet.

mojigato, ta *adj* - **1.** [beato] prudish - **2.** [con falsa humildad] sanctimonious.

mojón *sm* [piedra] milestone; [poste] milepost.

molar *fam vi* to be bloody gorgeous.

molcajete *sm Méx* mortar.

molde *sm* mould.

moldeado *sm* - **1.** [del pelo] soft perm - **2.** [de figura, cerámica] moulding.

moldear *vt* - **1.** [gen] to mould - **2.** [modelar] to cast - **3.** [cabello] to give a soft perm to.

mole ◇ *sf* hulk. ◇ *sm Méx* [salsa] *thick, cooked chilli sauce*; [guiso] *dish served in 'mole' sauce*.

molécula *sf* molecule.

moler *vt* - **1.** [gen] to grind; [aceitunas] to press; [trigo] to mill - **2.** *fam* [cansar] to wear out.

molestar *vt* - **1.** [perturbar] to annoy; ¿**le molesta que fume?** do you mind if I smoke?; **perdone que le moleste...** I'm sorry to bother you... - **2.** [doler] to hurt - **3.** [ofender] to offend. ➡ **molestarse** *vprnl* - **1.** [incomodarse] to bother; **molestarse en hacer algo** to bother to do sthg; **molestarse por alguien/algo** to put o.s. out for sb/sthg - **2.** [ofenderse]: **molestarse (por algo)** to take offence (at sthg).

molestia *sf* - **1.** [incomodidad] nuisance; **disculpen las molestias** we apologize for any inconvenience; **si no es demasiada molestia** if it's not too much trouble - **2.** [malestar] dis-comfort; **siento una molestia en el estómago** my stomach doesn't feel too good.

molesto, ta *adj* - **1.** [incordiante] annoying; [visita] inconvenient - **2.** [irritado]: **molesto (con)** annoyed (with) - **3.** [con malestar] in discom-fort.

molido, da *adj fam* [cansado] worn out; **estar molido de** to be worn out from.

molinero, ra *sm, f* miller.

molinillo *sm* grinder; **molinillo de café** coffee mill O grinder.

molino *sm* mill; **molino de viento** windmill.

molla *sf* [parte blanda] flesh.

molleja *sf* gizzard.

mollera *sf fam* [juicio] brains *pl*; **ser duro de mollera** [estúpido] to be thick in the head; [tes-tarudo] to be pig-headed.

molusco *sm* mollusc.

momentáneo, a *adj* [de un momento] mo-mentary; [pasajero] temporary.

momento *sm* [gen] moment; [periodo] time; **llegó un momento en que...** there came a time when...; **a cada momento** all the time; **al mo-mento** straightaway; **a partir de este momen-to** from this moment (on); **de momento, por el momento** for the time being O moment; **del momento** [actual] of the day; **de un momento a otro** any minute now; **dentro de un momen-to** in a moment; **desde el momento (en) que...** [tiempo] from the moment that...; [causa] see-ing as...; **en algún momento** sometime; **mo-mentos después** moments later; **¡un momen-to!** just a minute!; **momento decisivo** turning point.

momia *sf* mummy.

monada *sf* - **1.** [persona]: **su novia es una mo-nada** his girlfriend is gorgeous; **¡qué monada de bebé!** what a cute baby! - **2.** [cosa] lovely thing; **¡qué monada de falda!** what a lovely skirt! *⇒* **monadas** *sfpl* [gracias] antics; **hacer monadas** to monkey O clown around.

monaguillo *sm* altar boy.

monarca *sm* monarch.

monarquía *sf* monarchy; **monarquía absolu-ta/constitucional/parlamentaria** absolute/constitutional/parliamentary monarchy.

monárquico, ca *adj* monarchic.

monasterio *sm* [de monjes] monastery; [de monjas] convent.

Moncloa *sf*: **la Moncloa** residence of the Spanish premier.

monda *sf* [acción] peeling; [piel] peel; **ser la monda** *mfam* [extraordinario] to be amazing; [gracioso] to be a scream.

mondadientes *sm inv* toothpick.

mondadura *sf* [piel] peel.

mondar *vt* to peel. *⇒* **mondarse** *vprnl*: **mondarse (de risa)** *fam* to laugh one's head off.

moneda *sf* - **1.** [pieza] coin; **pagar a alguien con O en la misma moneda** to pay sb back in kind; **ser moneda corriente** to be common-place - **2.** [divisa] currency.

monedero *sm* - **1.** [gen] purse - **2.** [tarjeta]: **monedero electrónico** electronic purse.

monegasco, ca *adj* & *sm, f* Monegasque.

monetario, ria *adj* monetary.

mongólico, ca *sm, f* MED Down's syndrome person.

mongolismo *sm* Down's syndrome.

monigote *sm* - **1.** [muñeco] rag O paper doll - **2.** [dibujo] doodle - **3.** *fig* [persona] puppet.

monitor, ra *sm, f* [persona] instructor. *⇒* **monitor** *sm* INFORM & TECNOL monitor.

monja *sf* nun.

monje *sm* monk.

mono, na *⇔ adj* - **1.** [bonito] lovely - **2.** *Col* [rubio] blond(e). *⇔ sm, f* - **1.** [animal] monkey; **aunque la mona se vista de seda, mona se que-da** *prov* you can't make a silk purse out of a sow's ear *prov*; **mandar a alguien a freír mo-nas** *fam* to tell sb to get lost; **ser el último mo-no** to be bottom of the heap - **2.** *Col* [rubio] blond(e). *⇒* **mono** *sm* - **1.** [prenda - con pe-to] dungarees *pl*; [- con mangas] overalls *pl* - **2.** *fam* [abstinencia] cold turkey.

monóculo *sm* monocle.

monogamia *sf* monogamy.

monografía *sf* monograph.

monolingüe *adj* monolingual.

monólogo *sm* monologue; TEATRO soliloquy.

monopatín *sm* skateboard.

monopolio *sm* monopoly.

monopolizar *vt lit & fig* to monopolize.

monosílabo, ba *adj* monosyllabic. *⇒* **monosílabo** *sm* monosyllable.

monotonía *sf* [uniformidad] monotony.

monótono, na *adj* monotonous.

monovolumen *sm* people carrier.

monseñor *sm* Monsignor.

monserga *sf fam* drivel *(U)*; **déjate de mon-sergas, no me vengas con monsergas** don't give me that rubbish.

monstruo *⇔ adj inv* [grande] enormous, monster *(antes de s)*. *⇔ sm* - **1.** [gen] monster - **2.** [prodigio] giant, marvel.

monstruosidad *sf* - **1.** [crueldad] monstros-ity, atrocity - **2.** [fealdad] hideousness - **3.** [ano-malía] freak.

monstruoso, sa *adj* - **1.** [cruel] monstrous - **2.** [feo] hideous - **3.** [enorme] huge, enormous - **4.** [deforme] terribly deformed.

monta *sf* [importancia] importance; **de poca monta** of little importance.

montacargas *sm inv* goods lift *UK*, freight elevator *US*.

montaje *sm* - 1. [de máquina] assembly - 2. TEATRO staging - 3. FOTO montage - 4. CINE editing - 5. [farsa] put-up job.

montante *sm* - 1. [ventanuco] fanlight - 2. [importe] total; **montantes compensatorios** COM compensating duties - 3. *loc:* **coger el montante** to go away, to leave.

montaña *sf lit & fig* mountain; **ir de excursión a la montaña** to go on a trip to the mountains; **montaña rusa** roller coaster; **hacer una montaña de un grano de arena** to make a mountain out of a molehill.

montañero, ra *sm, f* mountaineer.

montañismo *sm* mountaineering.

montañoso, sa *adj* mountainous.

montar ⬦ *vt* - 1. [ensamblar - máquina, estantería] to assemble; [- tienda de campaña, tenderete] to put up - 2. [encajar]: **montar algo en algo** to fit sthg into sthg - 3. [organizar - negocio, piso] to set up - 4. [cabalgar] to ride - 5. [poner encima]: **montar a alguien en** to lift sb onto - 6. [CULIN - nata] to whip; [- claras, yemas] to beat - 7. TEATRO to stage - 8. CINE to cut, to edit. ⬦ *vi* - 1. [subir] to get on; [en coche] to get in; **montar en** [gen] to get onto; [coche] to get into; [animal] to mount - 2. [ir montado] to ride; **montar en bicicleta/a caballo** to ride a bicycle/a horse. ➠ **montarse** *vprnl* [gen] to get on; [en coche] to get in; [en animal] to mount; **montarse en** [gen] to get onto; [coche] to get into; [animal] to mount.

monte *sm* [elevación] mountain; [terreno] woodland; **monte bajo** scrub; **no todo el monte es orégano** *prov* life's not a bowl of cherries. ➠ **monte de piedad** *sm* state pawnbroker's.

montepío *sm* mutual aid society.

montés *adj* wild.

montículo *sm* hillock.

monto *sm* total.

montón *sm* - 1. [pila] heap, pile; **a O en montón** everything together *O* at once; **del montón** ordinary, run-of-the-mill - 2. [muchos] loads; **un montón de** loads of.

montura *sf* - 1. [cabalgadura] mount - 2. [arreos] harness; [silla] saddle - 3. [soporte - de gafas] frame.

monumental *adj* - 1. [ciudad, lugar] famous for its monuments - 2. [fracaso etc] monumental.

monumento *sm* monument.

monzón *sm* monsoon.

moña *sf fam* [borrachera]: **coger una moña** to get smashed.

moño *sm* - 1. [de pelo] bun *(of hair)*; **agarrarse del moño** [pegarse] to pull each other's hair out; **estar hasta el moño (de)** to be sick to death (of) - 2. *Amér* [lazo] bow.

moquear *vi* to have a runny nose.

moqueta *sf* fitted carpet.

mora *sf* - 1. [de la zarzamora] blackberry - 2. [del moral] mulberry.

morada *sf culto* dwelling.

morado, da *adj* purple. ➠ **morado** *sm* [color] purple.

moral ⬦ *adj* moral. ⬦ *sf* - 1. [ética] morality - 2. [ánimo] morale.

moraleja *sf* moral.

moralizar *vi* to moralize.

morbo *sm fam* [placer malsano] morbid pleasure.

morboso, sa *adj* morbid.

morcilla *sf* CULIN ≃ black pudding *UK*, ≃ blood sausage *US*; **¡que te/os den morcilla!** *mfam* you can stuff it, then!

mordaz *adj* caustic, biting.

mordaza *sf* gag.

mordedura *sf* bite.

morder ⬦ *vt* - 1. [con los dientes] to bite - 2. [gastar] to eat into. ⬦ *vi* to bite; **estar que muerde** to be hopping mad. ➠ **morderse** *vprnl:* **morderse la lengua/las uñas** to bite one's tongue/nails.

mordida *sf Amér C & Méx fam* [soborno] bribe.

mordisco *sm* bite.

mordisquear *vt* to nibble (at).

moreno, na ⬦ *adj* - 1. [pelo, piel] dark; [por el sol] tanned; **ponerse moreno** to get a tan - 2. [pan, azúcar] brown. ⬦ *sm, f* [de pelo] dark-haired person; [de piel] dark-skinned person.

morera *sf* white mulberry.

moretón *sm* bruise.

morfina *sf* morphine.

moribundo, da *adj* dying.

morir *vi* - 1. [gen] to die; **morir de algo** to die of sthg - 2. [río, calle] to come out - 3. [fuego] to die down; [luz] to go out; [día] to come to a close. ➠ **morirse** *vprnl* - 1. [fallecer]: **morirse (de)** to die (of) - 2. [sentir con fuerza]: **morirse de envidia/ira** to be burning with envy/rage; **me muero de ganas de ir a bailar** I'm dying to go dancing; **me muero de hambre/frío** I'm starving/freezing; **morirse por algo** to be dying for sthg; **morirse por alguien** to be crazy about sb.

mormón, ona *adj & sm, f* Mormon.

moro, ra ⬦ *adj* HIST Moorish. ⬦ *sm, f* - 1. HIST Moor; **moros y cristianos** *traditional Spanish festival involving mock battle*

between Moors and Christians - **2.** [árabe] Arab
(N.B.: the term 'moro' is considered to be ra-
cist).

morocho, cha ⬦ *adj Andes & R Plata* [per-
sona] dark-haired; *Ven* [mellizo] twin. ⬦ *sm, f*
Andes & R Plata [moreno] dark-haired person;
Ven [mellizo] twin.

moroso, sa ⬦ *adj* COM defaulting. ⬦ *sm, f*
COM defaulter, bad debtor.

morrear *mfam vt & vi* to snog.

morriña *sf* [por el país de uno] homesickness;
[por el pasado] nostalgia.

morro *sm* - **1.** [hocico] snout - **2.** *fam* [de coche,
avión] nose.

morsa *sf* walrus.

morse *sm (en aposición invariable)* Morse
(code).

mortadela *sf* Mortadella.

mortaja *sf* shroud.

mortal ⬦ *adj* mortal; [caída, enfermedad]
fatal; [aburrimiento, susto, enemigo] deadly.
⬦ *smf* mortal.

mortalidad *sf* mortality.

mortandad *sf* mortality.

mortero *sm* mortar.

mortífero, ra *adj* deadly.

mortificar *vt* to mortify.

mosaico, ca *adj* Mosaic. ➤ **mosaico** *sm*
mosaic.

mosca *sf* fly; **no se oía ni una mosca** you
could have heard a pin drop; **por si las moscas**
just in case; **¿qué mosca te ha picado?** what's
up with you? ➤ **mosca muerta** *smf* sly-
boots.

moscardón *sm* ZOOL blowfly.

moscón *sm* ZOOL bluebottle.

moscovita *adj & smf* Muscovite.

mosquearse *vprnl fam* [enfadarse] to get
cross; [sospechar] to smell a rat.

mosquete *sm* musket.

mosquetero *sm* musketeer.

mosquitero *sm* mosquito net.

mosquito *sm* mosquito.

mosso d'Esquadra *sm* member of the
Catalan police force.

mostacho *sm* moustache.

mostaza *sf* mustard.

mosto *sm* [residuo] must; [zumo de uva] grape
juice.

mostrador *sm* [en tienda] counter; [en bar]
bar.

mostrar *vt* to show. ➤ **mostrarse** *vprnl* to
appear, to show o.s.; **se mostró muy interesado** he expressed great interest.

mota *sf* [de polvo] speck; [en tela] dot.

mote *sm* - **1.** nickname; **poner un mote a alguien** to nickname sb - **2.** *Andes* [maíz] stewed
maize *UK* O corn *US*.

motel *sm* motel.

motín *sm* [del pueblo] uprising, riot; [de las tro-
pas] mutiny.

motivación *sf* motive, motivation *(U)*.

motivar *vt* - **1.** [causar] to cause; [impulsar] to
motivate - **2.** [razonar] to explain, to justify.

motivo *sm* - **1.** [causa] reason, cause; [de cri-
men] motive; **bajo ningún motivo** under no
circumstances; **dar motivo a** to give reason to;
tener motivos para to have reason to - **2.** ARTE,
LITER & MÚS motif.

moto *sf* motorbike *UK*, motorcycle.

motocicleta *sf* motorbike, motorcycle.

motociclismo *sm* motorcycling.

motociclista *smf* motorcyclist.

motoneta *sf* *Amér* (motor) scooter.

motonetista *smf* *Amér* scooter rider.

motor, motora O **motriz** *adj* motor.
➤ **motor** *sm* - **1.** [aparato] motor, engine;
motor fuera borda outboard motor - **2.** [fuerza]
dynamic force. ➤ **motora** *sf* motorboat.

motorismo *sm* motorcycling.

motorista *smf* motorcyclist.

motriz ▷ **motor**.

mousse [mus] *sm inv* CULIN mousse.

movedizo, za *adj* [movible] movable, easily
moved.

mover *vt* - **1.** [gen & INFORM] to move; [mecáni-
camente] to drive - **2.** [cabeza - afirmativamente]
to nod; [- negativamente] to shake - **3.** [suscitar]
to provoke - **4.** *fig* [empujar]: **mover a alguien
a algo/a hacer algo** to drive sb to sthg/to do
sthg. ➤ **mover a** *vi* - **1.** [incitar] to incite to
- **2.** [causar] to provoke, to cause. ➤ **moverse** *vprnl* - **1.** [gen] to move; [en la cama] to toss
and turn - **2.** [darse prisa] to get a move on.

movido, da *adj* - **1.** [debate, torneo] lively;
[persona] active, restless; [jornada, viaje] hectic
- **2.** FOTO blurred, fuzzy. ➤ **movida** *sf fam*
[ambiente] scene; **la movida madrileña** *the
Madrid scene of the late 1970s*.

móvil ⬦ *adj* mobile, movable. ⬦ *sm*
- **1.** [motivo] motive - **2.** [juguete] mobile.

movilidad *sf* mobility.

movilizar *vt* to mobilize.

movimiento *sm* - **1.** [gen & POLÍT] movement; **movimiento obrero/pacifista** working-
class/pacifist movement - **2.** FÍS & TECNOL motion; **movimiento continuo/de rotación**
perpetual/rotational motion; **movimiento sísmico** earth tremor - **3.** [circulación - gen] activity; [- de personal, mercancías] turnover; [- de
vehículos] traffic - **4.** [MÚS - parte de la obra]
movement.

moviola *sf* editing projector.

moza ▷ **mozo**.

mozárabe ◇ *adj* Mozarabic. ◇ *sm* [lengua] Mozarabic.

mozo, za ◇ *adj* [joven] young; [soltero] single. ◇ *sm, f* - **1.** young boy (*f* young girl), young lad (*f* young lass) - **2.** *Andes & R Plata* [camarero] waiter (*f* waitress). ▸ **mozo** *sm* - **1.** [trabajador] assistant (worker); **mozo de cordel** O **de cuerda** porter; **mozo de estación** (station) porter - **2.** [recluta] conscript.

MP3 (*abrev de* MPEG-1 Audio Layer-3) *sm* IN-FORM MP3.

mu *sm* [mugido] moo; **no decir ni mu** not to say a word.

mucamo, ma *sm, f Andes & R Plata* [en casa] maid; [en hotel] chamberperson (*f* chambermaid).

muchacho, cha *sm, f* boy (*f* girl). ▸ **muchacha** *sf* [sirvienta] maid.

muchedumbre *sf* [de gente] crowd, throng; [de cosas] great number, masses *pl*.

mucho, cha ◇ *adj* - **1.** (*en sing*) [gran cantidad] a lot of; (*pl*) many, a lot of; (*en interrogativas y negativas*) much, a lot of; **tengo mucho sueño** I'm very sleepy; **muchos días** several days; **no tengo mucho tiempo** I haven't got much time - **2.** (*en sing*) [demasiado]: **hay mucho niño aquí** there are too many kids here. ◇ *pron* (*en sing*) a lot; (*en pl*) many, a lot; **tengo mucho que contarte** I have a lot to tell you; **¿queda dinero? - no mucho** is there any money left? - not much O not a lot; **muchos piensan igual** a lot of O many people think the same. ▸ **mucho** *adv* - **1.** [gen] a lot; **habla mucho** he talks a lot; **me canso mucho** I get really O very tired; **me gusta mucho** I like it a lot O very much; **no me gusta mucho** I don't like it much; **(no) mucho más tarde** (not) much later - **2.** [largo tiempo]: **hace mucho que no vienes** I haven't seen you for a long time; **¿dura mucho la obra?** is the play long?; **mucho antes/después** long before/after - **3.** [frecuentemente]: **¿vienes mucho por aquí?** do you come here often? - **4.** *loc*: **como mucho** at the most; **con mucho** by far, easily; **ni con mucho** not by a long chalk; **ni mucho menos** by no means; **no está ni mucho menos decidido** it is by no means decided. ▸ **por mucho que** *loc conj* no matter how much, however much; **por mucho que insistas** no matter how much O however much you insist.

mucosidad *sf* mucus.

muda *sf* [ropa interior] change of underwear.

mudanza *sf* move; **estar de mudanza** to be moving.

mudar ◇ *vt* - **1.** [gen] to change; [casa] to move; **cuando mude la voz** when his voice breaks - **2.** [piel, plumas] to moult. ◇ *vi* [cambiar]: **mudar de** [opinión, color] to change; [domicilio] to move. ▸ **mudarse** *vprnl*: **mudarse (de casa)** to move (house); **mudarse (de ropa)** to change.

mudéjar *adj & smf* Mudejar.

mudo, da *adj* - **1.** [sin habla] dumb - **2.** [callado] silent, mute; **se quedó mudo** he was left speechless - **3.** [sin sonido] silent.

mueble ◇ *sm* piece of furniture; **los muebles** the furniture (*U*); **salvar los muebles** to save face. ◇ *adj* ▷ **bien**.

mueca *sf* [gen] face, expression; [de dolor] grimace.

muela *sf* [diente - gen] tooth; [- molar] molar; **muela del juicio** wisdom tooth.

muelle *sm* - **1.** [de colchón, reloj] spring - **2.** [en el puerto] dock, quay; [en el río] wharf.

muera ▷ **morir**.

muérdago *sm* mistletoe.

muermo *sm fam* bore, drag.

muerte *sf* - **1.** [gen] death; **a muerte** to the death, to the bitter end; **un susto de muerte** a terrible shock; **muerte natural/violenta** natural/violent death; **muerte súbita** [de bebé] cot death; FÚT sudden death; [en tenis] tiebreak, tiebreaker; **estar de muerte** *fam* [comida] to be yummy; [persona] to be gorgeous - **2.** [homicidio] murder.

muerto, ta ◇ *pp* ▷ **morir**. ◇ *adj* - **1.** [gen] dead; **caer muerto** to drop dead; **estar muerto (de cansancio)** to be dead tired; **estar muerto de miedo/frío** to be scared/freezing to death - **2.** *loc*: **no tener donde caerse muerto** not to have a penny to one's name. ◇ *sm, f* dead person; [cadáver] corpse; **cargar con el muerto** [trabajo, tarea] to be left holding the baby; [culpa] to get the blame; **el muerto al hoyo y el vivo al bollo** *prov* dead men have no friends *prov*.

muesca *sf* - **1.** [concavidad] notch, groove - **2.** [corte] nick.

muestra *sf* - **1.** [pequeña cantidad] sample; **para muestra (basta) un botón** one example is enough - **2.** [señal] sign, show; [prueba] proof; [de cariño, aprecio] token - **3.** [modelo] model, pattern - **4.** [exposición] show, exhibition.

muestrario *sm* collection of samples.

muestreo *sm* sample; [acción] sampling.

mugido *sm* [de vaca] moo, mooing (*U*); [de toro] bellow, bellowing (*U*).

mugir *vi* [vaca] to moo; [toro] to bellow.

mugre *sf* filth, muck.

mugriento, ta *adj* filthy.

mujer *sf* woman; [cónyuge] wife; **mujer fatal** femme fatale; **mujer de la limpieza** cleaning lady.

mujeriego, ga *adj* fond of the ladies. ◆ **mujeriego** *sm* womanizer.

mujerzuela *sf* despec loose woman.

mulato, ta *adj* & *sm, f* mulatto.

muleta *sf* - **1.** [para andar] crutch; *fig* prop, support - **2.** TAUROM muleta *(red cape hanging from a stick used to tease the bull)*.

mullido, da *adj* soft, springy.

mulo, la *sm, f* ZOOL mule.

multa *sf* fine; **poner una multa a alguien** to fine sb.

multar *vt* to fine.

multiconfesional *adj* [sociedad, organización] multifaith.

multicopista *sf* duplicator.

multimedia *adj inv* INFORM multimedia.

multimillonario, ria *sm, f* multimillionaire.

multinacional *adj* & *sf* multinational.

múltiple *adj* [variado] multiple. ◆ **múltiples** *adj pl* [numerosos] many, numerous.

multiplicación *sf* multiplication.

multiplicar *vt* & *vi* to multiply. ◆ **multiplicarse** *vprnl* - **1.** [persona] to do lots of things at the same time - **2.** BIOL to multiply.

múltiplo, pla *adj* multiple. ◆ **múltiplo** *sm* multiple; **mínimo común múltiplo** lowest common multiple.

multitud *sf* [de personas] crowd; **una multitud de cosas** loads of O countless things.

multitudinario, ria *adj* extremely crowded; [manifestación] mass *(antes de s)*.

multiuso *adj inv* multipurpose.

mundanal *adj* worldly.

mundano, na *adj* - **1.** [del mundo] worldly, of the world - **2.** [de la vida social] (high) society.

mundial ◇ *adj* [política, economía, guerra] world *(antes de s)*; [tratado, organización, fama] worldwide. ◇ *sm* World Championships *pl*; [en fútbol] World Cup.

mundo *sm* - **1.** [gen] world; **el otro mundo** the next world, the hereafter; **irse al otro mundo** to pass away; **por nada del mundo** not for (all) the world; **se le cayó el mundo encima** his world fell apart; **todo el mundo** everyone, everybody; **venir al mundo** to come into the world, to be born - **2.** [experiencia]**: ver** O **correr mundo** to see life.

munición *sf* ammunition.

municipal ◇ *adj* town *(antes de s)*, municipal; [elecciones] local; [instalaciones] public. ◇ *smf* ▷ **guardia**.

municipio *sm* - **1.** [corporación] town council - **2.** [territorio] town, municipality.

muñeco, ca *sm, f* [juguete] doll; [marioneta] puppet; **muñeco de peluche** cuddly O soft toy; **muñeco de trapo** rag doll. ◆ **muñeco** *sm fig* puppet. ◆ **muñeca** *sf* - **1.** ANAT wrist - **2.** *Andes* & *R Dom fam* [enchufe]**: tener muñeco** to have friends in high places. ◆ **muñeco de nieve** *sm* snowman.

muñequera *sf* wristband.

muñón *sm* stump.

mural ◇ *adj* [pintura] mural; [mapa] wall. ◇ *sm* mural.

muralla *sf* wall.

murciélago *sm* bat.

murmullo *sm* [gen] murmur, murmuring *(U)*; [de hojas] rustle, rustling *(U)*; [de insectos] buzz, buzzing *(U)*.

murmuración *sf* gossip *(U)*.

murmurar ◇ *vt* to murmur. ◇ *vi* - **1.** [susurrar - persona] to murmur, to whisper; [- agua, viento] to murmur, to gurgle - **2.** [rezongar, quejarse] to grumble.

muro *sm lit* & *fig* wall; **muro de las lamentaciones** Wailing Wall.

mus *sm inv* card game played in pairs with bidding and in which players communicate by signs.

musa *sf* [inspiración] muse.

musaraña *sf* ZOOL shrew; **pensar en las musarañas** to have one's head in the clouds.

muscular *adj* muscular.

musculatura *sf* muscles *pl*.

músculo *sm* muscle.

musculoso, sa *adj* muscular.

museo *sm* museum.

musgo *sm* moss.

música ▷ **músico**.

músico, ca ◇ *adj* musical. ◇ *sm, f* [persona] musician; **músico callejero** street musician, busker. ◆ **música** *sf* music; **poner música a algo** to set sthg to music; **música ligera/pop** light/pop music; **música ambiental** background music.

musitar *vt* to mutter, to mumble.

muslo *sm* thigh; [de pollo] drumstick.

mustio, tia *adj* - **1.** [flor, planta] withered, wilted - **2.** [persona] gloomy.

musulmán, ana *adj* & *sm, f* Muslim.

mutación *sf* [cambio] sudden change; BIOL mutation.

mutante *adj* & *smf* mutant.

mutar *vt* to mutate.

mutilado, da *adj* mutilated.

mutilar *vt* [gen] to mutilate; [estatua] to deface.

mutismo *sm* [silencio] silence.

mutua ▷ **mutuo**.

mútualidad sf [asociación] mutual benefit society.

mutuo, tua adj mutual. ◆ **mutua** sf mutual benefit society.

muy adv - **1.** [mucho] very; **muy bueno/cerca** very good/near; **muy de mañana** very early in the morning; **¡muy bien!** [vale] OK!, all right!; **¡qué bien!** very good!, well done!; **es muy hombre** he's a real man; **eso es muy de ella** that's just like her; **eso es muy de los americanos** that's typically American; **¡el muy idiota!** what an idiot! - **2.** [demasiado] too; **es muy joven para votar** she's too young to vote.

n, N sf [letra] n, N. ◆ **N** sm - **1.** (abrev de **norte**) N - **2.**: **el 20 N** 20th November, the date of Franco's death.

nabo sm turnip.

nácar sm mother-of-pearl.

nacer vi - **1.** [venir al mundo - niño, animal] to be born; [- planta] to sprout; [- pájaro] to hatch (out); **nacer de familia humilde** to be born into a poor family; **nacer para algo** to be born to be sthg; **ha nacido cantante** she's a born singer; **volver a nacer** to have a lucky escape - **2.** [surgir - pelo] to grow; [- río] to rise; [- costumbre, actitud, duda] to have its roots.

nacido, da ◇ adj born. ◇ sm, f: **los nacidos hoy** those born today; **recién nacido** newborn baby; **ser un mal nacido** to be a wicked O vile person.

naciente adj - **1.** [día] dawning; [sol] rising - **2.** [gobierno, estado] new, fledgling; [interés] growing.

nacimiento sm - **1.** [gen] birth; [de planta] sprouting - **2.** [de río] source - **3.** [origen] origin, beginning - **4.** [belén] Nativity scene.

nación sf [gen] nation; [territorio] country. ◆ **Naciones Unidas** sfpl United Nations.

nacional adj national; [mercado, vuelo] domestic; [asuntos] home (antes de s).

nacionalidad sf nationality; **doble nacionalidad** dual nationality.

nacionalismo sm nationalism.

nacionalista adj & smf nationalist.

nacionalizar vt - **1.** [banca, bienes] to nationalize - **2.** [persona] to naturalize. ◆ **nacionalizarse** vprnl to become naturalized.

nada ◇ pron nothing; (en negativas) anything; **no he leído nada de este autor** I haven't read anything by this author; **no hay nada como un buen libro** there is nothing like a good book; **nada más** nothing else, nothing more; **no quiero nada más** I don't want anything else; **te he traído un regalito de nada** I've brought you a little something; **de nada** [respuesta a 'gracias'] you're welcome; **esto no es nada** that's nothing. ◇ adv - **1.** [en absoluto] at all; **la película no me ha gustado nada** I didn't like the film at all; **no es nada extraño** it's not at all strange - **2.** [poco] a little, a bit; **no hace nada que salió** he left just a minute ago; **nada menos que** [cosa] no less than; [persona] none other than. ◇ sf: **la nada** nothingness, the void; **salir de la nada** to appear out of O from nowhere. ◆ **nada más** loc conj no sooner, as soon as; **nada más salir de casa se puso a llover** no sooner had I left the house than it started to rain, as soon as I left the house, it started to rain.

nadador, ra sm, f swimmer.

nadar vi [gen] to swim; [flotar] to float.

nadería sf trifle, little thing.

nadie pron nobody, no one; **casi nadie** hardly anybody; **no se lo dije a nadie** I didn't tell anybody; **no ha llamado nadie** nobody phoned.

nado ◆ **a nado** loc adv swimming.

náhuatl ◇ adj Nahuatl. ◇ smf Nahuatl (Indian).

naïf [na'if] adj naïve, primitivistic.

nailon, nilón, nylon® sm nylon.

naipe sm (playing) card. ◆ **naipes** smpl cards.

nalga sf buttock.

nana sf - **1.** [canción] lullaby - **2.** Col & Méx [niñera] nanny.

nanómetro sm nanometre.

naranja ◇ adj inv orange. ◇ sm [color] orange. ◇ sf [fruto] orange. ◆ **media naranja** sf fam other O better half.

naranjo sm [árbol] orange tree.

narciso sm BOT narcissus.

narcótico, ca adj narcotic. ◆ **narcótico** sm narcotic; [droga] drug.

narcotizar vt to drug.

narcotraficante smf drug trafficker.

narcotráfico sm drug trafficking.

nardo sm nard, spikenard.

narigudo, da adj big-nosed.

nariz sf - 1. [órgano] nose; **hablar por la nariz** to talk through one's nose; **tener la nariz tapada** to have a stuffed up O blocked nose - 2. [orificio] nostril - 3. [olfato] sense of smell - 4. loc: **de narices** fam [estupendo] great, brilliant; **estar hasta las narices (de algo)** fam to be fed up to the back teeth (with sthg); **meter las narices en algo** fam to poke O stick one's nose into sthg.

narración sf - 1. [cuento, relato] narrative, story - 2. [acción] narration.

narrador, ra sm, f narrator.

narrar vt [contar] to recount, to tell.

narrativo, va adj narrative. ◆ **narrativa** sf narrative.

nasal adj nasal.

nata sf - 1. fig [gen] cream; **nata batida** O **montada** whipped cream - 2. [de leche hervida] skin.

natación sf swimming.

natal adj [país] native; [ciudad, pueblo] home (antes de s).

natalidad sf birth rate.

natillas sfpl custard (U).

nativo, va adj & sm, f native.

nato, ta adj [gen] born; [cargo, título] ex officio.

natural ◇ adj - 1. [gen] natural; [flores, fruta, leche] fresh; **soy rubia natural** I'm a natural blonde; **al natural** [persona] in one's natural state; [fruta] in its own juice; **ser natural en alguien** to be natural O normal for sb - 2. [nativo] native; **ser natural de** to come from. ◇ smf [nativo] native. ◇ sm [talante] nature, disposition.

naturaleza sf - 1. [gen] nature; **por naturaleza** by nature - 2. [complexión] constitution.

naturalidad sf naturalness; **con naturalidad** naturally.

naturalizar vt to naturalize. ◆ **naturalizarse** vprnl to become naturalized.

naturista smf person favouring return to nature.

naufragar vi [barco] to sink, to be wrecked; [persona] to be shipwrecked.

naufragio sm [de barco] shipwreck.

náufrago, ga sm, f castaway.

náusea (gen pl) sf nausea (U), sickness (U); **me da náuseas** it makes me sick; **tener náuseas** to feel nauseated, to feel sick.

nauseabundo, da adj nauseating.

náutico, ca adj [gen] nautical; DEP water (antes de s). ◆ **náutica** sf navigation, seamanship.

navaja sf - 1. [cuchillo - pequeño] penknife; [- más grande] jackknife - 2. [molusco] razorshell.

navajero, ra sm, f thug who carries a knife.

naval adj naval.

Navarra n pr Navarre.

navarro, rra adj & sm, f Navarrese.

nave sf - 1. [barco] ship; **quemar las naves** to burn one's boats O bridges - 2. [vehículo] craft; **nave espacial** spaceship - 3. [de fábrica] shop, plant; [almacén] warehouse - 4. [de iglesia] nave.

navegación sf navigation.

navegador sm INFORM browser.

navegante smf navigator.

navegar ◇ vi [barco] to sail; [avión] to fly; **navegar por Internet** INFORM to surf the Net. ◇ vt [barco] to sail; [avión] to fly.

Navidad sf - 1. [día] Christmas (Day) - 2. (gen pl) [periodo] Christmas (time); **felices Navidades** Merry Christmas.

navideño, ña adj Christmas (antes de s).

naviero, ra adj shipping. ◆ **naviero** sm [armador] shipowner. ◆ **naviera** sf [compañía] shipping company.

navío sm large ship.

nazi adj & smf Nazi.

nazismo sm Nazism.

neblina sf mist.

nebuloso, sa adj - 1. [con nubes] cloudy; [de niebla] foggy - 2. [mirada, mirada] vague. ◆ **nebulosa** sf ASTRON nebula.

necedad sf - 1. [estupidez] stupidity, foolishness - 2. [dicho, hecho] stupid O foolish thing; **decir necedades** to talk nonsense.

necesario, ria adj necessary; **un mal necesario** a necessary evil; **es necesario hacerlo** it needs to be done; **no es necesario que lo hagas** you don't need to do it; **si fuera necesario** if need be.

neceser sm toilet bag O case.

necesidad sf - 1. [gen] need; **tener necesidad de algo** to need sthg; **hacer de la necesidad virtud** to make a virtue of necessity; **la necesidad aguza el ingenio** prov necessity is the mother of invention prov - 2. [obligación] necessity; **por necesidad** out of necessity - 3. [hambre] hunger. ◆ **necesidades** sfpl: **hacer (uno) sus necesidades** eufem to answer the call of nature.

necesitado, da ◇ adj needy. ◇ sm, f needy O poor person; **los necesitados** the poor.

necesitar vt to need; **necesito que me lo digas** I need you to tell me; **'se necesita piso'** 'flat wanted'. ◆ **necesitar de** vi to have need of.

necio, cia adj stupid, foolish; Méx [fastidioso] boring.

necrología sf obituary; [lista de esquelas] obituary column.

néctar sm nectar.

nectarina sf nectarine.

nefasto, ta adj [funesto] ill-fated; [dañino] bad, harmful; [pésimo] terrible, awful.

negación sf - **1.** [desmentido] denial - **2.** [negativa] refusal - **3.** [lo contrario] antithesis, negation - **4.** GRAM negative.

negado, da adj useless.

negar vt - **1.** [rechazar] to deny - **2.** [denegar] to refuse, to deny; **negarle algo a alguien** to refuse O deny sb sthg. ► **negarse** vprnl: **negarse (a)** to refuse (to).

negativo, va adj [gen] negative. ► **negativo** sm FOTO negative. ► **negativa** sf - **1.** [rechazo] refusal; **una negativa rotunda** a flat refusal - **2.** [mentís] denial.

negligencia sf negligence.

negligente adj negligent.

negociable adj negotiable.

negociación sf negotiation.

negociante sm, f [comerciante] businessman (f businesswoman).

negociar vi - **1.** [comerciar] to do business; **negociar con** to deal O trade with - **2.** [discutir] to negotiate. ◇ vt to negotiate.

negocio sm - **1.** [gen] business; **el mundo de los negocios** the business world - **2.** [transacción] deal, (business) transaction; **negocio sucio** shady deal, dirty business (U) - **3.** [operación ventajosa] good deal, bargain; **hacer negocio** to do well - **4.** [comercio] trade.

negra sf ▷ **negro**.

negrero, ra sm, f - **1.** HIST slave trader - **2.** [explotador] slave driver.

negrita, negrilla ▷ **letra**.

negro, gra ◇ adj - **1.** [gen] black - **2.** [furioso] furious; **ponerse negro** to get mad O angry - **3.** CINE: **cine negro** film noir. ◇ sm, f black man (f black woman). ► **negro** sm [color] black. ► **negra** sf - **1.** MÚS crotchet - **2.** loc: **tener la negra** fam to have bad luck.

negrura sf blackness.

nene, na sm, f fam [niño] baby.

nenúfar sm water lily.

neocelandés, esa = **neozelandés**.

neologismo sm neologism.

neón sm QUÍM neon.

neoyorquino, na ◇ adj New York (antes de s), of/relating to New York. ◇ sm, f New Yorker.

neozelandés, esa, **neocelandés, esa** sm, f New Zealander.

Nepal n pr: **el Nepal** Nepal.

Neptuno n pr Neptune.

nervio sm - **1.** ANAT nerve; **nervio óptico** optic nerve - **2.** [de carne] sinew - **3.** [vigor] energy, vigour; **sus niños son puro nervio** her kids never sit still for five minutes. ► **nervios** smpl [estado mental] nerves; **tener nervios** to be nervous; **poner los nervios de punta a alguien** to get on sb's nerves; **tener los nervios de punta** to be on edge.

nerviosismo sm nervousness, nerves pl.

nervioso, sa adj - **1.** [ANAT - sistema, enfermedad] nervous; [- tejido, célula, centro] nerve (antes de s) - **2.** [inquieto] nervous; **ponerse nervioso** to get nervous - **3.** [irritado] worked-up; **ponerse nervioso** to get uptight O worked up.

nervudo, da adj sinewy.

netiqueta sf INFORM netiquette.

neto, ta adj - **1.** [claro] clear, clean; [verdad] simple, plain - **2.** [peso, sueldo] net.

neumático, ca adj pneumatic. ► **neumático** sm tyre; **neumático de repuesto** spare tyre.

neumonía sf pneumonia.

neurálgico, ca adj - **1.** MED neuralgic - **2.** [importante] critical.

neurastenia sf nervous exhaustion.

neurología sf neurology.

neurólogo, ga sm, f neurologist.

neurona sf neuron, nerve cell.

neurosis sf inv neurosis.

neurótico, ca adj & sm, f neurotic.

neutral adj & smf neutral.

neutralidad sf neutrality.

neutralizar vt to neutralize.

neutro, tra adj - **1.** [gen] neutral - **2.** BIOL & GRAM neuter.

neutrón sm neutron.

nevado, da adj snowy. ► **nevada** sf snowfall.

nevar v impers to snow.

nevera sf fridge UK, icebox US.

nevería sf Caribe & Méx [heladería] ice cream parlour.

nevisca sf snow flurry.

nexo sm link, connection; [relación] relation, connection.

ni ◇ conj: **ni... ni...** neither... nor...; **ni mañana ni pasado** neither tomorrow nor the day after; **no... ni...** neither... nor..., not... or... (either); **no es alto ni bajo** he's neither tall nor short, he's not tall or short (either); **no es rojo ni verde ni azul** it's neither red nor green nor blue; **ni un/una...** not a single...; **no me quedaré ni un minuto más** I'm not staying a minute longer; **ni uno/una** not a single one; **no he aprobado ni una** I haven't passed a single one; **ni que** as if; **¡ni que yo fuera tonto!** as if I were that stupid! ◇ adv not even; **an-**

da tan atareado que ni tiene tiempo para comer he's so busy he doesn't even have time
to eat.

Nicaragua *n pr* Nicaragua.

nicaragüense *adj & smf* Nicaraguan.

nicho *sm* niche; **nicho ecológico** ecological
niche.

nicotina *sf* nicotine.

nido *sm* [gen] nest.

niebla *sf* [densa] fog; [neblina] mist; **hay niebla**
it's foggy.

nieto, ta *sm, f* grandson (*f* granddaughter).

nieve *sf* - 1. METEOR snow - 2. CULIN: **a punto de
nieve** beaten stiff - 3. *Caribe & Méx* [granizado]
drink of flavoured crushed ice. ❧ **nieves** *sfpl*
[nevada] snows, snowfall *sing*.

NIF (*abrev de* número de identificación fiscal)
sm ≃ National Insurance number *UK*.

Nilo *sm*: **el Nilo** the (river) Nile.

nilón = **nailon**.

nimiedad *sf* - 1. [cualidad] insignificance, triviality - 2. [dicho, hecho] trifle.

nimio, mia *adj* insignificant, trivial.

ninfa *sf* nymph.

ninfómana *sf* nymphomaniac.

ninguno, na ⟨⟩ *adj (antes de sm:* **ningún**)
no; **no dieron ninguna respuesta** no answer
was given; **no tengo ningún interés en hacerlo**
I've no interest in doing it, I'm not at all interested in doing it; **no tengo ningún hijo/nin-
guna buena idea** I don't have any children/
good ideas; **no tiene ninguna gracia** it's not
funny. ⟨⟩ *pron* [cosa] none, not any; [perso-
na] nobody, no one; **ninguno funciona** none
of them works; **no hay ninguno** there aren't
any, there are none; **ninguno lo sabrá** no one
O nobody will know; **ninguno de** none of;
ninguno de ellos none of them; **ninguno de
los dos** neither of them.

niña ▷ **niño**.

niñería *sf* - 1. [cualidad] childishness (*U*)
- 2. [tontería] silly O childish thing.

niñero, ra *adj* fond of children. ❧ **niñera**
sf nanny.

niñez *sf* childhood.

niño, ña ⟨⟩ *adj* young. ⟨⟩ *sm, f* [crío] child,
boy (*f* girl); [bebé] baby; **los niños** the children;
niño prodigio child prodigy; **ser el niño bonito
de alguien** to be sb's pet O blue-eyed boy.
❧ **niña** *sf* [del ojo] pupil.

nipón, ona *adj & sm, f* Japanese.

níquel *sm* nickel.

niquelar *vt* to nickel-plate.

niqui *sm* T-shirt.

níspero *sm* medlar.

nitidez *sf* clarity; [de imágenes, colores] sharpness.

nítido, da *adj* clear; [imágenes, colores] sharp.

nitrato *sm* nitrate.

nitrógeno *sm* nitrogen.

nivel *sm* - 1. [gen] level; [altura] height; **al nivel
de** level with; **al nivel del mar** at sea level;
nivel del agua water level - 2. [grado] level,
standard; **al mismo nivel (que)** on a level O par
(with); **a nivel europeo** at a European level;
nivel de vida standard of living; **niveles de audiencia** ratings.

nivelador, ra *adj* levelling. ❧ **niveladora**
sf bulldozer.

nivelar *vt* - 1. [allanar] to level - 2. [equilibrar]
to even out; FIN to balance.

no ⟨⟩ *adv* - 1. [expresa negación - gen] not;
[- en respuestas] no; [- con sustantivos] non-; **no
sé** I don't know; **no veo nada** I can't see anything; **no es fácil** it's not easy, it isn't easy; **no
tiene dinero** he has no money, he hasn't got
any money; **todavía no** not yet; **¿no vienes?** -
no, no creo aren't you coming? - no, I don't
think so; **no fumadores** non-smokers; **no bien**
as soon as; **no ya... sino que...** not only... but
(also)...; **¡a que no lo haces!** I bet you don't do
it!; **¿cómo no?** of course; **pues no, eso sí que
no** certainly not; **¡que no!** I said no! - 2. [expre-
sa duda, extrañeza]: **¿no irás a venir?** you're not
coming, are you?; **estamos de acuerdo, ¿no?**
we're agreed then, are we?; **es español, ¿no?**
he's Spanish, isn't he? ⟨⟩ *sm* no.

n.º (*abrev de* número) no.

nobiliario, ria *adj* noble.

noble *adj & smf* noble; **los nobles** the nobility.

nobleza *sf* nobility.

noche *sf* night; [atardecer] evening; **al caer la
noche** at nightfall; **ayer por la noche** last
night; **esta noche** tonight; **hacer noche en** to
stay the night in; **hacerse de noche** to get
dark; **por la noche, de noche** at night; **buenas
noches** [despedida] good night; [saludo] good
evening; **noche cerrada** dark night; **noche de
bodas** wedding night; **noche del estreno** first
O opening night; **noche toledana** sleepless
night; **de la noche a la mañana** overnight.

Nochebuena *sf* Christmas Eve.

nochero *sm* - 1. *C Sur* night watchman
- 2. *Amér* [mesita] bedside table.

Nochevieja *sf* New Year's Eve.

noción *sf* [concepto] notion; **tener noción (de)**
to have an idea (of). ❧ **nociones** *sfpl* [cono-
cimiento básico]: **tener nociones de** to have a
smattering of.

nocivo, va *adj* [gen] harmful; [gas] noxious.

noctámbulo, la *sm, f* night owl.

nocturno, na *adj* - 1. [club, tren, vuelo] night
(*antes de s*); [clase] evening (*antes de s*) - 2. [ani-
males, plantas] nocturnal.

nodriza *sf* wet nurse.

nómada ◇ *adj* nomadic. ◇ *smf* nomad.

nombramiento *sm* appointment.

nombrar *vt* - **1.** [citar] to mention - **2.** [designar] to appoint.

nombre *sm* - **1.** [gen] name; **conocer a alguien de nombre** to know somebody by name; **poner nombre a** to name; **sin nombre** nameless; **nombre artístico/comercial** stage/trade name; **nombre y apellidos** full name; **nombre compuesto** compound name; **nombre de dominio** [inform] domain name; **nombre de pila** first O Christian name; **nombre de soltera** maiden name; **en nombre de** on behalf of; **lo que hizo no tiene nombre** what he did is outrageous - **2.** [fama] reputation; **hacerse un nombre** to make a name for o.s.; **tener mucho nombre** to be renowned O famous - **3.** GRAM noun; **nombre abstracto/colectivo** abstract/collective noun.

nomenclatura *sf* nomenclature.

nómina *sf* - **1.** [lista de empleados] payroll - **2.** [hoja de salario] payslip.

nominal *adj* nominal.

nominar *vt* to nominate.

nomo, gnomo *sm* gnome.

non *sm* odd number. ◆ **nones** *adv* [no] no way.

nonagésimo, ma *num* ninetieth.

nordeste = **noreste**.

nórdico, ca *adj* - **1.** [del norte] northern, northerly - **2.** [escandinavo] Nordic.

noreste, nordeste ◇ *adj* [posición, parte] northeast, northeastern; [dirección, viento] northeasterly. ◇ *sm* north-east.

noria *sf* - **1.** [para agua] water wheel - **2.** [de feria] big wheel *UK*, Ferris wheel.

norma *sf* standard; [regla] rule; **es la norma hacerlo así** it's usual to do it this way; **tener por norma hacer algo** to make it a rule to do sthg; **normas de seguridad** safety regulations.

normal *adj* normal; **normal y corriente** run-of-the-mill; **es una persona normal y corriente** he's a perfectly ordinary person.

normalidad *sf* normality.

normalizar *vt* - **1.** [volver normal] to return to normal - **2.** [estandarizar] to standardize. ◆ **normalizarse** *vprnl* to return to normal.

normativo, va *adj* normative. ◆ **normativa** *sf* regulations *pl*.

noroeste ◇ *adj* [posición, parte] northwest, northwestern; [dirección, viento] northwesterly. ◇ *sm* northwest.

norte ◇ *adj* [posición, parte] north, northern; [dirección, viento] northerly. ◇ *sm* GEOGR north.

norteamericano, na *adj* & *sm, f* North American, American.

Noruega *n pr* Norway.

noruego, ga *adj* & *sm, f* Norwegian. ◆ **noruego** *sm* [lengua] Norwegian.

nos *pron pers* - **1.** *(complemento directo)* us; **le gustaría vernos** she'd like to see us - **2.** *(complemento indirecto)* (to) us; **nos lo dio** he gave it to us; **nos tiene miedo** he's afraid of us - **3.** *(reflexivo)* ourselves - **4.** *(recíproco)* each other; **nos enamoramos** we fell in love (with each other).

nosocomio *sm Amér* hospital.

nosotros, tras *pron pers* - **1.** *(sujeto)* we - **2.** *(predicado)*: **somos nosotros** it's us - **3.** *(después de prep,complemento)* us; **vente a comer con nosotros** come and eat with us - **4.** *loc*: **entre nosotros** between you and me, just between the two of us.

nostalgia *sf* [del pasado] nostalgia; [de país, amigos] homesickness.

nota *sf* - **1.** [gen & MÚS] note; **tomar nota de algo** [apuntar] to note sthg down; [fijarse] to take note of sthg; **tomar notas** to take notes; **nota al margen** marginal note; **nota dominante** prevailing mood - **2.** EDUC mark - **3.** [cuenta] bill - **4.** *loc*: **dar la nota** to make o.s. conspicuous.

notable ◇ *adj* remarkable, outstanding. ◇ *sm* EDUC merit, second class.

notar *vt* - **1.** [advertir] to notice; **te noto cansado** you look tired to me; **hacer notar algo** to point sthg out - **2.** [sentir] to feel; **noto un dolor raro** I can feel a strange pain. ◆ **notarse** *vprnl* to be apparent; **se nota que le gusta** you can tell she likes it.

notaría *sf* [oficina] notary's office.

notario, ria *sm, f* notary (public).

noticia *sf* news *(U)*; **una noticia** a piece of news; **¿tienes noticias suyas?** have you heard from him?; **noticia bomba** *fam* bombshell. ◆ **noticias** *sfpl*: **las noticias** RADIO & TV the news.

notificación *sf* notification.

notificar *vt* to notify, to inform.

notoriedad *sf* [fama] fame.

notorio, ria *adj* - **1.** [evidente] obvious - **2.** [conocido] widely-known.

novato, ta ◇ *adj* inexperienced. ◇ *sm, f* novice, beginner.

novecientos, tas *num* nine hundred; *ver también* **seis**.

novedad *sf* - **1.** [cualidad - de nuevo] newness; [- de novedoso] novelty - **2.** [cambio] change - **3.** [noticia] news *(U)*; **sin novedad** without incident; MIL all quiet. ◆ **novedades** *sfpl* [libros, discos] new releases; [moda] latest fashion *sing*.

novedoso, sa *adj* novel, new.

novel *adj* new, first-time.

novela *sf* novel; **novela policíaca** detective story.

novelesco, ca *adj* - **1**. [de la novela] fictional - **2**. [fantástico] fantastic.

novelista *smf* novelist.

noveno, na *num* ninth.

noventa *num* ninety; **los (años) noventa** the nineties; *ver también* **seis**.

noviar *vi* C Sur & Méx: **noviar con alguien** to go out with sb, to date sb *US*; **están noviando** they are going out together, they are dating *US*.

noviazgo *sm* engagement.

noviembre *sm* November; *ver también* **septiembre**.

novillada *sf* TAUROM bullfight with young bulls.

novillo, lla *sm, f* young bull or cow; **hacer novillos** *fam* to play truant *UK*, to play hooky *US*.

novio, via *sm, f* - **1**. [compañero] boyfriend (*f* girlfriend) - **2**. [prometido] fiancé (*f* fiancée) - **3**. [recién casado] bridegroom (*f* bride); **los novios** the newly-weds.

nubarrón *sm* storm cloud.

nube *sf* - **1**. *fig* [gen] cloud; **nube atómica** mushroom cloud; **nube de tormenta** thundercloud - **2**. [de personas, moscas] swarm - **3**. *loc*: **poner algo/a alguien por las nubes** to praise sthg/sb to the skies; **por las nubes** [caro] skyhigh, terribly expensive.

nublado, da *adj* - **1**. [encapotado] cloudy, overcast - **2**. *fig* [turbado] clouded.

nublar *vt* *lit & fig* to cloud. ➡ **nublarse** *vprnl* to cloud over.

nubosidad *sf* cloudiness, clouds *pl*.

nuca *sf* nape, back of the neck.

nuclear *adj* nuclear.

núcleo *sm* - **1**. [centro] nucleus; *fig* centre *UK*, center *US*; **núcleo de población** population centre *UK*, population center *US* - **2**. [grupo] core.

nudillo *sm* knuckle.

nudismo *sm* nudism.

nudo *sm* - **1**. [gen] knot; **se le hizo un nudo en la garganta** she got a lump in her throat - **2**. [cruce] junction - **3**. [vínculo] tie, bond - **4**. [punto principal] crux.

nudoso, sa *adj* knotty, gnarled.

nuera *sf* daughter-in-law.

nuestro, tra ◇ *adj poses* our; **nuestro coche** our car; **este libro es nuestro** this book is ours, this is our book; **un amigo nuestro** a friend of ours; **no es asunto nuestro** it's none of our business. ◇ *pron poses*: **el nuestro** ours; **el nuestro es rojo** ours is red; **ésta es la**

nuestra *fam* this is the chance we have been waiting for; **lo nuestro es el teatro** [lo que nos va] theatre is what we should be doing; **los nuestros** *fam* [nuestra familia] our folk; [nuestro bando] our lot, our side.

nueva ▷ **nuevo**.

Nueva York *n pr* New York.

Nueva Zelanda *n pr* New Zealand.

nueve *num* nine; *ver también* **seis**.

nuevo, va ◇ *adj* [gen] new; [patatas, legumbres] new, fresh; [vino] young; **esto es nuevo para mí, no lo sabía** that's news to me, I didn't know it; **ser nuevo en** to be new to; **estar/quedar como nuevo** to be as good as new. ◇ *sm, f* newcomer. ➡ **buena nueva** *sf* good news (*U*). ➡ **de nuevo** *loc adv* again.

nuez *sf* - **1**. BOT [gen] nut; [de nogal] walnut - **2**. ANAT Adam's apple. ➡ **nuez moscada** *sf* nutmeg.

nulidad *sf* - **1**. [no validez] nullity - **2**. [ineptitud] incompetence.

nulo, la *adj* - **1**. [sin validez] null and void - **2**. *fam* [incapacitado]: **nulo (para)** useless (at).

núm. (*abrev de* **número**) No.

numeración *sf* - **1**. [acción] numbering - **2**. [sistema] numerals *pl*, numbers *pl*.

numeral *adj* numeral.

numerar *vt* to number.

numérico, ca *adj* numerical.

número *sm* - **1**. [gen] number; **número de matrícula** AUTO registration number; **número de serie** serial number; **número de teléfono** telephone number; **número redondo** round number; **en números rojos** in the red; **hacer números** to reckon up - **2**. [tamaño, talla] size - **3**. [de publicación] issue; **número atrasado** back number - **4**. [de lotería] ticket - **5**. [de un espectáculo] turn, number; **montar el número** *fam* to make O cause a scene.

numeroso, sa *adj* numerous; **un grupo numeroso** a large group.

nunca *adv* (*en frases afirmativas*) never; (*en frases negativas*) ever; **casi nunca viene** he almost never comes, he hardly ever comes; **¿nunca le has visto?** have you never seen her?, haven't you ever seen her?; **más que nunca** more than ever; **nunca jamás** O **más** never more O again.

nuncio *sm* nuncio.

nupcial *adj* wedding (*antes de s*).

nupcias *sfpl* wedding *sing*, nuptials; **casarse en segundas nupcias** to remarry, to marry again.

nutria *sf* otter.

nutrición *sf* nutrition.

nutricionista *smf* Amér dietician.

nutrido, da *adj* - **1.** [alimentado] nourished; mal nutrido undernourished - **2.** [numeroso] large.

nutrir *vt* - **1.** [alimentar]: **nutrir (con** O **de)** to nourish O feed (with) - **2.** [fomentar] to feed, to nurture - **3.** [suministrar]: **nutrir (de)** to supply (with). ➡ **nutrirse** *vprnl* - **1.** [gen]: **nutrirse de** O **con** to feed on - **2.** [proveerse]: **nutrirse de** O **con** to supply O provide o.s. with.

nutritivo, va *adj* nutritious.

nylon® ['nailon] = **nailon**.

ñ, Ñ *sf* [letra] ñ, Ñ.

ñato, ta *adj* Andes & R Plata snub-nosed.

ñoñería, ñoñez *sf* inanity, insipidness *(U)*.

ñoño, ña *adj* - **1.** [remilgado] squeamish; [quejica] whining - **2.** [soso] dull, insipid.

ñudo *Amér* ➡ **al ñudo** *loc adv* in vain.

o¹ *(pl* **oes), O** *(pl* **Oes)** *sf* [letra] o, O.

o² *conj* or; **o... o** either... or; **o sea (que)** in other words.

O *sm (abrev de oeste)* W.

o/ *abrev de* **orden**.

oasis *sm inv* lit & fig oasis.

obcecar *vt* to blind. ➡ **obcecarse** *vprnl* to become stubborn; **obcecarse en hacer algo** to insist on doing sthg.

obedecer ◇ *vt*: **obedecer (a alguien)** to obey (sb). ◇ *vi* - **1.** [acatar] to obey; **hacerse**

obedecer to command obedience - **2.** [someterse]: **obedecer a** to respond to - **3.** [estar motivado]: **obedecer a** to be due to.

obediencia *sf* obedience.

obediente *adj* obedient.

obertura *sf* overture.

obesidad *sf* obesity.

obeso, sa *adj* obese.

óbice *sm*: **no ser óbice para** not to be an obstacle to.

obispo *sm* bishop.

objeción *sf* objection; **poner objeciones a** to raise objections to; **tener objeciones** to have objections; **objeción de conciencia** conscientious objection.

objetar *vt* to object to; **no tengo nada que objetar** I have no objection.

objetivo, va *adj* objective. ➡ **objetivo** *sm* - **1.** [finalidad] objective, aim - **2.** MIL target - **3.** FOTO lens.

objeto *sm* - **1.** [gen] object; **ser objeto de** to be the object of; **objeto volante no identificado** unidentified flying object; **objetos de valor** valuables; **objetos perdidos** lost property *(U)* - **2.** [propósito] purpose, object; **sin objeto** [inútilmente] to no purpose, pointlessly; **al** O **con objeto de** [para] in order to.

objetor, ra *sm, f* objector; **objetor de conciencia** conscientious objector.

oblicuo, cua *adj* [inclinado] oblique; [mirada] sidelong.

obligación *sf* - **1.** [gen] obligation, duty; **por obligación** out of a sense of duty - **2.** *(gen pl)* FIN bond, security.

obligar *vt*: **obligar a alguien (a hacer algo)** to oblige O force sb (to do sthg). ➡ **obligarse** *vprnl*: **obligarse a hacer algo** to undertake to do sthg.

obligatorio, ria *adj* obligatory, compulsory.

oboe *sm* [instrumento] oboe.

obra *sf* - **1.** [gen] work *(U)*; **es obra suya** it's his doing; **poner en obra** to put into effect; **obra de caridad** [institución] charity; **obras sociales** community work *(U)*; **por obra (y gracia) de** thanks to; **obras son amores y no buenas razones** *prov* actions speak louder than words *prov* - **2.** ARTE work (of art); TEATRO play; LITER book; MÚS opus; **obra maestra** masterpiece; **obras completas** complete works - **3.** CONSTR [lugar] building site; [reforma] alteration; **'obras'** [en carretera] 'roadworks'; **obras públicas** public works.

obrar ◇ *vi* - **1.** [actuar] to act - **2.** [causar efecto] to work, to take effect - **3.** [estar en poder]: **obrar en manos de** to be in the possession of. ◇ *vt* to work.

obrero, ra ⬦ *adj* [clase] working; [movimiento] labour *(antes de s)*. ⬦ *sm, f* [en fábrica] worker; [en obra] workman; **obrero cualificado** skilled worker.

obscenidad *sf* obscenity.

obsceno, na *adj* obscene.

obscurecer = **oscurecer**.

obscuridad = **oscuridad**.

obscuro, ra = **oscuro**.

obsequiar *vt*: **obsequiar a alguien con algo** to present sb with sthg.

obsequio *sm* gift, present.

observación *sf* - **1.** [gen] observation; **en O bajo observación** under observation - **2.** [comentario] remark, observation; **hacer una observación** to make a remark - **3.** [nota] note - **4.** [cumplimiento] observance.

observador, ra ⬦ *adj* observant. ⬦ *sm, f* observer.

observar *vt* - **1.** [contemplar] to observe, to watch - **2.** [advertir] to notice, to observe - **3.** [acatar - ley, normas] to observe; [- conducta, costumbre] to follow. ➤ **observarse** *vprnl* to be noticed.

observatorio *sm* observatory.

obsesión *sf* obsession.

obsesionar *vt* to obsess. ➤ **obsesionarse** *vprnl* to be obsessed.

obsesivo, va *adj* obsessive.

obseso, sa ⬦ *adj* obsessed. ⬦ *sm, f* obsessed O obsessive person.

obstaculizar *vt* to hinder, to hamper.

obstáculo *sm* obstacle; **un obstáculo para an** obstacle to; **poner obstáculos a algo/alguien** to hinder sthg/sb.

obstante ➤ **no obstante** *loc adv* nevertheless, however.

obstetricia *sf* obstetrics *(U)*.

obstinado, da *adj* [persistente] persistent; [terco] obstinate, stubborn.

obstinarse *vprnl* to refuse to give way; **obstinarse en** to persist in.

obstrucción *sf lit & fig* obstruction.

obstruir *vt* - **1.** [bloquear] to block, to obstruct - **2.** [obstaculizar] to obstruct, to impede. ➤ **obstruirse** *vprnl* to get blocked (up).

obtener *vt* [beca, cargo, puntos] to get; [premio, victoria] to win; [ganancias] to make; [satisfacción] to gain.

obturar *vt* to block.

obtuso, sa *adj* - **1.** [sin punta] blunt - **2.** [tonto] obtuse, stupid.

obús *(pl* obuses*) sm* [proyectil] shell.

obviar *vt* to avoid, to get round.

obvio, via *adj* obvious.

oca *sf* [ave] goose.

ocasión *sf* - **1.** [oportunidad] opportunity, chance - **2.** [momento] moment, time; [vez] occasion; **en dos ocasiones** on two occasions; **en alguna ocasión** sometimes; **en cierta ocasión** once; **en otra ocasión** some other time - **3.** [motivo] **con ocasión de** on the occasion of; **dar ocasión para algo/hacer algo** to give cause for sthg/to do sthg - **4.** [ganga] bargain; **de ocasión** [precio, artículos etc] bargain *(antes de s)*.

ocasional *adj* - **1.** [accidental] accidental - **2.** [irregular] occasional.

ocasionar *vt* to cause.

ocaso *sm* - **1.** [puesta del sol] sunset - **2.** [decadencia] decline.

occidental *adj* western.

occidente *sm* west. ➤ **Occidente** *sm* [bloque de países] the West.

OCDE *(abrev de* **Organización para la Cooperación y el Desarrollo Económico)** *sf* OECD.

Oceanía *n pr* Oceania.

océano *sm* ocean; [inmensidad] sea, host.

ochenta *num* eighty; **los (años) ochenta** the eighties; *ver también* **seis**.

ocho *num* eight; **de aquí en ocho días** [en una semana] a week today; *ver también* **seis**.

ochocientos, tas *num* eight hundred; *ver también* **seis**.

ocio *sm* [tiempo libre] leisure; [inactividad] idleness.

ocioso, sa *adj* - **1.** [inactivo] idle - **2.** [innecesario] unnecessary; [inútil] pointless.

ocre ⬦ *sm* ochre. ⬦ *adj inv* ochre.

octágono, na *adj* octagonal. ➤ **octágono** *sm* octagon.

octano *sm* octane.

octava ➤ **octavo**.

octavilla *sf* - **1.** [de propaganda política] pamphlet, leaflet - **2.** [tamaño] octavo.

octavo, va *num* eighth. ➤ **octavo** *sm* [parte] eighth. ➤ **octava** *sf* MÚS octave.

octeto *sm* INFORM byte.

octogenario, ria *adj* & *sm, f* octogenarian.

octogésimo, ma *num* eightieth.

octubre *sm* October; *ver también* **septiembre**.

ocular *adj* eye *(antes de s)*.

oculista *smf* ophthalmologist.

ocultar *vt* - **1.** [gen] to hide - **2.** [delito] to cover up. ➤ **ocultarse** *vprnl* to hide.

oculto, ta *adj* hidden.

ocupación *sf* - **1.** [gen] occupation; **ocupación ilegal de viviendas** squatting - **2.** [empleo] job.

ocupado, da *adj* - **1.** [persona] busy - **2.** [teléfono, lavabo etc] engaged - **3.** [lugar - gen, por ejército] occupied; [plaza] taken.

ocupante smf occupant; **ocupante ilegal de viviendas** squatter.

ocupar vt - 1. [gen] to occupy - 2. [superficie, espacio] to take up; [habitación, piso] to live in; [mesa] to sit at; [sillón] to sit in - 3. [actividad] to take up - 4. [cargo] to hold - 5. [dar trabajo a] to find O provide work for - 6. Amér C & Méx [usar] to use. ◆ **ocuparse** vprnl [encargarse]: **ocuparse de** [gen] to deal with; [niños, enfermos, finanzas] to look after.

ocurrencia sf - 1. [idea] bright idea - 2. [dicho gracioso] witty remark.

ocurrir vi - 1. [acontecer] to happen - 2. [pasar, preocupar]: **¿qué le ocurre a Juan?** what's up with Juan? ◆ **ocurrirse** vprnl [venir a la cabeza]: **no se me ocurre ninguna solución** I can't think of a solution; **¡ni se te ocurra!** don't even think about it!; **se me ocurre que...** it occurs to me that...

ODECA sf (abrev de **Organización de Estados Centroamericanos**) OCAS.

odiar vt & vi to hate.

odio sm hatred.

odioso, sa adj hateful, horrible.

odontólogo, ga sm, f dentist, dental surgeon.

OEA (abrev de **Organización de Estados Americanos**) sf OAS.

oeste ◇ adj [posición, parte] west, western; [dirección, viento] westerly. ◇ sm west.

ofender vt [injuriar] to insult; [palabras] to offend, to hurt. ◆ **ofenderse** vprnl: **ofenderse (por)** to take offence (at).

ofensa sf - 1. [acción]: **ofensa (a)** offence (against) - 2. [injuria] slight, insult.

ofensivo, va adj offensive. ◆ **ofensiva** sf offensive.

oferta sf - 1. [gen] offer; **'ofertas de trabajo'** 'situations vacant' - 2. ECON [suministro] supply; **la oferta y la demanda** supply and demand; **oferta monetaria** money supply - 3. [rebaja] bargain, special offer; **de oferta** bargain (antes de s), on offer - 4. FIN [proposición] bid, tender; **oferta pública de adquisición** COM takeover bid.

ofertar vt to offer.

oficial, la sm, f [obrero] journeyman; [aprendiz] trainee. ◆ **oficial** ◇ adj official. ◇ sm - 1. MIL officer - 2. [funcionario] clerk.

oficialismo sm Amér: **el oficialismo** [gobierno] the Government; [partidarios del gobierno] government supporters.

oficialista adj Amér pro-government.

oficiar vt to officiate at.

oficina sf office; **oficina de empleo** job centre; **oficina de turismo** tourist office.

oficinista smf office worker.

oficio sm - 1. [profesión manual] trade; **de oficio** by trade - 2. [trabajo] job - 3. [experiencia]: **tener mucho oficio** to be very experienced - 4. RELIG service.

oficioso, sa adj unofficial.

ofimática sf office automation.

ofrecer vt - 1. [gen] to offer; [fiesta] to give, to throw; **ofrecerle algo a alguien** to offer sb sthg - 2. [aspecto] to present. ◆ **ofrecerse** vprnl [presentarse] to offer, to volunteer; **ofrecerse a O para hacer algo** to offer to do sthg.

ofrecimiento sm offer.

ofrenda sf RELIG offering; [por gratitud, amor] gift.

ofrendar vt to offer up.

oftalmología sf ophthalmology.

ofuscar vt - 1. [deslumbrar] to dazzle - 2. [turbar] to blind. ◆ **ofuscarse** vprnl: **ofuscarse (con)** to be blinded (by).

ogro sm ogre.

oh interj: **¡oh!** oh!

oídas ◆ **de oídas** loc adv by hearsay.

oído sm - 1. [órgano] ear; **de oído** by ear; **hacer oídos sordos** to turn a deaf ear - 2. [sentido] (sense of) hearing; **ser duro de oído** to be hard of hearing.

oír ◇ vt - 1. [gen] to hear - 2. [atender] to listen to. ◇ vi to hear; **¡oiga, por favor!** excuse me!; **¡oye!** fam hey!

ojal sm buttonhole.

ojalá interj: **¡ojalá!** if only (that were so)!; **¡ojalá lo haga!** I hope she does it!; **¡ojalá fuera ya domingo!** I wish it were Sunday!

ojeada sf glance, look; **echar una ojeada a algo/alguien** to take a quick glance at sthg/sb, to take a quick look at sthg/sb.

ojear vt to have a look at.

ojera (gen pl) sf bags pl under the eyes.

ojeriza sf fam dislike; **tener ojeriza a alguien** to have it in for sb.

ojeroso, sa adj haggard.

ojo ◇ sm - 1. ANAT eye; **ojos saltones** popping eyes - 2. [agujero - de aguja] eye; [- de puente] span; **ojo de la cerradura** keyhole - 3. loc: **a ojo (de buen cubero)** roughly, approximately; **andar con (mucho) ojo** to be (very) careful; **comerse con los ojos a alguien** fam to drool over sb; **echar el ojo a algo** to have one's eye on sthg; **en un abrir y cerrar de ojos** in the twinkling of an eye; **estar ojo alerta** O **avizor** to be on the lookout; **mirar algo con buenos/malos ojos** to look favourably/unfavourably on sthg; **no pegar ojo** not to get a wink of sleep; **tener (buen) ojo** to have a good eye; **ojos que no ven, corazón que no siente** prov what the eye doesn't see, the heart doesn't grieve over. ◇ interj: **¡ojo!** be careful!, watch out!

okupa *smf mfam* squatter.

ola *sf* wave; **ola de calor** heatwave; **ola de frío** cold spell.

ole, olé *interj!* ¡olé! ¡bravo!

oleada *sf* - **1.** [del mar] swell - **2.** *fig* [avalancha] wave.

oleaje *sm* swell.

óleo *sm* oil (painting).

oleoducto *sm* oil pipeline.

oler ⬦ *vt* to smell. ⬦ *vi* - **1.** [despedir olor]: **oler (a)** to smell (of) - **2.** *fam* [indicando sospecha]: **oler a** to smack of. ➡ **olerse** *vprnl*: **olerse algo** *fam* to sense sthg.

olfatear *vt* - **1.** [olisquear] to sniff - **2.** [barruntar] to smell, to sense. ➡ **olfatear en** *vi* [indagar] to pry into.

olfato *sm* - **1.** [sentido] sense of smell - **2.** *fig* [sagacidad] nose, instinct; **tener olfato para algo** to be a good judge of sthg.

oligarquía *sf* oligarchy.

olimpiada, olimpíada *sf* Olympic Games *pl*; **las olimpiadas** the Olympics.

olisquear *vt* to sniff (at).

oliva *sf* olive.

olivar *sm* olive grove.

olivera *sf* olive tree.

olivo *sm* olive tree.

olla *sf* pot; **olla exprés** *O* **a presión** pressure cooker; **olla podrida** CULIN stew.

olmo *sm* elm (tree).

olor *sm* smell; **olor a** smell of.

oloroso, sa *adj* fragrant. ➡ **oloroso** *sm* oloroso (sherry).

OLP (*abrev de* **Organización para la Liberación de Palestina**) *sf* PLO.

olvidadizo, za *adj* forgetful.

olvidar *vt* - **1.** [gen] to forget - **2.** [dejarse] to leave; **olvidé las llaves en la oficina** I left my keys at the office. ➡ **olvidarse** *vprnl* - **1.** [gen] to forget; **olvidarse de algo/hacer algo** to forget sthg/to do sthg - **2.** [dejarse] to leave.

olvido *sm* - **1.** [de un nombre, hecho etc] forgetting; **caer en el olvido** to fall into oblivion - **2.** [descuido] oversight.

ombligo *sm* ANAT navel.

omisión *sf* omission.

omitir *vt* to omit.

ómnibus *sm inv* - **1.** omnibus; FERROC local train - **2.** *Cuba & Urug* [urbano] bus; *Andes, Cuba & Urug* [interurbano, internacional] intercity bus.

omnipotente *adj* omnipotent.

omnívoro, ra *adj* omnivorous.

omoplato, omóplato *sm* shoulder-blade.

OMS (*abrev de* **Organización Mundial de la Salud**) *sf* WHO.

once *num* eleven; *ver también* **seis**. ➡ **onces** *sm Andes* [por la mañana] elevenses; [por la tarde] tea.

ONCE (*abrev de* **Organización Nacional de Ciegos Españoles**) *sf* Spanish association for the blind, famous for its national lottery.

onceavo, va *num* eleventh.

onda *sf* wave; **onda eléctrica** *O* **hertziana** Hertzian wave; **onda expansiva** shock wave; **onda luminosa/sonora** light/sound wave; **estar en la onda** *fam* to be on the ball; **¿que onda?** *Méx & R Plata fam* how's it going?, how are things?

ondear *vi* to ripple.

ondulación *sf* [acción] rippling.

ondulado, da *adj* wavy.

ondular ⬦ *vi* [agua] to ripple; [terreno] to undulate. ⬦ *vt* to wave.

ONG (*abrev de* **organización no gubernamental**) *sf* NGO.

ónice, ónix *smf* onyx.

onomástico, ca *adj culto* onomastic. ➡ **onomástica** *sf culto* name day.

ONU (*abrev de* **Organización de las Naciones Unidas**) *sf* UN.

onza *sf* [unidad de peso] ounce.

OPA (*abrev de* **oferta pública de adquisición**) *sf* takeover bid.

opaco, ca *adj* opaque.

ópalo *sm* opal.

opción *sf* - **1.** [elección] option; **no hay opción** there is no alternative; **opciones sobre acciones** stock options - **2.** [derecho] right; **dar opción a** to give the right to; **tener opción a** [empleo, cargo] to be eligible for.

opcional *adj* optional.

OPEP (*abrev de* **Organización de Países Exportadores de Petróleo**) *sf* OPEC.

ópera *sf* opera; **ópera bufa** comic opera, opera buffa.

operación *sf* - **1.** [gen] operation; **operación quirúrgica** (surgical) operation - **2.** COM transaction.

operador, ra *sm, f* - **1.** INFORM & TELECOM operator - **2.** [de la cámara] cameraman; [del proyector] projectionist. ➡ **operador** *sm* MAT operator. ➡ **operador turístico** *sm* tour operator.

operar ⬦ *vt* - **1.** [enfermo]: **operar a alguien (de algo)** [enfermedad] to operate on sb (for sthg); **lo operaron del hígado** they've operated on his liver - **2.** [cambio etc] to bring about, to produce. ⬦ *vi* - **1.** [gen] to operate - **2.** [actuar] to act - **3.** COM & FIN to deal. ➡ **operarse** *vprnl* - **1.** [enfermo] to be operated on, to have an operation; **me voy a operar del hígado** I'm going to have an operation on my liver - **2.** [cambio etc] to occur.

operario, ria *sm, f* worker.

operativo, va *adj* operative. ◆ **operativo** *sm Amér* operation.

opereta *sf* operetta.

opinar ◇ *vt* to believe, to think. ◇ *vi* to give one's opinion.

opinión *sf* [parecer] opinion; **la opinión pública** public opinion.

opio *sm* opium.

opíparo, ra *adj* sumptuous.

oponente *smf* opponent.

oponer *vt* - **1.** [resistencia] to put up - **2.** [argumento, razón] to put forward, to give. ◆ **oponerse** *vprnl* - **1.** [no estar de acuerdo] to be opposed; **oponerse a algo** [desaprobar] to be opposed to sthg, to oppose sthg; [contradecir] to contradict sthg; **me opongo a creerlo** I refuse to believe it - **2.** [obstaculizar]: **oponerse a** to impede.

oporto *sm* port (wine).

oportunidad *sf* [ocasión] opportunity, chance; **darle una/otra oportunidad a alguien** to give sb a/another chance.

oportunismo *sm* opportunism.

oportunista *smf* opportunist.

oportuno, na *adj* - **1.** [pertinente] appropriate - **2.** [propicio] timely; **el momento oportuno** the right time.

oposición *sf* - **1.** [gen] opposition - **2.** [resistencia] resistance - **3.** *(gen pl)* [examen] public entrance examination; **oposición a profesor** public examination to be a teacher; **preparar oposiciones** to be studying for a public entrance examination.

opositar *vi*: **opositar (a)** to sit a public entrance examination (for).

opositor, ra *sm, f* - **1.** [a un cargo] *candidate in a public entrance examination* - **2.** [oponente] opponent.

opresión *sf fig* [represión] oppression.

opresivo, va *adj* oppressive.

opresor, ra *sm, f* oppressor.

oprimir *vt* - **1.** [apretar - botón etc] to press; [- garganta, brazo etc] to squeeze - **2.** [zapatos, cinturón] to pinch - **3.** *fig* [reprimir] to oppress - **4.** *fig* [angustiar] to weigh down on, to burden.

optar *vi* [escoger]: **optar (por algo)** to choose (sthg); **optar por hacer algo** to choose to do sthg; **optar entre** to choose between.

optativo, va *adj* optional.

óptico, ca ◇ *adj* optic. ◇ *sm, f* [persona] optician. ◆ **óptica** *sf* - **1.** FÍS optics *(U)* - **2.** [tienda] optician's (shop) - **3.** *fig* [punto de vista] point of view.

optimismo *sm* optimism.

optimista ◇ *adj* optimistic. ◇ *smf* optimist.

óptimo, ma ◇ *superl de* **bueno**. ◇ *adj* optimum.

opuesto, ta ◇ *pp* ▷ **oponer**. ◇ *adj* - **1.** [contrario] conflicting; **opuesto a** opposed O contrary to - **2.** [de enfrente] opposite.

opulencia *sf* [riqueza] opulence; [abundancia] abundance.

opulento, ta *adj* [rico] opulent.

oración *sf* - **1.** [rezo] prayer - **2.** GRAM sentence.

orador, ra *sm, f* speaker.

oral ◇ *adj* oral. ◇ *sm* ▷ **examen**.

órale *interj Méx fam* [de acuerdo] right!, sure!; [¡venga!] come on!

orangután *sm* orangutang.

orar *vi* to pray.

órbita *sf* - **1.** ASTRON orbit; **entrar/poner en órbita** to go/put into orbit - **2.** [de ojo] eye socket.

orca *sf* killer whale.

orden ◇ *sm* - **1.** [gen] order; **por orden** in order; **las fuerzas del orden** the forces of law and order; **orden de compra** COM purchase order; **orden público** law and order - **2.** [tipo] type, order; **problemas de orden económico** economic problems. ◇ *sf* order; **por orden de** by order of; **¡a la orden!** MIL (yes) sir!; **estar a la orden del día** to be the order of the day. ◆ **del orden de** *loc prep* around, approximately. ◆ **orden del día** *sm* agenda.

ordenado, da *adj* [lugar, persona] tidy.

ordenador *sm* INFORM computer; **ordenador personal** personal computer; **ordenador portátil** laptop computer.

ordenanza ◇ *sm* [de oficina] messenger. ◇ *sf (gen pl)* ordinance, law; **ordenanzas municipales** by-laws.

ordenar *vt* - **1.** [poner en orden - gen] to arrange; [- habitación, armario etc] to tidy (up) - **2.** [mandar] to order - **3.** RELIG to ordain - **4.** *Amér* [solicitar] to order. ◆ **ordenarse** *vprnl* RELIG to be ordained.

ordeñar *vt* to milk.

ordinariez *sf* commonness, coarseness.

ordinario, ria *adj* - **1.** [común] ordinary, usual - **2.** [vulgar] common, coarse - **3.** [no selecto] unexceptional - **4.** [no especial - presupuesto, correo] daily; [- tribunal] of first instance.

orégano *sm* oregano.

oreja *sf* ANAT ear.

orfanato, orfelinato *sm* orphanage.

orfandad *sf* orphanhood; *fig* abandonment.

orfebre *smf* [de plata] silversmith; [de oro] goldsmith.

orfebrería *sf* [obra - de plata] silver work; [- de oro] gold work.

orfelinato = **orfanato**.

orgánico, ca *adj* organic.

organigrama *sm* [gen & INFORM] flowchart.

organillo *sm* barrel organ.

organismo *sm* - **1.** BIOL organism - **2.** ANAT body - **3.** *fig* [entidad] organization, body.

organización *sf* organization; **Organización Mundial del Comercio** COM World Trade Organization.

organizar *vt* to organize.

órgano *sm* organ.

orgasmo *sm* orgasm.

orgía *sf* orgy.

orgullo *sm* pride.

orgulloso, sa *adj* proud.

orientación *sf* - **1.** [dirección - acción] guiding; [- rumbo] direction - **2.** [posicionamiento - acción] positioning; [- lugar] position - **3.** *fig* [información] guidance; **orientación profesional** careers advice *O* guidance.

oriental <> *adj* - **1.** [gen] eastern; [del Lejano Oriente] oriental - **2.** *Amér* [de Uruguay] Uruguayan. <> *smf* - **1.** oriental - **2.** *Amér* [de Uruguay] Uruguayan.

orientar *vt* - **1.** [dirigir] to direct; [casa] to build facing - **2.** *fig* [medidas etc]: **orientar hacia** to direct towards *O* at - **3.** *fig* [aconsejar] to give advice *O* guidance to.   **orientarse** *vprnl* - **1.** [dirigirse - foco etc]: **orientarse a** to point towards *O* at - **2.** [encontrar el camino] to get one's bearings - **3.** *fig* [encaminarse]: **orientarse hacia** to be aiming at.

oriente *sm* east.   **Oriente** *sm*: **el Oriente** the East, the Orient; **Oriente Medio/Próximo** Middle/Near East; **Lejano** *O* **Extremo Oriente** Far East.

orificio *sm* hole; TECNOL opening.

origen *sm* - **1.** [gen] origin; [ascendencia] origins *pl*, birth; **de origen español** of Spanish origin - **2.** [causa] cause; **dar origen a** to give rise to.

original <> *adj* - **1.** [gen] original - **2.** [raro] eccentric, different. <> *sm* original.

originalidad *sf* - **1.** [gen] originality - **2.** [extravagancia] eccentricity.

originar *vt* to cause.   **originarse** *vprnl* to be caused.

originario, ria *adj* [inicial, primitivo] original.

orilla *sf* - **1.** [ribera - de río] bank; [- de mar] shore; **a orillas de** [río] on the banks of; **a orillas del mar** by the sea - **2.** [borde] edge - **3.** [acera] pavement.

orillar *vt* [dificultad, obstáculo] to skirt around.

orín *sm* [herrumbre] rust.   **orines** *smpl* [orina] urine *(U)*.

orina *sf* urine.

orinal *sm* chamberpot.

orinar *vi* & *vt* to urinate.   **orinarse** *vprnl* to wet o.s.

oriundo, da *adj*: **oriundo de** native of.

ornamentación *sf* ornamentation.

ornamento *sm* [objeto] ornament.

ornar *vt* to decorate, to adorn.

ornitología *sf* ornithology.

oro *sm* gold; *fig* riches *pl*; **hacerse de oro** to make one's fortune; **pedir el oro y el moro** to ask the earth.   **oros** *smpl* [naipes] *suit of Spanish cards bearing gold coins.*   **oro negro** *sm* oil.

orografía *sf* [relieve] terrain.

orquesta *sf* - **1.** [músicos] orchestra; **orquesta de cámara/sinfónica** chamber/symphony orchestra - **2.** [lugar] orchestra pit.

orquestar *vt* to orchestrate.

orquestina *sf* dance band.

orquídea *sf* orchid.

ortiga *sf* (stinging) nettle.

ortodoxia *sf* orthodoxy.

ortodoxo, xa *adj* orthodox.

ortografía *sf* spelling.

ortográfico, ca *adj* spelling *(antes de s)*.

ortopedia *sf* orthopaedics *(U)*.

ortopédico, ca *adj* orthopaedic.

ortopedista *smf* orthopaedist.

oruga *sf* caterpillar.

orujo *sm* strong spirit made from grape pressings.

orzuelo *sm* stye.

os *pron pers* - **1.** *(complemento directo)* you; **me gustaría veros** I'd like to see you - **2.** *(complemento indirecto)* (to) you; **os lo dio** he gave it to you; **os tengo miedo** I'm afraid of you - **3.** *(reflexivo)* yourselves - **4.** *(recíproco)* each other; **os enamorasteis** you fell in love (with each other).

osadía *sf* - **1.** [valor] boldness, daring - **2.** [descaro] audacity, cheek.

osado, da *adj* - **1.** [valeroso] daring, bold - **2.** [descarado] impudent, cheeky.

osamenta *sf* skeleton.

osar *vi* to dare.

oscilación *sf* - **1.** [movimiento] swinging; FÍS oscillation - **2.** *fig* [variación] fluctuation.

oscilar *vi* - **1.** [moverse] to swing; FÍS to oscillate - **2.** *fig* [variar] to fluctuate.

oscurecer, obscurecer ⬦ *vt* - **1.** [privar de luz] to darken - **2.** *fig* [mente] to confuse, to cloud. ⬦ *v impers* [anochecer] to get dark. ⬧ **oscurecerse, obscurecerse** *vprnl* to grow dark.

oscuridad, obscuridad *sf* - **1.** [falta de luz] darkness - **2.** [zona oscura]: **en la oscuridad** in the dark - **3.** *fig* [falta de claridad] obscurity.

oscuro, ra, obscuro, ra *adj* - **1.** [gen] dark; **a oscuras** in the dark - **2.** [nublado] overcast - **3.** *fig* [inusual] obscure - **4.** *fig* [intenciones, asunto] shady.

óseo, a *adj* bone *(antes de s)*.

oso, osa *sm, f* bear (*f* she-bear); **oso de felpa** O **peluche** teddy bear; **oso hormiguero** anteater; **oso panda** panda; **oso polar** polar bear.

ostensible *adj* evident, clear.

ostentación *sf* ostentation, show.

ostentar *vt* [poseer] to hold, to have.

ostentoso, sa *adj* ostentatious.

osteópata *smf* osteopath.

ostra *sf* oyster; **aburrirse como una ostra** *fam* to be bored to death. ⬧ **ostras** *interj fam*: **¡ostras!** blimey!

OTAN *(abrev de* **Organización del Tratado del Atlántico Norte)** *sf* NATO.

OTI *(abrev de* **Organización de Televisiones Iberoamericanas)** *sf association of all Spanish-speaking television networks.*

otitis *sf inv* inflammation of the ear.

otoñal *adj* autumn *UK (antes de s)*, autumnal *UK*, fall *US (antes de s)*.

otoño *sm lit & fig* autumn *UK*, fall *US*.

otorgar *vt* to grant; [premio] to award, to present; DER to execute.

otorrino, na *sm, f fam* ear, nose and throat specialist.

otorrinolaringología *sf* ear, nose and throat medicine.

otro, tra ⬦ *adj* - **1.** [distinto] another, other; **otro chico** another boy; **el otro chico** the other boy; **(los) otros chicos** (the) other boys; **no hacer otra cosa que llorar** to do nothing but cry; **el otro día** [pasado] the other day - **2.** [nuevo] another; **estamos ante otro Dalí** this is another Dalí; **otros tres goles** another three goals. ⬦ *pron (sing)* another (one), *(pl)* others; **dame otro** give me another (one); **el otro** the other one; **(los) otros** (the) others; **yo no lo hice, fue otro** it wasn't me, it was somebody else; **otro habría abandonado, pero no él** anyone else would have given up, but not him; **¡otra!** [en conciertos] encore!, more!

output ['autput] *(pl* **outputs)** *sm* INFORM output *(U)*.

ovación *sf* ovation.

ovacionar *vt* to give an ovation to.

oval *adj* oval.

ovalado, da *adj* oval.

ovario *sm* ovary.

oveja *sf* sheep, ewe. ⬧ **oveja negra** *sf* black sheep.

overol, overoles *sm Amér* [ropa - con peto] dungarees *pl UK*, overalls *pl US*; [- para bebé] rompers *pl*.

ovillo *sm* ball *(of wool etc)*; **hacerse un ovillo** to curl up into a ball.

ovino, na *adj* ovine, sheep *(antes de s)*.

ovni ['ofni] *sm (abrev de* **objeto volador no identificado)** UFO.

ovulación *sf* ovulation.

ovular ⬦ *adj* ovular. ⬦ *vi* to ovulate.

oxidación *sf* rusting.

oxidar *vt* to rust; QUÍM to oxidize. ⬧ **oxidarse** *vprnl* to get rusty.

óxido *sm* - **1.** QUÍM oxide - **2.** [herrumbre] rust.

oxigenado, da *adj* - **1.** QUÍM oxygenated - **2.** [cabello] peroxided *(antes de s)*, bleached.

oxigenar *vt* QUÍM to oxygenate. ⬧ **oxigenarse** *vprnl* [airearse] to get a breath of fresh air.

oxígeno *sm* oxygen.

oye ▷ **oír**.

oyente *smf* - **1.** RADIO listener - **2.** [alumno] unregistered student.

ozono *sm* ozone.

p, P *sf* [letra] p, P.

p. - **1.** = **pág.** - **2.** *abrev de* **paseo**.

pabellón *sm* - **1.** [edificio] pavilion - **2.** [parte de un edificio] block, section - **3.** [en parques, jardines] summerhouse - **4.** [tienda de campaña] bell tent - **5.** [bandera] flag.

PAC *(abrev de* **Política Agrícola Común)** *sf* CAP.

pacer *vi* to graze.

pachá *(pl* **pachás** O **pachaes)** *sm* pasha; **vivir como un pachá** *fam* to live like a lord.

Pachamama *sf Andes* Mother Earth.

pachanga *sf fam* rowdy celebration.

pacharán *sm liqueur made from anis and sloes.*

pachorra *sf fam* calmness.

pachucho, cha *adj fam* under the weather.

paciencia *sf* patience; **perder la paciencia** to lose one's patience; **tener paciencia** to be patient.

paciente *adj & smf* patient.

pacificación *sf* pacification.

pacificar *vt* - 1. [país] to pacify - 2. [ánimos] to calm.

pacífico, ca *adj* [gen] peaceful; [persona] peaceable.

Pacífico *sm*: **el (océano) Pacífico** the Pacific (Ocean).

pacifismo *sm* pacifism.

pacifista *adj & smf* pacifist.

paco, ca *sm, f Andes & Pan fam* cop.

pacotilla *sf*: **de pacotilla** trashy, third-rate.

pactar *vt* to agree to. *vi*: **pactar (con)** to strike a deal (with).

pacto *sm* [gen] agreement, pact; [entre países] treaty.

padecer *vt* to suffer, to endure; [enfermedad] to suffer from. *vi* to suffer; [enfermedad]: **padecer de** to suffer from.

padecimiento *sm* suffering.

pádel ['paðel] *sm ball game for two or four players, played with a small rubber bat on a two-walled court.*

padrastro *sm* - 1. [pariente] stepfather - 2. [pellejo] hangnail.

padre *sm* [gen & RELIG] father. *adj inv* - 1. *Esp fam* [enorme] incredible - 2. *Méx fam* [estupendo] fantastic, great. **padres** *smpl* [padre y madre] parents.

padrenuestro (*pl* **padrenuestros**) *sm* Lord's Prayer.

padrino *sm* - 1. [de bautismo] godfather; [de boda] best man - 2. [en duelos, torneos etc] second - 3. *fig* [protector] patron. **padrinos** *smpl* [padrino y madrina] godparents.

padrísimo *adj Méx fam* great.

padrón *sm* [censo] census; [para votar] electoral roll *O* register.

padrote *sm Méx fam* pimp.

paella *sf* paella.

paellera *sf large frying pan or earthenware dish for cooking paella.*

pág., p. (*abrev de* **página**) p.

paga *sf* payment; [salario] salary, wages *pl*; [de niño] pocket money; **paga extra** *O* **extraordinaria** *bonus paid twice a year to Spanish workers.*

pagadero, ra *adj* payable; **pagadero a 90 días/a la entrega** payable within 90 days/on delivery.

pagano, na *adj & sm, f* pagan, heathen.

pagar *vt* [gen] to pay; [deuda] to pay off, to settle; [ronda, gastos, delito] to pay for; [ayuda, favor] to repay; **me las pagarás** *fam* you'll pay for this; **pagar el pato/los platos rotos** *fam* to carry the can. *vi* to pay; **pagar en efectivo** *O* **metálico** to pay (in) cash.

pagaré (*pl* **pagarés**) *sm* COM promissory note, IOU; **pagaré del Tesoro** Treasury note.

página *sf* page; **página inicial** *O* **de inicio** INFORM home page; **página Web** Web page; **las páginas amarillas** the Yellow Pages.

pago *sm* payment; *fig* reward, payment; **en pago de** [en recompensa por] as a reward for; [a cambio de] in return for; **pago anticipado/inicial** advance/down payment; **pago por visión** pay-per-view. **pagos** *smpl* [lugar]: **por estos pagos** around here.

pai *sm Amér C & Méx* pie.

paila *sf* - 1. *Andes, Amér C & Caribe* [sartén] frying pan - 2. *Chile* [huevos fritos] fried eggs *pl*.

paisaje *sm* [gen] landscape; [vista panorámica] scenery (*U*), view.

paisano, na *sm, f* [del mismo país] compatriot. **paisano** *sm* [civil] civilian; **de paisano** MIL in civilian clothes; **de paisano** [policía] in plain clothes.

Países Bajos *smpl*: **los Países Bajos** the Netherlands.

País Vasco *sm*: **el País Vasco** the Basque Country.

paja *sf* - 1. [gen] straw - 2. *fig* [relleno] waffle - 3. *vulg* [masturbación] wank.

pajar *sm* straw loft.

pájara *sf fig* crafty *O* sly woman.

pajarería *sf* pet shop.

pajarita *sf Esp* [corbata] bow tie.

pájaro *sm* ZOOL bird; **pájaro bobo** penguin; **pájaro carpintero** woodpecker; **pájaro de mal agüero** bird of ill omen; **más vale pájaro en mano que ciento volando** *prov* a bird in the hand is worth two in the bush; **matar dos pájaros de un tiro** to kill two birds with one stone; **tener pájaros en la cabeza** to be scatterbrained *O* empty-headed.

paje *sm* page.

pajilla, pajita *sf* (drinking) straw.

pajuerano, na *R Dom* *adj* [de pueblo] countrified. *sm, f* [palurdo] bumpkin, hick *US*.

Pakistán = Paquistán.

pala *sf* - 1. [herramienta] spade; [para recoger] shovel; CULIN slice - 2. [de frontón, ping-pong] bat - 3. [de remo, hélice] blade.

palabra *sf* - **1.** [gen] word; **de palabra** by word of mouth; **no tener palabra** to go back on one's word; **palabra divina** *O* **de Dios** word of God; **palabra de honor** word of honour - **2.** [habla] speech - **3.** [derecho de hablar] right to speak; **dar la palabra a alguien** to give the floor to sb - **4.** *loc*: **en cuatro** *O* **dos palabras** in a few words; **en una palabra** in a word.
➡ **palabras** *sfpl* [discurso] words.

palabrear *vt Amér fam* to agree on.

palabrería *sf fam* hot air.

palabrota *sf* swearword; **decir palabrotas** to swear.

palacete *sm* mansion, small palace.

palacio *sm* palace; **palacio de congresos** conference centre.

palada *sf* - **1.** [al cavar] spadeful, shovelful - **2.** [de remo] stroke.

paladar *sm* palate.

paladear *vt* to savour.

palanca *sf* [barra, mando] lever; **palanca de cambio** gear lever *O* stick, gearshift *US*; **palanca de mando** joystick.

palangana *sf* [para fregar] washing-up bowl; [para lavarse] wash bowl.

palco *sm* box *(at theatre)*; **palco de autoridades** VIP box.

Palestina *n pr* Palestine.

palestino, na *adj & sm, f* Palestinian.

paleta *sf* [gen] small shovel, small spade; [llana] trowel; CULIN slice; ARTE palette; [de ping-pong] bat; *Méx* [helado] ice lolly *UK*, Popsicle® *US*.

paletilla *sf* shoulder blade.

paleto, ta *Esp* ⟨⟩ *adj* coarse, uncouth. ⟨⟩ *sm, f* yokel, hick *US*.

paliar *vt* [atenuar] to ease, to relieve.

palidecer *vi* [ponerse pálido] to go *O* turn pale.

palidez *sf* paleness.

pálido, da *adj* pale; *fig* dull.

palillero *sm* toothpick holder.

palillo *sm* - **1.** [mondadientes] toothpick - **2.** [baqueta] drumstick - **3.** [para comida china] chopstick.

palique *sm Esp fam* chat, natter; **estar de palique** to chat, to natter.

paliza *sf* - **1.** [golpes, derrota] beating - **2.** [esfuerzo] hard grind.

palma *sf* - **1.** [de mano] palm - **2.** [palmera] palm (tree); [hoja de palmera] palm leaf.
➡ **palmas** *sfpl* [aplausos] applause *(U)*; **batir palmas** to clap (one's hands).

palmada *sf* - **1.** [golpe] pat; [más fuerte] slap - **2.** [aplauso] clap; **palmadas** clapping *(U)*.

palmar[1] *sm* palm grove.

palmar[2] *fam vi* to kick the bucket.

palmarés *sm* - **1.** [historial] record - **2.** [lista] list of winners.

palmear *vi* to clap, to applaud.

palmera *sf* [árbol] palm (tree); [datilera] date palm.

palmito *sm* - **1.** [árbol] palmetto, fan palm - **2.** CULIN palm heart.

palmo *sm* handspan; *fig* small amount; **palmo a palmo** bit by bit; **dejar a alguien con un palmo de narices** to let sb down.

palmotear *vi* to clap.

palo *sm* - **1.** [gen] stick; [de golf] club; [de portería] post; [de la escoba] handle - **2.** [mástil] mast - **3.** [golpe] blow *(with a stick)* - **4.** [de baraja] suit - **5.** *fig* [pesadez] bind, drag - **6.** *loc*: **a palo seco** [gen] without anything else; [bebida] neat.

paloma ▷ **palomo**.

palomar *sm* dovecote; [grande] pigeon shed.

palomilla *sf* - **1.** [insecto] grain moth - **2.** [tornillo] wing nut - **3.** [soporte] bracket.

palomita *sf*: **palomitas** popcorn *(U)*.

palomo, ma *sm, f* dove, pigeon; **paloma mensajera** carrier *O* homing pigeon.

palpable *adj* touchable, palpable; *fig* obvious, clear.

palpar ⟨⟩ *vt* - **1.** [tocar] to feel, to touch; MED to palpate - **2.** *fig* [percibir] to feel. ⟨⟩ *vi* to feel around.

palpitación *sf* beat, beating *(U)*; [con fuerza] throb, throbbing *(U)*. ➡ **palpitaciones** *sfpl* MED palpitations.

palpitante *adj* - **1.** [que palpita] beating; [con fuerza] throbbing - **2.** *fig* [interesante - interés, deseo, cuestión] burning.

palpitar *vi* [latir] to beat; [con fuerza] to throb.

palta *sf Andes & R Dom* avocado.

paludismo *sm* malaria.

palurdo, da *sm, f* yokel, hick *US*.

pamela *sf* sun hat.

pampa *sf*: **la pampa** the pampas *pl*.

pamplina *(gen pl) sf fam* trifle, unimportant thing.

pan *sm* - **1.** [alimento] bread; **pan integral** wholemeal bread; **pan lactal** *Arg* sliced bread; **pan moreno** *O* **negro** [integral] wholemeal bread; [con centeno] black *O* rye bread; **pan rallado** breadcrumbs *pl* - **2.** [hogaza] loaf - **3.** *loc*: **contigo pan y cebolla** I'll go through thick and thin with you; **llamar al pan pan y al vino vino** to call a spade a spade; **ser pan comido** to be a piece of cake, to be as easy as pie; **ser el pan nuestro de cada día** to be a regular occurrence, to be commonplace; **ser más bueno que el pan** to be kindness itself; **no sólo de pan vive el hombre** man cannot live on bread alone.

PAN *sm* - 1. *(abrev de* Partido Acción Nacional) Mexican political party - 2. *(abrev de* Partido de Avanzada Nacional) Guatemalan political party.

pana *sf* corduroy.

panacea *sf lit & fig* panacea.

panadería *sf* bakery, baker's.

panadero, ra *sm, f* baker.

panal *sm* honeycomb.

Panamá *n pr* Panama.

panameño, ña *adj & sm, f* Panamanian.

pancarta *sf* placard, banner.

panceta *sf* bacon.

pancho, cha *adj fam* calm, unruffled; **estar/quedarse tan pancho** to be/remain perfectly calm. ◆ **pancho** *sm R Dom* [comida] hot dog.

páncreas *sm inv* pancreas.

panda ◇ *sm* ▷ **oso**. ◇ *sf Esp* gang.

pandereta *sf* tambourine.

pandero *sm* MÚS tambourine.

pandilla *sf* gang.

panecillo *sm Esp* bread roll.

panecito *sm Amér* bread roll.

panegírico, ca *adj* panegyrical. ◆ **panegírico** *sm* panegyric.

panel *sm* - 1. [gen] panel - 2. [pared, biombo] screen - 3. [tablero] board; **panel solar** solar panel.

panera *sf* [para servir] bread basket; [para guardar] bread bin.

pánfilo, la *adj* simple, foolish.

panfleto *sm* pamphlet.

pánico *sm* panic.

panificadora *sf* (large) bakery.

panocha *sf* ear, cob.

panorama *sm* - 1. [vista] panorama - 2. *fig* [situación] overall state; [perspectiva] outlook.

panorámico, ca *adj* panoramic. ◆ **panorámica** *sf* panorama.

pantaletas *sfpl Amér C, Caribe & Méx* [bragas] panties, knickers *UK*.

pantalla *sf* - 1. [gen & INFORM] screen; **pantalla ancha** widescreen; **pantalla de cristal líquido** liquid crystal display; **la pequeña pantalla** the small screen, television - 2. [de lámpara] lampshade.

pantallazo *sm* screenshot.

pantalón *(gen pl) sm* trousers *pl*, pants *pl US*; **pantalón tejano** *O* **vaquero** jeans *pl*; **pantalón pitillo** drainpipe trousers *pl*.

pantano *sm* - 1. [ciénaga] marsh; [laguna] swamp - 2. [embalse] reservoir.

pantanoso, sa *adj* - 1. [cenagoso] marshy, boggy - 2. *fig* [difícil] tricky.

panteón *sm* pantheon; [familiar] mausoleum, vault.

pantera *sf* panther.

pantimedias *sfpl Méx* tights *UK*, pantyhose *US*.

pantorrilla *sf* calf.

pantufla *(gen pl) sf* slipper.

panty *(pl* pantys*) sm* tights *pl*.

panza *sf* belly.

pañal *sm* nappy *UK*, diaper *US*; **estar en pañales** [en sus inicios] to be in its infancy; [sin conocimientos] not to have a clue.

pañería *sf* [producto] drapery; [tienda] draper's (shop), dry-goods store *US*.

paño *sm* - 1. [tela] cloth, material - 2. [trapo] cloth; [para polvo] duster; [de cocina] tea towel - 3. [lienzo] panel. ◆ **paños** *smpl* [vestiduras] drapes; **en paños menores** in one's underwear.

pañoleta *sf* shawl, wrap.

pañuelo *sm* [de nariz] handkerchief; [para el cuello] scarf; [para la cabeza] headscarf; **pañuelo de papel** paper handkerchief, tissue.

papa *sf* potato; **no saber ni papa** *fam* not to have a clue. ◆ **Papa** *sm* Pope.

papá *sm fam* dad, daddy, pop *US*. ◆ **Papá Noel** *sm* Father Christmas.

papachador, ra *adj Méx* comforting.

papachar *vt Méx* to spoil.

papada *sf* [de persona] double chin; [de animal] dewlap.

papagayo *sm* - 1. [pájaro] parrot - 2. *Ven* [cometa] kite.

papalote *sm Amér C, Caribe & Méx* kite.

papamoscas *sm inv* flycatcher.

papanatas *smf inv fam* sucker.

papaya *sf* [fruta] papaya, pawpaw.

papel *sm* - 1. [gen] paper; [hoja] sheet of paper; **papel celofán** Cellophane; **papel confort** *Chile* toilet paper; **papel continuo** INFORM continuous paper; **papel de embalar** *O* **de embalaje** wrapping paper; **papel de fumar** cigarette paper; **papel de lija** sandpaper; **papel higiénico** toilet paper; **papel madera** *R Dom* cardboard; **papel milimetrado** graph paper; **papel pintado** wallpaper; **papel reciclado** recycled paper; **papel tapiz** INFORM wallpaper - 2. *fig* & CINE & TEATRO role, part; **desempeñar** *O* **hacer el papel de** to play the role *O* part of; **papel principal/secundario** main/minor part - 3. FIN stocks and shares *pl*; **papel moneda** paper money, banknotes *pl*. ◆ **papeles** *smpl* [documentos] papers.

papeleo *sm* paperwork, red tape.

papelera ▷ **papelero**.

papelería *sf* stationer's (shop).

papelero, ra *adj* paper *(antes de s)*. ◆ **papelera** *sf* [cesto - en oficina etc] wastepaper basket *O* bin; [- en la calle] litter bin.

papeleta *sf* - **1.** [boleto] ticket, slip (of paper); [de votación] ballot paper - **2.** EDUC *slip of paper with university exam results.*

paperas *sfpl* mumps.

papi *sm fam* daddy, dad.

papilla *sf* [para niños] baby food; **echar** *O* **arrojar la primera papilla** *fam* to be as sick as a dog; **hecho papilla** *fam* [cansado] shattered; [cosa] smashed to bits.

papiro *sm* papyrus.

paquete *sm* - **1.** [de libros, regalos etc] parcel; **paquete bomba** parcel bomb; **paquete postal** parcel - **2.** [de cigarrillos, klínex, folios etc] pack, packet; [de azúcar, arroz] bag - **3.** [de medidas] package; **paquete turístico** package tour - **4.** INFORM package.

Paquistán, Pakistán *n pr* Pakistan.

par <> *adj* - **1.** MAT even; **echar algo a pares o nones** *O* **decide something between two people by a game involving guessing the number of fingers that another person is holding out behind his/her back* - **2.** [igual] equal. <> *sm* - **1.** [pareja - de zapatos etc] pair - **2.** [dos - veces etc] couple - **3.** [número indeterminado] few, couple; **un par de copas** a couple of *O* a few drinks - **4.** [en golf] par - **5.** [noble] peer. ◆ **a la par** *loc adv* - **1.** [simultáneamente] at the same time - **2.** [a igual nivel] at the same level. ◆ **de par en par** *loc adj*: **abierto de par en par** wide open. ◆ **sin par** *loc adj* matchless.

para *prep* - **1.** [finalidad] for; **es para ti** it's for you; **una mesa para el salón** a table for the living room; **esta agua no es buena para beber** this water isn't fit for drinking *O* to drink; **te lo repetiré para que te enteres** I'll repeat it so you understand; **¿para qué?** what for? - **2.** [motivación] (in order) to; **para conseguir sus propósitos** in order to achieve his aims; **lo he hecho para agradarte** I did it to please you - **3.** [dirección] towards; **ir para casa** to head (for) home; **salir para el aeropuerto** to leave for the airport - **4.** [tiempo] for; **tiene que estar acabado para mañana** it has to be finished by *O* for tomorrow - **5.** [comparación]: **está muy delgado para lo que come** he's very thin considering how much he eats; **para ser verano hace mucho frío** considering it's summer, it's very cold - **6.** *(después de adj y antes de infinitivo)* [inminencia, propósito] to; **la comida está lista para servir** the meal is ready to be served; **el atleta está preparado para ganar** the athlete is ready to win. ◆ **para con** *loc prep* towards; **es buena para con los demás** she is kind towards other people.

parabién *(pl* parabienes*) sm* congratulations *pl.*

parábola *sf* - **1.** [alegoría] parable - **2.** GEOM parabola.

parabólico, ca *adj* parabolic.

parabrisas *sm inv* windscreen, windshield *US.*

paracaídas *sm inv* parachute.

paracaidista *smf* parachutist; MIL paratrooper.

parachoques *sm inv* AUTO bumper, fender *US;* FERROC buffer.

parada ▷ **parado.**

paradero *sm* - **1.** [de persona] whereabouts *pl* - **2.** *Chile, Col, Méx & Perú* [parada de autobús] bus stop.

paradisiaco, ca, paradisíaco, ca *adj* heavenly.

parado, da <> *adj* - **1.** [inmóvil - coche] stationary, standing; [- persona] still, motionless; [- fábrica, proyecto] at a standstill - **2.** *Esp* [sin empleo] unemployed - **3.** *loc:* **salir bien/mal parado de algo** to come off well/badly out of sthg. <> *sm, f Esp* [desempleado] unemployed person; **los parados** the unemployed. ◆ **parada** *sf* - **1.** [detención] stop, stopping *(U)* - **2.** DEP save - **3.** [de autobús] (bus) stop; [de taxis] taxi rank *UK O* stand *US;* [de metro] (underground) station; **parada discrecional** request stop - **4.** MIL parade.

paradoja *sf* paradox.

paradójico, ca *adj* paradoxical, ironical.

parador *sm* [hotel]: **parador (nacional)** *Esp state-owned luxury hotel, usually a building of historic or artistic importance.*

parafernalia *sf* paraphernalia.

parafrasear *vt* to paraphrase.

paráfrasis *sf inv* paraphrase.

paraguas *sm inv* umbrella.

Paraguay *n pr:* **(el) Paraguay** Paraguay.

paraguayo, ya *adj & sm, f* Paraguayan.

paragüero *sm* umbrella stand.

paraíso *sm* RELIG Paradise; *fig* paradise.

paraje *sm* spot, place.

paralelismo *sm* - **1.** GEOM parallelism - **2.** [semejanza] similarity, parallels *pl.*

paralelo, la *adj:* **paralelo (a)** parallel (to). ◆ **paralelo** *sm* GEOGR parallel. ◆ **paralela** *sf* GEOM parallel (line).

parálisis *sf inv* paralysis; **parálisis cerebral** cerebral palsy.

paralítico, ca *adj & sm, f* paralytic.

paralizar *vt* to paralyse. ◆ **paralizarse** *vprnl* to become paralysed; [producción etc] to come to a standstill.

parámetro *sm* parameter.

páramo *sm* moor, moorland *(U); fig* wilderness.

parangón *sm* paragon; **sin parangón** unparalleled.

paranoia *sf* paranoia.

paranormal *adj* paranormal.

parapente *sm* [deporte] parapenting, paragliding; |paracaídas| parapente.

parapetarse *vprnl llt & fig.* parapetarse **(tras)** to take refuge (behind).

parapeto *sm* [antepecho] parapet; [barandilla] bannister; [barricada] barricade.

parapléjico, ca *adj* & *sm, f* paraplegic.

parapsicología *sf* parapsychology.

parar ⬦ *vi* - 1. [gen] to stop; **parar de hacer algo** to stop doing sthg; **sin parar** non-stop - 2. [alojarse] to stay - 3. [recaer]: **parar en manos de alguien** to come into the possession of sb - 4. [acabar] to end up; **¿en qué parará este lío?** where will it all end? ⬦ *vt* - 1. [gen] to stop; [golpe] to parry - 2. [preparar] to prepare - 3. *Amér* [levantar] to raise. ⬥ **pararse** *vprnl* - 1. [detenerse] to stop - 2. *Amér* [ponerse de pie] to stand up - 3. *Méx & Ven* [salir de la cama] to get up.

pararrayos *sm inv* lightning conductor.

parásito, ta *adj* BIOL parasitic. ⬥ **parásito** *sm fig* & BIOL parasite. ⬥ **parásitos** *smpl* [interferencias] statics *pl*.

parasol *sm* parasol.

parcela *sf* - 1. [de tierra] plot (of land) - 2. [de saber] area.

parche *sm* - 1. [gen] patch - 2. [chapuza - para salir del paso] makeshift solution.

parchís *sm inv* ludo.

parcial ⬦ *adj* - 1. [no total] partial - 2. [no ecuánime] biased. ⬦ *sm* [examen] *end-of-term exam at university*.

parcialidad *sf* [tendenciosidad] bias, partiality.

parco, ca *adj* [escaso] meagre; [cena] frugal; [explicación] brief, concise.

pardillo, lla *Esp* ⬦ *adj* - 1. [ingenuo] naive - 2. [palurdo] countrified. ⬦ *sm, f* - 1. [ingenuo] naive person - 2. [palurdo] bumpkin, hick *US*.

pardo, da *adj* greyish-brown, dull brown.

parecer ⬦ *sm* - 1. [opinión] opinion - 2. [apariencia]: **de buen parecer** good-looking. ⬦ *vi* (antes de s) to look like; **parece un palacio** it looks like a palace. ⬦ *v cop* to look, to seem; **pareces cansado** you look O seem tired. ⬦ *v impers* - 1. [opinar]: **me parece que...** I think O it seems to me that...; **me parece que sí/no** I think/don't think so; **¿qué te parece?** what do you think (of it)? - 2. [tener aspecto de]: **parece que va a llover** it looks like it's going to rain; **parece que le gusta** it looks as if O it seems that she likes it; **eso parece** so it seems; **al parecer** apparently. ⬥ **parecerse** *vprnl*: **parecerse (en)** to be alike (in); **parecerse a alguien** [físicamente] to look like sb; [en carácter] to be like sb.

parecido, da *adj* similar; **bien parecido** [atractivo] good-looking. ⬥ **parecido** *sm*: **parecido (con/entre)** resemblance (to/between) ⬦ *sf* - 1. [gen] wall; **las paredes oyen** walls have ears; **subirse por las paredes** to hit the roof - 2. [de montaña] side.

paredón *sm* (thick) wall; [de fusilamiento] (execution) wall.

parejo, ja *adj*: **parejo (a)** similar (to). ⬥ **pareja** *sf* - 1. [gen] pair; [de novios] couple; **pareja de hecho** *common-law heterosexual or homosexual relationship*; **son una pareja de hecho** they live together as man and wife; **por parejas** in pairs - 2. [miembro del par - persona] partner.

parentela *sf fam* relations *pl*, family.

parentesco *sm* relationship.

paréntesis *sm inv* - 1. [signo] bracket; **entre paréntesis** in brackets, in parentheses - 2. [intercalación] digression - 3. [interrupción] break.

paria *smf* pariah.

parida *sf fam*: **eso es una parida** that's a load of nonsense; **decir paridas** to talk nonsense.

pariente, ta *sm, f* [familiar] relation, relative.

parir ⬦ *vi* to give birth. ⬦ *vt* to give birth to.

París *n pr* Paris.

parking ['parkin] (*pl* parkings) *sm* car park *UK*, parking lot *US*.

parlamentar *vi* to negotiate.

parlamentario, ria ⬦ *adj* parliamentary. ⬦ *sm, f* member of parliament.

parlamento *sm* POLIT parliament.

parlanchín, ina *fam* ⬦ *adj* chatty. ⬦ *sm, f* chatterbox.

parlante *adj* talking. ⬥ **parlante** *sm Amér* speaker.

parlotear *vi fam* to chatter.

paro *sm* - 1. *Esp* [desempleo] unemployment - 2. *Esp* [subsidio] unemployment benefit - 3. [cesación - acción] shutdown; [- estado] stoppage; **paro cardíaco** cardiac arrest - 4. *Amér* [huelga] strike.

parodia *sf* parody.

parodiar *vt* to parody.

parpadear *vi* - 1. [pestañear] to blink - 2. [centellear] to flicker.

párpado *sm* eyelid.

parque *sm* - 1. [gen] park; **parque acuático** waterpark; **parque de atracciones** amusement park; **parque comercial** retail park *UK*, shopping mall *US*; **parque eólico** wind farm; **parque nacional** national park; **parque tecnológico** science park; **parque temático** theme park; **(parque) zoológico** zoo - 2. [vehículos] fleet - 3. [para niños] playpen.

parqué, parquet [par'ke] (*pl* **parquets**) *sm* parquet (floor).

parqueadero *sm Amér* car park, parking lot *US*.

parquear *vt Amér* to park.

parquet = **parqué**.

parquímetro *sm* parking meter.

parra *sf* grapevine.

parrafada *sf* earful, dull monologue.

párrafo *sm* paragraph.

parranda *sf fam* [juerga]: **irse de parranda** to go out on the town.

parrilla *sf* [utensilio] grill; **a la parrilla** grilled, broiled *US*.

parrillada *sf* mixed grill.

párroco *sm* parish priest.

parroquia *sf* - **1.** [iglesia] parish church - **2.** [jurisdicción] parish - **3.** [clientela] clientele.

parroquiano, na *sm, f* - **1.** [feligrés] parishioner - **2.** [cliente] customer.

parsimonia *sf* deliberation; **con parsimonia** unhurriedly.

parte <> *sm* report; **dar parte (a alguien de algo)** to report (sthg to sb); **parte facultativo** O **médico** medical report; **parte meteorológico** weather forecast. <> *sf* [gen] part; [bando] side; DER party; **la mayor parte de la gente** most people; **la tercera parte de** a third of; **en alguna parte** somewhere; **no lo veo por ninguna parte** I can't find it anywhere; **en parte** to a certain extent, partly; **por mi parte** for my part; **por parte de padre/madre** on one's father's/mother's side; **por partes** bit by bit; **por una parte... por la otra...** on the one hand... on the other (hand)...; **tomar parte en algo** to take part in sthg. ◆ **de parte de** *loc prep* on behalf of, for; **¿de parte de (quién)?** TELECOM who is calling, please? ◆ **por otra parte** *loc adv* [además] what is more, besides.

partera *sf* midwife.

parterre *sm Esp* flowerbed.

partición *sf* [reparto] sharing out; [de territorio] partitioning.

participación *sf* - **1.** [colaboración] participation - **2.** [de lotería] share of a lottery ticket - **3.** [comunicación] notice.

participante *smf* participant.

participar <> *vi* [colaborar]: **participar (en)** to take part O participate (in); FIN to have a share (in). <> *vt*: **participar algo a alguien** to notify sb of sthg.

partícipe <> *adj*: **partícipe (de)** involved (in); **hacer partícipe de algo a alguien** [notificar] to notify sb of sthg; [compartir] to share sthg with sb. <> *smf* participant.

partícula *sf* particle.

particular <> *adj* - **1.** [gen] particular; **tiene su sabor particular** it has its own particular taste; **en particular** in particular - **2.** [no público - domicilio, clases etc] private - **3.** [no corriente - habilidad etc] uncommon. <> *smf* [persona] member of the public. <> *sm* [asunto] matter.

particularizar <> *vt* [caracterizar] to characterize. <> *vi* - **1.** [detallar] to go into details - **2.** [personalizar]: **particularizar en alguien** to single sb out.

partida *sf* - **1.** [marcha] departure - **2.** [en juego] game - **3.** [documento] certificate; **partida de defunción/matrimonio/nacimiento** death/marriage/birth certificate - **4.** [COM - mercancía] consignment; [- entrada] item, entry.

partidario, ria <> *adj*: **partidario de** in favour of, for. <> *sm, f* supporter.

partidista *adj* partisan, biased.

partido *sm* - **1.** POLÍT party - **2.** DEP match; **partido amistoso** friendly (match) - **3.** *loc*: **sacar partido de** to make the most of; **tomar partido por** to side with.

partir <> *vt* - **1.** [dividir] to divide, to split - **2.** [repartir] to share out - **3.** [romper] to break open; [cascar] to crack; [tronco, loncha etc] to cut. <> *vi* - **1.** [marchar] to leave, to set off - **2.** [basarse]: **partir de** to start from. ◆ **partirse** *vprnl* - **1.** [romperse] to split - **2.** [rajarse] to crack. ◆ **a partir de** *loc prep* starting from; **a partir de aquí** from here on.

partitura *sf* score.

parto *sm* birth; **estar de parto** to be in labour; **parto natural/prematuro** natural/premature birth.

parvulario *sm* nursery school, kindergarten.

pasa *sf* [fruta] raisin; **pasa de Corinto** currant; **pasa de Esmirna** sultana.

pasable *adj* passable.

pasada ▷ **pasado**.

pasadizo *sm* passage.

pasado, da *adj* - **1.** [gen] past; **pasado un año** a year later; **lo pasado, pasado está** let bygones be bygones - **2.** [último] last; **el año pasado** last year - **3.** [podrido] off, bad - **4.** [hecho - filete, carne] well done. ◆ **pasado** *sm* [gen] past; GRAM past (tense). ◆ **pasada** *sf* [con el trapo] wipe; [con la brocha] coat. ◆ **de pasada** *loc adv* in passing. ◆ **mala pasada** *sf* dirty trick.

pasador *sm* - **1.** [cerrojo] bolt - **2.** [para el pelo] slide.

pasaje *sm* - **1.** [billete] ticket - **2.** [pasajeros] passengers *pl* - **3.** [calle] passage - **4.** [fragmento] passage.

pasajero, ra <> *adj* passing. <> *sm, f* passenger.

pasamanos *sm inv* [de escalera interior] banister; [de escalera exterior] handrail.

pasamontañas *sm inv* balaclava (helmet).

pasapalos *smpl* *Méx & Ven* snacks, appetizers.

pasaporte *sm* passport.

pasapuré *sm* food mill.

pasapurés *sm inv* = **pasapuré**.

pasar <> *vt* - 1. [gen] to pass; [noticia, aviso] to pass on; ¿me pasas la sal? would you pass me the salt?; **pasar algo por** [filtrar] to pass sthg through - 2. [cruzar] to cross; **pasar la calle** to cross the road; **pasé el río a nado** I swam across the river - 3. [traspasar] to pass through - 4. [trasladar]: **pasar algo a** to move sthg to - 5. [llevar adentro] to show in; **el criado nos pasó al salón** the butler showed us into the living room - 6. [contagiar]: **pasar algo a alguien** to give sthg to sb, to infect sb with sthg; **me has pasado la tos** you've given me your cough - 7. [admitir - instancia etc] to accept - 8. [consentir]: **pasar algo a alguien** to let sb get away with sthg - 9. [rebasar - en el espacio] to go through; [- en el tiempo] to have been through; **pasar un semáforo en rojo** to go through a red light - 10. [emplear - tiempo] to spend; **pasó dos años en Roma** he spent two years in Rome - 11. [padecer] to go through, to suffer; **pasarlo mal** to have a hard time of it - 12. [sobrepasar]: **ya ha pasado los veinticinco** he's over twenty-five now; **mi hijo me pasa ya dos centímetros** my son is already two centimetres taller than me - 13. [adelantar - coche, contrincante etc] to overtake - 14. CINE to show. <> *vi* - 1. [gen] to pass, to go; **pasó por mi lado** he passed by my side; **el autobús pasa por mi casa** the bus goes past O passes in front of my house; **el Manzanares pasa por Madrid** the Manzanares goes O passes through Madrid; **he pasado por tu calle** I went your street; **pasar de... a...** to go O pass from... to...; **pasar de largo** to go by - 2. [entrar] to go/come in; **¡pase!** come in! - 3. [poder entrar]: **pasar (por)** to go (through); **por ahí no pasa** it won't go through there - 4. [ir un momento] to pop in; **pasaré por mi oficina/por tu casa** I'll pop into my office/ round to your place - 5. [suceder] to happen; ¿**qué pasa aquí?** what's going on here?; ¿**qué pasa?** what's the matter?; **pase lo que pase** whatever happens, come what may - 6. [terminarse] to be over; **pasó la Navidad** Christmas is over - 7. [transcurrir] to go by - 8. [cambiar - acción]: **pasar a** to move on to; **pasemos a otra cosa** let's move on to something else - 9. [conformarse]: **pasar (con/sin algo)** to make do (with/without sthg); **tendrá que pasar sin coche** she'll have to make do without a car - 10. [servir] to be all right, to be usable; **puede pasar** it'll do - 11. *fam* [prescindir]: **pasar de algo/alguien** to want nothing to do with sthg/sb; **paso de política** I'm not into politics - 12. [tolerar]: **pasar por algo** to put up with

sthg. ◆ **pasarse** *vprnl* - 1. [acabarse] to pass; **siéntate hasta que se te pase** sit down until you feel better - 2. [emplear - tiempo] to spend, to pass; **se pasaron el día hablando** they spent all day talking - 3. [desaprovecharse] to slip by; **se me pasó la oportunidad** I missed my chance - 4. [estropearse - comida] to go off; [- flores] to fade - 5. [cambiar de bando]: **pasarse a to** go over to - 6. [omitir] to miss out; **te has pasado una página** you've missed a page out - 7. [olvidarse]: **pasársele a alguien** to slip sb's mind; **se me pasó decírtelo** I forgot to mention it to you - 8. [no fijarse]: **pasársele a alguien** to escape sb's attention; **no se le pasa nada** he never misses a thing - 9. [excederse]: **pasarse de generoso/bueno** to be far too generous/kind - 10. *fam* [propasarse] to go over the top; **te has pasado diciéndole eso** what you said went too far O was over the top - 11. [divertirse]: ¿**qué tal te lo estás pasando?** how are you enjoying yourself?

pasarela *sf* - 1. [puente] footbridge; [para desembarcar] gangway - 2. [en un desfile] catwalk.

pasatiempo *sm* [hobby] pastime, hobby.

Pascua *sf* - 1. [de los judíos] Passover - 2. [de los cristianos] Easter; **hacer la Pascua a alguien** *fam* [ser pesado] to pester sb; [poner en apuros] to land sb in it. ◆ **Pascuas** *sfpl* [Navidad] Christmas *sing*; **¡felices Pascuas!** Merry Christmas!; **de Pascuas a Ramos** *fam* once in a blue moon.

pase *sm* - 1. [gen, DEP & TAUROM] pass - 2. *Esp* [proyección] showing, screening - 3. [desfile] parade; **pase de modelos** fashion parade.

pasear <> *vi* to go for a walk. <> *vt* to take for a walk; [perro] to walk; *fig* to show off, to parade.

paseo *sm* - 1. [acción - a pie] walk; [- en coche] drive; [- a caballo] ride; [- en barca] row; **dar un paseo** [a pie] to go for a walk - 2. [lugar] avenue; **paseo marítimo** promenade.

pasillo *sm* corridor.

pasión *sf* passion. ◆ **Pasión** *sf* RELIG: **la pasión** the Passion.

pasivo, va *adj* - 1. [gen & GRAM] passive - 2. [población etc] inactive. ◆ **pasivo** *sm* COM liabilities *pl*.

pasmado, da *adj* - 1. [asombrado] astonished, astounded - 2. [atontado] stunned.

pasmar *vt* to astound. ◆ **pasmarse** *vprnl* to be astounded.

pasmo *sm* astonishment.

pasmoso, sa *adj* astonishing.

paso *sm* - 1. [gen] step; [huella] footprint - 2. [acción] passing; [cruce] crossing; [camino de acceso] way through, thoroughfare; **abrir paso a alguien** *lit & fig* to make way for sb; **ceder el paso (a alguien)** to let sb past; AUTO to give way (to sb); **'ceda el paso'** 'give way'; **'prohi-**

bido el paso' 'no entry'; **paso elevado** fly-over; **paso a nivel** level crossing; **paso de cebra** zebra crossing - **3.** [forma de andar] walk; [ritmo] pace - **4.** [GEOGR - en montaña] pass; [- en el mar] strait - **5.** *(gen pl)* [gestión] step; [progreso] advance; **dar los pasos necesarios** to take the necessary steps - **6.** *loc*: **a cada paso** every other minute; **está a dos O cuatro pasos** it's just down the road; **estar de paso** to be passing through; **paso a paso** step by step; **salir del paso** to get out of trouble. ➡ **de paso** *loc adv* in passing.

pasodoble *sm* paso doble.

pasota *Esp fam* ◇ *adj* apathetic. ◇ *smf* dropout.

pasta *sf* - **1.** [masa] paste; [de papel] pulp; **pasta dentífrica** toothpaste - **2.** [CULIN - espagueti etc] pasta; [- de pasteles] pastry; [- de pan] dough - **3.** [pastelillo] pastry - **4.** *Esp fam* [dinero] dough - **5.** [encuadernación]: **en pasta** hardback.

pastar *vi* to graze.

pastel *sm* - **1.** [CULIN - dulce] cake; [- salado] pie - **2.** ARTE pastel.

pastelería *sf* - **1.** [establecimiento] cake shop, patisserie - **2.** [repostería] pastries *pl*.

pasteurizado, da [pasteuriˈθaðo, da] *adj* pasteurized.

pastiche *sm* pastiche.

pastilla *sf* - **1.** MED pill, tablet - **2.** [de jabón, chocolate] bar - **3.** [de caldo] cube.

pasto *sm* - **1.** [sitio] pasture - **2.** [hierba] fodder - **3.** *Amér* [hierba] lawn, grass - **4.** *loc*: **ser pasto de las llamas** to go up in flames.

pastón *sm fam*: **vale un pastón** it costs a bomb.

pastor, ra *sm, f* [de ganado] shepherd (*f* shepherdess). ➡ **pastor** *sm* - **1.** [sacerdote] minister - **2.** ▷ **perro**.

pastoso, sa *adj* - **1.** [blando] pasty; [arroz] sticky - **2.** [seco] dry.

pata ◇ *sf* - **1.** [pierna] leg - **2.** [pie - gen] foot; [- de perro, gato] paw; [- de vaca, caballo] hoof - **3.** *fam* [de persona] leg; **a cuatro patas** on all fours; **ir a la pata coja** to hop - **4.** [de mueble] leg; [de gafas] arm - **5.** *loc*: **meter la pata** to put one's foot in it; **poner/estar patas arriba** to turn/be upside down; **tener mala pata** to be unlucky. ◇ *sm Perú* [amigo] pal, mate *UK*, buddy *US*. ➡ **patas** *sfpl Chile fam* [poca vergüenza] cheek *(U)*. ➡ **pata de gallo** *sf* [en la cara] crow's feet *pl*.

patada *sf* kick; [en el suelo] stamp; **dar una patada a** to kick; **tratar a alguien a patadas** to treat sb like dirt.

patalear *vi* to kick about; [en el suelo] to stamp one's feet.

pataleo *sm* kicking *(U)*; [en el suelo] stamping *(U)*.

pataleta *sf* tantrum.

patán *sm* bumpkin.

patata *sf* potato; **patatas fritas** [de sartén] chips *UK*, French fries *US*; [de bolsa] crisps *UK*, chips *US*; **patata caliente** *fig* hot potato.

paté *sm* paté.

patear ◇ *vt* [dar un puntapié] to kick; [pisotear] to stamp on. ◇ *vi* [patalear] to stamp one's feet.

patentado, da *adj* patent, patented.

patente ◇ *adj* obvious; [demostración, prueba] clear. ◇ *sf* - **1.** [de invento] patent - **2.** *C Sur* [matrícula] number plate *UK*, license plate *US*.

paternal *adj* fatherly, paternal.

paternidad *sf* fatherhood; DER paternity.

paterno, na *adj* paternal.

patético, ca *adj* pathetic, moving.

patetismo *sm* pathos *(U)*.

patidifuso, sa *adj fam* stunned.

patilla *sf* - **1.** [de pelo] sideboard, sideburn - **2.** [de gafas] arm.

patín *sm* - **1.** [calzado - de cuchilla] ice skate; [- de ruedas] roller skate; [- en línea] roller blade - **2.** [patinete] scooter - **3.** [embarcación] pedal boat.

pátina *sf* patina.

patinaje *sm* skating.

patinar *vi* - **1.** [sobre hielo] to skate; [sobre ruedas] to roller-skate - **2.** [resbalar - coche] to skid; [- persona] to slip - **3.** *fam* [meter la pata] to put one's foot in it.

patinazo *sm* - **1.** [de coche] skid; [de persona] slip - **2.** *fam* [planchazo] blunder.

patinete *sm* scooter.

patio *sm* [gen] patio, courtyard; [de escuela] playground; [de cuartel] parade ground.

patitieso, sa *adj fam* - **1.** [de frío] frozen stiff - **2.** [de sorpresa] aghast, amazed.

pato, ta *sm, f* duck; **pagar el pato** to carry the can.

patológico, ca *adj* pathological.

patoso, sa *adj fam* clumsy.

patria ▷ **patrio**.

patriarca *sm* patriarch.

patrimonio *sm* - **1.** [bienes - heredados] inheritance; [- propios] wealth - **2.** *fig* [de una colectividad] exclusive birthright.

patrio, tria *adj* native. ➡ **patria** *sf* native country.

patriota *smf* patriot.

patriotismo *sm* patriotism.

patrocinador, ra *sm, f* sponsor.

patrocinar *vt* to sponsor.

patrocinio *sm* sponsorship.

patrón, ona *sm, f* - **1.** [de obreros] boss; [de criados] master (*f* mistress) - **2.** [de pensión etc] landlord (f landlady) - **3.** [santo] patron saint.

➤ **patrón** sm - **1.** [de barco] skipper - **2.** [en costura] pattern.

patronal ⟨⟩ adj [empresarial] management [antes de s]. ⟨⟩ sf - **1.** [de empresa] management - **2.** [de país] employers' organization.

patronato sm [gen] board; [con fines benéficos] trust.

patrono, na sm, f - **1.** [de empresa - encargado] boss; [- empresario] employer - **2.** [santo] patron saint.

patrulla sf patrol; **patrulla urbana** vigilante group.

patrullar vt & vi to patrol.

paulatino, na adj gradual.

pausa sf pause, break; MÚS rest; **con pausa** unhurriedly; **hacer una pausa** to pause; **pausa publicitaria** commercial break.

pausado, da adj deliberate, slow.

pauta sf - **1.** [gen] standard, model; **marcar la pauta** to set the standard - **2.** [en un papel] guideline.

pava ▷ **pavo**.

pavimentación sf [de carretera] road surfacing; [de acera] paving; [de suelo] flooring.

pavimento sm [de carretera] road surface; [de acera] paving; [de suelo] flooring.

pavo, va sm, f [ave] turkey; **pavo real** peacock (f peahen); **se le subió el pavo** she turned as red as a beetroot.

pavonearse vprnl despec: **pavonearse (de)** to boast O brag (about).

pavor sm terror.

paya sf Amér improvised poem accompanied by guitar.

payasada sf clowning (U); **hacer payasadas** to clown around.

payaso, sa sm, f clown.

payo, ya sm, f non-gipsy.

paz sf peace; [tranquilidad] peacefulness; **dejar a alguien en paz** to leave sb alone O in peace; **estar** O **quedar en paz** to be quits; **hacer las paces** to make (it) up; **poner paz entre** to reconcile, to make peace between; **que en paz descanse, que descanse en paz** may he/she rest in peace.

PC sm (abrev de **personal computer**) PC.

PD (abrev de **posdata**) PS.

pdo. abrev de **pasado**.

peaje sm toll.

peana sf pedestal.

peatón sm pedestrian.

peca sf freckle.

pecado sm sin; **estar en pecado** to be in sin; **morir en pecado** to die unrepentant; **pecado**

mortal mortal sin; **sería un pecado tirar este vestido** it would be a crime to throw out this dress.

pecador, ra sm, f sinner.

pecaminoso, sa adj sinful.

pecar vi RELIG to sin.

pecera sf fish tank; [redonda] fish bowl.

pecho sm - **1.** [tórax] chest; [de mujer] bosom - **2.** [mama] breast; **dar el pecho a** to breastfeed - **3.** Amér [en natación] breaststroke; **nadar pecho** to swim the breaststroke - **4.** loc: **a lo hecho, pecho** it's no use crying over spilt milk; **tomarse algo a pecho** to take sthg to heart.

pechuga sf [de ave] breast (meat).

pecoso, sa adj freckly.

pectoral adj ANAT pectoral, chest (antes de s).

peculiar adj - **1.** [característico] typical, characteristic - **2.** [curioso] peculiar.

peculiaridad sf - **1.** [cualidad] uniqueness - **2.** [detalle] particular feature O characteristic.

pedagogía sf education, pedagogy.

pedagogo, ga sm, f educator; [profesor] teacher.

pedal sm pedal; **pedal de embrague** clutch (pedal); **pedal de freno** brake pedal.

pedalear vi to pedal.

pedante adj pompous.

pedantería sf pomposity (U).

pedazo sm piece, bit; **a pedazos** in pieces O bits; **caerse a pedazos** to fall to pieces.

pedestal sm pedestal, stand; **poner/tener a alguien en un pedestal** to put sb on a pedestal.

pedestre adj on foot.

pediatra smf paediatrician.

pedicuro, ra sm, f chiropodist UK, podiatrist US.

pedido sm COM order; **hacer un pedido** to place an order.

pedigrí, pedigree [peðiˈɣri] sm pedigree.

pedir ⟨⟩ vt - **1.** [gen] to ask for; [en comercios, restaurantes] to order; **pedir a alguien que haga algo** to ask sb to do sthg; **pedir a alguien (en matrimonio)** to ask for sb's hand (in marriage); **pedir prestado algo a alguien** to borrow sthg from sb - **2.** [exigir] to demand - **3.** [requerir] to call for, to need - **4.** [poner precio]: **pedir (por)** to ask (for); **pide un millón por la moto** he's asking a million for the motorbike. ⟨⟩ vi [mendigar] to beg.

pedo sm fam [ventosidad] fart; **tirarse un pedo** to fart.

pedrada sf [golpe]: **a pedradas** by stoning; **matar a alguien a pedradas** to stone sb to death.

pedregullo sm R Dom gravel.

pedrería sf precious stones pl.

pedrusco *sm* rough stone.

pega *sf* [obstáculo] difficulty, hitch; **poner pegas (a)** to find problems (with).

pegadizo, za *adj* - **1.** [música] catchy - **2.** [contagioso] catching.

pegajoso, sa *adj* sticky; *despec* clinging.

pegamento *sm* glue.

pegar ⬦ *vt* - **1.** [adherir] to stick; [con pegamento] to glue; [póster, cartel] to fix, to put up; [botón] to sew on - **2.** [arrimar]: **pegar algo a** to put O place sthg against; **pega la silla a la pared** put the chair against the wall - **3.** [golpear] to hit - **4.** [propinar - bofetada, paliza etc] to give; [- golpe] to deal - **5.** [contagiar]: **pegar algo a alguien** to give sb sthg, to pass sthg on to sb. ⬦ *vi* - **1.** [adherir] to stick - **2.** [golpear] to hit - **3.** [armonizar] to go together, to match; **pegar con** to go with - **4.** [sol] to beat down. ➤ **pegarse** *vprnl* - **1.** [adherirse] to stick - **2.** [agredirse] to fight - **3.** [golpearse]: **pegarse (un golpe) con algo** to hit o.s. against sthg - **4.** [contagiarse - enfermedad] to be transmitted.

pegatina *sf* sticker.

pegote *sm fam* - **1.** [masa pegajosa] sticky mess - **2.** [chapucería] botch.

peinado *sm* hairdo; [estilo, tipo] hairstyle.

peinar *vt lit & fig* to comb. ➤ **peinarse** *vprnl* to comb one's hair.

peine *sm* comb; **pasarse el peine** to comb one's hair; **enterarse de O saber lo que vale un peine** *fam* to find out what's what O a thing or two.

peineta *sf* comb worn in the back of the hair.

p.ej. (*abrev de* **por ejemplo**) e.g.

Pekín *n pr* Peking, Beijing.

pela *sf fam* peseta; **no tengo pelas** I'm skint.

peladilla *sf* sugared almond.

pelado, da ⬦ *adj* - **1.** [cabeza] shorn - **2.** [piel, cara etc] peeling; [fruta] peeled - **3.** [habitación, monte, árbol] bare - **4.** [número] exact, round; **saqué un aprobado pelado** I passed, but only just - **5.** *fam* [sin dinero] broke, skint. ⬦ *sm, f Andes fam* [niño] kid. ➤ **pelado** *sm Esp* haircut.

pelaje *sm* [de gato, oso, conejo] fur; [de perro, caballo] coat.

pelar *vt* - **1.** [persona] to cut the hair of - **2.** [fruta, patatas] to peel; [guisantes, marisco] to shell - **3.** [aves] to pluck; [conejos etc] to skin. ➤ **pelarse** *vprnl* - **1.** [cortarse el pelo] to have one's hair cut - **2.** [piel, espalda etc] to peel.

peldaño *sm* step; [de escalera de mano] rung.

pelea *sf* - **1.** [a golpes] fight - **2.** [riña] row, quarrel.

pelear *vi* - **1.** [a golpes] to fight - **2.** [a gritos] to have a row O quarrel - **3.** [esforzarse] to struggle. ➤ **pelearse** *vprnl* - **1.** [a golpes] to fight - **2.** [a gritos] to have a row O quarrel.

pelele *sm fam despec* [persona] puppet.

peletería *sf* [tienda] fur shop, furrier's.

peliagudo, da *adj* tricky.

pelicano, pelícano *sm* pelican.

película *sf* [gen] film; **echar O poner una película** to show a film; **película muda/de terror** silent/horror film; **película del Oeste** western; **de película** amazing.

peligro *sm* danger; **correr peligro (de)** to be in danger (of); **estar/poner en peligro** to be/ put at risk; **en peligro de extinción** [especie, animal] endangered; **fuera de peligro** out of danger; **peligro de incendio** fire hazard; **¡peligro de muerte!** danger!

peligroso, sa *adj* dangerous.

pelín *sm fam* mite, tiny bit.

pelirrojo, ja ⬦ *adj* ginger, red-headed. ⬦ *sm, f* redhead.

pellejo *sm* [piel, vida] skin.

pellizcar *vt* [gen] to pinch.

pellizco *sm* pinch; **dar un pellizco a alguien** to give sb a pinch.

pelma, pelmazo, za *fam despec* ⬦ *adj* annoying, tiresome. ⬦ *sm, f* bore, pain.

pelo *sm* - **1.** [gen] hair - **2.** [de oso, conejo, gato] fur; [de perro, caballo] coat - **3.** [de una tela] nap - **4.** *loc*: **con pelos y señales** with all the details; **no tener pelos en la lengua** *fam* not to mince one's words; **poner a alguien los pelos de punta** *fam* to make sb's hair stand on end; **por los pelos, por un pelo** by the skin of one's teeth; **tomar el pelo a alguien** *fam* to pull sb's leg. ➤ **a contra pelo** *loc adv lit & fig* against the grain.

pelota ⬦ *sf* - **1.** [gen & DEP] ball; **jugar a la pelota** to play ball; **pelota vasca** pelota; **hacer la pelota (a alguien)** *fam* to suck up (to sb) - **2.** *fam* [cabeza] nut. ⬦ *smf* [persona] crawler, creep.

pelotera *sf fam* scrap, fight.

pelotón *sm* [de soldados] squad; [de gente] crowd; DEP pack.

pelotudo, da *R Dom fam* ⬦ *adj* stupid. ⬦ *sm, f* jerk.

peluca *sf* wig.

peluche *sm* plush.

peludo, da *adj* hairy.

peluquería *sf* - **1.** [establecimiento] hairdresser's (shop) - **2.** [oficio] hairdressing.

peluquero, ra *sm, f* hairdresser.

peluquín *sm* toupee; **¡ni hablar del peluquín!** *fam* it's out of the question!

pelusa *sf* - **1.** [de tela] fluff - **2.** [vello] down.

pelvis *sf inv* pelvis.

Pemex *smpl* (*abrev de* **Petróleos Mexicanos**) Mexican Oil.

pena sf - **1.** [lástima] shame, pity; **¡qué pena!** what a shame O pity!; **dar pena** to inspire pity; **el pobre me da pena** I feel sorry for the poor chap - **2.** [tristeza] sadness, sorrow - **3.** (gen pl) [desgracia] problem, trouble - **4.** (gen pl) [dificultad] struggle (U); **a duras penas** with great difficulty - **5.** [castigo] punishment; **so** O **bajo pena de** under penalty of; **pena capital** O **de muerte** death penalty - **6.** Amér [vergüenza] shame, embarrassment; **me da pena** I'm ashamed of it.

penacho sm - **1.** [de pájaro] crest - **2.** [adorno] plume.

penal <> adj criminal. <> sm prison.

penalidad (gen pl) sf suffering (U), hardship.

penalización sf - **1.** [acción] penalization - **2.** [sanción] penalty.

penalti, penalty sm DEP penalty.

penar <> vt [castigar] to punish. <> vi [sufrir] to suffer.

pender vi - **1.** [colgar]: **pender (de)** to hang (from) - **2.** [amenaza etc]: **pender sobre** to hang over.

pendiente <> adj - **1.** [por resolver] pending; [deuda] outstanding; **estar pendiente de** [atento a] to keep an eye on; [a la espera de] to be waiting for - **2.** [asignatura] failed. <> sm earring. <> sf slope.

pendón, ona sm, f fam libertine.

péndulo sm pendulum.

pene sm penis.

penene smf untenured teacher or lecturer.

penetración sf - **1.** [gen] penetration; **penetración de mercado** ECON market penetration - **2.** [sagacidad] astuteness.

penetrante adj - **1.** [intenso - dolor] acute; [- olor] sharp; [- frío] biting; [- mirada] penetrating; [- voz, sonido etc] piercing - **2.** [sagaz] sharp, penetrating.

penetrar <> vi: **penetrar en** [internarse en] to enter; [filtrarse por] to get into, to penetrate; [perforar] to pierce; [llegar a conocer] to get to the bottom of. <> vt - **1.** [introducirse en - arma, sonido etc] to pierce, to penetrate; [- humedad, líquido] to permeate; [- emoción, sentimiento] to pierce - **2.** [llegar a conocer - secreto etc] to get to the bottom of - **3.** [sexualmente] to penetrate.

penicilina sf penicillin.

península sf peninsula.

peninsular adj peninsular.

penitencia sf penance.

penitenciaría sf penitentiary.

penoso, sa adj - **1.** [trabajoso] laborious - **2.** [lamentable] distressing; [aspecto, espectáculo] sorry - **3.** Amér C, Caribe, Col & Méx [vergonzoso] shy.

pensador, ra sm, f thinker.

pensamiento sm - **1.** [gen] thought; [mente] mind; [idea] idea - **2.** BOT pansy.

pensar <> vi to think; **pensar bien/mal de alguien** to think well/ill of sb; **pensar en algo/en alguien/en hacer algo** to think about sthg/about sb/about doing sthg; **pensar sobre algo** to think about sthg; **piensa en un número/buen regalo** think of a number/good present; **dar que pensar a alguien** to give sb food for thought. <> vt - **1.** [reflexionar] to think about O over - **2.** [opinar, creer] to think; **pensar algo de alguien/algo** to think sthg of sb/sthg; **pienso que no vendrá** I don't think she'll come - **3.** [idear] to think up - **4.** [tener la intención de]: **pensar hacer algo** to intend to do sthg.

➤ **pensarse** vprnl: **pensarse algo** to think sthg over.

pensativo, va adj pensive, thoughtful.

pensión sf - **1.** [dinero] pension; **pensión de jubilación/de viudedad** retirement/widow's pension - **2.** [de huéspedes] = guest house; **media pensión** [en hotel] half board; **estar a media pensión** [en colegio] to have school dinners; **pensión completa** full board.

pensionista smf [jubilado] pensioner.

pentágono sm pentagon.

pentagrama sm MÚS stave.

penúltimo, ma adj & sm, f penultimate, last but one.

penumbra sf half-light.

penuria sf - **1.** [pobreza] penury, poverty - **2.** [escasez] paucity, dearth.

peña sf [grupo de amigos] circle, group; [club] club; [quinielística] pool.

peñasco sm large crag O rock.

peñón sm rock. ➤ **Peñón** sm: **el Peñón (de Gibraltar)** the Rock (of Gibraltar).

peón sm - **1.** [obrero] unskilled labourer - **2.** [en ajedrez] pawn.

peonza sf (spinning) top.

peor <> adj - **1.** (compar): **peor (que)** worse (than); **peor para él** that's his problem - **2.** (superl): **el/la peor...** the worst... <> pron: **el/la peor (de)** the worst (in); **el peor de todos** the worst of all; **lo peor fue que...** the worst thing was that... <> adv - **1.** (compar): **peor (que)** worse (than); **ahora veo peor** I see worse now; **estar peor** [enfermo] to get worse - **2.** (superl): worst; **el que lo hizo peor** the one who did it (the) worst.

pepinillo sm gherkin.

pepino sm BOT cucumber; **me importa un pepino** I couldn't care less.

pepita sf - **1.** [de fruta] pip - **2.** [de oro] nugget.

peppermint = **pipermín**.

pequeñez sf - **1.** [gen] smallness - **2.** fig [insignificancia] trifle; **discutir por pequeñeces** to argue over silly little things.

pequeño, ña adj small; **me queda pequeño** it's too small for me; [hermano] little; [posibilidad] slight; [ingresos, cifras etc] low.

pequinés sm [perro] Pekinese.

pera sf - 1. [fruta] pear - 2. [para ducha etc] (rubber) bulb - 3. C Sur [barbilla] chin - 4. loc: **pedir peras al olmo** to ask (for) the impossible; **ser la pera** fam to be the limit; **ser una pera en dulce** fam to be a gem.

peral sm pear tree.

percance sm mishap.

percatarse vprnl: **percatarse (de algo)** to notice (sthg).

percebe sm [pez] barnacle.

percepción sf [de los sentidos] perception; **percepción extrasensorial** extrasensory perception.

perceptible adj [por los sentidos] noticeable, perceptible.

percha sf - 1. [de armario] (coat) hanger - 2. [de pared] coat rack - 3. [para pájaros] perch.

perchero sm [de pared] coat rack; [de pie] coat stand.

percibir vt - 1. [con los sentidos] to perceive, to notice; [por los oídos] to hear; [ver] to see - 2. [cobrar] to receive, to get.

percusión sf percussion.

perdedor, ra sm, f loser.

perder ⬦ vt - 1. [gen] to lose; **llevas las de perder** you can't hope to win; **salir perdiendo** to come off worst - 2. [desperdiciar] to waste - 3. [tren, oportunidad] to miss. ⬦ vi - 1. [salir derrotado] to lose - 2. loc: **echar algo a perder** to spoil sthg; **echarse a perder** [alimento] to go off. ➠ **perderse** vprnl - 1. [gen] to get lost; **¡piérdete!** mfam get lost! - 2. [desaparecer] to disappear - 3. [desperdiciarse] to be wasted - 4. [desaprovechar]: **¡no te lo pierdas!** don't miss it! - 5. fig [por los vicios] to be beyond salvation.

perdición sf ruin, undoing.

pérdida sf - 1. [gen] loss; **no tiene pérdida** you can't miss it - 2. [de tiempo, dinero] waste - 3. [escape] leak. ➠ **pérdidas** sfpl - 1. FIN & MIL losses; **pérdidas humanas** loss of life - 2. [daños] damage (U).

perdidamente adv hopelessly.

perdido, da adj - 1. [extraviado] lost; [animal, bala] stray - 2. [sucio] filthy - 3. fam [de remate] complete, utter - 4. loc: **dar algo por perdido** to give sthg up for lost; **estar perdido** to be done for O lost.

perdigón sm pellet.

perdiz sf partridge.

perdón sm pardon, forgiveness; **no tener perdón** to be unforgivable; **¡perdón!** sorry!; **perdón, ¿me deja pasar?** excuse me, could you let me through?

perdonar ⬦ vt - 1. [gen] to forgive; **perdonarle algo a alguien** to forgive sb for sthg; **perdone que le moleste** sorry to bother you - 2. [eximir de - deuda, condena]: **perdonar algo a alguien** to let sb off sthg; **perdonarle la vida a alguien** to spare sb their life. ⬦ vi: **perdone, ¿cómo ha dicho?** excuse me, what did you say?

perdonavidas smf inv fam bully.

perdurar vi - 1. [durar mucho] to endure, to last - 2. [persistir] to persist.

perecedero, ra adj - 1. [productos] perishable - 2. [naturaleza] transitory.

perecer vi to perish, to die.

peregrinación sf RELIG pilgrimage.

peregrinaje sm RELIG pilgrimage.

peregrino, na ⬦ adj - 1. [ave] migratory - 2. fig [extraño] strange. ⬦ sm, f [persona] pilgrim.

perejil sm parsley.

perenne adj BOT perennial.

pereza sf idleness.

perezoso, sa adj [vago] lazy.

perfección sf perfection; **es de una gran perfección** it's exceptionally good.

perfeccionar vt - 1. [redondear] to perfect - 2. [mejorar] to improve.

perfeccionista adj & smf perfectionist.

perfecto, ta adj perfect.

perfidia sf perfidy, treachery.

perfil sm - 1. [contorno] outline, shape - 2. [de cara, cuerpo] profile; **de perfil** in profile - 3. fig [característica] characteristic - 4. fig [retrato moral] profile - 5. GEOM cross section.

perfilar vt to outline. ➠ **perfilarse** vprnl - 1. [destacarse] to be outlined - 2. [concretarse] to shape up.

perforación sf - 1. [gen & MED] perforation - 2. [taladro] bore-hole.

perforar vt [horadar] to perforate; [agujero] to drill; INFORM to punch.

perfume sm perfume.

perfumería sf - 1. [tienda, arte] perfumery - 2. [productos] perfumes pl.

pergamino sm parchment.

pericia sf skill.

periferia sf periphery; [alrededores] outskirts pl.

periférico, ca adj peripheral; [barrio] outlying.

perifollos smpl fam frills (and fripperies).

perífrasis sf inv: **perífrasis (verbal)** compound verb.

perilla sf goatee; **venir de perilla(s)** to be just the right thing.

perímetro sm perimeter.

periódico, ca adj [gen] periodic. ✹ **periódico** sm newspaper; **periódico dominical** Sunday paper.

periodismo sm journalism.

periodista smf journalist.

periodo, período sm period; DEP half.

peripecia sf incident, adventure.

peripuesto, ta adj fam dolled-up.

periquete sm: **en un periquete** fam in a jiffy.

periquito sm parakeet.

periscopio sm periscope.

peritar vt [casa] to value; [coche] to assess the damage to.

perito sm - 1. [experto] expert; **perito agrónomo** agronomist - 2. [ingeniero técnico] technician.

perjudicar vt to damage, to harm.

perjudicial adj: **perjudicial (para)** harmful (to).

perjuicio sm harm (U), damage (U).

perjurar vi [jurar en falso] to commit perjury.

perla sf pearl; **perla de cultivo** cultured pearl; fig [maravilla] gem, treasure; **de perlas** great, fine; **me viene de perlas** it's just the right thing.

perlé sm beading.

permanecer vi - 1. [en un lugar] to stay - 2. [en un estado] to remain, to stay.

permanencia sf - 1. [en un lugar] staying, continued stay - 2. [en un estado] continuation.

permanente ◇ adj permanent; [comisión] standing. ◇ sf perm; **hacerse la permanente** to have a perm.

permeable adj permeable.

permisible adj permissible, acceptable.

permisivo, va adj permissive.

permiso sm - 1. [autorización] permission; **con permiso** if I may, if you'll excuse me; **dar permiso para hacer algo** to give permission to do sthg - 2. [documento] licence, permit; **permiso de armas** gun licence; **permiso de conducir** driving licence UK, driver's license US; **permiso de residencia** residence permit - 3. [vacaciones] leave.

permitir vt to allow; **permitir a alguien hacer algo** to allow sb to do sthg; **¿me permite?** may I? ✹ **permitirse** vprnl to allow o.s. (the luxury of); **no puedo permitírmelo** I can't afford it.

permuta, permutación sf exchange.

pernicioso, sa adj damaging, harmful.

pero ◇ conj but; **la casa es vieja pero céntrica** the house may be old, but it's central; **pero ¿qué es tanto ruido?** what on earth is all this noise about? ◇ sm snag, fault; **poner peros a todo** to find fault with everything.

perol sm casserole (dish).

perorata sf long-winded speech.

perpendicular adj perpendicular; **ser perpendicular a algo** to be at right angles to sthg.

perpetrar vt to perpetrate, to commit.

perpetuar vt to perpetuate. ✹ **perpetuarse** vprnl to last, to endure.

perpetuo, tua adj - 1. [gen] perpetual - 2. [para toda la vida] lifelong; DER life (antes de s).

perplejo, ja adj perplexed, bewildered.

perra sf - 1. [rabieta] tantrum; **coger una perra** to throw a tantrum - 2. [dinero] penny; **estoy sin una perra** I'm flat broke - 3. ⊳ **perro**.

perrera ⊳ **perrero**.

perrería sf fam: **hacer perrerías a alguien** to play dirty tricks on sb.

perrero, ra sm, f [persona] dogcatcher. ✹ **perrera** sf - 1. [lugar] kennels pl - 2. [vehículo] dogcatcher's van.

perro, rra sm, f [animal] dog (f bitch); **perro callejero** stray dog; **perro de caza** hunting dog; **perro de compañía** pet dog; **perro faldero** lapdog; **perro lazarillo** guide dog; **perro lobo** alsatian; **perro pastor** sheepdog; **perro policía** police dog; **echar los perros a alguien** to have a go at sb; **ser perro viejo** to be an old hand. ✹ **perro caliente** sm hot dog.

persecución sf - 1. [seguimiento] pursuit - 2. [acoso] persecution.

perseguir vt - 1. [seguir, tratar de obtener] to pursue - 2. [acosar] to persecute - 3. [mala suerte, problema etc] to dog.

perseverante adj persistent.

perseverar vi: **perseverar (en)** to persevere (with), to persist (in).

persiana sf blind, shade US; **enrollarse como una persiana** fam to go on and on.

persistente adj persistent.

persistir vi: **persistir (en)** to persist (in).

persona sf - 1. [individuo] person; **cien personas** a hundred people; **de persona a persona** person to person; **en persona** in person; **por persona** per head; **ser buena persona** to be nice; **persona mayor** adult, grown-up - 2. DER party - 3. GRAM person.

personaje sm - 1. [persona importante] important person, celebrity; **ser todo un personaje** fam to be a real big shot - 2. [de obra] character.

personal ◇ adj [gen] personal; [teléfono, dirección] private, home (antes de s). ◇ sm [trabajadores] staff, personnel.

personalidad sf - 1. [características] personality - 2. [persona importante] important person, celebrity.

personalizar vi [nombrar] to name names.

personarse *vprnl* to turn up.

personero, ra *sm, f* Amér - **1.** [representante] representative - **2.** [portavoz] spokesperson.

personificar *vt* to personify.

perspectiva *sf* - **1.** [gen] perspective - **2.** [paisaje] view - **3.** [futuro] prospect; **en perspectiva** in prospect.

perspicacia *sf* insight, perceptiveness.

perspicaz *adj* sharp, perceptive.

persuadir *vt* to persuade; **persuadir a alguien para que haga algo** to persuade sb to do sthg. **persuadirse** *vprnl* to convince o.s.; **persuadirse de algo** to become convinced of sthg.

persuasión *sf* persuasion.

persuasivo, va *adj* persuasive.

pertenecer *vi* - **1.** [gen]: **pertenecer a** to belong to - **2.** [corresponder] to be a matter for.

perteneciente *adj*: **ser perteneciente a** to belong to.

pertenencia *sf* - **1.** [propiedad] ownership - **2.** [afiliación] membership. **pertenencias** *sfpl* [enseres] belongings.

pértiga *sf* - **1.** [vara] pole - **2.** DEP pole-vault.

pertinaz *adj* - **1.** [terco] stubborn - **2.** [persistente] persistent.

pertinente *adj* - **1.** [adecuado] appropriate - **2.** [relativo] relevant, pertinent.

pertrechos *smpl* - **1.** MIL supplies and ammunition - **2.** *fig* [utensilios] gear *(U)*.

perturbación *sf* - **1.** [desconcierto] disquiet, unease - **2.** [disturbio] disturbance; **perturbación del orden público** breach of the peace - **3.** MED mental imbalance.

perturbado, da *adj* - **1.** MED disturbed - **2.** [desconcertado] perturbed.

perturbador, ra *adj* unsettling. *sm, f* troublemaker.

perturbar *vt* - **1.** [trastornar] to disrupt - **2.** [inquietar] to disturb, to unsettle - **3.** [enloquecer] to perturb.

Perú *n pr*: **(el) Perú** Peru.

peruano, na *adj* & *sm, f* Peruvian.

perversión *sf* perversion.

perverso, sa *adj* depraved.

pervertido, da *sm, f* pervert.

pervertir *vt* to corrupt. **pervertirse** *vprnl* to be corrupted.

pesa *sf* - **1.** [gen] weight - **2.** *(gen pl)* DEP weights *pl*; **alzar pesas** to lift weights.

pesadez *sf* - **1.** [peso] weight - **2.** [sensación] heaviness - **3.** [molestia, fastidio] drag, pain - **4.** [aburrimiento] ponderousness.

pesadilla *sf* nightmare.

pesado, da *adj* - **1.** [gen] heavy - **2.** [caluroso] sultry - **3.** [lento] ponderous, sluggish - **4.** [duro] difficult, tough - **5.** [aburrido] boring - **6.** [molesto] annoying, tiresome; **¡qué pesado eres!** you're so annoying! *sm, f* bore, pain.

pesadumbre *sf* grief, sorrow.

pésame *sm* sympathy, condolences *pl*; **dar el pésame** to offer one's condolences; **mi más sentido pésame** my deepest sympathies.

pesar *sm* - **1.** [tristeza] grief - **2.** [arrepentimiento] remorse - **3.** *loc*: **a pesar mío** against my will. *vt* - **1.** [determinar el peso de] to weigh - **2.** [examinar] to weigh up. *vi* - **1.** [tener peso] to weigh - **2.** [ser pesado] to be heavy - **3.** [importar] to play an important part - **4.** [entristecer]: **me pesa tener que decirte esto** I'm sorry to have to tell you this. **a pesar de** *loc prep* despite; **a pesar de todo** in spite of everything. **a pesar de que** *loc conj* in spite of the fact that.

pesca *sf* - **1.** [acción] fishing; **ir de pesca** to go fishing; **pesca con caña** angling; **pesca con red** net fishing - **2.** [lo pescado] catch.

pescadería *sf* fishmonger's (shop).

pescadilla *sf* whiting.

pescado *sm* fish.

pescador, ra *sm, f* fisherman (*f* fisherwoman).

pescar *vt* - **1.** [peces] to catch - **2.** *fig* [enfermedad] to catch - **3.** *fam fig* [conseguir] to get o.s., to land - **4.** *fam fig* [atrapar] to catch. *vi* to fish, to go fishing.

pescuezo *sm* neck.

pese **pese a** *loc prep* despite; **pese a que** even though.

pesebre *sm* - **1.** [para los animales] manger - **2.** [belén] crib, Nativity scene.

pesero *sm* Amér C & Méx fixed-rate taxi service.

peseta *sf* [unidad] peseta. **pesetas** *sfpl fig* [dinero] money *(U)*.

pesetero, ra *adj* moneygrubbing.

pesimismo *sm* pessimism.

pesimista *adj* pessimistic. *smf* pessimist.

pésimo, ma *superl de* **malo**. *adj* terrible, awful.

peso *sm* - **1.** [gen] weight; **tiene un kilo de peso** it weighs a kilo; **peso atómico/molecular** atomic/molecular weight; **peso bruto/neto** gross/net weight; **peso muerto** dead weight - **2.** [moneda] peso - **3.** [de atletismo] shot - **4.** [balanza] scales *pl*.

pesquero, ra *adj* fishing. **pesquero** *sm* fishing boat.

pesquisa *sf* investigation, inquiry.

pestaña *sf* [de párpado] eyelash; **pestañas postizas** false eyelashes; **quemarse las pestañas** *fig* to burn the midnight oil.

pestañear *vi* to blink; **sin pestañear** without batting an eyelid.

peste *sf* - **1.** [enfermedad, plaga] plague; **peste bubónica** bubonic plague - **2.** *fam* [mal olor] stink, stench - **3.** *loc:* **decir pestes de alguien** to heap abuse on sb.

pesticida *sm* pesticide.

pestilencia *sf* stench.

pestillo *sm* [cerrojo] bolt; [mecanismo, en verjas] latch; **correr O echar el pestillo** to shoot the bolt.

petaca *sf* - **1.** [para cigarrillos] cigarette case; [para tabaco] tobacco pouch - **2.** [para bebidas] flask - **3.** *Méx* [maleta] suitcase. ◆ **petacas** *sfpl Méx fam* buttocks.

pétalo *sm* petal.

petanca *sf* game similar to bowls played in parks, on beach etc.

petardo *sm* [cohete] firecracker.

petate *sm* kit bag; **liar el petate** *fam* [marcharse] to pack one's bags and go; [morir] to kick the bucket.

petición *sf* - **1.** [acción] request; **a petición de** at the request of - **2.** DER [escrito] petition.

petiso, sa, **petizo, za** ◇ *adj Andes & R Dom fam* [person] short. ◇ *sm Andes & R Dom* [caballo] small horse.

peto *sm* [de prenda] bib; **pantalón con peto** overalls.

petrificar *vt lit & fig* to petrify.

petrodólar *sm* petrodollar.

petróleo *sm* oil, petroleum.

petrolero, ra *adj* oil *(antes de s)*. ◆ **petrolero** *sm* oil tanker.

petrolífero, ra *adj* oil *(antes de s)*.

petulante *adj* opinionated.

peúco *(gen pl) sm* bootee.

peyorativo, va *adj* pejorative.

pez *sm* fish; **pez de colores** goldfish; **pez de río** freshwater fish; **pez espada** swordfish; **estar pez (en algo)** to have no idea (about sthg). ◆ **pez gordo** *sm fam fig* big shot.

pezón *sm* [de pecho] nipple.

pezuña *sf* hoof.

piadoso, sa *adj* - **1.** [compasivo] kind-hearted - **2.** [religioso] pious.

pianista *smf* pianist.

piano *sm* piano.

pianola *sf* pianola.

piar *vi* to cheep, to tweet.

PIB *(abrev de producto interior bruto) sm* GDP.

pibe, ba *sm, f R Dom fam* kid.

pica *sf* - **1.** [naipe] spade - **2.** [lanza] pike; **poner una pica en Flandes** to do the impossible. ◆ **picas** *sfpl* [palo de baraja] spades.

picadero *sm* [de caballos] riding school.

picadillo *sm* - **1.** [de carne] mince; [de verdura] chopped vegetables *pl*; **hacer picadillo a alguien** *fam* to beat sb to a pulp - **2.** *Chile* [tapas] snacks, appetizers.

picado, da *adj* - **1.** [marcado - piel] pockmarked; [- fruta] bruised - **2.** [agujereado] perforated; **picado de polilla** moth-eaten - **3.** [triturado - alimento] chopped; [- carne] minced; [- tabaco] cut - **4.** [vino] sour - **5.** [diente] decayed - **6.** [mar] choppy - **7.** *fig* [enfadado] annoyed.

picador, ra *sm, f* TAUROM picador.

picadora *sf* mincer.

picadura *sf* - **1.** [de mosquito, serpiente] bite; [de avispa, ortiga, escorpión] sting - **2.** [tabaco] (cut) tobacco *(U)*.

picaflor *sm Amér* - **1.** [colibrí] hummingbird - **2.** [galanteador] womanizer.

picante ◇ *adj* - **1.** [comida etc] spicy, hot - **2.** *fig* [obsceno] saucy. ◇ *sm* [comida] spicy food; [sabor] spiciness.

picantería *sf Andes* cheap restaurant.

picaporte *sm* [aldaba] doorknocker; [barrita] latch.

picar ◇ *vt* - **1.** [suj: mosquito, serpiente] to bite; [suj: avispa, escorpión, ortiga] to sting - **2.** [escocer] to itch; **me pican los ojos** my eyes are stinging - **3.** [triturar - verdura] to chop; [- carne] to mince - **4.** [suj: ave] to peck - **5.** [aperitivo] to pick at - **6.** [tierra, piedra, hielo] to hack at - **7.** *fig* [enojar] to irritate - **8.** *fig* [estimular - persona, caballo] to spur on; [- curiosidad] to prick - **9.** [perforar - billete, ficha] to punch. ◇ *vi* - **1.** [alimento] to be spicy O hot - **2.** [pez] to bite - **3.** [escocer] to itch - **4.** [ave] to peck - **5.** [tomar un aperitivo] to nibble - **6.** [sol] to burn - **7.** [dejarse engañar] to take the bait. ◆ **picarse** *vprnl* - **1.** [vino] to turn sour - **2.** [mar] to get choppy - **3.** [diente] to get a cavity - **4.** [oxidarse] to go rusty - **5.** *fig* [enfadarse] to get annoyed O cross.

picardía *sf* - **1.** [astucia] craftiness - **2.** [travesura] naughty trick, mischief *(U)*.

picaresco, ca *adj* mischievous, roguish. ◆ **picaresca** *sf* - **1.** LITER picaresque literature - **2.** [modo de vida] roguery.

pícaro, ra *sm, f* - **1.** [astuto] sly person, rogue - **2.** [travieso] rascal; *ver también* **picaresca**.

picatoste *sm* crouton.

pichi *sm* pinafore (dress).

pichichi *sm* DEP top scorer.

pichincha *sf Bol & R Dom fam* bargain.

pichón *sm* ZOOL young pigeon.

picnic *(pl picnics) sm* picnic.

pico *sm* - **1.** [de ave] beak - **2.** [punta, saliente] corner - **3.** [herramienta] pick, pickaxe - **4.** [cumbre] peak - **5.** [cantidad indeterminada]: **cincuen-**

ta y pico fifty-odd, fifty-something; **llegó a las cinco y pico** he got there just after five - **6.** *fam* [boca] gob, mouth; **ser** *O* **tener un pico de oro** to be a smooth talker, to have the gift of the gab.

picor *sm* [del calor] burning; [que irrita] itch.

picoso, sa *adj Méx* spicy, hot.

picotear *vt* [suj: ave] to peck.

pida, pidiera *etc* ⊏▷ **pedir**.

pie *sm* - **1.** [gen & ANAT] foot; **a pie** on foot; **estar de** *O* **en pie** to be on one's feet *O* standing; **ponerse de** *O* **en pie** to stand up; **de pies a cabeza** *fig* from head to toe; **seguir en pie** [vigente] to be still valid; **en pie de igualdad** on an equal footing; **en pie de guerra** at war; **pie de foto** caption - **2.** [de micrófono, lámpara etc] stand; [de copa] stem - **3.** *loc*: **al pie de la letra** to the letter, word for word; **buscarle (los) tres pies al gato** to split hairs; **dar pie a alguien para que haga algo** to give sb cause to do sthg; **no tener ni pies ni cabeza** to make no sense at all; **no tenerse de** *O* **en pie** [por cansancio] not to be able to stand up a minute longer; *fig* [por ser absurdo] not to stand up; **pararle los pies a alguien** to put sb in their place; **tener un pie en la tumba** to have one foot in the grave.

piedad *sf* - **1.** [compasión] pity; **por piedad** for pity's sake; **tener piedad de** to take pity on - **2.** [religiosidad] piety.

piedra *sf* - **1.** [gen] stone; **piedra angular** *lit & fig* cornerstone; **piedra pómez** pumice stone; **piedra preciosa** precious stone; **piedra de toque** touchstone - **2.** [de mechero] flint.

piel *sf* - **1.** ANAT skin; **piel roja** redskin (*N.B.: the term 'piel roja' is considered to be racist*); **piel de gallina** goose bumps - **2.** [cuero] leather - **3.** [pelo] fur - **4.** [cáscara] skin, peel.

piensa *etc* ⊏▷ **pensar**.

pierda *etc* ⊏▷ **perder**.

pierna *sf* leg; **estirar las piernas** to stretch one's legs.

pieza *sf* - **1.** [gen] piece; [de mecanismo] part; **dejar/quedarse de una pieza** to leave/be thunderstruck - **2.** [obra dramática] play - **3.** [habitación] room.

pifiar *vt*: **pifiarla** *fam* to put one's foot in it.

pigmento *sm* pigment.

pijama *sm* pyjamas *pl*.

pila *sf* - **1.** [generador] battery - **2.** [montón] pile; **tiene una pila de deudas** he's up to his neck in debt - **3.** [fregadero] sink.

pilar *sm* *lit & fig* pillar.

píldora *sf* pill; [anticonceptivo]: **la píldora** the pill; **píldora del día siguiente** morning after pill; **dorar la píldora** to sugar the pill.

pileta *sf R Dom* [piscina] swimming pool; [en baño] washbasin; [en cocina] sink.

pillaje *sm* pillage.

pillar ⊂▷ *vt* - **1.** [gen] to catch - **2.** [chiste, explicación] to get - **3.** [atropellar] to knock down. ⊂▷ *vi fam* [hallarse]: **me pilla lejos** it's out of the way for me; **me pilla de camino** it's on my way; **no me pilla de nuevas** it doesn't surprise me. ◆ **pillarse** *vprnl* [dedos etc] to catch.

pillo, lla *fam* ⊂▷ *adj* - **1.** [travieso] mischievous - **2.** [astuto] crafty. ⊂▷ *sm, f* [pícaro] rascal.

pilotar *vt* [avión] to fly, to pilot; [coche] to drive; [barco] to steer.

piloto ⊂▷ *smf* [gen] pilot; [de coche] driver; **piloto automático** automatic pilot. ⊂▷ *sm* - **1.** [luz - de coche] tail light; [- de aparato] pilot lamp - **2.** *C Sur* [impermeable] raincoat. ⊂▷ *adj inv* pilot (*antes de s*).

piltrafa (*gen pl*) *sf* scrap; *fam* [persona débil] wreck.

pimentón *sm* - **1.** [dulce] paprika - **2.** [picante] cayenne pepper.

pimienta *sf* pepper; **pimienta blanca/negra** white/black pepper.

pimiento *sm* [fruto] pepper, capsicum; [planta] pimiento, pepper plant; **pimiento morrón** sweet pepper; **me importa un pimiento** *fam* I couldn't care less.

pimpollo *sm* - **1.** [de rama, planta] shoot; [de flor] bud - **2.** *fam fig* [persona atractiva] gorgeous person.

pinacoteca *sf* art gallery.

pinar *sm* pine wood *O* grove.

pinaza *sf* pine needles *pl*.

pincel *sm* [para pintar] paintbrush; [para maquillar etc] brush.

pinchadiscos *smf inv* disc jockey.

pinchar ⊂▷ *vt* - **1.** [punzar - gen] to prick; [- rueda] to puncture; [- globo, balón] to burst - **2.** [penetrar] to pierce - **3.** *fam* [teléfono] to tap - **4.** *fig* [irritar] to torment - **5.** *fig* [incitar]: **pinchar a alguien para que haga algo** to urge sb to do sthg. ⊂▷ *vi* - **1.** [rueda] to get a puncture - **2.** [barba] to be prickly. ◆ **pincharse** *vprnl* - **1.** [punzarse - persona] to prick o.s.; [- rueda] to get a puncture - **2.** [inyectarse]: **pincharse (algo)** [medicamento] to inject o.s. (with sthg); *fam* [droga] to shoot up (with sthg).

pinchazo *sm* - **1.** [punzada] prick - **2.** [marca] needle mark - **3.** [de neumático, balón etc] puncture, flat *US*.

pinche ⊂▷ *sm, f* kitchen boy (*f* kitchen maid). ⊂▷ *adj Méx fam* lousy, damn.

pinchito *sm* - **1.** CULIN [tapa] aperitif on a stick - **2.** CULIN [pincho moruno] shish kebab.

pincho *sm* - **1.** [punta] (sharp) point - **2.** [espina - de planta] prickle, thorn - **3.** CULIN aperitif on a stick; **pincho moruno** shish kebab.

pinga *sf Andes & Méx vulg* prick, cock.

pingajo *sm fam despec* rag.

ping-pong® [pin'pon] *sm* table-tennis.

pingüino *sm* penguin.

pinitos *smpl*: **hacer pinitos** *lit & fig* to take one's first steps.

pino *sm* pine; **en el quinto pino** in the middle of nowhere.

pinta ▷ **pinto**.

pintado, **da** *adj* - **1.** [coloreado] coloured; **'recién pintado'** 'wet paint' - **2.** [maquillado] made-up - **3.** [moteado] speckled. ▰ **pintada** *sf* [escrito] graffiti *(U)*.

pintalabios *sm inv* lipstick.

pintar ▷ *vt* - **1.** to paint; **pintar algo de negro** to paint sthg black - **2.** [significar, importar] to count; **aquí no pinto nada** there's no place for me here; **¿qué pinto yo en este asunto?** where do I come in? ▷ *vi* [con pintura] to paint. ▰ **pintarse** *vprnl* [maquillarse] to make o.s. up.

pinto, **ta** *adj* speckled, spotted. ▰ **pinta** *sf* - **1.** [lunar] spot - **2.** *fig* [aspecto] appearance; **tener pinta de algo** to look *O* seem like sthg; **tiene buena pinta** it looks good - **3.** [unidad de medida] pint - **4.** *Méx* [pintada] graffiti *(U)*.

pintor, **ra** *sm*, *f* painter.

pintoresco, **ca** *adj* picturesque; *fig* [extravagante] colourful.

pintura *sf* - **1.** ARTE painting; **pintura a la acuarela** watercolour; **pintura al óleo** oil painting - **2.** [materia] paint.

pinza *(gen pl)* *sf* - **1.** [gen] tweezers *pl*; [de tender ropa] peg, clothespin *US* - **2.** [de animal] pincer, claw - **3.** [pliegue] fold.

piña *sf* - **1.** [del pino] pine cone - **2.** [ananás] pineapple - **3.** *fig* [conjunto de gente] close-knit group.

piñata *sf* pot full of sweets which blindfolded children try to break open with sticks at parties.

piñón *sm* - **1.** [fruto] pine nut - **2.** [rueda dentada] pinion.

pío, **a** *adj* pious. ▰ **pío** *sm* cheep, cheeping *(U)*; [de gallina] cluck, clucking *(U)*; **no decir ni pío** *fig* not to make a peep.

piojo *sm* louse; **piojos** lice.

piola ▷ *adj* *Arg fam* - **1.** [astuto] shrewd - **2.** [estupendo] fabulous. ▷ *sf* *Amér* [cuerda] cord.

pionero, **ra** *sm*, *f* pioneer.

pipa *sf* - **1.** [para fumar] pipe - **2.** [pepita] seed, pip; **pipas (de girasol)** *sunflower seeds coated in salt* - **3.** *loc*: **pasarlo** *O* **pasárselo pipa** to have a whale of a time.

pipermín, **peppermint** [piper'min] *sm* peppermint liqueur.

pipí *sm fam* wee-wee; **hacer pipí** to have a wee-wee.

pique *sm* - **1.** [enfado] grudge - **2.** [rivalidad] rivalry - **3.** *loc*: **irse a pique** [barco] to sink; [negocio] to go under; [plan] to fail.

piquete *sm* [grupo]: **piquete de ejecución** firing squad; **piquete (de huelga)** picket.

pirado, **da** *adj fam* crazy.

piragua *sf* canoe.

piragüismo *sm* canoeing.

pirámide *sf* pyramid.

piraña *sf* piranha.

pirarse *vprnl fam* to clear off.

pirata ▷ *adj* pirate *(antes de s)*; [disco] bootleg. ▷ *smf lit & fig* pirate; **pirata informático** hacker.

piratear ▷ *vi* - **1.** [gen] to be involved in piracy - **2.** INFORM to hack. ▷ *vt* INFORM to hack into.

pirenaico, **ca** *adj* Pyrenean.

pírex, **pyrex**® *sm* Pyrex®.

Pirineos *smpl*: **los Pirineos** the Pyrenees.

piripi *adj fam* tipsy.

pirómano, **na** *sm*, *f* pyromaniac.

piropo *sm fam* flirtatious remark, ≃ wolf whistle.

pirotecnia *sf* pyrotechnics *(U)*.

pirrarse *vprnl fam*: **pirrarse por algo/alguien** to be dead keen on sthg/sb.

pirueta *sf* pirouette.

piruleta *sf* lollipop.

pirulí *(pl pirulís)* *sm* lollipop.

pis *(pl pises)* *sm fam* pee.

pisada *sf* - **1.** [acción] footstep; **seguir las pisadas de alguien** to follow in sb's footsteps - **2.** [huella] footprint.

pisapapeles *sm inv* paperweight.

pisar *vt* - **1.** [con el pie] to tread on - **2.** [uvas] to tread - **3.** *fig* [llegar a] to set foot in - **4.** *fig* [despreciar] to trample on - **5.** *fig* [anticiparse]: **pisar un contrato a alguien** to beat sb to a contract; **pisar una idea a alguien** to think of sthg before sb; **pisar fuerte** *fig* to be firing on all cylinders.

piscina *sf* swimming pool; **piscina al aire libre** open air swimming pool; **piscina climatizada** heated swimming pool.

Piscis ▷ *sm* [zodiaco] Pisces. ▷ *smf* [persona] Pisces.

piscolabis *sm inv fam* snack.

piso *sm* - **1.** [vivienda] flat - **2.** [planta] floor - **3.** [suelo - de carretera] surface; [- de edificio] floor - **4.** [capa] layer.

pisotear *vt* - **1.** [con el pie] to trample on - **2.** [humillar] to scorn.

pista *sf* - **1.** [gen] track; **pista de aterrizaje** runway; **pista de baile** dance floor; **pista cubierta**

indoor track; **pista de esquí** ski slope; **pista de hielo** ice rink; **pista de tenis** tennis court - **2.** *fig* [indicio] clue.

pistacho *sm* pistachio.

pisto *sm* ≃ ratatouille.

pistola *sf* - **1.** [arma - con cilindro] gun; [- sin cilindro] pistol - **2.** [pulverizador] spraygun; **pintar a pistola** to spray-paint.

pistolero, ra *sm, f* [persona] gunman. ➡ **pistolera** *sf* [funda] holster.

pistón *sm* - **1.** MECÁN piston - **2.** [MÚS - corneta] cornet; [- llave] key.

pitada *sf* *Amér fam* drag, puff.

pitar ⬦ *vt* - **1.** [arbitrar - partido] to referee; [- falta] to blow for - **2.** [abuchear]: **pitar a alguien** to whistle at sb in disapproval - **3.** *Amér fam* [fumar] to puff (on). ⬦ *vi* [tocar el pito] to blow a whistle; [del coche] to toot one's horn.

pitido *sm* whistle.

pitillera *sf* cigarette case.

pitillo *sm* [cigarrillo] cigarette.

pito *sm* - **1.** [silbato] whistle - **2.** [claxon] horn.

pitón *sm* [cuerno] horn.

pitonisa *sf* fortune-teller.

pitorrearse *vprnl fam*: **pitorrearse (de)** to take the mickey (out of).

pitorro *sm* spout.

piyama *sm o sf* *Amér* [pijama] pyjamas; **un piyama** a pair of pyjamas.

pizarra *sf* - **1.** [roca, material] slate - **2.** [encerado] blackboard, chalkboard *US*.

pizarrón *sm* *Amér* blackboard.

pizca *sf* *fam* - **1.** [gen] tiny bit; [de sal] pinch - **2.** *Méx* [cosecha] harvest, crop.

pizza ['pitsa] *sf* pizza.

pizzería [pitse'ria] *sf* pizzeria.

placa *sf* - **1.** [lámina] plate; [de madera] sheet; **placa solar** solar panel - **2.** [inscripción] plaque; [de policía] badge - **3.** [matrícula] number plate - **4.** [de cocina] ring - **5.** ELECTRÓN board - **6.**: **placa dental** dental plaque.

placenta *sf* placenta.

placentero, ra *adj* pleasant.

placer *sm* pleasure; **ha sido un placer (conocerle)** it has been a pleasure meeting you.

plácido, da *adj* [persona] placid; [día, vida, conversación] peaceful.

plafón *sm* ELECTR ceiling rose.

plaga *sf* - **1.** [gen] plague; AGRIC blight; [animal] pest - **2.** [epidemia] epidemic.

plagado, da *adj*: **plagado (de)** infested (with).

plagar *vt*: **plagar de** [propaganda etc] to swamp with; [moscas etc] to infest with.

plagiar *vt* [copiar] to plagiarize.

plagio *sm* [copia] plagiarism.

plan *sm* - **1.** [proyecto, programa] plan - **2.** *fam* [ligue] date - **3.** *fam* [modo, formal]: **lo dijo en plan serio** he was serious about it; **¡vaya plan de vida!** what a life!; **si te pones en ese plan...** if you're going to be like that about it...

plana ⊳ **plano**.

plancha *sf* - **1.** [para planchar] iron; **plancha de vapor** steam iron - **2.** [para cocinar] grill; **a la plancha** grilled - **3.** [placa] plate; [de madera] sheet - **4.** IMPR plate.

planchado *sm* ironing.

planchar *vt* to iron.

planeador *sm* glider.

planear ⬦ *vt* to plan. ⬦ *vi* - **1.** [hacer planes] to plan - **2.** [en el aire] to glide.

planeta *sm* planet.

planicie *sf* plain.

planificación *sf* planning; **planificación familiar** family planning.

planificar *vt* to plan.

planilla *sf* *Amér* [formulario] form.

plano, na *adj* flat. ➡ **plano** *sm* - **1.** [diseño, mapa] plan - **2.** [nivel, aspecto] level - **3.** CINE shot; **primer plano** close-up; **en segundo plano** *fig* in the background - **4.** GEOM plane. ➡ **plana** *sf* - **1.** [página] page; **en primera plana** on the front page - **2.** [loc]: **enmendarle la plana a alguien** to find fault with sb.

planta *sf* - **1.** BOT plant - **2.** [fábrica] plant; **planta depuradora** purification plant; **planta de envase** *O* **envasadora** packaging plant - **3.** [piso] floor; **planta baja** ground floor - **4.** [del pie] sole.

plantación *sf* - **1.** [terreno] plantation - **2.** [acción] planting.

plantado, da *adj* standing, planted; **dejar plantado a alguien** *fam* [cortar la relación] to walk out on sb; [no acudir] to stand sb up; **ser bien plantado** to be good-looking.

plantar *vt* - **1.** [sembrar] **plantar algo (de)** to plant sthg (with) - **2.** [fijar - tienda de campaña] to pitch; [- poste] to put in - **3.** *fam* [asestar] to deal, to land. ➡ **plantarse** *vprnl* - **1.** [gen] to plant o.s. - **2.** [en un sitio con rapidez]: **plantarse en** to get to, to reach.

planteamiento *sm* - **1.** [exposición] raising, posing - **2.** [enfoque] approach.

plantear *vt* - **1.** [exponer - problema] to pose; [- posibilidad, dificultad, duda] to raise - **2.** [enfocar] to approach. ➡ **plantearse** *vprnl*: **plantearse algo** to consider sthg, to think about sthg.

plantel *sm fig* [conjunto] group.

plantilla *sf* - **1.** [de empresa] staff - **2.** [suela interior] insole - **3.** [patrón] pattern, template.

plantón *sm*: **dar un plantón a alguien** *fam* to stand sb up.

plañidero, ra *adj* plaintive.

plañir *vi* to moan, to wail.

plasmar *vt* - **1.** *fig* [reflejar] to give shape to - ? [modelar] to shape, to mould. **plasmarse** *vprnl* to take shape.

plasta ◇ *adj mfam*: **ser plasta** to be a pain. ◇ *smf mfam* [pesado] pain, drag.

plástico, ca *adj* [gen] plastic. **plástico** *sm* [gen] plastic.

plastificar *vt* to plasticize.

plastilina® *sf* ≃ Plasticine®.

plata *sf* - **1.** [metal] silver; **plata de ley** sterling silver; **hablar en plata** *fam* to speak bluntly - **2.** [objetos de plata] silverware - **3.** *Amér* [dinero] money.

plataforma *sf* - **1.** [gen] platform; **plataforma espacial** space station; **plataforma petrolífera** oil rig - **2.** *fig* [punto de partida] launching pad - **3.** GEOL shelf.

platal *sm Amér fam*: **un platal** a fortune, loads of money.

plátano *sm* - **1.** [fruta] banana - **2.** [banano] banana tree; [árbol platanáceo] plane tree.

platea *sf* stalls *pl*.

plateado, da *adj* - **1.** [con plata] silver-plated - **2.** *fig* [color] silvery.

plática *sf Amér C & Méx* talk, chat.

platicar *vi Amér C & Méx* to talk, to chat.

platillo *sm* - **1.** [plato pequeño] small plate; [de taza] saucer - **2.** [de una balanza] pan - **3.** (*gen pl*) MÚS cymbal. **platillo volante** *sm* flying saucer.

platina *sf* [de microscopio] slide.

platino *sm* [metal] platinum. **platinos** *smpl* AUTO & MECÁN contact points.

plato *sm* - **1.** [recipiente] plate, dish; **lavar los platos** to do the washing-up; **pagar los platos rotos** to carry the can - **2.** [parte de una comida] course; **primer plato** first course, starter; **de primer plato** for starters; **segundo plato** second course, main course; **plato fuerte** [en una comida] main course; *fig* main part - **3.** [comida] dish; **plato combinado** *single-course meal which usually consists of meat or fish accompanied by chips and vegetables*; **plato principal** main course - **4.** [de tocadiscos, microondas] turntable.

plató *sm* set.

platónico, ca *adj* Platonic.

platudo, da *adj Amér fam* loaded, rolling in it.

plausible *adj* - **1.** [admisible] acceptable - **2.** [posible] plausible.

playa *sf* - **1.** [en el mar] beach; **ir a la playa de vacaciones** to go on holiday to the seaside - **2.**: **playa de estacionamiento** *Amér* car park *UK*, parking lot *US*.

play-back ['pleiβak] (*pl* **play-backs**) *sm*: **hacer play-back** to mime (the lyrics).

playero, ra *adj* beach (*antes de s*). **playera** *sf Amér C & Méx* [camiseta] T-shirt. **playeras** *stpl* - **1.** [de deporte] tennis shoes - **2.** [para la playa] canvas shoes.

plaza *sf* - **1.** [en una población] square; **plaza mayor** main square - **2.** [sitio] place - **3.** [asiento] seat; **de dos plazas** two-seater (*antes de s*) - **4.** [puesto de trabajo] position, job; **plaza vacante** vacancy - **5.** [mercado] market, marketplace - **6.** TAUROM: **plaza (de toros)** bullring.

plazo *sm* - **1.** [de tiempo] period (of time); **en un plazo de un mes** within a month; **mañana termina el plazo de inscripción** the deadline for registration is tomorrow; **a corto/largo plazo** [gen] in the short/long term; ECON short/long term - **2.** [de dinero] instalment; **a plazos** in instalments, on hire purchase.

plazoleta *sf* small square.

plebe *sf*: **la plebe** *lit & fig* the plebs.

plebeyo, ya *adj* - **1.** HIST plebeian - **2.** [vulgar] common.

plebiscito *sm* plebiscite.

plegable *adj* collapsible, foldaway; [chair] folding.

plegar *vt* to fold; [mesita, hamaca] to fold away.

plegaria *sf* prayer.

pleito *sm* - **1.** DER [litigio] legal action (*U*), lawsuit; [disputa] dispute - **2.** *Amér* [discusión] argument.

plenario, ria *adj* plenary.

plenilunio *sm* full moon.

plenitud *sf* [totalidad] completeness, fullness.

pleno, na *adj* full, complete; **en pleno día** in broad daylight; **en plena guerra** in the middle of the war; **le dio en plena cara** she hit him right in the face; **en pleno uso de sus facultades** in full command of his faculties; **en plena forma** on top form. **pleno** *sm* [reunión] plenary meeting.

pletórico, ca *adj*: **pletórico de** full of.

pliego *sm* - **1.** [hoja] sheet (of paper) - **2.** [carta, documento] *sealed document* O *letter*; **pliego de condiciones** specifications *pl*.

pliegue *sm* - **1.** [gen & GEOL] fold - **2.** [en un plisado] pleat.

plisado *sm* pleating.

plomería *sf Méx, R Plata & Ven* plumber's.

plomero *sm Amér C, Caribe, Méx & R Plata* plumber.

plomizo, za *adj* [color] leaden.

plomo *sm* - **1.** [metal] lead; **caer a plomo** to fall O drop like a stone - **2.** [pieza de metal] lead weight - **3.** [fusible] fuse.

pluma ◇ *sf* - **1.** [de ave] feather - **2.** [para escribir] (fountain) pen; HIST quill; **pluma estilográfica** fountain pen - **3.** *Caribe & Méx* [bolígrafo] ballpoint pen - **4.** *Caribe, Col & Méx* [grifo] tap. ◇ *adj inv* DEP featherweight.

plum-cake [pluŋ'keik] (*pl* **plum-cakes**) *sm* fruit cake.

plumero *sm* feather duster; **vérsele a alguien el plumero** *fam* to see through sb.

plumier (*pl* **plumiers**) *sm* pencil box.

plumilla *sf* nib.

plumón *sm* - **1.** [de ave] down - **2.** *Chile & Méx* [rotulador] felt-tip pen.

plural *adj* & *sm* plural.

pluralidad *sf* diversity.

pluralismo *sm* pluralism.

pluralizar *vi* to generalize.

pluriempleo *sm*: **hacer pluriempleo** to have more than one job.

plus (*pl* **pluses**) *sm* bonus.

pluscuamperfecto *adj* & *sm* pluperfect.

plusmarca *sf* record.

plusvalía *sf* ECON appreciation, added value.

Plutón *n pr* Pluto.

pluvial *adj* rain *(antes de s)*.

p.m. (*abrev de* **post merídiem**) p.m.

PNB (*abrev de* **producto nacional bruto**) *sm* GNP.

PNV (*abrev de* **Partido Nacionalista Vasco**) *sm* Basque nationalist party.

población *sf* - **1.** [ciudad] town, city; [pueblo] village - **2.** *Chile* [chabola] shanty town - **3.** [habitantes] population.

poblado, da *adj* - **1.** [habitado] inhabited; **una zona muy poblada** a densely populated area - **2.** *fig* [lleno] full; **poblado de algo** full of sthg; [barba, cejas] bushy. **poblado** *sm* settlement.

poblador, ra *sm, f* settler.

poblar *vt* - **1.** [establecerse en] to settle, to colonize - **2.** *fig* [llenar]: **poblar (de)** [plantas, árboles] to plant (with); [peces etc] to stock (with) - **3.** [habitar] to inhabit. **poblarse** *vprnl* - **1.** [colonizarse] to be settled with - **2.** *fig* [llenarse] to fill up; **poblarse (de)** to fill up (with).

pobre ◇ *adj* poor; **¡pobre hombre!** poor man!; **¡pobre de mí!** poor me! ◇ *smf* [gen] poor person; **los pobres** the poor, poor people; **¡el pobre!** poor thing!

pobreza *sf* [escasez] poverty; **pobreza de** lack O scarcity of.

pochismo *sm* *Méx fam* language mistake caused by English influence.

pocho, cha *adj* - **1.** [persona] off-colour - **2.** [fruta] over-ripe - **3.** *Méx fam* [americanizado] Americanized.

pocilga *sf* *lit & fig* pigsty.

pocillo *sm* *Amér* small cup.

pócima *sf* [poción] potion.

poción *sf* potion.

poco, ca ◇ *adj* little (*pl* few), not much (*pl* not many); **poca agua** not much water; **de poca importancia** of little importance; **hay pocos árboles** there aren't many trees; **pocas personas lo saben** few O not many people know it; **tenemos poco tiempo** we don't have much time; **hace poco tiempo** not long ago; **dame unos pocos días** give me a few days. ◇ *pron* little (*pl* few), not much (*pl* not many); **queda poco** there's not much left; **tengo muy pocos** I don't have very many, I have very few; **pocos hay que sepan tanto** not many people know so much; **un poco** a bit; **¿me dejas un poco?** can I have a bit?; **un poco de** a bit of; **un poco de sentido común** a bit of common sense; **unos pocos** a few. **poco** *adv* - **1.** [escasamente] not much; **este niño come poco** this boy doesn't eat much; **es poco común** it's not very common; **es un poco triste** it's rather sad; **por poco** almost, nearly - **2.** [brevemente]: **tardaré muy poco** I won't be long; **al poco de...** shortly after...; **dentro de poco** soon, in a short time; **hace poco** a little while ago, not long ago; **poco a poco** [progresivamente] little by little; **¡poco a poco!** [despacio] steady on!, slow down!

podar *vt* to prune.

podenco *sm* hound.

poder[1] *sm* - **1.** [gen] power; **estar en/hacerse con el poder** to be in/to seize power; **poder adquisitivo** purchasing power; **tener poder de convocatoria** to be a crowd-puller; **poderes fácticos** the church, military and press - **2.** [posesión]: **estar en poder de alguien** to be in sb's hands - **3.** (*gen pl*) [autorización] power, authorization; **dar poderes a alguien para que haga algo** to authorize sb to do sthg; **por poderes** by proxy.

poder[2] ◇ *vi* - **1.** [tener facultad] can, to be able to; **no puedo decírtelo** I can't tell you, I'm unable to tell you - **2.** [tener permiso] can, may; **no puedo salir por la noche** I'm not allowed to O I can't go out at night; **¿se puede fumar aquí?** may I smoke here? - **3.** [ser capaz moralmente] can; **no podemos portarnos así con él** we can't treat him like that - **4.** [tener posibilidad, ser posible] may, can; **podías haber cogido el tren** you could have caught the train; **puede estallar la guerra** war could O may break out; **¡hubiera podido invitarnos!** [expresa enfado] she could O might have invited us! - **5.** [ser capaz de dominar - enfermedad, rival]: **poder con** to be able to overcome - **6.** [ser capaz de realizar - tarea]: **poder con** to be able to cope with - **7.** *loc*: **a O hasta más no poder** as much as can be; **es avaro a más no poder** he's as miserly as can be; **no poder más** [estar cansado] to be too tired to carry on; [estar harto de comer] to be full (up); [estar enfadado] to have had enough; ¿se puede? may I come in?; **no poder con algo/alguien** [soportar] not to be able to stand sthg/sb; **no puedo con la hipocresía** I can't stand hypocrisy. <> *v impers* [ser posible] may; **puede que llueva** it may O might rain; **¿vendrás mañana? - puede** will you come tomorrow? - I may do; **puede ser** perhaps, maybe. <> *vt* [ser más fuerte que] to be stronger than.

poderío *sm* [poder] power.

poderoso, sa *adj* powerful.

podio, podium *sm* podium.

podólogo, ga *sm, f* chiropodist.

podrá ⊳ **poder**.

podrido, da <> *pp* ⊳ **pudrir**. <> *adj* - 1. rotten - 2. *R Dom* [persona]: **estoy podrido** I'm fed up.

poema *sm* poem.

poesía *sf* - 1. [género literario] poetry - 2. [poema] poem.

poeta *smf* poet.

poético, ca *adj* poetic.

poetisa *sf* female poet.

póker = póquer.

polaco, ca *adj & sm, f* Polish. ➡ **polaco** *sm* [lengua] Polish.

polar *adj* polar.

polarizar *vt fig* [miradas, atención, esfuerzo] to concentrate. ➡ **polarizarse** *vprnl* [vida política, opinión pública] to become polarized.

polaroid® *sf inv* Polaroid®.

polca *sf* polka.

polea *sf* pulley.

polémico, ca *adj* controversial. ➡ **polémica** *sf* controversy.

polemizar *vi* to argue, to debate.

polen *sm* pollen.

poleo *sm* pennyroyal.

poli *fam* <> *smf* cop. <> *sf* cops *pl*.

polichinela *sm* - 1. [personaje] Punchinello - 2. [títere] puppet, marionette.

policía <> *sm, f* policeman (*f* policewoman). <> *sf*: **la policía** the police.

policiaco, ca, policíaco, ca *adj* police (antes de s); [novela, película] detective (antes de s).

policial *adj* police (antes de s).

polideportivo, va *adj* multi-sport; [gimnasio] multi-use. ➡ **polideportivo** *sm* sports centre.

poliéster *sm inv* polyester.

polietileno *sm* polythene *UK*, polyethylene *US*.

polifacético, ca *adj* multifaceted, versatile.

poligamia *sf* polygamy.

polígamo, ma *adj* polygamous.

poligloto, ta, polígloto, ta *adj & sm, f* polyglot.

polígono *sm* - 1. GEOM polygon - 2. [terreno]: **polígono industrial/residencial** industrial/housing estate; **polígono de tiro** firing range.

polilla *sf* moth.

polipiel *sf* artificial skin.

Polisario (*abrev de* Frente Popular para la Liberación de Sakiet el Hamra y Río de Oro) *sm*: **el (Frente) Polisario** the Polisario Front.

politécnico, ca *adj* polytechnic. ➡ **politécnica** *sf* polytechnic.

político, ca *adj* - 1. [de gobierno] political - 2. [pariente]: **hermano político** brother-in-law; **familia política** in-laws *pl*. ➡ **político** *sm* politician. ➡ **política** *sf* - 1. [arte de gobernar] politics (*U*) - 2. [modo de gobernar, táctica] policy.

politizar *vt* to politicize. ➡ **politizarse** *vprnl* to become politicized.

polivalente *adj* [vacuna, suero] polyvalent; [edificio, sala] multipurpose.

póliza *sf* - 1. [de seguro] (insurance) policy - 2. [sello] stamp on a document showing that a certain tax has been paid.

polizón *sm* stowaway.

polla ⊳ **pollo**.

pollera *sf* C Sur skirt.

pollería *sf* poultry shop.

pollito *sm* chick.

pollo, lla *sm, f* ZOOL chick. ➡ **pollo** *sm* CULIN chicken. ➡ **polla** *sf vulg* cock, prick.

polo *sm* - 1. [gen] pole; **polo de atracción** O **atención** *fig* centre of attraction - 2. ELECTR terminal; **polo negativo/positivo** negative/positive terminal - 3. [helado] ice lolly - 4. [jersey] polo shirt - 5. DEP polo.

pololo, la *sm, f* Chile fam boyfriend (*f* girlfriend).

Polonia *n pr* Poland.

polución *sf* [contaminación] pollution.

polvareda *sf* dust cloud; **levantar una gran polvareda** *fig* to cause a commotion.

polvera *sf* powder compact.

polvo *sm* - 1. [en el aire] dust; **limpiar** O **quitar el polvo** to do the dusting - 2. [de un producto] powder; **en polvo** powdered; **polvos de talco** talcum powder; **polvos picapica** itching powder; **estar hecho polvo** *fam* to be knackered; **hacer polvo algo** to smash sthg; **limpio de polvo y paja** including all charges. ➡ **polvos** *smpl* [maquillaje] powder (*U*); **ponerse polvos** to powder one's face.

pólvora *sf* [sustancia explosiva] gunpowder; **correr como la pólvora** to spread like wildfire.

polvoriento, ta *adj* [superficie] dusty; [sustancia] powdery.

polvorín *sm* munitions dump.

polvorón *sm crumbly sweet made from flour, butter and sugar.*

pomada *sf* ointment.

pomelo *sm* [fruto] grapefruit.

pómez ⊳ **piedra**.

pomo *sm* knob.

pompa *sf* - **1.** [suntuosidad] pomp - **2.** [ostentación] show, ostentation - **3.**: **pompa (de jabón)** (soap) bubble. ◆ **pompas** *sfpl Méx fam* behind, bottom. ◆ **pompas fúnebres** *sfpl* [servicio] undertaker's *sing.*

pompis *sm inv fam* bottom, backside.

pompón *sm* pompom.

pomposo, sa *adj* - **1.** [suntuoso] sumptuous; [ostentoso] showy - **2.** [lenguaje] pompous.

pómulo *sm* [hueso] cheekbone.

ponchar *vt Amér C, Caribe & Méx* [rueda] to puncture.

ponchar *vt Amér C & Méx* [rueda] to puncture.

ponche *sm* punch.

poncho *sm* poncho.

ponderar *vt* - **1.** [alabar] to praise - **2.** [considerar] to weigh up.

ponencia *sf* [conferencia] lecture, paper; [informe] report.

poner ⟷ *vt* - **1.** [gen] to put; [colocar] to place, to put - **2.** [vestir]: **poner algo a alguien** to put sthg on sb - **3.** [contribuir, invertir] to put in; **poner dinero en el negocio** to put money into the business; **poner algo de mi/tu** *etc* **parte** to do my/your *etc* bit - **4.** [hacer estar de cierta manera]: **poner a alguien en un aprieto/de mal humor** to put sb in a difficult position/in a bad mood; **le has puesto colorado** you've made him blush - **5.** [calificar]: **poner a alguien de algo** to call sb sthg - **6.** [oponer]: **poner obstáculos a algo** to hinder sthg; **poner pegas a algo** to raise objections to sthg - **7.** [asignar - precio, medida] to fix, to settle; [- multa, tarea] to give; **le pusieron Mario** they called him Mario - **8.** [TELECOM - telegrama, fax] to send; [- conferencia] to make; **¿me pones con él?** can you put me through to him? - **9.** [conectar - televisión etc] to switch O put on; [- despertador] to set; [- instalación, gas] to put in - **10.** CINE, TEATRO & TV to show; **¿qué ponen en la tele?** what's on the telly? - **11.** [montar - negocio] to set up; **ha puesto una tienda** she has opened a shop - **12.** [decorar] to do up; **han puesto su casa con mucho lujo** they've done up their house in real style - **13.** [suponer] to suppose; **pongamos que sucedió así** (let's) suppose that's what happened; **pon que necesitemos cinco días** suppose we need five days; **poniendo que to-**

do salga bien assuming everything goes according to plan - **14.** [decir] to say; **¿qué pone ahí?** what does it say? - **15.** [huevo] to lay. ⟷ *vi* [ave] to lay (eggs). ◆ **ponerse** ⟷ *vprnl* - **1.** [colocarse] to put o.s.; **ponerse de pie** to stand up; **ponte en la ventana** stand by the window - **2.** [ropa, gafas, maquillaje] to put on - **3.** [estar de cierta manera] to go, to become; **se puso rojo de ira** he went red with anger; **se puso colorado** he blushed; **se puso muy guapa** she made herself attractive - **4.** [iniciar]: **ponerse a hacer algo** to start doing sthg - **5.** [de salud]: **ponerse malo** O **enfermo** to fall ill; **ponerse bien** to get better - **6.** [llenarse]: **ponerse de algo** to get covered in sthg; **se puso de barro hasta las rodillas** he got covered in mud up to the knees - **7.** [suj: astro] to set - **8.** [llegar]: **ponerse en** to get to. ⟷ *v impers Amér fam* [parecer]: **se me pone que...** it seems to me that...

pongo ⊳ **poner**.

poniente *sm* [occidente] West; [viento] west wind.

pontífice *sm* Pope, Pontiff.

pop *adj* pop.

popa *sf* stern.

popote *sm Méx* drinking straw.

populacho *sm despec* mob, masses *pl.*

popular *adj* - **1.** [del pueblo] of the people; [arte, música] folk - **2.** [famoso] popular.

popularidad *sf* popularity; **gozar de popularidad** to be popular.

popularizar *vt* to popularize. ◆ **popularizarse** *vprnl* to become popular.

popurrí *sm* potpourri.

póquer, póker *sm* [juego] poker.

por *prep* - **1.** [causa] because of; **se enfadó por tu comportamiento** she got angry because of your behaviour - **2.** *(antes de infinitivo)* [finalidad] (in order) to; *(antes de s, pron)* for; **lo hizo por complacerte** he did it to please you; **lo hice por ella** I did it for her - **3.** [medio, modo, agente] by; **por mensajero/fax** by courier/fax; **por escrito** in writing; **lo cogieron por el brazo** they took him by the arm; **el récord fue batido por el atleta** the record was broken by the athlete - **4.** [tiempo aproximado]: **creo que la boda será por abril** I think the wedding will be some time in April - **5.** [tiempo concreto]: **por la mañana/tarde** in the morning/afternoon; **por la noche** at night; **ayer salimos por la noche** we went out last night; **por unos días** for a few days - **6.** [lugar - aproximadamente en]: **¿por dónde vive?** whereabouts does he live?; **vive por las afueras** he lives somewhere on the outskirts; **había papeles por el suelo** there were papers all over the floor - **7.** [lugar - a través de] through; **iba paseando por el bosque/la calle** she was walking through the forest/along the street; **pasar por la aduana** to go through customs - **8.** [a cambio de, en lugar de] for; **lo ha comprado por poco dinero** she bought it for very little; **cambió el coche por la moto** he exchanged his car for a motorbike; **él lo hara por mí** he'll do it for me - **9.** [distribución] per; **dos euros por unidad** 2 euros each; **20 kms por hora** 20 km an *O* per hour - **10.** MAT: **dos por dos igual a cuatro** two times two is four - **11.** [en busca de] for; **baja por tabaco** go down to the shops for some cigarettes, go down to get some cigarettes; **a por** for; **vino a por las entradas** she came for the tickets - **12.** [concesión]: **por más** *O* **mucho que lo intentes no lo conseguirás** however hard you try *O* try as you might, you'll never manage it; **no me cae bien, por (muy) simpático que te parezca** you may think he's nice, but I don't like him. ➡ **por qué** *pron* why; **¿por qué lo dijo?** why did she say it?; **¿por qué no vienes?** why don't you come?

porcelana *sf* [material] porcelain, china.

porcentaje *sm* percentage; **trabaja a porcentaje** he works on a commission basis.

porche *sm* [soportal] arcade; [entrada] porch.

porción *sf* portion, piece.

pordiosero, ra *sm, f* beggar.

porfía *sf* [insistencia] persistence; [tozudez] stubbornness.

porfiar *vi* [empeñarse]: **porfiar en** to be insistent on.

pormenor *(gen pl)* *sm* detail; **entrar en pormenores** to go into detail.

porno *adj fam* porno.

pornografía *sf* pornography.

pornográfico, ca *adj* pornographic.

poro *sm* pore.

poroso, sa *adj* porous.

poroto *sm Andes & R Plata* kidney bean.

porque *conj* - **1.** [debido a que] because; **¿por qué lo hiciste? – porque sí** why did you do it? – just because - **2.** [para que] so that, in order that.

porqué *sm* reason; **el porqué de** the reason for.

porquería *sf* - **1.** [suciedad] filth - **2.** [cosa de mala calidad] rubbish *(U)*.

porra *sf* - **1.** [palo] club; [de policía] truncheon - **2.** *Méx* DEP [hinchada] supporters - **3.** *loc*: **mandar a alguien a la porra** *fam* to tell sb to go to hell; **¡y una porra!** like hell!

porrazo *sm* [golpe] bang, blow; [caída] bump.

porro *sm fam* [de droga] joint.

porrón *sm glass wine jar used for drinking wine from its long spout.*

portaaviones, portaviones *sm inv* aircraft carrier.

portada *sf* - **1.** [de libro] title page; [de revista] (front) cover; [de periódico] front page - **2.** [de disco] sleeve.

portador, ra *sm, f* carrier, bearer; **al portador** COM to the bearer.

portaequipajes *sm inv* - **1.** [maletero] boot *UK*, trunk *US* - **2.** [baca] roofrack.

portafolio *sm* = **portafolios**.

portafolios *sm inv* [carpeta] file; [maletín] attaché case.

portal *sm* - **1.** [entrada] entrance hall; [puerta] main door - **2.** INFORM [página web] portal.

portalámparas *sm inv* socket.

portamonedas *sm inv* purse.

portar *vt* to carry. ➡ **portarse** *vprnl* to behave; **se ha portado bien conmigo** she has treated me well; **portarse mal** to misbehave.

portátil *adj* portable.

portavoz *sm, f* [persona] spokesman *(f* spokeswoman).

portazo *sm*: **dar un portazo** to slam the door.

porte *sm* - **1.** *(gen pl)* [gasto de transporte] carriage; **porte debido/pagado** COM carriage due/paid - **2.** [transporte] carriage, transport - **3.** [aspecto] bearing, demeanour.

portento *sm* wonder, marvel.

portentoso, sa *adj* wonderful, amazing.

porteño, ña *adj* from the city of Buenos Aires.

portería *sf* - **1.** [de casa, colegio] caretaker's *UK o* super(intendant)'s *US* office *O* lodge; [de hotel, ministerio] porter's office *O* lodge - **2.** DEP goal, goalmouth.

portero, ra *sm, f* - **1.** [de casa, colegio] caretaker *UK*, super(intendant) *US*; [de hotel, ministerio] porter; **portero automático** *O* **electrónico** *O* **eléctrico** entry-phone - **2.** DEP goalkeeper.

pórtico *sm* - **1.** [fachada] portico - **2.** [arcada] arcade.

portuario, ria *adj* port *(antes de s)*; [de los muelles] dock *(antes de s)*; **trabajador portuario** docker.

Portugal *n pr* Portugal.

portugués, esa *adj* & *sm, f* Portuguese. ➡ **portugués** *sm* [lengua] Portuguese.

porvenir *sm* future.

pos ➡ **en pos de** *loc prep* - **1.** [detrás de] behind - **2.** [en busca de] after; **correr en pos de alguien** to run after sb.

posada *sf* - **1.** [fonda] inn, guest house - **2.** [hospedaje] lodging, accommodation.

posaderas *sfpl fam* backside *sing*, bottom *sing*.

posar ◇ *vt* to put *O* lay down; [mano, mirada] to rest. ◇ *vi* to pose. ➡ **posarse** *vprnl* - **1.** [gen] to settle - **2.** [pájaro] to perch; [nave, helicóptero] to come down.

posavasos *sm inv* coaster; [de cartón] beer mat.

posdata, postdata *sf* postscript.

pose *sf* pose; **adoptar una pose** to strike a pose.

poseedor, ra *sm, f* owner; [de cargo, acciones, récord] holder.

poseer *vt* [ser dueño de] to own; [estar en poder de] to have, to possess.

poseído, da *adj*: **poseído por** possessed by.

posesión *sf* possession.

posesivo, va *adj* possessive.

poseso, sa *sm, f* possessed person.

posgraduado, da, postgraduado, da *adj & sm, f* postgraduate.

posguerra, postguerra *sf* post-war period.

posibilidad *sf* possibility, chance; **cabe la posibilidad de que...** there is a chance that...

posibilitar *vt* to make possible.

posible *adj* possible; **es posible que llueva** it could rain; **dentro de lo posible, en lo posible** as far as possible; **de ser posible** if possible; **hacer (todo) lo posible** to do everything possible; **lo antes posible** as soon as possible; **¡no es posible!** surely not!

posición *sf* - 1. [gen] position; **en posición de descanso** standing at ease - 2. [categoría - social] status (U); **de buena posición** of high social status; [- económica] situation - 3. DEP position.

posicionarse *vprnl* to take a position O stance.

positivo, va *adj* [gen & ELECTR] positive.

poso *sm* sediment; *fig* trace.

posponer *vt* - 1. [relegar] to put behind, to relegate - 2. [aplazar] to postpone.

pospuesto, ta *pp* ⊳ **posponer**.

posta ⇒ **a posta** *loc adv* on purpose.

postal ◇ *adj* postal. ◇ *sf* postcard.

postdata = **posdata**.

poste *sm* post, pole; **poste de alta tensión** electricity pylon; DEP post.

póster *(pl* posters*) sm* poster.

postergar *vt* - 1. [retrasar] to postpone - 2. [relegar] to put behind, to relegate.

posteridad *sf* - 1. [generación futura] posterity - 2. [futuro] future.

posterior *adj* - 1. [en el espacio] rear, back - 2. [en el tiempo] subsequent, later.

posteriori ⇒ **a posteriori** *loc adv* later, afterwards.

posterioridad *sf*: **con posterioridad** later, subsequently.

postgraduado = **posgraduado**.

postguerra = **posguerra**.

postigo *sm* [contraventana] shutter.

postín *sm* showiness; **darse postín** to show off; **de postín** posh.

postizo, za *adj* [falso] false. ⇒ **postizo** *sm* hairpiece.

postor, ra *sm, f* bidder.

postre *sm* dessert, pudding; **para postre** *fig* to cap it all.

postrero, ra *adj (antes de sm sing:* postrer*) culto* last.

postrimerías *sfpl* final stages.

postulado *sm* postulate.

postular ◇ *vt* [exigir] to call for. ◇ *vi* [para colectas] to collect.

póstumo, ma *adj* posthumous.

postura *sf* - 1. [posición] position, posture - 2. [actitud] attitude, stance; **tomar postura** to adopt an attitude.

potable *adj* [bebible] drinkable; **agua potable** drinking water.

potaje *sm* [CULIN - guiso] vegetable stew; [- sopa] vegetable soup.

potasio *sm* potassium.

pote *sm* pot.

potencia *sf* [gen, MAT & POLÍT] power; **tiene mucha potencia** it's very powerful.

potencial ◇ *adj* [gen & FÍS] potential. ◇ *sm* - 1. [fuerza] power - 2. [posibilidades] potential - 3. GRAM conditional.

potenciar *vt* - 1. [fomentar] to encourage, to promote - 2. [reforzar] to boost.

potente *adj* powerful.

potra ⊳ **potro**.

potrero *sm Amér* [prado] field, pasture.

potro, tra *sm, f* ZOOL colt *(f* filly*). ⇒ **potro** *sm* DEP vaulting horse.

pozo *sm* well; [de mina] shaft.

PP *(abrev de* Partido Popular*) sm* Spanish political party to the right of the political spectrum.

ppp *(abrev de* puntos por pulgada*)* INFORM dpi.

práctica ⊳ **práctico**.

practicante ◇ *adj* practising. ◇ *smf* - 1. [de deporte] practitioner; [de religión] practising member of a church - 2. MED medical assistant.

practicar ◇ *vt* - 1. [gen] to practise; [deporte] to play - 2. [realizar] to carry out, to perform. ◇ *vi* to practise.

práctico, ca *adj* practical. ⇒ **práctica** *sf* - 1. [gen] practice; [de un deporte] playing; **llevar algo a la práctica, poner algo en práctica** to put sthg into practice; **en la práctica** in practice; **prácticas de tiro** target practice - 2. [clase no teórica] practical.

pradera *sf* large meadow, prairie.

prado *sm* meadow. ⇒ **Prado** *sm*: **el (Museo del) Prado** the Prado (Museum).

pragmático, ca ◇ *adj* pragmatic. ◇ *sm, f* [persona] pragmatist.

pral. *abrev de* **principal**.

praliné *sm* praline.

PRD *sm* (*abrev de* Partido de la Revolución Democrática) *Mexican political party*.

preacuerdo *sm* draft agreement.

preámbulo *sm* [introducción - de libro] foreword, preface; [- de congreso, conferencia] introduction.

precalentar *vt* - 1. CULIN to pre-heat - 2. DEP to warm up.

precario, ria *adj* precarious.

precaución *sf* - 1. [prudencia] caution, care - 2. [medida] precaution; **tomar precauciones** to take precautions.

precaver *vt* to guard against. ◆ **precaverse** *vprnl* to take precautions; **precaverse de** *O* **contra** to guard (o.s.) against.

precavido, da *adj* [prevenido] prudent; **es muy precavido** he always comes prepared.

precedente ◇ *adj* previous, preceding. ◇ *sm* precedent.

preceder *vt* to go before, to precede.

preceptivo, va *adj* obligatory, compulsory. ◆ **preceptiva** *sf* rules *pl*.

precepto *sm* precept; **fiestas de precepto** RELIG days of obligation.

preciado, da *adj* valuable, prized.

preciarse *vprnl* to have self-respect; **preciarse de** to be proud of.

precintar *vt* to seal.

precinto *sm* seal.

precio *sm lit & fig* price; **a cualquier precio** at any price; **poner precio a la cabeza de alguien** to put a price on sb's head; **¿qué precio tiene esto?** how much is this?; **subir/bajar los precios** to raise/lower prices; **al precio de** *fig* at the cost of; **precio de salida** starting price; **precio de venta (al público)** retail price.

preciosidad *sf* [cosa bonita]: **¡es una preciosidad!** it's lovely *O* beautiful!

precioso, sa *adj* - 1. [valioso] precious - 2. [bonito] lovely, beautiful.

precipicio *sm* precipice.

precipitación *sf* - 1. [apresuramiento] haste - 2. [lluvia] rainfall (*U*).

precipitado, da *adj* hasty.

precipitar *vt* - 1. [arrojar] to throw *O* hurl down - 2. [acelerar] to speed up. ◆ **precipitarse** *vprnl* - 1. [caer] to plunge (down) - 2. [acelerarse - acontecimientos etc] to speed up - 3. [apresurarse]: **precipitarse (hacia)** to rush (towards) - 4. [obrar irreflexivamente] to act rashly.

precisamente *adv* [justamente] ¡precisamente! exactly!, precisely!; **precisamente por eso** for that very reason; **precisamente tú lo sugeriste** in fact it was you who suggested it.

precisar *vt* - 1. [determinar] to fix, to set [aclarar] to specify exactly - 2. [necesitar] to need, to require.

precisión *sf* accuracy, precision.

preciso, sa *adj* - 1. [determinado, conciso] precise - 2. [necesario]: **ser preciso (para algo/hacer algo)** to be necessary (for sth/to do sth); **es preciso que vengas** you must come - 3. [justo] just; **en este preciso momento** at this very moment.

precocinado, da *adj* pre-cooked. ◆ **precocinado** *sm* pre-cooked dish.

preconcebido, da *adj* [idea] preconceived; [plan] drawn up in advance.

preconcebir *vt* to draw up in advance.

preconizar *vt* to recommend.

precoz *adj* [persona] precocious.

precursor, ra *sm, f* precursor.

predecesor, ra *sm, f* predecessor.

predecir *vt* to predict.

predestinado, da *adj*: **predestinado (a)** predestined (to).

predestinar *vt* to predestine.

predeterminar *vt* to predetermine.

predicado *sm* GRAM predicate.

predicador, ra *sm, f* preacher.

predicar *vt & vi* to preach.

predicción *sf* prediction; [del tiempo] forecast.

predicho, cha *pp* ⊳ **predecir**.

predilección *sf*: **predilección (por)** preference (for).

predilecto, ta *adj* favourite.

predisponer *vt*: **predisponer (a)** to predispose (to).

predisposición *sf* - 1. [aptitud]: **predisposición para** aptitude for - 2. [tendencia]: **predisposición a** predisposition to.

predispuesto, ta ◇ *pp* ⊳ **predisponer**. ◇ *adj*: **predispuesto (a)** predisposed (to).

predominante *adj* predominant; [viento, actitudes] prevailing.

predominar *vi*: **predominar (sobre)** to predominate *O* prevail (over).

predominio *sm* preponderance, predominance (*U*).

preelectoral *adj* pre-election (*antes de s*).

preeminente *adj* preeminent.

preescolar *adj* nursery (*antes de s*), preschool.

prefabricado, da *adj* prefabricated.

prefabricar vt to prefabricate.

prefacio sm preface.

preferencia sf preference; **con O de preferencia** preferably; **dar preferencia (a)** to give priority (to); **tener preferencia** AUTO to have right of way; **tener preferencia por** to have a preference for.

preferente adj preferential.

preferentemente adv preferably.

preferible adj: **preferible (a)** preferable (to).

preferido, da adj favourite.

preferir vt: **preferir algo (a algo)** to prefer sthg (to sthg); **prefiero que vengas** I'd rather you came.

prefijo sm - 1. GRAM prefix - 2. TELECOM (telephone) dialling code.

pregón sm [discurso] speech; [bando] proclamation.

pregonar vt - 1. [bando etc] to proclaim - 2. fig [secreto] to spread about.

pregunta sf question; **hacer una pregunta** to ask a question; **andar a la cuarta O última pregunta** to be broke.

preguntar ⬦ vt to ask; **preguntar algo a alguien** to ask sb sthg. ⬦ vi: **preguntar por** to ask about O after. ◆ **preguntarse** vprnl: **preguntarse (si)** to wonder (whether).

prehistoria sf prehistory.

prehistórico, ca adj prehistoric.

prejuicio sm prejudice.

preliminar ⬦ adj preliminary. ⬦ sm (gen pl) preliminary.

preludio sm [gen & MÚS] prelude.

premamá adj inv maternity.

prematrimonial adj premarital.

prematuro, ra adj premature.

premeditación sf premeditation.

premeditar vt to think out in advance.

premiar vt - 1. [recompensar] to reward - 2. [dar un premio a] to give a prize to.

premier (pl **premiers**) sm British prime minister.

premio sm [en competición] prize; [recompensa] reward; **premio gordo** first prize.

premisa sf premise.

premonición sf premonition.

premura sf [urgencia] haste.

prenatal adj prenatal, antenatal.

prenda sf - 1. [vestido] garment, article of clothing - 2. [garantía] pledge; **dejar algo en prenda** to leave sthg as a pledge - 3. [de un juego] forfeit; **jugar a las prendas** to play forfeits - 4. loc: **no soltar prenda** not to say a word.

prendarse vprnl to fall in love with.

prender ⬦ vt - 1. [arrestar] to arrest, to apprehend - 2. [sujetar] to fasten - 3. [encender] to light - 4. [agarrar] to grip. ⬦ vi [arder] to catch (fire). ◆ **prenderse** vprnl [arder] to catch fire.

prendido, da adj caught.

prensa sf - 1. [gen] press; **prensa del corazón** romantic magazines pl; **tener buena/mala prensa** fig to have a good/bad press - 2. [imprenta] printing press.

prensar vt to press.

preñado, da adj - 1. [mujer] pregnant; **quedarse preñada** to get pregnant - 2. fig [lleno]: **preñado de** full of.

preocupación sf concern, worry.

preocupado, da adj: **preocupado (por)** worried O concerned (about).

preocupar vt - 1. [inquietar] to worry - 2. [importar] to bother. ◆ **preocuparse** vprnl - 1. [inquietarse]: **preocuparse (por)** to worry (about), to be worried (about) - 2. [encargarse]: **preocuparse de algo** to take care of sthg; **preocuparse de hacer algo** to see to it that sthg is done; **preocuparse de que...** to make sure that...

preparación sf - 1. [gen] preparation - 2. [conocimientos] training.

preparado, da adj - 1. [dispuesto] ready; [de antemano] prepared - 2. CULIN ready-cooked. ◆ **preparado** sm [sustancia] preparation.

preparar vt - 1. [gen] to prepare; [trampa] to set, to lay; [maletas] to pack - 2. [examen] to prepare for - 3. DEP to train. ◆ **prepararse** vprnl: **prepararse (para algo)** to prepare o.s. O get ready (for sthg); **prepararse para hacer algo** to prepare O get ready to do sthg.

preparativo, va adj preparatory, preliminary. ◆ **preparativos** smpl preparations.

preposición sf preposition.

prepotente adj [arrogante] domineering.

prerrogativa sf prerogative.

presa sf - 1. [captura - de cazador] catch; [- de animal] prey; **hacer presa en alguien** to seize O grip sb; **ser presa de** to be prey to; **ser presa del pánico** to be panic-stricken - 2. [dique] dam.

presagiar vt [felicidad, futuro] to foretell; [tormenta, problemas] to warn of.

presagio sm - 1. [premonición] premonition - 2. [señal] omen.

prescindir ◆ **prescindir de** vi - 1. [renunciar a] to do without - 2. [omitir] to dispense with - 3. [no tener en cuenta] to disregard.

prescribir ⬦ vt to prescribe. ⬦ vi - 1. [ordenar] to prescribe - 2. DER to expire.

prescripción sf prescription.

prescrito, ta pp ⊳ **prescribir**.

presencia *sf* [asistencia, aspecto] presence; **en presencia de** in the presence of. ◆ **presencia de ánimo** *sf* presence of mind.

presencial ⌐ **testigo**.

presenciar *vt* [asistir] to be present at; [ser testigo de] to witness.

presentación *sf* - **1.** [gen] presentation - **2.** [entre personas] introduction.

presentador, ra *sm, f* presenter.

presentar *vt* - **1.** [gen] to present; [dimisión] to tender; [tesis, pruebas, propuesta] to submit; [solicitud, recurso, denuncia] to lodge; [moción] to propose; [libro, disco] to launch - **2.** [ofrecer - ventajas, novedades] to offer; [- disculpas, excusas] to make; [- respetos] to pay - **3.** [persona, amigos etc] to introduce - **4.** [enseñar] to show - **5.** [tener - aspecto etc] to have, to show; **presenta difícil solución** it's going to be difficult to solve - **6.** [proponer]: **presentar a alguien para** to propose sb for, to put sb forward for. ◆ **presentarse** *vprnl* - **1.** [aparecer] to turn up - **2.** [en juzgado, comisaría]: **presentarse (en)** to report (to); **presentarse a un examen** to sit an exam - **3.** [darse a conocer] to introduce o.s. - **4.** [para un cargo]: **presentarse (a)** to stand O run (for) - **5.** [futuro] to appear, to look - **6.** [problema etc] to arise.

presente ◇ *adj* - **1.** [gen] present; **aquí presente** here present - **2.** [en curso] current; **del presente mes** of this month. ◇ *smf* [escrito]: **por la presente le informo...** I hereby inform you... ◇ *sm* - **1.** [gen & GRAM] present - **2.** [regalo] gift, present - **3.** [corriente]: **el presente** [mes] the current month; [año] the current year.

presentimiento *sm* presentiment, feeling.

presentir *vt* to foresee; **presentir que algo va a pasar** to have a feeling that sthg is going to happen; **presentir lo peor** to fear the worst.

preservar *vt* to protect.

preservativo *sm* condom.

presidencia *sf* [de nación] presidency; [de asamblea, empresa] chairmanship.

presidenciable *smf Amér* potential presidential candidate.

presidente, ta *sm, f* [de nación] president; [de asamblea, empresa] chairman (*f* chairwoman); **presidente (del gobierno)** ≃ prime minister; **presidente de mesa** chief scrutineer.

presidiario, ria *sm, f* convict.

presidio *sm* prison.

presidir *vt* - **1.** [ser presidente de] to preside over; [reunión] to chair - **2.** [predominar] to dominate.

presión *sf* pressure; **presión fiscal** ECON tax burden.

presionar *vt* - **1.** [apretar] to press - **2.** *fig* [coaccionar] to pressurize.

preso, sa *sm, f* prisoner.

prestación *sf* [de servicio - acción] provision; [- resultado] service. ◆ **prestaciones** *sfpl* - **1.** [servicio social] benefits - **2.** [de coche etc] performance features.

prestado, da *adj* on loan; **dar prestado algo** to lend sthg; **vivir de prestado** to live off other people.

prestamista *smf* moneylender.

préstamo *sm* - **1.** [acción - de prestar] lending; [- de pedir prestado] borrowing - **2.** [cantidad] loan.

prestar *vt* - **1.** [dejar - dinero etc] to lend, to loan - **2.** [dar - ayuda etc] to give, to offer; [- servicio] to provide; [- atención] to pay; [- declaración, juramento] to make. ◆ **prestarse a** *vprnl* - **1.** [ofrecerse a] to offer to - **2.** [acceder a] to consent to - **3.** [dar motivo a] to be open to.

presteza *sf* promptness.

prestidigitador, ra *sm, f* conjurer.

prestigio *sm* prestige.

prestigioso, sa *adj* prestigious.

presto, ta *adj* [dispuesto]: **presto (a)** ready (to).

presumible *adj* probable, likely.

presumido, da *adj* conceited, vain.

presumir ◇ *vt* [suponer] to presume; **es de presumir que irán** presumably they'll go. ◇ *vi* - **1.** [jactarse] to show off - **2.** [ser vanidoso] to be conceited O vain.

presunción *sf* - **1.** [suposición] presumption - **2.** [vanidad] conceit, vanity.

presunto, ta *adj* presumed, supposed; [criminal, robo etc] alleged.

presuntuoso, sa *adj* [vanidoso] conceited; [pretencioso] pretentious.

presuponer *vt* to presuppose.

presupuesto, ta *pp* ⌐ **presuponer**. ◆ **presupuesto** *sm* - **1.** [cálculo] budget; [de costo] estimate; **presupuestos generales del Estado** ECON Spanish national budget - **2.** [suposición] assumption.

prêt-à-porter [pretapor'te] *sm* off-the-peg clothing.

pretencioso, sa *adj* [persona] pretentious; [cosa] showy.

pretender *vt* - **1.** [intentar]: **pretender hacer algo** to try to do sthg - **2.** [aspirar a]: **pretender hacer algo** to aspire O want to do sthg; **pretender que alguien haga algo** to want sb to do sthg; **¿qué pretendes decir?** what do you mean? - **3.** [afirmar] to claim - **4.** [cortejar] to court.

pretendido, da *adj* supposed.

pretendiente <> *smf* - 1. [aspirante]: **pretendiente (a)** candidate (for) - 2. [a un trono]: **pretendiente (a)** pretender (to). <> *sm* [a una mujer] suitor.

pretensión *sf* - 1. [intención] aim, intention - 2. [aspiración] aspiration - 3. [supuesto derecho]: **pretensión (a** O **sobre)** claim (to) - 4. [afirmación] claim - 5. *(gen pl)* [exigencia] demand - 6. *(gen pl)* [presuntuosidad] pretentiousness; **sin pretensiones** unpretentious.

pretérito, ta *adj* past. ◆ **pretérito** *sm* GRAM preterite, past.

pretexto *sm* pretext, excuse.

prevalecer *vi*: **prevalecer (sobre)** to prevail (over).

prevaler *vi*: **prevaler (sobre)** to prevail (over).

prevención *sf* [acción] prevention; [medida] precaution.

prevenido, da *adj* [previsor]: **ser prevenido** to be cautious - 2. [avisado, dispuesto]: **estar prevenido** to be prepared.

prevenir *vt* - 1. [evitar] to prevent; **más vale prevenir que curar** *prov* prevention is better than cure *prov* - 2. [avisar] to warn - 3. [prever] to foresee - 4. [predisponer]: **prevenir a alguien contra algo/alguien** to prejudice sb against sthg/sb.

preventivo, va *adj* [medicina, prisión] preventive; [medida] precautionary.

prever <> *vt* - 1. [conjeturar] to foresee - 2. [planear] to plan - 3. [predecir] to forecast. <> *vi*: **como era de prever** as was to be expected.

previniera *etc* ▷ **prevenir**.

previo, via *adj* prior; **previo pago de multa** on payment of a fine.

previó *etc* ▷ **prever**.

previsible *adj* foreseeable.

previsión *sf* - 1. [predicción] forecast - 2. [visión de futuro] foresight - 3. *Andes & R Plata* [social] social security.

previsor, ra *adj* prudent, farsighted.

previsto, ta <> *pp* ▷ **prever**. <> *adj* [conjeturado] predicted; [planeado] planned.

prieto, ta *adj* - 1. [ceñido] tight - 2. *Cuba & Méx fam* [moreno] dark-skinned.

prima ▷ **primo**.

primacía *sf* primacy; **tener primacía sobre algo** to take priority over sthg.

primar *vi*: **primar (sobre)** to have priority (over).

primario, ria *adj* primary; *fig* primitive.

primavera *sf* [estación] spring.

primaveral *adj* spring *(antes de s)*.

primer, primera ▷ **primero**.

primerizo, za *sm, f* [principiante] beginner.

primero, ra <> *num* & *adj (antes de sm sing:* **primer**) - 1. [para ordenar] first; **el primero de mayo** the first of May - 2. [en importancia] main, basic; **lo primero** the most important O main thing. <> *num m y f* - 1. [en orden]: **el primero** the first one; **llegó el primero** he came first; **es el primero de la clase** he's top of the class; **a primeros de mes** at the beginning of the month - 2. [mencionado antes]: **vinieron Pedro y Juan, el primero con...** Pedro and Juan arrived, the former with... ◆ **primero** <> *adv* - 1. [en primer lugar] first - 2. [antes, todo menos]: **primero morir que traicionarle** I'd rather die than betray him. <> *sm* - 1. [piso] first floor - 2. [curso] first year. ◆ **primera** *sf* - 1. AUTO first (gear) - 2. AERON & FERROC first class - 3. DEP first division - 4. *loc*: **de primera** first-class, excellent.

primicia *sf* scoop, exclusive.

primitivo, va *adj* - 1. [gen] primitive - 2. [original] original.

primo, ma *sm, f* - 1. [pariente] cousin; **primo hermano** first cousin - 2. *fam* [tonto] sucker; **hacer el primo** to be taken for a ride. ◆ **prima** *sf* - 1. [paga extra] bonus - 2. [de un seguro] premium. ◆ **prima dona** *sf* prima donna.

primogénito, ta *adj* & *sm, f* first-born.

primor *sm* fine thing.

primordial *adj* fundamental.

primoroso, sa *adj* - 1. [delicado] exquisite, fine - 2. [hábil] skilful.

princesa *sf* princess.

principado *sm* principality.

principal *adj* main, principal; [puerta] front.

príncipe *sm* prince.

principiante <> *adj* inexperienced. <> *smf* novice.

principio *sm* - 1. [comienzo] beginning, start; **a principios de** at the beginning of; **a principios de siglo** at the turn of the century; **en un principio** at first - 2. [fundamento, ley] principle; **en principio** in principle; **por principio** on principle - 3. [origen] origin, source - 4. [elemento] element. ◆ **principios** *smpl* - 1. [reglas de conducta] principles - 2. [nociones] rudiments.

pringar *vt* - 1. [ensuciar] to make greasy - 2. [mojar] to dip.

pringoso, sa *adj* [grasiento] greasy; [pegajoso] sticky.

pringue *sm* [suciedad] muck, dirt; [grasa] grease.

priori ◆ **a priori** *loc adv* in advance, a priori.

prioridad *sf* priority; AUTO right of way.

prioritario, ria *adj* priority *(antes de s)*.

prisa *sf* haste, hurry; **correr prisa** to be urgent; **darse prisa** to hurry (up); **meter prisa a alguien** to hurry O rush sb; **tener prisa** to be in a hurry.

prisión *sf* - 1. [cárcel] prison - 2. [encarcelamiento] imprisonment.

prisionero, ra *sm, f* prisoner; **hacer prisionero a alguien** to take sb prisoner.

prisma *sm* - 1. FÍS & GEOM prism - 2. *fig* [perspectiva] perspective.

prismáticos *smpl* binoculars.

privación *sf* [gen] deprivation; [de libertad] loss.

privado, da *adj* private; **en privado** in private.

privar *vt* [quitar]: **privar a alguien/algo de** to deprive sb/sthg of. ► **privarse de** *vprnl* to go without.

privativo, va *adj* exclusive.

privilegiado, da *adj* - 1. [favorecido] privileged - 2. [excepcional] exceptional.

privilegiar *vt* [persona] to favour.

privilegio *sm* privilege.

pro ◇ *prep* for, supporting; **una asociación pro derechos humanos** a human rights organization. ◇ *sm* advantage; **los pros y los contras** the pros and cons. ► **en pro de** *loc prep* for, in support of.

proa *sf* NÁUT prow, bows *pl*; AERON nose.

probabilidad *sf* probability; **con toda probabilidad** in all probability; [oportunidad] chance.

probable *adj* probable, likely; **es probable que llueva** it'll probably rain.

probador *sm* fitting room.

probar ◇ *vt* - 1. [demostrar, indicar] to prove - 2. [comprobar, testar] to, to check - 3. [experimentar] to try - 4. [degustar] to taste, to try. ◇ *vi*: **probar a hacer algo** to try to do sthg. ► **probarse** *vprnl* [ropa] to try on.

probeta *sf* test tube.

problema *sm* problem.

problemático, ca *adj* problematic. ► **problemática** *sf* problems *pl*.

procedencia *sf* - 1. [origen] origin - 2. [punto de partida] point of departure; **con procedencia de** (arriving) from.

procedente *adj* - 1. [originario]: **procedente de** [gen] originating in; AERON & FERROC (arriving) from - 2. [oportuno] appropriate; DER right and proper.

proceder ◇ *sm* conduct, behaviour. ◇ *vi* - 1. [originarse]: **proceder de** to come from - 2. [actuar]: **proceder (con)** to act (with) - 3. [empezar]: **proceder (a algo/a hacer algo)** to proceed (with sthg/to do sthg) - 4. [ser oportuno] to be appropriate.

procedimiento *sm* - 1. [método] procedure, method - 2. DER proceedings *pl*.

procesado, da *sm, f* accused, defendant.

procesador *sm* INFORM processor; **procesador Pentium**® Pentium® processor; **procesador de textos** word processor.

procesar *vt* - 1. DER to prosecute - 2. INFORM to process.

procesión *sf fig* & RELIG procession.

proceso *sm* - 1. [gen] process - 2. [desarrollo, intervalo] course - 3. [DER - juicio] trial; [- causa] lawsuit.

proclama *sf* proclamation.

proclamar *vt* - 1. [nombrar] to proclaim - 2. [anunciar] to declare. ► **proclamarse** *vprnl* - 1. [nombrarse] to proclaim o.s. - 2. [conseguir un título]: **proclamarse campeón** to become champion.

proclive *adj*: **proclive a** prone to.

procreación *sf* procreation.

procrear *vi* to procreate.

procurador, ra *sm, f* DER attorney.

procurar *vt* - 1. [intentar]: **procurar hacer algo** to try to do sthg; **procurar que...** to make sure that... - 2. [proporcionar] to get, to secure. ► **procurarse** *vprnl* to get, to obtain (for o.s.).

prodigar *vt*: **prodigar algo a alguien** to lavish sthg on sb.

prodigio *sm* [suceso] miracle; [persona] prodigy.

prodigioso, sa *adj* - 1. [sobrenatural] miraculous - 2. [extraordinario] wonderful.

pródigo, ga *adj* [generoso] generous, lavish.

producción *sf* - 1. [gen & CINE] production - 2. [productos] products *pl*.

producir *vt* - 1. [gen & CINE] to produce - 2. [causar] to cause, to give rise to - 3. [interés, fruto] to yield, to bear. ► **producirse** *vprnl* [ocurrir] to take place.

productividad *sf* productivity.

productivo, va *adj* productive; [que da beneficio] profitable.

producto *sm* - 1. [gen & MAT] product; AGRIC produce *(U)*; **producto acabado/manufacturado** finished/manufactured product; **producto de belleza** beauty product; **producto interior/nacional bruto** gross domestic/national product; **producto químico** chemical - 2. [ganancia] profit - 3. *fig* [resultado] result.

productor, ra ◇ *adj* producing. ◇ *sm, f* CINE [persona] producer. ► **productora** *sf* CINE [firma] production company.

proeza *sf* exploit, deed.

profanar *vt* to desecrate.

profano, **na** <> *adj* - **1**. [no sagrado] profane, secular - **2**. [ignorante] ignorant, uninitiated. <> *sm, f* layman (*f* laywoman).

profecía *sf* [predicción] prophecy.

proferir *vt* to utter; [insultos] to hurl.

profesar *vt* - **1**. [una religión] to follow; [una profesión] to practise - **2**. [admiración etc] to profess.

profesión *sf* profession.

profesional *adj* & *smf* professional.

profesionista *smf Méx* professional.

profesor, **ra** *sm, f* [gen] teacher; [de universidad] lecturer; [de autoescuela, esquí etc] instructor.

profesorado *sm* [plantilla] teaching staff, faculty *US*; [profesión] teachers *pl*, teaching profession.

profeta *sm* prophet.

profetisa *sf* prophetess.

profetizar *vt* to prophesy.

profiera *etc* ⊳ **proferir**.

prófugo, **ga** *adj* & *sm, f* fugitive.

profundidad *sf lit* & *fig* depth; **en profundidad** in depth; **tiene dos metros de profundidad** it's two metres deep.

profundizar <> *vt fig* to study in depth. <> *vi* to go into detail; **profundizar en** to study in depth.

profundo, **da** *adj* - **1**. [gen] deep - **2**. *fig* [respeto, libro, pensamiento] profound, deep; [dolor] intense.

profusión *sf* profusion.

progenitor, **ra** *sm, f* father (*f* mother). ➔ **progenitores** *smpl* parents.

programa *sm* - **1**. [gen] programme - **2**. [de actividades] schedule, programme; [de estudios] syllabus - **3**. INFORM program.

programación *sf* - **1**. INFORM programming - **2**. TV scheduling; **la programación del lunes** Monday's programmes.

programador, **ra** *sm, f* [persona] programmer.

programar *vt* - **1**. [vacaciones, reforma etc] to plan - **2**. CINE & TV to put on, to show - **3**. TECNOL to programme; INFORM to program.

progre *fam smf* progressive.

progresar *vi* to progress.

progresión *sf* [gen & MAT] progression; [mejora] progress, advance; **progresión aritmética/geométrica** arithmetic/geometric progression.

progresista *adj* & *smf* progressive.

progresivo, **va** *adj* progressive.

progreso *sm* progress; **hacer progresos** to make progress.

prohibición *sf* ban, banning (*U*).

prohibido, **da** *adj* prohibited, banned; **'prohibido aparcar/fumar'** 'no parking/smoking', 'parking/smoking prohibited'; **'prohibida la entrada'** 'no entry'; **'dirección prohibida'** AUTO 'no entry'.

prohibir *vt* - **1**. [gen] to forbid; **prohibir a alguien hacer algo** to forbid sb to do sthg; **'se prohíbe el paso'** 'no entry' - **2**. [por ley - de antemano] to prohibit; [- a posteriori] to ban.

prohibitivo, **va** *adj* prohibitive.

prójimo *sm* fellow human being.

prole *sf* offspring.

proletariado *sm* proletariat.

proletario, **ria** *adj* & *sm, f* proletarian.

proliferación *sf* proliferation.

proliferar *vi* to proliferate.

prolífico, **ca** *adj* prolific.

prolijo, **ja** *adj* [extenso] long-winded.

prólogo *sm* [de libro] preface, foreword; *fig* prelude.

prolongación *sf* extension.

prolongado, **da** *adj* long; *fig* [dilatado] lengthy.

prolongar *vt* [gen] to extend; [espera, visita, conversación] to prolong; [cuerda, tubo] to lengthen.

promedio *sm* average; **como promedio** on average.

promesa *sf* [compromiso] promise; **hacer una promesa** to make a promise; **romper una promesa** to break a promise.

prometer <> *vt* to promise. <> *vi* [tener futuro] to show promise. ➔ **prometerse** *vprnl* to get engaged.

prometido, **da** <> *sm, f* fiancé (*f* fiancée). <> *adj* [para casarse] engaged.

prominente *adj* - **1**. [abultado] protruding - **2**. [elevado, ilustre] prominent.

promiscuo, **cua** *adj* promiscuous.

promoción *sf* - **1**. [gen & DEP] promotion - **2**. [curso] class, year.

promocionar *vt* to promote.

promotor, **ra** *sm, f* promoter; [de una rebelión] instigator; **promotor inmobiliario** COM real estate developer.

promover *vt* - **1**. [iniciar - fundación etc] to set up; [- rebelión] to stir up - **2**. [impulsar] to stimulate - **3**. [ocasionar] to cause - **4**. [ascender] : **promover a alguien a** to promote sb to.

promulgar *vt* [ley] to enact.

pronombre *sm* pronoun.

pronosticar *vt* to predict, to forecast.

pronóstico *sm* - **1**. [predicción] forecast; **pronóstico del tiempo** weather forecast - **2**. MED prognosis; **de pronóstico grave** serious, in a serious condition.

pronto, ta adj quick, fast; [respuesta] prompt, early; [curación, tramitación] speedy. ◆ **pronto** ⬦ adv - **1.** [rápidamente] quickly; **tan pronto como** as soon as - **2.** [temprano] early; **salimos pronto** we left early - **3.** [dentro de poco] soon; **¡hasta pronto!** see you soon! ⬦ sm fam sudden impulse. ◆ **al pronto** loc adv at first. ◆ **de pronto** loc adv suddenly. ◆ **por lo pronto** loc adv - **1.** [de momento] for the time being - **2.** [para empezar] to start with.

pronunciación sf pronunciation.

pronunciado, da adj [facciones] pronounced; [curva] sharp; [pendiente, cuesta] steep; [nariz] prominent.

pronunciamiento sm - **1.** [sublevación] uprising - **2.** DER pronouncement.

pronunciar vt - **1.** [decir - palabra] to pronounce; [- discurso] to deliver, to make - **2.** DER to pass. ◆ **pronunciarse** vprnl - **1.** [definirse]: **pronunciarse (sobre)** to state an opinion (on) - **2.** [sublevarse] to revolt.

propagación sf - **1.** [gen] spreading (U) - **2.** BIOL & FÍS propagation.

propaganda sf - **1.** [publicidad] advertising (U) - **2.** [política, religiosa] propaganda.

propagar vt [gen] to spread; [razas, especies] to propagate. ◆ **propagarse** vprnl - **1.** [gen] to spread - **2.** BIOL & FÍS to propagate.

propasarse vprnl: **propasarse (con algo)** to go too far (with sthg); **propasarse con alguien** [sexualmente] to take liberties with sb.

propensión sf propensity, tendency.

propenso, sa adj: **propenso a algo/a hacer algo** prone to sthg/doing sthg.

propicio, cia adj - **1.** [favorable] propitious, favourable - **2.** [adecuado] suitable, appropriate.

propiedad sf - **1.** [derecho] ownership; [bienes] property; **propiedad privada** private property; **propiedad pública** public ownership - **2.** [facultad] property - **3.** [exactitud] accuracy; **usar una palabra con propiedad** to use a word properly.

propietario, ria sm, f [de bienes] owner.

propina sf tip; **dar de propina** to tip.

propinar vt [paliza] to give; [golpe] to deal.

propio, pia adj - **1.** [gen] own; **tiene coche propio** she has a car of her own, she has her own car; **por tu propio bien** for your own good - **2.** [peculiar]: **propio de** typical O characteristic of; **no es propio de él** it's not like him - **3.** [apropiado]: **propio (para)** suitable O right (for) - **4.** [en persona] himself (f herself); **el propio compositor** the composer himself.

proponer vt to propose; [candidato] to put forward. ◆ **proponerse** vprnl: **proponerse hacer algo** to plan O intend to do sthg.

proporción sf - **1.** [gen & MAT] proportion; **en proporción a** in proportion to - **2.** (gen pl) [importancia] extent, size. ◆ **proporciones** sfpl [tamaño] size sthg.

proporcionado, da adj: **proporcionado (a)** [estatura, sueldo] commensurate (with); [medidas] proportionate (to); **bien proporcionado** well-proportioned.

proporcionar vt - **1.** [facilitar]: **proporcionar algo a alguien** to provide sb with sthg - **2.** fig [conferir] to lend, to add.

proposición sf [propuesta] proposal.

propósito sm - **1.** [intención] intention - **2.** [objetivo] purpose. ◆ **a propósito** ⬦ loc adj [adecuado] suitable. ⬦ loc adv - **1.** [adrede] on purpose - **2.** [por cierto] by the way. ◆ **a propósito de** loc prep with regard to.

propuesta sf proposal; **a propuesta de** at the suggestion of; [de empleo] offer.

propuesto, ta pp ⬭ **proponer**.

propugnar vt to advocate, to support.

propulsar vt - **1.** [impeler] to propel - **2.** fig [promover] to promote.

propulsión sf propulsion; **propulsión a chorro** jet propulsion.

propulsor, ra sm, f [persona] promoter. ◆ **propulsor** sm - **1.** [dispositivo] engine - **2.** [combustible] propellent.

propusiera etc ⬭ **proponer**.

prórroga sf - **1.** [gen] extension; [de estudios, servicio militar] deferment - **2.** DEP extra time.

prorrogar vt [alargar] to extend; [aplazar] to defer, to postpone.

prorrumpir vi: **prorrumpir en** to burst into.

prosa sf LITER prose.

proscrito, ta ⬦ adj [prohibido] banned. ⬦ sm, f [desterrado] exile.

proseguir ⬦ vt to continue. ⬦ vi to go on, to continue.

prosiga etc ⬭ **proseguir**.

prosiguiera etc ⬭ **proseguir**.

prospección sf [gen] exploration; [petrolífera, minera] prospecting.

prospecto sm leaflet; COM & EDUC prospectus.

prosperar vi [mejorar] to prosper.

prosperidad sf - **1.** [mejora] prosperity - **2.** [éxito] success.

próspero, ra adj prosperous.

prostíbulo sm brothel.

prostitución sf [gen] prostitution.

prostituir vt lit & fig to prostitute. ◆ **prostituirse** vprnl to become a prostitute.

prostituta sf prostitute.

protagonista sm, f [gen] main character, hero (f heroine); TEATRO lead, leading role.

protagonizar *vt* - **1.** [obra, película] to play the lead in, to star in - **2.** *fig* [crimen] to be one of the main people responsible for; *fig* [hazaña] to play a leading part in.

protección *sf* protection; **bajo la protección de alguien** under the protection of sb; **protección de datos** INFORM data protection.

proteccionismo *sm* protectionism.

protector, ra ◇ *adj* protective. ◇ *sm, f* [persona] protector.

proteger *vt* [gen] to protect; **proteger algo de algo** to protect sthg from sthg. ◆ **protegerse** *vprnl* to take cover *O* refuge.

protegeslip *sm* panty pad *O* liner.

protegido, da *sm, f* protégé (*f* protégée).

proteína *sf* protein; **rico en proteínas** rich in protein.

prótesis *sf inv* MED prosthesis; [miembro] artificial limb.

protesta *sf* protest; DER objection.

protestante *adj* & *smf* Protestant.

protestar *vi* - **1.** [quejarse]: **protestar (por/contra)** to protest (about/against); **¡protesto!** DER objection! - **2.** [refunfuñar] to grumble.

protocolo *sm* - **1.** [gen & INFORM] protocol - **2.** [ceremonial] etiquette.

prototipo *sm* - **1.** [modelo] archetype - **2.** [primer ejemplar] prototype.

protuberancia *sf* protuberance, bulge.

provecho *sm* - **1.** [gen] benefit; **buen provecho** enjoy your meal!; **sacar provecho de** to make the most of, to take advantage of - **2.** [rendimiento] good effect.

provechoso, sa *adj* - **1.** [ventajoso] beneficial, advantageous - **2.** [lucrativo] profitable.

proveedor, ra *sm, f* supplier; **proveedor de servicios** service provider; **proveedor de acceso a Internet** Internet access provider.

proveer *vt* - **1.** [abastecer] to supply, to provide - **2.** [puesto, cargo] to fill. ◆ **proveerse de** *vprnl* - **1.** [ropa, víveres] to stock up on - **2.** [medios, recursos] to arm o.s. with.

provenir *vi*: **provenir de** to come from.

proverbial *adj* proverbial.

proverbio *sm* proverb.

providencia *sf* [medida] measure.

providencial *adj lit & fig* providential.

proviene *etc* ⊳ **provenir**.

provincia *sf* [división administrativa] province. ◆ **provincias** *sfpl* [no la capital] the provinces.

provinciano, na *adj* & *sm, f despec* provincial.

proviniera *etc* ⊳ **provenir**.

provisión *sf* - **1.** (gen pl) [suministro] supply, provision; [de una plaza] filling (*U*) - **2.** [disposición] measure.

provisional *adj* provisional.

provisorio, ria *adj Amér* provisional.

provisto, ta *pp* ⊳ **proveer**.

provocación *sf* [hostigamiento] provocation.

provocar *vt* - **1.** [incitar] to incite; **provocar a alguien a hacer algo** [gen] to cause sb to do sthg, to make sb do sthg; [matar, luchar etc] to provoke sb to do sthg - **2.** [irritar] to provoke - **3.** [ocasionar - gen] to cause - **4.** [excitar sexualmente] to arouse - **5.**: **¿te provoca hacerlo?** *Caribe, Col & Méx* [te apetece] would you like to do it?

provocativo, va *adj* provocative.

próximamente *adv* soon, shortly; CINE coming soon.

proximidad *sf* [cercanía] closeness, proximity. ◆ **proximidades** *sfpl* - **1.** [de ciudad] surrounding area *sing* - **2.** [de lugar] vicinity *sing*.

próximo, ma *adj* - **1.** [cercano] near, close; **próximo a algo** close to sthg; [casa, ciudad] nearby; **en fecha próxima** shortly - **2.** [siguiente] next; **el próximo año** next year.

proyección *sf* - **1.** [gen & GEOM] projection - **2.** CINE screening - **3.** *fig* [trascendencia] importance.

proyectar *vt* - **1.** [dirigir - focos etc] to shine, to direct - **2.** [mostrar - película] to screen; [- sombra] to cast; [- diapositivas] to show - **3.** [planear - viaje, operación, edificio] to plan; [- puente, obra] to design - **4.** [arrojar] to throw forwards.

proyectil *sm* projectile, missile.

proyecto *sm* - **1.** [intención] project - **2.** [plan] plan - **3.** [diseño - ARQUIT] design; TECNOL plan - **4.** [borrador] draft; **proyecto de ley** bill - **5.** EDUC: **proyecto fin de carrera** *design project forming part of doctoral thesis for architecture students etc*; **proyecto de investigación** [de un grupo] research project; [de una persona] dissertation.

proyector, ra *adj* projecting. ◆ **proyector** *sm* [de cine, diapositivas] projector.

prudencia *sf* [cuidado] caution, care; [previsión, sensatez] prudence; [moderación] moderation; **con prudencia** in moderation.

prudente *adj* - **1.** [cuidadoso] careful, cautious; [previsor, sensato] sensible - **2.** [razonable] reasonable.

prueba ◇ *v* ⊳ **probar**. ◇ *sf* - **1.** [demostración] proof; DER evidence, proof; **no tengo pruebas** I have no proof - **2.** [manifestación] sign, token; **en *O* como prueba de** in *O* as proof of - **3.** EDUC & MED test; **prueba de alcoholemia** Breathalyser®test; **prueba de acceso** entrance examination; **prueba de aptitud** aptitude test; **prueba del embarazo** pregnancy test - **4.** [comprobación] test; **a *O* de prue-**

ba [trabajador] on trial; [producto comprado] on approval; **poner a prueba** to (put to the) test - **5.** DEP event - **6.** IMPR proof.

PS (abrev de post scriptum) PS.

psicoanálisis, sicoanálisis sm inv psychoanalysis.

PSC sf (abrev de Partido Conservador o Partido Social Conservador) Colombian political party.

psicoanalista, sicoanalista smf psychoanalyst.

psicodélico, ca, sicodélico, ca adj psychedelic.

psicología, sicología sf lit & fig psychology.

psicológico, ca, sicológico, ca adj psychological.

psicólogo, ga, sicólogo, ga sm, f psychologist.

psicópata, sicópata smf psychopath.

psicosis, sicosis sf inv psychosis.

psicosomático, ca, sicosomático, ca adj psychosomatic.

psiquiatra, siquiatra smf psychiatrist.

psiquiátrico, ca, siquiátrico, ca adj psychiatric.

psíquico, ca, síquico, ca adj psychic.

PSOE [pe'soe] (abrev de Partido Socialista Obrero Español) sm major Spanish political party to the centre-left of the political spectrum.

pta. (abrev de peseta) pta.

púa sf - **1.** [de planta] thorn; [de erizo] quill; [de peine] tooth; [de tenedor] prong - **2.** MÚS plectrum.

pub [paβ] (pl pubs) sm bar.

pubertad sf puberty.

pubis sm inv pubes pl.

publicación sf publication; **publicación periódica** periodical.

publicar vt - **1.** [editar] to publish - **2.** [difundir] to publicize; [ley] to pass; [aviso] to issue.

publicidad sf - **1.** [difusión] publicity; **dar publicidad a algo** to publicize sthg - **2.** COM advertising; TV adverts pl, commercials pl.

publicitario, ria adj advertising (antes de s).

público, ca adj public; **ser público** [conocido] to be common knowledge; **en público** in public. ◆ **público** sm - **1.** CINE, TEATRO & TV audience; DEP crowd - **2.** [comunidad] public; **el gran público** the (general) public.

publirreportaje sm [anuncio de televisión] promotional film; [en revista] advertising spread.

pucha interj Andes & R Plata fam - **1.** [lamento, enojo] sugar! UK, shoot! US - **2.** [expresa sorpresa] wow! - **3.** [expresa enojo] damn!

puchero sm - **1.** [perola] cooking pot - **2.** [comida] stew ◆ **pucheros** smpl [gesto] pout sing; **hacer pucheros** to pout.

pucho sm C Sur fam [colilla] cigarette butt; [cigarillo] cigarette.

pudding = pudin.

púdico, ca adj - **1.** [recatado] modest - **2.** [tímido] bashful.

pudiente adj wealthy.

pudiera etc ▷ **poder.**

pudin (pl púdines), **pudding** ['puðin] (pl puddings) sm (plum) pudding.

pudor sm - **1.** [recato] (sense of) shame - **2.** [timidez] bashfulness.

pudoroso, sa adj - **1.** [recatado] modest - **2.** [tímido] bashful.

pudrir vt - **1.** [descomponerse] to rot - **2.** [fastidiar] to be fed up. ◆ **pudrirse** vprnl to rot.

puebla etc ▷ **poblar.**

pueblerino, na adj village (antes de s); despec provincial.

pueblo sm - **1.** [población - pequeña] village; [- grande] town - **2.** [nación] people.

pueda etc ▷ **poder.**

puente sm - **1.** [gen] bridge; **puente peatonal** footbridge; **tender un puente** to build bridges - **2.** [días festivos]: **hacer puente** to take an extra day off between two public holidays. ◆ **puente aéreo** sm [civil] air shuttle; [militar] airlift.

puenting sm bungee-jumping.

puerco, ca ◇ adj filthy. ◇ sm, f [animal] pig (f sow).

puercoespín sm porcupine.

puericultor, ra sm, f nursery nurse.

pueril adj fig childish.

puerro sm leek.

puerta sf - **1.** [de casa] door; [de jardín, ciudad etc] gate; **de puerta en puerta** from door to door; **llamar a la puerta** to knock on the door; **puerta de embarque** boarding gate; **puerta blindada/vidriera** reinforced/glass door - **2.** fig [posibilidad] gateway, opening - **3.** DEP goalmouth - **4.** loc: **a las puertas de** on the verge of.

puerto sm - **1.** [de mar] port; **puerto deportivo** marina; **puerto franco** O **libre** free port; **puerto pesquero** fishing port - **2.** [de montaña] pass - **3.** INFORM port; **puerto paralelo/serie/USB** parallel/serial/USB port - **4.** fig [refugio] haven.

Puerto Rico n pr Puerto Rico.

pues conj - **1.** [dado que] since, as - **2.** [por lo tanto] therefore, so; **creo, pues, que...** so, I think that... - **3.** [así que] so; **querías verlo, pues**

ahí está you wanted to see it, so here it is - **4.** [enfático]: ¡**pues ya está!** well, that's it!; ¡**pues claro!** but of course!

puesto, ta ◇ *pp* ▷ **poner**. ◆ *adj*: **ir muy puesto** to be all dressed up. ◆ **puesto** *sm* - **1.** [lugar] place - **2.** [empleo] post, position; **puesto de trabajo** job - **3.** [en fila, clasificación etc] place - **4.** [tenderete] stall, stand - **5.** MIL post; **puesto de mando/vigilancia** command/ sentry post; **puesto de policía** police station; **puesto de socorro** first-aid post. ◆ **puesta** *sf* [acción]: **puesta a punto** [de una técnica] perfecting; [de un motor] tuning; **puesta al día** updating; **puesta en escena** staging, production; **puesta en marcha** [de máquina] starting, start-up; [de acuerdo, proyecto] implementation; **puesta en práctica** implementation. ◆ **puesta de sol** *sf* sunset. ◆ **puesto que** *loc conj* since, as.

puf (*pl* **pufs**) *sm* pouf, pouffe. .

púgil *sm* boxer.

pugna *sf* fight, battle.

pugnar *vi fig* [esforzarse]: **pugnar por** to struggle O fight for.

puja *sf* [en subasta - acción] bidding; [- cantidad] bid.

pujar ◇ *vi* [en subasta] to bid higher. ◇ *vt* to bid.

pulcro, cra *adj* neat, tidy.

pulga *sf* flea.

pulgada *sf* inch.

pulgar ▷ **dedo**.

pulgón *sm* aphid.

pulimentar *vt* to polish.

pulir *vt* to polish. ◆ **pulirse** *vprnl* [gastarse] to blow.

pulmón *sm* lung; **a pleno pulmón** [gritar] at the top of one's voice; [respirar] deeply; **tener buenos pulmones** to have a powerful voice.

pulmonía *sf* pneumonia.

pulpa *sf* pulp.

púlpito *sm* pulpit.

pulpo *sm* [animal] octopus.

pulsación *sf* [del corazón] beat, beating *(U)*.

pulsador *sm* button, push button.

pulsar *vt* [botón, timbre etc] to press; [teclas de ordenador] to hit, to strike; [teclas de piano] to play; [cuerdas de guitarra] to pluck.

pulsera *sf* bracelet; **pulsera de tobillo** ankle bracelet.

pulso *sm* - **1.** [latido] pulse; **tomar el pulso a algo/alguien** *fig* to sound sthg/sb out - **2.** [firmeza]: **tener buen pulso** to have a steady hand; **a pulso** unaided; **ganarse algo a pulso** to deserve sthg.

pulular *vi* to swarm.

pulverizador, ra *adj* spray *(antes de s)*. ◆ **pulverizador** *sm* spray.

pulverizar *vt* - **1.** [líquido] to spray - **2.** [sólido] to reduce to dust; TECNOL to pulverize - **3.** *fig* [aniquilar] to pulverize.

puma *sm* puma.

punción *sf* puncture.

punta *sf* - **1.** [extremo - gen] point; [- de pan, pelo] end; [- de dedo, cuerno] tip; **de punta a punta** from one end to the other; **en punta** pointed; **en la otra punta de algo** at the other end of sthg; **sacar punta a (un lápiz)** to sharpen (a pencil); **a punta (de) pala** by the dozen O bucket; **tener algo en la punta de la lengua** *fig* to have sthg on the tip of one's tongue - **2.** [pizca] touch, bit; [de sal] pinch.

puntada *sf* [pespunte] stitch.

puntal *sm* [madero] prop; *fig* [apoyo] mainstay.

puntapié *sm* kick; **dar un puntapié a alguien** to kick sb; **tratar a alguien a puntapiés** *fig* to be nasty to sb.

puntear *vt* to pluck.

puntera ▷ **puntero**.

puntería *sf* - **1.** [destreza] marksmanship; **hacer puntería** to take aim - **2.** [orientación] aim.

puntero, ra ◇ *adj* leading. ◇ *sm, f* [líder] leader. ◆ **puntera** *sf* [de zapato] toecap.

puntiagudo, da *adj* pointed.

puntilla *sf* point lace; **dar la puntilla** *fig* to give the coup de grâce. ◆ **de puntillas** *loc adv* on tiptoe.

puntilloso, sa *adj* - **1.** [susceptible] touchy - **2.** [meticuloso] punctilious.

punto *sm* - **1.** [gen] point; **punto débil/fuerte** weak/strong point; *fig* backup, support; **punto culminante** high point; **puntos a tratar** matters to be discussed; **poner punto final a algo** to bring sthg to a close - **2.** [signo ortográfico] dot; **punto y coma** semi-colon; **puntos suspensivos** dots, suspension points; **dos puntos** colon - **3.** [marca] spot, dot - **4.** [lugar] spot, place; **punto de venta** COM point of sale - **5.** [momento] point, moment; **estar a punto** to be ready; **estar a punto de hacer algo** to be on the point of doing sthg - **6.** [estado] state, condition; **llegar a un punto en que...** to reach the stage where...; **estar en su punto** [gen] to be just right; [comida] to be done to a turn - **7.** [cláusula] clause - **8.** [puntada - en costura, cirugía] stitch; **punto de cruz** cross-stitch; **hacer punto** to knit; **un jersey de punto** a knitted jumper - **9.** [estilo de tejer] knitting; **punto de ganchillo** crochet - **10.** [objetivo] target. ◆ **en punto** *loc adv* on the dot. ◆ **hasta cierto punto** *loc adv* to some extent, up to a point. ◆ **punto de partida** *sm* starting point. ◆ **punto de vista** *sm* point of view. ◆ **punto muerto** *sm* - **1.** AUTO neutral - **2.** [en un proceso] deadlock; **estar en un punto muerto** to be deadlocked.

puntuación *sf* - **1.** [calificación] mark, [en concurso, competiciones] score - **2.** [ortográfica] punctuation.

puntual *adj* - **1.** [en el tiempo] punctual; **ser puntual** to be on time - **2.** [exacto, detallado] detailed - **3.** [aislado] isolated, one-off.

puntualidad *sf* [en el tiempo] punctuality.

puntualizar *vt* to specify, to clarify.

puntuar ◇ *vt* - **1.** [calificar] to mark; DEP to award marks to - **2.** [escrito] to punctuate. ◇ *vi* - **1.** [calificar] to mark - **2.** [entrar en el cómputo]: **puntuar (para)** to count (towards).

punzada *sf* [dolor intenso] stabbing pain (U); *fig* pang.

punzante *adj* - **1.** [que pincha] sharp - **2.** [intenso] sharp - **3.** [mordaz] caustic.

punzón *sm* punch.

puñado *sm* handful.

puñal *sm* dagger.

puñalada *sf* stab; [herida] stab wound.

puñeta ◇ *sf fam* [tontería]: **mandar a alguien a hacer puñetas** to tell sb to get lost; **en la quinta puñeta** in the back of beyond. ◇ *interj fam*: ¡**puñeta(s)!** damn it!

puñetazo *sm* punch; **lo derribó de un puñetazo** he knocked him to the ground.

puñetero, ra *fam* ◇ *adj* - **1.** [persona] damn; **tu puñetero marido** your damn husband - **2.** [cosa] tricky. ◇ *sm, f* pain.

puño *sm* - **1.** [mano cerrada] fist; **de su puño y letra** in his/her own handwriting; **meter O tener a alguien en un puño** to have sb under one's thumb - **2.** [de manga] cuff - **3.** [empuñadura - de espada] hilt; [- de paraguas] handle.

pupila *sf* pupil.

pupilo, la *sm, f* [discípulo] pupil.

pupitre *sm* desk.

puré *sm* CULIN purée; [sopa] thick soup; **puré de patatas** mashed potatoes *pl*; **hacer puré a alguien** to beat sb to a pulp.

pureza *sf* purity.

purga *sf fig* [depuración] purge.

purgante *adj & sm* purgative.

purgar *vt lit & fig* to purge.

purgatorio *sm* purgatory.

purificar *vt* to purify; [mineral, metal] to refine.

puritano, na *adj & sm, f* puritan.

puro, ra *adj* - **1.** [gen] pure; [oro] solid - **2.** [conducta, persona] chaste, innocent - **3.** [mero] sheer; [verdad] plain; **por pura casualidad** by pure chance. ◆ **puro** *sm* cigar.

púrpura ◇ *adj inv* purple. ◇ *sm* purple.

pus *sm* pus.

pusilánime *adj* cowardly.

puso ▷ **poner**.

puta ◇ *adj* ▷ **puto**. ◇ *sf vulg* whore; **ir de putas** to go whoring; **de puta madre** fucking brilliant.

puto, ta *adj vulg* [maldito] bloody. ◆ **puto** *sm vulg* male prostitute.

putrefacción *sf* rotting, putrefaction.

puzzle ['puθle], **puzle** *sm* jigsaw puzzle.

PVP (*abrev de* precio de venta al público) *sm* ≃ RRP.

PYME (*abrev de* **Pequeña y Mediana Empresa**) *sf* SME.

pyrex® = **pírex**.

pza. (*abrev de* plaza) Sq.

q, Q *sf* [letra] q, Q.

q.e.p.d. (*abrev de* que en paz descanse) RIP.

que ◇ *pron relat* - **1.** (*sujeto*) [persona] who, that; [cosa] that, which; **la mujer que me saluda** the woman (who O that is) waving to me; **el que me lo compró** the one who bought it from me; **la moto que me gusta** the motorbike (that) I like - **2.** (*complemento directo*) [persona] whom, that; [cosa] that, which; **el hombre que conociste ayer** the man (whom O that) you met yesterday; **ese coche es el que me quiero comprar** that car is the one (that O which) I want to buy - **3.** (*complemento indirecto*): **al/a la que** (to) whom; **ese es el chico al que presté dinero** that's the boy to whom I lent some money - **4.** (*complemento circunstancial*): **la playa a la que fui** the beach where O to which I went; **la mujer con la que hablas** the woman to whom you are talking; **la mesa sobre la que escribes** the table on which you are writing - **5.** (*complemento de tiempo*): **(en) que** when; **el día (en) que me fui** the day (when) I left. ◇ *conj* - **1.** (*con oraciones de sujeto*) that; **es importante que me escuches** it's important that you listen to me - **2.** (*con oraciones de complemento directo*) that; **me ha confesado que me quiere** he has told me that he loves me - **3.** (*compar*) than; **es más rápido**

que tú he's quicker than you; **antes morir que vivir la guerra** I'd rather die than live through a war - **4.** [expresa causa]: **hemos de esperar, que todavía no es la hora** we'll have to wait, as it isn't time yet - **5.** [expresa consecuencia] that; **tanto me lo pidió que se lo di** he asked me for it so insistently that I gave it to him - **6.** [expresa finalidad] so (that); **ven aquí que te vea** come over here so (that) I can see you - **7.** (+ subjuntivo) [expresa deseo] that; **quiero que lo hagas** I want you to do it; **espero que te diviertas** I hope (that) you have fun - **8.** (en oraciones exclamativas): ¡que te diviertas! have fun!; ¡que te doy un bofetón! do that again and I'll slap you! - **9.** (en oraciones interrogativas): ¿que quiere venir? pues que venga so she wants to come? then let her - **10.** [expresa disyunción] or; **quieras que no, harás lo que yo mando** you'll do what I tell you, whether you like it or not - **11.** [expresa hipótesis] if; **que no quieres hacerlo, pues no pasa nada** it doesn't matter if you don't want to do it - **12.** [expresa reiteración] and; **estaban charla que charla** they were talking and talking.

qué ◇ adj [gen] what; [al elegir, al concretar] which; **¿qué hora es?** what's the time?; **¿qué coche prefieres?** which car do you prefer?; **¿a qué distancia?** how far away? ◇ pron (interrogativo) what; **¿qué te dijo?** what did he tell you?; **no sé qué hacer** I don't know what to do; **¿qué?** [¿cómo?] sorry?, pardon? ◇ adv - **1.** [exclamativo] how; ¡qué horror! how awful!; ¡qué tonto eres! how stupid you are!, you're so stupid!; ¡qué casa más bonita! what a lovely house!; ¡y qué! so what? - **2.** [expresa gran cantidad]: ¡qué de...! what a lot of...!; ¡qué de gente hay aquí! what a lot of people there are here!, there are so many people here!

quebradero ➡ **quebradero de cabeza** sm headache, problem.

quebradizo, za adj - **1.** [frágil] fragile, brittle - **2.** [débil] frail - **3.** [voz] weak.

quebrado, da adj [terreno] rough, uneven; [perfil] rugged.

quebrantar vt - **1.** [incumplir - promesa, ley] to break; [- obligación] to fail in - **2.** [debilitar] to weaken; [moral, resistencia] to break. ➡ **quebrantarse** vprnl [debilitarse] to deteriorate.

quebranto sm [debilitamiento] weakening, debilitation.

quebrar ◇ vt [romper] to break. ◇ vi FIN to go bankrupt. ➡ **quebrarse** vprnl - **1.** [romperse] to break - **2.** [voz] to break, to falter.

quechua sm [idioma] Quechua.

quedar vi - **1.** [permanecer] to remain, to stay - **2.** [haber aún, faltar] to be left, to remain; **¿queda azúcar?** is there any sugar left?; **nos quedan 10 euros** we have 10 euros left; **¿cuánto queda para León?** how much further is it to

León?; **quedar por hacer** to remain to be done; **queda por fregar el suelo** the floor has still to be cleaned - **3.** [mostrarse]: **quedar como** to come across as; **quedar bien/mal (con alguien)** to make a good/bad impression (on sb) - **4.** [llegar a ser, resultar]: **el trabajo ha quedado perfecto** the job turned out perfectly; **el cuadro queda muy bien ahí** the picture looks great there - **5.** [acabar]: **quedar en** to end in; **quedar en nada** to come to nothing - **6.** [sentar] to look; **te queda un poco corto el traje** your suit is a bit too short; **quedar bien/mal a alguien** to look good/bad on sb; **quedar bien/mal con algo** to go well/badly with sthg - **7.** [citarse]: **quedar (con alguien)** to arrange to meet (sb); **hemos quedado el lunes** we've arranged to meet on Monday - **8.** [acordar]: **quedar en algo/en hacer algo** to agree on sthg/to do sthg; **quedar en que...** to agree that...; **¿en qué quedamos?** what's it to be, then? - **9.** fam [estar situado] to be; **¿por dónde queda?** whereabouts is it? ➡ **quedarse** vprnl - **1.** [permanecer - en un lugar] to stay, to remain - **2.** [terminar - en un estado]: **quedarse ciego/sordo** to go blind/deaf; **quedarse triste** to be feel sad; **quedarse sin dinero** to be left penniless; **la pared se ha quedado limpia** the wall is clean now - **3.** [comprar] to take; **me quedo éste** I'll take this one. ➡ **quedarse con** vprnl - **1.** [retener, guardarse] to keep - **2.** [preferir] to go for, to prefer.

quedo, da adj quiet, soft. ➡ **quedo** adv quietly, softly.

quehacer (gen pl) sm task; **quehaceres domésticos** housework (U).

queja sf - **1.** [lamento] moan, groan - **2.** [protesta] complaint; **presentar una queja** to lodge O make a complaint.

quejarse vprnl - **1.** [lamentar] to groan, to cry out; **quejarse de algo/alguien** to bemoan sthg/sb - **2.** [protestar] to complain; **quejarse de** to complain about.

quejica despec adj whining, whingeing.

quejido sm cry, moan.

quejoso, sa adj: **quejoso (de)** annoyed O upset (with).

quemado, da adj - **1.** [gen] burnt; **oler a quemado** to smell burning; [por agua hirviendo] scalded; [por electricidad] burnt-out; [fusible] blown - **2.** [por sol] sunburnt - **3.** Amér [bronceado] tanned - **4.** loc: **estar quemado** [agotado] to be burnt-out; [harto] to be fed up.

quemador sm burner.

quemadura sf [por fuego] burn; **quemadura en tercer grado** third-degree burning; [por agua hirviendo] scald.

quemar ◇ vt - **1.** [gen] to burn; [suj: agua hirviendo] to scald; [suj: electricidad] to blow - **2.** fig [malgastar] to fritter away - **3.** fig [desgastar] to burn out - **4.** *fig* [hartar] to make fed up. ◇ *vi* [estar caliente] to be (scalding) hot. ◆ **quemarse** *vprnl* - **1.** [por fuego] to burn down; [por agua hirviendo] to get scalded, [por calor] to burn; [por quemadura] to blister - **2.** [broncearse] to get burned - **3.** *fig* [desgastarse] to burn out - **4.** *fig* [hartarse] to get fed up.

quemarropa ◆ **a quemarropa** *loc adv* point-blank.

quemazón *sf* burning; [picor] itch.

quepa *etc* ▷ **caber**.

querella *sf* - **1.** DER [acusación] charge; **presentar una querella contra alguien** to bring an action against sb - **2.** [discordia] dispute.

querer ◇ *vt* - **1.** [gen] to want; **quiero una bicicleta** I want a bicycle; **¿quieren ustedes algo más?** would you like anything else?; **querer que alguien haga algo** to want sb to do sthg; **quiero que lo hagas tú** I want you to do it; **querer que pase algo** to want sthg to happen; **queremos que las cosas te vayan bien** we want things to go well for you; **quisiera hacerlo, pero...** I'd like to do it, but... - **2.** [amar] to love - **3.** [en preguntas - con amabilidad]: **¿quiere decirle a su amigo que pase?** could you tell your friend to come in, please? - **4.** [pedir - precio]: **querer algo (por)** to want sthg (for); **¿cuánto quieres por el coche?** how much do you want for the car? - **5.** *fig* & *irón* [dar motivos para]: **tú lo que quieres es que te pegue** you're asking for a smack - **6.** *loc*: **como quien no quiere la cosa** as if it were nothing; **quien bien te quiere te hará llorar** *prov* you have to be cruel to be kind *prov*. ◇ *vi* to want; **ven cuando quieras** come whenever you like O want; **no me voy porque no quiero** I'm not going because I don't want to; **queriendo** on purpose; **sin querer** accidentally; **querer decir** to mean; **¿qué quieres decir con eso?** what do you mean by that?; **querer es poder** where there's a will there's a way. ◇ *v impers* [haber atisbos]: **parece que quiere llover** it looks like rain. ◇ *sm* love. ◆ **quererse** *vprnl* to love each other.

querido, da ◇ *adj* dear. ◇ *sm, f* lover; [apelativo afectuoso] darling.

quesadilla *sf* *Amér C* & *Méx* filled fried tortilla.

queso *sm* cheese; **queso gruyère/parmesano/ roquefort** Gruyère/Parmesan/Roquefort (cheese); **queso de bola** Dutch cheese; **queso manchego** hard mild yellow cheese made in La Mancha; **queso para untar** cheese spread; **queso rallado** grated cheese; **dárselas con queso a alguien** to fool sb.

quicio *sm* jamb; **estar fuera de quicio** *fig* to be out of kilter; **sacar de quicio a alguien** *fig* to drive sb mad.

quiebra *sf* - **1.** [ruina] bankruptcy; **ir a la quiebra** to go bankrupt; [en bolsa] crash; **quiebra fraudulenta** DER fraudulent bankruptcy - **2.** *fig* [pérdida] collapse.

quiebro *sm* [ademán] swerve.

quien *pron* - **1.** *(relativo)* [sujeto] who; [complemento] whom; **fue mi hermano quien me lo explicó** it was my brother who explained it to me; **era Pepe a quien vi/de quien no me fiaba** it was Pepe (whom) I saw/didn't trust - **2.** *(indefinido)*: **quienes quieran verlo que se acerquen** whoever wants to see it will have to come closer; **hay quien lo niega** there are those who deny it - **3.** *loc*: **quien más quien menos** everyone.

quién *pron (interrogativo)* [sujeto] who; [complemento] who, whom; **¿quién es ese hombre?** who's that man?; **no sé quién viene** I don't know who is coming; **¿a quiénes has invitado?** who O whom have you invited?; **¿de quién es?** whose is it?; **¿quién es?** [en la puerta] who is it?; [al teléfono] who's calling?

quienquiera *(pl* **quienesquiera)** *pron* whoever; **quienquiera que venga** whoever comes.

quiera *etc* ▷ **querer**.

quieto, ta *adj* [parado] still; **¡estáte quieto!** keep still!; **¡quieto ahí!** don't move!

quietud *sf* - **1.** [inmovilidad] stillness - **2.** [tranquilidad] quietness.

quijada *sf* jaw.

quijotesco, ca *adj* quixotic.

quilate *sm* carat.

quilla *sf* NÁUT keel.

quilo *etc* = **kilo**.

quilombo *sm* - **1.** *mfam* [prostíbulo] whorehouse - **2.** *mfam* [lío] mess.

quimera *sf* fantasy.

quimérico, ca *adj* fanciful.

químico, ca ◇ *adj* chemical. ◇ *sm, f* [científico] chemist. ◆ **química** *sf* [ciencia] chemistry.

quina *sf* [bebida] quinine.

quincalla *sf* trinket.

quince *num* fifteen; **quince días** a fortnight; *ver también* **seis**.

quinceañero, ra *sm, f* teenager.

quinceavo, va *num* fifteenth.

quincena *sf* fortnight.

quincenal *adj* fortnightly.

quincuagésimo, ma *num* fiftieth.

quiniela *sf* [boleto] pools coupon. ◆ **quinielas** *sfpl* [apuestas] (football) pools; **jugar a las quinielas** to play the pools. ◆ **quiniela hípica** *sf* sweepstake.

quinientos, tas *num* five hundred; *ver también* **seis**.

quinina *sf* quinine.

quinqué *sm* oil lamp.

quinquenio *sm* [periodo] five-year period.

quinqui *smf fam* delinquent.

quinta ⊳ **quinto**.

quinteto *sm* quintet.

quinto, ta *num* fifth. ➡ **quinto** *sm* - 1. [parte] fifth - 2. MIL recruit. ➡ **quinta** *sf* - 1. [finca] country house - 2. MIL call-up year.

quintuplicar *vt* to increase fivefold. ➡ **quintuplicarse** *vprnl* to increase fivefold.

quiosco, kiosco *sm* kiosk; [de periódicos] newspaper stand; **quiosco de música** bandstand.

quiosquero, ra *sm, f* owner of a newspaper stand.

quirófano *sm* operating theatre.

quiromancia *sf* palmistry, chiromancy.

quiromasaje *sm* (manual) massage.

quirúrgico, ca *adj* surgical.

quisiera *etc* ⊳ **querer**.

quisque *sm*: **cada** *O* **todo quisque** every man Jack.

quisquilloso, sa *adj* - 1. [detallista] pernickety - 2. [susceptible] touchy.

quiste *sm* cyst.

quitaesmalte *sm* nail-polish remover.

quitaipón ➡ **de quitaipón** *loc adj* removable; [capucha] detachable.

quitamanchas *sm inv* stain remover.

quitanieves *sm inv* snow plough.

quitar *vt* - 1. [gen] to remove; [ropa, zapatos etc] to take off; **quitarle algo a alguien** to take sthg away from sb; **de quita y pon** removable; [capucha] detachable - 2. [dolor, ansiedad] to take away, to relieve; [sed] to quench - 3. [tiempo] to take up - 4. [robar] to take, to steal - 5. [impedir]: **esto no quita que sea un vago** that doesn't change the fact that he's a layabout - 6. [exceptuar]: **quitando el queso, me gusta todo** apart from cheese, I'll eat anything - 7. [desconectar] to switch off. ➡ **quitarse** *vprnl* - 1. [apartarse] to get out of the way - 2. [ropa] to take off - 3. [suj: mancha] to come out - 4. *loc*: **quitarse a alguien de encima** *O* **de en medio** to get rid of sb.

quitasol *sm* sunshade UK, parasol.

quite *sm* DEP parry; **estar al quite** to be on hand to help.

Quito *n pr* Quito.

quizá, quizás *adv* perhaps; **quizá llueva mañana** it might rain tomorrow; **quizá no lo creas** you may not believe it; **quizá sí** maybe; **quizá no** maybe not.

R

r, R *sf* [letra] r, R.

rábano *sm* radish; **coger el rábano por las hojas** to get the wrong end of the stick; **me importa un rábano** I couldn't care less, I don't give a damn.

rabí *sm* rabbi.

rabia *sf* - 1. [ira] rage; **me da rabia** it makes me mad - 2. [enfermedad] rabies.

rabiar *vi* - 1. [sufrir] to writhe in pain - 2. [enfadarse] to be furious.

rabieta *sf fam* tantrum; **tener una rabieta** to throw a tantrum.

rabillo *sm* corner; **mirar algo con el rabillo del ojo** to look at sthg out of the corner of one's eye.

rabioso, sa *adj* - 1. [furioso] furious - 2. [excesivo] terrible - 3. [enfermo de rabia] rabid - 4. [chillón] loud, gaudy.

rabo *sm* - 1. [de animal] tail; **rabo de buey** oxtail; **irse** *O* **salir con el rabo entre las piernas** to go off with one's tail between one's legs - 2. [de hoja, fruto] stem.

rácano, na *fam adj* [tacaño] mean, stingy.

RACE (*abrev de* **Real Automóvil Club de España**) *sm Spanish automobile association*, ≃ AA UK, ≃ AAA US.

racha *sf* - 1. [ráfaga] gust (of wind) - 2. [época] spell; [serie] string; **buena/mala racha** good/bad patch; **a rachas** in fits and starts.

racial *adj* racial.

racimo *sm* - 1. [de frutos] bunch - 2. [de flores] raceme.

raciocinio *sm* [razón] (power of) reason.

ración *sf* - 1. [porción] portion - 2. [en bar, restaurante] *large portion of a dish served as a snack*.

racional *adj* rational.

racionalizar *vt* to rationalize.

racionar *vt* to ration.

racismo *sm* racism.

racista *adj & smf* racist.

radar (*pl* **radares**) *sm* radar.

radiación *sf* radiation.

radiactivo, va, radioactivo, va *adj* radioactive.

radiador *sm* radiator.

radiante *adj* radiant; **lucía un sol radiante** it was brilliantly sunny.

radiar *vt* - **1.** [irradiar] to radiate - **2.** [por radio] to broadcast.

radical *adj* & *smf* radical.

radicar *vi*: **radicar en** [suj: problema etc] to lie in; [suj: población] to be [situated] in. ◆ **radicarse** *vprnl* [establecerse]: **radicarse (en)** to settle (in).

radio ◇ *sm* - **1.** ANAT & GEOM radius - **2.** [de rueda] spoke - **3.** QUÍM radium. ◇ *sf* radio; **oír algo por la radio** to hear sthg on the radio; **oír algo por radio macuto** *fam* to hear sthg on the bush telegraph; **radio digital** digital radio; **radio por Internet** Internet radio; **radio pirata** pirate radio station.

radioactivo = **radiactivo**.

radioaficionado, da *sm, f* radio ham.

radiocasete *sm* radio cassette (player).

radiocontrol *sm* remote control.

radiodespertador *sm* clock radio.

radiodifusión *sf* broadcasting.

radioescucha *smf inv* listener.

radiofónico, ca *adj* radio (antes de s).

radiografía *sf* [fotografía] X-ray; **hacerse una radiografía** to be X-rayed; [ciencia] radiography.

radionovela *sf* radio soap opera.

radiorreloj *sm* clock radio.

radiotaxi *sm* taxi (with radio link).

radioteléfono *sm* radiotelephone.

radioterapia *sf* radiotherapy.

radioyente *smf* listener.

RAE (abrev de **Real Academia Española**) *sf* institution that sets lexical and syntactic standards for Spanish.

raer *vt* to scrape (off).

ráfaga *sf* [de aire, viento] gust; [de disparos] burst; [de luces] flash.

raído, da *adj* threadbare; [por los bordes] frayed.

raigambre *sf* [tradición] tradition.

raíl, rail *sm* rail.

raíz (*pl* **raíces**) *sf* [gen & MAT] root; **raíz cuadrada/cúbica** square/cube root; **a raíz de** as a result of, following; **echar raíces** to put down roots.

raja *sf* - **1.** [porción] slice - **2.** [grieta] crack.

rajar *vt* - **1.** [partir] to crack; [melón] to slice - **2.** *mfam* [apuñalar] to slash. ◆ **rajarse** *vprnl* - **1.** [partirse] to crack - **2.** *fam* [echarse atrás] to chicken out.

rajatabla ◆ **a rajatabla** *loc adv* to the letter, strictly.

ralentí *sm* neutral.

rallado, da *adj* grated.

rallador *sm* grater.

ralladura (gen pl) *sf* grating.

rallar *vt* to grate.

rally ['rali] (*pl* **rallies**) *sm* rally.

RAM (abrev de **random access memory**) *sf* INFORM RAM.

rama *sf* branch; **andarse por las ramas** *fam* to beat about the bush; **irse por las ramas** *fam* to go off at a tangent.

ramaje *sm* branches *pl*.

ramal *sm* [de carretera, ferrocarril] branch.

ramalazo *sm* - **1.** *fam* [hecho que delata] giveaway sign; **tener un ramalazo** *fam* to be effeminate - **2.** [ataque] fit.

rambla *sf* - **1.** [avenida] avenue, boulevard - **2.** R Plata [paseo marítimo] seafront.

ramera *sf* whore, hooker *US*.

ramificación *sf* - **1.** [gen] ramification - **2.** [de carretera, ferrocarril, ciencia] branch.

ramificarse *vprnl* - **1.** [bifurcarse] to branch out - **2.** [subdividirse]: **ramificarse (en)** to subdivide (into).

ramillete *sm* bunch, bouquet.

ramo *sm* - **1.** [de flores] bunch, bouquet - **2.** [rama] branch; **el ramo de la construcción** the building industry.

rampa *sf* - **1.** [para subir y bajar] ramp - **2.** [cuesta] steep incline.

rana *sf* frog.

ranchero, ra *sm, f* rancher. ◆ **ranchera** *sf* - **1.** MÚS *popular Mexican song* - **2.** AUTO estate car.

rancho *sm* - **1.** [comida] mess - **2.** [granja] ranch - **3.** *loc*: **hacer rancho aparte** to keep to o.s. - **4.** C Sur & Ven [choza] shack, shanty; Ven [chabola] shanty town.

rancio, cia *adj* - **1.** [pasado] rancid - **2.** [antiguo] ancient - **3.** [añejo - vino] mellow.

rango *sm* - **1.** [social] standing - **2.** [jerárquico] rank.

ranking ['raŋkin] (*pl* **rankings**) *sm* ranking.

ranura *sf* groove; [de máquina tragaperras, cabina telefónica] slot.

rapaces ▷ **rapaz**.

rapapolvo *sm fam* ticking-off; **dar** O **echar un rapapolvo a alguien** to tick sb off.

rapar *vt* [barba, bigote] to shave off; [cabeza] to shave; [persona] to shave the hair of.

rapaz, za *sm, f fam* lad (f lass). ◆ **rapaz** *adj* - **1.** [que roba] rapacious, greedy - **2.** ZOOL ▷ **ave**. ◆ **rapaces** *sfpl* ZOOL birds of prey.

rape *sm* monkfish; **cortar el pelo al rape a alguien** to crop sb's hair.

rapé *sm* (en aposición invariable) snuff.

rapero, ra *sm, f* rapper.

rápidamente *adv* quickly.

rapidez *sf* speed.

rápido, da *adj* quick, fast; [coche] fast; [beneficio, decisión] quick. ◆ **rápido** ◇ *adv* quickly; **más rápido** quicker; **¡ven, rápido!** come, quick! ◇ *sm* [tren] express train. ◆ **rápidos** *smpl* [de río] rapids.

rapiña *sf* [robo] robbery with violence.

rapsodia *sf* rhapsody.

raptar *vt* to abduct, to kidnap.

rapto *sm* - **1.** [secuestro] abduction, kidnapping - **2.** [ataque] fit.

raqueta *sf* [para jugar - al tenis] racquet; [- al ping pong] bat.

raquítico, ca *adj* - **1.** MED rachitic - **2.** [insuficiente] miserable.

rareza *sf* - **1.** [poco común, extraño] rarity - **2.** [extravagancia] eccentricity.

raro, ra *adj* - **1.** [extraño] strange; **¡qué raro!** how odd O strange! - **2.** [excepcional] unusual, rare; [visita] infrequent - **3.** [extravagante] odd, eccentric - **4.** [escaso] rare; **rara vez** rarely.

ras *sm*: **a ras de** level with; **a ras de tierra** at ground level; **volar a ras de tierra** to fly low.

rasante *sf* [de carretera] gradient.

rascacielos *sm inv* skyscraper.

rascar ◇ *vt* - **1.** [con uñas, clavo] to scratch - **2.** [con espátula] to scrape (off); [con cepillo] to scrub. ◇ *vi* to be rough. ◆ **rascarse** *vprnl* to scratch o.s.

rasgar *vt* to tear; [sobre] to tear open.

rasgo *sm* - **1.** [característica] trait, characteristic - **2.** [trazo] flourish, stroke. ◆ **rasgos** *smpl* - **1.** [del rostro] features - **2.** [letra] handwriting *(U).* ◆ **a grandes rasgos** *loc adv* in general terms.

rasguear *vt* to strum.

rasguñar *vt* to scratch.

rasguño *sm* scratch.

raso, sa *adj* - **1.** [cucharada etc] level - **2.** [a poca altura] low - **3.** MIL: **soldado raso** private. ◆ **raso** *sm* [tela] satin.

raspa *sf* backbone (of fish).

raspadura *sf (gen pl)* scraping; [señal] scratch.

raspar *vt* - **1.** [rascar] to scrape (off) - **2.** [rasar] to graze, to shave. ◆ **rasparse** *vprnl* to scratch o.s.

rasposo, sa *adj* rough.

rastras ◆ **a rastras** *loc adv*: **llevar algo/a alguien a rastras** *lit & fig* to drag sthg/sb along.

rastreador, ra *sm, f* tracker.

rastrear *vt* [seguir las huellas de] to track.

rastrero, ra *adj* despicable.

rastrillo *sm* - **1.** [en jardinería] rake - **2.** [mercado] flea market; [benéfico] jumble sale - **3.** *Méx* [para afeitarse] safety razor.

rastro *sm* - **1.** [pista] trail; **perder el rastro de alguien** to lose track of sb; **sin dejar rastro** without trace - **2.** [vestigio] trace - **3.** [mercado] flea market.

rastrojo *sm* stubble.

rasurar *vt* to shave. ◆ **rasurarse** *vprnl* to shave.

rata *sf* rat.

ratero, ra *sm, f* petty thief.

ratificar *vt* to ratify. ◆ **ratificarse en** *vprnl* to stand by.

rato *sm* while; **estuvimos hablando mucho rato** we were talking for quite a while; **al poco rato (de)** shortly after; **pasar el rato** to kill time, to pass the time; **pasar un mal rato** to have a hard time of it; **ratos libres** spare time *(U);* **a ratos** at times; **un rato (largo)** *fig* really, terribly.

ratón *sm* [gen & INFORM] mouse.

ratonera *sf* - **1.** [para ratas] mousetrap - **2.** *fig* [trampa] trap.

raudal *sm* - **1.** [de agua] torrent - **2.** *fig* [montón] abundance; [de lágrimas] flood; [de desgracias] string; **a raudales** in abundance, by the bucket.

ravioli *(gen pl) sm* ravioli *(U).*

raya *sf* - **1.** [línea] line; [en tejido] stripe; **a rayas** striped - **2.** [del pelo] parting; **hacerse la raya** to part one's hair - **3.** [de pantalón] crease - **4.** *fig* [límite] limit; **pasarse de la raya** to overstep the mark; **mantener** O **tener a raya a alguien** to keep sb in line - **5.** [señal - en disco, pintura etc] scratch - **6.** [pez] ray - **7.** [guión] dash.

rayado, da *adj* - **1.** [a rayas - tela] striped; [- papel] ruled - **2.** [estropeado] scratched. ◆ **rayado** *sm* [rayas] stripes *pl.*

rayar ◇ *vt* - **1.** [marcar] to scratch - **2.** [trazar rayas] to rule lines on. ◇ *vi* - **1.** [aproximarse]: **rayar en algo** to border on sthg; **raya en los cuarenta** he's pushing forty - **2.** [alba] to break. ◆ **rayarse** *vprnl* to get scratched.

rayo *sm* - **1.** [de luz] ray; **rayo solar** sunbeam - **2.** FÍS beam, ray; **rayo láser** laser beam; **rayos infrarrojos/ultravioleta/uva** infrared/ultraviolet/UVA rays; **rayos X** X-rays; **caer como un rayo** *fig* to be a bombshell - **3.** METEOR bolt of lightning; **rayos** lightning *(U).*

rayón *sm* rayon.

rayuela *sf* hopscotch.

raza *sf* - **1.** [humana] race; **raza humana** human race - **2.** [animal] breed - **3.** *Perú fam* [cara] cheek, nerve.

razón *sf* - **1.** [gen] reason; **con razón no vino** no wonder he didn't come; **dar la razón a alguien** to say that sb is right; **en razón de** O **a** in view of; **razón de ser** raison d'être; **tener razón (en hacer algo)** to be right (to do sthg); **no tener razón** to be wrong; **razón de más pa-**

ra hacer algo all the more reason to do sthg; **y con razón** and quite rightly so - **2.** [información]: **se vende piso: razón aquí** flat for sale: enquire within; **dar razón de** to give an account of - **3.** MAT ratio. ❖ **a razón de** *loc adv* at a rate of.

razonable *adj* reasonable.

razonamiento *sm* reasoning *(U)*.

razonar ◇ *vt* [argumentar] to reason out. ◇ *vi* [pensar] to reason.

RDSI (*abrev de* **Red Digital de Servicios Integrados**) *sf* INFORM ISDN.

re *sm* MÚS D; [en solfeo] re.

reacción *sf* reaction; **reacción en cadena** chain reaction.

reaccionar *vi* to react; **reaccionar a algo** to react to sthg.

reaccionario, ria *adj & sm, f* reactionary.

reacio, cia *adj* stubborn.

reactivación *sf* revival.

reactor *sm* - **1.** [propulsor] reactor - **2.** [avión] jet (plane).

readmitir *vt* to accept *O* take back.

reafirmar *vt* to confirm. ❖ **reafirmarse** *vprnl* to assert o.s.; **reafirmarse en algo** to become confirmed in sthg.

reajuste *sm* - **1.** [cambio] readjustment; **reajuste ministerial** cabinet reshuffle - **2.** [ECON - de precios, impuestos] increase; [- de sector] streamlining; [- de salarios] reduction; **reajuste de plantilla** redundancies *pl.*

real *adj* - **1.** [verdadero] real - **2.** [de monarquía] royal.

realce *sm* - **1.** [esplendor] glamour; **dar realce a algo/alguien** to enhance sthg/sb - **2.** [en pintura] highlight.

realeza *sf* [monarcas] royalty.

realidad *sf* - **1.** [mundo real] reality; **realidad virtual** INFORM virtual reality - **2.** [verdad] truth; **en realidad** actually, in fact.

realista ◇ *adj* realistic. ◇ *smf* ARTE realist.

realización *sf* - **1.** [ejecución] carrying-out; [de proyecto, medidas] implementation; [de sueños, deseos] fulfilment - **2.** [obra] achievement - **3.** CINE production.

realizador, ra *sm, f* CINE & TV director.

realizar *vt* - **1.** [ejecutar - esfuerzo, viaje, inversión] to make; [- operación, experimento, trabajo] to perform; [- encargo] to carry out; [- plan, reformas] to implement - **2.** [hacer real] to fulfil, to realize - **3.** CINE to produce. ❖ **realizarse** *vprnl* - **1.** [en un trabajo] to find fulfilment - **2.** [hacerse real - sueño, predicción, deseo] to come true; [- esperanza, ambición] to be fulfilled - **3.** [ejecutarse] to be carried out.

realmente *adv* - **1.** [en verdad] in fact, actually - **2.** [muy] really, very.

realquilado, da *sm, f* sub-tenant.

realquilar *vt* to sublet.

realzar *vt* - **1.** [resaltar] to enhance - **2.** [en pintura] to highlight.

reanimar *vt* - **1.** [físicamente] to revive - **2.** [moralmente] to cheer up - **3.** MED to resuscitate.

reanudar *vt* [conversación, trabajo] to resume; [amistad] to renew.

reaparición *sf* reappearance.

rearme *sm* rearmament.

reavivar *vt* to revive.

rebaja *sf* - **1.** [acción] reduction - **2.** [descuento] discount; **hacer una rebaja** to give a discount. ❖ **rebajas** *sfpl* COM sales; **'grandes rebajas'** 'massive reductions'; **estar de rebajas** to have a sale on.

rebajado, da *adj* - **1.** [precio] reduced - **2.** [humillado] humiliated.

rebajar *vt* - **1.** [precio] to reduce; **te rebajo 2 euros** I'll knock 2 euros off for you - **2.** [persona] to humiliate - **3.** [intensidad] to tone down - **4.** [altura] to lower. ❖ **rebajarse** *vprnl* [persona] to humble o.s.; **rebajarse a hacer algo** to lower o.s. *O* stoop to do sthg; **rebajarse ante alguien** to humble o.s. before sb.

rebanada *sf* slice.

rebañar *vt* to scrape clean.

rebaño *sm* flock; [de vacas] herd.

rebasar *vt* to exceed, to surpass; [agua] to overflow; AUTO to overtake.

rebatir *vt* to refute.

rebeca *sf* cardigan.

rebelarse *vprnl* to rebel.

rebelde ◇ *adj* - **1.** [sublevado] rebel *(antes de s)* - **2.** [desobediente] rebellious. ◇ *smf* [sublevado, desobediente] rebel.

rebeldía *sf* - **1.** [cualidad] rebelliousness - **2.** [acción] (act of) rebellion.

rebelión *sf* rebellion; **rebelión militar** military uprising.

rebenque *sm* C Sur riding crop.

reblandecer *vt* to soften.

rebobinar *vt* to rewind.

rebosante *adj*: **rebosante (de)** brimming *O* overflowing (with).

rebosar ◇ *vt* to overflow with. ◇ *vi* to overflow; **rebosar de** to be overflowing with; *fig* [persona] to brim with.

rebotar *vi*: **rebotar (en)** to bounce (off), to rebound (off).

rebote *sm* - **1.** [bote] bounce, bouncing *(U)* - **2.** DEP rebound; **de rebote** on the rebound.

rebozado, da *adj* CULIN coated in batter *O* breadcrumbs.

rebozar *vt* CULIN to coat in batter *O* breadcrumbs.

rebuscado, da *adj* recherché, pretentious.

rebuznar *vi* to bray.

recabar *vt* [pedir] to ask for; [conseguir] to obtain.

recadero, ra *sm, f* messenger.

recado *sm* - **1.** [mensaje] message; **mandar recado de que...** to send word that... - **2.** [encargo] errand; **hacer recados** to run errands.

recaer *vi* - **1.** [enfermo] to have a relapse - **2.** [ir a parar]: **recaer sobre** to fall on - **3.** [reincidir]: **recaer en** to relapse into.

recaída *sf* relapse.

recalcar *vt* to stress, to emphasize.

recalcitrante *adj* recalcitrant.

recalentar *vt* - **1.** [volver a calentar] to warm up - **2.** [calentar demasiado] to overheat.

recámara *sf* - **1.** [de arma de fuego] chamber - **2.** *Amér C, Col & Méx* [dormitorio] bedroom.

recamarera *sf Amér C, Col & Méx* chambermaid.

recambio *sm* spare (part); [para pluma] refill; **de recambio** spare.

recapacitar *vi* to reflect, to think; **recapacitar sobre** to think about.

recapitulación *sf* recap, recapitulation.

recargado, da *adj* [estilo etc] overelaborate.

recargar *vt* - **1.** [volver a cargar - encendedor, recipiente] to refill; [- batería, pila] to recharge; [- fusil, camión] to reload; [- teléfono móvil] to top up - **2.** [cargar demasiado] to overload - **3.** [adornar en exceso] to overelaborate - **4.** [cantidad]: **recargar 20 euros a alguien** to charge sb 20 euros extra - **5.** [poner en exceso]: **recargar algo de algo** to put too much of sthg in sthg. ➠ **recargarse** *vprnl Méx* [apoyarse] to lean.

recargo *sm* extra charge, surcharge.

recatado, da *adj* [pudoroso] modest, demure.

recato *sm* [pudor] modesty, demureness.

recaudación *sf* - **1.** [acción] collection - **2.** [cantidad] takings *pl*; DEP gate; [de un cine] box-office takings.

recaudador, ra *sm, f*: **recaudador (de impuestos)** tax collector.

recaudar *vt* to collect.

recelar *vi*: **recelar de** to mistrust.

recelo *sm* mistrust, suspicion.

receloso, sa *adj* mistrustful, suspicious.

recepción *sf* [gen] reception.

recepcionista *smf* receptionist.

receptáculo *sm* receptacle.

receptivo, va *adj* receptive.

receptor, ra *sm, f* [persona] recipient. ➠ **receptor** *sm* [aparato] receiver.

recesión *sf* recession.

receta *sf* - **1.** *fig* & CULIN recipe - **2.** MED prescription.

rechazar *vt* - **1.** [gen & MED] to reject; [oferta] to turn down - **2.** [repeler - a una persona] to push away; MIL to repel.

rechazo *sm* - **1.** [gen & MED] rejection; [hacia una ley, un político] disapproval; **rechazo a hacer algo** refusal to do sthg - **2.** [negación] denial.

rechinar *vi* - **1.** [puerta] to creak; [dientes] to grind; [frenos, ruedas] to screech; [metal] to clank - **2.** [dando dentera] to grate.

rechistar *vi* to answer back.

rechoncho, cha *adj fam* chubby.

rechupete ➠ **de rechupete** *loc adv fam* [gen] brilliant, great; [comida] scrumptious.

recibidor *sm* entrance hall.

recibimiento *sm* reception, welcome.

recibir ◇ *vt* - **1.** [gen] to receive; [clase, instrucción] to have - **2.** [dar la bienvenida a] to welcome - **3.** [ir a buscar] to meet. ◇ *vi* [atender visitas] to receive visitors. ➠ **recibirse** *vprnl Amér*: **recibirse (de)** to graduate, to qualify (as).

recibo *sm* receipt; **acusar recibo de** to acknowledge receipt of; **no ser de recibo** to be unacceptable.

reciclaje *sm* - **1.** [de residuos] recycling - **2.** [de personas] retraining.

reciclar *vt* [residuos] to recycle.

recién *adv* - **1.** recently, newly; **el recién casado** the newly-wed; **los recién llegados** the newcomers; **el recién nacido** the newborn baby - **2.** *Amér* [hace poco] just; **recién llegó** he has just arrived.

reciente *adj* - **1.** [acontecimiento etc] recent - **2.** [pintura, pan etc] fresh.

recientemente *adv* recently.

recinto *sm* [zona cercada] enclosure; [área] place, area; [alrededor de edificios] grounds *pl*; **recinto ferial** fairground *(of trade fair)*.

recio, cia *adj* - **1.** [persona] robust - **2.** [voz] gravelly - **3.** [objeto] solid - **4.** [material, tela] tough, strong.

recipiente *sm* container, receptacle.

reciprocidad *sf* reciprocity.

recíproco, ca *adj* mutual, reciprocal.

recital *sm* - **1.** [de música clásica] recital; [de rock] concert - **2.** [de lectura] reading.

recitar *vt* to recite.

reclamación *sf* - **1.** [petición] claim, demand - **2.** [queja] complaint; **hacer una reclamación** to lodge a complaint.

reclamar ◇ *vt* [pedir, exigir] to demand, to ask for. ◇ *vi* [protestar]: **reclamar (contra)** to protest (against), to complain (about).

reclamo *sm* - **1.** [para atraer] inducement - **2.** [para cazar] decoy, lure - **3.** *Amér* [queja] complaint; *Amér* [reivindicación] claim.

reclinar *vt*: **reclinar algo (sobre)** to lean sthg (on). ➤ **reclinarse** *vprnl* to lean back; **reclinarse contra algo** to lean against sthg.

recluir *vt* to shut O lock away. ➤ **recluirse** *vprnl* to shut o.s. away.

reclusión *sf* - **1.** [encarcelamiento] imprisonment - **2.** *fig* [encierro] seclusion.

recluso, sa *sm, f* [preso] prisoner.

recluta *sm* [obligatorio] conscript; [voluntario] recruit.

reclutamiento *sm* [de soldados - obligatorio] conscription; [- voluntario] recruitment.

recobrar *vt* [gen] to recover; [conocimiento] to regain; [tiempo perdido] to make up for. ➤ **recobrarse** *vprnl*: **recobrarse (de)** to recover (from).

recodo *sm* bend.

recogedor *sm* dustpan.

recoger *vt* - **1.** [coger] to pick up - **2.** [ordenar, limpiar - mesa] to clear; [- habitación, cosas] to tidy O clear up - **3.** [ir a buscar] to pick up, to fetch - **4.** [albergar] to take in - **5.** [cosechar] to gather, to harvest; [fruta] to pick. ➤ **recogerse** *vprnl* - **1.** [a dormir, meditar] to retire - **2.** [cabello] to put up.

recogido, da *adj* - **1.** [lugar] withdrawn, secluded - **2.** [cabello] tied back. ➤ **recogida** *sf* - **1.** [gen] collection - **2.** [cosecha] harvest, gathering; [de fruta] picking.

recolección *sf* - **1.** [cosecha] harvest, gathering - **2.** [recogida] collection.

recolector, ra *sm, f* - **1.** [gen] collector - **2.** [de cosecha] harvester; [de fruta] picker.

recomendación *sf (gen pl)* - **1.** [gen] recommendation - **2.** [referencia] reference.

recomendado, da ◇ *sm, f* protégé (*f* protégée). ◇ *adj Amér* [correspondencia] registered.

recomendar *vt* to recommend; **recomendar a alguien que haga algo** to recommend that sb do sthg.

recompensa *sf* reward; **en recompensa por** in return for.

recompensar *vt* [premiar] to reward.

recomponer *vt* to repair, to mend.

recompuesto, ta *pp* ▷ **recomponer**.

reconciliación *sf* reconciliation.

reconciliar *vt* to reconcile. ➤ **reconciliarse** *vprnl* to be reconciled.

recóndito, ta *adj* hidden, secret.

reconfortar *vt* - **1.** [anímicamente] to comfort - **2.** [físicamente] to revitalize.

reconocer *vt* - **1.** [gen] to recognize - **2.** MED to examine - **3.** [terreno] to survey. ➤ **recono-**

cerse *vprnl* - **1.** [identificarse] to recognize each other - **2.** [confesarse]: **reconocerse culpable** to admit one's guilt.

reconocido, da *adj*   **1.** [admitido] recognized, acknowledged - **2.** [agradecido] grateful; **quedo muy reconocido** I am very much obliged to you.

reconocimiento *sm* - **1.** [gen] recognition; **reconocimiento del habla** INFORM & LING speech recognition - **2.** [agradecimiento] gratitude - **3.** MED examination - **4.** MIL reconnaissance.

reconquista *sf* reconquest, recapture. ➤ **Reconquista** *sf*: **la Reconquista** HIST the *Reconquest of Spain, when the Christian Kings retook the country from the Muslims.*

reconstruir *vt* - **1.** [edificio, país etc] to rebuild - **2.** [suceso] to reconstruct.

reconversión *sf* restructuring; **reconversión industrial** rationalization of industry.

recopilación *sf* [texto - de poemas, artículos] compilation, collection; [- de leyes] code.

recopilar *vt* - **1.** [recoger] to collect, to gather - **2.** [escritos, leyes] to compile.

récord (*pl* **records**) ◇ *sm* record; **batir un récord** to break a record. ◇ *adj inv* record.

recordar ◇ *vt* - **1.** [acordarse de] to remember; **recordar a alguien algo/que haga algo** to remind sb to do sthg - **2.** [traer a la memoria] to remind; **me recuerda a un amigo mío** he reminds me of a friend of mine. ◇ *vi* to remember; **si mal no recuerdo** as far as I can remember.

recordatorio *sm* [aviso] reminder.

recordman [re'korman] (*pl* **recordmen** O **recordmans**) *sm* record holder.

recorrer *vt* - **1.** [atravesar - lugar, país] to travel through O across, to cross; [- ciudad] to go round - **2.** [distancia] to cover - **3.** *fig* [con la mirada] to look over.

recorrida *sf Amér* [ruta, itinerario] route; [viaje] journey.

recorrido *sm* - **1.** [trayecto] route, path - **2.** [viaje] journey.

recortado, da *adj* - **1.** [cortado] cut - **2.** [borde] jagged.

recortar *vt* - **1.** [cortar - lo que sobra] to cut off O away; [- figuras de un papel] to cut out - **2.** [pelo, flequillo] to trim - **3.** *fig* [reducir] to cut. ➤ **recortarse** *vprnl* [figura etc] to stand out; **recortarse sobre algo** to stand out against sthg.

recorte *sm* - **1.** [pieza cortada] cut, trimming; [de periódico, revista] cutting - **2.** [reducción] cut, cutback; **recortes presupuestarios** budget cuts.

recostar *vt* to lean (back). ➤ **recostarse** *vprnl* to lie down.

recoveco *sm* - 1. [rincón] nook - 2. [curva] bend - 3. *fig* [lo más oculto]: **los recovecos del alma** the innermost recesses of the mind.

recreación *sf* re-creation.

recrear *vt* - 1. [volver a crear] to recreate - 2. [entretener] to amuse, to entertain. ➤ **recrearse** *vprnl* - 1. [entretenerse] to amuse o.s., to entertain o.s. - 2. [regodearse] to take delight O pleasure.

recreativo, va *adj* recreational.

recreo *sm* - 1. [entretenimiento] recreation, amusement - 2. [EDUC - en primaria] playtime *UK*, recess *US*; [- en secundaria] break *UK*, recess *US*.

recriminar *vt* to reproach.

recrudecerse *vprnl* to get worse.

recta ▷ **recto**.

rectángulo *sm* rectangle.

rectificar *vt* - 1. [error] to rectify, to correct - 2. [conducta, actitud etc] to improve - 3. [ajustar] to put right.

rectitud *sf* straightness; *fig* rectitude.

recto, ta *adj* - 1. [sin curvas, vertical] straight - 2. *fig* [íntegro] honourable. ➤ **recto** ◇ *sm* ANAT rectum. ◇ *adv* straight on O ahead. ➤ **recta** *sf* straight line.

rector, ra ◇ *adj* governing. ◇ *sm, f* [de universidad] vice-chancellor *UK*, president *US*. ➤ **rector** *sm* RELIG rector.

recuadro *sm* box.

recubrir *vt* [gen] to cover; [con pintura, barniz] to coat.

recuento *sm* recount.

recuerdo *sm* - 1. [rememoración] memory - 2. [objeto - de viaje] souvenir; [- de persona] keepsake; **de recuerdo** as a souvenir. ➤ **recuerdos** *smpl* [saludos] regards; **dale recuerdos de mi parte** give her my regards.

recular *vi* [retroceder] to go O move back.

recuperable *adj* [gen] recoverable; [fiestas, horas de trabajo] that can be made up later.

recuperación *sf* - 1. [de lo perdido, la salud, la economía] recovery; **recuperación de datos** INFORM data recovery - 2. [fisioterapia] physiotherapy.

recuperar *vt* [lo perdido] to recover; [horas de trabajo] to catch up; [conocimiento] to regain. ➤ **recuperarse** *vprnl* - 1. [enfermo] to recuperate, to recover - 2. [de una crisis] to recover; [negocio] to pick up; **recuperarse de algo** to get over sthg.

recurrir *vi* - 1. [buscar ayuda]: **recurrir a alguien** to turn to sb; **recurrir a algo** to resort to sthg - 2. DER to appeal; **recurrir contra algo** to appeal against sthg.

recurso *sm* - 1. [medio] resort; **como último recurso** as a last resort - 2. DER appeal. ➤ **recursos** *smpl* [fondos] resources; [financieros] means; **es una mujer llena de recursos** she's a resourceful woman; **sin recursos** with no means of support; **recursos propios** ECON equities.

red *sf* - 1. [malla] net; [para cabello] hairnet - 2. [sistema] network, system; [de electricidad, agua] mains *sing*; **red viaria** road network O system - 3. [organización - de espionaje] ring; [- de tiendas] chain - 4. INFORM network; **red local/neuronal** local (area)/neural network. ➤ **Red** *sf*: **la Red** the Net; **navegar por la Red** to surf the Net.

redacción *sf* - 1. [acción - gen] writing; [- de periódico etc] editing - 2. [estilo] wording - 3. [equipo de redactores] editorial team O staff - 4. [oficina] editorial office - 5. EDUC essay.

redactar *vt* to write (up); [carta] to draft.

redactor, ra *sm, f* [PRENSA - escritor] writer; [- editor] editor; **redactor jefe** editor-in-chief.

redada *sf* [de policía - en un solo lugar] raid; [- en varios lugares] round-up.

redención *sf* redemption.

redil *sm* fold, pen.

redimir *vt* - 1. [gen] to redeem - 2. [librar] to free, to exempt. ➤ **redimirse** *vprnl* to redeem o.s.

rédito *sm* interest (U), yield (U).

redoblar ◇ *vt* to redouble. ◇ *vi* to roll.

redomado, da *adj* out-and-out.

redondear *vt* - 1. [hacer redondo] to make round - 2. [negocio, acuerdo] to round off - 3. [cifra, precio] to round up/down.

redondel *sm* - 1. [gen] circle, ring - 2. TAUROM bullring.

redondo, da *adj* - 1. [circular, esférico] round; **a la redonda** around; **caerse redondo** *fig* to collapse in a heap; **girar en redondo** to turn around - 2. [perfecto] excellent.

reducción *sf* - 1. [gen] reduction; **reducción de gastos** reduction in costs - 2. [sometimiento] suppression.

reducido, da *adj* - 1. [pequeño] small - 2. [limitado] limited - 3. [estrecho] narrow.

reducir *vt* - 1. [gen] to reduce - 2. [someter - país, ciudad] to suppress; [- sublevados, atracadores] to bring under control - 3. MAT [convertir] to convert. ➤ **reducirse a** *vprnl* - 1. [limitarse a] to be reduced to - 2. [equivaler a] to boil O come down to.

reducto *sm* - 1. [fortificación] redoubt - 2. *fig* [refugio] stronghold, bastion.

redundancia *sf* redundancy; **y valga la redundancia** if you'll excuse the repetition.

redundante *adj* redundant, superfluous.

redundar *vi*: **redundar en algo** to have an effect on sthg; **redunda en beneficio nuestro** it is to our advantage.

reeditar *vt* to bring out a new edition of; [reimprimir] to reprint.

reelección *sf* re-election.

reembolsar, rembolsar *vt* [gastos] to reimburse; [fianza, dinero] to refund; [deuda] to repay.

reembolso, rembolso *sm* [de gastos] reimbursement; [de fianza, dinero] refund; [de deuda] repayment; **contra reembolso** cash on delivery.

reemplazar, remplazar *vt* [gen & INFORM] to replace; **reemplazar algo/alguien por algo/alguien** to replace sthg/sb with sthg/sb.

reemplazo, remplazo *sm* - 1. [gen & INFORM] replacement - 2. MIL call-up, draft.

reemprender *vt* to start again.

reencarnación *sf* reincarnation.

reencuentro *sm* reunion.

reestructurar *vt* to restructure.

ref. (*abrev de* **referencia**) ref.

refacción *sf Andes, Amér C, R Plata & Ven* repair; *Méx* [recambio] spare part.

refaccionar *vt Andes, Amér C & Ven* to repair.

refaccionaria *sf Amér* repair workshop.

referencia *sf* reference; **con referencia a** with reference to. ➡ **referencias** *sfpl* [informes] references; **tener buenas referencias** to have good references.

referéndum (*pl* **referendos** *O* **referéndum**) *sm* referendum; **convocar un referéndum** to call a referendum.

referente *adj*: **referente a** concerning, relating to; **en lo referente a** regarding.

referir *vt* - 1. [narrar] to tell, to recount - 2. [remitir]: **referir a alguien a** to refer sb to - 3. [relacionar]: **referir algo a** to relate sthg to. ➡ **referirse a** *vprnl* to refer to; **¿a qué te refieres?** what do you mean?; **por lo que se refiere a...** as far as... is concerned.

refilón ➡ **de refilón** *loc adv* - 1. [de lado] sideways; **mirar algo de refilón** to look at sthg out of the corner of one's eye - 2. *fig* [de pasada] briefly.

refinado, da *adj* refined.

refinamiento *sm* refinement.

refinar *vt* to refine.

refinería *sf* refinery.

reflector *sm* ELECTR spotlight; MIL searchlight.

reflejar *vt lit & fig* to reflect. ➡ **reflejarse** *vprnl lit & fig*: **reflejarse (en)** to be reflected (in).

reflejo, ja *adj* [movimiento, dolor] reflex (*antes de s*). ➡ **reflejo** *sm* - 1. [gen] reflection - 2. [destello] glint, gleam - 3. ANAT reflex. ➡ **reflejos** *smpl* [de peluquería] highlights.

reflexión *sf* reflection; **con reflexión** on reflection; **sin previa reflexión** without thinking.

reflexionar *vi* to reflect, to think; **reflexionar sobre algo** to think about sthg.

reflexivo, va *adj* - 1. [que piensa] thoughtful - 2. GRAM reflexive.

reflujo *sm* ebb (tide).

reforma *sf* - 1. [modificación] reform; **reforma agraria** agrarian reform - 2. [en local, casa etc] alterations *pl*; **hacer reformas** to renovate. ➡ **Reforma** *sf*: **la Reforma** RELIG the Reformation.

reformar *vt* - 1. [gen & RELIG] to reform - 2. [local, casa etc] to renovate. ➡ **reformarse** *vprnl* to mend one's ways.

reformatorio *sm* ≃ youth custody centre *UK*, ≃ borstal *UK*, reformatory *US*; [de menores de 15 años] ≃ remand home.

reforzar *vt* to reinforce.

refractario, ria *adj* - 1. [material] refractory - 2. [opuesto]: **refractario a** averse to.

refrán *sm* proverb, saying.

refregar *vt* - 1. [frotar] to scrub - 2. *fig* [reprochar]: **refregar algo a alguien** to reproach sb for sthg.

refrenar *vt* to curb, to restrain.

refrendar *vt* [aprobar] to approve.

refrescante *adj* refreshing.

refrescar ◇ *vt* - 1. [gen] to refresh; [bebidas] to chill - 2. *fig* [conocimientos] to brush up. ◇ *vi* - 1. [tiempo] to cool down - 2. [bebida] to be refreshing. ➡ **refrescarse** *vprnl* - 1. [tomar aire fresco] to get a breath of fresh air - 2. [beber algo] to have a drink - 3. [mojarse con agua fría] to splash o.s. down.

refresco *sm* - 1. [bebida] soft drink; **refrescos** refreshments - 2. [relevo]: **de refresco** new, fresh.

refriega *sf* scuffle; MIL skirmish.

refrigeración *sf* - 1. [aire acondicionado] air-conditioning - 2. [de alimentos] refrigeration - 3. [de máquinas] cooling.

refrigerador, ra *adj* cooling. ➡ **refrigerador** *sm* [de alimentos] refrigerator, fridge *UK*, icebox *US*.

refrigerar *vt* - 1. [alimentos] to refrigerate - 2. [local] to air-condition - 3. [máquina] to cool.

refrigerio *sm* snack.

refrito, ta *adj* [demasiado frito] over-fried; [frito de nuevo] re-fried. ➡ **refrito** *sm fig* [cosa rehecha] rehash.

refuerzo *sm* reinforcement.

refugiado, da *sm, f* refugee.

refugiar *vt* to give refuge to. ➡ **refugiarse** *vprnl* to take refuge; **refugiarse de algo** to shelter from sthg.

refugio *sm* - 1. [lugar] shelter, refuge; **refugio atómico** nuclear bunker - 2. *fig* [amparo, consuelo] refuge, comfort.

refulgir *vi* to shine brightly.

refunfuñar *vi* to grumble.

refutar *vt* to refute.

regadera *sf* - 1. [para regar] watering can - 2. *Col, Méx & Ven* [ducha] shower.

regadío *sm* irrigated land.

regalado, da *adj* - 1. [muy barato] dirt cheap - 2. [agradable] comfortable.

regalar *vt* - 1. [dar - de regalo] to give (as a present); [- gratis] to give away - 2. [agasajar]: **regalar a alguien con algo** to shower sb with sthg.

regaliz *sm* liquorice.

regalo *sm* - 1. [obsequio] present, gift; **un regalo del cielo** a godsend - 2. [placer] joy, delight.

regalón, ona *adj R Dom & Chile fam* spoilt.

regañadientes ◆ a regañadientes *loc adv fam* unwillingly, reluctantly.

regañar ◇ *vt* [reprender] to tell off. ◇ *vi* [pelearse] to fall out, to argue.

regañina *sf* [reprimenda] ticking off.

regar *vt* - 1. [con agua - planta] to water; [- calle] to hose down - 2. [suj: río] to flow through.

regata *sf* NÁUT regatta, boat race.

regatear ◇ *vt* - 1. [escatimar] to be sparing with; **no ha regateado esfuerzos** he has spared no effort - 2. DEP to beat, to dribble past - 3. [precio] to haggle over. ◇ *vi* - 1. [negociar el precio] to barter - 2. NÁUT to race.

regateo *sm* bartering, haggling.

regazo *sm* lap.

regeneración *sf* regeneration; [moral] reform.

regenerar *vt* to regenerate; [moralmente] to reform.

regentar *vt* [país] to run, to govern; [negocio] to run, to manage; [puesto] to hold.

regente ◇ *adj* regent. ◇ *sm, f* - 1. [de un país] regent - 2. [administrador - de tienda] manager; [- de colegio] governor - 3. *Méx* [alcalde] mayor (f mayoress).

regidor, ra *sm, f* TEATRO stage manager; CINE & TV assistant director.

régimen *(pl* **regímenes)** *sm* - 1. [sistema político] regime; **Antiguo régimen** ancien régime - 2. [normativa] rules *pl* - 3. [dieta] diet; **estar/ponerse a régimen** to be/go on a diet - 4. [de vida, lluvias etc] pattern; **régimen de vida** lifestyle.

regimiento *sm fig* & MIL regiment.

regio, gia *adj* - 1. *lit & fig* royal - 2. *Amér fam fig* fantastic.

regrón *sf* region; MIL district.

regir ◇ *vt* - 1. [reinar en] to rule, to govern - 2. [administrar] to run, to manage - 3. *fig* [determinar] to govern, to determine. ◇ *vi* [ley] to be in force, to apply. ◆ **regirse por** *vprnl* to trust in.

registradora *sf Amér* cash register.

registrar *vt* - 1. [inspeccionar - zona, piso] to search; [- persona] to frisk - 2. [nacimiento, temperatura etc] to register, to record. ◆ **registrarse** *vprnl* - 1. [suceder] to occur - 2. [observarse] to be recorded.

registro *sm* - 1. [oficina] registry (office); **registro civil** registry (office) - 2. [libro] register - 3. [inspección] search, searching (U) - 4. INFORM record - 5. LING & MÚS register.

regla *sf* - 1. [para medir] ruler, rule - 2. [norma] rule; **en regla** in order; **por regla general** as a rule - 3. MAT operation - 4. *fam* [menstruación] period.

reglamentación *sf* [acción] regulation; [reglas] rules *pl*, regulations *pl*.

reglamentar *vt* to regulate.

reglamentario, ria *adj* lawful; [arma, balón] regulation *(antes de s)*; DER statutory.

reglamento *sm* regulations *pl*, rules *pl*; **reglamento de tráfico** traffic regulations *pl*.

regocijar ◆ regocijarse *vprnl*: **regocijarse (de** *O* **con)** to rejoice (in).

regocijo *sm* joy, delight.

regodeo *sm* delight, pleasure; [malicioso] (cruel) delight *O* pleasure.

regordete *adj* chubby.

regresar ◇ *vi* [yendo] to go back, to return; [viniendo] to come back, to return. ◇ *vt Andes, Amér C, Caribe & Méx* [devolver] to give back.

regresión *sf* - 1. [de epidemia] regression - 2. [de exportaciones] drop, decline.

regresivo, va *adj* regressive.

regreso *sm* return; **estar de regreso** to be back.

reguero *sm* [de sangre, agua] trickle; [de harina etc] trail; **correr como un reguero de pólvora** to spread like wildfire.

regulación *sf* [gen] regulation; [de nacimientos, tráfico] control; [de mecanismo] adjustment.

regulador, ra *adj* regulatory.

regular ◇ *adj* - 1. [gen] regular; [de tamaño] medium; **de un modo regular** regularly - 2. [mediocre] average, fair - 3. [normal] normal, usual. ◇ *adv* all right; [de salud] so-so. ◇ *vt* [gen] to control, to regulate; [mecanismo] to adjust. ◆ **por lo regular** *loc adv* as a rule, generally.

regularidad *sf* regularity; **con regularidad** regularly.

regularizar *vt* [legalizar] to regularize.

regusto *sm* aftertaste; [semejanza, aire] flavour, hint.

rehabilitación *sf* - 1. [de personas] rehabilitation, [en un puesto] reinstatement - 2. [de local] restoration.

rehabilitar *vt* - 1. [personas] to rehabilitate; [en un puesto] to reinstate - 2. [local] to restore.

rehacer *vt* - 1. [volver a hacer] to redo, to do again - 2. [reconstruir] to rebuild - 3. INFORM redo. ◆ **rehacerse** *vprnl* [recuperarse] to recuperate, to recover.

rehecho, cha *pp* ▷ **rehacer**.

rehén *(pl* **rehenes)** *sm* hostage; **tomar como rehén** to take hostage.

rehogar *vt* to fry over a low heat.

rehuir *vt* to avoid.

rehusar *vt & vi* to refuse.

reimpresión *sf* [tirada] reprint; [acción] reprinting.

reina *sf* [monarca] queen; **reina de belleza** beauty queen; **reina madre** queen mother.

reinado *sm lit & fig* reign.

reinante *adj* - 1. [monarquía, persona] reigning, ruling - 2. [viento] prevailing; [frío, calor] current.

reinar *vi lit & fig* to reign.

reincidir *vi:* reincidir en [falta, error] to relapse into, to fall back into; [delito] to repeat.

reincorporar *vt* to reincorporate. ◆ **reincorporarse** *vprnl:* reincorporarse (a) to rejoin, to go back to.

reino *sm* BIOL & POLÍT kingdom; *fig* realm.

Reino Unido *n pr:* el Reino Unido the United Kingdom.

reinstalar *vt* to re-install.

reintegrar *vt* - 1. [a un puesto] to reinstate - 2. [dinero] to reimburse. ◆ **reintegrarse** *vprnl:* reintegrarse (a) to return (to).

reintegro *sm* - 1. [de dinero] reimbursement; BANCA withdrawal - 2. [en lotería] return of one's stake *(in lottery)*.

reír ◇ *vi* to laugh. ◇ *vt* to laugh at. ◆ **reírse** *vprnl:* reírse (de) to laugh (at).

reiterar *vt* to reiterate.

reiterativo, va *adj* repetitious.

reivindicación *sf* - 1. [de derechos] claim, demand - 2. [de atentado] claiming of responsibility.

reivindicar *vt* - 1. [derechos, salario etc] to claim, to demand - 2. [atentado] to claim responsibility for.

reivindicativo, va *adj:* plataforma reivindicativa (set of) demands; **jornada reivindicativa** day of protest.

reja *sf* [gen] bars *pl*; [en el suelo] grating; [celosía] grille.

rejego, ga *adj Amér fam* [terco] stubborn.

rejilla *sf* - 1. [enrejado] grid, grating; [de ventana] grille; [de cocina] grill *(on stove)*; [de horno] gridiron - 2. [para sillas, muebles] wickerwork - 3. [para equipaje] luggage rack.

rejón *sm* TAURÍM *type of "banderilla" used by mounted bullfighter.*

rejoneador, ra *sm, f* TAUROM *bullfighter on horseback who uses the "rejón".*

rejuntarse *vprnl fam* to live together.

rejuvenecer *vt & vi* to rejuvenate.

relación *sf* - 1. [nexo] relation, connection; con relación a, en relación con in relation to; tener relación con algo to bear a relation to sthg; relación precio-calidad value for money - 2. [comunicación, trato] relations *pl*, relationship - 3. [lista] list - 4. [descripción] account - 5. [informe] report - 6. *(gen pl)* [noviazgo] relationship - 7. MAT ratio; **en una relación de tres a uno** in a ratio of three to one. ◆ **relaciones** *sfpl* [contactos] connections.

relacionar *vt* [vincular] to relate, to connect. ◆ **relacionarse** *vprnl:* relacionarse (con) [alternar] to mix (with).

relajación *sf* relaxation.

relajar *vt* to relax. ◆ **relajarse** *vprnl* to relax.

relajo *sm Amér fam* [alboroto] racket, din.

relamer *vt* to lick repeatedly. ◆ **relamerse** *vprnl* - 1. [persona] to lick one's lips - 2. [animal] to lick its chops.

relamido, da *adj* prim and proper.

relámpago *sm* [descarga] flash of lightning, lightning *(U)*; [destello] flash.

relampaguear *vi fig* to flash.

relatar *vt* [suceso] to relate, to recount; [historia] to tell.

relatividad *sf* relativity.

relativo, va *adj* - 1. [gen] relative - 2. [escaso] limited.

relato *sm* [exposición] account, report; [cuento] tale.

relax *sm inv* - 1. [relajación] relaxation - 2. [sección de periódico] personal column.

relegar *vt:* relegar (a) to relegate (to); **relegar algo al olvido** to banish sthg from one's mind.

relevante *adj* outstanding, important.

relevar *vt* - 1. [sustituir] to relieve, to take over from - 2. [destituir]: **relevar (de)** to dismiss (from), to relieve (of) - 3. [eximir]: **relevar (de)** to free (from) - 4. [DEP - en partidos] to substitute; [- en relevos] to take over from. ◆ **relevarse** *vprnl* to take turns.

relevo *sm* - 1. MIL relief, changing - 2. DEP [acción] relay - 3. *loc:* tomar el relevo to take over. ◆ **relevos** *smpl* DEP [carrera] relay (race) *sing.*

relieve *sm* - 1. [gen, ARTE & GEOGR] relief; **bajo relieve** bas-relief - 2. [importancia] importance; **poner de relieve** to underline (the importance of).

religión *sf* religion.

religioso, sa ◇ *adj* religious. ◇ *sm, f* [monje] monk (*f* nun).

relinchar *vi* to neigh, to whinny.

reliquia *sf* relic; [familiar] heirloom.

rellano *sm* [de escalera] landing.

rellenar *vt* - 1. [volver a llenar] to refill - 2. [documento, formulario] to fill in *O* out - 3. [pollo, cojín etc] to stuff; [tarta, pastel] to fill.

relleno, na *adj* [gen] stuffed; [tarta, pastel] filled. ◈ **relleno** *sm* [de pollo] stuffing; [de pastel] filling.

reloj *sm* [de pared] clock; [de pulsera] watch; **reloj analógico/digital** analogue/digital watch; **reloj de arena** hourglass; **reloj de pulsera** watch, wristwatch; **hacer algo contra reloj** to do sthg against the clock; **ser como un reloj** *fig* to be like clockwork.

relojero, ra *sm, f* watchmaker.

reluciente *adj* shining, gleaming.

relucir *vi* lit & fig to shine; **sacar algo a relucir** to bring sthg up, to mention sthg; **salir a relucir** to come to the surface.

remachar *vt* - 1. [machacar] to rivet - 2. *fig* [recalcar] to drive home, to stress.

remache *sm* [clavo] rivet.

remanente *sm* - 1. [de géneros] surplus stock; [de productos agrícolas] surplus - 2. [en cuenta bancaria] balance.

remangar, arremangar *vt* to roll up. ◈ **remangarse** *vprnl* to roll up one's sleeves.

remanso *sm* still pool.

remar *vi* to row.

rematado, da *adj* utter, complete.

rematar ◇ *vt* - 1. [acabar] to finish; **y para rematarla** *fam* to cap it all - 2. [matar - persona] to finish off; [- animal] to put out of its misery - 3. DEP to shoot - 4. [liquidar, vender] to sell off cheaply - 5. *Amér* [subastar] to auction. ◇ *vi* [en fútbol] to shoot; [de cabeza] to head at goal.

remate *sm* - 1. [fin, colofón] end; **para remate** [colmo] to cap it all - 2. [en fútbol] shot; [de cabeza] header at goal. ◈ **de remate** *loc adv* totally, completely.

rembolsar = reembolsar.

rembolso = reembolso.

remedar *vt* to imitate; [por burla] to ape.

remediar *vt* [daño] to remedy, to put right; [problema] to solve; [peligro] to avoid.

remedio *sm* - 1. [solución] solution, remedy; **como último remedio** as a last resort; **no hay** *O* **queda más remedio que...** there's nothing

for it but...; **no tener más remedio** to have no alternative *O* choice - 2. [consuelo] consolation - 3. [medicamento] remedy, cure.

rememorar *vt* to remember, to recall.

remendar *vt* to mend, to darn.

remero, ra *sm, f* [persona] rower. ◈ **remera** *sf R Dom* [prenda] T-shirt.

remesa *sf* [de productos] consignment; [de dinero] remittance.

remeter *vt* to tuck in.

remezón *sm Andes & R Dom* earth tremor.

remiendo *sm* [parche] mend, darn.

remilgado, da *adj* - 1. [afectado] affected - 2. [escrupuloso] squeamish; [con comida] fussy.

remilgo *sm* - 1. [afectación] affectation - 2. [escrupulosidad] squeamishness; [con comida] fussiness.

reminiscencia *sf* reminiscence; **tener reminiscencias de** to be reminiscent of.

remiso, sa *adj*: **ser remiso a hacer algo** to be reluctant to do sthg.

remite *sm* sender's name and address.

remitente *smf* sender.

remitir ◇ *vt* - 1. [enviar] to send - 2. [traspasar]: **remitir algo a** to refer sthg to. ◇ *vi* - 1. [en texto]: **remitir a** to refer to - 2. [disminuir] to subside. ◈ **remitirse a** *vprnl* - 1. [atenerse a] to abide by - 2. [referirse a] to refer to.

remo *sm* - 1. [pala] oar - 2. [deporte] rowing.

remodelar *vt* [gen] to redesign; [gobierno] to reshuffle.

remojar *vt* [humedecer] to soak.

remojo *sm*: **poner en remojo** to leave to soak; **estar en remojo** to be soaking.

remolacha *sf* beetroot *UK*, beet *US*; [azucarera] (sugar) beet.

remolcador, ra *adj* [coche] tow *(antes de s)*; [barco] tug *(antes de s)*. ◈ **remolcador** *sm* [camión] breakdown lorry; [barco] tug, tugboat.

remolcar *vt* [coche] to tow; [barco] to tug.

remolino *sm* - 1. [de agua] eddy, whirlpool; [de viento] whirlwind; [de humo] cloud, swirl - 2. [de gente] throng, mass - 3. [de pelo] cowlick.

remolón, ona *adj* lazy.

remolque *sm* - 1. [acción] towing; **ir a remolque** *fig* [voluntariamente] to go in tow, to tag along; [obligado] to be dragged along - 2. [vehículo] trailer.

remontar *vt* [pendiente, río] to go up; [obstáculo] to overcome. ◈ **remontarse** *vprnl* - 1. [ave, avión] to soar, to climb high - 2. [gastos]: **remontarse a** to amount *O* come to - 3. *fig* [datar]: **remontarse a** to go *O* date back to.

remorder vt fig: **remorderle a alguien** to fill sb with remorse.

remordimiento sm remorse; **tener remordimientos de conciencia** to suffer pangs of conscience.

remoto, ta adj remote; **no tengo ni la más remota idea** I haven't got the faintest idea.

remover vt - **1.** [agitar - sopa, café] to stir; [- ensalada] to toss; [- bote, frasco] to shake; [- tierra] to dig up - **2.** [reavivar - recuerdos, pasado] to rake up - **3.** Amér [despedir] to dismiss, to sack. ◆ **removerse** vprnl to move about.

remplazar = **reemplazar**.

remplazo = **reemplazo**.

remuneración sf remuneration.

remunerar vt [pagar] to remunerate.

renacer vi - **1.** [gen] to be reborn; [flores, hojas] to grow again - **2.** [alegría, esperanza] to return, to revive.

renacimiento sm [gen] rebirth; [de flores, hojas] budding. ◆ **Renacimiento** sm: **el Renacimiento** the Renaissance.

renacuajo sm tadpole; fam fig tiddler.

renal adj renal, kidney (antes de s).

rencilla sf quarrel.

rencor sm resentment, bitterness.

rencoroso, sa adj resentful, bitter.

rendición sf surrender.

rendido, da adj - **1.** [agotado] exhausted; **caer rendido** to collapse - **2.** [sumiso] submissive; [admirador] devoted.

rendija sf crack, gap.

rendimiento sm - **1.** [de inversión, negocio] yield, return; [de trabajador, fábrica] productivity; [de tierra, cosecha] yield; **a pleno rendimiento** at full capacity - **2.** [de motor] performance.

rendir ◇ vt - **1.** [cansar] to tire out - **2.** [rentar] to yield - **3.** [vencer] to defeat, to subdue - **4.** [ofrecer] to give, to present; [pleitesía] to pay. ◇ vi [máquina] to perform well; [negocio] to be profitable; [fábrica, trabajador] to be productive. ◆ **rendirse** vprnl - **1.** [entregarse] to surrender - **2.** [ceder]: **rendirse a** to give in to - **3.** [desanimarse] to give in O up.

renegado, da adj & sm, f renegade.

renegar vi fam [gruñir] to grumble.

Renfe (abrev de Red Nacional de los Ferrocarriles Españoles) sf Spanish state railway network.

renglón sm line; COM item; **a renglón seguido** fig in the same breath, straight after.

reno sm reindeer.

renombrar vt INFORM to rename.

renombre sm renown, fame; **de renombre** famous.

renovación sf [de carné, contrato] renewal; [de mobiliario, local] renovation.

renovar vt - **1.** [cambiar - mobiliario, local] renovate; [- vestuario] to clear out; [- personal, plantilla] to shake out - **2.** [rehacer - carné, contrato, ataque] to renew ◆ **3.** [restaurar] to restore ◆ **4.** [innovar] to rethink, to revolutionize; POLÍT to reform.

renquear vi to limp, to hobble.

renta sf - **1.** [ingresos] income; **renta fija** fixed income; **renta variable/vitalicia** variable/life annuity - **2.** [alquiler] rent - **3.** [beneficios] return - **4.** [intereses] interest.

rentable adj profitable.

rentar ◇ vt - **1.** [rendir] to produce, to yield - **2.** Méx [alquilar] to rent. ◇ vi to be profitable.

rentista smf person of independent means.

renuncia sf [abandono] giving up; [dimisión] resignation; **presentar la renuncia** to resign.

renunciar vi - **1.** [abandonar] to give up - **2.** [dimitir] to resign. ◆ **renunciar a** vi - **1.** [prescindir de] to give up; [plan, proyecto] to drop; **renunciar al tabaco** to give up O stop smoking - **2.** [rechazar]: **renunciar (a hacer algo)** to refuse (to do sthg).

reñido, da adj - **1.** [enfadado]: **reñido (con)** on bad terms O at odds (with); **están reñidos** they've fallen out - **2.** [disputado] hard-fought - **3.** [incompatible]: **estar reñido con** to be incompatible with.

reñir ◇ vt - **1.** [regañar] to tell off - **2.** [disputar] to fight. ◇ vi [enfadarse] to argue, to fall out.

reo, a sm, f [culpado] offender, culprit; [acusado] accused, defendant.

reojo sm: **mirar algo de reojo** to look at sthg out of the corner of one's eye.

repantigarse vprnl to sprawl out.

reparación sf - **1.** [arreglo] repair, repairing (U); **en reparación** under repair - **2.** [compensación] reparation, redress.

reparador, ra adj [descanso, sueño] refreshing.

reparar ◇ vt [coche etc] to repair, to fix; [error, daño etc] to make amends for; [fuerzas] to restore. ◇ vi [advertir]: **reparar en algo** to notice sthg; **no reparar en gastos** to spare no expense.

reparo sm - **1.** [objeción] objection - **2.** [apuro]: **no tener reparos en** not to be afraid to.

repartición sf [reparto] sharing out.

repartidor, f sm, f [gen] distributor; [de butano, carbón] deliveryman (f deliverywoman); [de leche] milkman (f milkwoman); [de periódicos] paperboy (f papergirl).

repartir vt - **1.** [dividir - gen] to share out, to divide; [- territorio, nación] to partition - **2.** [distribuir - leche, periódicos, correo] to deliver;

[- naipes] to deal (out) - **3.** [asignar - trabajo, órdenes] to give out, to allocate; [- papeles] to assign.

reparto *sm* - **1.** [división] division, distribution; **reparto de beneficios** ECON profit sharing; **reparto de premios** prizegiving - **2.** [distribución - de leche, periódicos, correo] delivery - **3.** [asignación] allocation; **reparto a domicilio** home delivery - **4.** CINE & TEATRO cast.

repasador *sm* R Dom tea towel.

repasar *vt* - **1.** [revisar] to go over; [lección] to revise UK, to review US - **2.** [zurcir] to darn, to mend.

repaso *sm* [revisión] revision; [de ropa] darning, mending; **dar un repaso a algo** to look over sthg; **dar un último repaso a algo** to give sthg a final check; **curso de repaso** refresher course.

repatriar *vt* to repatriate.

repecho *sm* steep slope.

repelente *adj* - **1.** [desagradable, repugnante] repulsive - **2.** [ahuyentador] repellent.

repeler *vt* - **1.** [rechazar] to repel - **2.** [repugnar] to repulse, to disgust.

repelús *sm*: **me da repelús** it gives me the shivers.

repente *sm* [arrebato] fit. ◆ **de repente** *loc adv* suddenly.

repentino, na *adj* sudden.

repercusión *sf* - **1.** fig [consecuencia] repercussion - **2.** [resonancia] echoes *pl*.

repercutir *vi* fig [afectar]: **repercutir en** to have repercussions on.

repertorio *sm* - **1.** [obras] repertoire - **2.** fig [serie] selection.

repesca *sf* - **1.** EDUC resit - **2.** DEP repêchage.

repetición *sf* repetition; [de una jugada] action replay.

repetidor, ra *sm, f* EDUC student repeating a year. ◆ **repetidor** *sm* ELECTR repeater.

repetir ◇ *vt* to repeat; [ataque] to renew; [en comida] to have seconds of. ◇ *vi* - **1.** [alumno] to repeat a year - **2.** [sabor, alimento] **repetir (a alguien)** to repeat (on sb) - **3.** [comensal] to have seconds. ◆ **repetirse** *vprnl* - **1.** [fenómeno] to recur - **2.** [persona] to repeat o.s.

repicar *vi* [campanas] to ring.

repique *sm* peal, ringing *(U)*.

repiqueteo *sm* [de campanas] pealing; [de tambor] beating; [de timbre] ringing; [de lluvia, dedos] drumming.

repisa *sf* [estante] shelf; [sobre chimenea] mantelpiece.

replantear *vt* - **1.** [reenfocar] to reconsider, to restate - **2.** [volver a mencionar] to bring up again.

replegar *vt* [ocultar] to retract. ◆ **replegarse** *vprnl* [retirarse] to withdraw, to retreat.

repleto, ta *adj*: **repleto (de)** packed (with).

réplica *sf* - **1.** [respuesta] reply - **2.** [copia] replica.

replicar ◇ *vt* [responder] to answer; [objetar] to answer back, to retort. ◇ *vi* [objetar] to answer back.

repliegue *sm* - **1.** [retirada] withdrawal, retreat - **2.** [pliegue] fold.

repoblación *sf* [con gente] repopulation; [con peces] restocking; **repoblación forestal** reafforestation.

repoblar *vt* [con gente] to repopulate; [con peces] to restock; [con árboles] to replant.

repollo *sm* cabbage.

reponer *vt* - **1.** [gen] to replace - **2.** CINE & TEATRO to rerun; TV to repeat - **3.** [replicar]: **reponer que** to reply that.

reportaje *sm* RADIO & TV report; PRENSA article.

reportar *vt* - **1.** [traer] to bring - **2.** Méx [denunciar] to report; Andes, Amér C, Méx & Ven [informar] to report. ◆ **reportarse** *vprnl* Amér C, Méx & Ven: **reportarse (a)** to report (to).

reporte *sm* Amér C & Méx [informe] report; [noticia] news item O report.

reportero, ra, repórter *sm, f* reporter.

reposado, da *adj* relaxed, calm.

reposar *vi* - **1.** [descansar] to (have a) rest - **2.** [sedimentarse] to stand.

reposera *sf* R Dom sun-lounger UK, beach recliner US.

reposición *sf* - **1.** CINE rerun; TEATRO revival; TV repeat - **2.** [de existencias, pieza etc] replacement.

reposo *sm* [descanso] rest.

repostar ◇ *vi* [coche] to fill up; [avión] to refuel. ◇ *vt* - **1.** [gasolina] to fill up with - **2.** [provisiones] to stock up on.

repostería *sf* [oficio, productos] confectionery.

reprender *vt* [a niños] to tell off; [a empleados] to reprimand.

reprensión *sf* [a niños] telling-off; [a empleados] reprimand.

represalia *(gen pl) sf* reprisal; **tomar represalias** to retaliate, to take reprisals.

representación *sf* - **1.** [gen & COM] representation; **en representación de** on behalf of - **2.** TEATRO performance.

representante ◇ *adj* representative. ◇ *smf* - **1.** [gen & COM] representative; **representante de la ley** officer of the law - **2.** [de artista] agent.

representar *vt* - **1.** [gen & COM] to represent - **2.** [aparentar] to look; **representa unos 40**

años she looks about 40 - **3.** [significar] to mean; **representa el 50% del consumo interno** it accounts for 50% of domestic consumption - **4.** [TEATRO - función] to perform; [papel] to play.

representativo, va *adj* - **1.** [simbolizador]: **ser representativo de** to represent - **2.** [característico, relevante]: **representativo (de)** representative (of).

represión *sf* repression.

reprimenda *sf* reprimand.

reprimir *vt* [gen] to suppress; [minorías, disidentes] to repress. ◆ **reprimirse** *vprnl*: **reprimirse (de hacer algo)** to restrain o.s. (from doing sthg).

reprobar *vt* - **1.** to censure, to condemn - **2.** *Amér* [suspender] to fail.

reprochar *vt*: **reprochar algo a alguien** to reproach sb for sthg. ◆ **reprocharse** *vprnl*: **reprocharse algo (uno mismo)** to reproach o.s. for sthg.

reproche *sm* reproach.

reproducción *sf* reproduction.

reproducir *vt* [gen & ARTE] to reproduce; [gestos] to copy, to imitate. ◆ **reproducirse** *vprnl* - **1.** [volver a suceder] to recur - **2.** [procrear] to reproduce.

reptil *sm* reptile.

república *sf* republic.

República Checa *sf* Czech Republic.

República Dominicana *sf* Dominican Republic.

republicano, na *adj & sm, f* republican.

repudiar *vt* - **1.** [condenar] to repudiate - **2.** [rechazar] to disown.

repuesto, ta *◇ pp ▷* **reponer**. *◇ adj*: **repuesto (de)** recovered (from). ◆ **repuesto** *sm* [gen] reserve; AUTO spare part; **la rueda de repuesto** the spare wheel.

repugnancia *sf* disgust.

repugnante *adj* disgusting.

repugnar *vt*: **me repugna ese olor/su actitud** I find that smell/her attitude disgusting; **me repugna hacerlo** I'm loath to do it.

repujar *vt* to emboss.

repulsa *sf* [censura] condemnation.

repulsión *sf* repulsion.

repulsivo, va *adj* repulsive.

repuntar *vi Amér* [mejorar] to improve.

reputación *sf* reputation; **tener mucha reputación** to be very famous.

requerimiento *sm* - **1.** [demanda] entreaty; **a requerimiento de alguien** at sb's request - **2.** [DER - intimación] writ, injunction; [- aviso] summons *sing*.

requerir *vt* - **1.** [necesitar] to require - **2.** [ordenar] to demand - **3.** [pedir]: **requerir a alguien**

(para) que haga algo to ask sb to do sthg - **4.** DER to order. ◆ **requerirse** *vprnl* [ser necesario] to be required O necessary.

requesón *sm* cottage cheese.

requisa *sf* [requisición - MIL] requisition; [- en aduana] seizure.

requisito *sm* requirement; **requisito previo** prerequisite.

res *sf* - **1.** [animal] beast, animal - **2.** *Amér salvo C Sur*: **carne de res** beef. ◆ **reses** *smpl Amér* [ganado vacuno] cattle.

resabio *sm* - **1.** [sabor] nasty aftertaste - **2.** [vicio] persistent bad habit.

resaca *sf* - **1.** *fam* [de borrachera] hangover - **2.** [de las olas] undertow.

resalado, da *adj fam* charming.

resaltar *◇ vi* - **1.** [destacar] to stand out - **2.** [en edificios - decoración] to stand out. *◇ vt* [destacar] to highlight.

resarcir *vt*: **resarcir a alguien (de)** to compensate sb (for). ◆ **resarcirse** *vprnl* to be compensated; **resarcirse de** [daño, pérdida] to be compensated for; [desengaño, derrota] to make up for.

resbalada *sf Amér fam* slip.

resbaladizo, za *adj lit & fig* slippery.

resbalar *vi* - **1.** [deslizarse] to slide - **2.** [estar resbaladizo] to be slippery. ◆ **resbalarse** *vprnl* to slip (over).

resbalón *sm* slip; **dar** O **pegar un resbalón** to slip.

rescatar *vt* - **1.** [liberar, salvar] to rescue; [pagando rescate] to ransom - **2.** [recuperar - herencia etc] to recover.

rescate *sm* - **1.** [liberación, salvación] rescue - **2.** [dinero] ransom - **3.** [recuperación] recovery.

rescindir *vt* to rescind.

rescisión *sf* cancellation.

rescoldo *sm* ember; *fig* lingering feeling.

resecar *vt* [piel] to dry out. ◆ **resecarse** *vprnl* - **1.** [piel] to dry out - **2.** [tierra] to become parched.

reseco, ca *adj* - **1.** [piel, garganta, pan] very dry - **2.** [tierra] parched - **3.** [flaco] emaciated.

resentido, da *adj* bitter, resentful; **estar resentido con alguien** to be really upset with sb.

resentimiento *sm* resentment, bitterness.

resentirse *vprnl* - **1.** [debilitarse] to be weakened; [salud] to deteriorate - **2.** [sentir molestias]: **resentirse de** to be suffering from - **3.** [ofenderse] to be offended.

reseña *sf* [de libro, concierto] review; [de partido, conferencia] report.

reseñar *vt* - **1.** [criticar - libro, concierto] to review; [- partido, conferencia] to report on - **2.** [describir] to describe.

reserva *sf* - **1.** [de hotel, avión etc] reservation - **2.** [provisión] reserves *pl*; **tener algo de reserva** to keep sthg in reserve - **3.** [objeción] reservation - **4.** [de indígenas] reservation - **5.** [de animales] reserve; **reserva natural** nature reserve - **6.** MIL reserve. ► **reservas** *sfpl* - **1.** [energía acumulada] energy reserves - **2.** [recursos] resources.

reservado, da *adj* - **1.** [gen] reserved - **2.** [tema, asunto] confidential. ► **reservado** *sm* [en restaurante] private room; FERROC reserved compartment.

reservar *vt* - **1.** [habitación, asiento etc] to reserve, to book - **2.** [guardar - dinero, pasteles etc] to set aside; [- sorpresa] to keep - **3.** [callar - opinión, comentarios] to reserve. ► **reservarse** *vprnl* - **1.** [esperar]: **reservarse para** to save o.s. for - **2.** [guardar para sí - secreto] to keep to o.s.; [- dinero, derecho] to retain (for o.s.)

resfriado, da *adj*: **estar resfriado** to have a cold. ► **resfriado** *sm* cold; **pescar un resfriado** to catch a cold.

resfriar ► **resfriarse** *vprnl* [constiparse] to catch a cold.

resguardar *vt* & *vi*: **resguardar de** to protect against. ► **resguardarse** *vprnl*: **resguardarse de** [en un portal] to shelter from; [con abrigo, paraguas] to protect o.s. against.

resguardo *sm* - **1.** [documento] receipt - **2.** [protección] protection.

residencia *sf* - **1.** [estancia] stay - **2.** [localidad, domicilio] residence; **segunda residencia** second home; **residencia canina** kennels - **3.** [establecimiento - de estudiantes] hall of residence; [- de ancianos] old people's home; [- de oficiales] residence - **4.** [hospital] hospital - **5.** [permiso para extranjeros] residence permit.

residencial *adj* residential.

residente *adj* & *smf* resident.

residir *vi* - **1.** [vivir] to reside - **2.** [radicar]: **residir en** to lie in, to reside in.

residuo *sm* (*gen pl*) [material inservible] waste; QUÍM residue; **residuos nucleares** nuclear waste (U); **residuos tóxicos** toxic waste (U).

resignación *sf* resignation.

resignarse *vprnl*: **resignarse (a hacer algo)** to resign o.s. (to doing sthg).

resina *sf* resin.

resistencia *sf* - **1.** [gen, ELECTR & POLÍT] resistance; **ofrecer resistencia** to put up resistance - **2.** [de puente, cimientos] strength - **3.** [física - para correr etc] stamina.

resistente *adj* [gen] tough, strong; **resistente al calor** heat-resistant.

resistir ◇ *vt* - **1.** [dolor, peso, críticas] to withstand - **2.** [tentación, impulso, deseo] to resist - **3.** [tolerar] to tolerate, to stand - **4.** [ataque] to resist, to withstand. ◇ *vi* - **1.** [ejército, ciudad etc]: **resistir (a algo/a alguien)** to resist (sthg/sb) - **2.** [corredor etc] to keep going; **resistir a algo** to stand up to sthg, to withstand sthg - **3.** [mesa, dique etc] to take the strain; **resistir a algo** to withstand sthg - **4.** [mostrarse firmeante tentaciones etc] to resist (it); **resistir a algo** to resist sthg. ► **resistirse** *vprnl*: **resistirse (a algo)** to resist (sthg); **me resisto a creerlo** I refuse to believe it; **se le resisten las matemáticas** she just can't get the hang of maths.

resollar *vi* to gasp (for breath); [jadear] to pant.

resolución *sf* - **1.** [solución - de una crisis] resolution; [- de un crimen] solution - **2.** [firmeza] determination - **3.** [decisión] decision; DER ruling - **4.** [de Naciones Unidas etc] resolution.

resolver *vt* - **1.** [solucionar - duda, crisis] to resolve; [- problema, caso] to solve - **2.** [decidir]: **resolver hacer algo** to decide to do sthg - **3.** [partido, disputa, conflicto] to settle. ► **resolverse** *vprnl* - **1.** [solucionarse - duda, crisis] to be resolved; [- problema, caso] to be solved - **2.** [decidirse]: **resolverse a hacer algo** to decide to do sthg.

resonancia *sf* - **1.** [gen & FÍS] resonance (U) - **2.** *fig* [importancia] repercussions *pl*.

resonar *vi* to resound, to echo.

resoplar *vi* [de cansancio] to pant; [de enfado] to snort.

resoplido *sm* [por cansancio] pant; [por enfado] snort.

resorte *sm* spring; **saltar como movido por un resorte** to spring up; *fig* means *pl*; **tocar todos los resortes** to pull out all the stops.

respaldar *vt* to back, to support. ► **respaldarse** *vprnl fig* [apoyarse]: **respaldarse en** to fall back on.

respaldo *sm* - **1.** [de asiento] back - **2.** *fig* [apoyo] backing, support.

respectar *v impers*: **por lo que respecta a alguien/a algo, en lo que respecta a alguien/a algo** as far as sb/sthg is concerned.

respectivo, va *adj* respective; **en lo respectivo a** with regard to.

respecto *sm*: **al respecto, a este respecto** in this respect; **no sé nada al respecto** I don't know anything about it.

respetable *adj* - **1.** [venerable] respectable - **2.** [bastante] considerable.

respetar *vt* [gen] to respect; [la palabra] to honour.

respeto *sm*: **respeto (a O por)** respect (for); **es una falta de respeto** it shows a lack of respect; **por respeto a** out of consideration for.

respetuoso, sa *adj*: **respetuoso (con)** respectful (of).

respingo *sm* [movimiento] start, jump.

respingón, ona *adj* snub.

respiración *sf* breathing; MED respiration; **quedarse sin respiración** [asombrado] to be stunned.

respirar ⬦ *vt* [aire] to breathe. ⬦ *vi* to breathe; *fig* [sentir alivio] to breathe again; **no dejar respirar a alguien** *fig* not to allow sb a moment's peace; **sin respirar** [sin descanso] without a break; [atentamente] with great attention.

respiratorio, ria *adj* respiratory.

respiro *sm* - **1.** [descanso] rest - **2.** [alivio] relief, respite; **dar un respiro a alguien** *fam* to give sb a break.

resplandecer *vi* - **1.** [brillar] to shine - **2.** *fig* [destacar] to shine, to stand out.

resplandeciente *adj* shining; [sonrisa] beaming; [época] glittering; [vestimenta, color] resplendent.

resplandor *sm* - **1.** [luz] brightness; [de fuego] glow - **2.** [brillo] gleam.

responder ⬦ *vt* to answer. ⬦ *vi* - **1.** [contestar]: **responder (a algo)** to answer (sthg) - **2.** [reaccionar]: **responder (a)** to respond (to) - **3.** [responsabilizarse]: **responder de algo/por alguien** to answer for sthg/for sb - **4.** [replicar] to answer back.

respondón, ona *adj* insolent.

responsabilidad *sf* responsibility; DER liability; **exigir responsabilidades a alguien** to hold sb accountable; **tener la responsabilidad de algo** to be responsible for sthg; **responsabilidad civil/penal** DER civil/criminal liability; **responsabilidad limitada** limited liability.

responsabilizar *vt*: **responsabilizar a alguien (de algo)** to hold sb responsible (for sthg). ➧ **responsabilizarse** *vprnl*: **responsabilizarse (de)** to accept responsibility (for).

responsable ⬦ *adj* responsible; **responsable de** responsible for. ⬦ *smf* - **1.** [culpable] person responsible - **2.** [encargado] person in charge.

respuesta *sf* - **1.** [gen] answer, reply; [en exámenes] answer; **en respuesta a** in reply to - **2.** *fig* [reacción] response.

resquebrajar *vt* to crack. ➧ **resquebrajarse** *vprnl* to crack.

resquicio *sm* - **1.** [abertura] chink; [grieta] crack - **2.** *fig* [pizca] glimmer.

resta *sf* MAT subtraction.

restablecer *vt* to reestablish, to restore. ➧ **restablecerse** *vprnl* [curarse]: **restablecerse (de)** to recover (from).

restallar *vt* & *vi* [látigo] to crack; [lengua] to click.

restante *adj* remaining; **lo restante** the rest.

restar ⬦ *vt* - **1.** MAT to subtract - **2.** [disminuir]: **restar importancia a algo/méritos a alguien** to play down the importance of sthg/sb's qualities. ⬦ *vi* [faltar] to be left.

restauración *sf* restoration.

restaurante *sm* restaurant.

restaurar *vt* to restore.

restitución *sf* return.

restituir *vt* [devolver - objeto] to return; [- salud] to restore.

resto *sm*: **el resto** [gen] the rest; MAT the remainder. ➧ **restos** *smpl* - **1.** [sobras] leftovers - **2.** [cadáver] remains - **3.** [ruinas] ruins.

restregar *vt* to rub hard; [para limpiar] to scrub. ➧ **restregarse** *vprnl* [frotarse] to rub.

restricción *sf* restriction.

restrictivo, va *adj* restrictive.

restringir *vt* to limit, to restrict.

resucitar ⬦ *vt* [person] to bring back to life; [costumbre] to revive. ⬦ *vi* [persona] to rise from the dead.

resuello *sm* gasp, gasping (U); [jadeo] pant, panting (U).

resuelto, ta ⬦ *pp* ⬥ **resolver**. ⬦ *adj* [decidido] determined.

resulta *sf*: **de resultas de** as a result of.

resultado *sm* result; **dar buen/mal resultado** to be a success/failure.

resultante *adj* & *sf* resultant.

resultar ⬦ *vi* - **1.** [acabar siendo]: **resultar (ser)** to turn out (to be); **resultó ileso** he was uninjured; **nuestro equipo resultó vencedor** our team came out on top - **2.** [salir bien] to work (out), to be a success - **3.** [originarse]: **resultar de** to come of, to result from - **4.** [ser] to be; **resulta sorprendente** it's surprising; **me resultó imposible terminar antes** I was unable to finish earlier - **5.** [venir a costar]: **resultar a** to come to, to cost. ⬦ *v impers* [suceder]: **resultar que** to turn out that; **ahora resulta que no quiere alquilarlo** now it seems that she doesn't want to rent it.

resumen *sm* summary; **en resumen** in short.

resumidero *sm Amér* drain.

resumir *vt* to summarize; [discurso] to sum up. ➧ **resumirse en** *vprnl* - **1.** [sintetizarse en] to be able to be summed up in - **2.** [reducirse a] to boil down to.

resurgir *vi* to undergo a resurgence.

resurrección *sf* resurrection.

retablo *sm* altarpiece.

retaguardia *sf* [tropa] rearguard; [territorio] rear.

retahíla *sf* string, series.

retal *sm* remnant.

retardar *vt* [retrasar] to delay; [frenar] to hold up, to slow down.

retazo *sm* remnant; *fig* fragment.

rete *adv Amér fam* very.

retén *sm* - 1. reserve - 2. *Amér* [de menores] reformatory, reform school.

retención *sf* - 1. [en el sueldo] deduction - 2. *(gen pl)* [de tráfico] hold-up.

retener *vt* - 1. [detener] to hold back; [en comisaría] to detain - 2. [hacer permanecer] to keep - 3. [contener - impulso, ira] to hold back, to restrain - 4. [conservar] to retain - 5. [quedarse con] to hold on to, to keep - 6. [memorizar] to remember - 7. [deducir del sueldo] to deduct.

reticente *adj* [reacio] unwilling, reluctant.

retina *sf* retina.

retintín *sm* [ironía] sarcastic tone.

retirado, da *adj* - 1. [jubilado] retired - 2. [solitario, alejado] isolated, secluded. ➡ **retirada** *sf* - 1. MIL retreat; **batirse en retirada** to beat a retreat - 2. [de fondos, moneda, carné] withdrawal - 3. [de competición, actividad] withdrawal.

retirar *vt* - 1. [quitar - gen] to remove; [- dinero, moneda, carné] to withdraw; [- nieve] to clear - 2. [jubilar - a deportista] to force to retire; [- a empleado] to retire - 3. [retractarse de] to take back. ➡ **retirarse** *vprnl* - 1. [gen] to retire - 2. [de competición, elecciones] to withdraw; [de reunión] to leave - 3. [de campo de batalla] to retreat - 4. [apartarse] to move away.

retiro *sm* - 1. [jubilación] retirement; [pensión] pension - 2. [refugio, ejercicio] retreat.

reto *sm* challenge.

retocar *vt* to touch up.

retoño *sm* BOT sprout, shoot; *fig* offspring *(U)*.

retoque *sm* touching-up *(U)*; [de prenda de vestir] alteration; **dar los últimos retoques a** to put the finishing touches to.

retorcer *vt* [torcer - brazo, alambre] to twist; [- ropa, cuello] to wring. ➡ **retorcerse** *vprnl* [contraerse]: **retorcerse (de)** [risa] to double up (with); [dolor] to writhe about (in).

retorcido, da *adj* - 1. [torcido - brazo, alambre] twisted - 2. *fig* [rebuscado] complicated.

retornable *adj* returnable; **no retornable** non-returnable.

retornar *vt & vi* to return.

retorno *sm* [gen & INFORM] return; **retorno de carro** carriage return.

retortijón *(gen pl) sm* stomach cramp.

retozar *vi* to frolic; [amantes] to romp about.

retractarse *vprnl* [de una promesa] to go back on one's word; [de una opinión] to take back what one has said; **retractarse de** [lo dicho] to retract, to take back.

retraer *vt* [encoger] to retract. ➡ **retraerse** *vprnl* - 1. [encogerse] to retract - 2. [retroceder] to withdraw, to retreat.

retraído, da *adj* withdrawn, retiring.

retransmisión *sf* broadcast; **retransmisión en directo/diferido** live/recorded broadcast.

retransmitir *vt* to broadcast.

retrasado, da ◇ *adj* - 1. [país, industria] backward; [reloj] slow; [tren] late, delayed - 2. [en el pago, los estudios] behind - 3. MED retarded, backward. ◇ *sm, f*: **retrasado (mental)** mentally retarded person.

retrasar *vt* - 1. [aplazar] to postpone - 2. [demorar] to delay, to hold up - 3. [hacer más lento] to slow down, to hold up - 4. [en el pago, los estudios] to set back - 5. [reloj] to put back. ➡ **retrasarse** *vprnl* - 1. [llegar tarde] to be late - 2. [quedarse atrás] to fall behind - 3. [aplazarse] to be put off - 4. [reloj] to lose time.

retraso *sm* - 1. [por llegar tarde] delay; **llegar con (15 minutos de) retraso** to be (15 minutes) late - 2. [por sobrepasar una fecha]: **llevo en mi trabajo un retraso de 20 páginas** I'm 20 pages behind with my work - 3. [subdesarrollo] backwardness - 4. MED mental deficiency.

retratar *vt* - 1. [fotografiar] to photograph - 2. [dibujar] to do a portrait of - 3. *fig* [describir] to portray.

retrato *sm* - 1. [dibujo] portrait; [fotografía] photograph; **retrato robot** photofit picture; **ser el vivo retrato de alguien** to be the spitting image of sb - 2. *fig* [reflejo] portrayal.

retrete *sm* toilet.

retribución *sf* [pago] payment; [recompensa] reward.

retribuir *vt* - 1. [pagar] to pay; [recompensar] to reward - 2. *Amér* [favor, obsequio] to return.

retro *adj* old-fashioned.

retroactivo, va *adj* [ley] retroactive; [pago] backdated.

retroceder *vi* to go back; *fig* to back down.

retroceso *sm* [regresión - gen] backward movement; [- en negociaciones] setback; [- en la economía] recession.

retrógrado, da *adj & sm, f* reactionary.

retroproyector *sm* overhead projector.

retrospectivo, va *adj* retrospective.

retrovisor *sm* rear-view mirror.

retumbar *vi* [resonar] to resound.

reuma, reúma *sm o sf* rheumatism.

reumatismo *sm* rheumatism.

reunión *sf* meeting.

reunir *vt* - 1. [público, accionistas etc] to bring together - 2. [objetos, textos etc] to collect, to bring together; [fondos] to raise - 3. [requisitos] to meet; [cualidades] to possess, to combine. ➡ **reunirse** *vprnl* [congregarse] to meet.

revalidar *vt* - **1.** [ratificar] to confirm - **2.** *Amér* [estudios, diploma] to validate.

revalorizar *vt* - **1.** [aumentar el valor] to increase the value of; [moneda] to revalue - **2.** [restituir el valor] to reassess in a favourable light. ➤ **revalorizarse** *vprnl* [aumentar de valor] to appreciate; [moneda] to be revalued.

revancha *sf* - **1.** [venganza] revenge - **2.** DEP return match.

revelación *sf* revelation.

revelado *sm* FOTO developing.

revelador, ra *adj* [aclarador] revealing.

revelar *vt* - **1.** [declarar] to reveal - **2.** [evidenciar] to show - **3.** FOTO to develop. ➤ **revelarse** *vprnl*: revelarse como to show o.s. to be.

revendedor, ra *sm, f* ticket tout.

reventa *sf* resale; [de entradas] touting.

reventar ⟨⟩ *vt* - **1.** [explotar] to burst - **2.** [echar abajo] to break down; [con explosivos] to blow up. ⟨⟩ *vi* [explotar] to burst. ➤ **reventarse** *vprnl* [explotar] to explode; [rueda] to burst.

reventón *sm* [pinchazo] blowout, puncture UK, flat US.

reverberación *sf* [de sonido] reverberation; [de luz, calor] reflection.

reverberar *vi* [sonido] to reverberate; [luz, calor] to reflect.

reverdecer *vi* fig [amor] to revive.

reverencia *sf* - **1.** [respeto] reverence - **2.** [saludo - inclinación] bow; [- flexión de piernas] curtsy.

reverenciar *vt* to revere.

reverendo, da *adj* reverend. ➤ **reverendo** *sm* reverend.

reverente *adj* reverent.

reversible *adj* reversible.

reverso *sm* back, other side.

revertir *vi* - **1.** [volver, devolver] to revert - **2.** [resultar]: **revertir en** to result in; **revertir en beneficio/perjuicio de** to be to the advantage/ detriment of.

revés *sm* - **1.** [parte opuesta - de papel, mano] back; [- de tela] other O wrong side; **al revés** [- en sentido contrario] the wrong way round; [- en forma opuesta] the other way round; **del revés** [- lo de detrás, delante] the wrong way round, back to front; [- lo de dentro, fuera] inside out; [- lo de arriba, abajo] upside down - **2.** [bofetada] slap - **3.** DEP backhand - **4.** [contratiempo] setback.

revestimiento *sm* covering.

revestir *vt* - **1.** [recubrir]: **revestir (de)** [gen] to cover (with); [pintura] to coat (with); [forro] to line (with) - **2.** [poseer - solemnidad, gravedad etc] to take on, to have.

revisar *vt* - **1.** [repasar] to go over again - **2.** [inspeccionar] to inspect; [cuentas] to audit - **3.** [modificar] to revise.

revisión *sf* - **1.** [repaso] revision - **2.** [inspección] inspection; **revisión de cuentas** audit; **revisión médica** check-up - **3.** [modificación] amendment - **4.** [AUTO - puesta a punto] service; [- anual] ≈ MOT (test).

revisor, ra *sm, f* [en tren] ticket inspector, conductor US; [en autobús] (bus) conductor.

revista *sf* - **1.** [publicación] magazine; **revista del corazón** gossip magazine; **revista de modas** fashion magazine - **2.** [sección de periódico] section, review - **3.** [espectáculo teatral] revue - **4.** [inspección] inspection; **pasar revista a** MIL to inspect, to review; [examinar] to examine.

revistero *sm* [mueble] magazine rack.

revivir ⟨⟩ *vi* to revive. ⟨⟩ *vt* [recordar] to revive memories of.

revocar *vt* [gen] to revoke.

revolcar *vt* to upend. ➤ **revolcarse** *vprnl* to roll about.

revolotear *vi* to flutter (about).

revoltijo, revoltillo *sm* jumble.

revoltoso, sa *adj* - **1.** [travieso] mischievous - **2.** [sedicioso] rebellious.

revolución *sf* revolution.

revolucionar *vt* [transformar] to revolutionize.

revolucionario, ria *adj* & *sm, f* revolutionary.

revolver *vt* - **1.** [dar vueltas] to turn around; [líquido] to stir - **2.** [mezclar] to mix; [ensalada] to toss - **3.** [desorganizar] to mess up; [cajones] to turn out - **4.** [irritar] to upset. ➤ **revolver en** *vi* [cajones etc] to rummage around in. ➤ **revolverse** *vprnl* [volverse] to turn around.

revólver *sm* revolver.

revuelo *sm* [agitación] commotion; **armar un gran revuelo** to cause a great stir.

revuelto, ta ⟨⟩ *pp* ▷ **revolver**. ⟨⟩ *adj* - **1.** [desordenado] in a mess - **2.** [alborotado - época etc] turbulent - **3.** [clima] unsettled - **4.** [aguas] choppy. ➤ **revuelto** *sm* CULIN scrambled eggs *pl*. ➤ **revuelta** *sf* [disturbio] riot, revolt.

revulsivo, va *adj* fig stimulating, revitalizing. ➤ **revulsivo** *sm* fig kick-start.

rey *sm* king. ➤ **Reyes** *smpl*: **los Reyes** the King and Queen; **(Día de) Reyes** Twelfth Night.

reyerta *sf* fight, brawl.

rezagado, da *adj*: **ir rezagado** to lag behind.

rezar *vi* - **1.** [orar]: **rezar (a)** to pray (to); **rezar por algo/alguien** to pray for sthg/sb - **2.** [decir] to read, to say - **3.** [corresponderse]: **rezar con** to have to do with.

rezo *sm* [oración] prayer.

rezumar ◇ *vt* - 1. [transpirar] to ooze - 2. *fig* [manifestar] to be overflowing with. ◇ *vi* to ooze O seep out.

ría *sf* estuary.

riachuelo *sm* brook, stream.

riada *sf lit & fig* flood.

ribera *sf* [del río] bank; [del mar] shore.

ribete *sm* edging *(U)*, trimming *(U)*; *fig* touch, nuance.

ricino *sm* [planta] castor oil plant.

rico, ca ◇ *adj* - 1. [gen] rich - 2. [abundante]: **rico (en)** rich (in) - 3. [sabroso] delicious - 4. [simpático] cute. ◇ *sm, f* rich person; **los ricos** the rich.

rictus *sm inv* - 1. [de ironía] smirk - 2. [de desprecio] sneer - 3. [de dolor] wince.

ridiculez *sf* - 1. [payasada] silly thing, nonsense *(U)* - 2. [nimiedad] trifle; **cuesta una ridiculez** it costs next to nothing.

ridiculizar *vt* to ridicule.

ridículo, la *adj* ridiculous; [precio, suma] laughable, derisory. ➤ **ridículo** *sm* ridicule; **hacer el ridículo** to make a fool of o.s.; **poner** O **dejar en ridículo a alguien** to make sb look stupid; **quedar en ridículo** to look like a fool.

riego *sm* [de campo] irrigation; [de jardín] watering.

riel *sm* - 1. [de vía] rail - 2. [de cortina] (curtain) rail.

rienda *sf* [de caballería] rein; **dar rienda suelta a** *fig* to give free rein to. ➤ **riendas** *sfpl fig* [dirección] reins; **llevar** O **tener las riendas** to hold the reins, to be in control.

riesgo *sm* risk.

riesgoso, sa *adj Amér* risky.

rifa *sf* raffle.

rifar *vt* to raffle. ➤ **rifarse** *vprnl fig* to fight over.

rifle *sm* rifle.

rigidez *sf* - 1. [de un cuerpo, objeto etc] rigidity - 2. [del rostro] stoniness - 3. *fig* [severidad] strictness, harshness.

rígido, da *adj* - 1. [cuerpo, objeto etc] rigid - 2. [rostro] stony - 3. [severo - normas etc] harsh; [- carácter] inflexible.

rigor *sm* - 1. [severidad] strictness - 2. [exactitud] accuracy, rigour - 3. [inclemencia] harshness. ➤ **de rigor** *loc adj* usual.

riguroso, sa *adj* - 1. [severo] strict - 2. [exacto] rigorous - 3. [inclemente] harsh.

rimar *vt & vi* to rhyme; **rimar con algo** to rhyme with sthg.

rimbombante *adj* [estilo, frases] pompous.

rímel, rimmel® *sm* mascara.

rincón *sm* corner *(inside)*.

rinconera *sf* corner piece.

ring *(pl* **rings)** *sm* (boxing) ring.

rinoceronte *sm* rhinoceros.

riña *sf* [disputa] quarrel; [pelea] fight.

riñón *sm* kidney; **tener el riñón bien cubierto** *fig* to be well-heeled.

riñonera *sf* [pequeño bolso] bum bag *UK*, fanny pack *US*.

río *sm lit & fig* river; **a río revuelto, ganancia de pescadores** *prov* it's an ill wind that blows nobody any good *prov*; **cuando el río suena, agua lleva** *prov* there's no smoke without fire *prov*.

rioja *sm* Rioja (wine).

riojano, na *adj & sm, f* Riojan.

riqueza *sf* - 1. [fortuna] wealth - 2. [abundancia] richness.

risa *sf* laugh, laughter *(U)*; **me da risa** I find it funny; **¡qué risa!** how funny!; **de risa** funny.

risotada *sf* guffaw; **soltar una risotada** to laugh loudly.

ristra *sf lit & fig* string.

ristre ➤ **en ristre** *loc adv* at the ready.

risueño, ña *adj* [alegre] smiling.

ritmo *sm* - 1. [gen] rhythm; **al ritmo de** to the rhythm of; **llevar el ritmo** to keep time; **perder el ritmo** to get out of time; [cardíaco] beat - 2. [velocidad] pace.

rito *sm* - 1. RELIG rite - 2. [costumbre] ritual.

ritual *adj & sm* ritual.

rival *adj & smf* rival; **sin rival** unrivalled.

rivalidad *sf* rivalry.

rivalizar *vi*: **rivalizar (con)** to compete (with).

rizado, da *adj* - 1. [pelo] curly - 2. [mar] choppy. ➤ **rizado** *sm* [en peluquería]: **hacerse un rizado** to have one's hair curled.

rizar *vt* [pelo] to curl. ➤ **rizarse** *vprnl* [pelo] to curl.

rizo *sm* - 1. [de pelo] curl - 2. [del agua] ripple - 3. [de avión] loop - 4. *loc*: **rizar el rizo** to split hairs.

robar *vt* - 1. [gen] to steal; [casa] to burgle, burglarize *US*; **robar a alguien** to rob sb - 2. [en naipes] to draw - 3. [cobrar caro] to rob.

roble *sm* - 1. BOT oak - 2. *fig* [persona] strong person; **más fuerte que un roble** as strong as an ox.

robo *sm* [delito] robbery, theft; [en casa] burglary; **ser un robo** [precios etc] to be daylight robbery.

robot *(pl* **robots)** *sm* [gen & INFORM] robot.

robótica *sf* robotics *(U)*.

robustecer *vt* to strengthen. ➤ **robustecerse** *vprnl* to get stronger.

robusto, ta *adj* robust.

roca *sf* rock; **firme como una roca** solid as a rock.

rocalla *sf* rubble.

roce *sm* - **1.** [rozamiento - gen] rub, rubbing (U); [- suave] brush, brushing (U); FÍS friction - **2.** [desgaste] wear - **3.** [rasguño - en piel] graze; [- en zapato, puerta] scuffmark; [- en metal] scratch - **4.** [trato] close contact - **5.** [desavenencia] brush; **tener un roce con alguien** to have a brush with sb.

rociar *vt* - **1.** [arrojar gotas] to sprinkle; [con espray] to spray - **2.** [con vino] to wash down.

rocío *sm* dew.

rock, rock and roll *sm inv* rock and roll.

rockero, ra = **roquero**.

rocoso, sa *adj* rocky.

rodaballo *sm* turbot.

rodado, da *adj* - **1.** [piedra] rounded - **2.** [tráfico] road *(antes de s)* - **3.** *loc:* **estar muy rodado** [persona] to be very experienced; **venir rodado para** to be the perfect opportunity to.

rodaja *sf* slice.

rodaje *sm* - **1.** [filmación] shooting - **2.** [de motor] running-in - **3.** [experiencia] experience.

Ródano *sm:* **el Ródano** the (River) Rhône.

rodapié *sm* skirting board.

rodar ⬦ *vi* - **1.** [deslizar] to roll; **echar algo a rodar** *fig* to set sthg in motion - **2.** [circular] to travel, to go - **3.** [caer]: **rodar (por)** to tumble (down) - **4.** [ir de un lado a otro] to go around - **5.** CINE to shoot. ⬦ *vt* - **1.** CINE to shoot - **2.** [automóvil] to run in.

rodear *vt* - **1.** [gen] to surround; **le rodeó el cuello con los brazos** she put her arms around his neck; **rodear algo de algo** to surround sthg with sthg - **2.** [dar la vuelta a] to go around - **3.** [eludir] to skirt around. ⬦ **rodearse** *vprnl:* **rodearse de** to surround o.s. with.

rodeo *sm* - **1.** [camino largo] detour; **dar un rodeo** to make a detour - **2.** *(gen pl)* [evasiva] evasiveness (U) - **3.** [espectáculo] rodeo.

rodilla *sf* knee; **de rodillas** on one's knees.

rodillera *sf* [protección] knee pad.

rodillo *sm* [gen] roller; [para repostería] rolling pin.

rodríguez *sm inv* grass widower; **estar O quedarse de rodríguez** to be a grass widower.

roedor, ra *adj* ZOOL rodent *(antes de s)*. ⬦ **roedor** *sm* rodent.

roer *vt* - **1.** [con dientes] to gnaw (at) - **2.** *fig* [gastar] to eat away (at).

rogar *vt* [implorar] to beg; [pedir] to ask; **rogar a alguien que haga algo** to ask O beg sb to do sthg; **le ruego me perdone** I beg your pardon; **'se ruega silencio'** 'silence, please'.

rogativa *(gen pl) sf* rogation.

rojizo, za *adj* reddish.

rojo, ja ⬦ *adj* red; **ponerse rojo** [gen] to turn red; [ruborizarse] to blush. ⬦ *sm, f* POLÍT red. ⬦ **rojo** *sm* [color] red; **al rojo vivo** [en incandescencia] red hot, *fig* heated.

rol *(pl roles) sm* [papel] role.

rollizo, za *adj* chubby, plump.

rollo *sm* - **1.** [cilindro] roll; **rollo de primavera** CULIN spring roll - **2.** CINE roll - **3.** *fam* [discurso]: **el rollo de costumbre** the same old story; **tener mucho rollo** to witter on - **4.** *fam* [embuste] tall story - **5.** *fam* [pelmazo, pesadez] bore, drag.

ROM *(abrev de read-only memory) sf* INFORM ROM.

romance *sm* - **1.** LING Romance language - **2.** [idilio] romance.

románico, ca *adj* - **1.** ARQUIT & ARTE Romanesque - **2.** LING Romance.

romano, na *sm, f* Roman.

romanticismo *sm* - **1.** ARTE & LITER Romanticism - **2.** [sentimentalismo] romanticism.

romántico, ca *adj & sm, f* - **1.** ARTE & LITER Romantic - **2.** [sentimental] romantic.

rombo *sm* GEOM rhombus.

romería *sf* [peregrinación] pilgrimage.

romero, ra *sm, f* [peregrino] pilgrim. ⬦ **romero** *sm* BOT rosemary.

romo, ma *adj* [sin filo] blunt.

rompecabezas *sm inv* - **1.** [juego] jigsaw - **2.** *fam* [problema] puzzle.

rompeolas *sm inv* breakwater.

romper ⬦ *vt* - **1.** [gen] to break; [hacer añicos] to smash; [rasgar] to tear - **2.** [interrumpir - monotonía, silencio, hábito] to break; [- hilo del discurso] to break off; [- tradición] to put an end to - **3.** [terminar - relaciones etc] to break off. ⬦ *vi* - **1.** [terminar una relación]: **romper (con alguien)** to break O split up (with sb) - **2.** [olas, el día] to break; [hostilidades] to break out; **al romper el alba O día** at daybreak - **3.** [empezar]: **romper a hacer algo** to suddenly start doing sthg; **romper a llorar** to burst into tears; **romper a reír** to burst out laughing. ⬦ **romperse** *vprnl* [partirse] to break; [rasgarse] to tear; **se ha roto una pierna** he has broken a leg.

rompevientos *sm Amér* [anorak] anorak; *R Dom* [suéter] polo-neck jersey.

rompimiento *sm* - **1.** [breaking; [de relaciones] breaking-off - **2.** *Amér* [de relaciones, conversaciones] breaking-off; [de pareja] break-up; [de contrato] breach.

ron *sm* rum.

roncar *vi* to snore.

roncha *sf* red blotch.

ronco, ca *adj* - **1.** [afónico] hoarse; **se quedó ronco de tanto gritar** he shouted himself hoarse - **2.** [bronco] harsh.

ronda sf - **1.** [de vigilancia, visitas] rounds pl; **hacer la ronda** to do one's rounds - **2.** fam [de bebidas, en el juego etc] round - **3.** C Sur [corro] circle, ring.

rondar ⬦ vt - **1.** [vigilar] to patrol - **2.** [rayar - edad] to be around. ⬦ vi [merodear]: **rondar (por)** to wander O hang around.

ronquera sf hoarseness.

ronquido sm snore, snoring (U).

ronronear vi to purr.

ronroneo sm purr, purring (U).

roña ⬦ adj fam [tacaño] stingy. ⬦ sf - **1.** [suciedad] filth, dirt - **2.** [veterinaria] mange.

roñoso, sa ⬦ adj - **1.** [sucio] dirty - **2.** [tacaño] mean. ⬦ sm, f miser.

ropa sf clothes pl; **ropa blanca** linen; **ropa de abrigo** warm clothes pl; **ropa de cama** bed linen; **ropa hecha** ready-to-wear clothes; **ropa interior** underwear; **ropa sucia** laundry; **nadar y guardar la ropa** fig to cover one's back.

ropaje sm robes pl.

ropero sm - **1.** [armario] wardrobe - **2.** [habitación] walk-in wardrobe; TEATRO cloakroom.

roquero, ra, rockero, ra sm, f - **1.** [músico] rock musician - **2.** [fan] rock fan.

rosa ⬦ sf [flor] rose; **estar (fresco) como una rosa** to be as fresh as a daisy; **no hay rosa sin espinas** there's no rose without a thorn. ⬦ sm [color] pink. ⬦ adj inv [color] pink; **verlo todo de color (de) rosa** fig to see everything through rose-tinted spectacles. ➤ **rosa de los vientos** sf NÁUT compass.

rosado, da ⬦ adj pink. ⬦ sm [vino] rosé.

rosal sm [arbusto] rose bush.

rosario sm - **1.** RELIG rosary; **rezar el rosario** to say one's rosary - **2.** [sarta] string.

rosca sf - **1.** [de tornillo] thread - **2.** [forma - de anillo] ring; [- espiral] coil - **3.** CULIN ring doughnut.

rosco sm ring-shaped bread roll.

roscón sm ring-shaped cake; **roscón de reyes** cake eaten on 6th January.

rosetón sm [ventana] rose window.

rosquilla sf ring doughnut.

rosticería sf Chile shop selling roast chicken.

rostro sm face; **tener (mucho) rostro** fam fig to have a real nerve.

rotación sf - **1.** [giro] rotation; **rotación de cultivos** crop rotation - **2.** [alternancia] rota; **por rotación** in turn.

rotativo, va adj rotary, revolving. ➤ **rotativo** sm newspaper. ➤ **rotativa** sf rotary press.

roto, ta ⬦ pp ▷ **romper**. ⬦ adj - **1.** [gen] broken; [tela, papel] torn - **2.** fig [deshecho - vida etc] destroyed; [- corazón] broken - **3.** fig [exhausto] shattered. ⬦ sm, f Chile fam despec [trabajador] worker. ➤ **roto** sm [en tela] tear, rip.

rotonda sf - **1.** [glorieta] roundabout UK, traffic circle US - **2.** [plaza] circus.

rotoso, sa adj Andes & R Dom fam ragged.

rótula sf kneecap.

rotulador sm felt-tip pen; [fluorescente] marker pen.

rótulo sm - **1.** [letrero] sign - **2.** [encabezamiento] headline, title.

rotundo, da adj - **1.** [categórico - negativa, persona] categorical; [- lenguaje, estilo] emphatic - **2.** [completo] total.

rotura sf [gen] break, breaking (U); [de hueso] fracture; [en tela] rip, hole.

roulotte [ru'lot] sf caravan UK, trailer US.

rozadura sf - **1.** [señal] scratch, scrape - **2.** [herida] graze.

rozamiento sm [fricción] rub, rubbing (U); FÍS friction (U).

rozar vt - **1.** [gen] to rub; [suavemente] to brush; [suj: zapato] to graze - **2.** [pasar cerca de] to skim. ➤ **rozar con** vi - **1.** [tocar] to brush against - **2.** fig [acercarse a] to verge on. ➤ **rozarse** vprnl - **1.** [tocarse] to touch - **2.** [pasar cerca] to brush past each other - **3.** [herirse - rodilla etc] to graze - **4.** fig [tener trato]: **rozarse con** to rub shoulders with.

Rte. abrev de **remitente**.

RTVE (abrev de **Radiotelevisión Española**) sf Spanish state broadcasting company.

rubeola, rubéola sf German measles (U).

rubí (pl **rubíes** O **rubís**) sm ruby.

rubio, bia ⬦ adj - **1.** [pelo, persona] blond (f blonde), fair; **teñirse de rubio** to dye one's hair blond; **rubia platino** platinum blonde - **2.** [tabaco] Virginia (antes de s) - **3.** [cerveza] lager (antes de s). ⬦ sm, f [persona] blond (f blonde).

rubor sm - **1.** [vergüenza] embarrassment; **causar rubor** to embarrass - **2.** [sonrojo] blush.

ruborizar vt [avergonzar] to embarrass. ➤ **ruborizarse** vprnl to blush.

rúbrica sf - **1.** [de firma] flourish - **2.** [conclusión] final flourish; **poner rúbrica a algo** to complete sthg.

rubricar vt - **1.** fig [confirmar] to confirm - **2.** fig [concluir] to complete.

rucio, cia adj [gris] grey.

rudeza sf - **1.** [tosquedad] roughness - **2.** [grosería] coarseness.

rudimentario, ria adj rudimentary.

rudimentos smpl rudiments.

rudo, da adj - **1.** [tosco] rough - **2.** [brusco] sharp, brusque - **3.** [grosero] rude, coarse.

rueda *sf* - **1.** [pieza] wheel; **rueda delantera/ trasera** front/rear wheel; **rueda de repuesto** spare wheel; **comulgar con ruedas de molino** *fig* to be very gullible, ir sobre ruedas *fig* to go smoothly; **3.** [corro] circle. ▸ **rueda de prensa** *sf* press conference.

ruedo *sm* TAUROM bullring.

ruega *etc* ▷ **rogar**.

ruego *sm* request; **ruegos y preguntas** any other business.

rufián *sm* villain.

rugby *sm* rugby.

rugido *sm* [gen] roar; [de persona] bellow.

rugir *vi* [gen] to roar; [persona] to bellow.

rugoso, sa *adj* - **1.** [áspero - material, terreno] rough - **2.** [con arrugas - rostro etc] wrinkled; [- tejido] crinkled.

ruido *sm* - **1.** [gen] noise; [sonido] sound; **mucho ruido y pocas nueces** much ado about nothing - **2.** *fig* [escándalo] row; **hacer O meter ruido** to cause a stir.

ruidoso, sa *adj* [que hace ruido] noisy.

ruin *adj* - **1.** [vil] low, contemptible - **2.** [avaro] mean.

ruina *sf* - **1.** [gen] ruin; **dejar en O llevar a la ruina a alguien** to ruin sb; **estar en la ruina** to be ruined; **ser una ruina** to cost a fortune - **2.** [destrucción] destruction - **3.** [fracaso - persona] wreck; **estar hecho una ruina** to be a wreck. ▸ **ruinas** *sfpl* [históricas] ruins; **en ruinas** in ruins.

ruinoso, sa *adj* - **1.** [poco rentable] ruinous - **2.** [edificio] ramshackle.

ruiseñor *sm* nightingale.

ruleta *sf* roulette.

ruletear *vi Amér C & Méx fam* to drive a taxi.

ruletero *sm Amér C & Méx fam* taxi driver.

rulo *sm* [para el pelo] roller.

ruma *sf Andes & Ven* heap, pile.

Rumanía, Rumania *n pr* Romania.

rumano, na *adj & sm, f* Romanian. ▸ **rumano** *sm* [lengua] Romanian.

rumba *sf* rumba.

rumbo *sm* - **1.** [dirección] direction, course; **caminar sin rumbo fijo** to walk aimlessly; **ir con rumbo a** to be heading for; **perder el rumbo** [barco] to go off course; *fig* [persona] to lose one's way; **tomar otro rumbo** to take a different tack - **2.** *fig* [camino] path, direction.

rumiante *adj & sm* ruminant.

rumiar ◇ *vt* [suj: rumiante] to chew; *fig* to chew over. ◇ *vi* [masticar] to ruminate, to chew the cud.

rumor *sm* - **1.** [ruido sordo] murmur - **2.** [chisme] rumour; **corre el rumor de que** there's a rumour going around that.

rumorearse *v impers*: **rumorearse que...** to be rumoured that...

runrún *sm* [ruido confuso] hum, humming *(U)*.

rupestre *adj* cave *(antes de s)*.

ruptura *sf* [gen] break; [de relaciones, conversaciones] breaking-off; [de contrato] breach.

rural *adj* rural.

Rusia *n pr* Russia.

ruso, sa *adj & sm, f* Russian. ▸ **ruso** *sm* [lengua] Russian.

rústico, ca *adj* - **1.** [del campo] country *(antes de s)* - **2.** [tosco] rough, coarse. ▸ **en rústica** *loc adj* paperback.

ruta *sf* route; *fig* way, course.

rutina *sf* [gen & INFORM] routine; **por rutina** as a matter of course.

rutinario, ria *adj* routine.

s, S [letra] s, S.

s. *(abrev de siglo)* c *(century)*.

S - **1.** *(abrev de sur)* S - **2.** *(abrev de san)* St.

SA *(abrev de sociedad anónima) sf* ≃ Ltd, ≃ PLC.

sábado *sm* Saturday; **¿qué día es hoy? - (es) sábado** what day is it (today)? - (it's) Saturday; **cada sábado, todos los sábados** every Saturday; **cada dos sábados, un sábado sí y otro no** every other Saturday; **caer en sábado** to be on a Saturday; **te llamo el sábado** I'll call you on Saturday; **el próximo sábado, el sábado que viene** next Saturday; **el sábado pasado** last Saturday; **el sábado por la mañana/tarde/ noche** Saturday morning/afternoon/night; **en sábado** on Saturdays; **nací en sábado** I was born on a Saturday; **este sábado** [pasado] last Saturday; [próximo] this (coming) Saturday; **¿trabajas los sábados?** do you work (on) Saturdays?; **un sábado cualquiera** on any Saturday.

sábana *sf* sheet.

sabandija *sf fig* [persona] worm.

sabañón *sm* chilblain.

sabático, ca *adj* [del sábado] Saturday *(antes de s)*.

saber ⟨⟩ *sm* knowledge. ⟨⟩ *vt* - **1.** [conocer] to know; **ya lo sé** I know; **hacer saber algo a alguien** to inform sb of sthg, to tell sb sthg; **¿se puede saber qué haces?** would you mind telling me what you are doing? - **2.** [ser capaz de]: **saber hacer algo** to know how to do sthg, to be able to do sthg; **sabe hablar inglés/montar en bici** she can speak English/ride a bike - **3.** [enterarse] to learn, to find out; **lo supe ayer** I only found out yesterday - **4.** [entender de] to know about; **sabe mucha física** he knows a lot about physics. ⟨⟩ *vi* - **1.** [tener sabor]: **saber (a)** to taste (of); **saber bien/mal** to taste good/bad; **saber mal a alguien** *fig* to upset *O* annoy sb - **2.** [entender]: **saber de algo** to know about sthg - **3.** [tener noticia]: **saber de alguien** to hear from sb; **saber de algo** to learn of sthg - **4.** [parecer]: **eso me sabe a disculpa** that sounds like an excuse to me - **5.** *Andes, Arg & Chile fam* [soler]: **saber hacer algo** to be wont to do sthg - **6.** *loc*: **que yo sepa** as far as I know; **¡quién sabe!, ¡vete a saber!** who knows! ⟐ **saberse** *vprnl*: **saberse algo** to know sthg; **sabérselas todas** *fig* to know all the tricks. ⟐ **a saber** *loc adv* [es decir] namely.

sabiduría *sf* - **1.** [conocimientos] knowledge, learning - **2.** [prudencia] wisdom; **sabiduría popular** popular wisdom.

sabiendas ⟐ **a sabiendas** *loc adv* knowingly.

sabihondo = **sabiondo**.

sabio, bia *adj* - **1.** [sensato, inteligente] wise - **2.** [docto] learned.

sabiondo, da, sabihondo, da *adj & sm, f* know-all.

sablazo *sm fam fig* [de dinero] scrounging *(U)*; **dar un sablazo a alguien** to scrounge money off sb.

sable *sm* sabre.

sablear *vi fam* to scrounge money.

sabor *sm* - **1.** [gusto] taste, flavour; **tener sabor a algo** to taste of sthg; **dejar mal/buen sabor (de boca)** *fig* to leave a nasty taste in one's mouth/a warm feeling - **2.** *fig* [estilo] flavour.

saborear *vt lit & fig* to savour.

sabotaje *sm* sabotage.

sabotear *vt* to sabotage.

sabrá *etc* ⟿ **saber**.

sabroso, sa *adj* - **1.** [gustoso] tasty - **2.** *fig* [substancioso] tidy, considerable.

sabueso *sm* - **1.** [perro] bloodhound - **2.** *fig* [policía] sleuth.

saca *sf* sack.

sacacorchos *sm inv* corkscrew.

sacapuntas *sm inv* pencil sharpener.

sacar ⟨⟩ *vt* - **1.** [poner fuera, hacer salir] to take out; [lengua] to stick out; **sacar algo de** to take sthg out of; **nos sacaron algo de comer** they gave us something to eat; **sacar a alguien a bailar** to ask sb to dance - **2.** [quitar]: **sacar algo (de)** to remove sthg (from) - **3.** [librar, salvar]: **sacar a alguien de** to get sb out of - **4.** [conseguir]: **no sacas nada mintiéndole** you don't gain anything by lying to him - **5.** [obtener - carné, buenas notas] to get, to obtain; [- premio] to win; [- foto] to take; [- fotocopia] to make; [- dinero del banco] to withdraw - **6.** [sonsacar]: **sacar algo a alguien** to get sthg out of sb - **7.** [extraer - producto]: **sacar algo de** to extract sthg from - **8.** [fabricar] to produce - **9.** [crear - modelo, disco etc] to bring out - **10.** [exteriorizar] to show - **11.** [resolver - crucigrama etc] to do, to finish - **12.** [deducir] to gather, to understand; [conclusión] to come to - **13.** [mostrar] to show; **lo sacaron en televisión** he was on television - **14.** [comprar - entradas etc] to get, to buy - **15.** [prenda - de ancho] to let out; [- de largo] to let down - **16.** [aventajar]: **sacó tres minutos a su rival** he was three minutes ahead of his rival - **17.** [DEP - con la mano] to throw in; [- con la raqueta] to serve. ⟨⟩ *vi* DEP to put the ball into play; [con la raqueta] to serve. ⟐ **sacarse** *vprnl* [carné etc] to get. ⟐ **sacar adelante** *vt* - **1.** [hijos] to bring up - **2.** [negocio] to make a go of.

sacarina *sf* saccharine.

sacerdote, tisa *sm, f* [pagano] priest *(f* priestess). ⟐ **sacerdote** *sm* [cristiano] priest.

saciar *vt* [satisfacer - sed] to quench; [- hambre] to satisfy.

saco *sm* - **1.** [bolsa] sack, bag; **saco de dormir** sleeping bag - **2.** *Amér* [chaqueta] coat - **3.** *loc*: **dar por saco a alguien** *mfam* to screw sb; **entrar a saco en** to sack, to pillage; **mandar a alguien a tomar por saco** *mfam* to tell sb to get stuffed; **no echar algo en saco roto** to take good note of sthg.

sacramento *sm* sacrament.

sacrificar *vt* - **1.** [gen] to sacrifice; **sacrificar algo a** *lit & fig* to sacrifice sthg to - **2.** [animal - para consumo] to slaughter.

sacrificio *sm lit & fig* sacrifice.

sacrilegio *sm lit & fig* sacrilege.

sacristán, ana *sm, f* sacristan, sexton.

sacristía *sf* sacristy.

sacro, cra *adj* [sagrado] holy, sacred.

sacudida *sf* - **1.** [gen] shake; [de la cabeza] toss; [de tren, coche] jolt; **dar sacudidas** to jolt; **sacudida eléctrica** electric shock - **2.** [terremoto] tremor.

sacudir *vt* - **1.** [agitar] to shake - **2.** [golpear - alfombra etc] to beat - **3.** [hacer temblar] to shake - **4.** *fig* [conmover] to shake, to shock - **5.** *fam fig* [pegar] to smack.

sádico, ca ◇ *adj* sadistic. ◇ *sm, f* sadist.

sadismo *sm* sadism.

saeta *sf* - 1. [flecha] arrow - 2. MÚS *flamenco-style song sung on religious occasions.*

safari *sm* [expedición] safari; **ir de safari** to go on safari.

saga *sf* saga.

sagacidad *sf* astuteness.

sagaz *adj* astute, shrewd.

Sagitario ◇ *sm* [zodiaco] Sagittarius. ◇ *smf* [persona] Sagittarian.

sagrado, da *adj* holy, sacred; *fig* sacred.

Sáhara, Sahara *sm*: **el (desierto del) Sáhara** the Sahara (Desert).

sal *sf* CULIN & QUÍM salt; **la sal de la vida** *fig* the spark of life. ➡ **sales** *sfpl* - 1. [para reanimar] smelling salts - 2. [para baño] bath salts.

sala *sf* - 1. [habitación - gen] room; [- de una casa] lounge, living room; [- de hospital] ward; **sala de embarque** departure lounge; **sala de espera** waiting room; **sala de estar** lounge, living room; **sala de partos** delivery room - 2. [local - de conferencias, conciertos] hall; [- de cine, teatro] auditorium; **sala de fiestas** discotheque - 3. [DER -lugar] court (room); [- magistrados] bench.

salado, da *adj* - 1. [con sal] salted; [agua] salt *(antes de s)*; [con demasiada sal] salty - 2. *fig* [gracioso] witty - 3. *Amér C, Caribe & Méx* [desgraciado] unfortunate.

salamandra *sf* - 1. [animal] salamander - 2. [estufa] salamander stove.

salami, salame *sm C Sur* salami.

salar *vt* - 1. [para conservar] to salt - 2. [para cocinar] to add salt to.

salarial *adj* wage *(antes de s)*.

salario *sm* salary, wages *pl*; [semanal] wage.

salchicha *sf* sausage.

salchichón *sm* ≃ salami.

saldar *vt* - 1. [pagar - cuenta] to close; [- deuda] to settle - 2. *fig* [poner fin a] to settle - 3. COM to sell off. ➡ **saldarse** *vprnl* [acabar]: **saldarse con** to produce; **la pelea se saldó con 11 heridos** 11 people were injured in the brawl.

saldo *sm* - 1. [de cuenta] balance - 2. [de deudas] settlement - 3. *(gen pl)* [restos de mercancías] remnant; [rebajas] sale; **de saldo** bargain - 4. *fig* [resultado] balance.

saldrá *etc* ▷ **salir**.

saledizo, za *adj* projecting.

salero *sm* - 1. [recipiente] salt cellar *UK*, salt shaker *US* - 2. *fig* [gracia] wit; [donaire] charm.

salga *etc* ▷ **salir**.

salida *sf* - 1. [acción de partir - gen] leaving; [- de tren, avión] departure; **salidas nacionales/internacionales** domestic/international departures - 2. DEP start; **dar la salida** to start the race - 3. [lugar] exit, way out; **salida de emergencia/incendios** emergency/fire exit - 4. [momento]: **quedamos a la salida del trabajo** we agreed to meet after work - 5. [viaje] trip - 6. [aparición de sol, luna] rise; [- de revista, nuevo modelo] appearance - 7. [COM - posibilidades] market; [- producción] output - 8. *fig* [solución] way out; **si no hay otra salida** if there's no alternative - 9. *fig* [futuro - de carreras etc] opening, opportunity.

salido, da *adj* - 1. [saliente] projecting, sticking out; [ojos] bulging - 2. [animal] on heat - 3. *mfam* [persona] horny.

saliente ◇ *adj* POLÍT outgoing. ◇ *sm* projection.

salino, na *adj* saline.

salir *vi* - 1. [ir fuera] to go out; [venir fuera] to come out; **salir de** to go/come out of; **¿salimos al jardín?** shall we go out into the garden?; **¡sal aquí fuera!** come out here! - 2. [ser novios]: **salir (con alguien)** to go out (with sb) - 3. [marcharse]: **salir (de/para)** to leave (from/for); **salir corriendo** to go off like a shot - 4. [desembocar - calle]: **salir a** to open out onto - 5. [resultar] to turn out; **ha salido muy estudioso** he has turned out to be very studious; **¿qué salió en la votación?** what was the result of the vote?; **salir elegida actriz del año** to be voted actress of the year; **salir bien/mal** to turn out well/badly; **salir ganando/perdiendo** to come off well/badly - 6. [proceder]: **salir de** to come from; **el vino sale de la uva** wine comes from grapes - 7. [surgir - luna, estrellas, planta] to come out; [- sol] to rise; [- dientes] to come through; **le ha salido un sarpullido en la espalda** her back has come out in a rash - 8. [aparecer - publicación, producto, traumas] to come out; [- moda, ley] to come in; [- en imagen, prensa, televisión] to appear; **¡qué bien sales en la foto!** you look great in the photo!; **ha salido en los periódicos** it's in the papers; **hoy salió por la televisión** he was on television today; **salir de** CINE & TEATRO to appear as - 9. [costar]: **salir (a O por)** to work out (at); **salir caro** [de dinero] to be expensive; [por las consecuencias] to be costly - 10. [parecerse]: **salir a alguien** to turn out like sb, to take after sb - 11. [en juegos] to lead; **te toca salir a ti** it's your lead - 12. [quitarse - manchas] to come out - 13. [librarse]: **salir de** [gen] to get out of; [problema] to get round - 14. INFORM: **salir (de)** to quit, to exit. ➡ **salirse** *vprnl* - 1. [marcharse - de lugar, asociación etc]: **salirse (de)** to leave - 2. [filtrarse]: **salirse (por)** [líquido, gas] to leak O escape (through); [humo, aroma] to come out (through) - 3. [rebosar] to overflow; [leche] to boil over; **el río se salió del cauce** the river broke its banks - 4. [desviarse]: **salirse (de)** to come off; **el coche se salió de la carretera** the car came off O left the road - **5.** *fig* [escaparse]: **salirse de** [gen] to deviate from; [límites] to go beyond; **salirse del tema** to digress - **6.** *loc*: **salirse con la suya** to get one's own way. ➤ **salir adelante** *vi* - **1.** [persona, empresa] to get by - **2.** [proyecto, propuesta, ley] to be successful.

salitre *sm* saltpetre.

saliva *sf* saliva; **tragar saliva** *fig* to bite one's tongue.

salmo *sm* psalm.

salmón ◇ *sm* [pez] salmon. ◇ *adj* & *sm inv* [color] salmon (pink).

salmonete *sm* red mullet.

salmuera *sf* brine.

salobre *adj* salty.

salón *sm* - **1.** [habitación - en casa] lounge, sitting room; **salón comedor** living room-dining room; [- en residencia, edificio público] reception hall - **2.** [local - de sesiones etc] hall; **salón de actos** assembly hall - **3.** [feria] show, exhibition; **salón de exposiciones** exhibition hall - **4.** [establecimiento] shop; **salón de belleza/masaje** beauty/massage parlour; **salón de té** tearoom.

salpicadera *sf* *Méx* mudguard *UK*, fender *US*.

salpicadero *sm* dashboard.

salpicar *vt* [rociar] to splash.

salpimentar *vt* to season with salt and pepper.

salpullido = sarpullido.

salsa *sf* - **1.** [CULIN - gen] sauce; [- de carne] gravy; **salsa bearnesa/tártara** bearnaise/tartar sauce; **salsa rosa** thousand island dressing; **salsa de tomate** tomato sauce; **en su propia salsa** *fig* in one's element - **2.** *fig* [interés] spice - **3.** MÚS salsa.

salsera *sf* gravy boat.

saltamontes *sm inv* grasshopper.

saltar ◇ *vt* - **1.** [obstáculo] to jump (over) - **2.** [omitir] to skip, to miss out. ◇ *vi* - **1.** [gen] to jump; **saltar de alegría** to jump for joy; [a la comba] to skip; [al agua] to dive; **saltar sobre alguien** [abalanzarse] to set upon sb; **saltar de un tema a otro** to jump (around) from one subject to another - **2.** [levantarse] to jump up; **saltar de la silla** to jump out of one's seat - **3.** [salir para arriba - objeto] to jump (up); [- champán, aceite] to spurt (out); [- corcho, válvula] to pop out - **4.** [explotar] to explode, to blow up - **5.** [romperse] to break - **6.** [reaccionar violentamente] to explode. ➤ **saltarse** *vprnl* - **1.** [omitir] to skip, to miss out - **2.** [salir despedido] to pop off - **3.** [no respetar - cola, semáforo] to jump; [- ley, normas] to break.

salteado, da *adj* - **1.** CULIN sautéed - **2.** [espaciado] unevenly spaced.

salteador, ra *sm, f*: **salteador de caminos** highwayman.

saltear *vt* CULIN to sauté.

saltimbanqui *smf* acrobat.

salto *sm* - **1.** [gen & DEP] jump; [grande] leap; [al agua] dive; **levantarse de un salto** to leap to sb's feet; **dar** *O* **pegar un salto** to jump; [grande] to leap - **2.** *fig* [diferencia, omisión] gap - **3.** *fig* [progreso] leap forward. ➤ **salto de agua** *sm* waterfall. ➤ **salto de cama** *sm* negligée.

saltón, ona *adj* [ojos] bulging; [dientes] sticking out.

salubre *adj* healthy.

salud ◇ *sf* *lit* & *fig* health. ◇ *interj*: ¡salud! [para brindar] cheers!; ¡a su salud! your health!; [después de estornudar] bless you!

saludable *adj* - **1.** [sano] healthy - **2.** *fig* [provechoso] beneficial.

saludar *vt* to greet; MIL to salute; **saludar con la mano a alguien** to wave to sb; **saluda a Ana de mi parte** give my regards to Ana; **le saluda atentamente** yours faithfully. ➤ **saludarse** *vprnl* to greet one another.

saludo *sm* greeting; MIL salute; **retirarle el saludo a alguien** to stop speaking to sb; **Ana te manda saludos** [en cartas] Ana sends you her regards; [al teléfono] Ana says hello; **un saludo afectuoso** [en cartas] yours sincerely; **saludos** best regards.

salva *sf* MIL salvo; **una salva de aplausos** *fig* a round of applause.

salvación *sf* - **1.** [remedio]: **no tener salvación** to be beyond hope - **2.** [rescate] rescue - **3.** RELIG salvation.

salvado *sm* bran.

salvador, ra *sm, f* [persona] saviour. ➤ **Salvador** *sm* GEOGR: **El Salvador** El Salvador.

salvadoreño, ña *adj* & *sm, f* Salvadoran.

salvaguardar *vt* to safeguard.

salvaje ◇ *adj* - **1.** [gen] wild - **2.** [pueblo, tribu] savage. ◇ *smf* - **1.** [primitivo] savage - **2.** [bruto] maniac.

salvamanteles *sm inv* [llano] table mat; [con pies] trivet.

salvamento *sm* rescue, saving; **equipo de salvamento** rescue team.

salvar *vt* - **1.** [gen & INFORM] to save; **salvar algo/a alguien de algo** to save sthg/sb from sthg - **2.** [rescatar] to rescue - **3.** [superar - moralmente] to overcome; [- físicamente] to go over *O* around - **4.** [recorrer] to cover - **5.** [exceptuar]: **salvando algunos detalles** except for a few details. ➤ **salvarse** *vprnl* - **1.** [librarse] to escape - **2.** RELIG to be saved.

salvavidas ◇ *adj inv* life (antes de s). ◇ *sm* [chaleco] lifejacket; [flotador] lifebelt.

salvedad *sf* exception.

salvia *sf* sage.

salvo, va *adj* safe; **estar a salvo** to be safe; **poner algo a salvo** to put sthg in a safe place. ➡ **salvo** *adv* except; **salvo que** unless.

salvoconducto *sm* safe conduct, pass.

san *adj* Saint; **san José** Saint Joseph.

sanar ◇ *vt* [persona] to cure; [herida] to heal. ◇ *vi* [persona] to get better; [herida] to heal.

sanatorio *sm* sanatorium, nursing home.

sanción *sf* [castigo] punishment; ECON sanction.

sancionar *vt* [castigar] to punish.

sandalia *sf* sandal.

sandez *sf* silly thing, nonsense (U); **decir sandeces** to talk nonsense.

sandía *sf* watermelon.

sándwich ['sanwitʃ] (*pl* **sándwiches**) *sm* - 1. [con pan de molde] sandwich - 2. *Amér* [con pan de barra] filled baguette - 3. *C Sur* [feriado] day(s) taken off between two public holidays.

saneamiento *sm* - 1. [higienización - de edificio] disinfection - 2. *fig* & FIN [- de moneda etc] stabilization; [- de economía] putting back on a sound footing.

sanear *vt* - 1. [higienizar - tierras] to drain; [- un edificio] to disinfect - 2. *fig* & FIN [- moneda] to stabilize; [- economía] to put back on a sound footing.

sanfermines *smpl festival held in Pamplona when bulls are run through the streets of the town.*

sangrar ◇ *vi* to bleed. ◇ *vt* - 1. [sacar sangre] to bleed - 2. IMPR to indent.

sangre *sf* blood; **no llegó la sangre al río** it didn't get too nasty. ➡ **sangre fría** *sf* sangfroid; **a sangre fría** in cold blood.

sangría *sf* - 1. [bebida] sangria - 2. MED bloodletting - 3. *fig* [ruina] drain.

sangriento, ta *adj* [ensangrentado, cruento] bloody.

sanguijuela *sf lit & fig* leech.

sanguinario, ria *adj* bloodthirsty.

sanguíneo, a *adj* blood (antes de s).

sanidad *sf* - 1. [salubridad] health, healthiness - 2. [servicio] public health; [ministerio] health department.

sanitario, ria *adj* health (antes de s). ➡ **sanitarios** *smpl* [instalación] bathroom fittings *pl*.

San José *n pr* San José.

sano, na *adj* - 1. [saludable] healthy; **sano y salvo** safe and sound - 2. [positivo - principios, persona etc] wholesome; [- ambiente, educación] wholesome - 3. [entero] intact.

San Salvador *n pr* San Salvador.

santería *sf Amér* [tienda] *shop selling religious mementoes such as statues of saints.*

santero, ra *adj* pious.

Santiago (de Chile) *n pr* Santiago.

santiamén ➡ **en un santiamén** *loc adv* *fam* in a flash.

santidad *sf* saintliness, holiness.

santiguar *vt* to make the sign of the cross over. ➡ **santiguarse** *vprnl* [persignarse] to cross o.s.

santo, ta ◇ *adj* - 1. [sagrado] holy - 2. [virtuoso] saintly - 3. *fam fig* [dichoso] damn; **todo el santo día** all day long. ◇ *sm, f* RELIG saint. ➡ **santo** *sm* - 1. [onomástica] saint's day - 2. *loc:* **¿a santo de qué?** why on earth? ➡ **santo y seña** *sm* MIL password.

Santo Domingo *n pr* Santo Domingo.

santuario *sm* shrine; *fig* sanctuary.

saña *sf* viciousness, malice.

sapo *sm* toad; **echar sapos y culebras** *fig* to rant and rave.

saque *sm* - 1. [en fútbol]: **saque de banda** throw-in; **saque inicial** O **de centro** kick-off - 2. [en tenis etc] serve.

saquear *vt* - 1. [rapiñar - ciudad] to sack; [- tienda etc] to loot - 2. *fam* [vaciar] to ransack.

saqueo *sm* [de ciudad] sacking; [de tienda etc] looting.

sarao *sm* [fiesta] party.

sarcasmo *sm* sarcasm.

sarcástico, ca *adj* sarcastic.

sarcófago *sm* sarcophagus.

sardana *sf traditional Catalan dance and music.*

sardina *sf* sardine; **como sardinas en canasta** O **en lata** like sardines.

sardónico, ca *adj* sardonic.

sargento *smf* MIL ≃ sergeant.

sarpullido, salpullido *sm* rash.

sarro *sm* [de dientes] tartar.

sarta *sf lit & fig* string; **una sarta de mentiras** a pack of lies.

sartén *sf* frying pan; **tener la sartén por el mango** to be in control.

sastre, tra *sm, f* tailor.

sastrería *sf* [oficio] tailoring; [taller] tailor's (shop).

Satanás *sm* Satan.

satélite ◇ *sm* satellite. ◇ *adj fig* satellite (antes de s).

satén *sm* satin; [de algodón] sateen.

satinado, da *adj* glossy.

sátira *sf* satire.

satírico, ca ◇ *adj* satirical. ◇ *sm, f* satirist.

satirizar *vt* to satirize.

satisfacción *sf* satisfaction.

satisfacer vt - **1.** [gen] to satisfy; [sed] to quench - **2.** [deuda, pago] to pay, to settle - **3.** [ofensa, daño] to redress - **4.** [duda, pregunta] to answer - **5.** [cumplir - requisitos, exigencias] to meet.

satisfactorio, ria adj satisfactory.

satisfecho, cha ◇ pp ▷ **satisfacer**. ◇ adj satisfied; **satisfecho de sí mismo** self-satisfied; **darse por satisfecho** to be satisfied.

saturar vt to saturate. ◆ **saturarse** vprnl: **saturarse (de)** to become saturated (with).

saturnismo sm lead poisoning.

Saturno n pr Saturn.

sauce sm willow; **sauce llorón** weeping willow.

sauna sf sauna.

savia sf sap; fig vitality; **savia nueva** fig new blood.

saxo sm [instrumento] sax.

saxófono, saxofón sm [instrumento] saxophone.

sazón sf - **1.** [madurez] ripeness; **en sazón** ripe - **2.** [sabor] seasoning. ◆ **a la sazón** loc adv then, at that time.

sazonado, da adj seasoned.

sazonar vt to season.

scanner [es'kaner] = **escáner**.

scout [es'kaut] (pl **scouts**) sm scout.

SCT sf (abrev de **Secretaría de Comunicaciones y Transportes**) Mexican Department of Communication and Transport.

se pron pers - **1.** (reflexivo) [de personas] himself (f herself, pl themselves); [usted mismo] yourself (pl yourselves); [de cosas, animales] itself (pl themselves); **se está lavando, está lavándose** she is washing (herself); **se lavó los dientes** she cleaned her teeth; **espero que se diviertan** I hope you enjoy yourselves; **el perro se lame** the dog is licking itself; **se lame la herida** it's licking its wound; **se levantaron y se fueron** they got up and left - **2.** (reflexivo impersonal) oneself; **hay que afeitarse todos los días** one has to shave every day, you have to shave every day - **3.** (recíproco) each other, one another; **se aman** they love each other; **se escriben cartas** they write to each other - **4.** [en construcción pasiva]: **se ha suspendido la reunión** the meeting has been cancelled; **'se prohíbe fumar'** 'no smoking'; **'se habla inglés'** 'English spoken' - **5.** (impersonal): **en esta sociedad ya no se respeta a los ancianos** in our society old people are no longer respected; **se dice que...** it is said that..., people say that... - **6.** (en vez de 'le' o 'les' antes de 'lo', 'la', 'los' o 'las') (complemento indirecto) [gen] to him (f to her, pl to them); [de cosa, animal] to it (pl to them); [usted, ustedes] to you; **se lo dio** he gave it to him/her etc; **se lo dije, pero no me hizo caso** I told her, but she didn't listen; **si usted quiere, yo se lo arreglo en un minuto** if you like, I'll sort it out for you in a minute.

sé ▷ **saber**.

SE sf (abrev de **Secretaría de Economía**) Mexican Department of Economy.

sebo sm fat; [para jabón, velas] tallow.

secador sm dryer; **secador de pelo** hair-dryer.

secadora sf clothes O tumble dryer.

secar vt - **1.** [desecar] to dry - **2.** [enjugar] to wipe away; [con fregona] to mop up. ◆ **secarse** vprnl [gen] to dry up; [ropa, vajilla, suelo] to dry.

sección sf - **1.** [gen & GEOM] section - **2.** [departamento] department.

seccionar vt - **1.** [cortar] to cut; TECNOL to section - **2.** [dividir] to divide (up).

secesión sf secession.

seco, ca adj - **1.** [gen] dry; [plantas, flores] withered; [higos, pasas] dried; **lavar en seco** to dry-clean - **2.** [tajante] brusque - **3.** loc: **dejar a alguien seco** [matar] to kill sb stone dead; [pasmar] to stun sb; **parar en seco** to stop dead. ◆ **a secas** loc adv simply, just; **llámame Juan a secas** just call me Juan.

secretaría sf - **1.** [oficina, lugar] secretary's office - **2.** [organismo] secretariat; **secretaría general** general secretariat.

secretariado sm EDUC secretarial skills pl; **curso desecretariado** secretarial course.

secretario, ria sm, f secretary.

secreto, ta adj [gen] secret; [tono] confidential; **en secreto** in secret. ◆ **secreto** sm - **1.** [gen] secret; **guardar un secreto** to keep a secret; **secreto bancario** banking confidentiality; **declarar el secreto de sumario** to deny access to information regarding a judicial enquiry - **2.** [sigilo] secrecy.

secta sf sect.

sector sm - **1.** [gen] sector; [grupo] group - **2.** [zona] area.

secuaz smf despec minion.

secuela sf consequence.

secuencia sf sequence.

secuestrador, ra sm, f - **1.** [de persona] kidnapper - **2.** [de avión] hijacker.

secuestrar vt - **1.** [raptar] to kidnap - **2.** [avión] to hijack - **3.** [embargar] to seize.

secuestro sm - **1.** [rapto] kidnapping - **2.** [de avión, barco] hijack - **3.** [de bienes etc] seizure, confiscation.

secular adj - **1.** [seglar] secular, lay - **2.** [centenario] age-old.

secundar vt to support, to back (up); [propuesta] to second.

secundario, ria *adj* secondary. ➠ **secundaria** *sf* secondary education.

secuoya *sf* sequoia.

sed ◇ *v* ▷ **ser**. ◇ *sf* thirst; **el calor da sed** heat makes you thirsty; **tener sed** to be thirsty.

seda *sf* silk.

sedal *sm* fishing line.

sedante ◇ *adj* MED sedative; [música] soothing. ◇ *sm* sedative.

sede *sf* - 1. [emplazamiento] headquarters *pl*; [de gobierno] seat; **sede social** head office - 2. [de campeonato] host - 3. RELIG see. ➠ **Santa Sede** *sf*: **la Santa Sede** the Holy See.

sedentario, ria *adj* sedentary.

sedición *sf* sedition.

sediento, ta *adj* - 1. [de agua] thirsty - 2. *fig* [deseoso]: **sediento de** hungry for.

sedimentar *vt* to deposit. ➠ **sedimentarse** *vprnl* [líquido] to settle.

sedimento *sm* - 1. [poso] sediment - 2. GEOL deposit.

sedoso, sa *adj* silky.

seducción *sf* - 1. [cualidad] seductiveness - 2. [acción - gen] attraction, charm; [- sexual] seduction.

seducir *vt* - 1. [atraer] to attract, to charm; [sexualmente] to seduce - 2. [persuadir]: **seducir a alguien para que haga algo** to tempt sb to do sthg.

seductor, ra ◇ *adj* [gen] charming; [sexualmente] seductive; [persuasivo] tempting. ◇ *sm, f* seducer.

segador, ra *sm, f* [agricultor] reaper.

segar *vt* - 1. AGRIC to reap - 2. [cortar] to cut off - 3. *fig* [truncar] to put an end to.

seglar *sm* lay person.

segmento *sm* - 1. GEOM & ZOOL segment - 2. [trozo] piece - 3. [sector] sector.

segregación *sf* - 1. [separación, discriminación] segregation; **segregación racial** racial segregation - 2. [secreción] secretion.

segregar *vt* - 1. [separar, discriminar] to segregate - 2. [secretar] to secrete.

seguidilla *sf* - 1. (*gen pl*) [baile] *traditional Spanish dance* - 2. [cante] *mournful flamenco song*.

seguido, da *adj* - 1. [consecutivo] consecutive; **diez años seguidos** ten years in a row - 2. [sin interrupción - gen] one after the other; [- línea, pitido etc] continuous. ➠ **seguido** *adv* - 1. [inmediatamente después] straight after - 2. [en línea recta] straight on - 3. *Amér* [frecuentemente] often. ➠ **en seguida** *loc adv* straight away, at once; **en seguida nos vamos** we're going in a minute.

seguidor, ra *sm, f* follower.

seguimiento *sm* [de noticia] following; [de clientes] follow-up.

seguir ◇ *vt* - 1. [gen] to follow; **seguir de cerca algo** to follow sthg closely; **seguir de cerca a alguien** to tail sb - 2. [perseguir] to chase - 3. [reanudar] to continue, to resume. ◇ *vi* - 1. [sucederse]: **seguir a algo** to follow sthg; **a la tormenta siguió la lluvia** the storm was followed by rain - 2. [continuar] to continue, to go on; **seguir adelante** to carry on; **¡sigue! ¡no te pares!** go O carry on, don't stop!; **sigo trabajando en la fábrica** I'm still working at the factory; **debes seguir haciéndolo** you should keep on O carry on doing it; **sigo pensando que está mal** I still think it's wrong; **sigue enferma/en el hospital** she's still ill/at the hospital. ➠ **seguirse** *vprnl* to follow; **seguirse de algo** to follow O be deduced from sthg; **de esto se sigue que estás equivocado** it therefore follows that you are wrong.

según ◇ *prep* - 1. [de acuerdo con] according to; **según su opinión, ha sido un éxito** in his opinion O according to him, it was a success; **según yo/tú** *etc* in my/your *etc* opinion - 2. [dependiendo de] depending on; **según la hora que sea** depending on the time. ◇ *adv* - 1. [como] (just) as; **todo permanecía según lo recordaba** everything was just as she remembered it; **actuó según se le recomendó** he did as he had been advised - 2. [a medida que] as; **entrarás en forma según vayas entrenando** you'll get fit as you train - 3. [dependiendo]: **¿te gusta la música? - según** do you like music? - it depends; **lo intentaré según esté de tiempo** I'll try to do it, depending on how much time I have. ➠ **según que** *loc adv* depending on whether. ➠ **según qué** *loc adj* certain; **según qué días la clase es muy aburrida** some days the class is really boring.

segunda ▷ **segundo**.

segundero *sm* second hand.

segundo, da ◇ *num* & *adj* second. ◇ *num m y f* - 1. [en orden]: **el segundo** the second one; **llegó el segundo** he came second - 2. [mencionado antes]: **vinieron Pedro y Juan, el segundo con...** Pedro and Juan arrived, the latter with... - 3. [ayudante] number two; **segundo de abordo** NÁUT first mate. ➠ **segundo** *sm* - 1. [gen] second - 2. [piso] second floor. ➠ **segunda** *sf* - 1. AUTO second (gear); **meter la segunda** to go into second (gear) - 2. AERON & FERROC second class; **viajar en segunda** to travel second class - 3. DEP second division. ➠ **con segundas** *loc adv* with an ulterior motive.

seguramente *adv* probably; **seguramente iré, pero aún no lo sé** the chances are I'll go, but I'm not sure yet.

seguridad *sf* - 1. [fiabilidad, ausencia de peligro] safety; [protección, estabilidad] security; **de se-**

guridad [cinturón, cierre] safety *(antes de s)*; [puerta, guardia] security *(antes de s)*; **seguridad ciudadana** public safety; **seguridad vial** road safety - **2.** [certidumbre] certainty; **con seguridad** for sure, definitely - **3.** [confianza] confidence; **seguridad en sí mismo** self-confidence. ◆ **Seguridad Social** *sf* Social Security.

seguro, ra *adj* - **1.** [fiable, sin peligro] safe; [protegido, estable] secure - **2.** [infalible - prueba, negocio etc] reliable - **3.** [confiado] sure; **estar seguro de algo** to be sure about sthg - **4.** [indudable - nombramiento, fecha etc] definite, certain; **tener por seguro que** to be sure that - **5.** [con aplomo] self-confident; **estar seguro de sí mismo** to be self-confident. ◆ **seguro** ⬦ *sm* - **1.** [contrato] insurance (U); **seguro a todo riesgo/a terceros** comprehensive/third party insurance; **seguro de incendios/de vida** fire/life insurance; **seguro del coche** car insurance; **seguro de invalidez** *O* **incapacidad** disability insurance; **seguro mutuo** joint insurance; **seguro de vida** life insurance - **2.** [dispositivo] safety device; [de armas] safety catch - **3.** *Amér C & Méx* [imperdible] safety pin. ⬦ *adv* for sure, definitely; **seguro que vendrá** she's bound to come.

seis ⬦ *num & adj inv* - **1.** [para contar] six; **tiene seis años** she's six (years old) - **2.** [para ordenar] (number) six; **la página seis** page six. ⬦ *num m* - **1.** [número] six; **el seis** number six; **doscientos seis** two hundred and six; **treinta y seis** thirty-six - **2.** [en fechas] sixth; **el seis de agosto** the sixth of August - **3.** [en direcciones]: **calle Mayor (número) seis** number six calle Mayor - **4.** [en naipes] six; **el seis de diamantes** the six of diamonds; **echar** *O* **tirar un seis** to play a six. ⬦ *num & smpl* - **1.** [referido a grupos]: **invité a diez y sólo vinieron seis** I invited ten and only six came along; **somos seis** there are six of us; **de seis en seis** in sixes; **los seis** the six of them - **2.** [en temperaturas]: **estamos a seis bajo cero** the temperature is six below zero - **3.** [en puntuaciones]: **empatar a seis** to draw six all; **seis a cero** six-nil. ⬦ *num f pl* [hora]: **las seis** six o'clock; **son las seis** it's six o'clock.

seiscientos, tas *num* six hundred; *ver también* **seis**.

seísmo *sm* earthquake.

selección *sf* - **1.** [gen] selection; [de personal] recruitment - **2.** [equipo] team; **selección nacional** national team.

seleccionador, ra *sm, f* - **1.** DEP selector, ≃ manager - **2.** [de personal] recruiter.

seleccionar *vt* to pick, to select.

selectividad *sf* [examen] university entrance examination.

selectivo, va *adj* selective.

selecto, ta *adj* - **1.** [excelente] fine, excellent - **2.** [escogido] exclusive, select.

self-service [self'serβis] *sm inv* self-service restaurant.

sellar *vt* - **1.** [timbrar] to stamp - **2.** [lacrar] to seal.

sello *sm* - **1.** [gen] stamp - **2.** [tampón] rubber stamp - **3.** [lacre] seal - **4.** *Andes & Ven* [de monedas] tails - **5.** *fig* [carácter] hallmark.

selva *sf* [gen] jungle; [bosque] forest.

semáforo *sm* traffic lights *pl*.

semana *sf* week; **entre semana** during the week; **la semana próxima/que viene** next week; **semana laboral** working week. ◆ **Semana Santa** *sf* Easter; RELIG Holy Week.

semanada *sf Amér* (weekly) pocket money.

semanal *adj* weekly.

semanario, ria *adj* weekly. ◆ **semanario** *sm* [publicación semanal] weekly.

semántico, ca *adj* semantic. ◆ **semántica** *sf* semantics (U).

semblante *sm* countenance, face.

semblanza *sf* portrait, profile.

sembrado, da *adj fig* [lleno]: **sembrado de** scattered *O* plagued with.

sembrar *vt* - **1.** [plantar] to sow; **sembrar algo de algo** to sow sthg with sthg - **2.** *fig* [llenar] to scatter - **3.** *fig* [confusión, pánico etc] to sow.

semejante ⬦ *adj* - **1.** [parecido]: **semejante (a)** similar (to) - **2.** [tal] such; **jamás aceptaría semejante invitación** I would never accept such an invitation. ⬦ *sm (gen pl)* fellow (human) being.

semejanza *sf* similarity; **a semejanza de** similar to.

semejar *vt* to resemble. ◆ **semejarse** *vprnl* to be alike.

semen *sm* semen.

semental *sm* stud; [caballo] stallion.

semestral *adj* half-yearly, six-monthly.

semestre *sm* period of six months, semester US; **cada semestre** every six months.

semidirecto *adj* express.

semifinal *sf* semifinal.

semilla *sf* seed.

seminario *sm* - **1.** [escuela para sacerdotes] seminary - **2.** EDUC - curso, conferencia] seminar; [- departamento] department.

sémola *sf* semolina.

Sena *sm*: **el Sena** the (river) Seine.

senado *sm* senate.

senador, ra *sm, f* senator.

sencillez *sf* - **1.** [facilidad] simplicity - **2.** [modestia] unaffectedness - **3.** [discreción] plainness.

sencillo, lla *adj* - **1.** [fácil, sin lujo, llano] simple - **2.** [campechano] unaffected - **3.** [billete, unidad etc] single. ◆ **sencillo** *sm* - **1.** [disco] single - **2.** *Andes, Amér C & Méx fam* [cambio] loose change.

senda *sf* = **sendero.**

sendero *sm* path.

sendos, das *adj pl* each, respective; **llegaron los dos con sendos paquetes** they arrived each carrying a parcel, they both arrived with their respective parcels.

Senegal *n pr*: **(el) Senegal** Senegal.

senil *adj* senile.

sénior (*pl* **seniores**) *adj inv* & *sm* senior.

seno *sm* - **1.** [pecho] breast - **2.** [pechera] bosom; **en el seno de** *fig* within - **3.** [útero]: **seno (materno)** womb - **4.** *fig* [amparo, cobijo] refuge, shelter - **5.** ANAT [de la nariz] sinus.

sensación *sf* - **1.** [percepción] feeling, sensation - **2.** [efecto] sensation - **3.** [premonición] feeling.

sensacional *adj* sensational.

sensacionalista *adj* sensationalist.

sensatez *sf* wisdom, common sense.

sensato, ta *adj* sensible.

sensibilidad *sf* - **1.** [perceptibilidad] feeling - **2.** [sentimentalismo] sensitivity; **tener la sensibilidad a flor de piel** to be very sensitive - **3.** [don especial] feel - **4.** [de emulsión fotográfica, balanza etc] sensitivity.

sensibilizar *vt* - **1.** [concienciar] to raise the awareness of - **2.** FOTO to sensitize.

sensible *adj* - **1.** [gen] sensitive - **2.** [evidente] perceptible; [pérdida] significant.

sensiblero, ra *adj despec* mushy, sloppy.

sensitivo, va *adj* - **1.** [de los sentidos] sensory - **2.** [receptible] sensitive.

sensor *sm* sensor; **sensor de humo** smoke detector.

sensorial *adj* sensory.

sensual *adj* sensual.

sentado, da *adj* - **1.** [en asiento] seated; **estar sentado** to be sitting down - **2.** [establecido]: **dar algo por sentado** to take sthg for granted; **dejar sentado que...** to make it clear that...

sentar ◇ *vt* - **1.** [en asiento] to seat, to sit - **2.** [establecer] to establish. ◇ *vi* - **1.** [ropa, color] to suit - **2.** [comida]: **sentar bien/mal a alguien** to agree/disagree with sb - **3.** [vacaciones, medicamento]: **sentar bien a alguien** to do sb good - **4.** [comentario, consejo]: **le sentó mal** it upset her; **le sentó bien** she appreciated it. ◆ **sentarse** *vprnl* to sit down.

sentencia *sf* - **1.** DER sentence - **2.** [proverbio, máxima] maxim.

sentenciar *vt* DER: **sentenciar (a alguien a algo)** to sentence (sb to sthg).

sentido, da *adj* [profundo] heartfelt. ◆ **sentido** *sm* - **1.** [gen] sense; **en cierto sentido** in a sense; **en sentido literal** in a literal sense; **tener sentido** to make sense; **sentido común** common sense; **sentido del humor** sense of humour; **sexto sentido** sixth sense - **2.** [conocimiento] consciousness - **3.** [significado] meaning, sense; **doble sentido** double meaning - **4.** [dirección] direction; **de sentido único** one-way.

sentimental *adj* sentimental.

sentimentaloide *adj* mushy, sloppy.

sentimiento *sm* - **1.** [gen] feeling - **2.** [pena, aflicción]: **le acompaño en el sentimiento** my deepest sympathy.

sentir ◇ *vt* - **1.** [gen] to feel - **2.** [lamentar] to regret, to be sorry about; **siento que no puedas venir** I'm sorry you can't come; **lo siento (mucho)** I'm (really) sorry - **3.** [oír] to hear. ◇ *sm* feelings *pl*, sentiments *pl*. ◆ **sentirse** *vprnl* to feel; **me siento mareada** I feel sick.

seña *sf* [gesto, indicio, contraseña] sign, signal. ◆ **señas** *sfpl* - **1.** [dirección] address *sing*; **señas personales** (personal) description *sing* - **2.** [gesto, indicio] signs; **dar señas de algo** to show signs of sthg; **(hablar) por señas** (to talk) in sign language; **hacer señas (a alguien)** to signal (to sb) - **3.** [detalle] details; **para O por más señas** to be precise.

señal *sf* - **1.** [gen & TELECOM] signal; **señal de alarma/salida** alarm/starting signal; [de teléfono] tone; **señal de ocupado** engaged tone, búsy signal *US* - **2.** [indicio, símbolo] sign; **dar señales de vida** to show signs of life; **señal de la Cruz** sign of the Cross; **señal de tráfico** road sign; **en señal de** as a mark O sign of - **3.** [marca, huella] mark; **no dejó ni señal** she didn't leave a trace - **4.** [cicatriz] scar, mark - **5.** [fianza] deposit.

señalado, da *adj* [importante - fecha] special; [- personaje] distinguished.

señalar *vt* - **1.** [marcar, denotar] to mark; [hora, temperatura etc] to indicate, to say - **2.** [indicar - con el dedo, con un comentario] to point out - **3.** [fijar] to set, to fix.

señalización *sf* - **1.** [conjunto de señales] signs *pl*; **señalización vial** roadsigns *pl* - **2.** [colocación de señales] signposting.

señalizar *vt* to signpost.

señor, ra *adj* [refinado] noble, refined. ◆ **señor** *sm* - **1.** [tratamiento - antes de nombre, cargo] Mr; [- al dirigir la palabra] Sir; **el señor López** Mr López; **¡señor presidente!** Mr President!; **¿qué desea el señor?** what would you like, Sir?; **Muy señor mío** [en cartas] Dear Sir - **2.** [hombre] man - **3.** [caballero] gentleman - **4.** [dueño] owner - **5.** [amo - de criado] master. ◆ **señora** *sf* - **1.** [tratamiento - antes de nombre, cargo] Mrs; [- al dirigir la palabra] Madam; **la señora López** Mrs López; **¡señora presidenta!** Madam President!; **¿qué desea la señora?** what would you like, Madam?; **¡señoras y señores!...** Ladies and Gentlemen!...; **Estimada señora** [en cartas] Dear Madam - **2.** [mujer] lady; **señora de la limpieza** cleaning woman - **3.** [dama] lady - **4.** [dueña] owner - **5.** [ama - de criado] mistress - **6.** [esposa] wife. ➤ **señores** *smpl* [matrimonio]: **los señores Ruiz** Mr & Mrs Ruiz.

señoría *sf* lordship (*f* ladyship); **su señoría** [gen] his lordship; [a un noble] your lordship; [a un parlamentario] the right honourable gentleman/lady; [a un juez] your Honour.

señorial *adj* [majestuoso] stately.

señorío *sm* - **1.** [dominio] dominion, rule - **2.** [distinción] nobility.

señorito, ta *adj fam despec* [refinado] lordly. ➤ **señorito** *sm* - **1.** *desus* [hijo del amo] master - **2.** *fam despec* [niñato] rich kid. ➤ **señorita** *sf* - **1.** [soltera, tratamiento] Miss - **2.** [joven] young lady - **3.** [maestra]: **la señorita** miss, the teacher - **4.** *desus* [hija del amo] mistress.

señuelo *sm* - **1.** [reclamo] decoy - **2.** *fig* [trampa] bait, lure.

SEP *sf* (*abrev de* **Secretaría de Educación Pública**) *Mexican Department of Public Education.*

sepa *etc* ⊳ **saber.**

separación *sf* - **1.** [gen] separation - **2.** [espacio] space, distance.

separado, da *adj* - **1.** [gen] separate; **está muy separado de la pared** it's too far away from the wall; **por separado** separately - **2.** [del cónyuge] separated.

separar *vt* - **1.** [gen] to separate; **separar algo de** to separate sthg from - **2.** [desunir] to take off, to remove - **3.** [apartar - silla etc] to move away - **4.** [reservar] to put aside - **5.** [destituir]: **separar de** to remove *O* dismiss from. ➤ **separarse** *vprnl* - **1.** [apartarse] to move apart - **2.** [ir por distinto lugar] to part company - **3.** [matrimonio]: **separarse (de alguien)** to separate (from sb) - **4.** [desprenderse] to come away *O* off.

separatismo *sm* separatism.

separo *sm Méx* (prison) cell.

sepia *sf* [molusco] cuttlefish.

septentrional *adj* northern.

septiembre, setiembre *sm* September; **el 1 de septiembre** the 1st of September; **uno de los septiembres más lluviosos de la última década** one of the rainiest Septembers in the last decade; **a principios/mediados/finales de septiembre** at the beginning/in the middle/ at the end of September; **el pasado/próximo (mes de) septiembre** last/next September; **en septiembre** in September; **en pleno septiem-**

bre in mid-September; **este (mes de) septiembre** [pasado] (this) last September; [próximo] next September, this coming September; **para septiembre** by September.

séptimo, ma, sétimo, ma *num* seventh.

septuagésimo, ma *num* seventieth.

sepulcral *adj fig* [profundo - voz, silencio] lugubrious, gloomy.

sepulcro *sm* tomb.

sepultar *vt* to bury.

sepultura *sf* - **1.** [enterramiento] burial; **dar sepultura a alguien** to bury sb - **2.** [fosa] grave.

sepulturero, ra *sm, f* gravedigger.

sequedad *sf* - **1.** [falta de humedad] dryness - **2.** *fig* [antipatía] brusqueness.

sequía *sf* drought.

séquito *sm* [comitiva] retinue, entourage.

ser ⟨⟩ *v aux* (*antes de pp forma la voz pasiva*) to be; **fue visto por un testigo** he was seen by a witness. ⟨⟩ *v cop* - **1.** [gen] to be; **es alto/ gracioso** he is tall/funny; **es azul/difícil** it's blue/difficult; **es un amigo/el dueño** he is a friend/the owner - **2.** [empleo, dedicación] to be; **soy abogado/actriz** I'm a lawyer/an actress; **son estudiantes** they're students. ⟨⟩ *vi* - **1.** [gen] to be; **fue aquí** it was here; **lo importante es decidirse** the important thing is to reach a decision; **ser de** [estar hecho de] to be made of; [provenir de] to be from; [ser propiedad de] to belong to; [formar parte de] to be a member of; **¿de dónde eres?** where are you from?; **los juguetes son de mi hijo** the toys are my son's - **2.** [con precios, horas, números] to be; **¿cuánto es?** how much is it?; **son 30 euros** that'll be 30 euros; **¿qué (día) es hoy?** what day is it today?, what's today?; **mañana será 15 de julio** tomorrow (it) will be the 15th of July; **¿qué hora es?** what time is it?, what's the time?; **son las tres (de la tarde)** it's three o'clock (in the afternoon), it's three (pm) - **3.** [servir, ser adecuado]: **ser para** to be for; **este trapo es para (limpiar) las ventanas** this cloth is for (cleaning) the windows; **este libro es para niños** this book is (meant) for children - **4.** *(uso partitivo)*: **ser de los que...** to be one of those (people) who...; **ése es de los que están en huelga** he is one of those on strike. ⟨⟩ *v impers* - **1.** [expresa tiempo] to be; **es muy tarde** it's rather late; **era de noche/de día** it was night/day - **2.** [expresa necesidad, posibilidad]: **es de desear que...** it is to be hoped that...; **es de suponer que aparecerá** presumably, he'll turn up - **3.** [expresa motivo]: **es que no vine porque estaba enfermo** the reason I didn't come is that I was ill - **4.** *loc*: **a no ser que** unless; **como sea** one way or another, somehow or other; **de no ser por** had it not been for; **érase una vez, érase que se era** once upon a time; **no es para menos** not without reason; **o sea** that is (to say), I mean; **por si fuera poco** as if that wasn't enough. ◇ *sm* [ente] being; **ser humano/vivo** human/living being

Serbia *n pr* Serbia.

serenar *vt* [calmar] to calm. ◆ **serenarse** *vprnl* [calmarse] to calm down.

serenata *sf* MÚS serenade.

serenidad *sf* - 1. [tranquilidad] calm - 2. [quietud] tranquility.

sereno, na *adj* calm. ◆ **sereno** *sm* [vigilante] night watchman.

serial *sm* serial.

serie *sf* - 1. [gen & TV] series *sing*; [de hechos, sucesos] chain; [de mentiras] string - 2. [de sellos, monedas] set - 3. *loc*: **ser un fuera de serie** to be unique. ◆ **de serie** *loc adj* [equipamiento] (fitted) as standard. ◆ **en serie** *loc adv* [fabricación]: **fabricar en serie** to mass-produce.

seriedad *sf* - 1. [gravedad] seriousness - 2. [responsabilidad] sense of responsibility - 3. [formalidad - de persona] reliability.

serio, ria *adj* - 1. [gen] serious; **estar serio** to look serious - 2. [responsable, formal] responsible - 3. [sobrio] sober. ◆ **en serio** *loc adv* seriously; **lo digo en serio** I'm serious; **tomar(se) algo/a alguien en serio** to take sthg/sb seriously.

sermón *sm* lit & fig sermon; **echar un sermón por algo** to give a lecture for sthg.

seropositivo, va ◇ *adj* MED HIV-positive. ◇ *sm, f* MED HIV-positive person.

serpentear *vi* - 1. [río, camino] to wind - 2. [culebra] to wriggle.

serpentina *sf* streamer.

serpiente *sf* [culebra] snake; LITER serpent.

serranía *sf* mountainous region.

serrano, na *adj* - 1. [de la sierra] mountain *(antes de s)* - 2. [jamón] cured.

serrar *vt* to saw (up).

serrín *sm* sawdust.

serrucho *sm* handsaw.

servicial *adj* attentive, helpful.

servicio *sm* - 1. [gen] service; **fuera de servicio** out of order; **servicio de inteligencia** O **secreto** intelligence O secret service; **servicio de mesa** dinner service; **servicio militar** military service; **servicio de té** tea set - 2. [servidumbre] servants *pl* - 3. [turno] duty - 4. *(gen pl)* [WC] toilet, lavatory, bathroom US - 5. DEP serve, service.

servidor, ra *sm, f* - 1. [en cartas]: **su seguro servidor** yours faithfully - 2. [yo] yours truly, me. ◆ **servidor** *sm* INFORM server; **servidor seguro** secure server.

servidumbre *sf* - 1. [criados] servants *pl* - 2. [dependencia] servitude.

servil *adj* servile.

servilleta *sf* serviette, napkin.

servilletero *sm* serviette O napkin ring.

servir ◇ *vt* to serve; **sírvanos dos cervezas** bring us two beers; **¿te sirvo más patatas?** would you like some more potatoes?; **¿en qué puedo servirle?** what can I do for you? ◇ *vi* - 1. [gen] to serve; **servir en el gobierno** to be a government minister - 2. [valer, ser útil] to serve, to be useful; **no sirve para estudiar** he's no good at studying; **de nada sirve que se lo digas** it's no use telling him; **servir de algo** to serve as sthg. ◆ **servirse** *vprnl* - 1. [aprovecharse]: **servirse de** to make use of; **sírvase llamar cuando quiera** please call whenever you want - 2. [comida, bebida] to help o.s.

sésamo *sm* sesame.

sesenta *num* sixty; **los (años) sesenta** the sixties; *ver también* **seis**.

sesgo *sm* - 1. [oblicuidad] slant - 2. *fig* [rumbo] course, path - 3. [enfoque] bias.

sesión *sf* - 1. [reunión] meeting, session; DER sitting, session; **abrir/levantar la sesión** to open/to adjourn the meeting - 2. [proyección, representación] show, performance; **sesión continua** continuous showing; **sesión matinal** matinée; **sesión de tarde** afternoon matinée; **sesión de noche** evening showing - 3. [periodo] session.

seso *(gen pl) sm* - 1. [cerebro] brain - 2. [sensatez] brains *pl*, sense; **calentarse** O **devanarse los sesos** to rack one's brains; **sorber el seso** O **los sesos a alguien** to brainwash sb.

sesudo, da *adj* [inteligente] brainy.

set *(pl sets) sm* DEP set.

seta *sf* mushroom; **seta venenosa** toadstool.

setecientos, tas *num* seven hundred; *ver también* **seis**.

setenta *num* seventy; **los (años) setenta** the seventies; *ver también* **seis**.

setiembre = septiembre.

sétimo = séptimo.

seto *sm* fence; **seto vivo** hedge.

seudónimo *sm* pseudonym.

severidad *sf* - 1. [rigor] severity - 2. [intransigencia] strictness.

severo, ra *adj* - 1. [castigo] severe, harsh - 2. [persona] strict.

Sevilla *n pr* Seville.

sevillano, na *adj & sm, f* Sevillian. ◆ **sevillanas** *sfpl* Andalusian dance and song.

sexagésimo, ma *num* sixtieth.

sexista *adj & smf* sexist.

sexo *sm* [gen] sex; **sexo tántrico** tantric sex.

sexteto *sm* MÚS sextet.

sexto, ta *num* sixth.

sexual *adj* [gen] sexual; [educación, vida] sex *(antes de s)*.

sexualidad *sf* sexuality.

sha [sa, ʃa] *sm* shah.

shock = **choc**.

shorts [ʃorts] *smpl* shorts.

show [ʃou] *(pl* shows) *sm* show; **montar un show** *fig* to cause a scene.

si¹ *(pl* sis) *sm* MÚS B; [en solfeo] ti.

si² *conj* - **1.** *(condicional)* if; **si viene él yo me voy** if he comes, then I'm going; **si hubieses venido te habrías divertido** if you had come, you would have enjoyed yourself - **2.** *(en oraciones interrogativas indirectas)* if, whether; **ignoro si lo sabe** I don't know if O whether she knows - **3.** [expresa protesta] but; **¡si te dije que no lo hicieras!** but I told you not to do it!

sí *(pl* síes) ◇ *adv* - **1.** [afirmación] yes; **¿vendrás? - sí, iré** will you come? - yes, I will; **claro que sí** of course; **creo que sí** I think so; **¿están de acuerdo? - algunos sí** do they agree? - some do - **2.** [uso enfático]: **sí que** really, certainly; **sí que me gusta** I really O certainly like it - **3.** *loc:* **no creo que puedas hacerlo - ¡a que sí!** I don't think you can do it - I bet I can!; **¿sí?** [incredulidad] really? ◇ *pron pers* - **1.** *(reflexivo)* [de personas] himself (*f* herself, *pl* themselves); [usted] yourself (*pl* yourselves); [de cosas, animales] itself (*pl* themselves); **lo quiere todo para sí (misma)** she wants everything for herself; **se acercó la silla hacia sí** he drew the chair nearer (himself); **de (por) sí** [cosa] in itself - **2.** *(reflexivo impersonal)* oneself; **cuando uno piensa en sí mismo** when one thinks about oneself, when you think about yourself. ◇ *sm* consent; **dar el sí** to give one's consent.

siamés, esa *adj* Siamese. ◆ **siamés** *sm* [gato] Siamese.

Siberia *n pr:* (la) Siberia Siberia.

Sicilia *n pr* Sicily.

sicoanalista = **psicoanalista**.

sicodélico = **psicodélico**.

sicología = **psicología**.

sicológico = **psicológico**.

sicólogo, ga = **psicólogo**.

sicópata = **psicópata**.

sicosis = **psicosis**.

sicosomático = **psicosomático**.

sida *(abrev de* síndrome de inmunodeficiencia adquirida) *sm* AIDS.

siderurgia *sf* iron and steel industry.

siderúrgico, ca *adj* iron and steel *(antes de s)*.

sidra *sf* cider.

siega *sf* - **1.** [acción] reaping, harvesting - **2.** [época] harvest (time).

siembra *sf* - **1.** [acción] sowing - **2.** [época] sowing time.

siempre *adv* [gen] always; **como siempre** as usual; **de siempre** usual; **lo de siempre** the usual; **somos amigos de siempre** we've always been friends; **es así desde siempre** it has always been that way; **para siempre, para siempre jamás** for ever and ever. ◆ **siempre que** *loc conj* - **1.** [cada vez que] whenever - **2.** [con tal de que] provided that, as long as. ◆ **siempre y cuando** *loc conj* provided that, as long as.

sien *sf* temple.

sienta *etc* ▷ **sentar, sentir**.

sierra *sf* - **1.** [herramienta] saw - **2.** [cordillera] mountain range - **3.** [región montañosa] mountains *pl*.

siervo, va *sm, f* - **1.** [esclavo] serf - **2.** RELIG servant.

siesta *sf* siesta, nap; **dormir** O **echarse la siesta** to have an afternoon nap.

siete ◇ *num* seven. ◇ *sf* R Dom *fig*: **de la gran siete** amazing, incredible; **¡la gran siete!** *fam* sugar! *UK*, shoot! *US*; *ver también* **seis**.

sífilis *sf inv* syphilis.

sifón *sm* - **1.** [agua carbónica] soda (water) - **2.** [tubo] siphon.

sigilo *sm* [gen] secrecy; [al robar, escapar] stealth.

sigiloso, sa *adj* [discreto] secretive; [al robar, escapar] stealthy.

siglas *sfpl* acronym.

siglo *sm* - **1.** [cien años] century; **el siglo XX** the 20th century; **el siglo III antes de Cristo** the third century before Christ - **2.** *fig* [mucho tiempo]: **hace siglos que no la veo** I haven't seen her for ages.

signatura *sf* - **1.** [en biblioteca] catalogue number - **2.** [firma] signature.

significación *sf* - **1.** [importancia] significance - **2.** [significado] meaning.

significado, da *adj* important. ◆ **significado** *sm* [sentido] meaning.

significar ◇ *vt* - **1.** [gen] to mean - **2.** [expresar] to express. ◇ *vi* [tener importancia]: **no significa nada para mí** it means nothing to me.

significativo, va *adj* significant.

signo *sm* - **1.** [gen] sign; **signo de multiplicar/dividir** multiplication/division sign; **signo del zodiaco** sign of the zodiac - **2.** [en la escritura] mark; **signo de admiración/interrogación** exclamation/question mark - **3.** [símbolo] symbol.

sigo *etc* ▷ **seguir**.

siguiente <> *adj* - **1.** [en el tiempo, espacio] next - **2.** [a continuación] following. <> *smf* - **1.** [el que sigue]: **el siguiente** the next one; **¡el siguiente!** next, please! - **2.** [lo que sigue]: **lo siguiente** the following.

sílaba *sf* syllable.

silbar <> *vt* - **1.** [gen] to whistle - **2.** [abuchear] to hiss. <> *vi* - **1.** [gen] to whistle - **2.** [abuchear] to hiss - **3.** *fig* [oídos] to ring.

silbato *sm* whistle.

silbido, silbo *sm* - **1.** [gen] whistle - **2.** [para abuchear, de serpiente] hiss, hissing *(U)*.

silenciador *sm* silencer.

silenciar *vt* to hush up, to keep quiet.

silencio *sm* - **1.** [gen] silence; **guardar silencio (sobre algo)** to keep silent (about sthg); **reinaba el silencio más absoluto** there was complete silence; **romper el silencio** to break the silence - **2.** MÚS rest.

silencioso, sa *adj* silent, quiet.

silicona *sf* silicone.

silla *sf* - **1.** [gen] chair; **silla de ruedas** wheelchair; **silla eléctrica** electric chair; **silla de tijera** folding chair - **2.** [de caballo]: **silla (de montar)** saddle.

sillín *sm* saddle, seat.

sillón *sm* armchair.

silueta *sf* - **1.** [cuerpo] figure - **2.** [contorno] outline - **3.** [dibujo] silhouette.

silvestre *adj* wild.

simbólico, ca *adj* symbolic.

simbolizar *vt* to symbolize.

símbolo *sm* symbol.

simetría *sf* symmetry.

simiente *sf culto* seed.

símil *sm* - **1.** [paralelismo] similarity, resemblance - **2.** LITER simile.

similar *adj*: **similar (a)** similar (to).

similitud *sf* similarity.

simio, mia *sm, f* simian, ape.

simpatía *sf* - **1.** [cordialidad] friendliness - **2.** [cariño] affection; **coger simpatía a alguien** to take a liking to sb; **tener simpatía a, sentir simpatía por** to like - **3.** MED sympathy.

simpático, ca *adj* - **1.** [gen] nice, likeable; [abierto, cordial] friendly; **Juan me cae simpático** I like Juan - **2.** [anécdota, comedia etc] amusing, entertaining - **3.** [reunión, velada etc] pleasant, agreeable.

simpatizante *smf* sympathizer.

simpatizar *vi*: **simpatizar (con)** [persona] to hit it off (with); [cosa] to sympathize (with).

simple <> *adj* - **1.** [gen] simple - **2.** [fácil] easy, simple - **3.** [único, sin componentes] single; **dame una simple razón** give me one single reason - **4.** [mero] mere; **por simple estupidez** through sheer stupidity. <> *smf* [persona] simpleton.

simplemente *adv* simply.

simpleza *sf* - **1.** [de persona] simple-mindedness - **2.** [tontería] trifle.

simplicidad *sf* simplicity.

simplificar *vt* to simplify.

simplista *adj* simplistic.

simposio, simposium *sm* symposium.

simulacro *sm* simulation; **simulacro de combate** mock battle; **simulacro de incendio** fire drill.

simular *vt* - **1.** [sentimiento, desmayo etc] to feign; **simuló que no me había visto** he pretended not to have seen me - **2.** [enfermedad] to fake - **3.** [combate, salvamento] to simulate.

simultáneo, nea *adj* simultaneous.

sin *prep* without; **sin alcohol** alcohol-free; **estoy sin un euro** I'm penniless; **ha escrito cinco libros sin (contar) las novelas** he has written five books, not counting his novels; **está sin hacer** it hasn't been done yet; **estamos sin vino** we're out of wine; **sin que (+ subjuntivo)** without (+ gerundio); **sin que nadie se entera** without anyone noticing. **◆ sin embargo** *conj* however.

sinagoga *sf* synagogue.

sincerarse *vprnl*: **sincerarse (con alguien)** to open one's heart (to sb).

sinceridad *sf* sincerity; [llaneza, franqueza] frankness; **con toda sinceridad** in all honesty.

sincero, ra *adj* sincere; [abierto, directo] frank; **para ser sincero** to be honest.

síncope *sm* blackout; **le dio un síncope** she blacked out.

sincronizar *vt* [regular] to synchronize.

sindical *adj* (trade) union *(antes de s)*.

sindicalista *smf* trade unionist.

sindicato *sm* trade union, labor union *US*.

síndrome *sm* syndrome; **síndrome de abstinencia** withdrawal symptoms *pl*; **síndrome de clase turista** economy-class syndrome; **síndrome de Down** Down's syndrome; **síndrome de inmunodeficiencia adquirida** acquired immune deficiency syndrome; **síndrome premenstrual** premenstrual syndrome; **síndrome tóxico** *toxic syndrome caused by ingestion of adulterated rapeseed oil.*

sinfín *sm* vast number; **un sinfín de problemas** no end of problems.

sinfonía *sf* symphony.

sinfónico, ca *adj* symphonic. **◆ sinfónica** *sf* symphony orchestra.

Singapur *n pr* Singapore.

single ['siŋgel] *sm* - **1.** single - **2.** *C Sur* [habitación] single room.

singular ◇ *adj* - **1.** [raro] peculiar, odd - **2.** [único] unique - **3.** GRAM singular. ◇ *sm* GRAM singular; **en singular** in the singular.

singularidad *sf* - **1.** [rareza, peculiaridad] peculiarity - **2.** [exclusividad] uniqueness.

singularizar *vt* to distinguish, to single out. ➡ **singularizarse** *vprnl* to stand out; **singularizarse por algo** to stand out because of sthg.

siniestro, tra *adj* - **1.** [perverso] sinister - **2.** [desgraciado] disastrous. ➡ **siniestro** *sm* disaster; [accidente de coche] accident, crash; [incendio] fire.

sinnúmero *sm*: **un sinnúmero de** countless.

sino *conj* - **1.** [para contraponer] but; **no lo hizo él, sino ella** he didn't do it, she did; **no sólo es listo, sino también trabajador** he's not only clever but also hardworking - **2.** [para exceptuar] except, but; **¿quién sino tú lo haría?** who else but you would do it?; **no quiero sino que se haga justicia** I only want justice to be done.

sinónimo, ma *adj* synonymous; **ser sinónimo de algo** to be synonymous with sthg. ➡ **sinónimo** *sm* synonym.

sinopsis *sf inv* synopsis.

síntesis *sf inv* synthesis; **en síntesis** in short; **síntesis del habla** INFORM & LING speech synthesis.

sintético, ca *adj* [artificial] synthetic.

sintetizador, ra *adj* synthesizing. ➡ **sintetizador** *sm* synthesizer.

sintetizar *vt* - **1.** [resumir] to summarize - **2.** [fabricar artificialmente] to synthesize.

sintiera *etc* ⤷ **sentir**.

síntoma *sm* symptom.

sintonía *sf* - **1.** [música] signature tune - **2.** [conexión] tuning - **3.** *fig* [compenetración] harmony; **en sintonía con** in tune with.

sintonizar ◇ *vt* [conectar] to tune in to. ◇ *vi* - **1.** [conectar]: **sintonizar (con)** to tune in (to) - **2.** *fig* [compenetrarse]: **sintonizar en algo (con alguien)** to be on the same wavelength (as sb) about sthg.

sinuoso, sa *adj* - **1.** [camino] winding - **2.** [movimiento] sinuous.

sinvergüenza *smf* - **1.** [canalla] rogue - **2.** [fresco, descarado] cheeky person.

sionismo *sm* Zionism.

siquiatra = **psiquiatra**.

siquiátrico = **psiquiátrico**.

síquico = **psíquico**.

siquiera ◇ *conj* [aunque] even if; **ven siquiera por pocos días** do come, even if it's only for a few days. ◇ *adv* [por lo menos] at least; **dime siquiera tu nombre** (you could) at least tell me your name. ➡ **ni (tan) siquiera** *loc conj* not even; **ni (tan) siquiera me hablaron** they didn't even speak to me.

sirena *sf* - **1.** MITOL mermaid, siren - **2.** [señal] siren.

Siria *n pr* Syria.

sirimiri *sm* drizzle.

sirviente, ta *sm, f* servant.

sisa *sf* [en costura] dart; [de manga] armhole.

sisear *vt* & *vi* to hiss.

sísmico, ca *adj* seismic.

sistema *sm* - **1.** [gen & INFORM] system; **sistema monetario/nervioso/solar** monetary/nervous/solar system; **sistema métrico (decimal)** metric (decimal) system; **sistema monetario europeo** European Monetary System; **sistema montañoso** mountain chain O range; **sistema periódico de los elementos** periodic table of elements - **2.** [método, orden] method. ➡ **por sistema** *loc adv* systematically.

Sistema Ibérico *sm*: **el Sistema Ibérico** the Iberian mountain chain.

sistemático, ca *adj* systematic.

sistematizar *vt* to systematize.

sitiar *vt* [cercar] to besiege.

sitio *sm* - **1.** [lugar] place; **cambiar de sitio (con alguien)** to change places (with sb); **en otro sitio** elsewhere; **poner a alguien en su sitio** to put sb in his/her place - **2.** [espacio] room, space; **hacer sitio a alguien** to make room for sb; **ocupar sitio** to take up space - **3.** [cerco] siege - **4.** INFORM: **sitio Web** Web site - **5.** *Méx* [de taxi] taxi rank *UK* O stand *US*.

situación *sf* - **1.** [circunstancias] situation; [legal, social] status - **2.** [condición, estado] state, condition - **3.** [ubicación] location.

situado, da *adj* - **1.** [acomodado] comfortably off; **estar bien situado** to be well off - **2.** [ubicado] located.

situar *vt* - **1.** [colocar] to place, to put; [edificio, ciudad] to site, to locate - **2.** [en clasificación] to place, to rank - **3.** [localizar] to locate, to find. ➡ **situarse** *vprnl* - **1.** [colocarse] to take up position - **2.** [ubicarse] to be located - **3.** [acomodarse, establecerse] to get o.s. established - **4.** [en clasificación] to be placed; **se sitúa entre los mejores** he's (ranked) amongst the best.

skai [es'kai] = **escay**.

ski [es'ki] = **esquí**.

SL (*abrev de sociedad limitada*) *sf* ≃ Ltd.

slip [es'lip] *sm* briefs *pl*.

slogan [es'loɣan] = **eslogan**.

smoking [es'mokin] = **esmoquin**.

s/n (*abrev de sin número*) *abbreviation used in addresses after the street name, where the building has no number.*

snob = **esnob**.

snowboard *sm* snowboard *m*.

so <> *prep* under; **so pretexto de** under; **so pena de** under penalty of. <> *adv:* **¡so tonto!** you idiot! <> *interj:* **¡so!** whoa!

sobaco *sm* armpit.

sobado, da *adj* - **1.** [cuello, puños etc] worn, shabby; [libro] dog-eared - **2.** *fig* [argumento, excusa] hackneyed. **sobado** *sm* CULIN shortcrust pastry.

sobar *vt* - **1.** [tocar] to finger, to paw - **2.** *despec* [acariciar, besar] to touch up.

soberanía *sf* sovereignty.

soberano, na <> *adj* - **1.** [independiente] sovereign - **2.** *fig* [grande] massive; [paliza] thorough; [belleza, calidad] unrivalled. <> *sm, f* sovereign.

soberbio, bia *adj* - **1.** [arrogante] proud, arrogant - **2.** [magnífico] superb. **soberbia** *sf* - **1.** [arrogancia] pride, arrogance - **2.** [magnificencia] grandeur.

sobornar *vt* to bribe.

soborno *sm* - **1.** [acción] bribery - **2.** [dinero, regalo] bribe.

sobra *sf* excess, surplus; **lo sabemos de sobra** we know it only too well. **sobras** *sfpl* [de comida] leftovers.

sobrado, da *adj* - **1.** [de sobra] more than enough, plenty of - **2.** [de dinero] well off.

sobrante *adj* remaining.

sobrar *vi* - **1.** [quedar, restar] to be left over; **nos sobró comida** we had some food left over - **2.** [haber de más] to be more than enough; **parece que van a sobrar bocadillos** it looks like there are going to be too many sandwiches - **3.** [estar de más] to be superfluous; **lo que dices sobra** that goes without saying.

sobrasada *sf Mallorcan spiced sausage.*

sobre¹ *sm* - **1.** [para cartas] envelope - **2.** [para alimentos] sachet, packet.

sobre² *prep* - **1.** [encima de] on (top of); **el libro está sobre la mesa** the book is on (top of) the table - **2.** [por encima de] over, above; **el pato vuela sobre el lago** the duck is flying over the lake - **3.** [acerca de] about, on; **un libro sobre el amor** a book about *O* on love; **una conferencia sobre el desarme** a conference on disarmament - **4.** [alrededor de] about; **llegarán sobre las diez** they'll arrive at about ten o'clock - **5.** [acumulación] upon; **nos contó mentira sobre mentira** he told us lie upon lie *O* one lie after another - **6.** [cerca de] upon; **la desgracia estaba ya sobre nosotros** the disaster was already upon us.

sobrecarga *sf* - **1.** [exceso de carga] excess weight - **2.** [saturación] overload.

sobrecargo *sm* [de avión] purser.

sobrecoger *vt* - **1.** [asustar] to startle - **2.** [impresionar] to move. **sobrecogerse** *vprnl* - **1.** [asustarse] to be startled - **2.** [impresionarse] to be moved.

sobredosis *sf inv* overdose.

sobreentender = sobrentender.

sobregiro *sm* COM overdraft.

sobremesa *sf* after-dinner period; **de sobremesa** [programación etc] mid-afternoon *(antes de s).*

sobrenatural *adj* [extraordinario] supernatural.

sobrenombre *sm* nickname.

sobrentender, sobreentender *vt* to understand, to deduce. **sobrentenderse** *vprnl* to be inferred *O* implied.

sobrepasar *vt* - **1.** [exceder] to exceed - **2.** [aventajar]: **sobrepasar a alguien** to overtake sb. **sobrepasarse** *vprnl* to go too far.

sobrepeso *sm* excess weight.

sobreponer = superponer. **sobreponerse** *vprnl:* **sobreponerse a algo** to overcome sthg.

sobreproducción, superproducción *sf* ECON overproduction *(U).*

sobrepuesto, ta <> *adj* **= superpuesto**. <> *pp* ☞ **sobreponer**.

sobresaliente <> *adj* [destacado] outstanding. <> *sm* [en escuela] excellent, ≃ A; [en universidad] ≃ first class.

sobresalir *vi* - **1.** [en tamaño] to jut out - **2.** [en importancia] to stand out.

sobresaltar *vt* to startle. **sobresaltarse** *vprnl* to be startled, to start.

sobresalto *sm* start, fright.

sobrestimar *vt* to overestimate.

sobretodo *sm Amér* overcoat.

sobrevenir *vi* to happen, to ensue; **sobrevino la guerra** the war intervened.

sobreviviente = superviviente.

sobrevivir *vi* to survive.

sobrevolar *vt* to fly over.

sobriedad *sf* - **1.** [moderación] restraint, moderation - **2.** [no embriaguez] soberness.

sobrino, na *sm, f* nephew *(f* niece*).*

sobrio, bria *adj* - **1.** [moderado] restrained - **2.** [no excesivo] simple - **3.** [austero, no borracho] sober.

socarrón, ona *adj* sarcastic.

socavar *vt* [excavar por debajo] to dig under; *fig* [debilitar] to undermine.

socavón *sm* [hoyo] hollow; [en la carretera] pothole.

sociable *adj* sociable.

social *adj* - 1. [gen] social - 2. COM company (*antes de s*).

socialdemócrata *smf* social democrat.

socialismo *sm* socialism.

socialista *adj* & *smf* socialist.

sociedad *sf* - 1. [gen] society; **sociedad de consumo** consumer society; **sociedad deportiva** sports club; **sociedad literaria** literary society - 2. COM [empresa] company; **sociedad anónima** public (limited) company *UK*, incorporated company *US*; **sociedad (de responsabilidad) limitada** private limited company.

socio, cia *sm, f* - 1. COM partner - 2. [miembro] member.

sociología *sf* sociology.

sociólogo, ga *sm, f* sociologist.

socorrer *vt* to help.

socorrismo *sm* first aid; [en la playa] lifesaving.

socorrista *smf* first aid worker; [en la playa] lifeguard.

socorro <> *sm* help, aid. <> *interj*: ¡socorro! help!

soda *sf* [bebida] soda water, club soda *US*.

sodio *sm* sodium.

soez *adj* vulgar, dirty.

sofá *sm* sofa; **sofá cama** O **nido** sofa bed.

sofisticación *sf* sophistication.

sofisticado, da *adj* sophisticated.

sofocar *vt* - 1. [ahogar] to suffocate - 2. [incendio] to put out - 3. *fig* [rebelión] to quell - 4. *fig* [avergonzar] to mortify. ◆ **sofocarse** *vprnl* - 1. [ahogarse] to suffocate - 2. *fig* [irritarse]: **sofocarse (por)** to get hot under the collar (about).

sofoco *sm* - 1. [ahogo] breathlessness (*U*); [sonrojo, bochorno] hot flush - 2. *fig* [vergüenza] mortification - 3. *fig* [disgusto]: **llevarse un sofoco** to have a fit.

sofreír *vt* to fry lightly over a low heat.

sofrito, ta *pp* ⊳ **sofreír**. ◆ **sofrito** *sm* fried tomato and onion sauce.

software ['sofwer] *sm* INFORM software.

soga *sf* rope; [para ahorcar] noose.

sois ⊳ **ser**.

soja *sf* soya.

sol *sm* - 1. [astro] sun; **a pleno sol** in the sun; **al salir/ponerse el sol** at sunrise/sunset; **hace sol** it's sunny; **no dejar a alguien ni a sol ni a sombra** not to give sb a moment's peace - 2. [rayos, luz] sunshine, sun; **tomar el sol** to sunbathe - 3. MÚS G; [en solfeo] so - 4. [moneda] sol.

solamente *adv* only, just; **vino solamente él** only he came.

solapa *sf* - 1. [de prenda] lapel - 2. [de libro, sobre] flap.

solapado, da *adj* underhand, devious.

solar <> *adj* solar. <> *sm* undeveloped plot (of land).

solárium (*pl* **soláriums**), **solario** *sm* solarium.

solazar *vt* - 1. to amuse, to entertain - 2. [aliviar] to solace, to entertain.

soldada *sf* pay.

soldado *sm* soldier; **soldado raso** private.

soldador, ra *sm, f* [persona] welder. ◆ **soldador** *sm* [aparato] soldering iron.

soldar *vt* to solder, to weld.

soleado, da *adj* sunny.

soledad *sf* loneliness; **en soledad** alone; *culto* solitude.

solemne *adj* - 1. [con pompa] formal - 2. [grave] solemn - 3. *fig* [enorme] utter.

solemnidad *sf* [suntuosidad] pomp, solemnity; **de solemnidad** extremely.

soler *vi*: **soler hacer algo** to do sthg usually; **aquí suele llover mucho** it usually rains a lot here; **solíamos ir a la playa cada día** we used to go to the beach every day.

solera *sf* - 1. [tradición] tradition - 2. [del vino] sediment; **de solera** vintage - 3. *C Sur* [vestido] sundress - 4. *Chile* [de acera] kerb.

solfeo *sm* MÚS solfeggio, singing of scales.

solicitar *vt* - 1. [pedir] to request; [un empleo] to apply for; **solicitar algo a** O **de alguien** to request sthg of sb - 2. [persona] to pursue; **estar muy solicitado** to be very popular, to be much sought after.

solícito, ta *adj* solicitous, obliging.

solicitud *sf* - 1. [petición] request; **presentar una solicitud** to submit a request - 2. [documento] application - 3. [atención] care.

solidaridad *sf* solidarity; **en solidaridad con** in solidarity with.

solidario, ria *adj* - 1. [adherido]: **solidario (con)** sympathetic (to), supporting (of) - 2. [obligación, compromiso] mutually binding.

solidez *sf* [física] solidity.

solidificar *vt* to solidify. ◆ **solidificarse** *vprnl* to solidify.

sólido, da *adj* - 1. [gen] solid; [cimientos, fundamento] firm - 2. [argumento, conocimiento, idea] sound. ◆ **sólido** *sm* solid.

soliloquio *sm* soliloquy.

solista <> *adj* solo. <> *smf* soloist.

solitario, ria <> *adj* - 1. [sin compañía] solitary - 2. [lugar] lonely, deserted. <> *sm, f* [persona] loner. ◆ **solitario** *sm* [juego] patience.

sollozar *vi* to sob.

sollozo *sm* sob.

solo, la *adj* - 1. [sin nadie] alone; **dejar solo a alguien** to leave sb alone; **se quedó solo a temprana edad** he was on his own from an early age; **a solas** alone, by oneself - **2.** [sin nada] on its own; [café] black; [whisky] neat - **3.** [único] single, sole; **ni una sola gota** not a (single) drop; **dame una sola cosa** give me just one thing - **4.** [solitario] lonely. **solo** sm MÚS solo.

sólo adv only, just; **no sólo... sino (también)...** not only... but (also)...; **con sólo, sólo con** just by; **sólo que...** only...

solomillo sm sirloin.

soltar vt - **1.** [desasir] to let go of - **2.** [desatar - gen] to unfasten; [- nudo] to untie; [- hebilla, cordones] to undo - **3.** [dejar libre] to release - **4.** [desenrollar - cable etc] to let O pay out - **5.** [patada, grito, suspiro etc] to give; **no suelta ni un duro** you can't get a penny out of her - **6.** [decir bruscamente] to come out with. **soltarse** vprnl - **1.** [desasirse] to break free - **2.** [desatarse] to come undone - **3.** [desprenderse] to come off - **4.** [perder timidez] to let go.

soltero, ra ◇ adj single, unmarried. ◇ sm, f bachelor (f single woman).

solterón, ona ◇ adj unmarried. ◇ sm, f old bachelor (f spinster, old maid).

soltura sf - **1.** [gen] fluency - **2.** [seguridad de sí mismo] assurance.

soluble adj - **1.** [que se disuelve] soluble - **2.** [que se soluciona] solvable.

solución sf solution.

solucionar vt to solve; [disputa] to resolve.

solventar vt - **1.** [pagar] to settle - **2.** [resolver] to resolve.

solvente adj - **1.** [económicamente] solvent - **2.** fig [fuentes etc] reliable.

Somalia n pr Somalia.

sombra sf - **1.** [proyección - fenómeno] shadow; [- zona] shade; **dar sombra a** to cast a shadow over; **tener mala sombra** to be a nasty swine - **2.** [en pintura] shade - **3.** fig [anonimato] background; **permanecer en la sombra** to stay out of the limelight. **sombra de ojos** sf eyeshadow.

sombrero sm [prenda] hat; **quitarse el sombrero** fig to take one's hat off.

sombrilla sf sunshade, parasol; **me vale sombrilla** Méx fig I couldn't care less.

sombrío, bría adj - **1.** [oscuro] gloomy, dark - **2.** fig [triste] sombre, gloomy.

somero, ra adj superficial.

someter vt - **1.** [a rebeldes] to subdue - **2.** [presentar]: **someter algo a la aprobación de alguien** to submit sthg for sb's approval; **someter algo a votación** to put sthg to the vote - **3.** [subordinar] to subordinate - **4.** [a operación, interrogatorio etc]: **someter a alguien a algo** to subject sb to sthg. **someterse** vprnl - **1.** [rendirse] to surrender - **2.** [conformarse]: so-

meterse a algo to yield O bow to sthg - **3.** [a operación, interrogatorio etc]: **someterse a algo** to undergo sthg.

somier (pl **somieres**) sm [de muelles] bed springs pl; [de tablas] slats (of bed).

somnífero, ra adj somniferous. **somnífero** sm sleeping pill.

somos └➤ **ser**.

son sm - **1.** [sonido] sound; **bailar al son que le tocan** fig to toe the line - **2.** [estilo] way; **en son de** in the manner of; **en son de paz** in peace; └➤ **ser**.

sonajero sm rattle.

sonambulismo sm sleepwalking.

sonámbulo, la sm, f sleepwalker.

sonar[1] sm sonar.

sonar[2] vi - **1.** [gen] to sound; **suena a falso/chiste** it sounds false/like a joke; **(así O tal) como suena** literally, in so many words - **2.** [timbre] to ring - **3.** [hora]: **sonaron las doce** the clock struck twelve - **4.** [ser conocido, familiar] to be familiar; **me suena** it rings a bell; **no me suena su nombre** I don't remember hearing her name before - **5.** [pronunciarse - letra] to be pronounced - **6.** [rumorearse] to be rumoured. **sonarse** vprnl to blow one's nose.

sonda sf - **1.** MED & TECNOL probe - **2.** NÁUT sounding line - **3.** [en una mina] drill, bore.

sondear vt - **1.** [indagar] to sound out - **2.** [terreno] to test; [roca] to drill.

sondeo sm - **1.** [encuesta] (opinion) poll - **2.** [de un terreno] drilling (U) - **3.** NÁUT sounding.

sonido sm sound.

sonoro, ra adj - **1.** [gen] sound (antes de s); [película] talking - **2.** [ruidoso, resonante, vibrante] resonant.

sonreír vi [reír levemente] to smile. **sonreírse** vprnl to smile.

sonriente adj smiling.

sonrisa sf smile.

sonrojar vt to cause to blush. **sonrojarse** vprnl to blush.

sonrojo sm blush, blushing (U).

sonrosado, da adj rosy.

sonsacar vt: **sonsacar algo a alguien** [conseguir] to wheedle sthg out of sb; [hacer decir] to extract sthg from sb; **sonsacar a alguien** to pump sb for information.

sonso, sa ◇ adj Amér fam foolish, silly. ◇ sm, f fool, idiot.

soñador, ra sm, f dreamer.

soñar ◇ vt lit & fig to dream; **¡ni soñarlo!** not on your life! ◇ vi lit & fig: **soñar (con)** to dream (of O about).

soñoliento, ta adj sleepy, drowsy.

sopa *sf* - **1.** [guiso] soup - **2.** [de pan] *piece of soaked bread.*

sopapo *sm fam* slap.

sopero, ra *adj* soup *(antes de s).* ◆ **sopera** *sf* [recipiente] soup tureen.

sopesar *vt* to try the weight of; *fig* to weigh up.

sopetón ◆ **de sopetón** *loc adv* suddenly, abruptly.

soplar ◇ *vt* - **1.** [vela, fuego] to blow out - **2.** [ceniza, polvo] to blow off - **3.** [globo etc] to blow up - **4.** [vidrio] to blow - **5.** *fig* [pregunta, examen] to prompt. ◇ *vi* [gen] to blow.

soplete *sm* blowlamp.

soplido *sm* blow, puff.

soplo *sm* - **1.** [soplido] blow, puff - **2.** MED murmur - **3.** *fam* [chivatazo] tip-off.

soplón, ona *sm, f fam* grass.

soponcio *sm fam* fainting fit; **le dio un soponcio** [desmayo] she passed out; [ataque] she had a fit.

sopor *sm* drowsiness.

soporífero, ra *adj lit & fig* soporific.

soportar *vt* - **1.** [sostener] to support - **2.** [resistir, tolerar] to stand; **¡no le soporto!** I can't stand him! - **3.** [sobrellevar] to endure, to bear.

soporte *sm* - **1.** [apoyo] support - **2.** INFORM medium; **soporte físico** hardware; **soporte lógico** software.

soprano *smf* soprano.

sor *sf* RELIG sister.

sorber *vt* - **1.** [beber] to sip; [haciendo ruido] to slurp - **2.** [absorber] to soak up - **3.** [atraer] to draw O suck in.

sorbete *sm* sorbet.

sorbo *sm* [acción] gulp, swallow; **beber algo de un sorbo** to drink sthg in one gulp; [pequeño] sip; **beber a sorbos** to sip.

sordera *sf* deafness.

sórdido, da *adj* - **1.** [miserable] squalid - **2.** [obsceno, perverso] sordid.

sordo, da ◇ *adj* - **1.** [que no oye] deaf - **2.** [ruido, dolor] dull. ◇ *sm, f* [persona] deaf person; **los sordos** the deaf.

sordomudo, da ◇ *adj* deaf and dumb. ◇ *sm, f* deaf-mute.

sorna *sf* sarcasm.

soroche *sm Andes & Arg* altitude sickness.

sorprendente *adj* surprising.

sorprender *vt* - **1.** [asombrar] to surprise - **2.** [atrapar]: **sorprender a alguien (haciendo algo)** to catch sb (doing sthg) - **3.** [coger desprevenido] to catch unawares. ◆ **sorprenderse** *vprnl* to be surprised.

sorprendido, da *adj* surprised; **quedarse sorprendido** to be surprised.

sorpresa *sf* surprise.

sorpresivo, va *adj Amér* unexpected.

sortear *vt* - **1.** [rifar] to raffle - **2.** [echar a suertes] to draw lots for - **3.** *fig* [esquivar] to dodge.

sorteo *sm* - **1.** [lotería] draw - **2.** [rifa] raffle.

sortija *sf* ring.

sortilegio *sm* [hechizo] spell.

SOS *sm* SOS.

sosa *sf* soda.

sosegado, da *adj* calm.

sosegar *vt* to calm. ◆ **sosegarse** *vprnl* to calm down.

soseras *smf inv fam* dull person, bore.

sosias *sm inv* double, lookalike.

sosiego *sm* calm.

soslayo ◆ **de soslayo** *loc adv* [oblicuamente] sideways, obliquely; **mirar a alguien de soslayo** to look at sb out of the corner of one's eye.

soso, sa *adj* - **1.** [sin sal] bland, tasteless - **2.** [sin gracia] dull, insipid.

sospecha *sf* suspicion; **despertar sospechas** to arouse suspicion.

sospechar ◇ *vt* [creer, suponer] to suspect; **sospecho que no lo terminará** I doubt whether she'll finish it. ◇ *vi*: **sospechar de** to suspect.

sospechoso, sa ◇ *adj* suspicious. ◇ *sm, f* suspect.

sostén *sm* - **1.** [apoyo] support - **2.** [sustento] main support; [alimento] sustenance - **3.** [sujetador] bra.

sostener *vt* - **1.** [sujetar] to support, to hold up - **2.** [defender - idea, opinión, tesis] to defend; [- promesa, palabra] to stand by, to keep; **sostener que...** to maintain that... - **3.** [tener - conversación] to hold, to have; [- correspondencia] to keep up. ◆ **sostenerse** *vprnl* to hold o.s. up; [en pie] to stand up; [en el aire] to hang.

sostenido, da *adj* - **1.** [persistente] sustained - **2.** MÚS sharp.

sota *sf* ≃ jack.

sotana *sf* cassock.

sótano *sm* basement.

soterrar *vt* [enterrar] to bury; *fig* to hide.

soufflé [su'fle] *sm* soufflé.

soul *sm* MÚS soul (music).

soviético, ca ◇ *adj* - **1.** [del soviet] soviet - **2.** [de la URSS] Soviet. ◇ *sm, f* Soviet.

soy ▷ **ser.**

spaghetti [espa'yeti] = **espagueti.**

spanglish [es'panglis] *sm* Spanglish.

spot [es'pot], **espot** *sm* advertising spot, commercial.

spray [es'prai] = **espray.**

sprint [es'prin] = **esprint**.

squash [es'kuaʃ] *sm inv* squash.

Sr. (*abrev de señor*) Mr.

Sra. (*abrev de señora*) Mrs.

SRE *sf* (*abrev de* Secretaría de Relaciones Exteriores*) Mexican Department of Foreign Affairs.

Sres. (*abrev de señores*) Messrs.

Srta. (*abrev de señorita*) Miss.

Sta. (*abrev de santa*) St.

standard [es'tandar] = **estándar**.

starter [es'tarter] = **estárter**.

status [es'tatus] = **estatus**.

stereo [es'tereo] = **estéreo**.

Sto. (*abrev de santo*) St.

stock [es'tok] *sm* stock.

stop, estop [es'top] *sm* - 1. AUTO stop sign - 2. [en telegrama] stop.

stress [es'tres] = **estrés**.

strip-tease [es'triptis] *sm inv* striptease.

su (*pl* **sus**) *adj* poses [de él] his; [de ella] her; [de cosa, animal] its; [de uno] one's; [de ellos, ellas] their; [de usted, ustedes] your.

suave *adj* - 1. [gen] soft - 2. [liso] smooth - 3. [sabor, olor, color] delicate - 4. [apacible - persona, carácter] gentle; [- clima] mild - 5. [fácil - cuesta, tarea, ritmo] gentle; [- dirección de un coche] smooth.

suavidad *sf* - 1. [gen] softness - 2. [lisura] smoothness - 3. [de sabor, olor, color] delicacy - 4. [de carácter] gentleness - 5. [de clima] mildness - 6. [de cuesta, tarea, ritmo] gentleness; [de la dirección de un coche] smoothness.

suavizante *sm* conditioner; **suavizante para la ropa** fabric conditioner.

suavizar *vt* - 1. [gen] to soften; [ropa, cabello] to condition - 2. [ascensión, conducción, tarea] to ease; [clima] to make milder - 3. [sabor, olor, color] to tone down - 4. [alisar] to smooth.

subacuático, ca *adj* subaquatic.

subalquilar *vt* to sublet.

subalterno, na *sm, f* [empleado] subordinate.

subasta *sf* - 1. [venta pública] auction; **sacar algo a subasta** to put sthg up for auction - 2. [contrata pública] tender; **sacar algo a subasta** to put sthg out to tender.

subastar *vt* to auction.

subcampeón, ona *sm, f* runner-up.

subconsciente *adj* & *sm* subconscious.

subdesarrollado, da *adj* underdeveloped.

subdesarrollo *sm* underdevelopment.

subdirector, ra *sm, f* assistant manager.

subdirectorio *sm* INFORM subdirectory.

súbdito, ta *sm, f* - 1. [subordinado] subject - 2. [ciudadano] citizen, national.

subdivisión *sf* subdivision.

subestimar *vt* to underestimate; [infravalorar] to underrate. ➣ **subestimarse** *vprnl* to underrate o.s.

subido, da *adj* - 1. [intenso] strong, intense - 2. *fam* [atrevido] risqué. ➣ **subida** *sf* - 1. [cuesta] hill - 2. [ascensión] ascent, climb - 3. [aumento] increase, rise.

subir ◇ *vi* - 1. [a piso, azotea] to go/come up; [a montaña, cima] to climb - 2. [aumentar - precio, temperatura] to go up, to rise; [- cauce, marea] to rise - 3. [montar - en avión, barco] to get on; [- en coche] to get in; **sube al coche** get into the car - 4. [cuenta, importe]: **subir a** to come o amount to - 5. [de categoría] to be promoted. ◇ *vt* - 1. [ascender - calle, escaleras] to go/come up; [- pendiente, montaña] to climb - 2. [poner arriba] to lift up; [llevar arriba] to take/bring up - 3. [aumentar - precio, peso] to put up, to increase; [- volumen de radio etc] to turn up - 4. [montar]: **subir algo/a alguien a** to lift sthg/sb onto - 5. [alzar - mano, bandera, voz] to raise; [- persiana] to roll up; [- ventanilla] to wind up. ➣ **subirse** *vprnl* - 1. [ascender]: **subirse a** [árbol] to climb up; [mesa] to climb onto; [piso] to go/come up to - 2. [montarse]: **subirse a** [tren, avión] to get on, to board; [caballo, bicicleta] to mount; [coche] to get into; **el taxi paró y me subí** the taxi stopped and I got in - 3. [alzarse - pernera, mangas] to roll up; [- cremallera] to do up; [- pantalones, calcetines] to pull up.

súbito, ta *adj* sudden; **de súbito** suddenly.

subjetivo, va *adj* subjective.

sub júdice [suβ'dʒuðiθe] *adj* DER sub judice.

subjuntivo, va *adj* subjunctive. ➣ **subjuntivo** *sm* subjunctive.

sublevación *sf* uprising.

sublevamiento *sm* = **sublevación**.

sublevar *vt* - 1. [amotinar] to stir up - 2. [indignar] to infuriate. ➣ **sublevarse** *vprnl* [amotinarse] to rebel.

sublime *adj* sublime.

submarinismo *sm* skin-diving.

submarinista *smf* skin-diver.

submarino, na *adj* underwater. ➣ **submarino** *sm* submarine.

subnormal ◇ *adj* - 1. *despec* [minusválido] subnormal - 2. *fig* & *despec* [imbécil] moronic. ◇ *smf fig* & *despec* [imbécil] moron.

suboficial *sm* MIL non-commissioned officer.

subordinado, da *adj* & *sm, f* subordinate.

subordinar *vt* [gen & GRAM] to subordinate; **subordinar algo a algo** to subordinate sthg to sthg.

subproducto *sm* by-product.

subrayar *vt lit & fig* to underline.

subsanar *vt* - **1.** [solucionar] to resolve - **2.** [corregir] to correct.

subscribir = **suscribir**.

subscripción = **suscripción**.

subscriptor = **suscriptor**.

subsecretario, **ria** *sm, f* - **1.** [de secretario] assistant secretary - **2.** [de ministro] undersecretary.

subsidiario, **ria** *adj* DER ancillary.

subsidio *sm* benefit, allowance; **subsidio de invalidez** disability allowance; **subsidio de paro** unemployment benefit.

subsiguiente *adj* subsequent.

subsistencia *sf* [vida] subsistence. ◆ **subsistencias** *sfpl* [provisiones] provisions.

subsistir *vi* - **1.** [vivir] to live, to exist - **2.** [sobrevivir] to survive.

substancia = **sustancia**.

substancial = **sustancial**.

substancioso = **sustancioso**.

substantivo = **sustantivo**.

substitución = **sustitución**.

substituir = **sustituir**.

substituto = **sustituto**.

substracción = **sustracción**.

substraer = **sustraer**.

subsuelo *sm* subsoil.

subte *sm* R Dom metro, underground UK, subway US.

subterráneo, **a** *adj* subterranean, underground. ◆ **subterráneo** *sm* - **1.** underground tunnel - **2.** Arg [metro] underground.

subtítulo *sm* [gen & CINE] subtitle.

suburbio *sm* poor suburb.

subvención *sf* subsidy.

subvencionar *vt* to subsidize.

subversión *sf* subversion.

subversivo, **va** *adj* subversive.

subyacer *vi* [ocultarse]: **subyacer bajo algo** to underlie sthg.

subyugar *vt* - **1.** [someter] to subjugate - **2.** fig [dominar] to quell, to master - **3.** fig [atraer] to captivate.

succionar *vt* [suj: raíces] to suck up; [suj: bebé] to suck.

sucedáneo, **a** *adj* ersatz, substitute. ◆ **sucedáneo** *sm* substitute.

suceder ◇ *v impers* [ocurrir] to happen; **suceda lo que suceda** whatever happens. ◇ *vi* [venir después]: **suceder a** to come after, to follow; **a la guerra sucedieron años muy tristes** the war was followed by years of misery.

sucesión *sf* [gen] succession.

sucesivamente *adv* successively; **y así sucesivamente** and so on.

sucesivo, **va** *adj* - **1.** [consecutivo] successive, consecutive - **2.** [siguiente]: **en días sucesivos les informaremos** we'll let you know over the next few days; **en lo sucesivo** in future.

suceso *sm* - **1.** [acontecimiento] event - **2.** *(gen pl)* [hecho delictivo] crime; [incidente] incident; **sección de sucesos** accident and crime reports.

sucesor, **ra** *sm, f* successor.

suciedad *sf* - **1.** [cualidad] dirtiness *(U)* - **2.** [porquería] dirt, filth *(U)*.

sucinto, **ta** *adj* [conciso] succinct.

sucio, **cia** *adj* - **1.** [gen] dirty; [al comer, trabajar] messy; **en sucio** in rough - **2.** [juego] dirty.

suculento, **ta** *adj* tasty.

sucumbir *vi* - **1.** [rendirse, ceder]: **sucumbir (a)** to succumb (to) - **2.** [fallecer] to die - **3.** [desaparecer] to fall.

sucursal *sf* branch.

sudadera *sf* [prenda] sweatshirt.

Sudáfrica *n pr* South Africa.

sudafricano, **na** *adj & sm, f* South African.

Sudán *n pr* Sudan.

sudar *vi* [gen] to sweat.

sudeste, **sureste** ◇ *adj* [posición, parte] southeast, southeastern; [dirección, viento] southeasterly. ◇ *sm* southeast.

sudoeste, **suroeste** ◇ *adj* [posición, parte] southwest, southwestern; [dirección, viento] southwesterly. ◇ *sm* southwest.

sudor *sm* [gen] sweat *(U)*; **sudor frío** cold sweat.

sudoroso, **sa** *adj* sweaty.

Suecia *n pr* Sweden.

sueco, **ca** ◇ *adj* Swedish. ◇ *sm, f* [persona] Swede. ◆ **sueco** *sm* [lengua] Swedish.

suegro, **gra** *sm, f* father-in-law (*f* mother-in-law).

suela *sf* sole; **no llegarle a alguien a la suela del zapato** fig not to hold a candle to sb.

sueldo *sm* salary, wages *pl*; [semanal] wage.

suelo *sm* - **1.** [pavimento - en interiores] floor; [- en el exterior] ground; **caerse al suelo** to fall over; **besar el suelo** to fall flat on one's face - **2.** [terreno, territorio] soil; [para edificar] land - **3.** [base] bottom - **4.** *loc*: **echar por el suelo un plan** to ruin a project; **estar por los suelos** [persona, precio] to be at rock bottom; [productos] to be dirt cheap; **poner O tirar por los suelos** to run down, to criticize; ▷ **soler**.

suelto, **ta** *adj* - **1.** [gen] loose; [cordones] undone; **¿tienes cinco euros sueltos?** have you got five euros in loose change?; **andar suelto** [en libertad] to be free; [en fuga] to be at large; [con diarrea] to have diarrhoea - **2.** [separado] separate; [desparejado] odd; **no los vendemos sueltos** we don't sell them separately

- 3. [arroz] fluffy **- 4.** [lenguaje, estilo] fluent **- 5.** [desenvuelto] comfortable. ◆ **suelto** *sm* [calderilla] loose change.

suena etc ⟶ **sonar**.

sueño *sm* **- 1.** [ganas de dormir] sleepiness; [por medicamento etc] drowsiness; **¡qué sueño!** I'm really sleepy!; **tener sueño** to be sleepy **- 2.** [estado] sleep; **coger el sueño** to get to sleep **- 3.** [imagen mental, objetivo, quimera] dream; **en sueños** in a dream; **ni en sueños** *fig* no way, under no circumstances.

suero *sm* **- 1.** MED serum; **suero artificial** saline solution **- 2.** [de la leche] whey.

suerte *sf* **- 1.** [azar] chance; **echar** O **tirar algo a suertes** to draw lots for sthg; **la suerte está echada** the die is cast **- 2.** [fortuna] luck; **desear suerte a alguien** to wish sb luck; **estar de suerte** to be in luck; **por suerte** luckily; **¡qué suerte!** that was lucky!; **tener (buena) suerte** to be lucky; **tener mala suerte** to be unlucky **- 3.** [destino] fate; **tocar** O **caer en suerte a alguien** to fall to sb's lot; **traer mala suerte** to bring bad luck **- 4.** [situación] situation, lot **- 5.** *culto* [clase]: **toda suerte de** all manner of **- 6.** *culto* [manera] manner, fashion; **de suerte que** in such a way that.

suéter (*pl* **suéteres**) *sm* sweater.

suficiencia *sf* **- 1.** [capacidad] proficiency **- 2.** [presunción] smugness.

suficiente ◇ *adj* **- 1.** [bastante] enough; [medidas, esfuerzos] adequate; **no llevo (dinero) suficiente** I don't have enough (money) on me; **no tienes la estatura suficiente** you're not tall enough **- 2.** [presuntuoso] smug. ◇ *sm* [nota] pass.

sufragar ◇ *vt* [costes] to defray. ◇ *vi Amér* [votar] to vote.

sufragio *sm* suffrage.

sufragista *smf* suffragette.

sufrido, da *adj* **- 1.** [resignado] patient, uncomplaining; [durante mucho tiempo] long-suffering **- 2.** [resistente - tela] hardwearing; [- color] that does not show the dirt.

sufrimiento *sm* suffering.

sufrir ◇ *vt* **- 1.** [gen] to suffer; [accidente] to have **- 2.** [soportar] to bear, to stand; **tengo que sufrir sus manías** I have to put up with his idiosyncrasies **- 3.** [experimentar - cambios etc] to undergo. ◇ *vi* [padecer] to suffer; **sufrir de** [enfermedad] to suffer from; **sufrir del estómago** *etc* to have a stomach *etc* complaint.

sugerencia *sf* suggestion; **hacer una sugerencia** to make a suggestion.

sugerente *adj* evocative.

sugerir *vt* **- 1.** [proponer] to suggest; **sugerir a alguien que haga algo** to suggest that sb should do sthg **- 2.** [evocar] to evoke.

sugestión *sf* suggestion.

sugestionar *vt* to influence.

sugestivo, va *adj* **- 1.** [atrayente] attractive **- 2.** [que sugiere] stimulating, suggesting.

suiche *sm Col & Ven* switch.

suicida ◇ *adj* suicidal. ◇ *smf* [por naturaleza] suicidal person; [suicidado] person who has committed suicide.

suicidarse *vprnl* to commit suicide.

suicidio *sm* suicide.

Suiza *n pr* Switzerland.

suizo, za *adj* & *sm, f* Swiss.

sujeción *sf* **- 1.** [atadura] fastening **- 2.** [sometimiento] subjection.

sujetador *sm* bra.

sujetar *vt* **- 1.** [agarrar] to hold down **- 2.** [aguantar] to fasten; [papeles] to fasten together **- 3.** [someter] to subdue; [a niños] to control. ◆ **sujetarse** *vprnl* **- 1.** [agarrarse]: **sujetarse a** to hold on to, to cling to **- 2.** [aguantarse] to keep in place **- 3.** [someterse]: **sujetarse a** to keep O stick to.

sujeto, ta *adj* **- 1.** [agarrado - objeto] fastened **- 2.** [expuesto]: **sujeto a** subject to. ◆ **sujeto** *sm* **- 1.** [gen & GRAM] subject **- 2.** [individuo] individual; **sujeto pasivo** ECON taxpayer.

sulfato *sm* sulphate.

sulfurar *vt* [encolerizar] to infuriate. ◆ **sulfurarse** *vprnl* [encolerizarse] to get mad.

sultán *sm* sultan.

sultana *sf* sultana.

suma *sf* **- 1.** [MAT - acción] addition; [- resultado] total **- 2.** [conjunto - de conocimientos, datos] total, sum; [- de dinero] sum **- 3.** [resumen]: **en suma** in short.

sumamente *adv* extremely.

sumar *vt* **- 1.** MAT to add together; **sumar algo a algo** to add sthg to sthg; **tres y cinco suman ocho** three and five are O make eight **- 2.** [costar] to come to. ◆ **sumarse** *vprnl* **- 1.**: **sumarse (a)** [unirse] to join (in) **- 2.** [agregarse] to be in addition to.

sumario, ria *adj* **- 1.** [conciso] brief **- 2.** DER summary. ◆ **sumario** *sm* **- 1.** DER indictment **- 2.** [resumen] summary.

sumergible *adj* waterproof.

sumergir *vt* [hundir] to submerge; [con fuerza] to plunge; [bañar] to dip. ◆ **sumergirse** *vprnl* [hundirse] to submerge; [con fuerza] to plunge.

sumidero *sm* drain.

suministrador, ra *sm, f* supplier.

suministrar *vt* to supply; **suministrar algo a alguien** to supply sb with sthg.

suministro *sm* [gen] supply; [acto] supplying.

sumir *vt*: **sumir a alguien en** to plunge sb into. ◆ **sumirse en** *vprnl* - **1.** [depresión, sueño etc] to sink into - **2.** [estudio, tema] to immerse o.s. in.

sumisión *sf* - **1.** [obediencia - acción] submission; [- cualidad] submissiveness - **2.** [rendición] surrender.

sumiso, sa *adj* submissive.

sumo, ma *adj* - **1.** [supremo] highest, supreme - **2.** [gran] extreme, great.

sunnita ◇ *adj* Sunni. ◇ *smf* Sunnite.

suntuoso, sa *adj* sumptuous.

supeditar *vt*: **supeditar (a)** to subordinate (to); **estar supeditado a** to be dependent on. ◆ **supeditarse** *vprnl*: **supeditarse a** to submit to.

súper ◇ *sm fam* supermarket. ◇ *sf*: (gasolina) **súper** ≈ four-star (petrol).

superable *adj* surmountable.

superar *vt* - **1.** [mejorar] to beat; [récord] to break; **superar algo/a alguien en algo** to beat sthg/sb in sthg - **2.** [ser superior] to exceed, to surpass - **3.** [adelantar - corredor] to overtake, to pass - **4.** [época, técnica] **estar superado** to have been superseded - **5.** [vencer - dificultad etc] to overcome. ◆ **superarse** *vprnl* - **1.** [mejorar] to better o.s. - **2.** [lucirse] to excel o.s.

superávit *sm inv* surplus.

superdotado, da *sm, f* extremely gifted person.

superficial *adj lit & fig* superficial.

superficie *sf* - **1.** [gen] surface; **salir a la superficie** to surface - **2.** [área] area.

superfluo, flua *adj* superfluous; [gasto] unnecessary.

superior, ra *sm, f* RELIG superior (*f* mother superior). ◆ **superior** ◇ *adj* - **1.** [de arriba] top - **2.** [mayor] **superior (a)** higher (than) - **3.** [mejor] **superior (a)** superior (to) - **4.** [excelente] excellent - **5.** ANAT & GEOGR upper - **6.** EDUC higher. ◇ *sm (gen pl)* [jefe] superior.

superioridad *sf lit & fig* superiority; **superioridad sobre algo/alguien** superiority over sthg/sb.

superlativo, va *adj* - **1.** [belleza etc] exceptional - **2.** GRAM superlative.

supermercado *sm* supermarket.

superpoblación *sf* overpopulation.

superponer, sobreponer *vt fig* [anteponer]: **superponer algo a algo** to put sthg before sthg.

superpotencia *sf* superpower.

superpuesto, ta,　sobrepuesto, ta ◇ *adj* superimposed. ◇ *pp* ⊳ **superponer**.

supersónico, ca *adj* supersonic.

superstición *sf* superstition.

supersticioso, sa *adj* superstitious.

supervisar *vt* to supervise.

supervisor, ra *sm, f* supervisor.

supervivencia *sf* survival.

superviviente, sobreviviente ◇ *adj* surviving. ◇ *smf* survivor.

supiera *etc* ⊳ **saber**.

suplementario, ria *adj* supplementary, extra.

suplemento *sm* - **1.** [gen & PRENSA] supplement - **2.** [complemento] attachment.

suplente *smf* - **1.** [gen] stand-in - **2.** TEATRO understudy - **3.** DEP substitute.

supletorio, ria *adj* additional, extra. ◆ **supletorio** *sm* TELECOM extension.

súplica *sf* - **1.** [ruego] plea, entreaty - **2.** DER petition.

suplicar *vt* [rogar]: **suplicar algo (a alguien)** to plead for sthg (with sb); **suplicar a alguien que haga algo** to beg sb to do sthg.

suplicio *sm lit & fig* torture.

suplir *vt* - **1.** [sustituir]: **suplir algo/a alguien (con)** to replace sthg/sb (with) - **2.** [compensar]: **suplir algo (con)** to compensate for sthg (with).

supo ⊳ **saber**.

suponer ◇ *vt* - **1.** [creer, presuponer] to suppose - **2.** [implicar] to involve, to entail - **3.** [significar] to mean - **4.** [conjeturar] to imagine; **lo suponía** I guessed as much; **te suponía mayor** I thought you were older. ◇ *sm*: **ser un suponer** to be conjecture. ◆ **suponerse** *vprnl* to suppose; **se supone que es el mejor** he's supposed to be the best.

suposición *sf* assumption.

supositorio *sm* suppository.

supremacía *sf* supremacy.

supremo, ma *adj lit & fig* supreme.

supresión *sf* - **1.** [de ley, impuesto, derecho] abolition; [de sanciones, restricciones] lifting - **2.** [de palabras, texto] deletion - **3.** [de puestos de trabajo, proyectos] axing.

suprimir *vt* - **1.** [ley, impuesto, derecho] to abolish; [sanciones, restricciones] to lift - **2.** [palabras, texto] to delete - **3.** [puestos de trabajo, proyectos] to axe.

supuesto, ta ◇ *pp* ⊳ **suponer**. ◇ *adj* supposed; [culpable, asesino] alleged; [nombre] falso; **por supuesto** of course. ◆ **supuesto** *sm* assumption; **en el supuesto de que...** assuming...; **partimos del supuesto de que...** we work on the assumption that...

supurar *vi* to fester.

sur ◇ *adj* [posición, parte] south, southern; [dirección, viento] southerly. ◇ *sm* south.

surcar *vt* [tierra] to plough; [aire, agua] to cut O slice through.

surco *sm* - 1. [zanja] furrow - 2. [señal - de disco] groove; [- de rueda] rut - 3. [arruga] line, wrinkle.

sureño, ña ⬦ *adj* southern; [viento] southerly. ⬦ *sm, f* southerner.

sureste = **sudeste**.

surf, surfing *sm* surfing.

surgir *vi* - 1. [brotar] to spring forth - 2. [aparecer] to appear - 3. *fig* [producirse] to arise.

suroeste = **sudoeste**.

surrealista *adj* & *smf* surrealist.

surtido, da *adj* [variado] assorted. ⬦ **surtido** *sm* - 1. [gama] range - 2. [caja surtida] assortment.

surtidor *sm* [de gasolina] pump; [de un chorro] spout.

surtir *vt* [proveer]: **surtir a alguien (de)** to supply sb (with). ⬦ **surtirse de** *vprnl* [proveerse de] to stock up on.

susceptible *adj* - 1. [sensible] sensitive - 2. [propenso a ofenderse] touchy - 3. [posible]: **susceptible de** liable to.

suscitar *vt* to provoke; [interés, dudas, sospechas] to arouse.

suscribir, subscribir *vt* - 1. [firmar] to sign - 2. [ratificar] to endorse - 3. COM [acciones] to subscribe for. ⬦ **suscribirse, subscribirse** *vprnl* - 1. PRENSA: **suscribirse (a)** to subscribe (to) - 2. COM: **suscribirse a** to take out an option on.

suscripción, subscripción *sf* subscription.

suscriptor, ra, subscriptor, ra *sm, f* subscriber.

sushi *sm* CULIN sushi.

susodicho, cha *adj* above-mentioned.

suspender *vt* - 1. [colgar] to hang (up); **suspender algo de algo** to hang sthg from sthg - 2. EDUC to fail - 3. [interrumpir] to suspend; [sesión] to adjourn - 4. [aplazar] to postpone - 5. [de un cargo] to suspend.

suspense *sm* suspense.

suspensión *sf* - 1. [gen & AUTO] suspension - 2. [aplazamiento] postponement; [de reunión, sesión] adjournment.

suspenso, sa *adj* - 1. [colgado]: **suspenso de** hanging from - 2. [no aprobado]: **estar suspenso** to have failed - 3. *fig* [interrumpido]: **en suspenso** pending. ⬦ **suspenso** *sm* failure.

suspensores *smpl* Andes & Arg braces UK, suspenders US.

suspicacia *sf* suspicion.

suspicaz *adj* suspicious.

suspirar *vi* [dar suspiros] to sigh.

suspiro *sm* [aspiración] sigh.

sustancia, substancia *sf* - 1. [gen] substance; **sin sustancia** lacking in substance - 2. [esencia] essence - 3. [de alimento] nutritional value.

sustancial, substancial *adj* substantial, significant.

sustancioso, sa, substancioso, sa *adj* substantial.

sustantivación, substantivación *sf* nominalization.

sustantivar, substantivar *vi* nominalize.

sustantivo, va, substantivo, va *adj* GRAM noun (antes de s). ⬦ **sustantivo, substantivo** *sm* GRAM noun.

sustentar *vt* - 1. [gen] to support - 2. *fig* [mantener - argumento, teoría] to defend.

sustento *sm* - 1. [alimento] sustenance; [mantenimiento] livelihood - 2. [apoyo] support.

sustitución, substitución *sf* [cambio] replacement; **la sustitución de Elena por Luis** the substitution of Luis for Elena.

sustituir, substituir *vt*: **sustituir (por)** to replace (with); **sustituir a Elena por Luis** to replace Elena with Luis, to substitute Luis for Elena.

sustituto, ta, substituto, ta *sm, f* substitute, replacement.

susto *sm* fright; **darse** O **pegarse un susto** to get a fright.

sustracción, substracción *sf* - 1. [robo] theft - 2. MAT subtraction.

sustraer, substraer *vt* - 1. [robar] to steal - 2. MAT to subtract. ⬦ **sustraerse, substraerse** *vprnl*: **sustraerse a** O **de** [obligación, problema] to avoid.

susurrar *vt* & *vi* to whisper.

susurro *sm* whisper; *fig* murmur.

sutil *adj* [gen] subtle; [velo, tejido] delicate, thin; [brisa] gentle; [hilo, línea] fine.

sutileza *sf* subtlety; [de velo, tejido] delicacy, thinness; [de brisa] gentleness; [de hilo, línea] fineness.

sutura *sf* suture.

suyo, ya ⬦ *adj poses* [de él] his; [de ella] hers; [de uno] one's (own); [de ellos, ellas] theirs; [de usted, ustedes] yours; **este libro es suyo** this book is his/hers *etc*; **un amigo suyo** a friend of his/hers *etc*; **no es asunto suyo** it's none of his/her *etc* business; **es muy suyo** *fam fig* he/she is really selfish. ⬦ *pron poses* - 1.: **el suyo** [de él] his; [de ella] hers; [de cosa, animal] its (own); [de uno] one's own; [de ellos, ellas] theirs; [de usted, ustedes] yours - 2. *loc*: **de suyo** in itself; **hacer de las suyas** to be up to his/her *etc* usual tricks; **hacer suyo** to make one's own; **lo suyo es el teatro** he/she *etc* should be on the stage; **lo suyo sería volver** the proper thing to do would be to go back.

T

t¹, T *sf* [letra] t, T.

t² (*abrev de* **tonelada**) t.

tabacalero, ra *adj* tobacco (*antes de s*).

tabaco *sm* - 1. [planta] tobacco plant - 2. [picadura] tobacco; **tabaco negro/rubio** dark/Virginia tobacco - 3. [cigarrillos] cigarettes *pl*.

tábano *sm* horsefly.

tabarra *sf fam*: **dar la tabarra** to be a pest.

taberna *sf country-style bar, usually cheap*.

tabernero, ra *sm, f* [propietario] landlord (*f* landlady); [encargado] barman (*f* barmaid).

tabique *sm* [pared] partition (wall).

tabla *sf* - 1. [plancha] plank; **tabla de planchar** ironing board - 2. [pliegue] pleat - 3. [lista, gráfico] table; **tabla de multiplicación** O **pitagórica** multiplication O Pythagorean table; **tabla periódica** O **de los elementos** periodic table - 4. NÁUT [de surf, vela etc] board - 5. ARTE panel.
◆ **tablas** *sfpl* TEATRO stage *sing*, boards.

tablado *sm* [de teatro] stage; [de baile] dancefloor; [plataforma] platform.

tablao *sm* flamenco show.

tablero *sm* - 1. [gen] board - 2. [en baloncesto] backboard - 3.: **tablero (de mandos)** [de avión] instrument panel; [de coche] dashboard.

tableta *sf* - 1. MED tablet - 2. [de chocolate] bar.

tablón *sm* plank; [en el techo] beam; **tablón de anuncios** notice board.

tabú (*pl* **tabúes** O **tabús**) *adj & sm* taboo.

tabular *vt & vi* to tabulate.

taburete *sm* stool.

tacaño, ña *adj* mean, miserly.

tacha *sf* - 1. [defecto] flaw, fault; **sin tacha** faultless - 2. [clavo] tack.

tachar *vt* - 1. [lo escrito] to cross out - 2. *fig* [acusar]: **tachar a alguien de mentiroso** *etc* to accuse sb of being a liar *etc*.

tacho *sm Andes & R Plata* waste bin.

tachón *sm* - 1. [tachadura] correction, crossing out - 2. [clavo] stud.

tachuela *sf* tack.

tácito, ta *adj* tacit; [norma, regla] unwritten.

taciturno, na *adj* taciturn.

taco *sm* - 1. [tarugo] plug - 2. [cuña] wedge - 3. *fam fig* [palabrota] swearword; **soltar un taco** to swear - 4. [de billar] cue - 5. [de hojas, billetes de banco] wad; [de billetes de autobús, metro] book - 6. [de jamón, queso] hunk - 7. *Andes & R Plata* [tacón] heel - 8. [tortilla de maíz] taco.

tacón *sm* heel.

táctico, ca *adj* tactical. ◆ **táctica** *sf lit & fig* tactics *pl*.

tacto *sm* - 1. [sentido] sense of touch - 2. [textura] feel - 3. *fig* [delicadeza] tact.

tafetán *sm* taffeta.

Tailandia *n pr* Thailand.

taimado, da *adj* crafty.

Taiwán [tai'wan] *n pr* Taiwan.

tajada *sf* - 1. [rodaja] slice - 2. *fig* [parte] share; **sacar tajada de algo** to get sthg out of sthg.

tajante *adj* [categórico] categorical.

tajo *sm* - 1. [corte] deep cut - 2. [acantilado] precipice.

Tajo *sm*: **el (río) Tajo** the (River) Tagus.

tal ◇ *adj* - 1. [semejante, tan grande] such; **¡jamás se vio cosa tal!** you've never seen such a thing!; **lo dijo con tal seguridad que...** he said it with such conviction that...; **dijo cosas tales como...** he said such things as... - 2. [sin especificar] such and such; **a tal hora** at such and such a time - 3. [desconocido]: **un tal Pérez** a (certain) Mr Pérez. ◇ *pron* - 1. [alguna cosa] such a thing - 2. *loc*: **que sí tal que sí cual** this, that and the other; **ser tal para cual** to be two of a kind; **tal y cual, tal y tal** this and that; **y tal** [etcétera] and so on. ◇ *adv*: **¿qué tal?** how's it going?, how are you doing?; **¿qué tal fue el viaje?** how was the trip?; **déjalo tal cual** leave it just as it is. ◆ **con tal de** *loc prep* as long as, provided; **con tal de volver pronto...** as long as we're back early... ◆ **con tal (de) que** *loc conj* as long as, provided. ◆ **tal (y) como** *loc conj* just as O like. ◆ **tal que** *loc prep fam* [como por ejemplo] like.

taladrador, ra *adj* drilling. ◆ **taladradora** *sf* drill.

taladrar *vt* to drill; *fig* [suj: sonido] to pierce.

taladro *sm* - 1. [taladradora] drill - 2. [agujero] drill hole.

talante *sm* - 1. [humor] mood; **estar de buen talante** to be in good humour - 2. [carácter] character, disposition.

talar *vt* to fell.

talco *sm* talc, talcum powder.

talego *sm* - 1. [talega] sack - 2. *mfam* [mil pesetas] 1000 peseta note.

talento *sm* - 1. [don natural] talent; **de talento** talented - 2. [inteligencia] intelligence.

Talgo (*abrev de* **tren articulado ligero Goicoechea Oriol**) *sm Spanish intercity high-speed train*.

talibán ◇ *adj* taliban. ◇ *sm* taliban.

talismán *sm* talisman.

talla *sf* - 1. [medida] size; **¿qué talla usas?** what size are you? - 2. [estatura] height - 3. *fig* [capacidad] stature; **dar la talla** to be up to it - **4.** [ARTE - en madera] carving; [- en piedra] sculpture.

tallado, da *adj* [madera] carved; [piedras preciosas] cut.

tallar *vt* [esculpir - madera, piedra] to carve; [- piedra preciosa] to cut.

tallarín *(gen pl)* *sm* noodle.

talle *sm* - **1.** [cintura] waist - **2.** [figura, cuerpo] figure.

taller *sm* - **1.** [gen] workshop - **2.** AUTO garage - **3.** ARTE studio.

tallo *sm* stem; [brote] sprout, shoot.

talón *sm* - **1.** [gen & ANAT] heel; **talón de Aquiles** *fig* Achilles' heel; **pisarle a alguien los talones** to be hot on sb's heels - **2.** [cheque] cheque; [matriz] stub; **talón cruzado/devuelto/en blanco** crossed/bounced/blank cheque; **talón bancario** cashier's cheque *UK*, cashier's check *US*.

talonario *sm* [de cheques] cheque book; [de recibos] receipt book.

tamal *sm Amér* tamale.

tamaño, ña *adj* such; **¡cómo pudo decir tamaña estupidez!** how could he say such a stupid thing! ◆ **tamaño** *sm* size; **de gran tamaño** large; **de tamaño familiar** family-size; **de tamaño natural** life-size.

tambalearse *vprnl* - **1.** [bambolearse - persona] to stagger; [- mueble] to wobble; [- tren] to sway - **2.** *fig* [gobierno, sistema] to totter.

también *adv* also, too; **yo también** me too; **Juan está enfermo - Elena también** Juan is sick - so is Elena; **también a mí me gusta** I like it too, I also like it.

tambor *sm* - **1.** MÚS & TECNOL drum; [de pistola] cylinder - **2.** ANAT eardrum - **3.** AUTO brake drum.

Támesis *sm*: **el (río) Támesis** the (River) Thames.

tamiz *sm* [cedazo] sieve; **pasar algo por el tamiz** to sift sthg.

tamizar *vt* - **1.** [cribar] to sieve - **2.** *fig* [seleccionar] to screen.

tampoco *adv* neither, not... either; **ella no va y tú tampoco** she's not going and neither are you, she's not going and you aren't either.

tampón *sm* - **1.** [sello] stamp; [almohadilla] ink-pad - **2.** [para la menstruación] tampon.

tan *adv* - **1.** [mucho] so; **tan grande/deprisa** so big/quickly; **¡qué película tan larga!** what a long film!; **tan... que...** so... that...; **tan es así que...** so much so that... - **2.** [en comparaciones]: **tan... como...** as... as... ◆ **tan sólo** *loc adv* only.

tanda *sf* - **1.** [grupo, lote] group, batch - **2.** [serie] series; [de inyecciones] course - **3.** [turno de trabajo] shift.

tándem *(pl* **tándemes, tándems** *O* **tándem)** *sm* - **1.** [bicicleta] tandem - **2.** [pareja] duo, pair.

tangente *sf* tangent; **irse** *O* **salirse por la tangente** to go off at a tangent.

tangible *adj* tangible.

tango *sm* tango.

tanque *sm* - **1.** MIL tank - **2.** [vehículo cisterna] tanker - **3.** [depósito] tank.

tantear ◇ *vt* - **1.** [sopesar - peso, precio, cantidad] to try to guess; [- problema, posibilidades, ventajas] to weigh up - **2.** [probar, sondear] to test (out) - **3.** [toro, contrincante etc] to size up. ◇ *vi* - **1.** [andar a tientas] to feel one's way - **2.** [apuntar los tantos] to (keep) score.

tanteo *sm* - **1.** [prueba, sondeo] testing out; [de posibilidades, ventajas] weighing up; [de contrincante, puntos débiles] sizing up - **2.** [puntuación] score.

tanto, ta ◇ *adj* - **1.** [gran cantidad] so much *(pl* so many); **tanto dinero** so much money, such a lot of money; **tanta gente** so many people; **tiene tanto entusiasmo/tantos amigos que...** she has so much enthusiasm/so many friends that... - **2.** [cantidad indeterminada] so much *(pl* so many); **nos daban tantos euros al día** they used to give us so many euros per day; **cuarenta y tantos** forty-something, forty-odd; **nos conocimos en el sesenta y tantos** we met sometime in the Sixties - **3.** [en comparaciones]: **tanto... como** as much... as *(pl* as many... as).** ◇ *pron* - **1.** [gran cantidad] so much *(pl* so many); **¿cómo puedes tener tantos?** how can you have so many? - **2.** [cantidad indeterminada] so much *(pl* so many); **a tantos de agosto** on such and such a date in August - **3.** [igual cantidad] as much *(pl* as many); **había mucha gente aquí, allí no había tanta** there were a lot of people here, but not as many there; **otro tanto** as much again, the same again; **otro tanto le ocurrió a los demás** the same thing happened to the rest of them - **4.** *loc*: **ser uno de tantos** to be nothing special. ◆ **tanto** ◇ *sm* - **1.** [punto] point; [gol] goal; **marcar un tanto** to score - **2.** *fig* [ventaja] point; **apuntarse un tanto** to earn o.s. a point - **3.** [cantidad indeterminada]: **un tanto** so much, a certain amount; **tanto por ciento** percentage - **4.** *loc*: **estar al tanto (de)** to be on the ball (about). ◇ *adv* - **1.** [mucho]: **tanto (que...)** [cantidad] so much (that...); [tiempo] so long (that...); **no bebas tanto** don't drink so much; **tanto mejor/peor** so much the better/worse; **tanto más cuanto que...** all the more so because... - **2.** [en comparaciones]: **tanto como** as much as; **tanto hombres como mujeres** both men and women; **tanto si estoy como si no** whether I'm there or not - **3.** *loc*: **¡y tanto!** most certainly!, you bet! ◆ **tantas** *sfpl fam*: **eran las tantas** it was very late. ◆ **en tanto (que)** *loc conj* while. ◆ **entre**

tanto *loc adv* meanwhile. ➡ **por (lo) tanto** *loc conj* therefore, so. ➡ **tanto (es así) que** *loc conj* so much so that. ➡ **un tanto** *loc adv* [un poco] a bit, rather.

tanzano, na *adj & sm, f* Tanzanian.

tañido *sm* [de instumento] sound; [de campana] ringing.

tapa *sf* - 1. [de caja, baúl, recipiente] lid; **levantarse O volarse la tapa de los sesos** *fam* to blow one's brains out - 2. [aperitivo] snack, tapa; **irse de tapas** to go for some tapas - 3. [de libro] cover - 4. [de zapato] heel plate - 5. *Andes & R Dom* [de botella] top; [de frasco] stopper.

tapadera *sf* - 1. [tapa] lid - 2. [para encubrir] front.

tapar *vt* - 1. [cerrar - ataúd, cofre] to close (the lid of); [- olla, caja] to put the lid on; [- botella] to put the top on - 2. [ocultar, cubrir] to cover; [no dejar ver] to block out; [obstruir] to block - 3. [abrigar - con ropa] to wrap up; [- en la cama] to tuck in - 4. [encubrir] to cover up - 5. *Chile & Méx* [empaste] to fill. ➡ **taparse** *vprnl* - 1. [cubrirse] to cover (up) - 2. [abrigarse - con ropa] to wrap up; [- en la cama] to tuck o.s. in.

taparrabos *sm inv* - 1. [de hombre primitivo] loincloth - 2. *fam* [tanga] tanga briefs *pl*.

tapete *sm* - 1. [paño] runner; [de billar, para cartas] baize - 2. *Col & Méx* [alfombra] rug.

tapia *sf* (stone) wall.

tapiar *vt* - 1. [cercar] to wall in - 2. [enladrillar] to brick up.

tapicería *sf* - 1. [tela] upholstery - 2. [tienda - para muebles] upholsterer's - 3. [oficio - de muebles] upholstery - 4. [tapices] tapestries *pl*.

tapiz *sm* [para la pared] tapestry; *fig* [de nieve, flores] carpet.

tapizado *sm* - 1. [de mueble] upholstery - 2. [de pared] tapestries *pl*.

tapizar *vt* [mueble] to upholster; *fig* [campos, calles] to carpet, to cover.

tapón *sm* - 1. [para tapar - botellas, frascos] stopper; [- de corcho] cork; [- de metal, plástico] cap, top; [- de bañera, lavabo] plug - 2. [en el oído - de cerumen] wax *(U)* in the ear; [- de algodón] earplug - 3. [atasco] traffic jam - 4. [en baloncesto] block - 5. *Amér* [fusible] fuse.

taponar *vt* [cerrar - lavadero] to put the plug in; [- salida] to block; [- tubería] to stop up.

tapujo *sm*: **andarse con tapujos** [rodeos] to beat about the bush; **hacer algo sin tapujos** to do sthg openly.

taquería *sf Méx* [quiosco] taco stall; [restaurante] taco restaurant.

taquigrafía *sf* shorthand.

taquilla *sf* - 1. [ventanilla - gen] ticket office; CINE & TEATRO box office; **en taquilla** at the ticket/box office - 2. [recaudación] takings *pl* - 3. [armario] locker.

taquillero, ra ◇ *adj*: **es un espectáculo taquillero** the show is a box-office hit. ◇ *sm, f* ticket clerk.

taquimecanógrafo, fa *sm, f* shorthand typist.

tara *sf* - 1. [defecto] defect - 2. [peso] tare.

tarántula *sf* tarantula.

tararear *vt* to hum.

tardanza *sf* lateness.

tardar *vi* - 1. [llevar tiempo] to take; **esto va a tardar** this will take time; **tardó un año en hacerlo** she took a year to do it; **¿cuánto tardarás (en hacerlo)?** how long will you be (doing it)?, how long will it take you (to do it)? - 2. [retrasarse] to be late; [ser lento] to be slow; **¡no tardéis!** don't be long!; **tardar en hacer algo** to take a long time to do sthg; **no tardaron en hacerlo** they were quick to do it; **a más tardar** at the latest.

tarde ◇ *sf* [hasta las cinco] afternoon; [después de las cinco] evening; **por la tarde** [hasta las cinco] in the afternoon; [después de las cinco] in the evening; **buenas tardes** [hasta las cinco] good afternoon; [después de las cinco] good evening; **de tarde en tarde** from time to time; **muy de tarde en tarde** very occasionally. ◇ *adv* [gen] late; [en exceso] too late; **ya es tarde para eso** it's too late for that now; **tarde o temprano** sooner or later.

tardío, a *adj* [gen] late; [intento, decisión] belated.

tarea *sf* [gen] task; EDUC homework; **tareas de la casa** housework *(U)*.

tarifa *sf* - 1. [precio] charge; COM tariff; [en transportes] fare; **tarifa plana** flat rate - 2. *(gen pl)* [lista] price list.

tarima *sf* - 1. [estrado] platform - 2. [suelo] floorboards *pl*.

tarjeta *sf* [gen & INFORM] card; **tarjeta amarilla/roja** DEP yellow/red card; **tarjeta de cliente** store card; **tarjeta de crédito/débito** credit/debit card; **tarjeta de embarque** boarding pass; **tarjeta de felicitación** greetings card; **tarjeta postal** postcard; **tarjeta de recarga** top-up card; **tarjeta de sonido/vídeo** sound/video card; **tarjeta telefónica** postcard; **tarjeta de visita** visiting O calling card.

tarot *sm* tarot.

tarrina *sf* tub.

tarro *sm* [recipiente] jar.

tarta *sf* [gen] cake; [plana, con base de pasta dura] tart; [plana, con base de bizcocho] flan.

tartaleta *sf* tartlet.

tartamudear *vi* to stammer, to stutter.

tartamudo, da ◇ *adj* stammering. ◇ *sm, f* stammerer.

tartana *sf fam* [coche viejo] banger.

tártaro, ra <> *adj* [pueblo] Tartar. <> *sm, f* Tartar.

tartera *sf* [fiambrera] lunch box.

taruga *sm* - **1.** [de madera] block of wood; [de pan] chunk (of stale bread) - **2.** *fam* [necio] blockhead.

tasa *sf* - **1.** [índice] rate; **tasa de paro** *O* **desempleo** (level of) unemployment - **2.** [impuesto] tax; **tasas de aeropuerto** airport tax - **3.** EDUC: **tasas** fees - **4.** [tasación] valuation.

tasación *sf* valuation.

tasar *vt* - **1.** [valorar] to value - **2.** [fijar precio] to fix a price for.

tasca *sf* ≃ pub.

tatarabuelo, la *sm,　　　f*　　　great-great-grandfather (f grandmother).

tatuaje *sm* - **1.** [dibujo] tattoo - **2.** [acción] tattooing.

tatuar *vt* to tattoo.

taurino, na *adj* bullfighting (antes de s).

tauro <> *sm* [zodiaco] Taurus. <> *smf* [persona] Taurean.

tauromaquia *sf* bullfighting.

taxativo, va *adj* precise, exact.

taxi *sm* taxi.

taxidermista *smf* taxidermist.

taxímetro *sm* taximeter.

taxista *smf* taxi driver.

Tayikistán *sm* Tajikistan, Tadjikistan.

taza *sf* - **1.** [para beber] cup; **una taza de té** [recipiente] a teacup; [contenido] a cup of tea - **2.** [de retrete] bowl.

tazón *sm* bowl.

te *pron pers* - **1.** (complemento directo) you; **te gustaría verte** she'd like to see you - **2.** (complemento indirecto) (to) you; **te lo dio** he gave it to you; **te tiene miedo** he's afraid of you - **3.** (reflexivo) yourself - **4.** (valor impersonal) *fam*: **si te dejas pisar, estás perdido** if you let people walk all over you, you've had it.

té (pl tés) *sm* tea.

tea *sf* [antorcha] torch.

teatral *adj* - **1.** [de teatro - gen] theatre (antes de s); [- grupo] drama (antes de s) - **2.** [exagerado] theatrical.

teatro *sm* - **1.** [gen] theatre; **teatro de la ópera** opera house - **2.** *fig* [fingimiento] playacting.

tebeo ® *sm* (children's) comic; **estar más visto que el tebeo** to be old hat.

techo *sm* - **1.** [gen] roof; [dentro de casa] ceiling; **techo solar** AUTO sun roof; **bajo techo** under cover - **2.** *fig* [límite] ceiling. ⬥ **sin techo** *smf*: **los sin techo** the homeless.

techumbre *sf* roof.

tecla *sf* [gen, INFORM & MÚS] key.

teclado *sm* [gen & MÚS] keyboard.

teclear *vt & vi* [en ordenador etc] to type; [en piano] to play.

técnico, ca <> *adj* technical. <> *sm, f* - **1.** [mecánico] technician - **2.** [experto] expert - **3.** DEP [entrenador] coach, manager *UK*. ⬥ **técnica** *sf* - **1.** [gen] technique - **2.** [tecnología] technology.

tecnicolor *sm* Technicolor®.

tecnócrata *smf* technocrat.

tecnología *sf* technology; **tecnologías de la información** information technology; **tecnología punta** state-of-the-art technology.

tecnológico, ca *adj* technological.

tecolote *sm* Amér C & Méx [búho] owl; [policía] cop (on night patrol).

tedio *sm* boredom, tedium.

tedioso, sa *adj* tedious.

Tegucigalpa *n pr* Tegucigalpa.

teja *sf* [de tejado] tile; **color teja** brick red.

tejado *sm* roof.

tejano, na <> *adj* - **1.** [de Texas] Texan - **2.** [tela] denim. <> *sm, f* [persona] Texan. ⬥ **tejanos** *smpl* [pantalones] jeans.

tejemaneje *sm* *fam* - **1.** [maquinación] intrigue - **2.** [ajetreo] to-do, fuss.

tejer <> *vt* - **1.** [gen] to weave; [labor de punto] to knit - **2.** [telaraña] to spin. <> *vi* [hacer ganchillo] to crochet; [hacer punto] to knit.

tejido *sm* - **1.** [tela] fabric, material; [en industria] textile - **2.** ANAT tissue.

tejo *sm* - **1.** [juego] hopscotch - **2.** BOT yew.

tejón *sm* badger.

tel., teléf. (abrev de teléfono) tel.

tela *sf* - **1.** [tejido] fabric, material; [retal] piece of material; **tela de araña** cobweb; **tela metálica** wire netting - **2.** ARTE [lienzo] canvas - **3.** *fam* [dinero] dough - **4.** *loc*: **poner en tela de juicio** to call into question.

telar *sm* - **1.** [máquina] loom - **2.** (gen pl) [fábrica] textiles mill.

telaraña *sf* spider's web, cobweb; **la telaraña mundial** INFORM the (World Wide) Web.

tele *sf* *fam* telly.

telearrastre *sm* ski-tow.

telecomedia *sf* television comedy programme.

telecomunicación *sf* [medio] telecommunication. ⬥ **telecomunicaciones** *sfpl* [red] telecommunications.

telediario *sm* television news (U).

teledirigido, da *adj* remote-controlled.

teléf. (abrev de teléfono) = **tel.**

telefax *sm inv* telefax, fax.

teleférico *sm* cable-car.

telefilme, telefilm (pl telefilms) *sm* TV film.

telefonear vt & vi to phone.

telefónico, ca adj telephone (antes de s).

telefonista smf telephonist.

teléfono sm - 1. [gen] telephone, phone; **coger el teléfono** to answer the phone; **hablar por teléfono** to be on the phone; **llamar por teléfono** to phone; **teléfono fijo/inalámbrico/móvil** land line/cordless/mobile UK O cell US phone; **teléfono público** public phone; **teléfono WAP** WAP phone - 2.: **(número de) teléfono** telephone number.

telegrafía sf telegraphy.

telegráfico, ca adj lit & fig telegraphic.

telégrafo sm [medio, aparato] telegraph.

telegrama sm telegram.

telele sm: **le dio un telele** [desmayo] he had a fainting fit; [enfado] he had a fit.

telemando sm remote control.

telemática sf telematics (U).

telenovela sf television soap opera.

telepatía sf telepathy.

telescópico, ca adj telescopic.

telescopio sm telescope.

telesilla sm chair lift.

telespectador, ra sm, f viewer.

telesquí sm ski lift.

teletexto sm Teletext®.

teletienda sf home shopping programme.

teletipo sm - 1. [aparato] teleprinter - 2. [texto] Teletype®.

teletrabajo sm teleworking.

televenta sf - 1. [por teléfono] telesales pl - 2. [por televisión] TV advertising in which a phone number is given for clients to contact.

televidente smf viewer.

televisar vt to televise.

televisión sf - 1. [sistema, empresa] television; **televisión en blanco y negro/en color** black and white/colour television; **televisión digital** digital television; **televisión privada/pública** commercial/public television - 2. [televisor] television (set).

televisor sm television (set); **televisor de pantalla plana** flatscreen television.

télex sm inv telex.

telón sm [de escenario - delante] curtain; [- detrás] backcloth; **el telón de acero** HIST the Iron Curtain.

telonero, ra sm, f [cantante] support artist; [grupo] support band.

tema sm - 1. [asunto] subject - 2. MÚS [de composición, película] theme; [canción] song - 3. EDUC [de asignatura, oposiciones] topic; [en libro de texto] unit.

temario sm [de asignatura] curriculum; [de oposiciones] list of topics.

temático, ca adj thematic. ◆ **temática** sf subject matter.

temblar vi - 1. [tiritar]: **temblar (de)** [gen] to tremble (with); [de frío] to shiver (with); **tiemblo por lo que pueda pasarle** I shudder to think what could happen to him - 2. [vibrar - suelo, edificio, vehículo] to shudder, to shake; [- voz] to tremble, to shake.

temblor sm shaking (U), trembling (U).

tembloroso, sa adj trembling, shaky.

temer <> vt - 1. [tener miedo de] to fear, to be afraid of - 2. [sospechar] to fear. <> vi to be afraid; **no temas** don't worry; **temer por** to fear for. ◆ **temerse** vprnl: **temerse que** to be afraid that, to fear that; **me temo que no vendrá** I'm afraid she won't come.

temerario, ria adj rash; [conducción] reckless.

temeridad sf - 1. [cualidad] recklessness - 2. [acción] folly (U), reckless act.

temeroso, sa adj [receloso] fearful.

temible adj fearsome.

temor sm: **por temor a** O **de** for fear of.

temperamental adj - 1. [cambiante] temperamental - 2. [impulsivo] impulsive.

temperamento sm temperament.

temperatura sf temperature.

tempestad sf storm.

tempestuoso, sa adj lit & fig stormy.

templado, da adj - 1. [tibio - agua, bebida, comida] lukewarm - 2. GEOGR [clima, zona] temperate - 3. [nervios] steady; [persona, carácter] calm, composed.

templanza sf - 1. [serenidad] composure - 2. [moderación] moderation.

templar vt - 1. [entibiar - lo frío] to warm (up); [- lo caliente] to cool down - 2. [calmar - nervios, ánimos] to calm; [- ira] to restrain - 3. TECNOL [metal etc] to temper - 4. MÚS to tune. ◆ **templarse** vprnl [lo frío] to warm up; [lo caliente] to cool down.

temple sm - 1. [serenidad] composure - 2. TECNOL tempering - 3. ARTE tempera.

templete sm pavilion.

templo sm lit & fig temple; **como un templo** fig huge.

temporada sf - 1. [periodo concreto] season; [de exámenes] period; **de temporada** [fruta, trabajo] seasonal; **temporada alta/baja** high/low season; **temporada media** mid-season - 2. [periodo indefinido] (period of) time; **pasé una temporada en el extranjero** I spent some time abroad.

temporal <> adj - 1. [provisional] temporary - 2. [del tiempo] time (s) - 3. ANAT & RELIG temporal. <> sm [tormenta] storm; **capear el temporal** lit & fig to ride out the storm.

temporario, ria adj Amér temporary.

temporero, ra sm, f casual labourer.

temporizador sm timing device.

temprano, na adj early. ◆ **temprano** adv early.

ten ▷ **tener**. ◆ **ten con ten** sm tact.

tenacidad sf tenacity.

tenacillas sfpl tongs; [para vello] tweezers; [para rizar el pelo] curling tongs.

tenaz adj [perseverante] tenacious.

tenaza (gen pl) sf - 1. [herramienta] pliers pl - 2. [pinzas] tongs pl - 3. ZOOL pincer.

tendedero sm - 1. [cuerda] clothes line; [armazón] clothes horse - 2. [lugar] drying place.

tendencia sf tendency; **tendencia a hacer algo** tendency to do sthg; **nuevas tendencias** [en moda, arte] new trends.

tendencioso, sa adj tentendious.

tender vt - 1. [colgar - ropa] to hang out - 2. [tumbar] to lay (out) - 3. [extender] to stretch (out); [mantel] to spread - 4. [dar - cosa] to hand; [- mano] to hold out, to offer - 5. [entre dos puntos - cable, vía] to lay; [- puente] to build - 6. fig [preparar - trampa etc] to lay - 7. Amér [cama] to make; [mesa] to set, to lay. ◆ **tender a** vi - 1. [propender]: **tender a hacer algo** to tend to do something; **tender a la depresión** to have a tendency to get depressed - 2. MAT to approach. ◆ **tenderse** vprnl to stretch out, to lie down.

tenderete sm [puesto] stall.

tendero, ra sm, f shopkeeper.

tendido, da adj - 1. [extendido, tumbado] stretched out - 2. [colgado - ropa] hung out, on the line. ◆ **tendido** sm - 1. [instalación - de cable, vía] laying; **tendido eléctrico** electrical installation - 2. TAUROM front rows pl.

tendón sm tendon.

tendrá etc v ▷ **tener**.

tenebroso, sa adj dark, gloomy; fig shady, sinister.

tenedor[1] sm [utensilio] fork.

tenedor[2]**, ra** sm, f [poseedor] holder; **tenedor de libros** COM bookkeeper.

teneduría sf COM bookkeeping.

tenencia sf possession; **tenencia ilícita de armas** illegal possession of arms. ◆ **tenencia de alcaldía** sf deputy mayor's office.

tener ◇ v aux - 1. (antes de pp) [haber]: **teníamos pensado ir al teatro** we had thought of going to the theatre; **te lo tengo dicho** I've told you many times - 2. (antes de adj) [hacer estar]: **me tuvo despierto** it kept me awake; **eso la tiene despistada** that has confused her - 3. [expresa obligación]: **tener que hacer algo** to have to do sthg; **tiene que ser así** it has to be this way - 4. [expresa propósito]: **tenemos que ir a cenar un día** we ought to O should go for dinner some time. ◇ vt - 1. [gen] to have; **tengo un hermano** I have O I've got a brother; **tener fiebre** to have a temperature; **tuvieron una pelea** they had a fight; **tener un niño** to have a baby; **¡que tengan buen viaje!** have a good journey!; **hoy tengo clase** I have to go to school today - 2. [medida, edad, sensación, cualidad] to be; **tiene 3 metros de ancho** it's 3 metres wide; **¿cuántos años tienes?** how old are you?; **tiene diez años** she's ten (years old); **tener hambre/miedo** to be hungry/afraid; **tener mal humor** to be bad-tempered; **le tiene lástima** he feels sorry for her - 3. [sujetar] to hold; **¿puedes tenerme esto?** could you hold this for me, please?; **tenlo por el asa** hold it by the handle - 4. [tomar]: **ten el libro que me pediste** here's the book you asked me for; **¡aquí tienes!** here you are! - 5. [recibir] to get; **tuve un verdadero desengaño** I was really disappointed; **tendrá una sorpresa** he'll get a surprise - 6. [valorar]: **me tienen por tonto** they think I'm stupid; **tener a alguien en mucho** to think the world of sb - 7. [guardar, contener] to keep - 8. Amér [llevar]: **tengo tres años aquí** I've been here for three years - 9. loc: **no las tiene todas consigo** he is not too sure about it; **tener a bien hacer algo** to be kind enough to do sthg; **tener que ver con algo/alguien** [estar relacionado] to have something to do with sthg/sb; [ser equiparable] to be in the same league as sthg/sb. ◆ **tenerse** vprnl - 1. [sostenerse]: **tenerse de pie** to stand upright - 2. [considerarse]: **se tiene por listo** he thinks he's clever.

tengo ▷ **tener**.

tenia sf tapeworm.

teniente ◇ sm lieutenant; **teniente coronel/general** lieutenant colonel/general. ◇ adj fam [sordo] deaf (as a post).

tenis sm inv tennis; **tenis de mesa** table tennis.

tenista smf tennis player.

tenor sm - 1. MÚS tenor - 2. [estilo] tone. ◆ **a tenor de** loc prep in view of.

tensar vt [cable, cuerda] to tauten; [arco] to draw.

tensión sf - 1. [gen] tension; **tensión nerviosa** nervous tension - 2. TECNOL [estiramiento] stress - 3. MED: **tensión (arterial)** blood pressure; **tener la tensión alta/baja** to have high/low blood pressure; **tomar la tensión a alguien** to take sb's blood pressure - 4. ELECTR voltage; **alta tensión** high voltage.

tenso, sa adj taut; fig tense.

tentación sf temptation; **caer en la tentación** to give in to temptation; **tener la tentación de**

to be tempted to; **estos bombones son una tentación** these chocolates are really tempting.

tentáculo *sm* tentacle.

tentador, ra *adj* tempting.

tentar *vt* - **1.** [palpar] to feel - **2.** [atraer, incitar] to tempt.

tentativa *sf* attempt; **tentativa de asesinato** attempted murder; **tentativa de suicidio** suicide attempt.

tentempié *(pl* **tentempiés)** *sm* snack.

tenue *adj* - **1.** [tela, hilo, lluvia] fine - **2.** [luz, sonido, dolor] faint - **3.** [relación] tenuous.

teñir *vt* - **1.** [ropa, pelo]: **teñir algo (de rojo** *etc)* to dye sthg (red *etc)* - **2.** *fig* [matizar]: **teñir algo (de)** to tinge sthg (with). ⇒ **teñirse** *vprnl*: **teñirse (el pelo)** to dye one's hair.

teología *sf* theology; **teología de la liberación** liberation theology.

teólogo, ga *sm, f* theologian.

teorema *sm* theorem.

teoría *sf* theory; **en teoría** in theory.

teórico, ca ◇ *adj* theoretical; **clase teórica** theory class. ◇ *sm, f* [persona] theorist.

teorizar *vi* to theorize.

tequila *sm o sf* tequila.

terapéutico, ca *adj* therapeutic.

terapia *sf* therapy.

tercer ⊳ **tercero**.

tercera ⊳ **tercero**.

tercermundista *adj* third-world *(antes de s).*

tercero, ra *num (antes de sm sing:* **tercer)** third. ⇒ **tercero** *sm* - **1.** [piso] third floor - **2.** [curso] third year - **3.** [mediador, parte interesada] third party. ⇒ **tercera** *sf* AUTO third (gear).

terceto *sm* MÚS trio.

terciar ◇ *vt* [poner en diagonal - gen] to place diagonally; [- sombrero] to tilt. ◇ *vi* - **1.** [mediar]: **terciar (en)** to mediate (in) - **2.** [participar] to intervene, to take part. ⇒ **terciarse** *vprnl* to arise; **si se tercia** if the opportunity arises.

tercio *sm* - **1.** [tercera parte] third - **2.** TAUROM stage *(of bullfight).*

terciopelo *sm* velvet.

terco, ca *adj* stubborn.

tergal® *sm* Tergal®.

tergiversar *vt* to distort, to twist.

termal *adj* thermal.

termas *sfpl* [baños] hot baths, spa *sing.*

térmico, ca *adj* thermal.

terminación *sf* - **1.** [finalización] completion - **2.** [parte final] end - **3.** GRAM ending.

terminal ◇ *adj* [gen] final; [enfermo] terminal. ◇ *sm* ELECTR & INFORM terminal. ◇ *sf* [de aeropuerto] terminal; [de autobuses] terminus.

terminante *adj* categorical; [prueba] conclusive.

terminar ◇ *vt* to finish. ◇ *vi* - **1.** [acabar] to end; [tren] to stop, to terminate; **terminar en** [objeto] to end in - **2.** [ir a parar]: **terminar (de/en)** to end up (as/in); **terminar por hacer algo** to end up doing sthg. ⇒ **terminarse** *vprnl* - **1.** [finalizar] to finish - **2.** [agotarse] to run out; **se nos ha terminado la sal** we have run out of salt.

término *sm* - **1.** [fin, extremo] end; **poner término a algo** to put a stop to sthg - **2.** [territorio]: **término (municipal)** district - **3.** [plazo] period; **en el término de un mes** within (the space of) a month - **4.** [lugar, posición] place; **en primer término** ARTE & FOTO in the foreground; **en último término** ARTE & FOTO in the background; *fig* [si es necesario] as a last resort; [en resumidas cuentas] in the final analysis - **5.** [situación, punto] point; **término medio** [media] average; [compromiso] compromise, happy medium; **por término medio** on average - **6.** LING & MAT term; **a mí no me hables en esos términos** don't talk to me like that; **los términos del contrato** the terms of the contract; **en términos generales** generally speaking.

terminología *sf* terminology.

termo *sm* Thermos®(flask).

termómetro *sm* thermometer; **poner el termómetro a alguien** to take sb's temperature.

termostato *sm* thermostat.

terna *sf* POLÍT shortlist of three candidates.

ternasco *sf* suckling lamb.

ternero, ra *sm, f* [animal] calf. ⇒ **ternera** *sf* [carne] veal.

ternura *sf* tenderness.

terquedad *sf* stubbornness.

terracota *sf* terracotta.

terral, tierral *sm Amér* dust cloud.

terraplén *sm* embankment.

terráqueo, a *adj* Earth *(antes de s),* terrestrial.

terrateniente *smf* landowner.

terraza *sf* - **1.** [balcón] balcony - **2.** [de café] terrace, patio - **3.** [azotea] terrace roof - **4.** [bancal] terrace.

terremoto *sm* earthquake.

terrenal *adj* earthly.

terreno, na *adj* earthly. ⇒ **terreno** *sm* - **1.** [suelo - gen] land; GEOL terrain; AGRIC soil - **2.** [solar] plot (of land) - **3.** DEP: **terreno (de juego)** field, pitch - **4.** *fig* [ámbito] field.

terrestre *adj* - **1.** [del planeta] terrestrial - **2.** [de la tierra] land *(antes de s).*

terrible *adj* - **1.** [enorme, insoportable] terrible - **2.** [aterrador] terrifying.

terrícola *smf* earthling.

territorial *adj* territorial.

territorio *sm* territory; **por todo el territorio nacional** across the country, nationwide.

terrón *sm* - **1.** [de tierra] clod of earth - **2.** [de harina etc] lump.

terror *sm* [miedo, persona terrible] terror; CINE horror; **película de terror** horror movie; **dar terror** to terrify.

terrorífico, ca *adj* - **1.** [enorme, insoportable] terrible - **2.** [aterrador] terrifying.

terrorismo *sm* terrorism.

terrorista *adj* & *smf* terrorist.

terroso, sa *adj* - **1.** [parecido a la tierra] earthy - **2.** [con tierra] muddy.

terso, sa *adj* - **1.** [piel, superficie] smooth - **2.** [aguas, mar] clear - **3.** [estilo, lenguaje] polished.

tersura *sf* - **1.** [de piel, superficie] smoothness - **2.** [de aguas, mar] clarity.

tertulia *sf* regular meeting of people for informal discussion of a particular issue of common interest; **tertulia literaria** literary circle.

tesina *sf* (undergraduate) dissertation.

tesis *sf inv* [gen & UNIV] thesis.

tesitura *sf* [circunstancia] circumstances *pl*.

tesón *sm* - **1.** [tenacidad] tenacity, perseverance - **2.** [firmeza] firmness.

tesorero, ra *sm, f* treasurer.

tesoro *sm* - **1.** [botín] treasure - **2.** [hacienda pública] treasury, exchequer. ◆ **Tesoro** *sm* ECON: **el Tesoro (Público)** the Treasury.

test (*pl* **tests**) *sm* test.

testamentario, ria ◇ *adj* testamentary. ◇ *sm, f* executor.

testamento *sm* will; *fig* [artístico, intelectual] legacy; **hacer testamento** to write one's will. ◆ **Antiguo Testamento** *sm* Old Testament. ◆ **Nuevo Testamento** *sm* New Testament.

testar ◇ *vi* [hacer testamento] to make a will. ◇ *vt* [probar] to test.

testarudo, da *adj* stubborn.

testear *vt* C Sur to test.

testículo *sm* testicle.

testificar ◇ *vt* to testify; *fig* to testify to. ◇ *vi* to testify, to give evidence.

testigo ◇ *smf* [persona] witness; **testigo de cargo/descargo** witness for the prosecution/defence; **testigo ocular** O **presencial** eyewitness. ◇ *sm* DEP baton. ◆ **testigo de Jehová** *smf* Jehovah's Witness.

testimonial *adj* [documento, prueba etc] testimonial.

testimoniar *vt* to testify; *fig* to testify to.

testimonio *sm* - **1.** [relato] account; DER testimony; **prestar testimonio** to give evidence - **2.** [prueba] proof; **como testimonio de** as proof of; **dar testimonio de** to prove.

teta *sf* - **1.** *fam* [de mujer] tit - **2.** [de animal] teat.

tétanos *sm inv* tetanus.

tetera *sf* teapot.

tetilla *sf* - **1.** [de persona, animal] nipple - **2.** [de biberón] teat.

tetina *sf* teat.

tetrapléjico, ca *adj* & *sm, f* quadriplegic.

tétrico, ca *adj* gloomy.

textil *adj* & *sm* textile.

texto *sm* - **1.** [gen] text; **el Sagrado Texto** the Holy Scripture, the Bible - **2.** [pasaje] passage.

textual *adj* - **1.** [del texto] textual - **2.** [exacto] exact.

textura *sf* texture.

tez *sf* complexion.

ti *pron pers* (*después de prep*) - **1.** [gen] you; **siempre pienso en ti** I'm always thinking about you; **me acordaré de ti** I'll remember you - **2.** [reflexivo] yourself; **sólo piensas en ti (mismo)** you only think about yourself.

tía ▷ **tío.**

tianguis *sm inv Amér C & Méx* open-air market.

tibia *sf* shinbone, tibia.

tibieza *sf* [calidez] warmth; [falta de calor] lukewarmness.

tibio, bia *adj* - **1.** [cálido] warm; [falto de calor] tepid, lukewarm - **2.** *fig* [frío] lukewarm.

tiburón *sm* [gen] shark.

tic *sm* tic.

ticket = **tíquet.**

tictac *sm* tick tock.

tiempo *sm* - **1.** [gen] time; **al poco tiempo** soon afterwards; **a tiempo (de hacer algo)** in time (to do sthg); **con el tiempo** in time; **no me dio tiempo a terminarlo** I didn't have (enough) time to finish it; **estar a** O **tener tiempo de** to have time to; **fuera de tiempo** at the wrong moment; **ganar tiempo** to save time; **perder el tiempo** to waste time; **tiempo libre** O **de ocio** spare time; **a tiempo parcial** part-time; **en tiempos de Maricastaña** donkey's years ago; **matar el tiempo** to kill time - **2.** [periodo largo] long time; **con tiempo** in good time; **hace tiempo que** it is a long time since; **hace tiempo que no vive aquí** he hasn't lived here for some time; **tomarse uno su tiempo** to take one's time - **3.** [edad] age; **¿qué tiempo tiene?** how old is he? - **4.** [movimiento] movement; **motor de cuatro tiempos** four-stroke engine - **5.** METEOR weather; **hizo buen/mal tiempo** the weather was good/bad; **si el tiempo lo permite** O **no lo impide** weather permitting; **hace un tiempo de perros** it's a foul day - **6.** DEP half - **7.** GRAM tense - **8.** [MÚS - compás] time; [- ritmo] tempo.

tienda *sf* - **1.** [establecimiento] shop; **ir de tiendas** to go shopping; **tienda virtual** online retailer - **2.** [para acampar]: **tienda (de campaña)** tent.

tiene *v* ▷ **tener**.

tienta *v* ▷ **tentar**. ➡ **a tientas** *loc adv* blindly; **andar a tientas** to grope along.

tierno, na *adj* - **1.** [blando, cariñoso] tender - **2.** [del día] fresh.

tierra *sf* - **1.** [gen] land; **tierra adentro** inland; **tierra firme** terra firma; **tierra prometida** O **de promisión** Promised Land - **2.** [materia inorgánica] earth, soil; **un camino de tierra** a dirt track; **pista de tierra batida** clay court - **3.** [suelo] ground; **caer a tierra** to fall to the ground; **quedarse en tierra** [pasajero] to miss the plane/boat/train; **tomar tierra** to touch down - **4.** [patria] homeland, native land; **de la tierra** [vino, queso] local - **5.** ELECTR earth UK, ground US; **conectado a tierra** earthed UK, grounded US. ➡ **Tierra** *sf*: **la Tierra** the Earth.

tierral = **terral**.

tieso, sa *adj* - **1.** [rígido] stiff - **2.** [erguido] erect - **3.** *fam* [muerto] stone dead - **4.** *fam* [sin dinero] broke - **5.** *fig* [engreído] haughty.

tiesto *sm* flowerpot.

tifoideo, a *adj* typhoid *(antes de s)*.

tifón *sm* typhoon.

tifus *sm inv* typhus.

tigre *sm* tiger.

tigresa *sf* tigress.

tijera *(gen pl) sf* scissors *pl*; [de jardinero, esquilador] shears *pl*; **unas tijeras** a pair of scissors/shears; **de tijera** [escalera, silla] folding; **meter la tijera** *lit & fig* to cut.

tijereta *sf* [insecto] earwig.

tila *sf* [infusión] lime blossom tea.

tildar *vt*: **tildar a alguien de algo** to brand O call sb sthg.

tilde *sf* - **1.** [signo ortográfico] tilde - **2.** [acento gráfico] accent.

tiliches *smpl Amér C & Méx* bits and pieces.

tilín *sm* tinkle, tinkling *(U)*; **me hace tilín** *fam* I fancy him.

tilo *sm* [árbol] linden O lime tree.

timar *vt* [estafar]: **timar a alguien** to swindle sb; **timar algo a alguien** to swindle sb out of sthg.

timbal *sm* [MÚS - de orquesta] kettledrum.

timbre *sm* - **1.** [aparato] bell; **tocar el timbre** to ring the bell - **2.** [de voz, sonido] tone; TECNOL

timbre - **3.** [sello - de documentos] stamp; [- de impuestos] seal; *Amér C & Méx* [- de correos] stamp.

timidez *sf* shyness.

tímido, da *adj* shy.

timo *sm* [estafa] swindle.

timón *sm* - **1.** AERON & NÁUT rudder - **2.** *fig* [gobierno] helm; **llevar el timón de** to be at the helm of - **3.** *Andes & Cuba* [volante] steering wheel.

timonel, timonero *sm* NÁUT helmsman.

timorato, ta *adj* [mojigato] prudish.

tímpano *sm* ANAT eardrum.

tina *sf* - **1.** [tinaja] pitcher - **2.** [gran cuba] vat - **3.** *Amér C, Col & Méx* [bañera] bathtub.

tinaja *sf* (large) pitcher.

tinglado *sm* - **1.** [cobertizo] shed - **2.** [armazón] platform - **3.** *fig* [lío] fuss - **4.** *fig* [maquinación] plot.

tinieblas *sfpl* darkness *(U)*; *fig* confusion *(U)*, uncertainty *(U)*; **entre tinieblas** *lit & fig* in the dark.

tino *sm* - **1.** [puntería] good aim - **2.** *fig* [habilidad] skill - **3.** *fig* [juicio] sense, good judgment.

tinta *sf* ink; **tinta china** Indian ink; **cargar** O **recargar las tintas** to exaggerate; **saberlo de buena tinta** to have it on good authority; **sudar tinta** to sweat blood. ➡ **medias tintas** *sfpl*: **andarse con medias tintas** to be wishy-washy.

tinte *sm* - **1.** [sustancia] dye - **2.** [operación] dyeing - **3.** [tintorería] dry cleaner's - **4.** *fig* [tono] shade, tinge.

tintero *sm* [frasco] ink pot; [en la mesa] inkwell.

tintinear *vi* to jingle, to tinkle.

tinto, ta *adj* - **1.** [manchado] stained; **tinto en sangre** bloodstained - **2.** [vino] red. ➡ **tinto** *sm* - **1.** [vino] red wine - **2.** *Col & Ven* [café] black coffee.

tintorera *sf* ZOOL blue shark.

tintorería *sf* dry cleaner's.

tiña *sf* MED ringworm.

tío, a *sm, f* - **1.** [familiar] uncle *(f* aunt*)*; **el tío Sam** *fig* Uncle Sam - **2.** *fam* [individuo] guy *(f* bird*)* - **3.** *fam* [como apelativo] mate *(f* darling*)*.

tiovivo *sm* merry-go-round UK, carousel US.

tipear ◇ *vt Amér* to type. ◇ *vi* to type.

típico, ca *adj* typical; [traje, restaurante etc] traditional; **típico de** typical of.

tipificar *vt* - **1.** [gen & DER] to classify - **2.** [simbolizar] to typify.

tiple *smf* [cantante] soprano.

tipo, pa *sm, f* *fam* guy *(f* woman*)*. ➡ **tipo** *sm* - **1.** [clase] type, sort; **todo tipo de** all sorts of - **2.** [cuerpo - de mujer] figure; [- de hombre] build - **3.** ECON rate - **4.** IMPR & ZOOL type.

tipografía *sf* [procedimiento] printing.

tipográfico, ca *adj* typographical.

tipógrafo, fa *sm, f* printer

tíquet (*pl* **tíquets**), **ticket** ['tiket] (*pl* **tickets**) *sm* ticket.

tiquismiquis ◇ *adj inv fam* [maniático] pernickety. ◇ *smf inv fam* [maniático] fusspot. ◇ *smpl* - 1. [riñas] squabbles - 2. [bagatelas] trifles.

tira *sf* - 1. [banda cortada] strip - 2. [de viñetas] comic strip - 3. *loc*: **la tira de** *fam* loads *pl* of; **la tira** *Méx fam* [la policía] the cops, the fuzz *UK*. ◆ **tira y afloja** *sm* give and take.

tirabuzón *sm* [rizo] curl.

tirachinas *sm inv* catapult.

tiradero *sm Amér* rubbish dump.

tirado, da *adj* - 1. *fam* [barato] dirt cheap - 2. *fam* [fácil] simple, dead easy; **estar tirado** to be a cinch - 3. *loc*: **dejar tirado a alguien** *fam* to leave sb in the lurch. ◆ **tirada** *sf* - 1. [lanzamiento] throw - 2. [IMPR - número de ejemplares] print run; [- reimpresión] reprint; [- número de lectores] circulation - 3. [sucesión] series.

tirador, ra *sm, f* [con arma] marksman. ◆ **tirador** *sm* [mango] handle. ◆ **tiradores** *smpl Bol & R Dom* [tirantes] braces *UK*, suspenders *US*.

tiranía *sf* tyranny.

tirano, na ◇ *adj* tyrannical. ◇ *sm, f* tyrant.

tirante ◇ *adj* - 1. [estirado] taut - 2. *fig* [violento, tenso] tense. ◇ *sm* - 1. [de tela] strap - 2. ARQUIT brace. ◆ **tirantes** *smpl* [para pantalones] braces *UK*, suspenders *US*.

tirantez *sf fig* tension.

tirar ◇ *vt* - 1. [lanzar] to throw; **tirar algo a alguien/algo** [para hacer daño] to throw sthg at sb/sthg; **tírame una manzana** throw me an apple; **tírale un beso** blow him a kiss - 2. [dejar caer] to drop; [derramar] to spill; [volcar] to knock over - 3. [desechar, malgastar] to throw away - 4. [disparar] to fire; [bomba] to drop; [petardo, cohete] to let off; [foto] to take - 5. [derribar] to knock down - 6. [jugar - carta] to play; [- dado] to throw - 7. [DEP - falta, penalti etc] to take; [- balón] to pass - 8. [imprimir] to print - 9. *fam* [suspender] to fail. ◇ *vi* - 1. [estirar, arrastrar]: **tirar (de algo)** to pull (sthg); **tira y afloja** give and take - 2. [suj: prenda, pernera, manga] to be too tight - 3. [disparar] to shoot - 4. *fam* [atraer] to have a pull; **me tira la vida del campo** I feel drawn towards life in the country - 5. [cigarrillo, chimenea etc] to draw - 6. [dirigirse] to go, to head - 7. *fam* [apañárselas] to get by; **ir tirando** to get by; **voy tirando** I'm O.K., I've been worse - 8. [parecerse]: **tira a gris** it's greyish; **tira a su abuela** she takes after her grandmother; **tirando a** approaching, not far from - 9. [tender]: **tirar para algo** [persona] to have the makings of sthg; **este programa tira a (ser) hortera** this programme is a bit on the tacky side; **el tiempo tira a mejorar** the weather looks as if it's getting better - 10. [DEP - con el pie] to kick; [- con la mano] to throw; [- a meta, canasta etc] to shoot. ◆ **tirarse** *vprnl* - 1. [lanzarse]: **tirarse (a)** [al agua] to dive (into); [al vacío] to jump (into); **tirarse sobre alguien** to jump on top of sb - 2. [tumbarse] to stretch out - 3. [pasar tiempo] to spend.

tirita® *sf* (sticking) plaster *UK*, ≈ Bandaid® *US*.

tirilla® *sf* ≈ neckband.

tiritar *vi*: **tiritar (de)** to shiver (with).

tiro *sm* - 1. [gen] shot; **pegar un tiro a alguien** to shoot sb; **pegarse un tiro** to shoot o.s.; **ni a tiros** never in a million years - 2. [acción] shooting; **tiro al blanco** [deporte] target shooting; [lugar] shooting range; **tiro con arco** archery - 3. [huella, marca] bullet mark; [herida] gunshot wound - 4. [alcance] range; **a tiro de** within the range of; **a tiro de piedra** a stone's throw away; **ponerse/estar a tiro** [de arma] to come/be within range; *fig* [de persona] to come/be within one's reach - 5. [de chimenea, horno] draw - 6. [de caballos] team - 7. *fam* [de cocaína] line.

tiroides *sm o sf inv* thyroid (gland).

tirón *sm* - 1. [estirón] pull - 2. [robo] bagsnatching - 3. MED: **tirón (muscular)** strained muscle - 4. *fam* [popularidad] pull. ◆ **de un tirón** *loc adv* in one go.

tirotear ◇ *vt* to fire at. ◇ *vi* to shoot.

tiroteo *sm* [tiros] shooting; [intercambio de disparos] shootout.

tisana *sf* herbal tea.

tisis *sf inv* MED (pulmonary) tuberculosis.

titánico, ca *adj* titanic.

títere *sm lit & fig* puppet. ◆ **títeres** *smpl* [guiñol] puppet show *sing*.

titilar *vi* [estrella, luz] to flicker.

titiritero, ra *sm, f* - 1. [de títeres] puppeteer - 2. [acróbata] acrobat.

titubeante *adj* - 1. [actitud] hesitant; [voz] stuttering - 2. [al andar] tottering.

titubear *vi* [dudar] to hesitate; [al hablar] to stutter.

titubeo *(gen pl)* *sm* - 1. [duda] hesitation; [al hablar] stutter, stuttering *(U)* - 2. [al andar] tottering.

titulado, da *sm, f* [diplomado] holder of a qualification; [licenciado] graduate.

titular ◇ *adj* [profesor, médico] official. ◇ *smf* [poseedor] holder. ◇ *sm (gen pl)* PRENSA headline. ◇ *vt* [llamar] to title, to call. ◆ **titularse** *vprnl* - 1. [llamarse] to be titled *O* called - 2. [licenciarse]: **titularse (en)** to graduate (in) - 3. [diplomarse]: **titularse (en)** to obtain a qualification (in).

título sm - 1. [gen] title; **título de propiedad** title deed; **títulos de crédito** CINE credits - 2. [licenciatura] degree; [diploma] diploma; **tiene muchos títulos** she has a lot of qualifications - 3. fig [derecho] right; **a título de** as.

tiza sf chalk; **una tiza** a piece of chalk.

tiznar vt to blacken.

tizne sm o sf soot.

tizón sm burning stick O log.

tlapalería sf Méx ironmonger's (shop).

TLC, TLCAN sm (abrev de **Tratado de Libre Comercio de América del Norte**) NAFTA.

toalla sf [para secarse] towel; **toalla de ducha/manos** bath/hand towel; Amér **toalla higiénica** O **sanitaria** sanitary towel UK O napkin US; **arrojar** O **tirar la toalla** to throw in the towel.

toallero sm towel rail.

tobillo sm ankle.

tobogán sm [rampa] slide; [en parque de atracciones] helter-skelter; [en piscina] flume.

toca sf wimple.

tocadiscos sm inv record player.

tocado, da adj fam [chiflado] soft in the head. ➡ **tocado** sm [prenda] headgear (U).

tocador sm - 1. [mueble] dressing table - 2. [habitación - en lugar público] powder room; [- en casa] boudoir.

tocar <> vt - 1. [gen] to touch; [palpar] to feel - 2. [instrumento, canción] to play; [bombo] to bang; [sirena, alarma] to sound; [campana, timbre] to ring; **el reloj tocó las doce** the clock struck twelve - 3. [abordar - tema etc] to touch on - 4. fig [conmover] to touch. <> vi - 1. [entrar en contacto] to touch - 2. [estar próximo]: **tocar (con)** [gen] to be touching; [país, jardín] to border (on) - 3. [llamar - a la puerta, ventana] to knock - 4. [corresponder en reparto]: **tocar a alguien** to be due to sb; **tocamos a mil cada uno** we're due a thousand each; **le tocó la mitad** he got half of it; **te toca a ti hacerlo** [turno] it's your turn to do it; [responsabilidad] it's up to you to do it - 5. [caer en suerte]: **me ha tocado la lotería** I've won the lottery; **le ha tocado sufrir mucho** he has had to suffer a lot - 6. [llegar el momento]: **nos toca pagar ahora** it's time (for us) to pay now. ➡ **tocarse** vprnl to touch.

tocayo, ya sm, f namesake.

tocinería sf pork butcher's (shop).

tocino sm [para cocinar] lard; [para comer] fat (of bacon). ➡ **tocino de cielo** sm CULIN dessert made of syrup and eggs.

todavía adv - 1. [aún] still; [con negativo] yet, still; **todavía no lo he recibido** I still haven't got it, I haven't got it yet; **todavía ayer** as late as yesterday; **todavía no** not yet - 2. [sin embargo] still - 3. [incluso] even; **todavía mejor** even better.

todo, da <> adj - 1. [gen] all; **todo el mundo** everybody; **todo el libro** the whole book, all (of) the book; **todo el día** all day - 2. [cada, cualquier]: **todos los días/lunes** every day/Monday; **todo español** every Spaniard, all Spaniards - 3. [para enfatizar]: **es todo un hombre** he's every bit a man; **ya es toda una mujer** she's a big girl now; **fue todo un éxito** it was a great success. <> pron - 1. [todas las cosas] everything, all of them pl; **lo vendió todo** he sold everything, he sold it all; **todos están rotos** they're all broken, all of them are broken; **ante todo** [principalmente] above all; [en primer lugar] first of all; **con todo** despite everything; **sobre todo** above all; **está en todo** he/she always makes sure everything is just so; **todo lo más** at (the) most - 2. [todas las personas]: **todos** everybody; **todas vinieron** everybody O they all came. ➡ **todo** <> sm whole. <> adv completely, all. ➡ **del todo** loc adv: **no estoy del todo contento** I'm not entirely happy; **no lo hace mal del todo** she doesn't do it at all badly.

todopoderoso, sa adj almighty.

todoterreno sm all-terrain vehicle.

tofe sm coffee-flavoured toffee.

toga sf - 1. [manto] toga - 2. [traje] gown.

toldo sm [de tienda] awning; [de playa] sunshade.

tolerancia sf tolerance.

tolerante adj tolerant.

tolerar vt - 1. [consentir, aceptar] to tolerate; **tolerar que alguien haga algo** to tolerate sb doing sthg - 2. [aguantar] to stand.

toma sf - 1. [de biberón, papilla] feed; [de medicamento] dose - 2. [de sangre] sample - 3. [de ciudad etc] capture - 4. [de agua, aire] inlet; **toma de corriente** ELECTR socket; **toma de tierra** ELECTR earth - 5. CINE [de escena] take. ➡ **toma de posesión** sf - 1. [de gobierno, presidente] investiture - 2. [de cargo] undertaking.

tomar <> vt - 1. [gen] to take; [actitud, costumbre] to adopt - 2. [datos, información] to take down - 3. [medicina, drogas] to take; [comida, bebida] to have; **¿qué quieres tomar?** what would you like (to drink/eat)? - 4. [autobús, tren etc] to catch; [taxi] to take - 5. [considerar, confundir]: **tomar a alguien por algo/alguien** to take sb for sthg/sb - 6. loc: **tomarla con alguien** fam to have it in for sb; **¡toma!** [al dar algo] here you are!; [expresando sorpresa] well I never!; **¡toma (ésa)!** fam [expresa venganza] take that! <> vi - 1. [encaminarse] to go, to head - 2. Amér [beber alcohol] to drink. ➡ **tomarse** vprnl - 1. [comida, bebida] to have; [medicina, drogas] to take - 2. [interpretar] to take.

tomate sm [fruto] tomato.

tómbola sf tombola.

tomillo sm thyme.

tomo sm [volumen] volume.

ton ➡ **sin ton ni son** loc adv for no apparent reason.

tonada sf tune.

tonadilla sf ditty.

tonalidad sf [de color] tone.

tonel sm [recipiente] barrel.

tonelada sf ton.

tonelaje sm tonnage.

tónico, ca adj - 1. [reconstituyente] revitalizing - 2. GRAM & MÚS tonic. ➡ **tónico** sm [reconstituyente] tonic. ➡ **tónica** sf - 1. [bebida] tonic water - 2. [tendencia] trend - 3. MÚS tonic.

tonificar vt to invigorate.

tono sm - 1. [gen] tone; **fuera de tono** out of place - 2. [MÚS - tonalidad] key; [- altura] pitch - 3. [de color] shade; **tono de piel** complexion.

tonsura sf tonsure.

tontear vi [hacer el tonto] to fool about.

tontería sf - 1. [estupidez] stupid thing; **decir una tontería** to talk nonsense; **hacer una tontería** to do sthg foolish - 2. [cosa sin importancia o valor] trifle.

tonto, ta ⬦ adj stupid; **tonto de capirote** O **remate** daft as a brush. ⬦ sm, f idiot; **hacer el tonto** to play the fool; **hacerse el tonto** to act innocent. ➡ **a tontas y a locas** loc adv haphazardly.

top (pl **tops**) sm [prenda] short top.

topacio sm topaz.

topadora sf R Dom bulldozer.

topar vi [encontrarse]: **topar con alguien** to bump into sb; **topar con algo** to come across sthg.

tope ⬦ adj inv [máximo] top, maximum; [fecha] last. ⬦ sm - 1. [pieza] block; [para puerta] doorstop - 2. FERROC buffer - 3. [límite máximo] limit; [de plazo] deadline - 4. Méx [para velocidad] speed bump - 5. [freno]: **poner tope a** to rein in, to curtail - 6. loc: **estar hasta los topes** to be bursting at the seams. ➡ **a tope** ⬦ loc adv [de velocidad, intensidad] flat out. ⬦ loc adj fam [lleno - lugar] packed.

topetazo sm bump; **darse un topetazo** [en la cabeza] to bump o.s. on the head.

tópico, ca adj - 1. [manido] clichéd - 2. MED topical. ➡ **tópico** sm cliché.

topo sm - 1. fig & ZOOL mole - 2. [lunar] polka dot.

topógrafo, fa sm, f topographer.

topónimo sm place name.

toque sm - 1. [gen] touch; **dar los últimos toques a algo** to put the finishing touches to sthg - 2. [aviso] warning - 3. [sonido - de campana] chime, chiming (U); [- de tambor] beat, beating (U); [- de sirena etc] blast; **toque de diana** reveille; **toque de difuntos** death knell; **toque de queda** curfew.

toquetear vt [manosear - cosa] to fiddle with; [- persona] to fondle.

toquilla sf shawl.

tórax sm inv thorax.

torbellino sm - 1. [remolino - de aire] whirlwind; [- de agua] whirlpool; [- de polvo] dustcloud - 2. fig [mezcla confusa] spate.

torcedura sf [esguince] sprain.

torcer ⬦ vt - 1. [gen] to twist; [doblar] to bend - 2. [girar] to turn. ⬦ vi [girar] to turn. ➡ **torcerse** vprnl - 1. [retorcerse] to twist; [doblarse] to bend; **me tuerzo al andar/escribir** I can't walk/write in a straight line - 2. [dislocarse] to sprain - 3. [ir mal - negocios, día] to go wrong; [- persona] to go astray.

torcido, da adj [enroscado] twisted; [doblado] bent; [cuadro, corbata] crooked.

tordo, da adj dappled. ➡ **tordo** sm [pájaro] thrush.

torear ⬦ vt - 1. [lidiar] to fight (bulls) - 2. fig [eludir] to dodge - 3. fig [burlarse de]: **torear a alguien** to mess sb about. ⬦ vi [lidiar] to fight bulls.

toreo sm bullfighting.

torero, ra sm, f [persona] bullfighter. ➡ **torera** sf [prenda] bolero (jacket).

tormenta sf lit & fig storm.

tormento sm torment; **ser un tormento** [persona] to be a torment; [cosa] to be torture.

tormentoso, sa adj stormy; [sueño] troubled.

tornado sm tornado.

tornar culto ⬦ vt [convertir]: **tornar algo en (algo)** to turn sthg into (sthg). ⬦ vi - 1. [regresar] to return - 2. [volver a hacer]: **tornar a hacer algo** to do sthg again. ➡ **tornarse** vprnl [convertirse]: **tornarse (en)** to turn (into), to become.

torneado, da adj [cerámica] turned.

torneo sm tournament.

tornillo sm screw; [con tuerca] bolt; **le falta un tornillo** fam he has a screw loose.

torniquete sm MED tourniquet.

torno sm - 1. [de alfarero] (potter's) wheel - 2. [para pesos] winch. ➡ **en torno a** loc prep - 1. [alrededor de] around - 2. [acerca de] about; **girar en torno a** to be about.

toro sm bull. ➡ **toros** smpl [lidia] bullfight sing, bullfighting (U).

toronja sf grapefruit.

torpe adj - 1. [gen] clumsy - 2. [necio] slow, dim-witted.

torpedear vt to torpedo.

torpedero *sm* torpedo boat.

torpedo *sm* [proyectil] torpedo.

torpeza *sf* - 1. [gen] clumsiness; **fue una torpeza hacerlo/decirlo** it was a clumsy thing to do/say - 2. [falta de inteligencia] slowness.

torre *sf* - 1. [construcción] tower; ELECTR pylon; **torre (de apartamentos)** tower block; **torre de control** control tower; **torre de marfil** *fig* ivory tower; **torre de perforación** oil derrick - 2. [en ajedrez] rook, castle - 3. MIL turret.

torrefacto, ta *adj* high-roast *(antes de s)*.

torrencial *adj* torrential.

torrente *sm* torrent; **un torrente de** *fig* [gente, palabras etc] a stream O flood of; [dinero, energía] masses of; **un torrente de voz** a powerful voice.

torreta *sf* - 1. MIL turret - 2. ELECTR pylon.

torrezno *sm* chunk of fried bacon.

tórrido, da *adj lit & fig* torrid.

torrija *sf* French toast *(U) (dipped in milk o wine)*.

torsión *sf* - 1. [del cuerpo, brazo] twist, twisting *(U)* - 2. MECÁN torsion.

torso *sm culto* torso.

torta *sf* - 1. CULIN cake - 2. *Andes, Col, R Plata & Ven* [tarta] cake - 3. *fam* [bofetada] thump - 4. *fam* [accidente] crash. ◆ **ni torta** *loc adv fam* not a thing.

tortazo *sm* - 1. *fam* [bofetada] thump - 2. *fam* [accidente] crash; **darse** O **pegarse un tortazo** to crash.

tortícolis *sf inv* crick in the neck.

tortilla *sf* - 1. [de huevo] omelette; **tortilla (a la) española** Spanish O potato omelette; **tortilla (a la) francesa** French O plain omelette; **se dio la vuelta** O **se volvió la tortilla** the tables turned - 2. [de maíz] tortilla.

tórtola *sf* turtledove.

tortolito, ta *sm, f (gen pl) fam* [enamorado] lovebird.

tortuga *sf* - 1. [terrestre] tortoise; [marina] turtle; [fluvial] terrapin - 2. *fam* [persona o cosa lenta] snail.

tortuoso, sa *adj* - 1. [sinuoso] tortuous, winding - 2. *fig* [perverso] devious.

tortura *sf* torture.

torturar *vt* to torture.

tos *sf* cough; **tos ferina** whooping cough.

tosco, ca *adj* - 1. [basto] crude - 2. *fig* [ignorante] coarse.

toser *vi* to cough.

tostado, da *adj* - 1. [pan, almendras] toasted - 2. [color] brownish - 3. [piel] tanned. ◆ **tostada** *sf* piece of toast; **café con tostadas** coffee and toast.

tostador *sm* toaster.

tostadora *sf* = **tostador**.

tostar *vt* - 1. [dorar, calentar - pan, almendras] to toast; [- carne] to brown - 2. [broncear] to tan - 3. INFORM to burn. ◆ **tostarse** *vprnl* to get brown; **tostarse (al sol)** to sunbathe.

tostón *sm fam* [rollo, aburrimiento] bore, drag.

total ◇ *adj* - 1. [absoluto, completo] total - 2. *mfam* [estupendo] brill, ace. ◇ *sm* - 1. [suma] total - 2. [totalidad, conjunto] whole; **el total del grupo** the whole group; **en total** in all. ◇ *adv* anyway; **total que me marché** so anyway, I left.

totalidad *sf* whole; **en su totalidad** as a whole.

totalitario, ria *adj* totalitarian.

totalizar *vt* to amount to.

tóxico, ca *adj* toxic, poisonous. ◆ **tóxico** *sm* poison.

toxicómano, na *sm, f* drug addict.

toxina *sf* toxin.

tozudo, da *adj* stubborn.

traba *sf fig* [obstáculo] obstacle; **poner trabas (a alguien)** to put obstacles in the way (of sb).

trabajador, ra ◇ *adj* hard-working. ◇ *sm, f* worker.

trabajar ◇ *vi* - 1. [gen] to work; **trabajar de/en** to work as/in; **trabajar en una empresa** to work for a firm - 2. CINE & TEATRO to act. ◇ *vt* - 1. [hierro, barro, tierra] to work; [masa] to knead - 2. [mejorar] to work on O at.

trabajo *sm* - 1. [gen] work; **hacer un buen trabajo** to do a good job; **trabajo intelectual/físico** mental/physical effort; **trabajo manual** manual labour; **trabajos forzados** O **forzosos** hard labour *(U)*; **trabajos manuales** [en el colegio] arts and crafts - 2. [empleo] job; **no tener trabajo** to be out of work - 3. [estudio escrito] essay - 4. ECON & POLÍT labour - 5. *fig* [esfuerzo] effort.

trabajoso, sa *adj* - 1. [difícil] hard, difficult - 2. [molesto] tiresome.

trabalenguas *sm inv* tongue-twister.

trabar *vt* - 1. [sujetar] to fasten; [con grilletes] to shackle - 2. [unir] to join - 3. [iniciar - conversación, amistad] to strike up - 4. [obstaculizar] to hinder - 5. CULIN to thicken. ◆ **trabarse** *vprnl* - 1. [enredarse] to get tangled - 2. *loc*: **se le trabó la lengua** he got tongue-tied.

trabazón *sf* [de ideas, episodios] connection; [de discurso, novela] consistency.

trabucar *vt* to mix up. ◆ **trabucarse** *vprnl* [al hablar] to get tongue-tied.

tracción *sf* traction; **tracción a las cuatro ruedas** four-wheel drive.

tractor *sm* tractor.

tradición *sf* tradition.

tradicional *adj* traditional.

tradicionalismo *sm* traditionalism; POLÍT conservatism.

traducción *sf* translation; **traducción directa/inversa** translation into/out of one's own language.

traducir ⟨⟩ *vt* [a otro idioma] to translate. ⟨⟩ *vi*: **traducir (de/a)** to translate (from/into). ⬩ **traducirse** *vprnl* [a otro idioma]: **traducirse (por)** to be translated (by O as).

traductor, ra *sm, f* translator.

traer *vt* - **1.** [trasladar, provocar] to bring; [consecuencias] to carry, to have; **traer consigo** [implicar] to mean, to lead to - **2.** [llevar] to carry; **¿qué traes ahí?** what have you got there? - **3.** [llevar adjunto, dentro] to have; **trae un artículo interesante** it has an interesting article in it - **4.** [llevar puesto] to wear. ⬩ **traerse** *vprnl*: **traérselas** *fam fig* to be a real handful.

traficante *smf* [de drogas, armas etc] trafficker.

traficar *vi*: **traficar (en/con algo)** to traffic (in sthg).

tráfico *sm* [de vehículos] traffic; [de drogas, armas] trafficking, dealing.

tragaluz *sm* skylight.

traganíqueles *sf inv Amér fam* ⊳ **máquina**.

tragaperras *sf inv* slot machine.

tragar ⟨⟩ *vt* - **1.** [ingerir, creer] to swallow - **2.** [absorber] to swallow up - **3.** *fig* [soportar] to put up with. ⟨⟩ *vi* - **1.** [ingerir] to swallow - **2.** [aguantar] to grin and bear it; [acceder, ceder] to give in. ⬩ **tragarse** *vprnl fig* [soportarse]: **no se tragan** they can't stand each other.

tragedia *sf* tragedy.

trágico, ca *adj* tragic.

trago *sm* - **1.** [de líquido] mouthful; **dar un trago de algo** to take a swig of sthg; **de un trago** in one gulp - **2.** *fam* [copa] drink - **3.** *fam* [disgusto]: **ser un trago para alguien** to be tough on sb.

tragón, ona *fam* ⟨⟩ *adj* greedy. ⟨⟩ *sm, f* pig, glutton.

traición *sf* - **1.** [infidelidad] betrayal - **2.** DER treason.

traicionar *vt* [persona, país, ideales] to betray.

traicionero, ra *adj* [desleal] treacherous; DER treasonous.

traidor, ra ⟨⟩ *adj* treacherous; DER treasonous. ⟨⟩ *sm, f* traitor.

traiga *etc* ⊳ **traer**.

tráiler ['trailer] (*pl* **trailers**) *sm* - **1.** CINE trailer - **2.** AUTO articulated lorry - **3.** *Méx* [caravana] caravan UK, trailer US.

traje *sm* - **1.** [con chaqueta] suit; [de una pieza] dress; **ir de traje** to wear a suit; **traje de baño** swimsuit; **traje de ceremonia** O **de gala** dress suit, formal dress (*U*); **traje de chaqueta** woman's two-piece suit - **2.** [regional, de época etc] costume; **traje de luces** matador's outfit - **3.** [ropa] clothes *pl*; **traje de paisano** [de militar] civilian clothes, [de policía] plain clothes.

trajeado, da *adj fam* [arreglado] spruced up.

trajín *sm fam* [ajetreo] bustle.

trajinar *vi fam* to bustle about.

trajo ⊳ **traer**.

trama *sf* - **1.** [de hilos] weft - **2.** [argumento] plot - **3.** [conspiración] intrigue.

tramar *vt* [planear] to plot; [complot] to hatch; **estar tramando algo** to be up to something.

tramitar *vt* - **1.** [suj: autoridades - pasaporte, permiso] to take the necessary steps to obtain; [- solicitud, dimisión] to process - **2.** [suj: solicitante]: **tramitar un permiso/visado** to be in the process of applying for a licence/visa.

trámite *sm* [gestión] formal step; **de trámite** routine, formal. ⬩ **trámites** *smpl* - **1.** [proceso] procedure *sing* - **2.** [papeleo] paperwork (*U*).

tramo *sm* [espacio] section, stretch; [de escalera] flight (of stairs).

tramoya *sf* TEATRO stage machinery (*U*).

trampa *sf* - **1.** [para cazar] trap; *fig* [engaño] trick; **tender una trampa (a alguien)** to set O lay a trap (for sb); **hacer trampas** to cheat - **2.** *fam* [deuda] debt.

trampear *vi fam* [estafar] to swindle money.

trampilla *sf* [en el suelo] trapdoor.

trampolín *sm* [de piscina] diving board; [de esquí] ski jump; [en gimnasia] springboard.

tramposo, sa ⟨⟩ *adj* [fullero] cheating. ⟨⟩ *sm, f* [fullero] cheat.

tranca *sf* - **1.** [en puerta, ventana] bar - **2.** [arma] cudgel - **3.** *loc*: **a trancas y barrancas** with great difficulty.

trancarse *vprnl Amér* [atorarse] to get blocked, to get clogged up.

trance *sm* - **1.** [apuro] difficult situation; **estar en trance de hacer algo** to be about to do sthg; **pasar por un mal trance** to go through a bad patch - **2.** [estado hipnótico] trance.

tranquilidad *sf* peacefulness, calmness; **para mayor tranquilidad** to be on the safe side.

tranquilizante *sm* MED tranquilizer.

tranquilizar *vt* - **1.** [calmar] to calm (down) - **2.** [dar confianza] to reassure. ⬩ **tranquilizarse** *vprnl* - **1.** [calmarse] to calm down - **2.** [ganar confianza] to feel reassured.

tranquillo *sm Esp fam*: **coger el tranquillo a algo** to get the knack of sthg.

tranquilo, la *adj* - **1.** [sosegado - lugar, música] peaceful; [- persona, tono de voz, mar] calm; **¡(tú) tranquilo!** *fam* don't you worry! - **2.** [velada, charla, negocio) quiet - 3. [mente] untroubled; [conciencia] clear - 4. [despreocupado] casual, laid-back.

transacción sf COM transaction.

transar vi Amér [negociar] to come to an arrangement, to reach a compromise; [transigir] to compromise, to give in.

transatlántico, ca, trasatlántico, ca adj transatlantic. ➡ **transatlántico, trasatlántico** sm NÁUT (ocean) liner.

transbordador, trasbordador sm - 1. NÁUT ferry - 2. AERON: **transbordador (espacial)** space shuttle.

transbordar, trasbordar vi to change (trains etc).

transbordo, trasbordo sm: **hacer transbordo** to change (trains etc).

transcendencia = trascendencia.

transcendental = trascendental.

transcender = trascender.

transcribir, trascribir vt [escribir] to transcribe.

transcurrir, trascurrir vi - 1. [tiempo] to pass, to go by - 2. [ocurrir] to take place.

transcurso, trascurso sm - 1. [paso de tiempo] passing - 2. [periodo de tiempo]: **en el transcurso de** in the course of.

transeúnte smf [viandante] passer-by.

transexual adj & smf transsexual.

transferencia, trasferencia sf transfer.

transferir, trasferir vt to transfer.

transfigurarse, trasfigurarse vprnl to become transfigured.

transformación, trasformación sf - 1. [cambio, conversión] transformation - 2. [en rugby] conversion.

transformador, trasformador sm ELECTRÓN transformer.

transformar, trasformar vt - 1. [cambiar radicalmente]: **transformar algo/a alguien (en)** to transform sthg/sb (into) - 2. [convertir]: **transformar algo (en)** to convert sthg (into) - 3. [en rugby] to convert. ➡ **transformarse, trasformarse** vprnl - 1. [cambiar radicalmente] to be transformed - 2. [convertirse]: **transformarse en algo** to be converted into sthg.

tránsfuga, trásfuga smf POLÍT defector.

transfuguismo, trasfuguismo sm POLÍT defection.

transfusión, trasfusión sf transfusion.

transgredir, trasgredir vt to transgress.

transgresor, ra, trasgresor, ra sm, f transgressor.

transición sf transition; **periodo de transición** transition period; **transición democrática** transition to democracy.

transido, da adj: **transido (de)** stricken (with); **transido de pena** grief-stricken.

transigir vi - 1. [ceder] to compromise - 2. [ser tolerante] to be tolerant.

transistor sm transistor.

transitar vi to go (along).

tránsito sm - 1. [circulación - gen] movement; [- de vehículos] traffic; **pasajeros en tránsito a...** passengers with connecting flights to... - 2. [transporte] transit.

transitorio, ria adj [gen] transitory; [residencia] temporary; [régimen, medida] transitional, interim.

translúcido, da, traslúcido, da adj translucent.

transmisión, trasmisión sf - 1. [gen & AUTO] transmission - 2. RADIO & TV broadcast, broadcasting (U) - 3. [de herencia, poderes etc] transference.

transmisor, ra, trasmisor, ra adj transmission (antes de s). ➡ **transmisor, trasmisor** sm transmitter.

transmitir, trasmitir vt - 1. [gen] to transmit; [saludos, noticias] to pass on - 2. RADIO & TV to broadcast - 3. [ceder] to transfer.

transparencia, trasparencia sf transparency.

transparentarse, trasparentarse vprnl [tela] to be see-through; [vidrio, líquido] to be transparent.

transparente, trasparente adj [gen] transparent; [tela] see-through.

transpiración, traspiración sf perspiration.

transpirar, traspirar vi to perspire.

transponer, trasponer vt [cambiar] to switch. ➡ **transponerse, trasponerse** vprnl [adormecerse] to doze off.

transportador sm [para medir ángulos] protractor.

transportar, trasportar vt - 1. [trasladar] to transport - 2. [embelesar] to captivate. ➡ **transportarse, trasportarse** vprnl [embelesarse] to go into raptures.

transporte sm transport UK, transportation US; **transporte público O colectivo** public transport UK O transportation US.

transportista smf carrier.

transvase, trasvase sm - 1. [de líquido] decanting - 2. [de río] transfer.

transversal, trasversal adj transverse.

tranvía sm tram, streetcar US.

trapecio sm [de gimnasia] trapeze.

trapecista smf trapeze artist.

trapero, ra sm, f rag-and-bone man (f rag-and-bone woman).

trapío sm TAUROM good bearing.

trapisonda *sf fam* [enredo] scheme.

trapo *sm* - **1.** [trozo de tela] rag - **2.** [gamuza, bayeta] cloth; **pasar el trapo a algo** to wipe sthg with a cloth, poner a alguien como un trapo to tear sb to pieces. ➤ **trapos** *smpl fam* [ropa] clothes.

tráquea *sf* windpipe; MED trachea.

traqueteo *sm* [ruido] rattling.

tras *prep* - **1.** [detrás de] behind - **2.** [después de, en pos de] after; **uno tras otro** one after the other; **andar tras algo** to be after sthg.

trasatlántico, ca = transatlántico.

trasbordador = transbordador.

trasbordar = transbordar.

trasbordo = transbordo.

trascendencia, transcendencia *sf* importance; **tener una gran trascendencia** to be deeply significant.

trascendental, transcendental *adj* - **1.** [importante] momentous - **2.** [meditación] transcendental.

trascendente *adj* momentous.

trascender, transcender *vi* - **1.** [extenderse]: **trascender (a algo)** to spread (across sthg) - **2.** [filtrarse] to be leaked - **3.** [sobrepasar]: **trascender de** to transcend, to go beyond.

trascribir = transcribir.

trascurrir = transcurrir.

trascurso = transcurso.

trasegar *vt* [desordenar] to rummage about amongst.

trasero, ra *adj* back *(antes de s)*, rear *(antes de s)*. ➤ **trasero** *sm fam* backside, butt *US*.

trasferencia = transferencia.

trasferir = transferir.

trasfigurarse = transfigurarse.

trasfondo *sm* background; [de palabras, intenciones] undertone.

trasformación = transformación.

trasformador = transformador.

trasformar = transformar.

trásfuga = tránsfuga.

trasfusión = transfusión.

trasgredir = transgredir.

trasgresor, ra = transgresor.

trashumante *adj* seasonally migratory.

trasiego *sm* [movimiento] comings and goings *pl*.

traslación *sf* ASTRON passage.

trasladar *vt* - **1.** [desplazar] to move - **2.** [a empleado, funcionario] to transfer - **3.** [reunión, fecha] to postpone. ➤ **trasladarse** *vprnl* - **1.** [desplazarse] to go - **2.** [mudarse] to move; **me traslado de piso** I'm moving flat.

traslado *sm* - **1.** [de casa, empresa, muebles] move, moving *(U)* - **2.** [de trabajo] transfer - **3.** [de personas] movement.

traslúcido, da = translúcido.

trasluz *sm* reflected light; **al trasluz** against the light.

trasmisión = transmisión.

trasmisor, ra = transmisor.

trasmitir = transmitir.

trasnochar *vi* to stay up late.

traspapelar *vt* to mislay.

trasparencia = transparencia.

trasparentarse = transparentarse.

trasparente = transparente.

traspasar *vt* - **1.** [perforar, atravesar] to go through, to pierce; [suj: líquido] to soak through - **2.** [cruzar] to cross (over); [puerta] to pass through - **3.** [cambiar de sitio] to move - **4.** [vender - jugador] to transfer; [- negocio] to sell (as a going concern) - **5.** *fig* [exceder] to go beyond.

traspaso *sm* [venta - de jugador] transfer; [- de negocio] sale (as a going concern).

traspié *(pl* traspiés*)* *sm* - **1.** [resbalón] trip, stumble; **dar un traspié** to trip up - **2.** *fig* [error] slip.

traspiración = transpiración.

traspirar = transpirar.

trasplantar *vt* to transplant.

trasplante *sm* transplant, transplanting *(U)*.

trasponer = transponer.

trasportar = transportar.

trasquilar *vt* [esquilar] to shear.

trastabillar *vi* [tambalearse] to stagger; [tropezar] to stumble; [tartamudear] to stutter.

trastada *sf fam* dirty trick; **hacer una trastada a alguien** to play a dirty trick on sb.

traste *sm* - **1.** MÚS fret - **2.** *C Sur fam* [trasero] bottom - **3.** *Andes, Amér C, Caribe & Méx*: **trastes** utensils - **4.** *loc*: **dar al traste con algo** to ruin sthg; **irse al traste** to fall through.

trastero *sm* junk room.

trastienda *sf* backroom.

trasto *sm* - **1.** [utensilio inútil] piece of junk, junk *(U)* - **2.** *fam* [persona traviesa] menace, nuisance. ➤ **trastos** *smpl fam* [pertenencias, equipo] things, stuff *(U)*; **tirarse los trastos a la cabeza** to have a flaming row.

trastocar *vt* [cambiar] to turn upside down. ➤ **trastocarse** *vprnl* [enloquecer] to go mad.

trastornado, da *adj* disturbed, unbalanced.

trastornar *vt* - **1.** [volver loco] to drive mad - **2.** [inquietar] to worry, to trouble - **3.** [alterar] to turn upside down; [planes] to disrupt. ➤ **trastornarse** *vprnl* [volverse loco] to go mad.

trastorno *sm* - **1.** [mental] disorder; **trastorno bipolar** bipolar disorder; [digestivo] upset - **2.** [alteración - por huelga, nevada] disruption *(U)*; [- por guerra etc] upheaval.

trasvase = **transvase**.

tratable *adj* easy-going, friendly.

tratado *sm* - **1.** [convenio] treaty - **2.** [escrito] treatise.

tratamiento *sm* - **1.** [gen & MED] treatment - **2.** [título] title, form of address - **3.** INFORM processing; **tratamiento de datos/textos** data/word processing; **tratamiento por lotes** batch processing.

tratar <> *vt* - **1.** [gen & MED] to treat - **2.** [discutir] to discuss - **3.** INFORM to process - **4.** [dirigirse a]: **tratar a alguien de** [usted, tú etc] to address sb as. <> *vi* - **1.** [intentar]: **tratar de hacer algo** to try to do sthg - **2.** [versar]: **tratar de/sobre** to be about - **3.** [tener relación]: **tratar con alguien** to mix with sb, to have dealings with sb - **4.** [comerciar]: **tratar en** to deal in. ◈ **tratarse** *vprnl* - **1.** [relacionarse]: **tratarse con** to mix with, to have dealings with - **2.** [versar]: **tratarse de** to be about; **¿de qué se trata?** what's it about?

tratativas *sfpl* C Sur negotiation *sing*.

trato *sm* - **1.** [comportamiento] treatment; **de trato agradable** pleasant; **malos tratos** battering *(U)* (of child, wife) - **2.** [relación] dealings *pl* - **3.** [acuerdo] deal; **cerrar** O **hacer un trato** to do O make a deal; **¡trato hecho!** it's a deal! - **4.** [tratamiento] title, term of address.

trauma *sm* trauma.

traumatólogo, ga *sm, f* traumatologist.

través ◈ **a través de** *loc prep* - **1.** [de un lado a otro de] across, over - **2.** [por, por medio de] through. ◈ **de través** *loc adv* [transversalmente] crossways; [de lado] sideways.

travesaño *sm* - **1.** ARQUIT crosspiece - **2.** DEP crossbar - **3.** [de escalera] rung.

travesía *sf* - **1.** [viaje - por mar] voyage, crossing - **2.** [calle] cross-street.

travestido, da, travestí *(pl* travestís*)* *sm, f* transvestite.

travesura *sf* [acción] prank, mischief *(U)*; **hacer travesuras** to play pranks, to get up to mischief.

traviesa *sf* - **1.** FERROC sleeper *(on track)* - **2.** CONSTR crossbeam.

travieso, sa *adj* mischievous.

trayecto *sm* - **1.** [distancia] distance - **2.** [viaje] journey, trip - **3.** [ruta] route; **final de trayecto** end of the line.

trayectoria *sf* - **1.** [recorrido] trajectory - **2.** *fig* [evolución] path.

traza *sf* [aspecto] appearance *(U)*, looks *pl*; **tener trazas de hacer algo** to show signs of

doing sthg; **esto no tiene trazas de acabar pronto** this doesn't look as if it's going to finish soon.

trazado *sm* - **1.** [trazo] outline, sketching - **2.** [diseño] plan, design - **3.** [recorrido] route.

trazar *vt* - **1.** [dibujar] to draw, to trace; [ruta] to plot - **2.** [indicar, describir] to outline - **3.** [idear] to draw up.

trazo *sm* - **1.** [de dibujo, rostro] line - **2.** [de letra] stroke.

trébol *sm* [planta] clover. ◈ **tréboles** *smpl* [naipes] clubs.

trece *num* thirteen; *ver también* **seis**.

treceavo, va *num* thirteenth.

trecho *sm* [espacio] distance; [tiempo] time.

tregua *sf* truce; *fig* respite.

treinta *num* thirty; **los (años) treinta** the Thirties; *ver también* **seis**.

treintena *sf* thirty.

tremendo, da *adj* [enorme] tremendous, enormous.

trémulo, la *adj* [voz] trembling; [luz] flickering.

tren *sm* - **1.** [ferrocarril] train; **ir en tren** to go by train; **estar como (para parar) un tren** to be really gorgeous; **perder el tren** *fig* to miss the boat; **subirse al tren** *fig* to climb on the bandwagon - **2.** TECNOL line; **tren de aterrizaje** undercarriage, landing gear; **tren de lavado** car wash.

trenza *sf* - **1.** [de pelo] plait - **2.** [de fibras] braid.

trenzar *vt* - **1.** [pelo] to plait - **2.** [fibras] to braid.

trepa *smf fam* social climber.

trepador, ra <> *adj*: **planta trepadora** creeper. <> *sm, f fam* social climber.

trepar <> *vt* to climb. <> *vi* - **1.** [subir] to climb - **2.** *fam* [medrar] to be a social climber.

trepidar *vi* to shake, to vibrate.

tres *num* three; **ni a la de tres** for anything in the world, no way; *ver también* **seis**. ◈ **tres cuartos** *sm inv* [abrigo] three-quarter-length coat. ◈ **tres en raya** *sm* noughts and crosses *(U)* UK, tick-tack-toe US.

trescientos, tas *num* three hundred; *ver también* **seis**.

tresillo *sm* [sofá] three-piece suite.

treta *sf* trick.

triangular *adj* triangular.

triángulo *sm* GEOM & MÚS triangle; **triángulo equilátero/rectángulo** equilateral/right-angled triangle.

triates *smpl* Amér triplets.

tribu *sf* tribe.

tribulación *sf* tribulation.

tribuna *sf* - **1.** [estrado] rostrum, platform; [del jurado] jury box - **2.** [DEP - localidad] stand; [- graderío] grandstand - **3.** PRENSA: **tribuna de prensa** press box; **tribuna libre** open forum.

tribunal *sm* **1.** [gen] court **2.** [de examen] board of examiners; [de concurso] panel.

tributar *vt* [homenaje] to pay; [respeto, admiración] to have.

tributo *sm* - **1.** [impuesto] tax - **2.** *fig* [precio] price - **3.** [homenaje] tribute.

triciclo *sm* tricycle.

tricornio *sm* three-cornered hat.

tricotar *vt* & *vi* to knit.

tricotosa *sf* knitting machine.

tridimensional *adj* three-dimensional.

trifulca *sf fam* row, squabble.

trigésimo, ma *num* thirtieth.

trigo *sm* wheat.

trigonometría *sf* trigonometry.

trillado, da *adj fig* trite.

trilladora *sf* [máquina] threshing machine.

trillar *vt* to thresh.

trillizo, za *sm, f* triplet.

trillón *sm* trillion *UK*, quintillion *US*.

trilogía *sf* trilogy.

trimestral *adj* three-monthly, quarterly; [exámenes, notas] end-of-term *(antes de s)*.

trimestre *sm* three months *pl*, quarter; [en escuela, universidad] term.

trinar *vi* to chirp; **está que trina** *fig* she's fuming.

trincar *fam* ⟨⟩ *vt* - **1.** [agarrar] to grab - **2.** [detener] to nick, to arrest. ⟨⟩ *vi* [beber] to guzzle.

trinchar *vt* to carve.

trinchera *sf* - **1.** MIL trench - **2.** [abrigo] trench coat.

trineo *sm* [pequeño] sledge; [grande] sleigh.

Trinidad *sf*: **la (Santísima) Trinidad** the (Holy) Trinity.

Trinidad y Tobago *n pr* Trinidad and Tobago.

trino *sm* [de pájaros] chirp, chirping *(U)*; MÚS trill.

trío *sm* [gen] trio.

tripa *sf* - **1.** [intestino] gut, intestine - **2.** *fam* [barriga] gut, belly. ➤ **tripas** *sfpl fig* [interior] insides.

triple ⟨⟩ *adj* triple. ⟨⟩ *sm* - **1.** [tres veces]: **el triple** three times as much; **el triple de gente** three times as many people - **2.** [en baloncesto] three-pointer.

triplicado *sm* second copy, triplicate.

triplicar *vt* to triple, to treble. ➤ **triplicarse** *vprnl* to triple, to treble.

trípode *sm* tripod.

tripulación *sf* crew.

tripulante *smf* crew member.

tripular *vt* to man.

tris *sm*: **estar en un tris de (hacer algo)** to be within a whisker of (doing sthg).

triste *adj* - **1.** [gen] sad; [día, tiempo, paisaje] gloomy, dreary; **es triste que** it's a shame *O* pity that - **2.** *fig* [color, vestido, luz] pale - **3.** *(antes de s)* [humilde] poor; [sueldo] sorry, miserable; **ni un triste** *fig* not a single.

tristeza *sf* [gen] sadness; [de paisaje, día] gloominess, dreariness.

triturador *sm* [de basura] waste-disposal unit; [de papeles] shredder.

triturar *vt* - **1.** [moler, desmenuzar] to crush, to grind; [papel] to shred - **2.** [masticar] to chew.

triunfador, ra *sm, f* winner.

triunfal *adj* triumphant.

triunfar *vi* - **1.** [vencer] to win, to triumph - **2.** [tener éxito] to succeed, to be successful.

triunfo *sm* [gen] triumph; [en encuentro, elecciones] victory, win.

trivial *adj* trivial.

trivializar *vt* to trivialize.

trizas *sfpl*: **hacer trizas algo** [hacer añicos] to smash sthg to pieces; [desgarrar] to tear sthg to shreds; **estar hecho trizas** [persona] to be shattered.

trocar *vt* - **1.** [transformar]: **trocar algo (en algo)** to change sthg (into sthg) - **2.** [intercambiar] to swap.

trocear *vt* to cut up (into pieces).

trocha *sf* [senda] path; [atajo] shortcut.

troche ➤ **a troche y moche** *loc adv* haphazardly.

trofeo *sm* trophy.

troglodita *smf* - **1.** [cavernícola] cave dweller, troglodyte - **2.** *fam* [bárbaro, tosco] roughneck.

trola *sf fam* fib, lie.

trolebús *sm* trolleybus.

trombón *sm* [instrumento] trombone; [músico] trombonist.

trombosis *sf inv* thrombosis.

trompa *sf* - **1.** [de elefante] trunk; [de oso hormiguero] snout; [de insecto] proboscis - **2.** MÚS horn.

trompazo *sm fam* bang; **darse** *O* **pegarse un trompazo con** to bang into.

trompear *vt Amér fam* to punch. ➤ **trompearse** *vprnl Amér fam* to have a fight.

trompeta *sf* trumpet.

trompetista *smf* trumpeter.

trompicón *sm* [tropezón] stumble; **a trompicones** in fits and starts.

trompo *sm* - **1.** [juguete] spinning top - **2.** [giro] spin.

tronado, da *adj fam* [loco] nuts, crazy.

tronar <> *v impers* & *vi* to thunder. <> *vt* *Méx fam* [fracasar] to fail. ❧ **tronarse** *vprnl* *Amér fam* to shoot o.s.

tronchar *vt* [partir] to snap. ❧ **troncharse** *vprnl fam*: **troncharse (de risa)** to split one's sides laughing.

tronco, ca *sm, f mfam* [tipo] guy (f bird); [como apelativo] pal, mate. ❧ **tronco** *sm* ANAT & BOT trunk; [talado y sin ramas] log; **dormir como un tronco, estar hecho un tronco** to sleep like a log.

tronera *sf* - **1.** ARQUIT & HIST embrasure - **2.** [en billar] pocket.

trono *sm* throne; **subir al trono** to ascend the throne.

tropa *sf* (*gen pl*) MIL troops *pl*.

tropecientos, tas *adj fam* loads of.

tropel *sm* [de personas] mob, crowd.

tropero *sm* R Dom cowboy.

tropezar *vi* [con el pie]: **tropezar (con)** to trip O stumble (on). ❧ **tropezarse** *vprnl* [encontrarse] to bump into each other; **tropezarse con alguien** to bump into sb. ❧ **tropezar con** *vi* [problema, persona] to run into, to come across.

tropezón *sm* - **1.** [con el pie] trip, stumble; **dar un tropezón** to trip up, to stumble - **2.** *fig* [desacierto] slip-up. ❧ **tropezones** *smpl* CULIN small chunks.

tropical *adj* tropical.

trópico *sm* tropic.

tropiezo *sm* - **1.** [con el pie] trip, stumble; **dar un tropiezo** to trip up, to stumble - **2.** *fig* [equivocación] slip-up; [revés] setback.

troquel *sm* [molde] mould, die.

trotamundos *smf inv* globe-trotter.

trotar *vi* to trot; *fam fig* [de aquí para allá] to dash O run around.

trote *sm* [de caballo] trot; **al trote** at a trot.

troupe [trup, 'trupe] (*pl* troupes) *sf* troupe.

trovador *sm* troubadour.

trozar *vt* Amér [carne] to cut up; [res, tronco] to butcher, to cut up.

trozo *sm* [gen] piece; [de sendero, camino] stretch; [de obra, película] extract; **cortar algo en trozos** to cut sthg into pieces; **hacer algo a trozos** to do sthg in bits.

trucar *vt* to doctor; [motor] to soup up.

trucha *sf* [pez] trout.

truco *sm* - **1.** [trampa, engaño] trick; **truco de magia** magic trick - **2.** [habilidad, técnica] knack; **coger el truco** to get the knack; **truco publicitario** advertising gimmick.

truculento, ta *adj* horrifying, terrifying.

trueno *sm* METEOR clap of thunder, thunder (U).

trueque *sm* - **1.** COM & HIST barter - **2.** [intercambio] exchange, swap.

trufa *sf* [hongo, bombón] truffle.

truhán, ana *sm, f* rogue, crook.

truncar *vt* [frustrar - vida, carrera] to cut short; [- planes, ilusiones] to spoil, to ruin.

trusa *sf* Caribe [traje de baño] swimsuit; R Dom [faja] girdle.

tu (*pl* tus) *adj poses* (*antes de s*) your.

tú *pron pers* you; **es más alta que tú** she's taller than you; **de tú a tú** [lucha] evenly matched; **hablar** O **tratar de tú a alguien** to address sb as 'tú'.

tubérculo *sm* tuber, root vegetable.

tuberculosis *sf inv* tuberculosis.

tubería *sf* - **1.** [cañerías] pipes *pl*, pipework - **2.** [tubo] pipe.

tubo *sm* - **1.** [tubería] pipe; **tubo de escape** AUTO exhaust (pipe); **tubo del desagüe** drainpipe - **2.** [recipiente] tube; **tubo de ensayo** test tube - **3.** ANAT tract; **tubo digestivo** digestive tract, alimentary canal.

tuerca *sf* nut.

tuerto, ta *adj* [sin un ojo] one-eyed; [ciego de un ojo] blind in one eye.

tuétano *sm* ANAT (bone) marrow.

tufillo *sm* whiff.

tufo *sm* [mal olor] stench.

tugurio *sm* hovel.

tul *sm* tulle.

tulipa *sf* [de lámpara] tulip-shaped lampshade.

tulipán *sm* tulip.

tullido, da <> *adj* crippled. <> *sm, f* cripple, disabled person.

tumba *sf* grave, tomb; **ser (como) una tumba** to be as silent as the grave.

tumbar *vt* [derribar] to knock over O down. ❧ **tumbarse** *vprnl* [acostarse] to lie down.

tumbo *sm* jolt, jerk; **ir dando tumbos** *fig* [persona] to have a lot of ups and downs.

tumbona *sf* [en la playa] deck chair; [en el jardín] (sun) lounger.

tumor *sm* tumour.

tumulto *sm* - **1.** [disturbio] riot, disturbance - **2.** [alboroto] uproar, tumult; **un tumulto de gente** a crowd of people.

tumultuoso, sa *adj* - **1.** [conflictivo] tumultuous - **2.** [turbulento] rough, stormy.

tuna *sf* - **1.** = **tuno** - **2.** Amér C & Méx [fruta] prickly pear.

tunante, ta *sm, f* crook, scoundrel.

tunda *sf fam* [paliza] thrashing.

túnel *sm* tunnel; **salir del túnel** *fig* to turn the corner. ❧ **túnel de lavado** *sm* AUTO car wash.

Túnez *n pr* - **1.** [capital] Tunis - **2.** [país] Tunisia.

túnica *sf* tunic.

Tunicia *n pr* Tunisia.

tuno, na *sm, f* rogue, scoundrel. ▻ **tuna** *sf* group of student minstrels.

tuntún ▻ **al tuntún** *loc adv* without thinking.

tupé *sm* [cabello] quiff.

tupido, da *adj* thick, dense.

turba *sf* - **1.** [combustible] peat, turf - **2.** [muchedumbre] mob.

turbación *sf* - **1.** [desconcierto] upset, disturbance - **2.** [azoramiento] embarrassment.

turbante *sm* turban.

turbar *vt* - **1.** [alterar] to disturb - **2.** [emocionar] to upset - **3.** [desconcertar] to trouble, to disconcert. ▻ **turbarse** *vprnl* - **1.** [alterarse] to get upset - **2.** [aturdirse] to get embarrassed.

turbina *sf* turbine.

turbio, bia *adj* - **1.** [agua etc] cloudy - **2.** [vista] blurred - **3.** *fig* [negocio etc] shady - **4.** *fig* [época etc] turbulent.

turbulencia *sf* - **1.** [de fluido] turbulence - **2.** [alboroto] uproar, clamour.

turbulento, ta *adj* - **1.** [gen] turbulent - **2.** [revoltoso] unruly, rebellious.

turco, ca ◇ *adj* Turkish. ◇ *sm, f* [persona] Turk. ▻ **turco** *sm* [lengua] Turkish.

turismo *sm* - **1.** [gen] tourism; **hacer turismo (por)** to go touring (round); **turismo rural** rural tourism - **2.** AUTO private car.

turista *smf* tourist.

turístico, ca *adj* tourist *(antes de s)*.

turnarse *vprnl*: **turnarse (con alguien)** to take turns (with sb).

turno *sm* - **1.** [tanda] turn, go; **le ha llegado el turno de hacerlo** it's his turn to do it - **2.** [de trabajo] shift; **trabajar por turnos** to work shifts; **turno de día/noche** day/night shift.

turquesa ◇ *sf* [mineral] turquoise. ◇ *adj inv* [color] turquoise. ◇ *sm* [color] turquoise.

Turquía *n pr* Turkey.

turrón *sm* Christmas sweet similar to marzipan or nougat, made with almonds and honey.

tute *sm* [juego] card game similar to whist.

tutear *vt* to address as 'tú'. ▻ **tutearse** *vprnl* to address each other as 'tú'.

tutela *sf* - **1.** DER guardianship - **2.** [cargo]: **tutela (de)** responsibility (for); **bajo la tutela de** under the protection of.

tutelar ◇ *adj* DER tutelary. ◇ *vt* to act as guardian to.

tutor, ra *sm, f* - **1.** DER guardian - **2.** [profesor - privado] tutor; [- de un curso] form teacher.

tutoría *sf* DER guardianship.

tutú *sm* tutu.

tuviera *etc* ▻ **tener**.

tuyo, ya ◇ *adj poses* yours; **este libro es tuyo** this book is yours; **un amigo tuyo** a friend of yours; **no es asunto tuyo** it's none of your business. ◇ *pron poses*: **el tuyo** yours; **el tuyo es rojo** yours is red; **ésta es la tuya** *fam* this is the chance you've been waiting for; **lo tuyo es el teatro** [lo que haces bien] you should be on the stage; **los tuyos** *fam* [tu familia] your folks; [tu bando] your lot.

TV (*abrev de* **televisión**) *sf* TV.

TVE (*abrev de* **Televisión Española**) *sf* Spanish state television network.

u¹ (*pl* **úes**), **U** (*pl* **Úes**) *sf* [letra] u, U.

u² *conj* ('u' en vez de 'o' antes de palabras que empiezan por 'o' *u* 'ho') or; *ver también* **o²**.

ubicación *sf* position, location.

ubicar *vt* to place, to position; [edificio etc] to locate. ▻ **ubicarse** *vprnl* [edificio etc] to be situated.

ubre *sf* udder.

UCI (*abrev de* **unidad de cuidados intensivos**) *sf* ICU.

Ucrania *n pr* the Ukraine.

Ud., Vd. *abrev de* **usted**.

Uds., Vds. *abrev de* **usted**.

UE (*abrev de* **Unión Europea**) *sf* EU.

UEFA (*abrev de* **Unión de Asociaciones Europeas de Fútbol**) *sf* UEFA.

ufanarse *vprnl*: **ufanarse de** to boast about.

ufano, na *adj* - **1.** [satisfecho] proud, pleased - **2.** [engreído] boastful, conceited.

Uganda *n pr* Uganda.

UGT (*abrev de* **Unión General de los Trabajadores**) *sf* major socialist Spanish trade union.

UHF (*abrev de* **ultra high frequency**) *sf* UHF.

ujier (*pl* **ujieres**) *sm* usher.

újule *interj Amér*: ¡újule! wow!

úlcera *sf* MED ulcer.

ulcerar *vt* to ulcerate. ▻ **ulcerarse** *vprnl* MED to ulcerate.

ulterior *adj culto* [en el tiempo] subsequent, ulterior.

ulteriormente *adv culto* subsequently.

ultimador, ra *sm, f Amér* killer.

últimamente *adv* recently, of late.

ultimar *vt* - **1.** [gen] to conclude, to complete - **2.** *Amér* [matar] to kill.

ultimátum (*pl* ultimatos *O* ultimátum) *sm* ultimatum.

último, ma ⬥ *adj* - **1.** [gen] last; **por último** lastly, finally; **ser lo último** [lo final] to come last; [el último recurso] to be a last resort; [el colmo] to be the last straw - **2.** [más reciente] latest, most recent - **3.** [más remoto] furthest, most remote - **4.** [más bajo] bottom - **5.** [más alto] top - **6.** [de más atrás] back. ⬥ *sm, f* - **1.** [en fila, carrera etc]: **el último** the last (one); **llegar el último** to come last - **2.** *(en comparaciones, enumeraciones)*: **éste último...** the latter...

ultra *smf* POLÍT right-wing extremist.

ultraderecha *sf* extreme right (wing).

ultraizquierda *sf* extreme left (wing).

ultrajar *vt* to insult, to offend.

ultraje *sm* insult.

ultramar *sm* overseas *pl*; **de ultramar** overseas *(antes de s)*.

ultramarino, na *adj* overseas *(antes de s)*. ⬥ **ultramarinos** ⬥ *smpl* [comestibles] groceries. ⬥ *sm inv* [tienda] grocer's (shop) *sing*.

ultranza ⬥ **a ultranza** *loc adv* - **1.** [con decisión] to the death - **2.** [acérrimamente] out-and-out.

ultrasonido *sm* ultrasound.

ultratumba *sf*: **de ultratumba** from beyond the grave.

ultravioleta *adj inv* ultraviolet.

ulular *vi* - **1.** [viento, lobo] to howl - **2.** [búho] to hoot.

umbilical ⬥ **cordón**.

umbral *sm* - **1.** [gen] threshold - **2.** *fig* [límite] bounds *pl*, realms *pl*.

un, una ⬥ *art (antes de sf que empiece por 'a' o 'ha' tónica:* un*)* a, an *(ante sonido vocálico)*; **un hombre/coche** a man/car; **una mujer/mesa** a woman/table; **un águila/hacha** an eagle/axe; **una hora** an hour. ⬥ *adj* ⬥ **uno**.

unánime *adj* unanimous.

unanimidad *sf* unanimity; **por unanimidad** unanimously.

unción *sf* unction.

undécimo, ma *num* eleventh.

UNED *(abrev de* Universidad Nacional de Educación a Distancia) *sf Spanish open university*.

ungüento *sm* ointment.

únicamente *adv* only, solely.

único, ca *adj* - **1.** [sólo] only; **es lo único que quiero** it's all I want - **2.** [excepcional] unique - **3.** [precio, función, razón] single.

unicornio *sm* unicorn.

unidad *sf* - **1.** [gen, MAT & MIL] unit; **25 euros la unidad** 25 euros each; **unidad de cuidados intensivos** *O* **vigilancia intensiva** intensive care (unit); **unidad central de proceso** INFORM central processing unit; **unidad de disco** INFORM disk drive; **unidad monetaria** monetary unit - **2.** [cohesión, acuerdo] unity.

unido, da *adj* united; [familia, amigo] close.

unifamiliar *adj* detached; **vivienda unifamiliar house** *(detached or terraced)*.

unificar *vt* - **1.** [unir] to unite, to join; [países] to unify - **2.** [uniformar] to standardize.

uniformar *vt* - **1.** [igualar] to standardize - **2.** [poner uniforme] to put into uniform.

uniforme ⬥ *adj* uniform; [superficie] even. ⬥ *sm* uniform.

uniformidad *sf* uniformity; [de superficie] evenness.

unión *sf* - **1.** [gen] union; **en unión de** together with; **Unión Africana** African Union - **2.** [suma, adherimiento] joining together - **3.** TECNOL join, joint.

Unión Europea *sf*: **la Unión Europea** the European Union.

unir *vt* - **1.** [pedazos, habitaciones etc] to join - **2.** [empresas, estados, facciones] to unite - **3.** [comunicar - ciudades etc] to link - **4.** [suj: amistad, circunstancias etc] to bind - **5.** [casar] to join, to marry - **6.** [combinar] to combine; **unir algo a algo** to combine sthg with sthg - **7.** [mezclar] to mix *O* blend in. ⬥ **unirse** *vprnl* - **1.** [gen] to join together; **unirse a algo** to join sthg - **2.** [casarse]: **unirse en matrimonio** to be joined in wedlock.

unisexo, unisex *adj inv* unisex.

unísono ⬥ **al unísono** *loc adv* in unison.

unitario, ria *adj* - **1.** [de una unidad - estado, nación] single; [- precio] unit *(antes de s)* - **2.** POLÍT unitarian.

universal *adj* - **1.** [gen] universal - **2.** [mundial] world *(antes de s)*.

universidad *sf* university, college *US*, school *US*.

universitario, ria ⬥ *adj* university *(antes de s)*. ⬥ *sm, f* [estudiante] university student.

universo *sm* - **1.** ASTRON universe - **2.** *fig* [mundo] world.

unívoco, ca *adj* univocal, unambiguous.

uno, una ⬥ *adj* - **1.** [indefinido] one; **un día volveré** one *O* some day I'll return; **había unos coches mal aparcados** there were some badly parked cars; **había unos 12 muchachos** there were about *O* some 12 boys there - **2.** [numeral] one; **un hombre, un voto** one man, one voto; **la fila uno** row one. ➤ *pron* - **1.** [indefinido] one; **coge uno** take one; **uno de vosotros** one of you; **unos... otros...** some... others...; **uno a otro, unos a otros** each other, one another; **uno y otro** both; **unos y otros** all of them - **2.** *fam* [cierta persona] someone, somebody; **hablé con uno que te conoce** I spoke to someone who knows you; **me lo han contado unos** certain people told me so - **3.** [yo] one; **uno ya no está para estos trotes** one isn't really up to this sort of thing any more - **4.** *loc*: **a una** [en armonía, a la vez] together; **de uno en uno, uno a uno, uno por uno** one by one; **juntar varias cosas en una** to combine several things into one; **lo uno por lo otro** it all evens out in the end; **más de uno** many people; **una de dos** it's either one thing or the other; **unos cuantos** a few; **una y no más** once was enough, once bitten, twice shy. ➤ **uno** *sm* [número] (number) one; **el uno** number one; *ver también* **seis.** ➤ **una** *sf* [hora]: **la una** one o'clock.

untar *vt* - **1.** [pan, tostada]: **untar (con)** to spread (with); [piel, cara etc] to smear (with) - **2.** [máquina, bisagra etc] to grease.

untuoso, sa *adj* [graso] greasy, oily.

uña *sf* - **1.** [de mano] fingernail, nail; **ser uña y carne** to be as thick as thieves - **2.** [de pie] toenail - **3.** [garra] claw; **enseñar** *O* **sacar las uñas** to get one's claws out.

uralita® *sf* CONSTR *material made of asbestos and cement, usually corrugated and used mainly for roofing.*

uranio *sm* uranium.

Urano *n pr* Uranus.

urbanidad *sf* politeness, courtesy.

urbanismo *sm* town planning.

urbanización *sf* - **1.** [acción] urbanization - **2.** [zona residencial] (housing) estate.

urbanizar *vt* to develop, to urbanize.

urbano, na *adj* urban, city *(antes de s)*.

urbe *sf* large city.

urdir *vt* - **1.** [planear] to plot, to forge - **2.** [hilos] to warp.

urgencia *sf* - **1.** [cualidad] urgency - **2.** MED emergency; **de urgencia** emergency - **3.** [necesidad] urgent need; **en caso de urgencia** in case of emergency. ➤ **urgencias** *sfpl* MED casualty (department) *sing*; **ingresar por urgencias** to be admitted as an emergency.

urgente *adj* - **1.** [apremiante] urgent - **2.** MED emergency *(s)* - **3.** [correo] express.

urgir *vi* to be urgently necessary; **me urge hacerlo** I urgently need to do it; **urgir a alguien a que haga algo** to urge sb to do sthg.

urinario, ria *adj* urinary. ➤ **urinario** *sm* urinal, comfort station *US*.

URL *(abrev de* uniform resource locator*) sf* INFORM URL.

urna *sf* - **1.** [vasija] urn - **2.** [caja de cristal] glass case - **3.** [para votar] ballot box.

urraca *sf* magpie.

URSS *(abrev de* Unión de Repúblicas Socialistas Soviéticas*) sf* HIST USSR.

urticaria *sf* nettle rash.

Uruguay *n pr:* **(el) Uruguay** Uruguay.

uruguayo, ya *adj* & *sm, f* Uruguayan.

usado, da *adj* - **1.** [utilizado] used; **muy usado** widely used - **2.** [de segunda mano] second-hand - **3.** [gastado] worn-out, worn.

usanza *sf*: **a la vieja usanza** in the old way *O* style.

usar *vt* - **1.** [gen] to use; **usar algo/a alguien de** *O* **como algo** to use sthg/sb as sthg - **2.** [prenda] to wear. ➤ **usarse** *vprnl* - **1.** [emplearse] to be used - **2.** [estar de moda] to be worn.

USB *(abrev de* universal serial bus*) sm* INFORM USB.

usina *sf* Amér: **usina eléctrica** power station; **usina nuclear** nuclear power station.

uso *sm* - **1.** [gen] use; **al uso** fashionable; **al uso andaluz** in the Andalusian style; **'de uso externo'** MED 'for external use only' - **2.** *(gen pl)* [costumbre] custom - **3.** LING usage - **4.** [desgaste] wear and tear.

usted *pron pers* - **1.** [tratamiento de respeto - sing] you; [- pl]: **ustedes** you *pl*; **contesten ustedes a las preguntas** please answer the questions; **me gustaría hablar con usted** I'd like to talk to you; **¡oiga, usted!** hey, you!; **tratar a alguien de usted** to address sb using the 'usted' form - **2.** [tratamiento de respeto - posesivo]: **de usted/ustedes** yours.

usual *adj* usual.

usuario, ria *sm, f* user.

usufructo *sm* DER usufruct, use.

usura *sf* usury.

usurero, ra *sm, f* usurer.

usurpar *vt* to usurp.

utensilio *sm* [gen] tool, implement; CULIN utensil; **utensilios de pesca** fishing tackle.

útero *sm* womb, uterus.

útil ◇ *adj* [beneficiable, aprovechable] useful. ◇ *sm (gen pl)* [herramienta] tool; **útiles de jardinería** gardening tools; AGRIC implement; **útiles de labranza** agricultural implements.

utilidad *sf* - **1.** [cualidad] usefulness - **2.** [beneficio] profit.

utilitario, ria *adj* AUTO utility. ➤ **utilitario** *sm* AUTO utility car, compact *US*.

utilización *sf* use.

utilizar vt [gen] to use.

utopía sf utopia.

utópico, ca adj utopian.

UV (abrev de **ultravioleta**) UV.

uva sf grape; **uva de mesa** dessert grape; **uva moscatel** muscatel grape; **uva pasa** raisin; **estar de mala uva** to be in a bad mood; **tener mala uva** to be a nasty piece of work; **uvas de la suerte** grapes eaten for good luck as midnight chimes on New Year's Eve.

uy interj: ¡uy! ahh!, oh!

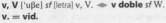

v, V ['uβe] sf [letra] v, V. ➡ **v doble** sf W.

v. = vid.

va ▷ **ir.**

vaca sf - 1. [animal] cow; **vaca lechera/sagrada** dairy/sacred cow; **ponerse como una vaca** to put on a lot of weight - 2. [carne] beef.

vacaciones sfpl holiday sing, holidays UK, vacation sing US; **estar/irse de vacaciones** to be/go on holiday.

vacante ◇ adj vacant. ◇ sf vacancy.

vaciar vt - 1. [gen]: **vaciar algo (de)** to empty sthg (of) - 2. [dejar hueco] to hollow (out) - 3. ARTE to cast, to mould.

vacilación sf - 1. [duda] hesitation; [al elegir] indecision - 2. [oscilación] swaying; [de la luz] flickering.

vacilante adj - 1. [gen] hesitant; [al elegir] indecisive - 2. [luz] flickering; [pulso] irregular; [paso] swaying, unsteady.

vacilar vi - 1. [dudar] to hesitate; [al elegir] to be indecisive - 2. [voz, principios, régimen] to falter - 3. [fluctuar - luz] to flicker; [- pulso] to be irregular - 4. [tambalearse] to wobble, to sway - 5. fam [chulear] to swank - 6. fam [bromear] to take the mickey.

vacilón, ona fam sm, f - 1. [chulo] show-off - 2. [bromista] tease. ➡ **vacilón** sm Amér C, Caribe & Méx [fiesta] party.

vacío, a adj empty. ➡ **vacío** sm - 1. FÍS vacuum; **envasar al vacío** to vacuum-pack; **vacío de poder** power vacuum - 2. [abismo, carencia] void - 3. [hueco] space, gap.

vacuna sf vaccine; **poner una vacuna a alguien** to vaccinate sb.

vacunar vt to vaccinate; **vacunar contra algo** to vaccinate against sthg.

vacuno, na adj bovine.

vadear vt to ford; fig to overcome.

vado sm - 1. [en acera] lowered kerb; 'vado permanente' 'keep clear' - 2. [de río] ford.

vagabundear vi [vagar]: **vagabundear (por)** to wander, to roam.

vagabundo, da ◇ adj [persona] vagrant; [perro] stray. ◇ sm, f tramp, bum US.

vagancia sf - 1. [holgazanería] laziness, idleness - 2. [vagabundeo] vagrancy.

vagar vi: **vagar (por)** to wander, to roam.

vagina sf vagina.

vago, ga adj - 1. [perezoso] lazy, idle - 2. [impreciso] vague.

vagón sm [de pasajeros] carriage, car US; [de mercancías] wagon.

vagoneta sf wagon.

vaguedad sf - 1. [cualidad] vagueness - 2. [dicho] vague remark.

vahído sm blackout, fainting fit.

vaho sm - 1. [vapor] steam - 2. [aliento] breath.

vaina sf - 1. [gen] sheath - 2. BOT - envoltura] pod - 3. Amér fam [engreído] pain in the neck; ¡qué vaina! Col, Méx & Ven mfam what a pain! - 4. Col, Perú & Ven [problema] pain - 5. Col, Perú & Ven [cosa] thing.

vainilla sf vanilla.

vaivén sm - 1. [balanceo - de barco] swaying, rocking; [- de péndulo, columpio] swinging - 2. [altibajo] ups-and-downs pl.

vajilla sf crockery; **una vajilla** a dinner service.

vale ◇ sm - 1. [bono] coupon, voucher - 2. [comprobante] receipt - 3. [pagaré] I.O.U. - 4. Méx & Ven fam [amigo] pal, mate UK, buddy US. ◇ interj ▷ **valer**.

valedero, ra adj valid.

valenciano, na adj & sm, f [de Valencia] Valencian.

valentía sf [valor] bravery.

valer ◇ vt - 1. [costar - precio] to cost; [tener un valor de] to be worth; ¿cuánto vale? [de precio] how much does it cost?, how much is it? - 2. [ocasionar] to earn - 3. [merecer] to deserve, to be worth - 4. [equivaler] to be equivalent O equal to. ◇ vi - 1. [merecer aprecio] to be worthy; **hacerse valer** to show one's worth - 2. [servir]: **valer para algo** to be for sthg; **eso aún vale** you can still use that; ¿para qué vale? what's it for? - 3. [ser válido] to be valid; [en juegos] to be allowed - 4. [ayudar] to help, to be of use - 5. [tener calidad] to be of worth; **no valer nada** to be worthless O use-

less - 6. [equivaler]: **valer por** to be worth - **7.** *loc:* **más vale tarde que nunca** better late than never; **más vale que te calles/vayas** it would be better if you shut up/left; **¿vale?** okay?, all right?; **¡vale okay!**, all right!
➥ **valerse** *vprnl* - **1.** [servirse]: **valerse de algo/alguien** to use sthg/sb - **2.** [desenvolverse]: **valerse (por sí mismo)** to manage on one's own - **3.** *Méx loc:* **¡no se vale!** that's not fair!

valeroso, sa *adj* brave, courageous.

valía *sf* value, worth.

validar *vt* to validate.

validez *sf* validity; **dar validez a** to validate.

válido, da *adj* valid.

valiente *adj* [valeroso] brave.

valija *sf* - **1.** [maleta] case, suitcase; **valija diplomática** diplomatic bag - **2.** [de correos] mailbag.

valioso, sa *adj* - **1.** [gen] valuable - **2.** [intento, esfuerzo] worthy.

valla *sf* - **1.** [cerca] fence - **2.** DEP hurdle.
➥ **valla publicitaria** *sf* billboard, hoarding.

vallar *vt* to put a fence round.

valle *sm* valley.

valor *sm* - **1.** [gen, MAT & MÚS] value; **joyas por valor de...** jewels worth...; **sin valor** worthless - **2.** [importancia] importance; **dar valor a** to give O attach importance to; **quitar valor a algo** to take away from sthg - **3.** [valentía] bravery. ➥ **valores** *smpl* - **1.** [principios] values - **2.** FIN securities, bonds; **valores en cartera** investments.

valoración *sf* - **1.** [de precio, pérdidas] valuation - **2.** [de mérito, cualidad, ventajas] evaluation, assessment.

valorar *vt* - **1.** [tasar, apreciar] to value - **2.** [evaluar] to evaluate, to assess.

vals (*pl* valses) *sm* waltz.

válvula *sf* valve. ➥ **válvula de escape** *sf fig* means of letting off steam.

vampiresa *sf fam* vamp, femme fatale.

vampiro *sm* [personaje] vampire.

vanagloriarse *vprnl:* **vanagloriarse (de)** to boast (about), to show off (about).

vandalismo *sm* vandalism.

vanguardia *sf* - **1.** MIL vanguard; **ir a la vanguardia de** *fig* to be at the forefront of - **2.** [cultural] avant-garde, vanguard; **de vanguardia** avant-garde.

vanidad *sf* - **1.** [orgullo] vanity - **2.** [inutilidad] futility.

vanidoso, sa *adj* vain, conceited.

vano, na *adj* - **1.** [gen] vain; **en vano** in vain - **2.** [vacío, superficial] shallow, superficial.

vapor *sm* - **1.** [emanación] vapour; [de agua] steam; **al vapor** CULIN steamed; **de vapor** [máquina etc] steam *(antes de s)*; **a todo vapor** at full speed - **2.** [barco] steamship.

vaporizador *sm* - **1.** [pulverizador] spray - **2.** [para evaporar] vaporizer.

vaporoso, sa *adj* [fino - tela etc] diaphanous.

vapulear *vt* to beat, to thrash; *fig* to slate.

vaquero, ra ⬦ *adj* cowboy *(antes de s)*. ⬦ *sm, f* [persona] cowboy (*f* cowgirl), cowherd. ➥ **vaqueros** *smpl* [pantalón] jeans.

vara *sf* - **1.** [rama, palo] stick - **2.** [de metal etc] rod - **3.** [insignia] staff.

variable *adj* changeable, variable.

variación *sf* variation; [del tiempo] change.

variado, da *adj* varied; [galletas, bombones] assorted.

variante ⬦ *adj* variant. ⬦ *sf* - **1.** [variación] variation; [versión] version - **2.** AUTO by-pass.

variar ⬦ *vt* - **1.** [modificar] to alter, to change - **2.** [dar variedad] to vary. ⬦ *vi* [cambiar]: **para variar** *irón* (just) for a change.

varicela *sf* chickenpox.

varicoso, sa *adj* varicose.

variedad *sf* variety. ➥ **variedades, varietés** *sfpl* TEATRO variety *(U)*, music hall *(U)*.

varilla *sf* - **1.** [barra larga] rod, stick - **2.** [tira larga - de abanico, paraguas] spoke, rib; [- de gafas] arm; [- de corsé] bone, stay.

vario, ria *adj* [variado] varied, different. ➥ **varios, rias** *adj* & *pron pl* several.

varita *sf* wand; **varita mágica** magic wand.

variz *(gen pl) sf* varicose vein.

varón *sm* [hombre] male, man; [chico] boy.

varonil *adj* masculine, male.

vasallo, lla *sm, f* [siervo] vassal.

vasco, ca *adj* & *sm, f* Basque. ➥ **vasco** *sm* [lengua] Basque.

vascuence *sm* [lengua] Basque.

vasectomía *sf* vasectomy.

vaselina® *sf* Vaseline®.

vasija *sf* vessel.

vaso *sm* - **1.** [recipiente, contenido] glass; **un vaso de plástico** a plastic cup - **2.** ANAT vessel; **vasos sanguíneos** blood vessels.

vástago *sm* - **1.** [descendiente] offspring *(U)* - **2.** [brote] shoot - **3.** [varilla] rod.

vasto, ta *adj* vast.

váter (*pl* váteres), **water** (*pl* wateres) *sm* toilet.

vaticinar *vt* to prophesy, to predict.

vatio, watio ['batjo] *sm* watt.

vaya *interj* - **1.** [sorpresa]: **¡vaya!** well! - **2.** [énfasis]: **¡vaya moto!** what a motorbike!; ➢ **ir**.

VB *abrev de* **visto bueno**.

Vd. *(abrev de usted)* = **Ud.**

Vda. *(abrev de viuda) abrev de* **viuda**.

Vds. *(abrev de ustedes)* = **Uds.**

ve ➢ **ir**.

véase ⊳ **ver**.

vecinal *adj* [camino, impuestos] local.

vecindad *sf* - **1.** [vecindario] neighbourhood - **2.** [alrededores] vicinity - **3.** *Méx* [vivienda] tenement house.

vecindario *sm* [de barrio] neighbourhood; [de población] community, inhabitants *pl*.

vecino, na ⊳ *adj* [cercano] neighbouring. ⊳ *sm, f* - **1.** [de la misma casa, calle] neighbour; [de un barrio] resident - **2.** [de una localidad] inhabitant.

vector *sm* vector.

veda *sf* - **1.** [prohibición] ban *(on hunting and fishing)*; **levantar la veda** to open the season - **2.** [periodo] close season.

vedado, da *adj* prohibited. ⇌ **vedado** *sm* reserve.

vedar *vt* to prohibit.

vedette [be'det] *sf* star.

vegetación *sf* vegetation.

vegetal ⊳ *adj* - **1.** BIOL vegetable, plant *(antes de s)* - **2.** [sandwich] salad *(antes de s)*. ⊳ *sm* vegetable.

vegetar *vi* to vegetate.

vegetariano, na *adj & sm, f* vegetarian.

vehemencia *sf* [pasión, entusiasmo] vehemence.

vehemente *adj* [apasionado, entusiasta] vehement.

vehículo *sm* [gen] vehicle; [de infección] carrier.

veinte *num* twenty; **los (años) veinte** the twenties; *ver también* **seis**.

veinteavo, va *num* twentieth.

veintena *sf* - **1.** [veinte] twenty - **2.** [aproximadamente]: **una veintena (de)** about twenty.

vejación *sf* humiliation.

vejamen *sm* = **vejación**.

vejestorio *sm despec* old fogey.

vejez *sf* old age.

vejiga *sf* bladder.

vela *sf* - **1.** [para dar luz] candle; **¿quién le ha dado vela en este entierro?** who asked you to stick your oar in?; **estar a dos velas** not to have two halfpennies to rub together - **2.** [de barco] sail - **3.** DEP sailing; **hacer vela** to go sailing - **4.** [vigilia] vigil; **pasar la noche en vela** [adrede] to stay awake all night; [desvelado] to have a sleepless night.

velada *sf* evening.

velado, da *adj* - **1.** [oculto] veiled, hidden - **2.** FOTO fogged.

velar ⊳ *vi* - **1.** [cuidar]: **velar por** to look after, to watch over - **2.** [no dormir] to stay awake. ⊳ *vt* - **1.** [de noche - muerto] to keep a vigil over - **2.** [ocultar] to mask, to veil. ⇌ **velarse** *vprnl* FOTO to get fogged.

veleidad *sf* - **1.** [inconstancia] fickleness - **2.** [antojo, capricho] whim, caprice.

velero *sm* sailing boat/ship.

veleta *sf* weather vane.

vello *sm* - **1.** [pelusilla] down - **2.** [pelo] hair; **vello púbico** pubic hair.

velloso, sa *adj* hairy.

velo *sm lit & fig* veil; **correr O echar un (tupido) velo sobre algo** to draw a veil over sthg.

velocidad *sf* - **1.** [gen] speed; **cobrar velocidad** to pick up speed; **perder velocidad** to lose speed; **velocidad máxima** top speed; TECNOL velocity; **a toda velocidad** at full speed; **de alta velocidad** high-speed; **velocidad punta** top speed - **2.** AUTO [marcha] gear; **cambiar de velocidad** to change gear.

velocímetro *sm* speedometer.

velódromo *sm* cycle track, velodrome.

veloz *adj* fast, quick.

ven ⊳ **venir**.

vena *sf* - **1.** [gen, ANAT & GEOL] vein - **2.** [inspiración] inspiration - **3.** [don] vein, streak; **tener vena de algo** to have a gift for doing sthg.

venado *sm* ZOOL deer; CULIN venison.

vencedor, ra ⊳ *adj* winning, victorious. ⊳ *sm, f* winner.

vencer ⊳ *vt* - **1.** [ganar] to beat, to defeat - **2.** [derrotar - suj: sueño, cansancio, emoción] to overcome - **3.** [aventajar]: **vencer a alguien a O en algo** to outdo sb at sthg - **4.** [superar - miedo, obstáculos] to overcome; [- tentación] to resist. ⊳ *vi* - **1.** [ganar] to win, to be victorious - **2.** [caducar - garantía, contrato, plazo] to expire; [- deuda, pago] to fall due; [- bono] to mature - **3.** [prevalecer] to prevail. ⇌ **vencerse** *vprnl* [estante etc] to give way, to collapse.

vencido, da *adj* - **1.** [derrotado] defeated; **darse por vencido** to give up - **2.** [caducado - garantía, contrato, plazo] expired; [- pago, deuda] due, payable.

vencimiento *sm* [término - de garantía, contrato, plazo] expiry; [- de pago, deuda] falling due.

venda *sf* bandage; **venda de gasa** gauze bandage; **tener una venda en O delante de los ojos** *fig* to be blind.

vendaje *sm* bandaging; **poner un vendaje a** to put on a dressing.

vendar *vt* to bandage; **vendar los ojos a alguien** to blindfold sb.

vendaval *sm* gale.

vendedor, ra *sm, f* [gen] seller; [en tienda] shop O sales assistant; [de coches, seguros] salesman (*f* saleswoman).

vender *vt lit & fig* to sell; **vender algo a O por** to sell sthg for. ⇌ **venderse** *vprnl* - **1.** [ser vendido] to be sold O on sale; **'se vende'** 'for sale' - **2.** [dejarse sobornar] to sell o.s., to be bribed.

vendimia *sf* grape harvest.

vendrá *etc* ⟶ **venir**.

veneno *sm* [gen] poison; [de serpiente, insecto] venom.

venenoso, sa *adj* - **1.** [gen] poisonous - **2.** *fig* [malintencionado] venomous.

venerable *adj* venerable.

venerar *vt* to venerate, to worship.

venéreo, a *adj* venereal.

venezolano, na *adj* & *sm, f* Venezuelan.

Venezuela *n pr* Venezuela.

venga *interj*: ¡venga! come on!

venganza *sf* vengeance, revenge.

vengar *vt* to avenge. ⟶ **vengarse** *vprnl*: **vengarse (de)** to take revenge (on).

vengativo, va *adj* vengeful, vindictive.

vengo ⟶ **venir**.

venia *sf* - **1.** [permiso] permission - **2.** DER [perdón] pardon; **con la venia** [tomando la palabra] by your leave.

venial *adj* petty, venial.

venida *sf* [llegada] arrival.

venidero, ra *adj* coming, future.

venir ⟨⟩ *vi* - **1.** [gen] to come; **venir a/de hacer algo** to come to do sthg/from doing sthg; **venir de algo** [proceder, derivarse] to come from sthg; **no me vengas con exigencias** don't come to me making demands; **venir a por algo** to come to pick up sthg; **el año que viene** next year - **2.** [llegar] to arrive; **vino a las doce** he arrived at twelve o'clock - **3.** [hallarse] to be; **su foto viene en primera página** his photo is *O* appears on the front page; **el texto viene en inglés** the text is in English - **4.** [acometer, sobrevenir]: **me viene sueño** I'm getting sleepy; **le vinieron ganas de reír** he was seized by a desire to laugh; **le vino una tremenda desgracia** he suffered a great misfortune - **5.** [ropa, calzado]: **venir a alguien** to fit sb; **¿qué tal te viene?** does it fit all right?; **el abrigo le viene pequeño** the coat is too small for her - **6.** [convenir]: **venir bien/mal a alguien** to suit/not to suit sb - **7.** [aproximarse]: **viene a costar un millón** it costs almost a million - **8.** *loc*: **¿a qué viene esto?** what do you mean by that?, what's that in aid of?; **venir a menos** [negocio] to go downhill; [persona] to go down in the world; **venir a parar en** to end in; **venir a ser** to amount to. ⟨⟩ *v aux* - **1.** *(antes de gerundio)* [haber estado]: **venir haciendo algo** to have been doing sthg - **2.** *(antes de participio)* [estar]: **los cambios vienen motivados por la presión de la oposición** the changes have resulted from pressure on the part of the opposition - **3.** *(antes de infinitivo)* [estar]: **esto viene a costar unos veinte euros** it costs almost twenty euros. ⟶ **venirse** *vprnl* - **1.** [volver]: **venirse (de)** to come back *O* return (from) - **2.** *loc*: **venirse abajo** [techo, estante etc] to collapse; [ilusiones] to be dashed.

venta *sf* - **1.** [acción] sale, selling, **estar en venta** to be for sale, **venta al contado** cash sale; **venta a plazos** sale by instalments - **2.** *(gen pl)* [cantidad] sales *pl*.

ventaja *sf* - **1.** [hecho favorable] advantage - **2.** [en competición] lead; **llevar ventaja a alguien** to have a lead over sb.

ventajoso, sa *adj* advantageous.

ventana *sf* [gen & INFORM] window.

ventanilla *sf* - **1.** [de vehículo, sobre] window - **2.** [taquilla] counter.

ventilación *sf* ventilation.

ventilador *sm* ventilator, fan.

ventilar *vt* - **1.** [airear] to air - **2.** [resolver] to clear up - **3.** [discutir] to air. ⟶ **ventilarse** *vprnl* [airearse] to air.

ventiscar, ventisquear *v impers* to blow a blizzard.

ventolera *sf* [viento] gust of wind.

ventosa *sf* [gen & ZOOL] sucker.

ventosidad *sf* wind, flatulence.

ventoso, sa *adj* windy.

ventrílocuo, cua *sm, f* ventriloquist.

ventura *sf* - **1.** [suerte] luck; **a la (buena) ventura** [al azar] at random, haphazardly; [sin nada previsto] without planning *O* a fixed plan - **2.** [casualidad] fate, fortune.

Venus *n pr* Venus.

ver ⟨⟩ *vi* - **1.** [gen] to see - **2.** *loc*: **a ver** [veamos] let's see; **¿a ver?** [mirando con interés] let me see, let's have a look; **¡a ver!** [¡pues claro!] what do you expect?; [al empezar algo] right!; **dejarse ver (por un sitio)** to show one's face (somewhere); **eso está por ver** that remains to be seen; **verás, iba a ir pero...** listen, I was thinking of coming but...; **ya veremos** we'll see. ⟨⟩ *vt* - **1.** [gen] to see; [mirar] to look at; [televisión, partido de fútbol] to watch; **¿ves algo?** can you see anything?; **he estado viendo tu trabajo** I've been looking at your work; **ya veo que estás de mal humor** I can see you're in a bad mood; **¿ves lo que quiero decir?** do you see what I mean?; **ir a ver lo que pasa** to go and see what's going on; **es una manera de ver las cosas** that's one way of looking at it; **yo no lo veo tan mal** I don't think it's that bad - **2.** *loc*: **eso habrá que verlo** that remains to be seen; **¡hay que ver qué lista es!** you wouldn't believe how clever she is!; **no puedo verle (ni en pintura)** *fam* I can't stand him; **si no lo veo, no lo creo** you'll never believe it; **ver venir a alguien** to see what sb is up to. ⟨⟩ *sm*: **estar de buen ver** to be good-looking. ⟶ **verse** *vprnl* - **1.** [mirarse, imaginarse] to see o.s.; **verse en el espejo** to see o.s. in the mirror - **2.** [percibirse]: **desde aquí se ve el mar** you can see the sea from here - **3**. [encontrarse] to meet, to see each other; **verse con alguien** to see sb; **hace mucho que no nos vemos** we haven't seen each other for a long time - **4**. [darse, suceder] to be seen - **5**. loc: **vérselas venir** fam to see it coming; **vérselas y deseárselas para hacer algo** to have a real struggle doing sthg. ◆ **véase** vprnl [en textos] see. ◆ **por lo visto, por lo que se ve** loc adv apparently.

vera sf - **1**. [orilla - de río, lago] bank; [- de camino] edge, side - **2**. fig [lado] side; **a la vera de** next to.

veracidad sf truthfulness.

veraneante smf holidaymaker, (summer) vacationer US.

veranear vi: **veranear en** to spend one's summer holidays in.

veraneo sm summer holidays pl; **de veraneo** holiday (antes de s).

veraniego, ga adj summer (antes de s).

verano sm summer.

veras sfpl truth (U); **de veras** [verdaderamente] really; [en serio] seriously.

veraz adj truthful.

verbal adj verbal.

verbena sf [fiesta] street party (on the eve of certain saints' days).

verbo sm GRAM verb.

verdad sf - **1**. [gen] truth; **a decir verdad** to tell the truth - **2**. [principio aceptado] fact - **3**. loc: **no te gusta, ¿verdad?** you don't like it, do you?; **está bueno, ¿verdad?** it's good, isn't it? ◆ **verdades** sfpl [opinión sincera] true thoughts; **cantar las verdades** fig to speak one's mind; **cantarle O decirle a alguien cuatro verdades** fig to tell sb a few home truths. ◆ **de verdad** ◇ loc adv - **1**. [en serio] seriously - **2**. [realmente] really. ◇ loc adj [auténtico] real.

verdadero, ra adj - **1**. [cierto, real] true, real; **fue un verdadero lío** it was a real mess - **2**. [sin falsificar] real - **3**. [enfático] real.

verde ◇ adj - **1**. [gen] green; **estar verde de envidia** to be green with envy; **poner verde a alguien** to criticize sb - **2**. [fruta] unripe, green - **3**. fig [obsceno] blue, dirty - **4**. fig [inmaduro - proyecto etc] in its early stages. ◇ sm [color] green. ◆ **Verdes** smpl [partido]: **los Verdes** the Greens.

verdor sm [color] greenness.

verdugo sm - **1**. [de preso] executioner; [que ahorca] hangman - **2**. [pasamontañas] balaclava helmet.

verdulería sf greengrocer's (shop).

verdulero, ra sm, f [tendero] greengrocer.

verdura sf vegetables pl, greens pl.

vereda sf - **1**. [senda] path; **hacer entrar O meter a alguien en vereda** to bring sb into line - **2**. C Sur & Perú [acera] pavement UK, sidewalk US.

veredicto sm verdict.

vergonzoso, sa adj - **1**. [deshonroso] shameful - **2**. [tímido] bashful.

vergüenza sf - **1**. [turbación] embarrassment; **dar vergüenza** to embarrass; **¡qué vergüenza!** how embarrassing!; **sentir vergüenza** to feel embarrassed - **2**. [timidez] bashfulness - **3**. [remordimiento] shame; **sentir vergüenza** to feel ashamed - **4**. [deshonra, escándalo] disgrace; **¡es una vergüenza!** it's disgraceful!

verídico, ca adj [cierto] true, truthful.

verificar vt - **1**. [comprobar - verdad, autenticidad] to check, to verify - **2**. [examinar - funcionamiento, buen estado] to check, to test - **3**. [confirmar - fecha, cita] to confirm - **4**. [llevar a cabo] to carry out. ◆ **verificarse** vprnl [tener lugar] to take place.

verja sf - **1**. [puerta] iron gate; **la verja de Gibraltar** the border between Spain and Gibraltar - **2**. [valla] railings pl - **3**. [enrejado] grille.

vermú, vermut (pl vermuts) sm - **1**. [bebida] vermouth - **2**. Andes & R Plata [en cine] early-evening showing; Andes & R Plata [en teatro] early-evening performance.

vernáculo, la adj vernacular.

verosímil adj - **1**. [creíble] believable, credible - **2**. [probable] likely, probable.

verruga sf wart.

versado, da adj: **versado (en)** versed (in).

versar vi: **versar sobre** to be about, to deal with.

versátil adj - **1**. [voluble] fickle - **2**. (considerado incorrecto) [polifacético] versatile.

versículo sm verse.

versión sf [gen] version; [en música pop] cover version; **versión original** CINE original (version).

verso sm - **1**. [género] verse; **verso blanco/libre** blank/free verse - **2**. [unidad rítmica] line (of poetry) - **3**. [poema] poem.

vértebra sf vertebra.

vertebrado, da adj vertebrate. ◆ **vertebrados** smpl ZOOL vertebrates.

vertedero sm [de basuras] rubbish tip O dump; [de agua] overflow.

verter vt - **1**. [derramar] to spill - **2**. [vaciar - líquido] to pour (out); [- recipiente] to empty - **3**. [tirar - basura, residuos] to dump - **4**. fig [decir] to tell. ◆ **verterse** vprnl [derramarse] to spill.

vertical ◇ adj GEOM vertical; [derecho] upright. ◇ sf GEOM vertical.

vértice sm [gen] vertex; [de cono] apex.

vertido sm - **1**. (gen pl) [residuo] waste (U) - **2**. [acción] dumping.

vertiente *sf* - **1.** [pendiente] slope - **2.** *fig* [aspecto] side, aspect.

vertiginoso, sa *adj* - **1.** [mareante] dizzy - **2.** *fig* [raudo] giddy.

vértigo *sm* [enfermedad] vertigo; [mareo] dizziness; **trepar me da vértigo** climbing makes me dizzy.

vesícula *sf*: **vesícula biliar** gall bladder.

vespertino, na *adj* evening *(antes de s)*.

vestíbulo *sm* [de casa] (entrance) hall; [de hotel, oficina] lobby, foyer.

vestido, da *adj* dressed; **ir vestido** to be dressed; **iba vestido de negro** he was dressed in black. ◆ **vestido** *sm* - **1.** [indumentaria] clothes *pl* - **2.** [prenda femenina] dress; **vestido de noche** evening dress.

vestidura *(gen pl) sf* clothes *pl*; RELIG vestments *pl*; **rasgarse las vestiduras** to make a fuss.

vestigio *sm* vestige; *fig* sign, trace.

vestimenta *sf* clothes *pl*, wardrobe.

vestir ◇ *vt* - **1.** [gen] to dress - **2.** [llevar puesto] to wear - **3.** [cubrir] to cover - **4.** *fig* [encubrir]: **vestir algo de** to invest sthg with. ◇ *vi* - **1.** [llevar ropa] to dress - **2.** *fig* [estar bien visto] to be the done thing. ◆ **vestirse** *vprnl* - **1.** [ponerse ropa] to get dressed, to dress; **vestirse de** to wear - **2.** [adquirir ropa]: **vestirse en** to buy one's clothes at.

vestuario *sm* - **1.** [vestimenta] clothes *pl*, wardrobe; TEATRO costumes *pl* - **2.** [para cambiarse] changing room; [de actores] dressing room.

veta *sf* - **1.** [filón] vein, seam - **2.** [faja, lista] grain.

vetar *vt* to veto.

veterano, na *adj & sm, f* veteran.

veterinario, ria ◇ *adj* veterinary. ◇ *sm, f* [persona] vet, veterinary surgeon. ◆ **veterinaria** *sf* [ciencia] veterinary science *O* medicine.

veto *sm* veto; **poner veto a algo** to veto sthg.

vetusto, ta *adj culto* ancient, very old.

vez *sf* - **1.** [gen] time; **una vez** once; **dos veces** twice; **tres veces** three times; **¿has estado allí alguna vez?** have you ever been there?; **a mi/ tu** *etc* **vez** in my/your *etc* turn; **a la vez (que)** at the same time (as); **cada vez (que)** every time; **cada vez más** more and more; **cada vez menos** less and less; **cada vez la veo más feliz** she seems happier and happier; **de una vez** in one go; **de una vez para siempre** *O* **por todas** once and for all; **muchas veces** often, a lot; **otra vez** again; **pocas veces, rara vez** rarely, seldom; **por última vez** for the last time; **una** *O* **alguna que otra vez** occasionally; **una vez más** once again; **una y otra vez** time and again; **érase una vez** once upon a time - **2.** [turno] turn; **pedir la vez** to ask who is last. ◆ **a ve-**

ces, algunas veces *loc adv* sometimes, at times. ◆ **de vez en cuando** *loc adv* from time to time, now and again. ◆ **en vez de** *loc prep* instead of. ◆ **tal vez** *loc adv* perhaps, maybe. ◆ **una vez que** *loc conj* once, after.

VHF *(abrev de* very high frequency) *sf* VHF.

VHS *(abrev de* video home system) *sm* VHS.

vía ◇ *sf* - **1.** [medio de transporte] route; **por vía aérea** [gen] by air; [correo] (by) airmail; **por vía marítima** by sea; **por vía terrestre** overland, by land; **vía fluvial** waterway - **2.** [calzada, calle] road; **vía pública** public thoroughfare - **3.** [FERROC - raíl] rails *pl*, track; [- andén] platform; **vía férrea** [ruta] railway line - **4.** [proceso]: **estar en vías de** to be in the process of; **país en vías de desarrollo** developing country; **una especie en vías de extinción** an endangered species - **5.** ANAT tract - **6.** [opción] channel, path; **por vía oficial/judicial** through official channels/the courts - **7.** [camino] way; **dar vía libre** [dejar paso] to give way; [dar libertad de acción] to give a free rein - **8.** DER procedure. ◇ *prep* via. ◆ **Vía Láctea** *sf* Milky Way.

viabilidad *sf* viability.

viable *adj fig* [posible] viable.

viaducto *sm* viaduct.

viajante *smf* travelling salesperson.

viajar *vi* - **1.** [trasladarse, irse]: **viajar (en)** to travel (by) - **2.** [circular] to run.

viaje *sm* - **1.** [gen] journey, trip; [en barco] voyage; **¡buen viaje!** have a good journey *O* trip!; **estar/ir de viaje** to be/go away (on a trip); **hay 11 días de viaje** it's an 11-day journey; **viaje de ida/de vuelta** outward/return journey; **viaje de ida y vuelta** return journey *O* trip; **viaje de negocios** business trip; **viaje de novios** honeymoon; **viaje organizado** package tour - **2.** *fig* [recorrido] trip. ◆ **viajes** *smpl* [singladuras] travels.

viajero, ra ◇ *adj* [persona] travelling; [ave] migratory. ◇ *sm, f* [gen] traveller; [en transporte público] passenger.

vial *adj* road *(antes de s)*.

viandante *smf* - **1.** [peatón] pedestrian - **2.** [transeúnte] passer-by.

viario, ria *adj* road *(antes de s)*.

víbora *sf* viper.

vibración *sf* vibration.

vibrante *adj* - **1.** [oscilante] vibrating - **2.** *fig* [emocionante] vibrant - **3.** [trémulo] quivering.

vibrar *vi* - **1.** [oscilar] to vibrate - **2.** *fig* [voz, rodillas etc] to shake - **3.** *fig* [público] to get excited.

vicaría *sf* [residencia] vicarage.

vicario *sm* vicar.

vicepresidente, ta *sm, f* [de país, asociación] vice-president; [de comité, empresa] vice-chairman.

viceversa *adv* vice versa.

viciado, da *adj* [aire] stuffy; [estilo] marred.

viciar *vt* [pervertir] to corrupt. ◆ **viciarse** *vprnl* [enviciarse] to take to vice.

vicio *sm* - 1. [mala costumbre] bad habit, vice; **llorar** *O* **quejarse de vicio** to complain for no (good) reason - 2. [libertinaje] vice - 3. [defecto físico, de dicción etc] defect.

vicioso, sa ◇ *adj* dissolute, depraved. ◇ *sm, f* dissolute person, depraved person.

vicisitud *sf* (gen pl) [avatar] vicissitude; **las vicisitud de la vida** life's ups and downs.

víctima *sf* victim; [en accidente, guerra] casualty; **ser víctima de** to be the victim of.

victimar *vt* Amér to kill, to murder.

victoria *sf* victory; **cantar victoria** to claim victory.

victorioso, sa *adj* victorious.

vid *sf* vine.

vid., v. (abrev de véase) v., vid.

vida *sf* life; **de por vida** for life; **en vida de** during the life *O* lifetime of; **en mi/tu** etc **vida** never in my/your etc life; **estar con vida** to be alive; **ganarse la vida** to earn a living; **pasar a mejor vida** to pass away; **pasarse la vida haciendo algo** to spend one's life doing sthg; **perder la vida** to lose one's life; **quitar la vida a alguien** to kill sb; **¡así es la vida!** that's life!, such is life!

vidente *smf* clairvoyant.

vídeo, video *sm* - 1. [gen] video; **grabar en vídeo** to videotape; **vídeo a la carta** video on demand - 2. [aparato reproductor] video, VCR *US*.

videocámara *sf* camcorder.

videocasete *sm* video, videocassette.

videoclip (pl videoclips) *sm* (pop) video.

videoclub (pl videoclubes *O* videoclubs) *sm* video club.

videojuego *sm* video game.

videotexto *sm* [por señal de televisión] teletext; [por línea telefónica] videotext, viewdata.

videotex *sm inv* = **videotexto**.

vidriero, ra *sm, f* - 1. [que fabrica cristales] glass merchant *O* manufacturer - 2. [que coloca cristales] glazier. ◆ **vidriera** *sf* - 1. [puerta] glass door; [ventana] glass window - 2. [en catedrales] stained glass window.

vidrio *sm* - 1. [material] glass - 2. Amér [de anteojos] glass - 3. Amér [de vehículo] window.

vidrioso, sa *adj* - 1. fig [tema, asunto] thorny, delicate - 2. fig [ojos] glazed.

vieira *sf* scallop.

viejo, ja ◇ *adj* old; **hacerse viejo** to get *O* grow old. ◇ *sm, f* - 1. [anciano] old man (f old

woman); **los viejos** the elderly; **viejo verde** dirty old man (f dirty old woman) - 2. fam [padres] old man (f old girl); **mis viejos** my folks - 3. Amér fam [amigo] mate, mate. ◆ **Viejo de Pascua** *sm* Chile: **Viejo de Pascua** *O* **Pascuero** Father Christmas.

viene ⮞ **venir**.

vienés, esa *adj* & *sm, f* Viennese.

viento *sm* - 1. [aire] wind; **hace viento** it's windy - 2. MÚS wind - 3. loc: **contra viento y marea** in spite of everything; **despedir** *O* **echar a alguien con viento fresco** to send sb packing; **mis esperanzas se las llevó el viento** my hopes flew out of the window; **viento en popa** splendidly.

vientre *sm* ANAT stomach.

viera ⮞ **ver**.

viernes *sm inv* Friday; ver también **sábado**. ◆ **Viernes Santo** *sm* RELIG Good Friday.

Vietnam *n pr* Vietnam.

vietnamita *adj* & *smf* Vietnamese.

viga *sf* [de madera] beam, rafter; [de metal] girder.

vigencia *sf* [de ley etc] validity; [de costumbre] use; **estar/entrar en vigencia** to be in/come into force.

vigente *adj* [ley etc] in force; [costumbre] in use.

vigésimo, ma *num* twentieth.

vigía *smf* lookout.

vigilancia *sf* - 1. [cuidado] vigilance, care; **estar bajo vigilancia** to be under surveillance - 2. [vigilantes] guards pl.

vigilante ◇ *adj* vigilant. ◇ *smf* guard; **vigilante nocturno** night watchman.

vigilar ◇ *vt* [enfermo] to watch over; [presos, banco] to guard; [niños, bolso] to keep an eye on; [proceso] to oversee. ◇ *vi* to keep watch.

vigilia *sf* [vela] wakefulness; **estar de vigilia** to be awake.

vigor *sm* - 1. [gen] vigour - 2. [vigencia]: **entrar en vigor** to come into force, to take effect.

vigorizar *vt* [fortalecer] to fortify.

vigoroso, sa *adj* [gen] vigorous, energetic.

vikingo, ga *adj* & *sm, f* Viking.

vil *adj* vile, despicable; [metal] base.

vileza *sf* - 1. [acción] vile *O* despicable act - 2. [cualidad] vileness.

villa *sf* - 1. [población] small town - 2. [casa] villa, country house - 3.: **villa miseria** Arg & Bol shanty town.

villancico *sm* [navideño] Christmas carol.

villano, na *sm, f* villain.

vilo ◆ **en vilo** loc adv - 1. [suspendido] in the air, suspended - 2. [inquieto] on tenterhooks; **tener a alguien en vilo** to keep sb in suspense.

vinagre *sm* vinegar.

vinagrera *sf* [vasija] vinegar bottle. ➤ **vinagreras** *sfpl* CULIN [convoy] cruet *sing*.

vinagreta *sf* vinaigrette, French dressing.

vinculación *sf* link, linking (U).

vincular *vt* - **1.** [enlazar] to link; **vincular algo con algo** to link sthg with O to sthg; [por obligación] to tie, to bind - **2.** DER to entail.

vínculo *sm* [lazo - entre hechos, países] link; [- personal, familiar] tie, bond.

vinícola *adj* [país, región] wine-producing *(antes de s)*; [industria] wine *(antes de s)*.

vinicultura *sf* wine producing.

vino *sm* wine; **vino blanco/tinto** white/red wine; **vino rosado** rosé; ▷ **venir**.

viña *sf* vineyard.

viñedo *sm* (large) vineyard.

viñeta *sf* - **1.** [de tebeo] (individual) cartoon - **2.** [de libro] vignette.

vio ▷ **ver**.

viola *sf* viola.

violación *sf* - **1.** [de ley, derechos] violation, infringement - **2.** [de persona] rape.

violador, ra *adj & sm, f* rapist.

violar *vt* - **1.** [ley, derechos, domicilio] to violate, to infringe - **2.** [persona] to rape.

violencia *sf* - **1.** [agresividad] violence; **violencia doméstica** domestic violence - **2.** [fuerza - de viento, pasiones] force - **3.** [incomodidad] embarrassment, awkwardness.

violentar *vt* - **1.** [incomodar] to embarrass - **2.** [forzar - domicilio] to break into. ➤ **violentarse** *vprnl* [incomodarse] to feel awkward.

violento, ta *adj* - **1.** [gen] violent; [goce] intense - **2.** [incómodo] awkward.

violeta ◇ *sf* [flor] violet. ◇ *adj inv & sm* [color] violet.

violín *sm* violin.

violón *sm* double bass.

violonchelo, violoncelo *sm* cello.

viperino, na *adj fig* venomous.

viraje *sm* - **1.** [giro - AUTO] turn; NÁUT tack - **2.** *fig* [cambio] change of direction.

virar ◇ *vt* [girar] to turn (round); NÁUT to tack. ◇ *vi* [girar] to turn (round).

virgen ◇ *adj* [gen] virgin; [cinta] blank; [película] unused. ◇ *smf* [persona] virgin. ◇ *sf* ARTE Madonna. ➤ **Virgen** *sf*: **la Virgen** RELIG the (Blessed) Virgin; **¡Virgen santa!** good heavens!

virgo *sm* [virginidad] virginity. ➤ **Virgo** ◇ *sm* [zodiaco] Virgo. ◇ *smf* [persona] Virgo.

virguería *sf fam* gem.

viril *adj* virile, manly.

virilidad *sf* virility.

virtual *adj* - **1.** [posible] possible, potential - **2.** [casi real] virtual.

virtud *sf* - **1.** [cualidad] virtue; **virtud cardinal/teologal** cardinal/theological virtue - **2.** [po-der] power; **tener la virtud de** to have the power O ability to. ➤ **en virtud de** *loc prep* by virtue of.

virtuoso, sa ◇ *adj* [honrado] virtuous. ◇ *sm, f* [genio] virtuoso.

viruela *sf* - **1.** [enfermedad] smallpox - **2.** [pústula] pockmark; **picado de viruelas** pockmarked.

virulé ➤ **a la virulé** *loc adj* - **1.** [torcido] crooked - **2.** [hinchado]: **un ojo a la virulé** a black eye.

virulencia *sf fig & MED* virulence.

virus *sm inv* [gen & INFORM] virus; **virus informático** computer virus.

viruta *sf* shaving.

visa *sf Amér* visa.

visado *sm* visa.

víscera *sf* internal organ; **vísceras** entrails.

visceral *adj fig & ANAT* visceral.

viscoso, sa *adj* [gen] viscous; [baboso] slimy. ➤ **viscosa** *sf* [tejido] viscose.

visera *sf* - **1.** [de gorra] peak - **2.** [de casco, suelta] visor - **3.** [de automóvil] sun visor.

visibilidad *sf* visibility.

visible *adj* visible; **estar visible** [presentable] to be decent O presentable.

visigodo, da *sm, f* Visigoth.

visillo *(gen pl)* *sm* net/lace curtain.

visión *sf* - **1.** [sentido, lo que se ve] sight - **2.** [alucinación, lucidez] vision; **ver visiones** to be seeing things - **3.** [punto de vista] (point of) view.

visionar *vt* to view privately.

visionario, ria *adj & sm, f* visionary.

visita *sf* - **1.** [gen] visit; [breve] call; **hacer una visita a alguien** to visit sb, to pay sb a visit - **2.** [visitante] visitor; **tener visita** O **visitas** to have visitors - **3.** [a página web] hit.

visitante *smf* visitor.

visitar *vt* [gen] to visit; [suj: médico] to call on.

vislumbrar *vt* - **1.** [entrever] to make out, to discern - **2.** [adivinar] to have an inkling of. ➤ **vislumbrarse** *vprnl* - **1.** [entreverse] to be barely visible - **2.** [adivinarse] to become a little clearer.

vislumbre *sm o sf lit & fig* glimmer.

viso *sm* - **1.** [aspecto]: **tener visos de** to seem; **tiene visos de hacerse realidad** it could become a reality - **2.** [reflejo - de tejido] sheen; [- de metal] glint.

visón *sm* mink.

víspera *sf* [día antes] day before, eve; **en vísperas de** on the eve of; **víspera de festivo** day prior to a public holiday.

vista ▷ **visto**.

vistazo *sm* glance, quick look.

visto, ta ◇ *pp* ▷ **ver**. ◇ *adj*: **estar bien/mal visto** to be considered good/frowned upon. ➤ **vista** ◇ *v* ▷ **vestir**.

◇ sf - 1. [sentido] sight, eyesight; [ojos] eyes pl - 2. [observación] watching - 3. [mirada] gaze; **alzar/bajar la vista** to look up/down; **fijar la vista en** to fix one's eyes on; **a primera O simple vista** [aparentemente] at first sight, on the face of it; **estar a la vista** [visible] to be visible; [muy cerca] to be staring one in the face - 4. [panorama] view - 5. DER hearing; **vista oral** hearing - 6. loc: **conocer a alguien de vista** to know sb by sight; **hacer la vista gorda** to turn a blind eye; **¡hasta la vista!** see you!; **no perder de vista a alguien/algo** [vigilar] not to let sb/sthg out of one's sight; [tener en cuenta] not to lose sight of sb/sthg; **perder de vista** [dejar de ver] to lose sight of; [perder contacto] to lose touch with; **saltar a la vista** to be blindingly obvious. ◆ **vistas** sfpl [panorama] view sing; **con vistas al mar** with a sea view. ◆ **visto bueno** sm: **el visto bueno** the go-ahead; **'visto bueno'** 'approved'. ◆ **a la vista** loc adv BANCA at sight. ◆ **con vistas a** loc prep with a view to. ◆ **en vista de** loc prep in view of. ◆ **en vista de que** loc conj since, seeing as. ◆ **por lo visto** loc adv apparently. ◆ **visto que** loc conj seeing O given that.

vistoso, sa adj eye-catching.

visual ◇ adj visual. ◇ sf line of sight.

visualizar vt - 1. [gen] to visualize - 2. INFORM to display.

vital adj [gen] vital; [ciclo] life (antes de s); [persona] full of life, vivacious.

vitalicio, cia adj for life, life (antes de s).

vitalidad sf vitality.

vitamina sf vitamin.

vitaminado, da adj vitamin-enriched.

vitamínico, ca adj vitamin (antes de s).

viticultor, ra sm, f wine grower.

viticultura sf wine growing, viticulture.

vitorear vt to cheer.

vítreo, a adj vitreous.

vitrina sf - 1. [en casa] display cabinet; [en tienda] showcase, glass case - 2. Andes & Ven [escaparate] (shop) window.

vituperar vt to criticize harshly.

viudedad sf - 1. [viudez - de mujer] widowhood; [- de hombre] widowerhood - 2.: (**pensión de**) **viudedad** widow's/widower's pension.

viudo, da sm, f widower (f widow).

viva ◇ sm cheer; **dar vivas** to cheer. ◇ interj: **¡viva!** hurrah!; **¡viva el rey!** long live the King!

vivac = vivaque.

vivacidad sf liveliness.

vivales smf inv crafty person.

vivamente adv - 1. [relatar, describir] vividly - 2. [afectar, emocionar] deeply.

vivaque, vivac sm bivouac.

vivaz adj - 1. [color, descripción] vivid - 2. [persona, discusión, ojos] lively - 3. [ingenio, inteligencia] alert, sharp.

vivencia (gen pl) sf experience.

víveres smpl provisions, supplies.

vivero sm - 1. [de plantas] nursery - 2. [de peces] fish farm; [de moluscos] bed.

viveza sf - 1. [de colorido, descripción] vividness - 2. [de persona, discusión, ojos] liveliness; [de ingenio, inteligencia] sharpness.

vívido, da adj vivid.

vividor, ra sm, f despec scrounger.

vivienda sf - 1. [alojamiento] housing - 2. [morada] dwelling.

viviente adj living.

vivir ◇ vt [experimentar] to experience, to live through. ◇ vi [gen] to live; [estar vivo] to be alive; **vivir para ver** who'd have thought it?

vivito adj: **vivito y coleando** fam alive and kicking.

vivo, va adj - 1. [existente - ser, lengua etc] living; **estar vivo** [persona, costumbre, recuerdo] to be alive - 2. [dolor, deseo, olor] intense; [luz, color, tono] bright - 3. [gestos, ojos, descripción] lively, vivid - 4. [activo - ingenio, niño] quick, sharp; [- ciudad] lively - 5. [genio] quick, hot. ◆ **vivos** smpl: **los vivos** the living. ◆ **en vivo** loc adv [en directo] live.

Vizcaya n pr Vizcaya; **Golfo de Vizcaya** Bay of Biscay.

vizconde, esa sm, f viscount (f viscountess).

vocablo sm word, term.

vocabulario sm [riqueza léxica] vocabulary.

vocación sf vocation.

vocacional adj vocational.

vocal ◇ adj vocal. ◇ sf vowel.

vocalizar vi to vocalize.

vocear ◇ vt - 1. [gritar] to shout O call out - 2. [llamar] to shout O call to - 3. [pregonar - mercancía] to hawk. ◇ vi [gritar] to shout.

vociferar vi to shout.

vodka ['boθka] sm o sf vodka.

vol. (abrev de volumen) vol.

volador, ra adj flying.

volandas ◆ **en volandas** loc adv in the air.

volante ◇ adj flying. ◇ sm - 1. [para conducir] (steering) wheel; **estar O ir al volante** to be at the wheel - 2. [de tela] frill, flounce - 3. [del médico] (referral) note - 4. [en bádminton] shuttlecock.

volar ◇ vt [en guerras, atentados] to blow up; [caja fuerte, puerta] to blow open; [edificio en ruinas] to demolish *(with explosives)*; [en cantera] to blast. ⬥ *vi* - **1.** [gen] to fly; [papeles etc] to blow away; **volar a** [una altura] to fly at; [un lugar] to fly to; **echarse a volar** to fly away **volar off** - **2.** *fam* [desaparecer] to disappear, to vanish.

volátil *adj fig* & QUIM volatile.

vol-au-vent = **volován**.

volcán *sm* volcano.

volcánico, ca *adj* volcanic.

volcar ⬥ *vt* - **1.** [tirar] to knock over; [carretilla] to tip up - **2.** [vaciar] to empty out. ⬥ *vi* [coche, camión] to overturn; [barco] to capsize. ⬥ **volcarse** *vprnl* [esforzarse] **volcarse (con/ en)** to bend over backwards (for/in).

volea *sf* volley.

voleibol *sm* volleyball.

voleo *sm* volley; **a** O **al voleo** [arbitrariamente] randomly, any old how.

volován (*pl* **volovanes**), **vol-au-vent** [bolo'βan] (*pl* **vol-au-vents**) *sm* vol-au-vent.

volquete *sm* dumper truck, dump truck US.

voltaje *sm* voltage.

voltear ⬥ *vt* - **1.** [heno, crepe, torero] to toss; [tortilla - con plato] to turn over; [mesa, silla] to turn upside-down - **2.** *Amér* [derribar] to knock over; *Andes, Amér C, Caribe* & *Méx* [volver] to turn. ⬥ *vi Méx* [torcer] to turn, to go round. ⬥ **voltearse** *vprnl Andes, Amér C, Caribe* & *Méx* [volverse] to turn around.

voltereta *sf* [en el suelo] handspring; [en el aire] somersault; **voltereta lateral** cartwheel.

voltio *sm* volt.

voluble *adj* changeable, fickle.

volumen *sm* - **1.** [gen & COM] volume; **a todo volumen** at full blast; **volumen de negocio** O **ventas** turnover - **2.** [espacio ocupado] size, bulk.

voluminoso, sa *adj* bulky.

voluntad *sf* - **1.** [determinación] will, willpower; **voluntad de hierro** iron will - **2.** [intención] intention; **buena voluntad** goodwill; **mala voluntad** ill will - **3.** [deseo] wishes *pl*, will; **contra la voluntad de alguien** against sb's will - **4.** [albedrío] free will; **a voluntad** [cuanto se quiere] as much as one likes; **por voluntad propia** of one's own free will.

voluntariado *sm* voluntary enlistment.

voluntario, ria ⬥ *adj* voluntary. ⬥ *sm, f* volunteer.

voluntarioso, sa *adj* [esforzado] willing.

voluptuoso, sa *adj* voluptuous.

volver ⬥ *vt* - **1.** [dar la vuelta a] to turn round; [lo de arriba abajo] to turn over - **2.** [poner del revés - boca abajo] to turn upside down; [- lo de dentro fuera] to turn inside out; [- lo de detrás delante] to turn back to front - **3.** [cabeza, ojos etc] to turn - **4.** [convertir en]: **eso le volvió un**

delincuente that made him a criminal, that turned him into a criminal. ⬥ *vi* [ir de vuelta] to go back, to return; [venir de vuelta] to come back, to return; **volver de** to come back from; **volver atrás** to turn back; **yo allí no vuelvo** I'm not going back there; **vuelve, no te vayas** come back, don't go; **volver en sí** to come to, to regain consciousness. ⬥ **volver a** *vi* [reanudar] to return to; **volver a hacer algo** [hacer otra vez] to do sthg again. ⬥ **volverse** *vprnl* - **1.** [darse la vuelta, girar la cabeza] to turn round - **2.** [ir de vuelta] to go back, to return; [venir de vuelta] to come back, to return - **3.** [convertirse en] to become; **volverse loco/pálido** to go mad/pale - **4.** *loc:* **volverse atrás** [de una afirmación, promesa] to go back on one's word; [de una decisión] to change one's mind, to back out; **volverse (en) contra (de) alguien** to turn against sb.

vomitar ⬥ *vt* [devolver] to vomit, to bring up. ⬥ *vi* to vomit, to be sick.

vómito *sm* [substancia] vomit *(U)*.

voraz *adj* - **1.** [persona, apetito] voracious - **2.** *fig* [fuego, enfermedad] raging.

vos *pron pers Amér* [tú - sujeto] you; [- objeto] you.

vosotros, tras *pron pers* you *pl*.

votación *sf* vote, voting *(U)*; **decidir algo por votación** to put sthg to the vote; **votación a mano alzada** show of hands.

votante *smf* voter.

votar ⬥ *vt* - **1.** [partido, candidato] to vote for; [ley] to vote on - **2.** [aprobar] to pass, to approve *(by vote)*. ⬥ *vi* to vote; **votar por** [emitir un voto por] to vote for; *fig* [estar a favor de] to be in favour of; **votar por que...** to vote (that)...; **votar en blanco** to return a blank ballot paper.

voto *sm* - **1.** [gen] vote - **2.** RELIG vow.

voy ▷ **ir**.

voz *sf* - **1.** [gen & GRAM] voice; **a media voz** in a low voice, under one's breath; **aclarar** O **aclararse la voz** to clear one's throat; **alzar** O **levantar la voz a alguien** to raise one's voice to sb; **en voz alta** aloud; **en voz baja** softly, in a low voice; **voz en off** CINE voice-over; TEATRO voice offstage - **2.** [grito] shout; **a voces** shouting; **dar voces** to shout - **3.** [vocablo] word - **4.** [derecho a expresarse] say, voice; **no tener ni voz ni voto** to have no say in the matter.

VPO (*abrev de* **vivienda de protección oficial**) *sf* ≈ council house/flat UK, ≈ public housing unit US.

vudú *(en aposición invariable) sm* voodoo.

vuelco *sm* upset; **dar un vuelco** [coche] to overturn; [relaciones] to change completely; [empresa] to go to ruin; **me dio un vuelco el corazón** my heart missed O skipped a beat.

vuelo *sm* - **1.** [gen & AERON] flight; **alzar** *O* **emprender** *O* **levantar el vuelo** [despegar] to take flight, to fly off; *fig* [irse de casa] to fly the nest; **coger algo al vuelo** [en el aire] to catch sthg in flight; *fig* [rápido] to catch on to sthg very quickly; **remontar el vuelo** to soar; **vuelo libre** hang gliding; **vuelo sin motor** gliding - **2.** [de vestido]: **una falda de vuelo** a full skirt.

vuelta *sf* - **1.** [gen] turn; [acción] turning; **dar una vuelta (a algo)** [recorriéndolo] to go round (sthg); **dar la vuelta al mundo** to go around the world; **darse la vuelta** to turn round; **dar vueltas (a algo)** [girándolo] to turn (sthg) round; **vuelta al ruedo** TAUROM bullfighter's lap of honour - **2.** DEP lap; **vuelta (ciclista)** tour - **3.** [regreso, devolución] return; **billete de ida y vuelta** return ticket; **a la vuelta** [volviendo] on the way back; [al llegar] on one's return; **estar de vuelta** to be back - **4.** [paseo]: **dar una vuelta** to go for a walk - **5.** [dinero sobrante] change - **6.** [ronda, turno] round - **7.** [parte opuesta] back, other side; **a la vuelta de la esquina** *lit & fig* round the corner; **a la vuelta de la página** over the page - **8.** [cambio, avatar] change - **9.** *loc*: **a vuelta de correo** by return of post; **dar la vuelta a la tortilla** *fam* to turn the tables; **dar una vuelta/dos** *etc* **vueltas de campana** [coche] to turn over once/twice *etc*; **darle vueltas a algo** to turn sthg over in one's mind; **estar de vuelta de algo** to be blasé about sthg; **no tiene vuelta de hoja** there are no two ways about it.

vuelto, ta ◇ *pp* ▷ **volver.** ◇ *adj* turned. ◆ **vuelto** *sm Amér* change.

vuestro, tra ◇ *adj poses*: your; **vuestro libro/amigo** your book/friend; **este libro es vuestro** this book is yours; **un amigo vuestro** a friend of yours; **no es asunto vuestro** it's none of your business. ◇ *pron poses*: **el vuestro** yours; **los vuestros están en la mesa** yours are on the table; **lo vuestro es el teatro** [lo que hacéis bien] you should be on the stage; **los vuestros** *fam* [vuestra familia] your folks; [vuestro bando] your lot.

vulgar *adj* - **1.** [no refinado] vulgar - **2.** [corriente, ordinario] ordinary, common; **vulgar y corriente** ordinary.

vulgaridad *sf* - **1.** [grosería] vulgarity; **hacer/decir una vulgaridad** to do/say sthg vulgar - **2.** [banalidad] banality.

vulgarizar *vt* to popularize.

vulgo *sm despec*: **el vulgo** [plebe] the masses *pl*; [no expertos] the lay public *(U)*.

vulnerable *adj* vulnerable.

vulnerar *vt* - **1.** [prestigio etc] to harm, to damage - **2.** [ley, pacto etc] to violate, to break.

vulva *sf* vulva.

w, W *sf* [letra] w, W.

walkie-talkie ['walki'talki] *(pl* **walkie-talkies)** *sm* walkie-talkie.

walkman® ['walkman] *(pl* **walkmans)** *sm* Walkman®.

Washington ['waʃiŋton] *n pr* Washington.

water ['bater] *(pl* **wateres)** = **váter**.

waterpolo [water'polo] *sm* water polo.

watio = **vatio**.

WC *(abrev de* **water closet)** *sm* WC.

web [weβ] *sf*: **la (World Wide) Web** the (World Wide) Web.

whisky ['wiski] = **güisqui**.

windsurf ['winsurf], **windsurfing** ['winsurfin] *sm* windsurfing.

WWW *(abrev de* **World Wide Web)** *sf* WWW.

x, X *sf* [letra] x, X. ◆ **X** *smf*: **la señora X** Mrs X.

xenofobia *sf* xenophobia.

xilofón, xilófono *sm* xylophone.

y¹, Y *sf* [letra] y, Y.

y² *conj* - **1.** [gen] and; **un ordenador y una impresora** a computer and a printer; **horas y horas de espera** hours and hours of waiting - **2.** [pero] and yet; **sabía que no lo conseguiría y seguía intentándolo** she knew she wouldn't manage it and yet she kept on trying - **3.** [en preguntas] what about; **¿y tu mujer?** what about your wife?

ya ◇ *adv* - **1.** [en el pasado] already; **ya me lo habías contado** you had already told me; **ya en 1926** as long ago as 1926 - **2.** [ahora] now; [inmediatamente] at once; **hay que hacer algo ya** something has to be done now/at once; **bueno, yo ya me voy** right, I'm off now; **ya no**

es así it's no longer like that - **3.** [en el futuro]: **ya te llamaré** I'll give you a ring some time; **ya hablaremos** we'll talk later; **ya nos habremos ido** we'll already have gone; **ya veras** you'll (soon) see - **4.** [refuerza al verbo]: **ya entiendo/lo sé** I understand/know. ◇ *conj* [distributiva]: **ya (sea) por... ya (sea) por...** whether for... or... ◇ *interj*: **¡ya!** [expresa asentimiento] right!; [expresa comprensión] yes!; **¡ya, ya!** *irón* sure!, yes, of course! ⬛ **ya no** *loc adv*: **ya no... sino** not only... but. ⬛ **ya que** *loc conj* since; **ya que has venido, ayúdame con esto** since you're here, give me a hand with this.

yacer *vi* to lie.

yacimiento *sm* - **1.** [minero] bed, deposit; **yacimiento de petróleo** oilfield - **2.** [arqueológico] site.

yanqui *smf* - **1.** HIST Yankee - **2.** *fam* [estadounidense] yank.

yate *sm* yacht.

yegua *sf* mare.

yema *sf* - **1.** [de huevo] yolk - **2.** [de planta] bud, shoot - **3.** [de dedo] fingertip.

Yemen *n pr*: **(el) Yemen** Yemen.

yen (*pl* **yenes**) *sm* yen.

yerba = **hierba**. ⬛ **yerba mate**: *R Dom* yerba maté.

yerbatero *sm Andes & Caribe* [curandero] healer; [vendedor de hierbas] herbalist.

yermo, ma *adj* [estéril] barren.

yerno *sm* son-in-law.

yeso *sm* - **1.** GEOL gypsum - **2.** CONSTR plaster - **3.** ARTE gesso.

yeyé *adj* sixties.

yo *pron pers* - **1.** *(sujeto)* I; **yo me llamo Luis** I'm called Luis - **2.** *(predicado)*: **soy yo** it's me - **3.** *loc*: **yo que tú/él** *etc* if I were you/him *etc*.

yodo, iodo *sm* iodine.

yoga *sm* yoga.

yogur (*pl* **yogures**)**, yogurt** (*pl* **yogurts**) *sm* yoghurt.

yonqui *smf fam* junkie.

yóquey (*pl* **yóqueys**)**, jockey** (*pl* **jockeys**) *sm* jockey.

yoyó *sm* yoyo.

yuca *sf* - **1.** BOT yucca - **2.** CULIN cassava.

yudo, judo ['juðo] *sm* judo.

yugo *sm lit & fig* yoke.

Yugoslavia *n pr* HIST Yugoslavia.

yugoslavo, va ◇ *adj* HIST Yugoslavian. ◇ *sm, f* Yugoslav.

yugular *adj* & *sf* jugular.

yunque *sm* anvil.

yuxtaponer *vt* to juxtapose.

yuxtaposición *sf* juxtaposition.

yuxtapuesto, ta *pp* ▷ **yuxtaponer**.

z, Z *sf* [letra] z, Z.

zafio, fia *adj* rough, uncouth.

zafiro *sm* sapphire.

zaga *sf* DEP defence; **a la zaga** behind, at the back; **no irle a la zaga a alguien** to be every bit O just as good as sb.

zaguán *sm* (entrance) hall.

Zaire *n pr* HIST Zaire.

zalamería (*gen pl*) *sf* flattery *(U)*; **hacerle zalamerías a alguien** to sweet talk sb.

zalamero, ra *sm, f* flatterer; *despec* smooth talker.

zamarra *sf* sheepskin jacket.

zambo, ba *sm, f* - **1.** [persona] knock-kneed person - **2.** *Amér* [hijo de persona negra y otra india] *person who has one black and one Indian parent*.

zambullir *vt* to dip, to submerge. ⬛ **zambullirse** *vprnl*: **zambullirse (en)** [agua] to dive (into); [actividad] to immerse o.s. (in).

zampar *fam vi* to gobble. ⬛ **zamparse** *vprnl* to wolf down.

zanahoria *sf* carrot.

zanca *sf* [de ave] leg, shank.

zancada *sf* stride.

zancadilla *sf* trip; **poner una** O **la zancadilla a alguien** [hacer tropezar] to trip sb up; [engañar] to trick sb.

zancadillear *vt* [hacer tropezar] to trip up.

zanco *sm* stilt.

zancudo, da *adj* long-legged. ⬛ **zancudo** *sm Amér* mosquito.

zángano, na *sm, f fam* [persona] lazy oaf. ⬛ **zángano** *sm* [abeja] drone.

zanja *sf* ditch.

zanjar *vt* [poner fin a] to put an end to; [resolver] to settle, to resolve.

zapallo *sm Andes & R Plata* [calabaza] pumpkin.

zapata *sf* [de freno] shoe.

zapateado *sm type of flamenco music and dance*.

zapatear *vi* to stamp one's feet.

zapatería *sf* - **1.** [oficio] shoemaking - **2.** [taller] shoemaker's - **3.** [tienda] shoe shop.

zapatero, ra *sm, f* - **1.** [fabricante] shoemaker - **2.** [vendedor] shoe seller.

zapatilla *sf* - **1**. [de baile] shoe, pump; [de estar en casa] slipper; [de deporte] sports shoe, trainer - **2**. [de grifo] washer.

zapato *sm* shoe; **zapato de salón** court shoe; **zapato de tacón** high heeled shoe.

zapping ['θapin] *sm inv* channel-hopping; **hacer zapping** to channel-hop.

zar, zarina *sm, f* tsar (*f* tsarina), czar (*f* czarina).

zarandear *vt* - **1**. [cosa] to shake - **2**. [persona] to jostle, to knock about.

zarpa *sf* [de animal - uña] claw; [- mano] paw.

zarpar *vi* to weigh anchor, to set sail; **zarpar rumbo a** to set sail for.

zarpazo *sm* clawing *(U)*.

zarza *sf* bramble, blackberry bush.

zarzal *sm* bramble patch.

zarzamora *sf* blackberry.

zarzaparrilla *sf* sarsaparilla.

zarzuela *sf* MÚS *Spanish light opera*.

zas *interj*: ¡zas! wham!, bang!

zenit = **cenit**.

zepelín (*pl* zepelines) *sm* zeppelin.

zigzag (*pl* zigzags *O* zigzagues) *sm* zigzag; **caminar en zigzag** to walk in a zigzag.

zigzaguear *vi* to zigzag.

zinc = **cinc**.

zíper *sm Amér C, Méx & Ven* zip UK, zipper US.

zócalo *sm* - **1**. [de pared] skirting board - **2**. [de edificio, pedestal] plinth - **3**. *Méx* [plaza] main square.

zoco *sm* souk, Arabian market.

zodiaco, zodíaco *sm* zodiac.

zombi, zombie *smf lit & fig* zombie.

zona *sf* zone, area; **zona de exclusión** exclusion zone; **zona eura** FIN euro zone; **zona verde** [grande] park; [pequeño] lawn.

zoo *sm* zoo.

zoología *sf* zoology.

zoológico, ca *adj* zoological. ◆ **zoológico** *sm* zoo.

zoólogo, ga *sm, f* zoologist.

zopenco, ca *fam sm, f* nitwit.

zoquete ◇ *sm C Sur* [calcetín] ankle sock. ◇ *smf* [tonto] blockhead.

zorro, rra *sm, f lit & fig* fox. ◆ **zorro** *sm* [piel] fox (fur).

zozobra *sf* anxiety, worry.

zozobrar *vi* - **1**. [naufragar] to be shipwrecked - **2**. *fig* [fracasar] to fall through.

zueco *sm* clog.

zulo *sm* hideout.

zulú (*pl* zulúes *O* zulús) *adj & sm, f* Zulu.

zumbar *vi* [gen] to buzz; [máquinas] to whirr, to hum; **me zumban los oídos** my ears are buzzing.

zumbido *sm* [gen] buzz, buzzing *(U)*; [de máquinas] whirr, whirring *(U)*.

zumo *sm* juice.

zurcido *sm* - **1**. [acción] darning - **2**. [remiendo] darn.

zurcir *vt* to darn.

zurdo, da *adj* [mano etc] left; [persona] left-handed. ◆ **zurda** *sf* [mano] left hand.

zurrar *vt* [pegar] to beat, to thrash.

zutano, na *sm, f* so-and-so, what's-his-name (*f* what's-her-name).

ENGLISH-SPANISH
INGLÉS-ESPAÑOL

A

a¹ *(pl* as *OR* a's), **A** *(pl* As *OR* A's) [eɪ] *n* [letter] a *f*, A *f*. ◆ **A** *n* - **1.** MUS la *m* - **2.** SCH [mark] ≃ sobresaliente *m*.

a² *(stressed* [eɪ]*, unstressed* [ə]*) (before vowel or silent 'h' an) indef art* - **1.** [gen] un (una); **a boy** un chico; **a table** una mesa; **an orange** una naranja; **an eagle** un águila; **a hundred/thousand pounds** cien/mil libras - **2.** [referring to occupation]: **to be a dentist/teacher** ser dentista/maestra - **3.** [to express prices, ratios etc] por; **£10 a person** 10 libras por persona; **50 kilometres an hour** 50 kilómetros por hora; **20p a kilo** 20 peniques el kilo; **twice a week/month** dos veces a la semana/al mes.

AA *n* - **1.** *(abbr of* **Automobile Association***)*, asociación británica del automóvil, ≃ RACE *m* - **2.** *(abbr of* **Alcoholics Anonymous***)* AA *mpl*.

AAA *n (abbr of* **American Automobile Association***)* asociación automovilística estadounidense, ≃ RACE *m*.

aback [ə'bæk] *adv*: **to be taken aback** quedarse desconcertado(da).

abandon [ə'bændən] ◇ *vt* [gen] abandonar; [soccer, rugby match] suspender. ◇ *n*: **with abandon** con desenfreno.

abashed [ə'bæʃt] *adj* avergonzado(da).

abate [ə'beɪt] *vi* [storm] amainar; [noise] disminuir; [fear] apaciguarse.

abattoir ['æbətwɑː'] *n* matadero *m*.

abbey ['æbɪ] *n* abadía *f*.

abbot ['æbət] *n* abad *m*.

abbreviate [ə'briːvɪeɪt] *vt* abreviar.

abbreviation [ə,briːvɪ'eɪʃn] *n* abreviatura *f*.

ABC *n lit* & *fig* abecé *m*.

abdicate ['æbdɪkeɪt] ◇ *vi* abdicar. ◇ *vt* [responsibility] abdicar de.

abdomen ['æbdəmen] *n* abdomen *m*.

abduct [əb'dʌkt] *vt* raptar.

aberration [,æbə'reɪʃn] *n* aberración *f*.

abeyance [ə'beɪəns] *n*: **in abeyance** [custom] en desuso; [law] en suspenso.

abhor [əb'hɔː'] *vt* aborrecer.

abide [ə'baɪd] *vt* soportar, aguantar. ◆ **abide by** *vt insep* [law, ruling] acatar; [principles, own decision] atenerse a.

ability [ə'bɪlətɪ] *n* [capability] capacidad *f*.

abject ['æbdʒekt] *adj* - **1.** [poverty] vil, indigente - **2.** [person] sumiso(sa); [apology] humillante.

ablaze [ə'bleɪz] *adj* [on fire] en llamas.

able ['eɪbl] *adj* - **1.** [capable]: **to be able to do sthg** poder hacer algo; **to feel able to do sthg** sentirse capaz de hacer algo - **2.** [skilful] capaz, competente.

ably ['eɪblɪ] *adv* competentemente.

abnormal [æb'nɔːml] *adj* anormal.

aboard [ə'bɔːd] ◇ *adv* a bordo. ◇ *prep* [ship, plane] a bordo de; [bus, train] en.

abode [ə'bəʊd] *n fml*: **of no fixed abode** sin domicilio fijo.

abolish [ə'bɒlɪʃ] *vt* abolir.

abolition [,æbə'lɪʃn] *n* abolición *f*.

abominable [ə'bɒmɪnəbl] *adj* abominable, deplorable.

aborigine [,æbə'rɪdʒənɪ] *n* aborigen *mf* de Australia.

abort [ə'bɔːt] *vt* - **1.** [pregnancy, plan, project] abortar; [pregnant woman] provocar el aborto a - **2.** COMPUT abortar.

abortion [ə'bɔːʃn] *n* aborto *m*; **to have an abortion** abortar.

abortive [ə'bɔ:tɪv] *adj* frustrado(da).

abound [ə'baʊnd] *vi* - **1.** [be plentiful] abundar - **2.** [be full]: **to abound with** *OR* **in** abundar en.

about [ə'baʊt] <> *adv* - **1.** [approximately] más o menos, como; **there were about fifty/a hundred** había (como) unos cincuenta/cien o así; **at about five o'clock** a eso de las cinco - **2.** [referring to place] por ahí; **to leave things lying about** dejar las cosas por ahí; **to walk about** ir andando por ahí; **to jump about** dar saltos - **3.** [on the point of]: **to be about to do sthg** estar a punto de hacer algo. <> *prep* - **1.** [relating to, concerning] sobre, acerca de; **a film about Paris** una película sobre París; **what is it about?** ¿de qué trata?; **there's something odd about that man** hay algo raro en ese hombre - **2.** [referring to place] por; **to wander about the streets** vagar por las calles.

about-turn *esp UK*, **about-face** *esp US n* MIL media vuelta *f*; *fig* cambio *m* radical.

above [ə'bʌv] <> *adv* - **1.** [on top, higher up] arriba; **the flat above** el piso de arriba; **see above** [in text] véase más arriba - **2.** [more, over]: **children aged five and above** niños de cinco años en adelante. <> *prep* - **1.** [on top of] encima de - **2.** [higher above than, over] por encima de - **3.** [more than, superior to] por encima de; **children above the age of 15** niños mayores de 15 años. ● **above all** *adv* sobre todo.

aboveboard [ə,bʌv'bɔ:d] *adj* limpio(pia).

abrasive [ə'breɪsɪv] *adj* - **1.** [substance] abrasivo(va) - **2.** [person] mordaz.

abreast [ə'brest] <> *adv*: **they were walking four abreast** caminaban en fila de a cuatro. <> *prep*: **to keep abreast of** mantenerse al día de.

abridged [ə'brɪdʒd] *adj* abreviado(da).

abroad [ə'brɔ:d] *adv* en el extranjero; **to go abroad** ir al extranjero.

abrupt [ə'brʌpt] *adj* - **1.** [sudden] repentino(na) - **2.** [brusque] brusco(ca).

abscess ['æbsɪs] *n* absceso *m*.

abscond [əb'skɒnd] *vi*: **to abscond (with/from)** escaparse *OR* fugarse (con/de).

abseil ['æbseɪl] *vi*: **to abseil (down sthg)** descolgarse *OR* descender haciendo rápel (por algo).

abseiling ['æbseɪlɪŋ] *n* rappel *m*.

absence ['æbsəns] *n* - **1.** [of person] ausencia *f* - **2.** [of thing] falta *f*.

absent ['æbsənt] *adj* [not present] ausente; **to be absent from** faltar a.

absentee [,æbsən'ti:] *n* ausente *mf*; **absentee ballot** *US* voto *m* por correo.

absent-minded [-'maɪndɪd] *adj* [person] despistado(da); [behaviour] distraído(da).

absolute ['æbsəlu:t] *adj* absoluto(ta); **that's absolute rubbish!** ¡menuda tontería es eso!

absolutely ['æbsəlu:tlɪ] <> *adv* [completely] absolutamente, completamente; **it was absolutely delicious** estuvo riquísimo. <> *excl* ¡desde luego!

absolve [əb'zɒlv] *vt*: **to absolve sb (from)** absolver a alguien (de).

absorb [əb'sɔ:b] *vt* [gen] absorber; **to be absorbed in sthg** *fig* estar absorto *OR* embebido en algo.

absorbent [əb'sɔ:bənt] *adj* absorbente; **absorbent cotton** *US* algodón *m* hidrófilo.

absorption [əb'sɔ:pʃn] *n* [of liquid] absorción *f*.

abstain [əb'steɪn] *vi* [refrain, not vote]: **to abstain (from)** abstenerse (de).

abstemious [æb'sti:mjəs] *adj fml* sobrio(bria), moderado(da).

abstention [əb'stenʃn] *n* abstención *f*.

abstract <> *adj* ['æbstrækt] abstracto(ta). <> *n* ['æbstrækt] [summary] resumen *m*, sinopsis *f*.

absurd [əb'sɜ:d] *adj* absurdo(da).

ABTA ['æbtə] (*abbr of* **Association of British Travel Agents**) *n* asociación británica de agencias de viajes.

abundant [ə'bʌndənt] *adj* abundante.

abuse <> *n* [ə'bju:s] (*U*) - **1.** [offensive remarks] insultos *mpl* - **2.** [misuse, maltreatment] abuso *m*. <> *vt* [ə'bju:z] - **1.** [insult] insultar - **2.** [maltreat, misuse] abusar de.

abusive [ə'bju:sɪv] *adj* [person] grosero(ra); [behaviour, language] insultante.

abysmal [ə'bɪzml] *adj* pésimo(ma), nefasto(ta).

abyss [ə'bɪs] *n* abismo *m*.

a/c (*abbr of* **account (current)**) c/c.

AC *n* (*abbr of* **alternating current**) CA *f*.

academic [,ækə'demɪk] <> *adj* - **1.** [of college, university] académico(ca) - **2.** [studious] estudioso(sa) - **3.** [hypothetical]: **that's completely academic now** eso carece por completo de relevancia. <> *n* - **1.** [university lecturer] profesor *m* universitario, profesora *f* universitaria - **2.** [intellectual] académico(ca).

academy [ə'kædəmɪ] *n* academia *f*.

ACAS ['eɪkæs] (*abbr of* **Advisory, Conciliation and Arbitration Service**) *n* organización británica para el arbitraje en conflictos laborales, ≃ IMAC *m*.

accede [æk'si:d] *vi* - **1.** [agree]: **to accede to** acceder a - **2.** [monarch]: **to accede to the throne** subir al trono.

accelerate [ək'seləreɪt] *vi* - **1.** [car, driver] acelerar - **2.** [inflation, growth] acelerarse.

acceleration [ək,selə'reɪʃn] n aceleración f.

accelerator [ək'seləreɪtər] n acelerador m.

accent ['æksent] n lit & fig acento m.

accept [ək'nent] vt **1.** [gen] aceptar - **2.** [difficult situation, problem] asimilar - **3.** [defeat, blame, responsibility] asumir - **4.** [agree]: **to accept that** admitir que - **5.** [subj: machine - coins, tokens] admitir.

acceptable [ək'septəbl] adj aceptable.

acceptance [ək'septəns] n - **1.** [gen] aceptación f - **2.** [of piece of work, article] aprobación f - **3.** [of defeat, blame, responsibility] reconocimiento m - **4.** [of person - as part of group etc] admisión f.

access ['ækses] n - **1.** [entry] acceso m - **2.** [opportunity to use or see] libre acceso m; **to have access to** tener acceso a.

accessible [ək'sesəbl] adj - **1.** [place] accesible - **2.** [service, book, film] asequible - **3.** [for the disabled] para discapacitados.

accessory [ək'sesərɪ] n - **1.** [of car, vacuum cleaner] accesorio m - **2.** LAW cómplice mf.
➠ **accessories** npl complementos mpl.

accident ['æksɪdənt] n accidente m; **to have an accident** [gen] tener un accidente; [in car] tener un accidente de coche; **it was an accident** fue sin querer; **by accident** [by chance] por casualidad.

accidental [,æksɪ'dentl] adj accidental.

accidentally [,æksɪ'dentəlɪ] adv - **1.** [by chance] por casualidad - **2.** [unintentionally] sin querer.

accident-prone adj propenso(sa) a los accidentes.

acclaim [ə'kleɪm] <> n (U) elogios mpl, alabanza f. <> vt elogiar, alabar.

acclimatize, -ise [ə'klaɪmətaɪz], **acclimate** ['æklɪmeɪt] US vi: **to acclimatize (to)** aclimatarse (a).

accolade ['ækəleɪd] n [praise] elogio m, halago m; [award] galardón m.

accommodate [ə'kɒmədeɪt] vt - **1.** [provide room for people - subj: person] alojar; [- subj: building, place] albergar - **2.** [oblige] complacer.

accommodating [ə'kɒmədeɪtɪŋ] adj complaciente, servicial.

accommodation UK [ə,kɒmə'deɪʃn] n [lodging] alojamiento m.

accommodations [ə,kɒmə'deɪʃnz] npl US = **accommodation**.

accompany [ə'kʌmpənɪ] vt acompañar.

accomplice [ə'kʌmplɪs] n cómplice mf.

accomplish [ə'kʌmplɪʃ] vt [aim, goal] conseguir, alcanzar; [task] realizar.

accomplished [ə'kʌmplɪʃt] adj [person] competente, experto(ta); [performance] logrado(da).

accomplishment [ə'kʌmplɪʃmənt] n - **1.** [action] realización f - **2.** [achievement] logro m.

accord [ə'kɔːd] <> n: **to do sthg of one's own accord** hacer algo por propia voluntad; **the situation improved of its own accord** la situación mejoró por sí sola. <> vt: **to accord sb sthg, to accord sthg to sb** conceder algo a alguien.

accordance [ə'kɔːdəns] n: **in accordance with** de acuerdo con, conforme a.

according [ə'kɔːdɪŋ] ➠ **according to** prep - **1.** [as stated or shown by] según; **to go according to plan** ir según lo planeado - **2.** [with regard to] de acuerdo con, conforme a.

accordingly [ə'kɔːdɪŋlɪ] adv - **1.** [appropriately] como corresponde - **2.** [consequently] por lo tanto.

accordion [ə'kɔːdjən] n acordeón m.

accost [ə'kɒst] vt abordar.

account [ə'kaʊnt] n - **1.** [with bank, shop etc] cuenta f - **2.** [report - spoken] relato m; [- written] informe m - **3.** [client] cuenta f, cliente m ▶▶▶ **to take account of sthg, to take sthg into account** tener en cuenta algo; **of no account** sin importancia; **it is of no account to me** me es indiferente; **on no account** bajo ningún pretexto OR concepto. ➠ **accounts** npl [of business] cuentas fpl. ➠ **by all accounts** adv a decir de todos, según todo el mundo. ➠ **on account of** prep debido a. ➠ **account for** vt insep - **1.** [explain] justificar - **2.** [represent] representar.

accountable [ə'kaʊntəbl] adj [responsible]: **accountable (for)** responsable (de).

accountancy [ə'kaʊntənsɪ] n contabilidad f.

accountant [ə'kaʊntənt] n contable mf, contador m, -ra f Amér.

accrue [ə'kruː] vi acumularse.

accumulate [ə'kjuːmjʊleɪt] <> vt acumular. <> vi [money, things] acumularse; [problems] amontonarse.

accuracy ['ækjʊrəsɪ] n - **1.** [of description, report] veracidad f - **2.** [of weapon, marksman] precisión f; [of typing, figures] exactitud f.

accurate ['ækjʊrət] adj - **1.** [description, report] veraz - **2.** [weapon, marksman, typist] preciso(sa); [figures, estimate] exacto(ta).

accurately ['ækjʊrətlɪ] adv - **1.** [truthfully] verazmente - **2.** [precisely] con precisión.

accusation [,ækju'zeɪʃn] n - **1.** [charge] acusación f - **2.** LAW denuncia f.

accuse [ə'kju:z] *vt*: to accuse sb of sthg/of doing sthg acusar a alguien de algo/de hacer algo.

accused [ə'kju:zd] (*pl* accused) *n* LAW: the accused el acusado, la acusada.

accustomed [ə'kʌstəmd] *adj*: accustomed to acostumbrado(da) a; to grow accustomed to acostumbrarse a.

ace [eɪs] <> *n* - 1. [playing card] as *m*; to be within an ace of *fig* estar al borde de - 2. [in tennis] ace *m*. <> *vt* US: to ace an exam bordar un examen.

ache [eɪk] <> *n* [pain] dolor *m*. <> *vi* [hurt] doler; my back aches me duele la espalda.

achieve [ə'tʃi:v] *vt* [success, goal, fame] alcanzar, lograr; [ambition] realizar.

achievement [ə'tʃi:vmənt] *n* - 1. [accomplishment] logro *m*, éxito *m* - 2. [act of achieving] consecución *f*, realización *f*.

Achilles' tendon [ə'kɪli:z-] *n* tendón *m* de Aquiles.

acid ['æsɪd] <> *adj* - 1. CHEM ácido(da) - 2. [sharp-tasting] agrio(agria) - 3. *fig* [person, remark] mordaz. <> *n* [chemical, drug] ácido *m*.

acid house *n* acid house *m*.

acid rain *n* lluvia *f* ácida.

acknowledge [ək'nɒlɪdʒ] *vt* - 1. [accept] reconocer - 2. [greet] saludar - 3. [letter etc]: to acknowledge receipt of acusar recibo de - 4. [recognize]: to acknowledge sb as reconocer OR considerar a alguien como.

acknowledg(e)ment [ək'nɒlɪdʒmənt] *n* - 1. [acceptance] reconocimiento *m* - 2. [confirmation of receipt] acuse *m* de recibo. ◆ **acknowledg(e)ments** *npl* agradecimientos *mpl*.

acne ['æknɪ] *n* acné *m*.

acorn ['eɪkɔ:n] *n* bellota *f*.

acoustic [ə'ku:stɪk] *adj* acústico(ca). ◆ **acoustics** *npl* acústica *f*.

acquaint [ə'kweɪnt] *vt* [make familiar]: to acquaint sb with sthg [information] poner a alguien al corriente de algo; [method, technique] familiarizar a alguien con algo.

acquaintance [ə'kweɪntəns] *n* [person] conocido *m*, -da *f*; to make sb's acquaintance *fml* conocer a alguien.

acquire [ə'kwaɪər] *vt* - 1. [buy, adopt] adquirir - 2. [obtain - information, document] procurarse.

acquisitive [ə'kwɪzɪtɪv] *adj* consumista.

acquit [ə'kwɪt] *vt* - 1. LAW: to acquit sb of sthg absolver a alguien de algo - 2. [perform]: to acquit o.s. well/badly hacer un buen/mal papel.

acquittal [ə'kwɪtl] *n* LAW absolución *f*.

acre ['eɪkər] *n* acre *m*.

acrid ['ækrɪd] *adj* lit & *fig* acre.

acrimonious [ˌækrɪ'məʊnjəs] *adj* [words] áspero(ra); [dispute] enconado(da).

acrobat ['ækrəbæt] *n* acróbata *mf*.

acronym ['ækrənɪm] *n* siglas *fpl*.

across [ə'krɒs] <> *adv* - 1. [from one side to the other] de un lado a otro - 2. [in measurements]: the river is 2 km across el río tiene 2 kms de ancho. <> *prep* - 1. [from one side to the other of] de un lado a otro de; to look across sthg mirar hacia el otro lado de algo - 2. [on the other side of] al otro lado de. ◆ **across from** *prep* enfrente de.

acrylic [ə'krɪlɪk] <> *adj* acrílico(ca). <> *n* acrílico *m*.

act [ækt] <> *n* - 1. [action, deed] acto *m*, acción *f*; to catch sb in the act coger a alguien con las manos en la masa - 2. [pretence] farsa *f* - 3. [in parliament] ley *f* - 4. [THEAT - part of play] acto *m*; [- routine, turn] número *m*. <> *vi* - 1. [gen] actuar; to act as [person] hacer de; [thing] actuar como - 2. [behave]: to act (as if/like) comportarse (como si/como) - 3. *fig* [pretend] fingir. <> *vt* [part - in play, film] interpretar.

acting ['æktɪŋ] <> *adj* [interim] en funciones. <> *n* actuación *f*; I like acting me gusta actuar.

action ['ækʃn] *n* - 1. [gen & MIL] acción *f*; to take action tomar medidas; to put sthg into action poner algo en práctica OR marcha; out of action [person] fuera de combate; [machine] averiado(da) - 2. [deed] acto *m*, acción *f* - 3. LAW demanda *f*.

activate ['æktɪveɪt] *vt* [device] activar; [machine] poner en funcionamiento.

active ['æktɪv] *adj* - 1. [person, campaigner, encouragement etc] activo(va) - 2. [volcano] en actividad; [bomb] activado(da); on active duty US MIL en servicio activo.

actively ['æktɪvlɪ] *adv* [encourage, discourage] activamente.

activity [æk'tɪvətɪ] *n* - 1. [movement, action] actividad *f* - 2. [pastime, hobby] afición *f*.

actor ['æktər] *n* actor *m*.

actress ['æktrɪs] *n* actriz *f*.

actual ['æktʃʊəl] *adj* [emphatic]: the actual cost is £10 el coste real es de 10 libras; the actual spot where it happened el sitio mismo en que ocurrió.

actually ['æktʃʊəlɪ] *adv* - 1. [really, in truth]: do you actually like him? ¿de verdad que te gusta?; no-one actually saw her en realidad, nadie la vio - 2. [by the way]: actually, I was there yesterday pues yo estuve ayer por allí.

acumen ['ækjʊmen] *n*: business acumen vista *f* para los negocios.

acute [ə'kju:t] *adj* - **1.** [illness, pain] agudo(da); [danger] extremo(ma) - **2.** [perceptive - person] perspicaz - **3.** [hearing, smell] muy fino(na).

ad [æd] *(abbr of advertisement)* n anuncio m

AD *(abbr of Anno Domini)* d. C.

adamant ['ædəmənt] *adj*: **to be adamant (that)** insistir (en que).

Adam's apple ['ædəmz-] n bocado m OR nuez f de Adán.

adapt [ə'dæpt] <> *vt* adaptar. <> *vi*: **to adapt (to)** adaptarse (a).

adaptable [ə'dæptəbl] *adj* [person] adaptable.

adapter, adaptor [ə'dæptər] n [ELEC - for several devices] ladrón m; [- for different socket] adaptador m.

add [æd] *vt* - **1.** [gen]: **to add sthg (to sthg)** añadir algo (a algo) - **2.** [numbers] sumar.
◆ **add on** *vt sep* [to bill, total]: **to add sthg on (to sthg)** añadir OR incluir algo (en algo).
◆ **add to** *vt insep* aumentar, acrecentar.
◆ **add up** <> *vt sep* [numbers] sumar. <> *vi inf* [make sense]: **it doesn't add up** no tiene sentido.

adder ['ædər] n víbora f.

addict ['ædıkt] n - **1.** [taking drugs] adicto m, -ta f; **drug addict** drogadicto m, -ta f, toxicómano m, -na f - **2.** *fig* [fan] fanático m, -ca f.

addicted [ə'dıktıd] *adj* - **1.** [to drug]: **addicted (to)** adicto(ta) (a) - **2.** *fig* [to food, TV]: **to be addicted (to)** ser un fanático (de).

addiction [ə'dıkʃn] n - **1.** [to drug]: **addiction (to)** adicción f (a) - **2.** *fig* [to food, TV]: **addiction (to)** vicio m (por).

addictive [ə'dıktıv] *adj lit & fig* adictivo(va).

addition [ə'dıʃn] n - **1.** MATHS suma f - **2.** [extra thing] adición f, añadido m - **3.** [act of adding] incorporación f; **in addition** además; **in addition to** además de.

additional [ə'dıʃənl] *adj* adicional.

additive ['ædıtıv] n aditivo m.

address [ə'dres] <> n - **1.** [of person, organization] dirección f, domicilio m - **2.** COMPUT dirección f - **3.** [speech] discurso m. <> *vt* - **1.** [letter, parcel, remark]: **to address sthg to** dirigir algo a - **2.** [meeting, conference] dirigirse a - **3.** [issue] abordar; **to address o.s. to sthg** enfrentarse a OR abordar algo.

address book n agenda f de direcciones.

adenoids ['ædınɔıdz] *npl* vegetaciones *fpl* (adenoideas).

adept ['ædept] *adj*: **to be adept (at sthg/at doing sthg)** ser experto(ta) (en algo/en hacer algo).

adequate ['ædıkwət] *adj* - **1.** [sufficient] suficiente - **2.** [good enough] aceptable.

adhere [əd'hıər] *vi* - **1.** [to surface, principle]: **to adhere (to)** adherirse (a) - **2.** [to rule, decision]: **to adhere to** respetar, observar.

adhesive [əd'hi:sıv] <> *adj* adhesivo(va); *adhesive tape* n cinta f adhesiva.

adhesive tape n cinta f adhesiva.

adjacent [ə'dʒeısənt] *adj*: **adjacent (to)** adyacente OR contiguo(gua) (a).

adjective ['ædʒıktıv] n adjetivo m.

adjoining [ə'dʒɔınıŋ] <> *adj* [table] adyacente; [room] contiguo(gua). <> *prep* junto a.

adjourn [ə'dʒɜ:n] *vt* [session] levantar; [meeting] interrumpir.

adjudge [ə'dʒʌdʒ] *vt* declarar.

adjudicate [ə'dʒu:dıkeıt] *vi* actuar como juez; **to adjudicate on** OR **upon sthg** emitir un fallo OR un veredicto sobre algo.

adjust [ə'dʒʌst] <> *vt* [machine, setting] ajustar; [clothing] arreglarse. <> *vi*: **to adjust (to)** adaptarse OR amoldarse (a).

adjustable [ə'dʒʌstəbl] *adj* [machine, chair] regulable.

adjustment [ə'dʒʌstmənt] n - **1.** [modification] modificación f, reajuste m; **to make an adjustment to sthg** hacer un reajuste a algo - **2.** *(U)* [change in attitude]: **adjustment (to)** adaptación f OR amoldamiento m (a).

ad lib [,æd'lıb] <> *adj* [improvised] improvisado(da). <> *adv* [without preparation] improvisando; [without limit] a voluntad. ◆ **ad-lib** *vi* improvisar.

administer [əd'mınıstər] *vt* [gen] administrar; [punishment] aplicar.

administration [əd,mını'streıʃn] n [gen] administración f; [of punishment] aplicación f.

administrative [əd'mınıstrətıv] *adj* administrativo(va).

admirable ['ædmərəbl] *adj* admirable.

admiral ['ædmərəl] n almirante m.

admiration [,ædmə'reıʃn] n admiración f.

admire [əd'maıər] *vt*: **to admire sb (for)** admirar a alguien (por).

admirer [əd'maıərər] n admirador m, -ra f.

admission [əd'mıʃn] n - **1.** [permission to enter] admisión f, ingreso m - **2.** [cost of entrance] entrada f - **3.** [of guilt, mistake] reconocimiento m; **by his/her etc own admission** como él mismo/ella misma etc reconoce.

admit [əd'mıt] <> *vt* - **1.** [acknowledge, confess]: **to admit (that)** admitir OR reconocer (que); **to admit doing sthg** reconocer haber hecho algo; **to admit defeat** *fig* darse por vencido - **2.** [allow to enter or join] admitir; **'admits two'** [on ticket] 'válido para dos (personas)'. <> *vi*: **to admit to sthg** [crime] confesar algo.

admittance [əd'mɪtəns] *n*: to gain admittance to conseguir entrar en; 'no admittance' 'prohibido el paso'.

admittedly [əd'mɪtɪdlɪ] *adv* sin duda.

admonish [əd'mɒnɪʃ] *vt* amonestar.

ad nauseam [,æd'nɔ:zɪæm] *adv* hasta la saciedad.

ado [ə'du:] *n*: without further OR more ado sin más preámbulos, sin mayor dilación.

adolescence [,ædə'lesns] *n* adolescencia *f*.

adolescent [,ædə'lesnt] <> *adj* - 1. [teenage] adolescente - 2. *pej* [immature] pueril. <> *n* [teenager] adolescente *mf*.

adopt [ə'dɒpt] *vt* & *vi* adoptar.

adoption [ə'dɒpʃn] *n* adopción *f*.

adore [ə'dɔ:r] *vt* - 1. [love deeply] adorar - 2. [like very much]: **I adore chocolate** me encanta el chocolate.

adorn [ə'dɔ:n] *vt* adornar.

adrenalin [ə'drenəlɪn] *n* adrenalina *f*.

Adriatic [,eɪdrɪ'ætɪk] *n*: **the Adriatic (Sea)** el (mar) Adriático.

adrift [ə'drɪft] <> *adj* [boat] a la deriva. <> *adv*: **to go adrift** *fig* irse a la deriva.

adult ['ædʌlt] <> *adj* - 1. [fully grown] adulto(ta) - 2. [mature] maduro(ra) - 3. [suitable for adults only] para adultos OR mayores. <> *n* adulto *m*, -ta *f*.

adultery [ə'dʌltərɪ] *n* adulterio *m*.

advance [əd'vɑ:ns] <> *n* - 1. [gen] avance *m* - 2. [money] anticipo *m*. <> *comp*: **advance notice** OR **warning** previo aviso *m*; **advance booking** reserva *f* anticipada. <> *vt* - 1. [improve] promover - 2. [bring forward in time] adelantar - 3. [give in advance]: **to advance sb sthg** adelantarle algo a alguien. <> *vi* avanzar. ◆ **advances** *npl*: **to make advances to sb** [sexual] hacerle proposiciones a alguien, insinuarse a alguien; [business] hacerle una propuesta a alguien. ◆ **in advance** *adv* [pay] por adelantado; [book] con antelación; [know, thank] de antemano.

advanced [əd'vɑ:nst] *adj* - 1. [developed] avanzado(da); **advanced in years** *euph* entrado(da) en años - 2. [student, pupil] adelantado(da); [studies] superior.

advantage [əd'vɑ:ntɪdʒ] *n*: **advantage (over)** ventaja *f* (sobre); **to be to one's advantage** ir en beneficio de uno; **to take advantage of sthg** aprovechar algo; **to have** OR **hold the advantage (over sb)** tener OR llevar ventaja (sobre alguien); **advantage Hewitt** [in tennis] ventaja de Hewitt.

advent ['ædvənt] *n* [arrival] advenimiento *m*. ◆ **Advent** *n* RELIG Adviento *m*.

adventure [əd'ventʃər] *n* aventura *f*.

adventure playground *n* UK parque *m* infantil.

adventurous [əd'ventʃərəs] *adj* - 1. [daring] aventurero(ra) - 2. [dangerous] arriesgado(da).

adverb ['ædvɜ:b] *n* adverbio *m*.

adverse ['ædvɜ:s] *adj* adverso(sa).

advert ['ædvɜ:t] *n* anuncio *m*.

advertise ['ædvətaɪz] <> *vt* anunciar. <> *vi* anunciarse, poner un anuncio; **to advertise for** buscar *(mediante anuncio)*.

advertisement [əd'vɜ:tɪsmənt] *n* anuncio *m*; **to be a great advertisement for** *fig* hacerle una propaganda excelente a.

advertiser ['ædvətaɪzər] *n* anunciante *mf*.

advertising ['ædvətaɪzɪŋ] *n* publicidad *f*.

advice [əd'vaɪs] *n* (U) consejos *mpl*; **to take sb's advice** seguir el consejo de alguien; **a piece of advice** un consejo; **to give sb advice** aconsejar a alguien.

advisable [əd'vaɪzəbl] *adj* aconsejable.

advise [əd'vaɪz] <> *vt* - 1. [give advice to]: **to advise sb to do sthg** aconsejar a alguien que haga algo; **to advise sb against sthg/against doing sthg** desaconsejar a alguien algo/que haga algo - 2. [professionally]: **to advise sb on sthg** asesorar a alguien en algo - 3. [recommend: caution] recomendar - 4. *fml* [inform]: **to advise sb (of sthg)** informar a alguien (de algo). <> *vi* - 1. [give advice]: **to advise against sthg** desaconsejar algo; **to advise against doing sthg** aconsejar no hacer algo - 2. [professionally]: **to advise on** asesorar en (materia de).

advisedly [əd'vaɪzɪdlɪ] *adv* [deliberately] deliberadamente; [after careful consideration] con conocimiento de causa.

adviser UK, **advisor** US [əd'vaɪzər] *n* [of politician etc] consejero *m*, -ra *f*; [financial, professional] asesor *m*, -ra *f*.

advisory [əd'vaɪzərɪ] *adj* [body] consultivo(va), asesor(ra); **in an advisory capacity** OR **role** en calidad de asesor.

advocate <> *n* ['ædvəkət] - 1. LAW abogado *m* defensor - 2. [supporter] defensor *m*, -ra *f*. <> *vt* ['ædvəkeɪt] abogar por.

Aegean [i:'dʒi:ən] *n*: **the Aegean (Sea)** el mar Egeo.

aerial ['eərɪəl] <> *adj* aéreo(a). <> *n* UK [antenna] antena *f*.

aerobics [eə'rəʊbɪks] *n* (U) aerobic *m*.

aerodynamic [,eərəʊdaɪ'næmɪk] *adj* aerodinámico(ca).

aeroplane ['eərəpleɪn] *n* UK avión *m*.

aerosol ['eərəsɒl] *n* aerosol *m*.

aesthetic, esthetic US [i:s'θetɪk] *adj* estético(ca).

afar [ə'fɑ:r] *adv*: **from afar** desde lejos.

affable ['æfəbl] *adj* afable.

affair [ə'feə^r] *n* - 1. [concern, matter] asunto *m* - 2. [extra-marital relationship] aventura *f* (amorosa) - 3. [event, do] acontecimiento *m*.

affect [ə'fekt] *vt* - 1. [influence, move emotionally] afectar - 2. [put on] fingir.

affected [ə'fektɪd] *adj* [insincere] afectado(da).

affection [ə'fekʃn] *n* cariño *m*, afecto *m*.

affectionate [ə'fekʃnət] *adj* cariñoso(sa).

affirm [ə'fɜːm] *vt* afirmar.

affix [ə'fɪks] *vt* fijar, pegar.

afflict [ə'flɪkt] *vt* aquejar, afligir; **to be afflicted with sthg** estar aquejido de algo.

affluence ['æfluəns] *n* prosperidad *f*.

affluent ['æfluənt] *adj* pudiente.

afford [ə'fɔːd] *vt* - 1. [gen]: **to be able to afford** poder permitirse (el lujo de); **we can't afford to let this happen** no podemos permitirnos el lujo de dejar que esto ocurra - 2. *fml* [provide, give] brindar.

affront [ə'frʌnt] *n* afrenta *f*.

Afghanistan [æf'gænɪstæn] *n* Afganistán.

afield [ə'fɪəld] *adv*: **further afield** más lejos.

afloat [ə'fləut] *adj lit & fig* a flote.

afoot [ə'fut] *adj* [plan] en marcha; **there is a rumour afoot that** corre el rumor de que.

afraid [ə'freɪd] *adj* - 1. [gen] asustado(da); **to be afraid of sb** tenerle miedo a alguien; **I'm afraid of them** me dan miedo; **to be afraid of sthg** tener miedo de algo; **to be afraid of doing** OR **to do sthg** tener miedo de hacer algo - 2. [in apologies]: **to be afraid that** temerse que.

afresh [ə'freʃ] *adv* de nuevo.

Africa ['æfrɪkə] *n* África.

African ['æfrɪkən] <> *adj* africano(na). <> *n* africano *m*, -na *f*.

African American *n* afroamericano *m*, -na *f*.

aft [ɑːft] *adv* en popa.

after ['ɑːftə^r] <> *prep* - 1. [gen] después de; **after all my efforts** después de todos mis esfuerzos; **after you!** ¡usted primero!; **day after day** día tras día; **the day after tomorrow** pasado mañana; **the week after next** no la semana que viene sino la otra - 2. *inf* [in search of]: **to be after sthg** buscar algo; **to be after sb** andar detrás de alguien - 3. [towards retreating person]: **to call after sb** llamar a alguien; **to run after sb** correr tras alguien - 4. *US* [telling the time]: **it's twenty after three** son las tres y veinte. <> *adv* más tarde, después. <> *conj* después (de) que; **after you had done it** después de que lo hubieras hecho. ◆ **afters** *npl* UK *inf* postre *m*. ◆ **after all** *adv* - 1. [in spite of everything] después de todo - 2. [it should be remembered] al fin y al cabo.

afterlife ['ɑːftəlaɪf] (*pl* **-lives** [-laɪvz]) *n* más allá *m*, vida *f* de ultratumba.

aftermath ['ɑːftəmæθ] *n* [time] periodo *m* posterior, [situation] situación *f* posterior.

afternoon [,ɑːftə'nuːn] *n* tarde *f*; **in the afternoon** por la tarde; **at three in the afternoon** a las tres de la tarde; **good afternoon** buenas tardes.

aftershave ['ɑːftəʃeɪv] *n* loción *f* para después del afeitado.

aftertaste ['ɑːftəteɪst] *n* - 1. [of food, drink] resabio *m* - 2. *fig* [of unpleasant experience] mal sabor *m* de boca.

afterthought ['ɑːftəθɔːt] *n* idea *f* a posteriori.

afterward(s) ['ɑːftəwəd(z)] *adv* después, más tarde.

again [ə'gen] *adv* [gen] otra vez, de nuevo; **never again** nunca jamás; **he's well again now** ya está bien; **to do sthg again** volver a hacer algo; **to say sthg again** repetir algo; **again and again** una y otra vez; **all over again** otra vez desde el principio; **time and again** una y otra vez ► **half as much again** la mitad otra vez; **twice as much again** dos veces lo mismo otra vez; **then** OR **there again** por otro lado, por otra parte.

against [ə'genst] <> *prep* contra; **I'm against it** estoy (en) contra (de) ello; **to lean against sthg** apoyarse en algo; **(as) against** a diferencia de. <> *adv* en contra.

age [eɪdʒ] <> *n* - 1. [gen] edad *f*; **to be of age** *US* ser mayor de edad; **to come of age** alcanzar la mayoría de edad; **to be under age** ser menor (de edad); **what age are you?** ¿qué edad tienes?; **to be forty years of age** tener cuarenta años (de edad); **at the age of thirty** a los treinta años - 2. [state of being old] vejez *f*. <> *vt & vi (cont* **ageing** OR **aging)** envejecer. ◆ **ages** *npl* [long time]: **ages ago** hace siglos; **I haven't seen her for ages** hace siglos que no la veo.

aged *npl* ['eɪdʒɪd]: **the aged** los ancianos.

age group *n* (grupo *m* de) edad *f*.

agency ['eɪdʒənsɪ] *n* - 1. [business] agencia *f* - 2. [organization, body] organismo *m*, instituto *m*.

agenda [ə'dʒendə] *n* - 1. [of meeting] orden *m* del día - 2. [intentions] intenciones *fpl*.

agent ['eɪdʒənt] *n* - 1. COMM [of company] representante *mf*; [of actor] agente *mf* - 2. [substance] agente *m* - 3. [secret agent] agente *m* (secreto).

aggravate ['ægrəveɪt] *vt* - 1. [make worse] agravar, empeorar - 2. [annoy] irritar.

aggregate ['ægrɪgət] <> *adj* total. <> *n* [total] total *m*.

aggressive [ə'gresɪv] *adj* - **1**. [belligerent - person] agresivo(va) - **2**. [forceful - person, campaign] audaz, emprendedor(ra).

aggrieved [ə'gri:vd] *adj* ofendido(da).

aghast [ə'gɑːst] *adj*: **aghast (at)** horrorizado(da) (ante).

agile [*UK* 'ædʒaɪl, *US* 'ædʒəl] *adj* ágil.

agitate ['ædʒɪteɪt] <> *vt* - **1**. [disturb, worry] inquietar - **2**. [shake about] agitar. <> *vi* [campaign]: **to agitate for/against** hacer campaña a favor de/en contra de.

AGM *n abbr of* **annual general meeting**.

agnostic [æg'nɒstɪk] <> *adj* agnóstico(ca). <> *n* agnóstico *m*, -ca *f*.

ago [ə'gəʊ] *adv*: **a long time/three days/three years ago** hace mucho tiempo/tres días/tres años.

agog [ə'gɒg] *adj* ansioso(sa), expectante.

agonizing ['ægənaɪzɪŋ] *adj* angustioso(sa).

agony ['ægənɪ] *n* - **1**. [physical pain] dolor *m* muy intenso; **to be in agony** morirse de dolor - **2**. [mental pain] angustia *f*; **to be in agony** estar angustiado.

agony aunt *n UK inf* consejera *f* sentimental.

agree [ə'gri:] <> *vi* - **1**. [be of same opinion]: **to agree (with sb about sthg)** estar de acuerdo (con alguien acerca de algo); **to agree on sthg** [reach agreement] ponerse de acuerdo en algo; **to agree on sthg** [be in agreement] estar de acuerdo en algo - **2**. [consent]: **to agree (to sthg)** acceder (a algo) - **3**. [approve]: **to agree with sthg** estar de acuerdo con algo - **4**. [be consistent] concordar - **5**. [food]: **to agree with sb** sentarle bien a alguien - **6**. GRAM: **to agree (with)** concordar (con). <> *vt* - **1**. [fix: date, time] acordar, convenir - **2**. [be of same opinion]: **to agree that** estar de acuerdo en que - **3**. [agree, consent]: **to agree to do sthg** acordar hacer algo - **4**. [concede]: **to agree (that)** reconocer que.

agreeable [ə'gri:əbl] *adj* - **1**. [pleasant] agradable - **2**. [willing]: **to be agreeable to sthg/doing sthg** estar conforme con algo/hacer algo.

agreed [ə'gri:d] <> *adj*: **to be agreed on sthg** estar de acuerdo sobre algo; **at the agreed time** a la hora acordada *OR* convenida. <> *adv* [admittedly] de acuerdo que.

agreement [ə'gri:mənt] *n* - **1**. [accord, settlement, contract] acuerdo *m*; **to be in agreement with** estar de acuerdo con - **2**. [consent] aceptación *f* - **3**. [consistency] correspondencia *f* - **4**. GRAM concordancia *f*.

agricultural [,ægrɪ'kʌltʃərəl] *adj* agrícola.

agriculture ['ægrɪkʌltʃər] *n* agricultura *f*.

aground [ə'graʊnd] *adv*: **to run aground** encallar.

ahead [ə'hed] *adv* - **1**. [in front] delante - **2**. [forwards] adelante, hacia delante; **go ahead!** ¡por supuesto!; **right** *OR* **straight ahead** todo recto *OR* de frente - **3**. [in football, rugby etc]: **to be ahead** ir ganando - **4**. [in better position] por delante; **to get ahead** [be successful] abrirse camino - **5**. [in time]: **to look** *OR* **think ahead** mirar hacia el futuro. <> **ahead of** *prep* - **1**. [in front of] frente a - **2**. [beating]: **to be two points ahead of** llevar dos puntos de ventaja a - **3**. [in better position than] por delante de - **4**. [in time] con anterioridad a; **ahead of schedule** por delante de lo previsto.

aid [eɪd] <> *n* ayuda *f*; **medical aid** asistencia *f* médica; **to go to the aid of sb** *OR* **to sb's aid** ir en auxilio de alguien; **in aid of** a beneficio de. <> *vt* [help] ayudar.

aide [eɪd] *n* POL ayudante *mf*.

AIDS, Aids [eɪdz] (*abbr of* **acquired immune deficiency syndrome**) <> *n* SIDA *m*. <> *comp*: **AIDS patient** sidoso *m*, -sa *f*.

ailing ['eɪlɪŋ] *adj* - **1**. [ill] achacoso(sa) - **2**. *fig* [economy] renqueante.

ailment ['eɪlmənt] *n* achaque *m*, molestia *f*.

aim [eɪm] <> *n* - **1**. [objective] objetivo *m* - **2**. [in firing gun] puntería *f*; **to take aim at** apuntar a. <> *vt* - **1**. [weapon]: **to aim sthg at** apuntar algo a - **2**. [plan, action]: **to be aimed at doing sthg** ir dirigido *OR* encaminado a hacer algo - **3**. [campaign, publicity, criticism]: **to aim sthg at sb** dirigir algo a alguien. <> *vi* - **1**. [point weapon]: **to aim (at)** apuntar (a algo) - **2**. [intend]: **to aim at** *OR* **for sthg** apuntar a *OR* pretender algo; **to aim to do sthg** pretender hacer algo.

aimless ['eɪmlɪs] *adj* sin un objetivo claro.

ain't [eɪnt] *inf* - **1**. (*abbr of* am not) ⊏⊐ **be** - **2**. (*abbr of* are not) ⊏⊐ **be** - **3**. (*abbr of* is not) ⊏⊐ **be** (*abbr of* have not) ⊏⊐ **have** - **5**. (*abbr of* has not) ⊏⊐ **have**.

air [eər] <> *n* - **1**. [gen] aire *m*; **into the air** al aire; **by air** en avión; **to clear the air** *fig* aclarar las cosas - **2**. RADIO & TV: **on the air** en el aire. <> *comp* aéreo(a). <> *vt* - **1**. [clothes, sheets] airear; [cupboard, room] ventilar - **2**. [views, opinions] expresar - **3**. *US* [broadcast] emitir. <> *vi* [clothes, sheets] airearse; [cupboard, room] ventilarse.

airbag ['eəbæg] *n* AUT airbag *m*.

airbase ['eəbeɪs] *n* base *f* aérea.

airbed ['eəbed] *n UK* colchón *m* inflable.

airborne ['eəbɔːn] *adj* - **1**. [troops] aerotransportado(da); [attack] aéreo(a) - **2**. [plane] en el aire, en vuelo.

air-conditioned [-kən'dɪʃnd] *adj* climatizado(da), con aire acondicionado.

air-conditioning [-kən'dɪʃnɪŋ] *n* aire *m* acondicionado.

aircraft ['eəkrɑːft] (*pl* **aircraft**) *n* [plane] avión *m*; [any flying machine] aeronave *f*.

aircraft carrier *n* portaaviones *m inv.*

air fluid ['oəfluːd] *n* campo *m* de aviación.

airforce ['eəfɔːs] *n*: **the airforce** las fuerzas aéreas.

airgun ['eəgʌn] *n* pistola *f* de aire comprimido.

airhostess ['eə,həustɪs] *n* azafata *f*, aeromoza *f Amér.*

airlift ['eəlɪft] <> *n* puente *m* aéreo. <> *vt* transportar por avión.

airline ['eəlaɪn] *n* línea *f* aérea.

airliner ['eəlaɪnə'] *n* avión *m* (grande) de pasajeros.

airlock ['eəlɒk] *n* - 1. [in tube, pipe] bolsa *f* de aire - 2. [airtight chamber] cámara *f* OR esclusa *f* de aire.

airmail ['eəmeɪl] *n*: **by airmail** por correo aéreo.

airplane ['eəpleɪn] *n* US avión *m*.

airport ['eəpɔːt] *n* aeropuerto *m*.

air raid *n* ataque *m* aéreo.

airsick ['eəsɪk] *adj*: **to be airsick** marearse *(en el avión).*

airspace ['eəspeɪs] *n* espacio *m* aéreo.

air steward *n* auxiliar *m* de vuelo, aeromozo *m Amér.*

airstrip ['eəstrɪp] *n* pista *f* de aterrizaje.

air terminal *n* terminal *f* aérea.

airtight ['eətaɪt] *adj* hermético(ca).

air-traffic controller *n* controlador aéreo *m*, controladora aérea *f*.

airy ['eərɪ] *adj* - 1. [room] espacioso(sa) y bien ventilado(da) - 2. [fanciful] ilusorio(ria) - 3. [nonchalant] despreocupado(da).

aisle [aɪl] *n* - 1. [in church] nave *f* lateral - 2. [in plane, theatre, supermarket] pasillo *m*.

ajar [ə'dʒɑː'] *adj* entreabierto(ta).

aka (*abbr of* **also known as**) alias.

akin [ə'kɪn] *adj*: **akin to sthg/to doing sthg** semejante a algo/a hacer algo.

alacrity [ə'lækrətɪ] *n* presteza *f*.

alarm [ə'lɑːm] <> *n* alarma *f*; **to raise** OR **sound the alarm** dar la (voz de) alarma. <> *vt* alarmar, asustar.

alarm clock *n* despertador *m*.

alarming [ə'lɑːmɪŋ] *adj* alarmante.

alas [ə'læs] <> *adv* desgraciadamente. <> *excl liter* ¡ay!

Albania [æl'beɪnjə] *n* Albania.

Albanian [æl'beɪnjən] <> *adj* albanés(esa). <> *n* - 1. [person] albanés *m*, -esa *f* - 2. [language] albanés *m*.

albeit [ɔːl'biːɪt] *conj fml* aunque, si bien.

album ['ælbəm] *n* - 1. [of stamps, photos] álbum *m* - 2. [record] elepé *m*.

alcohol ['ælkəhɒl] *n* alcohol *m*.

alcoholic [,ælkə'hɒlɪk] <> *adj* alcohólico(ca). <> *n* alcohólico *m*, -ca *f*.

alcopop ['ælkəʊpɒp] *n* refresco gaseoso que contiene un cierto porcentaje de alcohol.

alcove ['ælkəʊv] *n* hueco *m*.

alderman ['ɔːldəmən] (*pl* **-men** [-mən]) *n* ≃ concejal *m*, -la *f*.

ale [eɪl] *n* tipo de cerveza.

alert [ə'lɜːt] <> *adj* - 1. [vigilant] atento(ta) - 2. [perceptive] despierto(ta) - 3. [aware]: **to be alert to** ser consciente de. <> *n* [gen & MIL] alerta *f*; **to be on the alert** estar alerta. <> *vt* alertar; **to alert sb to sthg** alertar a alguien de algo.

A level (*abbr of* **Advanced level**) *n* UK SCH nivel escolar necesario para acceder a la universidad.

alfresco [æl'freskəʊ] *adj* & *adv* al aire libre.

algae ['ældʒiː] *npl* algas *fpl*.

algebra ['ældʒɪbrə] *n* álgebra *f*.

Algeria [æl'dʒɪərɪə] *n* Argelia.

alias ['eɪlɪəs] <> *adv* alias. <> *n* (*pl* **-es**) alias *m inv.*

alibi ['ælɪbaɪ] *n* coartada *f*.

alien ['eɪlɪən] <> *adj* - 1. [from outer space] extraterrestre - 2. [unfamiliar] extraño(ña), ajeno(na). <> *n* - 1. [from outer space] extraterrestre *mf* - 2. LAW [foreigner] extranjero *m*, -ra *f*.

alienate ['eɪljəneɪt] *vt* [make unsympathetic] ganarse la antipatía de.

alight [ə'laɪt] <> *adj* [on fire] ardiendo; **to set sthg alight** prender fuego a algo. <> *vi* (*pt* & *pp* **-ed**) *fml* - 1. [land] posarse - 2. [get off]: **to alight from** apearse de.

align [ə'laɪn] *vt* [line up] alinear.

alike [ə'laɪk] <> *adj* parecido(da). <> *adv* [treat] de la misma forma; **to look alike** parecerse.

alimony ['ælɪmənɪ] *n* pensión *f* alimenticia.

alive [ə'laɪv] *adj* - 1. [living] vivo(va) - 2. [active, lively] lleno(na) de vida.

alkali ['ælkəlaɪ] (*pl* **-s** OR **-ies**) *n* álcali *m*.

all [ɔːl] <> *adj* - 1. (with sing n) todo(da); **all the drink** toda la bebida; **all day** todo el día; **all night** toda la noche; **all the time** todo el tiempo OR el rato - 2. (with npl) todos(das); **all the boxes** todas las cajas; **all men** todos los hombres; **all three died** los tres murieron. <> *pron* - 1. (sing) [the whole amount] todo *m*, -da *f*; **she drank it all, she drank all of it** se lo bebió todo - 2. (pl) [everybody, everything] todos *mpl*, -das *f*; **all of them came, they all came** vinieron todos - 3. (with superl): **he's the cleverest of all** es el más listo de todos; **the**

most amazing thing of all lo más impresionante de todo; **best/worst of all...** lo mejor/peor de todo es que... ⬦ *adv* - **1.** [entirely] completamente; **I'd forgotten all about that** me había olvidado completamente de eso; **all alone** completamente solo(la) - **2.** [in sport, competitions]: **the score is two all** el resultado es de empate a dos - **3.** *(with compar)*: **to run all the faster** correr aun más rápido. ⬤ **all but** *adv* casi. ⬤ **all in all** *adv* en conjunto. ⬤ **all that** *adv*: **she's not all that pretty** no es tan guapa. ⬤ **in all** *adv* en total.

Allah ['ælə] *n* Alá *m*.

all-around *US* = **all-round**.

allay [ə'leɪ] *vt fml* [suspicions, doubts] despejar; [fears] apaciguar.

all clear *n* - **1.** [signal] señal *f* de cese de peligro - **2.** *fig* [go-ahead] luz *f* verde.

allegation [,ælɪ'geɪʃn] *n* acusación *f*.

allege [ə'ledʒ] *vt* alegar; **to be alleged to have done/said** ser acusado de haber hecho/dicho.

allegedly [ə'ledʒɪdlɪ] *adv* presuntamente.

allegiance [ə'liːdʒəns] *n* lealtad *f*.

allergy ['æladʒɪ] *n* alergia *f*.

alleviate [ə'liːvɪeɪt] *vt* aliviar.

alley(way) ['ælɪ(weɪ)] *n* callejuela *f*.

alliance [ə'laɪəns] *n* alianza *f*.

allied ['ælaɪd] *adj* - **1.** [powers, troops] aliado(da) - **2.** [subjects] afín.

alligator ['ælɪgeɪtə'] *(pl* alligator OR **-s)** *n* caimán *m*.

all-important *adj* crucial.

all-in *adj UK* [inclusive] todo incluido. ⬤ **all in** ⬦ *adj inf* [tired] hecho(cha) polvo. ⬦ *adv* [inclusive] todo incluido.

all-night *adj* [party etc] que dura toda la noche; [chemist, bar] abierto(ta) toda la noche.

allocate ['æləkeɪt] *vt*: **to allocate sthg to sb** [money, resources] destinar algo a alguien; [task, tickets, seats] asignar algo a alguien.

allot [ə'lɒt] *vt* [job, time] asignar; [money, resources] destinar.

allotment [ə'lɒtmənt] *n* - **1.** *UK* [garden] *parcela municipal arrendada para su cultivo* - **2.** [share - of money, resources] asignación *f*; [- of time] espacio *m* (de tiempo) concedido.

allow [ə'laʊ] *vt* - **1.** [permit] permitir, dejar - **2.** [set aside - money] destinar; [- time] dejar - **3.** [officially accept - subj: person] conceder; [- subj: law] admitir - **4.** [concede]: **to allow that** admitir OR reconocer que. ⬤ **allow for** *vt insep* contar con.

allowance [ə'laʊəns] *n* - **1.** [money received - from government] subsidio *m*; [- from employer] dietas *fpl* - **2.** *US* [pocket money] paga *f* - **3.** FIN

desgravación *f* - **4.**: **to make allowances for sthg/sb** [forgive] disculpar algo/a alguien; [take into account] tener en cuenta algo/a alguien.

alloy ['ælɔɪ] *n* aleación *f*.

all right ⬦ *adv* - **1.** [gen] bien - **2.** [only just acceptably] (más o menos) bien - **3.** [in answer - yes] vale, bueno. ⬦ *adj* - **1.** [gen] bien - **2.** [not bad]: **it's all right, but...** no está mal, pero... - **3.** [OK]: **sorry – that's all right** lo siento – no importa.

all-round *UK*, **all-around** *US adj* [multi-skilled] polifacético(ca).

all-terrain vehicle *n* todoterreno *m*.

all-time *adj* [favourite] de todos los tiempos; [high, low] histórico(ca).

allude [ə'luːd] *vi*: **to allude to** aludir a.

alluring [ə'ljʊərɪŋ] *adj* [person] atrayente; [thing] tentador(ra).

allusion [ə'luːʒn] *n* alusión *f*.

ally *n* ['ælaɪ] aliado *m*, -da *f*.

almighty [ɔːl'maɪtɪ] *adj inf* [very big] descomunal.

almond ['ɑːmənd] *n* [nut] almendra *f*.

almost ['ɔːlməʊst] *adv* casi.

alms [ɑːmz] *npl dated* limosna *f*.

aloft [ə'lɒft] *adv* [in the air] en lo alto.

alone [ə'ləʊn] ⬦ *adj* solo(la); **to be alone with** estar a solas con. ⬦ *adv* - **1.** [without others] solo(la) - **2.** [only] sólo
▶▶ **to leave sthg/sb alone** dejar algo/a alguien en paz. ⬤ **let alone** *conj* y mucho menos.

along [ə'lɒŋ] ⬦ *adv* - **1.** [forward] hacia delante; **to go OR walk along** avanzar; **she was walking along** iba andando - **2.** [to this or that place]: **to come along** venir; **to go along** ir. ⬦ *prep* [towards one end of, beside] por, a lo largo de. ⬤ **all along** *adv* todo el rato; **she knew all along** lo sabía desde el principio. ⬤ **along with** *prep* junto con.

alongside [ə,lɒŋ'saɪd] ⬦ *prep* - **1.** [next to] junto a - **2.** [together with] junto con. ⬦ *adv*: **to come alongside** ponerse a la misma altura.

aloof [ə'luːf] ⬦ *adj* frío(a), distante. ⬦ *adv* distante; **to remain aloof (from)** mantenerse a distancia (de).

aloud [ə'laʊd] *adv* en alto, en voz alta.

alphabet ['ælfəbet] *n* alfabeto *m*.

alphabetical [,ælfə'betɪkl] *adj* alfabético(ca); **in alphabetical order** en OR por orden alfabético.

Alps [ælps] *npl*: **the Alps** los Alpes.

already [ɔːl'redɪ] *adv* ya.

alright [,ɔːl'raɪt] = **all right**.

Alsatian [æl'seɪʃn] *n* [dog] pastor *m* alemán.

also ['ɔːlsəʊ] *adv* también.

altar ['ɔːltə'] *n* altar *m*.

alter ['ɔːltər] ◇ vt [modify] alterar, modificar. ◇ vi cambiar.

alteration [ˌɔːltəˈreɪʃn] n - 1. [gen] alteración f; **to make an alteration/alterations to** hacer una modificación/modificaciones en - 2. [to dress] arreglo m.

alternate ◇ adj [UK ɔːlˈtɜːnət, US ˈɒːltərnət] - 1. [by turns] alterno(na) - 2. [every other]: **on alternate days/weeks** cada dos días/semanas. ◇ n [UK ɔːlˈtɜːnət, US ˈɒːltərnət US sustituto(ta). ◇ vi [ˈɔːltəneɪt]: **to alternate (with/between)** alternar (con/entre).

alternating current [ˈɔːltəneɪtɪŋ-] n ELEC corriente f alterna.

alternative [ɔːlˈtɜːnətɪv] ◇ adj alternativo(va). ◇ n alternativa f, opción f; **to have no alternative (but to do sthg)** no tener más remedio (que hacer algo).

alternatively [ɔːlˈtɜːnətɪvlɪ] adv o bien.

alternator [ˈɔːltəneɪtər] n ELEC alternador m.

although [ɔːlˈðəʊ] conj aunque.

altitude [ˈæltɪtjuːd] n altitud f.

alto [ˈæltəʊ] (pl -s) n [female singer] contralto f; [male singer] contralto m.

altogether [ˌɔːltəˈgeðər] adv - 1. [completely] completamente; **not altogether** no del todo - 2. [considering all things] en conjunto - 3. [in total] en total.

aluminium UK [ˌæljʊˈmɪnɪəm], **aluminum** US [əˈluːmɪnəm] n aluminio m.

always [ˈɔːlweɪz] adv siempre.

am [æm] vb ⟾ **be**.

a.m. (abbr of ante meridiem): **at 3 a.m.** a las tres de la mañana.

AM (abbr of amplitude modulation) n AM f.

amalgamate [əˈmælgəmeɪt] ◇ vt [ideas] amalgamar; [companies, organizations] fusionar. ◇ vi [of ideas] amalgamarse; [of companies, organizations] fusionarse.

amass [əˈmæs] vt [fortune, wealth] amasar.

amateur [ˈæmətər] ◇ adj aficionado(da); pej chapucero(ra). ◇ n aficionado m, -da f; pej chapucero m, -ra f.

amateurish [ˌæməˈtɜːrɪʃ] adj chapucero(ra).

amaze [əˈmeɪz] vt asombrar.

amazed [əˈmeɪzd] adj asombrado(da).

amazement [əˈmeɪzmənt] n asombro m.

amazing [əˈmeɪzɪŋ] adj - 1. [surprising] asombroso(sa) - 2. [excellent] genial.

Amazon [ˈæməzn] n - 1. [river]: **the Amazon** el Amazonas - 2. [region]: **the Amazon (Basin)** la cuenca amazónica; **the Amazon rainforest** la selva amazónica.

ambassador [æmˈbæsədər] n embajador m, -ra f.

amber [ˈæmbər] ◇ adj - 1. [amber-coloured] de color ámbar - 2. UK [traffic light] ámbar. ◇ n ámbar m.

ambiguous [æmˈbɪgjʊəs] adj ambiguo(gua).

ambition [æmˈbɪʃn] n ambición f.

ambitious [æmˈbɪʃəs] adj ambicioso(sa).

amble [ˈæmbl] vi [walk] deambular.

ambulance [ˈæmbjʊləns] n ambulancia f.

ambush [ˈæmbʊʃ] ◇ n emboscada f. ◇ vt emboscar.

amenable [əˈmiːnəbl] adj receptivo(va); **amenable to** favorable a.

amend [əˈmend] vt [law] enmendar; [text] corregir; [schedule] modificar. ⟾ **amends** npl: **to make amends for sthg** reparar algo.

amendment [əˈmendmənt] n [change - to law] enmienda f; [- to text] corrección f; [- to schedule] modificación f.

amenities [əˈmiːnətɪz] npl [of town] facilidades fpl; [of building] comodidades fpl.

America [əˈmerɪkə] n América.

American [əˈmerɪkn] ◇ adj americano(na). ◇ n [person] americano m, -na f.

American Indian n amerindio m, -dia f.

amiable [ˈeɪmjəbl] adj amable, agradable.

amicable [ˈæmɪkəbl] adj amigable, amistoso(sa).

amid(st) [əˈmɪd(st)] prep fml entre, en medio de.

amiss [əˈmɪs] ◇ adj: **something's amiss** algo va mal. ◇ adv: **to take sthg amiss** tomarse algo a mal.

ammonia [əˈməʊnjə] n amoniaco m.

ammunition [ˌæmjʊˈnɪʃn] n (U) MIL municiones fpl.

amnesia [æmˈniːzjə] n amnesia f.

amnesty [ˈæmnəstɪ] n amnistía f.

amok [əˈmɒk], **amuck** adv: **to run amok** enloquecer atacando a gente de forma indiscriminada.

among(st) [əˈmʌŋ(st)] prep entre.

amoral [ˌeɪˈmɒrəl] adj amoral.

amorous [ˈæmərəs] adj apasionado(da).

amount [əˈmaʊnt] n cantidad f. ⟾ **amount to** vt insep - 1. [total] ascender a - 2. [be equivalent to] venir a ser.

amp [æmp] n abbr of **ampere**.

ampere [ˈæmpeər] n amperio m.

amphibian [æmˈfɪbɪən] n anfibio m.

ample [ˈæmpl] adj - 1. [enough] suficiente; [more than enough] sobrado(da); **to have ample time** tener tiempo de sobra - 2. [garment, room] amplio(plia); [stomach, bosom] abundante.

amplifier [ˈæmplɪfaɪər] n amplificador m.

amputate [ˈæmpjʊteɪt] vt & vi amputar.

Amsterdam [ˌæmstəˈdæm] *n* Amsterdam.

Amtrak [ˈæmtræk] *n organismo que regula y coordina las líneas férreas en Estados Unidos.*

amuck [əˈmʌk] = **amok**.

amuse [əˈmjuːz] *vt* - **1.** [make laugh, smile] divertir - **2.** [entertain] distraer; **to amuse o.s. (by doing sthg)** distraerse (haciendo algo).

amused [əˈmjuːzd] *adj* - **1.** [person, look] divertido(da); **I was not amused at** OR **by that** no me hizo gracia eso - **2.** [entertained]: **to keep o.s. amused** entretenerse, distraerse.

amusement [əˈmjuːzmənt] *n* - **1.** [enjoyment] regocijo *m*, diversión *f* - **2.** [diversion, game] atracción *f*.

amusement arcade *n* salón *m* de juegos.

amusement park *n* parque *m* de atracciones.

amusing [əˈmjuːzɪŋ] *adj* divertido(da).

an *(stressed* [æn], *unstressed* [ən]*)* ⊳ **a**.

anabolic steroid [ˌænəˈbɒlɪk-] *n* esteroide *m* anabolizante.

anaemic UK, **anemic** US [əˈniːmɪk] *adj* [ill] anémico(ca).

anaesthetic UK, **anesthetic** US [ˌænɪsˈθetɪk] *n* anestesia *f*.

analogue, analog US [ˈænəlɒg] ⊳ *adj* [watch, clock] analógico(ca). ⊳ *n fml* equivalente *m*.

analogy [əˈnælədʒɪ] *n* analogía *f*.

analyse UK, **analyze** US [ˈænəlaɪz] *vt* analizar.

analysis [əˈnæləsɪs] *(pl* **analyses** [əˈnæləsiːz]) *n* - **1.** [examination] análisis *m inv* - **2.** [psychoanalysis] psicoanálisis *m inv*.

analyst [ˈænəlɪst] *n* - **1.** [gen] analista *mf* - **2.** [psychoanalyst] psicoanalista *mf*.

analytic(al) [ˌænəˈlɪtɪk(l)] *adj* analítico(ca).

analyze US = **analyse**.

anarchist [ˈænəkɪst] *n* anarquista *mf*.

anarchy [ˈænəkɪ] *n* anarquía *f*.

anathema [əˈnæθəmə] *n*: **the idea is anathema to me** la idea me parece aberrante.

anatomy [əˈnætəmɪ] *n* anatomía *f*.

ANC *(abbr of* **African National Congress)** *n* ANC *m*.

ancestor [ˈænsestər] *n lit & fig* antepasado *m*.

anchor [ˈæŋkər] ⊳ *n* NAUT ancla *f*; **to drop anchor** echar el ancla; **to weigh anchor** levar anclas. ⊳ *vt* - **1.** [secure] sujetar - **2.** *esp US* TV presentar. ⊳ *vi* NAUT anclar.

anchovy [ˈæntʃəvɪ] *(pl* **anchovy** OR **-ies)** *n* [salted] anchoa *f*; [fresh, in vinegar] boquerón *m*.

ancient [ˈeɪnʃənt] *adj* - **1.** [gen] antiguo(gua) - **2.** *hum* [very old] vetusto(ta).

ancillary [ænˈsɪlərɪ] *adj* auxiliar.

and *(strong form* [ænd], *weak form* [ən]*) conj* - **1.** [gen] y; *(before 'i' or 'hi')* e; **fish and chips** pescado con patatas fritas; **faster and faster** cada vez más rápido; **it's nice and easy** es sencillito - **2.** [in numbers]: **one hundred and eighty** ciento ochenta; **one and a half** uno y medio; **2 and 2 is 4** 2 y 2 son 4 - **3.** [to]: **try and come** intenta venir; **come and see the kids** ven a ver a los niños; **wait and see** espera a ver. ◆ **and so on, and so forth** *adv* etcétera, y cosas así.

Andalusia [ˌændəˈluːzɪə] *n* Andalucía.

Andes [ˈændiːz] *npl*: **the Andes** los Andes.

Andorra [ænˈdɔːrə] *n* Andorra.

anecdote [ˈænɪkdəʊt] *n* anécdota *f*.

anemic US = **anaemic**.

anesthetic *etc* US = **anaesthetic**.

anew [əˈnjuː] *adv* de nuevo, nuevamente.

angel [ˈeɪndʒəl] *n* RELIG ángel *m*.

anger [ˈæŋgər] ⊳ *n* ira *f*, furia *f*. ⊳ *vt* enfadar.

angina [ænˈdʒaɪnə] *n* angina *f* de pecho.

angle [ˈæŋgl] *n* - **1.** [gen] ángulo *m* - **2.** [point of view] enfoque *m*.

angler [ˈæŋglər] *n* pescador *m*, -ra *f (con caña).*

Anglican [ˈæŋglɪkən] ⊳ *adj* anglicano(na). ⊳ *n* anglicano *m*, -na *f*.

angling [ˈæŋglɪŋ] *n* pesca *f* con caña.

Anglo-Saxon [ˌæŋgləʊˈsæksn] ⊳ *adj* anglosajón(ona). ⊳ *n* - **1.** [person] anglosajón *m*, -ona *f* - **2.** [language] anglosajón *m*.

angry [ˈæŋgrɪ] *adj* [person] enfadado(da); [letter, look, face] furioso(sa), airado(da); **to be angry at** OR **with sb** estar enfadado con alguien; **to get angry with sb** enfadarse con alguien.

anguish [ˈæŋgwɪʃ] *n* angustia *f*.

angular [ˈæŋgjʊlər] *adj* [face, body] anguloso(sa).

animal [ˈænɪml] ⊳ *adj* [instincts, kingdom] animal; [rights] de los animales. ⊳ *n* [creature] animal *m*; *pej* [person] animal *m*.

animate [ˈænɪmət] *adj* animado(da).

animated [ˈænɪmeɪtɪd] *adj* animado(da).

aniseed [ˈænɪsiːd] *n* anís *m*.

ankle [ˈæŋkl] ⊳ *n* tobillo *m*. ⊳ *comp*: **ankle boots** botines *mpl*; **ankle socks** calcetines *mpl* cortos.

annex *esp US* [ˈæneks] ⊳ *n* edificio *m* anejo. ⊳ *vt* anexionar.

annexe *esp UK* [ˈæneks] *n* edificio *m* anejo.

annihilate [əˈnaɪəleɪt] *vt* [destroy] aniquilar.

anniversary [ˌænɪˈvɜːsərɪ] *n* aniversario *m*.

announce [əˈnaʊns] *vt* anunciar.

announcement [əˈnaʊnsmənt] *n* anuncio *m*.

announcer [ə'naʊnsəʳ] n: radio/television announcer presentador m, -ra f OR locutor m, -ra f de radio/televisión.

annoy [ə'nɔɪ] vt fastidiar, molestar.

annoyance [ə'nɔɪəns] n molestia f.

annoyed [ə'nɔɪd] adj: to be annoyed at sthg/with sb estar molesto(ta) por algo/con alguien; to get annoyed at sthg/with sb molestarse por algo/con alguien.

annoying [ə'nɔɪɪŋ] adj fastidioso(sa).

annual ['ænjʊəl] <> adj anual. <> n - 1. [plant] planta f anual - 2. [book] anuario m.

annual general meeting n asamblea f general anual.

annul [ə'nʌl] vt anular.

annum ['ænəm] n: per annum al año.

anomaly [ə'nɒməlɪ] n anomalía f.

anonymous [ə'nɒnɪməs] adj anónimo(ma).

anorak ['ænəræk] n - 1. esp UK [garment] chubasquero m, anorak m - 2. UK inf [boring person] petardo m, -da f.

anorexia (nervosa) [,ænə'reksɪə(nɜ:'vəʊsə)] n anorexia f.

anorexic [,ænə'reksɪk] <> adj anoréxico(ca). <> n anoréxico m, -ca f.

another [ə'nʌðəʳ] <> adj otro(tra); another one otro(tra); in another few minutes en unos minutos más. <> pron otro m, -tra f; one after another uno tras otro, una tras otra; one another el uno al otro, la una a la otra; we love one another nos queremos.

answer ['ɑ:nsəʳ] <> n - 1. [gen] respuesta f; in answer to en respuesta a - 2. [to problem] solución f. <> vt - 1. [reply to] responder a, contestar a - 2. [respond to]: to answer the door abrir la puerta; to answer the phone coger OR contestar el teléfono. <> vi responder, contestar. ◆ **answer back** vt sep & vi replicar. ◆ **answer for** vt insep - 1. [accept responsibility for] responder por; they have a lot to answer for tienen mucho que explicar - 2. [suffer consequences of] responder de.

answerable ['ɑ:nsərəbl] adj: answerable (to sb/for sthg) responsable (ante alguien/de algo).

answering machine ['ɑ:nsərɪŋ-] n contestador m automático.

ant [ænt] n hormiga f.

antagonism [æn'tægənɪzm] n antagonismo m.

antagonize, -ise [æn'tægənaɪz] vt provocar la hostilidad de.

Antarctic [æn'tɑ:ktɪk] <> adj antártico(ca). <> n: the Antarctic el Antártico.

Antarctica [æn'tɑ:ktɪkə] n (la) Antártida.

antelope ['æntɪləʊp] (pl antelope OR -s) n antílope m.

antenatal [,ænti'neɪtl] adj prenatal.

antenatal clinic n clínica f de preparación al parto.

antenna [æn'tenə] n - 1. (pl -nae [-ni:]) [of insect] antena f - 2. (pl -s) US [aerial] antena f.

anthem ['ænθəm] n himno m.

anthology [æn'θɒlədʒɪ] n antología f.

antibiotic [,æntɪbaɪ'ɒtɪk] n antibiótico m.

antibody ['æntɪ,bɒdɪ] n anticuerpo m.

anticipate [æn'tɪsɪpeɪt] vt - 1. [expect] prever - 2. [look forward to] esperar ansiosamente - 3. [preempt] adelantarse a.

anticipation [æn,tɪsɪ'peɪʃn] n [excitement] expectación f; in anticipation of en previsión de.

anticlimax [ænti'klaɪmæks] n decepción f.

anticlockwise [,ænti'klɒkwaɪz] UK adv en sentido contrario al de las agujas del reloj.

antics ['æntɪks] npl payasadas fpl.

anticyclone [,ænti'saɪkləʊn] n anticiclón m.

antidepressant [,æntɪdɪ'presnt] n antidepresivo m.

antidote ['æntɪdəʊt] n lit & fig: antidote (to) antídoto m (contra).

antifreeze ['æntɪfri:z] n anticongelante m.

antihistamine [,æntɪ'hɪstəmɪn] n antihistamínico m.

antiperspirant [,ænti'pɜ:spərənt] n antitranspirante m.

antiquated ['æntɪkweɪtɪd] adj anticuado(da).

antique [æn'ti:k] <> adj [furniture, object] antiguo(gua). <> n antigüedad f.

antique shop n tienda f de antigüedades.

anti-Semitism [-'semɪtɪzm] n antisemitismo m.

antiseptic [,ænti'septɪk] <> adj antiséptico(ca). <> n antiséptico m.

antisocial [,ænti'səʊʃl] adj - 1. [against society] antisocial - 2. [unsociable] poco sociable.

anus ['eɪnəs] n ano m.

anvil ['ænvɪl] n yunque m.

anxiety [æŋ'zaɪətɪ] n - 1. [worry] ansiedad f, inquietud f - 2. [cause of worry] preocupación f - 3. [keenness] afán m, ansia f.

anxious ['æŋkʃəs] adj - 1. [worried] preocupado(da); to be anxious about estar preocupado por - 2. [keen]: to be anxious that/to do sthg estar ansioso(sa) por que/por hacer algo.

any ['enɪ] <> adj - 1. (with negative) ninguno(na); I haven't read any books no he leído ningún libro; I haven't got any money no tengo nada de dinero - 2. [some] algún(una); are there any cakes left? ¿queda algún pastel?; is there any milk left? ¿queda algo de leche?; have you got any money? ¿tienes dinero? - 3. [no matter which] cualquier; any box will do cualquier caja vale - 4. ⌐▷ **case**, **day**, **moment**, **rate**. ◇ *pron* - 1. *(with negative)* ninguno *m*, -na *f*; **I didn't get any** a mí no me tocó ninguno - 2. [some] alguno *m*, -na *f*; **can any of you do it?** ¿sabe alguno de vosotros hacerlo?; **I need some matches, do you have any?** necesito cerillas, ¿tienes? - 3. [no matter which] cualquiera; **take any you like** coge cualquiera que te guste. ◇ *adv* - 1. *(with negative)*: **I can't see it any more** ya no lo veo; **he's not feeling any better** no se siente nada mejor; **I can't stand it any longer** no lo aguanto más - 2. [some, a little]: **do you want any more potatoes?** ¿quieres más patatas?; **is that any better/different?** ¿es así mejor/diferente?

anybody ['enɪˌbɒdɪ] = **anyone**.

anyhow ['enɪhaʊ] *adv* - 1. [in spite of that] de todos modos - 2. [carelessly] de cualquier manera - 3. [in any case] en cualquier caso.

anyone ['enɪwʌn], **anybody** *pron* - 1. *(in negative sentences)* nadie; **I don't know anyone** no conozco a nadie - 2. *(in questions)* alguien - 3. [any person] cualquiera.

anyplace ['enɪpleɪs] *US* = **anywhere**.

anything ['enɪθɪŋ] *pron* - 1. *(in negative sentences)* nada; **I don't want anything** no quiero nada - 2. *(in questions)* algo; **would you like anything else?** ¿quiere algo más? - 3. [any object, event] cualquier cosa.

anyway ['enɪweɪ] *adv* - 1. [in any case] de todas formas *OR* maneras - 2. [in conversation] en cualquier caso.

anywhere ['enɪweə^r], **anyplace** *US* ['enɪpleɪs] *adv* - 1. *(in negative sentences)* en ningún sitio; **I didn't go anywhere** no fui a ninguna parte - 2. *(in questions)* en algún sitio; **did you go anywhere?** ¿fuiste a algún sitio? - 3. [wherever] cualquier sitio; **anywhere you like** donde quieras.

apart [ə'pɑːt] *adv* - 1. [separated]: **we're living apart** vivimos separados - 2. [aside] aparte; **joking apart** bromas aparte. ◄▬ **apart from** *prep* - 1. [except for] aparte de, salvo - 2. [as well as] aparte de.

apartheid [ə'pɑːtheɪt] *n* apartheid *m*.

apartment [ə'pɑːtmənt] *n esp US* piso *m*, apartamento *m*, departamento *m Amér*.

apartment building *n US* bloque *m* de pisos, bloque *m* de departamentos *Amér*.

apathy ['æpəθɪ] *n* apatía *f*.

ape [eɪp] ◇ *n* simio *m*. ◇ *vt pej* imitar.

aperitif [əperə'tiːf] *n* aperitivo *m*.

aperture ['æpə,tjʊə^r] *n* abertura *f*.

apex ['eɪpeks] (*pl* **-es** *OR* **apices**) *n* [top] vértice *m*.

APEX ['eɪpeks] (*abbr of* advance purchase excursion) *n UK* (tarifa *f*) APEX *f*.

apices ['eɪpɪsiːz] *pl* ⌐▷ **apex**.

apiece [ə'piːs] *adv* cada uno(na).

apocalypse [ə'pɒkəlɪps] *n* apocalipsis *m inv*.

apologetic [ə,pɒlə'dʒetɪk] *adj* [tone, look] lleno(na) de disculpas; **to be very apologetic (about)** no hacer más que disculparse (por).

apologize, -ise [ə'pɒlədʒaɪz] *vi*: **to apologize (to sb for sthg)** disculparse (ante alguien por algo); **I apologized to her** le pedí perdón.

apology [ə'pɒlədʒɪ] *n* disculpa *f*; **Tom sends his apologies** [can't come] Tom se excusa por no poder asistir.

apostle [ə'pɒsl] *n* RELIG apóstol *m*.

apostrophe [ə'pɒstrəfɪ] *n* apóstrofo *m*.

appal (*UK*), **appall** *US* [ə'pɔːl] *vt* horrorizar.

appalling [ə'pɔːlɪŋ] *adj* [shocking] horroroso(sa).

apparatus [,æpə'reɪtəs] (*pl* **apparatus** *OR* **-es**) *n* - 1. [equipment] aparatos *mpl*; **a piece of apparatus** un aparato - 2. POL aparato *m*.

apparel [ə'pærəl] *n US* ropa *f*.

apparent [ə'pærənt] *adj* - 1. [evident] evidente, patente - 2. [seeming] aparente.

apparently [ə'pærəntlɪ] *adv* - 1. [it seems] por lo visto - 2. [seemingly] aparentemente.

appeal [ə'piːl] ◇ *vi* - 1. [request]: **to appeal (to sb for sthg)** solicitar (de alguien algo) - 2. [to sb's honour, common sense]: **to appeal to sb** apelar a - 3. LAW: **to appeal (against)** apelar (contra) - 4. [attract, interest]: **to appeal (to)** atraer (a). ◇ *n* - 1. [request] llamamiento *m*, súplica *f*; [fundraising campaign] campaña *f* para recaudar fondos - 2. LAW apelación *f* - 3. [charm, interest] atractivo *m*.

appealing [ə'piːlɪŋ] *adj* [attractive] atractivo(va).

appear [ə'pɪə^r] *vi* - 1. [gen] aparecer - 2. [seem]: **to appear (to be/to do sthg)** parecer (ser/hacer algo); **it would appear that...** parece que... - 3. [in play, film, on TV]: **to appear on TV/in a film** salir en televisión/en una película - 4. LAW: **to appear (before)** comparecer (ante).

appearance [ə'pɪərəns] *n* - 1. [gen] aparición *f*; **to make an appearance** aparecer - 2. [of sportsman] actuación *f* - 3. [look - of person, place, object] aspecto *m*.

appease [ə'piːz] *vt* aplacar, apaciguar.

append [ə'pend] *vt fml* [add]: **to append sthg (to sthg)** agregar algo (a algo).

appendices [ə'pendɪsiːz] *npl* ⌐▷ **appendix**.

appendicitis [ə,pendɪ'saɪtɪs] *n* (*U*) apendicitis *f inv*.

appendix [ə'pendɪks] (*pl* **-dixes** *OR* **-dices**) *n* [gen & ANAT] apéndice *m*; **to have one's appendix out** *OR* **removed** operarse de apendicitis.

appetite ['æpɪtaɪt] *n* - 1. [for food] apetito *m*; **I no longer have any appetite for my food** ya no tengo ganas de comer - 2. *fig* [enthusiasm]: **appetite for** entusiasmo *m* por.

appetizer, -iser ['æpɪtaɪzə'] *n* aperitivo *m*.

appetizing, -ising ['æpɪtaɪzɪŋ] *adj* [food] apetitoso(sa).

applaud [ə'plɔːd] *vt* & *vi lit* & *fig* aplaudir.

applause [ə'plɔːz] *n* (*U*) aplausos *mpl*.

apple ['æpl] *n* manzana *f*.

apple tree *n* manzano *m*.

appliance [ə'plaɪəns] *n* aparato *m*.

applicable [ə'plɪkəbl] *adj*: **to be applicable (to)** aplicarse (a).

applicant ['æplɪkənt] *n*: **applicant (for)** solicitante *mf* (de).

application [,æplɪ'keɪʃn] *n* - 1. [gen] aplicación *f* - 2. [for job, college, club]: **application (for)** solicitud *f* (para) - 3. COMPUT aplicación *f*.

application form *n* impreso *m* de solicitud.

applied [ə'plaɪd] *adj* [science] aplicado(da).

apply [ə'plaɪ] *vt* - 1. [gen] aplicar; [brakes] echar; **to apply o.s. (to sthg)** aplicarse (en algo). *vi* - 1. [for work, grant] presentar una solicitud; **to apply to sb for sthg** solicitar a alguien algo - 2. [be relevant] aplicarse; **to apply to concernir a.**

appoint [ə'pɔɪnt] *vt* [to job, position]: **to appoint sb (to sthg)** nombrar a alguien (para algo).

appointment [ə'pɔɪntmənt] *n* - 1. [to job, position] nombramiento *m* - 2. [job, position] puesto *m*, cargo *m* - 3. [with businessman, lawyer] cita *f*; [with doctor, hairdresser] hora *f*; **to have an appointment** [with businessman] tener una cita; [with doctor] tener hora; **to make an appointment** concertar una cita.

apportion [ə'pɔːʃn] *vt* [money] repartir; [blame] adjudicar.

appraisal [ə'preɪzl] *n* evaluación *f*.

appreciable [ə'priːʃəbl] *adj* [difference] apreciable, sensible.

appreciate [ə'priːʃɪeɪt] *vt* - 1. [value, like] apreciar - 2. [recognize, understand] darse cuenta de - 3. [be grateful for] agradecer. *vi* FIN revalorizarse.

appreciation [ə,priːʃɪ'eɪʃn] *n* - 1. [liking] aprecio *m* - 2. [recognition, understanding] entendimiento *m* - 3. [gratitude] agradecimiento *m* - 4. FIN revalorización *f*.

appreciative [ə'priːʃjətɪv] *adj* [person, remark] agradecido(da); [audience] entendido(da).

apprehensive [,æprɪ'hensɪv] *adj* aprensivo(va).

apprentice [ə'prentɪs] *n* aprendiz *m*, -za *f*.

apprenticeship [ə'prentɪʃɪp] *n* aprendizaje *m*.

approach [ə'prəʊtʃ] *n* - 1. [arrival] llegada *f* - 2. [way in] acceso *m* - 3. [method] enfoque *m* - 4. [to person]: **to make approaches to sb** hacerle propuestas a alguien. *vt* - 1. [come near to] acercarse a - 2. [ask]: **to approach sb about sthg** dirigirse a alguien acerca de algo - 3. [problem, situation] abordar - 4. [level, speed] aproximarse a. *vi* acercarse.

approachable [ə'prəʊtʃəbl] *adj* accesible.

appropriate *adj* [ə'prəʊprɪət] apropiado(da), adecuado(da). *vt* [ə'prəʊprɪeɪt] LAW [take] apropiarse de.

approval [ə'pruːvl] *n* - 1. [admiration] aprobación *f* - 2. [official sanctioning] visto *m* bueno - 3. COMM: **on approval** a prueba.

approve [ə'pruːv] *vi* estar de acuerdo; **to approve of sthg/sb** ver con buenos ojos algo/a alguien. *vt* aprobar.

approx. [ə'prɒks] (*abbr of* **approximately**) aprox.

approximate *adj* [ə'prɒksɪmət] aproximado(da).

approximately [ə'prɒksɪmətlɪ] *adv* aproximadamente.

apricot ['eɪprɪkɒt] *n* [fruit] albaricoque *m*, chabacano *m Méx*, damasco *m Andes*.

April ['eɪprəl] *n* abril *m*; *see also* **September**.

April Fools' Day *n* primero *m* de abril, ≈ Día *m* de los Santos Inocentes.

apron ['eɪprən] *n* [clothing] delantal *m*, mandil *m*; **to be tied to sb's apron strings** *inf* estar pegado a las faldas de alguien.

apt [æpt] *adj* [pertinent] acertado(da).

aptitude ['æptɪtjuːd] *n* aptitud *f*.

aptly ['æptlɪ] *adv* apropiadamente.

aqualung ['ækwəlʌŋ] *n* escafandra *f* autónoma.

aquarium [ə'kweərɪəm] (*pl* -riums OR -ria [-rɪə]) *n* acuario *m*.

Aquarius [ə'kweərɪəs] *n* Acuario *m*.

aquatic [ə'kwætɪk] *adj* acuático(ca).

aqueduct ['ækwɪdʌkt] *n* acueducto *m*.

Arab ['ærəb] *adj* árabe. *n* [person] árabe *mf*.

Arabic ['ærəbɪk] *adj* árabe. *n* [language] árabe *m*.

Arabic numeral *n* número *m* arábigo.

arable ['ærəbl] *adj* cultivable.

arbitrary ['ɑːbɪtrərɪ] *adj* [random] arbitrario(ria).

arbitration [,ɑːbɪ'treɪʃn] *n* arbitraje *m*.

ARC (*abbr of* **AIDS-related complex**) *n* enfermedad relacionada con el sida.

arcade [ɑːˈkeɪd] n - 1. [shopping arcade] galería f comercial - 2. [covered passage] arcada f, galería f.

arcade game n videojuego m.

arch [ɑːtʃ] ◇ n - 1. ARCHIT arco m - 2. [of foot] puente m. ◇ vt arquear.

archaeologist, archeologist [,ɑːkɪˈɒlədʒɪst] n arqueólogo m, -ga f.

archaeology, archeology [,ɑːkɪˈɒlədʒɪ] n arqueología f.

archaic [ɑːˈkeɪɪk] adj arcaico(ca).

archbishop [,ɑːtʃˈbɪʃəp] n arzobispo m.

archenemy [,ɑːtʃˈenɪmɪ] n peor enemigo m, enemigo acérrimo.

archeologist = archaeologist.

archeology = archaeology.

archer [ˈɑːtʃər] n arquero m.

archery [ˈɑːtʃərɪ] n tiro m con arco.

archetypal [,ɑːkɪˈtaɪpl] adj arquetípico(ca).

architect [ˈɑːkɪtekt] n - 1. [of buildings] arquitecto m, -ta f - 2. fig [of plan, event] artífice mf.

architecture [ˈɑːkɪtektʃər] n [gen & COMPUT] arquitectura f.

archives [ˈɑːkaɪvz] npl [of documents] archivos mpl.

archway [ˈɑːtʃweɪ] n [passage] arcada f; [entrance] entrada f en forma de arco.

ardent [ˈɑːdənt] adj [supporter, admirer, desire] ardiente, ferviente.

arduous [ˈɑːdjʊəs] adj arduo(dua).

are (weak form [ər], strong form [ɑːr]) ▷ **be**.

area [ˈeərɪə] n - 1. [region, designated space] zona f, área f; **in the area** en la zona - 2. [of town] zona f, barrio m - 3. fig [approximate size, number]: **in the area of** del orden de, alrededor de - 4. [surface size] superficie f, área f - 5. [of knowledge, interest] campo m.

area code n US prefijo m (telefónico).

arena [əˈriːnə] n - 1. SPORT pabellón m - 2. fig [area of activity]: **she entered the political arena** saltó al ruedo político.

aren't [ɑːnt] (abbr of are not) ▷ **be**.

Argentina [,ɑːdʒənˈtiːnə] n (la) Argentina.

Argentine [ˈɑːdʒəntaɪn] adj argentino(na).

Argentinian [,ɑːdʒənˈtɪnɪən] ◇ adj argentino(na). ◇ n argentino m, -na f.

arguably [ˈɑːgjʊəblɪ] adv probablemente.

argue [ˈɑːgjuː] ◇ vi - 1. [quarrel]: **to argue (with sb about sthg)** discutir (con alguien de algo) - 2. [reason]: **to argue (for)** abogar (por); **to argue (against)** oponerse (a). ◇ vt: **to argue that** argumentar que.

argument [ˈɑːgjʊmənt] n - 1. [gen] discusión f; **to have an argument (with)** tener una discusión (con) - 2. [reason] argumento m.

argumentative [,ɑːgjʊˈmentətɪv] adj propenso(sa) a discutir.

arid [ˈærɪd] adj lit & fig árido(da).

Aries [ˈeəriːz] n Aries m.

arise [əˈraɪz] (pt arose, pp arisen [əˈrɪzn]) vi [appear]: **to arise (from)** surgir (de).

aristocrat [UK ˈærɪstəkræt, US əˈrɪstəkræt] n aristócrata mf.

arithmetic [əˈrɪθmətɪk] n aritmética f.

ark [ɑːk] n arca f.

arm [ɑːm] ◇ n - 1. [of person, chair, record player] brazo m; **arm in arm** del brazo; **to keep sb at arm's length** fig guardar las distancias con alguien - 2. [of garment] manga f. ◇ vt armar. ◇ vi armarse. ◆ **arms** npl [weapons] armas fpl.

armaments [ˈɑːməmənts] npl armamento m.

armband [ˈɑːmbænd] n - 1. [indicating mourning, rank] brazalete m - 2. [for swimming] flotador m (en los brazos).

armchair [ˈɑːmtʃeər] n sillón m.

armed [ɑːmd] adj - 1. [police, thieves] armado(da) - 2. fig [with information]: **armed with** provisto(ta) de.

armed forces npl fuerzas fpl armadas.

armhole [ˈɑːmhəʊl] n sobaquera f, sisa f.

armour UK, **armor** US [ˈɑːmər] n - 1. [for person] armadura f - 2. [for military vehicle] blindaje m.

armoured car [ɑːməd-] n MIL carro m blindado.

armoury UK, **armory** US [ˈɑːmərɪ] n arsenal m.

armpit [ˈɑːmpɪt] n sobaco m, axila f.

armrest [ˈɑːmrest] n brazo m.

arms control [ˈɑːmz-] n control m armamentístico.

army [ˈɑːmɪ] ◇ n lit & fig ejército m. ◇ comp del ejército, militar.

aroma [əˈrəʊmə] n aroma m.

arose [əˈrəʊz] pt ▷ **arise**.

around [əˈraʊnd] ◇ adv - 1. [about, round] por ahí; **to walk/look around** andar/mirar por ahí - 2. [on all sides] alrededor - 3. [present, available]: **is John around?** [there] ¿está John por ahí?; [here] ¿está John por aquí? - 4. [turn, look]: **to turn around** volverse; **to look around** volver la cabeza. ◇ prep - 1. [on all sides of] alrededor de - 2. [about, round - place] por - 3. [in the area of] cerca de - 4. [approximately] alrededor de.

arouse [əˈraʊz] vt [excite - feeling] despertar; [- person] excitar.

arrange [əˈreɪndʒ] vt - 1. [books, furniture] colocar; [flowers] arreglar - 2. [event, meeting, party] organizar; **to arrange to do sthg** acordar hacer algo; **we've arranged to meet at nine** hemos quedado a las nueve; **to arrange for sb to do sthg** hacer lo necesario para que alguien haga algo - **3.** MUS arreglar.

arrangement [ə'reɪndʒmənt] n - **1.** [agreement] acuerdo m; **to come to an arrangement** llegar a un acuerdo - **2.** [of furniture] disposición f; [of flowers] arreglo m - **3.** MUS arreglo m. ➤ **arrangements** npl preparativos mpl.

array [ə'reɪ] n [of objects] surtido m.

arrears [ə'rɪəz] npl [money owed] atrasos mpl; **in arrears** [retrospectively] con retraso; [late] atrasado en el pago.

arrest [ə'rest] ◇ n detención f, arresto m; **under arrest** detenido(da), bajo arresto. ◇ vt - **1.** [subj: police] detener - **2.** [sb's attention] captar - **3.** fml [stop] poner freno a.

arrival [ə'raɪvl] n llegada f; **late arrival** [of train, bus, mail] retraso m; **new arrival** [person] recién llegado m, recién llegada f; [baby] recién nacido m, recién nacida f.

arrive [ə'raɪv] vi - **1.** [gen] llegar; **to arrive at** [conclusion, decision] llegar a - **2.** [baby] nacer.

arrogant ['ærəgənt] adj arrogante.

arrow ['ærəʊ] n flecha f.

arse UK [ɑːs], **ass** US [æs] n v inf [bottom] culo m.

arsenic ['ɑːsnɪk] n arsénico m.

arson ['ɑːsn] n incendio m premeditado.

art [ɑːt] n arte m. ➤ **arts** npl - **1.** SCH & UNIV [humanities] letras fpl - **2.** [fine arts]: **the arts** las bellas artes. ➤ **arts and crafts** npl artesanía f.

artefact ['ɑːtɪfækt] = **artifact**.

artery ['ɑːtərɪ] n arteria f.

art gallery n [public] museo m (de arte); [commercial] galería f (de arte).

arthritis [ɑː'θraɪtɪs] n artritis f inv.

artichoke ['ɑːtɪtʃəʊk] n alcachofa f.

article ['ɑːtɪkl] n artículo m; **article of clothing** prenda f de vestir.

articulate ◇ adj [ɑː'tɪkjʊlət] [person] elocuente; [speech] claro(ra), bien articulado(da). ◇ vt [ɑː'tɪkjʊleɪt] [express clearly] expresar.

articulated lorry [ɑː'tɪkjʊleɪtɪd-] n UK camión m articulado.

artifact ['ɑːtɪfækt] n artefacto m.

artificial [ˌɑːtɪ'fɪʃl] adj artificial.

artillery [ɑː'tɪlərɪ] n [guns] artillería f.

artist ['ɑːtɪst] n artista mf.

artiste [ɑː'tiːst] n artista mf.

artistic [ɑː'tɪstɪk] adj - **1.** [gen] artístico(ca) - **2.** [good at art]: **to be artistic** tener sensibilidad artística.

artistry ['ɑːtɪstrɪ] n maestría f.

artless ['ɑːtlɪs] adj ingenuo(nua).

as (unstressed [əz], stressed [æz]) ◇ conj - **1.** [referring to time - while] mientras; [- when] cuando; **she told it to me as we walked along** me lo contó mientras paseábamos; **as time goes by** a medida que pasa el tiempo; **she rang (just) as I was leaving** llamó justo cuando iba a salir - **2.** [referring to manner, way] como; **do as I say** haz lo que te digo - **3.** [introducing a statement] como; **as you know,...** como (ya) sabes,... - **4.** [because] como, ya que ➤➤ **as it is** (ya) de por sí. ◇ prep como; **I'm speaking as a friend** te hablo como amigo; **she works as a nurse** trabaja de OR como enfermera; **as a boy, I lived in Spain** de niño vivía en España; **it came as a shock** fue una gran sorpresa. ◇ adv (in comparisons): **as... as** tan... como; **as tall as I am** tan alto como yo; **I've lived as long as she has** he vivido durante tanto tiempo como ella; **twice as big** el doble de grande; **it's just as fast** es igual de rápido; **as much as** tanto como; **as many as** tantos(tas) como; **as much wine as you like** tanto vino como quieras. ➤ **as for, as to** prep en cuanto a. ➤ **as from, as of** prep a partir de. ➤ **as if, as though** conj como si. ➤ **as to** prep UK con respecto a.

a.s.a.p. (abbr of **as soon as possible**) a la mayor brevedad posible.

asbestos [æs'bestəs] n amianto m, asbesto m.

ascend [ə'send] ◇ vt subir. ◇ vi ascender.

ascendant [ə'sendənt] n: **in the ascendant** en auge.

ascent [ə'sent] n - **1.** [climb] ascensión f - **2.** [upward slope] subida f, cuesta f - **3.** fig [progress] ascenso m.

ascertain [ˌæsə'teɪn] vt determinar.

ASCII ['æskɪ] (abbr of **American Standard Code for Information Interchange**) n ASCII m.

ascribe [ə'skraɪb] vt: **to ascribe sthg to** atribuir algo a.

ash [æʃ] n - **1.** [from cigarette, fire] ceniza f - **2.** [tree] fresno m.

ashamed [ə'ʃeɪmd] adj avergonzado(da), apenado(da) Andes, Amér C & Méx; **I'm ashamed to do it** me da vergüenza hacerlo; **I'm ashamed of...** me da vergüenza...

ashen-faced ['æʃn,feɪst] adj: **to be ashen-faced** tener la cara pálida.

ashore [ə'ʃɔːr] adv [swim] hasta la orilla; **to go ashore** desembarcar.

ashtray ['æʃtreɪ] n cenicero m.

Ash Wednesday n miércoles m inv de ceniza.

Asia [UK 'eɪʃə, US 'eɪʒə] n Asia.

Asian [UK 'eɪʃn, US 'eɪʒn] ◇ adj asiático(ca); **Asian American** americano(na) de origen asiático. ◇ n asiático m, -ca f.

aside [ə'saɪd] ⬦ *adv* - **1.** [to one side] a un lado; **to move aside** apartarse; **to brush** OR **sweep sthg aside** dejar algo aparte OR de lado - **2.** [apart] aparte; **aside from** aparte de. ⬦ *n* - **1.** [in play] aparte *m* - **2.** [remark] inciso *m*.

ask [ɑ:sk] ⬦ *vt* - **1.** [put - question]: **to ask a question** hacer una pregunta - **2.** [request, demand] pedir; **to ask sb (to do sthg)** pedir a alguien (que haga algo); **to ask sb for sthg** pedirle algo a alguien - **3.** [invite] invitar. ⬦ *vi* - **1.** [question] preguntar - **2.** [request] pedir. ⬥ **ask after** *vt insep* preguntar por. ⬥ **ask for** *vt insep* - **1.** [person] preguntar por - **2.** [thing] pedir. ⬥ **ask out** *vt sep* [ask to be boyfriend, girlfriend] pedir salir.

askance [ə'skæns] *adv*: **to look askance at sb** mirar a alguien con recelo.

askew [ə'skju:] *adj* torcido(da).

asking price ['ɑ:skɪŋ-] *n* precio *m* inicial.

asleep [ə'sli:p] *adj* dormido(da); **she's asleep** está·dormida OR durmiendo; **to fall asleep** quedarse dormido; **to be fast** OR **sound asleep** estar profundamente dormido.

asparagus [ə'spærəgəs] *n* (U) [plant] espárrago *m*; [shoots] espárragos *mpl*.

aspect ['æspekt] *n* - **1.** [of subject, plan] aspecto *m* - **2.** [appearance] cariz *m*, aspecto *m* - **3.** [of building] orientación *f*.

aspersions [ə'spɜ:ʃnz] *npl*: **to cast aspersions on sthg** poner en duda algo.

asphalt ['æsfælt] *n* asfalto *m*.

asphyxiate [əs'fɪksɪeɪt] *vt* asfixiar.

aspiration [,æspə'reɪʃn] *n* aspiración *f*.

aspire [ə'spaɪə] *vi*: **to aspire to** aspirar a.

aspirin ['æsprɪn] *n* aspirina *f*.

ass [æs] *n* - **1.** [donkey] asno *m*, -na *f* - **2.** *UK inf* [idiot] burro *m*, -rra *f* - **3.** *US v inf* = **arse**.

assailant [ə'seɪlənt] *n* agresor *m*, -ra *f*.

assassin [ə'sæsɪn] *n* asesino *m*, -na *f*.

assassinate [ə'sæsɪneɪt] *vt* asesinar.

assassination [ə,sæsɪ'neɪʃn] *n* asesinato *m*.

assault [ə'sɔ:lt] ⬦ *n* MIL: **assault (on)** ataque *m* (contra). ⬦ *vt* [physically] asaltar, agredir; [sexually] abusar de.

assemble [ə'sembl] ⬦ *vt* - **1.** [gather] juntar, reunir - **2.** [fit together] montar. ⬦ *vi* reunirse.

assembly [ə'semblɪ] *n* - **1.** [meeting, law-making body] asamblea *f* - **2.** [gathering together] reunión *f* - **3.** *UK* [at school] *reunión de todos los profesores y alumnos de un centro al comienzo de cada día escolar* - **4.** [fitting together] montaje *m*.

assembly line *n* cadena *f* de montaje.

assent [ə'sent] ⬦ *n* consentimiento *m*. ⬦ *vi*: **to assent (to)** asentir (a).

assert [ə'sɜ:t] *vt* - **1.** [fact, belief] afirmar - **2.** [authority] imponer.

assertive [ə'sɜ:tɪv] *adj* enérgico(ca).

assess [ə'ses] *vt* evaluar.

assessment [ə'sesmənt] *n* - **1.** [evaluation] evaluación *f* - **2.** [calculation] cálculo *m*.

assessor [ə'sesə] *n* tasador *m*, -ra *f*.

asset ['æset] *n* - **1.** [valuable quality - of person] cualidad *f* positiva; [- of thing] ventaja *f* - **2.** [valuable person] elemento *m* importante. ⬥ **assets** *npl* COMM activo *m*.

assign [ə'saɪn] *vt* - **1.** [gen]: **to assign sthg (to sb)** asignar algo (a alguien); **to assign sb to sthg** asignar a alguien algo; **to assign sb to do sthg** asignar a alguien que haga algo - **2.** [designate for specific use, purpose]: **to assign sthg (to)** destinar algo (a).

assignment [ə'saɪnmənt] *n* - **1.** [task] misión *f*; SCH trabajo *m* - **2.** [act of assigning] asignación *f*.

assimilate [ə'sɪmɪleɪt] *vt* - **1.** [learn] asimilar - **2.** [absorb]: **to assimilate sb (into)** integrar a alguien (en).

assist [ə'sɪst] ⬦ *vt*: **to assist sb (with sthg/in doing sthg)** ayudar a alguien (con algo/a hacer algo). ⬦ *vi* ayudar.

assistance [ə'sɪstəns] *n* ayuda *f*, asistencia *f*; **to be of assistance (to)** ayudar (a).

assistant [ə'sɪstənt] ⬦ *n* ayudante *mf*; **(shop) assistant** dependiente *m*, -ta *f*. ⬦ *comp* adjunto(ta); **assistant manager** director adjunto *m*, directora adjunta *f*; **assistant referee** árbitro *m*, asistente *f*.

associate ⬦ *adj* [ə'səʊʃɪət] asociado(da). ⬦ *n* [ə'səʊʃɪət] socio *m*, -cia *f*. ⬦ *vt* [ə'səʊʃɪeɪt] asociar; **to associate sthg/sb with** asociar algo/a alguien con; **to be associated with** [organization, plan, opinion] estar relacionado con; [people] estar asociado con. ⬦ *vi* [ə'səʊʃɪeɪt]: **to associate with sb** relacionarse con alguien.

association [ə,səʊsɪ'eɪʃn] *n* - **1.** [organization, act of associating] asociación *f*; **in association with** en colaboración con - **2.** [in mind] connotación *f*.

assorted [ə'sɔ:tɪd] *adj* - **1.** [of various types] variado(da) - **2.** [biscuits, sweets] surtido(da).

assortment [ə'sɔ:tmənt] *n* surtido *m*.

assume [ə'sju:m] *vt* - **1.** [suppose] suponer - **2.** [power, responsibility] asumir - **3.** [appearance, attitude] adoptar.

assumed name [ə'sju:md-] *n* nombre *m* falso.

assuming [ə'sju:mɪŋ] *conj* suponiendo que.

assumption [ə'sʌmpʃn] *n* - **1.** [supposition] suposición *f* - **2.** [of power] asunción *f*.

assurance [ə'ʃʊərəns] *n* - **1.** [promise] garantía *f* - **2.** [confidence] seguridad *f* de sí mismo - **3.** [insurance] seguro *m*.

assure [əˈʃʊəʳ] vt asegurar, garantizar; **to assure sb of sthg** garantizar a alguien algo; **to be assured of sthg** tener algo garantizado; **rest assured that...** ten por seguro que...

assured [əˈʃʊəd] adj [confident] seguro(ra).

asterisk [ˈæstərɪsk] n asterisco m.

astern [əˈstɜːn] adv NAUT a popa.

asthma [ˈæsmə] n asma f.

astonish [əˈstɒnɪʃ] vt asombrar.

astonishment [əˈstɒnɪʃmənt] n asombro m.

astound [əˈstaʊnd] vt asombrar.

astray [əˈstreɪ] adv: **to go astray** [become lost] extraviarse; **to lead sb astray** [into bad ways] llevar a alguien por el mal camino.

astride [əˈstraɪd] ◇ adv a horcajadas. ◇ prep a horcajadas en.

astrology [əˈstrɒlədʒɪ] n astrología f.

astronaut [ˈæstrənɔːt] n astronauta mf.

astronomical [ˌæstrəˈnɒmɪkl] adj lit & fig astronómico(ca).

astronomy [əˈstrɒnəmɪ] n astronomía f.

astute [əˈstjuːt] adj astuto(ta).

asylum [əˈsaɪləm] n - 1. [mental hospital] manicomio m - 2. [protection] asilo m.

asylum seeker [əˈsaɪləmˈsiːkəʳ] n peticionario m, -ria f de asilo.

at (unstressed [ət], stressed [æt]) prep - 1. [indicating place] en; **at my father's** en casa de mi padre; **standing at the window** de pie junto a la ventana; **at the bottom of the hill** al pie de la colina; **at school/work/home** en la escuela/el trabajo/casa - 2. [indicating direction] a - 3. [indicating a particular time]: **at a more suitable time** en un momento más oportuno; **at midnight/noon/eleven o'clock** a medianoche/mediodía/las once; **at night** por la noche; **at Christmas/Easter** en Navidades/Semana Santa - 4. [indicating speed, rate, price] a; **at 100 mph/high speed** a 100 millas por hora/gran velocidad; **at £50 (a pair)** a 50 libras (el par) - 5. [indicating particular state, condition]: **at peace/war** en paz/guerra; **she's at lunch** está comiendo; **to work hard at sthg** trabajar duro en algo - 6. [indicating a particular age] a; **at 52/your age** a los 52/tu edad - 7. (after adjectives): **delighted at** encantado con; **experienced at** experimentado en; **puzzled/horrified/fied at** perplejo/horrorizado ante; **he's good/bad at sport** se le dan bien/mal los deportes.
◆ **at all** adv - 1. (with negative): **not at all** [when thanked] de nada; [when answering a question] en absoluto; **she's not at all happy** no está nada contenta - 2. [in the slightest]: **anything at all will do** cualquier cosa valdrá; **do you know her at all?** ¿la conoces (de algo)?

ate [UK et, US eɪt] pt ▷ **eat**.

atheist [ˈeɪθɪɪst] n ateo m, -a f.

Athens [ˈæθɪnz] n Atenas.

athlete [ˈæθliːt] n atleta mf.

athletic [æθˈletɪk] adj atlético(ca). ◆ **athletics** npl atletismo m.

Atlantic [ətˈlæntɪk] ◇ adj atlántico(ca). ◇ n: **the Atlantic (Ocean)** el (océano) Atlántico.

atlas [ˈætləs] n atlas m inv.

ATM (abbr of **automatic teller machine**) n cajero automático.

atmosphere [ˈætmə,sfɪəʳ] n - 1. [of planet] atmósfera f - 2. [air in room, mood of place] ambiente m.

atmospheric [ˌætməsˈferɪk] adj - 1. [pressure, pollution] atmosférico(ca) - 2. [attractive, mysterious] sugerente.

atom [ˈætəm] n PHYS átomo m.

atom bomb, atomic bomb n bomba f atómica.

atomic [əˈtɒmɪk] adj atómico(ca).

atomic bomb = atom bomb.

atomizer, -iser [ˈætəmaɪzəʳ] n atomizador m.

atone [əˈtəʊn] vi: **to atone for** reparar.

A to Z n guía f alfabética; [map] callejero m.

atrocious [əˈtrəʊʃəs] adj [very bad] atroz.

atrocity [əˈtrɒsətɪ] n [terrible act] atrocidad f.

attach [əˈtætʃ] vt - 1. [with pin, clip]: **to attach sthg (to)** sujetar algo (a); [with string] atar algo (a) - 2. [document & COMPUT] adjuntar - 3. [importance, blame]: **to attach sthg (to sthg)** atribuir algo (a algo).

attaché case n maletín m.

attached [əˈtætʃt] adj [fond]: **to be attached to** tener cariño a.

attachment [əˈtætʃmənt] n - 1. [device] accesorio m - 2. COMPUT archivo m adjunto - 3. [fondness]: **attachment (to)** cariño m (por).

attack [əˈtæk] ◇ n: **attack (on)** ataque m (contra); **terrorist attack** atentado m terrorista; **to be under attack** estar siendo atacado. ◇ vt - 1. [gen] atacar - 2. [job, problem] acometer. ◇ vi atacar.

attacker [əˈtækəʳ] n atacante mf.

attain [əˈteɪn] vt lograr, alcanzar.

attainment [əˈteɪnmənt] n logro m.

attempt [əˈtempt] ◇ n: **attempt (at doing sthg)** intento m (de hacer algo); **attempt on sb's life** atentado m contra la vida de alguien. ◇ vt: **to attempt sthg/to do sthg** intentar algo/hacer algo.

attend [əˈtend] ◇ vt [go to] asistir a. ◇ vi - 1. [be present] asistir - 2. [pay attention]: **to attend (to)** atender (a). ◆ **attend to** vt insep - 1. [matter] ocuparse de - 2. [customer] atender a; [patient] asistir a.

attendance [ə'tendəns] *n* asistencia *f*; **the attendance for the match was over 10,000** más de 10.000 personas asistieron al partido.

attendant [ə'tendənt] <> *adj* concomitante. <> *n* [at museum] vigilante *mf*; [at petrol station, in swimming pool] encargado *m*, -da *f*.

attention [ə'tenʃn] <> *n (U)* - **1.** [gen] atención *f*; **to bring sthg to sb's attention, to draw sb's attention to sthg** llamar la atención de alguien sobre algo; **to attract** OR **catch sb's attention** atraer OR captar la atención de alguien; **to pay/pay no attention (to)** prestar/no prestar atención (a); **for the attention of** COMM a la atención de; **your attention please!** ¡atención! - **2.** [care] asistencia *f*. <> *excl* MIL ¡firmes!

attentive [ə'tentɪv] *adj* atento(ta).

attic ['ætɪk] *n* desván *m*, entretecho *m* Amér.

attitude ['ætɪtjuːd] *n* [posture] postura *f*.

attn. *(abbr of* for the attention of*)* a/a.

attorney [ə'tɜːnɪ] *n US* abogado *m*, -da *f*.

attorney general *(pl* **attorneys general***) n* fiscal *m* general del estado.

attract [ə'trækt] *vt* - **1.** [gen] atraer - **2.** [support, criticism] suscitar.

attraction [ə'trækʃn] *n* - **1.** [gen]: **attraction (to sb)** atracción *f* (hacia OR por alguien) - **2.** [attractiveness - of thing] atractivo *m*.

attractive [ə'træktɪv] *adj* atractivo(va).

attribute <> *vt* [ə'trɪbjuːt]: **to attribute sthg to** atribuir algo a. <> *n* ['ætrɪbjuːt] atributo *m*.

attrition [ə'trɪʃn] *n* desgaste *m*; **war of attrition** guerra de desgaste.

aubergine ['əʊbəʒiːn] *n UK* berenjena *f*.

auburn ['ɔːbən] *adj* castaño rojizo.

auction ['ɔːkʃn] <> *n* subasta *f*; **to put sthg up for auction** sacar algo a subasta. <> *vt* subastar.

auctioneer [,ɔːkʃə'nɪər] *n* subastador *m*, -ra *f*.

audacious [ɔː'deɪʃəs] *adj* [daring] audaz; [cheeky] atrevido(da).

audible ['ɔːdəbl] *adj* audible.

audience ['ɔːdjəns] *n* - **1.** [of play, film] público *m* - **2.** [formal meeting, TV viewers] audiencia *f*.

audiotypist ['ɔːdɪəʊ,taɪpɪst] *n* mecanógrafo *m*, -fa *f* por dictáfono.

audiovisual ['ɔːdɪəʊ-] *adj* audiovisual.

audit ['ɔːdɪt] <> *n* auditoría *f*. <> *vt* auditar.

audition [ɔː'dɪʃn] *n* prueba *f (a un artista)*.

auditor ['ɔːdɪtər] *n* auditor *m*, -ra *f*.

auditorium [,ɔːdɪ'tɔːrɪəm] *(pl* **-riums** OR **-ria** [-rɪə]*) n* auditorio *m*.

augment [ɔːg'ment] *vt* acrecentar.

augur ['ɔːgər] *vi*: **to augur well/badly** ser un buen/mal augurio.

August ['ɔːgəst] *n* agosto *m*; *see also* **September**.

Auld Lang Syne [,ɔːldlæŋ'saɪn] *n* canción escocesa en alabanza de los viejos tiempos que se canta tradicionalmente en Nochevieja.

aunt [ɑːnt] *n* tía *f*.

auntie, aunty ['ɑːntɪ] *n inf* tita *f*.

au pair [,əʊ'peər] *n* au pair *f*.

aura ['ɔːrə] *n* aura *f*, halo *m*.

aural ['ɔːrəl] *adj* auditivo(va).

auspices ['ɔːspɪsɪz] *npl*: **under the auspices of** bajo los auspicios de.

auspicious [ɔː'spɪʃəs] *adj* prometedor(ra).

Aussie ['ɒzɪ] *n inf* australiano *m*, -na *f*.

austere [ɒ'stɪər] *adj* austero(ra).

austerity [ɒ'sterətɪ] *n* austeridad *f*.

Australia [ɒ'streɪljə] *n* Australia.

Australian [ɒ'streɪljən] <> *adj* australiano(na). <> *n* australiano *m*, -na *f*.

Austria ['ɒstrɪə] *n* Austria.

Austrian ['ɒstrɪən] <> *adj* austriaco(ca). <> *n* austriaco *m*, -ca *f*.

authentic [ɔː'θentɪk] *adj* auténtico(ca).

author ['ɔːθər] *n* [by profession] escritor *m*, -ra *f*; [of particular book, text] autor *m*, -ra *f*.

authoritarian [ɔː,θɒrɪ'teərɪən] *adj* autoritario(ria).

authoritative [ɔː'θɒrɪtətɪv] *adj* - **1.** [person, voice] autoritario(ria) - **2.** [study] autorizado(da).

authority [ɔː'θɒrətɪ] *n* - **1.** [gen] autoridad *f*; **to be an authority on** ser una autoridad en - **2.** [permission] autorización *f*. ◆ **authorities** *npl*: **the authorities** las autoridades *fpl*.

authorize, -ise ['ɔːθəraɪz] *vt*: **to authorize (sb to do sthg)** autorizar (a alguien a hacer algo).

autism ['ɔːtɪzm] *n* autismo *m*.

autistic [ɔː'tɪstɪk] *adj* autista.

auto ['ɔːtəʊ] *(pl* **-s***) n US* coche *m*.

autobiography [,ɔːtəbaɪ'ɒgrəfɪ] *n* autobiografía *f*.

autocratic [,ɔːtə'krætɪk] *adj* autocrático(ca).

autograph ['ɔːtəgrɑːf] <> *n* autógrafo *m*. <> *vt* autografiar.

automate ['ɔːtəmeɪt] *vt* automatizar.

automatic [,ɔːtə'mætɪk] <> *adj* automático(ca). <> *n* - **1.** [car] coche *m* automático - **2.** [gun] arma *f* automática - **3.** [washing machine] lavadora *f* automática.

automatically [,ɔːtə'mætɪklɪ] *adv* automáticamente.

automation [,ɔːtə'meɪʃn] *n* automatización *f*.

automobile ['ɔ:təməbi:l] *n US* coche *m*, automóvil *m*.

autonomous [ɔ:'tɒnəməs] *adj* autónomo(ma).

autonomy [ɔ:'tɒnəmɪ] *n* autonomía *f*.

autopsy ['ɔ:tɒpsɪ] *n* autopsia *f*.

autumn ['ɔ:təm] *n* otoño *m*.

auxiliary [ɔ:g'zɪljərɪ] ◇ *adj* auxiliar. ◇ *n* [medical worker] auxiliar sanitario *m*, auxiliar sanitaria *f*.

Av. (*abbr of* avenue) Av.

avail [ə'veɪl] ◇ *n*: **to no avail** en vano. ◇ *vt*: **to avail o.s. of sthg** aprovechar algo.

available [ə'veɪləbl] *adj* - **1.** [product, service] disponible; **this product is no longer available** ya no comercializamos este producto - **2.** [person] libre, disponible.

avalanche ['ævəlɑ:nʃ] *n lit & fig* avalancha *f*, alud *m*.

avant-garde [,ævɒŋ'gɑ:d] *adj* de vanguardia, vanguardista.

avarice ['ævərɪs] *n* avaricia *f*.

Ave. (*abbr of* avenue) Avda.

avenge [ə'vendʒ] *vt* vengar.

avenue ['ævənju:] *n* - **1.** [wide road] avenida *f* - **2.** *fig* [method, means] vía *f*.

average ['ævərɪdʒ] ◇ *adj* - **1.** [mean, typical] medio(dia) - **2.** [mediocre] regular. ◇ *n* media *f*, promedio *m*; **on average** de media, por término medio. ◇ *vt* alcanzar un promedio de. ◆ **average out** *vi*: **to average out at** salir a una media de.

aversion [ə'vɜ:ʃn] *n* [dislike]: **aversion (to)** aversión *f* (a).

avert [ə'vɜ:t] *vt* - **1.** [problem, accident] evitar, prevenir - **2.** [eyes, glance] apartar, desviar.

aviary ['eɪvjərɪ] *n* pajarera *f*.

avid ['ævɪd] *adj*: **avid (for)** ávido(da) (de).

avocado [,ævə'kɑ:dəʊ] (*pl* -s OR -es) *n*: avocado (pear) aguacate *m*, palta *f Andes & R Plata*.

avoid [ə'vɔɪd] *vt*: **to avoid (sthg/doing sthg)** evitar(algo/hacer algo); **she's been avoiding me** ha estado esquivándome.

avoidance [ə'vɔɪdəns] ⊳ **tax avoidance**.

await [ə'weɪt] *vt* esperar, aguardar.

awake [ə'weɪk] ◇ *adj* [not sleeping] despierto(ta). ◇ *vt* (*pt* **awoke** OR **awaked**, *pp* **awoken**) *lit & fig* despertar. ◇ *vi lit & fig* despertarse.

awakening [ə'weɪknɪŋ] *n lit & fig* despertar *m*.

award [ə'wɔ:d] ◇ *n* - **1.** [prize] premio *m*, galardón *m* - **2.** [compensation] indemnización *f*.

◇ *vt*: **to award sb sthg, to award sthg to sb** [prize] conceder OR otorgar algo a alguien; [compensation] adjudicar algo a alguien.

aware [ə'weə'] *adj* - **1.** [conscious]: **aware of** consciente de; **to become aware of** darse cuenta de - **2.** [informed, sensitive] informado(da), al día; **aware of sthg** al día de algo; **to be aware that** estar informado de que.

awareness [ə'weənɪs] *n* conciencia *f*.

awash [ə'wɒʃ] *adj lit & fig*: **awash (with)** inundado(da) (de).

away [ə'weɪ] ◇ *adv* - **1.** [move, walk, drive]: **to walk away (from)** marcharse (de); **to drive away (from)** alejarse (de) (*en coche*); **to turn** OR **look away** apartar la vista - **2.** [at a distance - in space, time]: **away from** a distancia de; **4 miles away** a 4 millas de distancia; **a long way away** muy lejos; **the exam is two days away** faltan dos días para el examen - **3.** [not at home or office] fuera - **4.** [in safe place]: **to put sthg away** poner algo en su sitio - **5.** [indicating removal or disappearance]: **to fade away** desvanecerse; **to give sthg away** regalar algo; **to take sthg away from sb** quitarle algo a alguien - **6.** [continuously]: **he was working away when...** estaba muy concentrado trabajando cuando... ◇ *adj* SPORT [team, supporters] visitante; **away game** partido *m* fuera de casa.

awe [ɔ:] *n* sobrecogimiento *m*; **to be in awe of sb** sentirse intimidado por alguien.

awesome ['ɔ:səm] *adj* alucinante *Esp*, macanudo(da) *Andes & R Dom*, padrísimo(ma) *Méx*.

awful ['ɔ:fʊl] *adj* - **1.** [terrible] terrible, espantoso(sa); **I feel awful** me siento fatal - **2.** *inf* [very great] tremendo(da); **I like it an awful lot** me gusta muchísimo.

awfully ['ɔ:flɪ] *adv inf* [very] tremendamente.

awhile [ə'waɪl] *adv liter* un rato.

awkward ['ɔ:kwəd] *adj* - **1.** [clumsy - movement] torpe; [- person] desgarbado(da) - **2.** [embarrassed, embarrassing] incómodo(da) - **3.** [unreasonable] difícil - **4.** [inconvenient - shape, size] poco manejable; [- moment] inoportuno(na).

awning ['ɔ:nɪŋ] *n* toldo *m*.

awoke [ə'wəʊk] *pt* ⊳ **awake**.

awoken [ə'wəʊkn] *pp* ⊳ **awake**.

awry [ə'raɪ] ◇ *adj* torcido(da), ladeado(da). ◇ *adv*: **to go awry** salir mal.

axe *UK*, **ax** *US* [æks] ◇ *n* hacha *f*. ◇ *vt* [project, jobs] suprimir.

axes ['æksi:z] *npl* ⊳ **axis**.

axis ['æksɪs] (*pl* **axes**) *n* eje *m*.

axle ['æksl] *n* eje *m*.

aye [aɪ] ◇ *adv* sí. ◇ *n* sí *m*.

azalea [ə'zeɪljə] *n* azalea *f*.

Aztec ['æztek] ◇ *adj* azteca. ◇ *n* [person] azteca *mf*.

b (*pl* b's OR bs), **B** (*pl* B's OR Bs) [bi:] *n* [letter] b *f*, B *f*. ◆ **B** *n* - **1.** MUS si *m* - **2.** SCH [mark] ≃ bien *m*.

BA *n* (*abbr of* **Bachelor of Arts**), *(titular de una) licenciatura de letras.*

babble ['bæbl] *vi* [person] farfullar.

baboon [bə'bu:n] *n* babuino *m*.

baby ['beɪbɪ] ◇ *n* - **1.** [newborn child] bebé *m*; [infant] niño *m* - **2.** *inf* [term of affection] cariño *m*. ◇ *comp*: **baby brother** hermanito *m*; **baby sister** hermanita *f*.

baby buggy *n* - **1.** UK [foldable pushchair] sillita *f* de niño (con ruedas) - **2.** US = **baby carriage**.

baby carriage *n* US cochecito *m* de niños.

baby food *n* papilla *f*.

baby-sit *vi* cuidar a niños.

baby-sitter [-'sɪtəʳ] *n* canguro *mf*.

bachelor ['bætʃələʳ] *n* soltero *m*; **bachelor party** US despedida *f* de soltero.

Bachelor of Arts *n* ≃ licenciado *m* en Letras.

Bachelor of Science *n* ≃ licenciado *m* en Ciencias.

back [bæk] ◇ *adv* - **1.** [in position] atrás; **stand back!** ¡échense para atrás!; **to push back** empujar hacia atrás - **2.** [to former position or state] de vuelta; **to come back** volver; **to go back** volver; **to look back** volver la mirada; **to walk back** volver andando; **to give sthg back** devolver algo; **to be back (in fashion)** estar de vuelta; **he has been there and back** ha estado allí y ha vuelto; **I spent all day going back and forth** pasé todo el día yendo y viniendo - **3.** [in time]: **two weeks back** hace dos semanas; **it dates back to 1860** data de 1860; **back in March** allá en marzo - **4.** [phone, write] de vuelta; **to pay sb back** [give back money] devolverle el dinero a alguien. ◇ *n* - **1.** [of person] espalda *f*; [of animal] lomo *m*; **lying on one's back** tumbado de espaldas; **to break the back of** *fig* pasar lo peor OR la peor parte de - **2.** [of hand, cheque] dorso *m*; [of coin, page] reverso *m*; [of car, book, head] parte *f* trasera; [of chair] respaldo *m*; [of queue] final *m*; [of room, cupboard] fondo *m* - **3.** SPORT [player] defensa *m*. ◇ *adj* (*in compounds*) - **1.** [at the back - door, legs, seat] trasero(ra); [- page] último(ma) - **2.** [overdue - pay, rent] atrasado(da). ◇ *vt* - **1.** [support] respaldar - **2.** [bet on] apostar por - **3.** [strengthen with material] reforzar.

◇ *vi* [drive backwards] ir marcha atrás; [walk backwards] ir hacia atrás. ◆ **back to back** *adv* [with backs facing] espalda con espalda. ◆ **back to front** *adv* al revés. ◆ **back down** *vi* echarse OR volverse atrás. ◆ **back out** *vi* echarse OR volverse atrás. ◆ **back up** ◇ *vt sep* - **1.** [support] apoyar - **2.** COMPUT hacer una copia de seguridad de. ◇ *vi* - **1.** [reverse] ir marcha atrás - **2.** COMPUT hacer copias de seguridad.

backache ['bækeɪk] *n* dolor *m* de espalda.

backbencher [,bæk'bentʃəʳ] *n* UK diputado *sin cargo en el gabinete del gobierno o la oposición.*

backbone ['bækbəʊn] *n lit & fig* columna *f* vertebral.

backcloth ['bækklɒθ] UK = **backdrop**.

backdate [,bæk'deɪt] *vt*: **a pay rise backdated to March** un aumento de sueldo con efecto retroactivo desde marzo.

back door *n* puerta *f* trasera; **the team qualified through the back door** *fig* el equipo se clasificó por la puerta trasera.

backdrop ['bækdrɒp], **backcloth** *n lit & fig* telón *m* de fondo.

backfire [,bæk'faɪəʳ] *vi* - **1.** [motor vehicle] petardear - **2.** [go wrong]: **it backfired on him** le salió el tiro por la culata.

backgammon ['bæk,gæmən] *n* backgammon *m*.

background ['bækgraʊnd] *n* - **1.** [in picture, view] fondo *m*; **in the background** [of painting etc] al fondo; [out of the limelight] en la sombra - **2.** [of event, situation] trasfondo *m* - **3.** [upbringing] origen *m*; **family background** antecedentes *mpl* familiares - **4.** [knowledge, experience]: **a background in** conocimientos *mpl* de.

backhand ['bækhænd] *n* revés *m*.

backhanded ['bækhændɪd] *adj fig* equívoco(ca).

backhander ['bækhændəʳ] *n* UK *inf*: **to give sb a backhander** untarle la mano a alguien, coimear a alguien *Andes & R Dom*, morder a alguien *Amér C & Méx*.

backing ['bækɪŋ] *n* - **1.** [support] apoyo *m*, respaldo *m* - **2.** [lining] refuerzo *m* - **3.** MUS acompañamiento *m*.

backlash ['bæklæʃ] *n* reacción *f* violenta.

backlog ['bæklɒg] *n* acumulación *f*.

back number, **back issue** *n* número *m* atrasado.

backpack ['bækpæk] *n* mochila *f*.

back pay *n* (U) atrasos *mpl*.

back seat *n* asiento *m* trasero OR de atrás; **to take a back seat** *fig* situarse en segundo plano.

backside [,bæk'saɪd] *n inf* trasero *m*.

backstage [ˌbækˈsteɪdʒ] *adv* entre bastidores.

back street *n UK* calle *f* de barrio.

backstroke [ˈbækstrəʊk] *n* espalda *f (en natación)*; **to do the backstroke** nadar a espalda.

backup [ˈbækʌp] ◇ *adj* - **1.** [plan] de emergencia; [team] de apoyo - **2.** COMPUT de seguridad. ◇ *n* - **1.** [support] apoyo *m* - **2.** COMPUT copia *f* de seguridad.

backward [ˈbækwəd] ◇ *adj* - **1.** [movement, look] hacia atrás - **2.** [country, person] atrasado(da). ◇ *adv US* = **backwards**.

backwards [ˈbækwədz], **backward** *US adv* - **1.** [move, go] hacia atrás; **backwards and forwards** [movement] de un lado a otro - **2.** [back to front] al OR del revés.

backwater [ˈbæk,wɔːtəʳ] *n fig* páramo *m*, lugar *m* atrasado.

backyard [ˌbækˈjɑːd] *n* - **1.** *UK* [yard] patio *m* - **2.** *US* [garden] jardín *m* (trasero).

bacon [ˈbeɪkən] *n* bacon *m*, tocino *m*.

bacteria [bækˈtɪərɪə] *npl* bacterias *fpl*.

bad [bæd] *(comp* worse, *superl* worst*) adj* - **1.** [gen] malo(la); **he's bad at French** se le da mal el francés; **to have a bad back** estar mal de la espalda; **to go bad** [food] echarse a perder; **too bad!** ¡mala suerte!; **it's not bad (at all)** no está nada mal; **how are you? – not bad** ¿qué tal? – bien - **2.** [illness] grave - **3.** [guilty]: **to feel bad about sthg** sentirse mal por algo.

badge [bædʒ] *n* - **1.** [for decoration - metal, plastic] chapa *f*; [- sewn-on] insignia *f* - **2.** [for identification] distintivo *m*.

badger [ˈbædʒəʳ] ◇ *n* tejón *m*. ◇ *vt*: **to badger sb (to do sthg)** ponerse pesado(da) con alguien (para que haga algo).

badly [ˈbædlɪ] *(comp* worse, *superl* worst*) adv* - **1.** [not well] mal; **to think badly of sb** pensar mal de alguien - **2.** [seriously] gravemente; **I'm badly in need of help** necesito ayuda urgentemente.

badly-off *adj* - **1.** [poor] apurado(da) de dinero - **2.** [lacking]: **to be badly-off for sthg** estar OR andar mal de algo.

bad-mannered [-ˈmænəd] *adj* maleducado(da).

badminton [ˈbædmɪntən] *n* bádminton *m*.

bad-tempered [-ˈtempəd] *adj* - **1.** [by nature]: **to be bad-tempered** tener mal genio - **2.** [in a bad mood]: **to be bad-tempered** estar malhumorado(da).

baffle [ˈbæfl] *vt* desconcertar.

bag [bæg] ◇ *n* - **1.** [container, bagful] bolsa *f*; **to pack one's bags** *fig* hacer las maletas - **2.** [handbag] bolso *m*, cartera *f Andes & R Plata*. ◇ *vt UK inf* [reserve] pedirse, reservarse.

bags *npl* - **1.** [under eyes]: **to have bags under one's eyes** *inf* tener ojeras - **2.** [lots]: **bags of** *inf* un montón de.

bagel [ˈbeɪgəl] *n* bollo de pan en forma de rosca.

baggage [ˈbægɪdʒ] *n esp US* (U) equipaje *m*.

baggage reclaim *n* recogida *f* de equipajes.

baggy [ˈbægɪ] *adj* holgado(da).

bagpipes [ˈbægpaɪps] *npl* gaita *f*.

Bahamas [bəˈhɑːməz] *npl*: **the Bahamas** las Bahamas.

bail [beɪl] *n* (U) fianza *f*; **on bail** bajo fianza.
bail out ◇ *vt sep* - **1.** [pay bail for] obtener la libertad bajo fianza de - **2.** [rescue] sacar de apuros. ◇ *vi* [from plane] tirarse en paracaídas *(antes de que se estrelle el avión)*.

bailiff [ˈbeɪlɪf] *n* alguacil *m*.

bait [beɪt] ◇ *n lit* & *fig* cebo *m*; **to rise to** OR **take the bait** *fig* picarse, morder el anzuelo. ◇ *vt* - **1.** [put bait on] cebar - **2.** [tease, torment] hacer sufrir, cebarse con.

bake [beɪk] ◇ *vt* [food] cocer al horno. ◇ *vi* [food] cocerse al horno.

baked beans [beɪkt-] *npl* alubias *fpl* cocidas en salsa de tomate.

baked potato [beɪkt-] *n* patata *f* asada OR al horno.

baker [ˈbeɪkəʳ] *n* panadero *m*; **baker's (shop)** panadería *f*.

bakery [ˈbeɪkərɪ] *n* panadería *f*.

baking [ˈbeɪkɪŋ] *n* cocción *f*.

balaclava (helmet) [bæləˈklɑːvə-] *n* pasamontañas *m inv*.

balance [ˈbæləns] ◇ *n* - **1.** [equilibrium] equilibrio *m*; **to keep/lose one's balance** mantener/perder el equilibrio; **it caught me off balance** me pilló desprevenido(da) - **2.** *fig* [counterweight] contrapunto *m* - **3.** [of evidence etc] peso *m* - **4.** [scales] balanza *f*; **to be** OR **hang in the balance** estar en el aire - **5.** [of account] saldo *m*. ◇ *vt* - **1.** [keep in balance] poner en equilibrio - **2.** [compare] sopesar. ◇ *vi* - **1.** [maintain equilibrium] sostenerse en equilibrio - **2.** [in accounting] cuadrar. **on balance** *adv* tras pensarlo detenidamente.

balanced diet *n* dieta *f* equilibrada.

balance of payments *n* balanza *f* de pagos.

balance of trade *n* balanza *f* comercial.

balance sheet *n* balance *m*.

balcony [ˈbælkənɪ] *n* - **1.** [on building - big] terraza *f*; [- small] balcón *m* - **2.** [in theatre] anfiteatro *m*, galería *f*.

bald [bɔːld] *adj* - **1.** [without hair] calvo(va) - **2.** [tyre] desgastado(da) - **3.** *fig* [blunt] escueto(ta).

bale [beɪl] *n* bala *f*. ◆ **bale out** *vi UK* - **1.** [remove water] achicar agua - **2.** [from plane] tirarse en paracaídas *(antes de que se estrelle el avión)*.

Balearic Islands [ˌbælɪˈærɪk-], **Balearics** [ˌbælɪˈærɪks] *npl*: **the Balearic Islands** las Baleares.

baleful [ˈbeɪlfʊl] *adj* maligno(na).

balk, baulk [bɔːk] *vi*: **to balk (at doing sthg)** resistirse (a hacer algo).

Balkans [ˈbɔːlkənz], **Balkan States** *npl*: **the Balkans** los Balcanes.

ball [bɔːl] *n* - **1.** [for tennis, cricket] pelota *f*; [for golf, billiards] bola *f*; [for football, basketball, rugby] balón *m* - **2.** [round shape] bola *f* - **3.** [of foot] pulpejo *m* - **4.** [dance] baile *m*. ◆ **balls** *v inf* ◇ *npl* [testicles] pelotas *fpl*. ◇ *n (U)* [nonsense] gilipolleces *fpl*.

ballad [ˈbæləd] *n* balada *f*.

ballast [ˈbæləst] *n* lastre *m*.

ball bearing *n* cojinete *m* de bolas.

ball boy *n* recogepelotas *m inv*.

ballerina [ˌbæləˈriːnə] *n* bailarina *f*.

ballet [ˈbæleɪ] *n* ballet *m*.

ballet dancer *n* bailarín *m*, -ina *f*.

ball game *n US* [baseball match] partido *m* de béisbol.

balloon [bəˈluːn] *n* - **1.** [toy] globo *m* - **2.** [hot-air balloon] globo *m* (aerostático) - **3.** [in cartoon] bocadillo *m*.

ballot [ˈbælət] ◇ *n* [voting process] votación *f*. ◇ *vt*: **to ballot the members on an issue** someter un asunto a votación entre los afiliados.

ballot box *n* [container] urna *f*; **to decide sthg at the ballot box** decidir algo en las urnas.

ballot paper *n* voto *m*, papeleta *f*, balota *f Perú*, boleta *f* electoral *Méx & R Plata*.

ballpoint (pen) [ˈbɔːlpɔɪnt-] *n* bolígrafo *m*, pluma *f* atómica *Méx*, esfero *m Col*, birome *f R Plata*, lápiz *m* de pasta *Chile*.

ballroom [ˈbɔːlrʊm] *n* salón *m* de baile.

ballroom dancing *n (U)* baile *m* de salón.

balm [bɑːm] *n* bálsamo *m*.

balmy [ˈbɑːmɪ] *adj* apacible.

balti [ˈbɔːltɪ] *n* [pan] *cacerola utilizada en la cocina india*; [food] *plato indio sazonado con especias y preparado en un 'balti'*.

Baltic [ˈbɔːltɪk] ◇ *adj* báltico(ca). ◇ *n*: **the Baltic (Sea)** el (mar) Báltico.

Baltic Republic *n*: **the Baltic Republics** las repúblicas bálticas.

bamboo [bæmˈbuː] *n* bambú *m*.

bamboozle [bæmˈbuːzl] *vt inf* camelar, engatusar.

ban [bæn] ◇ *n*: **ban (on)** prohibición *f* (de). ◇ *vt*: **to ban (sb from doing sthg)** prohibir (a alguien hacer algo).

banal [bəˈnɑːl] *adj pej* banal.

banana [bəˈnɑːnə] *n* plátano *m*, banana *f Amér*.

band [bænd] *n* - **1.** [musical group - pop] grupo *m*; [- jazz, military] banda *f* - **2.** [of thieves etc] banda *f* - **3.** [strip] cinta *f*, tira *f* - **4.** [stripe, range] franja *f*. ◆ **band together** *vi* juntarse.

bandage [ˈbændɪdʒ] ◇ *n* venda *f*. ◇ *vt* vendar.

Band-Aid® *n US* ≃ tirita® *f Esp*, ≃ curita *f Amér*.

b and b, B and B *n abbr of* **bed and breakfast**.

bandit [ˈbændɪt] *n* bandido *m*, -da *f*.

bandstand [ˈbændstænd] *n* quiosco *m* de música.

bandwagon [ˈbændwægən] *n*: **to jump on the bandwagon** subirse *OR* apuntarse al carro.

bandy [ˈbændɪ] *adj* [legs] arqueado(da). ◆ **bandy about, bandy around** *vt sep* sacar a relucir.

bandy-legged [-ˌlegd] *adj* de piernas arqueadas.

bang [bæŋ] ◇ *n* - **1.** [blow] golpe *m* - **2.** [loud noise] estampido *m*, estruendo *m*. ◇ *vt* - **1.** [hit - drum, desk] golpear; [- knee, head] golpearse - **2.** [door] cerrar de golpe. ◇ *vi* golpear. ◇ *adv* [exactly]: **bang in the middle of** justo en mitad de; **bang on** [correct] muy acertado(da). ◆ **bangs** *npl US* flequillo *m*.

banger [ˈbæŋə*r*] *n UK* - **1.** *inf* [sausage] salchicha *f* - **2.** *inf* [old car] carraca *f*, cacharro *m* - **3.** [firework] petardo *m*.

Bangladesh [ˌbæŋɡləˈdeʃ] *n* Bangladesh.

bangle [ˈbæŋɡl] *n* brazalete *m*.

banish [ˈbænɪʃ] *vt lit & fig* desterrar.

banister [ˈbænɪstə*r*] *n* barandilla *f*, pasamanos *m inv*.

bank [bæŋk] ◇ *n* - **1.** [gen & FIN] banco *m* - **2.** [by river, lake] ribera *f*, orilla *f* - **3.** [slope] loma *f* - **4.** [of clouds etc] masa *f*. ◇ *vi* - **1.** FIN: **to bank with** tener una cuenta en - **2.** [plane] ladearse. ◆ **bank on** *vt insep* contar con.

bank account *n* cuenta *f* bancaria.

bank balance *n* saldo *m* bancario.

bank card = banker's card.

bank charges *npl* comisiones *fpl* bancarias.

bank details *npl* datos *mpl* bancarios.

bank draft *n* giro *m* bancario.

banker [ˈbæŋkə*r*] *n* banquero *m*, -ra *f*.

banker's card, bank card *n UK* tarjeta *f* de identificación bancaria.

bank holiday *n UK* día *m* festivo.

banking ['bæŋkɪŋ] n banca f.

bank manager n director m, ra f de banco.

bank note n billete m de banco.

bank rate n tipo m de interés bancario.

bankrupt ['bæŋkrʌpt] <> adj [financially] quebrado(da), en quiebra; **to go bankrupt** quebrar. <> vt llevar a la quiebra.

bankruptcy ['bæŋkrəptsɪ] n quiebra f, bancarrota f; fig [of ideas] falta f total.

bank statement n extracto m de cuenta.

banner ['bænər] n - 1. [carrying slogan] pancarta f - 2. [comput] banner m, pancarta f publicitaria.

banoffee [bə'nɒfiː] n (U) postre hecho con galletas, plátano, mantequilla y leche condensada.

banquet ['bæŋkwɪt] n banquete m.

banter ['bæntər] n (U) bromas fpl.

bap [bæp] n UK bollo m de pan.

baptism ['bæptɪzm] n bautismo m.

baptize, -ise [UK bæp'taɪz, US 'bæptaɪz] vt bautizar.

bar [bɑːr] <> n - 1. [of soap] pastilla f; [of gold] lingote m; [of wood] barrote m; [of metal] barra f; **a bar of chocolate** una chocolatina; **to be behind bars** estar entre rejas - 2. [drinking place] bar m - 3. [counter] barra f - 4. fig [obstacle] barrera f; [ban] prohibición f - 5. MUS compás m. <> vt - 1. [close with a bar] atrancar - 2. [block]: **to bar sb's way** impedir el paso a alguien - 3. [ban]: **to bar sb (from doing sthg)** prohibir a alguien (hacer algo); **to bar sb from somewhere** prohibir a alguien la entrada en un sitio. <> prep [except] menos, salvo; **bar none** sin excepción. ➡ **Bar** n LAW: **the Bar** UK conjunto de los abogados que ejercen en tribunales superiores; US la abogacía.

barbaric [bɑː'bærɪk] adj salvaje.

barbecue ['bɑːbɪkjuː] n barbacoa f.

barbed wire [bɑːbd-] n alambre m de espino.

barber ['bɑːbər] n barbero m; **barber's** peluquería f.

barbershop ['bɑːbəʃɒp] n US barbería f.

barbiturate [bɑː'bɪtjʊrət] n barbitúrico m.

bar code n código m de barras.

bare [beər] <> adj - 1. [without covering - legs, trees, hills] desnudo(da); [- feet] descalzo(za) - 2. [absolute, minimum] esencial - 3. [empty] vacío(a). <> vt descubrir; **to bare one's teeth** enseñar los dientes.

bareback ['beəbæk] adj & adv a pelo.

barefaced ['beəfeɪst] adj descarado(da).

barefoot(ed) [,beə'fʊt(ɪd)] adj & adv descalzo(za).

barely ['beəlɪ] adv [scarcely] apenas.

bargain ['bɑːgɪn] <> n - 1. [agreement] trato m, acuerdo m; **into the bargain** además - 2. [good buy] ganga f. <> vi: **to bargain (with sb for sthg)** negociar (con alguien para obtener algo). ➡ **bargain for, bargain on** vt insep contar con.

barge [bɑːdʒ] <> n barcaza f. <> vi inf: **to barge into** [person] chocarse con; [room] irrumpir en. ➡ **barge in** vi inf: **to barge in (on)** [conversation etc] entrometerse (en).

baritone ['bærɪtəʊn] n barítono m.

bark [bɑːk] <> n - 1. [of dog] ladrido m - 2. [of tree] corteza f. <> vi: **to bark (at)** ladrar (a).

barley ['bɑːlɪ] n cebada f.

barley sugar n UK azúcar m o f cande.

barley water n UK hordiate m.

barmaid ['bɑːmeɪd] n camarera f.

barman ['bɑːmən] (pl -men [-mən]) n camarero m, barman m.

barn [bɑːn] n granero m.

barometer [bə'rɒmɪtər] n barómetro m; fig [of public opinion etc] piedra f de toque.

baron ['bærən] n barón m; **press/oil baron** fig magnate m de la prensa/del petróleo.

baroness ['bærənɪs] n baronesa f.

barrack ['bærək] vt UK abroncar. ➡ **barracks** npl cuartel m.

barrage ['bærɑːʒ] n - 1. [of firing] descarga f, fuego m intenso de artillería - 2. [of questions] aluvión m, alud m - 3. UK [dam] presa f, dique m.

barrel ['bærəl] n - 1. [for beer, wine, oil] barril m - 2. [of gun] cañón m.

barren ['bærən] adj estéril.

barricade [,bærɪ'keɪd] <> n barricada f. <> vt levantar barricadas en.

barrier ['bærɪər] n lit & fig barrera f.

barring ['bɑːrɪŋ] prep salvo; **barring a miracle** a menos que ocurra un milagro.

barrister ['bærɪstər] n UK abogado m, -da f (de tribunales superiores).

barrow ['bærəʊ] n carrito m.

bartender ['bɑːtendər] n esp US camarero m, -ra f.

barter ['bɑːtər] <> n trueque m. <> vt: **to barter (sthg for sthg)** trocar (algo por algo).

base [beɪs] <> n base f. <> vt - 1. [place, establish] emplazar; **he's based in Paris** vive en París - 2. [use as starting point]: **to base sthg on** OR **upon** basar algo en. <> adj pej bajo(ja), vil.

baseball ['beɪsbɔːl] n béisbol m.

baseball cap n gorra f de visera.

basement ['beɪsmənt] n sótano m.

base rate n tipo m de interés base.

bases ['beɪsiːz] npl ▷ **basis**.

bash [bæʃ] *inf* <> *n* - 1. [attempt]: **to have a bash at** sthg intentar algo - 2. [party] juerga *f*. <> *vt* [hit - person, thing] darle un porrazo a; [- one's head, knee] darse un porrazo en.

bashful ['bæʃfʊl] *adj* [person] vergonzoso(sa); [smile] tímido(da).

basic ['beɪsɪk] *adj* básico(ca). ➡ **basics** *npl* - 1. [rudiments] principios *mpl* básicos - 2. [essentials] lo imprescindible.

basically ['beɪsɪklɪ] *adv* - 1. [essentially] esencialmente - 2. [really] en resumen.

basil ['bæzl] *n* albahaca *f*.

basin ['beɪsn] *n* - 1. *UK* [bowl] balde *m*, barreño *m* - 2. [wash basin] lavabo *m* - 3. GEOG cuenca *f*.

basis ['beɪsɪs] (*pl* **bases**) *n* base *f*; **on the basis of** de acuerdo con, a partir de; **on a weekly basis** semanalmente; **on a monthly basis** mensualmente.

bask [bɑːsk] *vi* [sunbathe]: **to bask in the sun** tostarse al sol.

basket ['bɑːskɪt] *n* - 1. [container] cesta *f* - 2. [in basketball] canasta *f*.

basketball ['bɑːskɪtbɔːl] *n* baloncesto *m*.

Basque [bɑːsk] <> *adj* vasco(ca). <> *n* - 1. [person] vasco *m*, -ca *f* - 2. [language] vascuence *m*, euskera *m*.

basmati (rice) [bæz'mɑːtɪ-] *n* (*U*) CULIN arroz *m* basmati.

bass [beɪs] <> *adj* bajo(ja). <> *n* - 1. [singer, bass guitar] bajo *m* - 2. [double bass] contrabajo *m* - 3. [on hi-fi, amplifier] graves *mpl*.

bass drum [beɪs-] *n* bombo *m*.

bass guitar [beɪs-] *n* bajo *m*.

bassoon [bə'suːn] *n* fagot *m*.

bastard ['bɑːstəd] *n* - 1. [illegitimate child] bastardo *m*, -da *f* - 2. *v inf pej* cabrón *m*, -ona *f*.

bastion ['bæstɪən] *n* bastión *m*.

bat [bæt] *n* - 1. [animal] murciélago *m* - 2. [for cricket, baseball] bate *m* - 3. [for table-tennis] pala *f*, paleta *f*.

batch [bætʃ] *n* - 1. [of bread] hornada *f* - 2. [of letters etc] remesa *f* - 3. [of work] montón *m* - 4. [of products] lote *m*.

bated ['beɪtɪd] *adj*: **with bated breath** con el aliento contenido.

bath [bɑːθ] <> *n* - 1. [bathtub] bañera *f*, bañadera *f* *Arg*, tina *f* *Amér* - 2. [act of washing] baño *m*, bañada *f* *Amér*; **to have** OR **take a bath** darse un baño, bañarse. <> *vt* bañar. ➡ **baths** *npl* *UK* [public swimming pool] piscina *f* municipal, alberca *f* municipal *Méx*, pileta *f* municipal *R Plata*.

bathe [beɪð] <> *vt* [wound] lavar. <> *vi* bañarse.

bathing ['beɪðɪŋ] *n* (*U*) baños *mpl*.

bathing cap *n* gorro *m* de baño.

bathing costume, bathing suit *n* traje *m* de baño, bañador *m*, malla *f* *Amér*.

bathrobe ['bɑːθrəʊb] *n* - 1. [made of towelling] albornoz *m* - 2. [dressing gown] batín *m*, bata *f*.

bathroom ['bɑːθrʊm] *n* - 1. *UK* [room with bath] (cuarto *m* de) baño *m* - 2. [toilet] servicio *m*.

bath towel *n* toalla *f* de baño.

bathtub ['bɑːθtʌb] *n* bañera *f*.

baton ['bætən] *n* - 1. [of conductor] batuta *f* - 2. [in relay race] testigo *m* - 3. *UK* [of policeman] porra *f*.

batsman ['bætsmən] (*pl* -men [-mən]) *n* bateador *m*.

battalion [bə'tæljən] *n* batallón *m*.

batten ['bætn] *n* listón *m* (de madera).

batter ['bætər] <> *n* pasta *f* para rebozar; *US* [for cakes] mezcla *f* pastelera. <> *vt* - 1. [child, woman] pegar - 2. [door, ship] golpear. ➡ **batter down** *vt sep* echar abajo.

battered ['bætəd] *adj* - 1. [child, woman] maltratado(da) - 2. [car, hat] abollado(da) - 3. [fish, vegetables etc] rebozado(da).

battery ['bætərɪ] *n* [of radio, toy] pila *f*; [of car, guns] batería *f*.

battle ['bætl] <> *n* - 1. [in war] batalla *f* - 2. [struggle]: **battle (for/against/with)** lucha *f* (por/contra/con). <> *vi*: **to battle (for/against/with)** luchar (por/contra/con).

battlefield ['bætlfiːld], **battleground** ['bætlgraʊnd] *n* *lit* & *fig* campo *m* de batalla.

battlements ['bætlmənts] *npl* almenas *fpl*.

battleship ['bætlʃɪp] *n* acorazado *m*.

bauble ['bɔːbl] *n* - 1. [ornament] baratija *f* - 2. [for Christmas tree] bola *f* de Navidad.

baulk [bɔːk] = **balk**.

bawdy ['bɔːdɪ] *adj* verde, picante.

bawl [bɔːl] *vi* - 1. [shout] vociferar - 2. [cry] berrear.

bay [beɪ] <> *n* - 1. [of coast] bahía *f* - 2. [for loading] zona *f* de carga y descarga - 3. [for parking] plaza *f*. ❱❱❱ **to keep** sthg/sb **at bay** mantener algo/a alguien a raya. <> *vi* aullar.

bay leaf *n* (hoja *f* de) laurel *m*.

bay window *n* ventana *f* saial.

bazaar [bə'zɑːr] *n* - 1. [market] bazar *m* - 2. *UK* [charity sale] mercadillo *m* benéfico.

B & B *abbr of* **bed and breakfast**.

BBC (*abbr of* **British Broadcasting Corporation**) *n* BBC *f*, *compañía estatal británica de radiotelevisión*.

BC (*abbr of* **before Christ**) a.C.

Bcc [ˌbiːsiːˈsiː] (*abbr of* **blind carbon copy**) *n* Cco.

be [biː] (*pt* **was** OR **were**, *pp* **been**) <> *aux vb* - 1. (*in combination with present participle: to* *form cont tense)* estar; **what is he doing?** ¿qué hace OR está haciendo?; **it's snowing** está nevando; **I'm leaving tomorrow** me voy mañana; **they've been promising it for years** han estado prometiéndolo durante años - **2.** *(in combination with pp: to form passive)* ser; **to be loved** ser amado; **there was no one to be seen** no se veía a nadie; **ten people were killed** murieron diez personas - **3.** *(in question tags)*: **you're not going now, are you?** no irás a marcharte ya ¿no?; **the meal was delicious, wasn't it?** la comida fue deliciosa ¿verdad? - **4.** *(followed by 'to' + infinitive)*: **I'm to be promoted** me van a ascender; **you're not to tell anyone** no debes decírselo a nadie. ◇ *cop vb* - **1.** *(with adj, n)* [indicating innate quality, permanent condition] ser; [indicating state, temporary condition] estar; **snow is white** la nieve es blanca; **she's intelligent/tall** es inteligente/alta; **to be a doctor/plumber** ser médico/fontanero; **I'm Welsh** soy galés; **1 and 1 are 2** 1 y 1 son 2; **your hands are cold** tus manos están frías; **I'm tired/angry** estoy cansado/enfadado; **he's in a difficult position** está en una situación difícil - **2.** [referring to health] estar; **she's ill/better** está enferma/mejor; **how are you?** ¿cómo estás?, ¿qué tal? - **3.** [referring to age]: **how old are you?** ¿qué edad OR cuántos años tienes?; **I'm 20 (years old)** tengo 20 años - **4.** [cost] ser, costar; **how much is it?** ¿cuánto es?; **that will be £10, please** son 10 libras; **apples are only 40p a kilo today** hoy las manzanas están a tan sólo 40 peniques el kilo. ◇ *vi* - **1.** [exist] ser, existir; **the worst prime minister that ever was** el peor primer ministro de todos los tiempos; **be that as it may** aunque así sea; **there is/are** hay; **is there life on Mars?** ¿hay vida en Marte? - **2.** [referring to place] estar; **Valencia is in Spain** Valencia está en España; **he will be here tomorrow** estará aquí mañana - **3.** [referring to movement] estar; **where have you been?** ¿dónde has estado? ◇ *impers vb* - **1.** [referring to time, dates] ser; **it's two o'clock** son las dos; **it's the 17th of February** estamos a 17 de febrero - **2.** [referring to distance]: **it's 3 km to the next town** hay 3 kms hasta el próximo pueblo - **3.** [referring to the weather]: **it's hot/cold/windy** hace calor/frío/viento - **4.** [for emphasis] ser; **it's me** soy yo.

beach [bi:tʃ] ◇ *n* playa *f*. ◇ *vt* varar.

beacon ['bi:kən] *n* - **1.** [warning fire] almenara *f* - **2.** [lighthouse] faro *m* - **3.** [radio beacon] radiofaro *m*.

bead [bi:d] *n* - **1.** [of wood, glass] cuenta *f*, abalorio *m* - **2.** [of sweat] gota *f*.

beagle ['bi:gl] *n* beagle *m*.

beak [bi:k] *n* pico *m*.

beaker ['bi:kər] *n* taza *f (sin asa)*.

beam [bi:m] ◇ *n* - **1.** [of wood, concrete] viga *f* - **2.** [of light] rayo *m*. ◇ *vt* [transmit]. ◇ *vi* - **1.** [smile] sonreír resplandeciente - **2.** [shine] resplandecer.

bean [bi:n] *n* CULIN [haricot] judía *f*, habichuela *f*, frijol *m Amér*, poroto *m Andes*, caraota *f Ven*; [of coffee] grano *m*.

beanbag ['bi:nbæg] *n* cojín grande relleno de bolitas de polietileno.

beanshoot ['bi:nʃu:t], **beansprout** ['bi:nspraut] *n* brote *m* de soja.

bear [beər] ◇ *n* [animal] oso *m*, -sa *f*. ◇ *vt* *(pt bore, pp borne)* - **1.** [carry] llevar - **2.** [support] soportar - **3.** [responsibility] cargar con - **4.** [marks, signs] llevar - **5.** [endure] aguantar - **6.** [fruit, crop] dar - **7.** [feeling] guardar, albergar. ◇ *vi*: **to bear left** torcer OR doblar a la izquierda; **to bring pressure/influence to bear on** ejercer presión/influencia sobre. ◆ **bear down** *vi*: **to bear down on** echarse encima de. ◆ **bear out** *vt sep* corroborar. ◆ **bear up** *vi* resistir. ◆ **bear with** *vt insep* tener paciencia con; **if you could just bear with me a moment...** si no le importa esperar un momento...

beard [bɪəd] *n* barba *f*.

bearer ['beərə] *n* - **1.** [of stretcher, news, cheque] portador *m*, -ra *f* - **2.** [of passport] titular *mf*.

bearing ['beərɪŋ] *n* - **1.** [connection]: **bearing (on)** relación *f* (con) - **2.** [deportment] porte *m* - **3.** [for shaft] cojinete *m* - **4.** [on compass] rumbo *m*; **to get one's bearings** orientarse; **to lose one's bearings** desorientarse.

beast [bi:st] *n* lit & fig bestia *f*.

beastly ['bi:stlɪ] *adj* dated atroz.

beat [bi:t] ◇ *n* - **1.** [of drum] golpe *m* - **2.** [of heart, pulse] latido *m* - **3.** MUS [rhythm] ritmo *m*; [individual unit of time] golpe *m (de compás)* - **4.** [of policeman] ronda *f*. ◇ *vt* *(pt beat, pp beaten)* - **1.** [hit - person] pegar; [- thing] golpear; [- carpet] sacudir - **2.** [wings, eggs, butter] batir - **3.** [defeat]: **to beat sb (at sthg)** ganar a alguien (a algo); **it beats me** inf no me lo explico - **4.** [be better than] ser mucho mejor que; **beat it!** inf ¡largo! ◇ *vi* *(pt beat, pp beaten)* - **1.** [rain] golpear - **2.** [heart, pulse] latir; [drums] redoblar. ◆ **beat off** *vt sep* [attackers] repeler. ◆ **beat up** *vt sep inf* dar una paliza a; **to beat o.s. up (about sth)** castigarse (por algo). ◆ **beat up on** *vt sep US inf* dar una paliza a.

beating ['bi:tɪŋ] *n* - **1.** [hitting] paliza *f* - **2.** [defeat] derrota *f*.

beautiful ['bju:tɪfʊl] *adj* - **1.** [person] guapo(pa) - **2.** [thing, animal] precioso(sa) - **3.** *inf* [very good - shot, weather] espléndido(da).

beautifully ['bju:təflɪ] *adv* - **1.** [attractively] bellamente - **2.** *inf* [very well] espléndidamente.

beauty ['bju:tɪ] *n* belleza *f*.

beauty parlour, beauty salon *n* salón *m* de belleza.

beauty salon = **beauty parlour**.

beauty spot *n* - 1. [picturesque place] bello paraje *m* - 2. [on skin] lunar *m*.

beaver ['bi:vəʳ] *n* castor *m*.

became [bɪ'keɪm] *pt* ▷ **become**.

because [bɪ'kɒz] *conj* porque. ◆ **because of** *prep* por, a causa de.

beck [bek] *n*: **to be at sb's beck and call** estar siempre a disposición de alguien.

beckon ['bekən] ◇ *vt* [signal to] llamar (con un gesto). ◇ *vi* [signal]: **to beckon to sb** llamar (con un gesto) a alguien.

become [bɪ'kʌm] (*pt* became, *pp* become) *vi* hacerse; **to become happy** ponerse contento; **to become suspicious** volverse receloso; **to become angry** enfadarse; **he became Prime Minister in 1991** en 1991 se convirtió en primer ministro.

becoming [bɪ'kʌmɪŋ] *adj* - 1. [attractive] favorecedor(ra) - 2. [appropriate] apropiado(da).

bed [bed] *n* - 1. [to sleep on] cama *f*; **to go to bed** irse a la cama; **to make the bed** hacer la cama; **to put sb to bed** acostar a alguien - 2. [flowerbed] macizo *m*; **a bed of roses** *fig* un lecho de rosas - 3. [of sea] fondo *m*; [of river] lecho *m*.

bed and breakfast *n* [service] cama *f* y desayuno; [hotel] ≃ pensión *f*.

bedclothes ['bedkləʊðz] *npl* ropa *f* de cama.

bedlam ['bedləm] *n* jaleo *m*, alboroto *m*.

bed linen *n* ropa *f* de cama.

bedraggled [bɪ'drægld] *adj* mojado y sucio(mojada y sucia).

bedridden ['bed,rɪdn] *adj* postrado(da) en cama.

bedroom ['bedrʊm] *n* - 1. [at home] dormitorio *m*, recámara *f Amér C & Méx* - 2. [in hotel] habitación *f*, recámara *f Amér C & Méx*.

bedside ['bedsaɪd] *n* [side of bed] lado *m* de la cama; [of ill person] lecho *m*; **bedside table** mesita *f* de noche.

bedsore ['bedsɔːʳ] *n* úlcera *f* por decúbito.

bedspread ['bedspred] *n* colcha *f*.

bedtime ['bedtaɪm] *n* hora *f* de irse a la cama.

bee [bi:] *n* abeja *f*.

beef [bi:f] *n* carne *f* de vaca, carne *f* de res *Amér*. ◆ **beef up** *vt sep inf* reforzar.

beefburger ['bi:f,bɜːgəʳ] *n* hamburguesa *f*.

beeline ['bi:laɪn] *n*: **to make a beeline for** *inf* irse derechito(ta) hacia.

been [bi:n] *pp* ▷ **be**.

beeper ['bi:pəʳ] *n* buscapersonas *m inv*.

beer [bɪəʳ] *n* cerveza *f*.

beet [bi:t] *n* - 1. [sugar beet] remolacha *f* azucarera - 2. *US* [beetroot] remolacha *f*, betabel *m Méx*, betarraga *f Chile*.

beetle ['bi:tl] *n* escarabajo *m*.

beetroot ['bi:tru:t] *n* remolacha *f*, betabel *m Méx*, betarraga *f Chile*.

before [bɪ'fɔːʳ] ◇ *adv* antes; **we went the year before** fuimos el año anterior. ◇ *prep* - 1. [in time] antes de; **they arrived before us** llegaron antes que nosotros - 2. [in space - facing] ante, delante de. ◇ *conj* antes de; **before it's too late** antes de que sea demasiado tarde.

beforehand [bɪ'fɔːhænd] *adv* con antelación, de antemano.

befriend [bɪ'frend] *vt* hacer *OR* entablar amistad con.

beg [beg] ◇ *vt* - 1. [money, food] mendigar, pedir - 2. [favour, forgiveness] suplicar; **to beg sb to do sthg** rogar a alguien que haga algo; **to beg sb for sthg** rogar algo a alguien. ◇ *vi* - 1. [for money, food]: **to beg (for sthg)** pedir *OR* mendigar (algo) - 2. [for favour, forgiveness]: **to beg (for sthg)** suplicar *OR* rogar (algo).

began [bɪ'gæn] *pt* ▷ **begin**.

beggar ['begəʳ] *n* [poor person] mendigo *m*, -ga *f*.

begin [bɪ'gɪn] (*pt* began, *pp* begun, *cont* -ning) ◇ *vt*: **to begin (doing *OR* to do sthg)** empezar *OR* comenzar (a hacer algo). ◇ *vi* empezar, comenzar; **to begin with** para empezar, de entrada.

beginner [bɪ'gɪnəʳ] *n* principiante *mf*.

beginning [bɪ'gɪnɪŋ] *n* comienzo *m*, principio *m*; **at the beginning of the month** a principios de mes.

begrudge [bɪ'grʌdʒ] *vt* - 1. [envy]: **to begrudge sb sthg** envidiar a alguien algo - 2. [give, do unwillingly]: **to begrudge doing sthg** hacer algo de mala gana *OR* a regañadientes.

begun [bɪ'gʌn] *pp* ▷ **begin**.

behalf [bɪ'hɑːf] *n*: **on behalf of** *UK*, **in behalf of** *US* en nombre *OR* en representación de.

behave [bɪ'heɪv] ◇ *vt*: **to behave o.s.** portarse bien. ◇ *vi* - 1. [in a particular way] comportarse, portarse - 2. [in an acceptable way] comportarse *OR* portarse bien.

behaviour *UK*, **behavior** *US* [bɪ'heɪvjəʳ] *n* comportamiento *m*, conducta *f*.

behead [bɪ'hed] *vt* decapitar.

beheld [bɪ'held] *pt & pp* ▷ **behold**.

behind [bɪ'haɪnd] ◇ *prep* - 1. [in space] detrás de - 2. [causing, responsible for] detrás de - 3. [in support of]: **we're behind you** nosotros te apoyamos - 4. [in time]: **to be behind schedule** ir retrasado(da) - 5. [less successful than] por detrás de. ◇ *adv* - 1. [in space] detrás - 2. [in time]: **to be behind (with)** ir atrasado(da) (con) **3.** [less successful] **por detrás.** ⬦ *n inf* trasero *m*

behold [bɪ'həʊld] (*pt & pp* beheld) *vt liter* contemplar.

beige [beɪʒ] *adj* beige.

being ['biːɪŋ] *n* - **1.** [creature] ser *m* - **2.** [state of existing]: **it is no longer in being** ya no existe; **to come into being** ver la luz, nacer.

belated [bɪ'leɪtɪd] *adj* tardío(a).

belch [beltʃ] ⬦ *vt* arrojar. ⬦ *vi* - **1.** [person] eructar - **2.** [smoke, fire] brotar.

beleaguered [bɪ'liːɡəd] *adj* - **1.** MIL asediado(da) - **2.** *fig* [harassed] acosado(da).

Belgian ['beldʒən] ⬦ *adj* belga. ⬦ *n* belga *mf*.

Belgium ['beldʒəm] *n* Bélgica.

Belgrade [ˌbel'ɡreɪd] *n* Belgrado.

belie [bɪ'laɪ] (*cont* belying) *vt* - **1.** [disprove] desmentir - **2.** [give false idea of] encubrir.

belief [bɪ'liːf] *n* - **1.** [faith, principle]: **belief (in)** creencia *f* (en) - **2.** [opinion] opinión *f*.

believe [bɪ'liːv] ⬦ *vt* creer; **believe it or not** lo creas o no. ⬦ *vi* [know to exist, be good]: **to believe in** creer en.

believer [bɪ'liːvə] *n* - **1.** [religious person] creyente *mf* - **2.** [in idea, action]: **believer in sthg** partidario *m*, -ria *f* de algo.

belittle [bɪ'lɪtl] *vt* menospreciar.

bell [bel] *n* [of church] campana *f*; [handbell] campanilla *f*; [handbell, on door, bike] timbre *m*.

belligerent [bɪ'lɪdʒərənt] *adj* - **1.** [at war] beligerante - **2.** [aggressive] belicoso(sa).

bellow ['beləʊ] *vi* - **1.** [person] rugir - **2.** [bull] bramar.

bellows ['beləʊz] *npl* fuelle *m*.

belly ['belɪ] *n* - **1.** [of person] barriga *f* - **2.** [of animal] vientre *m*.

bellyache ['belɪeɪk] *inf* ⬦ *n* dolor *m* de barriga. ⬦ *vi* gruñir.

belly button *n inf* ombligo *m*.

belong [bɪ'lɒŋ] *vi* - **1.** [be property]: **to belong to** pertenecer a - **2.** [be member]: **to belong to** ser miembro de - **3.** [be situated in right place]: **where does this book belong?** ¿dónde va este libro?; **he felt he didn't belong there** sintió que no encajaba allí.

belongings [bɪ'lɒŋɪŋz] *npl* pertenencias *fpl*.

beloved [bɪ'lʌvd] ⬦ *adj* querido(da). ⬦ *n* amado *m*, -da *f*.

below [bɪ'ləʊ] ⬦ *adv* - **1.** [gen] abajo; **the flat below** el piso de abajo - **2.** [in text] más abajo; **see below** véase más abajo - **3.** [with temperatures]: **thirty degrees below** treinta grados bajo cero. ⬦ *prep* - **1.** [lower than in position] (por) debajo de, bajo - **2.** [lower than in rank, number] por debajo de - **3.** [with temperatures]: **thirty degrees below zero** treinta grados bajo cero.

belt [belt] ⬦ *n* - **1.** [for clothing] cinturón *m* - **2.** TECH [wide] cinta *f*; [narrow] correa *f* - **3.** [of land, sea] franja *f*. ⬦ *vt inf* arrear. ⬦ *vi UK inf* ir a toda mecha.

beltway ['belt,weɪ] *n US* carretera *f* de circunvalación.

bemused [bɪ'mjuːzd] *adj* perplejo(ja).

bench [bentʃ] ⬦ *n* - **1.** [seat] banco *m* - **2.** [in lab, workshop] mesa *f* de trabajo - **3.** [in sport] banquillo *m*. ⬦ *vt* SPORT mandar al banquillo.

bend [bend] ⬦ *n* curva *f*; **round the bend** *inf* majareta, majara. ⬦ *vt* (*pt & pp* bent) doblar. ⬦ *vi* (*pt & pp* bent) [person] agacharse; [tree] doblarse; **to bend over backwards for** hacer todo lo humanamente posible por.

beneath [bɪ'niːθ] ⬦ *adv* debajo. ⬦ *prep* - **1.** [under] debajo de, bajo - **2.** [unworthy of] indigno(na) de.

benefactor ['benɪfæktə] *n* benefactor *m*.

beneficial [ˌbenɪ'fɪʃl] *adj*: **beneficial (to)** beneficioso(sa) (para).

beneficiary [ˌbenɪ'fɪʃərɪ] *n* - **1.** LAW [of will] beneficiario *m*, -ria *f* - **2.** [of change in law, new rule] beneficiado *m*, -da *f*.

benefit ['benɪfɪt] ⬦ *n* - **1.** [advantage] ventaja *f*; **for the benefit of** en atención a; **to be to sb's benefit, to be of benefit to sb** ir en beneficio de alguien - **2.** ADMIN [allowance of money] subsidio *m*; **to be on benefit** *UK* estar cobrando un subsidio estatal. ⬦ *vt* beneficiar. ⬦ *vi*: **to benefit from** beneficiarse de.

Benelux ['benɪlʌks] *n* (el) Benelux; **the Benelux countries** los países del Benelux.

benevolent [bɪ'nevələnt] *adj* benevolente.

benign [bɪ'naɪn] *adj* - **1.** [person] bondadoso(sa) - **2.** MED benigno(na).

bent [bent] ⬦ *pt & pp* ⊳ **bend**. ⬦ *adj* - **1.** [wire, bar] torcido(da) - **2.** [person, body] encorvado(da) - **3.** *UK inf* [dishonest] corrupto(ta) - **4.** [determined]: **to be bent on sthg/on doing sthg** estar empeñado(da) en algo/en hacer algo. ⬦ *n* [natural tendency] inclinación *f*; **bent for** don *m OR* talento *m* para.

bento box ['bentəʊ-] *n* plato en forma de caja con varios compartimentos típico de la comida japonesa.

bequest [bɪ'kwest] *n* legado *m*.

berate [bɪ'reɪt] *vt* regañar.

bereaved [bɪ'riːvd] (*pl* bereaved) *n*: **the bereaved** la familia del difunto.

beret ['bereɪ] *n* boina *f*.

berk [bɜːk] *n UK inf* imbécil *mf*.

Berlin [bɜː'lɪn] *n* Berlín.

berm [bɜːm] *n US* arcén *m*.

Bermuda [bəˈmjuːdə] *n* las Bermudas.

Bern [bɜːn] *n* Berna.

berry [ˈberɪ] *n* baya *f*.

berserk [bəˈzɜːk] *adj*: **to go berserk** ponerse hecho(cha) una fiera.

berth [bɜːθ] <> *n* - **1.** [in harbour] amarradero *m*, atracadero *m* - **2.** [in ship, train] litera *f*. <> *vt & vi* atracar.

beseech [bɪˈsiːtʃ] (*pt & pp* besought OR beseeched) *vt liter*: **to beseech (sb to do sthg)** suplicar (a alguien que haga algo).

beset [bɪˈset] (*pt & pp* beset) *adj*: **beset with** OR **by** [subj: person] acosado(da) por; [subj: plan] plagado(da) de.

beside [bɪˈsaɪd] *prep* - **1.** [next to] al lado de, junto a - **2.** [compared with] comparado(da) con ▸▸▸ **that's beside the point** eso no importa, eso no viene al caso; **to be beside o.s. with rage** estar fuera de sí; **to be beside o.s. with joy** estar loco(ca) de alegría.

besides [bɪˈsaɪdz] <> *adv* además. <> *prep* aparte de.

besiege [bɪˈsiːdʒ] *vt lit & fig* asediar.

besotted [bɪˈsɒtɪd] *adj*: **besotted with** embobado(da) con.

besought [bɪˈsɔːt] *pt & pp* ▷ **beseech**.

best [best] <> *adj* mejor; **best before...** [on packaging] consumir preferentemente antes de... <> *adv* mejor; **which did you like best?** ¿cuál te gustó más? <> *n*: **she's the best** es la mejor; **we're the best** somos los mejores; **to do one's best** hacerlo lo mejor que uno puede; **to make the best of sthg** sacarle el mayor partido posible a algo; **for the best** para bien. ▸ **at best** *adv* en el mejor de los casos.

best man *n* ≃ padrino *m* de boda.

bestow [bɪˈstəʊ] *vt fml*: **to bestow sthg on sb** [gift] otorgar OR conceder algo a alguien; [praise] dirigir algo a alguien; [title] conferir algo a alguien.

best-seller *n* [book] best seller *m*, éxito *m* editorial.

bet [bet] <> *n* - **1.** [gen]: **bet (on)** apuesta *f* (a) - **2.** *fig* [prediction] predicción *f*; **to hedge one's bets** cubrirse, guardarse las espaldas. <> *vt* (*pt & pp* bet OR -ted) apostar. <> *vi* (*pt & pp* bet OR -ted) - **1.** [gamble]: **to bet (on)** apostar (a) - **2.** [predict]: **to bet on sthg** contar con (que pase) algo; **you bet!** *inf* ¡ya lo creo!

betray [bɪˈtreɪ] *vt* - **1.** [person, trust, principles] traicionar - **2.** [secret] revelar - **3.** [feeling] delatar.

betrayal [bɪˈtreɪəl] *n* - **1.** [of person, trust, principles] traición *f* - **2.** [of secret] revelación *f*.

better [ˈbetər] <> *adj (compar of* good*)* mejor; **to get better** mejorar. <> *adv (compar of* well*)* - **1.** [in quality] mejor - **2.** [more]: **I like it better** me gusta más - **3.** [preferably]: **we had**

better be going más vale que nos vayamos ya. <> *n* [best one] mejor *mf*; **to get the better of sb** poder con alguien. <> *vt* mejorar; **to better o.s.** mejorarse.

better off *adj* - **1.** [financially] mejor de dinero - **2.** [in better situation]: **you'd be better off going by bus** sería mejor si vas en autobús.

betting [ˈbetɪŋ] *n (U)* apuestas *fpl*.

betting shop *n UK* casa *f* de apuestas.

between [bɪˈtwiːn] <> *prep* entre; **closed between 1 and 2** cerrado de 1 a 2. <> *adv*: **(in) between** en medio, entremedio.

beverage [ˈbevərɪdʒ] *n fml* bebida *f*.

beware [bɪˈweər] *vi*: **to beware (of)** tener cuidado (con).

bewildered [bɪˈwɪldəd] *adj* desconcertado(da).

bewitching [bɪˈwɪtʃɪŋ] *adj* hechizante.

beyond [bɪˈjɒnd] <> *prep* más allá de; **beyond midnight** pasada la medianoche. <> *adv* más allá.

bias [ˈbaɪəs] *n* - **1.** [prejudice] prejuicio *m* - **2.** [tendency] tendencia *f*, inclinación *f*.

biased [ˈbaɪəst] *adj* parcial; **to be biased towards/against** tener prejuicios en favor/en contra de.

bib [bɪb] *n* [for baby] babero *m*.

Bible [ˈbaɪbl] *n*: **the Bible** la Biblia.

bicarbonate of soda [baɪˈkɑːbənət-] *n* bicarbonato *m* sódico.

biceps [ˈbaɪseps] (*pl* biceps) *n* bíceps *m inv*.

bicker [ˈbɪkər] *vi* reñir.

bicycle [ˈbaɪsɪkl] <> *n* bicicleta *f*. <> *comp* de bicicleta.

bicycle path *n* camino *m* para bicicletas.

bicycle pump *n* bomba *f* de bicicleta.

bid [bɪd] <> *n* - **1.** [attempt]: **bid (for)** intento *m* (de hacerse con) - **2.** [at auction] puja *f* - **3.** [financial offer]: **bid (for sthg)** oferta *f* (para adquirir algo). <> *vt* (*pt & pp* bid) [money] ofrecer; [at auction] pujar.

bidder [ˈbɪdər] *n* postor *m*, -ra *f*.

bidding [ˈbɪdɪŋ] *n (U)* [at auction] puja *f*.

bide [baɪd] *vt*: **to bide one's time** esperar el momento oportuno.

bifocals [ˌbaɪˈfəʊklz] *npl* gafas *fpl* bifocales.

big [bɪg] *adj* - **1.** [large, important] grande, gran *(before singular nouns)*; **a big problem** un gran problema; **big problems** grandes problemas - **2.** [older] mayor - **3.** [successful] popular.

bigamy [ˈbɪgəmɪ] *n* bigamia *f*.

big deal *inf* <> *n*: **it's no big deal** no tiene (la menor) importancia. <> *excl* ¡y a mí qué!

Big Dipper [-ˈdɪpər] *n UK* [rollercoaster] montaña *f* rusa.

bigheaded [ˌbɪgˈhedɪd] *adj inf pej* creído(da).

bigot ['bɪgət] *n* intolerante *mf*.

bigoted ['bɪgətɪd] *adj* intolerante.

bigotry ['bɪgətrɪ] *n* intolerancia *f*.

big time *n inf*: **the big time** el éxito, la fama.

big toe *n* dedo *m* gordo (del pie).

big top *n* carpa *f*.

big wheel *n UK* [at fairground] noria *f*.

bike [baɪk] *n inf* [bicycle] bici *f*; [motorcycle] moto *f*.

bikeway ['baɪkweɪ] *n US* [lane] carril-bici *m*.

bikini [bɪ'ki:nɪ] *n* biquini *m*, bikini *m*.

bile [baɪl] *n* [fluid] bilis *f inv*.

bilingual [baɪ'lɪŋgwəl] *adj* bilingüe.

bill [bɪl] <> *n* - **1.** [statement of cost]: **bill (for)** [meal] cuenta *f* (de); [electricity, phone] factura *f* (de) - **2.** [in parliament] proyecto *m* de ley - **3.** [of show, concert] programa *m* - **4.** *US* [banknote] billete *m* - **5.** [poster]: **'post OR stick no bills'** 'prohibido fijar carteles' - **6.** [beak] pico *m*. <> *vt* [send a bill]: **to bill sb for** mandar la factura a alguien por. ⬥ **Bill** *n UK inf* [police]: **the Bill** la pasma.

billboard ['bɪlbɔ:d] *n* cartelera *f*.

billet ['bɪlɪt] *n* acantonamiento *m*.

billfold ['bɪlfəʊld] *n US* billetera *f*.

billiards ['bɪljədz] *n* billar *m*.

billion ['bɪljən] *num* - **1.** [thousand million] millar *m* de millones; **three billion** tres mil millones - **2.** *UK dated* [million million] billón *m*.

Bill of Rights *n*: **the Bill of Rights** *las diez primeras enmiendas de la Constitución estadounidense.*

bimbo ['bɪmbəʊ] *(pl -s OR -es) n inf pej* niña *f* mona.

bin [bɪn] *n* - **1.** *UK* [for rubbish] cubo *m* de la basura; [for paper] papelera *f* - **2.** [for grain, coal] depósito *m*.

bind [baɪnd] *vt (pt & pp bound)* - **1.** [tie up] atar - **2.** [unite - people] unir - **3.** [bandage] vendar - **4.** [book] encuadernar - **5.** [constrain] obligar.

binder ['baɪndə'] *n* [cover] carpeta *f*.

binding ['baɪndɪŋ] <> *adj* obligatorio(ria). <> *n* [on book] cubierta *f*, tapa *f*.

binge [bɪndʒ] *inf n*: **to go on a binge** irse de juerga.

bingo ['bɪŋgəʊ] *n* bingo *m*.

binoculars [bɪ'nɒkjʊləz] *npl* prismáticos *mpl*, gemelos *mpl*.

biochemistry [,baɪəʊ'kemɪstrɪ] *n* bioquímica *f*.

biodegradable [,baɪəʊdɪ'greɪdəbl] *adj* biodegradable.

bioethics [,baɪəʊ'eθɪks] *n (U)* bioética *f*.

biography [baɪ'ɒgrəfɪ] *n* biografía *f*.

biological [,baɪə'lɒdʒɪkl] *adj* biológico(ca).

biological mother *n* madre *f* biológica.

biology [baɪ'ɒlədʒɪ] *n* biología *f*.

bionic [baɪ'ɒnɪk] *adj* biónico(ca).

bionics [baɪ'ɒnɪks] *n (sing)* biónica *f*.

bioterrorism [,baɪəʊ'terərɪzm] *n* bioterrorismo *m*.

biowarfare [,baɪəʊ'wɔ:feə'] *n* guerra *f* biológica.

bipolar disorder [baɪ'pəʊlədɪs,ɔ:də'] *n* MED trastorno *m* bipolar.

birch [bɜ:tʃ] *n* [tree] abedul *m*.

bird [bɜ:d] *n* - **1.** [animal - large] ave *f*; [- small] pájaro *m* - **2.** *UK inf* [woman] tía *f*.

birdie ['bɜ:dɪ] *n* [in golf] birdie *m*.

bird's-eye view *n* vista *f* panorámica.

bird-watcher [-,wɒtʃə'] *n* observador *m*, -ra *f* de pájaros.

Biro® ['baɪərəʊ] *n* bolígrafo *m*, birome *f R Plata*, lápiz *m* de pasta *Chile*, esfero *m Col*, pluma *f* atómica *Méx*.

birth [bɜ:θ] *n* [gen] nacimiento *m*; [delivery] parto *m*; **by birth** de nacimiento; **to give birth (to)** dar a luz (a).

birth certificate *n* partida *f* de nacimiento.

birth control *n* control *m* de natalidad.

birthday ['bɜ:θdeɪ] *n* cumpleaños *m inv*.

birthmark ['bɜ:θmɑ:k] *n* antojo *m*.

birth mother *n* madre *f* biológica.

birthrate ['bɜ:θreɪt] *n* índice *m* de natalidad.

Biscay ['bɪskɪ] *n*: **the Bay of Biscay** el golfo de Vizcaya.

biscuit ['bɪskɪt] *n* [in UK] galleta *f*; *US* [scone] *masa cocida al horno que se suele comer con salsa de carne.*

bisect [baɪ'sekt] *vt* [gen] dividir en dos; MATHS bisecar.

bishop ['bɪʃəp] *n* - **1.** [in church] obispo *m* - **2.** [in chess] alfil *m*.

bison ['baɪsn] *(pl bison OR -s) n* bisonte *m*.

bit [bɪt] <> *pt* ⬥ **bite**. <> *n* - **1.** [piece] trozo *m*; **a bit of** un poco de; **a bit of advice** un consejo; **a bit of news** una noticia; **to take sthg to bits** desmontar algo - **2.** [amount]: **a bit of** un poco de; **a bit of shopping** algunas compras; **quite a bit of** bastante - **3.** [short time]: **(for) a bit** un rato - **4.** [of drill] broca *f* - **5.** [of bridle] bocado *m*, freno *m* - **6.** COMPUT bit *m*. ⬥ **a bit** *adv* un poco; **a bit easier** un poco más fácil. ⬥ **bit by bit** *adv* poco a poco.

bitch [bɪtʃ] <> *n* - **1.** [female dog] perra *f* - **2.** *v inf pej* [unpleasant woman] bruja *f*. <> *vi inf* [talk unpleasantly]: **to bitch about** poner a parir a.

bitchy ['bɪtʃɪ] *adj inf* malicioso(sa).

bite [baɪt] <> *n* - **1.** [by dog, person] mordisco *m*; [by insect, snake] picotazo *m* - **2.** *inf* [food]: **to have a bite (to eat)** comer algo

- 3. [wound - from dog] mordedura *f*; [- from insect, snake] picadura *f*. ⬦ *vt* (*pt* bit, *pp* bitten) **- 1.** [subj: person, animal] morder **- 2.** [subj: insect, snake] picar. ⬦ *vi* (*pt* bit, *pp* bitten) **- 1.** [animal, person]**: to bite (into sthg)** morder (algo) **- 2.** [insect, snake] picar **- 3.** [grip] agarrar.

biting ['baɪtɪŋ] *adj* **- 1.** [very cold] gélido(da), cortante **- 2.** [caustic] mordaz.

bitten ['bɪtn] *pp* ▷ **bite**.

bitter ['bɪtər] ⬦ *adj* **- 1.** [coffee, chocolate] amargo(ga) **- 2.** [icy] gélido(da) **- 3.** [causing pain] amargo(ga) **- 4.** [acrimonious] enconado(da) **- 5.** [resentful] amargado(da). ⬦ *n UK* [beer] *tipo de cerveza amarga*.

bitter lemon *n* bíter *m* de limón.

bitterness ['bɪtənɪs] *n* **- 1.** [of taste] amargor *m* **- 2.** [of wind, weather] gelidez *f* **- 3.** [resentment] amargura *f*.

bizarre [bɪ'zɑːr] *adj* [behaviour, appearance] extravagante; [machine, remark] singular, extraordinario(ria).

blab [blæb] *vi inf* irse de la lengua.

black [blæk] ⬦ *adj* **- 1.** [gen] negro(gra); **black and blue** amoratado(da); **black and white** [films, photos] en blanco y negro; [clearcut] extremadamente nítido(da) **- 2.** [coffee] solo; [milk] sin leche **- 3.** [angry] furioso(sa). ⬦ *n* **- 1.** [colour] negro *m* **- 2.** [person] negro *m*, -gra *f*

▶▶▶ **in black and white** [in writing] por escrito; **to be in the black** tener saldo positivo. ⬦ *vt UK* [boycott] boicotear. ◈ **black out** *vi* desmayarse.

blackberry ['blækbərɪ] *n* **- 1.** [fruit] mora *f* **- 2.** [bush] zarzamora *f*.

blackbird ['blækbɜːd] *n* mirlo *m*.

blackboard ['blækbɔːd] *n* pizarra *f*, pizarrón *m Amér*.

blackcurrant [,blæk'kʌrənt] *n* grosella *f* negra, casis *m*.

blacken ['blækn] *vt* **- 1.** [make dark] ennegrecer **- 2.** [tarnish] manchar.

black eye *n* ojo *m* morado.

blackhead ['blækhed] *n* barrillo *m*.

black ice *n* hielo transparente en las carreteras.

blackleg ['blækleg] *n pej* esquirol *m*.

blacklist ['blæklɪst] *n* lista *f* negra.

blackmail ['blækmeɪl] *lit & fig* ⬦ *n* chantaje *m*. ⬦ *vt lit & fig* chantajear.

black market *n* mercado *m* negro.

blackout ['blækaʊt] *n* **- 1.** [in wartime, power cut] apagón *m* **- 2.** [of news] censura *f* **- 3.** [fainting fit] desmayo *m*.

black pudding *n UK* morcilla *f*.

Black Sea *n*: **the Black Sea** el mar Negro.

black sheep *n* oveja *f* negra.

blacksmith ['blæksmɪθ] *n* herrero *m*.

black spot *n* punto *m* negro.

bladder ['blædər] *n* ANAT vejiga *f*.

blade [bleɪd] *n* **- 1.** [of knife, saw] hoja *f* **- 2.** [of propeller] aleta *f*, paleta *f* **- 3.** [of grass] brizna *f*, hoja *f*.

blame [bleɪm] ⬦ *n* culpa *f*; **to take the blame for** hacerse responsable de; **to be to blame for** ser el culpable de. ⬦ *vt* echar la culpa a, culpar.

bland [blænd] *adj* soso(sa).

blank [blæŋk] ⬦ *adj* **- 1.** [sheet of paper] en blanco; [wall] liso(sa) **- 2.** [cassette] virgen **- 3.** *fig* [look] vacío(a). ⬦ *n* **- 1.** [empty space] espacio *m* en blanco **- 2.** MIL [cartridge] cartucho *m* de fogueo.

blank cheque *n* cheque *m* en blanco; *fig* carta *f* blanca.

blanket ['blæŋkɪt] *n* **- 1.** [bed cover] manta *f*, frazada *f Amér* **- 2.** [layer] manto *m*.

blare [bleər] *vi* resonar, sonar.

blasé [*UK* 'blɑːzeɪ, *US* ,blɑː'zeɪ] *adj*: **to be blasé about** estar de vuelta de.

blasphemy ['blæsfəmɪ] *n* blasfemia *f*.

blast [blɑːst] ⬦ *n* **- 1.** [of bomb] explosión *f* **- 2.** [of wind] ráfaga *f*; **we had a blast** *US* lo pasamos genial. ⬦ *vt* [hole, tunnel] perforar *(con explosivos)*. ⬦ *excl UK inf* ¡maldita sea! ◈ **(at) full blast** *adv* a todo trapo.

blasted ['blɑːstɪd] *adj inf* maldito(ta).

blast-off *n* despegue *m*.

blatant ['bleɪtənt] *adj* descarado(da).

blaze [bleɪz] ⬦ *n* **- 1.** [fire] incendio *m* **- 2.** *fig* [of colour] explosión *f*; [of light] resplandor *m*; **a blaze of publicity** una ola de publicidad. ⬦ *vi lit & fig* arder.

blazer ['bleɪzər] *n* chaqueta de sport generalmente con la insignia de un equipo, colegio etc.

bleach [bliːtʃ] ⬦ *n* lejía *f*. ⬦ *vt* [hair] blanquear; [clothes] desteñir.

bleached [bliːtʃt] *adj* [hair] teñido(da) de rubio; [jeans] desteñido(da).

bleachers ['bliːtʃəz] *npl US* SPORT graderío *m* descubierto.

bleak [bliːk] *adj* **- 1.** [future] negro(gra) **- 2.** [place, person, face] sombrío(a) **- 3.** [weather] desapacible.

bleary-eyed [,blɪərɪ'aɪd] *adj* con los ojos nublados.

bleat [bliːt] *vi* **- 1.** [sheep] balar **- 2.** *fig* [person] quejarse.

bleed [bliːd] (*pt & pp* bled) ⬦ *vt* [radiator etc] purgar. ⬦ *vi* sangrar.

bleeper ['bliːpər] *n* busca *m*.

blemish ['blemɪʃ] *n* [mark] señal *f*, marca *f*; *fig* mancha *f*.

blend [blend] ◇ n - **1.** [mix] mezcla f - **2.** COMPUT degradado m. ◇ vt: **to blend (sth with sthg)** mezclar (algo con algo). ◇ vi **to blend (with) combinarse (con).**

blender ['blendər] n licuadora f.

bless [bles] (pt & pp -ed OR blest) vt RELIG bendecir

▶▶▶ **bless you!** [after sneezing] ¡jesús!; [thank you] ¡gracias!

blessing ['blesɪŋ] n - **1.** RELIG bendición f - **2.** fig [good wishes] aprobación f.

blest [blest] pt & pp ▭▷ **bless**.

blew [blu:] pt ▭▷ **blow**.

blight [blaɪt] vt [hopes, prospects] malograr, arruinar.

blimey ['blaɪmɪ] excl UK inf ¡ostias!

blind [blaɪnd] ◇ adj [unsighted, irrational] ciego(ga); **a blind man** un ciego; **to go blind** quedarse ciego. ◇ n [for window] persiana f. ◇ npl: **the blind** los ciegos. ◇ vt [permanently] dejar ciego(ga); [temporarily] cegar; **to blind sb to sthg** fig no dejar a alguien ver algo.

blind alley n lit & fig callejón m sin salida.

blind corner n curva f sin visibilidad.

blind date n cita f a ciegas.

blinders ['blaɪndəz] npl US anteojeras fpl.

blindfold ['blaɪndfəʊld] ◇ adv con los ojos vendados. ◇ n venda f. ◇ vt vendar los ojos a.

blindly ['blaɪndlɪ] adv - **1.** [unable to see] a ciegas - **2.** fig [guess] a boleo; [accept] ciegamente.

blindness ['blaɪndnɪs] n lit & fig: **blindness (to)** ceguera f (ante).

blind spot n - **1.** [when driving] ángulo m muerto - **2.** fig [inability to understand] punto m débil.

blink [blɪŋk] ◇ vt - **1.** [eyes]: **to blink one's eyes** parpadear - **2.** US AUT: **to blink one's lights** dar las luces (intermitentemente). ◇ vi parpadear.

blinkers ['blɪŋkəz] npl UK anteojeras fpl.

bliss [blɪs] n gloria f, dicha f.

blissful ['blɪsfʊl] adj dichoso(sa), feliz.

blister ['blɪstər] ◇ n ampolla f. ◇ vi ampollarse.

blithely ['blaɪðlɪ] adv alegremente.

blitz [blɪts] n MIL bombardeo m aéreo.

blizzard ['blɪzəd] n ventisca f (de nieve).

bloated ['bləʊtɪd] adj hinchado(da).

blob [blɒb] n - **1.** [drop] gota f - **2.** [indistinct shape] bulto m borroso.

bloc [blɒk] n bloque m.

block [blɒk] ◇ n - **1.** [gen] bloque m - **2.** US [of buildings] manzana f - **3.** [obstruction - physical or mental] bloqueo m. ◇ vt - **1.** [road] cortar; [pipe] obstruir; [sink, toilet] atascar; **my nose is blocked** tengo la nariz tapada - **2.** [view] ta-

par - **3.** [prevent] bloquear, obstaculizar - **4.** COMPUT: **to block a stretch of text** seleccionar un bloque de texto.

blockade [blɒ'keɪd] ◇ n bloqueo m. ◇ vt bloquear.

blockage ['blɒkɪdʒ] n obstrucción f.

blockbuster ['blɒkbʌstər] n inf [book] (gran) éxito m editorial; [film] (gran) éxito de taquilla.

block capitals npl mayúsculas fpl (de imprenta).

block letters npl mayúsculas fpl (de imprenta).

bloke [bləʊk] n UK inf tío m, tipo m.

blond [blɒnd] adj rubio(bia).

blonde [blɒnd] ◇ adj rubia, catira Col & Ven. ◇ n [woman] rubia f.

blood [blʌd] n sangre f; **in cold blood** a sangre fría; **new** OR **fresh blood** savia f nueva.

bloodbath (['blʌdbɑːθ], pl [-bɑːðz]) n matanza f, carnicería f.

blood cell n glóbulo m.

blood donor n donante mf de sangre.

blood group n grupo m sanguíneo.

bloodhound ['blʌdhaʊnd] n sabueso m.

blood poisoning n septicemia f.

blood pressure n tensión f arterial; **to have high/low blood pressure** tener la tensión alta/baja.

bloodshed ['blʌdʃed] n derramamiento m de sangre.

bloodshot ['blʌdʃɒt] adj inyectado(da) (de sangre).

bloodstream ['blʌdstriːm] n flujo m sanguíneo.

blood test n análisis m inv de sangre.

bloodthirsty ['blʌdˌθɜːstɪ] adj sanguinario(ria).

blood transfusion n transfusión f de sangre.

bloody ['blʌdɪ] ◇ adj - **1.** [war, conflict] sangriento(ta) - **2.** [face, hands] ensangrentado(da) - **3.** UK v inf maldito(ta), pinche Méx; **bloody hell!** ¡hostia! ◇ adv UK v inf: **he's bloody useless** es un puto inútil; **it's bloody brilliant** es de puta madre.

bloody-minded [-'maɪndɪd] adj UK inf puñetero(ra).

bloom [bluːm] ◇ n flor f; **in bloom** en flor. ◇ vi florecer.

blooming ['bluːmɪŋ] ◇ adj UK inf [to show annoyance] condenado(da). ◇ adv UK inf: **he's blooming useless** es un inútil del copón.

blossom ['blɒsəm] ◇ n flor f; **in blossom** en flor. ◇ vi lit & fig florecer.

blot [blɒt] ⬦ n [of ink] borrón m; fig mancha f. ⬦ vt - 1. [paper] emborronar - 2. [ink] secar. ◆ **blot out** vt sep [gen] cubrir, ocultar; [memories] borrar.

blotchy ['blɒtʃi] adj lleno(na) de manchas.

blotting paper ['blɒtɪŋ-] n (U) papel m secante.

blouse [blaʊz] n blusa f.

blow [bləʊ] ⬦ vi (pt blew, pp blown) - 1. [gen] soplar - 2. [in wind] salir volando, volar - 3. [fuse] fundirse. ⬦ vt (pt blew, pp blown) - 1. [subj: wind] hacer volar - 2. [whistle, horn] tocar, hacer sonar - 3. [bubbles] hacer - 4. [kiss] mandar - 5. [fuse] fundir - 6. [clear]: **to blow one's nose** sonarse la nariz - 7. inf [money] ventilarse; inf [chance] echar a perder. ⬦ n [hit, shock] golpe m. ◆ **blow out** ⬦ vt sep apagar. ⬦ vi - 1. [candle] apagarse - 2. [tyre] reventar. ◆ **blow over** vi - 1. [storm] amainar - 2. [scandal] calmarse. ◆ **blow up** ⬦ vt sep - 1. [inflate] inflar - 2. [destroy] volar - 3. [photograph] ampliar. ⬦ vi saltar por los aires.

blow-dry n secado m (con secador).

blowlamp UK ['bləʊlæmp], **blowtorch** esp US ['bləʊtɔ:tʃ] n soplete m.

blown [bləʊn] pp ⬌ **blow**.

blowout ['bləʊaʊt] n [of tyre] pinchazo m, reventón m.

blowtorch esp US = **blowlamp**.

blubber ['blʌbər] vi pej lloriquear.

bludgeon ['blʌdʒən] vt apalear.

blue [blu:] ⬦ adj - 1. [colour] azul - 2. inf [sad] triste - 3. [pornographic - film] equis (inv), porno; [- joke] verde. ⬦ n azul m; **out of the blue** en el momento menos pensado. ◆ **blues** npl: **the blues** MÚS el blues; inf [sad feeling] la depre.

bluebell ['blu:bel] n campanilla f.

blueberry ['blu:bəri] n arándano m.

bluebottle ['blu:ˌbɒtl] n moscardón m, moscón m.

blue cheese n queso m azul.

blue-collar adj: **blue-collar worker** obrero m, -ra f.

blue jeans npl US vaqueros mpl, tejanos mpl.

blueprint ['blu:prɪnt] n - 1. CONSTR cianotipo m - 2. fig [description] proyecto m.

bluff [blʌf] ⬦ adj brusco(ca). ⬦ n [deception] farol m. ⬦ vi tirarse un farol.

blunder ['blʌndər] ⬦ n metedura f de pata. ⬦ vi - 1. [make mistake] meter la pata - 2. [move clumsily] ir tropezando; **to blunder into sthg** tropezar con algo.

blunt [blʌnt] adj - 1. [knife, pencil] desafilado(da) - 2. [point, edge] romo(ma) - 3. [forthright] directo(ta), franco(ca).

blur [blɜ:r] ⬦ n imagen f borrosa. ⬦ vt - 1. [vision] nublar - 2. [distinction] desdibujar.

blurb [blɜ:b] n inf texto publicitario en la cubierta o solapa de un libro.

blurt [blɜ:t] ◆ **blurt out** vt sep espetar, decir de repente.

blush [blʌʃ] ⬦ n rubor m. ⬦ vi ruborizarse.

blusher ['blʌʃər] n colorete m.

blustery ['blʌstəri] adj borrascoso(sa).

BMX (abbr of **bicycle motorcross**) n ciclocross m.

BO n (abbr of **body odour**), olor a sudor.

boar [bɔ:r] n - 1. [male pig] verraco m - 2. [wild pig] jabalí m.

board [bɔ:d] ⬦ n - 1. [plank] tabla f - 2. [for notices] tablón m - 3. [for games] tablero m - 4. [blackboard] pizarra f - 5. COMPUT placa f - 6. [of company]: **board (of directors)** consejo m de administración - 7. [committee] comité m, junta f - 8. UK [at hotel, guesthouse]: **board and lodging** comida y habitación; **full board** pensión completa; **half board** media pensión - 9.: **on board** [ship, plane] a bordo; [bus, train] dentro ➤ **above board** en regla. ⬦ vt [ship, plane] embarcar en; [train, bus] subirse a.

boarder ['bɔ:dər] n - 1. [lodger] huésped mf - 2. [at school] interno m, -na f.

boarding card ['bɔ:dɪŋ-] n tarjeta f de embarque.

boardinghouse (['bɔ:dɪŋhaʊs], pl [-haʊzɪz]) n casa f de huéspedes.

boarding school ['bɔ:dɪŋ-] n internado m.

Board of Trade n UK: **the Board of Trade** ≃ el Ministerio de Comercio.

boardroom ['bɔ:drʊm] n sala f de juntas.

boast [bəʊst] ⬦ vt disfrutar de. ⬦ vi: **to boast (about)** alardear OR jactarse (de), compadrear (de) Amér.

boastful ['bəʊstfʊl] adj fanfarrón(ona).

boat [bəʊt] n [large] barco m; [small] barca f; **by boat** en barco.

boater ['bəʊtər] n [hat] canotié m.

boatswain ['bəʊsn], **bosun** n NÁUT contramaestre m.

bob [bɒb] ⬦ n - 1. [hairstyle] corte m de chico - 2. UK inf dated [shilling] chelín m - 3. = **bobsleigh**. ⬦ vi [boat] balancearse.

bobbin ['bɒbɪn] n bobina f.

bobby ['bɒbi] n UK inf poli m.

bobsleigh ['bɒbsleɪ], **bob** n bobsleigh m.

bode [bəʊd] vi liter: **to bode ill/well for** traer malos/buenos presagios para.

bodily ['bɒdɪlɪ] ⬦ adj corporal. ⬦ adv: **to lift/move sb bodily** levantar/mover a alguien por la fuerza.

body ['bɒdɪ] n - 1. [gen] cuerpo m - 2. [corpse] cadáver m - 3. [organization] entidad f; **a body of thought/opinion** una corriente de pensamiento/opinión - 4. [of car] carrocería f, [of plane] fuselaje m - 5. [item of clothing] body m.

body building n culturismo m.

bodyguard ['bɒdɪgɑːd] n guardaespaldas mf inv, guarura m Méx.

body language n lenguaje m corporal.

body odour n olor m corporal.

body piercing n piercing m.

bodywork ['bɒdɪwɜːk] n carrocería f.

bog [bɒg] n - 1. [marsh] cenagal m - 2. UK v inf [toilet] baño m.

bogged down [ˌbɒgd-] adj - 1. [in details, work]: **bogged down (in)** empantanado(da) (en) - 2. [in mud, snow]: **bogged down in** atascado(da) en.

boggle ['bɒgl] vi: **the mind boggles!** ¡es increíble!

bogus ['bəʊgəs] adj falso(sa).

boil [bɔɪl] <> n - 1. MED pústula f - 2. [boiling point]: **to bring sthg to the boil** hacer que algo hierva; **to come to the boil** romper a hervir. <> vt - 1. [water] hervir; **to boil the kettle** poner el agua a hervir - 2. [food] cocer. <> vi hervir. ◆ **boil down to** vt insep reducirse a. ◆ **boil over** vi fig [feelings] desbordarse.

boiled [bɔɪld] adj - 1. [gen] cocido(da); **boiled egg** [hard-boiled] huevo m duro; [soft-boiled] huevo m pasado por agua; **boiled sweets** UK caramelos mpl (duros).

boiler ['bɔɪləʳ] n caldera f.

boiler room n sala f de calderas.

boiler suit n UK mono m.

boiling ['bɔɪlɪŋ] adj inf [hot]: **I'm boiling** estoy asado(da) de calor; **it's boiling** hace un calor de muerte.

boiling point n punto m de ebullición.

boisterous ['bɔɪstərəs] adj ruidoso(sa), alborotador(ra).

bold [bəʊld] adj - 1. [brave, daring] audaz - 2. [lines, design] marcado(da) - 3. [colour] vivo(va) - 4. TYPO: **bold type** OR **print** negrita f.

Bolivia [bə'lɪvɪə] n Bolivia.

Bolivian [bə'lɪvɪən] <> adj boliviano(na). <> n boliviano m, -na f.

bollard ['bɒlɑːd] n [on road] poste m.

bollocks ['bɒləks] UK v inf npl cojones mpl.

bolster ['bəʊlstəʳ] vt reforzar. ◆ **bolster up** vt insep reforzar.

bolt [bəʊlt] <> n - 1. [on door, window] cerrojo m - 2. [type of screw] perno m. <> adv: **bolt upright** muy derecho(cha). <> vt - 1. [fasten together] atornillar - 2. [door, window] echar el cerrojo a - 3. [food] tragarse. <> vi salir disparado(da).

bomb [bɒm] <> n - 1. bomba f - 2. US inf [failure] desastre m. <> vt bombardear. <> vi US inf [fail] fracasar estrepitosamente.

bombard [bɒm'bɑːd] vt fig & MIL. to bombard (with) bombardear (a).

bombastic [bɒm'bæstɪk] adj grandilocuente, rimbombante.

bomb disposal squad n equipo m de artificieros.

bomber ['bɒməʳ] n - 1. [plane] bombardero m - 2. [person] terrorista mf que pone bombas.

bombing ['bɒmɪŋ] n bombardeo m.

bombshell ['bɒmʃel] n fig bombazo m; **a blonde bombshell** inf una rubia explosiva.

bona fide ['bəʊnə'faɪdɪ] adj auténtico(ca).

bond [bɒnd] <> n - 1. [between people] lazo m, vínculo m - 2. [binding promise] compromiso m - 3. FIN bono m. <> vt [glue] adherir; fig [people] unir.

bone [bəʊn] <> n [gen] hueso m; [of fish] raspa f, espina f; **to make no bones about doing sthg** no tener ningún reparo en hacer algo. <> vt [fish] quitar las espinas a; [meat] deshuesar.

bone-dry adj completamente seco(ca).

bone-idle adj haragán(ana), gandul(la).

bonfire ['bɒnfaɪəʳ] n hoguera f.

Bonn [bɒn] n Bonn.

bonnet ['bɒnɪt] n - 1. UK [of car] capó m - 2. [hat] toca f.

bonny ['bɒnɪ] adj Scotland majo(ja).

bonus ['bəʊnəs] (pl -es) n [extra money] prima f; [for increased productivity] plus m; fig beneficio m adicional.

bony ['bəʊnɪ] adj - 1. [person, hand] huesudo(da) - 2. [meat] lleno(na) de huesos; [fish] espinoso(sa).

boo [buː] <> excl ¡bu! <> n (pl -s) abucheo m. <> vt & vi abuchear.

boob [buːb] n inf [mistake] metedura f de pata. ◆ **boobs** npl UK v inf [woman's breasts] tetas fpl.

booby trap ['buːbɪ-] n [bomb] bomba f camuflada.

book [bʊk] <> n - 1. [for reading] libro m; **to throw the book at sb** castigar duramente a alguien - 2. [of stamps] librillo m; [of tickets, cheques] talonario m; [of matches] caja f (de solapa). <> vt - 1. [reserve] reservar; **to be fully booked** estar completo - 2. inf [subj: police] multar - 3. UK FTBL mostrar una tarjeta amarilla a. <> vi hacer reserva. ◆ **books** npl COMM libros mpl; **to be in sb's good/bad books** estar a bien/a mal con alguien. ◆ **book up** vt sep: **to be booked up** estar completo.

bookcase ['bʊkkeɪs] n estantería f.

bookie ['bʊkɪ] n inf corredor m, -ra f de apuestas.

booking ['bʊkɪŋ] n - 1. esp UK [reservation] reserva f - 2. UK FTBL tarjeta f amarilla.

booking office n esp UK taquilla f.

bookkeeping ['bʊk,kiːpɪŋ] n contabilidad f.

booklet ['bʊklɪt] n folleto m.

bookmaker ['bʊk,meɪkər] n corredor m, -ra f de apuestas.

bookmark ['bʊkmɑːk] n - 1. separador m - 2. COMPUT marcador m.

bookseller ['bʊk,selər] n librero m, -ra f.

bookshelf ['bʊkʃelf] (pl -shelves [-ʃelvz]) n [shelf] estante m; [bookcase] estantería f, librero m Chile & Méx.

bookshop UK ['bʊkʃɒp], **bookstore** US ['bʊkstɔːr] n librería f.

book token n esp UK vale m para comprar libros.

boom [buːm] ◇ n - 1. [loud noise] estampido m - 2. [increase] auge m, boom m - 3. [for TV camera, microphone] jirafa f. ◇ vi - 1. [make noise] tronar - 2. ECON estar en auge.

boon [buːn] n gran ayuda f.

boost [buːst] ◇ n - 1. [in profits, production] incremento m - 2. [to popularity, spirits] empujón m. ◇ vt - 1. [increase] incrementar - 2. [improve] levantar.

booster ['buːstər] n MED inyección f de refuerzo.

boot [buːt] ◇ n - 1. [item of footwear] bota f; [ankle boot] botín m - 2. UK [of car] maletero m, cajuela f Méx, baúl m Col & R Plata, maletera f Perú. ◇ vt - 1. inf [kick] dar una patada a - 2. COMPUT arrancar. ▸ **to boot** adv además. ▸ **boot out** vt sep inf echar, poner (de patitas) en la calle. ▸ **boot up** vt sep COMPUT arrancar.

booth [buːð] n - 1. [at fair] puesto m - 2. [for phoning, voting] cabina f.

booty ['buːtɪ] n - 1. botín m - 2. US inf [sexual intercourse]: **to get some booty** mojar el churro Esp OR bizcocho R Plata, echarse un caldito Méx.

booze [buːz] inf ◇ n (U) priva f. ◇ vi privar, empinar el codo.

bop [bɒp] inf ◇ n - 1. [disco] disco f - 2. [dance] baile m. ◇ vi bailar.

border ['bɔːdər] ◇ n - 1. [between countries] frontera f - 2. [edge] borde m - 3. [in garden] arriate m. ◇ vt - 1. [country] limitar con - 2. [edge] bordear. ▸ **border on** vt insep rayar en.

borderline ['bɔːdəlaɪn] ◇ adj: **a borderline case** un caso dudoso. ◇ n fig límite m.

bore [bɔːr] ◇ pt ▷ **bear**. ◇ n - 1. pej [person] pelmazo m, -za f; [situation, event] rollo m, lata f - 2. [of gun] calibre m. ◇ vt

- 1. [not interest] aburrir; **to bore sb stiff** OR **to tears** OR **to death** aburrir a alguien un montón - 2. [drill] horadar.

bored [bɔːd] adj aburrido(da); **to be bored stiff** OR **to tears** OR **to death** aburrirse como una ostra.

boredom ['bɔːdəm] n aburrimiento m.

boring ['bɔːrɪŋ] adj aburrido(da).

born [bɔːn] adj - 1. [given life] nacido(da); **to be born** nacer - 2. [natural] nato(ta).

borne [bɔːn] pp ▷ **bear**.

borough ['bʌrə] n [area of town] distrito m; [town] municipio m.

borrow ['bɒrəʊ] vt: **to borrow sthg from sb** coger OR tomar algo prestado a alguien; **can I borrow your bike?** ¿me prestas tu bici?

Bosnia ['bɒznɪə] n Bosnia.

Bosnia-Herzegovina [-,hɜːtsəgəˈviːnə] n Bosnia-Hercegovina.

Bosnian ['bɒznɪən] ◇ adj bosnio(nia). ◇ n bosnio m, -nia f.

bosom ['bʊzəm] n [of woman] busto m, pecho m.

boss [bɒs] ◇ n jefe m, -fa f. ◇ vt pej mangonear, dar órdenes a. ▸ **boss about, boss around** vt sep pej mangonear, dar órdenes a.

bossy ['bɒsɪ] adj mandón(ona).

bosun ['bəʊsn] = **boatswain**.

botany ['bɒtənɪ] n botánica f.

botch [bɒtʃ] ▸ **botch up** vt sep inf estropear, hacer chapuceramente.

both [bəʊθ] ◇ adj los dos, las dos, ambos(bas). ◇ pron: **both (of them)** los dos, las dos f, ambos mpl, -bas fpl; **both of us are coming** vamos los dos. ◇ adv: **she is both pretty and intelligent** es guapa e inteligente.

bother ['bɒðər] ◇ vt - 1. [worry] preocupar; [irritate] fastidiar; **I/she can't be bothered to do it** no tengo/tiene ganas de hacerlo - 2. [pester] molestar. ◇ vi: **to bother (doing** OR **to do sthg)** molestarse (en hacer algo); **to bother about** preocuparse por. ◇ n (U) - 1. [inconvenience] problemas mpl - 2. [pest, nuisance] molestia f.

bottle ['bɒtl] ◇ n - 1. [gen] botella f - 2. [of shampoo, medicine - plastic] bote m; [- glass] frasco m - 3. [for baby] biberón m - 4. (U) UK inf [courage] agallas fpl. ◇ vt [wine] embotellar. ▸ **bottle up** vt sep reprimir.

bottle bank n contenedor m de vidrio.

bottleneck ['bɒtlnek] n - 1. [in traffic] embotellamiento m - 2. [in production] atasco m.

bottle-opener n abrebotellas m inv.

bottom ['bɒtəm] ◇ adj - 1. [lowest] más bajo(ja), de abajo del todo - 2. [least successful] peor. ◇ n - 1. [lowest part - of glass, bottle] culo m; [- of bag, mine, sea] fondo m; [- of ladder,

hill] pie *m*; [- of page, list] final *m* - **2**. [farthest
point] final *m*, fondo *m* - **3**. [of class etc] par-
t*i*. *f* mán baja **4**. [buttock] trasero *m* **5**. [root]:
to get to the bottom of llegar al fondo de.
◆ **bottom out** *vi* tocar fondo.

bottom line *n fig:* **the bottom line is...** a fin
de cuentas...

bough [baʊ] *n* rama *f*.

bought [bɔːt] *pt* & *pp* ▷ **buy**.

boulder ['bəʊldər] *n* roca *f* grande y de forma redonda.

bounce [baʊns] ◇ *vi* - **1**. [gen] rebotar
- **2**. [person]: **to bounce (on sthg)** dar botes (en
algo) - **3**. [cheque] ser rechazado(da) por el
banco. ◇ *vt* botar. ◇ *n* bote *m*.

bouncer ['baʊnsər] *n inf* matón *m*, gorila *m*
(de un local).

bound [baʊnd] ◇ *pt* & *pp* ▷ **bind**.
◇ *adj* - **1**. [certain]: **it's bound to happen** seguro que va a pasar - **2**. [obliged]: **bound (by
sthg/to do sthg)** obligado(da) (por algo/a hacer algo); **I'm bound to say** OR **admit** tengo
que decir OR admitir - **3**. [for place]: **to be
bound for** ir rumbo a. ◇ *n* salto *m*. ◇ *vi* ir
dando saltos. ◆ **bounds** *npl* [limits] lími-
tes *mpl*; **out of bounds** (en) zona prohibida.

boundary ['baʊndərɪ] *n* [gen] límite *m*;
[between countries] frontera *f*.

bouquet [bəʊˈkeɪ] *n* [of flowers] ramo *m*.

bourbon ['bɜːbən] *n* bourbon *m*, whisky *m*
americano.

bourgeois ['bɔːʒwɑː] *adj* burgués(esa).

bout [baʊt] *n* - **1**. [attack] ataque *m*, acceso *m*
- **2**. [session] racha *f* - **3**. [boxing match] combate *m*.

bow¹ [baʊ] ◇ *n* - **1**. [act of bowing] reverencia *f* - **2**. [of ship] proa *f*. ◇ *vt* inclinar. ◇ *vi*
- **1**. [make a bow] inclinarse - **2**. [defer]: **to bow
to sthg** ceder OR doblegarse ante algo.

bow² [bəʊ] *n* - **1**. [weapon, for musical instru-
ment] arco *m* - **2**. [knot] lazo *m*.

bowels ['baʊəlz] *npl lit* & *fig* entrañas *fpl*.

bowl [bəʊl] ◇ *n* [gen] cuenco *m*, bol *m*; [for
soup] plato *m*; [for washing clothes] barreño *m*,
balde *m*. ◇ *vi* lanzar la bola. ◆ **bowls** *n* (U)
*juego similar a la petanca que se juega sobre
césped.* ◆ **bowl over** *vt sep* - **1**. [knock over]
atropellar - **2**. *fig* [surprise, impress] dejar atóni-
to(ta).

bow-legged [ˌbəʊˈlegɪd] *adj* de piernas arqueadas, estevado(da).

bowler ['bəʊlər] *n* - **1**. CRICKET lanzador *m* - **2**.:
bowler (hat) bombín *m*, sombrero *m* hongo.

bowling ['bəʊlɪŋ] *n* (U) bolos *mpl*.

bowling alley *n* - **1**. [building] bolera *f* - **2**. [al-
ley] calle *f*.

bowling green *n* campo de césped para jugar a los 'bowls'.

bow tie [bəʊ-] *n* pajarita *f*.

box [bɒks] ◇ *n* - **1**. [container, boxful] caja *f*;
[for jewels] estuche *m* - **2**. THEAT palco *m* - **3**. *UK
inf* [television]: **the box** la tele - **4**. [in printed
questionnaire etc] casilla *f*. ◇ *vt* [put in boxes]
encajonar. ◇ *vi* boxear.

boxer ['bɒksər] *n* - **1**. [fighter] boxeador *m*,
púgil *m* - **2**. [dog] boxer *m*.

boxer shorts *npl* calzoncillos *mpl*, boxers *mpl*.

boxing ['bɒksɪŋ] *n* boxeo *m*.

Boxing Day *n fiesta nacional en Inglaterra y
Gales el 26 de diciembre (salvo domingos) en
que tradicionalmente se da el aguinaldo.*

boxing glove *n* guante *m* de boxeo, guante *m* de box *Amér C* & *Méx*.

box office *n* taquilla *f*, boletería *f Amér*.

boxroom ['bɒksrʊm] *n UK* trastero *m*.

boy [bɔɪ] ◇ *n* - **1**. [male child] chico *m*, niño *m*, pibe *m R Plata* - **2**. *inf* [young man] chaval *m*. ◇ *excl*: **(oh) boy!** *US inf* ¡jolín!, ¡vaya,
vaya!

boycott ['bɔɪkɒt] ◇ *n* boicot *m*. ◇ *vt* boicotear.

boyfriend ['bɔɪfrend] *n* novio *m*.

boyish ['bɔɪɪʃ] *adj* [man] juvenil.

bra [brɑː] *n* sujetador *m*, sostén *m*.

brace [breɪs] ◇ *n* - **1**. [on teeth] aparato *m*
corrector - **2**. [pair] par *m*. ◇ *vt* [steady] tensar;
to brace o.s. (for) *lit* & *fig* prepararse (para).
◆ **braces** *npl UK* tirantes *mpl*, tiradores *mpl
Bol* & *R Plata*.

bracelet ['breɪslɪt] *n* brazalete *m*, pulsera *f*.

bracing ['breɪsɪŋ] *adj* tonificante.

bracken ['brækn] *n* helechos *mpl*.

bracket ['brækɪt] ◇ *n* - **1**. [support] soporte *m*, palomilla *f* - **2**. [parenthesis - round] paréntesis *m inv*; [- square] corchete *m*; **in brackets**
entre paréntesis - **3**. [group] sector *m*, banda *f*.
◇ *vt* [enclose in brackets] poner entre paréntesis.

brag [bræg] *vi* fanfarronear, jactarse.

braid [breɪd] ◇ *n* - **1**. [on uniform] galón *m*
- **2**. [hairstyle] trenza *f*. ◇ *vt* trenzar.

brain [breɪn] *n lit* & *fig* cerebro *m*. ◆ **brains**
npl cerebro *m*, seso *m*.

brainchild ['breɪntʃaɪld] *n inf* invención *f*,
idea *f*.

brainwash ['breɪnwɒʃ] *vt* lavar el cerebro a.

brainwave ['breɪnweɪv] *n* idea *f* genial.

brainy ['breɪnɪ] *adj inf* listo(ta).

brake [breɪk] ◇ *n lit* & *fig* freno *m*. ◇ *vi*
frenar.

brake light *n* luz *f* de freno.

bramble ['bræmbl] *n* [bush] zarza *f*, zarzamora *f*; [fruit] mora *f*.

bran [bræn] *n* salvado *m*.

branch [brɑ:ntʃ] <> n - 1. [of tree, subject] rama f - 2. [of river] afluente m; [of railway] ramal m - 3. [of company, bank] sucursal f. <> vi bifurcarse. ◆ **branch out** vi [person] ampliar horizontes; [firm] expandirse, diversificarse.

brand [brænd] <> n - 1. [of product] marca f - 2. fig [type] tipo m, estilo m - 3. [mark] hierro m. <> vt - 1. [cattle] marcar (con hierro) - 2. fig [classify]: **to brand sb (as sthg)** tildar a alguien (de algo).

brandish ['brændɪʃ] vt [weapon] blandir; [letter etc] agitar.

brand name n marca f.

brand-new adj flamante.

brandy ['brændɪ] n coñac m.

brash [bræʃ] adj pej enérgico e insolente.

brass [brɑ:s] n - 1. [metal] latón m - 2. MUS: **the brass** el metal.

brass band n banda f de metal.

brassiere [UK 'bræsɪə', US brə'zɪr] n sostén m, sujetador m.

brat [bræt] n inf pej mocoso m, -sa f.

bravado [brə'vɑ:dəʊ] n bravuconería f.

brave [breɪv] <> adj valiente. <> vt [weather, storm] desafiar; [sb's anger] hacer frente a.

bravery ['breɪvərɪ] n valentía f.

brawl [brɔ:l] n gresca f, reyerta f.

brawn [brɔ:n] n (U) - 1. [muscle] musculatura f, fuerza f física - 2. UK [meat] carne de cerdo en gelatina.

bray [breɪ] vi [donkey] rebuznar.

brazen ['breɪzn] adj [person] descarado(da); [lie] burdo(da).

brazier ['breɪzjə'] n brasero m.

Brazil [brə'zɪl] n (el) Brasil.

Brazilian [brə'zɪljən] <> adj brasileño(ña), brasilero(ra) Amér. <> n brasileño m, -ña f, brasilero m, -ra f Amér.

brazil nut n nuez f de Pará.

breach [bri:tʃ] <> n - 1. [act of disobedience] incumplimiento m; **breach of confidence** abuso m de confianza; **to be in breach of sthg** incumplir algo; **breach of contract** incumplimiento de contrato - 2. [opening, gap] brecha f - 3. fig [in friendship, marriage] ruptura f. <> vt - 1. [disobey] incumplir - 2. [make hole in] abrir (una) brecha en.

breach of the peace n alteración f del orden público.

bread [bred] n - 1. [food] pan m; **bread and butter** [buttered bread] pan con mantequilla; fig [main income] sustento m diario - 2. inf [money] pasta f.

bread bin UK, **bread box** US n panera f.

breadcrumbs ['bredkrʌmz] npl migas fpl (de pan); CULIN pan m rallado.

breadline ['bredlaɪn] n: **to be on the breadline** vivir en la miseria.

breadth [bretθ] n - 1. [in measurements] anchura f - 2. fig [scope] amplitud f.

breadwinner ['bred,wɪnə'] n: **he's the breadwinner** es el que mantiene a la familia.

break [breɪk] <> n - 1. [gap - in clouds] claro m; [- in transmission] corte m - 2. [fracture] fractura f - 3. [pause]: **break (from)** descanso m (de); **to have** OR **take a break** tomarse un descanso - 4. [playtime] recreo m - 5. inf [chance] oportunidad f; **a lucky break** un golpe de suerte. <> vt (pt **broke**, pp **broken**) - 1. [gen] romper; [arm, leg etc] romperse; **to break sb's hold** escaparse OR liberarse de alguien - 2. [machine] estropear - 3. [journey, contact] interrumpir - 4. [habit, health] acabar con; [strike] reventar - 5. [law, rule] violar; [appointment, word] faltar a - 6. [record] batir - 7. [tell]: **to break the news (of sthg to sb)** dar la noticia (de algo a alguien). <> vi (pt **broke**, pp **broken**) - 1. [come to pieces] romperse - 2. [stop working] estropearse - 3. [pause] parar; [weather] cambiar - 4. [start - day] romper; [- storm] estallar - 5. [escape]: **to break loose** OR **free** escaparse - 6. [voice] cambiar - 7. [news] divulgarse

▸▸▸ **to break even** salir sin pérdidas ni beneficios. ◆ **break away** vi escaparse; **to break away (from)** [end connection] separarse (de); POL escindirse (de). ◆ **break down** <> vt sep - 1. [destroy - gen] derribar; [- resistance] vencer - 2. [analyse] descomponer. <> vi - 1. [collapse, disintegrate, fail] venirse abajo - 2. [stop working] estropearse - 3. [lose emotional control] perder el control - 4. [decompose] descomponerse. ◆ **break in** <> vi - 1. [enter by force] entrar por la fuerza - 2. [interrupt]: **to break in (on sthg/sb)** interrumpir (algo/a alguien). <> vt sep - 1. [horse, shoes] domar - 2. [person] amoldar. ◆ **break into** vt insep - 1. [house, shop] entrar (por la fuerza) en; [box, safe] forzar - 2. [begin suddenly]: **to break into song/a run** echarse a cantar/correr. ◆ **break off** <> vt sep - 1. [detach] partir - 2. [end] romper; [holiday] interrumpir. <> vi - 1. [become detached] partirse - 2. [stop talking] interrumpirse. ◆ **break out** vi - 1. [fire, fighting, panic] desencadenarse; [war] estallar - 2. [escape]: **to break out (of)** escapar (de). ◆ **break up** <> vt sep - 1. [ice] hacer pedazos; [car] desguazar - 2. [relationship] romper; [talks] poner fin a; [fight] poner fin a; [crowd] disolver. <> vi - 1. [into smaller pieces] hacerse pedazos - 2. [relationship] deshacerse; [conference] concluir; [school, pupils] terminar; **to break up with sb** romper con alguien - 3. [crowd] disolverse.

breakage ['breɪkɪdʒ] n rotura f.

breakdown ['breɪkdaʊn] n - 1. [of car, train] avería f; [of talks, in communications] ruptura f; [of law and order] colapso m - 2. [analysis] desglose m.

breakfast ['brekfəst] n desayuno m; **to have breakfast** desayunar.

breakfast television n UK programación f matinal de televisión.

break-in n robo m (con allanamiento de morada).

breaking ['breɪkɪŋ] n: **breaking and entering** LAW allanamiento m de morada.

breakneck ['breɪknek] adj: **at breakneck speed** a (una) velocidad de vértigo.

breakthrough ['breɪkθruː] n avance m.

breakup ['breɪkʌp] n ruptura f.

breast [brest] n - **1.** [of woman] pecho m, seno m; [of man] pecho - **2.** [meat of bird] pechuga f.

breast-feed vt & vi amamantar.

breast milk n (U) leche f materna.

breaststroke ['breststrəʊk] n braza f.

breath [breθ] n - **1.** [act of breathing] respiración f; **to take a deep breath** respirar hondo; **to get one's breath back** recuperar el aliento; **to say sthg under one's breath** decir algo en voz baja - **2.** [air from mouth] aliento m; **out of breath** sin aliento.

breathalyse UK, **-yze** US ['breθəlaɪz] vt hacer la prueba del alcohol a.

breathe [briːð] <> vi respirar. <> vt - **1.** [inhale] respirar - **2.** [exhale] despedir. **breathe in** vt sep & vi aspirar. **breathe out** vi espirar.

breather ['briːðər] n inf respiro m.

breathing ['briːðɪŋ] n respiración f.

breathless ['breθlɪs] adj - **1.** [out of breath] jadeante - **2.** [with excitement] sin aliento (por la emoción).

breathtaking ['breθ,teɪkɪŋ] adj sobrecogedor(ra), impresionante.

breed [briːd] <> n - **1.** [of animal] raza f - **2.** fig [sort] especie f. <> vt (pt & pp bred [bred]) [animals] criar; [plants] cultivar. <> vi (pt & pp bred [bred]) procrear.

breeding ['briːdɪŋ] n - **1.** [of animals] cría f; [of plants] cultivo m - **2.** [manners] educación f.

breeze [briːz] <> n brisa f. <> vi: **to breeze in/out** entrar/salir como si tal cosa.

breezy ['briːzɪ] adj - **1.** [windy]: **it's breezy** hace aire - **2.** [cheerful] jovial, despreocupado(da).

brevity ['brevɪtɪ] n brevedad f.

brew [bruː] <> vt [beer] elaborar; [tea, coffee] preparar. <> vi - **1.** [tea] reposar - **2.** [trouble] fraguarse.

brewer ['bruːər] n cervecero m, -ra f.

brewery ['broərɪ] n fábrica f de cerveza.

bribe [braɪb] <> n soborno m. <> vt: **to bribe (sb to do sthg)** sobornar (a alguien para

que haga algo), coimear (a alguien para que haga algo) Andes & R Dom, mordar (a alguien para que haga algo) Méx.

bribery ['braɪbərɪ] n soborno m.

brick [brɪk] n ladrillo m.

bricklayer ['brɪk,leɪər] n albañil m.

bridal ['braɪdl] adj nupcial; **bridal dress** traje m de novia.

bride [braɪd] n novia f.

bridegroom ['braɪdgrom] n novio m.

bridesmaid ['braɪdzmeɪd] n dama f de honor.

bridge [brɪdʒ] <> n - **1.** [gen] puente m - **2.** [on ship] puente m de mando - **3.** [of nose] caballete m - **4.** [card game] bridge m. <> vt fig [gap] llenar.

bridle ['braɪdl] n brida f.

bridle path n camino m de herradura.

brief [briːf] <> adj - **1.** [short, to the point] breve; **in brief** en resumen - **2.** [clothes] corto(ta). <> n - **1.** LAW [statement] sumario m, resumen m - **2.** UK [instructions] instrucciones fpl. <> vt: **to brief sb (on)** informar a alguien (acerca de). **briefs** npl [underpants] calzoncillos mpl; [knickers] bragas fpl.

briefcase ['briːfkeɪs] n maletín m, portafolios m inv.

briefing ['briːfɪŋ] n [meeting] reunión f informativa; [instructions] instrucciones fpl.

briefly ['briːflɪ] adv - **1.** [for a short time] brevemente - **2.** [concisely] en pocas palabras.

brigade [brɪ'geɪd] n brigada f.

brigadier [,brɪgə'dɪər] n brigadier m, general m de brigada.

bright [braɪt] adj - **1.** [light] brillante; [day, room] luminoso(sa); [weather] despejado(da) - **2.** [colour] vivo(va) - **3.** [lively - eyes] brillante; [- smile] radiante - **4.** [intelligent - person] listo(ta); [- idea] genial - **5.** [hopeful] prometedor(ra).

brighten ['braɪtn] vi - **1.** [become lighter] despejarse - **2.** [become more cheerful] alegrarse. **brighten up** <> vt sep animar, alegrar. <> vi - **1.** [become more cheerful] animarse - **2.** [weather] despejarse.

brilliance ['brɪljəns] n - **1.** [cleverness] brillantez f - **2.** [of colour, light] brillo m.

brilliant ['brɪljənt] adj - **1.** [clever] genial - **2.** [colour] vivo(va) - **3.** [light, career, future] brillante - **4.** inf [wonderful] fenomenal, genial.

Brillo pad® ['brɪləʊ-] n estropajo m (jabonoso) de aluminio.

brim [brɪm] <> n - **1.** [edge] borde m - **2.** [of hat] ala f. <> vi lit & fig: **to brim with** rebosar de.

brine [braɪn] n - **1.** [for food] salmuera f - **2.** [sea water] agua f de mar.

bring [brɪŋ] (pt & pp **brought**) vt [gen] traer; **to bring sthg to an end** poner fin a algo. ➤ **bring about** vt sep producir. ➤ **bring around, bring round, bring to** vt sep [make conscious] reanimar. ➤ **bring back** vt sep - 1. [books etc] devolver; [person] traer de vuelta - 2. [memories] traer (a la memoria) - 3. [practice, hanging] volver a introducir; [fashion] recuperar. ➤ **bring down** vt sep - 1. [from upstairs] bajar - 2. [plane, bird] derribar; [government, tyrant] derrocar - 3. [prices] reducir. ➤ **bring forward** vt sep - 1. [meeting, elections etc] adelantar - 2. [in bookkeeping] sumar a la siguiente columna. ➤ **bring in** vt sep - 1. [introduce - law] implantar; [- bill] presentar - 2. [earn] ganar. ➤ **bring off** vt sep [plan] sacar adelante; [deal] cerrar. ➤ **bring out** vt sep - 1. [new product, book] sacar - 2. [the worst etc in sb] revelar, despertar. ➤ **bring round, bring to** vt sep = bring around. ➤ **bring up** vt sep - 1. [raise - children] criar - 2. [mention] sacar a relucir - 3. [vomit] devolver.

brink [brɪŋk] n: **on the brink of** al borde de.

brisk [brɪsk] adj - 1. [quick] rápido(da) - 2. [trade, business] boyante, activo(va) - 3. [efficient, confident - manner] enérgico(ca); [- person] eficaz.

bristle ['brɪsl] ⬦ n [gen] cerda f; [of person] pelillo m. ⬦ vi - 1. [stand up] erizarse, ponerse de punta - 2. [react angrily]: **to bristle (at)** enfadarse (por).

Brit [brɪt] n inf británico m, -ca f.

Britain ['brɪtn] n Gran Bretaña.

British ['brɪtɪʃ] ⬦ adj británico(ca). ⬦ npl: **the British** los británicos.

British Isles npl: **the British Isles** las Islas Británicas.

Briton ['brɪtn] n británico m, -ca f.

brittle ['brɪtl] adj quebradizo(za), frágil.

broach [brəʊtʃ] vt abordar.

B road n UK ≃ carretera f comarcal.

broad [brɔːd] ⬦ adj - 1. [shoulders, river, street] ancho(cha); [grin] amplio(plia) - 2. [range, interests] amplio(plia) - 3. [description, outline] general - 4. [hint] claro(ra) - 5. [accent] cerrado(da) ▸▸▸ **in broad daylight** a plena luz del día. ⬦ n US inf tía f, tipa f.

broad bean n haba f.

broadcast ['brɔːdkɑːst] ⬦ n emisión f. ⬦ vt (pt & pp **broadcast**) emitir.

broaden ['brɔːdn] ⬦ vt - 1. [road, pavement] ensanchar - 2. [scope, appeal] ampliar. ⬦ vi [river, road] ensancharse; [smile] hacerse más amplia.

broadly ['brɔːdlɪ] adv - 1. [gen] en general - 2. [smile] abiertamente.

broadsheet ['brɔːdʃiːt] n periódico de calidad (con hojas de gran tamaño).

broccoli ['brɒkəlɪ] n brécol m.

brochure ['brəʊʃə'] n folleto m.

broil [brɔɪl] vt US asar a la parrilla.

broke [brəʊk] ⬦ pt ⊳ **break**. ⬦ adj inf sin blanca, sin un duro.

broken ['brəʊkn] ⬦ pp ⊳ **break**. ⬦ adj - 1. [gen] roto(ta) - 2. [not working] estropeado(da) - 3. [interrupted - sleep] entrecortado(da); [- journey] discontinuo(nua).

broker ['brəʊkə'] n [of stock] corredor m; [of insurance] agente mf.

brolly ['brɒlɪ] n UK inf paraguas m inv.

bronchitis [brɒŋ'kaɪtɪs] n (U) bronquitis f inv.

bronze [brɒnz] n [metal, sculpture] bronce m.

brooch [brəʊtʃ] n broche m, alfiler m.

brood [bruːd] ⬦ n - 1. [of birds] nidada f - 2. inf [of children] prole f. ⬦ vi: **to brood (over OR about)** dar vueltas (a).

brook [brʊk] n arroyo m.

broom [bruːm] n - 1. [brush] escoba f - 2. [plant] retama f.

broomstick ['bruːmstɪk] n palo m de escoba.

Bros., bros. (abbr of **brothers**) Hnos.

broth [brɒθ] n caldo m.

brothel ['brɒθl] n burdel m.

brother ['brʌðə'] n [relative, monk] hermano m.

brother-in-law (pl **brothers-in-law**) n cuñado m.

brought [brɔːt] pt & pp ⊳ **bring**.

brow [braʊ] n - 1. [forehead] frente f - 2. [eyebrow] ceja f - 3. [of hill] cima f.

brown [braʊn] ⬦ adj - 1. [gen] marrón; [hair, eyes] castaño(ña) - 2. [tanned] moreno(na). ⬦ n marrón m. ⬦ vt [food] dorar.

brown bread n pan m integral.

brownie ['braʊnɪ-] n US bizcocho de chocolate y nueces.

brown paper n (U) papel m de embalar.

brown rice n arroz m integral.

brown sugar n azúcar m moreno.

browse [braʊz] ⬦ vi - 1. [person] echar un ojo, mirar; **to browse through** hojear - 2. COMPUT navegar. ⬦ vt COMPUT navegar por.

bruise [bruːz] ⬦ n cardenal m. ⬦ vt - 1. [person, arm] magullar; [fruit] magullar - 2. fig [feelings] herir.

brunch [brʌntʃ] n brunch m (combinación de desayuno y almuerzo que se toma tarde por la mañana).

brunette [bruː'net] n morena f.

brunt [brʌnt] *n*: **to bear** OR **take the brunt of** aguantar lo peor de.

brush [brʌʃ] <> *n* - **1.** [for hair, teeth] cepillo *m*; [for shaving, decorating] brocha *f*; [of artist] pincel *m*; [broom] escoba *f* - **2.** [encounter] roce *m*. <> *vt* - **1.** [clean with brush] cepillar; **to brush one's hair** cepillarse el pelo - **2.** [move with hand] quitar, apartar - **3.** [touch lightly] rozar. ◆ **brush aside** *vt sep* [dismiss] hacer caso omiso de. ◆ **brush off** *vt sep* [dismiss] hacer caso omiso de. ◆ **brush up** <> *vt sep* *fig* [revise] repasar. <> *vi*: **to brush up on** repasar.

brushwood ['brʌʃwʊd] *n* leña *f*.

brusque [bru:sk] *adj* brusco(ca).

Brussels ['brʌslz] *n* Bruselas.

brussels sprout *n* col *f* de Bruselas.

brutal ['bru:tl] *adj* brutal.

brute [bru:t] <> *adj* bruto(ta). <> *n* - **1.** [large animal] bestia *f*, bruto *m* - **2.** [bully] bestia *mf*.

BS *US* (*abbr of Bachelor of Science*) *n* (*titular de una*) *licenciatura de ciencias*.

BSc (*abbr of Bachelor of Science*) *n* (*titular de una*) *licenciatura de ciencias*.

BTW (*abbr of by the way*) *adv* por cierto.

bubble ['bʌbl] <> *n* [gen] burbuja *f*; [of soap] pompa *f*. <> *vi* - **1.** [produce bubbles] burbujear - **2.** [make a bubbling sound] borbotar.

bubble bath *n* espuma *f* de baño.

bubble gum *n* chicle *m* (de globo).

bubblejet printer ['bʌbldʒet-] *n* COMPUT impresora *f* de inyección.

buck [bʌk] <> *n* (*pl buck* OR **-s**) - **1.** [male animal] macho *m* - **2.** *esp US inf* [dollar] dólar *m* - **3.** *inf* [responsibility]: **to pass the buck to sb** echarle el muerto a alguien. <> *vt inf* [oppose] oponerse a, ir en contra de. <> *vi* corcovear. ◆ **buck up** *inf* <> *vt sep* [improve] mejorar; **buck your ideas up** más vale que espabiles. <> *vi* - **1.** [hurry up] darse prisa - **2.** [cheer up] animarse.

bucket ['bʌkɪt] *n* [container, bucketful] cubo *m*.

buckle ['bʌkl] <> *n* hebilla *f*. <> *vt* - **1.** [fasten] abrochar con hebilla - **2.** [bend] combar. <> *vi* [wheel] combarse; [knees] doblarse.

bud [bʌd] <> *n* [shoot] brote *m*; [flower] capullo *m*. <> *vi* brotar, echar brotes.

Buddha ['bʊdə] *n* Buda *m*.

Buddhism ['bʊdɪzm] *n* budismo *m*.

budding ['bʌdɪŋ] *adj* en ciernes.

buddy ['bʌdɪ] *n* *esp US inf* [friend] amiguete *m*, -ta *f*, colega *mf*.

budge [bʌdʒ] <> *vt* mover. <> *vi* [move] moverse; [give in] ceder.

budgerigar ['bʌdʒərɪgɑːr] *n* periquito *m*.

budget ['bʌdʒɪt] <> *adj* económico(ca). <> *n* presupuesto *m*. ◆ **budget for** *vt insep* contar con.

budgie ['bʌdʒɪ] *n inf* periquito *m*.

buff [bʌf] <> *adj* color de ante. <> *n inf* [expert] aficionado *m*, -da *f*.

buffalo ['bʌfələʊ] (*pl buffalo*, **-s** OR **-es**) *n* búfalo *m*.

buffer ['bʌfər] *n* - **1.** *UK* [for trains] tope *m* - **2.** *US* [of car] parachoques *m inv* - **3.** [protection] defensa *f*, salvaguarda *f* - **4.** COMPUT búfer *m*.

buffet[1] [*UK* 'bʊfeɪ, *US* bə'feɪ] *n* - **1.** [meal] bufé *m* - **2.** [cafeteria] cafetería *f*.

buffet[2] ['bʌfɪt] *vt* [physically] golpear.

buffet car ['bʊfeɪ-] *n* coche *m* restaurante.

bug [bʌg] <> *n* - **1.** *esp US* [small insect] bicho *m* - **2.** *inf* [illness] virus *m* - **3.** *inf* [listening device] micrófono *m* oculto - **4.** COMPUT error *m* - **5.** [enthusiasm] manía *f*. <> *vt* - **1.** *inf* [spy on - room] poner un micrófono oculto en; [- phone] pinchar - **2.** *esp US inf* [annoy] fastidiar, jorobar.

bugger ['bʌgər] *UK v inf n* - **1.** [unpleasant person] cabrón *m*, -ona *f* - **2.** [difficult, annoying task] coñazo *m*. ◆ **bugger off** *vi v inf*: **bugger off!** ¡vete a tomar por culo!

buggy ['bʌgɪ] *n* - **1.** [carriage] calesa *f* - **2.** [pushchair] sillita *f* de ruedas; *US* [pram] cochecito *m* de niño.

bugle ['bju:gl] *n* corneta *f*, clarín *m*.

build [bɪld] <> *vt* (*pt & pp built*) - **1.** [construct] construir - **2.** *fig* [form, create] crear. <> *n* complexión *f*, constitución *f*. ◆ **build (up)on** <> *vt insep* [further] desarrollar. <> *vt sep* [base on] fundar en. ◆ **build up** <> *vt sep* - **1.** [business - establish] poner en pie; [- promote] fomentar - **2.** [person] fortalecer. <> *vi* acumularse.

builder ['bɪldər] *n* constructor *m*, -ra *f*.

building ['bɪldɪŋ] *n* - **1.** [structure] edificio *m* - **2.** [profession] construcción *f*.

building and loan association *n US* ≃ caja *f* de ahorros.

building site *n* obra *f*.

building society *n UK* ≃ caja *f* de ahorros.

buildup ['bɪldʌp] *n* [increase] acumulación *f*; [of troops] concentración *f*.

built [bɪlt] *pt & pp* ⊳ **build**.

built-in *adj* - **1.** [physically integrated] empotrado(da) - **2.** [inherent] incorporado(da).

built-up *adj* urbanizado(da).

bulb [bʌlb] *n* - **1.** [for lamp] bombilla *f* - **2.** [of plant] bulbo *m* - **3.** [bulb-shaped part] parte *f* redondeada.

Bulgaria [bʌl'geərɪə] *n* Bulgaria.

Bulgarian [bʌl'geərɪən] <> adj búlgaro(ra). <> n - 1. [person] búlgaro m, -ra f - 2. [language] búlgaro m.

bulge [bʌldʒ] <> n [lump] protuberancia f, bulto m. <> vi: **to bulge (with)** rebosar (de), estar atestado(da) (de).

bulk [bʌlk] <> n - 1. [mass] bulto m, volumen m - 2. [large quantity]: **in bulk** a granel - 3. [majority, most of]: **the bulk of** la mayor parte de. <> adj a granel.

bulky ['bʌlkɪ] adj voluminoso(sa).

bull [bʊl] n - 1. [male cow] toro m - 2. [male animal] macho m.

bulldog ['bʊldɒg] n buldog m.

bulldozer ['bʊldəʊzər] n bulldozer m.

bullet ['bʊlɪt] n - 1. [of gun] bala f - 2. [typo] topo m.

bulletin ['bʊlətɪn] n - 1. [news] boletín m; [medical report] parte m - 2. [regular publication] boletín m, gaceta f.

bullfight ['bʊlfaɪt] n corrida f (de toros).

bullfighter ['bʊl,faɪtər] n torero m, -ra f.

bullfighting ['bʊl,faɪtɪŋ] n toreo m.

bullion ['bʊljən] n (U) lingotes mpl.

bullock ['bʊlək] n buey m, toro m castrado.

bullring ['bʊlrɪŋ] n - 1. [stadium] plaza f (de toros) - 2. [arena] ruedo m.

bull's-eye n diana f.

bully ['bʊlɪ] <> n abusón m, matón m. <> vt intimidar; **to bully sb into doing sthg** obligar a alguien con amenazas a hacer algo.

bum [bʌm] n - 1. esp UK v inf [bottom] cola f Amér., poto m Chile & Perú, traste m - 2. US inf pej [tramp] vagabundo m, -da f.

bumblebee ['bʌmblbiː] n abejorro m.

bump [bʌmp] <> n - 1. [lump - on head] chichón m; [- on road] bache m - 2. [knock, blow, noise] golpe m. <> vt [car] chocar con OR contra; [head, knee] golpearse en; **I bumped my head on the door** me di con la cabeza en la puerta. ◆ **bump into** vt insep [meet by chance] toparse con.

bumper ['bʌmpər] <> adj abundante; **bumper edition** edición especial. <> n - 1. AUT parachoques m inv - 2. US RAIL tope m.

bumptious ['bʌmpʃəs] adj pej engreído(da).

bumpy ['bʌmpɪ] adj - 1. [road] lleno(na) de baches - 2. [ride, journey] con muchas sacudidas.

bun [bʌn] n - 1. [cake, bread roll] bollo m - 2. [hairstyle] moño m. ◆ **buns** npl US inf trasero m, culo m.

bunch [bʌntʃ] <> n [of people] grupo m; [of flowers] ramo m; [of fruit] racimo m; [of keys] manojo m. <> vi agruparse. ◆ **bunches** npl [hairstyle] coletas fpl.

bundle ['bʌndl] <> n - 1. [of clothes] lío m, bulto m; [of notes, papers] fajo m; [of wood] haz m; **to be a bundle of nerves** fig ser un manojo de nervios - 2. COMPUT paquete m. <> vt [clothes] empaquetar de cualquier manera; [person] empujar. ◆ **bundle up** vt sep [put into bundles] liar.

bung [bʌŋ] <> n tapón m. <> vt UK inf - 1. [throw] tirar - 2. [pass] alcanzar.

bungalow ['bʌŋgələʊ] n bungalow m.

bungle ['bʌŋgl] vt chapucear.

bunion ['bʌnjən] n juanete m.

bunk [bʌŋk] n [bed] litera f.

bunk bed n litera f.

bunker ['bʌŋkər] n - 1. [shelter, in golf] bunker m - 2. [for coal] carbonera f.

bunny ['bʌnɪ] n: **bunny (rabbit)** conejito m, -ta f.

bunting ['bʌntɪŋ] n (U) [flags] banderitas fpl.

buoy [UK bɔɪ, US 'buːɪ] n boya f. ◆ **buoy up** vt sep [encourage] alentar.

buoyant ['bɔɪənt] adj - 1. [able to float] boyante - 2. [optimistic - gen] optimista; [- market] con tendencia alcista.

burden ['bɜːdn] <> n - 1. [heavy load] carga f - 2. fig [heavy responsibility]: **burden on** carga f para. <> vt: **to burden sb with** cargar a alguien con.

bureau ['bjʊərəʊ] (pl -x) n - 1. [government department] departamento m - 2. [office] oficina f - 3. UK [desk] secreter m; US [chest of drawers] cómoda f.

bureaucracy [bjʊə'rɒkrəsɪ] n burocracia f.

bureaux ['bjʊərəʊz] npl ▷ **bureau**.

burger ['bɜːgər] n hamburguesa f.

burglar ['bɜːglər] n ladrón m, -ona f.

burglar alarm n alarma f antirrobo.

burglarize US = **burgle**.

burglary ['bɜːglərɪ] n robo m (de una casa).

burgle ['bɜːgl], **burglarize** ['bɜːgləraɪz] US vt robar, desvalijar (una casa).

burial ['berɪəl] n entierro m.

burly ['bɜːlɪ] adj fornido(da).

Burma ['bɜːmə] n Birmania.

burn [bɜːn] <> vt (pt & pp **burnt** OR **-ed**) - 1. [gen] quemar - 2. [injure - by heat, fire] quemarse - 3. COMPUT tostar, grabar. <> vi (pt & pp **burnt** OR **-ed**) - 1. [gen] arder - 2. [be alight] estar encendido(da) - 3. [food] quemarse - 4. [cause burning sensation] escocer - 5. [become sunburnt] quemarse. <> n quemadura f. ◆ **burn down** vt sep incendiar. <> vi [be destroyed by fire] incendiarse.

burner ['bɜːnər] n quemador m.

Burns' Night n fiesta celebrada en Escocia el 25 de enero en honor del poeta escocés Robert Burns.

burnt [bɜːnt] *pt & pp* ▷ **burn**.

burp [bɜːp] *inf vi* eructar.

burqa [bʊːkə] *n* burqa *m*.

burrow ['bʌrəʊ] ◇ *n* madriguera *f*. ◇ *vi* - **1.** [dig] escarbar (un agujero) - **2.** *fig* [in order to search] hurgar.

bursar ['bɜːsə] *n* tesorero *m*, -ra *f*.

bursary ['bɜːsərɪ] *n UK* beca *f*.

burst [bɜːst] ◇ *vi* (*pt & pp* burst) - **1.** [gen] reventarse; [bag] romperse; [tyre] pincharse - **2.** [explode] estallar. ◇ *vt* (*pt & pp* burst) [gen] reventar; [tyre] pinchar. ◇ *n* [of gunfire, enthusiasm] estallido *m*. ◆ **burst into** *vt insep* - **1.** [tears, song]: **to burst into tears/song** romper a llorar/cantar - **2.** [flames] estallar en. ◆ **burst out** *vi* [begin suddenly]: **to burst out laughing/crying** echarse a reír/llorar.

bursting ['bɜːstɪŋ] *adj* - **1.** [full] lleno(na) a estallar - **2.** [with emotion]: **bursting with** rebosando de - **3.** [eager]: **to be bursting to do sthg** estar deseando hacer algo.

bury ['berɪ] *vt* - **1.** [in ground] enterrar - **2.** [hide - face, memory] ocultar.

bus [bʌs] ◇ *n* autobús *m*; **by bus** en autobús. ◇ *vt US*: **to bus tables** [in restaurant] recoger mesas.

bush [bʊʃ] *n* - **1.** [plant] arbusto *m* - **2.** [open country]: **the bush** el campo abierto, el monte. ▶▶▶ **to beat about the bush** andarse por las ramas.

bushy ['bʊʃɪ] *adj* poblado(da), espeso(sa).

business ['bɪznɪs] *n* - **1.** (U) [commerce, amount of trade] negocios *mpl*; **to be away on business** estar en viaje de negocios; **to mean business** *inf* ir en serio; **to go out of business** quebrar - **2.** [company] negocio *m*, empresa *f* - **3.** [concern, duty] oficio *m*, ocupación *f*; **to have no business doing** OR **to do sthg** no tener derecho a hacer algo; **mind your own business!** *inf* ¡no te metas donde no te llaman!; **that's none of your business** eso no es asunto tuyo - **4.** (U) [affair, matter] asunto *m*.

business class *n* clase *f* preferente.

businesslike ['bɪznɪslaɪk] *adj* formal y eficiente.

businessman ['bɪznɪsmæn] (*pl* -men [-men]) *n* empresario *m*, hombre *m* de negocios.

business studies *npl* empresariales *mpl*.

business trip *n* viaje *m* de negocios.

businesswoman ['bɪznɪs,wʊmən] (*pl* -women [-,wɪmɪn]) *n* empresaria *f*, mujer *f* de negocios.

busker ['bʌskə] *n UK* músico *m* ambulante OR callejero.

bus-shelter *n* marquesina *f* (*de parada de autobús*).

bus station *n* estación *f* OR terminal *f* de autobuses.

bus stop *n* parada *f* de autobús, paradero *m* *Amér C, Andes & Méx*.

bust [bʌst] (*pt & pp* -ed OR bust) ◇ *adj inf* - **1.** [broken] fastidiado(da), roto(ta) - **2.** [bankrupt]: **to go bust** quebrar. ◇ *n* [bosom, statue] busto *m*. ◇ *vt inf* [break] fastidiar, estropear.

bustle ['bʌsl] ◇ *n* bullicio *m*. ◇ *vi* apresurarse.

busy ['bɪzɪ] ◇ *adj* - **1.** [occupied] ocupado(da); **to be busy doing sthg** estar ocupado haciendo algo - **2.** [hectic - life, week] ajetreado(da); [- town, office] concurrido(da); [- road] con mucho tráfico - **3.** [active] activo(va). ◇ *vt*: **to busy o.s. (doing sthg)** ocuparse (haciendo algo).

busybody ['bɪzɪ,bɒdɪ] *n pej* entrometido *m*, -da *f*.

busy signal *n US* TELEC señal *f* de comunicando.

but [bʌt] ◇ *conj* pero; **we were poor but happy** éramos pobres pero felices; **she owns not one but two houses** tiene no una sino dos casas. ◇ *prep* menos, excepto; **everyone but Jane was there** todos estaban allí, menos Jane; **we've had nothing but bad weather** no hemos tenido más que mal tiempo; **he has no one but himself to blame** la culpa no es de otro más que él OR sino de él. ◇ *adv fml*: **had I but known** de haberlo sabido; **we can but try** por intentarlo que no quede. ◆ **but for** *conj* de no ser por.

butcher ['bʊtʃə] ◇ *n* - **1.** [occupation] carnicero *m*, -ra *f*; **butcher's (shop)** carnicería *f* - **2.** [indiscriminate killer] carnicero *m*, -ra *f*, asesino *m*, -na *f*. ◇ *vt* [animal - for meat] matar; *fig* [kill indiscriminately] hacer una carnicería con.

butler ['bʌtlə] *n* mayordomo *m*.

butt [bʌt] ◇ *n* - **1.** [of cigarette, cigar] colilla *f* - **2.** [of rifle] culata *f* - **3.** [for water] tina *f* - **4.** [of joke, remark] blanco *m* - **5.** *US inf* [bottom] trasero *m*, culo *m*. ◇ *vt* topetar. ◆ **butt in** *vi* [interrupt]: **to butt in on sb** cortar a alguien. ◆ **butt out** *vi US* dejar de entrometerse.

butter ['bʌtə] ◇ *n* mantequilla *f*. ◇ *vt* untar con mantequilla.

buttercup ['bʌtəkʌp] *n* ranúnculo *m*.

butter dish *n* mantequera *f*.

butterfly ['bʌtəflaɪ] *n* - **1.** [insect] mariposa *f* - **2.** [swimming style] (estilo *m*) mariposa *f*.

buttocks ['bʌtəks] *npl* nalgas *fpl*.

button ['bʌtn] ◇ *n* - **1.** [gen & COMPUT] botón *m* - **2.** *US* [badge] chapa *f*. ◇ *vt* = **button up**. ◆ **button up** *vt sep* abotonar, abrochar.

button mushroom *n* champiñón *m* pequeño.

44

buttress ['bʌtrɪs] n contrafuerte m.

buxom ['bʌksəm] adj [woman] maciza, pechugona.

buy [baɪ] ◇ vt (pt & pp **bought**) lit & fig comprar; **to buy sthg from sb** comprar algo a alguien; **to buy sb sthg** comprar algo a alguien, comprar algo para alguien. ◇ n compra f. ► **buy up** vt sep acaparar.

buyer ['baɪər] n [purchaser] comprador m, -ra f.

buyout ['baɪaʊt] n adquisición de la mayoría de las acciones de una empresa.

buzz [bʌz] ◇ n [of insect, machinery] zumbido m; [of conversation] rumor m; **to give sb a buzz** inf [on phone] dar un toque OR llamar a alguien. ◇ vi - **1.** [make noise] zumbar - **2.** fig [be active]: **to buzz (with)** bullir (de).

buzzer ['bʌzər] n timbre m.

buzzword ['bʌzwɜːd] n inf palabra f de moda.

by [baɪ] prep - **1.** [indicating cause, agent] por; **caused/written by** causado/escrito por; **a book by Joyce** un libro de Joyce - **2.** [indicating means, method, manner]: **to travel by bus/train/plane/ship** viajar en autobús/tren/avión/barco; **to pay by cheque** pagar con cheque; **he got rich by buying land** se hizo rico comprando terrenos; **by profession/trade** de profesión/oficio - **3.** [beside, close to] junto a; **by the sea** junto al mar - **4.** [past] por delante de; **to walk by sb/sthg** pasear por delante de alguien/algo; **we drove by the castle** pasamos por el castillo (conduciendo) - **5.** [via, through] por; **we entered by the back door** entramos por la puerta trasera - **6.** [with time - at or before, during] para; **I'll be there by eight** estaré allí para las ocho; **by now** ya; **by day/night** de día/noche - **7.** [according to] según; **by law/my standards** según la ley/mis criterios - **8.** [in division] entre; [in multiplication, measurements] por; **to divide 20 by 2** dividir 20 entre 2; **to multiply 20 by 2** multiplicar 20 por 2; **twelve feet by ten** doce pies por diez - **9.** [in quantities, amounts] por; **by the day/hour** por día/horas; **prices were cut by 50%** los precios fueron rebajados (en) un 50% - **10.** [indicating gradual change]: **day by day** día a día; **one by one** uno a uno - **11.** [to explain a word or expression]: **what do you mean by 'all right'?** ¿qué quieres decir con 'bien'?; **what do you understand by the word 'subsidiary'?** ¿qué entiendes por 'subsidiariedad'? ◀◀ **(all) by oneself** solo(la); **did you do it all by yourself?** ¿lo hiciste tú solo?

bye(-bye) [baɪ(baɪ)] excl inf ¡hasta luego!

bye-election = **by-election**.

byelaw ['baɪlɔː] = **bylaw**.

by-election, bye-election n elección f parcial.

bygone ['baɪɡɒn] adj pasado(da). ► **bygones** npl: **let bygones be bygones** lo pasado, pasado está.

bylaw, byelaw ['baɪlɔː] n reglamento m OR estatuto m local.

bypass ['baɪpɑːs] ◇ n - **1.** [road] carretera f de circunvalación - **2.** MED: **bypass (operation)** (operación f de) by-pass m. ◇ vt evitar.

by-product n - **1.** [product] subproducto m - **2.** [consequence] consecuencia f.

bystander ['baɪˌstændər] n espectador m, -ra f.

byte [baɪt] n COMPUT byte m.

byword ['baɪwɜːd] n: **to be a byword (for)** ser sinónimo de.

c¹ (pl **c's** OR **cs**), **C** (pl **C's** OR **Cs**) [siː] n [letter] c f, C f. ► **C** n - **1.** MUS do m - **2.** (abbr of **celsius, centigrade**) C.

c² (abbr of **cent(s)**) cént.

c. (abbr of **circa**) h.

c/a (abbr of **current account**) c/c.

cab [kæb] n - **1.** [taxi] taxi m - **2.** [of lorry] cabina f.

cabaret ['kæbəreɪ] n cabaret m.

cabbage ['kæbɪdʒ] n col f, repollo m.

cabin ['kæbɪn] n - **1.** [on ship] camarote m - **2.** [in aircraft] cabina f - **3.** [house] cabaña f.

cabinet ['kæbɪnɪt] n - **1.** [cupboard] armario m; [with glass pane] vitrina f - **2.** POL consejo m de ministros, gabinete m.

cable ['keɪbl] ◇ n - **1.** [rope, wire] cable m - **2.** [telegram] cablegrama m. ◇ vt cablegrafiar.

cable car n teleférico m.

cable television, cable TV n televisión f por cable.

cache [kæʃ] n - **1.** [store] alijo m - **2.** COMPUT caché f.

cache memory n COMPUT memoria f caché.

cackle ['kækl] vi - **1.** [hen] cacarear - **2.** [person] reírse.

cactus ['kæktəs] (*pl* **-tuses** OR **-ti** [-taɪ]) *n* cactus *m inv*.

cadet [kə'det] *n* cadete *m*.

cadge [kædʒ] *UK inf vt*: **to cadge sthg (off** OR **from sb)** gorronear algo (a alguien).

caesarean (section) *UK,* **cesarean (section)** *US* [sɪ'zeərɪən-] *n* cesárea *f*.

cafe, café ['kæfeɪ] *n* café *m*, cafetería *f*.

cafeteria [ˌkæfɪ'tɪərɪə] *n* (restaurante *m*) autoservicio *m*, cantina *f*.

caffeine ['kæfiːn] *n* cafeína *f*.

cage [keɪdʒ] *n* jaula *f*.

cagey ['keɪdʒɪ] (*comp* **-ier,** *superl* **-iest**) *adj inf* reservado(da).

cagoule [kə'guːl] *n UK* chubasquero *m*.

cajole [kə'dʒəʊl] *vt*: **to cajole sb (into doing sthg)** engatusar a alguien (para que haga algo).

cake [keɪk] *n* - **1.** [sweet food] pastel *m*, tarta *f*, torta *f Amér* - **2.** [of fish, potato] medallón *m* empanado - **3.** [of soap] pastilla *f*.

caked [keɪkt] *adj*: **caked with mud** cubierto(ta) de barro seco.

CAL (*abbr of* **computer assisted learning**) & (*abbr of* **computer aided learning**) *n* enseñanza *f* asistida por ordenador.

calcium ['kælsɪəm] *n* calcio *m*.

calculate ['kælkjʊleɪt] *vt* - **1.** [work out] calcular - **2.** [plan]: **to be calculated to do sthg** estar pensado(da) para hacer algo.

calculating ['kælkjʊleɪtɪŋ] *adj pej* calculador(ra).

calculation [ˌkælkjʊ'leɪʃn] *n* cálculo *m*.

calculator ['kælkjʊleɪtər] *n* calculadora *f*.

calendar ['kælɪndər] *n* calendario *m*.

calendar month *n* mes *m* civil.

calendar year *n* año *m* civil.

calf [kɑːf] (*pl* **calves**) *n* - **1.** [young animal - of cow] ternero *m*, -ra *f*, becerro *m*, -rra *f*; [- of other animals] cría *f* - **2.** [leather] piel *f* de becerro - **3.** [of leg] pantorrilla *f*.

calibre, caliber *US* ['kælɪbər] *n* - **1.** [quality] nivel *m* - **2.** [size] calibre *m*.

California [ˌkælɪ'fɔːnjə] *n* California.

calipers *US* = **callipers.**

call [kɔːl] *n* - **1.** [cry, attraction, vocation] llamada *f*, llamado *m Amér*; [cry of bird] reclamo *m* - **2.** TELEC llamada *f*, llamado *m Amér*; **to give sb a call** llamar a alguien - **3.** [visit] visita *f*; **to pay a call on sb** hacerle una visita a alguien - **4.** [demand]: **call for** llamamiento *m* a - **5.** [summons]: **on call** de guardia. <> *vt* - **1.** [gen & TELEC] llamar; **I'm called Joan** me llamo Joan; **what is it called?** ¿cómo se llama?; **he called my name** me llamó por el nombre; **we'll call it £10** dejémoslo en 10 libras - **2.** [announce - flight] anunciar; [- strike, meeting, elec-

tion] convocar. <> *vi* - **1.** [gen & TELEC] llamar; **who's calling?** ¿quién es? - **2.** [visit] pasar. ◆ **call at** *vt insep* [subj: train] efectuar parada en. ◆ **call back** <> *vt sep* - **1.** [on phone] volver a llamar - **2.** [ask to return] hacer volver. <> *vi* - **1.** [on phone] volver a llamar - **2.** [visit again] volver a pasarse. ◆ **call for** *vt insep* - **1.** [collect] ir a buscar - **2.** [demand] pedir. ◆ **call in** *vt sep* - **1.** [send for] llamar - **2.** [recall - product, banknotes] retirar; [- loan] exigir pago de. ◆ **call off** *vt sep* - **1.** [meeting, party] suspender; [strike] desconvocar - **2.** [dog etc] llamar *(para deje de atacar).* ◆ **call on** *vt insep* [visit] visitar. ◆ **call out** <> *vt sep* - **1.** [order to help - troops] movilizar; [- police, firemen] hacer intervenir - **2.** [cry out] gritar. <> *vi* gritar. ◆ **call round** *vi* pasarse. ◆ **call up** *vt sep* - **1.** MIL llamar a filas - **2.** *esp US* [on telephone] llamar (por teléfono).

CALL (*abbr of* **computer assisted (or aided) language learning**) *n* enseñanza *f* de idiomas asistida por ordenador.

call box *n UK* cabina *f* telefónica.

call centre *n* centro *m* de atención telefónica.

caller ['kɔːlər] *n* - **1.** [visitor] visita *f* - **2.** [on telephone] persona *f* que llama.

caller (ID) display *n* [on telephone] identificador *m* de llamada.

call-in *n US* RADIO & TV programa *m* a micrófono abierto.

calling ['kɔːlɪŋ] *n* - **1.** [profession] profesión *f* - **2.** [vocation] vocación *f*.

calling card *n US* tarjeta *f* de visita.

callipers *UK,* **calipers** *US* ['kælɪpəz] *npl* - **1.** MED aparato *m* ortopédico - **2.** [for measuring] calibrador *m*.

callous ['kæləs] *adj* despiadado(da).

calm [kɑːm] <> *adj* - **1.** [not worried or excited] tranquilo(la) - **2.** [evening, weather] apacible - **3.** [sea] en calma. <> *n* calma *f*. <> *vt* calmar. ◆ **calm down** <> *vt sep* calmar. <> *vi* calmarse.

Calor gas® ['kælər-] *n UK* (gas *m*) butano *m*.

calorie ['kælərɪ] *n* caloría *f*.

calves [kɑːvz] *npl* ▷ **calf.**

camber ['kæmbər] *n* [of road] peralte *m*.

Cambodia [kæm'bəʊdjə] *n* Camboya.

camcorder ['kæmˌkɔːdər] *n* camcorder *m*, videocámara *f*.

came [keɪm] *pt* ▷ **come.**

camel ['kæml] *n* camello *m*.

cameo ['kæmɪəʊ] (*pl* **-s**) *n* - **1.** [jewellery] camafeo *m* - **2.** [in acting] actuación *f* breve y memorable; [in writing] excelente descripción *f*.

camera ['kæmərə] *n* cámara *f*. ◆ **in camera** *adv fml* a puerta cerrada.

cameraman [ˈkæmərəmæn] (*pl* -men [-men]) *n* cámara *m*.

camouflage [ˈkæməflɑːʒ] <> *n* camuflaje *m*. <> *vt* camuflar.

camp [kæmp] <> *n* - 1. [gen & MIL] campamento *m* - 2. [temporary mass accommodation] campo *m*; **(summer) camp** *US* colonia *f*, campamento *m* de verano - 3. [faction] bando *m*. <> *vi* acampar. <> *adj inf* amanerado(da). **camp out** *vi* acampar (al aire libre).

campaign [kæmˈpeɪn] <> *n* campaña *f*. <> *vi*: **to campaign (for/against)** hacer campaña (a favor de/en contra de).

camp bed *n* cama *f* plegable.

camper [ˈkæmpər] *n* - 1. [person] campista *mf* - 2.: **camper (van)** autocaravana *f*.

campground [ˈkæmpgraʊnd] *n US* camping *m*.

camping [ˈkæmpɪŋ] *n* camping *m*; **to go camping** ir de acampada.

camping site, campsite [ˈkæmpsaɪt] *n* camping *m*.

campus [ˈkæmpəs] (*pl* -es) *n* campus *m inv*, ciudad *f* universitaria.

can¹ [kæn] <> *n* [for drink, food] lata *f*, bote *m*; [for oil, paint] lata; *US* [for garbage] cubo *m*. <> *vt* (*pt & pp* -ned, *cont* -ning) enlatar.

can² *(weak form* [kən], *strong form* [kæn], *conditional and preterite form* **could**; *negative form* **cannot** *and* **can't**) *modal vb* - 1. [be able to] poder; **can you come to lunch?** ¿puedes venir a comer?; **I can't OR cannot afford it** no me lo puedo permitir; **can you see/hear something?** ¿ves/oyes algo? - 2. [know how to] saber; **I can speak French** hablo francés, sé hablar francés; **I can play the piano** sé tocar el piano; **can you drive/cook?** ¿sabes conducir/cocinar? - 3. [indicating permission, in polite requests] poder; **you can use my car if you like** puedes utilizar mi coche si quieres; **can I speak to John, please?** ¿puedo hablar con John, por favor? - 4. [indicating disbelief, puzzlement]: **you can't be serious** estás de broma ¿no?; **what can she have done with it?** ¿qué puede haber hecho con ello? - 5. [indicating possibility] poder; **you could have done it** podrías haberlo hecho; **I could see you tomorrow** podríamos vernos mañana.

Canada [ˈkænədə] *n* (el) Canadá.

Canadian [kəˈneɪdjən] <> *adj* canadiense. <> *n* [person] canadiense *mf*.

canal [kəˈnæl] *n* canal *m*.

canary [kəˈneərɪ] *n* canario *m*.

Canary Islands, Canaries [kəˈneərɪz] *npl*: **the Canary Islands** las (islas) Canarias.

cancel [ˈkænsl] (*UK pt & pp* -**led**, *cont* -**ling**, *US pt & pp* -**ed**, *cont* -**ing**) *vt* - 1. [call off] cancelar, suspender - 2. [invalidate - cheque, debt] cancelar; [- order] anular. **cancel out** *vt sep* anular.

cancellation [ˌkænsəˈleɪʃn] *n* suspensión *f*.

cancer [ˈkænsər] *n* [disease] cáncer *m*. **Cancer** *n* Cáncer *m*.

candelabra [ˌkændɪˈlɑːbrə] *n* candelabro *m*.

candid [ˈkændɪd] *adj* franco(ca).

candidate [ˈkændɪdət] *n*: **candidate (for)** candidato *m*, -ta *f* (a).

candle [ˈkændl] *n* vela *f*.

candlelight [ˈkændllaɪt] *n*: **by candlelight** a la luz de una vela.

candlelit [ˈkændllɪt] *adj* [dinner] a la luz de las velas.

candlestick [ˈkændlstɪk] *n* candelero *m*.

candour *UK*, **candor** [ˈkændər] *US n* franqueza *f*, sinceridad *f*.

candy [ˈkændɪ] *n esp US* - 1. (U) [confectionery] golosinas *fpl*; **candy bar** chocolatina *f* - 2. [sweet] caramelo *m*.

candyfloss *UK* [ˈkændɪflɒs], **cotton candy** *US n* azúcar *m* hilado, algodón *m*.

cane [keɪn] *n* - 1. (U) [for making furniture, supporting plant] caña *f*, mimbre *m* - 2. [walking stick] bastón *m* - 3. [for punishment]: **the cane** la vara.

canine [ˈkeɪnaɪn] <> *adj* canino(na). <> *n*: **canine (tooth)** (diente *m*) canino *m*, colmillo *m*.

canister [ˈkænɪstər] *n* [for tea] bote *m*; [for film] lata *f*; [for gas] bombona *f*; **smoke canister** bote de humo.

cannabis [ˈkænəbɪs] *n* cannabis *m*.

canned [kænd] *adj* [food, drink] enlatado(da), en lata.

cannibal [ˈkænɪbl] *n* caníbal *mf*.

cannon [ˈkænən] *n* (*pl* **cannon** OR -s) cañón *m*.

cannonball [ˈkænənbɔːl] *n* bala *f* de cañón.

cannot [ˈkænɒt] *fml* (*abbr of* **can not**) ⊳ **can**.

canny [ˈkænɪ] *adj* [shrewd] astuto(ta).

canoe [kəˈnuː] *n* [gen] canoa *f*; SPORT piragua *f*.

canoeing [kəˈnuːɪŋ] *n* piragüismo *m*.

canon [ˈkænən] *n* - 1. [clergyman] canónigo *m* - 2. [general principle] canon *m*.

can opener *n esp US* abrelatas *m inv*.

canopy [ˈkænəpɪ] *n* [over bed, seat] dosel *m*.

can't [kɑːnt] (*abbr of* **cannot**) ⊳ **can**.

cantankerous [kænˈtæŋkərəs] *adj* [person] refunfuñón(ona), cascarrabias *(inv)*.

canteen [kænˈtiːn] *n* - 1. [restaurant] cantina *f* - 2. [set of cutlery] (juego *m* de) cubertería *f*.

canter ['kæntər] ◇ n medio galope m.
◇ vi ir a medio galope.

cantilever ['kæntɪliːvər] n voladizo m.

Cantonese [,kæntə'niːz] ◇ adj cantonés(esa). ◇ n - 1. [person] cantonés m, -esa f - 2. [language] cantonés m.

canvas ['kænvəs] n - 1. [cloth] lona f - 2. [for painting on, finished painting] lienzo m.

canvass ['kænvəs] ◇ vt - 1. POL [person] solicitar el voto a - 2. [opinion] pulsar. ◇ vi solicitar votos yendo de puerta en puerta.

canyon ['kænjən] n cañón m.

cap [kæp] ◇ n - 1. [hat - peaked] gorra f; [- with no peak] gorro m; **to go cap in hand to sb** acudir a alguien en actitud humilde - 2. [on bottle] tapón m; [on jar] tapa f; [on pen] capuchón m - 3. [limit] tope m - 4. UK [contraceptive device] diafragma m. ◇ vt - 1. [top]: **to be capped with** estar coronado(da) de - 2. [outdo]: **to cap it all** para colmo.

capability [,keɪpə'bɪlətɪ] n capacidad f.

capable ['keɪpəbl] adj - 1. [able]: **to be capable of sthg/of doing sthg** ser capaz de algo/de hacer algo - 2. [competent] competente.

capacity [kə'pæsɪtɪ] n - 1. [gen]: **capacity (for)** capacidad f (de); **seating capacity** aforo m - 2. [position] calidad f.

cape [keɪp] n - 1. GEOG cabo m - 2. [cloak] capa f.

caper ['keɪpər] n - 1. [food] alcaparra f - 2. inf [escapade] treta f.

capita ⊳ **per capita**.

capital ['kæpɪtl] ◇ adj - 1. [letter] mayúscula - 2. [punishable by death] capital. ◇ n - 1. [of country, main centre] capital f - 2.: **capital (letter)** mayúscula f - 3. [money] capital m; **to make capital (out) of** fig sacar partido de.

capital expenditure n (U) inversión f de capital.

capital gains tax n impuesto m sobre plusvalías.

capital goods npl bienes mpl de capital.

capitalism ['kæpɪtəlɪzm] n capitalismo m.

capitalist ['kæpɪtəlɪst] ◇ adj capitalista. ◇ n capitalista mf.

capitalize, -ise ['kæpɪtəlaɪz] vi: **to capitalize on sthg** aprovechar algo, capitalizar algo.

capital punishment n (U) pena f capital.

Capitol Hill ['kæpɪtl-] n el Capitolio.

capitulate [kə'pɪtjuleɪt] vi: **to capitulate (to)** capitular (ante).

Capricorn ['kæprɪkɔːn] n Capricornio m.

capsize [kæp'saɪz] ◇ vt hacer volcar OR zozobrar. ◇ vi volcar, zozobrar.

capsule ['kæpsjuːl] n cápsula f.

captain ['kæptɪn] n [gen] capitán m, -ana f; [of aircraft] comandante mf.

caption ['kæpʃn] n [under picture etc] leyenda f; [heading] encabezamiento m.

captivate ['kæptɪveɪt] vt cautivar.

captive ['kæptɪv] ◇ adj - 1. [imprisoned] en cautividad - 2. fig [market] asegurado(da). ◇ n cautivo m, -va f.

captivity [kæp'tɪvətɪ] n: **in captivity** en cautividad, en cautiverio.

captor ['kæptər] n apresador m, -ra f.

capture ['kæptʃər] ◇ vt - 1. [gen] capturar - 2. [audience, share of market] hacerse con; [city] tomar - 3. [scene, mood, attention] captar - 4. [comput] introducir. ◇ n [of person] captura f; [of city] toma f.

car [kɑːr] ◇ n - 1. [motorcar] coche m, automóvil m, carro m Amér, auto m - 2. [on train] vagón m, coche m. ◇ comp [door, tyre etc] del coche; INDUST del automóvil; [accident] de automóvil.

carafe [kə'ræf] n garrafa f.

car alarm n alarma f de coche.

caramel ['kærəmel] n - 1. [burnt sugar] caramelo m (líquido), azúcar m quemado - 2. [sweet] tofe m.

carat ['kærət] n UK quilate m.

caravan ['kærəvæn] n caravana f, roulotte f.

caravan site n UK camping m para caravanas OR roulottes.

carbohydrate [,kɑːbəʊ'haɪdreɪt] n CHEM hidrato m de carbono. **► carbohydrates** npl [in food] féculas fpl.

carbon ['kɑːbən] n - 1. [element] carbono m - 2. copia en papel carbón.

carbonated ['kɑːbəneɪtɪd] adj con gas.

carbon copy n [document] copia f en papel carbón; fig [exact copy] calco m.

carbon dioxide [-daɪ'ɒksaɪd] n bióxido m OR dióxido m de carbono.

carbon monoxide [-mɒ'nɒksaɪd] n monóxido m de carbono.

carbon paper, carbon n (U) papel m carbón.

car-boot sale n venta de objetos usados colocados en el portaequipajes del coche.

carburettor UK, **carburetor** US [,kɑːbə'retər] n carburador m.

carcass ['kɑːkəs] n [gen] cadáver m (de animal); [of bird] carcasa f; [at butcher's] canal m.

card [kɑːd] ◇ n - 1. [playing card] carta f, naipe m - 2. [for information, greetings, computers] tarjeta f; [for identification] carné m - 3. [postcard] postal f - 4. [cardboard] cartulina f. ◇ vt US [ask for ID] pedir el carné a. **► cards** npl las cartas, los naipes. **► on the cards** UK, **in the cards** US adv inf más que probable.

cardboard ['kɑːdbɔːd] ◇ n (U) cartón m. ◇ comp de cartón.

cardboard box *n* caja *f* de cartón.

cardiac ['kɑːdɪæk] *adj* cardíaco(ca).

cardigan ['kɑːdɪgən] *n* rebeca *f*.

cardinal ['kɑːdɪnl] <> *adj* capital. <> *n* RELIG cardenal *m*.

card index *n* UK fichero *m*.

cardphone ['kɑːdfəʊn] *n* tarjeta *f* telefónica.

card table *n* mesita *f* plegable *(para jugar a cartas)*.

care [keər] <> *n* - **1.** [gen] cuidado *m*; **medical care** asistencia *f* médica; **in sb's care** al cargo OR cuidado de alguien; **to be in/be taken into care** estar/ser internado en un centro de protección de menores; **to take care of** [person] cuidar de; [animal, machine] cuidar; [deal with] encargarse de; **take care!** [goodbye] ¡nos vemos!, ¡cuídate!; **to take care (to do sthg)** tener cuidado (de hacer algo) - **2.** [cause of worry] preocupación *f*. <> *vi* - **1.** [be concerned]: **to care (about)** preocuparse (de OR por) - **2.** [mind]: **I don't care** no me importa. ◈ **care of** *prep* al cuidado de, en casa de. ◈ **care for** *vt insep dated* [like]: **I don't care for cheese** no me gusta el queso.

career [kə'rɪər] <> *n* carrera *f*. <> *vi* ir a toda velocidad.

careers adviser *n* asesor *m*, -ra *f* de orientación profesional.

carefree ['keəfriː] *adj* despreocupado(da).

careful ['keəfʊl] *adj* [gen] cuidadoso(sa); [driver] prudente; [work] esmerado(da); **be careful!** ¡ten cuidado!; **to be careful with money** ser mirado OR cuidadoso con el dinero; **to be careful to do sthg** tener cuidado de hacer algo.

carefully ['keəflɪ] *adv* - **1.** [cautiously] cuidadosamente, con cuidado; [drive] con cuidado - **2.** [thoroughly] detenidamente.

careless ['keəlɪs] *adj* - **1.** [inattentive] descuidado(da) - **2.** [unconcerned] despreocupado(da).

caress [kə'res] <> *n* caricia *f*. <> *vt* acariciar.

caretaker ['keə,teɪkər] *n* UK conserje *mf*.

car ferry *n* transbordador *m* OR ferry *m* de coches.

cargo ['kɑːgəʊ] *(pl* -es OR -s*)* *n* carga *f*, cargamento *m*.

car hire *n* UK alquiler *m* OR renta *f* Méx de coches, arrendamiento *m* de autos.

Caribbean [UK kærɪ'bɪən, US kə'rɪbɪən] *n*: **the Caribbean (Sea)** el (mar) Caribe.

caring ['keərɪŋ] *adj* solícito(ta), dedicado(da).

carnage ['kɑːnɪdʒ] *n* carnicería *f*.

carnal ['kɑːnl] *adj liter* carnal.

carnation [kɑː'neɪʃn] *n* clavel *m*.

carnival ['kɑːnɪvl] *n* carnaval *m*.

carnivorous [kɑː'nɪvərəs] *adj* carnívoro(ra).

carol ['kærəl] *n* villancico *m*.

carousel [,kærə'sel] *n* - **1.** *esp* US [at fair] tiovivo *m* - **2.** [at airport] cinta *f* transportadora.

carp [kɑːp] <> *n* *(pl* carp OR -s*)* carpa *f*. <> *vi*: **to carp (about)** refunfuñar OR renegar (de).

car park *n* UK aparcamiento *m*, parqueadero *m* Col & Pan, estacionamiento *m* Amér.

carpenter ['kɑːpəntər] *n* carpintero *m*, -ra *f*.

carpentry ['kɑːpəntrɪ] *n* carpintería *f*.

carpet ['kɑːpɪt] <> *n* lit & fig alfombra *f*; **fitted carpet** moqueta *f*; **to sweep sthg under the carpet** fig echar tierra a algo. <> *vt* [fit with carpet] enmoquetar.

carpet slipper *n* zapatilla *f*.

carpet sweeper [-'swiːpər] *n* cepillo *m* mecánico (de alfombras).

car rental *n* US alquiler *m* OR renta *f* Méx de coches, arrendamiento *m* de autos.

carriage ['kærɪdʒ] *n* - **1.** [horsedrawn vehicle] carruaje *m* - **2.** UK [railway coach] vagón *m* - **3.** [transport of goods] transporte *m*; **carriage forward** UK porte a cuenta del destinatario - **4.** [on typewriter] carro *m*.

carriage return *n* retorno *m* de carro.

carriageway ['kærɪdʒweɪ] *n* UK calzada *f*.

carrier ['kærɪər] *n* - **1.** COMM transportista *mf* - **2.** [airline] aerolínea *f* - **3.** [of disease] portador *m*, -ra *f* - **4.** = **carrier bag**.

carrier bag *n* bolsa *f* *(de papel o plástico)*.

carrot ['kærət] *n* - **1.** [vegetable] zanahoria *f* - **2.** *inf* [incentive] aliciente *m*.

carry ['kærɪ] <> *vt* - **1.** [transport] llevar - **2.** [have about one's person] llevar encima - **3.** [disease] ser portador de - **4.** [involve] acarrear, conllevar - **5.** [motion, proposal] aprobar - **6.** [be pregnant with] estar embarazada de - **7.** MATHS llevarse. <> *vi* [sound] oírse. ◈ **carry away** *vt insep*: **to get carried away** exaltarse. ◈ **carry forward, carry over** *vt sep* llevar a la página siguiente. ◈ **carry off** *vt sep* - **1.** [make a success of] llevar a cabo - **2.** [win] llevarse. ◈ **carry on** *vt insep* - **1.** [continue] continuar, seguir; **to carry on doing sthg** continuar OR seguir haciendo algo - **2.** [conversation] mantener. <> *vi inf* [make a fuss] exagerar la nota. ◈ **carry out** *vt insep* - **1.** [perform] llevar a cabo - **2.** [fulfil] cumplir. ◈ **carry through** *vt sep* [accomplish] llevar a cabo.

carryall ['kærɪɔːl] *n* US bolsa *f* de viaje.

carrycot ['kærɪkɒt] *n* *esp* UK moisés *m*.

carry-out *n* US & Scotland comida *f* para llevar.

carsick ['kɑː,sɪk] *adj* mareado(da) *(al ir en coche)*.

cart [kɑːt] *n* - **1.** [for horse] carro *m*, carreta *f* - **2.** US [trolley] carrito *m*. ◇ *vt inf* acarrear.

carton ['kɑːtn] *n* - **1.** [strong cardboard box] caja *f* de cartón - **2.** [for liquids] cartón *m*, envase *m*.

cartoon [kɑː'tuːn] *n* - **1.** [satirical drawing] chiste *m* (en viñeta) - **2.** [comic strip] tira *f* cómica - **3.** [film] dibujos *mpl* animados.

cartridge ['kɑːtrɪdʒ] *n* - **1.** [for gun, camera & COMPUT] cartucho *m* - **2.** [for pen] recambio *m*.

cartwheel ['kɑːtwiːl] *n* voltereta *f* lateral.

carve [kɑːv] ◇ *vt* - **1.** [wood] tallar; [stone] esculpir - **2.** [meat] trinchar - **3.** [name, message] grabar. ◇ *vi* trinchar. ◆ **carve out** *vt sep* [niche, place] conquistar. ◆ **carve up** *vt sep* repartir.

carving ['kɑːvɪŋ] *n* - **1.** [art, work - wooden] tallado *m*; [- stone] labrado *m* - **2.** [object - wooden, stone] talla *f*.

carving knife *n* cuchillo *m* de trinchar.

car wash *n* lavado *m* de coches.

case [keɪs] *n* - **1.** [gen & GRAM] caso *m*; **to be the case** ser el caso; **in that/which case** en ese/cuyo caso; **as** OR **whatever the case may be** según sea el caso; **in case of** en caso de - **2.** [argument] argumentos *mpl*; **the case for/against (sthg)** los argumentos a favor/en contra (de algo) - **3.** LAW [trial, inquiry] pleito *m*, causa *f* - **4.** [container - of leather] funda *f*; [- of hard material] estuche *m* - **5.** UK [suitcase] maleta *f*, petaca *f* Méx, valija *f* R Plata. ◆ **in any case** *adv* en cualquier caso. ◆ **in case** *conj* & *adv* por si acaso; **in case she doesn't come** por si no viene.

cash [kæʃ] ◇ *n* - **1.** [notes and coins] (dinero *m*) efectivo *m*; **to pay (in) cash** pagar al contado OR en efectivo - **2.** *inf* [money] dinero *m* - **3.** [payment]: **cash in advance** pago *m* al contado por adelantado; **cash on delivery** entrega *f* contra reembolso. ◇ *vt* cobrar, hacer efectivo. ◆ **cash in** *vi*: **to cash in on** *inf* sacar partido de.

cash and carry *n* almacén de venta al por mayor.

cashbook ['kæʃbʊk] *n* libro *m* de caja.

cash box *n* caja *f* con cerradura *(para el dinero)*.

cash card *n* esp US tarjeta *f* de cajero automático.

cash desk *n* UK caja *f*.

cash dispenser [-dɪ'spensəʳ], **cash machine**, **cash point** *n* esp US cajero *m* automático.

cashew (nut) ['kæʃuː-] *n* (nuez *f* de) anacardo *m*.

cashier [kæ'ʃɪəʳ] *n* cajero *m*, -ra *f*.

cashless ['kæʃlɪs] *adj* sin dinero en efectivo.

cash machine = **cash dispenser**.

cashmere [kæʃ'mɪəʳ] *n* cachemira *f*.

cash point ['kæʃpɔɪnt] = **cash dispenser**.

cash register *n* caja *f* (registradora).

casing ['keɪsɪŋ] *n* [of electric cable] revestimiento *m*.

casino [kə'siːnəʊ] *(pl* -s*)* *n* casino *m*.

cask [kɑːsk] *n* tonel *m*, barril *m*.

casket ['kɑːskɪt] *n* - **1.** [for jewels] estuche *m* - **2.** US [coffin] ataúd *m*.

casserole ['kæsərəʊl] *n* - **1.** [stew] guiso *m* - **2.** [pan] cazuela *f*, cacerola *f*.

cassette [kæ'set] *n* cinta *f*, casete *f*.

cassette player *n* casete *m*, magnetófono *m*.

cassette recorder *n* casete *m*, magnetófono *m*.

cast [kɑːst] ◇ *n* [of play, film] reparto *m*. ◇ *vt* (*pt* & *pp* **cast**) - **1.** [look] echar, lanzar - **2.** [light] irradiar; [shadow] proyectar - **3.** [throw] arrojar, lanzar - **4.** [vote] emitir - **5.** [metal, statue] fundir. ◆ **cast off** *vi* NAUT soltar amarras.

castanets [ˌkæstə'nets] *npl* castañuelas *fpl*.

castaway ['kɑːstəweɪ] *n* náufrago *m*, -ga *f*.

caste [kɑːst] *n* casta *f*.

caster, castor ['kɑːstəʳ] *n* [wheel] ruedecilla *f*.

caster sugar, castor sugar *n* UK azúcar *m* extrafino.

casting vote *n* voto *m* de calidad.

cast iron *n* hierro *m* fundido.

castle ['kɑːsl] *n* - **1.** [building] castillo *m* - **2.** [in chess] torre *f*.

castor ['kɑːstəʳ] = **caster**.

castor oil *n* aceite *m* de ricino.

castor sugar = **caster sugar**.

castrate [kæ'streɪt] *vt* castrar.

casual ['kæʒʊəl] *adj* - **1.** [relaxed, indifferent] despreocupado(da) - **2.** *pej* [offhand] descuidado(da), informal - **3.** [chance - visitor] ocasional; [- remark] casual - **4.** [informal - clothes] de sport, informal - **5.** [irregular - labourer etc] eventual.

casually ['kæʒʊəlɪ] *adv* - **1.** [in a relaxed manner, indifferently] con aire despreocupado - **2.** [informally] informalmente.

casualty ['kæʒjʊəltɪ] *n* - **1.** [gen] víctima *f*; MIL baja *f* - **2.** (U) [ward] urgencias *fpl*.

casualty department *n* unidad *f* de urgencias.

cat [kæt] *n* - **1.** [domestic] gato *m*, -ta *f*; **to think that one is the cat's whiskers** UK creerse que uno es el oro y el moro - **2.** [wild] felino *m*.

Catalan ['kætəˌlæn] ◇ *adj* catalán(ana). ◇ *n* - **1.** [person] catalán *m*, -ana *f* - **2.** [language] catalán *m*.

catalogue *UK*, **catolog** *US* ['kætəlɒg] ◇ *n* - 1. [of items] catálogo *m* - 2. *fig* [series] serie *f*. ◇ *vt* - 1. [make official list of] catalogar - 2. *fig* [list] enumerar.

Catalonia [,kætə'ləʊnɪə] *n* Cataluña.

Catalonian [,kætə'ləʊnɪən] ◇ *adj* catalán(ana). ◇ *n* [person] catalán *m*, -ana *f*.

catalyst ['kætəlɪst] *n* lit & fig catalizador *m*.

catalytic convertor [,kætə'lɪtɪk kən'vɜ:tər] *n* catalizador *m*.

catapult ['kætəpʊlt] *UK n* - 1. [hand-held] tirachinas *m inv* - 2. HIST [machine] catapulta *f*.

cataract ['kætərækt] *n* [waterfall, in eye] catarata *f*.

catarrh [kə'tɑ:r] *n (U)* catarro *m*.

catastrophe [kə'tæstrəfɪ] *n* catástrofe *f*.

catch [kætʃ] ◇ *vt (pt & pp caught)* - 1. [gen] coger, agarrar *Amér*; [ball] atrapar - 2. [fish] pescar; [stop - person] parar - 3. [be in time for]: **I've got a train to catch** tengo que coger un tren; **to catch the (last) post** *UK* llegar a la (última) recogida del correo - 4. [hear clearly] entender, llegar a oír - 5. [interest, imagination] despertar - 6. [see]: **to catch sight OR a glimpse of** alcanzar a ver - 7. [hook - shirt etc] engancharse; [shut in door - finger] pillarse - 8. [strike] golpear. ◇ *vi (pt & pp caught)* - 1. [become hooked, get stuck] engancharse - 2. [start to burn] prenderse. ◇ *n* - 1. [of ball etc] parada *f* - 2. [of fish] pesca *f*, captura *f* - 3. [fastener - on door] pestillo *m*; [- on necklace] cierre *m* - 4. [snag] trampa *f*. ◆ **catch on** *vi* - 1. [become popular] hacerse popular - 2. *inf* [understand]: **to catch on (to)** caer en la cuenta (de). ◆ **catch out** *vt sep* [trick] pillar. ◆ **catch up** ◇ *vt sep* alcanzar. ◇ *vi*: **we'll soon catch up** pronto nos pondremos a la misma altura; **to catch up on** [sleep] recuperar; [work, reading] ponerse al día con. ◆ **catch up with** *vt insep* - 1. [group etc] alcanzar - 2. [criminal] pillar, descubrir.

catching ['kætʃɪŋ] *adj* contagioso(sa).

catchment area ['kætʃmənt-] *n UK* zona *f* de captación.

catchphrase ['kætʃfreɪz] *n* muletilla *f*.

catchy ['kætʃɪ] *adj* pegadizo(za).

categorically [,kætɪ'gɒrɪklɪ] *adv* [state] categóricamente; [deny] rotundamente.

category ['kætəgərɪ] *n* categoría *f*.

cater ['keɪtər] ◇ *vi* proveer comida. ◇ *vt US* [party, event] dar el servicio de comida y bebida de. ◆ **cater for** *vt insep UK* [tastes, needs] atender a; [social group] estar destinado(da) a; **I hadn't catered for that** no había contado con eso. ◆ **cater to** *vt insep* complacer.

caterer ['keɪtərər] *n* [firm] empresa *f* de hostelería.

catering ['keɪtərɪŋ] *n* [at wedding etc] servicio *m* de banquetes; [trade] hostelería *f*.

caterpillar ['kætəpɪlər] *n* oruga *f*.

caterpillar tracks *npl* (rodado *m* de) oruga *f*.

cathedral [kə'θi:drəl] *n* catedral *f*.

Catholic ['kæθlɪk] ◇ *adj* católico(ca). ◇ *n* católico *m*, -ca *f*. ◆ **catholic** *adj* diverso(sa).

Catseyes® ['kætsaɪz] *npl UK* catafaros *mpl*.

cattle ['kætl] *npl* ganado *m* (vacuno).

catty ['kætɪ] *adj inf pej* [spiteful] malintencionado(da).

catwalk ['kætwɔ:k] *n* pasarela *f*.

caucus ['kɔ:kəs] *n* [political group] comité *m*. ◆ **Caucus** *n US* congreso de los principales partidos estadounidenses.

caught [kɔ:t] *pt & pp* ▷ **catch**.

cauliflower ['kɒlɪ,flaʊər] *n* coliflor *f*.

cause [kɔ:z] ◇ *n* - 1. [gen] causa *f* - 2. [grounds]: **cause (for)** motivo *m* (para); **cause for complaint** motivo de queja; **cause to do sthg** motivo para hacer algo. ◇ *vt* causar; **to cause sb to do sthg** hacer que alguien haga algo.

caustic ['kɔ:stɪk] *adj* - 1. CHEM cáustico(ca) - 2. [comment] mordaz, hiriente.

caution ['kɔ:ʃn] ◇ *n* - 1. *(U)* [care] precaución *f*, cautela *f* - 2. [warning] advertencia *f*. ◇ *vt* - 1. [warn - against danger] prevenir; [- against behaving rudely etc] advertir - 2. *UK* [subj: policeman]: **to caution sb (for)** amonestar a alguien (por).

cautious ['kɔ:ʃəs] *adj* prudente, cauto(ta).

cavalier [,kævə'lɪər] *adj* arrogante, desdeñoso(sa).

cavalry ['kævlrɪ] *n* caballería *f*.

cave [keɪv] *n* cueva *f*. ◆ **cave in** *vi* [roof, ceiling] hundirse.

caveman ['keɪvmæn] *(pl -men [-men])* *n* cavernícola *mf*.

caviar(e) ['kævɪɑ:r] *n* caviar *m*.

cavity ['kævətɪ] *n* - 1. [in object, structure] cavidad *f* - 2. [in tooth] caries *f inv*.

cavort [kə'vɔ:t] *vi* retozar, brincar.

cc *n* - 1. (*abbr of* **cubic centimetre**) cc - 2. (*abbr of* **carbon copy**) cc.

CD *n* - 1. (*abbr of* **compact disc**) CD *m* - 2. (*abbr of* **Corps Diplomatique**) CD.

CD burner *n* grabadora *f* de CD.

CD player *n* reproductor *m* de CD.

CD-R (*abbr of* **compact disc recordable**) *n* CD-R *m*.

CD-R drive *n* grabadora *f* de CD-R.

CD ROM burner n estampadora f de CD.

CD-RW (*abbr of* compact disc rewritable) *n* CD RW *m*.

CD tower n torre f de almacenamiento de CDs.

cease [si:s] *fml* ⬦ *vt* cesar. ⬦ *vi* cesar.

cease-fire *n* alto *m* el fuego.

ceaseless ['si:slɪs] *adj fml* incesante.

cedar (tree) ['si:dər-] *n* cedro *m*.

ceiling ['si:lɪŋ] *n* - **1.** [of room] techo *m* - **2.** [limit] tope *m*, límite *m*.

celebrate ['selɪbreɪt] *vt* & *vi* celebrar.

celebrated ['selɪbreɪtɪd] *adj* célebre.

celebration [,selɪ'breɪʃn] *n* - **1.** (*U*) [activity, feeling] celebración *f* - **2.** [event] fiesta *f*, festejo *m*.

celebrity [sɪ'lebrətɪ] *n* celebridad *f*.

celery ['selərɪ] *n* apio *m*.

celibate ['selɪbət] *adj* célibe.

cell [sel] *n* - **1.** BIOL & POL célula *f* - **2.** COMPUT celda *f* - **3.** [prisoner's, nun's or monk's room] celda *f* - **4.** ELEC pila *f*.

cellar ['selər] *n* - **1.** [basement] sótano *m* - **2.** [stock of wine] bodega *f*.

cello ['tʃeləʊ] (*pl* **-s**) *n* violoncelo *m*.

Cellophane® ['seləfeɪn] *n* celofán® *m*.

Celsius ['selsɪəs] *adj* centígrado(da); **20 degrees Celsius** 20 grados centígrados.

Celt [kelt] *n* celta *mf*.

Celtic ['keltɪk] ⬦ *adj* celta. ⬦ *n* celta *m*.

cement [sɪ'ment] ⬦ *n* - **1.** [for concrete] cemento *m* - **2.** [glue] cola *f*. ⬦ *vt* - **1.** [glue] encolar - **2.** [agreement, relationship] cimentar, fortalecer.

cement mixer *n* hormigonera *f*.

cemetery ['semɪtrɪ] *n* cementerio *m*.

censor ['sensər] ⬦ *n* censor *m*, -ra *f*. ⬦ *vt* censurar.

censorship ['sensəʃɪp] *n* censura *f*.

censure ['senʃər] *vt* censurar.

census ['sensəs] (*pl* **-uses**) *n* censo *m*.

cent [sent] *n* centavo *m*.

centenary *UK* [sen'ti:nərɪ], **centennial** *US* [sen'tenjəl] *n* centenario *m*.

center *US* = **centre**.

centigrade ['sentɪgreɪd] *adj* centígrado(da); **20 degrees centigrade** 20 grados centígrados.

centilitre *UK*, **centiliter** *US* ['sentɪ,li:tər] *n* centilitro *m*.

centimetre *UK*, **centimeter** *US* ['sentɪ,mi:tər] *n* centímetro *m*.

centipede ['sentɪpi:d] *n* ciempiés *m inv*.

central ['sentrəl] *adj* - **1.** [gen] central; **in central Spain** en el centro de España - **2.** [easily reached] céntrico(ca).

Central America *n* Centroamérica.

Central Europe *n* Europa Central.

central heating *n* calefacción *f* central.

centralize, **-ise** ['sentrəlaɪz] *vt* centralizar.

central locking [-'lɒkɪŋ] *n* cierre *m* centralizado.

central reservation *n UK* mediana *f*.

centre *UK*, **center** *US* ['sentər] ⬦ *n* centro *m*; **centre of attention/gravity** centro de atención/gravedad; **the centre** POL el centro. ⬦ *adj* - **1.** [middle] central - **2.** POL centrista. ⬦ *vt* centrar.

centre back, **centre half** *n* defensa *mf* central.

centre forward *n* delantero *m*, -ra *f* centro (*inv*).

centre half = **centre back**.

century ['sentʃʊrɪ] *n* siglo *m*.

ceramic [sɪ'ræmɪk] *adj* de cerámica, cerámico(ca). ⬦ **ceramics** *n* cerámica *f*.

cereal ['sɪərɪəl] *n* - **1.** [crop] cereal *m* - **2.** [breakfast food] cereales *mpl*.

ceremonial [,serɪ'məʊnjəl] *adj* ceremonial.

ceremony ['serɪmənɪ] *n* ceremonia *f*; **to stand on ceremony** andarse con cumplidos *OR* ceremonias.

certain ['sɜ:tn] *adj* - **1.** [gen] seguro(ra); **he's certain to be late** (es) seguro que llega tarde; **to be certain (of)** estar seguro (de); **to make certain (of)** asegurarse (de); **for certain** con toda seguridad - **2.** [particular, some] cierto(ta); **to a certain extent** hasta cierto punto - **3.** [named person]: **a certain...** un(una) tal...

certainly ['sɜ:tnlɪ] *adv* desde luego; **certainly not!** ¡claro que no!

certainty ['sɜ:tntɪ] *n* seguridad *f*.

certificate [sə'tɪfɪkət] *n* [gen] certificado *m*; SCH & UNIV diploma *m*, título *m*; [of birth, death] partida *f*.

certified ['sɜ:tɪfaɪd] *adj* [document] certificado(da); [person] diplomado(da).

certified mail *n US* correo *m* certificado.

certified public accountant *n US* contable diplomado *m*, contable diplomada *f*, contador público *m*, contadora pública *f Amér*.

certify ['sɜ:tɪfaɪ] *vt* - **1.** [declare true] certificar - **2.** [declare insane] declarar demente.

cervical [sə'vaɪkl] *adj* cervical.

cervical smear *n* citología *f*, frotis *f* cervical.

cervix ['sɜ:vɪks] (*pl* **-ices** [-ɪsi:z]) *n* [of womb] cuello *m* del útero.

cesarean (section) = **caesarean (section)**.

cesspit ['sespɪt], **cesspool** ['sespu:l] *n* pozo *m* negro.

cf. (*abbr of* confer) cf., cfr.

CFC (*abbr of* chlorofluorocarbon) *n* CFC *m*.

Chad [tʃæd] *n* el Chad.

chafe [tʃeɪf] *vt* [rub] rozar.

chaffinch ['tʃæfɪntʃ] *n* pinzón *m*.

chain [tʃeɪn] ◇ *n* cadena *f*; **chain of mountains** cordillera *f*, cadena *f* montañosa; **chain of events** serie *f* OR cadena *f* de acontecimientos. ◇ *vt* [person, object] encadenar.

chain reaction *n* reacción *f* en cadena.

chain saw *n* motosierra *f*, sierra *f* mecánica.

chain-smoke *vi* fumar un cigarrillo tras otro.

chain store *n* tienda *f* (de una cadena).

chair [tʃeəʳ] ◇ *n* - 1. [gen] silla *f*; [armchair] sillón *m* - 2. [university post] cátedra *f* - 3. [of meeting] presidencia *f*. ◇ *vt* presidir.

chair lift *n* telesilla *m*.

chairman ['tʃeəmən] (*pl* **-men** [-mən]) *n* presidente *m*.

chairperson ['tʃeə,pɜːsn] (*pl* **-s**) *n* presidente *m*, -ta *f*.

chalet ['ʃæleɪ] *n* chalé *m*, chalet *m*.

chalk [tʃɔːk] *n* - 1. [for drawing] tiza *f*, gis *m* *Méx* - 2. [type of rock] creta *f*.

chalkboard ['tʃɔːkbɔːd] *n US* pizarra *f*.

challenge ['tʃælɪndʒ] ◇ *n* desafío *m*, reto *m*. ◇ *vt* - 1. [to fight, competition]: **to challenge sb (to sthg/to do sthg)** desafiar a alguien (a algo/a que haga algo) - 2. [question] poner en tela de juicio.

challenging ['tʃælɪndʒɪŋ] *adj* - 1. [task, job] estimulante, que supone un reto - 2. [look, tone of voice] desafiante.

chamber ['tʃeɪmbəʳ] *n* [room] cámara *f*.

chambermaid ['tʃeɪmbəmeɪd] *n* [at hotel] camarera *f*.

chamber music *n* música *f* de cámara.

chamber of commerce *n* cámara *f* de comercio.

chameleon [kə'miːljən] *n* camaleón *m*.

champagne [,ʃæm'peɪn] *n* champán *m*.

champion ['tʃæmpjən] *n* - 1. [of competition] campeón *m*, -ona *f* - 2. [of cause] defensor *m*, -ra *f*. ◇ *vt* defender.

championship ['tʃæmpjənʃɪp] *n* campeonato *m*.

chance [tʃɑːns] ◇ *n* - 1. [luck] azar *m*, suerte *f*; **by chance** por casualidad - 2. [likelihood] posibilidad *f*; **not to stand a chance (of)** no tener ninguna posibilidad (de); **by any chance** por casualidad, acaso - 3. [opportunity] oportunidad *f* - 4. [risk] riesgo *m*; **to take a chance (on)** correr un riesgo OR arriesgarse (con). ◇ *adj* fortuito(ta), casual. ◇ *vt* arriesgar; **to chance it** arriesgarse.

chancellor ['tʃɑːnsələʳ] *n* - 1. [chief minister] canciller *m* - 2. *US* UNIV ≃ rector *m*.

Chancellor of the Exchequer *n UK* Ministro *m*, -tra *f* de Economía y Hacienda.

chandelier [,ʃændə'lɪəʳ] *n* (lámpara *f* de) araña *f*.

change [tʃeɪndʒ] ◇ *n* - 1. [gen] cambio *m*; **change of clothes** muda *f*; **for a change** para variar - 2. [from payment] vuelta *f*, cambio *m*, vuelto *m* *Amér* - 3. [coins] suelto *m*, calderilla *f*, sencillo *m* *Andes*, feria *f* *Méx*, menudo *m* *Col* - 4. [money in exchange]: **have you got change for £5?** ¿tienes cambio de 5 libras? ◇ *vt* - 1. [gen] cambiar; **to change sthg into** transformar algo en; **to change pounds into euros** cambiar libras en *Esp* OR a euros; **to change direction** cambiar de rumbo; **to change one's mind** cambiar de idea OR de opinión - 2. [goods in shop] cambiar - 3. [switch - job, gear, train] cambiar de; **to change hands** COMM cambiar de mano; **to change one's shirt** cambiarse de camisa; **to get changed** cambiarse de ropa. ◇ *vi* - 1. [alter] cambiar; **to change into sthg** transformarse en algo - 2. [change clothes] cambiarse - 3. [change trains, buses] hacer transbordo. ◆ **change over** *vi* [convert]: **to change over to** cambiar a.

changeable ['tʃeɪndʒəbl] *adj* variable.

change machine *n* máquina *f* de cambio.

changeover ['tʃeɪndʒ,əʊvəʳ] *n*: **changeover (to)** cambio *m* (a).

changing ['tʃeɪndʒɪŋ] *adj* cambiante.

changing room *n* - 1. SPORT vestuario *m* - 2. [in clothes shop] probador *m*.

channel ['tʃænl] ◇ *n* canal *m*. ◇ *vt* (*UK* *pt* & *pp* **-led**, *cont* **-ling**, *US* *pt* & *pp* **-ed**, *cont* **-ing**) *lit* & *fig* canalizar. ◆ **Channel** *n*: **the (English) Channel** el Canal de la Mancha. ◆ **channels** *npl* [procedure] conductos *mpl*, medios *mpl*.

Channel Islands *npl*: **the Channel Islands** las islas del Canal de la Mancha.

Channel tunnel *n*: **the Channel tunnel** el túnel del Canal de la Mancha.

chant [tʃɑːnt] ◇ *n* - 1. RELIG canto *m* - 2. [of demonstrators] consigna *f*; [at sports match] cántico *m*. ◇ *vt* - 1. RELIG cantar - 2. [words] corear.

chaos ['keɪɒs] *n* caos *m inv*.

chaotic [keɪ'ɒtɪk] *adj* caótico(ca).

chap [tʃæp] *n UK inf* tipo *m*, tío *m*.

chapel ['tʃæpl] *n* capilla *f*.

chaperon(e) ['ʃæpərəʊn] ◇ *n* carabina *f*, acompañanta *f*. ◇ *vt* acompañar.

chaplain ['tʃæplɪn] *n* capellán *m*.

chapped [tʃæpt] *adj* agrietado(da).

chapter ['tʃæptəʳ] *n lit* & *fig* capítulo *m*.

char [tʃɑːʳ] ◇ *n UK* [cleaner] mujer *f* de la limpieza. ◇ *vt* [burn] carbonizar, calcinar.

character ['kærəktəʳ] *n* - 1. [nature, quality, letter] carácter *m*; **to be out of/in character (for)** no ser/ser típico (de) - 2. [in film, book, play] personaje *m* - 3. inf [person of stated kind] tipo *m* - 4. inf [person with strong personality]: **to be a character** ser todo un carácter.

characteristic [ˌkærəktəˈrɪstɪk] ⋄ *adj* característico(ca). ⋄ *n* característica *f*.

characterize, -ise [ˈkærəktəraɪz] *vt* [typify] caracterizar.

charade [ʃəˈrɑːd] *n* farsa *f*. ◆ **charades** *n* (U) charadas *fpl*.

charcoal [ˈtʃɑːkəʊl] *n* [for barbecue etc] carbón *m* (vegetal); [for drawing] carboncillo *m*.

charge [tʃɑːdʒ] ⋄ *n* - 1. [cost] precio *m*; **free of charge** gratis; **will that be cash or charge?** *US* ¿pagará en efectivo o con tarjeta? - 2. LAW cargo *m*, acusación *f* - 3. [responsibility]: **to have charge of sthg** tener algo al cargo de uno; **to take charge (of)** hacerse cargo (de); **to be in charge** ser el encargado(la encargada); **in charge of** encargado(da) de - 4. ELEC carga *f* - 5. MIL [of cavalry] carga *f*. ⋄ *vt* - 1. [customer, sum] cobrar; **to charge sthg to sb** cargar algo en la cuenta de alguien - 2. [attack] cargar contra - 3. [battery] cargar. ⋄ *vi* [rush] cargar; **to charge in/out** entrar/salir en tromba.

charge card *n* tarjeta de compra.

charger [ˈtʃɑːdʒəʳ] *n* [for batteries] cargador *m*.

chariot [ˈtʃærɪət] *n* carro *m*, cuadriga *f*.

charisma [kəˈrɪzmə] *n* carisma *m*.

charitable [ˈtʃærətəbl] *adj* - 1. [person, remark] caritativo(va) - 2. [organization] benéfico(ca).

charity [ˈtʃærətɪ] *n* - 1. [kindness, money] caridad *f* - 2. [organization] institución *f* benéfica.

charity shop *n UK* tienda de una entidad benéfica en la que se venden productos de segunda mano donados por simpatizantes.

charm [tʃɑːm] ⋄ *n* - 1. [appeal, attractiveness] encanto *m* - 2. [spell] hechizo *m* - 3. [on bracelet] dije *m*, amuleto *m*. ⋄ *vt* dejar encantado(da).

charming [ˈtʃɑːmɪŋ] *adj* encantador(ra).

chart [tʃɑːt] ⋄ *n* - 1. [diagram] gráfico *m* - 2. [map] carta *f*. ⋄ *vt* - 1. [plot, map] representar en un mapa - 2. *fig* [describe] trazar. ◆ **charts** *npl*: **the charts** la lista de éxitos.

charter [ˈtʃɑːtəʳ] ⋄ *n* [document] carta *f*. ⋄ *comp* chárter *(inv)*. ⋄ *vt* [plane, boat] fletar.

chartered accountant [ˈtʃɑːtəd-] *n UK* contable colegiado *m*, contable colegiada *f*, contador colegiado *m*, contadora colegiada *f Amér*.

charter flight *n* vuelo *m* chárter.

chase [tʃeɪs] ⋄ *n* [pursuit] persecución *f*. ⋄ *vt* - 1. [pursue] perseguir - 2. [drive away] ahuyentar - 3. [money, jobs] ir detrás de.

chasm [ˈkæzm] *n* [deep crack] sima *f*; *fig* [divide] abismo *m*.

chassis [ˈʃæsɪ] *(pl* chassis*)* *n* [of vehicle] chasis *m inv*.

chaste [tʃeɪst] *adj* casto(ta).

chat [tʃæt] ⋄ *n* [gen & COMPUT] charla *t*. ⋄ *vi* [gen & COMPUT] charlar. ◆ **chat up** *vt sep UK inf* intentar ligar con, tirarse un lance con.

chat line *n* línea *f* compartida.

chat room *n* COMPUT sala *f* de conversación.

chatter [ˈtʃætəʳ] ⋄ *n* - 1. [of person] cháchara *f* - 2. [of bird] gorjeo *m*; [of monkey] chillidos *mpl*. ⋄ *vi* - 1. [person] parlotear - 2. [teeth] castañetear.

chatterbox [ˈtʃætəbɒks] *n inf* parlanchín *m*, -ina *f*.

chatty [ˈtʃætɪ] *adj* - 1. [person] dicharachero(ra) - 2. [letter] informal.

chauffeur [ˈʃəʊfəʳ] *n* chófer *mf*.

chauvinist [ˈʃəʊvɪnɪst] *n* - 1. [sexist] sexista *mf*; **male chauvinist** machista *m* - 2. [nationalist] chovinista *mf*.

cheap [tʃiːp] ⋄ *adj* - 1. [inexpensive] barato(ta) - 2. [low - quality] de mala calidad - 3. [vulgar - joke etc] de mal gusto - 4. *US* [stingy] mezquino(na). ⋄ *adv* barato.

cheapen [ˈtʃiːpn] *vt* [degrade] rebajar.

cheaply [ˈtʃiːplɪ] *adv* barato.

cheat [tʃiːt] ⋄ *n* tramposo *m*, -sa *f*. ⋄ *vt* engañar, estafar. ⋄ *vi* [in exam] copiar; [at cards] hacer trampas.

check [tʃek] ⋄ *n* - 1. [inspection, test]: **check (on)** inspección *f* OR control *m* (de); **to keep a check on** controlar - 2. [restraint]: **check (on)** restricción *f* (en) - 3. *US* [cheque] cheque *m* - 4. *US* [bill] cuenta *f* - 5. *US* [tick] señal *f* de visto bueno - 6. [pattern] cuadros *mpl* - 7. [in chess] jaque *m*. ⋄ *vt* - 1. [test, verify] comprobar - 2. [inspect - machine, product] inspeccionar; [- ticket, passport] revisar, controlar - 3. [restrain, stop] refrenar. ⋄ *vi* comprobar; **to check (for/on sthg)** comprobar (algo). ◆ **check in** ⋄ *vt sep* [luggage, coat] facturar. ⋄ *vi* - 1. [at hotel] inscribirse, registrarse - 2. [at airport] facturar. ◆ **check out** ⋄ *vt sep* - 1. [luggage, coat] recoger - 2. [investigate] comprobar - 3. *inf* [look at] mirar. ⋄ *vi* [from hotel] dejar el hotel. ◆ **check up** *vi*: **to check up (on sthg)** informarse (acerca de algo); **to check up on sb** hacer averiguaciones sobre alguien.

checkbook *US* = **chequebook**.

checked [tʃekt] *adj* a cuadros.

checkered *US* = **chequered**.

checkers [ˈtʃekəz] *n* (U) *US* damas *fpl*.

check-in *n* facturación *f*.

check-in desk *n* mostrador *m* de facturación.

checking account [ˈtʃekɪŋ-] *n US* cuenta *f* corriente.

checkmate ['tʃekmeɪt] n jaque m mate.

checkout ['tʃekaʊt] n caja f.

checkpoint ['tʃekpɔɪnt] n control m.

checkup ['tʃekʌp] n chequeo m.

Cheddar (cheese) ['tʃedər-] n (queso m) cheddar m.

cheek [tʃiːk] n - 1. [of face] mejilla f - 2. inf [impudence] cara f, descaro m.

cheekbone ['tʃiːkbəʊn] n pómulo m.

cheeky ['tʃiːkɪ] adj descarado(da).

cheer [tʃɪər] ◇ n [shout] aclamación f; **cheers** vítores mpl. ◇ vt - 1. [shout approval, encouragement at] aclamar - 2. [gladden] animar. ◇ vi gritar con entusiasmo. ➡ **cheers** excl [when drinking] ¡salud!; UK inf [thank you] ¡gracias!; inf [goodbye] ¡hasta luego! ➡ **cheer up** ◇ vt sep animar. ◇ vi animarse.

cheerful ['tʃɪəfʊl] adj [gen] alegre.

cheerio [,tʃɪərɪ'əʊ] excl UK inf ¡hasta luego!

cheese [tʃiːz] n queso m.

cheeseboard ['tʃiːzbɔːd] n tabla f de quesos.

cheeseburger ['tʃiːz,bɜːgər] n hamburguesa f con queso.

cheesecake ['tʃiːzkeɪk] n pastel m OR tarta f de queso.

cheetah ['tʃiːtə] n guepardo m, onza f.

chef [ʃef] n chef m, jefe m de cocina.

chemical ['kemɪkl] ◇ adj químico(ca). ◇ n sustancia f química.

chemist ['kemɪst] n - 1. UK [pharmacist] farmacéutico m, -ca f; **chemist's (shop)** farmacia f - 2. [scientist] químico m, -ca f.

chemistry ['kemɪstrɪ] n [science] química f.

cheque UK, **check** US [tʃek] n cheque m, talón m.

chequebook UK, **checkbook** US ['tʃekbʊk] n talonario m de cheques, chequera f Amér.

cheque card n UK tarjeta f de identificación bancaria.

chequered UK ['tʃekəd], **checkered** US ['tʃekərd] adj - 1. [patterned] a cuadros - 2. [varied] lleno(na) de altibajos.

cherish ['tʃerɪʃ] vt - 1. [hope, memory] abrigar - 2. [privilege, right] apreciar - 3. [person, thing] tener mucho cariño a.

cherry ['tʃerɪ] n [fruit] cereza f; **cherry (tree)** cerezo m.

chess [tʃes] n ajedrez m.

chessboard ['tʃesbɔːd] n tablero m de ajedrez.

chest [tʃest] n - 1. ANAT pecho m; **to get sthg off one's chest** inf contar algo para desahogarse - 2. [box, trunk - gen] arca f, cofre m; [- for tools] caja f.

chestnut ['tʃesnʌt] ◇ adj [colour] castaño(ña). ◇ n [nut] castaña f; **chestnut (tree)** castaño m.

chest of drawers (pl chests of drawers) n cómoda f.

chew [tʃuː] vt - 1. [food] masticar - 2. [nails] morderse; [carpet] morder. ➡ **chew up** vt sep [food] masticar; [slippers] mordisquear; [tape] destrozar.

chewing gum ['tʃuːɪŋ-] n chicle m.

chic [ʃiːk] adj chic (inv), elegante.

chick [tʃɪk] n - 1. [baby bird] polluelo m - 2. inf [woman] nena f.

chicken ['tʃɪkɪn] n - 1. [bird] gallina f - 2. [food] pollo m - 3. inf [coward] gallina mf. ➡ **chicken out** vi inf: to chicken out (of sthg/of doing sthg) rajarse (a la hora de algo/de hacer algo).

chickenpox ['tʃɪkɪnpɒks] n varicela f.

chickpea ['tʃɪkpiː] n garbanzo m.

chicory ['tʃɪkərɪ] n achicoria f.

chief [tʃiːf] ◇ adj principal. ◇ n jefe m, -fa f.

Chief Executive n US [US president] presidente m, -ta f.

chief executive officer n US [head of company] director m, -ra f general.

chiefly ['tʃiːflɪ] adv - 1. [mainly] principalmente - 2. [especially, above all] por encima de todo.

chiffon ['ʃɪfɒn] n gasa f.

chilblain ['tʃɪlbleɪn] n sabañón m.

child [tʃaɪld] (pl children) n - 1. [boy, girl] niño m, -ña f - 2. [son, daughter] hijo m, -ja f.

child benefit n (U) UK subsidio pagado a todas las familias por cada hijo.

childbirth ['tʃaɪldbɜːθ] n (U) parto m.

childcare ['tʃaɪldkeər] n cuidado m de los niños.

childhood ['tʃaɪldhʊd] n infancia f, niñez f.

childish ['tʃaɪldɪʃ] adj pej infantil.

childlike ['tʃaɪldlaɪk] adj [person] como un niño; [smile, trust] de niño.

childminder ['tʃaɪld,maɪndər] n UK niñera f (durante el día).

childproof ['tʃaɪldpruːf] adj a prueba de niños.

children ['tʃɪldrən] npl ⊳ child.

children's home n hogar m infantil.

Chile ['tʃɪlɪ] n Chile.

Chilean ['tʃɪlɪən] ◇ adj chileno(na). ◇ n chileno m, -na f.

chili ['tʃɪlɪ] = chilli.

chill [tʃɪl] ◇ n - 1. [illness] resfriado m - 2. [in temperature]: there's a chill in the air hace un poco de fresco. ◇ vt - 1. [drink, food] (dejar) enfriar - 2. [person - with cold] enfriar; [- with fear] hacer sentir escalofríos. ➡ **chill out** vi inf relajarse.

chilli ['tʃɪlɪ] (pl -ies), **chili** (pl -ies) n guindilla f, chile m, ají m Andes & R Plata.

chilling ['tʃɪlɪŋ] *adj* [frightening] escalofriante.

chilly ['tʃɪlɪ] *adj* frío(a).

chime [tʃaɪm] ⬦ *n* [of clock] campanada *f*; [of bells] repique *m*. ⬦ *vt* [bell] repicar; [clock] sonar.

chimney ['tʃɪmnɪ] *n* chimenea *f*.

chimneypot ['tʃɪmnɪpɒt] *n* cañón *m* de chimenea.

chimneysweep ['tʃɪmnɪswi:p] *n* deshollinador *m*, -ra *f*.

chimp [tʃɪmp], **chimpanzee** [,tʃɪmpən'zi:] *n* chimpancé *mf*.

chin [tʃɪn] *n* barbilla *f*.

china ['tʃaɪnə] *n* porcelana *f*.

China ['tʃaɪnə] *n* la China.

Chinese [,tʃaɪ'ni:z] ⬦ *adj* chino(na). ⬦ *n*
- **1.** [person] chino *m*, -na *f* - **2.** [language] chino *m*. ⬦ *npl*: **the Chinese** los chinos.

Chinese leaves *npl* UK (hojas *fpl* de) col *f* china.

chink [tʃɪŋk] ⬦ *n* - **1.** [narrow opening] grieta *f*; [of light] resquicio *m* - **2.** [sound] tintineo *m*. ⬦ *vi* tintinear.

chip [tʃɪp] ⬦ *n* - **1.** UK [fried potato chip] patata *f* frita; US [potato crisp] patata *f* frita (de bolsa o de churrería) - **2.** [fragment - gen] pedacito *m*; [- of wood] viruta *f*; [- of stone] lasca *f* - **3.** [flaw - in cup, glass] desportilladura *f* - **4.** COMPUT chip *m* - **5.** [token] ficha *f*. ⬦ *vt* [damage] desportillar. **chip in** *vi* - **1.** [pay money] poner dinero - **2.** [in conversation] intervenir. **chip off** *vt sep* desconchar.

chipboard ['tʃɪpbɔ:d] *n* aglomerado *m*.

chip shop *n* UK tienda en la que se vende pescado y patatas fritas.

chiropodist [kɪ'rɒpədɪst] *n* podólogo *m*, -ga *f*, pedicuro *m*, -ra *f*.

chirp [tʃɜ:p] *vi* [bird] piar; [insect] chirriar.

chirpy ['tʃɜ:pɪ] *adj esp* UK *inf* alegre.

chisel ['tʃɪzl] *n* [for wood] formón *m*, escoplo *m*; [for stone] cincel *m*.

chit [tʃɪt] *n* [note] nota *f*.

chitchat ['tʃɪttʃæt] *n (U) inf* cháchara *f*.

chivalry ['ʃɪvlrɪ] *n* - **1.** *liter* [of knights] caballería *f* - **2.** [good manners] caballerosidad *f*.

chives ['tʃaɪvz] *npl* cebollana *f*.

chlorine ['klɔ:ri:n] *n* cloro *m*.

choc-ice ['tʃɒkaɪs] *n* UK bombón *m* helado.

chock [tʃɒk] *n* cuña *f*, calzo *m*.

chock-a-block, chock-full *adj inf*: **chock-a-block (with)** hasta los topes (de).

chocolate ['tʃɒklət] ⬦ *n* - **1.** [food, drink] chocolate *m* - **2.** [sweet] bombón *m*. ⬦ *comp* de chocolate.

choice [tʃɔɪs] ⬦ *n* - **1.** [gen] elección *f*; **to do sthg by** OR **from choice** elegir hacer algo
- **2.** [person chosen] preferido *m*, -da *f*; [thing chosen] alternativa *f* preferida - **3.** [variety, selection] surtido *m*. ⬦ *adj* de primera calidad.

choir ['kwaɪər] *n* coro *m*.

choirboy ['kwaɪəbɔɪ] *n* niño *m* de coro.

choke [tʃəʊk] ⬦ *n* AUT estárter *m*. ⬦ *vt*
- **1.** [subj: person] estrangular - **2.** [subj: fumes] asfixiar; [subj: fishbone etc] hacer atragantarse
- **3.** [block - pipes, gutter] atascar. ⬦ *vi* [on fishbone etc] atragantarse; [to death] asfixiarse.

cholera ['kɒlərə] *n* cólera *m*.

choose [tʃu:z] (*pt* chose, *pp* chosen) ⬦ *vt*
- **1.** [select] elegir, escoger; **there's little** OR **not much to choose between them** no se sabe cuál es mejor - **2.** [decide]: **to choose to do sthg** decidir hacer algo; **do whatever you choose** haz lo que quieras. ⬦ *vi* elegir, escoger.

choos(e)y ['tʃu:zɪ] (*comp* -ier, *superl* -iest) *adj* [gen] quisquilloso(sa); [about food] exigente, remilgado(da).

chop [tʃɒp] ⬦ *n* - **1.** CULIN chuleta *f* - **2.** [blow - with axe] hachazo *m*. ⬦ *vt* [vegetables, meat] picar; [wood] cortar. ⬦ *vi*: **to chop and change** cambiar cada dos por tres. **chops** *npl inf* morros *mpl*, jeta *f*. **chop down** *vt sep* talar. **chop up** *vt sep* [vegetables, meat] picar; [wood] cortar.

chopper ['tʃɒpər] *n* - **1.** [for wood] hacha *f*; [for meat] cuchillo *m* de carnicero - **2.** *inf* [helicopter] helicóptero *m*.

choppy ['tʃɒpɪ] *adj* picado(da).

chopsticks ['tʃɒpstɪks] *npl* palillos *mpl*.

chord [kɔ:d] *n* MUS acorde *m*.

chore [tʃɔ:r] *n* - **1.** [task] tarea *f*, faena *f* - **2.** *inf* [boring thing] lata *f*.

chortle ['tʃɔ:tl] *vi* reírse con satisfacción.

chorus ['kɔ:rəs] *n* - **1.** [part of song, refrain] estribillo *m* - **2.** [choir, group of singers or dancers] coro *m*.

chose [tʃəʊz] *pt* ⊳ **choose**.

chosen ['tʃəʊzn] *pp* ⊳ **choose**.

Christ [kraɪst] *n* Cristo *m*.

christen ['krɪsn] *vt* bautizar.

christening ['krɪsnɪŋ] *n* bautizo *m*.

Christian ['krɪstʃən] ⬦ *adj* cristiano(na). ⬦ *n* cristiano *m*, -na *f*.

Christianity [,krɪstɪ'ænətɪ] *n* cristianismo *m*.

Christian name *n* nombre *m* de pila.

Christmas ['krɪsməs] *n* Navidad *f*; **happy** OR **merry Christmas!** ¡Feliz Navidad!

Christmas card *n* crismas *m inv*.

Christmas carol *n* villancico *m*.

Christmas Day *n* día *m* de Navidad.

Christmas Eve *n* Nochebuena *f*.

Christmas pudding *n* UK pudín de frutas que se come caliente el día de Navidad.

Christmas tree n árbol m de Navidad.

chrome [krəʊm], **chromium** ['krəʊmɪəm] <> n cromo m. <> comp cromado(da).

chronic ['krɒnɪk] adj - 1. [illness, unemployment] crónico(ca) - 2. [liar, alcoholic] empedernido(da).

chronicle ['krɒnɪkl] n crónica f.

chronological [,krɒnə'lɒdʒɪkl] adj cronológico(ca).

chrysanthemum [krɪ'sænθəməm] (pl -s) n crisantemo m.

chubby ['tʃʌbɪ] adj [person, hands] rechoncho(cha); **to have chubby cheeks** ser mofletudo(da).

chuck [tʃʌk] vt inf - 1. [throw] tirar, arrojar; **to chuck sb out** echar a alguien - 2. [job, girlfriend] dejar. ◆ **chuck away, chuck out** vt sep inf tirar.

chuckle ['tʃʌkl] vi reírse entre dientes.

chug [tʃʌg] vi [train] traquetear; [car] resoplar.

chum [tʃʌm] n inf [gen] amiguete m, -ta f, manito m Méx; [at school] compañero m, -ra f.

chunk [tʃʌŋk] n [piece] trozo m.

church [tʃɜːtʃ] n iglesia f; **to go to church** ir a misa.

Church of England n: **the Church of England** la Iglesia Anglicana.

churchyard ['tʃɜːtʃjɑːd] n cementerio m, camposanto m.

churlish ['tʃɜːlɪʃ] adj descortés.

churn [tʃɜːn] <> n - 1. [for making butter] mantequera f - 2. [for transporting milk] lechera f. <> vt [stir up] agitar. ◆ **churn out** vt sep inf hacer como churros OR en cantidades industriales.

chute [ʃuːt] n [for water] vertedor m; [slide] tobogán m; [for waste] rampa f.

chutney ['tʃʌtnɪ] n salsa agridulce y picante de fruta y semillas.

CIA (abbr of **Central Intelligence Agency**) n CIA f.

CID (abbr of **Criminal Investigation Department**) n UK ≃ Brigada f de Policía Judicial.

cider ['saɪdər] n - 1. sidra f - 2. US [non-alcoholic] zumo m Esp OR jugo m Amér de manzana.

cigar [sɪ'gɑːr] n puro m.

cigarette [,sɪgə'ret] n cigarrillo m.

cigarette paper n papel m de fumar.

cinch [sɪntʃ] n inf: **it's a cinch** está tirado, es pan comido.

cinder ['sɪndər] n ceniza f.

Cinderella [,sɪndə'relə] n Cenicienta f.

cine-camera ['sɪnɪ-] n cámara f cinematográfica.

cine-film ['sɪnɪ-] n película f cinematográfica.

cinema ['sɪnəmə] n cine m.

cinnamon ['sɪnəmən] n canela f.

cipher, cypher ['saɪfər] n [secret writing system] código m, cifra f.

circa ['sɜːkə] prep hacia.

circle ['sɜːkl] <> n - 1. [gen] círculo m; **to go round in circles** dar (mil) vueltas al mismo tema - 2. [in theatre] anfiteatro m; [in cinema] entresuelo m. <> vt - 1. [draw a circle round] rodear con un círculo - 2. [move round] describir círculos alrededor de. <> vi dar vueltas.

circuit ['sɜːkɪt] n - 1. [gen] circuito m - 2. [of track] vuelta f.

circuitous [sə'kjuːɪtəs] adj tortuoso(sa).

circular ['sɜːkjʊlər] <> adj [gen] circular. <> n circular f.

circulate ['sɜːkjʊleɪt] <> vi - 1. [gen] circular - 2. [socialize] alternar. <> vt [rumour, document] hacer circular.

circulation [,sɜːkjʊ'leɪʃn] n - 1. [of blood, money] circulación f - 2. [of magazine, newspaper] tirada f.

circumcise ['sɜːkəmsaɪz] vt circuncidar.

circumference [sə'kʌmfərəns] n circunferencia f.

circumspect ['sɜːkəmspekt] adj circunspecto(ta).

circumstance ['sɜːkəmstəns] n circunstancia f; **circumstances** circunstancias fpl; **under OR in no circumstances** bajo ningún concepto; **in OR under the circumstances** dadas las circunstancias.

circumvent [,sɜːkəm'vent] vt fml burlar.

circus ['sɜːkəs] n - 1. [for entertainment] circo m - 2. [in place names] glorieta f.

CIS (abbr of **Commonwealth of Independent States**) n CEI f.

cistern ['sɪstən] n - 1. UK [in roof] depósito m de agua - 2. [in toilet] cisterna f.

cite [saɪt] vt citar.

citizen ['sɪtɪzn] n ciudadano m, -na f.

Citizens' Advice Bureau n oficina británica de información y asistencia al ciudadano.

Citizens' Band n banda de radio reservada para radioaficionados y conductores.

citizenship ['sɪtɪznʃɪp] n ciudadanía f.

citrus fruit ['sɪtrəs-] n cítrico m.

city ['sɪtɪ] n ciudad f. ◆ **City** n UK: **the City** la City (barrio financiero de Londres).

city centre n centro m de la ciudad.

city hall n US ayuntamiento m.

city technology college n UK centro de formación profesional financiado por la industria.

civic ['sɪvɪk] adj - 1. [duty, pride] cívico(ca) - 2. [leader, event] público(ca).

civic centre n UK zona de la ciudad donde se encuentran los edificios públicos.

civics ['sɪvɪks] n (U) SCH educación f cívica.

civil ['sɪvl] adj - 1. [involving ordinary citizens] civil - 2. [polite] cortés.

civil engineering n ingeniería f civil.

civilian [sɪ'vɪljən] <> n civil mf. <> comp [organization] civil; [clothes] de paisano.

civilization [,sɪvɪlaɪ'zeɪʃn] n civilización f.

civilized ['sɪvɪlaɪzd] adj civilizado(da).

civil law n derecho m civil.

civil liberties npl libertades fpl civiles.

civil rights npl derechos mpl civiles.

civil servant n funcionario m, -ria f público, -ca f.

civil service n administración f pública.

civil war n guerra f civil.

CJD (abbr of Creutzfeldt-Jakob disease) n enfermedad f de Creutzfeldt-Jakob.

clad [klæd] adj liter: clad in vestido(da) de.

claim [kleɪm] <> n - 1. [for pay, insurance, expenses] reclamación f - 2. [of right] reivindicación f; **to have a claim on sb** tener un derecho sobre alguien; **to lay claim to sthg** reclamar algo - 3. [assertion] afirmación f. <> vt - 1. [allowance, expenses, lost property] reclamar - 2. [responsibility, credit] atribuirse - 3. [maintain]: **to claim (that)** mantener que. <> vi: **to claim on one's insurance** reclamar al seguro.

claimant ['kleɪmənt] n [to throne] pretendiente mf; [of unemployment benefit] solicitante mf; LAW demandante mf.

clairvoyant [kleə'vɔɪənt] n clarividente mf.

clam [klæm] n almeja f.

clamber ['klæmbə'] vi trepar.

clammy ['klæmɪ] adj [hands] húmedo(da), pegajoso(sa); [weather] bochornoso(sa).

clamour UK, **clamor** US ['klæmə'] <> n (U) - 1. [noise] clamor m - 2. [demand]: **clamour (for)** demandas fpl (de). <> vi: **to clamour for sthg** exigir a voces algo.

clamp [klæmp] <> n [gen] abrazadera f; [for car wheel] cepo m. <> vt - 1. [with clamp] sujetar (con una abrazadera) - 2. [with wheel clamp] poner un cepo a. ◆ **clamp down** vi: **to clamp down on** poner freno a.

clan [klæn] n clan m.

clandestine [klæn'destɪn] adj clandestino(na).

clang [klæŋ] vi hacer un ruido metálico.

clap [klæp] <> vt: **to clap one's hands** dar palmadas. <> vi aplaudir.

clapping ['klæpɪŋ] n (U) aplausos mpl.

claret ['klærət] n burdeos m inv.

clarify ['klærɪfaɪ] vt aclarar.

clarinet [,klærə'net] n clarinete m.

clarity ['klærətɪ] n claridad f.

clash [klæʃ] <> n - 1. [difference - of interests] conflicto m; [- of personalities] choque m - 2. [fight, disagreement] **clash (with)** conflicto m (con) - 3. [noise] estruendo m. <> vi - 1. [fight, disagree]: **to clash (with)** enfrentarse (con) - 2. [opinions, policies] estar en desacuerdo - 3. [date, event]: **to clash (with)** coincidir (con) - 4. [colour]: **to clash (with)** desentonar (con).

clasp [klɑːsp] <> n [on necklace, bracelet] broche m; [on belt] cierre m. <> vt [person] abrazar; [thing] agarrar.

class [klɑːs] <> n - 1. [gen] clase f - 2. [category] clase f, tipo m. <> vt: **to class sb (as)** clasificar a alguien (de).

classic ['klæsɪk] <> adj [typical] clásico(ca). <> n clásico m.

classical ['klæsɪkl] adj clásico(ca).

classified ['klæsɪfaɪd] adj [secret] reservado(da), secreto(ta).

classified ad n anuncio m por palabras.

classify ['klæsɪfaɪ] vt clasificar.

classmate ['klɑːsmeɪt] n compañero m, -ra f de clase.

classroom ['klɑːsrʊm] n aula f, clase f.

classroom assistant n SCH ayudante mf del profesor.

classy ['klɑːsɪ] adj inf con clase.

clatter ['klætə'] n [gen] estrépito m; [of pots, pans, dishes] ruido m (de cacharros); [of hooves] chacoloteo m.

clause [klɔːz] n - 1. [in legal document] cláusula f - 2. GRAM oración f.

claw [klɔː] <> n - 1. [of animal, bird] garra f; [of cat] uña f - 2. [of crab, lobster] pinza f. <> vi: **to claw at sthg** [cat] arañar algo; [person] intentar agarrarse a algo.

clay [kleɪ] n arcilla f.

clean [kliːn] <> adj - 1. [gen] limpio(pia) - 2. [page] en blanco - 3. [environmentally-friendly] no contaminante - 4. [record, reputation] impecable; [driving licence] sin multas - 5. [joke] inocente - 6. [outline] nítido(da). <> vt & vi limpiar. ◆ **clean out** vt sep - 1. [clear out] limpiar el interior de - 2. inf [take everything from]: **the burglars cleaned us out** (los ladrones) nos limpiaron la casa. ◆ **clean up** vt sep [clear up] ordenar, limpiar; **to clean o.s. up** asearse.

cleaner ['kliːnə'] n - 1. [person] limpiador m, -ra f - 2. [substance] producto m de limpieza.

cleaning ['kliːnɪŋ] n limpieza f.

cleanliness ['klenlɪnɪs] n limpieza f.

cleanse [klenz] vt [gen] limpiar; [soul] purificar; **to cleanse sthg/sb of sthg** limpiar algo/a alguien de algo.

cleanser ['klenzə'] n crema f OR loción f limpiadora.

clean-shaven [-'ʃeɪvn] adj [never growing a beard] barbilampiño(ña); [recently shaved] bien afeitado(da).

clear [klɪər] ◇ adj - 1. [gen] claro(ra); [day, road, view] despejado(da); **to make sthg clear (to)** dejar algo claro (a); **it's clear that...** está claro que...; **are you clear about it?** ¿lo entiendes?; **to make o.s. clear** explicarse con claridad - 2. [transparent] transparente - 3. [well-defined] [sound, picture] nítido(da) - 4. [free of blemishes - skin] terso(sa) - 5. [free - time] libre - 6. [not touching]: **to be clear of the ground** no tocar el suelo - 7. [complete - day, week] entero(ra); [- profit] neto(ta). ◇ adv [out of the way]: **stand clear!** ¡aléjense!; **to jump/step clear** saltar/dar un paso para hacerse a un lado. ◇ vt - 1. [remove objects, obstacles from] despejar; [forest] talar; [pipe] desatascar; **they cleared the area of mines** limpiaron el área de minas; **to clear a space** hacer sitio; **to clear the table** quitar la mesa - 2. [remove] quitar - 3. [jump] saltar - 4. [pay] liquidar - 5. [authorize] aprobar - 6. [prove not guilty] declarar inocente; **to be cleared of sthg** salir absuelto de algo. ◇ vi despejarse. ◆ **clear away** vt sep poner en su sitio. ◆ **clear off** vi UK inf largarse. ◆ **clear out** vt sep limpiar a fondo. ◆ **clear up** ◇ vt sep - 1. [room, mess] limpiar; [toys, books] recoger - 2. [disagreement] aclarar; [mystery] resolver. ◇ vi - 1. [weather] despejarse; [infection] desaparecer - 2. [tidy up] ordenar, recoger.

clearance ['klɪərəns] n - 1. [removal - of rubbish, litter] despeje m, limpieza f; [of slums, houses] eliminación f - 2. [permission] autorización f, permiso m - 3. [free space] distancia f libre.

clear-cut adj [issue, plan] bien definido(da); [division] nítido(da).

clearing ['klɪərɪŋ] n claro m.

clearing bank n UK banco m de compensación.

clearly ['klɪəlɪ] adv - 1. [gen] claramente - 2. [plainly] obviamente.

clearway ['klɪəweɪ] n UK carretera donde no se puede parar.

cleavage ['kliːvɪdʒ] n [between breasts] escote m.

cleaver ['kliːvər] n cuchillo m OR cuchilla f de carnicero.

clef [klef] n clave f.

cleft [kleft] n grieta f.

clench [klentʃ] vt apretar.

clergy ['klɜːdʒɪ] npl: **the clergy** el clero.

clergyman ['klɜːdʒɪmən] (pl -men [-mən]) n clérigo m.

clerical ['klerɪkl] adj - 1. [work] de oficina; [worker] administrativo(va) - 2. [in church] clerical.

clerk [UK klɑːk, US klɜːrk] n - 1. [in office] oficinista mf - 2. [in court] secretario m - 3. US [shop assistant] dependiente m, -ta f.

clever ['klevər] adj - 1. [intelligent] listo(ta), inteligente - 2. [idea, invention] ingenioso(sa); [with hands] hábil.

cliché ['kliːʃeɪ] n cliché m.

click [klɪk] ◇ vt [fingers, tongue] chasquear. ◇ vi - 1. [heels] sonar con un taconazo; [camera] hacer clic - 2. inf [fall into place]: **suddenly, it clicked** de pronto, caí en la cuenta.

client ['klaɪənt] n cliente m, -ta f.

cliff [klɪf] n [on coast] acantilado m; [inland] precipicio m.

climate ['klaɪmɪt] n [weather] clima m; fig [atmosphere] ambiente m.

climax ['klaɪmæks] n [culmination] clímax m, culminación f.

climb [klaɪm] ◇ n [gen] subida f; [up mountain] escalada f. ◇ vt [stairs, ladder] subir; [tree] trepar a; [mountain] escalar. ◇ vi - 1. [clamber]: **to climb over sthg** trepar por algo; **to climb into sthg** meterse en algo - 2. [plant] trepar; [road, plane] subir - 3. [increase] subir.

climb-down n vuelta f atrás.

climber ['klaɪmər] n [mountaineer] alpinista mf, andinista mf Amér; [rock climber] escalador m, -ra f.

climbing ['klaɪmɪŋ] n montañismo m, andinismo m Amér.

clinch [klɪntʃ] vt [deal] cerrar.

cling [klɪŋ] (pt & pp clung) vi - 1. [hold tightly]: **to cling (to)** agarrarse (a) - 2. [clothes, person]: **to cling (to)** pegarse (a).

clingfilm ['klɪŋfɪlm] n UK film m de plástico adherente.

clinic ['klɪnɪk] n clínica f.

clinical ['klɪnɪkl] adj - 1. MED clínico(ca) - 2. [cold] frío(a).

clink [klɪŋk] vi tintinear.

clip [klɪp] ◇ n - 1. [for paper] clip m; [for hair] horquilla f; [on earring] cierre m - 2. [of film] fragmento m, secuencias fpl - 3. [cut]: **to give sb's hair a clip** cortarle el pelo a alguien. ◇ vt - 1. [fasten] sujetar - 2. [cut - lawn, newspaper cutting] recortar; [punch - tickets] picar.

clipboard ['klɪpbɔːd] n - 1. [for writing] tabloncillo m con pinza sujetapapeles - 2. COMPUT portapapeles m inv.

clippers ['klɪpəz] npl [for nails] cortaúñas m inv; [for hair] maquinilla f para cortar el pelo; [for hedges, grass] tijeras fpl de podar.

clipping ['klɪpɪŋ] n - 1. [from newspaper] recorte m - 2. [of nails] pedazo m.

clique [kliːk] n pej camarilla f.

cloak [kləʊk] n [garment] capa f.

cloakroom ['kləʊkrʊm] n - 1. [for clothes] guardarropa m - 2. UK [toilets] servicios mpl.

clock [klɒk] n - 1. [timepiece] reloj m; **round the clock** día y noche, las 24 horas - 2. [mileometer] cuentakilómetros m inv. ➡ **clock in**, **clock on** vi UK fichar (a la entrada). ➡ **clock off**, **clock out** vi UK fichar (a la salida).

clockwise ['klɒkwaɪz] adj & adv en el sentido de las agujas del reloj.

clockwork ['klɒkwɜːk] comp de cuerda.

clog [klɒg] vt atascar, obstruir. ➡ **clogs** npl zuecos mpl. ➡ **clog up** ◇ vt sep [drain, pipe] atascar; [eyes, nose] congestionar. ◇ vi atascarse.

close¹ [kləʊs] ◇ adj - 1. [near] cercano(na); **close to** cerca de; **close to tears/laughter** a punto de llorar/reír; **close up**, **close to** de cerca; **close by**, **close at hand** muy cerca; **we arrived on time, but it was a close shave** OR **thing** llegamos a tiempo, pero por los pelos - 2. [relationship, friend] íntimo(ma); **to be close to sb** estar muy unido(da) a alguien - 3. [relative, family] cercano(na); [resemblance]: **to bear a close resemblance to sb** parecerse mucho a alguien; [link, tie, cooperation] estrecho(cha) - 4. [questioning] minucioso(sa); [examination] detallado(da); [look] de cerca; **to keep a close watch on** vigilar de cerca - 5. [room, air] cargado(da); [weather] bochornoso(sa) - 6. [contest, race] reñido(da); [result] apretado(da). ◇ adv cerca; **close to** cerca de. ➡ **close on**, **close to** prep [almost] cerca de.

close² [kləʊz] ◇ vt - 1. [gen] cerrar - 2. [meeting, conference] clausurar; [discussion, speech] terminar - 3. [gap] reducir - 4. COMPUT [window, application] cerrar. ◇ vi - 1. [gen] cerrarse - 2. [shop] cerrar - 3. [meeting, film, day] terminar. ◇ n final m. ➡ **close down** ◇ vt sep cerrar (definitivamente). ◇ vi [factory etc] cerrarse (definitivamente).

closed [kləʊzd] adj cerrado(da).

close-knit [,kləʊs-] adj muy unido(da).

closely ['kləʊslɪ] adv - 1. [of connection, relation etc] estrechamente; **to be closely involved in sthg** estar muy metido en algo; [resemble] mucho - 2. [carefully] atentamente.

closet ['klɒzɪt] ◇ adj inf en secreto. ◇ n US armario m
▸▸▸ **to come out of the closet** salir del armario.

close-up ['kləʊs-] n primer plano m.

closing time n hora f de cierre.

closure ['kləʊʒə'] n cierre m.

clot [klɒt] ◇ n - 1. [in blood] coágulo m - 2. UK inf [fool] bobo m, -ba f. ◇ vi [blood] coagularse.

cloth [klɒθ] n - 1. (U) [fabric] tela f - 2. [piece of cloth] trapo m.

clothe [kləʊð] vt fml vestir.

clothes [kləʊðz] npl ropa f; **to put one's clothes on** ponerse la ropa, vestirse; **to take one's clothes off** quitarse la ropa, desvestirse.

clothes brush n cepillo m para la ropa.

clothesline ['kləʊðzlaɪn] n cuerda f para tender la ropa.

clothes peg UK, **clothespin** US ['kləʊðzpɪn] n pinza f (para la ropa).

clothing ['kləʊðɪŋ] n ropa f.

cloud [klaʊd] n nube f. ➡ **cloud over** vi lit & fig nublarse.

cloudy ['klaʊdɪ] adj - 1. [overcast] nublado(da) - 2. [murky] turbio(bia).

clout [klaʊt] inf n - 1. [blow] tortazo m - 2. (U) [influence] influencia f.

clove [kləʊv] n: **a clove of garlic** un diente de ajo. ➡ **cloves** npl [spice] clavos mpl.

clover ['kləʊvə'] n trébol m.

clown [klaʊn] n [performer] payaso m.

cloying ['klɔɪɪŋ] adj empalagoso(sa).

club [klʌb] ◇ n - 1. [organization, place] club m - 2. [nightclub] discoteca f - 3. [weapon] porra f, garrote m - 4.: **(golf) club** palo m de golf. ◇ vt apalear, aporrear. ➡ **clubs** npl [cards] tréboles mpl. ➡ **club together** vi UK recolectar dinero.

club car n US RAIL vagón m OR coche m club.

clubhouse ['klʌbhaʊs, pl -haʊzɪz] n [for golfers] (edificio m del) club m.

cluck [klʌk] vi [hen] cloquear.

clue [kluː] n - 1. [in crime] pista f; **not to have a clue (about)** no tener ni idea (de) - 2. [in crossword] pregunta f, clave f.

clued-up [kluːd-] adj UK inf al tanto.

clump [klʌmp] n [of bushes] mata f; [of trees, flowers] grupo m.

clumsy ['klʌmzɪ] adj - 1. [ungraceful] torpe - 2. [unwieldy] difícil de manejar - 3. [tactless] torpe, sin tacto.

clung [klʌŋ] pt & pt ▷ **cling**.

cluster ['klʌstə'] ◇ n [group] grupo m; [of grapes] racimo m. ◇ vi agruparse.

clutch [klʌtʃ] ◇ n AUT embrague m. ◇ vt [hand] estrechar; [arm, baby] agarrar. ◇ vi: **to clutch at sthg** tratar de agarrarse a algo.

clutter ['klʌtə'] ◇ n desorden m. ◇ vt cubrir desordenadamente.

cm (abbr of centimetre) cm.

CND (abbr of Campaign for Nuclear Disarmament) n organización británica contra el armamento nuclear.

CNG (abbr of compressed natural gas) n GNC m, gas m natural comprimido.

c/o (abbr of care of) c/d.

Co. - 1. (abbr of Company) Cía. **- 2.** abbr of County.

coach [kəʊtʃ] ⬦ *n* - **1.** [bus] autocar *m* - **2.** RAIL vagón *m* ⬦. [horsedrawn] carruaje *m* - **4.** SPORT **entrenador** *m*, -ra *f* - **5.** [tutor] profesor *m*, -ra *f* particular - **6.: coach (class)** *US* clase *t* turista. ⬦ *vt* - **1.** SPORT entrenar - **2.** [tutor] dar clases particulares a.

coal [kəʊl] *n* carbón *m*.

coalfield ['kəʊlfi:ld] *n* yacimiento *m* de carbón.

coalition [ˌkəʊə'lɪʃn] *n* coalición *f*.

coalman ['kəʊlmæn] (*pl* **-men** [-men]) *n* UK carbonero *m*.

coalmine ['kəʊlmaɪn] *n* mina *f* de carbón.

coarse [kɔːs] *adj* - **1.** [skin, hair, sandpaper] áspero(ra); [fabric] basto(ta) - **2.** [person, joke] ordinario(ria).

coast [kəʊst] ⬦ *n* costa *f*. ⬦ *vi* - **1.** [in car] ir en punto muerto - **2.** [progress easily]: **they coasted into the semifinals** se metieron en las semifinales sin ningún esfuerzo.

coastal ['kəʊstl] *adj* costero(ra).

coaster ['kəʊstə'] *n* [small mat] posavasos *m inv*.

coastguard ['kəʊstɡɑːd] *n* [person] guardacostas *mf inv*.

coastline ['kəʊstlaɪn] *n* litoral *m*.

coat [kəʊt] ⬦ *n* - **1.** [overcoat] abrigo *m*, sobretodo *m R Plata*; [for women] tapado *m R Plata*; [jacket] chaqueta *f* - **2.** [of animal] pelo *m*, pelaje *m* - **3.** [layer] capa *f*. ⬦ *vt*: **to coat sthg (with)** cubrir algo (de).

coat hanger *n* percha *f*, gancho *m Amér C, Andes & Méx.*

coating ['kəʊtɪŋ] *n* [of dust etc] capa *f*; [of chocolate, silver] baño *m*.

coat of arms (*pl* **coats of arms**) *n* escudo *m* de armas.

coax [kəʊks] *vt*: **to coax sb (to do OR into doing sthg)** engatusar a alguien (para que haga algo).

cob [kɒb] ⬢ **corn.**

cobbled ['kɒbld] *adj* adoquinado(da).

cobbler ['kɒblə'] *n* zapatero (remendón) *m*, zapatera (remendona) *f*.

cobbles ['kɒblz], **cobblestones** ['kɒblstəʊnz] *npl* adoquines *mpl*.

cobweb ['kɒbweb] *n* telaraña *f* (*abandonada*).

Coca-Cola® [ˌkəʊkə'kəʊlə] *n* Coca-Cola® *f*.

cocaine [kəʊ'keɪn] *n* cocaína *f*.

cock [kɒk] ⬦ *n* - **1.** [male chicken] gallo *m* - **2.** [male bird] macho *m* - **3.** *vulg* [penis] polla *f*. ⬦ *vt* - **1.** [gun] amartillar - **2.** [head] ladear. ⬢ **cock up** *vt sep UK v inf* jorobar.

cockerel ['kɒkrəl] *n* gallo *m* joven.

cockeyed ['kɒkaɪd] *adj inf* - **1.** [lopsided] torcido(da) - **2.** [foolish] disparatado(da).

cockle ['kɒkl] *n* berberecho *m*.

Cockney ['kɒknɪ] (*pl* **Cockneys**) *n* - **1.** [person] persona procedente del este de Londres - **2.** [dialect, accent] dialecto del este de Londres.

cockpit ['kɒkpɪt] *n* [in civil aviation] cabina *f*.

cockroach ['kɒkrəʊtʃ] *n* cucaracha *f*.

cocksure [ˌkɒk'ʃʊə'] *adj* presuntuoso(sa).

cocktail ['kɒkteɪl] *n* cóctel *m*.

cock-up *n v inf* pifia *f*.

cocky ['kɒkɪ] *adj inf* chulo(la).

cocoa ['kəʊkəʊ] *n* - **1.** [powder] cacao *m* - **2.** [drink] chocolate *m*.

coconut ['kəʊkənʌt] *n* coco *m*.

cod [kɒd] (*pl* **cod** OR **-s**) *n* bacalao *m*.

COD (*abbr of* cash on delivery) *entrega contra reembolso.*

code [kəʊd] ⬦ *n* - **1.** [gen] código *m* - **2.** [for telephone] prefijo *m*. ⬦ *vt* [encode] codificar, cifrar.

cod-liver oil *n* aceite *m* de hígado de bacalao.

coed [ˌkəʊ'ed] *adj* (*abbr of* coeducational) mixto(ta).

coerce [kəʊ'ɜːs] *vt*: **to coerce sb (into doing sthg)** coaccionar a alguien (para que haga algo).

coffee ['kɒfɪ] *n* café *m*.

coffee bar *n UK* cafetería *f*.

coffee break *n* descanso *m* para el café.

coffee morning *n UK* reunión matinal, generalmente benéfica, en la que se sirve café.

coffeepot ['kɒfɪpɒt] *n* cafetera *f* (*para servir*).

coffee shop *n* - **1.** *UK* [shop] cafetería *f* - **2.** *US* [restaurant] café *m*.

coffee table *n* mesita *f* baja (de salón).

coffin ['kɒfɪn] *n* ataúd *m*.

cog [kɒg] *n* [tooth on wheel] diente *m*; [wheel] rueda *f* dentada.

cognac ['kɒnjæk] *n* coñac *m*.

coherent [kəʊ'hɪərənt] *adj* coherente.

cohesive [kəʊ'hi:sɪv] *adj* [group] unido(da).

coil [kɔɪl] ⬦ *n* - **1.** [of rope, wire] rollo *m*; [of hair] tirabuzón *m*; [of smoke] espiral *f* - **2.** ELEC bobina *f* - **3.** *UK* [contraceptive device] DIU *m*, espiral *f*. ⬦ *vi* enrollarse, enroscarse. ⬦ *vt* enrollar, enroscar. ⬢ **coil up** *vt sep* enrollar.

coin [kɔɪn] ⬦ *n* moneda *f*. ⬦ *vt* [invent] acuñar.

coinage ['kɔɪnɪdʒ] *n* [currency] moneda *f*.

coin-box *n* depósito *m* de monedas.

coincide [ˌkəʊɪn'saɪd] *vi*: **to coincide (with)** coincidir (con).

coincidence [kəʊ'ɪnsɪdəns] *n* coincidencia *f*.

coincidental [kəʊˌɪnsɪ'dentl] *adj* fortuito(ta).

coke [kəʊk] *n* [fuel] coque *m*.

Coke® [kəʊk] *n* Coca-Cola® *f*.

cola ['kəʊlə] *n* (bebida *f* de) cola *f*.

colander ['kʌləndər] *n* colador *m*, escurridor *m*.

cold [kəʊld] <> *adj* frío(a); **it's cold** hace frío; **my hands are cold** tengo las manos frías; **I'm cold** tengo frío; **to get cold** enfriarse. <> *n* - **1.** [illness] resfriado *m*, constipado *m*; **to catch (a) cold** resfriarse, coger un resfriado - **2.** [low temperature] frío *m*.

cold-blooded [-'blʌdɪd] *adj* - **1.** [animal] de sangre fría - **2.** [person] despiadado(da); [killing] a sangre fría.

cold sore *n* calentura *f*.

cold war *n*: **the cold war** la guerra fría.

coleslaw ['kəʊlslɔ:] *n* ensalada de col, zanahoria, cebolla y mayonesa.

colic ['kɒlɪk] *n* cólico *m*.

collaborate [kə'læbəreɪt] *vi*: **to collaborate (with)** colaborar (con).

collapse [kə'læps] <> *n* - **1.** [of building] derrumbamiento *m*; [of roof] hundimiento *m* - **2.** [of marriage, system] fracaso *m*; [of government, currency] caída *f*; [of empire] derrumbamiento *m* - **3.** MED colapso *m*. <> *vi* - **1.** [building, person] derrumbarse; [roof, prices] hundirse; **to collapse with laughter** partirse de risa - **2.** [plan, business] venirse abajo - **3.** MED sufrir un colapso.

collapsible [kə'læpsəbl] *adj* plegable.

collar ['kɒlər] *n* - **1.** [on clothes] cuello *m* - **2.** [for dog] collar *m* - **3.** TECH collar *m*.

collarbone ['kɒləbəʊn] *n* clavícula *f*.

collate [kə'leɪt] *vt* - **1.** [compare] cotejar - **2.** [put in order] poner en orden.

collateral [kɒ'lætərəl] *n* garantía *f* subsidiaria, seguridad *f* colateral.

colleague ['kɒli:g] *n* colega *mf*.

collect [kə'lekt] <> *vt* - **1.** [gather together] reunir, juntar; **to collect o.s.** concentrarse - **2.** [as a hobby] coleccionar - **3.** [go to get - person, parcel] recoger - **4.** [money, taxes] recaudar. <> *vi* - **1.** [gather] congregarse, reunirse - **2.** [accumulate] acumularse - **3.** [for charity, gift] hacer una colecta. <> *adv* US TELEC: **to call (sb) collect** llamar (a alguien) a cobro revertido.

collection [kə'lekʃn] *n* - **1.** [of stamps, art etc] colección *f* - **2.** [of poems, stories etc] recopilación *f* - **3.** [of rubbish, mail] recogida *f*; [of taxes] recaudación *f* - **4.** [of money] colecta *f*.

collective [kə'lektɪv] <> *adj* colectivo(va). <> *n* colectivo *m*.

collector [kə'lektər] *n* - **1.** [as a hobby] coleccionista *mf* - **2.** [of taxes] recaudador *m*, -ra *f* - **3.** [of debts, rent] cobrador *m*, -ra *f*.

college ['kɒlɪdʒ] *n* - **1.** [for further education] instituto *m*, escuela *f* - **2.** US [university] universidad *f* - **3.** UK [of university] colegio universitario que forma parte de ciertas universidades - **4.** [organized body] colegio *m*.

college of education *n* UK escuela de formación de profesores de enseñanza primaria y secundaria.

collide [kə'laɪd] *vi*: **to collide (with)** [gen] chocar (con); [vehicles] colisionar OR chocar (con).

collie ['kɒlɪ] *n* collie *m*.

colliery ['kɒljərɪ] *n* mina *f* de carbón.

collision [kə'lɪʒn] *n* lit & fig: **to be on a collision course (with)** fig estar al borde del enfrentamiento (con).

colloquial [kə'ləʊkwɪəl] *adj* coloquial.

collude [kə'lu:d] *vi*: **to collude with** estar en connivencia con.

Colombia [kə'lɒmbɪə] *n* Colombia.

Colombian [kə'lɒmbɪən] <> *adj* colombiano(na). <> *n* colombiano *m*, -na *f*.

colon ['kəʊlən] *n* - **1.** ANAT colon *m* - **2.** [punctuation mark] dos puntos *mpl*.

colonel ['kɜ:nl] *n* coronel *mf*.

colonial [kə'ləʊnjəl] *adj* colonial.

colonize, -ise ['kɒlənaɪz] *vt* colonizar.

colony ['kɒlənɪ] *n* colonia *f*.

color US = **colour**.

colossal [kə'lɒsl] *adj* colosal.

colour UK, **color** US ['kʌlər] <> *n* color *m*. <> *adj* en color. <> *vt* - **1.** [give colour to] dar color a; [with pen, crayon] colorear - **2.** [dye] teñir - **3.** [affect] influenciar. <> *vi* [blush] ruborizarse.

colour bar *n* discriminación *f* racial.

colour-blind *adj* daltónico(ca).

coloured UK, **colored** US ['kʌləd] *adj* - **1.** [pens, sheets etc] de colores - **2.** [with stated colour]: **maroon-coloured** de color granate; **brightly-coloured** de vivos colores - **3.** [person - black] de color.

colourful UK, **colorful** US ['kʌləfʊl] *adj* - **1.** [brightly coloured] de vivos colores - **2.** [story] animado(da) - **3.** [person] pintoresco(ca) - **4.** [language] expresivo(va).

colouring UK, **coloring** US ['kʌlərɪŋ] *n* - **1.** [in food] colorante *m* - **2.** [complexion, hair] tez *f* - **3.** [of animal's skin] color *m*.

colour scheme *n* combinación *f* de colores.

colt [kəʊlt] *n* potro *m*.

column ['kɒləm] *n* - **1.** [gen] columna *f* - **2.** [of people, vehicles] hilera *f*.

columnist ['kɒləmnɪst] *n* columnista *mf*.

coma ['kəʊmə] *n* coma *m*.

comb [kəʊm] <> *n* peine *m*. <> *vt* lit & fig peinar.

combat ['kɒmbæt] ◇ n combate m. ◇ vt combatir.

combination [ˌkɒmbɪ'neɪʃn] n combinación f.

combine ◇ vt [kəm'baɪn]: to combine sthg (with) combinar algo (con). ◇ vi [kəm'baɪn] combinarse. ◇ n ['kɒmbaɪn] - 1. [group] grupo m - 2. = **combine harvester**.

combine harvester [-'hɑːvɪstər], **combine** n cosechadora f.

come [kʌm] vi (pt came, pp come) - 1. [move] venir; [arrive] llegar; **coming!** ¡ahora voy!; **the news came as a shock** la noticia constituyó un duro golpe; **he doesn't know whether he's coming or going** fig no sabe si va o viene - 2. [happen] pasar; **come what may** pase lo que pase - 3. [become]: **to come true** hacerse realidad; **to come unstuck** despegarse; **my shoelaces have come undone** se me han desatado los cordones - 4. [begin gradually]: **to come to do sthg** llegar a hacer algo - 5. [be placed in order]: **to come first/last in a race** llegar el primero/el último en una carrera; **she came second in the exam** quedó segunda en el examen; **P comes before Q** la P viene antes de la Q. ◈ **to come** adv: **in (the) days/years to come** en días/años venideros. ◈ **come about** vi [happen] pasar, ocurrir. ◈ **come along** vi - 1. [arrive by chance - opportunity] surgir; [- bus] aparecer, llegar - 2. [progress] ir; **the project is coming along nicely** el proyecto va muy bien. ◈ **come apart** vi deshacerse. ◈ **come back** vi - 1. [in talk, writing]: **to come back to sthg** volver a algo - 2. [memory]: **to come back to sb** volverle a la memoria a alguien. ◈ **come by** vt insep [get, obtain] conseguir. ◈ **come down** vi - 1. [from upstairs] bajar - 2. [decrease] bajar - 3. [descend - plane, parachutist] aterrizar; [- rain] caer. ◈ **come down to** vt insep reducirse a. ◈ **come down with** vt insep coger, agarrar (enfermedad). ◈ **come forward** vi presentarse. ◈ **come from** vt insep [noise etc] venir de; [person] ser de. ◈ **come in** vi - 1. [enter] entrar, pasar; **come in!** ¡pase! - 2. [arrive - train, letters, donations] llegar. ◈ **come in for** vt insep [criticism etc] recibir, llevarse. ◈ **come into** vt insep - 1. [inherit] heredar - 2. [begin to be]: **to come into being** nacer, ver la luz. ◈ **come off** ◇ vi - 1. [button] descoserse; [label] despegarse; [lid] soltarse; [stain] quitarse - 2. [plan, joke] salir bien. ◇ vt insep [medicine] dejar de tomar ▸▸▸ **come off it!** inf ¡venga ya! ◈ **come on** vi - 1. [start] empezar - 2. [start working - lights, heating] encenderse - 3. [progress] ir; **it's coming on nicely** va muy bien ▸▸▸ **come on!** [expressing encouragement, urging haste] ¡vamos!; [expressing disbelief] ¡venga ya! ◈ **come out** vi - 1. [screw, tooth] caerse

- 2. [stain] quitarse - 3. [become known] salir a la luz - 4. [appear - product, book, sun] salir; [- film] estrenarse - 5. [go on strike] ponerse en huelga - 6. [as homosexual] declararse homosexual. ◈ **come over** ◇ vt insep [subj: feeling] sobrevenir; **I don't know what has come over her** no sé qué le pasa. ◇ vi [to visit] pasarse. ◈ **come round** vi - 1. [to visit] pasarse - 2. [change opinion]: **to come round (to sthg)** terminar por aceptar (algo) - 3. [regain consciousness] volver en sí. ◈ **come through** vt insep [difficult situation, period] pasar por; [operation, war] sobrevivir a. ◈ **come to** ◇ vt insep - 1. [reach]: **to come to an end** tocar a su fin; **to come to a decision** alcanzar una decisión - 2. [amount to] ascender a; **the plan came to nothing** el plan se quedó en nada. ◇ vi [regain consciousness] volver en sí. ◈ **come under** vt insep - 1. [be governed by] estar bajo - 2. [suffer]: **to come under attack** ser atacado. ◈ **come up** vi - 1. [name, topic, opportunity] surgir - 2. [be imminent] estar al llegar - 3. [sun, moon] salir. ◈ **come up against** vt insep tropezar OR toparse con. ◈ **come up with** vt insep [idea] salir con; [solution] encontrar.

comeback ['kʌmbæk] n [return] reaparición f; **to make a comeback** [fashion] volver (a ponerse de moda); [actor] hacer una reaparición; [in match] recuperarse.

comedian [kə'miːdjən] n cómico m.

comedown ['kʌmdaʊn] n inf degradación f.

comedy ['kɒmədɪ] n - 1. [film, play] comedia f; [on television] serie f de humor - 2. [humorous entertainment] humorismo m - 3. [amusing nature] comicidad f.

comet ['kɒmɪt] n cometa m.

come-uppance [ˌkʌm'ʌpəns] n: **to get one's come-uppance** inf llevarse uno su merecido.

comfort ['kʌmfət] ◇ n - 1. [gen] comodidad f - 2. [solace] consuelo m. ◇ vt consolar, confortar.

comfortable ['kʌmftəbl] adj - 1. [gen] cómodo(da) - 2. [financially secure] acomodado(da) - 3. [victory, job, belief] fácil; [lead, majority] amplio(plia).

comfortably ['kʌmftəblɪ] adv - 1. [sit, sleep] cómodamente - 2. [without financial difficulty] sin aprietos - 3. [easily] fácilmente.

comfort station n US euph aseos mpl.

comic ['kɒmɪk] ◇ adj cómico(ca). ◇ n - 1. [comedian] cómico m, -ca f - 2. [magazine - for children] tebeo m; [- for adults] cómic m.

comical ['kɒmɪkl] adj cómico(ca).

comic strip n tira f cómica.

coming ['kʌmɪŋ] ◇ adj [future] próximo(ma). ◇ n: **comings and goings** idas fpl y venidas.

comma ['kɒmə] n coma f.

command [kə'mɑ:nd] ⬦ n - 1. [order] orden f - 2. (U) [control] mando m - 3. [of language, skill] dominio m, to have sthg at one's command dominar algo - 4. COMPUT comando m. ⬦ vt - 1. [order]: **to command sb (to do sthg)** ordenar OR mandar a alguien (que haga algo) - 2. MIL [control] comandar - 3. [deserve - respect, attention] hacerse acreedor(ra) de.

commandeer [,kɒmən'dɪəʳ] vt requisar.

commander [kə'mɑ:ndəʳ] n - 1. [in army] comandante mf - 2. [in navy] capitán m, -ana f de fragata.

commandment [kə'mɑ:ndmənt] n RELIG mandamiento m.

commando [kə'mɑ:ndəʊ] (pl -s OR -es) n comando m.

commemorate [kə'meməreɪt] vt conmemorar.

commemoration [kə,memə'reɪʃn] n conmemoración f.

commence [kə'mens] fml ⬦ vt: **to commence (doing sthg)** comenzar OR empezar (a hacer algo). ⬦ vi comenzar, empezar.

commend [kə'mend] vt - 1. [praise] alabar - 2. [recommend]: **to commend sthg (to)** recomendar algo (a).

commensurate [kə'menʃərət] adj fml: **commensurate with** acorde OR en proporción con.

comment ['kɒment] ⬦ n comentario m; **no comment** sin comentarios. ⬦ vi comentar; **to comment on** hacer comentarios sobre.

commentary ['kɒməntrɪ] n - 1. [on match, event] comentarios mpl - 2. [analysis] comentario m.

commentator ['kɒmənteɪtəʳ] n comentarista mf.

commerce ['kɒmɜ:s] n (U) comercio m.

commercial [kə'mɜ:ʃl] ⬦ adj comercial. ⬦ n anuncio m (televisivo o radiofónico).

commercial break n pausa f publicitaria.

commiserate [kə'mɪzəreɪt] vi: **I commiserated with her** le dije cuánto lo sentía.

commission [kə'mɪʃn] ⬦ n - 1. [money, investigative body] comisión f - 2. [piece of work] encargo m. ⬦ vt encargar; **to commission sb (to do sthg)** encargar a alguien (que haga algo).

commissionaire [kə,mɪʃə'neəʳ] n UK portero m (uniformado).

commissioner [kə'mɪʃnəʳ] n comisario m, -ria f.

commit [kə'mɪt] vt - 1. [crime, sin etc] cometer - 2. [pledge - money, resources] destinar; **to commit o.s. (to)** comprometerse (a) - 3. [consign - to mental hospital] ingresar; **to commit sb to prison** encarcelar a alguien; **to commit sthg to memory** aprender algo de memoria.

commitment [kə'mɪtmənt] n compromiso m.

committee [kə'mɪtɪ] n comisión f, comité m.

commodity [kə'mɒdətɪ] n producto m básico.

common ['kɒmən] ⬦ adj - 1. [gen]: **common (to)** común (a) - 2. [ordinary - man, woman] corriente, de la calle - 3. UK pej [vulgar] vulgar, ordinario(ria). ⬦ n campo m común. ➤ **in common** adv en común.

common law n derecho m consuetudinario. ➤ **common-law** adj [wife, husband] de hecho.

commonly ['kɒmənlɪ] adv generalmente, comúnmente.

Common Market n: **the Common Market** el Mercado Común.

commonplace ['kɒmənpleɪs] adj corriente, común.

common room n [for pupils] sala f de estudiantes; [for teachers] sala f de profesores.

Commons ['kɒmənz] npl UK: **the Commons** la Cámara de los Comunes.

common sense n sentido m común.

Commonwealth ['kɒmənwelθ] n: **the Commonwealth** la Commonwealth.

Commonwealth of Independent States n: **the Commonwealth of Independent States** la Comunidad de Estados Independientes.

commotion [kə'məʊʃn] n alboroto m.

communal ['kɒmjʊnl] adj comunal.

commune ⬦ n ['kɒmju:n] comuna f. ⬦ vi [kə'mju:n]: **to commune with** estar en comunión OR comulgar con.

communicate [kə'mju:nɪkeɪt] ⬦ vt transmitir, comunicar. ⬦ vi: **to communicate (with)** comunicarse (con).

communication [kə,mju:nɪ'keɪʃn] n - 1. [contact] comunicación f - 2. [letter, phone call] comunicado m.

communication cord n UK alarma f (de un tren o metro).

communion [kə'mju:njən] n [communication] comunión f. ➤ **Communion** n (U) RELIG comunión f.

communiqué [kə'mju:nɪkeɪ] n comunicado m.

Communism ['kɒmjʊnɪzm] n comunismo m.

Communist ['kɒmjʊnɪst] ⬦ adj comunista. ⬦ n comunista mf.

community [kə'mju:nətɪ] n comunidad f.

community centre n centro m social.

commutation ticket [,kɒmju:'teɪʃn-] n US abono m, boleto m de abono Amér.

commute [kə'mju:t] <> *vt* LAW conmutar. <> *vi* [to work] *viajar diariamente al lugar de trabajo*.

commuter [kə'mju:tə*r*] *n persona que viaja diariamente al lugar de trabajo*.

compact <> *adj* [kəm'pækt] [small and neat] compacto(ta). <> *n* ['kɒmpækt] - **1.** [for face powder] polvera *f* - **2.** US [car] utilitario *m*.

compact disc *n* compact disc *m*.

compact disc player *n* compact *m* (disc), reproductor *m* de discos compactos.

companion [kəm'pænjən] *n* compañero *m*, -ra *f*.

companionship [kəm'pænjənʃɪp] *n* [friendly relationship] compañerismo *m*.

company ['kʌmpənɪ] *n* [gen] compañía *f*; [business] empresa *f*, compañía *f*; **to keep sb company** hacer compañía a alguien; **to part company (with)** separarse (de).

company secretary *n secretario del consejo de administración*.

comparable ['kɒmprəbl] *adj*: **comparable (to OR with)** comparable (a).

comparative [kəm'pærətɪv] <> *adj* - **1.** [relative] relativo(va) - **2.** [study] comparado(da) - **3.** GRAM comparativo(va). <> *n* GRAM comparativo *m*.

comparatively [kəm'pærətɪvlɪ] *adv* relativamente.

compare [kəm'peə*r*] <> *vt*: **to compare sthg/sb (with), to compare sthg/sb (to)** comparar algo/a alguien (con); **compared with OR to** [as opposed to] comparado con; [in comparison with] en comparación con. <> *vi*: **to compare (with)** compararse (con); **to compare favourably/unfavourably with** ser mejor/peor que.

comparison [kəm'pærɪsn] *n* comparación *f*; **in comparison (with OR to)** en comparación (con).

compartment [kəm'pɑ:tmənt] *n* - **1.** [container] compartimento *m* - **2.** RAIL departamento *m*, compartimento *m*.

compass ['kʌmpəs] *n* [magnetic] brújula *f*. ➠ **compasses** *npl* compás *m*.

compassion [kəm'pæʃn] *n* compasión *f*.

compassionate [kəm'pæʃənət] *adj* compasivo(va).

compatible [kəm'pætəbl] *adj*: **compatible (with)** compatible (con).

compel [kəm'pel] *vt* [force] obligar; **to compel sb to do sthg** forzar OR obligar a alguien a hacer algo.

compelling [kəm'pelɪŋ] *adj* - **1.** [argument, reason] convincente - **2.** [book, film] absorbente.

compensate ['kɒmpenseɪt] <> *vt*: **to compensate sb for sthg** [financially] compensar OR indemnizar a alguien por algo. <> *vi*: **to compensate for sthg** compensar algo.

compensation [,kɒmpen'seɪʃn] *n* - **1.** [money]: **compensation (for)** indemnización *f* (por) - **2.** [way of compensating]: **compensation (for)** compensación *f* (por).

compete [kəm'pi:t] *vi* - **1.** [gen]: **to compete (for/in)** competir (por/en); **to compete (with OR against)** competir (con) - **2.** [be in conflict] rivalizar.

competence ['kɒmpɪtəns] *n* [proficiency] competencia *f*.

competent ['kɒmpɪtənt] *adj* competente, capaz.

competition [,kɒmpɪ'tɪʃn] *n* - **1.** [rivalry] competencia *f* - **2.** [competitors, rivals]: **the competition** la competencia - **3.** [race, sporting event] competición *f* - **4.** [contest] concurso *m*.

competitive [kəm'petətɪv] *adj* - **1.** [match, exam, prices] competitivo(va) - **2.** [person, spirit] competidor(ra).

competitor [kəm'petɪtə*r*] *n* competidor *m*, -ra *f*.

compile [kəm'paɪl] *vt* recopilar.

complacency [kəm'pleɪsnsɪ] *n* autocomplacencia *f*.

complacent [kəm'pleɪsnt] *adj* autocomplaciente.

complain [kəm'pleɪn] *vi* - **1.** [moan]: **to complain (about)** quejarse (de) - **2.** MED: **to complain of sthg** sufrir algo.

complaint [kəm'pleɪnt] *n* - **1.** [gen] queja *f* - **2.** MED problema *m*, dolencia *f*.

complement <> *n* ['kɒmplɪmənt] - **1.** [gen & GRAM] complemento *m* - **2.** [number]: **we offer a full complement of services** ofrecemos una gama completa de servicios. <> *vt* ['kɒmplɪ,ment] complementar.

complementary [,kɒmplɪ'mentərɪ] *adj* - **1.** [gen] complementario(ria) - **2.** [medicine] alternativo(va).

complete [kəm'pli:t] <> *adj* - **1.** [total] total - **2.** [lacking nothing] completo(ta); **bathroom complete with shower** baño con ducha - **3.** [finished] terminado(da). <> *vt* - **1.** [finish] terminar - **2.** [form] rellenar - **3.** [make whole - collection] completar; [- disappointment, amazement] colmar.

completely [kəm'pli:tlɪ] *adv* completamente.

completion [kəm'pli:ʃn] *n* finalización *f*, terminación *f*.

complex ['kɒmpleks] <> *adj* complejo(ja). <> *n* complejo *m*.

complexion [kəm'plekʃn] *n* [of face] tez *f*, cutis *m* inv.

compliance [kəm'plaɪəns] *n* [obedience]: compliance (with) cumplimiento *m* (de), acatamiento *m* (de).

complicate ['kɒmplɪkeɪt] *vt* complicar.

complicated ['kɒmplɪkeɪtɪd] *adj* complicado(da).

complication [ˌkɒmplɪ'keɪʃn] *n* complicación *f*.

compliment ◇ *n* ['kɒmplɪmənt] cumplido *m*; my compliments to the cook felicitaciones a la cocinera. ◇ *vt* ['kɒmplɪment]: to compliment sb (on) felicitar a alguien (por). ◆ compliments *npl fml* saludos *mpl*.

complimentary [ˌkɒmplɪ'mentərɪ] *adj* - 1. [remark] elogioso(sa); [person] halagador(ra) - 2. [drink, seats] gratis *(inv)*.

complimentary ticket *n* entrada *f* gratuita.

comply [kəm'plaɪ] *vi*: to comply with sthg [standards] cumplir (con) algo; [request] acceder a algo; [law] acatar algo.

component [kəm'pəʊnənt] *n* TECH pieza *f*; [element] elemento *m*.

compose [kəm'pəʊz] *vt* - 1. [constitute] componer; to be composed of estar compuesto OR componerse de - 2. [music, poem, letter] componer - 3. [calm]: to compose o.s. calmarse.

composed [kəm'pəʊzd] *adj* tranquilo(la).

composer [kəm'pəʊzər] *n* compositor *m*, -ra *f*.

composition [ˌkɒmpə'zɪʃn] *n* - 1. [gen] composición *f* - 2. [essay] redacción *f*.

compost [UK 'kɒmpɒst, US 'kɒmpəʊst] *n* compost *m*, abono *m*.

composure [kəm'pəʊʒər] *n* compostura *f*, calma *f*.

compound *n* ['kɒmpaʊnd] - 1. [gen & CHEM] compuesto *m* - 2. [enclosed area] recinto *m*.

compound fracture *n* fractura *f* complicada.

comprehend [ˌkɒmprɪ'hend] *vt* comprender.

comprehension [ˌkɒmprɪ'henʃn] *n* comprensión *f*.

comprehensive [ˌkɒmprɪ'hensɪv] ◇ *adj* - 1. [wide-ranging] completo(ta) - 2. [defeat, victory] rotundo(da) - 3. [insurance] a todo riesgo. ◇ *n UK* = comprehensive school.

comprehensive school, comprehensive *n* instituto de enseñanza media no selectiva en Gran Bretaña.

compress [kəm'pres] *vt* - 1. [squeeze, press & COMPUT] comprimir - 2. [shorten] reducir.

comprise [kəm'praɪz] *vt* - 1. [consist of] comprender - 2. [form] constituir.

compromise ['kɒmprəmaɪz] ◇ *n* arreglo *m*, término *m* medio. ◇ *vt* comprometer. ◇ *vi* llegar a un arreglo, transigir.

compulsion [kəm'pʌlʃn] *n* - 1. [strong desire] ganas *fpl* irrefrenables - 2. *(U)* [force] obligación *f*.

compulsive [kəm'pʌlsɪv] *adj* - 1. [gambler] empedernido(da); [liar] compulsivo(va) - 2. [fascinating, compelling] absorbente.

compulsory [kəm'pʌlsərɪ] *adj* [gen] obligatorio(ria); [redundancy, retirement] forzoso(sa).

computer [kəm'pjuːtər] *n* ordenador *m*, computadora *f Amér*.

computer game *n* juego *m* de ordenador.

computer-generated [kəmˌpjuːtə-'dʒenəreɪtɪd] *adj* generado(da) por ordenador.

computer graphics *npl* infografía *f*.

computerized [kəm'pjuːtəraɪzd] *adj* informatizado(da), computerizado(da).

computing [kəm'pjuːtɪŋ], **computer science** *n* informática *f*.

comrade ['kɒmreɪd] *n* camarada *mf*.

con [kɒn] *inf* ◇ *n* [trick] timo *m*. ◇ *vt* timar, estafar; to con sb out of sthg timarle algo a alguien; to con sb into doing sthg engañar a alguien para que haga algo.

concave [ˌkɒn'keɪv] *adj* cóncavo(va).

conceal [kən'siːl] *vt* [object, substance, information] ocultar; [feelings] disimular; to conceal sthg from sb ocultarle algo a alguien.

concede [kən'siːd] ◇ *vt* - 1. [defeat, a point] admitir, reconocer - 2. [goal] encajar. ◇ *vi* [gen] ceder; [in sports, chess] rendirse.

conceit [kən'siːt] *n* engreimiento *m*.

conceited [kən'siːtɪd] *adj* engreído(da).

conceive [kən'siːv] ◇ *vt* concebir. ◇ *vi* - 1. MED concebir - 2. [imagine]: to conceive of sthg imaginarse algo.

concentrate ['kɒnsəntreɪt] ◇ *vt* concentrar. ◇ *vi*: to concentrate (on) concentrarse (en).

concentration [ˌkɒnsən'treɪʃn] *n* concentración *f*.

concentration camp *n* campo *m* de concentración.

concept ['kɒnsept] *n* concepto *m*.

concern [kən'sɜːn] ◇ *n* - 1. [worry, anxiety] preocupación *f* - 2. [company] negocio *m*, empresa *f*. ◇ *vt* - 1. [worry] preocupar; to be concerned about preocuparse por - 2. [involve] concernir; those concerned los interesados; to be concerned with [subj: person] ocuparse de; to concern o.s. with sthg preocuparse de OR por algo; as far as... is concerned por lo que a... respecta.

concerned [kən'sɜːnd] *adj* [person] preocupado(da); [expression] de preocupación.

concerning [kən'sɜːnɪŋ] *prep* en relación con.

concert ['kɒnsət] n concierto m.

concerted [kən'sɜːtɪd] adj conjunto(ta).

concert hall n sala f de conciertos.

concertina [,kɒnsə'tiːnə] n concertina f.

concerto [kən'tʃeətəʊ] (pl -s) n concierto m.

concession [kən'seʃn] n - 1. [allowance, franchise] concesión f - 2. UK [special price] descuento m, rebaja f - 3. UK [reduced ticket - for cinema, theatre] entrada f con descuento; [- for public transport] billete m con descuento.

concise [kən'saɪs] adj conciso(sa).

conclude [kən'kluːd] <> vt - 1. [bring to an end] concluir, terminar - 2. [deduce]: **to conclude (that)** concluir que - 3. [agreement] llegar a; [business deal] cerrar; [treaty] firmar. <> vi terminar, concluir.

conclusion [kən'kluːʒn] n - 1. [decision] conclusión f - 2. [ending] conclusión f, final m - 3. [of business deal] cierre m; [of treaty, agreement] firma f.

conclusive [kən'kluːsɪv] adj concluyente.

concoct [kən'kɒkt] vt - 1. [excuse, story] ingeniar - 2. [food] confeccionar; [drink] preparar.

concoction [kən'kɒkʃn] n [drink] brebaje m; [food] mezcla f.

concourse ['kɒŋkɔːs] n [of station etc] vestíbulo m.

concrete ['kɒŋkriːt] <> adj [definite, real] concreto(ta). <> n hormigón m, concreto m Amér. <> comp [made of concrete] de hormigón.

concur [kən'kɜːr] vi [agree]: **to concur (with)** estar de acuerdo OR coincidir (con).

concurrently [kən'kʌrəntlɪ] adv simultáneamente, al mismo tiempo.

concussion [kən'kʌʃn] n conmoción f cerebral.

condemn [kən'dem] vt - 1. [gen]: **to condemn sb (for/to)** condenar a alguien (por/a) - 2. [building] declarar en ruinas.

condensation [,kɒnden'seɪʃn] n [on walls] condensación f; [on glass] vaho m.

condense [kən'dens] <> vt condensar. <> vi condensarse.

condensed milk [kən'denst-] n leche f condensada.

condescending [,kɒndɪ'sendɪŋ] adj altivo(va), condescendiente.

condition [kən'dɪʃn] <> n - 1. [state] estado m; **in good/bad condition** en buen/mal estado; **to be out of condition** no estar en forma - 2. MED [disease, complaint] afección f - 3. [provision] condición f; **on condition that** a condición de que; **on one condition** con una condición. <> vt [gen] condicionar.

conditional [kən'dɪʃənl] <> adj condicional; **to be conditional on OR upon** depender de. <> n: **the conditional** el condicional.

conditioner [kən'dɪʃnər] n suavizante m.

condolences [kən'dəʊlənsɪz] npl pésame m; **to offer one's condolences** dar el pésame.

condom ['kɒndəm] n preservativo m, condón m.

condominium [,kɒndə'mɪnɪəm] n US - 1. [apartment] piso m, apartamento m - 2. [apartment block] bloque m de pisos OR apartamentos.

condone [kən'dəʊn] vt perdonar.

conducive [kən'djuːsɪv] adj: **conducive to** favorable para.

conduct <> n ['kɒndʌkt] - 1. [behaviour] conducta f - 2. [carrying out] dirección f. <> vt [kən'dʌkt] - 1. [carry out] dirigir, llevar a cabo - 2. [behave]: **to conduct o.s. well/badly** comportarse bien/mal - 3. MUS dirigir - 4. PHYS conducir.

conducted tour [kən'dʌktɪd-] n visita f con guía.

conductor [kən'dʌktər] n - 1. [of orchestra, choir] director m, -ra f - 2. [on bus] cobrador m - 3. US [on train] revisor m, -ra f.

conductress [kən'dʌktrɪs] n [on bus] cobradora f.

cone [kəʊn] n - 1. [shape] cono m - 2. [for ice cream] cucurucho m - 3. [from tree] piña f.

confectioner [kən'fekʃnər] n confitero m, -ra f; **confectioner's (shop)** confitería f.

confectionery [kən'fekʃnərɪ] n (U) dulces mpl, golosinas fpl.

confederation [kən,fedə'reɪʃn] n confederación f.

confer [kən'fɜːr] <> vt fml: **to confer sthg (on)** otorgar OR conferir algo (a). <> vi: **to confer (with)** consultar (con).

conference ['kɒnfərəns] n congreso m, conferencia f.

confess [kən'fes] <> vt confesar. <> vi - 1. [to crime & RELIG] confesarse; **to confess to sthg** confesar algo - 2. [admit]: **to confess to sthg** admitir algo.

confession [kən'feʃn] n confesión f.

confetti [kən'fetɪ] n confeti m.

confide [kən'faɪd] vi: **to confide (in)** confiarse (a).

confidence ['kɒnfɪdəns] n - 1. [self-assurance] confianza f OR seguridad f (en sí mismo/misma) - 2. [trust] confianza f; **to have confidence in sb** tener confianza en alguien - 3. [secrecy]: **in confidence** en secreto - 4. [secret] intimidad f, secreto m.

confidence trick n timo m, estafa f.

confident ['kɒnfɪdənt] *adj* - **1.** [self-assured - person] seguro de sí mismo(segura de sí misma), [smile, attitude] confiado(da) - **2.** [sure]: **confident (of)** seguro(ra) (de).

confidential [ˌkɒnfɪ'denʃl] *adj* [gen] confidencial; [secretary, clerk] de confianza.

confine [kən'faɪn] *vt* - **1.** [limit, restrict] limitar, restringir; **to be confined to** limitarse a - **2.** [shut up] recluir, encerrar.

confined [kən'faɪnd] *adj* [space] reducido(da).

confinement [kən'faɪnmənt] *n* [imprisonment] reclusión *f*.

confines ['kɒnfaɪnz] *npl* confines *mpl*.

confirm [kən'fɜ:m] *vt* confirmar.

confirmation [ˌkɒnfə'meɪʃn] *n* confirmación *f*.

confirmed [kən'fɜ:md] *adj* [non-smoker] inveterado(da); [bachelor] empedernido(da).

confiscate ['kɒnfɪskeɪt] *vt* confiscar.

conflict ⬦ *n* ['kɒnflɪkt] conflicto *m*. ⬦ *vi* [kən'flɪkt]: **to conflict (with)** estar en desacuerdo (con).

conflicting [kən'flɪktɪŋ] *adj* contrapuesto(ta).

conform [kən'fɔ:m] *vi* - **1.** [behave as expected] amoldarse a las normas sociales - **2.** [be in accordance]: **to conform (to OR with)** [expectations] corresponder (a); [rules] ajustarse (a).

confound [kən'faʊnd] *vt* [confuse, defeat] confundir, desconcertar.

confront [kən'frʌnt] *vt* - **1.** [problem, task] hacer frente a - **2.** [subj: problem, task] presentarse a - **3.** [enemy etc] enfrentarse con - **4.** [challenge]: **to confront sb (with)** poner a alguien cara a cara (con).

confrontation [ˌkɒnfrʌn'teɪʃn] *n* enfrentamiento *m*, confrontación *f*.

confuse [kən'fju:z] *vt* - **1.** [bewilder] desconcertar, confundir - **2.** [mix up]: **to confuse (with)** confundir (con) - **3.** [complicate, make less clear] complicar.

confused [kən'fju:zd] *adj* - **1.** [person] confundido(da), desconcertado(da) - **2.** [reasoning, situation] confuso(sa).

confusing [kən'fju:zɪŋ] *adj* confuso(sa).

confusion [kən'fju:ʒn] *n* - **1.** [gen] confusión *f* - **2.** [of person] desconcierto *m*.

congeal [kən'dʒi:l] *vi* [fat] solidificarse; [blood] coagularse.

congenial [kən'dʒi:njəl] *adj* ameno(na), agradable.

congested [kən'dʒestɪd] *adj* - **1.** [road] congestionado(da); [area] superpoblado(da) - **2.** MED congestionado(da).

congestion [kən'dʒestʃn] *n* [of traffic & MED] congestión *f*.

conglomerate [kən'glɒmərət] *n* COMM conglomerado *m*.

congratulate [kən'grætʃʊleɪt] *vt*: **to congratulate sb (on)** felicitar a alguien (por).

congratulations [kənˌgrætʃʊ'leɪʃənz] ⬦ *npl* felicitaciones *fpl*. ⬦ *excl* ¡enhorabuena!

congregate ['kɒŋgrɪgeɪt] *vi* [people] congregarse; [animals] juntarse.

congregation [ˌkɒŋgrɪ'geɪʃn] *n* RELIG feligreses *mpl*.

congress ['kɒŋgres] *n* congreso *m*. ⬥ **Congress** *n* [in US]: **(the) Congress** el Congreso.

congressman ['kɒŋgresmən] (*pl* **-men** [-mən]) *n* US congresista *m*.

conifer ['kɒnɪfər] *n* conífera *f*.

conjugate ['kɒndʒʊgeɪt] *vt* conjugar.

conjugation [ˌkɒndʒʊ'geɪʃn] *n* conjugación *f*.

conjunction [kən'dʒʌŋkʃn] *n* - **1.** GRAM conjunción *f* - **2.** [combination]: **in conjunction with** juntamente con.

conjunctivitis [kənˌdʒʌŋktɪ'vaɪtɪs] *n* conjuntivitis *f inv*.

conjure ['kʌndʒər] *vi* hacer juegos de manos. ⬥ **conjure up** *vt sep* [evoke] evocar.

conjurer, conjuror ['kʌndʒərər] *n* prestidigitador *m*, -ra *f*.

conk [kɒŋk] *n inf* [nose] napia *f*. ⬥ **conk out** *vi inf* - **1.** [break down] escacharrarse - **2.** [fall asleep] quedarse roque.

conker ['kɒŋkər] *n* UK castaña *f* (del castaño de Indias).

conman ['kɒnmæn] (*pl* **-men** [-men]) *n* estafador *m*, timador *m*.

connect [kə'nekt] ⬦ *vt* - **1.** [join]: **to connect sthg (to)** conectar algo (a); **to get connected** conectarse - **2.** [on telephone]: **I'll connect you now** ahora le paso OR pongo - **3.** [associate]: **to connect sthg/sb (with)** asociar algo/a alguien (con) - **4.** ELEC: **to connect sthg to** conectar algo a. ⬦ *vi* [train, plane, bus]: **to connect (with)** enlazar (con).

connected [kə'nektɪd] *adj* [related]: **connected (with)** relacionado(da) (con).

connection, connexion [kə'nekʃn] *n* - **1.** [gen, ELEC & COMPUT]: **connection (between/with)** conexión *f* (entre/con); **in connection with** con relación OR respecto a - **2.** [plane, train, bus] enlace *m* - **3.** [professional acquaintance] contacto *m*; **to have good connections** tener mucho enchufe.

connive [kə'naɪv] *vi* - **1.** [plot]: **to connive (with)** confabularse (con) - **2.** [allow to happen]: **to connive at sthg** hacer la vista gorda con algo.

connoisseur [ˌkɒnə'sɜ:r] *n* entendido *m*, -da *f*.

conquer ['kɒŋkəʳ] *vt* - **1.** [take by force] conquistar - **2.** [gain control of, overcome] vencer.

conqueror ['kɒŋkərəʳ] *n* conquistador *m*, -ra *f*.

conquest ['kɒŋkwest] *n* conquista *f*.

cons [kɒnz] *npl* - **1.** *UK inf*: **all mod cons** con todas las comodidades - **2.** ⊳ **pro.**

conscience ['kɒnʃəns] *n* conciencia *f*.

conscientious [,kɒnʃi'enʃəs] *adj* concienzudo(da).

conscious ['kɒnʃəs] *adj* - **1.** [gen] consciente; **to be conscious of** ser consciente de; **to become conscious of** darse cuenta de - **2.** [intentional] deliberado(da).

consciousness ['kɒnʃəsnɪs] *n* - **1.** [gen] conciencia *f* - **2.** [state of being awake] conocimiento *m*; **to lose/regain consciousness** perder/recobrar el conocimiento.

conscript *n* recluta *mf*.

conscription [kən'skrɪpʃn] *n* servicio *m* militar obligatorio.

consecutive [kən'sekjutɪv] *adj* consecutivo(va); **on three consecutive days** tres días seguidos.

consent [kən'sent] ◇ *n (U)* - **1.** [permission] consentimiento *m* - **2.** [agreement]: **by general OR common consent** de común acuerdo. ◇ *vi*: **to consent (to)** consentir (en).

consequence ['kɒnsɪkwəns] *n* - **1.** [result] consecuencia *f*; **in consequence** por consiguiente - **2.** [importance] importancia *f*.

consequently ['kɒnsɪkwəntlɪ] *adv* por consiguiente.

conservation [,kɒnsə'veɪʃn] *n* [gen] conservación *f*; [environmental protection] protección *f* del medio ambiente.

conservative [kən'sɜːvətɪv] *adj* - **1.** [not modern] conservador(ra) - **2.** [estimate, guess] moderado(da). ◆ **Conservative** ◇ *adj* POL conservador(ra). ◇ *n* POL conservador *m*, -ra *f*.

Conservative Party *n*: **the Conservative Party** el Partido Conservador.

conservatory [kən'sɜːvətrɪ] *n pequeña habitación acristalada adosada a una casa.*

conserve ◇ *n* ['kɒnsɜːv] compota *f*. ◇ *vt* [kən'sɜːv] [energy, supplies] ahorrar; [nature, wildlife] conservar.

consider [kən'sɪdəʳ] *vt* - **1.** [gen] considerar; **to consider doing sthg** considerar hacer algo; **to consider whether to do sthg** pensarse si hacer algo; **to consider o.s. lucky** considerarse afortunado(da) - **2.** [take into account] tener en cuenta; **all things considered** teniéndolo todo en cuenta.

considerable [kən'sɪdrəbl] *adj* considerable.

considerably [kən'sɪdrəblɪ] *adv* considerablemente, sustancialmente.

considerate [kən'sɪdərət] *adj* considerado(da).

consideration [kən,sɪdə'reɪʃn] *n* - **1.** [gen] consideración *f* - **2.** [factor] factor *m* - **3.** [amount of money] retribución *f*.

considering [kən'sɪdərɪŋ] ◇ *prep* habida cuenta de. ◇ *conj* después de todo.

consign [kən'saɪn] *vt*: **to consign sthg/sb to** relegar algo/a alguien a.

consignment [,kən'saɪnmənt] *n* remesa *f*.

consist [kən'sɪst] ◆ **consist in** *vt insep* consistir en. ◆ **consist of** *vt insep* constar de.

consistency [kən'sɪstənsɪ] *n* - **1.** [coherence - of behaviour, policy] consecuencia *f*, coherencia *f*; [of work, performances] regularidad *f* - **2.** [texture] consistencia *f*.

consistent [kən'sɪstənt] *adj* - **1.** [regular] constante - **2.** [coherent]: **consistent (with)** consecuente (con).

consolation [,kɒnsə'leɪʃn] *n* consuelo *m*.

console ◇ *n* ['kɒnsəʊl] consola *f*. ◇ *vt* [kən'səʊl] consolar.

consonant ['kɒnsənənt] *n* consonante *f*.

consortium [kən'sɔːtjəm] *(pl* -tiums *OR* -tia [-tjə]) *n* consorcio *m*.

conspicuous [kən'spɪkjʊəs] *adj* [building] visible; [colour] llamativo(va).

conspiracy [kən'spɪrəsɪ] *n* conspiración *f*.

conspire [kən'spaɪəʳ] ◇ *vt*: **to conspire to do sthg** conspirar para hacer algo. ◇ *vi* - **1.** [plan secretly]: **to conspire (against/with)** conspirar (contra/con) - **2.** [combine] confabularse.

constable ['kʌnstəbl] *n* policía *mf*.

constabulary [kən'stæbjʊlərɪ] *n policía f (de una zona determinada).*

constant ['kɒnstənt] ◇ *adj* [gen] constante. ◇ *n* constante *f*.

constantly ['kɒnstəntlɪ] *adv* [forever] constantemente.

consternation [,kɒnstə'neɪʃn] *n* consternación *f*.

constipated ['kɒnstɪpeɪtɪd] *adj* estreñido(da).

constipation [,kɒnstɪ'peɪʃn] *n* estreñimiento *m*.

constituency [kən'stɪtjʊənsɪ] *n* [area] distrito *m* electoral.

constituent [kən'stɪtjʊənt] *n* - **1.** [element] componente *m o f* - **2.** [voter] votante *mf*.

constitute ['kɒnstɪtjuːt] *vt* constituir.

constitution [,kɒnstɪ'tjuːʃn] *n* constitución *f*.

constraint [kən'streɪnt] n - **1.** [restriction]: **constraint (on)** limitación f (de) - **2.** [coercion] coacción f.

construct vt [kən'strʌkt] lit & fig construir.

construction [kən'strʌkʃn] n construcción f.

constructive [kən'strʌktɪv] adj constructivo(va).

construe [kən'struː] vt fml: **to construe sthg as** interpretar algo como.

consul ['kɒnsəl] n cónsul mf.

consulate ['kɒnsjulət] n consulado m.

consult [kən'sʌlt] <> vt consultar. <> vi: **to consult with sb** consultar a OR con alguien.

consultant [kən'sʌltənt] n - **1.** [expert] asesor m, -ra f - **2.** UK [hospital doctor] (médico) especialista m, (médica) especialista f.

consultation [,kɒnsəl'teɪʃn] n - **1.** [gen] consulta f - **2.** [discussion] discusión f.

consulting room [kən'sʌltɪŋ-] n consultorio m, consulta f.

consume [kən'sjuːm] vt lit & fig consumir.

consumer [kən'sjuːmər] n consumidor m, -ra f.

consumer goods npl bienes mpl de consumo.

consumer society n sociedad f de consumo.

consummate <> adj [kən'sʌmət] - **1.** [skill, ease] absoluto(ta) - **2.** [liar, politician, snob] consumado(da). <> vt ['kɒnsəmeɪt] [marriage] consumar.

consumption [kən'sʌmpʃn] n [use] consumo m.

contact ['kɒntækt] <> n contacto m; **in contact (with)** en contacto (con); **to lose contact with** perder (el) contacto con; **to make contact with** ponerse en contacto con. <> vt ponerse en contacto con.

contact lens n lentilla f, lente f de contacto.

contagious [kən'teɪdʒəs] adj contagioso(sa).

contain [kən'teɪn] vt contener; **to contain o.s.** contenerse.

container [kən'teɪnər] n - **1.** [box, bottle etc] recipiente m, envase m - **2.** [for transporting goods] contenedor m.

contaminate [kən'tæmɪneɪt] vt contaminar.

cont'd (abbr of continued): **'cont'd page 30** sigue en la página 30.

contemplate ['kɒntempleɪt] <> vt - **1.** [consider] considerar, pensar en; **to contemplate doing sthg** contemplar la posibilidad de hacer algo - **2.** fml [look at] contemplar. <> vi reflexionar.

contemporary [kən'tempərərɪ] <> adj contemporáneo(a). <> n contemporáneo m, -a f.

contempt [kən'tempt] n - **1.** [scorn]: **contempt (for)** desprecio m OR desdén m (por); **to hold sb in contempt** despreciar a alguien - **2.** LAW desacato m.

contemptuous [kən'temptʃuəs] adj despreciativo(va); **to be contemptuous of sthg** despreciar algo.

contend [kən'tend] <> vi - **1.** [deal]: **to contend with** enfrentarse a - **2.** [compete]: **to contend for/against** competir por/contra. <> vt fml: **to contend that** sostener OR afirmar que.

contender [kən'tendər] n [gen] contendiente mf; [for title] aspirante mf.

content <> adj [kən'tent]: **content (with)** contento(ta) OR satisfecho(cha) (con). <> n ['kɒntent] contenido m. <> vt [kən'tent]: **to content o.s. with sthg/with doing sthg** contentarse con algo/con hacer algo. ◆ **contents** npl - **1.** [of container, letter etc] contenido m - **2.** [heading in book] índice m.

contented [kən'tentɪd] adj satisfecho(cha), contento(ta).

contention [kən'tenʃn] n fml - **1.** [argument, assertion] argumento m - **2.** (U) [disagreement] disputas fpl.

contest <> n ['kɒntest] - **1.** [competition] concurso m; [in boxing] combate m - **2.** [for power, control] lucha f. <> vt [kən'test] - **1.** [seat, election] presentarse como candidato(ta) a - **2.** [dispute - statement] disputar; [- decision] impugnar.

contestant [kən'testənt] n [in quiz show] concursante mf; [in race] participante mf; [in boxing match] contrincante mf.

context ['kɒntekst] n contexto m.

continent ['kɒntɪnənt] n continente m. ◆ **Continent** n UK: **the Continent** Europa continental.

continental [,kɒntɪ'nentl] adj - **1.** GEOG continental - **2.** UK [European] de Europa continental.

continental breakfast n desayuno m continental.

continental quilt n UK edredón m.

contingency [kən'tɪndʒənsɪ] n contingencia f.

contingency plan n plan m de emergencia.

continual [kən'tɪnjuəl] adj continuo(nua), constante.

continually [kən'tɪnjuəlɪ] adv continuamente, constantemente.

continuation [kən,tɪnju'eɪʃn] n continuación f.

continue [kən'tɪnju:] ◇ vt: **to continue (doing** OR **to do sthg)** continuar (haciendo algo); **'to be continued'** 'continuará'. ◇ vi: **to continue (with sthg)** continuar (con algo).

continuous [kən'tɪnjʊəs] adj continuo(nua).

continuously [kən'tɪnjʊəslɪ] adv continuamente, ininterrumpidamente.

contort [kən'tɔ:t] vt retorcer.

contortion [kən'tɔ:ʃn] n contorsión f.

contour ['kɒn,tʊər] n - 1. [outline] contorno m - 2. [on map] curva f de nivel.

contraband ['kɒntrəbænd] ◇ adj de contrabando. ◇ n contrabando m.

contraception [,kɒntrə'sepʃn] n anticoncepción f.

contraceptive [,kɒntrə'septɪv] ◇ adj anticonceptivo(va). ◇ n anticonceptivo m.

contract ◇ n ['kɒntrækt] contrato m. ◇ vt [kən'trækt] - 1. [through legal agreement]: **to contract sb (to do sthg)** contratar a alguien (para hacer algo) - 2. fml [illness, disease] contraer. ◇ vi [kən'trækt] [decrease in size, length] contraerse.

contraction [kən'trækʃn] n contracción f.

contractor [kən'træktər] n contratista mf.

contradict [,kɒntrə'dɪkt] vt contradecir.

contradiction [,kɒntrə'dɪkʃn] n contradicción f.

contraflow ['kɒntrəfləʊ] n habilitación del carril contrario.

contraption [kən'træpʃn] n chisme m, artilugio m.

contrary ['kɒntrərɪ] ◇ adj - 1. [opposite] contrario(ria); **contrary to** en contra de - 2. [kən'treərɪ] [awkward] puñetero(ra). ◇ n: **the contrary** lo contrario; **on the contrary** al contrario. ◆ **contrary to** prep en contra de.

contrast ◇ n ['kɒntrɑ:st]: **contrast (between)** contraste m (entre); **by** OR **in contrast** en cambio; **to be a contrast (to** OR **with)** contrastar (con). ◇ vt [kən'trɑ:st]: **to contrast sthg with** contrastar algo con. ◇ vi [kən'trɑ:st]: **to contrast (with)** contrastar (con).

contravene [,kɒntrə'vi:n] vt contravenir.

contribute [kən'trɪbju:t] ◇ vt [give] contribuir, aportar. ◇ vi - 1. [gen]: **to contribute (to)** contribuir (a) - 2. [write material]: **to contribute to** colaborar con.

contribution [,kɒntrɪ'bju:ʃn] n - 1. [gen]: **contribution (to)** contribución f (a) - 2. [article] colaboración f - 3. [to social security] cotización f.

contributor [kən'trɪbjʊtər] n - 1. [of money] contribuyente mf - 2. [to magazine, newspaper] colaborador m, -ra f.

contrive [kən'traɪv] fml vt [engineer] maquinar, idear.

contrived [kən'traɪvd] adj inverosímil.

control [kən'trəʊl] ◇ n - 1. [gen & COMPUT] control m; [on spending] restricción f; **beyond** OR **outside one's control** fuera del control de uno; **in control of** al mando de; **to be in control of the situation** dominar la situación - 2. [of emotions] dominio m. ◇ vt - 1. [gen] controlar; **to control o.s.** dominarse, controlarse - 2. [operate - machine, plane] manejar; [- central heating] regular. ◆ **controls** npl [of machine, vehicle] mandos mpl.

controller [kən'trəʊlər] n FIN interventor m, -ra f; RADIO & TV director m, -ra f.

control panel n tablero m de instrumentos OR de mandos.

control tower n torre f de control.

controversial [,kɒntrə'vɜ:ʃl] adj polémico(ca).

controversy ['kɒntrəvɜ:sɪ, UK kən'trɒvəsɪ] n polémica f, controversia f.

convalesce [,kɒnvə'les] vi convalecer.

convene [kən'vi:n] ◇ vt convocar. ◇ vi reunirse.

convenience [kən'vi:njəns] n comodidad f, conveniencia f; **do it at your convenience** hágalo cuando le venga bien; **at your earliest convenience** en cuanto le sea posible.

convenience store n tienda f de ultramarinos (que abre hasta tarde).

convenient [kən'vi:njənt] adj - 1. [suitable] conveniente; **is Monday convenient?** ¿te viene bien el lunes? - 2. [handy - size] práctico(ca); [- position] adecuado(da); **convenient for** [well-situated] bien situado(da) para.

convent ['kɒnvənt] n convento m.

convention [kən'venʃn] n convención f.

conventional [kən'venʃənl] adj convencional.

converge [kən'vɜ:dʒ] vi lit & fig: **to converge (on)** converger (en).

conversant [kən'vɜ:sənt] adj fml: **conversant with** familiarizado(da) con.

conversation [,kɒnvə'seɪʃn] n conversación f.

conversational [,kɒnvə'seɪʃənl] adj coloquial.

converse ◇ n ['kɒnvɜ:s]: **the converse** lo contrario OR opuesto. ◇ vi [kən'vɜ:s] fml: **to converse (with)** conversar (con).

conversely [kən'vɜ:slɪ] adv fml a la inversa.

conversion [kən'vɜ:ʃn] n [gen, COMPUT & RELIG] conversión f.

convert ◇ vt [kən'vɜ:t] - 1. [gen & COMPUT]: **to convert sthg (to** OR **into)** convertir algo (en)

- 2. [change belief of]: **to convert sb (to)** convertir a alguien (a). ◇ *n* ['kɒnvɜːt] converso *m*, -sa *f*.

convertible [kən'vɜːtəbl] ◇ *adj* **- 1.** [sofa]: **convertible sofa** sofá-cama *m* **- 2.** [currency] convertible **- 3.** [car] descapotable. ◇ *n* (coche *m*) descapotable *m*.

convex [kɒn'veks] *adj* convexo(xa).

convey [kən'veɪ] *vt* **- 1.** *fml* [transport] transportar **- 2.** [express]: **to convey sthg (to)** transmitir algo (a).

convict ◇ *n* ['kɒnvɪkt] presidiario *m*, -ria *f*. ◇ *vt* [kən'vɪkt]: **to convict sb of** condenar a alguien por.

conviction [kən'vɪkʃn] *n* **- 1.** [belief, fervour] convicción *f* **- 2.** LAW condena *f*.

convince [kən'vɪns] *vt*: **to convince sb (of sthg/to do sthg)** convencer a alguien (de algo/para que haga algo).

convincing [kən'vɪnsɪŋ] *adj* convincente.

convoluted ['kɒnvəluːtɪd] *adj* [tortuous] enrevesado(da).

convoy ['kɒnvɔɪ] *n* convoy *m*.

convulse [kən'vʌls] *vt*: **to be convulsed with** [pain] retorcerse de; [laughter] troncharse de.

convulsion [kən'vʌlʃn] *n* MED convulsión *f*.

coo [kuː] *vi* arrullar.

cook [kʊk] ◇ *n* cocinero *m*, -ra *f*. ◇ *vt* [gen] cocinar, guisar; [prepare] preparar. ◇ *vi* **- 1.** [prepare food] cocinar, guisar **- 2.** [subj: food] cocerse. ◆ **cook up** *vt sep* [plan, deal] tramar, urdir; [excuse] inventarse.

cookbook ['kʊk,bʊk] = **cookery book**.

cooker ['kʊkə'] *n esp UK* cocina *f (aparato)*.

cookery ['kʊkərɪ] *n* cocina *f (arte)*.

cookery book, cookbook *n* libro *m* de cocina.

cookie ['kʊkɪ] *n* **- 1.** *US* [biscuit] galleta *f* **- 2.** COMPUT cookie *m*.

cooking ['kʊkɪŋ] *n* [food] cocina *f*.

cool [kuːl] ◇ *adj* **- 1.** [not warm] fresco(ca); [lukewarm] tibio(bia); **it's cool** hace fresco **- 2.** [calm] tranquilo(la) **- 3.** [unfriendly] frío(a) **- 4.** *inf* [hip] guay, chachi. ◇ *vt* refrescar. ◇ *vi* [become less warm] enfriarse. ◇ *n*: **to keep/lose one's cool** mantener/perder la calma. ◆ **cool down** *vi* **- 1.** [become less warm] enfriarse **- 2.** [become less angry] calmarse.

cool box *n* nevera *f* portátil.

coop [kuːp] *n* gallinero *m*. ◆ **coop up** *vt sep inf* encerrar.

cooperate [kəʊ'ɒpəreɪt] *vi*: **to cooperate (with)** cooperar (con).

cooperation [kəʊ,ɒpə'reɪʃn] *n* cooperación *f*.

cooperative [kəʊ'ɒpərətɪv] ◇ *adj* **- 1.** [helpful] servicial **- 2.** [collective] cooperativo(va). ◇ *n* cooperativa *f*.

coordinate ◇ *n* [kəʊ'ɔːdɪnət] coordenada *f*. ◇ *vt* [kəʊ'ɔːdɪneɪt] coordinar. ◆ **coordinates** *npl* [clothes] conjuntos *mpl*.

coordination [kəʊ,ɔːdɪ'neɪʃn] *n* coordinación *f*.

cop [kɒp] *n inf* poli *mf*; **the cops** la poli.

cope [kəʊp] *vi* arreglárselas; **to cope with** [work] poder con; [problem, situation] hacer frente a.

copier ['kɒpɪə'] *n* fotocopiadora *f*.

cop-out *n inf* escaqueo *m*.

copper ['kɒpə'] *n* **- 1.** [metal] cobre *m* **- 2.** *UK inf* [policeman] poli *mf*, paco *m*, -ca *f Andes*.

coppice ['kɒpɪs], **copse** [kɒps] *n* bosquecillo *m*.

copy ['kɒpɪ] ◇ *n* **- 1.** [imitation, duplicate] copia *f* **- 2.** [of book, magazine] ejemplar *m*. ◇ *vt* **- 1.** [imitate & COMPUT] copiar **- 2.** [photocopy] fotocopiar.

copyright ['kɒpɪraɪt] *n (U)* derechos *mpl* de autor.

coral ['kɒrəl] *n* coral *m*.

cord [kɔːd] *n* **- 1.** [string] cuerda *f*; [for tying clothes] cordón *m* **- 2.** [cable] cable *m*, cordón *m* **- 3.** [fabric] pana *f*. ◆ **cords** *npl* pantalones *mpl* de pana.

cordial ['kɔːdjəl] ◇ *adj* cordial. ◇ *n* refresco *m (hecho a base de concentrado de fruta)*.

cordon ['kɔːdn] *n* cordón *m*. ◆ **cordon off** *vt sep* acordonar.

corduroy ['kɔːdərɔɪ] *n* pana *f*.

core [kɔːr] ◇ *n* **- 1.** [of fruit] corazón *m* **- 2.** [of Earth, nuclear reactor, group] núcleo *m* **- 3.** [of issue, matter] meollo *m*. ◇ *vt* quitar el corazón de.

Corfu [kɔː'fuː] *n* Corfú.

corgi ['kɔːgɪ] *(pl* -s*) n* corgi *mf*.

coriander [,kɒrɪ'ændə'] *n* cilantro *m*.

cork [kɔːk] *n* corcho *m*.

corkscrew ['kɔːkskruː] *n* sacacorchos *m inv*.

corn [kɔːn] *n* **- 1.** *UK* [wheat, barley, oats] cereal *m* **- 2.** *US* [maize] maíz *m*, choclo *m Andes & R Plata*; **corn on the cob** mazorca *f* **- 3.** [callus] callo *m*.

cornea ['kɔːnɪə] *(pl* -s*) n* córnea *f*.

corned beef [kɔːnd-] *n* fiambre de carne de vaca cocinada y enlatada.

corner ['kɔːnə'] ◇ *n* **- 1.** [angle - of street, page, screen] esquina *f*; [- of room, cupboard] rincón *m*; [- of mouth] comisura *f*; **just around the corner** a la vuelta de la esquina **- 2.** [bend -

in street, road] curva f - **3.** [faraway place] rincón m - **4.** [in football] córner m. <> vt - **1.** [trap] arrinconar - **2.** [monopolize] acaparar.

corner shop n pequeña tienda de barrio que vende comida, artículos de limpieza etc.

cornerstone ['kɔ:nəstəʊn] n fig piedra f angular.

cornet ['kɔ:nɪt] n - **1.** [instrument] corneta f - **2.** UK [ice-cream cone] cucurucho m.

cornflakes ['kɔ:nfleɪks] npl copos mpl de maíz, cornflakes mpl.

cornflour UK ['kɔ:nflaʊə'], **cornstarch** US ['kɔ:nstɑ:tʃ] n harina f de maíz, maicena® f.

Cornwall ['kɔ:nwɔ:l] n Cornualles.

corny ['kɔ:nɪ] adj inf trillado(da).

coronary ['kɒrənrɪ], **coronary thrombosis** [-θrɒm'bəʊsɪs] (pl coronary thromboses [-θrɒm'bəʊsi:z]) n trombosis f inv coronaria, infarto m.

coronation [,kɒrə'neɪʃn] n coronación f.

coroner ['kɒrənə'] n juez de instrucción que investiga los casos de muerte sospechosa.

Corp. (abbr of corporation) Corp.

corporal ['kɔ:pərəl] n cabo mf.

corporal punishment n castigo m corporal.

corporate ['kɔ:pərət] adj - **1.** [business] corporativo(va); [strategy, culture] empresarial - **2.** [collective] colectivo(va).

corporation [,kɔ:pə'reɪʃn] n - **1.** [company] ≈ sociedad f anónima - **2.** UK [council] ayuntamiento m.

corps [kɔ:'] (pl corps) n cuerpo m.

corpse [kɔ:ps] n cadáver m.

correct [kə'rekt] <> adj - **1.** [accurate - time, amount, forecast] exacto(ta); [- answer, spelling, information] correcto(ta) - **2.** [socially acceptable] correcto(ta) - **3.** [appropriate, required] apropiado(da). <> vt corregir.

correction [kə'rekʃn] n corrección f.

correctly [kə'rektlɪ] adv - **1.** [gen] correctamente; **I don't think I can have heard you correctly** no estoy segura de haberte oído bien - **2.** [appropriately, as required] apropiadamente.

correlation [,kɒrə'leɪʃn] n: **correlation (between)** correlación f (entre).

correspond [,kɒrɪ'spɒnd] vi - **1.** [correlate]: **to correspond (with OR to)** corresponder (con OR a) - **2.** [match]: **to correspond (with OR to)** coincidir (con) - **3.** [write letters]: **to correspond (with)** cartearse (con).

correspondence [,kɒrɪ'spɒndəns] n: **correspondence (with/between)** correspondencia f (con/entre).

correspondence course n curso m por correspondencia.

correspondent [,kɒrɪ'spɒndənt] n [reporter] corresponsal mf.

corridor ['kɒrɪdɔ:'] n pasillo m.

corroborate [kə'rɒbəreɪt] vt corroborar.

corrode [kə'rəʊd] <> vt corroer. <> vi corroerse.

corrosion [kə'rəʊʒn] n corrosión f.

corrugated ['kɒrəgeɪtɪd] adj ondulado(da).

corrugated iron n chapa f ondulada.

corrupt [kə'rʌpt] <> adj [gen & COMPUT] corrupto(ta). <> vt [gen & COMPUT] corromper; **to corrupt a minor** pervertir a un menor.

corruption [kə'rʌpʃn] n corrupción f.

corset ['kɔ:sɪt] n corsé m.

Corsica ['kɔ:sɪkə] n Córcega.

cortege, cortège [kɔ:'teɪʒ] n cortejo m.

cosh [kɒʃ] <> n porra f. <> vt aporrear.

cosmetic [kɒz'metɪk] <> n cosmético m. <> adj fig superficial.

cosmopolitan [kɒzmə'pɒlɪtn] adj cosmopolita.

cosset ['kɒsɪt] vt mimar.

cost [kɒst] <> n coste m, costo m; **at cost** [comm] a precio de coste; **at no extra cost** sin costo adicional; **at the cost of** a costa de; **at all costs** a toda costa. <> vt (pt & pp cost OR -ed) - **1.** [gen] costar; **it cost us £20/a lot of effort** nos costó 20 libras/mucho esfuerzo; **how much does it cost?** ¿cuánto cuesta OR vale? - **2.** [estimate] presupuestar, preparar un presupuesto de. ◆ **costs** npl LAW litisexpensas fpl.

co-star ['kəʊ-] n coprotagonista mf.

Costa Rica [,kɒstə'ri:kə] n Costa Rica.

Costa Rican [,kɒstə'ri:kən] <> adj costarricense. <> n costarricense mf.

cost-effective adj rentable.

costing ['kɒstɪŋ] n cálculo m del coste.

costly ['kɒstlɪ] adj costoso(sa).

cost of living n: **the cost of living** el coste de la vida.

costume ['kɒstju:m] n - **1.** [gen] traje m - **2.** [swimming costume] traje m de baño.

costume jewellery n (U) bisutería f.

cosy UK, **cozy** US ['kəʊzɪ] <> adj - **1.** [warm and comfortable - room] acogedor(ra) - **2.** [intimate] agradable, amigable. <> n funda f para tetera.

cot [kɒt] n - **1.** UK [for child] cuna f - **2.** US [folding bed] cama f plegable.

cottage ['kɒtɪdʒ] n casa f de campo, chalé m.

cottage cheese n queso m fresco.

cottage pie n UK pastel de carne picada con una capa de puré de patatas.

cotton ['kɒtn] *n* - **1**. [fabric, plant] algodón *m* - **2**. [thread] hilo *m* (de algodón). ◆ **cotton on** *vi inf*: to cotton on (to) caer en la cuenta (de).

cotton candy *n US* azúcar *m* hilado, algodón *m*.

cotton wool *n* algodón *m* (hidrófilo).

couch [kaʊtʃ] ◇ *n* - **1**. [sofa] sofá *m* - **2**. [in doctor's surgery] diván *m*. ◇ *vt*: **to couch sthg in** formular algo en.

couchette [ku:'ʃet] *n UK* litera *f*.

cough [kɒf] ◇ *n* tos *f*; **to have a cough** tener tos. ◇ *vi* toser.

cough mixture, cough syrup *n UK* jarabe *m* para la tos.

cough sweet *n UK* caramelo *m* para la tos.

cough syrup = cough mixture.

could [kʊd] *pt, cond* ▷ **can²**.

couldn't ['kʊdnt] *(abbr of could not)* ▷ **can²**.

could've ['kʊdəv] *(abbr of could have)* ▷ **can²**.

council ['kaʊnsl] *n* - **1**. [of a town] ayuntamiento *m*; [of a county] ≃ diputación *f* - **2**. [group, organization] consejo *m* - **3**. [meeting] junta *f*, consejo *m*.

council estate *n* urbanización de viviendas de protección oficial.

council house *n UK* ≃ casa *f* de protección oficial.

councillor ['kaʊnsələr] *n* concejal *m*, -la *f*.

council tax *n UK* impuesto municipal basado en el valor de la propiedad, ≃ contribución *f* urbana.

counsel ['kaʊnsəl] *n* - **1**. *(U) fml* [advice] consejo *m*; **to keep one's own counsel** reservarse su opinión - **2**. [lawyer] abogado *m*, -da *f*.

counsellor *UK*, **counselor** *US* ['kaʊnsələr] *n* - **1**. [gen] consejero *m*, -ra *f* - **2**. [therapist] psicólogo *m*, -ga *f* - **3**. *US* [lawyer] abogado *m*, -da *f*.

count [kaʊnt] ◇ *n* - **1**. [total] total *m*; [of votes] recuento *m*; **to keep/lose count of** llevar/perder la cuenta de - **2**. [aristocrat] conde *m*. ◇ *vt* - **1**. [add up] contar; [total, cost] calcular - **2**. [consider]: **to count sb as** considerar a alguien como - **3**. [include] incluir, contar. ◇ *vi* contar; **to count (up) to** contar hasta; **to count for nothing** no contar para nada. ◆ **count against** *vt insep* perjudicar. ◆ **count (up)on** *vt insep* contar con. ◆ **count up** *vt insep* contar.

countdown ['kaʊntdaʊn] *n* cuenta *f* atrás.

counter ['kaʊntər] ◇ *n* - **1**. [total] mostrador *m*; [in bank] ventanilla *f*; **over the counter** sin receta médica - **2**. [in board game] ficha *f*. ◇ *vt*: **to counter sthg with** responder a algo mediante; **to counter sthg by doing sthg** contrarrestar algo haciendo algo. ◆ **counter to** *adv* contrario a.

counteract [,kaʊntə'rækt] *vt* contrarrestar.

counterattack [,kaʊntərə'tæk] ◇ *n* contraataque *m*. ◇ *vt & vi* contraatacar.

counterclockwise [,kaʊntə'klɒkwaɪz] *adv US* en sentido opuesto a las agujas del reloj.

counterfeit ['kaʊntəfɪt] ◇ *adj* falsificado(da). ◇ *vt* falsificar.

counterfoil ['kaʊntəfɔɪl] *n* matriz *f*.

countermand [,kaʊntə'mɑːnd] *vt* revocar.

counterpart ['kaʊntəpɑːt] *n* homólogo *m*, -ga *f*.

counterproductive [,kaʊntəprə'dʌktɪv] *adj* contraproducente.

countess ['kaʊntɪs] *n* condesa *f*.

countless ['kaʊntlɪs] *adj* innumerables.

country ['kʌntrɪ] ◇ *n* - **1**. [nation] país *m* - **2**. [population]: **the country** el pueblo - **3**. [countryside]: **the country** el campo - **4**. [terrain] terreno *m*. ◇ *comp* campestre.

country dancing *n (U)* baile *m* tradicional.

country house *n* casa *f* solariega.

countryman ['kʌntrɪmən] *(pl* -men [-mən]*) n* [from same country] compatriota *m*.

country park *n UK* parque natural abierto al público.

countryside ['kʌntrɪsaɪd] *n* [land] campo *m*; [landscape] paisaje *m*.

county ['kaʊntɪ] *n* condado *m*.

county council *n UK* organismo que gobierna un condado, ≃ diputación *f* provincial.

coup [ku:] *n* - **1**. [rebellion]: **coup (d'état)** golpe *m* (de estado) - **2**. [masterstroke] éxito *m*.

couple ['kʌpl] ◇ *n* - **1**. [two people in relationship] pareja *f* - **2**. [two objects, people]: **a couple (of)** un par (de) - **3**. [a few - objects, people]: **a couple (of)** un par (de), unos (unas). ◇ *vt* [join]: **to couple sthg (to)** enganchar algo (con).

coupon ['ku:pɒn] *n* [gen] vale *m*, cupón *m*; [for pools] boleto *m*.

courage ['kʌrɪdʒ] *n* valor *m*.

courageous [kə'reɪdʒəs] *adj* valiente.

courgette [kɔː'ʒet] *n UK* calabacín *m*, calabacita *f Méx*, zapallito *m* (italiano).

courier ['kʊrɪər] *n* - **1**. [on holiday] guía *mf* - **2**. [to deliver letters, packages] mensajero *m*, -ra *f*.

course [kɔːs] *n* - **1**. [gen] curso *m*; [of lectures] ciclo *m*; UNIV carrera *f*; **course of treatment** MED tratamiento *m*; **to change course** cambiar de rumbo; **to run OR take its course** seguir su curso; **off course** fuera de su rumbo; **course (of action)** camino *m* (a seguir); **in the course of** a lo largo de - **2**. [of meal] plato *m* - **3**. SPORT [for golf] campo *m*; [for race] circuito *m*. ◆ **of**

course *adv* - **1.** [inevitably, not surprisingly] naturalmente - **2.** [certainly] claro; **of course not** claro que no.

coursebook ['kɔːsbʊk] *n* libro *m* de texto.

coursework ['kɔːswɜːk] *n (U)* trabajo *m* realizado durante el curso.

court [kɔːt] ◇ *n* - **1.** [place of trial, judge, jury etc] tribunal *m* - **2.** SPORT cancha *f*, pista *f* - **3.** [of king, queen etc] corte *f*. ◇ *vi dated* [go out together] cortejarse.

courteous ['kɜːtjəs] *adj* cortés.

courtesy ['kɜːtɪsɪ] ◇ *n* cortesía *f*. ◇ *comp* de cortesía. ➡ **(by) courtesy of** *prep* [the author] con permiso de; [a company] por cortesía OR gentileza de.

courthouse ['kɔːthaʊs, *pl* -haʊzɪz] *n* US palacio *m* de justicia.

courtier ['kɔːtjəʳ] *n* cortesano *m*.

court-martial *n* (*pl* **court-martials** OR **courts-martial**) consejo *m* de guerra.

courtroom ['kɔːtrʊm] *n* sala *f* del tribunal.

courtyard ['kɔːtjɑːd] *n* patio *m*.

cousin ['kʌzn] *n* primo *m*, -ma *f*.

cove [kəʊv] *n* cala *f*, ensenada *f*.

covenant ['kʌvənənt] *n* - **1.** [of money] *compromiso escrito para el pago regular de una contribución especialmente con fines caritativos* - **2.** [agreement] convenio *m*.

cover ['kʌvəʳ] ◇ *n* - **1.** [covering] cubierta *f*; [lid] tapa *f*; [for seat, typewriter] funda *f* - **2.** [blanket] manta *f*; **under the covers** debajo de las sábanas - **3.** [of book] tapa *f*, cubierta *f*; [of magazine - at the front] portada *f*; [- at the back] contraportada *f* - **4.** [protection, shelter] refugio *m*; **under cover** [from weather] a cubierto - **5.** [concealment] tapadera *f*; **under cover of** al amparo OR abrigo de - **6.** [insurance] cobertura *f*. ◇ *vt* - **1.** [gen]: **to cover sthg (with)** cubrir algo (de); [with lid] tapar algo (con) - **2.** [include] abarcar - **3.** [report on] informar sobre - **4.** [discuss, deal with] abarcar. ➡ **cover up** *vt sep* - **1.** [place sthg over] tapar - **2.** [conceal] encubrir.

coverage ['kʌvərɪdʒ] *n* [of news] cobertura *f* informativa.

cover charge *n* cubierto *m*.

covering ['kʌvərɪŋ] *n* - **1.** [for floor etc] cubierta *f* - **2.** [of snow, dust] capa *f*.

covering letter UK, **cover letter** US *n* [with CV] carta *f* de presentación; [with parcel, letter] nota *f* aclaratoria.

cover note *n* UK póliza *f* provisional.

covert ['kʌvət] *adj* [operation] encubierto(ta), secreto(ta); [glance] furtivo(va).

cover-up *n* encubrimiento *m*.

covet ['kʌvɪt] *vt* codiciar.

cow [kaʊ] ◇ *n* - **1.** [female type of cattle] vaca *f* - **2.** [female elephant, whale, seal] hembra *f* - **3.** UK inf pej [woman] bruja *f*. ◇ *vt* acobardar, intimidar.

coward ['kaʊəd] *n* cobarde *mf*.

cowardly ['kaʊədlɪ] *adj* cobarde.

cowboy ['kaʊbɔɪ] *n* [cattlehand] vaquero *m*, tropero *m* R Plata.

cower ['kaʊəʳ] *vi* encogerse.

cox [kɒks], **coxswain** ['kɒksən] *n* timonel *mf*.

coy [kɔɪ] *adj* tímido(da).

cozy US = **cosy**.

crab [kræb] *n* cangrejo *m*.

crab apple *n* manzana *f* silvestre.

crack [kræk] ◇ *n* - **1.** [split - in wood, ground] grieta *f*; [- in glass, pottery] raja *f* - **2.** [gap] rendija *f* - **3.** [sharp noise - of whip] chasquido *m*; [- of twigs] crujido *m* - **4.** *inf* [attempt]: **to have a crack at sthg** intentar algo - **5.** [cocaine] crack *m*. ◇ *adj* de primera. ◇ *vt* - **1.** [cause to split] romper, partir - **2.** [egg, nut] cascar - **3.** [whip etc] chasquear - **4.** [bang]: **to crack one's head** golpearse la cabeza - **5.** [code] dar con la clave de; [problem] resolver - **6.** *inf* [tell - joke] contar. ◇ *vi* - **1.** [split - skin, wood, ground] agrietarse; [- pottery, glass] partirse - **2.** [break down] hundirse - **3.** [make sharp noise - whip] chasquear; [- twigs] crujir - **4.** UK inf [act quickly]: **to get cracking** ponerse manos a la obra. ➡ **crack down** *vi*: **to crack down (on)** tomar medidas severas (contra). ➡ **crack up** *vi* - **1.** [under pressure] venirse abajo - **2.** *inf* [laugh] partirse de risa.

cracker ['krækəʳ] *n* - **1.** [biscuit] galleta *f* (salada) - **2.** UK [for Christmas] *cilindro de papel que produce un estallido al abrirlo y que tiene dentro un regalito de Navidad*.

crackers ['krækəz] *adj* UK inf majareta.

crackle ['krækl] *vi* [fire] crujir, chasquear; [radio] sonar con interferencias.

cradle ['kreɪdl] ◇ *n* [baby's bed, birthplace] cuna *f*. ◇ *vt* acunar, mecer.

craft [krɑːft] *n* - **1.** [trade] oficio *m*; [skill] arte *m* - **2.** (*pl* **craft**) [boat] embarcación *f*. ➡ **crafts** *npl* artesanía *f*.

craftsman ['krɑːftsmən] (*pl* **-men** [-mən]) *n* artesano *m*.

craftsmanship ['krɑːftsmənʃɪp] *n (U)* - **1.** [skill] destreza *f*, habilidad *f* - **2.** [skilled work] artesanía *f*.

crafty ['krɑːftɪ] *adj* astuto(ta).

crag [kræg] *n* peñasco *m*.

cram [kræm] ◇ *vt* - **1.** [push - books, clothes] embutir; [people] apiñar - **2.** [overfill]: **to cram**

sth with atiborrar OR atestar algo de; **to be crammed (with)** estar repleto(ta) (de). ❖ *vi* [study] **empollar.**

cramp [kræmp] *n* calambre *m*; **stomach cramps** retortijones *mpl* de vientre.

cranberry ['krænbəri] *n* arándano *m* (agrio).

crane [kreɪn] *n* - **1.** [machine] grúa *f* - **2.** [bird] grulla *f*.

crank [kræŋk] ❖ *n* - **1.** [handle] manivela *f* - **2.** *inf* [eccentric] majareta *mf*. ❖ *vt* [wind] girar.

crankshaft ['kræŋkʃɑːft] *n* cigüeñal *m*.

cranny ['kræni] ▷ **nook**.

crap [kræp] *v inf* ❖ *n* (U) [gen] mierda *f*. ❖ *adj* UK de mierda, muy chungo(ga).

crash [kræʃ] ❖ *n* - **1.** [accident] choque *m* - **2.** [loud noise] estruendo *m* - **3.** FIN crac *m*. ❖ *vt* [plane] estrellar. ❖ *vi* - **1.** [collide - two vehicles] chocar; [one vehicle - into wall etc] estrellarse - **2.** FIN quebrar - **3.** COMPUT colgarse, bloquearse. ⬥ **crash out** *vi* dormir.

crash course *n* curso *m* acelerado, cursillo *m* intensivo de introducción.

crash helmet *n* casco *m* protector.

crash-land *vi* realizar un aterrizaje forzoso.

crass [kræs] *adj* burdo(da); **a crass error** un craso error.

crate [kreɪt] *n* caja *f* (para embalaje o transporte).

crater ['kreɪtər] *n* cráter *m*.

cravat [krə'væt] *n* pañuelo *m* (de hombre).

crave [kreɪv] ❖ *vt* ansiar. ❖ *vi*: **to crave for sthg** ansiar algo.

crawl [krɔːl] ❖ *vi* - **1.** [baby] andar a gatas - **2.** [insect, person] arrastrarse - **3.** [move slowly, with difficulty] avanzar lentamente. ❖ *n* [swimming stroke]: **the crawl** el crol.

crayon ['kreɪɒn] *n* (barra *f* de) cera *f*.

craze [kreɪz] *n* moda *f*.

crazy ['kreɪzi] *adj inf* - **1.** [mad - person] loco(ca); [- idea] disparatado(da); **like crazy** como un loco - **2.** [enthusiastic]: **to be crazy about** estar loco(ca) por.

creak [kriːk] *vi* [floorboard, bed] crujir; [door, hinge] chirriar.

cream [kriːm] ❖ *adj* [in colour] (color) crema (inv). ❖ *n* - **1.** [food] nata *f* - **2.** [cosmetic, mixture for food] crema *f* - **3.** [colour] (color *m*) crema *m* - **4.** [elite]: **the cream** la flor y nata, la crema.

cream cake *n* UK pastel *m* de nata, pastel *m* de crema *Amér*, masa *f* de crema *R Plata*.

cream cheese *n* queso *m* cremoso OR blanco.

cream cracker *n* UK galleta *f* sin azúcar (que generalmente se come con queso).

cream tea *n* UK merienda a base de de té con bollos con nata y mermelada.

crease [kriːs] ❖ *n* [deliberate - in shirt] pliegue *m*; [- in trousers] raya *f*; [accidental] arruga *f*. ❖ *vt* arrugar. ❖ *vi* [gen] arrugarse; [forehead] fruncirse.

create [kriː'eɪt] *vt* [gen] crear; [interest] producir.

creation [kriː'eɪʃn] *n* creación *f*.

creative [kriː'eɪtɪv] *adj* [gen] creativo(va); [energy] creador(ra); **creative writing** creación *f* literaria.

creature ['kriːtʃər] *n* criatura *f*; **a creature of habit** un animal de costumbres.

crèche [kreʃ] *n* UK guardería *f* (infantil).

credence ['kriːdns] *n*: **to give OR lend credence to** dar crédito a.

credentials [krɪ'denʃlz] *npl* credenciales *fpl*.

credibility [,kredə'bɪlətɪ] *n* credibilidad *f*.

credit ['kredɪt] ❖ *n* - **1.** [financial aid] crédito *m*; **to be in credit** tener saldo acreedor OR positivo; **on credit** a crédito - **2.** (U) [praise] reconocimiento *m*; **to do sb credit** decir mucho en favor de alguien; **to give sb credit for** reconocer a alguien el mérito de - **3.** [towards qualification, degree] crédito *m* - **4.** [money credited] saldo *m* acreedor OR positivo. ❖ *vt* - **1.** FIN [add] abonar; **we'll credit your account** lo abonaremos en su cuenta - **2.** [believe] creer - **3.** [give the credit to]: **to credit sb with** atribuir a alguien el mérito de. ⬥ **credits** *npl* [on film] títulos *mpl*.

credit card *n* tarjeta *f* de crédito.

credit note *n* [from shop] vale *m* de compra.

creditor ['kredɪtər] *n* acreedor *m*, -ra *f*.

creed [kriːd] *n* credo *m*.

creek [kriːk] *n* - **1.** [inlet] cala *f* - **2.** US [stream] riachuelo *m*.

creep [kriːp] ❖ *vi* (*pt & pp* **crept**) - **1.** [person] deslizarse, andar con sigilo - **2.** [insect] arrastrarse; [traffic etc] avanzar lentamente - **3.** *inf* [grovel]: **to creep (to sb)** hacer la pelota (a alguien). ❖ *n inf* - **1.** [unctuous person] pelotillero *m*, -ra *f* - **2.** [horrible person] asqueroso *m*, -sa *f*. ⬥ **creeps** *npl*: **to give sb the creeps** *inf* ponerle a alguien la piel de gallina.

creeper ['kriːpər] *n* enredadera *f*.

creepy ['kriːpɪ] *adj inf* horripilante.

creepy-crawly [-'krɔːlɪ] (*pl* -ies) *n inf* bicho *m*.

cremate [krɪ'meɪt] *vt* incinerar.

crematorium [,kremə'tɔːrɪəm] (*pl* -riums OR -ria [-rɪə]) UK, **crematory** ['kremətrɪ] US *n* crematorio *m*.

crepe [kreɪp] *n* - **1.** [cloth] crespón *m* - **2.** [rubber] crepé *m* - **3.** [thin pancake] crep *f*.

crepe bandage *n* UK venda *f* de gasa.

crepe paper *n* (U) papel *m* crespón.

crept [krept] *pt* & *pp* ▷ **creep**.

crescendo [krɪ'ʃendəʊ] (*pl* -s) *n* crescendo *m*.

crescent ['kresnt] *n* - 1. [shape] medialuna *f* - 2. [street] *calle en forma de medialuna*.

cress [kres] *n* berro *m*.

crest [krest] *n* - 1. [on bird's head, of wave] cresta *f* - 2. [of hill] cima *f*, cumbre *f* - 3. [on coat of arms] blasón *m*.

crestfallen ['krest,fɔːln] *adj* alicaído(da).

Crete [kriːt] *n* Creta.

cretin ['kretɪn] *n inf* [idiot] cretino *m*, -na *f*.

Creutzfeldt-Jakob disease [,krɔɪtsfelt'jækɒb-] *n* enfermedad *f* de Creutzfeldt-Jakob.

crevasse [krɪ'væs] *n* grieta *f*, fisura *f*.

crevice ['krevɪs] *n* grieta *f*, hendidura *f*.

crew [kruː] *n* - 1. [of ship, plane] tripulación *f* - 2. [on film set etc] equipo *m*.

crew cut *n* rapado *m*, corte *m* al cero.

crew-neck(ed) [-nek(t)] *adj* con cuello redondo.

crib [krɪb] *n* - 1. [cot] cuna *f* - 2. US inf [place] casa *f*, cantón *f* Méx.

crick [krɪk] *n* [in neck] tortícolis *f inv*.

cricket ['krɪkɪt] *n* - 1. [game] cricket *m* - 2. [insect] grillo *m*.

crime [kraɪm] ◇ *n* - 1. [serious offence] crimen *m*; [less serious offence] delito *m* - 2. [criminal behaviour - serious] criminalidad *f*; [- less serious] delincuencia *f* - 3. [immoral act] crimen *m*. ◇ *comp*: **crime novel** novela *f* policíaca; **crimes against humanity** crímenes contra la humanidad.

criminal ['krɪmɪnl] ◇ *adj* LAW [act, behaviour] criminal, delictivo(va); [law] penal; [lawyer] criminalista. ◇ *n* [serious] criminal *mf*; [less serious] delincuente *mf*.

crimson ['krɪmzn] ◇ *adj* [in colour] carmesí. ◇ *n* carmesí *m*.

cringe [krɪndʒ] *vi* - 1. [out of fear] encogerse - 2. *inf* [with embarrassment] sentir vergüenza ajena.

crinkle ['krɪŋkl] *vt* arrugar.

cripple ['krɪpl] ◇ *n dated* & *offens* tullido *m*, -da *f*. ◇ *vt* - 1. MED dejar inválido(da) - 2. [country, industry] paralizar.

crisis ['kraɪsɪs] (*pl* crises ['kraɪsiːz]) *n* crisis *f inv*.

crisp [krɪsp] *adj* - 1. [pastry, bacon, snow] crujiente; [banknote, vegetables, weather] fresco(ca) - 2. [brisk] directo(ta). ▶ **crisps** *npl* UK patatas *fpl* fritas (*de bolsa*).

crisscross ['krɪskrɒs] *adj* entrecruzado(da).

criterion [kraɪ'tɪərɪən] (*pl* -ria [-rɪə] OR -rions) *n* criterio *m*.

critic ['krɪtɪk] *n* crítico *m*, -ca *f*.

critical ['krɪtɪkl] *adj* [gen] crítico(ca); [illness] grave; **to be critical of** criticar.

critically ['krɪtɪklɪ] *adv* [gen] críticamente; **critically important** de vital importancia; **critically acclaimed** aclamado(da) por la crítica; [ill] gravemente.

criticism ['krɪtɪsɪzm] *n* crítica *f*.

criticize, -ise ['krɪtɪsaɪz] *vt* & *vi* criticar.

croak [krəʊk] *vi* - 1. [frog] croar; [raven] graznar - 2. [person] ronquear.

Croat ['krəʊæt], **Croatian** [krəʊ'eɪʃn] ◇ *adj* croata. ◇ *n* - 1. [person] croata *mf* - 2. [language] croata *m*.

Croatia [krəʊ'eɪʃə] *n* Croacia.

Croatian = **Croat**.

crochet ['krəʊʃeɪ] *n* ganchillo *m*.

crockery ['krɒkərɪ] *n* loza *f*, vajilla *f*.

crocodile ['krɒkədaɪl] (*pl* crocodile OR -s) *n* cocodrilo *m*.

crocus ['krəʊkəs] (*pl* -es) *n* azafrán *m* (*planta*).

croft [krɒft] *n* UK pequeña granja que proporciona sustento a la familia propietaria.

crony ['krəʊnɪ] *n inf* amiguete *m*.

crook [krʊk] *n* - 1. [criminal] ratero *m*, -ra *f* - 2. *inf* [dishonest person] ladrón *m*, -ona *f*, sinvergüenza *mf* - 3. [shepherd's staff] cayado *m*.

crooked ['krʊkɪd] *adj* - 1. [teeth, tie] torcido(da) - 2. [back] encorvado(da); [path] sinuoso(sa) - 3. *inf* [dishonest - person, policeman] corrupto(ta).

crop [krɒp] ◇ *n* - 1. [kind of plant] cultivo *m* - 2. [harvested produce] cosecha *f* - 3. [whip] fusta *f*. ◇ *vt* [cut short] cortar (muy corto). ▶ **crop up** *vi* surgir.

croquette [krɒ'ket] *n* croqueta *f*.

cross [krɒs] ◇ *adj* enfadado(da); **to get cross (with)** enfadarse (con). ◇ *n* - 1. [gen] cruz *f* - 2. [hybrid] cruce *m*; **a cross between** [combination] una mezcla de - 3. SPORT centro *m*. ◇ *vt* - 1. [gen & FIN] cruzar - 2. [face - subj: expression] reflejarse en - 3. SPORT centrar - 4. [oppose] contrariar - 5. RELIG: **to cross o.s.** santiguarse. ◇ *vi* [intersect] cruzarse. ▶ **cross off, cross out** *vt sep* tachar.

crossbar ['krɒsbɑːr] *n* - 1. [on goal] travesaño *m* - 2. [on bicycle] barra *f*.

cross-Channel *adj* [ferry] que hace la travesía del Canal de la Mancha; [route] a través del Canal de la Mancha.

cross-country ◇ *adj* & *adv* a campo traviesa. ◇ *n* cross *m*.

cross-examine *vt* interrogar (*para comprobar veracidad*).

cross-eyed ['krɒsaɪd] *adj* bizco(ca).

crossfire ['krɒs.faɪər] *n* fuego *m* cruzado.

crossing ['krɒsɪŋ] *n* - **1.** [on road] cruce *m*, paso *m* de peatones; [on railway line] paso a nivel - **2.** [sea journey] travesía *f*.

crossing guard *n* - **1.** *US* persona encargada de ayudar a cruzar la calle a los colegiales; [on railway line] paso a nivel - **2.** [sea journey] travesía *f*.

cross-legged ['krɒslegd] *adv* con las piernas cruzadas.

cross-purposes *npl*: **I think we're at cross-purposes** creo que estamos hablando de cosas distintas.

cross-reference *n* remisión *f*, referencia *f*.

crossroads ['krɒsrəʊdz] (*pl* **crossroads**) *n* cruce *m*.

cross-section *n* - **1.** [drawing] sección *f* transversal - **2.** [sample] muestra *f* representativa.

crosswalk ['krɒswɔːk] *n US* paso *m* de peatones.

crosswind ['krɒswɪnd] *n* viento *m* de costado.

crosswise ['krɒswaɪz], **crossways** *adv* en diagonal.

crossword (puzzle) ['krɒswɜːd-] *n* crucigrama *m*.

crotch [krɒtʃ] *n* entrepierna *f*.

crotchety ['krɒtʃɪtɪ] *adj UK inf* refunfuñón(ona).

crouch [kraʊtʃ] *vi* [gen] agacharse; [ready to spring] agazaparse.

crow [krəʊ] <> *n* corneja *f*. <> *vi* - **1.** [cock] cantar - **2.** *inf* [gloat] darse pisto.

crowbar ['krəʊbɑːr] *n* palanca *f*.

crowd [kraʊd] <> *n* - **1.** [mass of people] multitud *f*, muchedumbre *f*; [at football match etc] público *m* - **2.** [particular group] gente *f*. <> *vi* agolparse, apiñarse; **to crowd in/out** entrar/salir en tropel. <> *vt* - **1.** [room, theatre etc] llenar - **2.** [people] meter, apiñar.

crowded ['kraʊdɪd] *adj*: **crowded (with)** repleto(ta) OR abarrotado(da) (de).

crown [kraʊn] <> *n* - **1.** [of royalty, on tooth] corona *f* - **2.** [of hat] copa *f*; [of head] coronilla *f*; [of hill] cumbre *f*, cima *f*. <> *vt* [gen] coronar; **to crown it all** para colmo. **Crown** *n*: **the Crown** [monarchy] la Corona.

crown jewels *npl* joyas *fpl* de la corona.

crown prince *n* príncipe *m* heredero.

crow's feet *npl* patas *fpl* de gallo.

crucial ['kruːʃl] *adj* crucial.

crucifix ['kruːsɪfɪks] *n* crucifijo *m*.

Crucifixion [ˌkruːsɪˈfɪkʃn] *n*: **the Crucifixion** la Crucifixión.

crude [kruːd] *adj* - **1.** [rubber, oil, joke] crudo(da) - **2.** [person, behaviour] basto(ta) - **3.** [drawing, sketch] tosco(ca).

crude oil *n* crudo *m*.

cruel [krʊəl] *adj* [gen] cruel; [blow] duro(ra); [winter] crudo(da).

cruelty ['krʊəltɪ] *n (U)* crueldad *f*.

cruet ['kruːɪt] *n* vinagreras *fpl*.

cruise [kruːz] <> *n* crucero *m*. <> *vi* - **1.** [sail] hacer un crucero - **2.** [drive, fly] ir a velocidad de crucero.

cruiser ['kruːzər] *n* - **1.** [warship] crucero *m* - **2.** [cabin cruiser] yate *m (para cruceros)*.

crumb [krʌm] *n* - **1.** [of food] miga *f*, migaja *f* - **2.** [of information] pizca *f*.

crumble ['krʌmbl] <> *n* postre a base de compota de fruta con masa quebrada dulce por encima. <> *vt* desmigajar. <> *vi* - **1.** [building, cliff] desmoronarse; [plaster] caerse - **2.** *fig* [relationship, hopes] venirse abajo.

crumbly ['krʌmblɪ] *adj* que se desmigaja con facilidad.

crumpet ['krʌmpɪt] *n* - **1.** [food] *bollo que se come tostado* - **2.** *(U) inf* [women] tías *fpl*.

crumple ['krʌmpl] *vt* [dress, suit] arrugar; [letter] estrujar.

crunch [krʌntʃ] <> *n* crujido *m*. <> *vt* [with teeth] ronzar.

crunchy ['krʌntʃɪ] *adj* crujiente.

crusade [kruːˈseɪd] *n lit & fig* cruzada *f*.

crush [krʌʃ] <> *n* - **1.** [crowd] gentío *m* - **2.** *inf* [infatuation]: **to have a crush on sb** estar colado(da) OR loco(ca) por alguien. <> *vt* - **1.** [squash] aplastar - **2.** [grind - garlic, grain] triturar; [- ice] picar; [- grapes] exprimir - **3.** [destroy] demoler.

crust [krʌst] *n* - **1.** [on bread, of snow, earth] corteza *f* - **2.** [on pie] parte *f* dura.

crutch [krʌtʃ] *n* - **1.** [stick] muleta *f*; *fig* [support] apoyo *m* - **2.** [crotch] entrepierna *f*.

crux [krʌks] *n*: **the crux of the matter** el quid de la cuestión.

cry [kraɪ] <> *n* - **1.** [weep] llorera *f* - **2.** [shout] grito *m*. <> *vi* - **1.** [weep] llorar - **2.** [shout] gritar. **cry off** *vi* volverse atrás.

cryogenics [ˌkraɪəˈdʒenɪks] *n (sing)* criogenia *f*.

crystal ['krɪstl] *n* cristal *m*.

crystal clear *adj* - **1.** [transparent] cristalino(na) - **2.** [clearly stated] claro(ra) como el agua.

CTC *n abbr of* **city technology college**.

cub [kʌb] *n* - **1.** [young animal] cachorro *m* - **2.** [boy scout] lobato *m*, *boy scout de entre 8 y 11 años*.

Cuba ['kjuːbə] *n* Cuba.

Cuban ['kju:bən] <> adj cubano(na). <> n [person] cubano m, -na f.

cubbyhole ['kʌbɪhəʊl] n [room] cuchitril m; [cupboard] armario m.

cube [kju:b] <> n [gen] cubo m; [of sugar] terrón m. <> vt - 1. MATHS elevar al cubo - 2. [cut up] cortar en dados.

cubic ['kju:bɪk] adj cúbico(ca).

cubicle ['kju:bɪkl] n [at swimming pool] caseta f; [in shop] probador m; [in toilets] cubículo m.

Cub Scout n lobato m, boy scout de entre 8 y 11 años.

cuckoo ['kʊku:] n cuco m, cuclillo m.

cuckoo clock n reloj m de cuco.

cucumber ['kju:kʌmbə'] n pepino m.

cuddle ['kʌdl] <> n abrazo m. <> vt abrazar. <> vi abrazarse.

cuddly toy ['kʌdlɪ-] n muñeco m de peluche.

cue [kju:] n - 1. RADIO, THEAT & TV entrada f; on cue justo en aquel instante - 2. fig [stimulus, signal] señal f - 3. [in snooker, pool] taco m.

cuff [kʌf] n - 1. [of sleeve] puño m; off the cuff [speech, remarks] improvisado(da), sacado(da) de la manga - 2. US [of trouser leg] vuelta f - 3. [blow] cachete m.

cuff link n gemelo m, collera f Andes.

cuisine [kwɪ'zi:n] n cocina f.

cul-de-sac ['kʌldəsæk] n callejón m sin salida.

cull [kʌl] vt - 1. [animals] sacrificar (selectivamente) - 2. fml [information, facts] recoger.

culminate ['kʌlmɪneɪt] vi: to culminate in culminar en.

culmination [,kʌlmɪ'neɪʃn] n culminación f.

culottes [kju:'lɒts] npl falda f pantalón.

culpable ['kʌlpəbl] adj fml: culpable (of) culpable (de); culpable homicide homicidio m involuntario.

culprit ['kʌlprɪt] n culpable mf.

cult [kʌlt] <> n RELIG culto m. <> comp [series, movie] de culto.

cultivate ['kʌltɪveɪt] vt - 1. [gen] cultivar - 2. [get to know - person] hacer amistad con.

cultivated ['kʌltɪveɪtɪd] adj - 1. [cultured] culto(ta) - 2. [land] cultivado(da).

cultivation [,kʌltɪ'veɪʃn] n (U) cultivo m.

cultural ['kʌltʃərəl] adj cultural.

culture ['kʌltʃə'] n - 1. [gen] cultura f - 2. [of bacteria] cultivo m.

cultured ['kʌltʃəd] adj culto(ta).

cumbersome ['kʌmbəsəm] adj - 1. [package] abultado(da); [machinery] aparatoso(sa) - 2. [system] torpe.

cunning ['kʌnɪŋ] <> adj [gen] astuto(ta); [device, idea] ingenioso(sa). <> n (U) astucia f.

cup [kʌp] <> n - 1. [gen] taza f - 2. [prize, of bra] copa f. <> vt ahuecar.

cupboard ['kʌbəd] n armario m.

cupcake ['kʌpkeɪk] n US magdalena f.

cup tie n UK partido m de copa.

curate ['kjʊərət] n coadjutor m, -ra f.

curator [,kjʊə'reɪtə'] n conservador m, -ra f.

curb [kɜ:b] <> n - 1. [control]: curb (on) control m OR restricción f (de); to put a curb on sthg poner freno a algo - 2. US [in road] bordillo m, bordo m de la banqueta Méx, cordón m de la vereda R Plata, cuneta f Chile, sardinel m Col. <> vt controlar, contener.

curdle ['kɜ:dl] vi [milk] cuajarse; fig [blood] helarse.

cure [kjʊə'] <> n - 1. MED: cure (for) cura f (para) - 2. [solution]: cure (for) remedio m (a). <> vt - 1. MED curar - 2. [problem, inflation] remediar - 3. [food, tobacco] curar; [leather] curtir.

cure-all n panacea f.

curfew ['kɜ:fju:] n toque m de queda.

curio ['kjʊərɪəʊ] (pl -s) n curiosidad f.

curiosity [,kjʊərɪ'ɒsətɪ] n curiosidad f.

curious ['kjʊərɪəs] adj curioso(sa); to be curious about sentir curiosidad por.

curl [kɜ:l] <> n [of hair] rizo m. <> vt - 1. [hair] rizar - 2. [twist] enroscar. <> vi - 1. [hair] rizarse - 2. [paper] abarquillarse. ← **curl up** vi [person, animal] acurrucarse; [leaf, paper] abarquillarse.

curler ['kɜ:lə'] n rulo m.

curling tongs npl tenacillas fpl de rizar.

curly ['kɜ:lɪ] adj [hair] rizado(da); [pig's tail] enroscado(da).

currant ['kʌrənt] n pasa f de Corinto.

currency ['kʌrənsɪ] n - 1. FIN moneda f; foreign currency divisa f - 2. fml [acceptability]: to gain currency ganar aceptación.

current ['kʌrənt] <> adj [price, method, girlfriend] actual; [year] en curso; [issue] último(ma); [ideas, expressions, customs] corriente. <> n corriente f.

current account n UK cuenta f corriente.

current affairs npl temas mpl de actualidad.

currently ['kʌrəntlɪ] adv actualmente.

curriculum [kə'rɪkjələm] (pl -lums OR -la [-lə]) n [course of study] plan m de estudios, temario m.

curriculum vitae [-'vi:taɪ] (pl curricula vitae) n UK currículum m (vitae).

curry ['kʌrɪ] n curry m.

curse [kɜ:s] <> n - 1. [evil charm] maldición f - 2. [swearword] taco m, palabrota f. <> vt maldecir. <> vi [swear] soltar tacos.

cursor ['kɜ:sə'] n COMPUT cursor m.

cursory ['kɜ:sərɪ] adj superficial.

curt [kɜ:t] adj brusco(ca), seco(ca).

curtail [kɜ:'teɪl] *vt* - **1.** [visit] acortar - **2.** [expenditure] **reducir**; [rights] **restringir**.

curtain ['kɜ:tn] *n* - **1.** [gen] cortina *f* - **2.** [in theatre] telón *m*.

curts(e)y ['kɜ:tsɪ] ⟨⟩ *n* reverencia *f (de mujer)*. ⟨⟩ *vi (pt & pp* **curtsied**) hacer una reverencia *(una mujer)*.

curve [kɜ:v] ⟨⟩ *n* curva *f*. ⟨⟩ *vi* [river] hacer una curva; [surface] curvarse.

cushion ['kʊʃn] *n* - **1.** [for sitting on] cojín *m* - **2.** [protective layer] colchón *m*. ⟨⟩ *vt lit & fig* amortiguar.

cushy ['kʊʃɪ] *adj inf* cómodo(da); **a cushy job** *OR* **number** un chollo (de trabajo).

custard ['kʌstəd] *n (U)* natillas *fpl*.

custodian [kʌ'stəʊdjən] *n* - **1.** [of building, museum] conservador *m*, -ra *f* - **2.** [of tradition, values] guardián *m*, -ana *f*.

custody ['kʌstədɪ] *n* custodia *f*; **to take sb into custody** detener a alguien; **in custody** bajo custodia.

custom ['kʌstəm] ⟨⟩ *n* - **1.** [tradition, habit] costumbre *f* - **2.** *(U) fml* [trade] clientela *f*. ⟨⟩ *adj* hecho(cha) de encargo. ➡ **customs** *n* [place] aduana *f*.

customary ['kʌstəmrɪ] *adj* acostumbrado(da), habitual.

customer ['kʌstəmər] *n* - **1.** [client] cliente *mf* - **2.** *inf* [person] tipo *m*.

customize, -ise ['kʌstəmaɪz] *vt* [gen & COMPUT] personalizar.

Customs and Excise *n (U) UK* oficina del gobierno encargada de la recaudación de derechos arancelarios.

customs duty *n (U)* derechos *mpl* de aduana, aranceles *mpl*.

customs officer *n* agente *mf* de aduanas.

cut [kʌt] ⟨⟩ *n* - **1.** [gen] corte *m* - **2.** [reduction]: **cut (in)** reducción *f* (de); **wage cut** recorte *m* salarial - **3.** *inf* [share] parte *f*. ⟨⟩ *vt (pt & pp* **cut**) - **1.** [gen & COMPUT] cortar; [one's finger etc] cortarse; **to cut sb's hair** cortarle el pelo a alguien; **to cut a hole** hacer un agujero; **to cut class** *US* faltar a clase; **to cut o.s.** cortarse - **2.** [spending, staff etc] reducir, recortar; [text] acortar - **3.** *inf* [lecture] fumarse. ⟨⟩ *vi (pt & pp* **cut**) [gen & COMPUT] cortar. ➡ **cut back** *vt sep* - **1.** [plant] podar - **2.** [expenditure, budget] recortar. ➡ **cut down** ⟨⟩ *vt sep* - **1.** [chop down] cortar, talar - **2.** [reduce] reducir. ⟨⟩ *vi*: **to cut down on smoking** *OR* **cigarettes** fumar menos. ➡ **cut in** *vi* - **1.** [interrupt]: **to cut in (on sb)** cortar *OR* interrumpir (a alguien) - **2.** [in car] colarse. ➡ **cut off** *vt sep* - **1.** [gen] cortar - **2.** [interrupt] interrumpir - **3.** [town, village] quedarse incomunicado(da) (de). ➡ **cut out** *vt sep* - **1.** [remove] recortar - **2.** [dress, pattern etc] cortar; **to be cut out for sth** *fig* [person] estar hecho(cha) para algo - **3.** [stop]: **to cut out smoking** *OR* **cigarettes** dejar de fumar; **cut it out!** *inf* ¡hasta ya! - **4.** [exclude - light etc] eliminar; **to cut sb out of one's will** desheredar a alguien. ➡ **cut up** *vt sep* [chop up] cortar, desmenuzar.

cutback ['kʌtbæk] *n*: **cutback (in)** recorte *m OR* reducción *f* (en).

cute [kju:t] *adj* [appealing] mono(na), lindo(da).

cuticle ['kju:tɪkl] *n* cutícula *f*.

cutlery ['kʌtlərɪ] *n (U)* cubertería *f*.

cutlet ['kʌtlɪt] *n* chuleta *f*.

cutout ['kʌtaʊt] *n* - **1.** [on machine] cortacircuitos *m inv* - **2.** [shape] recorte *m*.

cut-price, cut-rate *US adj* de oferta.

cutthroat ['kʌtθrəʊt] *adj* [ruthless] encarnizado(da).

cutting ['kʌtɪŋ] ⟨⟩ *adj* [sarcastic] cortante, hiriente. ⟨⟩ *n* - **1.** [of plant] esqueje *m* - **2.** [from newspaper] recorte *m* - **3.** *UK* [for road, railway] desmonte *m*.

CV *(abbr of* **curriculum vitae***) n UK* CV *m*.

cwt. *abbr of* **hundredweight**.

cyanide ['saɪənaɪd] *n* cianuro *m*.

cybercafe ['saɪbəˌkæfeɪ] *n* cibercafé *m*.

cybercrime ['saɪbəkraɪm] *n* ciberdelito *m*.

cyberspace ['saɪbəspeɪs] *n* ciberespacio *m*.

cycle ['saɪkl] ⟨⟩ *n* - **1.** [series of events, poems, songs] ciclo *m* - **2.** [bicycle] bicicleta *f*. ⟨⟩ *comp*: **cycle lane** carril *m* bici; **cycle path** carril *m* bici. ⟨⟩ *vi* ir en bicicleta.

cycling ['saɪklɪŋ] *n* ciclismo *m*; **to go cycling** ir en bicicleta.

cyclist ['saɪklɪst] *n* ciclista *mf*.

cygnet ['sɪgnɪt] *n* pollo *m* de cisne.

cylinder ['sɪlɪndər] *n* - **1.** [shape, engine component] cilindro *m* - **2.** [container - for gas] bombona *f*.

cynic ['sɪnɪk] *n* cínico *m*, -ca *f*.

cynical ['sɪnɪkl] *adj* cínico(ca).

cynicism ['sɪnɪsɪzm] *n* cinismo *m*.

cypress ['saɪprəs] *n* ciprés *m*.

Cypriot ['sɪprɪət] ⟨⟩ *adj* chipriota. ⟨⟩ *n* chipriota *mf*.

Cyprus ['saɪprəs] *n* Chipre *m*.

cyst [sɪst] *n* quiste *m*.

cystitis [sɪs'taɪtɪs] *n* cistitis *f inv*.

czar [zɑ:r] *n zar m*; **government drugs czar** *UK* jefe *m*, -fa *f* de la lucha contra el narcotráfico.

Czech [tʃek] ⟨⟩ *adj* checo(ca). ⟨⟩ *n* - **1.** [person] checo *m*, -ca *f* - **2.** [language] checo *m*.

Czech Republic *n*: **the Czech Republic** la República Checa.

d (*pl* **d's** OR **ds**), **D** [di:] (*pl* **D's** OR **Ds**) *n* [letter] d *f*, D *f*. ◆ **D** *n* - **1.** MUS re *m* - **2.** SCH ≃ suspenso *m* - **3.** US *abbr of* **Democrat**, **Democratic**.

D.A. *n* US *abbr of* **district attorney**.

dab [dæb] ◇ *n* [small amount] toque *m*, pizca *f*; [of powder] pizca *f*. ◇ *vt* - **1.** [skin, wound] dar ligeros toques en - **2.** [cream, ointment]: **to dab sthg on** OR **onto** aplicar algo sobre.

dabble ['dæbl] *vi*: **to dabble (in)** pasar el tiempo OR entretenerse (con).

dachshund ['dækshʊnd] *n* perro *m* salchicha.

dad [dæd], **daddy** ['dædɪ] *n inf* papá *m*.

daddy longlegs [-'lɒŋlegz] (*pl* **daddy longlegs**) *n* típula *f*.

daffodil ['dæfədɪl] *n* narciso *m*.

daft [dɑːft] *adj* UK *inf* tonto(ta).

dagger ['dægə*r*] *n* daga *f*, puñal *m*.

daily ['deɪlɪ] ◇ *adj* diario(ria). ◇ *adv* diariamente; **twice daily** dos veces al día. ◇ *n* [newspaper] diario *m*.

dainty ['deɪntɪ] *adj* delicado(da), fino(na).

dairy ['deərɪ] *n* - **1.** [on farm] vaquería *f* - **2.** [shop] lechería *f* - **3.** [factory] central *f* lechera.

dairy farm *n* vaquería *f*.

dairy products *npl* productos *mpl* lácteos.

dais ['deɪɪs] *n* tarima *f*, estrado *m*.

daisy ['deɪzɪ] *n* margarita *f* (*flor*).

daisy wheel *n* margarita *f* (*de máquina de escribir*).

dale [deɪl] *n* valle *m*.

dam [dæm] ◇ *n* [across river] presa *f*. ◇ *vt* represar.

damage ['dæmɪdʒ] ◇ *n* - **1.** [physical harm]: **damage (to)** daño *m* (a); **to cause damage to sthg** ocasionar daños a algo - **2.** [harmful effect]: **damage (to)** perjuicio *m* (a). ◇ *vt* dañar.
◆ **damages** *npl* LAW daños *mpl* y perjuicios.

damn [dæm] ◇ *adj inf* maldito(ta). ◇ *adv inf* tela de, muy; **don't be so damn stupid** no seas tan rematadamente estúpido. ◇ *n inf*: **I don't give** OR **care a damn (about it)** me importa un bledo. ◇ *vt* - **1.** [gen & RELIG] condenar - **2.** *v inf* [curse]: **damn it!** ¡maldita sea!

damned [dæmd] *inf* ◇ *adj* maldito(ta); **I'm damned if I know why she did it** que me maten si sé por qué lo hizo; **well I'll be** OR **I'm damned!** ¡ostras! ◇ *adv* tela de, muy.

damning ['dæmɪŋ] *adj* condenatorio(ria).

damp [dæmp] ◇ *adj* húmedo(da). ◇ *n* humedad *f*. ◇ *vt* [make wet] humedecer.

dampen ['dæmpən] *vt* - **1.** [make wet] humedecer - **2.** *fig* [emotion] apagar.

damson ['dæmzn] *n* (ciruela *f*) damascena *f*.

dance [dɑːns] ◇ *n* baile *m*. ◇ *vt* bailar. ◇ *vi* - **1.** [to music] bailar - **2.** [move quickly and lightly] agitarse, moverse.

dancer ['dɑːnsə*r*] *n* bailarín *m*, -ina *f*.

dancing ['dɑːnsɪŋ] *n* (*U*) baile *m*.

dandelion ['dændɪlaɪən] *n* diente *m* de león.

dandruff ['dændrʌf] *n* caspa *f*.

Dane [deɪn] *n* danés *m*, -esa *f*.

danger ['deɪndʒə*r*] *n*: **danger (to)** peligro *m* (para); **in/out of danger** en/fuera de peligro; **to be in danger of doing sthg** correr el riesgo de hacer algo.

dangerous ['deɪndʒərəs] *adj* peligroso(sa).

dangle ['dæŋgl] ◇ *vt* colgar; *fig*: **to dangle sthg before sb** tentar a alguien con algo. ◇ *vi* colgar, pender.

Danish ['deɪnɪʃ] ◇ *adj* danés(esa). ◇ *n* - **1.** [language] danés *m* - **2.** US = **Danish pastry**. ◇ *npl* [people]: **the Danish** los daneses.

Danish pastry, **Danish** *n* pastel de hojaldre con crema o manzana o almendras etc.

dank [dæŋk] *adj* húmedo(da) e insalubre.

dapper ['dæpə*r*] *adj* pulcro(cra).

dappled ['dæpld] *adj* - **1.** [light] moteado(da) - **2.** [horse] rodado(da).

dare [deə*r*] ◇ *vt* - **1.** [be brave enough]: **to dare to do sthg** atreverse a hacer algo, osar hacer algo - **2.** [challenge]: **to dare sb to do sthg** desafiar a alguien a hacer algo
▸▸▸ **I dare say (...)** supongo OR me imagino (que...) ◇ *vi* atreverse, osar; **how dare you!** ¿cómo te atreves? ◇ *n* desafío *m*, reto *m*.

daredevil ['deə,devl] *n* temerario *m*, -ria *f*.

daring ['deərɪŋ] ◇ *adj* atrevido(da), audaz. ◇ *n* audacia *f*.

dark [dɑːk] ◇ *adj* - **1.** [night, colour, hair] oscuro(ra); **it's getting dark** está oscureciendo; **it was already dark** ya era de noche - **2.** [person, skin] moreno(na) - **3.** [thoughts, days, mood] sombrío(a), triste - **4.** [idea, comment, side of character etc] siniestro(tra). ◇ *n* - **1.** [darkness]: **the dark** la oscuridad; **to be in the dark about sthg** estar a oscuras sobre algo - **2.** [night]: **before/after dark** antes/después del anochecer.

darken ['dɑːkn] ◇ *vt* oscurecer. ◇ *vi* [become darker] oscurecerse.

dark glasses *npl* gafas *fpl* oscuras, anteojos *mpl* OR lentes *mpl* oscuros *Amér*.

darkness ['dɑːknɪs] *n* oscuridad *f*.

darkroom ['dɑːkrʊm] n PHOT cuarto m oscuro.

darling ['dɑːlɪŋ] ⋄ adj [dear] querido(da). ⋄ n - 1. [loved person] encanto m - 2. inf [addressing any woman] maja f.

darn [dɑːn] ⋄ adj inf maldito(ta), condenado(da). ⋄ adv inf tela de, muy; **don't be so darn stupid** no seas tan rematadamente estúpido. ⋄ vt zurcir. ⋄ excl inf ¡maldita sea!

dart [dɑːt] ⋄ n [arrow] dardo m. ⋄ vi precipitarse. ⬧ **darts** n (U) [game] dardos mpl.

dartboard ['dɑːtbɔːd] n blanco m, diana f.

dash [dæʃ] ⋄ n - 1. [of liquid] gotas fpl, chorrito m; [of colour] toque m - 2. [in punctuation] guión m. ⋄ vt - 1. liter [throw] arrojar - 2. [hopes] frustrar, malograr. ⋄ vi ir de prisa.

dashboard ['dæʃbɔːd] n salpicadero m.

dashing ['dæʃɪŋ] adj gallardo(da).

data ['deɪtə] n (U) datos mpl.

database ['deɪtəbeɪs] n COMPUT base f de datos.

data management n COMPUT gestión f de datos.

data processing n proceso m de datos.

data protection n COMPUT protección f de datos.

date [deɪt] ⋄ n - 1. [in time] fecha f; **to date** hasta la fecha - 2. [appointment] cita f - 3. US [person] pareja f (con la que se sale) - 4. [performance] actuación f - 5. [fruit] dátil m. ⋄ vt - 1. [establish the date of] datar - 2. [mark with the date] fechar - 3. US [go out with] salir con.

dated ['deɪtɪd] adj anticuado(da).

date of birth n fecha f de nacimiento.

daub [dɔːb] vt: **to daub sthg with** embadurnar algo con.

daughter ['dɔːtər] n hija f.

daughter-in-law (pl **daughters-in-law** OR **daughter-in-laws**) n nuera f.

daunting ['dɔːntɪŋ] adj amedrantador(ra).

dawdle ['dɔːdl] vi remolonear.

dawn [dɔːn] ⋄ n - 1. [of day] amanecer m, alba f - 2. [of era, period] albores mpl. ⋄ vi [day] amanecer. ⬧ **dawn (up)on** vt insep: **it dawned on me that...** caí en la cuenta de que...

day [deɪ] n - 1. [gen] día m; **I work an eight-hour day** trabajo una jornada de ocho horas; **the day before/after** el día anterior/siguiente; **the day before yesterday** anteayer; **the day after tomorrow** pasado mañana; **any day now** cualquier día de estos; **from day to day** de un día para otro - 2. [period in history]: **in those days** en aquellos tiempos; **these days** hoy día. ⬧ **days** adv de día.

daybreak ['deɪbreɪk] n amanecer m, alba f; **at daybreak** al amanecer.

daydream ['deɪdriːm] ⋄ n sueño m, ilusión f. ⋄ vi soñar despierto(ta).

daylight ['deɪlaɪt] n - 1. [light] luz f del día; **in broad daylight** a plena luz del día; **it was still daylight** todavía era de día - 2. [dawn] amanecer m.

day off (pl **days off**) n día m libre.

day return n UK billete m de ida y vuelta (en el día).

daytime ['deɪtaɪm] ⋄ n (U) día m. ⋄ comp de día, diurno(na).

day-to-day adj cotidiano(na).

daytrader ['deɪtreɪdər] n [St Ex] operador m, -ra f de posiciones diarias.

day trip n excursión f (de un día).

daze [deɪz] ⋄ n: **in a daze** aturdido(da). ⋄ vt lit & fig aturdir.

dazzle ['dæzl] vt lit & fig deslumbrar.

DC n - 1. (abbr of direct current) CC f - 2. abbr of **District of Columbia**.

D-day ['diːdeɪ] n el día D.

DEA (abbr of Drug Enforcement Administration) n organismo estadounidense para la lucha contra la droga.

deacon ['diːkn] n diácono m.

deactivate [ˌdiːˈæktɪveɪt] vt desactivar.

dead [ded] ⋄ adj - 1. [person, animal, plant] muerto(ta); **a dead body** un cadáver; **to be dead on arrival** ingresar cadáver - 2. [numb - leg, arm] entumecido(da); **my arm has gone dead** se me ha dormido el brazo - 3. [telephone] cortado(da); [car battery] descargado(da) - 4. [silence] absoluto(ta) - 5. [lifeless - town, party] sin vida. ⋄ adv - 1. [directly, precisely] justo - 2. [completely] totalmente, completamente; **to be dead set on sthg** estar decidido a hacer algo; **'dead slow'** 'al paso' - 3. inf [very] la mar de, muy - 4. [suddenly]: **to stop dead** parar en seco. ⋄ npl: **the dead** los muertos.

deaden ['dedn] vt atenuar.

dead end n lit & fig callejón m sin salida.

dead heat n empate m.

deadline ['dedlaɪn] n [period] plazo m; [date] fecha f tope.

deadlock ['dedlɒk] n punto m muerto.

dead loss n inf - 1. [person] inútil mf - 2. [thing] inutilidad f.

deadly ['dedlɪ] ⋄ adj - 1. [gen] mortal - 2. [accuracy] absoluto(ta). ⋄ adv [boring] mortalmente, terriblemente; [serious] totalmente.

deadpan ['dedpæn] adj [expression] inexpresivo(va), serio(ria); [humour] socarrón(ona).

deaf [def] <> *adj* [unable to hear] sordo(da). <> *npl*: **the deaf** los sordos.

deaf-and-dumb *adj* sordomudo(da).

deafen ['defn] *vt* ensordecer.

deaf-mute *n* sordomudo *m*, -da *f*.

deafness ['defnis] *n* sordera *f*.

deal [di:l] (*pt* & *pp* **dealt**) <> *n* - 1. [quantity]: **a good** OR **great deal (of)** mucho - 2. [agreement] acuerdo *m*; [business agreement] trato *m*; **to do** OR **strike a deal with sb** hacer un trato con alguien; **it's a deal!** ¡trato hecho! - 3. *inf* [treatment] trato *m*; **big deal!** ¡vaya cosa! - 4. [price]: **to get a good deal on sthg** conseguir algo a un precio barato. <> *vt* - 1. [strike]: **to deal sb/sthg a blow, to deal a blow to sb/sthg** *lit* & *fig* asestar un golpe a alguien/algo - 2. [cards] repartir, dar. <> *vi* - 1. [in cards] repartir, dar - 2. [in drugs] traficar con droga. ► **deal in** *vt insep* COMM comerciar en. ► **deal out** *vt sep* repartir. ► **deal with** *vt insep* - 1. [handle - situation, problem] hacer frente a, resolver; [- customer] tratar con - 2. [be about] tratar de - 3. [be faced with] enfrentarse a.

dealer ['di:lər] *n* - 1. [trader] comerciante *mf* - 2. [in drugs, arms] traficante *mf* - 3. [in cards] repartidor *m*, -ra *f*.

dealing ['di:lɪŋ] *n* comercio *m*. ► **dealings** *npl* [personal] trato *m*; [in business] tratos *mpl*.

dealt [delt] *pt* & *pp* ⊳ **deal**.

dean [di:n] *n* - 1. [of university] ≈ decano *m* - 2. [of church] deán *m*.

dear [dɪər] <> *adj* - 1. [loved] querido(da); **dear to sb** preciado(da) para alguien - 2. [expensive] caro(ra) - 3. [in letter]: **Dear Sir** Estimado señor, Muy señor mío; **Dear Madam** Estimada señora; **Dear Daniela** Querida Daniela. <> *n*: **my dear** cariño *m*, -ña *f*. <> *excl*: **oh dear!** ¡vaya por Dios!

dearly ['dɪəlɪ] *adv* [very much]: **I love you dearly** te quiero muchísimo; **I would dearly love to...** me encantaría...

death [deθ] *n* muerte *f*; **to frighten sb to death** dar un susto de muerte a alguien.

death certificate *n* partida *f* OR certificado *m* de defunción.

death duty UK, **death tax** US *n* impuesto *m* de sucesiones.

deathly ['deθlɪ] <> *adj* [silence] sepulcral. <> *adv*: **he was deathly pale** estaba pálido como un muerto.

death penalty *n* pena *f* de muerte.

death rate *n* índice *m* OR tasa *f* de mortalidad.

death tax US = **death duty**.

death trap *n* *inf* trampa *f* mortal, sitio *m* muy peligroso.

debar [di:'bɑːr] *vt*: **to debar sb from** [place] prohibir a alguien la entrada en; **to debar sb from doing sthg** prohibir a alguien hacer algo.

debase [dɪ'beɪs] *vt*: **to debase o.s.** rebajarse.

debate [dɪ'beɪt] <> *n* debate *m*; **that's open to debate** eso es discutible. <> *vt* - 1. [issue] discutir, debatir - 2. [what to do]: **to debate (whether to do sthg)** pensarse (si hacer algo). <> *vi* discutir, debatir.

debating society [dɪ'beɪtɪŋ-] *n* asociación *que organiza debates en una universidad.*

debauchery [dɪ'bɔːtʃərɪ] *n* depravación *f*, libertinaje *m*.

debit ['debɪt] <> *n* debe *m*, débito *m*. <> *vt*: **to debit sb** OR **sb's account with an amount, to debit an amount to sb** adeudar OR cargar una cantidad en la cuenta de alguien.

debit card *n* tarjeta *f* de débito.

debit note *n* nota *f* de cargo.

debris ['deɪbriː] *n* (U) [of building] escombros *mpl*; [of aircraft] restos *mpl*.

debt [det] *n* deuda *f*; **to be in debt (to sb)** tener una deuda (con alguien); **to get into debt** endeudarse; **to be in sb's debt** *fig* estar en deuda con alguien.

debt collector *n* cobrador *m*, -ra *f* de morosos.

debtor ['detər] *n* deudor *m*, -ra *f*.

debug [,di:'bʌg] *vt* COMPUT depurar.

debunk [,di:'bʌŋk] *vt* desmentir.

debut ['deɪbjuː] *n* debut *m*.

decade ['dekeɪd] *n* década *f*.

decadent ['dekədənt] *adj* decadente.

decaffeinated [dɪ'kæfɪneɪtɪd] *adj* descafeinado(da).

decamp [dɪ'kæmp] *vi* *inf* escabullirse.

decanter [dɪ'kæntər] *n* licorera *f*.

decathlon [dɪ'kæθlɒn] *n* decatlón *m*.

decay [dɪ'keɪ] <> *n* (U) - 1. [of tooth] caries *f inv*; [of body, plant] descomposición *f* - 2. *fig* [of building] deterioro *m*; [of society] degradación *f*. <> *vi* - 1. [tooth] picarse; [body, plant] pudrirse - 2. *fig* [building] deteriorarse; [society] degradarse.

deceased [dɪ'siːst] *fml* *n* (*pl* **deceased**): **the deceased** el difunto(la difunta).

deceit [dɪ'siːt] *n* engaño *m*.

deceitful [dɪ'siːtfʊl] *adj* [person, smile] embustero(ra); [behaviour] falso(sa).

deceive [dɪ'siːv] *vt* engañar; **to deceive o.s.** engañarse (a uno mismo/una misma).

December [dɪ'sembər] *n* diciembre *m*; *see also* **September**.

decency ['diːsnsɪ] *n* - 1. [respectability] decencia *f* - 2. [consideration]: **to have the decency to do sthg** tener la delicadeza de hacer algo.

decent ['diːsnt] *adj* - 1. [gen] decente - 2. [considerate]: **that's very decent of you** es muy amable de tu parte.

deception [dɪ'sepʃn] *n* engaño *m*.

deceptive [dɪ'septɪv] *adj* engañoso(sa).

decide [dɪ'saɪd] <> *vt* - 1. [gen]: **to decide (to do sthg)** decidir (hacer algo); **to decide (that)** decidir que - 2. [person] hacer decidirse - 3. [issue, case] resolver. <> *vi* decidir; **I couldn't decide** no me decidía; **I decided against doing it** decidí no hacerlo. **decide (up)on** *vt insep* decidirse por.

decided [dɪ'saɪdɪd] *adj* - 1. [advantage, improvement] indudable - 2. [person] decidido(da); [opinion] categórico(ca).

decidedly [dɪ'saɪdɪdlɪ] *adv* - 1. [clearly] decididamente - 2. [resolutely] con decisión.

deciduous [dɪ'sɪdjʊəs] *adj* de hoja caduca.

decimal ['desɪml] <> *adj* decimal. <> *n* (número *m*) decimal *m*.

decimal point *n* coma *f* decimal.

decimate ['desɪmeɪt] *vt* diezmar.

decipher [dɪ'saɪfər] *vt* descifrar.

decision [dɪ'sɪʒn] *n* decisión *f*; **to make a decision** tomar una decisión.

decisive [dɪ'saɪsɪv] *adj* - 1. [person] decidido(da) - 2. [factor, event] decisivo(va).

deck [dek] *n* - 1. [of ship] cubierta *f*; [of bus] piso *m* - 2. [of cards] baraja *f* - 3. *US* [of house] entarimado *m* (junto a una casa).

deckchair ['dektʃeər] *n* tumbona *f*.

declaration [,deklə'reɪʃn] *n* declaración *f*.

Declaration of Independence *n*: **the Declaration of Independence** la declaración de independencia estadounidense de 1776.

declare [dɪ'kleər] *vt* declarar.

decline [dɪ'klaɪn] <> *n* declive *m*; **in decline** en decadencia; **on the decline** en declive. <> *vt* [offer] declinar; [request] denegar; **to decline to do sthg** rehusar hacer algo. <> *vi* - 1. [number, importance] disminuir - 2. [refuse] negarse.

decode [,diː'kəʊd] *vt* descodificar.

decompose [,diːkəm'pəʊz] *vi* descomponerse.

decongestant [,diːkən'dʒestənt] *n* descongestionante *m*.

décor ['deɪkɔːr] *n* decoración *f*.

decorate ['dekəreɪt] *vt* - 1. [make pretty]: **decorate sthg (with)** decorar algo (de) - 2. [with paint] pintar; [with wallpaper] empapelar - 3. [with medal] condecorar.

decoration [,dekə'reɪʃn] *n* - 1. [gen] decoración *f* - 2. [ornament] adorno *m* - 3. [medal] condecoración *f*.

decorator ['dekəreɪtər] *n* [painter] pintor *m*, -ra *f*; [paperhanger] empapelador *m*, -ra *f*.

decorum [dɪ'kɔːrəm] *n* decoro *m*.

decoy <> *n* ['diːkɔɪ] señuelo *m*, <> *vt* [dɪ'kɔɪ] atraer (mediante un señuelo).

decrease <> *n* ['diːkriːs]: **decrease (in)** disminución *f* (de), reducción *f* (de). <> *vt* & *vi* [dɪ'kriːs] disminuir.

decree [dɪ'kriː] <> *n* - 1. [order, decision] decreto *m* - 2. *US* [judgment] sentencia *f*, fallo *m*. <> *vt* decretar.

decree nisi [-'naɪsaɪ] (*pl* **decrees nisi**) *n UK* LAW sentencia *f* provisional de divorcio.

decrepit [dɪ'krepɪt] *adj* - 1. [person] decrépito(ta) - 2. [thing] deteriorado(da).

dedicate ['dedɪkeɪt] *vt* - 1. dedicar; **to dedicate o.s. to sthg** consagrarse OR dedicarse a algo - 2. *US* [open for public use] inaugurar.

dedication [,dedɪ'keɪʃn] *n* - 1. [commitment] dedicación *f* - 2. [in book] dedicatoria *f*.

deduce [dɪ'djuːs] *vt*: **to deduce (sthg from sthg)** deducir (algo de algo).

deduct [dɪ'dʌkt] *vt*: **to deduct (from)** deducir (de), descontar (de).

deduction [dɪ'dʌkʃn] *n* deducción *f*.

deed [diːd] *n* - 1. [action] acción *f*, obra *f* - 2. LAW escritura *f*.

deem [diːm] *vt fml* estimar; **to deem it wise to do sthg** estimar prudente hacer algo.

deep [diːp] <> *adj* - 1. [gen] profundo(da); **to be 10 feet deep** tener 10 pies de profundidad - 2. [sigh, breath, bowl] hondo(da); **to take a deep breath** respirar hondo - 3. [colour] intenso(sa) - 4. [sound, voice] grave. <> *adv* [dig, cut] hondo; **to go** OR **run deep** estar muy arraigado(da).

deepen ['diːpn] <> *vt* [hole, channel] ahondar. <> *vi* - 1. [river, sea] ahondarse - 2. [crisis, recession] agudizarse; [emotion, darkness] hacerse más intenso(sa).

deep freeze *n* congelador *m*.

deeply ['diːplɪ] *adv* [gen] profundamente; [dig, breathe, sigh] hondo.

deep-sea *adj*: **deep-sea diving** buceo *m* de profundidad.

deer [dɪər] (*pl* **deer**) *n* ciervo *m*.

deface [dɪ'feɪs] *vt* pintarrajear.

defamatory [dɪ'fæmətrɪ] *adj fml* difamatorio(ria).

default [dɪ'fɔːlt] <> *n* - 1. [on payment, agreement] incumplimiento *m*; [failure to attend] incomparecencia *f* (del contrario); **by default** [win] por incomparecencia - 2. COMPUT: **default (setting)** configuración *f* por defecto. <> *vi* incumplir un compromiso; **to default on sthg** incumplir algo.

defeat [dɪ'fiːt] <> *n* derrota *f*; **to admit defeat** darse por vencido(da). <> *vt* [team, opponent] derrotar; [motion] rechazar; [plans] frustrar.

defeatist [dɪ'fi:tɪst] *adj* derrotista.

defect <> *n* ['di:fekt] [fault] defecto *m*. <> *vi* [dɪ'fekt] POL desertar; **to defect to the other side** pasarse al otro bando.

defective [dɪ'fektɪv] *adj* defectuoso(sa).

defence *UK,* **defense** *US* [dɪ'fens] *n* defensa *f*.

defenceless *UK,* **defenseless** *US* [dɪ'fenslɪs] *adj* indefenso(sa).

defend [dɪ'fend] *vt* defender.

defendant [dɪ'fendənt] *n* acusado *m*, -da *f*.

defender [dɪ'fendər] *n* - 1. [gen] defensor *m*, -ra *f* - 2. SPORT defensa *mf*.

defense *US* = **defence**.

defenseless *US* = **defenceless**.

defensive [dɪ'fensɪv] <> *adj* - 1. [weapons, tactics] defensivo(va) - 2. [person]: **to be defensive** ponerse a la defensiva. <> *n*: **on the defensive** a la defensiva.

defer [dɪ'fɜ:r] <> *vt* aplazar. <> *vi*: **to defer to sb** deferir con OR a alguien.

deferential [,defə'renʃl] *adj* deferente.

defiance [dɪ'faɪəns] *n* desafío *m*; **in defiance of** en desafío de, a despecho de.

defiant [dɪ'faɪənt] *adj* desafiante.

deficiency [dɪ'fɪʃnsɪ] *n* - 1. [lack] escasez *f* - 2. [inadequacy] deficiencia *f*.

deficient [dɪ'fɪʃnt] *adj* - 1. [lacking]: **to be deficient in** ser deficitario(ria) en, estar falto(ta) de - 2. [inadequate] deficiente.

deficit ['defɪsɪt] *n* déficit *m*.

defile [dɪ'faɪl] *vt* [desecrate] profanar; *fig* [mind, purity] corromper.

define [dɪ'faɪn] *vt* definir.

definite ['defɪnɪt] *adj* - 1. [plan, date, answer] definitivo(va) - 2. [improvement, difference] indudable - 3. [sure - person] seguro(ra); **I am quite definite (about it)** estoy bastante seguro (de ello) - 4. [categorical] tajante, concluyente.

definitely ['defɪnɪtlɪ] *adv* - 1. [without doubt] sin duda - 2. [for emphasis] desde luego, con (toda) seguridad; **definitely not** desde luego que no.

definition [defɪ'nɪʃn] *n* - 1. [gen] definición *f*; **by definition** por definición - 2. [clarity] nitidez *f*.

deflate [dɪ'fleɪt] <> *vt* [balloon] desinflar; *fig* [person] bajar los humos a. <> *vi* desinflarse.

deflation [dɪ'fleɪʃn] *n* ECON deflación *f*.

deflect [dɪ'flekt] *vt* [gen] desviar; [criticism] soslayar.

defogger [,di:'fɒgər] *n* US AUT dispositivo *m* antivaho, luneta *f* térmica.

deformed [dɪ'fɔ:md] *adj* deforme.

defragment [,di:fræg'ment] *vt* COMPUT desfragmentar.

defraud [dɪ'frɔ:d] *vt* defraudar, estafar.

defibrillator [di:'fɪbrɪleɪtər] *n* MED desfibrilador *m*.

defrost [,di:'frɒst] <> *vt* - 1. [gen] descongelar - 2. US AUT [demist] desempañar. <> *vi* descongelarse.

deft [deft] *adj* habilidoso(sa), diestro(tra).

defunct [dɪ'fʌŋkt] *adj* [body, organization] desaparecido(da); [plan] desechado(da).

defuse [,di:'fju:z] *vt* UK - 1. [bomb] desactivar - 2. [situation] distender.

defy [dɪ'faɪ] *vt* - 1. [disobey - person, authority] desobedecer; [law, rule] violar - 2. [challenge]: **to defy sb to do sthg** retar OR desafiar a alguien a hacer algo - 3. [attempts, efforts] hacer inútil; **to defy description** ser indescriptible; **to defy explanation** ser inexplicable.

degenerate <> *adj* [dɪ'dʒenərət] degenerado(da). <> *vi* [dɪ'dʒenəreɪt]: **to degenerate (into)** degenerar (en).

degrading [dɪ'greɪdɪŋ] *adj* denigrante.

degree [dɪ'gri:] *n* - 1. [unit of measurement, amount] grado *m*; **a degree of risk** un cierto riesgo; **by degrees** paulatinamente, poco a poco - 2. [qualification] título *m* universitario, ≃ licenciatura *f*; **to have/take a degree (in sthg)** tener/hacer una licenciatura (en algo) - 3. [course] ≃ carrera *f*.

dehydrated [,di:haɪ'dreɪtɪd] *adj* deshidratado(da).

de-ice [di:'aɪs] *vt* quitar el hielo de.

deign [deɪn] *vt*: **to deign to do sthg** dignarse a hacer algo.

deity ['di:ɪtɪ] *n* deidad *f*.

dejected [dɪ'dʒektɪd] *adj* abatido(da).

delay [dɪ'leɪ] <> *n* retraso *m*. <> *vt* retrasar; **to delay starting sthg** retrasar el comienzo de algo. <> *vi*: **to delay (in doing sthg)** retrasarse (en hacer algo).

delayed [dɪ'leɪd] *adj*: **to be delayed** [person] retrasarse; [train, flight] llevar retraso.

delectable [dɪ'lektəbl] *adj* - 1. [food] deleitable - 2. [person] apetecible.

delegate <> *n* ['delɪgət] delegado *m*, -da *f*. <> *vt* ['delɪgeɪt]: **to delegate sthg (to sb)** delegar algo (en alguien); **to delegate sb to do sthg** delegar a alguien para hacer algo.

delegation [,delɪ'geɪʃn] *n* delegación *f*.

delete [dɪ'li:t] *vt* [gen & COMPUT] borrar, suprimir; [cross out] tachar.

delete key *n* COMPUT tecla *f* de borrado.

deli ['delɪ] *n inf abbr of* **delicatessen**.

deliberate <> *adj* [dɪ'lɪbərət] - 1. [intentional] deliberado(da) - 2. [slow] pausado(da). <> *vi* [dɪ'lɪbəreɪt] *fml* deliberar.

deliberately [dɪ'lɪbərətlɪ] *adv* - 1. [on purpose] adrede - 2. [slowly] pausadamente.

delicacy ['delɪkəsɪ] n - 1. [gracefulness, tact] delicadeza f - 2. [food] exquisitez f, manjar m.

delicate ['delɪkət] adj - 1. [gen] delicado(da) - 2. [subtle - colour, taste] suave, sutil - 3. [tactful] delicado(da), prudente; [instrument] sensible.

delicatessen [,delɪkə'tesn] n ≃ charcutería f, ≃ (tienda f de) ultramarinos m inv.

delicious [dɪ'lɪʃəs] adj delicioso(sa).

delight [dɪ'laɪt] ⟨⟩ n [great pleasure] gozo m, regocijo m; **to our delight** para gran alegría nuestra; **to take delight in doing sthg** disfrutar haciendo algo. ⟨⟩ vt encantar. ⟨⟩ vi: **to delight in sthg/in doing sthg** disfrutar con algo/haciendo algo.

delighted [dɪ'laɪtɪd] adj encantado(da), muy contento(ta); **delighted by** OR **with** encantado con; **to be delighted to do sthg/that** estar encantado de hacer algo/de que; **I'd be delighted (to come)** me encantaría (ir).

delightful [dɪ'laɪtfʊl] adj [gen] encantador(ra); [meal] delicioso(sa); [view] muy agradable.

delinquent [dɪ'lɪŋkwənt] ⟨⟩ adj [behaviour] delictivo(va); [child] delincuente. ⟨⟩ n delincuente mf.

delirious [dɪ'lɪrɪəs] adj [with fever] delirante; fig [ecstatic] enfervorizado(da).

deliver [dɪ'lɪvəʳ] vt - 1. [hand over] entregar; [distribute] repartir; **to deliver sthg to sb** entregar algo a alguien - 2. [give - speech, verdict, lecture] pronunciar; [- message, warning, ultimatum] transmitir; [- blow, kick] asestar - 3. [service] prestar - 4. [baby] traer al mundo - 5. fml [free] liberar, libertar - 6. US POL [votes] captar.

delivery [dɪ'lɪvərɪ] n - 1. [handing over] entrega f; [distribution] reparto m - 2. [goods delivered] partida f - 3. [way of speaking] (estilo m de) discurso m - 4. [birth] parto m.

delude [dɪ'luːd] vt engañar; **to delude o.s.** engañarse (a uno mismo/una misma).

deluge ['deljuːdʒ] n [flood] diluvio m; fig [huge number] aluvión m.

delusion [dɪ'luːʒn] n espejismo m, engaño m.

de luxe [də'lʌks] adj de lujo.

delve [delv] vi: **to delve (into)** [bag, cupboard] hurgar (en); fig [mystery] profundizar (en).

demand [dɪ'mɑːnd] ⟨⟩ n - 1. [claim, firm request] exigencia f, reclamación f; **on demand** a petición - 2. [need ECON]: **demand for** demanda f de; **in demand** solicitado(da). ⟨⟩ vt [gen] exigir; [pay rise] reivindicar, demandar; **to demand to do sthg** exigir hacer algo.

demanding [dɪ'mɑːndɪŋ] adj - 1. [exhausting] que exige mucho esfuerzo - 2. [not easily satisfied] exigente.

demean [dɪ'miːn] vt: **to demean o.s.** humillarse, rebajarse.

demeaning [dɪ'miːnɪŋ] adj denigrante.

demeanour UK, **demeanor** US [dɪ'miːnəʳ] n (U) fml comportamiento m.

demented [dɪ'mentɪd] adj demente.

demise [dɪ'maɪz] n fml - 1. [death] defunción f - 2. [end] desaparición f.

demister [,diː'mɪstəʳ] n UK AUT dispositivo m antivaho, luneta f térmica.

demo ['deməʊ] (abbr of **demonstration**) n inf - 1. mani f - 2. MUS maqueta f.

democracy [dɪ'mɒkrəsɪ] n democracia f.

democrat ['deməkræt] n demócrata mf. ➡ **Democrat** n US demócrata mf.

democratic [demə'krætɪk] adj democrático(ca). ➡ **Democratic** adj US demócrata.

Democratic Party n US Partido m Demócrata.

demolish [dɪ'mɒlɪʃ] vt [building] demoler; [argument, myth] destrozar.

demonstrate ['demənstreɪt] ⟨⟩ vt - 1. [prove] demostrar - 2. [show] hacer una demostración de. ⟨⟩ vi manifestarse; **to demonstrate for/against sthg** manifestarse a favor/en contra de algo.

demonstration [demən'streɪʃn] n - 1. [of machine, product] demostración f - 2. [public meeting] manifestación f.

demonstrator ['demənstreɪtəʳ] n - 1. [in march] manifestante mf - 2. [of machine, product] demostrador m, -ra f comercial.

demoralized [dɪ'mɒrəlaɪzd] adj desmoralizado(da).

demote [,diː'məʊt] vt descender de categoría.

demure [dɪ'mjʊəʳ] adj recatado(da).

den [den] n [lair] guarida f.

denial [dɪ'naɪəl] n - 1. [refutation] negación f, rechazo m; **she's in denial about her drink problem** se niega a aceptar que tiene un problema con la bebida - 2. [of rumour] desmentido m - 3. [refusal] denegación f.

denier ['denɪəʳ] n denier m.

denigrate ['denɪgreɪt] vt fml desacreditar.

denim ['denɪm] n tela f vaquera. ➡ **denims** npl (pantalones mpl) vaqueros mpl.

denim jacket n cazadora f vaquera.

Denmark ['denmɑːk] n Dinamarca.

denomination [dɪ,nɒmɪ'neɪʃn] n - 1. [religious group] confesión f - 2. [of money] valor m.

denounce [dɪ'naʊns] vt denunciar.

dense [dens] adj - 1. [gen] denso(sa); [trees] tupido(da) - 2. inf [stupid] bruto(ta).

density ['densətɪ] n densidad f.

dent [dent] ⟨⟩ n [on car] abolladura f. ⟨⟩ vt [car] abollar.

dental ['dentl] adj dental.

dental floss n hilo m OR seda f dental.

dental surgeon n odontólogo m, -ga f.

dentist ['dentɪst] n dentista mf; **to go to the dentist's** ir al dentista.

dentures ['dentʃəz] npl dentadura f postiza.

deny [dɪ'naɪ] vt - **1.** [refute] negar, rechazar; **to deny doing sthg** negar haber hecho algo - **2.** [rumour] desmentir - **3.** fml [refuse]: **to deny sb sthg** denegar algo a alguien.

deodorant [di:'əʊdərənt] n desodorante m.

depart [dɪ'pɑːt] vi fml - **1.** [leave]: **to depart (from)** salir (de); **this train will depart from Platform 2** este tren efectuará su salida por la vía 2 - **2.** [differ]: **to depart from sthg** apartarse de algo.

department [dɪ'pɑːtmənt] n - **1.** [gen] departamento m - **2.** [in government] ministerio m.

department store n grandes almacenes mpl.

departure [dɪ'pɑːtʃər] n - **1.** [of train, plane] salida f; [of person] marcha f, partida f - **2.** [change]: **departure (from)** abandono m (de); **a new departure** un nuevo enfoque.

departure lounge n [in airport] sala f de embarque; [in coach station] vestíbulo m de salidas.

depend [dɪ'pend] vi: **to depend on** depender de; **you can depend on me** puedes confiar en mí; **it depends** depende; **depending on** según, dependiendo de.

dependable [dɪ'pendəbl] adj fiable.

dependant [dɪ'pendənt] n: **my dependants** las personas a mi cargo.

dependent [dɪ'pendənt] adj - **1.** [gen]: **to be dependent (on)** depender (de) - **2.** [addicted] adicto(ta).

depict [dɪ'pɪkt] vt [in picture] retratar.

deplete [dɪ'pliːt] vt mermar, reducir.

deplorable [dɪ'plɔːrəbl] adj deplorable.

deplore [dɪ'plɔːr] vt deplorar.

deploy [dɪ'plɔɪ] vt desplegar.

depopulation [di:,pɒpjʊ'leɪʃn] n despoblación f.

deport [dɪ'pɔːt] vt deportar.

depose [dɪ'pəʊz] vt deponer.

deposit [dɪ'pɒzɪt] <> n - **1.** GEOL yacimiento m - **2.** [sediment] poso m, sedimento m - **3.** [payment into bank] ingreso m - **4.** [down payment - on house, car] entrada f; [- on hotel room] señal f, adelanto m; [- on hired goods] fianza f; [- on bottle] dinero m del envase OR casco. <> vt - **1.** [put down] depositar - **2.** [in bank] ingresar.

deposit account n UK cuenta f de ahorro a plazo fijo.

depot ['depəʊ] n - **1.** [storage facility] almacén m; [for weapons] depósito m - **2.** [for buses] cochera f - **3.** US [bus or train terminus] terminal f.

depreciate [dɪ'priːʃɪeɪt] vi depreciarse.

depress [dɪ'pres] vt - **1.** [person] deprimir - **2.** [economy] desactivar - **3.** [price, share value] reducir.

depressed [dɪ'prest] adj deprimido(da).

depressing [dɪ'presɪŋ] adj deprimente.

depression [dɪ'preʃn] n - **1.** [gen & ECON] depresión f; **to suffer from depression** sufrir depresiones - **2.** fml [in pillow] hueco m.

deprivation [,deprɪ'veɪʃn] n - **1.** [poverty] miseria f - **2.** [lack] privación f.

deprive [dɪ'praɪv] vt: **to deprive sb of sthg** privar a alguien de algo.

depth [depθ] n profundidad f; **in depth** a fondo; **to be out of one's depth** [in water] no hacer pie; **he was out of his depth with that job** ese trabajo le venía grande. ➡ **depths** npl: **in the depths of winter** en pleno invierno; **to be in the depths of despair** estar en un abismo de desesperación.

deputation [,depjʊ'teɪʃn] n delegación f.

deputize, -ise ['depjʊtaɪz] vi: **to deputize (for)** actuar en representación (de). -ise

deputy ['depjʊtɪ] <> adj: **deputy head** subdirector m, -ra f; **deputy prime minister** vicepresidente m, -ta f del gobierno. <> n - **1.** [second-in-command] asistente mf, suplente mf - **2.** POL diputado m, -da f - **3.** US [deputy sheriff] ayudante mf del sheriff.

derail [dɪ'reɪl] vt & vi [train] descarrilar.

deranged [dɪ'reɪndʒd] adj perturbado(da), trastornado(da).

derby [UK 'dɑːbɪ, US 'dɜːrbɪ] n - **1.** [sports event] derby m (local) - **2.** US [hat] sombrero m hongo.

deregulate [,di:'regjʊleɪt] vt liberalizar.

derelict ['derəlɪkt] adj abandonado(da), en ruinas.

deride [dɪ'raɪd] vt mofarse de.

derisory [də'raɪzərɪ] adj - **1.** [puny, trivial] irrisorio(ria) - **2.** [derisive] burlón(ona).

derivative [dɪ'rɪvətɪv] n derivado m.

derive [dɪ'raɪv] <> vt - **1.** [draw, gain]: **to derive sthg from sthg** encontrar algo en algo - **2.** [come]: **to be derived from** derivar de. <> vi: **to derive from** derivar de.

derogatory [dɪ'rɒgətrɪ] adj despectivo(va).

derrick ['derɪk] n - **1.** [crane] grúa f - **2.** [over oil well] torre f de perforación.

derv [dɜːv] n UK gasóleo m, gasoil m.

descend [dɪ'send] <> vt fml [go down] descender por. <> vi - **1.** fml [go down] descender - **2.** [subj: silence, gloom]: **to descend**

(on sthg/sb) invadir (algo/a alguien) · 2. [stoop]: **to descend to sthg/to doing sthg** rehajarse a algo/a hacer algo.

descendant [dɪ'sendənt] *n* descendiente *mf*.

descended [dɪ'sendɪd] *adj*: **to be descended from** ser descendiente de, descender de.

descent [dɪ'sent] *n* - 1. [downwards movement] descenso *m*, bajada *f* - 2. [origin] ascendencia *f*.

describe [dɪ'skraɪb] *vt* describir; **to describe o.s. as** definirse como.

description [dɪ'skrɪpʃn] *n* - 1. [account] descripción *f* - 2. [type]: **of all descriptions** de todo tipo.

desecrate ['desɪkreɪt] *vt* profanar.

desert ◇ *n* ['dezət] GEOG desierto *m*. ◇ *vt* [dɪ'zɜːt] abandonar. ◇ *vi* MIL desertar.

deserted [dɪ'zɜːtɪd] *adj* [place] desierto(ta).

deserter [dɪ'zɜːtər] *n* desertor *m*, -ra *f*.

desert island ['dezət-] *n* isla *f* desierta.

deserve [dɪ'zɜːv] *vt* merecer.

deserving [dɪ'zɜːvɪŋ] *adj* encomiable; **deserving of** *fml* merecedor(ra) de.

design [dɪ'zaɪn] ◇ *n* - 1. [gen] diseño *m*; [of garment] corte *m* - 2. [pattern] dibujo *m* - 3. *fml* [intention] designio *m*; **by design** adrede; **to have designs on** tener las miras puestas en. ◇ *vt* - 1. [gen] diseñar - 2. [conceive, intend] concebir.

designate ◇ *adj* ['dezɪgnət] designado(da). ◇ *vt* ['dezɪgneɪt] designar; **to designate sb as sthg/to do sthg** designar a alguien algo/para hacer algo.

designer [dɪ'zaɪnər] ◇ *adj* [clothes, drugs] de diseño; [glasses] de marca. ◇ *n* [gen] diseñador *m*, -ra *f*; THEAT escenógrafo *m*, -fa *f*.

desirable [dɪ'zaɪərəbl] *adj* - 1. *fml* [appropriate] deseable, conveniente - 2. [attractive] atractivo(va), apetecible.

desire [dɪ'zaɪər] ◇ *n*: **desire (for sthg/to do sthg)** deseo *m* (de algo/de hacer algo). ◇ *vt* desear.

desk [desk] *n* - 1. [gen] mesa *f*, escritorio *m*; [in school] pupitre *m* - 2. [service area]: **information desk** (mostrador *m* de) información *f*.

desktop publishing *n* COMPUT autoedición *f*.

desolate ['desələt] *adj* [place, person] desolado(da); [feeling] desolador(ra).

despair [dɪ'speər] ◇ *n* desesperación *f*; **to do sthg in despair** hacer algo desesperadamente. ◇ *vi* desesperarse; **to despair of sb** desesperarse con alguien; **to despair of sthg/doing sthg** perder la esperanza de algo/hacer algo.

despairing [dɪ'speərɪŋ] *adj* [attempt] desesperado(da); [look, cry] de desesperación.

despatch [dɪ'spætʃ] = **dispatch**.

desperate ['desprət] *adj* desesperado(da); **to be desperate for sthg** necesitar algo desesperadamente.

desperately ['desprətlɪ] *adv* - 1. [want, fight, love] desesperadamente - 2. [ill] gravemente; [poor, unhappy, shy] tremendamente.

desperation [,despə'reɪʃn] *n* desesperación *f*; **in desperation** con desesperación.

despicable [dɪ'spɪkəbl] *adj* despreciable.

despise [dɪ'spaɪz] *vt* despreciar.

despite [dɪ'spaɪt] *prep* a pesar de, pese a.

despondent [dɪ'spɒndənt] *adj* descorazonado(da).

dessert [dɪ'zɜːt] *n* postre *m*.

dessertspoon [dɪ'zɜːtspuːn] *n* [spoon] cuchara *f* de postre.

destination [,destɪ'neɪʃn] *n* destino *m*.

destined ['destɪnd] *adj* - 1. [fated, intended]: **destined for sthg/to do sthg** destinado(da) a algo/a hacer algo - 2. [bound]: **destined for** con destino a.

destiny ['destɪnɪ] *n* destino *m*.

destitute ['destɪtjuːt] *adj* indigente.

de-stress [diː'stres] *vi* desestresarse.

destroy [dɪ'strɔɪ] *vt* - 1. [ruin] destruir - 2. [defeat] aplastar - 3. [put down] matar, sacrificar.

destruction [dɪ'strʌkʃn] *n* destrucción *f*.

detach [dɪ'tætʃ] *vt* - 1. [pull off]: **to detach sthg (from)** quitar OR separar algo (de) - 2. [disassociate]: **to detach o.s. from sthg** distanciarse de algo.

detachable [dɪ'tætʃəbl] *adj* [handle etc] de quita y pon; [collar] postizo(za).

detached [dɪ'tætʃt] *adj* [objective] objetivo(va); [aloof] distante.

detached house *n* casa *f* OR chalé *m* individual.

detachment [dɪ'tætʃmənt] *n* - 1. [objectivity] objetividad *f*; [aloofness] distanciamiento *m* - 2. MIL destacamento *m*.

detail ['diːteɪl] ◇ *n* - 1. [small point] detalle *m* - 2. (U) [facts, points] detalles *mpl*; **to go into detail** entrar en detalles; **in detail** con detalle - 3. MIL destacamento *m*. ◇ *vt* [list] detallar.
⬥ **details** *npl* [information] información *f*; [personal] datos *mpl*.

detailed ['diːteɪld] *adj* detallado(da).

detain [dɪ'teɪn] *vt* [gen] retener; [in police station] detener.

detect [dɪ'tekt] *vt* [gen] detectar; [difference] notar, percibir.

detection [dɪ'tekʃn] (U) *n* - 1. [gen] detección *f* - 2. [of crime] investigación *f*; [of drugs] descubrimiento *m*.

detective [dɪ'tektɪv] *n* [private] detective *mf*; [policeman] agente *mf*.

detective novel n novela f policíaca.

détente [dei'tɒnt] n POL distensión f.

detention [dɪ'tenʃn] n - 1. [of suspect, criminal] detención f, arresto m - 2. [at school] *castigo consistente en tener que quedarse en la escuela después de clase.*

deter [dɪ'tɜ:ʳ] vt: **to deter sb (from doing sthg)** disuadir a alguien (de hacer algo).

detergent [dɪ'tɜ:dʒənt] n detergente m.

deteriorate [dɪ'tɪərɪəreɪt] vi [health, economy] deteriorarse; [weather] empeorar.

determination [dɪ,tɜ:mɪ'neɪʃn] n determinación f.

determine [dɪ'tɜ:mɪn] vt determinar; **to determine to do sthg** fml decidir OR resolver hacer algo.

determined [dɪ'tɜ:mɪnd] adj decidido(da); **determined to do sthg** decidido(da) OR resuelto(ta) a hacer algo.

deterrent [dɪ'terənt] n elemento m de disuasión; **to serve as a deterrent** tener un efecto disuasorio; **nuclear deterrent** armas fpl nucleares disuasorias.

detest [dɪ'test] vt detestar.

detonate ['detəneɪt] <> vt hacer detonar. <> vi detonar.

detour ['di:,tuəʳ] n desvío m; **to make a detour** dar un rodeo.

detox ['di:tɒks] n desintoxicación f.

detract [dɪ'trækt] vi: **to detract from sthg** [gen] mermar algo, aminorar algo; [achievement] restar importancia a algo.

detriment ['detrɪmənt] n: **to the detriment of** en detrimento de.

detrimental [,detrɪ'mentl] adj perjudicial.

deuce [dju:s] n (U) TÉNIS deuce m, cuarenta f.

devaluation [,di:vælju'eɪʃn] n devaluación f.

devastated ['devəsteɪtɪd] adj [area, city] asolado(da); fig [person] desolado(da).

devastating ['devəsteɪtɪŋ] adj - 1. [destructive - hurricane etc] devastador(ra) - 2. [effective - remark, argument] abrumador(ra) - 3. [upsetting - news, experience] desolador(ra) - 4. [attractive] imponente, irresistible.

develop [dɪ'veləp] <> vt - 1. [idea, argument, product, method] desarrollar - 2. [land] urbanizar; [region] desarrollar - 3. [illness] contraer; [habit] adquirir; **to develop a fault** estropearse - 4. PHOT revelar. <> vi - 1. [grow] desarrollarse; **to develop into sthg** transformarse en algo - 2. [appear] presentarse.

developing country [dɪ'veləpɪŋ-] n país m en vías de desarrollo.

development [dɪ'veləpmənt] (U) n - 1. [growth] desarrollo m - 2. [of design] elaboración f; [of product] desarrollo m - 3. [developed land] urbanización f - 4. [new event] (nuevo) acontecimiento m; **recent developments** la evolución reciente - 5. [advance - in science etc] avance m.

device [dɪ'vaɪs] n - 1. [gen] dispositivo m - 2. COMPUT dispositivo m periférico.

devil ['devl] n diablo m, demonio m; **poor devil** pobre diablo; **you lucky devil!** ¡vaya suerte que tienes!; **who/where/why the devil...?** ¿quién/dónde/por qué demonios...?
➤ **Devil** n [Satan]: **the Devil** el Diablo, el Demonio.

devious ['di:vjəs] adj - 1. [person, scheme] retorcido(da); [means] enrevesado(da) - 2. [route] sinuoso(sa).

devise [dɪ'vaɪz] vt [instrument, system] diseñar; [plan] concebir.

devoid [dɪ'vɔɪd] adj fml: **devoid of** desprovisto(ta) de.

devolution [,di:və'lu:ʃn] n POL ≃ autonomía f, ≃ traspaso m de competencias.

devote [dɪ'vəut] vt: **to devote sthg to** dedicar OR consagrar algo a.

devoted [dɪ'vəutɪd] adj [lovers] unido(da); [follower, admirer] ferviente; **to be devoted to sb** tenerle mucho cariño a alguien.

devotee [,devə'ti:] n [fan] devoto m, -ta f, admirador m, -ra f.

devotion [dɪ'vəuʃn] (U) n - 1. [commitment]: **devotion (to)** dedicación f (a) - 2. [to family, lover & RELIG] devoción f.

devour [dɪ'vauəʳ] vt lit & fig devorar.

devout [dɪ'vaut] adj RELIG devoto(ta).

dew [dju:] n rocío m.

dexterity [dek'sterətɪ] n destreza f.

diabetes [,daɪə'bi:ti:z] n diabetes f inv.

diabetic [,daɪə'betɪk] <> adj [person] diabético(ca). <> n diabético m, -ca f.

diabolic(al) [,daɪə'bɒlɪk(l)] adj inf [very bad] pésimo(ma).

diagnose ['daɪəgnəuz] vt MED diagnosticar; **she was diagnosed as having cancer** le diagnosticaron cáncer.

diagnosis [,daɪəg'nəusɪs] (pl -oses [-əusi:z]) n MED [verdict] diagnóstico m; [science, activity] diagnosis f inv.

diagonal [daɪ'ægənl] <> adj diagonal. <> n diagonal f.

diagram ['daɪəgræm] n diagrama m.

dial ['daɪəl] <> n - 1. [of watch, clock] esfera f - 2. [of meter] cuadrante m - 3. [of telephone] disco m; [of radio] dial m. <> vt (UK & US) [number] marcar.

dialect ['daɪəlekt] n dialecto m.

dialling code ['daɪəlɪŋ-] n UK prefijo m (telefónico).

dialling tone *UK* [ˈdaɪəlɪŋ-], **dial tone** *US* n señal f de llamada.

dialogue *UK*, **dialog** *US* [ˈdaɪəlɒg] n diálogo m.

dial tone *US* = **dialling tone**.

dialysis [daɪˈælɪsɪs] n diálisis f inv.

diameter [daɪˈæmɪtəʳ] n diámetro m.

diamond [ˈdaɪəmənd] n - 1. [gem, playing card, in baseball] diamante m - 2. [shape] rombo m. ◆ **diamonds** npl diamantes mpl.

diaper [ˈdaɪpəʳ] n *US* pañal m.

diaphragm [ˈdaɪəfræm] n diafragma m.

diarrh(o)ea [ˌdaɪəˈrɪə] n diarrea f.

diary [ˈdaɪərɪ] n - 1. [appointment book] agenda f - 2. [journal] diario m.

dice [daɪs] ◇ n (pl dice) dado m. ◇ vt cortar en cuadraditos.

dictate vt [dɪkˈteɪt]: **to dictate sthg (to sb)** dictar algo (a alguien).

dictation [dɪkˈteɪʃn] n dictado m.

dictator [dɪkˈteɪtəʳ] n dictador m, -ra f.

dictatorship [dɪkˈteɪtəʃɪp] n dictadura f.

dictionary [ˈdɪkʃənrɪ] n diccionario m.

did [dɪd] pt ▷ **do**.

diddle [ˈdɪdl] vt inf timar.

didn't [ˈdɪdnt] (abbr of did not) ▷ **do**.

die [daɪ] ◇ vi (pt & pp died, cont dying) - 1. [gen] morir; **to be dying** estar muriéndose; **to be dying for sthg/to do sthg** morirse por algo/por hacer algo - 2. liter [feeling, fire] extinguirse. ◇ n (pl dice) esp *US* [dice] dado m. ◆ **die away** vi desvanecerse. ◆ **die down** vi [wind] amainar; [sound] apaciguarse; [fire] remitir; [excitement, fuss] calmarse. ◆ **die out** vi extinguirse.

diehard [ˈdaɪhɑːd] n intransigente mf.

diesel [ˈdiːzl] n - 1. [fuel] gasóleo m, gasoil m - 2. [vehicle] vehículo m diésel.

diesel engine n AUT motor m diésel; RAIL locomotora f diésel.

diesel fuel, diesel oil n gasóleo m.

diet [ˈdaɪət] ◇ n - 1. [eating pattern] dieta f - 2. [to lose weight] régimen m; **to be on a diet** estar a régimen. ◇ comp [low-calorie] light (inv). ◇ vi estar a régimen.

differ [ˈdɪfəʳ] vi - 1. [be different] ser diferente; **to differ from sthg** distinguirse OR diferir de algo - 2. [disagree]: **to differ with sb (about sthg)** disentir OR discrepar de alguien (en algo).

difference [ˈdɪfrəns] n diferencia f; **it didn't make any difference** [changed nothing] no cambió nada.

different [ˈdɪfrənt] adj: **different (from)** diferente OR distinto(ta) (de).

differentiate [ˌdɪfəˈrenʃɪeɪt] ◇ vt: **to differentiate (sthg from sthg)** diferenciar OR distinguir (algo de algo). ◇ vi: **to differentiate between** diferenciar OR distinguir entre.

difficult [ˈdɪfɪkəlt] adj difícil.

difficulty [ˈdɪfɪkəltɪ] n dificultad f; **to have difficulty in doing sthg** tener dificultad en OR para hacer algo.

diffident [ˈdɪfɪdənt] adj retraído(da).

diffuse vt [dɪˈfjuːz] difundir.

dig [dɪg] ◇ vt (pt & pp dug) - 1. [hole - with spade] cavar; [- with hands, paws] escarbar - 2. [garden] cavar en; [mine] excavar - 3. [press]: **to dig sthg into** clavar OR hundir algo en. ◇ vi (pt & pp dug) - 1. [with spade] cavar; [with hands, paws] escarbar - 2. [press]: **to dig into** clavarse OR hundirse en. ◇ n - 1. [unkind remark] pulla f - 2. ARCHAEOL excavación f. ◆ **dig out** vt sep inf [find - letter, object] desempolvar; [- information] encontrar. ◆ **dig up** vt sep [body, treasure, information] desenterrar; [plant, tree] arrancar.

digest ◇ n [ˈdaɪdʒest] compendio m. ◇ vt [dɪˈdʒest] lit & fig digerir.

digestion [dɪˈdʒestʃn] n digestión f.

digestive biscuit [dɪˈdʒestɪv-] n *UK* galleta f integral.

digit [ˈdɪdʒɪt] n - 1. [figure] dígito m - 2. [finger, toe] dedo m.

digital [ˈdɪdʒɪtl] adj digital.

digital camera n cámara f digital.

digital radio n radio f digital.

digital television, digital TV n televisión f digital.

dignified [ˈdɪgnɪfaɪd] adj [gen] digno(na); [ceremonious] ceremonioso(sa).

dignity [ˈdɪgnətɪ] n dignidad f.

digress [daɪˈgres] vi apartarse del tema; **to digress from** apartarse OR desviarse de.

digs [dɪgz] npl *UK* inf alojamiento m; **to live in digs** vivir en un cuarto de alquiler.

dike, dyke [daɪk] n [wall, bank] dique m.

dilapidated [dɪˈlæpɪdeɪtɪd] adj [building] derruido(da); [car] destartalado(da).

dilate [daɪˈleɪt] vi dilatarse.

dilemma [dɪˈlemə] n dilema m.

diligent [ˈdɪlɪdʒənt] adj diligente.

dilute [daɪˈluːt] vt diluir.

dim [dɪm] ◇ adj - 1. [light] tenue; [room] sombrío(bría) - 2. [eyesight] débil - 3. [memory] vago(ga) - 4. inf [stupid] tonto(ta), torpe. ◇ vt atenuar. ◇ vi [light] atenuarse.

dime [daɪm] n *US* moneda de diez centavos.

dimension [dɪˈmenʃn] n dimensión f.

diminish [dɪˈmɪnɪʃ] vt & vi disminuir.

diminutive [dɪˈmɪnjʊtɪv] fml ◇ adj diminuto(ta). ◇ n GRAM diminutivo m.

dimmers ['dɪməz] *npl US* [dipped headlights] luces *fpl* cortas OR de cruce; [parking lights] luces *fpl* de posición OR situación.

dimple ['dɪmpl] *n* hoyuelo *m*.

din [dɪn] *n inf* estrépito *m*.

dine [daɪn] *vi fml* cenar. **dine out** *vi* cenar fuera.

diner ['daɪnəʳ] *n* - **1.** [person] comensal *mf* - **2.** US [restaurant - cheap] restaurante *m* barato; [- on the road] ≃ restaurante *m* OR parador *m* de carretera.

dinghy ['dɪŋgɪ] *n* [sailing boat] bote *m*; [made of rubber] lancha *f* neumática.

dingy ['dɪndʒɪ] *adj* [room, street] lóbrego(ga); [clothes, carpet] deslustrado(da).

dining car ['daɪnɪŋ-] *n* vagón *m* restaurante, coche *m* comedor *Amér.*

dining room ['daɪnɪŋ-] *n* comedor *m*.

dinner ['dɪnəʳ] *n* - **1.** [evening meal] cena *f*; [midday meal] comida *f*, almuerzo *m*; **to have dinner** [in the evening] cenar; [at lunchtime] comer, almorzar - **2.** [formal event] cena *f* de gala, banquete *m*.

dinner jacket *n* esmoquin *m*.

dinner party *n* cena *f* (*en casa con amigos*).

dinnertime ['dɪnətaɪm] *n* [in the evening] la hora de la cena; [at midday] la hora del almuerzo OR de la comida.

dinosaur ['daɪnəsɔːʳ] *n* [reptile] dinosaurio *m*.

dint [dɪnt] *n fml*: **by dint of** a base de.

dip [dɪp] ◇ *n* - **1.** [in road, ground] pendiente *f* - **2.** [sauce] salsa *f* - **3.** [swim] chapuzón *m*; **to go for/take a dip** ir a darse/darse un chapuzón. ◇ *vt* - **1.** [into liquid]: **to dip sthg in OR into sthg** mojar algo en algo - **2.** UK [headlights]: **to dip one's lights** poner las luces de cruce. ◇ *vi* descender suavemente.

diploma [dɪ'pləumə] (*pl* -s) *n* diploma *m*.

diplomacy [dɪ'pləuməsɪ] *n* diplomacia *f*.

diplomat ['dɪpləmæt] *n* - **1.** [official] diplomático *m*, -ca *f* - **2.** [tactful person] persona *f* diplomática.

diplomatic [ˌdɪplə'mætɪk] *adj* diplomático(ca).

dipstick ['dɪpstɪk] *n* AUT varilla *f* del aceite (*para medir el nivel*).

dire ['daɪəʳ] *adj* - **1.** [consequences] grave; [warning] serio(ria); [need, poverty] extremo(ma) - **2.** UK *inf* [terrible] fatal.

direct [dɪ'rekt] ◇ *adj* directo(ta). ◇ *vt* - **1.** [gen]: **to direct sthg at sb** dirigir algo a alguien - **2.** [person to place]: **to direct sb (to)** indicar a alguien el camino (a) - **3.** [order]: **to direct sb to do sthg** mandar a alguien hacer algo. ◇ *adv* directamente.

direct current *n* corriente *f* continua.

direct debit *n* UK domiciliación *f* (de pago).

direction [dɪ'rekʃn] *n* dirección *f*; **sense of direction** sentido *m* de la orientación. **directions** *npl* - **1.** [instructions to place] señas *fpl*, indicaciones *fpl* - **2.** [instructions for use] modo *m* de empleo.

directly [dɪ'rektlɪ] *adv* - **1.** [gen] directamente - **2.** [immediately] inmediatamente - **3.** [very soon] pronto, en breve.

director [dɪ'rektəʳ] *n* director *m*, -ra *f*.

directory [dɪ'rektərɪ] *n* - **1.** [gen] guía *f* (alfabética) - **2.** COMPUT directorio *m*.

directory assistance *n* US (servicio *m* de) información *f* telefónica.

directory enquiries *n* UK (servicio *m* de) información *f* telefónica.

dirt [dɜːt] *n* (U) - **1.** [mud, dust] suciedad *f* - **2.** [earth] tierra *f*.

dirty ['dɜːtɪ] ◇ *adj* - **1.** [gen] sucio(cia); **to get dirty** ensuciarse - **2.** [joke] verde; [film] pornográfico(ca); [book, language] obsceno(na); **dirty word** palabrota *f*. ◇ *vt* ensuciar.

disability [ˌdɪsə'bɪlətɪ] *n* discapacidad *f*, minusvalía *f*; **people with disabilities** los discapacitados, los minusválidos.

disabled [dɪs'eɪbld] ◇ *adj* [person] discapacitado(da), minusválido(da); **disabled toilet** servicio *m* para discapacitados OR minusválidos. ◇ *npl*: **the disabled** los minusválidos, los discapacitados.

disadvantage [ˌdɪsəd'vɑːntɪdʒ] *n* desventaja *f*; **to be at a disadvantage** estar en desventaja.

disagree [ˌdɪsə'griː] *vi* - **1.** [have different opinions]: **to disagree (with)** no estar de acuerdo (con) - **2.** [conflict] contradecirse, no concordar - **3.** [subj: food, drink]: **to disagree with sb** sentar mal a alguien.

disagreeable [ˌdɪsə'griːəbl] *adj* desagradable.

disagreement [ˌdɪsə'griːmənt] *n* - **1.** [fact of disagreeing] desacuerdo *m* - **2.** [argument] discusión *f*.

disallow [ˌdɪsə'lau] *vt* - **1.** *fml* [appeal, claim] rechazar - **2.** [goal] anular.

disappear [ˌdɪsə'pɪəʳ] *vi* desaparecer.

disappearance [ˌdɪsə'pɪərəns] *n* desaparición *f*.

disappoint [ˌdɪsə'pɔɪnt] *vt* [person] decepcionar; [expectations, hopes] defraudar.

disappointed [ˌdɪsə'pɔɪntɪd] *adj* - **1.** [person]: **disappointed (in OR with sthg)** decepcionado(da) (con algo) - **2.** [expectations, hopes] defraudado(da).

disappointing [ˌdɪsə'pɔɪntɪŋ] *adj* decepcionante.

disappointment [ˌdɪsə'pɔɪntmənt] *n* decepción *f*, desilusión *f*; **to be a disappointment** ser decepcionante

disapproval [ˌdɪsə'pru:vl] *n* desaprobación *f*.

disapprove [ˌdɪsə'pru:v] *vi* estar en contra; **to disapprove of sthg** desaprobar algo; **to disapprove of sb** no ver con buenos ojos a alguien.

disarm [dɪs'ɑ:m] ◇ *vt lit* & *fig* desarmar. ◇ *vi* desarmarse.

disarmament [dɪs'ɑ:məmənt] *n* desarme *m*.

disarray [ˌdɪsə'reɪ] *n*: **in disarray** [clothes, hair] en desorden; [army, political party] sumido(da) en el desconcierto.

disaster [dɪ'zɑ:stər] *n* [gen] desastre *m*; [earthquake, eruption] catástrofe *f*.

disastrous [dɪ'zɑ:strəs] *adj* desastroso(sa).

disband [dɪs'bænd] ◇ *vt* disolver, disgregar. ◇ *vi* disolverse, disgregarse.

disbelief [ˌdɪsbɪ'li:f] *n*: **in OR with disbelief** con incredulidad.

disc *UK*, **disk** *US* [dɪsk] *n* disco *m*.

discard [dɪs'kɑ:d] *vt* [old clothes etc] desechar; [possibility] descartar.

discern [dɪ's3:n] *vt* - 1. [gen] discernir; [improvement] percibir - 2. [figure, outline] distinguir.

discerning [dɪ's3:nɪŋ] *adj* refinado(da); [audience] entendido(da).

discharge ◇ *n* ['dɪstʃɑ:dʒ] - 1. [of patient] alta *f*; [of prisoner, defendant] puesta *f* en libertad; [of soldier] licencia *f* - 2. [of gas, smoke] emisión *f*; [of sewage] vertido *m* - 3. [MED - from wound] supuración *f* - 4. ELEC descarga *f*. ◇ *vt* [dɪs'tʃɑ:dʒ] - 1. [patient] dar de alta; [prisoner, defendant] poner en libertad; [soldier] licenciar - 2. *fml* [duty etc] cumplir - 3. [gas, smoke] despedir; [sewage] verter; [cargo] descargar.

disciple [dɪ'saɪpl] *n* [follower & RELIG] discípulo *m*, -la *f*.

discipline ['dɪsɪplɪn] ◇ *n* disciplina *f*. ◇ *vt* - 1. [control] disciplinar - 2. [punish] castigar.

disc jockey *n* pinchadiscos *mf inv*.

disclaim [dɪs'kleɪm] *vt fml* negar.

disclose [dɪs'kləʊz] *vt* revelar.

disclosure [dɪs'kləʊʒər] *n* revelación *f*.

disco ['dɪskəʊ] (*pl* -s) (*abbr of* **discotheque**) *n* - 1. [place] discoteca *f*; [event] baile *m* - 2. [type of music] música *f* disco.

discomfort [dɪs'kʌmfət] *n* - 1. [uncomfortableness] incomodidad *f* - 2. [pain] molestia *f*.

disconcert [ˌdɪskən's3:t] *vt* desconcertar.

disconnect [ˌdɪskə'nekt] ◇ *vt* - 1. [detach] quitar, separar - 2. [from gas, electricity - appliance] desconectar; [- house, subscriber] cortar el suministro a - 3. [on phone - person] cortar la línea a. ◇ *vi* [from Internet] desconectarse.

disconsolate [dɪs'kɒnsələt] *adj* desconsolado(da).

discontent [ˌdɪskən'tent] *n*: **discontent (with)** descontento *m* (ta) (con).

discontented [ˌdɪskən'tentɪd] *adj* descontento(ta).

discontinue [ˌdɪskən'tɪnju:] *vt* interrumpir.

discord ['dɪskɔ:d] *n* - 1. [disagreement] discordia *f* - 2. MUS disonancia *f*.

discotheque ['dɪskəʊtek] *n* discoteca *f*.

discount ◇ *n* ['dɪskaʊnt] descuento *m*; **at a discount** con descuento. ◇ *vt* [*UK* dɪs'kaʊnt, *US* 'dɪskaʊnt] [report, claim] descartar.

discourage [dɪ'skʌrɪdʒ] *vt* - 1. [dispirit] desanimar - 2. [crime, behaviour] impedir; [thieves, tourists] ahuyentar; **to discourage sb from doing sthg** disuadir a alguien de hacer algo.

discover [dɪ'skʌvər] *vt* descubrir.

discovery [dɪ'skʌvərɪ] *n* descubrimiento *m*.

discredit [dɪs'kredɪt] ◇ *n* descrédito *m*. ◇ *vt* - 1. [person, organization] desacreditar - 2. [idea, report] refutar.

discreet [dɪ'skri:t] *adj* discreto(ta).

discrepancy [dɪ'skrepənsɪ] *n*: **discrepancy (in/between)** discrepancia *f* (en/entre).

discretion [dɪ'skreʃn] (*U*) *n* - 1. [tact] discreción *f* - 2. [judgment] criterio *m*; **at the discretion of** a voluntad de.

discriminate [dɪ'skrɪmɪneɪt] *vi* - 1. [distinguish]: **to discriminate (between)** discriminar OR distinguir (entre) - 2. [treat unfairly]: **to discriminate against sb** discriminar a alguien.

discriminating [dɪ'skrɪmɪneɪtɪŋ] *adj* refinado(da); [audience] entendido(da).

discrimination [dɪˌskrɪmɪ'neɪʃn] *n* - 1. [prejudice]: **discrimination (against)** discriminación *f* (hacia) - 2. [judgment] (buen) gusto *m*.

discus ['dɪskəs] (*pl* -es) *n* [object] disco *m* (*en atletismo*); **the discus** [competition] el lanzamiento de disco.

discuss [dɪ'skʌs] *vt* [subj: book, lecture] tratar de.

discussion [dɪ'skʌʃn] *n* discusión *f*.

disdain [dɪs'deɪn] *fml* ◇ *n*: **disdain (for)** desdén *m* OR desprecio *m* (hacia). ◇ *vt* desdeñar, despreciar.

disease [dɪ'zi:z] *n lit* & *fig* enfermedad *f*.

disembark [ˌdɪsɪm'bɑ:k] *vi* desembarcar.

disenchanted [ˌdɪsɪn'tʃɑ:ntɪd] *adj*: **disenchanted (with)** desencantado(da) (con).

disengage [ˌdɪsɪn'geɪdʒ] *vt* TECH [gears] quitar; [clutch] soltar.

disfavour UK, **disfavor** US [dɪs'feɪvər] n - **1.** [disapproval] desaprobación f - **2.** [state of being disapproved of] desgracia f.

disfigure [dɪs'fɪgər] vt desfigurar.

disgrace [dɪs'greɪs] <> n vergüenza f; **he's a disgrace to his family** es una deshonra para su familia; **to be in disgrace** [child, pet] estar castigado(da). <> vt deshonrar.

disgraceful [dɪs'greɪsfʊl] adj vergonzoso(sa); **it's disgraceful** es una vergüenza.

disgruntled [dɪs'grʌntld] adj disgustado(da).

disguise [dɪs'gaɪz] <> n disfraz m. <> vt disfrazar.

disgust [dɪs'gʌst] <> n: disgust (at) [physical] asco m (hacia); [moral] indignación f (ante). <> vt [physically] repugnar; [morally] indignar.

disgusting [dɪs'gʌstɪŋ] adj [physically] asqueroso(sa); [morally] indignante.

dish [dɪʃ] n - **1.** [container] fuente f - **2.** US [plate] plato m - **3.** [course] plato m. ◆ **dishes** npl platos mpl; **to do** OR **wash the dishes** fregar (los platos). ◆ **dish out** vt sep inf repartir. ◆ **dish up** vt sep inf servir.

dish aerial UK, **dish antenna** US n (antena f) parabólica f.

dishcloth ['dɪʃklɒθ] n [for washing, wiping] bayeta f; [for drying] paño m (de cocina).

disheartened [dɪs'hɑːtnd] adj descorazonado(da).

dishevelled UK, **disheveled** US [dɪ'ʃevəld] adj desaliñado(da); [hair] despeinado(da).

dishonest [dɪs'ɒnɪst] adj deshonesto(ta), nada honrado(da).

dishonor US = **dishonour**.

dishonour UK, **dishonor** US [dɪs'ɒnər] fml <> n deshonra f. <> vt deshonrar.

dishonourable UK, **dishonorable** US [dɪs'ɒnərəbl] adj deshonroso(sa).

dish soap n US lavavajillas m inv (detergente).

dish towel n US paño m (de cocina).

dishwasher ['dɪʃ,wɒʃər] n - **1.** [machine] lavavajillas m inv (electrodoméstico) - **2.** [person] lavaplatos mf inv.

dishwashing liquid n US lavavajillas m inv (detergente).

disillusioned [,dɪsɪ'luːʒnd] adj desilusionado(da).

disincentive [,dɪsɪn'sentɪv] n traba f.

disinclined [,dɪsɪn'klaɪnd] adj: **to be disinclined to do sthg** no tener ganas de hacer algo.

disinfect [,dɪsɪn'fekt] vt desinfectar.

disinfectant [,dɪsɪn'fektənt] n desinfectante m.

disintegrate [dɪs'ɪntɪgreɪt] vi lit & fig desintegrarse.

disinterested [,dɪs'ɪntrəstɪd] adj - **1.** [objective] desinteresado(da) - **2.** inf [uninterested]: **disinterested (in)** indiferente (a).

disjointed [dɪs'dʒɔɪntɪd] adj deslabazado(da).

disk [dɪsk] n - **1.** COMPUT disco m; [diskette] disquete m - **2.** US = **disc**.

disk drive n COMPUT disquetera f, unidad f de disco.

diskette [dɪsk'et] n disquete m.

dislike [dɪs'laɪk] <> n - **1.** [feeling]: **dislike (for)** [things] aversión f (a); [people] antipatía f (por); **to take a dislike to** cogerle manía a - **2.** [thing not liked]: **her likes and dislikes** las cosas que le gustan y las que no le gustan. <> vt: **I dislike her** no me gusta; **I dislike them** no me gustan.

dislocate ['dɪsləkeɪt] vt MED dislocar; **to dislocate one's shoulder** dislocarse el hombro.

dislodge [dɪs'lɒdʒ] vt: **to dislodge sthg/sb (from)** sacar algo/a alguien (de).

disloyal [,dɪs'lɔɪəl] adj: **disloyal (to)** desleal (a).

dismal ['dɪzml] adj - **1.** [weather, future] sombrío(a); [place, atmosphere] deprimente - **2.** [attempt, failure] lamentable.

dismantle [dɪs'mæntl] vt [machine] desmontar; [organization] desmantelar.

dismay [dɪs'meɪ] <> n (U) consternación f; **to my/his** etc **dismay** para mi/su etc consternación. <> vt consternar.

dismiss [dɪs'mɪs] vt - **1.** [refuse to take seriously] desechar - **2.** [from job]: **to dismiss sb (from)** despedir a alguien (de) - **3.** [allow to leave]: **to dismiss sb** dar a alguien permiso para irse.

dismissal [dɪs'mɪsl] n [from job] despido m.

dismount [,dɪs'maʊnt] vi: **to dismount (from sthg)** desmontar (de algo).

disobedience [,dɪsə'biːdjəns] n desobediencia f.

disobedient [,dɪsə'biːdjənt] adj: **disobedient (to)** desobediente (con).

disobey [,dɪsə'beɪ] vt & vi desobedecer.

disorder [dɪs'ɔːdər] n - **1.** [disarray]: **in disorder** en desorden - **2.** (U) [rioting] disturbios mpl - **3.** MED [physical] afección f, dolencia f; [mental] trastorno m.

disorderly [dɪs'ɔːdəli] adj - **1.** [untidy] desordenado(da) - **2.** [unruly - behaviour] incontrolable(da).

disorganized, -ised [dɪs'ɔːgənaɪzd] adj desorganizado(da).

disorientated UK [dɪs'ɔːrɪənteɪtɪd], **disoriented** US [dɪs'ɔːrɪəntɪd] adj desorientado(da).

disown [dɪs'əʊn] vt [gen] renegar de; [statement] no reconocer como propio(pia).

disparaging [dɪ'spærɪdʒɪŋ] *adj* menospre-
ciativo(va).

dispassionate [dɪ'spæʃnət] *adj* desapasio-
nado(da).

dispatch, despatch [dɪ'spætʃ] ◇ *n*
- **1.** [message] despacho *m* - **2.** [sending] envío *m*. ◇ *vt* [goods, parcel] expedir; [message,
messenger, troops] enviar.

dispel [dɪ'spel] *vt* disipar.

dispensary [dɪ'spensərɪ] *n* dispensario *m*.

dispense [dɪ'spens] *vt* - **1.** [advice] ofrecer;
[justice] administrar - **2.** [drugs, medicine] despachar. ◆ **dispense with** *vt insep* prescindir
de.

disperse [dɪ'spɜːs] ◇ *vt* dispersar. ◇ *vi*
dispersarse.

dispirited [dɪ'spɪrɪtɪd] *adj* desanimado(da).

displace [dɪs'pleɪs] *vt* [supplant] reemplazar,
sustituir.

display [dɪ'spleɪ] ◇ *n* - **1.** [arrangement - in
shop window] escaparate *m*; [- in museum] exposición *f*; [- on stall, pavement] muestrario *m*
- **2.** [demonstration, public event] demostración *f*
- **3.** [sporting] exhibición *f* - **4.** COMPUT pantalla *f*.
◇ *vt* - **1.** [arrange] exponer - **2.** [show] demostrar - **3.** [on screen] mostrar.

displease [dɪs'pliːz] *vt* [annoy] disgustar; [an-
ger] enfadar.

displeasure [dɪs'pleʒəʳ] *n* [annoyance] disgusto *m*; [anger] enfado *m*.

disposable [dɪ'spəʊzəbl] *adj* desechable;
disposable income poder *m* adquisitivo.

disposal [dɪ'spəʊzl] *n* - **1.** [removal] eliminación *f* - **2.** US trituradora *f* de basuras - **3.** [avail-
ability]: **to have sthg at one's disposal** disponer
de algo.

dispose [dɪ'spəʊz] ◆ **dispose of** *vt insep*
[rubbish] deshacerse de; [problem] quitarse de
encima OR de en medio.

disposed [dɪ'spəʊzd] *adj* [willing]: **to be disposed to do sthg** estar dispuesto(ta) a hacer
algo.

disposition [ˌdɪspə'zɪʃn] *n* [temperament] carácter *m*.

disprove [ˌdɪs'pruːv] *vt* refutar.

dispute [dɪ'spjuːt] ◇ *n* - **1.** [quarrel] disputa *f* - **2.** *(U)* [disagreement] conflicto *m*, desacuerdo *m*; **in dispute** [people] en desacuerdo; [matter] en litigio, en entredicho - **3.** INDUST
conflicto *m* laboral. ◇ *vt* cuestionar.

disqualify [ˌdɪs'kwɒlɪfaɪ] *vt* - **1.** [subj: authority, illness etc]: **to disqualify sb (from doing
sthg)** incapacitar a alguien (para hacer algo)
- **2.** SPORT descalificar - **3.** UK [from driving] retirar el permiso de conducir a.

disquiet [dɪs'kwaɪət] *n* inquietud *f*.

disregard [ˌdɪsrɪ'gɑːd] ◇ *n*: **disregard (for)**
indiferencia *f* (a), despreocupación *f* (por)
◇ *vt* hacer caso omiso de.

disrepair [ˌdɪsrɪ'peəʳ] *n*: **in a state of disrepair** deteriorado(da).

disreputable [dɪs'repjʊtəbl] *adj* [person,
company] de mala fama; [behaviour] vergonzante.

disrepute [ˌdɪsrɪ'pjuːt] *n*: **to bring sthg into
disrepute** desprestigiar OR desacreditar algo.

disrupt [dɪs'rʌpt] *vt* [meeting] interrumpir;
[transport system] trastornar, perturbar; [class]
revolucionar, enredar en.

disruption [dɪs'rʌpʃn] *n* [of meeting] interrupción *f*; [of transport system] trastorno *m*.

dissatisfaction ['dɪsˌsætɪs'fækʃn] *n*
descontento *m*.

dissatisfied [ˌdɪs'sætɪsfaɪd] *adj*: **dissatisfied (with)** insatisfecho(cha) OR desconten-
to(ta) (con).

dissect [dɪ'sekt] *vt* MED disecar; *fig* [study]
analizar minuciosamente.

disseminate [dɪ'semɪneɪt] *vt* difundir.

dissent [dɪ'sent] ◇ *n* [gen] disconformi-
dad *f*, disentimiento *m*; SPORT: **he was booked
for dissent** lo amonestaron por protestar.
◇ *vi*: **to dissent (from)** disentir (de).

dissertation [ˌdɪsə'teɪʃn] *n* - **1.** US [doctoral]
tesis *f inv* - **2.** UK [lower degree] tesina *f*.

disservice [ˌdɪs'sɜːvɪs] *n*: **to do sb a disservice** hacer un flaco servicio a alguien.

dissident ['dɪsɪdənt] *n* disidente *mf*.

dissimilar [ˌdɪ'sɪmɪləʳ] *adj*: **dissimilar (to)**
distinto(ta) (de).

dissipate ['dɪsɪpeɪt] *vt* - **1.** [heat, fears] disipar
- **2.** [efforts, money] desperdiciar.

dissociate [dɪ'səʊʃɪeɪt] *vt* disociar.

dissolute ['dɪsəluːt] *adj* disoluto(ta).

dissolve [dɪ'zɒlv] ◇ *vt* disolver. ◇ *vi*
- **1.** [substance] disolverse - **2.** *fig* [disappear]
desvanecerse, desaparecer.

dissuade [dɪ'sweɪd] *vt*: **to dissuade sb (from
doing sthg)** disuadir a alguien (de hacer algo).

distance ['dɪstəns] *n* distancia *f*; **at a distance** a distancia; **from a distance** desde lejos;
in the distance a lo lejos.

distance learning *n* enseñanza *f* a distancia.

distant ['dɪstənt] *adj* - **1.** [place, time, relative]
lejano(na); **distant from** distante de - **2.** [per-
son, manner] frío(a), distante.

distaste [dɪs'teɪst] *n*: **distaste (for)** desagrado *m* (por).

distasteful [dɪs'teɪstfʊl] *adj* desagradable.

distended [dɪ'stendɪd] *adj* dilatado(da).

distil UK, **distill** US [dɪ'stɪl] *vt* [liquid] destilar.

distillery [dɪ'stɪlərɪ] n destilería f.

distinct [dɪ'stɪŋkt] adj - 1. [different]: **distinct (from)** distinto(ta) (de); **as distinct from** a diferencia de - 2. [clear - improvement] notable, visible; [- possibility] claro(ra).

distinction [dɪ'stɪŋkʃn] n - 1. [difference, excellence] distinción f - 2. [in exam result] sobresaliente m.

distinctive [dɪ'stɪŋktɪv] adj característico(ca), particular.

distinguish [dɪ'stɪŋgwɪʃ] vt [gen]: **to distinguish sthg (from)** distinguir algo (de).

distinguished [dɪ'stɪŋgwɪʃt] adj distinguido(da).

distinguishing [dɪ'stɪŋgwɪʃɪŋ] adj distintivo(va).

distort [dɪ'stɔːt] vt - 1. [shape, face] deformar; [sound] distorsionar - 2. [truth, facts] tergiversar.

distracted [dɪ'stræktɪd] adj ausente.

distraction [dɪ'strækʃn] n [interruption, diversion] distracción f.

distraught [dɪ'strɔːt] adj consternado(da).

distress [dɪ'stres] <> n - 1. [anxiety] angustia f; [pain] dolor m - 2. [danger, difficulty] peligro m. <> vt afligir, apenar.

distressing [dɪ'stresɪŋ] adj angustioso(sa).

distribute [dɪ'strɪbjuːt] vt distribuir, repartir.

distribution [ˌdɪstrɪ'bjuːʃn] n distribución f.

distributor [dɪ'strɪbjʊtəʳ] n - 1. COMM distribuidor m, -ra f - 2. AUT delco® m.

district ['dɪstrɪkt] n - 1. [area - of country] zona f, región f; [- of town] barrio m - 2. [administrative area] distrito m.

district attorney n US fiscal mf (del distrito).

district council n UK ADMIN ≃ municipio m.

district nurse n UK enfermera encargada de atender a domicilio a los pacientes de una zona.

distrust [dɪs'trʌst] <> n desconfianza f. <> vt desconfiar de.

disturb [dɪ'stɜːb] vt - 1. [interrupt - person] molestar; [- concentration, sleep] perturbar - 2. [upset, worry] inquietar - 3. [alter - surface, arrangement] alterar; [- papers] desordenar.

disturbance [dɪ'stɜːbəns] n - 1. [fight] tumulto m; **there were a number of minor disturbances throughout the night** se produjeron algunos disturbios durante la noche - 2. [interruption] interrupción f - 3. [of mind, emotions] trastorno m.

disturbed [dɪ'stɜːbd] adj - 1. [upset, ill] trastornado(da) - 2. [worried] inquieto(ta).

disturbing [dɪ'stɜːbɪŋ] adj inquietante.

disuse [ˌdɪs'juːs] n: **to fall into disuse** [regulation] caer en desuso; [building, mine] verse paulatinamente abandonado(da).

disused [ˌdɪs'juːzd] adj abandonado(da).

ditch [dɪtʃ] <> n [gen] zanja f; [by road] cuneta f. <> vt inf - 1. [end relationship with] romper con - 2. [get rid of] deshacerse de.

dither ['dɪðəʳ] vi vacilar.

ditto ['dɪtəʊ] adv ídem.

dive [daɪv] <> vi (UK pt & pp -d, US pt -d OR **dove**, pp -d) - 1. [into water - person] zambullirse, tirarse al agua; [- submarine, bird, fish] sumergirse - 2. [with breathing apparatus] bucear - 3. [through air - person] lanzarse; [- plane] caer en picado - 4. [into bag, cupboard]: **to dive into** meter la mano en. <> n - 1. [of person - into water] zambullida f - 2. [of submarine] inmersión f - 3. [of person - through air] salto m; SPORT [- by goalkeeper] estirada f; **it was a dive** se ha tirado - 4. [of plane] picado m - 5. inf pej [bar, restaurant] garito m, antro m.

diver ['daɪvəʳ] n [underwater] buceador m, -ra f; [professional] buzo m; [from diving board] saltador m, -ra f (de trampolín).

diverge [daɪ'vɜːdʒ] vi - 1. [gen]: **to diverge (from)** divergir (de) - 2. [disagree] discrepar.

diversify [daɪ'vɜːsɪfaɪ] <> vt diversificar. <> vi diversificarse.

diversion [daɪ'vɜːʃn] n - 1. [of traffic, river, funds] desvío m - 2. [distraction] distracción f.

diversity [daɪ'vɜːsətɪ] n diversidad f.

divert [daɪ'vɜːt] vt - 1. [traffic, river, funds] desviar - 2. [person, attention] distraer.

divide [dɪ'vaɪd] <> vt: **to divide sthg (between OR among)** dividir algo (entre); **to divide sthg into** dividir algo en; **to divide sthg by** dividir algo entre OR por; **divide 3 into 89** divide 89 entre 3. <> vi - 1. [river, road, wall] bifurcarse - 2. [group] dividirse.

dividend ['dɪvɪdend] n FIN dividendo m; [profit] beneficio m.

divine [dɪ'vaɪn] adj divino(na).

diving ['daɪvɪŋ] (U) n - 1. [into water] salto m - 2. [with breathing apparatus] buceo m.

divingboard ['daɪvɪŋbɔːd] n trampolín m.

divinity [dɪ'vɪnətɪ] n - 1. [godliness, deity] divinidad f - 2. [study] teología f.

division [dɪ'vɪʒn] n - 1. [gen] división f - 2. [of labour, responsibility] reparto m.

divorce [dɪ'vɔːs] <> n divorcio m. <> vt [husband, wife] divorciarse de. <> vi divorciarse.

divorced [dɪ'vɔːst] adj divorciado(da).

divorcee [dɪvɔː'siː] n divorciado m, -da f.

divulge [daɪ'vʌldʒ] vt divulgar, revelar.

DIY abbr of **do-it-yourself**.

dizzy ['dɪzɪ] *adj* - 1. [because of illness etc] mareado(da) - 2. [because of heights]: **to feel dizzy** sentir vértigo.

DJ *n abbr of* **disc jockey**.

DNA (*abbr of* **deoxyribonucleic acid**) *n* ADN *m*.

DNS (*abbr of* **Domain Name System**) *n* COMPUT DNS *m*.

do [du:] <> *aux vb* (*pt* **did**) - 1. (*in negatives*): **don't leave it there** no lo dejes ahí - 2. (*in questions*): **what did he want?** ¿qué quería?; **do you think she'll come?** ¿crees que vendrá? - 3. (*referring back to previous vb*): **do you think so?** – **yes, I do** ¿tú crees? – sí; **she reads more than I do** lee más que yo; **so do I/they** yo/ellos también - 4. (*in question tags*): **you know her, don't you?** la conoces, ¿no?; **so you think you can dance, do you?** así que te crees que sabes bailar, ¿no? - 5. (*for emphasis*): **I did tell you but you've forgotten** sí que te lo dije, pero te has olvidado; **do come in** ¡pase, por favor! <> *vt* (*pt* **did**, *pp* **done**) - 1. [gen] hacer; **she does aerobics/gymnastics** hace aerobic/gimnasia; **to do the cooking/cleaning** hacer la comida/limpieza; **to do one's hair** peinarse; **to do one's teeth** lavarse los dientes; **he did his duty** cumplió con su deber; **what can I do for you?** ¿en qué puedo servirle?; **what can we do?** ¿qué le vamos a hacer? - 2. [referring to job]: **what do you do?** ¿a qué te dedicas? - 3. [study] hacer; **I did physics at school** hice física en la escuela - 4. [travel at a particular speed] ir a; **the car can do 110 mph** el coche alcanza las 110 millas por hora - 5. [be good enough for]: **will that do you?** ¿te vale eso? <> *vi* (*pt* **did**, *pp* **done**) - 1. [gen] hacer; **do as she says** haz lo que te dice; **they're doing really well** les va muy bien; **he could do better** lo podría hacer mejor; **how did you do in the exam?** ¿qué tal te salió el examen? - 2. [be good enough, sufficient] servir, valer; **this kind of behaviour won't do** ese tipo de comportamiento no es aceptable; **that will do (nicely)** con eso vale; **that will do!** [showing annoyance] ¡basta ya! ▸ **how do you do?** [greeting] ¿cómo está usted?; [answer] mucho gusto. <> *n* [party] fiesta *f*. ◆ **dos** *npl* (*pl* **dos** OR **do's**): **dos and don'ts** normas *fpl* básicas. ◆ **do away with** *vt insep* [disease, poverty] acabar con; [law, reforms] suprimir. ◆ **do down** *vt sep inf*: **to do sb down** menospreciar a alguien; **to do o.s. down** menospreciarse. ◆ **do over** *vt sep US* volver a hacer. ◆ **do up** *vt sep* - 1. [fasten - shoelaces, tie] atar; [- coat, buttons] abrochar; **do your shoes up** átate los zapatos; **do your coat up** abróchate el abrigo - 2. [decorate] renovar, redecorar; **to do o.s. up** arreglarse - 3. [wrap up] envolver. ◆ **do with** *vt insep* - 1. [need]: **I could do with a drink/new car** no me vendría

mal una copa/un coche nuevo - 2. [have connection with]: **that has nothing to do with it** eso no tiene nada que ver (con ello). ◆ **do without** <> *vt insep* pasar sin; **I can do without your sarcasm** podrías ahorrarte tu sarcasmo. <> *vi* apañárselas.

Doberman ['dəʊbəmən] (*pl* -s) *n*: **Doberman (pinscher)** dóberman *m*.

docile [*UK* 'dəʊsaɪl, *US* 'dɒsəl] *adj* dócil.

dock [dɒk] <> *n* - 1. [in harbour] dársena *f*, muelle *m* - 2. [in court] banquillo *m* (de los acusados). <> *vi* [ship] atracar; [spacecraft] acoplarse.

docker ['dɒkər], **dockworker** ['dɒk,wɜːkər] *n* estibador *m*.

docklands ['dɒkləndz] *npl UK* barrio *m* portuario.

dockyard ['dɒkjɑːd] *n* astillero *m*.

doctor ['dɒktər] <> *n* - 1. [of medicine] médico *m*, -ca *f*; **to go to the doctor's** ir al médico - 2. [holder of PhD] doctor *m*, -ra *f*. <> *vt* - 1. [results, text] amañar - 2. [food, drink] adulterar.

doctorate ['dɒktərət], **doctor's degree** *n* doctorado *m*.

doctrine ['dɒktrɪn] *n* doctrina *f*.

document *n* ['dɒkjʊmənt] [gen & COMPUT] documento *m*.

documentary [,dɒkjʊ'mentərɪ] <> *adj* documental. <> *n* documental *m*.

dodge [dɒdʒ] <> *n inf* [fraud] artimaña *f*. <> *vt* esquivar. <> *vi* echarse a un lado.

dodgy ['dɒdʒɪ] *adj UK inf* [business, plan] arriesgado(da); [brakes, weather, situation] chungo(ga).

doe [dəʊ] *n* - 1. [female deer] gama *f* - 2. [female rabbit] coneja *f*.

does (*weak form* [dəz], *strong form* [dʌz]) *vb* ▷ **do**.

doesn't ['dʌznt] (*abbr of* **does not**) ▷ **do**.

dog [dɒg] <> *n* - 1. [animal] perro *m* - 2. *US* [hot dog] perrito *m* caliente. <> *vt* - 1. [subj: person] seguir - 2. [subj: problems, bad luck] perseguir.

dog collar *n* - 1. [of dog] collar *m* de perro - 2. [of priest] alzacuello *m*.

dog-eared [-ɪəd] *adj* manoseado(da).

dogged ['dɒgɪd] *adj* tenaz.

dogsbody ['dɒgz,bɒdɪ] *n UK inf* último mono *m*, burro *m* de carga.

doing ['duːɪŋ] *n*: **this is all your doing** es de tu entera responsabilidad. ◆ **doings** *npl* actividades *fpl*.

do-it-yourself *n* bricolaje *m*.

doldrums ['dɒldrəmz] *npl fig*: **to be in the doldrums** [trade] estar estancado(da); [person] estar abatido(da).

dole [dəʊl] n (subsidio m de) paro m; **to be on the dole** estar parado(da). ◆ **dole out** vt sep distribuir, repartir.

doleful ['dəʊlfʊl] adj lastimero(ra).

doll [dɒl] n [toy] muñeca f.

dollar ['dɒlə'] n dólar m.

dolphin ['dɒlfɪn] n delfín m.

domain [də'meɪn] n - **1.** [sphere of interest] campo m, ámbito m - **2.** [land] dominios mpl - **3.** COMPUT dominio m.

dome [dəʊm] n [roof] cúpula f; [ceiling] bóveda f.

domestic [də'mestɪk] <> adj - **1.** [internal - policy, flight] nacional - **2.** [chores, water supply, animal] doméstico(ca) - **3.** [home-loving] hogareño(ña), casero(ra). <> n [servant] criado m, -da f.

domestic appliance n electrodoméstico m.

dominant ['dɒmɪnənt] adj dominante.

dominate ['dɒmɪneɪt] vt dominar.

domineering [,dɒmɪ'nɪərɪŋ] adj dominante.

dominion [də'mɪnjən] n - **1.** (U) [power] dominio m - **2.** [land] dominios mpl.

domino ['dɒmɪnəʊ] (pl -es) n dominó m. ◆ **dominoes** npl dominó m.

don [dɒn] n UK UNIV profesor m, -ra f de universidad.

donate [də'neɪt] vt donar.

done [dʌn] <> pp ▷ do. <> adj - **1.** [finished] listo(ta) - **2.** [cooked] hecho(cha); **well-done** muy hecho. <> adv [to conclude deal]: done! ¡(trato) hecho!

donkey ['dɒŋkɪ] (pl donkeys) n burro m.

donor ['dəʊnə'] n donante mf.

donor card n carné m de donante.

don't [dəʊnt] (abbr of do not) ▷ do.

donut ['dəʊnʌt] n US [with hole] donut® m.

doodle ['duːdl] vi garabatear.

doom [duːm] n perdición f, fatalidad f.

doomed [duːmd] adj [plan, mission] condenado(da) al fracaso.

door [dɔːr] n - **1.** [gen] puerta f; **to open the door to** fig abrir la puerta a - **2.** [doorway] entrada f.

doorbell ['dɔːbel] n timbre m (de la puerta).

doorknob ['dɔːnɒb] n pomo m.

doorman ['dɔːmən] (pl -men [-mən]) n portero m.

doormat ['dɔːmæt] n [mat] felpudo m.

doorstep ['dɔːstep] n peldaño m de la puerta.

doorway ['dɔːweɪ] n entrada f.

dope [dəʊp] <> n inf - **1.** [cannabis] maría f - **2.** [for athlete, horse] estimulante m - **3.** [fool] bobo m, -ba f. <> vt drogar, dopar.

dopey ['dəʊpɪ] (comp -ier, superl -iest) adj inf - **1.** [groggy] atontado(da), grogui - **2.** [stupid] bobo(ba).

dormant ['dɔːmənt] adj [volcano] inactivo(va).

dormitory ['dɔːmətrɪ] n dormitorio m (colectivo).

Dormobile® ['dɔːmə,biːl] n combi m.

DOS [dɒs] (abbr of disk operating system) n DOS m.

dose [dəʊs] n lit & fig dosis f inv.

dosser ['dɒsə'] n UK inf gandul m, -la f.

dosshouse ['dɒshaʊs, pl -haʊzɪz] n UK inf pensión f de mala muerte.

dot [dɒt] <> n punto m; **on the dot** en punto. <> vt salpicar.

dotcom ['dɒtkɒm] adj puntocom.

dote [dəʊt] ◆ **dote (up)on** vt insep adorar.

dot-matrix printer n COMPUT impresora f matricial.

double ['dʌbl] <> adj - **1.** [gen] doble - **2.** [repeated] repetido(da); **it's double the price** cuesta el doble; **double three eight two** treinta y tres, ochenta y dos. <> adv - **1.** [twice] el doble; **to cost double** costar el doble - **2.** [in two - fold] en dos; **to bend double** doblarse, agacharse. <> n - **1.** [twice as much] el doble - **2.** [drink] doble m - **3.** [lookalike] doble mf. <> vt doblar. <> vi [increase twofold] doblarse. ◆ **doubles** npl TENNIS dobles mpl.

double-barrelled UK, **double-barreled** US [-'bærəld] adj - **1.** [shotgun] de dos cañones - **2.** [name] con dos apellidos unidos con guión.

double bass [-beɪs] n contrabajo m.

double bed n cama f de matrimonio.

double-breasted [-'brestɪd] adj cruzado(da).

double-check vt & vi verificar dos veces.

double chin n papada f.

double-click <> n COMPUT doble clic m. <> vt COMPUT hacer doble clic en. <> vi COMPUT hacer doble clic.

double cream n nata f enriquecida.

double-cross vt traicionar.

double-decker [-'dekə'] n autobús m de dos pisos.

double-dutch n UK hum: **it's double-dutch to me** me suena a chino.

double-glazing [-'gleɪzɪŋ] n doble acristalamiento m.

double room n habitación f doble.

double vision n visión f doble.

doubly ['dʌblɪ] adv doblemente.

doubt [daʊt] <> n duda f; **there is no doubt that** no hay OR cabe duda de que; **without (a) doubt** sin duda (alguna); **to be in doubt about sthg** estar dudando acerca de algo; **to**

cast doubt on poner en duda; **no doubt** sin duda. ⬦ vt - **1.** [not trust] dudar de - **2.** [consider unlikely] dudar; **I doubt it** lo dudo; **to doubt whether** OR **if** dudar que.

doubtful ['dautful] adj - **1.** [gen] dudoso(sa) - **2.** [unsure] incierto(ta); **to be doubtful about** OR **of** tener dudas acerca de.

doubtless ['dautlıs] adv sin duda.

dough [dəu] n (U) - **1.** [for baking] masa f, pasta f - **2.** v inf [money] pasta f.

doughnut ['dəunʌt] n [without hole] buñuelo m; [with hole] donut® m.

douse [daus] vt - **1.** [put out] apagar - **2.** [drench] mojar, empapar.

dove[1] [dʌv] n paloma f.

dove[2] [dəuv] US pt ⬑ **dive**.

dovetail ['dʌvteıl] vt & vi encajar.

dowdy ['daudı] adj poco elegante.

down [daun] ⬦ adv - **1.** [downwards] (hacia) abajo; **to fall down** caer; **to bend down** agacharse; **down here/there** aquí/allí abajo - **2.** [along]: **I'm going down the pub** voy a acercarme al pub - **3.** [southwards] hacia el sur; **we're going down to Brighton** vamos a bajar a Brighton - **4.** [lower in amount]: **prices are coming down** los precios van bajando - **5.** [including]: **down to the last detail** hasta el último detalle - **6.** [as deposit]: **to pay £5 down** pagar 5 libras ahora (y el resto después). ⬦ prep - **1.** [downwards]: **they ran down the hill** corrieron cuesta abajo; **he walked down the stairs** bajó la escalera; **rain poured down the window** la lluvia resbalaba por la ventana - **2.** [along]: **she was walking down the street** iba andando por la calle. ⬦ adj - **1.** [depressed] deprimido(da) - **2.** [not in operation]: **the computer is down again** el ordenador se ha estropeado otra vez. ⬦ n [feathers] plumón m; [hair] pelusa f, vello m; US [in American football] cada uno de los cuatro intentos de avance que tiene el equipo atacante. ⬦ vt - **1.** [knock over] derribar - **2.** [swallow] beberse de un trago. ⬤ **downs** npl UK montes, especialmente los del sur de Inglaterra. ⬤ **down with** excl: **down with the King!** ¡abajo el rey!

down-and-out n vagabundo m, -da f.

down-at-heel adj esp UK desastrado(da).

downbeat ['daunbi:t] adj inf pesimista.

downcast ['daunkɑ:st] adj fml [sad] alicaído(da), triste.

downfall ['daunfɔ:l] n [of person] ruina f; [of regime] caída f.

downhearted [,daun'hɑ:tıd] adj desanimado(da).

downhill [,daun'hıl] ⬦ adj cuesta abajo. ⬦ adv - **1.** [downwards] cuesta abajo - **2.** [worse]: **to be going downhill** ir cuesta abajo. ⬦ n [skiing] descenso m.

Downing Street ['daunıŋ-] n calle londinense donde se encuentran las residencias del Primer Ministro y del ministro de Finanzas; por extensión designa al gobierno británico.

down payment n entrada f.

downpour ['daunpɔ:r] n chaparrón m.

downright ['daunraıt] ⬦ adj patente, manifiesto(ta). ⬦ adv completamente.

downstairs [,daun'steəz] ⬦ adj de abajo. ⬦ adv abajo; **to come/go downstairs** bajar (la escalera).

downstream [,daun'stri:m] adv río OR aguas abajo.

down-to-earth adj realista.

downtown [,daun'taun] US ⬦ adj del centro (de la ciudad). ⬦ n centro m (urbano). ⬦ adv [live] en el centro; [go] al centro; **he gave me a lift downtown** me llevó OR me dio Amér C, Méx & Perú un aventón al centro.

downturn ['dauntɜ:n] n bajón m.

down under adv en/a Australia o Nueva Zelanda.

downward ['daunwəd] ⬦ adj - **1.** [towards the ground] hacia abajo - **2.** [decreasing] descendente. ⬦ adv US = **downwards**.

downwards ['daunwədz], **downward** adv [gen] hacia abajo; **face downwards** boca abajo.

dowry ['dauərı] n dote f.

doze [dəuz] ⬦ n sueñecito m; **to have a doze** echar una cabezada. ⬦ vi dormitar. ⬤ **doze off** vi quedarse adormilado(da).

dozen ['dʌzn] ⬦ num adj: **a dozen eggs** una docena de huevos. ⬦ n docena f; **50p a dozen** 50 peniques la docena. ⬤ **dozens** npl inf: **dozens of** montones mpl de.

dozy ['dəuzı] adj - **1.** [sleepy] soñoliento(ta), amodorrado(da) - **2.** UK inf [stupid] tonto(ta).

Dr. - 1. (abbr of **Doctor**) Dr - **2.** (abbr of **Drive**) ≃ c/.

drab [dræb] adj [colour] apagado(da); [building, clothes] soso(sa); [lives] monótono(na).

draft [drɑ:ft] ⬦ n - **1.** [early version] borrador m - **2.** [money order] letra f de cambio, giro m - **3.** US MIL: **the draft** la llamada a filas - **4.** US = **draught**. ⬦ vt - **1.** [write] redactar, hacer un borrador de - **2.** US MIL llamar a filas - **3.** [transfer - staff etc] transferir.

draftsman US = **draughtsman**.

drafty US = **draughty**.

drag [dræg] ⬦ vt - **1.** [gen & COMPUT] arrastrar; **to drag and drop sthg** arrastrar y soltar algo - **2.** [lake, river] dragar. ⬦ vi - **1.** [dress, coat] arrastrarse - **2.** [time, play] ir muy despacio. ⬦ n inf - **1.** [bore - thing] rollo m; [- person] pesado m, -da f - **2.** [on cigarette] calada f - **3.** [cross-dressing]: **in drag** vestido de mujer. ⬤ **drag on** vi ser interminable.

dragon ['drægən] *n* - **1.** [beast] dragón *m*
- **2.** *inf* [woman] bruja *f*.

dragonfly ['drægnflaɪ] *n* libélula *f*.

drain [dreɪn] ⬦ *n* [for water] desagüe *m*; [for
sewage] alcantarilla *f*; [grating] sumidero *m*.
⬦ *vt* - **1.** [marsh, field] drenar; [vegetables]
escurrir - **2.** [energy, resources] agotar - **3.** [drink,
glass] apurar. ⬦ *vi* - **1.** [dishes] escurrirse
- **2.** [colour, blood, tension] desaparecer poco a
poco.

drainage ['dreɪnɪdʒ] *n* - **1.** [pipes, ditches] alcantarillado *m* - **2.** [of land] drenaje *m*.

draining board *UK* ['dreɪnɪŋ-], **drain-
board** *US* ['dreɪnbɔːrd] *n* escurridero *m*.

drainpipe ['dreɪnpaɪp] *n* tubo *m* de desagüe.

dram [dræm] *n* chupito *m*.

drama ['drɑːmə] *n* - **1.** [gen] drama *m* - **2.** [sub-
ject] teatro *m* - **3.** [excitement] dramatismo *m*.

dramatic [drə'mætɪk] *adj* - **1.** [concerned with
theatre] dramático(ca) - **2.** [gesture, escape, im-
provement] espectacular.

dramatist ['dræmətɪst] *n* dramaturgo *m*,
-ga *f*.

dramatize, -ise ['dræmətaɪz] *vt* - **1.** [rewrite
as play] adaptar - **2.** *pej* [make exciting] dramatizar.

drank [dræŋk] *pt* ⊳ **drink**.

drape [dreɪp] *vt*: **to drape sthg over sthg** cubrir algo con algo; **draped with** *OR* **in** cubierto
con. ⬥ **drapes** *npl US* cortinas *fpl*.

draper ['dreɪpər] *n* pañero *m*, -ra *f*.

drastic ['dræstɪk] *adj* [extreme, urgent, notice-
able] drástico(ca).

draught *UK*, **draft** *US* [drɑːft] *n* - **1.** [air cur-
rent] corriente *f* de aire - **2.** [beer]: **on draught**
de barril. ⬥ **draughts** *n UK* (U) damas *fpl*.

draught beer *n UK* cerveza *f* de barril.

draughtboard ['drɑːftbɔːd] *n UK* tablero *m*
de damas.

draughtsman *UK*, **draftsman** *US*
['drɑːftsmən] (*pl* **-men** [-mən]) *n* delineante *mf*.

draughty *UK*, **drafty** *US* ['drɑːftɪ] *adj* que
tiene corrientes de aire; **it's draughty** hay corriente.

draw [drɔː] ⬦ *vt* (*pt* **drew**, *pp* **drawn**)
- **1.** [sketch] dibujar; [line, circle] trazar; [a picture]
hacer - **2.** [pull - cart etc] tirar de; **she drew the
comb through her hair** se pasó el peine por el
pelo - **3.** [curtains - open] descorrer; [- close] correr - **4.** [gun, sword] sacar - **5.** [pension, benefit]
percibir - **6.** [cheque] librar - **7.** [conclusion] sacar, llegar a - **8.** [distinction, comparison] establecer - **9.** [attract - criticism, praise, person] atraer;
to be *OR* **feel drawn to** sentirse atraído(da) a
OR por. ⬦ *vi* (*pt* **drew**, *pp* **drawn**) - **1.** [sketch]
dibujar - **2.** [move] moverse; **to draw away** alejarse; **to draw closer** acercarse; **to draw to an**
end *OR* **a close** llegar a su fin - **3.** SPORT: **to draw
(with)** empatar (con). ⬦ *n* - **1.** SPORT empate *m* - **2.** [lottery] sorteo *m*. ⬥ **draw out** *vt sep*
- **1.** [encourage to talk] hacer hablar - **2.** [pro-
long] prolongar - **3.** [money] sacar. ⬥ **draw
up** ⬦ *vt sep* [draft] preparar, redactar. ⬦ *vi*
[stop] pararse.

drawback ['drɔːbæk] *n* inconveniente *m*,
desventaja *f*.

drawbridge ['drɔːbrɪdʒ] *n* puente *m* levadi-
zo.

drawer [drɔːr] *n* [in desk, chest] cajón *m*.

drawing ['drɔːɪŋ] *n* dibujo *m*.

drawing board *n* tablero *m* de delineante.

drawing pin *n UK* chincheta *f*.

drawing room *n* salón *m*.

drawl [drɔːl] *n* manera lenta y poco clara de
hablar, alargando las vocales.

drawn [drɔːn] *pp* ⊳ **draw**.

dread [dred] ⬦ *n* pavor *m*. ⬦ *vt*: **to dread
(doing sthg)** temer (hacer algo).

dreadful ['dredfʊl] *adj* - **1.** [very unpleasant -
pain, weather] terrible - **2.** [poor - play, English]
horrible, fatal - **3.** [for emphasis - waste, bore] es-
pantoso(sa).

dreadfully ['dredfʊlɪ] *adv* terriblemente.

dream [driːm] ⬦ *n lit* & *fig* sueño *m*; **bad
dream** pesadilla *f*. ⬦ *adj* ideal. ⬦ *vt*
(*pt* & *pp* **-ed** *OR* **dreamt**): **to dream (that)** soñar
que; **I never dreamt this would happen** ja-
más creí *OR* imaginé que esto pudiera suce-
der. ⬦ *vi* (*pt* & *pp* **-ed** *OR* **dreamt**) *lit* & *fig*: **to
dream of doing sthg** soñar con hacer algo; **to
dream (of** *OR* **about)** soñar (con); **I wouldn't
dream of it** ¡ni hablar!, ¡de ninguna manera!
⬥ **dream up** *vt sep* inventar, idear.

dreamt [dremt] *pp* ⊳ **dream**.

dreamy ['driːmɪ] *adj* - **1.** [distracted] soña-
dor(ra) - **2.** [peaceful, dreamlike] de ensueño.

dreary ['drɪərɪ] *adj* - **1.** [weather, day] triste
- **2.** [job, life] monótono(na); [persona] gris.

dredge [dredʒ] *vt* dragar. ⬥ **dredge up**
vt sep - **1.** [with dredger] sacar del agua (*al dragar*) - **2.** *fig* [from past] sacar a relucir.

dregs [dregz] *npl* - **1.** [of liquid] posos *mpl*
- **2.** *fig* [of society] escoria *f*.

drench [drentʃ] *vt* empapar; **drenched to the
skin** calado(da) hasta los huesos; **to be
drenched in** *OR* **with** estar empapado(da) en.

dress [dres] ⬦ *n* - **1.** [woman's garment] vestido *m* - **2.** (U) [clothing] traje *m*. ⬦ *vt*
- **1.** [clothe] vestir; **to be dressed in** ir vesti-
do(da) de; **to be dressed** estar vestido(da); **to
get dressed** vestirse - **2.** [bandage] vendar
- **3.** CULIN aliñar. ⬦ *vi* - **1.** [put on clothing] vestirse - **2.** [wear clothes] vestir; **to dress well/
badly** vestir bien/mal.

dress circle *n* palco *m* de platea.

dresser ['dresər] n - **1.** [for dishes] aparador m - **2.** US [chest of drawers] cómoda f.

dressing ['dresɪŋ] n - **1.** [bandage] vendaje m - **2.** [for salad] aliño m - **3.** US [for turkey etc] relleno m.

dressing gown n bata f.

dressing room n THEAT camerino m; SPORT vestuario m.

dressing table n tocador m.

dressmaker ['dres,meɪkər] n costurero m, -ra f, modisto m, -ta f.

dressmaking ['dres,meɪkɪŋ] n costura f.

dress rehearsal n ensayo m general.

dressy ['dresɪ] adj elegante.

drew [druː] pt ⊳ **draw**.

dribble ['drɪbl] ◇ n - **1.** [saliva] baba f - **2.** [trickle] hilo m. ◇ vt SPORT [ball] regatear. ◇ vi - **1.** [drool] babear - **2.** [spill] gotear, caer gota a gota.

dried [draɪd] adj [gen] seco(ca); [milk, eggs] en polvo.

drier ['draɪər] = **dryer**.

drift [drɪft] ◇ n - **1.** [trend, movement] movimiento m, tendencia f; [of current] flujo m - **2.** [meaning] sentido m - **3.** [mass - of snow] ventisquero m; [- of sand, leaves] montículo m. ◇ vi - **1.** [boat] ir a la deriva - **2.** [snow, sand, leaves] amontonarse.

driftwood ['drɪftwʊd] n madera f de deriva.

drill [drɪl] ◇ n - **1.** [tool - gen] taladro m; [- bit] broca f; [- dentist's] fresa f; [- in mine, oilfield] perforadora f - **2.** [exercise - for fire, battle] simulacro m. ◇ vt - **1.** [tooth, wood, oil well] perforar - **2.** [instruct - people, pupils] adiestrar, entrenar; [- soldiers] instruir; **to drill sthg into sb** inculcar algo en alguien. ◇ vi: **to drill into/for** perforar en/en busca de.

drink [drɪŋk] ◇ n - **1.** [gen] bebida f; **a drink of water** un trago de agua - **2.** [alcoholic beverage] copa f; **would you like a drink?** ¿quieres tomar algo (de beber)?; **to have a drink** tomar algo, tomar una copa. ◇ vt (pt **drank**, pp **drunk**) beber. ◇ vi (pt **drank**, pp **drunk**) beber; **to drink to sb/sb's success** beber a la salud de alguien/por el éxito de alguien.

drink-driving UK, **drunk-driving** US n conducción f en estado de embriaguez.

drinker ['drɪŋkər] n - **1.** [of alcohol] bebedor m, -ra f - **2.** [of tea, coffee]: **tea/coffee drinker** persona que bebe té/café.

drinking water ['drɪŋkɪŋ-] n agua f potable.

drip [drɪp] ◇ n - **1.** [drop] gota f; [drops] goteo m - **2.** MED gota a gota m inv. ◇ vi [liquid, tap, nose] gotear.

drip-dry adj de lava y pon.

drive [draɪv] ◇ n - **1.** [outing] paseo m (en coche); **to go for a drive** ir a dar una vuelta en coche - **2.** [journey] viaje m (en coche) - **3.** [urge]

instinto m - **4.** [campaign] campaña f - **5.** [energy] vigor m, energía f - **6.** [road to house] camino m (de entrada) - **7.** [street] calle f - **8.** [in golf, tennis] drive m - **9.** COMPUT unidad f de disco. ◇ vt (pt **drove**, pp **driven**) - **1.** [vehicle] conducir, manejar Amér - **2.** [passenger] llevar (en coche) - **3.** [fuel, power] impulsar - **4.** [force to move - gen] arrastrar; [- cattle] arrear; **it drove people from their homes** obligó a la gente a abandonar sus hogares - **5.** [motivate] motivar - **6.** [force]: **to drive sb to do sthg** conducir OR llevar a alguien a hacer algo; **to drive sb to despair** hacer desesperar a alguien; **to drive sb mad** OR **crazy** volver loco a alguien - **7.** [hammer] clavar. ◇ vi (pt **drove**, pp **driven**) AUT conducir, manejar Amér; **I don't drive** no sé conducir; **I drove there** fui en coche.

drive-by n (pl **drive-bys**) tiroteo OR asesinato desde un vehículo.

drivel ['drɪvl] n (U) inf tonterías fpl.

driven ['drɪvn] pp ⊳ **drive**.

driver ['draɪvər] n [gen] conductor m, -ra f; RAIL maquinista mf; [of racing car] piloto mf.

driver's license US = **driving licence**.

drive shaft n (eje m de) transmisión f.

driveway ['draɪvweɪ] n camino m (de entrada).

driving ['draɪvɪŋ] ◇ adj [rain] torrencial; [wind] huracanado(da). ◇ n (U) conducción f, el conducir.

driving instructor n profesor m, -ra f de autoescuela.

driving lesson n clase f de conducir OR conducción.

driving licence UK, **driver's license** US n carné m OR permiso m de conducir.

driving mirror n retrovisor m.

driving school n autoescuela f.

driving test n examen m de conducir.

drizzle ['drɪzl] ◇ n llovizna f. ◇ impers vb lloviznar.

droll [drəʊl] adj gracioso(sa).

drone [drəʊn] n - **1.** [hum] zumbido m - **2.** [bee] zángano m.

drool [druːl] vi - **1.** [dribble] babear - **2.** fig [admire]: **he was drooling over her** se le caía la baba con ella.

droop [druːp] vi [shoulders] encorvarse; [eyelids] cerrarse; [head] inclinarse; [flower] marchitarse.

drop [drɒp] ◇ n - **1.** [of liquid, milk, whisky] gota f - **2.** [sweet] pastilla f - **3.** [decrease]: **drop (in)** [price] caída f (de); [temperature] descenso m (de); [demand, income] disminución f (en) - **4.** [distance down] caída f. ◇ vt - **1.** [let fall - gen] dejar caer; [- bomb] lanzar - **2.** [decrease] reducir - **3.** [voice] bajar - **4.** [abandon - subject, course] dejar; [- charges] retirar; [- person, lover] abandonar; [- player] excluir, no seleccionar - **5.** [utter - hint, remark] lanzar, soltar - **6.** [write]: **to drop sb a line** mandar unas líneas a alguien - **7.** [let out of car] dejar. ⬦ *vi* - **1.** [fall down] caer; **it dropped onto the ground** se cayó al suelo; **to drop to one's knees** arrodillarse; **we walked until we dropped** estuvimos andando hasta no poder más - **2.** [fall away - ground] ceder - **3.** [decrease - temperature, price, voice] bajar; [- attendance, demand, unemployment] disminuir; [- wind] amainar. ➡ **drops** *npl* MED gotas *fpl*. ➡ **drop in** *vi inf*: **to drop in on** pasarse por casa de. ➡ **drop off** ⬦ *vt sep* [person, letter] dejar. ⬦ *vi* - **1.** [fall asleep] quedarse dormido(da) - **2.** [grow less] bajar. ➡ **drop out** *vi*: **to drop out (of OR from)** [school, college] dejar de asistir (a); [competition] retirarse (de).

dropout ['drɒpaʊt] *n* [from society] marginado *m*, -da *f*; [from university] persona *f* que ha dejado los estudios.

droppings ['drɒpɪŋz] *npl* excrementos *mpl* (de animal).

drought [draʊt] *n* sequía *f*.

drove [drəʊv] *pt* ⬦ **drive**.

drown [draʊn] ⬦ *vt* [kill] ahogar. ⬦ *vi* ahogarse.

drowsy ['draʊzɪ] *adj* [person] somnoliento(ta).

drudgery ['drʌdʒərɪ] *n* trabajo pesado y monótono.

drug [drʌg] ⬦ *n* - **1.** [medicine] medicamento *m* - **2.** [narcotic] droga *f*; **to be on OR take drugs** drogarse. ⬦ *vt* - **1.** [person] drogar - **2.** [food, drink] echar droga a.

drug abuse *n* consumo *m* de drogas.

drug addict *n* drogadicto *m*, -ta *f*.

drugstore ['drʌgstɔːr] *n US* farmacia *f (que también vende productos de perfumería, cosméticos, periódicos etc)*.

drum [drʌm] ⬦ *n* - **1.** [instrument, of machine] tambor *m*; **drums** batería *f* - **2.** [container, cylinder] bidón *m*. ⬦ *vt* [fingers] tamborilear con. ⬦ *vi* [rain, hoofs] golpetear. ➡ **drum up** *vt sep* intentar conseguir.

drummer ['drʌmər] *n* [in orchestra] tambor *mf*; [in pop group] batería *mf*.

drumstick ['drʌmstɪk] *n* - **1.** [for drum] palillo *m* - **2.** [food] muslo *m*.

drunk [drʌŋk] ⬦ *pp* ⬦ **drink**. ⬦ *adj* [on alcohol] borracho(cha); **to get drunk** emborracharse; **to be drunk** estar borracho(cha). ⬦ *n* borracho *m*, -cha *f*.

drunkard ['drʌŋkəd] *n* borracho *m*, -cha *f*.

drunk-driving *US* = **drink-driving**.

drunken ['drʌŋkn] *adj* - **1.** [person] borracho(cha) - **2.** [talk, steps, stupor] de borracho(cha).

drunken driving = **drink-driving**.

dry [draɪ] ⬦ *adj* - **1.** [gen] seco(ca) - **2.** [day] sin lluvia - **3.** [earth, soil] árido(da). ⬦ *vt* [gen] secar; [hands, hair] secarse; **to dry o.s.** secarse; **to dry one's eyes** secarse las lágrimas. ⬦ *vi* secarse. ➡ **dry up** ⬦ *vt sep* secar. ⬦ *vi* - **1.** [river, well] secarse - **2.** [stop - supply] agotarse - **3.** [stop speaking] quedarse en blanco - **4.** [dry dishes] secar.

dry cleaner *n*: **dry cleaner's (shop)** tintorería *f*.

dryer ['draɪər] *n* [for clothes] secadora *f*.

dry land *n* tierra *f* firme.

dry rot *n* putrefacción *f* de la madera.

dry ski slope *n* pista *f* de esquí artificial.

drysuit ['draɪsuːt] *n* traje *m* de neopreno.

DSS *(abbr of Department of Social Security) n ministerio británico de la seguridad social.*

DTI *(abbr of Department of Trade and Industry) n ministerio británico de comercio e industria.*

DTP *(abbr of desktop publishing) n* autoed. *f.*

dual ['djuːəl] *adj* doble.

dual carriageway *n UK* carretera de dos sentidos y doble vía separados, ≃ autovía *f.*

dubbed [dʌbd] *adj* - **1.** CIN doblado(da) - **2.** [nicknamed] apodado(da).

dubious ['djuːbjəs] *adj* - **1.** [questionable - person, deal, reasons] sospechoso(sa); [- honour, distinction] paradójico(ca) - **2.** [uncertain, undecided] dudoso(sa).

Dublin ['dʌblɪn] *n* Dublín *n*.

duchess ['dʌtʃɪs] *n* duquesa *f*.

duck [dʌk] ⬦ *n* - **1.** [bird] pato *m*, -ta *f*; **to take to sthg like a duck to water** encontrarse en seguida en su salsa con algo - **2.** [food] pato *m*. ⬦ *vt* - **1.** [lower] agachar, bajar - **2.** [try to avoid - duty] esquivar. ⬦ *vi* [lower head] agacharse.

duckling ['dʌklɪŋ] *n* patito *m*.

duct [dʌkt] *n* conducto *m*.

dud [dʌd] ⬦ *adj* [gen] falso(sa); [mine] que no estalla; [cheque] sin fondos. ⬦ *n persona o cosa inútil.*

dude [djuːd] *n US inf* [man] tipo *m*, tío *m Esp*; [term of address] colega *m Esp*, tío *m Esp*, mano *m Andes, Amér C & Méx*, flaco *m R Plata*.

due [djuː] ⬦ *adj* - **1.** [expected] esperado(da); **it's due out in May** saldrá en mayo; **she's due back soon** volverá dentro de poco; **the train's due in half an hour** el tren debe llegar dentro de media hora - **2.** [appropriate] debido(da); **with all due respect** sin ganas de ofender; **in due course** [at appropriate time] a su debido tiempo; [eventually] al final - **3.** [owed, owing] pagadero(ra); **I'm due a bit of luck** ya sería hora que tuviera un poco de suerte; **to be due to** deberse a. ⬦ *n* [deserts]: **to give sb their due**

hacer justicia a alguien. <> adv: **due north/ south** derecho hacia el norte/sur. ➡ **dues** npl cuota f. ➡ **due to** prep debido a

duel ['dju:əl] n duelo m.

duet [dju:'et] n dúo m.

duffel bag, duffle bag ['dʌfl-] n morral m.

duffel coat, duffle coat ['dʌfl-] n trenca f.

duffle bag ['dʌfl-] = **duffel bag**.

duffle coat ['dʌfl-] = **duffel coat**.

dug [dʌg] pt & pp ▷ **dig**.

duke [dju:k] n duque m.

dull [dʌl] <> adj - 1. [boring] aburrido(da) - 2. [listless] torpe - 3. [dim] apagado(da) - 4. [cloudy] gris, triste - 5. [thud, boom, pain] sordo(da). <> vt [senses] embotar, entorpecer; [pain] aliviar; [pleasure, memory] enturbiar.

duly ['dju:lɪ] adv - 1. [properly] debidamente - 2. [as expected] como era de esperar.

dumb [dʌm] adj - 1. [unable to speak] mudo(da); **to be struck dumb** quedarse de una pieza - 2. esp US inf [stupid] estúpido(da).

dummy ['dʌmɪ] <> adj falso(sa). <> n - 1. [of ventriloquist] muñeco m; [in shop window] maniquí m - 2. [copy] imitación f - 3. UK [for baby] chupete m - 4. SPORT amago m - 5. inf [idiot] imbécil mf.

dump [dʌmp] <> n - 1. [for rubbish] basurero m, vertedero m - 2. [for ammunition] depósito m - 3. COMPUT volcado m de memoria - 4. inf [ugly place - house] casucha f. <> vt - 1. [put down - sand, load] descargar; [- bags, washing] dejar - 2. [dispose of] deshacerse de. <> vi vulgar jiñar.

dumper (truck) UK ['dʌmpər-], **dump truck** US n volquete m.

dumping ['dʌmpɪŋ] n [of rubbish] vertido m; 'no dumping' 'prohibido verter basura'.

dumpling ['dʌmplɪŋ] n bola de masa que se guisa al vapor con carne y verduras.

dump truck US = **dumper (truck)**.

dumpy ['dʌmpɪ] adj inf bajito y regordete (bajita y regordeta).

dunce [dʌns] n zoquete mf.

dune [dju:n] n duna f.

dung [dʌŋ] n [of animal] excremento m; [used as manure] estiércol m.

dungarees [ˌdʌŋgə'ri:z] npl UK [for work] mono m, overol m Amér; [fashion garment] pantalones mpl de peto, mameluco m.

dungeon ['dʌndʒən] n calabozo m.

duo ['dju:əʊ] n dúo m.

dupe [dju:p] <> n primo m, -ma f, inocente mf. <> vt: **to dupe sb (into doing sthg)** embaucar a alguien (para que haga algo).

duplex ['dju:pleks] n US - 1. [apartment] dúplex m - 2. [house] casa f adosada.

duplicate <> adj ['dju:plɪkət] duplicado(da) <> n ['dju:plɪkət] copia f, duplicado m; **in duplicate** por duplicado. <> vt ['dju:plɪkeɪt] [copy] duplicar.

durable ['djʊərəbl] adj duradero(ra).

duration [djʊ'reɪʃn] n duración f; **for the duration of** durante.

duress [djʊ'res] n: **under duress** bajo coacción.

Durex® ['djʊəreks] n [condom] preservativo m, condón m.

during ['djʊərɪŋ] prep durante.

dusk [dʌsk] n crepúsculo m, anochecer m.

dust [dʌst] <> n polvo m; **to gather dust** [get dusty] cubrirse de polvo; fig [be ignored] quedar arrinconado(da). <> vt - 1. [clean] quitar el polvo a, limpiar - 2. [cover with powder]: **to dust sthg (with)** espolvorear algo (con).

dustbin ['dʌstbɪn] n UK cubo m de la basura.

dustcart ['dʌstkɑ:t] n UK camión m de la basura.

dustcloth ['dʌstklɒθ] n US trapo m del polvo.

duster ['dʌstər] n [cloth] bayeta f, trapo m (del polvo).

dust jacket, dust cover n sobrecubierta f.

dustman ['dʌstmən] (pl -men [-mən]) n UK basurero m.

dustpan ['dʌstpæn] n recogedor m.

dusty ['dʌstɪ] adj [covered in dust] polvoriento(ta).

Dutch [dʌtʃ] <> adj holandés(esa). <> n [language] holandés m. <> npl: **the Dutch** los holandeses.

Dutch elm disease n hongo que ataca los olmos.

dutiful ['dju:tɪfʊl] adj obediente, sumiso(sa).

duty ['dju:tɪ] n - 1. (U) [moral, legal responsibility] deber m; **to do one's duty** cumplir con su deber - 2. [work] servicio m - 3. [tax] impuesto m. ➡ **duties** npl tareas fpl.

duty-free <> adj libre de impuestos. <> n (U) inf artículos mpl libres de impuestos.

duvet ['du:veɪ] n UK edredón m.

duvet cover n UK funda f del edredón.

DVD (abbr of Digital Versatile Disk) n DVD m.

DVD player n reproductor m de DVD.

DVD recorder n grabador m de DVD.

DVD ROM (abbr of Digital Versatile Disk read only memory) n DVD ROM m.

dwarf [dwɔ:f] <> n (pl -s OR dwarves [dwɔ:vz]) enano m, -na f. <> vt achicar, empequeñecer.

dwell [dwel] vi (pt & pp -ed OR dwelt) liter morar, habitar. ➡ **dwell on** vt insep darle vueltas a.

dwelling ['dwelɪŋ] n liter morada f.

dwelt [dwelt] pt & pp ⊳ **dwell**.

dwindle ['dwɪndl] vi ir disminuyendo.

dye [daɪ] ◇ n tinte m. ◇ vt teñir; **to dye one's hair** teñirse el pelo.

dying ['daɪɪŋ] ◇ cont ⊳ **die**. ◇ adj - **1.** [person, animal] moribundo(da) - **2.** [activity, practice] en vías de desaparición.

dyke [daɪk] = **dike**.

dynamic [daɪ'næmɪk] adj dinámico(ca).

dynamite ['daɪnəmaɪt] n lit & fig dinamita f.

dynamo ['daɪnəməʊ] (pl -s) n dinamo f.

dynasty [UK 'dɪnəstɪ, US 'daɪnəstɪ] n dinastía f.

dysfunctional [dɪs'fʌŋkʃənəl] adj disfuncional.

dyslexia [dɪs'leksɪə] n dislexia f.

dyslexic [dɪs'leksɪk] adj disléxico(ca).

e (pl e's OR es), **E** (pl E's OR Es) [i:] n [letter] e f, E f. ◆ **E** n - **1.** MUS mi m - **2.** SCH [mark] ≃ suspenso m - **3.** (abbr of east) E m - **4.** inf [drug] (abbr of ecstasy) éxtasis m inv.

each [i:tʃ] ◇ adj cada. ◇ pron cada uno m, una f; **one each** uno cada uno; **each of us/the boys** cada uno de nosotros/los niños; **two of each** dos de cada (uno); **each other** el uno al otro; **they kissed each other** se besaron; **we know each other** nos conocemos.

e-account n cuenta f electrónica.

eager ['i:gər] adj [pupil] entusiasta; [smile, expression] de entusiasmo; **to be eager for sthg/ to do sthg** estar ansioso(sa) por algo/por hacer algo.

eagle ['i:gl] n águila f.

ear [ɪər] n - **1.** [outer part] oreja f; [inner part] oído m; **to have** OR **keep one's ear to the ground** inf mantenerse al corriente - **2.** [of corn] espiga f.

earache ['ɪəreɪk] n dolor m de oídos.

eardrum ['ɪədrʌm] n tímpano m.

earl [ɜ:l] n conde m.

earlier ['ɜ:lɪər] ◇ adj anterior. ◇ adv antes; **earlier on** antes.

earliest ['ɜ:lɪəst] ◇ adj primero(ra). ◇ n: **at the earliest** como muy pronto.

earlobe ['ɪələʊb] n lóbulo m (de la oreja).

early ['ɜ:lɪ] ◇ adj - **1.** [before expected time, in day] temprano(na); **she was early** llegó temprano; **I'll take an early lunch** almorzaré pronto OR temprano; **to get up early** madrugar - **2.** [at beginning]: **early morning** la madrugada; **in the early 1950s** a principios de los años 50. ◇ adv - **1.** [before expected time] temprano, pronto; **we got up early** nos levantamos temprano; **it arrived ten minutes early** llegó con diez minutos de adelanto - **2.** [at beginning]: **as early as 1920** ya en 1920; **early this morning** esta mañana temprano; **early in the year** a principios de año; **early on** temprano.

early retirement n prejubilación f, jubilación f anticipada.

earmark ['ɪəmɑ:k] vt: **to be earmarked for** estar destinado(da) a.

earn [ɜ:n] vt - **1.** [be paid] ganar - **2.** [generate - subj: business, product] generar - **3.** fig [gain - respect, praise] ganarse.

earnest ['ɜ:nɪst] adj [gen] serio(ria); [wish] sincero(ra). ◆ **in earnest** adv [seriously] en serio.

earnings ['ɜ:nɪŋz] npl [of person] ingresos mpl; [of company] ganancias fpl.

earphones ['ɪəfəʊnz] npl auriculares mpl.

earplugs ['ɪəplʌgz] npl tapones mpl para los oídos.

earring ['ɪərɪŋ] n pendiente m, arete m Amér.

earshot ['ɪəʃɒt] n: **within/out of earshot** al alcance/fuera del alcance del oído.

earth [ɜ:θ] ◇ n - **1.** [gen] tierra f; **to cost the earth** UK costar un dineral - **2.** [in electric plug, appliance] toma f de tierra. ◇ vt UK: **to be earthed** estar conectado(da) a tierra.

earthenware ['ɜ:θnweər] n loza f.

earthquake ['ɜ:θkweɪk] n terremoto m.

earthworm ['ɜ:θwɜ:m] n lombriz f (de tierra).

earthy ['ɜ:θɪ] adj - **1.** [rather crude] natural, desinhibido(da) - **2.** [of, like earth] terroso(sa).

earwig ['ɪəwɪg] n tijereta f.

ease [i:z] ◇ n (U) - **1.** [lack of difficulty] facilidad f; **with ease** con facilidad - **2.** [comfort] comodidad f; **at ease** cómodo(da); **ill at ease** incómodo(da). ◇ vt - **1.** [pain, grief] calmar, aliviar; [problems, tension] atenuar - **2.** [move carefully]: **to ease sthg open** abrir algo con cuidado; **to ease o.s. out of sthg** levantarse despacio de algo. ◇ vi [problem] atenuarse; [pain] calmarse; [rain, wind] amainar; [grip] relajarse. ◆ **ease off** vi [problem] atenuarse; [pain] calmarse; [rain, wind] amainar. ➡ **ease up** *vi* **1.** *inf* [treat less severely]: **to ease up on sb** no ser tan duro(ra) con alguien - **2.** [rain, wind] amainar - **3.** [relax - person] tomarse las cosas con más calma.

easel ['iːzl] *n* caballete *m*.

easily ['iːzɪlɪ] *adv* - **1.** [without difficulty] fácilmente - **2.** [without doubt] sin lugar a dudas - **3.** [in a relaxed manner] tranquilamente, relajadamente.

east [iːst] ◇ *n* - **1.** [direction] este *m* - **2.** [region]: **the east** el este. ◇ *adj* oriental; [wind] del este. ◇ *adv*: **east (of)** al este (de). ➡ **East** *n*: **the East** POL el Este; [Asia] el Oriente.

East End *n*: **the East End** el este de Londres.

Easter ['iːstər] *n* - **1.** [period] Semana *f* Santa - **2.** [festival] Pascua *f*.

Easter egg *n* huevo *m* de Pascua.

easterly ['iːstəlɪ] *adj* del este.

eastern ['iːstən] *adj* del este, oriental. ➡ **Eastern** *adj* [gen & POL] del Este; [from Asia] oriental.

East German ◇ *adj* de Alemania Oriental. ◇ *n* [person] alemán *m*, -ana *f* oriental.

East Germany *n*: **(the former) East Germany** (la antigua) Alemania Oriental.

eastward ['iːstwəd] ◇ *adj* hacia el este. ◇ *adv* = **eastwards**.

eastwards ['iːstwədz], **eastward** *adv* hacia el este.

easy ['iːzɪ] *adj* - **1.** [not difficult] fácil - **2.** [life, time] cómodo(da) - **3.** [manner] relajado(da).

easy chair *n* [armchair] sillón *m*.

easygoing [ˌiːzɪ'gəʊɪŋ] *adj* [person] tolerante; [manner] relajado(da).

easy-peasy *n* *inf hum* chupado(da).

eat [iːt] (*pt* ate, *pp* eaten) *vt* & *vi* comer. ➡ **eat away**, **eat into** *vt sep* - **1.** [corrode] corroer - **2.** [deplete] mermar.

eaten ['iːtn] *pp* ⊳ **eat**.

eau de cologne [ˌəʊdəkə'ləʊn] *n* (agua *f* de) colonia *f*.

eaves ['iːvz] *npl* alero *m*.

eavesdrop ['iːvzdrɒp] *vi*: **to eavesdrop (on)** escuchar secretamente (a).

e-banking *n* banca *f* electrónica.

ebb [eb] ◇ *n* reflujo *m*. ◇ *vi* [tide, sea] bajar.

ebony ['ebənɪ] *n* ébano *m*.

e-business *n* - **1.** [company] empresa *f* electrónica - **2.** [electronic commerce] comercio *m* electrónico.

EC (*abbr of* European Community) *n* CE *f*.

e-cash *n* dinero *m* electrónico.

eccentric [ɪk'sentrɪk] ◇ *adj* excéntrico(ca). ◇ *n* excéntrico *m*, -ca *f*.

echo ['ekəʊ] ◇ *n lit* & *fig* eco *m*. ◇ *vt* [words] repetir; [opinion] hacerse eco de. ◇ *vi* resonar.

eclipse [ɪ'klɪps] ◇ *n lit* & *fig* eclipse *m*; **a total/partial eclipse** un eclipse total/parcial. ◇ *vt fig* eclipsar.

eco- ['iːkəʊ] (*abbr of* ecology or ecological) *prefix* eco-.

eco-friendly ['iːkəʊ'frendlɪ] *adj* ecológico(ca).

ecological [ˌiːkə'lɒdʒɪkl] *adj* - **1.** [pattern, balance, impact] ecológico(ca) - **2.** [group, movement, person] ecologista.

ecology [ɪ'kɒlədʒɪ] *n* ecología *f*.

e-commerce *n* comercio *m* electrónico.

economic [ˌiːkə'nɒmɪk] *adj* - **1.** [of money, industry] económico(ca) - **2.** [profitable] rentable.

Economic and Monetary Union *n* Unión *f* Económica y Monetaria.

economical [ˌiːkə'nɒmɪkl] *adj* económico(ca); **to be economical with the truth** no decir toda la verdad.

economics [ˌiːkə'nɒmɪks] ◇ *n* (U) economía *f*. ◇ *npl* [of plan, business] aspecto *m* económico.

economize, -ise [ɪ'kɒnəmaɪz] *vi*: **to economize (on)** economizar (en).

economy [ɪ'kɒnəmɪ] *n* economía *f*.

economy class *n* clase *f* turista.

economy-class syndrome *n* síndrome *m* de la clase turista.

ecotax ['iːkəʊtæks] *n* ecotasa *f*.

ecotourism [ˌiːkəʊ'tʊərɪzm] *n* ecoturismo *m*.

ecstasy ['ekstəsɪ] *n* - **1.** [great happiness] éxtasis *m inv* - **2.** [drug] éxtasis *m inv*.

ecstatic [ek'stætɪk] *adj* extático(ca).

Ecuador ['ekwədɔːr] *n* (el) Ecuador.

Ecuadoran [ˌekwə'dɔːrən], **Ecuadorian** [ˌekwə'dɔːrɪən] ◇ *adj* ecuatoriano(na). ◇ *n* ecuatoriano *m*, -na *f*.

eczema ['eksɪmə] *n* eczema *m*.

Eden ['iːdn] *n*: **(the Garden of) Eden** (el jardín del) Edén *m*.

edge [edʒ] ◇ *n* - **1.** [of cliff, table, garden] borde *m*; **to be on the edge of** estar al borde de - **2.** [of coin] canto *m*; [of knife] filo *m*. ◇ *vi*: **to edge away/closer** ir alejándose/acercándose poco a poco. ➡ **on edge** *adj* con los nervios de punta.

edgeways ['edʒweɪz], **edgewise** ['edʒwaɪz] *adv* de lado.

edgy ['edʒɪ] *adj* nervioso(sa).

edible ['edɪbl] *adj* comestible.

edict ['iːdɪkt] *n* edicto *m*.

Edinburgh ['edɪnbrə] *n* Edimburgo.

edit ['edɪt] *vt* - **1.** [correct - text] corregir, revisar - **2.** COMPUT editar - **3.** [select material for - book] editar - **4.** CIN, RADIO & TV montar - **5.** [run - newspaper, magazine] dirigir.

edition [ɪ'dɪʃn] *n* edición *f*.

editor ['edɪtər] *n* - **1.** [of newspaper, magazine] director *m*, -ra *f* - **2.** [of section of newspaper, programme, text] redactor *m*, -ra *f* - **3.** [compiler - of book] editor *m*, -ra *f* - **4.** CIN, RADIO & TV montador *m*, -ra *f* - **5.** COMPUT editor *m*.

editorial [ˌedɪ'tɔːrɪəl] ◇ *adj* editorial; **editorial staff** redacción *f*. ◇ *n* editorial *m*.

educate ['edʒʊkeɪt] *vt* - **1.** [at school, college] educar - **2.** [inform] informar.

education [ˌedʒʊ'keɪʃn] *n (U)* - **1.** [activity, sector] enseñanza *f* - **2.** [process or result of teaching] educación *f*.

educational [ˌedʒʊ'keɪʃənl] *adj* educativo(va); [establishment] docente.

EEC (*abbr of* **European Economic Community**) *n* CEE *f*.

eel [i:l] *n* anguila *f*.

efface [ɪ'feɪs] *vt* borrar.

effect [ɪ'fekt] ◇ *n* efecto *m*; **to have an effect on** tener OR surtir efecto en; **to do sthg for effect** hacer algo para causar efecto; **to take effect** [law, rule] entrar en vigor; [drug] hacer efecto; **words to that effect** palabras por el estilo. ◇ *vt* efectuar, llevar a cabo. ◆ **effects** *npl*: **(special) effects** efectos *mpl* especiales.

effective [ɪ'fektɪv] *adj* - **1.** [successful] eficaz - **2.** [actual, real] efectivo(va) - **3.** [law, ceasefire] operativo(va).

effectively [ɪ'fektɪvlɪ] *adv* - **1.** [well, successfully] eficazmente - **2.** [in fact] de hecho.

effectiveness [ɪ'fektɪvnɪs] *n* eficacia *f*.

effeminate [ɪ'femɪnət] *adj pej* afeminado(da).

effervescent [ˌefə'vesənt] *adj* efervescente.

efficiency [ɪ'fɪʃənsɪ] *n* [gen] eficiencia *f*; [of machine] rendimiento *m*.

efficient [ɪ'fɪʃənt] *adj* [gen] eficiente; [machine] de buen rendimiento.

effluent ['eflʊənt] *n* aguas *fpl* residuales.

effort ['efət] *n* - **1.** [gen] esfuerzo *m*; **to be worth the effort** merecer la pena; **to make the effort to do sthg** hacer el esfuerzo de hacer algo; **to make an/no effort to do sthg** hacer un esfuerzo/no hacer ningún esfuerzo por hacer algo - **2.** *inf* [result of trying] tentativa *f*.

effortless ['efətlɪs] *adj* sin gran esfuerzo.

effusive [ɪ'fjuːsɪv] *adj* efusivo(va).

e.g. (*abbr of* **exempli gratia**) *adv* p. ej.

egg [eg] *n* [gen] huevo *m*. ◆ **egg on** *vt sep* incitar.

eggcup ['egkʌp] *n* huevera *f*.

eggplant ['egplɑːnt] *n US* berenjena *f*.

eggshell ['egʃel] *n* cáscara *f* de huevo.

egg white *n* clara *f* (de huevo).

egg yolk [-jəʊk] *n* yema *f* (de huevo).

ego ['iːgəʊ] (*pl* -**s**) *n* - **1.** [opinion of self] amor *m* propio - **2.** [psych] ego *m*.

egoism ['iːgəʊɪzm] *n* egoísmo *m*.

egoistic [ˌiːgəʊ'ɪstɪk] *adj* egoísta.

egotistic(al) [ˌiːgə'tɪstɪk(l)] *adj* egotista.

Egypt ['iːdʒɪpt] *n* Egipto.

Egyptian [ɪ'dʒɪpʃn] ◇ *adj* egipcio(cia). ◇ *n* [person] egipcio *m*, -cia *f*.

eiderdown ['aɪdədaʊn] *n esp UK* edredón *m*.

eight [eɪt] *num* ocho; *see also* **six**.

eighteen [ˌeɪ'tiːn] *num* dieciocho; *see also* **six**.

eighth [eɪtθ] *num* octavo(va); *see also* **sixth**.

eighty ['eɪtɪ] *num* ochenta; *see also* **sixty**.

Eire ['eərə] *n* Eire.

either ['aɪðər, 'iːðər] ◇ *adj* - **1.** [one or the other] cualquiera de los dos; **she couldn't find either jumper** no podía encontrar ninguno de los dos jerseys; **you can do it either way** lo puedes hacer como quieras; **I don't care either way** me da igual - **2.** [each] cada; **on either side** a ambos lados. ◇ *pron*: **either (of them)** cualquiera de ellos(ellas); **I don't like either (of them)** no me gusta ninguno de ellos (ninguna de ellas). ◇ *adv* (*in negatives*) tampoco; **she can't and I can't either** ella no puede y yo tampoco. ◇ *conj*: **either... or** o... o; **either you or me** o tú o yo; **I don't like either him or his wife** no me gusta ni él ni su mujer.

eject [ɪ'dʒekt] *vt* - **1.** [object] expulsar - **2.** [person]: **to eject sb (from)** expulsar a alguien (de).

eke [iːk] ◆ **eke out** *vt sep* [money, supply] estirar.

elaborate ◇ *adj* [ɪ'læbrət] [ceremony] complicado(da); [carving] trabajado(da); [explanation, plan] detallado(da). ◇ *vi* [ɪ'læbəreɪt]: **to elaborate on sthg** ampliar algo, explicar algo con más detalle.

elapse [ɪ'læps] *vi* transcurrir.

elastic [ɪ'læstɪk] ◇ *adj* - **1.** [gen] elástico(ca) - **2.** *fig* [flexible] flexible. ◇ *n* elástico *m*.

elasticated [ɪ'læstɪkeɪtɪd] *adj* elástico(ca).

elastic band *n UK* gomita *f*.

elated [ɪ'leɪtɪd] *adj* eufórico(ca).

elbow ['elbəʊ] *n* codo *m*.

elder ['eldər] ◇ *adj* mayor. ◇ *n* - **1.** [older person] mayor *mf* - **2.** [of tribe, church] anciano *m* - **3.**: **elder (tree)** saúco *m*.

elderly ['eldəlɪ] ◇ *adj* mayor, anciano(na). ◇ *npl*: **the elderly** los ancianos.

eldest ['eldɪst] *adj* mayor.

elect [ɪ'lekt] ◇ *adj* electo(ta); **the president elect** el presidente electo. ◇ *vt* - **1.** [by voting] elegir; **to elect sb (as) sthg** elegir a alguien (como) algo - **2.** *fml* [choose]: **to elect to do sthg** optar por OR decidir hacer algo.

election [ɪ'lekʃn] *n* elección *f.*

electioneering [ɪ,lekʃə'nɪərɪŋ] *n pej* electoralismo *m.*

elector [ɪ'lektər] *n* elector *m*, -ra *f.*

electorate [ɪ'lektərət] *n*: **the electorate** el electorado.

electric [ɪ'lektrɪk] *adj* [gen] eléctrico(ca). ➡ **electrics** *npl* UK *inf* sistema *m* eléctrico.

electrical [ɪ'lektrɪkl] *adj* eléctrico(ca).

electrical shock US = **electric shock**.

electric blanket *n* manta *f* eléctrica, frazada *f* eléctrica *Amér*, cobija *f* eléctrica *Amér*.

electric cooker *n* cocina *f* eléctrica.

electric fire *n* estufa *f* eléctrica.

electrician [,ɪlek'trɪʃn] *n* electricista *mf.*

electricity [,ɪlek'trɪsətɪ] *n* electricidad *f.*

electric shock UK, **electrical shock** US *n* descarga *f* eléctrica.

electrify [ɪ'lektrɪfaɪ] *vt* - **1.** [rail line] electrificar - **2.** *fig* [excite] electrizar.

electrocute [ɪ'lektrəkju:t] *vt* electrocutar; **to electrocute o.s., to be electrocuted** electrocutarse.

electrolysis [,ɪlek'trɒləsɪs] *n* electrólisis *f inv.*

electron [ɪ'lektrɒn] *n* electrón *m.*

electronic [,ɪlek'trɒnɪk] *adj* electrónico(ca). ➡ **electronics** ◇ *n (U)* [technology] electrónica *f.* ◇ *npl* [equipment] sistema *m* electrónico.

electronic banking *n* banca *f* electrónica.

electronic data processing *n* proceso *m* electrónico de datos.

electronic mail *n* correo *m* electrónico.

electronic mailbox *n* buzón *m* electrónico.

electronic tag *n* brazalete *m* electrónico *(que permite conocer la localización de presos en libertad condicional).*

electronic tagging *n* sistema electrónico *que permite conocer la localización de presos en libertad condicional gracias al brazalete electrónico que están obligados a llevar.*

elegant ['elɪgənt] *adj* elegante.

element ['elɪmənt] *n* - **1.** [gen] elemento *m* - **2.** [amount, proportion] toque *m* - **3.** [in heater, kettle] resistencia *f.* ➡ **elements** *npl* - **1.** [basics] elementos *mpl* - **2.** [weather]: **the elements** los elementos.

elementary [,elɪ'mentərɪ] *adj* elemental; **elementary education** enseñanza *f* primaria.

elementary school *n* US escuela *f* primaria.

elephant ['elɪfənt] *(pl* **elephant** OR **-s)** *n* elefante *m.*

elevate ['elɪveɪt] *vt*: **to elevate sthg/sb (to** OR **into)** elevar algo/a alguien (a la categoría de)

elevator ['elɪveɪtər] *n* US ascensor *m*, elevador *m* *Méx.*

eleven [ɪ'levn] *num* once *m; see also* **six.**

elevenses [ɪ'levnzɪz] *n (U)* UK tentempié *m (que se toma sobre las once de la mañana).*

eleventh [ɪ'levnθ] *num* undécimo(ma); *see also* **sixth.**

elicit [ɪ'lɪsɪt] *vt fml* - **1.** [response, reaction]: **to elicit sthg (from sb)** provocar algo (en alguien) - **2.** [information]: **to elicit sthg (from sb)** sacar algo (a alguien).

eligible ['elɪdʒəbl] *adj* [suitable, qualified] elegible; **to be eligible for sthg/to do sthg** reunir los requisitos para algo/para hacer algo.

eliminate [ɪ'lɪmɪneɪt] *vt* eliminar; **to be eliminated from sthg** ser eliminado(da) de algo.

elite [ɪ'li:t] ◇ *adj* selecto(ta). ◇ *n* élite *f.*

elitist [ɪ'li:tɪst] *pej adj* elitista.

elk [elk] *(pl* **elk** OR **-s)** *n* - **1.** [in Europe] alce *m* - **2.** [in North America] ciervo *m* canadiense.

elm [elm] *n*: **elm (tree)** olmo *m.*

elocution [,elə'kju:ʃn] *n* dicción *f.*

elongated ['i:lɒŋgeɪtɪd] *adj* alargado(da).

elope [ɪ'ləʊp] *vi*: **to elope (with)** fugarse (con).

eloquent ['eləkwənt] *adj* elocuente.

El Salvador [,el'sælvədɔ:r] *n* El Salvador.

else [els] *adv*: **anything else?** ¿algo más?; **I don't need anything else** no necesito nada más; **everyone else** todos los demás(todas las demás); **everywhere else** en OR a cualquier otra parte; **little else** poco más; **nothing/nobody else** nada/nadie más; **someone/something else** otra persona/cosa; **somewhere else** en OR a otro sitio; **who else?** ¿quién si no?; **who else came?** ¿quién más vino?; **what else?** ¿qué más?; **where else?** ¿en OR a qué otro sitio? ➡ **or else** *conj* [or if not] si no, de lo contrario.

elsewhere [els'weər] *adv* a OR en otro sitio.

elude [ɪ'lu:d] *vt* [gen] escaparse a, eludir a; [blow] esquivar.

elusive [ɪ'lu:sɪv] *adj* [person, success] esquivo(va); [quality] difícil de encontrar.

emaciated [ɪ'meɪʃɪeɪtɪd] *adj* demacrado(da).

e-mail *(abbr of* **electronic mail)** *n* COMPUT correo *m* electrónico; **e-mail account** cuenta *f* de correo electrónico; **e-mail address** dirección *f* electrónica; **e-mail phone** teléfono *m* con correo electrónico.

emanate ['eməneɪt] *fml vi*: **to emanate from** emanar de.

emancipate [ɪ'mænsɪpeɪt] *vt*: **to emancipate sb (from)** emancipar a alguien (de).

embankment [ɪm'bæŋkmənt] n - 1. RAIL terraplén m - 2. [of river] dique m.

embark [ɪm'bɑːk] vi embarcar; **to embark on** fig embarcarse en.

embarkation [ˌembɑː'keɪʃn] n [gen] embarque m; [of troops] embarco m.

embarrass [ɪm'bærəs] vt - 1. [gen] avergonzar; **it embarrasses me** me da vergüenza - 2. [financially] poner en un aprieto.

embarrassed [ɪm'bærəst] adj [ashamed] avergonzado(da); [uneasy] violento(ta).

embarrassing [ɪm'bærəsɪŋ] adj embarazoso(sa), violento(ta); **how embarrassing!** ¡qué vergüenza!

embarrassment [ɪm'bærəsmənt] n [feeling] vergüenza f, pena f Andes, Amér C & Méx.

embassy ['embəsɪ] n embajada f.

embedded [ɪm'bedɪd] adj [buried & COMPUT]: **embedded (in)** incrustado(da) (en).

embellish [ɪm'belɪʃ] vt: **to embellish sthg (with)** adornar algo (con).

embers ['embəz] npl rescoldos mpl.

embezzle [ɪm'bezl] vt malversar.

embittered [ɪm'bɪtəd] adj amargado(da), resentido(da).

emblem ['embləm] n emblema m.

embody [ɪm'bɒdɪ] vt personificar, encarnar; **to be embodied in sthg** estar plasmado en algo.

embossed [ɪm'bɒst] adj - 1. [heading, design]: **embossed (on)** [paper] estampado(da) (en); [leather, metal] repujado(da) (en) - 2. [paper]: **embossed (with)** estampado(da) (con) - 3. [leather, metal]: **embossed (with)** repujado(da) (con).

embrace [ɪm'breɪs] <> n abrazo m. <> vt - 1. [hug] abrazar, dar un abrazo a - 2. fml [convert to] convertirse a - 3. fml [include] abarcar. <> vi abrazarse.

embroider [ɪm'brɔɪdər] vt - 1. SEW bordar - 2. pej [embellish] adornar.

embroidery [ɪm'brɔɪdərɪ] n (U) bordado m.

embroil [ɪm'brɔɪl] vt: **to get/be embroiled (in)** enredarse/estar enredado(da) (en).

embryo ['embrɪəʊ] (pl -s) n embrión m.

emerald ['emərəld] <> adj [colour] esmeralda m inv; **the Emerald Isle** Irlanda. <> n [stone] esmeralda f.

emerge [ɪ'mɜːdʒ] <> vi - 1. [gen]: **to emerge (from)** salir (de) - 2. [come into existence, become known] surgir, emerger. <> vt: **it emerged that...** resultó que...

emergence [ɪ'mɜːdʒəns] n surgimiento m, aparición f.

emergency [ɪ'mɜːdʒənsɪ] <> adj [case, exit] de emergencia; [ward, services] de urgencia; [supplies] de reserva; [meeting] extraordinario(ria). <> n emergencia f.

emergency exit n salida f de emergencia.

emergency landing n aterrizaje m forzoso.

emergency services npl servicios mpl de urgencia.

emery board ['emərɪ-] n lima f de uñas.

emigrant ['emɪgrənt] n emigrante mf.

emigrate ['emɪgreɪt] vi: **to emigrate (to/from)** emigrar (a/de).

eminent ['emɪnənt] adj eminente.

emission [ɪ'mɪʃn] n emisión f.

emit [ɪ'mɪt] vt [gen] emitir; [smell, smoke] despedir.

emoticon [ɪ'məʊtɪkɒn] n COMPUT emoticono m.

emotion [ɪ'məʊʃn] n emoción f.

emotional [ɪ'məʊʃənl] adj - 1. [gen] emotivo(va) - 2. [needs, problems] emocional; **to get emotional** emocionarse.

empathize, -ise ['empəθaɪz] vi: **to empathize (with)** identificarse (con).

emperor ['empərər] n emperador m.

emphasis ['emfəsɪs] (pl -ases [-əsiːz]) n: **emphasis (on)** énfasis m inv (en); **to lay OR place emphasis on** poner énfasis en, hacer hincapié en.

emphasize, -ise ['emfəsaɪz] vt [word, syllable] acentuar; [point, fact, feature] subrayar, hacer hincapié en; **to emphasize that...** subrayar que...

emphatic [ɪm'fætɪk] adj [denial] rotundo(da), categórico(ca); [victory] convincente.

emphatically [ɪm'fætɪklɪ] adv - 1. [deny] rotundamente, enfáticamente; [win] convincentemente - 2. [certainly] ciertamente.

empire ['empaɪər] n imperio m.

employ [ɪm'plɔɪ] vt - 1. [give work to] emplear; **to be employed as** estar empleado(da) de - 2. fml [use] utilizar, emplear; **to employ sthg as sthg/to do sthg** utilizar algo de algo/para hacer algo.

employee [ɪm'plɔɪiː] n empleado m, -da f.

employer [ɪm'plɔɪər] n - 1. [individual] patrono m, -na f, empresario m, -ria f - 2. [company]: **one of the country's biggest employers** una de las empresas que más trabajadores tiene en el país.

employment [ɪm'plɔɪmənt] n empleo m; **to be in employment** tener trabajo.

employment agency n agencia f de trabajo.

empower [ɪm'paʊər] vt fml: **to be empowered to do sthg** estar autorizado(da) a OR para hacer algo.

empress ['emprɪs] n emperatriz f.

empty ['emptɪ] <> adj - 1. [gen] vacío(a); [town] desierto(ta) - 2. pej [words, threat, promise] vano(na). <> vt vaciar. <> vi vaciarse. <> n inf casco m.

empty-handed [-ˈhændɪd] *adv* con las manos vacías.

EMS (*abbr of* European Monetary System) *n* SME *m*.

EMU (*abbr of* Economic and Monetary Union) *n* UEM *f*.

emulate [ˈemjʊleɪt] *vt* emular.

emulsion [ɪˈmʌlʃn] *n*: **emulsion (paint)** pintura *f* al agua.

enable [ɪˈneɪbl] *vt* COMPUT ejecutar.

enact [ɪˈnækt] *vt* - **1.** LAW promulgar - **2.** [act] representar.

enamel [ɪˈnæml] *n* - **1.** [gen] esmalte *m* - **2.** [paint] pintura *f* de esmalte.

encampment [ɪnˈkæmpmənt] *n* campamento *m*.

encapsulate [ɪnˈkæpsjʊleɪt] *vt*: **to encapsulate sthg (in)** sintetizar algo (en).

encase [ɪnˈkeɪs] *vt*: **encased in** revestido(da) de.

enchanted [ɪnˈtʃɑːntɪd] *adj*: **enchanted (by** OR **with)** encantado(da) (con).

enchanting [ɪnˈtʃɑːntɪŋ] *adj* encantador(ra).

encircle [ɪnˈsɜːkl] *vt* rodear.

enclose [ɪnˈkləʊz] *vt* - **1.** [surround, contain] rodear; **enclosed by** OR **with** rodeado de; **an enclosed space** un espacio cerrado - **2.** [put in envelope] adjuntar; **'please find enclosed...'** 'envío adjunto...'

enclosure [ɪnˈkləʊʒəʳ] *n* - **1.** [place] recinto *m* (vallado) - **2.** [in letter] anexo *m*.

encompass [ɪnˈkʌmpəs] *vt fml* [include] abarcar.

encore [ˈɒŋkɔːʳ] ◇ *n* bis *m*. ◇ *excl* ¡otra!

encounter [ɪnˈkaʊntəʳ] ◇ *n* encuentro *m*. ◇ *vt fml* encontrarse con.

encourage [ɪnˈkʌrɪdʒ] *vt* - **1.** [give confidence to]: **to encourage sb (to do sthg)** animar a alguien (a hacer algo) - **2.** [foster] fomentar.

encouragement [ɪnˈkʌrɪdʒmənt] *n* [confidence boosting] aliento *m*; [fostering] fomento *m*.

encroach [ɪnˈkrəʊtʃ] *vi*: **to encroach on** OR **upon** [rights, territory] usurpar; [privacy, time] invadir.

encrypt [ɪnˈkrɪpt] *vt* COMPUT encriptar.

encyclop(a)edia [ɪn,saɪkləˈpiːdjə] *n* enciclopedia *f*.

end [end] ◇ *n* - **1.** [last part, finish] fin *m*, final *m*; **at the end of May/2002** a finales de mayo/2002; **at the end of the week** al final de la semana; **my patience is at an end** se me está agotando la paciencia; **to be at the end of one's tether** UK OR **rope** US estar hasta la coronilla; **to bring sthg to an end** poner fin a algo; **to come to an end** llegar a su fin; **'the end'** [in films] 'FIN'; **at the end of the day** *fig* a fin de cuentas, al fin y al cabo; **in the end** al final

- **2.** [of two-ended thing] extremo *m*; [of pointed thing] punta *f*; [of stadium] fondo *m*; [of phone line] lado *m*; **and to end** extremo con extremo; **to turn sthg on its end** poner algo boca abajo; **cigarette end** colilla *f* - **3.** *fml* [purpose] fin *m*. ◇ *vt*: **to end sthg (with)** terminar algo (con). ◇ *vi* [finish] acabarse, terminarse. ◆ **on end** *adv* - **1.** [upright - hair] de punta; [- object] de pie - **2.** [continuously]: **for days on end** durante días y días. ◆ **end up** *vi* acabar, terminar; **to end up doing sthg** acabar OR terminar por hacer algo/haciendo algo; **to end up in** ir a parar a.

endanger [ɪnˈdeɪndʒəʳ] *vt* poner en peligro.

endearing [ɪnˈdɪərɪŋ] *adj* simpático(ca).

endeavour UK, **endeavor** US [ɪnˈdevəʳ] *fml* ◇ *n* esfuerzo *m*. ◇ *vt*: **to endeavour to do sthg** procurar hacer algo.

ending [ˈendɪŋ] *n* final *m*, desenlace *m*.

endive [ˈendaɪv] *n* - **1.** [curly lettuce] escarola *f* - **2.** [chicory] endibia *f*, achicoria *f*.

endless [ˈendlɪs] *adj* [gen] interminable; [patience, resources] inagotable.

endorse [ɪnˈdɔːs] *vt* - **1.** [approve] apoyar, respaldar - **2.** [cheque] endosar.

endorsement [ɪnˈdɔːsmənt] *n* - **1.** [approval] apoyo *m*, respaldo *m* - **2.** UK [on driving licence] *nota de sanción que consta en el carné de conducir*.

endoscope [ˈendəskəʊp] *n* MED endoscopio *m*.

endow [ɪnˈdaʊ] *vt* - **1.** *fml* [equip]: **to be endowed with** estar dotado(da) de - **2.** [donate money to] donar fondos a.

endurance [ɪnˈdjʊərəns] *n* resistencia *f*.

endure [ɪnˈdjʊəʳ] ◇ *vt* soportar, aguantar. ◇ *vi fml* perdurar.

endways [ˈendweɪz] *adv* - **1.** [not sideways] de frente - **2.** [with ends touching] extremo con extremo.

enemy [ˈenɪmɪ] *n* enemigo *m*, -ga *f*.

energetic [,enəˈdʒetɪk] *adj* - **1.** [lively, physically taxing] enérgico(ca) - **2.** [enthusiastic] activo(va), vigoroso(sa).

energy [ˈenədʒɪ] *n* energía *f*.

enforce [ɪnˈfɔːs] *vt* [law] hacer cumplir, aplicar; [standards] imponer.

enforced [ɪnˈfɔːst] *adj* forzoso(sa).

engage [ɪnˈgeɪdʒ] ◇ *vt* - **1.** [attract] atraer; **to engage sb in conversation** entablar conversación con alguien - **2.** [TECH - clutch] pisar; [- gear] meter - **3.** *fml* [employ] contratar; **to be engaged in** OR **on** dedicarse a. ◇ *vi* [be involved]: **to engage in** [gen] dedicarse a; [conversation] entablar.

engaged [ɪnˈgeɪdʒd] *adj* - **1.** [to be married]: **engaged (to)** prometido(da) (con); **to get en-**

gaged prometerse - **2.** [busy, in use] ocupado(da); **engaged in sthg** ocupado en algo - **3.** TELEC comunicando.

engaged tone n UK señal f de comunicando.

engagement [ɪn'geɪdʒmənt] n - **1.** [to be married] compromiso m; [period] noviazgo m - **2.** [appointment] cita f.

engagement ring n anillo m de compromiso.

engaging [ɪn'geɪdʒɪŋ] adj atractivo(va).

engender [ɪn'dʒendər] vt fml engendrar.

engine ['endʒɪn] n - **1.** [of vehicle] motor m - **2.** RAIL locomotora f, máquina f.

engine driver n UK maquinista mf.

engineer [,endʒɪ'nɪər] ◇ n - **1.** [gen] ingeniero m, -ra f - **2.** US [engine driver] maquinista mf. ◇ vt - **1.** [construct] construir - **2.** [contrive] tramar.

engineering [,endʒɪ'nɪərɪŋ] n ingeniería f.

England ['ɪŋglənd] n Inglaterra.

English ['ɪŋglɪʃ] ◇ adj inglés(esa). ◇ n [language] inglés m. ◇ npl [people]: **the English** los ingleses.

English breakfast n desayuno m inglés.

English Channel n: **the English Channel** el canal de la Mancha.

Englishman ['ɪŋglɪʃmən] (pl -men [-mən]) n inglés m.

Englishwoman ['ɪŋglɪʃ,wʊmən] (pl -women [-,wɪmɪn]) n inglesa f.

engrave [ɪn'greɪv] vt lit & fig: **to engrave sthg (on)** grabar algo (en).

engraving [ɪn'greɪvɪŋ] n grabado m.

engrossed [ɪn'grəʊst] adj: **to be engrossed (in)** estar absorto(ta) (en).

engulf [ɪn'gʌlf] vt: **to be engulfed in** [flames etc] verse devorado(da) por; [fear, despair] verse sumido(da) en.

enhance [ɪn'hɑːns] vt [gen] aumentar; [status, position] elevar; [beauty] realzar.

enjoy [ɪn'dʒɔɪ] vt - **1.** [like] disfrutar de; **did you enjoy the film/book?** ¿te gustó la película/el libro?; **she enjoys reading** le gusta leer; **enjoy your meal!** ¡que aproveche!, ¡buen provecho!; **to enjoy o.s.** pasarlo bien, divertirse - **2.** fml [possess] gozar OR disfrutar de.

enjoyable [ɪn'dʒɔɪəbl] adj agradable.

enjoyment [ɪn'dʒɔɪmənt] n [pleasure] placer m.

enlarge [ɪn'lɑːdʒ] vt [gen, PHOT & POL] ampliar.

enlargement [ɪn'lɑːdʒmənt] n [gen, PHOT & POL] ampliación f.

enlighten [ɪn'laɪtn] vt fml iluminar.

enlightened [ɪn'laɪtnd] adj amplio(plia) de miras.

enlightenment [ɪn'laɪtnmənt] n (U) aclaración f. ➠ **Enlightenment** n: **the Enlightenment** la Ilustración.

enlist [ɪn'lɪst] ◇ vt - **1.** [person] alistar, reclutar - **2.** [support] obtener. ◇ vi MIL: **to enlist (in)** alistarse (en).

enmity ['enmətɪ] n enemistad f.

enormity [ɪ'nɔːmətɪ] n [extent] enormidad f.

enormous [ɪ'nɔːməs] adj enorme.

enough [ɪ'nʌf] ◇ adj bastante, suficiente; **do you have enough glasses?** ¿tienes suficientes vasos? ◇ pron bastante; **is this enough?** ¿basta con eso?; **more than enough** más que suficiente; **to have had enough (of)** [expressing annoyance] estar harto(ta) (de). ◇ adv bastante, suficientemente; **I was stupid enough to believe her** fui lo bastante tonto como para creerla; **he was good enough to lend me his car** fml tuvo la bondad de dejarme su coche; **strangely enough** curiosamente.

enquire [ɪn'kwaɪər] vi [ask for information] informarse; **to enquire about sthg** informarse de algo; **to enquire when/how/whether...** preguntar cuándo/cómo/si... ➠ **enquire into** vt insep investigar.

enquiry [ɪn'kwaɪərɪ] n - **1.** [question] pregunta f; **'Enquiries'** 'Información' - **2.** [investigation] investigación f.

enraged [ɪn'reɪdʒd] adj enfurecido(da).

enrol, **enroll** US [ɪn'rəʊl] ◇ vt matricular. ◇ vi: **to enrol (on)** matricularse (en).

en route [,ɒn'ruːt] adv: **en route (from/to)** en el camino (de/a).

ensign ['ensaɪn] n - **1.** [flag] bandera f - **2.** US [sailor] ≃ alférez m de fragata.

ensue [ɪn'sjuː] vi fml seguir; [war] sobrevenir.

ensure [ɪn'ʃʊər] vt: **to ensure (that)** asegurar que.

ENT (abbr of Ear, Nose & Throat) n otorrinolaringología f.

entail [ɪn'teɪl] vt [involve] conllevar, suponer.

enter ['entər] ◇ vt - **1.** [gen] entrar en - **2.** [join - profession, parliament] ingresar en; [- university] matricularse en; [- army, navy] alistarse en - **3.** [become involved in - politics etc] meterse en; [- race, examination etc] inscribirse en - **4.** [register]: **to enter sthg/sb for sthg** inscribir algo/a alguien en algo - **5.** [write down] apuntar - **6.** [appear in] presentarse OR aparecer en. ◇ vi - **1.** [come or go in] entrar - **2.** [participate]: **to enter (for sthg)** inscribirse (en algo). ➠ **enter into** vt insep entrar en; [agreement] comprometerse a; [conversation, negotiations] entablar.

enter key n COMPUT tecla f enter.

enterprise ['entəpraɪz] n - **1.** [project, company] empresa f - **2.** [initiative] iniciativa f.

enterprise zone n zona del Reino Unido donde se fomenta la actividad industrial y empresarial.

enterprising [ˈentəˌpraɪzɪŋ] adj emprendedor(ra).

entertain [ˌentəˈteɪn] vt - **1.** [amuse] divertir, entretener - **2.** [invite] recibir (en casa) - **3.** fml [idea, proposal] considerar.

entertainer [ˌentəˈteɪnər] n artista mf.

entertaining [ˌentəˈteɪnɪŋ] adj divertido(da), entretenido(da).

entertainment [ˌentəˈteɪnmənt] n - **1.** (U) [amusement] diversión f - **2.** [show] espectáculo m.

enthral UK, **enthrall** US [ɪnˈθrɔːl] vt embelesar.

enthusiasm [ɪnˈθjuːzɪæzm] n - **1.** [passion, eagerness]: **enthusiasm (for)** entusiasmo m (por) - **2.** [interest] pasión f, interés m.

enthusiast [ɪnˈθjuːzɪæst] n entusiasta mf.

enthusiastic [ɪnˌθjuːzɪˈæstɪk] adj [person] entusiasta; [cry, response] entusiástico(ca).

entice [ɪnˈtaɪs] vt seducir, atraer; **nothing could entice me to do that** no haría eso de ninguna manera.

entire [ɪnˈtaɪər] adj entero(ra); **the entire evening** toda la noche.

entirely [ɪnˈtaɪəlɪ] adv completamente; **I'm not entirely sure** no estoy del todo seguro.

entirety [ɪnˈtaɪrətɪ] n fml: **in its entirety** en su totalidad.

entitle [ɪnˈtaɪtl] vt [allow]: **to entitle sb to sthg** dar a alguien derecho a algo; **to entitle sb to do sthg** autorizar a alguien a hacer algo.

entitled [ɪnˈtaɪtld] adj - **1.** [allowed]: **to be entitled to sthg/to do sthg** tener derecho a algo/a hacer algo - **2.** [book, song, film] titulado(da).

entourage [ˌɒntʊˈrɑːʒ] n séquito m.

entrails [ˈentreɪlz] npl entrañas fpl.

entrance ◇ n [ˈentrəns]: **entrance (to)** entrada f (a OR de); **to gain entrance to** fml [building] lograr acceso a; [society, university] lograr el ingreso en. ◇ vt [ɪnˈtrɑːns] encantar, hechizar.

entrance examination n examen m de ingreso.

entrance fee n [for museum] (precio m de) entrada f.

entrant [ˈentrənt] n participante mf.

entreat [ɪnˈtriːt] vt: **to entreat sb (to do sthg)** suplicar OR rogar a alguien (que haga algo).

entrepreneur [ˌɒntrəprəˈnɜːr] n empresario m, -ria f.

entrust [ɪnˈtrʌst] vt: **to entrust sthg to sb, to entrust sb with sthg** confiar algo a alguien.

entry [ˈentrɪ] n - **1.** [gen]: **entry (into)** entrada f (en); **'no entry'** 'se prohíbe la entrada', 'prohibido el paso' - **2.** fig [joining - of group, society] ingreso m - **3.** [in competition] participante mf - **4.** [in diary] anotación f; [in ledger] partida f.

entry form n boleto m OR impreso m de inscripción.

envelop [ɪnˈveləp] vt: **to envelop sthg/sb in** envolver algo/a alguien en.

envelope [ˈenvələʊp] n sobre m.

envious [ˈenvɪəs] adj [person] envidioso(sa); [look] de envidia; **to be envious of** tener envidia de.

environment [ɪnˈvaɪərənmənt] n - **1.** [natural world]: **the environment** el medio ambiente; **Department of the Environment** UK ministerio m del medio ambiente - **2.** [surroundings] entorno m - **3.** [atmosphere] ambiente m.

environmental [ɪnˌvaɪərənˈmentl] adj - **1.** [gen] medioambiental; **environmental pollution** contaminación f del medio ambiente - **2.** [group, campaigner] ecologista.

environmentally [ɪnˌvaɪərənˈmentəlɪ] adv ecológicamente; **environmentally friendly** ecológico(ca).

envisage [ɪnˈvɪzɪdʒ], **envision** US [ɪnˈvɪʒn] vt prever.

envoy [ˈenvɔɪ] n enviado m, -da f.

envy [ˈenvɪ] ◇ n envidia f. ◇ vt: **to envy (sb sthg)** envidiar (algo a alguien).

epic [ˈepɪk] ◇ adj épico(ca). ◇ n [poem, work] epopeya f; [film] película f épica.

epidemic [ˌepɪˈdemɪk] n epidemia f.

epileptic [ˌepɪˈleptɪk] ◇ adj epiléptico(ca). ◇ n epiléptico m, -ca f.

episode [ˈepɪsəʊd] n - **1.** [event] episodio m - **2.** [of story, TV series] capítulo m.

epistle [ɪˈpɪsl] n epístola f.

epitaph [ˈepɪtɑːf] n epitafio m.

epitome [ɪˈpɪtəmɪ] n: **the epitome of** [person] la personificación de; [thing] el vivo ejemplo de.

epitomize, -ise [ɪˈpɪtəmaɪz] vt [subj: person] personificar; [subj: thing] representar el paradigma de.

epoch [ˈiːpɒk] n época f.

equable [ˈekwəbl] adj [calm, reasonable] ecuánime.

equal [ˈiːkwəl] ◇ adj igual; **equal to** [sum] igual a; **to be equal to** [task etc] estar a la altura de. ◇ n igual mf; **to treat sb as an equal** tratar a alguien de igual a igual. ◇ vt (UK pt & pp -led, cont -ling, US pt & pp -ed, cont -ing) - **1.** MATHS ser igual a - **2.** [person, quality] igualar.

equality [iːˈkwɒlətɪ] n igualdad f.

equalize, -ise [ˈiːkwəlaɪz] vi SPORT empatar.

equalizer [ˈiːkwəlaɪzər] n SPORT gol m del empate.

equally ['i:kwəlɪ] *adv* - **1**. [gen] igualmente; **equally important** de igual importancia - **2**. [share, divide] a partes iguales, por igual - **3**. [just as likely] de igual modo.

equal opportunities *npl* igualdad *f* de oportunidades.

equanimity [,ekwə'nɪmətɪ] *n* ecuanimidad *f*.

equate [ɪ'kweɪt] *vt*: **to equate sthg with** equiparar algo con.

equation [ɪ'kweɪʒn] *n* ecuación *f*.

equator [ɪ'kweɪtər] *n*: **the Equator** el Ecuador.

equilibrium [,i:kwɪ'lɪbrɪəm] *n* equilibrio *m*.

equip [ɪ'kwɪp] *vt* - **1**. [provide with equipment]: **to equip sthg (with)** equipar algo (con); **to equip sb (with)** proveer a alguien (de) - **2**. [prepare]: **to be equipped for** estar preparado(da) para.

equipment [ɪ'kwɪpmənt] *n* (*U*) equipo *m*.

equitable ['ekwɪtəbl] *adj* equitativo(va).

equity ['ekwətɪ] *n* (*U*) FIN [of company] capital *m* social; [of shareholders] fondos *mpl* propios. ➡ **equities** *npl* FIN acciones *fpl* ordinarias.

equivalent [ɪ'kwɪvələnt] ⬦ *adj* equivalente; **to be equivalent to** equivaler a. ⬦ *n* equivalente *m*.

equivocal [ɪ'kwɪvəkl] *adj* equívoco(ca).

er [ɜːr] *excl* ¡ejem!

era ['ɪərə] (*pl* -s) *n* era *f*, época *f*.

eradicate [ɪ'rædɪkeɪt] *vt* erradicar.

erase [ɪ'reɪz] *vt* lit & fig borrar.

eraser [ɪ'reɪzər] *n* *esp* US goma *f* de borrar.

erect [ɪ'rekt] ⬦ *adj* [person, posture] erguido(da). ⬦ *vt* - **1**. [building, statue] erigir, levantar - **2**. [tent] montar.

erection [ɪ'rekʃn] *n* - **1**. (*U*) [of building, statue] construcción *f* - **2**. [erect penis] erección *f*.

ERM (*abbr of* **Exchange Rate Mechanism**) *n* mecanismo *de tipos de cambio del SME*.

ermine ['ɜːmɪn] *n* armiño *m*.

erode [ɪ'rəʊd] *vt* - **1**. [rock, soil] erosionar; [metal] desgastar - **2**. [confidence, rights] mermar.

erosion [ɪ'rəʊʒn] *n* - **1**. [of rock, soil] erosión *f*; [of metal] desgaste *m* - **2**. [of confidence, rights] merma *f*.

erotic [ɪ'rɒtɪk] *adj* erótico(ca).

err [ɜːr] *vi* equivocarse, errar.

errand ['erənd] *n* recado *m*, mandado *m*; **to go on OR run an errand** hacer un recado.

erratic [ɪ'rætɪk] *adj* irregular.

error ['erər] *n* error *m*; **to make an error** cometer un error; **spelling error** falta *f* de ortografía; **in error** por equivocación.

erupt [ɪ'rʌpt] *vi* [volcano] entrar en erupción; *fig* [violence, war] estallar.

eruption [ɪ'rʌpʃn] *n* - **1**. [of volcano] erupción *f* - **2**. [of violence, war] estallido *m*.

escalate ['eskəleɪt] *vi* - **1**. [conflict] intensificarse - **2**. [costs] ascender.

escalator ['eskəleɪtər] *n* escalera *f* mecánica.

escapade [,eskə'peɪd] *n* aventura *f*.

escape [ɪ'skeɪp] ⬦ *n* - **1**. [gen] fuga *f* - **2**. [leakage - of gas, water] escape *m*. ⬦ *vt* - **1**. [avoid] escapar a, eludir - **2**. [subj: fact, name]: **her name escapes me right now** ahora mismo no me sale su nombre. ⬦ *vi* - **1**. [gen]: **to escape (from)** escaparse (de) - **2**. [survive] escapar.

escapism [ɪ'skeɪpɪzm] *n* (*U*) evasión *f*.

escort ⬦ *n* ['eskɔːt] - **1**. [guard] escolta *f* - **2**. [companion] acompañante *mf*. ⬦ *vt* [ɪ'skɔːt] escoltar.

ESF [i:es'ef] (*abbr of* **European Social Fund**) *n* FSE *m*.

Eskimo ['eskɪməʊ] *n* (*pl* -s) [person] esquimal *mf*.

espadrille [,espə'drɪl] *n* alpargata *f*.

especially [ɪ'speʃəlɪ] *adv* - **1**. [more than usually, specifically] especialmente - **2**. [in particular] sobre todo.

espionage ['espɪə,nɑːʒ] *n* espionaje *m*.

esplanade [,esplə'neɪd] *n* paseo *m* marítimo.

Esquire [ɪ'skwaɪər] *n* Sr. Don; **B. Jones Esquire** Sr. Don B. Jones.

essay ['eseɪ] *n* - **1**. SCH redacción *f*; UNIV trabajo *m* - **2**. LIT ensayo *m*.

essence ['esns] *n* esencia *f*.

essential [ɪ'senʃl] *adj* - **1**. [absolutely necessary]: **essential (to OR for)** esencial OR indispensable (para) - **2**. [basic] fundamental, esencial. ➡ **essentials** *npl* [most important elements] los elementos esenciales.

essentially [ɪ'senʃəlɪ] *adv* [basically] esencialmente.

establish [ɪ'stæblɪʃ] *vt* - **1**. [gen] establecer - **2**. [facts, cause] verificar.

establishment [ɪ'stæblɪʃmənt] *n* establecimiento *m*. ➡ **Establishment** *n*: **the Establishment** el sistema.

estate [ɪ'steɪt] *n* - **1**. [land, property] finca *f* - **2**. : **(housing) estate** urbanización *f* - **3**. : **(industrial) estate** polígono *m* industrial - **4**. LAW [inheritance] herencia *f*.

estate agency *n* UK agencia *f* inmobiliaria.

estate agent *n* UK agente inmobiliario *m*, agente inmobiliaria *f*.

estate car *n* UK ranchera *f*.

esteem [ɪ'stiːm] ⬦ *n* estima *f*. ⬦ *vt* estimar, apreciar.

esthetic US = **aesthetic**.

estimate <> n ['estimət] - **1.** [calculation, judgment] cálculo m, estimación f - **2.** [written quote] presupuesto m. <> vt ['estimeit] estimar.

estimation [,esti'meiʃn] n - **1.** [opinion] juicio m - **2.** [calculation] cálculo m.

Estonia [e'stəʊnɪə] n Estonia.

estranged [ɪ'streɪndʒd] adj [from husband, wife] separado(da); **his estranged son** su hijo, con el que no se habla.

estuary ['estjʊərɪ] n estuario m.

e-tailer ['i:teɪlər] n tienda f electrónica.

etc. (abbr of **etcetera**) etc.

etching ['etʃɪŋ] n aguafuerte m o f.

eternal [ɪ'tɜːnl] adj [gen] eterno(na); fig [complaints, whining] perpetuo(tua).

eternity [ɪ'tɜːnətɪ] n eternidad f.

ethic ['eθɪk] n ética f. <> **ethics** <> n (U) [study] ética f. <> npl [morals] moralidad f.

ethical ['eθɪkl] adj ético(ca).

Ethiopia [,i:θɪ'əʊpɪə] n Etiopía.

ethnic ['eθnɪk] adj - **1.** [traditions, groups, conflict] étnico(ca) - **2.** [food] típico de una cultura distinta a la occidental.

ethos ['i:θɒs] n código m de valores.

etiquette ['etɪket] n etiqueta f.

e-trade n (U) comercio m electrónico.

EU (abbr of **European Union**) n UE f.

euphemism ['ju:fəmɪzm] n eufemismo m.

euphoria [ju:'fɔːrɪə] n euforia f.

euro ['jʊərəʊ] n [currency] euro m.

Eurocheque ['jʊərəʊ,tʃek] n eurocheque m.

Europe ['jʊərəp] n Europa f.

European [,jʊərə'pi:ən] <> adj europeo(a). <> n europeo m, -a f.

European Central Bank n: **the European Central Bank** el Banco Central Europeo.

European Commission n: **the European Commission** la Comisión Europea.

European Community n: **the European Community** la Comunidad Europea.

European Monetary System n: **the European Monetary System** el Sistema Monetario Europeo.

European Union n: **the European Union** la Unión Europea.

Eurosceptic ['jʊərəʊ,skeptɪk] <> adj euroescéptico(ca). <> n euroescéptico m, -ca f.

Eurostar ['jʊərəʊstɑː] n Eurostar m.

euro zone n FIN zona f euro.

euthanasia [,ju:θə'neɪzjə] n eutanasia f.

evacuate [ɪ'vækjʊeɪt] vt evacuar.

evade [ɪ'veɪd] vt [gen] eludir; [taxes] evadir.

evaluate [ɪ'væljʊeɪt] vt evaluar.

evaporate [ɪ'væpəreɪt] vi [liquid] evaporarse; fig [feeling] desvanecerse.

evaporated milk [ɪ'væpəreɪtd-] n leche f evaporada.

evasion [ɪ'veɪʒn] n - **1.** [of responsibility, payment etc] evasión f - **2.** [lie] evasiva f.

evasive [ɪ'veɪsɪv] adj evasivo(va).

eve [i:v] n: **on the eve of** en la víspera de.

even ['i:vn] <> adj - **1.** [regular] uniforme, constante - **2.** [calm] sosegado(da) - **3.** [flat, level] llano(na), liso(sa) - **4.** [equal - contest, teams] igualado(da); [- chance] igual; **to get even with** ajustarle las cuentas a - **5.** [number] par. <> adv - **1.** [gen] incluso, hasta; **even now/then** incluso ahora/entonces; **not even** ni siquiera - **2.** [in comparisons] aun; **even more** aun más. <> **even if** conj aunque, así Amér. <> **even so** conj aun así. <> **even though** conj aunque. <> **even out** vi igualarse.

evening ['i:vnɪŋ] n - **1.** [end of day - early part] tarde f; [- later part] noche f; **in the evening** por la tarde/noche - **2.** [event, entertainment] velada f. <> **evenings** adv [early] por la tarde; [late] por la noche.

evening class n clase f nocturna.

evening dress n - **1.** [worn by man] traje m de etiqueta - **2.** [worn by woman] traje m de noche.

event [ɪ'vent] n - **1.** [happening] acontecimiento m, suceso m; **in the event of** en caso de; **in the event that it rains** (en) caso de que llueva - **2.** SPORT prueba f. <> **in any event** adv en todo caso. <> **in the event** adv UK al final.

eventful [ɪ'ventfʊl] adj accidentado(da).

eventual [ɪ'ventʃʊəl] adj final.

eventuality [ɪ,ventʃʊ'ælətɪ] n eventualidad f.

eventually [ɪ'ventʃʊəlɪ] adv finalmente.

ever ['evər] adv - **1.** [at any time] alguna vez; **have you ever done it?** ¿lo has hecho alguna vez?; **the best ever** el mejor de todos los tiempos; **hardly ever** casi nunca - **2.** [all the time] siempre; **all he ever does is complain** no hace más que quejarse; **as ever** como siempre; **for ever** para siempre - **3.** [for emphasis]: **ever so** big muy grande; **ever such a mess** un lío tan grande; **why/how ever did you do it?** ¿por qué/cómo diablos lo hiciste?; **what ever can it be?** ¿qué diablos puede ser? <> **ever since** <> adv desde entonces. <> conj desde que. <> prep desde.

evergreen ['evəgri:n] <> adj de hoja perenne. <> n árbol m de hoja perenne.

everlasting [,evə'lɑːstɪŋ] adj eterno(na).

every ['evrɪ] adj cada; **every day** cada día, todos los días; **every week** todas las semanas. <> **every now and then, every so often** adv de vez en cuando. <> **every other** adj: **every other day** un día sí y otro no, cada dos días.

everybody ['evrɪ,bɒdɪ] = **everyone**.

everyday ['evrɪdeɪ] *adj* diario(ria), cotidiano(na).

everyone ['evrɪwʌn], **everybody** *pron* todo el mundo, todos(das).

everyplace *US* = **everywhere**.

everything ['evrɪθɪŋ] *pron* todo; **money isn't everything** el dinero no lo es todo.

everywhere ['evrɪweəʳ], **everyplace** *US* ['evrɪˌpleɪs] *adv* en OR por todas partes; [with verbs of motion] a todas partes; **everywhere you go** dondequiera que vayas.

evict [ɪ'vɪkt] *vt*: **to evict sb from** desahuciar a alguien de.

evidence ['evɪdəns] *(U) n* - 1. [proof] pruebas *fpl* - 2. LAW [of witness] declaración *f*; **to give evidence** dar testimonio.

evident ['evɪdənt] *adj* evidente, manifiesto(ta).

evidently ['evɪdəntlɪ] *adv* - 1. [seemingly] por lo visto, al parecer - 2. [obviously] evidentemente.

evil ['iːvl] <> *adj* [person] malo(la), malvado(da); [torture, practice] perverso(sa), vil. <> *n* - 1. [evil quality] maldad *f* - 2. [evil thing] mal *m*.

evocative [ɪ'vɒkətɪv] *adj* evocador(ra).

evoke [ɪ'vəuk] *vt* - 1. [memory, emotion] evocar - 2. [response] producir.

evolution [ˌiːvə'luːʃn] *n* - 1. BIOL evolución *f* - 2. [development] desarrollo *m*.

evolve [ɪ'vɒlv] <> *vt* desarrollar. <> *vi* - 1. BIOL: **to evolve (into/from)** evolucionar (en/de) - 2. [develop] desarrollarse.

ewe [juː] *n* oveja *f*.

ex [eks] *n inf* [former spouse, lover etc] ex *mf*.

ex- [eks] *prefix* ex-.

exacerbate [ɪg'zæsəbeɪt] *vt* exacerbar.

exact [ɪg'zækt] <> *adj* exacto(ta); **to be exact** para ser exactos. <> *vt*: **to exact sthg (from)** arrancar algo (a).

exacting [ɪg'zæktɪŋ] *adj* - 1. [job, work] arduo(dua) - 2. [standards] severo(ra); [person] exigente.

exactly [ɪg'zæktlɪ] <> *adv* [precisely] exactamente; **it's exactly ten o'clock** son las diez en punto; **not exactly** [not really] no precisamente; [as reply] no exactamente. <> *excl* ¡exacto!

exaggerate [ɪg'zædʒəreɪt] *vt & vi* exagerar.

exaggeration [ɪgˌzædʒə'reɪʃn] *n* exageración *f*.

exalted [ɪg'zɔːltɪd] *adj* [person, position] elevado(da).

exam [ɪg'zæm] *(abbr of* **examination***) n* examen *m*.

examination [ɪgˌzæmɪ'neɪʃn] *n* - 1. = **exam** - 2. [inspection] inspección *f*, examen *m* - 3. MED reconocimiento *m* - 4. [consideration] estudio *m*.

examine [ɪg'zæmɪn] *vt* - 1. [gen] examinar - 2. MED reconocer - 3. [consider - idea, proposal] estudiar - 4. LAW interrogar.

examiner [ɪg'zæmɪnəʳ] *n* examinador *m*, -ra *f*.

example [ɪg'zɑːmpl] *n* ejemplo *m*; **for example** por ejemplo; **to make an example of sb** imponer un castigo ejemplar a alguien.

exasperate [ɪg'zæspəreɪt] *vt* exasperar.

exasperation [ɪgˌzæspə'reɪʃn] *n* exasperación *f*.

excavate ['ekskəveɪt] *vt* excavar.

exceed [ɪk'siːd] *vt* - 1. [amount, number] exceder, sobrepasar - 2. [limit, expectations] rebasar.

exceedingly [ɪk'siːdɪŋlɪ] *adv* extremadamente.

excel [ɪk'sel] <> *vi*: **to excel (in** OR **at)** sobresalir (en). <> *vt*: **to excel o.s.** *UK* lucirse.

excellence ['eksələns] *n* excelencia *f*.

excellent ['eksələnt] *adj* excelente.

except [ɪk'sept] <> *prep & conj*: **except (for)** excepto, salvo. <> *vt*: **to except sb (from)** exceptuar OR excluir a alguien (de).

excepting [ɪk'septɪŋ] *prep* excepto, salvo.

exception [ɪk'sepʃn] *n* - 1. [exclusion]: **exception (to)** excepción *f* (a); **with the exception of** a excepción de - 2. [offence]: **to take exception to** ofenderse por.

exceptional [ɪk'sepʃənl] *adj* excepcional.

excerpt ['eksɜːpt] *n*: **excerpt (from)** extracto *m* (de).

excess <> *adj* [ɪk'ses] excedente. <> *n* ['ekses] exceso *m*.

excess baggage, **excess luggage** *n* exceso *m* de equipaje.

excess fare *n UK* suplemento *m*.

excessive [ɪk'sesɪv] *adj* excesivo(va).

exchange [ɪks'tʃeɪndʒ] <> *n* - 1. [gen] intercambio *m*; **in exchange (for)** a cambio (de) - 2. FIN cambio *m* - 3. TELEC: **(telephone) exchange** central *f* telefónica - 4. *fml* [conversation]: **a heated exchange** una acalorada discusión. <> *vt* [swap] intercambiar; [goods in shop] cambiar; **to exchange sthg for sthg** cambiar algo por algo; **to exchange sthg with sb** intercambiar algo con alguien.

exchange rate *n* FIN tipo *m* de cambio.

Exchequer [ɪks'tʃekəʳ] *n UK*: **the Exchequer** ≃ Hacienda.

excise ['eksaɪz] *n (U)* impuestos *mpl* sobre el consumo interior.

excite [ɪk'saɪt] *vt* [suspicion, interest] despertar.

excited [ɪk'saɪtɪd] *adj* emocionado(da).

excitement [ɪk'saɪtmənt] *n* emoción *f*.

exciting [ɪk'saɪtɪŋ] *adj* emocionante.

exclaim [ɪk'skleɪm] ◇ *vt* exclamar. ◇ *vi*: **to exclaim (at)** exclamar (ante).

exclamation [ˌeksklə'meɪʃn] *n* exclamación *f*.

exclamation mark *UK*, **exclamation point** *US n* signo *m* de admiración.

exclude [ɪk'sklu:d] *vt*: **to exclude sthg/sb (from)** excluir algo/a alguien (de).

excluding [ɪk'sklu:dɪŋ] *prep* sin incluir, con excepción de.

exclusive [ɪk'sklu:sɪv] ◇ *adj* - 1. [sole] exclusivo(va) - 2. [high-class] selecto(ta). ◇ *n* [news story] exclusiva *f*. ► **exclusive of** *prep* excluyendo.

excrement ['ekskrɪmənt] *n* excremento *m*.

excruciating [ɪk'skru:ʃɪeɪtɪŋ] *adj* insoportable.

excursion [ɪk'skɜ:ʃn] *n* excursión *f*.

excuse ◇ *n* [ɪk'skju:s] excusa *f*; **to make an excuse** dar una excusa, excusarse. ◇ *vt* [ɪk'skju:z] - 1. [gen]: **to excuse o.s. (for doing sthg)** excusarse OR disculparse (por haber hecho algo) - 2. [let off]: **to excuse sb (from)** dispensar a alguien (de) ► **excuse me** [to attract attention] oiga (por favor); [when coming past] con permiso; [apologizing] perdone; *US* [pardon me?] ¿perdón?, ¿cómo?

ex-directory *adj UK* que no figura en la guía telefónica.

execute ['eksɪkju:t] *vt* [gen & COMPUT] ejecutar.

execution [ˌeksɪ'kju:ʃn] *n* ejecución *f*.

executioner [ˌeksɪ'kju:ʃnər] *n* verdugo *m*.

executive [ɪg'zekjʊtɪv] ◇ *adj* [decision-making] ejecutivo(va). ◇ *n* - 1. [person] ejecutivo *m*, -va *f* - 2. [committee] ejecutiva *f*, órgano *m* ejecutivo.

executive director *n* director ejecutivo *m*, directora ejecutiva *f*.

executor [ɪg'zekjʊtər] *n* albacea *m*.

exemplify [ɪg'zemplɪfaɪ] *vt* ejemplificar.

exempt [ɪg'zempt] ◇ *adj*: **exempt (from)** exento(ta) (de). ◇ *vt*: **to exempt sthg/sb (from)** eximir algo/a alguien (de).

exercise ['eksəsaɪz] ◇ *n* - 1. [gen] ejercicio *m* - 2. MIL maniobra *f*. ◇ *vt* - 1. [dog] llevar de paseo; [horse] entrenar - 2. *fml* [power, right] ejercer; [caution, restraint] mostrar. ◇ *vi* hacer ejercicio.

exercise book *n* cuaderno *m* de ejercicios.

exert [ɪg'zɜ:t] *vt* ejercer; **to exert o.s.** esforzarse.

exertion [ɪg'zɜ:ʃn] *n* esfuerzo *m*.

exhale [eks'heɪl] ◇ *vt* exhalar, despedir. ◇ *vi* espirar.

exhaust [ɪg'zɔ:st] ◇ *n* (U) [fumes] gases *mpl* de combustión; **exhaust (pipe)** tubo *m* de escape. ◇ *vt* agotar.

exhausted [ɪg'zɔ:stɪd] *adj* [person] agotado(da).

exhausting [ɪg'zɔ:stɪŋ] *adj* agotador(ra).

exhaustion [ɪg'zɔ:stʃn] *n* agotamiento *m*.

exhaustive [ɪg'zɔ:stɪv] *adj* exhaustivo(va).

exhibit [ɪg'zɪbɪt] ◇ *n* - 1. ART objeto *m* expuesto; *US* [exhibition] exposición *f* - 2. LAW prueba *f* (instrumental). ◇ *vt* - 1. *fml* [feeling] mostrar, manifestar - 2. ART exponer.

exhibition [ˌeksɪ'bɪʃn] *n* - 1. ART exposición *f* - 2. [of feeling] manifestación *f*.

exhilarating [ɪg'zɪləreɪtɪŋ] *adj* estimulante.

exile ['eksaɪl] ◇ *n* - 1. [condition] exilio *m*; **in exile** en el exilio - 2. [person] exiliado *m*, -da *f*. ◇ *vt*: **to exile sb (from/to)** exiliar a alguien (de/a).

exist [ɪg'zɪst] *vi* existir.

existence [ɪg'zɪstəns] *n* existencia *f*; **to be in existence** existir; **to come into existence** nacer.

existing [ɪg'zɪstɪŋ] *adj* existente, actual.

exit ['eksɪt] ◇ *n* salida *f*. ◇ *vi* [gen & COMPUT] salir; THEAT hacer mutis.

exodus ['eksədəs] *n* éxodo *m*.

exonerate [ɪg'zɒnəreɪt] *vt*: **to exonerate sb (from)** exonerar a alguien (de).

exorbitant [ɪg'zɔ:bɪtənt] *adj* [cost] excesivo(va); [demand, price] exorbitante.

exotic [ɪg'zɒtɪk] *adj* exótico(ca).

expand [ɪk'spænd] ◇ *vt* ampliar. ◇ *vi* extenderse, ampliarse; [materials, fluids] expandirse, dilatarse. ► **expand (up)on** *vt insep* desarrollar.

expanse [ɪk'spæns] *n* extensión *f*.

expansion [ɪk'spænʃn] *n* expansión *f*.

expect [ɪk'spekt] ◇ *vt* - 1. [gen] esperar; **to expect sb to do sthg** esperar que alguien haga algo; **to expect sthg (from sb)** esperar algo (de alguien); **to expect the worst** esperarse lo peor; **as expected** como era de esperar - 2. [suppose] imaginarse, suponer; **I expect so** supongo que sí. ◇ *vi* - 1. [anticipate]: **to expect to do sthg** esperar hacer algo - 2. [be pregnant]: **to be expecting** estar embarazada OR en estado.

expectancy ► **life expectancy**.

expectant [ɪk'spektənt] *adj* expectante.

expectant mother *n* futura madre *f*.

expectation [ˌekspek'teɪʃn] *n* esperanza *f*; **against all expectation** OR **expectations**, **contrary to all expectation** OR **expectations** contrariamente a lo que se esperaba; **to live up to/fall short of expectations** estar/no estar a la altura de lo esperado.

expedient [ɪk'spiːdjənt] *fml* ⟨⟩ *adj* conveniente. ⟨⟩ *n* recurso *m*.

expedition [ˌekspɪ'dɪʃn] *n* - **1.** [journey] expedición *f* - **2.** [outing] salida *f*.

expel [ɪk'spel] *vt* - **1.** [person]: **to expel sb (from)** expulsar a alguien (de) - **2.** [gas, liquid]: **to expel sthg (from)** expeler algo (de).

expend [ɪk'spend] *vt*: **to expend sthg (on)** emplear algo (en).

expendable [ɪk'spendəbl] *adj* reemplazable.

expenditure [ɪk'spendɪtʃər] *n (U)* gasto *m*.

expense [ɪk'spens] *n (U)* gasto *m*; **to go to great expense (to do sthg)** incurrir en grandes gastos (para hacer algo); **at the expense of** [sacrificing] a costa de; **at sb's expense** *lit* & *fig* a costa de alguien; **to spare no expense** no repararse en gastos. ➡ **expenses** *npl* COMM gastos *mpl*.

expense account *n* cuenta *f* de gastos.

expensive [ɪk'spensɪv] *adj* caro(ra).

experience [ɪk'spɪərɪəns] ⟨⟩ *n* experiencia *f*. ⟨⟩ *vt* experimentar.

experienced [ɪk'spɪərɪənst] *adj*: **experienced (at OR in)** experimentado(da) (en).

experiment [ɪk'sperɪmənt] ⟨⟩ *n* experimento *m*. ⟨⟩ *vi*: **to experiment (with/on)** experimentar (con), hacer experimentos (con).

expert ['eksp3ːt] ⟨⟩ *adj*: **expert (at sthg/at doing sthg)** experto(ta) (en algo/en hacer algo); **expert advice** la opinión de un experto. ⟨⟩ *n* experto *m*, -ta *f*.

expertise [ˌeksp3ː'tiːz] *n (U)* pericia *f*.

expire [ɪk'spaɪər] *vi* [licence, membership] caducar; [lease, deadline] vencer.

expiry [ɪk'spaɪərɪ] *n* [of licence, membership] caducación *f*; [of lease, deadline] vencimiento *m*.

explain [ɪk'spleɪn] ⟨⟩ *vt*: **to explain sthg (to sb)** explicar algo (a alguien). ⟨⟩ *vi* explicar; **to explain to sb about sthg** explicarle algo a alguien.

explanation [ˌeksplə'neɪʃn] *n*: **explanation (for)** explicación *f* (de).

explicit [ɪk'splɪsɪt] *adj* explícito(ta).

explode [ɪk'spləʊd] ⟨⟩ *vt* [bomb] hacer explotar; [building etc] volar; *fig* [theory] reventar. ⟨⟩ *vi lit* & *fig* estallar.

exploit ⟨⟩ *n* ['eksplɔɪt] proeza *f*, hazaña *f*. ⟨⟩ *vt* [ɪk'splɔɪt] explotar.

exploitation [ˌeksplɔɪ'teɪʃn] *n (U)* explotación *f*.

exploration [ˌeksplə'reɪʃn] *n* exploración *f*.

explore [ɪk'splɔːr] *vt* & *vi lit* & *fig* explorar.

explorer [ɪk'splɔːrər] *n* explorador *m*, -ra *f*.

explosion [ɪk'spləʊʒn] *n* explosión *f*.

explosive [ɪk'spləʊsɪv] ⟨⟩ *adj* explosivo(va). ⟨⟩ *n* explosivo *m*.

exponent [ɪk'spəʊnənt] *n* - **1.** [supporter] partidario *m*, -ria *f* - **2.** [expert] experto *m*, -ta *f*.

export ⟨⟩ *n* ['ekspɔːt] - **1.** [act] exportación *f* - **2.** [exported product] artículo *m* de exportación. ⟨⟩ *comp* de exportación. ⟨⟩ *vt* [ɪk'spɔːt] COMM & COMPUT exportar.

exporter [ek'spɔːtər] *n* exportador *m*, -ra *f*.

expose [ɪk'spəʊz] *vt* - **1.** [to sunlight, danger etc & PHOT] exponer; **to be exposed to sthg** estar OR verse expuesto a algo - **2.** [reveal, uncover] descubrir.

exposed [ɪk'spəʊzd] *adj* [land, house, position] expuesto(ta), al descubierto.

exposure [ɪk'spəʊʒər] *n* - **1.** [to light, radiation] exposición *f* - **2.** MED hipotermia *f* - **3.** PHOT [time] (tiempo *m* de) exposición *f*; [photograph] fotografía *f* - **4.** [publicity] publicidad *f*.

exposure meter *n* fotómetro *m*.

expound [ɪk'spaʊnd] *fml vt* exponer.

express [ɪk'spres] ⟨⟩ *adj* - **1.** UK [letter, delivery] urgente - **2.** [train, coach] rápido(da) - **3.** *fml* [specific] expreso(sa). ⟨⟩ *adv* urgente. ⟨⟩ *n* [train] expreso *m*. ⟨⟩ *vt* expresar; **to express o.s.** expresarse.

expression [ɪk'spreʃn] *n* expresión *f*.

expressive [ɪk'spresɪv] *adj* [full of feeling] expresivo(va).

expressly [ɪk'spreslɪ] *adv* [specifically] expresamente.

expressway [ɪk'spresweɪ] *n US* autopista *f*.

exquisite [ɪk'skwɪzɪt] *adj* exquisito(ta).

ext., extn. *(abbr of* **extension***)* ext.

extend [ɪk'stend] ⟨⟩ *vt* - **1.** [gen] extender; [house] ampliar; [road, railway] prolongar; [visa, deadline] prorrogar - **2.** [offer - welcome, help] brindar; [- credit] conceder. ⟨⟩ *vi* - **1.** [become longer] extenderse - **2.** [from surface, object] sobresalir.

extension [ɪk'stenʃn] *n* - **1.** [gen & TELEC] extensión *f* - **2.** [to building] ampliación *f* - **3.** [of visit] prolongación *f*; [of deadline, visa] prórroga *f* - **4.** ELEC: **extension (lead)** alargador *m*.

extension cable *n* alargador *m*.

extensive [ɪk'stensɪv] *adj* [gen] extenso(sa); [changes] profundo(da); [negotiations] amplio(plia).

extensively [ɪk'stensɪvlɪ] *adv* [gen] extensamente; [change] profundamente; **to use sthg extensively** hacer (un) gran uso de algo.

extent [ɪk'stent] *n* - **1.** [size] extensión *f* - **2.** [of problem, damage] alcance *m* - **3.** [degree]: **to what extent...?** ¿hasta qué punto...?; **to the extent that** [in that, in so far as] en la medida en que; [to the point where] hasta tal punto que; **to some/a certain extent** hasta cierto punto; **to a large OR great extent** en gran medida.

extenuating circumstances [ɪk'sten-jʊeɪtɪŋ-] *npl* circunstancias *fpl* atenuantes.

exterior [ɪk'stɪərɪər] ⬦ *adj* exterior. ⬦ *n* exterior *m*.

exterminate [ɪk'stɜːmɪneɪt] *vt* exterminar.

external [ɪk'stɜːnl] *adj* externo(na).

extinct [ɪk'stɪŋkt] *adj* extinto(ta).

extinguish [ɪk'stɪŋgwɪʃ] *vt fml* [gen] extinguir; [cigarette] apagar.

extinguisher [ɪk'stɪŋgwɪʃər] *n* extintor *m*.

extn. = **ext**.

extol *UK*, **extoll** *US* [ɪk'stəʊl] *vt* [merits, values] ensalzar.

extort [ɪk'stɔːt] *vt*: **to extort sthg from sb** [confession, promise] arrancar algo a alguien; [money] sacar algo a alguien.

extortionate [ɪk'stɔːʃnət] *adj* desorbitado(da), exorbitante.

extra ['ekstrə] ⬦ *adj* [additional] adicional; [spare] de más; **take extra care** pon sumo cuidado. ⬦ *n* - **1.** [addition] extra *m* - **2.** [additional charge] suplemento *m* - **3.** CIN & THEAT extra *mf*. ⬦ *adv* extra; **to pay/charge extra** pagar/cobrar un suplemento; **be extra careful** pon sumo cuidado.

extra- ['ekstrə] *prefix* extra-.

extract ⬦ *n* ['ekstrækt] - **1.** [from book, piece of music] fragmento *m* - **2.** CHEM extracto *m*. ⬦ *vt* [ɪk'strækt]: **to extract sthg (from)** [gen] extraer algo (de); [confession] arrancar algo (de).

extradite ['ekstrədaɪt] *vt*: **to extradite sb (from/to)** extraditar a alguien (de/a).

extramarital [,ekstrə'mærɪtl] *adj* extramatrimonial.

extramural [,ekstrə'mjʊərəl] *adj* UNIV *fuera de la universidad pero organizado por ella*.

extraordinary [ɪk'strɔːdnrɪ] *adj* extraordinario(ria).

extraordinary general meeting *n* junta *f* (general) extraordinaria.

extravagance [ɪk'strævəgəns] *n* - **1.** *(U)* [excessive spending] derroche *m*, despilfarro *m* - **2.** [luxury] extravagancia *f*.

extravagant [ɪk'strævəgənt] *adj* - **1.** [wasteful] derrochador(ra) - **2.** [expensive] caro(ra) - **3.** [exaggerated] extravagante.

extreme [ɪk'striːm] ⬦ *adj* extremo(ma). ⬦ *n* [furthest limit] extremo *m*.

extremely [ɪk'striːmlɪ] *adv* [very] sumamente, extremadamente.

extremist [ɪk'striːmɪst] ⬦ *adj* extremista. ⬦ *n* extremista *mf*.

extricate ['ekstrɪkeɪt] *vt*: **to extricate sthg from** lograr sacar algo de; **to extricate o.s. from** lograr salirse de.

extrovert ['ekstrəvɜːt] ⬦ *adj* extrovertido(da). ⬦ *n* extrovertido *m*, -da *f*.

exultant [ɪg'zʌltənt] *adj* [person] jubiloso(sa); [cry] de júbilo.

eye [aɪ] ⬦ *n* ojo *m*; **before my eye (very)** eyes ante mis etc propios ojos; **to have an eye for sthg** tener buen ojo para algo; **to keep one's eyes open for, to keep an eye out for** estar atento(ta) a. ⬦ *vt* (*cont* eyeing OR eying) mirar.

eyeball ['aɪbɔːl] *n* globo *m* ocular.

eyebath ['aɪbɑːθ] *n* lavaojos *m inv*.

eyebrow ['aɪbraʊ] *n* ceja *f*.

eyebrow pencil *n* delineador *m* de cejas.

eye candy *n* *(U)* *inf hum & pej* persona o cosa atractiva superficialmente pero sin mucho contenido.

eyedrops ['aɪdrɒps] *npl* colirio *m*.

eyelash ['aɪlæʃ] *n* pestaña *f*.

eyelid ['aɪlɪd] *n* párpado *m*.

eyeliner ['aɪ,laɪnər] *n* lápiz *m* de ojos.

eye-opener *n* *inf* [revelation] revelación *f*; [surprise] sorpresa *f*.

eye shadow *n* sombra *f* de ojos.

eyesight ['aɪsaɪt] *n* vista *f*.

eyesore ['aɪsɔːr] *n* monstruosidad *f*.

eyestrain ['aɪstreɪn] *n* vista *f* cansada.

eye test *n* revisión *f* ocular.

eyewitness [,aɪ'wɪtnɪs] *n* testigo *mf* ocular.

e-zine ['iːziːn] *n* fanzine *m* electrónico.

f (*pl* **f's** OR **fs**), **F** (*pl* **F's** OR **Fs**) [ef] *n* [letter] f *f*, F *f*. ◆ **F** ⬦ *n* - **1.** MUS fa *m* - **2.** SCH ≃ muy deficiente *m*. ⬦ *adj* (*abbr of* **Fahrenheit**) F.

fab [fæb] *adj inf* genial.

fable ['feɪbl] *n* [traditional story] fábula *f*.

fabric ['fæbrɪk] *n* - **1.** [cloth] tela *f*, tejido *m* - **2.** [of building, society] estructura *f*.

fabrication [,fæbrɪ'keɪʃn] *n* - **1.** [lying, lie] invención *f* - **2.** [manufacture] fabricación *f*.

fabulous ['fæbjʊləs] *adj inf* [excellent] fabuloso(sa).

facade [fə'sɑːd] *n* fachada *f*.

face [feɪs] ⬦ *n* - **1.** [of person] cara *f*, rostro *m*; **face to face** cara a cara; **to look sb in the**

face mirar a alguien a la cara; **to lose face** quedar mal; **to save face** salvar las apariencias; **face time** US [meeting] tiempo m de contacto personal; **in your face** inf atrevido(da) - 2. [expression] semblante m - 3. [person] cara f - 4. [of cliff, mountain, coin] cara f; [of building] fachada f - 5. [of clock, watch] esfera f - 6. [appearance, nature] aspecto m - 7. [surface] superficie f; **on the face of it** a primera vista. ⬦ vt - 1. [point towards] mirar a - 2. [confront, accept, deal with] hacer frente a; **let's face it** no nos engañemos - 3. inf [cope with] aguantar, soportar. ⬦ vi: **to face forwards/south** mirar hacia delante/al sur. ⬦ **face down** adv boca abajo. ⬦ **face up** adv boca arriba. ⬦ **in the face of** prep [in spite of] ante. ⬦ **face up to** vt insep hacer frente a.

facecloth ['feɪsklɒθ] n UK toallita f (para lavarse).

face cream n crema f facial.

face-lift n [on face] lifting m; **to have a face-lift** hacerse un lifting; fig [on building etc] lavado m de cara.

face powder n (U) polvos mpl (para la cara).

face-saving [-'seɪvɪŋ] adj para salvar las apariencias.

facet ['fæsɪt] n faceta f.

facetious [fə'siːʃəs] adj guasón(ona).

face value n [of coin, stamp] valor m nominal; **to take sthg at face value** tomarse algo literalmente.

facility [fə'sɪlətɪ] n [feature] prestación f. ⬦ **facilities** npl [amenities] instalaciones fpl; [services] servicios mpl.

facing ['feɪsɪŋ] adj opuesto(ta).

facsimile [fæk'sɪmɪlɪ] n facsímil m.

fact [fækt] n - 1. [piece of information] dato m; [established truth] hecho m; **to know sthg for a fact** saber algo a ciencia cierta - 2. (U) [truth] realidad f. ⬦ **in fact** conj & adv de hecho, en realidad.

fact of life n: **it's a fact of life** es un hecho indiscutible. ⬦ **facts of life** npl euph: **to tell sb (about) the facts of life** contar a alguien cómo nacen los niños.

factor ['fæktər] n factor m.

factory ['fæktərɪ] n fábrica f.

fact sheet n UK hoja f informativa.

factual ['fæktʃuəl] adj basado(da) en hechos reales.

faculty ['fækltɪ] n - 1. [gen] facultad f - 2. US [in college]: **the faculty** el profesorado.

fad [fæd] n [of society] moda f pasajera; [of person] capricho m.

fade [feɪd] ⬦ vt descolorar, desteñir. ⬦ vi - 1. [jeans, curtains, paint] descolorarse, desteñirse; [flower] marchitarse - 2. [light, sound, smile] irse apagando - 3. [memory, feeling, interest] desvanecerse.

faeces UK, **feces** US ['fiːsiːz] npl heces fpl.

fag [fæg] n inf - 1. UK [cigarette] pitillo m - 2. US pej [homosexual] marica m, joto m Méx.

Fahrenheit ['færənhaɪt] adj Fahrenheit (inv).

fail [feɪl] ⬦ vt - 1. [exam, test, candidate] suspender - 2. [not succeed]: **to fail to do sthg** no lograr hacer algo - 3. [neglect]: **to fail to do sthg** no hacer algo - 4. [let down] fallar. ⬦ vi - 1. [not succeed] fracasar; **if all else fails** en último extremo - 2. [not pass exam] suspender - 3. [stop functioning] fallar - 4. [weaken] debilitarse.

failing ['feɪlɪŋ] ⬦ n [weakness] fallo m. ⬦ prep a falta de; **failing that** en su defecto.

failure ['feɪljər] n - 1. [lack of success, unsuccessful thing] fracaso m - 2. [person] fracasado m, -da f - 3. [in exam] suspenso m - 4. [act of neglecting]: **her failure to do it** el que no lo hiciera - 5. [breakdown, malfunction] avería f, fallo m.

faint [feɪnt] ⬦ adj - 1. [weak, vague] débil; [outline] impreciso(sa); [memory, longing] vago(ga); [trace, hint, smell] leve - 2. [chance] reducido(da) - 3. [dizzy] mareado(da). ⬦ vi desmayarse.

fair [feər] ⬦ adj - 1. [just] justo(ta); **it's not fair!** ¡no hay derecho! - 2. [quite large] considerable - 3. [quite good] bastante bueno(na); **'fair'** SCH 'regular' - 4. [hair] rubio(bia) - 5. [skin, complexion] claro(ra) - 6. [weather] bueno(na) - 7. liter [beautiful] hermoso(sa). ⬦ n - 1. UK [funfair] feria f - 2. [trade fair] feria f. ⬦ adv [fairly] limpio. ⬦ **fair enough** adv UK inf vale.

fair-haired [-'heəd] adj rubio(bia).

fairly ['feəlɪ] adv - 1. [moderately] bastante - 2. [justly] justamente.

fairness ['feənɪs] n [justness] justicia f.

fair play n juego m limpio.

fairy ['feərɪ] n hada f.

fairy tale n cuento m de hadas.

faith [feɪθ] n fe f; **in good/bad faith** de buena/mala fe.

faithful ['feɪθfʊl] ⬦ adj fiel. ⬦ npl RELIG: **the faithful** los fieles.

faithfully ['feɪθfʊlɪ] adv fielmente; **'Yours faithfully'** UK [in letter] 'le saluda atentamente'.

fake [feɪk] ⬦ adj falso(sa). ⬦ n - 1. [object, painting] falsificación f - 2. [person] impostor m, -ra f. ⬦ vt - 1. [results, signature] falsificar - 2. [illness, emotions] fingir. ⬦ vi [pretend] fingir.

falcon ['fɔːlkən] n halcón m.

Falkland Islands ['fɔːklənd-], **Falklands** ['fɔːkləndz] *npl*: **the Falkland Islands** las (islas) Malvinas.

fall [fɔːl] ◇ *vi* (*pt* fell, *pp* fallen) - 1. [gen] caer; **he fell off the chair** se cayó de la silla; **she fell backwards** se cayó hacia atrás; **to fall to bits** OR **pieces** hacerse pedazos; **to fall flat** *fig* no causar el efecto deseado - 2. [decrease] bajar - 3. [become]: **to fall asleep** dormirse; **to fall ill** ponerse enfermo(ma); **to fall in love** enamorarse. ◇ *n* - 1. [gen] caída *f* - 2. METEOR: **a fall of snow** una nevada - 3. [MIL - of city] caída *f* - 4. [decrease]: **fall (in)** descenso *m* (de) - 5. *US* [autumn] otoño *m*. ◆ **falls** *npl* cataratas *fpl*. ◆ **fall apart** *vi* [book, chair] romperse; *fig* [country, person] desmoronarse. ◆ **fall back** *vi* [person, crowd] echarse atrás, retroceder. ◆ **fall back on** *vt insep* [resort to] recurrir a. ◆ **fall behind** *vi* - 1. [in race] quedarse atrás - 2. [with rent, work] retrasarse. ◆ **fall for** *vt insep* - 1. *inf* [fall in love with] enamorarse de - 2. [trick, lie] tragarse. ◆ **fall in** *vi* - 1. [roof, ceiling] desplomarse, hundirse - 2. MIL formar filas. ◆ **fall off** *vi* - 1. [branch, handle] desprenderse - 2. [demand, numbers] disminuir. ◆ **fall out** *vi* - 1. [hair, tooth]: **his hair is falling out** se le está cayendo el pelo - 2. [argue] pelearse, discutir - 3. MIL romper filas. ◆ **fall over** *vi* [person, object etc] caerse. ◆ **fall through** *vi* [plan, deal] fracasar.

fallacy ['fæləsɪ] *n* concepto *m* erróneo, falacia *f*.

fallen ['fɔːln] *pp* ▷ **fall**.

fallible ['fæləbl] *adj* falible.

fallout ['fɔːlaʊt] *n* (U) - 1. [radiation] lluvia *f* radiactiva - 2. [consequences] secuelas *fpl*.

fallout shelter *n* refugio *m* atómico.

fallow ['fæləʊ] *adj* en barbecho.

false [fɔːls] *adj* [gen] falso(sa); [eyelashes, nose] postizo(za).

false alarm *n* falsa alarma *f*.

false teeth *npl* dentadura *f* postiza.

falsify ['fɔːlsɪfaɪ] *vt* [facts, accounts] falsificar.

falter ['fɔːltər] *vi* vacilar.

fame [feɪm] *n* fama *f*.

familiar [fə'mɪljər] *adj* - 1. [known] familiar, conocido(da); **to be familiar to sb** serle familiar a alguien - 2. [conversant]: **familiar with** familiarizado(da) con; **to be on familiar terms with sb** tener trato informal con alguien - 3. *pej* [too informal - tone, manner] demasiado amistoso(sa).

familiarity [fə,mɪlɪ'ærətɪ] *n* (U) [knowledge]: **familiarity with** conocimiento *m* de.

familiarize, -ise [fə'mɪljəraɪz] *vt*: **to familiarize o.s./sb with sthg** familiarizarse/familiarizar a alguien con algo.

family ['fæmlɪ] *n* familia *f*.

family credit *n* (U) *UK* ≃ prestación *f* OR ayuda *f* familiar.

family doctor *n* médico *m* de cabecera.

family planning *n* planificación *f* familiar.

famine ['fæmɪn] *n* hambruna *f*.

famished ['fæmɪʃt] *adj* *inf* [very hungry] muerto(ta) de hambre, famélico(ca).

famous ['feɪməs] *adj*: **famous (for)** famoso(sa) (por).

fan [fæn] ◇ *n* - 1. [of paper, silk] abanico *m* - 2. [electric or mechanical] ventilador *m* - 3. [of musician, artist etc] fan *mf*, admirador *m*, -ra *f*; [of music, art etc] aficionado *m*, -da *f*; FTBL hincha *mf*. ◇ *vt* - 1. [cool] abanicar - 2. [stimulate - fire, feelings] avivar. ◆ **fan out** *vi* desplegarse en abanico.

fanatic [fə'nætɪk] *n* fanático *m*, -ca *f*.

fan belt *n* correa *f* del ventilador.

fanciful ['fænsɪfʊl] *adj* [odd] rocambolesco(ca).

fancy ['fænsɪ] ◇ *vt* - 1. *inf* [feel like]: **I fancy a cup of tea/going to the cinema** me apetece una taza de té/ir al cine - 2. *inf* [desire]: **do you fancy her?** ¿te gusta? - 3. [imagine]: **fancy that!** ¡imagínate!, ¡mira por donde! - 4. *dated* [think] creer. ◇ *n* [desire, liking] capricho *m*; **to take a fancy to** encapricharse con. ◇ *adj* - 1. [elaborate] elaborado(da) - 2. [expensive] de lujo, caro(ra); [prices] exorbitante.

fancy dress *n* (U) disfraz *m*.

fancy-dress party *n* fiesta *f* de disfraces.

fanfare ['fænfeər] *n* fanfarria *f*.

fang [fæŋ] *n* colmillo *m*.

fan heater *n* convector *m*.

fanny ['fænɪ] *n* *US* *inf* [buttocks] culo *m*.

fantasize, -ise ['fæntəsaɪz] *vi* fantasear; **to fantasize about sthg/about doing sthg** soñar con algo/con hacer algo.

fantastic [fæn'tæstɪk] *adj* [gen] fantástico(ca).

fantasy ['fæntəsɪ] *n* fantasía *f*.

fantasy football *n* (U) ≃ la liga fantástica®.

fao (*abbr of* for the attention of) a/a.

far [fɑːr] ◇ *adv* - 1. [in distance, time] lejos; **is it far?** ¿está lejos?; **how far is it?** ¿a qué distancia está?; **how far is it to Prague?** ¿cuánto hay de aquí a Praga?; **so far** por ahora, hasta ahora; **far and wide** por todas partes; **as far as** hasta - 2. [in degree or extent]: **how far have you got?** ¿hasta dónde has llegado?; **he's not far wrong** OR **out** OR **off** no anda del todo descaminado; **as far as I know** que yo sepa; **as far as I'm concerned** por OR en lo que a mí respecta; **as far as possible** en (la medida de) lo posible; **far and away, by far** con mucho; **far from it** en absoluto, todo lo contrario; **so far** [until now] hasta el momento; [to a certain ex-

tent] hasta un cierto punto. ⬦ *adj*
(*comp* **farther** OR **further**, *superl* **farthest** OR
furthest) [extreme] extremo(ma).

faraway ['fɑːrəweɪ] *adj* - **1.** [land etc] lejano(na) - **2.** [look, expression] ausente.

farce [fɑːs] *n lit* & *fig* farsa *f*.

farcical ['fɑːsɪkl] *adj* absurdo(da).

fare [feəʳ] *n* - **1.** [payment] (precio *m* del) billete *m*; [in taxi] tarifa *f*; [passenger] pasajero *m*, -ra *f (de taxi)* - **2.** (*U*) *fml* [food] comida *f*.

Far East *n*: **the Far East** el Extremo Oriente.

farewell [,feə'wel] ⬦ *n* despedida *f*. ⬦ *excl liter* ¡vaya con Dios!

farm [fɑːm] ⬦ *n* [smaller] granja *f*, chacra *f Amér*; [larger] hacienda *f*. ⬦ *vt* [land] cultivar; [livestock] criar.

farmer ['fɑːməʳ] *n* [on smaller farm] granjero *m*, -ra *f*, chacarero *m*, -ra *f Amér*; [on larger farm] agricultor *m*, -ra *f*.

farmhand ['fɑːmhænd], **farm labourer**, **farm worker** *n* peón *m*.

farmhouse ['fɑːmhaʊs, *pl* -haʊzɪz] *n* granja *f*, caserío *m*.

farming ['fɑːmɪŋ] (*U*) *n* - **1.** AGRIC & INDUST agricultura *f* - **2.** [act - of crops] cultivo *m*; [- of animals] cría *f*, crianza *f*.

farm labourer = **farmhand**.

farmland ['fɑːmlænd] *n* (*U*) tierras *fpl* de labranza.

farmstead ['fɑːmsted] *n US* granja *f*.

farm worker = **farmhand**.

farmyard ['fɑːmjɑːd] *n* corral *m*.

far-reaching [-'riːtʃɪŋ] *adj* trascendental, de amplio alcance.

farsighted [,fɑː'saɪtɪd] *adj* - **1.** [gen] con visión de futuro - **2.** *US* [long-sighted] présbita.

fart [fɑːt] *v inf* ⬦ *n* [flatulence] pedo *m*. ⬦ *vi* tirarse un pedo.

farther ['fɑːðəʳ] *compar* ▷ **far**.

farthest ['fɑːðəst] *superl* ▷ **far**.

fascinate ['fæsɪneɪt] *vt* fascinar.

fascinating [,'fæsɪneɪtɪŋ] *adj* fascinante.

fascination [,fæsɪ'neɪʃn] *n* fascinación *f*.

fascism ['fæʃɪzm] *n* fascismo *m*.

fashion ['fæʃn] ⬦ *n* - **1.** [clothing, style, vogue] moda *f* - **2.** [manner] manera *f*. ⬦ *vt fml* - **1.** [make] elaborar - **2.** *fig* [mould] forjar.

fashionable ['fæʃnəbl] *adj* de moda.

fashion show *n* pase *m* OR desfile *m* de modelos.

fast [fɑːst] ⬦ *adj* - **1.** [rapid] rápido(da) - **2.** [clock, watch]: **her watch is two minutes fast** su reloj va dos minutos adelantado - **3.** [dye, colour] que no destiñe. ⬦ *adv* - **1.** [rapidly] rápido, rápidamente; **how fast were they going?** ¿a qué velocidad conducían? - **2.** [firmly]: **stuck fast** bien pegado(da); **to hold**

fast to sthg [person, object] agarrarse fuerte a algo; [principles] mantenerse fiel a algo; **fast asleep** profundamente dormido. ⬦ *n* ayuno *m*. ⬦ *vi* ayunar.

fasten ['fɑːsn] *vt* - **1.** [gen] sujetar; [clothes, belt] abrochar; **he fastened his coat** se abrochó el abrigo - **2.** [attach]: **to fasten sthg to sthg** fijar algo a algo.

fastener ['fɑːsnəʳ] *n* cierre *m*; [zip] cremallera *f*.

fastening ['fɑːsnɪŋ] *n* [of door, window] cerrojo *m*, pestillo *m*.

fast food *n* (*U*) comida *f* rápida.

fastidious [fə'stɪdɪəs] *adj* [fussy] quisquilloso(sa).

fat [fæt] ⬦ *adj* - **1.** [gen] gordo(da); **to get fat** engordar - **2.** [meat] con mucha grasa - **3.** [book, package] grueso(sa). ⬦ *n* - **1.** [gen] grasa *f* - **2.** [for cooking] manteca *f*.

fatal ['feɪtl] *adj* - **1.** [mortal] mortal - **2.** [serious] fatal, funesto(ta).

fatality [fə'tælətɪ] *n* [accident victim] víctima *f* mortal.

fate [feɪt] *n* - **1.** [destiny] destino *m*; **to tempt fate** tentar a la suerte - **2.** [result, end] suerte *f*, final *m*.

fateful ['feɪtfʊl] *adj* fatídico(ca).

fat-free *adj* sin grasas.

father ['fɑːðəʳ] *n lit* & *fig* padre *m*.

Father Christmas *n UK* Papá *m* Noel.

father-in-law (*pl* **fathers-in-law** OR **father-in-laws**) *n* suegro *m*.

fatherly ['fɑːðəlɪ] *adj* paternal.

fathom ['fæðəm] ⬦ *n* braza *f*. ⬦ *vt*: **to fathom sthg/sb (out)** llegar a comprender algo/a alguien.

fatigue [fə'tiːg] *n* fatiga *f*.

fatten ['fætn] *vt* engordar.

fattening ['fætnɪŋ] *adj* que engorda.

fatty ['fætɪ] ⬦ *adj* graso(sa). ⬦ *n inf pej* gordinflón *m*, -ona *f*.

fatuous ['fætjʊəs] *adj* necio(cia).

faucet ['fɔːsɪt] *n US* grifo *m*, llave *f Amér*, canilla *f R Plata*, paja *f Amér C*, caño *m Perú*.

fault [fɔːlt] ⬦ *n* - **1.** [responsibility] culpa *f*; **it's my fault** es culpa mía; **to be at fault** tener la culpa - **2.** [mistake, imperfection] defecto *m*; **to find fault with** encontrar defectos a - **3.** GEOL falla *f* - **4.** [in tennis] falta *f*. ⬦ *vt*: **to fault sb (on sthg)** criticar a alguien (en OR por algo).

faultless ['fɔːltlɪs] *adj* impecable.

faulty ['fɔːltɪ] *adj* [machine, system] defectuoso(sa); [reasoning, logic] imperfecto(ta).

fauna ['fɔːnə] *n* fauna *f*.

faux pas [,fəʊ'pɑː] (*pl* **faux pas**) *n* plancha *f*.

favour *UK*, **favor** *US* ['feɪvəʳ] ⬦ *n* [gen] favor *m*; **in sb's favour** a favor de alguien; **to be**

in/out of favour (with) ser/dejar de ser popular (con); **to rule in sb's favour** fallar a favor de alguien. ◇ vt. **1.** [prefer] decantarse por, preferir - **2.** [treat better, help] favorecer. ◆ **in favour** adv [in agreement] a favor. ◆ **in favour of** prep - **1.** [in preference to] en favor de - **2.** [in agreement with]: **to be in favour of sthg/of doing sthg** estar a favor de algo/de hacer algo.

favourable UK, **favorable** US ['feɪvrəbl] adj [positive] favorable.

favourite UK, **favorite** US ['feɪvrɪt] ◇ adj favorito(ta). ◇ n favorito m, -ta f. ◆ **favorites** npl COMPUT favoritos mpl.

favouritism UK, **favoritism** US ['feɪvrɪtɪzm] n favoritismo m.

fawn [fɔːn] ◇ adj beige (inv). ◇ n [animal] cervato m, cervatillo m. ◇ vi: **to fawn on sb** adular a alguien.

fax [fæks] ◇ n fax m. ◇ vt - **1.** [send fax to] mandar un fax a - **2.** [send by fax] enviar por fax.

fax machine, facsimile machine n fax m.

FBI (abbr of Federal Bureau of Investigation) n FBI m.

fear [fɪər] ◇ n - **1.** [gen] miedo m, temor m; **for fear of** por miedo a - **2.** [risk] peligro m. ◇ vt - **1.** [be afraid of] temer - **2.** [anticipate] temerse; **to fear (that)...** temerse que...

fearful ['fɪəful] adj - **1.** fml [frightened] temeroso(sa) - **2.** [frightening] terrible.

fearless ['fɪəlɪs] adj intrépido(da).

feasible ['fiːzəbl] adj factible, viable.

feast [fiːst] ◇ n [meal] banquete m, festín m. ◇ vi: **to feast on** OR **off sthg** darse un banquete a base de algo.

feat [fiːt] n hazaña f.

feather ['feðər] n pluma f.

feature ['fiːtʃər] ◇ n - **1.** [characteristic] característica f - **2.** [of face] rasgo m - **3.** GEOG accidente m geográfico - **4.** [article] artículo m de fondo - **5.** RADIO & TV [programme] programa m especial - **6.** CIN = **feature film.** ◇ vt [subj: film] tener como protagonista a; [subj: exhibition] tener como atracción principal a. ◇ vi: **to feature (in)** aparecer OR figurar (en).

feature film n largometraje m.

February ['februərɪ] n febrero m; see also **September.**

feces US = **faeces.**

fed [fed] pt & pp ⊳ **feed.**

federal ['fedrəl] adj federal.

federation [ˌfedə'reɪʃn] n federación f.

fed up adj: **fed up (with)** harto(ta) (de).

fee [fiː] n [to lawyer, doctor etc] honorarios mpl, membership fee cuota f de socio, entrance fee entrada f, school fees (price in mth) matrícula f.

feeble ['fiːbəl] adj - **1.** [weak] débil - **2.** [poor, silly] pobre, flojo(ja).

feed [fiːd] ◇ vt (pt & pp fed) [gen] alimentar; [animal] dar de comer a. ◇ vi comer. ◇ n - **1.** [of baby] toma f - **2.** [animal food] pienso m.

feedback ['fiːdbæk] n (U) - **1.** [reaction] reacciones fpl - **2.** COMPUT & ELEC realimentación f; [on guitar etc] feedback m.

feeding bottle ['fiːdɪŋ-] n UK biberón m.

feel [fiːl] ◇ vt (pt & pp felt) - **1.** [touch] tocar - **2.** [sense, notice, experience] sentir; **I felt myself blushing** noté que me ponía colorado(da) - **3.** [believe] creer; **to feel (that)** creer OR pensar que ◇ **not to feel o.s.** no encontrarse bien. ◇ vi (pt & pp felt) - **1.** [have sensation]: **to feel hot/cold/sleepy** tener calor/frío/sueño; **how do you feel?** ¿cómo te encuentras? - **2.** [have emotion]: **to feel safe/happy** sentirse seguro/feliz - **3.** [seem] parecer (al tacto) - **4.** [by touch]: **to feel for sthg** buscar algo a tientas - **5.** [be in mood]: **do you feel like a drink/eating out?** ¿te apetece una copa/comer fuera? ◇ n - **1.** [sensation, touch] tacto m, sensación f - **2.** [atmosphere] atmósfera f.

feeler ['fiːlər] n antena f.

feeling ['fiːlɪŋ] n - **1.** [emotion] sentimiento m - **2.** [sensation] sensación f - **3.** [intuition] presentimiento m - **4.** [opinion] opinión f - **5.** [understanding] apreciación f, entendimiento m. ◆ **feelings** npl sentimientos mpl.

feet [fiːt] npl ⊳ **foot.**

feign [feɪn] vt fml fingir, aparentar.

fell [fel] ◇ pt ⊳ **fall.** ◇ vt [tree] talar. ◆ **fells** npl GEOG monte m.

fellow ['feləu] ◇ adj: **fellow students/prisoners** compañeros de clase/celda; **fellow citizens** conciudadanos. ◇ n - **1.** dated [man] tipo m - **2.** [comrade, peer] camarada mf - **3.** [of a society] miembro m - **4.** [of college] miembro m del claustro de profesores.

fellowship ['feləuʃɪp] n - **1.** [comradeship] camaradería f - **2.** [society] asociación f - **3.** [grant] beca f de investigación.

felony ['felənɪ] n US LAW crimen m, delito m grave.

felt [felt] ◇ pt & pp ⊳ **feel.** ◇ n (U) fieltro m.

felt-tip pen n rotulador m.

female ['fi:meɪl] <> adj [animal, plant, connector] hembra; [figure, sex] femenino(na). <> n - 1. [female animal] hembra f - 2. [woman] mujer f.

feminine ['femɪnɪn] <> adj femenino(na). <> n GRAM femenino m.

feminist ['femɪnɪst] n feminista mf.

fence [fens] <> n valla f; **to sit on the fence** fig nadar entre dos aguas. <> vt [surround] cercar.

fencing ['fensɪŋ] n SPORT esgrima f.

fend [fend] vi: **to fend for o.s.** valerse por sí mismo(ma). ◆ **fend off** vt sep [blows] defenderse de, desviar; [questions, reporters] eludir.

fender ['fendər] n - 1. [round fireplace] guardafuego m - 2. [on boat] defensa f - 3. US [on car] guardabarros m inv.

ferment <> n ['fɜ:ment] [unrest] agitación f. <> vi [fə'ment] fermentar.

fern [fɜ:n] n helecho m.

ferocious [fə'rəʊʃəs] adj feroz.

ferret ['ferɪt] n hurón m. ◆ **ferret about, ferret around** vi inf rebuscar.

ferris wheel ['ferɪs-] n esp US noria f.

ferry ['ferɪ] <> n [large, for cars] transbordador m, ferry m; [small] barca f. <> vt llevar, transportar.

ferryboat ['ferɪbəʊt] n transbordador m, ferry m.

fertile ['fɜ:taɪl] adj fértil.

fertilizer ['fɜ:tɪlaɪzər] n abono m.

fervent ['fɜ:vənt] adj ferviente.

fester ['festər] vi lit & fig enconarse.

festival ['festəvl] n - 1. [event, celebration] festival m - 2. [holiday] día m festivo.

festive ['festɪv] adj festivo(va).

festive season n: **the festive season** las Navidades.

festivities [fes'tɪvətɪz] npl festividades fpl.

festoon [fe'stu:n] vt engalanar.

fetch [fetʃ] vt - 1. [go and get] ir a buscar - 2. inf [raise - money] venderse por.

fetching ['fetʃɪŋ] adj atractivo(va).

fete, fête [feɪt] n fiesta f benéfica.

fetish ['fetɪʃ] n - 1. [object of sexual obsession] fetiche m - 2. [mania] obsesión f, manía f.

fetus ['fi:təs] US = **foetus**.

feud [fju:d] <> n enfrentamiento m duradero. <> vi pelearse.

feudal ['fju:dl] adj feudal.

fever ['fi:vər] n lit & fig fiebre f; **to have a fever** tener fiebre.

feverish ['fi:vərɪʃ] adj lit & fig febril.

few [fju:] <> adj pocos(cas); **the next few weeks** las próximas semanas; **a few** algunos(nas); **a few more potatoes** algunas patatas más; **quite a few, a good few** bastantes; **few and far between** escasos, contados. <> pron pocos mpl, -cas f; **a few (of them)** algunos mpl, -nas f; **quite a few** bastantes mpl & fpl.

fewer ['fju:ər] <> adj menos. <> pron menos.

fewest ['fju:əst] adj menos.

fiancé [fɪ'ɒnseɪ] n prometido m.

fiancée [fɪ'ɒnseɪ] n prometida f.

fiasco [fɪ'æskəʊ] (UK -s, US -es) n fiasco m.

fib [fɪb] inf n bola f, trola f.

fibre UK, **fiber** US ['faɪbər] n fibra f.

fibreglass UK, **fiberglass** US ['faɪbəɡlɑ:s] n (U) fibra f de vidrio.

fickle ['fɪkl] adj voluble.

fiction ['fɪkʃn] n - 1. [stories] (literatura f de) ficción f - 2. [fabrication] ficción f.

fictional ['fɪkʃənl] adj - 1. [literary] novelesco(ca) - 2. [invented] ficticio(cia).

fictitious [fɪk'tɪʃəs] adj [false] ficticio(cia).

fiddle ['fɪdl] n - 1. [violin] violín m - 2. UK inf [fraud] timo m.

fiddly ['fɪdlɪ] adj UK [job] delicado(da); [gadget] intrincado(da).

fidget ['fɪdʒɪt] vi no estarse quieto(ta).

field [fi:ld] n [gen & COMPUT] campo m; **in the field** sobre el terreno.

field day n: **to have a field day** disfrutar de lo lindo.

field glasses npl prismáticos mpl.

field marshal n mariscal m de campo.

field trip n salida f para realizar trabajo de campo.

fieldwork ['fi:ldwɜ:k] n (U) trabajo m de campo.

fiend [fi:nd] n [cruel person] malvado m, -da f.

fiendish ['fi:ndɪʃ] adj - 1. [evil] malévolo(la) - 2. inf [very difficult] endiablado(da).

fierce [fɪəs] adj [gen] feroz; [temper] endiablado(da); [loyalty] ferviente; [heat] asfixiante.

fiery ['faɪərɪ] adj - 1. [burning] ardiente - 2. [volatile - temper] endiablado(da); [- speech] encendido(da); [- person] apasionado(da).

fifteen [fɪf'ti:n] num quince; see also **six**.

fifth [fɪfθ] num quinto(ta); see also **sixth**.

fifty ['fɪftɪ] num cincuenta; see also **sixty**.

fifty-fifty <> adj al cincuenta por ciento; **a fifty-fifty chance** unas posibilidades del cincuenta por ciento. <> adv: **to go fifty-fifty** ir a medias.

fig [fɪɡ] n higo m.

fight [faɪt] <> n [physical, verbal] pelea f; fig [struggle] lucha f; **to have a fight (with)** pelearse (con); **to put up a fight** oponer resistencia.

⬥ vt (pt & pp **fought**) [gen] luchar contra; [in punch up] **pelearse con;** [battle, campaign] librar; [war] luchar en. ⬥ vi (pt & pp **fought**) - 1. [in punch-up] pelearse; [in war] luchar - 2. fig [battle, struggle]: **to fight (for/against)** luchar (por/contra) - 3. [argue]: **to fight (about OR over)** pelearse OR discutir (por). ⬥ **fight back** ⬥ vt insep [tears, feelings] reprimir, contener. ⬥ vi defenderse.

fighter ['faɪtə'] n - 1. [plane] caza m - 2. [soldier] combatiente mf - 3. [boxer] púgil mf - 4. [combative person] luchador m, -ra f.

fighting ['faɪtɪŋ] n (U) [on streets, terraces] peleas fpl; [in war] combates mpl.

figment ['fɪgmənt] n: **to be a figment of sb's imagination** ser producto de la imaginación de alguien.

figurative ['fɪgərətɪv] adj figurado(da).

figure [UK 'fɪgə', US 'fɪgjər] ⬥ n - 1. [statistic, number] cifra f; **to put a figure on sthg** dar un número exacto de algo - 2. [shape of person, personality] figura f - 3. [diagram] figura f. ⬥ vt esp US [suppose] figurarse, suponer. ⬥ vi [feature] figurar. ⬥ **figure out** vt sep [reason, motives] figurarse; [problem etc] resolver; [amount, quantity] calcular; **to figure out how to do sthg** dar con la manera de hacer algo.

figurehead ['fɪgəhed] n [leader without real power] testaferro m.

figure of speech n forma f de hablar.

Fiji ['fiːdʒiː] n Fiji.

file [faɪl] ⬥ n - 1. [folder] carpeta f - 2. [report] expediente m; **on file, on the files** archivado - 3. COMPUT archivo m - 4. [tool] lima f - 5. [line]: **in single file** en fila india. ⬥ vt - 1. [put in file] archivar - 2. LAW presentar - 3. [shape, smooth] limar. ⬥ vi [walk in single line] ir en fila.

filet US = **fillet**.

filing cabinet ['faɪlɪŋ-] n archivador m.

Filipino [,fɪlɪ'piːnəʊ] ⬥ adj filipino(na). ⬥ n (pl -s) filipino m, -na f.

fill [fɪl] ⬥ vt - 1. [gen]: **to fill sthg (with)** llenar algo (de) - 2. [gap, hole, crack] rellenar; [tooth] empastar - 3. [need, vacancy etc] cubrir; [time] ocupar. ⬥ n: **to eat one's fill** comer hasta hartarse; **to have had one's fill of sthg** estar harto a la coronilla de algo. ⬥ **fill in** vt sep - 1. [complete] rellenar - 2. [inform]: **to fill sb in (on)** poner a alguien al corriente (de). ⬥ **fill out** vt sep [complete] rellenar. ⬥ **fill up** ⬥ vt sep llenar (hasta arriba). ⬥ vi - 1. [gen] llenarse - 2. [buy petrol] repostar.

fillet UK, **filet** US ['fɪlɪt] ⬥ n filete m. ⬥ vt cortar en filetes.

fillet steak n filete m, bife m de lomo R Plata.

filling ['fɪlɪŋ] ⬥ adj [satisfying] que llena mucho. ⬥ n - 1. [in tooth] empaste m Esp - 2. [in cake, sandwich] relleno m.

filling station n estación f de servicio OR de nafta R Plata.

film [fɪlm] ⬥ n - 1. [gen] película f - 2. (U) [art of cinema] cine m. ⬥ vt & vi filmar, rodar.

film noir ['nwaː'] (pl **films noirs**) n CIN cine m negro.

film star n estrella f de cine.

Filofax® ['faɪləʊfæks] n agenda f de anillas.

filter ['fɪltə'] ⬥ n filtro m. ⬥ vt [purify] filtrar.

filter coffee n café m de filtro.

filter lane n UK carril m de giro.

filter-tipped [-'tɪpt] adj con filtro.

filth [fɪlθ] n (U) - 1. [dirt] suciedad f - 2. [obscenity] obscenidades fpl.

filthy ['fɪlθɪ] adj - 1. [very dirty] mugriento(ta), sucísimo(ma) - 2. [obscene] obsceno(na).

fin [fɪn] n [on fish] aleta f.

final ['faɪnl] ⬥ adj - 1. [last] último(ma) - 2. [at end] final - 3. [definitive] definitivo(va). ⬥ n final f. ⬥ **finals** npl UNIV exámenes mpl finales.

finale [fɪ'nɑːlɪ] n final m.

finalize, -ise ['faɪnəlaɪz] vt ultimar.

finally ['faɪnəlɪ] adv - 1. [at last] por fin - 2. [lastly] finalmente, por último.

finance ⬥ n ['faɪnæns] (U) - 1. [money management] finanzas fpl - 2. [money] fondos mpl. ⬥ vt [faɪ'næns] financiar. ⬥ **finances** npl finanzas fpl.

financial [fɪ'nænʃl] adj financiero(ra).

find [faɪnd] ⬥ vt (pt & pp **found**) - 1. [gen] encontrar - 2. [realize - fact] darse cuenta de, descubrir - 3. LAW: **to be found guilty/not guilty (of)** ser declarado(da) culpable/inocente (de). ⬥ n hallazgo m, descubrimiento m. ⬥ **find out** ⬥ vi - 1. [become aware] enterarse - 2. [obtain information] informarse. ⬥ vt insep [truth] descubrir; [fact] averiguar. ⬥ vt sep [person] descubrir.

findings ['faɪndɪŋz] npl conclusiones fpl.

fine [faɪn] ⬥ adj - 1. [excellent] excelente - 2. [perfectly satisfactory]: **it's/that's fine** está bien; **how are you? – fine thanks** ¿qué tal? – muy bien - 3. [weather] bueno(na); **it will be fine tomorrow** mañana hará buen día - 4. [thin, smooth, delicate] fino(na) - 5. [minute - detail, distinction] sutil; [- adjustment, tuning] milimétrico(ca). ⬥ adv [well] bien; [very well] muy bien. ⬥ n multa f. ⬥ vt multar.

fine arts npl bellas artes fpl.

finery ['faɪnərɪ] n (U) galas fpl.

finesse [fɪ'nes] n finura f, delicadeza f.

fine-tune ['faɪntjuːn] vt poner a punto.

finger ['fɪŋgər] <> n dedo m. <> vt acariciar con los dedos.

fingernail ['fɪŋgəneɪl] n uña f (de las manos).

fingerprint ['fɪŋgəprɪnt] n huella f dactilar OR digital.

fingertip ['fɪŋgətɪp] n punta f del dedo.

finicky ['fɪnɪkɪ] adj pej [person] melindroso(sa); [task] delicado(da).

finish ['fɪnɪʃ] <> n - 1. [end] final m; [in race] meta f - 2. [surface texture] acabado m. <> vt: **to finish sthg/doing sthg** acabar OR terminar algo/de hacer algo. <> vi terminar. ◆ **finish off** vt sep [food, task] acabar OR terminar del todo. ◆ **finish up** vi acabar, terminar.

finishing line ['fɪnɪʃɪŋ-] n línea f de meta.

finishing school ['fɪnɪʃɪŋ-] n colegio privado donde se prepara a las alumnas de clase alta para entrar en sociedad.

finite ['faɪnaɪt] adj - 1. [limited] finito(ta) - 2. GRAM conjugado(da).

Finland ['fɪnlənd] n Finlandia f.

Finn [fɪn] n [person] finlandés m, -esa f.

Finnish ['fɪnɪʃ] <> adj finlandés(esa). <> n [language] finlandés m.

fir [fɜːr], **fir tree** n abeto m.

fire ['faɪər] <> n - 1. [gen] fuego m; **on fire** en llamas; **to catch fire** prender; **to open fire (on sb)** abrir fuego (contra alguien); **to set fire to** prender fuego a - 2. [blaze] incendio m - 3. UK [heater]: **(electric/gas) fire** estufa f (eléctrica/de gas). <> vt - 1. [shoot] disparar; **to fire a shot** disparar - 2. esp US [dismiss] despedir. <> vi: **to fire (on OR at)** disparar (contra).

fire alarm n alarma f antiincendios.

firearm ['faɪərɑːm] n arma f de fuego.

firebomb ['faɪəbɒm] n bomba f incendiaria.

fire brigade UK, **fire department** US n cuerpo m de bomberos.

fire door n puerta f cortafuegos.

fire engine n coche m de bomberos.

fire escape n escalera f de incendios.

fire exit n salida f de incendios.

fire extinguisher n extintor m.

fireguard ['faɪəgɑːd] n pantalla f (de chimenea).

firehouse ['faɪəhaʊs] n US cuartel m de bomberos.

firelighter ['faɪəlaɪtər] n pastilla f para encender el fuego.

fireman ['faɪəmən] (pl -men [-mən]) n bombero m.

fireplace ['faɪəpleɪs] n chimenea f.

fireproof ['faɪəpruːf] adj ignífugo(ga), resistente al fuego.

fireside ['faɪəsaɪd] n: **by the fireside** al calor de la chimenea.

fire station n parque m de bomberos.

firewall ['faɪəwɔːl] n COMPUT cortafuego m.

firewood ['faɪəwʊd] n leña f.

firework ['faɪəwɜːk] n fuego m de artificio. ◆ **fireworks** npl fuegos mpl artificiales.

firing ['faɪərɪŋ] n (U) MIL disparos mpl.

firing squad n pelotón m de ejecución OR fusilamiento.

firm [fɜːm] <> adj - 1. [gen] firme; **to stand firm** mantenerse firme - 2. FIN [steady] estable. <> n empresa f.

first [fɜːst] <> adj primero(ra); **the first day** el primer día; **for the first time** por primera vez; **first thing (in the morning)** a primera hora (de la mañana). <> adv - 1. [gen] primero; **to come first** quedar primero(ra); **first of all** en primer lugar - 2. [for the first time] por primera vez. <> n - 1. [person] primero m, -ra f - 2. [unprecedented event] acontecimiento m sin precedentes - 3. UK UNIV ≃ sobresaliente m. ◆ **at first** adv al principio. ◆ **at first hand** adv de primera mano.

first aid n (U) [treatment] primeros auxilios mpl; [technique] socorrismo m.

first-aid kit n botiquín m de primeros auxilios.

first-class <> adj - 1. [excellent] de primera - 2. [letter, ticket] de primera clase. <> adv [travel] en primera clase.

first floor n - 1. UK [above ground level] primer piso m - 2. US [at ground level] planta f baja.

firsthand [,fɜːst'hænd] <> adj de primera mano. <> adv directamente.

first lady n primera dama f.

firstly ['fɜːstlɪ] adv en primer lugar.

first name n nombre m de pila.

first-rate adj de primera.

fir tree ['fɜːtriː] = **fir**.

fish [fɪʃ] <> n (pl fish) - 1. [animal] pez m - 2. (U) [food] pescado m. <> vt pescar en. <> vi [for fish]: **to fish (for sthg)** pescar (algo).

fish and chips npl pescado m frito con patatas fritas.

fish and chip shop n UK tienda f de pescado frito con patatas fritas.

fishbowl ['fɪʃbəʊl] n pecera f.

fishcake ['fɪʃkeɪk] n pastelillo m de pescado.

fisherman ['fɪʃəmən] (pl -men [-mən]) n pescador m.

fish farm n piscifactoría f.

fish fingers UK, **fish sticks** US npl palitos mpl de pescado.

fishing ['fɪʃɪŋ] n pesca f; **to go fishing** ir de pesca.

fishing boat n barco m pesquero.

fishing line n sedal m.

fishing net n red f de pesca.

fishing rod n caña f de pesca.

fishmonger ['fɪʃˌmʌŋgəʳ] n esp UK pescadero m, -ra f; **fishmonger's (shop)** pescadería f.

fish sticks US = **fish fingers**.

fishy ['fɪʃɪ] adj - 1. [smell, taste] a pescado - 2. inf [suspicious] sospechoso(sa).

fist [fɪst] n puño m.

fit [fɪt] <> adj - 1. [suitable]: **to see** OR **think fit to do sthg** creer conveniente hacer algo; **do as you think fit** haz lo que te parezca conveniente - 2. [healthy] en forma; **to keep fit** mantenerse en forma. <> n - 1. [of clothes, shoes etc]: **it's a good fit** le/te etc sienta OR va bien - 2. [bout, seizure] ataque m; **he had a fit** lit & fig le dio un ataque; **in fits and starts** a trompicones. <> vt - 1. [be correct size for] sentar bien a, ir bien a - 2. [place]: **to fit sthg into** encajar algo en - 3. [provide]: **to fit sthg with** equipar algo con; **to have an alarm fitted** poner una alarma - 4. [be suitable for] corresponder a. <> vi - 1. [clothes, shoes] estar bien de talla - 2. [part - when assembling etc]: **this bit fits in here** esta pieza encaja aquí - 3. [have enough room] caber. ⬤ **fit in** <> vt sep [accommodate] hacer un hueco a. <> vi - 1. [subj: person]: **to fit in (with)** adaptarse (a) - 2. [be compatible]: **it doesn't fit in with our plans** no encaja con nuestros planes.

fitful ['fɪtfʊl] adj irregular, intermitente.

fitment ['fɪtmənt] n accesorio m.

fitness ['fɪtnɪs] (U) n - 1. [health] buen estado m físico - 2. [suitability]: **fitness (for)** idoneidad f (para).

fitted carpet ['fɪtəd-] n moqueta f.

fitted kitchen ['fɪtəd-] n UK cocina f amueblada a medida.

fitter ['fɪtəʳ] n [mechanic] (mecánico m) ajustador m.

fitting ['fɪtɪŋ] <> adj fml adecuado(da). <> n - 1. [part] accesorio m - 2. [for clothing] prueba f. ⬤ **fittings** npl accesorios mpl.

fitting room n probador m.

five [faɪv] num cinco; see also **six**.

fiver ['faɪvəʳ] n UK inf (billete de) cinco libras.

fix [fɪks] <> vt - 1. [attach, decide on] fijar; **to fix sthg (to)** fijar algo (a) - 2. [repair] arreglar, refaccionar Amér - 3. inf [rig] amañar - 4. esp US [prepare - food, drink] preparar. <> n - 1. inf [difficult situation]: **to be in a fix** estar en un aprieto - 2. drug sl dosis f inv. ⬤ **fix up** vt sep - 1. [provide]: **to fix sb up with** proveer a alguien de - 2. [arrange] organizar, preparar.

fixation [fɪk'seɪʃn] n: **fixation (on** OR **about)** fijación f (con).

fixed [fɪkst] adj fijo(ja).

fixture ['fɪkstʃəʳ] n - 1. [furniture] instalación f fija. 2. [permanent feature] rasgo m característico 3. [sports event] encuentro m.

fizz [fɪz] vi burbujear.

fizzle ['fɪzl] ⬤ **fizzle out** vi [firework, fire] apagarse; [enthusiasm] disiparse.

fizzy ['fɪzɪ] adj [gen] gaseoso(sa); [water, soft drink] con gas.

flabbergasted ['flæbəgɑːstɪd] adj pasmado(da).

flabby ['flæbɪ] adj fofo(fa).

flag [flæg] <> n [banner] bandera f. <> vi decaer. ⬤ **flag down** vt sep [taxi] parar.

flagpole ['flægpəʊl] n asta f (de bandera).

flagrant ['fleɪgrənt] adj flagrante.

flagstone ['flægstəʊn] n losa f.

flair [fleəʳ] n - 1. [ability] don m; **to have a flair for sthg** tener un don para algo - 2. [style] estilo m.

flak [flæk] n (U) - 1. [gunfire] fuego m antiaéreo - 2. inf [criticism] críticas fpl.

flake [fleɪk] <> n [of skin] escama f; [of snow] copo m; [of paint] desconchón m. <> vi [skin] descamarse; [paint, plaster] desconcharse.

flamboyant [flæm'bɔɪənt] adj - 1. [person, behaviour] extravagante - 2. [clothes, design] vistoso(sa).

flame [fleɪm] n llama f; **in flames** en llamas.

flamingo [flə'mɪŋgəʊ] (pl -s OR -es) n flamenco m.

flammable ['flæməbl] adj inflamable.

flan [flæn] n tarta f (de fruta etc).

flank [flæŋk] <> n - 1. [of animal] costado m, ijada f - 2. [of army] flanco m. <> vt: **to be flanked by** estar flanqueado(da) por.

flannel ['flænl] n - 1. [fabric] franela f - 2. UK [facecloth] toallita f (de baño para lavarse).

flap [flæp] <> n [of pocket, book, envelope] solapa f; [of skin] colgajo m. <> vt agitar; [wings] batir. <> vi [flag, skirt] ondear; [wings] aletear.

flapjack ['flæpdʒæk] n - 1. UK [biscuit] galleta f de avena - 2. US [pancake] torta f, crepe f.

flare [fleəʳ] <> n [signal] bengala f. <> vi - 1. [burn brightly]: **to flare (up)** llamear - 2. [intensify]: **to flare (up)** estallar. ⬤ **flares** npl UK pantalones mpl de campana.

flash [flæʃ] <> n - 1. [of light] destello m; **a flash of lightning** un relámpago, un refucilo R Plata - 2. PHOT flash m - 3. [of genius, inspiration etc] momento m; [of anger] acceso m; **in a flash** en un instante. <> vt - 1. [shine in specified direction] dirigir; [switch on briefly] encender intermitentemente - 2. [a smile, look] lanzar - 3. [show - picture, image] mostrar; [- information, news] emitir. <> vi - 1. [light] destellar - 2. [eyes] brillar - 3. [rush]: **to flash by** OR **past** pasar como un rayo.

flashback ['flæʃbæk] n flashback m.

flashbulb ['flæʃbʌlb] n flash m.

flashgun ['flæʃgʌn] n disparador m de flash.

flashlight ['flæʃlaɪt] n US [torch] linterna f.

flashy ['flæʃɪ] adj inf chulo(la); pej ostentoso(sa).

flask [flɑːsk] n - 1. [thermos flask] termo® m - 2. [used in chemistry] matraz m - 3. [hip flask] petaca f.

flat [flæt] <> adj - 1. [surface, ground] llano(na); [feet] plano(na) - 2. [shoes] bajo(ja), de piso Méx - 3. [tyre] desinflado(da), ponchado(da) Méx - 4. [refusal, denial] rotundo(da) - 5. [business, trade] flojo(ja); [voice, tone] monótono(na); [colour] soso(sa); [performance, writing] desangelado(da) - 6. MUS [lower than correct note] desafinado(da); [lower than stated note] bemol (inv) - 7. [fare, price] único(ca) - 8. [beer, lemonade] muerto(ta) - 9. [battery] descargado(da). <> adv - 1. [level]: **to lie flat** estar totalmente extendido(da); **to fall flat on one's face** [person] caerse de bruces - 2. [of time]: **in five minutes flat** en cinco minutos justos. <> n - 1. UK [apartment] piso m, apartamento m, departamento m Amér - 2. US [tyre] pinchazo m - 3. MUS bemol m. ◆ **flat out** adv a toda velocidad.

flatly ['flætlɪ] adv - 1. [refuse, deny] de plano, rotundamente - 2. [speak, perform] monótonamente.

flatmate ['flætmeɪt] n UK compañero m, -ra f de piso.

flat rate n tarifa f plana.

flatten ['flætn] vt - 1. [surface, paper, bumps] allanar, aplanar; [paper] alisar - 2. [building, city] arrasar. ◆ **flatten out** <> vi allanarse, nivelarse. <> vt sep allanar.

flatter ['flætər] vt - 1. [subj: person, report] adular, halagar - 2. [subj: clothes, colour, photograph] favorecer.

flattering ['flætərɪŋ] adj - 1. [remark, interest] halagador(ra) - 2. [clothes, colour, photograph] favorecedor(ra).

flattery ['flætərɪ] n (U) halagos mpl.

flaunt [flɔːnt] vt ostentar, hacer gala de.

flavour UK, **flavor** US ['fleɪvər] <> n - 1. [taste] sabor m - 2. fig [atmosphere] aire m, sabor m. <> vt condimentar.

flavouring UK, **flavoring** US ['fleɪvərɪŋ] n (U) condimento m; **artificial flavouring** aromatizante m artificial.

flaw [flɔː] n [fault] desperfecto m.

flawless ['flɔːlɪs] adj impecable.

flax [flæks] n lino m.

flea [fliː] n pulga f; **to send sb away with a flea in his/her ear** echar una buena reprimenda a alguien.

flea market n rastro m.

fleck [flek] n mota f.

fled [fled] pt & pp ▷ **flee**.

flee [fliː] (pt & pp fled) <> vt huir de. <> vi: **to flee (from/to)** huir (de/a).

fleece [fliːs] <> n - 1. vellón m - 2. [garment] forro m polar. <> vt inf [cheat] desplumar.

fleet [fliːt] n - 1. [of ships] flota f - 2. [of cars, buses] parque m (móvil).

fleeting ['fliːtɪŋ] adj fugaz.

Fleet Street n calle londinense que antiguamente era el centro de la prensa británica y cuyo nombre todavía se utiliza para referirse a ésta.

Flemish ['flemɪʃ] <> adj flamenco(ca). <> n [language] flamenco m. <> npl: **the Flemish** los flamencos.

flesh [fleʃ] n - 1. [of body] carne f; **in the flesh** en persona - 2. [of fruit, vegetable] pulpa f.

flesh wound n herida f superficial.

flew [fluː] pt ▷ **fly**.

flex [fleks] <> n ELEC cable m, cordón m. <> vt flexionar.

flexible ['fleksəbl] adj flexible.

flexitime ['fleksɪtaɪm] n (U) horario m flexible.

flick [flɪk] <> n - 1. [of whip, towel] golpe m rápido - 2. [with finger] toba f. <> vt [switch] apretar, pulsar. ◆ **flick through** vt insep hojear.

flicker ['flɪkər] vi [eyes, flame] parpadear.

flick knife n UK navaja f automática.

flight [flaɪt] n - 1. [gen] vuelo m; **flight of fancy** OR **of the imagination** vuelo de la imaginación - 2. [of steps, stairs] tramo m - 3. [of birds] bandada f - 4. [escape] huida f, fuga f.

flight attendant n auxiliar mf de vuelo.

flight crew n tripulación f de vuelo.

flight deck n - 1. [of plane] cabina f del piloto - 2. [of aircraft carrier] cubierta f de vuelo.

flight recorder n caja f negra.

flimsy ['flɪmzɪ] adj - 1. [dress, material] muy ligero(ra) - 2. [structure] débil, poco sólido(da) - 3. [excuse] flojo(ja).

flinch [flɪntʃ] vi - 1. [shudder] estremecerse; **without flinching** sin pestañear - 2. [be reluctant]: **to flinch (from sthg/from doing sthg)** retroceder (ante algo/ante hacer algo); **without flinching** sin inmutarse.

fling [flɪŋ] <> n [affair] aventura f (amorosa). <> vt (pt & pp flung) arrojar.

flint [flɪnt] n - 1. [rock] sílex m - 2. [in lighter] piedra f.

flip [flɪp] vt - 1. [turn] dar la vuelta a; **to flip sthg open** abrir algo de golpe - 2. [switch] pulsar. ◆ **flip through** vt insep hojear.

flip-flop n [shoe] chancleta f.

flippant ['flɪpənt] adj frívolo(la).

flipper ['flɪpər] n aleta f.

flirt [flɜːt] ◇ n coqueto m, ta f, ◇ vi [with person]: **to flirt (with)** flirtear OR coquetear (con).

flirtatious [flɜː'teɪʃəs] adj coqueto(ta).

flit [flɪt] vi [bird] revolotear.

float [fləʊt] ◇ n - 1. [for fishing line] corcho m - 2. [for swimming] flotador m - 3. [in procession] carroza f - 4. [supply of change] cambio m. ◇ vt [on water] hacer flotar. ◇ vi flotar.

flock [flɒk] n - 1. [of sheep] rebaño m; [of birds] bandada f - 2. fig [of people] multitud f, tropel m.

flog [flɒg] vt - 1. [whip] azotar - 2. UK inf [sell] vender.

flood [flʌd] n - 1. [of water] inundación f - 2. [of letters, people] aluvión m, riada f.

flooding ['flʌdɪŋ] n (U) inundación f.

floodlight ['flʌdlaɪt] n foco m.

floor [flɔːr] ◇ n - 1. [of room, forest] suelo m; [of club, disco] pista f - 2. [of sea, valley] fondo m - 3. [of building] piso m, planta f. ◇ vt - 1. [knock down] derribar - 2. [baffle] desconcertar, dejar perplejo(ja).

floorboard ['flɔːbɔːd] n tabla f (del suelo).

floor show n espectáculo m de cabaré.

flop [flɒp] inf n [failure] fracaso m.

floppy ['flɒpɪ] adj caído(da), flojo(ja).

floppy (disk) n disco m flexible.

flora ['flɔːrə] n flora f.

florid ['flɒrɪd] adj - 1. [extravagant] florido(da) - 2. [red] rojizo(za).

florist ['flɒrɪst] n florista mf; **florist's (shop)** floristería f.

flotsam ['flɒtsəm] n (U): **flotsam and jetsam** restos mpl de un naufragio; fig desechos mpl de la humanidad.

flounce [flaʊns] ◇ n SEW volante m. ◇ vi: **to flounce out** salir airadamente.

flounder ['flaʊndər] vi - 1. [move with difficulty] debatirse - 2. [when speaking] titubear.

flour ['flaʊər] n harina f.

flourish ['flʌrɪʃ] ◇ vi florecer. ◇ vt agitar. ◇ n: **to do sthg with a flourish** hacer algo exageradamente.

flout [flaʊt] vt desobedecer.

flow [fləʊ] ◇ n flujo m; **traffic flow** circulación f. ◇ vi - 1. [gen] fluir, correr - 2. [hair, clothes] ondear.

flow chart, flow diagram n organigrama m, cuadro m sinóptico.

flower ['flaʊər] ◇ n lit & fig flor f. ◇ vi lit & fig florecer.

flowerbed ['flaʊəbed] n arriate m.

flowerpot ['flaʊəpɒt] n tiesto m.

flowery ['flaʊərɪ] adj - 1. [patterned] de flores, floreado(da) - 2. pej [elaborate] florido(da).

flown [fləʊn] pp ▷ **fly**.

flu [fluː] n gripe f.

fluctuate ['flʌktʃʊeɪt] vi fluctuar.

fluency ['fluːənsɪ] n soltura f, fluidez f.

fluent ['fluːənt] adj - 1. [in foreign language]: **to be fluent in French, to speak fluent French** dominar el francés - 2. [style] fluido(da).

fluff [flʌf] n pelusa f.

fluffy ['flʌfɪ] adj [jumper] de pelusa; [toy] de peluche.

fluid ['fluːɪd] ◇ n fluido m, líquido m. ◇ adj - 1. [flowing] fluido(da) - 2. [situation, opinion] incierto(ta).

fluid ounce n onza f líquida (unos 30 ml).

fluke [fluːk] n inf chiripa f; **by a fluke** por OR de chiripa.

flummox ['flʌməks] vt UK inf desconcertar.

flung [flʌŋ] pt & pp ▷ **fling**.

flunk [flʌŋk] vt & vi esp US inf catear. ◆ **flunk out** vi US inf ser expulsado(da).

fluorescent [fluə'resnt] adj fluorescente.

fluoride ['fluəraɪd] n fluoruro m.

flurry ['flʌrɪ] n - 1. [shower] ráfaga f - 2. [burst] torbellino m.

flush [flʌʃ] ◇ adj [level]: **flush with** nivelado(da) con. ◇ n - 1. [lavatory mechanism] cadena f - 2. [blush] rubor m - 3. [sudden feeling] arrebato m. ◇ vt [force out of hiding]: **to flush sb out** hacer salir a alguien. ◇ vi [blush] ruborizarse.

flushed [flʌʃt] adj - 1. [red-faced] encendido(da) - 2. [excited]: **flushed (with)** enardecido(da) (por).

flustered ['flʌstəd] adj aturullado(da).

flute [fluːt] n MUS flauta f.

flutter ['flʌtər] ◇ n - 1. [of wings] aleteo m; [of eyelashes] pestañeo m - 2. inf [of excitement] arranque m. ◇ vi - 1. [bird] aletear - 2. [flag, dress] ondear.

flux [flʌks] n [change]: **to be in a state of flux** cambiar constantemente.

fly [flaɪ] ◇ n - 1. [insect] mosca f - 2. [of trousers] bragueta f. ◇ vt (pt flew, pp flown) - 1. [plane] pilotar; [kite, model aircraft] hacer volar - 2. [passengers, supplies] transportar en avión - 3. [flag] ondear. ◇ vi (pt flew, pp flown) - 1. [bird, plane] volar; **to send sthg/ sb flying, to knock sthg/sb flying** inf mandar algo/a alguien por los aires - 2. [travel by plane] ir en avión - 3. [pilot a plane] pilotar - 4. [flag] ondear. ◆ **fly away** vi irse volando.

fly-fishing n pesca f con mosca.

flying ['flaɪɪŋ] ⬦ adj [able to fly] volador(ra), volante. ⬦ n: **I hate/love flying** odio/me encanta ir en avión; **her hobby is flying** es aficionada a la aviación.

flying colours npl: **to pass (sthg) with flying colours** salir airoso(sa) (de algo).

flying picket n piquete m volante.

flying saucer n platillo m volante.

flying squad n brigada f volante.

flying start n: **to get off to a flying start** empezar con muy buen pie.

flying visit n visita f relámpago.

flyover ['flaɪ,əʊvə'] n UK paso m elevado.

flysheet ['flaɪʃiːt] n doble techo m.

fly spray n matamoscas m inv (en aerosol).

FM (abbr of frequency modulation) FM f.

foal [fəʊl] n potro m.

foam [fəʊm] ⬦ n - 1. [bubbles] espuma f - 2.: **foam (rubber)** gomaespuma f. ⬦ vi hacer espuma.

fob [fɒb] ➡ **fob off** vt sep: **to fob sb off (with sthg)** quitarse a alguien de encima (con algo); **to fob sthg off on sb** endosar a alguien algo.

focal point ['fəʊkl-] n punto m focal OR central.

focus ['fəʊkəs] ⬦ n (pl -cuses OR -ci [-saɪ]) [gen] foco m; **in focus** enfocado; **out of focus** desenfocado. ⬦ vt - 1. [eyes, lens, rays] enfocar - 2. [attention] fijar, centrar. ⬦ vi - 1. [eyes, lens]: **to focus (on sthg)** enfocar (algo) - 2. [attention]: **to focus on sthg** centrarse en algo.

fodder ['fɒdə'] n forraje m.

foe [fəʊ] n liter enemigo m, -ga f.

foetus, fetus ['fiːtəs] n feto m.

fog [fɒg] n niebla f.

foggy ['fɒgɪ] adj [day] de niebla; **it's foggy** hay niebla.

foghorn ['fɒghɔːn] n sirena f (de niebla).

fog lamp n faro m antiniebla.

foible ['fɔɪbl] n manía f.

foil [fɔɪl] ⬦ n (U) [metal sheet] papel m de aluminio OR de plata. ⬦ vt frustrar.

fold [fəʊld] ⬦ vt [sheet, blanket] doblar; [chair, pram] plegar; **to fold one's arms** cruzar los brazos. ⬦ vi - 1. [table, chair etc] plegarse - 2. inf [collapse] venirse abajo. ⬦ n - 1. [in material, paper] pliegue m - 2. [for animals] redil m. ➡ **fold up** ⬦ vt sep - 1. [bend] doblar - 2. [close up] plegar. ⬦ vi - 1. [bend] doblarse - 2. [close up] plegarse - 3. [collapse] venirse abajo.

folder ['fəʊldə'] n [gen & COMPUT] carpeta f.

folding ['fəʊldɪŋ] adj plegable; [ladder] de tijera.

foliage ['fəʊlɪɪdʒ] n follaje m.

folk [fəʊk] ⬦ adj popular. ⬦ npl [people] gente f. ⬦ n = **folk music**. ➡ **folks** npl inf [parents] padres mpl.

folklore ['fəʊklɔːr] n folclore m.

folk music, folk n - 1. [traditional] música f folclórica OR popular - 2. [contemporary] música f folk.

folk song n - 1. [traditional] canción f popular - 2. [contemporary] canción f folk.

follow ['fɒləʊ] ⬦ vt - 1. [gen] seguir - 2. [understand] comprender. ⬦ vi - 1. [gen] seguir - 2. [be logical] ser lógico(ca); **it follows that** se deduce que - 3. [understand] comprender. ➡ **follow up** vt sep - 1. [monitor] hacer un seguimiento de - 2. [continue]: **to follow sthg up with** proseguir algo con.

follower ['fɒləʊə'] n partidario m, -ria f.

following ['fɒləʊɪŋ] ⬦ adj siguiente. ⬦ n partidarios mpl; [of team] afición f. ⬦ prep tras.

folly ['fɒlɪ] n (U) [foolishness] locura f.

fond [fɒnd] adj - 1. [affectionate] afectuoso(sa), cariñoso(sa) - 2. [having a liking]: **to be fond of sb** tener cariño a alguien; **to be fond of sthg/of doing sthg** ser aficionado(da) a algo/a hacer algo.

fondle ['fɒndl] vt acariciar.

font [fɒnt] n - 1. [in church] pila f bautismal - 2. COMPUT fuente f.

food [fuːd] n comida f.

food mixer n batidora f eléctrica.

food poisoning [-'pɔɪznɪŋ] n intoxicación f alimenticia.

food processor [-,prəʊsesə'] n robot m de cocina.

foodstuffs ['fuːdstʌfs] npl comestibles mpl.

fool [fuːl] ⬦ n - 1. [idiot] idiota mf, imbécil mf; **to act OR play the fool** hacer el tonto - 2. UK [dessert] mousse de fruta con nata. ⬦ vt [deceive] engañar; **to fool sb into doing sthg** embaucar a alguien para que haga algo. ⬦ vi bromear. ➡ **fool about, fool around** vi - 1. [behave foolishly]: **to fool about (with sthg)** hacer el tonto (con algo) - 2. [be unfaithful]: **to fool around (with sb)** tontear (con alguien).

foolhardy ['fuːl,hɑːdɪ] adj temerario(ria).

foolish ['fuːlɪʃ] adj tonto(ta).

foolproof ['fuːlpruːf] adj infalible.

foot [fʊt] n - 1. [gen] pie m; [of bird, animal] pata f; **to be on one's feet** estar de pie; **to get to one's feet** levantarse; **on foot** a pie, andando; **to put one's foot in it** meter la pata; **to put one's feet up** descansar - 2. (pl feet) [unit of measurement] = 30,48 cm pie m.

footage ['fʊtɪdʒ] n (U) secuencias fpl.

football ['fʊtbɔːl] n - **1.** [game - soccer] fútbol m; [- American football] fútbol m americano - **2.** [ball] balón m.

footballer ['fʊtbɔːləʳ], **football player** n UK futbolista mf.

football ground n UK estadio m de fútbol.

football pitch n UK campo m de fútbol.

football player = **footballer**.

footbrake ['fʊtbreɪk] n freno m de pedal.

footbridge ['fʊtbrɪdʒ] n puente m peatonal, pasarela f.

foothills ['fʊthɪlz] npl estribaciones fpl.

foothold ['fʊthəʊld] n punto m de apoyo para el pie; **to get a foothold** [on mountain, rockface] encontrar un punto de apoyo; [in organization, company] afianzarse.

footing ['fʊtɪŋ] n - **1.** [foothold] equilibrio m; **to lose one's footing** perder el equilibrio - **2.** [basis] base f; **on an equal footing (with)** en pie de igualdad (con).

footlights ['fʊtlaɪts] npl candilejas fpl.

footnote ['fʊtnəʊt] n nota f a pie de página.

footpath ['fʊtpɑːθ, pl -pɑːðz] n senda f.

footprint ['fʊtprɪnt] n huella f, pisada f.

footstep ['fʊtstep] n - **1.** [sound] paso m - **2.** [footprint] pisada f; **to follow in sb's footsteps** seguir los pasos de alguien.

footwear ['fʊtweəʳ] n calzado m.

for [fɔːʳ] <> prep - **1.** [indicating intention, destination, purpose] para; **this is for you** esto es para ti; **I'm going for the paper** voy (a) por el periódico; **the plane for Paris** el avión para OR de París; **it's time for bed** es hora de irse a la cama; **to go for a walk** ir a dar un paseo; **what's it for?** ¿para qué es OR sirve? - **2.** [representing, on behalf of] por; **the MP for Barnsley** el diputado por Barnsley; **let me do it for you** deja que lo haga por ti; **he plays for England** juega en la selección inglesa; **to work for sb** trabajar para - **3.** [because of] por; **a prize for bravery** un premio a la valentía; **to jump for joy** dar saltos de alegría; **for fear of failing** por miedo al fracaso - **4.** [with regard to] para; **to be ready for sthg** estar listo(ta) para algo; **it's not for me to say** no me toca a mí decidir; **he looks young for his age** parece más joven de lo que es; **to feel sorry/glad for sb** sentirlo/alegrarse por alguien - **5.** [indicating amount of time, space] para; **there's no time/room for it** no hay tiempo/sitio para eso - **6.** [indicating period of time - during] durante; [- by, in time for] para; **she cried for two hours** estuvo llorando durante dos horas; **I've lived here for three years** llevo tres años viviendo aquí, he vivido aquí (durante) tres años; **I've worked here for years** trabajo aquí desde hace años; **I'll do it for tomorrow** lo tendré hecho para mañana - **7.** [indicating distance] en; **there were roadworks for 50 miles** había obras en 50 millas; **we walked for miles** andamos millas y millas - **8.** [indicating particular occasion] para; **I got it for my birthday** me lo regalaron para OR por mi cumpleaños; **for the first time** por vez primera - **9.** [indicating amount of money, price] por; **I bought/sold it for £10** lo compré/vendí por 10 libras; **they're 50p for ten** son 50 peniques los diez - **10.** [in favour of, in support of] a favor de; **to vote for sthg/sb** votar por algo/a alguien - **11.** [in ratios] por - **12.** [indicating meaning]: **P for Peter** P de Pedro; **what's the Greek for 'mother'?** ¿cómo se dice 'madre' en griego? <> conj fml [as, since] ya que. ⇒ **for all** <> prep - **1.** [in spite of] a pesar de; **for all your moaning** a pesar de lo mucho que te quejas - **2.** [considering how little] para; **for all the good it has done me** para lo que me ha servido. <> conj: **for all I care, she could be dead** por mí, como si se muere; **for all I know** por lo que yo sé, que yo sepa.

forage ['fɒrɪdʒ] vi [search]: **to forage (for sthg)** buscar (algo).

foray ['fɒreɪ] n lit & fig: **foray (into)** incursión f (en).

forbad [fə'bæd], **forbade** [fə'beɪd] pt ▷ **forbid**.

forbid [fə'bɪd] (pt -bade OR -bad, pp forbid OR -bidden) vt: **to forbid sb (to do sthg)** prohibir a alguien (hacer algo).

forbidden [fə'bɪdn] adj prohibido(da).

forbidding [fə'bɪdɪŋ] adj [building, landscape] inhóspito(ta); [person, expression] severo(ra), austero(ra).

force [fɔːs] <> n fuerza f; **sales force** personal m de ventas; **security forces** fuerzas fpl de seguridad; **by force** a la fuerza; **to be in/come into force** estar/entrar en vigor; **in force** [in large numbers] en masa, en gran número. <> vt forzar; **to force one's way through/into** abrirse paso a la fuerza a través de/para entrar en. ⇒ **forces** npl: **the forces** las fuerzas armadas; **to join forces (with)** unirse (con).

force-feed vt alimentar a la fuerza.

forceful ['fɔːsfʊl] adj [person, impression] fuerte; [support, recommendation] enérgico(ca); [speech, idea, argument] contundente.

forceps ['fɔːseps] npl fórceps m inv.

forcibly ['fɔːsəblɪ] adv - **1.** [using physical force] por la fuerza - **2.** [remind] vivamente; [express, argue] convincentemente.

ford [fɔːd] n vado m.

fore [fɔːʳ] n: **to come to the fore** emerger, empezar a destacar.

forearm ['fɔːrɑːm] n antebrazo m.

foreboding [fɔː'bəʊdɪŋ] n - **1.** [presentiment] presagio m - **2.** [apprehension] desasosiego m.

forecast ['fɔːkɑːst] ⟷ n [prediction] predicción f, previsión f; [of weather] pronóstico m. ⟷ vt (pt & pp **forecast** OR **-ed**) [predict] predecir; [weather] pronosticar.

foreclose [fɔː'kləuz] ⟷ vi: **to foreclose on sb** privar a alguien del derecho a redimir su hipoteca. ⟷ vt ejecutar.

forecourt ['fɔːkɔːt] n patio m.

forefinger ['fɔː,fɪŋgəʳ] n (dedo m) índice m.

forefront ['fɔːfrʌnt] n: **in** OR **at the forefront of** en OR a la vanguardia de.

forego [fɔː'gəu] = **forgo**.

foregone conclusion ['fɔːgɒn-] n: **it's a foregone conclusion** es un resultado conocido de antemano.

foreground ['fɔːgraund] n primer plano m.

forehand ['fɔːhænd] n [stroke] golpe m natural, drive m.

forehead ['fɔːhed] n frente f.

foreign ['fɒrən] adj - 1. [from abroad] extranjero(ra) - 2. [external - policy, trade] exterior; [- correspondent, holiday] en el extranjero - 3. [unwanted, harmful] extraño(ña) - 4. [alien, untypical]: **foreign (to sb/sthg)** ajeno(na) (a alguien/algo).

foreign affairs npl asuntos mpl exteriores.

foreign currency n (U) divisa f.

foreigner ['fɒrənəʳ] n extranjero m, -ra f.

foreign minister n ministro m, -tra f de asuntos exteriores.

Foreign Office n UK: **the Foreign Office** el Ministerio de Asuntos Exteriores británico.

Foreign Secretary n UK Ministro m, -tra f de Asuntos Exteriores.

foreleg ['fɔːleg] n pata f delantera.

foreman ['fɔːmən] (pl **-men** [-mən]) n - 1. [of workers] encargado m - 2. [of jury] presidente m.

foremost ['fɔːməust] ⟷ adj primero(ra). ⟷ adv: **first and foremost** ante todo, por encima de todo.

forensic [fə'rensɪk] adj forense.

forerunner ['fɔː,rʌnəʳ] n [precursor] precursor m, -ra f.

foresee [fɔː'siː] (pt **-saw** [-'sɔː], pp **-seen**) vt prever.

foreseeable [fɔː'siːəbl] adj previsible; **for** OR **in the foreseeable future** en un futuro próximo.

foreseen [fɔː'siːn] pp ⊳ **foresee**.

foreshadow [fɔː'ʃædəu] vt presagiar.

foresight ['fɔːsaɪt] n (U) previsión f.

forest ['fɒrɪst] n bosque m.

forestall [fɔː'stɔːl] vt anticiparse a.

forestry ['fɒrɪstrɪ] n silvicultura f.

foretaste ['fɔːteɪst] n anticipo m.

foretell [fɔː'tel] (pt & pp **-told**) vt predecir.

forever [fə'revəʳ] adv - 1. [eternally] para siempre - 2. inf [incessantly] siempre, continuamente.

forewarn [fɔː'wɔːn] vt prevenir.

foreword ['fɔːwɜːd] n prefacio m.

forfeit ['fɔːfɪt] ⟷ n [penalty] precio m; [in game] prenda f. ⟷ vt renunciar a, perder.

forgave [fə'geɪv] pt ⊳ **forgive**.

forge [fɔːdʒ] ⟷ n fragua f. ⟷ vt - 1. [gen] fraguar - 2. [falsify] falsificar. ⬦ **forge ahead** vi hacer grandes progresos.

forger ['fɔːdʒəʳ] n falsificador m, -ra f.

forgery ['fɔːdʒərɪ] n falsificación f.

forget [fə'get] (pt **-got**, pp **-gotten**) ⟷ vt: **to forget (to do sthg)** olvidar (hacer algo). ⟷ vi: **to forget (about sthg)** olvidarse (de algo).

forgetful [fə'getful] adj olvidadizo(za).

forget-me-not n nomeolvides m inv.

forgive [fə'gɪv] (pt **-gave**, pp **-given**) vt: **to forgive sb (for sthg/for doing sthg)** perdonar a alguien (algo/por haber hecho algo).

forgiveness [fə'gɪvnɪs] n perdón m.

forgo, forego [fɔː'gəu] (pt **-went**, pp **-gone** [-'gɒn]) vt sacrificar, renunciar a.

forgot [fə'gɒt] pt ⊳ **forget**.

forgotten [fə'gɒtn] pp ⊳ **forget**.

fork [fɔːk] ⟷ n - 1. [for food] tenedor m - 2. [for gardening] horca f - 3. [in road etc] bifurcación f. ⟷ vi bifurcarse. ⬦ **fork out** inf vi: **to fork out for sthg** soltar pelas para algo.

forklift truck ['fɔːklɪft-] n carretilla f elevadora.

forlorn [fə'lɔːn] adj - 1. [person, expression] consternado(da) - 2. [place, landscape] desolado(da) - 3. [hope, attempt] desesperado(da).

form [fɔːm] ⟷ n - 1. [shape, type] forma f; **in the form of** en forma de - 2. [fitness]: **on form** UK, **in form** US en forma; **off form** en baja forma - 3. [document] impreso m, formulario m - 4. [figure - of person] figura f - 5. UK [class] clase f. ⟷ vt formar; [plan] concebir; [impression, idea] formarse. ⟷ vi formarse.

formal ['fɔːml] adj - 1. [gen] formal; [education] convencional - 2. [clothes, wedding, party] de etiqueta.

formality [fɔː'mælɪtɪ] n formalidad f.

format ['fɔːmæt] ⟷ n [gen & COMPUT] formato m; [of meeting] plan m. ⟷ vt COMPUT formatear.

formation [fɔː'meɪʃn] n formación f.

formative ['fɔːmətɪv] adj formativo(va).

former ['fɔːməʳ] ⟷ adj - 1. [previous] antiguo(gua); **in former times** antiguamente - 2. [first of two] primero(ra). ⟷ n: **the former** el primero(la primera)/los primeros(las primeras).

formerly ['fɔ:məlɪ] adv antiguamente.

formidable ['fɔ:mɪdəbl] adj - **1.** [frightening] imponente, temible - **2.** [impressive] formidable.

formula ['fɔ:mjʊlə] (pl -as OR -ae [-i:]) n - **1.** [gen] fórmula f - **2.** [baby milk] leche f maternizada.

formulate ['fɔ:mjʊleɪt] vt formular.

forsake [fə'seɪk] (pt forsook, pp forsaken) vt liter abandonar.

forsaken [fə'seɪkn] adj abandonado(da).

forsook [fə'sʊk] pt ▷ **forsake**.

fort [fɔ:t] n fuerte m, fortaleza f; **to hold the fort (for sb)** quedarse al cargo (en lugar de alguien).

forte ['fɔ:tɪ] n fuerte m.

forth [fɔ:θ] adv liter - **1.** [outwards, onwards] hacia adelante; **to go forth** partir - **2.** [into future]: **from that day forth** desde aquel día en adelante.

forthcoming [fɔ:θ'kʌmɪŋ] adj - **1.** [election, events] próximo(ma); [book] de próxima aparición - **2.** [person] abierto(ta).

forthright ['fɔ:θraɪt] adj [person, manner, opinions] directo(ta), franco(ca); [opposition] rotundo(da).

forthwith [,fɔ:θ'wɪθ] adv fml inmediatamente.

fortified wine ['fɔ:tɪfaɪd-] n vino m licoroso.

fortify ['fɔ:tɪfaɪ] vt - **1.** MIL fortificar - **2.** [person, resolve] fortalecer.

fortnight ['fɔ:tnaɪt] n quincena f; **in a fortnight** en quince días.

fortnightly ['fɔ:t,naɪtlɪ] ◇ adj quincenal. ◇ adv quincenalmente.

fortress ['fɔ:trɪs] n fortaleza f.

fortunate ['fɔ:tʃnət] adj afortunado(da).

fortunately ['fɔ:tʃnətlɪ] adv afortunadamente.

fortune ['fɔ:tʃu:n] n - **1.** [money, luck] fortuna f - **2.** [future]: **to tell sb's fortune** decir a alguien la buenaventura.

fortune-teller [-,telə'] n adivino m, -na f.

forty ['fɔ:tɪ] num cuarenta; see also **sixty**.

forum ['fɔ:rəm] (pl -s) n lit & fig foro m.

forward ['fɔ:wəd] ◇ adj - **1.** [towards front - movement] hacia adelante; [near front - position etc] delantero(ra) - **2.** [towards future]: **forward planning** planificación f (de futuro) - **3.** [advanced]: **we're no further forward** no hemos adelantado (nada) - **4.** [impudent] atrevido(da). ◇ adv [ahead] hacia adelante; **to go OR move forward** avanzar. ◇ n SPORT delantero m, -ra f. ◇ vt [letter, e-mail] remitir; **'please forward'** 'remítase al destinatario'.

forwarding address ['fɔ:wədɪŋ-] n nueva dirección f (para reenvío de correo).

forwards ['fɔ:wədz] = **forward**.

forward slash n TYPO barra f inclinada.

forwent [fɔ:'went] pt ▷ **forgo**.

fossil ['fɒsl] n fósil m.

foster ['fɒstə'] vt - **1.** [child] acoger - **2.** [idea, arts, relations] promover.

foster child n menor mf en régimen de acogida.

foster parents npl familia f de acogida.

fought [fɔ:t] pt & pp ▷ **fight**.

foul [faʊl] ◇ adj - **1.** [unclean - smell] fétido(da); [- taste] asqueroso(sa); [- water, language] sucio(cia) - **2.** [very unpleasant] horrible; **to fall foul of sb** ponerse a mal con alguien. ◇ n falta f. ◇ vt - **1.** [make dirty] ensuciar - **2.** SPORT cometer una falta contra.

found [faʊnd] ◇ pt & pp ▷ **find**. ◇ vt: **to found sthg (on)** fundar algo (en).

foundation [faʊn'deɪʃn] n - **1.** [organization, act of establishing] fundación f - **2.** [basis] fundamento m, base f - **3.** [make-up]: **foundation (cream)** crema f base. ◆ **foundations** npl fig & CONSTR cimientos mpl.

founder ['faʊndə'] ◇ n fundador m, -ra f. ◇ vi lit & fig hundirse, irse a pique.

foundry ['faʊndrɪ] n fundición f.

fountain ['faʊntɪn] n - **1.** [structure] fuente f - **2.** [jet] chorro m.

fountain pen n (pluma f) estilográfica f.

four [fɔ:'] num cuatro; **on all fours** a gatas; see also **six**.

four-letter word n palabrota f, taco m.

four-poster (bed) n cama f de columnas.

foursome ['fɔ:səm] n grupo m de cuatro personas.

fourteen [,fɔ:'ti:n] num catorce; see also **six**.

fourth [fɔ:θ] num cuarto(ta); see also **sixth**.

Fourth of July n: **the Fourth of July** el cuatro de julio, día de la independencia de los Estados Unidos.

four-wheel drive n [system] tracción f a las cuatro ruedas; [car] todoterreno m.

fowl [faʊl] (pl fowl OR -s) n ave f de corral.

fox [fɒks] ◇ n zorro m. ◇ vt [perplex] dejar perplejo(ja).

foxglove ['fɒksglʌv] n dedalera f.

foyer ['fɔɪeɪ] n vestíbulo m.

fracas [UK 'fræka:; US 'freɪkəs] (pl UK fracas, US fracases) n fml riña f, gresca f.

fraction ['frækʃn] n - **1.** MATHS quebrado m, fracción f - **2.** [small part] fracción f.

fractionally ['frækʃnəlɪ] adv ligeramente.

fracture ['fræktʃə'] ◇ n fractura f. ◇ vt fracturar.

fragile ['frædʒaɪl] adj frágil.

fragment n ['frægmənt] [of glass, text] fragmento m; [of paper, plastic] trozo m.

fragrance ['freɪgrəns] n fragancia f.

fragrant ['freɪgrənt] adj fragante.

frail [freɪl] adj frágil.

frame [freɪm] <> n - 1. [of picture, door] marco m; [of glasses] montura f; [of chair, bed] armadura f; [of bicycle] cuadro m; [of boat] armazón m o f - 2. [physique] cuerpo m. <> vt - 1. [put in a frame] enmarcar - 2. [express] formular, expresar - 3. inf [set up] tender una trampa a, amañar la culpabilidad de.

frame of mind n estado m de ánimo.

framework ['freɪmwɜːk] n - 1. [physical structure] armazón m o f, esqueleto m - 2. [basis] marco m.

France [frɑːns] n Francia f.

franchise ['fræntʃaɪz] n - 1. POL sufragio m, derecho m de voto - 2. COMM concesión f, licencia f exclusiva.

frank [fræŋk] <> adj franco(ca). <> vt franquear.

frankly ['fræŋklɪ] adv francamente.

frantic ['fræntɪk] adj frenético(ca).

fraternity [frə'tɜːnətɪ] n - 1. fml [community] cofradía f - 2. US [in university] asociación de estudiantes que suele funcionar como club social - 3. (U) fml [friendship] fraternidad f.

fraternize, -ise ['frætənaɪz] vi: to fraternize (with) fraternizar (con).

fraud [frɔːd] n - 1. (U) [deceit] fraude m - 2. pej [impostor] farsante mf.

fraught [frɔːt] adj - 1. [full]: fraught with lleno(na) OR cargado(da) de - 2. UK [frantic] tenso(sa).

fray [freɪ] <> vt fig [nerves] crispar, poner de punta. <> vi - 1. [sleeve, cuff] deshilacharse - 2. fig [temper, nerves] crisparse. <> n liter: to enter the fray saltar a la palestra.

frayed [freɪd] adj [sleeve, cuff] deshilachado(da).

freak [friːk] <> adj imprevisible. <> n - 1. [strange creature - in appearance] monstruo m; [- in behaviour] estrafalario m, -ria f - 2. [unusual event] anormalidad f, caso m insólito - 3. inf [fanatic]: film/fitness freak fanático m, -ca f del cine/ejercicio. ◆ **freak out** inf vi flipar, alucinar.

freckle ['frekl] n peca f.

free [friː] <> adj (comp freer, superl freest) - 1. [gen]: free (from OR of) libre (de); to be free to do sthg ser libre de hacer algo; feel free! ¡adelante!, ¡cómo no!; to set free liberar - 2. [not paid for] gratis (inv), gratuito(ta); free of charge gratis (inv) - 3. [unattached] suelto(ta) - 4. [generous]: to be free with sthg no regatear

algo. <> adv - 1. [without payment]: (for) free gratis - 2. [run] libremente - 3. [loose]: to pull/cut sthg free soltar algo tirando/cortando. <> vt (pt & pp freed) - 1. [release] liberar, libertar; to free sb of sthg librar a alguien de algo - 2. [make available] dejar libre - 3. [extricate - person] rescatar; [- one's arm, oneself] soltar.

freedom ['friːdəm] n libertad f; freedom from indemnidad f ante OR de.

Freefone®, **freephone** ['friːfəʊn] n (U) UK teléfono m OR número m gratuito.

free-for-all n refriega f.

free gift n obsequio m.

freehand ['friːhænd] adj & adv a pulso.

freehold ['friːhəʊld] n propiedad f absoluta.

free house n pub no controlado por una compañía cervecera.

free kick n tiro m libre.

freelance ['friːlɑːns] <> adj free-lance. <> adv como free-lance. <> n free-lance mf.

freely ['friːlɪ] adv - 1. [readily - admit, confess] sin reparos; [- available] fácilmente - 2. [openly] abiertamente, francamente - 3. [without restrictions] libremente - 4. [generously] liberalmente.

Freemason ['friːˌmeɪsn] n francmasón m, masón m.

freephone ['friːfəʊn] = **freefone**.

Freepost® ['friːpəʊst] n franqueo m pagado.

free-range adj de granja.

freestyle ['friːstaɪl] n [in swimming] estilo m libre.

free trade n libre cambio m.

freeway ['friːweɪ] n US autopista f.

freewheel [ˌfriːˈwiːl] vi [on bicycle] andar sin pedalear; [in car] ir en punto muerto.

free will n libre albedrío m; to do sthg of one's own free will hacer algo por voluntad propia.

freeze [friːz] <> vt (pt froze, pp frozen) - 1. [gen] helar - 2. [food, wages, prices] congelar - 3. [assets] bloquear. <> vi (pt froze, pp frozen) - 1. [gen] helarse - 2. COMPUT bloquearse. <> impers vb METEOR helar. <> n - 1. [cold weather] helada f - 2. [of wages, prices] congelación f.

freeze-dried [-'draɪd] adj liofilizado(da).

freezer ['friːzər] n congelador m.

freezing ['friːzɪŋ] <> adj - 1. [gen] helado(da) - 2. [weather] muy frío(a); it's freezing in here hace un frío espantoso aquí. <> n = **freezing point**.

freezing point n punto m de congelación.

freight [freɪt] n (U) - 1. [goods] mercancías fpl, flete m - 2. [transport] transporte m.

freight train n (tren m de) mercancías m inv.

French [frentʃ] ◇ *adj* francés(esa). ◇ *n* [language] francés *m*. ◇ *npl*: **the French** los franceses.

French bean *n* judía *f* verde, ejote *m* Amér C & Méx, chaucha *f* R Plata, poroto *m* verde Chile, habichuela *f* Col, vainita *f* Ven.

French bread *n* (U) pan *m* de barra.

French dressing *n* [vinaigrette] vinagreta *f*.

French fries, fries *npl esp US* patatas *fpl* fritas *(de sartén)*.

Frenchman ['frentʃmən] (*pl* -men [-mən]) *n* francés *m*.

French stick *n UK* barra *f* de pan.

French windows *npl* puertaventanas *fpl*.

Frenchwoman ['frentʃ,wumən] (*pl* -women [-,wimin]) *n* francesa *f*.

frenetic [frə'netik] *adj* frenético(ca).

frenzy ['frenzi] *n* frenesí *m*.

frequency ['fri:kwənsi] *n* frecuencia *f*.

frequent ◇ *adj* ['fri:kwənt] frecuente. ◇ *vt* [fri'kwent] frecuentar.

frequently ['fri:kwəntli] *adv* a menudo.

fresh [freʃ] *adj* - **1.** [gen] fresco(ca); [flavour, taste] refrescante - **2.** [bread] del día - **3.** [not canned] natural - **4.** [water] dulce - **5.** [pot of tea, fighting] nuevo(va).

freshen ['freʃn] ◇ *vt* [air] refrescar. ◇ *vi* [wind] soplar más fuerte. ◆ **freshen up** *vi* [person] refrescarse.

fresher ['freʃər] *n UK* estudiante *mf* de primer año.

freshly ['freʃli] *adv* recién.

freshman ['freʃmən] (*pl* -men [-mən]) *n* estudiante *mf* de primer año.

freshness ['freʃnis] *n* (U) - **1.** [of food] frescura *f* - **2.** [originality] novedad *f*, originalidad *f* - **3.** [brightness] pulcritud *f* - **4.** [refreshing quality] frescor *m*.

freshwater ['freʃ,wɔ:tər] *adj* de agua dulce.

fret [fret] *vi* preocuparse.

friar ['fraiər] *n* fraile *m*.

friction ['frikʃn] *n* fricción *f*.

Friday ['fraidi] *n* viernes *m inv*; *see also* **Saturday**.

fridge [fridʒ] *n esp UK* nevera *f*, refrigerador *m* Amér, heladera *f* R Plata, refrigeradora *f* Col & Perú.

fridge-freezer *n UK* combi *m*, nevera *f* congeladora.

fried [fraid] *adj* frito(ta).

friend [frend] *n* [close acquaintance] amigo *m*, -ga *f*; **to be friends with sb** ser amigo de alguien; **to make friends (with)** hacerse amigo (de), trabar amistad (con).

friendly ['frendli] *adj* - **1.** [person] amable, simpático(ca); [attitude, manner, welcome]

amistoso(sa); **to be friendly with sb** llevarse bien con alguien - 2. [nation] amigo(ga) - 3. [argument, game] amistoso(sa).

friendship ['frendʃip] *n* amistad *f*.

fries [fraiz] = **French fries**.

frieze [fri:z] *n* friso *m*.

fright [frait] *n* - **1.** [fear] miedo *m*; **to take fright** espantarse, asustarse - **2.** [shock] susto *m*.

frighten ['fraitn] *vt* asustar; **to frighten sb into doing sthg** atemorizar a alguien para que haga algo.

frightened ['fraitnd] *adj* asustado(da); **to be frightened of sthg/of doing sthg** tener miedo a algo/a hacer algo.

frightening ['fraitniŋ] *adj* aterrador(ra), espantoso(sa).

frightful ['fraitful] *adj dated* terrible.

frigid ['fridʒid] *adj* [sexually] frígido(da).

frill [fril] *n* - **1.** [decoration] volante *m* - **2.** *inf* [extra] adorno *m*.

fringe [frindʒ] ◇ *n* - **1.** [decoration] flecos *mpl* - **2.** *UK* [of hair] flequillo *m* - **3.** [edge] periferia *f* - **4.** [extreme] margen *m*. ◇ *vt* [edge] bordear.

fringe benefit *n* beneficio *m* complementario.

frisk [frisk] *vt* cachear, registrar.

frisky ['friski] *adj inf* retozón(ona), juguetón(ona).

fritter ['fritər] *n* buñuelo *m*. ◆ **fritter away** *vt sep*: **to fritter money/time away on sthg** malgastar dinero/tiempo en algo.

frivolous ['frivələs] *adj* frívolo(la).

frizzy ['frizi] *adj* crespo(pa), ensortijado(da).

fro [frəu] ▷ **to**.

frock [frɒk] *n dated* vestido *m*.

frog [frɒg] *n* [animal] rana *f*.

frogman ['frɒgmən] (*pl* -men) *n* hombre *m* rana.

frolic ['frɒlik] *vi* (*pt & pp* -ked, *cont* -king) retozar, triscar.

from (*weak form* [frəm], *strong form* [frɒm]) *prep* - **1.** [indicating source, origin, removal] de; **where are you from?** ¿de dónde eres?; **I got a letter from her today** hoy me ha llegado una carta suya; **a flight from Paris** un vuelo de París; **to translate from Spanish into English** traducir del español al inglés; **he's not back from work yet** aún no ha vuelto del trabajo; **to take sthg away from sb** quitar algo a alguien - **2.** [indicating a deduction]: **take 15 (away) from 19** quita 15 a 19; **to deduct sthg from sthg** deducir OR descontar algo de algo - **3.** [indicating escape, separation] de; **he ran away from home** huyó de casa - **4.** [indicating position] desde; **seen from above/below** visto desde arriba/abajo; **a light bulb hung from the ceiling** una bombilla colgaba del techo - **5.** [indicating distance] de; **it's 60 km from here** está a 60 kms de aquí - **6.** [indicating material object is made out of] de; **it's made from wood/plastic** está hecho(cha) de madera/plástico - **7.** [starting at a particular time] desde; **closed from 1 pm to 5 pm** cerrado de 13h a 14h; **from the moment I saw him** desde el momento en que lo vi - **8.** [indicating difference, change] de; **to be different from** ser diferente de; **from... to de...** a; **the price went up from £100 to £150** el precio subió de 100 a 150 libras - **9.** [because of, as a result of] de; **to die from cold** morir de frío; **to suffer from cold/hunger** padecer frío/hambre - **10.** [on the evidence of] por; **to speak from personal experience** hablar por propia experiencia - **11.** [indicating lowest amount]: **prices range from £5 to £500** los precios oscilan entre 5 y 500 libras; **it could take anything from 15 to 20 weeks** podría llevar de 15 a 20 semanas.

front [frʌnt] ◇ *n* - **1.** [gen] parte *f* delantera; [of building] fachada *f*; [of queue] principio *m*; [of dress, shirt] parte *f* de delante - **2.** METEOR, MIL & POL frente *m* - **3.** [on coast]: **(sea) front** paseo *m* marítimo - **4.** [outward appearance] fachada *f*. ◇ *adj* [gen] delantero(ra); [page] primero(ra). ➡ **in front** *adv* - **1.** [further forward] delante - **2.** [winning] ganando. ➡ **in front of** *prep* delante de. ➡ **front onto** *vt insep* [be opposite] dar a.

front bench [ˌfrʌntˈbentʃ] *n* UK *en la Cámara de los Comunes, cada una de las dos filas de escaños ocupadas respectivamente por los ministros del gobierno y los principales líderes de la oposición mayoritaria.*

front door *n* puerta *f* principal.

frontier [UK ˈfrʌnˌtɪər, US frʌnˈtɪər] *n lit & fig* frontera *f*.

front man *n* - **1.** [of group] portavoz *mf* - **2.** [of programme] presentador *m* - **3.** [of rock band] líder *m*.

front room *n* sala *f* de estar.

front-runner *n* favorito *m*, -ta *f*.

front-wheel drive *n* [vehicle] vehículo *m* de tracción delantera.

frost [frɒst] *n* - **1.** [layer of ice] escarcha *f* - **2.** [weather] helada *f*.

frostbite [ˈfrɒstbaɪt] *n (U)* MED congelación *f*.

frosted [ˈfrɒstɪd] *adj* - **1.** [glass] esmerilado(da) - **2.** US CULIN escarchado(da).

frosty [ˈfrɒstɪ] *adj* - **1.** [very cold] de helada - **2.** [covered with frost] escarchado(da) - **3.** *fig* [unfriendly] glacial.

froth [frɒθ] ◇ *n* espuma *f*. ◇ *vi* hacer espuma.

frown [fraʊn] *vi* fruncir el ceño. ➡ **frown (up)on** *vt insep* desaprobar.

froze [frəʊz] *pt* ▷ **freeze**.

frozen [ˈfrəʊzn] ◇ *pp* ▷ **freeze**. ◇ *adj* - **1.** [gen] helado(da) - **2.** [foodstuffs] congelado(da).

frugal [ˈfruːgl] *adj* frugal.

fruit [fruːt] *n (pl* fruit OR fruits*)* - **1.** [food] fruta *f* - **2.** [result] fruto *m*.

fruitcake [ˈfruːtkeɪk] *n* pastel *m* de frutas.

fruiterer [ˈfruːtərər] *n* UK frutero *m*, -ra *f*; **fruiterer's (shop)** frutería *f*.

fruitful [ˈfruːtfʊl] *adj* [successful] fructífero(ra).

fruition [fruːˈɪʃn] *n*: **to come to fruition** [plan] realizarse; [hope] cumplirse.

fruit juice *n* zumo *m* de fruta.

fruitless [ˈfruːtlɪs] *adj* infructuoso(sa).

fruit machine *n* UK máquina *f* tragaperras.

fruit salad *n* macedonia *f* (de frutas).

frumpy [ˈfrʌmpɪ] *adj* anticuado(da) en la manera de vestir.

frustrate [frʌˈstreɪt] *vt* frustrar.

frustrated [frʌˈstreɪtɪd] *adj* frustrado(da).

frustration [frʌˈstreɪʃn] *n* frustración *f*.

fry [fraɪ] ◇ *vt* [food] freír. ◇ *vi* [food] freírse.

frying pan [ˈfraɪɪŋ-] *n* sartén *f*.

FSA [ˌefesˈeɪ] *(abbr of* food standards agency*) n* UK *agencia gubernamental encargada de la seguridad alimentaria.*

ft. *abbr of* **foot**.

FTP *(abbr of* File Transfer Protocol*) n* COMPUT FTP *m*.

fuck [fʌk] *vulg vt & vi* joder, follar, chingar *Méx*. ➡ **fuck off** *vi vulg*: **fuck off!** ¡vete a tomar por culo!

fudge [fʌdʒ] *n (U)* [sweet] *dulce de azúcar, leche y mantequilla.*

fuel [fjʊəl] ◇ *n* combustible *m*. ◇ *vt (UK pt & pp* -led, *cont* -ling, *US pt & pp* -ed, *cont* -ing*)* - **1.** [supply with fuel] alimentar - **2.** [increase] agravar.

fuel tank *n* depósito *m* de gasolina.

fugitive [ˈfjuːdʒətɪv] *n* fugitivo *m*, -va *f*.

fulfil, fulfill US [fʊlˈfɪl] *vt* [promise, duty, threat] cumplir; [hope, ambition] realizar; [obligation] cumplir con; [role] desempeñar; [requirement] satisfacer.

fulfilment, fulfillment US [fʊlˈfɪlmənt] *n* - **1.** [satisfaction] satisfacción *f*, realización *f (de uno mismo)* - **2.** [of promise, duty, threat] cumplimiento *m*; [of hope, ambition] realización *f*; [of role] desempeño *m*; [of requirement] satisfacción *f*.

full [fʊl] ◇ *adj* - **1.** [filled]: **full (of)** lleno(na) (de); **I'm full!** [after meal] ¡no puedo más! - **2.** [schedule] completo(ta) - **3.** [complete - recovery, employment, control] pleno(na); [- name, price, fare] completo(ta); [- explanation, information] detallado(da); [- member, professor] numerario(ria); **three full weeks** tres semanas enteras - **4.** [maximum - volume, power etc] máximo(ma); **at full speed** a toda velocidad - **5.** [plump] grueso(sa) - **6.** [wide] holgado(da), amplio(plia). <> *adv* [very]: **to know sthg full well** saber algo perfectamente. <> *n*: **to pay in full** pagar el total; **write your name in full** escriba su nombre y apellidos.

full-blown [-'bləʊn] *adj* [gen] auténtico(ca); [AIDS]: **to have full-blown AIDS** haber desarrollado el SIDA por completo.

full board *n* pensión *f* completa.

full-fledged *US* = **fully-fledged.**

full moon *n* luna *f* llena.

full-scale *adj* - **1.** [life-size] de tamaño natural - **2.** [complete] a gran escala.

full stop *n* punto *m*.

full time *n* UK SPORT final *m* del (tiempo reglamentario del) partido. <> **full-time** *adj* & *adv* a tiempo completa.

full up *adj* lleno(na).

fully ['fʊlɪ] *adv* - **1.** [completely] completamente - **2.** [thoroughly] detalladamente.

fully-fledged UK, **full-fledged** US [-'fledʒd] *adj fig* hecho(cha) y derecho(cha); [member] de pleno derecho.

fulsome ['fʊlsəm] *adj* exagerado(da); **to be fulsome in one's praise (of sthg/sb)** colmar de elogios (algo/a alguien).

fumble ['fʌmbl] *vi* hurgar.

fume [fjuːm] *vi* [with anger] rabiar. <> **fumes** *npl* humo *m*.

fumigate ['fjuːmɪgeɪt] *vt* fumigar.

fun [fʌn] *n* (*U*) - **1.** [pleasure, amusement] diversión *f*; **my uncle/parachuting is great fun** mi tío/el paracaidismo es muy divertido; **to have fun** divertirse; **have fun!** ¡que te diviertas!; **for fun, for the fun of it** por diversión - **2.** [playfulness]: **he's full of fun** le encanta todo lo que sea diversión - **3.** [at sb else's expense]: **to make fun of sb, to poke fun at sb** reírse OR burlarse de alguien.

function ['fʌŋkʃn] <> *n* - **1.** [gen & MATHS] función *f*; **function key** COMPUT tecla *f* de función - **2.** [formal social event] acto *m*. <> *vi* funcionar; **to function as** hacer de.

functional ['fʌŋkʃnəl] *adj* - **1.** [practical] funcional - **2.** [operational] en funcionamiento.

fund [fʌnd] <> *n* fondo *m*. <> *vt* financiar. <> **funds** *npl* fondos *mpl*.

fundamental [,fʌndə'mentl] *adj*: **fundamental (to)** fundamental (para).

funding ['fʌndɪŋ] *n* - **1.** [financing] financiación *f* - **2.** [funds] fondos *mpl*.

funeral ['fjuːnərəl] *n* funeral *m*.

funeral parlour *n* funeraria *f*.

funfair ['fʌnfeə] *n* feria *f*.

fungus ['fʌŋɡəs] (*pl* -gi [-gaɪ] OR -guses) *n* hongo *m*.

funnel ['fʌnl] *n* - **1.** [for pouring] embudo *m* - **2.** [on ship] chimenea *f*.

funny ['fʌnɪ] *adj* - **1.** [amusing] divertido(da); **I don't think that's funny** no me hace gracia - **2.** [odd] raro(ra) - **3.** [ill] pachucho(cha).

fur [fɜːr] *n* - **1.** [on animal] pelaje *m*, pelo *m* - **2.** [garment] (prenda *f* de) piel *f*.

fur coat *n* abrigo *m* de piel OR pieles.

furious ['fjʊərɪəs] *adj* - **1.** [very angry] furioso(sa) - **2.** [frantic] frenético(ca).

furlong ['fɜːlɒŋ] *n* 201,17 *metros*.

furnace ['fɜːnɪs] *n* horno *m*.

furnish ['fɜːnɪʃ] *vt* - **1.** [fit out] amueblar - **2.** *fml* [provide - goods, explanation] proveer; [- proof] aducir; **to furnish sb with sthg** proporcionar algo a alguien.

furnished ['fɜːnɪʃt] *adj* amueblado(da).

furnishings ['fɜːnɪʃɪŋz] *npl* mobiliario *m*.

furniture ['fɜːnɪtʃər] *n* (*U*) muebles *mpl*, mobiliario *m*; **a piece of furniture** un mueble.

furrow ['fʌrəʊ] *n lit & fig* surco *m*.

furry ['fɜːrɪ] *adj* - **1.** [animal] peludo(da) - **2.** [toy] de peluche.

further ['fɜːðər] <> *compar* ⊳ **far.** <> *adv* - **1.** [in distance] más lejos; **how much further is it?** ¿cuánto queda?; **further on** más adelante - **2.** [in degree, extent, time] más; **further on/back** más adelante/atrás - **3.** [in addition] además. <> *adj* otro(tra); **until further notice** hasta nuevo aviso; **nothing further** nada más. <> *vt* promover, fomentar.

further education *n* UK estudios postescolares no universitarios.

furthermore [,fɜːðə'mɔːr] *adv* lo que es más.

furthest ['fɜːðɪst] <> *superl* ⊳ **far.** <> *adj* - **1.** [in distance] más lejano(na) - **2.** [greatest - in degree, extent] extremo(ma). <> *adv* - **1.** [in distance] más lejos - **2.** [to greatest degree, extent] más.

furtive ['fɜːtɪv] *adj* furtivo(va).

fury ['fjʊərɪ] *n* furia *f*.

fuse *esp* UK, **fuze** US [fjuːz] <> *n* - **1.** ELEC fusible *m* - **2.** [of firework] mecha *f*. <> *vt* fundir. <> *vi* [gen & ELEC] fundirse.

fuse-box *n* caja *f* de fusibles.

fused [fjuːzd] *adj* [fitted with a fuse] con fusible.

fuselage ['fjuːzəlɑːʒ] *n* fuselaje *m*.

fuss [fʌs] <> *n* (*U*) - **1.** [excitement, anxiety] jaleo *m*; **to make a fuss** armar un escándalo - **2.** [complaints] protestas *fpl*. <> *vi* apurarse, angustiarse.

fussy ['fʌsɪ] *adj* - **1.** [fastidious] quisquilloso(sa); **I'm not fussy** me da lo mismo - **2.** [overdecorated] recargado(da).

futile ['fju:taɪl] *adj* inútil, vano(na).

futon ['fu:tɒn] *n* futón *m*.

future ['fju:tʃər] ◇ *n* futuro *m*; **in future** de ahora en adelante; **in the future** en el futuro; **in the not too distant future** en un futuro próximo; **future (tense)** futuro *m*. ◇ *adj* futuro(ra).

fuzzy ['fʌzɪ] *adj* - **1.** [hair] crespo(pa) - **2.** [photo, image] borroso(sa).

G

g¹ (*pl* **g's** OR **gs**), **G** (*pl* **G's** OR **Gs**) [dʒi:] *n* [letter] g *f*, G f. **G** *n* - **1.** MUS sol *m* - **2.** (*abbr of* **good**) B.

g² *n* (*abbr of* **gram**) g. *m*

gab [gæb] ⊃ **gift**.

gabble ['gæbl] ◇ *vt* & *vi* farfullar, balbucir. ◇ *n* farfulleo *m*.

gable ['geɪbl] *n* aguilón *m*.

gadget ['gædʒɪt] *n* artilugio *m*.

Gaelic ['geɪlɪk] *n* [language] gaélico *m*.

gaffe [gæf] *n* metedura *f* de pata.

gag [gæg] ◇ *n* - **1.** [for mouth] mordaza *f* - **2.** *inf* [joke] chiste *m*. ◇ *vt* amordazar.

gaiety ['geɪətɪ] *n* alegría *f*, regocijo *m*.

gaily ['geɪlɪ] *adv* alegremente.

gain [geɪn] ◇ *n* - **1.** [profit] beneficio *m*, ganancia *f* - **2.** [improvement] mejora *f* - **3.** [increase] aumento *m*. ◇ *vt* [gen] ganar. ◇ *vi* - **1.** [advance]: **to gain in sthg** ganar algo - **2.** [benefit]: **to gain (from** OR **by)** beneficiarse (de) - **3.** [watch, clock] adelantarse. **gain on** *vt insep* ganar terreno a.

gait [geɪt] *n* forma *f* de andar.

gal. *abbr of* **gallon**.

gala ['gɑ:lə] *n* [celebration] fiesta *f*.

galaxy ['gæləksɪ] *n* galaxia *f*.

gale [geɪl] *n* vendaval *m*.

gall [gɔ:l] *n* [nerve]: **to have the gall to do sthg** tener el descaro de hacer algo.

gallant *adj* - **1.** ['gælənt] [courageous] valiente, valeroso(sa) - **2.** [gə'lænt, 'gælənt] [polite to women] galante.

gall bladder *n* vesícula *f* biliar.

gallery ['gælərɪ] *n* - **1.** [for exhibiting art] museo *m*; [for selling art] galería *f* - **2.** [in courtroom, parliament] tribuna *f* - **3.** [in theatre] paraíso *m*.

galley ['gælɪ] (*pl* **galleys**) *n* - **1.** [ship] galera *f* - **2.** [kitchen] cocina *f*.

galling ['gɔ:lɪŋ] *adj* indignante.

gallivant [,gælɪ'vænt] *vi inf* andar por ahí holgazaneando.

gallon ['gælən] *n* [in UK] = 4,546 litros galón *m*; [in US] = 3,785 litros galón *m*.

gallop ['gæləp] ◇ *n* galope *m*. ◇ *vi lit* & *fig* galopar.

gallows ['gæləʊz] (*pl* **gallows**) *n* horca *f*.

gallstone ['gɔ:lstəʊn] *n* cálculo *m* biliar.

galore [gə'lɔ:r] *adj* en abundancia.

galvanize, -ise ['gælvənaɪz] *vt* - **1.** TECH galvanizar - **2.** [impel]: **to galvanize sb into action** impulsar a alguien a la acción.

gambit ['gæmbɪt] *n* táctica *f*.

gamble ['gæmbl] ◇ *n* [calculated risk] riesgo *m*. ◇ *vi* - **1.** [bet] jugar; **to gamble on** [race etc] apostar a; [stock exchange] jugar a - **2.** [take risk]: **to gamble on** contar de antemano con que.

gambler ['gæmblər] *n* jugador *m*, -ra *f*.

gambling ['gæmblɪŋ] *n* (U) juego *m*.

game [geɪm] ◇ *n* - **1.** [gen] juego *m* - **2.** [of football, rugby etc] partido *m*; [of snooker, chess, cards] partida *f* - **3.** [hunted animals] caza *f*. ◇ *adj* - **1.** [brave] valiente - **2.** [willing]: **game (for sthg/to do sthg)** dispuesto(ta) (a algo/a hacer algo). **games** ◇ *n* (U) [at school] deportes *mpl*. ◇ *npl* [sporting contest] juegos *mpl*.

gamekeeper ['geɪm,ki:pər] *n* guarda *mf* de caza.

game reserve *n* coto *m* de caza.

games console *n* consola *f* de juegos.

gaming ['geɪmɪŋ] *n* (U) juegos *mpl*.

gammon ['gæmən] *n* jamón *m*.

gamut ['gæmət] *n* gama *f*; **to run the gamut of sthg** recorrer toda la gama de algo.

gang [gæŋ] *n* - **1.** [of criminals] banda *f* - **2.** [of young people] pandilla *f*. **gang up** *vi inf*: **to gang up (on sb)** confabularse (contra alguien).

gangland ['gæŋlænd] *n* (U) mundo *m* del hampa.

gangrene ['gæŋgri:n] *n* gangrena *f*.

gangster ['gæŋstər] *n* gángster *m*.

gangway ['gæŋweɪ] *n* UK [aisle] pasillo *m*.

gantry ['gæntrɪ] *n* pórtico *m* (*para grúas*).

gaol [dʒeɪl] UK = **jail**.

gap [gæp] n - **1.** [empty space, in market] hueco m, [in traffic, trees, clouds] claro m, [in tout] es pacio m en blanco - **2.** [interval] intervalo m - **3.** fig [in knowledge, report] laguna f - **4.** fig [great difference] desfase m.

gape [geɪp] vi [person] mirar boquiabierto(ta).

gaping ['geɪpɪŋ] adj -, **1.** [open-mouthed] boquiabierto(ta) - **2.** [wound] abierto(ta); [hole] enorme.

garage [UK 'gæra:ʒ, 'gærɪdʒ, US gə'ra:ʒ] n - **1.** [for keeping car] garaje m - **2.** UK [for fuel] gasolinera f - **3.** [for car repair] taller m - **4.** UK [for selling cars] concesionario m de automóviles.

garbage ['ga:bɪdʒ] n (U) esp US - **1.** [refuse] basura f - **2.** inf [nonsense] tonterías fpl.

garbage can n US cubo m de la basura.

garbage truck n US camión m de la basura.

garbled ['ga:bld] adj confuso(sa).

garden ['ga:dn] n jardín m.

garden centre n centro m de jardinería.

gardener ['ga:dnəʳ] n jardinero m, -ra f.

gardening ['ga:dnɪŋ] n jardinería f; **to do some gardening** trabajar en el jardín.

gargle ['ga:gl] vi hacer gárgaras.

gargoyle ['ga:gɔɪl] n gárgola f.

garish ['geərɪʃ] adj chillón(ona).

garland ['ga:lənd] n guirnalda f.

garlic ['ga:lɪk] n ajo m.

garlic bread n pan m de ajo.

garment ['ga:mənt] n prenda f (de vestir).

garnish ['ga:nɪʃ] vt guarnecer.

garrison ['gærɪsn] n guarnición f.

garrulous ['gærələs] adj parlanchín(ina).

garter ['ga:təʳ] n - **1.** [band round leg] liga f - **2.** US [suspender] portaligas m inv.

gas [gæs] <> n (pl -es OR -ses) - **1.** [gen] gas m - **2.** US [petrol] gasolina f, bencina f Chile, nafta f R Plata. <> vt asfixiar con gas.

gas cooker, gas stove n UK cocina f de gas, estufa f de gas Amér C, Col & Méx.

gas cylinder n bombona f de gas, garrafa f de gas R Plata, balón m de gas Chile.

gas fire n UK estufa f de gas.

gas gauge n US indicador m del nivel de gasolina OR bencina Chile OR nafta R Plata.

gash [gæʃ] <> n raja f. <> vt rajar.

gasket ['gæskɪt] n junta f.

gasman ['gæsmæn] (pl -men [-men]) n hombre m del gas.

gas mask n máscara f antigás.

gas meter n contador m OR medidor m Amér del gas.

gasoline ['gæsəli:n] n US gasolina f.

gasp [ga:sp] <> n - **1.** [pant] resuello m - **2.** [of shock, surprise] grito m ahogado. <> vi - **1.** [breathe quickly] resollar, jadear - **2.** [in shock, surprise] ahogar un grito.

gas pedal n US acelerador m.

gas station n US gasolinera f, grifo m Perú, bomba f Chile, Col & Ven, estación f de nafta R Plata.

gas stove = **gas cooker.**

gas tank n US depósito m de gasolina, tanque m de gasolina Perú OR de bencina Chile OR de nafta R Plata.

gas tap n llave f del gas.

gastroenteritis ['gæstrəʊ,entə'raɪtɪs] n (U) gastroenteritis f inv.

gastronomy [gæs'trɒnəmɪ] n gastronomía f.

gasworks ['gæswɜ:ks] (pl gasworks) n fábrica f de gas.

gate [geɪt] n - **1.** [gen] puerta f; [metal] verja f - **2.** SPORT [takings] taquilla f; [attendance] entrada f.

gatecrash ['geɪtkræʃ] inf vi colarse.

gateway ['geɪtweɪ] n - **1.** [entrance] puerta f, pórtico m - **2.** COMPUT pasarela f.

gather ['gæðəʳ] <> vt - **1.** [collect] recoger; **to gather together** reunir - **2.** [dust] llenarse de - **3.** [increase - speed, strength] ganar, cobrar - **4.** [understand]: **to gather (that)** deducir que - **5.** [cloth] fruncir. <> vi [people, animals] reunirse; [clouds] acumularse.

gathering ['gæðərɪŋ] n [meeting] reunión f.

gauche [gəʊʃ] adj torpe.

gaudy ['gɔ:dɪ] adj chillón(ona), llamativo(va).

gauge, gage US [geɪdʒ] <> n - **1.** [for fuel, temperature] indicador m; [for width of tube, wire] calibrador m - **2.** [calibre] calibre m - **3.** RAIL ancho m de vía. <> vt lit & fig calibrar.

gaunt [gɔ:nt] adj - **1.** [person, face] demacrado(da) - **2.** [building, landscape] adusto(ta).

gauntlet ['gɔ:ntlɪt] n guante m; **to run the gauntlet of sthg** exponerse a algo; **to throw down the gauntlet (to sb)** arrojar el guante (a alguien).

gauze [gɔ:z] n gasa f.

gave [geɪv] pt ⊳ **give.**

gawky ['gɔ:kɪ] adj desgarbado(da).

gawp [gɔ:p] vi: **to gawp (at sthg/sb)** mirar boquiabierto(ta) (algo/a alguien).

gay [geɪ] <> adj - **1.** [homosexual] gay, homosexual - **2.** [cheerful, lively, bright] alegre. <> n gay mf.

gaze [geɪz] <> n mirada f fija. <> vi: **to gaze (at sthg/sb)** mirar fijamente (algo/a alguien).

gazelle [gə'zel] (pl gazelle OR -s) n gacela f.

gazetteer [,gæzɪ'tɪəʳ] n índice m geográfico.

gazump [gə'zʌmp] *vt UK inf*: **to gazump sb** acordar vender una casa a alguien y luego vendérsela a otro a un precio más alto.

GB *n* - **1.** (*abbr of* Great Britain) GB *f* - **2.** COMPUT (*abbr of* gigabyte) GB *m*.

GCSE (*abbr of* General Certificate of Secondary Education) *n* examen final de enseñanza secundaria en Gran Bretaña.

GDP (*abbr of* gross domestic product) *n* PIB *m*.

gear [gɪər] ⬦ *n* - **1.** [mechanism] engranaje *m* - **2.** [speed - of car, bicycle] marcha *f*; **in gear** con una marcha metida; **out of gear** en punto muerto; **to change gear** cambiar de marcha - **3.** (*U*) [equipment, clothes] equipo *m* - **4.** (*U*) *inf* [stuff, possessions] bártulos *mpl*. ⬦ *vt*: **to gear sthg to** orientar OR encaminar algo hacia. ➡ **gear up** *vi*: **to gear up for sthg/to do sthg** hacer preparativos para algo/para hacer algo.

gearbox ['gɪəbɒks] *n* caja *f* de cambios.

gear lever, gear stick *UK*, **gear shift** *US n* palanca *f* de cambios.

gear wheel *n* rueda *f* dentada.

geek [giːk] *n esp US inf* lelo *m*, -la *f*, tontaina *mf*; **a computer geek** un monstruo de la informática.

geese [giːs] *npl* ⬥ **goose.**

gel [dʒel] ⬦ *n* [for shower] gel *m*; [for hair] gomina *f*. ⬦ *vi* - **1.** [thicken] aglutinarse - **2.** [plan] cuajar; [idea, thought] tomar forma.

gelatin ['dʒelətɪn], **gelatine** [,dʒelə'tiːn] *n* gelatina *f*.

gelignite ['dʒelɪgnaɪt] *n* gelignita *f*.

gem [dʒem] *n* [precious stone] gema *f*; [jewel, special person, thing] joya *f*.

Gemini ['dʒemɪnaɪ] *n* Géminis *m inv*.

gender ['dʒendər] *n* - **1.** GRAM género *m* - **2.** [sex] sexo *m*.

gene [dʒiːn] *n* gen *m*.

general ['dʒenərəl] ⬦ *adj* general. ⬦ *n* general *m*. ➡ **in general** *adv* - **1.** [as a whole] en general - **2.** [usually] por lo general.

general anaesthetic *n* anestesia *f* general.

general delivery *n US* lista *f* de correos.

general election *n* elecciones *fpl* generales.

generalization [,dʒenərəlaɪ'zeɪʃn] *n* generalización *f*.

general knowledge *n* cultura *f* general.

generally ['dʒenərəlɪ] *adv* en general.

general practitioner *n* médico *m*, -ca *f* de cabecera.

general public *n*: **the general public** el gran público.

generate ['dʒenəreɪt] *vt* generar.

generation [,dʒenə'reɪʃn] *n* generación *f*.

generator ['dʒenəreɪtər] *n* generador *m*.

generosity [,dʒenə'rɒsətɪ] *n* generosidad *f*.

generous ['dʒenərəs] *adj* generoso(sa); [cut of clothes] amplio(plia).

genetic [dʒɪ'netɪk] *adj* genético(ca). ➡ **genetics** *n* (*U*) genética *f*.

genetically modified [dʒɪ'netɪkəlɪ'mɒdɪfaɪd] *adj* modificado(da) genéticamente, transgénico(ca).

genial ['dʒiːnjəl] *adj* cordial, afable.

genitals ['dʒenɪtlz] *npl* genitales *mpl*.

genius ['dʒiːnjəs] (*pl* -es) *n* genio *m*.

gent [dʒent] *n inf* caballero *m*. ➡ **gents** *n UK* [toilets] servicio *m* de caballeros.

genteel [dʒen'tiːl] *adj* fino(na), refinado(da).

gentle ['dʒentl] *adj* - **1.** [kind] tierno(na), dulce - **2.** [breeze, movement, slope] suave - **3.** [scolding] ligero(ra); [hint] sutil.

gentleman ['dʒentlmən] (*pl* -men [-mən]) *n* - **1.** [well-behaved man] caballero *m* - **2.** [man] señor *m*, caballero *m*.

gently ['dʒentlɪ] *adv* - **1.** [kindly] dulcemente - **2.** [softly, smoothly] suavemente - **3.** [carefully] con cuidado.

gentry ['dʒentrɪ] *n* alta burguesía *f*.

genuine ['dʒenjuɪn] *adj* - **1.** [real] auténtico(ca) - **2.** [sincere] sincero(ra).

geography [dʒɪ'ɒgrəfɪ] *n* geografía *f*.

geology [dʒɪ'ɒlədʒɪ] *n* geología *f*.

geometric(al) [,dʒɪə'metrɪk(l)] *adj* geométrico(ca).

geometry [dʒɪ'ɒmətrɪ] *n* geometría *f*.

geranium [dʒɪ'reɪnjəm] (*pl* -s) *n* geranio *m*.

gerbil ['dʒɜːbɪl] *n* jerbo *m*, gerbo *m*.

geriatric [,dʒerɪ'ætrɪk] ⬦ *adj* [of old people] geriátrico(ca). ⬦ *n* - **1.** MED anciano *m*, -na *f* - **2.** *inf* [very old person] vejestorio *m*.

germ [dʒɜːm] *n fig & BIOL* germen *m*; MED microbio *m*.

German ['dʒɜːmən] ⬦ *adj* alemán(ana). ⬦ *n* - **1.** [person] alemán *m*, -ana *f* - **2.** [language] alemán *m*.

German measles *n* rubéola *f*.

Germany ['dʒɜːmənɪ] *n* Alemania.

germinate ['dʒɜːmɪneɪt] *vt & vi lit & fig* germinar.

gerund ['dʒerənd] *n* gerundio *m*.

gesticulate [dʒes'tɪkjuleɪt] *vi* gesticular.

gesture ['dʒestʃər] ⬦ *n* gesto *m*. ⬦ *vi*: **to gesture to** OR **towards sb** hacer gestos a alguien.

get [get] (*UK pt & pp* got, *US pt* got, *pp* gotten) ⬦ *vt* - **1.** [bring, fetch] traer; **can I get you something to eat/drink?** ¿te traigo algo de comer/beber?; **I'll get my coat** voy a por el abrigo; **could you get me the boss, please?** [when phoning] póngame con el jefe - **7.** [door, phone] contestar a - **8.** [obtain] conseguir; **she got top marks** sacó las mejores notas - **4.** [buy] comprar - **5.** [receive] recibir; **what did you get for your birthday?** ¿qué te regalaron para tu cumpleaños?; **she gets a good salary** gana un buen sueldo; **we don't get much rain** no llueve mucho - **6.** [catch - bus, criminal, illness] coger, agarrar *Amér*; **I've got a cold** estoy resfriado; **he got cancer** contrajo cáncer - **7.** [cause to do]: **to get sb to do sthg** hacer que alguien haga algo; **I'll get my sister to help** le pediré a mi hermana que ayude - **8.** [cause to be done]: **to get sthg done** mandar hacer algo; **have you got the car fixed yet?** ¿te han arreglado ya el coche? - **9.** [cause to become]: **to get sthg ready** preparar algo; **to get sthg dirty** ensuciar algo - **10.** [cause to move]: **can you get it through the gap?** ¿puedes meterlo por el hueco?; **to get sthg/sb out of sthg** conseguir sacar algo/a alguien de algo - **11.** [experience - a sensation]: **do you get the feeling he doesn't like us?** ¿no te da la sensación de que no le gustamos? - **12.** [understand] entender; **I don't get it** *inf* no me aclaro, no lo entiendo; **he didn't seem to get the point** no pareció captar el sentido - **13.** *inf* [annoy] poner negro(gra) - **14.** [find]: **you get a lot of artists here** hay mucho artista por aquí. ⬦ *vi* - **1.** [become] ponerse; **to get angry/pale** ponerse furioso/pálido; **to get ready** prepararse; **to get dressed** vestirse; **I'm getting cold/bored** me estoy enfriando/aburriendo; **it's getting late** se está haciendo tarde - **2.** [arrive] llegar; **how do I get there?** ¿cómo se llega (allí)?; **to get home** llegar a casa; **I only got back yesterday** regresé justo ayer - **3.** [eventually succeed]: **to get to do sthg** llegar a hacer algo; **did you get to see him?** ¿conseguiste verlo? - **4.** [progress] llegar; **how far have you got?** ¿cuánto llevas?, ¿hasta dónde has llegado?; **now we're getting somewhere** ahora sí que vamos por buen camino; **we're getting nowhere** así no llegamos a ninguna parte. ⬦ *aux vb*: **to get excited** emocionarse; **someone could get hurt** alguien podría resultar herido; **I got beaten up** me zurraron; **let's get going** OR **moving** pongámonos en marcha. ⬩ **get about** *vi* - **1.** [move from place to place] salir a menudo - **2.** [circulate - news etc] difundirse; = **get around**. ⬩ **get along** *vi* - **1.** [manage] arreglárselas - **2.** [progress]: **how are you getting along?** ¿cómo te va? - **3.** [have a good relationship]: **to get along (with sb)** llevarse bien (con alguien). ⬩ **get around, get round** ⬦ *vt insep* [overcome - problem] evitar; [- obstacle] sortear. ⬦ *vi* [circulate - news etc] difundirse; = **get about**. ⬩ **get at** *vt insep* - **1.** [reach] llegar a, alcanzar - **2.** [imply] referirse a - **3.** *inf* [criticize]: **stop getting at me!** ¡deja ya de meterte conmigo! ⬩ **get away**

vi - **1.** [leave] salir, irse - **2.** [go on holiday]: **I really need to get away** necesito unas buenas vacaciones - **3.** [escape] escaparse. ⬩ **get away with** *vt insep* salir impune de; **she lets him get away with everything** ella se lo consiente todo. ⬩ **get back** ⬦ *vt sep* [recover, regain] recuperar. ⬦ *vi* - **1.** [move away] echarse atrás, apartarse - **2.** [return] volver. ⬩ **get back to** *vt insep* - **1.** [return to previous state, activity] volver a - **2.** *esp US inf* [phone back]: **I'll get back to you later** te llamo de vuelta más tarde. ⬩ **get by** *vi* apañárselas. ⬩ **get down** *vt sep* - **1.** [depress] deprimir - **2.** [fetch from higher level] bajar - **3.** [write down] anotar. ⬩ **get down to** *vt insep*: **to get down to doing sthg** ponerse a hacer algo. ⬩ **get in** *vi* - **1.** [enter] entrar - **2.** [arrive] llegar. ⬩ **get into** *vt insep* - **1.** [car] subir a - **2.** [become involved in] meterse en - **3.** [enter into a particular situation, state]: **to get into a panic** OR **state** ponerse nerviosísimo(ma); **to get into trouble** meterse en líos; **to get into the habit of doing sthg** adquirir el hábito OR coger la costumbre de hacer algo - **4.** [be accepted as a student at]: **she managed to get into Oxford** consiguió entrar en Oxford. ⬩ **get off** ⬦ *vt sep* - **1.** [remove] quitar - **2.** [prevent from being punished] librar. ⬦ *vt insep* - **1.** [go away from] irse OR salirse de; **get off my land!** ¡fuera de mis tierras! - **2.** [train, bus, table] bajarse de. ⬦ *vi* - **1.** [leave bus, train] bajarse, desembarcarse *Amér* - **2.** [escape punishment] escaparse; **he got off lightly** salió bien librado - **3.** [depart] irse, salir. ⬩ **get off with** *vt insep UK inf* ligar con. ⬩ **get on** ⬦ *vt insep* [bus, train, horse] subirse a. ⬦ *vi* - **1.** [enter bus, train] subirse, montarse - **2.** [have good relationship] llevarse bien - **3.** [progress]: **how are you getting on?** ¿cómo te va? - **4.** [proceed]: **to get on with sthg** seguir OR continuar con algo - **5.** [be successful professionally] triunfar. ⬩ **get out** ⬦ *vt sep* [remove - object, prisoner] sacar; [- stain etc] quitar; **she got a pen out of her bag** sacó un bolígrafo del bolso. ⬦ *vi* - **1.** [leave] salir; **get out!** ¡vete de aquí! - **2.** [leave car, bus, train] bajarse - **3.** [become known - news] difundirse, filtrarse. ⬩ **get out of** *vt insep* - **1.** [car, bus, train] bajar de; [bed] levantarse de - **2.** [escape from] escapar OR huir de - **3.** [avoid]: **to get out of (doing) sthg** librarse de (hacer) algo. ⬩ **get over** ⬦ *vt insep* - **1.** [recover from] recuperarse de - **2.** [overcome] superar. ⬦ *vt sep* [communicate] hacer comprender. ⬩ **get round** *vt insep* = **get around**. ⬩ **get through** ⬦ *vt insep* - **1.** [job, task] terminar - **2.** [exam] aprobar - **3.** [food, drink] consumir - **4.** [unpleasant situation] sobrevivir a. ⬦ *vi* TELEC conseguir comunicar. ⬩ **get to** ⬦ *vt insep inf* [annoy] fastidiar, molestar. ⬦ *vi* [end up] ir a parar. ⬩ **get together** ⬦ *vt sep* [organize - project, demonstration] or-

ganizar, montar; [- team] juntar; [- report] preparar. <> vi juntarse, reunirse. ◆ **get up**
<> vi levantarse. <> vt insep [organize - peti-
tion etc] preparar, organizar. ◆ **get up to**
vt insep inf hacer, montar.

getaway ['getəweɪ] n fuga f, huida f; **to
make one's getaway** darse a la fuga.

get-together n inf reunión f.

geyser ['gi:zər] n - 1. [hot spring] géiser m
- 2. UK [water heater] calentador m de agua.

Ghana ['gɑːnə] n Ghana.

ghastly ['gɑːstlɪ] adj - 1. inf [very bad, unpleas-
ant] horrible, espantoso(sa) - 2. [horrifying] horripilante - 3. [ill] fatal.

gherkin ['gɜːkɪn] n pepinillo m.

ghetto ['getəʊ] (pl -s OR -es) n gueto m.

ghetto blaster [-'blɑːstər] n inf radiocasete
portátil de gran tamaño y potencia.

ghost [gəʊst] n [spirit] fantasma m.

giant ['dʒaɪənt] <> adj gigantesco(ca). <> n
gigante m.

gibberish ['dʒɪbərɪʃ] n galimatías m inv.

gibe [dʒaɪb] <> n pulla f. <> vi: **to gibe (at)**
mofarse (de).

giblets ['dʒɪblɪts] npl menudillos mpl.

Gibraltar [dʒɪ'brɔːltər] n Gibraltar; **the Rock
of Gibraltar** el Peñón.

giddy ['gɪdɪ] adj mareado(da); **to be giddy**
[have vertigo] tener vértigo.

gift [gɪft] n - 1. [present] regalo m, obsequio m
- 2. [talent] don m; **to have a gift for sthg/for
doing sthg** tener un don especial para algo/
para hacer algo; **to have the gift of the gab**
tener un pico de oro.

gift certificate US = **gift token**.

gifted ['gɪftɪd] adj - 1. [talented] dotado(da)
- 2. [extremely intelligent] superdotado(da).

gift token, gift certificate, gift voucher
n UK vale m OR cupón m para regalo.

gig [gɪg] n inf [concert] concierto m.

gigabyte ['gaɪgəbaɪt] n COMPUT gigabyte m.

gigantic [dʒaɪ'gæntɪk] adj gigantesco(ca).

giggle ['gɪgl] n - 1. [laugh] risita f, risa f
tonta - 2. UK inf [fun]: **it's a real giggle** es la
mar de divertido; **to do sthg for a giggle** hacer
algo por puro cachondeo. <> vi [laugh] soltar
risitas.

gilded ['gɪldɪd] = **gilt**.

gill [dʒɪl] n [unit of measurement] = 0,142 litros.

gills [gɪlz] npl [of fish] agallas fpl.

gilt [gɪlt], **gilded** <> adj dorado(da). <> n
dorado m.

gilt-edged adj FIN de máxima garantía.

gimmick ['gɪmɪk] n pej artilugio m innecesario; **advertising gimmick** reclamo m publicitario.

gin [dʒɪn] n ginebra f; **gin and tonic** gin-
tonic m.

ginger ['dʒɪndʒər] <> adj UK [hair] berme-
jo(ja); **to have ginger hair** ser pelirrojo(ja); [cat]
de color bermejo. <> n jengibre m.

ginger ale n [mixer] ginger-ale m.

ginger beer n [slightly alcoholic] refresco m de
jengibre.

gingerbread ['dʒɪndʒəbred] n - 1. [cake]
pan m de jengibre - 2. [biscuit] galleta f de jengibre.

ginger-haired [-'heəd] adj pelirrojo(ja).

gingerly ['dʒɪndʒəlɪ] adv con mucho tiento.

gipsy, gypsy ['dʒɪpsɪ] <> adj gitano(na).
<> n UK gitano m, -na f.

giraffe [dʒɪ'rɑːf] (pl giraffe OR -s) n jirafa f.

girder ['gɜːdər] n viga f.

girdle ['gɜːdl] n [corset] faja f.

girl [gɜːl] n - 1. [child] niña f - 2. [young woman]
chica f - 3. [daughter] niña f, chica f - 4. inf [fe-
male friend]: **the girls** las amigas, las chicas.

girlfriend ['gɜːlfrend] n - 1. [female lover] novia f - 2. [female friend] amiga f.

girl guide UK, **girl scout** US n [individual] ex-
ploradora f.

giro ['dʒaɪrəʊ] (pl -s) n UK - 1. (U) [system] giro m - 2.: **giro (cheque)** cheque m para giro
bancario.

girth [gɜːθ] n - 1. [circumference] circunferencia f - 2. [of horse] cincha f.

gist [dʒɪst] n: **the gist of** lo esencial de; **to get
the gist (of sthg)** entender el sentido (de algo).

give [gɪv] <> vt (pt gave, pp given) - 1. [gen]
dar; [time, effort] dedicar; [attention] prestar; **to
give sb/sthg sthg, to give sthg to sb/sthg** dar
algo a alguien/algo; **he was given twenty
years** [sentenced to] le cayeron veinte años
- 2. [as present]: **to give sb sthg, to give sthg to
sb** regalar algo a alguien - 3. [hand over]: **to give
sb sthg, to give sthg to sb** entregar OR dar algo a alguien. <> vi (pt gave, pp given) [col-
lapse, break] romperse, ceder; [stretch] dar de
sí. ◆ **give or take** prep más o menos; **in
half an hour give or take five minutes** dentro
de media hora, cinco minutos más o cinco
minutos menos. ◆ **give away** vt sep - 1. [as
present] regalar - 2. [reveal] revelar, descubrir
- 3. [bride] llevar al altar. ◆ **give back** vt sep
[return] devolver, regresar Méx. ◆ **give in**
vi - 1. [admit defeat] rendirse, darse por venci-
do(da) - 2. [agree unwillingly]: **to give in to sthg**
ceder ante algo. ◆ **give off** vt insep [pro-
duce, emit] despedir. ◆ **give out** <> vt sep
[distribute] repartir, distribuir. <> vi [supply,
strength] agotarse, acabarse; [legs, machine] fallar. ◆ **give up** <> vt sep - 1. [stop] abando-

nar; **to give up chocolate** dejar de comer chocolate - **2.** [job] dejar ◇ *vi* rendirse, darse por vencido(da).

given ['gɪvn] ◇ *adj* - **1.** [set, fixed] dado(da) - **2.** [prone]: **to be given to sthg/to doing sthg** ser dado(da) a algo/a hacer algo. ◇ *prep* [taking into account] dado(da); **given that** dado que.

given name *n esp US* nombre *m* de pila.

glacier ['glæsjər] *n* glaciar *m*.

glad [glæd] *adj* - **1.** [happy, pleased] alegre, contento(ta); **to be glad about/that** alegrarse de/de que - **2.** [willing]: **to be glad to do sthg** tener gusto en hacer algo.

glad-hand ['glædhænd] *vt inf pej* dar la mano efusivamente a.

gladly ['glædlɪ] *adv* - **1.** [happily, eagerly] alegremente - **2.** [willingly] con mucho gusto.

glamor *US* = **glamour**.

glamorous ['glæmərəs] *adj* atractivo(va), lleno(na) de encanto.

glamour *UK*, **glamor** *US* ['glæmər] *n* encanto *m*, atractivo *m*, sofisticación *f*.

glance [glɑːns] ◇ *n* [quick look] mirada *f*, vistazo *m*; **to cast OR take a glance at sthg** echar un vistazo a algo; **at a glance** de un vistazo; **at first glance** a primera vista. ◇ *vi* [look quickly]: **to glance at sb** lanzar una mirada a alguien; **to glance at OR through sthg** hojear algo. ◆ **glance off** *vt insep* rebotar en.

glancing ['glɑːnsɪŋ] *adj* de refilón.

gland [glænd] *n* glándula *f*.

glandular fever ['glændjʊlər-] *n* mononucleosis *f inv* infecciosa.

glare [gleər] ◇ *n* - **1.** [scowl] mirada *f* asesina - **2.** [blaze, dazzle] resplandor *m*, deslumbramiento *m* - **3.** *(U) fig* [of publicity] foco *m*. ◇ *vi* [blaze, dazzle] brillar.

glaring ['gleərɪŋ] *adj* - **1.** [very obvious] flagrante - **2.** [blazing, dazzling] deslumbrante.

glasnost ['glæznɒst] *n* glasnost *f*.

glass [glɑːs] ◇ *n* - **1.** [material] vidrio *m*, cristal *m* - **2.** [drinking vessel, glassful] vaso *m*; [with stem] copa *f*. ◇ *comp* de vidrio *OR* cristal. ◆ **glasses** *npl* [spectacles] gafas *fpl*.

glassware ['glɑːsweər] *n (U)* cristalería *f*.

glassy ['glɑːsɪ] *adj* - **1.** [smooth, shiny] cristalino(na) - **2.** [blank, lifeless] vidrioso(sa).

glaze [gleɪz] ◇ *n* [on pottery] vidriado *m*; [on food] glaseado *m*. ◇ *vt* - **1.** [pottery] vidriar; [food] glasear - **2.** [window] acristalar.

glazier ['gleɪzjər] *n* vidriero *m*, -ra *f*.

gleam [gliːm] ◇ *n* destello *m*; [of hope] rayo *m*. ◇ *vi* relucir.

gleaming ['gliːmɪŋ] *adj* reluciente.

glean [gliːn] *vt* [gather] recoger; [information] extraer.

glee [gliː] *n (U)* [joy, delight] alegría *f*, regocijo *m*.

glen [glen] *n Scotland* cañada *f*.

glib [glɪb] *adj pej* de mucha labia.

glide [glaɪd] *vi* - **1.** [move smoothly] deslizarse - **2.** [fly] planear.

glider ['glaɪdər] *n* [plane] planeador *m*.

gliding ['glaɪdɪŋ] *n* [sport] vuelo *m* sin motor.

glimmer ['glɪmər] *n* - **1.** [faint light] luz *f* tenue - **2.** *fig* [trace, sign] atisbo *m*; [of hope] rayo *m*.

glimpse [glɪmps] ◇ *n* - **1.** [look, sight] vislumbre *f*; **to catch a glimpse of sthg/sb** entrever algo/a alguien - **2.** [idea, perception] asomo *m*, atisbo *m*. ◇ *vt* entrever, vislumbrar.

glint [glɪnt] ◇ *n* - **1.** [flash] destello *m* - **2.** [in eyes] brillo *m*. ◇ *vi* destellar.

glisten ['glɪsn] *vi* relucir, brillar.

glitter ['glɪtər] *vi* relucir, brillar.

gloat [gləʊt] *vi*: **to gloat (over sthg)** regodearse (con algo).

global ['gləʊbl] *adj* [worldwide] mundial, global; **the global village** la aldea global.

globalization [ˌgləʊbəlaɪˈzeɪʃn] *n* globalización *f*.

global warming [-'wɔːmɪŋ] *n* calentamiento *m* global.

globe [gləʊb] *n* - **1.** [gen] globo *m* - **2.** [spherical map] globo *m* (terráqueo).

gloom [gluːm] *n (U)* - **1.** [darkness] penumbra *f* - **2.** [unhappiness] pesimismo *m*, melancolía *f*.

gloomy ['gluːmɪ] *adj* - **1.** [dark, cloudy] oscuro(ra) - **2.** [unhappy] melancólico(ca) - **3.** [without hope - report, forecast] pesimista; [- situation, prospects] desalentador(ra).

glorious ['glɔːrɪəs] *adj* magnífico(ca).

glory ['glɔːrɪ] *n* - **1.** [gen] gloria *f* - **2.** [beauty, splendour] esplendor *m*. ◆ **glory in** *vt insep* [relish] disfrutar de, regocijarse con.

gloss [glɒs] *n* - **1.** [shine] lustre *m*, brillo *m* - **2.**: **gloss (paint)** pintura *f* esmalte. ◆ **gloss over** *vt insep* tocar muy por encima.

glossary ['glɒsərɪ] *n* glosario *m*.

glossy ['glɒsɪ] *adj* - **1.** [smooth, shiny] lustroso(sa) - **2.** [on shiny paper] de papel satinado.

glove [glʌv] *n* guante *m*.

glove compartment *n* guantera *f*.

glow [gləʊ] ◇ *n* [light] fulgor *m*. ◇ *vi* [gen] brillar.

glower ['glaʊər] *vi*: **to glower (at sthg/sb)** mirar con furia (algo/a alguien).

glucose ['gluːkəʊs] *n* glucosa *f*.

glue [gluː] ◇ *n* [paste] pegamento *m*; [for glueing wood, metal etc] cola *f*. ◇ *vt* (*cont* **glueing** *OR* **gluing**) [paste] pegar (con pegamento); [wood, metal etc] encolar; **to be glued to sthg** [absorbed by] estar pegado(da) a algo.

glum [glʌm] *adj* [unhappy] sombrío(a).

glut [glʌt] *n* superabundancia *f*.

glutton ['glʌtn] *n* [greedy person] glotón *m*, -ona *f*; **to be a glutton for punishment** ser un masoquista.

GM [dʒiː'em] (*abbr of* **genetically modified**) *adj* transgénico(ca), modificado(da) genéticamente; **GM foods** alimentos transgénicos; **GM products** productos modificados genéticamente.

GMO (*abbr of* **genetically modified organism**) *n* OMG *m*.

gnarled [nɑːld] *adj* nudoso(sa).

gnash [næʃ] *vt*: **to gnash one's teeth** hacer rechinar los dientes.

gnat [næt] *n* mosquito *m*.

gnaw [nɔː] *vt* [chew] roer; **to gnaw (away) at** sb corroer a alguien.

gnome [nəʊm] *n* gnomo *m*.

GNP (*abbr of* **gross national product**) *n* PNB *m*.

GNVQ (*abbr of* **General National Vocational Qualification**) *n* SCH *curso de formación profesional de dos años de duración para los mayores de 16 años en Inglaterra y Gales.*

go [gəʊ] <> *vi* (*pt* **went**, *pp* **gone**) - 1. [move, travel, attend] ir; **where are you going?** ¿adónde vas?; **he's gone to Portugal** se ha ido a Portugal; **we went by bus/train** fuimos en autobús/tren; **to go and do sthg** ir a hacer algo; **where does this path go?** ¿adónde lleva este camino?; **to go right/left** girar a la derecha/izquierda; **to go swimming/shopping** ir a nadar/de compras; **to go for a walk/run** ir a dar un paseo/a correr - 2. [depart - person] irse, marcharse; [- bus] salir; **I must go, I have to go** tengo que irme; **it's time we went** es hora de irse OR marcharse; **let's go!** ¡vámonos! - 3. [pass - time] pasar; **the time went slowly/quickly** el tiempo pasaba lentamente/rápido - 4. [progress] ir; **to go well/badly** ir bien/mal; **how's it going?** *inf* [how are you?] ¿qué tal? - 5. [belong, fit] ir; **the plates go in the cupboard** los platos van en el armario; **it won't go into the suitcase** no cabe en la maleta - 6. [become] ponerse; **to go grey** ponerse gris; **to go mad** volverse loco(c a); **to go blind** quedarse ciego(ga) - 7. [indicating intention, certainty, expectation]: **what are you going to do now?** ¿qué vas a hacer ahora?; **he said he was going to be late** dijo que llegaría tarde; **it's going to rain/snow** va a llover/nevar - 8. [match, be compatible]: **to go (with)** ir bien (con); **this blouse goes well with the skirt** esta blusa va muy bien OR hace juego con la falda - 9. [function, work] funcionar - 10. [bell, alarm] sonar - 11. [start] empe-

zar - 12. [stop working] estropearse; **the fuse must have gone** se ha debido de fundir el fusible - 13. [deteriorate]: **her sight/hearing is going** está perdiendo la vista/el oído - 14. [be disposed of]: **he'll have to go** habrá que despedirlo; **everything must go!** ¡gran liquidación! - 15. *inf* [expressing irritation, surprise]: **now what's he gone and done?** ¿qué leches ha hecho ahora? - 16. [in division]: **three into two won't go** tres no es divisible por dos. <> *n* (*pl* **goes**) [turn] turno *m*; **it's my go** me toca a mí

▸▸▸ **to have a go at sb** *inf* echar una bronca a alguien; **to be on the go** *inf* no parar, estar muy liado(da). ▸ **to go** *adv* [remaining]: **there are only three days to go** sólo quedan tres días. ▸ **go about** <> *vt insep* - 1. [perform] hacer, realizar; **to go about one's business** ocuparse uno de sus asuntos - 2. [tackle]: **to go about doing sthg** apañárselas para hacer algo; **how do you intend going about it?** ¿cómo piensas hacerlo? <> *vi* = **go around**. ▸ **go ahead** *vi* - 1. [begin]: **to go ahead (with sthg)** seguir adelante (con algo); **go ahead!** ¡adelante! - 2. [take place] celebrarse - 3. [in match, contest] ponerse por delante. ▸ **go along** *vi* [proceed]: **as you go along** a medida que lo vayas haciendo. ▸ **go along with** *vt insep* estar de acuerdo con. ▸ **go around, go round, go about** *vi* [joke, illness, story] correr (por ahí). ▸ **go away** *vi* - 1. [person, animal] irse; **go away!** ¡vete! - 2. [pain] desaparecer. ▸ **go back** *vi* - 1. [return] volver - 2. [clocks] atrasarse. ▸ **go back on** *vt insep* [one's word, promise] faltar a. ▸ **go back to** *vt insep* - 1. [return to activity] continuar OR seguir con; **to go back to sleep** volver a dormir - 2. [date from] remontarse a. ▸ **go by** <> *vi* [time, people, vehicles] pasar. <> *vt insep* - 1. [be guided by] guiarse por - 2. [judge from]: **going by her accent, I'd say she was French** a juzgar por su acento yo diría que es francesa. ▸ **go down** <> *vi* - 1. [descend] bajar - 2. [get lower - prices, temperature, swelling] bajar - 3. [be accepted]: **to go down well/badly** tener una buena/mala acogida - 4. [sun] ponerse - 5. [tyre, balloon] deshincharse - 6. [be relegated] descender. <> *vt insep* bajar. ▸ **go for** *vt insep* - 1. [choose] decidirse por - 2. [be attracted to]: **I don't really go for men like him** no me gustan mucho los hombres como él - 3. [attack] lanzarse sobre, atacar - 4. [try to obtain - record, job] ir a por. ▸ **go forward** *vi* [clocks] adelantarse. ▸ **go in** *vi* entrar. ▸ **go in for** *vt insep* - 1. [competition, exam] presentarse a - 2. *inf* [enjoy]: **I don't really go in for classical music** no me va la música clásica. ▸ **go into** *vt insep* - 1. [enter] entrar en - 2. [investigate] investigar - 3. [take up as a profession] dedicarse a. ▸ **go off** <> *vi* - 1. [explode - bomb] estallar; [- gun] dispararse - 2. [alarm] sonar - 3. [go

bad - food] estropearse; [- milk] cortarse
- 4 [lights, heating] apagarse. ◇ vt insep inf [lose interest in] perder el gusto a OR el interés en OR por. ◆ **go on** ◇ vi - **1.** [take place] pasar, ocurrir - **2.** [continue]: **to go on (doing sthg)** seguir (haciendo algo) - **3.** [heating etc] encenderse - **4.** [talk for too long]: **to go on (about)** no parar de hablar (de). ◇ vt insep [be guided by] guiarse por. ◇ excl ¡venga!, ¡vamos! ◆ **go on at** vt insep [nag] dar la lata a. ◆ **go out** vi - **1.** [leave house] salir; **to go out for a meal** cenar fuera - **2.** [tide] bajar - **3.** [light, fire, cigarette] apagarse. ◆ **go over** vt insep - **1.** [examine] repasar - **2.** [repeat] repetir. ◆ **go round** vi [revolve] girar, dar vueltas, = **go around**. ◆ **go through** vt insep - **1.** [penetrate] atravesar - **2.** [experience] pasar por, experimentar - **3.** [study, search through] registrar; **she went through his pockets** le miró en los bolsillos. ◆ **go through with** vt insep llevar a cabo. ◆ **go towards** vt insep contribuir a. ◆ **go under** vi lit & fig hundirse. ◆ **go up** ◇ vi - **1.** [rise - person, prices, temperature, balloon] subir - **2.** [be built] levantarse, construirse. ◇ vt insep subir. ◆ **go without** ◇ vt insep prescindir de. ◇ vi apañárselas.

goad [gəʊd] vt [provoke] aguijonear, incitar.

go-ahead ◇ adj [dynamic] dinámico(ca). ◇ n (U) [permission] luz f verde.

goal [gəʊl] n - **1.** SPORT [point scored] gol m; [area between goalposts] portería f, arco m Amér - **2.** [aim] objetivo m, meta f.

goalkeeper ['gəʊl,kiːpər] n portero m, -ra f, arquero m, -ra f Amér.

goalmouth ['gəʊlmaʊθ, pl -maʊðz] n portería f, meta f, arco m Amér.

goalpost ['gəʊlpəʊst] n poste m (de la portería).

goat [gəʊt] n [animal] cabra f.

goatee [gəʊˈtiː] n perilla f.

gob [gɒb] v inf n UK [mouth] pico m.

gobble ['gɒbl] vt [food] engullir, tragar. ◆ **gobble down, gobble up** vt sep engullir, tragar.

go-between n intermediario m, -ria f.

gobsmacked ['gɒbsmækt] adj UK inf alucinado(da), flipado(da).

go-cart = **go-kart**.

god [gɒd] n dios m. ◆ **God** ◇ n Dios m; **God knows** sabe Dios; **for God's sake** ¡por el amor de Dios!; **thank God** ¡gracias a Dios! ◇ excl: **(my) God!** ¡Dios (mío)!

godchild ['gɒdtʃaɪld] (pl -**children** [-,tʃɪldrən]) n ahijado m, -da f.

goddaughter ['gɒd,dɔːtər] n ahijada f.

goddess ['gɒdɪs] n diosa f.

godfather ['gɒd,fɑːðər] n padrino m.

godforsaken ['gɒdfə,seɪkn] adj dejado(da) de la mano de Dios.

godmother ['gɒd,mʌðər] n madrina f.

godsend ['gɒdsend] n: **to be a godsend** venir como agua de mayo.

godson ['gɒdsʌn] n ahijado m.

goes [gəʊz] ▷ **go**.

goggles ['gɒglz] npl [for swimming] gafas fpl submarinas; [for skiing] gafas de esquí; [for welding] gafas de protección.

going ['gəʊɪŋ] ◇ adj - **1.** UK [available] disponible - **2.** [rate] actual. ◇ n (U) - **1.** [rate of advance] marcha f - **2.** [conditions] condiciones fpl.

go-kart, go-cart [-kɑːt] n kart m.

gold [gəʊld] ◇ adj [gold-coloured] dorado(da). ◇ n [gen] oro m. ◇ comp [made of gold] de oro.

golden ['gəʊldən] adj - **1.** [made of gold] de oro - **2.** [gold-coloured] dorado(da).

goldfish ['gəʊldfɪʃ] (pl **goldfish**) n pez m de colores.

gold leaf n pan m de oro.

gold medal n medalla f de oro.

goldmine ['gəʊldmaɪn] n lit & fig mina f de oro.

gold-plated [-'pleɪtɪd] adj chapado(da) en oro.

goldsmith ['gəʊldsmɪθ] n orfebre mf.

golf [gɒlf] n golf m.

golf ball n [for golf] pelota f de golf.

golf club n - **1.** [society, place] club m de golf - **2.** [stick] palo m de golf.

golf course n campo m de golf.

golfer ['gɒlfər] n golfista mf.

gone [gɒn] ◇ pp ▷ **go**. ◇ adj: **those days are gone** esos tiempos ya pasaron. ◇ prep [past]: **it was gone six already** ya eran las seis pasadas.

gong [gɒŋ] n gong m.

good [gʊd] ◇ adj (comp **better**, superl **best**) - **1.** [gen] bueno(na); **it's good to see you** me alegro de verte; **she's good at it** se le da bien; **he's a very good singer** canta muy bien; **to be good with** saber manejárselas con; **she's good with her hands** es muy mañosa; **it's good for you** es bueno, es beneficioso; **to feel good** sentirse fenomenal; **it's good that...** está bien que...; **to look good** [attractive] estar muy guapo(pa); [appetizing, promising] tener buena pinta; **it looks good on you** te queda bien; **good looks** atractivo m; **be good!** ¡sé bueno!, ¡pórtate bien!; **good!** ¡muy bien!, ¡estupendo! - **2.** [kind] amable; **to be good to sb** ser amable con alguien; **to be good enough to do sthg** ser tan amable de hacer algo; **that was very good of him** fue muy amable de su parte. ◇ n - 1. (U) [benefit] bien m; it will do him good le hará bien - 2. [use] beneficio m, provecho m; what's the good of...? ¿de OR para qué sirve...?; it's no good no sirve para nada - 3. [morally correct behaviour] el bien; to be up to no good estar tramando algo malo. ◇ adv - 1. [expresses approval] estupendo - 2. US inf [well] bien. ▪ goods npl - 1. [COMM - for sale] productos mpl; [- when transported] mercancías fpl; to come up with OR deliver the goods UK inf cumplir (lo prometido) - 2. ECON bienes mpl. ▪ as good as adv casi, prácticamente; it's as good as new está como nuevo. ▪ for good adv [forever] para siempre. ▪ good afternoon excl ¡buenas tardes! ▪ good evening excl [in the evening] ¡buenas tardes!; [at night] ¡buenas noches! ▪ good morning excl ¡buenos días!, ¡buen día! Amér ▪ good night excl ¡buenas noches!

goodbye [,gʊd'baɪ] ◇ excl ¡adiós!; to say goodbye despedirse. ◇ n adiós m.

Good Friday n Viernes m Santo.

good-humoured [-'hju:məd] adj jovial.

good-looking [-'lʊkɪŋ] adj [person] guapo(pa).

good-natured [-'neɪtʃəd] adj bondadoso(sa).

goodness ['gʊdnɪs] ◇ n (U) - 1. [kindness] bondad f - 2. [nutritive quality] alimento m. ◇ excl: (my) goodness! ¡Dios mío!; for goodness' sake! ¡por Dios!; thank goodness ¡gracias a Dios!

goods train [gʊdz-] n UK mercancías m inv.

goodwill [,gʊd'wɪl] n - 1. [kind feelings] buena voluntad f - 2. COMM fondo m de comercio.

goody ['gʊdɪ] inf n [person] bueno m, -na f.

goose [gu:s] (pl geese) n [bird] ganso m, oca f.

gooseberry ['gʊzbərɪ] n [fruit] grosella f silvestre, uva f espina.

goosebumps US ['gu:sbʌmps] inf npl = gooseflesh.

gooseflesh ['gu:sfleʃ] n carne f de gallina.

gore [gɔ:r] ◇ n liter [blood] sangre f (derramada). ◇ vt cornear.

gorge [gɔ:dʒ] ◇ n cañón m. ◇ vt: to gorge o.s. on OR with atracarse de.

gorgeous ['gɔ:dʒəs] adj - 1. [lovely] magnífico(ca), espléndido(da) - 2. inf [good-looking]: to be gorgeous estar como un tren.

gorilla [gə'rɪlə] n gorila mf.

gormless ['gɔ:mlɪs] adj UK inf memo(ma), lerdo(da).

gorse [gɔ:s] n (U) tojo m.

gory ['gɔ:rɪ] adj [death, scene] sangriento(ta); [details, film] escabroso(sa).

gosh [gɒʃ] excl inf ¡joroba!, ¡caray!

go-slow n UK huelga f de celo.

gospel ['gɒspl] n [doctrine] evangelio m. ▪ Gospel n [in Bible] Evangelio m.

gossip ['gɒsɪp] ◇ n - 1. [conversation] cotilleo m - 2. [person] cotilla mf, chismoso m, -sa f. ◇ vi cotillear.

gossip column n ecos mpl de sociedad.

got [gɒt] pt & pp ▷ get.

gotten ['gɒtn] pp US ▷ get.

goulash ['gu:læʃ] n gulasch m.

gourmet ['gʊəmeɪ] ◇ n gastrónomo m, -ma f. ◇ comp para OR de gastrónomos.

gout [gaʊt] n gota f.

govern ['gʌvən] ◇ vt - 1. POL gobernar - 2. [control] dictar. ◇ vi POL gobernar.

governess ['gʌvənɪs] n institutriz f.

government ['gʌvnmənt] ◇ n gobierno m. ◇ comp gubernamental.

governor ['gʌvənər] n - 1. US POL gobernador m, -ra f - 2. [of school, bank, prison] director m, -ra f.

gown [gaʊn] n - 1. [dress] vestido m, traje m - 2. [of judge etc] toga f.

GP (abbr of general practitioner) n médico m, -ca f de cabecera.

grab [græb] ◇ vt - 1. [snatch away] arrebatar; [grip] agarrar, asir; to grab sthg off sb arrebatar algo a alguien - 2. inf [appeal to] seducir. ◇ vi: to grab at sthg intentar agarrar algo.

grace [greɪs] ◇ n - 1. (U) [elegance] elegancia f, gracia f - 2. (U) [delay] prórroga f - 3. [prayer]: to say grace bendecir la mesa. ◇ vt fml - 1. [honour] honrar - 2. [decorate] adornar, embellecer.

graceful ['greɪsfʊl] adj - 1. [beautiful] elegante - 2. [gracious] cortés.

gracious ['greɪʃəs] ◇ adj - 1. [polite] cortés - 2. [elegant] elegante. ◇ excl: (good) gracious! ¡Dios mío!

grade [greɪd] ◇ n - 1. [level, quality] clase f, calidad f - 2. US [class] curso m, clase f - 3. [mark] nota f. ◇ vt - 1. [classify] clasificar - 2. [mark, assess] calificar.

grade crossing n US paso m a nivel.

grade school n US escuela f primaria.

gradient ['greɪdjənt] n pendiente f.

grad school n US escuela f de posgrado.

gradual ['grædʒʊəl] adj gradual.

gradually ['grædʒʊəlɪ] adv gradualmente.

graduate ◇ n ['grædʒʊət] - 1. [person with a degree] licenciado m, -da f, egresado m, -da f Amér - 2. US [of high school] ≃ bachiller m. ◇ vi ['grædʒʊeɪt] - 1. [with a degree]: to graduate (from) licenciarse (por), licensiarse (en) Amér, egresar (de) Amér - 2. US [from high school]: to graduate (from) ≃ obtener el título de bachiller (en).

graduation [ˌgrædʒʊ'eɪʃn] n graduación f, egreso m Amér.

graffiti [grə'fiːtɪ] n (U) pintada f.

graft [grɑːft] n - **1.** MED & BOT injerto m **2.** UK inf [hard work] curro m muy duro - **3.** US inf [corruption] chanchullos mpl.

grain [greɪn] n - **1.** [seed, granule] grano m - **2.** (U) [crop] cereales mpl - **3.** fig [small amount] pizca f - **4.** [pattern] veta f.

gram, gramme [græm] n gramo m.

grammar ['græmə'] n gramática f.

grammar checker n COMPUT corrector m de gramática.

grammar school n [in UK] colegio subvencionado para mayores de once años con un programa de asignaturas tradicional; [in US] escuela f primaria.

grammatical [grə'mætɪkl] adj - **1.** [of grammar] gramatical - **2.** [correct] (gramaticalmente) correcto(ta).

gramme [græm] UK = gram.

gramophone ['græməfəʊn] dated n gramófono m.

gran [græn] n UK inf abuelita f, yaya f, mamá f grande Méx.

grand [grænd] ◇ adj - **1.** [impressive] grandioso(sa) - **2.** [ambitious] ambicioso(sa) - **3.** [important] distinguido(da) - **4.** inf dated [excellent] fenomenal. ◇ n inf [thousand pounds or dollars]**: a grand** mil libras/dólares; **five grand** cinco mil libras/dólares.

grandchild ['græntʃaɪld] (pl -children [-ˌtʃɪldrən]) n nieto m, -ta f.

grand(d)ad ['grændæd] n inf abuelito m, yayo m, papá m grande Méx.

granddaughter ['grænˌdɔːtə'] n nieta f.

grandeur ['grændʒə'] n - **1.** [splendour] grandiosidad f - **2.** [status] grandeza f.

grandfather ['grændˌfɑːðə'] n abuelo m.

grandma ['grænmɑː] n inf abuelita f, yaya f, mamá f grande Méx.

grandmother ['grænˌmʌðə'] n abuela f.

grandpa ['grænpɑː] n inf abuelito m, yayo m, papá m grande Méx.

grandparents ['grænˌpeərənts] npl abuelos mpl.

grand piano n piano m de cola.

grand slam n SPORT [in tennis] gran slam m; [in rugby] gran slam m.

grandson ['grænsʌn] n nieto m.

grandstand ['grændstænd] n tribuna f.

grand total n [total number] cantidad f total; [total sum, cost] importe m total.

granite ['grænɪt] n granito m.

granny ['grænɪ] n inf abuelita f, yaya f, mamá f grande Méx.

grant [grɑːnt] ◇ n subvención f; [for study] beca f. ◇ vt fml - **1.** [gen] conceder; **to take something for granted** no apreciar algo lo suficiente en lo que vale; **it is taken for granted that...** se da por sentado que... - **2.** [admit - truth, logic] admitir, aceptar.

granulated sugar ['grænjʊleɪtd-] n azúcar m granulado.

granule ['grænjuːl] n gránulo m.

grape [greɪp] n uva f.

grapefruit ['greɪpfruːt] (pl grapefruit OR -s) n pomelo m, toronja f Amér.

grapevine ['greɪpvaɪn] n - **1.** [plant] vid f; [against wall] parra f - **2.** [information channel]**: I heard on the grapevine that...** me ha dicho un pajarito que...

graph [grɑːf] n gráfico m, gráfica f.

graphic ['græfɪk] adj lit & fig gráfico(ca). ◆ **graphics** npl - **1.** [pictures] ilustraciones fpl - **2.** COMPUT gráficos mpl.

graphite ['græfaɪt] n grafito m.

graph paper n (U) papel m cuadriculado.

grapple ['græpl] ◆ **grapple with** vt insep - **1.** [person] forcejear con - **2.** [problem] esforzarse por resolver.

grasp [grɑːsp] ◇ n - **1.** [grip] agarre m, asimiento m - **2.** [understanding] comprensión f; **to have a good grasp of something** dominar algo. ◇ vt - **1.** [grip, seize] agarrar, asir - **2.** [understand] comprender - **3.** [opportunity] aprovechar.

grasping ['grɑːspɪŋ] adj pej avaro(ra).

grass [grɑːs] n - **1.** [plant] hierba f, pasto m Amér, zacate f Méx; [lawn] césped m; [pasture] pasto m, pasto m Amér, grama f Amér C & Ven; **'keep off the grass'** 'prohibido pisar el césped' - **2.** inf [marijuana] hierba f, maría f.

grasshopper ['grɑːsˌhɒpə'] n saltamontes m inv.

grass roots ◇ npl bases fpl. ◇ comp de base.

grass snake n culebra f.

grate [greɪt] ◇ n parrilla f, rejilla f. ◇ vt rallar. ◇ vi rechinar, chirriar; **to grate on sb's nerves** poner a alguien los nervios de punta.

grateful ['greɪtfʊl] adj [gen] agradecido(da); [smile, letter] de agradecimiento; **to be grateful to sb (for something)** estar agradecido a alguien (por algo); **I'm very grateful to you** te lo agradezco mucho; **I'd be grateful if you could do it by tomorrow** te agradecería si lo hicieras para mañana.

grater ['greɪtə'] n rallador m.

gratify ['grætɪfaɪ] vt - **1.** [please - person]**: to be gratified** estar satisfecho(cha) - **2.** [satisfy - wish] satisfacer.

grating ['greɪtɪŋ] <> adj chirriante. <> n [grille] reja f, enrejado m.

gratuitous [grə'tjuːɪtəs] adj fml gratuito(ta).

grave [greɪv] <> adj grave. <> n sepultura f, tumba f.

gravel ['grævl] n grava f, gravilla f.

gravestone ['greɪvstəun] n lápida f (sepulcral).

graveyard ['greɪvjɑːd] n cementerio m.

gravity ['grævətɪ] n gravedad f.

gravy ['greɪvɪ] n (U) [meat juice] salsa f OR jugo m de carne.

gray US = **grey**.

graze [greɪz] <> vt - 1. [feed on] pacer OR pastar en - 2. [skin, knee etc] rasguñar - 3. [touch lightly] rozar. <> vi pacer, pastar. <> n rasguño m.

grease [griːs] <> n grasa f. <> vt engrasar.

greaseproof paper [,griːspruːf-] n (U) UK papel m de cera (para envolver).

greasy ['griːzɪ] adj grasiento(ta); [inherently] graso(sa).

great [greɪt] <> adj - 1. [gen] grande; [heat] intenso(sa); **with great care** con mucho cuidado; **a great deal of...** un montón de... - 2. inf [splendid] estupendo(da), fenomenal; **we had a great time** lo pasamos en grande; **great!** ¡estupendo! <> adv: **great big** enorme. <> n grande mf.

Great Britain n Gran Bretaña.

greatcoat ['greɪtkəut] n gabán m.

Great Dane n gran danés m.

great-grandchild n bisnieto m, -ta f.

great-grandfather n bisabuelo m.

great-grandmother n bisabuela f.

greatly ['greɪtlɪ] adv enormemente.

greatness ['greɪtnɪs] n grandeza f.

Greece [griːs] n Grecia.

greed [griːd] n (U): **greed (for)** [food] glotonería f (con); [money] codicia f (de); [power] ambición f (de).

greedy ['griːdɪ] adj - 1. [for food] glotón(ona) - 2. [for money, power]: **greedy for** codicioso(sa) OR ávido(da) de.

Greek [griːk] <> adj griego(ga). <> n - 1. [person] griego m, -ga f - 2. [language] griego m.

green [griːn] <> adj - 1. [gen] verde - 2. [environmentalist] verde, ecologista - 3. inf [inexperienced] novato(ta) - 4. inf [ill, pale] pálido(da). <> n - 1. [colour] verde m - 2. [in village] parque m comunal - 3. [in golf] green m. <> **Green** n POL verde mf, ecologista mf; **the Greens** los verdes. <> **greens** npl [vegetables] verdura f.

greenback ['griːnbæk] n US inf billete m (dólar estadounidense).

green belt n UK cinturón m verde.

green card n - 1. UK [for vehicle] seguro que cubre a los conductores en el extranjero - 2. US [work permit] permiso m de trabajo.

greenery ['griːnərɪ] n vegetación f.

greenfly ['griːnflaɪ] (pl **greenfly** OR **-ies**) n pulgón m.

greengrocer ['griːnˌgrəusər] n verdulero m, -ra f; **greengrocer's (shop)** verdulería f.

greenhouse ['griːnhaus, pl -hauzɪz] n invernadero m.

greenhouse effect n: **the greenhouse effect** el efecto invernadero.

greenhouse gas n gas m invernadero.

Greenland ['griːnlənd] n Groenlandia.

green salad n ensalada f verde.

greet [griːt] vt - 1. [say hello to] saludar - 2. [receive] recibir.

greeting ['griːtɪŋ] n saludo m. <> **greetings** npl: **Christmas/birthday greetings!** ¡feliz navidad/cumpleaños!; **greetings from...** recuerdos de...

greetings card UK ['griːtɪŋz-], **greeting card** US n tarjeta f de felicitación.

grenade [grə'neɪd] n: **(hand) grenade** granada f (de mano).

grew [gruː] pt ▷ **grow**.

grey UK, **gray** US [greɪ] <> adj lit & fig gris; **a grey hair** una cana. <> n gris m.

grey-haired [-'heəd] adj canoso(sa).

greyhound ['greɪhaund] n galgo m.

grid [grɪd] n - 1. [grating] reja f, enrejado m - 2. [system of squares] cuadrícula f.

griddle ['grɪdl] n plancha f.

gridlock ['grɪdlɒk] n US embotellamiento m, atasco m.

grief [griːf] n (U) - 1. [sorrow] dolor m, pesar m - 2. inf [trouble] problemas mpl ▷▷▷ **to come to grief** [person] sufrir un percance; [plans] irse al traste; **good grief!** ¡madre mía!

grievance ['griːvns] n (motivo m de) queja f.

grieve [griːv] vi: **to grieve (for)** llorar (por).

grievous ['griːvəs] adj fml grave.

grievous bodily harm n (U) lesiones fpl graves.

grill [grɪl] <> n - 1. [on cooker] grill m; [for barbecue] parrilla f - 2. [food] parrillada f. <> vt - 1. [on cooker] asar al grill; [on barbecue] asar a la parrilla - 2. inf [interrogate] someter a un duro interrogatorio.

grille [grɪl] n [on radiator, machine] rejilla f; [on window, door] reja f.

grim [grɪm] *adj* - **1.** [expression] adusto(ta); [determination] inexorable - **2.** [place, facts, prospect] desolador(ra).

grimace [grɪˈmeɪs] ⬦ *n* mueca *f*. ⬦ *vi* hacer una mueca.

grime [graɪm] *n* mugre *f*.

grimy [ˈgraɪmɪ] *adj* mugriento(ta).

grin [grɪn] ⬦ *n* sonrisa *f* (abierta). ⬦ *vi*: to **grin (at)** sonreír (a).

grind [graɪnd] ⬦ *vt* (*pt & pp* **ground**) [crush] moler. ⬦ *vi* (*pt & pp* **ground**) [scrape] rechinar, chirriar. ⬦ *n* [hard, boring work] rutina *f*.
⬦ **grind down** *vt sep* [oppress] oprimir, acogotar. ⬦ **grind up** *vt sep* pulverizar.

grinder [ˈgraɪndər] *n* molinillo *m*.

grip [grɪp] ⬦ *n* - **1.** [grasp, hold]: to **have a grip (on sthg/sb)** tener (algo/a alguien) bien agarrado - **2.** [control, domination]: **grip on** control *m* de, dominio *m* de; **in the grip of sthg** en las garras de algo, dominado(da) por algo; **to get to grips with** llegar a controlar; **to get a grip on** o.s. calmarse, controlarse; **to lose one's grip** *fig* perder el control - **3.** [adhesion] sujeción *f*, adherencia *f* - **4.** [handle] asidero *m* - **5.** [bag] bolsa *f* de viaje. ⬦ *vt* - **1.** [grasp] agarrar, asir; [hand] apretar; [weapon] empuñar - **2.** [seize] apoderarse de. ⬦ *vi* adherirse.

gripe [graɪp] *inf* ⬦ *n* [complaint] queja *f*. ⬦ *vi*: to **gripe (about)** quejarse (de).

gripping [ˈgrɪpɪŋ] *adj* apasionante.

grisly [ˈgrɪzlɪ] *adj* [horrible, macabre] espeluznante.

gristle [ˈgrɪsl] *n* cartílago *m*, ternilla *f*.

grit [grɪt] ⬦ *n* - **1.** [stones] grava *f*; [sand, dust] arena *f* - **2.** *inf* [courage] valor *m*. ⬦ *vt* echar arena en (*las calles*).

gritty [ˈgrɪtɪ] *adj inf* [brave] valiente.

groan [grəʊn] ⬦ *n* gemido *m*. ⬦ *vi* - **1.** [moan] gemir - **2.** [creak] crujir.

grocer [ˈgrəʊsər] *n* tendero *m*, -ra *f*, abarrotero *m*, -ra *f* *Amér*; **grocer's (shop)** tienda *f* de comestibles OR ultramarinos, supermercado *m*, abarrotería *f* *Amér C*.

groceries [ˈgrəʊsərɪz] *npl* [foods] comestibles *mpl*, abarrotes *mpl Amér*.

grocery [ˈgrəʊsərɪ] *n US* [shop] tienda *f* de comestibles OR ultramarinos, supermercado *m*, abarrotería *f Amér*.

groggy [ˈgrɒgɪ] *adj* atontado(da).

groin [grɔɪn] *n* ingle *f*.

groom [gru:m] ⬦ *n* - **1.** [of horses] mozo *m* de cuadra - **2.** [bridegroom] novio *m*. ⬦ *vt* - **1.** [brush] cepillar, almohazar - **2.** [prepare]: to **groom sb (for sthg)** preparar a alguien (para algo).

groove [gru:v] *n* [deep line] ranura *f*; [in record] surco *m*.

grope [grəʊp] ⬦ *vt* - **1.** [try to find]: to **grope one's way** andar a tientas - **2.** [fondle] meter mano a. ⬦ *vi*: to **grope (about) for sthg** [object] buscar algo a tientas; [solution, remedy] buscar algo a ciegas.

gross [grəʊs] ⬦ *adj* - **1.** [total] bruto(ta) - **2.** *fml* [serious, inexcusable] grave - **3.** [coarse, vulgar] basto(ta), vulgar - **4.** *inf* [obese] obeso(sa) - **5.** *inf* [revolting] asqueroso(sa). ⬦ *n* (*pl* **gross** OR **-es**) gruesa *f*. ⬦ *vt* ganar en bruto.

grossly [ˈgrəʊslɪ] *adv* [seriously] enormemente.

grotesque [grəʊˈtesk] *adj* grotesco(ca).

grotto [ˈgrɒtəʊ] (*pl* **-es** OR **-s**) *n* gruta *f*.

grotty [ˈgrɒtɪ] *adj UK inf* asqueroso(sa).

ground [graʊnd] ⬦ *pt & pp* ⊢ **grind**. ⬦ *n* - **1.** [surface of earth] suelo *m*; [soil] tierra *f*; **above/below ground** sobre/bajo tierra; **on the ground** en el suelo - **2.** [area of land] terreno *m*; SPORT campo *m* - **3.** [subject area] terreno *m*; **to break fresh** OR **new ground** abrir nuevas fronteras - **4.** [advantage]: **to gain/lose ground** ganar/perder terreno. ⬦ *vt* - **1.** [base]: **to be grounded on** OR **in sthg** basarse en algo - **2.** [aircraft, pilot] hacer permanecer en tierra - **3.** *US inf* [child] castigar sin salir - **4.** *US* ELEC: **to be grounded** estar conectado(da) a tierra.
⬦ **grounds** *npl* - **1.** [reason]: **grounds (for sthg/for doing sthg)** motivos *mpl* (para algo/para hacer algo); **on the grounds that** aduciendo que, debido a que - **2.** [around house] jardines *mpl*; [of public building] terrenos *mpl* - **3.** [of coffee] posos *mpl*.

ground crew, ground staff *n* personal *m* de tierra.

ground floor *n* planta *f* baja; **ground floor flat** (piso *m*) bajo *m*.

grounding [ˈgraʊndɪŋ] *n*: **grounding (in)** base *f* (de), conocimientos *mpl* básicos (de).

groundless [ˈgraʊndlɪs] *adj* infundado(da).

groundsheet [ˈgraʊndʃiːt] *n* lona *f* impermeable (*para camping etc*).

groundskeeper [ˈgraʊnzkiːpər] *n* SPORT jardinero *m*, -ra *f*.

ground staff *n* - **1.** [at sports ground] personal *m* al cargo de las instalaciones - **2.** *UK* = **ground crew**.

groundwork [ˈgraʊndwɜːk] *n* (U) trabajo *m* preliminar.

group [gruːp] ⬦ *n* grupo *m*. ⬦ *vt* agrupar. ⬦ *vi*: to **group (together)** agruparse.

groupie [ˈgruːpɪ] *n inf* groupie *mf*.

grouse [graʊs] ⬦ *n* (*pl* **grouse** OR **-s**) [bird] urogallo *m*. ⬦ *vi inf* quejarse.

grove [grəʊv] *n* [of trees] arboleda *f*.

grovel [ˈgrɒvl] (*pt & pp* **-ed**, *cont* **-ing**) *vi lit & fig*: to **grovel (to)** arrastrarse (ante).

grow [grəʊ] ◇ vi (pt **grew**, pp **grown**) - 1. [gen] crecer - 2. [become] volverse, ponerse; **to grow dark** oscurecer; **to grow old** envejecer. ◇ vt (pt **grew**, pp **grown**) - 1. [plants] cultivar - 2. [hair, beard] dejarse crecer. ❧ **grow on** vt insep inf: **it's growing on me** me gusta cada vez más. ❧ **grow out of** vt insep - 1. [become too big for]: **he has grown out of his clothes** se le ha quedado pequeña la ropa - 2. [lose - habit] perder; **he'll grow out of it** ya se le pasará. ❧ **grow up** vi crecer; **when I grow up** cuando sea mayor; **I grew up in Ireland** me crié en Irlanda; **grow up!** ¡no seas niño!

grower ['grəʊər] n cultivador m, -ra f.

growl [graʊl] vi [dog, person] gruñir; [engine] rugir.

grown [grəʊn] ◇ pp ⊳ **grow**. ◇ adj adulto(ta).

grown-up n persona f mayor.

growth [grəʊθ] n - 1. [gen]: **growth (of OR in)** crecimiento m (de) - 2. MED tumor m.

grub [grʌb] n - 1. [insect] larva f, gusano m - 2. inf [food] manduca f, papeo m.

grubby ['grʌbɪ] adj sucio(cia), mugriento(ta).

grudge [grʌdʒ] ◇ n rencor m; **to bear sb a grudge, to bear a grudge against sb** guardar rencor a alguien. ◇ vt: **to grudge sb sthg** conceder algo a alguien a regañadientes; **to grudge doing sthg** hacer algo a regañadientes.

gruelling UK, **grueling** US ['grʊəlɪŋ] adj agotador(ra).

gruesome ['gru:səm] adj horripilante.

gruff [grʌf] adj - 1. [hoarse] bronco(ca) - 2. [rough, unfriendly] hosco(ca).

grumble ['grʌmbl] vi - 1. [complain] quejarse, refunfuñar - 2. [stomach] gruñir, hacer ruido.

grumpy ['grʌmpɪ] adj inf gruñón(ona).

grunt [grʌnt] vi gruñir.

G-string n taparrabos m inv, tanga m.

guarantee [,gærən'ti:] ◇ n garantía f. ◇ vt garantizar.

guard [gɑːd] ◇ n - 1. [person] guardia mf; [in prison] carcelero m, -ra f - 2. [group of guards, operation] guardia f; **to be on/stand guard** estar de/hacer guardia; **to catch sb off guard** coger a alguien desprevenido - 3. UK RAIL jefe m de tren - 4. [protective device - for body] protector m; [- for machine] cubierta f protectora. ◇ vt - 1. [protect, hide] guardar - 2. [prevent from escaping] vigilar.

guard dog n perro m guardián.

guarded ['gɑːdɪd] adj cauteloso(sa).

guardian ['gɑːdjən] n - 1. [of child] tutor m, -ra f - 2. [protector] guardián m, -ana f, protector m, -ra f.

guardrail ['gɑːdreɪl] n US [on road] barrera f de protección.

guard's van n UK furgón m de cola.

Guatemala [,gwɑːtə'mɑːlə] n Guatemala.

Guatemalan [,gwɑːtə'mɑːlən] ◇ adj guatemalteco(ca). ◇ n guatemalteco m, -ca f.

guerilla [gə'rɪlə] = **guerrilla**.

Guernsey ['gɜːnzɪ] n [place] Guernsey.

guerrilla, guerilla [gə'rɪlə] n guerrillero m, -ra f.

guerrilla warfare n (U) guerra f de guerrillas.

guess [ges] ◇ n suposición f, conjetura f; **to take a guess** intentar adivinar. ◇ vt adivinar; **guess what?** ¿sabes qué? ◇ vi - 1. [conjecture] adivinar; **to guess at sthg** tratar de adivinar algo; **to guess right** acertar; **to guess wrong** equivocarse; **to keep sb guessing** tener a alguien en la incertidumbre - 2. [suppose]: **I guess (so)** supongo OR me imagino que sí.

guesswork ['geswɜːk] n (U) conjeturas fpl, suposiciones fpl.

guest [gest] n - 1. [at home, on programme] invitado m, -da f - 2. [at hotel] huésped mf.

guesthouse ['gesthaʊs, pl -haʊzɪz] n casa f de huéspedes.

guestroom ['gestrʊm] n cuarto m de los invitados.

guffaw [gʌ'fɔː] ◇ n carcajada f. ◇ vi reírse a carcajadas.

guidance ['gaɪdəns] n (U) - 1. [help] orientación f - 2. [leadership] dirección f.

guide [gaɪd] ◇ n - 1. [person] guía mf - 2. [book] guía f. ◇ vt - 1. [show by leading] guiar - 2. [control] conducir, dirigir - 3. [influence]: **to be guided by** guiarse por. ❧ **Guides** n = **Girl Guides**.

guide book n guía f.

guide dog n perro m lazarillo.

guidelines ['gaɪdlaɪnz] npl directrices fpl.

guild [gɪld] n - 1. HIST gremio m - 2. [association] corporación f.

guile [gaɪl] n (U) astucia f.

guillotine ['gɪlə,ti:n] n [gen] guillotina f.

guilt [gɪlt] n - 1. [remorse] culpa f - 2. LAW culpabilidad f.

guilty ['gɪltɪ] adj [gen]: **guilty (of)** culpable (de).

guinea pig ['gɪnɪ-] n lit & fig conejillo m de Indias.

guise [gaɪz] n fml apariencia f.

guitar [gɪ'tɑːr] n guitarra f.

guitarist [gɪ'tɑːrɪst] n guitarrista mf.

gulf [gʌlf] n - 1. [sea] golfo m - 2. [chasm] sima f, abismo m - 3. [big difference]: **gulf (between)** abismo m (entre). ❧ **Gulf** n: **the Gulf** el Golfo.

gull [gʌl] n gaviota f.

gullet ['gʌlɪt] n esotago m.

gullible ['gʌləbl] adj crédulo(la).

gully ['gʌlɪ] n barranco m.

gulp [gʌlp] ◇ n trago m. ◇ vt [liquid] tragarse; [food] engullir. ◇ vi tragar saliva. ◆ **gulp down** vt sep [liquid] tragarse; [food] engullir.

gum [gʌm] ◇ n - 1. [chewing gum] chicle m - 2. [adhesive] pegamento m - 3. ANAT encía f. ◇ vt pegar, engomar.

gumboots ['gʌmbuːts] npl UK botas fpl de agua OR de goma.

gun [gʌn] n - 1. [pistol] pistola f; [rifle] escopeta f, fusil m; [artillery] cañón m - 2. [tool] pistola f. ◆ **gun down** vt sep abatir (a tiros).

gunboat ['gʌnbəʊt] n cañonero m.

gunfire ['gʌnfaɪər] n (U) disparos mpl, tiroteo m.

gunman ['gʌnmən] (pl -men [-mən]) n pistolero m.

gunpoint ['gʌnpɔɪnt] n: **at gunpoint** a punta de pistola.

gunpowder ['gʌn,paʊdər] n pólvora f.

gunshot ['gʌnʃɒt] n tiro m, disparo m.

gunsmith ['gʌnsmɪθ] n armero m.

gurgle ['gɜːgl] vi - 1. [water] gorgotear - 2. [baby] gorjear.

guru ['gʊruː] n lit & fig gurú m.

gush [gʌʃ] ◇ n chorro m. ◇ vi - 1. [flow out] chorrear, manar - 2. pej [enthuse] ser muy efusivo(va).

gusset ['gʌsɪt] n escudete m.

gust [gʌst] n ráfaga f, racha f.

gusto ['gʌstəʊ] n: **with gusto** con deleite.

gut [gʌt] ◇ n - 1. MED intestino m - 2. [strong thread] sedal m. ◇ vt - 1. [animal] destripar; [fish] limpiar - 2. [subj: fire] destruir el interior de. ◆ **guts** npl inf - 1. [intestines] tripas fpl - 2. [courage] agallas fpl.

gutter ['gʌtər] n - 1. [ditch] cuneta f - 2. [on roof] canalón m.

gutter press n pej prensa f amarilla OR sensacionalista.

guy [gaɪ] n - 1. inf [man] tipo m, tío m, chavo m Méx - 2. UK [dummy] muñeco que se quema la noche de Guy Fawkes.

Guy Fawkes' Night n UK fiesta que se celebra el 5 de noviembre en que se encienden hogueras y se lanzan fuegos artificiales.

guy rope n viento m, cuerda f (de tienda de campaña).

guzzle ['gʌzl] ◇ vt zamparse. ◇ vi zampar.

gym [dʒɪm] n inf - 1. [gymnasium] gimnasio m - 2. [exercises] gimnasia f.

gymnasium [dʒɪm'neɪzjəm] (pl -siums OR -sia [-zjə]) n gimnasio m.

gymnast ['dʒɪmnæst] n gimnasta mf.

gymnastics [dʒɪm'næstɪks] n (U) gimnasia f.

gym shoes npl zapatillas fpl de gimnasia.

gymslip ['dʒɪm,slɪp] n UK bata f de colegio.

gynaecologist UK, **gynecologist** US [,gaɪnə'kɒlədʒɪst] n ginecólogo m, -ga f.

gynaecology UK, **gynecology** US [,gaɪnə'kɒlədʒɪ] n ginecología f.

gypsy ['dʒɪpsɪ] = **gipsy**.

gyrate [dʒaɪ'reɪt] vi girar.

h (pl h's OR hs), **H** (pl H's OR Hs) [eɪtʃ] n [letter] h f, H f.

haberdashery ['hæbədæʃərɪ] n - 1. UK [selling sewing materials] mercería f - 2. US [selling men's clothing] tienda f de ropa para caballeros.

habit ['hæbɪt] n - 1. [custom] costumbre f, hábito m; **to make a habit of sthg** tomar algo por costumbre; **to make a habit of doing sthg** tener por costumbre hacer algo; **to have a drug habit** ser drogadicto(ta) - 2. [garment] hábito m.

habitat ['hæbɪtæt] n hábitat m.

habitual [hə'bɪtʃʊəl] adj - 1. [usual] habitual, acostumbrado(da) - 2. [smoker, gambler] empedernido(da).

hack [hæk] ◇ n pej [writer] escritorzuelo m, -la f; [journalist] gacetillero m, -ra f. ◇ vt [cut] cortar en tajos, acuchillar. ◆ **hack into** vt insep piratear.

hacker ['hækər] n: **(computer) hacker** pirata mf informático.

hackneyed ['hæknɪd] adj pej trillado(da), gastado(da).

hacksaw ['hæksɔː] n sierra f para metales.

had [weak form [həd], strong form [hæd]] pt & pp ▷ **have**.

haddock ['hædək] (pl haddock) n eglefino m.

hadn't ['hædnt] (abbr of had not) ▷ **have**.

haemophiliac [ˌhiːməˈfɪliæk] = **hemophiliac**.

haemorrhage [ˈhemərɪdʒ] = **hemorrhage**.

haemorrhoids [ˈhemərɔɪdz] = **hemorrhoids**.

haggard [ˈhægəd] *adj* ojeroso(sa).

haggis [ˈhægɪs] *n plato típico escocés hecho con las asaduras del cordero.*

haggle [ˈhægl] *vi:* **to haggle (with sb over** OR **about sthg)** regatear (algo con alguien).

Hague [heɪg] *n:* **The Hague** La Haya.

hail [heɪl] ◇ *n* - **1.** METEOR granizo *m*, pedrisco *m* - **2.** *fig* [large number] lluvia *f*. ◇ *vt* - **1.** [call] llamar; [taxi] parar - **2.** [acclaim]: **to hail sb as sthg** aclamar a alguien algo; **to hail sthg as sthg** ensalzar algo catalogándolo de algo. ◇ *impers vb:* **it's hailing** está granizando.

hailstone [ˈheɪlstəʊn] *n* granizo *m*, piedra *f*.

hair [heər] *n* - **1.** (U) [gen] pelo *m*; **to do one's hair** arreglarse el pelo - **2.** [on person's skin] vello *m*.

hairbrush [ˈheəbrʌʃ] *n* cepillo *m* (para el pelo).

haircut [ˈheəkʌt] *n* corte *m* de pelo.

hairdo [ˈheəduː] (*pl* **-s**) *n inf* peinado *m*.

hairdresser [ˈheəˌdresər] *n* peluquero *m*, -ra *f*; **hairdresser's (salon)** peluquería *f*.

hairdryer [ˈheəˌdraɪər] *n* secador *m* (de pelo).

hair gel *n* gomina *f*.

hairgrip [ˈheəgrɪp] *n* UK horquilla *f*.

hairpin [ˈheəpɪn] *n* horquilla *f* de moño.

hairpin bend *n* curva *f* muy cerrada.

hair-raising [-ˌreɪzɪŋ] *adj* espeluznante.

hair remover [-rɪˌmuːvər] *n* depilatorio *m*.

hair slide *n* UK pasador *m*.

hairspray [ˈheəspreɪ] *n* laca *f* (para el pelo).

hairstyle [ˈheəstaɪl] *n* peinado *m*.

hairy [ˈheərɪ] *adj* - **1.** [covered in hair] peludo(da) - **2.** *inf* [scary] espeluznante, espantoso(sa).

Haiti [ˈheɪtɪ] *n* Haití.

hake [heɪk] (*pl* **hake** OR **-s**) *n* merluza *f*.

half [*UK* hɑːf, *US* hæf] ◇ *adj* medio(dia); **half a dozen/mile** media docena/milla; **half an hour** media hora. ◇ *adv* - **1.** [gen]: **half naked/Spanish** medio desnudo/español; **half full/open** medio lleno/abierto; **half and half** mitad y mitad; **not half!** UK *inf* ¡y cómo! - **2.** [by half]: **half as big (as)** la mitad de grande (que) - **3.** [in telling the time]: **half past nine, half after nine** US las nueve y media; **it's half past** son y media. ◇ *n* - **1.** (*pl* **halves**) [one of two parts] mitad *f*; **one half of the group** una mitad del grupo; **in half** por la mitad, en dos; **to go halves (with sb)** ir a medias (con alguien)

- **2.** (*pl* **halfs**) [fraction, halfback, child's ticket] medio *m* - **3.** (*pl* **halves**) [of sports match] tiempo *m*, mitad *f* - **4.** (*pl* **halfs**) [of beer] media pinta *f*. ◇ *pron* la mitad; **half of it/them** la mitad.

halfback [ˈhɑːfbæk] *n* [in rugby] medio *m*.

half board *n* media pensión *f*.

half-breed ◇ *adj* mestizo(za). ◇ *n* mestizo *m*, -za *f* (*atención: el término 'half-breed' se considera racista*).

half-caste [-kɑːst] ◇ *adj* mestizo(za). ◇ *n* mestizo *m*, -za *f* (*atención: el término 'half-caste' se considera racista*).

half-hearted [-ˈhɑːtɪd] *adj* poco entusiasta.

half hour *n* media hora *f*.

half-mast *n*: **at half-mast** [flag] a media asta.

half moon *n* media luna *f*.

half note *n* US MUS blanca *f*.

halfpenny [ˈheɪpnɪ] (*pl* **-pennies** OR **-pence**) *n* medio penique *m*.

half-price *adj* a mitad de precio.

half term *n* UK cortas vacaciones escolares a mitad de trimestre.

half time *n* (U) descanso *m*.

halfway [hɑːfˈweɪ] ◇ *adj* intermedio(dia). ◇ *adv* - **1.** [in space]: **I was halfway down the street** llevaba la mitad de la calle andada - **2.** [in time]: **the film was halfway through** la película iba por la mitad.

halibut [ˈhælɪbət] (*pl* **halibut** OR **-s**) *n* fletán *m*.

hall [hɔːl] *n* - **1.** [entrance to house] vestíbulo *m*; [corridor] pasillo *m* - **2.** [public building, large room] sala *f* - **3.** UK UNIV colegio *m* mayor - **4.** [country house] mansión *f*, casa *f* solariega.

hallmark [ˈhɔːlmɑːk] *n* - **1.** [typical feature] sello *m* distintivo - **2.** [on metal] contraste *m*.

hallo [həˈləʊ] = **hello.**

hall of residence (*pl* **halls of residence**) *n* UK residencia *f* universitaria, colegio *m* mayor.

Hallowe'en [ˌhæləʊˈiːn] *n fiesta celebrada la noche del 31 de octubre.*

hallucinate [həˈluːsɪneɪt] *vi* alucinar.

hallway [ˈhɔːlweɪ] *n* [entrance to house] vestíbulo *m*; [corridor] pasillo *m*.

halo [ˈheɪləʊ] (*pl* **-es** OR **-s**) *n* halo *m*, aureola *f*.

halt [hɔːlt] ◇ *n* [stop]: **to grind to a halt** [vehicle] ir parando lentamente; [process] paralizarse; **to call a halt to** poner fin a. ◇ *vt* [person] parar, detener; [development, activity] interrumpir. ◇ *vi* [person, train] pararse, detenerse; [development, activity] interrumpirse.

halterneck [ˈhɔːltənek] *adj* escotado(da) por detrás.

halve [*UK* hɑːv, *US* hæv] *vt* - **1.** [reduce by half] reducir a la mitad - **2.** [divide] partir en dos.

halves [UK hɑːvz, US hævz] pl ▷ **half**.

ham [hæm] ◇ n [meat] jamón m. ◇ comp de jamón.

hamburger ['hæmbɜːgəʳ] n - **1.** [burger] hamburguesa f - **2.** [US] US [mince] carne f picada.

hamlet ['hæmlɪt] n aldea f.

hammer ['hæməʳ] ◇ n [gen & SPORT] martillo m. ◇ vt - **1.** [with tool] martillear - **2.** [with fist] aporrear - **3.** inf [defeat] dar una paliza a. ◇ vi [with fist]: **to hammer (on sthg)** aporrear (algo). ◆ **hammer out** vt insep [solution, agreement] alcanzar con esfuerzo.

hammock ['hæmək] n hamaca f, chinchorro m Méx.

hamper ['hæmpəʳ] ◇ n - **1.** [for food] cesta f - **2.** US [for laundry] cesto m de la ropa sucia. ◇ vt obstaculizar.

hamster ['hæmstəʳ] n hámster m.

hamstring ['hæmstrɪŋ] n tendón m de la corva.

hand [hænd] ◇ n - **1.** [gen] mano f; **to hold hands** ir cogidos de la mano; **hand in hand** [people] (cogidos) de la mano; **by hand** a mano; **in the hands of** en manos de; **to force sb's hand** apretar las tuercas a alguien; **to get OR lay one's hands on sthg** hacerse con algo; **to get OR lay one's hands on sb** pillar a alguien; **to give sb a free hand** dar carta blanca a alguien; **to go hand in hand** [things] ir de la mano; **to have one's hands full** estar muy ocupado(da); **to have time in hand** tener tiempo de sobra; **to overplay one's hand** fig extralimitarse; **to take sb in hand** hacerse cargo OR ocuparse de alguien - **2.** [influence] influencia f; **to have a hand in sthg/in doing sthg** intervenir en algo/al hacer algo - **3.** [worker - on farm] bracero m, peón m; [- on ship] tripulante mf - **4.** [of clock, watch] manecilla f, aguja f - **5.** [handwriting] letra f - **6.** [applause]: **a big hand** un gran aplauso. ◇ vt: **to hand sthg to sb, to hand sb sthg** dar OR entregar algo a alguien. ◆ **(close) at hand** adv cerca. ◆ **on hand** adv al alcance de la mano. ◆ **on the other hand** conj por otra parte. ◆ **out of hand** adv [completely] terminantemente. ◆ **to hand** adv a mano. ◆ **hand back** vt sep devolver. ◆ **hand down** vt sep [heirloom] dejar en herencia; [knowledge] transmitir. ◆ **hand in** vt sep [essay, application] entregar; [resignation] presentar. ◆ **hand out** vt sep repartir, distribuir. ◆ **hand over** ◇ vt sep - **1.** [baton, money] entregar - **2.** [responsibility, power] ceder. ◇ vi: **to hand over (to)** dar paso (a).

handbag ['hændbæg] n bolso m, bolsa f Méx, cartera f Andes.

handball ['hændbɔːl] n balonmano m.

handbook ['hændbʊk] n manual m.

handbrake ['hændbreɪk] n freno m de mano.

handcuffs ['hændkʌfs] npl esposas fpl.

handful ['hændfʊl] n [gen] puñado m.

handgun ['hændgʌn] n pistola f.

handheld PC ['hændheld-] n ordenador m de bolsillo, asistente m personal.

handicap ['hændɪkæp] ◇ n - **1.** [disability] discapacidad f, minusvalía f - **2.** [disadvantage] desventaja f, obstáculo m - **3.** SPORT hándicap m. ◇ vt estorbar.

handicapped ['hændɪkæpt] ◇ adj discapacitado(da), minusválido(da). ◇ npl: **the handicapped** los discapacitados, los minusválidos.

handicraft ['hændɪkrɑːft] n [skill] artesanía f.

handiwork ['hændɪwɜːk] n (U) [doing, work] obra f.

handkerchief ['hæŋkətʃɪf] (pl -chiefs OR -chieves [-tʃiːvz]) n pañuelo m.

handle ['hændl] ◇ n [of tool, broom, knife] mango m; [of door, window] manilla f; [of suitcase, cup, jug] asa f; [of racket] empuñadura f. ◇ vt [gen] manejar; [order, complaint, application] encargarse de; [negotiations, takeover] conducir; [people] tratar.

handlebars ['hændlbɑːz] npl manillar m, manubrio m Amér.

handler ['hændləʳ] n - **1.** [of animal] adiestrador m, -ra f - **2.** [at airport]: **(baggage) handler** mozo m de equipajes.

hand luggage n UK equipaje m de mano.

handmade [ˌhænd'meɪd] adj hecho(cha) a mano.

handout ['hændaʊt] n - **1.** [gift] donativo m - **2.** [leaflet] hoja f (informativa); [in class] notas fpl.

handrail ['hændreɪl] n pasamano m.

handset ['hændset] n auricular m (de teléfono); **to lift/replace the handset** descolgar/colgar (el teléfono).

hands free kit n kit m manos libres.

handshake ['hændʃeɪk] n apretón m de manos.

handsome ['hænsəm] adj - **1.** [man] guapo, atractivo - **2.** [literary] [woman] bella - **3.** [reward, profit] considerable.

handstand ['hændstænd] n pino m.

handwriting ['hændˌraɪtɪŋ] n letra f, caligrafía f.

handy ['hændɪ] adj inf - **1.** [useful] práctico(ca); **to come in handy** venir bien - **2.** [skilful] mañoso(sa) - **3.** [near] a mano, cerca; **to keep sthg handy** tener algo a mano.

handyman ['hændɪmæn] (pl -men [-men]) n: **a good handyman** un manitas.

hang [hæŋ] <> vt - **1.** (pt & pp hung) [fasten] colgar; [washing] tender; [wallpaper] poner - **2.** (pt & pp hung OR hanged) [execute] ahorcar; **to hang o.s.** ahorcarse. <> vi - **1.** (pt & pp hung) [be fastened] colgar, pender - **2.** (pt & pp hung OR hanged) [be executed] ser ahorcado(da) - **3.** (pt & pp hung) US inf: **I'm going to hang with my friends tonight** voy a ir por ahí esta noche con los amigos - **4.** COMPUT colgarse. <> n: **to get the hang of sthg** inf coger el tranquillo a algo. ◆ **hang about, hang around, hang round** vi - **1.** [spend time] pasar el rato; **they didn't hang about** se pusieron en marcha sin perder un minuto - **2.** [wait] esperar; **hang about!** ¡un momento! ◆ **hang on** vi - **1.** [keep hold]: **to hang on (to)** agarrarse (a) - **2.** inf [continue waiting] esperar, aguardar - **3.** [persevere] resistir. ◆ **hang out** vi inf [spend time] pasar el rato. ◆ **hang round** vi = **hang about.** ◆ **hang up** <> vt sep colgar. <> vi colgar. ◆ **hang up on** vt insep: **to hang up on sb** colgarle a alguien.

hangar ['hæŋəʳ] n hangar m.

hanger ['hæŋəʳ] n percha f.

hanger-on (pl hangers-on) n lapa f, parásito m.

hang gliding n vuelo m con ala delta.

hangover ['hæŋ,əʊvəʳ] n [from drinking] resaca f.

hang-up n inf complejo m.

hanker ['hæŋkəʳ] ◆ **hanker after, hanker for** vt insep anhelar.

hankie, hanky ['hæŋkɪ] (abbr of handkerchief) n inf pañuelo m.

haphazard [,hæp'hæzəd] adj [arrangement] caótico(ca).

hapless ['hæplɪs] adj liter desventurado(da).

happen ['hæpən] vi - **1.** [occur] pasar, ocurrir; **to happen to sb** pasarle OR sucederle a alguien - **2.** [chance]: **I happened to be looking out of the window...** dio la casualidad de que estaba mirando por la ventana...; **do you happen to have a pen on you?** ¿no tendrás un boli por casualidad?; **as it happens...** da la casualidad de que...

happening ['hæpənɪŋ] n suceso m, acontecimiento m.

happily ['hæpɪlɪ] adv - **1.** [with pleasure] alegremente, felizmente - **2.** [willingly] con mucho gusto - **3.** [fortunately] afortunadamente.

happiness ['hæpɪnɪs] n [state] felicidad f; [feeling] alegría f.

happy ['hæpɪ] adj - **1.** [gen contented] feliz; [pleased] contento(ta); [cheerful] alegre; **happy Christmas/birthday!** ¡feliz navidad/cumpleaños!; **to be happy with/about sthg** estar contento con algo - **2.** [causing contentment] feliz, alegre - **3.** [fortunate] feliz, oportuno(na)

- **4.** [willing]: **to be happy to do sthg** estar más que dispuesto(ta) a hacer algo; **I'd be happy to do it** yo lo haría con gusto.

happy-go-lucky adj despreocupado(da).

happy medium n término m medio.

harangue [həˈræŋ] <> n arenga f. <> vt arengar.

harass ['hærəs] vt acosar.

harbour UK, **harbor** US ['hɑːbəʳ] <> n puerto m. <> vt - **1.** [feeling] abrigar - **2.** [person] dar refugio a, encubrir.

hard [hɑːd] <> adj - **1.** [gen] duro(ra); [frost] fuerte; **to go hard** endurecerse; **to be hard on sb/sthg** [subj: person] ser duro con alguien/algo; [subj: work, strain] perjudicar a alguien/algo; [subj: result] ser inmerecido(da) para alguien/algo - **2.** [difficult] difícil; **hard of hearing** duro de oído - **3.** [forceful - push, kick etc] fuerte - **4.** [fact, news] concreto(ta) - **5.** UK [extreme]: **hard left/right** extrema izquierda/derecha. <> adv - **1.** [try, rain] mucho; [work] duro; [listen] atentamente; [think] detenidamente - **2.** [push, kick] fuerte, con fuerza ▸▸ **to be hard pushed** OR **put** OR **pressed to do sthg** vérselas y deseárselas para hacer algo; **to feel hard done by** sentirse tratado injustamente.

hardback ['hɑːdbæk] n edición f en pasta dura.

hardboard ['hɑːdbɔːd] n madera f conglomerada.

hard-boiled adj lit & fig duro(ra).

hard cash n dinero m contante y sonante.

hard copy n COMPUT copia f impresa.

hard disk n COMPUT disco m duro.

hard drive n COMPUT unidad f de disco duro.

harden ['hɑːdn] <> vt - **1.** [gen] endurecer - **2.** [resolve, opinion] reforzar. <> vi - **1.** [gen] endurecerse - **2.** [resolve, opinion] reforzarse.

hard-headed [-'hedɪd] adj realista.

hard-hearted [-'hɑːtɪd] adj insensible.

hard labour n (U) trabajos mpl forzados.

hard-liner n partidario m, -ria f de la línea dura.

hardly ['hɑːdlɪ] adv apenas; **hardly ever/anything** casi nunca/nada; **that's hardly fair** eso no es justo; **I'm hardly a communist, am I?** ¡pues sí que tengo yo mucho que ver con el comunismo!

hardness ['hɑːdnɪs] n - **1.** [firmness] dureza f - **2.** [difficulty] dificultad f.

hardship ['hɑːdʃɪp] n - **1.** (U) [difficult conditions] privaciones fpl - **2.** [difficult circumstance] infortunio m.

hard shoulder n UK AUT arcén m, acotamiento m Méx, berma f Andes, banquina f R Plata, hombrillo m Ven.

hard up adj inf: to be hard up andar mal de dinero; to be hard up for sthg andar escaso(sa) de algo.

hardware ['hɑːdweəʳ] (U) n - **1.** [tools, equipment] artículos mpl de ferretería - **2.** COMPUT hardware m.

hardware store n US ferretería f.

hardwearing [,hɑːd'weərɪŋ] adj UK resistente.

hardworking [,hɑːd'wɜːkɪŋ] adj trabajador(ra).

hardy ['hɑːdɪ] adj - **1.** [person, animal] fuerte, robusto(ta) - **2.** [plant] resistente.

hare [heəʳ] n liebre f.

harebrained ['heə,breɪnd] adj inf atolondrado(da).

harelip [,heə'lɪp] n labio m leporino.

haricot (bean) ['hærɪkəʊ-] n judía f, alubia f, frijol m Amér, poroto m Andes, caraota f Ven.

Harley Street ['hɑːlɪ-] n calle londinense famosa por sus médicos especialistas.

harm [hɑːm] <> n daño m; there's no harm in trying/asking no se pierde nada por intentarlo/preguntar; to be out of harm's way estar a salvo; to come to no harm [person] salir sano y salvo; [thing] no dañarse. <> vt [gen] hacer daño a, dañar; [reputation, chances, interests] dañar.

harmful ['hɑːmfʊl] adj: harmful (to) perjudicial OR dañino(na) (para); [substance] nocivo(va) (para).

harmless ['hɑːmlɪs] adj inofensivo(va).

harmonica [hɑː'mɒnɪkə] n armónica f.

harmonize, -ise ['hɑːmənaɪz] <> vi: to harmonize (with) armonizar (con). <> vt armonizar.

harmony ['hɑːmənɪ] n armonía f.

harness ['hɑːnɪs] <> n [for horse] arreos mpl, guarniciones fpl. <> vt - **1.** [horse] enjaezar - **2.** [use] aprovechar.

harp [hɑːp] n arpa f. ◆ **harp on** vi: to harp on (about sthg) dar la matraca (con algo).

harpoon [hɑː'puːn] n arpón m.

harpsichord ['hɑːpsɪkɔːd] n clavicémbalo m.

harrowing ['hærəʊɪŋ] adj pavoroso(sa).

harsh [hɑːʃ] adj - **1.** [life, conditions, winter] duro(ra) - **2.** [punishment, decision, person] severo(ra) - **3.** [texture, taste, voice] áspero(ra); [light, sound] violento(ta).

harvest ['hɑːvɪst] <> n [gen] cosecha f, pizca f Méx; [of grapes] vendimia f. <> vt cosechar.

has (weak form [həz], strong form [hæz]) 3rd person sing ⊳ **have**.

has-been n inf pej vieja gloria f.

hash [hæʃ] n [meat] picadillo m (de carne).

hashish ['hæʃiːʃ] n hachís m.

hasn't [hæznt] (abbr of had not) ⊳ **have**.

⊳ **have**.

hassle ['hæsl] inf <> n (U) [annoyance] rollo m, lío m. <> vt dar la lata a.

haste [heɪst] n prisa f; to make haste dated darse prisa, apresurarse.

hasten ['heɪsn] fml <> vt acelerar. <> vi: to hasten (to do sthg) apresurarse (a hacer algo).

hastily ['heɪstɪlɪ] adv - **1.** [quickly] de prisa, precipitadamente - **2.** [rashly] a la ligera, sin reflexionar.

hasty ['heɪstɪ] adj - **1.** [quick] apresurado(da), precipitado(da) - **2.** [rash] irreflexivo(va).

hat [hæt] n sombrero m.

hatch [hætʃ] <> vi [chick] romper el cascarón, salir del huevo. <> vt - **1.** [chick, egg] incubar - **2.** fig [scheme, plot] tramar. <> n [for serving food] ventanilla f.

hatchback ['hætʃ,bæk] n coche m con puerta trasera.

hatchet ['hætʃɪt] n hacha f.

hatchway ['hætʃ,weɪ] n escotilla f.

hate [heɪt] <> n odio m. <> vt odiar; to hate doing sthg odiar hacer algo.

hateful ['heɪtfʊl] adj odioso(sa).

hatred ['heɪtrɪd] n odio m.

hat trick n SPORT tres tantos marcados por un jugador en el mismo partido.

haughty ['hɔːtɪ] adj altanero(ra), altivo(va).

haul [hɔːl] <> n - **1.** [of stolen goods] botín m; [of drugs] alijo m - **2.** [distance]: long haul largo camino m, largo trayecto m. <> vt [pull] tirar, arrastrar.

haulage ['hɔːlɪdʒ] n transporte m.

haulier UK ['hɔːlɪəʳ], **hauler** US ['hɔːlər] n transportista mf.

haunch [hɔːntʃ] n - **1.** [of person] asentaderas fpl; to squat on one's haunches ponerse en cuclillas - **2.** [of animal] pernil m.

haunt [hɔːnt] <> n sitio m favorito. <> vt - **1.** [subj: ghost - house] aparecer en; [- person] aparecerse a - **2.** [subj: memory, fear, problem] atormentar.

have [hæv] <> aux vb (pt & pp had) (to form perfect tenses) haber; to have eaten haber comido; he hasn't gone yet, has he? no se habrá ido ya ¿no?; I've finished – have you? he terminado – ¿ah sí?; no, he hasn't (done it) no, no lo ha hecho; yes, he has (done it) sí, lo ha hecho; I was out of breath, having run all the way estaba sin aliento después de haber corrido todo el camino. <> vt (pt & pp had) - **1.** [possess, receive]: to have (got) tener; I have no money, I haven't got any money no tengo dinero; he has big hands tiene las manos grandes; do you have a car?, have you got a car? ¿tienes coche? - **2.** [experience, suffer] tener; **I had an accident** tuve un accidente; **to have a cold** tener un resfriado - **3.** *(referring to an action, instead of another vb)*: **to have a look** mirar, echar una mirada; **to have a swim** darse un baño, nadar; **to have breakfast** desayunar; **to have lunch** comer; **to have dinner** cenar; **to have a cigarette** fumarse un cigarrillo; **to have an operation** operarse - **4.** [give birth to]: **to have a baby** tener un niño - **5.** [cause to be done]: **to have sb do sthg** hacer que alguien haga algo; **to have sthg done** hacer que se haga algo; **to have one's hair cut** (ir a) cortarse el pelo - **6.** [be treated in a certain way]: **I had my car stolen** me robaron el coche - **7.** *inf* [cheat]: **you've been had** te han timado ▸▸◂ **to have had it** [car, machine] estar para el arrastre. ◇ *modal vb (pt & pp had)* [be obliged]: **to have (got) to do sthg** tener que hacer algo. ▸ **have off** *vt sep* [as holiday] tener libre. ▸ **have on** *vt sep* - **1.** [be wearing] llevar (puesto) - **2.** [tease] tomar el pelo a - **3.** [have to do]: **have you got anything on Friday?** ¿estás libre OR haces algo el viernes? ▸ **have out** *vt sep* [have removed]: **to have one's tonsils out** operarse de las amígdalas.

haven ['heɪvn] *n fig* refugio *m*, asilo *m*.

haven't ['hævnt] *(abbr of have not)* ⊳ **have**.

haversack ['hævəsæk] *n* mochila *f*.

havoc ['hævək] *n* estragos *mpl*.

Hawaii [hə'waɪi:] *n* Hawai.

hawk [hɔ:k] *n lit & fig* halcón *m*; **to watch sb like a hawk** observar a alguien con ojos de lince.

hawker ['hɔ:kər] *n* vendedor *m*, -ra *f* ambulante.

hay [heɪ] *n* heno *m*.

hay fever *n (U)* fiebre *f* del heno.

haystack ['heɪstæk] *n* almiar *m*.

haywire ['heɪwaɪər] *adj inf*: **to go haywire** [person] volverse majareta; [plan] liarse, embrollarse; [computer, TV etc] changarse.

hazard ['hæzəd] ◇ *n* riesgo *m*, peligro *m*. ◇ *vt* [guess, suggestion] aventurar.

hazardous ['hæzədəs] *adj* peligroso(sa).

hazard warning lights *npl UK* luces *fpl* de emergencia.

haze [heɪz] *n* neblina *f*.

hazel ['heɪzl] *adj* color avellana *(inv)*.

hazelnut ['heɪzlˌnʌt] *n* avellana *f*.

hazy ['heɪzɪ] *adj* - **1.** [misty] neblinoso(sa) - **2.** [vague] vago(ga), confuso(sa).

he [hi:] ◇ *pers pron* él; **he's tall/happy** es alto/feliz; **he can't do it** él no puede hacerlo; **there he is** allí está. ◇ *comp*: **he-goat** macho cabrío *m*.

head [hed] ◇ *n* - **1.** ANAT & COMPUT cabeza *f*; **a OR per head** por persona, por cabeza; **to be**

soft in the head estar mal de la sesera; **to be off one's head** *UK*, **to be out of one's head** *US* estar como una cabra; **it was over my head** no me enteré de nada; **it went to her head** se le subió a la cabeza; **to keep/lose one's head** no perder/perder la cabeza; **to laugh one's head off** reír a mandíbula batiente - **2.** [mind, brain] talento *m*, aptitud *f*; **she has a head for figures** se le dan bien las cuentas - **3.** [top - gen] cabeza *f*; [- of bed] cabecera *f* - **4.** [of flower] cabezuela *f*; [of cabbage] cogollo *m* - **5.** [on beer] espuma *f* - **6.** [leader] jefe *m*, -fa *f* - **7.** [head teacher] director *m*, -ra *f* (de colegio). ◇ *vt* - **1.** [procession, convoy, list, page] encabezar - **2.** [organization, delegation] dirigir - **3.** FTBL cabecear. ◇ *vi*: **to head north/for home** dirigirse hacia el norte/a casa. ▸ **heads** *npl* [on coin] cara *f*; **heads or tails?** ¿cara o cruz? ▸ **head for** *vt insep* - **1.** [place] dirigirse a - **2.** *fig* [trouble, disaster] ir camino de.

headache ['hedeɪk] *n* - **1.** MED dolor *m* de cabeza; **I have a headache** me duele la cabeza - **2.** *fig* [problem] quebradero *m* de cabeza.

headband ['hedbænd] *n* cinta *f*, banda *f* *(para el pelo)*.

head boy *n UK* [at school] *alumno delegado principal que suele representar a sus condiscípulos en actos escolares.*

headdress ['hed,dres] *n* tocado *m*.

header ['hedər] *n* - **1.** FTBL cabezazo *m* - **2.** TYPO encabezamiento *m*.

headfirst [,hed'fɜ:st] *adv* de cabeza.

head girl *n UK* [in school] *alumna delegada principal que suele representar a sus condiscípulas en actos escolares.*

heading ['hedɪŋ] *n* encabezamiento *m*.

headlamp ['hedlæmp] *n UK* faro *m*.

headland ['hedlənd] *n* cabo *m*, promontorio *m*.

headlight ['hedlaɪt] *n* faro *m*.

headline ['hedlaɪn] *n* titular *m*.

headlong ['hedlɒŋ] *adv* - **1.** [headfirst] de cabeza - **2.** [quickly, unthinkingly] precipitadamente.

headmaster [,hed'mɑ:stər] *n* director *m* (de colegio).

headmistress [,hed'mɪstrɪs] *n* directora *f* (de colegio).

head office *n* oficina *f* central.

head of state *n* jefe *m* de Estado.

head-on ◇ *adj* de frente, frontal. ◇ *adv* de frente.

headphones ['hedfəʊnz] *npl* auriculares *mpl*.

headquarter [hed'kwɔ:tər] *vt*: **to be headquartered in** tener la sede en.

headquarters [,hed'kwɔ:təz] *npl* (oficina *f*) central *f*, sede *f*; MIL cuartel *m* general.

headrest ['hedrest] n reposacabezas m inv.

headroom ['hedrʊm] n (U) [in car] espacio m entre la cabeza y el techo; [below bridge] altura f libre, gálibo m.

headscarf ['hedskɑːf] (pl -scarves [-skɑːvz] OR -scarfs) n pañuelo m (para la cabeza).

headset ['hedset] n auriculares mpl con micrófono.

head start n: head start (on OR over) ventaja f (con respecto a).

headstrong ['hedstrɒŋ] adj obstinado(da).

head waiter n maître m, capitán m de meseros Méx.

headway ['hedweɪ] n: to make headway avanzar, hacer progresos.

headwind ['hedwɪnd] n viento m de proa.

heady ['hedɪ] adj - 1. [exciting] emocionante - 2. [causing giddiness] embriagador(ra).

heal [hiːl] ◇ vt - 1. [person] curar; [wound] cicatrizar - 2. fig [troubles, discord] remediar. ◇ vi [wound] cicatrizar.

healing ['hiːlɪŋ] n curación f.

health [helθ] n - 1. [gen] salud f - 2. fig [of country, organization] buen estado m.

health care n asistencia f sanitaria.

health centre n ambulatorio m, centro m sanitario.

health food n comida f dietética.

health food shop n tienda f de dietética.

health service n servicio m sanitario de la Seguridad Social, ≃ INGS m.

healthy ['helθɪ] adj - 1. [gen] sano(na), saludable - 2. [profit] pingüe - 3. [attitude, respect] natural, sano(na).

heap [hiːp] ◇ n montón m, pila f. ◇ vt [pile up]: to heap sthg (on OR onto sthg) amontonar algo (sobre algo). ◆ heaps npl inf montones fpl.

hear [hɪəʳ] (pt & pp heard [hɜːd]) ◇ vt - 1. [gen] oír; I hear (that...) me dicen que... - 2. LAW ver. ◇ vi [gen] oír; have you heard about that job yet? ¿sabes algo del trabajo ese?; to hear from sb tener noticias de alguien ▸▸▸ to have heard of haber oído hablar de; I won't hear of it! ¡de eso ni hablar!

hearing ['hɪərɪŋ] n - 1. [sense] oído m; in OR within sb's hearing al alcance del oído de alguien; hard of hearing duro de oído - 2. LAW vista f; to give sb a fair hearing fig dar a alguien la oportunidad de que se exprese.

hearing aid n audífono m.

hearsay ['hɪəseɪ] n (U) habladurías fpl.

hearse [hɜːs] n coche m fúnebre.

heart [hɑːt] n - 1. [gen] corazón m; from the heart con toda sinceridad - 2. [courage]: I didn't have the heart to tell her no tuve valor para decírselo; to lose heart descorazonarse - 3. [centre - of issue, problem] quid m; [- of city etc] centro m; [- of lettuce] cogollo m. ◆ hearts npl corazones mpl. ◆ at heart adv en el fondo. ◆ by heart adv de memoria.

heartache ['hɑːteɪk] n dolor m.

heart attack n infarto m.

heartbeat ['hɑːtbiːt] n latido m.

heartbroken ['hɑːtˌbrəʊkn] adj desolado(da), abatido(da).

heartburn ['hɑːtbɜːn] n ardor m de estómago.

heart failure n paro m cardíaco.

heartfelt ['hɑːtfelt] adj sincero(ra), de todo corazón.

hearth [hɑːθ] n hogar m.

heartless ['hɑːtlɪs] adj cruel.

heartwarming ['hɑːtˌwɔːmɪŋ] adj gratificante, grato(ta).

hearty ['hɑːtɪ] adj - 1. [laughter] bonachón(ona); [welcome, congratulations, thanks] cordial; [person] fuerte(ta) - 2. [meal] abundante; [appetite] bueno(na) - 3. [dislike, distrust] profundo(da).

heat [hiːt] ◇ n - 1. [gen] calor m - 2. [specific temperature] temperatura f - 3. fig [pressure] tensión f; in the heat of the moment en el calor del momento - 4. [eliminating round] serie f, prueba f eliminatoria. ◇ vt calentar. ◆ heat up ◇ vt sep calentar. ◇ vi calentarse.

heated ['hiːtɪd] adj - 1. [swimming pool] climatizado(da) - 2. [debate, argument] acalorado(da).

heater ['hiːtəʳ] n calentador m, estufa f.

heath [hiːθ] n [place] brezal m.

heathen ['hiːðn] n pagano m, -na f.

heather ['heðəʳ] n brezo m.

heating ['hiːtɪŋ] n calefacción f.

heatstroke ['hiːtstrəʊk] n (U) insolación f.

heat wave n ola f de calor.

heave [hiːv] ◇ vt - 1. [pull] tirar de, arrastrar; [push] empujar - 2. inf [throw] tirar. ◇ vi - 1. [pull] tirar - 2. [rise and fall - waves] ondular; [- chest] palpitar.

heaven ['hevn] n [Paradise] cielo m; it was heaven [delightful] fue divino. ◆ heavens npl: the heavens liter los cielos; (good) heavens! ¡cielos!

heavenly ['hevnlɪ] adj inf dated [delightful] divino(na).

heavily ['hevɪlɪ] adv - 1. [smoke, drink] mucho; [rain] con fuerza; heavily in debt con muchas deudas - 2. [solidly]: heavily built corpulento(a) - **3.** [breathe, sigh] profundamente - **4.** [sit, move, fall] pesadamente - **5.** [speak] pesarosamente.

heavy ['hevɪ] *adj* - **1.** [gen] pesado(da); [solid] sólido(da); **how heavy is it?** ¿cuánto pesa?; **heavy build** corpulencia *f* - **2.** [traffic, rain, fighting] intenso(sa); **to be a heavy smoker/drinker** ser un fumador/bebedor empedernido - **3.** [losses, responsibility] grande - **4.** [soil, mixture] denso(sa) - **5.** [blow] duro(ra); [fine, defeat] duro(ra) - **6.** [busy - schedule, day] apretado(da) - **7.** [work] duro(ra) - **8.** [weather, air, day] cargado(da).

heavy cream *n US* nata *f* para montar.

heavy goods vehicle *n UK* vehículo *m* (de transporte) pesado.

heavyweight ['hevɪweɪt] ◇ *adj* SPORT de los pesos pesados. ◇ *n* SPORT peso *m* pesado.

Hebrew ['hi:bru:] ◇ *adj* hebreo(a). ◇ *n* - **1.** [person] hebreo *m*, -a *f* - **2.** [language] hebreo *m*.

Hebrides ['hebrɪdi:z] *npl*: **the Hebrides** las Hébridas.

heck [hek] *excl*: **what/where/why the heck...?** ¿qué/dónde/por qué demonios...?; **a heck of a lot of** la mar de.

heckle ['hekl] *vt & vi* interrumpir con exabruptos.

hectic ['hektɪk] *adj* ajetreado(da).

he'd [hi:d] - **1.** *(abbr of* he had*)* ▷ **have** - **2.** *(abbr of* he would*)* ▷ **would**.

hedge [hedʒ] ◇ *n* seto *m*. ◇ *vi* [prevaricate] contestar con evasivas.

hedgehog ['hedʒhɒg] *n* erizo *m*.

heed [hi:d] ◇ *n*: **to pay heed to sb** hacer caso a alguien; **to take heed of sthg** tener algo en cuenta. ◇ *vt fml* tener en cuenta.

heedless ['hi:dlɪs] *adj*: **to be heedless of sthg** no hacer caso de algo.

heel [hi:l] *n* - **1.** [of foot] talón *m* - **2.** [of shoe] tacón *m*, taco *m* *Amér*.

hefty ['heftɪ] *adj inf* - **1.** [person] fornido(da) - **2.** [salary, fee, fine] considerable, importante.

heifer ['hefər] *n* vaquilla *f*.

height [haɪt] *n* - **1.** [gen] altura *f*; [of person] estatura *f*; **5 metres in height** 5 metros de altura; **to gain/lose height** ganar/perder altura - **2.** [zenith]: **the height of** [gen] el punto álgido de; [ignorance, bad taste] el colmo de.

heighten ['haɪtn] ◇ *vt* intensificar, aumentar. ◇ *vi* intensificarse, aumentar.

heir [eər] *n* heredero *m*.

heiress ['eərɪs] *n* heredera *f*.

heirloom ['eəlu:m] *n* reliquia *f* de familia.

heist [haɪst] *n inf* golpe *m*, robo *m*.

held [held] *pt & pp* ▷ **hold**.

helicopter ['helɪkɒptər] *n* helicóptero *m*.

helium ['hi:lɪəm] *n* helio *m*.

hell [hel] ◇ *n* infierno *m*; **one OR a hell of a mess** *inf* un lío de mil demonios; **it was hell** *inf* fue un infierno; **to do sthg for the hell of it** *inf* hacer algo porque sí; **to give sb hell** *inf* hacérselas pasar canutas a alguien; **go to hell!** *v inf* ¡vete al infierno!; **neighbours from hell** *inf* vecinos infernales; **boyfriend from hell** *inf* novio infernal. ◇ *excl inf* ¡hostias!

he'll [hi:l] - **1.** *(abbr of* he will*)* ▷ **will** - **2.** *(abbr of* he shall*)* ▷ **shall**.

hellish ['helɪʃ] *adj* diabólico(ca).

hello [hə'ləʊ], **hallo, hullo** *excl* - **1.** [as greeting] ¡hola!; [on phone - when answering] ¡diga!, ¡bueno! *Méx*, ¡hola! *R Plata*, ¡aló! *Andes*; [- when calling] ¡oiga!, ¡hola! *R Plata*, ¡aló! *Andes* - **2.** [to attract attention] ¡oiga!

helm [helm] *n lit & fig* timón *m*.

helmet ['helmɪt] *n* casco *m*.

help [help] ◇ *n* - **1.** [gen & COMPUT] ayuda *f*; **with the help of** con la ayuda de; **to be a help** ser una ayuda; **to be of help** ayudar - **2.** *(U)* [emergency aid] socorro *m*, ayuda *f*. ◇ *vt* - **1.** [assist]: **to help sb (to) do sthg/with sthg** ayudar a alguien (a hacer algo/con algo); **can I help you?** [in shop, bank] ¿en qué puedo servirle? - **2.** [avoid]: **I can't help it/feeling sad** no puedo evitarlo/evitar que me dé pena; **it can't be helped** ¿qué se le va a hacer? - **3.** [with food, drink]: **to help o.s. (to sthg)** servirse (algo). ◇ *vi*: **to help (with)** ayudar (con). ◇ *excl* ¡socorro!, ¡auxilio! ⬅ **help out** *vt sep* echar una mano a. ◇ *vi* echar una mano.

helper ['helpər] *n* - **1.** [gen] ayudante *mf* - **2.** *US* [to do housework] mujer *f OR* señora *f* de la limpieza.

helpful ['helpfʊl] *adj* - **1.** [willing to help] servicial, atento(ta) - **2.** [providing assistance] útil.

helping ['helpɪŋ] *n* ración *f*; **would you like a second helping?** ¿quiere repetir?

helpless ['helplɪs] *adj* [child] indefenso(sa); [look, gesture] impotente.

helpline ['helplaɪn] *n* servicio *m* de asistencia telefónica.

help menu *n* COMPUT menú *m* de ayuda.

Helsinki ['helsɪŋkɪ] *n* Helsinki.

hem [hem] *n* dobladillo *m*. ⬅ **hem in** *vt sep* rodear, cercar.

hemisphere ['hemɪˌsfɪər] *n* [of earth & ANAT] hemisferio *m*.

hemline ['hemlaɪn] *n* bajo *m* (de falda etc).

hemophiliac, haemophiliac [ˌhi:mə'fɪliæk] *n* hemofílico *m*, -ca *f*.

hemorrhage, haemorrhage ['hemərɪdʒ] *n* hemorragia *f*.

hemorrhoids, haemorrhoids ['hemərɔɪdz] *npl* hemorroides *fpl*.

hen [hen] *n* - **1.** [female chicken] gallina *f* - **2.** [female bird] hembra *f*.

hence [hens] *adv fml* - **1.** [therefore] por lo tanto, así pues - **2.** [from now]: **five years hence** de aquí a cinco años.

henceforth [,hens'fɔ:θ] *adv fml* de ahora en adelante.

henchman ['hentʃmən] (*pl* -**men** [-mən]) *n pej* esbirro *m*.

henpecked ['henpekt] *adj pej*: **a henpecked husband** un calzonazos.

hepatitis [,hepə'taɪtɪs] *n* hepatitis *f inv*.

her [hɜ:r] <> *pers pron* - **1.** (*direct - unstressed*) la; (*- stressed*) ella; [referring to ship, car etc] lo; **I know her** la conozco; **I like her** me gusta; **it's her** es ella; **if I were** OR **was her** si (yo) fuera ella; **you can't expect her to do it** no esperarás que ella lo haga; **fill her up!** AUT ¡llénemelo!, ¡lleno, por favor! - **2.** (*indirect - gen*) le; (*- with other 3rd person pronouns*) se; **he sent her a letter** le mandó una carta; **we spoke to her** hablamos con ella; **I gave it to her** se lo di - **3.** (*after prep, in comparisons etc*) ella; **I'm shorter than her** yo soy más bajo que ella. <> *poss adj* su, sus (*pl*); **her coat** su abrigo; **her children** sus niños; **her name is Sarah** se llama Sarah; **it wasn't her fault** no fue culpa suya OR su culpa; **she washed her hair** se lavó el pelo.

herald ['herəld] <> *vt fml* - **1.** [signify, usher in] anunciar - **2.** [proclaim] proclamar. <> *n* - **1.** [messenger] heraldo *m* - **2.** [sign] anuncio *m*.

herb [UK hɜ:b, US ɜ:rb] *n* hierba *f* (*aromática o medicinal*).

herd [hɜ:d] <> *n* [of cattle, goats] rebaño *m*; [of elephants] manada *f*. <> *vt fig* [push] conducir (en grupo) bruscamente.

here [hɪər] *adv* aquí; **here he is/they are** aquí está/están; **here it is** aquí está; **here is the book** aquí tienes el libro; **here are the keys** aquí tienes las llaves; **here you are** [when giving] aquí tienes; **here and there** aquí y allá.

hereabouts UK ['hɪərə,baʊts], **hereabout** US [,hɪərə'baʊt] *adv* por aquí.

hereafter [,hɪər'ɑ:ftər] <> *adv fml* [from now on] de ahora en adelante; [later on] más tarde. <> *n*: **the hereafter** el más allá, la otra vida.

hereby [,hɪə'baɪ] *adv fml* - **1.** [in documents] por la presente - **2.** [when speaking]: **I hereby declare you the winner** desde este momento te declaro vencedor.

hereditary [hɪ'redɪtrɪ] *adj* hereditario(ria).

heresy ['herəsɪ] *n fig* & RELIG herejía *f*.

herewith [,hɪə'wɪð] *adv fml* [with letter]: **'please find herewith...'** 'le mando adjunto...'

heritage ['herɪtɪdʒ] *n* patrimonio *m*.

hermetically [hɜ:'metɪklɪ] *adv*: **hermetically sealed** cerrado(da) herméticamente.

hermit ['hɜ:mɪt] *n* ermitaño *m*, -ña *f*.

hernia ['hɜ:njə] *n* hernia *f*.

hero ['hɪərəʊ] (*pl* -**es**) *n* - **1.** [gen] héroe *m* - **2.** US [sandwich] bocadillo hecho con una barra de pan larga y estrecha, relleno de varios ingredientes.

heroic [hɪ'rəʊɪk] *adj* heroico(ca).

heroin ['herəʊɪn] *n* heroína *f* (*droga*); **heroin addict** heroinómano *m*, -na *f*.

heroine ['herəʊɪn] *n* heroína *f*.

heron ['herən] (*pl* **heron** OR -**s**) *n* garza *f* real.

herring ['herɪŋ] (*pl* **herring** OR -**s**) *n* arenque *m*.

hers [hɜ:z] *poss pron* suyo(suya); **that money is hers** ese dinero es suyo; **those keys are hers** esas llaves son suyas; **it wasn't his fault, it was hers** no fue culpa de él sino de ella; **a friend of hers** un amigo suyo, un amigo de ella; **mine is good, but hers is bad** el mío es bueno pero el suyo es malo.

herself [hɜ:'self] *pron* - **1.** (*reflexive*) se; (*after prep*) sí misma; **with herself** consigo misma - **2.** (*for emphasis*) ella misma; **she did it herself** lo hizo ella sola.

he's [hi:z] - **1.** (*abbr of he is*) [▷] **be** - **2.** (*abbr of he has*) [▷] **have**.

hesitant ['hezɪtənt] *adj* - **1.** [unsure of oneself] indeciso(sa), inseguro(ra) - **2.** [faltering, slow to appear] vacilante.

hesitate ['hezɪteɪt] *vi* vacilar, dudar.

hesitation [,hezɪ'teɪʃn] *n* vacilación *f*.

heterogeneous [,hetərə'dʒi:njəs] *adj fml* heterogéneo(a).

heterosexual [,hetərəʊ'sekʃʊəl] <> *adj* heterosexual. <> *n* heterosexual *mf*.

hey [heɪ] *excl* ¡eh!, ¡oye!

heyday ['heɪdeɪ] *n* apogeo *m*, auge *m*.

hi [haɪ] *excl inf* [hello] ¡hola!

hiatus [haɪ'eɪtəs] (*pl* -**es**) *n fml* [pause] interrupción *f*.

hibernate ['haɪbəneɪt] *vi* hibernar.

hiccough, hiccup ['hɪkʌp] <> *n* - **1.** [caused by wind] hipo *m*; **to have (the) hiccoughs** tener hipo - **2.** *fig* [difficulty] contratiempo *m*. <> *vi* hipar.

hid [hɪd] *pt* [▷] **hide**.

hidden ['hɪdn] <> *pp* [▷] **hide**. <> *adj* oculto(ta).

hide [haɪd] <> *vt* (*pt* **hid**, *pp* **hidden**) - **1.** [conceal] esconder, ocultar; **to hide sthg (from sb)** esconder OR ocultar algo (a alguien) - **2.** [cover] tapar, ocultar. <> *vi* (*pt* **hid**, *pp* **hidden**) esconderse. <> *n* - **1.** [animal skin] piel *f* - **2.** [for watching birds, animals] puesto *m*.

hide-and-seek *n* escondite *m*.

hideaway ['haɪdəweɪ] *n inf* escondite *m*.

hideous ['hɪdɪəs] *adj* horrible.

hiding ['haɪdɪŋ] n - 1. [concealment]: **in hiding** escondido(da) - 2. inf [beating]: **to give sb/ get a (good) hiding** darle a alguien/recibir una (buena) paliza.

hiding place n escondite m.

hierarchy ['haɪərɑːkɪ] n jerarquía f.

hi-fi ['haɪfaɪ] <> adj de alta fidelidad. <> n equipo m de alta fidelidad.

high [haɪ] <> adj - 1. [gen] alto(ta); [altitude] grande; **it's 6 metres high** tiene 6 metros de alto OR altura; **how high is it?** ¿cuánto mide?; **temperatures in the high 20s** temperaturas cercanas a los 30 grados; **at high speed** a gran velocidad - 2. [wind] fuerte - 3. [risk, quality] grande - 4. [ideals, principles, tone] elevado(da) - 5. [high-pitched] agudo(da) - 6. inf colocado(da). <> adv alto; **he threw the ball high in the air** lanzó la pelota muy alto. <> n - 1. [highest point] punto m álgido - 2. [weather front] anticiclón m; [top temperature] máxima f.

highbrow ['haɪbraʊ] adj culto(ta), intelectual.

high chair n trona f.

high-class adj [superior] de (alta) categoría.

High Court n UK tribunal m supremo.

higher ['haɪər] adj [exam, qualification] superior. ➠ **Higher** n: **Higher (Grade)** en Escocia, examen realizado al final de la enseñanza secundaria.

higher education n enseñanza f superior.

high-handed [-'hændɪd] adj despótico(ca).

high jump n salto m de altura; **you're** OR **you'll be for the high jump** UK inf te la vas a cargar.

Highlands ['haɪləndz] npl: **the Highlands** [of Scotland] las Tierras Altas de Escocia.

highlight ['haɪlaɪt] <> n [of event, occasion] punto m culminante. <> vt - 1. [visually] resaltar, marcar - 2. [emphasize] destacar, resaltar. ➠ **highlights** npl - 1. [in hair] reflejos mpl - 2. [of match] mejores momentos mpl.

highlighter (pen) ['haɪlaɪtər-] n rotulador m, marcador m.

highly ['haɪlɪ] adv - 1. [very, extremely] muy; **highly paid** bien pagado(da) - 2. [favourably]: **to speak highly of sb** hablar muy bien de alguien; **to think highly of sb** tener a alguien en mucha estima.

highly-strung adj muy nervioso(sa).

Highness ['haɪnɪs] n: **His/Her/Your (Royal) Highness** Su Alteza f (Real); **their (Royal) Highnesses** Sus Altezas (Reales).

high-pitched [-'pɪtʃt] adj agudo(da).

high point n [of occasion] momento m OR punto m culminante.

high-powered [-'paʊəd] adj - 1. [powerful] de gran potencia - 2. [prestigious - activity, place] prestigioso(sa); [- person] de altos vuelos.

high-ranking [-'ræŋkɪŋ] adj [in army etc] de alta graduación; [in government]: **high-ranking official** alto cargo m.

high-rise adj: **high-rise building** torre f.

high school n ≃ instituto m de bachillerato.

high season n temporada f alta.

high street <> adj UK [bank] comercial. <> n calle f mayor OR principal.

high tech, hi-tech [-'tek] adj de alta tecnología.

high tide n [of sea] marea f alta.

highway ['haɪweɪ] n - 1. US [main road between cities] autopista f - 2. UK [any main road] carretera f.

Highway Code n UK: **the Highway Code** el código de la circulación.

hijack ['haɪdʒæk] vt [aircraft] secuestrar.

hijacker ['haɪdʒækər] n secuestrador m, -ra f (de un avión).

hike [haɪk] <> n [long walk] caminata f; **to go for** OR **on a hike** ir de excursión. <> vi [go for walk] ir de excursión.

hiker ['haɪkər] n excursionista mf.

hiking ['haɪkɪŋ] n excursionismo m; **to go hiking** ir de excursión.

hilarious [hɪ'leərɪəs] adj desternillante.

hill [hɪl] n - 1. [mound] colina f - 2. [slope] cuesta f.

hillside ['hɪlsaɪd] n ladera f.

hilly ['hɪlɪ] adj montañoso(sa).

hilt [hɪlt] n puño m, empuñadura f.

him [hɪm] pers pron - 1. (direct - unstressed) lo, le; (- stressed) él; **I know him** lo OR le conozco; **I like him** me gusta; **it's him** es él; **if I were** OR **was him** si (yo) fuera él; **you can't expect him to do it** no esperarás que él lo haga - 2. (indirect - gen) le; (- with other 3rd person pronouns) se; **she sent him a letter** le mandó una carta; **we spoke to him** hablamos con él; **I gave it to him** se lo di - 3. (after prep, in comparisons etc) él; **I'm shorter than him** yo soy más bajo que él.

Himalayas [ˌhɪmə'leɪəz] npl: **the Himalayas** el Himalaya.

himself [hɪm'self] pron - 1. (reflexive) se; (after prep) sí mismo; **with himself** consigo mismo - 2. (for emphasis) él mismo; **he did it himself** lo hizo él solo.

hind [haɪnd] <> adj trasero(ra). <> n (pl hind OR -s) cierva f.

hinder ['hɪndər] vt [gen] estorbar; [progress, talks, attempts] entorpecer.

Hindi ['hɪndɪ] n [language] hindi m.

hindrance ['hɪndrəns] n [obstacle] obstáculo m, impedimento m; [person] estorbo m.

hindsight ['haɪndsaɪt] n: **with the benefit of hindsight** ahora que se sabe lo que pasó.

Hindu ['hɪndu:] ◇ *adj* hindú. ◇ *n* (*pl* -s) hindú *mf*.

hinge [hɪndʒ] *n* [on door, window] bisagra *f*.
hinge (up)on *vt insep* [depend on] depender de.

hint [hɪnt] ◇ *n* - **1.** [indication] indirecta *f*; **to drop a hint** lanzar una indirecta - **2.** [piece of advice] consejo *m* - **3.** [small amount, suggestion] asomo *m*; [of colour] pizca *f*. ◇ *vi*: **to hint at sthg** insinuar algo. ◇ *vt*: **to hint that** insinuar que.

hip [hɪp] ◇ *n* ANAT cadera *f*. ◇ *adj inf* moderno(na).

hippie, hippy ['hɪpɪ] *n* hippy *mf*.

hippopotamus [,hɪpə'pɒtəməs] (*pl* -muses OR -mi [-maɪ]) *n* hipopótamo *m*.

hippy ['hɪpɪ] = **hippie**.

hire ['haɪər] ◇ *n* (*U*) [of car, equipment] alquiler *m*; **for hire** [taxi] libre; **'boats for hire'** 'se alquilan barcos'. ◇ *vt* - **1.** [rent] alquilar - **2.** [employ] contratar. **hire out** *vt sep* [car, equipment] alquilar; [one's services] ofrecer.

hire car *n* UK coche *m* de alquiler.

hire purchase *n* (*U*) UK compra *f* a plazos; **to buy sthg on hire purchase** comprar algo a plazos.

his [hɪz] ◇ *poss adj* su, sus (*pl*); **his house** su casa; **his children** sus niños; **his name is Joe** se llama Joe; **it wasn't his fault** no fue culpa suya OR su culpa; **he washed his hair** se lavó el pelo. ◇ *poss pron* suyo(suya); **that money is his** ese dinero es suyo; **those keys are his** esas llaves son suyas; **it wasn't her fault, it was his** no fue culpa de ella sino de él; **a friend of his** un amigo suyo, un amigo de él; **mine is good, but his is bad** el mío es bueno pero el suyo es malo.

Hispanic [hɪ'spænɪk] ◇ *adj* hispánico(ca). ◇ *n esp* US hispano *m*, -na *f*.

hiss [hɪs] ◇ *n* - **1.** [of person] bisbiseo *m*, siseo *m* - **2.** [of steam, gas, snake] silbido *m*. ◇ *vi* - **1.** [person] bisbisear, sisear; [to express disapproval] silbar, abuchear - **2.** [steam, gas, snake] silbar.

historic [hɪ'stɒrɪk] *adj* [significant] histórico(ca).

historical [hɪ'stɒrɪkəl] *adj* histórico(ca).

history ['hɪstərɪ] ◇ *n* - **1.** [gen] historia *f* - **2.** [past record & COMPUT] historial *m*. ◇ *comp* [book, teacher, programme] de historia.

hit [hɪt] ◇ *n* - **1.** [blow] golpe *m* - **2.** [successful strike] impacto *m* - **3.** [success, record] éxito *m* - **4.** COMPUT visita *f*. ◇ *comp* de éxito. ◇ *vt* (*pt & pp* hit) - **1.** [subj: person] pegar, golpear - **2.** [crash into] chocar contra OR con - **3.** [reach] alcanzar; [bull's-eye] dar en - **4.** [affect badly] afectar - **5.** [occur to]: **the solution hit me** se me ocurrió la solución.

hit-and-miss = **hit-or-miss**.

hit-and-run *adj* [driver] que se da a la fuga después de; [accident] en el cual el conductor se da a la fuga, [crime] en que el conductor se da a la fuga.

hitch [hɪtʃ] ◇ *n* [problem, snag] problema *m*, pega *f*. ◇ *vt* - **1.** [catch]: **to hitch a lift** conseguir que le lleven a uno en coche - **2.** [fasten]: **to hitch sthg on** OR **onto sthg** enganchar algo a algo. ◇ *vi* [hitchhike] hacer autoestop. **hitch up** *vt sep* [clothes] subirse.

hitchhike ['hɪtʃhaɪk] *vi* hacer autoestop.

hitchhiker ['hɪtʃhaɪkər] *n* autoestopista *mf*.

hi-tech [,haɪ'tek] = **high tech**.

hitherto [,hɪðə'tu:] *adv fml* hasta ahora.

hit-or-miss, hit-and-miss *adj* azaroso(sa).

HIV (*abbr of* human immunodeficiency virus) *n* VIH *m*; **to be HIV-positive** ser seropositivo(va).

hive [haɪv] *n* [for bees] colmena *f*; **a hive of activity** un enjambre, un centro de actividad. **hive off** *vt sep* [separate] transferir.

HNC (*abbr of* Higher National Certificate) *n* diploma técnico en Gran Bretaña.

HND (*abbr of* Higher National Diploma) *n* diploma técnico superior en Gran Bretaña.

hoard [hɔ:d] ◇ *n* [store] acopio *m*. ◇ *vt* [collect, save] acumular; [food] acaparar.

hoarding ['hɔ:dɪŋ] *n* UK [for advertisements, posters] valla *f* publicitaria.

hoarfrost ['hɔ:frɒst] *n* escarcha *f*.

hoarse [hɔ:s] *adj* - **1.** [voice] ronco(ca) - **2.** [person] afónico(ca).

hoax [həʊks] *n* engaño *m*; **hoax call** falsa alarma telefónica.

hob [hɒb] *n* UK [on cooker] encimera *f*.

hobble ['hɒbl] *vi* [limp] cojear.

hobby ['hɒbɪ] *n* [leisure activity] hobby *m*, afición *f*.

hobbyhorse ['hɒbɪhɔ:s] *n* - **1.** [toy] caballo *m* de juguete - **2.** [favourite topic] caballo *m* de batalla.

hobo ['həʊbəʊ] (*pl* -es OR -s) *n* US [tramp] vagabundo *m*, -da *f*.

hockey ['hɒkɪ] *n* - **1.** [on grass] hockey *m* sobre hierba - **2.** US [ice hockey] hockey *m* sobre hielo.

hoe [həʊ] ◇ *n* azada *f*. ◇ *vt* remover con la azada.

hog [hɒg] ◇ *n* US [pig] cerdo *m*, puerco *m*; **to go the whole hog** *fig* tirar la casa por la ventana. ◇ *vt inf* [monopolize] acaparar.

Hogmanay ['hɒgməneɪ] *n* denominación escocesa de la Nochevieja.

hoist [hɔɪst] ◇ *n* [pulley, crane] grúa *f*; [lift] montacargas *m inv*. ◇ *vt* izar.

hold [həʊld] ◇ *vt* (*pt & pp* held) - **1.** [have hold of] tener cogido(da) - **2.** [keep in position] sujetar - **3.** [sustain, support] sostener, aguantar - **4.** [embrace] abrazar - **5.** [as prisoner] detener - **6.** [keep] guardar - **7.** [maintain - interest etc] mantener - **8.** [have, possess] poseer - **9.** [contain - gen] contener; [- number of people] tener cabida para; [- fears, promise etc] guardar - **10.** [conduct, stage - event] celebrar; [- conversation] mantener; [- inquiry] realizar - **11.** fml [consider] considerar; **to hold sthg dear** apreciar mucho algo - **12.** [on telephone]: **please hold the line** no cuelgue por favor - **13.** MIL ocupar, tener

▸▸▸ **hold it** OR **everything!** ¡para!, ¡espera!; **to hold one's own** defenderse. <> vi (pt & pp **held**) - **1.** [luck, weather] continuar así; [promise, offer] seguir en pie; **to hold still** OR **steady** estarse quieto - **2.** [on phone] esperar. <> n - **1.** [grasp, grip]: **to have a firm hold on sthg** tener algo bien agarrado; **to take** OR **lay hold of sthg** agarrar algo; **to get hold of sthg** [obtain] hacerse con algo - **2.** [of ship, aircraft] bodega f - **3.** [control, influence] dominio m. ▸ **hold back** vt sep - **1.** [tears, anger] contener, reprimir - **2.** [secret] ocultar. ▸ **hold down** vt sep [job] conservar. ▸ **hold off** vt sep [fend off] rechazar. ▸ **hold on** vi - **1.** [wait] esperar; [on phone] no colgar - **2.** [grip]: **to hold on (to sthg)** agarrarse (a algo). ▸ **hold out** <> vt sep [hand] tender; [arms] extender. <> vi [last] durar. ▸ **hold up** <> vt sep - **1.** [raise] levantar, alzar - **2.** [delay] retrasar. <> vi [theory, facts] tenerse en pie.

holdall ['hɔ:ldɔ:l] n UK bolsa f de viaje.

holder ['hɔuldə'] n - **1.** [container] soporte m; [for candle] candelero m; [for cigarette] boquilla f - **2.** [owner] titular mf; [of ticket, record, title] poseedor m, -ra f.

holding ['hɔuldɪŋ] n - **1.** [investment] participación f - **2.** [farm] propiedad f, terreno m de cultivo.

holdup ['hɔuldʌp] n - **1.** [delay] retraso m - **2.** [robbery] atraco m a mano armada.

hole [hɔul] n - **1.** [gen] agujero m; [in ground, road etc] hoyo m; [of animal] madriguera f - **2.** [in golf] hoyo m - **3.** [horrible place] cuchitril m.

holiday ['hɔlɪdeɪ] n - **1.** [vacation] vacaciones fpl; **to be/go on holiday** estar/ir de vacaciones - **2.** [public holiday] fiesta f, día m festivo. ▸ **holidays** in US: **the holidays** las fiestas OR vacaciones (de Navidad); **happy holidays!** ¡felices fiestas!

holiday camp n UK colonia f veraniega.

holiday home n UK casa f para las vacaciones.

holidaymaker ['hɔlɪdeɪ,meɪkə'] n UK turista mf.

holistic [hɔu'lɪstɪk] adj holístico(ca).

Holland ['hɔlənd] n Holanda.

holler ['hɔlə'] vt & vi esp US inf gritar.

hollow ['hɔləu] <> adj - **1.** [not solid] hueco(ca) - **2.** [cheeks, eyes] hundido(da) - **3.** [resonant] sonoro(ra), resonante - **4.** [false, meaningless] vano(na); [laugh] falso(sa). <> n hueco m; [in ground] depresión f, hondonada f. ▸ **hollow out** vt sep - **1.** [make hollow] dejar hueco(ca) - **2.** [make by hollowing] hacer ahuecando.

holly ['hɔlɪ] n acebo m.

holocaust ['hɔləkɔ:st] n holocausto m. ▸ **Holocaust** n: **the Holocaust** el Holocausto.

holster ['hɔulstə'] n pistolera f.

holy ['hɔulɪ] adj - **1.** [sacred] sagrado(da); [water] bendito(ta) - **2.** [pure and good] santo(ta).

Holy Ghost n: **the Holy Ghost** el Espíritu Santo.

Holy Spirit n: **the Holy Spirit** el Espíritu Santo.

homage ['hɔmɪdʒ] n (U) fml homenaje m; **to pay homage to** rendir homenaje a.

home [hɔum] <> n - **1.** [house, flat] casa f; **away from home** [not in & SPORT] fuera de casa; **to make one's home somewhere** establecerse en algún sitio; **it's a home from home** UK OR **home away from home** US me siento como en mi propia casa - **2.** [own country] tierra f; [own city] ciudad f natal - **3.** [family] hogar m; **to leave home** independizarse, irse de casa - **4.** [place of origin] cuna f - **5.** [institution] residencia f. <> adj - **1.** [not foreign] nacional - **2.** [in one's own home - cooking] casero(ra); [- life] familiar; [- improvements] en la casa; [- delivery] a domicilio - **3.** SPORT de casa. <> adv [to one's house] a casa; [at one's house] en casa. ▸ **at home** adv - **1.** [in one's house, flat] en casa - **2.** [comfortable]: **at home (with)** a gusto (con); **to make o.s. at home** acomodarse; **make yourself at home** estás en tu casa - **3.** [in one's own country] en mi país.

home address n domicilio m particular.

home brew n [beer] cerveza f casera.

home computer n ordenador m doméstico.

home economics n (U) economía f doméstica.

home help n UK asistente empleado por el ayuntamiento para ayudar en las tareas domésticas a enfermos y ancianos.

homeland ['hɔumlænd] n - **1.** [country of birth] tierra f natal, patria f - **2.** [in South Africa] homeland m, territorio donde se confinaba a la población negra.

homeless ['hɔumlɪs] adj sin hogar.

homely ['hɔumlɪ] adj - **1.** [simple] sencillo(lla) - **2.** [unattractive] feúcho(cha).

homemade [,hɔum'meɪd] adj [food] casero(ra); [clothes] de fabricación casera.

Home Office n UK: the Home Office el Ministerio del Interior británico.

homeopathy [ˌhəʊmɪˈɒpəθɪ] n homeopatía f.

home page n [on Internet] página f inicial OR
de inicio.

Home Secretary n UK: the Home Secretary
el Ministro del Interior británico.

homesick [ˈhəʊmsɪk] adj nostálgico(ca); **to
be homesick** tener morriña.

hometown [ˈhəʊmtaʊn] n pueblo m/ciu-
dad f natal.

homeward [ˈhəʊmwəd] <> adj de regreso
OR vuelta (a casa). <> adv = **homewards**.

homewards [ˈhəʊmwədz], **homeward**
adv hacia casa.

homework [ˈhəʊmwɜːk] n (U) lit & fig deberes mpl.

homey, homy [ˈhəʊmɪ] US <> adj confortable, agradable. <> n inf [friend] amiguete m,
-ta f.

homicide [ˈhɒmɪsaɪd] n homicidio m.

homogeneous [ˌhɒməˈdʒiːnjəs] adj homo-
géneo(a).

homosexual [ˌhɒməˈsekʃʊəl] <> adj homosexual. <> n homosexual mf.

homy = **homey**.

Honduran [hɒnˈdjʊərən] <> adj hondure-
ño(ña). <> n hondureño m, -ña f.

Honduras [hɒnˈdjʊərəs] n Honduras.

hone [həʊn] vt - 1. [sharpen] afilar - 2. [develop,
refine] afinar.

honest [ˈɒnɪst] adj - 1. [trustworthy, legal]
honrado(da) - 2. [frank] franco(ca), sincero(ra);
to be honest... si he de serte franco...

honestly [ˈɒnɪstlɪ] <> adv - 1. [truthfully]
honradamente - 2. [expressing sincerity] de verdad, en serio. <> excl [expressing impatience,
disapproval] ¡será posible!

honesty [ˈɒnɪstɪ] n - 1. [trustworthiness] honradez f - 2. [frankness] sinceridad f; **in all honesty...** si he de serte franco...

honey [ˈhʌnɪ] n - 1. [food] miel f - 2. esp US
[form of address] cielo m, mi vida f.

honeycomb [ˈhʌnɪkəʊm] n panal m.

honeymoon [ˈhʌnɪmuːn] n luna f de miel;
fig periodo m idílico.

honeysuckle [ˈhʌnɪˌsʌkl] n madreselva f.

Hong Kong [ˌhɒŋˈkɒŋ] n Hong Kong.

honk [hɒŋk] <> vi - 1. [motorist] tocar el claxon - 2. [goose] graznar. <> vt tocar.

honor US = **honour**.

honorary [UK ˈɒnərərɪ, US ɒnəˈreərɪ] adj
- 1. [given as an honour] honorario(ria) - 2. [un-
paid] honorífico(ca).

honour UK, **honor** US [ˈɒnər] <> n - 1. [gen]
honor m, honra f; **in honour of** en honor de

- 2. [source of pride - person] honra f. <> vt
- 1. [promise, agreement] cumplir, [debt] satisfacer; [cheque] pagar, [obligation, word] (cumplir con
our to] honrar. <> **honours** npl - 1. [tokens of
respect] honores mpl - 2. UK UNIV: **honours degree** licenciatura de cuatro años necesaria para
acceder a un máster.

honourable UK, **honorable** US [ˈɒnrəbl]
adj - 1. [proper] honroso(sa) - 2. [morally upright]
honorable.

hood [hʊd] n - 1. [on cloak, jacket] capucha f
- 2. [of pram, convertible car] capota f; [for cooker]
campana f - 3. US [car bonnet] capó m.

hoodlum [ˈhuːdləm] n US inf matón m.

hoof [huːf, hʊf] (pl -s OR hooves) n [of horse]
casco m; [of cow etc] pezuña f.

hook [hʊk] <> n - 1. [gen] gancho m; **off the
hook** [phone] descolgado(da) - 2. [for catching
fish] anzuelo m - 3. [fastener] corchete m. <> vt
- 1. [attach with hook] enganchar - 2. [fish]
pescar, coger. <> **hook up** vt sep: **to hook
sthg up to sthg** conectar algo a algo; **to hook
with sb** reunirse OR juntarse con alguien, ligar
con alguien.

hooked [hʊkt] adj - 1. [nose] aguileño(ña)
- 2. inf [addicted]: **to be hooked (on)** estar en-
ganchado(da) (a).

hook(e)y [ˈhʊkɪ] n US inf: **to play hookey** hacer novillos.

hooligan [ˈhuːlɪgən] n gamberro m.

hoop [huːp] n aro m.

hooray [hʊˈreɪ] = **hurray**.

hoot [huːt] <> n [of owl] grito m, ululato m;
[of horn] bocinazo m; **a hoot of laughter** una
carcajada. <> vi [owl] ulular; [horn] sonar; **to
hoot with laughter** reírse a carcajadas. <> vt
tocar.

hooter [ˈhuːtər] n [horn] claxon® m, bocina f.

Hoover® [ˈhuːvər] n UK aspiradora f.
<> **hoover** vt pasar la aspiradora por.

hooves [huːvz] npl ▷ **hoof**.

hop [hɒp] vi - 1. [person] saltar a la pata coja
- 2. [bird etc] dar saltitos - 3. [move nimbly] ponerse de un brinco. <> **hops** npl lúpulo m.

hope [həʊp] <> vi: **to hope (for sthg)** esperar
(algo). <> vt: **to hope (that)** esperar que. <> n
esperanza f; **in the hope of** con la esperanza
de; **to raise sb's hopes** dar esperanzas a alguien.

hopeful [ˈhəʊpfʊl] adj - 1. [optimistic] optimista; **to be hopeful of sthg/of doing sthg** tener esperanzas de algo/hacer algo - 2. [prom-
ising] prometedor(ra).

hopefully [ˈhəʊpfəlɪ] adv - 1. [in a hopeful
way] esperanzadamente - 2. [with luck] con
suerte; **hopefully not** espero que no.

hopeless ['həʊplɪs] *adj* - **1.** [despairing] desesperado(da) - **2.** [impossible] imposible - **3.** *inf* [useless] inútil.

hopelessly ['həʊplɪslɪ] *adv* - **1.** [despairingly] desesperadamente - **2.** [completely] totalmente.

horizon [hə'raɪzn] *n* [of sky] horizonte *m*; **on the horizon** en el horizonte; *fig* a la vuelta de la esquina.

horizontal [ˌhɒrɪ'zɒntl] *adj* horizontal.

hormone ['hɔːməʊn] *n* hormona *f*.

horn [hɔːn] *n* - **1.** [of animal] cuerno *m* - **2.** MUS [instrument] trompa *f* - **3.** [on car] claxon® *m*, bocina *f*; [on ship] sirena *f* - **4.** *US inf* [telephone] teléfono *m*.

hornet ['hɔːnɪt] *n* avispón *m*.

horny ['hɔːnɪ] *adj* - **1.** [scale, body, armour] córneo(a); [hand] calloso(sa) - **2.** *v inf* [sexually excited] cachondo(da), caliente.

horoscope ['hɒrəskəʊp] *n* horóscopo *m*.

horrendous [hɒ'rendəs] *adj* horrendo(da).

horrible ['hɒrəbl] *adj* - **1.** [gen] horrible - **2.** [nasty, mean] malo(la).

horrid ['hɒrɪd] *adj esp UK* [person] antipático(ca); [idea, place] horroroso(sa).

horrific [hɒ'rɪfɪk] *adj* horrendo(da).

horrify ['hɒrɪfaɪ] *vt* horrorizar.

horror ['hɒrər] *n* horror *m*; **to have a horror of sthg** tener horror a algo.

horror film *n* película *f* de terror OR de miedo.

hors d'oeuvre [ɔː'dɜːvr] (*pl* hors d'oeuvres [ɔː'dɜːvr]) *n* entremeses *mpl*.

horse [hɔːs] *n* [animal] caballo *m*.

horseback ['hɔːsbæk] <> *adj*: horseback riding equitación *f*. <> *n*: on horseback a caballo.

horse chestnut *n* [nut] castaña *f* de Indias; horse chestnut (tree) castaño *m* de Indias.

horseman ['hɔːsmən] (*pl* -men [-mən]) *n* jinete *m*.

horsepower ['hɔːsˌpaʊər] *n* (*U*) caballos *mpl* de vapor.

horse racing *n* (*U*) carreras *fpl* de caballos.

horseradish ['hɔːsˌrædɪʃ] *n* rábano *m* silvestre.

horserider ['hɔːsraɪdər] *n esp US* jinete *m*, amazona *f*.

horse riding *n* equitación *f*; **to go horse riding** montar a caballo.

horseshoe ['hɔːsʃuː] *n* herradura *f*.

horsewoman ['hɔːsˌwʊmən] (*pl* -women [-ˌwɪmɪn]) *n* amazona *f*.

horticulture ['hɔːtɪkʌltʃər] *n* horticultura *f*.

hose [həʊz] *n* [hosepipe] manguera *f*.

hosepipe ['həʊzpaɪp] *n* manguera *f*.

hosiery ['həʊzɪərɪ] *n* (*U*) medias *fpl* y calcetines.

hospice ['hɒspɪs] *n* hospital *m* para enfermos terminales.

hospitable [hɒ'spɪtəbl] *adj* hospitalario(ria).

hospital ['hɒspɪtl] *n* hospital *m*.

hospitality [ˌhɒspɪ'tælətɪ] *n* hospitalidad *f*.

host [həʊst] <> *n* - **1.** [person, place, organization] anfitrión *m*, -ona *f* - **2.** [compere] presentador *m*, -ra *f* - **3.** *liter* [large number]: **a host of** una multitud de - **4.** RELIG hostia *f* - **5.** COMPUT host *m*, anfitrión *m*. <> *vt* - **1.** [show] presentar; [event] ser el anfitrión de - **2.** COMPUT albergar, hospedar.

hostage ['hɒstɪdʒ] *n* rehén *m*; **to be taken/held hostage** ser cogido(da)/mantenido(da) como rehén.

hostel ['hɒstl] *n* albergue *m*.

hostess ['həʊstes] *n* - **1.** [at party] anfitriona *f* - **2.** [in club etc] chica *f* de alterne.

host family *n* familia *f* de acogida.

hostile [*UK* 'hɒstaɪl, *US* 'hɒstl] *adj* - **1.** [antagonistic, enemy]: **hostile (to)** hostil (hacia) - **2.** [unfavourable] adverso(sa).

hostility [hɒ'stɪlətɪ] *n* [antagonism] hostilidad *f*. ◆ **hostilities** *npl* hostilidades *fpl*.

hot [hɒt] *adj* - **1.** [gen] caliente; **I'm hot** tengo calor - **2.** [weather, climate] caluroso(sa); **it's (very) hot** hace (mucho) calor - **3.** [spicy] picante, picoso(sa) *Méx* - **4.** *inf* [expert]: **hot on** OR **at** experto(ta) en - **5.** [recent] caliente, último(ma) - **6.** [temper] vivo(va).

hot-air balloon *n* aeróstato *m*, globo *m*.

hotbed ['hɒtbed] *n* semillero *m*.

hot-cross bun *n* *bollo a base de especias y pasas con una cruz dibujada en una cara que se come en Semana Santa.*

hot dog *n* perrito *m* caliente.

hotel [həʊ'tel] *n* hotel *m*.

hot flush *UK*, **hot flash** *US* *n* sofoco *m*.

hotheaded [ˌhɒt'hedɪd] *adj* irreflexivo(va).

hothouse ['hɒthaʊs, *pl* -haʊzɪz] *n* [greenhouse] invernadero *m*.

hot line *n* [for politician] teléfono *m* rojo.

hotly ['hɒtlɪ] *adv* - **1.** [passionately] acaloradamente - **2.** [closely]: **we were hotly pursued** nos pisaban los talones.

hotplate ['hɒtpleɪt] *n* - **1.** [for cooking] placa *f* - **2.** [for keeping food warm] calientaplatos *m inv*.

hot-tempered *adj* iracundo(da).

hot-water bottle *n* bolsa *f* de agua caliente.

hound [haʊnd] <> *n* [dog] perro *m* de caza, sabueso *m*. <> *vt* - **1.** [persecute] acosar

- 2. [drive]**: to hound sb out (of somewhere)** conseguir echar a alguien (de algún sitio) acosándolo.

hour ['aʊər] *n* **- 1.** [gen] hora *f*; **half an hour** media hora; **70 miles per** OR **an hour** 70 millas por hora; **to pay by the hour** pagar por horas; **on the hour** a la hora en punto cada hora **- 2.** liter [important time] momento *m*. ➤ **hours** *npl* [of business] horas *fpl*.

hourly ['aʊəlɪ] *adj* & *adv* **- 1.** [every hour] cada hora **- 2.** [per hour] por hora.

house <> *n* [haʊs, *pl* 'haʊzɪz] **- 1.** [gen] casa *f*; **it's on the house** la casa invita, es cortesía de la casa; **to put** OR **set one's house in order** poner las cosas en orden **- 2.** POL cámara *f* **- 3.** [in theatre] audiencia *f*; **to bring the house down** *inf* ser un exitazo, ser muy aplaudido(da). <> *vt* [haʊz] [person, family] alojar; [department, library, office] albergar. <> *adj* **- 1.** [within business] de la empresa **- 2.** [wine] de la casa.

house arrest *n*: **under house arrest** bajo arresto domiciliario.

houseboat ['haʊsbəʊt] *n* casa *f* flotante.

housebreaking ['haʊs,breɪkɪŋ] *n* allanamiento *m* de morada.

housecoat ['haʊskəʊt] *n* bata *f*.

household ['haʊshəʊld] <> *adj* **- 1.** [domestic] doméstico(ca), de la casa **- 2.** [word, name] conocido(da) por todos. <> *n* hogar *m*.

housekeeper ['haʊs,kiːpər] *n* ama *f* de llaves.

housekeeping ['haʊs,kiːpɪŋ] *n* (U) **- 1.** [work] quehaceres *mpl* domésticos **- 2.**: **housekeeping (money)** dinero *m* para los gastos de la casa.

house music *n* música *f* house.

House of Commons *n* UK: **the House of Commons** la Cámara de los Comunes.

House of Lords *n* UK: **the House of Lords** la Cámara de los Lores.

House of Representatives *n* US: **the House of Representatives** la Cámara de los Representantes.

houseplant ['haʊsplɑːnt] *n* planta *f* interior.

Houses of Parliament *n*: **the Houses of Parliament** el Parlamento británico.

housewarming (party) ['haʊs,wɔːmɪŋ-] *n* fiesta *f* de inauguración de una casa.

housewife ['haʊswaɪf] (*pl* **-wives** [-waɪvz]) *n* ama *f* de casa.

housework ['haʊswɜːk] *n* (U) quehaceres *mpl* domésticos.

housing ['haʊzɪŋ] *n* [houses] vivienda *f*; [act of accommodating] alojamiento *m*.

housing association *n* UK cooperativa *f* de viviendas.

housing benefit *n* (U) subsidio estatal para ayudar al pago del alquiler y de otros gastos.

housing estate UK, **housing project** US *n* urbanización generalmente de protección oficial, ≃ fraccionamiento *m* Méx.

hovel ['hɒvl] *n* casucha *f*, tugurio *m*.

hover ['hɒvər] *vi* [fly] cernerse.

hovercraft ['hɒvəkrɑːft] (*pl* **hovercraft** OR **-s**) *n* aerodeslizador *m*.

how [haʊ] *adv* **- 1.** [gen] cómo; **how do you do it?** ¿cómo se hace?; **I found out how he did it** averigué cómo lo hizo; **how are you?** ¿cómo estás?; **how do you do?** mucho gusto **- 2.** [referring to degree, amount]: **how high is it?** ¿cuánto mide de alto OR de altura?; **he asked how high it was** preguntó cuánto medía de alto; **how expensive is it?** ¿qué precio tiene?, ¿es muy caro?; **how far is it to Paris?** ¿a qué distancia está París de aquí?; **how long have you been waiting?** ¿cuánto llevas esperando?; **how many people came?** ¿cuánta gente vino?; **how old are you?** ¿qué edad OR cuántos años tienes? **- 3.** [in exclamations] qué; **how nice/awful!** ¡qué bonito/horrible!; **how I hate doing it!** ¡cómo OR cuánto odio tener que hacerlo! ➤ **how about** *adv*: **how about a drink?** ¿qué tal una copa?; **how about you?** ¿qué te parece?, ¿y tú? ➤ **how much** <> *pron* cuánto(ta); **how much does it cost?** ¿cuánto cuesta? <> *adj* cuánto(ta); **how much bread?** ¿cuánto pan?

however [haʊ'evər] <> *adv* **- 1.** [nevertheless] sin embargo, no obstante **- 2.** [no matter how]: **however difficult it may be** por (muy) difícil que sea; **however many times** OR **much I told her** por mucho que se lo dijera **- 3.** [how] cómo; **however did you know?** ¿cómo lo sabías? <> *conj* comoquiera que; **however you want** como quieras.

howl [haʊl] <> *n* **- 1.** [of animal] aullido *m* **- 2.** [of person - in pain, anger] alarido *m*, grito *m*; **a howl of laughter** una carcajada. <> *vi* **- 1.** [animal] aullar **- 2.** [person - in pain, anger] gritar; **to howl with laughter** reírse a carcajadas **- 3.** [wind] bramar.

hp (*abbr of* horsepower) CV *m*, cv *m*.

HP *n* (*abbr of* hire purchase) **- 1.** UK: **to buy sthg on HP** comprar algo a plazos **- 2.** = **hp**.

HQ *n abbr of* **headquarters**.

HTML (*abbr of* hypertext markup language) *n* COMPUT HTML *m*.

hub [hʌb] *n* **- 1.** [of wheel] cubo *m* **- 2.** [of activity] centro *m*, eje *m*.

hubbub ['hʌbʌb] *n* alboroto *m*.

hubcap ['hʌbkæp] *n* tapacubos *m inv*.

huddle ['hʌdl] *vi* **- 1.** [crouch, curl up] acurrucarse **- 2.** [cluster] apretarse unos contra otros, apiñarse.

hue [hjuː] *n* **- 1.** [shade] tono *m*, matiz *m* **- 2.** [colour] color *m*.

huff [hʌf] *n*: **in a huff** mosqueado(da).

hug [hʌg] <> n abrazo m. <> vt - 1. [embrace, hold] abrazar; **to hug sthg to o.s.** abrazar algo fuertemente - 2. [stay close to] ceñirse OR ir pegado a.

huge [hju:dʒ] adj enorme.

hulk [hʌlk] n - 1. [of ship] casco m abandonado - 2. [person] tiarrón m, -ona f.

hull [hʌl] n casco m.

hullo [hə'ləʊ] = **hello**.

hum [hʌm] <> vi - 1. [buzz] zumbar - 2. [sing] canturrear, tararear - 3. [be busy] bullir, hervir. <> vt tararear, canturrear.

human ['hju:mən] <> adj humano(na). <> n: **human (being)** (ser m) humano m.

humane [hju:'meɪn] adj humano(na).

humanitarian [hju:,mænɪ'teərɪən] adj humanitario(ria).

humanity [hju:'mænətɪ] n humanidad f. ▶ **humanities** npl: **the humanities** las humanidades.

human race n: **the human race** la raza humana.

human rights npl derechos mpl humanos.

humble ['hʌmbl] <> adj humilde. <> vt fml humillar.

humbug ['hʌmbʌg] n - 1. (U) dated [hypocrisy] farsa f, hipocresía f - 2. UK [sweet] caramelo m de menta.

humdrum ['hʌmdrʌm] adj rutinario(ria), aburrido(da).

humid ['hju:mɪd] adj húmedo(da).

humidity [hju:'mɪdətɪ] n humedad f.

humiliate [hju:'mɪlɪeɪt] vt humillar.

humiliation [hju:,mɪlɪ'eɪʃn] n humillación f.

humility [hju:'mɪlətɪ] n humildad f.

humor US = **humour**.

humorous ['hju:mərəs] adj - 1. [remark, situation] gracioso(sa) - 2. [play, publication] humorístico(ca).

humour UK, **humor** US ['hju:mər] <> n - 1. [sense of fun, mood] humor m; **in good/bad humour** fml de buen/mal humor - 2. [funny side] gracia f. <> vt complacer.

hump [hʌmp] n - 1. [hill] montículo m - 2. [on back] joroba f, giba f.

humpbacked bridge ['hʌmpbækt-] n puente m peraltado.

hunch [hʌntʃ] <> n inf presentimiento m. <> vt encorvar.

hunchback ['hʌntʃbæk] n jorobado m, -da f.

hunched [hʌntʃt] adj encorvado(da).

hundred ['hʌndrəd] num cien; a OR one hundred cien; a OR one hundred and eighty ciento ochenta; three hundred trescientos; five hundred quinientos; see also six. ▶ **hundreds** npl centenares mpl.

hundredth ['hʌndrətθ] <> num adj centésimo(ma). <> num n [fraction] centésimo m; a hundredth of a second una centésima; see also **sixth**.

hundredweight ['hʌndrədweɪt] n [in UK] = 50,8 kg; [in US] = 45,3 kg.

hung [hʌŋ] pt & pp ⊳ **hang**.

Hungarian [hʌŋ'geərɪən] <> adj húngaro(ra). <> n - 1. [person] húngaro m, -ra f - 2. [language] húngaro m.

Hungary ['hʌŋgərɪ] n Hungría.

hunger ['hʌŋgər] n - 1. [for food] hambre f - 2. liter [for change, knowledge etc] sed f. ▶ **hunger after, hunger for** vt insep liter anhelar, ansiar.

hunger strike n huelga f de hambre.

hung over adj inf: **to be hung over** tener resaca.

hungry ['hʌŋgrɪ] adj [for food] hambriento(ta); **to be/go hungry** tener/pasar hambre.

hung up adj inf acomplejado(da).

hunk [hʌŋk] n - 1. [large piece] pedazo m, trozo m - 2. inf [attractive man] tío m bueno, macizo m.

hunt [hʌnt] <> n - 1. [of animals, birds] caza f; UK [foxhunting party] partida f de caza - 2. [for person, clue etc] busca f, búsqueda f. <> vi [for animals, birds] cazar. <> vt - 1. [animals, birds] cazar - 2. [person] perseguir.

hunter ['hʌntər] n [of animals, birds] cazador m, -ra f.

hunting ['hʌntɪŋ] n - 1. [of animals] caza f; **to go hunting** ir de caza OR cacería - 2. UK [of foxes] caza f del zorro.

hurdle ['hɜ:dl] <> n - 1. [in race] valla f - 2. [obstacle] obstáculo m. <> vt saltar.

hurl [hɜ:l] vt - 1. [throw] lanzar, arrojar - 2. [shout] proferir, soltar.

hurray, hooray [hʊ'reɪ] excl ¡hurra!

hurricane ['hʌrɪkən] n huracán m.

hurried ['hʌrɪd] adj [hasty] apresurado(da).

hurriedly ['hʌrɪdlɪ] adv apresuradamente.

hurry ['hʌrɪ] <> n prisa f; **to be in a hurry** tener prisa; **to be in no hurry to do sthg** [unwilling] no tener ningunas ganas de hacer algo. <> vt [person] meter prisa a; [work, speech] apresurar. <> vi: **to hurry (to do sthg)** apresurarse (a hacer algo). ▶ **hurry up** vi darse prisa.

hurt [hɜ:t] <> vt (pt & pp hurt) - 1. [physically - person] hacer daño a; [- one's leg, arm] hacerse daño en; **nobody was hurt** nadie resultó herido; **to hurt o.s.** hacerse daño - 2. [emotionally] herir - 3. [harm] perjudicar. <> vi (pt & pp hurt) - 1. [gen] doler; **my head hurts** me duele la cabeza - 2. [cause physical pain, do harm] hacer daño. <> adj - 1. [injured] herido(da) - 2. [offended] dolido(da); [feelings] herido(da).

hurtful ['hɜːtfʊl] *adj* hiriente.

hurtle ['hɜːtl] *vi* **to hurtle past** pasar como un rayo.

husband ['hʌzbənd] *n* marido *m*.

hush [hʌʃ] <> *n* silencio *m*. <> *excl* ¡silencio!, ¡a callar!

husk [hʌsk] *n* [of seed, grain] cáscara *f*.

husky ['hʌskɪ] <> *adj* [hoarse] ronco(ca). <> *n* husky *m*, perro *m* esquimal.

hustle ['hʌsl] <> *vt* [hurry] meter prisa a. <> *n*: **hustle (and bustle)** bullicio *m*, ajetreo *m*.

hut [hʌt] *n* **- 1.** [rough house] cabaña *f*, choza *f* **- 2.** [shed] cobertizo *m*.

hutch [hʌtʃ] *n* conejera *f*.

hyacinth ['haɪəsɪnθ] *n* jacinto *m*.

hydrant ['haɪdrənt] *n* boca *f* de riego; [for fire] boca *f* de incendio.

hydraulic [haɪ'drɔːlɪk] *adj* hidráulico(ca).

hydroelectric [,haɪdrəʊɪ'lektrɪk] *adj* hidroeléctrico(ca).

hydrofoil ['haɪdrəfɔɪl] *n* embarcación *f* con hidroala.

hydrogen ['haɪdrədʒən] *n* hidrógeno *m*.

hyena [haɪ'iːnə] *n* hiena *f*.

hygiene ['haɪdʒiːn] *n* higiene *f*.

hygienic [haɪ'dʒiːnɪk] *adj* higiénico(ca).

hymn [hɪm] *n* himno *m*.

hype [haɪp] *inf n* bombo *m*, publicidad *f* exagerada.

hyperactive [,haɪpər'æktɪv] *adj* hiperactivo(va).

hyperlink ['haɪpə,lɪŋk] *n* COMPUT hiperenlace *m*.

hypermarket ['haɪpə,mɑːkɪt] *n* hipermercado *m*.

hyphen ['haɪfn] *n* guión *m*.

hypnosis [hɪp'nəʊsɪs] *n* hipnosis *f inv*.

hypnotic [hɪp'nɒtɪk] *adj* hipnótico(ca).

hypnotize, -ise ['hɪpnətaɪz] *vt* hipnotizar.

hypochondriac [,haɪpə'kɒndriæk] *n* hipocondríaco *m*, -ca *f*.

hypocrisy [hɪ'pɒkrəsɪ] *n* hipocresía *f*.

hypocrite ['hɪpəkrɪt] *n* hipócrita *mf*.

hypocritical [,hɪpə'krɪtɪkl] *adj* hipócrita.

hypothesis [haɪ'pɒθɪsɪs] (*pl* **-theses** [-θɪsiːz]) *n* hipótesis *f inv*.

hypothetical [,haɪpə'θetɪkl] *adj* hipotético(ca).

hysteria [hɪs'tɪərɪə] *n* histeria *f*.

hysterical [hɪs'terɪkl] *adj* **- 1.** [frantic] histérico(ca) **- 2.** *inf* [very funny] tronchante.

hysterics [hɪs'terɪks] *npl* **- 1.** [panic, excitement] histeria *f*, histerismo *m* **- 2.** *inf* [fits of laughter]: **to be in hysterics** troncharse OR partirse de risa.

i (*pl* **i's** OR **is**), **I**[1] (*pl* **I's** OR **Is**) [aɪ] *n* [letter] i *f*, I *f*.

I[2] [aɪ] *pers pron* yo; **I'm happy** soy feliz; **I'm leaving** me voy; **she and I were at college together** ella y yo fuimos juntos a la universidad; **it is I** *fml* soy yo; **I can't do that** yo no puedo hacer eso.

ice [aɪs] <> *n* **- 1.** [frozen water] hielo *m* **- 2.** *UK* [ice cream] helado *m*. <> *vt* CULIN glasear, alcorzar. ◆ **ice over, ice up** *vi* helarse.

iceberg ['aɪsbɜːg] *n* iceberg *m*.

iceberg lettuce *n* lechuga *f* iceberg.

icebox ['aɪsbɒks] *n* **- 1.** *UK* [in refrigerator] congelador *m* **- 2.** *US* [refrigerator] refrigerador *m*.

ice cream *n* helado *m*.

ice cube *n* cubito *m* de hielo.

ice hockey *n* hockey *m* sobre hielo.

Iceland ['aɪslənd] *n* Islandia.

Icelandic [aɪs'lændɪk] <> *adj* islandés(esa). <> *n* [language] islandés *m*.

ice lolly *n UK* polo *m*.

ice pick *n* pico *m* para el hielo.

ice rink *n* pista *f* de (patinaje sobre) hielo.

ice skate *n* patín *m* de cuchilla. ◆ **ice-skate** *vi* patinar sobre hielo.

ice-skating *n* patinaje *m* sobre hielo.

icicle ['aɪsɪkl] *n* carámbano *m*.

icing ['aɪsɪŋ] *n* glaseado *m*.

icing sugar *n UK* azúcar *m* glas.

icon, ikon ['aɪkɒn] *n* COMPUT & RELIG icono *m*.

icy ['aɪsɪ] *adj* **- 1.** [gen] helado(da) **- 2.** *fig* [unfriendly] glacial.

I'd [aɪd] **- 1.** (*abbr of* **I had**) ▷ **have** **- 2.** (*abbr of* **I would**) ▷ **would**.

ID <> *n abbr of* **identification.** <> *abbr of* **Idaho**.

idea [aɪ'dɪə] *n* **- 1.** [gen] idea *f*; **to have an idea of sthg** tener (alguna) idea de algo; **to have no idea** no tener ni idea; **to get the idea** *inf* captar la idea, hacerse una idea **- 2.** [intuition, feeling] sensación *f*, impresión *f*; **to have an idea (that)...** tener la sensación de que...

ideal [aɪ'dɪəl] <> *adj*: **ideal (for)** ideal (para). <> *n* ideal *m*.

ideally [aɪ'dɪəlɪ] *adv* **- 1.** [perfectly] idealmente; [suited] perfectamente **- 2.** [preferably] a ser posible.

identical [aɪ'dentɪkl] *adj* idéntico(ca).

identification [aɪ,dentɪfɪ'keɪʃn] n - 1. [gen]: **identification (with)** identificación f (con) - 2. [documentation] documentación f.

identify [aɪ'dentɪfaɪ] <> vt identificar; **to identify sb with sthg** relacionar a alguien con algo. <> vi: **to identify with sb/sthg** identificarse con alguien/algo.

Identikit picture® [aɪ'dentɪkɪt-] n fotorrobot f.

identity [aɪ'dentətɪ] n identidad f.

identity card, ID card n carné m OR documento m de identidad, cédula f de identidad Amér.

ideology [,aɪdɪ'ɒlədʒɪ] n ideología f.

idiom ['ɪdɪəm] n - 1. [phrase] locución f, modismo m - 2. fml [style] lenguaje m.

idiomatic [,ɪdɪə'mætɪk] adj natural.

idiosyncrasy [,ɪdɪə'sɪŋkrəsɪ] n rareza f, manía f.

idiot ['ɪdɪət] n [fool] idiota mf.

idiotic [,ɪdɪ'ɒtɪk] adj idiota.

idle ['aɪdl] <> adj - 1. [lazy] perezoso(sa), vago(ga) - 2. [not working - machine, factory] parado(da); [- person] desocupado(da), sin trabajo - 3. [rumour] infundado(da); [threat, boast] vano(na); [curiosity] que no viene a cuento. <> vi estar en punto muerto. ◆ **idle away** vt sep desperdiciar.

idol ['aɪdl] n ídolo m.

idolize, -ise ['aɪdəlaɪz] vt idolatrar.

idyllic [ɪ'dɪlɪk] adj idílico(ca).

i.e. (abbr of id est) i.e., es decir.

if [ɪf] conj - 1. [gen] si; **if I were you** yo que tú, yo en tu lugar - 2. [though] aunque; **he's clever, if a little arrogant** es listo, aunque algo arrogante. ◆ **if not** conj - 1. [otherwise] si no, de lo contrario - 2. [not to say] por no decir; **it was cheeky, if not downright rude of him** fue mucha caradura de su parte, por no decir grosería. ◆ **if only** <> conj - 1. [naming a reason] aunque sólo sea; **at least he got me a present, if only a little one** por lo menos me han comprado un regalo, aunque sea pequeño - 2. [expressing regret] si; **if only I'd been quicker!** ¡ojalá hubiera sido más rápido! <> excl ¡ojalá!

igloo ['ɪgluː] (pl -s) n iglú m.

ignite [ɪg'naɪt] <> vt encender. <> vi encenderse.

ignition [ɪg'nɪʃn] n - 1. [act of igniting] ignición f - 2. [in car] encendido m; **to switch on the ignition** arrancar (el motor).

ignition key n llave f de contacto.

ignorance ['ɪgnərəns] n ignorancia f.

ignorant ['ɪgnərənt] adj - 1. [uneducated, rude] ignorante - 2. fml [unaware]: **to be ignorant of sthg** ignorar algo.

ignore [ɪg'nɔːr] vt [thing] no hacer caso de, ignorar; [person] no hacer caso a, ignorar.

ilk [ɪlk] n: **of that ilk** [of that sort] de ese tipo.

ill [ɪl] <> adj - 1. [unwell] enfermo(ma); **to feel ill** encontrarse mal; **to be taken OR to fall ill** caer OR ponerse enfermo(ma) - 2. [bad] malo(la). <> adv [badly] mal.

I'll [aɪl] - 1. (abbr of I will) ▷ **will** - 2. (abbr of I shall) ▷ **shall**.

ill-advised [-əd'vaɪzd] adj [action] poco aconsejable; [person] imprudente.

ill at ease adj incómodo(da).

illegal [ɪ'liːgl] adj ilegal.

illegible [ɪ'ledʒəbl] adj ilegible.

illegitimate [,ɪlɪ'dʒɪtɪmət] adj ilegítimo(ma).

ill-equipped [-ɪ'kwɪpt] adj: **to be ill-equipped to do sthg** estar mal preparado(da) para hacer algo.

ill-fated [-'feɪtɪd] adj infausto(ta).

ill feeling n resentimiento m.

ill health n mala salud f.

illicit [ɪ'lɪsɪt] adj ilícito(ta).

illiteracy [ɪ'lɪtərəsɪ] n analfabetismo m.

illiterate [ɪ'lɪtərət] <> adj analfabeto(ta). <> n analfabeto m, -ta f.

illness ['ɪlnɪs] n enfermedad f.

illogical [ɪ'lɒdʒɪkl] adj ilógico(ca).

ill-suited adj: **ill-suited (for)** poco adecuado(da) (para).

ill-timed [-'taɪmd] adj inoportuno(na).

ill-treat vt maltratar.

illuminate [ɪ'luːmɪneɪt] vt - 1. [light up] iluminar - 2. [explain] ilustrar, aclarar.

illumination [ɪ,luːmɪ'neɪʃn] n [lighting] alumbrado m, iluminación f. ◆ **illuminations** npl UK iluminaciones fpl, alumbrado m decorativo.

illusion [ɪ'luːʒn] n - 1. [gen] ilusión f; **to be under the illusion that** creer equivocadamente que - 2. [magic trick] truco m de ilusionismo.

illustrate ['ɪləstreɪt] vt ilustrar.

illustration [,ɪlə'streɪʃn] n ilustración f.

illustrious [ɪ'lʌstrɪəs] adj fml ilustre.

ill will n rencor m, animadversión f; **to bear sb ill will** guardar rencor a alguien.

I'm [aɪm] (abbr of I am) ▷ **be**.

image ['ɪmɪdʒ] n imagen f.

imagery ['ɪmɪdʒrɪ] n (U) imágenes fpl.

imaginary [ɪ'mædʒɪnrɪ] adj imaginario(ria).

imagination [ɪ,mædʒɪ'neɪʃn] n imaginación f.

imaginative [ɪ'mædʒɪnətɪv] adj imaginativo(va).

imagine [ɪ'mædʒɪn] vt - 1. [gen] imaginar; **imagine never having to work!** ¡imagina que nunca tuvieras que trabajar!; **imagine (that)!** ¡imagínate!; **I can't imagine what he means** no tengo ni idea de que quiere decir - 2. [suppose]. **to imagine (that)** imaginarse que.

imbalance [,ɪm'bæləns] *n* desequilibrio *m*.

imbecile ['ɪmbɪsiːl] *n* imbécil *mf*.

IMF (*abbr of* **International Monetary Fund**) *n* FMI *m*.

IMHO (*abbr of* **in my humble opinion**) *adv inf* en mi humilde opinión.

imitate ['ɪmɪteɪt] *vt* imitar.

imitation [,ɪmɪ'teɪʃn] ◇ *n* imitación *f*. ◇ *adj* de imitación; **imitation jewellery** bisutería *f*.

immaculate [ɪ'mækjʊlət] *adj* - 1. [clean and tidy] inmaculado(da); [taste] exquisito(ta) - 2. [performance, timing] impecable.

immaterial [,ɪmə'tɪərɪəl] *adj* [irrelevant, unimportant] irrelevante.

immature [,ɪmə'tjʊər] *adj* inmaduro(ra); [animal] joven.

immediate [ɪ'miːdjət] *adj* - 1. [gen] inmediato(ta); **in the immediate future** en un futuro inmediato; **in the immediate vicinity** en las inmediaciones - 2. [family] más cercano(na).

immediately [ɪ'miːdjətlɪ] ◇ *adv* - 1. [at once] inmediatamente - 2. [directly] directamente. ◇ *conj* en cuanto.

immense [ɪ'mens] *adj* inmenso(sa).

immerse [ɪ'mɜːs] *vt* - 1. [plunge]: **to immerse sthg in sthg** sumergir algo en algo - 2. [involve]: **to immerse o.s. in sthg** enfrascarse en algo.

immersion heater [ɪ'mɜːʃn-] *n* calentador *m* de inmersión.

immigrant ['ɪmɪɡrənt] *n* inmigrante *mf*.

immigration [,ɪmɪ'ɡreɪʃn] *n* inmigración *f*.

imminent ['ɪmɪnənt] *adj* inminente.

immobilize, -ise [ɪ'məʊbɪlaɪz] *vt* inmovilizar.

immobilizer [ɪ'məʊbɪlaɪzər] *n* AUTO inmovilizador *m*.

immoral [ɪ'mɒrəl] *adj* inmoral.

immortal [ɪ'mɔːtl] *adj* inmortal.

immortalize, -ise [ɪ'mɔːtəlaɪz] *vt* inmortalizar.

immune [ɪ'mjuːn] *adj* - 1. [gen & MED]: **immune (to)** inmune (a) - 2. [exempt]: **immune (from)** exento(ta) (de).

immunity [ɪ'mjuːnətɪ] *n* - 1. [gen & MED]: **immunity (to)** inmunidad *f* (a) - 2. [exemption]: **immunity (from)** exención *f* (de).

immunize, -ise ['ɪmjuːnaɪz] *vt*: **to immunize sb (against sthg)** inmunizar a alguien (contra algo).

imp [ɪmp] *n* - 1. [creature] duendecillo *m* - 2. [naughty child] diablillo *m*.

impact ◇ *n* ['ɪmpækt] impacto *m*; **to make an impact on OR upon** causar impacto en. ◇ *vt* [ɪm'pækt] [influence] influenciar.

impair [ɪm'peər] *vt* [sight, hearing] dañar, debilitar; [movement] entorpecer; [ability, efficiency] mermar; [prospects] perjudicar.

impart [ɪm'pɑːt] *vt fml* - 1. [information]: **to impart sthg (to sb)** comunicar algo (a alguien) - 2. [feeling, quality]: **to impart sthg (to sthg)** conferir algo (a algo).

impartial [ɪm'pɑːʃl] *adj* imparcial.

impassable [ɪm'pɑːsəbl] *adj* intransitable, impracticable.

impasse [æm'pɑːs] *n* impasse *m*, callejón *m* sin salida.

impassive [ɪm'pæsɪv] *adj* impasible.

impatience [ɪm'peɪʃns] *n* impaciencia *f*.

impatient [ɪm'peɪʃnt] *adj* impaciente; **to be impatient to do sthg** estar impaciente por hacer algo; **to be impatient for sthg** esperar algo con impaciencia; **to get impatient** impacientarse.

impeccable [ɪm'pekəbl] *adj* impecable.

impede [ɪm'piːd] *vt* dificultar.

impediment [ɪm'pedɪmənt] *n* - 1. [obstacle] impedimento *m*, obstáculo *m* - 2. [disability] defecto *m*.

impel [ɪm'pel] *vt*: **to impel sb to do sthg** impulsar a alguien a hacer algo.

impending [ɪm'pendɪŋ] *adj* inminente.

imperative [ɪm'perətɪv] ◇ *adj* [need] apremiante; **it is imperative that...** es imprescindible que... ◇ *n* imperativo *m*.

imperfect [ɪm'pɜːfɪkt] ◇ *adj* [not perfect] imperfecto(ta). ◇ *n* GRAM: **imperfect (tense)** (pretérito *m*) imperfecto *m*.

imperial [ɪm'pɪərɪəl] *adj* - 1. [of an empire or emperor] imperial - 2. [system of measurement]: **imperial system** sistema anglosajón de medidas.

imperialism [ɪm'pɪərɪəlɪzm] *n* imperialismo *m*.

impersonal [ɪm'pɜːsnl] *adj* impersonal.

impersonate [ɪm'pɜːsəneɪt] *vt* [try to pass as] hacerse pasar por; [do impression of] imitar.

impersonation [ɪm,pɜːsə'neɪʃn] *n* - 1. [pretending to be]: **charged with impersonation of a policeman** acusado de hacerse pasar por policía - 2. [impression] imitación *f*; **to do impersonations (of)** imitar (a), hacer imitaciones (de).

impertinent [ɪm'pɜːtɪnənt] *adj* impertinente, insolente.

impervious [ɪm'pɜːvjəs] *adj* [not influenced]: **impervious to** insensible a.

impetuous [ɪm'petʃʊəs] *adj* impetuoso(sa).

impetus ['ɪmpɪtəs] *n* (U) - 1. [momentum] ímpetu *m* - 2. [stimulus] impulso *m*.

impinge [ɪmˈpɪndʒ] *vi*: **to impinge on** sthg/sb afectar algo/a alguien.

implant <> *n* [ˈɪmplɑːnt] implante *m*. <> *vt* [ɪmˈplɑːnt] - 1. [fix - idea etc]: **to implant** sthg **in** OR **into** inculcar algo en - 2. MED: **to implant** sthg **in** OR **into** implantar algo en.

implausible [ɪmˈplɔːzəbl] *adj* inverosímil.

implement <> *n* [ˈɪmplɪmənt] herramienta *f*. <> *vt* [ˈɪmplɪment] llevar a cabo, poner en práctica.

implication [ˌɪmplɪˈkeɪʃn] *n* - 1. [involvement] implicación *f* - 2. [inference] consecuencia *f*; **by implication** de forma indirecta.

implicit [ɪmˈplɪsɪt] *adj* - 1. [gen]: **implicit (in)** implícito(ta) (en) - 2. [complete - belief] absoluto(ta); [- faith] incondicional.

implore [ɪmˈplɔːr] *vt*: **to implore sb (to do sthg)** suplicar a alguien (que haga algo).

imply [ɪmˈplaɪ] *vt* - 1. [suggest] insinuar, dar a entender - 2. [involve] implicar, suponer.

impolite [ˌɪmpəˈlaɪt] *adj* maleducado(da), descortés.

import <> *n* [ˈɪmpɔːt] - 1. [act of importing, product] importación *f* - 2. *fml* [meaning] sentido *m*, significado *m*. <> *vt* [ɪmˈpɔːt] [gen & COMPUT] importar.

importance [ɪmˈpɔːtns] *n* importancia *f*.

important [ɪmˈpɔːtnt] *adj*: **important (to)** importante (para); **it's not important** no importa.

importer [ɪmˈpɔːtər] *n* importador *m*, -ra *f*.

impose [ɪmˈpəʊz] <> *vt*: **to impose sthg (on)** imponer algo (a). <> *vi*: **to impose (on)** abusar (de), molestar (a).

imposing [ɪmˈpəʊzɪŋ] *adj* imponente, impresionante.

imposition [ˌɪmpəˈzɪʃn] *n* - 1. [enforcement] imposición *f* - 2. [cause of trouble] molestia *f*.

impossible [ɪmˈpɒsəbl] *adj* - 1. [gen] imposible - 2. [person, behaviour] inaguantable, insufrible.

impostor, imposter US [ɪmˈpɒstər] *n* impostor *m*, -ra *f*.

impotent [ˈɪmpətənt] *adj* impotente.

impound [ɪmˈpaʊnd] *vt* incautarse.

impoverished [ɪmˈpɒvərɪʃt] *adj* [country, people, imagination] empobrecido(da).

impracticable [ɪmˈpræktɪkəbl] *adj* impracticable, irrealizable.

impractical [ɪmˈpræktɪkl] *adj* poco práctico(ca).

impregnable [ɪmˈpregnəbl] *adj lit* & *fig* incontestable.

impregnate [ˈɪmpregneɪt] *vt* - 1. [introduce substance into]: **to impregnate sthg (with)** impregnar OR empapar algo (de) - 2. *fml* [fertilize] fecundar.

impress [ɪmˈpres] <> *vt* - 1. [produce admiration in] impresionar; **I was favourably impressed** me causó buena impresión - 2. [stress]: **to impress sthg on sb** hacer comprender a alguien la importancia de algo. <> *vi* [create good impression] causar buena impresión; [show off] impresionar.

impression [ɪmˈpreʃn] *n* - 1. [gen] impresión *f*; **to make an impression** impresionar; **to make a good/bad impression** causar una buena/mala impresión; **to be under the impression that** tener la impresión de que - 2. [imitation] imitación *f*.

impressive [ɪmˈpresɪv] *adj* impresionante.

imprint [ˈɪmprɪnt] *n* - 1. [mark] huella *f*, impresión *f* - 2. [publisher's name] pie *m* de imprenta.

imprison [ɪmˈprɪzn] *vt* encarcelar.

improbable [ɪmˈprɒbəbl] *adj* [event] improbable; [story, excuse] inverosímil; [clothes, hat] estrafalario(ria); [contraption] extraño(ña).

impromptu [ɪmˈprɒmptjuː] *adj* improvisado(da).

improper [ɪmˈprɒpər] *adj* - 1. [unsuitable] impropio(pia) - 2. [incorrect, illegal] indebido(da) - 3. [rude] indecoroso(sa).

improve [ɪmˈpruːv] <> *vi* mejorar; **to improve on** OR **upon** sthg mejorar algo. <> *vt* mejorar.

improvement [ɪmˈpruːvmənt] *n* - 1. [gen]: **improvement (in/on)** mejora *f* (en/con respecto a); **to be an improvement on** sthg ser mejor que algo - 2. [in health] mejoría *f* - 3. [to home] reforma *f*.

improvise [ˈɪmprəvaɪz] *vt* & *vi* improvisar.

impudent [ˈɪmpjʊdənt] *adj* insolente.

impulse [ˈɪmpʌls] *n* impulso *m*; **on impulse** sin pensar.

impulsive [ɪmˈpʌlsɪv] *adj* impulsivo(va).

impunity [ɪmˈpjuːnətɪ] *n*: **with impunity** impunemente.

impurity [ɪmˈpjʊərətɪ] *n* impureza *f*.

in [ɪn] <> *prep* - 1. [indicating place, position] en; **in a box/the garden/the lake** en una caja/el jardín/el lago; **to be in hospital/prison** estar en el hospital/la cárcel; **in here/there** aquí/allí dentro - 2. [wearing]: **she was still in her nightclothes** todavía llevaba su ropa de dormir - 3. [at a particular time]: **at four o'clock in the morning/afternoon** a las cuatro de la mañana/tarde; **in the morning/afternoon** por la mañana/tarde; **in 2006/May/the spring** en 2006/mayo/primavera - 4. [within] en; **he learned to type in two weeks** aprendió a escribir a máquina en dos semanas; **I'll be ready in five minutes** estoy listo en cinco minutos - 5. [during] desde hace; **it's my first decent meal in weeks** es lo primero decente que como desde hace OR en semanas - **6.** [indicating situation, circumstances]: **to live/die in poverty** vivir/morir en la pobreza; **in danger/difficulty** en peligro/dificultades; **in the sun** al sol; **in the rain** bajo la lluvia; **a rise in prices** un aumento de los precios - **7.** [indicating manner, condition] en; **in a loud/soft voice** en voz alta/baja; **in pencil/ink** a lápiz/bolígrafo; **in this way** de este modo - **8.** [indicating emotional state] con - **9.** [specifying area of activity]: **advances in medicine** avances en la medicina; **he's in computers** se dedica a informática - **10.** [with numbers - showing quantity, age]: **in large/small quantities** en grandes/pequeñas cantidades; **in (their) thousands** a OR por millares; **she's in her sixties** anda por los sesenta - **11.** [describing arrangement]: **in a line/circle** en línea/círculo; **to stand in twos** estar en pares OR parejas - **12.** [as regards] en; **in these matters** en estos temas; **two metres in length/width** dos metros de largo/ancho; **a change in direction** un cambio de dirección - **13.** [in ratios]: **one in ten** uno de cada diez; **five pence in the pound** cinco peniques por libra - **14.** *(after superl)* de; **the best in the world** el mejor del mundo - **15.** *(+ present participle)*: **in doing sthg** al hacer algo

▶▶ **there's nothing in it for us** no tiene ninguna ventaja para nosotros. ◇ *adv* - **1.** [inside] dentro; **to jump in** saltar adentro; **do come in** pasa por favor - **2.** [at home, work]: **is Judith in?** ¿está Judith?; **I'm staying in tonight** esta noche no salgo - **3.** [of train, boat, plane]: **is the train in yet?** ¿ha llegado el tren? - **4.** [of tide]: **the tide's in** la marea está alta

▶▶ **you're in for a surprise** te vas a llevar una sorpresa. ◇ *adj inf* de moda. ◆ **ins** *npl*: **the ins and outs** los detalles, los pormenores.

in. *abbr of* **inch.**

inability [,ɪnə'bɪlətɪ] *n*: **inability (to do sthg)** incapacidad *f* (de hacer algo).

inaccessible [,ɪnək'sesəbl] *adj* inaccesible.

inaccurate [ɪn'ækjʊrət] *adj* inexacto(ta).

inadequate [ɪn'ædɪkwət] *adj* - **1.** [insufficient] insuficiente - **2.** [person] incapaz.

inadvertently [,ɪnəd'vɜ:təntlɪ] *adv* sin querer, accidentalmente.

inadvisable [,ɪnəd'vaɪzəbl] *adj* poco aconsejable.

inane [ɪ'neɪn] *adj* necio(cia).

inanimate [ɪn'ænɪmət] *adj* inanimado(da).

inappropriate [,ɪnə'prəʊprɪət] *adj* [remark, clothing] impropio(pia); [time] inoportuno(na).

inarticulate [,ɪnɑː'tɪkjʊlət] *adj* [person] que no se expresa bien; [speech] mal pronunciado(da) OR expresado(da).

inasmuch [,ɪnəz'mʌtʃ] ◆ **inasmuch as** *conj* en la medida en que.

inaudible [ɪ'nɔːdɪbl] *adj* inaudible.

inauguration [ɪ,nɔːgjʊ'reɪʃn] *n* - **1.** [of leader, president] investidura *f* - **2.** [of building, system] inauguración *f*.

in-between *adj* intermedio(dia).

inborn [,ɪn'bɔːn] *adj* innato(ta).

inbound ['ɪnbaʊnd] *adj* de llegada.

in-box *n* [for e-mail] buzón *m* de entrada.

inbred [,ɪn'bred] *adj* - **1.** [closely related] endogámico(ca) - **2.** [inborn] innato(ta).

inbuilt [,ɪn'bɪlt] *adj* [in person] innato(ta); [in thing] inherente.

inc. *(abbr of* inclusive*)* inclus.

Inc. [ɪŋk] *(abbr of* incorporated*)* US ≃ S.A.

incapable [ɪn'keɪpəbl] *adj* - **1.** [unable]: **to be incapable of sthg/of doing sthg** ser incapaz de algo/de hacer algo - **2.** [useless] incompetente.

incapacitated [,ɪnkə'pæsɪteɪtɪd] *adj* incapacitado(da).

incarcerate [ɪn'kɑːsəreɪt] *vt fml* encarcelar.

incarnation [,ɪnkɑː'neɪʃn] *n* - **1.** [personification] personificación *f* - **2.** [existence] encarnación *f*.

incendiary device [ɪn'sendjərɪ-] *n* artefacto *m* incendiario.

incense ◇ *n* ['ɪnsens] incienso *m*. ◇ *vt* [ɪn'sens] enfurecer, indignar.

incentive [ɪn'sentɪv] *n* incentivo *m*.

incentive scheme *n* plan *m* de incentivos.

incentivize [ɪn'sentɪvaɪz] *vt* incentivar.

inception [ɪn'sepʃn] *n fml* inicio *m*.

incessant [ɪn'sesnt] *adj* incesante, constante.

incessantly [ɪn'sesntlɪ] *adv* incesantemente, constantemente.

incest ['ɪnsest] *n* incesto *m*.

inch [ɪntʃ] ◇ *n* = 2,54 cm pulgada *f*; **to be within an inch of doing sthg** estar en un tris de hacer algo. ◇ *vi*: **to inch forward** avanzar poco a poco.

incidence ['ɪnsɪdəns] *n* [of disease, theft] índice *m*.

incident ['ɪnsɪdənt] *n* incidente *m*, suceso *m*.

incidental [,ɪnsɪ'dentl] *adj* accesorio(ria).

incidentally [,ɪnsɪ'dentəlɪ] *adv* por cierto, a propósito.

incinerate [ɪn'sɪnəreɪt] *vt* incinerar.

incipient [ɪn'sɪpɪənt] *adj fml* incipiente.

incisive [ɪn'saɪsɪv] *adj* [comment, person] incisivo(va); [mind] penetrante.

incite [ɪn'saɪt] *vt* incitar; **to incite sb to do sthg** incitar a alguien a que haga algo.

inclination [,ɪnklɪ'neɪʃn] *n* - **1.** (U) [liking, preference] inclinación *f*, propensión *f* - **2.** [tendency]: **inclination to do sthg** tendencia *f* a hacer algo.

incline <> n ['ɪnklaɪn] pendiente f. <> vt [ɪn'klaɪn] [head] inclinar, ladear.

inclined [ɪn'klaɪnd] adj - 1. [tending]: **to be inclined to sthg** ser propenso(sa) OR tener tendencia a algo; **to be inclined to do sthg** tener tendencia a hacer algo; **I'm inclined to agree** creo que estoy de acuerdo - 2. fml [wanting]: **to be inclined to do sthg** estar dispuesto(ta) a hacer algo - 3. [sloping] inclinado(da).

include [ɪn'kluːd] vt - 1. [gen] incluir - 2. [with letter] adjuntar.

included [ɪn'kluːdɪd] adj incluido(da).

including [ɪn'kluːdɪŋ] prep incluyendo; **six died, including a child** murieron seis personas, incluyendo a un niño.

inclusive [ɪn'kluːsɪv] adj - 1. [including everything] inclusivo(va); **one to nine inclusive** uno a nueve inclusive - 2. [including all costs]: **inclusive of VAT** con el IVA incluido; **£150 inclusive** 150 libras todo incluido.

inclusivity [ˌɪnkluː'sɪvɪtɪ] n política f de inclusión.

incoherent [ˌɪnkəʊ'hɪərənt] adj incoherente.

income ['ɪŋkʌm] n (U) [gen] ingresos mpl; [from property] renta f; [from investment] réditos mpl.

income support n (U) UK subsidio para personas con muy bajos ingresos o desempleados sin derecho a subsidio de paro, ≈ salario m social.

income tax n impuesto m sobre la renta.

incompatible [ˌɪnkəm'pætɪbl] adj [gen & COMPUT]: **incompatible (with)** incompatible (con).

incompetent [ɪn'kɒmpɪtənt] adj incompetente, incapaz.

incomplete [ˌɪnkəm'pliːt] adj incompleto(ta).

incomprehensible [ɪn,kɒmprɪ'hensəbl] adj incomprensible.

inconceivable [ˌɪnkən'siːvəbl] adj inconcebible.

inconclusive [ˌɪnkən'kluːsɪv] adj [evidence, argument] poco convincente; [meeting, outcome] sin conclusión clara.

incongruous [ɪn'kɒŋgrʊəs] adj incongruente.

inconsequential [ˌɪnkɒnsɪ'kwenʃl] adj intrascendente, de poca importancia.

inconsiderable [ˌɪnkən'sɪdərəbl] adj: **not inconsiderable** nada insignificante OR despreciable.

inconsiderate [ˌɪnkən'sɪdərət] adj desconsiderado(da).

inconsistency [ˌɪnkən'sɪstənsɪ] n - 1. [between theory and practice] inconsecuen-

cia f; [between statements etc] falta f de correspondencia - 2. [contradictory point] contradicción f.

inconsistent [ˌɪnkən'sɪstənt] adj - 1. [translation, statement]: **inconsistent (with)** incoherente OR incongruente (con) - 2. [group, government, person] inconsecuente - 3. [erratic] irregular, desigual.

inconspicuous [ˌɪnkən'spɪkjʊəs] adj discreto(ta).

inconvenience [ˌɪnkən'viːnjəns] <> n - 1. [difficulty, discomfort] molestia f, incomodidad f; **we apologize for any inconvenience caused** disculpen las molestias - 2. [inconvenient thing] inconveniente m. <> vt incomodar.

inconvenient [ˌɪnkən'viːnjənt] adj [time] inoportuno(na); [location] incómodo(da); **that date is inconvenient** esa fecha no me viene bien.

incorporate [ɪn'kɔːpəreɪt] vt - 1. [integrate]: **to incorporate sthg/sb (in OR into)** incorporar algo/a alguien (en) - 2. [include] incluir, comprender.

incorporated [ɪn'kɔːpəreɪtɪd] adj COMM: **incorporated company** sociedad f anónima.

incorrect [ˌɪnkə'rekt] adj incorrecto(ta).

incorrigible [ɪn'kɒrɪdʒəbl] adj incorregible.

increase <> n ['ɪnkriːs]: **increase (in)** [gen] aumento m (de); [in price, temperature] subida f (de); **to be on the increase** ir en aumento. <> vt [ɪn'kriːs] - 1. [gen] aumentar, incrementar - 2. [price] subir. <> vi [ɪn'kriːs] [gen] aumentar; [price, temperature] subir.

increasing [ɪn'kriːsɪŋ] adj creciente.

increasingly [ɪn'kriːsɪŋlɪ] adv cada vez más.

incredible [ɪn'kredəbl] adj increíble.

incredibly [ɪn'kredəblɪ] adv increíblemente.

incredulous [ɪn'kredjʊləs] adj incrédulo(la).

increment ['ɪnkrɪmənt] n incremento m.

incriminating [ɪn'krɪmɪneɪtɪŋ] adj comprometedor(ra).

incubator ['ɪnkjʊbeɪtə'] n [for baby] incubadora f.

incumbent [ɪn'kʌmbənt] fml <> adj: **to be incumbent on OR upon sb to do sthg** incumbir a alguien hacer algo. <> n titular mf.

incur [ɪn'kɜː'] vt [wrath, criticism] incurrir en, atraerse; [debt] contraer; [expenses] incurrir en.

indebted [ɪn'detɪd] adj - 1. [grateful]: **indebted (to)** en deuda (con) - 2. [owing money]: **indebted (to)** endeudado(da) (con).

indecent [ɪn'diːsnt] adj - 1. [improper] indecente - 2. [unreasonable, excessive] desmedido(da).

indecent assault n abusos mpl deshonestos.

indecent exposure n exhibicionismo m.

indecisive [ˌɪndɪ'saɪsɪv] adj - **1.** [person] indeciso(sa) - **2.** [result] no decisivo(va).

indeed [ɪn'diːd] adv - **1.** [certainly] ciertamente; **are you coming? – indeed I am** ¿vienes tú? – por supuesto que sí - **2.** [in fact] de hecho - **3.** [for emphasis] realmente; **very big indeed** grandísimo(ma); **very few indeed** poquísimos(mas) - **4.** [to express surprise, disbelief]: **indeed?** ¿ah sí? - **5.** [what is more] es más.

indefinite [ɪn'defɪnɪt] adj - **1.** [time, number] indefinido(da) - **2.** [answer, opinion] impreciso(sa) - **3.** GRAM indeterminado(da), indefinido(da).

indefinitely [ɪn'defɪnətlɪ] adv - **1.** [for unfixed period] indefinidamente - **2.** [imprecisely] de forma imprecisa.

indemnity [ɪn'demnɪtɪ] n - **1.** [insurance] indemnidad f - **2.** [compensation] indemnización f.

indent [ɪn'dent] <> n [in text] sangrado m. <> vt - **1.** [dent] mellar - **2.** [text] sangrar.

independence [ˌɪndɪ'pendəns] n independencia f; **to gain independence** independizarse.

Independence Day n el Día de la Independencia.

independent [ˌɪndɪ'pendənt] adj: **independent (of)** independiente (de).

independent school n UK colegio m privado.

in-depth adj a fondo, exhaustivo(va).

indescribable [ˌɪndɪ'skraɪbəbl] adj indescriptible.

indestructible [ˌɪndɪ'strʌktəbl] adj indestructible.

index ['ɪndeks] n (pl -es OR indices) índice m.

index card n ficha f.

index finger n (dedo m) índice m.

index-linked [-lɪŋkt] adj indexado(da).

India ['ɪndjə] n (la) India.

Indian ['ɪndjən] <> adj - **1.** [from India] indio(dia), hindú - **2.** [from the Americas] indio(dia). <> n - **1.** [from India] indio m, -dia f, hindú mf - **2.** [from the Americas] indio m, -dia f.

Indian Ocean n: **the Indian Ocean** el océano Índico.

indicate ['ɪndɪkeɪt] <> vt indicar. <> vi [when driving]: **to indicate left/right** indicar a la izquierda/derecha.

indication [ˌɪndɪ'keɪʃn] n - **1.** [suggestion, idea] indicación f - **2.** [sign] indicio m.

indicative [ɪn'dɪkətɪv] <> adj: **indicative of sthg** indicativo(va) de algo. <> n GRAM indicativo m.

indicator ['ɪndɪkeɪtər] n - **1.** [sign, criterion] indicador m - **2.** [on car] intermitente m.

indices ['ɪndɪsiːz] npl ⊏➤ **index**.

indict [ɪn'daɪt] vt: **to indict sb (for)** acusar a alguien (de).

indictment [ɪn'daɪtmənt] n - **1.** LAW acusación f - **2.** [criticism] crítica f severa.

indifference [ɪn'dɪfrəns] n indiferencia f.

indifferent [ɪn'dɪfrənt] adj - **1.** [uninterested]: **indifferent (to)** indiferente (a) - **2.** [mediocre] mediocre.

indigenous [ɪn'dɪdʒɪnəs] adj indígena.

indigestion [ˌɪndɪ'dʒestʃn] n (U) indigestión f.

indignant [ɪn'dɪgnənt] adj: **indignant (at)** indignado(da) (por).

indignity [ɪn'dɪgnɪtɪ] n indignidad f.

indigo ['ɪndɪgəʊ] <> adj (color) añil. <> n añil m.

indirect [ˌɪndɪ'rekt] adj indirecto(ta).

indiscreet [ˌɪndɪ'skriːt] adj indiscreto(ta).

indiscriminate [ˌɪndɪ'skrɪmɪnət] adj indiscriminado(da).

indispensable [ˌɪndɪ'spensəbl] adj indispensable, imprescindible.

indisputable [ˌɪndɪ'spjuːtəbl] adj incuestionable.

indistinct [ˌɪndɪ'stɪŋkt] adj [memory] confuso(sa); [words] imperceptible; [picture, marking] borroso(sa).

indistinguishable [ˌɪndɪ'stɪŋgwɪʃəbl] adj: **indistinguishable (from)** indistinguible (de).

individual [ˌɪndɪ'vɪdʒʊəl] <> adj - **1.** [gen] individual - **2.** [tuition] particular - **3.** [approach, style] personal. <> n individuo m.

individually [ˌɪndɪ'vɪdʒʊəlɪ] adv [separately] individualmente, por separado.

indoctrination [ɪnˌdɒktrɪ'neɪʃn] n adoctrinamiento m.

Indonesia [ˌɪndə'niːzjə] n Indonesia.

indoor ['ɪndɔːr] adj [gen] interior; [shoes] de andar por casa; [plant] de interior; [sports] en pista cubierta; **indoor swimming pool** piscina f cubierta.

indoors [ˌɪn'dɔːz] adv [gen] dentro; [at home] en casa.

induce [ɪn'djuːs] vt - **1.** [persuade]: **to induce sb to do sthg** inducir OR persuadir a alguien a que haga algo - **2.** [labour, sleep, anger] provocar.

inducement [ɪn'djuːsmənt] n [incentive] incentivo m, aliciente m.

induction [ɪn'dʌkʃn] n - 1. [into official position]: **induction into** introducción f OR inducción f a - 2. ELEC & MED inducción f - 3. [introduction to job] introducción f.

induction course n cursillo m introductorio.

indulge [ɪn'dʌldʒ] ⟨⟩ vt - 1. [whim, passion] satisfacer - 2. [child, person] consentir. ⟨⟩ vi: **to indulge in sthg** permitirse algo.

indulgence [ɪn'dʌldʒəns] n - 1. [act of indulging] indulgencia f - 2. [special treat] capricho m.

indulgent [ɪn'dʌldʒənt] adj indulgente.

industrial [ɪn'dʌstrɪəl] adj industrial.

industrial action n huelga f; **to take industrial action** declararse en huelga.

industrial estate UK, **industrial park** US n polígono m industrial.

industrialist [ɪn'dʌstrɪəlɪst] n industrial mf.

industrial park US = **industrial estate**.

industrial relations npl relaciones fpl laborales.

industrial revolution n revolución f industrial.

industrious [ɪn'dʌstrɪəs] adj diligente, trabajador(ra).

industry ['ɪndəstrɪ] n - 1. [gen] industria f; **the tourist industry** el sector turístico - 2. fml [hard work] laboriosidad f.

inebriated [ɪ'niːbrɪeɪtɪd] adj fml ebrio(ebria).

inedible [ɪn'edɪbl] adj - 1. [that cannot be eaten] no comestible - 2. [bad-tasting] incomible.

ineffective [,ɪnɪ'fektɪv] adj ineficaz, inútil.

ineffectual [,ɪnɪ'fektʃʊəl] adj inútil.

inefficiency [,ɪnɪ'fɪʃnsɪ] n ineficiencia f.

inefficient [,ɪnɪ'fɪʃnt] adj ineficiente.

ineligible [ɪn'elɪdʒəbl] adj inelegible; **to be ineligible for** no tener derecho a.

inept [ɪ'nept] adj inepto(ta); **inept at** incapaz para.

inequality [,ɪnɪ'kwɒlətɪ] n desigualdad f.

inert [ɪ'nɜːt] adj inerte.

inertia [ɪ'nɜːʃə] n inercia f.

inescapable [,ɪnɪ'skeɪpəbl] adj ineludible.

inevitable [ɪn'evɪtəbl] adj inevitable.

inevitably [ɪn'evɪtəblɪ] adv inevitablemente.

inexcusable [,ɪnɪk'skjuːzəbl] adj inexcusable, imperdonable.

inexpensive [,ɪnɪk'spensɪv] adj barato(ta), económico(ca).

inexperienced [,ɪnɪk'spɪərɪənst] adj inexperto(ta).

inexplicable [,ɪnɪk'splɪkəbl] adj inexplicable.

infallible [ɪn'fæləbl] adj infalible.

infamous ['ɪnfəməs] adj infame.

infancy ['ɪnfənsɪ] n primera infancia f; **to be in its infancy** fig dar sus primeros pasos.

infant ['ɪnfənt] n - 1. [baby] bebé m - 2. [young child] niño pequeño m, niña pequeña f.

infantry ['ɪnfəntrɪ] n infantería f.

infant school n UK colegio m preescolar (para niños de entre 4 y 7 años).

infatuated [ɪn'fætjʊeɪtɪd] adj: **infatuated (with)** encaprichado(da) (con).

infatuation [ɪn,fætjʊ'eɪʃn] n: **infatuation (with)** encaprichamiento m (con).

infect [ɪn'fekt] vt [wound] infectar.

infection [ɪn'fekʃn] n - 1. [disease] infección f - 2. [spreading of germs] contagio m.

infectious [ɪn'fekʃəs] adj - 1. [disease] infeccioso(sa) - 2. [laugh, attitude] contagioso(sa).

infer [ɪn'fɜːr] vt - 1. [deduce]: **to infer (that)** deducir OR inferir que; **to infer sthg (from sthg)** deducir OR inferir algo (de algo) - 2. inf [imply] insinuar.

inferior [ɪn'fɪərɪər] ⟨⟩ adj: **inferior (to)** inferior (a). ⟨⟩ n [in status] inferior mf.

inferiority [ɪn,fɪərɪ'ɒrətɪ] n inferioridad f.

inferiority complex n complejo m de inferioridad.

inferno [ɪn'fɜːnəʊ] (pl -s) n [hell] infierno m; **the building was an inferno** el edificio sufría un pavoroso incendio.

infertile [ɪn'fɜːtaɪl] adj estéril.

infested [ɪn'festɪd] adj: **infested with** infestado(da) de.

infighting ['ɪn,faɪtɪŋ] n (U) disputas fpl internas.

infiltrate ['ɪnfɪltreɪt] vt infiltrar.

infinite ['ɪnfɪnət] adj infinito(ta).

infinitive [ɪn'fɪnɪtɪv] n infinitivo m; **in the infinitive** en infinitivo.

infinity [ɪn'fɪnətɪ] n - 1. MATHS infinito m - 2. [incalculable number]: **an infinity (of)** infinidad f (de).

infirm [ɪn'fɜːm] ⟨⟩ adj achacoso(sa). ⟨⟩ npl: **the infirm** los enfermos.

infirmary [ɪn'fɜːmərɪ] n - 1. [hospital] hospital m - 2. [room] enfermería f.

infirmity [ɪn'fɜːmətɪ] n - 1. [illness] dolencia f - 2. [state] enfermedad f.

inflamed [ɪn'fleɪmd] adj MED inflamado(da).

inflammable [ɪn'flæməbl] adj [burning easily] inflamable.

inflammation [,ɪnflə'meɪʃn] n MED inflamación f.

inflatable [ɪn'fleɪtəbl] *adj* inflable, hinchable.

inflate [ɪn'fleɪt] ⋄ *vt* - 1. [gen] inflar, hinchar - 2. [prices] inflar. ⋄ *vi* inflarse, hincharse.

inflation [ɪn'fleɪʃn] *n* ECON inflación *f*.

inflationary [ɪn'fleɪʃnrɪ] *adj* ECON inflacionista.

inflict [ɪn'flɪkt] *vt*: to inflict sthg on sb infligir algo a alguien.

influence ['ɪnfluəns] ⋄ *n*: influence (on OR over sb) influencia *f* (sobre alguien); influence (on sthg) influencia (en algo); to be a bad influence on sb tener mala influencia en alguien; under the influence of [person, group] bajo la influencia de; [alcohol, drugs] bajo los efectos de. ⋄ *vt* influenciar.

influential [ˌɪnflu'enʃl] *adj* influyente.

influenza [ˌɪnflu'enzə] *n fml* gripe *f*.

influx ['ɪnflʌks] *n* afluencia *f*.

inform [ɪn'fɔːm] *vt*: to inform sb (of/about sthg) informar a alguien (de/sobre algo).
➡ **inform on** *vt insep* delatar.

informal [ɪn'fɔːml] *adj* informal; [language] familiar.

informant [ɪn'fɔːmənt] *n* - 1. [informer] delator *m*, -ra *f* - 2. [of researcher] informante *mf*.

information [ˌɪnfə'meɪʃn] *n (U)*: information (on OR about) información *f* OR datos *mpl* (sobre); a piece of information un dato; for your information para tu información.

information desk *n* (mostrador *m* de) información *f*.

information technology *n* informática *f*.

informative [ɪn'fɔːmətɪv] *adj* informativo(va).

informer [ɪn'fɔːməʳ] *n* delator *m*, -ra *f*.

infrared [ˌɪnfrə'red] *adj* infrarrojo(ja).

infrastructure ['ɪnfrə,strʌktʃəʳ] *n* infraestructura *f*.

infringe [ɪn'frɪndʒ] ⋄ *vt* - 1. [rule] infringir - 2. [right] vulnerar. ⋄ *vi*: to infringe on sthg vulnerar algo.

infringement [ɪn'frɪndʒmənt] *n* - 1. [of rule] infracción *f* - 2. [of right] violación *f*.

infuriating [ɪn'fjʊərɪeɪtɪŋ] *adj* exasperante.

ingenious [ɪn'dʒiːnjəs] *adj* ingenioso(sa).

ingenuity [ˌɪndʒɪ'njuːətɪ] *n* ingenio *m*, inventiva *f*.

ingenuous [ɪn'dʒenjʊəs] *adj fml* ingenuo(nua).

ingot ['ɪŋɡət] *n* lingote *m*.

ingrained [ɪn'ɡreɪnd] *adj* - 1. [ground in] incrustado(da) - 2. [deeply rooted] arraigado(da).

ingratiating [ɪn'ɡreɪʃɪeɪtɪŋ] *adj* obsequioso(sa), lisonjero(ra).

ingredient [ɪn'ɡriːdjənt] *n* ingrediente *m*.

inhabit [ɪn'hæbɪt] *vt* habitar.

inhabitant [ɪn'hæbɪtənt] *n* habitante *mf*.

inhale [ɪn'heɪl] ⋄ *vt* inhalar. ⋄ *vi* [gen] respirar; [smoker] tragarse el humo.

inhaler [ɪn'heɪləʳ] *n* MED inhalador *m*.

inherent [ɪn'hɪərənt, ɪn'herənt] *adj*: inherent (in) inherente (a).

inherently [ɪn'hɪərəntlɪ, ɪn'herəntlɪ] *adv* intrínsecamente.

inherit [ɪn'herɪt] *vt*: to inherit sthg (from sb) heredar algo (de alguien).

inheritance [ɪn'herɪtəns] *n* herencia *f*.

inhibit [ɪn'hɪbɪt] *vt* - 1. [restrict] impedir - 2. [person] cohibir.

inhibition [ˌɪnhɪ'bɪʃn] *n* inhibición *f*.

inhospitable [ˌɪnhɒ'spɪtəbl] *adj* - 1. [unwelcoming] inhospitalario(ria) - 2. [harsh] inhóspito(ta).

in-house ⋄ *adj* [journal, report] de circulación interna; [worker] de plantilla; [training] en el lugar de trabajo. ⋄ *adv* en la misma empresa.

inhuman [ɪn'hjuːmən] *adj* - 1. [cruel] inhumano(na) - 2. [not human] infrahumano(na).

initial [ɪ'nɪʃl] ⋄ *adj* inicial. ⋄ *vt* (UK pt & pp -led, cont -ling, US pt & pp -ed, cont -ing) poner las iniciales a. ➡ **initials** *npl* [of person] iniciales *fpl*.

initially [ɪ'nɪʃəlɪ] *adv* inicialmente.

initiate [ɪ'nɪʃɪeɪt] *vt* iniciar.

initiative [ɪ'nɪʃətɪv] *n* iniciativa *f*.

injection [ɪn'dʒekʃn] *n* inyección *f*.

injunction [ɪn'dʒʌŋkʃn] *n* interdicto *m*.

injure ['ɪndʒəʳ] *vt* [gen] herir; SPORT lesionar; [reputation] dañar; [chances] perjudicar.

injured ['ɪndʒəd] *adj* [gen] herido(da); SPORT lesionado(da); [reputation] dañado(da).

injury ['ɪndʒərɪ] *n* - 1. [wound] herida *f*; [to muscle, broken bone] lesión *f* - 2. *(U)* [physical harm] lesiones *fpl*.

injury time *n* (tiempo *m* de) descuento *m*.

injustice [ɪn'dʒʌstɪs] *n* injusticia *f*; to do sb an injustice ser injusto(ta) con alguien.

ink [ɪŋk] *n* tinta *f*.

ink-jet printer *n* COMPUT impresora *f* de chorro de tinta.

inkling ['ɪŋklɪŋ] *n*: to have an inkling of sthg tener una vaga idea de algo.

inlaid [ˌɪn'leɪd] *adj* incrustado(da); inlaid with [jewels] con incrustaciones de.

inland ⋄ *adj* ['ɪnlənd] interior. ⋄ *adv* [ɪn'lænd] [go] hacia el interior; [remain] en el interior.

Inland Revenue *n* UK: the Inland Revenue ≃ Hacienda *f*.

in-laws *npl* suegros *mpl*.

inlet ['ɪnlet] *n* - **1.** [stretch of water] entrante *m* - **2.** [way in] entrada *f*, admisión *f*.

in-line skating *n* SPORT patinaje *m* en línea.

inmate ['ɪnmeɪt] *n* [of prison] preso *m*, -sa *f*; [of mental hospital] interno *m*, -na *f*.

inn [ɪn] *n* fonda *f*; [pub] *pub decorado a la vieja usanza.*

innate [ˌɪ'neɪt] *adj* innato(ta).

inner ['ɪnəʳ] *adj* - **1.** [gen] interior - **2.** [feelings] íntimo(ma); [fears, doubts, meaning] interno(na).

inner city *n* núcleo *m* urbano deprimido.

inner tube *n* cámara *f* (de aire).

inning ['ɪnɪŋ] *n* [in baseball] entrada *f*, inning *m*.

innings ['ɪnɪŋz] (*pl* innings) *n* [in cricket] entrada *f*, turno *m*; **to have had a good innings** *fig* haber tenido una vida larga y provechosa.

innocence ['ɪnəsəns] *n* inocencia *f*.

innocent ['ɪnəsənt] ◇ *adj*: **innocent (of)** inocente (de). ◇ *n* [naive person] inocente *mf*.

innocuous [ɪ'nɒkjuəs] *adj* inocuo(cua).

innovation [ˌɪnə'veɪʃn] *n* innovación *f*.

innovative ['ɪnəvətɪv] *adj* innovador(ra).

innuendo [ˌɪnju:'endəʊ] (*pl* -es OR -s) *n* - **1.** [individual remark] insinuación *f*, indirecta *f* - **2.** (*U*) [style of speaking] insinuaciones *fpl*, indirectas *fpl*.

inoculate [ɪ'nɒkjuleɪt] *vt*: **to inoculate sb (against sthg)** inocular a alguien (contra algo).

in-patient *n* paciente interno *m*, paciente interna *f*.

input ['ɪnpʊt] ◇ *n* - **1.** [contribution] aportación *f*, contribución *f* - **2.** COMPUT & ELEC entrada *f*. ◇ *vt* (*pt & pp* input OR -ted) COMPUT introducir.

inquest ['ɪnkwest] *n* investigación *f* judicial.

inquire [ɪn'kwaɪəʳ] ◇ *vi* [ask for information] informarse, preguntar; **to inquire about sthg** informarse de algo. ◇ *vt*: **to inquire when/if/how...** preguntar cuándo/si/cómo... ◆ **inquire after** *vt insep* preguntar por. ◆ **inquire into** *vt insep* investigar.

inquiry [ɪn'kwaɪərɪ] *n* - **1.** [question] consulta *f*, pregunta *f*; **'Inquiries'** 'Información' - **2.** [investigation] investigación *f*.

inquiry desk *n* (mostrador *m* de) información *f*.

inquisitive [ɪn'kwɪzətɪv] *adj* curioso(sa).

inroads ['ɪnrəʊdz] *npl*: **to make inroads into** [savings, supplies] mermar; [market, enemy territory] abrirse paso en.

insane [ɪn'seɪn] *adj* [mad] demente; *fig* [jealousy, person] loco(ca); **to drive sb insane** volver loco a alguien.

insanity [ɪn'sænətɪ] *n* MED demencia *f*; [craziness] locura *f*.

insatiable [ɪn'seɪʃəbl] *adj* insaciable.

inscription [ɪn'skrɪpʃn] *n* - **1.** [engraved] inscripción *f* - **2.** [written] dedicatoria *f*.

inscrutable [ɪn'skru:təbl] *adj* inescrutable.

insect ['ɪnsekt] *n* insecto *m*.

insecticide [ɪn'sektɪsaɪd] *n* insecticida *m*.

insect repellent *n* loción *f* antiinsectos.

insecure [ˌɪnsɪ'kjuəʳ] *adj* - **1.** [not confident] inseguro(ra) - **2.** [not safe] poco seguro(ra).

insensible [ɪn'sensəbl] *adj fml* - **1.** [unconscious] inconsciente - **2.** [unaware]: **to be insensible of sthg** no ser consciente de algo - **3.** [unable to feel]: **to be insensible to sthg** ser insensible a algo.

insensitive [ɪn'sensətɪv] *adj*: **insensitive (to)** insensible (a).

inseparable [ɪn'seprəbl] *adj*: **inseparable (from)** inseparable (de).

insert ◇ *vt* [ɪn'sɜ:t]: **to insert sthg (in OR into)** [hole] introducir algo (en); [text] insertar algo (en). ◇ *n* ['ɪnsɜ:t] PRESS encarte *m*.

insertion [ɪn'sɜ:ʃn] *n* inserción *f*.

inshore ◇ *adj* ['ɪnʃɔ:ʳ] costero(ra). ◇ *adv* [ɪn'ʃɔ:ʳ] hacia la orilla OR la costa.

inside [ɪn'saɪd] ◇ *prep* dentro de; **inside three months** en menos de tres meses. ◇ *adv* - **1.** [be, remain] dentro; [go, move, look] adentro; **come inside!** ¡metéos dentro! - **2.** *fig* [feel, hurt etc] por dentro. ◇ *adj* interior; **inside leg measurement** medida *f* de la entrepierna. ◇ *n* interior *m*; **from the inside** desde dentro; **to overtake on the inside** [of road] adelantar por dentro; **inside out** [wrong way] al revés; **to turn sthg inside out** [clothing] dar la vuelta a algo; **to know sthg inside out** conocer algo de arriba abajo OR al dedillo. ◆ **insides** *npl inf* tripas *fpl*. ◆ **inside of** *prep* US [building, object] dentro de.

inside lane *n* AUT carril *m* de dentro; SPORT calle *f* de dentro.

insight ['ɪnsaɪt] *n* - **1.** (*U*) [power of understanding] perspicacia *f* - **2.** [understanding] idea *f*.

insignificant [ˌɪnsɪg'nɪfɪkənt] *adj* insignificante.

insincere [ˌɪnsɪn'sɪəʳ] *adj* insincero(ra).

insinuate [ɪn'sɪnjueɪt] *vt pej*: **to insinuate (that)** insinuar (que).

insipid [ɪn'sɪpɪd] *adj pej* soso(sa), insípido(da).

insist [ɪn'sɪst] ◇ *vt*: **to insist that** insistir en que. ◇ *vi*: **to insist on sthg** exigir algo; **to insist on doing sthg** insistir (en hacer algo).

insistent [ɪn'sɪstənt] *adj* - **1.** [determined] insistente; **to be insistent on sthg** insistir en algo - **2.** [continual] persistente.

insofar [ˌɪnsəʊ'fɑ:ʳ] ◆ **insofar as** *conj* en la medida en que.

Insole ['ɪnsəʊl] n plantilla f.

insolent ['ɪnsələnt] adj insolente.

insolvent [ɪn'sɒlvənt] adj insolvente.

insomnia [ɪn'sɒmnɪə] n insomnio m.

inspect [ɪn'spekt] vt inspeccionar; [troops] pasar revista a.

inspection [ɪn'spekʃn] n inspección f; [of troops] revista. f; **on closer inspection** tras un examen más detallado.

inspector [ɪn'spektər] n inspector m, -ra f; [on bus, train] revisor m, -ra f.

inspiration [,ɪnspə'reɪʃn] n - 1. [gen] inspiración f - 2. [source of inspiration]: **inspiration (for)** fuente f de inspiración (para).

inspirational [,ɪnspə'reɪʃnl] adj inspirador(ra).

inspire [ɪn'spaɪər] vt - 1. [stimulate, encourage]: **to inspire sb (to do sthg)** alentar OR animar a alguien (a hacer algo) - 2. [fill]: **to inspire sb with sthg, to inspire sthg in sb** inspirar algo a alguien.

install UK, **instal** US [ɪn'stɔːl] vt [gen & COMPUT] instalar.

installation [,ɪnstə'leɪʃn] n [gen & COMPUT] instalación f.

installment US = **instalment**.

installment plan n US compra f a plazos.

instalment UK, **installment** US [ɪn'stɔːlmənt] n - 1. [payment] plazo m; **in instalments** a plazos - 2. TV & RADIO episodio m; [of novel] entrega f.

instance ['ɪnstəns] n [example, case] ejemplo m; **for instance** por ejemplo; **in the first instance** fml en primer lugar; **in this instance** en este caso.

instant ['ɪnstənt] ◇ adj instantáneo(a). ◇ n [moment] instante m; **at that** OR **the same instant** en aquel mismo instante; **the instant (that)...** en cuanto...; **this instant** ahora mismo.

instantly ['ɪnstəntlɪ] adv en el acto.

instead [ɪn'sted] adv en cambio; **I came instead** yo vine en su lugar; **if you haven't got any sugar, you can use honey instead** si no tiene azúcar, utilice miel en su lugar. ◆ **instead of** prep en lugar de, en vez de; **I came instead of her** yo vine en su lugar.

instep ['ɪnstep] n [of foot] empeine m.

instigate ['ɪnstɪgeɪt] vt iniciar; **to instigate sb to do sthg** instigar a alguien a hacer algo.

instil UK, **instill** US [ɪn'stɪl] vt: **to instil sthg in** OR **into sb** inculcar algo a alguien.

instinct ['ɪnstɪŋkt] n instinto m; **my first instinct was...** mi primer impulso fue...

instinctive [ɪn'stɪŋktɪv] adj instintivo(va).

institute ['ɪnstɪtjuːt] ◇ n instituto m. ◇ vt [proceedings] ... entablar; [system] establecer, instituir.

institution [,ɪnstɪ'tjuːʃn] n - 1. [gen] institución f - 2. [home - for children, old people] asilo m; [- for mentally-handicapped] hospital m psiquiátrico.

institutional racism, institutionalized racism [,ɪnstɪ'tjuːʃnəlaɪzd-] n racismo m institucional.

instruct [ɪn'strʌkt] vt - 1. [tell, order]: **to instruct sb to do sthg** mandar OR ordenar a alguien que haga algo - 2. [teach]: **to instruct sb (in sthg)** instruir a alguien (en algo).

instruction [ɪn'strʌkʃn] n [gen & COMPUT] instrucción f. ◆ **instructions** npl [for use] instrucciones fpl.

instructor [ɪn'strʌktər] n - 1. [gen] instructor m - 2. [in skiing] monitor m - 3. [in driving] profesor m - 4. US [at college] profesor m, -ra f.

instrument ['ɪnstrʊmənt] n instrumento m.

instrumental [,ɪnstrʊ'mentl] adj [important, helpful]: **to be instrumental in sthg** jugar un papel fundamental en algo.

instrument panel n tablero m de instrumentos.

insubordinate [,ɪnsə'bɔːdɪnət] adj insubordinado(da).

insubstantial [,ɪnsəb'stænʃl] adj [frame, structure] endeble; [meal] poco sustancioso(sa).

insufficient [,ɪnsə'fɪʃnt] adj: **insufficient (for)** insuficiente (para).

insular ['ɪnsjʊlər] adj [narrow-minded] estrecho(cha) de miras.

insulate ['ɪnsjʊleɪt] vt aislar.

insulating tape ['ɪnsjʊleɪtɪŋ-] n UK cinta f aislante.

insulation [,ɪnsjʊ'leɪʃn] n [electrical] aislamiento m; [against the cold] aislamiento m térmico.

insulin ['ɪnsjʊlɪn] n insulina f.

insult ◇ vt [ɪn'sʌlt] [with words] insultar; [with actions] ofender. ◇ n ['ɪnsʌlt] [remark] insulto m; [action] ofensa f.

insuperable [ɪn'suːprəbl] adj fml insalvable, insuperable.

insurance [ɪn'ʃʊərəns] n - 1. [against fire, accident, theft]: **insurance (against)** seguro m (contra) - 2. fig [safeguard, protection]: **insurance (against)** prevención f (contra).

insurance policy n póliza f de seguros.

insure [ɪn'ʃʊər] ◇ vt - 1. [against fire, accident, theft]: **to insure sthg/sb (against)** asegurar algo/a alguien (contra) - 2. US [make certain] asegurar. ◇ vi [prevent]: **to insure (against)** prevenir OR prevenirse (contra).

insurer [ɪn'ʃʊərər] n asegurador m, -ra f.

insurmountable [ˌɪnsəˈmaʊntəbl] *adj fml* infranqueable, insuperable.

intact [ɪnˈtækt] *adj* intacto(ta).

intake [ˈɪnteɪk] *n* - 1. [of food, drink] ingestión *f*; [of air] inspiración *f* - 2. [in army] reclutamiento *m*; [in organization] número *m* de ingresos.

integral [ˈɪntɪɡrəl] *adj* integrante; **to be integral to** ser parte integrante de.

integrate [ˈɪntɪɡreɪt] <> *vi*: **to integrate (with OR into)** integrarse (en). <> *vt*: **to integrate sthg/sb with sthg, to integrate sthg/sb into sthg** integrar algo/a alguien en algo.

integrity [ɪnˈteɡrətɪ] *n* integridad *f*.

intellect [ˈɪntəlekt] *n* [mind, cleverness] intelecto *m*, inteligencia *f*.

intellectual [ˌɪntəˈlektjʊəl] <> *adj* intelectual. <> *n* intelectual *mf*.

intelligence [ɪnˈtelɪdʒəns] *n* (U) - 1. [ability to think] inteligencia *f* - 2. [information] información *f* secreta - 3. [information service] servicio *m* secreto OR de espionaje.

intelligent [ɪnˈtelɪdʒənt] *adj* [gen & COMPUT] inteligente.

intend [ɪnˈtend] *vt* pretender; **to intend doing OR to do sthg** tener la intención de hacer algo; **what do you intend to do?** ¿qué piensas hacer?; **later than I had intended** más tarde de lo que había pensado; **to be intended for/as sthg** [project, book] estar pensado para/como algo; **the flowers were intended for you** las flores eran para ti.

intended [ɪnˈtendɪd] *adj* [effect, result] pretendido(da).

intense [ɪnˈtens] *adj* - 1. [extreme, profound] intenso(sa) - 2. [serious - person] muy serio(ria).

intensely [ɪnˈtenslɪ] *adv* - 1. [very - boring, irritating] enormemente - 2. [very much - suffer] intensamente; [- dislike] profundamente.

intensify [ɪnˈtensɪfaɪ] <> *vt* intensificar. <> *vi* intensificarse.

intensity [ɪnˈtensətɪ] *n* intensidad *f*.

intensive [ɪnˈtensɪv] *adj* [concentrated] intensivo(va).

intensive care *n* (U): **(in) intensive care** (bajo) cuidados *mpl* intensivos.

intent [ɪnˈtent] <> *adj* - 1. [absorbed] atento(ta) - 2. [determined]: **to be intent on OR upon doing sthg** estar empeñado(da) en hacer algo. <> *n fml* intención *f*; **to all intents and purposes** para todos los efectos.

intention [ɪnˈtenʃn] *n* intención *f*; **to have no intention of** no tener la menor intención de.

intentional [ɪnˈtenʃənl] *adj* deliberado(da), intencionado(da); **it wasn't intentional** fue sin querer.

intently [ɪnˈtentlɪ] *adv* atentamente.

interact [ˌɪntərˈækt] *vi* - 1. [communicate, work together]: **to interact (with sb)** relacionarse (con alguien) - 2. [react]: **to interact (with sthg)** interaccionar (con algo).

interactivity [ˌɪntəræktˈɪvɪtɪ] *n* interactividad *f*.

intercede [ˌɪntəˈsiːd] *vi fml*: **to intercede (with/for)** interceder (ante/por).

intercept [ˌɪntəˈsept] *vt* interceptar.

interchange <> *n* [ˈɪntətʃeɪndʒ] - 1. [exchange] intercambio *m* - 2. [on motorway] enlace *m*. <> *vt* [ˌɪntəˈtʃeɪndʒ] intercambiar.

interchangeable [ˌɪntəˈtʃeɪndʒəbl] *adj*: **interchangeable (with)** intercambiable (con).

intercity [ˌɪntəˈsɪtɪ] *n* [train] tren *m* interurbano.

intercom [ˈɪntəkɒm] *n* [for block of flats] portero *m* automático; [within a building] interfono *m*.

intercourse [ˈɪntəkɔːs] *n* (U): **sexual intercourse** relaciones *fpl* sexuales, coito *m*.

interest [ˈɪntrəst] <> *n* - 1. [gen]: **interest (in)** interés *m* (en OR por); **that's of no interest** eso no tiene interés; **in the interest OR interests of** [in order to benefit] en interés de; [in order to achieve] en pro de; **to take an interest in sthg** interesarse por algo - 2. FIN interés *m*; **to pay the interest on a loan** pagar los intereses de un préstamo - 3. [hobby] afición *f*. <> *vt* interesar; **to interest sb in sthg/in doing sthg** interesar a alguien en algo/en hacer algo.

interested [ˈɪntrəstɪd] *adj* interesado(da); **I'm not interested** no me interesa; **to be interested in sthg/in doing sthg** estar interesado en algo/en hacer algo; **I'm interested in that subject** me interesa el tema.

interesting [ˈɪntrəstɪŋ] *adj* interesante.

interest rate *n* tipo *m* de interés.

interface *n* COMPUT interfaz *f*, interface *m*.

interfere [ˌɪntəˈfɪər] *vi* - 1. [meddle]: **to interfere (with OR in sthg)** entrometerse OR interferir (en algo) - 2. [damage] interferir; **to interfere with sthg** [career, routine] interferir en algo; [work, performance] interrumpir algo.

interference [ˌɪntəˈfɪərəns] *n* (U) - 1. [meddling]: **interference (with OR in)** intromisión *f* OR interferencia *f* (en) - 2. [on radio, TV, telephone] interferencia *f*.

interim [ˈɪntərɪm] <> *adj* [report] parcial; [measure] provisional; [government] interino(na). <> *n*: **in the interim** entre tanto.

interior [ɪnˈtɪərɪər] <> *adj* - 1. [inner] interior - 2. POL [minister, department] del Interior. <> *n* interior *m*.

interior decorator, interior designer *n* interiorista *mf*.

interlock [ˌɪntəˈlɒk] *vi* [fingers] entrelazarse; [cogs] engranar.

interloper ['ɪntələʊpə'] n intruso m, -sa f

interlude [ˈɪntəluːd] *n* - **1.** [period] intervalo *m* - **2.** [interval] intermedio *m*.

intermediary [ˌɪntəˈmiːdjəri] n intermediario m, -ria f.

intermediate [ˌɪntəˈmiːdjət] adj intermedio(dia).

interminable [ɪnˈtɜːmɪnəbl] adj interminable.

intermission [ˌɪntəˈmɪʃn] n [of film] descanso m; [of play, opera, ballet] entreacto m.

intermittent [ˌɪntəˈmɪtənt] adj intermitente.

intern <> vt [ɪnˈtɜːn] recluir, internar. <> n [ˈɪntɜːn] esp US médico m interno residente.

internal [ɪnˈtɜːnl] adj - **1.** [gen] interno(na) - **2.** [within a country] interior, nacional; **internal flight** vuelo m nacional.

internally [ɪnˈtɜːnəlɪ] adv - **1.** [gen] internamente - **2.** [within a country] a nivel nacional.

Internal Revenue Service n US: **the Internal Revenue Service** ≃ la Agencia Triburaria *Esp*, ≃ la Dirección General Impositiva *Amér*.

international [ˌɪntəˈnæʃənl] <> adj internacional. <> n UK - **1.** SPORT [match] encuentro m internacional - **2.** SPORT [player] internacional mf.

Internet [ˈɪntənet] n: **the Internet** Internet f; **on the Internet** en Internet.

Internet access n acceso m a Internet.

Internet access provider n proveedor m de acceso a Internet.

Internet café n cibercafé m.

Internet connection n conexión f a Internet.

Internet radio n radio f por Internet.

Internet Service Provider n proveedor m de servicios Internet.

Internet start-up company n empresa f electrónica aparecida con Internet.

Internet television, Internet TV n televisión f por Internet.

interpret [ɪnˈtɜːprɪt] <> vt interpretar. <> vi hacer de intérprete.

interpreter [ɪnˈtɜːprɪtə'] n [person] intérprete mf.

interrelate [ˌɪntərɪˈleɪt] vi: **to interrelate (with)** interrelacionarse (con).

interrogate [ɪnˈterəgeɪt] vt [gen & COMPUT] interrogar.

interrogation [ɪnˌterəˈgeɪʃn] n interrogatorio m.

interrogation mark n US signo m de interrogación.

interrogative [ˌɪntəˈrɒgətɪv] adj GRAM interrogativo(va).

interrupt [ˌɪntəˈrʌpt] vt & vi interrumpir.

interruption [ˌɪntəˈrʌpʃn] n interrupción f.

intersect [ˌɪntəˈsekt] <> vi cruzarse. <> vt cruzar.

intersection [ˌɪntəˈsekʃn] n US [of roads] cruce m, intersección f.

intersperse [ˌɪntəˈspɜːs] vt: **to be interspersed with** OR **by** estar entremezclado con.

interstate [ˈɪntəsteɪt] n US autopista f interestatal.

interval [ˈɪntəvl] n - **1.** [gen & MUS]: **interval (between)** intervalo m (entre); **at intervals** [now and again] a ratos; **at regular intervals** a intervalos regulares; **at monthly/yearly intervals** a intervalos de un mes/un año - **2.** UK [at play, concert] intermedio m, descanso m.

intervene [ˌɪntəˈviːn] vi - **1.** [gen]: **to intervene (in)** intervenir (en) - **2.** [prevent thing from happening] interponerse; **the war intervened** sobrevino la guerra - **3.** [pass] transcurrir.

intervention [ˌɪntəˈvenʃn] n intervención f.

interview [ˈɪntəvjuː] <> n [gen] entrevista f; [with police] interrogatorio m. <> vt [gen] entrevistar; [subj: policeman] interrogar.

interviewer [ˈɪntəvjuːə'] n entrevistador m, -ra f.

intestine [ɪnˈtestɪn] n intestino m.

intimacy [ˈɪntɪməsɪ] n: **intimacy (between/with)** intimidad f (entre/con).

intimate <> adj [ˈɪntɪmət] - **1.** [gen] íntimo(ma) - **2.** [knowledge] profundo(da). <> vt [ˈɪntɪmeɪt] fml: **to intimate (that)** dar a entender (que).

intimidate [ɪnˈtɪmɪdeɪt] vt intimidar.

into [ˈɪntʊ] prep - **1.** [inside] en; **to go into a room** entrar en una habitación; **to put sthg into sthg** meter algo en algo; **to get into a car** subir a un coche - **2.** [against] con; **to bump/crash into** tropezar/chocar con - **3.** [referring to change in condition etc]: **to turn** OR **develop into** convertirse en; **to translate sthg into Spanish** traducir algo al español - **4.** [concerning] en relación con; **research into electronics** investigación en torno a la electrónica - **5.** [in expressions of time]: **fifteen minutes into the game** a los quince minutos de empezar el partido; **well into the spring** hasta bien entrada la primavera - **6.** MATHS: **to divide 4 into 8** dividir 8 entre 4.

intolerable [ɪnˈtɒlrəbl] adj fml [position, conditions] intolerable; [boredom, pain] inaguantable.

intolerance [ɪnˈtɒlərəns] n intolerancia f.

intolerant [ɪnˈtɒlərənt] adj intolerante.

intoxicated [ɪnˈtɒksɪkeɪtɪd] adj - **1.** [drunk] embriagado(da) - **2.** fig [excited]: **intoxicated (by** OR **with)** ebrio(ebria) (de).

intractable [ɪn'træktəbl] *adj fml* - **1.** [stubborn] intratable - **2.** [insoluble] inextricable, insoluble.

intransitive [ɪn'trænzətɪv] *adj* intransitivo(va).

intravenous [ˌɪntrə'viːnəs] *adj* intravenoso(sa).

in-tray *n* bandeja *f* de entrada.

intricate ['ɪntrɪkət] *adj* intrincado(da).

intrigue [ɪn'triːg] ⟨⟩ *n* intriga *f*. ⟨⟩ *vt* intrigar.

intriguing [ɪn'triːgɪŋ] *adj* intrigante.

intrinsic [ɪn'trɪnsɪk] *adj* intrínseco(ca).

introduce [ˌɪntrə'djuːs] *vt* - **1.** [present - person, programme] presentar; **to introduce sb (to sb)** presentar a alguien (a alguien); **to introduce o.s.** presentarse - **2.** [bring in]: **to introduce sthg (to OR into)** introducir algo (en) - **3.** [show for first time]: **to introduce sb to sthg** iniciar a alguien en algo.

introduction [ˌɪntrə'dʌkʃn] *n* - **1.** [gen]: **introduction (to sthg)** introducción *f* (a algo) - **2.** [of people]: **introduction (to sb)** presentación *f* (a alguien).

introductory [ˌɪntrə'dʌktrɪ] *adj* [chapter] introductorio(ria); [remarks] preliminar; [price, offer] de lanzamiento.

introvert ['ɪntrəvɜːt] *n* introvertido *m*, -da *f*.

introverted ['ɪntrəvɜːtɪd] *adj* introvertido(da).

intrude [ɪn'truːd] *vi* [interfere]: **to intrude (on OR upon sb)** inmiscuirse (en los asuntos de alguien); **to intrude (on OR upon sthg)** inmiscuirse (en algo); [disturb] molestar.

intruder [ɪn'truːdər] *n* intruso *m*, -sa *f*.

intrusive [ɪn'truːsɪv] *adj* [interfering] entrometido(da); [unwanted] indeseado(da).

intuition [ˌɪntjuː'ɪʃn] *n* intuición *f*.

inundate ['ɪnʌndeɪt] *vt* - **1.** *fml* [flood] inundar - **2.** [overwhelm] desbordar; **to be inundated with** verse desbordado por.

invade [ɪn'veɪd] *vt* invadir.

invalid ⟨⟩ *adj* [ɪn'vælɪd] - **1.** [marriage, vote, ticket] nulo(la) - **2.** [argument, result] que no es válido(da). ⟨⟩ *n* ['ɪnvəlɪd] inválido *m*, -da *f*.

invaluable [ɪn'væljuəbl] *adj*: **invaluable (to)** [information, advice] inestimable (para); [person] valiosísimo(ma) (para).

invariably [ɪn'veərɪəblɪ] *adv* siempre, invariablemente.

invasion [ɪn'veɪʒn] *n* invasión *f*.

invent [ɪn'vent] *vt* inventar.

invention [ɪn'venʃn] *n* - **1.** [gen] invención *f* - **2.** [ability to invent] inventiva *f*.

inventive [ɪn'ventɪv] *adj* [person, mind] inventivo(va); [solution] ingenioso(sa).

inventor [ɪn'ventər] *n* inventor *m*, -ra *f*.

inventory ['ɪnventrɪ] *n* - **1.** [list] inventario *m* - **2.** [goods] existencias *fpl*.

invert [ɪn'vɜːt] *vt* invertir.

inverted commas [ɪn'vɜːtɪd-] *npl UK* comillas *fpl*; **in inverted commas** entre comillas.

invest [ɪn'vest] ⟨⟩ *vt* [money, time, energy]: **to invest sthg (in)** invertir algo (en). ⟨⟩ *vi lit* & *fig*: **to invest (in)** invertir (en).

investigate [ɪn'vestɪgeɪt] *vt* & *vi* investigar.

investigation [ɪnˌvestɪ'geɪʃn] *n* [enquiry, examination]: **investigation (into)** investigación *f* (en).

investment [ɪn'vestmənt] *n* inversión *f*.

investor [ɪn'vestər] *n* inversor *m*, -ra *f*.

inveterate [ɪn'vetərət] *adj* [liar] incorregible; [reader, smoker] empedernido(da).

invidious [ɪn'vɪdɪəs] *adj* [task, role] desagradable; [comparison] odioso(sa).

invigilate [ɪn'vɪdʒɪleɪt] *vt* & *vi UK* vigilar *(en un examen)*.

invigorating [ɪn'vɪgəreɪtɪŋ] *adj* [bath, walk] vigorizante; [experience] estimulante.

invincible [ɪn'vɪnsɪbl] *adj* - **1.** [unbeatable] invencible - **2.** [determination] inalterable.

invisible [ɪn'vɪzɪbl] *adj* invisible.

invitation [ˌɪnvɪ'teɪʃn] *n* invitación *f*; **an invitation to sthg/to do sthg** una invitación a algo/a hacer algo.

invite [ɪn'vaɪt] *vt* - **1.** [gen]: **to invite sb (to sthg/to do sthg)** invitar a alguien (a algo/a hacer algo) - **2.** [ask for, provoke] buscarse.

inviting [ɪn'vaɪtɪŋ] *adj* tentador(ra).

invoice ['ɪnvɔɪs] ⟨⟩ *n* factura *f*. ⟨⟩ *vt* - **1.** [send invoice to] mandar la factura a - **2.** [prepare invoice for] facturar.

invoke [ɪn'vəʊk] *vt fml* [quote as justification] acogerse a.

involuntary [ɪn'vɒləntrɪ] *adj* involuntario(ria).

involve [ɪn'vɒlv] *vt* - **1.** [entail, require]: **to involve sthg/doing sthg** conllevar algo/hacer algo; **it involves working weekends** supone OR implica trabajar los fines de semana - **2.** [concern, affect] afectar a; **to be involved in sthg** [accident, crash] verse envuelto en algo.

involved [ɪn'vɒlvd] *adj* - **1.** [complex] enrevesado(da) - **2.** [participating]: **to be involved in** estar metido(da) en; **he didn't want to get involved** no quería tener nada que ver - **3.** [in a relationship]: **to be/get involved with sb** estar liado(da)/liarse con alguien.

involvement [ɪn'vɒlvmənt] *n* - **1.**: **involvement (in)** [crime] implicación *f* (en); [running sthg] participación *f* (en) - **2.** [concern, enthusiasm]: **involvement (in)** compromiso *m* (con) - **3.** (U) [relationship] relación *f* sentimental.

inward ['ɪnwəd] ◇ adj ▪ 1 [inner] inter-
ɪɪɪʆɪɪə] ▪ ? [[ɔwɔɾdʒ ʃ] iɪɪʌʆdɪ bɑcɪɑ ɑl ɪɪɪtərɪɔr
◇ adv US = **inwards**.

inwards, inward ['ɪnwədz] adv hacia dentro.

in-your-face adj inf impactante.

iodine [UK 'aɪədiːn, US 'aɪədaɪn] n yodo m.

iota [aɪ'əʊtə] n pizca f, ápice m.

IOU (abbr of **I owe you**) n pagaré.

IQ (abbr of **intelligence quotient**) n C.I. m

IRA ◇ n (abbr of **Irish Republican Army**)
IRA m. ◇ n US (abbr of **Individual Retirement Account**) cuenta f de retiro OR jubilación individual.

Iran [ɪ'rɑːn] n (el) Irán.

Iranian [ɪ'reɪnjən] ◇ adj iraní. ◇ n [per-
son] iraní mf.

Iraq [ɪ'rɑːk] n (el) Irak.

Iraqi [ɪ'rɑːkɪ] ◇ adj iraquí. ◇ n [person] iraquí mf.

irate [aɪ'reɪt] adj iracundo(da), airado(da).

Ireland ['aɪələnd] n Irlanda.

iris ['aɪərɪs] (pl -es) n ▪ 1. [flower] lirio m ▪ 2. [of
eye] iris m inv.

Irish ['aɪrɪʃ] ◇ adj irlandés(esa). ◇ n [lan-
guage] irlandés m. ◇ npl [people]: **the Irish** los
irlandeses.

Irishman ['aɪrɪʃmən] (pl -men [-mən]) n irlandés m.

Irish Sea n: **the Irish Sea** el mar de Irlanda.

Irishwoman ['aɪrɪʃˌwʊmən] (pl -women
[-ˌwɪmɪn]) n irlandesa f.

irksome ['ɜːksəm] adj fastidioso(sa).

iron ['aɪən] ◇ adj lit & fig de hierro. ◇ n
▪ 1. [metal, nutrient] hierro m ▪ 2. [for clothes]
plancha f ▪ 3. [golf club] hierro m. ◇ vt & vi
planchar. ▪ **iron out** vt sep fig [overcome]
resolver.

Iron Curtain n: **the Iron Curtain** el telón de
acero.

ironic(al) [aɪ'rɒnɪk(l)] adj irónico(ca).

ironing ['aɪənɪŋ] n ▪ 1. [work] planchado m
▪ 2. [clothes to be ironed] ropa f para planchar.

ironing board n tabla f de planchar.

ironmonger ['aɪənˌmʌŋgəʳ] n UK ferrete-
ro m, -ra f; **ironmonger's (shop)** ferretería f.

irony ['aɪrənɪ] n ironía f.

irrational [ɪ'ræʃənl] adj irracional.

irreconcilable [ɪˌrekən'saɪləbl] adj [com-
pletely different] irreconciliable.

irregular [ɪ'regjʊləʳ] adj [gen & GRAM] irregular.

irrelevant [ɪ'reləvənt] adj irrelevante, que
no viene al caso; **that's irrelevant** eso no viene
al caso.

irreparable [ɪ'repərəbl] adj irreparable.

irreplaceable [ˌɪrɪ'pleɪsəbl] adj irreempla-
zable, insustituible.

irrepressible [ˌɪrɪ'presəbl] adj [onthuciacm]
ɪrrəprɪmiblə; [nɔrɔɔl] ɪmpɔɾɔblə

irresistible [ˌɪrɪ'zɪstəbl] adj irresistible.

irrespective [ˌɪrɪ'spektɪv] ▪ **irrespective
of** prep independientemente de.

irresponsible [ˌɪrɪ'spɒnsəbl] adj irresponsable.

irrigate ['ɪrɪgeɪt] vt regar, irrigar.

irrigation [ˌɪrɪ'geɪʃn] n riego m.

irritable ['ɪrɪtəbl] adj [person] irritable; [an-
swer, tone] irritado(da).

irritate ['ɪrɪteɪt] vt irritar.

irritating ['ɪrɪteɪtɪŋ] adj irritante.

irritation [ɪrɪ'teɪʃn] n ▪ 1. [anger, soreness]
irritación f ▪ 2. [cause of anger] motivo m de
irritación.

IRS (abbr of **Internal Revenue Service**) n US:
the IRS ≃ Hacienda f.

is [ɪz] vb ▷ **be**.

ISDN (abbr of **Integrated Services Delivery
Network**) n COMPUT RDSI f.

Islam ['ɪzlɑːm] n [religion] islam m.

Islamic fundamentalist [ɪz'læmɪk
ˌfʌndə'mentəlɪst] n fundamentalista mf islá-
mico, -ca f.

Islamist ['ɪzləmɪst] adj & n islamista mf.

island ['aɪlənd] n ▪ 1. [in water] isla f ▪ 2. [in
traffic] isleta f, refugio m.

islander ['aɪləndəʳ] n isleño m, -ña f.

isle [aɪl] n [as part of name] isla f; liter [island]
ínsula f.

Isle of Man n: **the Isle of Man** la isla de Man.

Isle of Wight [-waɪt] n: **the Isle of Wight** la
isla de Wight.

isn't ['ɪznt] (abbr of **is not**) ▷ **be**.

isobar ['aɪsəbɑːʳ] n isobara f.

isolate ['aɪsəleɪt] vt: **to isolate sb (from)**
[physically] aislar a alguien (de); [socially] marginar a alguien (de).

isolated ['aɪsəleɪtɪd] adj aislado(da).

ISP (abbr of **Internet Service Provider**) n
PSI m.

Israel ['ɪzreɪəl] n Israel.

Israeli [ɪz'reɪlɪ] ◇ adj israelí. ◇ n israelí mf.

issue ['ɪʃuː] ◇ n ▪ 1. [important subject] cuestión f, tema m; **at issue** en cuestión; **to avoid
the issue** evitar el tema; **to make an issue of
sthg** darle demasiada importancia a algo
▪ 2. [of newspaper, magazine] número m ▪ 3. [of
stamps, shares, banknotes] emisión f. ◇ vt
▪ 1. [statement, warning] hacer público(ca); [de-
cree] promulgar ▪ 2. [stamps, shares, banknotes]
emitir ▪ 3. [give]: **to issue sthg to sb, to issue sb
with sthg** [passport, document] expedir algo a
alguien; [ticket] proporcionar algo a alguien.

isthmus ['ɪsməs] n istmo m.

it [ɪt] pron - 1. [referring to specific thing or person - subj] él m, ella f; [- direct object] lo m, la f; [- indirect object] le; **it is in my hand** está en mi mano; **did you find it?** ¿lo encontraste?; **give it to me** dámelo; **he gave it a kick** le dio una patada - 2. (with prepositions) él m, ella f; [meaning 'this matter' etc] ello; **as if his life depended on it** como si le fuera la vida en ello; **in it** dentro; **have you been to it before?** ¿has estado antes?; **on it** encima; **to talk about it** hablar de él/ella/ello; **under/beneath it** debajo; **beside it** al lado; **from/of it** de él/ella/ello; **over it** por encima - 3. (impersonal use): **it was raining** llovía; **it is cold today** hace frío hoy; **it's two o'clock** son las dos; **who is it? - it's Mary/me** ¿quién es? - soy Mary/yo; **what day is it?** ¿a qué (día) estamos hoy?; **it's Monday** es lunes; **it says here that...** aquí dice que...

IT n abbr of **information technology**.

Italian [ɪ'tæljən] ⬥ adj italiano(na). ⬥ n - 1. [person] italiano m, -na f - 2. [language] italiano m.

italic [ɪ'tælɪk] adj cursiva. ➤ **italics** npl cursiva f.

Italy ['ɪtəlɪ] n Italia.

itch [ɪtʃ] ⬥ n picor m, picazón f. ⬥ vi - 1. [be itchy - person] tener picazón; [- arm, leg etc] picar; **my arm is itching** me pica el brazo - 2. fig [be impatient]: **to be itching to do sthg** estar deseando hacer algo.

itchy ['ɪtʃɪ] adj [garment, material] que pica; **I've got an itchy arm** me pica el brazo.

it'd ['ɪtəd] - 1. (abbr of it had) ⟾ **have** - 2. (abbr of it would) ⟾ **would**.

item ['aɪtəm] n - 1. [in collection] artículo m; [on list, agenda] punto m - 2. [article in newspaper] artículo m; **news item** noticia f.

itemize, -ise ['aɪtəmaɪz] vt detallar.

itinerary [aɪ'tɪnərərɪ] n itinerario m.

it'll [ɪtl] - 1. (abbr of it will) ⟾ **will** - 2. (abbr of it shall) ⟾ **shall**.

its [ɪts] poss adj su, sus (pl); **the dog broke its leg** el perro se rompió la pata.

it's [ɪts] - 1. (abbr of it is) ⟾ **be** - 2. (abbr of it has) ⟾ **have**.

itself [ɪt'self] pron - 1. (reflexive) se; (after prep) sí mismo(ma); **with itself** consigo mismo(ma) - 2. (for emphasis): **the town itself is lovely** el pueblo en sí es muy bonito; **in itself** en sí; **it's simplicity itself** es la sencillez misma.

I've [aɪv] (abbr of I have) ⟾ **have**.

ivory ['aɪvərɪ] n marfil m.

ivy ['aɪvɪ] n hiedra f.

Ivy League n US grupo de ocho prestigiosas universidades del este de los EE.UU.

j (pl **j's** OR **js**), **J** (pl **J's** OR **Js**) [dʒeɪ] n [letter] j f, J f.

jab [dʒæb] ⬥ n - 1. [with elbow] codazo m; [in boxing] golpe m corto - 2. UK inf [injection] pinchazo m. ⬥ vt: **to jab sthg into** clavar algo en; **to jab sthg at** apuntarle algo a.

jabber ['dʒæbər] vi charlotear.

jack [dʒæk] n - 1. [device] gato m - 2. ELEC [plug] clavija f; [socket] clavijero m - 3. [French deck playing card] ≈ jota f; [Spanish deck playing card] ≈ sota f. ➤ **jack up** vt sep - 1. [lift with a jack] levantar con gato - 2. [force up] subir.

jackal ['dʒækəl] n chacal m.

jackdaw ['dʒækdɔ:] n grajilla f.

jacket ['dʒækɪt] n - 1. [garment] chaqueta f, americana f, saco m Amér - 2. [potato skin] piel f - 3. [book cover] sobrecubierta f - 4. US [of record] cubierta f.

jacket potato n patata f asada con piel.

jackhammer ['dʒæk,hæmər] n US martillo m neumático.

jack knife n navaja f. ➤ **jack-knife** vi: **the lorry jack-knifed** derrapó la parte delantera del camión.

jack plug n clavija f.

jackpot ['dʒækpɒt] n (premio m) gordo m.

jaded ['dʒeɪdɪd] adj [tired] agotado(da); [bored] hastiado(da).

jagged ['dʒægɪd] adj dentado(da).

jail, gaol [dʒeɪl] ⬥ n cárcel f; **in jail** en la cárcel. ⬥ vt encarcelar.

jailer ['dʒeɪlər] n carcelero m, -ra f.

jam [dʒæm] ⬥ n - 1. [preserve] mermelada f - 2. [of traffic] embotellamiento m, atasco m - 3. MUS sesión improvisada de jazz o rock - 4. inf [difficult situation]: **to get into/be in a jam** meterse/estar en un apuro. ⬥ vt - 1. [place roughly] meter a la fuerza - 2. [fix] sujetar; **jam the door shut** atranca la puerta - 3. [pack tightly] apiñar - 4. [fill] abarrotar, atestar - 5. TELEC bloquear - 6. [cause to stick] atascar; **it's jammed** se ha atascado - 7. RADIO interferir. ⬥ vi - 1. [stick] atascarse - 2. MUS improvisar.

Jamaica [dʒə'meɪkə] n Jamaica.

jam-packed [-'pækt] adj inf a tope.

jangle ['dʒæŋgl] vi tintinear.

janitor ['dʒænɪtər] n US & Scotland conserje m, portero m.

January ['dʒænjʊərɪ] n enero m; see also **September**.

Japan [dʒə'pæn] n (ol) Japón.

Japanese [ˌdʒæpə'niːz] — adj Japonés(esa). — n (pl Japanese) [language] japonés m. — npl: **the Japanese** los japoneses.

jar [dʒɑːʳ] — n tarro m. — vt [shake] sacudir. — vi - **1.** [upset]: **to jar (on sb)** poner los nervios de punta (a alguien) - **2.** [clash - opinions] discordar; [- colours] desentonar.

jargon ['dʒɑːgən] n jerga f.

jaundice ['dʒɔːndɪs] n ictericia f.

jaundiced ['dʒɔːndɪst] adj fig [attitude, view] desencantado(da).

jaunt [dʒɔːnt] n excursión f.

jaunty ['dʒɔːntɪ] adj [hat, wave] airoso(sa); [person] vivaz, desenvuelto(ta).

javelin ['dʒævlɪn] n jabalina f.

jaw [dʒɔː] n [of person, animal] mandíbula f.

jawbone ['dʒɔːbəʊn] n [of person, animal] mandíbula f, maxilar m.

jay [dʒeɪ] n arrendajo m.

jaywalker ['dʒeɪwɔːkəʳ] n peatón m imprudente.

jazz [dʒæz] n MUS jazz m. ◆ **jazz up** vt sep inf alegrar, avivar.

jazzy ['dʒæzɪ] adj [bright] llamativo(va).

jealous ['dʒeləs] adj - **1.** [envious]: **to be jealous (of)** tener celos OR estar celoso(sa) (de) - **2.** [possessive]: **to be jealous (of)** ser celoso(sa) (de).

jealousy ['dʒeləsɪ] n (U) celos mpl.

jeans [dʒiːnz] npl vaqueros mpl.

jeep [dʒiːp] n jeep m, campero m Amér.

jeer [dʒɪəʳ] — vt [boo] abuchear; [mock] mofarse de. — vi: **to jeer (at sb)** [boo] abuchear (a alguien); [mock] mofarse (de alguien).

Jehovah's Witness [dʒɪ'həʊvəz-] n testigo mf de Jehová.

Jell-O® ['dʒeləʊ] n US jalea f, gelatina f.

jelly ['dʒelɪ] n - **1.** [dessert] jalea f, gelatina f - **2.** [jam] mermelada f.

jellyfish ['dʒelɪfɪʃ] (pl jellyfish OR -es) n medusa f.

jeopardize, -ise ['dʒepədaɪz] vt poner en peligro, arriesgar.

jerk [dʒɜːk] — n - **1.** [of head] movimiento m brusco; [of arm] tirón m; [of vehicle] sacudida f - **2.** v inf [fool] idiota mf, majadero m, -ra f. — vi [person] saltar; [vehicle] dar sacudidas.

jersey ['dʒɜːzɪ] (pl jerseys) n - **1.** [sweater] jersey m - **2.** [in cycling] maillot m.

Jersey ['dʒɜːzɪ] n Jersey.

jest [dʒest] n: **in jest** en broma.

Jesus (Christ) ['dʒiːzəs-] — n Jesús m, Jesucristo m. — excl inf ¡Santo Dios!

jet [dʒet] n - **1.** [aircraft] reactor m - **2.** [stream] chorro m - **3.** [nozzle, outlet] boquilla f.

jet black adj negro(gra) azabache.

jet engine n reactor m.

jetfoil ['dʒetfɔɪl] n hidroplano m.

jet lag n desfase m horario.

jetsam ['dʒetsəm] ⊳ **flotsam**.

jettison ['dʒetɪsən] vt [cargo] deshacerse de; fig [ideas] desechar.

jetty ['dʒetɪ] n embarcadero m.

Jew [dʒuː] n judío m, -a f.

jewel ['dʒuːəl] n - **1.** [gemstone] piedra f preciosa - **2.** [jewellery] joya f.

jewel case n US caja f (de CD).

jeweller UK, **jeweler** US ['dʒuːələʳ] n joyero m, -ra f; **jeweller's (shop)** joyería f.

jewellery UK, **jewelry** US ['dʒuːəlrɪ] n (U) joyas fpl, alhajas fpl.

Jewess ['dʒuːɪs] n judía f.

Jewish ['dʒuːɪʃ] adj judío(a).

jib [dʒɪb] n - **1.** [beam] aguilón m - **2.** [sail] foque m.

jibe [dʒaɪb] n pulla f, burla f.

jiffy ['dʒɪfɪ] n inf: **in a jiffy** en un segundo.

Jiffy bag® n sobre m acolchado.

jig [dʒɪg] n giga f.

jigsaw (puzzle) ['dʒɪgsɔː-] n rompecabezas m inv, puzzle m.

jilt [dʒɪlt] vt dejar plantado(da).

jingle ['dʒɪŋgl] — n - **1.** [sound] tintineo m - **2.** [song] sintonía f (de anuncio publicitario). — vi tintinear.

jinx [dʒɪŋks] n gafe m.

jitters ['dʒɪtəz] npl inf: **to have the jitters** estar como un flan.

job [dʒɒb] n - **1.** [paid employment] trabajo m, empleo m - **2.** [task & COMPUT] tarea f; **to make a good job of sthg** hacer un buen trabajo con algo - **3.** [difficult task]: **we had a job doing it** nos costó mucho hacerlo - **4.** [function] cometido m - **5.** UK phr: **it's a good job that...** inf menos mal que...; **that's just the job** inf eso me viene de perilla.

Jobcentre n UK oficina f de empleo.

jobless ['dʒɒblɪs] adj desempleado(da).

Job Seekers Allowance n UK subsidio m de desempleo.

jobsharing ['dʒɒbʃeərɪŋ] n (U) empleo m compartido.

jockey ['dʒɒkɪ] — n (pl -s) jockey m, jinete m. — vi: **to jockey for position** competir por colocarse en mejor posición.

jocular ['dʒɒkjʊləʳ] adj - **1.** [cheerful] bromista - **2.** [funny] jocoso(sa).

jodhpurs ['dʒɒdpəz] npl pantalón m de montar.

jog [dʒɒg] ⬦ n trote m; **to go for a jog** hacer footing. ⬦ vt golpear ligeramente. ⬦ vi hacer footing.

jogging ['dʒɒgɪŋ] n footing m.

john [dʒɒn] n US inf [toilet] wáter m.

join [dʒɔɪn] ⬦ n juntura f. ⬦ vt - **1.** [unite] unir, juntar - **2.** [get together with] reunirse con - **3.** [become a member of - political party, trade union] afiliarse a; [- club] hacerse socio de; [- army] alistarse en - **4.** [take part in] unirse a; **to join the queue** UK, **to join the line** US meterse en la cola. ⬦ vi - **1.** [rivers] confluir; [edges, pieces] unirse, juntarse - **2.** [become a member - of political party, trade union] afiliarse; [- of club] hacerse socio; [- of army] alistarse. ⬥ **join in** vt insep participar en, tomar parte en. ⬦ vi participar, tomar parte. ⬥ **join up** vi MIL alistarse.

joiner ['dʒɔɪnər] n carpintero m.

joinery ['dʒɔɪnərɪ] n carpintería f.

joint [dʒɔɪnt] ⬦ adj [responsibility] compartido(da); [effort] conjunto(ta); **joint owner** copropietario m, -ria f. ⬦ n - **1.** ANAT articulación f - **2.** [place where things are joined] juntura f - **3.** UK [of meat - uncooked] corte m para asar; [- cooked] asado m - **4.** inf pej [place] antro m - **5.** inf [cannabis cigarette] porro m.

joint account n cuenta f conjunta.

jointly ['dʒɔɪntlɪ] adv conjuntamente.

joist [dʒɔɪst] n vigueta f.

joke [dʒəʊk] ⬦ n [funny story] chiste m; [funny action] broma f; **to be a joke** [person] ser un inútil; [situation] ser una tomadura de pelo; **it's no joke** [not easy] no es (nada) fácil. ⬦ vi bromear; **you're joking** estás de broma; **I'm not joking** hablo en serio.

joker ['dʒəʊkər] n - **1.** [funny person] bromista mf - **2.** [useless person] inútil mf - **3.** [playing card] comodín m.

jolly ['dʒɒlɪ] ⬦ adj [person, laugh] alegre; [time] divertido(da). ⬦ adv UK inf muy.

jolt [dʒəʊlt] ⬦ n - **1.** liter sacudida f - **2.** fig susto m. ⬦ vt [jerk] sacudir, zarandear.

Jordan ['dʒɔːdn] n Jordania.

jostle ['dʒɒsl] ⬦ vt empujar, dar empujones a. ⬦ vi empujar, dar empujones.

jot [dʒɒt] n pizca f. ⬥ **jot down** vt sep apuntar, anotar.

jotter ['dʒɒtər] n bloc m.

journal ['dʒɜːnl] n - **1.** [magazine] revista f, boletín m - **2.** [diary] diario m.

journalism ['dʒɜːnəlɪzm] n periodismo m.

journalist ['dʒɜːnəlɪst] n periodista mf.

journey ['dʒɜːnɪ] ⬦ n (pl -s) viaje m. ⬦ vi viajar.

jovial ['dʒəʊvjəl] adj jovial.

jowls [dʒaʊlz] npl carrillos mpl.

joy [dʒɔɪ] n - **1.** [happiness] alegría f, regocijo m - **2.** [cause of joy] placer m.

joyful ['dʒɔɪfʊl] adj alegre.

joyous ['dʒɔɪəs] adj jubiloso(sa).

joyride ['dʒɔɪraɪd] ⬦ n vuelta f en un coche robado. ⬦ vi (pt -rode, pp -ridden) darse una vuelta en un coche robado.

joystick ['dʒɔɪstɪk] n [of aircraft] palanca f de mando; [for video games, computers] joystick m.

JP n abbr of **Justice of the Peace**.

Jr. US (abbr of **Junior**) jr; **Mark Andrews Jr.** Mark Andrews, hijo.

jubilant ['dʒuːbɪlənt] adj [person] jubiloso(sa); [shout] alborozado(da).

jubilee ['dʒuːbɪliː] n aniversario m.

judge [dʒʌdʒ] ⬦ n [gen & LAW] juez mf; **to be a good judge of character** tener buen ojo para la gente. ⬦ vt - **1.** [gen & LAW] juzgar - **2.** [age, distance] calcular. ⬦ vi juzgar.

judg(e)ment ['dʒʌdʒmənt] n - **1.** LAW fallo m, sentencia f; **to pass judgement (on sb)** pronunciar sentencia (sobre alguien) - **2.** [opinion] juicio m - **3.** [ability to form opinion] juicio m; **against my better judgement** en contra de lo que me dicta el juicio.

judiciary [dʒuː'dɪʃərɪ] n: **the judiciary** [part of government] el poder judicial; [judges] la judicatura.

judicious [dʒuː'dɪʃəs] adj juicioso(sa).

judo ['dʒuːdəʊ] n judo m.

jug [dʒʌg] n jarra f.

juggernaut ['dʒʌgənɔːt] n camión m grande.

juggle ['dʒʌgl] ⬦ vt - **1.** [throw] hacer juegos malabares con - **2.** [rearrange] jugar con. ⬦ vi hacer juegos malabares.

juggler ['dʒʌglər] n malabarista mf.

jugular (vein) ['dʒʌgjʊlər-] n yugular f.

juice [dʒuːs] n - **1.** [from fruit, vegetables] zumo m - **2.** [from meat] jugo m.

juicer ['dʒuːsər] n exprimidor m.

juicy ['dʒuːsɪ] adj - **1.** [gen] jugoso(sa) - **2.** inf [scandalous] picante.

jukebox ['dʒuːkbɒks] n máquina f de discos.

July [dʒuː'laɪ] n julio m; see also **September**.

jumble ['dʒʌmbl] ⬦ n [mixture] revoltijo m. ⬦ vt: **to jumble (up)** revolver.

jumble sale n UK rastrillo m benéfico.

jumbo jet ['dʒʌmbəʊ-] n jumbo m.

jumbo-sized ['dʒʌmbəʊsaɪzd] adj gigante.

jump [dʒʌmp] ⬦ n - **1.** [act of jumping] salto m - **2.** [start, surprised movement] sobresalto m - **3.** [fence in horsejumping] obstáculo m - **4.** [rapid increase] incremento m, salto m. ⬦ vt - **1.** [cross by jumping] saltar - **2.** [attack] asaltar - **3.** [miss out] saltarse. ⬦ vi - **1.** [spring]

saltar - ? [make a sudden movement] **sobresal** rarse - r [increase rapidly] aumentar de golpe.
◆ **jump at** vt insep no dejar escapar.

jumper ['dʒʌmpə*] n - 1. UK [pullover] jersey m - 2. US [dress] pichi m.

jumper cables npl US cables mpl de empalme (de batería).

jump leads npl cables mpl de empalme (de batería).

jump-start vt [by pushing] arrancar empujando; [using jump leads] arrancar haciendo un puente.

jumpsuit ['dʒʌmpsuːt] n mono m.

jumpy ['dʒʌmpɪ] adj inquieto(ta).

junction ['dʒʌŋkʃn] n [of roads] cruce m; UK [on motorway] salida f; [of railway lines] empalme m.

June [dʒuːn] n junio m; see also **September**.

jungle ['dʒʌŋgl] n lit & fig selva f.

junior ['dʒuːnjə*] ◇ adj - 1. [partner, member] de menor antigüedad, júnior (inv); [officer] subalterno(na) - 2. [after name]: **Mark Andrews junior** Mark Andrews, hijo. ◇ n - 1. [person of lower rank] subalterno m, -na f - 2. [younger person]: **he's my junior** soy mayor que él - 3. US SCH & UNIV alumno de penúltimo año.

junior high school n US ≃ instituto m de bachillerato (13-15 años).

junior school n UK ≃ escuela f primaria.

junk [dʒʌŋk] inf n (U) [unwanted things] trastos mpl.

junk food n pej comida f basura.

junkie ['dʒʌŋkɪ] n inf yonqui mf.

junk mail n (U) pej propaganda f (por correo).

junk shop n tienda f de objetos usados.

Jupiter ['dʒuːpɪtə*] n Júpiter m.

jurisdiction [,dʒʊərɪs'dɪkʃn] n jurisdicción f.

juror ['dʒʊərə*] n jurado m.

jury ['dʒʊərɪ] n jurado m; **the jury is still out on that** eso está por ver.

just [dʒʌst] ◇ adv - 1. [recently]: **he has just left/moved** acaba de salir/mudarse - 2. [at that moment]: **we were just leaving when...** justo íbamos a salir cuando...; **I'm just about to do it** voy a hacerlo ahora; **I couldn't do it just then** no lo podía hacer en aquel momento; **just as I was leaving** justo en el momento en que salía; **just recently** hace muy poco; **just yesterday** ayer mismo - 3. [only, simply] sólo, solamente; **he's just a child** no es más que un niño; **'just add water'** 'simplemente añada un poco de agua'; **if you need help, just ask** si necesitas ayuda, no tienes más que pedirla; **just a minute OR moment OR second** un momento - 4. [almost not] apenas; **I (only) just did it** conseguí hacerlo por muy poco - 5. [for emphasis]:

I just know it! ¡estoy seguro!; **just imagine!** ¡imagínatelo!; **just look at what you've done!** ¡mira lo que has hecho! - 6. [exactly, precisely] exactamente, precisamente; **just what I need** justo lo que necesito; **just here/there** aquí/allí mismo - 7. [in requests]: **could you just open your mouth?** ¿podrías abrir la boca un momento, por favor? ◇ adj justo(ta). ◆ **just about** adv - 1. [nearly] casi - 2. [more or less] más o menos. ◆ **just as** adv: **just as... as** tan... como, igual de... que. ◆ **just now** adv - 1. [a short time ago] hace un momento - 2. [at this moment] justo ahora, ahora mismo.

justice ['dʒʌstɪs] n justicia f; **to do justice to sthg** [to a job] estar a la altura de algo; [to a meal] hacerle los honores a algo.

Justice of the Peace (pl **Justices of the Peace**) n juez mf de paz.

justifiable ['dʒʌstɪfaɪəbl] adj justificable.

justify ['dʒʌstɪfaɪ] vt - 1. [explain]: **to justify (sthg/doing sthg)** justifica (algo/el haber hecho algo) - 2. TYPO justificar.

justly ['dʒʌstlɪ] adv justamente.

jut [dʒʌt] vi: **to jut (out)** sobresalir.

juvenile ['dʒuːvənaɪl] ◇ adj - 1. LAW juvenil - 2. pej [childish] infantil. ◇ n LAW menor mf (de edad).

juxtapose [,dʒʌkstə'pəʊz] vt: **to juxtapose sthg (with)** yuxtaponer algo (a).

k (pl **k's** OR **ks**), **K** (pl **K's** OR **Ks**) [keɪ] n [letter] k f, K f. ◆ **K** n - 1. (abbr of **kilobyte(s)**) K - 2. abbr of **thousand**.

kaleidoscope [kə'laɪdəskəʊp] n lit & fig caleidoscopio m.

kangaroo [,kæŋgə'ruː] n canguro m.

kaput [kə'pʊt] adj inf escacharrado(da).

karaoke [kɑːrɑː'əʊkɪ] n karaoke m.

karat ['kærət] n US quilate m.

karate [kə'rɑːtɪ] n kárate m.

Katmandu [,kætmæn'duː] n Katmandú.

kayak ['kaɪæk] n kayac m.

Kb n COMPUT Kb.

kcal (*abbr of* **kilocalorie**) kcal.

kebab [kɪ'bæb] *n* pincho *m* moruno.

keel [ki:l] *n* quilla *f*; **on an even keel** en equilibrio estable.

keen [ki:n] *adj* - 1. [enthusiastic] entusiasta; **to be keen on sthg** ser aficionado(da) a algo; **she is keen on you** tú le gustas; **I'm not keen on the idea** no me entusiasma la idea; **to be keen to do** OR **on doing sthg** tener ganas de hacer algo - 2. [intense - interest, desire] profundo(da); [- competition] reñido(da) - 3. [sharp - sense of smell, hearing, vision] agudo(da); [- eye, ear] fino(na); [- mind] agudo.

keep [ki:p] <> *vt* (*pt & pp* **kept**) - 1. [maintain in a particular place or state or position] mantener; **to keep sb waiting/awake** tener a alguien esperando/despierto; **to keep sb talking** darle conversación a alguien - 2. [retain] quedarse con; **keep the change** quédese con la vuelta - 3. [put aside, store] guardar; **to keep sthg for sb** guardar algo para alguien - 4. [detain] detener - 5. [fulfil, observe - appointment] acudir a; [- promise, vow] cumplir - 6. [not disclose]: **to keep sthg from sb** ocultar algo a alguien; **to keep sthg to o.s.** no contarle algo a nadie - 7. [in writing - record, account] llevar; [- diary] escribir; [- note] tomar - 8. [own - animals, shop] tener. <> *vi* (*pt & pp* **kept**) - 1. [remain] mantenerse; **to keep quiet** callarse; **to keep still** estarse quieto - 2. [continue]: **to keep doing sthg** [repeatedly] no dejar de hacer algo; [without stopping] continuar OR seguir haciendo algo; **to keep going** seguir adelante - 3. [continue in a particular direction] continuar, seguir; **to keep left/right** circular por la izquierda/derecha - 4. [food] conservarse - 5. UK [be in a particular state of health] estar, andar. <> *n* [food, board etc]: **to earn one's keep** ganarse el pan. ◆ **keeps** *n*: **for keeps** para siempre. ◆ **keep back** <> *vt sep* [information] ocultar; [money, salary] retener. <> *vi* no acercarse. ◆ **keep off** *vt insep* [subject] evitar; **'keep off the grass'** 'no pisar la hierba'. ◆ **keep on** <> *vi* - 1. [continue]: **to keep on doing sthg** [continue to do] continuar OR seguir haciendo algo; [do repeatedly] no dejar de hacer algo - 2. [talk incessantly]: **to keep on (about)** seguir dale que te pego (con). <> *vt sep* [not sack] mantener en el puesto. ◆ **keep out** <> *vt sep* no dejar pasar. <> *vi*: **'keep out'** 'prohibida la entrada'. ◆ **keep to** *vt insep* - 1. [follow] ceñirse a - 2. [fulfil, meet] cumplir. ◆ **keep up** <> *vt sep* mantener. <> *vi* [maintain pace, level etc] mantener el ritmo; **to keep up with sb/sthg** seguir el ritmo de alguien/algo.

keeper ['ki:pər] *n* - 1. [of park, zoo] guarda *mf* - 2. UK [goalkeeper] guardameta *m*.

keep-fit UK *n* (U) ejercicios *mpl* de mantenimiento.

keeping ['ki:pɪŋ] *n* - 1. [care]: **in sb's keeping** al cuidado de alguien; **in safe keeping** en lugar seguro - 2. [conformity, harmony]: **in/out of keeping (with)** de acuerdo/en desacuerdo (con).

keepsake ['ki:pseɪk] *n* recuerdo *m*.

keg [keg] *n* barrilete *m*.

kennel ['kenl] *n* - 1. [for dog] caseta *f* del perro - 2. US = **kennels**. ◆ **kennels** *npl* UK residencia *f* para perros.

Kenya ['kenjə] *n* Kenia.

Kenyan ['kenjən] <> *adj* keniano(na). <> *n* keniano *m*, -na *f*.

kept [kept] *pt & pp* ▷ **keep**.

kerb [kɜ:b] *n* UK bordillo *m*, cuneta *f* Chile.

kernel ['kɜ:nl] *n* [of nut, fruit] pepita *f*.

kerosene ['kerəsi:n] *n* queroseno *m*.

kestrel ['kestrəl] *n* cernícalo *m*.

ketchup ['ketʃəp] *n* catsup *m*.

kettle ['ketl] *n* tetera *f* para hervir; **to put the kettle on** poner el agua a hervir.

key [ki:] <> *n* - 1. [for lock] llave *f* - 2. [of typewriter, computer, piano] tecla *f* - 3. [explanatory list] clave *f* - 4. [solution, answer]: **the key (to)** la clave (de) - 5. MUS [scale of notes] tono *m*; **off key** desafinado(da). <> *adj* clave (*inv*).

keyboard ['ki:bɔ:d] *n* teclado *m*.

keyboard shortcut *n* atajo *m* de teclado.

key card *n* tarjeta *f* de acceso.

keyed up [ki:d-] *adj* nervioso(sa).

keyhole ['ki:həʊl] *n* ojo *m* de la cerradura.

keyhole surgery *n* cirugía *f* endoscópica.

keynote ['ki:nəʊt] *comp*: **keynote speech** discurso *m* principal.

keypad ['ki:pæd] *n* teclado *m* numérico.

key ring *n* llavero *m*.

kg (*abbr of* **kilogram**) kg *m*.

khaki ['kɑ:kɪ] <> *adj* caqui. <> *n* caqui *m*. ◆ **khakis** *npl* US pantalones *mpl* de soldado.

kick [kɪk] <> *n* - 1. [from person] patada *f*, puntapié *m*; [from animal] coz *f* - 2. *inf* [excitement]: **to do sthg for kicks** hacer algo para divertirse. <> *vt* - 1. [hit once with foot] dar una patada OR un puntapié a; [hit repeatedly with foot] dar patadas OR puntapiés a - 2. *inf* [give up] dejar. <> *vi* [person] dar patadas; [animal] dar coces, cocear. ◆ **kick about, kick around** *vi* UK *inf* andar rondando por ahí. ◆ **kick back** *vi* US [relax] relajarse. ◆ **kick in** *vi* [drug] surtir efecto. ◆ **kick off** *vi* [football] hacer el saque inicial. ◆ **kick out** *vt sep* *inf* echar, poner de patitas en la calle.

kid [kɪd] <> *n* - 1. *inf* [child] crío *m*, -a *f* - 2. [young person] chico *m*, -ca *f*, chaval *m*, -la *f* - 3. [young goat] cabrito *m* - 4. [leather] cabritilla *f*. <> *comp* *inf* [brother, sister] menor. <> *vt* *inf* **1.** [tease] tomar el pelo u **2.** [delude]: **to kid sb** hacer ilusionarse a alguien **to be kidding** estar de broma.

kidnap ['kɪdnæp] (*UK pt* & *pp* **-ped**, *cont* **-ping**, *US pt* & *pp* **-ed**, *cont* **-ing**) *vt* secuestrar, raptar, plagiar *Amér*.

kidnapping *UK*, **kidnaping** *US* ['kɪdnæpɪŋ] *n* secuestro *m*, rapto *m*, plagio *m Amér*.

kidney ['kɪdnɪ] (*pl* **kidneys**) *n* ANAT & CULIN riñón *m*.

kidney bean *n* judía *f* pinta, frijol *m Amér* OR poroto *m Andes* rojo *(con forma de riñón)*, caraota *f* roja *(con forma de riñón) Ven*.

kill [kɪl] ⬦ *vt* - **1.** [gen] matar; **he was killed in an accident** murió en un accidente - **2.** *fig* [cause to end, fail] poner fin a - **3.** [occupy]: **to kill time** matar el tiempo. ⬦ *vi* matar. ⬦ *n* [killing]: **we watched the wolves move in for the kill** vimos cómo los lobos se preparaban para caer sobre su presa.

killer ['kɪlə'] *n* [person, animal] asesino *m*, -na *f*.

killing ['kɪlɪŋ] *n* asesinato *m*.

killjoy ['kɪldʒɔɪ] *n* aguafiestas *mf inv*.

kiln [kɪln] *n* horno *m*.

kilo ['kiːləʊ] (*pl* **-s**) (*abbr of* **kilogram**) *n* kilo *m*.

kilobyte ['kɪləbaɪt] *n* kilobyte *m*.

kilogram(me) ['kɪləgræm] *n* kilogramo *m*.

kilohertz ['kɪləhɜːtz] (*pl* **kilohertz**) *n* kilohercio *m*.

kilometre *UK* ['kɪlə,miːtə'], **kilometer** *US* [kɪ'lɒmɪtə'] *n* kilómetro *m*.

kilowatt ['kɪləwɒt] *n* kilovatio *m*.

kilt [kɪlt] *n* falda *f* escocesa.

kin [kɪn] ▷ **kith**.

kind [kaɪnd] ⬦ *adj* [person, gesture] amable; [thought] considerado(da). ⬦ *n* tipo *m*, clase *f*; **a kind of** una especie de; **all kinds of** todo tipo de; **kind of** *esp US inf* bastante; **nothing of the kind** nada por el estilo; **they're two of a kind** son tal para cual.

kindergarten ['kɪndə,gɑːtn] *n* jardín *m* de infancia.

kind-hearted [-'hɑːtɪd] *adj* bondadoso(sa).

kindle ['kɪndl] *vt* - **1.** [fire] encender - **2.** *fig* [idea, feeling] despertar.

kindly ['kaɪndlɪ] ⬦ *adj* amable, bondadoso(sa). ⬦ *adv* - **1.** [gently, favourably] amablemente; **to look kindly on sthg/sb** mirar algo/a alguien con buenos ojos - **2.** [please]: **will you kindly...?** ¿sería tan amable de...?

kindness ['kaɪndnɪs] *n* - **1.** [gentleness] amabilidad *f* - **2.** [helpful act] favor *m*.

kindred ['kɪndrɪd] *adj* [similar] afín; **kindred spirit** alma *f* gemela.

king [kɪŋ] *n* rey *m*.

kingdom ['kɪŋdəm] *n* reino *m*.

kingfisher ['kɪŋ,fɪʃə'] *n* martín *m* pescador.

king size(d) ['kɪŋsaɪz(d)] *adj* [cigarette] extralargo; [bed] gigante; [bed] extragrande.

kinky ['kɪŋkɪ] *adj inf* morboso(sa), pervertido(da).

kiosk ['kiːɒsk] *n* - **1.** [small shop] quiosco *m* - **2.** *UK* [telephone box] cabina *f* telefónica.

kip [kɪp] *UK inf* ⬦ *n* sueñecito *m*. ⬦ *vi* dormir.

kipper ['kɪpə'] *n* arenque *m* ahumado.

kiss [kɪs] ⬦ *n* beso *m*. ⬦ *vt* besar; **to kiss sb goodbye** dar un beso de despedida a alguien. ⬦ *vi* besarse.

kiss of life *n* [to resuscitate sb]: **the kiss of life** la respiración boca a boca.

kit [kɪt] *n* - **1.** [set of implements] equipo *m* - **2.** *UK* [clothes] equipo *m* - **3.** [to be assembled] modelo *m* para armar, kit *m*.

kit bag *n* macuto *m*, petate *m*.

kitchen ['kɪtʃɪn] *n* cocina *f*.

kitchen sink *n* fregadero *m*.

kitchen unit *n* módulo *m* de cocina.

kite [kaɪt] *n* [toy] cometa *f*.

kitesurfing ['kaɪtsɜːfɪŋ] *n* kitesurf *m*.

kith [kɪθ] *n*: **kith and kin** parientes *mpl* y amigos.

kitten ['kɪtn] *n* gatito *m*.

kitty ['kɪtɪ] *n* [for bills, drinks] fondo *m* común; [in card games] bote *m*, puesta *f*.

kiwi ['kiːwiː] *n* - **1.** [bird] kiwi *m* - **2.** *inf* [New Zealander] neocelandés *m*, -esa *f*.

kiwi (fruit) *n* kiwi *m*.

km (*abbr of* **kilometre**) km.

km/h (*abbr of* **kilometres per hour**) km/h.

knack [næk] *n*: **it's easy once you've got the knack** es fácil cuando le coges el tranquillo; **he has the knack of appearing at the right moment** tiene el don de aparecer en el momento adecuado.

knackered ['nækəd] *adj UK inf* - **1.** [exhausted] hecho(cha) polvo - **2.** [broken] cascado(da).

knapsack ['næpsæk] *n* mochila *f*.

knead [niːd] *vt* amasar.

knee [niː] ⬦ *n* rodilla *f*. ⬦ *vt* dar un rodillazo a.

kneecap ['niːkæp] *n* rótula *f*.

kneel [niːl] *vi* (*UK* **knelt**, *US* **-ed** OR **knelt**) [go down on knees] arrodillarse; [be on knees] estar de rodillas. ◆ **kneel down** *vi* arrodillarse.

knelt [nelt] *pt* & *pp* ▷ **kneel**.

knew [njuː] *pt* ▷ **know**.

knickers ['nɪkəz] *npl* - **1.** *UK* [underwear] bragas *fpl*, calzones *mpl Amér*, pantaletas *fpl Amér C & Méx*, bombacha *f R Plata*, blúmer *m Amér C* - **2.** *US* [knickerbockers] bombachos *mpl*.

knick-knack ['nɪknæk] *n* baratija *f*.

knife [naɪf] ◇ *n* (*pl* **knives**) cuchillo *m*. ◇ *vt* acuchillar.

knight [naɪt] ◇ *n* - **1.** HIST caballero *m* - **2.** [knighted man] *hombre con el título de 'Sir'* - **3.** [in chess] caballo *m*. ◇ *vt* conceder el título de 'Sir' a.

knighthood ['naɪthʊd] *n* - **1.** [present-day title] título *m* de 'Sir' - **2.** HIST título *m* de caballero.

knit [nɪt] ◇ *vt* (*UK pt & pp* **-ted**, *US pt & pp* **knit** OR **-ted**) [make with wool] tejer, tricotar. ◇ *vi* - **1.** [with wool] hacer punto - **2.** [join] soldarse.

knitting ['nɪtɪŋ] *n* (*U*) - **1.** [activity] labor *f* de punto - **2.** [work produced] punto *m*, calceta *f*.

knitting needle *n* aguja *f* de hacer punto.

knitwear ['nɪtweəʳ] *n* (*U*) género *m* OR ropa *f* de punto.

knives [naɪvz] *npl* ▷ **knife**.

knob [nɒb] *n* - **1.** [on door, drawer, bedstead] pomo *m* - **2.** [on TV, radio etc] botón *m*.

knock [nɒk] ◇ *n* - **1.** [hit] golpe *m* - **2.** *inf* [piece of bad luck] revés *m*. ◇ *vt* - **1.** [hit hard] golpear; **to knock sb over** [gen] hacer caer a alguien; AUT atropellar a alguien - **2.** [make by hitting] hacer, abrir - **3.** *inf* [criticize] poner por los suelos. ◇ *vi* - **1.** [on door]: **to knock (at** OR **on)** llamar (a) - **2.** [car engine] golpetear.
◆ **knock down** *vt sep* - **1.** [subj: car, driver] atropellar - **2.** [building] derribar. ◆ **knock off** *vi inf* [stop working] parar de currar. ◆ **knock out** *vt sep* - **1.** [subj: person, punch] dejar sin conocimiento; [subj: boxer] dejar fuera de combate; [subj: drug] dejar dormido a - **2.** [eliminate from competition] eliminar.

knocker ['nɒkəʳ] *n* [on door] aldaba *f*.

knock-kneed [-'niːd] *adj* patizambo(ba).

knock-on effect *n UK* reacción *f* en cadena; **to have a knock-on effect on sthg** repercutir en algo.

knockout ['nɒkaʊt] *n* K.O. *m*

knot [nɒt] ◇ *n* - **1.** [gen] nudo *m*; **to tie/untie a knot** hacer/deshacer un nudo; **to tie the knot** *inf* [marry] casarse - **2.** [of people] corrillo *m*. ◇ *vt* anudar.

knotty ['nɒtɪ] *adj* intrincado(da).

know [nəʊ] ◇ *vt* (*pt* **knew**, *pp* **known**) - **1.** [gen]: **to know (that)** saber (que); [language] saber hablar; **to know sthg backwards** saberse algo al dedillo; **to get to know sthg** enterarse de algo; **to let sb know (about)** avisar a alguien (de) - **2.** [be familiar with - person, place] conocer; **to get to know sb** llegar a conocer a alguien. ◇ *vi* (*pt* **knew**, *pp* **known**) - **1.** [have knowledge] saber - **2.** [be knowledgeable]: **to know about sthg** saber de algo. ◇ *n*: **to be in the know** estar enterado(da).

know-all, know-it-all *n UK* sabelotodo *mf*.

know-how *n* conocimientos *mpl*, know-how *m*.

knowing ['nəʊɪŋ] *adj* cómplice.

knowingly ['nəʊɪŋlɪ] *adv* - **1.** [in knowing manner] con complicidad - **2.** [intentionally] a sabiendas.

know-it-all = know-all.

knowledge ['nɒlɪdʒ] *n* (*U*) - **1.** [awareness] conocimiento *m*; **to the best of my knowledge** por lo que yo sé - **2.** [facts known by individual] conocimientos *mpl*.

knowledgeable ['nɒlɪdʒəbl] *adj* entendido(da).

known [nəʊn] *pp* ▷ **know**.

knuckle ['nʌkl] *n* - **1.** [on hand] nudillo *m* - **2.** [of pork] codillo *m*.

koala (bear) [kəʊ'ɑːlə-] *n* koala *m*.

Koran [kɒ'rɑːn] *n*: **the Koran** el Corán.

Korea [kə'rɪə] *n* Corea.

Korean [kə'rɪən] ◇ *adj* coreano(na). ◇ *n* - **1.** [person] coreano *m*, -na *f* - **2.** [language] coreano *m*.

kosher ['kəʊʃəʳ] *adj* - **1.** [meat] kosher, permitido(da) por la religión judía - **2.** *inf* [reputable] limpio(pia), legal.

Kosovo ['kʊsəvəʊ] *n* Kosovo *m*.

kung fu [,kʌŋ'fuː] *n* kung-fu *m*.

Kurd [kɜːd] *n* kurdo *m*, -da *f*.

Kuwait [kjuː'weɪt] *n* Kuwait.

l [¹](*pl* **l's** OR **ls**), **L** (*pl* **L's** OR **Ls**) [el] *n* [letter] l *f*, L *f*.

l [²](*abbr of* litre) l.

lab [læb] *inf* = **laboratory**.

label ['leɪbl] ◇ *n* - **1.** [identification] etiqueta *f* - **2.** [of record] sello *m* discográfico. ◇ *vt* (*UK pt & pp* **-led**, *cont* **-ling**, *US pt & pp* **-ed**, *cont* **-ing**) [fix label to] etiquetar.

labor *US* = **labour**.

laboratory [*UK* lə'bɒrətrɪ, *US* 'læbrə,tɔːrɪ], **lab** *n* laboratorio *m*.

laborious [lə'bɔːrɪəs] *adj* laborioso(sa).

labor union *n US* sindicato *m*.

labour UK, **labor** US ['leɪbə'] ⬦ n - 1. [work] trabajo m; [task] [piece of work] tarea f - 3. [workers] mano f de obra - 4. [giving birth] parto m. ⬦ vi - 1. [work] trabajar - 2. [work with difficulty]: **to labour at** OR **over** trabajar afanosamente en. ➡ **Labour** ⬦ adj POL laborista. ⬦ n (U) UK POL los laboristas.

laboured UK, **labored** US ['leɪbəd] adj [style] trabajoso(sa); [gait, breathing] penoso(sa), fatigoso(sa).

labourer UK, **laborer** US ['leɪbərə'] n obrero m, -ra f.

Labour Party n UK: **the Labour Party** el partido Laborista.

Labrador ['læbrədɔː'] n [dog] labrador m.

labyrinth ['læbərɪnθ] n laberinto m.

lace [leɪs] ⬦ n - 1. [fabric] encaje m - 2. [shoelace] cordón m. ⬦ vt - 1. [shoe, boot] atar - 2. [drink, food]: **coffee laced with brandy** café con unas gotas de coñac. ➡ **lace up** vt sep atar.

lack [læk] ⬦ n falta f; **for** OR **through lack of** por falta de; **there was no lack of excitement** no faltó emoción. ⬦ vt carecer de. ⬦ vi: **to be lacking** in carecer de; **to be lacking** faltar.

lackadaisical [,lækə'deɪzɪkl] adj pej apático(ca).

lacklustre UK, **lackluster** US ['læk,lʌstə'] adj pej soso(sa), apagado(da).

laconic [lə'kɒnɪk] adj lacónico(ca).

lacquer ['lækə'] n laca f.

lad [læd] n inf [boy] chaval m; **come on lads!** ¡vamos chicos!

ladder ['lædə'] ⬦ n - 1. [for climbing] escalera f - 2. UK [in tights] carrera f. ⬦ vt UK [tights] hacerse una carrera en.

laden ['leɪdn] adj: **laden (with)** cargado(da) (de).

ladies UK ['leɪdɪz], **ladies' room** US n lavabo m de señoras.

ladle ['leɪdl] ⬦ n cucharón m. ⬦ vt servir con cucharón.

lady ['leɪdɪ] ⬦ n - 1. [woman] señora f - 2. [woman of high status] dama f. ⬦ comp mujer; **lady doctor** doctora f. ➡ **Lady** n [woman of noble rank] lady f.

ladybird UK ['leɪdɪbɜːd], **ladybug** US ['leɪdɪbʌg] n mariquita f.

lady-in-waiting [-'weɪtɪŋ] (pl **ladies-in-waiting**) n dama f de honor.

ladylike ['leɪdɪlaɪk] adj elegante, propio(pia) de una señora.

lag [læg] ⬦ vi - 1. [move more slowly]: **to lag (behind)** rezagarse - 2. [develop more slowly]: **to lag (behind)** andar a la zaga. ⬦ vt [pipes] revestir. ⬦ n [delay] retraso m, demora f.

lager ['lɑːgə'] n cerveza f rubia.

lagoon [lə'guːn] n laguna f.

laid [leɪd] pt & pp ⬅ **lay**.

laid-back adj inf relajado(da).

lain [leɪn] pp ⬅ **lie**.

lair [leə'] n guarida f.

laity ['leɪətɪ] n RELIG: **the laity** los seglares, los legos.

lake [leɪk] n lago m.

Lake District n: **the Lake District** el Distrito de los Lagos al noroeste de Inglaterra.

lamb [læm] n cordero m.

lambswool ['læmzwʊl] ⬦ n lana f de cordero. ⬦ comp de lana de cordero.

lame [leɪm] adj - 1. [person, horse] cojo(ja) - 2. [excuse, argument] pobre.

lament [lə'ment] ⬦ n lamento m. ⬦ vt lamentar.

lamentable ['læməntəbl] adj lamentable.

laminated ['læmɪneɪtɪd] adj - 1. [gen] laminado(da) - 2. [ID card] plastificado(da).

lamp [læmp] n lámpara f.

lampoon [læm'puːn] ⬦ n pasquín m, sátira f. ⬦ vt satirizar.

lamppost ['læmppəʊst] n farol m.

lampshade ['læmpʃeɪd] n pantalla f (de lámpara).

lance [lɑːns] ⬦ n lanza f. ⬦ vt abrir con lanceta.

lance corporal n soldado m de primera.

land [lænd] ⬦ n - 1. [gen] tierra f - 2. [property] tierras fpl, finca f. ⬦ vt - 1. [unload] desembarcar - 2. [plane] hacer aterrizar - 3. [catch - fish] pescar - 4. inf [obtain] conseguir, pillar - 5. inf [place]: **to land sb in sthg** meter a alguien en algo; **to land sb with sb/sthg** cargar a alguien con alguien/algo. ⬦ vi - 1. [by plane] aterrizar, tomar tierra - 2. [from ship] desembarcar - 3. [fall] caer - 4. [end up] ir a parar. ➡ **land up** vi inf: **to land up (in)** ir a parar (a).

landfill site ['lændfɪl-] n vertedero m de basuras.

landing ['lændɪŋ] n - 1. [of stairs] rellano m - 2. [of aeroplane] aterrizaje m - 3. [of person] desembarco m.

landing card n tarjeta f de desembarque.

landing gear n (U) tren m de aterrizaje.

landing stage n desembarcadero m.

landing strip n pista f de aterrizaje.

landlady ['lænd,leɪdɪ] n - 1. [of rented room or building] casera f - 2. [of hotel, pub] patrona f.

landlord ['lændlɔːd] n - 1. [of rented room or building] dueño m, casero m - 2. [of pub] patrón m.

landmark ['lændmɑːk] n - 1. [prominent feature] punto m de referencia - 2. fig [in history] hito m.

landowner ['lænd,əʊnəʳ] *n* terratenien-te *mf*.

landscape ['lændskeɪp] *n* paisaje *m*.

landslide ['lændslaɪd] *n* - **1.** [of earth, rocks] desprendimiento *m* de tierras - **2.** POL victoria *f* arrolladora OR aplastante.

lane [leɪn] *n* - **1.** [road in country] camino *m* - **2.** [road in town] callejuela *f*, callejón *m* - **3.** [for traffic] carril *m*; **'keep in lane'** *cartel que prohibe el cambio de carril* - **4.** [in swimming pool, race track] calle *f* - **5.** [for shipping, aircraft] ruta *f*.

language ['læŋgwɪdʒ] *n* - **1.** [gen] idioma *m*, lengua *f* - **2.** [faculty or style of communication & COMPUT] lenguaje *m*.

language laboratory *n* laboratorio *m* de idiomas.

languid ['læŋgwɪd] *adj* lánguido(da).

languish ['læŋgwɪʃ] *vi* [in misery] languide-cer; [in prison] pudrirse.

lank [læŋk] *adj* lacio(cia).

lanky ['læŋkɪ] *adj* larguirucho(cha).

lantern ['læntən] *n* farol *m*.

lap [læp] ◇ *n* - **1.** [of person] regazo *m* - **2.** [of race] vuelta *f*. ◇ *vt* - **1.** [subj: animal] beber a lengüetadas - **2.** [overtake in race] doblar. ◇ *vi* [water, waves] romper con suavidad.

lapel [lə'pel] *n* solapa *f*.

Lapland ['læplænd] *n* Laponia.

lapse [læps] ◇ *n* - **1.** [slip-up] fallo *m*, lapsus *m inv* - **2.** [in behaviour] desliz *m* - **3.** [of time] lapso *m*, periodo *m*. ◇ *vi* - **1.** [membership] caducar; [treatment, agreement] cumplir, expirar - **2.** [standards, quality] bajar momentáneamente; [tradition] extinguirse - **3.** [subj: person]: **to lapse into** terminar cayendo en.

lap-top (computer) *n* COMPUT ordenador *m* portátil.

larceny ['lɑːsənɪ] *n (U)* latrocinio *m*.

lard [lɑːd] *n* manteca *f* de cerdo.

larder ['lɑːdəʳ] *n* despensa *f*.

large [lɑːdʒ] *adj* [gen] grande; [family] numeroso(sa); [sum] importante. ◆ **at large** *adv* - **1.** [as a whole] en general - **2.** [escaped prisoner, animal] suelto(ta). ◆ **by and large** *adv* en general.

largely ['lɑːdʒlɪ] *adv* [mostly] en gran parte; [chiefly] principalmente.

lark [lɑːk] *n* - **1.** [bird] alondra *f* - **2.** *inf* [joke] broma *f*. ◆ **lark about** *vi* hacer el tonto.

laryngitis [,lærɪn'dʒaɪtɪs] *n (U)* laringitis *f inv*.

larynx ['lærɪŋks] *n* laringe *f*.

lasagna, lasagne [lə'zænjə] *n (U)* lasaña *f*.

laser ['leɪzəʳ] *n* láser *m*.

laser printer *n* COMPUT impresora *f* láser.

lash [læʃ] ◇ *n* - **1.** [eyelash] pestaña *f* - **2.** [blow with whip] latigazo *m*. ◇ *vt* - **1.** *lit &* *fig* [whip] azotar - **2.** [tie]: **to lash sthg (to)** amarrar algo (a). ◆ **lash out** *vi* - **1.** [attack]: **to lash out at sb** [physically] soltar un golpe a alguien; [verbally] arremeter contra alguien - **2.** *UK inf* [spend money]: **to lash out (on sthg)** tirar la casa por la ventana (con algo).

lass [læs] *n* chavala *f*, muchacha *f*.

lasso [læ'suː] *n (pl -s)* lazo *m*.

last [lɑːst] ◇ *adj* último(ma); **last month/ Tuesday** el mes/martes pasado; **last March** en marzo del año pasado; **last but one** penúlti-mo(ma); **last but two** antepenúltimo(ma); **last night** anoche. ◇ *adv* - **1.** [most recently] por última vez; **when I last called him** la última vez que lo llamé - **2.** [finally, in final position] en último lugar; **he arrived last** llegó el último; **last but not least** por último, pero no por ello menos importante. ◇ *pron*: **the year/Saturday before last** no el año/sábado pasado, sino el anterior; **the last but one** el penúltimo (la penúltima); **the night before last** anteanoche; **the time before last** la vez anterior a la pasada; **to leave sthg till last** dejar algo para el final. ◇ *n*: **the last I saw/heard of him** la última vez que lo vi/que oí de él. ◇ *vi* durar; [food] conservarse. ◆ **at (long) last** *adv* por fin.

last-ditch *adj* último(ma), desesperado(da).

lasting ['lɑːstɪŋ] *adj* [peace, effect] durade-ro(ra).

lastly ['lɑːstlɪ] *adv* - **1.** [to conclude] por último - **2.** [at the end] al final.

last-minute *adj* de última hora.

latch [lætʃ] *n* pestillo *m*. ◆ **latch onto** *vt insep inf* [person] pegarse OR engancharse a; [idea] pillar.

late [leɪt] ◇ *adj* - **1.** [not on time] con retraso; **to be late (for)** llegar tarde (a); **the flight is twenty minutes late** el vuelo lleva veinte minutos de retraso; **the bus was an hour late** el autobús llegó con una hora de retraso - **2.** [near end of]: **in the late afternoon** al final de la tarde; **in late December** a finales de diciembre; **it's getting late** se está haciendo tarde - **3.** [later than normal] tardío(a); **we had a late breakfast** desayunamos tarde - **4.** [former]: **the late president** el ex-presidente - **5.** [dead] difunto(ta). ◇ *adv* - **1.** [gen] tarde; **they are open late** abren hasta tarde - **2.** [near end of period]: **late in the day** al final del día; **late in August** a finales de agosto. ◆ **of late** *adv* últimamente.

latecomer ['leɪt,kʌməʳ] *n* persona *f* que llega tarde.

lately ['leɪtlɪ] *adv* últimamente.

latent ['leɪtənt] *adj* latente.

later ['leɪtəʳ] ◇ *adj* - **1.** [date, edition] posterior - **2.** [near end of]: **in the later 15th century**

a finales del siglo XVI. ◇ *adv* [at a later time] later (...) más tarde; ... later than Friday el viernes como muy tarde.

lateral ['lætərəl] *adj* lateral.

latest ['leɪtɪst] ◇ *adj* [most recent] último(ma). ◇ *n*: **at the latest** a más tardar, como muy tarde.

lathe [leɪð] *n* torno *m*.

lather ['lɑ:ðəʳ] ◇ *n* espuma *f* (de jabón). ◇ *vt* enjabonar.

Latin ['lætɪn] ◇ *adj* **- 1.** [temperament, blood] latino(na) - **2.** [studies] de latín. ◇ *n* [language] latín *m*.

Latin America *n* Latinoamérica *f*, América *f* Latina.

Latin American ◇ *adj* latinoamericano(na). ◇ *n* [person] latinoamericano *m*, -na *f*.

latitude ['lætɪtju:d] *n* GEOG latitud *f*.

latter ['lætəʳ] ◇ *adj* **- 1.** [near to end] último(ma) - **2.** [second] segundo(da). ◇ *n*: **the** latter éste *m*, -ta *f*.

latterly ['lætəlɪ] *adv* últimamente.

lattice ['lætɪs] *n* enrejado *m*, celosía *f*.

Latvia ['lætvɪə] *n* Letonia.

laudable ['lɔ:dəbl] *adj* loable.

laugh [lɑ:f] ◇ *n* **- 1.** [sound] risa *f* **- 2.** *inf* [fun, joke]: **to have a laugh** divertirse; **to do sthg for laughs** OR **a laugh** hacer algo para divertirse OR en cachondeo. ◇ *vi* reírse. **laugh at** *vt insep* [mock] reírse de. **laugh off** *vt sep* [dismiss] tomarse a risa.

laughable ['lɑ:fəbl] *adj pej* [absurd] ridículo(la), risible.

laughing stock ['lɑ:fɪŋ-] *n* hazmerreír *m*.

laughter ['lɑ:ftəʳ] *n (U)* risa *f*.

launch [lɔ:ntʃ] ◇ *n* **- 1.** [of boat, ship] botadura *f* **- 2.** [of rocket, missile, product] lanzamiento *m* **- 3.** [boat] lancha *f*. ◇ *vt* **- 1.** [boat, ship] botar - **2.** [missile, attack, product & COMPUT] lanzar - **3.** [company] fundar.

launch(ing) pad ['lɔ:ntʃ(ɪŋ)-] *n* plataforma *f* de lanzamiento.

launder ['lɔ:ndəʳ] *vt* **- 1.** [wash] lavar - **2.** *inf* [money] blanquear.

laund(e)rette [lɔ:n'dret], **Laundromat**® US ['lɔ:ndrəmæt] *n* lavandería *f* (automática).

laundry ['lɔ:ndrɪ] *n* **- 1.** [clothes - about to be washed] colada *f*, ropa *f* sucia; [- newly washed] ropa *f* limpia - **2.** [business, room] lavandería *f*.

laureate ['lɔ:rɪət] ▷ **poet laureate**.

lava ['lɑ:və] *n* lava *f*.

lavatory ['lævətrɪ] *n* **- 1.** [receptacle] wáter *m* - **2.** [room] servicio *m*.

lavender ['lævəndəʳ] *n* **- 1.** [plant] lavanda *f* - **2.** [colour] color *m* lavanda.

lavish ['lævɪʃ] ◇ *adj* **1.** [person] pródigo(ga); [gift, reward] suntuoso(sa): **to be lavish with** [praise, attention] ser pródigo en; [money] ser desprendido(da) con - **2.** [sumptuous] espléndido(da), suntuoso(sa). ◇ *vt*: **to lavish sthg on** [praise, care] prodigar algo a; [time, money] gastar algo en.

law [lɔ:] *n* **- 1.** [gen] ley *f*; **against the law** ilegal; **to break the law** infringir OR violar la ley; **law and order** el orden público **- 2.** [set of rules, study, profession] derecho *m*.

law-abiding [-ə,baɪdɪŋ] *adj* observante de la ley.

law court *n* tribunal *m* de justicia.

law enforcement officer *n* agente *mf* de policía.

law firm *n* bufete *m* de abogados.

lawful ['lɔ:fʊl] *adj fml* legal, lícito(ta).

lawn [lɔ:n] *n* [grass] césped *m*, pasto *m* Amér, grama *f* Amér C & Ven.

lawnmower ['lɔ:n,məʊəʳ] *n* cortacésped *mf*.

lawn tennis *n* tenis *m* sobre hierba.

law school *n* facultad *f* de derecho; **he went to law school** estudió derecho.

lawsuit ['lɔ:su:t] *n* pleito *m*.

lawyer ['lɔ:jəʳ] *n* abogado *m*, -da *f*.

lax [læks] *adj* [discipline, morals] relajado(da); [person] negligente; [security] poco riguroso(sa).

laxative ['læksətɪv] *n* laxante *m*.

lay [leɪ] ◇ *pt* ▷ **lie**. ◇ *vt* (*pt & pp* laid) **- 1.** [put, place] colocar, poner; **to lay o.s. open to sthg** exponerse a algo **- 2.** [prepare - plans] hacer **- 3.** [put in position - bricks] poner; [- cable, trap] tender; [- foundations] echar; **to lay the table** poner la mesa **- 4.** [egg] poner **- 5.** [blame, curse]: **to lay sthg on sb** echar algo a alguien. ◇ *adj* **- 1.** [not clerical] laico(ca) **- 2.** [untrained, unqualified] lego(ga). **lay aside** *vt sep* **- 1.** [store for future - food] guardar; [- money] ahorrar **- 2.** [prejudices, reservations] dejar a un lado. **lay down** *vt sep* **- 1.** [set out] imponer, establecer **- 2.** [put down - arms] deponer, entregar; [- tools] dejar. **lay off** ◇ *vt sep* [make redundant] despedir. ◇ *vt insep inf* [stop, give up]: **to lay off (doing sthg)** dejar (de hacer algo). ◇ *vi inf*: **lay off!** ¡déjame en paz! **lay on** *vt sep* [transport, entertainment] organizar; [food] preparar. **lay out** *vt sep* **- 1.** [arrange, spread out] disponer **- 2.** [plan, design] diseñar el trazado de.

layabout ['leɪəbaʊt] *n* UK inf holgazán *m*, -ana *f*, gandul *m*, -la *f*.

lay-by (*pl* lay-bys) *n* UK área *f* de descanso.

layer ['leɪəʳ] ◇ *n* **- 1.** [of substance, material] capa *f* **- 2.** *fig* [level] nivel *m*. ◇ *vt* [hair] cortar a capas.

layman ['leɪmən] (*pl* -men [-mən]) *n* - 1. [untrained, unqualified person] lego *m*, -ga *f* - 2. RELIG laico *m*, -ca *f*.

layout ['leɪaʊt] *n* [of building, garden] trazado *m*, diseño *m*; [of text] presentación *f*, composición *f*; [of.page & COMPUT] diseño *m*.

laze [leɪz] *vi*: to laze (about OR around) gandulear, holgazanear.

lazy ['leɪzɪ] *adj* - 1. [person] perezoso(sa), vago(ga) - 2. [stroll, gesture] lento(ta); [afternoon] ocioso(sa).

lazybones ['leɪzɪbəʊnz] (*pl* lazybones) *n inf* gandul *m*, -la *f*.

lb (*abbr of pound*) lb.

LCD *n abbr of* liquid crystal display.

lead¹ [li:d] ◇ *n* - 1. [winning position] delantera *f*; to be in OR have the lead llevar la delantera, ir en cabeza; to take the lead ponerse a la cabeza - 2. [amount ahead]: to have a lead of... llevar una ventaja de... - 3. [initiative, example] ejemplo *m*; to take the lead [do sthg first] tomar la delantera - 4. THEAT: (to play) the lead (hacer) el papel principal - 5. [clue] pista *f* - 6. [for dog] correa *f* - 7. [wire, cable] cable *m*. ◇ *adj* [singer, actor] principal; [guitar, guitarist] solista; [story in newspaper] más destacado(da). ◇ *vt* (*pt & pp* led) - 1. [be in front of] encabezar - 2. [take, guide, direct] conducir - 3. [be in charge of, take the lead in] dirigir; [debate] moderar - 4. [life] llevar - 5. [cause]: to lead sb to do sthg llevar a alguien a hacer algo; we were led to believe that... nos dieron a entender que... ◇ *vi* (*pt & pp* led) - 1. [go]: to lead (to) conducir OR llevar (a) - 2. [give access to]: to lead (to OR into) dar (a) - 3. [be winning] ir en cabeza - 4. [result in]: to lead to conducir a - 5. [in cards] salir. ➡ **lead up to** *vt insep* - 1. [build up to] conducir a, preceder a - 2. [plan to introduce] apuntar a.

lead² [led] *n* - 1. [metal] plomo *m* - 2. [in pencil] mina *f*.

leaded ['ledɪd] *adj* - 1. [petrol] con plomo - 2. [window] emplomado(da).

leader ['li:dər] *n* - 1. [of party etc, in competition] líder *mf* - 2. UK [in newspaper] editorial *m*, artículo *m* de fondo.

leadership ['li:dəʃɪp] *n* (U) - 1. [people in charge]: the leadership los líderes - 2. [position of leader] liderazgo *m* - 3. [qualities of leader] dotes *fpl* de mando.

lead-free [led-] *adj* sin plomo.

lead guitar *n* guitarra *f* solista.

leading ['li:dɪŋ] *adj* - 1. [major - athlete, writer] destacado(da); [- company] principal - 2. [at front] que va en cabeza.

leading lady *n* primera actriz *f*.

leading light *n* figura *f* destacada.

leading man *n* primer actor *m*.

leaf [li:f] *n* (*pl* leaves) - 1. [of tree, book] hoja *f* - 2. [of table] hoja *f* abatible. ➡ **leaf through** *vt insep* hojear.

leaflet ['li:flɪt] *n* [small brochure] folleto *m*; [piece of paper] octavilla *f*.

league [li:g] *n* [gen & SPORT] liga *f*; to be in league with [work with] estar confabulado con.

leak [li:k] ◇ *n* - 1. [hole - in tank, bucket] agujero *m*; [- in roof] gotera *f* - 2. [escape] escape *m*, fuga *f* - 3. [of information] filtración *f*. ◇ *vt* [information] filtrar. ◇ *vi* - 1. [bucket] tener un agujero; [roof] tener goteras; [boot] calar - 2. [water, gas] salirse, escaparse; to leak (out) from salirse de. ➡ **leak out** *vi* [liquid] escaparse.

leakage ['li:kɪdʒ] *n* fuga *f*, escape *m*.

lean [li:n] ◇ *adj* - 1. [person] delgado(da) - 2. [meat] magro(gra) - 3. [winter, year] de escasez. ◇ *vt* (*pt & pp* leant OR -ed) [support, prop]: to lean sthg against apoyar algo contra. ◇ *vi* (*pt & pp* leant OR -ed) - 1. [bend, slope] inclinarse; to lean out of the window asomarse a la ventana - 2. [rest]: to lean on/against apoyarse en/contra.

leaning ['li:nɪŋ] *n*: leaning (towards) inclinación *f* (hacia OR por).

leant [lent] *pt & pp* ➡ **lean**.

lean-to (*pl* lean-tos) *n* cobertizo *m*.

leap [li:p] ◇ *n* salto *m*. ◇ *vi* (*pt & pp* leapt OR -ed) [gen] saltar; [prices] dispararse.

leapfrog ['li:pfrɒg] ◇ *n* pídola *f*, rango *m* R Plata. ◇ *vt* saltar.

leapt [lept] *pt & pp* ➡ **leap**.

leap year *n* año *m* bisiesto.

learn [lɜ:n] (*pt & pp* -ed OR learnt) ◇ *vt* - 1. [acquire knowledge of, memorize] aprender; to learn (how) to do sthg aprender a hacer algo - 2. [hear]: to learn (that) enterarse de (que). ◇ *vi* [acquire knowledge] aprender.

learned ['lɜ:nɪd] *adj* erudito(ta).

learner ['lɜ:nər] *n* [beginner] principiante *mf*; [student] estudiante *mf*.

learner (driver) *n* conductor *m* principiante OR en prácticas.

learner's permit *n* US carné *m* de conducir provisional.

learning ['lɜ:nɪŋ] *n* saber *m*, erudición *f*.

learning disability *n* discapacidad *f* para el aprendizaje.

learnt [lɜ:nt] *pt & pp* ➡ **learn**.

lease [li:s] ◇ *n* LAW contrato *m* de arrendamiento, arriendo *m*; to give sb a new lease of life UK OR on life US darle nueva vida a alguien. ◇ *vt* arrendar; to lease sthg from/to sb arrendar algo de/a alguien.

leasehold ['li:shəʊld] ◇ *adj* arrendado(da). ◇ *adv* en arriendo.

leash [li:ʃ] n [for dog] correa f.

least [li:st] (superl of little) ◇ adj [smallest in amount, degree] menor; **he earns the least money** es el que menos dinero gana. ◇ pron [smallest amount]: **the least** lo menos; **it's the least (that) he can do** es lo menos que puede hacer; **not in the least** en absoluto; **to say the least** por no decir otra cosa. ◇ adv [to the smallest amount, degree] menos. ◆ **at least** adv por lo menos. ◆ **least of all** adv y menos (todavía). ◆ **not least** adv sobre todo.

leather ['leðər] ◇ n piel f, cuero m. ◇ comp [jacket, trousers] de cuero; [shoes, bag] de piel.

leave [li:v] ◇ vt (pt & pp left) - 1. [gen] dejar; **he left it to her to decide** dejó que ella decidiera; **to leave sb alone** dejar a alguien en paz - 2. [go away from - place] irse de; [- house, room, work] salir de; [- wife] abandonar; **to leave home** irse de casa - 3. [not take, forget] dejarse - 4. [bequeath]: **to leave sb sthg, to leave sthg to sb** dejarle algo a alguien. ◇ vi (pt & pp left) [bus, train, plane] salir; [person] irse, marcharse. ◇ n [time off, permission] permiso m; **to be on leave** estar de permiso. ◆ **leave behind** vt sep - 1. [abandon] dejar - 2. [forget] dejarse - 3. [walking, in race]: **to get left behind** quedarse atrás. ◆ **leave out** vt sep - 1. [omit] omitir - 2. [exclude] excluir.

leave of absence n excedencia f.

leaves [li:vz] npl ▷ leaf.

Lebanon ['lebənən] n: (the) Lebanon (el) Líbano.

lecherous ['letʃərəs] adj lascivo(va).

lecture ['lektʃər] ◇ n - 1. [talk - at university] clase f; [- at conference] conferencia f; **to give a lecture (on)** [- at university] dar una clase (sobre); [- at conference] dar una conferencia (sobre) - 2. [criticism, reprimand] sermón m. ◇ vt [scold] echar un sermón a. ◇ vi [give talk]: **to lecture (on/in)** [at university] dar clases (de/en); [at conference] dar una conferencia (sobre/en).

lecturer ['lektʃərər] n [at university] profesor m, -ra f de universidad.

led [led] pt & pp ▷ lead¹.

ledge [ledʒ] n - 1. [of window] alféizar m - 2. [of mountain] saliente m.

ledger ['ledʒər] n libro m mayor.

leech [li:tʃ] n lit & fig sanguijuela f.

leek [li:k] n puerro m.

leer [lɪər] vi: **to leer at sb** mirar lascivamente a alguien.

leeway ['li:weɪ] n [room to manoeuvre] libertad f [de acción OR movimientos].

left [left] ◇ pt & pp ▷ leave. ◇ adj - 1. [remaining]: **to be left** quedar; **there's no wine left** no queda vino - 2. [not right] izquier-

do(da). ◇ adv a la izquierda. ◇ n izquierda f; **on OR to the left** a la izquierda. ◆ **Left** n POL: **the Left** la izquierda.

left-hand adj izquierdo(da); **the left-hand side** el lado izquierdo, la izquierda.

left-handed [-'hændɪd] adj - 1. [person] zurdo(da) - 2. [implement] para zurdos.

left luggage (office) n UK consigna f.

leftover ['leftəʊvər] adj sobrante. ◆ **leftovers** npl sobras fpl.

left wing n POL izquierda f. ◆ **left-wing** adj izquierdista.

leg [leg] n - 1. [of person] pierna f; **to pull sb's leg** tomarle el pelo a alguien - 2. [of animal] pata f - 3. [of trousers] pernera f, pierna f - 4. CULIN [of lamb, pork] pierna f; [of chicken] muslo m - 5. [of furniture] pata f - 6. [of journey] etapa f; [of cup tie] partido m.

legacy ['legəsɪ] n lit & fig legado m.

legal ['li:gl] adj - 1. [lawful] legal - 2. [concerning the law] jurídico(ca), legal.

legalize, -ise ['li:gəlaɪz] vt legalizar.

legal tender n moneda f de curso legal.

legend ['ledʒənd] n lit & fig leyenda f.

leggings ['legɪŋz] npl mallas fpl.

legible ['ledʒəbl] adj legible.

legislation [,ledʒɪs'leɪʃn] n legislación f.

legislature ['ledʒɪsleɪtʃər] n asamblea f legislativa.

legitimate [lɪ'dʒɪtɪmət] adj legítimo(ma).

legless ['leglɪs] adj UK inf [drunk] trompa, como una cuba.

legroom ['legrʊm] n (U) espacio m para las piernas.

leg-warmers [-,wɔːməz] npl calentadores mpl.

leisure [UK 'leʒər, US 'li:ʒər] n ocio m; **do it at your leisure** hazlo cuando tengas tiempo.

leisure centre n centro m deportivo y cultural.

leisurely [UK 'leʒəlɪ, US 'li:ʒərlɪ] adj lento(ta).

leisure time n tiempo m libre.

lemon ['lemən] n [fruit] limón m.

lemonade [,lemə'neɪd] n - 1. UK [fizzy drink] gaseosa f - 2. [made with fresh lemons] limonada f.

lemongrass ['lemʊngrɑːs] n (U) hierba f limonera.

lemon juice n zumo m de limón.

lemon sole n mendo m limón.

lemon squeezer [-'skwiːzər] n exprimidor m, exprimelimones pl inv.

lemon tea n té m con limón.

lend [lend] (pt & pp lent) vt - 1. [loan] prestar, dejar; **to lend sb sthg, to lend sthg to sb** prestarle algo a alguien - **2.** [offer]: **to lend sthg (to sb)** prestar algo (a alguien); **to lend sb a hand** echar una mano a alguien; **to lend itself to sthg** prestarse a algo - **3.** [add]: **to lend sthg to** prestar algo a.

lending rate ['lendɪŋ-] *n* tipo *m* de interés (en un crédito).

length [leŋθ] *n* - **1.** [measurement] longitud *f*, largo *m*; **what length is it?** ¿cuánto mide de largo?; **it's a metre in length** tiene un metro de largo - **2.** [whole distance, size] extensión *f* - **3.** [duration] duración *f* - **4.** [of swimming pool] largo *m* - **5.** [piece - of string, wood] trozo *m*; [- of cloth] largo *m*. ◆ **at length** *adv* - **1.** [eventually] por fin - **2.** [in detail - speak] largo y tendido; [- discuss] con detenimiento.

lengthen ['leŋθən] ◇ *vt* alargar. ◇ *vi* alargarse.

lengthways ['leŋθweɪz] *adv* a lo largo.

lengthy ['leŋθɪ] *adj* [stay, visit] extenso(sa); [discussions, speech] prolongado(da).

lenient ['li:njənt] *adj* indulgente.

lens [lenz] *n* - **1.** [in glasses] lente *f*; [in camera] objetivo *m* - **2.** [contact lens] lentilla *f*, lente *f* de contacto.

lent [lent] *pt* & *pp* ⊏▷ **lend**.

Lent [lent] *n* Cuaresma *f*.

lentil ['lentɪl] *n* lenteja *f*.

Leo ['li:əʊ] *n* Leo *m*.

leopard ['lepəd] *n* leopardo *m*.

leotard ['li:ətɑːd] *n* malla *f*.

leper ['lepər] *n* leproso *m*, -sa *f*.

leprosy ['leprəsɪ] *n* lepra *f*.

lesbian ['lezbɪən] *n* lesbiana *f*.

less [les] *(compar of little)* ◇ *adj* menos; **less... than** menos... que; **less and less...** cada vez menos... ◇ *pron* menos; **the less you work, the less you earn** cuanto menos trabajas, menos ganas; **it costs less than you think** cuesta menos de lo que piensas; **no less than** nada menos que. ◇ *adv* menos; **less than five** menos de cinco; **less often** menos; **less and less** cada vez menos. ◇ *prep* [minus] menos.

lessen ['lesn] ◇ *vt* aminorar, reducir. ◇ *vi* aminorarse, reducirse.

lesser ['lesər] *adj* menor.

lesson ['lesn] *n* - **1.** [class] clase *f* - **2.** [warning experience] lección *f*; **to teach sb a lesson** darle una buena lección a alguien.

lest [lest] *conj fml* para que no; **lest we forget** no sea que nos olvidemos.

let [let] *vt* *(pt & pp* **let**) - **1.** [allow]: **to let sb do sthg** dejar a alguien hacer algo; **to let sb know sthg** avisar a alguien de algo; **to let go of sthg/sb** soltar algo/a alguien; **to let sthg/sb go** [release] liberar a algo/alguien, soltar a algo/alguien; **to let o.s. go** [relax] soltarse el pelo; [become slovenly] abandonarse - **2.** [in verb forms]: **let's go!** ¡vamos!; **let's see** veamos; **let him wait!** ¡déjale que espere! - **3.** [rent out - house, room] alquilar; [- land] arrendar; **'to let'** 'se alquila'. ◆ **let alone** *adv* ni mucho menos. ◆ **let down** *vt sep* - **1.** [deflate] desinflar - **2.** [disappoint] fallar, defraudar. ◆ **let in** *vt sep* - **1.** [admit] dejar entrar - **2.** [leak] dejar pasar. ◆ **let off** *vt sep* - **1.** [excuse]: **to let sb off sthg** eximir a alguien de algo - **2.** [not punish] perdonar - **3.** [cause to explode - bomb] hacer estallar; [- gun] disparar - **4.** [gas] despedir. ◆ **let on** *vi*: **don't let on!** ¡no cuentes nada! ◆ **let out** *vt sep* - **1.** [allow to go out] dejar salir - **2.** [emit - sound] soltar. ◆ **let up** *vi* - **1.** [heat, rain] amainar - **2.** [person] parar.

letdown ['letdaʊn] *n inf* chasco *m*.

lethal ['li:θl] *adj* letal, mortífero(ra).

lethargic [lə'θɑːdʒɪk] *adj* - **1.** [mood] letárgico(ca); [person] aletargado(da) - **2.** [apathetic] apático(ca).

let's [lets] *(abbr of let us)* ⊏▷ **let**.

letter ['letər] *n* - **1.** [written message] carta *f* - **2.** [of alphabet] letra *f*; **to the letter** *fig* al pie de la letra.

letter bomb *n* carta *f* bomba.

letterbox ['letəbɒks] *n UK* buzón *m*.

letter of credit *n* carta *f* de crédito.

lettuce ['letɪs] *n* lechuga *f*.

letup ['letʌp] *n* tregua *f*, respiro *m*.

leuk(a)emia [lu:'ki:mɪə] *n* leucemia *f*.

level ['levl] ◇ *adj* - **1.** [equal in speed, score] igualado(da); **they are level** van igualados; [equal in height] nivelado(da); **to be level (with sthg)** estar al mismo nivel (que algo) - **2.** [flat - floor, surface] liso(sa), llano(na). ◇ *n* - **1.** [gen] nivel *m*; **to be on the level** *inf* ser de fiar - **2.** [storey] piso *m* - **3.** *US* [spirit level] nivel *m* de burbuja de aire. ◇ *vt* *(UK pt & pp* **-led**, *cont* **-ling**, *US pt & pp* **-ed**, *cont* **-ing)** - **1.** [make flat] allanar - **2.** [demolish - building] derribar; [- forest] arrasar. ◆ **level off, level out** *vi* - **1.** [stabilize, slow down] estabilizarse - **2.** [ground] nivelarse; [plane] enderezarse. ◆ **level with** *vt insep inf* ser sincero(ra) con.

level crossing *n UK* paso *m* a nivel.

level-headed [-'hedɪd] *adj* sensato(ta).

lever [*UK* 'li:vər, *US* 'levər] *n* - **1.** [handle, bar] palanca *f* - **2.** *fig* [tactic] resorte *m*.

leverage [*UK* 'li:vərɪdʒ, *US* 'levərɪdʒ] *n (U)* - **1.** [force] fuerza *f* de apalanque - **2.** *fig* [influence] influencia *f*.

levy ['levɪ] ◇ *n*: **levy (on)** [financial contribution] contribución *f* (a OR para); [tax] tasa *f* OR impuesto *m* (sobre). ◇ *vt* - **1.** [impose] imponer - **2.** [collect] recaudar.

lewd [lju:d] *adj* [person, look] lascivo(va); [behaviour, song] obsceno(na); [joke] verde.

liability [ˌlaɪə'bɪlətɪ] n - **1**. [legal responsibility]: **liability (for)** responsabilidad f (de OR por) - **2**. [hindrance] estorbo m. ◆ **liabilities** npl FIN pasivo m.

liable ['laɪəbl] adj - **1**. [likely]: **that's liable to happen** eso pueda que ocurra - **2**. [prone]: **to be liable to** ser propenso(sa) a - **3**. [legally responsible]: **to be liable (for)** ser responsable (de).

liaise [lɪ'eɪz] vi: **to liaise (with)** estar en contacto (con).

liaison [lɪ'eɪzɒn] n [contact, co-operation]: **liaison (with/between)** coordinación f (con/entre), enlace m (con/entre).

liar ['laɪər] n mentiroso m, -sa f.

libel ['laɪbl] ◇ n libelo m. ◇ vt (UK & US) calumniar.

liberal ['lɪbərəl] ◇ adj - **1**. [tolerant] liberal - **2**. [generous, abundant] generoso(sa). ◇ n liberal mf. ◆ **Liberal** ◇ adj POL liberal. ◇ n POL liberal mf.

Liberal Democrat UK ◇ adj demócrata liberal. ◇ n demócrata liberal mf.

liberate ['lɪbəreɪt] vt liberar.

liberation [ˌlɪbə'reɪʃn] n liberación f.

liberty ['lɪbətɪ] n libertad f; **at liberty** en libertad; **to be at liberty to do sthg** ser libre de hacer algo.

Libra ['li:brə] n Libra f.

librarian [laɪ'breərɪən] n bibliotecario m, -ria f.

library ['laɪbrərɪ] (pl -ies) n [public institution] biblioteca f.

libretto [lɪ'bretəʊ] (pl -s) n libreto m.

Libya ['lɪbɪə] n Libia.

lice [laɪs] npl ⊳ **louse**.

licence, license¹ US ◇ n - **1**. [gen] permiso m, licencia f; **under license** con autorización OR permiso oficial - **2**. AUT carné OR permiso m de conducir. ◇ vt US = **license**.

licence fee n UK TV impuesto anual que tienen que pagar todos los hogares con un televisor y que se usa para financiar la televisión pública.

licence number n AUT matrícula f.

license US, **licence** ['laɪsəns] ◇ vt [person, organization] dar licencia a; [activity] autorizar. ◇ n US = **licence**.

licensed ['laɪsənst] adj - **1**. [person]: **to be licensed to do sthg** estar autorizado(da) para hacer algo - **2**. [object] registrado(da), con licencia - **3**. UK [premises] autorizado(da) a vender alcohol.

license plate n US (placa f de) matrícula f.

lick [lɪk] ◇ n inf [small amount]: **a lick of paint** una mano de pintura. ◇ vt lit & fig lamer.

licorice ['lɪkərɪs] = **liquorice**.

lid [lɪd] n - **1**. [cover] tapa f - **2**. [eyelid] párpado m.

lie [laɪ] ◇ n mentira f; **to tell lies** contar mentiras, mentir. ◇ vi - **1**. (pt lied, pp lied, cont lying) [tell lie] mentir; **to lie to sb** mentirle a alguien - **2**. (pt lay, pp lain, cont lying) [lie down] tumbarse, echarse; [be buried] yacer; **to be lying** estar tumbado(da) - **3**. (pt lay, pp lain, cont lying) [be situated] hallarse; **there is snow lying on the ground** hay nieve en el suelo; **he is lying in fourth place** se encuentra en cuarto lugar - **4**. (pt lay, pp lain, cont lying) [be - solution, attraction] hallarse, encontrarse - **5**. (pt lay, pp lain, cont lying): **to lie low** permanecer escondido(da). ◆ **lie about, lie around** vi estar OR andar tirado(da). ◆ **lie down** vi tumbarse, echarse; **not to take sthg lying down** no quedarse cruzado de brazos ante algo. ◆ **lie in** vi UK quedarse en la cama hasta tarde.

Liechtenstein ['lɪktən,staɪn] n Liechtenstein.

lie-down n UK: **to have a lie-down** echarse un rato.

lie-in n UK: **to have a lie-in** quedarse en la cama hasta tarde.

lieu [lju:, lu:] ◆ **in lieu** adv: **in lieu of** en lugar de.

lieutenant [UK lef'tenənt, US lu:'tenənt] n - **1**. MIL teniente m - **2**. [deputy] lugarteniente mf - **3**. US [police officer] oficial mf de policía.

life [laɪf] (pl lives) n [gen] vida f; **that's life!** ¡así es la vida!; **for life** de por vida, para toda la vida; **to breathe life into sthg** infundir una nueva vida a algo.

life assurance = **life insurance**.

life belt n flotador m, salvavidas m inv.

lifeboat ['laɪfbəʊt] n [on a ship] bote m salvavidas; [on shore] lancha f de salvamento.

life buoy n flotador m, salvavidas m inv.

life cycle n ciclo m vital.

life expectancy n expectativa f de vida.

lifeguard ['laɪfgɑːd] n socorrista mf.

life imprisonment [-ɪm'prɪznmənt] n cadena f perpetua.

life insurance, life assurance n (U) seguro m de vida.

life jacket n chaleco m salvavidas.

lifeless ['laɪflɪs] adj - **1**. [dead] sin vida - **2**. [listless] insulso(sa).

lifelike ['laɪflaɪk] adj realista, natural.

lifeline ['laɪflaɪn] n - **1**. [rope] cuerda f OR cable m (de salvamento) - **2**. [something vital for survival] cordón m umbilical.

lifelong ['laɪflɒŋ] adj de toda la vida.

life preserver [-prɪ,zɜːvər] n US - 1. [life jacket] chaleco m salvavidas - 2. [life belt] flotador m, salvavidas m inv.

life raft n balsa f salvavidas.

lifesaver ['laɪf,seɪvər] n [person] socorrista mf.

life sentence n (condena f a) cadena f perpetua.

life-size(d) [-saɪz(d)] adj (de) tamaño natural.

lifespan ['laɪfspæn] n vida f.

lifestyle ['laɪfstaɪl] n estilo m OR modo m de vida.

life-support system n aparato m de respiración artificial.

lifetime ['laɪftaɪm] n vida f.

lift [lɪft] <> n - 1. [ride - in car etc]: **to give sb a lift (somewhere)** acercar OR llevar a alguien (a algún sitio), dar (un) aventón a alguien (a algún sitio) Col & Méx - 2. UK [elevator] ascensor m, elevador m Méx. <> vt - 1. [gen] levantar; **to lift sthg down** bajar algo; **to lift sthg out of sthg** sacar algo de algo - 2. [plagiarize] copiar. <> vi [disappear - mist] disiparse.

lift-off n despegue m.

light [laɪt] <> adj - 1. [gen] ligero(ra); [rain] fino(na); [traffic] ligero(ra) - 2. [not strenuous - duties, responsibilities] simple; [- work] suave; [- punishment] leve - 3. [low-calorie, low-alcohol] light - 4. [bright] luminoso(sa), lleno(na) de luz; **it's growing light** se hace de día - 5. [pale - colour] claro(ra). <> n - 1. [brightness, source of light] luz f - 2. [for cigarette, pipe] fuego m, lumbre f; **have you got a light?** ¿tienes fuego? - 3. [perspective]: **to see sthg/sb in a different light** ver algo/a alguien de otra manera distinta

▸▸▸ **to bring sthg to light** sacar algo a la luz; **to come to light** salir a la luz (pública); **to set light to** prender fuego a; **to throw OR cast OR shed light on** arrojar luz sobre. <> vt (pt & pp lit OR -ed) - 1. [ignite] encender - 2. [illuminate] iluminar. <> vi (pt & pp lit OR -ed) prenderse. <> adv [travel] con poco equipaje.

⯈ **light up** <> vt sep [illuminate] iluminar. <> vi - 1. [look happy] iluminarse, encenderse - 2. inf [start smoking] encender un cigarrillo.

light bulb n bombilla f, foco m Méx, bombillo m Amér C & Col, bombita f R Plata, bujía f Amér C, ampolleta f Chile.

lighten ['laɪtn] <> vt - 1. [make brighter - room] iluminar - 2. [make less heavy] aligerar. <> vi [brighten] aclararse.

lighter ['laɪtər] n [cigarette lighter] encendedor m, mechero m.

light-headed [-'hedɪd] adj [dizzy] mareado(da); [emotionally] exaltado(da).

light-hearted [-'hɑːtɪd] adj - 1. [cheerful] alegre - 2. [amusing] frívolo(la).

lighthouse ['laɪthaʊs, pl -haʊzɪz] n faro m.

lighting ['laɪtɪŋ] n iluminación f; **street lighting** alumbrado m público.

lightly ['laɪtlɪ] adv - 1. [gently] suavemente - 2. [slightly] ligeramente - 3. [frivolously] a la ligera.

light meter n fotómetro m.

lightning ['laɪtnɪŋ] n (U): **a flash of lightning** un relámpago; **a bolt of lightning** un rayo; **it was struck by lightning** lo alcanzó un rayo.

lightweight ['laɪtweɪt] <> adj [object] ligero(ra). <> n [boxer] peso m ligero.

likable, likeable ['laɪkəbl] adj simpático(ca).

like [laɪk] <> prep - 1. [gen] como; (in questions or indirect questions) cómo; **what did it taste like?** ¿a qué sabía?; **what did it look like?** ¿cómo era?; **tell me what it's like** dime cómo es; **something like £100** algo así como cien libras; **something like that** algo así, algo por el estilo - 2. [in the same way as] como, igual que; **like this/that** así - 3. [typical of] propio(pia) OR típico(ca) de; **it's not like them** no es su estilo. <> vt - 1. [find pleasant, approve of]: **I like cheese** me gusta el queso; **I like it/them** me gusta/gustan; **I don't like it/them** no me gusta/gustan; **he likes doing OR to do sthg** (a él) le gusta hacer algo - 2. [want] querer; **would you like some more?** ¿quieres un poco más?; **I'd like to come tomorrow** querría OR me gustaría venir mañana; **I'd like you to come to dinner** me gustaría que vinieras a cenar; **whenever you like** cuando quieras; **I don't like to bother her** no quiero molestarla; [in shops, restaurants]: **I'd like a kilo of apples/the soup** póngame un kilo de manzanas/la sopa. <> n: **the like of sb/sthg** alguien/algo del estilo. ⯈ **likes** npl [things one likes] gustos mpl, preferencias fpl.

likeable ['laɪkəbl] = likable.

likelihood ['laɪklɪhʊd] n probabilidad f.

likely ['laɪklɪ] adj - 1. [probable] probable; **rain is likely** es probable que llueva; **he's likely to come** es probable que venga - 2. [suitable] indicado(da).

liken ['laɪkn] vt: **to liken sthg/sb to** comparar algo/a alguien con.

likeness ['laɪknɪs] n - 1. [resemblance]: **likeness (to)** parecido m (con) - 2. [portrait] retrato m.

likewise ['laɪkwaɪz] adv [similarly] de la misma forma; **to do likewise** hacer lo mismo.

liking ['laɪkɪŋ] n: **to have a liking for sthg** tener afición f por OR a algo; **to take a liking to sb** tomar OR coger cariño m a alguien; **to be to sb's liking** ser del gusto de alguien; **for my/his liking** etc para mi/su gusto etc.

lilac ['laɪlək] ◇ adj |colour| lila ◇ n - **1.** [tree, flower] lila f - **2.** [colour] lila m.

Lilo® ['laɪləʊ] (pl -s) n UK colchoneta f, colchón m hinchable.

lily ['lɪlɪ] n lirio m, azucena f.

lily of the valley (pl lilies of the valley) n lirio m de los valles.

limb [lɪm] n - **1.** [of body] miembro m - **2.** [of tree] rama f.

limber ['lɪmbər] ◆ **limber up** vi desentumecerse.

limbo ['lɪmbəʊ] (pl -s) n (U) [uncertain state]: **to be in limbo** estar en un estado de incertidumbre.

lime [laɪm] n - **1.** [fruit] lima f - **2.** [drink]: **lime (juice)** lima f - **3.** CHEM cal f.

limelight ['laɪmlaɪt] n: **in the limelight** en (el) candelero.

limerick ['lɪmərɪk] n copla humorística de cinco versos.

limestone ['laɪmstəʊn] n (U) (piedra f) caliza f.

limey ['laɪmɪ] (pl limeys) n US inf término peyorativo que designa a un inglés.

limit ['lɪmɪt] ◇ n [gen] límite m ▶▶▶ **off limits** en zona prohibida; **within limits** dentro de un límite. ◇ vt limitar.

limitation [ˌlɪmɪ'teɪʃn] n limitación f.

limited ['lɪmɪtɪd] adj [restricted] limitado(da); **to be limited to** estar limitado a.

limited (liability) company n sociedad f limitada.

limousine ['lɪməziːn] n limusina f.

limp [lɪmp] ◇ adj flojo(ja). ◇ vi cojear.

limpet ['lɪmpɪt] n lapa f.

line [laɪn] ◇ n - **1.** [gen & MIL] línea f - **2.** [row] fila f; **in a line** en fila - **3.** esp US [queue] cola f - **4.** [course - direction] línea f; [- of action] camino m; **what's his line of business?** ¿a qué negocios se dedica? - **5.** [length - of rope, for washing] cuerda f; [- for fishing] sedal m; [- of wire] hilo m - **6.** TELEC: **(telephone) line** línea f (telefónica); **hold the line, please** no cuelgue, por favor; **the line is busy** está comunicando; **it's a bad line** hay interferencias; **your wife is on the line for you** su mujer al teléfono - **7.** [on page] línea f, renglón m; [of poem, song] verso m; [letter]: **to drop sb a line** inf mandar unas letras a alguien - **8.** [wrinkle] arruga f - **9.** [borderline] límite m - **10.** COMM línea f; **line of credit** línea f de crédito. ◇ vt [coat, curtains] forrar; [drawer] cubrir el interior de. ◆ **out of line** adv: **to be out of line** estar fuera de lugar. ◆ **line up** ◇ vt sep - **1.** [make into a row or queue] alinear - **2.** [arrange] programar, organizar. ◇ vi [form a queue] alinearse.

lined [laɪnd] adj - **1.** [of paper] de rayas - **2.** [wrinkled] arrugado(da).

line dancing n baile en el que los participantes se colocan en fila y se mueven al mismo tiempo que los otros.

linen ['lɪnɪn] n - **1.** [cloth] lino m - **2.** [tablecloths, sheets] ropa f blanca OR de hilo; **bed linen** ropa f de cama.

liner ['laɪnər] n [ship] transatlántico m.

linesman ['laɪnzmən] (pl -men [-mən]) n juez m de línea.

lineup ['laɪnʌp] n - **1.** [of players, competitors] alineación f - **2.** US [identification parade] rueda f de identificación.

linger ['lɪŋgər] vi - **1.** [remain - over activity] entretenerse; [- in a place] rezagarse - **2.** [persist] persistir.

lingerie ['lænʒərɪ] n ropa f interior femenina.

lingo ['lɪŋgəʊ] (pl -es) n inf [foreign language] idioma m; [jargon] jerga f.

linguist ['lɪŋgwɪst] n - **1.** [someone good at languages]: **he's a good linguist** tiene facilidad para las lenguas - **2.** [student or teacher of linguistics] lingüista mf.

linguistics [lɪŋ'gwɪstɪks] n (U) lingüística f.

lining ['laɪnɪŋ] n - **1.** [gen & AUT] forro m - **2.** [of stomach, nose] paredes fpl interiores.

link [lɪŋk] ◇ n - **1.** [of chain] eslabón m - **2.** [connection] conexión f, enlace m; **links (between/with)** lazos mpl (entre/con), vínculos mpl (entre/con). ◇ vt - **1.** [connect - cities] comunicar; [- computers] conectar; [- facts] relacionar; **to link sthg with** OR **to relacionar** OR **asociar algo con** - **2.** [join - arms] enlazar. ◇ vi COMPUT: **to link to sth** enlazar con algo. ◆ **link up** vt sep: **to link sthg up (with)** conectar algo (con).

links [lɪŋks] (pl links) n campo m de golf (cerca del mar).

lino ['laɪnəʊ], **linoleum** [lɪ'nəʊljəm] n linóleo m.

lintel ['lɪntl] n dintel m.

lion ['laɪən] n león m.

lioness ['laɪənes] n leona f.

lip [lɪp] n - **1.** [of mouth] labio m - **2.** [of cup] borde m; [of jug] pico m.

liposuction ['lɪpəʊˌsʌkʃən] n liposucción f.

lip-read vi leer los labios.

lip salve [-sælv] n UK vaselina® f, cacao m.

lip service n: **to pay lip service to sthg** hablar en favor de algo sin hacer nada al respeto.

lipstick ['lɪpstɪk] n - **1.** [container] lápiz m OR barra f de labios - **2.** [substance] carmín m.

liqueur [lɪ'kjʊər] n licor m.

liquid ['lɪkwɪd] ◇ adj líquido(da). ◇ n líquido m.

liquidation [ˌlɪkwɪ'deɪʃn] n liquidación f; **to go into liquidation** ir a la quiebra.

liquid crystal display *n* pantalla *f* de cristal líquido.

liquidize, -ise ['lɪkwɪdaɪz] *vt UK* licuar.

liquidizer ['lɪkwɪdaɪzər] *n UK* licuadora *f*.

liquor ['lɪkər] *n (U) esp US* alcohol *m*, bebida *f* alcohólica.

liquorice, licorice ['lɪkərɪʃ, 'lɪkərɪs] *n (U)* regaliz *m*.

liquor store *n US* tienda donde se venden bebidas alcohólicas para llevar.

lisp [lɪsp] ⬦ *n* ceceo *m*. ⬦ *vi* cecear.

list [lɪst] ⬦ *n* lista *f*. ⬦ *vt* - 1. [in writing] hacer una lista de - 2. [in speech] enumerar. ⬦ *vi* NAUT escorar.

listed building [,lɪstɪd-] *n UK* edificio declarado de interés histórico y artístico.

listen ['lɪsn] *vi* - 1. [give attention]: **to listen (to sthg/sb)** escuchar (algo/a alguien); **to listen for** estar atento a - 2. [heed advice]: **to listen (to sb/sthg)** hacer caso (a alguien/de algo); **to listen to reason** atender a razones.

listener ['lɪsnər] *n* [to radio] radioyente *mf*.

listeria [lɪs'tɪːərɪə] *n* - 1. [illness] listeriosis *f inv* - 2. [bacteria] listeria *f*.

listless ['lɪstlɪs] *adj* apático(ca).

lit [lɪt] *pt & pp* ▷ **light**.

litany ['lɪtənɪ] (*pl* **-ies**) *n lit & fig* letanía *f*.

liter *US* = **litre**.

literacy ['lɪtərəsɪ] *n* alfabetización *f*.

literal ['lɪtərəl] *adj* literal.

literally ['lɪtərəlɪ] *adv* literalmente.

literary ['lɪtərərɪ] *adj* [gen] literario(ria).

literate ['lɪtərət] *adj* - 1. [able to read and write] alfabetizado(da) - 2. [well-read] culto(ta), instruido(da).

literature ['lɪtrətʃər] *n* - 1. [novels, plays, poetry] literatura *f* - 2. [books on a particular subject] publicaciones *fpl* - 3. [printed information] documentación *f*.

lithe [laɪð] *adj* ágil.

Lithuania [,lɪθjʊ'eɪnɪə] *n* Lituania.

litigation [,lɪtɪ'geɪʃn] *n fml* litigio *m*.

litre *UK*, **liter** *US* ['liːtər] *n* litro *m*.

litter ['lɪtər] ⬦ *n* - 1. [waste material] basura *f* - 2. [newborn animals] camada *f*. ⬦ *vt*: **to litter sthg (with)** ensuciar algo (de); **papers littered the floor** había papeles esparcidos por el suelo.

litterbin ['lɪtə,bɪn] *n UK* papelera *f*.

little ['lɪtl] ⬦ *adj* - 1. [small in size, younger] pequeño(ña); **a little dog** un perrito; **you poor little thing!** ¡pobrecillo! - 2. [short in length] corto(ta); **a little while** un ratito - 3. (*comp* less, *superl* least) [not much] poco(ca); **a little bit** un poco; **he speaks little English** habla poco inglés; **he speaks a little English** habla un poco de inglés. ⬦ *pron*: **I understood very little** en-

tendí muy poco; **a little** un poco; **a little under half** algo menos de la mitad. ⬦ *adv* poco; **little by little** poco a poco.

little finger *n* dedo *m* meñique.

live[1] [lɪv] ⬦ *vi* [gen] vivir. ⬦ *vt* vivir; **to live a quiet life** llevar una vida tranquila. ⬦ **live down** *vt sep* lograr hacer olvidar. ⬦ **live off** *vt insep* [savings, land] vivir de; [people] vivir a costa de. ⬦ **live on** ⬦ *vt insep* - 1. [survive on] vivir con OR de - 2. [eat] vivir de. ⬦ *vi* [memory, feeling] permanecer, perdurar. ⬦ **live together** *vi* vivir juntos. ⬦ **live up to** *vt insep* estar a la altura de. ⬦ **live with** *vt insep* - 1. [live in same house as] vivir con - 2. [accept - situation, problem] aceptar.

live[2] [laɪv] *adj* - 1. [living] vivo(va) - 2. [coals] encendido(da) - 3. [bomb] sin explotar; [ammunition] real - 4. ELEC cargado(da) - 5. [broadcast, performance] en directo.

livelihood ['laɪvlɪhʊd] *n* sustento *m*, medio *m* de vida.

lively ['laɪvlɪ] *adj* - 1. [person, debate, time] animado(da) - 2. [mind] agudo(da), perspicaz - 3. [colours] vivo(va).

liven ['laɪvn] ⬦ **liven up** ⬦ *vt sep* animar. ⬦ *vi* animarse.

liver ['lɪvər] *n* hígado *m*.

livery ['lɪvərɪ] *n* [of servant] librea *f*; [of company] uniforme *m*.

lives [laɪvz] *npl* ▷ **life**.

livestock ['laɪvstɒk] *n* ganado *m*.

livid ['lɪvɪd] *adj* - 1. [angry] furioso(sa) - 2. [blue-grey] lívido(da).

living ['lɪvɪŋ] ⬦ *adj* [relatives, language] vivo(va); [artist etc] contemporáneo(a). ⬦ *n* - 1. [means of earning money]: **what do you do for a living?** ¿cómo te ganas la vida?; **to earn a living** ganarse la vida - 2. [lifestyle] vida *f*.

living conditions *npl* condiciones *fpl* de vida.

living room *n* sala *f* de estar, salón *m*.

living standards *npl* nivel *m* de vida.

lizard ['lɪzəd] *n* [small] lagartija *f*; [big] lagarto *m*.

llama ['lɑːmə] (*pl* **llama** OR **-s**) *n* llama *f*.

load [ləʊd] ⬦ *n* - 1. [thing carried] carga *f* - 2. [amount of work]: **a heavy/light load** mucho/poco trabajo - 3. [large amount]: **loads/a load of** *inf* montones OR un montón de; **it was a load of rubbish** *inf* fue una porquería. ⬦ *vt* - 1. [gen & COMPUT]: **to load sthg/sb (with)** cargar algo/a alguien (de) - 2. [camera, video recorder]: **he loaded the camera with a film** cargó la cámara con una película. ⬦ **load up** *vt sep & vi* cargar.

loaded ['ləʊdɪd] *adj* - 1. [dice] trucado(da); [question, statement] con doble sentido OR intención - 2. *inf* [rich] forrado(da).

loading bay ['ləʊdɪŋ-] n zona f de carga y descarga.

loaf [ləʊf] (pl loaves) n [of bread] pan m; a loaf of bread un pan.

loafer ['ləʊfəʳ] n [shoe] mocasín m.

loan [ləʊn] ◇ n préstamo m; on loan prestado(da). ◇ vt prestar; to loan sthg to sb, to loan sb sthg prestar algo a alguien.

loath, loth [ləʊθ] adj: to be loath to do sthg ser reacio(cia) a hacer algo.

loathe [ləʊð] vt: to loathe (doing sthg) aborrecer OR detestar (hacer algo).

loathsome ['ləʊðsəm] adj [person, behaviour] odioso(sa); [smell] repugnante.

loaves [ləʊvz] npl ⊳ loaf.

lob [lɒb] n TENNIS lob m.

lobby ['lɒbɪ] ◇ n - 1. [hall] vestíbulo m - 2. [pressure group] grupo m de presión, lobby m. ◇ vt (pt & pp -ied) ejercer presión (política) sobre.

lobe [ləʊb] n lóbulo m.

lobster ['lɒbstəʳ] n langosta f.

local ['ləʊkl] ◇ adj local. ◇ n inf - 1. [person]: the locals [in village] los lugareños; [in town] los vecinos del lugar - 2. UK [pub] bar m del barrio - 3. US [bus, train] omnibús m.

local authority n UK autoridad f local.

local call n llamada f local.

local government n gobierno m municipal.

locality [ləʊ'kælətɪ] n localidad f.

locally ['ləʊkəlɪ] adv - 1. [on local basis] en el lugar - 2. [nearby] por la zona.

locate [UK ləʊ'keɪt, US 'ləʊkeɪt] vt - 1. [find] localizar - 2. [situate] ubicar.

location [ləʊ'keɪʃn] n - 1. [place] ubicación f, situación f - 2. [finding] localización f - 3. CIN: on location en exteriores.

loch [lɒk, lɒx] n Scotland lago m.

lock [lɒk] ◇ n - 1. [of door] cerradura f; [of bicycle] candado m - 2. [on canal] esclusa f - 3. AUT [steering lock] ángulo m de giro - 4. liter [of hair] mechón m. ◇ vt - 1. [with key] cerrar con llave; [with padlock] cerrar con candado - 2. [keep safely] poner bajo llave - 3. [immobilize] bloquear. ◇ vi - 1. [with key, padlock] cerrarse - 2. [become immobilized] bloquearse. ◆ **lock in** vt sep encerrar. ◆ **lock out** vt sep - 1. [accidentally] dejar fuera al cerrar accidentalmente la puerta; to lock o.s. out quedarse fuera (por olvidarse la llave dentro) - 2. [deliberately] dejar fuera a. ◆ **lock up** vt sep - 1. [person - in prison] encerrar; [- in asylum] internar - 2. [house] cerrar (con llave).

locker ['lɒkəʳ] n taquilla f, armario m.

locker room n US vestuario m con taquillas.

locket ['lɒkɪt] n guardapelo m.

locksmith ['lɒksmɪθ] n cerrajero m, -ra f.

locomotive [ˌləʊkə'məʊtɪv] n locomotora f.

locum ['ləʊkəm] (pl -s) n interino m, -na f.

locust ['ləʊkəst] n langosta f (insecto).

lodge [lɒdʒ] ◇ n - 1. [caretaker's etc room] portería f - 2. [of manor house] casa f del guarda - 3. [for hunting] refugio m - 4. [of freemasons] logia f. ◇ vi - 1. [stay]: to lodge (with sb) alojarse (con alguien) - 2. [become stuck] alojarse. ◇ vt fml [appeal, complaint] presentar.

lodger ['lɒdʒəʳ] n huésped mf.

lodging ['lɒdʒɪŋ] n ⊳ **board**. ◆ **lodgings** npl habitación f (alquilada).

loft [lɒft] n [in house] desván m, entretecho m Chile & Col; [for hay] pajar m; US [warehouse apartment] almacén reformado y convertido en apartamento.

lofty ['lɒftɪ] adj - 1. [noble] noble, elevado(da) - 2. pej [haughty] arrogante, altanero(ra) - 3. liter [high] elevado(da).

log [lɒg] ◇ n - 1. [of wood] tronco m; [for fire] leño m - 2. [written record - of ship] diario m de a bordo; COMPUT registro m. ◇ vt registrar. ◆ **log in** vi COMPUT entrar. ◆ **log off** vi COMPUT salir. ◆ **log on** vi COMPUT entrar. ◆ **log out** vi COMPUT salir.

logbook ['lɒgbʊk] n - 1. [of ship] diario m de a bordo; [of plane] diario m de vuelo - 2. [of car] documentación f.

loggerheads ['lɒgəhedz] n: to be at loggerheads estar a matar.

logic ['lɒdʒɪk] n lógica f.

logical ['lɒdʒɪkl] adj lógico(ca).

logistics [lə'dʒɪstɪks] ◇ n (U) logística f. ◇ npl logística f.

logo ['ləʊgəʊ] (pl -s) n logotipo m.

loin [lɔɪn] n lomo m.

loiter ['lɔɪtəʳ] vi [for bad purpose] merodear; [hang around] vagar.

loll [lɒl] vi - 1. [sit, lie about] repantigarse - 2. [hang down] colgar.

lollipop ['lɒlɪpɒp] n pirulí m.

lollipop lady n UK mujer encargada de parar el tráfico en un paso de cebra para que crucen los niños.

lollipop man n UK hombre encargado de parar el tráfico en un paso de cebra para que crucen los niños.

lolly ['lɒlɪ] n inf - 1. [lollipop] pirulí m - 2. UK [ice lolly] polo m.

London ['lʌndən] n Londres.

Londoner ['lʌndənəʳ] n londinense mf.

lone [ləʊn] adj solitario(ria).

loneliness ['ləʊnlɪnɪs] n soledad f.

lonely ['ləʊnlɪ] adj - 1. [person] solo(la) - 2. [time, childhood, place] solitario(ria).

lonesome ['ləʊnsəm] adj US inf - 1. [person] solo(la) - 2. [place] solitario(ria).

long [lɒŋ] <> *adj* largo(ga); **the table is 5m long** la mesa mide *OR* tiene 5m de largo; **two days long** de dos días de duración; **the journey is 50km long** el viaje es de 50 km; **the book is 500 pages long** el libro tiene 500 páginas; **a long time** mucho tiempo; **a long way from** muy lejos de. <> *adv* mucho tiempo; **how long will it take?** ¿cuánto se tarda?; **how long will you be?** ¿cuánto tardarás?; **how long have you been waiting?** ¿cuánto tiempo llevas esperando?; **how long have you known them?** ¿cuánto hace que los conoces?; **how long is the journey?** ¿cuánto hay de viaje?; **I'm no longer young** ya no soy joven; **I can't wait any longer** no puedo esperar más; **as long as a week** hasta una semana; **so long** *inf* hasta luego *OR* pronto; **before long** pronto; **for long** mucho tiempo. <> *vt*: **to long to do sthg** desear ardientemente hacer algo. ◆ **as long as, so long as** *conj* mientras; **as long as you do it, so will I** siempre y cuando tú lo hagas, yo también lo haré. ◆ **long for** *vt insep* desear ardientemente.

long-distance *adj* [runner] de fondo; [lorry driver] para distancias grandes.

long-distance call *n* conferencia *f* (telefónica) *Esp*, llamada *f* de larga distancia.

longhand ['lɒŋhænd] *n* escritura *f* a mano.

long-haul *adj* de larga distancia.

longing ['lɒŋɪŋ] <> *adj* anhelante. <> *n* - 1. [desire] anhelo *m*, deseo *m*; [nostalgia] nostalgia *f*, añoranza *f* - 2. [strong wish]: **(a) longing (for)** (un) ansia *f* (de).

longitude ['lɒndʒɪtjuːd] *n* longitud *f*.

long jump *n* salto *m* de longitud.

long-life *adj* de larga duración.

longlist ['lɒŋlɪst] *n* selección *f* inicial.

long-playing record [-'pleɪɪŋ-] *n* elepé *m*.

long-range *adj* - 1. [missile, bomber] de largo alcance - 2. [plan, forecast] a largo plazo.

long shot *n* posibilidad *f* remota.

longsighted [,lɒŋ'saɪtɪd] *adj* présbita.

long-standing *adj* antiguo(gua).

longsuffering [,lɒŋ'sʌfərɪŋ] *adj* sufrido(da).

long term *n*: **in the long term** a largo plazo.

long wave *n* (U) onda *f* larga.

long weekend *n* puente *m*.

longwinded [,lɒŋ'wɪndɪd] *adj* prolijo(ja).

loo [luː] *n* (pl **-s**) *n UK inf* wáter *m*.

look [lʊk] <> *n* - 1. [with eyes] mirada *f*; **to give sb a look** mirar a alguien; **to take** *OR* **have a look (at sthg)** mirar algo; **let her have a look** déjale ver; **to have a look through sthg** ojear algo - 2. [search]: **to have a look (for sthg)** buscar (algo) - 3. [appearance] aspecto *m*; **his new look** su nuevo look; **I don't like the look**

of it no me gusta nada; **by the look** *OR* **looks of it, it has been here for ages** parece que hace años que está aquí. <> *vi* - 1. [with eyes]: **to look (at sthg/sb)** mirar (algo/a alguien) - 2. [search]: **to look (for sthg/sb)** buscar (algo/a alguien) - 3. [building, window]: **to look (out) onto** dar a - 4. [have stated appearance] verse; [seem] parecer. <> *vt* - 1. [look at] mirar - 2. [appear]: **to look one's age** representar la edad que se tiene. ◆ **looks** *npl* belleza *f*. ◆ **look after** *vt insep* - 1. [take care of] cuidar - 2. [be responsible for] encargarse de. ◆ **look at** *vt insep* - 1. [see, glance at] mirar; [examine] examinar; [check over] echar un vistazo a - 2. [judge, evaluate] ver. ◆ **look down on** *vt insep* [condescend to] despreciar. ◆ **look for** *vt insep* buscar. ◆ **look forward to** *vt insep* esperar (con ilusión); **to be looking forward to doing sthg** estar deseando hacer algo. ◆ **look into** *vt insep* [problem, possibility] estudiar; [issue] investigar. ◆ **look on** *vi* mirar, observar. ◆ **look out** *vi* [be careful] tener cuidado; **look out!** ¡cuidado! ◆ **look out for** *vt insep* estar atento(ta) a. ◆ **look over** *vt sep* mirar por encima. ◆ **look round** <> *vt insep* [shop] echar un vistazo a; [castle, town] visitar. <> *vi* - 1. [turn head] volver la cabeza - 2. [in shop] mirar. ◆ **look to** *vt insep* - 1. [turn to] recurrir a - 2. [think about] pensar en. ◆ **look up** <> *vt sep* - 1. [in book] buscar - 2. [visit - person] ir a ver *OR* visitar. <> *vi* [improve] mejorar. ◆ **look up to** *vt insep* respetar, admirar.

lookout ['lʊkaʊt] *n* - 1. [place] puesto *m* de observación - 2. [person] centinela *mf* - 3. [search]: **to be on the lookout for** estar al acecho de.

loom [luːm] <> *n* telar *m*. <> *vi* [rise up] surgir *OR* aparecer amenazante. ◆ **loom up** *vi* divisarse sombríamente.

loony ['luːnɪ] *inf* <> *adj* majara. <> *n* majara *mf*.

loop [luːp] *n* - 1. [shape] lazo *m* - 2. COMPUT bucle *m*.

loophole ['luːphəʊl] *n* laguna *f*.

loose [luːs] *adj* - 1. [not firmly fixed] flojo(ja) - 2. [unattached - paper, sweets, hair, knot] suelto(ta) - 3. [clothes, fit] holgado(da) - 4. *dated* [promiscuous] promiscuo(cua) - 5. [inexact - translation] impreciso(sa).

loose change *n* (dinero *m*) suelto *m*.

loose end *n*: **to be at a loose end** *UK*, **to be at loose ends** *US* no tener nada que hacer.

loosely ['luːslɪ] *adv* - 1. [not firmly] holgadamente, sin apretar - 2. [inexactly] vagamente.

loosen ['luːsn] *vt* aflojar. ◆ **loosen up** *vi* - 1. [before game, race] desentumecerse - 2. *inf* [relax] relajarse.

loot [luːt] <> *n* botín *m*. <> *vt* saquear.

loofing ['lu:fiŋ] n saquco m.

lop [lɒp] vt podar. ◆ **lop off** vt sep cortar.

lop-sided [-'saɪdɪd] adj - **1.** [uneven] ladeado(da), torcido(da) - **2.** fig [biased] desequilibrado(da).

lord [lɔːd] n UK [man of noble rank] noble m. ◆ **Lord** n - **1.** RELIG: **the Lord** [God] el Señor; **good Lord!** UK ¡Dios mío! - **2.** [in titles] lord m; [as form of address]: **my Lord** [bishop] su Ilustrísima; [judge] su Señoría. ◆ **Lords** npl UK POL: **the Lords** la Cámara de los Lores.

Lordship ['lɔːdʃɪp] n: **your/his Lordship** su Señoría f.

lore [lɔːʳ] n (U) saber m OR tradición f popular.

lorry ['lɒrɪ] n UK camión m.

lorry driver n UK camionero m, -ra f.

lose [luːz] (pt & pp lost) ◇ vt perder; **to lose one's way** perderse; **my watch has lost ten minutes** mi reloj se ha atrasado diez minutos; **to lose o.s. in sthg** fig quedarse absorto(ta) en algo. ◇ vi [fail to win] perder.

loser ['luːzəʳ] n - **1.** [of competition] perdedor m, -ra f - **2.** inf pej [unsuccessful person] desgraciado m, -da f.

loss [lɒs] n - **1.** [gen] pérdida f; **to make a loss** sufrir pérdidas - **2.** [failure to win] derrota f.

lost [lɒst] ◇ pt & pp ▷ **lose.** ◇ adj - **1.** [unable to find way] perdido(da); **to get lost** perderse; **get lost!** inf ¡vete a la porra! - **2.** [that cannot be found] extraviado(da), perdido(da).

lost-and-found office n US oficina f de objetos perdidos.

lost property office n UK oficina f de objetos perdidos.

lot [lɒt] n - **1.** [large amount]: **a lot of, lots of** mucho(cha); **a lot of people** mucha gente, muchas personas; **a lot of problems** muchos problemas; **the lot** todo - **2.** [group, set] lote m - **3.** [destiny] destino m, suerte f - **4.** US [of land] terreno m; [car park] aparcamiento m - **5.** [at auction] partida f, lote m
▸▸▸ **to draw lots** echar a suerte. ◆ **a lot** adv mucho; **quite a lot** bastante; **such a lot** tanto.

lotion ['ləʊʃn] n loción f.

lottery ['lɒtərɪ] n lotería f.

lottery ticket n billete m de lotería.

loud [laʊd] ◇ adj - **1.** [voice, music] alto(ta); [bang, noise] fuerte; [person] ruidoso(sa) - **2.** [emphatic]: **to be loud in one's criticism of** ser enérgico(ca) en la crítica de - **3.** [too bright] chillón(ona). ◇ adv fuerte; **out loud** en voz alta.

loudhailer [,laʊd'heɪləʳ] n UK megáfono m.

loudly ['laʊdlɪ] adv - **1.** [shout] a voz en grito; [talk] ... ... - ... [garishly] con colores chillones OR llamativos.

loudspeaker [,laʊd'spiːkəʳ] n altavoz m.

lounge [laʊndʒ] ◇ n - **1.** [in house] salón m - **2.** [in airport] sala f de espera. ◇ vi repantigarse.

lounge bar n UK salón-bar m.

louse [laʊs] n (pl lice) [insect] piojo m.

lousy ['laʊzɪ] adj inf [poor quality] fatal, pésimo(ma).

lout [laʊt] n gamberro m.

louvre UK, **louver** US ['luːvəʳ] n persiana f.

lovable ['lʌvəbl] adj adorable.

love [lʌv] ◇ n - **1.** [gen] amor m; **give her my love** dale un abrazo de mi parte; **she sends her love from** [at end of letter] un abrazo de; **to be in love (with)** estar enamorado(da) (de); **to fall in love with sb** enamorarse de alguien; **to make love** hacer el amor - **2.** [liking, interest] pasión f; **a love of** OR **for** una pasión por - **3.** inf [form of address] cariño m - **4.** TENNIS: **30 love** 30 a nada. ◇ vt - **1.** [sexually, sentimentally] amar, querer - **2.** [son, daughter, parents, friend] querer - **3.** [like]: **I love football** me encanta el fútbol; **I love going to** OR **to go to the theatre** me encanta ir al teatro.

love affair n aventura f amorosa.

love life n vida f amorosa.

lovely ['lʌvlɪ] adj - **1.** [beautiful - person] encantador(ra); [- dress, place] precioso(sa) - **2.** [pleasant] estupendo(da).

lover ['lʌvəʳ] n - **1.** [sexual partner] amante mf - **2.** [enthusiast] amante mf, aficionado m, -da f.

loving ['lʌvɪŋ] adj cariñoso(sa).

low [ləʊ] ◇ adj - **1.** [gen] bajo(ja); **in the low twenties** 20 y algo; **a low trick** una mala jugada - **2.** [little remaining] escaso(sa) - **3.** [unfavourable - opinion] malo(la); [- esteem] poco(ca) - **4.** [dim] tenue - **5.** [dress, neckline] escotado(da) - **6.** [depressed] deprimido(da). ◇ adv - **1.** [gen] bajo; **the batteries are running low** las pilas están acabándose; **morale is running very low** la moral está por los suelos; **low paid** mal pagado - **2.** [speak] en voz baja. ◇ n - **1.** [low point] punto m más bajo - **2.** METEOR [low pressure area] área f de bajas presiones; [lowest temperature] mínima f.

low-calorie adj light (inv), bajo(ja) en calorías.

low-cut adj escotado(da).

lower ['ləʊəʳ] ◇ adj inferior. ◇ vt - **1.** [gen] bajar; [flag] arriar - **2.** [reduce] reducir.

low-fat adj bajo(ja) en grasas.

low-key adj discreto(ta).

lowly ['ləʊlɪ] *adj* humilde.

low-lying *adj* bajo(ja).

loyal ['lɔɪəl] *adj* leal, fiel.

loyalty ['lɔɪəltɪ] *n* lealtad *f*.

lozenge ['lɒzɪndʒ] *n* - 1. [tablet] pastilla *f* - 2. [shape] rombo *m*.

LP (*abbr of* **long-playing record**) *n* LP *m*.

LPG [ˌelpiːˈdʒiː] (*abbr of* **liquified petroleum gas**) *n* GLP *m*.

L-plate *n* UK placa *f* L (de prácticas).

Ltd, ltd (*abbr of* **limited**) S.L.

lubricant ['luːbrɪkənt] *n* lubricante *m*.

lubricate ['luːbrɪkeɪt] *vt* lubricar.

lucid ['luːsɪd] *adj* - 1. [clear] claro(ra) - 2. [not confused] lúcido(da).

luck [lʌk] *n* suerte *f*; **good/bad luck** [good, bad fortune] buena/mala suerte; **good luck!** [said to express best wishes] ¡suerte!; **bad OR hard luck!** ¡mala suerte!; **to be in luck** estar de suerte; **to try one's luck at sthg** probar suerte a OR con algo; **with (any) luck** con un poco de suerte.

luckily ['lʌkɪlɪ] *adv* afortunadamente.

lucky ['lʌkɪ] *adj* - 1. [fortunate - person] afortunado(da); [- event] oportuno(na); **to be lucky** [person] tener suerte; **it's lucky he came** fue una suerte que llegara - 2. [bringing good luck] que trae buena suerte.

lucrative ['luːkrətɪv] *adj* lucrativo(va).

ludicrous ['luːdɪkrəs] *adj* absurdo(da).

lug [lʌg] *vt inf* arrastrar.

luggage ['lʌgɪdʒ] *n* UK equipaje *m*.

luggage rack *n* UK [of car] baca *f*; [in train] portaequipajes *m inv*.

lukewarm ['luːkwɔːm] *adj* - 1. [tepid] tibio(bia), templado(da) - 2. [unenthusiastic] indiferente.

lull [lʌl] ◇ *n*: **the lull before the storm** *fig* la calma antes de la tormenta. ◇ *vt*: **to lull sb into a false sense of security** infundir una sensación de falsa seguridad a alguien; **to lull sb to sleep** adormecer OR hacer dormir a alguien.

lullaby ['lʌləbaɪ] *n* nana *f*, canción *f* de cuna.

lumber ['lʌmbə*ʳ*] *n (U)* - 1. US [timber] maderos *mpl* - 2. UK [bric-a-brac] trastos *mpl*.

➤ **lumber with** *vt sep UK inf*: **to lumber sb with sthg** cargar a alguien con algo.

lumberjack ['lʌmbədʒæk] *n* leñador *m*, -ra *f*.

luminous ['luːmɪnəs] *adj* luminoso(sa).

lump [lʌmp] ◇ *n* - 1. [of coal, earth] trozo *m*; [of sugar] terrón *m*; [in sauce] grumo *m* - 2. [on body] bulto *m* - 3. *fig* [in throat] nudo *m*. ◇ *vt*: **to lump sthg together** [things] amontonar algo; [people, beliefs] agrupar OR juntar algo.

lump sum *n* suma *f* OR cantidad *f* global.

lumpy ['lʌmpɪ] (*comp* **-ier**, *superl* **-iest**) *adj* [sauce] grumoso(sa); [mattress] lleno(na) de bultos.

lunacy ['luːnəsɪ] *n* locura *f*.

lunar ['luːnə*ʳ*] *adj* lunar.

lunatic ['luːnətɪk] *n* - 1. *pej* [fool] idiota *mf* - 2. [insane person] loco *m*, -ca *f*.

lunch [lʌntʃ] ◇ *n* comida *f*, almuerzo *m*; **to have lunch** almorzar, comer; **why don't we do lunch some time?** ¿por qué no almorzamos juntos algún día de estos? ◇ *vi* almorzar, comer.

luncheon ['lʌntʃən] *n* comida *f*, almuerzo *m*.

luncheon meat *n* carne de cerdo en lata troceada.

luncheon voucher *n* UK vale *m* del almuerzo.

lunch hour *n* hora *f* del almuerzo.

lunchtime ['lʌntʃtaɪm] *n* hora *f* del almuerzo.

lung [lʌŋ] *n* pulmón *m*.

lunge [lʌndʒ] *vi* lanzarse; **to lunge at sb** arremeter contra alguien.

lurch [lɜːtʃ] ◇ *n* [of boat] bandazo *m*; [of person] tumbo *m*; **to leave sb in the lurch** dejar a alguien en la estacada. ◇ *vi* [boat] dar bandazos; [person] tambalearse.

lure [ljʊə*ʳ*] ◇ *n* atracción *f*. ◇ *vt* atraer.

lurid ['ljʊərɪd] *adj* - 1. [brightly coloured] chillón(ona) - 2. [shockingly unpleasant] espeluznante - 3. [sensational] escabroso(sa).

lurk [lɜːk] *vi* - 1. [person] estar al acecho - 2. [memory, danger, fear] ocultarse.

luscious ['lʌʃəs] *adj lit & fig* apetitoso(sa).

lush [lʌʃ] *adj* [luxuriant] exuberante.

lust [lʌst] *n* - 1. [sexual desire] lujuria *f* - 2. [strong desire]: **lust for sthg** ansia *f* de algo.

➤ **lust after, lust for** *vt insep* - 1. [desire - wealth, success] codiciar - 2. [desire sexually] desear.

lusty ['lʌstɪ] *adj* vigoroso(sa).

Luxembourg ['lʌksəmˌbɜːg] *n* Luxemburgo.

luxuriant [lʌgˈʒʊərɪənt] *adj* exuberante.

luxurious [lʌgˈʒʊərɪəs] *adj* [gen] lujoso(sa); [lifestyle] de lujo.

luxury ['lʌkʃərɪ] ◇ *n* lujo *m*. ◇ *comp* de lujo.

LW (*abbr of* **long wave**) *n* OL *f*.

Lycra® ['laɪkrə] *n* lycra® *f*.

lying ['laɪɪŋ] ◇ *adj* mentiroso(sa). ◇ *n (U)* mentiras *fpl*.

lynch [lɪntʃ] *vt* linchar.

lyric ['lɪrɪk] *adj* lírico(ca).

lyrical ['lɪrɪkl] *adj* [poetic] lírico(ca).

lyrics ['lɪrɪks] *npl* letra *f*.

m¹ (*pl* m's *OR* ms), **M** (*pl* M's *OR* Ms) [em] *n* [letter] m f, M f. ◆ **M** *abbr of* **motorway**.

m² - **1.** (*abbr of* metre) m - **2.** (*abbr of* million) m - **3.** *abbr of* **mile**.

MA *n abbr of* **Master of Arts**.

mac [mæk] (*abbr of* mackintosh) *n UK inf* [coat] impermeable m.

macaroni [,mækə'rəʊnɪ] *n (U)* macarrones *mpl*.

mace [meɪs] *n* - **1.** [ornamental rod] maza f - **2.** [spice] macis f *inv*.

machine [mə'ʃiːn] ◇ *n* - **1.** [power-driven device] máquina f - **2.** [organization] aparato m. ◇ *vt* - **1.** SEW coser a máquina - **2.** TECH producir a máquina.

machinegun [mə'ʃiːngʌn] *n* [with tripod] ametralladora f; [hand-held] metralleta f.

machine language *n* COMPUT lenguaje m máquina.

machinery [mə'ʃiːnərɪ] *n lit* & *fig* maquinaria f.

macho ['mætʃəʊ] *adj inf* macho.

mackerel ['mækrəl] (*pl* mackerel *OR* -s) *n* caballa f.

mackintosh ['mækɪntɒʃ] *n UK* impermeable m.

mad [mæd] *adj* - **1.** [gen] loco(ca); [attempt, idea] disparatado(da); **to be mad about sb/sthg** estar loco(ca) por alguien/algo; **to go mad** volverse loco - **2.** [furious] furioso(sa) - **3.** [hectic] desenfrenado(da).

Madagascar [,mædə'gæskəʳ] *n* Madagascar.

madam ['mædəm] *n* - **1.** [woman] señora f - **2.** [in brothel] madam f.

madcap ['mædkæp] *adj* descabellado(da).

mad cow disease *n* el mal de las vacas locas.

madden ['mædn] *vt* volver loco(ca).

made [meɪd] *pt* & *pp* ▷ **make**.

Madeira [mə'dɪərə] *n* - **1.** [wine] madeira m, madera m - **2.** GEOG Madeira.

made-to-measure *adj* hecho(cha) a la medida.

made-up *adj* - **1.** [with make-up - face, person] maquillado(da); [- lips, eyes] pintado(da) - **2.** [invented] inventado(da).

madly ['mædlɪ] *adv* [frantically] enloquecidamente; **madly in love** locamente enamorado.

madman ['mædmən] (*pl* -men [-mən]) *n* loco m.

madness [mædnɪs] *n lit* & *fig* locura f.

Madrid [mə'drɪd] *n* Madrid.

Mafia ['mæfɪə] *n*: **the Mafia** la mafia.

magazine [,mægə'ziːn] *n* - **1.** [periodical] revista f - **2.** [news programme] magazín m - **3.** [on a gun] recámara f.

maggot ['mægət] *n* gusano m, larva f.

magic ['mædʒɪk] ◇ *adj* [gen] mágico(ca). ◇ *n* magia f.

magical ['mædʒɪkl] *adj lit* & *fig* mágico(ca).

magician [mə'dʒɪʃn] *n* - **1.** [conjuror] prestidigitador m, -ra f - **2.** [wizard] mago m.

magistrate ['mædʒɪstreɪt] *n* juez mf de primera instancia.

magistrates' court *n UK* juzgado m de primera instancia.

magnanimous [mæg'nænɪməs] *adj* magnánimo(ma).

magnate ['mægneɪt] *n* magnate mf.

magnesium [mæg'niːzɪəm] *n* magnesio m.

magnet ['mægnɪt] *n* imán m.

magnetic [mæg'netɪk] *adj* - **1.** [attracting iron] magnético(ca) - **2.** *fig* [appealingly forceful] carismático(ca).

magnetic tape *n* cinta f magnética.

magnificent [mæg'nɪfɪsənt] *adj* [building, splendour] grandioso(sa); [idea, book, game] magnífico(ca).

magnify ['mægnɪfaɪ] *vt* - **1.** [in vision] aumentar, ampliar - **2.** [in the mind] exagerar.

magnifying glass ['mægnɪfaɪɪŋ-] *n* lupa f.

magnitude ['mægnɪtjuːd] *n* magnitud f.

magpie ['mægpaɪ] *n* urraca f.

mahogany [mə'hɒgənɪ] *n* - **1.** [wood] caoba f - **2.** [colour] caoba m.

maid [meɪd] *n* [in hotel] camarera f; [domestic] criada f.

maiden ['meɪdn] ◇ *adj* inaugural. ◇ *n liter* doncella f.

maiden aunt *n* tía f soltera.

maiden name *n* nombre m de soltera.

mail [meɪl] ◇ *n* - **1.** [system] correo m; **by mail** por correo - **2.** [letters, parcels received] correspondencia f. ◇ *vt esp US* [send] mandar por correo; [put in mail box] echar al buzón.

mailbox ['meɪlbɒks] *n* - **1.** *US* [letterbox] buzón m - **2.** COMPUT buzón m.

mailing list ['meɪlɪŋ-] *n* [for mailshots] lista f de distribución de publicidad *OR* información; COMPUT lista f de correo.

mailman ['meɪlmən] (*pl* -men [-mən]) *n US* cartero m.

mail order *n* venta f por correo.

mailshot ['meɪlʃɒt] n folleto m de publicidad (por correo).

maim [meɪm] vt mutilar.

main [meɪn] ◇ adj principal. ◇ n [pipe] tubería f principal; [wire] cable m principal. ▪ **mains** npl: **the mains** [gas, water] la tubería principal; [electricity] la red eléctrica. ▪ **in the main** adv por lo general.

main course n plato m fuerte.

mainframe (computer) ['meɪnfreɪm-] n unidad f central.

mainland ['meɪnlənd] ◇ adj continental; **mainland Spain** la Península. ◇ n: **on the mainland** en tierra firme.

mainly ['meɪnlɪ] adv principalmente.

main road n carretera f principal.

mainstay ['meɪnsteɪ] n fundamento m.

mainstream ['meɪnstriːm] ◇ adj [gen] predominante; [taste] corriente; [political party] convencional. ◇ n: **the mainstream** la tendencia general.

maintain [meɪn'teɪn] vt - 1. [gen] mantener - 2. [support, provide for] sostener - 3. [assert]: **to maintain (that)** sostener que.

maintenance ['meɪntənəns] n - 1. [gen] mantenimiento m - 2. [money] pensión f alimenticia.

maize [meɪz] n maíz m.

majestic [mə'dʒestɪk] adj majestuoso(sa).

majesty ['mædʒəstɪ] n [grandeur] majestad f. ▪ **Majesty** n: **His/Her/Your Majesty** Su Majestad.

major ['meɪdʒər] ◇ adj - 1. [important] importante; [main] principal; **of major importance** de gran importancia - 2. MUS mayor. ◇ n MIL comandante m; US [subject] especialidad f.

Majorca [mə'jɔːkə, mə'dʒɔːkə] n Mallorca f.

majority [mə'dʒɒrətɪ] n mayoría f.

make [meɪk] ◇ vt (pt & pp made) - 1. [produce] hacer; **she makes her own clothes** se hace su propia ropa - 2. [perform - action] hacer; **to make a speech** pronunciar OR dar un discurso; **to make a decision** tomar una decisión; **to make a mistake** cometer un error; **to make a payment** efectuar un pago - 3. [cause to be, cause to do] hacer; **it makes me sick** me pone enfermo; **it makes me want to...** me da ganas de...; **it made him angry** hizo que se enfadara; **you made me jump!** ¡vaya susto que me has dado!; **to make sb happy** hacer a alguien feliz; **to make sb sad** entristecer a alguien - 4. [force]: **to make sb do sthg** hacer que alguien haga algo, obligar a alguien a hacer algo - 5. [construct]: **it's made of wood/metal** está hecho de madera/metal; **made in Spain** fabricado en España - 6. [add up to] hacer, ser; **2 and 2 make 4** 2 y 2 hacen OR son 4 - 7. [calculate]

calcular; **I make it 50/six o'clock** calculo que serán 50/las seis; **what time do you make it?** ¿qué hora tienes? - 8. [earn] ganar; **to make a profit** obtener beneficios; **to make a loss** sufrir pérdidas - 9. [have the right qualities for] ser; **she'd make a good doctor** seguro que sería una buena doctora - 10. [reach] llegar a - 11. [gain - friend, enemy] hacer; **to make friends with sb** hacerse amigo de alguien

▶▶ **to make it** [arrive in time] conseguir llegar a tiempo; [be a success] alcanzar el éxito; [be able to attend] venir/ir; [survive] vivir. ◇ n [brand] marca f. ▪ **make for** vt insep - 1. [move towards] dirigirse a OR hacia - 2. [contribute to] contribuir a. ▪ **make into** vt sep: **to make sthg into sthg** convertir algo en algo. ▪ **make of** vt sep - 1. [understand] entender; **what do you make of this word?** ¿qué entiendes tú por esta palabra? - 2. [have opinion of] opinar de. ▪ **make off** vi darse a la fuga. ▪ **make out** ◇ vt sep - 1. [see] distinguir; [hear] entender, oír - 2. [understand - word, number] descifrar; [- person, attitude] comprender - 3. [fill out - form] rellenar; [- cheque, receipt] extender; [- list] hacer - 4. inf [pretend]: **to make o.s. out to be sthg** dárselas de algo. ◇ vi US inf [sexually] darse el lote, fajar Méx. ▪ **make up** ◇ vt sep - 1. [compose, constitute] componer, constituir - 2. [invent] inventar - 3. [apply cosmetics to] maquillar - 4. [prepare - parcel, prescription, bed] preparar - 5. [make complete - amount] completar; [- difference] cubrir; [- deficit, lost time] recuperar. ◇ n US [test] **examen que se realiza más tarde si no se pude hacer en su día.** ▪ **make up for** vt insep compensar.

make-believe n (U) fantasías fpl.

makeover ['meɪkəʊvər] n [of person] cambio m de imagen; [of home, garden] reforma f completa.

maker ['meɪkər] n [of film, programme] creador m, -ra f; [of product] fabricante mf.

makeshift ['meɪkʃɪft] adj [temporary] provisional; [improvized] improvisado(da).

make-up n - 1. [cosmetics] maquillaje m; **make-up remover** loción f OR leche f desmaquilladora - 2. [person's character] carácter m - 3. [structure] estructura f; [of team] composición f.

making ['meɪkɪŋ] n [of product] fabricación f; [of film] rodaje m; [of decision] toma f; **this is history in the making** esto pasará a la historia; **your problems are of your own making** tus problemas te los has buscado tú mismo; **to be the making of sb/sthg** ser la causa del éxito de alguien/algo; **to have the makings of** tener madera de.

malaise [mæ'leɪz] n fml malestar m.

malaria [mə'leərɪə] n malaria f.

Malaya [mə'leɪə] n Malaya.

Malaysia [mə'leɪzɪə] n Malaisia.

male [meɪl] <> adj - **1.** [animal] macho
- **2.** [human] masculino(na), varón - **3.** [concerning men] masculino(na). <> n - **1.** [animal] macho m - **2.** [human] varón m.

male nurse n enfermero m.

malevolent [mə'levələnt] adj malévolo(la).

malfunction [mæl'fʌŋkʃn] <> n fallo m.
<> vi averiarse.

malice ['mælɪs] n malicia f.

malicious [mə'lɪʃəs] adj malicioso(sa).

malign [mə'laɪn] <> adj maligno(na), perjudicial. <> vt fml difamar.

malignant [mə'lɪgnənt] adj - **1.** MED maligno(na) - **2.** fml [full of hate] malvado(da).

mall [mɔːl] n esp US: **(shopping) mall** centro m comercial peatonal.

mallet ['mælɪt] n mazo m.

malnutrition [,mælnjuː'trɪʃn] n malnutrición f.

malpractice [,mæl'præktɪs] n (U) LAW negligencia f.

malt [mɔːlt] n - **1.** [grain] malta f - **2.** [whisky] whisky m de malta - **3.** US leche malteada con helado.

Malta ['mɔːltə] n Malta.

mammal ['mæml] n mamífero m.

mammogram ['mæməgræm] n MED mamografía f.

mammoth ['mæməθ] <> adj descomunal.
<> n mamut m.

man [mæn] <> n (pl **men**) - **1.** [gen] hombre m; **the man in the street** el hombre de la calle, el ciudadano de a pie; **to be man enough to do sthg** ser lo suficientemente hombre para hacer algo - **2.** [humankind] el hombre. <> vt [gen] manejar; [ship, plane] tripular; **manned 24 hours a day** [telephone] en servicio las 24 horas del día.

manage ['mænɪdʒ] <> vi - **1.** [cope] poder
- **2.** [survive] apañárselas. <> vt - **1.** [succeed]:
to manage to do sthg conseguir hacer algo
- **2.** [company] dirigir, llevar; [money] administrar, manejar; [pop star] representar; [time] organizar - **3.** [cope with] poder con; **can you manage that box?** ¿puedes con la caja?

manageable ['mænɪdʒəbl] adj [task] factible, posible; [children] dominable; [inflation, rate] controlable.

management ['mænɪdʒmənt] n - **1.** [control, running] gestión f - **2.** [people in control] dirección f.

manager ['mænɪdʒəʳ] n - **1.** [of company] director m, -ra f; [of shop] jefe m, -fa f; [of pop star] manager mf - **2.** SPORT ≃ entrenador m.

manageress [,mænɪdʒə'res] n UK [of company] directora f; [of shop] jefa f.

managerial [,mænɪ'dʒɪərɪəl] adj directivo(va).

managing director ['mænɪdʒɪŋ-] n director m, -ra f gerente.

mandarin ['mændərɪn] n [fruit] mandarina f.

mandate ['mændeɪt] n - **1.** [elected right or authority] mandato m; **to have a mandate to do sthg** tener autoridad para hacer algo - **2.** [task] misión f.

mandatory ['mændətrɪ] adj obligatorio(ria).

mane [meɪn] n [of horse] crin f; [of lion] melena f.

maneuver US = **manoeuvre**.

manfully ['mænfʊlɪ] adv valientemente.

mangle ['mæŋgl] vt [crush] aplastar; [tear to pieces] despedazar.

mango ['mæŋgəʊ] (pl **-es** OR **-s**) n mango m.

mangy ['meɪndʒɪ] adj sarnoso(sa).

manhandle ['mæn,hændl] vt [person]: **they manhandled her into the van** la metieron en el camión a empujones.

manhole ['mænhəʊl] n boca f (del alcantarillado).

manhood ['mænhʊd] n - **1.** [state] virilidad f
- **2.** [time] edad f adulta.

manhour ['mæn,aʊəʳ] n hora f hombre.

mania ['meɪnjə] n - **1.** [excessive liking]: **mania (for)** pasión f (por) - **2.** PSYCHOL manía f.

maniac ['meɪnɪæk] n - **1.** [madman] maníaco m, -ca f - **2.** [fanatic] fanático m, -ca f.

manic ['mænɪk] adj maníaco(ca).

manicure ['mænɪ,kjʊəʳ] n manicura f.

manifest ['mænɪfest] fml <> adj manifiesto(ta). <> vt manifestar.

manifesto [,mænɪ'festəʊ] (pl **-s** OR **-es**) n manifiesto m.

manipulate [mə'nɪpjʊleɪt] vt - **1.** [control for personal benefit] manipular - **2.** [controls, lever] manejar.

mankind [mæn'kaɪnd] n la humanidad.

manly ['mænlɪ] adj varonil, viril.

man-made adj [environment, problem, disaster] producido(da) por el hombre; [fibre, lake, goods] artificial.

manner ['mænəʳ] n - **1.** [method] manera f, forma f - **2.** [bearing, attitude] actitud f - **3.** liter [type, sort] tipo m, clase f. ◆ **manners** npl modales mpl; **it's good/bad manners to do sthg** es de buena/mala educación hacer algo.

mannerism ['mænərɪzm] n costumbre f (típica de uno).

mannish ['mænɪʃ] adj [woman] hombruno(na).

manoeuvre UK, **maneuver** US [mə'nu:vər] ◇ n lit & fig maniobra f. ◇ vt maniobrar. ◇ vi maniobrar.

manor ['mænər] n [house] casa f solariega.

manpower ['mæn,pauər] n [manual workers] mano f de obra; [white-collar workers] personal m.

mansion ['mænʃn] n [manor] casa f solariega; [big house] casa grande.

manslaughter ['mæn,slɔ:tər] n homicidio m involuntario.

mantelpiece ['mæntlpi:s] n repisa f (de la chimenea).

manual ['mænjuəl] ◇ adj manual. ◇ n manual m.

manual worker n obrero m, -ra f.

manufacture [,mænju'fæktʃər] ◇ n fabricación f. ◇ vt [make] fabricar.

manufacturer [,mænju'fæktʃərər] n fabricante mf.

manure [mə'njuər] n estiércol m.

manuscript ['mænjuskrıpt] n - 1. [gen] manuscrito m - 2. [in exam] hoja f de examen.

many ['menı] ◇ adj (comp more, superl most) muchos(chas); many people muchas personas, mucha gente; how many? ¿cuántos(tas) ?; I wonder how many people went me pregunto cuánta gente fue; too many demasiados(das); there weren't too many students no había muchos estudiantes; as many... as tantos(tas)... como; they have three times as many soldiers as us tienen el triple de soldados que nosotros; so many tantos(tas); I've never seen so many people nunca había visto tanta gente; a good OR great many muchísimos(mas). ◇ pron muchos(chas); twice as many el doble; four times as many cuatro veces esa cantidad.

map n mapa m. ◆ **map out** vt sep [map] planear, planificar.

maple ['meıpl] n arce m.

mar [ma:r] vt deslucir.

marathon ['mærəθn] n maratón m.

marauder [mə'rɔ:dər] n merodeador m, -ra f.

marble ['ma:bl] n - 1. [stone] mármol m - 2. [for game] canica f.

march [ma:tʃ] ◇ n - 1. MIL marcha f - 2. [of demonstrators] marcha f (de protesta) - 3. [steady progress] avance m. ◇ vi - 1. [in formation, in protest] marchar - 2. [speedily]: **to march up to sb** abordar a alguien decididamente. ◇ vt llevar por la fuerza.

March [ma:tʃ] n marzo m; see also **September**.

marcher ['ma:tʃər] n [protester] manifestante mf.

mare [meər] n yegua f.

margarine [,ma:dʒə'ri:n, ,ma:gə'ri:n] n margarina f.

marge [ma:dʒ] n inf margarina f.

margin ['ma:dʒın] n [gen] margen m.

marginal ['ma:dʒınl] adj - 1. [unimportant] marginal - 2. UK POL: **marginal seat** OR **constituency** escaño vulnerable a ser perdido en las elecciones por tener una mayoría escasa.

marginally ['ma:dʒınəlı] adv ligeramente.

marigold ['mærıgəuld] n caléndula f.

marihuana, marijuana [,mærı'wa:nə] n marihuana f.

marine [mə'ri:n] ◇ adj marino(na). ◇ n soldado m de infantería de marina.

marital ['mærıtl] adj matrimonial.

marital status n estado m civil.

maritime ['mærıtaım] adj marítimo(ma).

mark [ma:k] ◇ n - 1. [stain] mancha f; [scratch] marca f - 2. [written symbol - on paper] marca f; [- in the sand] señal f - 3. [in exam] nota f; [point] punto m; **to get good marks** sacar buenas notas - 4. [stage, level]: **once past the halfway mark** una vez llegado a medio camino - 5. [sign - of respect] señal f; [- of illness, old age] huella f - 6. [currency] marco m. ◇ vt - 1. [stain] manchar; [scratch] marcar - 2. [label - with initials etc] señalar - 3. [exam, essay] puntuar, calificar - 4. [identify - place] señalar; [- beginning, end] marcar - 5. [commemorate] conmemorar - 6. [characterize] caracterizar - 7. SPORT marcar. ◆ **mark off** vt sep [cross off] poner una marca en.

marked [ma:kt] adj [improvement] notable; [difference] acusado(da).

marker ['ma:kər] n - 1. [sign] señal f - 2. SPORT marcador m, -ora f.

marker pen n rotulador m.

market ['ma:kıt] ◇ n mercado m. ◇ vt comercializar.

market garden n esp UK [small] huerto m; [large] huerta f.

marketing ['ma:kıtıŋ] n [subject] marketing m; [selling] comercialización f.

marketplace ['ma:kıtpleıs] n lit & fig mercado m.

market research n estudio m de mercados.

market value n valor m actual OR en venta.

marking ['ma:kıŋ] n - 1. [of exams etc] corrección f - 2. SPORT marcaje m. ◆ **markings** npl [of flower, animal] pintas fpl; [on road] señales fpl.

marksman ['ma:ksmən] (pl **-men** [-mən]) n tirador m.

marmalade ['ma:məleıd] n mermelada f (de cítricos).

maroon [mə'ru:n] adj granate.

marooned [mə'ru:nd] *adj* incomunica-
do(da), aislada(da).

marquee [mɑː'kɪ] *n* carpa *f*, toldo *m* grande;
US [of building] marquesina *f*.

marriage ['mærɪdʒ] *n* - **1.** [act] boda *f*
- **2.** [state, institution] matrimonio *m*.

marriage bureau *n* UK agencia *f* matrimonial.

marriage certificate *n* certificado *m* de
matrimonio.

marriage guidance *n* asesoría *f* matrimonial.

married ['mærɪd] *adj* - **1.** [person] casado(da);
a married couple un matrimonio - **2.** [life] matrimonial.

marrow ['mærəʊ] *n* - **1.** UK [vegetable] calabacín *m* grande - **2.** [in bones] médula *f*.

marry ['mærɪ] <> *vt* - **1.** [take as husband or
wife] casarse con; **to get married** casarse
- **2.** [sanction marriage of] casar. <> *vi* casarse.

Mars [mɑːz] *n* Marte *m*.

marsh [mɑːʃ] *n* - **1.** [area of land] zona *f* pan-
tanosa - **2.** [type of land] pantano *m*.

marshal ['mɑːʃl] <> *n* - **1.** MIL mariscal *m*
- **2.** [steward] oficial *m*, miembro *mf* del servicio de orden - **3.** US [officer] jefe *m*, -fa *f* de
policía. <> *vt* (UK *pt & pp* -**led**, *cont* -**ling**, US
pt & pp -**ed**, *cont* -**ing**) [people] dirigir, conducir; [thoughts] ordenar.

martial arts [ˌmɑːʃl-] *npl* artes *fpl* marciales.

martial law [ˌmɑːʃl-] *n* ley *f* marcial.

martyr ['mɑːtər] *n* mártir *mf*.

martyrdom ['mɑːtədəm] *n* martirio *m*.

marvel ['mɑːvl] <> *n* maravilla *f*. <> *vi* (UK
pt & pp -**led**, *cont* -**ling**, US *pt & pp* -**ed**,
cont -**ing**): **to marvel (at)** maravillarse OR
asombrarse (ante).

marvellous UK, **marvelous** US ['mɑːvələs]
adj maravilloso(sa).

Marxism ['mɑːksɪzm] *n* marxismo *m*.

Marxist ['mɑːksɪst] <> *adj* marxista. <> *n*
marxista *mf*.

marzipan ['mɑːzɪpæn] *n* mazapán *m*.

mascara [mæs'kɑːrə] *n* rímel *m*.

masculine ['mæskjʊlɪn] *adj* [gen] masculi-
no(na); [woman, appearance] hombruno(na).

mash [mæʃ] <> *n* inf puré *m* de patatas.
<> *vt* hacer puré.

mask [mɑːsk] <> *n* lit & fig máscara *f*. <> *vt*
- **1.** [to hide] enmascarar - **2.** [cover up] ocultar,
disfrazar.

masochist ['mæsəkɪst] *n* masoquista *mf*.

mason ['meɪsn] *n* - **1.** [stonemason] cantero *m*
- **2.** [freemason] masón *m*.

masonry ['meɪsnrɪ] *n* [stones] albañilería *f*.

masquerade [ˌmæskə'reɪd] *vi*: **to masquerade as** hacerse pasar por.

mass [mæs] <> *n* - **1.** [gen] masa *f* - **2.** [large
amount] montón *m* - **3.** [religious ceremony] misa *f*. <> *adj* [unemployment] masivo(va); [com-
munication] de masas. <> *vi* agruparse, concentrarse. ◆ **masses** *npl* - **1.** inf [lots]
montones *mpl* - **2.** [workers]: **the masses** las
masas.

massacre ['mæsəkər] <> *n* matanza *f*, masacre *f*. <> *vt* masacrar.

massage [UK 'mæsɑːʒ, US mə'sɑːʒ] <> *n*
masaje *m*. <> *vt* dar un masaje a.

massive ['mæsɪv] *adj* [gen] enorme; [majority]
aplastante.

mass media *n & npl*: **the mass media** los medios de comunicación de masas.

mass production *n* producción *f* OR fabricación *f* en serie.

mast [mɑːst] *n* - **1.** [on boat] mástil *m* - **2.** RADIO
& TV poste *m*, torre *f*.

master ['mɑːstər] <> *n* - **1.** [of people, animals]
amo *m*, dueño *m*; [of house] señor *m* - **2.** fig
[of situation] dueño *m*, -ña *f* - **3.** UK [teacher -
primary school] maestro *m*; [- secondary school]
profesor *m* - **4.** [of recording] original *m*. <> *adj*
maestro(tra). <> *vt* - **1.** [situation] dominar,
controlar; [difficulty] superar - **2.** [technique etc]
dominar.

master key *n* llave *f* maestra.

masterly ['mɑːstəlɪ] *adj* magistral.

mastermind ['mɑːstəmaɪnd] <> *n* cerebro *m*. <> *vt* ser el cerebro de, dirigir.

Master of Arts (*pl* **Masters of Arts**) *n* - **1.** [de-
gree] máster *m* en Letras - **2.** [person] licenciado *m*, -da *f* con máster en Letras.

Master of Science (*pl* **Masters of Science**) *n*
- **1.** [degree] máster *m* en Ciencias - **2.** [person]
licenciado *m*, -da *f* con máster en Ciencias.

masterpiece ['mɑːstəpiːs] *n* lit & fig obra *f*
maestra.

master's degree *n* máster *m*.

mastery ['mɑːstərɪ] *n* dominio *m*.

mat [mæt] *n* - **1.** [rug] alfombrilla *f*; [beer mat]
posavasos *m* inv; [tablemat] salvamanteles *m*
inv - **2.** [doormat] felpudo *m*.

match [mætʃ] <> *n* - **1.** [game] partido *m*
- **2.** [for lighting] cerilla *f* - **3.** [equal]: **to be a
match for** estar a la altura de; **to be no match
for** no poder competir con. <> *vt* - **1.** [be the
same as] coincidir con - **2.** [pair off]: **to match
sthg (to)** emparejar algo (con) - **3.** [be equal
with] competir con - **4.** [go well with] hacer juego con. <> *vi* - **1.** [be the same] coincidir - **2.** [go
together well] hacer juego, combinar.

matchbox ['mætʃbɒks] *n* caja *f* de cerillas.

matching ['mætʃɪŋ] *adj* a juego.

mate [meɪt] <> *n* - **1.** inf [friend] amigo *m*,
-ga *f*, compañero *m*, -ra *f* - **2.** US [spouse] esposo *m*, -sa *f* - **3.** UK inf [term of address] colega *m*

- 4. [of animal] macho *m*, hembra *f* - **5.** NAUT: **(first) mate** (primer) oficial *m*. <> *vi* [animals]: **to mate (with)** aparearse (con).

material [mə'tɪərɪəl] <> *adj* - **1.** [physical] material - **2.** [important] sustancial. <> *n* - **1.** [substance] material *m* - **2.** [type of substance] materia *f* - **3.** [fabric] tela *f*, tejido *m* - **4.** [type of fabric] tejido *m* - **5.** (U) [ideas, information] información *f*, documentación *f*. ◆ **materials** *npl*: **building materials** materiales *mpl* de construcción; **writing materials** objetos *mpl* de escritorio; **cleaning materials** productos *mpl* de limpieza.

materialistic [mə,tɪərɪə'lɪstɪk] *adj* materialista.

maternal [mə'tɜːnl] *adj* [gen] maternal; [grandparent] materno(na).

maternity [mə'tɜːnətɪ] *n* maternidad *f*.

maternity dress *n* vestido *m* premamá.

maternity hospital *n* hospital *m* de maternidad.

maternity leave *n* baja *f* por maternidad.

math US = **maths**.

mathematical [,mæθə'mætɪkl] *adj* matemático(ca).

mathematics [,mæθə'mætɪks] *n* (U) matemáticas *fpl*.

maths UK [mæθs], **math** US [mæθ] (*abbr of* mathematics) *inf n* (U) mates *fpl*.

matinée [ˈmætɪneɪ] *n* [at cinema] primera sesión *f*; [at theatre] función *f* de tarde.

mating season [ˈmeɪtɪŋ-] *n* época *f* de celo.

matrices [ˈmeɪtrɪsiːz] *npl* ⊏▷ **matrix**.

matriculation [mə,trɪkjʊ'leɪʃn] *n* matrícula *f*.

matrimonial [,mætrɪ'məʊnjəl] *adj* matrimonial.

matrimony [ˈmætrɪmənɪ] *n* (U) matrimonio *m*.

matrix [ˈmeɪtrɪks] (*pl* matrices OR -es) *n* matriz *f*.

matron [ˈmeɪtrən] *n* - **1.** UK [in hospital] enfermera *f* jefa - **2.** [in school] mujer a cargo de la enfermería.

matronly [ˈmeɪtrənlɪ] *adj euph* [figure] corpulenta y de edad madura.

matt UK, **matte** US [mæt] *adj* mate.

matted [ˈmætɪd] *adj* enmarañado(da).

matter [ˈmætər] <> *n* - **1.** [question, situation] asunto *m*; **the fact** OR **truth of the matter is (that)...** la verdad es que...; **that's another** OR **a different matter** es otra cuestión OR cosa; **as a matter of course** automáticamente; **to make matters worse** para colmo de desgracias; **a matter of opinion** una cuestión de opiniones - **2.** [trouble, cause of pain]: **what's the matter (with it/her)?** ¿qué (le) pasa?;

something's the matter with my car algo le pasa a mi coche - **3.** PHYS materia *f* - **4.** (U) [material] material *m*. <> *vi* [be important] importar; **it doesn't matter** no importa. ◆ **as a matter of fact** *adv* en realidad. ◆ **for that matter** *adv* de hecho. ◆ **no matter** *adv*: **no matter how hard I try** por mucho que lo intente; **no matter what he does** haga lo que haga; **we must win, no matter what** tenemos que ganar como sea.

Matterhorn [ˈmætə,hɔːn] *n*: **the Matterhorn** el monte Cervino.

matter-of-fact *adj* pragmático(ca).

mattress [ˈmætrɪs] *n* colchón *m*.

mature [mə'tjʊər] <> *adj* [person, wine] maduro(ra); [cheese] curado(da). <> *vi* - **1.** [gen] madurar - **2.** [wine] envejecer.

mature student *n* UK UNIV estudiante *mf* adulto, -ta *f*.

maul [mɔːl] *vt* [savage] herir gravemente.

mauve [məʊv] *adj* malva.

max. [mæks] (*abbr of* maximum) máx.

maxim [ˈmæksɪm] (*pl* -s) *n* máxima *f*.

maximum [ˈmæksɪməm] <> *adj* máximo(ma). <> *n* (*pl* maxima OR -s) máximo *m*; **at the maximum** como máximo.

may [meɪ] *modal vb* poder; **the coast may be seen** se puede ver la costa; **you may like it** puede OR es posible que te guste; **I may come, I may not** puede que venga, puede que no; **will you do it? – I may do** ¿lo harás? – puede que sí; **it may be done in two different ways** puede hacerse de dos maneras (distintas); **may I come in?** ¿se puede (pasar)?; **may I?** ¿me permite?; **if I may so me permite; it may be cheap, but it's good** puede que sea barato, pero es bueno; **may all your dreams come true!** ¡que todos tus sueños se hagan realidad!; **be that as it may** aunque así sea; **come what may** pase lo que pase.

May [meɪ] *n* mayo *m*; *see also* **September**.

maybe [ˈmeɪbiː] *adv* - **1.** [perhaps] quizás, tal vez; **maybe she'll come** tal vez venga - **2.** [approximately] más o menos.

May Day *n* Primero *m* de Mayo.

mayhem [ˈmeɪhem] *n* alboroto *m*.

mayonnaise [,meɪə'neɪz] *n* mayonesa *f*.

mayor [meər] *n* alcalde *m*, -esa *f*.

mayoress [ˈmeərɪs] *n* alcaldesa *f*.

maze [meɪz] *n lit* & *fig* laberinto *m*.

MB (*abbr of* megabyte) MB *m*.

MD *n abbr of* **managing director**.

me [miː] *pers pron* - **1.** (*direct, indirect*) me; **can you see/hear me?** ¿me ves/oyes?; **it's me** soy yo; **they spoke to me** hablaron conmigo; **she gave it to me** me lo dio; **give it to me!** ¡dámelo! - **2.** (*stressed*): **you can't expect me to do it** no esperarás que yo lo haga - **3.** (*after* *prep*] mí; **they went with/without me** fueron conmigo/sin mí **- 4.** *(in comparisons)* yo, she's shorter than me (ella) es más baja que yo.

meadow ['medəʊ] *n* prado *m*, pradera *f*.

meagre *UK*, **meager** *US* ['miːgər] *adj* miserable, escaso(sa).

meal [miːl] *n* comida *f*.

mealtime ['miːltaɪm] *n* hora *f* de la comida.

mean [miːn] ⟨⟩ *vt* (*pt & pp* meant) **- 1.** [signify] significar, querer decir; **what does that word mean?** ¿qué quiere decir esa palabra?; **it means nothing to me** no significa nada para mí **- 2.** [have in mind] querer decir, referirse a; **what do you mean?** ¿qué quieres decir?; **do you know what I mean?** ¿sabes?; **to be meant for** estar destinado(da) a; **to be meant to do sthg** deber hacer algo; **that's not meant to be there** eso no debería estar allí; **it was meant to be a surprise** se suponía que era una sorpresa; **it was meant to be a joke** era solamente una broma; **to mean well** tener buenas intenciones **- 3.** [be serious about:] **I mean it** hablo OR lo digo en serio **- 4.** [be important, matter] significar; **it means a lot to us** significa mucho para nosotros **- 5.** [entail] suponer, implicar ▸▸▸ **I mean** quiero decir, o sea. ⟨⟩ *adj* **- 1.** [miserly] tacaño(ña) **- 2.** [unkind] mezquino(na), malo(la); **to be mean to sb** ser malo con alguien **- 3.** [average] medio(dia). ⟨⟩ *n* [average] promedio *m*, media *f*.

meander [mɪ'ændər] *vi* **- 1.** [river, road] serpentear **- 2.** [walk aimlessly] vagar; [write, speak aimlessly] divagar.

meaning ['miːnɪŋ] *n* **- 1.** [sense - of a word etc] significado *m* **- 2.** [significance] intención *f*, sentido *m* **- 3.** [purpose, point] propósito *m*, razón *f* de ser.

meaningful ['miːnɪŋfʊl] *adj* **- 1.** [expressive] significativo(va) **- 2.** [profound] profundo(da).

meaningless ['miːnɪŋlɪs] *adj* **- 1.** [without meaning, purpose] sin sentido **- 2.** [irrelevant, unimportant] irrelevante.

means [miːnz] ⟨⟩ *n* [method, way] medio *m*; **we have no means of doing it** no tenemos manera de hacerlo; **by means of** por medio de; **by legal means** legalmente. ⟨⟩ *npl* [money] recursos *mpl*. ▸ **by all means** *adv* por supuesto. ▸ **by no means** *adv* en absoluto.

meant [ment] *pt & pp* ⊳ **mean**.

meantime ['miːn,taɪm] *n*: **in the meantime** mientras tanto.

meanwhile ['miːn,waɪl] *adv* mientras tanto.

measles ['miːzlz] *n*: **(the) measles** sarampión *m*.

measly ['miːzlɪ] *adj inf* raquítico(ca).

measure ['meʒər] ⟨⟩ *n* **- 1.** [step, action] medida *f* **- 2.** [of alcohol] medida *f* **- 3.** [indication,

sign]: **a measure of** una muestra de **- 4.** *US* MUS compás *m*. ⟨⟩ *vt* [object] medir; [damage, impact etc] [...]

measurement ['meʒəmənt] *n* medida *f*.

meat [miːt] *n* **- 1.** [foodstuff] carne *f*; **cold meat** fiambre *m* **- 2.** [substance, content] sustancia *f*.

meatball ['miːtbɔːl] *n* albóndiga *f*.

meat pie *n UK* empanada *f* de carne.

meaty ['miːtɪ] *adj fig* sustancioso(sa).

Mecca ['mekə] *n* GEOG La Meca; *fig* meca *f*.

mechanic [mɪ'kænɪk] *n* mecánico *m*, -ca *f*. ▸ **mechanics** ⟨⟩ *n* (*U*) [study] mecánica *f*. ⟨⟩ *npl fig* mecanismos *mpl*.

mechanical [mɪ'kænɪkl] *adj* [worked by machinery, routine] mecánico(ca).

mechanism ['mekənɪzm] *n lit & fig* mecanismo *m*.

medal ['medl] *n* medalla *f*.

medallion [mɪ'dæljən] *n* medallón *m*.

meddle ['medl] *vi*: **to meddle (in)** entrometerse (en); **to meddle with sthg** manosear algo.

media ['miːdjə] ⟨⟩ *pl* ⊳ **medium**. ⟨⟩ *n & npl*: **the media** los medios de comunicación.

mediaeval [,medɪ'iːvl] = **medieval**.

median ['miːdjən] ⟨⟩ *adj* mediano(na). ⟨⟩ *n US* [of road] mediana *f*.

mediate ['miːdɪeɪt] *vi*: **to mediate (for/between)** mediar (por/entre).

mediator ['miːdɪeɪtər] *n* mediador *m*, -ra *f*.

Medicaid ['medɪkeɪd] *n US sistema estatal de ayuda médica*.

medical ['medɪkl] ⟨⟩ *adj* médico(ca). ⟨⟩ *n* reconocimiento *m* médico.

Medicare ['medɪkeər] *n US ayuda médica estatal para ancianos*.

medicated ['medɪkeɪtɪd] *adj* medicinal.

medicine ['medsɪn] *n* **- 1.** [treatment of illness] medicina *f*; **Doctor of Medicine** UNIV doctor *m*, -ra *f* en medicina **- 2.** [substance] medicina *f*, medicamento *m*.

medieval, mediaeval [,medɪ'iːvl] *adj* medieval.

mediocre [,miːdɪ'əʊkər] *adj* mediocre.

meditate ['medɪteɪt] *vi*: **to meditate (on OR upon)** meditar (sobre).

Mediterranean [,medɪtə'reɪnjən] ⟨⟩ *n* [sea]: **the Mediterranean (Sea)** el (mar) Mediterráneo. ⟨⟩ *adj* mediterráneo(a).

medium ['miːdjəm] ⟨⟩ *adj* mediano(na). ⟨⟩ *n* **- 1.** (*pl* media) [way of communicating] medio *m* **- 2.** (*pl* mediums) [spiritualist] médium *mf*.

medium-sized [-saɪzd] *adj* de tamaño mediano.

medium wave *n* onda *f* media.

medley ['medlɪ] (*pl* **medleys**) *n* - **1.** [mixture] mezcla *f* - **2.** [selection of music] popurrí *m*.

meek [mi:k] *adj* sumiso(sa), dócil.

meet [mi:t] ◇ *vt* (*pt & pp* **met**) - **1.** [by chance] encontrarse con; [for first time, come across] conocer; [by arrangement, for a purpose] reunirse con - **2.** [go to meet - person] ir/venir a buscar - **3.** [need, demand, condition] satisfacer; [target] cumplir con; [deadline] cumplir - **4.** [deal with - problem, challenge] hacer frente a - **5.** [costs, debts] pagar - **6.** [experience - problem, situation] encontrarse con - **7.** [hit, touch] darse OR chocar contra - **8.** [join] juntarse OR unirse con - **9.** [play against] enfrentarse con. ◇ *vi* (*pt & pp* **met**) - **1.** [by chance] encontrarse; [by arrangement] verse; [for a purpose] reunirse - **2.** [get to know sb] conocerse; **shall we meet at eight?** ¿quedamos a las ocho? - **3.** [hit in collision] chocar; [touch] tocar - **4.** [eyes] **their eyes met** sus miradas se cruzaron - **5.** [join - roads etc] juntarse - **6.** [play each other] enfrentarse. ◇ *n US* [meeting] encuentro *m*. ◆ **meet up** *vi*: **to meet up (with sb)** quedar (con alguien); **we're meeting up for lunch** hemos quedado para comer. ◆ **meet with** *vt insep* - **1.** [problems, resistance]: **meet with refusal** ser rechazado(da); **to meet with success** tener éxito; **to meet with failure** fracasar - **2.** *US* [by arrangement] reunirse con.

meeting ['mi:tɪŋ] *n* - **1.** [for discussions, business] reunión *f* - **2.** [by chance, in sport] encuentro *m*; [by arrangement] cita *f*; [formal] entrevista *f*.

megabyte ['megəbaɪt] *n* COMPUT megabyte *m*, mega *m*.

megaphone ['megəfəʊn] *n* megáfono *m*.

melancholy ['melənkəlɪ] ◇ *adj* melancólico(ca). ◇ *n* melancolía *f*.

mellow ['meləʊ] ◇ *adj* [sound, colour, light] suave; [wine] añejo(ja). ◇ *vi* [sound, light] suavizarse; [person] ablandarse.

melody ['melədɪ] *n* melodía *f*.

melon ['melən] *n* melón *m*.

melt [melt] ◇ *vt* - **1.** [make liquid] derretir - **2.** *fig* [soften] ablandar. ◇ *vi* - **1.** [become liquid] derretirse - **2.** *fig* [soften] ablandarse - **3.** [disappear]: **to melt away** [savings] esfumarse; [anger] desvanecerse. ◆ **melt down** *vt sep* fundir.

meltdown ['meltdaʊn] *n* - **1.** [act of melting] fusión *f* - **2.** [incident] fuga *f* radiactiva.

melting pot ['meltɪŋ-] *n fig* crisol *m*.

member ['membər] *n* - **1.** [of social group] miembro *mf* - **2.** [of party, union] afiliado *m*, -da *f*; [of organization, club] socio *m*, -cia *f* - **3.** [limb, penis] miembro *m*.

Member of Congress (*pl* **Members of Congress**) *n* miembro *mf* del Congreso (*de los Estados Unidos*).

Member of Parliament (*pl* **Members of Parliament**) *n UK* diputado *m*, -da *f* (*del parlamento británico*).

membership ['membəʃɪp] *n* - **1.** [of party, union] afiliación *f*; [of club] calidad *f* de socio - **2.** [number of members - of party, union] número *m* de afiliados - **3.** [people themselves]: **the membership** [of organization] los miembros; **the** [of party, union] los afiliados; [of club] los socios.

membership card *n* [of party, union] carnet *m* de afiliado, -da *f*; [of club] carnet *m* de socio, -cia *f*.

memento [mɪ'mentəʊ] (*pl* **-s**) *n* recuerdo *m*.

memo ['meməʊ] (*pl* **-s**) *n* memorándum *m*.

memoirs ['memwɑ:z] *npl* memorias *fpl*.

memorandum [,memə'rændəm] (*pl* **-da** [-də] OR **-dums**) *n fml* memorándum *m*.

memorial [mɪ'mɔ:rɪəl] ◇ *adj* conmemorativo(va). ◇ *n* monumento *m* conmemorativo.

memorize, -ise ['meməraɪz] *vt* memorizar, aprender de memoria.

memory ['memərɪ] *n* - **1.** [faculty, of computer] memoria *f* - **2.** [thing or things remembered] recuerdo *m*; **from memory** de memoria.

men [men] *npl* ▷ **man**.

menace ['menəs] ◇ *n* - **1.** [threat] amenaza *f*; [danger] peligro *m* - **2.** *inf* [nuisance, pest] pesadez *f*. ◇ *vt* amenazar.

menacing ['menəsɪŋ] *adj* amenazador(ra).

mend [mend] ◇ *n inf*: **to be on the mend** ir recuperándose. ◇ *vt* [shoes, toy] arreglar; [socks] zurcir; [clothes] remendar.

menial ['mi:njəl] *adj* servil, de baja categoría.

meningitis [,menɪn'dʒaɪtɪs] *n* (*U*) meningitis *f inv*.

menopause ['menəpɔ:z] *n*: **the menopause** la menopausia.

men's room *n US*: **the men's room** los servicios de caballeros.

menstruation [,menstrʊ'eɪʃn] *n* menstruación *f*.

menswear ['menzweər] *n* ropa *f* de caballeros.

mental ['mentl] *adj* mental.

mental hospital *n* hospital *m* psiquiátrico.

mentality [men'tælətɪ] *n* mentalidad *f*.

mentally handicapped ['mentəlɪ-] *npl*: **the mentally handicapped** los disminuidos psíquicos.

mention ['menʃn] ◇ *vt*: **to mention sthg (to)** mencionar algo (a); **not to mention** sin mencionar, además de; **don't mention it!** ¡de nada!, ¡no hay de qué! ◇ *n* mención *f*.

menu ['menju:] *n* - **1.** [in restaurant] carta *f* - **2.** COMPUT menú *m*.

meow *US* = **miaow**.

MEP (abbr of Member of the European Parliament) n eurodiputado m, -da f.

mercenary ['mɜːsɪnrɪ] ◇ adj mercenario(ria). ◇ n mercenario m, -ria f.

merchandise ['mɜːtʃəndaɪz] n (U) mercancías fpl, géneros mpl.

merchant ['mɜːtʃənt] ◇ adj [seaman, ship] mercante. ◇ n comerciante mf.

merchant bank n UK banco m mercantil.

merchant navy UK, **merchant marine** US n marina f mercante.

merciful ['mɜːsɪfʊl] adj - **1.** [showing mercy] compasivo(va) - **2.** [fortunate] afortunado(da).

merciless ['mɜːsɪlɪs] adj despiadado(da).

mercury ['mɜːkjʊrɪ] n mercurio m.

Mercury ['mɜːkjʊrɪ] n Mercurio m.

mercy ['mɜːsɪ] n - **1.** [kindness, pity] compasión f; **to have mercy on** apiadarse de; **to beg for mercy** pedir clemencia; **at the mercy of** fig a merced de - **2.** [blessing] suerte f.

mere [mɪəʳ] adj simple, mero(ra); **she's a mere child** no es más que una niña.

merely ['mɪəlɪ] adv simplemente, sólo.

merge [mɜːdʒ] ◇ vt - **1.** [gen] mezclar - **2.** COMM & COMPUT fusionar. ◇ vi - **1.** [join, combine]: **to merge (with)** [company] fusionarse (con); [roads, branches] unirse OR convergir (con) - **2.** [blend - colours] fundirse; **to merge into** confundirse con.

merger ['mɜːdʒəʳ] n COMM fusión f.

meringue [mə'ræŋ] n merengue m.

merit ['merɪt] ◇ n mérito m. ◇ vt merecer, ser digno(na) de. ◆ **merits** npl ventajas fpl; **to judge sthg on its merits** evaluar OR juzgar algo según sus méritos.

mermaid ['mɜːmeɪd] n sirena f.

merry ['merɪ] adj - **1.** [gen] alegre - **2.** [party] animado(da); **Merry Christmas!** ¡feliz Navidad! - **3.** inf [tipsy] achispado(da).

merry-go-round n tiovivo m.

mesh [meʃ] ◇ n malla f. ◇ vi fig encajar.

mesmerize, -ise ['mezməraɪz] vt: **to be mesmerized (by)** estar fascinado(da) (por).

mess [mes] n - **1.** [untidy state] desorden m; **to make a mess of sthg** hacer algo muy mal - **2.** [muddle, problematic situation] lío m - **3.** MIL [room] comedor m; [food] rancho m. ◆ **mess about, mess around** inf ◇ vt sep vacilar. ◇ vi - **1.** [waste time] pasar el rato; [fool around] hacer el tonto - **2.** [interfere]: **to mess about with sthg** manosear algo. ◆ **mess up** vt sep inf - **1.** [clothes] ensuciar; [room] desordenar - **2.** [plan, evening] echar a perder.

message ['mesɪdʒ] n - **1.** [piece of information] mensaje m, recado m - **2.** [of book etc] mensaje m.

messenger ['mesɪndʒəʳ] n mensajero m, -ra f.

Messrs, Messrs. ['mesəz] (abbr of messieurs) Sres.

messy ['mesɪ] adj [dirty] sucio(cia); [untidy] desordenado(da).

met [met] pt & pp ▷ **meet**.

metal ['metl] ◇ n metal m. ◇ comp de metal, metálico(ca).

metallic [mɪ'tælɪk] adj - **1.** [gen] metálico(ca) - **2.** [paint, finish] metalizado(da).

metalwork ['metlwɜːk] n [craft] metalistería f.

metaphor ['metəfəʳ] n metáfora f.

mete [miːt] ◆ **mete out** vt sep: **to mete sthg out to sb** imponer algo a alguien.

meteor ['miːtɪəʳ] n bólido m.

meteorology [,miːtjə'rɒlədʒɪ] n meteorología f.

meter ['miːtəʳ] n - **1.** [device] contador m - **2.** US = **metre**.

method ['meθəd] n método m.

methodical [mɪ'θɒdɪkl] adj metódico(ca).

Methodist ['meθədɪst] ◇ adj metodista. ◇ n metodista mf.

meths [meθs] n UK inf alcohol m metilado OR desnaturalizado.

methylated spirits ['meθɪleɪtɪd-] n alcohol m metilado OR desnaturalizado.

meticulous [mɪ'tɪkjʊləs] adj meticuloso(sa), minucioso(sa).

metre UK, **meter** US ['miːtəʳ] n metro m.

metric ['metrɪk] adj métrico(ca).

metronome ['metrənəʊm] n metrónomo m.

metropolitan [,metrə'pɒlɪtn] adj [of a metropolis] metropolitano(na).

mettle ['metl] n: **to be on one's mettle** estar dispuesto(ta) a hacer lo mejor posible; **he showed OR proved his mettle** mostró su valor.

mew [mjuː] = **miaow**.

mews [mjuːz] (pl **mews**) n UK callejuela de antiguas caballerizas convertidas en viviendas de lujo.

Mexican ['meksɪkn] ◇ adj mexicano(na), mejicano(na). ◇ n mexicano m, -na f, mejicano m, -na f.

Mexico ['meksɪkəʊ] n México, Méjico.

MI5 (abbr of Military Intelligence 5) n organismo británico de contraespionaje.

MI6 (abbr of Military Intelligence 6) n organismo británico de espionaje.

miaow UK [miː'aʊ], **meow** US [mɪ'aʊ] ◇ n maullido m. ◇ vi maullar.

mice [maɪs] npl ▷ **mouse**.

mickey ['mɪkɪ] *n UK inf*: **to take the mickey out of sb** tomar el pelo a alguien; **to take the mickey out of sthg** burlarse de algo.

microchip ['maɪkrəʊtʃɪp] *n* COMPUT microchip *m*.

microcomputer [,maɪkrəʊkəm'pju:təʳ] *n* microordenador *m*, microcomputadora *f Amér*.

microfilm ['maɪkrəʊfɪlm] *n* microfilm *m*.

microphone ['maɪkrəfəʊn] *n* micrófono *m*.

micro scooter *n* patinete *m*.

microscope ['maɪkrəskəʊp] *n* microscopio *m*.

microscopic [,maɪkrə'skɒpɪk] *adj lit & fig* microscópico(ca).

microwave ['maɪkrəweɪv] <> *n*: **microwave (oven)** microondas *m inv*. <> *vt* cocinar en el microondas.

mid- [mɪd] *prefix* medio(dia); **(in) mid-morning** a media mañana; **(in) mid-August** a mediados de agosto; **(in) mid-winter** en pleno invierno; **she's in her mid-twenties** tiene unos 25 años.

midair [mɪd'eəʳ] *n*: **in midair** en el aire.

midday ['mɪdeɪ] *n* mediodía *m*.

middle ['mɪdl] <> *adj* [gen] del medio. <> *n* - **1.** [of room, town etc] medio *m*, centro *m*; **in the middle of the month/the 19th century** a mediados del mes/del siglo XIX; **in the middle of the week** a mitad de semana; **to be in the middle of doing sthg** estar haciendo algo; **in the middle of the night** en plena noche - **2.** [waist] cintura *f*.

middle-aged *adj* de mediana edad.

Middle Ages *npl*: **the Middle Ages** la Edad Media.

middle-class *adj* de clase media.

middle classes *npl*: **the middle classes** la clase media.

Middle East *n*: **the Middle East** el Oriente Medio.

middleman ['mɪdlmæn] (*pl* -men [-men]) *n* intermediario *m*.

middle name *n* segundo nombre *m (en un nombre compuesto)*.

middleweight ['mɪdlweɪt] *n* peso *m* medio.

middling ['mɪdlɪŋ] *adj* regular.

midfield [,mɪd'fi:ld] *n* FTBL centro *m* del campo.

midge [mɪdʒ] *n* (tipo *m* de) mosquito *m*.

midget ['mɪdʒɪt] *n* enano *m*, -na *f*.

midi system ['mɪdɪ-] *n* minicadena *f*.

Midlands ['mɪdləndz] *npl*: **the Midlands** *la región central de Inglaterra*.

midnight ['mɪdnaɪt] *n* medianoche *f*.

midriff ['mɪdrɪf] *n* diafragma *m*.

midst [mɪdst] *n*: **in the midst of** en medio de.

midsummer ['mɪd,sʌməʳ] *n* pleno verano *m*.

midway [,mɪd'weɪ] *adv* - **1.** [in space]: **midway (between)** a medio camino (entre) - **2.** [in time]: **midway (through)** a la mitad (de).

midweek <> *adj* [mɪd'wi:k] de entre semana. <> *adv* ['mɪdwi:k] entre semana.

midwife ['mɪdwaɪf] (*pl* -wives [-waɪvz]) *n* comadrona *f*.

midwifery ['mɪd,wɪfərɪ] *n* obstetricia *f*.

might [maɪt] <> *modal vb* - **1.** [expressing possibility]: **he might be armed** podría estar armado; **I might do it** puede que OR quizás lo haga; **I might come, I might not** puede que venga, puede que no; **will you do it? – I might do** ¿lo harás? – puede que sí; **we might have been killed, had we not been careful** si no hubiéramos tenido cuidado, podríamos haber muerto; **will you tell them? – I might as well** ¿se lo dirás? – ¿por qué no? - **2.** [expressing suggestion]: **you might have told me!** ¡podrías habérmelo dicho!; **it might be better to wait** quizás sea mejor esperar - **3.** *fml* [asking permission]: **he asked if he might leave the room** pidió permiso para salir - **4.** [expressing concession]: **you might well be right, but...** puede que tengas razón, pero...

▸▸ **I might have known** OR **guessed** podría haberlo sospechado. <> *n (U)* fuerza *f*, poder *m*.

mighty ['maɪtɪ] <> *adj* [strong] fuerte; [powerful] poderoso(sa). <> *adv esp US* muy.

migraine ['mi:greɪn, 'maɪgreɪn] *n* jaqueca *f*.

migrant ['maɪgrənt] <> *adj* [workers] inmigrante. <> *n* [person] emigrante *mf*.

migrate [UK maɪ'greɪt, US 'maɪgreɪt] *vi* emigrar.

mike [maɪk] (*abbr of* **microphone**) *n inf* micro *m*.

mild [maɪld] *adj* - **1.** [taste, disinfectant, wind] suave; [effect, surprise, illness, punishment] leve - **2.** [person, nature] apacible; [tone of voice] sereno(na) - **3.** [climate] templado(da).

mildew ['mɪldju:] *n* [gen] moho *m*; [on plants] añublo *m*.

mildly ['maɪldlɪ] *adv* - **1.** [gen] ligeramente, levemente; **to put it mildly** por no decir más - **2.** [talk] suavemente.

mile [maɪl] *n* milla *f*; **it's miles away** [place] está muy lejos; **to be miles away** *fig* estar en la luna.

mileage ['maɪlɪdʒ] *n* distancia *f* en millas.

mileometer, milometer [maɪ'lɒmɪtəʳ] *n* cuentamillas *m inv*, ≃ cuentakilómetros *m inv*.

milestone ['maɪlstəʊn] *n* - **1.** [marker stone] mojón *m* - **2.** *fig* [event] hito *m*.

militant ['mɪlɪtənt] <> *adj* militante. <> *n* militante *mf*.

military ['mɪlɪtrɪ] ◇ *adj* militar. ◇ *n*: **the military** los militares, las fuerzas armadas.

militia [mɪ'lɪʃə] *n* milicia *f*.

milk [mɪlk] ◇ *n* leche *f*. ◇ *vt* - **1**. [cow etc] ordeñar - **2**. [use to own ends] sacar todo el jugo a; **they milked him for every penny he had** le chuparon hasta el último centavo.

milk chocolate *n* chocolate *m* con leche.

milkman ['mɪlkmən] (*pl* -**men** [-mən]) *n* lechero *m*.

milk shake *n* batido *m*.

milky ['mɪlkɪ] *adj* - **1**. *UK* [with milk] con mucha leche - **2**. [pale white] lechoso(sa).

Milky Way *n*: **the Milky Way** la Vía Láctea.

mill [mɪl] ◇ *n* - **1**. [flour-mill] molino *m* - **2**. [factory] fábrica *f* - **3**. [grinder] molinillo *m*. ◇ *vt* moler. ◆ **mill about, mill around** *vi* arremolinarse.

millennium [mɪ'lenɪəm] (*pl* -**nnia** [-nɪə]) *n* milenio *m*.

miller ['mɪlə^r] *n* molinero *m*, -ra *f*.

millet ['mɪlɪt] *n* mijo *m*.

milligram(me) ['mɪlɪgræm] *n* miligramo *m*.

millimetre *UK*, **millimeter** *US* ['mɪlɪ,miːtə^r] *n* milímetro *m*.

millinery ['mɪlɪnrɪ] *n* sombrerería *f* (de señoras).

million ['mɪljən] *n* millón *m*; **four million dollars** cuatro millones de dólares.

millionaire [,mɪljə'neə^r] *n* millonario *m*.

millstone ['mɪlstəʊn] *n* piedra *f* de molino, muela *f*.

milometer [maɪ'lɒmɪtə^r] = **mileometer**.

mime [maɪm] ◇ *n* [acting] mímica *f*. ◇ *vt* describir con gestos. ◇ *vi* hacer mímica.

mimic ['mɪmɪk] ◇ *n* imitador *m*, -ra *f*. ◇ *vt* (*pt & pp* -**ked**, *cont* -**king**) imitar.

mimicry ['mɪmɪkrɪ] *n* imitación *f*.

min. [mɪn] - **1**. (*abbr of* **minute**) min - **2**. (*abbr of* **minimum**) mín.

mince [mɪns] ◇ *n UK* carne *f* picada. ◇ *vt* picar. ◇ *vi* andar con afectación.

mincemeat ['mɪnsmiːt] *n* [fruit] *mezcla de fruta confitada y especias*.

mince pie *n* [sweet cake] *pastelillo navideño de fruta confitada y frutos secos*.

mincer ['mɪnsə^r] *n* máquina *f* de picar carne.

mind [maɪnd] ◇ *n* - **1**. [gen] mente *f*; **state of mind** estado *m* de ánimo; **to calculate sthg in one's mind** calcular algo mentalmente; **to come into** OR **to cross sb's mind** pasársele a alguien por la cabeza; **the first thing that came into my mind** lo primero que me vino a la mente; **to have sthg on one's mind** estar preocupado por algo; **to keep an open mind** tener una actitud abierta; **that was a load** OR **weight off my mind** me quité un peso de en-

cima; **are you out of your mind?** ¿estás loco?; **to make one's mind up** decidirse - **2**. [attention] atención *f*; **to put one's mind to sthg** poner empeño en algo - **3**. [opinion]: **to change one's mind** cambiar de opinión; **to my mind** en mi opinión; **to be in two minds about sthg** no estar seguro(ra) de algo; **to speak one's mind** hablar sin rodeos - **4**. [memory] memoria *f* - **5**. [intention]: **to have sthg in mind** tener algo en mente; **to have a mind to do sthg** estar pensando en hacer algo; **nothing could be further from my mind** nada más lejos de mis intenciones. ◇ *vi* [be bothered]: **do you mind?** ¿te importa?; **I don't mind...** no me importa...; **which do you want? – I don't mind** ¿cuál prefieres? – me da igual; **never mind** [don't worry] no te preocupes; [it's not important] no importa. ◇ *vt* - **1**. [be bothered about, dislike]: **do you mind if I leave?** ¿te molesta si me voy?; **I don't mind waiting** no me importa esperar; **I wouldn't mind a...** no me vendría mal un... - **2**. [pay attention to] tener cuidado con; **mind you don't fall** ten cuidado no te vayas a caer - **3**. [take care of] cuidar - **4**. [concentrate on]: **mind your own business!** ¡métete en tus asuntos! ◆ **mind you** *adv*: **he's a bit deaf; mind you, he is old** está un poco sordo; te advierto que es ya mayor.

minder ['maɪndə^r] *n UK inf* [bodyguard] guardaespaldas *m* & *f inv*.

mindful ['maɪndfʊl] *adj*: **mindful of** consciente de.

mindless ['maɪndlɪs] *adj* - **1**. [stupid] absurdo(da), sin sentido - **2**. [not requiring thought] aburrido(da).

mine[1] [maɪn] *poss pron* mío (mía); **that money is mine** ese dinero es mío; **his car hit mine** su coche chocó contra el mío; **it wasn't your fault, it was mine** la culpa no fue tuya sino mía; **a friend of mine** un amigo mío.

mine[2] [maɪn] ◇ *n* mina *f*. ◇ *vt* - **1**. [excavate - coal] extraer - **2**. [lay mines in] minar.

minefield ['maɪnfiːld] *n lit & fig* campo *m* de minas.

miner ['maɪnə^r] *n* minero *m*, -ra *f*.

mineral ['mɪnərəl] ◇ *adj* mineral. ◇ *n* mineral *m*.

mineral water *n* agua *f* mineral.

minesweeper ['maɪn,swiːpə^r] *n* dragaminas *m inv*.

mingle ['mɪŋgl] *vi* - **1**. [combine]: **to mingle (with)** mezclarse (con) - **2**. [socially]: **to mingle (with)** alternar (con).

miniature ['mɪnətʃə^r] ◇ *adj* en miniatura. ◇ *n* - **1**. [painting] miniatura *f* - **2**. [of alcohol] botellín *f* de licor en miniatura.

minibus ['mɪnɪbʌs] (*pl* -**es**) *n* microbús *m*.

minicab ['mınıkæb] *n UK* taxi *que se puede pedir por teléfono, pero no se puede parar en la calle.*

minidish ['mınıdıʃ] *n* miniparabólica *f*.

minima ['mınımə] *pl* ⊳ **minimum**.

minimal ['mınıml] *adj* mínimo(ma).

minimum ['mınıməm] ◇ *adj* mínimo(ma). ◇ *n* (*pl* **-mums** OR **-ma**) mínimo *m*.

mining ['maınıŋ] ◇ *n* minería *f*. ◇ *adj* minero(ra).

miniskirt ['mınıskɜːt] *n* minifalda *f*.

minister ['mınıstə'] *n* - **1.** POL: **minister (for)** ministro *m*, -tra *f* (de) - **2.** RELIG pastor *m*, -ra *f*.
◆ **minister to** *vt insep* [needs] atender a.

ministerial [,mını'stıərıəl] *adj* ministerial.

minister of state *n*: **minister of state (for)** secretario *m*, -ria *f* de estado (para).

ministry ['mınıstrı] *n* - **1.** POL ministerio *m* - **2.** RELIG: **the ministry** el clero.

mink [mıŋk] (*pl* mink) *n* visón *m*.

minnow ['mınəʊ] *n* - **1.** [fish] pececillo *m* (de agua dulce) - **2.** [team] comparsa *f*.

minor ['maınə'] ◇ *adj* [gen] menor; [injury] leve. ◇ *n* menor *mf* (de edad); *US* [subject] subespecialidad *f*.

minority [maı'nɒrətı] *n* minoría *f*; **to be in a** OR **the minority** estar en la minoría, ser minoría.

mint [mınt] ◇ *n* - **1.** [herb] menta *f*, hierbabuena *f* - **2.** [peppermint] pastilla *f* de menta - **3.** [for coins]: **the mint** la Casa de la Moneda; **in mint condition** en perfecto estado, como nuevo(va). ◇ *vt* acuñar.

minus ['maınəs] ◇ *prep* - **1.** MATHS [less]: **4 minus 2 is 2** 4 menos 2 es 2 - **2.** [in temperatures]: **it's minus 5°C** estamos a 5 grados bajo cero. ◇ *n* (*pl* **-es**) - **1.** MATHS signo *m* (de) menos - **2.** [disadvantage] desventaja *f*.

minus sign *n* signo *m* (de) menos.

minute¹ ['mınıt] *n* minuto *m*; **at any minute** en cualquier momento; **at the minute** en este momento; **just a minute** un momento; **this minute** ahora mismo. ◆ **minutes** *npl* acta *f*; **to take (the) minutes** levantar OR tomar acta.

minute² [maı'njuːt] *adj* [very small] diminuto(ta).

miracle ['mırəkl] *n lit & fig* milagro *m*.

miraculous [mı'rækjʊləs] *adj* milagroso(sa).

mirage [mı'rɑːʒ] *n lit & fig* espejismo *m*.

mire [maıə'] *n* fango *m*, lodo *m*.

mirror ['mırə'] ◇ *n* espejo *m*. ◇ *vt* reflejar.

mirth [mɜːθ] *n* risa *f*.

misadventure [,mısəd'ventʃə'] *n* desgracia *f*; **death by misadventure** LAW muerte *f* accidental.

misapprehension ['mıs,æprı'henʃn] *n* - **1.** [misunderstanding] malentendido *m* - **2.** [mistaken belief] creencia *f* errónea.

misappropriation ['mısə,prəʊprı'eıʃn] *n*: **misappropriation (of)** malversación *f* (de).

misbehave [,mısbı'heıv] *vi* portarse mal.

miscalculate [,mıs'kælkjʊleıt] *vt & vi* calcular mal.

miscarriage [,mıs'kærıdʒ] *n* [at birth] aborto *m* (natural).

miscarriage of justice *n* error *m* judicial.

miscellaneous [,mısə'leınjəs] *adj* diverso(sa).

mischief ['mıstʃıf] *n* (*U*) - **1.** [playfulness] picardía *f* - **2.** [naughty behaviour] travesuras *fpl* - **3.** [harm] daño *m*.

mischievous ['mıstʃıvəs] *adj* - **1.** [playful] lleno(na) de picardía - **2.** [naughty] travieso(sa).

misconception [,mıskən'sepʃn] *n* concepto *m* erróneo.

misconduct [,mıs'kɒndʌkt] *n* mala conducta *f*.

misconstrue [,mıskən'struː] *vt fml* malinterpretar.

miscount [,mıs'kaʊnt] *vt & vi* contar mal.

misdeed [,mıs'diːd] *n liter* fechoría *f*.

misdemeanour *UK*, **misdemeanor** *US* [,mısdı'miːnə'] *n fml* delito *m* menor.

miser ['maızə'] *n* avaro *m*, -ra *f*.

miserable ['mızrəbl] *adj* - **1.** [unhappy] infeliz, triste - **2.** [wretched, poor] miserable - **3.** [weather] horrible - **4.** [pathetic] lamentable.

miserly ['maızəlı] *adj* miserable, mezquino(na).

misery ['mızərı] *n* - **1.** [unhappiness] desdicha *f* - **2.** [suffering] sufrimiento *m*.

misfire [,mıs'faıə'] *vi* - **1.** [car engine] no arrancar - **2.** [plan] fracasar.

misfit ['mısfıt] *n* inadaptado *m*, -da *f*.

misfortune [mıs'fɔːtʃuːn] *n* - **1.** [bad luck] mala suerte *f* - **2.** [piece of bad luck] desgracia *f*.

misgivings [mıs'gıvıŋz] *npl* recelos *mpl*.

misguided [,mıs'gaıdıd] *adj* [person] descaminado(da); [attempt] equivocado(da).

mishandle [,mıs'hændl] *vt* - **1.** [person, animal] maltratar - **2.** [affair] llevar mal.

mishap ['mıshæp] *n* contratiempo *m*.

misinterpret [,mısın'tɜːprıt] *vt* malinterpretar.

misjudge [,mıs'dʒʌdʒ] *vt* - **1.** [guess wrongly] calcular mal - **2.** [appraise wrongly] juzgar mal.

mislay [,mıs'leı] (*pt & pp* -**laid**) *vt* extraviar.

mislead [,mıs'liːd] (*pt & pp* -**led**) *vt* engañar.

misleading [,mıs'liːdıŋ] *adj* engañoso(sa).

misled [,mıs'led] *pt & pp* ⊳ **mislead**.

misnomer [ˌmɪsˈnəʊməʳ] n término m equivocado.

misplace [ˌmɪsˈpleɪs] vt extraviar.

misprint [ˈmɪsprɪnt] n errata f, error m de imprenta.

miss [mɪs] ◇ vt - **1.** [fail to see - TV programme, film] perderse; [- error, person in crowd] no ver - **2.** [fail to hear] no oír - **3.** [omit] saltarse - **4.** [shot] fallar; [ball] no dar a - **5.** [feel absence of] echar de menos OR en falta - **6.** [opportunity] perder, dejar pasar; [turning] pasarse - **7.** [train, bus] perder - **8.** [appointment] faltar a; [deadline] no cumplir - **9.** [avoid] evitar. ◇ vi fallar. ◇ n fallo m; **to give sthg a miss** inf pasar de algo. ◆ **miss out** ◇ vt sep pasar por alto. ◇ vi: **to miss out (on sthg)** perderse (algo).

Miss [mɪs] n señorita f; **Miss Brown** la señorita Brown.

misshapen [ˌmɪsˈʃeɪpn] adj deforme.

missile [UK ˈmɪsaɪl, US ˈmɪsəl] n - **1.** [weapon] misil m - **2.** [thrown object] proyectil m.

missing [ˈmɪsɪŋ] adj - **1.** [lost] perdido(da), extraviado(da) - **2.** [not present] ausente; **to be missing** faltar.

mission [ˈmɪʃn] n misión f.

missionary [ˈmɪʃənrɪ] n misionero m, -ra f.

mist [mɪst] n [gen] neblina f; [at sea] bruma f. ◆ **mist over, mist up** vi [windows, spectacles] empañarse; [eyes] llenarse de lágrimas.

mistake [mɪˈsteɪk] ◇ n error m; **to make a mistake** equivocarse, cometer un error; **by mistake** por error. ◇ vt (pt -took, pp -taken) [misunderstand] entender mal.

mistaken [mɪˈsteɪkn] ◇ pp ▷ **mistake**. ◇ adj equivocado(da); **to be mistaken about sb/sthg** estar equivocado respecto a alguien/algo.

mister [ˈmɪstəʳ] n inf amigo m. ◆ **Mister** n señor m; **mister Brown** el señor Brown.

mistletoe [ˈmɪsltəʊ] n muérdago m.

mistook [mɪˈstʊk] pt ▷ **mistake**.

mistreat [ˌmɪsˈtriːt] vt maltratar.

mistress [ˈmɪstrɪs] n - **1.** [female lover] amante f - **2.** UK [school teacher - primary] maestra f; [- secondary] profesora f - **3.** [woman in control] señora f.

mistrust [ˌmɪsˈtrʌst] ◇ n desconfianza f, recelo m. ◇ vt desconfiar de.

misty [ˈmɪstɪ] adj [gen] neblinoso(sa); [at sea] brumoso(sa).

misunderstand [ˌmɪsʌndəˈstænd] (pt & pp -stood) vt & vi entender mal.

misunderstanding [ˌmɪsʌndəˈstændɪŋ] n malentendido m.

misunderstood [ˌmɪsʌndəˈstʊd] pt & pp ▷ **misunderstand**.

misuse ◇ n [ˌmɪsˈjuːs] uso m indebido. ◇ vt [ˌmɪsˈjuːz] hacer uso indebido de.

miter US = **mitre**.

mitigate [ˈmɪtɪgeɪt] vt fml mitigar.

mitre, **mitor** [US] [ˈmaɪtəʳ] n [hat] mitra f.

mitt [mɪt] n manopla f; US [for baseball] guante m.

mitten [ˈmɪtn] n manopla f.

mix [mɪks] ◇ vt: **to mix sthg (with)** mezclar algo (con). ◇ vi - **1.** [substances] mezclarse; [activities] ir bien juntos(tas) - **2.** [socially]: **to mix with** alternar con. ◇ n mezcla f. ◆ **mix up** vt sep - **1.** [confuse] confundir - **2.** [disorder] mezclar.

mixed [mɪkst] adj - **1.** [of different kinds] surtido(da), variado(da) - **2.** [of different sexes] mixto(ta).

mixed-ability adj UK [class, group] con alumnos de varios niveles.

mixed grill n parrillada f mixta.

mixed up adj - **1.** [confused] confuso(sa); **to get mixed up** confundirse - **2.** [involved]: **mixed up in** [fight, crime] involucrado(da) en.

mixer [ˈmɪksəʳ] n - **1.** [for food] batidora f; [for cement] hormigonera f - **2.** [for music] mesa f de mezclas - **3.** [non-alcoholic drink] bebida no alcohólica para mezclar con bebidas alcohólicas.

mixture [ˈmɪkstʃəʳ] n [gen] mezcla f; [for sweets] surtido m.

mix-up n inf confusión f.

mm (abbr of millimetre) mm.

MMR [ˌememˈɑːʳ] (abbr of measles, mumps & rubella) n MED sarampión, paperas y rubeola.

moan [məʊn] ◇ n [of pain, sadness] gemido m. ◇ vi - **1.** [in pain, sadness] gemir - **2.** inf [complain]: **to moan (about)** quejarse (de).

moat [məʊt] n foso m.

mob [mɒb] ◇ n muchedumbre f. ◇ vt asediar.

mobile [ˈməʊbaɪl] ◇ adj [able to move] móvil. ◇ n móvil m.

mobile home n caravana f.

mobile phone n teléfono m móvil.

mobilize, -ise [ˈməʊbɪlaɪz] vt movilizar.

mock [mɒk] ◇ adj fingido(da); **mock (exam)** simulacro m de examen. ◇ vt burlarse de. ◇ vi burlarse.

mockery [ˈmɒkərɪ] n burlas fpl; **to make a mockery of sthg** poner en ridículo algo.

mod cons [ˌmɒd-] (abbr of modern conveniences) npl UK inf: **all mod cons** con todas las comodidades.

mode [məʊd] n modo m.

model [ˈmɒdl] ◇ n - **1.** [gen] modelo m - **2.** [small copy] maqueta f - **3.** [for painter, in fashion] modelo mf. ◇ adj - **1.** [exemplary] modelo (inv) - **2.** [reduced-scale] en miniatura. ◇ vt (UK pt & pp -led, cont -ling, US pt & pp -ed, cont -ing) - **1.** [shape] modelar - **2.** [wear] lucir (en pase de modelos) - **3.** [copy]: **to model**

o.s. on sb tener a alguien como modelo - **4.** COMPUT simular por ordenador. <> *vi (UK pt & pp* -**led**, *cont* -**ling**, *US pt & pp* -**ed**, *cont* -**ing**) trabajar de modelo.

modem ['məʊdem] *n* COMPUT módem *m*.

moderate <> *adj* ['mɒdərət] moderado(da). <> *n* ['mɒdərət] POL moderado *m*, -da *f*. <> *vt* ['mɒdəreɪt] moderar. <> *vi* ['mɒdəreɪt] [in debate] hacer de moderador.

moderation [,mɒdə'reɪʃn] *n* moderación *f*; **in moderation** con moderación.

modern ['mɒdən] *adj* moderno(na).

modernize, -ise ['mɒdənaɪz] <> *vt* modernizar. <> *vi* modernizarse.

modern languages *npl* lenguas *fpl* modernas.

modest ['mɒdɪst] *adj* - **1.** [gen] modesto(ta) - **2.** [improvement] ligero(ra); [price] módico(ca).

modesty ['mɒdɪstɪ] *n* modestia *f*.

modicum ['mɒdɪkəm] *n fml*: **a modicum of** un mínimo de.

modify ['mɒdɪfaɪ] *vt* modificar.

module ['mɒdjuːl] *n* módulo *m*.

mogul ['məʊgl] *n* magnate *mf*.

mohair ['məʊheəʳ] *n* mohair *m*.

moist [mɔɪst] *adj* húmedo(da).

moisten ['mɔɪsn] *vt* humedecer.

moisture ['mɔɪstʃəʳ] *n* humedad *f*.

moisturizer ['mɔɪstʃəraɪzəʳ] *n* (crema *f*) hidratante *m*.

molar ['məʊləʳ] *n* muela *f*.

molasses [mə'læsɪz] *n (U)* melaza *f*.

mold *US* = **mould**.

mole [məʊl] *n* - **1.** [animal, spy] topo *m* - **2.** [spot] lunar *m*.

molecule ['mɒlɪkjuːl] *n* molécula *f*.

molest [mə'lest] *vt* - **1.** [sexually] abusar sexualmente de - **2.** [annoy] molestar.

mollusc, mollusk *US* ['mɒləsk] *n* molusco *m*.

mollycoddle ['mɒlɪ,kɒdl] *vt inf* mimar.

molt *US* = **moult**.

molten ['məʊltn] *adj* fundido(da).

mom [mɒm] *n US inf* mamá *f*.

moment ['məʊmənt] *n* momento *m*; **at any moment** de un momento a otro; **at the moment** en este momento; **for the moment** de momento.

momentarily ['məʊməntərɪlɪ] *adv* - **1.** [for a short time] momentáneamente - **2.** *US* [soon] pronto.

momentary ['məʊməntrɪ] *adj* momentáneo(a).

momentous [mə'mentəs] *adj* trascendental.

momentum [mə'mentəm] *n (U)* - **1.** PHYS momento *m* - **2.** *fig* [speed, force] ímpetu *m*, impulso *m*; **to gather momentum** cobrar intensidad.

momma ['mɒmə], **mommy** ['mɒmɪ] *n US* mamá *f*.

Monaco ['mɒnəkəʊ] *n* Mónaco.

monarch ['mɒnək] *n* monarca *mf*.

monarchy ['mɒnəkɪ] *n* - **1.** [gen] monarquía *f* - **2.** [royal family]: **the monarchy** la familia real.

monastery ['mɒnəstrɪ] *n* monasterio *m*.

Monday ['mʌndɪ] *n* lunes *m inv*; *see also* **Saturday**.

monetary ['mʌnɪtrɪ] *adj* monetario(ria).

money ['mʌnɪ] *n* dinero *m*; **to make money** hacer dinero; **we got our money's worth** sacamos provecho a nuestro dinero; **for my money** en mi opinión.

money belt *n* cinturón *m* monedero.

moneybox ['mʌnɪbɒks] *n* hucha *f*.

moneylender ['mʌnɪ,lendəʳ] *n* prestamista *mf*.

money order *n* giro *m* postal.

money-spinner [-,spɪnəʳ] *n esp UK inf* mina *f* (de dinero).

mongol ['mɒŋgəl] *dated & offens n* mongólico *m*, -ca *f*.

Mongolia [mɒŋ'gəʊlɪə] *n* Mongolia.

mongrel ['mʌŋgrəl] *n* perro *m* cruzado.

monitor ['mɒnɪtəʳ] <> *n* [gen & COMPUT] monitor *m*. <> *vt* - **1.** [check] controlar - **2.** [listen in to] escuchar.

monk [mʌŋk] *n* monje *m*.

monkey ['mʌŋkɪ] *(pl* **monkeys**) *n* mono *m*.

monkey nut *n* cacahuete *m*.

monkey wrench *n* llave *f* inglesa.

mono ['mɒnəʊ] *adj* mono *(inv)*.

monochrome ['mɒnəkrəʊm] *adj* monocromo(ma).

monocle ['mɒnəkl] *n* monóculo *m*.

monologue, monolog *US* ['mɒnəlɒg] *n* monólogo *m*.

monopolize, -ise [mə'nɒpəlaɪz] *vt* monopolizar.

monopoly [mə'nɒpəlɪ] *n*: **monopoly (on OR of)** monopolio *m* (de).

monotone ['mɒnətəʊn] *n*: **in a monotone** con voz monótona.

monotonous [mə'nɒtənəs] *adj* monótono(na).

monotony [mə'nɒtənɪ] *n* monotonía *f*.

monsoon [mɒn'suːn] *n* monzón *m*.

monster ['mɒnstəʳ] *n* [imaginary creature, cruel person] monstruo *m*.

monstrosity [mɒn'strɒsətɪ] *n* monstruosidad *f*.

monstrous ['mɒnstrəs] *adj* - **1.** [very unfair, frightening, ugly] monstruoso(sa) - **2.** [very large] gigantesco(ca).

month [mʌnθ] *n* mes *m*.

monthly ['mʌnθlɪ] ◇ *adj* mensual. ◇ *adv* mensualmente.

monument ['mɒnjʊmənt] *n* monumento *m*.

monumental [,mɒnjʊ'mentl] *adj* - **1.** [gen] monumental - **2.** [error] descomunal.

moo [mu:] *vi* mugir.

mood [mu:d] *n* [of individual] humor *m*; [of public, voters] disposición *f*; **in a (bad) mood** de mal humor; **in a good mood** de buen humor.

moody ['mu:dɪ] *adj pej* - **1.** [changeable] de humor variable - **2.** [bad-tempered] malhumorado(da).

moon [mu:n] *n* luna *f*.

moonlight ['mu:nlaɪt] *n* luz *f* de la luna.

moonlighting ['mu:nlaɪtɪŋ] *n* pluriempleo *m*.

moonlit ['mu:nlɪt] *adj* [night] de luna; [landscape] iluminado(da) por la luna.

moor [mɔːr] ◇ *n esp UK* páramo *m*. ◇ *vt* amarrar. ◇ *vi* echar las amarras.

Moor [mɔːr] *n* moro *m*, -ra *f*.

Moorish ['mɔːrɪʃ] *adj* moro(ra), morisco(ca).

moorland ['mɔːlənd] *n esp UK* páramo *m*, brezal *m*.

moose [mu:s] (*pl* **moose**) *n* [North American] alce *m*.

mop [mɒp] ◇ *n* - **1.** [for cleaning] fregona *f* - **2.** *inf* [of hair] pelambrera *f*. ◇ *vt* - **1.** [clean with mop] pasar la fregona por - **2.** [dry with cloth - sweat] enjugar. **mop up** *vt sep* [clean up] limpiar.

mope [məʊp] *vi pej* estar deprimido(da).

moped ['məʊped] *n* ciclomotor *m*, motoneta *f Amér*.

moral ['mɒrəl] ◇ *adj* moral. ◇ *n* [lesson] moraleja *f*. **morals** *npl* [principles] moral *f*.

morale [mə'rɑːl] *n* (*U*) moral *f*.

morality [mə'rælətɪ] *n* - **1.** [gen] moralidad *f* - **2.** [system of principles] moral *f*.

morass [mə'ræs] *n* cenagal *m*.

morbid ['mɔːbɪd] *adj* morboso(sa).

more [mɔːr] ◇ *adv* - **1.** (*with adj and adverbs*) más; **more important (than)** más importante (que) - **2.** [to a greater degree] más; **we were more hurt than angry** más que enfadados estábamos heridos; **I couldn't agree more** estoy totalmente de acuerdo. ◇ *adj* más; **more food than drink** más comida que bebida; **more than 70 people died** más de 70 personas murieron; **have some more tea** toma un poco más de té; **I finished two more chapters today** acabé otros dos capítulos hoy. ◇ *pron* más; **more than five** más de cinco;

he's got more than I have él tiene más que yo; **I don't want any more** no quiero más; **there's no more (left)** no queda nada (más); **(and) what's more** (y lo que) es más. **any more** *adv*: **not... any more** ya no...; **she doesn't live here any more** ya no vive aquí. **more and more** *adv, adj* & *pron* cada vez más. **more or less** *adv* más o menos.

moreover [mɔː'rəʊvər] *adv fml* además.

morgue [mɔːg] *n* depósito *m* de cadáveres.

Mormon ['mɔːmən] *n* mormón *m*, -ona *f*.

morning ['mɔːnɪŋ] *n* - **1.** [first part of day] mañana *f*; **in the morning** por la mañana; **six o'clock in the morning** las seis de la mañana; **on Monday morning** el lunes por la mañana - **2.** [between midnight and dawn] madrugada *f* - **3.** [tomorrow morning]: **in the morning** mañana por la mañana. **mornings** *adv US* por la mañana.

Moroccan [mə'rɒkən] ◇ *adj* marroquí. ◇ *n* marroquí *mf*.

Morocco [mə'rɒkəʊ] *n* Marruecos *m*.

moron ['mɔːrɒn] *n inf* imbécil *mf*.

morose [mə'rəʊs] *adj* malhumorado(da).

morphine ['mɔːfiːn] *n* morfina *f*.

Morse (code) [mɔːs-] *n* (código *m*) morse *m*.

morsel ['mɔːsl] *n* bocado *m*.

mortal ['mɔːtl] ◇ *adj* [gen] mortal. ◇ *n* mortal *mf*.

mortality [mɔː'tælətɪ] *n* mortalidad *f*.

mortar ['mɔːtər] *n* - **1.** [cement mixture] argamasa *f* - **2.** [gun, bowl] mortero *m*.

mortgage ['mɔːgɪdʒ] ◇ *n* hipoteca *f*. ◇ *vt* hipotecar.

mortified ['mɔːtɪfaɪd] *adj* muerto(ta) de vergüenza.

mortuary ['mɔːtʃʊərɪ] *n* depósito *m* de cadáveres.

mosaic [mə'zeɪɪk] *n* mosaico *m*.

Moslem ['mɒzləm] = **Muslim**.

mosque [mɒsk] *n* mezquita *f*.

mosquito [mə'skiːtəʊ] (*pl* **-es** OR **-s**) *n* mosquito *m*, zancudo *m Amér*.

moss [mɒs] *n* musgo *m*.

most [məʊst] (*superl of* **many**) ◇ *adj* - **1.** [the majority of] la mayoría de; **most people** la mayoría de la gente - **2.** [largest amount of]: **(the) most** más; **who has got (the) most money?** ¿quién es el que tiene más dinero? ◇ *pron* - **1.** [the majority]: **most (of)** la mayoría (de); **most are women** la mayoría son mujeres; **most of the time** la mayor parte del tiempo - **2.** [largest amount]: **I earn (the) most** soy el que más dinero gana; **the most I've ever won** lo máximo que he ganado; **most of the time** la mayor parte del tiempo; **at most** como mucho

▶▶▶ **to make the most of sthg** sacarle el mayor partido a algo. ◇ *adv* - **1.** [to the greatest extent]: **(the) most** el/la/lo más; **the most handsome man** el hombre más guapo; **what I like most** lo que más me gusta; **most often** más a menudo - **2.** *fml* [very] muy; **most certainly** con toda seguridad - **3.** *US* [almost] casi.

mostly ['məʊstlɪ] *adv* [in the main part] principalmente; [usually] normalmente.

MOT (*abbr of* Ministry of Transport test) *n* ≈ ITV f.

motel [məʊ'tel] *n* motel *m*.

moth [mɒθ] *n* polilla f.

mothball ['mɒθbɔːl] *n* bola f de naftalina.

mother ['mʌðər] ◇ *n* madre f. ◇ *vt pej* [spoil] mimar.

motherhood ['mʌðəhʊd] *n* maternidad f.

mother-in-law (*pl* **mothers-in-law** OR **mother-in-laws**) *n* suegra f.

motherly ['mʌðəlɪ] *adj* maternal.

mother-of-pearl *n* nácar *m*.

mother-to-be (*pl* **mothers-to-be**) *n* futura madre f.

mother tongue *n* lengua f materna.

motif [məʊ'tiːf] *n* ART & MUS motivo *m*.

motion ['məʊʃn] ◇ *n* - **1.** [gen] movimiento *m*; **to go through the motions (of doing sthg)** (hacer algo para) cubrir el expediente - **2.** [proposal] moción f. ◇ *vt*: **to motion sb to do sthg** indicar a alguien con un gesto que haga algo. ◇ *vi*: **to motion to sb** hacer una señal (con la mano) a alguien.

motionless ['məʊʃənlɪs] *adj* inmóvil.

motion picture *n US* película f.

motivated ['məʊtɪveɪtɪd] *adj* motivado(da).

motivation [,məʊtɪ'veɪʃn] *n* motivación f.

motive ['məʊtɪv] *n* [gen] motivo *m*; [for crime] móvil *m*.

motley ['mɒtlɪ] *adj pej* variopinto(ta).

motor ['məʊtər] ◇ *adj UK* [industry, accident] automovilístico(ca); [mechanic] de automóviles. ◇ *n* - **1.** [engine] motor *m* - **2.** *UK inf* [car] coche *m*.

motorbike ['məʊtəbaɪk] *n* moto f.

motorboat ['məʊtəbəʊt] *n* lancha f motora.

motorcar ['məʊtəkɑːr] *n* automóvil *m*.

motorcycle ['məʊtə,saɪkl] *n* motocicleta f.

motorcyclist ['məʊtə,saɪklɪst] *n* motociclista mf.

motoring ['məʊtərɪŋ] *n* automovilismo *m*.

motorist ['məʊtərɪst] *n* automovilista mf, conductor m, -ra f.

motor racing *n* (*U*) carreras *fpl* de coches, automovilismo *m* deportivo.

motor scooter *n* Vespa® f, escúter *m*.

motorsport ['məʊtəspɔːt] *n* carreras *fpl* de coches.

motor vehicle *n* vehículo *m* de motor.

motorway ['məʊtəweɪ] *UK n* autopista f.

mottled ['mɒtld] *adj* moteado(da).

motto ['mɒtəʊ] (*pl* **-s** OR **-es**) *n* lema *m*.

mould, mold *US* [məʊld] ◇ *n* - **1.** [growth] moho *m* - **2.** [shape] molde *m*. ◇ *vt lit & fig* moldear.

moulding, molding *US* ['məʊldɪŋ] *n* [decoration] moldura f.

mouldy, moldy *US* ['məʊldɪ] *adj* mohoso(sa).

moult *UK*, **molt** *US* [məʊlt] *vi* [bird] mudar la pluma; [dog] mudar el pelo.

mound [maʊnd] *n* - **1.** [small hill] montículo *m* - **2.** [untidy pile] montón *m*.

mount [maʊnt] ◇ *n* - **1.** [gen] montura f; [for photograph] marco *m*; [for jewel] engaste *m* - **2.** [mountain] monte *m*. ◇ *vt* - **1.** [horse, bike] subirse a, montar en - **2.** [attack] lanzar - **3.** [exhibition] montar - **4.** [jewel] engastar; [photograph] enmarcar. ◇ *vi* [increase] aumentar.

mountain ['maʊntɪn] *n lit & fig* montaña f.

mountain bike *n* bicicleta f de montaña.

mountaineer [,maʊntɪ'nɪər] *n* montañero m, -ra f, andinista mf *Amér*.

mountaineering [,maʊntɪ'nɪərɪŋ] *n* montañismo *m*, andinismo m *Amér*.

mountainous ['maʊntɪnəs] *adj* montañoso(sa).

mourn [mɔːn] ◇ *vt* [person] llorar por; [thing] lamentarse de. ◇ *vi*: **to mourn for sb** llorar la muerte de alguien.

mourner ['mɔːnər] *n* doliente mf.

mournful ['mɔːnfʊl] *adj* [face, voice] afligido(da), lúgubre; [sound] lastimero(ra).

mourning ['mɔːnɪŋ] *n* luto *m*; **in mourning** de luto.

mouse [maʊs] (*pl* **mice**) *n* ZOOL & COMPUT ratón *m*.

mousetrap ['maʊstræp] *n* ratonera f.

mousse [muːs] *n* - **1.** [food] mousse *m* - **2.** [for hair] espuma f.

moustache *UK* [mə'stɑːʃ], **mustache** *US* ['mʌstæʃ] *n* bigote *m*.

mouth *n* [maʊθ] [gen] boca f; [of river] desembocadura f.

mouthful ['maʊθfʊl] *n* [of food] bocado *m*; [of drink] trago *m*.

mouthorgan ['maʊθ,ɔːgən] *n* armónica f.

mouthpiece ['maʊθpiːs] *n* - **1.** [of telephone] micrófono *m* - **2.** [of musical instrument] boquilla f - **3.** [spokesperson] portavoz mf.

mouthwash ['maʊθwɒʃ] *n* elixir *m* bucal.

mouth-watering [-,wɔːtərɪŋ] *adj* muy apetitoso(sa).

movable ['mu:vəbl] *adj* movible.

move [mu:v] ◇ *n* - **1**. [movement] movimiento *m*; **on the move** [travelling around] viajando; [beginning to move] en marcha; **to get a move on** *inf* espabilarse, darse prisa - **2**. [change - of house] mudanza *f*; [- of job] cambio *m* - **3**. [in board game] jugada *f* - **4**. [course of action] medida *f*. ◇ *vt* - **1**. [shift] mover; **to move sthg closer** acercar algo - **2**. [change - house] mudarse de; [- job] cambiar de - **3**. [transfer, postpone] trasladar - **4**. [affect] conmover - **5**. [in debate - motion] proponer - **6**. [cause]: **to move sb to do sthg** mover OR llevar a alguien a hacer algo. ◇ *vi* - **1**. [gen] moverse; [events] cambiar; **move closer** acércate - **2**. [change house] mudarse; [change job] cambiar de trabajo. ◆ **move about, move around** *vi* - **1**. [fidget] ir de aquí para allá - **2**. [travel] viajar. ◆ **move along** ◇ *vt sep* dispersar. ◇ *vi* - **1**. [move towards front or back] hacerse a un lado - **2**. [move away - crowd, car] circular. ◆ **move around** *vi* = **move about**. ◆ **move away** *vi* - **1**. [walk away] apartarse - **2**. [go to live elsewhere] marcharse. ◆ **move in** *vi* - **1**. [to new house] instalarse - **2**. [take control, attack] intervenir. ◆ **move on** *vi* - **1**. [go away] marcharse - **2**. [progress] avanzar. ◆ **move out** *vi* mudarse; **my girlfriend moved out yesterday** mi novia se fue a vivir a otra casa ayer. ◆ **move over** *vi* hacer sitio. ◆ **move up** *vi* [on bench etc] hacer sitio.

moveable = **movable**.

movement ['mu:vmənt] *n* [gen] movimiento *m*.

movie ['mu:vɪ] *n esp US* película *f*.

movie camera *n* cámara *f* cinematográfica.

moving ['mu:vɪŋ] *adj* - **1**. [touching] conmovedor(ra) - **2**. [not fixed] móvil.

mow [məʊ] *vt* (*pt* -ed, *pp* -ed OR mown) [grass, lawn] cortar; [corn] segar. ◆ **mow down** *vt sep* acribillar.

mower ['məʊər] *n* cortacésped *mf*.

mown [məʊn] *pp* ➩ **mow**.

MP *n* - **1**. (*abbr of* Military Police) PM *f* - **2**. *UK abbr of* **Member of Parliament**.

MPEG (*abbr of* Moving Pictures Expert Group) *n* [comput] MPEG *m*.

mpg (*abbr of* miles per gallon) millas/galón.

mph (*abbr of* miles per hour) mph.

Mr ['mɪstər] *n* Sr.; **Mr Jones** el Sr. Jones.

Mrs ['mɪsɪz] *n* Sra.; **Mrs Jones** la Sra. Jones.

MRSA [,emɑ:res'eɪ] (*abbr of* methicillin resistant Staphylococcus aureus) *n* MED estafilococo *m* áureo resistente a la meticilina.

Ms [mɪz] *n* abreviatura utilizada delante de un apellido de mujer cuando no se quiere especificar si está casada o no.

MS, ms *n abbr of* **multiple sclerosis**.

MSc (*abbr of* Master of Science) *n* (titular *mf* de un) máster *m* en Ciencias.

msg [emes'dʒi:] (*abbr of* **message**) *n* msj.

much [mʌtʃ] ◇ *adj* (*comp* more, *superl* most) mucho(cha); **there isn't much rice left** no queda mucho arroz; **after much thought** tras mucho reflexionar; **as much time as...** tanto tiempo como...; **twice as much flour** el doble de harina; **how much...?** ¿cuánto(ta)...?; **so much** tanto(ta); **too much** demasiado(da). ◇ *pron* mucho; **have you got much?** ¿tienes mucho?; **I don't see much of him** no lo veo mucho; **much of the time** una buena parte del tiempo; **I don't think much of it** no me parece gran cosa; **this isn't much of a party** esta fiesta no es nada del otro mundo; **as much as** tanto como; **twice as much** el doble; **I thought as much** ya me lo imaginaba; **how much?** ¿cuánto?; **so much for** tanto con; **too much** demasiado. ◇ *adv* mucho; **I don't go out much** no salgo mucho; **much too cold** demasiado frío; **they are much the same** son muy parecidos; **thank you very much** muchas gracias; **as much as** tanto como; **so much** tanto; **he is not so much stupid as lazy** más que tonto es vago; **without so much as...** sin siquiera...; **too much** demasiado. ◆ **much as** *conj*: **much as (I like him)** por mucho OR más que (me guste).

muck [mʌk] *inf n* (U) - **1**. [dirt] mugre *f*, porquería *f* - **2**. [manure] estiércol *m*. ◆ **muck about, muck around** *UK inf vi* hacer el indio OR tonto. ◆ **muck up** *vt sep UK inf* fastidiar.

mucky ['mʌkɪ] *adj* mugriento(ta).

mucus ['mju:kəs] *n* mucosidad *f*.

mud [mʌd] *n* barro *m*, lodo *m*.

muddle ['mʌdl] ◇ *n* - **1**. [disorder] desorden *m* - **2**. [confusion] lío *m*, confusión *f*; **to be in a muddle** estar hecho un lío; **to get into a muddle** hacerse un lío. ◇ *vt* - **1**. [put into disorder] desordenar - **2**. [confuse] liar, confundir. ◆ **muddle along** *vi* apañárselas más o menos. ◆ **muddle through** *vi* arreglárselas. ◆ **muddle up** *vt sep* [put into disorder] desordenar; [confuse] liar, confundir.

muddy ['mʌdɪ] *adj* [gen] lleno(na) de barro; [river] cenagoso(sa).

mudguard ['mʌdgɑ:d] *n* guardabarros *m inv*, tapabarro *m Andes*.

mudslinging ['mʌd,slɪŋɪŋ] *n* (U) *fig* insultos *mpl*, improperios *mpl*.

muesli ['mju:zlɪ] *n UK* muesli *m*.

muff [mʌf] ◇ *n* manguito *m*. ◇ *vt inf* [catch] fallar; [chance] dejar escapar.

muffin ['mʌfɪn] *n* - **1**. *UK* [eaten with butter] *especie de bollo de pan que se come caliente* - **2**. *US* [cake] *especie de magdalena que se come caliente*.

muffle ['mʌfl] *vt* [sound] amortiguar.

muffler ['mʌflər] *n US* [for car] silenciador *m*.

mug [mʌg] <> *n* - **1.** [cup] taza *f* (alta) - **2.** inf [fool] primo *m*, -ma *f* - **3.** inf [face] jeta *f*. <> *vt* asaltar, atracar.

mugging ['mʌgɪŋ] *n* [attack] atraco *m*.

muggy ['mʌgɪ] *adj* bochornoso(sa).

mule [mjuːl] *n* mula *f*.

mull [mʌl] ◆ **mull over** *vt sep* reflexionar sobre.

mulled [mʌld] *adj*: **mulled wine** vino caliente con azúcar y especias.

multicoloured *UK*, **multicolored** *US* [,mʌltɪ'kʌləd] *adj* multicolor.

multifaith ['mʌltɪfeɪθ] *adj* [society, organization] multiconfesional.

multigym [mʌltɪ'dʒɪm] *n* multiestación *f* (de musculación).

multilateral [,mʌltɪ'lætərəl] *adj* multilateral.

multinational [,mʌltɪ'næʃənl] *n* multinacional *f*.

multiple ['mʌltɪpl] <> *adj* múltiple. <> *n* múltiplo *m*.

multiple sclerosis [-sklɪ'rəʊsɪs] *n* esclerosis *f inv* múltiple.

multiplex cinema ['mʌltɪpleks-] *n* (cine *m*) multisalas *m inv*.

multiplication [,mʌltɪplɪ'keɪʃn] *n* multiplicación *f*.

multiply ['mʌltɪplaɪ] <> *vt* multiplicar. <> *vi* [increase, breed] multiplicarse.

multistorey *UK*, **multistory** *US* [,mʌltɪ'stɔːrɪ] *adj* de varias plantas.

multitude ['mʌltɪtjuːd] *n* multitud *f*.

multi-user *adj* COMPUT multiusuario.

mum [mʌm] *UK inf* <> *n* mamá *f*. <> *adj*: **to keep mum** no decir ni pío.

mumble ['mʌmbl] <> *vt* mascullar. <> *vi* musitar, hablar entre dientes.

mummy ['mʌmɪ] *n* - **1.** *UK inf* [mother] mamá *f* - **2.** [preserved body] momia *f*.

mumps [mʌmps] *n* (U) paperas *fpl*.

munch [mʌntʃ] *vt* & *vi* masticar.

mundane [mʌn'deɪn] *adj* prosaico(ca).

municipal [mjuː'nɪsɪpl] *adj* municipal.

municipality [mjuː,nɪsɪ'pælətɪ] *n* municipio *m*.

mural ['mjuːərəl] *n* mural *m*.

murder ['mɜːdər] <> *n* asesinato *m*. <> *vt* - **1.** [kill] asesinar - **2.** inf [defeat] dar una paliza a.

murderer ['mɜːdərər] *n* asesino *m*.

murderous ['mɜːdərəs] *adj* asesino(na).

murky ['mɜːkɪ] *adj* - **1.** [water, past] turbio(bia) - **2.** [night, street] sombrío(a), lúgubre.

murmur ['mɜːmər] <> *n* [low sound] murmullo *m*. <> *vt* & *vi* murmurar.

muscle ['mʌsl] *n* - **1.** MED músculo *m* - **2.** fig [power] poder *m*. ◆ **muscle in** *vi* entrometerse.

muscular ['mʌskjʊlər] *adj* - **1.** [of muscles] muscular - **2.** [strong] musculoso(sa).

muse [mjuːz] <> *n* musa *f*. <> *vi* meditar.

museum [mjuː'ziːəm] *n* museo *m*.

mushroom ['mʌʃrʊm] <> *n* [button] champiñón *m*; [field] seta *f*; BOT hongo *m*, callampa *f* Chile. <> *vi* extenderse rápidamente.

music ['mjuːzɪk] *n* música *f*.

musical ['mjuːzɪkl] <> *adj* - **1.** [gen] musical - **2.** [talented in music] con talento para la música. <> *n* musical *m*.

musical instrument *n* instrumento *m* musical.

music centre *n* cadena *f* (musical).

music hall *n UK* [building] teatro *m* de variedades OR de revista; [genre] music-hall *m*.

musician [mjuː'zɪʃn] *n* músico *m*, -ca *f*.

Muslim, Moslem ['mʊzlɪm] <> *adj* musulmán(ana). <> *n* musulmán *m*, -ana *f*.

muslin ['mʌzlɪn] *n* muselina *f*.

mussel ['mʌsl] *n* mejillón *m*.

must [mʌst] <> *aux vb* - **1.** [have to, intend to] deber, tener que; **I must go** tengo que OR debo irme; **if I must** si no hay más remedio - **2.** [as suggestion] tener que; **you must come and see us** tienes que venir a vernos - **3.** [to express likelihood] deber (de); **it must be true** debe (de) ser verdad; **they must have known** deben de haberlo sabido. <> *n inf*: **binoculars are a must** unos prismáticos son imprescindibles.

mustache *US* = **moustache**.

mustard ['mʌstəd] *n* mostaza *f*.

muster ['mʌstər] *vt* reunir; **to muster the courage to do sthg** armarse de valor para hacer algo.

must've ['mʌstəv] *(abbr of must have)* ▷ **must**.

musty ['mʌstɪ] *adj* [room] que huele a cerrado; [book] que huele a viejo.

mute [mjuːt] <> *adj* mudo(da). <> *n* [person] mudo *m*, -da *f*.

muted ['mjuːtɪd] *adj* - **1.** [not bright] apagado(da) - **2.** [subdued] contenido(da).

mutilate ['mjuːtɪleɪt] *vt* mutilar.

mutiny ['mjuːtɪnɪ] <> *n* motín *m*. <> *vi* amotinarse.

mutter ['mʌtər] <> *vt* musitar, mascullar. <> *vi* murmurar.

mutton ['mʌtn] *n* (carne *f* de) carnero *m*.

mutual ['mjuːtʃʊəl] *adj* - **1.** [reciprocal] mutuo(tua) - **2.** [common] común.

mutually ['mjuːtʃʊəlɪ] *adv* mutuamente.

muzzle ['mʌzl] ◇ n - **1.** [animal's nose and jaws] hocico m, morro m - **2.** [wire guard] bo[zal m] - **3.** [of gun] boca f. ◇ vt [put muzzle on] poner bozal a.

MW (abbr of medium wave) OM f.

my [maɪ] poss adj - **1.** [gen] mi, mis (pl); my house/sister mi casa/hermana; my children mis hijos; my name is Sarah me llamo Sarah; it wasn't my fault no fue culpa mía OR mi culpa; I washed my hair me lavé el pelo - **2.** [in titles]: my Lord milord; my Lady milady.

myriad ['mɪrɪəd] liter adj innumerables.

myself [maɪ'self] pron - **1.** (reflexive) me; (after prep) mí mismo(ma); with myself conmigo mismo - **2.** (for emphasis) yo mismo(ma); I did it myself lo hice yo solo(la).

mysterious [mɪ'stɪərɪəs] adj misterioso(sa).

mystery ['mɪstərɪ] n misterio m.

mystery shopping n compra f oculta.

mystical ['mɪstɪkl] adj místico(ca).

mystified ['mɪstɪfaɪd] adj desconcertado(da), perplejo(ja).

mystifying ['mɪstɪfaɪɪŋ] adj desconcertante.

mystique [mɪ'stiːk] n misterio m.

myth [mɪθ] n mito m.

mythical ['mɪθɪkl] adj - **1.** [imaginary] mítico(ca) - **2.** [untrue] falso(sa).

mythology [mɪ'θɒlədʒɪ] n [collection of myths] mitología f.

n (pl n's OR ns), **N** (pl N's OR Ns) [en] n [letter] n f, N f. ◆ **N** (abbr of north) N.

n/a, N/A (abbr of not applicable) no corresponde.

nab [næb] vt inf - **1.** [arrest] pillar - **2.** [get quickly] coger.

nag [næg] vt [subj: person] dar la lata a.

nagging ['nægɪŋ] adj - **1.** [thought, doubt] persistente - **2.** [person] gruñón(ona).

nail [neɪl] ◇ n - **1.** [for fastening] clavo m - **2.** [of finger, toe] uña f. ◇ vt: to nail sthg to

sthg clavar algo en OR a algo. ◆ **nail down** vt sep - **1.** [fasten] clavar - **2.** [person]: I couldn't nail him down no me pudo hacerle concretar.

nailbrush ['neɪlbrʌʃ] n cepillo m de uñas.

nail file n lima f de uñas.

nail polish n esmalte m para las uñas.

nail scissors npl tijeras fpl para las uñas.

nail varnish n esmalte m para las uñas.

nail varnish remover [-rɪ'muːvər] n quitaesmaltes m inv.

naive, naïve [naɪ'iːv] adj ingenuo(nua).

naked ['neɪkɪd] adj - **1.** [gen] desnudo(da); naked flame llama f sin protección - **2.** [blatant - hostility, greed] abierto(ta); [- facts] sin tapujos - **3.** [unaided]: with the naked eye a simple vista.

name [neɪm] ◇ n [gen] nombre m; [surname] apellido m; what's your name? ¿cómo te llamas?; my name is John me llamo John; by name por el nombre; it's in my wife's name está a nombre de mi mujer; in the name of en nombre de; to call sb names llamar de todo a alguien; to have a good name tener buena fama. ◇ vt - **1.** [christen] poner nombre a; we named him Jim le llamamos Jim; what's your name after sb UK, to name sb for sb US poner a alguien el nombre de alguien - **2.** [identify] nombrar - **3.** [date, price] poner, decir - **4.** [appoint] nombrar.

nameless ['neɪmlɪs] adj [unknown - person, author] anónimo(ma).

namely ['neɪmlɪ] adv a saber.

namesake ['neɪmseɪk] n tocayo m, -ya f.

nanny ['nænɪ] n niñera f.

nanometre ['nænəʊˌmiːtər], **nanometer** US n nanómetro m.

nap [næp] ◇ n siesta f; to take OR have a nap echar una siesta. ◇ vi: we were caught napping inf nos pillaron desprevenidos.

nape [neɪp] n: nape of the neck nuca f.

napkin ['næpkɪn] n servilleta f.

nappy ['næpɪ] n UK pañal m.

nappy liner n parte desechable de un pañal de gasa.

narcissi [nɑː'sɪsaɪ] npl ▷ **narcissus**.

narcissus [nɑː'sɪsəs] (pl -cissuses OR -cissi) n narciso m.

narcotic [nɑː'kɒtɪk] ◇ adj narcótico(ca). ◇ n narcótico m.

narrative ['nærətɪv] ◇ adj narrativo(va). ◇ n - **1.** [account] narración f - **2.** [art of narrating] narrativa f.

narrator [UK nə'reɪtər, US 'næreɪtər] n narrador m, -ra f.

narrow ['nærəʊ] ◇ adj - **1.** [not wide] estrecho(cha) - **2.** [limited] estrecho(cha) de miras - **3.** [victory, defeat] por un estrecho margen;

[majority] escaso(sa); [escape, miss] por muy poco. ⟨⟩ vi - 1. [become less wide] estrecharse - 2. [eyes] entornarse - 3. [gap] reducirse.
⇒ **narrow down** vt sep reducir.

narrowly ['nærəʊlı] adv [barely] por muy poco.

narrow-minded [-'maındıd] adj estrecho(cha) de miras.

nasal ['neızl] adj nasal.

nasty ['nɑːstı] adj - 1. [unkind] malintencionado(da) - 2. [smell, taste, feeling] desagradable; [weather] horrible - 3. [problem, decision] peliagudo(da) - 4. [injury, disease] doloroso(sa); [accident] grave; [fall] malo(la).

nation ['neıʃn] n nación f.

national ['næʃənl] ⟨⟩ adj nacional. ⟨⟩ n súbdito m, -ta f.

national anthem n himno m nacional.

national dress n traje m típico (de un país).

National Health Service n UK: the National Health Service organismo gestor de la salud pública, ≃ INGS.

National Insurance n UK ≃ Seguridad f Social.

nationalism ['næʃnəlızm] n nacionalismo m.

nationalist ['næʃnəlıst] ⟨⟩ adj nacionalista. ⟨⟩ n nacionalista mf.

nationality [,næʃə'nælətı] n nacionalidad f.

nationalize, -ise ['næʃnəlaız] vt nacionalizar.

national park n parque m nacional.

national service n UK MIL servicio m militar.

National Trust n UK: the National Trust organización británica encargada de la preservación de edificios históricos y lugares de interés, ≃ el Patrimonio Nacional.

nationwide ['neıʃənwaıd] ⟨⟩ adj de ámbito nacional. ⟨⟩ adv [travel] por todo el país; [be broadcast] a todo el país.

native ['neıtıv] ⟨⟩ adj - 1. [country, area] natal - 2. [speaker] nativo(va); **native language** lengua f materna - 3. [plant, animal]: **native (to)** originario(ria) (de). ⟨⟩ n [of country, area] natural mf, nativo m, -va f.

Native American n indio americano m, india americana f.

Nativity [nə'tıvətı] n: the Nativity la Natividad.

NATO ['neıtəʊ] (abbr of North Atlantic Treaty Organization) n la OTAN.

natural ['nætʃrəl] adj - 1. [gen] natural - 2. [comedian, musician] nato(ta).

natural disaster n desastre m natural.

natural gas n gas m natural.

naturalize, -ise ['nætʃrəlaız] vt naturalizar; **to be naturalized** naturalizarse.

naturally ['nætʃrəlı] adv - 1. [as expected, understandably] naturalmente - 2. [unaffectedly] con naturalidad - 3. [instinctively] por naturaleza; **to come naturally to sb** ser innato en alguien.

natural wastage n (U) reducción de plantilla por jubilación escalonada.

nature ['neıtʃər] n - 1. [gen] naturaleza f; **matters of this nature** asuntos de esta índole - 2. [disposition] modo m de ser, carácter m; **by nature** por naturaleza.

nature reserve n reserva f natural.

naughty ['nɔːtı] adj - 1. [badly behaved] travieso(sa), malo(la) - 2. [rude] verde.

nausea ['nɔːsjə] n náuseas fpl.

nauseam ['nɔːzıæm] ⊳ **ad nauseam**.

nauseating ['nɔːsıeıtıŋ] adj lit & fig nauseabundo(da).

nautical ['nɔːtıkl] adj náutico(ca), marítimo(ma).

naval ['neıvl] adj naval.

nave [neıv] n nave f.

navel ['neıvl] n ombligo m.

navigate ['nævıgeıt] ⟨⟩ vt - 1. [steer] pilotar, gobernar - 2. [travel safely across] surcar, navegar por. ⟨⟩ vi [in plane, ship] dirigir, gobernar; [in car] dar direcciones.

navigation [,nævı'geıʃn] n navegación f.

navigator ['nævıgeıtər] n oficial mf de navegación, navegante mf.

navvy ['nævı] n UK inf peón m caminero.

navy ['neıvı] ⟨⟩ n armada f. ⟨⟩ adj [in colour] azul marino (inv).

navy blue adj azul marino (inv).

Nazi ['nɑːtsı] ⟨⟩ adj nazi. ⟨⟩ n (pl -s) nazi mf.

NB (abbr of nota bene) N.B.

near [nıər] ⟨⟩ adj - 1. [close in distance, time] cercano(na); **the near side** el lado más cercano; **in the near future** en un futuro próximo - 2. [related] cercano(na), próximo(ma) - 3. [almost happened]: **it was a near thing** por poco faltó. ⟨⟩ adv - 1. [close in distance, time] cerca; **nowhere near** ni de lejos, ni mucho menos; **to draw OR come near** acercarse - 2. [almost] casi. ⟨⟩ prep - 1. [close in position]: **near (to)** cerca de; **to go near sthg** acercarse a algo - 2. [close in time]: **it's getting near (to) Christmas** ya estamos casi en Navidades; **near the end** casi al final; **nearer the time** cuando se acerque la fecha - 3. [on the point of]: **near (to)** al borde de - 4. [similar to]: **near (to)** cerca de. ⟨⟩ vt acercarse OR aproximarse a. ⟨⟩ vi acercarse, aproximarse.

nearby [nıə'baı] ⟨⟩ adj cercano(na). ⟨⟩ adv cerca.

nearly ['nıəlı] adv casi; **I nearly fell** por poco me caigo.

near miss n - 1. [nearly a hit]: **it was a near miss** falló por poco - 2. [nearly a collision] inci ( )

nearside ['nɪəsaɪd] <> adj [right-hand drive] del lado izquierdo; [left-hand drive] del lado derecho. <> n [right-hand drive] lado m izquierdo; [left-hand drive] lado derecho.

nearsighted [,nɪə'saɪtɪd] adj US miope, corto(ta) de vista.

neat [niːt] adj - 1. [tidy, precise - gen] pulcro(cra); [- room, house] arreglado(da); [- handwriting] esmerado(da) - 2. [smart] arreglado(da), pulcro(cra) - 3. [skilful] hábil - 4. [undiluted] solo(la) - 5. US inf [very good] guay.

neatly ['niːtlɪ] adv - 1. [tidily, smartly] con pulcritud; [write] con esmero - 2. [skilfully] hábilmente.

nebulous ['nebjʊləs] adj fml nebuloso(sa).

necessarily [UK 'nesəsrəlɪ, US ,nesə'serəlɪ] adv necesariamente.

necessary ['nesəsrɪ] adj - 1. [required] necesario(ria) - 2. [inevitable] inevitable.

necessity [nɪ'sesətɪ] n necesidad f; **of necessity** por fuerza, por necesidad. ◆ **necessities** npl artículos mpl de primera necesidad.

neck [nek] <> n [of person, bottle, dress] cuello m; [of animal] pescuezo m, cuello. <> vi inf pegarse el lote.

necklace ['neklɪs] n collar m.

neckline ['neklaɪn] n escote m.

necktie ['nektaɪ] n US corbata f.

nectarine ['nektəriːn] n nectarina f.

née [neɪ] adj de soltera.

need [niːd] <> n: **need (for sthg/to do sthg)** necesidad f (de algo/de hacer algo); **there's no need for you to cry** no hace falta que llores; **if need be** si hace falta; **in need** necesitado(da). <> vt - 1. [require] necesitar; **I need a haircut** me hace falta un corte de pelo; **the floor needs cleaning** hay que limpiar el suelo; **that's all we need!** ¡sólo nos faltaba eso! - 2. [be obliged]: **to need to do sthg** tener que hacer algo. <> modal vb: **to need to do sthg** necesitar hacer algo; **need we go?** ¿tenemos que irnos?; **it need not happen** no tiene por qué ser así.

needle ['niːdl] <> n aguja f. <> vt inf pinchar.

needless ['niːdlɪs] adj innecesario(ria); **needless to say...** está de más decir que...

needlework ['niːdlwɜːk] n - 1. [embroidery] bordado m - 2. (U) [activity] costura f.

needn't ['niːdnt] (abbr of need not) ▷ **need**.

needy ['niːdɪ] adj necesitado(da).

negative ['negətɪv] <> adj negativo(va). <> n - 1. PHOT negativo m - 2. LING negación f, ( )

neglect [nɪ'glekt] <> n [of garden, work] descuido m; [of duty] incumplimiento m; **a state of neglect** un estado de abandono. <> vt - 1. [ignore] desatender - 2. [duty, work] no cumplir con.

neglectful [nɪ'glektfʊl] adj descuidado(da), negligente; **to be neglectful of sthg/sb** desatender algo/a alguien.

negligee ['neglɪʒeɪ] n salto m de cama.

negligence ['neglɪdʒəns] n negligencia f.

negligible ['neglɪdʒəbl] adj insignificante.

negotiate [nɪ'gəʊʃɪeɪt] <> vt - 1. [obtain through negotiation] negociar - 2. [obstacle] salvar, franquear; [bend] tomar. <> vi: **to negotiate (with sb for sthg)** negociar (con alguien algo).

negotiation [nɪ,gəʊʃɪ'eɪʃn] n negociación f. ◆ **negotiations** npl negociaciones fpl.

Negress ['niːgrɪs] n negra f.

Negro ['niːgrəʊ] <> adj negro(gra). <> n (pl -es) negro m, -gra f.

neigh [neɪ] vi relinchar.

neighbour UK, **neighbor** US ['neɪbər] n vecino m, -na f.

neighbourhood UK, **neighborhood** US ['neɪbəhʊd] n - 1. [of town] barrio m, vecindad f - 2. [approximate figure]: **in the neighbourhood of** alrededor de.

neighbouring UK, **neighboring** US ['neɪbərɪŋ] adj vecino(na).

neighbourly UK, **neighborly** US ['neɪbəlɪ] adj [advice] de buen vecino.

neither ['naɪðər, 'niːðər] <> adv: **I don't drink - me neither** no bebo - yo tampoco; **the food was neither good nor bad** la comida no era ni buena ni mala; **to be neither here nor there** no tener nada que ver. <> pron ninguno(na); **neither of us/them** ninguno de nosotros/ellos. <> adj: **neither cup is blue** ninguna de las dos tazas es azul. <> conj: **neither... nor...** ni... ni...; **she could neither eat nor sleep** no podía ni comer ni dormir.

neon ['niːɒn] n neón m.

neon light n luz f de neón.

nephew ['nefjuː] n sobrino m.

Neptune ['neptjuːn] n Neptuno m.

nerve [nɜːv] n - 1. ANAT nervio m - 2. [courage] valor m; **to keep one's nerve** mantener la calma, no perder los nervios; **to lose one's nerve** echarse atrás, perder el valor - 3. [cheek] cara f; **to have the nerve to do sthg** tener la cara de hacer algo. ◆ **nerves** npl nervios mpl.

nerve-racking [-,rækɪŋ] adj crispante.

nervous ['nɜ:vəs] *adj* - **1.** ANAT & PSYCHOL nervioso(sa) - **2.** [apprehensive] inquieto(ta), aprensivo(va).

nervous breakdown *n* crisis *f inv* nerviosa.

nest [nest] ◇ *n* nido *m*; **wasps' nest** avispero *m*; **nest of tables** mesas *fpl* nido. ◇ *vi* anidar.

nest egg *n* ahorros *mpl*.

nestle ['nesl] *vi* [settle snugly - in chair] arrellanarse; [- in bed] acurrucarse.

net [net] ◇ *adj* [weight, price, loss] neto(ta). ◇ *n* red *f*. ◇ *vt* - **1.** [catch] coger con red - **2.** [acquire] embolsarse.

Net [net] *n* COMPUT: **the Net** la Red; **to surf the Net** navegar por la Red.

netball ['netbɔ:l] *n* deporte parecido al baloncesto femenino.

net curtains *npl* visillos *mpl*.

Netherlands ['neðələndz] *npl*: **the Netherlands** los Países Bajos.

netiquette ['netɪket] *n* COMPUT netiqueta *f*.

netting ['netɪŋ] *n* red *f*, malla *f*.

nettle ['netl] *n* ortiga *f*.

network ['netwɜ:k] ◇ *n* - **1.** [gen & COMPUT] red *f* - **2.** RADIO & TV [station] cadena *f*. ◇ *vt* COMPUT conectar a la red.

neurosis [,njʊə'rəʊsɪs] (*pl* -ses [-si:z]) *n* neurosis *f inv*.

neurotic [,njʊə'rɒtɪk] ◇ *adj* neurótico(ca). ◇ *n* neurótico *m*, -ca *f*.

neuter ['nju:tə'] ◇ *adj* neutro(tra). ◇ *vt* castrar.

neutral ['nju:trəl] ◇ *adj* - **1.** [gen] neutro(tra) - **2.** [non-allied] neutral. ◇ *n* AUT punto *m* muerto.

neutrality [nju:'trælətɪ] *n* neutralidad *f*.

neutralize, -ise ['nju:trəlaɪz] *vt* neutralizar.

never ['nevə'] *adv* - **1.** [not time] nunca, jamás; **I've never done it** no lo he hecho nunca; **never again** nunca más; **never ever** nunca jamás, nunca en la vida; **well I never!** ¡vaya!, ¡caramba! - **2.** *inf* [as negative] no; **I never knew** no lo sabía; **you never did!** ¡no (me digas)!

never-ending *adj* inacabable.

nevertheless [,nevəðə'les] *adv* sin embargo, no obstante.

new [nju:] *adj* nuevo(va); [baby] recién nacido (recién nacida); **to be new to sthg** ser nuevo(va) en algo; **as good as new** como nuevo.

▸ **news** *n* (U) noticias *fpl*; **a piece of news** una noticia; **the news** [gen] las noticias; [on TV] el telediario; **that's news to me** me coge de nuevas; **to break the news to sb** dar la noticia a alguien.

newborn ['nju:bɔ:n] *adj* recién nacido (recién nacida).

newcomer ['nju:,kʌmə'] *n*: **newcomer (to)** recién llegado *m*, recién llegada *f* (a).

New Delhi *n* Nueva Delhi.

newfangled [,nju:'fæŋgld] *adj inf pej* moderno(na).

new-found *adj* [gen] recién descubierto (recién descubierta); [friend] reciente.

newly ['nju:lɪ] *adv* recién.

newlyweds ['nju:lɪwedz] *npl* recién casados *mpl*.

new moon *n* luna *f* nueva.

news agency *n* agencia *f* de noticias.

newsagent UK ['nju:zeɪdʒənt], **newsdealer** US ['nju:zdi:lər] *n* [person] vendedor *m*, -ra *f* de periódicos; **newsagent's (shop)** *tienda en la que se vende prensa así como tabaco y chucherías*.

newscaster ['nju:zkɑ:stə'] *n* presentador *m*, -ra *f*, locutor *m*, -ra *f*.

newsdealer US = **newsagent**.

newsflash ['nju:zflæʃ] *n* noticia *f* de última hora.

newsletter ['nju:z,letə'] *n* boletín *m*.

newspaper ['nju:z,peɪpə'] *n* - **1.** [publication, company] periódico *m*; [daily] diario *m* - **2.** [paper] papel *m* de periódico.

newsprint ['nju:zprɪnt] *n* papel *m* de periódico.

newsreader ['nju:z,ri:də'] *n* presentador *m*, -ra *f*, locutor *m*, -ra *f*.

newsreel ['nju:zri:l] *n* noticiario *m* cinematográfico.

newsstand ['nju:zstænd] *n* US quiosco *m* de periódicos.

newt [nju:t] *n* tritón *m*.

new technology *n* nueva tecnología *f*.

new town *n* UK ciudad nueva construida por el gobierno.

New Year *n* Año *m* Nuevo; **Happy New Year!** ¡Feliz Año Nuevo!

New Year's Day *n* el día de Año Nuevo.

New Year's Eve *n* Nochevieja *f*.

New York [-'jɔ:k] *n* - **1.** [city]: **New York (City)** Nueva York - **2.** [state]: **New York (State)** (el estado de) Nueva York.

New Zealand [-'zi:lənd] *n* Nueva Zelanda.

New Zealander [-'zi:ləndə'] *n* neozelandés *m*, -esa *f*.

next [nekst] ◇ *adj* - **1.** [in time] próximo(ma); **the next day** el día siguiente; **next Tuesday/year** el martes/el año que viene; **next week** la semana próxima OR que viene; **the next week** los próximos siete días - **2.** [in space - page etc] siguiente; [- room, house] de al lado. ◇ *pron* el siguiente (la siguiente); **who's next?** ¿quién es el siguiente?; **next,**

please! ¡el siguiente, por favor!; **the day after next** pasado mañana; **the week after next** la semana que viene no, la otra ◇ *adv* - **1.** [afterwards] después; **what should I do next?** ¿qué hago ahora?; **it's my go next** ahora me toca a mí - **2.** [again] de nuevo; **when do they next play?** ¿cuándo vuelven a jugar? - **3.** [with superlatives]: **next best/biggest** *etc* el segundo mejor/más grande *etc.* ◇ *prep US* al lado de, junto a. ◈ **next to** *prep* al lado de, junto a; **next to nothing** casi nada; **in next to no time** en un abrir y cerrar de ojos.

next door *adv* (en la casa de) al lado. ◈ **next-door** *adj*: **next-door neighbour** vecino *m*, -na *f* de al lado.

next of kin *n* pariente más cercano *m*, pariente más cercana *f*.

NHS (*abbr of* **National Health Service**) *n*: **the National Health Service** organismo gestor de la salud pública, ≃ INGS.

NI ◇ *n abbr of* **National Insurance**. ◇ *abbr of* **Northern Ireland**.

nib [nɪb] *n* plumilla *f*.

nibble [ˈnɪbl] *vt* mordisquear.

Nicaragua [ˌnɪkəˈrægjʊə] *n* Nicaragua.

Nicaraguan [ˌnɪkəˈrægjʊən] ◇ *adj* nicaragüense. ◇ *n* nicaragüense *mf*.

nice [naɪs] *adj* - **1.** [attractive] bonito(ta); **you look nice** estás guapa; [good] bueno(na); **it smells nice** huele bien - **2.** [kind] amable; [friendly] agradable, simpático(ca), dije *Amér*; **that was nice of you** fue muy amable de tu parte; **to be nice to sb** ser bueno con alguien - **3.** [pleasant] agradable; **to have a nice time** pasarlo bien.

nice-looking [-ˈlʊkɪŋ] *adj* [person] guapo(pa); [car, room] bonito(ta).

nicely [ˈnaɪslɪ] *adv* - **1.** [well, attractively] bien - **2.** [politely] educadamente, con educación - **3.** [satisfactorily] bien; **that will do nicely** esto irá de perlas.

niche [niːʃ] *n* - **1.** [in wall] nicho *m*, hornacina *f* - **2.** [in life] hueco *m* - **3.** COMM nicho *m*.

nick [nɪk] ◇ *n* [cut] cortecito *m*; [notch] muesca *f*. ▶▶▶ **in the nick of time** justo a tiempo. ◇ *vt* - **1.** [cut] cortar; [make notch in] mellar - **2.** *UK inf* [steal] birlar.

nickel [ˈnɪkl] *n* - **1.** [metal] níquel *m* - **2.** *US* [coin] moneda *f* de cinco centavos.

nickname [ˈnɪkneɪm] ◇ *n* apodo *m*. ◇ *vt* apodar.

nicotine [ˈnɪkətiːn] *n* nicotina *f*.

niece [niːs] *n* sobrina *f*.

Nigeria [naɪˈdʒɪərɪə] *n* Nigeria.

Nigerian [naɪˈdʒɪərɪən] ◇ *adj* nigeriano(na). ◇ *n* nigeriano *m*, -na *f*.

niggle [ˈnɪgl] *vt UK* - **1.** [worry] inquietar - **2.** [criticize] meterse con.

night [naɪt] ◇ *n* noche *f*; [evening] tarde *f*; **last night** anoche, ayer por la noche; **tomorrow night** mañana por la noche; **at night** por la noche, de noche; **night and day, day and night** noche y día, día y noche; **to have an early/a late night** irse a dormir pronto/tarde. ◈ **nights** *adv* - **1.** *US* [at night] por las noches - **2.** *UK* [nightshift]: **to work nights** hacer el turno de noche.

nightcap [ˈnaɪtkæp] *n* [drink] *bebida que se toma antes de ir a dormir.*

nightclub [ˈnaɪtklʌb] *n* club *m* nocturno.

nightdress [ˈnaɪtdres] *n* camisón *m*.

nightfall [ˈnaɪtfɔːl] *n* anochecer *m*.

nightgown [ˈnaɪtgaʊn] *n* camisón *m*.

nightie [ˈnaɪtɪ] *n inf* camisón *m*.

nightingale [ˈnaɪtɪŋgeɪl] *n* ruiseñor *m*.

nightlife [ˈnaɪtlaɪf] *n* vida *f* nocturna.

nightly [ˈnaɪtlɪ] ◇ *adj* nocturno(na), de cada noche. ◇ *adv* cada noche.

nightmare [ˈnaɪtmeər] *n lit & fig* pesadilla *f*.

night porter *n* recepcionista *mf* del turno de noche.

night school *n* (U) escuela *f* nocturna.

night shift *n* turno *m* de noche.

nightshirt [ˈnaɪtʃɜːt] *n* camisa *f* de dormir (masculina).

nighttime [ˈnaɪttaɪm] *n* noche *f*.

nil [nɪl] *n* - **1.** [nothing] nada *f* - **2.** *UK* SPORT cero *m*; **five nil** cinco a cero.

Nile [naɪl] *n*: **the Nile** el Nilo.

nimble [ˈnɪmbl] *adj* - **1.** [person, fingers] ágil - **2.** [mind] rápido(da).

nine [naɪn] *num* nueve; *see also* **six**.

nineteen [ˌnaɪnˈtiːn] *num* diecinueve; *see also* **six**.

ninety [ˈnaɪntɪ] *num* noventa; *see also* **sixty**.

ninth [naɪnθ] *num* noveno(na); *see also* **sixth**.

nip [nɪp] ◇ *n* [of drink] trago *m*. ◇ *vt* [pinch] pellizcar; [bite] mordisquear.

nipple [ˈnɪpl] *n* - **1.** [of woman] pezón *m* - **2.** [of baby's bottle, man] tetilla *f*.

nit [nɪt] *n* [in hair] liendre *f*.

nitpicking [ˈnɪtpɪkɪŋ] *inf n* (U): **that's just nitpicking** no son más que nimiedades.

nitrogen [ˈnaɪtrədʒən] *n* nitrógeno *m*.

nitty-gritty [ˌnɪtɪˈgrɪtɪ] *n inf*: **to get down to the nitty-gritty** ir al grano.

no [nəʊ] ◇ *adv* [gen] no; **to say no** decir que no; **you're no better than me** tú no eres mejor que yo. <> *adj* no; **I have no time** no tengo tiempo; **there are no taxis** no hay taxis; **a woman with no money** una mujer sin dinero; **that's no excuse** esa no es excusa que valga; **he's no fool** no es ningún tonto; **she's no friend of mine** no es amiga mía; **'no smoking/parking/cameras'** 'prohibido fumar/aparcar/hacer fotos'. <> *n* (*pl* **-es**) no *m*; **he/she won't take no for an answer** no acepta una respuesta negativa.

No., no. (*abbr of* number) n.º

nobility [nə'bɪlətɪ] *n* nobleza *f*.

noble ['nəubl] <> *adj* noble. <> *n* noble *mf*.

nobody ['nəubədɪ], **no one** <> *pron* nadie. <> *n pej* don nadie *m*.

nocturnal [nɒk'tɜːnl] *adj* nocturno(na).

nod [nɒd] <> *vt*: **to nod one's head** [in agreement] asentir con la cabeza; [to indicate sthg] indicar con la cabeza; [as greeting] saludar con la cabeza. <> *vi* - **1.** [in agreement] asentir con la cabeza - **2.** [to indicate sthg] indicar con la cabeza - **3.** [as greeting] saludar con la cabeza.
♦ **nod off** *vi* quedarse dormido(da).

noise [nɔɪz] *n* ruido *m*; **to make a noise** hacer ruido.

noisy ['nɔɪzɪ] *adj* ruidoso(sa); **it was very noisy** había mucho ruido.

no-man's-land *n* tierra *f* de nadie.

nominal ['nɒmɪnl] *adj* nominal.

nominate ['nɒmɪneɪt] *vt* - **1.** [propose]: **to nominate sb (for** OR **as)** proponer a alguien (por OR como) - **2.** [appoint]: **to nominate sb (to** sthg) nombrar a alguien (algo).

nomination [ˌnɒmɪ'neɪʃn] *n* - **1.** [proposal] nominación *f* - **2.** [appointment]: **nomination (to** sthg) nombramiento *m* (a algo).

nominee [ˌnɒmɪ'niː] *n* candidato *m*, -ta *f*.

non- [nɒn] *prefix* no.

nonalcoholic [ˌnɒnælkə'hɒlɪk] *adj* sin alcohol.

nonaligned [ˌnɒnə'laɪnd] *adj* no alineado(da).

nonchalant [UK 'nɒnʃələnt, US ˌnɒnʃə'lɑːnt] *adj* despreocupado(da).

noncommittal [ˌnɒnkə'mɪtl] *adj* evasivo(va).

nonconformist [ˌnɒnkən'fɔːmɪst] <> *adj* inconformista. <> *n* inconformista *mf*.

nondescript [UK 'nɒndɪskrɪpt, US ˌnɒndɪ'skrɪpt] *adj* anodino(na), soso(sa).

none [nʌn] <> *pron* - **1.** [not any] nada; **there is none left** no queda nada; **it's none of your business** no es asunto tuyo - **2.** [not one - object, person] ninguno(na); **none of us/the books** ninguno de nosotros/de los libros; **I had none** no tenía ninguno. <> *adv*: **I'm none the worse/better** no me ha perjudicado/ayudado en nada; **I'm none the wiser** no me ha aclarado nada. ♦ **none too** *adv* no demasiado; **none too soon** justo a tiempo.

nonentity [nɒ'nentətɪ] *n* cero *m* a la izquierda.

nonetheless [ˌnʌnðə'les] *adv* sin embargo, no obstante.

non-event *n* chasco *m*.

nonexistent [ˌnɒnɪg'zɪstənt] *adj* inexistente.

nonfiction [ˌnɒn'fɪkʃn] *n* no ficción *f*.

no-nonsense *adj* práctico(ca).

nonpayment [ˌnɒn'peɪmənt] *n* impago *m*.

nonplussed, nonplused US [ˌnɒn'plʌst] *adj* perplejo(ja).

nonreturnable [ˌnɒnrɪ'tɜːnəbl] *adj* no retornable, sin retorno.

nonsense ['nɒnsəns] <> *n* (*U*) - **1.** [gen] tonterías *fpl*; **it is nonsense to suggest that...** es absurdo sugerir que... - **2.** [incomprehensible words] galimatías *m inv*. <> *excl* ¡tonterías!

nonsensical [nɒn'sensɪkl] *adj* disparatado(da), absurdo(da).

nonsmoker [ˌnɒn'sməukəʳ] *n* no fumador *m*, no fumadora *f*.

nonstick [ˌnɒn'stɪk] *adj* antiadherente.

nonstop [ˌnɒn'stɒp] <> *adj* [activity, rain] continuo(nua), incesante; [flight] sin escalas. <> *adv* sin parar.

noodles ['nuːdlz] *npl* tallarines *mpl* chinos.

nook [nuk] *n* [of room]: **every nook and cranny** todos los recovecos.

noon [nuːn] *n* mediodía *m*.

no one *pron* = **nobody**.

noose [nuːs] *n* [loop] nudo *m* corredizo; [for hanging] soga *f*.

no-place US = **nowhere**.

nor [nɔːʳ] *conj* - **1.** ⊳ **neither** - **2.** [and not] ni; **I don't smoke – nor do I** no fumo – yo tampoco; **I don't know, nor do I care** ni lo sé, ni me importa.

norm [nɔːm] *n* norma *f*; **the norm** lo normal.

normal ['nɔːml] <> *adj* normal. <> *n*: **above normal** por encima de lo normal; **to return to normal** volver a la normalidad.

normality [nɔː'mælɪtɪ], **normalcy** US ['nɔːmlsɪ] *n* normalidad *f*.

normally ['nɔːməlɪ] *adv* normalmente.

north [nɔːθ] <> *n* - **1.** [direction] norte *m* - **2.** [region]: **the North** el norte. <> *adj* del norte; **North London** el norte de Londres. <> *adv*: **north (of)** al norte (de).

North Africa *n* África del Norte.

North America *n* Norteamérica.

North American <> *adj* norteamericano(na). <> *n* norteamericano *m*, -na *f*.

northeast [,nɔːθ'iːst] <> *n* - **1.** [direction] nordeste *m* - **2.** [region]: **the Northeast** el nordeste. <> *adj* del nordeste. <> *adv*: **northeast (of)** al nordeste (de).

northerly ['nɔːðəlɪ] *adj* del norte.

northern ['nɔːðən] *adj* del norte, norteño(ña); **northern France** el norte de Francia.

Northern Ireland *n* Irlanda del Norte.

northernmost ['nɔːðənməʊst] *adj* más septentrional OR al norte.

North Korea *n* Corea del Norte.

North Pole *n*: **the North Pole** el Polo Norte.

North Sea *n*: **the North Sea** el Mar del Norte.

northward ['nɔːθwəd] <> *adj* hacia el norte. <> *adv* = **northwards**.

northwards ['nɔːθwədz], **northward** *adv* hacia el norte.

northwest [,nɔːθ'west] <> *n* - **1.** [direction] noroeste *m* - **2.** [region]: **the Northwest** el noroeste. <> *adj* del noroeste. <> *adv*: **northwest (of)** al noroeste (de).

Norway ['nɔːweɪ] *n* Noruega.

Norwegian [nɔː'wiːdʒən] <> *adj* noruego(ga). <> *n* - **1.** [person] noruego *m*, -ga *f* - **2.** [language] noruego *m*.

nose [nəʊz] *n* [of person] nariz *f*; [of animal] hocico *m*; [of plane, car] morro *m*; **to keep one's nose out of sthg** no meter las narices en algo; **to poke** OR **stick one's nose in** *inf* meter las narices; **to turn up one's nose at sthg** hacerle ascos a algo. ► **nose about, nose around** *vi* curiosear.

nosebleed ['nəʊzbliːd] *n* hemorragia *f* nasal.

nosedive ['nəʊzdaɪv] <> *n* [of plane] picado *m*. <> *vi lit & fig* bajar en picado.

nosey ['nəʊzɪ] = **nosy**.

no-smoking *adj* [area, carriage] para no fumadores; [flight] de no fumadores.

nostalgia [nɒ'stældʒə] *n*: **nostalgia (for)** nostalgia *f* (de).

nostril ['nɒstrəl] *n* ventana *f* de la nariz.

nosy ['nəʊzɪ], **nosey** *adj* fisgón(ona), entrometido(da).

not [nɒt] *adv* no; **this is not the first time** no es la primera vez; **it's green, isn't it?** es verde, ¿no?; **not me** yo no; **I hope/think not** espero/creo que no; **not even a...** ni siquiera un(una)...; **not all** OR **every** no todos(das); **not always** no siempre; **not that...** no es que...; **not at all** [no] en absoluto; [to acknowledge thanks] de nada.

notable ['nəʊtəbl] *adj* notable; **to be notable for sthg** destacar por algo.

notably ['nəʊtəblɪ] *adv* - **1.** [in particular] especialmente - **2.** [noticeably] marcadamente.

notary ['nəʊtərɪ] *n*: **notary (public)** notario *m*, -ria *f*.

notch [nɒtʃ] *n* [cut] muesca *f*.

note [nəʊt] <> *n* - **1.** [gen] nota *f*; **to make a note of sthg** tomar nota de algo - **2.** [paper money] billete *m* - **3.** [tone] tono *m*. <> *vt* - **1.** [observe] notar; **please note that...** tenga en cuenta que... - **2.** [mention] mencionar. ► **notes** *npl* [written record] apuntes *mpl*; **to take notes** tomar apuntes; [in book] notas *fpl*. ► **note down** *vt sep* anotar, apuntar.

notebook ['nəʊtbʊk] *n* - **1.** [for taking notes] libreta *f*, cuaderno *m* - **2.** COMPUT: **notebook (computer)** ordenador *m* portátil.

noted ['nəʊtɪd] *adj* destacado(da); **to be noted for** distinguirse por.

notepad ['nəʊtpæd] *n* bloc *m* de notas.

notepaper ['nəʊtpeɪpə*r*] *n* papel *m* de escribir OR de cartas.

noteworthy ['nəʊt,wɜːðɪ] *adj* digno(na) de mención.

nothing ['nʌθɪŋ] <> *pron* nada; **I've got nothing to do** no tengo nada que hacer; **for nothing** [free] gratis; [for no purpose] en vano, en balde; **he's nothing if not generous** otra cosa no será pero desde luego generoso sí que es; **nothing but** tan sólo. <> *adv*: **to be nothing like sb/sthg** no parecerse en nada a alguien/algo; **I'm nothing like finished** no he terminado ni mucho menos.

notice ['nəʊtɪs] <> *n* - **1.** [on wall, door] cartel *m*; [in newspaper] anuncio *m* - **2.** [attention] atención *f*; **to take notice (of)** hacer caso (de), prestar atención (a); **he/she didn't take a blind bit of notice** no hizo ni el más mínimo caso - **3.** [warning] aviso *m*; **at short notice** casi sin previo aviso; **until further notice** hasta nuevo aviso; **without notice** sin previo aviso - **4.** [at work]: **to be given one's notice** ser despedido(da); **to hand in one's notice** presentar la dimisión. <> *vt* - **1.** [sense, smell] notar; [see] fijarse en, ver; **to notice sb doing sthg** fijarse en alguien que está haciendo algo - **2.** [realize] darse cuenta de. <> *vi* darse cuenta.

noticeable ['nəʊtɪsəbl] *adj* notable.

notice board *n* tablón *m* de anuncios.

notify ['nəʊtɪfaɪ] *vt*: **to notify sb (of sthg)** notificar OR comunicar (algo) a alguien.

notion ['nəʊʃn] *n* noción *f*. ► **notions** *npl* US artículos *mpl* de mercería.

notorious [nəʊ'tɔːrɪəs] *adj* famoso(sa), célebre.

notwithstanding [,nɒtwɪθ'stændɪŋ] *fml* <> *prep* a pesar de. <> *adv* sin embargo.

nougat ['nuːgɑː] *n* dulce hecho a base de nueces y frutas.

nought [nɔːt] *num* cero.

noun [naʊn] *n* nombre *m*, sustantivo *m*.

nourish ['nʌrɪʃ] *vt* - 1. [feed] nutrir - 2. [entertain] alimentar, albergar.

nourishing ['nʌrɪʃɪŋ] *adj* nutritivo(va).

nourishment ['nʌrɪʃmənt] *n* alimento *m*, sustento *m*.

novel ['nɒvl] <> *adj* original. <> *n* novela *f*.

novelist ['nɒvəlɪst] *n* novelista *mf*.

novelty ['nɒvltɪ] *n* - 1. [gen] novedad *f* - 2. [cheap object] baratija *f* (poco útil).

November [nə'vembər] *n* noviembre *m*; *see also* **September**.

novice ['nɒvɪs] *n* - 1. [inexperienced person] principiante *mf* - 2. RELIG novicio *m*, -cia *f*.

now [naʊ] <> *adv* - 1. [at this time, at once] ahora; **do it now** hazlo ahora; **he's been away for two weeks now** lleva dos semanas fuera; **any day now** cualquier día de éstos; **any time now** en cualquier momento; **for now** por ahora, por el momento; **now and then** OR **again** de vez en cuando - 2. [nowadays] hoy día - 3. [at a particular time in the past] entonces - 4. [to introduce statement] vamos a ver. <> *conj*: **now (that)** ahora que, ya que. <> *n* ahora; **five days from now** de aquí a cinco días; **from now on** a partir de ahora; **they should be here by now** ya deberían estar aquí; **up until now** hasta ahora.

nowadays ['naʊədeɪz] *adv* hoy en día, actualmente.

nowhere *UK* ['nəʊweər], **no-place** *US adv* [be] en ninguna parte; [go] a ninguna parte; **nowhere else** en ninguna otra parte; **to appear out of** OR **from nowhere** salir de la nada; **to be getting nowhere** no estar avanzando nada, no ir a ninguna parte; **(to be) nowhere near (as... as...)** (no ser) ni mucho menos (tan... como...)

nozzle ['nɒzl] *n* boquilla *f*.

nuance [njuː'ɑːns] *n* matiz *m*.

nuclear ['njuːklɪər] *adj* nuclear.

nuclear bomb *n* bomba *f* atómica.

nuclear disarmament *n* desarme *m* nuclear.

nuclear energy *n* energía *f* nuclear.

nuclear power *n* energía *f* nuclear.

nuclear power station *n* central *f* nuclear.

nuclear reactor *n* reactor *m* nuclear.

nucleus ['njuːklɪəs] (*pl* **-lei** [-lɪaɪ]) *n* lit & fig núcleo *m*.

nude [njuːd] <> *adj* desnudo(da). <> *n* ART desnudo *m*; **in the nude** desnudo(da).

nudge [nʌdʒ] *vt* [with elbow] dar un codazo a.

nudist ['njuːdɪst] *n* nudista *mf*.

nudity ['njuːdətɪ] *n* desnudez *f*.

nugget ['nʌgɪt] *n* [of gold] pepita *f*.

nuisance ['njuːsns] *n* [thing] fastidio *m*, molestia *f*; [person] pesado *m*; **to make a nuisance of o.s.** dar la lata.

nuke [njuːk] *inf* <> *n* bomba *f* atómica. <> *vt* - 1. MIL atacar con arma nuclear - 2. [cook in microwave] cocinar en el microondas.

null [nʌl] *adj*: **null and void** nulo(la) y sin efecto.

numb [nʌm] <> *adj* entumecido(da); **to be numb with cold** estar helado(da) de frío; **to be numb with fear** estar paralizado(da) de miedo. <> *vt* entumecer.

number ['nʌmbər] <> *n* - 1. [gen] número *m*; **a number of** varios(rias); **a large number of** gran número de; **large numbers of** grandes cantidades de; **any number of** la mar de - 2. [of car] matrícula *f*. <> *vt* - 1. [amount to] ascender a - 2. [give a number to] numerar - 3. [include]: **to be numbered among** figurar entre.

number one <> *adj* principal, número uno. <> *n inf* [oneself] uno mismo (una misma).

numberplate ['nʌmbəpleɪt] *n* matrícula *f* (de vehículo).

Number Ten *n* el número 10 de Downing Street, residencia oficial del primer ministro británico.

numeral ['njuːmərəl] *n* número *m*, cifra *f*.

numerate ['njuːmərət] *adj UK* competente en aritmética.

numerical [njuː'merɪkl] *adj* numérico(ca).

numerous ['njuːmərəs] *adj* numeroso(sa).

nun [nʌn] *n* monja *f*.

nurse [nɜːs] <> *n* MED enfermero *m*, -ra *f*; [nanny] niñera *f*. <> *vt* - 1. [care for] cuidar, atender - 2. [try to cure - a cold] curarse - 3. *fig* [nourish] abrigar - 4. [subj: mother] amamantar.

nursery ['nɜːsərɪ] *n* - 1. [at home] cuarto *m* de los niños; [away from home] guardería *f* - 2. [for plants] semillero *m*, vivero *m*.

nursery rhyme *n* poema *m* OR canción *f* infantil.

nursery school *n* parvulario *m*.

nursery slopes *npl* pista *f* para principiantes.

nursing ['nɜːsɪŋ] *n* [profession] profesión *f* de enfermera; [of patient] asistencia *f*, cuidado *m*.

nursing home *n* [for old people] clínica *f* de reposo (privada); [for childbirth] clínica *f* (privada) de maternidad.

nurture ['nɜːtʃər] *vt* - 1. [child, plant] criar - 2. [plan, feelings] alimentar.

nut [nʌt] *n* - 1. [to eat] nuez *f* - 2. [of metal] tuerca *f*; **the nuts and bolts** *fig* lo esencial, lo básico - 3. *inf* [mad person] chiflado *m*, -da *f*.
◆ **nuts** *inf* <> *adj*: **to be nuts** estar chalado(da). <> *excl US* ¡maldita sea!

nutcrackers ['nʌt,krækəz] *npl* cascanueces *m inv.*

nutmeg ['nʌtmeg] *n* nuez *f* moscada.

nutritious [nju:'trɪʃəs] *adj* nutritivo(va).

nutshell ['nʌtʃel] *n*: **in a nutshell** en una palabra.

nuzzle ['nʌzl] ⟨⟩ *vt* rozar con el hocico. ⟨⟩ *vi*: **to nuzzle (up) against** arrimarse a.

NVQ (*abbr of* **National Vocational Qualification**) *n* título de formación profesional en Inglaterra y Gales.

nylon ['naɪlɒn] ⟨⟩ *n* nylon *m.* ⟨⟩ *comp* de nylon.

o (*pl* **o's** OR **os**), **O** (*pl* **O's** OR **Os**) [əʊ] *n* - **1.** [letter] o *f*, O *f* - **2.** [zero] cero *m.*

oak [əʊk] ⟨⟩ *n* roble *m.* ⟨⟩ *comp* de roble.

OAP *n abbr of* **old age pensioner**.

oar [ɔːr] *n* remo *m*; **to put** OR **stick one's oar in** entrometerse.

oasis [əʊ'eɪsɪs] (*pl* **oases** [əʊ'eɪsi:z]) *n lit & fig* oasis *m inv.*

oatcake ['əʊtkeɪk] *n* galleta *f* de avena.

oath [əʊθ] *n* - **1.** [promise] juramento *m*; **on** OR **under oath** bajo juramento - **2.** [swearword] palabrota *f.*

oatmeal ['əʊtmiːl] US *n* [flakes] copos *mpl* de avena; [porridge] avena *f.*

oats [əʊts] *npl* [grain] avena *f.*

obedience [ə'biːdjəns] *n*: **obedience (to sb)** obediencia *f* (a alguien).

obedient [ə'biːdjənt] *adj* obediente.

obese [əʊ'biːs] *adj fml* obeso(sa).

obey [ə'beɪ] *vt & vi* obedecer.

obituary [ə'bɪtʃʊərɪ] *n* nota *f* necrológica, necrología *f.*

object ⟨⟩ *n* ['ɒbdʒɪkt] - **1.** [gen & COMPUT] objeto *m* - **2.** [aim] objeto *m*, propósito *m* - **3.** GRAM complemento *m.* ⟨⟩ *vt* [ɒb'dʒekt] objetar. ⟨⟩ *vi* [ɒb'dʒekt]: **to object (to sthg/to doing sthg)** oponerse (a algo/a hacer algo); **I object to that comment** me parece muy mal ese comentario.

objection [əb'dʒekʃn] *n* objeción *f*, reparo *m*; **to have no objection (to sthg/to doing sthg)** no tener inconveniente (en algo/en hacer algo).

objectionable [əb'dʒekʃənəbl] *adj* [person] desagradable; [behaviour] censurable.

objective [əb'dʒektɪv] ⟨⟩ *adj* objetivo(va). ⟨⟩ *n* objetivo *m.*

obligation [,ɒblɪ'geɪʃn] *n* - **1.** [compulsion] obligación *f*; **to be under an obligation to do sthg** tener la obligación de hacer algo - **2.** [duty] deber *m.*

obligatory [ə'blɪgətrɪ] *adj* obligatorio(ria).

oblige [ə'blaɪdʒ] *vt* - **1.** [force]: **to oblige sb to do sthg** obligar a alguien a hacer algo - **2.** *fml* [do a favour to] hacer un favor a; **I would be much obliged if...** le estaría muy agradecido si...

obliging [ə'blaɪdʒɪŋ] *adj* servicial, atento(ta).

oblique [ə'bliːk] ⟨⟩ *adj* - **1.** [indirect - reference] indirecto(ta) - **2.** [slanting] oblicuo(cua). ⟨⟩ *n* TYPO barra *f.*

obliterate [ə'blɪtəreɪt] *vt* arrasar.

oblivion [ə'blɪvɪən] *n* olvido *m.*

oblivious [ə'blɪvɪəs] *adj* inconsciente; **to be oblivious to** OR **of sthg** no ser consciente de algo.

oblong ['ɒblɒŋ] ⟨⟩ *adj* rectangular, oblongo(ga). ⟨⟩ *n* rectángulo *m.*

obnoxious [əb'nɒkʃəs] *adj* detestable.

oboe ['əʊbəʊ] *n* oboe *m.*

obscene [əb'siːn] *adj* obsceno(na).

obscure [əb'skjʊər] ⟨⟩ *adj lit & fig* oscuro(ra). ⟨⟩ *vt* - **1.** [make difficult to understand] oscurecer - **2.** [hide] esconder.

obsequious [əb'siːkwɪəs] *adj fml & pej* servil.

observance [əb'zɜːvns] *n* observancia *f*, cumplimiento *m.*

observant [əb'zɜːvnt] *adj* observador(ra).

observation [,ɒbzə'veɪʃn] *n* - **1.** [by police] vigilancia *f*; [by doctor] observación *f* - **2.** [comment] comentario *m.*

observatory [əb'zɜːvətrɪ] *n* observatorio *m.*

observe [əb'zɜːv] *vt* - **1.** [gen] observar - **2.** [obey] cumplir con, observar.

observer [əb'zɜːvər] *n* observador *m*, -ra *f.*

obsess [əb'ses] *vt* obsesionar; **to be obsessed by** OR **with** estar obsesionado con.

obsessive [əb'sesɪv] *adj* obsesivo(va).

obsolescent [,ɒbsə'lesnt] *adj* obsolescente.

obsolete ['ɒbsəliːt] *adj* obsoleto(ta).

obstacle ['ɒbstəkl] *n* - **1.** [object] obstáculo *m* - **2.** [difficulty] estorbo *m.*

obstetrics [ɒbˈstetrɪks] *n* obstetricia *f*.

obstinate [ˈɒbstənət] *adj* - **1.** [stubborn] obstinado(da), terco(ca) - **2.** [persistent] tenaz.

obstruct [əbˈstrʌkt] *vt* - **1.** [block] obstruir, bloquear - **2.** [hinder] estorbar.

obstruction [əbˈstrʌkʃn] *n* [gen & SPORT] obstrucción *f*; [blockage] atasco *m*.

obtain [əbˈteɪn] *vt* obtener, conseguir.

obtainable [əbˈteɪnəbl] *adj* que se puede conseguir, disponible.

obtrusive [əbˈtruːsɪv] *adj* [smell] penetrante; [colour] chillón(ona); [person] entrometido(da).

obtuse [əbˈtjuːs] *adj lit* & *fig* obtuso(sa).

obvious [ˈɒbvɪəs] *adj* obvio(via), evidente.

obviously [ˈɒbvɪəslɪ] *adv* - **1.** [of course] evidentemente, obviamente; **obviously not** claro que no - **2.** [clearly] claramente.

occasion [əˈkeɪʒn] *n* - **1.** [time] vez *f*, ocasión *f*; **on one occasion** una vez, en una ocasión; **on several occasions** varias veces, en varias ocasiones; **on occasion** *fml* de vez en cuando - **2.** [important event] acontecimiento *m*; **to rise to the occasion** ponerse a la altura de las circunstancias - **3.** *fml* [opportunity] ocasión *f*.

occasional [əˈkeɪʒənl] *adj* [trip, drink] esporádico(ca); [showers] ocasional.

occasionally [əˈkeɪʒnəlɪ] *adv* de vez en cuando.

occult [ɒˈkʌlt] *adj* oculto(ta).

occupant [ˈɒkjʊpənt] *n* - **1.** [of building, room] inquilino *m*, -na *f* - **2.** [of chair, vehicle] ocupante *mf*.

occupation [ˌɒkjʊˈpeɪʃn] *n* - **1.** [job] empleo *m*, ocupación *f* - **2.** [pastime] pasatiempo *m* - **3.** MIL [of country, building] ocupación *f*.

occupational hazard *n*: **occupational hazards** gajes *mpl* del oficio.

occupational therapy *n* terapia *f* ocupacional.

occupier [ˈɒkjʊpaɪəʳ] *n* inquilino *m*, -na *f*.

occupy [ˈɒkjʊpaɪ] *vt* - **1.** [gen] ocupar - **2.** [live in] habitar - **3.** [entertain]: **to occupy o.s.** entretenerse.

occur [əˈkɜːʳ] *vi* - **1.** [happen] ocurrir, suceder - **2.** [be present] encontrarse.

occurrence [əˈkʌrəns] *n* [event] acontecimiento *m*.

ocean [ˈəʊʃn] *n* océano *m*.

oceangoing [ˈəʊʃn͵gəʊɪŋ] *adj* marítimo(ma).

ochre *UK*, **ocher** *US* [ˈəʊkəʳ] *adj* ocre.

o'clock [əˈklɒk] *adv*: **it's one o'clock** es la una; **it's two/three o'clock** son las dos/las tres; **at one/two o'clock** a la una/las dos.

octave [ˈɒktɪv] *n* octava *f*.

October [ɒkˈtəʊbəʳ] *n* octubre *m*; *see also* **September**.

octopus [ˈɒktəpəs] (*pl* **-pi** [-paɪ] *OR* **-puses**) *n* pulpo *m*.

OD *abbr of* **overdose, overdrawn**.

odd [ɒd] *adj* - **1.** [strange] raro(ra), extraño(ña) - **2.** [not part of pair] sin pareja - **3.** [number] impar - **4.** *inf* [leftover] sobrante - **5.** *inf* [occasional]: **I play the odd game** juego alguna que otra vez - **6.** *inf* [approximately]: **30 odd years** 30 y tantos *OR* y pico años. ➤ **odds** *npl* - **1.**: **the odds** [probability] las probabilidades; [in betting] las apuestas; **the odds are that...** lo más probable es que...; **against all odds** contra viento y marea - **2.** [bits]: **odds and ends** chismes *mpl*, cosillas *fpl*

▸▸▸ **to be at odds with sthg** no concordar con algo; **to be at odds with sb** estar reñido con alguien.

oddity [ˈɒdɪtɪ] (*pl* **-ies**) *n* rareza *f*.

odd jobs *npl* chapuzas *fpl*.

oddly [ˈɒdlɪ] *adv* extrañamente; **oddly enough** aunque parezca mentira.

oddments [ˈɒdmənts] *npl* retales *mpl*.

odds-on [ˈɒdz-] *adj inf*: **the odds-on favourite** el favorito indiscutible.

odometer [əʊˈdɒmɪtəʳ] *n US* cuentakilómetros *m inv*.

odour *UK*, **odor** *US* [ˈəʊdəʳ] *n* [gen] olor *m*; [of perfume] fragancia *f*.

of (*unstressed* [əv], *stressed* [ɒv]) *prep* - **1.** [gen] de; **the cover of a book** la portada de un libro; **a cousin of mine** un primo mío; **both of us** nosotros dos, los dos; **the worst of them** el peor de ellos; **to die of sthg** morir de algo - **2.** [expressing quantity, referring to container] de; **thousands of people** miles de personas; **there are three of us** somos tres; **a cup of coffee** un café, una taza de café - **3.** [indicating amount, age, time] de; **a child of five** un niño de cinco (años); **at the age of five** a los cinco años; **an increase of 6%** un incremento del 6%; **the 12th of February** el 12 de febrero - **4.** [made from]: **a dress of silk** un vestido de seda; **to be made of sthg** estar hecho de algo - **5.** [with emotions, opinions]: **fear of ghosts** miedo a los fantasmas; **love of good food** amor por la buena mesa; **it was very kind of you** fue muy amable de *OR* por tu parte.

off [ɒf] ⟨⟩ *adv* - **1.** [away]: **to drive off** alejarse conduciendo; **to turn off** salir de la carretera; **I'm off!** ¡me voy! - **2.** [at a distance - in time]: **it's two days off** quedan dos días; **that's a long time off** aún queda mucho para eso; [- in space]: **it's ten miles off** está a diez millas; **far off** lejos - **3.** [so as to remove]: **to take sthg off** [gen] quitar algo; [one's clothes] quitarse algo;

to cut sthg off cortar algo; **could you help me off with my coat?** ¿me ayudas a quitarme el abrigo? **- 4.** [so as to complete]: **to finish off** [rr]-minar, acabar; **to kill off** rematar **- 5.** [not at work] libre; **a day off** un día libre; **time off** tiempo *m* libre **- 6.** [so as to separate]: **to fence off** vallar; **to wall off** tapiar **- 7.** [so as to stop working]: **to turn off** [light, radio] apagar; [water, tap] cerrar **- 8.** [discounted]: **£10 off** 10 libras de descuento **- 9.** [having money]: **to be well/ badly off** andar bien/mal de dinero. ⬦ *prep* **- 1.** [away from]: **to get off sthg** bajarse de algo; **to keep off sthg** mantenerse alejado de algo; **'keep off the grass'** 'prohibido pisar el césped' **- 2.** [close to]: **just off the coast** muy cerca de la costa; **it's off Oxford Street** está al lado de Oxford Street **- 3.** [removed from]: **to cut a slice off sthg** cortar un pedazo de algo; **take your hands off me!** ¡quítame las manos de encima! **- 4.** [not attending]: **to be off work/duty** no estar trabajando/de servicio; **a day off work** un día de vacaciones **- 5.** *inf* [no longer liking]: **she's off coffee/her food** no le apetece café/comer **- 6.** [deducted from]: **there's 10% off the price** hay un 10% de rebaja sobre el precio **- 7.** *inf* [from]: **I bought it off him** se lo compré a él. ⬦ *adj* **- 1.** [gone bad - meat, cheese] pasado(da), estropeado(da); [- milk] cortado(da) **- 2.** [light, radio, device] apagado(da); [water, electricity] desconectado(da); [tap] cerrado(da) **- 3.** [cancelled] suspendido(da).

offal [ˈɒfl] *n (U)* asaduras *fpl*.

off-chance *n*: **on the off-chance** por si acaso.

off colour *adj* indispuesto(ta).

off duty *adj* [policeman] fuera de servicio; [soldier] de permiso.

offence *UK*, **offense** *US* [əˈfens] *n* **- 1.** [crime] delito *m* **- 2.** [cause of upset] ofensa *f*; **to cause sb offence** ofender a alguien; **to take offence** ofenderse.

offend [əˈfend] *vt* ofender.

offender [əˈfendər] *n* **- 1.** [criminal] delincuente *mf* **- 2.** [culprit] culpable *mf*.

offense *US n* **- 1.** = **offence - 2.** [ˈɒfens] SPORT ataque *m*.

offensive [əˈfensɪv] ⬦ *adj* **- 1.** [remark, behaviour] ofensivo(va); [smell] repugnante **- 2.** [aggressive] atacante. ⬦ *n* MIL ofensiva *f*.

offer [ˈɒfər] ⬦ *n* oferta *f*; **on offer** [available] disponible; [at a special price] en oferta. ⬦ *vt* ofrecer; **to offer sthg to sb, to offer sb sthg** ofrecer algo a alguien; [be willing]: **to offer to do sthg** ofrecerse a hacer algo. ⬦ *vi* [volunteer] ofrecerse.

offering [ˈɒfərɪŋ] *n* **- 1.** [thing offered] ofrecimiento *m*; [gift] regalo *m* **- 2.** [sacrifice] ofrenda *f*.

off-guard *adj* desprevenido(da).

offhand [ˌɒfˈhænd] ⬦ *adj* frío(a), indiferente. ⬦ *adv* de improviso.

office [ˈɒfɪs] *n* **- 1.** [gen] oficina *f*; [room] despacho *m*, oficina *f* **- 3.** *US* [of doctor, dentist] consulta *f*, consultorio *m* **- 4.** [position of authority] cargo *m*; **in office** [political party] en el poder; [person] en el cargo; **to take office** [political party] subir al poder; [person] asumir el cargo.

office automation *n* ofimática *f*.

office block *n* bloque *m* de oficinas.

office hours *npl* horas *fpl* de oficina.

officer [ˈɒfɪsər] *n* **- 1.** MIL oficial *mf* **- 2.** [in organization, trade union] delegado *m*, -da *f* **- 3.** [in police force] agente *mf*.

office worker *n* oficinista *mf*.

official [əˈfɪʃl] ⬦ *adj* oficial. ⬦ *n* [of government] funcionario *m*, -ria *f*; [of trade union] representante *mf*.

officialdom [əˈfɪʃldəm] *n* burocracia *f*.

offing [ˈɒfɪŋ] *n*: **to be in the offing** estar al caer OR a la vista.

off-licence *n UK* tienda donde se venden bebidas alcohólicas para llevar.

off-line ⬦ *adj* **- 1.** [printer] desconectado(da) **- 2.** [operation] fuera de línea. ⬦ *adv*: **to go off-line** desconectarse.

off-peak *adj* [electricity, phone call, travel] de tarifa reducida; [period] económico(ca).

off-putting [-ˌpʊtɪŋ] *adj* **- 1.** [unpleasant] repelente **- 2.** [distracting]: **it's very off-putting** me distrae mucho.

off season *n*: **the off season** la temporada baja.

offset [ˈɒfset] (*pt & pp* **offset**) *vt* compensar, contrarrestar.

offshoot [ˈɒfʃuːt] *n* retoño *m*.

offshore [ˈɒfʃɔːr] ⬦ *adj* [wind] costero(ra); [fishing] de bajura; [oil rig] marítimo(ma); [banking] en bancos extranjeros. ⬦ *adv* mar adentro; **two miles offshore** a dos millas de la costa.

offside ⬦ *adj* [ˌɒfˈsaɪd] **- 1.** [part of vehicle - right-hand drive] izquierdo(da); [- left-hand drive] derecho(cha) **- 2.** SPORT fuera de juego. ⬦ *adv* [ˌɒfˈsaɪd] SPORT fuera de juego.

offspring [ˈɒfsprɪŋ] (*pl* **offspring**) *n* **- 1.** [of people *fml* & *hum* [- child] descendiente *mf*; [- children] descendencia *f* **- 2.** [of animals] crías *fpl*.

offstage [ˌɒfˈsteɪdʒ] *adj & adv* entre bastidores.

off-the-peg *adj UK* confeccionado(da).

off-the-record ⬦ *adj* extraoficial. ⬦ *adv* extraoficialmente.

off-white *adj* blancuzco(ca).

often ['ɒfn, 'ɒftn] *adv* [many times] a menudo; **how often do you go?** ¿cada cuánto OR con qué frecuencia vas?; **I don't often see him** no lo veo mucho; **I don't do it as often as I used to** no lo hago tanto como antes. ◆ **as often as not** *adv* muchas veces. ◆ **every so often** *adv* cada cierto tiempo. ◆ **more often than not** *adv* la mayoría de las veces.

ogle ['əʊgl] *vt pej* comerse con los ojos.

oh [əʊ] *excl* - **1.** [to introduce comment] ¡ah!; **oh really?** ¿de verdad? - **2.** [expressing joy, surprise, fear] ¡oh!; **oh no!** ¡no!

oil [ɔɪl] ⟨⟩ *n* - **1.** [gen] aceite *m* - **2.** [petroleum] petróleo *m*. ⟨⟩ *vt* engrasar.

oilcan ['ɔɪlkæn] *n* aceitera *f*.

oilfield ['ɔɪlfiːld] *n* yacimiento *m* petrolífero.

oil filter *n* filtro *m* del aceite.

oil-fired [-,faɪəd] *adj* de fuel-oil.

oil painting *n* (pintura *f* al) óleo *m*.

oilrig ['ɔɪlrɪg] *n* plataforma *f* petrolífera.

oilskins ['ɔɪlskɪnz] *npl* [coat] impermeable *m*, chubasquero *m*.

oil slick *n* marea *f* negra.

oil tanker *n* - **1.** [ship] petrolero *m* - **2.** [lorry] camión *m* cisterna.

oil well *n* pozo *m* petrolífero OR de petróleo.

oily ['ɔɪlɪ] *adj* [food] aceitoso(sa); [rag, cloth] grasiento(ta); [skin, hair] graso(sa).

ointment ['ɔɪntmənt] *n* pomada *f*, ungüento *m*.

OK, okay [,əʊ'keɪ] *inf* ⟨⟩ *adj*: **I'm OK** estoy bien; **the food was OK** la comida no estuvo mal; **is it OK with you?** ¿te parece bien? ⟨⟩ *excl* - **1.** [gen] vale, de acuerdo - **2.** [to introduce new topic] bien, vale. ⟨⟩ *vt* (*pt & pp* OKed, *cont* OKing) dar el visto bueno a.

old [əʊld] ⟨⟩ *adj* - **1.** [gen] viejo(ja); **how old are you?** ¿cuántos años tienes?, ¿qué edad tienes?; **I'm 20 years old** tengo 20 años; **an old woman** una vieja; **old people** las personas mayores; **when I'm older** cuando sea mayor - **2.** [former] antiguo(gua). ⟨⟩ *npl*: **the old** los ancianos.

old age *n* la vejez.

old age pensioner *n* UK pensionista *mf*, jubilado *m*, -da *f*.

Old Bailey [-'beɪlɪ] *n*: **the Old Bailey** *el juzgado criminal central de Inglaterra.*

old-fashioned [-'fæʃnd] *adj* - **1.** [outmoded] pasado(da) de moda, anticuado(da) - **2.** [traditional] tradicional.

old people's home *n* residencia *f* OR hogar *m* de ancianos.

O level *n* UK examen y calificación sobre una asignatura concreta que se pasaba a los 16 años.

olive ['ɒlɪv] *n* [fruit] aceituna *f*, oliva *f*.

olive oil *n* aceite *m* de oliva.

Olympic [ə'lɪmpɪk] *adj* olímpico(ca). ◆ **Olympics** *npl*: **the Olympics** los Juegos Olímpicos.

Olympic Games *npl*: **the Olympic Games** los Juegos Olímpicos.

ombudsman ['ɒmbʊdzmən] (*pl* **-men** [-mən]) *n* ≃ defensor *m* del pueblo.

omelet(te) ['ɒmlɪt] *n* tortilla *f*.

omen ['əʊmen] *n* presagio *m*.

ominous ['ɒmɪnəs] *adj* siniestro(tra), de mal agüero.

omission [ə'mɪʃn] *n* omisión *f*.

omit [ə'mɪt] *vt* omitir; [name - from list] pasar por alto; **to omit to do sthg** no hacer algo.

omnibus ['ɒmnɪbəs] *n* - **1.** [book] antología *f* - **2.** UK RADIO & TV *programa que emite todos los capítulos de la semana seguidos.*

on [ɒn] ⟨⟩ *prep* - **1.** [indicating position - gen] en; [- on top of] sobre, en; **on a chair** en OR sobre una silla; **on the wall/ground** en la pared/el suelo; **he was lying on his side/back** estaba tumbado de costado/de espaldas; **on the left/right** a la izquierda/derecha; **I haven't got any money on me** no llevo nada de dinero encima - **2.** [indicating means]: **it runs on diesel** funciona con diesel; **on TV/the radio** en la tele/la radio; **she's on the telephone** está al teléfono; **he lives on fruit** vive (a base) de fruta; **to hurt o.s. on sthg** hacerse daño con algo - **3.** [indicating mode of transport]: **to travel on a bus/train/ship** viajar en autobús/tren/barco; **I was on the bus** iba en el autobús; **to get on a bus/train/ship** subirse a un autobús/tren/barco; **on foot** a pie; **on horseback** a caballo - **4.** [indicating time, activity]: **on Thursday** el jueves; **on Thursdays** los jueves; **on my birthday** el día de mi cumpleaños; **on the 10th of February** el 10 de febrero; **on the 10th** el día 10; **on my return, on returning** al volver; **on business/holiday** de negocios/vacaciones - **5.** [concerning] sobre, acerca de; **a book on astronomy** un libro acerca de OR sobre astronomía - **6.** [indicating influence] en, sobre; **the impact on the environment** el impacto en OR sobre el medio ambiente - **7.** [using, supported by]: **to be on social security** cobrar dinero de la seguridad social; **he's on tranquillizers** está tomando tranquilizantes; **to be on drugs** [addicted] drogarse - **8.** [earning]: **she's on £25,000 a year** gana 25.000 libras al año - **9.** [referring to musical instrument] con; **on the violin** con el violín; **on the piano** al piano - **10.** *inf* [paid by]: **the drinks are on me** yo pago las copas, a las copas invito yo. ⟨⟩ *adv* - **1.** [indicating covering, clothing]: **put the lid on** pon la tapa; **what did she have on?** ¿qué llevaba encima OR puesto?; **put your coat on** ponte el abrigo - **2.** [being shown]: **what's on at the cinema?** ¿qué echan OR ponen en el cine? - **3.** [working - machine] funcionando; [- radio, TV, light] encendido(da); [- tap] abierto(ta); [- brakes] puesto(ta); **turn on the power** pulse el botón de encendido - **4.** [indicating continuing action]: **we talked/worked on into the night** seguimos hablando/trabajando hasta bien entrada la noche; **he kept on walking** siguió caminando - **5.** [forward]: **send my mail on (to me)** reenvíame el correo; **later on** más tarde, después; **earlier on** antes - **6.** inf [referring to behaviour]: **it's just not on!** ¡es una pasada! ⮞ **from... on** adv: from now on de ahora en adelante; **from that moment/time on** desde aquel momento. ⮞ **on and off** adv de vez en cuando. ⮞ **on to, onto** (only written as onto for senses 4 and 5) prep - **1.** [to a position on top of] encima de, sobre; **she jumped on to the chair** salto encima de OR sobre la silla - **2.** [to a position on a vehicle]: **to get on to a bus/train/plane** subirse a un autobús/tren/avión - **3.** [to a position attached to] a; **stick the photo on to the page** pega la foto a la hoja - **4.** [aware of wrongdoing]: **to be onto sb** andar detrás de alguien - **5.** [into contact with]: **get onto the factory** ponte en contacto con la fábrica.

once [wʌns] ⬥ adv - **1.** [on one occasion] una vez; **once a week** una vez a la semana; **once again** OR **more** otra vez; **for once** por una vez; **more than once** más de una vez; **once and for all** de una vez por todas; **once or twice** alguna que otra vez; **once in a while** de vez en cuando - **2.** [previously] en otro tiempo, antiguamente; **once upon a time** érase una vez. ⬥ conj una vez que; **once you have done it** una vez que lo hayas hecho. ⮞ **at once** adv - **1.** [immediately] en seguida, inmediatamente - **2.** [at the same time] a la vez, al mismo tiempo; **all at once** de repente, de golpe.

oncoming [ˈɒnˌkʌmɪŋ] adj [traffic] que viene en dirección contraria.

one [wʌn] ⬥ num [the number 1] un (una); **I only want one** sólo quiero uno; **one fifth** un quinto, una quinta parte; **one of my friends** uno de mis amigos; **(number) one** el uno. ⬥ adj - **1.** [only] único(ca); **it's her one ambition** es su única ambición - **2.** [indefinite]: **one of these days** un día de éstos. ⬥ pron - **1.** [referring to a particular thing or person] uno (una); **I want the red one** yo quiero el rojo; **the one with the blond hair** la del pelo rubio; **which one do you want?** ¿cuál quieres?; **this one** éste (ésta); **that one** ése (ésa); **another one** otro (otra); **she's the one I told you about** es (ésa) de la que te hablé - **2.** fml [you, anyone] uno (una); **to do one's duty** cumplir uno con su

deber. ⮞ **for one** adv: **I for one remain unconvinced** yo, por lo menos OR por mi parte, sigo poco convencido.

one-armed bandit n (máquina f) tragaperras f inv.

one-man adj individual, en solitario.

one-man band n [musician] hombre m orquesta.

one-off inf ⬥ adj excepcional. ⬥ n caso m excepcional.

one-on-one US = **one-to-one**.

one-parent family n familia f monoparental.

oneself [wʌnˈself] pron - **1.** (reflexive, after prep) uno mismo (una misma); **to buy presents for oneself** hacerse regalos a sí mismo; **to take care of oneself** cuidarse - **2.** (for emphasis): **by oneself** [without help] solo(la).

one-sided [-ˈsaɪdɪd] adj - **1.** [unequal] desigual - **2.** [biased] parcial.

one-to-one UK, **one-on-one** US adj [relationship] entre dos; [discussion] cara a cara; [tuition] individual.

one-touch dialling UK, **one-touch dialing** US n marcación f automática.

one-upmanship [ˌwʌnˈʌpmənʃɪp] n habilidad para colocarse en una situación de ventaja.

one-way adj - **1.** [street] de dirección única - **2.** [ticket] de ida.

ongoing [ˈɒnˌgəʊɪŋ] adj [gen] en curso; [problem, situation] pendiente.

onion [ˈʌnjən] n cebolla f.

online [ˈɒnlaɪn] ⬥ adj COMPUT en línea; **to be online** estar conectado a Internet. ⬥ adv en línea; **to go online** conectarse a Internet.

online banking n banca f en línea.

online shopping n compras fpl en línea.

onlooker [ˈɒnˌlʊkəʳ] n espectador m, -ra f.

only [ˈəʊnlɪ] ⬥ adj único(ca); **to be an only child** ser hijo único. ⬥ adv [exclusively] sólo, solamente; **I was only too willing to help** estaba encantado de poder ayudar; **I only wish I could!** ¡ojalá pudiera!; **it's only natural** es completamente normal; **it's only to be expected** no es de sorprender; **not only... but** no sólo... sino; **only just** apenas. ⬥ conj sólo que; **I would go, only I'm too tired** iría, lo que pasa es que estoy muy cansado.

onset [ˈɒnset] n comienzo m.

onshore [ˈɒnʃɔːʳ] adj [wind] procedente del mar; [oil production] en tierra firme.

onslaught [ˈɒnslɔːt] n lit & fig acometida f.

onto (unstressed before consonant [ˈɒntə], unstressed before vowel [ˈɒntʊ], stressed [ˈɒntuː]) = **on to**.

onus ['əʊnəs] *n* responsabilidad *f*.

onward ['ɒnwəd] <> *adj* [in space] hacia delante; [in time] progresivo(va). <> *adv* = **onwards**.

onwards, onward ['ɒnwədz] *adv* [in space] adelante, hacia delante; [in time]: **from now/then onwards** de ahora/allí en adelante.

ooze [u:z] <> *vt fig* rebosar. <> *vi*: **to ooze (from OR out of)** rezumar (de); **to ooze with sthg** *fig* rebosar OR irradiar algo.

opaque [əʊ'peɪk] *adj* - **1.** [not transparent] opaco(ca) - **2.** *fig* [obscure] oscuro(ra).

open ['əʊpn] <> *adj* - **1.** [gen] abierto(ta); [curtains] descorrido(da); [view, road] despejado(da) - **2.** [receptive]: **to be open to** [ideas, suggestions] estar abierto a; [blame, criticism, question] prestarse a - **3.** [frank] sincero(ra), franco(ca) - **4.** [uncovered - car] descubierto(ta) - **5.** [available - subj: choice, chance]: **to be open to sb** estar disponible para alguien. <> *n* - **1.**: **in the open** [fresh air] al aire libre; **to bring sthg out into the open** sacar a luz algo - **2.** SPORT **open** *m*, abierto *m*. <> *vt* - **1.** [gen] abrir; **to open fire** abrir fuego - **2.** [curtains] correr - **3.** [inaugurate - public area, event] inaugurar - **4.** [negotiations] entablar. <> *vi* - **1.** [door, flower] abrirse - **2.** [shop, office] abrir - **3.** [event, play] dar comienzo. ◆ **open on to** *vt insep* dar a. ◆ **open up** <> *vt sep* abrir. <> *vi* - **1.** [become available] surgir - **2.** [unlock door] abrir.

opener ['əʊpnə'] *n* [gen] abridor *m*; [for tins] abrelatas *m inv*; [for bottles] abrebotellas *m inv*.

opening ['əʊpnɪŋ] <> *adj* inicial. <> *n* - **1.** [beginning] comienzo *m*, principio *m* - **2.** [gap - in fence] abertura *f* - **3.** [opportunity] oportunidad *f* - **4.** [job vacancy] puesto *m* vacante.

opening hours *npl* horario *m* (de apertura).

openly ['əʊpənlɪ] *adv* abiertamente.

open-minded [-'maɪndɪd] *adj* sin prejuicios.

open-plan *adj* de planta abierta.

Open University *n* UK: **the Open University** ≃ la Universidad Nacional de Educación a Distancia.

opera ['ɒpərə] *n* ópera *f*.

opera house *n* teatro *m* de la ópera.

operate ['ɒpəreɪt] <> *vt* - **1.** [machine] hacer funcionar - **2.** [business, system] dirigir; [service] proporcionar. <> *vi* - **1.** [carry out trade, business] operar, actuar - **2.** [function] funcionar - **3.** MED: **to operate (on sb/sthg)** operar (a alguien/de algo).

operating theatre UK, **operating room** US ['ɒpəreɪtɪŋ-] *n* quirófano *m*.

operation [,ɒpə'reɪʃn] *n* - **1.** [planned activity - police, rescue, business] operación *f*; [- military] maniobra *f* - **2.** [running - of business] adminis-

tración *f* - **3.** [functioning - of machine] funcionamiento *m*; **to be in operation** [- machine] estar funcionando; [- law, system] estar en vigor - **4.** MED operación *f*, intervención *f* quirúrgica; **to have an operation (for/on)** operarse (de).

operational [,ɒpə'reɪʃənl] *adj* [ready for use] en funcionamiento.

operative ['ɒprətɪv] <> *adj* en vigor, vigente. <> *n* [worker] operario *m*, -ria *f*; [spy] agente *mf*.

operator ['ɒpəreɪtə'] *n* - **1.** TELEC operador *m*, -ra *f*, telefonista *mf* - **2.** [worker] operario *m*, -ria *f* - **3.** [company] operadora *f*.

opinion [ə'pɪnjən] *n* opinión *f*; **to be of the opinion that** opinar OR creer que; **in my opinion** a mi juicio, en mi opinión; **what is her opinion of...?** ¿qué opina de...?

opinionated [ə'pɪnjəneɪtɪd] *adj pej* dogmático(ca).

opinion poll *n* sondeo *m*, encuesta *f*.

opponent [ə'pəʊnənt] *n* - **1.** POL adversario *m*, -ria *f*; [of system, approach] opositor *m*, -ora *f* - **2.** SPORT contrincante *mf*.

opportune ['ɒpətju:n] *adj* oportuno(na).

opportunist [,ɒpə'tju:nɪst] *n* oportunista *mf*.

opportunity [,ɒpə'tju:nətɪ] *n* oportunidad *f*, ocasión *f*; **to take the opportunity to do OR of doing sthg** aprovechar la ocasión de OR para hacer algo.

oppose [ə'pəʊz] *vt* oponerse a.

opposed [ə'pəʊzd] *adj* opuesto(ta); **to be opposed to** oponerse a; **as opposed to** en vez de, en lugar de; **I like beer as opposed to wine** me gusta la cerveza y no el vino.

opposing [ə'pəʊzɪŋ] *adj* opuesto(ta), contrario(ria).

opposite ['ɒpəzɪt] <> *adj* - **1.** [facing - side, house] de enfrente; [- end] opuesto(ta) - **2.** [very different]: **opposite (to)** opuesto(ta) OR contrario(ria) (a). <> *adv* enfrente. <> *prep* enfrente de. <> *n* contrario *m*.

opposite number *n* homólogo *m*, -ga *f*.

opposition [,ɒpə'zɪʃn] *n* - **1.** [gen] oposición *f* - **2.** [opposing team]: **the opposition** los contrincantes. ◆ **Opposition** *n* UK POL: **the Opposition** la oposición.

oppress [ə'pres] *vt* - **1.** [persecute] oprimir - **2.** [depress] agobiar.

oppressive [ə'presɪv] *adj* - **1.** [unjust] tiránico(ca), opresivo(va) - **2.** [stifling] agobiante, sofocante - **3.** [causing unease] opresivo(va), agobiante.

opt [ɒpt] <> *vt*: **to opt to do sthg** optar por OR elegir hacer algo. <> *vi*: **to opt for sthg** optar por OR elegir algo. ◆ **opt in** *vi*: **to opt**

in (to sthg) decidir participar (en algo).
◆ **opt out** *vi* **to opt out (of sthg)** decidir no [participar (en algo)].

optical ['ɒptɪkl] *adj* óptico(ca).

optician [ɒp'tɪʃn] *n* óptico *m*, -ca *f*; **the optician's (shop)** la óptica.

optimist ['ɒptɪmɪst] *n* optimista *mf*.

optimistic [,ɒptɪ'mɪstɪk] *adj* optimista.

optimum ['ɒptɪməm] *adj* óptimo(ma).

option ['ɒpʃn] *n* opción *f*; **to have the option to do** OR **of doing sthg** tener la opción OR la posibilidad de hacer algo; **to have no option** no tener otra opción.

optional ['ɒpʃənl] *adj* facultativo(va), optativo(va); **optional extra** extra *m* opcional.

or [ɔːʳ] *conj* - **1.** [gen] o; *(before 'o' or 'ho')* u; **or (else)** de lo contrario, si no - **2.** *(after negative)*: **he cannot read or write** no sabe ni leer ni escribir.

oral ['ɔːrəl] ◇ *adj* - **1.** [spoken] oral - **2.** [relating to the mouth] bucal. ◇ *n* examen *m* oral.

orally ['ɔːrəlɪ] *adv* - **1.** [in spoken form] oralmente - **2.** [via the mouth] por vía oral.

orange ['ɒrɪndʒ] ◇ *adj* naranja *(inv)*. ◇ *n* [fruit] naranja *f*.

orator ['ɒrətəʳ] *n* orador *m*, -ra *f*.

orbit ['ɔːbɪt] ◇ *n* órbita *f*; **to put sthg into orbit (around)** poner algo en órbita (alrededor de). ◇ *vt* girar alrededor de.

orchard ['ɔːtʃəd] *n* huerto *m*.

orchestra ['ɔːkɪstrə] *n* - **1.** orquesta *f* - **2.** [in theatre] platea *f* OR patio *m* de butacas.

orchestral [ɔː'kestrəl] *adj* orquestal.

orchid ['ɔːkɪd] *n* orquídea *f*.

ordain [ɔː'deɪn] *vt* - **1.** *fml* [decree] decretar - **2.** RELIG: **to be ordained** ordenarse (sacerdote).

ordeal [ɔː'diːl] *n* calvario *m*.

order ['ɔːdəʳ] ◇ *n* - **1.** [instruction] orden *f* - **2.** COMM [request] pedido *m*; **to order** por encargo - **3.** [in restaurant] ración *f* - **4.** [sequence, discipline, system] orden *m*; **in order** en orden; **out of order** desordenado(da); **in order of importance** por orden de importancia - **5.** [fitness for use]: **in working order** en funcionamiento; **'out of order'** 'no funciona'; **to be out of order** [not working] estar estropeado(da); [incorrect behaviour] ser improcedente; **in order** [correct] en regla - **6.** RELIG orden *f*. ◇ *vt* - **1.** [command]: **to order sb (to do sthg)** ordenar a alguien (que haga algo); **to order that** ordenar que - **2.** [request - drink, taxi] pedir - **3.** COMM pedir, encargar - **4.** [put in order] ordenar. ◆ **in the order of** *UK*, **on the order of** *US prep* del orden de. ◆ **in order that** *conj* para que. ◆ **in order to** *conj* para. ◆ **order about, order around** *vt sep* mangonear.

order form *n* hoja *f* de pedido.

orderly ['ɔːdəlɪ] ◇ *adj* [person, crowd] disciplinado (da); [room] ordenado(da). ◇ *n* - **1.** [in hospital] auxiliar *mf* sanitario - **2.** [in army] ordenanza *mf*.

ordinarily ['ɔːdənrəlɪ] *adv* ordinario.

ordinary ['ɔːdənrɪ] ◇ *adj* - **1.** [normal] corriente, normal - **2.** *pej* [unexceptional] mediocre, ordinario(ria). ◇ *n*: **out of the ordinary** fuera de lo común.

ordnance ['ɔːdnəns] *n (U)* - **1.** [military supplies] pertrechos *mpl* de guerra - **2.** [artillery] artillería *f*.

ore [ɔːʳ] *n* mineral *m*.

oregano [,ɒrɪ'gɑːnəʊ] *n* orégano *m*.

organ ['ɔːgən] *n* [gen, ANAT & MUS] órgano *m*.

organic [ɔː'gænɪk] *adj* - **1.** [gen] orgánico(ca) - **2.** [food] ecológico(ca), orgánico(ca).

organization [,ɔːgənaɪ'zeɪʃn] *n* organización *f*.

organize, -ise ['ɔːgənaɪz] *vt* organizar.

organizer ['ɔːgənaɪzəʳ] *n* organizador *m*, -ra *f*.

orgasm ['ɔːgæzm] *n* orgasmo *m*.

orgy ['ɔːdʒɪ] *n lit & fig* orgía *f*.

Orient ['ɔːrɪənt] *n*: **the Orient** el Oriente.

oriental [,ɔːrɪ'entl] ◇ *adj* oriental. ◇ *n* oriental *mf* *(atención: el término 'oriental' se considera racista)*.

orienteering [,ɔːrɪən'tɪərɪŋ] *n* deporte *m* de orientación.

origami [,ɒrɪ'gɑːmɪ] *n* papiroflexia *f*.

origin ['ɒrɪdʒɪn] *n* origen *m*; **country of origin** país *m* de origen. ◆ **origins** *npl* origen *m*.

original [ə'rɪdʒənl] ◇ *adj* original; **the original owner** el primer propietario. ◇ *n* original *m*.

originally [ə'rɪdʒənəlɪ] *adv* [at first] originariamente; [with originality] originalmente.

originate [ə'rɪdʒəneɪt] ◇ *vt* originar, producir. ◇ *vi*: **to originate (in)** nacer OR surgir (de); **to originate from** nacer OR surgir de.

Orkney Islands ['ɔːknɪ-], **Orkneys** ['ɔːknɪz] *npl*: **the Orkney Islands** las Orcadas.

ornament ['ɔːnəmənt] *n* adorno *m*.

ornamental [,ɔːnə'mentl] *adj* ornamental, decorativo(va).

ornate [ɔː'neɪt] *adj* [style] recargado(da); [decoration, vase] muy vistoso(sa).

ornithology [,ɔːnɪ'θɒlədʒɪ] *n* ornitología *f*.

orphan ['ɔːfn] ◇ *n* huérfano *m*, -na *f*. ◇ *vt*: **to be orphaned** quedarse huérfano.

orphanage ['ɔːfənɪdʒ] *n* orfelinato *m*.

orthodox ['ɔːθədɒks] *adj* ortodoxo(xa).

orthopaedic, orthopedic [,ɔːθə'piːdɪk] *adj* ortopédico(ca).

orthopedic [ˌɔːθəˈpiːdɪk] = **orthopaedic**.

oscillate [ˈɒsɪleɪt] *vi lit* & *fig*: **to oscillate (between)** oscilar (entre).

Oslo [ˈɒzləʊ] *n* Oslo.

ostensible [ɒˈstensəbl] *adj* aparente.

ostentatious [ˌɒstənˈteɪʃəs] *adj* ostentoso(sa).

osteopath [ˈɒstɪəpæθ] *n* osteópata *mf*.

ostracize, -ise [ˈɒstrəsaɪz] *vt* [colleague etc] marginar, hacer el vacío a; POL condenar al ostracismo.

ostrich [ˈɒstrɪtʃ] *n* avestruz *m*.

other [ˈʌðər] ◇ *adj* otro (otra); **the other one** el otro (la otra); **the other three** los otros tres; **the other day** el otro día; **the other week** hace unas semanas. ◇ *pron* - **1.** [different one]: **others** otros(otras) - **2.** [remaining, alternative one]: **the other** el otro (la otra); **the others** los otros (las otras), los demás (las demás); **one after the other** uno tras otro; **one or other** uno u otro; **to be none other than** no ser otro sino. **something or other** *pron* una cosa u otra. **somehow or other** *adv* de una u otra forma. **other than** *conj* excepto, salvo; **other that** por lo demás.

otherwise [ˈʌðəwaɪz] ◇ *adv* - **1.** [or else] si no - **2.** [apart from that] por lo demás - **3.** [differently] de otra manera; **deliberately or otherwise** adrede o no. ◇ *conj* si no, de lo contrario.

otter [ˈɒtər] *n* nutria *f*.

ouch [aʊtʃ] *excl* ¡ay!

ought [ɔːt] *aux vb* deber; **you ought to go/to be nicer** deberías irte/ser más amable; **she ought to pass the exam** debería aprobar el examen; **it ought to be fun** promete ser divertido.

ounce [aʊns] *n* [unit of measurement] = *28,35g*, ≈ onza *f*.

our [ˈaʊər] *poss adj* nuestro(tra), nuestros(tras) *(pl)*; **our money** nuestro dinero; **our house** nuestra casa; **our children** nuestros hijos; **it wasn't our fault** no fue culpa nuestra OR nuestra culpa; **we washed our hair** nos lavamos el pelo.

ours [ˈaʊəz] *poss pron* nuestro(tra); **that money is ours** ese dinero es nuestro; **those keys are ours** esas llaves son nuestras; **it wasn't our fault, it was OURS** no fue culpa de ellos sino de nosotros; **a friend of ours** un amigo nuestro; **their car hit ours** suyo coche chocó contra el nuestro.

ourselves [aʊəˈselvz] *pron* - **1.** *(reflexive)* nos *mpl* & *fpl*; *(after prep)* nosotros *mpl*, nosotras *f* - **2.** *(for emphasis)* nosotros mismos *mpl*, nosotras mismas *f*; **we did it by ourselves** lo hicimos nosotros solos.

oust [aʊst] *vt fml*: **to oust sb (from)** [job] desbancar a alguien (de); [land] desalojar a alguien (de).

out [aʊt] *adv* - **1.** [not inside, out of doors] fuera; **we all went out** todos salimos fuera; **I'm going out for a walk** voy a salir a dar un paseo; **they ran out** salieron corriendo; **he poured the water out** sirvió el agua - **2.** [away from home, office] fuera; **John's out at the moment** John está fuera ahora mismo - **3.** [extinguished] apagado(da); **the fire went out** el fuego se apagó - **4.** [of tides]: **the tide had gone out** la marea estaba baja - **5.** [out of fashion] pasado(da) de moda - **6.** [published, released - book] publicado(da); **they've a new record out** han sacado un nuevo disco - **7.** [in flower] en flor - **8.** *inf* [on strike] en huelga. **out of** *prep* - **1.** [away from, outside] fuera de; **to go out of the room** salir de la habitación - **2.** [indicating cause] por; **out of spite/love** por rencor/amor - **3.** [indicating origin, source] de; **a page out of a book** una página de un libro; **to get information out of sb** sacar información a alguien - **4.** [without] sin; **we're out of sugar** estamos sin azúcar, se nos ha acabado el azúcar - **5.** [made from] de; **it's made out of plastic** está hecho de plástico - **6.** [sheltered from] a resguardo de - **7.** [to indicate proportion]: **one out of ten people** una de cada diez personas; **ten out of ten** [mark] diez de OR sobre diez.

out-and-out *adj* [disgrace, lie] infame; [liar, crook] redomado(da).

outback [ˈaʊtbæk] *n*: **the outback** los llanos del interior de Australia.

outboard (motor) [ˈaʊtbɔːd-] *n* (motor *m*) fueraborda *m*.

outbreak [ˈaʊtbreɪk] *n* [of war] comienzo *m*; [of crime] ola *f*; [of illness] epidemia *f*; [of spots] erupción *f*.

outburst [ˈaʊtbɜːst] *n* - **1.** [sudden expression of emotion] explosión *f*, arranque *m* - **2.** [sudden occurrence] estallido *m*.

outcast [ˈaʊtkɑːst] *n* marginado *m*, -da *f*, paria *mf*.

outcome [ˈaʊtkʌm] *n* resultado *m*.

outcrop [ˈaʊtkrɒp] *n* afloramiento *m*.

outcry [ˈaʊtkraɪ] *n* protestas *fpl*.

outdated [ˌaʊtˈdeɪtɪd] *adj* anticuado(da), pasado(da) de moda.

outdid [ˌaʊtˈdɪd] *pt* ▷ **outdo**.

outdo [ˌaʊtˈduː] (*pt* -**did**, *pp* -**done** [-dʌn]) *vt* aventajar, superar.

outdoor [ˈaʊtdɔːr] *adj* [life, swimming pool] al aire libre; [clothes] de calle.

outdoors [aʊtˈdɔːz] *adv* al aire libre.

outer [ˈaʊtər] *adj* exterior, externo(na).

outer space *n* espacio *m* exterior.

outfit ['aʊtfɪt] n - 1. [clothes] conjunto m, traje m - 2. inf [organization] equipo m. ◆ **outfitter** ['aʊtfɪtəʳ] n tienda f de confección.

outgoing ['aʊt,gəʊɪŋ] adj - 1. [chairman] saliente - 2. [sociable] extrovertido(da). ◆ **outgoings** npl UK gastos mpl.

outgrow [,aʊt'grəʊ] (pt -grew, pp -grown) vt - 1. [grow too big for]: **he has outgrown his shirts** las camisas se le han quedado pequeñas - 2. [grow too old for] ser demasiado mayor para.

outhouse ['aʊthaʊs, pl -haʊzɪz] n dependencia f.

outing ['aʊtɪŋ] n [trip] excursión f.

outlandish [aʊt'lændɪʃ] adj estrafalario(ria).

outlaw ['aʊtlɔː] ◇ n proscrito m, -ta f. ◇ vt [make illegal] ilegalizar.

outlay ['aʊtleɪ] n desembolso m.

outlet ['aʊtlet] n - 1. [for emotions] salida f - 2. [for water] desagüe m; [for gas] salida f - 3. [shop] punto m de venta - 4. US ELEC toma f de corriente.

outline ['aʊtlaɪn] ◇ n - 1. [brief description] esbozo m, resumen m; **in outline** en líneas generales - 2. [silhouette] contorno m. ◇ vt [describe briefly] esbozar, resumir.

outlive [,aʊt'lɪv] vt [subj: person] sobrevivir a.

outlook ['aʊtlʊk] n - 1. [attitude, disposition] enfoque m, actitud f - 2. [prospect] perspectiva f (de futuro).

outlying ['aʊt,laɪŋ] adj [remote] lejano(na), remoto(ta); [on edge of town] periférico(ca).

outmoded [,aʊt'məʊdɪd] adj anticuado(da), pasado(da) de moda.

outnumber [,aʊt'nʌmbəʳ] vt exceder en número.

out-of-date adj - 1. [clothes, belief] anticuado(da), pasado(da) de moda - 2. [passport, season ticket] caducado(da).

out of doors adv al aire libre.

out-of-the-way adj [far away] remoto(ta); [unusual] poco común.

outpatient ['aʊt,peɪʃnt] n paciente externo m, paciente externa f.

outpost ['aʊtpəʊst] n puesto m avanzado.

output ['aʊtpʊt] n - 1. [production] producción f, rendimiento m - 2. [COMPUT - printing out] salida f; [- printout] impresión f.

outrage ['aʊtreɪdʒ] ◇ n - 1. [anger] indignación f - 2. [atrocity] atrocidad f, escándalo m. ◇ vt ultrajar, atropellar.

outrageous [aʊt'reɪdʒəs] adj - 1. [offensive, shocking] indignante, escandaloso(sa) - 2. [very unusual] extravagante.

outright ◇ adj ['aʊtraɪt] - 1. [categoric] categórico(ca) - 2. [total - disaster] completo(ta); [- victory, winner] indiscutible. ◇ adv [,aʊt'raɪt] - 1. [ask] abiertamente; [deny] categóricamente - 2. [win] total mente; [be killed] en el acto.

outset ['aʊtset] n: **at the outset** al principio; **from the outset** desde el principio.

outside ◇ adj ['aʊtsaɪd] - 1. [gen] exterior - 2. [opinion, criticism] independiente - 3. [chance] remoto(ta). ◇ adv [,aʊt'saɪd] fuera; **to go/run/look outside** ir/correr/mirar fuera. ◇ prep ['aʊtsaɪd] fuera de; **we live half an hour outside London** vivimos a media hora de Londres. ◇ n ['aʊtsaɪd] [exterior] exterior m. ◆ **outside of** prep US [apart from] aparte de.

outside lane n carril m de adelantamiento.

outside line n línea f exterior.

outsider [,aʊt'saɪdəʳ] n - 1. [stranger] forastero m, -ra f - 2. [in horse race] caballo que no es uno de los favoritos.

outsize ['aʊtsaɪz] adj - 1. [bigger than usual] enorme - 2. [clothes] de talla muy grande.

outskirts ['aʊtskɜːts] npl: **the outskirts** las afueras.

outsource ['aʊtsɔːs] vt COMM subcontratar.

outspoken [,aʊt'spəʊkn] adj franco(ca).

outstanding [,aʊt'stændɪŋ] adj - 1. [excellent] destacado(da) - 2. [not paid, unfinished] pendiente.

outstay [,aʊt'steɪ] vt: **to outstay one's welcome** quedarse más tiempo de lo debido.

outstretched [,aʊt'stretʃt] adj extendido(da).

outstrip [,aʊt'strɪp] vt lit & fig aventajar, dejar atrás.

outward ['aʊtwəd] ◇ adj - 1. [journey] de ida - 2. [composure, sympathy] aparente - 3. [sign, proof] visible, exterior. ◇ adv US = **outwards**.

outwardly ['aʊtwədlɪ] adv [apparently] aparentemente, de cara al exterior.

outwards UK ['aʊtwədz], **outward** US adv hacia fuera.

outweigh [,aʊt'weɪ] vt pesar más que.

outwit [,aʊt'wɪt] vt ser más listo(ta) que.

oval ['əʊvl] ◇ adj oval, ovalado(da). ◇ n óvalo m.

Oval Office n: **the Oval Office** el Despacho Oval, oficina que tiene el presidente de Estados Unidos en la Casa Blanca.

ovary ['əʊvərɪ] n ovario m.

ovation [əʊ'veɪʃn] n ovación f; **a standing ovation** una ovación de gala (con el público en pie).

oven ['ʌvn] n horno m.

ovenproof ['ʌvnpruːf] adj refractario(ria).

over ['əʊvə'] ◇ *prep* - **1.** [directly above, on top of] encima de; **a fog hung over the river** una espesa niebla flotaba sobre el río; **put your coat over the chair** pon el abrigo encima de la silla - **2.** [to cover] sobre; **she wore a veil over her face** un velo le cubría el rostro - **3.** [on other side of] al otro lado de; **he lives over the road** vive enfrente - **4.** [across surface of] por encima de; **they sailed over the ocean** cruzaron el océano en barco - **5.** [more than] más de; **over and above** además de - **6.** [senior to] por encima de - **7.** [with regard to] por; **a fight over a woman** una pelea por una mujer - **8.** [during] durante; **over the weekend** (en) el fin de semana. ◇ *adv* - **1.** [short distance away]: **over here** aquí; **over there** allí - **2.** [across]: **to cross over** cruzar; **to go over** ir - **3.** [down]: **to fall over** caerse; **to push over** empujar, tirar - **4.** [round]: **to turn sthg over** dar la vuelta a algo; **to roll over** darse la vuelta - **5.** [more] más - **6.** [remaining]: **to be (left) over** quedar, sobrar - **7.** [at sb's house]: **invite them over** invítalos a casa - **8.** RADIO: **over (and out)!** ¡cambio (y cierro)! - **9.** [involving repetitions]: **(all) over again** otra vez desde el principio; **over and over (again)** una y otra vez. ◇ *adj* [finished] terminado(da). ⟜ **all over** ◇ *prep* por todo(da). ◇ *adv* [everywhere] por todas partes. ◇ *adj* [finished] terminado(da).

overall ◇ *adj* ['əʊvərɔːl] [general] global, total. ◇ *adv* [ˌəʊvər'ɔːl] en conjunto. ◇ *n* ['əʊvərɔːl] - **1.** [gen] guardapolvo *m* - **2.** US [for work] mono *m*. ⟜ **overalls** *npl* - **1.** [for work] mono *m* - **2.** US [dungarees] pantalones *mpl* de peto.

overawe [ˌəʊvər'ɔː] *vt* intimidar.

overbalance [ˌəʊvə'bæləns] *vi* perder el equilibrio.

overbearing [ˌəʊvə'beərɪŋ] *adj pej* despótico(ca).

overboard ['əʊvəbɔːd] *adv*: **to fall overboard** caer al agua OR por la borda; **to go overboard (about sb/sthg)** *inf* [be over-enthusiastic about] ponerse como loco(ca) (con alguien/algo).

overbook [ˌəʊvə'bʊk] *vi* hacer overbooking.

overcame [ˌəʊvə'keɪm] *pt* ⟞ **overcome**.

overcast ['əʊvəkɑːst] *adj* cubierto(ta), nublado(da).

overcharge [ˌəʊvə'tʃɑːdʒ] *vt*: **to overcharge sb (for sthg)** cobrar a alguien en exceso (por algo).

overcoat ['əʊvəkəʊt] *n* abrigo *m*.

overcome [ˌəʊvə'kʌm] (*pt* -**came**, *pp* -**come**) *vt* [deal with] vencer, superar.

overcrowded [ˌəʊvə'kraʊdɪd] *adj* [room] atestado(da) de gente; [country] superpoblado(da).

overcrowding [ˌəʊvə'kraʊdɪŋ] *n* [of country] superpoblación *f*; [of prison] hacinamiento *m*.

overdo [ˌəʊvə'duː] (*pt* -**did** [-dɪd], *pp* -**done**) *vt* - **1.** [exaggerate] exagerar - **2.** [overcook] hacer demasiado.

overdone [ˌəʊvə'dʌn] ◇ *pp* ⟞ **overdo**. ◇ *adj* muy hecho(cha).

overdose *n* ['əʊvədəʊs] sobredosis *f inv*.

overdraft ['əʊvədrɑːft] *n* [sum owed] saldo *m* deudor; [loan arranged] (giro *m* OR crédito *m* en) descubierto *m*.

overdrawn [ˌəʊvə'drɔːn] *adj*: **to be overdrawn** tener un saldo deudor.

overdue [ˌəʊvə'djuː] *adj* - **1.** [late]: **to be overdue** [train] ir con retraso; [library book] estar con el plazo de préstamo caducado; **I'm overdue (for) a bit of luck** va siendo hora de tener un poco de suerte - **2.** [awaited]: **(long) overdue** (largamente) esperado(da), ansiado(da) - **3.** [unpaid] vencido(da) y sin pagar.

overestimate [ˌəʊvər'estɪmeɪt] *vt* sobreestimar.

overflow ◇ *vi* [ˌəʊvə'fləʊ] - **1.** [spill over] rebosar; [river] desbordarse - **2.** [go beyond limits]: **to overflow (into)** rebosar (hacia) - **3.** [be very full]: **to be overflowing (with)** rebosar (de). ◇ *n* ['əʊvəfləʊ] [pipe] cañería *f* de desagüe.

overgrown [ˌəʊvə'grəʊn] *adj* cubierto(ta) de matojos.

overhaul ◇ *n* ['əʊvəhɔːl] - **1.** [of car, machine] revisión *f* - **2.** [of method, system] repaso *m* general. ◇ *vt* [ˌəʊvə'hɔːl] revisar.

overhead ◇ *adj* ['əʊvəhed] aéreo(a). ◇ *adv* [ˌəʊvə'hed] por lo alto, por encima. ◇ *n* ['əʊvəhed] (U) US gastos *mpl* generales. ⟜ **overheads** *npl* gastos *mpl* generales.

overhead projector *n* retroproyector *m*.

overhear [ˌəʊvə'hɪə'] (*pt & pp* -**heard** [-hɜːd]) *vt* oír por casualidad.

overheat [ˌəʊvə'hiːt] *vi* recalentarse.

overjoyed [ˌəʊvə'dʒɔɪd] *adj*: **to be overjoyed (at sthg)** estar encantado(da) (con algo).

overkill ['əʊvəkɪl] *n* exageración *f*, exceso *m*.

overladen [ˌəʊvə'leɪdn] *pp* ⟞ **overload**.

overland ['əʊvəlænd] ◇ *adj* terrestre. ◇ *adv* por tierra.

overlap *vi* [ˌəʊvə'læp] [cover each other] superponerse.

overleaf [ˌəʊvə'liːf] *adv* al dorso.

overload [ˌəʊvə'ləʊd] (*pp* -**loaded** OR -**laden**) *vt* sobrecargar.

overlook [ˌəʊvə'lʊk] *vt* - **1.** [look over] mirar OR dar a - **2.** [disregard, miss] pasar por alto - **3.** [forgive] perdonar.

overnight ◇ *adj* ['əʊvənaɪt] - **1.** [for all of night] de noche, nocturno(na) - **2.** [for a night's stay - clothes] para una noche - **3.** [very sudden] súbito(ta) <> *adv* [**at night**] **- 1.** [for all of night] durante la noche ∎ **2.** [very suddenly] de la noche a la mañana.

overpass [ˈəʊvəpɑːs] *n US* paso *m* elevado.

overpower [ˌəʊvəˈpaʊər] *vt* **- 1.** [in fight] vencer, subyugar **- 2.** *fig* [overwhelm] sobreponerse a, vencer.

overpowering [ˌəʊvəˈpaʊərɪŋ] *adj* arrollador(ra), abrumador(ra).

overran [ˌəʊvəˈræn] *pt* ▷ **overrun**.

overrated [ˌəʊvəˈreɪtɪd] *adj* sobreestimado(da).

override [ˌəʊvəˈraɪd] (*pt* **-rode**, *pp* **-ridden**) *vt* **- 1.** [be more important than] predominar sobre **- 2.** [overrule] desautorizar.

overriding [ˌəʊvəˈraɪdɪŋ] *adj* predominante.

overrode [ˌəʊvəˈrəʊd] *pt* ▷ **override**.

overrule [ˌəʊvəˈruːl] *vt* [person] desautorizar; [decision] anular; [request] denegar.

overrun [ˌəʊvəˈrʌn] <> *vt* (*pt* **-ran**, *pp* **-run**) **- 1.** MIL [enemy, army] apabullar, arrasar; [country] ocupar, invadir **- 2.** *fig* [cover]: **to be overrun with** estar invadido(da) de. <> *vi* (*pt* **-ran**, *pp* **-run**) rebasar el tiempo previsto.

oversaw [ˌəʊvəˈsɔː] *pt* ▷ **oversee**.

overseas <> *adj* [ˈəʊvəsiːz] **- 1.** [in or to foreign countries - market] exterior; [- sales, aid] al extranjero; [- network, branches] en el extranjero **- 2.** [from abroad] extranjero(ra). <> *adv* [ˌəʊvəˈsiːz] [go, travel] al extranjero; [study, live] en el extranjero.

oversee [ˌəʊvəˈsiː] (*pt* **-saw**, *pp* **-seen** [-ˈsiːn]) *vt* supervisar.

overseer [ˈəʊvəˌsiːər] *n* supervisor *m*, -ra *f*.

overshadow [ˌəʊvəˈʃædəʊ] *vt* **- 1.** [be more important than]: **to be overshadowed by** ser eclipsado(da) por **- 2.** [mar]: **to be overshadowed by sthg** ser ensombrecido(da) por algo.

overshoot [ˌəʊvəˈʃuːt] (*pt & pp* **-shot**) *vt* [go past] pasarse.

oversight [ˈəʊvəsaɪt] *n* descuido *m*.

oversleep [ˌəʊvəˈsliːp] (*pt & pp* **-slept** [-ˈslept]) *vi* no despertarse a tiempo, quedarse dormido(da).

overspill [ˈəʊvəspɪl] *n* exceso *m* de población.

overstep [ˌəʊvəˈstep] *vt* pasar de; **to overstep the mark** pasarse de la raya.

overt [ˈəʊvɜːt] *adj* abierto(ta), evidente.

overtake [ˌəʊvəˈteɪk] *vt* (*pt* **-took**, *pp* **-taken** [-ˈteɪkn]) **- 1.** AUT adelantar **- 2.** [subj: event] coger de improviso.

overthrow *vt* [ˌəʊvəˈθrəʊ] (*pt* **-threw**, *pp* **-thrown**) [oust] derrocar.

overtime [ˈəʊvətaɪm] <> *n (U)* **- 1.** [extra work] horas *fpl* extra **- 2.** *US* SPORT (tiempo *m* de) descuento *m*. <> *adv* **to work overtime** trabajar horas extra.

overtones [ˈəʊvətəʊnz] *npl* matiz *m*.

overtook [ˌəʊvəˈtʊk] *pt* ▷ **overtake**.

overture [ˈəʊvəˌtjʊər] *n* MUS obertura *f*.

overturn [ˌəʊvəˈtɜːn] <> *vt* **- 1.** [turn over] volcar **- 2.** [overrule] rechazar **- 3.** [overthrow] derrocar, derrumbar. <> *vi* [vehicle] volcar; [boat] zozobrar.

overweight [ˌəʊvəˈweɪt] *adj* grueso(sa), gordo(da).

overwhelm [ˌəʊvəˈwelm] *vt* **- 1.** [make helpless] abrumar **- 2.** [defeat] aplastar.

overwhelming [ˌəʊvəˈwelmɪŋ] *adj* **- 1.** [despair, kindness] abrumador(ra) **- 2.** [defeat, majority] aplastante.

overwork [ˌəʊvəˈwɜːk] <> *n* trabajo *m* excesivo. <> *vt* [give too much work to] hacer trabajar demasiado.

overwrought [ˌəʊvəˈrɔːt] *adj fml* nerviosísimo(ma), sobreexcitado(da).

owe [əʊ] *vt*: **to owe sthg to sb, to owe sb sthg** deber algo a alguien.

owing [ˈəʊɪŋ] *adj* que se debe. ◆ **owing to** *prep* debido a.

owl [aʊl] *n* búho *m*, lechuza *f*.

own [əʊn] <> *adj*: **my/your/his** *etc* **own car** mi/tu/su *etc* propio coche. <> *pron*: **my own** el mío (la mía); **his/her own** el suyo (la suya); **a house of my/his own** mi/su propia casa; **on one's own** solo(la); **to get one's own back** *inf* tomarse la revancha, desquitarse. <> *vt* poseer, tener. ◆ **own up** *vi*: **to own up (to sthg)** confesar (algo).

owner [ˈəʊnər] *n* propietario *m*, -ria *f*.

ownership [ˈəʊnəʃɪp] *n* propiedad *f*.

ox [ɒks] (*pl* **oxen**) *n* buey *m*.

Oxbridge [ˈɒksbrɪdʒ] *n (U)* las universidades de Oxford y Cambridge.

oxen [ˈɒksn] *npl* ▷ **ox**.

oxtail soup [ˈɒksteɪl-] *n* sopa *f* de rabo de buey.

oxygen [ˈɒksɪdʒən] *n* oxígeno *m*.

oxygen mask *n* máscara *f* de oxígeno.

oxygen tent *n* tienda *f* de oxígeno.

oyster [ˈɔɪstər] *n* ostra *f*.

oz. *abbr of* **ounce**.

ozone [ˈəʊzəʊn] *n* ozono *m*.

ozone-friendly *adj* que no daña a la capa de ozono.

ozone layer *n* capa *f* de ozono.

p

p [(pl p's OR ps), **P** (pl P's OR Ps) [pi:] n [letter] p f, P f.

p² - 1. (abbr of **page**) p., pág. - 2. UK abbr of **penny, pence**.

pa [pɑː] n esp US inf papá m.

p.a. (abbr of **per annum**) p.a.

PA ◇ n - 1. UK abbr of **personal assistant** - 2. abbr of **public-address system**. ◇ abbr of **Pennsylvania**.

pace [peɪs] ◇ n paso m, ritmo m; **to keep pace (with sthg)** [change, events] mantenerse al corriente (de algo); **to keep pace (with sb)** seguir el ritmo (a alguien). ◇ vi: **to pace (up and down)** pasearse de un lado a otro.

pacemaker ['peɪs,meɪkər] n - 1. MED marcapasos m inv - 2. [in race] liebre f.

Pacific [pə'sɪfɪk] ◇ adj del Pacífico. ◇ n: **the Pacific (Ocean)** el (océano) Pacífico.

pacifier ['pæsɪfaɪər] n US [for child] chupete m.

pacifist ['pæsɪfɪst] n pacifista mf.

pacify ['pæsɪfaɪ] vt [person, mob] calmar, apaciguar.

pack [pæk] ◇ n - 1. [bundle] lío m, fardo m; [rucksack] mochila f - 2. esp US [packet] paquete m - 3. [of cards] baraja f - 4. [of dogs] jauría f; [of wolves] manada f; pej [of people] banda f; **a pack of lies** una sarta de mentira. ◇ vt - 1. [for journey - bags, suitcase] hacer; [- clothes etc] meter (en la maleta) - 2. [put in parcel] empaquetar; [put in container] envasar - 3. [fill] llenar, abarrotar; **to be packed into sthg** estar apretujados dentro de algo. ◇ vi hacer las maletas. ► **pack in** inf ◇ vt sep UK [stop] dejar; **pack it in!** ¡déjalo!, ¡ya basta! ◇ vi [break down] escacharrarse. ► **pack off** vt sep inf enviar, mandar.

package ['pækɪdʒ] ◇ n [gen & COMPUT] paquete m. ◇ vt [wrap up] envasar.

package deal n convenio m OR acuerdo m global.

package tour n vacaciones fpl con todo incluido.

packaging ['pækɪdʒɪŋ] n [wrapping] envasado m.

packed [pækt] adj: **packed (with)** repleto(ta) (de).

packed lunch n UK almuerzo preparado de antemano que se lleva uno al colegio, a la oficina etc.

packed-out adj UK inf a tope.

packet ['pækɪt] n [gen] paquete m; [of crisps, sweets] bolsa f.

packing ['pækɪŋ] n - 1. [protective material] embalaje m - 2. [for journey]: **to do the packing** hacer el equipaje.

packing case n cajón m de embalaje.

pact [pækt] n pacto m.

pad [pæd] ◇ n - 1. [of material] almohadilla f - 2. [of cotton wool] tampón m - 3. [of paper] bloc m - 4. [of spacecraft]: **(launch) pad** plataforma f (de lanzamiento) - 5. inf dated [home] casa f. ◇ vt acolchar, rellenar. ◇ vi [walk softly] andar con suavidad.

padding ['pædɪŋ] n (U) - 1. [in jacket, chair] relleno m - 2. [in speech] paja f.

paddle ['pædl] ◇ n - 1. [for canoe, dinghy] pala f, canalete m; US [for table tennis] pala f - 2. [walk in sea] paseo m por la orilla. ◇ vt UK remar en. ◇ vi - 1. [in canoe] remar - 2. [person - in sea] pasear por la orilla.

paddle boat, paddle steamer n vapor m de paletas OR ruedas.

paddling pool ['pædlɪŋ-] n UK [inflatable] piscina f inflable.

paddock ['pædək] n - 1. [small field] potrero m, corral m - 2. [at racecourse] paddock m.

paddy field ['pædɪ-] n arrozal m.

padlock ['pædlɒk] ◇ n candado m. ◇ vt cerrar con candado.

paediatrics [,piːdɪ'ætrɪks] UK = **pediatrics**.

pagan ['peɪgən] ◇ adj pagano(na). ◇ n pagano m, -na f.

page [peɪdʒ] ◇ n [of book, newspaper] página f. ◇ vt - 1. [in hotel, airport] llamar por megafonía - 2. [using an electronic pager] llamar por el busca.

pageant ['pædʒənt] n desfile m.

pageantry ['pædʒəntrɪ] n boato m.

paid [peɪd] ◇ pt & pp ▷ **pay**. ◇ adj [holiday, leave] pagado(da); [work, staff] remunerado(da); **badly/well paid** mal/bien pagado.

pail [peɪl] n cubo m.

pain [peɪn] n - 1. [ache] dolor m; **to be in pain** sufrir dolor - 2. [mental suffering] pena f, sufrimiento m - 3. inf [annoyance - person] pesado m, -da f; [- thing] pesadez f. ► **pains** npl [effort, care] esfuerzos mpl; **to be at pains to do sthg** afanarse por hacer algo.

pained [peɪnd] adj apenado(da).

painful ['peɪnfʊl] adj [back, eyes] dolorido(da); [injury, exercise, memory] doloroso(sa).

painfully ['peɪnfʊlɪ] adv - 1. [causing pain] dolorosamente - 2. [extremely] terriblemente.

painkiller ['peɪn,kɪlər] n analgésico m.

painless ['peɪnlɪs] adj - **1.** [physically] indoloro(ra) - **2.** [emotionally] sin complicaciones.

painstaking ['peɪnz,teɪkɪŋ] adj meticuloso(sa), minucioso(sa).

paint [peɪnt] <> n pintura f. <> vt pintar; **to paint the ceiling white** pintar el techo de blanco; **to paint one's lips/nails** pintarse los labios/las uñas. <> vi pintar.

paintbrush ['peɪntbrʌʃ] n - **1.** ART pincel m - **2.** [of decorator] brocha f.

painter ['peɪntər] n pintor m, -ra f; **painter and decorator** pintor m, -ra f y decorador, -ra f.

painting ['peɪntɪŋ] n - **1.** [picture] cuadro m, pintura f - **2.** (U) [art form, trade] pintura f.

paint stripper n quitapinturas f inv.

paintwork ['peɪntwɜːk] n (U) pintura f.

pair [peər] n - **1.** [of shoes, socks, wings] par m; [of aces] pareja f - **2.** [two-part object]: **a pair of scissors** unas tijeras; **a pair of trousers** unos pantalones - **3.** [couple - of people] pareja f.

pajamas [pəˈdʒɑːməz] esp US = **pyjamas**.

Pakistan [UK ,pɑːkɪˈstɑːn, US ,pækɪˈstæn] n (el) Paquistán.

Pakistani [UK ,pɑːkɪˈstɑːn, US ,pækɪˈstænɪ] <> adj paquistaní. <> n paquistaní mf.

pal [pæl] n inf [friend] amiguete m, -ta f, colega mf.

palace ['pælɪs] n palacio m.

palatable ['pælətəbl] adj - **1.** [pleasant to taste] sabroso(sa) - **2.** [acceptable] aceptable.

palate ['pælət] n paladar m.

palaver [pəˈlɑːvər] n UK inf [fuss] follón m.

pale [peɪl] <> adj - **1.** [colour, clothes, paint] claro(ra); [light] tenue - **2.** [person, skin] pálido(da); **to turn pale** palidecer. <> vi palidecer.

Palestine ['pælɪˌstaɪn] n Palestina.

Palestinian [,pæləˈstɪnɪən] <> adj palestino(na). <> n [person] palestino m, -na f.

palette ['pælət] n paleta f.

palings ['peɪlɪŋz] npl empalizada f.

pall [pɔːl] <> n - **1.** [of smoke] nube f, cortina f - **2.** US [coffin] féretro m. <> vi hacerse pesado(da).

pallet ['pælɪt] n palet m.

palliative care n (U) MED cuidados mpl paliativos.

pallor ['pælər] n liter palidez f.

palm [pɑːm] n - **1.** [tree] palmera f - **2.** [of hand] palma f; **to read sb's palm** leerle la mano a alguien. ◆ **palm off** vt sep inf: **to palm sthg off on sb** endosar algo a alguien; **to palm sthg off as** hacer pasar algo por.

Palm Sunday n Domingo m de Ramos.

palm tree n palmera f.

palpable ['pælpəbl] adj palpable.

paltry ['pɔːltrɪ] adj mísero(ra).

pamper ['pæmpər] vt mimar.

pamphlet ['pæmflɪt] n [publicity, information] folleto m; [political] panfleto m.

pan [pæn] <> n - **1.** [saucepan] cazuela f, cacerola f; [frying pan] sartén f - **2.** US [for bread, cakes etc] molde m. <> vt inf [criticize] poner por los suelos. <> vi CIN: **the camera pans right/left** la cámara se mueve hacia la derecha/la izquierda. ◆ **pan out** vi inf [happen succesfully] resultar, salir.

panacea [,pænəˈsɪə] n: **a panacea (for)** la panacea (de).

Panama ['pænə,mɑː] n Panamá.

Panama Canal n: **the Panama Canal** el canal de Panamá.

pancake ['pænkeɪk] n torta f, crepe f, panqueque m, panqué m Amér C & Col, crepa f Méx, panqueca f Ven.

Pancake Day n UK ≃ Martes m inv de Carnaval.

panda ['pændə] (pl panda OR -s) n panda m.

Panda car n UK coche m patrulla, auto m patrulla Amér C, Méx & Chile, patrullero m, patrulla f Col & Méx.

pandemonium [,pændɪˈməʊnjəm] n pandemónium m, jaleo m; **it was pandemonium** fue un auténtico pandemónium.

pander ['pændər] vi: **to pander to** complacer a.

pane [peɪn] n (hoja f de) cristal m.

panel ['pænl] n - **1.** [group of people] equipo m; [in debates] mesa f - **2.** [of wood, metal] panel m - **3.** [of a machine] tablero m, panel m.

panelling UK, **paneling** US ['pænəlɪŋ] n (U) [on a ceiling] artesonado m; [on a wall] paneles mpl.

pang [pæŋ] n punzada f.

panic ['pænɪk] <> n pánico m; **to be in a panic about sthg** ponerse muy nervioso por algo. <> vi (pt & pp -ked, cont -king) aterrarse; **don't panic** que no cunda el pánico.

panicky ['pænɪkɪ] adj: **he feels panicky** tiene pánico; **she got panicky** le entró el pánico.

panic-stricken adj preso(sa) OR víctima del pánico.

panorama [,pænəˈrɑːmə] n panorama m.

pant [pænt] vi jadear.

panther ['pænθər] (pl panther OR -s) n pantera f.

panties ['pæntɪz] npl US bragas fpl, calzones mpl Amér, pantaletas fpl Amér C & Méx, bombacha f R Plata, blúmer m Amér C.

pantihose ['pæntɪhəʊz] = **panty hose**.

pantomime ['pæntəmaɪm], **panto** n - **1.** UK obra musical humorística para niños celebrada en Navidad - **2.** [mime] pantomima f.

pantry ['pæntrɪ] n despensa f.

pants [pænts] <> npl - 1. UK [underpants] calzoncillos mpl - 2. US [trousers] pantalones mpl. <> adj UK inf [bad]: **to be pants** ser un churro.

pantsuit ['pæntsuːt] n traje m pantalón.

panty hose, pantihose ['pæntɪ-] npl US medias fpl.

papa [UK pə'pɑː, US 'pæpə] n papá m.

paper ['peɪpəʳ] <> n - 1. (U) [material] papel m; **piece of paper** [sheet] hoja f de papel; [scrap] trozo m de papel - 2. [newspaper] periódico m - 3. UK [in exam] examen m - 4. [essay - gen] estudio m, ensayo m; [- for conference] ponencia f. <> adj [made of paper] de papel. <> vt empapelar. ⬧ **papers** npl [official documents] documentación f.

paperback ['peɪpəbæk] n libro m en rústica.

paper clip n clip m.

paper handkerchief n pañuelo m de papel, klínex® m inv.

paper knife n abrecartas m inv.

paper shop n UK quiosco m de periódicos.

paper towel n toallita f de papel.

paper tray n bandeja f de papel.

paperweight ['peɪpəweɪt] n pisapapeles m inv.

paperwork ['peɪpəwɜːk] n papeleo m.

papier-mâché [ˌpæpjeɪ'mæʃeɪ] n cartón m piedra.

paprika ['pæprɪkə] n pimentón m.

Pap smear, Pap test n US citología f.

par [pɑːʳ] n - 1. [parity]: **on a par with** al mismo nivel que - 2. GOLF par m; **under/over par** bajo/sobre par.

parable ['pærəbl] n parábola f.

parachute ['pærəʃuːt] n paracaídas m inv.

parade [pə'reɪd] <> n [procession] desfile m; **on parade** MIL pasando revista. <> vt - 1. [soldiers] hacer desfilar; [criminals, captives] pasear - 2. fig [flaunt] hacer alarde de. <> vi desfilar.

paradise ['pærədaɪs] n fig paraíso m.

paradox ['pærədɒks] n paradoja f.

paradoxically [ˌpærə'dɒksɪklɪ] adv paradójicamente.

paraffin ['pærəfɪn] n parafina f.

paragliding ['pærəˌglaɪdɪŋ] n parapente m.

paragraph ['pærəgrɑːf] n párrafo m.

Paraguay ['pærəgwaɪ] n (el) Paraguay.

Paraguayan [ˌpærə'gwaɪən] <> adj paraguayo(ya). <> n paraguayo m, -ya f.

paralegal [ˌpærə'liːgl] n US ayudante de un abogado.

parallel ['pærəlel] <> adj: **parallel (to OR with)** paralelo(la) (a). <> n - 1. [parallel line, surface] paralela f - 2. [something, someone similar]: **to have no parallel** no tener precedente - 3. [similarity] semejanza f - 4. GEOG paralelo m.

paralyse UK, **paralyze** US ['pærəlaɪz] vt lit & fig paralizar.

paralysis [pə'rælɪsɪs] (pl -lyses [-lɪsiːz]) n parálisis f inv.

paramedic [ˌpærə'medɪk] n esp US auxiliar sanitario m, auxiliar sanitaria f.

parameter [pə'ræmɪtəʳ] n parámetro m.

paramount ['pærəmaʊnt] adj vital, fundamental; **of paramount importance** de suma importancia.

paranoid ['pærənɔɪd] adj paranoico(ca).

paraphernalia [ˌpærəfə'neɪljə] n parafernalia f.

parasite ['pærəsaɪt] n parásito m, -ta f.

parasol ['pærəsɒl] n sombrilla f.

paratrooper ['pærətruːpəʳ] n paracaidista mf (del ejército).

parcel ['pɑːsl] n paquete m. ⬧ **parcel up** vt sep (UK pt & pp -led, cont -ling, US pt & pp -ed, cont -ing) UK empaquetar.

parcel post n (servicio m de) paquete m postal.

parched [pɑːtʃt] adj - 1. [throat, mouth] muy seco(ca); [lips] quemado(da) - 2. inf [very thirsty] seco(ca).

parchment ['pɑːtʃmənt] n [paper] pergamino m.

pardon ['pɑːdn] <> n - 1. LAW perdón m, indulto m - 2. [forgiveness] perdón m; **I beg your pardon?** [showing surprise, asking for repetition] ¿perdón?, ¿cómo (dice)?; **I beg your pardon** [to apologize] le ruego me disculpe, perdón. <> vt - 1. [forgive]: **to pardon sb (for sthg)** perdonar a alguien (por algo); **pardon?** ¿perdón?, ¿cómo (dice)?; **pardon me** [touching sb accidentally, belching] discúlpeme, perdón; [excuse me] con permiso - 2. LAW indultar.

parent ['peərənt] n [father] padre m; [mother] madre f. ⬧ **parents** npl padres mpl.

parental [pə'rentl] adj de los padres.

parenthesis [pə'renθɪsɪs] (pl -theses [-θɪsiːz]) n paréntesis m inv; **in parenthesis** entre paréntesis.

parish ['pærɪʃ] n - 1. [of church] parroquia f - 2. UK [area of local government] ≃ municipio m.

parity ['pærətɪ] n: **parity (with/between)** igualdad f (con/entre).

park [pɑːk] <> n parque m. <> vt & vi aparcar, estacionar Amér, parquear Amér.

park-and-ride n aparcamiento m disuasorio Esp.

parking ['pɑːkɪŋ] n aparcamiento m Esp, estacionamiento m Amér; **'no parking'** 'prohibido aparcar'.

parking lot n US aparcamiento m (al aire libre).

parking meter n parquímetro m.

parking ticket n multa f por aparcamiento indebido, multa f por estacionamiento indebido Amér.

parlance ['pɑːləns] n: in common/legal parlance en el habla común/legal, en el lenguaje común/legal.

parliament ['pɑːləmənt] n - 1. [assembly, institution] parlamento m - 2. [session] legislatura f.

parliamentary [ˌpɑːlə'mentəri] adj parlamentario(ria).

parlour UK, **parlor** US ['pɑːlər] n dated salón m.

parochial [pə'rəʊkjəl] adj - 1. pej de miras estrechas - 2.: **parochial school** US colegio m privado religioso.

parody ['pærədi] ◇ n parodia f. ◇ vt parodiar.

parole [pə'rəʊl] n libertad f condicional (bajo palabra); **on parole** en libertad condicional.

parquet ['pɑːkeɪ] n parqué m.

parrot ['pærət] n loro m.

parry ['pæri] vt [blow] parar; [attack] desviar.

parsimonious [ˌpɑːsɪ'məʊnjəs] adj fml & pej mezquino(na), tacaño(ña).

parsley ['pɑːsli] n perejil m.

parsnip ['pɑːsnɪp] n chirivía f.

parson ['pɑːsn] n párroco m.

part [pɑːt] ◇ n - 1. [gen] parte f; **the best OR better part of** la mayor parte de; **for the most part** en su mayoría - 2. [component] pieza f - 3. THEAT papel m - 4. [involvement]: **part (in)** participación f (en); **to play an important part (in)** desempeñar OR jugar un papel importante (en); **to take part (in)** tomar parte (en) - 5. US [hair parting] raya f. ◇ adv en parte. ◇ vt - 1. [lips, curtains] abrir - 2. [hair] peinar con raya. ◇ vi - 1. [leave one another] separarse - 2. [separate - lips, curtains] abrirse. ➡ **part with** vt insep separarse de.

part exchange n UK sistema de pagar parte de algo con un artículo usado; **in part exchange** como parte del pago.

partial ['pɑːʃl] adj - 1. [incomplete, biased] parcial - 2. [fond]: **partial to** amigo(ga) de, aficionado(da) a.

participant [pɑː'tɪsɪpənt] n participante mf.

participate [pɑː'tɪsɪpeɪt] vi: **to participate (in)** participar (en).

participation [pɑːˌtɪsɪ'peɪʃn] n participación f.

participle ['pɑːtɪsɪpl] n participio m.

particle ['pɑːtɪkl] n partícula f.

particular [pə'tɪkjʊlər] adj - 1. [specific, individual] en particular OR especial; **did you want any particular colour?** ¿quería algún color en particular? - 2. [extra, greater] especial - 3. [difficult] exigente. ➡ **particulars** npl [of person] datos mpl; [of thing] detalles mpl. ➡ **in particular** adv en particular.

particularly [pə'tɪkjʊləli] adv especialmente.

parting ['pɑːtɪŋ] n - 1. [separation] despedida f - 2. UK [in hair] raya f.

partisan [ˌpɑːtɪ'zæn] ◇ adj partidista. ◇ n [freedom fighter] partisano m, -na f.

partition [pɑː'tɪʃn] ◇ n - 1. [wall] tabique m; [screen] separación f - 2. COMPUT partición f. ◇ vt - 1. [room] dividir con tabiques - 2. [country] dividir - 3. COMPUT crear particiones en.

partly ['pɑːtli] adv en parte.

partner ['pɑːtnər] n - 1. [spouse, lover] pareja f - 2. [in an activity] compañero m, -ra f - 3. [in a business] socio m, -cia f - 4. [ally] colega mf.

partnership ['pɑːtnəʃɪp] n - 1. [relationship] asociación f - 2. [business] sociedad f.

partridge ['pɑːtrɪdʒ] n perdiz f.

part-time ◇ adj a tiempo parcial. ◇ adv a tiempo parcial.

party ['pɑːti] n - 1. POL partido m - 2. [social gathering] fiesta f - 3. [group] grupo m - 4. LAW parte f.

party line n - 1. POL línea f (política) del partido - 2. TELEC línea f (telefónica) compartida.

pass [pɑːs] ◇ n - 1. [in football, rugby, hockey] pase m; [in tennis] passing-shot m - 2. [document, permit] pase m; **travel pass** tarjeta f OR abono m de transportes - 3. UK [successful result] aprobado m - 4. [route between mountains] puerto m
▸▸▸ **to make a pass at sb** intentar ligar con alguien. ◇ vt - 1. [gen] pasar - 2. [move past - thing] pasar por (delante de); [- person] pasar delante de; **to pass sb in the street** cruzarse con alguien - 3. AUT adelantar - 4. [exceed] sobrepasar - 5. [exam, candidate, law] aprobar - 6. [opinion, judgement] formular; [sentence] dictar. ◇ vi - 1. [gen] pasar - 2. AUT adelantar - 3. [in exam] aprobar - 4. [occur] transcurrir. ➡ **pass as, pass for** vt insep pasar por. ➡ **pass away, pass on** vi fallecer. ➡ **pass by** ◇ vt sep [subj: people] hacer caso omiso a; [subj: events, life] pasar desapercibido(da) a. ◇ vi pasar cerca. ➡ **pass for** vt insep = **pass as**. ➡ **pass on** ◇ vt sep: **to pass sthg on (to)** pasar algo (a). ◇ vi - 1. [move on] continuar - 2. = **pass away**. ➡ **pass out** vi - 1. [faint] desmayarse - 2. UK MIL graduarse. ➡ **pass over** vt insep pasar por alto. ➡ **pass up** vt sep dejar pasar OR escapar.

passable ['pɑːsəbl] *adj* - **1.** [satisfactory] pasable - **2.** [not blocked] transitable.

passage ['pæsɪdʒ] *n* - **1.** [corridor - between houses] pasadizo *m*, pasaje *m*; [- between rooms] pasillo *m* - **2.** [of music, speech] pasaje *m* - **3.** *fml* [of vehicle, person, time] paso *m* - **4.** [sea journey] travesía *f*.

passageway ['pæsɪdʒweɪ] *n* [between houses] pasadizo *m*, pasaje *m*; [between rooms] pasillo *m*.

passbook ['pɑːsbʊk] *n* ≃ cartilla *f* OR libreta *f* de banco.

passenger ['pæsɪndʒəʳ] *n* pasajero *m*, -ra *f*.

passerby [,pɑːsə'baɪ] (*pl* **passersby** [,pɑːsəz'baɪ]) *n* transeúnte *mf*.

passing ['pɑːsɪŋ] ◇ *adj* [fad] pasajero(ra); [remark] de pasada. ◇ *n* transcurso *m*. ➡ **in passing** *adv* de pasada.

passion ['pæʃn] *n*: **passion (for)** pasión *f* (por).

passionate ['pæʃənət] *adj* apasionado(da).

passive ['pæsɪv] *adj* pasivo(va).

Passover ['pɑːs,əʊvəʳ] *n*: **(the) Passover** (la) Pascua judía.

passport ['pɑːspɔːt] *n* pasaporte *m*; **passport to sthg** *fig* pasaporte a algo.

passport control *n* UK control *m* de pasaportes.

password ['pɑːswɜːd] *n* [gen & COMPUT] contraseña *f*.

past [pɑːst] ◇ *adj* - **1.** [former] anterior - **2.** [most recent] último(ma); **over the past week** durante la última semana - **3.** [finished] terminado(da). ◇ *adv* - **1.** [telling the time]: **it's ten past** son y diez - **2.** [beyond, in front] por delante; **to walk/run past** pasar andando/corriendo. ◇ *n* - **1.** [time]: **the past** el pasado - **2.** [personal history] pasado *m*. ◇ *prep* - **1.** [telling the time]: **it's five/half/a quarter past ten** son las diez y cinco/media/cuarto - **2.** [alongside, in front of] por delante de; **to walk/run past sthg** pasar algo andando/corriendo - **3.** [beyond] más allá de; **it's past the bank** está pasado el banco.

pasta ['pæstə] *n* (*U*) pasta *f*.

paste [peɪst] ◇ *n* - **1.** [smooth mixture] pasta *f* - **2.** [food] paté *m* - **3.** [glue] engrudo *m*. ◇ *vt* [labels, stamps] pegar; [surface] engomar, engrudar; COMPUT pegar.

pastel ['pæstl] ◇ *adj* pastel (*inv*). ◇ *n* ART [crayon] pastel *m*.

pasteurize, -ise ['pɑːstʃəraɪz] *vt* pasteurizar.

pastille ['pæstɪl] *n* UK pastilla *f*.

pastime ['pɑːstaɪm] *n* pasatiempo *m*.

pastor ['pɑːstəʳ] *n* RELIG pastor *m*.

past participle *n* participio *m* pasado.

pastry ['peɪstrɪ] *n* - **1.** [mixture] pasta *f*, masa *f* - **2.** [cake] pastel *m*.

past tense *n*: **the past tense** el pasado.

pasture ['pɑːstʃəʳ] *n* pasto *m*.

pasty [¹['peɪstɪ] *adj* pálido(da).

pasty [²['pæstɪ] *n* UK empanada *f*.

pat [pæt] ◇ *n* [of butter etc] porción *f*. ◇ *vt* [gen] golpear ligeramente; [dog] acariciar; **to pat sb on the back/hand** darle a alguien una palmadita en la espalda/la mano.

patch [pætʃ] ◇ *n* - **1.** [for mending] remiendo *m*; [on elbow] codera *f*; [to cover eye] parche *m* - **2.** [part of surface] área *f* - **3.** [area of land] bancal *m*, parcela *f* - **4.** [period of time] periodo *m* - **5.** COMPUT parche *m*. ◇ *vt* remendar. ➡ **patch up** *vt sep* - **1.** [mend] reparar - **2.** [resolve - relationship] salvar; **we have patched things up** hemos hecho las paces.

patchwork ['pætʃwɜːk] *adj* de trozos de distintos colores y formas.

patchy ['pætʃɪ] *adj* - **1.** [uneven - fog, sunshine] irregular; [- colour] desigual - **2.** [incomplete] deficiente, incompleto(ta) - **3.** [good in parts] irregular.

pâté ['pæteɪ] *n* paté *m*.

patent [UK 'peɪtənt, US 'pætənt] ◇ *adj* [obvious] patente, evidente. ◇ *n* patente *f*. ◇ *vt* patentar.

patent leather *n* charol *m*.

paternal [pə'tɜːnl] *adj* [love, attitude] paternal; [grandmother, grandfather] paterno(na).

paternity [pə'tɜːnətɪ] *n* paternidad *f*.

path [pɑːθ, *pl* pɑːðz] *n* - **1.** [track, way ahead] camino *m* - **2.** COMPUT camino *m* - **3.** [trajectory - of bullet] trayectoria *f*; [- of flight] rumbo *m* - **4.** [course of action] curso *m*.

pathetic [pə'θetɪk] *adj* - **1.** [causing pity] patético(ca), lastimoso(sa) - **2.** [attempt, person] inútil; [actor, film] malísimo(ma).

pathname ['pɑːθneɪm] *n* camino *m*.

pathological [,pæθə'lɒdʒɪkl] *adj* patológico(ca).

pathology [pə'θɒlədʒɪ] *n* patología *f*.

pathos ['peɪθɒs] *n* patetismo *m*.

pathway ['pɑːθweɪ] *n* camino *m*, sendero *m*.

patience ['peɪʃns] *n* - **1.** [quality] paciencia *f* - **2.** UK [card game] solitario *m*.

patient ['peɪʃnt] ◇ *adj* paciente. ◇ *n* paciente *mf*.

patio ['pætɪəʊ] (*pl* -s) *n* [paved] área pavimentada al lado de una casa utilizada para el esparcimiento.

patriotic [UK ,pætrɪ'ɒtɪk, US ,peɪtrɪ'ɒtɪk] *adj* patriótico(ca).

patrol [pə'trəʊl] ◇ *n* patrulla *f*. ◇ *vt* patrullar.

patrol car *n* coche *m* patrulla, auto *m* patrulla *Amér (, Méx & Chile*, patrullero *m*, patrulla *f* Col & Méx.

patrolman [pə'trəʊlmən] (*pl* -men [-mən]) *n* US policía *m*, guardia *m*.

patron ['peɪtrən] *n* - **1.** [of arts] mecenas *mf inv* - **2.** UK [of charity, campaign] patrocinador *m*, -ra *f* - **3.** *fml* [customer] cliente *mf*.

patronize, -ise ['pætrənaɪz] *vt* - **1.** *pej* [talk down to] tratar con aire paternalista OR condescendiente - **2.** *fml* [back financially] patrocinar.

patronizing ['pætrənaɪzɪŋ] *adj pej* paternalista, condescendiente.

patter ['pætər] ⟨⟩ *n* - **1.** [of raindrops] repiqueteo *m*; [of feet] pasitos *mpl* - **2.** [sales talk] charlatanería *f*. ⟨⟩ *vi* [dog, feet] corretear; [rain] repiquetear.

pattern ['pætən] *n* - **1.** [design] dibujo *m*, diseño *m* - **2.** [of life, work] estructura *f*; [of illness, events] desarrollo *m*, evolución *f* - **3.** [for sewing, knitting] patrón *m* - **4.** [model] modelo *m*.

paunch [pɔːntʃ] *n* barriga *f*, panza *f*.

pauper ['pɔːpər] *n* indigente *mf*.

pause [pɔːz] ⟨⟩ *n* pausa *f*. ⟨⟩ *vi* - **1.** [stop speaking] hacer una pausa - **2.** [stop moving, doing sthg] detenerse.

pave [peɪv] *vt* pavimentar; **to pave the way for** preparar el terreno para.

pavement ['peɪvmənt] *n* - **1.** UK [at side of road] acera *f*, andén *m* Amér C & Col, vereda *f* Perú, banqueta *f* Amér C & Méx - **2.** US [roadway] calzada *f*.

pavilion [pə'vɪljən] *n* - **1.** UK [at sports field] vestuarios *mpl* - **2.** [at exhibition] pabellón *m*.

paving ['peɪvɪŋ] *n (U)* pavimento *m*.

paving stone *n* losa *f*.

paw [pɔː] *n* [of dog] pata *f*; [of lion, cat] zarpa *f*.

pawn [pɔːn] ⟨⟩ *n* - **1.** [chesspiece] peón *m* - **2.** [unimportant person] marioneta *f*. ⟨⟩ *vt* empeñar.

pawnbroker ['pɔːn,brəʊkər] *n* prestamista *mf*.

pawnshop ['pɔːnʃɒp] *n* monte *m* de piedad.

pay [peɪ] ⟨⟩ *vt* (*pt & pp* **paid**) - **1.** [gen] pagar; **to pay sb for sthg** pagar a alguien por algo; **he paid £20 for it** pagó 20 libras por ello - **2.** [compliment, visit] hacer; [respects] ofrecer; [attention] prestar; [homage] rendir. ⟨⟩ *vi* (*pt & pp* **paid**) - **1.** [gen] pagar; **to pay by credit card** pagar con tarjeta de crédito; **it pays well** está bien pagado; **to pay dearly for sthg** pagar caro (por) algo - **2.** [be profitable] ser rentable. ⟨⟩ *n* sueldo *m*, paga *f*. ◆ **pay back** *vt sep* - **1.** [money] devolver, reembolsar; [person] devolver el dinero a - **2.** [revenge oneself]: **to pay sb back (for sthg)** hacer pagar a alguien (por algo). ◆ **pay for** *vt insep* pagar. ◆ **pay off**

⟨⟩ *vt sep* - **1.** [repay - debt] liquidar, saldar - **2.** [dismiss] despedir con indemnización - **3.** [bribe] comprar, pagar o *inf* [efforts] dar fruto. ◆ **pay up** *vi* pagar.

payable ['peɪəbl] *adj* - **1.** [to be paid] pagadero(ra) - **2.** [on cheque]: **payable to** a favor de.

pay-as-you-go *n* pago *m* por uso.

paycheck ['peɪtʃek] *n* US paga *f*.

payday ['peɪdeɪ] *n* día *m* de paga.

payee [peɪ'iː] *n* beneficiario *m*, -ria *f*.

pay envelope *n* US sobre *m* de paga.

payment ['peɪmənt] *n* pago *m*.

pay packet *n* UK - **1.** [envelope] sobre *m* de paga - **2.** [wages] paga *f*.

pay-per-view *n* pago *m* por visión.

pay phone, pay station *n* teléfono *m* público.

pay rise *n* aumento *m* de sueldo.

payroll ['peɪrəʊl] *n* nómina *f*.

payslip ['peɪslɪp] *n* UK hoja *f* de paga.

pay station US = **pay phone**.

pay TV *n* televisión *f* de pago.

pc (*abbr of* per cent) p.c.

PC *n* - **1.** (*abbr of* **personal computer**) PC *m* - **2.** UK *abbr of* **police constable**.

PDF (*abbr of* portable document format) *n* COMPUT PDF *m*.

PE (*abbr of* physical education) *n* educación *f* física.

pea [piː] *n* guisante *m*, arveja *f* Andes, Col & Ven, chícharo *m* Amér C & Méx, petipuá *m* Ven.

peace [piːs] *n* - **1.** [gen] paz *f* - **2.** [quiet] calma *f*, tranquilidad *f* - **3.** [freedom from disagreement] orden *m*; **to make (one's) peace (with)** hacer las paces (con).

peaceable ['piːsəbl] *adj* [not aggressive] pacífico(ca).

peaceful ['piːsfʊl] *adj* - **1.** [quiet, calm] tranquilo(la) - **2.** [not aggressive] pacífico(ca).

peacetime ['piːstaɪm] *n (U)* tiempos *mpl* de paz.

peach [piːtʃ] ⟨⟩ *adj* [in colour] de color melocotón OR durazno Amér. ⟨⟩ *n* - **1.** [fruit] melocotón *m*, durazno *m* Amér - **2.** [colour] color *m* melocotón OR durazno Amér.

peacock ['piːkɒk] *n* pavo *m* real.

peak [piːk] ⟨⟩ *n* - **1.** [mountain top] pico *m*, cima *f* - **2.** [highest point] apogeo *m* - **3.** [of cap] visera *f*. ⟨⟩ *adj* [season] alto(ta); [condition] perfecto(ta). ⟨⟩ *vi* alcanzar el máximo.

peaked [piːkt] *adj* con visera.

peak period *n* UK [of electricity etc] periodo *m* de tarifa máxima; [of traffic] horas *fpl* punta.

peak rate *n* tarifa *f* máxima.

peal [piːl] ◇ n [of bells] repique m; **peal (of laughter)** carcajada f. ◇ vi repicar.

peanut ['piːnʌt] n cacahuete m, maní m Amér, cacahuate m Méx.

peanut butter n manteca f de cacahuete OR de maní R Plata, mantequilla f de maní Amér OR de cacahuate Méx.

pear [peəʳ] n pera f.

pearl [pɜːl] n perla f.

peasant ['peznt] n [in countryside] campesino m, -na f.

peat [piːt] n turba f.

pebble ['pebl] n guijarro m.

peck [pek] ◇ n - 1. [with beak] picotazo m - 2. [kiss] besito m. ◇ vt [with beak] picotear. ◇ vi picotear.

pecking order ['pekɪŋ-] n jerarquía f.

peckish ['pekɪʃ] adj UK inf: **to feel peckish** estar algo hambriento(ta).

peculiar [pɪ'kjuːljəʳ] adj - 1. [odd] singular, extraño(ña) - 2. UK [slightly ill] raro(ra), indispuesto(ta) - 3. [characteristic]: **to be peculiar to** ser propio(pia) de.

peculiarity [pɪˌkjuːlɪ'ærətɪ] n - 1. [eccentricity] extravagancia f - 2. [characteristic] peculiaridad f.

pedal ['pedl] ◇ n pedal m. ◇ vi (UK pt & pp -led, cont -ling, US pt & pp -ed, cont -ing) pedalear.

pedal bin n UK cubo de basura con pedal.

pedantic [pɪ'dæntɪk] adj pej puntilloso(sa).

peddle ['pedl] vt [drugs] traficar con; [wares] vender de puerta en puerta.

pedestal ['pedɪstl] n pedestal m.

pedestrian [pɪ'destrɪən] ◇ adj pej pedestre. ◇ n peatón m.

pedestrian crossing n UK paso m de peatones.

pediatrics, paediatrics [ˌpiːdɪ'ætrɪks] n pediatría f.

pedigree ['pedɪgriː] ◇ adj de raza. ◇ n - 1. [of animal] pedigrí m - 2. [of person] linaje m.

pedlar UK, **peddler** US ['pedləʳ] n vendedor m, -ra f ambulante.

pee [piː] inf ◇ n pis m. ◇ vi mear.

peek [piːk] inf ◇ n mirada f, ojeada f. ◇ vi mirar a hurtadillas.

peel [piːl] ◇ n [gen] piel f; [of orange, lemon] corteza f; [once removed] mondaduras fpl. ◇ vt pelar. ◇ vi [walls, paint] desconcharse; [wallpaper] despegarse; [skin, nose] pelarse.

peelings ['piːlɪŋz] npl peladuras fpl.

peep [piːp] ◇ n - 1. [look] mirada f, ojeada f - 2. inf [sound] pío m. ◇ vi [look] mirar furtivamente. ➧ **peep out** vi asomar.

peephole ['piːphəʊl] n mirilla f.

peer [pɪəʳ] ◇ n - 1. [noble] par m - 2. [equal] igual m. ◇ vi mirar con atención.

peerage ['pɪərɪdʒ] n - 1. [rank] rango m de par - 2. [group]: **the peerage** la nobleza.

peeress ['pɪərɪs] n paresa f.

peer group n grupo generacional o social.

peeved [piːvd] adj inf disgustado(da).

peevish ['piːvɪʃ] adj malhumorado(da).

peg [peg] n - 1. UK [for washing line] pinza f - 2. [on tent] estaca f - 3. [hook] gancho m.

pejorative [pɪ'dʒɒrətɪv] adj peyorativo(va), despectivo(va).

pekinese [ˌpiːkə'niːz], **pekingese** [ˌpiːkɪŋ'iːz] n (pl pekinese) [dog] pekinés m.

pelican ['pelɪkən] (pl pelican OR -s) n pelícano m.

pelican crossing n UK paso de peatones con semáforo accionado por el usuario.

pellet ['pelɪt] n - 1. [small ball] bolita f - 2. [for gun] perdigón m.

pelmet ['pelmɪt] n UK galería f (de cortinas).

pelt [pelt] ◇ n [animal skin] piel f. ◇ vt: **to pelt sb with sthg** acribillar a alguien con algo, arrojar algo a alguien. ◇ vi - 1. [rain]: **it was pelting down** OR **with rain** llovía a cántaros - 2. [run very fast] correr a toda pastilla.

pelvis ['pelvɪs] (pl -vises OR -ves [-viːz]) n pelvis f.

pen [pen] ◇ n - 1. [ballpoint] bolígrafo m, lapicera f R Plata & Chile; [fountain pen] pluma f; [felt-tip] rotulador m - 2. [enclosure] redil m, corral m. ◇ vt [enclose] encerrar.

penal ['piːnl] adj penal.

penalize, -ise UK ['piːnəlaɪz] vt [gen] penalizar; SPORT penalizar, castigar.

penalty ['penltɪ] n - 1. [punishment] pena f; **to pay the penalty (for sthg)** fig pagar las consecuencias (de algo) - 2. [fine] multa f - 3. SPORT penalty m; **penalty (kick)** FTBL penalty m; RUGBY golpe m de castigo.

penance ['penəns] n penitencia f.

pence [pens] UK npl ➧ **penny**.

penchant [UK pɑ̃ʃɑ̃, US 'pentʃənt] n: **to have a penchant for sthg** tener debilidad por algo; **to have a penchant for doing sthg** tener propensión a hacer algo.

pencil ['pensl] n lápiz m; **in pencil** a lápiz. ➧ **pencil in** vt sep [date, appointment] apuntar provisionalmente.

pencil case n estuche m, plumero m Esp.

pencil sharpener n sacapuntas m inv.

pendant ['pendənt] n [jewel on chain] colgante m.

pending ['pendɪŋ] fml ◇ adj - 1. [waiting to be dealt with] pendiente - 2. [about to happen] inminente. ◇ prep a la espera de.

pendulum ['pendjʊləm] (pl -s) n [of clock] péndulo m.

penetrate ['penɪtreɪt] vt - **1.** [barrier] atravesar, [subj: wind, rain, sharp object] penetrar en **2.** [infiltrate - organization] infiltrarse en.

pen friend n UK amigo m, -ga f por correspondencia.

penguin ['peŋgwɪn] n pingüino m.

penicillin [ˌpenɪ'sɪlɪn] n penicilina f.

peninsula [pə'nɪnsjʊlə] (pl -s) n península f.

penis ['pi:nɪs] (pl penises ['pi:nɪsɪz]) n pene m.

penitentiary [ˌpenɪ'tenʃərɪ] n US penitenciaría f.

penknife ['pennaɪf] (pl -knives [-naɪvz]) n navaja f.

pen name n seudónimo m.

pennant ['penənt] n banderín m.

penniless ['penɪlɪs] adj sin dinero.

penny ['penɪ] n - **1.** (pl -ies) UK [coin] penique m; US centavo m - **2.** (pl pence) UK [value] penique m.

pen pal n inf amigo m, -ga f por correspondencia.

pension ['penʃn] n - **1.** [gen] pensión f - **2.** [disability pension] subsidio m.

pensioner ['penʃənəʳ] n: (old-age) pensioner pensionista mf.

pensive ['pensɪv] adj pensativo(va).

pentagon ['pentəgən] n pentágono m. ▶ **Pentagon** n US: the Pentagon el Pentágono, sede del ministerio de Defensa estadounidense.

Pentecost ['pentɪkɒst] n Pentecostés m.

penthouse ['penthaʊs, pl -haʊzɪz] n ático m.

pent up ['pent-] adj reprimido(da).

penultimate [pe'nʌltɪmət] adj penúltimo(ma).

people ['pi:pl] ◇ n [nation, race] pueblo m. ◇ npl - **1.** [gen] gente f; [individuals] personas fpl; a table for eight people una mesa para ocho personas; people say that... dice la gente que...; young people los jóvenes - **2.** [inhabitants] habitantes mpl - **3.** POL: the people el pueblo. ◇ vt: to be peopled by OR with estar poblado(da) de.

pep [pep] n inf vitalidad f. ▶ **pep up** vt sep [person] animar; [food] alegrar.

pepper ['pepəʳ] n - **1.** [spice] pimienta f - **2.** [vegetable] pimiento m; red/green pepper pimiento rojo/verde.

peppermint ['pepəmɪnt] n - **1.** [sweet] pastilla f de menta - **2.** [herb] menta f.

pepper pot UK, **peppershaker** US n pimentero m.

pep talk n inf palabras fpl de ánimo.

per [pɜːʳ] prep [expressing rate, ratio] por; per hour/kilo/person por hora/kilo/persona; per

day al día; as per instructions de acuerdo con OR según las instrucciones; as per usual como de costumbre.

per annum adv al OR por año.

per capita [pə'kæpɪtə] ◇ adj per cápita. ◇ adv por cabeza.

perceive [pə'si:v] vt - **1.** [notice] percibir, apreciar - **2.** [understand, realize] advertir, apreciar - **3.** [see]: to perceive sthg/sb as ver algo/a alguien como.

per cent adv por ciento; fifty per cent of the population el cincuenta por ciento de la población.

percentage [pə'sentɪdʒ] n porcentaje m.

perception [pə'sepʃn] n - **1.** [noticing] percepción f - **2.** [insight] perspicacia f - **3.** [opinion] idea f.

perceptive [pə'septɪv] adj perspicaz.

perch [pɜːtʃ] ◇ n - **1.** [for bird] percha f, vara f - **2.** (pl perch) [fish] perca f. ◇ vi: to perch (on) [bird] posarse (en); [person] sentarse (en).

percolator ['pɜːkəleɪtəʳ] n cafetera f eléctrica.

percussion [pə'kʌʃn] n MUS percusión f.

perennial [pə'renjəl] ◇ adj [gen & BOT] perenne. ◇ n BOT planta f perenne.

perfect ◇ adj ['pɜːfɪkt] perfecto(ta); he's a perfect stranger to me me es completamente desconocido. ◇ n ['pɜːfɪkt] GRAM: the perfect (tense) el perfecto. ◇ vt [pə'fekt] perfeccionar.

perfection [pə'fekʃn] n perfección f; to perfection a la perfección.

perfectionist [pə'fekʃənɪst] n perfeccionista mf.

perfectly ['pɜːfɪktlɪ] adv - **1.** [for emphasis] absolutamente; perfectly well perfectamente bien - **2.** [to perfection] perfectamente.

perforate ['pɜːfəreɪt] vt perforar.

perform [pə'fɔːm] ◇ vt - **1.** [carry out] llevar a cabo, realizar; [duty] cumplir - **2.** [music, dance] interpretar; [play] representar. ◇ vi - **1.** [function - car, machine] funcionar; [- person, team] desenvolverse - **2.** [actor] actuar; [singer, dance] interpretar.

performance [pə'fɔːməns] n - **1.** [carrying out] realización f; [of duty] cumplimiento m - **2.** [show] representación f - **3.** [of actor, singer etc] interpretación f, actuación f - **4.** [of car, engine] rendimiento m.

performer [pə'fɔːməʳ] n [actor, singer etc] intérprete mf.

perfume ['pɜːfjuːm] n perfume m.

perfunctory [pə'fʌŋktərɪ] adj superficial.

perhaps [pə'hæps] adv - **1.** [maybe] quizás, quizá; perhaps she'll do it quizás ella lo haga; perhaps so/not tal vez sí/no - **2.** [in polite requests, suggestions, remarks]: perhaps you could help? ¿te importaría ayudar?; **perhaps you should start again** ¿por qué no empiezas de nuevo? - **3.** [approximately] aproximadamente.

peril ['perɪl] n liter peligro m.

perimeter [pə'rɪmɪtər] n perímetro m; **perimeter fence** OR **wall** cerca f.

period ['pɪərɪəd] <> n - **1.** [of time] período m, periodo m - **2.** HIST época f - **3.** SCH clase f, hora f - **4.** [menstruation] período m; **to be on one's period** tener el periodo - **5.** US [full stop] punto m - **6.** SPORT tiempo m. <> comp de época.

periodic [ˌpɪərɪ'ɒdɪk], **periodical** adj periódico(ca).

periodical [ˌpɪərɪ'ɒdɪkl] <> adj = **periodic**. <> n [magazine] revista f.

peripheral [pə'rɪfərəl] <> adj - **1.** [of little importance] marginal - **2.** [at edge] periférico(ca). <> n COMPUT periférico m.

perish ['perɪʃ] vi - **1.** [die] perecer - **2.** [decay] deteriorarse.

perishable ['perɪʃəbl] adj perecedero(ra). ➡ **perishables** npl productos mpl perecederos.

perjury ['pɜːdʒərɪ] n LAW perjurio m.

perk [pɜːk] n inf extra m, beneficio m adicional. ➡ **perk up** vi animarse.

perky ['pɜːkɪ] adj inf alegre, animado(da).

perm [pɜːm] n permanente f.

permanent ['pɜːmənənt] <> adj - **1.** [gen] permanente; [job, address] fijo(ja) - **2.** [continuous, constant] constante. <> n US [perm] permanente f.

permeate ['pɜːmɪeɪt] vt impregnar.

permissible [pə'mɪsəbl] adj permisible.

permission [pə'mɪʃn] n: **permission (to do sthg)** permiso m (para hacer algo).

permissive [pə'mɪsɪv] adj permisivo(va).

permit <> vt [pə'mɪt] permitir; **to permit sb sthg/to do sthg** permitir a alguien algo/hacer algo. <> vi [pə'mɪt]: **if time permits** si hay tiempo. <> n ['pɜːmɪt] permiso m.

pernicious [pə'nɪʃəs] adj fml pernicioso(sa).

pernickety [pə'nɪkətɪ] adj inf quisquilloso(sa).

perpendicular [ˌpɜːpən'dɪkjʊlər] <> adj - **1.** MATHS: **perpendicular (to)** perpendicular (a) - **2.** [upright] vertical. <> n MATHS perpendicular f.

perpetrate ['pɜːpɪtreɪt] vt fml perpetrar.

perpetual [pə'petʃʊəl] adj - **1.** pej [constant] constante - **2.** [everlasting] perpetuo(tua).

perplex [pə'pleks] vt dejar perplejo(ja).

perplexing [pə'pleksɪŋ] adj desconcertante.

persecute ['pɜːsɪkjuːt] vt perseguir.

perseverance [ˌpɜːsɪ'vɪərəns] n perseverancia f.

persevere [ˌpɜːsɪ'vɪər] vi: **to persevere (with sthg/in doing sthg)** perseverar (en algo/en hacer algo).

Persian ['pɜːʃn] adj persa.

persist [pə'sɪst] vi - **1.** [problem, rain] persistir - **2.** [person]: **to persist in doing sthg** empeñarse en hacer algo.

persistence [pə'sɪstəns] n - **1.** [continuation] persistencia f - **2.** [determination] perseverancia f.

persistent [pə'sɪstənt] adj - **1.** [constant] continuo(nua) - **2.** [determined] persistente.

person ['pɜːsn] (pl people OR persons) fml n - **1.** [man, woman] persona f; **in person** en persona - **2.** [body]: **to have sthg about one's person** llevar algo encima - **3.** GRAM persona f; **in the first person** en primera persona.

personable ['pɜːsnəbl] adj agradable.

personal ['pɜːsənl] adj - **1.** [gen] personal - **2.** [private - life, problem] privado(da) - **3.** pej [rude] ofensivo(va); **to be personal** hacer alusiones personales.

personal assistant n secretario m, -ria f personal.

personal column n sección f de asuntos personales.

personal computer n ordenador m personal.

personality [ˌpɜːsə'nælətɪ] n personalidad f.

personally ['pɜːsnəlɪ] adv - **1.** [gen] personalmente - **2.** [in person] en persona.

personal loan n crédito m personal.

personal organizer n agenda f (personal).

personal property n (U) bienes mpl muebles.

personal stereo n walkman® m inv.

personify [pə'sɒnɪfaɪ] vt personificar.

personnel [ˌpɜːsə'nel] <> n (U) [department] departamento m de personal. <> npl [staff] personal m.

perspective [pə'spektɪv] n perspectiva f; **to get sthg in perspective** fig poner algo en perspectiva.

Perspex® ['pɜːspeks] n UK ≃ plexiglás® m.

perspiration [ˌpɜːspə'reɪʃn] n transpiración f.

persuade [pə'sweɪd] vt: **to persuade sb (of sthg/to do sthg)** persuadir a alguien (de algo/a hacer algo); **to persuade sb that** convencer a alguien (de) que.

persuasion [pə'sweɪʒn] n - **1.** [act of persuading] persuasión f - **2.** [belief] creencia f.

persuasive [pə'sweɪsɪv] adj persuasivo(va).

pert [pɜːt] adj - **1.** [person] vivaracho(cha) - **2.** [part of body] respingón(ona).

pertain [pə'teɪn] *vi fml*: **pertaining to** relacionado(da) con.

pertinent ['pɜːtɪnənt] *adj* pertinente.

perturb [pə'tɜːb] *vt fml* perturbar.

Peru [pə'ruː] *n* (el) Perú.

peruse [pə'ruːz] *vt* [read carefully] leer detenidamente; [browse through] leer por encima.

Peruvian [pə'ruːvjən] <> *adj* peruano(na). <> *n* [person] peruano *m*, -na *f*.

pervade [pə'veɪd] *vt* impregnar.

perverse [pə'vɜːs] *adj* [delight, enjoyment] perverso(sa); [contrary] puñetero(ra).

perversion [UK pə'vɜːʃn, US pər'vɜːrʒn] *n* - 1. [sexual deviation] perversión *f* - 2. [of justice, truth] tergiversación *f*.

pervert <> *n* ['pɜːvɜːt] pervertido *m*, -da *f*. <> *vt* [pə'vɜːt] - 1. [course of justice] tergiversar - 2. [corrupt sexually] pervertir.

pessimist ['pesɪmɪst] *n* pesimista *mf*.

pessimistic [,pesɪ'mɪstɪk] *adj* pesimista.

pest [pest] *n* - 1. [insect] insecto *m* nocivo; [animal] animal *m* nocivo - 2. *inf* [annoying person] pesado *m*, -da *f*; [annoying thing] lata *f*.

pester ['pestər] *vt* dar la lata a.

pet [pet] <> *adj* [subject, theory] preferido(da); **pet hate** gran fobia *f*. <> *n* - 1. [domestic animal] animal *m* doméstico - 2. [favourite person] preferido *m*, -da *f*. <> *vt* acariciar. <> *vi* pegarse el lote.

petal ['petl] *n* pétalo *m*.

peter ['piːtər] ◆ **peter out** *vi* [supplies, interest] agotarse; [path] desaparecer.

petite [pə'tiːt] *adj* [woman] chiquita.

petition [pɪ'tɪʃn] <> *n* petición *f*. <> *vi* LAW: **to petition for divorce** pedir el divorcio.

petrified ['petrɪfaɪd] *adj* [terrified] petrificado(da).

petrol ['petrəl] *n* UK gasolina *f*, nafta *f R Plata*, bencina *f Chile*.

petrol bomb *n* UK bomba *f* de gasolina.

petrol can *n* UK lata *f* de gasolina OR de nafta *R Plata* OR de bencina *Chile*.

petroleum [pɪ'trəʊljəm] *n* petróleo *m*.

petrol pump *n* UK surtidor *m* de gasolina OR de nafta *R Plata* OR de bencina *Chile*, bomba *f Chile, Col & Ven*.

petrol station *n* UK gasolinera *f*, grifo *m Perú*, bomba *f Chile, Col & Ven*, estación *f* de nafta *R Plata*.

petrol tank *n* UK depósito *m* de gasolina, tanque *m* de gasolina *Amér* OR de bencina *Chile* OR de nafta *R Plata*.

pet shop *n* pajarería *f*.

petticoat ['petɪkəʊt] *n* [underskirt] enaguas *fpl*; [full-length] combinación *f*.

petty ['petɪ] *adj* - 1. [small-minded] mezquino(na) - 2. [trivial] insignificante.

petty cash *n* dinero *m* para gastos menores.

petty officer *n* sargento *m* de la marina.

petulant ['petjʊlənt] *adj* caprichoso(sa).

pew [pjuː] *n* banco *m*.

pewter ['pjuːtər] *n* peltre *m*.

phantom ['fæntəm] <> *adj* ilusorio(ria). <> *n* [ghost] fantasma *m*.

pharmaceutical [,fɑːmə'sjuːtɪkl] *adj* farmacéutico(ca).

pharmacist ['fɑːməsɪst] *n* farmacéutico *m*, -ca *f*.

pharmacy ['fɑːməsɪ] *n* [shop] farmacia *f*.

phase [feɪz] <> *n* fase *f*. <> *vt* escalonar. ◆ **phase in** *vt sep* introducir progresivamente. ◆ **phase out** *vt sep* retirar progresivamente.

PhD (*abbr of* **Doctor of Philosophy**) *n* - 1. [qualification] doctorado *m* - 2. [person] doctor *m*, -ra *f*.

pheasant ['feznt] (*pl* **pheasant** OR **-s**) *n* faisán *m*.

phenomena [fɪ'nɒmɪnə] *npl* ▷ **phenomenon**.

phenomenal [fɪ'nɒmɪnl] *adj* extraordinario(ria).

phenomenon [fɪ'nɒmɪnən] (*pl* **-mena**) *n lit & fig* fenómeno *m*.

phial ['faɪəl] *n* frasco *m* (pequeño).

philanthropist [fɪ'lænθrəpɪst] *n* filántropo *m*, -pa *f*.

philately [fɪ'lætəlɪ] *n* filatelia *f*.

Philippine ['fɪlɪpiːn] *adj* filipino(na). ◆ **Philippines** *npl*: **the Philippines** las Filipinas.

philosopher [fɪ'lɒsəfər] *n* filósofo *m*, -fa *f*.

philosophical [,fɪlə'sɒfɪkl] *adj* filosófico(ca).

philosophy [fɪ'lɒsəfɪ] *n* filosofía *f*.

phlegm [flem] *n* [mucus, composure] flema *f*.

phlegmatic [fleg'mætɪk] *adj* flemático(ca).

phobia ['fəʊbjə] *n* fobia *f*; **to have a phobia about sthg** tener fobia a algo.

phone [fəʊn] <> *n* teléfono *m*; **to be on the phone** [speaking] estar al teléfono; UK [connected to network] tener teléfono; **to talk about sthg on the phone** discutir algo por teléfono. <> *vt & vi* llamar, telefonear. ◆ **phone in** *vi* llamar. ◆ **phone up** *vt sep & vi* llamar.

phone book *n* guía *f* telefónica.

phone booth *n* teléfono *m* público.

phone box *n* UK cabina *f* telefónica.

phone call *n* llamada *f* telefónica; **to make a phone call** hacer una llamada.

phonecard ['fəʊnkɑːd] *n* tarjeta *f* telefónica.

phone-in *n* RADIO & TV *programa con llamadas de los oyentes*.

phone number *n* número *m* de teléfono.

phonetics [fə'netɪks] *n (U)* fonética *f*.

phoney *UK*, **phony** *US* ['fəʊnɪ] <> *adj* (*comp* -ier, *superl* -iest) *inf* falso(sa). <> *n* farsante *mf*.

phosphorus ['fɒsfərəs] *n* fósforo *m*.

photo ['fəʊtəʊ] *n* foto *f*; **to take a photo (of)** sacar una foto (de).

photocopier ['fəʊtəʊ,kɒpɪəʳ] *n* fotocopiadora *f*.

photocopy ['fəʊtəʊ,kɒpɪ] <> *n* fotocopia *f*. <> *vt* fotocopiar.

photograph ['fəʊtəgrɑːf] <> *n* fotografía *f*; **to take a photograph (of)** sacar una fotografía (de). <> *vt* fotografiar.

photographer [fə'tɒgrəfəʳ] *n* fotógrafo *m*, -fa *f*.

photography [fə'tɒgrəfɪ] *n (U)* fotografía *f*.

photoshoot ['fəʊtəʊʃuːt] *n* sesión *f* fotográfica.

phrasal verb ['freɪzl-] *n* verbo *m* con preposición.

phrase [freɪz] <> *n* - 1. [group of words] locución *f*, frase *f* - 2. [expression] expresión *f*. <> *vt* [apology, refusal] expresar; [letter] redactar.

phrasebook ['freɪzbʊk] *n* guía *f* de conversación.

physical ['fɪzɪkl] <> *adj* físico(ca). <> *n* [examination] examen *m* médico.

physical education *n* educación *f* física.

physically ['fɪzɪklɪ] *adv* físicamente.

physically handicapped *npl*: **the physically handicapped** los discapacitados físicos.

physician [fɪ'zɪʃn] *n* médico *mf*.

physicist ['fɪzɪsɪst] *n* físico *m*, -ca *f*.

physics ['fɪzɪks] *n (U)* física *f*.

physiotherapy [,fɪzɪəʊ'θerəpɪ] *n* fisioterapia *f*.

physique [fɪ'ziːk] *n* físico *m*.

pianist ['pɪənɪst] *n* pianista *mf*.

piano [pɪ'ænəʊ] (*pl* -s) *n* [instrument] piano *m*.

piccolo ['pɪkələʊ] (*pl* -s) *n* flautín *m*.

pick [pɪk] <> *n* - 1. [tool] piqueta *f* - 2. [for guitar] púa *f* - 3. [selection]: **take your pick** escoge el que quieras - 4. [best]: **the pick of** lo mejor de. <> *vt* - 1. [team, winner] seleccionar; [time, book, dress] elegir; **to pick one's way across OR through** andar con tiento por - 2. [fruit, flowers] coger - 3. [remove - hairs etc]: **to pick sthg off sthg** quitar algo de algo - 4. [nose] hurgarse; [teeth] mondarse; [scab, spot] arrancarse - 5. [provoke]: **to pick a fight/quarrel (with)** buscar pelea/bronca (con) - 6. [open - lock] forzar (con ganzúa). <> **pick on** *vt insep* meterse con. <> **pick out** *vt sep* - 1. [recognize] reconocer - 2. [identify] identificar - 3. [select]

escoger. <> **pick up** <> *vt sep* - 1. [gen] recoger; **to pick up the pieces** *fig* volver a la normalidad - 2. [lift up] levantar; [the phone] descolgar - 3. [buy, acquire] adquirir; **to pick up speed** cobrar velocidad - 4. [illness, bug] contraer - 5. [learn - tips, language] aprender; [- habit] adquirir - 6. *inf* [find partner] ligar con - 7. RADIO & TELEC captar - 8. [start again] reanudar. <> *vi* - 1. [improve] mejorar - 2. [start again] seguir - 3. [wind] aumentar.

pickaxe *UK*, **pickax** *US* ['pɪkæks] *n* piqueta *f*.

picket ['pɪkɪt] <> *n* piquete *m*. <> *vt* formar piquetes en.

picket line *n* piquete *m* (de huelga).

pickle ['pɪkl] <> *n* - 1. [vinegar preserve] encurtido *m*; [sweet vegetable sauce] *salsa espesa agridulce con trozos de cebolla etc*; *US* [cucumber] pepinillos *mpl* en vinagre - 2. *inf* [difficult situation]: **to be in a pickle** estar en un lío. <> *vt* encurtir.

pickpocket ['pɪk,pɒkɪt] *n* carterista *mf*.

pick-up *n* - 1. [of record player] fonocaptor *m* - 2. [truck] furgoneta *f*.

picnic ['pɪknɪk] <> *n* comida *f* campestre, picnic *m*. <> *vi* (*pt & pp* -ked, *cont* -king) ir de merienda al campo.

pictorial [pɪk'tɔːrɪəl] *adj* ilustrado(da).

picture ['pɪktʃəʳ] <> *n* - 1. [painting] cuadro *m*; [drawing] dibujo *m* - 2. [photograph] foto *f*; [illustration] ilustración *f* - 3. [on TV] imagen *f* - 4. [cinema film] película *f* - 5. [in mind] idea *f*, imagen *f* - 6. [situation] situación *f* ⟩⟩⟩ **to get the picture** *inf* entenderlo; **to be in/out of the picture** estar/no estar en el ajo. <> *vt* - 1. [in mind] imaginarse - 2. [in media]: **to be pictured** aparecer en la foto. <> **pictures** *npl UK*: **the pictures** el cine.

picture book *n* libro *m* ilustrado.

picturesque [,pɪktʃə'resk] *adj* pintoresco(ca).

pie [paɪ] *n* [sweet] tarta *f* (*cubierta de hojaldre*); [savoury] empanada *f*, pastel *m*.

piece [piːs] *n* - 1. [individual part or portion] trozo *m*, pedazo *m*; **to come to pieces** deshacerse; **to take sthg to pieces** desmontar algo; **to tear sthg to pieces** hacer trizas algo; **in pieces** en pedazos; **to go to pieces** *fig* venirse abajo - 2. (*with U*) [individual object]: **piece of furniture** mueble *m*; **piece of clothing** prenda *f* de vestir; **piece of fruit** fruta *f*; **piece of luggage** bulto *m* de equipaje; **piece of advice** consejo *m*; **piece of news** noticia *f*; **a piece of information** una información; **piece of luck** golpe *m* de suerte - 3. [in board game] pieza *f*; [in draughts] ficha *f* - 4. [of journalism] artículo *m* - 5. [coin] moneda *f*. <> **piece together** *vt sep* [discover] componer.

piecemeal ['piːsmiːl] ⬦ adj poco sistemático(ca). ⬦ adv [gradually] por etapas.

piecework ['piːswɜːk] n U trabajo m a destajo.

pie chart n gráfico m de sectores.

pier [pɪəʳ] n - 1. [at seaside] paseo marítimo en un malecón - 2. [for landing boat] embarcadero m.

pierce [pɪəs] vt - 1. [subj: bullet, needle] perforar; **to have one's ears pierced** hacerse agujeros en las orejas - 2. [subj: voice, scream] romper.

piercing ['pɪəsɪŋ] adj - 1. [scream] desgarrador(ra); [sound, voice] agudo(da) - 2. [wind] cortante - 3. [look, eyes] penetrante.

piety ['paɪətɪ] n piedad f.

pig [pɪg] n - 1. [animal] cerdo m, puerco m, chancho m Amér - 2. inf pej [greedy eater] tragón m, -ona f - 3. inf pej [unkind person] cerdo m, -da f, chancho m, -cha f Amér - 4. inf pej [policeman] madero m.

pigeon ['pɪdʒɪn] (pl pigeon OR -s) n paloma f.

pigeonhole ['pɪdʒɪnhəʊl] ⬦ n [compartment] casilla f. ⬦ vt [classify] encasillar.

piggybank ['pɪgɪbæŋk] n hucha f con forma de cerdito.

pigheaded [ˌpɪg'hedɪd] adj cabezota.

pigment ['pɪgmənt] n pigmento m.

pigpen US = pigsty.

pigskin ['pɪgskɪn] n piel f de cerdo.

pigsty ['pɪgstaɪ], **pigpen** US ['pɪgpen] n lit & fig pocilga f.

pigtail ['pɪgteɪl] n [girl's] trenza f; [Chinese, bullfighter's] coleta f.

pike [paɪk] n - 1. (pl pike OR -s) [fish] lucio m - 2. (pl -s) [weapon] pica f.

Pilates [pɪ'lɑːtiːz] n Pilates m.

pilchard ['pɪltʃəd] n sardina f.

pile [paɪl] ⬦ n - 1. [heap] montón m - 2. [neat stack] pila f - 3. [of carpet, fabric] pelo m. ⬦ vt amontonar. ➤ **piles** npl MED almorranas fpl. ➤ **pile into** vt insep inf meterse atropelladamente en. ➤ **pile up** ⬦ vt sep amontonar. ⬦ vi - 1. [form a heap] amontonarse - 2. [mount up] acumularse.

pileup ['paɪlʌp] n accidente m en cadena.

pilfer ['pɪlfəʳ] ⬦ vt sisar. ⬦ vi: **to pilfer (from)** sisar (de).

pilgrim ['pɪlgrɪm] n peregrino m, -na f.

pilgrimage ['pɪlgrɪmɪdʒ] n peregrinación f.

pill [pɪl] n - 1. MED píldora f, pastilla f - 2. [contraceptive]: **the pill** la píldora (anticonceptiva); **to be on the pill** tomar la píldora.

pillage ['pɪlɪdʒ] vt saquear.

pillar ['pɪləʳ] n lit & fig pilar m.

pillar box n UK buzón m.

pillion ['pɪljən] n: **to ride pillion** ir en el asiento trasero (de una moto).

pillow ['pɪləʊ] n - 1. [for bed] almohada f - 2. US [on sofa, chair] cojín m.

pillowcase ['pɪləʊkeɪs], **pillowslip** ['pɪləʊslɪp] n funda f de almohada.

pilot ['paɪlət] ⬦ n - 1. AERON & NAUT piloto m - 2. TV programa m piloto. ⬦ comp [project, study] piloto (inv), de prueba. ⬦ vt AERON & NAUT pilotar.

pilot burner, pilot light n piloto m, luz f indicadora.

pilot study n estudio m piloto.

pimp [pɪmp] n inf chulo m, padrote m Méx.

pimple ['pɪmpl] n grano m.

pin [pɪn] ⬦ n - 1. [for sewing] alfiler m; **pins and needles** hormigueo m - 2. [of plug] clavija f; COMPUT pin m - 3. TECH clavija f. ⬦ vt - 1. [fasten]: **to pin sthg to OR on** [sheet of paper] clavar con alfileres algo en; [medal, piece of cloth] prender algo en - 2. [trap]: **to pin sb against OR to** inmovilizar a alguien contra - 3. [apportion]: **to pin sthg on OR upon sb** cargar algo a alguien. ➤ **pin down** vt sep [identify] determinar, identificar.

pinafore ['pɪnəfɔːʳ] n - 1. [apron] delantal m - 2. UK [dress] pichi m.

pinball ['pɪnbɔːl] n millón m, flípper m.

pincers ['pɪnsəz] npl - 1. [tool] tenazas fpl - 2. [front claws] pinzas fpl.

pinch [pɪntʃ] ⬦ n - 1. [nip] pellizco m - 2. [small quantity] pizca f. ⬦ vt - 1. [nip] pellizcar; [subj: shoes] apretar - 2. inf [steal] mangar. ⬦ vi [shoes] apretar. ➤ **at a pinch** UK, **in a pinch** US adv si no hay más remedio.

pincushion ['pɪnˌkʊʃn] n acerico m.

pine [paɪn] ⬦ n pino m. ⬦ vi: **to pine for** suspirar por. ➤ **pine away** vi morirse de pena.

pineapple ['paɪnæpl] n piña f, ananá m R Plata.

pinetree ['paɪntriː] n pino m.

ping [pɪŋ] n [of metal] sonido m metálico.

Ping-Pong® [-pɒŋ] n ping-pong® m.

pink [pɪŋk] ⬦ adj rosa. ⬦ n - 1. [colour] rosa m - 2. [flower] clavel m.

pink pound UK, **pink dollar** US n: **the pink pound** el poder adquisitivo de los homosexuales.

pinnacle ['pɪnəkl] n - 1. [high point] cumbre f - 2. [mountain peak] cima f; [spire] pináculo m.

pinpoint ['pɪnpɔɪnt] vt determinar, identificar.

pin-striped [-ˌstraɪpt] adj a rayas.

pint [paɪnt] n UK [unit of measurement] = 0,568 litros; US = 0,473 litros, ≃ pinta f.

pioneer [ˌpaɪə'nɪəʳ] n pionero m, -ra f.

pious ['paɪəs] *adj* - **1.** [religious] piadoso(sa) - **2.** *pej* [sanctimonious] mojigato(ta).

pip [pɪp] *n* - **1.** [seed] pepita *f* - **2.** *UK* [bleep] señal *f*.

pipe [paɪp] <> *n* - **1.** [for gas, water] tubería *f* - **2.** [for smoking] pipa *f*. <> *vt* [transport via pipes] conducir por tuberías. ◆ **pipes** *npl* MUS gaita *f*. ◆ **pipe down** *vi inf* cerrar la boca. ◆ **pipe up** *vi inf*: **to pipe up with a suggestion** saltar con una sugerencia.

pipe cleaner *n* limpiapipas *m inv*.

pipe dream *n* sueño *m* imposible.

pipeline ['paɪplaɪn] *n* tubería *f*; [for gas] gasoducto *m*; [for oil] oleoducto *m*.

piper ['paɪpər] *n* gaitero *m*, -ra *f*.

piping hot ['paɪpɪŋ-] *adj* humeante, calentito(ta).

piquant ['piːkənt] *adj* - **1.** [food] picante - **2.** [story] intrigante; [situation] que suscita un placer mordaz.

pique [piːk] <> *n* resentimiento *m*. <> *vt* - **1.** [upset] ofender - **2.** [arouse] despertar.

pirate ['paɪrət] <> *adj* [gen & COMPUT] pirata. <> *n* [sailor] pirata *mf*. <> *vt* piratear.

pirate radio *n UK* radio *f* pirata.

pirouette [,pɪrʊ'et] *n* pirueta *f*.

Pisces ['paɪsiːz] *n* Piscis *m inv*.

piss [pɪs] *v inf* <> *n* [urine] meada *f*. <> *vi* mear. ◆ **piss about, piss around** *UK v inf* <> *vt sep* vacilar. <> *vi* [waste time] tocarse los huevos; [fool around] hacer el gilipollas.

pissed [pɪst] *adj vulg UK* [drunk] pedo *(inv)*.

pissed off *adj vulg*: **to be** *OR* **to feel pissed off** estar cabreado(da).

pistol ['pɪstl] *n* pistola *f*.

piston ['pɪstən] *n* pistón *m*, émbolo *m*.

pit [pɪt] <> *n* - **1.** [large hole] hoyo *m* - **2.** [small hole - in metal, glass] señal *f*, marca *f*; [- on face] picadura *f*, piquete *m Méx* - **3.** [for orchestra] foso *m* de la orquesta - **4.** [mine] mina *f* - **5.** *US* [of fruit] hueso *m*, cuesco *m*, carozo *m R Plata*, pepa *f Col*. <> *vt*: **to be pitted against** ser enfrentado(da) con. ◆ **pits** *npl* [in motor racing]: **the pits** los box.

pitch [pɪtʃ] <> *n* - **1.** SPORT campo *m* - **2.** MUS tono *m* - **3.** [level, degree] grado *m*, punto *m* - **4.** *UK* [selling place] puesto *m* - **5.** *inf* [sales talk] labia *f* de comerciante. <> *vt* - **1.** [throw] lanzar, arrojar - **2.** [design]: **to be pitched in order to do sthg** estar diseñado para hacer algo - **3.** [speech] dar un tono a - **4.** [tent] montar, poner. <> *vi* - **1.** [ball] tocar el suelo; **to pitch forwards** [person] precipitarse hacia delante - **2.** [ship, plane] dar un bandazo.

pitch-black *adj* negro(gra) como boca de lobo.

pitched battle [,pɪtʃt-] *n* HIST batalla *f* campal; *fig* [bitter struggle] lucha *f* encarnizada.

pitcher ['pɪtʃər] *n* [jug] cántaro *m*.

pitchfork ['pɪtʃfɔːk] *n* horca *f*.

piteous ['pɪtɪəs] *adj* lastimero(ra).

pitfall ['pɪtfɔːl] *n* peligro *m*, escollo *m*.

pith [pɪθ] *n* piel *f* blanca.

pithy ['pɪθɪ] *adj* conciso(sa) y contundente.

pitiful ['pɪtɪfʊl] *adj* [condition, excuse, effort] lamentable; [person, appearance] lastimoso(sa).

pitiless ['pɪtɪlɪs] *adj* [person] despiadado(da).

pit stop *n* [in motor racing] parada *f* en boxes.

pittance ['pɪtəns] *n* miseria *f*.

pity ['pɪtɪ] <> *n* [compassion] compasión *f*; [shame] pena *f*, lástima *f*; **what a pity!** ¡qué pena!; **to take** *OR* **have pity on** compadecerse de. <> *vt* compadecerse de, sentir pena por.

pivot ['pɪvət] *n* - **1.** TECH pivote *m*, eje *m* - **2.** *fig* [person] eje *m*.

pizza ['piːtsə] *n* pizza *f*.

placard ['plækɑːd] *n* pancarta *f*.

placate [plə'keɪt] *vt* aplacar, apaciguar.

place [pleɪs] <> *n* - **1.** [gen] lugar *m*, sitio *m*; **place of birth** lugar de nacimiento; **it's good in places** tiene algunas partes buenas - **2.** [proper position] sitio *m*; **to put sb in their place** poner a alguien en su sitio - **3.** [suitable occasion, time] momento *m* - **4.** [home] casa *f* - **5.** [specific seat] asiento *m*; [in queue] sitio *m*; THEAT localidad *f* - **6.** [setting at table] cubierto *m* - **7.** [on course, at university] plaza *f* - **8.** [on committee, in team] puesto *m* - **9.** [role, function] papel *m*; **to have an important place in** desempeñar un papel importante en; **put yourself in my place** ponte en mi lugar - **10.** [position, rank] lugar *m*, posición *f* - **11.** [in book] página *f*; [in speech]: **to lose one's place** no saber (uno) dónde estaba - **12.** MATHS: **decimal place** punto *m* decimal - **13.** [instance]: **in the first place** [from the start] desde el principio; **in the first place... and in the second place...** [firstly, secondly] en primer lugar... y en segundo lugar... ◆◆◆ **to take place** tener lugar; **to take the place of** sustituir a. <> *vt* - **1.** [position, put] colocar, poner - **2.** [lay, apportion]: **to place emphasis on** poner énfasis en; **to place pressure on** ejercer presión sobre - **3.** [identify]: **I recognize the face, but I can't place her** me suena su cara, pero no sé de qué - **4.** [bet, order etc] hacer - **5.** [in horse racing]: **to be placed** llegar entre los tres primeros. ◆ **all over the place** *adv* por todas partes. ◆ **in place** *adv* - **1.** [in proper position] en su sitio - **2.** [established, set up] en marcha *OR* funcionamiento; **everything is now in place** los preparativos ya están finalizados. ◆ **in place of** *prep* en lugar de. ◆ **out of place** *adv* - **1.** [in wrong position]: **to be out of place** no estar en su sitio - **2.** [inappropriate, unsuitable] fuera de lugar.

place mat n mantel m individual.

placement ['pleɪsmənt] n colocación f

placid ['plæsɪd] adj - 1. [quiet, tranquil] - ble - 2. [peaceful] tranquilo(la).

plagiarize, -ise ['pleɪdʒəraɪz] vt plagiar.

plague [pleɪg] ◇ n - 1. [attack of disease] peste f - 2. [disease]: **(the) plague** la peste; **to avoid sb/sthg like the plague** huir de alguien/algo como de la peste - 3. [of rats, insects] plaga f. ◇ vt: **to plague sb with** [complaints, requests] acosar a alguien con; [questions] acribillar a alguien a; **to be plagued by** [ill health] estar acosado de; [doubts] estar atormentado de.

plaice [pleɪs] (pl plaice) n platija f.

plaid [plæd] n tejido m escocés.

Plaid Cymru [ˌplaɪd'kʌmrɪ] n UK POL partido nacionalista galés.

plain [pleɪn] ◇ adj - 1. [not patterned] liso(sa) - 2. [simple - gen] sencillo(lla); [- yoghurt] natural - 3. [clear] evidente, claro(ra); **to make sthg plain to sb** dejar algo bien claro a alguien - 4. [speaking, statement] franco(ca) - 5. [absolute - madness etc] auténtico(ca) - 6. [not pretty] sin atractivo. ◇ adv inf completamente. ◇ n GEOG llanura f, planicie f.

plain chocolate n UK chocolate m amargo.

plain-clothes adj vestido(da) de paisano.

plain flour n UK harina f (sin levadura).

plainly ['pleɪnlɪ] adv - 1. [upset, angry] evidentemente - 2. [visible, audible] claramente - 3. [frankly] francamente - 4. [simply] sencillamente.

plaintiff ['pleɪntɪf] n demandante mf.

plait [plæt] ◇ n trenza f. ◇ vt trenzar.

plan [plæn] ◇ n - 1. [strategy] plan m; **to go according to plan** salir según lo previsto - 2. [of story, essay] esquema m - 3. [of building etc] plano m. ◇ vt - 1. [organize] planear - 2. [career, future, economy] planificar - 3. [design, devise] trazar un esquema OR boceto de. ◇ vi hacer planes. ➤ **plans** npl planes mpl; **to have plans for** tener planes para. ➤ **plan on** vt insep: **to plan on doing sthg** pensar hacer algo.

plane [pleɪn] ◇ adj plano(na). ◇ n - 1. [aircraft] avión m - 2. GEOM [flat surface] plano m - 3. fig [level - intellectual] plano m - 4. [tool] cepillo m - 5. [tree] plátano m.

planet ['plænɪt] n planeta m.

plank [plæŋk] n [piece of wood] tablón m, tabla f.

planning ['plænɪŋ] n [gen] planificación f.

planning permission n permiso m de construcción OR de obras.

plant [plɑ:nt] ◇ n - 1. BOT planta f - 2. [factory] planta f, fábrica f - 3. [heavy machinery] maquinaria f. ◇ vt - 1. [seed, tree, vegetable]: **to plant sthg (in)** plantar algo (en) - 2. [bomb, bug] colocar secretamente.

plantation [plæn'teɪʃn] n plantación f.

plaque [plɑ:k] n [gen & MED] placa f.

plaster [ˈplɑːstə] ◇ n - 1. [for wall, ceiling] yeso m - 2. [for broken bones] escayola f - 3. UK [bandage] tirita® f. ◇ vt [put plaster on] enyesar.

plaster cast n - 1. [for broken bones] escayola f - 2. [model, statue] vaciado m en yeso.

plastered ['plɑ:stəd] adj inf [drunk] cocido(da).

plasterer ['plɑ:stərə] n yesero m, -ra f.

plastic ['plæstɪk] ◇ adj [made from plastic] de plástico. ◇ n plástico m.

Plasticine® ['plæstɪsi:n] n UK plastilina® f.

plastic surgery n cirugía f plástica.

plate [pleɪt] ◇ n - 1. [dish, plateful] plato m; **to hand sthg on a plate to sb** ponerle algo a alguien en bandeja de plata - 2. [on machinery, wall, door] placa f - 3. (U) [metal covering]: **gold/silver plate** chapa f de oro/plata - 4. [photograph] lámina f - 5. [in dentistry] dentadura f postiza. ◇ vt: **to be plated (with)** estar chapado(da) (en OR de).

plateau ['plætəʊ] (pl -s OR -x [-z]) n [high, flat land] meseta f.

plate glass n vidrio m cilindrado.

platform ['plætfɔ:m] n - 1. [gen & COMPUT] plataforma f; [stage] estrado m; [at meeting] tribuna f - 2. RAIL andén m; **platform 12** la vía 12 - 3. POL programa m electoral.

platinum ['plætɪnəm] n platino m.

platitude ['plætɪtjuːd] n tópico m.

platoon [plə'tu:n] n pelotón m.

platter ['plætə] n [dish] fuente f.

plausible ['plɔ:zəbl] adj plausible, admisible.

play [pleɪ] ◇ n - 1. (U) [amusement] juego m; **at play** jugando - 2. [piece of drama] obra f - 3. [game]: **play on words** juego m de palabras - 4. TECH juego m. ◇ vt - 1. [game, sport] jugar a; [match] jugar; [in specific position] jugar de - 2. [play game against]: **to play sb (at sthg)** jugar contra alguien (a algo) - 3. [perform for amusement]: **to play a joke on** gastar una broma a; **to play a dirty trick on** jugar una mala pasada a - 4. [act - part, character] representar; **to play a part OR role in** fig desempeñar un papel en; **to play the fool** hacer el tonto - 5. [instrument, tune] tocar; [record, cassette] poner ▶▶▶ **to play it safe** actuar sobre seguro. ◇ vi - 1. [gen]: **to play (with/against)** jugar (con/contra); **to play for sb/a team** jugar para alguien/con un equipo - 2. [be performed, shown - play] representarse; [- film] exhibirse - 3. [MUS - person] tocar; [- music] sonar. ➤ **play along** vi: **to play along (with)** seguir la corriente (a). ➤ **play down** vt sep quitar importancia a.

play up ◇ vt sep [emphasize] hacer resaltar. ◇ vi [machine, part of body, child] dar guerra.

play-act vi fingir, hacer comedia.

playboy ['pleɪbɔɪ] n playboy m.

player ['pleɪəʳ] n - 1. [of sport, game] jugador m, -ra f - 2. MUS intérprete mf - 3. THEAT actor m, actriz f - 4. [important person or organization] protagonista mf.

playful ['pleɪfʊl] adj juguetón(ona).

playground ['pleɪgraʊnd] n - 1. [at school] patio m de recreo - 2. [in park] zona f de juegos.

playgroup ['pleɪgru:p] n jardín m de infancia, guardería f.

playing card ['pleɪɪŋ-] n naipe m, carta f.

playing field ['pleɪɪŋ-] n campo m de juego.

playmate ['pleɪmeɪt] n compañero m, -ra f de juego.

play-off n partido m de desempate.

playpen ['pleɪpen] n parque m (de niños) (tipo cuna).

playschool ['pleɪsku:l] n jardín m de infancia, guardería f.

plaything ['pleɪθɪŋ] n lit & fig juguete m.

playtime ['pleɪtaɪm] n recreo m.

playwright ['pleɪraɪt] n dramaturgo m, -ga f.

plc abbr of **public limited company**.

plea [pli:] n - 1. [appeal] súplica f, petición f - 2. LAW declaración por parte del acusado de culpabilidad o inocencia.

plead [pli:d] ◇ vt (pt & pp -ed OR pled) - 1. LAW [one's cause] defender - 2. [give as excuse] pretender. ◇ vi (pt & pp -ed OR pled) - 1. [beg]: **to plead (with sb to do sthg)** rogar OR implorar (a alguien que haga algo); **to plead for sthg** pedir algo - 2. LAW declarar.

pleasant ['pleznt] adj - 1. [smell, taste, view] agradable; [surprise, news] grato(ta) - 2. [person, smile, face] simpático(ca).

pleasantry ['plezntrɪ] n: **to exchange pleasantries** intercambiar cumplidos.

please [pli:z] ◇ vt complacer, agradar; **he always pleases himself** él siempre hace lo que le da la gana; **please yourself!** ¡como quieras! ◇ vi - 1. [give satisfaction] satisfacer, agradar - 2. [think appropriate]: **to do as one pleases** hacer como a uno le parezca. ◇ adv por favor.

pleased [pli:zd] adj: **to be pleased (about/with)** estar contento(ta) (por/con); **to be pleased for sb** alegrarse por alguien; **to be very pleased with o.s.** estar muy satisfecho de sí mismo; **pleased to meet you!** ¡encantado(da) de conocerle!, ¡mucho gusto!

pleasing ['pli:zɪŋ] adj agradable, grato(ta).

pleasure ['pleʒəʳ] n - 1. [feeling of happiness] gusto m - 2. [enjoyment] diversión f - 3. [delight] placer m; **it's a pleasure, my pleasure** no hay de qué.

pleat [pli:t] ◇ n pliegue m. ◇ vt plisar.

pled [pled] pt & pp ▷ **plead**.

pledge [pledʒ] ◇ n - 1. [promise] promesa f - 2. [token] señal f, prenda f. ◇ vt - 1. [promise] prometer - 2. [commit]: **to pledge sb to sthg** hacer jurar a alguien algo; **to pledge o.s. to** comprometerse a - 3. [pawn] empeñar.

plentiful ['plentɪfʊl] adj abundante.

plenty ['plentɪ] ◇ n (U) abundancia f. ◇ pron: **we've got plenty** tenemos de sobra; **that's plenty** es más que suficiente; **plenty of** mucho(cha).

pliable ['plaɪəbl], **pliant** ['plaɪənt] adj flexible.

pliers ['plaɪəz] npl alicates mpl.

plight [plaɪt] n grave situación f.

plimsoll ['plɪmsəl] n UK playera f, zapato m de tenis.

plinth [plɪnθ] n [for statue] peana f; [for pillar] plinto m.

PLO (abbr of **Palestine Liberation Organization**) n OLP f.

plod [plɒd] vi - 1. [walk slowly] caminar con paso cansino - 2. [work steadily]: **to plod away at sthg** trabajar pacientemente en algo.

plodder ['plɒdəʳ] n pej persona f mediocre pero voluntariosa (en el trabajo).

plonk [plɒŋk] n (U) UK inf [wine] vino m peleón. **plonk down** vt sep inf dejar caer.

plot [plɒt] ◇ n - 1. [plan] complot m, conspiración f - 2. [story] argumento m, trama f - 3. [of land] parcela f. ◇ vt - 1. [plan] tramar, urdir - 2. [on map, graph] trazar. ◇ vi: **to plot (to do sthg)** tramar (hacer algo); **to plot against** conspirar contra.

plotter ['plɒtəʳ] n - 1. [schemer] conspirador m, -ra f - 2. COMPUT plotter m.

plough UK, **plow** US [plaʊ] ◇ n arado m. ◇ vt arar. **plough into** ◇ vt sep [invest] invertir. ◇ vt insep [hit] chocar contra.

ploughman's ['plaʊmənz] (pl **ploughman's**) n UK: **ploughman's (lunch)** queso, cebolletas y ensalada con pan.

plow US = **plough**.

ploy [plɔɪ] n táctica f, estratagema f.

pls (abbr of **please**) adv xfa, pf.

pluck [plʌk] ◇ vt - 1. [fruit, flower] coger - 2. [pull sharply] arrancar - 3. [bird] desplumar - 4. [eyebrows] depilar - 5. [instrument] puntear. ◇ n dated valor m. **pluck up** vt insep: **to pluck up the courage to do sthg** armarse de valor para hacer algo.

plucky ['plʌkɪ] adj dated valiente.

plug [plʌg] ◇ *n* - **1.** ELEC enchufe *m* - **2.** [for bath or sink] tapón *m.* ◇ *vt* - **1.** [hole, leak] tapar - **2.** *inf* [mention favourably] dar publicidad a. ◆ **plug in** *vt sep* enchufar.

plughole ['plʌghəʊl] *n* desagüe *m.*

plug-in *n* COMPUT plug-in *m.*

plum [plʌm] ◇ *adj* - **1.** [colour] de color ciruela - **2.** [choice]: **plum job** chollo *m.* ◇ *n* [fruit] ciruela *f.*

plumb [plʌm] ◇ *adv* - **1.** *UK* [exactly]: **plumb in the middle** justo en medio - **2.** *US* [completely] completamente. ◇ *vt*: **to plumb the depths of** alcanzar las cotas más bajas de.

plumber ['plʌmər] *n* fontanero *m,* -ra *f Esp,* plomero *m,* -ra *f Amér,* gásfiter *mf Chile,* gásfitero *m,* -ra *f Perú.*

plumbing ['plʌmɪŋ] *n (U)* - **1.** [fittings] tuberías *fpl* - **2.** [work] fontanería *f,* plomería *f Amér.*

plume [plu:m] *n* - **1.** [feather] pluma *f* - **2.** [decoration, of smoke] penacho *m.*

plummet ['plʌmɪt] *vi* caer en picado.

plump [plʌmp] *adj* regordete(ta). ◆ **plump for** *vt insep* optar OR decidirse por. ◆ **plump up** *vt sep* ahuecar.

plum pudding *n* budín navideño con pasas.

plunder ['plʌndər] ◇ *n* - **1.** [stealing, raiding] saqueo *m,* pillaje *m* - **2.** [stolen goods] botín *m.* ◇ *vt* saquear.

plunge [plʌndʒ] ◇ *n* [dive] zambullida *f;* **to take the plunge** [get married] dar el paso decisivo; [take risk] lanzarse. ◇ *vt* - **1.** [knife etc]: **to plunge sthg into** hundir algo en - **2.** [into darkness, water]: **to plunge sthg into** sumergir algo en. ◇ *vi* - **1.** [dive] zambullirse - **2.** [decrease] bajar vertiginosamente.

plunger ['plʌndʒər] *n* [for blocked pipes] desatascador *m.*

pluperfect [,plu:'pɜ:fɪkt] *n*: **pluperfect (tense)** (pretérito *m*) pluscuamperfecto *m.*

plural ['plʊərəl] ◇ *adj* [gen] plural. ◇ *n* plural *m;* **in the plural** en plural.

plus [plʌs] ◇ *adj* [or more]: **35-plus** 35 o más. ◇ *n (pl* **-es** OR **-ses**) - **1.** MATHS [sign] signo *m* más - **2.** [bonus] ventaja *f.* ◇ *prep* más. ◇ *conj* además.

plush [plʌʃ] *adj* lujoso(sa).

plus sign *n* signo *m* más.

Pluto ['plu:təʊ] *n* [planet] Plutón *m.*

plutonium [plu:'təʊnɪəm] *n* plutonio *m.*

ply [plaɪ] ◇ *vt* - **1.** [trade] ejercer - **2.** [supply, provide]: **to ply sb with sthg** [questions] acosar a alguien con algo; [food, drink] no parar de ofrecer a alguien algo. ◇ *vi* navegar.

plywood ['plaɪwʊd] *n* contrachapado *m.*

p.m., pm *(abbr of* **post meridiem***):* **at 3 p.m.** a las tres de la tarde.

PM *n abbr of* **prime minister**.

PMT, PMS *(abbr of* **premenstrual tension, premenstrual syndrome***)* *n* tensión *f* premenstrual.

pneumatic [nju:'mætɪk] *adj* [tyre, chair] neumático(ca).

pneumatic drill *n* martillo *m* neumático.

pneumonia [nju:'məʊnjə] *n (U)* pulmonía *f.*

poach [pəʊtʃ] ◇ *vt* - **1.** [game] cazar furtivamente; [fish] pescar furtivamente - **2.** [copy] plagiar - **3.** CULIN [salmon] cocer; [egg] escalfar. ◇ *vi* [for game] cazar furtivamente; [for fish] pescar furtivamente.

poacher ['pəʊtʃər] *n* [hunter] cazador furtivo *m,* cazadora furtiva *f;* [fisherman] pescador furtivo *m,* pescadora furtiva *f.*

poaching ['pəʊtʃɪŋ] *n* [for game] caza *f* furtiva; [for fish] pesca *f* furtiva.

PO Box *(abbr of* **Post Office Box***)* *n* apdo. *m,* casilla *f* (de correos) *Andes.*

pocket ['pɒkɪt] ◇ *n* - **1.** [in clothes] bolsillo *m;* **to be £10 out of pocket** salir perdiendo 10 libras; **to pick sb's pocket** vaciar a alguien el bolsillo - **2.** [in car door etc] bolsa *f,* bolsillo *m* - **3.** [of resistance] foco *m;* [of air] bolsa *f;* [on pool, snooker table] tronera *f.* ◇ *vt* - **1.** [place in pocket] meterse en el bolsillo - **2.** [steal] birlar. ◇ *adj* de bolsillo.

pocketbook ['pɒkɪtbʊk] *n* - **1.** [notebook] libreta *f* - **2.** *US* [handbag] bolso *m;* [wallet] cartera *f.*

pocketknife ['pɒkɪtnaɪf] *(pl* **-knives** [-naɪvz]*) n* navaja *f* (de bolsillo).

pocket money *n* - **1.** [from parents] propina *f* - **2.** [for minor expenses] dinero *m* para gastar.

pockmark ['pɒkmɑ:k] *n* marca *f,* señal *f.*

pod [pɒd] *n* [of plants] vaina *f.*

podgy ['pɒdʒɪ], **pudgy** *adj inf* gordinflón(ona).

podiatrist [pə'daɪətrɪst] *n US* podólogo *m,* -ga *f.*

podium ['pəʊdɪəm] *(pl* **-diums** OR **-dia** [-dɪə]*) n* podio *m.*

poem ['pəʊɪm] *n* poema *m,* poesía *f.*

poet ['pəʊɪt] *n* poeta *mf.*

poetic [pəʊ'etɪk] *adj* poético(ca).

poet laureate *n* poeta de la corte británica que escribe poemas para ocasiones oficiales.

poetry ['pəʊɪtrɪ] *n* poesía *f.*

poignant ['pɔɪnjənt] *adj* patético(ca), conmovedor(ra).

point [pɔɪnt] ◇ *n* - **1.** [gen] punto *m;* **a sore point** *fig* un asunto espinoso OR delicado - **2.** [in time] momento *m;* **at that point** en ese momento - **3.** [tip] punta *f* - **4.** [detail, argument]: **to make a point** hacer una observación; **to have a point** tener razón - **5.** [main idea]: **the point is...** lo fundamental es...; **that's the**

whole point de eso se trata; **to miss the point of** no coger la idea de; **to get** OR **come to the point** ir al grano; **it's beside the point** no viene al caso - **6.** [feature] aspecto *m*; **weak/strong point** punto *m* débil/fuerte - **7.** [purpose] sentido *m*; **what's the point?** ¿para qué?; **there's no point in it** no tiene sentido - **8.** [decimal point] coma *f*; **two point six** dos coma seis - **9.** UK ELEC toma *f* de corriente - **10.** GEOG punta *f*

▶▶ **to make a point of doing sthg** preocuparse de hacer algo. ◇ *vt*: **to point a gun at sthg/sb** apuntar a algo/alguien con una pistola; **to point one's finger at sthg/sb** señalar algo/a alguien con el dedo. ◇ *vi* - **1.** [indicate with finger]: **to point at sthg/sb, to point to sthg/sb** señalar algo/a alguien con el dedo - **2.** *fig* [suggest]: **everything points to her guilt** todo indica que ella es la culpable. ◆ **points** *npl* - **1.** UK RAIL agujas *fpl* - **2.** AUT platinos *mpl*.

◆ **up to a point** *adv* hasta cierto punto.
◆ **on the point of** *prep*: **to be on the point of doing sthg** estar a punto de hacer algo.
◆ **point out** *vt sep* [person, object, fact] señalar, indicar; [mistake] hacer notar.

point-blank *adv* - **1.** [refuse, deny] categóricamente - **2.** [at close range] a quemarropa.

pointed ['pɔɪntɪd] *adj* - **1.** [sharp, angular] en punta, puntiagudo(da) - **2.** [cutting, incisive] intencionado(da).

pointer ['pɔɪntə'] *n* - **1.** [piece of advice] consejo *m* - **2.** [needle] aguja *f* - **3.** COMPUT puntero *m*.

pointless ['pɔɪntlɪs] *adj* sin sentido; **it's pointless** no tiene sentido.

point of view (*pl* points of view) *n* - **1.** [opinion] punto *m* de vista - **2.** [aspect, perspective] perspectiva *f*.

poise [pɔɪz] *n* [self-assurance] aplomo *m*, serenidad *f*; [elegance] elegancia *f*.

poised [pɔɪzd] *adj* - **1.** [ready]: **to be poised for sthg** estar preparado(da) para algo - **2.** [calm and dignified] sereno(na).

poison ['pɔɪzn] ◇ *n* veneno *m*. ◇ *vt* [generally - intentionally] envenenar; [- unintentionally] intoxicar.

poisoning ['pɔɪznɪŋ] *n* [intentional] envenenamiento *m*; [unintentional] intoxicación *f*.

poisonous ['pɔɪznəs] *adj* - **1.** [substance, gas] tóxico(ca) - **2.** [snake] venenoso(sa).

poke [pəʊk] ◇ *vt* - **1.** [with finger, stick] empujar; [with elbow] dar un codazo a; [fire] atizar; **to poke sb in the eye** meter el dedo en el ojo de alguien - **2.** [push, stuff]: **to poke sthg into** meter algo en. ◇ *vi* [protrude]: **to poke out of sthg** sobresalir por algo. ◆ **poke about, poke around** *vi inf* fisgonear, hurgar.

poker ['pəʊkə'] *n* - **1.** [game] póker *m* - **2.** [for fire] atizador *m*.

poker-faced [-ˌfeɪst] *adj* con cara inexpresiva.

poky ['pəʊkɪ] *adj pej*: **a poky little room** un cuartucho.

Poland ['pəʊlənd] *n* Polonia.

polar ['pəʊlə'] *adj* polar.

Polaroid® ['pəʊlərɔɪd] *n* - **1.** [camera] polaroid® *f* - **2.** [photograph] fotografía *f* polaroid.

pole [pəʊl] *n* - **1.** [rod, post] poste *m*; [for tent, flag] mástil *m*; **telegraph pole** poste *m* telegráfico - **2.** ELEC & GEOG polo *m*; **to be poles apart** *fig* ser polos opuestos.

Pole [pəʊl] *n* polaco *m*, -ca *f*.

pole vault *n*: **the pole vault** el salto con pértiga.

police [pə'li:s] ◇ *npl* [police force]: **the police** la policía. ◇ *vt* mantener el orden en, vigilar.

police car *n* coche *m* patrulla, auto *m* patrulla *Amér C, Chile & Méx*, patrullero *m*, patrulla *f Col & Méx*.

police constable *n* UK policía *mf*.

police force *n* cuerpo *m* de policía.

policeman [pə'li:smən] (*pl* -men [-mən]) *n* policía *m*.

police officer *n* agente *mf* de policía.

police record *n*: **(to have a) police record** (tener) antecedentes *mpl* policiales.

police station *n* comisaría *f* (de policía).

policewoman [pə'li:sˌwʊmən] (*pl* -women [-ˌwɪmɪn]) *n* (mujer *f*) policía *f*.

policy ['pɒləsɪ] *n* - **1.** [plan, practice] política *f* - **2.** [document, agreement] póliza *f*.

polio ['pəʊlɪəʊ] *n* polio *f*.

polish ['pɒlɪʃ] ◇ *n* - **1.** [for floor, furniture] cera *f*; [for shoes] betún *m*; [for metal] abrillantador *m*; [for nails] esmalte *m* - **2.** [shine] brillo *m*, lustre *m* - **3.** *fig* [refinement] refinamiento *m*. ◇ *vt* [stone, wood] pulir; [floor] encerar; [shoes, car] limpiar; [cutlery, silver, glasses] sacar brillo a. ◆ **polish off** *vt sep inf* [food] zamparse; [job] despachar.

Polish ['pəʊlɪʃ] ◇ *adj* polaco(ca). ◇ *n* [language] polaco *m*. ◇ *npl*: **the Polish** los polacos.

polished ['pɒlɪʃt] *adj* - **1.** [person, manner] refinado(da) - **2.** [performance, speech] esmerado(da).

polite [pə'laɪt] *adj* educado(da), cortés.

politic ['pɒlətɪk] *adj fml* oportuno(na), conveniente.

political [pə'lɪtɪkl] *adj* [concerning politics] político(ca).

politically correct [pəˌlɪtɪklɪ-] *adj* políticamente correcto(ta).

politician [ˌpɒlɪ'tɪʃn] *n* político *m*, -ca *f*.

politics ['pɒlətɪks] ◇ n (U) política f. ◇ npl - 1. [personal beliefs] ideas fpl políticas - 2. [of a group, society] política f.

polka ['pɒlkə] n polca f.

polka dot n lunar m (en un vestido).

poll [pəʊl] ◇ n [vote] votación f, [of opinion] encuesta f. ◇ vt - 1. [people] sondear - 2. [votes] obtener. ◆ **polls** npl: **the polls** los comicios.

pollen ['pɒlən] n polen m.

polling booth ['pəʊlɪŋ-] n cabina f electoral.

polling day ['pəʊlɪŋ-] n UK día m de las elecciones.

polling station ['pəʊlɪŋ-] n colegio m OR centro m electoral.

pollute [pə'luːt] vt contaminar.

pollution [pə'luːʃn] n (U) - 1. [process of polluting] contaminación f - 2. [impurities] sustancias fpl contaminantes.

polo ['pəʊləʊ] n polo m.

polo neck UK n - 1. [neck] cuello m alto - 2. [jumper] jersey m de cuello alto.

polyethylene US = polythene.

Polynesia [ˌpɒlɪ'niːʒə] n Polinesia.

polystyrene [ˌpɒlɪ'staɪriːn] n poliestireno m.

polytechnic [ˌpɒlɪ'teknɪk] n UK escuela f politécnica.

polythene UK ['pɒlɪθiːn], **polyethylene** US ['pɒlɪ'eθɪliːn] n polietileno m.

polythene bag n UK bolsa f de plástico.

pomegranate ['pɒmɪˌgrænɪt] n granada f.

pomp [pɒmp] n pompa f.

pompom ['pɒmpɒm] n borla f, pompón m.

pompous ['pɒmpəs] adj - 1. [self-important] presumido(da) - 2. [style] pomposo(sa); [building] ostentoso(sa).

pond [pɒnd] n estanque m.

ponder ['pɒndər] vt considerar.

ponderous ['pɒndərəs] adj - 1. [speech, book] pesado(da) - 2. [action, walk] lento(ta) y torpe.

pong [pɒŋ] UK inf n (olor m a) peste f.

pontoon [pɒn'tuːn] n - 1. [bridge] pontón m - 2. UK [game] veintiuna f.

pony ['pəʊnɪ] n poni m.

ponytail ['pəʊnɪteɪl] n coleta f (de caballo).

pony-trekking [-ˌtrekɪŋ] n (U): **to go pony-trekking** hacer una excursión en poni.

poodle ['puːdl] n caniche m.

pool [puːl] ◇ n - 1. [of water, blood, ink] charco m; [pond] estanque m - 2. [swimming pool] piscina f - 3. [of light] foco m - 4. COMM [fund] fondo m común - 5. [of people, things]: **typing pool** servicio m de mecanografía; **car pool** parque m móvil - 6. [game] billar m americano.

◇ vt [resources, funds] juntar; [knowledge] poner en común. ◆ **pools** npl UK: **the pools** las quinielas.

poor [pɔːr] ◇ adj - 1. [gen] pobre; **poor old John!** ¡el pobre de John!; **you poor thing!** ¡pobrecito! - 2. [quality, result] malo(la) - 3. [prospects, chances] escaso(sa). ◇ npl: **the poor** los pobres.

poorly ['pɔːlɪ] ◇ adj UK pachucho(cha). ◇ adv mal; **poorly off** pobre.

pop [pɒp] ◇ n - 1. [music] (música f) pop m - 2. (U) inf [fizzy drink] gaseosa f - 3. esp US inf [father] papá m - 4. [sound] pequeña explosión f. ◇ vt [balloon, bubble] pinchar. ◇ vi - 1. [balloon] reventar; [cork, button] saltar - 2. [eyes] salirse de las órbitas - 3. [ears]: **her ears popped** se le destaparon los oídos - 4. [go quickly]: **I'm just popping round to the shop** voy un momento a la tienda. ◆ **pop in** vi entrar un momento. ◆ **pop up** vi aparecer de repente.

pop concert n concierto m de música pop.

popcorn ['pɒpkɔːn] n palomitas fpl (de maíz).

pope [pəʊp] n papa m.

pop group n grupo m (de música) pop.

poplar ['pɒplər] n álamo m.

poppy ['pɒpɪ] n amapola f.

Popsicle® ['pɒpsɪkl] n US polo m.

populace ['pɒpjʊləs] n: **the populace** [masses] el populacho; [people] el pueblo.

popular ['pɒpjʊlər] adj - 1. [gen] popular; [person] estimado(da) - 2. [belief, attitude, discontent] generalizado(da) - 3. [newspaper, politics] para las masas.

popularize, -ise ['pɒpjʊləraɪz] vt - 1. [make popular] popularizar - 2. [simplify] vulgarizar.

population [ˌpɒpjʊ'leɪʃn] n población f.

porcelain ['pɔːsəlɪn] n porcelana f.

porch [pɔːtʃ] n - 1. [entrance] porche m, pórtico m - 2. US [verandah] porche m.

porcupine ['pɔːkjʊpaɪn] n puerco m espín.

pore [pɔːr] n poro m. ◆ **pore over** vt insep estudiar esmeradamente.

pork [pɔːk] n carne f de cerdo.

pork pie n empanada f de carne de cerdo.

pornography [pɔː'nɒgrəfɪ] n pornografía f.

porous ['pɔːrəs] adj poroso(sa).

porridge ['pɒrɪdʒ] n papilla f OR gachas fpl de avena.

port [pɔːt] n - 1. [coastal town, harbour] puerto m - 2. NAUT [left-hand side] babor m - 3. [drink] oporto m - 4. COMPUT puerto m.

portable ['pɔːtəbl] adj portátil.

portent ['pɔːtənt] n liter presagio m.

porter [ˈpɔːtəʳ] n - 1. UK [in block of flats] portero m, -ra f; [in public building, hotel] conserje mf - 2. [for luggage] mozo m.

portfolio [ˌpɔːtˈfəʊljəʊ] (pl -s) n - 1. ART, FIN & POL cartera f - 2. [sample of work] carpeta f.

porthole [ˈpɔːthəʊl] n portilla f.

portion [ˈpɔːʃn] n - 1. [part, section] porción f - 2. [of chips, vegetables etc] ración f.

portly [ˈpɔːtlɪ] adj corpulento(ta).

port of call n - 1. NAUT puerto m de escala - 2. fig [on journey] escala f.

portrait [ˈpɔːtrɪt] n - 1. [picture] retrato m - 2. COMPUT formato m vertical.

portray [pəˈtreɪ] vt - 1. [represent - in a play, film] representar - 2. [describe] describir - 3. [paint] retratar.

Portugal [ˈpɔːtʃʊgl] n Portugal.

Portuguese [ˌpɔːtʃʊˈgiːz] <> adj portugués(esa). <> n [language] portugués m. <> npl: the Portuguese los portugueses.

posh [pɒʃ] adj inf - 1. [hotel, area etc] de lujo, elegante - 2. UK [person, accent] afectado(da).

position [pəˈzɪʃn] <> n - 1. [gen] posición f - 2. [right place] sitio m, lugar m - 3. [status] rango m - 4. [job] puesto m - 5. [in a race, competition] lugar m - 6. [state, situation] situación f; to be in a/no position to do sthg estar/no estar en condiciones de hacer algo - 7. [stance, opinion]: position on postura f respecto a. <> vt colocar.

positive [ˈpɒzətɪv] adj - 1. [gen] positivo(va); the test was positive la prueba dio positivo - 2. [sure]: to be positive (about) estar seguro(ra) (de) - 3. [optimistic, confident]: to be positive (about) ser optimista (respecto a) - 4. [definite - action] decisivo(va); [- decision] categórico(ca) - 5. [irrefutable - evidence, fact] irrefutable; [- proof] concluyente.

posse [ˈpɒsɪ] n US - 1. [to pursue criminal] grupo m de hombres a caballo - 2. [group] grupo m.

possess [pəˈzes] vt - 1. [gen] poseer - 2. [subj: emotion] adueñarse de.

possession [pəˈzeʃn] n posesión f; to have sthg in one's possession, to be in possession of sthg tener (posesión de) algo. ◆ **possessions** npl bienes mpl.

possessive [pəˈzesɪv] adj - 1. [gen] posesivo(va) - 2. pej [selfish] egoísta.

possibility [ˌpɒsəˈbɪlətɪ] n posibilidad f; there's a possibility that... es posible que...

possible [ˈpɒsəbl] adj - 1. [gen] posible; as soon as possible cuanto antes; as much as possible [quantity] todo lo posible; [to the greatest possible extent] en la medida de lo posible; I go as often as possible voy siempre que puedo; it's possible that she'll come es posible que venga - 2. [viable - plan etc] viable, factible.

possibly [ˈpɒsəblɪ] adv - 1. [perhaps] posiblemente, quizás - 2. [within one's power]: could you possibly help me? ¿te importaría ayudarme? - 3. [to show surprise]: how could he possibly do that? ¿cómo demonios pudo hacer eso? - 4. [for emphasis]: I can't possibly do it no puedo hacerlo de ninguna manera.

post [pəʊst] <> n - 1. [service]: the post el correo; by post por correo - 2. (U) [letters etc] cartas fpl - 3. [delivery] reparto m - 4. UK [collection] colecta f - 5. [pole] poste m - 6. [position, job] puesto m - 7. MIL puesto m. <> vt - 1. [put in letterbox] echar al correo; [send by mail] mandar por correo - 2. [transfer] enviar, destinar - 3. COMPUT [message, query] enviar.

postage [ˈpəʊstɪdʒ] n franqueo m, porte m; postage and packing gastos mpl de envío.

postal [ˈpəʊstl] adj postal.

postal order n giro m postal.

postal vote n voto m por correo.

postbox [ˈpəʊstbɒks] n UK buzón m.

postcard [ˈpəʊstkɑːd] n postal f.

postcode [ˈpəʊstkəʊd] n UK código m postal.

postdate [ˌpəʊstˈdeɪt] vt poner posfecha a; a postdated cheque extender un cheque con fecha posterior.

poster [ˈpəʊstəʳ] n cartel m, póster m.

poste restante [ˌpəʊstˈrestɑːnt] n esp UK lista f de correos.

posterior [pɒˈstɪərɪəʳ] n hum trasero m.

postgraduate [ˌpəʊstˈgrædʒʊət] n posgraduado m, -da f.

posthumous [ˈpɒstjʊməs] adj póstumo(ma).

postman [ˈpəʊstmən] (pl -men [-mən]) n cartero m.

postmark [ˈpəʊstmɑːk] n matasellos m inv.

postmortem [ˌpəʊstˈmɔːtəm] n [autopsy] autopsia f.

post office n - 1. [organization]: the Post Office ≃ Correos m inv - 2. [building] oficina f de correos.

post office box n apartado m de correos, casilla f de correos Andes & R Plata.

postpone [ˌpəʊstˈpəʊn] vt posponer.

postscript [ˈpəʊstskrɪpt] n [additional message] posdata f; fig [additional information] nota f final.

posture [ˈpɒstʃəʳ] n lit & fig postura f; posture on sthg postura hacia algo.

postwar [ˌpəʊstˈwɔːr] adj de (la) posguerra.

posy [ˈpəʊzɪ] n ramillete m.

pot [pɒt] <> n - 1. [for cooking] olla f - 2. [for tea] tetera f; [for coffee] cafetera f - 3. [for plant] bote *m*; [for jam] tarro *m* - **4.** [flowerpot] tiesto *m*, maceta *f* • **5.** *(UI) inf* [cannabis] maría *f*, hierba *f*.

▶▶ **to go to pot** ir al traste. ◇ *vt* plantar (en un tiesto).

potassium [pəˈtæsɪəm] *n* potasio *m*.

potato [pəˈteɪtəʊ] (*pl* **-es**) *n* patata *f*.

potato peeler [-ˌpiːləʳ] *n* pelapatatas *m inv Esp*, pelapapas *m inv Amér*.

potent [ˈpəʊtənt] *adj* - **1.** [powerful, influential] poderoso(sa) - **2.** [drink, drug] fuerte - **3.** [sexually capable] potente.

potential [pəˈtenʃl] ◇ *adj* potencial, posible. ◇ *n* (*U*) potencial *m*; **to have potential** tener posibilidades, prometer.

potentially [pəˈtenʃəlɪ] *adv* en potencia.

pothole [ˈpɒthəʊl] *n* - **1.** [in road] bache *m* - **2.** [underground] cueva *f*.

potholing [ˈpɒtˌhəʊlɪŋ] *n UK* espeleología *f*.

potion [ˈpəʊʃn] *n* poción *f*.

potluck [ˌpɒtˈlʌk] *n*: **to take potluck** [gen] elegir a ojo; [at meal] conformarse con lo que haya.

potshot [ˈpɒtˌʃɒt] *n*: **to take a potshot (at sthg/sb)** disparar (a algo/alguien) sin apuntar.

potted [ˈpɒtɪd] *adj* - **1.** [plant] en tiesto - **2.** [meat, fish] en conserva.

potter [ˈpɒtəʳ] *n* alfarero *m*, -ra *f*. ▶▶ **potter about, potter around** *vi UK* entretenerse.

pottery [ˈpɒtərɪ] *n* - **1.** [gen] cerámica *f*, alfarería *f* - **2.** [factory] fábrica *f* de cerámica.

potty [ˈpɒtɪ] *UK inf* ◇ *adj* [person] chalado(da). ◇ *n* orinal *m*.

pouch [paʊtʃ] *n* - **1.** [small bag] bolsa *f* pequeña; [for tobacco] petaca *f* - **2.** [on animal's body] bolsa *f* (abdominal).

poultry [ˈpəʊltrɪ] ◇ *n* [meat] carne *f* de pollería. ◇ *npl* [birds] aves *fpl* de corral.

pounce [paʊns] *vi* [leap]: **to pounce (on OR upon)** abalanzarse (sobre).

pound [paʊnd] ◇ *n* - **1.** [unit of money, weight] libra *f* - **2.** [for cars] depósito *m* (de coches); [for dogs] perrera *f*. ◇ *vt* - **1.** [hammer on] golpear, aporrear - **2.** [pulverize] machacar. ◇ *vi* - **1.** [hammer]: **to pound on sthg** golpear OR aporrear algo - **2.** [beat, throb] palpitar; **her heart was pounding** le palpitaba el corazón.

pound sterling *n* libra *f* esterlina.

pour [pɔːʳ] ◇ *vt* [cause to flow]: **to pour sthg (into)** echar OR verter algo (en); **to pour sthg down the sink** tirar algo por el fregadero; **to pour sb a drink, to pour a drink for sb** servirle una copa a alguien; **can I pour you a cup of tea?** ¿quieres que te sirva una taza de té? ◇ *vi* [liquid] chorrear; [smoke] salir a borbotones. ◇ *impers vb* [rain hard] llover a cántaros; **it's pouring (down)** está lloviendo a cántaros.

▶▶ **pour in** *vi* llegar a raudales. ▶▶ **pour out** ◇ *vt sep* - **1.** [empty] echar, vaciar - **2.** [serve] servir. ◇ *vi* [information] salir en avalancha.

pouring [ˈpɔːrɪŋ] *adj* [rain] torrencial.

pout [paʊt] *vi* [showing displeasure] hacer pucheros; [being provocative] hacer un gesto provocador con los labios.

poverty [ˈpɒvətɪ] *n lit & fig* pobreza *f*.

poverty-stricken *adj* necesitado(da).

powder [ˈpaʊdəʳ] ◇ *n* polvo *m*; [make-up] polvos *mpl*. ◇ *vt* poner polvos en; **to powder o.s.** darse polvos, empolvarse.

powder compact *n* polvera *f*.

powdered [ˈpaʊdəd] *adj* [in powder form] en polvo.

powder puff *n* borla *f*.

powder room *n* servicios *mpl* de señoras.

power [ˈpaʊəʳ] ◇ *n* - **1.** (*U*) [authority, control] poder *m*; **to have power over sb** tener poder sobre alguien; **to come to/take power** llegar al/hacerse con el poder; **to be in power** estar en el poder - **2.** [ability] facultad *f*; **it isn't within my power to do it** no está dentro de mis posibilidades hacerlo; **I'll do everything in my power to help** haré todo lo que pueda por ayudar - **3.** [legal authority] autoridad *f*, competencia *f*; **to have the power to do sthg** tener autoridad para hacer algo - **4.** [physical strength] fuerza *f* - **5.** [energy - solar, steam etc] energía *f* - **6.** [electricity] corriente *f* - **7.** [powerful nation, person, group] potencia *f* - **8.** [phr]: **to do sb a power of good** sentar de maravilla a alguien. ◇ *vt* impulsar.

powerboat [ˈpaʊəbəʊt] *n* motora *f*.

power cut *n* apagón *m*.

power failure *n* corte *m* de corriente.

powerful [ˈpaʊəfʊl] *adj* - **1.** [gen] poderoso(sa) - **2.** [blow, voice, drug] potente - **3.** [speech, film] conmovedor(ra).

powerless [ˈpaʊəlɪs] *adj* - **1.** [helpless] impotente - **2.** [unable]: **to be powerless to do sthg** no poder hacer algo.

power point *n UK* toma *f* (de corriente).

power station *n* central *f* eléctrica.

power steering *n* dirección *f* asistida.

pp (*abbr of* per procurationem) p.p.

p & p *abbr of* **postage and packing**.

PR *n abbr of* **proportional representation**. *abbr of* **public relations**.

practicable [ˈpræktɪkəbl] *adj* factible.

practical [ˈpræktɪkl] ◇ *adj* - **1.** [gen] práctico(ca) - **2.** [skilled with hands] hábil, mañoso(sa). ◇ *n* práctica *f*.

practicality [ˌpræktɪˈkælətɪ] *n* viabilidad *f*.

practical joke *n* broma *f* pesada.

practically ['præktɪklɪ] *adv* - **1.** [in a practical way] de manera práctica - **2.** [almost] prácticamente, casi.

practice ['præktɪs] *n* - **1.** [training, training session] práctica *f*; SPORT entrenamiento *m*; MUS ensayo *m*; **I'm out of practice** me falta práctica; **practice makes perfect** se aprende a base de práctica - **2.** [reality]: **to put sthg into practice** llevar algo a la práctica - **3.** [habit, regular activity] costumbre *f* - **4.** [of profession] ejercicio *m* - **5.** [business - of doctor] consulta *f*; [- of lawyer] bufete *m*, despacho *m*.

practicing US = **practising**.

practise, practice US ['præktɪs] <> *vt* - **1.** SPORT entrenar; MUS & THEAT ensayar - **2.** [religion, economy, safe sex] practicar - **3.** [medicine, law] ejercer. <> *vi* - **1.** [train - gen] practicar; SPORT entrenarse - **2.** [as doctor] practicar; [as lawyer] ejercer.

practising, practicing US ['præktɪsɪŋ] *adj* - **1.** [Catholic, Jew etc] practicante - **2.** [doctor, lawyer] en ejercicio - **3.** [homosexual] activo(va).

practitioner [præk'tɪʃnəʳ] *n*: **medical practitioner** médico *m*, -ca *f*.

prairie ['preərɪ] *n* pradera *f*, prado *m*.

praise [preɪz] <> *n (U)* elogio *m*, alabanza *f*. <> *vt* elogiar, alabar.

praiseworthy ['preɪz,wɜːðɪ] *adj* encomiable.

pram [præm] *n* cochecito *m* de niño.

prance [prɑːns] *vi* - **1.** [person] ir dando brincos - **2.** [horse] hacer cabriolas.

prank [præŋk] *n* travesura *f*; **to play a prank on sb** gastarle una broma pesada a alguien.

prawn [prɔːn] *n* gamba *f*.

pray [preɪ] *vi* rezar, orar; **to pray to sb** rogar a alguien.

prayer [preəʳ] *n* - **1.** RELIG oración *f* - **2.** *fig* [strong hope] ruego *m*, súplica *f*.

prayer book *n* misal *m*.

preach [priːtʃ] <> *vt* [gen] predicar; [sermon] dar. <> *vi* - **1.** RELIG: **to preach (to)** predicar (a) - **2.** *pej* [pontificate]: **to preach (at)** sermonear (a).

preacher ['priːtʃəʳ] *n* - **1.** predicador *m*, -ra *f* - **2.** US [minister] pastor *m*, -ra *f*.

precarious [prɪ'keərɪəs] *adj* precario(ria).

precaution [prɪ'kɔːʃn] *n* precaución *f*.

precede [prɪ'siːd] *vt* preceder.

precedence ['presɪdəns] *n*: **to take precedence over** tener prioridad sobre.

precedent ['presɪdənt] *n* precedente *m*.

precinct ['priːsɪŋkt] *n* - **1.** UK [shopping area] zona *f* comercial - **2.** US [district] distrito *m*.
➤ **precincts** *npl* recinto *m*.

precious ['preʃəs] *adj* - **1.** [gen] precioso(sa) - **2.** [memories, possessions] preciado(da) - **3.** [af-

fected] afectado(da) - **4.** *iro*: **I've heard enough about your precious dog!** ¡ya estoy cansado de tu dichoso perro!

precipice ['presɪpɪs] *n lit* & *fig* precipicio *m*.

precipitate *vt* [prɪ'sɪpɪteɪt] precipitar.

precise [prɪ'saɪs] *adj* preciso(sa), exacto(ta).

precisely [prɪ'saɪslɪ] *adv* - **1.** [with accuracy] exactamente - **2.** [exactly, literally] precisamente - **3.** [as confirmation]: **precisely!** ¡eso es!, ¡exactamente!

precision [prɪ'sɪʒn] *n* precisión *f*.

preclude [prɪ'kluːd] *vt fml* evitar, impedir; [possibility] excluir; **to preclude sthg/sb from doing sthg** impedir que algo/alguien haga algo.

precocious [prɪ'kəʊʃəs] *adj* precoz.

preconceived [,priːkən'siːvd] *adj* preconcebido(da).

precondition [,priːkən'dɪʃn] *n fml*: **precondition (for)** requisito *m* previo (para).

predator ['predətəʳ] *n* depredador *m*, -ra *f*; *fig* buitre *mf*.

predecessor ['priːdɪsesəʳ] *n* antecesor *m*, -ra *f*.

predicament [prɪ'dɪkəmənt] *n* apuro *m*.

predict [prɪ'dɪkt] *vt* predecir, pronosticar.

predictable [prɪ'dɪktəbl] *adj* - **1.** [result etc] previsible - **2.** [film, book, person] poco original.

prediction [prɪ'dɪkʃn] *n* pronóstico *m*.

predispose [,priːdɪs'pəʊz] *vt*: **to be predisposed to sthg/to do sthg** [by nature] estar predispuesto(ta) a algo/a hacer algo.

predominant [prɪ'dɒmɪnənt] *adj* predominante.

predominantly [prɪ'dɒmɪnəntlɪ] *adv* fundamentalmente.

preempt [,priː'empt] *vt* [make ineffective] adelantarse a.

preemptive [,priː'emptɪv] *adj* preventivo(va).

preen [priːn] *vt* - **1.** [subj: bird] arreglar (con el pico); **to preen itself** atusarse las plumas - **2.** *fig* [subj: person]: **to preen o.s.** acicalarse.

prefab ['priːfæb] *n inf* casa *f* prefabricada.

preface ['prefɪs] *n*: **preface (to)** prólogo *m* OR prefacio *m* (a).

prefect ['priːfekt] *n* UK [pupil] delegado *m*, -da *f* de curso.

prefer [prɪ'fɜːʳ] *vt*: **to prefer sthg (to)** preferir algo (a); **to prefer to do sthg** preferir hacer algo.

preferable ['prefrəbl] *adj*: **to be preferable (to)** ser preferible (a).

preferably ['prefrəblɪ] *adv* preferentemente.

preference ['prefərəns] *n*: preference (for) preferencia *f* (por); to give sb preference, to give preference to sb dar preferencia a alguien.

preferential [,prefə'renʃl] *adj* preferente.

prefix ['priːfɪks] *n* prefijo *m*.

pregnancy ['pregnənsɪ] *n* embarazo *m*.

pregnant ['pregnənt] *adj* - **1.** [woman] embarazada - **2.** [animal] preñada.

prehistoric [,priːhɪ'stɒrɪk] *adj* prehistórico(ca).

prejudice ['predʒudɪs] <> *n*: prejudice (against) prejuicio *m* (contra); prejudice in favour of predisposición *f* a favor de. <> *vt* - **1.** [bias]: to prejudice sb (in favour of/against) predisponer a alguien (a favor de/en contra de) - **2.** [harm] perjudicar.

prejudiced ['predʒudɪst] *adj* parcial; to be prejudiced in favour of/against estar predispuesto a favor de/en contra de.

preliminary [prɪ'lɪmɪnərɪ] *adj* preliminar.

prelude ['prelju:d] *n* [event]: prelude (to) preludio *m* (a).

premarital [,priː'mærɪtl] *adj* prematrimonial.

premature ['premə,tjuəʳ] *adj* prematuro(ra).

premeditated [,priː'medɪteɪtɪd] *adj* premeditado(da).

premenstrual syndrome, premenstrual tension [priː'menstruəl-] *n* síndrome *m* premenstrual.

premier ['premjəʳ] <> *adj* primero(ra). <> *n* primer ministro *m*, primera ministra *f*.

premiere ['premɪeəʳ] *n* estreno *m*.

premise ['premɪs] *n* premisa *f*. premises *npl* local *m*; on the premises en el local.

premium ['priːmjəm] *n* prima *f*; to put OR place a high premium on sthg dar gran importancia a algo.

premium bond *n* UK boleto numerado emitido por el Estado que autoriza a participar en sorteos mensuales de dinero hasta su amortización.

premonition [,premə'nɪʃn] *n* premonición *f*.

pre-nup ['priːnʌp] *(abbr of* pre-nuptual contract*) n informal* acuerdo *m* prenupcial.

preoccupied [priː'ɒkjupaɪd] *adj*: preoccupied (with) preocupado(da) (por).

prep [prep] *(abbr of* preparation*) n (U)* UK *inf* tarea *f*, deberes *mpl*.

prepaid ['priːpeɪd] *adj* [post paid] porte pagado.

preparation [,prepə'reɪʃn] *n* [act of preparing] preparación *f*. preparations *npl* preparativos *mpl*; to make preparations for hacer preparativos para los preparativos para.

preparatory [prɪ'pærətrɪ] *adj* preparatorio(ria), preliminar.

preparatory school *n* [in UK] *colegio de pago para niños de 7 a 12 años;* [in US] *escuela privada de enseñanza secundaria y preparación para estudios superiores.*

prepare [prɪ'peəʳ] <> *vt* preparar. <> *vi*: to prepare for sthg/to do sthg prepararse para algo/para hacer algo.

prepared [prɪ'peəd] *adj* - **1.** [gen] preparado(da); to be prepared for sthg estar preparado para algo - **2.** [willing]: to be prepared to do sthg estar dispuesto(ta) a hacer algo.

preposition [,prepə'zɪʃn] *n* preposición *f*.

preposterous [prɪ'pɒstərəs] *adj* absurdo(da).

prep school *n inf abbr of* **preparatory school**.

prerequisite [,priː'rekwɪzɪt] *n*: prerequisite (for) requisito *m* (para).

prerogative [prɪ'rɒgətɪv] *n* prerrogativa *f*.

Presbyterian [,prezbɪ'tɪərɪən] <> *adj* presbiteriano(na). <> *n* presbiteriano *m*, -na *f*.

preschool ['priː,skuːl] <> *adj* preescolar. <> *n* US parvulario *m*.

prescribe [prɪ'skraɪb] *vt* - **1.** MED recetar - **2.** [order] ordenar, mandar.

prescription [prɪ'skrɪpʃn] *n* receta *f*; on prescription con receta médica.

presence ['prezns] *n* presencia *f*; to make one's presence felt hacer sentir la presencia de uno.

presence of mind *n* aplomo *m*.

present <> *adj* ['preznt] - **1.** [current] actual - **2.** [in attendance] presente; to be present at sthg asistir a algo, estar presente en algo. <> *n* ['preznt] - **1.** [current time]: the present el presente; at present actualmente - **2.** LING: present (tense) (tiempo *m*) presente *m* - **3.** [gift] regalo *m*; to give sb a present dar un regalo a alguien. <> *vt* [prɪ'zent] - **1.** [gen] presentar; to present sb with sthg, to present sthg to sb [challenge, opportunity] representar algo para alguien; to present sb to sb presentar a alguien a alguien; to present o.s. [arrive] presentarse - **2.** [give]: to present sb with sthg, to present sthg to sb [as present] obsequiar algo a alguien; [at ceremony] entregar algo a alguien - **3.** [play etc] representar.

presentable [prɪ'zentəbl] *adj* presentable; to look presentable tener un aspecto presentable; to make o.s. presentable arreglarse.

presentation [,prezn'teɪʃn] n - **1.** [gen] presentación f - **2.** [ceremony] entrega f - **3.** [performance] representación f.

present day n: **the present day** el presente. ➡ **present-day** adj de hoy en día.

presenter [prɪ'zentər] n UK presentador m, -ra f.

presently ['prezntlɪ] adv - **1.** [soon] dentro de poco - **2.** [now] actualmente.

preservation [,prezə'veɪʃn] n preservación f, conservación f.

preservative [prɪ'zɜ:vətɪv] n conservante m.

preserve [prɪ'zɜ:v] ◇ vt conservar. ◇ n [jam] mermelada f. ➡ **preserves** npl [jam] confituras fpl; [vegetables] conserva f.

preset [,pri:'set] (pt & pp **preset**) vt programar.

president ['prezɪdənt] n presidente m, -ta f.

presidential [,prezɪ'denʃl] adj presidencial.

press [pres] ◇ n - **1.** [push]: **to give sthg a press** apretar algo - **2.** [newspapers, reporters]: **the press** la prensa; **to get a good/bad press** tener buena/mala prensa - **3.** [machine] prensa f; **to go to press** entrar en prensa - **4.** [with iron] planchado m; **to give sthg a press** dar un planchado a algo. ◇ vt - **1.** [gen] apretar; **to press sthg against sthg** apretar algo contra algo - **2.** [grapes, flowers] prensar - **3.** [iron] planchar - **4.** [urge]: **to press sb for sthg** presionar a alguien en busca de algo - **5.** [pursue - claim] insistir en; **to press charges against sb** LAW demandar a alguien. ◇ vi - **1.** [gen]: **to press (on sthg)** apretar (algo) - **2.** [crowd]: **to press forward** empujar hacia adelante. ➡ **press for** vt insep exigir, reclamar. ➡ **press on** vi [continue]: **to press on (with)** seguir adelante (con).

press agency n agencia f de prensa.

press conference n rueda f de prensa.

pressed [prest] adj: **to be pressed (for time/ money)** andar escaso(sa) (de tiempo/de dinero).

pressing ['presɪŋ] adj apremiante.

press officer n jefe m, -fa f de prensa.

press release n comunicado m de prensa.

press-stud n UK automático m.

press-up n UK flexión f.

pressure ['preʃər] n presión f.

pressure cooker n olla f a presión.

pressure gauge n manómetro m.

pressure group n grupo m de presión.

pressurize, -ise ['preʃəraɪz] vt - **1.** TECH presurizar - **2.** UK [force]: **to pressurize sb to do** OR **into doing sthg** presionar a alguien para que haga algo.

prestige [pre'sti:ʒ] n prestigio m.

presumably [prɪ'zju:məblɪ] adv: **presumably you've read it** supongo que los has leído.

presume [prɪ'zju:m] vt suponer; **he is presumed dead** se supone que está muerto.

presumption [prɪ'zʌmpʃn] n - **1.** [assumption] suposición f; [of innocence] presunción f - **2.** (U) [audacity] presunción f, osadía f.

presumptuous [prɪ'zʌmptʃʊəs] adj presuntuoso(sa).

pretence, pretense US [prɪ'tens] n fingimiento m, simulación f; **to make a pretence of doing sthg** fingir hacer algo; **under false pretences** con engaños, con falsos pretextos.

pretend [prɪ'tend] ◇ vt: **to pretend to do sthg** fingir hacer algo; **she pretended not to notice** hizo como si no se hubiera dado cuenta; **don't pretend you didn't know!** ¡no finjas que no lo sabías! ◇ vi fingir, simular. ◇ adj inf de mentira.

pretense US = **pretence**.

pretension [prɪ'tenʃn] n pretensión f; **to have pretensions to sthg** tener pretensiones de algo.

pretentious [prɪ'tenʃəs] adj pretencioso(sa).

pretext ['pri:tekst] n pretexto m; **on** OR **under the pretext that.../of doing sthg** con el pretexto de que.../de hacer algo.

pretty ['prɪtɪ] ◇ adj bonito(ta). ◇ adv bastante; **pretty much** más o menos; **pretty well** [almost] casi.

prevail [prɪ'veɪl] vi - **1.** [be widespread] predominar, imperar - **2.** [triumph]: **to prevail (over)** prevalecer (sobre) - **3.** [persuade]: **to prevail on** OR **upon sb to do sthg** persuadir a alguien para que haga algo.

prevailing [prɪ'veɪlɪŋ] adj predominante.

prevalent ['prevələnt] adj predominante.

prevent [prɪ'vent] vt impedir; [event, illness, accident] evitar; **to prevent sthg (from) happening** impedir OR evitar que algo pase; **to prevent sb (from) doing sthg** impedir a alguien que haga algo.

preventive [prɪ'ventɪv], **preventative** adj preventivo(va).

preview ['pri:vju:] n - **1.** [film] avance m - **2.** [exhibition] preestreno m.

previous ['pri:vjəs] adj previo(via), anterior.

previously ['pri:vjəslɪ] adv - **1.** [formerly] anteriormente - **2.** [before]: **two years previously** dos años antes.

prewar [,pri:'wɔ:r] adj de preguerra.

prey [preɪ] n presa f, víctima f. ➡ **prey on** vt insep - **1.** [live off] cazar, alimentarse de - **2.** [trouble]: **to prey on sb's mind** atormentar a alguien.

price [praɪs] ◇ n lit & fig precio m; **to go up/down in price** subir/bajar de precio; **you**

can't put a price on health la salud no tiene precio; to pay the price for sthg pagar el precio de algo; at any price a todo costo, a cualquier precio; at a price a un alto precio; to pay a high price for sthg pagar algo caro. ◇ vt poner precio a; to be wrongly priced tener el precio equivocado; to price o.s. out of the market salirse del mercado por vender demasiado caro.

priceless ['praɪslɪs] adj lit & fig que no tiene precio, inestimable.

price list n lista f OR tarifa f de precios.

price tag n [label] etiqueta f (del precio).

pricey ['praɪsɪ] (comp -ier, superl -iest) adj caro(ra).

prick [prɪk] ◇ n - 1. [wound] pinchazo m - 2. vulg [penis] polla f - 3. vulg [stupid person] gilipollas mf inv. ◇ vt - 1. [gen] pinchar - 2. [sting] picar. ◆ **prick up** vt insep: to prick up one's ears [subj: animal] levantar las orejas; [subj: person] aguzar el oído.

prickle ['prɪkl] ◇ n - 1. [thorn] espina f - 2. [sensation] comezón f. ◇ vi picar.

prickly ['prɪklɪ] adj - 1. [thorny] espinoso(sa) - 2. fig [touchy] susceptible, enojadizo(za).

prickly heat n (U) sarpullido por causa del calor.

pride [praɪd] ◇ n orgullo m. ◇ vt: to pride o.s. on sthg enorgullecerse de algo.

priest [priːst] n sacerdote m.

priestess ['priːstɪs] n sacerdotisa f.

priesthood ['priːsthʊd] n - 1. [position, office]: the priesthood el sacerdocio - 2. [priests collectively]: the priesthood el clero.

prig [prɪg] n mojigato m, -ta f.

prim [prɪm] adj remilgado(da); prim and proper remilgado(da).

primarily ['praɪmərɪlɪ] adv principalmente.

primary ['praɪmərɪ] ◇ adj - 1. [main] principal - 2. SCH primario(ria). ◇ n US POL primaria f.

primary school n escuela f primaria.

primate ['praɪmeɪt] n ZOOL primate m.

prime [praɪm] ◇ adj - 1. [main] primero(ra), principal - 2. [excellent] excelente; [quality] primero(ra). ◇ n: to be in one's prime estar en la flor de la vida. ◇ vt - 1. [surface] preparar - 2. [gun, pump] cebar.

prime minister n primer ministro m, primera ministra f.

primer ['praɪmər] n - 1. [paint] imprimación f - 2. [textbook] cartilla f.

primeval, primaeval [praɪ'miːvl] adj [ancient] primitivo(va).

primitive ['prɪmɪtɪv] adj [tribe, species etc] primitivo(va); [accommodation, sense of humour] rudimentario(ria).

primrose ['prɪmrəʊz] n primavera f, prímula f.

Primus stove® ['praɪməs-] n hornillo m de camping.

prince [prɪns] n príncipe m.

princess [prɪn'ses] n princesa f.

principal ['prɪnsəpl] ◇ adj principal. ◇ n SCH director m, -ra f.

principle ['prɪnsəpl] n - 1. [gen] principio m; to be against sb's principles ir contra los principios de alguien - 2. (U) [integrity] principios mpl; on principle, as a matter of principle por principio. ◆ **in principle** adv en principio.

print [prɪnt] ◇ n - 1. (U) [type] caracteres mpl (de imprenta); **in print** [available] disponible; [in printed characters] en letra impresa; to be out of print estar agotado - 2. [piece of artwork] grabado m - 3. [reproduction] reproducción f - 4. [photograph] fotografía f - 5. [fabric] estampado m - 6. [mark of foot etc] huella f. ◇ vt - 1. TYPO imprimir - 2. [produce by printing - book, newspaper] tirar - 3. [publish] publicar - 4. [decorate - cloth etc] estampar - 5. [write in block letters] escribir con letra de imprenta. ◇ vi imprimir. ◆ **print out** vt sep COMPUT imprimir.

printer ['prɪntər] n - 1. [person] impresor m, -ra f; [firm] imprenta f - 2. [machine] impresora f.

printer cable n cable m de impresora.

printing ['prɪntɪŋ] n - 1. (U) [act of printing] impresión f - 2. [trade] imprenta f.

printout ['prɪntaʊt] n COMPUT salida f de impresora.

prior ['praɪər] ◇ adj [previous] previo(via); without prior notice sin previo aviso; to have prior commitments tener compromisos previos; to have a prior engagement tener un compromiso previo. ◇ n [monk] prior m. ◆ **prior to** prep antes de; prior to doing sthg con anterioridad a hacer algo.

priority [praɪ'ɒrətɪ] n prioridad f; to have OR take priority (over) tener prioridad (sobre).

prise [praɪz] vt: to prise sthg open/away abrir/separar algo haciendo palanca.

prison ['prɪzn] ◇ n cárcel f, prisión f; to be in prison estar en la cárcel; to be sentenced to 5 years in prison ser condenado a cinco años de cárcel. ◇ comp: to be given a prison sentence ser condenado a una pena de cárcel; a prison officer un funcionario de prisiones.

prisoner ['prɪznər] n - 1. [convict] preso m, -sa f - 2. [captive] prisionero m, -ra f.

prisoner of war (pl prisoners of war) n prisionero m, -ra f de guerra.

privacy [UK 'prɪvəsɪ, US 'praɪvəsɪ] n intimidad f.

private ['praɪvɪt] ◇ *adj* - **1.** [gen] privado(da); [class] particular; [telephone call, belongings] personal - **2.** [thoughts, plans] secreto(ta); **a private joke** un chiste que entienden unos pocos - **3.** [secluded] retirado(da) - **4.** [unsociable - person] reservado(da). ◇ *n* - **1.** [soldier] soldado *m* raso - **2.: (to do sthg) in private** [in secret] (hacer algo) en privado.

private enterprise *n (U)* empresa *f* privada.

private education *n (U)* enseñanza *f* privada.

private eye *n* detective privado *m*, -da *f*.

privately ['praɪvɪtlɪ] *adv* - **1.** [not by the state] de forma privada; **privately owned** de propiedad privada - **2.** [confidentially] en privado.

private property *n* propiedad *f* privada.

private school *n* colegio *m* privado.

privatize, -ise ['praɪvɪtaɪz] *vt* privatizar.

privet ['prɪvɪt] *n* alheña *f*.

privilege ['prɪvɪlɪdʒ] *n* privilegio *m*.

privy ['prɪvɪ] *adj*: **to be privy to sthg** estar enterado(da) de algo.

Privy Council *n* UK: **the Privy Council** en *Gran Bretaña, consejo privado que asesora al monarca*.

prize [praɪz] ◇ *adj* de primera. ◇ *n* premio *m*. ◇ *vt*: **to be prized** ser apreciado(da).

prize-giving [-ˌɡɪvɪŋ] *n* UK entrega *f* de premios.

prizewinner ['praɪzˌwɪnəʳ] *n* premiado *m*, -da *f*.

pro [prəʊ] (*pl* -s) *n* - **1.** *inf* [professional] profesional *mf* - **2.** [advantage]: **the pros and cons** los pros y los contras.

PRO [ˌpiːɑːˈrəʊ] *n* - **1.** UK (*abbr of* Public Record Office) registro *m* del Reino Unido - **2.** (*abbr of* public relations officer) *jefe de relaciones públicas*.

probability [ˌprɒbəˈbɪlətɪ] *n* probabilidad *f*.

probable ['prɒbəbl] *adj* probable; **it is not very probable that it will happen** no es muy probable que ocurra.

probably ['prɒbəblɪ] *adv* probablemente.

probation [prəˈbeɪʃn] *n* - **1.** [of prisoner] libertad *f* condicional; **to put sb on probation** poner a alguien en libertad condicional - **2.** [trial period] periodo *m* de prueba; **to be on probation** estar en periodo de prueba.

probe [prəʊb] ◇ *n* - **1.** [investigation]: **probe (into)** investigación *f* (sobre) - **2.** MED & AERON sonda *f*. ◇ *vt* - **1.** [investigate] investigar - **2.** [with tool] sondar; [with finger, stick] hurgar en.

problem ['prɒbləm] *n* problema *m*; **no problem!** *inf* ¡por supuesto!, ¡desde luego!

procedure [prəˈsiːdʒəʳ] *n* procedimiento *m*.

proceed *vi* [prəˈsiːd] - **1.** [do subsequently]: **to proceed to do sthg** proceder a hacer algo - **2.** *fml* [advance] avanzar. ◆ **proceeds** *npl* ['prəʊsiːdz] ganancias *fpl*, beneficios *mpl*.

proceedings [prəˈsiːdɪŋz] *npl* - **1.** [series of events] acto *m* - **2.** [legal action] proceso *m*; **to start proceedings against sb** entablar proceso contra alguien.

process ['prəʊses] ◇ *n* proceso *m*; **in the process** en el intento. ◇ *vt* - **1.** [gen & COMPUT] procesar - **2.** [application] tramitar.

processing ['prəʊsesɪŋ] *n* - **1.** [gen & COMPUT] procesamiento *m* - **2.** [of applications etc] tramitación *f*.

procession [prəˈseʃn] *n* desfile *m*; [religious] procesión *f*.

proclaim [prəˈkleɪm] *vt* [gen] proclamar; [law] promulgar.

procrastinate [prəˈkræstɪneɪt] *vi* andarse con dilaciones.

procure [prəˈkjʊəʳ] *vt* [obtain] obtener.

prod [prɒd] *vt* [push, poke] dar empujoncitos a.

prodigal ['prɒdɪgl] *adj* [son, daughter] pródigo(ga).

prodigy ['prɒdɪdʒɪ] *n* [person] prodigio *m*; **a child prodigy** un niño prodigio.

produce ◇ *n* [prəˈdjuːs] *(U)* productos *mpl* agrícolas; **'produce of France'** 'producto de Francia'. ◇ *vt* [prəˈdjuːs] - **1.** [gen] producir; [offspring, flowers] engendrar - **2.** [bring out] mostrar, enseñar - **3.** THEAT poner en escena.

producer [prəˈdjuːsəʳ] *n* - **1.** [gen] productor *m*, -ra *f* - **2.** THEAT director *m*, -ra *f* de escena.

product ['prɒdʌkt] *n* producto *m*.

production [prəˈdʌkʃn] *n* - **1.** [gen] producción *f*; **to put/go into production** empezar a fabricar/fabricarse - **2.** *(U)* THEAT puesta *f* en escena.

production line *n* cadena *f* de producción.

productive [prəˈdʌktɪv] *adj* - **1.** [efficient] productivo(va) - **2.** [rewarding] provechoso(sa).

productivity [ˌprɒdʌkˈtɪvətɪ] *n* productividad *f*.

profane [prəˈfeɪn] *adj* [disrespectful] obsceno(na).

profession [prəˈfeʃn] *n* profesión *f*; **by profession** de profesión.

professional [prəˈfeʃnl] ◇ *adj* profesional. ◇ *n* profesional *mf*.

professor [prəˈfesəʳ] *n* - **1.** UK [head of department] catedrático *m*, -ca *f* - **2.** US & Canada [lecturer] profesor *m*, -ra *f* (de universidad).

proficiency [prəˈfɪʃənsɪ] *n*: **proficiency (in)** competencia *f* (en).

profile ['prəʊfaɪl] *n* perfil *m*; **high profile** notoriedad *f*.

profit ['prɒfɪt] <> *n* - 1. [financial gain] beneficio *m*, ganancia *f*; **to make a profit** sacar un beneficio; **to sell sthg at a profit** vender algo con beneficios - 2. [advantage] provecho *m*. <> *vi*: **to profit (from OR by)** sacar provecho (de).

profitability [,prɒfɪtə'bɪlətɪ] *n* rentabilidad *f*.

profitable ['prɒfɪtəbl] *adj* - 1. [making a profit] rentable - 2. [beneficial] provechoso(sa).

profiteering [,prɒfɪ'tɪərɪŋ] *n* especulación *f*.

profit-related pay *n* remuneración *f* vinculada a los beneficios.

profound [prə'faʊnd] *adj* profundo(da).

profusely [prə'fju:slɪ] *adv* profusamente; **to apologise profusely** pedir disculpas cumplidamente.

profusion [prə'fju:ʒn] *n* profusión *f*.

progeny ['prɒdʒənɪ] *n* progenie *f*.

prognosis [prɒg'nəʊsɪs] (*pl* **-noses** [-'nəʊsi:z]) *n* pronóstico *m*.

program ['prəʊgræm] <> *n* - 1. COMPUT programa *m* - 2. US = **programme**. <> *vt* (*pt & pp* **-med** OR **-ed**, *cont* **-ming** OR **ing**) - 1. COMPUT programar - 2. US = **programme**. <> *vi* (*pt & pp* **-med** OR **-ed**, *cont* **-ming** OR **ing**) COMPUT programar.

programer US = **programmer**.

programme UK, **program** US ['prəʊgræm] <> *n* programa *m*. <> *vt*: **to programme sthg (to do sthg)** programar algo (para que haga algo).

programmer UK, **programer** US ['prəʊgræmər] *n* COMPUT programador *m*, -ra *f*.

programming ['prəʊgræmɪŋ] *n* programación *f*.

progress <> *n* ['prəʊgres] - 1. [gen] progreso *m*; **in progress** en curso; **to make progress** hacer progresos - 2. [forward movement] avance *m*. <> *vi* [prə'gres] - 1. [gen] progresar; **as the year progressed** conforme avanzaba el año; [pupil etc] hacer progresos - 2. [move forward] avanzar.

progressive [prə'gresɪv] *adj* - 1. [enlightened] progresista - 2. [gradual] progresivo(va).

prohibit [prə'hɪbɪt] *vt* prohibir; **to prohibit sb from doing sthg** prohibirle a alguien hacer algo; **fishing is prohibited** prohibido pescar.

project <> *n* ['prɒdʒekt] - 1. [plan, idea] proyecto *m* - 2. SCH: **project (on)** estudio *m* OR trabajo *m* (sobre) - 3. US: **the projects** urbanización con viviendas de protección oficial. <> *vt* [prə'dʒekt] - 1. [gen] proyectar - 2. [estimate -

statistic, costs] estimar - 3. [company, person] dar una imagen de; [image] proyectar. <> *vi* [prə'dʒekt] proyectarse.

projectile [prə'dʒektaɪl] *n* proyectil *m*.

projection [prə'dʒekʃn] *n* - 1. [gen] proyección *f* - 2. [protrusion] saliente *m*.

projector [prə'dʒektər] *n* proyector *m*.

proletariat [,prəʊlɪ'teərɪət] *n* proletariado *m*.

prolific [prə'lɪfɪk] *adj* prolífico(ca).

prologue, prolog US ['prəʊlɒg] *n* prólogo *m*; **to be the OR a prologue to sthg** *fig* ser el prólogo a algo.

prolong [prə'lɒŋ] *vt* prolongar.

prom [prɒm] *n* - 1. *abbr of* **promenade concert** - 2. UK *inf* [road by sea] (*abbr of* **promenade**) paseo *m* marítimo - 3. US [ball] baile *m* de gala (en la escuela).

promenade [,prɒmə'nɑ:d] *n* UK [by sea] paseo *m* marítimo.

promenade concert *n* UK concierto sinfónico en donde parte del público está de pie.

prominent ['prɒmɪnənt] *adj* - 1. [important] destacado(da), importante - 2. [noticeable] prominente.

promiscuous [prɒ'mɪskjʊəs] *adj* promiscuo(cua).

promise ['prɒmɪs] <> *n* promesa *f*. <> *vt*: **to promise (to do sthg)** prometer (hacer algo); **to promise sb sthg** prometer a alguien algo. <> *vi*: **I promise** te lo prometo.

promising ['prɒmɪsɪŋ] *adj* prometedor(ra).

promontory ['prɒməntrɪ] (*pl* **-ies**) *n* promontorio *m*.

promote [prə'məʊt] *vt* - 1. [foster] fomentar, promover - 2. [push, advertise] promocionar - 3. [in job]: **to promote sb (to sthg)** ascender a alguien (a algo) - 4. SPORT: **to be promoted** subir.

promoter [prə'məʊtər] *n* - 1. [organizer] organizador *m*, -ra *f* - 2. [supporter] promotor *m*, -ra *f*.

promotion [prə'məʊʃn] *n* - 1. [in job] ascenso *m*; **to get OR be given promotion** conseguir un ascenso - 2. [advertising] promoción *f* - 3. [campaign] campaña *f* de promoción.

prompt [prɒmpt] <> *adj* rápido(da); **the injury requires prompt treatment** las heridas requieren un tratamiento inmediato; **to be prompt in doing sthg** hacer algo con prontitud. <> *adv* en punto; **at 2 o'clock prompt** a las dos en punto. <> *vt* - 1. [motivate]: **to prompt sb (to do sthg)** inducir OR impulsar a alguien (a hacer algo) - 2. THEAT apuntar. <> *n* THEAT [line] apunte *m*.

promptly ['prɒmptlɪ] *adv* - 1. [reply, react, pay] inmediatamente, rápidamente - 2. [arrive, leave] puntualmente.

prone [prəʊn] *adj* - **1.** [susceptible]: **to be prone to sthg/to do sthg** ser propenso(sa) a algo/a hacer algo - **2.** [lying flat] boca abajo.

prong [prɒŋ] *n* diente *m*, punta *f*.

pronoun ['prəʊnaʊn] *n* pronombre *m*.

pronounce [prə'naʊns] <> *vt* - **1.** [gen] pronunciar - **2.** [declare] declarar. <> *vi*: **to pronounce on sthg** pronunciarse sobre algo.

pronounced [prə'naʊnst] *adj* pronunciado(da), marcado(da).

pronouncement [prə'naʊnsmənt] *n* declaración *f*.

pronunciation [prə,nʌnsɪ'eɪʃn] *n* pronunciación *f*.

proof [pruːf] <> *n* - **1.** [gen & TYPO] prueba *f* - **2.** [of alcohol]: **to be 10% proof** tener 10 grados. <> *adj* [secure]: **proof against** a prueba de.

prop [prɒp] <> *n* - **1.** [physical support] puntal *m*, apoyo *m* - **2.** *fig* [supporting thing, person] sostén *m*. <> *vt*: **to prop sthg on OR against sthg** apoyar algo contra algo. ◆ **props** *npl* accesorios *mpl*. ◆ **prop up** *vt sep* - **1.** [physically support] apuntalar - **2.** *fig* [sustain] apoyar.

propaganda [,prɒpə'gændə] *n* propaganda *f*.

propel [prə'pel] *vt* propulsar, impulsar.

propeller [prə'pelər] *n* hélice *f*.

propelling pencil [prə'pelɪŋ-] *n* UK portaminas *m inv*.

propensity [prə'pensətɪ] *n fml*: **to have a propensity to do sthg** tener propensión a hacer algo.

proper ['prɒpər] *adj* - **1.** [real] de verdad - **2.** [correct - gen] correcto(ta); [- time, place, equipment] adecuado(da).

properly ['prɒpəlɪ] *adv* - **1.** [satisfactorily, correctly] bien - **2.** [decently] correctamente.

proper noun *n* nombre *m* propio.

property ['prɒpətɪ] *n* - **1.** [gen] propiedad *f* - **2.** [estate] finca *f* - **3.** *fml* [house] inmueble *m*.

property owner *n* propietario *m*, -ria *f* de un inmueble.

prophecy ['prɒfɪsɪ] *n* profecía *f*.

prophesy ['prɒfɪsaɪ] *vt* profetizar.

prophet ['prɒfɪt] *n* profeta *mf*.

proportion [prə'pɔːʃn] *n* - **1.** [part] parte *f* - **2.** [ratio, comparison] proporción *f* - **3.** [correct relationship]: **out of proportion** desproporcionado(da); **to get things out of proportion** *fig* sacar las cosas fuera de quicio; **to keep things in proportion** *fig* no exagerar; **sense of proportion** *fig* sentido *m* de la medida.

proportional [prə'pɔːʃənl] *adj*: **proportional (to)** proporcional (a), en proporción (a).

proportional representation *n* representación *f* proporcional.

proportionate [prə'pɔːʃnət] *adj*: **proportionate (to)** proporcional (a).

proposal [prə'pəʊzl] *n* - **1.** [plan, suggestion] propuesta *f* - **2.** [offer of marriage] proposición *f*.

propose [prə'pəʊz] <> *vt* - **1.** [suggest] proponer; [motion] presentar; **to propose doing sthg** proponer hacer algo - **2.** [intend]: **to propose doing OR to do sthg** tener la intención de hacer algo. <> *vi* [make offer of marriage] declararse.

proposition [,prɒpə'zɪʃn] *n* [suggestion] propuesta *f*; **to make sb a proposition** hacer una propuesta a alguien.

proprietor [prə'praɪətər] *n* propietario *m*, -ria *f*.

propriety [prə'praɪətɪ] *n* (U) *fml* - **1.** [moral correctness] propiedad *f* - **2.** [rightness] conveniencia *f*, oportunidad *f*.

pro rata [-'rɑːtə] *adj* & *adv* a prorrata.

prose [prəʊz] *n* - **1.** (U) LIT prosa *f* - **2.** SCH traducción *f* inversa.

prosecute ['prɒsɪkjuːt] <> *vt* procesar, enjuiciar. <> *vi* - **1.** [bring a charge] entablar una acción judicial - **2.** [represent in court] representar al demandante.

prosecution [,prɒsɪ'kjuːʃn] *n* - **1.** [gen] procesamiento *m* - **2.** [lawyers]: **the prosecution** la acusación.

prosecutor ['prɒsɪkjuːtər] *n esp* US fiscal *mf*.

prospect <> *n* [-'prɒspekt] - **1.** [gen] perspectiva *f*; **it was a pleasant prospect** era una perspectiva agradable; **they were faced with the prospect of losing their jobs** tenían que hacer frente a la perspectiva de perder sus trabajos - **2.** [possibility] posibilidad *f*. <> *vi* [prə'spekt]: **to prospect (for)** hacer prospecciones (de). ◆ **prospects** *npl*: **prospects (for)** perspectivas *fpl* (de); **job prospects** perspectivas laborales.

prospecting [prə'spektɪŋ] *n* (U) prospecciones *fpl*.

prospective [prə'spektɪv] *adj* posible.

prospector [prə'spektər] *n* prospector *m*, -ra *f*.

prospectus [prə'spektəs] *(pl -es) n* prospecto *m*, folleto *m* informativo.

prosper ['prɒspər] *vi* prosperar.

prosperity [prɒ'sperətɪ] *n* prosperidad *f*.

prosperous ['prɒspərəs] *adj* próspero(ra).

prostitute ['prɒstɪtjuːt] *n* prostituta *f*.

prostrate *adj* ['prɒstreɪt] postrado(da).

protagonist [prə'tægənɪst] *n* - **1.** *fml* [supporter] partidario *m*, -ria *f* - **2.** [main character] protagonista *mf*.

protect [prə'tekt] *vt*: **to protect sthg/sb (against/from)** proteger algo/a alguien (contra/de).

protection [prə'tekʃn] n: protection (from) protección (f) (contra/de).

protective [prə'tektɪv] adj protector(ra); **to feel protective towards sb** tener sentimientos protectores hacia alguien.

protégé ['prɒteʒeɪ] n protegido m.

protein ['prəʊtiːn] n proteína f.

protest ◇ n ['prəʊtest] protesta f; **under protest** bajo protesta; **without protest** sin protestar. ◇ vt [prə'test] - 1. [complain]: **to protest that** quejarse de - 2. [state] manifestar, aseverar; **he protested his innocence** declaró su inocencia - 3. US [oppose] protestar en contra de. ◇ vi [prə'test]: **to protest (about/against/at)** protestar (por/en contra de/por).

Protestant ['prɒtɪstənt] ◇ adj protestante. ◇ n protestante mf.

protester [prə'testər] n manifestante mf.

protest march n manifestación f.

protocol ['prəʊtəkɒl] n protocolo m.

prototype ['prəʊtətaɪp] n prototipo m.

protracted [prə'træktɪd] adj prolongado(da).

protrude [prə'truːd] vi: **to protrude (from)** sobresalir (de).

protruding [prə'truːdɪŋ] adj [chin] prominente; [teeth] salido(da); [eyes] saltón(ona).

protuberance [prə'tjuːbərəns] n protuberancia f.

proud [praʊd] adj - 1. [gen] orgulloso(sa); **to be proud of** estar orgulloso(sa) de; **that's nothing to be proud of!** ¡yo no estaría orgulloso de eso!; **to be proud of o.s.** estar orgulloso de uno mismo; **to be proud to do sthg** tener el honor de hacer algo - 2. pej [arrogant] soberbio(bia), arrogante.

prove [pruːv] ◇ vt (pp -d OR proven) - 1. [show to be true] probar, demostrar - 2. [show oneself to be]: **to prove o.s. to be sthg** resultar ser algo; **to prove o.s.** demostrar (uno) sus cualidades. ◇ vi (pp -d OR proven) resultar; **to prove (to be) interesting/difficult** resultar interesante/difícil.

proven ['pruːvn, 'prəʊvn] ◇ pp ⊳ **prove**. ◇ adj probado(da).

proverb ['prɒvɜːb] n refrán m.

provide [prə'vaɪd] vt proporcionar, proveer; **to provide sb with sthg** proporcionar a alguien algo; **to provide sthg for sb** ofrecer algo a alguien. ◆ **provide for** vt insep - 1. [support] mantener - 2. fml [make arrangements for] tomar medidas para.

provided [prə'vaɪdɪd], **providing** ◆ **provided (that)** conj con tal de (de) que; **you should pass, provided you work hard** aprobarás, con tal de que trabajes duro.

providing [prə'vaɪdɪŋ] ◆ **providing (that)** conj = provided.

province ['prɒvɪns] n - 1. [part of country] provincia f - 2. [area of activity] campo m, competencia f.

provincial [prə'vɪnʃl] adj - 1. [of a province] provincial - 2. pej [narrow-minded] provinciano(na).

provision [prə'vɪʒn] n - 1. [gen] suministro m - 2. [in agreement, law] disposición f. ◆ **provisions** npl [supplies] víveres mpl.

provisional [prə'vɪʒənl] adj provisional.

proviso [prə'vaɪzəʊ] (pl -s) n condición f; **with the proviso that...** con la condición de que...

provocative [prə'vɒkətɪv] adj - 1. [controversial] provocador(ra) - 2. [sexy] provocativo(va).

provoke [prə'vəʊk] vt provocar; **to provoke sb to do sthg** OR **into doing sthg** provocar a alguien a que haga algo.

prow [praʊ] n proa f.

prowess ['praʊɪs] n fml proezas fpl.

prowl [praʊl] ◇ n: **on the prowl** merodeando. ◇ vt merodear por. ◇ vi merodear.

prowler ['praʊlər] n merodeador m, -ra f.

proxy ['prɒksɪ] n: **by proxy** por poderes.

prudent ['pruːdnt] adj prudente.

prudish ['pruːdɪʃ] adj mojigato(ta).

prune [pruːn] ◇ n [fruit] ciruela f pasa. ◇ vt podar.

pry [praɪ] vi fisgonear.

PS (abbr of postscript) n P.D.

psalm [sɑːm] n salmo m.

pseudonym ['sjuːdənɪm] n seudónimo m.

psyche ['saɪkɪ] n psique f.

psychiatric [ˌsaɪkɪ'ætrɪk] adj psiquiátrico(ca).

psychiatrist [saɪ'kaɪətrɪst] n psiquiatra mf.

psychiatry [saɪ'kaɪətrɪ] n psiquiatría f.

psychic ['saɪkɪk] adj - 1. [clairvoyant] clarividente - 2. [mental] psíquico(ca).

psychoanalysis [ˌsaɪkəʊə'næləsɪs] n psicoanálisis m inv.

psychoanalyst [ˌsaɪkəʊ'ænəlɪst] n psicoanalista mf.

psychological [ˌsaɪkə'lɒdʒɪkl] adj psicológico(ca).

psychologist [saɪ'kɒlədʒɪst] n psicólogo m, -ga f.

psychology [saɪ'kɒlədʒɪ] n psicología f.

psychopath ['saɪkəpæθ] n psicópata mf.

psychotic [saɪ'kɒtɪk] ◇ adj psicótico(ca). ◇ n psicótico m, -ca f.

pt abbr of **pint, point**.

PTO (abbr of please turn over) sigue.

pub [pʌb] (abbr of public house) n pub m (británico).

puberty ['pjuːbətɪ] *n* pubertad *f*.

pubic ['pjuːbɪk] *adj* púbico(ca).

public ['pʌblɪk] ⟨⟩ *adj* público(ca); **to go public** COMM constituirse en sociedad anónima (con cotización en Bolsa). ⟨⟩ *n* público *m*; **in public** en público; **the public** el gran público.

public-address system *n* sistema *m* de megafonía.

publican ['pʌblɪkən] *n* UK patrón *m*, -ona *f* de un 'pub'.

publication [ˌpʌblɪ'keɪʃn] *n* publicación *f*.

public bar *n* UK en ciertos pubs y hoteles, bar de sencilla decoración con precios más bajos que los del 'saloon bar'.

public company *n* sociedad *f* anónima (con cotización en Bolsa).

public convenience *n* UK aseos *mpl* públicos.

public holiday *n* fiesta *f* nacional, (día *m*) feriado *m* Amér.

public house *n* UK *fml* pub *m* (británico).

publicity [pʌb'lɪsɪtɪ] *n* publicidad *f*.

publicize, -ise ['pʌblɪsaɪz] *vt* divulgar.

public limited company *n* sociedad *f* anónima (con cotización en Bolsa).

public opinion *n* (U) opinión *f* pública.

public prosecutor *n* fiscal *mf* del Estado.

public relations ⟨⟩ *n* (U) relaciones *fpl* públicas. ⟨⟩ *npl* relaciones *fpl* públicas.

public school *n* - 1. UK [private school] colegio *m* privado - 2. US [state school] escuela *f* pública.

public-spirited *adj* con sentido cívico.

public transport *n* transporte *m* público.

publish ['pʌblɪʃ] *vt* - 1. [gen] publicar - 2. [make known] hacer público(ca).

publisher ['pʌblɪʃəʳ] *n* [person] editor *m*, -ra *f*; [firm] editorial *f*.

publishing ['pʌblɪʃɪŋ] *n* (U) industria *f* editorial.

pub lunch *n* almuerzo servido en un 'pub'.

pucker ['pʌkəʳ] *vt* fruncir.

pudding ['pʊdɪŋ] *n* - 1. [sweet] pudín *m*; [savoury] pastel *m* - 2. (U) UK [course] postre *m*.

puddle ['pʌdl] *n* charco *m*.

Puerto Rico [ˌpwɜːtəʊ'riːkəʊ] *n* Puerto Rico.

puff [pʌf] ⟨⟩ *n* - 1. [of cigarette, pipe] calada *f* - 2. [gasp] jadeo *m* - 3. [of air] soplo *m*; [of smoke] bocanada *f*. ⟨⟩ *vt* echar. ⟨⟩ *vi* - 1. [smoke]: **to puff at** OR **on** dar caladas a *f* - 2. [pant] jadear. ⟨⟩ **puff out** *vt sep* - 1. [cheeks, chest] hinchar; [feathers] ahuecar - 2. [smoke] echar.

puffed [pʌft] *adj* [swollen]: **puffed (up)** hinchado(da).

puffin ['pʌfɪn] *n* frailecillo *m*.

puff pastry, puff paste US *n* hojaldre *m*.

puffy ['pʌfɪ] *adj* hinchado(da).

pugnacious [pʌg'neɪʃəs] *adj fml* pugnaz.

pull [pʊl] ⟨⟩ *vt* - 1. [gen] tirar de; [trigger] apretar - 2. [tooth, cork] sacar, extraer - 3. [muscle] sufrir un tirón en - 4. [attract] atraer - 5. [gun] sacar y apuntar. ⟨⟩ *vi* tirar. ⟨⟩ *n* - 1. [tug with hand] tirón *m* - 2. (U) [influence] influencia *f*. ⟨⟩ **pull apart** *vt sep* - 1. [machine etc] desmontar - 2. [toy, book etc] hacer pedazos. ⟨⟩ **pull at** *vt insep* dar tirones de. ⟨⟩ **pull away** *vi* [from roadside] alejarse (de la acera). ⟨⟩ **pull down** *vt sep* [building] derribar. ⟨⟩ **pull in** *vi* [train] pararse (en el andén). ⟨⟩ **pull off** *vt sep* [succeed in] conseguir llevar a cabo. ⟨⟩ **pull out** ⟨⟩ *vt sep* - 1. [troops] retirar - 2. [tooth] sacar. ⟨⟩ *vi* - 1. [vehicle] alejarse (de la acera) - 2. [withdraw] retirarse. ⟨⟩ **pull over** *vi* AUT hacerse a un lado. ⟨⟩ **pull through** *vi* recobrarse. ⟨⟩ **pull together** *vt sep*: **to pull o.s. together** calmarse, serenarse. ⟨⟩ **pull up** ⟨⟩ *vt sep* [move closer] acercar. ⟨⟩ *vi* parar, detenerse.

pulley ['pʊlɪ] (*pl* pulleys) *n* polea *f*.

pullover ['pʊlˌəʊvəʳ] *n* jersey *m*.

pulp [pʌlp] *n* - 1. [soft mass] papilla *f* - 2. [of fruit] pulpa *f* - 3. [of wood] pasta *f* de papel.

pulpit ['pʊlpɪt] *n* púlpito *m*.

pulsate [pʌl'seɪt] *vi* palpitar.

pulse [pʌls] ⟨⟩ *n* - 1. [in body] pulso *m*; **to take sb's pulse** tomarle el pulso a alguien - 2. TECH impulso *m*. ⟨⟩ *vi* latir. ⟨⟩ **pulses** *npl* [food] legumbres *fpl*.

puma ['pjuːmə] (*pl* puma OR -s) *n* puma *m*.

pumice (stone) ['pʌmɪs-] *n* piedra *f* pómez.

pummel ['pʌml] (UK) (US) *vt* aporrear.

pump [pʌmp] ⟨⟩ *n* - 1. [machine] bomba *f* - 2. [for petrol] surtidor *m*. ⟨⟩ *vt* [convey by pumping] bombear. ⟨⟩ **pumps** *npl* [shoes] zapatillas *fpl* de tenis. ⟨⟩ **pump up** *vt* [inflate] inflar.

pumpkin ['pʌmpkɪn] *n* calabaza *f*, zapallo *m* Perú, auyama *f* Col.

pun [pʌn] *n* juego *m* de palabras.

punch [pʌntʃ] ⟨⟩ *n* - 1. [blow] puñetazo *m* - 2. [tool - for leather etc] punzón *m*; [- for tickets] máquina *f* para picar billetes - 3. [drink] ponche *m*. ⟨⟩ *vt* - 1. [hit] dar un puñetazo a - 2. [ticket] picar - 3. [hole] perforar.

Punch-and-Judy show [-'dʒuːdɪ-] *n* teatro de guiñol para niños con personajes arquetípicos y representado normalmente en la playa.

punch(ed) card [pʌntʃ(t)-] *n* tarjeta *f* perforada.

punch line *n* remate *m* (de un chiste).

punch-up *n* UK *inf* pelea *f*.

punchy ['pʌntʃɪ] *adj inf* efectista, resultón(ona).

punctual ['pʌŋktʃʊəl] *adj* puntual.

punctuation [ˌpʌŋktʃʊ'eɪʃən] *n* puntuación *f*.

punctuation mark *n* signo *m* de puntuación.

puncture ['pʌŋktʃər] <> *n* pinchazo *m*; **to have a puncture** pinchar; [in skin] punción *f*. <> *vt* pinchar.

pundit ['pʌndɪt] *n* experto *m*, -ta *f*.

pungent ['pʌndʒənt] *adj* [strong-smelling] penetrante, fuerte.

punish ['pʌnɪʃ] *vt*: **to punish sb (for sthg/for doing sthg)** castigar a alguien (por algo/por haber hecho algo).

punishing ['pʌnɪʃɪŋ] *adj* penoso(sa).

punishment ['pʌnɪʃmənt] *n* [for crime] castigo *m*.

punk [pʌŋk] <> *adj* punk. <> *n* - **1.** [music]: **punk (rock)** punk *m* - **2.** [person]: **punk (rocker)** punki *mf* - **3.** US *inf* [lout] gamberro *m*.

punt [pʌnt] *n* batea *f*.

punter ['pʌntər] *n* UK - **1.** [gambler] apostante *mf* - **2.** *inf* [customer] cliente *m*, -ta *f*.

puny ['pju:nɪ] *adj* [person, limbs] enclenque, raquítico(ca); [effort] penoso(sa), lamentable.

pup [pʌp] *n* - **1.** [young dog] cachorro *m* - **2.** [young seal, otter] cría *f*.

pupil ['pju:pl] *n* - **1.** [student] alumno *m*, -na *f* - **2.** [follower] pupilo *m*, -la *f* - **3.** [of eye] pupila *f*.

puppet ['pʌpɪt] *n* lit & fig títere *m*.

puppy ['pʌpɪ] *n* cachorro *m*, perrito *m*.

purchase ['pɜːtʃəs] *fml* <> *n* compra *f*, adquisición *f*. <> *vt* comprar, adquirir.

purchaser ['pɜːtʃəsər] *n* comprador *m*, -ra *f*.

purchasing power ['pɜːtʃəsɪŋ-] *n* poder *m* adquisitivo.

pure [pjʊər] *adj* puro(ra).

puree ['pjʊəreɪ] *n* puré *m*; **tomato puree** concentrado *m* de tomate.

purely ['pjʊəlɪ] *adv* puramente; **purely and simply** pura y simplemente.

purge [pɜːdʒ] <> *n* POL purga *f*. <> *vt*: **to purge sthg (of)** purgar algo (de).

purify ['pjʊərɪfaɪ] *vt* purificar.

purist ['pjʊərɪst] *n* purista *mf*.

puritan ['pjʊərɪtən] <> *adj* puritano(na). <> *n* puritano *m*, -na *f*.

purity ['pjʊərətɪ] *n* pureza *f*.

purl [pɜːl] *n* (U) punto *m* del revés.

purple ['pɜːpl] *adj* morado(da).

purport [pə'pɔːt] *vi* fml: **to purport to do/be sthg** pretender hacer/ser algo.

purpose ['pɜːpəs] *n* [gen] propósito *m*; **what is the purpose of your visit?** ¿cuál es el objeto de tu visita?; **for one's own purposes** por su propio interés; **it serves no purpose** carece de

sentido; **it has served its purpose** ha servido; **to no purpose** en vano. **on purpose** *adv* a propósito, adrede.

purposeful ['pɜːpəsfʊl] *adj* resuelto(ta).

purr [pɜːr] *vi* - **1.** [cat, person] ronronear - **2.** [engine, machine] zumbar.

purse [pɜːs] <> *n* - **1.** [for money] monedero *m* - **2.** US [handbag] bolso *m*, bolsa *f* Méx, cartera *f* Andes. <> *vt* fruncir (con desagrado); **she pursed her lips** frunció los labios.

purser ['pɜːsər] *n* contador *m*, -ra *f*.

pursue [pə'sju:] *vt* - **1.** [follow] perseguir - **2.** fml [policy] llevar a cabo; [aim, pleasure etc] ir en pos de, buscar; [topic, question] profundizar en; [hobby, studies] dedicarse a.

pursuer [pə'sju:ər] *n* perseguidor *m*, -ra *f*.

pursuit [pə'sju:t] *n* - **1.** (U) fml [attempt to achieve] búsqueda *f* - **2.** [chase, in cycling] persecución *f* - **3.** [occupation, activity] ocupación *f*; **leisure pursuit** pasatiempo *m*.

pus [pʌs] *n* pus *m*.

push [pʊʃ] <> *vt* - **1.** [shove] empujar; **to push sthg into sthg** meter algo en algo; **to push sthg open/shut** abrir/cerrar algo empujándolo - **2.** [press - button] apretar, pulsar - **3.** [encourage]: **to push sb (to do sthg)** empujar a alguien (a hacer algo) - **4.** [force]: **to push sb (into doing sthg)** obligar a alguien (a hacer algo) - **5.** *inf* [promote] promocionar. <> *vi* [press forward] empujar; [on button] apretar, pulsar. <> *n* lit & fig empujón *m*; **at the push of a button** con sólo apretar un botón; **to give sb the push** *inf* [end relationship] dar calabazas a alguien; [from job] dar la patada a alguien; **at a push** apurando mucho. **push around** *vt sep* *inf* mandonear. **push for** *vt insep* [demand] reclamar. **push in** *vi* [in queue] colarse. **push off** *vi* *inf* largarse. **push on** *vi* seguir adelante sin parar. **push through** *vt sep* [law etc] conseguir que se apruebe.

pushchair ['pʊʃtʃeər] *n* UK silla *f* (de paseo).

pushed [pʊʃt] *adj* inf: **to be pushed for sthg** andar corto(ta) de algo; **to be hard pushed to do sthg** tenerlo difícil para hacer algo.

pusher ['pʊʃər] *n* inf camello *m*.

pushover ['pʊʃˌəʊvər] *n* inf: **it's a pushover** está chupado.

push-up *n* esp US flexión *f*.

pushy ['pʊʃɪ] *adj* pej agresivo(va), insistente.

puss [pʊs], **pussy (cat)** ['pʊsɪ-] *n* inf gatito *m*, minino *m*.

put [pʊt] (*pt & pp* put) *vt* - **1.** [gen] poner; **to put sthg into sthg** meter algo en algo - **2.** [place exactly] colocar - **3.** [send - to prison etc] meter; **to put the children to bed** acostar a los niños - **4.** [express] expresar, formular; **to put it bluntly** hablando claro - **5.** [ask - question] ha-

cer; [- proposal] presentar; **to put it to sb that...**
sugerir a alguien que... - **6.** [estimate]: **to put
sthg at** calcular algo en - **7.** [invest]: **to put
money into a project** invertir dinero en un
proyecto; **to put money into an account** ingresar dinero en una cuenta; **to put a lot of effort
into sthg** esforzarse mucho con algo - **8.** [apply]: **to put pressure on** presionar a. ◆ **put
across, put over** vt sep transmitir; **to put o.s.
across** hacerse entender. ◆ **put away** vt sep
[tidy away] poner en su sitio, guardar. ◆ **put
back** vt sep - **1.** [replace] devolver a su sitio
- **2.** [postpone] aplazar; [schedule] retrasar
- **3.** [clock, watch] atrasar. ◆ **put by** vt sep
ahorrar. ◆ **put down** vt sep - **1.** [lay down]
dejar - **2.** [phone] colgar - **3.** [quell] sofocar, reprimir - **4.** UK [animal] sacrificar - **5.** [write down]
apuntar. ◆ **put down to** vt sep achacar a.
◆ **put forward** vt sep - **1.** [plan, theory, name]
proponer; [proposal] presentar - **2.** [clock, meeting, event] adelantar. ◆ **put in** vt sep
- **1.** [spend - time] dedicar - **2.** [submit] presentar - **3.** [install] instalar. ◆ **put off** vt sep
- **1.** [postpone] posponer, aplazar - **2.** [cause to
wait] hacer esperar - **3.** [distract] distraer
- **4.** [discourage] disuadir - **5.** [cause to dislike]: **to
put sb off sthg** quitarle a alguien las ganas
de algo. ◆ **put on** vt sep - **1.** [wear] ponerse
- **2.** [show, play] representar; [exhibition] hacer;
[transport] organizar - **3.** [gain]: **to put on
weight** engordar - **4.** [radio, light] encender; **to
put on the brakes** frenar - **5.** [record, tape] poner - **6.** [start cooking] empezar a hacer OR cocinar; **to put the kettle on** poner el agua a
hervir - **7.** [bet] apostar por - **8.** [add] añadir
- **9.** [feign - air, accent] fingir. ◆ **put out** vt sep
- **1.** [place outside] sacar - **2.** [issue - statement]
hacer público - **3.** [extinguish, switch off] apagar
- **4.** [prepare for use - clothes] sacar - **5.** [extend -
hand, leg] extender; [- tongue] sacar - **6.** [upset]: **to be put out** estar disgustado(da) - **7.** [inconvenience] causar molestias a. ◆ **put
through** vt sep TELEC [call] poner; **to put sb
through to sb** poner a alguien con alguien.
◆ **put up** ◇ vt sep - **1.** [build] construir;
[tent] montar - **2.** [umbrella] abrir; [flag] izar
- **3.** [raise - hand] levantar - **4.** [poster] fijar;
[painting] colgar - **5.** [provide - money] poner
- **6.** [propose - candidate] proponer - **7.** [increase] subir, aumentar - **8.** [provide accommodation for] alojar. ◇ vt insep [resistance] ofrecer;
to put up a fight ofrecer resistencia. ◆ **put
up with** vt insep aguantar.

putrid ['pju:trɪd] adj fml putrefacto(ta).

putt [pʌt] n putt m.

putting green ['pʌtɪŋ-] n césped abierto al
público en el que se puede jugar a golf con el
putter.

putty ['pʌtɪ] n masilla f.

puzzle ['pʌzl] ◇ n - **1.** [toy, game] rompecabezas m inv - **2.** [mystery] misterio m, enigma m. ◇ vt dejar perplejo, desconcertar.
◇ vi: **to puzzle over sthg** romperse la cabeza
con algo. ◆ **puzzle out** vt sep descifrar.

puzzling ['pʌzlɪŋ] adj desconcertante.

pyjamas, pajamas [pə'dʒɑːməz] npl pijama m; **a pair of pyjamas** un pijama.

pylon ['paɪlən] n torre f (de conducción eléctrica).

pyramid ['pɪrəmɪd] n pirámide f.

Pyrenees [ˌpɪrə'niːz] npl: **the Pyrenees** los
Pirineos.

Pyrex® ['paɪreks] n pírex® m.

python ['paɪθn] (pl python OR -s) n pitón m.

q (pl q's OR qs), **Q** (pl Q's OR Qs) [kjuː] n [letter] q f, Q f.

quack [kwæk] n - **1.** [noise] graznido m (de pato) - **2.** inf [doctor] matasanos m inv.

quad [kwɒd] n abbr of **quadrangle**.

quadrangle ['kwɒdræŋgl] n - **1.** [figure] cuadrángulo m - **2.** [courtyard] patio m.

quadruple [kwɒ'druːpl] ◇ vt cuadruplicar.
◇ vi cuadruplicarse.

quadruplets ['kwɒdruplɪts] npl cuatrillizos mpl, -zas f.

quads [kwɒdz] npl inf cuatrillizos mpl,
-zas f.

quagmire ['kwægmaɪəʳ] n lodazal m.

quail [kweɪl] ◇ n (pl quail OR -s) codorniz f.
◇ vi liter amedrentarse.

quaint [kweɪnt] adj - **1.** [picturesque] pintoresco(ca) - **2.** [odd] singular.

quake [kweɪk] ◇ n inf terremoto m. ◇ vi
temblar, estremecerse.

Quaker ['kweɪkəʳ] n cuáquero m, -ra f.

qualification [ˌkwɒlɪfɪ'keɪʃn] n - **1.** [examination, certificate] título m - **2.** [ability, skill] aptitud f - **3.** [qualifying statement] condición f.

qualified ['kwɒlıfaıd] *adj* - **1.** [trained] cualificado(da); **to be qualified to do sthg** estar cualificado para hacer algo - **2.** [limited] limitado(da).

qualify ['kwɒlıfaı] <> *vt* - **1.** [modify] matizar - **2.** [entitle]: **to qualify sb to do sthg** capacitar a alguien para hacer algo. <> *vi* - **1.** [pass exams] sacar el título - **2.** [be entitled]: **to qualify (for)** tener derecho (a) - **3.** SPORT clasificarse.

quality ['kwɒlıtı] <> *n* - **1.** [standard] calidad *f* - **2.** [characteristic] cualidad *f*. <> *comp* de calidad.

qualms [kwɑ:mz] *npl* escrúpulos *mpl*.

quandary ['kwɒndərı] *n*: **to be in a quandary about** OR **over sthg** estar en un dilema sobre algo.

quantify ['kwɒntıfaı] *vt* cuantificar.

quantity ['kwɒntətı] *n* cantidad *f*.

quantity surveyor *n* aparejador *m*, -ra *f*.

quarantine ['kwɒrənti:n] *n* cuarentena *f*.

quark [kwɑ:k] *n* CULIN *tipo de queso blando bajo en grasas.*

quarrel ['kwɒrəl] <> *n* pelea *f*; **to have no quarrel with sb/sthg** no tener nada en contra de alguien/algo. <> *vi* (*UK pt* & *pp* **-led**, *cont* **-ling**, *US pt* & *pp* **-ed**, *cont* **-ing**) pelearse; **to quarrel with sb** pelearse con alguien; **to quarrel with sthg** no estar de acuerdo con algo.

quarrelsome ['kwɒrəlsəm] *adj* pendenciero(ra).

quarry ['kwɒrı] *n* - **1.** [place] cantera *f* - **2.** [prey] presa *f*.

quart [kwɔ:t] *n* cuarto *m* de galón.

quarter ['kwɔ:tə'] *n* - **1.** [fraction] cuarto *m* - **2.** [in telling time]: **a quarter past two** UK, **quarter after two** US las dos y cuarto - **3.** [of year] trimestre *m* - **4.** US [coin] moneda *f* de 25 centavos - **5.** [four ounces] cuatro onzas *fpl* - **6.** [area in town] barrio *m* - **7.** [group of people] lugar *m*, parte *f*. <> **quarters** *npl* [rooms] residencia *f*, alojamiento *m*. <> **at close quarters** *adv* muy de cerca.

quarterfinal [,kwɔ:tə'faınl] *n* cuarto *m* de final.

quarterly ['kwɔ:təlı] <> *adj* trimestral. <> *adv* trimestralmente. <> *n* trimestral *f*.

quartermaster ['kwɔ:tə,mɑ:stə'] *n* oficial *m* de intendencia.

quartet [kwɔ:'tet] *n* cuarteto *m*.

quartz [kwɔ:ts] *n* cuarzo *m*.

quartz watch *n* reloj *m* de cuarzo.

quash [kwɒʃ] *vt* - **1.** [reject] anular, invalidar - **2.** [quell] reprimir, sofocar.

quasi- ['kweızaı] *prefix* cuasi-.

quaver ['kweıvə'] <> *n* MUS corchea *f*. <> *vi* temblar.

quay [ki:] *n* muelle *m*.

quayside ['ki:saıd] *n* muelle *m*.

queasy ['kwi:zı] *adj* mareado(da).

queen [kwi:n] *n* - **1.** [gen] reina *f* - **2.** [playing card] dama *f*.

Queen Mother *n*: **the Queen Mother** la reina madre.

queer [kwıə'] <> *adj* - **1.** [odd] raro(ra), extraño(ña) - **2.** *inf pej* [homosexual] marica. <> *n inf pej* marica *m*.

quell [kwel] *vt* - **1.** [rebellion] sofocar, reprimir - **2.** [feelings] dominar, contener.

quench [kwentʃ] *vt* apagar.

querulous ['kwerʊləs] *adj fml* quejumbroso(sa).

query ['kwıərı] <> *n* pregunta *f*, duda *f*. <> *vt* poner en duda.

quest [kwest] *n liter*: **quest (for)** búsqueda *f* (de).

question ['kwestʃn] <> *n* - **1.** [query, problem in exam] pregunta *f* - **2.** [doubt] duda *f*; **to bring sthg into question** hacer reflexionar sobre algo; **to call sthg into question** poner algo en duda; **without question** sin duda; **beyond question** fuera de toda duda - **3.** [issue, matter] cuestión *f*, asunto *m*. <> *vt* - **1.** [ask questions to] preguntar; [interrogate] interrogar - **2.** [express doubt about] cuestionar. <> **in question** *adv*: **the matter in question** el asunto en cuestión. <> **out of the question** *adv* imposible; **that's out of the question!** ¡ni hablar!

questionable ['kwestʃənəbl] *adj* [gen] cuestionable; [taste] dudoso(sa).

question mark *n* (signo *m* de) interrogación *f*.

questionnaire [,kwestʃə'neə'] *n* cuestionario *m*.

queue [kju:] UK <> *n* cola *f*. <> *vi*: **to queue (up for sthg)** hacer cola (para algo).

quibble ['kwıbl] *pej vi* quejarse por tonterías; **to quibble over** OR **about** quejarse tontamente por OR de.

quiche [ki:ʃ] *n* quiche *f*.

quick [kwık] <> *adj* - **1.** [gen] rápido(da); **be quick!** ¡date prisa!; **could we have a quick word?** ¿podríamos hablar un momento? - **2.** [clever - person] espabilado(da); [- wit] agudo(da) - **3.** [irritable]: **a quick temper** un genio vivo. <> *adv* rápidamente.

quicken ['kwıkn] <> *vt* [one's pace] apretar, acelerar. <> *vi* acelerarse.

quickly ['kwıklı] *adv* - **1.** [rapidly] rápidamente, de prisa - **2.** [without delay] rápidamente, en seguida.

quicksand ['kwɪksænd] *n* arenas *fpl* movedizas.

quick-witted [-'wɪtɪd] *adj* agudo(da).

quid [kwɪd] (*pl* quid) *n* UK *inf* libra *f* (esterlina).

quiet ['kwaɪət] <> *adj* - 1. [silent - gen] silencioso(sa); [- room, place] tranquilo(la); **to be quiet** [make no noise] no hacer ruido; **be quiet!** ¡cállate!; **in a quiet voice** en voz baja; **to keep quiet about sthg** guardar silencio sobre algo - 2. [not talkative] callado(da); **to go quiet** callarse - 3. [tranquil, uneventful] tranquilo(la) - 4. [unpublicized - wedding etc] privado(da), íntimo(ma). <> *n* tranquilidad *f*, silencio *m*; **on the quiet** a escondidas. <> *vt US* tranquilizar.
 quiet down <> *vt sep* tranquilizar. <> *vi* tranquilizarse.

quieten ['kwaɪətn] *vt* tranquilizar.
 quieten down <> *vt sep* tranquilizar. <> *vi* tranquilizarse.

quietly ['kwaɪətlɪ] *adv* - 1. [without noise] silenciosamente, sin hacer ruido; **to speak quietly** hablar en voz baja - 2. [without moving] sin moverse - 3. [without excitement] tranquilamente - 4. [without fuss] discretamente.

quilt [kwɪlt] *n* edredón *m*.

quinine [kwɪ'niːn] *n* quinina *f*.

quins UK [kwɪnz], **quints** US [kwɪnts] *npl inf* quintillizos *mpl*, -zas *f*.

quintet [kwɪn'tet] *n* quinteto *m*.

quints US = **quins**.

quintuplets [kwɪn'tjuːplɪts] *npl* quintillizos *mpl*, -zas *f*.

quip [kwɪp] *n* ocurrencia *f*, salida *f*.

quirk [kwɜːk] *n* - 1. [habit] manía *f*, rareza *f* - 2. [strange event] extraña coincidencia *f*.

quit [kwɪt] <> *vt* (*UK* quit OR -ted, *US* quit) - 1. [resign from] dejar, abandonar - 2. [stop]: **to quit doing sthg** dejar de hacer algo - 3. COMPUT salir de. <> *vi* (*UK* quit OR -ted, *US* quit) - 1. [resign] dimitir - 2. COMPUT salir.

quite [kwaɪt] *adv* - 1. [completely] totalmente, completamente - 2. [fairly] bastante; **quite a lot of people** bastante gente - 3. [after negative]: **it's not quite big enough** no es todo lo grande que tendría que ser; **I'm not quite sure** no estoy del todo seguro; **I don't quite understand/know** no entiendo/sé muy bien - 4. [to emphasize]: **quite a...** todo un (toda una)...; **quite the opposite** todo lo contrario - 5. [to express agreement]: **quite (so)!** ¡efectivamente!, ¡desde luego!

quits [kwɪts] *adj inf*: **to be quits (with sb)** estar en paz (con alguien); **to call it quits** dejarlo así.

quiver ['kwɪvəʳ] <> *n* [for arrows] carcaj *m*. <> *vi* temblar, estremecerse.

quiz [kwɪz] <> *n* (*pl* -zes) - 1. [gen] concurso *m* - 2. US SCH control *m*. <> *vt*: **to quiz sb (about)** interrogar a alguien (sobre).

quizzical ['kwɪzɪkl] *adj* burlón(ona).

quota ['kwəʊtə] *n* cuota *f*.

quotation [kwəʊ'teɪʃn] *n* - 1. [citation] cita *f* - 2. COMM presupuesto *m*.

quotation marks *npl* comillas *fpl*.

quote [kwəʊt] <> *n* - 1. [citation] cita *f* - 2. COMM presupuesto *m*. <> *vt* - 1. [cite] citar - 2. [figures, example, price] dar; **he quoted £100** fijó un precio de 100 libras. <> *vi* - 1. [cite]: **to quote (from)** citar (de) - 2. COMM: **to quote for** dar un presupuesto por.

quotient ['kwəʊʃnt] *n* cociente *m*.

R

r (*pl* r's OR rs), **R** (*pl* R's OR Rs) [ɑːʳ] *n* [letter] r *f*, R *f*.

rabbi ['ræbaɪ] *n* rabino *m*.

rabbit ['ræbɪt] *n* conejo *m*.

rabbit hutch *n* conejera *f*.

rabble ['ræbl] *n* chusma *f*, populacho *m*.

rabies ['reɪbiːz] *n* rabia *f*.

RAC (*abbr of* Royal Automobile Club) *n* asociación británica del automóvil, ≃ RACE *m*.

race [reɪs] <> *n* - 1. *lit* & *fig* [competition] carrera *f* - 2. [people, descent] raza *f*. <> *vt* - 1. [compete against] competir con *(corriendo)*; **they raced each other to the door** echaron una carrera hasta la puerta - 2. [cars, pigeons] hacer carreras de; [horses] hacer correr. <> *vi* - 1. [rush] ir corriendo - 2. [beat fast] acelerarse.

race car US = **racing car**.

racecourse ['reɪskɔːs] *n* hipódromo *m*.

race driver US = **racing driver**.

racehorse ['reɪshɔːs] *n* caballo *m* de carreras.

racetrack ['reɪstræk] *n* [for horses] hipódromo *m*; [for cars] autódromo *m*.

racewalking ['reɪswɔːkɪŋ] *n* marcha *f* atlética.

racial ['reɪʃl] *adj* racial.

racial discrimination n discriminación f racial.

racing ['reɪsɪŋ] n carreras fpl, motor racing carreras de coches.

racing car UK, **race car** US n coche m de carreras, auto m de carrera Amér.

racing driver UK, **race driver** US n piloto mf de carreras.

racism ['reɪsɪzm], **racialism** n racismo m.

racist ['reɪsɪst] <> adj racista. <> n racista mf.

rack [ræk] <> n - 1. [for magazines] revistero m; [for bottles] botellero m; [for plates] escurreplatos m inv; [for clothes] percha f - 2. [for luggage] portaequipajes m inv. <> vt: to be racked by OR with liter estar transido(da) de; to rack one's brains UK devanarse los sesos.

racket, racquet ['rækɪt] n - 1. SPORT raqueta f - 2. [noise] jaleo m, alboroto m - 3. [swindle] timo m - 4. [illegal activity] negocio m sucio.

racquet ['rækɪt] n = racket.

racy ['reɪsɪ] adj entretenido(da) y picante.

radar ['reɪdɑ:r] n radar m.

radiant ['reɪdjənt] adj - 1. [happy] radiante - 2. liter [brilliant] resplandeciente.

radiate ['reɪdɪeɪt] <> vt lit & fig irradiar. <> vi - 1. [be emitted] ser irradiado(da) - 2. [spread from centre] salir, extenderse.

radiation [,reɪdɪ'eɪʃn] n radiación f.

radiator ['reɪdɪeɪtər] n radiador m.

radical ['rædɪkl] <> adj radical. <> n POL radical mf.

radically ['rædɪklɪ] adv radicalmente.

radii ['reɪdɪaɪ] npl ⊳ radius.

radio ['reɪdɪəʊ] <> n (pl -s) radio f. <> comp de radio, radiofónico(-s).

radioactive [,reɪdɪəʊ'æktɪv] adj radiactivo(va).

radio alarm n radiodespertador m.

radio-controlled [-kən'trəʊld] adj teledirigido(da).

radiography [,reɪdɪ'ɒɡrəfɪ] n radiografía f.

radiology [,reɪdɪ'ɒlədʒɪ] n radiología f.

radiotherapy [,reɪdɪəʊ'θerəpɪ] n radioterapia f.

radish ['rædɪʃ] n rábano m.

radius ['reɪdɪəs] (pl radii) n [gen & ANAT] radio m.

RAF [ɑ:reɪ'ef, ræf] n abbr of **Royal Air Force**.

raffle ['ræfl] <> n rifa f, sorteo m. <> comp: raffle ticket boleto m. <> vt rifar.

raft [rɑ:ft] n [craft] balsa f.

rafter ['rɑ:ftər] n viga f (de armadura de tejado).

rag [ræg] n - 1. [piece of cloth] trapo m - 2. pej [newspaper] perioducho m. ⬛ **rags** npl [clothes] harapos mpl.

rag-and-bone man n trapero m.

rag doll n muñeca f de trapo.

rage [reɪdʒ] <> n - 1. [fury] rabia f, ira f - 2. inf [fashion]: it's all the rage es la última moda. <> vi - 1. [behave angrily] estar furioso(sa) - 2. [subj: storm, sea] enfurecerse; [subj: disease] hacer estragos; [subj: argument, controversy] continuar con violencia.

ragged ['rægɪd] adj - 1. [wearing torn clothes] andrajoso(sa), harapiento(ta) - 2. [torn] hecho(cha) jirones.

rag week n UK semana en que los universitarios organizan actividades divertidas con fines benéficos.

raid [reɪd] <> n - 1. [attack] incursión f - 2. [forced entry - by robbers] asalto m; [- by police] redada f. <> vt - 1. [attack] atacar por sorpresa - 2. [subj: robbers] asaltar; [subj: police] hacer una redada en.

raider ['reɪdər] n [attacker] invasor m, -ra f.

rail [reɪl] n - 1. [on staircase] barandilla f - 2. [bar] barra f; towel rail toallero m - 3. (U) [form of transport] ferrocarril m; by rail por ferrocarril - 4. [of railway line] carril m, riel m.

railcard ['reɪlkɑ:d] n UK tarjeta que permite algunos descuentos al viajar en tren.

railing ['reɪlɪŋ] n reja f.

railway UK ['reɪlweɪ], **railroad** US ['reɪlrəʊd] n - 1. [company] ferrocarril m - 2. [route] línea f de ferrocarril.

railway line n [route] línea f de ferrocarril; [track] vía f férrea.

railwayman ['reɪlweɪmən] (pl -men [-mən]) n UK ferroviario m.

railway station n estación f de ferrocarril.

railway track n vía f férrea.

rain [reɪn] <> n lluvia f; in the rain bajo la lluvia. <> impers vb METEOR llover. <> vi caer.

rainbow ['reɪnbəʊ] n arco m iris.

rain check n esp US: I'll take a rain check (on that) no lo quiero ahora, pero igual me apunto la próxima vez.

raincoat ['reɪnkəʊt] n impermeable m.

raindrop ['reɪndrɒp] n gota f de lluvia.

rainfall ['reɪnfɔ:l] n pluviosidad f.

rain forest n bosque m tropical.

rainy ['reɪnɪ] adj lluvioso(sa).

raise [reɪz] <> vt - 1. [lift up] levantar; [flag] izar - 2. [increase - level] aumentar; to raise one's voice levantar la voz - 3. [improve] elevar - 4. [obtain - from donations] recaudar; [- by selling, borrowing] conseguir - 5. [memory, thoughts] traer; [doubts, fears] levantar

- **6.** [bring up, breed] criar - **7.** [crops] cultivar - **8.** [mention] plantear - **9.** [build] construir. ⬦ *n US* aumento *m*.

raisin ['reɪzn] *n* pasa *f*.

rake [reɪk] ⬦ *n* [implement] rastrillo *m*. ⬦ *vt* [smooth] rastrillar.

rally ['rælɪ] ⬦ *n* - **1.** [meeting] mitin *m* - **2.** [car race] rally *m* - **3.** [in tennis etc] peloteo *m*. ⬦ *vt* reunir. ⬦ *vi* - **1.** [come together] reunirse - **2.** [recover] recuperarse. ◆ **rally round** ⬦ *vt insep* formar una piña con. ⬦ *vi inf* formar una piña.

ram [ræm] ⬦ *n* carnero *m*. ⬦ *vt* - **1.** [crash into] embestir - **2.** [force] embutir.

RAM [ræm] (*abbr of* random access memory) *n* COMPUT RAM *f*.

ramble ['ræmbl] ⬦ *n* paseo *m* por el campo. ⬦ *vi* - **1.** [walk] pasear - **2.** [talk] divagar. ◆ **ramble on** *vi* divagar sin parar.

rambler ['ræmblər] *n* [walker] excursionista *mf*.

rambling ['ræmblɪŋ] *adj* - **1.** [building, house] laberíntico(ca) - **2.** [speech, writing] incoherente.

ramp [ræmp] *n* - **1.** [slope] rampa *f* - **2.** AUT [in road] rompecoches *m inv*.

rampage [ræm'peɪdʒ] *n*: **to go on the rampage** desbandarse.

rampant ['ræmpənt] *adj* desenfrenado(da).

ramparts ['ræmpɑːts] *npl* murallas *fpl*.

ramshackle ['ræm,ʃækl] *adj* destartalado(da).

ran [ræn] *pt* ▷ **run**.

ranch [rɑːntʃ] *n* rancho *m*.

rancher ['rɑːntʃər] *n* ranchero *m*, -ra *f*.

rancid ['rænsɪd] *adj* rancio(cia).

rancour *UK*, **rancor** *US* ['ræŋkər] *n* rencor *m*.

random ['rændəm] ⬦ *adj* - **1.** [arbitrary] hecho(cha) al azar - **2.** TECH aleatorio(ria). ⬦ *n*: **at random** al azar.

random access memory *n* COMPUT memoria *f* de acceso aleatorio.

R and R (*abbr of* rest and recreation) *n US* permiso militar.

randy ['rændɪ] *adj inf* cachondo(da), caliente.

rang [ræŋ] *pt* ▷ **ring**.

range [reɪndʒ] ⬦ *n* - **1.** [of missile, telescope] alcance *m*; [of ship, plane] autonomía *f*; **to be out of/within range** estar fuera del/al alcance; **at close range** de cerca - **2.** [variety] gama *f* - **3.** [of prices, salaries] escala *f* - **4.** [of mountains] cordillera *f* - **5.** [shooting area] campo *m* de tiro - **6.** [of voice] registro *m*. ⬦ *vt* alinear. ⬦ *vi* [vary]: **to range from... to..., to range**

between... and... oscilar *OR* fluctuar entre... y...; **prices ranging from $20 to $100** precios que van desde veinte hasta cien dólares.

ranger ['reɪndʒər] *n* guardabosques *mf inv*.

rank [ræŋk] ⬦ *adj* - **1.** [utter, absolute - bad luck, outsider] absoluto(ta); [- disgrace, injustice] flagrante - **2.** [foul] pestilente. ⬦ *n* - **1.** [position, grade] grado *m*, rango *m* - **2.** [social class] clase *f*, categoría *f*; **the rank and file** las bases - **3.** [row] fila *f*. ⬦ *vt* [class]: **to be ranked** estar clasificado(da). ⬦ *vi*: **to rank as** estar considerado(da) (como); **to rank among** encontrarse entre. ◆ **ranks** *npl* - **1.** MIL: **the ranks** los soldados rasos - **2.** *fig* [members] filas *fpl*.

rankle ['ræŋkl] *vi* doler.

ransack ['rænsæk] *vt* [search] registrar a fondo; [plunder] saquear.

ransom ['rænsəm] *n* rescate *m*; **to hold sb to ransom** *fig* hacer chantaje a alguien.

rant [rænt] *vi* despotricar.

rap [ræp] ⬦ *n* - **1.** [knock] golpecito *m* - **2.** [type of music] rap *m* - **3.** *US* [legal charge] acusación *f*; **rap sheet** antecedentes *mpl* penales. ⬦ *vt* dar un golpecito en.

rape [reɪp] ⬦ *n* - **1.** [crime] violación *f* - **2.** BOT colza *f*. ⬦ *vt* [person] violar.

rapeseed oil ['reɪpsiːd-] *n* aceite *m* de colza.

rapid ['ræpɪd] *adj* rápido(da). ◆ **rapids** *npl* rápidos *mpl*.

rapidly ['ræpɪdlɪ] *adv* rápidamente.

rapist ['reɪpɪst] *n* violador *m*, -ra *f*.

rapport [ræ'pɔːr] *n* compenetración *f*.

rapture ['ræptʃər] *n* arrobamiento *m*; **to go into raptures over** *OR* **about** deshacerse en elogios a.

rapturous ['ræptʃərəs] *adj* muy entusiasta.

rare [reər] *adj* - **1.** [scarce] poco común, raro(ra) - **2.** [infrequent] poco frecuente, raro(ra) - **3.** [exceptional] raro(ra), excepcional - **4.** CULIN poco hecho(cha).

rarely ['reəlɪ] *adv* raras veces.

raring ['reərɪŋ] *adj*: **to be raring to go** estar ansioso(sa) por empezar.

rarity ['reərətɪ] *n* rareza *f*.

rascal ['rɑːskl] *n* pícaro *m*, -ra *f*.

rash [ræʃ] ⬦ *adj* precipitado(da). ⬦ *n* - **1.** MED erupción *f* (cutánea), sarpullido *m* - **2.** [spate] aluvión *m*.

rasher ['ræʃər] *n* loncha *f*.

rasp [rɑːsp] *n* - **1.** [harsh sound] chirrido *m* - **2.** [tool] lima *f* gruesa.

raspberry ['rɑːzbərɪ] *n* [fruit] frambuesa *f*.

rat [ræt] *n* [animal] rata *f*.

rate [reɪt] ⬦ *n* - **1.** [speed] ritmo *m*; **at this rate** a este paso - **2.** [of birth, death] índice *m*; [of unemployment, inflation] tasa *f* - **3.** [price] precio *m*, tarifa *f*; [of interest] tipo *m*. ⬦ *vt*

- **1.** [consider]: **to rate sthg/sb (as/among)** considerar algo/a alguien (como/entre) - **2.** UK inf [have a good opinion of] valorar mucho. ■ [deserve] merecer. ◆ **rates** npl UK ≈ contribución f urbana. ◆ **at any rate** adv - **1.** [at least] al menos - **2.** [anyway] de todos modos.

ratepayer ['reɪtˌpeɪəʳ] n UK contribuyente mf.

rather ['rɑːðəʳ] adv - **1.** [to quite a large extent] bastante - **2.** [to a great extent] muy - **3.** [to a limited extent] algo; **he's rather like you** se parece (en) algo a ti - **4.** [as preference]: **I would rather wait** preferiría esperar; **I'd rather not stay** prefiero no quedarme; **would you like to come? – I'd rather not** ¿quieres venir? – mejor no - **5.** [more exactly]: **or rather...** o más bien..., o mejor dicho... - **6.** [on the contrary]: **(but) rather...** (sino) más bien OR por el contrario... ◆ **rather than** conj en vez de.

ratify ['rætɪfaɪ] vt ratificar.

rating ['reɪtɪŋ] n [standing] clasificación f.

ratio ['reɪʃɪəʊ] (pl -s) n proporción f, relación f.

ration ['ræʃn] ◇ n ración f. ◇ vt racionar. ◆ **rations** npl [supplies] víveres mpl.

rational ['ræʃənl] adj racional.

rationale [ˌræʃə'nɑːl] n lógica f, razones fpl.

rationalize, -ise ['ræʃənəlaɪz] vt racionalizar.

rat race n mundo despiadadamente competitivo de los negocios.

rattle ['rætl] ◇ n - **1.** [of engine, metal] traqueteo m; [of chains] crujido m; [of glass] tintineo m; [of typewriter] repiqueteo m - **2.** [for baby] sonajero m. ◇ vt - **1.** [make rattle] hacer sonar - **2.** [unsettle] desconcertar. ◇ vi golpetear; [chains] crujir; [glass] tintinear.

rattlesnake ['rætlsneɪk], **rattler** US ['rætləʳ] n serpiente f de cascabel.

raucous ['rɔːkəs] adj ronco(ca) y estridente.

ravage ['rævɪdʒ] vt estragar, asolar. ◆ **ravages** npl estragos mpl.

rave [reɪv] ◇ n [party] macrofiesta f tecno. ◇ vi - **1.** [talk angrily]: **to rave at sb** increpar a alguien; **to rave against sb/sthg** despotricar contra alguien/algo - **2.** [talk enthusiastically]: **to rave about sthg** deshacerse en alabanzas sobre algo.

raven ['reɪvn] n cuervo m.

ravenous ['rævənəs] adj [person, animal] famélico(ca); [appetite] voraz.

ravine [rə'viːn] n barranco m.

raving ['reɪvɪŋ] adj [lunatic] de atar; [fantasy] delirante.

ravioli [ˌrævɪ'əʊlɪ] n (U) raviolis mpl.

ravishing ['rævɪʃɪŋ] adj [sight, beauty] de ensueño; [person] bellísimo(ma).

raw [rɔː] adj - **1.** [uncooked] crudo(da) - **2.** [untreated - silk] crudo(da); [- sewage] sin tratar; [- spirit] puro(ra) - **3.** [painful] en carne viva - **4.** [inexperienced] novato(ta) - **5.** [cold] crudo(da).

raw deal n: **to get a raw deal** recibir un trato injusto.

raw material n materia f prima.

ray [reɪ] n rayo m; **ray of hope** resquicio m de esperanza.

rayon ['reɪɒn] n rayón m.

raze [reɪz] vt arrasar.

razor ['reɪzəʳ] n [wet shaver] navaja f; [electric machine] maquinilla f de afeitar.

razor blade n hoja f de afeitar.

RC abbr of **Roman Catholic**.

Rd abbr of **road**.

R & D (abbr of **research and development**) n I + D f.

re [riː] prep Ref.

RE n (abbr of **religious education**) religión f.

reach [riːtʃ] ◇ n alcance m; **he has a long reach** tiene los brazos largos; **within (sb's) reach** [easily touched] al alcance (de alguien); [easily travelled to] a poca distancia (de alguien); **out of OR beyond sb's reach** fuera del alcance de alguien. ◇ vt - **1.** [gen] alcanzar, llegar a - **2.** [arrive at - place etc] llegar a - **3.** [get by stretching - object, shelf] alcanzar - **4.** [contact] localizar. ◇ vi: **I can't reach** no llego; **to reach out/across** alargar la mano; **to reach down** agacharse.

react [rɪ'ækt] vi - **1.** [respond]: **to react (to)** reaccionar (a OR ante) - **2.** [rebel]: **to react against** reaccionar en contra de - **3.** CHEM: **to react with** reaccionar con.

reaction [rɪ'ækʃn] n: **reaction (to/against)** reacción f (a/contra).

reactionary [rɪ'ækʃənrɪ] ◇ adj reaccionario(ria). ◇ n reaccionario m, -ria f.

reactor [rɪ'æktəʳ] n reactor m.

read [riːd] ◇ vt (pt & pp read [red]) - **1.** [gen & COMPUT] leer; **she can't read my writing** no entiende mi letra - **2.** [subj: sign, words] poner, decir - **3.** [subj: thermometer, meter etc] marcar - **4.** [interpret] interpretar - **5.** UK UNIV estudiar. ◇ vi (pt & pp read [red]) - **1.** [person] leer - **2.** [read aloud]: **to read to sb** leerle a alguien - **3.** [piece of writing]: **to read well** estar bien escrito. ◆ **read out** vt sep leer en voz alta. ◆ **read through** vt sep leer. ◆ **read up on** vt insep leer OR documentarse sobre.

readable ['riːdəbl] adj ameno(na).

reader ['riːdəʳ] n - **1.** [person who reads] lector m, -ra f - **2.** COMPUT lector m.

readership ['riːdəʃɪp] n [total number of readers] lectores mpl.

readily ['redɪlɪ] *adv* - **1.** [willingly] de buena gana - **2.** [easily] fácilmente.

reading ['riːdɪŋ] *n* - **1.** [gen] lectura *f* - **2.** [recital] recital *m*.

readjust [ˌriːə'dʒʌst] *vt* reajustar. ⟨⟩ *vi*: **to readjust (to)** volverse a adaptar (a).

readout ['riːdaʊt] *n* COMPUT visualización *f*.

ready ['redɪ] ⟨⟩ *adj* - **1.** [prepared] listo(ta), preparado(da); **to be ready for sthg/to do sthg** estar listo para algo/para hacer algo; **to get ready** [prepare] prepararse; [for going out] arreglarse - **2.** [willing]: **to be ready to do sthg** estar dispuesto(ta) a hacer algo - **3.** [in need of]: **to be ready for sthg** necesitar algo - **4.** [likely]: **to be ready to do sthg** estar a punto de hacer algo - **5.** [smile] pronto(ta). ⟨⟩ *vt* preparar; **to ready o.s. for sthg** prepararse para algo.

ready cash *n* dinero *m* contante.

ready-made *adj* [products] hecho(cha); [clothes] confeccionado(da).

ready money *n* dinero *m* contante.

ready-to-wear *adj* confeccionado(da).

reafforestation ['riːəˌfɒrɪ'steɪʃn], **reforestation** *n* repoblación *f* forestal.

real ['rɪəl] ⟨⟩ *adj* - **1.** [not imagined, actual] real; **the real thing** lo auténtico; **for real** de verdad; **in real terms** en términos reales - **2.** [genuine, proper] auténtico(ca); **a real friend** un amigo de verdad. ⟨⟩ *adv US* muy.

real estate *n* propiedad *f* inmobiliaria.

real estate agent *n US* agente inmobiliario *m*, agente inmobiliaria *f*.

realign [ˌriːə'laɪn] *vt* volver a alinear.

realism ['rɪəlɪzm] *n* realismo *m*.

realistic [ˌrɪə'lɪstɪk] *adj* realista.

reality [rɪ'ælətɪ] *n* realidad *f*.

reality TV *n* (U) reality shows *mpl*.

realization [ˌrɪəlaɪ'zeɪʃn] *n* - **1.** [recognition] comprensión *f* - **2.** [achievement] consecución *f*.

realize, -ise ['rɪəlaɪz] *vt* - **1.** [become aware of] darse cuenta de - **2.** [produce, achieve, make profit of] realizar.

really ['rɪəlɪ] ⟨⟩ *adv* - **1.** [for emphasis] de verdad; **really good** buenísimo; **did you like it? – not really** ¿te gustó? – la verdad es que no - **2.** [actually, honestly] realmente - **3.** [to sound less negative] en realidad. ⟨⟩ *excl* - **1.** [expressing doubt]: **really?** [in affirmatives] ¿ah sí?; [in negatives] ¿ah no? - **2.** [expressing surprise, disbelief]: **really?** ¿de verdad?, ¿seguro?

realm [relm] *n* - **1.** [field] campo *m*, esfera *f* - **2.** [kingdom] reino *m*.

realtor ['rɪəltər] *n US* agente inmobiliario *m*, agente inmobiliaria *f*.

reap [riːp] *vt lit & fig* cosechar.

reappear [ˌriːə'pɪər] *vi* reaparecer.

rear [rɪər] ⟨⟩ *adj* trasero(ra), de atrás. ⟨⟩ *n* [back] parte *f* de atrás; **to bring up the rear** cerrar la marcha. ⟨⟩ *vt* criar. ⟨⟩ *vi*: **to rear (up)** encabritarse.

rearm [riː'ɑːm] *vi* rearmarse.

rearmost ['rɪəməʊst] *adj* último(ma).

rearrange [ˌriːə'reɪndʒ] *vt* - **1.** [room, furniture] colocar de otro modo; [system, plans] reorganizar - **2.** [meeting] volver a concertar.

rearview mirror ['rɪəvjuː-] *n* (espejo *m*) retrovisor *m*.

reason ['riːzn] ⟨⟩ *n* - **1.** [cause]: **reason (for)** razón *f* (de); **I don't know the reason why** no sé por qué; **by reason of** *fml* a causa de; **for some reason** por alguna razón - **2.** [justification]: **to have reason to do sthg** tener motivos para hacer algo - **3.** [rationality] razón *f*; **it stands to reason** es lógico; **to listen to reason** avenirse a razones. ⟨⟩ *vt* & *vi* razonar.
➤ **reason with** *vt insep* razonar con.

reasonable ['riːznəbl] *adj* razonable.

reasonably ['riːznəblɪ] *adv* razonablemente.

reasoned ['riːznd] *adj* razonado(da).

reasoning ['riːznɪŋ] *n* razonamiento *m*.

reassess [ˌriːə'ses] *vt* reconsiderar.

reassurance [ˌriːə'ʃʊərəns] *n* - **1.** (U) [comfort] palabras *fpl* tranquilizadoras - **2.** [promise] promesa *f*.

reassure [ˌriːə'ʃʊər] *vt* tranquilizar.

reassuring [ˌriːə'ʃʊərɪŋ] *adj* tranquilizador(ra).

rebate ['riːbeɪt] *n* - **1.** [refund] devolución *f* - **2.** [discount] bonificación *f*.

rebel ⟨⟩ *n* ['rebl] rebelde *mf*. ⟨⟩ *vi* [rɪ'bel]: **to rebel (against)** rebelarse (contra), alebrestarse (contra) *Col, Méx & Ven*.

rebellion [rɪ'beljən] *n* rebelión *f*.

rebellious [rɪ'beljəs] *adj* rebelde.

rebound ⟨⟩ *n* ['riːbaʊnd]: **on the rebound** [ball] de rebote *m*. ⟨⟩ *vi* [ˌrɪ'baʊnd] [bounce back] rebotar.

re-brand *vt* relanzar con otra marca.

rebuff [rɪ'bʌf] *n* [slight] desaire *m*; [refusal] negativa *f*.

rebuild [ˌriː'bɪld] (*pt & pp* **-built**) *vt* reconstruir.

rebuke [rɪ'bjuːk] ⟨⟩ *n* reprimenda *f*. ⟨⟩ *vt*: **to rebuke sb (for)** reprender a alguien (por).

rebuttal [riː'bʌtl] *n* refutación *f*.

recalcitrant [rɪ'kælsɪtrənt] *adj* recalcitrante.

recall [rɪ'kɔːl] ⟨⟩ *n* [memory] memoria *f*. ⟨⟩ *vt* - **1.** [remember] recordar, acordarse de - **2.** [ambassador] retirar; [goods] retirar del mercado.

recant [rɪ'kænt] *vi* [deny statement] retractarse; [deny religion] renegar de la fe.

recap ['ri:kæp] *vt* ⟨> *vi* resumir, ▪▪▪▪▪▪ tulación *f.* ⟨> *vt* [summarize] recapitular, resumir. ⟨> *vi* recapitular, resumir.

recapitulate [,ri:kə'pɪtjʊleɪt] *vt* & *vi* recapitular, resumir.

recd, rec'd (*abbr of* received) rbdo.

recede [ri:'si:d] *vi* - 1. [person, car] alejarse; [coastline] retroceder - 2. *fig* [disappear] esfumarse.

receding [rɪ'si:dɪŋ] *adj* [chin, forehead] hundida; **to have a receding hairline** tener entradas.

receipt [rɪ'si:t] *n* recibo *m*; **to acknowledge receipt** acusar recibo. ◆ **receipts** *npl* recaudación *f.*

receive [rɪ'si:v] *vt* - 1. [gen] recibir; **I received a fine** me pusieron una multa - 2. [reaction] tener; [injury, setback] sufrir - 3. [greet]: **to be well/badly received** tener una buena/mala acogida.

receiver [rɪ'si:vər] *n* - 1. [of telephone] auricular *m* - 2. [radio, TV set] receptor *m* - 3. [criminal] perista *mf* - 4. FIN síndico *m*, -ca *f.*

recent ['ri:snt] *adj* reciente.

recently ['ri:sntlɪ] *adv* recientemente.

receptacle [rɪ'septəkl] *n* receptáculo *m.*

reception [rɪ'sepʃn] *n* - 1. [gen] recepción *f* - 2. [welcome] recibimiento *m.*

reception desk *n* recepción *f.*

receptionist [rɪ'sepʃənɪst] *n* recepcionista *mf.*

recess ['ri:ses, UK rɪ'ses] *n* - 1. [vacation] periodo *m* vacacional; **to be in recess** estar clausurado(da) - 2. [alcove] nicho *m*, hueco *m* - 3. *US* SCH recreo *m.* ◆ **recesses** *npl* [of mind, heart] recovecos *mpl*; [of building] escondrijos *mpl.*

recession [rɪ'seʃn] *n* recesión *f.*

recharge [,ri:'tʃɑːdʒ] *vt* recargar.

recipe ['resɪpɪ] *n* fig & CULIN receta *f.*

recipient [rɪ'sɪpɪənt] *n* [of letter, cheque] destinatario *m*, -ria *f.*

reciprocal [rɪ'sɪprəkl] *adj* recíproco(ca).

recital [rɪ'saɪtl] *n* recital *m.*

recite [rɪ'saɪt] *vt* - 1. [poem] recitar - 2. [list] enumerar.

reckless ['reklɪs] *adj* [gen] imprudente; [driver, driving] temerario(ria).

reckon ['rekn] *vt* - 1. *inf* [think]: **to reckon (that)** pensar que - 2. [consider, judge]: **to be reckoned to be sthg** ser considerado(da) algo - 3. [calculate] calcular. ◆ **reckon on** *vt insep* contar con. ◆ **reckon with** *vt insep* [expect] contar con.

reckoning ['rekənɪŋ] *n* [calculation] cálculo *m.*

reclaim [rɪ'kleɪm] *vt* - 1. [claim back] reclamar - 2. [recover] recuperar; **to reclaim land from the sea** ganarle tierras al mar.

recline [rɪ'klaɪn] *vi* reclinarse.

reclining [rɪ'klaɪnɪŋ] *adj* [seat] reclinable.

recluse [rɪ'klu:s] *n* solitario *m*, -ria *f.*

recognition [,rekəg'nɪʃn] *n* reconocimiento *m*; **to have changed beyond** OR **out of all recognition** estar irreconocible; **in recognition of** en reconocimiento a.

recognizable ['rekəgnaɪzəbl] *adj* reconocible.

recognize, -ise ['rekəgnaɪz] *vt* reconocer.

recoil ⟨> *vi* [rɪ'kɔɪl] [draw back] retroceder, echarse atrás. ⟨> *n* ['ri:kɔɪl] [of gun] retroceso *m.*

recollect [,rekə'lekt] *vt* & *vi* recordar.

recollection [,rekə'lekʃn] *n* recuerdo *m.*

recommend [,rekə'mend] *vt* recomendar.

recompense ['rekəmpens] ⟨> *n*: **recompense (for)** compensación *f* OR indemnización *f* (por). ⟨> *vt*: **to recompense sb (for)** recompensar a alguien (por).

reconcile ['rekənsaɪl] *vt* - 1. [find agreement between] conciliar - 2. [make friendly again] reconciliar; **to be reconciled with sb** reconciliarse con alguien - 3. [accept]: **to reconcile o.s. to** resignarse a.

reconditioned [,ri:kən'dɪʃnd] *adj* reparado(da).

reconnaissance [rɪ'kɒnɪsəns] *n* reconocimiento *m.*

reconnoitre *UK*, **reconnoiter** *US* [,rekə'nɔɪtər] ⟨> *vt* reconocer. ⟨> *vi* hacer un reconocimiento.

reconsider [,ri:kən'sɪdər] *vt* & *vi* reconsiderar.

reconstruct [,ri:kən'strʌkt] *vt* [building, crime] reconstruir.

record ⟨> *n* ['rekɔ:d] - 1. [of event, piece of information & COMPUT] registro *m*; [of meeting] actas *fpl*; **to go/be on record as saying that...** declarar/haber declarado públicamente que...; **off the record** confidencial - 2. [vinyl disc] disco *m* - 3. [best achievement] récord *m* - 4. [past results] resultados *mpl* - 5. HIST historial *m*; **criminal record** antecedentes *mpl* penales. ⟨> *vt* [rɪ'kɔ:d] - 1. [write down] anotar - 2. [document] documentar - 3. [put on tape] grabar. ⟨> *vi* [rɪ'kɔ:d] grabar. ⟨> *adj* ['rekɔ:d] récord (*inv*).

recorded delivery [rɪ'kɔ:dɪd-] *n* correo *m* certificado.

recorder [rɪ'kɔ:dər] *n* [musical instrument] flauta *f.*

record holder *n* plusmarquista *mf.*

recording [rɪ'kɔ:dɪŋ] *n* grabación *f.*

record player n tocadiscos m inv.

recount ⋄ n ['ri:kaʊnt] segundo recuento m. ⋄ vt - 1. [rɪ'kaʊnt] [narrate] narrar - 2. [ˌri:'kaʊnt] [count again] volver a contar.

recoup [rɪ'ku:p] vt recuperar.

recourse [rɪ'kɔ:s] n fml: **to have recourse to** recurrir a.

recover [rɪ'kʌvəʳ] ⋄ vt - 1. [retrieve, recoup] recuperar - 2. [regain - calm etc] recobrar. ⋄ vi: **to recover (from)** recuperarse (de).

recovery [rɪ'kʌvərɪ] n recuperación f.

recreation [ˌrekrɪ'eɪʃn] n [leisure] esparcimiento m, recreo m.

recrimination [rɪˌkrɪmɪ'neɪʃn] n recriminación f.

recruit [rɪ'kru:t] ⋄ n recluta mf. ⋄ vt - 1. [gen] reclutar; **to recruit sb (for sthg/to do sthg)** reclutar a alguien (para algo/para hacer algo) - 2. [find, employ] contratar. ⋄ vi buscar empleados nuevos.

recruitment [rɪ'kru:tmənt] n [gen] reclutamiento m; [of staff] contratación f.

rectangle ['rek,tæŋgl] n rectángulo m.

rectangular [rek'tæŋgjʊləʳ] adj rectangular.

rectify ['rektɪfaɪ] vt rectificar.

rector ['rektəʳ] n - 1. [priest] párroco m - 2. Scotland [head - of school] director m, -ra f; [- of college, university] rector m, -ra f.

rectory ['rektərɪ] n rectoría f.

recuperate [rɪ'ku:pəreɪt] ⋄ vt recuperar. ⋄ vi: **to recuperate (from)** recuperarse (de).

recur [rɪ'kɜ:ʳ] vi repetirse.

recurrence [rɪ'kʌrəns] n repetición f.

recurrent [rɪ'kʌrənt] adj que se repite.

recycle [ˌri:'saɪkl] vt reciclar.

recycle bin n COMPUT papelera f.

red [red] ⋄ adj rojo(ja); **to go red** [with embarrassment] ponerse colorado(da). ⋄ n [colour] rojo m; **to be in the red** inf estar en números rojos.

red card n FTBL: **to show sb the red card** mostrarle a alguien (la) tarjeta roja.

red carpet n: **to roll out the red carpet for sb** recibir a alguien con todos los honores. ➥ **red-carpet** adj: **to give sb the red-carpet treatment** dispensar a alguien un gran recibimiento.

Red Cross n: **the Red Cross** la Cruz Roja.

redcurrant ['redkʌrənt] n - 1. [fruit] grosella f - 2. [bush] grosellero m.

redden ['redn] ⋄ vt [make red] teñir de rojo. ⋄ vi [flush] enrojecer.

redecorate [ˌri:'dekəreɪt] vt & vi volver a pintar (o empapelar).

redeem [rɪ'di:m] vt - 1. [save, rescue] salvar, rescatar - 2. RELIG redimir - 3. fml [at pawnbroker's] desempeñar.

redeeming [rɪ'di:mɪŋ] adj: **his only redeeming feature** lo único que le salva.

redeploy [ˌri:dɪ'plɔɪ] vt reorganizar.

red-faced [-'feɪst] adj - 1. [flushed] rojo(ja), colorado(da) - 2. [with embarrassment] rojo(ja) de vergüenza.

red-haired [-'heəd] adj pelirrojo(ja).

red-handed [-'hændɪd] adj: **to catch sb red-handed** coger a alguien con las manos en la masa.

redhead ['redhed] n pelirrojo m, -ja f.

red herring n fig [unhelpful clue] pista f falsa; [means of distracting attention] ardid m para distraer la atención.

red-hot adj [metal, person, passion] al rojo (vivo).

redid [ˌri:'dɪd] pt ⊳ **redo**.

redirect [ˌri:dɪ'rekt] vt - 1. [retarget] redirigir - 2. [divert] desviar - 3. [forward] reexpedir.

rediscover [ˌri:dɪs'kʌvəʳ] vt - 1. [re-experience] volver a descubrir - 2. [make popular, famous again]: **to be rediscovered** ser descubierto(ta) de nuevo.

red light n [traffic signal] semáforo m rojo.

red-light district n barrio m chino.

redo [ˌri:'du:] (pt -did, pp -done) vt - 1. [do again] volver a hacer - 2. COMPUT rehacer.

redolent ['redələnt] adj liter [reminiscent]: **to be redolent of sthg** evocar algo.

redouble [ˌri:'dʌbl] vt: **to redouble one's efforts (to do sthg)** redoblar esfuerzos (para hacer algo).

redraft [ˌri:'drɑ:ft] vt volver a redactar.

redress [rɪ'dres] fml ⋄ n (U) reparación f. ⋄ vt: **to redress the balance (between)** equilibrar la balanza (entre).

red tape n fig papeleo m.

reduce [rɪ'dju:s] ⋄ vt reducir; **to be reduced to doing sthg** verse rebajado OR forzado a hacer algo; **it reduced me to tears** me hizo llorar. ⋄ vi US [diet] (intentar) adelgazar.

reduction [rɪ'dʌkʃn] n - 1. [gen]: **reduction (in)** reducción f (de) - 2. COMM: **reduction (of)** descuento m (de).

redundancy [rɪ'dʌndənsɪ] n UK [job loss] despido m.

redundant [rɪ'dʌndənt] adj - 1. UK [jobless]: **to be made redundant** perder el empleo; **to make sb redundant** despedir a alguien - 2. [not required - equipment, factory] innecesario(ria); [- comment] redundante.

reed [ri:d] n - 1. [plant] carrizo m, cañavera f - 2. [of musical instrument] lengüeta f.

reef [ri:f] n arrecife m.

reek [ri:k] vi: **to reek (of)** apestar (a).

reel [ri:l] ◇ n - **1.** [of cotton, on fishing rod] carrete m - **2.** [of film] rollo m. ◇ vi - **1.** [stagger] tambalearse - **2.** [be dizzy]: **to reel from sthg** quedarse atónito(ta) por algo. ◆ **reel in** vt sep sacar enrollando el carrete (en pesca). ◆ **reel off** vt sep recitar al corrido.

reenact [,ri:ɪn'ækt] vt representar de nuevo.

ref [ref] n - **1.** inf SPORT (abbr of referee) árbitro m - **2.** ADMIN (abbr of reference) ref.

refectory [rɪ'fektərɪ] n refectorio m.

refer [rɪ'fɜːr] vt - **1.** [send, direct]: **to refer sb to** [to place] enviar a alguien a; [to source of information] remitir a alguien a - **2.** [report, submit]: **to refer sthg to** remitir algo a. ◆ **refer to** vt insep - **1.** [mention, speak about] referirse a - **2.** [consult] consultar.

referee [,refə'ri:] ◇ n - **1.** SPORT árbitro m - **2.** UK [for job application] persona que proporciona referencias de alguien para un trabajo. ◇ vt & vi SPORT arbitrar.

reference ['refrəns] n - **1.** [mention, reference number]: **to make reference to** hacer referencia a; **with reference to** fml con referencia a - **2.** (U) [for advice, information]: consulta f (a) - **3.** [for job - letter] referencia f; [- person] persona que proporciona referencias de alguien para un trabajo.

reference book n libro m de consulta.

reference number n número m de referencia.

referendum [,refə'rendəm] (pl -s OR -da [-də]) n referéndum m.

refill ◇ n ['ri:fɪl] [for pen] recambio m; inf [of drink]: **would you like a refill?** ¿te apetece otra copa? ◇ vt [,ri:'fɪl] volver a llenar.

refine [rɪ'faɪn] vt - **1.** [oil, food] refinar - **2.** [plan, speech] pulir.

refined [rɪ'faɪnd] adj - **1.** [oil, food, person] refinado(da) - **2.** [equipment, theory] perfeccionado(da).

refinement [rɪ'faɪnmənt] n - **1.** [improvement]: **refinement (on)** mejora f (de) - **2.** (U) [gentility] refinamiento m.

reflect [rɪ'flekt] ◇ vt - **1.** [gen] reflejar - **2.** [think, consider]: **to reflect that...** considerar que... ◇ vi: **to reflect (on OR upon)** reflexionar (sobre).

reflection [rɪ'flekʃn] n - **1.** [gen] reflejo m - **2.** [criticism]: **reflection on** crítica f de - **3.** [thinking] reflexión f; **on reflection** pensándolo bien.

reflector [rɪ'flektər] n reflector m.

reflex ['ri:fleks] n: **reflex (action)** (acto m) reflejo m.

reflexive [rɪ'fleksɪv] adj GRAM reflexivo(va).

reforestation [ri:,fɒrɪ'steɪʃn] = **reafforestation**.

reform [rɪ'fɔːm] ◇ n reforma f. ◇ vt reformar. ◇ vi reformarse.

Reformation [,refə'meɪʃn] n: **the Reformation** la Reforma.

reformatory [rɪ'fɔːmətrɪ] n US reformatorio m.

reformer [rɪ'fɔːmər] n reformador m, -ra f.

refrain [rɪ'freɪn] n [chorus] estribillo m.

refresh [rɪ'freʃ] vt [gen & COMPUT] refrescar; **to refresh sb's memory** refrescarle la memoria a alguien.

refreshed [rɪ'freʃt] adj descansado(da).

refresher course [rɪ'freʃər-] n cursillo m de reciclaje (en el mismo trabajo).

refreshing [rɪ'freʃɪŋ] adj [change, honesty, drink] refrescante; [sleep] vigorizante.

refreshments [rɪ'freʃmənts] npl refrigerio m.

refrigerator [rɪ'frɪdʒəreɪtər] n nevera f, refrigerador m Amér, heladera f R Plata, refrigeradora f Col & Perú.

refuel [,ri:'fjʊəl] ◇ vt (UK pt & pp -led, cont -ling, US pt & pp -ed, cont -ing) llenar de carburante. ◇ vi (UK pt & pp -led, cont -ling, US pt & pp -ed, cont -ing) repostar.

refuge ['refju:dʒ] n refugio m; **to seek OR take refuge (in)** fig buscar refugio (en).

refugee [,refjʊ'dʒi:] n refugiado m, -da f.

refund ◇ n ['ri:fʌnd] reembolso m. ◇ vt [rɪ'fʌnd]: **to refund sthg to sb, to refund sb sthg** reembolsar algo a alguien.

refurbish [,ri:'fɜːbɪʃ] vt [building] restaurar; [office, shop] renovar.

refusal [rɪ'fju:zl] n - **1.** [disagreement, saying no]: **refusal (to do sthg)** negativa f (a hacer algo) - **2.** [withholding, denial] denegación f - **3.** [non-acceptance]: **to meet with refusal** ser rechazado(da).

refuse¹ [rɪ'fju:z] ◇ vt - **1.** [withhold, deny]: **to refuse sb sthg, to refuse sthg to sb** denegar a alguien algo - **2.** [decline, reject] rechazar - **3.** [not agree, be completely unwilling]: **to refuse to do sthg** negarse a hacer algo. ◇ vi negarse.

refuse² ['refju:s] n [rubbish] basura f.

refuse collection ['refju:s-] n recogida f de basuras.

refute [rɪ'fju:t] vt fml refutar.

regain [rɪ'geɪn] vt [leadership, first place] recuperar; [health, composure] recobrar.

regal ['ri:gl] adj regio(gia).

regalia [rɪ'geɪljə] n (U) ropaje m.

regard [rɪ'gɑːd] ◇ n - **1.** fml [respect, esteem]: **regard (for)** estima f OR respeto m (por); **to hold sthg/sb in high regard** tener algo/a alguien en gran estima - **2.** [aspect]: **in this/that regard** a este/ese respecto - **3.** [consideration]: **with no regard for** sin ninguna consideración por. ⬦ *vt* - **1.** [consider]: **to regard o.s. as sthg** considerarse algo - **2.** [look at, view]: **to regard sb/sthg with** ver a alguien/algo con; **to be highly regarded** estar muy bien considerado.

➤ **regards** *npl* [in greetings] recuerdos *mpl*; **give them my regards** salúdales de mi parte. ➤ **as regards** *prep* en cuanto a, por lo que se refiere a. ➤ **in regard to, with regard to** *prep* respecto a, en cuanto a.

regarding [rɪ'gɑːdɪŋ] *prep* respecto a, en cuanto a.

regardless [rɪ'gɑːdlɪs] *adv* a pesar de todo. ➤ **regardless of** *prep* sin tener en cuenta; **regardless of the cost** cueste lo que cueste.

regime [reɪ'ʒiːm] *n* régimen *m*.

regiment ['redʒɪmənt] *n* MIL regimiento *m*.

region ['riːdʒən] *n* región *f*; **in the region of** alrededor de.

regional ['riːdʒənl] *adj* regional.

register ['redʒɪstər] ⬦ *n* [gen] registro *m*; [at school] lista *f*. ⬦ *vt* - **1.** [record - gen] registrar; [- car] matricular - **2.** [express] mostrar, reflejar. ⬦ *vi* - **1.** [be put on official list]: **to register (as/for)** inscribirse (como/para) - **2.** [book in - at hotel] registrarse; [- at conference] inscribirse - **3.** *inf* [be noticed]: **I told him but it didn't seem to register** se lo dije, pero no pareció que lo captara.

registered ['redʒɪstəd] *adj* - **1.** [officially listed] inscrito(ta) oficialmente - **2.** [letter, parcel] certificado(da).

registered trademark *n* marca *f* registrada.

registrar ['redʒɪstrɑːr] *n* - **1.** [keeper of records] registrador *m*, -ra *f* oficial - **2.** UNIV secretario *m*, -ria *f* general - **3.** [doctor] médico *m*, -ca *f* de hospital.

registration [,redʒɪ'streɪʃn] *n* - **1.** [gen] registro *m* - **2.** AUT = **registration number**.

registration number, registration *n* AUT número *m* de matrícula; COMPUT número *m* de registro.

registry ['redʒɪstrɪ] *n* registro *m*.

registry office *n* registro *m* civil.

regret [rɪ'gret] *n* - **1.** *fml* [sorrow] pesar *m* - **2.** [sad feeling]: **I've no regrets about it** no lo lamento en absoluto.

regretfully [rɪ'gretfʊlɪ] *adv* con pesar; **regretfully, we have to announce...** lamentamos tener que anunciar...

regrettable [rɪ'gretəbl] *adj* lamentable.

regroup [,riː'gruːp] *vi* reagruparse.

regular ['regjʊlər] ⬦ *adj* - **1.** [gen] regular - **2.** [customer] habitual - **3.** [time, place] acostumbrado(da); [problem] usual, normal - **4.** US [size] normal, mediano(na) - **5.** US [pleasant] legal. ⬦ *n* cliente *m* habitual.

regularly ['regjʊləlɪ] *adv* - **1.** [gen] con regularidad - **2.** [equally spaced] de manera uniforme.

regulate ['regjʊleɪt] *vt* regular.

regulation [,regjʊ'leɪʃn] *n* - **1.** [rule] regla *f*, norma *f* - **2.** (*U*) [control] regulación *f*.

rehabilitate [,riːə'bɪlɪteɪt] *vt* rehabilitar.

rehearsal [rɪ'hɜːsl] *n* ensayo *m*.

rehearse [rɪ'hɜːs] *vt* ensayar.

reign [reɪn] *lit* & *fig* ⬦ *n* reinado *m*. ⬦ *vi*: **to reign (over)** reinar (sobre).

reimburse [,riːɪm'bɜːs] *vt*: **to reimburse sb (for sthg)** reembolsar a alguien (algo).

rein [reɪn] *n fig*: **to keep a tight rein on sb/ sthg** tener muy controlado(da) a álguien/algo. ➤ **reins** *npl* [for horse] riendas *fpl*.

reindeer ['reɪn,dɪər] (*pl* **reindeer**) *n* reno *m*.

reinforce [,riːɪn'fɔːs] *vt* reforzar.

reinforced concrete [,riːɪn'fɔːst-] *n* cemento *m* OR hormigón *m* armado.

reinforcement [,riːɪn'fɔːsmənt] *n* refuerzo *m*. ➤ **reinforcements** *npl* refuerzos *mpl*.

re-install *vt* reinstalar.

reinstate [,riːɪn'steɪt] *vt* - **1.** [give job back to] restituir OR reintegrar en su puesto a - **2.** [bring back] restablecer.

reissue [riː'ɪʃuː] *vt* [gen] reeditar; [film] reestrenar.

reiterate [riː'ɪtəreɪt] *vt fml* reiterar.

reject ⬦ *n* ['riːdʒekt] - **1.** [thing]: **rejects** artículos *mpl* defectuosos - **2.** *inf* [person] desecho *m*. ⬦ *vt* [rɪ'dʒekt] rechazar.

rejection [rɪ'dʒekʃn] *n* rechazo *m*.

rejoice [rɪ'dʒɔɪs] *vi*: **to rejoice (at** OR **in)** alegrarse OR regocijarse (con).

rejuvenate [rɪ'dʒuːvəneɪt] *vt* rejuvenecer.

rekindle [,riː'kɪndl] *vt* reavivar.

relapse [rɪ'læps] ⬦ *n* recaída *f*. ⬦ *vi*: **to relapse into** volver a caer en.

relate [rɪ'leɪt] ⬦ *vt* - **1.** [connect]: **to relate sthg (to)** relacionar algo (con) - **2.** [tell] contar, relatar. ⬦ *vi* - **1.** [be connected]: **to relate to** estar relacionado(da) con - **2.** [concern]: **to relate to** referirse a - **3.** [empathize]: **to relate (to sb)** tener mucho en común (con alguien). ➤ **relating to** *prep* concerniente OR referente a.

related [rɪ'leɪtɪd] *adj* - **1.** [in same family] emparentado(da); **to be related to sb** ser pariente de alguien - **2.** [connected] relacionado(da).

relation [rɪ'leɪʃn] *n* - **1.** [connection]: **relation (to/between)** relación *f* (con/entre); **to bear no relation to** no tener nada que ver con - **2.** [family member] pariente *mf*, familiar *mf*. ➤ **relations** *npl* [family, race, industrial] relaciones *fpl*.

relationship [rɪ'leɪʃnʃɪp] n - 1. [gen] relación f; **a good relationship** buenas relaciones f; [in family] relación(ones) f.

relative ['relətɪv] <> adj relativo(va). <> n pariente mf, familiar mf. ◆ **relative to** prep fml con relación a.

relatively ['relətɪvlɪ] adv relativamente.

relax [rɪ'læks] <> vt - 1. [gen] relajar - 2. [loosen - grip] aflojar. <> vi - 1. [gen] relajarse - 2. [loosen] aflojarse.

relaxation [,ri:læk'seɪʃn] n - 1. [recreation] relajación f, esparcimiento m - 2. [slackening - of discipline] relajación f.

relaxed [rɪ'lækst] adj relajado(da).

relaxing [rɪ'læksɪŋ] adj relajante.

relay ['ri:leɪ] <> n - 1. SPORT: **relay (race)** carrera f de relevos; **in relays** fig por turnos - 2. RADIO & TV retransmisión f. <> vt (pt & pp -ed) [broadcast] retransmitir.

release [rɪ'li:s] <> n - 1. [setting free] puesta f en libertad, liberación f - 2. [relief] alivio m - 3. [statement] comunicado m - 4. [emitting - of gas] escape m; [- of heat, pressure] emisión f - 5. [thing issued - of film] estreno m; [- of record] publicación f. <> vt - 1. [lift restriction on]: **to release sb from** liberar a alguien de - 2. [make available - funds, resources] entregar - 3. [let go - rope, reins, brake, person] soltar; [- grip] aflojar; [- mechanism, trigger] disparar - 4. [emit - gas, heat] despedir - 5. [issue - film] estrenar; [- record] sacar.

relegate ['relɪgeɪt] vt - 1. [demote]: **to relegate sthg/sb (to)** relegar algo/a alguien (a) - 2. UK FTBL: **to be relegated** descender (a una división inferior).

relent [rɪ'lent] vi [person] ablandarse; [wind, storm] remitir, aminorar.

relentless [rɪ'lentlɪs] adj implacable.

relevant ['reləvənt] adj - 1. [connected]: **relevant (to)** pertinente (a) - 2. [important]: **relevant (to)** importante OR relevante (para) - 3. [appropriate] pertinente, oportuno(na).

reliable [rɪ'laɪəbl] adj - 1. [dependable] fiable - 2. [information] fidedigno(na).

reliably [rɪ'laɪəblɪ] adv - 1. [dependably] sin fallar - 2. [correctly]: **to be reliably informed about sthg** saber algo de fuentes fidedignas.

reliant [rɪ'laɪənt] adj: **to be reliant on sb/sthg** depender de alguien/de algo.

relic ['relɪk] n - 1. [gen] reliquia f - 2. [custom still in use] vestigio m.

relief [rɪ'li:f] n - 1. [comfort] alivio m - 2. [for poor, refugees] ayuda f - 3. (U) US [social security] subsidio m.

relieve [rɪ'li:v] vt - 1. [ease, lessen] aliviar - 2. [take away from]: **to relieve sb of sthg** liberar a alguien de algo.

religion [rɪ'lɪdʒn] n religión f.

religious [rɪ'lɪdʒəs] adj religioso(sa).

relinquish [rɪ'lɪŋkwɪʃ] vt [power, claim] ceder; [title] renunciar a; **to relinquish one's hold on sthg** soltar algo.

relish ['relɪʃ] <> n - 1. [enjoyment]: **with (great) relish** con (gran) deleite - 2. [pickle] salsa rojiza agridulce con pepinillo etc. <> vt disfrutar con.

relocate [,ri:ləʊ'keɪt] <> vt trasladar. <> vi trasladarse.

reluctance [rɪ'lʌktəns] n reticencia f.

reluctant [rɪ'lʌktənt] adj reacio(cia); **to be reluctant to do sthg** estar poco dispuesto a hacer algo.

reluctantly [rɪ'lʌktəntlɪ] adv con desgana.

rely [rɪ'laɪ] ◆ **rely on** vt insep - 1. [count on] contar con; **to be able to rely on sb/sthg to do sthg** poder estar seguro de que alguien/algo hará algo - 2. [be dependent on]: **to rely on sb/sthg for sthg** depender de alguien/algo para algo.

remain [rɪ'meɪn] <> vt continuar como; **to remain the same** continuar siendo igual. <> vi - 1. [stay] quedarse, permanecer - 2. [survive - custom, problem] quedar, continuar. ◆ **remains** npl restos mpl.

remainder [rɪ'meɪndər] n - 1. [rest]: **the remainder** el resto - 2. MATHS resto m.

remaining [rɪ'meɪnɪŋ] adj restante.

remand [rɪ'mɑːnd] <> n LAW: **on remand** detenido(da) en espera de juicio. <> vt LAW: **to be remanded in custody** estar bajo custodia.

remark [rɪ'mɑːk] <> n [comment] comentario m. <> vt: **to remark (that)** comentar que.

remarkable [rɪ'mɑːkəbl] adj - 1. [fantastic] extraordinario(ria) - 2. [surprising] sorprendente.

remarry [,ri:'mærɪ] vi volver a casarse.

remedial [rɪ'mi:djəl] adj - 1. SCH [class, teacher] de refuerzo; [pupil] atrasado(da) - 2. [corrective] correctivo(va).

remedy ['remədɪ] <> n lit & fig: **remedy (for)** remedio m (para). <> vt remediar.

remember [rɪ'membər] <> vt [gen] recordar, acordarse de; **to remember to do sthg** acordarse de hacer algo; **to remember doing sthg** recordar OR acordarse de haber hecho algo; **he remembered me in his will** me dejó algo en su testamento. <> vi [gen] recordar, acordarse.

remembrance [rɪ'membrəns] n fml: **in remembrance of** en conmemoración de.

Remembrance Day n en Gran Bretaña, día en conmemoración de los caídos en las dos guerras mundiales.

remind [rɪ'maɪnd] *vt*: to remind sb (about sthg/to do sthg) recordar a alguien (algo/que haga algo); **she reminds me of my sister** me recuerda a mi hermana.

reminder [rɪ'maɪndə'] *n* - 1. [to jog memory] recordatorio *m*, recuerdo *m* - 2. [letter, note] notificación *f*, aviso *m*.

reminisce [,remɪ'nɪs] *vi*: to reminisce (about sthg) rememorar (algo).

reminiscent [,remɪ'nɪsnt] *adj* [similar to]: to be reminiscent of evocar, recordar a.

remiss [rɪ'mɪs] *adj* negligente, remiso(sa); **it was remiss of me** fue una negligencia por mi parte.

remit[1] [rɪ'mɪt] *vt* [money] remitir.

remit[2] ['ri:mɪt] *n* [responsibility] misión *f*.

remittance [rɪ'mɪtns] *n* giro *m*.

remnant ['remnənt] *n* - 1. [remaining part] resto *m* - 2. [of cloth] retal *m*.

remold *US* = **remould**.

remorse [rɪ'mɔːs] *n* (U) remordimientos *mpl*.

remorseful [rɪ'mɔːsful] *adj* lleno(na) de remordimientos.

remorseless [rɪ'mɔːslɪs] *adj* - 1. [pitiless] despiadado(da) - 2. [unstoppable] implacable.

remote [rɪ'məut] *adj* - 1. [place, time possibility] remoto(ta) - 2. [from reality etc]: **remote (from)** apartado(da) OR alejado(da) (de).

remote access *n* acceso *m* remoto.

remote control *n* telemando *m*, mando *m* a distancia.

remotely [rɪ'məutlɪ] *adv* - 1. [in the slightest]: **not remotely** ni remotamente, en lo más mínimo - 2. [far off] muy lejos.

remould *UK*, **remold** *US* ['ri:məuld] *n* neumático *m* recauchutado.

removable [rɪ'mu:vəbl] *adj* - 1. [detachable] separable - 2. [hard disk] extraíble.

removal [rɪ'mu:vl] *n* - 1. (U) [act of removing] separación *f*, extracción *f*; [of threat, clause] supresión *f* - 2. *UK* [change of house] mudanza *f*.

removal van *n UK* camión *m* de mudanzas.

remove [rɪ'mu:v] *vt* - 1. [take away, clean away]: to remove sthg (from) quitar algo (de) - 2. [clothing, shoes] quitarse - 3. [from a job, post]: to remove sb (from) destituir a alguien (de) - 4. [problem, controls] eliminar; [suspicion] disipar.

remuneration [rɪ,mju:nə'reɪʃn] *n fml* remuneración *f*.

render ['rendə'] *vt* - 1. [make]: to render sb speechless dejar a alguien boquiabierto - 2. [give - help, service] prestar.

rendering ['rendərɪŋ] *n* - 1. [rendition] interpretación *f* - 2. [of carcass] transformación *f*.

rendezvous ['rɒndɪvu:] (*pl* rendezvous) *n* [meeting] cita *f*.

renegade ['renɪgeɪd] <> *adj* renegado(da). <> *n* renegado *m*, -da *f*.

renew [rɪ'nju:] *vt* - 1. [attempt, attack] reemprender - 2. [relationship] reanudar - 3. [licence, contract, passport] renovar - 4. [strength, interest] reavivar.

renewable [rɪ'nju:əbl] *adj* renovable.

renewal [rɪ'nju:əl] *n* - 1. [of activity] reanudación *f* - 2. [of contract, licence, passport] renovación *f*.

renounce [rɪ'nauns] *vt* renunciar a.

renovate ['renəveɪt] *vt* reformar, renovar.

renown [rɪ'naun] *n* renombre *m*.

renowned [rɪ'naund] *adj*: renowned (for) célebre (por).

rent [rent] <> *n* alquiler *m*. <> *vt* alquilar, rentar *Méx*. <> *vi US* [property] alquilarse; **this apartment rents for $300 a month** este departamento se alquila por 300 dólares al mes.

rental ['rentl] <> *adj* de alquiler. <> *n* alquiler *m*.

renunciation [rɪ,nʌnsɪ'eɪʃn] *n* renuncia *f*.

reorganize, -ise [,ri:'ɔːgənaɪz] *vt* reorganizar.

rep [rep] *n abbr of* **representative, repertory**.

repaid [ri:'peɪd] *pt & pp* ⊳ **repay**.

repair [rɪ'peə'] <> *n* reparación *f*, refacción *f Amér*. <> *vt* reparar, refaccionar *Amér*.

repair kit *n* caja de herramientas de una bicicleta.

repartee [,repɑː'ti:] *n* intercambio *m* de réplicas ingeniosas.

repatriate [,ri:'pætrɪeɪt] *vt* repatriar.

repay [ri:'peɪ] (*pt & pp* repaid) *vt* - 1. [money] devolver; [debt, person] pagar - 2. [thank] devolver el favor a.

repayment [ri:'peɪmənt] *n* - 1. [act of paying back] devolución *f* - 2. [sum] pago *m*.

repeal [rɪ'pi:l] <> *n* revocación *f*, abrogación *f*. <> *vt* revocar, abrogar.

repeat [rɪ'pi:t] <> *vt* - 1. [gen] repetir - 2. [TV, radio programme] volver a emitir. <> *n* - 1. [recurrence] repetición *f* - 2. [of programme] reposición *f*.

repeatedly [rɪ'pi:tɪdlɪ] *adv* repetidamente.

repel [rɪ'pel] *vt* repeler.

repellent [rɪ'pelənt] <> *adj* repelente. <> *n* espray *m* antiinsectos.

repent [rɪ'pent] <> *vt* arrepentirse de. <> *vi*: to repent of arrepentirse de.

repentance [rɪ'pentəns] *n* arrepentimiento *m*.

repercussions [,ri:pə'kʌʃnz] *npl* repercusiones *fpl*.

repertoire ['repətwɑ:ʳ] *n* repertorio *m*.

repertory ['repətrɪ] *n* repertorio *m*

repetition [ˌrepɪ'tɪʃn] *n* repetición *t*.

repetitious [ˌrepɪ'tɪʃəs], **repetitive** [rɪ'petɪtɪv] *adj* repetitivo(va).

repetitive strain injury *n (U)* lesión *f* por movimiento repetitivo.

replace [rɪ'pleɪs] *vt* - **1.** [take the place of] sustituir - **2.** [change for something else]: **to replace sthg (with)** cambiar algo (por) - **3.** [change for somebody else]: **to replace sb (with)** sustituir a alguien (por) - **4.** [supply another]: **they replaced it** me dieron otro - **5.** [put back] poner en su sitio.

replacement [rɪ'pleɪsmənt] *n* - **1.** [act of substituting] sustitución *f* - **2.** [something new]: **replacement (for)** sustituto *m*, -ta *f* (para) - **3.** [somebody new]: **replacement (for)** sustituto *m*, -ta *f* OR suplente *mf* (de) - **4.** [another one]: **they gave me a replacement** me dieron otro.

replay ◇ *n* ['ri:pleɪ] repetición *f*. ◇ *vt* [ˌri:'pleɪ] [film, tape] volver a poner.

replenish [rɪ'plenɪʃ] *vt*: **to replenish sthg (with)** reaprovisionar OR reponer algo (de).

replica ['replɪkə] *n* réplica *f*.

reply [rɪ'plaɪ] ◇ *n*: **reply (to)** respuesta *f* (a). ◇ *vt* responder, contestar. ◇ *vi*: **to reply (to sb/sthg)** responder (a alguien/algo).

reply coupon *n* cupón *m* de respuesta.

report [rɪ'pɔ:t] ◇ *n* - **1.** [gen] informe *m*; PRESS & TV reportaje *m*; [shorter] información *f* - **2.** UK SCH boletín *m* de evaluación, boletín *m* de calificaciones OR notas. ◇ *vt* - **1.** [say, make known]: **to report that** informar que, reportar que *Amér*; **to report sthg (to)** informar de algo (a), reportar algo (a) *Amér* - **2.** [losses] anunciar - **3.** [complain about] denunciar; **to report sb (to sb for sthg)** denunciar a alguien (a alguien por algo), reportar a alguien (a alguien por algo) *Amér*. ◇ *vi* [give account]: **to report on** informar sobre.

report card *n* US boletín *m* de evaluación, boletín *m* de calificaciones OR notas.

reportedly [rɪ'pɔ:tɪdlɪ] *adv* según se afirma.

reporter [rɪ'pɔ:təʳ] *n* reportero *m*, -ra *f*.

repose [rɪ'pəʊz] *n liter* reposo *m*.

repossess [ˌri:pə'zes] *vt* requisar la posesión de.

reprehensible [ˌreprɪ'hensəbl] *adj fml* reprensible.

represent [ˌreprɪ'zent] *vt* [gen] representar; [person, country] representar a; **to be well OR strongly represented** estar bien representado(da).

representation [ˌreprɪzen'teɪʃn] *n* representación *f*. ◆ **representations** *npl fml*: **to make representations to sb** presentar una queja a.

representative [ˌreprɪ'zentətɪv] ◇ *adj*: **representative (of)** representativo(va) (de). ◇ *n* representante *mf*.

repress [rɪ'pres] *vt* reprimir.

repression [rɪ'preʃn] *n* represión *f*.

reprieve [rɪ'pri:v] *n* - **1.** [delay] tregua *f* - **2.** [of death sentence] indulto *m*.

reprimand ['reprɪmɑ:nd] ◇ *n* reprensión *f*. ◇ *vt* reprender.

reprisal [rɪ'praɪzl] *n* represalia *f*.

reproach [rɪ'prəʊtʃ] ◇ *n* reproche *m*. ◇ *vt*: **to reproach sb (for OR with sthg)** reprochar a alguien (algo).

reproachful [rɪ'prəʊtʃfʊl] *adj* de reproche.

reproduce [ˌri:prə'dju:s] ◇ *vt* reproducir. ◇ *vi* BIOL reproducirse.

reproduction [ˌri:prə'dʌkʃn] *n* reproducción *f*.

reproof [rɪ'pru:f] *n fml* - **1.** [words of blame] reprobación *f* - **2.** [disapproval] reproche *m*.

reptile ['reptaɪl] *n* reptil *m*.

republic [rɪ'pʌblɪk] *n* república *f*.

republican [rɪ'pʌblɪkən] ◇ *adj* republicano(na). ◇ *n* republicano *m*, -na *f*. ◆ **Republican** ◇ *adj* [in US, Northern Ireland] republicano(na); **the Republican Party** [in US] el partido republicano. ◇ *n* [in US, Northern Ireland] republicano *m*, -na *f*.

repudiate [rɪ'pju:dɪeɪt] *vt fml* [person, violence] repudiar; [accusation] rechazar.

repulse [rɪ'pʌls] *vt* rechazar.

repulsive [rɪ'pʌlsɪv] *adj* repulsivo(va).

reputable ['repjʊtəbl] *adj* de buena fama OR reputación.

reputation [ˌrepjʊ'teɪʃn] *n* reputación *f*; **to have a reputation for sthg/for being sthg** tener fama de algo/de ser algo.

reputed [rɪ'pju:tɪd] *adj* supuesto(ta); **to be reputed to be/do sthg** tener fama de ser/hacer algo.

reputedly [rɪ'pju:tɪdlɪ] *adv* según se dice.

request [rɪ'kwest] ◇ *n*: **request (for)** petición *f* (de); **on request** a petición del interesado; **at sb's request** a petición de alguien. ◇ *vt* solicitar, pedir; **to request sb to do sthg** rogar a alguien que haga algo.

request stop *n* UK parada *f* discrecional.

require [rɪ'kwaɪəʳ] *vt* - **1.** [need] necesitar, requerir - **2.** [demand] requerir; **to require sb to do sthg** exigir a alguien que haga algo.

requirement [rɪ'kwaɪəmənt] *n* requisito *m*.

requisition [ˌrekwɪ'zɪʃn] *vt* requisar.

rerun *n* ['ri:,rʌn] - **1.** [film, programme] reposición *f* - **2.** [repeated situation] repetición *f*.

resat [,ri:'sæt] *pt* & *pp* ⊏> **resit**.

rescind [rɪ'sɪnd] *vt* LAW [contract] rescindir; [law] revocar.

rescue ['reskju:] <> *n* rescate *m*; **to go** OR **come to sb's rescue** ir OR acudir al rescate de alguien. <> *vt*: **to rescue sb/sthg (from)** rescatar a alguien/algo (de).

rescuer ['reskjuəʳ] *n* rescatador *m*, -ra *f*.

research [,rɪ'sɜ:tʃ] <> *n* (U): **research (on** OR **into)** investigación *f* (de OR sobre); **research and development** investigación y desarrollo. <> *vt* investigar.

researcher [rɪ'sɜ:tʃəʳ] *n* investigador *m*, -ra *f*.

resemblance [rɪ'zembləns] *n* parecido *m*, semejanza *f*.

resemble [rɪ'zembl] *vt* parecerse a.

resent [rɪ'zent] *vt*: **to resent sb** tener celos de alguien.

resentful [rɪ'zentful] *adj* [person] resentido(da); [look] de resentimiento.

resentment [rɪ'zentmənt] *n* resentimiento *m*.

reservation [,rezə'veɪʃn] *n* - **1.** [booking] reserva *f* - **2.** [uncertainty]: **without reservation** sin reserva - **3.** US [for Native Americans] reserva *f*. ➡ **reservations** *npl* [doubts] reservas *fpl*.

reserve [rɪ'zɜ:v] <> *n* - **1.** [gen] reserva *f*; **in reserve** en reserva - **2.** SPORT suplente *mf*. <> *vt* - **1.** [save, book] reservar - **2.** [retain]: **to reserve the right to do sthg** reservarse el derecho a hacer algo.

reserved [rɪ'zɜ:vd] *adj* reservado(da).

reservoir ['rezəvwɑːʳ] *n* [lake] pantano *m*, embalse *m*.

reset [,ri:'set] (*pt* & *pp* reset) *vt* [clock] poner en hora; [meter, controls, computer] reinicializar.

reshape [,ri:'ʃeɪp] *vt* [policy, thinking] reformar, rehacer.

reshuffle [,ri:'ʃʌfl] *n* remodelación *f*; **cabinet reshuffle** remodelación del gabinete.

reside [rɪ'zaɪd] *vi fml* [live] residir.

residence ['rezɪdəns] *n* - **1.** *fml* [house] residencia *f* - **2.** [state of residing]: **to be in residence (at)** residir (a).

residence permit *n* permiso *m* de residencia.

resident ['rezɪdənt] <> *adj* - **1.** [settled, living] residente - **2.** [on-site, live-in] que vive en su lugar de trabajo. <> *n* residente *mf*.

residential [,rezɪ'denʃl] *adj* [live-in] en régimen de internado.

residential area *n* zona *f* residencial.

residue ['rezɪdju:] *n* residuo *m*.

resign [rɪ'zaɪn] <> *vt* - **1.** [give up] dimitir de, renunciar a - **2.** [accept calmly]: **to resign o.s. to sthg** resignarse a algo. <> *vi* [quit]: **to resign (from)** dimitir (de).

resignation [,rezɪg'neɪʃn] *n* - **1.** [from job] dimisión *f* - **2.** [calm acceptance] resignación *f*.

resigned [rɪ'zaɪnd] *adj*: **resigned (to)** resignado(da) (a).

resilient [rɪ'zɪlɪənt] *adj* [person] resistente, fuerte; [rubber] elástico(ca).

resin ['rezɪn] *n* resina *f*.

resist [rɪ'zɪst] *vt* - **1.** [refuse to give in to - temptation] resistir - **2.** [refuse to accept] resistir, oponerse a - **3.** [fight against] resistir a.

resistance [rɪ'zɪstəns] *n*: **resistance (to)** resistencia *f* (a).

resit UK <> *n* ['ri:sɪt] (examen *m* de) repesca *f*. <> *vt* [,ri:'sɪt] (*pt* & *pp* -sat) volver a presentarse a.

resolute ['rezəlu:t] *adj* resuelto(ta), determinado(da).

resolution [,rezə'lu:ʃn] *n* - **1.** [gen] resolución *f* - **2.** [vow, promise] propósito *m*.

resolve [rɪ'zɒlv] <> *n* (U) resolución *f*. <> *vt* - **1.** [vow, promise]: **to resolve that** resolver que; **to resolve to do sthg** resolver hacer algo - **2.** [solve] resolver.

resort [rɪ'zɔːt] *n* - **1.** [for holidays] lugar *m* de vacaciones - **2.** [solution]: **as a** OR **in the last resort** como último recurso. ➡ **resort to** *vt insep* recurrir a.

resound [rɪ'zaʊnd] *vi* - **1.** [noise] resonar - **2.** [place]: **the room resounded with laughter** la risa resonaba por la habitación.

resounding [rɪ'zaʊndɪŋ] *adj* - **1.** [loud - noise, knock] retumbante; [- crash] estruendoso(sa) - **2.** [very great] clamoroso(sa).

resource [rɪ'sɔːs] *n* recurso *m*.

resourceful [rɪ'sɔːsful] *adj* [person] de recursos; [solution] ingenioso(sa).

respect [rɪ'spekt] <> *n* - **1.** [gen]: **respect (for)** respeto *m* (por); **with respect** con respeto - **2.** [aspect] aspecto *m*; **in this respect** a este respecto; **in that respect** en cuanto a eso. <> *vt* [admire] respetar; **to respect sb for sthg** respetar a alguien por algo. ➡ **respects** *npl*: **to pay one's respects (to)** presentar uno sus respetos (a). ➡ **with respect to** *prep* con respecto a.

respectable [rɪ'spektəbl] *adj* respetable.

respectful [rɪ'spektful] *adj* respetuoso(sa).

respective [rɪ'spektɪv] *adj* respectivo(va).

respectively [rɪ'spektɪvlɪ] *adv* respectivamente.

respite ['respaɪt] *n* - **1.** [lull] respiro *m* - **2.** [delay] aplazamiento *m*.

resplendent [rɪ'splendənt] *adj* resplandeciente.

respond [rɪ'spɒnd] *vi*: **to respond (to)** responder (a).

response [rɪ'spɒns] *n* respuesta *f*.

responsibility [rɪ,spɒnsə'bɪlətɪ] *n*: **responsibility (for)** responsabilidad *f* (de); **to claim responsibility for sthg** reivindicar algo.

responsible [rɪ'spɒnsəbl] *adj* - **1.** [gen] responsable; **responsible (for)** responsable (de)
- **2.** [answerable]: **responsible to sb** responsable
ante alguien - **3.** [job, position] de responsabilidad.

responsibly [rɪ'spɒnsəblɪ] *adv* de manera
responsable.

responsive [rɪ'spɒnsɪv] *adj* - **1.** [quick to re-
act]: **to be responsive** responder muy bien
- **2.** [aware]: **responsive (to)** sensible *OR* per-
ceptivo(va) (a).

rest [rest] <> *n* - **1.** [remainder]: **the rest (of)**
el resto (de); **the rest of us** los demás - **2.** [re-
laxation, break] descanso *m*; **to have a rest**
descansar - **3.** [support - for feet] descanso *m*;
[- for head] respaldo *m*. <> *vt* -.**1.** [relax - eyes,
feet] descansar - **2.** [support] apoyar, descansar. <> *vi* - **1.** [relax, be still] descansar - **2.** [de-
pend]: **to rest on** *OR* **upon** depender de - **3.** [be
supported] apoyarse, descansar
▸▸▸ **rest assured that...** tenga la seguridad de
que...

restaurant ['restərɒnt] *n* restaurante *m*.

restaurant car *n UK* coche *m OR* vagón *m*
restaurante, coche *m* comedor.

restful ['restfʊl] *adj* tranquilo(la), apacible.

rest home *n* [for the elderly] asilo *m* de ancianos; [for the sick] casa *f* de reposo.

restive ['restɪv] *adj* inquieto(ta).

restless ['restlɪs] *adj* - **1.** [bored, dissatisfied]
impaciente, desasosegado(da) - **2.** [fidgety] in-
quieto(ta), agitado(da) - **3.** [sleepless] agita-
do(da).

restoration [,restə'reɪʃn] *n* restauración *f*.

restore [rɪ'stɔːr] *vt* - **1.** [reestablish] restablecer
- **2.** [to a previous position or condition]: **to restore
sb to sthg** restaurar a alguien en algo; **to restore sthg to sthg** volver a poner algo en algo
- **3.** [renovate] restaurar - **4.** [give back] devolver.

restrain [rɪ'streɪn] *vt* controlar; **to restrain
o.s. from doing sthg** contenerse para no hacer
algo.

restrained [rɪ'streɪnd] *adj* comedido(da).

restraint [rɪ'streɪnt] *n* - **1.** [rule, check] restricción *f* - **2.** [control] control *m*.

restrict [rɪ'strɪkt] *vt* [limit] restringir, limitar;
to restrict o.s. to sthg limitarse a algo.

restriction [rɪ'strɪkʃn] *n* restricción *f*.

restrictive [rɪ'strɪktɪv] *adj* restrictivo(va).

rest room *n US* aseos *mpl*.

result [rɪ'zʌlt] <> *n* resultado *m*; **as a result**
como resultado. <> *vi* - **1.** [cause]: **to result
(in sthg)** tener como resultado (algo) - **2.** [be
caused]: **to result (from)** resultar (de).

resume [rɪ'zjuːm] <> *vt* [start again] reanudar. <> *vi* volver a empezar.

résumé ['rezjuːmeɪ] *n* - **1.** [summary] resumen *m* - **2.** *US* [of career, qualifications] currículum *m* (vitae).

resumption [rɪ'zʌmpʃn] *n* reanudación *f*.

resurgence [rɪ'sɜːdʒəns] *n* resurgimiento *m*.

resurrection [,rezə'rekʃn] *n* resurrección *f*.

resuscitate [rɪ'sʌsɪteɪt] *vt* resucitar.

retail ['riːteɪl] <> *n* venta *f* al por menor *OR*
al detalle. <> *vt* vender al por menor. <> *vi*:
to retail for tener un precio de venta al público de. <> *adv* al por menor.

retailer ['riːteɪlər] *n* minorista *mf*, detallista *mf*.

retail price *n* precio *m* de venta al público.

retain [rɪ'teɪn] *vt* retener.

retainer [rɪ'teɪnər] *n* [fee] anticipo *m*.

retaliate [rɪ'tælɪeɪt] *vi* - **1.** [react] responder
- **2.** [take reprisals] tomar represalias.

retaliation [rɪ,tælɪ'eɪʃn] *n (U)* represalias *fpl*.

retarded [rɪ'tɑːdɪd] *adj* retrasado(da).

retch [retʃ] *vi* tener arcadas.

retentive [rɪ'tentɪv] *adj* retentivo(va).

reticent ['retɪsənt] *adj* reservado(da).

retina ['retɪnə] *(pl* -nas *OR* -nae [-niː]) *n* retina *f*.

retinue ['retɪnjuː] *n* séquito *m*.

retire [rɪ'taɪər] *vi* - **1.** [from work] jubilarse
- **2.** *fml* [to another place, to bed] retirarse.

retired [rɪ'taɪəd] *adj* jubilado(da).

retirement [rɪ'taɪəmənt] *n* [act] jubilación *f*;
[time] retiro *m*.

retiring [rɪ'taɪərɪŋ] *adj* [shy] retraído(da).

retort [rɪ'tɔːt] <> *n* [sharp reply] réplica *f*.
<> *vt*: **to retort (that)** replicar (que).

retrace [rɪ'treɪs] *vt*: **to retrace one's steps**
desandar lo andado.

retract [rɪ'trækt] <> *vt* - **1.** [withdraw, take
back] retractarse de - **2.** [pull in - claws] retraer.
<> *vi* [subj: claws] meterse, retraerse; [subj:
wheels] replegarse.

retrain [,riː'treɪn] *vt* reciclar.

retraining [,riː'treɪnɪŋ] *n* reciclaje *m*.

retread ['riːtred] *n* neumático *m* recauchutado.

retreat [rɪ'triːt] <> *n* - **1.** MIL: **retreat (from)**
retirada *f* (de) - **2.** [peaceful place] refugio *m*.
<> *vi* [move away]: **to retreat (from)** [gen] reti-
rarse (de); [from a person] apartarse (de).

retribution [ˌretrɪˈbjuːʃn] *n* (U) castigo *m* merecido.

retrieval [rɪˈtriːvl] *n* [gen & COMPUT] recuperación *f*.

retrieve [rɪˈtriːv] *vt* - **1.** [get back] recobrar - **2.** COMPUT recuperar - **3.** [rescue - situation] salvar.

retriever [rɪˈtriːvər] *n* perro *m* cobrador.

retrograde [ˈretrəɡreɪd] *adj fml* [gen] retrógrado(da); [step] hacia atrás.

retrospect [ˈretrəspekt] *n*: in retrospect retrospectivamente, mirando hacia atrás.

retrospective [ˌretrəˈspektɪv] *adj* - **1.** [gen] retrospectivo(va) - **2.** [law, pay rise] con efecto retroactivo.

return [rɪˈtɜːn] ◇ *n* - **1.** (U) [arrival back] vuelta *f*, regreso *m* - **2.** UK [ticket] billete *m* de ida y vuelta - **3.** [profit] ganancia *f*, rendimiento *m*. ◇ *vt* - **1.** [book, visit, compliment, call] devolver - **2.** [reciprocate] corresponder a - **3.** [replace] devolver a su sitio - **4.** LAW [verdict] pronunciar - **5.** POL [candidate] elegir. ◇ *vi*: to return (from/to) volver (de/a). ◆ returns *npl* COMM réditos *mpl*
▸▸▸ many happy returns (of the day)! ¡feliz cumpleaños! ◆ in return *adv* a cambio. ◆ in return for *prep* a cambio de.

return (key) *n* COMPUT tecla *f* de retorno.

return ticket *n* UK billete *m* de ida y vuelta *Esp*, boleto *m* de ida y vuelta *Amér*, boleto *m* redondo *Méx*.

reunification [ˌriːjuːnɪfɪˈkeɪʃn] *n* reunificación *f*.

reunion [ˌriːˈjuːnjən] *n* reunión *f*.

reunite [ˌriːjuːˈnaɪt] *vt* [factions, parts] reunir; [people]: to be reunited with volver a encontrarse con.

rev [rev] *inf* ◇ *n* (abbr of revolution) revolución *f* (motriz). ◇ *vt*: to rev sthg (up) acelerar algo. ◇ *vi* [subj: person]: to rev (up) acelerar el motor.

revamp [ˌriːˈvæmp] *vt inf* renovar.

reveal [rɪˈviːl] *vt* revelar.

revealing [rɪˈviːlɪŋ] *adj* - **1.** [comment, silence] revelador(ra) - **2.** [garment] atrevido(da).

reveille [UK rɪˈvælɪ, US ˈrevəlɪ] *n* toque *m* de diana.

revel [ˈrevl] (UK pt & pp -led, cont -ling, US pt & pp -ed, cont -ing) *vi*: to revel in deleitarse en.

revelation [ˌrevəˈleɪʃn] *n* revelación *f*.

revenge [rɪˈvendʒ] *n* venganza *f*; to take revenge (on sb) vengarse (de alguien).

revenue [ˈrevənjuː] *n* ingresos *mpl*.

reverberate [rɪˈvɜːbəreɪt] *vi* - **1.** [reecho] resonar - **2.** [have repercussions] repercutir.

reverberations [rɪˌvɜːbəˈreɪʃnz] *npl* - **1.** [echoes] reverberaciones *fpl* - **2.** [repercussions] repercusiones *fpl*.

revere [rɪˈvɪər] *vt* venerar.

reverence [ˈrevərəns] *n* reverencia *f*.

Reverend [ˈrevərənd] *n* reverendo *m*.

reverie [ˈrevərɪ] *n* ensueño *m*.

reversal [rɪˈvɜːsl] *n* - **1.** [turning around] cambio *m* total - **2.** [ill fortune] contratiempo *m*.

reverse [rɪˈvɜːs] ◇ *adj* inverso(sa). ◇ *n* - **1.** AUT: reverse (gear) marcha *f* atrás - **2.** [opposite]: the reverse lo contrario - **3.** [opposite side, back]: the reverse [gen] el revés; [of coin] el reverso; [of piece of paper] el dorso. ◇ *vt* - **1.** AUT dar marcha atrás a - **2.** [change usual order] invertir - **3.** [change to opposite] cambiar completamente - **4.** UK TELEC: to reverse the charges llamar a cobro revertido. ◇ *vi* AUT dar marcha atrás.

reverse-charge call *n* UK llamada *f* a cobro revertido, llamada *f* por cobrar *Chile & Méx*.

reversing light [rɪˈvɜːsɪŋ-] *n* UK luz *f* de marcha atrás.

revert [rɪˈvɜːt] *vi*: to revert to volver a.

review [rɪˈvjuː] ◇ *n* - **1.** [examination] revisión *f* - **2.** [critique] reseña *f*. ◇ *vt* - **1.** [reexamine] revisar - **2.** [consider] reconsiderar - **3.** [write an article on] reseñar - **4.** US [study again] repasar.

reviewer [rɪˈvjuːər] *n* crítico *m*, -ca *f*.

revile [rɪˈvaɪl] *vt liter* injuriar.

revise [rɪˈvaɪz] ◇ *vt* - **1.** [reconsider] revisar - **2.** [rewrite] modificar, corregir - **3.** UK [study] repasar. ◇ *vi* UK: to revise (for sthg) repasar (para algo).

revision [rɪˈvɪʒn] *n* - **1.** [alteration] corrección *f*, modificación *f* - **2.** UK [study] repaso *m*.

revitalize, -ise [ˌriːˈvaɪtəlaɪz] *vt* revivificar.

revival [rɪˈvaɪvl] *n* - **1.** [of person] resucitación *f*; [of economy] reactivación *f* - **2.** [of play] reposición *f*.

revive [rɪˈvaɪv] ◇ *vt* - **1.** [person, plant, hopes] resucitar; [economy] reactivar - **2.** [tradition, memories] restablecer; [play] reponer. ◇ *vi* reponerse.

revolt [rɪˈvəʊlt] ◇ *n* rebelión *f*. ◇ *vt* repugnar. ◇ *vi*: to revolt (against) rebelarse OR sublevarse (contra).

revolting [rɪˈvəʊltɪŋ] *adj* repugnante, asqueroso(sa).

revolution [ˌrevəˈluːʃn] *n* revolución *f*.

revolutionary [ˌrevəˈluːʃnərɪ] ◇ *adj* revolucionario(ria). ◇ *n* revolucionario *m*, -ria *f*.

revolve [rɪˈvɒlv] *vi* [go round] girar; to revolve around OR round *lit & fig* girar en torno a.

revolver [rɪˈvɒlvər] *n* revólver *m*.

revolving [rɪ'vɒlvɪŋ] *adj* giratorio(ria).

revolving door *n* puerta *f* giratoria.

revue [rɪ'vjuː] *n* revista *f* (teatral).

revulsion [rɪ'vʌlʃn] *n* asco *m*, repugnancia *f*.

reward [rɪ'wɔːd] ⬦ *n* recompensa *f*. ⬦ *vt*: **to reward sb (for/with)** recompensar a alguien (por/con).

rewarding [rɪ'wɔːdɪŋ] *adj* gratificador(ra).

rewind [,riː'waɪnd] (*pt & pp* **rewound**) *vt* rebobinar.

rewire [,riː'waɪəʳ] *vt* cambiar la instalación eléctrica de.

reword [,riː'wɜːd] *vt* expresar de otra forma.

rewound [,riː'waʊnd] *pt & pp* ⊳ **rewind**.

rewritable [,riː'raɪtəbl] *adj* COMPUT regrabable.

rewrite [,riː'raɪt] (*pt* **rewrote** [,riː'rəʊt], *pp* **rewritten** [,riː'rɪtn]) *vt* volver a escribir.

rhapsody ['ræpsədɪ] *n* MUS rapsodia *f*.

rhetoric ['retərɪk] *n* retórica *f*.

rhetorical question [rɪ'tɒrɪkl-] *n* pregunta *f* retórica (*a la que no se espera contestación*).

rheumatism ['ruːmətɪzm] *n* reumatismo *m*.

Rhine [raɪn] *n*: **the Rhine** el Rin.

rhino ['raɪnəʊ] (*pl* **rhino** OR -s), **rhinoceros** [raɪ'nɒsərəs] (*pl* **rhinoceros** OR -es) *n* rinoceronte *m*.

Rhode Island [rəʊd-] *n* Rhode Island.

rhododendron [,rəʊdə'dendrən] *n* rododendro *m*.

Rhône [rəʊn] *n*: **the (River) Rhône** el (río) Ródano.

rhubarb ['ruːbɑːb] *n* ruibarbo *m*.

rhyme [raɪm] ⬦ *n* - 1. [gen] rima *f* - 2. [poem] poesía *f*, versos *mpl*. ⬦ *vi*: **to rhyme (with)** rimar (con).

rhythm ['rɪðm] *n* ritmo *m*.

rib [rɪb] *n* - 1. ANAT costilla *f* - 2. [of umbrella] varilla *f*.

ribbed [rɪbd] *adj* [sweater] de canalé.

ribbon ['rɪbən] *n* cinta *f*.

rice [raɪs] *n* arroz *m*.

rice pudding *n* arroz *m* con leche.

rich [rɪtʃ] ⬦ *adj* - 1. [gen] rico(ca) - 2. [full]: **to be rich in** abundar en - 3. [fertile] fértil - 4. [indigestible] pesado(da). ⬦ *npl*: **the rich** los ricos. ➡ **riches** *npl* - 1. [natural resources] riquezas *fpl* - 2. [wealth] riqueza *f*.

richly ['rɪtʃlɪ] *adv* - 1. [rewarded] muy generosamente - 2. [plentifully] copiosamente.

richness ['rɪtʃnɪs] *n* - 1. [gen] riqueza *f* - 2. [fertility] fertilidad *f* - 3. [indigestibility] pesadez *f*.

rickety ['rɪkətɪ] *adj* desvencijado(da).

rickshaw ['rɪkʃɔː] *n* jinrikisha *f*.

ricochet ['rɪkəʃeɪ] ⬦ *n* rebote *m*. ⬦ *vi* (*pt & pp* -ed OR -ted, *cont* -ing OR -ting), **to ricochet (off)** rebotar (de).

rid [rɪd] *vt* (*pt* **rid** OR -**ded**, *pp* **rid**, *cont* -**ding**): **to get rid of** deshacerse de.

ridden ['rɪdn] *pp* ⊳ **ride**.

riddle ['rɪdl] *n* - 1. [verbal puzzle] acertijo *m* - 2. [mystery] enigma *m*.

riddled ['rɪdld] *adj*: **to be riddled with** [mistakes] estar plagado(da) de.

ride [raɪd] ⬦ *n* - 1. [gen] paseo *m*; **to go for a ride** [on horseback] darse un paseo a caballo; [on bike] darse un paseo en bicicleta; [in car] darse una vuelta en coche; **to take sb for a ride** *inf fig* embaucar a alguien - 2. [journey] viaje *m*; **it's a short car ride away** está a poca distancia en coche - 3. [at fair] atracción *f*. ⬦ *vt* (*pt* **rode**, *pp* **ridden**) - 1. [horse] montar a - 2. [bicycle, motorbike] montar en; **he rode his bike to the station** fue a la estación en bici - 3. US [bus, train] ir en; [elevator] subir/bajar en - 4. [distance] recorrer. ⬦ *vi* (*pt* **rode**, *pp* **ridden**) - 1. [on horseback] montar a caballo; **she rode over to see me** vino a verme a caballo - 2. [on bicycle] ir en bici; [on motorbike] ir en moto - 3. [in car]: **we rode to London in a jeep** fuimos a Londres en jeep.

rider ['raɪdəʳ] *n* - 1. [on horseback] jinete *m*, amazona *f* - 2. [on bicycle] ciclista *mf*; [on motorbike] motorista *mf*.

ridge [rɪdʒ] *n* - 1. [on mountain] cresta *f* - 2. [on flat surface] rugosidad *f*.

ridicule ['rɪdɪkjuːl] ⬦ *n* (*U*) burlas *fpl*. ⬦ *vt* burlarse de.

ridiculous [rɪ'dɪkjʊləs] *adj* ridículo(la).

riding ['raɪdɪŋ] *n* equitación *f*; **to go riding** ir a montar a caballo.

riding school *n* escuela *f* de equitación.

rife [raɪf] *adj* extendido(da); **to be rife with** estar lleno de.

riffraff ['rɪfræf] *n* gentuza *f*.

rifle ['raɪfl] ⬦ *n* fusil *m*, rifle *m*. ⬦ *vt* desvalijar.

rifle range *n* campo *m* de tiro.

rift [rɪft] *n* - 1. GEOL hendidura *f*, grieta *f* - 2. [quarrel] desavenencia *f* - 3. POL: **rift between/in** escisión *f* entre/en.

rig [rɪg] ⬦ *n* - 1.: (oil) rig [onshore] torre *f* de perforación; [offshore] plataforma *f* petrolífera - 2. US [truck] camión *m*. ⬦ *vt* [falsify] amañar, falsificar. ➡ **rig up** *vt sep* construir, armar.

rigging ['rɪgɪŋ] *n* cordaje *m*.

right [raɪt] ⬦ *adj* - 1. [correct] correcto(ta); **to be right (about)** tener razón (respecto a); **that's right** sí; **to get sthg right** acertar en algo - 2. [morally correct, satisfactory, well] bien; **to be right to do sthg** hacer bien en hacer algo; **something isn't right with it** le pasa algo

- **3.** [appropriate] apropiado(da); **it's just right** es perfecto; **the right moment** el momento oportuno - **4.** [uppermost]: **right side** cara f anterior OR de arriba - **5.** [on right-hand side] derecho(cha). ◇ n - **1.** (U) [moral correctness] el bien; **to be in the right** tener razón - **2.** [entitlement, claim] derecho m; **by rights** en justicia - **3.** [right-hand side] derecha f; **on the right** a la derecha. ◇ adv - **1.** [correctly] bien, correctamente - **2.** [to right-hand side] a la derecha - **3.** [emphatic use]: **right here** aquí mismo; **right at the top** arriba del todo; **right in the middle** justo en el medio; **she crashed right into the tree** chocó de frente contra el árbol - **4.** [completely] completamente - **5.** [immediately]: **I'll be right back** ahora mismo vuelvo; **right before/after (sthg)** justo antes/después (de algo); **right now** ahora mismo, ahorita Amér C & Méx; **right away** en seguida, luego Amér. ◇ vt - **1.** [correct] corregir, rectificar - **2.** [make upright] enderezar. ◇ excl ¡bien! ◆ **Right** n POL: **the Right** la derecha.

right angle n ángulo m recto; **at right angles (to)** en ángulo recto (con).

righteous ['raɪtʃəs] adj [anger] justo(ta); [person] honrado(da).

rightful ['raɪtfʊl] adj legítimo(ma).

right-hand adj derecho(cha); **the right-hand side** el lado derecho, la derecha.

right-hand drive n vehículo f con el volante a la derecha.

right-handed [-'hændɪd] adj diestro(tra).

right-hand man n brazo m derecho.

rightly ['raɪtlɪ] adv - **1.** [correctly] correctamente - **2.** [appropriately] debidamente, bien - **3.** [morally] con razón.

right of way n - **1.** AUT prioridad f - **2.** [access] derecho m de paso.

right-on adj inf progre.

right wing n: **the right wing** la derecha. ◆ **right-wing** adj derechista.

rigid ['rɪdʒɪd] adj - **1.** [stiff] rígido(da) - **2.** [harsh, unbending] inflexible.

rigmarole ['rɪgmərəʊl] n inf pej - **1.** [process] ritual m - **2.** [story] galimatías m inv.

rigor US = **rigour**.

rigorous ['rɪgərəs] adj riguroso(sa).

rigour UK, **rigor** US ['rɪgər] n [firmness] rigor m.

rile [raɪl] vt irritar, sacar de quicio.

rim [rɪm] n - **1.** [of container] borde m - **2.** [of spectacles] montura f.

rind [raɪnd] n [of bacon, cheese] corteza f; [of orange, lemon] cáscara f.

ring [rɪŋ] ◇ n - **1.** [telephone call]: **to give sb a ring** llamar a alguien (por teléfono) - **2.** [sound of doorbell] timbrazo m - **3.** [on finger, around planet] anillo m - **4.** [metal hoop] aro m; [for cur-

tains, drinks can] anilla f - **5.** [circle - of trees] círculo m; [- of people] corro m - **6.** [for boxing] cuadrilátero m; [at circus] pista f - **7.** [illegal group] red f. ◇ vt - **1.** (pt rang, pp rung) UK [phone] llamar por teléfono, telefonear - **2.** (pt rang, pp rung) [bell] tocar - **3.** (pt & pp ringed) [draw a circle round] señalar con un círculo - **4.** (pt rang, pp rung) [surround] rodear. ◇ vi (pt rang, pp rung) - **1.** UK [phone] llamar por teléfono, telefonear - **2.** [bell] sonar - **3.** [to attract attention]: **to ring (for)** llamar (para) - **4.** [resound]: **to ring with** resonar con.
◆ **ring back** vt sep & vi UK llamar más tarde. ◆ **ring off** vi UK colgar. ◆ **ring up** vt sep UK [telec] llamar (por teléfono).

ring binder n carpeta f de anillas.

ringing ['rɪŋɪŋ] n [of bell] repique m, tañido m; [in ears] zumbido m.

ringing tone n tono m de llamada.

ringleader ['rɪŋ,li:dər] n cabecilla mf.

ringlet ['rɪŋlɪt] n rizo m, tirabuzón m.

ring-pull n anilla f.

ring road n UK carretera f de circunvalación.

ring tone n [for mobile phone] melodía f.

rink [rɪŋk] n pista f.

rinse [rɪns] vt - **1.** [dishes, vegetables] enjuagar; [clothes] aclarar - **2.** [wash out]: **to rinse one's mouth out** enjuagarse la boca.

riot ['raɪət] ◇ n disturbio m; **to run riot** desbocarse. ◇ vi amotinarse.

rioter ['raɪətər] n amotinado m, -da f.

riotous ['raɪətəs] adj desenfrenado(da).

riot police npl brigada f antidisturbios.

rip [rɪp] ◇ n rasgón m. ◇ vt - **1.** [tear] rasgar, desgarrar - **2.** [remove violently] quitar de un tirón. ◇ vi rasgarse, romperse.

RIP (abbr of rest in peace) RIP.

ripe [raɪp] adj maduro(ra); **to be ripe (for sthg)** estar listo (para algo).

ripen ['raɪpn] vt & vi madurar.

rip-off n inf estafa f.

ripple ['rɪpl] ◇ n - **1.** [in water] onda f, rizo m - **2.** [of laughter, applause] murmullo m. ◇ vt rizar.

rise ◇ n - **1.** UK [increase in salary] aumento m - **2.** [to fame, power, of practice] ascenso m ⫸ **to give rise to sthg** dar origen a algo. ◇ vi [raɪz] (pt rose, pp risen ['rɪzn]) - **1.** [gen] elevarse - **2.** [price, wage, temperature] subir - **3.** [sun, moon] salir - **4.** [stand up, get out of bed] levantarse - **5.** [street, ground] subir - **6.** [respond]: **to rise to** reaccionar ante - **7.** [rebel] sublevarse - **8.** [move up in status] ascender; **to rise to power/fame** ascender al poder/a la gloria.

rising ['raɪzɪŋ] ◇ adj - **1.** [sloping upwards] ascendente - **2.** [number, rate] creciente; [temperature, prices] en aumento - **3.** [increasingly successful] en alza. ◇ n rebelión f.

risk [rɪsk] ◇ n [gen] riesgo m; [danger] peligro m ▪ a health risk un peligro para la salud; to run the risk of sthg/of doing sthg correr el riesgo de algo/de hacer algo; to take a risk arriesgarse; at your own risk bajo tu cuenta y riesgo; at risk en peligro. ◇ vt - 1. [put in danger] arriesgar - 2. [take the chance of]: to risk doing sthg correr el riesgo de hacer algo.

risky ['rɪskɪ] adj peligroso(sa), arriesgado(da).

risqué ['ri:skeɪ] adj subido(da) de tono.

rissole ['rɪsəʊl] n UK especie de albóndiga de carne o verduras.

rite [raɪt] n rito m.

ritual ['rɪtʃʊəl] ◇ adj ritual. ◇ n ritual m.

rival ['raɪvl] ◇ adj rival. ◇ n rival mf. ◇ vt (UK pt & pp -led, cont -ling, US pt & pp -ed, cont -ing) rivalizar con.

rivalry ['raɪvlrɪ] n rivalidad f.

river ['rɪvəʳ] n río m.

river bank n orilla f OR margen f del río.

riverbed ['rɪvəbed] n cauce m OR lecho m del río.

riverside ['rɪvəsaɪd] n: the riverside la ribera OR orilla del río.

rivet ['rɪvɪt] ◇ n remache m. ◇ vt - 1. [fasten] remachar - 2. fig [fascinate]: to be riveted by sthg estar fascinado(da) con algo.

Riviera [,rɪvɪ'eərə] n: the French Riviera la Riviera francesa.

road [rəʊd] n [major] carretera f; [street] calle f; [path, minor thoroughfare] camino m; to be on the road to recovery estar en vías de recuperación; on the road [car] en circulación; [person] viajando; [rock band] de gira.

roadblock ['rəʊdblɒk] n control m.

road hog n inf pej conductor rápido y negligente.

road map n mapa m de carreteras.

road rage n violencia f en carretera.

road safety n seguridad f en carretera.

roadside ['rəʊdsaɪd] n: the roadside el borde de la carretera.

road sign n señal f de tráfico.

road tax n impuesto m de circulación.

roadtrip ['rəʊdtrɪp] n US viaje m hecho en automóvil.

roadway ['rəʊdweɪ] n calzada f.

road works npl obras fpl.

roadworthy ['rəʊd,wɜːðɪ] adj apto(ta) para circular.

roam [rəʊm] ◇ vt vagar por. ◇ vi vagar.

roar [rɔːʳ] ◇ vi [make a loud noise] rugir; to roar with laughter reírse a carcajadas. ◇ vt rugir, decir a voces. ◇ n - 1. [of traffic] fragor m - 2. [of lion, person] rugido m.

roaring ['rɔːrɪŋ] adj - 1. [loud] clamoroso(sa) - 2. [fire] muy vivo(va) - 3. [as emphasis]: to do a roaring trade in sthg vender algo como rosquillas.

roast [rəʊst] ◇ adj asado(da). ◇ n asado m. ◇ vt - 1. [potatoes, meat] asar - 2. [nuts, coffee beans] tostar.

roast beef n rosbif m.

rob [rɒb] vt robar; [bank] atracar; to rob sb of sthg lit & fig robar a alguien algo.

robber ['rɒbəʳ] n ladrón m, -ona f; [of bank] atracador m, -ra f.

robbery ['rɒbərɪ] n robo m; [of bank] atraco m.

robe [rəʊb] n - 1. [towelling] albornoz m - 2. [of student] toga f - 3. [of priest] sotana f - 4. US [dressing gown] bata f.

robin ['rɒbɪn] n petirrojo m.

robot ['rəʊbɒt] n robot m.

robust [rəʊ'bʌst] adj robusto(ta), fuerte.

rock [rɒk] ◇ n - 1. (U) [substance, boulder] roca f - 2. [stone] piedra f - 3. [crag] peñasco m - 4. [music] rock m - 5. UK [sweet] palo m de caramelo. ◇ comp [concert, group, singer] de rock. ◇ vt [cause to move] mecer, balancear. ◇ vi mecerse. ▪ Rock n inf [Gibraltar]: the Rock el Peñón. ▪ on the rocks adv - 1. [drink] con hielo - 2. [marriage, relationship] que va mal.

rock and roll, rock'n'roll n rock and roll m.

rock bottom n: to hit rock bottom tocar fondo. ▪ rock-bottom adj: rock-bottom prices precios muy bajos.

rockery ['rɒkərɪ] n jardín m de rocas.

rocket ['rɒkɪt] n - 1. [vehicle, weapon, firework] cohete m - 2. [plant] roqueta f.

rocket launcher [-,lɔːntʃəʳ] n lanzacohetes m inv.

rocking chair ['rɒkɪŋ-] n mecedora f.

rocking horse ['rɒkɪŋ-] n caballo m de balancín.

rock'n'roll [,rɒkən'rəʊl] = rock and roll.

rocky ['rɒkɪ] adj [full of rocks] rocoso(sa).

Rocky Mountains npl: the Rocky Mountains las montañas Rocosas.

rod [rɒd] n [wooden] vara f; [metal] barra f; [for fishing] caña f.

rode [rəʊd] pt ▷ ride.

rodent ['rəʊdənt] n roedor m.

roe [rəʊ] n hueva f; hard roe hueva f; soft roe lecha f.

roe deer n corzo m.

rogue [rəʊg] n [likeable rascal] picaruelo m, -la f.

role [rəʊl] n fig & THEAT papel m.

role model n modelo m a seguir.

roll [rəʊl] ◇ n - **1.** [gen] rollo m; [of paper, banknotes] fajo m; [of cloth] pieza f - **2.** [of bread] panecillo m - **3.** [list] lista f; [payroll] nómina f - **4.** [of drums] redoble m; [of thunder] retumbo m. ◇ vt - **1.** [turn over] hacer rodar - **2.** [roll up] enrollar - **3.** [cigarette] liar. ◇ vi - **1.** [ball, barrel] rodar - **2.** [vehicle] ir, avanzar - **3.** [ship] balancearse - **4.** [thunder] retumbar; [drum] redoblar. ➤ **roll about, roll around** vi: to roll about OR around (on) rodar (por). ➤ **roll in** vi inf llegar a raudales. ➤ **roll over** vi darse la vuelta. ➤ **roll up** ◇ vt sep - **1.** [make into roll] enrollar - **2.** [sleeves] remangarse. ◇ vi - **1.** [vehicle] llegar - **2.** inf [person] presentarse, aparecer.

roll call n: to take a roll call pasar lista.

roller ['rəʊlə'] n - **1.** [cylinder] rodillo m - **2.** [curler] rulo m.

Rollerblades® ['rəʊlə,bleɪdz] npl patines mpl en línea.

rollerblade ['rəʊləbleɪd] vi patinar (con patines en línea).

rollerblading ['rəʊlə,bleɪdɪŋ] n patinaje m (con patines en línea); **to go rollerblading** ir a patinar (con patines en línea).

roller coaster n montaña f rusa.

roller skate n patín m de ruedas.

rolling ['rəʊlɪŋ] adj [undulating] ondulante ➤➤ **to be rolling in it** inf nadar en la abundancia.

rolling pin n rodillo m (de cocina).

rolling stock n material m rodante.

roll-on adj [deodorant etc] de bola.

ROM [rɒm] (abbr of read only memory) n ROM f.

Roman ['rəʊmən] ◇ adj romano(na). ◇ n romano m, -na f.

Roman Catholic ◇ adj católico (romano)(católica (romana)). ◇ n católico (romano) m, católica (romana) f.

romance [rəʊ'mæns] n - **1.** [romantic quality] lo romántico - **2.** [love affair] amorío m - **3.** [in fiction - modern] novela f romántica. ◇ adj: Romance Languages lenguas fpl romance.

Romania, Rumania [ru:'meɪnjə] n Rumanía.

Romanian, Rumanian [ru:'meɪnjən] ◇ adj rumano(na). ◇ n - **1.** [person] rumano m, -na f - **2.** [language] rumano m.

Roman numerals npl números mpl romanos.

romantic [rəʊ'mæntɪk] adj romántico(ca).

romp [rɒmp] ◇ n retozo m, jugueteo m. ◇ vi retozar, juguetear.

rompers ['rɒmpəz] npl pelele m.

romper suit ['rɒmpə'-] n UK = rompers.

roof [ru:f] n - **1.** [of building] tejado m; [of vehicle] techo m; **to go through OR hit the roof** [person] subirse por las paredes - **2.** [of mouth] paladar m.

roofing ['ru:fɪŋ] n techumbre f.

roof rack n baca f, portaequipajes m inv.

rooftop ['ru:ftɒp] n tejado m.

rook [rʊk] n - **1.** [bird] grajo m - **2.** [chess piece] torre f.

rookie ['rʊkɪ] n - **1.** US inf [novice] novato m, -ta f - **2.** US inf [military recruit] novato m, -ta f.

room [ru:m, rʊm] ◇ n - **1.** [in house, building] habitación f - **2.** [for conferences etc] sala f - **3.** [bedroom] habitación f, cuarto m - **4.** (U) [space] sitio m, espacio m. ◇ vi sep US: room with compartir alojamiento con.

rooming house ['ru:mɪŋ-] n US casa f de huéspedes, pensión f.

roommate ['ru:mmeɪt] n compañero m, -ra f de habitación.

room service n servicio m de habitación.

roomy ['ru:mɪ] adj espacioso(sa), amplio(plia).

roost [ru:st] n percha f, palo m.

rooster ['ru:stə'] n gallo m.

root [ru:t] ◇ n lit & fig raíz f. ◇ vi [pig etc] hozar; [person] hurgar, escarbar. ➤ **roots** npl [origins] raíces fpl. ➤ **root for** vt insep US inf apoyar a. ➤ **root out** vt sep [eradicate] desarraigar.

rope [rəʊp] ◇ n [thin] cuerda f; [thick] soga f; NAUT maroma f, cable m; **to know the ropes** saber de qué va el asunto; **to show sb the ropes** poner a alguien al tanto. ◇ vt atar con cuerda. ➤ **rope in** vt sep inf arrastrar OR enganchar a; **to rope sb in to do sthg** liar a alguien para hacer algo.

rosary ['rəʊzərɪ] n rosario m.

rose [rəʊz] ◇ pt ▷ **rise.** ◇ adj [pink] rosa, color de rosa. ◇ n [flower] rosa f.

rosé ['rəʊzeɪ] n rosado m.

rosebud ['rəʊzbʌd] n capullo m de rosa.

rose bush n rosal m.

rosemary ['rəʊzmərɪ] n romero m.

rosette [rəʊ'zet] n [badge] escarapela f.

roster ['rɒstə'] n lista f.

rostrum ['rɒstrəm] (pl -trums OR -tra [-trə]) n tribuna f.

rosy ['rəʊzɪ] adj - **1.** [pink] sonrosado(da) - **2.** [hopeful] prometedor(ra).

rot [rɒt] ◇ n (U) - **1.** [of wood, food] podredumbre f; [in society, organization] decadencia f - **2.** UK dated [nonsense] tonterías fpl. ◇ vt pudrir. ◇ vi pudrirse.

rota ['rəʊtə] n lista f (de turnos).

rotary ['rəʊtərɪ] <> *adj* giratorio(ria), rotativo(va). <> *n US* [roundabout] glorieta *f*, rotonda *f*.   circulación glorietal.

rotate [rəʊ'teɪt] <> *vt* [turn] hacer girar, dar vueltas a. <> *vi* [turn] girar, dar vueltas.

rotation [rəʊ'teɪʃn] *n* [gen] rotación *f*.

rote [rəʊt] *n*: by rote de memoria.

rotten ['rɒtn] *adj* - 1. [decayed] podrido(da) - 2. *inf* [poor-quality] malísimo(ma), fatal - 3. *inf* [unpleasant] despreciable - 4. *inf* [unwell]: to feel rotten sentirse fatal OR muy mal.

rouge [ruːʒ] *n* colorete *m*.

rough [rʌf] <> *adj* - 1. [not smooth - surface, skin] áspero(ra); [- ground, road] desigual - 2. [not gentle] bruto(ta) - 3. [crude, not refined - person, manner] grosero(ra), tosco(ca); [- shelter] precario(ria); [- living conditions] duro(ra) - 4. [approximate - plan, sketch] a grandes rasgos; [- estimate, translation] aproximado(da); to write a rough draft of sthg escribir un borrador de algo - 5. [unpleasant] duro(ra), difícil - 6. [wind] violento(ta); [sea] picado(da); [weather, day] tormentoso(sa) - 7. [harsh - wine, voice] áspero(ra) - 8. [violent - area] peligroso(sa); [- person] violento(ta). <> *adv*: to sleep rough dormir al raso. <> *n* - 1. GOLF: the rough el rough - 2. [undetailed form]: in rough en borrador. <> *vt*: to rough it vivir sin comodidades.

roughage ['rʌfɪdʒ] *n* (U) fibra *f*.

rough and ready *adj* tosco(ca).

roughen ['rʌfn] *vt* poner áspero(ra).

roughly ['rʌflɪ] *adv* - 1. [approximately] más o menos - 2. [not gently] brutalmente - 3. [crudely] toscamente.

roulette [ruː'let] *n* ruleta *f*.

round [raʊnd] <> *adj* redondo(da). <> *prep* - 1. [surrounding] alrededor de; the reeds round the pond las cañas alrededor del estanque; she put her arm round his shoulder le puso el brazo al hombro - 2. [near] cerca de; round here por aquí - 3. [all over - the world etc] por todo(da); we went round the museum dimos una vuelta por el museo - 4. [in circular movement]: round (and round) alrededor de - 5. [in measurements]: she's 30 inches round the waist mide 30 pulgadas de cintura - 6. [at or to the other side of]: they were waiting round the corner esperaban a la vuelta de la esquina; to drive round the corner doblar la esquina; we went round the lake rodeamos el lago - 7. [so as to avoid]: he drove round the pothole condujo esquivando el bache. <> *adv* - 1. [on all sides]: all round por todos lados - 2. [near]: round about alrededor, en las proximidades - 3. [all over]: to travel round viajar por ahí - 4. [in circular movement]: she passed round a plate of biscuits pasó un plato de galletas; round (and round) en redondo; to go OR spin

round girar - 5. [to the other side] al otro lado: we went round to the back of the house illimos iiaa vuelta hasta la parte de atrás de la casa - 6. [at or to nearby place]: he came round to see us vino a vernos. <> *n* - 1. [of talks, drinks, sandwiches] ronda *f*; a round of toast una tostada; a round of applause una salva de aplausos - 2. [in championship] vuelta *f* - 3. [of doctor] visitas *fpl*; [of milkman, postman] recorrido *m* - 4. [of ammunition] cartucho *m* - 5. [in boxing] asalto *m* - 6. [in golf] vuelta *f*. <> *vt* doblar.
  rounds *npl* [of postman] recorrido *m*; [of doctor] visitas *fpl*; he's out on his rounds está visitando pacientes; to do OR go the rounds [joke, rumour] divulgarse; [illness] estar rodando.   **round off** *vt sep* terminar.   **round up** *vt sep* - 1. [sheep] recoger; [people] reunir - 2. MATHS redondear al alza.

roundabout ['raʊndəbaʊt] *n UK* - 1. [on road] glorieta *f*, rotonda *f* - 2. [at fairground] tiovivo *m*.

rounders ['raʊndəz] *n UK juego parecido al béisbol.*

roundly ['raʊndlɪ] *adv* rotundamente.

round-shouldered [-'ʃəʊldəd] *adj* cargado(da) de espaldas.

round table *n* mesa *f* redonda.

round trip *n* viaje *m* de ida y vuelta.

roundup ['raʊndʌp] *n* - 1. [summary] resumen *m*; news roundup resumen *m* informativo - 2. [of criminals] redada *f*.

rouse [raʊz] *vt* - 1. *fml* [wake up] despertar - 2. [impel]: to rouse sb/o.s. to do sthg animar a alguien/animarse a hacer algo - 3. [excite] excitar; it roused his interest le despertó el interés.

rousing ['raʊzɪŋ] *adj* [speech] conmovedor(ra); [cheer] entusiasta.

rout [raʊt] <> *n* derrota *f* aplastante. <> *vt* derrotar, aplastar.

route [ruːt] *n* [gen] ruta *f*; [of bus] línea *f*, recorrido *m*; [of ship] rumbo *m*; [for deliveries] recorrido *m*, itinerario *m*; [main road] carretera *f* principal.

route map *n* plano *m* (del camino).

routine [ruː'tiːn] <> *adj* rutinario(ria); (to have) a routine checkup (hacerse) un reconocimiento médico rutinario. <> *n* rutina *f*.

roving ['rəʊvɪŋ] *adj* itinerante; a roving reporter un periodista ambulante.

row¹[rəʊ] <> *n* - 1. [line] fila *f*, hilera *f* - 2. [succession] serie *f*; three in a row tres seguidos. <> *vt* [boat] remar. <> *vi* remar.

row²[raʊ] <> *n* - 1. [quarrel] pelea *f*, bronca *f* - 2. *inf* [noise] estruendo *m*, ruido *m*. <> *vi* [quarrel] reñir, pelearse.

rowboat ['rəʊbəʊt] *n US* bote *m* de remos.

rowdy ['raʊdɪ] *adj* [noisy] ruidoso(sa); [quarrelsome] pendenciero(ra).

row house [rəʊ-] *n US* casa *f* adosada.

rowing ['rəʊɪŋ] *n* remo *m*.

rowing boat *n UK* bote *m* de remo.

royal ['rɔɪəl] <> *adj* real. <> *n inf* miembro *m* de la familia real.

Royal Air Force *n*: **the Royal Air Force** las Fuerzas Aéreas de Gran Bretaña.

royal family *n* familia *f* real.

Royal Mail *n UK*: **the Royal Mail** ≃ Correos *m*.

Royal Navy *n*: **the Royal Navy** la Armada de Gran Bretaña.

royalty ['rɔɪəltɪ] *n* realeza *f*. ◆ **royalties** *npl* derechos *mpl* de autor.

rpm (*abbr of* **revolutions per minute**) r.p.m. *fpl*

RSPCA (*abbr of* **Royal Society for the Prevention of Cruelty to Animals**) *n sociedad británica protectora de animales*, ≃ SPA *f*.

RSVP (*abbr of* **répondez s'il vous plaît**) s.r.c.

Rt Hon (*abbr of* **Right Honourable**) su Sría.

rub [rʌb] <> *vt*: **to rub sthg (against** OR **on)** frotar algo (en OR contra); **to rub sthg on** OR **onto** frotar algo en; **to rub sb up the wrong way** *UK*, **to rub sb the wrong way** *US* sacar a alguien de quicio. <> *vi*: **to rub (against sthg)** rozar (algo); **to rub (together)** rozarse. ◆ **rub off on** *vt insep* [subj: quality] influir en. ◆ **rub out** *vt sep* [erase] borrar.

rubber ['rʌbə^r] *n* - 1. [substance] goma *f*, caucho *m* - 2. *UK* [eraser] goma *f* de borrar - 3. *US inf* [condom] goma *f* - 4. [in bridge] partida *f*.

rubber band *n US* goma *f* elástica.

rubber plant *n* ficus *m inv*.

rubber stamp *n* estampilla *f Esp*, sello *m* de goma, timbre *m* de goma *Chile*. ◆ **rubber-stamp** *vt* aprobar oficialmente.

rubbish ['rʌbɪʃ] *n* (*U*) - 1. [refuse] basura *f* - 2. *inf fig* [worthless matter] porquería *f* - 3. *inf* [nonsense] tonterías *fpl*; **don't talk rubbish** no digas tonterías.

rubbish bin *n UK* cubo *m* de la basura.

rubbish dump *n UK* vertedero *m*, basurero *m*.

rubble ['rʌbl] *n* (*U*) escombros *mpl*.

ruby ['ruːbɪ] *n* rubí *m*.

rucksack ['rʌksæk] *n* mochila *f*.

ructions ['rʌkʃnz] *npl inf* bronca *f*.

rudder ['rʌdə^r] *n* timón *m*.

ruddy ['rʌdɪ] *adj* [reddish] rojizo(za).

rude [ruːd] *adj* - 1. [impolite - person, manners, word] grosero(ra), liso(sa) *Arg & Perú*; [- joke] verde - 2. [shocking] violento(ta), brusco(ca).

rudimentary [ˌruːdɪ'mentərɪ] *adj* rudimentario(ria).

rueful ['ruːfʊl] *adj* arrepentido(da).

ruffian ['rʌfjən] *n* rufián *m*.

ruffle ['rʌfl] *vt* - 1. [hair] despeinar; [water] agitar; [feathers] encrespar - 2. [composure, nerves] encrespar - 3. [person] poner nervioso(sa) a.

rug [rʌg] *n* - 1. [carpet] alfombra *f* - 2. [blanket] manta *f* de viaje.

rugby ['rʌgbɪ] *n* rugby *m*.

rugged ['rʌgɪd] *adj* - 1. [wild, inhospitable] escabroso(sa) - 2. [sturdy] fuerte - 3. [roughly handsome] duro y atractivo (dura y atractiva); **his rugged good looks** sus rasgos recios.

rugger ['rʌgə^r] *n UK inf* rugby *m*.

ruin ['ruːɪn] <> *n* ruina *f*. <> *vt* - 1. [destroy] estropear - 2. [spoil] arruinar - 3. [bankrupt] arruinar. ◆ **in ruin(s)** *adv* en ruinas.

rule [ruːl] <> *n* - 1. [regulation, guideline] regla *f*, norma *f*; **to break the rules** violar las normas; **to obey the rules** obedecer las normas - 2. [norm]: **the rule** la regla, la norma; **as a rule** por regla general - 3. [government] dominio *m*; **to be under Roman rule** estar bajo dominio romano - 4. [ruler] regla *f*. <> *vt* - 1. *fml* [control] regir - 2. [govern] gobernar - 3. [decide]: **to rule that** decidir OR ordenar que. <> *vi* - 1. [give decision] decidir, fallar - 2. *fml* [be paramount] ser primordial - 3. [govern] gobernar. ◆ **rule out** *vt sep* descartar.

ruled [ruːld] *adj* rayado(da).

ruler ['ruːlə^r] *n* - 1. [for measurement] regla *f* - 2. [monarch] soberano *m*, -na *f*.

ruling ['ruːlɪŋ] <> *adj* en el poder. <> *n* fallo *m*, decisión *f*.

rum [rʌm] *n* ron *m*.

Rumania [ruː'meɪnjə] = **Romania**.

Rumanian [ruː'meɪnjən] = **Romanian**.

rumble ['rʌmbl] <> *n* [gen] estruendo *m*; [of stomach] ruido *m*. <> *vi* [gen] retumbar; [stomach] hacer ruido.

rummage ['rʌmɪdʒ] *vi* hurgar, rebuscar; **to rummage around in sthg** revolver en algo.

rumour *UK*, **rumor** *US* ['ruːmə^r] *n* rumor *m*; **there's a rumour going around that...** se rumorea que...

rumoured *UK*, **rumored** *US* ['ruːməd] *adj*: **to be rumoured** rumorearse; **she is rumoured to be very rich** se rumorea que es muy rica.

rump [rʌmp] *n* - 1. [of animal] grupa *f*, ancas *fpl* - 2. *inf* [of person] trasero *m*.

rump steak *n* filete *m* de lomo, churrasco *m* de cuadril *R Plata*.

rumpus ['rʌmpəs] *n inf* lío *m*, jaleo *m*.

run [rʌn] <> *n* - 1. [on foot] carrera *f*; **to go for a run** ir a correr; **on the run** en fuga - 2. [journey

- in car] paseo *m* OR vuelta *f* (en coche); **to go for a run** ir a dar una vuelta, [- In tralle slllll ‖ ||. [saltar of mlll], dl|l|l|||l] xF||lf |), [- of luck] racha *f* - **4.** THEAT: **the play had a 6-week run** la obra estuvo en cartelera 6 semanas - **5.** [great demand]: **a run on sthg** una gran demanda de algo - **6.** [in tights] carrera *f* - **7.** [in cricket, baseball] carrera *f* - **8.** [for skiing etc] pista *f*. ◇ *vt* (*pt* **ran**, *pp* **run**) - **1.** [on foot] correr - **2.** [manage - business] dirigir, administrar; [- life, event] organizar - **3.** [operate - computer program, machine, film] poner - **4.** [have and use - car etc] hacer funcionar - **5.** [open - tap] abrir; **to run a bath** llenar la bañera - **6.** [publish] publicar. ◇ *vi* (*pt* **ran**, *pp* **run**) - **1.** [on foot] correr - **2.** *esp US* [in election]: **to run (for)** presentarse como candidato(ta) (a); **he's running for president** se presenta a la presidencia - **3.** [factory, machine] funcionar; [engine] estar encendido(da); **to run on** OR **off sthg** funcionar con algo; **it runs on diesel/off the mains** funciona con diesel/electricidad; **to run smoothly** ir bien - **4.** [bus, train] ir - **5.** [flow] correr - **6.** [tap] gotear; **somebody has left the tap running** alguien se ha dejado el grifo abierto; [nose] moquear; **my nose is running** me moquea la nariz; [eyes] llorar - **7.** [colour] desteñir. ◆ **run across** *vt insep* [meet] encontrarse con. ◆ **run away** *vi* [flee]: **to run away (from)** huir OR fugarse (de). ◆ **run down** ◇ *vt sep* - **1.** [run over] atropellar - **2.** [criticize] hablar mal de. ◇ *vi* [battery] acabarse; [clock] pararse; [project, business] debilitarse. ◆ **run into** *vt insep* - **1.** [problem] encontrar; [person] tropezarse con - **2.** [in vehicle] chocar con. ◆ **run off** ◇ *vt sep* [copies, photocopies] sacar. ◇ *vi*: **to run off (with)** fugarse (con). ◆ **run out** *vi* - **1.** [become used up] acabarse - **2.** [expire] caducar. ◆ **run out of** *vt insep* quedarse sin. ◆ **run over** *vt sep* atropellar. ◆ **run through** *vt insep* - **1.** [be present in] recorrer, atravesar; **the vein of humour which ran through her work** el tono de humor que está presente en su trabajo - **2.** [practise] ensayar - **3.** [read through] echar un vistazo a. ◆ **run to** *vt insep* [amount to] ascender a; **the bill ran to thousands** la cuenta subía a varios miles. ◆ **run up** *vt insep* [amass] incurrir en; **he ran up a huge bill** acumuló una factura enorme. ◆ **run up against** *vt insep* tropezar con.

runaway [ˈrʌnəweɪ] ◇ *adj* - **1.** [gen] fugitivo(va); [horse] desbocado(da); [train] fuera de control; [inflation] desenfrenado(da) - **2.** [victory] fácil. ◇ *n* fugitivo *m*, -va *f*.

rundown [ˈrʌndaʊn] *n* [report] informe *m*, resumen *m*; **to give sb a rundown on sthg** poner a alguien al tanto de algo. ◆ **run-down** *adj* - **1.** [dilapidated] en ruinas - **2.** [tired] agotado(da); **to feel run-down** sentirse débil.

rung [rʌŋ] ◇ *pp* ▷ **ring**. ◇ *n lit* & *fig* peldaño *m*.

runner [ˈrʌnəʳ] *n* - **1.** [athlete] corredor *m*, -ra *f* - **2.** [smuggler] contrabandista *mf* - **3.** [on sledge] carril *m*; [of drawer, sliding seat] carro *m*.

runner bean *n UK* judía *f* verde, chaucha *f R Plata*, vainita *f Ven*, ejote *m Amér C & Méx*, poroto *m* verde *Chile*.

runner-up (*pl* **runners-up**) *n* subcampeón *m*, -ona *f*.

running [ˈrʌnɪŋ] ◇ *adj* - **1.** [continuous] continuo(nua) - **2.** [consecutive] seguidos(das); **four days running** cuatro días consecutivos - **3.** [water] corriente. ◇ *n* - **1.** [act of running] el correr; **to go running** hacer footing - **2.** SPORT carreras *fpl* - **3.** [management] dirección *f*, organización *f* - **4.** [operation] funcionamiento *m* ▶▶ **to be in/out of the running (for sthg)** tener/no tener posibilidades (de algo).

runny [ˈrʌnɪ] *adj* - **1.** [sauce, gravy] derretido(da) - **2.** [nose] que moquea; [eyes] llorosos(as).

run-of-the-mill *adj* normal y corriente.

runt [rʌnt] *n* - **1.** [animal] cría *f* más pequeña y débil - **2.** *pej* [person] renacuajo *m*.

run-up *n* - **1.** [preceding time] periodo *m* previo; **the run-up to the elections** el periodo previo a las elecciones - **2.** SPORT carrerilla *f*.

runway [ˈrʌnweɪ] *n* pista *f*.

rupture [ˈrʌptʃəʳ] ◇ *n* MED hernia *f*. ◇ *vt* romper.

rural [ˈrʊərəl] *adj* rural.

ruse [ruːz] *n* ardid *m*.

rush [rʌʃ] ◇ *n* - **1.** [hurry] prisa *f*; **to be in a rush** tener prisa - **2.** [busy period] hora *f* punta - **3.** [surge - of air] ráfaga *f*; [- of water] torrente *m*; [- mental] arrebato *m*; **to make a rush for sthg** ir en desbandada hacia algo; **there was a rush for the exit** la gente salió apresuradamente. ◇ *vt* - **1.** [hurry] apresurar; **to rush sb into doing sthg** apresurar a alguien para que haga algo - **2.** [send quickly] llevar rápidamente; **he was rushed to hospital** lo llevaron al hospital a toda prisa. ◇ *vi* - **1.** [hurry] ir de prisa, correr; **to rush into sthg** meterse de cabeza en algo; **there's no need to rush** no hay ninguna prisa; **he rushed to help her** corrió a ayudarla - **2.** [surge] precipitarse. ◆ **rushes** *npl* BOT juncos *mpl*.

rush hour *n* hora *f* punta, hora *f* pico *Amér*, hora *f* peack *Chile*.

rusk [rʌsk] *n* galleta que se da a los niños pequeños para que se acostumbren a masticar.

Russia [ˈrʌʃə] *n* Rusia.

Russian [ˈrʌʃn] ◇ *adj* ruso(sa). ◇ *n* - **1.** [person] ruso *m*, -sa *f* - **2.** [language] ruso *m*.

rust [rʌst] ◇ *n* óxido *m*. ◇ *vi* oxidarse.

rustic [ˈrʌstɪk] *adj* rústico(ca).

rustle ['rʌsl] ⬦ *vt* - **1.** [paper] hacer crujir - **2.** *US* [cattle] robar. ⬦ *vi* [wind, leaves] susurrar; [paper] crujir.

rusty ['rʌstɪ] *adj lit* & *fig* oxidado(da); **my French is a bit rusty** hace mucho que no practico el francés.

rut [rʌt] *n* [track] rodada *f*; **to get into/be in a rut** *fig* caer/estar metido en una rutina; **to get out of a rut** salir de la rutina.

ruthless ['ru:θlɪs] *adj* despiadado(da).

RV *n US* (*abbr of* recreational vehicle) casaremolque *f*.

rye [raɪ] *n* [grain] centeno *m*.

rye bread *n* pan *m* de centeno.

s (*pl* ss *OR* s's), **S** (*pl* Ss *OR* S's) [es] *n* [letter] s *f*, S *f*. ◆ **S** (*abbr of* south) S.

Sabbath ['sæbəθ] *n*: **the Sabbath** [for Christians] el domingo; [for Jews] el sábado.

sabbatical [sə'bætɪkl] *n* sabático *m*; **on sabbatical** de sabático.

sabotage ['sæbətɑ:ʒ] ⬦ *n* sabotaje *m*. ⬦ *vt* sabotear.

saccharin(e) ['sækərɪn] *n* sacarina *f*.

sachet ['sæʃeɪ] *n* bolsita *f*.

sack [sæk] ⬦ *n* - **1.** [bag] saco *m* - **2.** *UK inf* [dismissal]: **to get** *OR* **be given the sack** ser despedido(da); **to give sb the sack** despedir a alguien. ⬦ *vt UK inf* despedir.

sacking ['sækɪŋ] *n* - **1.** [fabric] harpillera *f* - **2.** [dismissal] despido *m*.

sacred ['seɪkrɪd] *adj lit* & *fig* sagrado(da).

sacrifice ['sækrɪfaɪs] *fig* ⬦ *n* RELIG sacrificio *m*; **to make sacrifices** sacrificarse. ⬦ *vt* RELIG sacrificar.

sacrilege ['sækrɪlɪdʒ] *n fig* & RELIG sacrilegio *m*.

sacrosanct ['sækrəʊsæŋkt] *adj* sacrosanto(ta).

sad [sæd] *adj* triste.

sadden ['sædn] *vt* entristecer.

saddle ['sædl] ⬦ *n* - **1.** [for horse] silla *f* (de montar) - **2.** [of bicycle, motorcycle] sillín *m*,

asiento *m*. ⬦ *vt* - **1.** [horse] ensillar - **2.** *fig* [burden]: **to saddle sb with sthg** cargar a alguien con algo; **she was saddled with an elderly relative** le encajaron un pariente anciano.

saddlebag ['sædlbæg] *n* alforja *f*.

sadistic [sə'dɪstɪk] *adj* sádico(ca).

sadly ['sædlɪ] *adv* tristemente.

sadness ['sædnɪs] *n* tristeza *f*.

s.a.e., sae *n abbr of* **stamped addressed envelope**.

safari [sə'fɑːrɪ] *n* safari *m*.

safe [seɪf] ⬦ *adj* - **1.** [gen] seguro(ra); **a safe place** un lugar seguro; **is this ladder safe?** ¿es segura esta escalera?; **you're safe now** ahora estás seguro; **safe and sound** sano y salvo (sana y salva) - **2.** [without harm] sano y salvo (sana y salva) - **3.** [not causing disagreement]: **it's safe to say that...** se puede afirmar con seguridad que...; **to be on the safe side** por mayor seguridad - **4.** [reliable] digno(na) de confianza. ⬦ *n* caja *f* (de caudales).

safe-conduct *n* salvoconducto *m*.

safe-deposit box, safety-deposit box *n* caja *f* de seguridad.

safeguard ['seɪfgɑ:d] ⬦ *n* salvaguardia *f*, protección *f*; **as a safeguard** como protección; **a safeguard against sthg** una protección contra algo. ⬦ *vt*: **to safeguard sthg/sb (against sthg)** salvaguardar *OR* proteger algo/a alguien (contra algo).

safekeeping [,seɪf'ki:pɪŋ] *n*: **she gave me the letter for safekeeping** me dio la carta para que se la guardara en un lugar seguro.

safely ['seɪflɪ] *adv* - **1.** [with no danger] con seguridad - **2.** [not in danger] seguramente - **3.** [unharmed] sano y salvo (sana y salva) - **4.** [for certain]: **I can safely say that...** puedo decir con toda confianza que...

safe sex *n* sexo *m* sin riesgo.

safety ['seɪftɪ] *n* seguridad *f*.

safety belt *n* cinturón *m* de seguridad.

safety pin *n* imperdible *m*, seguro *m Méx*.

saffron ['sæfrən] *n* [spice] azafrán *m*.

sag [sæg] *vi* [sink downwards] hundirse, combarse.

sage [seɪdʒ] ⬦ *adj* sabio(bia). ⬦ *n* - **1.** [herb] salvia *f* - **2.** [wise man] sabio *m*.

Sagittarius [,sædʒɪ'teərɪəs] *n* Sagitario *m*.

Sahara [sə'hɑːrə] *n*: **the Sahara (Desert)** el (desierto del) Sáhara.

said [sed] *pt* & *pp* ▷ **say**.

sail [seɪl] ⬦ *n* - **1.** [of boat] vela *f*; **to set sail** zarpar - **2.** [journey by boat] paseo *m* en barco de vela; **to go for a sail** salir a hacer una excursión en barco de vela. ⬦ *vt* - **1.** [boat, ship] gobernar - **2.** [sea] cruzar. ⬦ *vi* - **1.** [travel by boat] navegar - **2.** [move - boat]: **the ship sailed**

across the ocean el barco cruzó el océano - **3.** [leave by boat] zarpar; **we sail at 10 am** zarpamos a las 10 de la mañana. ➤ **sail through** vt insep hacer con facilidad.

sailboat US = **sailing boat**.

sailing ['seɪlɪŋ] n - **1.** (U) SPORT vela f - **2.** [trip by ship] travesía f.

sailing boat UK, **sailboat** US ['seɪlbəʊt] n barco m de vela.

sailing ship n (buque m) velero m.

sailor ['seɪlə'] n marinero m, -ra f.

saint [seɪnt] n fig & RELIG santo m, -ta f; **he's no saint** no es ningún santo; **to have the patience of a saint** tener más paciencia que un santo.

saintly ['seɪntlɪ] adj santo(ta), piadoso(sa).

sake [seɪk] n: **for the sake of** por (el bien de); **for God's** OR **heaven's sake** ¡por el amor de Dios!

salad ['sæləd] n ensalada f.

salad bowl n ensaladera f.

salad cream n UK salsa parecida a la mahonesa para aderezar la ensalada.

salad dressing n aliño m (para la ensalada).

salami [sə'lɑːmɪ] n salami m.

salary ['sælərɪ] n sueldo m.

sale [seɪl] n - **1.** [gen] venta f; **on sale** en venta; **(up) for sale** en venta; **'for sale'** 'se vende' - **2.** [at reduced prices] liquidación f, saldo m. ➤ **sales** npl - **1.** ECON ventas fpl - **2.** [at reduced prices]: **the sales** las rebajas.

saleroom UK ['seɪlrʊm], **salesroom** US ['seɪlzrʊm] n sala f de subastas.

sales assistant ['seɪlz-], **salesclerk** US ['seɪlzklɜːrk] n dependiente m, -ta f.

salesman ['seɪlzmən] (pl -men [-mən]) n [in shop] dependiente m, vendedor m; [travelling] viajante m.

sales rep n inf representante mf.

salesroom US = **saleroom**.

saleswoman ['seɪlz,wʊmən] (pl -women [-,wɪmɪn]) n [in shop] dependienta f, vendedora f; [travelling] viajante f.

salient ['seɪljənt] adj fml sobresaliente.

saliva [sə'laɪvə] n saliva f.

sallow ['sæləʊ] adj cetrino(na).

salmon ['sæmən] (pl salmon OR -s) n salmón m.

salmonella [,sælmə'nelə] n salmonelosis f inv.

salon ['sælɒn] n salón m.

saloon [sə'luːn] n - **1.** UK [car] (coche m) utilitario m - **2.** US [bar] bar m - **3.** UK [in pub]: **saloon (bar)** en ciertos pubs y hoteles, bar elegante con precios más altos que los del 'public bar' - **4.** [in ship] salón m.

salt [sɔːlt, sɒlt] ◇ n sal f; **to take sthg with a pinch of salt** considerar algo con cierta reserva. ◇ vt [food] salar; [roads] echar sal en (las carreteras etc para evitar que se hielen). ➤ **salt away** vt sep inf ahorrar.

salt cellar UK, **salt shaker** US [-,ʃeɪkə'] n salero m.

saltwater ['sɔːlt,wɔːtə'] adj de agua salada.

salty ['sɔːltɪ] adj salado(da), salobre.

salutary ['sæljʊtrɪ] adj saludable.

salute [sə'luːt] ◇ n - **1.** [with hand] saludo m - **2.** MIL [firing of guns] salva f, saludo m. ◇ vt - **1.** MIL [with hand] saludar - **2.** [acknowledge formally] reconocer.

Salvadorean, Salvadorian [,sælvə-'dɔːrɪən] ◇ adj salvadoreño(ña). ◇ n salvadoreño m, -ña f.

salvage ['sælvɪdʒ] ◇ n (U) - **1.** [rescue of ship] salvamento m - **2.** [property rescued] objetos mpl recuperados OR rescatados. ◇ vt lit & fig: **to salvage sthg (from)** salvar algo (de).

salvation [sæl'veɪʃn] n salvación f.

Salvation Army n: **the Salvation Army** el Ejército de Salvación.

same [seɪm] ◇ adj mismo(ma); **the same colour as his** el mismo color que el suyo; **at the same time** [simultaneously] al mismo tiempo; [yet] aún así; **one and the same** el mismo(la misma). ◇ pron: **the same** el mismo (la misma); **she did the same** hizo lo mismo; **the ingredients are the same** los ingredientes son los mismos OR iguales; **his car is the same as yours** su coche es el mismo que el tuyo; **I'll have the same (again)** tomaré lo mismo (que antes); **all** OR **just the same** [nevertheless, anyway] de todos modos; **it's all the same to me** me da igual; **it's not the same** no es lo mismo; **happy Christmas! – the same to you!** ¡feliz Navidad! – ¡igualmente! ◇ adv: **the same** lo mismo.

sample ['sɑːmpl] ◇ n muestra f; **a free sample** una muestra gratuita. ◇ vt [food, wine, attractions] probar.

sanatorium (pl -riums OR -ria [-rɪə]), **sanitorium** US (pl -riums OR -ria [-rɪə]) [,sænə'tɔːrɪəm] n sanatorio m.

sanctimonious [,sæŋktɪ'məʊnjəs] adj pej santurrón(ona).

sanction ['sæŋkʃn] ◇ n sanción f. ◇ vt sancionar.

sanctity ['sæŋktətɪ] n santidad f.

sanctuary ['sæŋktʃʊərɪ] n - **1.** [for wildlife] reserva f; **a bird sanctuary** una reserva de aves - **2.** [refuge] refugio m - **3.** [holy place] santuario m.

sand [sænd] ◇ n arena f. ◇ vt lijar; **to sand down a surface** lijar una superficie.

sandal ['sændl] *n* sandalia *f*; **a pair of sandals** unas sandalias.

sandalwood ['sændlwʊd] *n* sándalo *m*.

sandbox *US* = **sandpit**.

sandcastle ['sænd,kɑːsl] *n* castillo *m* de arena.

sand dune *n* duna *f*.

sandpaper ['sænd,peɪpər] ⬦ *n (U)* papel *m* de lija. ⬦ *vt* lijar.

sandpit *UK* ['sændpɪt], **sandbox** *US* ['sændbɒks] *n* cuadro *m* de arena.

sandstone ['sændstəʊn] *n* piedra *f* arenisca.

sandwich ['sænwɪdʒ] ⬦ *n* [made with roll etc] bocadillo *m*; [made with sliced bread] sandwich *m* frío; **a cheese sandwich** un sandwich de queso. ⬦ *vt fig* apretujar; **she was sandwiched between two businessmen** quedó atrapada entre dos hombres de negocios.

sandwich board *n* cartelón *m* (de hombre-anuncio).

sandwich course *n UK curso universitario que incluye un cierto tiempo de experiencia profesional.*

sandy ['sændɪ] *adj* - 1. [covered in sand] arenoso(sa) - 2. [sand-coloured] rojizo(za).

sane [seɪn] *adj* - 1. [not mad] cuerdo(da) - 2. [sensible] prudente, sensato(ta).

sang [sæŋ] *pt* ⟶ **sing**.

sanitary ['sænɪtrɪ] *adj* - 1. [connected with health] sanitario(ria) - 2. [clean, hygienic] higiénico(ca).

sanitary towel, sanitary napkin *US n* [disposable] compresa *f*, toalla *f* higiénica *Amér*.

sanitation [,sænɪ'teɪʃn] *n* sanidad *f*.

sanitorium *US* = **sanatorium**.

sanity ['sænətɪ] *n* - 1. [saneness] cordura *f* - 2. [good sense] sensatez *f*.

sank [sæŋk] *pt* ⟶ **sink**.

Santa (Claus) ['sæntə(,klɔːz)] *n* Papá *m* Noel.

sap [sæp] ⬦ *n* [of plant] savia *f*. ⬦ *vt* [weaken] minar.

sapling ['sæplɪŋ] *n* árbol *m* nuevo, arbolito *m*.

sapphire ['sæfaɪər] *n* zafiro *m*.

Saran wrap® [sə'ræn-] *n US* plástico *m* transparente *(para envolver alimentos)*.

sarcastic [sɑː'kæstɪk] *adj* sarcástico(ca).

sardine [sɑː'diːn] *n* sardina *f*; **to be packed in like sardines** ir como sardinas en lata.

sardonic [sɑː'dɒnɪk] *adj* sardónico(ca).

SAS (*abbr of* **Special Air Service**) *n unidad especial del ejército británico encargada de operaciones de sabotaje.*

SASE *n US abbr of* **self-addressed stamped envelope**.

sash [sæʃ] *n* faja *f*.

sat [sæt] *pt* & *pp* ⟶ **sit**.

SAT [sæt] *n* - 1. (*abbr of* **Standard Assessment Test**) *examen de aptitud que se realiza a los siete, once y catorce años en Inglaterra y Gales* - 2. (*abbr of* **Scholastic Aptitude Test**) *examen de ingreso a la universidad en Estados Unidos.*

Satan ['seɪtn] *n* Satanás *m*.

satchel ['sætʃəl] *n* cartera *f*.

satellite ['sætəlaɪt] *n lit* & *fig* satélite *m*.

satellite TV *n* televisión *f* por satélite.

satin ['sætɪn] ⬦ *n* satén *m*, raso *m*. ⬦ *comp* de satén, de raso.

satire ['sætaɪər] *n* sátira *f*.

satisfaction [,sætɪs'fækʃn] *n* satisfacción *f*; **to do sthg to sb's satisfaction** hacer algo a la satisfacción OR al gusto de alguien.

satisfactory [,sætɪs'fæktərɪ] *adj* satisfactorio(ria).

satisfied ['sætɪsfaɪd] *adj* satisfecho(cha); **you're never satisfied!** ¡nunca te conformas con nada!; **a satisfied smile** una sonrisa de satisfacción.

satisfy ['sætɪsfaɪ] *vt* - 1. [gen] satisfacer - 2. [convince] convencer - 3. [requirements] cumplir, satisfacer.

satisfying ['sætɪsfaɪɪŋ] *adj* - 1. [pleasant] satisfactorio(ria) - 2. [filling] sustancioso(sa); **a satisfying meal** una comida sustanciosa.

satsuma [,sæt'suːmə] *n* satsuma *f*.

saturate ['sætʃəreɪt] *vt* - 1. [drench]: **to saturate sthg (with)** empapar algo (de); **he was saturated with sweat** estaba empapado de sudor - 2. [fill completely] saturar.

Saturday ['sætədɪ] ⬦ *n* sábado *m*; **what day is it?** – **it's Saturday** ¿a qué estamos hoy? – estamos a sábado; **on Saturday** el sábado; **on Saturdays** los sábados; **last Saturday** el sábado pasado; **this Saturday** este sábado, el sábado que viene; **next Saturday** el sábado de la semana que viene; **every Saturday** todos los sábados; **every other Saturday** cada dos sábados, un sábado sí y otro no; **the Saturday before** el sábado anterior; **the Saturday after next** no este sábado sino el siguiente; **the Saturday before last** hace dos sábados. ⬦ *comp* del sábado.

Saturn ['sætən] *n* Saturno *m*.

sauce [sɔːs] *n* CULIN salsa *f*.

saucepan ['sɔːspən] *n* [with two handles] cacerola *f*; [with one long handle] cazo *m*.

saucer ['sɔːsər] *n* platillo *m*.

saucy ['sɔːsɪ] *adj inf* descarado(da), fresco(ca).

Saudi Arabia [,saʊdɪə'reɪbjə] *n* Arabia Saudí.

Saudi (Arabian) ['saʊdɪ-] ⬦ *adj* saudí, saudita. ⬦ *n* [person] saudí *mf*, saudita *mf*.

sauna ['sɔːnə] n sauna f.

saunter ['sɔːntər] vi pasearse (tranquilamente); **he sauntered into the room** entró desenfadadamente en la habitación.

sausage ['sɒsɪdʒ] n salchicha f.

sausage roll n UK salchicha envuelta en masa como de empanadilla.

sauté [UK 'səʊteɪ, US sɔːʊ'teɪ] vt (pt & pp **sautéed** OR **sautéd**) saltear.

savage ['sævɪdʒ] <> adj [cruel, fierce] feroz, salvaje. <> n pej salvaje mf. <> vt - 1. [subj: animal] embestir, atacar - 2. [subj: person] atacar con ferocidad.

save [seɪv] <> vt - 1. [rescue] salvar, rescatar; **to save sb from sthg** salvar a alguien de algo - 2. [prevent waste of - time, money, energy] ahorrar - 3. [set aside - money] ahorrar; [- food, strength] guardar; **why don't you save some of your sweets for later?** ¿por qué no te guardas algunos caramelos para más tarde?; **will you save me some soup?** ¿me guardarás algo de sopa?; **save your strength for later** ahorra fuerzas para más tarde - 4. [avoid] evitar; **it saves having to go to the bank** ahorra tener que ir al banco; **to save sb from doing sthg** evitar a alguien (el) hacer algo - 5. SPORT parar - 6. COMPUT guardar

▶▶▶ **to save face** salvar las apariencias. <> vi ahorrar. <> n SPORT parada f. <> prep fml: **save (for)** excepto. ▶▶ **save up** vi ahorrar.

saving grace ['seɪvɪŋ-] n lo único positivo.

savings ['seɪvɪŋz] npl ahorros mpl.

savings account n cuenta f de ahorros.

savings bank n ≃ caja f de ahorros.

saviour UK, **savior** US ['seɪvjər] n salvador m, -ra f.

savour UK, **savor** US ['seɪvər] vt lit & fig saborear.

savoury UK, **savory** US ['seɪvərɪ] <> adj - 1. [not sweet] salado(da) - 2. US [tasty] sabroso(sa) - 3. [respectable, pleasant] agradable; **not a very savoury character** un personaje no muy honesto. <> n comida f de aperitivo.

saw [sɔː] <> pt ▷ **see**. <> n sierra f. <> vt (UK -ed, pp sawn, US -ed) serrar.

sawdust ['sɔːdʌst] n serrín m.

sawed-off shotgun US = **sawn-off shotgun**.

sawmill ['sɔːmɪl] n aserradero m.

sawn [sɔːn] pp UK ▷ **saw**.

sawn-off shotgun UK, **sawed-off shotgun** US ['sɔːd-] n arma f de cañones recortados.

saxophone ['sæksəfəʊn] n saxofón m.

say [seɪ] <> vt (pt & pp **said**) - 1. [gen] decir; **she said that...** dijo que...; **you should have said so!** ¡haberlo dicho!; **to say sthg again** repetir algo; **you can say that again!** ¡ya lo creo!;

to say yes decir que sí; **he's said to be good** se dice que es bueno; **let's say you were to win** pongamos que ganaras, suñi úe say 9.30? ¿qué tal a las 9.30?; **that goes without saying** ni que decir tiene; **to say the least** por no decir otra cosa; **I'll say this for him/her...** hay que decir OR admitir que él/ella...; **it has a lot to be said for it** tiene muy buenos puntos en su favor - 2. [indicate - clock, meter] marcar. <> n: **to have a/no say in sthg** tener/no tener voz y voto en algo; **let me have my say** déjame decir lo que pienso. ▶▶ **that is to say** adv es decir.

saying ['seɪɪŋ] n dicho m.

scab [skæb] n - 1. MED costra f - 2. pej [nonstriker] esquirol m.

scaffold ['skæfəʊld] n - 1. [around building] andamio m - 2. [for execution] cadalso m.

scaffolding ['skæfəldɪŋ] n (U) andamios mpl, andamiaje m.

scald [skɔːld] vt escaldar.

scale [skeɪl] <> n - 1. [of map] escala f; **to scale** a escala; **not drawn to scale** no hecho(cha) a escala - 2. [size, extent] tamaño m, escala f; **on a large scale** a gran escala - 3. [on measuring equipment] escala f - 4. [music] escala f - 5. [of fish, snake] escama f. <> vt - 1. [climb] escalar - 2. [remove scales from] escamar. ▶▶ **scales** npl - 1. [for weighing food] balanza f - 2. [for weighing person] báscula f; **bathroom scales** báscula de baño. ▶▶ **scale down** vt insep reducir.

scale model n maqueta f.

scallop ['skɒləp] <> n ZOOL vieira f. <> vt [decorate edge of] festonear.

scalp [skælp] <> n cuero m cabelludo. <> vt cortar la cabellera a.

scalpel ['skælpəl] n bisturí m.

scaly ['skeɪlɪ] adj [skin] escamoso(sa).

scamper ['skæmpər] vi corretear.

scampi ['skæmpɪ] n (U): **(breaded) scampi** gambas fpl a la gabardina.

scan [skæn] <> n exploración f ultrasónica. <> vt - 1. [examine carefully] examinar - 2. [glance at] dar un vistazo a - 3. ELECTRON & TV registrar.

scandal ['skændl] n - 1. [scandalous event, outrage] escándalo m - 2. [scandalous talk] habladurías fpl.

scandalize, -ise ['skændəlaɪz] vt escandalizar.

Scandinavia [,skændɪ'neɪvjə] n Escandinavia.

Scandinavian [,skændɪ'neɪvjən] <> adj escandinavo(va). <> n [person] escandinavo m, -va f.

scant [skænt] adj escaso(sa).

scanty ['skæntɪ] adj [amount, resources] escaso(sa); [dress] ligero(ra); [meal] insuficiente.

scapegoat ['skeɪpgəʊt] *n* cabeza *f* de turco.

scar [skɑ:r] *n* - **1.** [physical] cicatriz *f* - **2.** *fig* [mental] señal *f*.

scarce ['skeəs] *adj* escaso(sa).

scarcely ['skeəslɪ] *adv* apenas; **scarcely anyone/ever** casi nadie/nunca.

scare [skeər] <> *n* - **1.** [sudden fear] susto *m*, sobresalto *m* - **2.** [public fear] temor *m* - **3.** [panic]: **there was a bomb scare** hubo una amenaza de bomba. <> *vt* asustar, sobresaltar.
➣ **scare away, scare off** *vt sep* ahuyentar.

scarecrow ['skeəkrəʊ] *n* espantapájaros *m inv*.

scared ['skeəd] *adj* - **1.** [frightened] asustado(da); **don't be scared** no te asustes; **to be scared stiff** *OR* **to death** estar muerto de miedo - **2.** [worried]: **to be scared that** tener miedo que.

scarf [skɑ:f] <> *n* (*pl* -**s** *OR* **scarves**) [for neck] bufanda *f*, [for head] pañuelo *m* de cabeza. <> *vt US* [eat]: **scarf (down)** zamparse.

scarlet ['skɑ:lət] *adj* color escarlata.

scarlet fever *n* escarlatina *f*.

scarves [skɑ:vz] *npl* ⊳ **scarf**.

scathing ['skeɪðɪŋ] *adj* mordaz; **to be scathing about sthg/sb** criticar duramente algo/a alguien.

scatter ['skætər] <> *vt* esparcir, desparramar. <> *vi* dispersarse.

scatterbrained ['skætəbreɪnd] *adj inf* atolondrado(da).

scavenger ['skævɪndʒər] *n* - **1.** [animal] carroñero *m*, -ra *f* - **2.** [person] persona *f* que rebusca en las basuras.

scenario [sɪ'nɑ:rɪəʊ] (*pl* -**s**) *n* - **1.** [possible situation] situación *f* hipotética - **2.** [of film, play] resumen *m* del argumento.

scene [si:n] *n* - **1.** [gen, theatre] escena *f*; **behind the scenes** entre bastidores - **2.** [painting of place] panorama *m*, paisaje *m* - **3.** [location] sitio *m*; **the scene of the crime** la escena del crimen - **4.** [show of emotion] jaleo *m*, escándalo *m*
▶▶▶ **to set the scene** [for person] describir la escena; [for event] crear el ambiente propicio.

scenery ['si:nərɪ] *n (U)* - **1.** [of countryside] paisaje *m* - **2.** THEAT decorado *m*.

scenic ['si:nɪk] *adj* [view] pintoresco(ca); [tour] turístico(ca).

scent [sent] *n* - **1.** [smell - of flowers] fragancia *f*; [- of animal] rastro *m* - **2.** *fig* [track] pista *f*; **to lose the scent** perder la pista; **to throw sb off the scent** burlar a alguien - **3.** [perfume] perfume *m*.

scepter *US* = **sceptre**.

sceptic *UK*, **skeptic** *US* ['skeptɪk] *n* escéptico *m*, -ca *f*.

sceptical *UK*, **skeptical** *US* ['skeptɪkl] *adj* escéptico(ca); **to be sceptical about** tener muchas dudas acerca de.

sceptre *UK*, **scepter** *US* ['septər] *n* cetro *m*.

schedule [*UK* 'ʃedju:l, *US* 'skedʒʊl] <> *n* - **1.** [plan] programa *m*, plan *m*; **on schedule** sin retraso; **ahead of schedule** con adelanto; **behind schedule** con retraso - **2.** [of prices, contents] lista *f*; [of times] horario *m*. <> *vt*: **to schedule sthg (for)** fijar algo (para).

scheduled flight [*UK* 'ʃedju:ld-, *US* 'skedʒʊld-] *n* vuelo *m* regular.

scheme [ski:m] <> *n* - **1.** [plan] plano *m*, proyecto *m*; **pension scheme** plan *m* de pensiones - **2.** *pej* [dishonest plan] intriga *f* - **3.** [arrangement, decoration - of room] disposición *f*; **colour scheme** combinación *f* de colores. <> *vi pej*: **to scheme (to do sthg)** intrigar (para hacer algo).

scheming ['ski:mɪŋ] *adj* intrigante.

schism ['sɪzm, 'skɪzm] *n* cisma *f*.

schizophrenic [,skɪtsə'frenɪk] *adj* esquizofrénico(ca).

scholar ['skɒlər] *n* - **1.** [expert] erudito *m*, -ta *f* - **2.** *dated* [student] alumno *m*, -na *f*.

scholarship ['skɒləʃɪp] *n* - **1.** [grant] beca *f* - **2.** [learning] erudición *f*.

school [sku:l] *n* - **1.** [for children] colegio *m*, escuela *f*; **to go to school** ir al colegio, ir a la escuela; **the children are at school** los niños están en el colegio; **art school** escuela *f* de arte; **driving school** autoescuela *f*; **law/medical school** facultad *f* de derecho/medicina - **2.** *US* [university] universidad *f*.

school age *n* edad *f* escolar.

schoolbook ['sku:lbʊk] *n* libro *m* de texto.

schoolboy ['sku:lbɔɪ] *n* colegial *m*.

schoolchild ['sku:ltʃaɪld] (*pl* -**children** [-tʃɪldrən]) *n* colegial *m*, -la *f*.

schooldays ['sku:ldeɪz] *npl* años *mpl* de colegio.

schoolgirl ['sku:lgɜ:l] *n* colegiala *f*.

schooling ['sku:lɪŋ] *n* educación *f* escolar.

school-leaver [-,li:vər] *n UK* joven que ha terminado la enseñanza.

schoolmaster ['sku:l,mɑ:stər] *n dated* [at primary school] maestro *m*; [at secondary school] profesor *m*.

schoolmistress ['sku:l,mɪstrɪs] *n dated* [at primary school] maestra *f*; [at secondary school] profesora *f*.

school of thought *n* corriente *f* de opinión.

schoolteacher ['sku:l,ti:tʃər] *n* [primary] maestro *m*, -tra *f*; [secondary] profesor *m*, -ra *f*.

school year *n* año *m* escolar.

schooner ['sku:nər] *n* - **1.** [ship] goleta *f* - **2.** *UK* [sherry glass] copa *f* larga (para jerez).

sciatica [saɪ'ætɪkə] *n* ciática *f*.

science ['saɪəns] *n* ciencia *f*; his best subject is science su mejor asignatura son las ciencias.

science fiction *n* ciencia *f* ficción.

scientific [ˌsaɪən'tɪfɪk] *adj* científico(ca).

scientist ['saɪəntɪst] *n* científico *m*, -ca *f*.

scintillating ['sɪntɪleɪtɪŋ] *adj* brillante, chispeante.

scissors ['sɪzəz] *npl* tijeras *fpl*; **a pair of scissors** unas tijeras.

sclerosis = multiple sclerosis.

scoff [skɒf] <> *vt UK inf* zamparse, tragarse. <> *vi*: **to scoff (at sb/sthg)** mofarse OR burlarse (de alguien/de algo).

scold [skəʊld] *vt* regañar, reñir.

scone [skɒn] *n* bollo tomado con té a la hora de la merienda.

scoop [skuːp] <> *n* - 1. [utensil - for sugar] cucharita *f* plana; [- for ice cream] pinzas *fpl (de helado)*; [- for flour] paleta *f* - 2. PRESS exclusiva *f*; **to make a scoop** conseguir una exclusiva. <> *vt* - 1. [with hands] recoger - 2. [with utensil] recoger con cucharilla. ◆ **scoop out** *vt sep* sacar con cuchara.

scooter ['skuːtə'] *n* - 1. [toy] patinete *m* - 2. [motorcycle] Vespa® *f*, motoneta *f Amér*.

scope [skəʊp] *n (U)* - 1. [opportunity] posibilidades *fpl*; **there is scope for improvement** se puede mejorar - 2. [range] alcance *m*.

scorch [skɔːtʃ] *vt* [dress, fabric, grass] chamuscar; [face, skin] quemar.

scorching ['skɔːtʃɪŋ] *adj inf* abrasador(ra).

score [skɔː'] <> *n* - 1. [in test] calificación *f*, nota *f*; [in competition, game] puntuación *f*; **are you keeping (the) score?** ¿llevas el tanteo? - 2. SPORT resultado *m*; **what's the score?** ¿cómo van?; **the final score was 2 all** el resultado final fue empate a dos - 3. *dated* [twenty] veintena *f* - 4. MUS partitura *f* - 5. [subject]: **on that score** a ese respecto, por lo que se refiere a eso

▸▸▸ **to have a score to settle with sb** tener una cuenta que saldar con alguien; **to know the score** conocer el percal. <> *vt* - 1. SPORT marcar - 2. [achieve - success, victory] obtener - 3. [cut] grabar. <> *vi* - 1. SPORT marcar - 2. [in test etc] obtener una puntuación; **you scored well in part one** obtuviste una buena puntuación en la primera parte. ◆ **score out** *vt sep UK* tachar.

scoreboard ['skɔːbɔːd] *n* marcador *m*.

scorer ['skɔːrə'] *n* - 1. [official] tanteador *m*, -ra *f* - 2. [player - in football] goleador *m*, -ra *f*; [- in other sports] marcador *m*, -ra *f*.

scorn [skɔːn] <> *n* menosprecio *m*, desdén *m*; **to pour scorn on sthg/sb** despreciar algo/a alguien. <> *vt* menospreciar, desdeñar.

scornful ['skɔːnfʊl] *adj* despectivo(va).

Scorpio ['skɔːpɪəʊ] *(pl -s) n* Escorpión *m*.

scorpion ['skɔːpɪən] *n* alacrán *m*.

Scot [skɒt] *n* escocés *m*, -esa *f*.

scotch [skɒtʃ] *vt* [rumour] desmentir; [idea] desechar.

Scotch [skɒtʃ] *n* whisky *m* escocés.

Scotch tape® *n US* cinta *f* Scotch® *Amér*.

scot-free *adj inf*: **to get off scot-free** salir impune.

Scotland ['skɒtlənd] *n* Escocia.

Scots [skɒts] <> *adj* escocés(esa). <> *n* [dialect] escocés *m*.

Scotsman ['skɒtsmən] *(pl -men* [-mən]*)* *n* escocés *m*.

Scotswoman ['skɒtswʊmən] *(pl -women* [-ˌwɪmɪn]*)* *n* escocesa *f*.

Scottish ['skɒtɪʃ] *adj* escocés(esa).

Scottish National Party *n*: **the Scottish National Party** el Partido Nacionalista Escocés.

scoundrel ['skaʊndrəl] *n dated* sinvergüenza *m*, canalla *m*.

scour [skaʊə'] *vt* - 1. [clean] fregar, restregar - 2. [search] registrar, batir; **they scoured the countryside looking for the little girl** peinaron el campo en busca de la niña.

scourge [skɜːdʒ] *n* [cause of suffering] azote *m*.

scout [skaʊt] *n* MIL explorador *m*. ◆ **Scout** *n* [boy scout] explorador *m*. ◆ **scout around** *vi*: **to scout around (for)** explorar el terreno (en busca de).

scowl [skaʊl] *vi* fruncir el ceño.

scrabble ['skræbl] *vi* - 1. [scramble, scrape] escarbar; **to scrabble up/down** subir/bajar escarbando - 2. [feel around]: **to scrabble around for sthg** hurgar en busca de algo.

Scrabble® ['skræbl] *n* Scrabble® *m*.

scraggy ['skrægɪ] *adj inf* flaco(ca).

scramble ['skræmbl] <> *n* [rush] pelea *f*; **he got hurt in the scramble for the door** resultó herido en la desbandada que hubo hacia la puerta. <> *vi* - 1. [climb] trepar - 2. [move clumsily]: **to scramble to one's feet** levantarse rápidamente y tambaleándose.

scrambled eggs ['skræmbld-] *npl* huevos *mpl* revueltos.

scrap [skræp] <> *n* - 1. [small piece] trozo *m*, pedazo *m* - 2. *(U)* [metal] chatarra *f*; **he sold it for scrap** lo vendió para chatarra - 3. *inf* [fight, quarrel] pelotera *f*; **to have a scrap** pelearse. <> *vt* desechar, descartar. ◆ **scraps** *npl* [food] sobras *fpl*.

scrapbook ['skræpbʊk] *n* álbum *m* de recortes.

scrap dealer *n* chatarrero *m*, -ra *f*.

scrape [skreɪp] <> *n* - 1. [noise] chirrido *m* - 2. *dated* [difficult situation] apuro *m*. <> *vt*

- 1. [remove]: **to scrape sthg off sthg** raspar algo de algo **- 2.** [vegetables] raspar **- 3.** [car, bumper, glass] rayar; [knee, elbow, skin] rasguñar. ⬦ *vi* [rub]: **to scrape against/on sthg** rozar contra/ en algo. ◆ **scrape through** *vt insep* [exam] aprobar por los pelos.

scraper ['skreɪpəʳ] *n* raspador *m*.

scrap merchant *n* UK chatarrero *m*, -ra *f*.

scrap paper UK, **scratch paper** US *n* (U) papel *m* usado.

scrapyard ['skræpjɑːd] *n* [gen] depósito *m* de chatarra; [for cars] cementerio *m* de coches.

scratch [skrætʃ] ⬦ *n* **- 1.** [wound] arañazo *m*, rasguño *m* **- 2.** [mark] raya *f*, surco *m*. ▸▸▸ **to do sthg from scratch** hacer algo partiendo desde el principio; **to be up to scratch** estar a la altura requerida. ⬦ *vt* **- 1.** [wound] arañar, rasguñar **- 2.** [mark] rayar **- 3.** [rub - head, leg] rascar; **he scratched his head** se rascó la cabeza. ⬦ *vi* [rub] rascarse.

scratch card *n* tarjeta con una zona que hay que rascar para ver si contiene premio.

scratch paper US = **scrap paper.**

scrawl [skrɔːl] ⬦ *n* garabatos *mpl*. ⬦ *vt* garabatear.

scrawny ['skrɔːnɪ] *adj* flaco(ca).

scream [skriːm] ⬦ *n* **- 1.** [cry, shout] grito *m*, chillido *m* **- 2.** [noise] chirrido *m*. ⬦ *vt* vociferar. ⬦ *vi* [person] chillar; **to scream at sb** gritar a alguien.

scree [skriː] *n* montón de piedras desprendidas de la ladera de una montaña.

screech [skriːtʃ] ⬦ *n* **- 1.** [of person] chillido *m*; [of bird] chirrido *m* **- 2.** [of car, tyres] chirrido *m*, rechinar *m*. ⬦ *vt* gritar. ⬦ *vi* **- 1.** [person, bird] chillar **- 2.** [car, tyres] chirriar, rechinar.

screen [skriːn] ⬦ *n* **- 1.** TV, CIN & COMPUT pantalla *f* **- 2.** [panel] biombo *m*. ⬦ *vt* **- 1.** [show in cinema] proyectar **- 2.** [broadcast on TV] emitir **- 3.** [candidate, patient] examinar; **to screen sb for sthg** hacer un chequeo a alguien para algo.

screen break *n* COMPUT salto *m* de pantalla.

screening ['skriːnɪŋ] *n* **- 1.** [of film] proyección *f* **- 2.** [of TV programme] emisión *f* **- 3.** [for security] examen *m* **- 4.** MED [examination] chequeo *m*.

screenplay ['skriːnpleɪ] *n* guión *m*.

screenshot ['skriːnʃɒt] *n* pantallazo *m*, captura *f* de pantalla.

screw [skruː] ⬦ *n* [for fastening] tornillo *m*. ⬦ *vt* **- 1.** [fix]: **to screw sthg to** atornillar algo a **- 2.** [twist] enroscar; **to screw a lid on** poner la tapa de rosca **- 3.** *vulg* [woman] follar, coger *Amér*. ◆ **screw up** *vt sep* **- 1.** [sheet of paper etc] arrugar **- 2.** [eyes] entornar; [face] arrugar **- 3.** *v inf* [ruin] jorobar.

screwdriver ['skruː,draɪvəʳ] *n* destornillador *m*.

scribble ['skrɪbl] ⬦ *n* garabato *m*. ⬦ *vt* & *vi* garabatear.

script [skrɪpt] *n* **- 1.** [of play, film etc] guión *m* **- 2.** [system of writing] escritura *f* **- 3.** [handwriting] letra *f*.

Scriptures ['skrɪptʃəz] *npl*: **the Scriptures** las Sagradas Escrituras.

scriptwriter ['skrɪpt,raɪtəʳ] *n* guionista *mf*.

scroll [skrəʊl] ⬦ *n* rollo *m* de pergamino/papel. ⬦ *vt* COMPUT desplazar.

scrounge [skraʊndʒ] *inf vt* gorronear.

scrounger ['skraʊndʒəʳ] *n* *inf* gorrón *m*, -ona *f*.

scrub [skrʌb] ⬦ *n* **- 1.** [rub] restregón *m*; **give it a good scrub** dale un buen fregado **- 2.** [undergrowth] maleza *f*. ⬦ *vt* restregar.

scruff [skrʌf] *n*: **by the scruff of the neck** por el pescuezo.

scruffy ['skrʌfɪ] *adj* [person] dejado(da); [clothes] andrajoso(sa); [room] desordenado(da).

scrum(mage) ['skrʌm(ɪdʒ)] *n* RUGBY melé *f*.

scrunchie ['skrʌntʃɪ], **scrunchy** *n* coletero *m*.

scruples ['skruːplz] *npl* escrúpulos *mpl*.

scrutinize, -ise ['skruːtɪnaɪz] *vt* escudriñar.

scrutiny ['skruːtɪnɪ] *n* (U) escrutinio *m*, examen *m*; **to be open to public scrutiny** estar expuesto(ta) al examen del público; **to come under the scrutiny of** ser cuidadosamente examinado(da) por.

scuff [skʌf] *vt* [damage - shoes] pelar; [- furniture, floor] rayar.

scuffle ['skʌfl] *n* refriega *f*, reyerta *f*; **there were scuffles between the police and demonstrators** hubo enfrentamientos entre la policía y los manifestantes.

scullery ['skʌlərɪ] *n* trascocina *f*.

sculptor ['skʌlptəʳ] *n* escultor *m*, -ra *f*.

sculpture ['skʌlptʃəʳ] *n* escultura *f*.

scum [skʌm] *n* (U) **- 1.** [froth] espuma *f* **- 2.** *v inf pej* [worthless people] escoria *f*; **to be the scum of the earth** ser la escoria de la sociedad.

scupper ['skʌpəʳ] *vt* *fig* & NAUT hundir.

scurrilous ['skʌrələs] *adj* *fml* injurioso(sa), difamatorio(ria).

scurry ['skʌrɪ] *vi*: **to scurry off** OR **away** escabullirse.

scuttle ['skʌtl] ⬦ *n* cubo *m* del carbón. ⬦ *vi* [rush]: **to scuttle off** OR **away** escabullirse.

scythe [saɪð] *n* guadaña *f*.

SDLP (*abbr of* Social Democratic and Labour Party) *n* partido político norirlandés que defiende la integración pacífica en la república de Irlanda.

sea [si:] *n* - 1. [not land] mar *m* o *f*; **at sea** en el mar; **by sea** en barco; **by the sea** a orillas del mar; **out to sea** [away from shore] mar adentro; [across the water] hacia el mar - 2. [not ocean] mar *m*
▶▶▶ **to be all at sea** estar totalmente perdido(da).

sea bass *n* lubina *f*.

seabed ['si:bed] *n*: **the seabed** el lecho marino.

seaboard ['si:bɔ:d] *n fml* litoral *m*.

sea breeze *n* brisa *f* marina.

seafood ['si:fu:d] *n* (U) mariscos *mpl*.

seafront ['si:frʌnt] *n* paseo *m* marítimo.

seagull ['si:gʌl] *n* gaviota *f*.

seal [si:l] ◇ *n* - 1. (*pl* **seal** OR **-s**) [animal] foca *f* - 2. [official mark] sello *m*; **she has given it her seal of approval** le ha dado el visto bueno; **to put** OR **set the seal on sthg** sellar algo - 3. [on bottle, meter] precinto *m*; [on letter] sello *m*. ◇ *vt* - 1. [envelope] sellar, cerrar - 2. [opening, tube, crack] tapar, cerrar. ◆ **seal off** *vt sep* [entrance, exit] cerrar; [area] acordonar.

sea level *n* nivel *m* del mar.

sea lion (*pl* **sea lion** OR **-s**) *n* león *m* marítimo.

seam [si:m] *n* - 1. SEW costura *f* - 2. [of coal] veta *f*.

seaman ['si:mən] (*pl* **-men** [-mən]) *n* marinero *m*.

seamy ['si:mɪ] *adj* sórdido(da).

séance ['seɪɒns] *n* sesión *f* de espiritismo.

seaplane ['si:pleɪn] *n* hidroavión *m*.

seaport ['si:pɔ:t] *n* puerto *m* de mar.

search [sɜ:tʃ] ◇ *n* [gen] búsqueda *f*; [of room, drawer] registro *m*; [of person] cacheo *m*; **search for sthg** búsqueda de algo; **in search of** en busca de. ◇ *vt* [gen] registrar; [one's mind] escudriñar; **to search sthg for sthg** buscar algo en algo. ◇ *vi*: **to search (for sthg/sb)** buscar (algo/a alguien); **he was searched at the airport** lo registraron en el aeropuerto.

search engine *n* COMPUT motor *m* de búsqueda.

searching ['sɜ:tʃɪŋ] *adj* [question] agudo(da); [look] penetrante.

searchlight ['sɜ:tʃlaɪt] *n* reflector *m*.

search party *n* equipo *m* de búsqueda.

search warrant *n* mandamiento *m* de registro.

seashell ['si:ʃel] *n* concha *f* (marina).

seashore ['si:ʃɔ:r] *n*: **the seashore** la orilla del mar.

seasick ['si:sɪk] *adj* mareado(da); **to be/feel seasick** estar/sentirse mareado(da).

seaside ['si:saɪd] *n*: **the seaside** la playa.

seaside resort *n* lugar *m* de veraneo (en la playa).

season ['si:zn] ◇ *n* - 1. [of year] estación *f*; **the four seasons** las cuatro estaciones - 2. [particular period] época *f*; **the planting season** la época de plantar; **the football season** la temporada futbolística; **the holiday season** la temporada de vacaciones; **to book a holiday out of season** reservar unas vacaciones fuera de temporada - 3. [of fruit etc]: **out of/in season** fuera de/en sazón; **plums are in season** las ciruelas están en temporada - 4. [of talks, films] temporada *f* - 5. ZOOL: **to be in season** estar en celo. ◇ *vt* sazonar; **season to taste** sazonar a gusto; **season with salt and pepper** salpimentar.

seasonal ['si:zənl] *adj* [work] temporal; [change] estacional.

seasoned ['si:znd] *adj* [experienced] veterano(na); **to be a seasoned traveller** ser un viajero experimentado.

seasoning ['si:znɪŋ] *n* condimento *m*.

season ticket *n* abono *m*.

seat [si:t] ◇ *n* - 1. [in room, on train] asiento *m*; **is this seat taken?** ¿está ocupado este asiento?; **take a seat, please** siéntese por favor; **there only are a few seats left** sólo quedan unos pocos asientos - 2. [of trousers, skirt] trasero *m* - 3. POL [in parliament] escaño *m* - 4. [centre] sede *f*; **the seat of government** la sede del gobierno. ◇ *vt* - 1. [sit down] sentar; **be seated!** ¡siéntese! - 2. [subj: building, vehicle] tener cabida para.

seat belt *n* cinturón *m* de seguridad.

seating ['si:tɪŋ] *n* (U) [capacity] asientos *mpl*.

seawater ['si:,wɔ:tər] *n* agua *f* de mar.

seaweed ['si:wi:d] *n* (U) alga *f* marina.

seaworthy ['si:,wɜ:ðɪ] *adj* en condiciones de navegar.

sec. (*abbr of* second) seg.

secede [sɪ'si:d] *vi fml*: **to secede (from sthg)** separarse (de algo).

secluded [sɪ'klu:dɪd] *adj* apartado(da).

seclusion [sɪ'klu:ʒn] *n* aislamiento *m*; **to live in seclusion** vivir aislado(da).

second ['sekənd] ◇ *n* - 1. [of time] segundo *m*; **can you wait a second?** ¿podrías esperar un momento? - 2. [second gear] segunda *f* - 3. *UK* UNIV ≃ licenciatura *f* con notable. ◇ *num* segundo(da); **to ask for a second chance/opinion** pedir una segunda oportunidad/opinión; **Elizabeth the Second** Isabel II. ◇ *vt* secundar; *see also* **sixth**. ◆ **seconds**

npl - **1.** COMM artículos *mpl* defectuosos - **2.** [of food]: **to have seconds** repetir *(en una comida)*; **are there any seconds?** ¿se puede repetir?

secondary ['sekəndrı] *adj* - **1.** [SCH - school] secundario(ria); [- education] medio(dia) - **2.** [less important]: **to be secondary to** ser secundario(ria) a.

secondary school *n* escuela *f* de enseñanza media.

second-class ['sekənd-] <> *adj* - **1.** [gen] de segunda clase; **to be a second-class citizen** ser un ciudadano de segunda (clase); **second-class mail** *servicio postal más barato y lento que el de primera clase* - **2.** UK UNIV: **second-class degree** *nota global de licenciatura equivalente a un notable o un aprobado alto.* <> *adv*: **to travel second-class** viajar en segunda; **to send a letter second-class** *enviar una carta utilizando el correo de segunda clase.*

second hand ['sekənd-] *n* [of clock] segundero *m.*

second-hand ['sekənd-] <> *adj* [goods, information] de segunda mano. <> *adv* [not new] de segunda mano.

secondly ['sekəndlı] *adv* en segundo lugar.

secondment [sɪ'kɒndmənt] *n* UK traslado *m* temporal.

second-rate ['sekənd-] *adj pej* de segunda categoría, mediocre.

second thought ['sekənd-] *n*: **to have second thoughts about sthg** tener dudas acerca de algo; **on second thoughts** *UK*, **on second thought** *US* pensándolo bien.

secrecy ['si:krəsı] *n (U)* secreto *m*; **to be shrouded in secrecy** estar rodeado de un gran secreto.

secret ['si:krıt] <> *adj* secreto(ta). <> *n* secreto *m*; **in secret** en secreto; **to keep a secret** guardar un secreto; **to tell sb a secret** contar a alguien un secreto; **to make no secret of sthg** no ocultar algo; **the secret of happiness** la clave de la felicidad.

secretarial [ˌsekrə'teərıəl] *adj* [course, training] de secretariado; [staff] administrativo(va).

secretary [*UK* 'sekrətrı, *US* 'sekrə,terı] *n* - **1.** [gen] secretario *m*, -ria *f* - **2.** POL [minister] ministro *m.*

Secretary of State *n* - **1.** *UK:* **Secretary of State (for)** ministro *m* (de) - **2.** *US* ministro *m* estadounidense de Asuntos Exteriores.

secretive ['si:krətıv] *adj* [person] reservado(da); [organization] secreto(ta).

secretly ['si:krıtlı] *adv* [hope, think] secretamente; [tell] en secreto; **she was secretly pleased** aunque no lo expresara, estaba contenta.

sect [sekt] *n* secta *f.*

sectarian [sek'teərıən] *adj* sectario(ria).

section ['sekʃn] *n* sección *f.*

sector ['sektə'] *n* sector *m.*

secular ['sekjʊlə'] *adj* [education, life] laico(ca), secular; [music] profano(na).

secure [sɪ'kjʊə'] <> *adj* [gen] seguro(ra). <> *vt* - **1.** [obtain] conseguir, obtener - **2.** [make safe] proteger - **3.** [fasten] cerrar bien.

security [sɪ'kjʊərətı] *n* - **1.** seguridad *f* - **2.** [for loan] garantía *f.* ➡ **securities** *npl* FIN valores *mpl.*

security guard *n* guardia *m* jurado OR de seguridad.

sedan [sɪ'dæn] *n US* (coche *m*) utilitario *m.*

sedate [sɪ'deɪt] <> *adj* sosegado(da). <> *vt* sedar.

sedation [sɪ'deɪʃn] *n (U)* sedación *f*; **to be under sedation** estar sedado(da).

sedative ['sedətıv] *n* sedante *m.*

sediment ['sedımənt] *n* sedimento *m.*

seduce [sɪ'dju:s] *vt*: **to seduce sb (into doing sthg)** seducir a alguien (a hacer algo).

seductive [sɪ'dʌktıv] *adj* seductor(ra).

see [si:] *(pt* saw, *pp* seen) <> *vt* - **1.** [gen] ver - **2.** [visit - friend, doctor] ir a ver, visitar; **see you soon/later/tomorrow!** ¡hasta pronto/luego/mañana!; **see you!** ¡hasta luego!; **see below/p 10** véase más abajo/pág. 10 - **3.** [accompany]: **to see sb to the door** acompañar a alguien a la puerta - **4.** [make sure]: **to see (to it) that...** encargarse de que... <> *vi* [gen] ver; [understand] entender; **I can't see no veo**; **to see if one can do sthg** ver si uno puede hacer algo; **let's see, let me see** vamos a ver, veamos; **you see...** verás, es que...; **I see** ya veo. ➡ **seeing as, seeing that** *conj inf* como. ➡ **see about** *vt insep* [arrange] encargarse de. ➡ **see off** *vt sep* - **1.** [say goodbye to] despedir - **2.** *UK* [chase away] ahuyentar. ➡ **see through** *vt insep* [person] ver claramente las intenciones de; **I can see right through her** veo claramente sus intenciones. ➡ **see to** *vt insep* ocuparse de.

seed [si:d] *n* [of plant] semilla *f*; **to go to seed** *fig* venirse abajo. ➡ **seeds** *npl fig* [of doubt] semilla *f*; [of idea] germen *m.*

seedling ['si:dlıŋ] *n* plantón *m.*

seedy ['si:dı] *adj* [room, area] sórdido(da); [person] desaliñado(da).

seek [si:k] *(pt & pp* sought) *fml vt* - **1.** [look for, try to obtain] buscar - **2.** [ask for] solicitar.

seem [si:m] <> *vi* parecer; **it seems (to be) good** parece (que es) bueno; **I can't seem to do it** no puedo hacerlo (por mucho que lo intente). <> *impers vb*: **it seems (that)** parece que; **it seems to me that** me parece que.

seemingly ['si:mıŋlı] *adv* aparentemente.

seen [si:n] *pp* ▷ **see.**

seep [si:p] *vi* rezumar, filtrarse.

seesaw ['si:sɔ:] *n* balancín *m*.

seethe [si:ð] *vi* - **1.** [person] rabiar - **2.** [place]: **to be seething with** estar o rebosar de.

see-through *adj* transparente.

segment ['segmənt] *n* - **1.** [proportion, section] segmento *m* - **2.** [of fruit] gajo *m*.

segregate ['segrɪgeɪt] *vt* segregar.

Seine [seɪn] *n*: **the (River) Seine** el (río) Sena.

seize [si:z] *vt* - **1.** [grab] agarrar, coger - **2.** [capture - control, power, town] tomar, hacerse con - **3.** [arrest] detener - **4.** [take advantage of] aprovechar. ◆ **seize (up)on** *vt insep* valerse de. ◆ **seize up** *vi* agarrotarse.

seizure ['si:ʒər] *n* - **1.** MED ataque *m* - **2.** [taking, capturing] toma *f*.

seldom ['seldəm] *adv* raramente.

select [sɪ'lekt] <> *adj* selecto(ta). <> *vt* - **1.** [gen] elegir, escoger - **2.** [team & COMPUT] seleccionar.

selection [sɪ'lekʃn] *n* - **1.** [gen] selección *f* - **2.** [fact of being selected] elección *f* - **3.** [in shop] surtido *m*; **we have a wide selection of ties** tenemos una amplia selección de corbatas.

selective [sɪ'lektɪv] *adj* selectivo(va).

self [self] (*pl* **selves**) *n* uno mismo *m*, una misma *f*; **she's not her usual self** no estaba como de costumbre; **the self** el yo.

self-addressed stamped envelope [-ə,drest'stæmpt-] *n* US sobre con sus señas y franqueo.

self-assured *adj* seguro de sí mismo (segura de sí misma).

self-catering *adj* sin pensión; **a self-catering holiday/chalet** unas vacaciones/un chalet sin servicio de comidas.

self-centred [-'sentəd] *adj* egocéntrico(ca).

self-confessed [-kən'fest] *adj* confeso(sa).

self-confident *adj* [person] seguro de sí mismo (segura de sí misma); [attitude, remark] lleno(na) de seguridad.

self-conscious *adj* cohibido(da).

self-contained [-kən'teɪnd] *adj* independiente; **a self-contained flat** un apartamento independiente.

self-control *n* control *m* de sí mismo/misma.

self-defence *n* defensa *f* propia; **in self-defence** en defensa propia.

self-discipline *n* autodisciplina *f*.

self-employed [-ɪm'plɔɪd] *adj* autónomo(ma), que trabaja por cuenta propia.

self-esteem *n* amor *m* propio.

self-evident *adj* evidente, patente.

self-explanatory *adj* evidente.

self-government *n* autogobierno *m*.

self-important *adj pej* engreído(da).

self-indulgent *adj pej*: **a self-indulgent person** una persona autocomplaciente; **to be self-indulgent** con autocomplacencia.

self-interest *n* (U) *pej* interés *m* propio.

selfish ['selfɪʃ] *adj* egoísta.

selfishness ['selfɪʃnɪs] *n* egoísmo *m*.

selfless ['selflɪs] *adj* desinteresado(da).

self-made *adj*: **a self-made man** un hombre hecho a sí mismo.

self-opinionated *adj pej* que siempre tiene que decir la suya.

self-pity *n pej* lástima *f* de uno mismo/una misma.

self-portrait *n* autorretrato *m*.

self-possessed [-pə'zest] *adj* dueño de sí mismo (dueña de sí misma).

self-raising flour UK [-,reɪzɪŋ-], **self-rising flour** US *n* harina *f* con levadura.

self-reliant *adj* independiente.

self-respect *n* amor *m* propio.

self-respecting [-rɪs'pektɪŋ] *adj* que se precie, digno(na); **no self-respecting person would eat this rubbish** nadie con un mínimo de dignidad se comería esa basura.

self-restraint *n* dominio *m* de sí mismo/misma.

self-righteous *adj pej* santurrón(ona).

self-rising flour US = **self-raising flour**.

self-sacrifice *n* abnegación *f*.

self-satisfied *adj pej* [person] satisfecho de sí mismo (satisfecha de sí misma); [smile] lleno(na) de suficiencia.

self-service *comp* de autoservicio; **a self-service restaurant** un autoservicio.

self-sufficient *adj*: **self-sufficient (in)** autosuficiente (en).

self-taught *adj* autodidacta.

sell [sel] <> *vt* (*pt & pp* **sold**) [gen] vender; **to sell sthg to sb, to sell sb sthg** vender algo a alguien; **to sell sthg for** vender algo por. <> *vi* (*pt & pp* **sold**) - **1.** [subj: businessman, firm] vender - **2.** [subj: merchandise] venderse; **this model sells well** este modelo se vende muy bien; **to sell (for** OR **at)** venderse (a). ◆ **sell off** *vt sep* liquidar. ◆ **sell out** <> *vt sep* [performance]: **to have sold out** estar agotado(da). <> *vi* - **1.** [shop]: **to sell out (of sthg)** agotar las existencias (de algo) - **2.** [be disloyal, unprincipled] venderse.

sell-by date *n* UK fecha *f* de caducidad; **to be past its sell-by date** haber caducado.

seller ['selər] *n* vendedor *m*, -ra *f*.

selling price *n* precio *m* de venta.

Sellotape® ['seləteɪp] *n* UK celo® *m*, cinta *f* Scotch® Amér.

sell-out *n* [performance, match] lleno *m*.

selves [selvz] *npl* ▷ **self**.

semaphore ['seməfɔːr] *n (U)* semáforo *m*.

semblance ['sembləns] *n fml* apariencia *f*.

semen ['siːmen] *n* semen *m*.

semester [sɪ'mestər] *n* semestre *m*.

semicircle ['semɪ,sɜːkl] *n* semicírculo *m*; **arranged in a semicircle** poner en semicírculo.

semicolon [,semɪ'kəʊlən] *n* punto *m* y coma.

semidetached [,semɪdɪ'tætʃt] <> *adj* adosado(da). <> *n UK* casa *f* adosada (a otra).

semifinal [,semɪ'faɪnl] *n* semifinal *f*.

seminar ['seminɑːr] *n* seminario *m*.

seminary ['semɪnərɪ] *n* RELIG seminario *m*.

semiskilled [,semɪ'skɪld] *adj* semicualificado(da).

semolina [,semə'liːnə] *n* sémola *f*.

Senate ['senɪt] *n* POL: **the (United States) Senate** el Senado (de los Estados Unidos).

senator ['senətər] *n* senador *m*, -ra *f*.

send [send] *pt & pp* **sent** *vt* - **1.** [gen] mandar; **to send sb sthg, to send sthg to sb** mandar a alguien algo; **send me a postcard!** ¡mándame una postal!; **send them my best wishes** enviales saludos - **2.** [tell to go] enviar, mandar; **she sent her son to the shop for a newspaper** envió a su hijo a comprar un periódico en la tienda; **he was sent to prison** fue encarcelado. **send for** *vt insep* [person] mandar llamar a. **send in** *vt sep* mandar, enviar. **send off** *vt sep* - **1.** [by post] mandar (por correo) - **2.** SPORT expulsar. **send off for** *vt insep* [goods, information] pedir, encargar. **send up** *vt sep UK inf* [imitate] parodiar.

sender ['sendər] *n* remitente *mf*.

send-off *n* despedida *f*.

senile ['siːnaɪl] *adj* senil.

senior ['siːnjər] <> *adj* - **1.** [highest-ranking] superior, de rango superior - **2.** SCH [pupil] mayor; [class, common room] de los mayores; **senior year** *US último curso de la enseñanza secundaria y de la universidad en Estados Unidos.* <> *n* - **1.** [older person]: **I'm five years his senior** le llevo cinco años - **2.** SCH mayor *mf*.

senior citizen *n* ciudadano *m*, -na *f* de la tercera edad.

sensation [sen'seɪʃn] *n* sensación *f*; **to cause a sensation** causar sensación.

sensational [sen'seɪʃənl] *adj* [gen] sensacional.

sensationalist [sen'seɪʃnəlɪst] *adj pej* sensacionalista.

sense [sens] <> *n* - **1.** [faculty, meaning] sentido *m*; **to make sense of sthg** entender algo; **I can't make any sense of this** no entiendo esto - **2.** [feeling - of guilt, terror] sentimiento *m*; [- of urgency] sensación *f*; [- of honour, duty] sentido *m* - **3.** [natural ability]: **business sense** talento *m* para los negocios; **sense of humour/style** sentido *m* del humor/estilo - **4.** [wisdom, reason] juicio *m*, sentido *m* común; **there's no OR little sense in arguing** no tiene sentido discutir. <> *vt* sentir, percibir; **to sense (that)** percibir OR sentir que. **in a sense** *adv* en cierto sentido.

senseless ['senslɪs] *adj* - **1.** [stupid] sin sentido - **2.** [unconscious] inconsciente; **the blow knocked him senseless** el golpe lo dejó inconsciente.

sensibilities [,sensɪ'bɪlətɪz] *npl* [delicate feelings] sensibilidad *f*; **to offend sb's sensibilities** herir la sensibilidad de alguien.

sensible ['sensəbl] *adj* [person, decision] sensato(ta); [clothes] práctico(ca).

sensitive ['sensɪtɪv] *adj* - **1.** [understanding]: **sensitive (to)** comprensivo(va) (hacia) - **2.** [easily hurt, touchy]: **sensitive (to/about)** susceptible (a/acerca de) - **3.** [controversial] delicado(da) - **4.** [easily damaged, tender] sensible; **to have sensitive skin** tener la piel sensible; **sensitive to heat/light** sensible al calor/la luz - **5.** [responsive - instrument] sensible.

sensual ['sensjʊəl] *adj* sensual.

sensuous ['sensjʊəs] *adj* sensual.

sent [sent] *pt & pp* > **send**.

sentence ['sentəns] <> *n* - **1.** [group of words] frase *f*, oración *f* - **2.** LAW sentencia *f*; **a prison sentence** una condena de cárcel. <> *vt*: **to sentence sb (to)** condenar a alguien (a); **he was sentenced to death/3 years** lo condenaron a muerte/tres años de cárcel.

sentiment ['sentɪmənt] *n* - **1.** [feeling] sentimiento *m* - **2.** [opinion] opinión *f*.

sentimental [,sentɪ'mentl] *adj* sentimental.

sentry ['sentrɪ] *n* centinela *m*.

separate <> *adj* ['seprət] - **1.** [not joined, apart]: **separate (from)** separado(da) (de) - **2.** [individual, distinct] distinto(ta). <> *vt* ['sepəreɪt] - **1.** [keep or move apart]: **to separate sthg/sb (from)** separar algo/a alguien (de) - **2.** [distinguish]: **to separate sthg/sb from** diferenciar algo/a alguien de - **3.** [divide]: **to separate sthg/sb into** dividir algo/a alguien en. <> *vi* ['sepəreɪt] - **1.** [gen]: **to separate (from)** separarse (de) - **2.** [divide]: **to separate (into)** dividirse (en). **separates** *npl UK* piezas *fpl* (de vestir que combinan).

separately ['seprətlɪ] *adv* - **1.** [on one's own] independientemente - **2.** [one by one] por separado.

separation [,sepə'reɪʃn] *n* separación *f*.

September [sep'tembər] *n* septiembre *m*, setiembre *m*; **1 September 1992** [in letters etc] 1 de septiembre de 1992; **by/in September** para/en septiembre; **last/this/next September** en septiembre del año pasado/de este año/del año que viene; **every September** todos los años en septiembre; **during September** en septiembre, durante el mes de septiembre; **at the beginning/end of September** a principios/finales de septiembre; **in the middle of September** a mediados de septiembre.

septic ['septɪk] *adj* séptico(ca).

septic tank *n* fosa *f* séptica.

sequel ['si:kwəl] *n* - **1.** [book, film]: **sequel (to)** continuación *f* (de) - **2.** [consequence]: **sequel (to)** secuela *f* (de).

sequence ['si:kwəns] *n* - **1.** [series] sucesión *f* - **2.** [order, of film] secuencia *f*.

Serb = Serbian.

Serbia ['sɜ:bjə] *n* Serbia.

Serbian ['sɜ:bjən], **Serb** [sɜ:b] ⟨⟩ *adj* serbio(bia). ⟨⟩ *n* - **1.** [person] serbio *m*, -bia *f* - **2.** [dialect] serbio *m*.

serene [sɪ'ri:n] *adj* sereno(na).

sergeant ['sɑ:dʒənt] *n* - **1.** MIL sargento *m* - **2.** [in police] ≃ subinspector *m* de policía.

sergeant major *n* sargento *m* mayor.

serial ['sɪərɪəl] *n* serial *m*.

serial cable *n* COMPUT cable *m* de serie.

serial number *n* número *m* de serie.

series ['sɪəri:z] (*pl* **series**) *n* serie *f*; **a series of disasters** una serie de catástrofes; **a TV series** una serie televisiva.

serious ['sɪərɪəs] *adj* - **1.** [gen] serio(ria); **are you serious?** ¿hablas en serio? - **2.** [very bad] grave.

seriously ['sɪərɪəslɪ] *adv* - **1.** [honestly] en serio - **2.** [very badly] gravemente; **to be seriously ill** estar gravemente enfermo - **3.** [in a considered, earnest, solemn manner] seriamente ►►► **to take sthg/sb seriously** tomar algo/a alguien en serio.

seriousness ['sɪərɪəsnɪs] *n* - **1.** [gravity] gravedad *f* - **2.** [solemnity] seriedad *f*.

sermon ['sɜ:mən] *n pej* & RELIG sermón *m*.

serrated [sɪ'reɪtɪd] *adj* dentado(da).

servant ['sɜ:vənt] *n* sirviente *m*, -ta *f*.

serve [sɜ:v] ⟨⟩ *vt* - **1.** [work for] servir - **2.** [have effect]: **to serve to do sthg** servir para hacer algo - **3.** [fulfil]: **to serve a purpose** cumplir un propósito - **4.** [provide for] abastecer - **5.** [food, drink]: **to serve sthg to sb, to serve sb sthg** servir algo a alguien; **dinner will be served at 8** la cena será servida a las 8 - **6.** [customer] despachar, servir; **are you being served?** ¿lo atienden? - **7.** LAW: **to serve sb with sthg, to serve sthg on sb** entregar a alguien algo - **8.** [prison sentence] cumplir; [apprenticeship] hacer; [term of office] ejercer - **9.** SPORT servir, sacar ►►► **that serves you right!** ¡bien merecido lo tienes! ⟨⟩ *vi* - **1.** [work, give food or drink] servir

- **2.** [function]: **to serve as** servir de - **3.** [in shop, bar etc] despachar - **4.** SPORT sacar. ⟨⟩ *n* sa[...] saque *m*; [...] sep servir.

service ['sɜ:vɪs] ⟨⟩ *n* - **1.** [gen] servicio *m*; **in service** en funcionamiento; **out of service** fuera de servicio; **bus/train service** servicio de autobús/tren - **2.** [mechanical check] revisión *f* - **3.** RELIG oficio *m*, servicio *m*; **to hold a service** celebrar un oficio - **4.** [set - of plates etc] servicio *m*, juego *m*; **dinner service** servicio de mesa - **5.** SPORT saque *m* - **6.** [use]: **to be of service (to sb)** servir (a alguien); **to do sb a service** hacer un favor a alguien. ⟨⟩ *vt* [car, machine] revisar. ►► **services** *npl* - **1.** [on motorway] área *f* de servicios - **2.** [armed forces]: **the services** las fuerzas armadas - **3.** [efforts, work] servicios *mpl*.

serviceable ['sɜ:vɪsəbl] *adj* útil, práctico(ca).

service area *n* área *f* de servicios.

service charge *n* servicio *m*.

serviceman ['sɜ:vɪsmən] (*pl* **-men** [-mən]) *n* militar *m*.

service provider *n* proveedor *m* de servicios.

service station *n* estación *f* de servicio.

serviette [,sɜ:vɪ'et] *n* servilleta *f*.

serving dish *n* fuente *f*.

serving spoon *n* cuchara *f* de servir.

sesame ['sesəmɪ] *n* sésamo *m*.

session ['seʃn] *n* - **1.** [gen] sesión *f*; **in session** en sesión - **2.** US [school term] trimestre *m*.

set [set] ⟨⟩ *adj* - **1.** [fixed - expression, amount] fijo(ja); [- pattern, method] establecido(da) - **2.** UK SCH [text etc] asignado(da) - **3.** [ready, prepared]: **set (for sthg/to do sthg)** listo(ta) (para algo/para hacer algo). ⟨⟩ *n* - **1.** [collection - gen] juego *m*; [- of stamps] serie *f* - **2.** [TV, radio] aparato *m* - **3.** THEAT decorado *m*; CIN plató *m* - **4.** TENNIS set *m* - **5.** [hairdressing] marcado *m*. ⟨⟩ *vt* (*pt* & *pp* **set**) - **1.** [position, place] poner, colocar - **2.** [fix, insert]: **to set sthg in** OR **into** montar algo en - **3.** [cause to be or start]: **to set free** poner en libertad; **to set fire to** prender fuego a; **to set sb thinking** hacer pensar a alguien - **4.** [trap, table, essay] poner - **5.** [alarm, meter] poner - **6.** [time, wage] fijar - **7.** [example] dar; **to set a good example** dar ejemplo; [precedent] sentar; [trend] imponer, dictar - **8.** [target] fijar - **9.** MED [bones, leg] componer - **10.** [book, play, film] situar, ambientar; **the series is set in London** la serie está ambientada en Londres. ⟨⟩ *vi* (*pt* & *pp* **set**) - **1.** [sun] ponerse - **2.** [jelly] cuajarse; [glue, cement] secarse. ►► **set about** *vt insep* [start - task] comenzar; [- problem] atacar; **to set about doing sthg** ponerse a hacer algo. ►► **set aside** *vt sep* - **1.** [keep, save] reservar - **2.** [dismiss - enmity, differences] dejar de lado. ►► **set back** *vt sep* [delay] retrasar. **set off** <> vt sep - **1.** [initiate, cause] provocar - **2.** [ignite - bomb] hacer estallar. <> vi ponerse en camino. **set out** <> vt sep - **1.** [arrange] disponer - **2.** [explain] exponer. <> vi - **1.** [on journey] ponerse en camino - **2.** [intend]: **to set out to do sthg** proponerse a hacer algo. **set up** vt sep - **1.** [business] poner, montar; [committee, organization] crear; [procedure] establecer; [interview, meeting] organizar; **to set up house OR home** instalarse - **2.** [statue, roadblock] levantar - **3.** [prepare for use] preparar - **4.** inf [frame] tenderle una trampa a.

setback ['setbæk] n revés m, contratiempo m.

set menu n menú m del día.

settee [se'ti:] n sofá m.

setting ['setɪŋ] n - **1.** [surroundings] escenario m - **2.** [of dial, control] posición f.

settle ['setl] <> vt - **1.** [conclude, decide] resolver; **that settles it, she can move out!** ¡no se hable más, que se vaya! - **2.** [pay] ajustar, saldar - **3.** [calm - nerves] tranquilizar; **this should settle your stomach** esto te va a asentará el estómago. <> vi - **1.** [stop travelling] instalarse - **2.** [make o.s. comfortable] acomodarse - **3.** [dust, sediment] depositarse; **the snow has settled** la nieve ha cuajado - **4.** [calm down - person] calmarse. **settle down** vi - **1.** [concentrate on]: **to settle down (for sthg)** prepararse (para algo) - **2.** [become respectable] sentar la cabeza - **3.** [calm oneself] calmarse. **settle for** vt insep conformarse con. **settle in** vi [in new home] instalarse; [in new job] adaptarse. **settle on** vt insep [choose] decidirse por. **settle up** vi: **to settle up (with sb)** ajustar las cuentas (con alguien).

settlement ['setlmənt] n - **1.** [agreement] acuerdo m - **2.** [village] poblado m.

settler ['setlər] n colono m.

set-up n inf - **1.** [system, organization] sistema m - **2.** [frame, trap] trampa f.

seven ['sevn] num siete; see also **six**.

seventeen [ˌsevn'ti:n] num diecisiete; see also **six**.

seventeenth [ˌsevn'ti:nθ] num decimoséptimo(ma); see also **sixth**.

seventh ['sevnθ] num séptimo(ma); see also **sixth**.

seventy ['sevntɪ] num setenta; see also **sixty**.

sever ['sevər] vt - **1.** [cut through] cortar - **2.** [finish completely] romper.

several ['sevrəl] <> adj varios(rias). <> pron varios mpl, -rias f.

severance ['sevrəns] n fml ruptura f.

severance pay n despido m.

severe [sɪ'vɪər] adj [gen] severo(ra); [pain] fuerte, agudo(da).

severity [sɪ'verətɪ] n [gen] gravedad f; [of shortage, problem] severidad f.

sew [səʊ] vt & vi (UK pp sewn, US pp sewed OR sewn) coser. **sew up** vt sep [cloth] coser.

sewage ['su:ɪdʒ] n (U) aguas fpl residuales.

sewer ['suər] n alcantarilla f, cloaca f.

sewing ['səʊɪŋ] n (U) - **1.** [activity] labor f de costura - **2.** [items] costura f.

sewing machine n máquina f de coser.

sewn [səʊn] pp ▷ **sew**.

sex [seks] n sexo m; **to have sex** tener relaciones sexuales.

sexist ['seksɪst] <> adj sexista. <> n sexista mf.

sexual ['sekʃʊəl] adj sexual.

sexual harassment n acoso m sexual.

sexual intercourse n (U) relaciones fpl sexuales.

sexy ['seksɪ] adj inf sexi (inv).

shabby ['ʃæbɪ] adj - **1.** [clothes, briefcase] desastrado(da); [street] de aspecto abandonado - **2.** [person] andrajoso(sa).

shack [ʃæk] n chabola f.

shackle ['ʃækl] vt [enchain] poner grilletes a. **shackles** npl [metal rings] grilletes mpl.

shade [ʃeɪd] <> n - **1.** (U) [shadow] sombra f; **in the shade** a la sombra - **2.** [lampshade] pantalla f - **3.** [of colour, meaning] matiz m - **4.** US [blind] persiana f - **5.** [little bit]: **a shade too big** un poquito grande. <> vt [from light] dar sombra a; **the car was shaded from the sun** el coche estaba protegido del sol. **shades** npl inf [sunglasses] gafas fpl de sol.

shadow ['ʃædəʊ] <> n - **1.** [dark shape, form] sombra f - **2.** [darkness] oscuridad f ▸▸▸ **there's not a OR the shadow of a doubt** no hay la menor duda; **to be scared of your own shadow** tener miedo hasta de su propia sombra. <> vt [subj: detective] seguir.

shadow cabinet n gobierno m en la sombra (directiva del principal partido de la oposición en Gran Bretaña).

shadowy ['ʃædəʊɪ] adj - **1.** [dark] sombrío(a) - **2.** [hard to see] vago(ga).

shady ['ʃeɪdɪ] adj - **1.** [sheltered from sun] sombreado(da) - **2.** inf [dishonest - businessman] sospechoso(sa); [- deal] turbio(bia).

shaft [ʃɑːft] n - **1.** [vertical passage] pozo m - **2.** [of lift] hueco m - **3.** [tech - rod] eje m - **4.** [of light] rayo m - **5.** [of spear] asta f.

shaggy ['ʃægɪ] adj [dog] peludo(da).

shake [ʃeɪk] <> vt (pt shook, pp shaken ['ʃeɪkən]) - **1.** [move vigorously] sacudir; **to shake sb's hand** dar OR estrechar la mano a

alguien; **to shake hands** darse OR estrecharse la mano; **he shook hands with her la dio
la mano; to shake one's head** [ʌ ʌʃʌɪʌl]
gar con la cabeza; [in disbelief] mover la cabeza mostrando incredulidad; **he shook his fist
at them** amenazar a alguien con el puño
- 2. [bottle, aerosol] agitar; **shake well before using** agitar antes de usar - 3. [shock] trastornar, conmocionar; **the disaster which shook
the city** el desastre que sacudió la ciudad.
◇ vi (pt **shook**, pp **shaken** ['ʃeɪkən])
- 1. [tremble] temblar; **to shake with fear** temblar de miedo - 2. inf [shake hands]: **let's shake
on it** venga esa mano. ◆ **shake off** vt sep
[pursuer] deshacerse de; [cold] quitarse de encima; [illness] superar. ◆ **shake up** vt sep
[contents of bottle etc] agitar; [organisation] res-
tructurar, reorganizar; [person]: **she wasn't
hurt, just a bit shaken up** no resultó herida,
sólo un poco conmocionada.

shaken ['ʃeɪkn] pp ▷ **shake**.

shaky ['ʃeɪkɪ] adj - 1. [weak, nervous] temblo-
roso(sa); **to feel shaky** encontrarse nervioso
- 2. [unconfident, insecure - start] incierto(ta);
[- argument] poco sólido(da) - 3. [wobbly - chair,
table] inestable; [- handwriting] tembloro-
so(sa).

shall (weak form [ʃəl], strong form [ʃæl])
aux vb - 1. (1st person sing, 1st person pl) [to express future tense]: **we shall be there tomorrow**
mañana estaremos ahí; **I shan't be home till
ten** no estaré en casa hasta las diez - 2. (esp 1st
person sing & 1st person pl) [in questions]: **shall
we go for a walk?** ¿vamos a dar una vuelta?;
shall I give her a ring? ¿la llamo?; **I'll do that,
shall I?** hago esto, ¿vale? - 3. [in orders]: **you
shall do as I tell you!** ¡harás lo que yo te diga!;
no one shall leave until I say so que nadie salga hasta que yo lo diga.

shallow ['ʃæləʊ] adj - 1. [in size] poco profun-
do(da) - 2. pej [superficial] superficial.

sham [ʃæm] ◇ n farsa f. ◇ vi fingir.

shambles ['ʃæmblz] n desbarajuste m, follón m.

shame [ʃeɪm] ◇ n - 1. (U) [remorse] vergüenza f, pena f Andes, Amér C & Méx - 2. [dishon-
our]: **to bring shame on** OR **upon sb** deshonrar a alguien - 3. [pity]: **what a shame!** ¡qué
pena OR lástima!; **it's a shame** es una pena OR
lástima. ◇ vt - 1. [fill with shame] avergonzar,
apenar Andes, Amér C & Méx - 2. [force by making ashamed]: **to shame sb into doing sthg** conseguir que alguien haga algo avergonzándole
OR avergonzándolo Amér.

shamefaced [,ʃeɪm'feɪst] adj avergonza-
do(da).

shameful ['ʃeɪmfʊl] adj vergonzoso(sa).

shameless ['ʃeɪmlɪs] adj desvergonza-
do(da).

shampoo [ʃæm'puː] ◇ n (pl -s) [liquid]
champú m. ◇ vt lavar (con champú).
shampoo [ʃæm'puː] n (pl -s) lavado m.

shandy ['ʃændɪ] n cerveza f con gaseosa,
clara f.

shan't [ʃɑːnt] (abbr of shall not) ▷ **shall**.

shantytown ['ʃæntɪtaʊn] n barrio m de chabolas, cantegril m Amér.

shape [ʃeɪp] ◇ n - 1. [form] forma f; **it's oval
in shape** tenía forma ovalada; **biscuits in the
shape of stars** galletas con forma de estrellas
- 2. [silhouette] figura f - 3. [structure] configuración f; **to take shape** tomar forma - 4. [form,
health]: **to be in good/bad shape** [person] estar/
no estar en forma; [business etc] estar en buen/
mal estado; **to get back in shape** ponerse en
forma; **to lick** OR **knock sb into shape** poner a
alguien a punto. ◇ vt - 1. [mould]: **to shape
sthg (into)** dar a algo forma (de) - 2. [cause to
develop] desarrollar. ◆ **shape up** vi [develop]
desarrollarse.

-shaped ['ʃeɪpt] suffix: **egg/star-shaped** en
forma de huevo/estrella.

shapeless ['ʃeɪplɪs] adj sin forma.

shapely ['ʃeɪplɪ] adj bien hecho(cha).

share [ʃeəʳ] ◇ n - 1. [portion]: **share (of** OR
in) parte f (de) - 2. [contribution, quota]: **to have/
do one's share of sthg** tener/hacer la parte
que a uno le toca de algo. ◇ vt [gen]: **to share
sthg (with)** compartir algo (con); **we share a
love of opera** nos une la pasión por la ópera.
◇ vi compartir. ◆ **shares** npl acciones fpl.
◆ **share out** vt sep repartir, distribuir.

shareholder ['ʃeə,həʊldəʳ] n accionista mf.

shark [ʃɑːk] n (pl shark OR -s) n tiburón m; fig
estafador m, -ra f.

sharp [ʃɑːp] ◇ adj - 1. [not blunt] afila-
do(da) - 2. [well-defined - outline] definido(da);
[- photograph] nítido(da); [- contrast] marca-
do(da) - 3. [intelligent, keen - person] listo(ta);
[- eyesight] penetrante; [- hearing] fino(na);
[- intelligence] vivo(va) - 4. [abrupt, sudden]
brusco(ca) - 5. [quick, firm - blow] seco(ca)
- 6. [angry, severe] cortante - 7. [piercing, acute -
sound, cry, pain] agudo(da); [- cold, wind] penetrante - 8. [acid] ácido(da) - 9. MUS desafina-
do(da); **F sharp** fa m sostenido. ◇ adv
- 1. [punctually]: **at seven o'clock sharp** a las siete en punto - 2. [quickly, suddenly] bruscamente. ◇ n MUS sostenido m.

sharpen ['ʃɑːpn] vt - 1. [make sharp] afilar;
[pencil] sacar punta a - 2. [make keener, quicker,
greater] agudizar.

sharpener ['ʃɑːpnəʳ] n [for pencils] sacapuntas m inv; [for knives] afilador m.

sharp-eyed [-'aɪd] adj perspicaz.

sharply ['ʃɑːplɪ] adv - 1. [distinctly] claramente - 2. [suddenly] repentinamente - 3. [harshly] duramente.

shat [ʃæt] pt & pp ⊳ **shit**.

shatter ['ʃætəʳ] ⋄ vt - 1. [smash] hacer añicos - 2. [hopes etc] echar por tierra. ⋄ vi hacerse añicos.

shattered ['ʃætəd] adj - 1. [shocked, upset] destrozado(da) - 2. UK inf [very tired] hecho(cha) polvo.

shave [ʃeɪv] ⋄ n afeitado m; **to have a shave** afeitarse. ⋄ vt - 1. [face, body] afeitar - 2. [cut pieces off] raspar. ⋄ vi afeitarse.

shaver ['ʃeɪvəʳ] n maquinilla f (de afeitar) eléctrica.

shaving brush ['ʃeɪvɪŋ-] n brocha f de afeitar.

shaving cream ['ʃeɪvɪŋ-] n crema f dé afeitar.

shaving foam ['ʃeɪvɪŋ-] n espuma f de afeitar.

shavings ['ʃeɪvɪŋz] npl virutas fpl.

shawl [ʃɔːl] n chal m.

she [ʃiː] ⋄ pers pron - 1. [referring to woman, girl, animal] ella; **she's tall** es alta; **I don't like it, but she does** no me gusta, pero a ella sí; **she can't do it** ella no puede hacerlo; **there she is** allí está - 2. [referring to boat, car, country]: **she's a fine ship** es un buen barco. ⋄ comp: **she-elephant** elefanta f; **she bear** osa f.

sheaf [ʃiːf] (pl sheaves) n - 1. [of papers, letters] fajo m - 2. [of corn, grain] gavilla f.

shear [ʃɪəʳ] vt (pp -ed OR shorn) [sheep] esquilar. ◈ **shears** npl [for garden] tijeras fpl de podar. ◈ **shear off** vi romperse.

sheath [ʃiːθ] (pl -s) n - 1. [covering for knife] vaina f - 2. UK [condom] preservativo m.

sheaves [ʃiːvz] npl ⊳ **sheaf**.

shed [ʃed] ⋄ n cobertizo m. ⋄ vt (pt & pp shed) - 1. [skin] mudar de; [leaves] despojarse de - 2. [discard] deshacerse de - 3. [accidentally lose]: **a lorry has shed its load on the M1** un camión ha perdido su carga en la M1 - 4. [tears, blood] derramar.

she'd (weak form [ʃɪd], strong form [ʃiːd]) - 1. (abbr of she had) ⊳ **have** - 2. (abbr of she would) ⊳ **would**.

sheen [ʃiːn] n brillo m, lustre m.

sheep [ʃiːp] (pl sheep) n [animal] oveja f.

sheepdog ['ʃiːpdɒg] n perro m pastor.

sheepish ['ʃiːpɪʃ] adj avergonzado(da).

sheepskin ['ʃiːpskɪn] n piel f de carnero.

sheer [ʃɪəʳ] adj - 1. [absolute] puro(ra) - 2. [very steep - cliff] escarpado(da); [- drop] vertical - 3. [tights] transparente.

sheet [ʃiːt] n - 1. [for bed] sábana f - 2. [of paper] hoja f - 3. [of glass, metal, wood] lámina f.

sheik(h) [ʃeɪk] n jeque m.

shelf [ʃelf] (pl shelves) n estante m; **it's on the top shelf** está en el estante de arriba.

shell [ʃel] ⋄ n - 1. [of egg, nut] cáscara f - 2. [of tortoise, crab] caparazón m; [of snail, mussels] concha f - 3. [on beach] concha f - 4. [of building] esqueleto m; [of boat] casco m; [of car] armazón m, chasis m inv - 5. MIL [missile] proyectil m. ⋄ vt - 1. [peas] desvainar; [nuts, eggs] quitar la cáscara a - 2. MIL [fire shells at] bombardear.

she'll [ʃiːl] - 1. (abbr of she will) ⊳ **will** - 2. (abbr of she shall) ⊳ **shall**.

shellfish ['ʃelfɪʃ] (pl shellfish) n - 1. [creature] crustáceo m - 2. (U) [food] mariscos mpl.

shell suit n UK chandal m (de nailon).

shelter ['ʃeltəʳ] ⋄ n [building, protection] refugio m; **to seek shelter** buscar refugio; **to take shelter (from)** refugiarse (de); **to run for shelter** correr a refugiarse; **nuclear shelter** refugio nuclear; **bus shelter** marquesina f. ⋄ vt - 1. [protect]: **to be sheltered by/from** estar protegido(da) por/de - 2. [provide place to live for] dar asilo OR cobijo a - 3. [hide] proteger, esconder. ⋄ vi: **to shelter from/in** resguardarse de/en, protegerse de/en.

sheltered ['ʃeltəd] adj [place, existence] protegido(da).

shelve [ʃelv] vt dar carpetazo a.

shelves [ʃelvz] npl ⊳ **shelf**.

shepherd ['ʃepəd] ⋄ n pastor m. ⋄ vt fig acompañar.

shepherd's pie ['ʃepədz-] n carne picada cubierta de puré de patatas.

sheriff ['ʃerɪf] n sheriff m.

sherry ['ʃerɪ] n jerez m.

she's [ʃiːz] - 1. (abbr of she is) ⊳ **be** - 2. (abbr of she has) ⊳ **have**.

Shetland ['ʃetlənd] n: **(the) Shetland (Islands)** las islas Shetland.

shield [ʃiːld] ⋄ n [armour, sports trophy] escudo m. ⋄ vt: **to shield sb (from)** proteger a alguien (de)

shift [ʃɪft] ⋄ n - 1. [slight change] cambio m; **a shift in sthg** un cambio en algo - 2. [period of work, workers] turno m; **the night shift** el turno de noche. ⋄ vt - 1. [furniture etc] cambiar de sitio, mover - 2. [attitude, belief] cambiar de. ⋄ vi - 1. [person] moverse; [wind, opinion] cambiar - 2. US AUT cambiar de marcha.

shiftless ['ʃɪftlɪs] adj vago(ga).

shifty ['ʃɪftɪ] adj inf [person] con pinta deshonesta; [behaviour] sospechoso(sa); [look] huidizo(za).

shilling ['ʃɪlɪŋ] n chelín m.

shilly-shally ['ʃɪlɪˌʃælɪ] (pt & pp -ied) vi titubear, vacilar.

shimmer ['ʃɪmər] *vi* rielar, brillar con luz trémula.

shin [ʃɪn] *n* espinilla *f.*

shinbone ['ʃɪnbəʊn] *n* espinilla *f.*

shine [ʃaɪn] <> *n* brillo *m.* <> *vt* (*pt & pp* **shone**) [torch, lamp] dirigir; **she shone a torch into his eyes** la enfocó en los ojos con una linterna. <> *vi* (*pt & pp* **shone**) [gen] brillar.

shingle ['ʃɪŋgl] *n* - **1.** (*U*) [on beach] guijarros *mpl* - **2.** *US* [nameplate] placa *f* con el nombre; **to hang out one's shingle** abrir un despacho/consultorio. ◆ **shingles** *n* (*U*) herpes *m inv.*

shin pad *n* espinillera *f.*

ship [ʃɪp] <> *n* barco *m*, buque *m.* <> *vt* enviar por barco.

shipbuilding ['ʃɪp,bɪldɪŋ] *n* construcción *f* naval.

shipment ['ʃɪpmənt] *n* envío *m.*

shipper ['ʃɪpər] *n* compañía *f* naviera.

shipping ['ʃɪpɪŋ] *n* (*U*) - **1.** [transport] envío *m*, transporte *m* - **2.** [ships] barcos *mpl*, buques *mpl.*

shipshape ['ʃɪpʃeɪp] *adj* en orden.

shipwreck ['ʃɪprek] <> *n* - **1.** [destruction of ship] naufragio *m* - **2.** [wrecked ship] barco *m* náufrago. <> *vt*: **to be shipwrecked** naufragar.

shipyard ['ʃɪpjɑːd] *n* astillero *m.*

shire [ʃaɪər] *n* [county] condado *m.*

shirk [ʃɜːk] *vt* eludir.

shirt [ʃɜːt] *n* camisa *f.*

shirtsleeves ['ʃɜːtsliːvz] *npl*: **to be in (one's) shirtsleeves** ir en mangas de camisa.

shit [ʃɪt] *vulg* <> *n* - **1.** [excrement] mierda *f* - **2.** (*U*) [nonsense] gilipolleces *fpl.* <> *vi* (*pt & pp* **shit, -ted** *OR* **shat**) cagar. <> *excl* ¡mierda!

shiver ['ʃɪvər] <> *n* escalofrío *m*; **to give sb the shivers** dar escalofríos a alguien; **it sent shivers down her spine** le puso los pelos de punta. <> *vi*: **to shiver (with)** [fear] temblar *OR* estremecerse (de); [cold] tiritar (de).

shoal [ʃəʊl] *n* banco *m.*

shock [ʃɒk] <> *n* - **1.** [unpleasant surprise, reaction, emotional state] susto *m*; **it came as a shock** fue un duro golpe - **2.** (*U*) MED: **to be suffering from shock, to be in shock** estar en un estado de choque - **3.** [impact] choque *m* - **4.** [electric shock] descarga *f* *OR* sacudida *f* (eléctrica); **to get a shock from sthg** recibir una descarga de algo. <> *vt* - **1.** [upset] conmocionar - **2.** [offend] escandalizar.

shock absorber [-əb,zɔːbər] *n* amortiguador *m.*

shocking ['ʃɒkɪŋ] *adj* - **1.** [very bad] pésimo(ma) - **2.** [behaviour, film] escandaloso(sa), indecoroso(sa).

shod [ʃɒd] <> *pt & pp* ⊳ **shoe**. <> *adj* calzado(da).

shoddy ['ʃɒdɪ] *adj* [work] chapucero(ra); [goods] de pacotilla; *fig* [treatment] vil, despreciable.

shoe [ʃuː] <> *n* zapato *m.* <> *vt* (*pt & pp* **shod** *OR* **shoed**, *cont* **shoeing**) herrar.

shoebrush ['ʃuːbrʌʃ] *n* cepillo *m* para los zapatos.

shoehorn ['ʃuːhɔːn] *n* calzador *m.*

shoelace ['ʃuːleɪs] *n* cordón *m* del zapato.

shoe polish *n* betún *m.*

shoe shop *n* zapatería *f.*

shoestring ['ʃuːstrɪŋ] *n fig*: **on a shoestring** con cuatro cuartos, con muy poco dinero.

shone [ʃɒn] *pt & pp* ⊳ **shine**.

shoo [ʃuː] <> *vt* [animal] espantar, ahuyentar; **he shooed the cat away** echó al gato; [person] mandar a otra parte. <> *excl* ¡fuera!

shook [ʃʊk] *pt* ⊳ **shake**.

shoot [ʃuːt] <> *n* - **1.** *UK* [hunting expedition] cacería *f* - **2.** [new growth] brote *m*, retoño *m.* <> *vt* (*pt & pp* **shot**) - **1.** [fire gun at] disparar contra, abalear *Andes, Amér C & Ven*; [injure] herir a tiros; [kill] matar a tiros; **to shoot o.s.** pegarse un tiro; **he was shot in the leg** le dispararon en la pierna; **to shoot the breeze** *US* estar de cháchara - **2.** *UK* [hunt] cazar - **3.** [arrow] disparar - **4.** CIN rodar, filmar. <> *vi* (*pt & pp* **shot**) - **1.** [fire gun]: **to shoot (at)** disparar (contra); **don't shoot!** ¡no dispare! - **2.** *UK* [hunt] cazar - **3.** [move quickly]: **to shoot in/out/past** entrar/salir/pasar disparado(da) - **4.** CIN rodar, filmar - **5.** SPORT chutar; **he shot at goal** chutó a puerta. ◆ **shoot down** *vt sep* - **1.** [plane] derribar - **2.** [person] matar a tiros. ◆ **shoot up** *vi* - **1.** [child, plant] crecer rápidamente - **2.** [prices] dispararse.

shooting ['ʃuːtɪŋ] *n* - **1.** [killing] asesinato *m* (*a tiros*) - **2.** (*U*) [hunting] caza *f*, cacería *f.*

shooting star *n* estrella *f* fugaz.

shop [ʃɒp] <> *n* [store] tienda *f.* <> *vi* comprar; **to go shopping** ir de compras.

shop assistant *n* *UK* dependiente *m*, -ta *f.*

shop floor *n*: **the shop floor** el personal, los obreros.

shopkeeper ['ʃɒp,kiːpər] *n* tendero *m*, -ra *f.*

shoplifting ['ʃɒp,lɪftɪŋ] *n* (*U*) robo *m* en una tienda.

shopper ['ʃɒpər] *n* comprador *m*, -ra *f.*

shopping ['ʃɒpɪŋ] *n* (*U*) - **1.** [purchases] compras *fpl* - **2.** [act of shopping] compra *f*; **to do some/the shopping** hacer algunas compras/la compra.

shopping bag n bolsa f de la compra.

shopping basket n UK - 1. [in supermarket] cesta f - 2. [for online shopping] cesta f de la compra.

shopping cart n US - 1. [in supermarket] carrito m de la compra - 2. [for online shopping] cesta f de la compra.

shopping centre UK, **shopping mall** US, **shopping plaza** US [-ˌplɑːzə] n centro m comercial.

shopsoiled UK ['ʃɒpsɔɪld], **shopworn** US ['ʃɒpwɔːn] adj deteriorado(da).

shop steward n enlace mf sindical.

shopwindow [ˌʃɒp'wɪndəu] n escaparate m.

shopworn US = shopsoiled.

shore [ʃɔːr] n - 1. [of sea, lake, river] orilla f - 2. [land]: **on shore** en tierra. ◆ **shore up** vt sep apuntalar.

shorn [ʃɔːn] ◇ pp ▷ **shear**. ◇ adj [grass, hair] corto(ta); [head] rapado(da).

short [ʃɔːt] ◇ adj - 1. [gen] corto(ta); **a short time ago** hace poco - 2. [not tall] bajo(ja) - 3. [curt]: **to be short (with sb)** ser seco(ca) (con alguien); **to have a short temper** tener mal genio - 4. [lacking] escaso(sa); **to be short on sthg** no andar sobrado de algo; **to be short of sthg** OR andar mal de - 5. [be shorter form]: **to be short for** ser el diminutivo de. ◇ adv - 1. [out of]: **we are running short of water** se nos está acabando el agua - 2. [suddenly, abruptly]: **to cut sthg short** interrumpir algo; **we had to cut short our trip to Cyprus** tuvimos que interrumpir nuestro viaje a Chipre; **to stop short** parar en seco OR de repente; **to bring** OR **pull sb up short** hacer a alguien parar en seco. ◇ n - 1. UK [alcoholic drink] chupito m - 2. [film] cortometraje m. ◆ **shorts** npl - 1. [gen] pantalones mpl cortos - 2. US [underwear] calzoncillos mpl. ◆ **for short** adv para abreviar. ◆ **in short** adv en resumen. ◆ **nothing short of** prep: **it was nothing short of madness/a disgrace** fue una auténtica locura/vergüenza. ◆ **short of** prep - 1. [just before] cerca de - 2. [without]: **short of asking, I can't see how you'll find out** salvo que preguntes, no sé cómo lo vas a averiguar.

shortage ['ʃɔːtɪdʒ] n falta f, escasez f; **there was a paper shortage** había falta OR escasez de papel.

shortbread ['ʃɔːtbred] n especie de torta hecha de azúcar, harina y mantequilla.

short-change vt [in shop] dar mal el cambio a; fig [reward unfairly] estafar.

short circuit n cortocircuito m.

shortcomings ['ʃɔːtˌkʌmɪŋz] npl defectos mpl.

shortcrust pastry ['ʃɔːtkrʌst-] n pasta f quebrada.

short cut n - 1. [quick way] atajo m; **to take a short cut** tomar un atajo - 2. [quick method] método m rápido.

shorten ['ʃɔːtn] ◇ vt acortar. ◇ vi acortarse.

shortfall ['ʃɔːtfɔːl] n: **shortfall (in** OR **of)** déficit m (de).

shorthand ['ʃɔːthænd] n [writing system] taquigrafía f.

shorthand typist n UK taquimecanógrafo m, -fa f.

short list n UK [for job] lista f de candidatos seleccionados.

shortly ['ʃɔːtlɪ] adv [soon] dentro de poco; **shortly before/after** poco antes/después de.

shortsighted [ˌʃɔːt'saɪtɪd] adj [myopic] miope, corto(ta) de vista; fig [lacking foresight] corto de miras.

short-staffed [-'stɑːft] adj: **to be short-staffed** estar falto(ta) de personal.

shortstop ['ʃɔːtstɒp] n US [baseball] jugador que intenta interceptar bolas entre la segunda y tercera base.

short story n cuento m.

short-tempered [-'tempəd] adj de mal genio.

short-term adj a corto plazo.

short wave n (U) onda f corta.

shot [ʃɒt] ◇ pt & pp ▷ **shoot**. ◇ n - 1. [gunshot] tiro m, disparo m; **he fired two shots** disparó dos tiros; **like a shot** [quickly] disparado(da) - 2. [marksman] tirador m, -ra f; **to be a good shot** ser un buen tirador - 3. [in football] chut m, tiro m; [in golf, tennis] golpe m; **good shot!** ¡buen golpe! - 4. [photograph] foto f - 5. CIN plano m, toma f - 6. inf [try, go] intento m; **go on, have a shot** venga, inténtalo; **to have a shot at (doing) sthg** intentar (hacer) algo - 7. [injection] inyección f.

shotgun ['ʃɒtgʌn] n escopeta f.

should [ʃʊd] aux vb - 1. [be desirable]: **we should leave now** deberíamos irnos ya OR ahora - 2. [seeking advice, permission]: **should I go too?** ¿voy yo también? - 3. [as suggestion]: **I should deny everything** yo lo negaría todo - 4. [indicating probability]: **she should be home soon** tiene que llegar a casa pronto - 5. [have been expected]: **they should have won the match** tendrían que OR deberían haber ganado el partido - 6. [indicating intention, wish]: **I should like to come with you me gustaría ir contigo - 7. (as conditional): if you should see Mary, could you ask her to phone me?** si vieras a Mary, ¿le podrías pedir que me llamara?; **should you decide to accept the job...** si decide aceptar el trabajo... - 8. (in 'that' clauses): **we**

decided that you should do it decidimos que lo hicieras tú - **9.** [expressing uncertain opinion]: **I should think he's about 50 (years old)** yo diría que tiene unos 50 (años) - **10.** [expressing indignation]: **he tidied up afterwards – so he should!** después lo limpió – ¡era lo menos que podía hacer!; **I should hope so!** ¡eso espero!; **I should think so, too!** ¡es lo mínimo que podía hacer!

shoulder ['ʃəʊldər] ◇ n - **1.** [part of body, clothing] hombro m - **2.** CULIN espaldilla f, paleta f Amér. ◇ vt [accept - responsibility] cargar con; **to shoulder the blame** asumir la responsabilidad.

shoulder blade n omóplato m.

shoulder strap n - **1.** [on dress] tirante m, bretel m - **2.** [on bag] correa f, bandolera f.

shouldn't ['ʃʊdnt] (abbr of should not) ▷ **should**.

should've ['ʃʊdəv] (abbr of should have) ▷ **should**.

shout [ʃaʊt] ◇ n grito m; **to let out a shout** lanzar un grito. ◇ vt gritar. ◇ vi: **to shout (at)** gritar (a). ◆ **shout down** vt sep acallar a gritos.

shouting ['ʃaʊtɪŋ] n (U) gritos mpl.

shove [ʃʌv] ◇ n: **to give sthg/sb a shove** dar a algo/a alguien un empujón. ◇ vt empujar; **to shove sthg/sb in** meter algo/a alguien a empujones. ◆ **shove off** vi inf [go away] largarse.

shovel ['ʃʌvl] ◇ n pala f. ◇ vt (UK pt & pp -led, cont -ling, US pt & pp -ed, cont -ing) remover con la pala OR a paletadas; **to shovel food into one's mouth** fig zamparse la comida.

show [ʃəʊ] ◇ n - **1.** [display, demonstration] demostración f; **a show of strength** una demostración de fuerte - **2.** [piece of entertainment - at theatre] espectáculo m; [- on radio, TV] programa m - **3.** [performance] función f - **4.** [of dogs, flowers, art] exposición f. ◇ vt (pp shown OR -ed) - **1.** [gen] mostrar - **2.** [escort]: **to show sb to the door** llevar OR acompañar a alguien hasta algo; **he showed us to our seats** nos llevó a nuestros asientos - **3.** [make visible, reveal] dejar ver; **white clothes show the dirt** la ropa blanca deja ver la suciedad; **come on, show yourself!** venga, ¡déjate ver! - **4.** [indicate - increase, profit, loss] arrojar, registrar - **5.** [broadcast - film] poner; [- TV programme] poner, emitir. ◇ vi (pp shown OR -ed) - **1.** [indicate, make clear] indicar, mostrar - **2.** [be visible] verse; **does it show?** ¿se ve? - **3.** [film]: **it is showing at the Odeon** lo ponen en el Odeon. ◆ **show off** ◇ vt sep lucir, presumir de. ◇ vi presumir. ◆ **show out** vt sep acompañar hasta la puerta; **show the gentlemen out, please** acompañe a los caba-

lleros hasta la puerta, por favor. ◆ **show up** ◇ vt sep poner en evidencia. ◇ vi - **1.** [stand out] resaltar - **2.** [turn up] aparecer.

show business n (U) mundo m del espectáculo.

showdown ['ʃəʊdaʊn] n: **to have a showdown with** enfrentarse abiertamente a OR con.

shower ['ʃaʊər] ◇ n - **1.** [device] ducha f - **2.** [wash]: **to have OR take a shower** ducharse - **3.** [of rain] chubasco m, chaparrón m. ◇ vt - **1.** [sprinkle] rociar - **2.** [bestow]: **to shower sb with sthg, to shower sthg on OR upon sb** [presents, compliments] colmar a alguien de algo; [insults] acribillar a alguien a algo. ◇ vi [wash] ducharse.

shower cap n gorro m de ducha.

showing ['ʃəʊɪŋ] n [of film] pase m, proyección f; [of paintings] exposición f.

show jumping [-,dʒʌmpɪŋ] n concurso m hípico de salto.

shown [ʃəʊn] pp ▷ **show**.

show-off n inf presumido m, -da f.

showpiece ['ʃəʊpiːs] n pieza f de mayor interés.

showroom ['ʃəʊrʊm] n salón m OR sala f de exposición.

shrank [ʃræŋk] pt ▷ **shrink**.

shrapnel ['ʃræpnl] n metralla f.

shred [ʃred] ◇ n [small piece - of material] jirón m; [- of paper] pedacito m; fig [scrap] pizca f; **there isn't a shred of truth in what he says** no hay una pizca de verdad en lo que dice; **to be in shreds** lit & fig estar hecho(cha) pedazos. ◇ vt [paper] hacer trizas; [food] rallar.

shredder ['ʃredər] n [for paper] destructora f; [for food] rallador m.

shrewd [ʃruːd] adj astuto(ta).

shriek [ʃriːk] ◇ n chillido m, grito m. ◇ vi: **to shriek (with OR in)** chillar (de).

shrill [ʃrɪl] adj [high-pitched] estridente, agudo(da).

shrimp [ʃrɪmp] n US gamba f, camarón m Amér.

shrine [ʃraɪn] n santuario m.

shrink [ʃrɪŋk] ◇ vt (pt shrank, pp shrunk) encoger. ◇ vi (pt shrank, pp shrunk) - **1.** [become smaller] encoger - **2.** fig [contract, diminish] disminuir - **3.** [recoil]: **to shrink away from** retroceder OR arredrarse ante - **4.** [be reluctant]: **to shrink from sthg** eludir algo.

shrinkage ['ʃrɪŋkɪdʒ] n [loss in size] encogimiento m; fig [contraction] reducción f.

shrink-wrap vt precintar o envasar con plástico termoretráctil.

shrivel ['ʃrɪvl] (*UK pt* & *pp* **-led**, *cont* **-ling**, *US pt* & *pp* **-ed**, *cont* **-ing**) ◇ *vt*: **to shrivel (up)** secar, marchitar. ◇ *vi*: **to shrivel (up)** secarse, marchitarse.

shroud [ʃraʊd] ◇ *n* [cloth] mortaja *f*, sudario *m*. ◇ *vt*: **to be shrouded in sthg** estar envuelto(ta) en algo.

Shrove Tuesday ['ʃrəʊv-] *n* martes *m inv* de carnaval.

shrub [ʃrʌb] *n* arbusto *m*.

shrubbery ['ʃrʌbərɪ] *n* (zona *f* de) arbustos *mpl*.

shrug [ʃrʌg] ◇ *vt*: **to shrug one's shoulders** encogerse de hombros. ◇ *vi* encogerse de hombros. ◆ **shrug off** *vt sep* quitar importancia a.

shrunk [ʃrʌŋk] *pp* ▷ **shrink**.

shudder ['ʃʌdəʳ] *vi* [tremble]: **to shudder (with)** estremecerse (de).

shuffle ['ʃʌfl] *vt* - **1.** [feet] arrastrar - **2.** [cards] barajar - **3.** [sheets of paper] revolver.

shun [ʃʌn] *vt* rehuir, esquivar.

shunt [ʃʌnt] *vt* RAIL cambiar de vía; *fig* [move] llevar (de un sitio a otro).

shut [ʃʌt] ◇ *adj* cerrado(da). ◇ *vt* (*pt* & *pp* **shut**) cerrar. ◇ *vi* (*pt* & *pp* **shut**) - **1.** [close] cerrarse - **2.** [close for business] cerrar. ◆ **shut away** *vt sep* guardar bajo llave. ◆ **shut down** *vt sep* & *vi* cerrar. ◆ **shut out** *vt sep* [person, cat] dejar fuera a; [light, noise] no dejar entrar. ◆ **shut up** *inf* ◇ *vt sep* [silence] hacer callar. ◇ *vi* callarse; **shut up!** ¡cállate!

shutter ['ʃʌtəʳ] *n* - **1.** [on window] postigo *m* - **2.** [in camera] obturador *m*.

shuttle ['ʃʌtl] ◇ *adj*: **shuttle service** [of planes] puente *m* aéreo; [of buses, trains] servicio *m* regular. ◇ *n* [plane] avión *m* (de puente aéreo).

shuttlecock ['ʃʌtlkɒk] *n* volante *m*.

shy [ʃaɪ] ◇ *adj* [timid] tímido(da). ◇ *vi* espantarse.

Siberia [saɪ'bɪərɪə] *n* Siberia.

sibling ['sɪblɪŋ] *n* hermano *m*, -na *f*.

Sicily ['sɪsɪlɪ] *n* Sicilia.

sick [sɪk] *adj* - **1.** [ill] enfermo(ma) - **2.** [nauseous]: **to feel sick** marearse - **3.** [vomiting]: **to be sick** *UK* devolver, vomitar - **4.** [fed up]: **to be sick of sthg/of doing sthg** estar harto(ta) de algo/de hacer algo; **to be sick and tired of (doing) sthg** estar hasta la coronilla de (hacer) algo - **5.** [joke] de mal gusto.

sickbay ['sɪkbeɪ] *n* enfermería *f*.

sicken ['sɪkn] ◇ *vt* poner enfermo(ma), asquear. ◇ *vi UK*: **to be sickening for sthg** estar cogiendo algo.

sickening ['sɪknɪŋ] *adj* - **1.** [disgusting] asqueroso(sa) - **2.** [infuriating] exasperante.

sickle ['sɪkl] *n* hoz *f*.

sick leave *n* (*U*) baja *f* por enfermedad.

sickly ['sɪklɪ] *adj* - **1.** [unhealthy] enfermizo(za) - **2.** [unpleasant] nauseabundo(da).

sickness ['sɪknɪs] *n* - **1.** [illness] enfermedad *f* - **2.** (*U*) *UK* [nausea, vomiting] mareo *m*.

sick pay *n* (*U*) paga *f* por enfermedad.

side [saɪd] ◇ *n* - **1.** [gen] lado *m*; **at** OR **by one's side** al lado de uno; **on every side, on all sides** por todos los lados; **from side to side** de un lado a otro; **side by side** juntos, uno al lado de otro; **to put sthg to** OR **on one side** poner algo a un lado - **2.** [of person] costado *m*; [of animal] ijada *f* - **3.** [edge] lado *m*, borde *m* - **4.** [of hill, valley] falda *f*, ladera *f* - **5.** [bank] orilla *f* - **6.** [page] cara *f* - **7.** [participant - in war, game] lado *m*, bando *m*; [- in sports match] equipo *m* - **8.** [viewpoint] punto *m* de vista; **you should try to see both sides** deberías considerar las dos caras de la situación; **to take sb's side** ponerse del lado OR de parte de alguien; **to take sides** tomar partido; **to be on sb's side** estar del lado OR de parte de alguien; **whose side are you on?** ¿de parte de quién estás? - **9.** [aspect] aspecto *m*; **it does have its comical side** tiene su lado cómico; **to be on the safe side** para estar seguro. ◇ *adj* lateral. ◆ **side with** *vt insep* ponerse de parte de.

sideboard ['saɪdbɔːd] *n* aparador *m*.

sideboards ['saɪdbɔːdz] *UK*, **sideburns** ['saɪdbɜːnz] *US npl* patillas *fpl*.

side effect *n fig* & MED efecto *m* secundario.

sidelight ['saɪdlaɪt] *n* luz *f* lateral.

sideline ['saɪdlaɪn] *n* - **1.** [extra business] negocio *m* suplementario - **2.** [on tennis court] línea *f* lateral; [on football pitch] línea de banda.

sidelong ['saɪdlɒŋ] *adj* & *adv* de reojo OR soslayo; **to give sb a sidelong glance** mirar a alguien de reojo OR soslayo.

sidesaddle ['saɪd,sædl] *adv*: **to ride sidesaddle** montar a sentadillas OR mujeriegas.

sideshow ['saɪdʃəʊ] *n* barraca *f* OR caseta *f* de feria.

sidestep ['saɪdstep] *vt* - **1.** [in football, rugby] regatear - **2.** *fig* [problem, question] esquivar.

side street *n* calle *f* lateral.

sidetrack ['saɪdtræk] *vt*: **to be sidetracked** desviarse OR salirse del tema; **I keep getting sidetracked** me distraigo continuamente.

sidewalk ['saɪdwɔːk] *n US* acera *f*, andén *m Amér C* & *Col*, vereda *f Perú*, banqueta *f Méx*.

sideways ['saɪdweɪz] ◇ *adj* [movement] hacia un lado; [glance] de soslayo. ◇ *adv* [move] de lado; [look] de reojo.

siding ['saɪdɪŋ] *n* vía *f* muerta.

sidle ['saɪdl] ◆ **sidle up** *vi*: **to sidle up to** acercarse furtivamente a.

siege [si:dʒ] n - **1.** [by army] sitio m, cerco m - **2.** [by police] cerco m policial.

sieve [sɪv] <> n [utensil] colador m; **to have a head** OR **memory like a sieve** tener muy mala memoria. <> vt [soup] colar; [flour, sugar] tamizar.

sift [sɪft] <> vt - **1.** [sieve] tamizar - **2.** fig [examine carefully] examinar cuidadosamente. <> vi: **to sift through sthg** examinar cuidadosamente algo.

sigh [saɪ] <> n suspiro m. <> vi suspirar.

sight [saɪt] <> n - **1.** [vision] vista f - **2.** [act of seeing]: **her first sight of the sea** la primera vez que vio el mar; **in sight** a la vista; **to disappear out of sight** perderse de vista; **at first sight** a primera vista; **it was love at first sight** fue un flechazo - **3.** [something seen] espectáculo m - **4.** [on gun] mira f; **to set one's sights on sthg** echarle el ojo a algo; **it's not a pretty sight** no es muy agradable de ver. <> vt divisar, avistar. ➤ **sights** npl atracciones fpl turísticas.

sightseeing ['saɪt,si:ɪŋ] n (U) recorrido m turístico; **to go sightseeing** hacer turismo.

sightseer ['saɪt,si:ər] n turista mf.

sign [saɪn] <> n - **1.** [written symbol] signo m - **2.** [horoscope]: **sign of the zodiac** signo del zodiaco - **3.** [gesture] señal f - **4.** [of pub, shop] letrero m; [on road] señal f; [notice] cartel m - **5.** [indication] señal f, indicio m; **it's a good sign** es una buena señal. <> vt firmar. <> vi firmar. ➤ **sign on** vi - **1.** [enrol, register]: **to sign on (for)** [army] alistarse (en); [job] firmar el contrato (de); [course] matricularse (en) - **2.** [register as unemployed] firmar para cobrar el paro. ➤ **sign up** <> vt sep [employee] contratar; [recruit] alistar. <> vi: **to sign up (for)** [army] alistarse (en); [job] firmar el contrato (de); [course] matricularse (en).

signal ['sɪgnl] <> n señal f. <> vt (UK pt & pp -led, cont -ling, US pt & pp -ed, cont -ing) - **1.** [indicate] indicar - **2.** [tell]: **to signal sb (to do sthg)** hacer señas a alguien (para que haga algo). <> vi (UK pt & pp -led, cont -ling, US pt & pp -ed, cont -ing) - **1.** AUT señalizar - **2.** [indicate]: **to signal for sthg** pedir algo por señas.

signalman ['sɪgnlmən] (pl -men [-mən]) n RAIL guardavía m.

signature ['sɪgnətʃər] n firma f.

signature tune n sintonía f.

signet ring ['sɪgnɪt-] n (anillo m de) sello m.

significance [sɪg'nɪfɪkəns] n trascendencia f, importancia f; **to attach significance to sthg** atribuir importancia a algo; **to be of little/great/no significance** ser de poca/mucha/ninguna importancia.

significant [sɪg'nɪfɪkənt] adj - **1.** [considerable, meaningful] significativo(va) - **2.** [important] trascendente.

signify ['sɪgnɪfaɪ] vt significar.

signpost ['saɪnpəʊst] n letrero m indicador.

Sikh [si:k] <> adj sij. <> n [person] sij mf.

silence ['saɪləns] <> n silencio m; **to do sthg in silence** hacer algo en silencio. <> vt [person, critic] acallar; [gun] silenciar.

silencer ['saɪlənsər] n silenciador m.

silent ['saɪlənt] adj - **1.** [gen] silencioso(sa) - **2.** [not revealing anything]: **to be silent about** quedar en silencio respecto a; **to remain silent** permanecer callado(da) - **3.** CIN & LING mudo(da); **a silent movie** una película muda; **a silent b** una b muda.

silhouette [,sɪluː'et] n silueta f.

silicon chip [,sɪlɪkən-] n chip m de silicio.

silk [sɪlk] <> n seda f. <> comp de seda; **a silk blouse** una blusa de seda.

silky ['sɪlkɪ] adj [hair, dress, skin] sedoso(sa); [voice] aterciopelado(da).

sill [sɪl] n [of window] alféizar m.

silly ['sɪlɪ] adj estúpido(da); **that was a silly thing to say** qué tontería has dicho.

silo ['saɪləʊ] (pl -s) n silo m.

silt [sɪlt] n cieno m, légamo m.

silver ['sɪlvər] <> adj - **1.** [in colour] plateado(da) - **2.** [made of silver] de plata. <> n (U) - **1.** [metal, silverware] plata f - **2.** [coins] monedas fpl plateadas.

silver foil, silver paper n (U) papel m de plata.

silver-plated [-'pleɪtɪd] adj plateado(da).

silversmith ['sɪlvəsmɪθ] n platero m, -ra f.

silver surfer [-'sɜːfər] n inf internauta mf de la tercera edad.

silverware ['sɪlvəweər] n (U) - **1.** [dishes etc] plata f - **2.** US [cutlery] cubertería f de plata.

similar ['sɪmɪlər] adj: **similar (to)** parecido(da) OR similar (a).

similarly ['sɪmɪləlɪ] adv [likewise] asimismo; [equally] igualmente.

simmer ['sɪmər] vt & vi hervir a fuego lento.

simpering ['sɪmpərɪŋ] adj [person] que sonríe con cara de tonto(ta); [smile] bobo(ba).

simple ['sɪmpl] adj - **1.** [gen] sencillo(lla) - **2.** dated [mentally retarded] simple - **3.** [plain - fact] mero(ra); [- truth] puro(ra).

simple-minded [-'maɪndɪd] adj simple.

simplicity [sɪm'plɪsətɪ] n sencillez f.

simplify ['sɪmplɪfaɪ] vt simplificar.

simply ['sɪmplɪ] adv - **1.** [merely] sencillamente, simplemente - **2.** [in a simple way] de manera sencilla.

simulate ['sɪmjʊleɪt] vt simular.

simultaneous [UK ,sɪməl'teɪnjəs, US ,saɪməl'teɪnjəs] adj simultáneo(a).

sin [sɪn] <> n pecado m. <> vi: **to sin (against)** pecar (contra).

since [sɪns] <> *adv* desde entonces; **we haven't been there since** no hemos vuelto allí desde entonces. <> *prep* desde; **since last Tuesday** desde el último martes; **since then** desde entonces; **he has worked here since 1975** trabaja aquí desde 1975. <> *conj* - **1.** [in time] desde que; **she's been miserable ever since she married him** desde que se casó con él ha sido desdichada; **it's ages since I saw you** hace siglos que no te veo - **2.** [because] ya que, puesto que.

sincere [sɪnˈsɪəʳ] *adj* sincero(ra).

sincerely [sɪnˈsɪəlɪ] *adv* sinceramente; **Yours sincerely** [at end of letter] atentamente.

sincerity [sɪnˈserətɪ] *n* sinceridad *f*.

sinew [ˈsɪnjuː] *n* tendón *m*.

sinful [ˈsɪnfʊl] *adj* - **1.** [person] pecador(ra) - **2.** [thought, act] pecaminoso(sa).

sing [sɪŋ] (*pt* sang, *pp* sung) *vt* & *vi* cantar; **to sing along with sb** cantar a coro con alguien.

Singapore [ˌsɪŋəˈpɔːʳ] *n* Singapur.

singe [sɪndʒ] *vt* chamuscar.

singer [ˈsɪŋəʳ] *n* cantante *mf*; **she's a good singer** canta muy bien.

singing [ˈsɪŋɪŋ] *n* (U) canto *m*.

single [ˈsɪŋgl] <> *adj* - **1.** [only one] solo(la); **not a single person was there** no había ni una sola persona - **2.** [individual]: **every single penny** todos y cada uno de los peniques - **3.** [unmarried] soltero(ra); **he's single** está soltero - **4.** *UK* [one-way] de ida. <> *n* - **1.** *UK* [one-way ticket] billete *m* de ida - **2.** MUS [record] sencillo *m*, single *m*. ➡ **singles** *npl* TENNIS (partido *m*) individual *m*. ➡ **single out** *vt sep*: **to single sb out (for)** escoger a alguien (para).

single bed *n* cama *f* individual.

single-breasted [-ˈbrestɪd] *adj* recto(ta).

single-click <> *n* clic *m*. <> *vi* hacer clic. <> *vt* hacer clic en.

single cream *n UK* nata *f* líquida.

single file *n*: **in single file** en fila india.

single-handed [-ˈhændɪd] *adv* sin ayuda.

single-minded [-ˈmaɪndɪd] *adj* resuelto(ta).

single parent *n* padre *m* soltero, madre *f* soltera; **he's a single parent** es padre soltero.

single-parent family *n* familia *f* monoparental.

single room *n* habitación *f* individual.

singlet [ˈsɪŋglɪt] *n UK* camiseta *f* sin mangas.

singular [ˈsɪŋgjʊləʳ] <> *adj* singular. <> *n* singular *m*; **in the singular** en singular.

sinister [ˈsɪnɪstəʳ] *adj* siniestro(tra).

sink [sɪŋk] <> *n* - **1.** [in kitchen] fregadero *m* - **2.** [in bathroom] lavabo *m*. <> *vt* (*pt* sank, *pp* sunk) - **1.** [cause to go under water] hundir - **2.** [cause to penetrate]: **to sink sthg into** [knife,

claws] clavar algo en; [teeth] hincar algo en; **he sank his teeth into the steak** le hincó los dientes al filete. <> *vi* (*pt* sank, *pp* sunk) - **1.** [go down - ship, sun] hundirse - **2.** [slump - person] hundirse; **she sank into a chair** se desplomó en una silla - **3.** [decrease] bajar. ➡ **sink in** *vi* hacer mella; **it hasn't sunk in yet** todavía no lo tiene asumido.

sink unit *n* fregadero *m* (con mueble debajo).

sinner [ˈsɪnəʳ] *n* pecador *m*, -ra *f*.

sinus [ˈsaɪnəs] (*pl* -es) *n* seno *m*.

sip [sɪp] <> *n* sorbo *m*. <> *vt* beber a sorbos.

siphon, syphon [ˈsaɪfn] *n* sifón *m*. ➡ **siphon off** *vt sep* - **1.** [liquid] sacar con sifón - **2.** *fig* [funds] desviar.

sir [sɜːʳ] *n* - **1.** [form of address] señor *m*; **thank you, sir** gracias, señor; [in letter]: **Dear sir**, Estimado Señor - **2.** [in titles]: **Sir Philip Holden** Sir Philip Holden.

siren [ˈsaɪərən] *n* [alarm] sirena *f*.

sirloin (steak) [ˈsɜːlɔɪn] *n* solomillo *m*, (filete *m*) de lomo *m* *Andes, Col & Ven*.

sissy [ˈsɪsɪ] *n inf* mariquita *m*.

sister [ˈsɪstəʳ] *n* - **1.** [gen] hermana *f* - **2.** *UK* [senior nurse] enfermera *f* jefe.

sister-in-law (*pl* sisters-in-law OR sister-in-laws) *n* cuñada *f*.

sit [sɪt] (*pt* & *pp* sat) <> *vi* - **1.** [be seated, sit down] sentarse - **2.** [be member]: **to sit on** ser miembro de - **3.** [be in session] reunirse. <> *vt UK* [exam] presentarse a. ➡ **sit about, sit around** *vi* estar sentado(da) sin hacer nada. ➡ **sit down** *vi* sentarse; **sit down, please** siéntese, por favor; **she was sitting down** estaba sentada. ➡ **sit in on** *vt insep* estar presente en (sin tomar parte). ➡ **sit through** *vt insep* aguantar (hasta el final). ➡ **sit up** *vi* - **1.** [sit upright] incorporarse; **sit up straight!** siéntate derecho - **2.** [stay up] quedarse levantado(da); **we sat up until midnight** nos quedamos levantados hasta la medianoche.

sitcom [ˈsɪtkɒm] *n inf* comedia *f* de situación.

site [saɪt] <> *n* [place] sitio *m*, lugar *m*; [of construction work] obra *f*. <> *vt* situar.

sit-in *n* sentada *f*; **to stage a sit-in** protagonizar una sentada.

sitting [ˈsɪtɪŋ] *n* - **1.** [serving of meal] turno *m* (para comer) - **2.** [session] sesión *f*.

sitting room *n* sala *f* de estar.

situated [ˈsɪtjʊeɪtɪd] *adj* [located]: **to be situated** estar situado(da).

situation [ˌsɪtjʊˈeɪʃn] *n* - **1.** [gen] situación *f* - **2.** [job]: **'Situations Vacant'** *UK* 'Ofertas de trabajo'.

six [sɪks] <> *num adj* seis (*inv*); **she's six (years old)** tiene seis años. <> *num n* - **1.** [the number six] seis *m inv*; **two hundred and six** doscientos seis; **six comes before seven** el seis ~~୲ ୲୲ ଐ୍ୱ॓ ॑ ୲ୱ॑॓ ଐ ॓॑ ୰ ୲ୱ ॓॑॓ୱ॓ ॑ ॑॓ ॑॓ୱ॑~~ **(thirty)** son las seis (y media); **we arrived at six** llegamos a las seis - 3. [in addresses]: **six Peyton Place** Peyton Place número seis - 4. [in scores]: **six-nil** seis a cero. ◇ *num pron* seis *mf*; **there are six of us** somos seis.

sixteen [sɪks'tiːn] *num* dieciséis; *see also* **six**.

sixteenth [sɪks'tiːnθ] *num* decimosexto(ta); *see also* **sixth**.

sixth [sɪksθ] ◇ *num adj* sexto(ta). ◇ *num adv* sexto(ta). ◇ *num pron* sexto *m*, -ta *f*. ◇ *n* - 1. [fraction]: **a sixth** OR **one sixth of** un sexto de, la sexta parte de - 2. [in dates]: **the sixth** el (día) seis; **the sixth of September** el seis de septiembre.

sixth form *n* UK SCH *curso optativo de dos años de enseñanza secundaria con vistas al examen de ingreso a la universidad*, ≃ COU *m*.

sixth form college *n* UK *centro público para alumnos de 16 a 18 años donde se preparan para los 'A levels' o para exámenes de formación profesional*.

sixty ['sɪkstɪ] *num* sesenta; *see also* **six**. ◆ **sixties** *npl* - 1. [decade]: **the sixties** los años sesenta - 2. [in ages]: **to be in one's sixties** estar en los sesenta.

size [saɪz] *n* - 1. [gen] tamaño *m*; **what size do you take?** ¿cuál es su talla?; **what size shoes do you take?** ¿qué número calza? - 2. [of clothes] talla *f*; [of shoes] número *m*. ◆ **size up** *vt sep* [situation] evaluar; [person] calar.

sizeable ['saɪzəbl] *adj* considerable.

sizzle ['sɪzl] *vi* chisporrotear.

skate [skeɪt] ◇ *n* - 1. *(pl* -s) [ice skate, roller skate] patín *m* - 2. *(pl* skate) [fish] raya *f*. ◇ *vi* [on skates] patinar.

skateboard ['skeɪtbɔːd] *n* monopatín *m*.

skater ['skeɪtər] *n* patinador *m*, -ra *f*.

skating ['skeɪtɪŋ] *n* patinaje *m*.

skating rink *n* pista *f* de patinaje.

skeleton ['skelɪtn] *n* ANAT esqueleto *m*; **to have a skeleton in the cupboard** *fig* guardar un secreto vergonzante.

skeleton key *n* llave *f* maestra.

skeleton staff *n* personal *m* mínimo.

skeptic US = **sceptic**.

sketch [sketʃ] ◇ *n* - 1. [drawing, brief outline] esbozo *m*, bosquejo *m* - 2. [humorous scene] sketch *m*. ◇ *vt* esbozar.

sketchbook ['sketʃbʊk] *n* cuaderno *m* de dibujo.

sketchpad ['sketʃpæd] *n* bloc *m* de dibujo.

sketchy ['sketʃɪ] *adj* incompleto(ta).

skewer ['skjʊər] *n* brocheta *f*.

ski [skiː] ◇ *n* patinazo *m*. ◇ *vi* (*pt & pp* skied, *cont* skiing) esquiar.

ski boots *npl* botas *fpl* de esquí.

skid [skɪd] ◇ *n* patinazo *m*. ◇ *vi* patinar.

skier ['skiːər] *n* esquiador *m*, -ra *f*.

skies [skaɪz] *npl* ⊏▷ **sky**.

skiing ['skiːɪŋ] *n* (U) esquí *m*; **to go skiing** ir a esquiar.

ski jump *n* - 1. [slope] pista *f* para saltos de esquí - 2. [event] saltos *mpl* de esquí.

skilful, skillful US ['skɪlfʊl] *adj* hábil.

ski lift *n* telesilla *m*.

skill [skɪl] *n* - 1. (U) [expertise] habilidad *f*, destreza *f* - 2. [craft, technique] técnica *f*.

skilled [skɪld] *adj* - 1. [skilful] habilidoso(sa); **to be skilled (in** OR **at doing sthg)** ser experto(ta) (en hacer algo) - 2. [trained] cualificado(da).

skillful US = **skilful**.

skim [skɪm] ◇ *vt* - 1. [remove - cream] desnatar - 2. [fly above] volar rozando. ◇ *vi*: **to skim through sthg** hojear algo, leer algo por encima.

skimmed milk [skɪmd-] *n* leche *f* desnatada.

skimp [skɪmp] ◇ *vt* [gen] escatimar; [work] hacer de prisa y corriendo. ◇ *vi*: **to skimp on sthg** [gen] escatimar algo; [work] hacer algo de prisa y corriendo.

skimpy ['skɪmpɪ] *adj* [clothes] muy corto y estrecho (muy corta y estrecha); [meal, facts] escaso(sa).

skin [skɪn] ◇ *n* - 1. [gen] piel *f*; [on face] cutis *m*; **to save** OR **protect one's own skin** salvar el pellejo - 2. [on milk, pudding] nata *f*; [on paint] capa *f*, película *f*. ◇ *vt* - 1. [animal] despellejar - 2. [knee, elbow etc] rasguñarse.

skincare ['skɪnkeər] *n* (U) cuidado *m* de la piel.

skin-deep *adj* superficial.

skin diving *n* buceo *m*, submarinismo *m* (sin traje ni escafandra).

skinny ['skɪnɪ] ◇ *adj inf* flaco(ca). ◇ *n* US: **the skinny** información *f* confidencial.

skin-tight *adj* muy ajustado(da).

skip [skɪp] ◇ *n* - 1. [little jump] brinco *m*, saltito *m* - 2. UK [large container] contenedor *m*, container *m*. ◇ *vt* [miss out] saltarse. ◇ *vi* - 1. [move in little jumps] ir dando brincos - 2. UK [jump over rope] saltar a la comba.

ski pants *npl* pantalones *mpl* de esquí.

ski pole *n* bastón *m* para esquiar.

skipper ['skɪpər] *n* NAUT & SPORT capitán *m*, -ana *f*.

skipping rope ['skɪpɪŋ-] *n* UK comba *f*, cuerda *f* de saltar.

skirmish ['skɜːmɪʃ] *n lit & fig* escaramuza *f*.

skirt [skɜːt] ⬦ n - **1.** falda f - **2.** US: **(bed) skirt** volante m. ⬦ vt - **1.** [border] rodear, bordear - **2.** [go round - obstacle] sortear; [- person, group] esquivar - **3.** [avoid dealing with] eludir.
➤ **skirt round** vt insep - **1.** [obstacle] sortear - **2.** [issue, problem] evitar, eludir.

skit [skɪt] n: **skit (on)** parodia f (de).

skittle ['skɪtl] n UK bolo m. ➤ **skittles** n (U) bolos mpl.

skive [skaɪv] vi UK inf: **to skive (off)** escaquearse.

skulk [skʌlk] vi esconderse.

skull [skʌl] n [gen] calavera f; ANAT cráneo m.

skunk [skʌŋk] n mofeta f.

sky [skaɪ] n cielo m.

skylight ['skaɪlaɪt] n claraboya f.

sky marshal n US policía destinado en un avión para evitar secuestros.

skyscraper ['skaɪˌskreɪpər] n rascacielos m inv.

slab [slæb] n [of stone] losa f; [of cheese] pedazo m; [of chocolate] tableta f.

slack [slæk] ⬦ adj - **1.** [rope, cable] flojo(ja) - **2.** [business] inactivo(va) - **3.** [person - careless] descuidado(da). ⬦ n [in rope] parte f floja; **to take up the slack** tensar la cuerda.

slacken ['slækn] ⬦ vt [speed, pace] reducir; [rope] aflojar. ⬦ vi [speed, pace] reducirse.

slag [slæg] n [waste material] escoria f.

slagheap ['slæghiːp] n escorial m.

slain [sleɪn] pp ▷ **slay**.

slam [slæm] ⬦ vt - **1.** [shut] cerrar de golpe; **she slammed the door** dio un portazo - **2.** [place with force]: **to slam sthg on** OR **onto sthg** dar un golpe con algo contra algo violentamente; **he slammed his fist on the desk** dio un puñetazo en la mesa. ⬦ vi [shut] cerrarse de golpe.

slander ['slɑːndər] ⬦ n calumnia f, difamación f. ⬦ vt calumniar, difamar.

slang [slæŋ] n argot m, jerga f.

slant [slɑːnt] ⬦ n - **1.** [diagonal angle] inclinación f - **2.** [perspective] enfoque m. ⬦ vi inclinarse.

slanting ['slɑːntɪŋ] adj inclinado(da).

slap [slæp] ⬦ n [in face] bofetada f; [on back] palmada f; **it was a slap in the face** fig fue una bofetada; **he gave him a slap on the back** le dio una palmadita en la espalda. ⬦ vt - **1.** [person, face] abofetear; **she slapped him round the face** lo abofeteó, le dio una bofetada; [back] dar una palmada a - **2.** [place with force]: **he slapped the folder on the desk** dejó la carpeta en la mesa dando un golpetazo; **she slapped some paste on the wallpaper** embadurnó el papel pintado con cola. ⬦ adv inf [directly] de narices; **he walked slap into a lamppost** se dio de lleno con una farola.

slapstick ['slæpstɪk] n (U) payasadas fpl; **slapstick comedy** astracanada f.

slap-up adj UK inf: **slap-up meal** comilona f.

slash [slæʃ] ⬦ n - **1.** [long cut] raja f, tajo m - **2.** esp US [oblique stroke] barra f oblicua; **forward slash** barra inclinada. ⬦ vt - **1.** [material, tyre] rasgar; **she slashed her wrists** se cortó las venas - **2.** inf [prices etc] recortar drásticamente.

slasher movie n inf película f sanguinaria.

slat [slæt] n tablilla f.

slate [sleɪt] ⬦ n pizarra f. ⬦ vt [criticize] poner por los suelos.

slaughter ['slɔːtər] ⬦ n lit & fig matanza f. ⬦ vt matar.

slaughterhouse ['slɔːtəhaʊs, pl -haʊzɪz] n matadero m.

slave [sleɪv] ⬦ n esclavo m, -va f; **to be a slave to** fig ser un esclavo de. ⬦ vi [work hard] trabajar como un negro; **to slave over a hot stove** hum pasarse el día bregando en la cocina.

slavery ['sleɪvərɪ] n lit & fig esclavitud f.

Slavic ['slɑːvɪk] adj eslavo m, -va f.

slay [sleɪ] (pt **slew**, pp **slain**) vt liter asesinar, matar.

sleazy ['sliːzɪ] adj [disreputable] de mala muerte.

sledge [sledʒ], **sled** US [sled] n trineo m.

sledgehammer ['sledʒˌhæmər] n almádena f.

sleek [sliːk] adj - **1.** [hair] suave y brillante; [fur] lustroso(sa) - **2.** [shape] de línea depurada.

sleep [sliːp] ⬦ n sueño m. ⬦ vi (pt & pp **slept**) dormir. ➤ **sleep in** vi levantarse tarde. ➤ **sleep with** vt insep euph acostarse con.

sleeper ['sliːpər] n - **1.** [person]: **to be a heavy/light sleeper** tener el sueño profundo/ligero - **2.** [sleeping compartment] coche-cama m - **3.** [train] tren m nocturno (con literas) - **4.** UK [on railway track] traviesa f.

sleeping bag ['sliːpɪŋ-] n saco m de dormir.

sleeping car ['sliːpɪŋ-] n coche-cama m, coche m dormitorio.

sleeping pill ['sliːpɪŋ-] n pastilla f para dormir.

sleepless ['sliːpləs] adj [night] en blanco.

sleepwalk ['sliːpwɔːk] vi [be a sleepwalker] ser somnámbulo(la); [walk in one's sleep] andar mientras uno duerme.

sleepy ['sliːpɪ] adj [person] soñoliento(ta).

sleet [sliːt] ⬦ n aguanieve f. ⬦ impers vb: **it's sleeting** cae aguanieve.

sleeve [sliːv] n - **1.** [of garment] manga f; **to have sthg up one's sleeve** guardar una carta en la manga - **2.** [for record] cubierta f.

sleigh [sleɪ] n trineo m.

sleight of hand [ˌslaɪt-] n (U) lit & fig juego m de manos.

slender ['slendər] adj - **1.** [thin] esbelto(ta) - **2.** [scarce] escaso(sa).

slept [slept] pt & pp ⊳ **sleep**.

S-level (abbr of Special level) n UK SCH examen que se realiza al mismo tiempo que el A-level, pero de un nivel superior.

slew [slu:] ◇ pt ⊳ **slay**. ◇ vi girar bruscamente.

slice [slaɪs] ◇ n - **1.** [of bread] rebanada f; [of cheese] loncha f; [of sausage] raja f; [of lemon] rodaja f; [of meat] tajada f - **2.** [of market, glory] parte f. ◇ vt [gen] cortar; [bread] rebanar.

slick [slɪk] adj - **1.** [smooth, skilful] logrado(da) - **2.** pej [superficial - talk] aparentemente brillante; [- person] de labia fácil.

slide [slaɪd] ◇ n - **1.** [decline] descenso m - **2.** PHOT diapositiva f - **3.** [in playground] tobogán m - **4.** UK [for hair] pasador m. ◇ vt (pt & pp slid [slɪd]) deslizar. ◇ vi (pt & pp slid [slɪd]) - **1.** [slip] resbalar - **2.** [glide] deslizarse - **3.** [decline gradually] caer.

sliding door [ˌslaɪdɪŋ-] n puerta f corredera.

sliding scale [ˌslaɪdɪŋ-] n escala f móvil.

slight [slaɪt] ◇ adj - **1.** [improvement, hesitation etc] ligero(ra); [wound] superficial; **not in the slightest** fml en absoluto - **2.** [slender] menudo(da). ◇ n desaire m. ◇ vt menospreciar, desairar.

slightly ['slaɪtlɪ] adv [to small extent] ligeramente.

slim [slɪm] ◇ adj - **1.** [person, object] delgado(da) - **2.** [chance, possibility] remoto(ta). ◇ vi (intentar) adelgazar.

slime [slaɪm] n [in pond etc] lodo m, cieno m; [of snail, slug] baba f.

slimming ['slɪmɪŋ] n adelgazamiento m.

sling [slɪŋ] ◇ n - **1.** [for injured arm] cabestrillo m - **2.** [for carrying things] braga f, honda f. ◇ vt (pt & pp slung) - **1.** [hang roughly] colgar descuidadamente - **2.** inf [throw] tirar.

slip [slɪp] ◇ n - **1.** [mistake] descuido m, desliz m; **a slip of the pen/tongue** un lapsus - **2.** [of paper - gen] papelito m; [- form] hoja f - **3.** [underskirt] enaguas fpl

▸▸▸ **to give sb the slip** inf dar esquinazo a alguien. ◇ vt: **to slip sthg into** meter algo rápidamente en. ◇ vi - **1.** [lose one's balance] resbalar, patinar - **2.** [slide] escurrirse, resbalar - **3.** [decline] empeorar. ▸ **slip up** vi cometer un error (poco importante).

slipped disc [ˌslɪpt-] n hernia f discal.

slipper ['slɪpər] n zapatilla f.

slippery ['slɪpərɪ] adj resbaladizo(za).

slip road n UK [for joining motorway] acceso m; [for leaving motorway] salida f.

slipshod ['slɪpʃɒd] adj chapucero(ra).

slip up n inf desliz m; **to make a slip-up** cometer un desliz.

slipway ['slɪpweɪ] n grada f.

slit [slɪt] ◇ n ranura f, hendidura f. ◇ vt (pt & pp slit) abrir, cortar (a lo largo).

slither ['slɪðər] vi deslizarse; **it slithered away** se marchó deslizándose.

sliver ['slɪvər] n [of glass] esquirla f; [of wood] astilla f; [of cheese, ham] tajada f muy fina.

slob [slɒb] n inf guarro m, -rra f.

slog [slɒg] inf ◇ n [work] curro m, trabajo m pesado. ◇ vi [work]: **to slog (away) at** trabajar sin descanso en.

slogan ['sləʊgən] n eslogan m.

slop [slɒp] ◇ vt derramar. ◇ vi derramarse.

slope [sləʊp] ◇ n cuesta f, pendiente f. ◇ vi inclinarse; **the road slopes down to the beach** la carretera desciende hasta la playa.

sloping ['sləʊpɪŋ] adj [gen] inclinado(da); [ground] en pendiente.

sloppy ['slɒpɪ] adj [person] descuidado(da); [work] chapucero(ra); [appearance] dejado(da).

slot [slɒt] n - **1.** [opening] ranura f - **2.** [groove] muesca f - **3.** [place in schedule] espacio m.

slot machine n - **1.** [vending machine] máquina f automática (de bebidas, cigarrillos etc) - **2.** [arcade machine] máquina f tragaperras.

slouch [slaʊtʃ] vi ir con los hombros caídos.

Slovakia [slə'vækɪə] n Eslovaquia.

slovenly ['slʌvnlɪ] adj [unkempt] desaliñado(da); [careless] descuidado(da).

slow [sləʊ] ◇ adj - **1.** [not fast] lento(ta); **to be a slow reader** leer despacio - **2.** [not prompt]: **to be slow to do sthg** tardar en hacer algo; **to be slow to anger** tarda en enfadarse - **3.** [clock etc] atrasado(da); **my watch is a few minutes slow** mi reloj va atrasado unos cuantos minutos - **4.** [not intelligent] corto(ta) (de alcances) - **5.** [not hot]: **bake in a slow oven** cocinar a horno moderado. ◇ vt aminorar, ralentizar. ◇ vi ir más despacio. ▸ **slow down, slow up** ◇ vt sep [growth] retrasar; [car] reducir la velocidad de. ◇ vi - **1.** [walker] ir más despacio; [car] reducir la velocidad - **2.** [take it easy] tomarse las cosas con calma.

slowdown ['sləʊdaʊn] n - **1.** [slackening off] ralentización f - **2.** US [go-slow] huelga f de celo.

slowly ['sləʊlɪ] adv despacio, lentamente.

slow motion n: **in slow motion** a cámara lenta.

sludge [slʌdʒ] n (U) [mud] fango m, lodo m; [sewage] aguas fpl residuales.

slug [slʌg] n - **1.** [insect] babosa f - **2.** US inf [bullet] bala f.

sluggish ['slʌgɪʃ] *adj* [movement, activity] lento(ta); [feeling] aturdido(da).

sluice [slu:s] *n* [passage] canal *m* de desagüe; [gate] compuerta *f*.

slum [slʌm] *n* [area] barrio *m* bajo.

slumber ['slʌmbə'] *liter vi* dormir.

slump [slʌmp] <> *n* - 1. [decline]: **slump (in)** bajón *m* (en) - 2. ECON crisis *f* económica. <> *vi* - 1. [fall in value] dar un bajón - 2. [fall heavily - person] desplomarse, dejarse caer; **they found him slumped on the floor** lo encontraron desplomado en el suelo.

slung [slʌŋ] *pt* & *pp* ⊳ **sling**.

slur [slɜːʳ] <> *n* [insult] agravio *m*; **to cast a slur on sb** manchar la reputación de alguien. <> *vt* mascullar.

slush [slʌʃ] *n* nieve *f* medio derretida.

slush fund, slush money US *n* fondos utilizados para actividades corruptas.

slut [slʌt] *n* - 1. *inf* [dirty or untidy woman] marrana *f* - 2. *v inf* [sexually immoral woman] ramera *f*.

sly [slaɪ] *adj* (*comp* **slyer** OR **slier**, *superl* **slyest** OR **sliest**) - 1. [look, smile] furtivo(va) - 2. [person] astuto(ta).

smack [smæk] <> *n* - 1. [slap] cachete *m* - 2. [impact] golpe *m*. <> *vt* - 1. [slap] pegar, dar un cachete a - 2. [place violently] tirar de golpe. <> *vi*: **to smack of sthg** oler a algo.

small [smɔːl] *adj* [gen] pequeño(ña); [person] bajo(ja); [matter, attention] de poca importancia; [importance] poco(ca); **to make sb feel small** hacer que alguien se sienta muy poca cosa; **to get smaller** empequeñecer.

small ads [-ædz] *npl* UK anuncios *mpl* clasificados.

small change *n* cambio *m*, suelto *m*, calderilla *f* Esp, sencillo *m* Andes, feria *f* Méx, menudo *m* Col.

smallholder ['smɔːlˌhəʊldəʳ] *n* UK minifundista *mf*.

small hours *npl* primeras horas *fpl* de la madrugada; **in the small hours** en la madrugada.

smallpox ['smɔːlpɒks] *n* viruela *f*.

small print *n*: **the small print** la letra pequeña.

small talk *n* (U) conversación *f* trivial.

smarmy ['smɑːmɪ] *adj* cobista.

smart [smɑːt] <> *adj* - 1. [neat, stylish] elegante - 2. *esp* US [clever] inteligente - 3. [fashionable, exclusive] elegante - 4. [quick, sharp] rápido(da). <> *vi* - 1. [eyes, wound] escocer - 2. [person] sentir resquemor. ⊶ **smarts** *n* US [intelligence] mollera *f*.

smart drug *n* droga *f* inteligente, nootrópico *m*.

smarten ['smɑːtn] ⊶ **smarten up** *vt sep* arreglar; **to smarten o.s. up** arreglarse.

smash [smæʃ] <> *n* - 1. [sound] estrépito *m* - 2. *inf* [car crash] accidente *m* - 3. TENNIS mate *m*, smash *m*. <> *vt* - 1. [break into pieces] romper, hacer pedazos - 2. *fig* [defeat] aplastar. <> *vi* - 1. [break into pieces] romperse, hacerse pedazos - 2. [crash, collide]: **to smash through sthg** romper algo atravesándolo; **to smash into sthg** chocar violentamente con algo.

smashing ['smæʃɪŋ] *adj inf* fenomenal.

smattering ['smætərɪŋ] *n* nociones *fpl*; **he has a smattering of Spanish** tiene nociones de español.

smear [smɪəʳ] <> *n* - 1. [dirty mark] mancha *f* - 2. [smear test] citología *f*, Papanicolau *m* Amér - 3. [slander] calumnia *f*, difamación *f*. <> *vt* - 1. [smudge] manchar - 2. [spread]: **to smear sthg onto sthg** untar algo con algo; **the screen was smeared with grease** la pantalla estaba embadurnada de grasa - 3. [slander] calumniar, difamar.

smell [smel] <> *n* - 1. [odour] olor *m* - 2. [sense of smell] olfato *m*. <> *vt* (*pt* & *pp* **-ed** OR **smelt**) *lit* & *fig* oler. <> *vi* (*pt* & *pp* **-ed** OR **smelt**) - 1. [gen] oler; **to smell of/like** oler a/como; **to smell good/bad** oler bien/mal - 2. [smell unpleasantly] apestar.

smelly ['smelɪ] *adj* maloliente.

smelt [smelt] <> *pt* & *pp* ⊳ **smell**. <> *vt* fundir.

smile [smaɪl] <> *n* sonrisa *f*. <> *vi* sonreír; **to smile at sb** sonreírle a algn.

smirk [smɜːk] *n* sonrisa *f* desdeñosa.

smock [smɒk] *n* blusón *m*.

smog [smɒg] *n* niebla *f* baja, smog *m*.

smoke [sməʊk] <> *n* [gen] humo *m*; **to go up in smoke** ser consumido(da) por las llamas. <> *vt* - 1. [cigarette, cigar] fumar; **to smoke a pipe** fumar en pipa - 2. [fish, meat, cheese] ahumar. <> *vi* - 1. [smoke tobacco] fumar; **I don't smoke** no fumo - 2. [give off smoke] echar humo.

smoked [sməʊkt] *adj* ahumado(da).

smoker ['sməʊkəʳ] *n* - 1. [person] fumador *m*, -ra *f* - 2. RAIL [compartment] compartimiento *m* de fumadores.

smokescreen ['sməʊkskriːn] *n fig* cortina *f* de humo.

smoke shop *n* US estanco *m*.

smoke signal *n* señal *f* de humo.

smoking ['sməʊkɪŋ] *n*: **smoking is bad for you** fumar es malo; **to give up smoking** dejar de fumar; **'no smoking'** 'prohibido fumar'.

smoking gun *n fig* [clue] pista *f*.

smoky ['sməʊkɪ] *adj* - **1.** [full of smoke] lleno(na) de humo - **2.** [taste, colour] ahumado(da).

smolder *US* = **smoulder**.

smooth [smu:ð] ⟨⟩ *adj* - **1.** [surface] liso(sa); [skin] terso(sa) - **2.** [mixture, gravy] sin grumos - **3.** [movement, taste] suave - **4.** [flight, ride] tranquilo(la) - **5.** *pej* [person, manner] meloso(sa) - **6.** [trouble-free] sin problemas. ⟨⟩ *vt* alisar. ⬤ **smooth out** *vt sep* - **1.** [table cloth, crease] alisar - **2.** [difficulties] allanar.

smother ['smʌðər] *vt* - **1.** [cover thickly]: **to smother sthg in** *OR* **with** cubrir algo de - **2.** [kill] asfixiar - **3.** [extinguish] sofocar, apagar - **4.** *fig* [control] contener; **to smother a yawn** contener un bostezo.

smoulder *UK*, **smolder** *US* ['sməʊldər] *vi* - **1.** [fire] arder sin llama - **2.** *fig* [person, feelings] arder.

SMS (*abbr of* **short message service**) *n* COMPUT servicio *m* de mensajes cortos.

smudge [smʌdʒ] ⟨⟩ *n* [dirty mark] mancha *f*; [ink blot] borrón *m*. ⟨⟩ *vt* [by blurring] emborronar; [by dirtying] manchar.

smug [smʌg] *adj pej* pagado(da) *OR* satisfecho(cha) de sí mismo(ma).

smuggle ['smʌgl] *vt* [across frontiers] pasar de contrabando.

smuggler ['smʌglər] *n* contrabandista *mf*.

smuggling ['smʌglɪŋ] *n* (*U*) contrabando *m*.

smutty ['smʌtɪ] *adj inf pej* guarro(rra).

snack [snæk] *n* bocado *m*, piscolabis *m inv*.

snack bar *n* bar *m*, cafetería *f*.

snag [snæg] ⟨⟩ *n* [problem] pega *f*. ⟨⟩ *vi*: **to snag (on)** engancharse (en).

snail [sneɪl] *n* caracol *m*; **at a snail's pace** a paso de tortuga.

snail mail *n* correo *m* caracol.

snake [sneɪk] *n* [large] serpiente *f*; [small] culebra *f*.

snap [snæp] ⟨⟩ *adj* repentino(na); **a snap decision** una decisión repentina. ⟨⟩ *n* - **1.** [act or sound] crujido *m*, chasquido *m* - **2.** *inf* [photograph] foto *f*. ⟨⟩ *vt* - **1.** [break] partir (en dos) - **2.** [move with a snap]: **to snap sthg open** abrir algo de golpe. ⟨⟩ *vi* - **1.** [break] partirse (en dos) - **2.** [attempt to bite]: **to snap at sthg/sb** intentar morder algo/a alguien - **3.** [speak sharply]: **to snap (at sb)** contestar bruscamente *OR* de mala manera a alguien. ⬤ **snap up** *vt sep* no dejar escapar.

snappy ['snæpɪ] *adj inf* - **1.** [stylish] con estilo - **2.** [quick] rápido(da); **make it snappy!** ¡date prisa! - **3.** [irritable] arisco(ca).

snapshot ['snæpʃɒt] *n* foto *f*.

snare [sneər] *n* trampa *f*.

snarl [snɑ:l] *vi* gruñir.

snatch [snætʃ] ⟨⟩ *n* [of conversation, song] fragmento *m*. ⟨⟩ *vt* [grab] agarrar; **to snatch sthg from sb** arrancarle *OR* arrebatarle algo a alguien.

sneak [sni:k] ⟨⟩ *n* *UK inf* acusica *mf*, chivato *m*, -ta *f*. ⟨⟩ *vt* (*US pt* & *pp* **snuck**) pasar a escondidas; **she tried to sneak the cakes out of the cupboard** intentó sacar los pasteles del armario a hurtadillas; **she sneaked him into her bedroom** lo coló en su dormitorio. ⟨⟩ *vi* (*US pt* & *pp* **snuck**): **to sneak in/out** entrar/salir a escondidas; **he sneaked in without paying** se coló sin pagar; **don't try and sneak off!** ¡no intentes escabullirte!

sneakers ['sni:kəz] *npl US* zapatos *mpl* de lona.

sneaky ['sni:kɪ] *adj inf* solapado(da).

sneer [snɪər] *vi* [smile unpleasantly] sonreír con desprecio.

sneeze [sni:z] *vi* estornudar.

snide [snaɪd] *adj* sarcástico(ca).

sniff [snɪf] ⟨⟩ *vt* - **1.** [smell] oler - **2.** [drug] esnifar. ⟨⟩ *vi* [to clear nose] sorber por la nariz.

snigger ['snɪgər] ⟨⟩ *n* risa *f* disimulada. ⟨⟩ *vi* reírse por lo bajo.

snip [snɪp] ⟨⟩ *n* *inf* [bargain] ganga *f*. ⟨⟩ *vt* cortar con tijeras.

sniper ['snaɪpər] *n* francotirador *m*, -ra *f*.

snippet ['snɪpɪt] *n* retazo *m*; **snippet of information** un dato aislado.

snivel ['snɪvl] (*UK*) (*US*) *vi* lloriquear.

snob [snɒb] *n* esnob *mf*.

snobbish ['snɒbɪʃ], **snobby** ['snɒbɪ] *adj* esnob.

snooker ['snu:kər] *n* snooker *m*, juego parecido al billar.

snoop [snu:p] *vi inf*: **to snoop (around)** fisgonear.

snooty ['snu:tɪ] *adj* engreído(da).

snooze [snu:z] ⟨⟩ *n* cabezada *f*; **to have a snooze** echar una cabezada. ⟨⟩ *vi* dormitar.

snore [snɔ:r] ⟨⟩ *n* ronquido *m*. ⟨⟩ *vi* roncar.

snoring ['snɔ:rɪŋ] *n* (*U*) ronquidos *mpl*.

snorkel ['snɔ:kl] *n* tubo *m* respiratorio.

snort [snɔ:t] ⟨⟩ *n* resoplido *m*. ⟨⟩ *vi* resoplar.

snout [snaʊt] *n* hocico *m*.

snow [snəʊ] ⟨⟩ *n* nieve *f*. ⟨⟩ *impers vb* nevar; **it's snowing** está nevando.

snowball ['snəʊbɔ:l] ⟨⟩ *n* bola *f* de nieve. ⟨⟩ *vi fig* aumentar rápidamente.

snowboard ['snəʊbɔ:d] *n* snowboard *m*.

snowboarding ['snəʊbɔ:dɪŋ] *n* snowboard *m*; **to go snowboarding** hacer snowboard.

snowbound ['snəʊbaʊnd] *adj* bloqueado(da) por la nieve.

snowdrift ['snəʊdrɪft] *n* montón *m* de nieve.

snowdrop ['snəʊdrɒp] *n* campanilla *f* blanca.

snowfall ['snəʊfɔːl] *n* nevada *f*.

snowflake ['snəʊfleɪk] *n* copo *m* de nieve.

snowman ['snəʊmæn] (*pl* -men [-men]) *n* muñeco *m* de nieve.

snowplough *UK*, **snowplow** *US* ['snəʊplaʊ] *n* quitanieves *m inv*.

snowshoe ['snəʊʃuː] *n* raqueta *f* de nieve.

snowstorm ['snəʊstɔːm] *n* tormenta *f* de nieve.

SNP *n abbr of* **Scottish National Party**.

Snr, snr (*abbr of* **senior**) sén.

snub [snʌb] <> *n* desaire *m*. <> *vt* desairar.

snuck [snʌk] *US pt* & *pp* ⊳ **sneak**.

snuff [snʌf] *n* [tobacco] rapé *m*.

snug [snʌg] *adj* - 1. [person] cómodo y calentito (cómoda y calentita); [feeling] de bienestar - 2. [place] acogedor(ra) - 3. [close-fitting] ajustado(da).

snuggle ['snʌgl] *vi*: **to snuggle up to sb** arrimarse a alguien acurrucándose.

so [səʊ] <> *adv* - 1. [to such a degree] tan; **so difficult (that)** tan difícil (que); **don't be so stupid!** ¡no seas bobo!; **I wish he wouldn't talk so much** ojalá no hablara tanto; **I've never seen so much money/many cars** en mi vida he visto tanto dinero/tantos coches; **thank you so much** muchísimas gracias; **it's about so high** es así de alto - 2. [in referring back to previous statement, event etc]: **so what's the point then?** entonces ¿qué sentido tiene?; **so you knew already?** ¿así que ya lo sabías?; **I don't think so** no creo, me parece que no; **I'm afraid so** me temo que sí; **if so** si es así, de ser así; **is that so?** ¿es cierto?, ¿es así? - 3. [also] también; **so can I** y yo (también puedo); **so do I** y yo (también); **she speaks French and so does her husband** ella habla francés y su marido también - 4. [in such a way]: **(like) so** así, de esta forma - 5. [in expressing agreement]: **so there is!** ¡pues (sí que) es verdad!, ¡sí que lo hay, sí!; **so I see** ya lo veo - 6. [unspecified amount, limit]: **they pay us so much a week** nos pagan tanto a la semana; **it's not so much the money as the time involved** no es tanto el dinero como el tiempo que conlleva; **they didn't so much as say thank you** ni siquiera dieron las gracias; **or so** o así. <> *conj* - 1. [with the result that, therefore] así que, por lo tanto - 2. [to introduce a statement] (bueno) pues; **so what have you been up to?** bueno, ¿y qué has estado haciendo?; **so that's who she is!** ¡anda! ¡o sea que ella!; **so what?** *inf* ¿y qué?; **so there** *inf* ¡(y si no te gusta,) te chinchas! ◆ **and so on, and so forth** *adv* y cosas por el estilo. ◆ **so as** *conj* para; **we didn't knock so as not to disturb them** no llamamos para no molestarlos. ◆ **so far** *conj* [up to now] hasta ahora; **so far, so good** por ahora todo bien. ◆ **so that** *conj* para que; **he lied so that she would go free** mintió para que ella saliera en libertad.

soak [səʊk] <> *vt* - 1. [leave immersed] poner en remojo - 2. [wet thoroughly] empapar. <> *vi* - 1. [become thoroughly wet]: **to leave sthg to soak, to let sthg soak** dejar algo en remojo - 2. [spread]: **to soak into** OR **through sthg** calar algo. ◆ **soak up** *vt sep* [liquid] absorber.

soaking ['səʊkɪŋ] *adj* empapado(da); **to be soaking wet** estar empapado.

so-and-so *n inf* - 1. [to replace a name] fulano *m*, -na *f* de tal - 2. [annoying person] hijo *m*, -ja *f* de tal.

soap [səʊp] *n* - 1. (*U*) [for washing] jabón *m* - 2. TV culebrón *m*.

soap flakes *npl* escamas *fpl* de jabón.

soap opera *n* culebrón *m*.

soap powder *n* jabón *m* en polvo.

soapy ['səʊpɪ] *adj* [full of soap] jabonoso(sa).

soar [sɔːr] *vi* - 1. [bird] remontar el vuelo - 2. [rise into the sky] elevarse - 3. [increase rapidly] alcanzar cotas muy altas.

sob [sɒb] <> *n* sollozo *m*. <> *vi* sollozar.

sober ['səʊbər] *adj* - 1. [gen] sobrio(bria) - 2. [serious] serio(ria). ◆ **sober up** *vi* pasársele a uno la borrachera.

sobering ['səʊbərɪŋ] *adj* que hace reflexionar; **it was a sobering thought** dio mucho que pensar.

so-called [-kɔːld] *adj* - 1. [expressing scepticism] mal llamado(da), supuesto(ta) - 2. [widely known as] así llamado(da).

soccer ['sɒkər] *n* (*U*) fútbol *m*.

sociable ['səʊʃəbl] *adj* sociable.

social ['səʊʃl] *adj* social.

social club *n* club *m* social.

socialism ['səʊʃəlɪzm] *n* socialismo *m*.

socialist ['səʊʃəlɪst] <> *adj* socialista. <> *n* socialista *mf*.

socialize, -ise ['səʊʃəlaɪz] *vi*: **to socialize (with)** alternar (con).

social security *n* seguridad *f* social.

social services *npl* servicios *mpl* sociales.

social worker *n* asistente *m*, -ta *f* social.

society [sə'saɪətɪ] *n* - 1. [gen] sociedad *f* - 2. [club, organization] sociedad *f*, asociación *f*.

sociology [,səʊsɪ'ɒlədʒɪ] *n* sociología *f*.

sock [sɒk] *n* calcetín *m*, media *f* Amér.

socket ['sɒkɪt] *n* - 1. ELEC enchufe *m* - 2. [of eye] cuenca *f*; [of joint] glena *f*.

sod [sɒd] *n* - 1. [of turf] tepe *m* - 2. *v inf* [person] cabroncete *m*.

soda ['səʊdə] *n* - 1. [gen] soda *f* - 2. *US* [fizzy drink] gaseosa *f*.

soda water *n* soda *f*.

codden ['ɒndn] *adj* empapado(da).

sodium ['səʊdɪəm] *n* sodio *m*.

sofa ['səʊfə] *n* sofá *m*.

soft [sɒft] *adj* - **1.** [pliable, not stiff, not strict] blando(da); **to go soft** ablandarse - **2.** [smooth, gentle, not bright] suave.

soft drink *n* refresco *m*.

soften ['sɒfn] ⟨⟩ *vt* suavizar. ⟨⟩ *vi* - **1.** [substance] ablandarse - **2.** [expression] suavizarse.

softhearted [,sɒft'hɑːtɪd] *adj* de buen corazón.

softly ['sɒftlɪ] *adv* - **1.** [gently] con delicadeza - **2.** [quietly, not brightly] suavemente - **3.** [leniently] con indulgencia.

soft-spoken *adj* de voz suave.

software ['sɒftweəʳ] *n* COMPUT software *m*.

soggy ['sɒgɪ] *adj inf* empapado(da).

soil [sɔɪl] ⟨⟩ *n* [earth] tierra *f*, suelo *m*. ⟨⟩ *vt* ensuciar.

soiled [sɔɪld] *adj* sucio(cia).

solace ['sɒləs] *n liter* consuelo *m*.

solar ['səʊləʳ] *adj* solar; **solar eclipse** eclipse de sol.

solar power *n* energía *f* solar.

sold [səʊld] *pt & pp* ⊳ **sell**.

solder ['səʊldəʳ] ⟨⟩ *n (U)* soldadura *f*. ⟨⟩ *vt* soldar.

soldier ['səʊldʒəʳ] *n* soldado *m*.

sold out *adj* agotado(da); **the theatre was sold out** se agotaron las localidades; **all the shops were sold out of lemons** se habían agotado los limones en todas las tiendas.

sole [səʊl] ⟨⟩ *adj* - **1.** [only] único(ca) - **2.** [exclusive] exclusivo(va) - **1.** (*pl* -s) [of foot] planta *f*; [of shoe] suela *f* - **2.** (*pl* sole) [fish] lenguado *m*.

solemn ['sɒləm] *adj* solemne.

solicit [sə'lɪsɪt] ⟨⟩ *vt fml* [request] solicitar. ⟨⟩ *vi* [prostitute] ofrecer sus servicios.

solicitor [sə'lɪsɪtəʳ] *n UK* LAW *abogado que lleva casos administrativos y legales, pero que no acude a los tribunales superiores.*

solid ['sɒlɪd] ⟨⟩ *adj* - **1.** [gen] sólido(da) - **2.** [rock, wood, gold] macizo(za) - **3.** [reliable, respectable] serio(ria), formal - **4.** [without interruption] sin interrupción; **it rained for two solid weeks** llovió sin parar durante dos semanas. ⟨⟩ *n* sólido *m*; **to be on solids** [baby] estar tomando alimentos sólidos.

solidarity [,sɒlɪ'dærətɪ] *n* solidaridad *f*.

solitaire [,sɒlɪ'teəʳ] *n* - **1.** [jewel, board game] solitario *m* - **2.** *US* [card game] solitario *m*.

solitary ['sɒlɪtrɪ] *adj* solitario(ria).

solitary confinement *n*: **to be in solitary confinement** estar incomunicado(da) (en la cárcel).

solitude ['sɒlɪtjuːd] *n* soledad *f*.

solo ['səʊləʊ] ⟨⟩ *adj & adv* a solas. ⟨⟩ *n* (*pl* -s) solo *m*.

soloist ['səʊləʊɪst] *n* solista *mf*.

soluble ['sɒljʊbl] *adj* soluble.

solution [sə'luːʃn] *n*: **solution (to)** solución *f* (a).

solve [sɒlv] *vt* resolver.

solvent ['sɒlvənt] ⟨⟩ *adj* FIN solvente. ⟨⟩ *n* disolvente *m*.

Somalia [sə'mɑːlɪə] *n* Somalia.

sombre *UK*, **somber** *US* ['sɒmbəʳ] *adj* sombrío(a).

some [sʌm] ⟨⟩ *adj* - **1.** [a certain amount, number of]: **would you like some coffee?** ¿quieres café?; **give me some money** dame algo de dinero; **there are some good articles in it** tiene algunos artículos buenos; **I bought some socks** [one pair] me compré unos calcetines; [more than one pair] me compré calcetines - **2.** [fairly large number or quantity of]: **I've known him for some years** lo conozco desde hace bastantes años; **I had some difficulty getting here** me costó lo mío llegar aquí - **3.** *(contrastive use)* [certain] algunos(as); **some jobs are better paid than others** algunos trabajos están mejor pagados que otros; **some people say that...** los hay que dicen que...; **in some ways** en cierto modo - **4.** [in imprecise statements] algún(una); **there must be some mistake** debe haber un *OR* algún error; **she married some writer or other** se casó con no sé qué escritor; **someday** algún día - **5.** *inf* [very good]: **that's some car he's got** ¡menudo coche tiene!; **some help you are!** *iro* [not very good] ¡menuda *OR* valiente ayuda me das! ⟨⟩ *pron* - **1.** [a certain amount]: **can I have some?** [money, milk, coffee etc] ¿puedo coger un poco?; **some of** parte de - **2.** [a certain number] algunos(as); **can I have some?** [books, potatoes etc] ¿puedo coger algunos?; **some (of them) left early** algunos se fueron temprano; **some say he lied** hay quien dice que mintió. ⟨⟩ *adv* - **1.** unos(as); **there were some 7,000 people there** habría unas 7.000 personas - **2.** *US* [slightly] algo, un poco; **shall I turn it up some?** ¿lo subo algo o un poco?

somebody ['sʌmbədɪ] *pron* alguien; **somebody or other** alguien.

someday ['sʌmdeɪ] *adv* algún día.

somehow ['sʌmhaʊ], **someway** *US* ['sʌmweɪ] *adv* - **1.** [by some action] de alguna manera; **somehow or other** de un modo u otro - **2.** [for some reason] por alguna razón.

someone ['sʌmwʌn] *pron* alguien; **someone or other** alguien, no sé quien.

someplace *US* = **somewhere**.

somersault ['sʌməsɔːlt] *n* [in air] salto *m* mortal; [on ground] voltereta *f*.

something ['sʌmθɪŋ] ⬦ *pron* algo; **or something** *inf* o algo así; **something or other** alguna cosa. ⬦ *adv*: **something like**, **something in the region of** algo así como.

sometime ['sʌmtaɪm] *adv* en algún momento; **sometime or other** en algún momento; **sometime next week** durante la semana que viene.

sometimes ['sʌmtaɪmz] *adv* a veces.

someway *US* = **somehow**.

somewhat ['sʌmwɒt] *adv fml* algo.

somewhere *UK* ['sʌmweəʳ], **someplace** *US* ['sʌmpleɪs] *adv* - **1.** [unknown place - with verbs of position] en alguna parte; [- with verbs of movement] a alguna parte; **it's somewhere else** está en otra parte; **it's somewhere in the kitchen** está en alguna parte de la cocina; **shall we go somewhere else?** ¿nos vamos a otra parte?; **I need somewhere to spend the night** necesito un lugar donde pasar la noche - **2.** [in approximations]: **somewhere between five and ten** entre cinco y diez; **somewhere around 20** alrededor de 20; **he's somewhere in his fifties** tiene cincuenta años y pico.

son [sʌn] *n* hijo *m*.

song [sɒŋ] *n* - **1.** [gen] canción *f*; **to make a song and dance about sthg** *inf* armar la de Dios es Cristo sobre algo - **2.** [of bird] canto *m*.

sonic ['sɒnɪk] *adj* sónico(ca).

son-in-law (*pl* sons-in-law *OR* son-in-laws) *n* yerno *m*.

sonnet ['sɒnɪt] *n* soneto *m*.

sonny ['sʌnɪ] *n inf* hijo *m*, chico *m*.

soon [su:n] *adv* pronto; **how soon will it be ready?** ¿para cuándo estará listo?; **soon after** poco después; **as soon as** tan pronto como; **as soon as possible** cuanto antes; **see you soon** hasta pronto.

sooner ['su:nəʳ] *adv* - **1.** [in time] antes; **no sooner did he arrive than...** apenas había llegado cuando...; **no sooner said than done** dicho y hecho; **sooner or later** (más) tarde o (más) temprano; **the sooner the better** cuanto antes mejor - **2.** [expressing preference]: **I'd sooner (not)...** preferiría (no)...

soot [sʊt] *n* hollín *m*.

soothe [su:ð] *vt* - **1.** [pain] aliviar - **2.** [nerves etc] calmar.

sophisticated [sə'fɪstɪkeɪtɪd] *adj* [gen] sofisticado(da).

sophomore ['sɒfəmɔːʳ] *n US* estudiante *mf* del segundo curso.

soporific [ˌsɒpə'rɪfɪk] *adj* soporífico(ca).

sopping ['sɒpɪŋ] *adj*: **sopping (wet)** chorreando.

soppy ['sɒpɪ] *adj inf pej* sentimentaloide.

soprano [sə'prɑːnəʊ] (*pl* -s) *n* soprano *f*.

sorbet ['sɔːbeɪ] *n* sorbete *m*; **lemon sorbet** sorbete de limón.

sorcerer ['sɔːsərəʳ] *n* brujo *m*, -ja *f*.

sordid ['sɔːdɪd] *adj* - **1.** [immoral] obsceno(na) - **2.** [dirty, unpleasant] sórdido(da).

sore [sɔːʳ] ⬦ *adj* - **1.** [painful] dolorido(da); **to have a sore throat** tener dolor de garganta - **2.** *US* [upset] enfadado(da); **to get sore** enfadarse. ⬦ *n* llaga *f*, úlcera *f*.

sorely ['sɔːlɪ] *adv liter* enormemente.

sorrow ['sɒrəʊ] *n* pesar *m*, pena *f*.

sorry ['sɒrɪ] ⬦ *adj* - **1.** [expressing apology]: **to be sorry about sthg** sentir *OR* lamentar algo; **I'm sorry for what I did** siento lo que hice; **I'm sorry** lo siento; **I'm sorry if I'm disturbing you** *OR* **to disturb you** siento molestarte - **2.** [expressing shame, disappointment]: **to be sorry that** sentir que; **we were sorry about his resignation** sentimos que dimitiera; **to be sorry for** arrepentirse de - **3.** [expressing regret]: **I'm sorry to have to say that...** siento tener que decir que... - **4.** [expressing pity]: **to be** *OR* **feel sorry for o.s.** sentir lástima de uno mismo (una misma) - **5.** [expressing polite disagreement]: **I'm sorry, but...** perdón, pero... - **6.** [poor, pitiable] lamentable, penoso(sa); **it was a sorry sight** tenía un aspecto horrible. ⬦ *excl* - **1.** [I apologise]: **sorry!** ¡perdón! - **2.** [pardon]: **sorry?** ¿perdón? - **3.** [to correct oneself]: **a girl, sorry, a woman** una chica, perdón, una mujer.

sort [sɔːt] ⬦ *n* tipo *m*, clase *f*; **what sort of computer have you got?** ¿qué tipo de ordenador tienes?; **all sorts of** todo tipo de; **sort of** más o menos, así así; **a sort of** una especie de; **she did nothing of the sort** no hizo nada por el estilo. ⬦ *vt* clasificar. ➤ **sort out** *vt sep* - **1.** [classify] clasificar - **2.** [solve] solucionar, resolver.

sorting office ['sɔːtɪŋ-] *n* oficina de clasificación del correo.

SOS *n* SOS *m*; **to send an SOS** lanzar un SOS.

so-so *adj* & *adv inf* así así.

soufflé ['su:fleɪ] *n* suflé *m*; **a cheese soufflé** un suflé de queso.

sought [sɔːt] *pt* & *pp* ⮞ **seek**.

soul [səʊl] *n* - **1.** [gen] alma *f* - **2.** [music] música *f* soul.

soul-destroying [-dɪˌstrɔɪɪŋ] *adj* desmoralizador(ra).

soulful ['səʊlfʊl] *adj* lleno(na) de sentimiento.

sound [saʊnd] ⬦ *adj* - **1.** [healthy] sano(na) - **2.** [sturdy] sólido(da) - **3.** [reliable] fiable, seguro(ra). ⬦ *adv*: **to be sound asleep** estar profundamente dormido(da). ⬦ *n* - **1.** [gen] sonido *m* - **2.** [particular noise] ruido *m* - **3.** [impression]: **by the sound of it** por lo que parece. ◇ *vt* [bell etc] hacer sonar, tocar. ◇ *vi* - **1.** [gen] sonar - **2.** [give impression]: **it sounds interesting** parece interesante; **it sounds like fun** suena divertido. ➤ **sound out** *vt sep*: **to sound sb out (on** OR **about)** sondear a alguien (sobre).

sound barrier *n* barrera *f* del sonido.

sound card *n* COMPUT tarjeta *f* de sonido.

sound effects *npl* efectos *mpl* sonoros.

sounding ['saʊndɪŋ] *n* NAUT sondeo *m* marino.

soundly ['saʊndlɪ] *adv* - **1.** [severely - beat] totalmente - **2.** [deeply] profundamente.

soundproof ['saʊndpruːf] *adj* insonorizado(da).

soundtrack ['saʊndtræk] *n* banda *f* sonora.

soup [suːp] *n* [thick] sopa *f*; [clear] caldo *m*.

soup plate *n* plato *m* hondo OR sopero.

soup spoon *n* cuchara *f* sopera.

sour [saʊəʳ] ◇ *adj* - **1.** [acidic] ácido(da) - **2.** [milk, person, reply] agrio(gria). ◇ *vt* agriar.

source [sɔːs] *n* - **1.** [gen] fuente *f* - **2.** [cause] origen *m*.

sour grapes *n* (*U*) *inf*: **it's sour grapes!** ¡están verdes!

south [saʊθ] ◇ *n* - **1.** [direction] sur *m* - **2.** [region]: **the South** el sur. ◇ *adj* del sur. ◇ *adv*: **south (of)** al sur (de).

South Africa *n*: **(the Republic of) South Africa** (la República de) Suráfrica.

South African ◇ *adj* surafricano(na). ◇ *n* [person] surafricano *m*, -na *f*.

South America *n* Sudamérica.

South American ◇ *adj* sudamericano(na). ◇ *n* [person] sudamericano *m*, -na *f*.

southeast [ˌsaʊθiːst] ◇ *n* - **1.** [direction] sudeste *m* - **2.** [region]: **the Southeast** el sudeste. ◇ *adj* del sudeste. ◇ *adv*: **southeast (of)** hacia el sudeste (de).

southerly ['sʌðəlɪ] *adj* del sur.

southern ['sʌðən] *adj* del sur, sureño(ña); **the southern hemisphere** el hemisferio sur.

South Korea *n* Corea del Sur.

South Pole *n*: **the South Pole** el polo Sur.

southward ['saʊθwəd] ◇ *adj* sur. ◇ *adv* = **southwards**.

southwards ['saʊθwədz], **southward** *adv* hacia el sur.

southwest [ˌsaʊθwest] ◇ *n* - **1.** [direction] suroeste *m* - **2.** [region]: **the Southwest** el suroeste. ◇ *adj* del suroeste. ◇ *adv*: **southwest (of)** hacia el suroeste (de).

souvenir [ˌsuːvəˈnɪəʳ] *n* recuerdo *m*.

sovereign ['sɒvrɪn] ◇ *adj* soberano(na). ◇ *n* - **1.** [ruler] soberano *m*, -na *f* - **2.** [coin] soberano *m*.

Soviet ['saʊvɪət] ◇ *adj* soviético(ca). ◇ *n* [person] soviético *m*, -ca *f*.

Soviet Union *n*: **the (former) Soviet Union** la (antigua) Unión Soviética.

sow[1] [saʊ] (*pt* -ed, *pp* sown OR -ed) *vt lit & fig* sembrar.

sow[2] [saʊ] *n* cerda *f*, puerca *f*, chancha *f* *Amér*.

sown [saʊn] *pp* ▷ **sow**[1].

soya ['sɔɪə] *n* soja *f*.

soy(a) bean ['sɔɪ(ə)-] *n esp US* semilla *f* de soja, frijol *m* de soja *Amér*, porot *m* de soja *Andes*.

spa [spɑː] *n* balneario *m*.

spa bath *n* bañera *f* de hidromasaje.

space [speɪs] ◇ *n* espacio *m*; **there isn't enough space for it** no hay suficiente espacio para ello; **in the space of 30 minutes** en el espacio de 30 minutos. ◇ *vt* espaciar. ➤ **space out** *vt sep* [arrange with spaces between] espaciar.

spacecraft ['speɪskrɑːft] (*pl* spacecraft) *n* nave *f* espacial.

spaceman ['speɪsmæn] (*pl* -men [-men]) *n* *inf* astronauta *m*.

spaceship ['speɪsʃɪp] *n* nave *f* espacial.

space shuttle *n* transbordador *m* espacial.

spacesuit ['speɪssuːt] *n* traje *m* espacial.

spacing ['speɪsɪŋ] *n* TYPO espacio *m*; **double spacing** doble espacio.

spacious ['speɪʃəs] *adj* espacioso(sa).

spade [speɪd] *n* [tool] pala *f*. ➤ **spades** *npl* picas *fpl*.

spaghetti [spəˈgetɪ] *n* (*U*) espaguetis *mpl*.

Spain [speɪn] *n* España.

spam [spæm] ◇ *n* COMPUT correo *m* basura. ◇ *vt* COMPUT enviar correo basura a.

spammer ['spæməʳ] *n* COMPUT spammer *m*.

spamming ['spæmɪŋ] *n* (*U*) COMPUT spamming *m*, envío *m* de correo basura.

span [spæn] ◇ *pt* ▷ **spin**. ◇ *n* - **1.** [in time] lapso *m*, periodo *m* - **2.** [range] gama *f* - **3.** [of wings] envergadura *f* - **4.** [of bridge, arch] ojo *m*. ◇ *vt* - **1.** [in time] abarcar - **2.** [bridge etc] cruzar, atravesar.

Spaniard ['spænjəd] *n* español *m*, -la *f*.

spaniel ['spænjəl] *n* perro *m* de aguas.

Spanish ['spænɪʃ] ◇ *adj* español(la). ◇ *n* [language] español *m*, castellano *m*. ◇ *npl* [people]: **the Spanish** los españoles.

spank [spæŋk] *vt* zurrar.

spanner ['spænəʳ] *n* llave *f* inglesa.

spar [spɑːʳ] ◇ *n* palo *m*, verga *f*. ◇ *vi* [in boxing]: **to spar (with)** entrenarse (con).

spare [speəʳ] ◇ *adj* - **1.** [surplus] de sobra - **2.** [free - chair, time] libre; **I've got a spare pen you can borrow** tengo un bolígrafo de sobra que te puedo prestar; **have you got a spare minute?** ¿tienes un minuto?; **there's one going spare** sobra uno - **3.** *inf* [crazy]: **to go spare** volverse loco(ca). <> *n* - **1.** [extra one]: I always carry a spare siempre llevo uno de sobra - **2.** *inf* [part] pieza *f* de recambio *OR* repuesto. <> *vt* - **1.** [time] conceder; [money] dejar; **we can't spare any time/money** no tenemos tiempo/dinero; **to spare** de sobra - **2.** [not harm - person, life] perdonar; [- company, city] salvar; **they spared his life** le perdonaron la vida - **3.** [not use, not take]: **to spare no expense/effort** no escatimar gastos/esfuerzos - **4.** [save from]: **to spare sb sthg** ahorrarle a alguien algo; **you've spared me the trouble** me has ahorrado la molestia.

spare part *n* AUT pieza *f* de recambio *OR* repuesto.

spare time *n* tiempo *m* libre.

spare wheel *n* rueda *f* de recambio.

sparing ['speəriŋ] *adj*: **to be sparing with** *OR* **of** ser parco(ca) en.

sparingly ['speəriŋli] *adv* con moderación.

spark [spɑ:k] *n lit & fig* chispa *f*.

sparkle ['spɑ:kl] <> *n* (U) [of diamond] destello *m*; [of eyes] brillo *m*. <> *vi* [star, jewels] centellear; [eyes] brillar.

sparkling wine ['spɑ:klıŋ-] *n* vino *m* espumoso.

spark plug *n* bujía *f*.

sparrow ['spærəu] *n* gorrión *m*.

sparse [spɑ:s] *adj* escaso(sa).

spasm ['spæzm] *n* - **1.** MED [state] espasmo *m* - **2.** MED [attack] acceso *m*.

spastic ['spæstık] *n* MED espástico *m*, -ca *f*.

spat [spæt] *pt & pp* ⇨ **spit**.

spate [speıt] *n* cadena *f*, serie *f*.

spatter ['spætər] *vt* salpicar.

spawn [spɔ:n] <> *n* (U) huevas *fpl*. <> *vt fig* engendrar. <> *vi* desovar, frezar.

speak [spi:k] <> *vt* (*pt* spoke, *pp* spoken) - **1.** [say] decir; **to speak one's mind** decir lo que se piensa - **2.** [language] hablar; **can you speak French?** ¿hablas francés? <> *vi* (*pt* spoke, *pp* spoken) hablar; **to speak to** *OR* **with** hablar con; **to speak to sb (about)** hablar con alguien (de); **to speak about** hablar de; **nobody/nothing to speak of** nadie/nada especial; **we aren't speaking** [we aren't friends] no nos hablamos. ⇨ **so to speak** *adv* por así decirlo. ⇨ **speak for** *vt insep* [represent] hablar en nombre de. ⇨ **speak up** *vi* - **1.** [speak out]: **to speak up for** salir en defensa de - **2.** [speak louder] hablar más alto.

speaker ['spi:kər] *n* - **1.** [person talking] persona *f* que habla - **2.** [person making a speech - at meal etc] orador *m*, -ra *f*; [- at conference] conferenciante *mf* - **3.** [of a language] hablante *mf*; **English speakers** angloparlantes - **4.** [of radio] altavoz *m*.

speaking ['spi:kıŋ] <> *adv*: **generally speaking** en general; **legally speaking** desde una perspectiva legal. <> *adj*: **we are not on speaking terms** no nos dirigimos la palabra.

spear [spıər] <> *n* [gen] lanza *f*; [for hunting] jabalina *f*. <> *vt* [animal] atravesar; [piece of food] pinchar.

spearhead ['spıəhed] *vt* encabezar.

spec [spek] *n* UK *inf*: **to buy on spec** comprar sin garantías.

special ['speʃl] *adj* - **1.** [gen] especial - **2.** [particular, individual] particular.

special delivery *n* correo *m* urgente.

specialist ['speʃəlıst] <> *adj* [doctor] especialista; [literature] especializado(da). <> *n* especialista *mf*.

speciality [,speʃı'ælətı], **specialty** US ['speʃltı] *n* especialidad *f*.

specialize, -ise ['speʃəlaız] *vi*: **to specialize (in)** especializarse (en).

specially ['speʃəlı] *adv* especialmente.

special needs *npl*: **special needs children** niños con necesidades especiales.

specialty US = **speciality**.

species ['spi:ʃi:z] (*pl* species) *n* especie *f*.

specific [spə'sıfık] *adj* - **1.** [particular] determinado(da) - **2.** [precise] específico(ca) - **3.** [unique]: **specific to** específico(ca) de.

specifically [spə'sıfıklı] *adv* - **1.** [particularly] expresamente - **2.** [precisely] específicamente.

specify ['spesıfaı] *vt*: **to specify (that)** especificar (que).

specimen ['spesımən] *n* - **1.** [example] espécimen *m*, ejemplar *m* - **2.** [sample] muestra *f*.

speck [spek] *n* - **1.** [small stain] manchita *f* - **2.** [small particle] mota *f*.

speckled ['spekld] *adj*: **speckled (with)** moteado(da) (de), con manchas (de).

specs [speks] *npl* UK *inf* [glasses] gafas *fpl*.

spectacle ['spektəkl] *n* [sight] espectáculo *m*; **to make a spectacle of o.s.** dar el espectáculo. ⇨ **spectacles** *npl* UK gafas *fpl*.

spectacular [spek'tækjulər] *adj* espectacular.

spectator [spek'teıtər] *n* espectador *m*, -ra *f*.

spectre UK, **specter** US ['spektər] *n lit & fig* fantasma *m*.

spectrum ['spektrəm] (*pl* -tra [-trə]) *n* - **1.** [gen] espectro *m* - **2.** *fig* [variety] gama *f*.

speculation [,spekju'leıʃn] *n* especulación *f*.

sped [sped] *pt & pp* ⇨ **speed**.

speech [spi:tʃ] *n* - **1.** [gen] habla *f* - **2.** [formal talk] discurso *m*; **to give** *OR* **make a speech (on**

sthg to sb) pronunciar un discurso (sobre algo a alguien) **- 3.** [manner of speaking] manera f de hablar **4.** [dialect] dialecto m, hablla f.

speechless ['spi:tʃlis] *adj*: **to be speechless (with)** enmudecer (de).

speed [spi:d] ⇔ *n* **- 1.** [rate of movement] velocidad f; **at top speed** a toda velocidad; **at a speed of 30 mph** a una velocidad de 30 millas por hora **- 2.** [rapidity] rapidez f. ⇔ *vi* (*pt & pp* **sped** *OR* **speed**) **- 1.** [move fast]: **to speed (along/away/by)** ir/alejarse/pasar a toda velocidad; **to speed by** [hours, years] pasar volando **- 2.** AUT [go too fast] conducir con exceso de velocidad. **◆ speed up** ⇔ *vt sep* [gen] acelerar; [person] meter prisa a. ⇔ *vi* [gen] acelerarse; [person] darse prisa.

speedboat ['spi:dbəʊt] *n* lancha f motora.

speed-dial button *n* [on phone, fax] botón *m* de marcado abreviado.

speed-dialling UK, **speed-dialing** US *n* (U) TELEC marcado *m* rápido.

speeding ['spi:dɪŋ] *n* (U) exceso *m* de velocidad.

speed limit *n* límite *m* de velocidad.

speedometer [spɪ'dɒmɪtər] *n* velocímetro *m*.

speedway ['spi:dweɪ] *n* **- 1.** (U) SPORT carreras *fpl* de moto **- 2.** US [road] autopista f.

speedy ['spi:dɪ] *adj* rápido(da).

spell [spel] ⇔ *n* **- 1.** [of time] temporada f; [of weather] racha f; **sunny spells** intervalos de sol; **to go through a good/bad spell** pasar una buena/mala racha **- 2.** [enchantment] hechizo *m*; **to cast** *OR* **put a spell on sb** hechizar a alguien **- 3.** [magic words] conjuro *m*. ⇔ *vt* (*UK pt & pp* **spelt** *OR* **-ed**, *US pt & pp* **-ed**) **- 1.** [form by writing] deletrear; **how do you spell that?** ¿cómo se escribe eso? **- 2.** *fig* [signify] significar; **to spell trouble** augurar problemas. ⇔ *vi* (*UK pt & pp* **spelt** *OR* **-ed**, *US pt & pp* **-ed**) escribir correctamente; **I can't spell** cometo muchas faltas de ortografía. **◆ spell out** *vt sep* **- 1.** [read aloud] deletrear **- 2.** [explain]: **to spell sthg out (for** *OR* **to sb)** decir algo por las claras (a alguien).

spellbound ['spelbaʊnd] *adj* hechizado(da), embelesado(da); **to hold sb spellbound** tener hechizado(da) a alguien.

spellcheck ['speltʃek] *vt* COMPUT pasar el corrector ortográfico a.

spellchecker ['speltʃekər] *n* COMPUT corrector *m* ortográfico.

spelling ['spelɪŋ] *n* ortografía f; **the right/ wrong spelling** la grafía correcta/incorrecta; **to be good at spelling** tener buena ortografía; **spelling mistake** falta f de ortografía.

spelt [spelt] *UK pt & pp* ⊳ **spell**.

spend [spend] (*pt & pp* **spent**) *vt* **- 1.** [gen] gastar; **to spend sthg on** gastar algo en **- 2.** [time, life] pasar; **to spend time doing sthg** pasar el tiempo haciendo algo.

spendthrift ['spendθrɪft] *n* derrochador *m*, -ra f.

spent [spent] ⇔ *pt & pp* ⊳ **spend**. ⇔ *adj* [matches, ammunition] usado(da); [patience] agotado(da).

sperm [spɜːm] (*pl* **sperm** *OR* **-s**) *n* esperma *m*.

spew [spju:] *vt* arrojar, escupir.

sphere [sfɪər] *n* **- 1.** [gen] esfera f **- 2.** [of people] círculo *m*.

spice [spaɪs] *n* CULIN especia f.

spick-and-span [,spɪkən'spæn] *adj* inmaculado(da).

spicy ['spaɪsɪ] *adj fig* [hot and peppery] picante; [with spices] con muchas especias.

spider ['spaɪdər] *n* araña f.

spike [spaɪk] *n* **- 1.** [on railing etc] punta f; [on wall] clavo *m* **- 2.** [on plant] pincho *m*; [of hair] pelo *m* de punta.

spill [spɪl] ⇔ *vt* (*UK pt & pp* **spilt** *OR* **-ed**, *US pt & pp* **-ed**) derramar, verter. ⇔ *vi* (*UK pt & pp* **spilt** *OR* **-ed**, *US pt & pp* **-ed**) [flow] derramarse, verterse.

spilt [spɪlt] *UK pt & pp* ⊳ **spill**.

spin [spɪn] ⇔ *n* **- 1.** [turn] vuelta f **- 2.** AERON barrena f **- 3.** *inf* [in car] vuelta f; **to go for a spin** ir a dar una vuelta. ⇔ *vt* (*pt* **span** *OR* **spun**, *pp* **spun**) **- 1.** [cause to rotate] girar, dar vueltas a **- 2.** [clothes, washing] centrifugar **- 3.** [wool, yarn] hilar. ⇔ *vi* (*pt* **span** *OR* **spun**, *pp* **spun**) [rotate] girar, dar vueltas; **to spin out of control** [vehicle] comenzar a dar trompos. **◆ spin out** *vt sep* [story] alargar, prolongar; [money] estirar.

spinach ['spɪnɪdʒ] *n* (U) espinacas *fpl*.

spinal column ['spaɪnl-] *n* columna f vertebral.

spinal cord *n* médula f espinal.

spindly ['spɪndlɪ] *adj* larguirucho(cha).

spin-dryer *n* UK centrifugadora f.

spine [spaɪn] *n* **- 1.** ANAT espina f dorsal **- 2.** [of book] lomo *m* **- 3.** [spike, prickle] espina f, púa f.

spinning ['spɪnɪŋ] *n* hilado *m*.

spinning top *n* peonza f.

spin-off *n* [by-product] resultado *m* *OR* efecto *m* indirecto.

spinster ['spɪnstər] *n* soltera f.

spiral ['spaɪərəl] ⇔ *adj* en espiral. ⇔ *n* [curve] espiral f. ⇔ *vi* (*UK pt & pp* **-led**, *cont* **-ling**, *US pt & pp* **-ed**, *cont* **-ing**) [move in spiral curve] moverse en espiral.

spiral staircase *n* escalera f de caracol.

spire [spaɪər] *n* aguja f.

spirit ['spɪrɪt] *n* **- 1.** [gen] espíritu *m* **- 2.** [vigour] vigor *m*, valor *m*. **◆ spirits** *npl*

- 1. [mood] humor *m*; **to be in high/low spirits** estar exultante/alicaído **- 2.** [alcohol] licores *mpl*.

spirited ['spɪrɪtɪd] *adj* enérgico(ca).

spirit level *n* nivel *m* de burbuja de aire.

spiritual ['spɪrɪtʃʊəl] *adj* espiritual.

spit [spɪt] ◇ *n* **- 1.** [saliva] saliva *f* **- 2.** [skewer] asador *m*. ◇ *vi* (*UK pt & pp* **spat**, *US pt & pp* **spit**) escupir. ◇ *impers vb UK* [rain lightly]: **it's spitting** está chispeando.

spite [spaɪt] ◇ *n* rencor *m*. ◇ *vt* fastidiar, molestar. ◆ **in spite of** *prep* a pesar de.

spiteful ['spaɪtfʊl] *adj* [person, behaviour] rencoroso(sa); [action, remark] malintencionado(da).

spittle ['spɪtl] *n* saliva *f*.

splash [splæʃ] ◇ *n* **- 1.** [sound] chapoteo *m* **- 2.** [of colour, light] mancha *f*. ◇ *vt* salpicar. ◇ *vi* **- 1.** [person]: **to splash about** OR **around** chapotear **- 2.** [water, liquid]: **to splash on** OR **against sthg** salpicar algo. ◆ **splash out** *vi inf*: **to splash out (on sthg)** gastar un dineral (en algo).

spleen [spliːn] *n* ANAT bazo *m*; *fig* [anger] cólera *f*.

splendid ['splendɪd] *adj* **- 1.** [marvellous] espléndido(da) **- 2.** [magnificent, beautiful] magnífico(ca).

splint [splɪnt] *n* tablilla *f*.

splinter ['splɪntər] ◇ *n* [of wood] astilla *f*; [of glass, metal] fragmento *m*. ◇ *vi* astillarse.

split [splɪt] ◇ *n* **- 1.** [crack - in wood] grieta *f*; [- in garment] desgarrón *m* **- 2.** [division]: **split (in)** escisión *f* (en) **- 3.** [difference]: **split (between)** diferencia *f* (entre). ◇ *vt* (*pt & pp* **split**) **- 1.** [tear] desgarrar, rasgar; [crack] agrietar **- 2.** [break in two] partir **- 3.** [party, organization] escindir **- 4.** [share] repartir. ◇ *vi* (*pt & pp* **split**) **- 1.** [break up - road] bifurcarse; [- object] partirse **- 2.** [party, organization] escindirse **- 3.** [wood] agrietarse; [fabric] desgarrarse. ◆ **split up** *vi* separarse.

split second *n* fracción *f* de segundo; **for a split second** por una fracción de segundo.

splutter ['splʌtər] *vi* **- 1.** [person] balbucear **- 2.** [fire, oil] chisporrotear.

spoil [spɔɪl] *vt* (*pt & pp* **-ed** OR **spoilt**) **- 1.** [ruin] estropear, echar a perder **- 2.** [child etc] mimar. ◆ **spoils** *npl* botín *m*.

spoiled [spɔɪld] = **spoilt**.

spoilsport ['spɔɪlspɔːt] *n* aguafiestas *m & f inv*.

spoilt [spɔɪlt] ◇ *pt & pp* ▷ **spoil**. ◇ *adj* mimado(da), consentido(da), regalón(ona) *R Plata & Chile*.

spoke [spəʊk] ◇ *pt* ▷ **speak**. ◇ *n* radio *m*.

spoken ['spəʊkn] *pp* ▷ **speak**.

spokesman ['spəʊksmən] (*pl* **-men** [-mən]) *n* portavoz *m*.

spokeswoman ['spəʊks,wʊmən] (*pl* **-women** [-,wɪmɪn]) *n* portavoz *f*.

sponge [spʌndʒ] ◇ *n* **- 1.** [for cleaning, washing] esponja *f* **- 2.** [cake] bizcocho *m*. ◇ *vt* limpiar con una esponja. ◇ *vi inf*: **to sponge off** vivir a costa de.

sponge bag *n UK* neceser *m*.

sponge cake *n* bizcocho *m*, bizcochuelo *m* *Ven*.

sponsor ['spɒnsər] ◇ *n* patrocinador *m*, -ra *f*. ◇ *vt* **- 1.** [gen] patrocinar **- 2.** [support] respaldar.

sponsored walk [,spɒnsəd-] *n* marcha *f* benéfica.

sponsorship ['spɒnsəʃɪp] *n* patrocinio *m*.

spontaneous [spɒn'teɪnjəs] *adj* espontáneo(a).

spooky ['spuːkɪ] *adj inf* escalofriante.

spool [spuːl] *n* [gen & COMPUT] bobina *f*.

spoon [spuːn] *n* **- 1.** [piece of cutlery] cuchara *f* **- 2.** [spoonful] cucharada *f*.

spoon-feed *vt* [feed with spoon] dar de comer con cuchara a.

spoonful ['spuːnfʊl] (*pl* **-s** OR **spoonsful** ['spuːnzfʊl]) *n* cucharada *f*.

sporadic [spə'rædɪk] *adj* esporádico(ca).

sport [spɔːt] *n* [game] deporte *m*.

sporting ['spɔːtɪŋ] *adj lit & fig* deportivo(va); **to give sb a sporting chance** dar a alguien la oportunidad de ganar.

sports car ['spɔːts-] *n* coche *m* deportivo, auto *m* sport, carro *m* sport *Amér*.

sports jacket ['spɔːts-] *n* chaqueta *f* de esport.

sportsman ['spɔːtsmən] (*pl* **-men** [-mən]) *n* deportista *m*.

sportsmanship ['spɔːtsmənʃɪp] *n* deportividad *f*.

sportswear ['spɔːtsweər] *n* ropa *f* deportiva.

sportswoman ['spɔːts,wʊmən] (*pl* **-women** [-,wɪmɪn]) *n* deportista *f*.

sports utility vehicle *n US* todoterreno *m* utilitario.

sporty ['spɔːtɪ] *adj inf* [fond of sports] aficionado(da) a los deportes.

spot [spɒt] ◇ *n* **- 1.** [stain] mancha *f*, mota *f*; [dot] punto *m* **- 2.** [pimple] grano *m* **- 3.** [drop] gota *f* **- 4.** *inf* [bit, small amount] pizca *f* **- 5.** [place] lugar *m*; **on the spot** en el lugar; **to do sthg on the spot** hacer algo en el acto **- 6.** RADIO & TV espacio *m*. ◇ *vt* [notice] notar, ver.

spot check *n* control *m* aleatorio.

spotless ['spɒtlɪs] *adj* [thing] inmaculado(da); [reputation] intachable.

spotlight ['spɒtlaɪt] *n* [lamp] foco *m*, reflector *m*; [in theatre, home] foco *m*, reflector *m* de luz; **to be in the spotlight** *fig* ser el centro de atención.

spotted ['spɒtɪd] *adj* de lunares.

spotty ['spɒtɪ] *adj* UK [skin] con granos.

spouse [spaʊs] *n* cónyuge *mf*.

spout [spaʊt] <> *n* [of teapot] pitorro *m*; [of jug] pico *m*. <> *vi*: **to spout from** OR **out of** [liquid] salir a chorros de; [smoke, flames] salir incesantemente de.

sprain [spreɪn] <> *n* torcedura *f*. <> *vt* torcerse.

sprang [spræŋ] *pt* ▷ **spring**.

sprawl [sprɔːl] *vi* [sit] repantigarse, arrellanarse; [lie] echarse, tumbarse.

spray [spreɪ] <> *n* - **1**. [small drops - of liquid] rociada *f*; [- of sea] espuma *f*; [- of aerosol] pulverización *f* - **2**. [pressurized liquid] espray *m* - **3**. [can, container - gen] atomizador *m*; [- for garden] pulverizador *m* - **4**. [of flowers] ramo *m*. <> *vt* rociar, vaporizar.

spread [spred] <> *n* - **1**. [soft food]: **cheese spread** queso *m* para untar - **2**. [of fire, disease] propagación *f*. <> *vt* (*pt & pp* **spread**) - **1**. [rug, tablecloth] extender; [map] desplegar - **2**. [legs, fingers etc] estirar - **3**. [butter, jam] untar; [glue] repartir; **to spread sthg over sthg** extender algo por algo - **4**. [disease] propagar; [news] difundir, diseminar - **5**. [wealth, work] repartir equitativamente. <> *vi* (*pt & pp* **spread**) - **1**. [disease, fire, news] extenderse, propagarse - **2**. [gas, cloud] esparcirse. ◆ **spread out** *vi* diseminarse, dispersarse.

spread-eagled [-,iːgld] *adj* despatarrado(da).

spreadsheet ['spredʃiːt] *n* COMPUT hoja *f* de cálculo electrónica.

spree [spriː] *n*: **a killing spree** una matanza; **to go on a shopping spree** salir a comprar a lo loco.

sprightly ['spraɪtlɪ] *adj* ágil, activo(va).

spring [sprɪŋ] <> *n* - **1**. [season] primavera *f* - **2**. [coil] muelle *m* - **3**. [jump] salto *m* - **4**. [water source] manantial *m*, vertiente *f* R Plata. <> *vi* (*pt* **sprang**, *pp* **sprung**) - **1**. [jump] saltar - **2**. [move suddenly] moverse de repente; **to spring into action** OR **to life** entrar inmediatamente en acción. ◆ **spring up** *vi* surgir de repente.

springboard ['sprɪŋbɔːd] *n lit & fig* trampolín *m*.

spring-clean *vt* limpiar a fondo.

spring onion *n* UK cebolleta *f*.

springtime ['sprɪŋtaɪm] *n*: **in (the) springtime** en primavera.

springy ['sprɪŋɪ] *adj* [carpet, mattress, grass] mullido(da), [rubber] elástico(ca).

sprinkle ['sprɪŋkl] *vt* [cloth, road] salpicar; **to sprinkle sthg over** OR **on sthg, to sprinkle sthg with sthg** rociar algo sobre algo.

sprinkler ['sprɪŋklə'] *n* aspersor *m*.

sprint [sprɪnt] <> *n* - **1**. SPORT esprint *m* - **2**. [fast run] carrera *f*. <> *vi* SPORT esprintar; [run fast] correr a toda velocidad.

sprout [spraʊt] <> *n* - **1**. CULIN: **(Brussels) sprouts** coles *fpl* de Bruselas - **2**. [shoot] brote *m*, retoño *m*. <> *vt* [plant] echar. <> *vi* - **1**. [plants, vegetables] crecer - **2**. [leaves, shoots] brotar.

spruce [spruːs] <> *adj* pulcro(cra). <> *n* picea *f*. ◆ **spruce up** *vt sep* arreglar.

sprung [sprʌŋ] *pp* ▷ **spring**.

spry [spraɪ] *adj* ágil, activo(va).

spun [spʌn] *pt & pp* ▷ **spin**.

spur [spɜːr] <> *n* - **1**. [incentive]: **spur (to sthg)** estímulo *m* (para conseguir algo) - **2**. [on rider's boot] espuela *f*. <> *vt* [encourage]: **to spur sb to do sthg** animar a alguien a hacer algo. ◆ **on the spur of the moment** *adv* sin pensarlo dos veces. ◆ **spur on** *vt sep*: **to spur sb on** animar a alguien.

spurious ['spʊərɪəs] *adj* falso(sa).

spurn [spɜːn] *vt* rechazar.

spurt [spɜːt] <> *n* - **1**. [of water] chorro *m*; [of flame] llamarada *f* - **2**. [of activity, effort] arranque *m* - **3**. [of speed] acelerón *m*. <> *vi* [gush]: **to spurt (out of** OR **from)** [liquid] salir a chorros de; [flame] salir incesantemente de.

spy [spaɪ] <> *n* espía *mf*. <> *vt inf* divisar. <> *vi*: **to spy (on)** espiar (a), aguaitar (a) *Amér*.

spying ['spaɪɪŋ] *n* espionaje *m*.

Sq., sq. *abbr of* **square**.

squabble ['skwɒbl] <> *n* riña *f*. <> *vi*: **to squabble (about** OR **over)** reñir (por).

squad [skwɒd] *n* - **1**. [of police] brigada *f* - **2**. MIL pelotón *m* - **3**. [SPORT - of club] plantilla *f*, equipo *m* completo; [- of national team] seleccionado *m*; **the England squad** el equipo inglés.

squadron ['skwɒdrən] *n* [of planes] escuadrilla *f*; [of warships] escuadra *f*; [of soldiers] escuadrón *m*.

squalid ['skwɒlɪd] *adj* [filthy] miserable, sórdido(da).

squall [skwɔːl] *n* [storm] turbión *m*.

squalor ['skwɒlə'] *n* (U) miseria *f*.

squander ['skwɒndə'] *vt* [opportunity] desaprovechar; [money] despilfarrar; [resources] malgastar.

square [skweə'] <> *adj* - **1**. [gen] cuadrado(da); **4 square metres** 4 metros cuadrados; **the kitchen is 4 metres square** la cocina mide

4 metros por 4 - **2.** [not owing money]: **we're square now** ya estamos en paz. ◇ *n* - **1.** [shape] cuadrado *m* - **2.** [in town, city] plaza *f* - **3.** *inf* [unfashionable person] carroza *mf*. ◇ *vt* - **1.** MATHS elevar al cuadrado - **2.** [balance, reconcile]: **how can you square that with your principles?** ¿cómo encajas esto con tus principios? ➡ **square up** *vi* [settle up]: **to square up with** saldar cuentas con.

squarely ['skweəlɪ] *adv* [directly] justo, exactamente.

square meal *n* comida *f* satisfactoria.

squash [skwɒʃ] ◇ *n* - **1.** [game] squash *m* - **2.** *UK* [drink] zumo *m* - **3.** *US* [vegetable] cucurbitácea *f*. ◇ *vt* [squeeze, flatten] aplastar.

squat [skwɒt] ◇ *adj* achaparrado(da). ◇ *vi* [crouch]: **to squat (down)** agacharse, ponerse en cuclillas.

squatter ['skwɒtər] *n UK* ocupante *mf* ilegal, squatter *mf*.

squawk [skwɔ:k] *n* [of bird] graznido *m*.

squeak [skwi:k] *n* - **1.** [of animal] chillido *m* - **2.** [of hinge] chirrido *m*.

squeal [skwi:l] *vi* - **1.** [person, animal] chillar, gritar - **2.** [brakes] chirriar.

squeamish ['skwi:mɪʃ] *adj* aprensivo(va).

squeeze [skwi:z] ◇ *n* [pressure] apretón *m*. ◇ *vt* - **1.** [press firmly] apretar - **2.** [force out - toothpaste] sacar (estrujando); [- juice] exprimir - **3.** [cram]: **to squeeze sthg into sthg** [into place] conseguir meter algo en algo; [into time] arreglárselas para hacer algo en algo.

squelch [skwelʃ] *vi*: **to squelch through mud** cruzar el barro chapoteando.

squid [skwɪd] (*pl* squid OR -s) *n* - **1.** ZOOL calamar *m* - **2.** (U) [food] calamares *mpl*.

squiggle ['skwɪgl] *n* garabato *m*.

squint [skwɪnt] ◇ *n* estrabismo *m*, bizquera *f*. ◇ *vi*: **to squint at** mirar con los ojos entrecerrados.

squire ['skwaɪər] *n* [landowner] terrateniente *mf*.

squirm [skwɜ:m] *vi* [wriggle] retorcerse.

squirrel [*UK* 'skwɪrəl, *US* 'skwɜ:rəl] *n* ardilla *f*.

squirt [skwɜ:t] ◇ *vt* [force out] sacar a chorro de. ◇ *vi*: **to squirt out of** salir a chorro.

Sr *abbr of* **senior**.

Sri Lanka [ˌsri:'læŋkə] *n* Sri Lanka.

St - **1.** (*abbr of* **saint**) Sto.(Sta.) - **2.** (*abbr of* **Street**) c/.

stab [stæb] ◇ *n* - **1.** [with knife] puñalada *f* - **2.** *inf* [attempt]: **to have a stab (at sthg)** probar (a hacer algo) - **3.** [twinge] punzada *f*. ◇ *vt* - **1.** [with knife] apuñalar - **2.** [jab] pinchar.

stable ['steɪbl] ◇ *adj* - **1.** [unchanging] estable - **2.** [not moving] fijo(ja) - **3.** MED [condition] estacionario(ria); [mental health] equilibrado(da). ◇ *n* [building] cuadra *f*.

stack [stæk] ◇ *n* [pile] pila *m*. ◇ *vt* [pile up] apilar.

stadium ['steɪdjəm] (*pl* -diums OR -dia [-djə]) *n* estadio *m*.

staff [stɑ:f] ◇ *n* [employees] empleados *mpl*, personal *m*. ◇ *vt*: **the shop is staffed by women** la tienda está llevada por una plantilla de mujeres.

stag [stæg] (*pl* stag OR -s) *n* ciervo *m*, venado *m*.

stage [steɪdʒ] ◇ *n* - **1.** [part of process, phase] etapa *f* - **2.** [in theatre, hall] escenario *m*, escena *f* - **3.** [acting profession]: **the stage** el teatro. ◇ *vt* - **1.** THEAT representar - **2.** [event, strike] organizar.

stagecoach ['steɪdʒkəʊtʃ] *n* diligencia *f*.

stage fright *n* miedo *m* al público.

stage-manage *vt* - **1.** THEAT dirigir - **2.** *fig* [orchestrate] urdir, maquinar.

stagger ['stægər] ◇ *vt* - **1.** [astound] dejar atónito(ta); **to be staggered by sthg** quedarse pasmado(da) por algo - **2.** [arrange at different times] escalonar. ◇ *vi* tambalearse.

stagnant ['stægnənt] *adj lit & fig* estancado(da).

stagnate [stæg'neɪt] *vi* estancarse.

stag party *n* despedida *f* de soltero.

staid [steɪd] *adj* recatado y conservador (recatada y conservadora).

stain [steɪn] ◇ *n* mancha *f*. ◇ *vt* manchar.

stained glass [ˌsteɪnd-] *n* (U) vidrio *m* de color; **stained glass window** vidriera *f*.

stainless steel [ˌsteɪnlɪs-] *n* acero *m* inoxidable.

stain remover [-rɪˌmu:vər] *n* quitamanchas *m inv*.

stair [steər] *n* peldaño *m*, escalón *m*. ➡ **stairs** *npl* escaleras *fpl*, escalera *f*.

staircase ['steəkeɪs] *n* escalera *f*.

stairway ['steəweɪ] *n* escalera *f*.

stairwell ['steəwel] *n* hueco *m* OR caja *f* de la escalera.

stake [steɪk] ◇ *n* - **1.** [share]: **to have a stake in** tener intereses en - **2.** [wooden post] estaca *f* - **3.** [in gambling] apuesta *f*. ◇ *vt* - **1.** [risk]: **to stake sthg (on OR upon)** arriesgar OR jugarse algo (en) - **2.** [in gambling] apostar. ➡ **at stake** *adv*: **to be at stake** estar en juego.

stale [steɪl] *adj* [bread] duro(ra); [food] pasado(da); [air] viciado(da).

stalemate ['steɪlmeɪt] *n* - **1.** [deadlock] punto *m* muerto - **2.** CHESS tablas *fpl*.

stalk [stɔːk] ◇ *n* - **1.** [of flower, plant] tallo *m*
- **2.** [of leaf, fruit] pecíolo *m*, rabillo *m*. ◇ *vt*
[hunt] acechar, seguir sigilosamente. ◇ *vi*. to
stalk in/out entrar/salir con paso airado.

stall [stɔːl] ◇ *n* [in market, at exhibition] puesto *m*, caseta *f*. ◇ *vt* AUT calar. ◇ *vi* - **1.** AUT
calarse - **2.** [delay] andar con evasivas.
➤ **stalls** *npl* UK platea *f*.

stallion ['stæljən] *n* semental *m*.

stalwart ['stɔːlwət] *n* partidario *m*, -ria *f* incondicional.

stamina ['stæmɪnə] *n* resistencia *f*.

stammer ['stæmər] ◇ *n* tartamudeo *m*.
◇ *vi* tartamudear.

stamp [stæmp] ◇ *n* - **1.** [gen] sello *m*, estampilla *f* Amér, timbre *m* Méx - **2.** [tool] tampón *m*. ◇ *vt* - **1.** [mark by stamping] timbrar,
sellar - **2.** [stomp]: to stamp one's feet patear.
◇ *vi* - **1.** [stomp] patalear - **2.** [tread heavily]: to
stamp on sthg pisotear OR pisar algo.

stamp album *n* álbum *m* de sellos OR de
estampillas Amér OR de timbres Méx.

stamp collecting [-kə,lektɪŋ] *n* filatelia *f*.

stamped addressed envelope
['stæmptə,drest-] *n* UK sobre con sus señas y
franqueo.

stampede [stæm'piːd] ◇ *n* lit & fig estampida *f*. ◇ *vi* salir de estampida.

stance [stæns] *n* - **1.** [way of standing] postura *f* - **2.** [attitude]: stance (on) postura *f* (ante).

stand [stænd] ◇ *n* - **1.** [stall] puesto *m*;
[selling newspapers] quiosco *m* - **2.** [supporting
object] soporte *m*; coat stand perchero *m*
- **3.** SPORT tribuna *f*; the stands las gradas
- **4.** [act of defence]: to make a stand resistir al
enemigo - **5.** [publicly stated view] postura *f*
- **6.** US LAW estrado *m*. ◇ *vt* (pt & pp stood)
- **1.** [place upright] colocar (verticalmente)
- **2.** [withstand, tolerate] soportar; I can't stand
that woman no soporto a esa mujer; he can't
stand being beaten odia perder. ◇ *vi*
(pt & pp stood) - **1.** [be upright - person] estar de
pie; [- object] estar (en posición vertical); try to
stand still procura no moverte; he doesn't let
anything stand in his way no deja que nada
se interponga en su camino - **2.** [get to one's
feet] ponerse de pie, levantarse - **3.** [liquid] reposar - **4.** [still be valid] seguir vigente OR en pie
- **5.** [be in particular state]: as things stand tal
como están las cosas - **6.** UK POL [be a candid-
ate] presentarse; to stand for Parliament presentarse para las elecciones al Parlamento
- **7.** US AUT: 'no standing' 'prohibido aparcar'.
➤ **stand back** *vi* echarse para atrás.
➤ **stand by** ◇ *vt insep* - **1.** [person] seguir al
lado de - **2.** [promise, decision] mantener. ◇ *vi*
- **1.** [in readiness]: to stand by (for sthg/to do
sthg) estar preparado(da) (para algo/para hacer algo) - **2.** [remain inactive] quedarse sin ha-

cer nada. ➤ **stand down** *vi* [resign] retirarse.
➤ **stand for** *vt insep* - **1.** [signify] significar;
PTO stands for please turn over PTO quiere
decir 'sigue en la página siguiente' - **2.** [toler-
ate] aguantar, tolerar; I won't stand for it! ¡no
pienso aguantarlo! ➤ **stand in** *vi*: to stand
in for sb sustituir a alguien. ➤ **stand out**
vi sobresalir, destacarse. ➤ **stand up**
◇ *vt sep inf* [boyfriend etc] dejar plantado(da).
◇ *vi* [rise from seat] levantarse. ➤ **stand up
for** *vt insep* salir en defensa de. ➤ **stand
up to** *vt insep* - **1.** [weather, heat etc] resistir
- **2.** [person] hacer frente a.

standard ['stændəd] ◇ *adj* - **1.** [normal] corriente, estándar - **2.** [accepted] estableci-
do(da). ◇ *n* - **1.** [acceptable level] nivel *m*; to
be of a high standard ser de un excelente nivel; it's below standard está por debajo del
nivel exigido - **2.** [point of reference - moral] criterio *m*; [- technical] norma *f* - **3.** [flag] estandarte *m*. ➤ **standards** *npl* [principles] valores *mpl* morales.

standard lamp *n* UK lámpara *f* de pie.

standard of living (*pl* standards of living) *n*
nivel *m* de vida.

standby ['stændbaɪ] (*pl* standbys) ◇ *n* recurso *m*; to be on standby estar prepara-
do(da). ◇ *comp*: standby ticket billete *m* en
lista de espera.

stand-in *n* [stuntman] doble *mf*; [temporary re-
placement] sustituto *m*, -ta *f*.

standing ['stændɪŋ] ◇ *adj* [permanent] permanente. ◇ *n* - **1.** [reputation] reputación *f*
- **2.** [duration] duración *f*; friends of 20 years'
standing amigos desde hace 20 años.

standing order *n* domiciliación *f* de pago
Esp, débito *m* bancario Amér.

standing room *n* (U) [on bus] sitio *m* para
estar de pie, sitio *m* para ir parado Amér; [at
theatre, sports ground] localidades *fpl* de pie.

standoffish [,stænd'ɒfɪʃ] *adj* distante.

standpoint ['stændpɔɪnt] *n* punto *m* de vista.

standstill ['stændstɪl] *n*: at a standstill [not
moving] parado(da); fig [not active] en un punto
muerto; to come to a standstill [stop moving]
pararse; fig [cease] llegar a un punto muerto.

stand-up *adj* US [decent, honest]: a stand-up
guy un tipo decente.

stank [stæŋk] *pt* ▷ **stink**.

staple ['steɪpl] ◇ *adj* [principal] básico(ca),
de primera necesidad. ◇ *n* - **1.** [item of sta-
tionery] grapa *f* - **2.** [principal commodity] producto *m* básico OR de primera necesidad.
◇ *vt* grapar, corchetear Chile.

stapler ['steɪplə'] *n* grapadora *f*.

star [stɑːʳ] ◇ n [gen] estrella f. ◇ comp estelar. ◇ vi: **to star (in)** hacer de protagonista en. ◆ **stars** npl horóscopo m.

starboard ['stɑːbəd] ◇ adj de estribor. ◇ n: **to starboard** a estribor.

starch [stɑːtʃ] n - 1. [gen] almidón m - 2. [in potatoes etc] fécula f.

stardom ['stɑːdəm] n estrellato m.

stare [steəʳ] ◇ n mirada f fija. ◇ vi: **to stare (at sthg/sb)** mirar fijamente (algo/a alguien).

stark [stɑːk] ◇ adj - 1. [landscape, decoration, room] austero(ra) - 2. [harsh - reality] crudo(da). ◇ adv: **stark naked** en cueros.

starling ['stɑːlɪŋ] n estornino m.

starry ['stɑːrɪ] adj estrellado(da).

starry-eyed [-'aɪd] adj [optimism etc] iluso(sa); [lovers] encandilado(da).

Stars and Stripes n: **the Stars and Stripes** la bandera de las barras y estrellas.

start [stɑːt] ◇ n - 1. [beginning] principio m, comienzo m; **at the start of the year** a principios de año - 2. [jerk, jump] sobresalto m - 3. [starting place] salida f - 4. [time advantage] ventaja f; **to have a start on sb** llevar ventaja a alguien; ◇ vt - 1. [begin] empezar, comenzar; **to start doing** OR **to do sthg** empezar a hacer algo - 2. [turn on - machine, engine] poner en marcha; [- vehicle] arrancar - 3. [set up] formar, crear; [business] montar. ◇ vi - 1. [begin] empezar, comenzar; **to start with sb/ sthg** empezar por alguien/algo; **don't start!** inf ¡no empieces! - 2. [machine, tape] ponerse en marcha; [vehicle] arrancar - 3. [begin journey] ponerse en camino - 4. [jerk, jump] sobresaltarse. ◆ **start off** ◇ vt sep [discussion, rumour] desencadenar; [meeting] empezar; [person]: **this should be enough to start you off** con esto tienes suficiente para empezar. ◇ vi - 1. [begin] empezar, comenzar - 2. [leave on journey] salir, ponerse en camino. ◆ **start out** vi - 1. [originally be] empezar, comenzar; **she started out as a journalist** empezó como periodista - 2. [leave on journey] salir/ponerse en camino. ◆ **start up** ◇ vt sep - 1. [business] montar; [shop] poner; [association] crear - 2. [car, engine] arrancar. ◇ vi - 1. [begin] empezar - 2. [car, engine] arrancar.

starter ['stɑːtəʳ] n - 1. UK [of meal] primer plato m, entrada f - 2. AUT (motor m de) arranque m - 3. [person participating in race] participante mf.

starting point ['stɑːtɪŋ-] n lit & fig punto m de partida.

startle ['stɑːtl] vt asustar.

startling ['stɑːtlɪŋ] adj asombroso(sa).

start-up n nueva empresa f.

starvation [stɑː'veɪʃn] n hambre f, inanición f.

starve [stɑːv] ◇ vt [deprive of food] privar de comida. ◇ vi - 1. [have no food] pasar hambre; **to starve to death** morirse de hambre - 2. inf [be hungry]: **I'm starving!** ¡me muero de hambre!

state [steɪt] ◇ n estado m; **not to be in a fit state to do sthg** no estar en condiciones de hacer algo; **to be in a state** [nervous] tener los nervios de punta; [untidy] estar hecho un asco. ◇ comp [ceremony] oficial, de Estado; [control, ownership] estatal. ◇ vt - 1. [gen] indicar; [reason, policy] plantear; [case] exponer - 2. [time, date, amount] fijar. ◆ **State** n: **the State** el Estado. ◆ **States** npl: **the States** los Estados Unidos.

State Department n US ≃ Ministerio m de Asuntos Exteriores.

stately ['steɪtlɪ] adj majestuoso(sa).

statement ['steɪtmənt] n - 1. [gen] declaración f - 2. [from bank] extracto m OR estado m de cuenta.

state of mind (pl states of mind) n estado m de ánimo.

statesman ['steɪtsmən] (pl -men [-mən]) n estadista m.

static ['stætɪk] ◇ adj estático(ca). ◇ n (U) interferencias fpl, parásitos mpl.

static electricity n electricidad f estática.

station ['steɪʃn] ◇ n - 1. [gen] estación f - 2. RADIO emisora f - 3. [centre of activity] centro m, puesto m - 4. fml [rank] rango m. ◇ vt - 1. [position] situar, colocar - 2. MIL estacionar, apostar.

stationary ['steɪʃnərɪ] adj inmóvil.

stationer's (shop) ['steɪʃnəʳz] n papelería f.

stationery ['steɪʃnərɪ] n (U) objetos mpl de escritorio.

stationmaster ['steɪʃn,mɑːstəʳ] n jefe m de estación.

station wagon n US ranchera f.

statistic [stə'tɪstɪk] n estadística f. ◆ **statistics** n (U) estadística f.

statistical [stə'tɪstɪkl] adj estadístico(ca).

statue ['stætʃuː] n estatua f.

stature ['stætʃəʳ] n - 1. [height] estatura f, talla f - 2. [importance] categoría f.

status ['steɪtəs] n (U) - 1. [position, condition] condición f, estado m - 2. [prestige] prestigio m, estatus m inv.

status bar n COMPUT barra f de estado.

status symbol n símbolo m de posición social.

statute ['stætjuːt] n estatuto m.

statutory ['stætjʊtrɪ] *adj* reglamentario(ria).

staunch [stɔ:ntʃ] ⟨⟩ *adj* fiel, leal. ⟨⟩ *vt* restañar.

stave [steɪv] *n* MUS pentagrama *m*. ⬤ **stave off** *vt sep* (*pt & pp* **-d** OR **stove**) [disaster, defeat] retrasar; [hunger, illness] aplacar temporalmente.

stay [steɪ] ⟨⟩ *vi* - **1.** [not move away] quedarse, permanecer; **to stay put** permanecer en el mismo sitio - **2.** [as visitor] alojarse - **3.** [continue, remain] permanecer; **to stay out of sthg** mantenerse al margen de algo. ⟨⟩ *n* estancia *f*. ⬤ **stay in** *vi* quedarse en casa. ⬤ **stay on** *vi* permanecer, quedarse. ⬤ **stay out** *vi* [from home] quedarse fuera. ⬤ **stay up** *vi* quedarse levantado(da).

staying power ['steɪɪŋ-] *n* resistencia *f*.

stead [sted] *n*: **to stand sb in good stead** servir de mucho a alguien.

steadfast ['stedfɑ:st] *adj* [supporter] fiel; [gaze] fijo(ja); [resolve] inquebrantable.

steadily ['stedɪlɪ] *adv* - **1.** [gradually] constantemente - **2.** [regularly - breathe, move] normalmente - **3.** [calmly - look] fijamente, [- speak] con tranquilidad.

steady ['stedɪ] ⟨⟩ *adj* - **1.** [gradual] gradual - **2.** [regular, constant] constante, continuo(nua) - **3.** [not shaking] firme - **4.** [voice] sereno(na); [stare] fijo(ja) - **5.** [relationship] estable, serio(ria); [boyfriend, girlfriend] formal; **a steady job** un trabajo fijo - **6.** [reliable, sensible] sensato(ta). ⟨⟩ *vt* - **1.** [stop from shaking] mantener firme; **to steady o.s.** dejar de temblar - **2.** [nerves, voice] dominar, controlar; **to steady o.s.** controlar los nervios.

steak [steɪk] *n* - **1.** (U) [meat] bistec *m*, filete *m*, bife *m* Andes & R Dom - **2.** [piece of meat, fish] filete *m*.

steal [sti:l] ⟨⟩ *vt* (*pt* **stole**, *pp* **stolen**) [gen] robar; [idea] apropiarse de. ⟨⟩ *vi* (*pt* **stole**, *pp* **stolen**) [move secretly] moverse sigilosamente; **he stole into the bedroom** entró sigilosamente en el dormitorio.

stealthy ['stelθɪ] *adj* cauteloso(sa), sigiloso(sa).

steam [sti:m] ⟨⟩ *n* (U) vapor *m*, vaho *m*. ⟨⟩ *vt* CULIN cocer al vapor. ⟨⟩ *vi* [water, food] echar vapor. ⬤ **steam up** ⟨⟩ *vt sep* [mist up] empañar. ⟨⟩ *vi* empañarse.

steamboat ['sti:mbəʊt] *n* buque *m* de vapor.

steam engine *n* máquina *f* de vapor.

steamer ['sti:mə⟩] *n* [ship] buque *m* de vapor.

steamroller ['sti:m,rəʊlə⟩] *n* apisonadora *f*.

steamy ['sti:mɪ] *adj* - **1.** [full of steam] lleno(na) de vaho - **2.** *inf* [erotic] caliente, erótico(ca).

steel [sti:l] *n* acero *m*.

steelworks ['sti:lwɜ:ks] ⟨*pl* **steelworks**⟩ *n* fundición *f* de acero.

steep [sti:p] ⟨⟩ *adj* - **1.** [hill, road] empinado(da) - **2.** [considerable - increase, fall] considerable - **3.** *inf* [expensive] muy caro(ra), abusivo(va). ⟨⟩ *vt* remojar.

steeple ['sti:pl] *n* aguja *f* (de un campanario).

steeplechase ['sti:pltʃeɪs] *n* carrera *f* de obstáculos.

steer ['stɪə⟩] ⟨⟩ *n* buey *m*. ⟨⟩ *vt* - **1.** [vehicle] conducir - **2.** [person, discussion etc] dirigir. ⟨⟩ *vi*: **the car steers well** el coche se conduce bien; **to steer clear of sthg/sb** evitar algo/a alguien.

steering ['stɪərɪŋ] *n* (U) dirección *f*.

steering wheel *n* volante *m*, timón *m* Andes.

stem [stem] ⟨⟩ *n* - **1.** [of plant] tallo *m* - **2.** [of glass] pie *m* - **3.** GRAM raíz *f*. ⟨⟩ *vt* [flow] contener; [blood] restañar. ⬤ **stem from** *vt insep* derivarse de.

stem cell *n* MED célula *f* madre.

stench [stentʃ] *n* hedor *m*.

stencil ['stensl] ⟨⟩ *n* plantilla *f*. ⟨⟩ *vt* (UK *pt & pp* **-led**, *cont* **-ling**, US *pt & pp* **-ed**, *cont* **-ing**) estarcir.

stenographer [stə'nɒɡrəfə⟩] *n* US taquígrafo *m*, -fa *f*.

step [step] ⟨⟩ *n* - **1.** [gen] paso *m*; **step by step** paso a paso - **2.** [action] medida *f* - **3.** [stair, rung] peldaño *m*. ⟨⟩ *vi* - **1.** [move foot] dar un paso; **he stepped off the bus** se bajó del autobús - **2.** [tread]: **to step on sthg** pisar algo; **to step in sthg** meter el pie en algo. ⬤ **steps** *npl* - **1.** escaleras *fpl* - **2.** UK [stepladder] escalera *f* de tijera. ⬤ **step down** *vi* [leave job] renunciar. ⬤ **step in** *vi* intervenir. ⬤ **step up** *vt sep* aumentar.

stepbrother ['step,brʌðə⟩] *n* hermanastro *m*.

stepdaughter ['step,dɔ:tə⟩] *n* hijastra *f*.

stepfather ['step,fɑ:ðə⟩] *n* padrastro *m*.

stepladder ['step,lædə⟩] *n* escalera *f* de tijera.

stepmother ['step,mʌðə⟩] *n* madrastra *f*.

stepping-stone ['stepɪŋ-] *n* [in river] pasadera *f*.

stepsister ['step,sɪstə⟩] *n* hermanastra *f*.

stepson ['stepsʌn] *n* hijastro *m*.

stereo ['sterɪəʊ] ⟨⟩ *adj* estéreo (*inv*). ⟨⟩ *n* (*pl* **-s**) - **1.** [record player] equipo *m* estereofónico - **2.** [stereo sound] estéreo *m*.

stereotype ['sterɪətaɪp] *n* estereotipo *m*.

sterile ['steraɪl] *adj* - **1.** [germ-free] esterilizado(da) - **2.** [unable to produce offspring] estéril.

sterilize, -ise ['sterəlaɪz] *vt* esterilizar.

sterling ['stɜ:lɪŋ] ◇ *adj* - **1.** FIN esterlina - **2.** [excellent] excelente. ◇ *n (U)* libra *f* esterlina.

sterling silver *n* plata *f* de ley.

stern [stɜ:n] ◇ *adj* severo(ra). ◇ *n* popa *f*.

steroid ['stɪərɔɪd] *n* esteroide *m*.

stethoscope ['steθəskəʊp] *n* estetoscopio *m*.

stew [stju:] ◇ *n* estofado *m*, guisado *m*. ◇ *vt* [meat, vegetables] estofar, guisar; [fruit] hacer una compota de.

steward ['stjʊəd] *n* [on plane] auxiliar *m* de vuelo; [on ship, train] camarero *m*.

stewardess ['stjʊədɪs] *n* auxiliar *f* de vuelo, azafata *f*.

stick [stɪk] ◇ *n* - **1.** [of wood, for playing sport] palo *m* - **2.** [of dynamite] cartucho *m*; [of rock] barra *f* - **3.** [walking stick] bastón *m*. ◇ *vt* (*pt & pp* **stuck**) - **1.** [push]: **to stick sthg through sthg** atravesar algo con algo - **2.** *inf* [put] meter - **3.** *UK inf* [tolerate] soportar, aguantar. ◇ *vi* (*pt & pp* **stuck**) - **1.** [adhere]: **to stick (to)** pegarse (a) - **2.** [jam] atrancarse. ❧ **stick out** ◇ *vt sep* - **1.** [make protrude] sacar; **to stick one's tongue out** sacar la lengua - **2.** [endure] aguantar. ◇ *vi* [protrude] sobresalir. ❧ **stick to** *vt insep* - **1.** [follow closely] seguir - **2.** [principles] ser fiel a; [promise, agreement] cumplir con; [decision] atenerse a. ❧ **stick up** *vi* salir, sobresalir. ❧ **stick up for** *vt insep* defender.

sticker ['stɪkər] *n* [piece of paper] pegatina *f*.

sticking plaster ['stɪkɪŋ-] *n* [tape] esparadrapo *m* *Amér*, tela *f* emplástica.

stickler ['stɪklər] *n*: **stickler for sthg** maniático *m*, -ca *f* de algo.

stick shift *n US* palanca *f* de cambios.

stick-up *n inf* atraco *m* a mano armada.

sticky ['stɪkɪ] *adj* - **1.** [tacky] pegajoso(sa) - **2.** [adhesive] adhesivo(va) - **3.** *inf* [awkward] engorroso(sa).

stiff [stɪf] ◇ *adj* - **1.** [inflexible] rígido(da) - **2.** [door, drawer] atascado(da) - **3.** [aching] agarrotado(da); **to have a stiff neck** tener tortícolis; **to be stiff** tener agujetas - **4.** [formal - person, manner] estirado(da); [- smile] rígido(da) - **5.** [severe, intense] severo(ra) - **6.** [difficult - task] duro(ra). ◇ *adv inf*: **bored/frozen stiff** muerto(ta) de aburrimiento/frío.

stiffen ['stɪfn] *vi* - **1.** [become inflexible] endurecerse - **2.** [bones] entumecerse; [muscles] agarrotarse - **3.** [become more severe, intense] intensificarse.

stifle ['staɪfl] *vt* - **1.** [prevent from breathing] ahogar, sofocar - **2.** [yawn etc] reprimir.

stifling ['staɪflɪŋ] *adj* sofocante.

stigma ['stɪgmə] *n* estigma *m*.

stile [staɪl] *n* escalones *mpl* para pasar una valla.

stiletto heel [stɪ'letəʊ-] *n UK* tacón *m* fino OR de aguja.

still [stɪl] ◇ *adv* - **1.** [up to now, up to then, even now] todavía - **2.** [to emphasize remaining amount] aún; **I've still got two left** aún me quedan dos - **3.** [nevertheless, however] sin embargo, no obstante - **4.** [with comparatives] aún - **5.** [motionless] sin moverse. ◇ *adj* - **1.** [not moving] inmóvil - **2.** [calm, quiet] tranquilo(la), sosegado(da) - **3.** [not windy] apacible - **4.** [not fizzy] sin gas. ◇ *n* - **1.** PHOT vista *f* fija - **2.** [for making alcohol] alambique *m*.

stillborn ['stɪlbɔ:n] *adj* nacido muerto (nacida muerta).

still life (*pl* **-s**) *n* bodegón *m*, naturaleza *f* muerta.

stilted ['stɪltɪd] *adj* forzado(da).

stilts [stɪlts] *npl* - **1.** [for person] zancos *mpl* - **2.** [for building] pilotes *mpl*.

stimulate ['stɪmjʊleɪt] *vt* [gen] estimular; [interest] excitar.

stimulating ['stɪmjʊleɪtɪŋ] *adj* [physically] estimulante; [mentally] interesante.

stimulus ['stɪmjʊləs] (*pl* **-li** [-laɪ]) *n* estímulo *m*.

sting [stɪŋ] ◇ *n* - **1.** [by bee] picadura *f* - **2.** [of bee] aguijón *m* - **3.** [sharp pain] escozor *m*; **to take the sting out of sthg** suavizar algo. ◇ *vt* (*pt & pp* **stung**) - **1.** [bee, nettle] picar - **2.** [cause sharp pain to] escocer. ◇ *vi* (*pt & pp* **stung**) picar.

stingy ['stɪndʒɪ] *adj inf* tacaño(ña), roñoso(sa).

stink [stɪŋk] ◇ *n* peste *f*, hedor *m*. ◇ *vi* (*pt* **stank** OR **stunk**, *pp* **stunk**) [have unpleasant smell] apestar, heder.

stinking ['stɪŋkɪŋ] *inf fig* ◇ *adj* asqueroso(sa). ◇ *adv*: **to have a stinking cold** tener un resfriado horrible.

stint [stɪnt] ◇ *n* periodo *m*. ◇ *vi*: **to stint on sthg** escatimar algo.

stipulate ['stɪpjʊleɪt] *vt* estipular.

stir [stɜ:r] ◇ *n* [public excitement] revuelo *m*; **to cause a stir** causar revuelo. ◇ *vt* - **1.** [mix] remover - **2.** [move gently] agitar, mover - **3.** [move emotionally] conmover. ◇ *vi* [move gently] moverse, agitarse. ❧ **stir up** *vt sep* - **1.** [water, sediment] levantar - **2.** [cause] [excitement, hatred etc] provocar.

stirrup ['stɪrəp] *n* estribo *m*.

stitch [stɪtʃ] ◇ *n* - **1.** SEW puntada *f* - **2.** [in knitting] punto *m* - **3.** MED punto *m* (de sutura) - **4.** [stomach pain]: **to have a stitch** sentir pinchazos (en el estómago). ◇ *vt* - **1.** SEW coser - **2.** MED suturar.

stoat [stəʊt] *n* armiño *m*.

stock [stɒk] ◇ *n* - **1.** [supply] reserva *f* - **2.** *(U)* COMM [reserves] existencias *fpl*; [selection] surtido *m*; **in stock** en existencia, en almacén; **out of stock** agotado(da) - **5.** FIN [of company] capital *m*; stocks and shares acciones *fpl*, valores *mpl* - **4.** [ancestry] linaje *m*, estirpe *f* - **5.** CULIN caldo *m* - **6.** [livestock] ganado *m*, ganadería *f* ▶▶▶ **to take stock (of sthg)** evaluar (algo). ◇ *adj* estereotipado(da). ◇ *vt* - **1.** COMM abastecer de, tener en el almacén - **2.** [shelves] llenar; [lake] repoblar. ◆ **stock up** *vi*: **to stock up (with)** abastecerse (de).

stockbroker ['stɒk,brəʊkər] *n* corredor *m*, -ra *f* de bolsa.

stock cube *n* UK pastilla *f* de caldo.

stock exchange *n* bolsa *f*.

stockholder ['stɒk,həʊldər] *n* US accionista *mf*.

stocking ['stɒkɪŋ] *n* [for woman] media *f*.

stockist ['stɒkɪst] *n* UK distribuidor *m*, -ra *f*.

stock market *n* bolsa *f*, mercado *m* de valores.

stock phrase *n* frase *f* estereotipada.

stockpile ['stɒkpaɪl] ◇ *n* reservas *fpl*. ◇ *vt* almacenar, acumular.

stocktaking ['stɒk,teɪkɪŋ] *n (U)* inventario *m*, balance *m*.

stocky ['stɒkɪ] *adj* corpulento(ta), robusto(ta).

stodgy ['stɒdʒɪ] *adj* [indigestible] indigesto(ta).

stoical ['stəʊɪkl] *adj* estoico(ca).

stoke [stəʊk] *vt* [fire] avivar, alimentar.

stole [stəʊl] ◇ *pt* ▷ **steal**. ◇ *n* estola *f*.

stolen ['stəʊln] *pp* ▷ **steal**.

stolid ['stɒlɪd] *adj* impasible.

stomach ['stʌmək] ◇ *n* - **1.** [organ] estómago *m*; **to do sthg on an empty stomach** hacer algo con el estómago vacío - **2.** [abdomen] vientre *m*. ◇ *vt* tragar, aguantar; **I can't stomach him** no lo trago.

stomachache ['stʌməkeɪk] *n* dolor *m* de estómago.

stomach upset [-'ʌpset] *n* trastorno *m* gástrico.

stone [stəʊn] *(pl -s)* ◇ *n* - **1.** [mineral] piedra *f* - **2.** [jewel] piedra *f* preciosa - **3.** [seed] hueso *m* - **4.** *(pl* stone*)* UK [unit of measurement] = 6,35 *kilos*. ◇ *vt* apedrear.

stone-cold *adj* helado(da).

stonewashed ['stəʊnwɒʃt] *adj* lavado(da) a la piedra.

stonework ['stəʊnwɜːk] *n* mampostería *f*.

stood [stʊd] *pt & pp* ▷ **stand**.

stool [stuːl] *n* [seat] taburete *m*.

stoop [stuːp] ◇ *n* [bent back]: **to walk with a stoop** caminar encorvado(da). ◇ *vi* - **1.** [bend] inclinarse, agacharse - **2.** [hunch shoulders] encorvarse.

stop [stɒp] ◇ *n* [gen] parada *f*; **to put a stop to sthg** poner fin a algo. ◇ *vt* - **1.** [gen] parar; **to stop doing sthg** dejar de hacer algo - **2.** [prevent] impedir - **3.** [cause to stop moving] detener. ◇ *vi* [gen] pararse; [rain, music] cesar; **to stop at nothing (to do sthg)** no reparar en nada (para hacer algo). ◆ **stop off** *vi* hacer una parada. ◆ **stop up** *vt sep* [block] taponar, tapar.

stopgap ['stɒpgæp] *n* [thing] recurso *m* provisional; [person] sustituto *m*, -ta *f*.

stopover ['stɒp,əʊvər] *n* [gen] parada *f*; [of plane] escala *f*.

stoppage ['stɒpɪdʒ] *n* - **1.** [strike] paro *m*, huelga *f* - **2.** UK [deduction] retención *f*.

stopper ['stɒpər] *n* tapón *m*.

stop press *n* noticias *fpl* de última hora.

stopwatch ['stɒpwɒtʃ] *n* cronómetro *m*.

storage ['stɔːrɪdʒ] *n* almacenamiento *m*.

storage heater *n* UK *calentador por almacenamiento térmico.*

store [stɔːr] ◇ *n* - **1.** *esp* US [shop] tienda *f* - **2.** [supply] provisión *f*, reserva *f* - **3.** [place of storage] almacén *m*. ◇ *vt* - **1.** [gen & COMPUT] almacenar - **2.** [keep] guardar. ◆ **store up** *vt sep* [provisions, goods] almacenar; [information] acumular.

storekeeper ['stɔː,kiːpər] *n* US tendero *m*, -ra *f*.

storeroom ['stɔːrʊm] *n* [gen] almacén *m*; [for food] despensa *f*.

storey UK *(pl* storeys*)*, **story** US *n* planta *f*.

stork [stɔːk] *n* cigüeña *f*.

storm [stɔːm] ◇ *n* - **1.** [bad weather] tormenta *f* - **2.** [violent reaction] torrente *m*. ◇ *vt* MIL asaltar. ◇ *vi* - **1.** [go angrily]: **to storm out** salir echando pestes - **2.** [say angrily] vociferar.

stormy ['stɔːmɪ] *adj* - **1.** [weather] tormentoso(sa) - **2.** [meeting] acalorado(da); [relationship] tempestuoso(sa).

story ['stɔːrɪ] *n* - **1.** [tale] cuento *m* - **2.** [history] historia *f* - **3.** [news article] artículo *m* - **4.** US = **storey**.

storybook ['stɔːrɪbʊk] *adj* de cuento.

storyteller ['stɔːrɪ,telər] *n* [teller of story] narrador *m*, -ra *f*, cuentista *mf*.

stout [staʊt] ◇ *adj* - **1.** [rather fat] corpulento(ta) - **2.** [strong, solid] fuerte, sólido(da) - **3.** [resolute] firme. ◇ *n (U)* cerveza *f* negra.

stove [stəʊv] ◇ *pt & pp* ▷ **stave**. ◇ *n* [for heating] estufa *f*; [for cooking] cocina *f*.

stow [stəʊ] *vt*: **to stow sthg (away)** guardar algo.

stowaway ['stəʊəweɪ] n polizón m.

straddle ['strædl] vt [person] sentarse a horcajadas sobre.

straggle ['strægl] vi - 1. [sprawl] desparramarse - 2. [dawdle] rezagarse.

straggler ['stræglər] n rezagado m, -da f.

straight [streɪt] ◇ adj - 1. [not bent] recto(ta); **sit up straight!** ¡siéntate derecho! - 2. [hair] liso(sa) - 3. [honest, frank] sincero(ra) - 4. [tidy] arreglado(da) - 5. [choice, swap] simple, fácil - 6. [alcoholic drink] solo(la). ◇ adv - 1. [in a straight line - horizontally] directamente; [- vertically] recto(ta); **straight ahead** todo recto; **it was heading straight for me** venía directo hacia mí - 2. [directly] directamente; [immediately] inmediatamente; **come straight home** ven directamente a casa - 3. [frankly] francamente - 4. [tidy] en orden - 5. [undiluted] solo(la)
▶▶ **let's get things straight** vamos a aclarar las cosas; **to go straight** [criminal] dejar la mala vida. ◆ **straight off** adv en el acto. ◆ **straight out** adv sin tapujos.

straight away [ˌstreɪtə'weɪ] adv en seguida.

straighten ['streɪtn] vt - 1. [tidy - room] ordenar; [- hair, dress] poner bien - 2. [make straight - horizontally] poner recto(ta); [- vertically] enderezar. ◆ **straighten out** vt sep [mess] arreglar; [problem] resolver.

straight face n: **to keep a straight face** aguantar la risa.

straightforward [ˌstreɪt'fɔːwəd] adj - 1. [easy] sencillo(lla) - 2. [frank - answer] directo(ta); [- person] sincero(ra).

strain [streɪn] ◇ n - 1. [weight] peso m; [pressure] presión f - 2. [mental stress] tensión f nerviosa; **to be under a lot of strain** estar muy agobiado(da) - 3. [physical injury] torcedura f. ◇ vt - 1. [overtax - budget] estirar - 2. [use hard]: **to strain one's eyes/ears** aguzar la vista/el oído - 3. [injure - eyes] cansar; [- muscle, back] torcerse - 4. [drain] colar. ◇ vi: **to strain to do sthg** esforzarse por hacer algo. ◆ **strains** npl liter [of music] acordes mpl.

strained [streɪnd] adj - 1. [worried] preocupado(da) - 2. [unfriendly] tirante, tenso(sa) - 3. [insincere] forzado(da).

strainer ['streɪnər] n colador m.

strait [streɪt] n estrecho m. ◆ **straits** npl: **in dire** OR **desperate straits** en un serio aprieto.

straitjacket ['streɪtˌdʒækɪt] n [garment] camisa f de fuerza.

straitlaced [ˌstreɪt'leɪst] adj pej mojigato(ta).

strand [strænd] n [thin piece] hebra f; **a strand of hair** un pelo del cabello.

stranded ['strændɪd] adj [ship] varado(da); [person] colgado(da).

strange [streɪndʒ] adj - 1. [unusual] raro(ra), extraño(ña) - 2. [unfamiliar] desconocido(da).

stranger ['streɪndʒər] n - 1. [unfamiliar person] extraño m, -ña f, desconocido m, -da f; **to be a/no stranger to sthg** no estar/estar familiarizado con algo - 2. [outsider] forastero m, -ra f.

strangle ['stræŋgl] vt [kill] estrangular.

stranglehold ['stræŋglhəʊld] n fig [strong influence] dominio m absoluto.

strap [stræp] ◇ n [of handbag, watch, case] correa f; [of dress, bra] tirante m, bretel m. ◇ vt [fasten] atar con correa.

strapping ['stræpɪŋ] adj robusto(ta).

strategic [strə'tiːdʒɪk] adj estratégico(ca).

strategy ['strætɪdʒɪ] n estrategia f.

straw [strɔː] n - 1. AGRIC paja f - 2. [for drinking] pajita f, paja f
▶▶ **the last straw** el colmo.

strawberry ['strɔːbərɪ] ◇ n fresa f, frutilla f Bol, Ecuad, Andes & R Dom. ◇ comp de fresa, de frutilla f Bol, Ecuad, Andes & R Dom.

stray [streɪ] ◇ adj - 1. [animal - without owner] callejero(ra); [- lost] extraviado(da) - 2. [bullet] perdido(da). ◇ vi - 1. [from path] desviarse; [from group] extraviarse - 2. [thoughts, mind] perderse.

streak [striːk] ◇ n - 1. [of hair] mechón m; **to have streaks in one's hair** tener un mechón en el pelo; [of lightning] rayo m - 2. [in character] vena f. ◇ vi [move quickly] ir como un rayo.

stream [striːm] ◇ n - 1. [small river] riachuelo m - 2. [of liquid, smoke] chorro m; [of light] raudal m - 3. [current] corriente f - 4. [of people, cars] torrente m - 5. [continuous series] sarta f, serie f - 6. UK SCH grupo m. ◇ vi - 1. [liquid, smoke, light]: **to stream into** entrar a raudales en; **to stream out of** brotar de - 2. [people, cars]: **to stream into** entrar atropelladamente en; **to stream out of** salir atropelladamente de - 3. [phr]: **to have a streaming cold** tener un resfriado horrible. ◇ vt UK SCH agrupar de acuerdo con el rendimiento escolar.

streamer ['striːmər] n [for party] serpentina f.

streamlined ['striːmlaɪnd] adj - 1. [aerodynamic] aerodinámico(ca) - 2. [efficient] racional.

street [striːt] n calle f; **to be streets ahead of sb** UK estar muy por delante de alguien; **to be on the streets** estar en la calle.

streetcar ['striːtkɑːr] n US tranvía m.

street lamp, street light n farola f.

street plan n plano m (de la ciudad).

streetwise ['striːtwaɪz] adj inf espabilado(da).

strength [streŋθ] n - 1. [physical or mental power] fuerza f - 2. [power, influence] poder m

- **3.** [quality] punto *m* fuerte - **4.** [solidity - of material structure] solidez *f* - **5.** [intensity - of feel·ing, smell, mind] intensidad *f*; [- of accent, wind] fuerza *f*; [- of drug] potencia *f* - **6.** [credibility, weight] peso *m*, fuerza *f*.

strengthen ['streŋθn] *vt* - **1.** [gen] fortalecer - **2.** [reinforce - argument, bridge] reforzar - **3.** [intensify] acentuar, intensificar - **4.** [make closer] estrechar.

strenuous ['strenjʊəs] *adj* agotador(ra).

stress [stres] ◇ *n* - **1.** [emphasis]: **stress (on)** hincapié *m* OR énfasis *m inv* (en) - **2.** [tension, anxiety] estrés *m* - **3.** [physical pressure]: **stress (on)** presión *f* (en) - **4.** LING [on word, syllable] acento *m*. ◇ *vt* - **1.** [emphasize] recalcar, subrayar - **2.** *inf* estresar - **3.** LING [word, syllable] acentuar. ◇ *vi inf* estresarse. ◆ **stress out** *vt inf* estresar.

stress-buster *n informal* eliminador *m* de estrés.

stressful ['stresfʊl] *adj* estresante.

stress management *n* control *m* del estrés.

stretch [stretʃ] ◇ *n* - **1.** [of land, water] extensión *f*; [of road, river] tramo *m*, trecho *m* - **2.** [of time] periodo *m* - **3.** [to move one's body]: **to have a stretch** estirarse. ◇ *vt* - **1.** [gen] estirar; **I'm going to stretch my legs** voy a estirar las piernas - **2.** [overtax - person] extender - **3.** [challenge] hacer rendir al máximo. ◆ **stretch out** ◇ *vt sep* [foot, leg] estirar; [hand, arm] alargar. ◇ *vi* - **1.** [lie down] tumbarse - **2.** [reach out] estirarse.

stretcher ['stretʃə'] *n* camilla *f*.

stretch limo ['stretʃ'lɪməʊ] *n inf* limusina *f* ampliada.

strew [stru:] (*pp* **strewn** [stru:n] OR **-ed**) *vt*: **to be strewn on/over** estar esparcido(da) sobre/por; **to be strewn with** estar cubierto(ta) de.

stricken ['strɪkn] *adj*: **to be stricken by** OR **with** [illness] estar aquejado(da) de; [drought, famine] estar asolado(da) por; [grief] estar afligido(da) por; [doubts, horror] estar atenazado(da) por; **she was stricken with remorse** le remordía la conciencia.

strict [strɪkt] *adj* - **1.** [gen] estricto(ta) - **2.** [precise] exacto(ta), estricto(ta).

strictly ['strɪktlɪ] *adv* - **1.** [severely] severamente - **2.** [absolutely - prohibited] terminantemente; [- confidential] absolutamente - **3.** [exactly] exactamente; **strictly speaking** en el sentido estricto de la palabra - **4.** [exclusively] exclusivamente; **this is strictly between you and me** esto debe quedar exclusivamente entre tú y yo.

stride [straɪd] ◇ *n* zancada *f*; **to take sthg in one's stride** tomarse algo con calma. ◇ *vi* (*pt* **strode**, *pp* **stridden** ['strɪdn]): **to stride**

along andar a zancadas; **he strode off down the road** marchó calle abajo dando grandes zancadas.

strident ['straɪdnt] *adj* - **1.** [harsh] estridente - **2.** [vociferous] exaltado(da).

strife [straɪf] *n* (U) *fml* conflictos *mpl*.

strike [straɪk] ◇ *n* - **1.** [refusal to work etc] huelga *f*; **to be (out) on strike** estar en huelga; **to go on strike** declararse en huelga - **2.** MIL ataque *m* - **3.** [find] descubrimiento *m*. ◇ *vt* (*pt & pp* **struck**) - **1.** *fml* [hit - deliberately] golpear, pegar; [- accidentally] chocar contra - **2.** [disaster, earthquake] asolar; [lightning] fulminar; **she was struck by lightning** le alcanzó un rayo - **3.** [thought, idea] ocurrírsele a - **4.** [deal, bargain] cerrar - **5.** [match] encender. ◇ *vi* (*pt & pp* **struck**) - **1.** [stop working] estar en huelga - **2.** *fml* [hit accidentally]: **to strike against** chocar contra - **3.** [hurricane, disaster] sobrevenir; [lightning] caer - **4.** *fml* [attack] atacar - **5.** [chime] dar la hora; **the clock struck six** el reloj dio las seis. ◆ **strike down** *vt sep* fulminar. ◆ **strike out** *vt sep* tachar. ◆ **strike up** *vt insep* - **1.** [friendship] trabar; [conversation] entablar - **2.** [tune] empezar a tocar.

striker ['straɪkə'] *n* - **1.** [person on strike] huelguista *mf* - **2.** FTBL delantero *m*, -ra *f*.

striking ['straɪkɪŋ] *adj* - **1.** [noticeable, unusual] chocante, sorprendente - **2.** [attractive] llamativo(va), atractivo(va).

string [strɪŋ] *n* - **1.** [thin rope] cuerda *f*; **a (piece of) string** un cordón; **to pull strings** utilizar uno sus influencias - **2.** [of beads, pearls] sarta *f* - **3.** [series] serie *f*, sucesión *f* - **4.** [of musical instrument] cuerda *f*. ◆ **strings** *npl* MUS: **the strings** los instrumentos de cuerda. ◆ **string out** (*pt & pp* **strung out**) *vt insep*: **to be strung out** alinearse. ◆ **string together** *vt sep* [words] encadenar.

string bean *n* judía *f* verde, chaucha *f R Plata*, vainita *f Ven*, poroto *m* verde *Chile*, habichuela *f Col*.

stringed instrument ['strɪŋd-] *n* instrumento *m* de cuerda.

stringent ['strɪndʒənt] *adj* estricto(ta), severo(ra).

strip [strɪp] ◇ *n* - **1.** [narrow piece] tira *f*; **to tear a strip off sb, to tear sb off a strip** UK echarle una bronca a alguien - **2.** [narrow area] franja *f* - **3.** UK SPORT camiseta *f*, colores *mpl*. ◇ *vt* - **1.** [undress] desnudar - **2.** [paint, wallpaper] quitar. ◇ *vi* [undress] desnudarse. ◆ **strip off** *vi* desnudarse.

strip cartoon *n* UK historieta *f*, tira *f* cómica.

stripe [straɪp] *n* - **1.** [band of colour] raya *f*, franja *f* - **2.** [sign of rank] galón *m*.

striped [straɪpt] *adj* a rayas.

strip lighting n alumbrado m fluorescente.

stripper ['strɪpər] n - 1. [performer of striptease] artista mf de striptease - 2. [for paint] disolvente m.

striptease ['striptiːz] n striptease m.

strive [straɪv] (pt strove, pp striven ['strɪvn]) vi fml: **to strive for sthg** luchar por algo; **to strive to do sthg** esforzarse por hacer algo.

strode [strəʊd] pt ⊳ **stride**.

stroke [strəʊk] ◇ n - 1. MED apoplejía f, derrame m cerebral - 2. [of pen] trazo m; [of brush] pincelada f - 3. [style of swimming] estilo m - 4. [in tennis, golf etc] golpe m - 5. [of clock] campanada f - 6. UK TYPO [oblique] barra f - 7. [piece]: **a stroke of genius** una genialidad; **a stroke of luck** un golpe de suerte; **at a stroke** de una vez, de golpe. ◇ vt acariciar.

stroll [strəʊl] ◇ n paseo m; **to go for a stroll** dar un paseo. ◇ vi pasear.

stroller ['strəʊlər] n US [for baby] sillita f (de niño).

strong [strɒŋ] adj - 1. [gen] fuerte; **to be still going strong** [person] conservarse bien; [group] seguir en la brecha; [object] estar todavía en forma - 2. [material, structure] sólido(da), resistente - 3. [feeling, belief] profundo(da); [opposition, denial] firme; [support] acérrimo(ma); [accent] marcado(da) - 4. [discipline, policy] estricto(ta) - 5. [argument] convincente - 6. [in numbers]: **the crowd was 2,000 strong** la multitud constaba de 2.000 personas - 7. [good, gifted]: **one's strong point** el punto fuerte de uno - 8. [concentrated] concentrado(da).

strongbox ['strɒŋbɒks] n caja f fuerte.

stronghold ['strɒŋhəʊld] n fig [bastion] bastión m, baluarte m.

strongly ['strɒŋlɪ] adv - 1. [sturdily] fuertemente - 2. [in degree] intensamente - 3. [fervently]: **to support/oppose sthg strongly** apoyar/oponerse a algo totalmente; **I feel very strongly about that** eso me preocupa muchísimo.

strong room n cámara f acorazada.

strove [strəʊv] pt ⊳ **strive**.

struck [strʌk] pt & pp ⊳ **strike**.

structure ['strʌktʃər] n - 1. [arrangement] estructura f - 2. [building] construcción f.

struggle ['strʌgl] ◇ n - 1. [great effort]: **struggle (for sthg/to do sthg)** lucha f (por algo/por hacer algo) - 2. [fight, tussle] forcejeo m. ◇ vi - 1. [make great effort]: **to struggle (for sthg/to do sthg)** luchar (por algo/por hacer algo) - 2. [to free o.s.]: **to struggle free** forcejear para soltarse.

strum [strʌm] vt & vi rasguear.

strung [strʌŋ] pt & pp ⊳ **string**.

strut [strʌt] ◇ n CONSTR puntal m. ◇ vi andar pavoneándose.

stub [stʌb] ◇ n - 1. [of cigarette] colilla f; [of pencil] cabo m - 2. [of ticket] resguardo m; [of cheque] matriz f. ◇ vt: **to stub one's toe on** darse con el pie en. ◆ **stub out** vt sep apagar.

stubble ['stʌbl] n - 1. (U) [in field] rastrojo m - 2. [on chin] barba f incipiente OR de tres días.

stubborn ['stʌbən] adj [person] terco(ca), testarudo(da).

stuck [stʌk] ◇ pt & pp ⊳ **stick**. ◇ adj - 1. [jammed - lid, window] atascado(da) - 2. [unable to progress] atascado(da) - 3. [stranded] colgado(da) - 4. [in a meeting, at home] encerrado(da).

stuck-up adj inf pej engreído(da).

stud [stʌd] n - 1. [metal decoration] tachón m - 2. [earring] pendiente m - 3. UK [on boot, shoe] taco m - 4. [horse] semental m.

studded ['stʌdɪd] adj: **studded (with)** tachonado(da) (con).

student ['stjuːdnt] ◇ n - 1. [at college, university] estudiante mf - 2. [scholar] estudioso m, -sa f. ◇ comp estudiantil.

studio ['stjuːdɪəʊ] (pl -s) n estudio m.

studio flat UK, **studio apartment** US n estudio m.

studious ['stjuːdjəs] adj estudioso(sa).

studiously ['stjuːdjəslɪ] adv cuidadosamente.

study ['stʌdɪ] ◇ n estudio m. ◇ vt - 1. [learn] estudiar - 2. [examine - report, sb's face] examinar, estudiar. ◇ vi estudiar. ◆ **studies** npl estudios mpl.

stuff [stʌf] ◇ n (U) inf - 1. [things, belongings] cosas fpl - 2. [substance]: **what's that stuff in your pocket?** ¿qué es eso que llevas en el bolsillo? ◇ vt - 1. [push, put] meter - 2. [fill, cram]: **to stuff sthg (with)** [box, room] llenar algo (de); [pillow, doll] rellenar algo (de) - 3. CULIN rellenar.

stuffed [stʌft] adj - 1. [filled, crammed]: **stuffed with** atestado(da) de - 2. inf [person - with food] lleno(na), inflado(da) - 3. CULIN relleno(na) - 4. [preserved - animal] disecado(da).

stuffing ['stʌfɪŋ] n (U) relleno m.

stuffy ['stʌfɪ] adj - 1. [atmosphere] cargado(da); [room] mal ventilado(da) - 2. [old-fashioned] retrógrado(da), carca.

stumble ['stʌmbl] vi [trip] tropezar. ◆ **stumble across, stumble on** vt insep [thing] dar con; [person] encontrarse con.

stumbling block ['stʌmblɪŋ-] n obstáculo m, escollo m.

stump [stʌmp] ◇ n [of tree] tocón m; [of limb] muñón m. ◇ vt - 1. [question, problem] dejar perplejo(ja); **I'm stumped** no tengo ni idea; **he was stumped for an answer** no sabía qué contestar - 2. US POL [constituency, state] recorrer en campaña electoral.

stun [stʌn] *vt lit* & *fig* aturdir.

▉▉▉▉▉▉ ▐▐ ▐▐▐ ▐▐ ▐▐ ▐▐▐ ▐ ▪ ▪ ▐▐▐▐▐

stunk [stʌŋk] *pt* & *pp* ⊳ **stink**.

stunning ['stʌnɪŋ] *adj* - 1. [very beautiful] imponente - 2. [shocking] pasmoso(sa).

stunt [stʌnt] ⟨⟩ *n* - 1. [for publicity] truco *m* publicitario - 2. CIN escena *f* arriesgada OR peligrosa. ⟨⟩ *vt* atrofiar.

stunted ['stʌntɪd] *adj* esmirriado(da).

stunt man *n* especialista *m*, doble *m*.

stupefy ['stju:pɪfaɪ] *vt* - 1. [tire, bore] aturdir, atontar - 2. [surprise] dejar estupefacto(ta).

stupendous [stju:'pendəs] *adj inf* [wonderful] estupendo(da); [very large] enorme.

stupid ['stju:pɪd] *adj* - 1. [foolish] estúpido(da) - 2. *inf* [annoying] puñetero(ra).

stupidity [stju:'pɪdətɪ] *n* (U) estupidez *f*.

sturdy ['stɜ:dɪ] *adj* [person, shoulders] fuerte; [furniture, bridge] firme, sólido(da).

stutter ['stʌtər] ⟨⟩ *vi* tartamudear. ⟨⟩ *vt* decir tartamudeando.

sty [staɪ] *n* [pigsty] pocilga *f*.

stye [staɪ] *n* orzuelo *m*.

style [staɪl] ⟨⟩ *n* - 1. [characteristic manner] estilo *m* - 2. (U) [smartness, elegance] clase *f* - 3. [design] modelo *m*. ⟨⟩ *vt* [hair] peinar.

stylish ['staɪlɪʃ] *adj* elegante, con estilo.

stylist ['staɪlɪst] *n* [hairdresser] peluquero *m*, -ra *f*.

stylus ['staɪləs] (*pl* -es) *n* [on record player] aguja *f*.

suave [swɑ:v] *adj* [well-mannered] afable, amable; [obsequious] zalamero(ra).

sub [sʌb] *n inf* SPORT (*abbr of* **substitute**) reserva *mf*.

subconscious [,sʌb'kɒnʃəs] *adj* subconsciente.

subcontract [,sʌbkən'trækt] *vt* subcontratar.

subdivide [,sʌbdɪ'vaɪd] *vt* subdividir.

subdue [səb'dju:] *vt* - 1. [enemy, nation] sojuzgar - 2. [feelings] contener.

subdued [səb'dju:d] *adj* - 1. [person] apagado(da) - 2. [colour, light] tenue.

subject ⟨⟩ *adj* ['sʌbdʒekt] [affected]: **subject to** [taxes, changes, law] sujeto(ta) a; [illness] proclive a. ⟨⟩ *n* ['sʌbdʒekt] - 1. [topic] tema *m*; **don't change the subject** no cambies de tema - 2. GRAM sujeto *m* - 3. SCH & UNIV asignatura *f* - 4. [citizen] súbdito *m*, -ta *f*. ⟨⟩ *vt* [səb'dʒekt] [bring under control] someter, dominar. **⬗ subject to** *prep* dependiendo de.

subjective [səb'dʒektɪv] *adj* subjetivo(va).

subject matter ['sʌbdʒekt-] *n* (U) tema *m*, contenido *m*.

subjunctive [səb'dʒʌŋktɪv] *n* GRAM: **subjunctive (mood)** (modo *m*) subjuntivo *m*.

sublet [,sʌb'let] (*pt* & *pp* **sublet**) *vt* & *vi* subarrendar.

sublime [sə'blaɪm] *adj* [wonderful] sublime.

submachine gun [,sʌbmə'ʃi:n-] *n* metralleta *f*.

submarine [,sʌbmə'ri:n] *n* - 1. submarino *m* - 2. US [sandwich] bocadillo OR sandwich hecho con una barra de pan larga y estrecha.

submerge [səb'mɜ:dʒ] ⟨⟩ *vt* - 1. [in water] sumergir - 2. *fig* [in activity]: **to submerge o.s. in sthg** dedicarse de lleno a algo. ⟨⟩ *vi* sumergirse.

submission [səb'mɪʃn] *n* - 1. [capitulation] sumisión *f* - 2. [presentation] presentación *f*.

submissive [səb'mɪsɪv] *adj* sumiso(sa).

submit [səb'mɪt] ⟨⟩ *vt* presentar. ⟨⟩ *vi*: **to submit (to sb)** rendirse (a alguien); **to submit (to sthg)** someterse (a algo).

subnormal [,sʌb'nɔ:ml] *adj* subnormal.

subordinate [sə'bɔ:dɪnət] ⟨⟩ *adj fml* [less important]: **subordinate (to)** subordinado(da) (a). ⟨⟩ *n* subordinado *m*, -da *f*.

subpoena [sə'pi:nə] ⟨⟩ *n* LAW citación *f*. ⟨⟩ *vt* LAW citar.

subscribe [səb'skraɪb] *vi* - 1. [to magazine, newspaper]: **to subscribe (to)** suscribirse (a) - 2. [to belief]: **to subscribe to** estar de acuerdo con.

subscriber [səb'skraɪbər] *n* - 1. [to magazine, newspaper] suscriptor *m*, -ra *f* - 2. [to service] abonado *m*, -da *f*.

subscription [səb'skrɪpʃn] *n* [to magazine] suscripción *f*; [to service] abono *m*; [to society, club] cuota *f*; **to take out a subscription to sthg** suscribirse a algo.

subsequent ['sʌbsɪkwənt] *adj* subsiguiente, posterior; **subsequent to this** con posterioridad a esto.

subsequently ['sʌbsɪkwəntlɪ] *adv* posteriormente.

subservient [səb'sɜ:vjənt] *adj* [servile]: **subservient (to sb)** servil (ante alguien).

subside [səb'saɪd] *vi* - 1. [anger] apaciguarse; [pain] calmarse; [grief] pasarse; [storm, wind] amainar - 2. [noise] apagarse - 3. [river] bajar, descender; [building, ground] hundirse.

subsidence [səb'saɪdns, 'sʌbsɪdns] *n* CONSTR hundimiento *m*.

subsidiary [səb'sɪdjərɪ] ⟨⟩ *adj* secundario(ria). ⟨⟩ *n*: **subsidiary (company)** filial *f*.

subsidize, -ise ['sʌbsɪdaɪz] *vt* subvencionar.

subsidy ['sʌbsɪdɪ] *n* subvención *f*.

substance ['sʌbstəns] *n* - 1. [gen] sustancia *f* - 2. [essence] esencia *f*.

substantial [səb'stænʃl] adj - 1. [large, considerable] sustancial, considerable; [meal] abundante - 2. [solid] sólido(da).

substantially [səb'stænʃəlɪ] adv - 1. [quite a lot] sustancialmente, considerablemente - 2. [fundamentally] esencialmente; [for the most part] en gran parte.

substantiate [səb'stænʃɪeɪt] vt fml justificar.

substitute ['sʌbstɪtjuːt] <> n - 1. [replacement]: **substitute (for)** sustituto m, -ta f (de) - 2. SPORT suplente mf, reserva mf. <> vt: **to substitute sthg/sb for** sustituir algo/a alguien por.

subtitle ['sʌbˌtaɪtl] n subtítulo m.

subtle ['sʌtl] adj - 1. [gen] sutil; [taste, smell] delicado(da) - 2. [plan, behaviour] ingenioso(sa).

subtlety ['sʌtltɪ] n - 1. [gen] sutileza f; [of taste, smell] delicadeza f - 2. [of plan, behaviour] ingenio m.

subtract [səb'trækt] vt: **to subtract sthg (from)** restar algo (de).

subtraction [səb'trækʃn] n resta f.

suburb ['sʌbɜːb] n barrio m residencial. **suburbs** npl: **the suburbs** las afueras.

suburban [sə'bɜːbn] adj - 1. [of suburbs] de los barrios residenciales - 2. pej [boring] convencional, burgués(esa).

suburbia [sə'bɜːbɪə] n (U) barrios mpl residenciales.

subversive [səb'vɜːsɪv] <> adj subversivo(va). <> n subversivo m, -va f.

subway ['sʌbweɪ] n - 1. UK [underground walkway] paso m subterráneo - 2. US [underground railway] metro m, subte(rráneo) m R Plata.

succeed [sək'siːd] <> vt suceder a; **to succeed sb to the throne** suceder a alguien en el trono. <> vi - 1. [gen] tener éxito - 2. [achieve desired result]: **to succeed in sthg/in doing sthg** conseguir algo/hacer algo - 3. [plan, tactic] salir bien - 4. [go far in life] triunfar.

success [sək'ses] n - 1. [gen] éxito m; **to be a success** tener éxito - 2. [in career, life] triunfo m.

successful [sək'sesful] adj [gen] de éxito; [attempt] logrado(da).

succession [sək'seʃn] n sucesión f; **to follow in quick OR close succession** sucederse rápidamente.

successive [sək'sesɪv] adj sucesivo(va); **he won on 3 successive years** ganó durante tres años consecutivos.

succinct [sək'sɪŋkt] adj sucinto(ta).

succumb [sə'kʌm] vi: **to succumb (to)** sucumbir (a).

such [sʌtʃ] <> adj - 1. [like that] semejante, tal; **such stupidity** tal OR semejante estupidez;

there's no such thing no existe nada semejante - 2. [like this]: **have you got such a thing as a tin opener?** ¿tendrías acaso un abrelatas?; **such words as 'duty' and 'honour'** palabras (tales) como 'deber' y 'honor' - 3. [whatever]: **I've spent such money as I had** he gastado el poco dinero que tenía - 4. [so great, so serious]: **there are such differences that...** las diferencias son tales que...; **such... that...** tal... que. <> adv tan; **such a lot of books** tantos libros; **such nice people** una gente tan amable; **such a good car** un coche tan bueno; **such a long time** tanto tiempo. <> pron: **and such (like)** y otros similares OR por el estilo. **as such** pron propiamente dicho(cha). **such and such** adj: **at such and such a time** a tal hora.

suck [sʌk] <> vt - 1. [by mouth] chupar - 2. [machine] aspirar. <> vi US v inf [be bad] [book, film]: **that really sucks!** ¡es una mierda!

sucker ['sʌkər] n - 1. [of animal] ventosa f - 2. inf [gullible person] primo m, -ma f, ingenuo m, -nua f; **to be a sucker for punishment** ser un masoquista.

suction ['sʌkʃn] n [gen] succión f; [by machine] aspiración f.

Sudan [suː'dɑːn] n (el) Sudán.

sudden ['sʌdn] adj [quick] repentino(na); [unforeseen] inesperado(da); **all of a sudden** de repente.

suddenly ['sʌdnlɪ] adv de repente.

suds [sʌdz] npl espuma f del jabón.

sue [suː] vt: **to sue sb (for)** demandar a alguien (por).

suede [sweɪd] n [for jacket, shoes] ante m; [for gloves] cabritilla f.

suet ['suɪt] n sebo m.

suffer ['sʌfər] <> vt sufrir. <> vi - 1. [gen] sufrir - 2. [experience negative effects] salir perjudicado(da) - 3. MED: **to suffer from** [illness] sufrir OR padecer de,

sufferer ['sʌfrər] n enfermo m, -ma f; **cancer sufferer** enfermo de cáncer; **hay fever sufferer** persona que padece fiebre del heno.

suffering ['sʌfrɪŋ] n [gen] sufrimiento m; [pain] dolor m.

suffice [sə'faɪs] vi fml ser suficiente, bastar.

sufficient [sə'fɪʃnt] adj fml suficiente, bastante.

sufficiently [sə'fɪʃntlɪ] adv fml suficientemente, bastante.

suffocate ['sʌfəkeɪt] <> vt asfixiar, ahogar. <> vi asfixiarse, ahogarse.

suffrage ['sʌfrɪdʒ] n sufragio m.

suffuse [sə'fjuːz] vt: **suffused with** bañado de.

sugar ['ʃugər] <> n azúcar m o f. <> vt echar azúcar a.

sugar beet n remolacha f (azucarera).

sugarcane ['ʃʊgəkeɪn] n (U) caña f de azúcar.

sugary ['ʃʊgərɪ] adj [high in sugar] azucarado(da), dulce.

suggest [sə'dʒest] vt - 1. [propose] sugerir; **to suggest doing sthg** sugerir hacer algo - 2. [imply] insinuar.

suggestion [sə'dʒestʃn] n - 1. [proposal] sugerencia f - 2. [implication] insinuación f; **there was no suggestion of murder** no había nada que indicara que fuera un asesinato.

suggestive [sə'dʒestɪv] adj [implying sexual connotation] provocativo(va), insinuante.

suicide ['su:ɪsaɪd] n lit & fig suicidio m; **to commit suicide** suicidarse.

suit [su:t] <> n - 1. [clothes - for men] traje m; [- for women] traje de chaqueta - 2. [in cards] palo m - 3. LAW pleito m. <> vt - 1. [look attractive on] favorecer, sentar bien a; **it suits you** te favorece, te sienta bien - 2. [be convenient or agreeable to] convenir; **that suits me fine** por mí, estupendo - 3. [be appropriate to] ser adecuado(da) para; **that job suits you perfectly** ese trabajo te va de perlas.

suitable ['su:təbl] adj adecuado(da); **the most suitable person** la persona más indicada.

suitably ['su:təblɪ] adv adecuadamente.

suitcase ['su:tkeɪs] n maleta f, petaca f Méx, valija f R Plata.

suite [swi:t] n - 1. [of rooms] suite f - 2. [of furniture] juego m; **dining-room suite** comedor m.

suited ['su:tɪd] adj: **suited to/for** adecuado(da) para; **the couple are ideally suited** forman una pareja perfecta.

suitor ['su:tər] n dated pretendiente m.

sulfur US = **sulphur**.

sulk [sʌlk] vi estar de mal humor.

sulky ['sʌlkɪ] adj malhumorado(da).

sullen ['sʌlən] adj hosco(ca), antipático(ca).

sulphur UK, **sulfur** US ['sʌlfər] n azufre m.

sultana [səl'tɑ:nə] n UK [dried grape] pasa f de Esmirna.

sultry ['sʌltrɪ] adj [hot] bochornoso(sa), sofocante.

sum [sʌm] n suma f. **◆ sum up** vt sep & vi [summarize] resumir.

summarize, -ise ['sʌməraɪz] vt & vi resumir.

summary ['sʌmərɪ] n resumen m.

summer ['sʌmər] <> n verano m. <> comp de verano.

summerhouse ['sʌməhaʊs, pl -haʊzɪz] n cenador m.

summer school n escuela f de verano.

summertime ['sʌmətaɪm] n: **(the) summertime** (el) verano.

summit ['sʌmɪt] n - 1. [mountain-top] cima f, cumbre f - 2. [meeting] cumbre f.

summon ['sʌmən] vt [person] llamar; [meeting, council] ▬ **summon up** vt sep [courage] armarse de; **to summon up the strength to do sthg** reunir fuerzas para hacer algo.

summons ['sʌmənz] <> n (pl summonses) LAW citación f. <> vt LAW citar.

sump [sʌmp] n cárter m.

sumptuous ['sʌmptʃʊəs] adj suntuoso(sa).

sun [sʌn] n sol m; **in the sun** al sol; **everything under the sun** todo lo habido y por haber.

sunbathe ['sʌnbeɪð] vi tomar el sol.

sunbed ['sʌnbed] n camilla f de rayos ultravioletas.

sunburn ['sʌnbɜːn] n (U) quemadura f de sol.

sunburned ['sʌnbɜːnd], **sunburnt** ['sʌnbɜːnt] adj quemado(da) por el sol.

Sunday ['sʌndɪ] n domingo m; **Sunday lunch** comida del domingo que generalmente consiste en carne asada, patatas asadas etc; see also **Saturday**.

Sunday school n catequesis f inv.

sundial ['sʌndaɪəl] n reloj m de sol.

sundown ['sʌndaʊn] n anochecer m.

sundries ['sʌndrɪz] npl fml [gen] artículos mpl diversos; FIN gastos mpl diversos.

sundry ['sʌndrɪ] adj fml diversos(sas); **all and sundry** todos sin excepción.

sunflower ['sʌn,flaʊər] n girasol m.

sung [sʌŋ] pp ▷ **sing**.

sunglasses ['sʌn,glɑːsɪz] npl gafas fpl de sol.

sunk [sʌŋk] pp ▷ **sink**.

sunlight ['sʌnlaɪt] n luz f del sol; **in direct sunlight** a la luz directa del sol.

sunny ['sʌnɪ] adj - 1. [day] de sol; [room] soleado(da) - 2. [cheerful] alegre.

sunrise ['sʌnraɪz] n - 1. (U) [time of day] amanecer m - 2. [event] salida f del sol.

sunroof ['sʌnruːf] n [on car] techo m corredizo; [on building] azotea f.

sunset ['sʌnset] n - 1. (U) [time of day] anochecer m - 2. [event] puesta f del sol.

sunshade ['sʌnʃeɪd] n sombrilla f.

sunshine ['sʌnʃaɪn] n (luz f del) sol m.

sunstroke ['sʌnstrəʊk] n (U) insolación f; **to get sunstroke** coger una insolación.

suntan ['sʌntæn] <> n bronceado m; **to have a suntan** estar bronceado(da); **to get a suntan** broncearse. <> comp [lotion, cream] bronceador(ra).

suntrap ['sʌntræp] n lugar m muy soleado.

super ['su:pər] <> adj - 1. inf [wonderful] estupendo(da), fenomenal - 2. [better than normal - size etc] superior. <> n US inf [of apartment building] portero m, -ra f.

superannuation [ˌsuːpəˌrænjʊ'eɪʃn] n (U) jubilación f, pensión f.

superb [suː'pɜːb] adj excelente, magnífico(ca).

supercilious [ˌsuːpə'sɪlɪəs] adj altanero(ra).

superficial [ˌsuːpə'fɪʃl] adj superficial.

superfluous [suː'pɜːflʊəs] adj superfluo(flua).

superhuman [ˌsuːpə'hjuːmən] adj sobrehumano(na).

superimpose [ˌsuːpərɪm'pəʊz] vt: to superimpose sthg on superponer OR sobreponer algo a.

superintendent [ˌsuːpərɪn'tendənt] n - 1. UK [of police] ≃ subjefe m (de policía) - 2. fml [of department] supervisor m, -ra f - 3. US inf [of apartment building] portero m, -ra f.

superior [suː'pɪərɪəʳ] ◇ adj - 1. [gen]: superior (to) superior (a) - 2. pej [arrogant] altanero(ra), arrogante. ◇ n superior mf.

superlative [suː'pɜːlətɪv] ◇ adj [of the highest quality] supremo(ma). ◇ n GRAM superlativo m.

supermarket ['suːpəˌmɑːkɪt] n supermercado m.

supernatural [ˌsuːpə'nætʃrəl] adj sobrenatural.

superpower ['suːpəˌpaʊəʳ] n superpotencia f.

supersede [ˌsuːpə'siːd] vt suplantar.

supersonic [ˌsuːpə'sɒnɪk] adj supersónico(ca).

superstitious [ˌsuːpə'stɪʃəs] adj supersticioso(sa).

superstore ['suːpəstɔːʳ] n hipermercado m.

supertanker ['suːpəˌtæŋkəʳ] n superpetrolero m.

supervise ['suːpəvaɪz] vt [person] vigilar; [activity] supervisar.

supervisor ['suːpəvaɪzəʳ] n [gen] supervisor m, -ra f; [of thesis] director m, -ra f.

supper ['sʌpəʳ] n [evening meal] cena f.

supple ['sʌpl] adj flexible.

supplement ◇ n ['sʌplɪmənt] suplemento m. ◇ vt ['sʌplɪment] complementar.

supplementary [ˌsʌplɪ'mentərɪ] adj suplementario(ria).

supplier [sə'plaɪəʳ] n proveedor m, -ra f.

supply [sə'plaɪ] ◇ n - 1. [gen] suministro m; [of jokes etc] surtido m - 2. (U) ECON oferta f; supply and demand la oferta y la demanda. ◇ vt: to supply sthg (to) suministrar OR proveer algo (a); to supply sthg with sthg suministrar a algo de algo. ➠ **supplies** npl MIL pertrechos mpl; [food] provisiones fpl; [for office etc] material m.

support [sə'pɔːt] ◇ n - 1. (U) [physical, moral, emotional] apoyo m; in support of en apoyo de - 2. (U) [financial] ayuda f - 3. (U) [intellectual] respaldo m - 4. TECH soporte m. ◇ vt - 1. [physically] sostener - 2. [emotionally, morally, intellectually] apoyar - 3. [financially - oneself, one's family] mantener; [- company, organization] financiar; to support o.s. ganarse la vida - 4. SPORT seguir.

supporter [sə'pɔːtəʳ] n - 1. [gen] partidario m, -ria f - 2. SPORT hincha mf.

support group n grupo m de apoyo.

suppose [sə'pəʊz] ◇ vt suponer. ◇ vi suponer; I suppose (so) supongo (que sí); I suppose not supongo que no.

supposed [sə'pəʊzd] adj - 1. [doubtful] supuesto(ta) - 2. [intended]: he was supposed to be here at eight debería haber estado aquí a las ocho - 3. [reputed]: it's supposed to be very good se supone OR se dice que es muy bueno.

supposedly [sə'pəʊzɪdlɪ] adv según cabe suponer.

supposing [sə'pəʊzɪŋ] conj: supposing your father found out? ¿y si se entera tu padre?

suppress [sə'pres] vt - 1. [uprising] reprimir - 2. [emotions] contener.

supreme [sʊ'priːm] adj supremo(ma).

Supreme Court n: the Supreme Court [in US] el Tribunal Supremo (de los Estados Unidos).

surcharge ['sɜːtʃɑːdʒ] n: surcharge (on) recargo m (en).

sure [ʃʊəʳ] ◇ adj - 1. [gen] seguro(ra); I'm not sure why he said that no estoy seguro de por qué dijo eso - 2. [certain - of outcome]: to be sure of poder estar seguro(ra) de; make sure (that) you do it asegúrate de que lo haces - 3. [confident]: to be sure of o.s. estar seguro(ra) de uno mismo. ◇ adv - 1. esp US inf [yes] por supuesto, pues claro - 2. US [really] realmente. ➠ for sure adv a ciencia cierta; I don't know for sure no lo sé con total seguridad. ➠ sure enough adv efectivamente.

surely ['ʃʊəlɪ] adv sin duda; surely you remember him? ¡no me digas que no te acuerdas de él!

surety ['ʃʊərətɪ] n (U) fianza f.

surf [sɜːf] ◇ n espuma f (de las olas). ◇ vt COMPUT: to surf the Net navegar por Internet.

surface ['sɜːfɪs] ◇ n - 1. [gen] superficie f - 2. fig [immediately visible part]: on the surface a primera vista; below OR beneath the surface debajo de las apariencias. ◇ vi [gen] salir a la superficie.

surface mail n correo m por vía terrestre/marítima.

surfboard ['sɜːfbɔːd] n plancha f OR tabla f de surf.

surfeit ['sɜːfɪt] n fml exceso m.

surfing ['sɜ:fɪŋ] *n* surf *m*.

surge [sɜ:dʒ] <> *n* - 1. [of waves, people] oleada *f*; [of electricity] sobrecarga *f* momentánea - 2. [of emotion] arrebato *m* - 3. [of interest, support, sales] aumento *m* súbito. <> *vi* [people, vehicles] avanzar en masa; [sea] encresparse; **the angry mob surged forward** la multitud encolerizada avanzó en tropel.

surgeon ['sɜ:dʒən] *n* cirujano *m*, -na *f*.

surgery ['sɜ:dʒərɪ] *n* - 1. *(U)* MED [performing operations] cirugía *f* - 2. UK MED [place] consultorio *m*; [consulting period] consulta *f*.

surgical ['sɜ:dʒɪkl] *adj* [gen] quirúrgico(ca).

surgical spirit *n* UK alcohol *m* de 90°.

surly ['sɜ:lɪ] *adj* hosco(ca), malhumorado(da).

surmount [sɜ:'maʊnt] *vt* [overcome] superar, vencer.

surname ['sɜ:neɪm] *n* apellido *m*.

surpass [sə'pɑ:s] *vt fml* [exceed] superar, sobrepasar.

surplus ['sɜ:pləs] <> *adj* excedente, sobrante. <> *n* [gen] excedente *m*, sobrante *m*; [in budget] superávit *m*.

surprise [sə'praɪz] <> *n* sorpresa *f*; **to take sb by surprise** coger a alguien desprevenido. <> *vt* sorprender.

surprised [sə'praɪzd] *adj* [person, expression] asombrado(da); **we were really surprised** nos quedamos sorprendidos; **I'm surprised you're still here** me sorprende que todavía estés aquí; **she was surprised to find the house empty** se sorprendió al encontrar la casa vacía.

surprising [sə'praɪzɪŋ] *adj* sorprendente.

surrender [sə'rendər] <> *n* rendición *f*. <> *vi lit & fig*: **to surrender (to)** rendirse OR entregarse (a).

surreptitious [ˌsʌrəp'tɪʃəs] *adj* subrepticio(cia).

surrogate ['sʌrəgeɪt] <> *adj* sustitutorio(ria). <> *n* sustituto *m*, -ta *f*.

surrogate mother *n* madre *f* de alquiler.

surround [sə'raʊnd] *vt lit & fig* rodear; **to be surrounded by** estar rodeado(da) de.

surrounding [sə'raʊndɪŋ] *adj* - 1. [area, countryside] circundante - 2. [controversy, debate] relacionado(da).

surroundings [sə'raʊndɪŋz] *npl* [physical] alrededores *mpl*; [social] entorno *m*.

surveillance [sɜ:'veɪləns] *n* vigilancia *f*.

survey <> *n* ['sɜ:veɪ] - 1. [of public opinion, population] encuesta *f* - 2. [of land] medición *f*; [of building] inspección *f*. <> *vt* [sə'veɪ] - 1. [contemplate] contemplar - 2. [investigate statistically] hacer un estudio de - 3. [examine - land] medir; [- building] inspeccionar.

surveyor [sə'veɪər] *n* [of property] perito *m* tasador de la propiedad; [of land] agrimensor *m*, -ra *f*.

survival [sə'vaɪvl] *n* [gen] supervivencia *f*.

survive [sə'vaɪv] <> *vt* sobrevivir a. <> *vi* - 1. [person] sobrevivir; **how are you? – surviving** ¿cómo estás? – voy tirando - 2. [custom, project] perdurar.

survivor [sə'vaɪvər] *n* [person who escapes death] superviviente *mf*; **there were no survivors** no hubo supervivientes.

susceptible [sə'septəbl] *adj* - 1. [to pressure, flattery]: **susceptible (to)** sensible (a) - 2. MED: **susceptible (to)** propenso(sa) (a).

suspect <> *adj* ['sʌspekt] sospechoso(sa). <> *n* ['sʌspekt] sospechoso *m*, -sa *f*. <> *vt* [sə'spekt] - 1. [distrust] sospechar - 2. [think likely] imaginar; **I suspect he's right** imagino que tiene razón - 3. [consider guilty]: **to suspect sb (of)** considerar a alguien sospechoso(sa) (de). ➡ **suspected** *pp*: **to have a suspected heart attack** haber sufrido un posible infarto; **the suspected culprits** los presuntos culpables.

suspend [sə'spend] *vt* [gen] suspender; [payments, work] interrumpir; [schoolchild] expulsar temporalmente.

suspended sentence [sə'spendɪd-] *n* condena *f* condicional.

suspender belt [sə'spendər-] *n* UK liguero *m*.

suspenders [sə'spendəz] *npl* - 1. UK [for stockings] ligas *fpl* - 2. US [for trousers] tirantes *mpl*, tiradores *mpl* Bol & R Plata, suspensores *mpl* Andes & Arg.

suspense [sə'spens] *n* [gen] incertidumbre *f*; CIN suspense *m*; **to keep sb in suspense** mantener a alguien en vilo.

suspension [sə'spenʃn] *n* - 1. [gen & AUT] suspensión *f* - 2. [from job, school] expulsión *f* temporal.

suspension bridge *n* puente *m* colgante.

suspicion [sə'spɪʃn] *n* - 1. [gen] sospecha *f*; [distrust] recelo *m*; **on suspicion of** bajo sospecha de; **to be under suspicion** estar bajo sospecha; **to arouse suspicion** levantar sospechas - 2. [small amount] pizca *f*.

suspicious [sə'spɪʃəs] *adj* - 1. [having suspicions] receloso(sa) - 2. [causing suspicion] sospechoso(sa).

sustain [sə'steɪn] *vt* - 1. [gen] sostener - 2. *fml* [injury, damage] sufrir.

sustenance ['sʌstɪnəns] *n (U) fml* sustento *m*.

SW (*abbr of* short wave) OC.

swab [swɒb] *n* (trozo *m* de) algodón *m*.

swagger ['swægər] *vi* pavonearse.

Swahili [swɑ:'hi:lɪ] *n* suahili *m*.

swallow ['swɒləʊ] <> *n* [bird] golondrina *f.* <> *vt* [food, drink] tragar. <> **swallow up** *vt sep* [salary, time] tragarse.

swam [swæm] *pt* ▷ **swim**.

swamp [swɒmp] <> *n* pantano *m*, ciénaga *f.* <> *vt* - **1.** [flood - boat] hundir; [- land] inundar - **2.** [overwhelm]: **to swamp sthg (with)** [office] inundar algo (de); **to swamp sb (with)** agobiar a alguien (con); **we were swamped with applications** nos vimos inundados de solicitudes.

swan [swɒn] *n* cisne *m.*

swap [swɒp], **swop** *vt* - **1.** [of one thing]: **to swap sthg (for/with)** cambiar algo (por/con) - **2.** *fig* [stories, experiences] intercambiar.

swarm [swɔ:m] <> *n* [of bees] enjambre *m; fig* [of people] multitud *f.* <> *vi* - **1.** *fig* [people] ir en tropel - **2.** *fig* [place]: **to be swarming (with)** estar abarrotado(da) (de).

swarthy ['swɔ:ðɪ] *adj* moreno(na).

swastika ['swɒstɪkə] *n* esvástica *f*, cruz *f* gamada.

swat [swɒt] *vt* aplastar.

sway [sweɪ] <> *vt* [influence] convencer. <> *vi* balancearse.

swear [sweəʳ] <> *vt* (*pt* swore, *pp* sworn): **I could have sworn I saw him** juraría que lo vi. <> *vi* (*pt* swore, *pp* sworn) - **1.** [state emphatically] jurar; **I couldn't swear to it** no me atrevería a jurarlo - **2.** [use swearwords] decir tacos, jurar; **to swear at sb** insultar a alguien.

swearword ['sweəwɜ:d] *n* palabrota *f.*

sweat [swet] <> *n* [perspiration] sudor *m.* <> *vi* [perspire] sudar. <> *vt* - **1.** MED: **to sweat out a cold** quitarse un resfriado sudando - **2.** [in difficult situation]: **to sweat it out** aguantar.

sweater ['swetəʳ] *n* suéter *m*, jersey *m.*

sweatshirt ['swetʃɜ:t] *n* sudadera *f.*

sweaty ['swetɪ] *adj* [skin] sudoroso(sa); [clothes] sudado(da).

swede [swi:d] *n UK* nabo *m* sueco.

Swede [swi:d] *n* sueco *m*, -ca *f.*

Sweden ['swi:dn] *n* Suecia.

Swedish ['swi:dɪʃ] <> *adj* sueco(ca). <> *n* [language] sueco *m.* <> *npl*: **the Swedish** los suecos.

sweep [swi:p] <> *n* [movement - of broom] barrido *m;* [- of arm, hand] movimiento *m OR* gesto *m* amplio. <> *vt* (*pt & pp* swept) - **1.** [with brush] barrer - **2.** [with light-beam] rastrear; [with eyes] recorrer. <> *vi* (*pt & pp* swept) - **1.** [wind, rain]: **to sweep over OR across sthg** azotar algo - **2.** [person]: **to sweep past** pasar como un rayo. <> **sweep away** *vt sep* [destroy] destruir completamente. <> **sweep up** *vt sep & vi* barrer.

sweeping ['swi:pɪŋ] *adj* - **1.** [effect, change] radical - **2.** [statement] demasiado general - **3.** [curve] amplio(plia) - **4.** [gesture] amplio(plia).

sweet [swi:t] <> *adj* - **1.** [gen] dulce; [sugary] azucarado(da) - **2.** [smell - of flowers, air] fragante, perfumado(da) - **3.** [sound] melodioso(sa) - **4.** [character, person] amable - **5.** *US inf* genial. <> *n UK* - **1.** [candy] caramelo *m*, golosina *f* - **2.** [dessert] postre *m.* <> *excl US inf* genial.

sweet corn *n* maíz *m.*

sweeten ['swi:tn] *vt* endulzar.

sweetheart ['swi:thɑ:t] *n* - **1.** [term of endearment] cariño *m* - **2.** [boyfriend or girlfriend] amor *m*, novio *m*, -via *f.*

sweetness ['swi:tnɪs] *n* - **1.** [gen] dulzura *f* - **2.** [of taste] dulzor *m.*

sweet pea *n* guisante *m* de olor, alverjilla *f Andes, Col & Ven*, chícharo *m* de olor *Amér C & Méx*, arvejilla *f R Plata*, clarín *m Chile.*

swell [swel] <> *vi* (*pp* swollen *OR* -ed) - **1.** [become larger]: **to swell (up)** hincharse - **2.** [population, sound] aumentar. <> *vt* (*pp* swollen *OR* -ed) [numbers etc] aumentar. <> *n* [of sea] oleaje *m.* <> *adj US inf* estupendo(da).

swelling ['swelɪŋ] *n* hinchazón *f;* **the swelling has gone down** ha bajado la hinchazón.

sweltering ['sweltərɪŋ] *adj* - **1.** [weather] abrasador(ra), sofocante - **2.** [person] achicharrado(da).

swept [swept] *pt & pp* ▷ **sweep**.

swerve [swɜ:v] *vi* virar bruscamente.

swift [swɪft] <> *adj* - **1.** [fast] rápido(da) - **2.** [prompt] pronto(ta). <> *n* [bird] vencejo *m.*

swig [swɪg] *inf n* trago *m;* **to take a swig of sthg** tomar un trago de algo.

swill [swɪl] <> *n* [pig food] bazofia *f.* <> *vt UK* [wash] enjuagar.

swim [swɪm] <> *n* baño *m;* **to go for a swim** ir a nadar *OR* a darse un baño. <> *vi* (*pt* swam, *pp* swum) - **1.** [in water] nadar - **2.** [head, room] dar vueltas. <> *vt* (*pt* swam, *pp* swum): **to swim the English Channel** cruzar el canal de la Mancha a nado; **I swam 20 lengths** nadé veinte largos.

swimmer ['swɪməʳ] *n* nadador *m*, -ra *f;* **she's a good swimmer** nada bien.

swimming ['swɪmɪŋ] *n* natación *f;* **to go swimming** ir a nadar.

swimming cap *n* gorro *m* de baño.

swimming costume *n UK* bañador *m*, traje *m* de baño.

swimming pool *n* piscina *f*, alberca *f Méx*, pileta *f R Plata.*

swimming trunks *npl* bañador *m.*

swimsuit ['swɪmsuːt] n bañador m Esp, traje m de baño, malla f R Plata, vestido m de baño Col.

swindle ['swɪndl] ◇ n estafa f, timo m. ◇ vt estafar, timar; **to swindle sb out of sthg** estafar a alguien algo.

swine [swaɪn] n inf pej [person] cerdo m, -da f, canalla mf.

swing [swɪŋ] ◇ n - 1. [child's toy] columpio m - 2. [change] viraje m; **a swing towards the Conservatives** un giro hacia los conservadores - 3. [sway] meneo m, balanceo m
▶▶ **to be in full swing** estar en plena marcha. ◇ vt (pt & pp swung) - 1. [move back and forth] balancear - 2. [move in a curve - car etc] hacer virar bruscamente. ◇ vi (pt & pp swung) - 1. [move back and forth] balancearse, oscilar - 2. [move in a curve] girar - 3. [turn]: **to swing (round)** volverse, girarse - 4. [change] virar, cambiar.

swing bridge n puente m giratorio.

swing door n puerta f oscilante.

swingeing ['swɪndʒɪŋ] adj esp UK severo(ra).

swipe [swaɪp] ◇ vt inf [steal] birlar. ◇ vi: **to swipe at sthg** intentar golpear algo.

swirl [swɜːl] vi arremolinarse.

swish [swɪʃ] vt [tail] agitar, menear.

Swiss [swɪs] ◇ adj suizo(za). ◇ n [person] suizo m, -za f. ◇ npl: **the Swiss** los suizos.

switch [swɪtʃ] ◇ n - 1. [control device] interruptor m - 2. [change] cambio m completo, viraje m. ◇ vt - 1. [change] cambiar de; **to switch one's attention to sthg** dirigir la atención a OR hacia algo - 2. [swap] intercambiar.
▶ **switch off** vt sep [light, radio etc] apagar; [engine] parar. ▶ **switch on** vt sep [light, radio etc] encender; [engine] poner en marcha.

Switch® [swɪtʃ] n UK tarjeta f de débito Switch®.

switchboard ['swɪtʃbɔːd] n centralita f, conmutador m Amér.

Switzerland ['swɪtsələnd] n Suiza.

swivel ['swɪvl] ◇ vt (UK pt & pp -led, cont -ling, US pt & pp -ed, cont -ing) hacer girar. ◇ vi (UK pt & pp -led, cont -ling, US pt & pp -ed, cont -ing) girar.

swivel chair n silla f giratoria.

swollen ['swəʊln] ◇ pp ▷ swell. ◇ adj - 1. [ankle, leg etc] hinchado(da); **my eyes were swollen** tenía los ojos hinchados - 2. [river] crecido(da).

swoop [swuːp] ◇ n [raid] redada f; **a swoop on a flat** una redada en un apartamento. ◇ vi - 1. [move downwards] caer en picado - 2. [move quickly] atacar por sorpresa.

swop [swɒp] = swap.

sword [sɔːd] n espada f.

swordfish ['sɔːdfɪʃ] (pl swordfish OR -es) n pez m espada.

swore [swɔːr] pt ▷ swear.

sworn [swɔːn] ◇ pp ▷ swear. ◇ adj LAW jurado(da).

swot [swɒt] UK inf ◇ n pej empollón m, -ona f. ◇ vi: **to swot (for)** empollar (para).

swum [swʌm] pp ▷ swim.

swung [swʌŋ] pt & pp ▷ swing.

sycamore ['sɪkəmɔːr] n - 1. sicomoro m - 2. US [plane tree] plátano m.

syllable ['sɪləbl] n sílaba f.

syllabus ['sɪləbəs] (pl -buses OR -bi [-baɪ]) n programa m (de estudios).

symbol ['sɪmbl] n símbolo m.

symbolize, -ise ['sɪmbəlaɪz] vt simbolizar.

symmetry ['sɪmətrɪ] n simetría f.

sympathetic [ˌsɪmpə'θetɪk] adj - 1. [understanding] comprensivo(va) - 2. [willing to support] favorable; **sympathetic to** bien dispuesto(ta) hacia.

sympathize, -ise ['sɪmpəθaɪz] vi - 1. [feel sorry]: **to sympathize (with)** compadecerse (de) - 2. [understand]: **to sympathize (with sthg)** comprender (algo) - 3. [support]: **to sympathize with sthg** apoyar algo.

sympathizer, -iser ['sɪmpəθaɪzər] n simpatizante mf.

sympathy ['sɪmpəθɪ] n - 1. [understanding]: **sympathy (for)** comprensión f (hacia); [compassion] compasión f (por) - 2. [agreement] solidaridad f. ◆ **sympathies** npl [to bereaved person] pésame m.

symphony ['sɪmfənɪ] n sinfonía f.

symposium [sɪm'pəʊzjəm] (pl -siums OR -sia [-zjə]) n fml simposio m.

symptom ['sɪmptəm] n lit & fig síntoma m.

synagogue ['sɪnəgɒg] n sinagoga f.

syndicate n ['sɪndɪkət] sindicato m.

syndrome ['sɪndrəʊm] n síndrome m.

synonym ['sɪnənɪm] n: **synonym (for OR of)** sinónimo m (de).

synopsis [sɪ'nɒpsɪs] (pl -ses [-siːz]) n sinopsis f inv.

syntax ['sɪntæks] n sintaxis f inv.

synthesis ['sɪnθəsɪs] (pl -ses [-siːz]) n síntesis f inv.

synthetic [sɪn'θetɪk] adj - 1. [man-made] sintético(ca) - 2. pej [insincere] artificial.

syphilis ['sɪfɪlɪs] n sífilis f inv.

syphon ['saɪfn] = siphon.

Syria ['sɪrɪə] n Siria.

syringe [sɪ'rɪndʒ] n jeringa f, jeringuilla f.

syrup ['sɪrəp] n (U) - 1. CULIN almíbar m - 2. MED jarabe m; **cough syrup** jarabe para la tos.

system ['sɪstəm] n [gen] sistema m; [of central heating etc] instalación f; **to get sthg out of one's system** inf sacarse algo de encima.

systematic [,sɪstə'mætɪk] adj sistemático(ca).

system disk n COMPUT disco m del sistema.

systems analyst ['sɪstəmz-] n COMPUT analista mf de sistemas.

t (pl **t's** OR **ts**), **T** (pl **T's** OR **Ts**) [ti:] n [letter] t f, T f.

ta [tɑ:] excl UK inf ¡gracias!

tab [tæb] n - **1.** [of cloth] etiqueta f - **2.** [of metal, card etc] lengüeta f - **3.** US [bill] cuenta f; **to pick up the tab** inf pagar la cuenta ▸▸▸ **to keep tabs on sb** vigilar de cerca a alguien.

tabby ['tæbɪ] n: **tabby (cat)** gato m atigrado.

table ['teɪbl] ⬦ n - **1.** [piece of furniture] mesa f; [small] mesilla f - **2.** [diagram] tabla f. ⬦ vt UK [propose] presentar.

tablecloth ['teɪblklɒθ] n mantel m.

table lamp n lámpara f de mesa.

tablemat ['teɪblmæt] n salvamanteles m inv.

tablespoon ['teɪblspu:n] n - **1.** [spoon] cuchara f grande - **2.** [spoonful] cucharada f (grande).

tablet ['tæblɪt] n - **1.** [pill, piece of soap] pastilla f - **2.** [piece of stone] lápida f.

table tennis n tenis m de mesa.

table wine n vino m de mesa.

tabloid ['tæblɔɪd] n: **the tabloids** los periódicos sensacionalistas; **tabloid (newspaper)** tabloide m.

tabulate ['tæbjʊleɪt] vt tabular.

tacit ['tæsɪt] adj fml tácito(ta).

taciturn ['tæsɪtɜ:n] adj fml taciturno(na).

tack [tæk] ⬦ n - **1.** [nail] tachuela f - **2.** fig [course of action] táctica f. ⬦ vt - **1.** [fasten with nail] fijar con tachuelas - **2.** [in sewing] hilvanar. ⬦ vi NAUT virar.

tackle ['tækl] ⬦ n - **1.** FTBL entrada f - **2.** RUGBY placaje m - **3.** (U) [equipment] equipo m, aparejos mpl - **4.** [for lifting] aparejo m. ⬦ vt - **1.** [deal with - job] emprender; [- problem] abordar - **2.** FTBL entrar - **3.** RUGBY placar - **4.** [attack] atacar, arremeter.

tacky ['tækɪ] adj - **1.** inf [cheap and nasty] cutre; [ostentatious and vulgar] hortera - **2.** [sticky] pegajoso(sa).

tact [tækt] n (U) tacto m, discreción f.

tactful ['tæktfʊl] adj discreto(ta).

tactic ['tæktɪk] n táctica f. ⬅ **tactics** n (U) MIL táctica f.

tactical ['tæktɪkl] adj estratégico(ca); [weapons] táctico(ca).

tactless ['tæktlɪs] adj indiscreto(ta).

tadpole ['tædpəʊl] n renacuajo m.

tag [tæg] n [of cloth, paper] etiqueta f; **price tag** etiqueta del precio. ⬅ **tag question** n cláusula f final interrogativa. ⬅ **tag along** vi inf: **to tag along (with)** pegarse (a), engancharse (a).

tail [teɪl] ⬦ n [gen] cola f; [of coat, shirt] faldón m. ⬦ vt inf [follow] seguir de cerca. ⬅ **tails** npl - **1.** [formal dress] frac m - **2.** [side of coin] cruz f. ⬅ **tail off** vi [voice] ir debilitándose; [sound] ir disminuyendo.

tailback ['teɪlbæk] n UK cola f.

tailcoat ['teɪl,kəʊt] n frac m.

tail end n parte f final.

tailgate ['teɪlgeɪt] ⬦ n US [of car] puerta f trasera de un vehículo. ⬦ vt conducir pegado a, pisar los talones a.

tailor ['teɪlə(r)] ⬦ n sastre m. ⬦ vt adaptar; **it can be tailored to your needs** se puede adaptar a sus necesidades.

tailor-made adj hecho(cha) a la medida.

tailwind ['teɪlwɪnd] n viento m de cola.

tainted ['teɪntɪd] adj - **1.** [reputation] manchado(da) - **2.** US [food] estropeado(da).

Taiwan [,taɪ'wɑ:n] n Taiwán.

take [teɪk] ⬦ vt (pt took, pp taken) - **1.** [gen] tomar; **do you take sugar?** ¿tomas azúcar?; **to take control/command** tomar control/el mando; **to take a photo** hacer OR tomar una foto; **to take a walk** dar un paseo; **to take a bath** bañarse; **to take a test** hacer un examen; **to take pity on sb** compadecerse de alguien; **to take offence** ofenderse; **to be taken ill** ponerse enfermo; **take the second turning on the right** toma el segundo giro a la derecha - **2.** [bring, carry, accompany] llevar - **3.** [steal] quitar, robar - **4.** [buy] coger, quedarse con; [rent] alquilar; **I'll take the red one** me quedo con el rojo - **5.** [take hold of] coger; **to take sb prisoner** capturar a alguien - **6.** [accept - offer, cheque, criticism] aceptar; [- advice] seguir; [- responsibility, blame] asumir; **the machine only takes 50p pieces** la máquina sólo admite monedas de 50 ~~peniques~~; ~~take my~~ ~~word for it~~, créeme - **7.** [have room for - passengers, goods] tener cabida para - **8.** [bear - pain etc] soportar, aguantar; **some people can't take a joke** hay gente que no sabe aguantar una broma - **9.** [require - time, courage] requerir; [- money] costar; **it will take a week/three hours** llevará una semana/tres horas; **it only took me 5 minutes** sólo me llevó cinco minutos; **it takes guts to do that** hay que tener agallas para hacer eso; **it took 5 people to move the piano** hicieron falta 5 personas para mover el piano - **10.** [travel by - means of transport, route] tomar, coger - **11.** [wear - shoes] calzar; [- clothes] usar - **12.** [consider] considerar; **take John for instance...** tomemos a John, por ejemplo...; **to take sb for a fool/a policeman** tomar a alguien por tonto/por un policía - **13.** [assume] **I take it (that)...** supongo que... <> *n* CIN toma *f*. ◆ **take after** *vt insep* parecerse a. ◆ **take apart** *vt sep* [dismantle] desmontar. ◆ **take away** *vt sep* - **1.** [remove] quitar - **2.** [deduct] restar, sustraer. ◆ **take back** *vt sep* - **1.** [return] devolver - **2.** [accept - faulty goods] aceptar la devolución de - **3.** [admit as wrong] retirar - **4.** [in memories]: **it takes me back to when I was a teenager** me hace volver a mi adolescencia. ◆ **take down** *vt sep* - **1.** [dismantle] desmontar - **2.** [write down] tomar nota de. ◆ **take in** *vt sep* - **1.** [deceive] engañar; **to be taken in by sb** ser engañado por alguien - **2.** [understand] comprender, asimilar; **I can't take it all in** no consigo asimilarlo todo - **3.** [include] incluir, abarcar - **4.** [provide accommodation for] acoger. ◆ **take off** <> *vt sep* - **1.** [clothes, glasses] quitarse - **2.** [have as holiday] tomarse - **3.** UK *inf* [imitate] imitar. <> *vi* - **1.** [plane] despegar - **2.** [go away suddenly] irse, marcharse. ◆ **take on** *vt sep* - **1.** [accept - work, job] aceptar; [- responsibility] asumir - **2.** [employ] emplear, coger - **3.** [confront] desafiar. ◆ **take out** *vt sep* [from container, pocket] sacar. ◆ **take over** <> *vt sep* - **1.** [company, business] absorber, adquirir; [country, government] apoderarse de - **2.** [job] asumir. <> *vi* - **1.** [take control] tomar el poder - **2.** [in job] entrar en funciones. ◆ **take to** *vt insep* - **1.** [feel a liking for - person] coger cariño a; [- activity] aficionarse a - **2.** [begin]: **to take to doing sthg** empezar a hacer algo. ◆ **take up** *vt sep* - **1.** [begin]: **to take up singing** dedicarse a cantar; [job] aceptar, tomar - **2.** [use up - time, space] ocupar; [- effort] requerir. ◆ **take up on** *vt sep* [accept]: **to take sb up on an offer** aceptar una oferta de alguien.

takeaway UK ['teɪkə,weɪ], **takeout** US ['teɪkaʊt] *n* [food] comida *f* para llevar.

taken ['teɪkn] *pp* ▷ **take**.

takeoff ['teɪkɒf] *n* [of plane] despegue *m*.

~~takeout~~ US = ~~takeaway~~.

takeover ['teɪk,əʊvər] *n* [of company] adquisición *t*.

takings *npl* [of shop] venta *f*; [of show] recaudación *f*.

talc [tælk], **talcum (powder)** ['tælkəm-] *n* talco *m*.

tale [teɪl] *n* - **1.** [fictional story] cuento *m* - **2.** [anecdote] anécdota *f*.

talent ['tælənt] *n*: **talent (for sthg)** talento *m* (para algo).

talented ['tæləntɪd] *adj* con talento.

talk [tɔːk] <> *n* - **1.** [conversation] conversación *f*, plática *f* Amér C & Méx; **to have a talk** conversar - **2.** (U) [gossip] habladurías *fpl* - **3.** [lecture] charla *f*, conferencia *f*, plática *f* Amér C & Méx; **to give a talk on sthg** dar una charla sobre algo. <> *vi* - **1.** [gen] hablar; **to talk to/of** hablar OR plática Amér C & Méx con/de; **talking of Sarah, I met her mum yesterday** hablando de Sarah, ayer me encontré a su madre; **to talk on** OR **about** hablar OR plática Amér C & Méx acerca de OR sobre; **they aren't talking to each other** no se hablan - **2.** [gossip] chismorrear. <> *vt* hablar de. ◆ **talks** *npl* conversaciones *fpl*. ◆ **talk into** *vt sep*: **to talk sb into doing sthg** convencer a alguien para que haga algo. ◆ **talk out of** *vt sep*: **to talk sb out of doing sthg** disuadir a alguien de que haga algo. ◆ **talk over** *vt sep* discutir, hablar de.

talkative ['tɔːkətɪv] *adj* hablador(ra).

talk show US *n* programa *m* de entrevistas.

talk time *n* (U) [on mobile phone] tiempo *m* de conversación.

tall [tɔːl] *adj* alto(ta); **she's 2 metres tall** mide 2 metros; **how tall is he?** ¿cuánto mide?

tall story *n* cuento *m* (increíble).

tally ['tælɪ] <> *n* cuenta *f*; **to keep a tally** llevar la cuenta. <> *vi* concordar.

talon ['tælən] *n* garra *f*.

tambourine [,tæmbə'riːn] *n* pandereta *f*.

tame [teɪm] <> *adj* - **1.** [domesticated] doméstico(ca) - **2.** *pej* [unexciting] soso(sa). <> *vt* - **1.** [domesticate] domesticar - **2.** [bring under control] dominar.

tamper ['tæmpər] ◆ **tamper with** *vt insep* [lock] intentar forzar; [records, file] falsear; [machine] manipular.

tampon ['tæmpɒn] *n* tampón *m*.

tan [tæn] <> *adj* de color marrón claro. <> *n* bronceado *m*; **to get a tan** broncearse. <> *vi* broncearse.

tang [tæŋ] *n* [smell] olor *m* fuerte; [taste] sabor *m* fuerte.

tangent ['tændʒənt] *n* GEOM tangente *f*; **to go off at a tangent** salirse por la tangente.

tangerine [,tæn'dʒəri:n] n mandarina f.

tangible ['tændʒəbl] adj tangible.

tangle ['tæŋgl] n [mass] maraña f; fig [mess] enredo m, embrollo m.

tank [tæŋk] n - 1. [container] depósito m, tanque m - 2. MIL tanque m, carro m de combate.

tanker ['tæŋkər] n - 1. [ship - gen] barco m cisterna, tanque m; [- for oil] petrolero m - 2. [truck] camión m cisterna.

tanned [tænd] adj bronceado(da).

Tannoy® ['tænɔɪ] n (sistema m de) altavoces mpl; his name was called out over the Tannoy su nombre sonó por megafonía.

tantalizing ['tæntəlaɪzɪŋ] adj tentador(ra).

tantamount ['tæntəmaunt] adj: tantamount to equivalente a.

tantrum ['tæntrəm] (pl -s) n rabieta f; to throw a tantrum coger una rabieta.

Tanzania [,tænzə'nɪə] n Tanzania.

tap [tæp] <> n - 1. [device] grifo m, llave f Amér, canilla f R Plata, paja f Amér C, caño f Perú - 2. [light blow] golpecito m - 3. [phr]: to be on tap [beer, water] ser de barril. <> vt - 1. [hit] golpear ligeramente - 2. [strength, resources] utilizar, usar - 3. [phone] intervenir.
➡ **taps** n US MIL [at funeral] toque m de difuntos.

tap dancing n claqué m.

tape [teɪp] <> n - 1. [cassette, magnetic tape, strip of cloth] cinta f - 2. [adhesive plastic] cinta f adhesiva. <> vt - 1. [on tape recorder, video recorder] grabar - 2. [with adhesive tape] pegar con cinta adhesiva.

tape measure n cinta f métrica.

taper ['teɪpər] <> n [candle] vela f. <> vi afilarse.

tape recorder n magnetófono m.

tapestry ['tæpɪstrɪ] n - 1. [piece of work] tapiz m - 2. [craft] tapicería f.

tar [tɑːr] n alquitrán m.

target ['tɑːgɪt] n - 1. [of missile, goal, aim] objetivo m - 2. [in archery, shooting, of criticism] blanco m; to be on target to do sthg llevar el ritmo adecuado para hacer algo.

tariff ['tærɪf] n tarifa f.

Tarmac® ['tɑːmæk] n [material] alquitrán m.
➡ **tarmac** n AERON: the tarmac la pista.

tarnish ['tɑːnɪʃ] vt [make dull] deslustrar; fig [damage] empañar, manchar.

tarpaulin [tɑː'pɔːlɪn] n lona f alquitranada.

tart [tɑːt] <> adj [bitter] agrio(agria). <> n - 1. [sweet pastry] tarta f - 2. v inf [prostitute] furcia f, fulana f. ➡ **tart up** vt sep UK inf pej emperejilar.

tartan ['tɑːtn] <> n tartán m. <> comp de tartán.

tartar(e) sauce ['tɑːtər-] n salsa f tártara.

task [tɑːsk] n tarea f.

task force n MIL destacamento m de fuerzas.

tassel ['tæsl] n borla f.

taste [teɪst] <> n - 1. [physical sense, discernment] gusto m; in bad/good taste de mal/buen gusto - 2. [flavour] sabor m - 3. [try]: have a taste pruébalo - 4. fig [for success, fast cars etc]: taste (for) afición f (a), gusto m (por) - 5. fig [experience] experiencia f. <> vt - 1. [notice flavour of] notar un sabor a; I can't taste the lemon in it no noto el sabor a limón - 2. [test, try] probar - 3. fig [experience] conocer. <> vi saber; to taste of OR like saber a.

tasteful ['teɪstful] adj de buen gusto.

tasteless ['teɪstlɪs] adj - 1. [offensive, cheap and unattractive] de mal gusto - 2. [without flavour] insípido(da), soso(sa).

tasty ['teɪstɪ] adj sabroso(sa).

tatters ['tætəz] npl: in tatters [clothes] andrajoso(sa); fig [confidence, reputation] por los suelos.

tattoo [tə'tuː] <> n (pl -s) - 1. [design] tatuaje m - 2. UK [military display] desfile m militar. <> vt tatuar.

tatty ['tætɪ] adj UK inf pej desastrado(da).

taught [tɔːt] pt & pp ▷ **teach**.

taunt [tɔːnt] <> vt zaherir a. <> n pulla f.

Taurus ['tɔːrəs] n Tauro m.

taut [tɔːt] adj tenso(sa).

tawdry ['tɔːdrɪ] adj pej de oropel.

tax [tæks] <> n impuesto m. <> vt - 1. [goods, profits] gravar - 2. [business, person] imponer contribuciones a - 3. [strain, test] poner a prueba.

taxable ['tæksəbl] adj imponible.

tax allowance n desgravación f fiscal.

taxation [tæk'seɪʃn] n (U) - 1. [system] sistema m tributario - 2. [amount] impuestos mpl.

tax avoidance [-ə'vɔɪdəns] n evasión f fiscal.

tax collector n recaudador m, -ra f de impuestos.

tax disc n UK pegatina del impuesto de circulación.

tax evasion n fraude m fiscal, evasión f de impuestos.

tax-exempt US = **tax-free**.

tax-free UK, **tax-exempt** US adj exento(ta) de impuestos.

taxi ['tæksɪ] <> n taxi m. <> vi [plane] rodar por la pista.

taxi driver n taxista mf.

tax inspector n ≃ inspector m de Hacienda.

taxi rank UK, **taxi stand** n parada f de taxis.

taxpayer ['tæks,peɪəʳ] n contribuyente mf.

tax relief n (U) desgravación f fiscal.

tax return n declaración f de renta.

TB n abbr of **tuberculosis**.

tea [tiː] n - **1.** [drink, leaves] té m - **2.** UK [afternoon snack] té m, merienda f - **3.** UK [evening meal] merienda cena f.

teabag ['tiːbæg] n bolsita f de té.

tea break n UK descanso m (durante la jornada laboral).

teach [tiːtʃ] ⬦ vt (pt & pp **taught**) - **1.** [give lessons to - student] dar clases a; **to teach sb sthg** enseñar algo a alguien; **to teach (sb) that** inculcar a alguien que; **that will teach you a lesson!** ¡eso te enseñará! - **2.** [give lessons in] [subject] dar clases de. ⬦ vi (pt & pp **taught**) ser profesor(ra).

teacher ['tiːtʃəʳ] n [at primary school] maestro m, -tra f; [at secondary school] profesor m, -ra f.

teacher training college UK, **teachers college** US n escuela f normal.

teaching ['tiːtʃɪŋ] n enseñanza f.

tea cloth n UK [tea towel] paño m de cocina.

tea cosy UK, **tea cozy** US n cubretetera f.

teacup ['tiːkʌp] n taza f de té.

teak [tiːk] n teca f.

team [tiːm] n equipo m.

teammate ['tiːmmeɪt] n compañero m, -ra f de equipo.

teamwork ['tiːmwɜːk] n (U) trabajo m en equipo.

teapot ['tiːpɒt] n tetera f.

tear[1] [tɪəʳ] n lágrima f; **in tears** llorando.

tear[2] [teəʳ] ⬦ vt (pt **tore**, pp **torn**) - **1.** [rip] rasgar, romper; **to tear sthg to pieces** fig poner algo por los suelos - **2.** [remove roughly] arrancar; **she tore a page out of her exercise book** arrancó una página de su libro de ejercicios. ⬦ vi (pt **tore**, pp **torn**) - **1.** [rip] romperse, rasgarse - **2.** inf [move quickly]: **he tore out of the house** salió de la casa a toda pastilla; **they were tearing along** iban a toda pastilla. ⬦ n rasgón m, desgarrón m. ◆ **tear apart** vt sep - **1.** [rip up] despedazar - **2.** [upset greatly] desgarrar. ◆ **tear down** vt sep [building, statue] echar abajo. ◆ **tear up** vt sep hacer pedazos.

teardrop ['tɪədrɒp] n lágrima f.

tearful ['tɪəful] adj [person] lloroso(sa).

tear gas [tɪəʳ-] n (U) gas m lacrimógeno.

tearoom ['tiːrʊm] n salón m de té.

tease [tiːz] vt - **1.** [mock]: **to tease sb (about)** tomar el pelo a alguien (acerca de) - **2.** US [hair] cardarse.

tea service, tea set n servicio m OR juego m de té.

teaspoon ['tiːspuːn] n - **1.** [utensil] cucharilla f - **2.** [amount] cucharadita f.

teat [tiːt] n - **1.** [of animal] tetilla f - **2.** [of bottle] tetina f.

teatime ['tiːtaɪm] n UK hora f del té.

tea towel n paño m de cocina.

technical ['teknɪkl] adj técnico(ca).

technical college n UK ≃ centro m de formación profesional.

technicality [,teknɪ'kælətɪ] n detalle m técnico.

technically ['teknɪklɪ] adv - **1.** [gen] técnicamente - **2.** [theoretically] teóricamente, en teoría.

technician [tek'nɪʃn] n técnico m, -ca f.

technique [tek'niːk] n técnica f.

techno ['teknəʊ] n MUS tecno m.

technological [,teknə'lɒdʒɪkl] adj tecnológico(ca).

technology [tek'nɒlədʒɪ] n tecnología f.

technophobe ['teknəfəʊb] n tecnófobo m, -ba f.

teddy ['tedɪ] n: **teddy (bear)** oso m de peluche.

tedious ['tiːdjəs] adj tedioso(sa).

tee [tiː] n tee m.

teem [tiːm] vi - **1.** [rain] llover a cántaros - **2.** [be busy]: **to be teeming with** estar inundado(da) de.

teenage ['tiːneɪdʒ] adj adolescente.

teenager ['tiːn,eɪdʒəʳ] n adolescente mf, quinceañero m, -ra f.

teens [tiːnz] npl adolescencia f; **he's in his teens** es adolescente.

tee-shirt n camiseta f.

teeter ['tiːtəʳ] vi lit & fig tambalearse.

teeth [tiːθ] npl ⬐ **tooth**.

teethe [tiːð] vi echar los dientes.

teething troubles ['tiːðɪŋ-] npl fig problemas mpl iniciales.

teetotaller UK, **teetotaler** US [tiː'təʊtləʳ] n abstemio m, -mia f.

TEFL ['tefl] (abbr of teaching of English as a foreign language) n enseñanza de inglés para extranjeros.

tel. (abbr of telephone) tfno.

telebanking ['telɪbæŋkɪŋ] n FIN banca f telefónica.

telecoms ['telɪkɒmz] npl = **telecommunications**.

telecommunications ['telɪkə,mjuːnɪ'keɪʃnz] npl telecomunicaciones fpl.

telegram ['telɪgræm] n telegrama m.

telegraph ['telɪgrɑːf] n telégrafo m.

telegraph pole, telegraph post UK n poste m de telégrafos.

telepathy [tɪ'lepəθɪ] n telepatía f.

telephone ['telɪfəʊn] <> n teléfono m. <> vt & vi telefonear.

telephone banking n banca f telefónica.

telephone book n guía f telefónica.

telephone booth n teléfono m público.

telephone box n UK cabina f (telefónica).

telephone call n llamada f telefónica, llamado m telefónico Amér.

telephone directory n guía f telefónica.

telephone number n número m de teléfono.

telephonist [tɪ'lefənɪst] n UK telefonista mf.

telephoto lens [,telɪ'fəʊtəʊ-] n teleobjetivo m.

telescope ['telɪskəʊp] n telescopio m.

teletext ['telɪtekst] n teletexto m.

televideo [telɪ'vɪdɪəʊ] n televídeo m.

televise ['telɪvaɪz] vt televisar.

television ['telɪ,vɪʒn] n televisión f; to watch television ver la televisión.

television set n televisor m, (aparato m de) televisión f.

teleworker ['telɪwɔ:kər] n teletrabajador m, -ra f.

telex ['teleks] <> n télex m. <> vt [message] transmitir por télex; [person] mandar un télex a.

tell [tel] <> vt (pt & pp told) - 1. [gen] decir; to tell sb (that) decir a alguien que; to tell sb sthg, to tell sthg to sb decir a alguien algo - 2. [joke, story] contar - 3. [judge, recognize]: to tell what sb is thinking saber en qué está pensando alguien; to tell the time decir la hora - 4. [differentiate]: to tell the difference between A and B distinguir entre A y B; it's hard to tell one from another son difíciles de distinguir. <> vi (pt & pp told) [have effect] surtir efecto. ◆ **tell apart** vt sep distinguir; I can't tell them apart no consigo distinguirlos. ◆ **tell off** vt sep esp US reñir, reprender.

telling ['telɪŋ] adj [remark, incident] revelador(ra).

telltale ['telteɪl] <> adj revelador(ra). <> n chivato m, -ta f, acusica mf.

telly ['telɪ] (abbr of television) n UK inf tele f.

temp [temp] <> n UK inf (abbr of temporary (employee)) trabajador m, -ra f temporal. <> vi: she's temping tiene un trabajo temporal.

temper ['tempər] <> n - 1. [state of mind, mood] humor m; to keep one's temper mantener la calma; to lose one's temper enfadarse, perder la paciencia - 2. [angry state]: to be in a

temper estar de mal humor - 3. [temperament] temperamento m. <> vt fml templar, suavizar.

temperament ['temprəmənt] n temperamento m.

temperamental [,temprə'mentl] adj [volatile] temperamental.

temperate ['temprət] adj templado(da).

temperature ['temprətʃər] n temperatura f; to take sb's temperature tomarle a alguien la temperatura; to have a temperature tener fiebre.

tempestuous [tem'pestjʊəs] adj lit & fig tempestuoso(sa).

template ['templɪt] n plantilla f.

temple ['templ] n - 1. RELIG templo m - 2. ANAT sien f.

temporarily [,tempə'rerəlɪ] adv temporalmente, provisionalmente.

temporary ['tempərərɪ] adj [gen] temporal, temporario Amér, provisional, provisorio Andes, Col & Ven; [improvement, problem] pasajero(ra).

tempt [tempt] vt [entice]: to be OR feel tempted to do sthg estar OR sentirse tentado de hacer algo.

temptation [temp'teɪʃn] n tentación f.

tempting ['temptɪŋ] adj tentador(ra).

ten [ten] num diez; see also **six**.

tenable ['tenəbl] adj [reasonable, credible] sostenible.

tenacious [tɪ'neɪʃəs] adj tenaz.

tenancy ['tenənsɪ] n [period - of house] alquiler m; [- of land] arrendamiento m.

tenant ['tenənt] n [of house] inquilino m, -na f; [of pub] arrendatario m, -ria f.

tend [tend] vt - 1. [look after] cuidar - 2. US: to tend bar atender en el bar.

tendency ['tendənsɪ] n [leaning, inclination] inclinación f.

tender ['tendər] <> adj [gen] tierno(na); [sore] dolorido(da). <> n - 1. COMM propuesta f, oferta f - 2.: (legal) tender moneda f de curso legal. <> vt fml [resignation] presentar.

tendon ['tendən] n tendón m.

tenement ['tenəmənt] n bloque de viviendas modestas.

tenet ['tenɪt] n fml principio m.

tennis ['tenɪs] n tenis m.

tennis ball n pelota f de tenis.

tennis court n pista f de tenis.

tennis match n partido m de tenis.

tennis player n tenista mf.

tennis racket n raqueta f de tenis.

tenor ['tenər] n [singer] tenor m.

tense [tens] ◇ adj tenso(sa). ◇ n tiempo m. ◇ vt tensar

tension ['tenʃn] n tensión f.

tent [tent] n tienda f (de campaña), carpa f Amér.

tentacle ['tentəkl] n tentáculo m.

tentative ['tentətɪv] adj - 1. [person] indeciso(sa); [step, handshake] vacilante - 2. [suggestion, conclusion etc] provisional.

tenterhooks ['tentəhʊks] npl: to be on tenterhooks estar sobre ascuas.

tenth [tenθ] num décimo(ma); see also sixth.

tent peg n estaca f.

tent pole n mástil m de tienda.

tenuous ['tenjʊəs] adj [argument] flojo(ja); [evidence, connection] débil, insignificante; [hold] ligero(ra).

tenure ['tenjər] n - 1. (U) fml [of property] arrendamiento m - 2. [of job] ocupación f, ejercicio m.

tepid ['tepɪd] adj [liquid] tibio(bia).

term [tɜːm] ◇ n - 1. [word, expression] término m - 2. SCH & UNIV trimestre m - 3. POL mandato m; term of office mandato - 4. [period of time] periodo m; in the long/short term a largo/corto plazo. ◇ vt: to term sthg sthg calificar algo de algo. ◆ **terms** npl - 1. [of contract, agreement] condiciones fpl - 2. [basis]: on equal OR the same terms en condiciones de igualdad; to be on speaking terms (with sb) hablarse (con alguien); to come to terms with sthg aceptar algo. ◆ **in terms of** prep por lo que se refiere a.

terminal ['tɜːmɪnl] ◇ adj MED incurable, terminal. ◇ n - 1. [transport] terminal f - 2. COMPUT terminal m.

terminate ['tɜːmɪneɪt] ◇ vt fml [gen] poner fin a; [pregnancy] interrumpir. ◇ vi - 1. [bus, train] finalizar el trayecto - 2. [contract] terminarse.

termini ['tɜːmɪnaɪ] npl ⊳ terminus.

terminus ['tɜːmɪnəs] (pl -ni OR -nuses) n (estación f) terminal f.

terrace ['terəs] n - 1. [gen] terraza f - 2. UK [of houses] hilera f de casas adosadas. ◆ **terraces** npl FTBL: the terraces las gradas.

terraced ['terəst] adj - 1. [hillside] a terrazas - 2. [house, housing] adosado(da).

terraced house n UK casa f adosada.

terrain [te'reɪn] n terreno m.

terrible ['terəbl] adj - 1. [crash, mess, shame] terrible, espantoso(sa) - 2. [unwell, unhappy, very bad] fatal.

terribly ['terəblɪ] adv [sing, play, write] malísimamente; [injured, sorry, expensive] terriblemente.

terrier ['terɪər] n terrier m.

terrific [tə'rɪfɪk] adj - 1. [wonderful] estupendo(da) - 2. [enormous] enorme.

terrified ['terɪfaɪd] adj aterrorizado(da); **to be terrified (of)** tener terror (a).

terrifying ['terɪfaɪɪŋ] adj aterrador(ra).

territory ['terətrɪ] n - 1. [political area] territorio m - 2. [terrain] terreno m - 3. [area of knowledge] esfera f.

terror ['terər] n [fear] terror m; **to live in terror** vivir aterrorizado(da); **they ran out of the house in terror** salieron de la casa aterrorizados.

terrorism ['terərɪzm] n terrorismo m.

terrorist ['terərɪst] n terrorista mf.

terrorize, -ise ['terəraɪz] vt aterrorizar.

terse [tɜːs] adj seco(ca).

Terylene® ['terɪliːn] n terylene® m.

test [test] ◇ n - 1. [trial] prueba f; **to put sthg to the test** poner algo a prueba - 2. [examination] examen m, prueba f - 3. MED [of blood, urine] análisis m inv; [of eyes] revisión f. ◇ vt - 1. [try out] probar, poner a prueba - 2. [examine] examinar; **to test sb on** examinar a alguien de.

testament ['testəmənt] n [will] testamento m.

test-drive vt someter a prueba de carretera.

testicles ['testɪklz] npl testículos mpl.

testify ['testɪfaɪ] ◇ vi - 1. LAW prestar declaración - 2. [be proof]: **to testify to sthg** dar fe de OR atestiguar algo. ◇ vt: **to testify that** declarar que.

testimony [UK 'testɪmənɪ, US 'testəməʊnɪ] n LAW testimonio m, declaración f.

testing ['testɪŋ] adj duro(ra).

test match n UK SPORT partido m internacional.

test pilot n piloto mf de pruebas.

test tube n probeta f.

test-tube baby n bebé mf probeta.

tetanus ['tetənəs] n tétanos m inv.

tether ['teðər] ◇ vt atar. ◇ n: **to be at the end of one's tether** estar uno que ya no puede más.

text [tekst] ◇ n - 1. [gen] texto m - 2. [textbook] libro m de texto - 3. [sent by mobile phone] mensaje m de texto, SMS m. ◇ vt enviar un mensaje de texto a. ◇ vi enviar mensajes de texto.

textbook ['tekstbʊk] n libro m de texto.

textile ['tekstaɪl] n textil m, tejido m.

texting ['tekstɪŋ] n inf mensajes fpl de texto.

text message n [on mobile phone] mensaje m de texto.

text messaging [-'mesɪdʒɪŋ] n [on mobile phone] mensajería f de texto.

texture ['tekstʃəʳ] n textura f.

Thai [taɪ] ◇ adj tailandés(esa). ◇ n - **1.** [person] tailandés m, -esa f - **2.** [language] tailandés m.

Thailand ['taɪlænd] n Tailandia.

Thames [temz] n: **the Thames** el Támesis.

than (weak form [ðən], strong form [ðæn]) ◇ prep que; **you're older than me** eres mayor que yo; **you're older than I thought** eres mayor de lo que pensaba. ◇ conj que; **I'd sooner read than sleep** prefiero leer que dormir; **no sooner did he arrive than she left** tan pronto llegó él, ella se fue; **more than three/once** más de tres/de una vez; **rather than stay, he chose to go** en vez de quedarse, prefirió irse.

thank [θæŋk] vt: **to thank sb (for sthg)** dar las gracias a alguien (por algo), agradecer a alguien (algo); **thank God OR goodness OR heavens!** ¡gracias a Dios!, ¡menos mal! ➧ **thanks** ◇ npl agradecimiento m; **they left without a word of thanks** se marcharon sin dar las gracias. ◇ excl ¡gracias!; **thanks a lot** muchas gracias; **would you like a biscuit? – no thanks** ¿quieres una galleta? – no, gracias; **thanks for** gracias por. ➧ **thanks to** prep gracias a.

thankful ['θæŋkfʊl] adj - **1.** [relieved] aliviado(da) - **2.** [grateful]: **thankful (for)** agradecido(da) (por).

thankless ['θæŋklɪs] adj ingrato(ta).

Thanksgiving ['θæŋks,gɪvɪŋ] n US Día m de Acción de Gracias (el cuarto jueves de noviembre).

thank you excl ¡gracias!; **thank you very much** muchas gracias; **thank you for** gracias por; **to say thank you (for sthg)** dar gracias (por algo); **tea? – no thank you** ¿té? – no, gracias.

that ([ðæt], weak form of pron and conj [ðət]) ◇ pron (pl those) - **1.** (demonstrative use: pl 'those') ése m, ésa f, ésos mpl, ésas fpl; (indefinite) eso; **that sounds familiar** eso me resulta familiar; **who's that?** [who is it?] ¿quién es?; **what's that?** ¿qué es eso?; **that's a shame** is una pena; **is that Maureen?** [asking someone else] ¿es ésa Maureen?; [asking person in question] ¿eres Maureen?; **like that** así; **do you like these or those?** ¿te gustan éstos o ésos? - **2.** [further away in distance, time] aquél m, aquélla f, aquéllos mpl, aquéllas fpl; (indefinite) aquello; **that was the life!** ¡aquello sí que era vida!; **all those who helped me** todos aquellos que me ayudaron - **3.** (to introduce relative clauses) que; **a path that led into the woods** un sendero que conducía al bosque; **everything that I have done** todo lo que he hecho; **the room that I sleep in** el cuarto donde OR en (el) que duermo; **the day that he arrived** el día en que llegó; **the firm that he's applying to** la empresa a la que solicita trabajo. ◇ adj (demonstrative: pl 'those') ese(esa), esos(esas) (pl); [further away in distance, time] aquel(aquella), aquellos(aquellas) (pl); **those chocolates are delicious** esos bombones están exquisitos; **I'll have that book at the back** yo cogeré aquel libro del fondo; **later that day** más tarde ese/aquel mismo día. ◇ adv tan; **it wasn't that bad** no estuvo tan mal; **it doesn't cost that much** no cuesta tanto; **it was that big** fue así de grande. ◇ conj que; **he recommended that I phone you** aconsejó que te telefoneara; **it's time that we were leaving** deberíamos irnos ya, ya va siendo hora de irse. ➧ **that is** adv es decir.

thatched [θætʃt] adj con techo de paja.

that's [ðæts] (abbr of that is) ➞ **that**.

thaw [θɔː] ◇ vt [snow, ice] derretir; [frozen food] descongelar. ◇ vi [snow, ice] derretirse; [frozen food] descongelarse; fig [people, relations] distenderse. ◇ n deshielo m.

the (weak form [ðə], before vowel [ðɪ], strong form [ðiː]) def art - **1.** [gen] el(la); (pl) los(las); (before f nouns beginning with stressed 'a' or 'ha' = **el**; 'a' + 'el' = **al**; 'de' + 'el' = **del**): **the boat** el barco; **the Queen** la reina; **the men** los hombres; **the women** las mujeres; **the water** el agua; **to the end of the world** al fin del mundo; **to play the piano** tocar el piano; **the Joneses are coming to supper** los Jones vienen a cenar - **2.** (with an adj to form a n): **the old/young** los viejos/jóvenes; **the impossible** lo imposible - **3.** [in dates]: **the twelfth of May** el doce de mayo; **the forties** los cuarenta - **4.** (in comparisons): **the more I see her, the less I like her** cuanto más la veo, menos me gusta; **the sooner the better** cuanto antes mejor - **5.** [in titles]: **Catherine the Great** Catalina la Grande; **George the First** Jorge Primero.

theatre, theater US ['θɪətəʳ] n - **1.** [for plays etc] teatro m - **2.** UK [in hospital] quirófano m - **3.** US [cinema] cine m.

theatregoer, theatergoer US ['θɪətə,gəʊəʳ] n aficionado m, -da f al teatro.

theatrical [θɪ'ætrɪkl] adj lit & fig teatral.

theft [θeft] n [more serious] robo m; [less serious] hurto m.

their [ðeəʳ] poss adj su, sus (pl); **their house** su casa; **their children** sus hijos; **it wasn't their fault** no fue culpa suya OR su culpa; **they washed their hair** se lavaron el pelo.

theirs [ðeəz] poss pron suyo(suya); **that money is theirs** ese dinero es suyo; **our car was theirs** nuestro coche chocó contra el suyo; **it**

wasn't our fault, it was theirs no fue culpa nuestra sino suya OR de ellos; a friend of theirs un amigo suyo OR de ellos.

them (weak form [ðəm], strong form [ðem]) pers pron pl - **1.** (direct) los mpl, las fpl; **I know them** los conozco; **I like them** me gustan; **if I were OR was them** si (yo) fuera ellos - **2.** (indirect - gen) les; (- with other 3rd person pronouns) se mpl & fpl; **she sent them a letter** les mandó una carta; **we spoke to them** hablamos con ellos; **I gave it to them** se lo di (a ellos) - **3.** (stressed, after prep, in comparisons etc) ellos mpl, ellas fpl; **you can't expect them to do it** no esperarás que **ellos** lo hagan; **with/ without them** con/sin ellos; **a few of them** unos pocos; **some of them** algunos; **all of them** todos ellos; **we're not as wealthy as them** no somos tan ricos como ellos.

theme [θi:m] n - **1.** (gen) tema m - **2.** [signature tune] sintonía f.

theme pub n UK pub m temático.

theme tune n tema m musical.

themselves [ðem'selvz] pron - **1.** (reflexive) se; (after prep) sí; **they enjoyed themselves** se divirtieron; **they were talking amongst themselves** hablaban entre ellos - **2.** (for emphasis) ellos mismos mpl, ellas mismas fpl; **they did it themselves** lo hicieron ellos mismos - **3.** [alone] solos(las); **they organized it (by) themselves** lo organizaron ellas solas - **4.** [their usual selves]: **the boys aren't themselves today** hoy los chicos no se están portando como de costumbre.

then [ðen] <> adv - **1.** [not now] entonces; **it starts at 8 – I'll see you then** empieza a las 8 – hasta las 8, entonces; **up until then he had always trusted her** hasta entonces siempre había confiado en ella; **from then on** desde entonces - **2.** [next, afterwards] luego, después - **3.** [in that case] entonces; **I'll do it straight away then** entonces lo voy a hacer ahora mismo; **all right then** de acuerdo, pues - **4.** [therefore] entonces, por lo tanto; **then it must have been her!** ¡entonces tiene que haber sido ella! - **5.** [furthermore, also] además. <> adj entonces; **the then headmistress** la entonces directora; **then again** pero por otra parte.

theology [θɪ'ɒlədʒɪ] n teología f.

theoretical [θɪə'retɪkl] adj teórico(ca).

theorize, -ise ['θɪəraɪz] vi: **to theorize (about sthg)** teorizar (sobre algo).

theory ['θɪərɪ] n teoría f; **in theory** en teoría.

therapeutic cloning n MED clonación f terapéutica.

therapist ['θerəpɪst] n terapeuta mf.

therapy ['θerəpɪ] n terapia f.

there [ðeə'] <> pron [indicating existence]: **there is/are** hay; **there's someone at the door** hay alguien en la puerta; **there must be some** mistake debe (de) haber un error; **there are five of us** somos cinco. <> adv - **1.** [referring to place - near speaker] ahí; [- further away] allí, allá; **I'm going there next week** voy para allá OR allí la semana que viene; **there it is** ahí está, over there por allí; **it's six miles there and back** hay seis millas entre ir y volver; **we're nearly there** ya casi hemos llegado - **2.** [in existence, available] ahí; **is anybody there?** ¿hay alguien ahí?; **is John there, please?** [when telephoning] ¿está John? <> excl: **there, I knew he'd turn up** ¡mira!, sabía que aparecería; **there, there (don't cry)** ¡venga, venga (no llores)! ➤ **there and then, then and there** adv en el acto.

thereabouts [,ðeərə'bauts], **thereabout** US [,ðeərə'baut] adv: **or thereabouts** o por ahí.

thereafter [,ðeər'ɑ:ftər] adv fml después, a partir de entonces.

thereby [,ðeər'baɪ] adv fml de ese modo.

therefore ['ðeəfɔ:r] adv por lo tanto.

there's [ðeəz] (abbr of there is) ⊳ **there**.

thermal ['θɜ:ml] adj térmico(ca).

thermometer [θə'mɒmɪtər] n termómetro m.

Thermos (flask)® ['θɜ:məs-] n termo m.

thermostat ['θɜ:məstæt] n termostato m.

thesaurus [θɪ'sɔ:rəs] (pl -es) n diccionario m de sinónimos y voces afines.

these [ði:z] pl ⊳ **this**.

thesis ['θi:sɪs] (pl theses ['θi:si:z]) n tesis f inv.

they [ðeɪ] pers pron pl - **1.** (gen) ellos mpl, ellas fpl; **they're pleased** (ellos) están satisfechos; **they're pretty earrings** son unos pendientes bonitos; **they can't do it** ellos no pueden hacerlo; **there they are** allí están - **2.** [unspecified people]: **they say it's going to snow** dicen que va a nevar.

they'd [ðeɪd] - **1.** (abbr of they had) ⊳ **have** - **2.** (abbr of they would) ⊳ **would**.

they'll [ðeɪl] - **1.** (abbr of they will) ⊳ **will** - **2.** (abbr of they shall) ⊳ **shall**.

they're [ðeər] (abbr of they are) ⊳ **be**.

they've [ðeɪv] (abbr of they have) ⊳ **have**.

thick [θɪk] <> adj - **1.** [not thin] grueso(sa); **it's 3 cm thick** tiene 3 cm de grueso; **how thick is it?** ¿qué espesor tiene? - **2.** [dense - hair, liquid, fog] espeso(sa) - **3.** inf [stupid] necio(cia). <> n: **to be in the thick of** estar en el centro OR meollo de.

thicken ['θɪkn] <> vt espesar. <> vi [gen] espesarse.

thicket ['θɪkɪt] n matorral m.

thickness ['θɪknɪs] n espesor m.

thickset [,θɪk'set] *adj* fornido(da).

thick-skinned [-'skɪnd] *adj* insensible.

thief [θi:f] (*pl* **thieves**) *n* ladrón *m*, -ona *f*.

thieve [θi:v] *vt & vi* robar, hurtar.

thieves [θi:vz] *npl* ⊳ **thief**.

thigh [θaɪ] *n* muslo *m*.

thimble ['θɪmbl] *n* dedal *m*.

thin [θɪn] *adj* - **1.** [not thick] delgado(da), fino(na) - **2.** [skinny] delgado(da), flaco(ca) - **3.** [watery] claro(ra), aguado(da) - **4.** [sparse - crowd, vegetation, mist] poco denso (poco densa); [- hair] ralo(la). ◆ **thin down** *vt sep* [liquid] aclarar.

thing [θɪŋ] *n* - **1.** [gen] cosa *f*; **the next thing on the list** lo siguiente de la lista; **the (best) thing to do would be...** lo mejor sería...; **first thing in the morning** a primer hora de la mañana; **last thing at night** a última hora de la noche; **the main thing** lo principal; **the whole thing is a shambles** es un auténtico desastre; **it's a good thing you were there** menos mal que estabas allí; **I thought the same thing** lo mismo pensé yo; **the thing is...** el caso es que...; **to make a thing (out) of sthg** *inf* exagerar algo - **2.** [anything]: **not a thing** nada; **I didn't do a thing** no hice nada - **3.** [person]: **poor thing!** ¡pobrecito! *m*, -ta *f*. ◆ **things** *npl* - **1.** [clothes, possessions] cosas *fpl*; **things aren't what they used to be** las cosas ya no son lo que eran - **2.** *inf* [life]: **how are things?** ¿qué tal (van las cosas)?

think [θɪŋk] ◇ *vt* (*pt & pp* **thought**) - **1.** [believe]: **to think (that)** creer OR pensar que; **I think so** creo que sí; **I don't think so** creo que no - **2.** [have in mind] pensar; **what are you thinking?** ¿en qué piensas?; **I didn't think to ask her** no se me ocurrió preguntárselo - **3.** [imagine] entender, hacerse una idea de; **I can't think what might have happened to them** no quiero ni pensar lo que les podría haber ocurrido; **I thought so** ya me lo imaginaba - **4.** [in polite requests]: **do you think you could help me?** ¿cree que podría ayudarme? ◇ *vi* (*pt & pp* **thought**) - **1.** [use mind] pensar; **to think aloud** pensar en voz alta - **2.** [have stated opinion]: **what do you think of OR about his new film?** ¿qué piensas de su nueva película?; **to think a lot of sthg/sb** tener en mucha estima algo/a alguien ▸▸▸ **to think twice** pensárselo dos veces. ◆ **think about** *vt insep* pensar en; **I'll have to think about it** tendré que pensarlo. ◆ **think of** *vt insep* - **1.** [consider]: **to think of doing sthg** pensar en hacer algo - **2.** [remember] acordarse de - **3.** [conceive] pensar en; **how did you think of (doing) that?** ¿cómo se te ocurrió (hacer) esto? ◆ **think out, think**

through *vt sep* [plan] elaborar; [problem] examinar. ◆ **think over** *vt sep* pensarse. ◆ **think up** *vt sep* idear.

think tank *n* grupo de expertos convocados por una organización para aconsejar sobre un tema determinado.

third [θɜːd] ◇ *num adj* tercer(ra). ◇ *num n* - **1.** [fraction] tercio *m* - **2.** [in order] tercero *m*, -ra *f* - **3.** UNIV ≃ aprobado *m* (en un título universitario); *see also* **sixth**.

thirdly ['θɜːdlɪ] *adv* en tercer lugar.

third party insurance *n* seguro *m* a terceros.

third-rate *adj pej* de poca categoría.

Third World *n*: **the Third World** el Tercer Mundo.

thirst [θɜːst] *n lit & fig*: **thirst (for)** sed *f* (de).

thirsty ['θɜːstɪ] *adj* [parched]: **to be** OR **feel thirsty** tener sed.

thirteen [,θɜː'tiːn] *num* trece; *see also* **six**.

thirty ['θɜːtɪ] *num* treinta; *see also* **sixty**.

this [ðɪs] ◇ *pron* (*pl* **these**) [gen] éste *m*, ésta *f*, éstos *mpl*, éstas *fpl*; (indefinite) esto; **this is/these are for you** esto es/éstos son para ti; **this can't be true** esto no puede ser cierto; **do you prefer these or those?** ¿prefieres éstos o aquéllos?; **this is Daphne Logan** [introducing another person] ésta es OR te presento a Daphne Logan; [introducing oneself on phone] soy Daphne Logan; **what's this?** ¿qué es eso? ◇ *adj* - **1.** [gen] este(esta), estos(estas) *(pl)*; **this country** este país; **these thoughts** estos pensamientos; **I prefer this one** prefiero éste; **this morning/week** esta mañana/semana; **this Sunday/summer** este domingo/verano - **2.** *inf* [a certain] un(una); **there's this woman I know** hay una tía que conozco. ◇ *adv*: **it was this big** era así de grande; **you'll need about this much** te hará falta un tanto así.

thistle ['θɪsl] *n* cardo *m*.

thong [θɒŋ] *n* - **1.** [of leather] correa *f* - **2.** [underwear] tanga *f*.

thorn [θɔːn] *n* [prickle] espina *f*.

thorough ['θʌrə] *adj* - **1.** [investigation etc] exhaustivo(va) - **2.** [person, work] minucioso(sa).

thoroughbred ['θʌrəbred] *n* pura sangre *mf*.

thoroughfare ['θʌrəfeəʳ] *n fml* calle *f* mayor.

thoroughly ['θʌrəlɪ] *adv* - **1.** [fully, in detail] a fondo - **2.** [completely, utterly] completamente.

those [ðəʊz] *pl* ⊳ **that**.

though, tho' [ðəʊ] ◇ *conj* aunque; **even though** aunque; **as though** como si. ◇ *adv* sin embargo; **she still likes him though** y sin embargo le sigue gustando.

thought [θɔːt] ◇ *pt & pp* ⊳ **think**. ◇ *n* - **1.** [notion, idea] idea *f* - **2.** [act of thinking]: **after**

much thought después de pensarlo mucho

● **5.** [philosophy, thinking] pensamiento *m*

● **thoughts** *fpl* **4.** [reflections] reflexiones *fpl* **2.** [views] opiniones *fpl*; **what are your thoughts on the subject?** ¿qué piensas sobre el tema?

thoughtful ['θɔ:tful] *adj* - **1.** [pensive] pensativo(va) - **2.** [considerate] considerado(da); **that was thoughtful of her** fue muy considerada.

thoughtless ['θɔ:tlɪs] *adj* desconsiderado(da).

thousand ['θaʊznd] *num* mil; **a OR one thousand** mil; **two thousand** dos mil; **thousands of miles de; they came in their thousands** vinieron miles de ellos; *see also* **six.**

thousandth ['θaʊzntθ] ◇ *num adj* milésimo(ma). ◇ *num n* [fraction] milésima *f*; *see also* **sixth.**

thrash [θræʃ] *vt lit & fig* dar una paliza a.

● **thrash about, thrash around** *vi* agitarse violentamente. ● **thrash out** *vt sep* darle vueltas a, discutir.

thread [θred] ◇ *n* - **1.** [of cotton, argument] hilo *m* - **2.** [of screw] rosca *f*, filete *m*. ◇ *vt* [needle] enhebrar.

threadbare ['θredbeər] *adj* raído(da).

threat [θret] *n*: **threat (to/of)** amenaza *f* (para/de); **they were just empty threats** no eran más que amenazas vanas.

threaten ['θretn] ◇ *vt* amenazar; **to threaten sb (with)** amenazar a alguien (con). ◇ *vi* amenazar.

three [θri:] *num* tres; *see also* **six.**

three-dimensional [-dɪ'menʃənl] *adj* tridimensional.

threefold ['θri:fəʊld] ◇ *adj* triple. ◇ *adv* tres veces.

three-piece *adj* de tres piezas; **three-piece suite** tresillo *m*.

three-ply *adj* [wood] de tres capas; [rope, wool] de tres hebras.

three-quarter length *adj*: **three-quarter length jacket** tres cuartos *m*.

thresh [θreʃ] *vt* trillar.

threshold ['θreʃhəʊld] *n* - **1.** [doorway] umbral *m* - **2.** [level] límite *m*; **the pain threshold** el umbral del dolor.

threw [θru:] *pt* ▷ **throw.**

thrifty ['θrɪftɪ] *adj* [person] ahorrativo(va); [meal] frugal.

thrill [θrɪl] ◇ *n* - **1.** [sudden feeling] estremecimiento *m* - **2.** [exciting experience]: **it was a thrill to see it** fue emocionante verlo. ◇ *vt* entusiasmar.

thrilled [θrɪld] *adj*: **thrilled (with sthg/to do sthg)** encantado(da) (de algo/de hacer algo).

thriller ['θrɪlər] *n* novela *f*/película *f*/obra *f* de suspense.

thrilling ['θrɪlɪŋ] *adj* emocionante.

thrive [θraɪv] (*pt* **throve** *OR* **thrived**) *vi* [plant] crecer mucho; [person] rebosar de salud, [business] prosperar.

thriving ['θraɪvɪŋ] *adj* [plant] que crece bien.

throat [θrəʊt] *n* garganta *f*; **to have a sore throat** tener dolor de garganta.

throb [θrɒb] *vi* - **1.** [heart, pulse] latir; [head] palpitar - **2.** [engine, music] vibrar, resonar.

throes [θrəʊz] *npl*: **to be in the throes of** estar en medio de.

throne [θrəʊn] *n* trono *m*; **to be on the throne** ocupar el trono.

throng [θrɒŋ] ◇ *n* multitud *f*. ◇ *vt* llegar en tropel a.

throttle ['θrɒtl] ◇ *n* válvula *f* reguladora. ◇ *vt* [strangle] estrangular.

through, thru [θru:] ◇ *adj* [finished]: **to be through with sthg** haber terminado algo. ◇ *adv* - **1.** [in place] de parte a parte, de un lado a otro; **they let us through** nos dejaron pasar; **I read it through** lo leí hasta el final - **2.** [in time] hasta el final. ◇ *prep* - **1.** [relating to place, position] a través de; **to cut/travel through sthg** cortar/viajar por algo - **2.** [during] durante; **all through the night** durante toda la noche; **to go through an experience** pasar por una experiencia - **3.** [because of] a causa de, por - **4.** [by means of] gracias a, por medio de; **I got it through a friend** lo conseguí a través de un amigo - **5.** *US* [up to and including]: **Monday through Friday** de lunes a viernes. ● **through and through** *adv* de pies a cabeza.

throughout [θru:'aʊt] ◇ *prep* - **1.** [during] a lo largo de, durante todo (durante toda) - **2.** [everywhere in] por todo (da). ◇ *adv* - **1.** [all the time] todo el tiempo - **2.** [everywhere] por todas partes.

throve [θrəʊv] *pt* ▷ **thrive.**

throw [θrəʊ] ◇ *vt* (*pt* **threw**, *pp* **thrown**) - **1.** [gen] tirar; [ball, hammer, javelin] lanzar; **to throw o.s. into sthg** *fig* meterse de lleno en algo - **2.** [horse] derribar, desmontar - **3.** *fig* [confuse] desconcertar. ◇ *n* lanzamiento *m*, tiro *m*. ● **throw away** *vt sep* [discard] tirar; *fig* [waste] desperdiciar. ● **throw out** *vt sep* - **1.** [discard] tirar - **2.** [force to leave] echar. ● **throw up** *vi inf* [vomit] vomitar.

throwaway ['θrəʊə,weɪ] *adj* - **1.** [bottle, product] desechable - **2.** [remark, gesture] hecho(cha) como quien no quiere la cosa.

throw-in *n UK* FTBL saque *m* de banda.

thrown [θrəʊn] *pp* ▷ **throw.**

thru [θru:] *US inf* = **through.**

thrush [θrʌʃ] *n* - **1.** [bird] tordo *m* - **2.** MED [vaginal] candidiasis *f*.

thrust [θrʌst] ⬦ n - 1. [of sword] estocada f; [of knife] cuchillada f; [of troops] arremetida f - 2. TECH (fuerza f de) propulsión f - 3. [main meaning] esencia f. ⬦ vt (pt & pp thrust) [shove]: **he thrust the knife into his enemy** hundió el cuchillo en el cuerpo de su enemigo.

thud [θʌd] vi dar un golpe seco.

thug [θʌg] n matón m.

thumb [θʌm] ⬦ n [of hand] pulgar m; fig **tocarse** OR **rascarse la barriga**. ⬦ vt inf [hitch]: **to thumb a lift** hacer dedo. ➡ **thumb through** vt insep hojear.

thumbs down [ˌθʌmz-] n: **to get** OR **be given the thumbs down** [plan] ser rechazado(da); [play] ser recibido(da) con descontento.

thumbs up [ˌθʌmz-] n: **we got** OR **were given the thumbs up** nos dieron luz verde OR el visto bueno.

thumbtack ['θʌmtæk] n US chincheta f.

thump [θʌmp] ⬦ n - 1. [blow] puñetazo m - 2. [thud] golpe m seco. ⬦ vt [punch] dar un puñetazo a. ⬦ vi [heart, head] latir con fuerza.

thunder ['θʌndər] ⬦ n (U) - 1. METEOR truenos mpl - 2. fig [loud sound] estruendo m. ⬦ impers vb METEOR **tronar**. ⬦ vi [make loud sound] retumbar.

thunderbolt ['θʌndəbəʊlt] n rayo m.

thunderclap ['θʌndəklæp] n trueno m.

thunderstorm ['θʌndəstɔːm] n tormenta f.

thundery ['θʌndəri] adj tormentoso(sa).

Thursday ['θɜːzdɪ] n jueves m inv; see also **Saturday**.

thus [ðʌs] adv fml - 1. [therefore] por consiguiente, así que - 2. [in this way] así, de esta manera.

thwart [θwɔːt] vt frustrar.

thyme [taɪm] n tomillo m.

thyroid ['θaɪrɔɪd] n tiroides m inv.

tiara [tɪˈɑːrə] n tiara f.

Tibet [tɪˈbet] n (el) Tibet.

tic [tɪk] n tic m.

tick [tɪk] ⬦ n - 1. [written mark] marca f OR señal f de visto bueno - 2. [sound] tictac m - 3. inf [credit]: **on tick** a crédito. ⬦ vt marcar (con una señal). ⬦ vi [make ticking sound] hacer tictac. ➡ **tick off** vt sep - 1. [mark off] marcar (con una señal de visto bueno) - 2. [tell off]: **to tick sb off (for sthg)** echar una bronca a alguien (por algo) - 3. US inf [irritate] fastidiar. ➡ **tick over** vi funcionar al ralentí.

ticket ['tɪkɪt] n - 1. [for bus, train etc] billete m, boleto m Amér; [for cinema, football match] entrada f - 2. [for traffic offence] multa f, parte m Chile.

ticket collector n UK revisor m, -ra f.

ticket inspector n UK revisor m, -ra f.

ticket machine n máquina f automática para la venta de billetes OR boletos Amér.

ticket office n taquilla f, boletería f Amér.

tickle ['tɪkl] vt - 1. [touch lightly] hacer cosquillas a - 2. fig [amuse] divertir.

ticklish ['tɪklɪʃ] adj [sensitive to touch]: **to be ticklish** tener cosquillas.

tidal ['taɪdl] adj de la marea.

tidal wave n maremoto m.

tidbit US = **titbit**.

tiddlywinks ['tɪdlɪwɪŋks], **tiddledywinks** US ['tɪdldɪwɪŋks] n juego m de la pulga.

tide [taɪd] n - 1. [of sea] marea f; **high/low tide** marea alta/baja; **the tide is in/out** ha subido/bajado la marea; **the tide is coming in/going out** la marea está subiendo/bajando - 2. fig [of protest, feeling] oleada f; **the rising tide of crime** la creciente oleada de crímenes.

tidy ['taɪdɪ] ⬦ adj - 1. [room, desk etc] ordenado(da) - 2. [person, dress, hair] arreglado(da). ⬦ vt ordenar, arreglar. ➡ **tidy up** vt sep ordenar, arreglar.

tie [taɪ] ⬦ n - 1. [necktie] corbata f - 2. [string, cord] atadura f - 3. [bond, link] vínculo m, lazo m - 4. SPORT [draw] empate m. ⬦ vt (pt & pp tied, cont tying) - 1. [attach, fasten]: **to tie sthg (to** OR **onto sthg)** atar algo (a algo); **to tie sthg round/with sthg** atar algo a/con algo - 2. [do up - shoelaces] atar; [- knot] hacer - 3. fig [link]: **to be tied to** estar ligado(da) a. ⬦ vi (pt & pp tied, cont tying) [draw]: **to tie (with)** empatar (con). ➡ **tie down** vt sep fig atar. ➡ **tie in with** vt insep concordar con. ➡ **tie up** vt sep - 1. [gen] atar - 2. fig [money, resources] inmovilizar - 3. fig [link]: **to be tied up with** estar ligado(da) a.

tiebreak(er) ['taɪbreɪk(ər)] n - 1. TENNIS muerte f súbita, tiebreak m - 2. [in game, competition] pregunta adicional para romper un empate.

tiepin ['taɪpɪn] n alfiler m de corbata.

tier [tɪər] n [of seats] hilera f; [of cake] piso m.

tiff [tɪf] n pelea f (de poca importancia).

tiger ['taɪgər] n tigre m.

tight [taɪt] ⬦ adj - 1. [gen] apretado(da); [shoes] estrecho(cha) - 2. [string, skin] tirante - 3. [budget, schedule] ajustado(da) - 4. [rules, restrictions] riguroso(sa) - 5. [corner, bend] cerrado(da) - 6. [match, finish] reñido(da) - 7. inf [drunk] cocido(da) - 8. inf [miserly] agarrado(da). ⬦ adv - 1. [hold, squeeze] con fuerza; **to hold tight** agarrarse (fuerte); **to shut** OR **close sthg tight** cerrar algo bien - 2. [pull, stretch] de modo tirante. ➡ **tights** npl medias fpl.

tighten ['taɪtn] ⬦ vt - 1. [hold, grip]: **to tighten one's hold** OR **grip on sthg** coger con más fuerza algo - **2.** [rope, chain] tensar - **3.** [knot] apretar; [bolt] apretar - **4.** [rules, system] intensificar - **v̇** [rope, chain] tensarse.

tightfisted [,taɪt'fɪstɪd] *adj inf pej* agarrado(da).

tightly ['taɪtlɪ] *adv* - **1.** [hold, squeeze] con fuerza; [fasten] bien - **2.** [pack] apretadamente.

tightrope ['taɪtrəʊp] *n* cuerda *f* floja; **to be on OR walking a tightrope** andar OR bailar en la cuerda floja.

tile [taɪl] *n* - **1.** [on roof] teja *f* - **2.** [on floor] baldosa *f*; [on wall] azulejo *m*.

tiled [taɪld] *adj* [roof] tejado(da); [floor] embaldosado(da); [wall]·alicatado(da).

till [tɪl] *prep* hasta; **till now/then** hasta ahora/entonces. *conj* hasta que; **wait till he arrives** espera hasta que llegue. *n* caja *f* (registradora).

tiller ['tɪlər] *n* NAUT caña *f* del timón.

tilt [tɪlt] *vt* inclinar. *vi* inclinarse.

timber ['tɪmbər] *n* - **1.** (U) [wood] madera *f* *(para la construcción)* - **2.** [beam - of ship] cuaderna *f*; [- of house] viga *f*.

time [taɪm] *n* - **1.** [gen] tiempo *m*; **ahead of time** temprano; **in good time** con tiempo; **on time** puntualmente; **to take time** llevar tiempo; **it's (about) time to...** ya es hora de...; **to have no time for** no poder con, no aguantar; **to pass the time** pasar el rato; **to play for time** intentar ganar tiempo - **2.** [as measured by clock] hora *f*; **what time is it?, what's the time?** ¿qué hora es?; **the time is three o'clock** son las tres; **in a week's/year's time** dentro de una semana/un año - **3.** [length of time] rato *m*; **it was a long time before he came** pasó mucho tiempo antes de que viniera; **for a time** durante un tiempo - **4.** [point in time in past, era] época *f*; **at that time** en aquella época - **5.** [occasion] vez *f*; **three times a week** tres veces a la semana; **from time to time** de vez en cuando - **6.** MUS compás *m*; **to keep time** llevar el compás. *vt* - **1.** [schedule] programar - **2.** [race, runner] cronometrar - **3.** [arrival, remark] elegir el momento oportuno para. **times** *n*: **four times as much as me** cuatro veces más que yo. *prep* MATHS: **4 times 5** 4 por 5. **about time** *adv*: **it's about time** ya va siendo hora. **at a time** *adv*: **for months at a time** durante meses seguidos; **one at a time** de uno en uno. **at times** *adv* a veces. **at the same time** *adv* al mismo tiempo. **for the time being** *adv* de momento. **in time** *adv* - **1.** [not late]: **in time (for)** a tiempo (para) - **2.** [eventually] con el tiempo.

time bomb *n* [bomb] bomba *f* de relojería; *fig* [dangerous situation] bomba *f*.

time lag *n* intervalo *m*.

timeless ['taɪmlɪs] *adj* eterno(na).

time limit *n* plazo *m*.

timely ['taɪmlɪ] *adj* oportuno(na).

time off *n* tiempo *m* libre.

time out *n US* SPORT tiempo *m* muerto.

timer ['taɪmər] *n* temporizador *m*.

time scale *n* tiempo *m* de ejecución.

time-share *n UK* multipropiedad *f*.

time switch *n* interruptor *m* de reloj.

timetable ['taɪm,teɪbl] *n* - **1.** [of buses, trains, school] horario *m* - **2.** [schedule of events] programa *m*.

time zone *n* huso *m* horario.

timid ['tɪmɪd] *adj* tímido(da).

timing ['taɪmɪŋ] *n* (U) - **1.** [judgment]: **she made her comment with perfect timing** su comentario fue hecho en el momento más oportuno - **2.** [scheduling]: **the timing of the election is crucial** es crucial que las elecciones se celebren en el momento oportuno - **3.** [measuring] cronometraje *m*.

timpani ['tɪmpənɪ] *npl* timbales *mpl*.

tin [tɪn] *n* - **1.** [metal] estaño *m*; **tin plate** hojalata *f* - **2.** *UK* [can, container] lata *f*.

tin can *n* lata *f*.

tinfoil ['tɪnfɔɪl] *n* (U) papel *m* de aluminio.

tinge [tɪndʒ] *n* - **1.** [of colour] matiz *m* - **2.** [of feeling] ligera sensación *f*.

tinged [tɪndʒd] *adj*: **tinged with** con un toque de.

tingle ['tɪŋgl] *vi*: **my feet are tingling** siento hormigueo en los pies.

tinker ['tɪŋkər] *vi* hacer chapuzas; **to tinker with** enredar con.

tinkle ['tɪŋkl] *vi* [ring] tintinear.

tinned [tɪnd] *adj UK* enlatado(da), en conserva.

tin opener *n UK* abrelatas *m inv*.

tinsel ['tɪnsl] *n* (U) oropel *m*.

tint [tɪnt] *n* tinte *m*, matiz *m*.

tinted ['tɪntɪd] *adj* [glasses, windows] tintado(da), ahumado(da).

tiny ['taɪnɪ] *adj* diminuto(ta), pequeñito(ta).

tip [tɪp] *n* - **1.** [end] punta *f* - **2.** *UK* [dump] vertedero *m* - **3.** [gratuity] propina *f* - **4.** [piece of advice] consejo *m*. *vt* - **1.** [tilt] inclinar, ladear - **2.** [spill, pour] vaciar, verter - **3.** [give a gratuity to] dar una propina a. *vi* - **1.** [tilt] inclinarse, ladearse - **2.** [spill] derramarse. **tip over** *vt sep* volcar. *vi* volcarse.

tip-off *n* información *f* (confidencial).

tipped [tɪpt] *adj* [cigarette] con filtro.

tipsy ['tɪpsɪ] *adj inf dated* piripi.

tiptoe ['tɪptəʊ] *n*: **on tiptoe** de puntillas.

tip-top *adj inf dated* de primera.

tire ['taɪər] *n US* = **tyre**. *vt* cansar. *vi*: **to tire (of)** cansarse (de).

tired ['taɪəd] *adj*: **tired (of sthg/of doing sthg)** cansado(da) (de algo/de hacer algo).

tireless ['taɪəlɪs] *adj* incansable.

tiresome ['taɪəsəm] *adj* pesado(da).

tiring ['taɪərɪŋ] *adj* cansado(da).

tissue ['tɪʃuː] *n* - 1. [paper handkerchief] pañuelo *m* de papel - 2. (*U*) BIOL tejido *m* - 3. [paper] papel *m* de seda.

tissue paper *n* (*U*) papel *m* de seda.

tit [tɪt] *n* - 1. [bird] herrerillo *m* - 2. *vulg* [breast] teta *f*.

titbit *UK* ['tɪtbɪt], **tidbit** *US* ['tɪdbɪt] *n* - 1. [of food] golosina *f* - 2. *fig* [of news] noticia *f* breve e interesante.

tit for tat [-'tæt] *n*: **it's tit for tat** donde las dan las toman.

titillate ['tɪtɪleɪt] *vt & vi* excitar.

title ['taɪtl] *n* título *m*.

title deed *n* título *m* de propiedad.

title role *n* papel *m* principal.

titter ['tɪtə'] *vi* reírse por lo bajo.

TM *abbr of* **trademark**.

to (*unstressed before consonant* [tə], *unstressed before vowel* [tʊ], *stressed* [tuː]) <> *prep* - 1. [indicating place, direction] a; **to go to Liverpool/Spain/school** ir a Liverpool/España/la escuela; **to go to the doctor's/John's** ir al médico/a casa de John; **the road to Glasgow** la carretera de Glasgow; **to the left/right** a la izquierda/derecha; **to the east/west** hacia el este/oeste - 2. (*to express indirect object*) a; **to give sthg to sb** darle algo a alguien; **to talk to sb** hablar con alguien; **a threat to sb** una amenaza para alguien; **we were listening to the radio** escuchábamos la radio - 3. [as far as] hasta, a; **to count to ten** contar hasta diez; **we work from nine to five** trabajamos de nueve a cinco - 4. [in expressions of time]: **it's ten/a quarter to three** son las tres menos diez/cuarto - 5. [per] por; **40 miles to the gallon** un galón (por) cada 40 millas - 6. [of] de; **the key to the car** la llave del coche - 7. [for] para; **a letter to my daughter** una carta para *OR* a mi hija - 8. [indicating reaction, effect]: **to my surprise** para sorpresa mía - 9. [in stating opinion]: **it seemed quite unnecessary to me/him** *etc* para mí/él *etc* aquello parecía del todo innecesario - 10. [indicating state, process]: **to lead to trouble** traer problemas. <> *adv* [shut]: **push the door to** cierra la puerta. <> *with inf* - 1. (*forming simple infinitive*): **to walk** andar - 2. (*following another vb*): **to begin to do sthg** empezar a hacer algo; **to try/want to do sthg** intentar/querer hacer algo; **to hate to have to do sthg** odiar tener que hacer algo - 3. (*following an adj*): **difficult to do** difícil de hacer; **ready to go** listos para marchar - 4. (*indicating purpose*) para; **I'm doing it to help you** lo hago para ayudarte; **he came to see me** vino a verme - 5. (*substituting for a relative clause*): **I have a lot to do** tengo mucho que hacer; **he told me to leave me** dijo que me fuera - 6. (*to avoid repetition of infinitive*): **I meant to call him but I forgot to** tenía intención de llamarle pero se me olvidó - 7. [in comments]: **to be honest...** para ser honesto...; **to sum up...** resumiendo... <>> **to and fro** *adv* de un lado para otro, de aquí para allá.

toad [təʊd] *n* sapo *m*.

toadstool ['təʊdstuːl] *n* seta *f* venenosa.

toast [təʊst] <> *n* - 1. (*U*) [bread] pan *m* tostado; **a slice of toast** una tostada - 2. [drink] brindis *m*. <> *vt* - 1. [bread] tostar - 2. [person] brindar por.

toasted sandwich [ˌtəʊstɪd-] *n* sándwich *m* tostado.

toaster ['təʊstə'] *n* tostador *m*, -ra *f*.

tobacco [tə'bækəʊ] *n* tabaco *m*.

toboggan [tə'bɒgən] *n* tobogán *m*, trineo *m*.

today [tə'deɪ] <> *n* - 1. [this day] hoy *m*; **today's date** la fecha de hoy; **what is today's date?** ¿qué día es hoy?; **today's paper** el periódico de hoy; **as from today** a partir de hoy - 2. [nowadays] hoy (en día). <> *adv* - 1. [this day] hoy; **what's the date today?, what date is it today** ¿qué fecha es hoy?; **today is the 6th of January** hoy es el 6 de enero; **what day is it today?** ¿qué día es hoy?; **it's Sunday today** hoy es domingo; **a week ago today** hoy hace una semana; **a week (from) today** de aquí a una semana - 2. [nowadays] hoy (en día).

toddler ['tɒdlə'] *n* niño pequeño *m*, niña pequeña *f* (que empieza a andar).

toddy ['tɒdɪ] *n* ponche *m*.

to-do (*pl* -s) *n* *inf* jaleo *m*.

toe [təʊ] <> *n* - 1. [of foot] dedo *m* (del pie) - 2. [of sock] punta *f*; [of shoe] puntera *f*. <> *vt*: **to toe the line** acatar las normas.

toenail ['təʊneɪl] *n* uña *f* del dedo del pie.

toffee ['tɒfɪ] *n* caramelo *m*.

toga ['təʊgə] *n* toga *f*.

together [tə'geðə'] *adv* - 1. [gen] juntos(tas); **all together** todos juntos; **to stick together** pegar; **to go (well) together** combinar bien - 2. [at the same time] a la vez, juntos(tas). <>> **together with** *prep* junto con.

toil [tɔɪl] *fml* <> *n* trabajo *m* duro. <> *vi* trabajar sin descanso.

toilet ['tɔɪlɪt] *n* [at home] wáter *m*, lavabo *m*; [in public place] servicios *mpl*, lavabo *m*; **to go to the toilet** ir al wáter.

toilet bag *n* neceser *m*.

toilet paper *n* (*U*) papel *m* higiénico.

toiletries ['tɔɪlɪtrɪz] *npl* artículos *mpl* de tocador.

toilet roll *n* [roll] rollo *m* de papel higiénico.

toilet water n (agua f de) colonia f.

token ['təʊkn] ◇ adj simbólico(ca) ◇ n - 1. [voucher] vale m; [disk] ficha f - 2. [symbol] muestra f, símbolo m; **as a token of our appreciation** como muestra de nuestro agradecimiento. ◆ **by the same token** adv del mismo modo.

told [təʊld] pt & pp ▷ **tell**.

tolerable ['tɒlərəbl] adj tolerable, pasable.

tolerance ['tɒlərəns] n tolerancia f.

tolerant ['tɒlərənt] adj tolerante.

tolerate ['tɒləreɪt] vt - 1. [put up with] soportar, tolerar - 2. [permit] tolerar.

toll [təʊl] ◇ n - 1. [number]: **death toll** número m de víctimas - 2. [fee] peaje m ▷▷▷ **to take its toll** hacer mella. ◇ vi tocar, doblar.

toll-free US adv: **to call a number toll-free** llamar a un número gratis.

tomato [UK təˈmɑːtəʊ, US təˈmeɪtəʊ] (pl -es) n tomate m, jitomate m Amér C & Méx.

tomb [tuːm] n tumba f, sepulcro m.

tomboy ['tɒmbɔɪ] n niña f poco femenina.

tombstone ['tuːmstəʊn] n lápida f.

tomcat ['tɒmkæt] n gato m (macho).

tomorrow [təˈmɒrəʊ] ◇ n lit & fig mañana f; **tomorrow is Sunday** mañana es domingo; **the day after tomorrow** pasado mañana; **tomorrow night** mañana por la noche; **he was drinking like there was no tomorrow** bebía como si se fuera a acabar el mundo; **tomorrow's world** el futuro. ◇ adv mañana; **see you tomorrow** hasta mañana; **a week (from) tomorrow** dentro de una semana, a partir de mañana; **it happened a year ago tomorrow** mañana hará un año que ocurrió.

ton [tʌn] (pl ton OR -s) n - 1. UK [imperial] = 1016 kg; US = 907,2 kg, ≃ tonelada f - 2. [metric] = 1000 kg tonelada f. ◆ **tons** npl inf: **tons (of)** un montón (de).

tone [təʊn] n - 1. [gen] tono m - 2. [on phone] señal f. ◆ **tone down** vt sep suavizar, moderar. ◆ **tone up** vt sep poner en forma.

tone-deaf adj que no tiene (buen) oído.

tongs [tɒŋz] npl [for coal] tenazas fpl; [for sugar] pinzas fpl, tenacillas fpl.

tongue [tʌŋ] n - 1. [gen] lengua f - 2. [of shoe] lengüeta f.

tongue-in-cheek adj: **it was only tongue-in-cheek** no iba en serio.

tongue-tied [-,taɪd] adj incapaz de hablar (por timidez o nervios).

tongue twister [-,twɪstər] n trabalenguas m inv.

tonic ['tɒnɪk] n - 1. [gen] tónico m - 2. [tonic water] tónica f.

tonic water n agua f tónica.

tonight [təˈnaɪt] ◇ n esta noche f. ◇ adv esta noche.

tonnage ['tʌnɪdʒ] n tonelaje m.

tonne [tʌn] (pl tonne OR -s) n tonelada f métrica.

tonsil ['tɒnsl] n amígdala f; **to have one's tonsils out** operarse de las amígdalas.

tonsil(l)itis [,tɒnsɪˈlaɪtɪs] n (U) amigdalitis f inv.

too [tuː] adv - 1. [also] también; **me too** yo también - 2. [excessively] demasiado; **too much** demasiado; **too many things** demasiadas cosas; **it finished all OR only too soon** terminó demasiado pronto; **I'd be only too happy to help me** encantaría ayudarte; **not too...** no muy...

took [tʊk] pt ▷ **take**.

tool [tuːl] n [implement] herramienta f; **garden tools** útiles mpl del jardín.

tool bar n COMPUT barra f de herramientas.

tool box n caja f de herramientas.

tool kit n juego m de herramientas.

toot [tuːt] ◇ n bocinazo m. ◇ vi tocar la bocina.

tooth [tuːθ] (pl teeth) n [in mouth, of saw, gear wheel] diente m; **to brush one's teeth** cepillarse OR lavarse los dientes; **he had a tooth out** le sacaron un diente.

toothache ['tuːθeɪk] n dolor m de muelas.

toothbrush ['tuːθbrʌʃ] n cepillo m de dientes.

toothpaste ['tuːθpeɪst] n pasta f de dientes.

toothpick ['tuːθpɪk] n palillo m.

top [tɒp] ◇ adj - 1. [highest - step, floor] de arriba; [- object on pile] de encima - 2. [most important, successful] importante; **to be a top model** ser top model; **she got the top mark** sacó la mejor nota - 3. [maximum] máximo(ma); **at top speed** a máxima velocidad; **to be top secret** ser altamente confidencial. ◇ n - 1. [highest point] parte f superior OR de arriba; [of list] cabeza f, principio m; [of tree] copa f; [of hill, mountain] cumbre f, cima f; **at the top of the stairs** en lo alto de la escalera; **from top to bottom** de pies a cabeza; **on top** encima; **to go over the top** UK pasarse (de la raya); **at the top of one's voice** a voz en grito - 2. [lid, cap - of jar, box] tapa f; [- of bottle, tube] tapón m; [- of pen] capuchón m - 3. [upper side] superficie f - 4. [blouse] blusa f; [T-shirt] camiseta f; [of pyjamas] parte f de arriba - 5. [toy] peonza f - 6. [most important level] cúpula f - 7. [of league, table, scale] cabeza f. ◇ vt - 1. [be first in] estar a la cabeza de - 2. [better] superar - 3. [exceed] exceder. ◆ **on top of** prep - 1. [in space] encima de; **to be feeling on top of the**

world estar en la gloria - **2.** [in addition to] además de. ◆ **top up** *UK*, **top off** *US vt sep* volver a llenar.

top floor *n* último piso *m*.

top hat *n* sombrero *m* de copa.

top-heavy *adj* demasiado pesado(da) en la parte de arriba.

topic ['tɒpɪk] *n* tema *m*, asunto *m*.

topical ['tɒpɪkl] *adj* actual.

topless ['tɒplɪs] *adj* en topless.

top-level *adj* de alto nivel.

topmost ['tɒpməʊst] *adj* más alto(ta).

topping ['tɒpɪŋ] *n* capa *f*; **with a topping of cream** cubierto de nata.

topple ['tɒpl] ◇ *vt* [government, pile] derribar; [president] derrocar. ◇ *vi* venirse abajo.

top-secret *adj* sumamente secreto (sumamente secreta).

topsy-turvy [,tɒpsɪ'tɜ:vɪ] ◇ *adj* [messy] patas arriba *(inv)*. ◇ *adv* [messily] en desorden, de cualquier manera.

top-up *n*: **can I give you a top-up?** ¿quieres que te ponga más?

top-up card *n* [for mobile phone] tarjeta *f* de recarga.

torch [tɔ:tʃ] *n* - **1.** *UK* [electric] linterna *f* - **2.** [burning] antorcha *f*.

tore [tɔ:ʳ] *pt* ▷ **tear²**.

torment ◇ *n* ['tɔ:ment] tormento *m*; **she waited in torment** esperaba atormentada. ◇ *vt* [tɔ:'ment] - **1.** [worry greatly] atormentar - **2.** [annoy] fastidiar.

torn [tɔ:n] *pp* ▷ **tear²**.

tornado [tɔ:'neɪdəʊ] *(pl* **-es** OR **-s)** *n* tornado *m*.

torpedo [tɔ:'pi:dəʊ] *n* *(pl* **-es)** torpedo *m*.

torrent ['tɒrənt] *n* torrente *m*.

torrid ['tɒrɪd] *adj* [hot] tórrido(da); *fig* [passionate] apasionado(da).

tortoise ['tɔ:təs] *n* tortuga *f* (de tierra).

tortoiseshell ['tɔ:təʃel] ◇ *adj*: **tortoiseshell cat** gato *m* pardo atigrado. ◇ *n (U)* [material] carey *m*, concha *f*.

torture ['tɔ:tʃəʳ] ◇ *n* tortura *f*. ◇ *vt* torturar.

Tory ['tɔ:rɪ] ◇ *adj* tory, del partido conservador (británico). ◇ *n* tory *mf*, miembro *m* del partido conservador (británico).

toss [tɒs] ◇ *vt* - **1.** [throw carelessly] tirar - **2.** [move from side to side - head, boat] sacudir - **3.** [salad] remover; [pancake] dar la vuelta en el aire - **4.** [coin]: **to toss a coin** echar a cara o cruz. ◇ *vi* [move rapidly]: **to toss and turn** dar vueltas (en la cama). ◆ **toss up** *vi* jugar a cara o cruz.

tot [tɒt] *n* - **1.** *inf* [small child] nene *m*, nena *f* - **2.** [of drink] trago *m*.

total ['təʊtl] ◇ *adj* total. ◇ *n* total *m*. ◇ *vt* (*UK pt* & *pp* **-led**, *cont* **-ling**, *US pt* & *pp* **-ed**, *cont* **-ing**) [add up] sumar. ◇ *vi* (*UK pt* & *pp* **-led**, *cont* **-ling**, *US pt* & *pp* **-ed**, *cont* **-ing**) [amount to] ascender a.

totalitarian [,təʊtælɪ'teərɪən] *adj* totalitario(ria).

totally ['təʊtəlɪ] *adv* [entirely] totalmente.

totter ['tɒtəʳ] *vi lit* & *fig* tambalearse.

touch [tʌtʃ] ◇ *n* - **1.** [sense, act of feeling] tacto *m* - **2.** [detail, skill, knack] toque *m*; **to put the finishing touches to sthg** dar el último toque a algo - **3.** [contact]: **to get/keep in touch (with)** ponerse/mantenerse en contacto (con); **to lose touch (with)** perder el contacto (con); **to be out of touch (with)** no estar al tanto de - **4.** SPORT: **in touch** fuera de banda - **5.** [small amount]: **a touch (of)** un poquito (de). ◇ *vt* - **1.** [gen] tocar; **you haven't touched your food** no has tocado la comida - **2.** [emotionally] conmover - **3.** [equal] igualar; **nobody can touch her for professionalism** nadie la iguala en profesionalismo. ◇ *vi* [be in contact] tocarse. ◆ **touch down** *vi* [plane] aterrizar. ◆ **touch on** *vt insep* tratar por encima.

touch-and-go *adj* dudoso(sa), poco seguro (poco segura).

touchdown ['tʌtʃdaʊn] *n* - **1.** [of plane] aterrizaje *m* - **2.** [in American football] ensayo *m*.

touched [tʌtʃt] *adj* [grateful] emocionado(da).

touching ['tʌtʃɪŋ] *adj* conmovedor(ra).

touchline ['tʌtʃlaɪn] *n* línea *f* de banda.

touchscreen ['tʌtʃskri:n] *n* pantalla *f* táctil.

touchy ['tʌtʃɪ] *adj* - **1.** [person]: **touchy (about)** susceptible (con) - **2.** [subject, question] delicado(da).

tough [tʌf] *adj* - **1.** [resilient] fuerte - **2.** [hardwearing] resistente - **3.** [meat, regulations, policies] duro(ra) - **4.** [difficult to deal with] difícil - **5.** [rough - area] peligroso(sa).

toughen ['tʌfn] *vt* endurecer.

toupee ['tu:peɪ] *n* peluquín *m*.

tour [tʊəʳ] ◇ *n* - **1.** [long journey] viaje *m* largo; **to go on a tour of Germany** hacer un recorrido por Alemania - **2.** [of pop group etc] gira *f* - **3.** [for sightseeing] recorrido *m*, visita *f*. ◇ *vt* [museum] visitar; [country] recorrer, viajar por. ◇ *vi* estar de gira.

Tourette's Syndrome, Tourette syndrome *n* MED síndrome *m* de Tourette.

touring ['tʊərɪŋ] *n* viajes *mpl* turísticos.

tourism ['tʊərɪzm] *n* turismo *m*.

tourist ['tʊərɪst] *n* turista *mf*.

tourist (information) office *n* oficina *f* de turismo.

tournament ['tɔ:nəmənt] *n* torneo *m*.

tour operator *n* touroperador *m*.

tousled ['tauzl] *adj* despeinado(da), alborotado(da).

tout [taut] ⟨⟩ *n* revendedor *m*, -ra *f*. ⟨⟩ *vt* revender. ⟨⟩ *vi*: **to tout for sthg** solicitar algo; **to tout for business** tratar de captar clientes.

tow [təu] ⟨⟩ *n*: **to give sb a tow** remolcar a alguien; **in tow with sb** acompañado de alguien. ⟨⟩ *vt* remolcar.

towards *UK* [tə'wɔːdz], **toward** *US* [tə'wɔːd] *prep* - **1.** [gen] hacia - **2.** [for the purpose or benefit of] para.

towel ['tauəl] *n* toalla *f*.

towelling *UK*, **toweling** *US* ['tauəlɪŋ] *n (U)* (tejido *m* de) toalla *f*.

towel rail *n* toallero *m*.

tower ['tauər] ⟨⟩ *n* torre *f*; **a tower of strength** *UK* un firme apoyo OR pilar. ⟨⟩ *vi*: **to tower over sb** ser mucho más alto(ta) que alguien.

tower block *n UK* bloque *m* (*de pisos u oficinas*).

towering ['tauərɪŋ] *adj* altísimo(ma).

town [taun] *n* - **1.** [gen] ciudad *f*; [smaller] pueblo *m* - **2.** [centre of town, city] centro *m* de la ciudad; **to go out on the town** irse de juerga; **to go to town** *fig* [to put in a lot of effort] emplearse a fondo; [spend a lot of money] tirar la casa por la ventana.

town centre *n* centro *m* (de la ciudad).

town council *n* ayuntamiento *m*.

town hall *n* ayuntamiento *m*.

town plan *n* plano *m* de la ciudad.

town planning *n* [study] urbanismo *m*.

township ['taunʃɪp] *n* - **1.** [in South Africa] zona urbana asignada por el gobierno para la población negra - **2.** [in US] = municipio *m*.

towpath ['təupɑːθ, *pl* -pɑːðz] *n* camino *m* de sirga.

towrope ['təurəup] *n* cable *m* de remolque.

tow truck *n US* (coche *m*) grúa *f*.

toxic ['tɒksɪk] *adj* tóxico(ca).

toy [tɔɪ] *n* juguete *m*. ⬥ **toy with** *vt insep* [idea] acariciar; [food, coin etc] jugetear con.

toy shop *n* juguetería *f*.

trace [treɪs] ⟨⟩ *n* - **1.** [evidence, remains] rastro *m*, huella *f*; **there's no trace of her** no hay rastro de ella - **2.** [small amount] pizca *f*. ⟨⟩ *vt* - **1.** [find] localizar, encontrar - **2.** [follow progress of] describir - **3.** [on paper] calcar.

tracing paper ['treɪsɪŋ-] *n (U)* papel *m* de calcar.

track [træk] ⟨⟩ *n* - **1.** [path] sendero *m* - **2.** SPORT pista *f* - **3.** RAIL vía *f* - **4.** [mark, trace] rastro *m*, huella *f* - **5.** [on record, tape] canción *f* **to be on the right/wrong track** ir por el buen/mal camino. ⟨⟩ *vt* [follow] seguir la pista de. ⬥ **track down** *vt sep* localizar.

track record *n* historial *m*; **to have a good track record** tener un buen historial.

tracksuit ['træksuːt] *n* chandal *m*, equipo *m* de deportes, buzo *m* *Chile & Perú*, pants *mpl Méx*, sudadera *f Col*, jogging *m R Plata*.

tract [trækt] *n* - **1.** [pamphlet] artículo *m* breve - **2.** [of land, forest] extensión *f*.

traction ['trækʃn] *n* tracción *f*; **to have one's leg in traction** tener la pierna escayolada en alto.

tractor ['træktər] *n* tractor *m*.

trade [treɪd] ⟨⟩ *n* - **1.** (U) [commerce] comercio *m* - **2.** [job] oficio *m*; **by trade** de oficio. ⟨⟩ *vt* [exchange]: **to trade sthg (for)** cambiar algo (por). ⟨⟩ *vi* COMM: **to trade (with)** comerciar (con). ⬥ **trade in** *vt sep* [exchange] dar como entrada.

trade fair *n* feria *f* de muestras.

trade-in *n* artículo usado que se entrega como entrada al comprar un artículo nuevo.

trademark ['treɪdmɑːk] *n* COMM marca *f* comercial.

trade name *n* COMM nombre *m* comercial.

trader ['treɪdər] *n* comerciante *mf*.

tradesman ['treɪdzmən] (*pl* -men [-mən]) *n* [trader] comerciante *m*; [shopkeeper] tendero *m*.

trade(s) union *n UK* sindicato *m*.

trade(s) unionist *n UK* sindicalista *mf*.

trading ['treɪdɪŋ] *n (U)* comercio *m*.

trading estate *n UK* polígono *m* industrial.

trading standards officer *n funcionario del organismo británico que vela por el cumplimiento de las normas comerciales*.

tradition [trə'dɪʃn] *n* tradición *f*.

traditional [trə'dɪʃənl] *adj* tradicional.

traffic ['træfɪk] ⟨⟩ *n* - **1.** [vehicles] tráfico *m* - **2.** [illegal trade]: **traffic (in)** tráfico *m* (de). ⟨⟩ *vi* (*pt & pp* -ked, *cont* -king): **to traffic in** traficar con.

traffic circle *n US* glorieta *f*.

traffic jam *n* embotellamiento *m*.

trafficker ['træfɪkər] *n*: **trafficker (in)** traficante *mf* (de).

traffic lights *npl* semáforos *mpl*.

traffic warden *n UK* ≃ guardia *mf* de tráfico.

tragedy ['trædʒədɪ] *n* tragedia *f*.

tragic ['trædʒɪk] *adj* trágico(ca).

trail [treɪl] ⟨⟩ *n* - **1.** [path] sendero *m*, camino *m*; **to blaze a trail** *fig* marcar la pauta - **2.** [trace, track] rastro *m*, huellas *fpl*; **a trail of**

smoke un rastro de humo; **they left a trail of clues** dejaron un rastro de pistas; **to be on the trail of sb/sthg** seguir la pista de alguien/algo; **they are hot on his trail** le están pisando los talones. ◇ vt - **1.** [drag] arrastrar - **2.** [lose to] ir por detrás de. ◇ vi - **1.** [drag] arrastrarse - **2.** [move slowly] andar con desgana - **3.** [lose] ir perdiendo. ➡ **trail away, trail off** vi apagarse.

trailer ['treɪlə'] n - **1.** [vehicle for luggage] remolque m - **2.** esp US [for living in] roulotte m, caravana f - **3.** CIN trailer m.

train [treɪn] ◇ n - **1.** RAIL tren m; **to go by train** ir en tren - **2.** [of dress] cola f. ◇ vt - **1.** [teach]: **to train sb (to do sthg)** enseñar a alguien (a hacer algo); **to train sb in sthg** preparar a alguien para algo - **2.** [for job]: **to train sb (as sthg)** formar OR preparar a alguien (como algo) - **3.** [animal] amaestrar - **4.** SPORT: **to train sb (for)** entrenar a alguien (para) - **5.** [aim - gun] apuntar. ◇ vi - **1.** [for job] estudiar; **to train as** formarse OR prepararse como; **to train to be a teacher** estudiar para ser profesor - **2.** SPORT: **to train (for)** entrenarse (para).

trained [treɪnd] adj cualificado(da).

trainee [treɪ'niː] n aprendiz m, -za f.

trainer ['treɪnə'] n - **1.** [of animals] amaestrador m, -ra f - **2.** SPORT entrenador m, -ra f. ➡ **trainers** npl UK zapatillas fpl de deporte.

training ['treɪnɪŋ] n (U) - **1.** [for job]: **training (in)** formación f OR preparación f (para) - **2.** SPORT entrenamiento m; **to be in training (for sthg)** estar entrenando para algo.

training college n UK [gen] centro m de formación especializada; [for teachers] escuela f normal.

training shoes npl UK zapatillas fpl de deporte.

train of thought n hilo m del razonamiento.

traipse [treɪps] vi andar con desgana.

trait [treɪt] n rasgo m, característica f.

traitor ['treɪtə'] n: **traitor (to)** traidor m, -ra f (a).

trajectory [trə'dʒektəri] n trayectoria f.

tram [træm], **tramcar** ['træmkɑː'] n UK tranvía m.

tramp [træmp] ◇ n - **1.** [homeless person] vagabundo m, -da f - **2.** US inf [woman] fulana f. ◇ vi andar pesadamente.

trample ['træmpl] vt pisar, pisotear; **to be trampled underfoot** ser pisoteado(da).

trampoline ['træmpəliːn] n cama f elástica.

trance [trɑːns] n trance m; **to go into a trance** entrar en trance.

tranquil ['træŋkwɪl] adj liter tranquilo(la), apacible.

tranquillizer UK, **tranquilizer** US ['træŋkwɪlaɪzə'] n tranquilizante m.

transaction [træn'zækʃn] n transacción f; **money transactions** transacciones de dinero.

transcend [træn'send] vt fml ir más allá de.

transcript ['trænskrɪpt] n US expediente m académico.

transfer ◇ n ['trænsfɜː'] - **1.** [gen] transferencia f - **2.** [for job] traslado m - **3.** SPORT traspaso m - **4.** [design] calcomanía f. ◇ vt [træns'fɜːr] - **1.** [from one place to another] trasladar - **2.** [from one person to another] transferir. ◇ vi [træns'fɜːr] [to different job etc]: **he transferred to a different department** lo trasladaron a otro departamento.

transfix [træns'fɪks] vt [immobilize] paralizar; **transfixed with** paralizado(da) por.

transform [træns'fɔːm] vt: **to transform sthg/sb (into)** transformar algo/a alguien (en).

transfusion [træns'fjuːʒn] n transfusión f.

transient ['trænzɪənt] adj fml [fleeting] transitorio(ria), pasajero(ra).

transistor [træn'zɪstə'] n transistor m.

transistor radio n dated transistor m.

transit ['trænsɪt] n US transporte m; **in transit** en tránsito.

transition [træn'zɪʃn] n: **transition (from sthg to sthg)** transición f (de algo a algo).

transitive ['trænzɪtɪv] adj GRAM transitivo(va).

transitory ['trænzɪtrɪ] adj transitorio(ria).

translate [træns'leɪt] vt [languages] traducir.

translation [træns'leɪʃn] n traducción f.

translator [træns'leɪtə'] n traductor m, -ra f.

transmission [trænz'mɪʃn] n transmisión f.

transmit [trænz'mɪt] vt transmitir.

transmitter [trænz'mɪtə'] n ELECTRON transmisor m.

transparency [trans'pærənsɪ] n - **1.** [quality] transparencia f - **2.** [slide] diapositiva f.

transparent [træns'pærənt] adj - **1.** [seethrough] transparente - **2.** [obvious] claro(ra).

transpire [træn'spaɪə'] fml ◇ vt: **it transpires that...** resulta que... ◇ vi [happen] ocurrir.

transplant n ['trænsplɑːnt] trasplante m; **he had a heart transplant** le hicieron un trasplante de corazón.

transport ◇ n ['trænspɔːt] transporte m. ◇ vt [træn'spɔːt] transportar.

transportation [,trænspɔː'teɪʃn] n esp US transporte m.

transport cafe ['trænspɔːt-] n UK bar m de camioneros.

transpose [træns'pəuz] vt [change round] invertir.

trap [træp] ⬦ *n* trampa *f*, to lay a trap [for] tender una **trampa** (a). ⬦ *vt* - **1.** [catch - animals, birds] **coger con trampa** - **2.** [trick] atrapar, engañar - **3.** [finger]: **she trapped her fingers in the door** le pilló los dedos en la puerta.

trapdoor [ˌtræp'dɔːʳ] *n* [gen] trampilla *f*, trampa; THEAT escotillón *m*.

trapeze [trə'piːz] *n* trapecio *m*.

trappings ['træpɪŋz] *npl* atributos *mpl*.

trash [træʃ] *n* US lit & fig basura *f*.

trashcan ['træʃkæn] *n* US cubo *m* de la basura.

traumatic [trɔː'mætɪk] *adj* traumático(ca).

travel ['trævl] ⬦ *n* (U) viajes *mpl*. ⬦ *vt* (UK *pt* & *pp* -led, *cont* -ling, US *pt* & *pp* -ed, *cont* -ing) [place] viajar por; [distance] recorrer. ⬦ *vi* (UK *pt* & *pp* -led, *cont* -ling, US *pt* & *pp* -ed, *cont* -ing) viajar.

travel agency *n* agencia *f* de viajes.

travel agent *n* empleado *m*, -da *f* de una agencia de viajes; **travel agent's** agencia *f* de viajes.

traveller UK, **traveler** US ['trævləʳ] *n* [person on journey] viajero *m*, -ra *f*; UK (new age) **traveller** persona que vive en un vehículo y lleva un estilo de vida itinerante.

traveller's cheque *n* cheque *m* de viajero.

travelling UK, **traveling** US ['trævlɪŋ] *adj* [theatre, showman] ambulante.

travelsick ['trævəlsɪk] *adj* que se marea al viajar; **to be** OR **feel travelsick** estar mareado(da).

travesty ['trævəstɪ] *n* burda parodia *f*.

trawler ['trɔːləʳ] *n* trainera *f*.

tray [treɪ] *n* bandeja *f*.

treacherous ['tretʃərəs] *adj* - **1.** [plan, action] traicionero(ra); [person] traidor(ra) - **2.** [dangerous] peligroso(sa).

treachery ['tretʃərɪ] *n* traición *f*.

treacle ['triːkl] *n* UK melaza *f*.

tread [tred] ⬦ *n* - **1.** [on tyre, shoe] banda *f* - **2.** [sound of walking] pasos *mpl*. ⬦ *vi* (*pt* trod, *pp* **trodden**) [walk] andar; **to tread carefully** *fig* andar con pies de plomo.

treason ['triːzn] *n* traición *f*.

treasure ['treʒəʳ] ⬦ *n* lit & fig tesoro *m*. ⬦ *vt* guardar como oro en paño.

treasurer ['treʒərəʳ] *n* tesorero *m*, -ra *f*.

treasury ['treʒərɪ] *n* [room] habitación donde se guarda el tesoro de un castillo, de una catedral etc. ◆ **Treasury** *n*: **the Treasury** ≃ el Ministerio de Hacienda.

treat [triːt] ⬦ *vt* - **1.** [gen] tratar; **to treat sb well/badly** tratar bien/mal a alguien; **to treat sth as a joke** tomarse algo como si fuera broma; **to treat sb for sth** MED tratar a alguien de algo - **2.** [give sth special]: **to treat sb (to)** invi-

tar a alguien (a). ⬦ *n* [something special] regalo *m*; **he took me out to dinner as a treat** me invitó a cenar.

treatise ['triːtɪs] *n* fml: **treatise (on)** tratado *m* (sobre).

treatment ['triːtmənt] *n* - **1.** MED: **treatment (for)** tratamiento *m* (para) - **2.** [manner of dealing] trato *m*.

treaty ['triːtɪ] *n* tratado *m*.

treble ['trebl] ⬦ *adj* - **1.** MUS de tiple - **2.** [with numbers] triple. ⬦ *vt* triplicar. ⬦ *vi* triplicarse.

treble clef *n* clave *f* de sol.

tree [triː] *n* BOT & COMPUT árbol *m*.

tree-hugger *n* inf hum pej ecologista *mf*.

treetop ['triːtɒp] *n* copa *f* (de árbol).

tree-trunk *n* tronco *m* (de árbol).

trek [trek] *n* viaje *m* largo y difícil.

trellis ['trelɪs] *n* enrejado *m*, espaldera *f*.

tremble ['trembl] *vi* temblar; **to tremble with cold/fear** temblar de frío/miedo.

tremendous [trɪ'mendəs] *adj* - **1.** [impressive, large] enorme, tremendo(da) - **2.** inf [really good] estupendo(da).

tremor ['tremər] *n* - **1.** [of person, body, voice] estremecimiento *m* - **2.** [small earthquake] temblor *m*.

trench [trentʃ] *n* - **1.** [narrow channel] zanja *f* - **2.** MIL trinchera *f*.

trench coat *n* trinchera *f*, gabardina *f*, impermeable *m*.

trend [trend] *n* [tendency] tendencia *f*; [fashion] moda *f*; **to set a trend** establecer una moda.

trendy ['trendɪ] inf *adj* [person] moderno(na); [clothes] de moda.

trepidation [ˌtrepɪ'deɪʃn] *n* fml: **in** OR **with trepidation** con ansiedad OR agitación.

trespass ['trespəs] *vi* entrar ilegalmente; **to trespass on** entrar ilegalmente en; **'no trespassing'** 'prohibido el paso'.

trespasser ['trespəsər] *n* intruso *m*, -sa *f*; **'trespassers will be prosecuted'** 'los intrusos serán sancionados por la ley'.

trestle ['tresl] *n* caballete *m*.

trestle table *n* mesa *f* de caballete.

trial ['traɪəl] *n* - **1.** LAW juicio *m*, proceso *m*; **to be on trial (for)** ser procesado(da) (por); **to be brought to trial** ser llevado(da) a juicio - **2.** [test, experiment] prueba *f*; **on trial** de prueba; **by trial and error** a base de probar - **3.** [unpleasant experience] suplicio *m*, fastidio *m*.

triangle ['traɪæŋgl] *n* GEOM & MUS triángulo *m*.

tribe [traɪb] *n* tribu *f*.

tribunal [traɪ'bjuːnl] *n* tribunal *m*.

tributary ['trɪbjʊtrɪ] *n* afluente *m*.

tribute ['trɪbju:t] *n* - **1.** [credit] tributo *m*; **to be a tribute to** hacer honor a - **2.** (U) [respect, admiration]: **to pay tribute (to)** rendir homenaje (a).

trice [traɪs] *n*: **in a trice** en un dos por tres.

trick [trɪk] <> *n* - **1.** [to deceive] truco *m*; [to trap] trampa *f*; [joke] broma *f*; **to play a trick on sb** gastarle una broma a alguien - **2.** [in magic] juego *m* (de manos) - **3.** [knack] truco *m*; **that should do the trick** eso es lo que necesitamos. <> *vt* engañar; **to trick sb into doing sthg** engañar a alguien para que haga algo.

trickery ['trɪkərɪ] *n* (U) engaño *m*.

trickle ['trɪkl] <> *n* [of liquid] hilo *m*. <> *vi* - **1.** [liquid] resbalar *(formando un hilo)* - **2.** [people, things]: **to trickle in/out** llegar/salir poco a poco.

tricky ['trɪkɪ] *adj* [difficult] difícil.

tricycle ['traɪsɪkl] *n* triciclo *m*.

tried [traɪd] *adj*: **tried and tested** probado(da).

trifle ['traɪfl] *n* - **1.** UK CULIN *postre de bizcocho con gelatina, crema, frutas y nata* - **2.** [unimportant thing] nadería *f*. **a trifle** *adv fml* un poco, ligeramente.

trifling ['traɪflɪŋ] *adj pej* trivial.

trigger ['trɪgər] *n* [on gun] gatillo *m*. **trigger off** *vt sep* desencadenar.

trill [trɪl] *n* trino *m*.

trim [trɪm] <> *adj* - **1.** [neat and tidy] limpio y arreglado (limpia y arreglada) - **2.** [slim] esbelto(ta). <> *n* [of hair] recorte *m*. <> *vt* - **1.** [nails, moustache] recortar - **2.** [decorate]: **to trim sthg (with)** adornar algo (con).

trimmings ['trɪmɪŋz] *npl* - **1.** [on clothing] adornos *mpl* - **2.** [with food] guarnición *f*.

trinket ['trɪŋkɪt] *n* baratija *f*.

trio ['tri:əʊ] (*pl* -s) *n* trío *m*.

trip [trɪp] <> *n* drug sl [gen] viaje *m*; **to be (away) on a trip** estar de viaje; **a trip to London/the seaside** un viaje a Londres/la costa. <> *vt* [make stumble] hacer la zancadilla a. <> *vi* [stumble] tropezar; **to trip over sthg** tropezar con algo. **trip up** *vt sep* [make stumble] hacer tropezar, hacer la zancadilla a.

tripe [traɪp] (U) *n* - **1.** CULIN callos *mpl* - **2.** *inf* [nonsense] tonterías *fpl*.

triple ['trɪpl] <> *adj* triple. <> *adv*: **triple the quantity** el triple. <> *vt* triplicar. <> *vi* triplicarse.

triple jump *n*: **the triple jump** el triple salto.

triplets ['trɪplɪts] *npl* trillizos *mpl*, -zas *fpl*.

triplicate ['trɪplɪkət] *n*: **in triplicate** por triplicado.

tripod ['traɪpɒd] *n* trípode *m*.

trite [traɪt] *adj pej* trillado(da).

triumph ['traɪəmf] <> *n* triunfo *m*. <> *vi*: **to triumph (over)** triunfar (sobre).

trivia ['trɪvɪə] *n* (U) trivialidades *fpl*.

trivial ['trɪvɪəl] *adj pej* trivial.

trod [trɒd] *pt* ▷ **tread**.

trodden ['trɒdn] *pp* ▷ **tread**.

trolley ['trɒlɪ] (*pl* trolleys) *n* - **1.** UK [for shopping, food, drinks] carrito *m* - **2.** US [tram] tranvía *m*.

trolley case *n* maleta *f* tipo carrito.

trombone [trɒm'bəʊn] *n* trombón *m*.

troop [tru:p] <> *n* [of people] grupo *m*, bandada *f*. <> *vi* ir en grupo. **troops** *npl* tropas *fpl*. **troop in** *vi* entrar en tropel. **troop out** *vi* salir en tropel.

trooper ['tru:pər] *n* - **1.** MIL soldado *m* de caballería - **2.** US [policeman] *miembro de la policía estatal*.

trophy ['trəʊfɪ] *n* SPORT trofeo *m*.

tropical ['trɒpɪkl] *adj* tropical.

tropics ['trɒpɪks] *npl*: **the tropics** el trópico.

trot [trɒt] <> *n* - **1.** [of horse] trote *m* - **2.** [of person] paso *m* rápido. <> *vi* - **1.** [horse] trotar - **2.** [person] andar con pasos rápidos. **on the trot** *adv inf*: **three times on the trot** tres veces seguidas.

trouble ['trʌbl] <> *n* (U) - **1.** [bother] molestia *f*; [difficulty, main problem] problema *m*; **to tell sb one's troubles** contarle a alguien sus problemas; **would it be too much trouble to ask you to...?** ¿tendría inconveniente en...?; **to be in trouble** tener problemas; **to have trouble doing sthg** tener problemas haciendo algo; **what seems to be the trouble?** ¿cuál es el problema? - **2.** [pain] dolor *m*; [illness] enfermedad *f*; **heart trouble** problemas cardiacos; **back trouble** problemas de espalda; **I'm having trouble with my leg** me está molestando la pierna - **3.** [violence, unpleasantness] problemas *mpl*. <> *vt* - **1.** [worry, upset] preocupar - **2.** [disturb, give pain to] molestar. **troubles** *npl* - **1.** [problems, worries] problemas *mpl* - **2.** POL conflicto *m*.

troubled ['trʌbld] *adj* - **1.** [worried, upset] preocupado(da) - **2.** [disturbed, problematic] agitado(da), turbulento(da).

troublemaker ['trʌbl,meɪkər] *n* alborotador *m*, -ra *f*.

troubleshooter ['trʌbl,ʃu:tər] *n* [in organizations] *persona contratada para resolver problemas*.

troublesome ['trʌblsəm] *adj* molesto(ta).

trough [trɒf] *n* - **1.** [for drinking] abrevadero *m*; [for eating] comedero *m* - **2.** [low point] punto *m* más bajo.

troupe [tru:p] *n* compañía *f*.

trousers ['traʊzəz] *npl* pantalones *mpl*.

trousseau ['tru:səʊ] (pl -x [-z] OR -s) n trousseau m.

trout [traʊt] (pl trout OR -s) n trucha f.

trowel ['traʊəl] n - 1. [for the garden] desplantador m - 2. [for cement, plaster] paleta f, palustre m.

truant ['tru:ənt] n [child] alumno m, -na f que hace novillos; **to play truant** hacer novillos.

truce [tru:s] n: **truce (between)** tregua f (entre).

truck [trʌk] n - 1. [lorry] camión m - 2. RAIL vagón m de mercancías.

truck driver n esp US camionero m, -ra f.

trucker ['trʌkər] n US camionero m, -ra f.

truck farm n US puesto de verduras y frutas para la venta.

truculent ['trʌkjʊlənt] adj agresivo(va), pendenciero(ra).

trudge [trʌdʒ] vi caminar con dificultad.

true [tru:] adj - 1. [gen] verdadero(ra); **it's true** es verdad; **to come true** hacerse realidad - 2. [genuine] auténtico(ca); [friend] de verdad - 3. [exact] exacto(ta).

truffle ['trʌfl] n trufa f.

truly ['tru:lɪ] adv verdaderamente; **yours truly** le saluda atentamente.

trump [trʌmp] n triunfo m (en cartas).

trumped-up ['trʌmpt-] adj pej inventado(da).

trumpet ['trʌmpɪt] n trompeta f.

truncheon ['trʌntʃən] n porra f.

trundle ['trʌndl] vi rodar lentamente; **he trundled along to the post office** se arrastró lentamente hasta correos.

trunk [trʌŋk] n - 1. [of tree, person] tronco m - 2. [of elephant] trompa f - 3. [box] baúl m - 4. US [of car] maletero m, cajuela f Méx, baúl m Col & R Plata, maletera f Perú. ◆ **trunks** npl bañador m (de hombre) Esp, traje m de baño (de hombre).

trunk call n UK conferencia f Esp, llamada f interurbana.

trunk road n ≃ carretera f nacional.

truss [trʌs] ◇ n MED braguero m. ◇ vt: **truss (up)** atar.

trust [trʌst] ◇ vt - 1. [believe in] confiar en - 2. [have confidence in]: **to trust sb to do sthg** confiar en alguien para que haga algo - 3. [entrust]: **to trust sb with sthg** confiar algo a alguien - 4. [accept as safe, reliable] fiarse de. ◇ n - 1. (U) [faith, responsibility]: **trust (in)** confianza f (en); **to put** OR **place one's trust in** confiar en - 2. FIN trust m; **in trust** en fideicomiso.

trusted ['trʌstɪd] adj de confianza.

trustee [trʌs'ti:] n FIN & LAW fideicomisario m, -ria f.

trust fund n fondo m de fideicomiso.

trusting ['trʌstɪŋ] adj confiado(da).

trustworthy ['trʌst,wɜːðɪ] adj digno(na) de confianza.

truth [tru:θ] n verdad f; **in (all) truth** en verdad, verdaderamente.

truthful ['tru:θfʊl] adj - 1. [person] sincero(ra) - 2. [story] verídico(ca).

try [traɪ] ◇ vt - 1. [attempt] intentar; **to try to do sthg** tratar de OR intentar hacer algo - 2. [sample, test] probar - 3. LAW [case] ver; [criminal] juzgar, procesar - 4. [put to the test - person] acabar con la paciencia de; [- patience] acabar con. ◇ vi intentar. ◇ n - 1. [attempt] intento m, tentativa f; **to have a try at sthg** intentar hacer algo - 2. [sample, test]: **to give sthg a try** probar algo - 3. RUGBY ensayo m. ◆ **try on** vt sep probarse. ◆ **try out** ◇ vt sep [car, machine] probar; [plan] poner a prueba; **to try sthg out on sb** probar algo con alguien. ◇ vi: **to try out for** US presentarse a una prueba de selección para.

trying ['traɪɪŋ] adj difícil, pesado(da).

T-shirt n camiseta f, remera f R Plata, playera f Méx, polera f Chile.

T-square n escuadra f en forma de T.

tub [tʌb] n - 1. [container - small] bote m; [- large] tina f - 2. inf [bath] bañera f.

tubby ['tʌbɪ] adj inf regordete(ta).

tube [tju:b] n - 1. [cylinder, container] tubo m - 2. ANAT conducto m - 3. UK inf RAIL metro m, subte m; **by tube** en metro.

tuberculosis [tju:,bɜ:kjʊ'ləʊsɪs] n tuberculosis f.

tubing ['tju:bɪŋ] n (U) tubos mpl.

tubular ['tju:bjʊlər] adj tubular.

tuck [tʌk] vt [place neatly] meter. ◆ **tuck away** vt sep [money etc] guardar. ◆ **tuck in** ◇ vt sep - 1. [person - in bed] arropar - 2. [clothes] meterse. ◇ vi inf comer con apetito. ◆ **tuck up** vt sep arropar; **to tuck sb up in bed** arropar a alguien en la cama.

tuck shop n UK confitería f (emplazada cerca de un colegio).

Tuesday ['tju:zdɪ] n martes m inv; see also **Saturday**.

tuft [tʌft] n [of hair] mechón m; [of grass] manojo m.

tug [tʌg] ◇ n - 1. [pull] tirón m - 2. [boat] remolcador m. ◇ vt tirar de. ◇ vi: **to tug (at)** tirar (de).

tug-of-war n juego m de la cuerda (en el que dos equipos compiten tirando de ella).

tuition [tju:'ɪʃn] n enseñanza f; **private tuition** clases fpl particulares.

tulip ['tju:lɪp] n tulipán m.

tumble ['tʌmbl] ◇ vi [person] caerse (rodando). ◇ n caída f. ◆ **tumble to** vt insep UK inf caerse en la cuenta de.

tumbledown ['tʌmbldaʊn] *adj* ruinoso(sa).

tumble-dryer [-,draɪəʳ] *n* secadora *f*.

tumbler ['tʌmbləʳ] *n* [glass] vaso *m*.

tummy ['tʌmɪ] *n inf* barriga *f*.

tumour *UK*, **tumor** *US* ['tju:məʳ] *n* tumor *m*.

tuna [*UK* 'tju:nə, *US* 'tu:nə] (*pl* **tuna** OR **-s**) *n* atún *m*.

tune [tju:n] ◇ *n* - 1. [song, melody] melodía *f* - 2. [harmony]: **in tune** MUS afinado(da); **out of tune** MUS desafinado(da). ◇ *vt* - 1. MUS afinar - 2. RADIO & TV sintonizar - 3. [engine] poner a punto. ➤ **tune in** *vi* RADIO & TV: **to tune in (to sthg)** sintonizar (algo). ➤ **tune up** *vi* MUS concertar OR afinar los instrumentos.

tuneful ['tju:nfʊl] *adj* melodioso(sa).

tuner ['tju:nəʳ] *n* - 1. RADIO & TV sintonizador *m* - 2. MUS afinador *m*, -ra *f*.

tunic ['tju:nɪk] *n* túnica *f*.

tuning fork ['tju:nɪŋ-] *n* diapasón *m*.

Tunisia [tju:'nɪzɪə] *n* Túnez.

tunnel ['tʌnl] ◇ *n* túnel *m*. ◇ *vi* (*UK pt & pp* **-led**, *cont* **-ling**, *US pt & pp* **-ed**, *cont* **-ing**) hacer un túnel.

turban ['tɜ:bən] *n* turbante *m*.

turbine ['tɜ:baɪn] *n* turbina *f*.

turbocharged ['tɜ:bəʊtʃɑ:dʒd] *adj* provisto(ta) de turbina; [car] turbo (*inv*).

turbodiesel [,tɜ:bəʊ'di:zl] *n* turbodiésel *m*.

turbulence ['tɜ:bjʊləns] *n* (*U*) *lit & fig* turbulencia *f*.

turbulent ['tɜ:bjʊlənt] *adj lit & fig* turbulento(ta).

tureen [tə'ri:n] *n* sopera *f*.

turf [tɜ:f] ◇ *n* (*pl* **-s** OR **turves**) - 1. [grass surface] césped *m* - 2. [clod] tepe *m*. ◇ *vt* encespedar. ➤ **turf out** *vt sep UK inf* [person] dar la patada a, echar; [old clothes] tirar.

turgid ['tɜ:dʒɪd] *adj fml* [over-solemn] ampuloso(sa).

Turk [tɜ:k] *n* turco *m*, -ca *f*.

turkey ['tɜ:kɪ] (*pl* **turkeys**) *n* pavo *m*.

Turkey ['tɜ:kɪ] *n* Turquía.

Turkish ['tɜ:kɪʃ] ◇ *adj* turco(ca). ◇ *n* [language] turco *m*. ◇ *npl* [people]: **the Turkish** los turcos.

Turkish delight *n* rahat lokum *m*, *dulce de una sustancia gelatinosa, cubierto de azúcar glas*.

turmoil ['tɜ:mɔɪl] *n* confusión *f*, alboroto *m*; **the country was in turmoil** reinaba la confusión en el país.

turn [tɜ:n] ◇ *n* - 1. [in road, river] curva *f* - 2. [of knob, wheel] vuelta *f* - 3. [change] cambio *m* - 4. [in game] turno *m*; **it's my turn** me toca a mí; **in turn** sucesivamente, uno tras otro;

to take (it in) turns (to do sthg) turnarse (en hacer algo) - 5. [performance] número *m* - 6. MED ataque *m*. ➤➤ **to do sb a good turn** hacerle un favor a alguien. ◇ *vt* - 1. [chair, page, omelette] dar la vuelta a - 2. [knob, wheel] girar - 3. [corner] doblar - 4. [thoughts, attention]: **to turn sthg to** dirigir algo hacia - 5. [change]: **to turn sthg into** convertir OR transformar algo en - 6. [cause to become]: **the cold turned his fingers blue** se le pusieron los dedos azules por el frío; **to turn sthg inside out** volver algo del revés. ◇ *vi* - 1. [car] girar; [road] torcer; [person] volverse, darse la vuelta - 2. [wheel] dar vueltas - 3. [turn page over]: **turn to page two** pasen a la página dos - 4. [thoughts, attention]: **to turn to** dirigirse hacia - 5. [seek consolation]: **to turn to sb/ sthg** buscar consuelo en alguien/algo; **she has nobody to turn to** no tiene a quien acudir - 6. [change]: **to turn into** convertirse OR transformarse en - 7. [become]: **it turned black** se volvió negro - 8. [go sour] cortarse. ➤ **turn around** *vt sep* = **turn round**. ➤ **turn away** *vt sep* [refuse entry to] no dejar entrar. ➤ **turn back** ◇ *vt sep* [person, vehicle] hacer volver. ◇ *vi* volver, volverse. ➤ **turn down** *vt sep* - 1. [offer, person] rechazar - 2. [volume, heating] bajar. ➤ **turn in** *vi inf* [go to bed] irse a dormir. ➤ **turn off** ◇ *vt insep* [road, path] desviarse de. ◇ *vt sep* [radio, heater] apagar; [engine] parar; [gas, tap] cerrar. ◇ *vi* [leave road] desviarse. ➤ **turn on** ◇ *vt sep* - 1. [radio, TV, engine] encender; [gas, tap] abrir - 2. *inf* [excite sexually] poner cachondo(da). ◇ *vt insep* [attack] atacar. ➤ **turn out** ◇ *vt sep* - 1. [extinguish] apagar - 2. [empty - pockets, bag] vaciar. ◇ *vt insep*: **to turn out to** be resultar ser. ◇ *vi* - 1. [end up] salir - 2. [arrive]: **to turn out (for)** venir OR presentarse (a). ➤ **turn over** ◇ *vt sep* - 1. [turn upside down] dar la vuelta a; [page] volver - 2. [consider] darle vueltas a - 3. *UK* RADIO & TV cambiar - 4. [hand over]: **to turn sthg/sb over (to)** entregar algo/a alguien (a). ◇ *vi* [roll over] darse la vuelta. ➤ **turn round**, **turn around** ◇ *vt sep* - 1. [gen] dar la vuelta a - 2. [knob, key] hacer girar. ◇ *vi* [person] darse la vuelta, volverse. ➤ **turn up** ◇ *vt sep* [volume, heating] subir. ◇ *vi inf* aparecer.

turning ['tɜ:nɪŋ] *n* [in road] bocacalle *f*.

turning point *n* momento *m* decisivo.

turnip ['tɜ:nɪp] *n* nabo *m*.

turnout ['tɜ:naʊt] *n* número *m* de asistentes, asistencia *f*.

turnover ['tɜ:n,əʊvəʳ] *n* (*U*) - 1. [of personnel] movimiento *m* de personal - 2. *UK* FIN volumen *m* de ventas, facturación *f*.

turnpike ['tɜ:npaɪk] *n US* autopista *f* de peaje.

turnstile ['tɜ:nstaɪl] *n* torniquete *m*.

turntable ['tɜːn,teɪbl] n plato m giratório.

turn up n UR [on trousers] vuelta f, **a turn-up for the books** int una auténtica sorpresa.

turpentine ['tɜːpəntaɪn] n trementina f.

turquoise ['tɜːkwɔɪz] <> adj turquesa. <> n [mineral, gem] turquesa f.

turret ['tʌrɪt] n torreta f, torrecilla f.

turtle ['tɜːtl] (pl turtle OR -s) n tortuga f (marina).

turtleneck ['tɜːtlnek] n cuello m (de) cisne.

turves [tɜːvz] UK npl ▷ turf.

tusk [tʌsk] n colmillo m.

tussle ['tʌsl] <> n lucha f, pelea f. <> vi: to **tussle (over)** pelearse (por).

tutor ['tjuːtər] n - **1.** [private] profesor particular m, profesora particular f, tutor m, -ra f - **2.** UNIV profesor universitario m, profesora universitaria f (de un grupo pequeño).

tutorial [tjuːˈtɔːrɪəl] n tutoría f, clase f con grupo reducido.

tuxedo [tʌkˈsiːdəʊ] (pl -s) n esmoquin m.

TV (abbr of **television**) <> n televisión f; **on TV** en la televisión. <> comp de televisión.

TV movie n telefilm m.

twang [twæŋ] n - **1.** [of guitar] tañido m; [of string, elastic] sonido m vibrante - **2.** [accent] gangueo m, acento m nasal.

tweed [twiːd] n tweed m.

tweenage ['twiːneɪdʒ] adj inf preadolescente.

tweezers ['twiːzəz] npl pinzas fpl.

twelfth [twelfθ] num duodécimo(ma); see also **sixth**.

twelve [twelv] num doce; see also **six**.

twentieth ['twentɪəθ] num vigésimo(ma); see also **sixth**.

twenty ['twentɪ] num veinte; see also **sixty**.

twenty-one [twentɪ'wʌn] n US [game] veintiuna f.

twice [twaɪs] num adv dos veces; **twice a week** dos veces por semana; **it costs twice as much** cuesta el doble; **twice as big** el doble de grande; **he's twice her age** le dobla en edad; **think twice** piénsalo dos veces.

twiddle ['twɪdl] <> vt dar vueltas a; to **twiddle one's thumbs** fig holgazanear. <> vi: to **twiddle with** juguetear con.

twig [twɪg] n ramita f.

twilight ['twaɪlaɪt] n crepúsculo m.

twin [twɪn] <> adj gemelo(la). <> n gemelo m, -la f.

twin-bedded [-ˈbedɪd] adj de dos camas.

twine [twaɪn] <> n (U) bramante m. <> vt: to **twine sthg round sthg** enrollar algo en algo.

twinge [twɪndʒ] n [of pain] punzada f; [of guilt] remordimiento m.

twinkle ['twɪŋkl] vi - **1.** [star] centellear, parpadear - **2.** [eyes] brillar.

twin room n habitación f con dos camas.

twin town n ciudad f hermanada.

twirl [twɜːl] <> vt dar vueltas a. <> vi dar vueltas rápidamente.

twist [twɪst] <> n - **1.** [in road] vuelta f, recodo m; [in river] meandro m - **2.** [of head, lid, knob] giro m - **3.** [shape] espiral f - **4.** fig [in plot] giro m imprevisto. <> vt - **1.** [cloth, rope] retorcer; [hair] enroscar - **2.** [face etc] torcer - **3.** [dial, lid] dar vueltas a; [head] volver - **4.** [ankle, knee etc] torcerse - **5.** [misquote] tergiversar. <> vi - **1.** [person] retorcerse; [road, river] serpentear - **2.** [face] contorsionarse; [frame, rail] torcerse - **3.** [turn - head, hand] volverse.

twit [twɪt] n UK inf imbécil mf.

twitch [twɪtʃ] <> n contorsión f; **nervous twitch** tic m (nervioso). <> vi contorsionarse.

two [tuː] num dos; to **break in two** partirse en dos; to **do sthg in twos** hacer algo en pares; to **put two and two together** atar cabos; see also **six**.

two-door adj [car] de dos puertas.

twofaced [,tuːˈfeɪst] adj pej hipócrita.

twofold ['tuːfəʊld] <> adj doble; **a twofold increase** un incremento del doble. <> adv: to **increase twofold** duplicarse.

two-piece adj [suit] de dos piezas.

twosome ['tuːsəm] n inf pareja f.

two-way adj [traffic] en ambas direcciones; [agreement, cooperation] mutuo(tua).

two-way street n calle f de doble sentido.

tycoon [taɪˈkuːn] n magnate m; **an oil tycoon** un magnate del petróleo.

type [taɪp] <> n - **1.** [gen] tipo m - **2.** (U) TYPO tipo m, letra f; **in bold/italic type** en negrita/ cursiva. <> vt - **1.** [on typewriter] escribir a máquina, mecanografiar - **2.** [on computer] escribir en el ordenador; to **type sthg into sthg** entrar algo en algo. <> vi escribir a máquina.

typecast ['taɪpkɑːst] (pt & pp **typecast**) vt: to **typecast sb (as)** encasillar a alguien (como).

typeface ['taɪpfeɪs] n tipo m, letra f.

typescript ['taɪpskrɪpt] n copia f mecanografiada.

typeset ['taɪpset] (pt & pp **typeset**) vt componer.

typewriter ['taɪp,raɪtər] n máquina f de escribir.

typhoid (fever) ['taɪfɔɪd-] n fiebre f tifoidea.

typhoon [taɪˈfuːn] n tifón m.

typical ['tɪpɪkl] adj: **typical (of)** típico(ca) (de).

typing ['taɪpɪŋ] *n* mecanografía *f*.

typist ['taɪpɪst] *n* mecanógrafo *m*, -fa *f*.

typography [taɪ'pɒgrəfɪ] *n* [process, job] tipografía *f*.

tyranny ['tɪrənɪ] *n* tiranía *f*.

tyrant ['taɪrənt] *n* tirano *m*, -na *f*.

tyre UK, **tire** US ['taɪə'] *n* neumático *m*.

tyre pressure *n* presión *f* de los neumáticos.

u (*pl* u's OR us), **U** (*pl* U's OR Us) [ju:] *n* [letter] u *f*, U *f*.

U-bend *n* sifón *m*.

UCAS ['ju:kæs] (*abbr of* **Universities and Colleges Admissions Service**) *n* UK UNIV & SCH *organización que coordina las admisiones y matrículas en las universidades británicas*.

udder ['ʌdə'] *n* ubre *f*.

UFO (*abbr of* **unidentified flying object**) *n* OVNI *m*.

Uganda [ju:'gændə] *n* Uganda.

ugh [ʌg] *excl* ¡puf!

ugly ['ʌglɪ] *adj* - **1.** [unattractive] feo(a) - **2.** *fig* [unpleasant] desagradable.

UHF (*abbr of* **ultra-high frequency**) UHF.

UK (*abbr of* **United Kingdom**) *n* RU *m*; **the UK** el Reino Unido.

Ukraine [ju:'kreɪn] *n*: **the Ukraine** Ucrania.

ulcer ['ʌlsə'] *n* úlcera *f*.

ulcerated ['ʌlsəreɪtɪd] *adj* ulceroso(sa).

Ulster ['ʌlstə'] *n* (el) Úlster.

ulterior [ʌl'tɪərɪə'] *adj*: **ulterior motive** motivo *m* oculto.

ultimata [ʌltɪ'meɪtə] *npl* ▷ **ultimatum**.

ultimate ['ʌltɪmət] ◇ *adj* - **1.** [final, longterm] final, definitivo(va) - **2.** [most powerful] máximo(ma). ◇ *n*: **the ultimate in** el colmo de.

ultimately ['ʌltɪmətlɪ] *adv* finalmente, a la larga.

ultimatum [ʌltɪ'meɪtəm] (*pl* **-s** OR **-ta**) *n* ultimátum *m*; **to issue an ultimatum to sb** dar un ultimátum a alguien.

ultrasound ['ʌltrəsaʊnd] *n* ultrasonido *m*.

ultraviolet [ʌltrə'vaɪələt] *adj* ultravioleta.

umbilical cord [ʌm'bɪlɪkl-] *n* cordón *m* umbilical.

umbrella [ʌm'brelə] ◇ *n* - **1.** [for rain] paraguas *m inv* - **2.** [on beach] parasol *m* - **3.**: **under the umbrella of** *fig* bajo la protección de. ◇ *adj* que engloba a otros(otras).

umpire ['ʌmpaɪə'] *n* árbitro *m*.

umpteen [ʌmp'ti:n] *num adj inf*: **umpteen times** la tira de veces.

umpteenth [ʌmp'ti:nθ] *num adj inf* enésimo(ma); **for the umpteenth time** por enésima vez.

UN (*abbr of* **United Nations**) *n*: **the UN** la ONU.

unabated [ʌnə'beɪtɪd] *adj* incesante; **to continue unabated** continuar sin cesar.

unable [ʌn'eɪbl] *adj*: **to be unable to do sthg** no poder hacer algo.

unacceptable [ʌnək'septəbl] *adj* inaceptable.

unaccompanied [ʌnə'kʌmpənɪd] *adj* - **1.** [child] que no va acompañado(da); [luggage] desatendido(da) - **2.** [song] sin acompañamiento.

unaccountably [ʌnə'kaʊntəblɪ] *adv* inexplicablemente.

unaccounted [ʌnə'kaʊntɪd] *adj*: **12 people are unaccounted for** hay 12 personas aún sin localizar.

unaccustomed [ʌnə'kʌstəmd] *adj* [unused]: **to be unaccustomed to** no estar acostumbrado(da) a.

unadulterated [ʌnə'dʌltəreɪtɪd] *adj* - **1.** [unspoilt] sin adulterar - **2.** [absolute] completo(ta), absoluto(ta).

unanimous [ju:'nænɪməs] *adj* unánime.

unanimously [ju:'nænɪməslɪ] *adv* unánimemente.

unanswered [ʌn'ɑ:nsəd] *adj* sin contestar.

unappetizing, -ising [ʌn'æpɪtaɪzɪŋ] *adj* poco apetitoso(sa).

unarmed [ʌn'ɑ:md] *adj* desarmado(da).

unarmed combat *n* lucha *f* OR combate *m* a brazo partido.

unashamed [ʌnə'ʃeɪmd] *adj* descarado(da).

unassuming [ʌnə'sju:mɪŋ] *adj* sin pretensiones.

unattached [ʌnə'tætʃt] *adj* - **1.** [not fastened, linked] independiente; **unattached to** que no está ligado a - **2.** [without partner] libre, sin compromiso.

unattended [ʌnə'tendɪd] *adj* desatendido(da); **to leave sthg unattended** dejar algo desatendido.

unattractive [,Anə'træktıv] *adj* poco atrac-
tivo(va).

unauthorized, -ised [,An'ɔ:θəraızd] *adj* no
autorizado(da).

unavailable [,Anə'veıləbl] *adj*: **to be unavailable** no estar disponible; **he was unavailable for comment** no quiso hacer ningún comentario.

unavoidable [,Anə'vɔıdəbl] *adj* inevitable,
ineludible; **unavoidable delays** retrasos inevi-
tables.

unaware [,Anə'weər] *adj* inconsciente; **to be
unaware of** no ser consciente de.

unawares [,Anə'weəz] *adv*: **to catch** OR **take
sb unawares** coger a alguien desapreveni-
do(da).

unbalanced [,An'bælənst] *adj* desequilibra-
do(da).

unbearable [An'beərəbl] *adj* insoportable,
inaguantable.

unbeatable [,An'bi:təbl] *adj* [gen] insuperable; [prices, value] inmejorable.

unbeknown(st) [,Anbı'nəʊn(st)] *adv*: **unbe-
known(st) to** sin conocimiento de.

unbelievable [,Anbı'li:vəbl] *adj* increíble.

unbending [,An'bendıŋ] *adj* resoluto(ta).

unbias(s)ed [,An'baıəst] *adj* imparcial.

unborn [,An'bɔ:n] *adj* [child] no nacido(da)
aún.

unbreakable [,An'breıkəbl] *adj* irrompible.

unbridled [,An'braıdld] *adj* desmesura-
do(da), desenfrenado(da).

unbutton [,An'bAtn] *vt* desabrochar.

uncalled-for [,An'kɔ:ld-] *adj* injusto(ta), in-
merecido(da).

uncanny [An'kænı] *adj* extraño(ña).

unceasing [,An'si:sıŋ] *adj fml* incesante.

unceremonious ['An,serı'məʊnjəs] *adj*
[curt] brusco(ca).

uncertain [An'sɜ:tn] *adj* [gen] incierto(ta);
[undecided, hesitant] indeciso(sa); **it's uncertain
whether they will accept the proposals** no se
sabe si aceptarán las propuestas; **in no uncertain terms** de forma vehemente.

unchanged [,An'tʃeındʒd] *adj* sin alterar.

unchecked [,An'tʃekt] <> *adj* [unrestrained]
desenfrenado(da). <> *adv* [unrestrained] libremente, sin restricciones.

uncivilized, -ised [,An'sıvılaızd] *adj* [society]
incivilizado(da); [person] inculto(ta).

uncle ['Aŋkl] *n* tío *m*.

unclear [,An'klıər] *adj* poco claro(ra); **to be
unclear about sthg** no tener claro algo.

uncomfortable [,An'kAmftəbl] *adj* - 1. [gen]
incómodo(da) - 2. *fig* [fact, truth] inquietante,
desagradable.

uncommon [An'kɒmən] *adj* [rare] poco común, raro(ra).

uncompromising [An'kɒmprəmaızıŋ] *adj*
inflexible, intransigente.

unconcerned [,Ankən'sɜ:nd] *adj* [not
anxious] indiferente.

unconditional [,Ankən'dıʃənl] *adj* incondicional.

unconscious [An'kɒnʃəs] <> *adj* inconsciente; **to be unconscious of sthg** ser inconsciente de OR ignorar algo; **he was
knocked unconscious by a falling brick** un ladrillo que caía lo dejó inconsciente. <> *n* inconsciente *m*.

unconsciously [An'kɒnʃəslı] *adv* in-
conscientemente.

uncontrollable [,Ankən'trəʊləbl] *adj* [gen]
incontrolable; [desire, hatred] irrefrenable;
[laughter] incontenible.

unconventional [,Ankən'venʃnl] *adj* poco
convencional.

unconvinced [,Ankən'vınst] *adj*: **to remain
unconvinced** seguir sin convencerse.

uncouth [An'ku:θ] *adj* grosero(ra).

uncover [An'kAvər] *vt* [gen] descubrir; [jar, tin
etc] destapar.

undecided [,Andı'saıdıd] *adj* - 1. [person] in-
deciso(sa) - 2. [issue] pendiente.

undeniable [,Andı'naıəbl] *adj* innegable.

under ['Andər] <> *prep* - 1. [beneath] debajo
de, abajo de *Amér* - 2. [with movement] bajo;
put it under the table ponlo debajo de OR bajo
la mesa; **they walked under the bridge** pasaron bajo OR por debajo del puente - 3. [sub-
ject to, undergoing, controlled by] bajo; **under the
circumstances** dadas las circunstancias; **under discussion** en proceso de discusión; **he has
20 men under him** tiene 20 hombres a su cargo - 4. [less than] menos de; **children under the
age of 14** niños menores de 14 años - 5. [ac-
cording to] según - 6. [in headings, classifica-
tions]: **he filed it under 'D'** lo archivó en la 'D'
- 7. [name, title]: **under an alias** bajo nombre
supuesto. <> *adv* - 1. [gen] debajo; **to go under** [business] irse a pique - 2. [less]: **children of
12 years and under** niños menores de 13
años; **£5 or under** cinco libras o menos
- 3. [under water] bajo el agua.

underage [Andər'eıdʒ] *adj* [person] menor de
edad; [sex, drinking] en menores de edad.

undercarriage ['Andə,kærıdʒ] *n* tren *m* de
aterrizaje.

undercharge [,Andə'tʃɑ:dʒ] *vt* cobrar menos del precio estipulado a.

underclothes ['Andəkləʊðz] *npl* ropa *f* interior.

undercoat ['Andəkəʊt] *n* [of paint] primera
mano *f* OR capa *f*.

undercover [ˌʌndəˈkʌvəʳ] *adj* secreto(ta).

undercurrent [ˈʌndəˌkʌrənt] *n fig* sentimiento *m* oculto.

undercut [ˌʌndəˈkʌt] (*pt & pp* **undercut**) *vt* [in price] vender más barato que.

underdeveloped [ˌʌndədɪˈveləpt] *adj* subdesarrollado(da).

underdog [ˈʌndədɒg] *n*: **the underdog** el que lleva las de perder.

underdone [ˌʌndəˈdʌn] *adj* poco hecho(cha).

underestimate *vt* [ˌʌndərˈestɪmeɪt] subestimar.

underexposed [ˌʌndərɪkˈspəʊzd] *adj* PHOT subexpuesto(ta).

underfed [ˈʌndəˈfed] *adj* desnutrido(da).

underfoot [ˌʌndəˈfʊt] *adv* debajo de los pies; **it's wet underfoot** el suelo está mojado.

undergo [ˌʌndəˈgəʊ] (*pt* **-went**, *pp* **-gone**) *vt* [pain, change, difficulties] sufrir, experimentar; [operation, examination] someterse a.

undergraduate [ˌʌndəˈgrædʒʊət] *n* estudiante universitario no licenciado *m*, estudiante universitaria no licenciada *f*.

underground ◇ *adj* [ˈʌndəgraʊnd] - **1.** [below the ground] subterráneo(a) - **2.** *fig* [secret, illegal] clandestino(na). ◇ *adv* [ˌʌndəˈgraʊnd]: **to go underground** pasar a la clandestinidad. ◇ *n* [ˈʌndəgraʊnd] - **1.** *UK* [railway system] metro *m*, subte(rráneo) *m R Plata* - **2.** [activist movement] movimiento *m* clandestino.

undergrowth [ˈʌndəgrəʊθ] *n (U)* maleza *f*.

underhand [ˌʌndəˈhænd] *adj* turbio(bia), poco limpio(pia).

underline [ˌʌndəˈlaɪn] *vt* subrayar.

underlying [ˌʌndəˈlaɪɪŋ] *adj* subyacente.

undermine [ˌʌndəˈmaɪn] *vt fig* minar, socavar; **to undermine sb's confidence/authority** minar la confianza/autoridad de alguien.

underneath [ˌʌndəˈniːθ] ◇ *prep* - **1.** [beneath] debajo de - **2.** [with movement] bajo. ◇ *adv* [under, below] debajo. ◇ *adj inf* inferior, de abajo. ◇ *n* [underside]: **the underneath** la superficie inferior.

underpaid *adj* [ˈʌndəpeɪd] mal pagado(da).

underpants [ˈʌndəpænts] *npl* calzoncillos *mpl*.

underpass [ˈʌndəpɑːs] *n* paso *m* subterráneo.

underprivileged [ˌʌndəˈprɪvɪlɪdʒd] *adj* desvalido(da), desamparado(da).

underrated [ˌʌndəˈreɪtɪd] *adj* subestimado(da), infravalorado(da).

undershirt [ˈʌndəʃɜːt] *n US* camiseta *f*.

underside [ˈʌndəsaɪd] *n*: **the underside** la superficie inferior.

underskirt [ˈʌndəskɜːt] *n* enaguas *fpl*.

understand [ˌʌndəˈstænd] (*pt & pp* **-stood**) ◇ *vt* - **1.** [gen] comprender, entender; **is that understood?** ¿queda claro? - **2.** [know all about] entender de - **3.** *fml* [be informed]: **to understand that** tener entendido que - **4.** [assume]: **it is understood that...** se entiende que... ◇ *vi* comprender, entender.

understandable [ˌʌndəˈstændəbl] *adj* comprensible.

understanding [ˌʌndəˈstændɪŋ] ◇ *n* - **1.** [knowledge] entendimiento *m*, comprensión *f* - **2.** [sympathy] comprensión *f* mutua - **3.** [informal agreement] acuerdo *m*; **we have a little understanding** tenemos un pequeño acuerdo. ◇ *adj* comprensivo(va).

understatement [ˌʌndəˈsteɪtmənt] *n* - **1.** [inadequate statement] atenuación *f*; **it's an understatement to say he's fat** decir que es gordo es quedarse corto - **2.** *(U)* [quality of understating]: **he's a master of understatement** puede quitarle importancia a cualquier cosa.

understood [ˌʌndəˈstʊd] *pt & pp* ▷ **understand**.

understudy [ˈʌndəˌstʌdɪ] *n* suplente *mf*.

undertake [ˌʌndəˈteɪk] (*pt* **-took**, *pp* **-taken**) *vt* - **1.** [task] emprender; [responsibility, control] asumir, tomar - **2.** [promise]: **to undertake to do sthg** comprometerse a hacer algo.

undertaker [ˈʌndəˌteɪkəʳ] *n* director *m*, -ra *f* de pompas fúnebres.

undertaking [ˌʌndəˈteɪkɪŋ] *n* - **1.** [task] tarea *f*, empresa *f* - **2.** [promise] promesa *f*.

undertone [ˈʌndətəʊn] *n* - **1.** [quiet voice] voz *f* baja; **in an undertone** en voz baja - **2.** [vague feeling] matiz *m*.

undertook [ˌʌndəˈtʊk] *pt* ▷ **undertake**.

underwater [ˌʌndəˈwɔːtəʳ] ◇ *adj* submarino(na). ◇ *adv* bajo el agua.

underwear [ˈʌndəweəʳ] *n* ropa *f* interior.

underwent [ˌʌndəˈwent] *pt* ▷ **undergo**.

underworld [ˈʌndəˌwɜːld] *n* [criminal society]: **the underworld** el hampa, los bajos fondos.

underwriter [ˈʌndəˌraɪtəʳ] *n* asegurador *m*, -ra *f*.

undeserving [ˌʌndɪˈzɜːvɪŋ] *adj* [person]: **to be undeserving of sthg** no merecer algo.

undid [ˌʌnˈdɪd] *pt* ▷ **undo**.

undies [ˈʌndɪz] *npl inf* paños *mpl* menores.

undisputed [ˌʌndɪˈspjuːtɪd] *adj* indiscutible.

undistinguished [ˌʌndɪˈstɪŋgwɪʃt] *adj* mediocre.

undo [ˌʌnˈduː] (*pt* **-did**, *pp* **-done**) *vt* - **1.** [unfasten - knot] desatar, desanudar; [- button, clasp] desabrochar; [- parcel] abrir - **2.** [nullify] anular, deshacer - **3.** COMPUT deshacer.

undoing [ˌʌn'duːɪŋ] n (U) fml **ruina** f, perdición f. It was his undoing fue su perdición.

undone [ˌʌn'dʌn] <> pp ⊳ **undo**. <> adj
- **1.** [coat] desabrochado(da); [shoes] desatado(da); **to come undone** desatarse - **2.** fml [not
done] por hacer.

undoubted [ʌn'daʊtɪd] adj indudable.

undoubtedly [ʌn'daʊtɪdlɪ] adv fml indudablemente, sin duda (alguna).

undress [ˌʌn'dres] <> vt desnudar. <> vi
desnudarse.

undue [ˌʌn'djuː] adj fml indebido(da).

undulate ['ʌndjʊleɪt] vi fml ondular.

unduly [ˌʌn'djuːlɪ] adv fml indebidamente.

unearth [ˌʌn'ɜːθ] vt [dig up] desenterrar; fig
[discover] descubrir.

unearthly [ʌn'ɜːθlɪ] adj inf [hour] intempestivo(va).

unease [ʌn'iːz] n malestar m.

uneasy [ʌn'iːzɪ] adj - **1.** [person, feeling] intranquilo(la) - **2.** [peace] inseguro(ra).

uneconomic ['ʌnˌiːkə'nɒmɪk] adj poco rentable.

uneducated [ˌʌn'edjʊkeɪtɪd] adj ignorante,
inculto(ta).

unemployed [ˌʌnɪm'plɔɪd] <> adj parado(da), desempleado(da). <> npl: the unemployed los parados.

unemployment [ˌʌnɪm'plɔɪmənt] n desempleo m, paro m.

unemployment benefit UK, **unemployment compensation** US n subsidio m de
desempleo OR paro.

unerring [ˌʌn'ɜːrɪŋ] adj infalible.

uneven [ˌʌn'iːvn] adj - **1.** [not flat - road] lleno(na) de baches; [- land] escabroso(sa)
- **2.** [inconsistent, unfair] desigual.

unexpected [ˌʌnɪk'spektɪd] adj inesperado(da).

unexpectedly [ˌʌnɪk'spektɪdlɪ] adv inesperadamente.

unfailing [ʌn'feɪlɪŋ] adj indefectible.

unfair [ˌʌn'feəʳ] adj injusto(ta).

unfaithful [ˌʌn'feɪθfʊl] adj [sexually] infiel.

unfamiliar [ˌʌnfə'mɪljəʳ] adj - **1.** [not well-
known] desconocido(da) - **2.** [not acquainted]:
to be unfamiliar with sthg/sb desconocer algo/a alguien.

unfashionable [ˌʌn'fæʃnəbl] adj [clothes,
ideas] pasado(da) de moda; [area of town] poco
popular.

unfasten [ˌʌn'fɑːsn] vt [garment, buttons] desabrochar; [rope, tie] desatar, soltar; [door] abrir.

unfavourable UK, **unfavorable** US
[ˌʌn'feɪvrəbl] adj desfavorable.

unfeeling [ʌn'fiːlɪŋ] adj insensible.

unfinished [ˌʌn'fɪnɪʃt] adj sin terminar.

unfit [ˌʌn'fɪt] adj - **1.** [injured] lesionado(da);
[in poor shape] que... no... en forma - **2.** [not
suitable - thing] impropio(pia); [- person]: **unfit
to** incapaz de; **unfit for** no apto para.

unfold [ʌn'fəʊld] <> vt - **1.** [open out] desplegar, desdoblar - **2.** [explain] revelar. <> vi [become clear] revelarse.

unforeseen [ˌʌnfɔː'siːn] adj imprevisto(ta).

unforgettable [ˌʌnfə'getəbl] adj inolvidable.

unforgivable [ˌʌnfə'gɪvəbl] adj imperdonable.

unfortunate [ʌn'fɔːtʃnət] adj - **1.** [unlucky]
desgraciado(da), desdichado(da) - **2.** [regrettable] inoportuno(na).

unfortunately [ʌn'fɔːtʃnətlɪ] adv desgraciadamente, desafortunadamente.

unfounded [ˌʌn'faʊndɪd] adj infundado(da).

unfriendly [ˌʌn'frendlɪ] adj poco amistoso(sa).

unfurnished [ˌʌn'fɜːnɪʃt] adj desamueblado(da).

ungainly [ʌn'geɪnlɪ] adj desgarbado(da).

ungodly [ˌʌn'gɒdlɪ] adj inf [hour] intempestivo(va); **at an ungodly hour** a una hora intempestiva.

ungrateful [ʌn'greɪtfʊl] adj desagradecido(da), ingrato(ta).

unhappy [ʌn'hæpɪ] adj - **1.** [sad] triste;
[wretched] desdichado(da), infeliz - **2.** [uneasy]:
to be unhappy (with OR about) estar inquieto(ta) (por) - **3.** fml [unfortunate] desafortunado(da).

unharmed [ˌʌn'hɑːmd] adj [person] ileso(sa); [thing] indemne; **he escaped unharmed**
salió ileso.

unhealthy [ʌn'helθɪ] adj - **1.** [in bad health]
enfermizo(za) - **2.** [causing bad health] insalubre - **3.** fig [interest etc] morboso(sa).

unheard-of [ʌn'hɜːd-] adj - **1.** [unknown,
completely absent] inaudito(ta) - **2.** [unprecedented] sin precedente.

unhook [ˌʌn'hʊk] vt - **1.** [unfasten hooks of]
desabrochar - **2.** [remove from hook] descolgar,
desenganchar.

unhurt [ˌʌn'hɜːt] adj ileso(sa).

unhygienic [ˌʌnhaɪ'dʒiːnɪk] adj antihigiénico(ca).

unidentified flying object n objeto m volador no identificado.

unification [ˌjuːnɪfɪ'keɪʃn] n unificación f.

uniform ['juːnɪfɔːm] <> adj uniforme,
constante. <> n uniforme m.

unify ['juːnɪfaɪ] vt unificar, unir.

unilateral [ˌjuːnɪ'lætərəl] adj unilateral.

unimportant [ˌʌnɪm'pɔːtənt] *adj* sin importancia, insignificante.

uninhabited [ˌʌnɪn'hæbɪtɪd] *adj* deshabitado(da).

uninjured [ˌʌn'ɪndʒəd] *adj* ileso(sa).

uninstall [ˌʌnɪn'stɔːl] *vt* desinstalar.

unintelligent [ˌʌnɪn'telɪdʒənt] *adj* poco inteligente.

unintentional [ˌʌnɪn'tenʃənl] *adj* involuntario(ria).

union ['juːnjən] ◇ *n* - **1.** [trade union] sindicato *m* - **2.** [alliance] unión *f*, alianza *f*. ◇ *comp* sindical.

Union Jack *n*: the Union Jack la bandera del Reino Unido.

unique [juː'niːk] *adj* - **1.** [gen] único(ca) - **2.** *fml* [peculiar, exclusive]: **unique to** peculiar de.

unison ['juːnɪzn] *n* unísono *m*.

unit ['juːnɪt] *n* - **1.** [gen] unidad *f* - **2.** [piece of furniture] módulo *m*, elemento *m*.

unite [juː'naɪt] ◇ *vt* [gen] unir; [country] unificar. ◇ *vi* unirse, juntarse.

united [juː'naɪtɪd] *adj* unido(da).

United Kingdom *n*: the United Kingdom el Reino Unido.

United Nations *n*: the United Nations las Naciones Unidas.

United States *n*: the United States (of America) los Estados Unidos (de América).

unit trust *n* UK fondo *m* de inversión mobiliaria.

unity ['juːnətɪ] *n* (U) unidad *f*, unión *f*.

universal [ˌjuːnɪ'vɜːsl] *adj* universal.

universe ['juːnɪvɜːs] *n*: the universe el universo.

university [ˌjuːnɪ'vɜːsətɪ] ◇ *n* universidad *f*. ◇ *comp* universitario(ria); **university student** (estudiante) universitario *m*, (estudiante) universitaria *f*.

unjust [ˌʌn'dʒʌst] *adj* injusto(ta).

unkempt [ˌʌn'kempt] *adj* [person] desaseado(da); [hair] despeinado(da); [clothes] descuidado(da).

unkind [ʌn'kaɪnd] *adj* [uncharitable] poco amable, cruel.

unknown [ˌʌn'nəʊn] *adj* desconocido(da); **unknown to him** sin que él lo supiera.

unlawful [ˌʌn'lɔːfʊl] *adj* ilegal, ilícito(ta).

unleaded [ˌʌn'ledɪd] *adj* sin plomo.

unleash [ˌʌn'liːʃ] *vt liter* desatar.

unless [ən'les] *conj* a menos que; **unless I say so** a menos que yo lo diga; **unless I'm mistaken** si no me equivoco.

unlike [ˌʌn'laɪk] *prep* - **1.** [different from] distinto(ta) a, diferente a - **2.** [differently from] a

diferencia de - **3.** [not typical of] poco característico(ca) de; **that's unlike him** no es propio de él.

unlikely [ʌn'laɪklɪ] *adj* - **1.** [not probable] poco probable; **it's unlikely that he'll come now**, **he's unlikely to come now** ahora es poco probable que venga; **to be highly unlikely** ser muy poco probable - **2.** [bizarre] inverosímil.

unlisted [ʌn'lɪstɪd] *adj* US [phone number] que no figura en la guía telefónica.

unload [ˌʌn'ləʊd] *vt* [goods, car] descargar.

unlock [ˌʌn'lɒk] *vt* abrir (con llave).

unlucky [ʌn'lʌkɪ] *adj* - **1.** [unfortunate] desgraciado(da); **to be unlucky** tener mala suerte - **2.** [number, colour etc] de la mala suerte; **to be unlucky** traer mala suerte.

unmarried [ˌʌn'mærɪd] *adj* que no se ha casado.

unmetered [ʌn'miːtəd] *adj* ilimitado(da).

unmistakable [ˌʌnmɪ'steɪkəbl] *adj* inconfundible.

unmitigated [ʌn'mɪtɪgeɪtɪd] *adj* absoluto(ta).

unnatural [ʌn'nætʃrəl] *adj* - **1.** [unusual, strange] anormal - **2.** [affected] afectado(da).

unnecessary [ʌn'nesəsərɪ] *adj* innecesario(ria).

unnerving [ˌʌn'nɜːvɪŋ] *adj* desconcertante.

unnoticed [ˌʌn'nəʊtɪst] *adj* inadvertido(da), desapercibido(da); **to go unnoticed** pasar desapercibido(da).

unobtainable [ˌʌnəb'teɪnəbl] *adj* inasequible.

unobtrusive [ˌʌnəb'truːsɪv] *adj* discreto(ta).

unofficial [ˌʌnə'fɪʃl] *adj* extraoficial.

unorthodox [ˌʌn'ɔːθədɒks] *adj* poco ortodoxo(xa).

unpack [ˌʌn'pæk] ◇ *vt* - **1.** [box] desempaquetar, desembalar; [suitcases] deshacer - **2.** [clothes] sacar (de la maleta). ◇ *vi* deshacer las maletas.

unpalatable [ʌn'pælətəbl] *adj* [food] incomible; [drink] imbebible; *fig* [difficult to accept] desagradable.

unparalleled [ʌn'pærəleld] *adj* incomparable, sin precedente.

unpleasant [ʌn'pleznt] *adj* - **1.** [disagreeable] desagradable - **2.** [unfriendly, rude - person] antipático(ca); [- remark] mezquino(na).

unplug [ʌn'plʌg] *vt* desenchufar, desconectar.

unpopular [ˌʌn'pɒpjʊlər] *adj* poco popular; **she was unpopular with the other girls** las otras chicas no le tenían mucho aprecio.

unprecedented [ʌn'presɪdəntɪd] *adj* sin precedentes, inaudito(ta).

unpredictable [ˌʌnprɪˈdɪktəbl] *adj* imprevisible.

unprofessional [ˌʌnprəˈfeʃənl] *adj* poco profesional.

unqualified [ˌʌnˈkwɒlɪfaɪd] *adj* - **1.** [not qualified] sin título, no cualificado(da) - **2.** [total, complete] incondicional.

unquestionable [ˌʌnˈkwestʃənəbl] *adj* incuestionable, indiscutible.

unquestioning [ʌnˈkwestʃənɪŋ] *adj* incondicional.

unravel [ʌnˈrævl] (*UK pt* & *pp* -**led**, *cont* -**ling**, *US pt* & *pp* -**ed**, *cont* -**ing**) *vt lit* & *fig* desenmarañar.

unreal [ˌʌnˈrɪəl] *adj* irreal.

unrealistic [ˌʌnrɪəˈlɪstɪk] *adj* [person] poco realista; [idea, plan] impracticable.

unreasonable [ʌnˈriːznəbl] *adj* - **1.** [person, behaviour, decision] poco razonable - **2.** [demand, price] excesivo(va).

unrelated [ˌʌnrɪˈleɪtɪd] *adj*: **to be unrelated (to)** no tener conexión (con).

unrelenting [ˌʌnrɪˈlentɪŋ] *adj* implacable, inexorable.

unreliable [ˌʌnrɪˈlaɪəbl] *adj* que no es de fiar.

unremitting [ˌʌnrɪˈmɪtɪŋ] *adj* incesante.

unrequited [ˌʌnrɪˈkwaɪtɪd] *adj* no correspondido(da).

unreserved [ˌʌnrɪˈzɜːvd] *adj* [wholehearted] incondicional, absoluto(ta).

unresolved [ˌʌnrɪˈzɒlvd] *adj* sin resolver, pendiente.

unrest [ˌʌnˈrest] *n (U)* malestar *m*, inquietud *f*.

unrivalled *UK*, **unrivaled** *US* [ʌnˈraɪvld] *adj* incomparable, sin par.

unroll [ˌʌnˈrəʊl] *vt* desenrollar.

unruly [ʌnˈruːlɪ] *adj* - **1.** [person, behaviour] revoltoso(sa) - **2.** [hair] rebelde.

unsafe [ˌʌnˈseɪf] *adj* [gen] inseguro(ra); [risky] arriesgado(da).

unsaid [ˌʌnˈsed] *adj*: **to leave sthg unsaid** dejar algo sin decir.

unsatisfactory [ˈʌnˌsætɪsˈfæktərɪ] *adj* insatisfactorio(ria).

unsavoury, **unsavory** *US* [ˌʌnˈseɪvərɪ] *adj* desagradable.

unscathed [ˌʌnˈskeɪðd] *adj* ileso(sa).

unscrew [ˌʌnˈskruː] *vt* - **1.** [lid, top] abrir - **2.** [sign, hinge] desatornillar.

unscrupulous [ʌnˈskruːpjʊləs] *adj* desaprensivo(va), poco escrupuloso(sa).

unseemly [ʌnˈsiːmlɪ] *adj* indecoroso(sa).

unselfish [ʌnˈselfɪʃ] *adj* altruista.

unsettle [ʌnˈsetl] *vt* perturbar.

unsettled [ʌnˈsetld] *adj* **1.** [person] nervioso(sa), intranquil(la) **2.** [weather] variable **- 3.** [argument, matter, debt] pendiente **- 4.** [situation] inestable.

unshak(e)able [ʌnˈʃeɪkəbl] *adj* inquebrantable.

unshaven [ˌʌnˈʃeɪvn] *adj* sin afeitar.

unsightly [ʌnˈsaɪtlɪ] *adj* [building] feo(a); [scar, bruise] desagradable.

unskilled [ˌʌnˈskɪld] *adj* [person] no cualificado(da); [work] no especializado(da).

unsociable [ʌnˈsəʊʃəbl] *adj* poco sociable.

unsocial [ˌʌnˈsəʊʃl] *adj*: **to work unsocial hours** trabajar a horas intempestivas.

unsound [ˌʌnˈsaʊnd] *adj* - **1.** [conclusion, method] erróneo(a) - **2.** [building, structure] defectuoso(sa).

unspeakable [ʌnˈspiːkəbl] *adj* [crime] incalificable; [pain] indecible.

unstable [ˌʌnˈsteɪbl] *adj* inestable.

unsteady [ˌʌnˈstedɪ] *adj* [gen] inestable; [hands, voice] tembloroso(sa); [footsteps] vacilante.

unstoppable [ˌʌnˈstɒpəbl] *adj* irrefrenable.

unstuck [ˌʌnˈstʌk] *adj*: **to come unstuck** [notice, stamp, label] despegarse, desprenderse; *fig* [plan, system, person] fracasar.

unsubscribe [ˌʌnsəbˈskraɪb] *vi*: **to unsubscribe (from sth)** cancelar la suscripción (de algo).

unsuccessful [ˌʌnsəkˈsesfʊl] *adj* [person] fracasado(da); [attempt, meeting] infructuoso(sa); **to be unsuccessful** [person] no tener éxito.

unsuccessfully [ˌʌnsəkˈsesfʊlɪ] *adv* sin éxito, en vano.

unsuitable [ˌʌnˈsuːtəbl] *adj* inadecuado(da), inapropiado(da); **he is unsuitable for the job** no es la persona indicada para el trabajo; **I'm afraid 3 o'clock would be unsuitable** lo siento, pero no me va bien a las 3.

unsure [ˌʌnˈʃɔːʳ] *adj* - **1.** [not confident]: **to be unsure of o.s.** sentirse inseguro(ra) - **2.** [not certain]: **to be unsure (about OR of)** no estar muy seguro (de).

unsuspecting [ˌʌnsəˈspektɪŋ] *adj* desprevenido(da), confiado(da).

unsympathetic [ˈʌnˌsɪmpəˈθetɪk] *adj*: **unsympathetic to** indiferente a.

untangle [ˌʌnˈtæŋgl] *vt* desenmarañar.

untapped [ˌʌnˈtæpt] *adj* sin explotar.

untenable [ˌʌnˈtenəbl] *adj* insostenible.

unthinkable [ʌnˈθɪŋkəbl] *adj* impensable, inconcebible.

untidy [ʌnˈtaɪdɪ] *adj* [room, desk] desordenado(da); [person, appearance] desaliñado(da).

untie [ˌʌnˈtaɪ] (*cont* **untying**) *vt* desatar.

until [ən'tɪl] ⬦ *prep* hasta; **until now/then** hasta ahora/entonces. ⬦ *conj* - 1. [gen] hasta que; **wait until everybody is there** espera a que haya llegado todo el mundo - 2. *(after negative)*: **don't leave until you've finished** no te vayas hasta que hayas terminado.

untimely [ʌn'taɪmlɪ] *adj* - 1. [premature] prematuro(ra) - 2. [inappropriate] inoportuno(na).

untold [ˌʌn'təʊld] *adj* [incalculable, vast] incalculable; [suffering, joy] indecible.

untoward [ˌʌntə'wɔːd] *adj* [event] adverso(sa); [behaviour] fuera de lugar.

untrue [ˌʌn'truː] *adj* [not true] falso(sa).

unused *adj* - 1. [ˌʌn'juːzd] [not previously used] nuevo(va), sin usar - 2. [ʌn'juːst] [unaccustomed]: **to be unused to sthg/to doing sthg** no estar acostumbrado(da) a algo/a hacer algo.

unusual [ʌn'juːʒl] *adj* [rare] insólito(ta), poco común.

unusually [ʌn'juːʒəlɪ] *adv* - 1. [exceptionally] extraordinariamente; **the exam was unusually difficult** el examen fue extraordinariamente difícil - 2. [surprisingly] sorprendentemente.

unveil [ˌʌn'veɪl] *vt* - 1. [statue, plaque] descubrir - 2. *fig* [plans, policy] revelar.

unwanted [ˌʌn'wɒntɪd] *adj* [clothes, furniture] superfluo(flua); [child, pregnancy] no deseado(da).

unwavering [ʌn'weɪvərɪŋ] *adj* [determination, feeling] firme, inquebrantable; [concentration] constante; [gaze] fijo(ja).

unwelcome [ʌn'welkəm] *adj* inoportuno(na).

unwell [ˌʌn'wel] *adj*: **to be/feel unwell** estar/ sentirse mal.

unwieldy [ʌn'wiːldɪ] *adj* - 1. [object] abultado(da); [tool] poco manejable - 2. *fig* [system, organization] poco eficiente.

unwilling [ˌʌn'wɪlɪŋ] *adj*: **to be unwilling to do sthg** no estar dispuesto a hacer algo.

unwind [ˌʌn'waɪnd] (*pt & pp* **unwound**) ⬦ *vt* desenrollar. ⬦ *vi fig* [person] relajarse.

unwise [ˌʌn'waɪz] *adj* imprudente.

unwitting [ʌn'wɪtɪŋ] *adj fml* inconsciente.

unworkable [ˌʌn'wɜːkəbl] *adj* impracticable.

unworthy [ʌn'wɜːðɪ] *adj* [undeserving]: **to be unworthy of** no ser digno(na) de.

unwound [ˌʌn'waʊnd] *pt & pp* ⊳ **unwind**.

unwrap [ˌʌn'ræp] *vt* [present] desenvolver; [parcel] desempaquetar.

unwritten law [ˌʌn'rɪtn-] *n* ley *f* no escrita.

up [ʌp] ⬦ *adv* - 1. [towards a higher position] hacia arriba; [in a higher position] arriba; **to throw sthg up** lanzar algo hacia arriba; **she's**

up in her room está arriba en su cuarto; **we'll be up in just a moment** subiremos en un minuto; **we walked up to the top** subimos hasta arriba del todo; **put it up there** ponlo ahí arriba - 2. [northwards]: **I'm going up to York next week** voy a subir a York la semana próxima; **up north** en el norte - 3. [along a road or river] adelante; **their house is 100 metres further up** su casa está a 100 metros más adelante. ⬦ *prep* - 1. [towards a higher position]: **we went up the mountain** subimos por la montaña; **let's go up this road** vamos por esta carretera; **I went up the stairs** subí las escaleras - 2. [in a higher position] en lo alto de; **up a tree** en un árbol - 3. [at far end of] al final de; **they live up the road from us** viven más adelante en nuestra misma calle - 4. [against current of river]: **up the Amazon** Amazonas arriba. ⬦ *adj* - 1. [out of bed] levantado(da); **I was up at six today** hoy me levanté a las seis - 2. [at an end] terminado(da) - 3. *inf* [wrong]: **is something up?** ¿pasa algo?, ¿algo va mal?; **what's up?** ¿qué pasa? ⬦ *n*: **ups and downs** altibajos *mpl*. ◆ **up and down** ⬦ *adv*: **to jump up and down** saltar para arriba y para abajo; **to walk up and down** andar para un lado y para otro. ⬦ *prep*: **we walked up and down the avenue** estuvimos caminando arriba y abajo de la avenida. ◆ **up to** *prep* - 1. [indicating level] hasta; **it could take up to six weeks** podría tardar hasta seis semanas; **it's not up to standard** no tiene el nivel necesario - 2. [well or able enough for]: **to be up to doing sthg** sentirse con fuerzas (como) para hacer algo; **my French isn't up to much** mi francés no es gran cosa - 3. *inf* [secretly doing something]: **what are you up to?** ¿qué andas tramando? - 4. [indicating responsibility]: **it's not up to me to decide** no depende de mí el decidir. ◆ **up until** *prep* hasta.

up-and-coming *adj* prometedor(ra).

upbringing ['ʌpˌbrɪŋɪŋ] *n* educación *f*.

update [ˌʌp'deɪt] *vt* actualizar.

upheaval [ʌp'hiːvl] *n* trastorno *m*, agitación *f*.

upheld [ʌp'held] *pt & pp* ⊳ **uphold**.

uphill [ˌʌp'hɪl] ⬦ *adj* [rising] empinado(da), cuesta arriba; *fig* [difficult] arduo(dua), difícil. ⬦ *adv* cuesta arriba.

uphold [ʌp'həʊld] (*pt & pp* -**held**) *vt* sostener, apoyar.

upholstery [ʌp'həʊlstərɪ] *n* tapicería *f*.

upkeep ['ʌpkiːp] *n* mantenimiento *m*.

uplifting [ʌp'lɪftɪŋ] *adj* inspirador(ra).

up-market *adj* de clase superior.

upon [ə'pɒn] *prep fml* en, sobre; **upon entering the room** al entrar en el cuarto; **question upon question** pregunta tras pregunta; **summer is upon us** ya tenemos el verano encima.

upper ['ʌpər] ⬦ *adj* superior. ⬦ *n* [of shoe] pala *f*.

upper class *n*: **the upper class** la clase alta.
◆ **upper-class** *adj* de clase alta.

upper hand *n*: **to have/gain the upper hand (in)** llevar/empezar a llevar la ventaja (en).

uppermost ['ʌpəməʊst] *adj* - 1. [highest] más alto(ta) - 2. [most important]: **to be uppermost in one's mind** ser lo más importante para uno.

upright ['ʌpraɪt] ⬦ *adj* - 1. [erect - person, chair] derecho(cha) - 2. [standing vertically - object] vertical - 3. *fig* [honest] recto(ta), honrado(da). ⬦ *adv* erguidamente. ⬦ *n* poste *m*.

uprising ['ʌp,raɪzɪŋ] *n* sublevación *f*.

uproar ['ʌprɔːr] *n* - 1. (U) [commotion] alboroto *m* - 2. [protest] escándalo *m*.

uproot [,ʌp'ruːt] *vt* - 1. [person] desplazar, mudar - 2. BOT [plant] desarraigar.

upset [ʌp'set] ⬦ *adj* - 1. [distressed] disgustado(da); **to get upset** disgustarse - 2. MED: **to have an upset stomach** sentirse mal del estómago. ⬦ *n*: **to have a stomach upset** sentirse mal del estómago. ⬦ *vt* (*pt & pp* **upset**) - 1. [distress] disgustar, perturbar - 2. [mess up] dar al traste con - 3. [overturn, knock over] volcar.

upshot ['ʌpʃɒt] *n* resultado *m*.

upside down [,ʌpsaɪd-] ⬦ *adj* al revés. ⬦ *adv* al revés; **to turn sthg upside down** revolver algo, desordenar algo.

upstairs [,ʌp'steəz] ⬦ *adj* de arriba. ⬦ *adv* arriba. ⬦ *n* el piso de arriba.

upstart ['ʌpstɑːt] *n* advenedizo *m*, -za *f*.

upstream [,ʌp'striːm] *adv* río arriba.

upsurge ['ʌpsɜːdʒ] *n*: **upsurge of** OR **in** aumento *m* considerable de.

uptake ['ʌpteɪk] *n*: **to be quick on the uptake** cogerlas al vuelo; **to be slow on the uptake** ser un poco torpe.

uptight [ʌp'taɪt] *adj inf* tenso(sa), nervioso(sa).

up-to-date *adj* - 1. [modern] moderno(na) - 2. [most recent] actual, al día - 3. [informed]: **to keep up-to-date with** mantenerse al día de.

upturn ['ʌptɜːn] *n*: **upturn (in)** mejora *f* (de).

upward ['ʌpwəd] ⬦ *adj* hacia arriba. ⬦ *adv US* = **upwards**.

upwards ['ʌpwədz], **upward** *adv* hacia arriba. ◆ **upwards of** *prep* más de.

uranium [jʊ'reɪnjəm] *n* uranio *m*.

Uranus ['jʊərənəs] *n* Urano *m*.

urban ['ɜːbən] *adj* urbano(na).

urbane [ɜː'beɪn] *adj* cortés, urbano(na).

urchin ['ɜːtʃɪn] *n dated* pilluelo *m*, -la *f*.

Urdu ['ʊədu:] *n* urdu *m*.

urge [ɜːdʒ] ⬦ *n* impulso *m*, deseo *m*; **to have an urge to do sthg** desear ardientemente

hacer algo. ⬦ *vt* - 1. [try to persuade]: **to urge sb to do sthg** instar a alguien a hacer algo - 2. [advocate] recomendar encarecidamente.

urgency ['ɜːdʒənsɪ] *n* (U) urgencia *f*.

urgent ['ɜːdʒənt] *adj* - 1. [pressing] urgente - 2. [desperate] apremiante.

urinal [,jʊə'raɪnl] *n* [place] urinario *m*; [vessel] orinal *m*.

urinate ['jʊərɪneɪt] *vi* orinar.

urine ['jʊərɪn] *n* orina *f*.

URL (*abbr of* **uniform resource locator**) *n* COMPUT URL *m*.

urn [ɜːn] *n* - 1. [for ashes] urna *f* - 2. [for tea, coffee] *cilindro o barril con grifo para servir té o café en grandes cantidades.*

Uruguay ['jʊərəgwaɪ] *n* Uruguay.

Uruguayan [,jʊərə'gwaɪən] ⬦ *adj* uruguayo(ya). ⬦ *n* uruguayo *m*, -ya *f*.

us [ʌs] *pers pron* - 1. (*direct, indirect*) nos; **can you see/hear us?** ¿puedes vernos/oírnos?; **it's us** somos nosotros; **he sent us a letter** nos mandó una carta; **she gave it to us** nos lo dio - 2. (*stressed, after prep, in comparisons etc*) nosotros(tras); **you can't expect us to do it** no esperarás que lo hagamos **nosotros**; **with/without us** con/sin nosotros; **they are more wealthy than us** son más ricos que nosotros; **all of us** todos (nosotros); **some of us** algunos de nosotros.

US (*abbr of* **United States**) *n* EEUU *mpl*.

USA *n* (*abbr of* **United States of America**) EEUU *mpl*.

usage ['juːzɪdʒ] *n* uso *m*.

USB port *n* COMPUT puerto *m* USB.

use ⬦ *n* [juːs] uso *m*; **to be in use** usarse; **to be out of use** no usarse; **'out of use'** 'no funciona'; **to let sb have the use of sthg** dejar a alguien usar algo; **to be of/no use** ser útil/inútil; **what's the use (of doing sthg)?** ¿de qué sirve (hacer algo)? ⬦ *aux vb* [juːs] soler, acostumbrar; **I used to go swimming** solía OR acostumbraba ir a nadar; **he used to be fat** antes estaba gordo. ⬦ *vt* [juːz] - 1. [utilize, employ] usar, emplear - 2. [exploit] usar, manejar. ◆ **use up** *vt sep* agotar.

used *adj* - 1. [juːzd] [dirty, second-hand] usado(da) - 2. [juːst] [accustomed]: **to be used to** estar acostumbrado(da) a; **to get used to** acostumbrarse a.

useful ['juːsfʊl] *adj* - 1. [handy] útil - 2. [helpful - person] valioso(sa).

useless ['juːslɪs] *adj* - 1. [gen] inútil - 2. *inf* [hopeless] incompetente.

user ['juːzər] *n* usuario *m*, -ria *f*.

user-friendly *adj* fácil de utilizar.

usher ['ʌʃər] ⬦ *n* [at wedding] ujier *m*; [at theatre, concert] acomodador *m*, -ra *f*. ⬦ *vt*: **to usher sb in** hacer pasar a alguien; **to usher sb out** acompañar a alguien hasta la puerta.

usherette [,ʌʃə'ret] *n* acomodadora *f*.

USSR (*abbr of* Union of Soviet Socialist Republics) *n*: **the (former) USSR** la (antigua) URSS.

usual ['juːʒəl] *adj* habitual; **as usual** [as normal] como de costumbre; [as often happens] como siempre.

usually ['juːʒəlɪ] *adv* por regla general; **we usually go to church on Sunday** solemos ir a misa el domingo.

usurp [juː'zɜːp] *vt fml* usurpar.

utensil [juː'tensl] *n* utensilio *m*.

uterus ['juːtərəs] (*pl* -ri [-raɪ] OR -ruses) *n* útero *m*.

utility [juː'tɪlətɪ] *n* - **1.** [gen] utilidad *f* - **2.** [public service] servicio *m* público. ◆ **utilities** *n US* [service charges] empresa *f* de servicios públicos.

utility room *n* trascocina *f*.

utilize, -ise ['juːtəlaɪz] *vt* utilizar.

utmost ['ʌtməʊst] ◇ *adj* mayor, supremo(ma). ◇ *n*: **to do one's utmost** hacer lo imposible; **to the utmost** al máximo, a más no poder.

utter ['ʌtər] ◇ *adj* puro(ra), completo(ta). ◇ *vt* [word] pronunciar; [sound, cry] emitir.

utterly ['ʌtəlɪ] *adv* completamente.

U-turn *n lit & fig* giro *m* de 180°; **to do a U-turn** [in car] cambiar de sentido; *fig* dar un giro radical.

v¹ (*pl* v's OR vs), **V** (*pl* V's OR Vs) [viː] *n* [letter] v *f*, V *f*.

v² - **1.** (*abbr of* verse) v - **2.** (*abbr of* volt) v - **3.** [cross-reference] (*abbr of* vide) v. - **4.** *abbr of* versus.

vacancy ['veɪkənsɪ] *n* - **1.** [job, position] vacante *f* - **2.** [room available] habitación *f* libre; **'no vacancies'** 'completo'.

vacant ['veɪkənt] *adj* - **1.** [room, chair, toilet] libre - **2.** [job, post] vacante - **3.** [look, expression] distraído(da).

vacant lot *n* terreno *m* disponible.

vacate [və'keɪt] *vt* - **1.** [job, post] dejar vacante - **2.** [room, seat, premises] desocupar.

vacation [və'keɪʃn] *US* ◇ *n* vacaciones *fpl*; **to be on vacation** estar de vacaciones. ◇ *vi* pasar las vacaciones.

vacationer [və'keɪʃənər] *n US*: **summer vacationer** veraneante *mf*.

vaccinate ['væksɪneɪt] *vt*: **to vaccinate sb (against sthg)** vacunar a alguien (de OR contra algo).

vaccine [*UK* 'væksiːn, *US* væk'siːn] *n* vacuna *f*.

vacuum ['vækjʊəm] ◇ *n* - **1.** *fig* & TECH vacío *m* - **2.** [cleaner] aspiradora *f*. ◇ *vt* pasar la aspiradora por.

vacuum cleaner *n* aspiradora *f*.

vacuum-packed *adj* envasado(da) al vacío.

vagina [və'dʒaɪnə] *n* vagina *f*.

vagrant ['veɪgrənt] *n* vagabundo *m*, -da *f*.

vague [veɪg] *adj* - **1.** [imprecise] vago(ga), impreciso(sa) - **2.** [person] poco claro(ra) - **3.** [feeling] leve - **4.** [evasive] evasivo(va) - **5.** [absentminded] distraído(da) - **6.** [outline] borroso(sa).

vaguely ['veɪglɪ] *adv* - **1.** [imprecisely] vagamente - **2.** [slightly, not very] levemente.

vain [veɪn] *adj* - **1.** *pej* [conceited] vanidoso(sa) - **2.** [futile] vano(na). ◆ **in vain** *adv* en vano.

valentine card ['væləntaɪn-] *n* tarjeta *f* que se manda el Día de los Enamorados.

valet ['væleɪ, 'vaelɪt] *n* ayuda *m* de cámara.

valiant ['væljənt] *adj* valeroso(sa).

valid ['vælɪd] *adj* - **1.** [argument, explanation] válido(da) - **2.** [ticket, driving licence] en vigor; **to be valid for six months** ser válido(da) durante seis meses.

valley ['vælɪ] (*pl* valleys) *n* valle *m*.

valour *UK*, **valor** *US* ['vælər] *n* (U) *fml & liter* valor *m*.

valuable ['væljʊəbl] *adj* valioso(sa). ◆ **valuables** *npl* objetos *mpl* de valor.

valuation [,væljʊ'eɪʃn] *n* - **1.** [pricing, estimated price] valuación *f* - **2.** [opinion, judging of worth] valoración *f*.

value ['væljuː] ◇ *n* valor *m*; **to be good value** estar muy bien de precio; **to be value for money** estar muy bien de precio; **to take sthg/sb at face value** tomarse algo/a alguien en su sentido literal. ◇ *vt* - **1.** [estimate price of] valorar, tasar; **a necklace valued at £300** un collar valorado en 300 libras - **2.** [cherish] apreciar. ◆ **values** *npl* [morals] valores *mpl* morales.

value-added tax [-ædɪd-] *n* impuesto *m* sobre el valor añadido.

valued ['væljuːd] *adj* apreciado(da).

valve ['vælv] *n* [in pipe, tube] válvula *f*.

van [væn] *n* - 1. AUT furgoneta *f*, camioneta *f* - 2. UK RAIL furgón *m*.

vandal ['vændl] *n* vándalo *m*, gamberro *m*, -rra *f*.

vandalism ['vændəlɪzm] *n* vandalismo *m*, gamberrismo *m*.

vandalize, -ise ['vændəlaɪz] *vt* destruir, destrozar.

vanguard ['vænɡɑ:d] *n* vanguardia *f*; **in the vanguard of** a la vanguardia de.

vanilla [və'nɪlə] *n* vainilla *f*.

vanish ['vænɪʃ] *vi* desaparecer.

vanity ['vænətɪ] *n pej* vanidad *f*.

vantage point ['vɑ:ntɪdʒ,pɔɪnt] *n* posición *f* ventajosa.

vapour *UK*, **vapor** *US* ['veɪpər] *n* (U) vapor *m*.

variable ['veərɪəbl] *adj* variable.

variance ['veərɪəns] *n fml*: **at variance (with)** en desacuerdo (con).

variation [,veərɪ'eɪʃn] *n*: **variation (in/on)** variación *f* (en/sobre).

varicose veins ['værɪkəʊs-] *npl* varices *fpl*.

varied ['veərɪd] *adj* variado(da).

variety [və'raɪətɪ] *n* - 1. [gen] variedad *f*; **for a variety of reasons** por razones varias - 2. (U) THEAT variedades *fpl*.

variety show *n* espectáculo *m* de variedades.

various ['veərɪəs] *adj* - 1. [several] varios(rias) - 2. [different] diversos(sas).

varnish ['vɑ:nɪʃ] <> *n* barniz *m*. <> *vt* [with varnish] barnizar; [with nail varnish] pintar.

vary ['veərɪ] <> *vt* variar. <> *vi*: **to vary (in/ with)** variar (de/con).

vase [*UK* vɑ:z, *US* veɪz] *n* florero *m*.

Vaseline® ['væsəli:n] *n* vaselina® *f*.

vast [vɑ:st] *adj* enorme, inmenso(sa).

vat [væt] *n* cuba *f*, tina *f*.

VAT [væt vi:eɪ'ti:] (*abbr of* **value added tax**) *n* IVA *m*.

Vatican ['vætɪkən] *n*: **the Vatican** el Vaticano.

vault [vɔ:lt] <> *n* - 1. [in bank] cámara *f* acorazada - 2. [in church] cripta *f* - 3. [roof] bóveda *f*. <> *vt* saltar. <> *vi*: **to vault over sthg** saltar por encima de algo.

VCR (*abbr of* **video cassette recorder**) *n US* aparato *m* de vídeo.

VD (*abbr of* **venereal disease**) *n* ETS *f*.

VDU (*abbr of* **visual display unit**) *n* monitor *m*.

veal [vi:l] *n* (U) ternera *f*.

veer [vɪər] *vi* virar.

vegan ['vi:ɡən] *n* vegetariano que no consume ningún producto que provenga de un animal, como huevos, leche etc.

vegetable ['vedʒtəbl] <> *n* - 1. BOT vegetal *m* - 2. [food] hortaliza *f*, legumbre *f*; **vegetables** verduras *fpl*. <> *adj* vegetal.

vegetarian [,vedʒɪ'teərɪən] <> *adj* vegetariano(na). <> *n* vegetariano *m*, -na *f*.

vegetation [,vedʒɪ'teɪʃn] *n* vegetación *f*.

veggieburger ['vedʒɪbɜ:ɡər] *n* hamburguesa *f* vegetariana.

vehement ['vi:əmənt] *adj* [person, denial] vehemente; [attack, gesture] violento(ta).

vehicle ['vi:əkl] *n* [for transport] vehículo *m*.

veil [veɪl] <> *n lit & fig* velo *m*. <> *vt* cubrir con un velo.

vein [veɪn] *n* - 1. ANAT & BOT vena *f* - 2. [of mineral] filón *m*, veta *f*.

velocity [vɪ'lɒsətɪ] *n* velocidad *f*.

velvet ['velvɪt] *n* terciopelo *m*.

vendetta [ven'detə] *n* enemistad *f* mortal.

vending machine ['vendɪŋ-] *n* máquina *f* de venta.

vendor ['vendɔ:r] *n* vendedor *m*, -ra *f*.

veneer [və'nɪər] *n* [of wood] chapa *f*; *fig* [appearance] apariencia *f*; **a veneer of** una apariencia de.

venereal disease [vɪ'nɪərɪəl-] *n* enfermedad *f* venérea.

venetian blind *n* persiana *f* veneciana.

Venezuela [,venɪz'weɪlə] *n* Venezuela.

Venezuelan [,venɪz'weɪlən] <> *adj* venezolano(na). <> *n* venezolano *m*, -na *f*.

vengeance ['vendʒəns] *n* venganza *f*; **with a vengeance** con creces.

venison ['venɪzn] *n* carne *f* de venado.

venom ['venəm] *n* [poison] veneno *m*; *fig* [spite] malevolencia *f*.

vent [vent] <> *n* [opening] abertura *f* de escape; [grille] rejilla *f* de ventilación; **to give vent to sthg** dar rienda suelta a algo. <> *vt*: **to vent sthg (on)** desahogar algo (contra).

ventilate ['ventɪleɪt] *vt* ventilar.

ventilator ['ventɪleɪtər] *n* ventilador *m*.

ventriloquist [ven'trɪləkwɪst] *n* ventrílocuo *m*, -cua *f*.

venture ['ventʃər] <> *n* empresa *f*. <> *vt* aventurar; **to venture an opinion** aventurarse a dar una opinión; **to venture to do sthg** aventurarse a hacer algo. <> *vi* - 1. [go somewhere dangerous]: **she ventured outside** se atrevió a salir - 2. [take a risk]: **to venture into** lanzarse a.

venue ['venju:] *n* lugar *m* (en que se celebra algo).

Venus ['vi:nəs] *n* [planet] Venus *m*.

veranda(h) [vəˈrændə] *n* veranda *f*.

verb [vɜːb] *n* verbo *m*.

verbal [ˈvɜːbl] *adj* verbal.

verbatim [vɜːˈbeɪtɪm] <> *adj* literal. <> *adv* literalmente, palabra por palabra.

verbose [vɜːˈbəʊs] *adj fml* [person] verboso(sa); [report] prolijo(ja).

verdict [ˈvɜːdɪkt] *n* - **1.** LAW veredicto *m*, fallo *m*; **a verdict of guilty/not guilty** un veredicto de culpabilidad/inocencia - **2.** [opinion]: **verdict (on)** juicio *m* OR opinión *f* (sobre).

verge [vɜːdʒ] *n* - **1.** [edge, side] borde *m* - **2.** [brink]: **on the verge of sthg** al borde de algo; **to be on the verge of doing sthg** estar a punto de hacer algo. ➡ **verge (up)on** *vt insep* rayar en.

verify [ˈverɪfaɪ] *vt* - **1.** [check] verificar, comprobar - **2.** [confirm] confirmar.

veritable [ˈverɪtəbl] *adj hum* & *fml* verdadero(ra).

vermin [ˈvɜːmɪn] *npl* [insects] bichos *mpl*; [animals] alimañas *fpl*.

vermouth [ˈvɜːməθ] *n* vermut *m*.

versa ⊳ **vice versa**.

versatile [ˈvɜːsətaɪl] *adj* - **1.** [person] polifacético(ca) - **2.** [machine, tool] que tiene muchos usos.

verse [vɜːs] *n* - **1.** (U) [poetry] versos *mpl*, poesía *f* - **2.** [stanza] estrofa *f* - **3.** [in Bible] versículo *m*.

versed [vɜːst] *adj*: **well versed in** versado(da) en.

version [ˈvɜːʃn] *n* versión *f*.

versus [ˈvɜːsəs] *prep* SPORT contra.

vertebra [ˈvɜːtɪbrə] (*pl* **-brae** [-briː]) *n* vértebra *f*.

vertical [ˈvɜːtɪkl] *adj* vertical.

vertigo [ˈvɜːtɪɡəʊ] *n* vértigo *m*.

verve [vɜːv] *n* brío *m*, entusiasmo *m*.

very [ˈverɪ] <> *adv* - **1.** [as intensifier] muy; **he's not very intelligent** no es muy inteligente; **very much** mucho; **I don't go out very often** OR much no salgo mucho; **is it good? – not very** ¿es bueno? – no mucho - **2.** [emphatic]: **the very same/next day** justo ese mismo día/al día siguiente; **the very first** el primero de todos; **the very best** el mejor (de todos); **at the very least** como muy poco; **a house of my very own** mi propia casa. <> *adj*: **in the very middle of the picture** en el mismísimo centro del cuadro; **the very thing I was looking for** justo lo que estaba buscando; **the very thought makes me ill** sólo con pensarlo me pongo enfermo; **fighting for his very life** luchando por su propia vida; **the very idea!** ¡va-

ya idea! ➡ **very well** *adv* muy bien; **you can't very well stop him now** es un poco tarde para impedírselo.

vessel [ˈvesl] *n fml* - **1.** [boat] nave *f* - **2.** [container] vasija *f*, recipiente *m*.

vest [vest] *n* - **1.** UK [undershirt] camiseta *f* - **2.** US [waistcoat] chaleco *m*.

vested interest [ˈvestɪd-] *n*: **vested interest (in)** intereses *mpl* creados (en).

vestibule [ˈvestɪbjuːl] *n fml* [entrance hall] vestíbulo *m*.

vestige [ˈvestɪdʒ] *n fml* vestigio *m*.

vestry [ˈvestrɪ] *n* sacristía *f*.

vet [vet] <> *n* UK (*abbr of* **veterinary surgeon**) veterinario *m*, -ria *f*. <> *vt* someter a una investigación.

veteran [ˈvetrən] *n* veterano *m*, -na *f*.

veterinarian [ˌvetərɪˈneərɪən] *n* US veterinario *m*, -ria *f*.

veterinary surgeon [ˈvetərɪnrɪ-] *n* UK *fml* veterinario *m*, -ria *f*.

veto [ˈviːtəʊ] <> *n* (*pl* **-es**) veto *m*. <> *vt* vetar.

vex [veks] *vt fml* molestar.

vexed question [ˌvekst-] *n* manzana *f* de la discordia.

vg (*abbr of* **very good**) MB.

VGA (*abbr of* **video graphics array**) *n* COMPUT VGA *m*.

VHF (*abbr of* **very high frequency**) VHF.

VHS (*abbr of* **video home system**) *n* VHS *m*.

via [ˈvaɪə] *prep* - **1.** [travelling through] vía - **2.** [by means of] a través de, por.

viable [ˈvaɪəbl] *adj* viable.

vibrate [vaɪˈbreɪt] *vi* vibrar.

vicar [ˈvɪkər] *n* [in Church of England] párroco *m*; [in Roman Catholic Church] vicario *m*.

vicarage [ˈvɪkərɪdʒ] *n* casa *f* del párroco.

vicarious [vɪˈkeərɪəs] *adj* indirecto(ta).

vice [vaɪs] *n* - **1.** [immorality, moral fault] vicio *m* - **2.** [tool] torno *m* de banco.

vice-chairman *n* vicepresidente *m*.

vice-chancellor *n* UNIV rector *m*, -ra *f*.

vice-president *n* vicepresidente *m*, -ta *f*.

vice versa [ˌvaɪsɪˈvɜːsə] *adv* viceversa.

vicinity [vɪˈsɪnətɪ] *n*: **in the vicinity (of)** cerca (de).

vicious [ˈvɪʃəs] *adj* [dog] furioso(sa); [person, ruler] cruel; [criticism, attack] despiadado(da).

vicious circle *n* círculo *m* vicioso.

victim [ˈvɪktɪm] *n* víctima *f*.

victimize, -ise [ˈvɪktɪmaɪz] *vt* [retaliate against] tomar represalias contra; [pick on] mortificar.

victor [ˈvɪktər] *n liter* vencedor *m*, -ra *f*.

victorious [vik'tɔːrɪəs] *adj* victorioso(sa).

victory ['vɪktərɪ] *n*: **victory (over)** victoria *f* (sobre).

video ['vɪdɪəʊ] <> *n* (*pl* -s) - 1. [recording, medium, machine] vídeo *m* - 2. [cassette] videocasete *m*. <> *vt* - 1. [using video recorder] grabar en vídeo - 2. [using camera] hacer un vídeo de.

video camera *n* videocámara *f*.

video cassette *n* videocasete *m*.

videoconference ['vɪdɪəʊ‚kɒnfərəns] *n* videoconferencia *f*.

videoconferencing ['vɪdɪəʊ‚kɒnfərənsɪŋ] *n* (U) videoconferencias *fpl*.

video game *n* videojuego *m*.

video on demand *n* (U) TV vídeo *m* a la carta.

videorecorder ['vɪdɪəʊrɪ‚kɔːdər] *n* vídeo *m*.

video shop *n* tienda *f* de vídeos.

videotape ['vɪdɪəʊteɪp] *n* videocinta *f*.

vie [vaɪ] (*pt* & *pp* vied, *cont* vying) *vi*: **to vie (with sb for sthg/to do sthg)** competir (con alguien por algo/para hacer algo).

Vietnam [*UK* ‚vjet'næm, *US* ‚vjet'nɑːm] *n* (el) Vietnam.

Vietnamese [‚vjetnə'miːz] <> *adj* vietnamita. <> *n* - 1. [person] vietnamita *mf* - 2. [language] vietnamita *m*.

view [vjuː] <> *n* - 1. [opinion] parecer *m*, opinión *f*; **in my view** en mi opinión - 2. [attitude]: **view (of)** actitud *f* (frente a) - 3. [scene] vista *f*, panorama *m* - 4. [field of vision] vista *f*; **to come into view** aparecer. <> *vt* - 1. [consider] ver, considerar - 2. *fml* [examine, look at - stars etc] observar; [- house, flat] visitar, ver. ◆ **in view of** *prep* en vista de. ◆ **with a view to** *conj* con miras OR vistas a.

viewer ['vjuːər] *n* - 1. [person] espectador *m*, -ra *f* - 2. [apparatus] visionador *m*.

viewfinder ['vjuː‚faɪndər] *n* visor *m*.

viewpoint ['vjuːpɔɪnt] *n* - 1. [opinion] punto *m* de vista - 2. [place] mirador *m*.

vigil ['vɪdʒɪl] *n* - 1. [watch] vigilia *f*; **to keep (a) vigil** observar vigilia - 2. RELIG Vigilia *f*.

vigilante [‚vɪdʒɪ'læntɪ] *n* persona que extraoficialmente patrulla un área para protegerla tomándose la justicia en sus manos.

vigorous ['vɪgərəs] *adj* enérgico(ca).

vile [vaɪl] *adj* [person, act] vil, infame; [food, smell] repugnante; [mood] de perros.

villa ['vɪlə] *n* [in country] villa *f*; [in town] chalet *m*.

village ['vɪlɪdʒ] *n* aldea *f*, pueblecito *m*.

villager ['vɪlɪdʒər] *n* aldeano *m*, -na *f*.

villain ['vɪlən] *n* - 1. [of film, book] malo *m*, -la *f* - 2. *dated* [criminal] criminal *mf*.

vinaigrette [‚vɪnɪ'gret] *n* vinagreta *f*.

vindicate ['vɪndɪkeɪt] *vt* justificar.

vindictive [vɪn'dɪktɪv] *adj* vengativo(va).

vine [vaɪn] *n* [on ground] vid *f*; [climbing plant] parra *f*.

vinegar ['vɪnɪgər] *n* vinagre *m*.

vineyard ['vɪnjəd] *n* viña *f*, viñedo *m*.

vintage ['vɪntɪdʒ] <> *adj* - 1. [wine] añejo(ja) - 2. [classic] clásico(ca) - 3. [outstanding]: **a vintage year** un año excepcional. <> *n* cosecha *f* (de vino).

vintage wine *n* vino *m* añejo.

vinyl ['vaɪnɪl] *n* vinilo *m*.

viola [vɪ'əʊlə] *n* viola *f*.

violate ['vaɪəleɪt] *vt* - 1. [law, treaty, rights] violar, infringir - 2. [peace, privacy] invadir.

violence ['vaɪələns] *n* violencia *f*.

violent ['vaɪələnt] *adj* - 1. [gen] violento(ta) - 2. [emotion, anger] intenso(sa); **to have a violent dislike for sb** sentir una enorme antipatía hacia alguien.

violet ['vaɪələt] <> *adj* violeta, violado(da). <> *n* [flower] violeta *f*.

violin [‚vaɪə'lɪn] *n* violín *m*.

violinist [‚vaɪə'lɪnɪst] *n* violinista *mf*.

VIP (*abbr of* very important person) *n* VIP *mf*.

viper ['vaɪpər] *n* víbora *f*.

virgin ['vɜːdʒɪn] <> *adj liter* - 1. [spotless] virgen - 2. [olive oil] virgen. <> *n* virgen *mf*.

Virgo ['vɜːgəʊ] (*pl* -s) *n* Virgo *m*.

virile ['vɪraɪl] *adj* viril.

virtually ['vɜːtʃʊəlɪ] *adv* prácticamente.

virtual reality *n* realidad *f* virtual.

virtue ['vɜːtjuː] *n* - 1. [morality, good quality] virtud *f* - 2. [benefit] ventaja *f*. ◆ **by virtue of** *prep fml* en virtud de.

virtuous ['vɜːtʃʊəs] *adj* virtuoso(sa).

virus ['vaɪrəs] *n* COMPUT & MED virus *m*.

visa ['viːzə] *n* visado *m*, visa *f* Amér.

vis-à-vis [‚viːzɑː'viː] *prep fml* con relación a.

viscose ['vɪskəʊs] *n* viscosa *f*.

visibility [‚vɪzɪ'bɪlətɪ] *n* visibilidad *f*.

visible ['vɪzəbl] *adj* visible.

vision ['vɪʒn] *n* - 1. (U) [ability to see] visión *f*, vista *f* - 2. *fig* [foresight] clarividencia *f* - 3. [impression, dream] visión *f*.

visit ['vɪzɪt] <> *n* visita *f*; **to pay sb a visit** hacer una visita a alguien; **on a visit** de visita. <> *vt* visitar.

visiting hours ['vɪzɪtɪŋ-] *npl* horas *fpl* de visita.

visitor ['vɪzɪtər] *n* - 1. [to one's home, hospital] visita *f*; **we've got visitors** [at home] tenemos visitas - 2. [to museum, town etc] visitante *mf*.

visitors' book *n* libro *m* de visitas.

visor ['vaɪzəʳ] n visera f.

vista ['vɪstə] n [view] vista f, perspectiva f; fig [wide range] perspectiva.

visual ['vɪʒʊəl] adj [gen] visual; [of the eyes] ocular.

visual aids npl medios mpl visuales.

visual display unit n monitor m.

visualize, -ise ['vɪʒʊəlaɪz] vt visualizar; **to visualize (sb) doing sthg** imaginar (a alguien) haciendo algo.

vital ['vaɪtl] adj - **1.** [essential] vital, esencial - **2.** [full of life] enérgico(ca).

vitally ['vaɪtəlɪ] adv sumamente.

vital statistics npl inf medidas fpl (del cuerpo de la mujer).

vitamin [UK 'vɪtəmɪn, US 'vaɪtəmɪn] n vitamina f; **vitamin C** vitamina C.

vitamin pill n pastilla f vitamínica.

vivacious [vɪ'veɪʃəs] adj vivaz.

vivid ['vɪvɪd] adj - **1.** [colour] vivo(va) - **2.** [description, memory] vívido(da).

vividly ['vɪvɪdlɪ] adv - **1.** [brightly] con colores muy vivos - **2.** [clearly] vívidamente.

vixen ['vɪksn] n zorra f.

VLF (abbr of very low frequency) VLF.

V-neck n [sweater, dress] jersey m con cuello de pico.

vocabulary [və'kæbjʊlərɪ] n vocabulario m.

vocal ['vəʊkl] adj - **1.** [outspoken] vociferante - **2.** [of the voice] vocal.

vocal cords npl cuerdas fpl vocales.

vocalist ['vəʊkəlɪst] n [in orchestra] vocalista mf; [in pop group] cantante mf.

vocation [vəʊ'keɪʃn] n vocación f.

vocational [vəʊ'keɪʃənl] adj profesional.

vociferous [və'sɪfərəs] adj fml ruidoso(sa).

vodka ['vɒdkə] n [drink] vodka m.

vogue [vəʊg] n moda f; **in vogue** en boga, de moda.

voice [vɔɪs] <> n voz f; **to give voice to** expresar. <> vt [opinion, emotion] expresar.

voice mail n correo m de voz; **to send/receive voice mail** mandar/recibir un mensaje de correo de voz; **to check one's voice mail** verificar el correo de voz.

void [vɔɪd] <> adj - **1.** [invalid] inválido(da), ▷ **null** - **2.** fml [empty]: **void of** falto(ta) de. <> n liter vacío m.

volatile [UK 'vɒlətaɪl, US 'vɒlətl] adj [situation] volátil; [person] voluble.

vol-au-vent ['vɒləʊvɑ̃] n volován m.

volcano [vɒl'keɪnəʊ] (pl -es OR -s) n volcán m.

volition [və'lɪʃn] n fml: **of one's own volition** por voluntad propia.

volley ['vɒlɪ] <> n (pl volleys) - **1.** [of gunfire] ráfaga f - **2.** fig [rapid succession] torrente m - **3.** SPORT volea f. <> vt volear.

volleyball ['vɒlɪbɔːl] n voleibol m.

volt [vəʊlt] n voltio m.

voltage ['vəʊltɪdʒ] n voltaje m.

voluble ['vɒljʊbl] adj fml locuaz.

volume ['vɒljuːm] n volumen m; **to speak volumes** decir mucho.

voluntarily [UK ˌvɒləntrɪlɪ, US ˌvɒlən'terəlɪ] adv voluntariamente.

voluntary ['vɒləntrɪ] adj voluntario(ria); **voluntary organization** organización f benéfica.

volunteer [ˌvɒlən'tɪəʳ] <> n [person who volunteers] voluntario m, -ria f. <> vt - **1.** [offer of one's free will]: **to volunteer to do sthg** ofrecerse para hacer algo - **2.** [information, advice] dar, ofrecer. <> vi - **1.** [freely offer one's services]: **to volunteer (for)** ofrecerse (para) - **2.** MIL alistarse.

vomit ['vɒmɪt] <> n vómito m. <> vi vomitar.

vote [vəʊt] <> n - **1.** [gen] voto m - **2.** [session, ballot, result] votación f; **to put sthg to the vote, to take a vote on sthg** someter algo a votación - **3.** [votes cast]: **the vote** los votos. <> vt - **1.** [person, leader] elegir - **2.** [choose]: **to vote to do sthg** votar hacer algo. <> vi: **to vote (for/against)** votar (a favor de/en contra de).

vote of thanks (pl votes of thanks) n palabras fpl de agradecimiento.

voter ['vəʊtəʳ] n votante mf.

voting ['vəʊtɪŋ] n votación f.

vouch [vaʊtʃ] ◆ **vouch for** vt insep - **1.** [person] responder por - **2.** [character, accuracy] dar fe de.

voucher ['vaʊtʃəʳ] n vale m.

vow [vaʊ] <> n RELIG voto m; [solemn promise] promesa f solemne. <> vt: **to vow to do sthg** jurar hacer algo; **to vow that** jurar que.

vowel ['vaʊəl] n vocal f.

voyage ['vɔɪɪdʒ] n viaje m.

vs abbr of **versus**.

VSO (abbr of Voluntary Service Overseas) n organización británica de voluntarios que ayuda a países en vías de desarrollo.

vulgar ['vʌlgəʳ] adj - **1.** [in bad taste] ordinario(ria) - **2.** [offensive] grosero(ra).

vulnerable ['vʌlnərəbl] adj: **vulnerable (to)** vulnerable (a).

vulture ['vʌltʃəʳ] n lit & fig buitre m.

w (*pl* **w's** OR **ws**), **W** (*pl* **W's** OR **Ws**) ['dʌblju:] *n* [letter] w f, W f. ◆ **W - 1.** (*abbr of* west) O - 2. (*abbr of* watt) w.

wad [wɒd] *n* - **1.** [of paper] taco *m* - **2.** [of banknotes, documents] fajo *m* - **3.** [of cotton, cotton wool, tobacco] bola f.

waddle ['wɒdl] *vi* caminar como un pato.

wade [weɪd] *vi* caminar por el agua. ◆ **wade through** *vt insep fig:* he was wading through the documents le costaba mucho leer los documentos.

wading pool ['weɪdɪŋ-] *n US* piscina f para niños.

wafer ['weɪfər] *n* [thin biscuit] barquillo *m*.

waffle ['wɒfl] ◇ *n* - **1.** CULIN gofre *m* - **2.** *UK inf* [vague talk] paja f. ◇ *vi* enrollarse; **to waffle on about sthg** enrollarse sobre algo.

waft [wɑːft wɒft] *vi* flotar.

wag [wæg] ◇ *vt* menear; **the dog was wagging its tail** el perro meneaba la cola. ◇ *vi* menearse.

wage [weɪdʒ] ◇ *n* [gen] salario *m*; [daily] jornal *m*. ◇ *vt*: **to wage war** hacer la guerra. ◆ **wages** *npl* [gen] salario *m*; [daily] jornal *m*.

wage earner [-ˌɜːnər] *n* asalariado *m*, -da f.

wage packet *n UK* - **1.** [envelope] sobre *m* de pago - **2.** *fig* [pay] paga f.

wager ['weɪdʒər] *n* apuesta f.

waggle ['wægl] *inf vt* menear.

waggon ['wægən] *UK* = **wagon**.

wagon, waggon ['wægən] *n* - **1.** [horse-drawn vehicle] carro *m* - **2.** *UK* RAIL vagón *m*.

wail [weɪl] ◇ *n* lamento *m*, gemido *m*. ◇ *vi* lamentarse, gemir.

waist [weɪst] *n* cintura f.

waistcoat ['weɪskəʊt] *n esp US* chaleco *m*.

waistline ['weɪstlaɪn] *n* cintura f, talle *m*.

wait [weɪt] ◇ *n* espera f; **to lie in wait for sb** estar al acecho de alguien. ◇ *vi*: **to wait (for sthg/sb)** esperar (algo/a alguien); **to wait and see** esperar y ver lo que pasa; **wait a minute** OR **second** OR **moment!** [interrupting sb] ¡espera un minuto OR segundo OR momento!; [interrupting o.s.] ¡espera!; **keys cut while you wait** se hacen llaves en el acto. ◆ **wait for** *vt insep* esperar. ◆ **wait on** *vt insep* [serve food to] servir. ◆ **wait up** *vi* - **1.** quedarse despierto(ta) esperando - **2.** *US:* **wait up!** ¡un momento!

waiter ['weɪtər] *n* camarero *m*.

['weɪtɪŋ-] *n* lista f de espera.

waiting room ['weɪtɪŋ-] *n* sala f de espera.

waitress ['weɪtrɪs] *n* camarera f.

waive [weɪv] *vt fml* [rule] no aplicar.

wake [weɪk] ◇ *n* [of ship, boat] estela f; **in the wake of** *fig* tras. ◇ *vt* (*pt* **woke** OR **-d**, *pp* **woken** OR **-d**) despertar. ◇ *vi* (*pt* **woke** OR **-d**, *pp* **woken** OR **-d**) despertarse. ◆ **wake up** ◇ *vt sep* despertar. ◇ *vi* [wake] despertarse.

waken ['weɪkən] *fml* ◇ *vt* despertar. ◇ *vi* despertarse.

Wales [weɪlz] *n* (el país de) Gales.

walk [wɔːk] ◇ *n* - **1.** [way of walking] andar *m*, paso *m* - **2.** [journey on foot] paseo *m*; **to go for a walk** dar un paseo; **it's ten minutes' walk away** está a diez minutos andando. ◇ *vt* - **1.** [dog] pasear - **2.** [streets] andar por; [distance] recorrer, andar. ◇ *vi* - **1.** [move on foot] andar, caminar - **2.** [for pleasure] pasear. ◆ **walk out** *vi* - **1.** [leave suddenly] salirse - **2.** [go on strike] declararse en huelga. ◆ **walk out on** *vt insep* abandonar.

walker ['wɔːkər] *n* caminante *mf*, paseante *mf*.

walkie-talkie [ˌwɔːkɪ'tɔːkɪ] *n* walki-talki *m*.

walking ['wɔːkɪŋ] ◇ *n* (U) [for sport] marcha f; [for pleasure] andar *m*; **he does a lot of walking** camina mucho. ◇ *adj*: **he's a walking disaster** *hum* es un desastre andante.

walking shoes *npl* zapatos *mpl* para caminar.

walking stick *n* bastón *m*.

Walkman® ['wɔːkmən] *n* walkman® *m*.

walk of life (*pl* **walks of life**) *n*: **people from all walks of life** gente de toda condición.

walkout ['wɔːkaʊt] *n* huelga f.

walkover ['wɔːkˌəʊvər] *n* victoria f fácil.

walkup [':wɔːkʌp] *n US* [building] edificio *m* sin ascensor f.

walkway ['wɔːkweɪ] *n* [on ship, machine] pasarela f; [between buildings] paso *m*.

wall [wɔːl] *n* - **1.** [inside building, of cell, stomach] pared f - **2.** [outside] muro *m*; **to drive sb up the wall** volverle loco a alguien; **it's like talking to a brick wall** le entra por un oído y le sale por el otro.

wallchart ['wɔːltʃɑːt] *n* (gráfico *m*) mural *m*.

walled [wɔːld] *adj* amurallado(da).

wallet ['wɒlɪt] *n* cartera f, billetera f.

wallflower ['wɔːlˌflaʊər] *n* - **1.** [plant] alhelí *m* - **2.** *inf fig* [person] persona tímida que queda al margen de una fiesta.

wallop ['wɒləp] *inf vt* [child] pegar una torta a; [ball] golpear fuerte.

wallow ['wɒləʊ] *vi* [in liquid] revolcarse.

wallpaper ['wɔ:l,peɪpəʳ] ◇ n - **1.** [on walls] papel m pintado - **2.** COMPUT papel m tapiz. ◇ vt empapelar.

Wall Street n Wall Street f, zona financiera neoyorquina.

wally ['wɒlɪ] n UK inf imbécil mf.

walnut ['wɔ:lnʌt] n - **1.** [nut] nuez f - **2.** [wood, tree] nogal m.

walrus ['wɔ:lrəs] (pl walrus OR -es) n morsa f.

waltz [wɔ:ls] ◇ n vals m. ◇ vi [dance] bailar el vals.

wan [wɒn] adj pálido(da).

wand [wɒnd] n: **(magic) wand** varita f mágica.

wander ['wɒndəʳ] vi vagar; **my mind kept wandering** se me iba la mente en otras cosas.

wane [weɪn] vi [influence, interest] disminuir, decrecer.

wangle ['wæŋgl] vt inf agenciarse.

want [wɒnt] ◇ n fml - **1.** [need] necesidad f - **2.** [lack] falta f; **for want of** por OR a falta de - **3.** [deprivation] indigencia f, miseria f. ◇ vt [desire] querer; **to want to do sthg** querer hacer algo.

wanted ['wɒntɪd] adj: **to be wanted (by the police)** ser buscado(da) (por la policía).

wanton ['wɒntən] adj fml gratuito(ta), sin motivo.

WAP [wæp] (abbr of wireless application protocol) n WAP m.

war [wɔ:ʳ] ◇ n lit & fig guerra f; **to be at war** estar en guerra; **the war on drugs** la guerra contra las drogas; **to have been in the wars** UK estar maltrecho. ◇ vi estar en guerra.

ward [wɔ:d] n - **1.** [in hospital] sala f - **2.** UK POL distrito m electoral - **3.** LAW pupilo m, -la f.
◆ **ward off** vt insep protegerse de.

warden ['wɔ:dn] n - **1.** [of park] guarda mf - **2.** UK [of youth hostel, hall of residence] encargado m, -da f - **3.**: **(traffic) warden** ≃ guardia mf de tráfico - **4.** US [prison governor] director m, -ra f.

warder ['wɔ:dəʳ] n [in prison] carcelero m, -ra f.

wardrobe ['wɔ:drəʊb] n - **1.** [piece of furniture] armario m, guardarropa m - **2.** [collection of clothes] guardarropa m, vestuario m.

warehouse ['weəhaʊs, pl -haʊzɪz] n almacén m.

wares [weəz] npl liter mercancías fpl.

warfare ['wɔ:feəʳ] n (U) guerra f.

warhead ['wɔ:hed] n ojiva f, cabeza f.

warily ['weərɪlɪ] adv con cautela.

warm [wɔ:m] ◇ adj - **1.** [pleasantly hot - gen] caliente; [- weather, day] caluroso(sa); [luke-warm] tibio(bia), templado(da); **it's/I'm warm** hace/tengo calor; **to get warm** [person, room] calentarse; **they tried to keep warm** intentaron mantenerse calientes - **2.** [clothes etc] que abriga - **3.** [colour, sound] cálido(da) - **4.** [friendly - person, atmosphere, smile] afectuoso(sa); [- congratulations] efusivo(va). ◇ vt calentar.
◆ **warm up** ◇ vt sep calentar. ◇ vi - **1.** [gen] entrar en calor; [weather, room, engine] calentarse - **2.** [sportsperson] calentar.

warm-hearted [-'hɑ:tɪd] adj afectuoso(sa).

warmly ['wɔ:mlɪ] adv - **1.** [in warm clothes]: **to dress warmly** vestirse con ropa de abrigo - **2.** [in a friendly way] calurosamente.

warmth [wɔ:mθ] n - **1.** [heat] calor m - **2.** [of clothes] abrigo m - **3.** [friendliness] cordialidad f.

warn [wɔ:n] vt prevenir, advertir; **to warn sb of sthg** prevenir a alguien algo; **to warn sb not to do sthg, warn sb against doing sthg** advertir a alguien que no haga algo.

warning ['wɔ:nɪŋ] n aviso m, advertencia f; **to give sb a warning** hacer una advertencia a alguien; **without warning** sin previo aviso.

warning light n piloto m.

warning triangle n UK triángulo m de avería.

warp [wɔ:p] vi alabearse.

warrant ['wɒrənt] ◇ n orden f OR mandamiento m judicial. ◇ vt fml merecer.

warranty ['wɒrəntɪ] n garantía f; **to be under warranty** estar en garantía.

warren ['wɒrən] n red f de madrigueras.

warrior ['wɒrɪəʳ] n guerrero m, -ra f.

warship ['wɔ:ʃɪp] n buque m de guerra.

wart [wɔ:t] n verruga f.

wartime ['wɔ:taɪm] n tiempos mpl de guerra.

wary ['weərɪ] adj: **wary (of)** receloso(sa) (de).

was (weak form [wəz], strong form [wɒz]) pt ▷ **be**.

wash [wɒʃ] ◇ n - **1.** [act of washing] lavado m; **to have a wash** lavarse; **to give sthg a wash** lavar algo - **2.** [things to wash] ropa sucia - **3.** [from boat] estela f. ◇ vt - **1.** [gen] lavar; [hands, face] lavarse; **she's washing her hair** se está lavando el pelo - **2.** [carry - subj: waves etc] arrastrar, llevarse; **it was washed ashore** el mar lo arrastró hasta la costa. ◇ vi - **1.** [clean oneself] lavarse - **2.** [waves, oil]: **to wash over sthg** bañar algo.
◆ **wash away** vt sep - **1.** [water, waves] llevarse, barrer - **2.** [dirt] quitar.
◆ **wash up** ◇ vt sep UK [dishes] lavar, fregar. ◇ vi - **1.** UK [wash the dishes] fregar OR lavar los platos - **2.** US [wash o.s.] lavarse.

washable ['wɒʃəbl] adj lavable.

washbasin *UK* ['wɒʃ,beɪsn], **washbowl** *US* ['wɒʃbəʊl] *n* lavabo *m*.

washcloth ['wɒʃ,klɒθ] *n US* toallita *f* para lavarse la cara.

washer ['wɒʃər] *n* TECH arandela *f*.

washing ['wɒʃɪŋ] *n (U)* - **1.** [operation] colada *f*; **to do the washing** hacer la colada - **2.** [clothes - dirty] ropa *f* sucia OR para lavar; [- clean] colada *f*; **to hang up the washing** tender la colada.

washing line *n* tendedero *m*.

washing machine *n* lavadora *f*.

washing powder *n UK* detergente *m*, jabón *m* en polvo.

Washington ['wɒʃɪŋtən] *n* [town]: **Washington D.C.** ciudad *f* de Washington.

washing-up *n* - **1.** *UK* [crockery, pans etc] platos *mpl* para fregar - **2.** [operation] fregado *m*; **to do the washing-up** fregar los platos.

washing-up liquid *n UK* lavavajillas *m inv*.

washout ['wɒʃaʊt] *n inf* desastre *m*.

washroom ['wɒʃrʊm] *n US* aseos *mpl*.

wasn't [wɒznt] *(abbr of was not)* ▷ **be**.

wasp [wɒsp] *n* [insect] avispa *f*.

wastage ['weɪstɪdʒ] *n* desperdicio *m*.

waste [weɪst] ▷ *adj* [land] yermo(ma); [material, fuel] de desecho. ▷ *n* - **1.** [misuse, incomplete use] desperdicio *m*, derroche *m*; **a waste of time** una pérdida de tiempo - **2.** *(U)* [refuse] desperdicios *mpl*; [chemical, toxic etc] residuos *mpl*. ▷ *vt* [time] perder; [money] malgastar, derrochar; [food, energy, opportunity] desperdiciar. ◆ **wastes** *npl liter* yermos *mpl*.

wastebasket *US* = **wastepaper basket**.

waste disposal unit *n* triturador *m* de basuras.

wasteful ['weɪstfʊl] *adj* derrochador(ra).

waste ground *n (U)* descampados *mpl*.

wastepaper basket [,weɪst'peɪpər-], **wastepaper bin** [,weɪst'peɪpər-], **wastebasket** *US* ['weɪst,bɑːskɪt] *n* papelera *f*.

watch [wɒtʃ] ▷ *n* - **1.** [timepiece] reloj *m* - **2.** [act of watching]: **to keep watch** estar de guardia; **to keep watch on sthg/sb** vigilar algo/a alguien - **3.** MIL [group of people] guardia *f*. ▷ *vt* - **1.** [look at - gen] mirar; [- sunset] contemplar; [- football match, TV] ver - **2.** [spy on] vigilar - **3.** [be careful about] tener cuidado con, vigilar; **watch what you say** ten cuidado con lo que dices. ▷ *vi* mirar, observar. ◆ **watch out** *vi* tener cuidado.

watchdog ['wɒtʃdɒg] *n* - **1.** [dog] perro *m* guardián - **2.** *fig* [organization] comisión *f* de vigilancia.

watchful ['wɒtʃfʊl] *adj* atento(ta).

watchmaker ['wɒtʃ,meɪkər] *n* relojero *m*, -ra *f*.

watchman ['wɒtʃmən] *(pl* -men [-mən]*) n* vigilante *m*.

water ['wɔːtər] ▷ *n* [gen] agua *f*. ▷ *vt* regar. ▷ *vi* - **1.** [eyes]: **my eyes are watering** me lloran los ojos - **2.** [mouth]: **my mouth is watering** se me hace la boca agua. ◆ **waters** *npl* aguas *fpl*. ◆ **water down** *vt sep* [dilute] diluir, aguar.

water bottle *n* cantimplora *f*.

watercolour ['wɔːtə,kʌlər] *n* acuarela *f*.

watercress ['wɔːtəkres] *n* berro *m*.

waterfall ['wɔːtəfɔːl] *n* cascada *f*, salto *m* de agua.

water heater *n* calentador *m* de agua.

waterhole ['wɔːtəhəʊl] *n* balsa *f* (donde acuden a beber los animales).

watering can ['wɔːtərɪŋ-] *n* regadera *f*.

water level *n* nivel *m* del agua.

water lily *n* nenúfar *m*.

waterline ['wɔːtəlaɪn] *n* NAUT línea *f* de flotación.

waterlogged ['wɔːtəlɒgd] *adj* inundado(da).

water main *n* cañería *f* principal.

watermark ['wɔːtəmɑːk] *n* - **1.** [in paper] filigrana *f* - **2.** [showing water level] marca *f* del nivel del agua.

watermelon ['wɔːtə,melən] *n* sandía *f*.

water polo *n* water-polo *m*.

waterproof ['wɔːtəpruːf] ▷ *adj* impermeable. ▷ *n* impermeable *m*.

watershed ['wɔːtəʃed] *n fig* momento *m* decisivo.

water skiing *n* esquí *m* acuático.

water tank *n* reserva *f* de agua.

watertight ['wɔːtətaɪt] *adj* [waterproof] hermético(ca).

waterway ['wɔːtəweɪ] *n* vía *f* navegable.

waterworks ['wɔːtəwɜːks] *(pl* **waterworks**) *n* [building] central *f* de agua.

watery ['wɔːtərɪ] *adj* - **1.** [food] soso(sa); [drink] aguado(da) - **2.** [pale] desvaído(da).

watt [wɒt] *n* vatio *m*.

wave [weɪv] ▷ *n* - **1.** [of hand] ademán *m* OR señal *f* (con la mano) - **2.** [of water] ola *f* - **3.** [of emotion, nausea, panic] arranque *m*; [of immigrants, crime etc] oleada *f* - **4.** [of light, sound, heat] onda *f* - **5.** [in hair] ondulación *f*. ▷ *vt* - **1.** [move about as signal] agitar - **2.** [signal to] hacer señales OR señas a; **she waved them in** les hizo una señal para que entraran. ▷ *vi* - **1.** [with hand - in greeting] saludar con la mano; [- to say goodbye] decir adiós con la mano;

to wave at OR **to sb** saludar a alguien con la mano; **he waved hello to us** nos saludó con la mano - **2.** [flag] ondear; [trees] agitarse.

wavelength ['weɪvleŋθ] n longitud f de onda; **to be on the same wavelength** fig estar en la misma onda.

waver ['weɪvəʳ] vi - **1.** [falter - resolution, confidence] flaquear - **2.** [hesitate] dudar, vacilar - **3.** [fluctuate] oscilar.

wavy ['weɪvɪ] adj ondulado(da).

wax [wæks] <> n cera f. <> vt encerar.

wax paper n esp US papel m de cera.

waxworks ['wækswɜ:ks] (pl waxworks) n museo m de cera.

way [weɪ] <> n - **1.** [manner, method] manera f, modo m; **in the same way** del mismo modo, igualmente; **this/that way** así; **in a way** en cierto modo; **to be in a bad way** estar bastante mal - **2.** [route, path] camino m; **to lose one's way** perderse; **to find one's way around** orientarse; **the way back** OR **home** el camino de vuelta a casa; **way in** entrada f; **way out** salida f; **it's out of my way** no me pilla de camino; **it's out of the way** [place] está algo aislado; **on the** OR **on one's way** de camino; **I'm on my way** voy de camino; **across** OR **over the way** enfrente; **to be under way** fig [meeting] estar en marcha; **to get under way** [meeting] ponerse en marcha; **to be in the way** estar en medio; **to get in the way** ponerse en medio; **to get out of the way** quitarse de en medio; **to get sthg out of the way** [task] quitarse algo de encima; **to go out of one's way to do sthg** tomarse muchas molestias para hacer algo; **to keep out of the way** mantenerse alejado; **to make way for** dar paso a - **3.** [direction] dirección f; **come this way** ven por aquí; **go that way** ve por ahí; **which way do we go?** ¿hacia dónde vamos?; **which way is it to the cathedral?** ¿por dónde se va a la catedral?; **the wrong way up** OR **round** al revés; **the right way up** OR **round** del derecho - **4.** [distance]: **all the way** todo el camino OR trayecto; **it's a long way away** está muy lejos; **we have a long way to go** queda mucho camino por recorrer; **to go a long way towards doing sthg** fig contribuir enormemente a hacer algo; **we've come a long way since then** fig hemos avanzado mucho desde entonces

▸▸▸ **to give way** [under weight, pressure] ceder; **'give way'** UK AUT 'ceda el paso'; **no way!** ¡ni hablar! <> adv inf [far] mucho; **it's way too big** es tela de grande. ▸ **ways** npl [customs, habits] costumbres fpl, hábitos mpl. ▸ **by the way** adv por cierto.

waylay [,weɪ'leɪ] (pt & pp -laid) vt abordar.

wayward ['weɪwəd] adj [person, behaviour] incorregible.

WC (abbr of **water closet**) WC.

we [wi:] pers pron nosotros mpl, -tras f; **we can't do it** nosotros no podemos hacerlo; **here we are** aquí estamos; **as we say in France** como decimos en Francia; **we British** nosotros los británicos.

weak [wi:k] adj - **1.** [gen] débil; **to grow weak** debilitarse - **2.** [material, structure] frágil - **3.** [argument, tea etc] flojo(ja).

weaken ['wi:kn] <> vt debilitar. <> vi - **1.** [become less determined] ceder, flaquear - **2.** [physically] debilitarse.

weakling ['wi:klɪŋ] n pej enclenque mf.

weakness ['wi:knɪs] n - **1.** [gen] debilidad f; **to have a weakness for sthg** tener debilidad por algo - **2.** [imperfect point] defecto m.

wealth [welθ] n - **1.** [riches] riqueza f - **2.** [abundance] profusión f; **a wealth of sthg** abundancia de algo.

wealthy ['welθɪ] adj rico(ca).

wean [wi:n] vt [from mother's milk] destetar.

weapon ['wepən] n arma f.

weaponry ['wepənrɪ] n (U) armamento m.

weapons of mass destruction npl armas fpl de destrucción masiva.

wear [weəʳ] <> n (U) - **1.** [use] uso m; **I've had a lot of wear out of this jacket** le he sacado mucho partido a esta chaqueta; **to be the worse for wear** [thing] estar deteriorado; [person] estar hecho un trapo - **2.** [damage] desgaste m; **wear and tear** desgaste - **3.** [type of clothes] ropa f; **children's wear** ropa de niños; **evening wear** ropa de noche. <> vt (pt **wore**, pp **worn**) - **1.** [clothes, hair, perfume] llevar; [shoes] calzar; **to wear red** vestirse de rojo - **2.** [damage] desgastar; **to wear a hole in sthg** acabar haciendo un agujero en algo. <> vi (pt **wore**, pp **worn**) - **1.** [deteriorate] desgastarse - **2.** [last]: **to wear well/badly** durar mucho/poco. ▸ **wear away** <> vt sep desgastar. <> vi desgastarse. ▸ **wear down** vt sep - **1.** [reduce size of] desgastar - **2.** [weaken] agotar. ▸ **wear off** vi desaparecer, disiparse. ▸ **wear out** <> vt sep - **1.** [shoes, clothes] gastar - **2.** [person] agotar. <> vi gastarse.

weary ['wɪərɪ] adj fatigado(da), cansado(da); **to be weary of sthg/of doing sthg** estar cansado de algo/de hacer algo.

weasel ['wi:zl] n comadreja f.

weather ['weðəʳ] <> n tiempo m; **what's the weather like?** ¿qué tal tiempo hace?; **to make heavy weather of sthg** complicar algo innecesariamente; **to be under the weather** no encontrarse muy bien. <> vt [crisis etc] superar.

weather-beaten [-,bi:tn] adj [face, skin] curtido(da).

weathercock ['weðəkɒk] n veleta f.

weather forecast n parte m meteorológico.

weatherman [ˈweðəmæn] (pl man [-mən]) n hombre m del tiempo.

weather vane [-veɪn] n veleta f.

weave [wiːv] ⬦ vt (pt wove, pp woven) [using loom] tejer. ⬦ vi (pt wove, pp woven) [move]: **to weave through** colarse por entre; **to weave in and out of the traffic** avanzar zigzagueando en el tráfico.

weaver [ˈwiːvəʳ] n tejedor m, -ra f.

weaving [ˈwiːvɪŋ] n tejeduría f.

web [web] n - **1.** [cobweb] telaraña f - **2.** fig [of lies etc] urdimbre f - **3.** COMPUT: **the Web** la Web.

web browser n COMPUT navegador m.

webcam [ˈwebkæm] n cámara f web.

web designer n diseñador m, -ra f de páginas Web.

web page n página f web.

web site n sitio m Web.

wed [wed] (pt & pp -ded OR wed) liter ⬦ vt desposar. ⬦ vi desposarse.

we'd [wiːd] - **1.** (abbr of we had) ▷ **have** - **2.** (abbr of we would) ▷ **would**.

wedding [ˈwedɪŋ] n boda f, casamiento m.

wedding anniversary n aniversario m de boda.

wedding cake n tarta f nupcial.

wedding dress n traje m de novia.

wedding ring n anillo m de boda, argolla f Amér.

wedge [wedʒ] ⬦ n - **1.** [for steadying or splitting] cuña f - **2.** [triangular slice] porción f, trozo m. ⬦ vt: **to wedge sthg open/shut** dejar algo abierto/cerrado con una cuña.

Wednesday [ˈwenzdɪ] n miércoles m inv; see also **Saturday**.

wee [wiː] ⬦ adj Scotland pequeño(ña). ⬦ n v inf pipí m; **to do a wee** hacer pipí. ⬦ vi v inf hacer pipí.

weed [wiːd] ⬦ n - **1.** [wild plant] mala hierba f - **2.** UK inf [feeble person] canijo m, -ja f. ⬦ vt desherbar, escardar.

weedkiller [ˈwiːdˌkɪləʳ] n herbicida m.

weedy [ˈwiːdɪ] adj UK inf [feeble] enclenque.

week [wiːk] n [gen] semana f; **a week on Saturday, Saturday week** del sábado en ocho días; **this/next week** esta/la próxima semana; **in 2 weeks' time** en dos semanas; **we haven't seen him for weeks** hace semanas que no lo vemos.

weekday [ˈwiːkdeɪ] n día m laborable.

weekend [ˌwiːkˈend] n fin m de semana.

weekly [ˈwiːklɪ] ⬦ adj semanal. ⬦ adv semanalmente. ⬦ n semanario m.

weep [wiːp] ⬦ vt (pt & pp wept) derramar. ⬦ vi (pt & pp wept) llorar.

weeping willow [ˌwiːpɪŋ-] n sauce m llorón.

weigh [weɪ] vt - **1.** [gen] pesar - **2.** [consider carefully] sopesar; **she weighed her words** sopesó sus palabras. ➡ **weigh down** vt sep - **1.** [physically] sobrecargar - **2.** [mentally]: **to be weighed down by OR with** estar abrumado(da) de OR por. ➡ **weigh up** vt sep - **1.** [consider carefully] sopesar - **2.** [size up] hacerse una idea de.

weight [weɪt] n - **1.** [gen] peso m; **to put on OR gain weight** engordar; **to lose weight** adelgazar; **to pull one's weight** poner (uno) de su parte - **2.** [metal object] pesa f.

weighted [ˈweɪtɪd] adj: **to be weighted in favour of/against** inclinarse a favor/en contra de.

weighting [ˈweɪtɪŋ] n prima por vivir en una ciudad con alto coste de vida.

weightlifting [ˈweɪtˌlɪftɪŋ] n levantamiento m de pesos, halterofilia f.

weighty [ˈweɪtɪ] adj [serious] de peso.

weir [wɪəʳ] n presa f, dique m.

weird [wɪəd] adj raro(ra), extraño(ña).

welcome [ˈwelkəm] ⬦ adj - **1.** [guest] bienvenido(da); **to make sb welcome** acoger bien a alguien - **2.** [free]: **you're welcome to come** si quieres, puedes venir - **3.** [appreciated]: **to be welcome** ser de agradecer - **4.** [in reply to thanks]: **you're welcome** de nada. ⬦ n bienvenida f; **to give sb a warm welcome** dar una calurosa bienvenida a alguien. ⬦ vt - **1.** [receive] dar la bienvenida a - **2.** [approve, support] recibir bien. ⬦ excl ¡bienvenido(da) !

weld [weld] ⬦ n soldadura f. ⬦ vt soldar.

welfare [ˈwelfeəʳ] ⬦ adj de asistencia social. ⬦ n - **1.** [state of wellbeing] bienestar m - **2.** US [income support] subsidio m de la seguridad social; **to be on welfare** recibir un subsidio.

well [wel] ⬦ adj (comp better, superl best) bien; **to be well** [healthy] estar bien (de salud); **I don't feel well** no me siento bien; **to get well** mejorarse; **all is well** todo va bien; **(it's) just as well** menos mal; **it would be as well to check first** sería mejor comprobar primero. ⬦ adv - **1.** [satisfactorily, thoroughly] bien; **to go well** ir bien; **he's doing very well at his new school** le va muy bien en el nuevo colegio; **well done!** ¡muy bien!; **well and truly** completamente; **to be well out of sthg** inf tener la suerte de haberse salido de algo - **2.** [definitely, certainly] claramente, definitivamente; **it was well worth it** sí que valió la pena - **3.** [as emphasis]: **you know perfectly well (that)** sabes de sobra (que) - **4.** [very possibly]: **it could well rain** es muy posible que llueva. ⬦ n pozo m. ⬦ excl - **1.** [gen] bueno; **oh well!** ¡en fin!

- **2.** [in surprise] ¡vaya! ◆ **as well** adv - **1.** [in addition] también - **2.** [with same result]: **you may** OR **might as well (do it)** ¿y por qué no (lo haces)? ◆ **as well as** conj además de. ◆ **well up** vi brotar.

we'll [wiːl] - **1.** (abbr of we will) ▷ **will²** - **2.** (abbr of we shall) ▷ **shall**.

well-advised [-əd'vaɪzd] adj sensato(ta); **you would be well-advised to do it** sería aconsejable que lo hicieras.

well-behaved [-bɪ'heɪvd] adj formal, bien educado(da); **to be well-behaved** portarse bien.

wellbeing [ˌwel'biːɪŋ] n bienestar m.

well-built adj fornido(da).

well-done adj [thoroughly cooked] muy hecho(cha).

well-dressed [-'drest] adj bien vestido(da).

well-earned [-'ɜːnd] adj bien merecido(da).

well-heeled [-'hiːld] adj inf ricachón(ona).

wellington boots ['welɪŋtən-], **wellingtons** ['welɪŋtənz] npl botas fpl de agua.

well-kept adj - **1.** [neat, tidy] bien cuidado(da) - **2.** [not revealed] bien guardado(da).

well-known adj conocido(da).

well-mannered [-'mænəd] adj de buenos modales.

well-meaning adj bienintencionado(da).

well-nigh [-naɪ] adv casi.

well-off adj [rich] acomodado(da), rico(ca).

well-read [-'red] adj instruido(da), culto(ta).

well-rounded [-'raʊndɪd] adj [varied] completo(ta).

well-timed adj oportuno(na).

well-to-do adj adinerado(da).

wellwisher ['wel,wɪʃər] n simpatizante mf (que da muestras de apoyo).

Welsh [welʃ] ◇ adj galés(esa). ◇ n [language] galés m. ◇ npl: **the Welsh** los galeses.

Welshman ['welʃmən] (pl -men [-mən]) n galés m.

Welshwoman ['welʃ,wʊmən] (pl -women [-,wɪmɪn]) n galesa f.

went [went] pt ▷ **go**.

wept [wept] pt & pp ▷ **weep**.

were [wɜːr] pt ▷ **be**.

we're [wɪər] (abbr of we are) ▷ **be**.

weren't [wɜːnt] (abbr of were not) ▷ **be**.

west [west] ◇ n - **1.** [direction] oeste m - **2.** [region]: **the West** el Oeste. ◇ adj del oeste. ◇ adv: **west (of)** al oeste (de). ◆ **West** n POL: **the West** el Occidente.

West Bank n: **the West Bank** Cisjordania.

West Country n UK: **the West Country** el sudoeste de Inglaterra.

West End n UK: **the West End** zona central de Londres, famosa por sus teatros, tiendas etc.

westerly ['westəlɪ] adj [wind] del oeste.

western ['westən] ◇ adj occidental. ◇ n [film] película f del oeste, western m.

West German ◇ adj de la Alemania Occidental. ◇ n [person] alemán m, -ana f occidental.

West Germany n: **(the former) West Germany** (la antigua) Alemania Occidental.

West Indian ◇ adj antillano(na). ◇ n [person] antillano m, -na f.

West Indies [-'ɪndiːz] npl: **the West Indies** las Antillas.

Westminster ['westmɪnstər] n barrio londinense en que se encuentra el parlamento británico.

westward ['westwəd] ◇ adj hacia el oeste. ◇ adv = **westwards**.

westwards ['westwədz], **westward** adv hacia el oeste.

wet [wet] ◇ adj - **1.** [soaked] mojado(da); [damp] húmedo(da); **to get wet** mojarse - **2.** [rainy] lluvioso(sa) - **3.** [paint, cement] fresco(ca); **wet paint** recién pintado(da) - **4.** UK inf pej [weak, feeble] ñoño(ña). ◇ n inf POL político conservador moderado. ◇ vt (pt & pp **wet** OR **-ted**) [soak] mojar; [dampen] humedecer.

wet blanket n inf pej aguafiestas mf.

wet suit n traje m de submarinista.

we've [wiːv] (abbr of = we have), = **have**.

whack [wæk] inf n [hit] castañazo m.

whale [weɪl] n [animal] ballena f.

wharf [wɔːf] (pl **-s** OR **wharves** [wɔːvz]) n muelle m, embarcadero m.

what [wɒt] ◇ adj - **1.** (in direct, indirect questions) qué; **what kind of car has she got?** ¿qué coche tiene?; **what shape is it?** ¿qué forma tiene?; **he asked me what shape it was** me preguntó qué forma tenía; **what colour is it?** ¿de qué color es? - **2.** (in exclamations) qué; **what a surprise!** ¡qué sorpresa!; **what a stupid idea!** ¡qué idea más tonta! ◇ pron - **1.** (interrogative) qué; **what are they doing?** ¿qué hacen?; **she asked me what they were doing** me preguntó qué estaban haciendo; **what are they talking about?** ¿de qué están hablando?; **what is it called?** ¿cómo se llama?; **what does it cost?** ¿cuánto cuesta?; **what is it like?** ¿cómo es?; **what's the Spanish for 'book'?** ¿cómo se dice 'book' en español?; **what is this for?** ¿para qué es esto?; **what about another drink/going out for a meal?** ¿qué tal otra copa/si salimos a comer?; **what**

about me? ¿y yo qué?; **what it nobody comes!** ¿y si no viene nadie, qué? - **2.** (relative) lo que; **I saw what happened/he did** yo vi lo que ocurrió/hizo; **I don't know what to do** no sé qué hacer; **what we need is...** lo que nos hace falta es... <> excl [expressing disbelief] ¿qué?; **what, no milk!** ¿cómo? ¿que no hay leche?

whatever [wɒt'evər] <> adj cualquier; **eat whatever food you find** come lo que encuentres; **no chance whatever** ni la más remota posibilidad; **nothing whatever** nada en absoluto. <> pron - **1.** [no matter what]: **whatever they may offer** ofrezcan lo que ofrezcan; **whatever you like** lo que (tú) quieras; **don't touch this, whatever you do** hagas lo que hagas, no toques esto; **whatever happens** pase lo que pase; **whatever the weather** haga el tiempo que haga - **2.** [indicating surprise]: **whatever do you mean?** ¿qué quieres decir? - **3.** [indicating ignorance]: **he told me to get a D.R.V., whatever that is** OR **may be** me dijo que consiguiera un D.R.V., sea lo que sea eso; **or whatever** o lo que sea.

whatsoever [,wɒtsəʊ'evər] adj: **nothing whatsoever** nada en absoluto; **none whatsoever** ni uno.

wheat [wi:t] n trigo m.

wheedle ['wi:dl] vt decir con zalamería; **to wheedle sb into doing sthg** camelar OR engatusar a alguien para que haga algo; **to wheedle sthg out of sb** sonsacarle algo a alguien.

wheel [wi:l] <> n - **1.** [gen] rueda f - **2.** [steering wheel] volante m; **to be at the wheel** estar al volante. <> vt empujar (algo sobre ruedas). <> vi - **1.** [move in circle] dar vueltas - **2.** [turn round]: **to wheel round** darse la vuelta.

wheelbarrow ['wi:l,bærəʊ] n carretilla f.

wheelchair ['wi:l,tʃeər] n silla f de ruedas.

wheelclamp ['wi:l,klæmp] n cepo m.

wheeze [wi:z] vi resollar.

whelk [welk] n buccino m.

when [wen] <> adv (in direct, indirect questions) cuándo; **when does the plane arrive?** ¿cuándo llega el avión?; **he asked me when I would be in London** me preguntó cuándo estaría en Londres; **I don't know when I'll be back** no sé cuándo volveré; **that was when I knew for sure that...** fue entonces cuando me di cuenta que...; **say when!** ¡di basta! <> conj cuando; **tell me when you've read it** avísame cuando lo hayas leído; **on the day when it happened** el día (en) que pasó; **use less oil when frying food** utiliza menos aceite al freír comida; **how can I buy it when I can't afford it?** ¿cómo voy a comprarlo si no tengo dinero?

when [wen] conj [no matter when] cuando; [every time] cada vez que; **whenever you like** cuando quieras; **whenever I call him he runs away** siempre que le llamo se marcha corriendo. <> adv cuando sea.

where [weər] <> adv (in direct, indirect questions) dónde; **where do you live?** ¿dónde vives?; **do you know where he lives?** ¿sabes dónde vive?; **where are you from?** ¿de dónde eres?; **where are we going?** ¿adónde vamos?; **I don't know where to start** no sé por dónde empezar. <> conj - **1.** [referring to place, situation] donde; **this is where...** es aquí donde...; **go where you like** vete (a) donde quieras - **2.** [if]: **where possible** siempre que sea posible.

whereabouts <> adv [,weərə'baʊts] (por) dónde. <> npl ['weərəbaʊts] paradero m; **to know sb's whereabouts** conocer el paradero de alguien.

whereas [weər'æz] conj mientras que.

whereby [weə'baɪ] conj fml por el/la cual.

whereupon [,weərə'pɒn] conj fml tras OR con lo cual.

wherever [weər'evər] <> conj [no matter where] dondequiera que; **wherever you go** dondequiera que vayas; **sit wherever you like** siéntate donde quieras. <> adv - **1.** [no matter where] en cualquier parte - **2.** [indicating surprise]: **wherever did you hear that?** ¿dónde habrás oído eso?

wherewithal ['weəwɪðɔ:l] n fml: **to have the wherewithal to do sthg** disponer de los medios para hacer algo.

whet [wet] vt: **to whet sb's appetite (for sthg)** despertar el interés de alguien (por algo).

whether ['weðər] conj - **1.** [indicating choice, doubt] si; **she doesn't know whether to go or stay** no sabe si quedarse o marcharse; **I doubt whether she'll do it** dudo que lo haga - **2.** [no matter if]: **whether I want to or not** tanto si quiero como si no, quiera o no quiera.

which [wɪtʃ] <> adj - **1.** (in direct, indirect questions) qué; **which house is yours?** ¿cuál es tu casa?, ¿qué casa es la tuya?; **which one?** ¿cuál?; **which ones?** ¿cuáles? - **2.** [to refer back to]: **in which case** en cuyo caso; **we won't arrive until 6, by which time it will be dark** no llegaremos hasta la 6, hora a la cual ya será de noche. <> pron - **1.** (in direct, indirect questions) cuál, cuáles (pl); **which do you prefer?** ¿cuál prefieres?; **I can't decide which to have** no sé cuál coger - **2.** (in relative clause replacing n) que; **the table, which was made of wood,...** la mesa, que OR la cual era de madera,...; **the world in which we live** el mundo en que OR en el cual vivimos - **3.** (to refer back to

382

a clause) lo cual; **she denied it, which surprised me** lo negó, lo cual me sorprendió; **before which** antes de lo cual.

whichever [wɪtʃ'evər] <> adj - **1.** [no matter which]: **whichever route you take** vayas por donde vayas - **2.** [the one which]: **whichever colour you prefer** el color que prefieras. <> pron el que (la que), los que (las que) *(pl)*; **take whichever you like** coge el que quieras.

whiff [wɪf] *n* [smell] olorcillo *m*; **she caught a whiff of his aftershave** le llegó el olorcillo de su aftershave.

while [waɪl] <> *n* rato *m*; **it's a long while since I did that** hace mucho que no hago eso; **for a while** un rato; **after a while** después de un rato; **in a while** dentro de poco; **once in a while** de vez en cuando. <> conj - **1.** [during the time that] mientras - **2.** [whereas] mientras que - **3.** [although] aunque. ◆ **while away** *vt sep* pasar; **to while away the time** pasar el rato.

whilst [waɪlst] *conj fml* - **1.** [during the time that] mientras - **2.** [whereas] mientras que - **3.** [although] aunque.

whim [wɪm] *n* capricho *m*.

whimper ['wɪmpər] *vt & vi* gimotear.

whimsical ['wɪmzɪkl] *adj* [idea, story] fantasioso(sa); [look] juguetón(ona).

whine [waɪn] *vi* [child, dog] gemir; [siren] ulular.

whinge [wɪndʒ] *vi UK inf*: **to whinge (about)** quejarse (de).

whip [wɪp] <> *n* - **1.** [for hitting] látigo *m*; [for horse] fusta *f* - **2.** *UK* POL miembro de un partido encargado de asegurar que otros miembros voten en el parlamento. <> *vt* - **1.** [gen] azotar - **2.** [take quickly]: **to whip sthg out/off** sacar/quitar algo rápidamente - **3.** [whisk] batir.

whipped cream [wɪpt-] *n* nata *f* montada.

whip-round *n UK inf*: **to have a whip-round** hacer una colecta.

whirl [wɜːl] <> *n fig* [of activity, events] torbellino *m*. <> *vt*: **to whirl sb/sthg round** hacer dar vueltas a alguien/algo. <> *vi* [move around] arremolinarse; [dancers] girar vertiginosamente.

whirlpool ['wɜːlpuːl] *n* remolino *m*.

whirlpool bath *n* bañera *f* de hidromasaje.

whirlwind ['wɜːlwɪnd] *n* torbellino *m*.

whirr [wɜːr] *vi* zumbar.

whisk [wɪsk] <> *n* CULIN varilla *f*. <> *vt* - **1.** [move quickly]: **to whisk sthg away/out** llevarse/sacar algo rápidamente; **we were whisked off to visit the museum** nos llevaron rápidamente a visitar el museo - **2.** CULIN batir.

whisker ['wɪskər] *n* (pelo *m* del) bigote *m*. ◆ **whiskers** *npl* [of person] patillas *fpl*; [of cat] bigotes *mpl*.

whisky *UK*, **whiskey** *(pl -s) US & Ireland* ['wɪskɪ] *n* whisky *m*.

whisper ['wɪspər] <> *vt* susurrar. <> *vi* cuchichear.

whistle ['wɪsl] <> *n* - **1.** [sound] silbido *m*, pitido *m* - **2.** [device] silbato *m*, pito *m*. <> *vt* silbar. <> *vi* [person] silbar, chiflar *Amér*; [referee] pitar; [bird] piar.

white [waɪt] <> *adj* - **1.** [gen] blanco(ca); **to go** OR **turn white** ponerse blanco - **2.** [coffee, tea] con leche. <> *n* - **1.** [colour] blanco *m* - **2.** [person] blanco *m*, -ca *f* - **3.** [of egg] clara *f* - **4.** [of eye] blanco *m*.

white-collar *adj* de oficina; **white-collar worker** oficinista *mf*.

white elephant *n fig* mamotreto *m* (caro e inútil).

Whitehall ['waɪthɔːl] *n* calle londinense en que se encuentra la Administración británica; por extensión ésta.

white-hot *adj* incandescente.

White House *n*: **the White House** la Casa Blanca.

white lie *n* mentira *f* piadosa.

whiteness ['waɪtnɪs] *n* blancura *f*.

white paper *n* POL libro *m* blanco.

white sauce *n* (salsa *f*) bechamel *f*.

white spirit *n UK especie de aguarrás*.

whitewash ['waɪtwɒʃ] <> *n* - **1.** (U) [paint] blanqueo *m*, lechada *f* (de cal) - **2.** *pej* [cover-up] encubrimiento *m*. <> *vt* [paint] blánquear.

whiting ['waɪtɪŋ] *(pl whiting* OR *-s) n* pescadilla *f*.

Whitsun ['wɪtsn] *n* [day] Pentecostés *m*.

whittle ['wɪtl] *vt* [reduce]: **to whittle down** OR **away** reducir gradualmente.

whiz, whizz [wɪz] *vi*: **to whiz past** OR **by** pasar muy rápido OR zumbando.

whiz(z) kid *n inf* genio *m*, prodigio *m*.

who [huː] *pron* - **1.** (in direct, indirect questions) quién, quiénes *(pl)*; **who are you?** ¿quién eres tú?; **who is it?** [at door etc] ¿quién es?; **who did you see?** ¿a quién viste?; **I didn't know who she was** no sabía quién era - **2.** (in relative clauses) que; **he's the doctor who treated me** es el médico que me atendió; **those who are in favour** los que están a favor.

who'd [huːd] - **1.** (abbr of who had) ▷ **have** - **2.** (abbr of who would) ▷ **would**.

whodun(n)it [ˌhuːˈdʌnɪt] *n inf* historia *f* policíaca de misterio.

whoever [huːˈevəʳ] *pron* - **1.** [unknown person] quienquiera; quienesquiera *(pl)*; **whoever finds it** quienquiera que lo encuentre; **tell whoever you like** díselo a quien quieras - **2.** [indicating surprise, astonishment]: **whoever can that be?** ¿quién podrá ser? - **3.** [no matter who]: **come in, whoever you are** pasa, seas quién seas.

whole [həʊl] ◇ *adj* - **1.** [entire, complete] entero(ra); **we've had enough of the whole thing** ya estamos hartos de todo esto - **2.** [for emphasis]: **a whole lot taller** muchísimo más alto; **a whole new idea** una idea totalmente nueva. ◇ *n* - **1.** [all]: **the whole of the school/summer** el colegio/verano entero - **2.** [unit, complete thing] todo *m*. ➡ **as a whole** *adv* en conjunto. ➡ **on the whole** *adv* en general.

wholefood [ˈhəʊlfuːd] *n* UK comida *f* integral.

whole-hearted [-ˈhɑːtɪd] *adj* incondicional.

wholemeal UK [ˈhəʊlmiːl], **whole wheat** US *adj* integral.

wholesale [ˈhəʊlseɪl] ◇ *adj* - **1.** COMM al por mayor - **2.** *pej* [indiscriminate] indiscriminado(da). ◇ *adv* - **1.** COMM al por mayor - **2.** *pej* [indiscriminately] indiscriminadamente.

wholesaler [ˈhəʊl,seɪləʳ] *n* mayorista *mf*.

wholesome [ˈhəʊlsəm] *adj* sano(na).

whole wheat US = **wholemeal**.

who'll [huːl] - **1.** *(abbr of who will)* ▷ **will²** - **2.** *(abbr of who shall)* ▷ **shall**.

wholly [ˈhəʊlɪ] *adv* completamente.

whom [huːm] *pron* - **1.** *(in direct, indirect questions) fml* quién, quiénes *(pl)*; **from whom did you receive it?** ¿de quién lo recibiste?; **for/of/to whom** por/de/a quién - **2.** *(in relative clauses)* que; **the man whom I saw** el hombre que vi; **the man to whom I gave it** el hombre al que se lo di; **several people came, none of whom I knew** vinieron varias personas, de las que no conocía a ninguna.

whooping cough [ˈhuːpɪŋ-] *n* tos *f* ferina.

whopping [ˈwɒpɪŋ] *inf* ◇ *adj* enorme. ◇ *adv*: **a whopping great lorry/lie, a whopping big lorry/lie** un camión/una mentira enorme.

whore [hɔːʳ] *n pej* puta *f*.

who're [ˈhuːəʳ] *(abbr of who are)* ▷ **be**.

whose [huːz] ◇ *pron (in direct, indirect questions)* de quién, de quiénes *(pl)*; **whose is this?** ¿de quién es esto?; **I wonder whose they are** me pregunto de quién serán. ◇ *adj* - **1.** *(in direct, indirect questions)* de quién; **whose car is that?** ¿de quién es ese coche? - **2.** *(in relative clauses)* cuyo(ya), cuyos(yas) *(pl)*; **that's the boy whose father's an MP** ese

on el chico cuyo padre es diputado; **the woman whose daughters are twins** la mujer cuyas hijas son gemelas.

who's who [huːz-] *n* [book] Quién es Quién *m*.

who've [huːv] *(abbr of who have)* ▷ **have**.

why [waɪ] ◇ *adv* por qué; **why did you lie to me?** ¿por qué me mentiste?; **why don't you all come?** ¿por qué no venís todos?; **why not?** ¿por qué no? ◇ *conj* por qué; **I don't know why he said that** no sé por qué dijo eso. ◇ *pron*: **there are several reasons why he left** hay varias razones por las que se marchó; **that's why she did it** por eso es por lo que lo hizo; **I don't know the reason why** no se por qué razón. ◇ *excl* ¡hombre!, ¡vaya! ➡ **why ever** *adv*: **why ever did you do that?** ¿pero por qué has hecho eso?

wick [wɪk] *n* mecha *f*; **to get on sb's wick** UK *inf fig* sacar de quicio a alguien.

wicked [ˈwɪkɪd] *adj* - **1.** [evil] malvado(da) - **2.** [mischievous, devilish] travieso(sa).

wicker [ˈwɪkəʳ] *adj* de mimbre.

wickerwork [ˈwɪkəwɜːk] *n (U)* artículos *mpl* de mimbre.

wicket [ˈwɪkɪt] *n* CRICKET [stumps] palos *mpl*.

wide [waɪd] ◇ *adj* - **1.** [broad] ancho(cha); **how wide is it?** ¿cuánto mide de ancho?; **it's 50 cm wide** tiene 50 cm de ancho - **2.** [range, choice etc] amplio(plia) - **3.** [gap, difference, implications] grande, considerable - **4.** [off-target] desviado(da). ◇ *adv* - **1.** [broadly]: **to open/spread sthg wide** abrir/desplegar algo completamente - **2.** [off target]: **to go** OR **be wide** salir desviado.

wide-angle lens *n* gran angular *m*.

wide awake *adj* completamente despierto(ta).

widely [ˈwaɪdlɪ] *adv* - **1.** [travel, read] extensamente; **to be widely read/travelled** haber leído/viajado mucho - **2.** [believed, known, loved] generalmente; **there is a widely held view that...** existe la creencia generalizada de que... - **3.** [differ, vary] mucho.

widen [ˈwaɪdn] *vt* [gen] ampliar; [road, bridge] ensanchar.

wide open *adj* - **1.** [window, door] abierto(ta) de par en par - **2.** [eyes] completamente abierto(ta).

wide-ranging [-ˈreɪndʒɪŋ] *adj* [changes, survey, consequences] de gran alcance; [discussion, interests] de gran variedad; [selection] amplio(plia).

widescreen [ˈwaɪdskriːn] *adj* [television] de pantalla ancha.

widescreen TV ['waɪdskriː-] *n* televisor *m* panorámico, televisor *m* de pantalla ancha.

widespread ['waɪdspred] *adj* extendido(da), general.

widow ['wɪdəʊ] *n* [woman] viuda *f*.

widowed ['wɪdəʊd] *adj* viudo(da).

widower ['wɪdəʊəʳ] *n* viudo *m*.

width [wɪdθ] *n* - **1.** [breadth] anchura *f*; **it's 50 cm in width** tiene 50 cm de ancho - **2.** [in swimming pool] ancho *m*.

wield [wiːld] *vt* - **1.** [weapon] esgrimir; [implement] manejar - **2.** [power] ejercer.

wife [waɪf] (*pl* **wives**) *n* mujer *f*, esposa *f*.

wig [wɪg] *n* peluca *f*.

wiggle ['wɪgl] *inf vt* menear; [hips etc] contonear.

wild [waɪld] *adj* - **1.** [gen] salvaje; [plant, flower] silvestre; [bull] bravo(va) - **2.** [landscape, scenery] agreste - **3.** [weather, sea] borrascoso(sa) - **4.** [crowd, laughter, applause] frenético(ca) - **5.** [hair] alborotado(da) - **6.** [hope, idea, plan] descabellado(da) - **7.** [guess, exaggeration] extravagante. ➡ **wilds** *npl*: **the wilds** las tierras remotas.

wilderness ['wɪldənɪs] *n* - **1.** [barren land] yermo *m*, desierto *m* - **2.** [overgrown land] jungla *f*.

wild-goose chase *n inf* búsqueda *f* infructuosa.

wildlife ['waɪldlaɪf] *n* (*U*) fauna *f*.

wildly ['waɪldlɪ] *adv* - **1.** [enthusiastically] frenéticamente - **2.** [without discipline, inaccurately] a lo loco - **3.** [very] extremadamente.

wilful *UK*, **willful** *US* ['wɪlful] *adj* - **1.** [stubborn] que siempre se tiene que salir con la suya - **2.** [deliberate] deliberado(da).

will¹ [wɪl] ⬦ *n* - **1.** [gen] voluntad *f* - **2.** [document] testamento *m*; **to make a will** hacer testamento. ⬦ *vt*: **to will sthg to happen** desear mucho que ocurra algo; **to will sb to do sthg** desear mucho que alguien haga algo.

will² [wɪl] *modal vb* - **1.** [to express future tense]: **they say it will rain tomorrow** dicen que lloverá *OR* va a llover mañana; **we will have arrived by midday** habremos llegado a mediodía; **when will we get paid?** ¿cuándo nos pagarán?; **will they come? - yes, they will/no, they won't** ¿vendrán? - sí/no; **you will come, won't you?** (*emphatic*) vas a venir, ¿no? - **2.** [indicating willingness]: **will you have some more tea?** ¿te apetece más té?; **I won't do it** no lo haré - **3.** [in commands, requests]: **you will leave this house at once** vas a salir de esta casa ahora mismo; **close that window, will you?** cierra la ventana, ¿quieres?; **will you be quiet!** ¿queréis hacer el favor de callaros? - **4.** [indicating possibility, what usually happens]: **the hall will hold up to 1,000 people** la sala tiene cabi-

da para 1.000 personas - **5.** [expressing an assumption]: **that'll be your father** ese va a ser *OR* será tu padre - **6.** [indicating irritation]: **well, if you will leave your toys everywhere...** normal, si vais dejando los juguetes por todas partes...; **she will keep phoning me** ¡y venga a llamarme!

wilful *US* = **wilful**.

willing ['wɪlɪŋ] *adj* [eager] servicial.

willingly ['wɪlɪŋlɪ] *adv* de buena gana.

willow (tree) ['wɪləʊ-] *n* sauce *m*.

willpower ['wɪl,paʊəʳ] *n* fuerza *f* de voluntad.

willy-nilly [,wɪlɪ'nɪlɪ] *adv* [carelessly] a la buena de Dios.

wilt [wɪlt] *vi* [plant] marchitarse; [person] desfallecer, extenuarse.

wily ['waɪlɪ] *adj* astuto(ta).

wimp [wɪmp] *n inf pej* blandengue *mf*.

win [wɪn] ⬦ *n* victoria *f*, triunfo *m*. ⬦ *vt* (*pt & pp* **won**) ganar. ⬦ *vi* (*pt & pp* **won**) ganar; **you/I etc can't win** no hay manera. ➡ **win over, win round** *vt sep* convencer.

wince [wɪns] *vi* hacer una mueca de dolor; **to wince at/with sthg** estremecerse ante/de algo.

winch [wɪntʃ] *n* torno *m*.

wind¹ [wɪnd] ⬦ *n* - **1.** METEOR viento *m* - **2.** [breath] aliento *m*, resuello *m* - **3.** (*U*) [in stomach] gases *mpl*; **to break wind** *euph* ventosear. ⬦ *vt* [knock breath out of] dejar sin aliento.

wind² [waɪnd] ⬦ *vt* (*pt & pp* **wound**) - **1.** [string, thread] enrollar; **to wind sthg around sthg** enrollar algo alrededor de algo - **2.** [clock, watch] dar cuerda a. ⬦ *vi* (*pt & pp* **wound**) serpentear. ➡ **wind down** ⬦ *vt sep* - **1.** [car window] bajar - **2.** [business] cerrar poco a poco. ⬦ *vi* [person] relajarse, descansar. ➡ **wind up** ⬦ *vt sep* - **1.** [finish - activity] finalizar, concluir; [business] liquidar - **2.** [clock, watch] dar cuerda a - **3.** [car window] subir - **4.** *UK inf* [annoy] vacilar, tomar el pelo a. ⬦ *vi inf* [end up] terminar, acabar; **to wind up doing sthg** acabar haciendo algo.

windfall ['wɪndfɔːl] *n* [unexpected gift] dinero *m* llovido del cielo.

wind farm [wɪnd-] *n* parque *m* eólico.

winding ['waɪndɪŋ] *adj* tortuoso(sa).

wind instrument [wɪnd-] *n* instrumento *m* de viento.

windmill ['wɪndmɪl] *n* molino *m* de viento.

window ['wɪndəʊ] *n* - **1.** [gen & COMPUT] ventana *f* - **2.** AUT ventanilla *f* - **3.** [of shop] escaparate *m*.

window box *n* jardinera *f* (de ventana).

window cleaner n - 1. [person] limpiacristales m & f inv - 2. [product] limpiacristales m inv.

window ledge n alféizar m.

window pane n cristal m (de la ventana).

windowsill ['wɪndəʊsɪl] n alféizar m.

windpipe ['wɪndpaɪp] n tráquea f.

windscreen UK ['wɪndskriːn], **windshield** US ['wɪndʃiːld] n parabrisas m inv.

windscreen washer n lavaparabrisas m inv.

windscreen wiper n limpiaparabrisas m inv.

windshield US = **windscreen**.

windsurfing ['wɪnd,sɜːfɪŋ] n windsurf m.

windswept ['wɪndswept] adj [scenery] azotado(da) por el viento.

wind turbine [wɪnd-] n aerogenerador m.

windy ['wɪndɪ] adj [day, weather] ventoso(sa), de mucho viento; [place] expuesto(ta) al viento; **it's windy** hace viento.

wine [waɪn] n vino m; **red/white wine** vino tinto/blanco.

wine bar n UK bar de cierta elegancia especializado en vinos y que a veces suele servir comidas.

wine cellar n bodega f.

wineglass ['waɪnglɑːs] n copa f OR vaso m (de vino).

wine list n lista f de vinos.

wine merchant n UK vinatero m, -ra f.

wine tasting [-,teɪstɪŋ] n cata f de vinos.

wine waiter n sommelier m.

wing [wɪŋ] n - 1. [gen] ala f - 2. AUT guardabarros m inv - 3. SPORT [side of pitch] banda f; [winger] extremo m. ◆ **wings** npl THEAT: **the wings** los bastidores.

winger ['wɪŋəʳ] n SPORT extremo m.

wing mirror n retrovisor m.

wink [wɪŋk] n guiño m; **not to sleep a wink, not to get a wink of sleep** inf no pegar ojo.

winkle ['wɪŋkl] n bígaro m.

Winnebago® [,wɪnɪ'beɪgəʊ] n autocaravana f.

winner ['wɪnəʳ] n ganador m, -ra f.

winning ['wɪnɪŋ] adj - 1. [team, competitor] vencedor(ra); [goal, point] de la victoria; [ticket, number] premiado(da) - 2. [smile, ways] atractivo(va). ◆ **winnings** npl ganancias fpl.

winning post n meta f.

winter ['wɪntəʳ] ◇ n (U) invierno m. ◇ comp de invierno, invernal.

winter sports npl deportes mpl de invierno.

wintertime ['wɪntətaɪm] n (U) invierno m.

wintfiry ['wɪntrɪ] adj [gen] de invierno, invernal. [informal] frío (a fría).

wipe [waɪp] ◇ n: **give the table a wipe** pásale un trapo a la mesa. ◇ vt [rub to clean] limpiar, pasar un trapo a; [rub to dry] secar. ◆ **wipe out** vt sep - 1. [erase] borrar - 2. [eradicate] aniquilar. ◆ **wipe up** vt sep empapar, limpiar.

wire ['waɪəʳ] ◇ n - 1. [gen] alambre m; ELEC cable m - 2. US [telegram] telegrama m. ◇ vt - 1. [ELEC - house] poner la instalación eléctrica de; [- plug] conectar el cable a - 2. US [send telegram to] enviar un telegrama a.

wirefree ['waɪəfriː] adj inalámbrico(ca).

wireless ['waɪəlɪs] n dated radio f.

wiring ['waɪərɪŋ] n (U) instalación f eléctrica.

wiry ['waɪərɪ] adj - 1. [hair] estropajoso(sa) - 2. [body, man] nervudo(da).

wisdom ['wɪzdəm] n - 1. [learning] sabiduría f - 2. [good sense] sensatez f.

wisdom tooth n muela f del juicio.

wise [waɪz] adj - 1. [learned] sabio(bia); **she's no wiser** OR **none the wiser** sigue sin entender - 2. [sensible] prudente.

wisecrack ['waɪzkræk] n pej broma f, chiste m.

wish [wɪʃ] ◇ n: **to do sthg against sb's wishes** hacer algo en contra de los deseos de alguien. ◇ vt: **to wish to do sthg** fml desear hacer algo; **to wish sb sthg** desear a alguien algo; **I wish (that) you had told me before!** ¡ojalá me lo hubieras dicho antes!; **I wish (that) you would shut up** ¿por qué no te calles? ◇ vi [by magic]: **to wish for sthg** pedir (como deseo) algo. ◆ **wishes** npl: **(with) best wishes** [in letter] muchos recuerdos.

wishful thinking [,wɪʃfʊl-] n (U): **it's just wishful thinking** no son más que (vanas) ilusiones.

wishy-washy ['wɪʃɪ,wɒʃɪ] adj inf pej soso(sa), insípido(da).

wisp [wɪsp] n - 1. [of hair] mechón m; [of grass] brizna f - 2. [cloud] nubecilla f; [of smoke] voluta f.

wistful ['wɪstfʊl] adj melancólico(ca).

wit [wɪt] n - 1. [humour] ingenio m, agudeza f - 2. [intelligence]: **to have the wit to do sthg** tener el buen juicio de hacer algo. ◆ **wits** npl: **to be scared out of one's wits** inf estar muerto de miedo.

witch [wɪtʃ] n bruja f.

with [wɪð] prep - 1. [in company of] con; **we stayed with them for a week** estuvimos con ellos una semana; **with me** conmigo; **with you** contigo - 2. [indicating opposition] con - 3. [indicating means, manner, feelings] con; **I washed it**

with detergent lo lavé con detergente; **he filled it with wine** lo llenó de vino; **covered with mud** cubierto de barro; **she was trembling with fear** temblaba de miedo; **"all right", she said with a smile** "vale", dijo con una sonrisa - **4.** [having - gen] con; **a man with a beard** un hombre con barba; **the woman with the black hair/big dog** la señora del pelo negro/perro grande; **I'm married with six children** estoy casado con seis hijos - **5.** [regarding] con; **he's very mean with money** es muy tacaño con el dinero - **6.** [because of] con; **with the weather as it is, we have decided to stay at home** con el tiempo como está hemos decidido quedarnos en casa; **with my luck, I'll probably lose** con la suerte que tengo seguro que pierdo - **7.** [indicating understanding]: **are you with me?** ¿me sigues? - **8.** [indicating support] con; **I'm with Dad on this** en eso estoy con papá.

withdraw [wɪð'drɔ:] ◇ vt (pt -drew, pp -drawn) - **1.** [gen]: **to withdraw sthg (from)** retirar algo (de) - **2.** [money] sacar. ◇ vi (pt -drew, pp -drawn): **to withdraw (from/to)** retirarse (de/a); **to withdraw into o.s.** encerrarse en uno mismo.

withdrawal [wɪð'drɔ:əl] n - **1.** [gen & MIL] retirada f - **2.** [retraction] retractación f - **3.** FIN reintegro m.

withdrawal symptoms npl síndrome m de abstinencia.

withdrawn [wɪð'drɔ:n] ◇ pp ▷ **withdraw**. ◇ adj [shy, quiet] reservado(da).

withdrew [wɪð'dru:] pt ▷ **withdraw**.

wither [ˈwɪðər] vi - **1.** [dry up] marchitarse - **2.** [become weak] debilitarse.

withhold [wɪð'həʊld] (pt & pp -held [-'held]) vt [gen] retener; [consent, permission] negar.

within [wɪ'ðɪn] ◇ prep - **1.** [gen] dentro de; **within reach** al alcance de la mano; **within sight of** a la vista de - **2.** [less than - distance] a menos de; [- time] en menos de; **it's within walking distance** se puede ir andando; **he was within five seconds of the leader** estaba a cinco segundos del líder; **within the next six months** en los próximos seis meses; **it arrived within a week** llegó en menos de una semana. ◇ adv dentro.

without [wɪð'aʊt] ◇ prep sin; **without sthg/doing sthg** sin algo/hacer algo; **without making any mistakes** sin cometer ningún error; **it happened without my realizing** pasó sin que me diera cuenta. ◇ adv: **to go** OR **do without sthg** pasar sin algo.

withstand [wɪð'stænd] (pt & pp -stood [-'stʊd]) vt resistir, aguantar.

witness [ˈwɪtnɪs] ◇ n - **1.** [person] testigo mf; **to be witness to sthg** ser testigo de algo

- **2.** [testimony]: **to bear witness to sthg** atestiguar algo, dar fe de algo. ◇ vt - **1.** [see] presenciar - **2.** [countersign] firmar (como testigo).

witness box UK, **witness stand** US n tribuna f (de los testigos).

witticism [ˈwɪtɪsɪzm] n ocurrencia f.

witty [ˈwɪtɪ] adj ingenioso(sa), ocurrente.

wives [waɪvz] npl ▷ **wife**.

wizard [ˈwɪzəd] n - **1.** [magician] mago m (en cuentos) - **2.** [skilled person] genio m.

wobble [ˈwɒbl] vi [gen] tambalearse; [furniture] cojear; [legs] temblar.

woe [wəʊ] n liter aflicción f.

woke [wəʊk] pt ▷ **wake**.

woken [ˈwəʊkn] pp ▷ **wake**.

wolf [wʊlf] n (pl wolves) ZOOL lobo m.

wolves [wʊlvz] npl ▷ **wolf**.

woman [ˈwʊmən] (pl women) ◇ n - **1.** [female] mujer f - **2.** [womanhood] la mujer. ◇ comp: **woman doctor** médica f.

womanly [ˈwʊmənlɪ] adj femenino(na).

womb [wu:m] n matriz f, útero m.

women [ˈwɪmɪn] npl ▷ **woman**.

women's lib [-'lɪb] n liberación f de la mujer.

women's liberation n liberación f de la mujer.

won [wʌn] pt & pp ▷ **win**.

wonder [ˈwʌndər] ◇ n - **1.** [amazement] asombro m, admiración f - **2.** [cause for surprise]: **it's a wonder (that)…** es un milagro que… - **3.** [amazing thing, person] maravilla f; **to work** OR **do wonders** hacer maravillas OR milagros. ◇ vt - **1.** [speculate]: **to wonder (if** OR **whether)** preguntarse (si) - **2.** [in polite requests]: **I wonder if** OR **whether I could ask you a question?** ¿le importaría que le hiciera una pregunta? - **3.** [be surprised]: **I wonder (that) she hasn't left him** me pregunto cómo es que todavía no lo ha dejado. ◇ vi [speculate]: **I was only wondering** preguntaba sólo por curiosidad; **to wonder about sthg** preguntarse por algo.

wonderful [ˈwʌndəfʊl] adj maravilloso(sa), estupendo(da).

wonderfully [ˈwʌndəfʊlɪ] adv - **1.** [very well] estupendamente - **2.** [very] extremadamente.

won't [wəʊnt] (abbr of will not) ▷ **will**[2].

woo [wu:] vt - **1.** liter [court] cortejar - **2.** [try to win over] granjearse el apoyo de.

wood [wʊd] n - **1.** [timber] madera f; [for fire] leña f - **2.** [group of trees] bosque m; **I can't see the wood for the trees** UK los árboles no me dejan ver el bosque. ◆ **woods** npl bosque m.

wooded ['wudid] *adj* arbolado(da).

wooden ['wudn] *adj* - **1.** [of wood] de madera - **2.** *pej* [actor] envarado(da).

woodpecker ['wud,pekə'] *n* pájaro *m* carpintero.

woodwind ['wudwind] *n*: **the woodwind** los instrumentos de viento de madera.

woodwork ['wudwɜːk] *n* carpintería *f*.

woodworm ['wudwɜːm] *n* carcoma *f*.

wool [wul] *n* lana *f*; **to pull the wool over sb's eyes** *inf fig* dar a alguien gato por liebre.

woollen *UK*, **woolen** *US* ['wulən] *adj* de lana. ◆ **woollens** *npl* géneros *mpl* de lana.

woolly ['wuli] *adj* - **1.** [woollen] de lana - **2.** *inf* [fuzzy, unclear] confuso(sa).

word [wɜːd] ◇ *n* - **1.** LING palabra *f*; **we couldn't understand a word he said** no entendimos ni una sola palabra de lo que dijo; **word for word** palabra por palabra; **in other words** en otras palabras; **in a word** en una palabra; **too... for words** de lo más...; **she doesn't mince her words** no tiene pelos en la lengua; **I couldn't get a word in edgeways** no pude meter baza - **2.** *(U)* [news] noticia *f*; **there is no word from them** no hemos tenido noticias de ellos; **word has it that...** se rumorea que... - **3.** [promise] palabra *f*; **to be as good as one's word, to be true to one's word** cumplir lo prometido. ◇ *vt* redactar, expresar.

wording ['wɜːdɪŋ] *n (U)* términos *mpl*, forma *f* (de expresión).

word processing *n (U)* proceso *m* de textos.

word processor [-'prəusesə'] *n* procesador *m* de textos.

wore [wɔː'] *pt* ▷ **wear**.

work [wɜːk] ◇ *n* - **1.** *(U)* [employment] trabajo *m*, empleo *m*; **to be out of work** estar desempleado; **at work** en el trabajo - **2.** [activity, tasks] trabajo *m*; **at work** trabajando; **to have one's work cut out doing sthg** *OR* **to do sthg** tenerlo muy difícil para hacer algo - **3.** [of art, literature etc] obra *f* - **4.** [handiwork] obra *f*; **it was the work of a psychopath** fue obra de un psicópata. ◇ *vt* - **1.** [employees, subordinates] hacer trabajar; **she works herself too hard** trabaja demasiado - **2.** [machine] manejar, operar - **3.** [wood, metal, land] trabajar. ◇ *vi* - **1.** [person]: **to work (on sthg)** trabajar (en algo); **he works as a gardener** trabaja de jardinero; **to work for sb** trabajar para alguien - **2.** [machine, system, idea] funcionar - **3.** [drug] surtir efecto - **4.** [become by movement]: **to work loose** soltarse; **to work free** desprenderse. ◆ **works** ◇ *n* [factory] fábrica *f*. ◇ *npl* [mechanism] mecanismo *m*. ◆ **work on** *vt insep* - **1.** [pay attention to] trabajar en - **2.** [take as basis] partir de. ◆ **work out** ◇ *vt sep* - **1.** [plan, schedule] elaborar - **2.** [total, amount]

calcular; [answer] dar con. ◇ *vi* - **1.** [figure etc]: **to work out at** salir a - **2.** [turn out] resolverse - **3.** [be successful] salir bien - **4.** [train, exercise] hacer ejercicio. ◆ **work up** *vt sep* - **1.** [excite]: **to work o.s. up into a frenzy** ponerse frenético(ca) - **2.** [generate] despertar; **I can't work up much enthusiasm** no consigo entusiasmarme; **to work up an appetite** abrir el apetito.

workable ['wɜːkəbl] *adj* factible, viable.

workaholic [,wɜːkə'hɒlɪk] *n* adicto *m*, -ta *f* al trabajo.

workday ['wɜːkdeɪ], **working day** *n* [not weekend] día *m* laborable.

worked up [,wɜːkt-] *adj* nervioso(sa); **to get worked up** alterarse.

worker ['wɜːkə'] *n* [person who works] trabajador *m*, -ra *f*; [manual worker] obrero *m*, -ra *f*; **a hard/fast worker** una persona que trabaja mucho/a prisa; **office worker** oficinista *mf*.

workforce ['wɜːkfɔːs] *n* mano *f* de obra.

working ['wɜːkɪŋ] *adj* - **1.** [in operation] funcionando - **2.** [having employment] empleado(da); **a working mother** una madre trabajadora - **3.** [relating to work - gen] laboral; [- day] laborable. ◆ **workings** *npl* mecanismo *m*.

working class *n*: **the working class** la clase obrera. ◆ **working-class** *adj* obrero(ra).

working order *n*: **to be in (good) working order** funcionar (bien).

workload ['wɜːkləud] *n* cantidad *f* de trabajo.

workman ['wɜːkmən] *(pl* **-men** [-mən]*)* *n* obrero *m*.

workmanship ['wɜːkmənʃɪp] *n* artesanía *f*.

workmate ['wɜːkmeɪt] *n* compañero *m*, -ra *f* de trabajo, colega *mf*.

work permit [-,pɜːmɪt] *n* permiso *m* de trabajo.

workplace ['wɜːkpleɪs] *n* lugar *m* de trabajo.

workshop ['wɜːkʃɒp] *n* taller *m*.

workspace ['wɜːkspeɪs] *n* COMPUT espacio *m* de trabajo.

workstation ['wɜːk,steɪʃn] *n* COMPUT estación *f* de trabajo.

worktop ['wɜːktɒp] *n UK* mármol *m*, encimera *f*.

work-to-rule *n UK* huelga *f* de celo.

world [wɜːld] ◇ *n* mundo *m*; **the best in the world** el mejor del mundo; **the highest mountain in the world** la montaña más alta del mundo; **all over the world** por todo el mundo; **to think the world of sb** querer a alguien con locura; **a world of difference** una diferencia enorme; **to see the world** ver mundo; **it's a small world** el mundo es un pañuelo; **the antique world** el mundo antiguo; **what is the world coming to?** ¿a dónde vamos a ir a parar?; **they are worlds apart** hay un abismo entre ellos; **to have all the time in the world** tener todo el tiempo del mundo. ◇ *comp* mundial.

world-class *adj* de primera categoría.

world-famous *adj* famoso(sa) en el mundo entero.

worldly ['wɜːldlɪ] *adj liter* mundano(na).

World Trade Organization *n* Organización *f* Mundial del Comercio.

World War I *n* la Primera Guerra Mundial.

World War II *n* la Segunda Guerra Mundial.

worldwide ['wɜːldwaɪd] ◇ *adj* mundial. ◇ *adv* en todo el mundo.

World Wide Web *n*: **the World Wide Web** la (World Wide) Web.

worm [wɜːm] *n* [animal] gusano *m*; [earthworm] lombriz *f* (de tierra).

worn [wɔːn] ◇ *pp* ▷ **wear**. ◇ *adj* - **1.** [threadbare] gastado(da) - **2.** [tired] ajado(da).

worn-out *adj* - **1.** [old, threadbare]: **to be worn-out** estar ya para tirar - **2.** [tired] agotado(da).

worried ['wʌrɪd] *adj* preocupado(da).

worry ['wʌrɪ] ◇ *n* preocupación *f*. ◇ *vt* [trouble] preocupar. ◇ *vi*: **to worry (about)** preocuparse (por); **not to worry!** ¡no importa!

worrying ['wʌrɪɪŋ] *adj* preocupante.

worrywort ['wʌrɪwɔːrt] *n US inf* angustias *mf inv Esp*, angustiado *m*, -da *f*.

worse [wɜːs] ◇ *adj* peor; **to get worse** empeorar; **to get worse and worse** ir cada vez peor; **to go from bad to worse** ir de mal en peor; **to make things worse** empeorar las cosas; **they are none the worse for their adventure** se sienten perfectamente a pesar de su aventura. ◇ *adv* peor; **worse off** [gen] en peor situación; [financially] peor económicamente; **you could do worse than marry him** no harías tan mal casándote con él. ◇ *n*: **worse was to come** lo peor estaba aún por venir; **a change for the worse** un cambio para peor; **to take a turn for the worse** empeorar.

worsen ['wɜːsn] *vt* & *vi* empeorar.

worship ['wɜːʃɪp] ◇ *vt* (*UK pt* & *pp* **-ped**, *cont* **-ping**, *US pt* & *pp* **-ed**, *cont* **-ing**) *lit* & *fig* adorar. ◇ *n lit* & *fig*: **worship (of)** culto *m* (a), adoración *f* (por). ▶ **Worship** *n*: **Your/Her/His Worship** su señoría; **his Worship the Mayor** el Excelentísimo Señor alcalde.

worst [wɜːst] ◇ *adj* peor; **the worst thing is...** lo peor es que...; **worst of all** lo peor de todo. ◇ *adv* peor; **the worst affected area** la región más afectada. ◇ *n*: **the worst** [thing] lo peor; [person] el peor *m*, la peor *f*; **this is communism at its worst** esto es la peor manifestación del comunismo; **to fear the worst** temer lo peor; **if the worst comes to the worst** en último extremo; **to bring out the worst in sb** sacar lo peor de alguien. ◆ **at (the) worst** *adv* en el peor de los casos.

worth [wɜːθ] ◇ *prep* - **1.** [having the value of]: **it's worth £50** vale 50 libras; **how much is it worth?** ¿cuánto vale?; **it isn't worth that much** no vale tanto - **2.** [deserving of] digno(na) de; **the museum is worth visiting** OR **a visit, it's worth visiting the museum** el museo merece una visita; **it's not worth it** no vale la pena; **it's worth a try** vale la pena intentarlo; **for what it's worth, I think that...** por si mi opinión sirve de algo, creo que... ◇ *n* - **1.** [amount]: **£50,000 worth of antiques** antigüedades por valor de 50.000 libras; **a month's worth of groceries** provisiones para un mes - **2.** *fml* [value] valor *m*.

worthless ['wɜːθlɪs] *adj* - **1.** [object] sin valor - **2.** [person] despreciable.

worthwhile [,wɜːθ'waɪl] *adj* que vale la pena; [cause] noble, digno(na).

worthy ['wɜːðɪ] *adj* - **1.** [gen] digno(na) - **2.** [good but unexciting] encomiable.

would [wʊd] *modal vb* - **1.** (*in reported speech*): **she said she would come** dijo que vendría - **2.** (*in conditional phrases*): **if she couldn't come she would tell us** si no pudiera venir nos lo diría; **what would you do?** ¿qué harías?; **if he had known, he would have resigned** si lo hubiera sabido, habría dimitido - **3.** (*indicating willingness*): **she wouldn't go** no quiso/quería ir; **he would do anything for her** haría cualquier cosa por ella - **4.** (*in polite questions*): **would you like a drink?** ¿quieres beber algo?; **would you mind closing the window?** ¿le importaría cerrar la ventana?; **help me shut this suitcase, would you?** ayúdame a cerrar esta maleta, ¿quieres? - **5.** [indicating inevitability]: **he would say that, wouldn't he?** hombre, era de esperar que dijera eso, ¿no? - **6.** [expressing opinions]: **I would have thought (that) it would be easy** hubiera pensado que sería fácil; **I would prefer...** preferiría...; **I would like...** quisiera..., quiero... - **7.** [giving advice]: **I would report it if I were you** yo en tu lugar lo denunciaría - **8.** [indicating habit]: **he would smoke a cigar after dinner** solía fumar un puro después de la cena; **she would often complain about the neighbours** se quejaba a menudo de los vecinos - **9.** [in conjectures]: **it would have been around 2 o'clock** serían las dos.

would-be *adj*: **a would-be author** un aspirante a literato.

wouldn't ['wʊdnt] (*abbr of* **would not**) ▷ **would**.

would've ['wʊdəv] (*abbr of* = would have), = **would**.

wound [wuːnd] *n* herida *f*. *vt lit & fig* herir.

wound [waʊnd] *pt & pp* > **wind**.

wove [wəʊv] *pt* > **weave**.

woven ['wəʊvn] *pp* > **weave**.

WP *abbr of* **word processing, word processor**.

wrangle ['ræŋgl] *n* disputa *f*. *vi*: **to wrangle (with sb over sthg)** discutir OR pelearse (con alguien por algo).

wrap [ræp] *vt* - 1. [cover] envolver; **to wrap sthg in sthg** envolver algo en algo; **to wrap sthg around** OR **round sthg** liar algo alrededor de algo - 2. [encircle]: **he wrapped his hands around it** lo rodeó con sus manos. *n* - 1. [garment] echarpe *m*; **to keep sthg under wraps** *fig* mantener algo en secreto - 2. US [food] *tipo de bocadillo servido en una torta de maíz y doblado por la mitad*. **wrap up** *vt sep* [cover] envolver. *vi* [put warm clothes on]: **wrap up well** OR **warmly** abrígate bien.

wrapper ['ræpər] *n* envoltorio *m*.

wrapping ['ræpɪŋ] *n* envoltorio *m*.

wrapping paper *n* (U) papel *m* de envolver.

wrath [rɒθ] *n liter* ira *f*, cólera *f*.

wreak [riːk] *vt* causar; **to wreak havoc** hacer estragos.

wreath [riːθ] *n* corona *f* (de flores).

wreck [rek] *n* - 1. [of car, plane] restos *mpl* del siniestro; [of ship] restos del naufragio - 2. *inf* [person] guiñapo *m*; **to be a nervous wreck** estar hecho(cha) un manojo de nervios. *vt* - 1. [destroy] destrozar - 2. NAUT hacer naufragar; **to be wrecked** naufragar - 3. [spoil] dar al traste con; [health] acabar con.

wreckage ['rekɪdʒ] *n* (U) [of plane, car] restos *mpl*; [of building] escombros *mpl*.

wren [ren] *n* chochín *m*.

wrench [rentʃ] *n* - 1. US [tool] llave *f* inglesa - 2. [injury] torcedura *f*. *vt* - 1. [pull violently]: **to wrench sthg (off)** arrancar algo; **to wrench sthg open** abrir algo de un tirón - 2. [twist and injure] torcer.

wrestle ['resl] *vi lit & fig*: **to wrestle (with)** luchar (con).

wrestler ['reslər] *n* luchador *m*, -ra *f*.

wrestling ['reslɪŋ] *n* lucha *f* libre.

wretch [retʃ] *n* desgraciado *m*, -da *f*.

wretched ['retʃɪd] *adj* - 1. [miserable] miserable - 2. *inf* [damned] maldito(ta).

wriggle ['rɪgl] *vi* - 1. [move about] menearse - 2. [twist] escurrirse, deslizarse.

wring [rɪŋ] (*pt & pp* **wrung**) *vt* - 1. [wet clothes] estrujar, escurrir 2. [neck] retorcer.

wringing ['rɪŋɪŋ] *adj*: **wringing (wet)** empapado(da).

wrinkle ['rɪŋkl] *n* arruga *f*. *vt* arrugar. *vi* arrugarse.

wrist [rɪst] *n* muñeca *f*.

wristwatch ['rɪstwɒtʃ] *n* reloj *m* de pulsera.

writ [rɪt] *n* mandato *m* judicial.

write [raɪt] (*pt* **wrote**, *pp* **written**) *vt* - 1. [gen & COMPUT] escribir; **to write sb a letter** escribirle una carta a alguien - 2. US [person] escribir a. *vi* [gen & COMPUT] escribir; **to write (to sb)** UK escribir (a alguien). **write away** *vi*: **to write away for sthg** escribir pidiendo algo. **write back** *vt sep & vi* contestar. **write down** *vt sep* apuntar. **write off** *vt sep* - 1. [plan, hopes] abandonar - 2. [debt] cancelar, anular - 3. [person - as failure] considerar un fracaso - 4. UK *inf* [wreck] cargarse. **write up** *vt sep* redactar.

write-off *n*: **the car was a write-off** el coche quedó totalmente destrozado.

writer ['raɪtər] *n* - 1. [as profession] escritor *m*, -ra *f* - 2. [of letter, article, story] autor *m*, -ra *f*.

writhe [raɪð] *vi* retorcerse.

writing ['raɪtɪŋ] *n* - 1. (U) [handwriting] letra *f*, caligrafía *f* - 2. [something written] escrito *m*; **to put sthg in writing** poner algo por escrito - 3. [activity] escritura *f*.

writing paper *n* (U) papel *m* de carta.

written ['rɪtn] *pp* > **write**. *adj* - 1. [not oral] escrito(ta) - 2. [official] por escrito.

wrong [rɒŋ] *adj* - 1. [not normal, not satisfactory] malo(la); **the clock's wrong** el reloj anda mal; **what's wrong?** ¿qué pasa?; **there's nothing wrong** no pasa nada; **there's nothing wrong with me** no me pasa nada - 2. [not suitable, not correct] equivocado(da); [moment, time] inoportuno(na); [answer] incorrecto(ta); **he has given me the wrong change** me ha dado el cambio equivocado; **I think we've gone the wrong way** creo que nos hemos equivocado de camino; **I always seem to say the wrong thing** parece que siempre digo lo que no debo; **to be wrong** [person] equivocarse; **to be wrong about sthg/sb** equivocarse con respecto a algo/alguien; **to be wrong to do sthg** cometer un error al hacer algo - 3. [morally bad] malo(la); **it's wrong to steal/lie** robar/mentir está mal; **what's wrong with being a communist?** ¿qué tiene de malo ser comunista? *adv* [incorrectly] mal; **to get sthg wrong** entender mal algo. *n* - 1. [evil] mal *m*; **to be in the wrong** haber hecho mal - 2. [injustice] injusticia *f*. *vt* ser injusto(ta) con, agraviar.

wrongful ['rɒŋfʊl] *adj* [dismissal] improcedente; [arrest, imprisonment] ilegal.

wrongly ['rɒŋlɪ] *adv* equivocadamente.

wrote [rəʊt] *pt* ⊏⟩ **write**.

wrought iron [rɔːt-] *n* hierro *m* forjado.

wrung [rʌŋ] *pt* & *pp* ⊏⟩ **wring**.

wry [raɪ] *adj* [amused] irónico(ca).

WTO [ˌdʌbljuːtiːˈəʊ] (*abbr of* World Trade Organization) *n* OMC *f*.

WWW (*abbr of* World Wide Web) *n* WWW *f*.

x (*pl* x's OR xs), **X** (*pl* X's OR Xs) [eks] *n* [letter] x *f inv*, X *f inv.*

xenophobia [ˌzenəˈfəʊbjə] *n* xenofobia *f.*

Xmas ['eksməs] *n* Navidad *f.*

XML [ˌeksemˈel] (*abbr of* Extensible Markup Language) *n* COMPUT XML *m.*

X-ray ⟨⟩ *n* - 1. [ray] rayo *m* X - 2. [picture] radiografía *f*; **to have a chest X-ray** hacerse una radiografía. ⟨⟩ *vt* examinar con rayos X, radiografiar.

xylophone ['zaɪləfəʊn] *n* xilofón *m.*

y (*pl* y's OR ys), **Y** (*pl* Y's OR Ys) [waɪ] *n* [letter] y *f*, Y *f.*

yacht [jɒt] *n* yate *m*; [for racing] balandro *m.*

yachting ['jɒtɪŋ] *n* balandrismo *m.*

yachtsman ['jɒtsmən] (*pl* -men [-mən]) *n* balandrista *m.*

Yank [jæŋk] *n inf pej* [estadounidense] yanqui *mf.*

Yankee ['jæŋkɪ] *n US término usado para designar a una persona del noreste de los EEUU.*

yap [jæp] *vi* [dog] ladrar.

yard [jɑːd] *n* - 1. [unit of measurement] = 91,44 cm yarda *f* - 2. [walled area] patio *m* - 3. [shipyard] astillero *m*; **builder's/goods yard** depósito *m* de materiales/de mercancías - 4. *US* [attached to house] jardín *m.*

yardstick ['jɑːdstɪk] *n* criterio *m*, pauta *f.*

yarn [jɑːn] *n* [thread] hilo *m*, hilaza *f.*

yawn [jɔːn] ⟨⟩ *n* [when tired] bostezo *m.* ⟨⟩ *vi* - 1. [when tired] bostezar - 2. [gap, chasm] abrirse.

yd *abbr of* yard.

yeah [jeə] *adv inf* sí.

year [jɪə] *n* - 1. [gen] año *m*; **he's 25 years old** tiene 25 años; **all (the) year round** todo el año; **over the years** con los años - 2. SCH curso *m*; **he's in (his) first year** está en primero. ➡ **years** *npl* [ages] años *mpl*; **it's years since I last saw you** hace siglos que no te veo.

yearly ['jɪəlɪ] ⟨⟩ *adj* anual. ⟨⟩ *adv* - 1. [once a year] una vez al año - 2. [every year] cada año.

yearn [jɜːn] *vi*: **to yearn for sthg/to do sthg** ansiar algo/hacer algo.

yearning ['jɜːnɪŋ] *n*: **yearning (for sb/sthg)** anhelo *m* (de alguien/algo).

yeast [jiːst] *n* levadura *f.*

yell [jel] ⟨⟩ *n* grito *m*, alarido *m.* ⟨⟩ *vt* & *vi* vociferar.

yellow ['jeləʊ] ⟨⟩ *adj* [in colour] amarillo(lla). ⟨⟩ *n* amarillo *m.*

yellow card *n* FTBL tarjeta *f* amarilla.

yelp [jelp] ⟨⟩ *n* aullido *m.* ⟨⟩ *vi* aullar.

yes [jes] ⟨⟩ *adv* sí; **to say yes** decir que sí; **to say yes to sthg** consentir algo; **does he speak English? – yes, he does** ¿habla inglés? – sí; **he doesn't speak English – yes he does!** no habla inglés – sí, sí que habla. ⟨⟩ *n* sí *m.*

yesterday ['jestədɪ] ⟨⟩ *n* ayer *m.* ⟨⟩ *adv* ayer; **yesterday afternoon** ayer por la tarde; **the day before yesterday** antes de ayer, anteayer.

yet [jet] ⟨⟩ *adv* - 1. [gen] todavía, aún; **have you had lunch yet?** ¿has comido ya?; **their worst defeat yet** la mayor derrota que han sufrido hasta la fecha; **as yet** de momento, hasta ahora; **not yet** todavía OR aún no - 2. [even]: **yet another car** otro coche más; **yet again** otra vez más; **yet more** aún más. ⟨⟩ *conj* pero, sin embargo.

yew [juː] *n* tejo *m.*

Yiddish ['jɪdɪʃ] ⟨⟩ *adj* yídish *(inv).* ⟨⟩ *n* yídish *m.*

yield [jiːld] ⟨⟩ *n* - 1. AGRIC cosecha *f* - 2. FIN rédito *m.* ⟨⟩ *vt* - 1. [gen] producir, dar - 2. [give up] ceder. ⟨⟩ *vi* - 1. [shelf, lock etc] ceder

- 2. *fml* [person, enemy] rendirse; **to yield to sb/ sthg** claudicar ante alguien/algo **- 3.** *US* AUT [give way]**: 'yield'** 'ceda el paso'.

YMCA (*abbr of* **Young Men's Christian Association**) *n* asociación internacional de jóvenes cristianos.

yoga [ˈjəʊgə] *n* yoga *m*.

yoghourt, yoghurt, yogurt [*UK* ˈjɒgət, *US* ˈjəʊgərt] *n* yogur *m*.

yoke [jəʊk] *n lit* & *fig* yugo *m*.

yolk [jəʊk] *n* yema *f*.

you [ju:] *pers pron* **- 1.** (*subject - sing*) tú, vos (+ *pl vb*) *Amér C & R Plata*; (- *formal use*) usted; (- *pl*) vosotros *mpl*, -tras *f Esp*; (- *formal use*) ustedes (*pl*); **you're a good cook** eres/usted es un buen cocinero; **are you French?** ¿eres/es usted francés?; **you idiot!** ¡imbécil!; **there you are** [you've appeared] ¡ya estás/está usted aquí!; [have this] ahí tienes/tiene; **that jacket isn't really you** esa chaqueta no te/le pega **- 2.** (*direct object - unstressed - sing*) te; (- *pl*) os *OR* los/las *Amér*; (- *formal use*) le *m OR* lo *Amér*, la *f*; (- *pl*) les *mpl OR* los *Amér*, las *fpl*; **I can see you** te/os *OR* los/las *Amér* veo; **yes, Madam, I understand you** sí, señora, la comprendo **- 3.** (*direct object - stressed*)**: I don't expect you to do it** no te voy a pedir que tú lo hagas **- 4.** (*indirect object - sing*) te; (- *pl*) os *OR* los *Amér*; (- *formal use*) le; (- *pl*) les; **she gave it to you** te/os *OR* se *Amér* lo dio; **can I get you a chair, sir?** ¿le traigo una silla, señor? **- 5.** (*after prep, in comparisons etc - sing*) ti *OR* vos *Amér C & R Plata*; (- *pl*) vosotros *mpl*, -tras *f OR* ustedes *Amér*; (- *formal use*) usted; (- *pl*) ustedes; **we shall go with/without you** iremos contigo/sin ti *OR* vos *Amér C & R Plata*, iremos con/sin vosotros *OR* ustedes *Amér* (*pl*); **I'm shorter than you** soy más bajo que tú *OR* vos *Amér C & R Plata*/vosotros *OR* ustedes *Amér* **- 6.** [anyone, one] uno; **you wouldn't have thought so** uno no lo habría pensado; **exercise is good for you** el ejercicio es bueno.

you'd [ju:d] **- 1.** (*abbr of* **you had**) ▷ **have - 2.** (*abbr of* **you would**) ▷ **would**.

you'll [ju:l] **- 1.** (*abbr of* **you will**) ▷ **will² - 2.** (*abbr of* **you shall**) ▷ **shall**.

young [jʌŋ] ◇ *adj* [not old] joven; **his younger sister** su hermana pequeña; **I'm younger than her** soy más joven que ella; **I'm two years younger than her** soy dos años menor que ella; **the younger generation** la generación más joven. ◇ *npl* **- 1.** [young people]**: the young** los jóvenes **- 2.** [baby animals] crías *fpl*.

youngster [ˈjʌŋstər] *n* joven *mf*.

your [jɔ:r] *poss adj* **- 1.** (*everyday use - referring to one person*) tu; (- *referring to more than one person*) vuestro(tra); **your dog** tu/ vuestro perro; **your children** tus/vuestros ni-

ños; **what's your name?** ¿cómo te llamas?; **it wasn't your fault** no fue culpa tuya/vuestra; **you didn't wash your hair** no te lavaste/no os lavasteis el pelo; **your dog su; your dog su pelo**, what are your names? ¿cuáles son sus nombres? **- 3.** (*impersonal - one's*)**: your attitude changes as you get older** la actitud de uno cambia con la vejez; **it's good for your teeth/hair** es bueno para los dientes/el pelo; **your average Englishman** el inglés medio.

you're [jɔ:r] (*abbr of* **you are**) ▷ **be**.

yours [jɔ:z] *poss pron* **- 1.** (*everyday use - referring to one person*) tuyo (tuya); (- *referring to more than one person*) vuestro (vuestra); **that money is yours** ese dinero es tuyo/vuestro; **those keys are yours** esas llaves son tuyas/vuestras; **my car hit yours** mi coche chocó contra el tuyo/el vuestro; **it wasn't her fault, it was yours** no fue culpa de ella sino tuya/vuestra; **a friend of yours** un amigo tuyo/vuestro **- 2.** (*formal use*) suyo (suya). ▬ **Yours** *adv*: **Yours faithfully/sincerely** [in letter] atentamente.

yourself [jɔ:'self] (*pl* **-selves** [-'selvz]) *pron* **- 1.** (*as reflexive - sing*) te; (- *pl*) os; (- *formal use*) se; **did you hurt yourself?** ¿te hiciste/se hizo daño? **- 2.** (*after prep - sing*) ti mismo (ti misma); (- *pl*) vosotros mismos (vosotras mismas); (- *formal use*) usted mismo (usted misma); **with yourself** contigo mismo/misma **- 3.** (*for emphasis*)**: you yourself** tú mismo (tú misma); (*formal use*) usted mismo(ma); **you yourselves** vosotros mismos (vosotras mismas); (*formal use*) ustedes mismos(mas) **- 4.** [without help] solo(la); **did you do it (by) yourself?** ¿lo hiciste solo?

youth [ju:θ] *n* **- 1.** [gen] juventud *f*; **in his youth** en su juventud **- 2.** [boy, young man] joven *m*.

youth club *n* club *m* juvenil.

youthful [ˈju:θfʊl] *adj* juvenil.

youth hostel *n* albergue *m* juvenil.

you've [ju:v] (*abbr of* **you have**) ▷ **have**.

Yugoslav *adj* = **Yugoslavian**.

Yugoslavia [ˌju:gəˈslɑ:vɪə] *n* Yugoslavia.

Yugoslavian [ˌju:gəˈslɑ:vɪən], **Yugoslav** [ˌju:gəˈslɑ:v] ◇ *adj* yugoslavo(va). ◇ *n* yugoslavo *m*, -va *f*.

yuppie, yuppy [ˈjʌpɪ] (*abbr of* **young upwardly mobile professional**) *n* yuppy *mf*.

YWCA (*abbr of* **Young Women's Christian Association**) *n* asociación internacional de jóvenes cristianas.

z *(pl* z's *OR* zs)**, Z** *(pl* Z's *OR* Zs) [UK zed, US zi:]
n [letter] z f, Z f.

Zambia ['zæmbɪə] *n* Zambia.

zany ['zeɪnɪ] *adj inf* [humour, trick] disparata-
do(da); [person] loco(ca).

zeal [zi:l] *n fml* celo m.

zealous ['zeləs] *adj fml* entusiasta.

zebra [UK 'zebrə, US 'zi:brə] *(pl* zebra *OR* -s)
n cebra f.

zebra crossing *n UK* paso m cebra.

zenith [UK 'zenɪθ, US 'zi:nəθ] *n fig &* ASTRON
cenit m.

zero [UK 'zɪərəʊ, US 'zi:rəʊ] ◇ *adj* cero
(inv), nulo(la). ◇ *n (pl* zero *OR* -es) cero m;
below zero bajo cero.

zest [zest] *n (U)* - **1.** [enthusiasm] entusiasmo m; **her zest for life** su entusiasmo por vivir
- **2.** [of orange, lemon] cáscara f.

zigzag ['zɪgzæg] ◇ *n* zigzag m. ◇ *vi* zigzaguear.

Zimbabwe [zɪm'bɑːbwɪ] *n* Zimbabue.

zinc [zɪŋk] *n* cinc m, zinc m.

zip [zɪp] *n* - **1.** *UK* [fastener] cremallera f, cierre m *Amér,* zíper m *Amér C, Méx & Ven,* cierre m relámpago *Perú OR* eclair *Chile* - **2.** COM-
PUT comprimir. ➤ **zip up** *vt sep* cerrar la
cremallera *OR* el cierre *Amér OR* zíper *Amér C,*
Méx & Ven de.

zip code *n US* código m postal.

Zipdisk® *n* COMPUT disco m Zip®.

zip fastener *UK n* cremallera f.

zipper ['zɪpər] *n US* cremallera f.

zodiac ['zəʊdɪæk] *n*: **the zodiac** el zodiaco.

zone [zəʊn] *n* zona f.

zoo [zu:] *n* zoo m.

zoology [zəʊ'ɒlədʒɪ] *n* zoología f.

zoom [zu:m] *vi inf* [move quickly]: **to zoom
past** pasar zumbando.

zoom lens *n* zoom m.

zucchini [zu:'ki:nɪ] *(pl* zucchini) *n US* calabacín m, calabacita f *Méx,* zapallito m (italiano).

Achevé d'imprimer par Maury-Imprimeur
45300 Malesherbes en janvier 2008
N° de projet : 11006784
Dépôt légal : janvier 2008 - N° d'imprimeur : 133967

Imprimé en France - (Printed in France)